D0305655

ANNUAL BIBLIOGRAPHY OF ENGLISH LANGUAGE AND LITERATURE FOR 2006

GENERAL EDITOR

GERARD LOWE

ANNUAL

BIBLIOGRAPHY
OF
ENGLISH LANGUAGE AND LITERATURE FOR 2006

VOLUME 81

ACADEMIC EDITOR
JENNIFER FELLOWS

AMERICAN EDITORS
BRUCE T. SAJDAK
and
JAMES R. KELLY

Published by
Maney Publishing
for the
Modern Humanities Research Association
2007

The *Annual Bibliography*
of English Language and Literature
may be ordered from Maney Publishing,
Hudson Road, Leeds LS9 7DL

Unsolicited offprints, photocopies or other material for reporting, and correspondence about such matters, ought to be sent direct to the Academic Editor, *Annual Bibliography of English Language and Literature,* University Library, West Road, Cambridge CB3 9DR, England
(e-mail: abell@bibl.org)
(http://www.mhra.org.uk/Publications/Journals/abell.html)

ISBN 978-1-905981-53-3
ISSN 0066-3786

Printed in Great Britain by
MANEY PUBLISHING
HUDSON ROAD LEEDS LS9 7DL

PREFACE

As ever, I should like to thank all those who have helped to produce the current volume of the Annual Bibliography: our contributors worldwide and, in strictly alphabetical order, Ann Keith, James Kelly, Lucy Lewis, Gerard Lowe and Bruce Sajdak.

My pleasure in expressing my annual gratitude is mingled with sadness as I report the death of Elizabeth Erskine, who started work on the *Annual Bibliography* in the mid-1970s, when it was produced from Sheffield under the editorship of Derek Roper, and who moved with it to Cambridge, working with Mike Smith and eventually taking over the editorship. Her wit and intelligence enlivened the *Annual Bibliography* office for many years; we shall not see her like again.

If Elizabeth was one of the longest-serving *Annual Bibliography* staff, Ron Dobler, who retires from the US team after some thirty-five years, must surely hold the record for length of service as a field contributor. We thank him for all his bibliographical work over the years and wish him all the very best for the future. As he departs, we welcome Robert Desmarais as a contributor for Canada.

Finally, we are always glad to hear from potential contributors and to be alerted to any errors or omissions.

3 August 2007 JENNIFER FELLOWS

USA:

*Michael Adams, Mina Rees Library, City University of New York

Stephen Adams, Westfield State College, Westfield, MA

Robert Armitage, New York Public Library, New York

*Candace R. Benefiel, Stirling C. Evans Library, Texas A&M University, College Station

Karen W. Brown, Thomas Cooper Library, University of South Carolina, Columbia

Gerald T. Burke, University Library, Albany, NY

Dan Coffey, Parks Library, Iowa State University, Ames

Angela Courtney, Main Library, Indiana University, Bloomington

Charlotte Cubbage, Northwestern University Library, Evanston, IL

Christine DeZelar-Tiedman, University of Minnesota Libraries, Minneapolis

*G. Ronald Dobler, Morehead State University, Morehead, KY

Marie Garrett, University of Tennessee Libraries, Knoxville

* Marc Glasser, Salem State University, Salem, MA

*Lila M. Harper, Central Washington State University, Ellensburg

*Styron Harris, East Tennessee State University, Johnson City

Susan Hopwood , Marquette University Libraries, Milwaukee, WI

Emily J. Horning, Sterling Memorial Library, Yale University, New Haven, CT

*Cecile M. Jagodzinski, Main Library, Indiana University, Bloomington

Naomi Lederer, Morgan Library, Colorado State University, Fort Collins

Leslie Madden, Georgia State University Library, Atlanta

Diane Maher, Copley Library, University of San Diego, CA

Fred Muratori, Olin Library, Cornell University, Ithaca, NY

Kristin Nielsen, University of Georgia Libraries, Athens

Darby Orcutt, North Carolina State University Library, Raleigh

Michael Rodriguez, Michigan State University Library, East Lansing

Yvonne Schofer, Memorial Library, University of Wisconsin, Madison

Jane Segal, Fondren Library, Rice University, Houston, TX

Jen Stevens, George Mason University Library, Fairfax, VA

*Glenn Ellen Starr Stilling, Belk Library, Appalachian State University, Boone, NC

Laura Taddeo, University at Buffalo Libraries, Buffalo, NY

*Stephen L. Thompson, Rockefeller Library, Brown University, Providence, RI

*Markel D. Tumlin, University Library, San Diego State University, San Diego, CA

Sharon Verba, Thomas Cooper Library, University of South Carolina, Columbia

Tammy J. Eschedor Voelker, Main Library, Kent State University, Kent, OH

* Senior contributor

CONTENTS

SOURCES AND ABBREVIATIONS 2006

What follows is a list of the periodicals consulted in the compilation of the Bibliography; an asterisk indicates that relevant items have been found and are indexed in this volume. The editors are always glad to hear of journals requiring coverage.

*1650–1850	1650–1850: ideas, aesthetics, and inquiries in the early modern era (New York)
*4thG	Fourth Genre: explorations in nonfiction (East Lansing, MI)
*AAR	African American Review (Indiana State Univ., Terre Haute)
*A/B	A/B: Auto/Biography Studies (Univ. of North Carolina, Chapel Hill)
*ABR	American Benedictine Review (Assumption Abbey, Richardton, ND)
*Acme	Acme: annali della Facoltà di Lettere e Filosofia dell'Università degli Studi di Milano (Milan)
*Àcoma	Àcoma: rivista internazionale di studi nordamericani (Milan)
*ACPQ	American Catholic Philosophical Quarterly (American Catholic Philosophical Assn, Washington, DC)
AcqL	Acquisitions Librarian (Binghamton, NY)
ADEB	ADE Bulletin (Modern Language Assn of America, New York)
*ADS	Australasian Drama Studies (Univ. of Queensland, St Lucia)
*Aethlon	Aethlon: the journal of sport literature (East Tennessee State Univ., Johnson City)
AFSN	American Folklore Society News (American Folklore Soc., Ohio State Univ., Columbus)
*AfSR	African Studies Review (Dept of Anthropology, Univ. of Massachusetts, Amherst)
*Agenda	Agenda (London)
Agni	Agni (Boston Univ., Boston, MA)
*AH	American Heritage (Soc. of American Historians, New York)
AI	American Imago (Assn for Applied Psychoanalysis) (Baltimore, MD)
*AICRJ	American Indian Culture and Research Journal (American Indian Studies Center, Univ. of California, Los Angeles)
*AIQ	American Indian Quarterly (Southwestern American Indian Soc.; Soc. for American Indian Studies & Research, Lincoln, NE)
*AJ	Age of Johnson (New York)
*AJH	American Jewish History: an American Jewish History Society quarterly publication (Baltimore, MD)
*AL	American Literature: a journal of literary history, criticism, and bibliography (Durham, NC)
*AlaR	Alabama Review: a quarterly journal of Alabama history (Alabama Historical Assn, Tuscaloosa)
*Albion	Albion: a quarterly journal concerned with British studies (Dept of History, Appalachian State Univ., Boone, NC; North American Conference on British Studies)
*ALR	American Literary Realism (Champaign, IL)
*ALS	Australian Literary Studies (Univ. of Queensland, St Lucia)
*AmBR	American Book Review (Illinois State Univ., Normal)
*AmDr	American Drama (Dept of English, Helen Weinberger Center, McMicken College of Arts and Sciences, Univ. of Cincinnati, OH)
*AmerJ	Amerasia Journal (Univ. of California, Los Angeles)
*AmJ	American Journalism: a journal of media history (Sacramento, CA)
AmJP	American Journal of Psychoanalysis (New York)
*AmLH	American Literary History (Cary, NC; Oxford)
*AmP	American Periodicals: a journal of history, criticism and bibliography (Research Soc. for American Periodicals) (Columbus, OH)

*Amphora	Amphora (Alcuin Soc., Vancouver)
*AmQ	American Quarterly (American Studies Assn) (Baltimore, MD)
*AmS	American Studies: a tri-annual interdisciplinary journal (Mid-America American Studies Assn; Univ. of Kansas, Lawrence)
*Amst	Amerikastudien / American Studies (Heidelberg)
*ANCW	America: the national Catholic weekly (New York)
*Anglophonia	Anglophonia: French journal of English studies (Univ. of Toulouse–Le Mirail)
*AngP	Anglistica Pisana (Pisa)
*ANQ	ANQ: a quarterly journal of short articles, notes, and reviews (Univ. of Kentucky, Lexington)
*AnthQ	Anthropological Quarterly (Washington, DC)
Anthrop	Anthropologica (Wilfrid Laurier Univ., Waterloo, Ont.)
*Anthropoetics	Anthropoetics: the electronic journal of generative anthropology (Univ. of California, Los Angeles) (http://www.humnet.ucla.edu/humnet/anthropoetics/home.html)
*Antipodes	Antipodes: a North American journal of Australian literature (American Assn of Australian Literary Studies, Brooklyn, NY)
ApalR	Apalachee Review (Tallahassee, FL)
*AppalJ	Appalachian Journal: a regional studies review (Boone, NC)
*AppH	Appalachian Heritage (Appalachian Center, Berea College, Berea, KY)
*AppL	Applied Linguistics (Oxford)
*APQ	American Philosophical Quarterly (Bowling Green State Univ., Bowling Green, OH)
*APR	American Poetry Review (Philadelphia, PA)
*AQ	Arizona Quarterly: a journal of American literature, culture and theory (Univ. of Arizona, Tucson)
*AR	Antioch Review (Yellow Springs, OH)
*ARAL	Annual Review of Applied Linguistics (Cambridge; New York)
*Arc	Arc: Canada's national poetry magazine (Ottawa)
Arion	Arion (Boston, MA)
*ArkR	Arkansas Review: a journal of Delta studies (Arkansas State Univ., Springdale)
*ArMJ	Arthur Miller Journal (English Dept, St Francis College, Brooklyn, New York)
ARSCJ	Association for Recorded Sound Collection Journal (Toronto)
*Arthuriana	Arthuriana (International Arthurian Soc. – North American Branch) (Southern Methodist Univ., Dallas, TX)
*AS	American Speech: a quarterly of linguistic usage (American Dialect Soc.) (Durham, NC)
*ASch	American Scholar (Washington, DC)
*ASSA	Applied Semiotics / Semiotique appliquée: a learned journal of literary research on the World Wide Web (Univ. of Toronto) (http://www.chass.utoronto.ca/french/as-sa/)
ATJ	Asian Theatre Journal (Assn for Asian Performance, Honolulu, HI)
*Atl	Atlantis: journal of the Spanish Association for Anglo-American studies (Univ. de La Laguna, Tenerife)
Atlantis	Atlantis: a women's studies journal (Mount Saint Vincent Univ., Halifax, N.S.)
*AtlR	Atlanta Review (Atlanta, GA)
*ATQ	American Transcendental Quarterly: 19th century American literature and culture (Univ. of Rhode Island, Kingston)
AU	Art & Understanding (Albany, NY)

*AUMLA	AUMLA: journal of the Australasian Universities Language and Literature Association: a journal of literary criticism and linguistics (Christchurch, New Zealand)
*Auto/Biography	Auto/Biography: an international and interdisciplinary journal (London)
*Aztlan	Aztlan: a journal of Chicano studies (Los Angeles, CA)
*B2	Boundary 2: an international journal of literature and culture (Durham, NC)
*BaumB	Baum Bugle (Kalamazoo, MI)
BCCB	Bulletin of the Center for Children's Books (Graduate School of Library and Information Science, Univ. of Illinois at Urbana–Champaign)
*BCS	B.C. Studies (Vancouver)
*BecC	Beckett Circle: newsletter of the Samuel Beckett Society (Dept of English, Univ. of Wisconsin, Madison)
*BELL	BELL: Belgian essays on language and literature (Belgian Assn of Anglicists in Higher Education, Liège)
*BH	Book History (University Park, PA)
*BHM	Bulletin of the History of Medicine (Baltimore, MD)
*Biography	Biography: an interdisciplinary quarterly (Center for Biographical Research, Univ. of Hawaii, Honolulu)
*BJ	Byron Journal (Byron Soc., London)
*BJA	British Journal of Aesthetics (Oxford)
*BJECS	British Journal for Eighteenth-Century Studies (Voltaire Foundation, Oxford)
*BJJ	Ben Jonson Journal: literary contexts in the age of Elizabeth, James, and Charles (Las Vegas, NV)
*BkCan	Books in Canada
*BkW	Book World (Washington, DC)
*Blake	Blake: an illustrated quarterly (Rochester Univ., Rochester, NY)
*BLR	Bodleian Library Record (Oxford)
Blueline	Blueline (State Univ. of New York, Potsdam)
*Book	Book: newsletter of the Program in the History of the Book in American Culture (Worcester, MA)
*BosR	Boston Review: a political and literary forum (Cambridge, MA)
BPJ	Beloit Poetry Journal (Beloit, WI)
*BrC	Brilliant Corners: a journal of jazz and literature (Lycoming College, Williamsport, PA)
*BRev	Bloomsbury Review: a book magazine (Denver, CO)
*Brick	Brick (Toronto)
*BrSt	Brontë Studies: the journal of the Brontë Society (Brontë Soc., Haworth) (Leeds)
*BSANZB	Bibliographical Society of Australia and New Zealand Bulletin (Victoria Univ. of Wellington, Wellington, New Zealand)
*BSch	Black Scholar: journal of Black studies and research (Black World Foundation, Oakland, CA)
*BSJ	Baker Street Journal: an irregular quarterly of Sherlockiana (Indianapolis, IN)
*BStE	Brno Studies in English (Univ. Masarykova, Brno) (Prague)
*BurB	Burroughs Bulletin (Univ. of Louisville, KY)
BWR	Black Warrior Review (Univ. of Alabama, Tuscaloosa)
BYUS	Brigham Young University Studies: a multidisciplinary Latter-Day Saint journal (Provo, UT)

*Callaloo	Callaloo: a journal of African-American and African arts and letters (Univ. of Virginia, Charlottesville) (Baltimore, MD)
Calyx	Calyx: a journal of art and literature by women (Corvallis, OR)
*CamQ	Cambridge Quarterly (Cambridge Quarterly Assn, Clare College, Cambridge) (Oxford)
*CanJAS	Canadian Journal of African Studies (Toronto)
*CanJFS	Canadian Journal of Film Studies / Revue canadienne d'études cinématographiques (McGill Univ., Montreal)
*CanJNS	Canadian Journal of Native Studies (Canadian Indian/Native Studies Assn, Brandon Univ., Brandon, Man.)
CanJP	Canadian Journal of Philosophy (Calgary, Alta)
*CanL	Canadian Literature / Littérature canadienne: a quarterly of criticism and review (Univ. of British Columbia, Vancouver)
*CanP	Canadian Poetry (Univ. of Western Ontario, London)
*CanTR	Canadian Theatre Review (School of Literatures and Performing Studies in English, Univ. of Guelph, Ont.)
*CapR	Capilano Review (Capilano College, West Vancouver, B.C.)
CaribS	Caribbean Studies (Puerto Rico Univ., San Juan)
*CaroQ	Carolina Quarterly (Univ. of North Carolina, Chapel Hill)
*CarQ	Caribbean Quarterly (Univ. of the West Indies, Kingston, Jamaica)
*Carrollian	Carrollian (Lewis Carroll Soc., Clifford, Herefordshire)
*CathHR	Catholic Historical Review (Catholic Univ. of America, Washington, DC)
*CathS	Cather Studies (Univ. of Nebraska, Lincoln)
*CC	Cross Currents (Assn for Religion and Intellectual Life, College of New Rochelle, NY)
*CEACrit	CEA Critic (Dept of English, Widener Univ., Chester, PA)
*CEAF	CEA Forum (Youngstown State Univ., Youngstown, OH)
*CEl	Cahiers élisabéthains: late medieval and Renaissance English studies (Centre d'Études et de Recherches Élisabéthaines de l'Univ. Paul-Valéry, Montpellier)
*CFMB	Canadian Folk Music Bulletin (Calgary, Alta)
*CH	California History (California Historical Soc., San Francisco)
*Chasqui	Chasqui: revista de literatura latino americana (Provo, UT)
*ChattR	Chattahoochee Review (DeKalb Community College, Dunwoody, GA)
*ChauR	Chaucer Review: a journal of medieval studies and literary criticism (University Park, PA)
Chelsea	Chelsea (New York)
*ChildLit	Children's Literature: annual of the Modern Language Association Division on Children's Literature and the Children's Literature Association (New Haven, CT)
*ChiR	Chicago Review (Division of the Humanities, Univ. of Chicago, Chicago, IL)
*CHist	Church History (American Soc. of Church History, Chicago, IL)
*CHR	Canadian Historical Review (Univ. of Toronto)
*Chronicles	Chronicles: a magazine of American culture (Rockford, IL)
*ChronOkla	Chronicles of Oklahoma (Oklahoma Historical Soc., Oklahoma City)
*Cineaction	Cineaction (Toronto)
*Cineaste	Cineaste (Union City, NJ)
*Cithara	Cithara: essays in the Judaeo-Christian tradition (St Bonaventure Univ., St Bonaventure, NY)
CJ	Classical Journal (Univ. of Colorado, Boulder)

*CK	Common Knowledge (New York)
*CL	Comparative Literature (Univ. of Oregon, Eugene)
*CLAJ	CLA Journal (College Language Assn, Morehouse College, Atlanta, GA)
*CLAQ	Children's Literature Association Quarterly (Battle Creek, MI)
*CLCWeb	CLCWeb: computers, literature, and culture, a WWWeb journal (Purdue Univ., West Lafayette, IN) (http://clcwebjournal.lib.purdue.edu/)
*CLIN	Cuadernos de literatura inglesa y norteamericana (Facultad de Filosofía y Letras, Pontificia Univ. Católica Argentina (Buenos Aires)
*CLIO	CLIO: a journal of literature, history, and the philosophy of history (Indiana Univ.–Purdue Univ., Fort Wayne)
*CLS	Comparative Literature Studies (Pennsylvania State Univ., University Park)
*Clues	Clues: a journal of detection (Bowling Green State Univ., OH)
*ColB	Coleridge Bulletin: the journal of the Friends of Coleridge (Nether Stowey, Som.)
*ColJR	Columbia Journalism Review (Columbia Univ., New York)
*ColLit	College Literature (West Chester Univ., PA)
ColoH	Colorado Heritage (Colorado Historical Soc., Denver)
ColoR	Colorado Review: a journal of contemporary literature (Colorado State Univ., Fort Collins)
ColUL	College and Undergraduate Libraries (Binghamton, NY)
ComCog	Communication and Cognition (Ghent, Belgium)
*Comitatus	Comitatus: a journal of medieval and Renaissance studies (Center for Medieval and Renaissance Studies, Univ. of California, Los Angeles)
CommEd	Communication Education (National Communication Assn, Annandale, VA)
ComMon	Communication Monographs (Falls Creek, VA)
*CommRev	Common Review: the magazine of the Great Books Foundation (Chicago, IL)
*Comparatist	Comparatist: journal of the Southern Comparative Literature Association (Fairfax, VA)
*CompCrit	Comparative Criticism: an annual journal (Cambridge)
*CompDr	Comparative Drama (Western Michigan Univ., Kalamazoo)
*CompLing	Computational Linguistics (Assn for Computational Linguistics, Cambridge, MA)
*ComQ	Communication Quarterly (Eastern Communication Assn, Salisbury State Univ., Salisbury, MD)
ComR	Communication Research (Thousand Oaks, CA)
*Configurations	Configurations: a journal of literature, science, and technology (Soc. for Literature and Science; Georgia Inst. of Technology) (Baltimore, MD)
*Confrontation	Confrontation (English Dept, C. W. Post College of Long Island Univ., Brookville, NY)
Conjunctions	Conjunctions (New York)
*ConLett	Confronto letterario (Pavia)
*ConLit	Contemporary Literature (Univ. of Wisconsin, Madison)
*Connotations	Connotations: a journal for critical debate (Münster; New York)
*ConnR	Connecticut Review (Connecticut State Univ. System, Hartford)
*Conradian	Conradian: journal of the Joseph Conrad Society (UK) (Amsterdam; Atlanta, GA)

*Conradiana	Conradiana: a journal of Joseph Conrad studies (Texas Tech Univ., Lubbock)
*ConS	Concord Saunterer (Thoreau Lyceum, Concord, MA)
*Contagion	Contagion: journal of violence, mimesis, and culture (Loyola Univ., Chicago, IL)
*ContRev	Contemporary Review (London)
CP	Classical Philology (Chicago, IL)
*CRAS	Canadian Review of American Studies (Carleton Univ., Ottawa)
*Cresset	Cresset: a review of literature, arts and public affairs (Valparaiso Univ., Valparaiso, IN)
*Criticism	Criticism: a quarterly for literature and the arts (Wayne State Univ., Detroit, MI)
*CritP	Critique: revue générale des publications françaises et étrangères (Paris)
*CritQ	Critical Quarterly (Oxford)
CritR	Critical Review: an interdisciplinary journal of politics and society (Newton, CT)
*CritS	Critical Survey (New York; Oxford)
*CritW	Critique: studies in contemporary fiction (Washington, DC)
*CrN	Creative Nonfiction (Pittsburgh, PA)
*CSL	CSL: bulletin of the New York C. S. Lewis Society (Glendale, NY)
*CSR	Christian Scholar's Review (Holland, MI)
*CulL	Cultural Logic: an electronic journal of Marxist theory and practice (Wichita, KS) (http://eserver.org/clogic/default.html)
*Culture	Culture: annali dell'Istituto di Lingue della Facoltà di Scienze Politiche dell'Univ. degli Studi di Milano (Milan)
CurA	Current Anthropology: a world journal of the human sciences (St Louis, MO)
*CVE	Cahiers victoriens et édouardiens (Univ. Paul-Valéry, Montpellier)
*CW	Classical World (Pennsylvania State Univ., College Park)
Cweal	Commonweal (Commonweal Foundation, New York)
CWH	Civil War History: a journal of the Middle Period (Dept of History, Kent State Univ., Kent, OH)
*DalR	Dalhousie Review (Dalhousie Univ., Halifax, N.S.)
*DarkM	Dark Man: the journal of Robert E. Howard studies (Rock Valley College, Rockville, IL)
*Descant	Descant (Toronto)
*DeusL	Deus Loci: the Lawrence Durrell quarterly (Okagan Univ., Kelowna, B.C.)
*Diacritics	Diacritics: a review of contemporary criticism (Dept of Romance Studies, Cornell Univ., Ithaca, NY) (Baltimore, MD)
*Dia-keimena	Dia-keimena / Inter-textes (Centre for Comparative Literature, Aristotle Univ. of Thessaloniki)
*Dic	Dictionaries: journal of the Dictionary Society of North America (Madison, WI)
*Dickensian	Dickensian (Dickens Fellowship, Eliot College, Univ. of Kent, Canterbury)
*DickQ	Dickens Quarterly: a scholarly journal devoted to the study of the life, times, & works of Charles Dickens (Univ. of Massachusetts, Amherst)
*Discourse	Discourse: journal for theoretical studies in media and culture (Wayne State Univ., Detroit, MI)
*DLS	Doris Lessing Studies (Brooklyn, NY)
*DNR	Dime Novel Roundup: a magazine devoted to the collecting, conservation and study of old-time dime and nickel novels, popular story papers, series books, and pulp magazines (Dundas, MN)

*DQ	Denver Quarterly (Dept of English, Univ. of Denver, CO)
*Dramatist	Dramatist (New York)
*DSA	Dickens Studies Annual: essays on Victorian fiction (Graduate Center, City Univ. of New York)
DSNA	DSNA: Dictionary Society of North America newsletter (Madison, WI)
*EA	Études anglaises: Grande-Bretagne, États-Unis (Paris)
*EAL	Early American Literature (Chapel Hill, NC)
*EAPR	Edgar Allan Poe Review (Poe Studies Assn, Ohio Univ., Athens)
*EArtsS	Essays in Arts and Sciences (Univ. of New Haven, West Haven, CT)
*EC	Essays in Criticism: a quarterly journal founded by F. W. Bateson (Oxford)
*ECent	Eighteenth Century: theory and interpretation (Texas Tech Univ., Lubbock)
*ECF	Eighteenth-Century Fiction (McMaster Univ., Hamilton, Ont.)
*ECI	Eighteenth-Century Ireland / Iris an dá chultúr (Eighteenth-Century Ireland Soc., Dublin)
*ECL	Eighteenth-Century Life (College of William and Mary, Williamsburg, VA)
*ECN	Eighteenth-Century Novel (New York)
*ECS	Eighteenth-Century Studies (American Soc. for Eighteenth Century Studies, Wake Forest Univ., Winston-Salem, NC)
*EDISB	Emily Dickinson International Society Bulletin (Lexington, KY)
*EDJ	Emily Dickinson Journal (Emily Dickinson International Soc.) (Baltimore, MD)
*EDS	English Dance and Song (English Folk Dance and Song Soc., London)
*EGN	Ellen Glasgow Newsletter (Austin, TX)
*EI	Éire-Ireland: a journal of Irish studies (Irish American Cultural Inst., St Paul, MN)
*EIUC	Estudios ingleses de la Universidad Complutense (Madrid)
*EJES	European Journal of English Studies (Lisse)
*ELH	ELH: journal of English literary history (Baltimore, MD)
*ELN	English Language Notes (Univ. of Colorado, Boulder)
*ELT	English Literature in Transition (1880–1920) (Univ. of North Carolina, Greensboro)
*EMS	Essays in Medieval Studies: proceedings of the Illinois Medieval Association (West Virginia Univ., Morgantown)
*Eng	English (English Assn, Leicester)
*EngAot	English in Aotearoa (Wellington, New Zealand)
*EngS	English Studies: a journal of English language and literature (Lisse, The Netherlands)
*EOR	Eugene O'Neill Review (Suffolk Univ., Boston, MA)
Epoch	Epoch (Cornell Univ., Ithaca, NY)
*EREA	EREA: revue d'études anglophones (Univ. de Provence (Aix-Marseille 1), Aix-en-Provence) (www.e-rea.org)
*ERec	English Record (New York State English Council, Schenectady)
*ERR	European Romantic Review (North American Soc. for the Study of Romanticism, San Francisco, CA)
*ESA	English Studies in Africa: a journal of the humanities (Univ. of the Witwatersrand, South Africa)
*ESCan	English Studies in Canada (Assn of Canadian College and University Teachers of English, Carleton Univ., Ottawa)

*ESQ	ESQ: a journal of the American renaissance (Washington State Univ., Pullman)
*Esquire	Esquire (New York)
*EtBr	Études britanniques contemporaines (Univ. Paul-Valéry, Montpellier)
*EtCan	Études canadiennes: revue interdisciplinaire des études canadiennes en France (Assn Française d'Études Canadiennes, Talence)
*ETh	Early Theatre: a journal associated with the Records of Early English Drama (Hamilton, Ont.)
Ethnology	Ethnology: an international journal of cultural and social anthropology (Pittsburgh Univ., Pittsburgh, PA)
Ethnomusicology	Ethnomusicology: journal of the Society for Ethnomusicology (Univ. of Illinois, Urbana)
EtLitt	Études littéraires (Univ. Laval, Que.)
*EurJAC	European Journal of American Culture (Exeter)
*EWN	Evelyn Waugh Newsletter and Studies (Evelyn Waugh Soc., Lock Haven College, PA)
*EWR	Edith Wharton Review (Kean Univ., Union, NJ)
*EWW	English World-Wide: a journal of varieties of English (Amsterdam; Philadelphia, PA)
*Exemplaria	Exemplaria: a journal of theory in medieval and Renaissance studies (Asheville, NC)
*Exp	Explicator (Helen Dwight Reid Educational Foundation, Washington, DC)
*ExRC	Explorations in Renaissance Culture (Dept of English, Southwest Missouri State Univ., Springfield)
*Extrapolation	Extrapolation (Kent State Univ., Kent, OH)
*FCS	Fifteenth-Century Studies (Univ. of Virginia, Charlottesville) (Columbia, SC)
*FDR	Field Day Review (Field Day: Dublin & Keough Institute for Irish Studies, Univ. of Notre Dame: Notre Dame, IN)
*FemSt	Feminist Studies (Univ. of Maryland, College Park)
Fence	Fence (New York)
Field	Field: contemporary poetry and poetics (Oberlin College, OH)
*FilCr	Film Criticism (Allegheny College, Meadville, PA)
*FilmH	Film and History: an interdisciplinary journal of film and television studies (Popular Culture Center, Cleveland, OK)
*FilmQ	Film Quarterly (Univ. of California, Berkeley)
*FiveP	Five Points: a journal of literature and art (Atlanta, GA)
*FJ	Faulkner Journal (Dept of English, Univ. of Akron, OH)
*FJCM	Framework: the journal of cinema and media (Wayne State Univ., Detroit, MI)
FlR	Florida Review (Univ. of Central Florida, Orlando)
*FLS	Foreign Literature Studies (Wuhan, China)
*FMJ	Folk Music Journal: the journal of traditional music and dance (London)
*FMLS	Forum for Modern Language Studies (Univ. of St Andrews) (Oxford)
*FOAFN	FOAFtale News (International Soc. for Contemporary Legend Research, Memorial Univ. of Newfoundland, St John's)
*FolkL	Folk Life: journal of ethnological studies (Soc. for Folk Life Studies, Leeds)
*Folklore	Folklore (Folklore Soc., University College, London)
*FOR	Flannery O'Connor Review (Dept of English and Speech, Georgia College & State Univ., Milledgeville)
FoxM	Foxfire Magazine (Mountain City, GA)

*Frontiers	Frontiers: a journal of women studies (Washington State Univ., Pullman)
*GaR	Georgia Review (Univ. of Georgia, Athens)
*Gastronomica	Gastronomica: the journal of food and culture (Berkeley, CA)
*GavB	Gávea-Brown: revista bilingue de letras e estudios Luso-Americanos (Brown Univ., Providence, RI)
*GBB	George Borrow Bulletin (George Borrow Soc., Wallingford, Oxon.)
*GEGHLS	George Eliot – George Henry Lewes Studies (Northern Illinois Univ., DeKalb)
*GenI	Gender Issues (Rutgers Univ., New Brunswick, NJ)
*Genre	Genre: forms of discourse and culture (Dept of English, Univ. of Oklahoma, Norman)
*GER	George Eliot Review (George Eliot Fellowship, Coventry)
*GetR	Gettysburg Review (Gettysburg College, Gettysburg, PA)
*GissJ	Gissing Journal (Bradford)
*GLQ	GLQ: a journal of lesbian and gay studies (Durham, NC)
*GLRW	Gay and Lesbian Review Worldwide (Boston, MA)
*GothS	Gothic Studies (Manchester)
*GPQ	Great Plains Quarterly (Center for Great Plains Studies, Univ. of Nebraska, Lincoln)
*Gramma	Gramma: periodiko theorias & kritikes (Dept of English, Aristotle Univ., Thessaloniki)
*GT	Glimmer Train (Portland, OR)
GWR	G.W. Review (Marvin Center, George Washington Univ., Washington, DC)
*HAge	Heroic Age: journal of early medieval Northwestern Europe (Belleville, IL) (http://members.aol.com/heroicage1/homepage.html)
*HarSJ	Hardy Society Journal (Thomas Hardy Soc., Dorchester)
*HC	Hollins Critic (Hollins Univ., Hollins, VA)
*HemR	Hemingway Review (Hemingway Soc., Nantucket, MA)
*HGP	Heritage of the Great Plains (Emporia State Univ., Emporia, KS)
*Historian	Historian (Univ. of South Florida, Tampa)
*HJEJ	Henry James E-Journal (New Paltz, NY)
*HJR	Henry James Review (Henry James Soc., Univ. of Louisville, KY) (Baltimore, MD)
*HJS	Hypermedia Joyce Studies (http://www.geocities.com/hypermedia_joyce/archive.html)
*HLQ	Huntington Library Quarterly: studies in English and American history and literature (Henry E. Huntington Library and Art Gallery, San Marino, CA)
*HopQ	Hopkins Quarterly (St Joseph's Univ., Philadelphia, PA)
*HR	Hudson Review: a magazine of literature and the arts (New York)
*HTR	Harvard Theological Review (Cambridge, MA)
*Humanist	Humanist: a magazine of critical inquiry and social concern (American Humanist Assn, Amherst, NY)
*Humor	Humor: international journal of humor research (The Hague)
*HWSJ	Henry Williamson Society Journal (Chichester)
*Hypatia	Hypatia: a journal of feminist philosophy (Univ. of Oregon, Eugene)
*IE	Indiana English (Indiana State Univ., Terre Haute)
*IFR	International Fiction Review (Dept of Culture and Language Studies, Univ. of New Brunswick, Fredericton)

*IGSJ	Ivor Gurney Society Journal (Ivor Gurney Soc., School of English, Univ. of Birmingham)
IHI	Iowa Heritage Illustrated (State Historical Soc. of Iowa, Iowa City)
*IJES	International Journal of English Studies (Univ. de Murcia)
*IJPP	Interpretation: a journal of political philosophy (Queen's College, City Univ. of New York, Flushing)
*ILS	Irish Literary Supplement (Wading River, NY)
*IMR	Iron Mountain Review (Emory, VA)
*Indice	Indice (Turin)
*IndS	Independent Shavian (Bernard Shaw Soc., New York)
*InR	Indiana Review (Bloomington, IN)
Interpretation	Interpretation: a journal of Bible and theology (Union Theological Seminar in Virginia, Richmond)
*Intertexts	Intertexts (Texas Tech Univ., Lubbock)
*IowaR	Iowa Review (Univ. of Iowa, Iowa City)
*Iris	Iris: a journal about women (Univ. of Virginia, Charlottesville)
*Isis	Isis: an international review devoted to the history of science and its cultural influences (History of Science Soc.) (Chicago, IL)
*ISLE	ISLE: interdisciplinary studies in literature and environment (Assn for the Study of Literature and Environment, Univ. of Nevada, Reno)
*ISR	Irish Studies Review (Bath)
*ItalA	Italian Americana (State Univ. of New York, Buffalo)
*JAAH	Journal of African American History (Assn for the Study of African American Life and History, Silver Spring, MD)
*JAAL	Journal of Adolescent and Adult Literacy (International Reading Assn, Newark, DE)
*JAAR	Journal of the American Academy of Religion (Whittier College, Whittier, CA)
*JAAS	Journal of Asian American Studies (Assn for Asian American Studies) (Baltimore, MD)
*JAC	Journal of American Culture: studies of a civilization (American Culture Assn, Bowling Green State Univ., Bowling Green, OH)
JACJ	JAC: a journal of composition theory (Dept of English, Iowa State Univ., Ames)
*JADT	Journal of American Drama and Theatre (Graduate School, City Univ. of New York)
*JAE	Journal of Aesthetic Education (Univ. of Illinois, Champaign)
*JAF	Journal of American Folklore: journal of the American Folklore Society (Arlington, VA)
*JAH	Journal of American History (Indiana Univ., Bloomington)
JAMLS	Journal of Arts Management, Law, and Society (Washington, DC)
JAMS	Journal of the American Musicological Society (Stanford Univ., Stanford, CA)
*JAR	Journal of Anthropological Research (Univ. of New Mexico, Albuquerque)
*JArizH	Journal of Arizona History (Arizona Historical Soc., Tucson)
*JAStud	Journal of American Studies (Cambridge)
*JBecS	Journal of Beckett Studies (Florida State Univ., Tallahassee)
*JBJ	John Buchan Journal (John Buchan Soc., Bridge of Weir, Renfrewshire)
*JBlaS	Journal of Black Studies (Thousand Oaks, CA)
*JCarL	Journal of Caribbean Literatures (Dept of English, Univ. of Northern Iowa, Cedar Falls)
*JCG	Journal of Cultural Geography (Bowling Green State Univ., Bowling Green, OH)

JCI	Journal of Communication Inquiry (Univ. of Iowa, Iowa City)
*JCL	Journal of Commonwealth Literature (East Grinstead, W. Sussex)
*JCPS	Journal of Commonwealth and Postcolonial Studies (Georgia Southern Univ., Statesboro)
*JDJ	John Donne Journal: studies in the age of Donne (John Donne Soc., Raleigh, NC)
*JDN	James Dickey Newsletter (DeKalb Community College, Dunwoody, GA)
*JDTC	Journal of Dramatic Theory and Criticism (Univ. of Kansas, Lawrence)
*JEBS	Journal of the Early Book Society for the Study of Manuscripts and Printing History (New York)
JECS	Journal of Early Christian Studies (North American Patristics Soc.) (Baltimore, MD)
*JEGP	Journal of English and Germanic Philology: a quarterly devoted to the English, German, and Scandinavian languages and literatures (Champaign, IL)
*JEL	Journal of English Linguistics (Thousand Oaks, CA)
*JEMCS	Journal for Early Modern Cultural Studies (Bloomington, IN)
*Jezikoslovlje	Jezikoslovlje (Osijek, Croatia)
*JFA	Journal of the Fantastic in the Arts (International Assn for the Fantastic in the Arts) (Boca Raton, FL)
*JFR	Journal of Folklore Research (Indiana Univ. Folklore Inst., Bloomington)
*JFV	Journal of Film and Video (University Film and Video Assn, California State Univ., Los Angeles)
JGE	Journal of General Education (Pennsylvania State Univ., University Park)
*JHI	Journal of the History of Ideas (Rutgers Univ., New Brunswick, NJ)
*JHM	Journal of the History of Medicine and Allied Sciences (New Haven, CT)
*JHo	Journal of Homosexuality (Binghamton, NY)
*JHS	Journal of the History of Sexuality (Univ. of Chicago, IL)
*JJLS	James Joyce Literary Supplement (Miami Univ., Coral Gables, FL)
*JLesS	Journal of Lesbian Studies (Binghamton, NY)
*JLS	Journal of Literary Semantics: an international review (Heidelberg)
JLSP	Journal of Language and Social Psychology (Univ. of California, Santa Barbara)
*JMCQ	Journalism and Mass Communication Quarterly (Assn for Education in Journalism and Mass Communication, Columbia, SC)
*JMEMS	Journal of Medieval and Early Modern Studies (Durham, NC)
*JMH	Journal of Modern History (Chicago, IL)
*JML	Journal of Modern Literature (Foundation for Modern Literature, Bloomington, IN)
*JMMLA	Journal of the Midwest Modern Language Association (Univ. of Iowa, Iowa City)
*JNT	Journal of Narrative Theory (Soc. for the Study of Narrative Literature, Eastern Michigan Univ., Ypsilanti)
*JNZL	Journal of New Zealand Literature (Dept of English, Univ. of Otago, Dunedin)
*JoH	Journalism History (Univ. of Nevada, Las Vegas)
*Journeys	Journeys: the international journal of travel and travel writing (London)

*JPC	Journal of Popular Culture (Popular Culture Center, Bowling Green State Univ., OH)
*JPCL	Journal of Pidgin and Creole Languages (Amsterdam)
*JPFT	Journal of Popular Film and Television (Helen Dwight Reid Educational Foundation) (Washington, DC)
JPH	Journal of Presbyterian History (Presbyterian Historical Soc., Philadelphia, PA)
*JPHS	Journal of the Printing Historical Society (London)
*JPRS	Journal of Pre-Raphaelite Studies (Strong College, York Univ., Toronto)
*JPW	Journal of Postcolonial Writing (Abingdon, Oxon.)
*JR	Journal of Religion (Chicago, IL)
*JRS	Journal of Ritual Studies (Pittsburgh Univ., Pittsburgh, PA)
*JSchP	Journal of Scholarly Publishing (North York, Ont.)
*JSH	Journal of Southern History (Rice Univ., Houston, TX)
*JSoc	Journal of Sociolinguistics (Oxford)
*JSSE	Journal of the Short Story in English / Les Cahiers de la nouvelle (Univ. d'Angers)
*JSwest	Journal of the Southwest (Univ. of Arizona, Tucson)
*JTLBS	Journal of the Thomas Lovell Beddoes Society (Belper, Derbyshire)
*JudQ	Judaism: a quarterly journal of Jewish life and thought (Univ. of California, Santa Cruz)
*JVC	Journal of Victorian Culture (Edinburgh)
*JWIL	Journal of West Indian Literature (Univ. of West Indies)
*JWMS	Journal of the William Morris Society (Hammersmith)
Kalliope	Kalliope: a journal of women's literature & art (Florida Community College, Jacksonville)
KenEB	Kentucky English Bulletin (Bowling Green, KY)
*KenPR	Kentucky Philological Review (Highland Heights, KY)
*KJ	Kipling Journal (Kipling Soc., Brighton)
*KnLet	Knight Letter (Lewis Carroll Soc. of North America, Nappa, CA)
*KR	Kenyon Review (Kenyon College, Gambier, OH)
*KSJ	Keats–Shelley Journal: Keats, Shelley, Byron, Hunt, and their circles (Keats–Shelley Assn of America, New York)
*KSR	Keats–Shelley Review (Keats–Shelley Memorial Assn, Windsor)
*Lang	Language: journal of the Linguistic Society of America (Baltimore, MD)
*LauR	Laurel Review (Northwest Missouri State Univ., Maryville)
*LawL	Law and Literature (Berkeley, CA)
LB	Living Blues: a journal of the African American Blues tradition (University, MS)
*Legacy	Legacy: a journal of American women writers (Pennsylvania State Univ., University Park)
*Leviathan	Leviathan: a journal of Melville studies (Melville Soc.; Hofstra Univ., Hempstead, NY)
LH	Lincoln Herald (Harrogate, TN)
*LibC	Libraries & Culture: a journal of library history (Austin, TX)
*Library	Library: the transactions of the Bibliographical Society (Oxford)
*LIT	LIT: literature, interpretation, theory (Reading)
*LitB	Literature and Belief (Provo, UT)
*LitFQ	Literature/Film Quarterly (Salisbury State Univ., Salisbury, MD)
*LitH	Literature and History (Univ. of Manchester)
*LitIm	Literary Imagination: the review of the Association of Literary Scholars and Critics (Athens, GA)

*LitMed	Literature and Medicine (Baltimore, MD)
*LitR	Literary Review: an international journal of contemporary writing (Fairleigh Dickinson Univ., Madison, NJ)
*LitTheol	Literature & Theology: an interdisciplinary journal of theory and criticism (Oxford)
*LittPr	Litteraria Pragensia: studies in literature and culture (Czech Academy of Sciences) (Amsterdam; Philadelphia, PA)
LJH	Lamar Journal of the Humanities (College of Arts and Sciences, Lamar Univ., Beaumont, TX)
*LProv	Lettore di provincia (Ravenna)
*LPub	Learned Publishing: the journal of the Association of Learned and Professional Society Publishers (London)
LQ	Library Quarterly: a journal of investigation in library and information sciences (Chicago, IL)
*LRB	London Review of Books (London)
*LRC	Literary Review of Canada: a review of Canadian books on culture, politics and society (Toronto)
*LSE	Leeds Studies in English (Univ. of Leeds)
*LU	Lion and the Unicorn: a critical journal of children's literature (Baltimore, MD)
*Lumen	Lumen (Edmonton, Alta)
MacGuffin	MacGuffin (Dept of English, Schoolcraft College, Livonia, MI)
*MÆ	Medium Ævum (Soc. for the Study of Medieval Languages and Literature, Oxford)
*MaHR	Massachusetts Historical Review (Massachusetts Historical Soc., Boston)
*MarvT	Marvels & Tales: journal of fairy-tale studies (Wayne State Univ., Detroit, MI)
*MassR	Massachusetts Review: a quarterly of literature, the arts, and public affairs (Univ. of Massachusetts, Amherst)
*MatC	Material Culture: journal of the Pioneer American Society (Normal, IL)
*Meanjin	Meanjin (Univ. of Melbourne, Parkville, Vic.)
*MedRen	Medieval and Renaissance Drama in England (Madison, NJ)
*MELUS	MELUS (Univ. of Southern California, Los Angeles)
*Menckeniana	Menckeniana: a quarterly review (Enoch Pratt Free Library, Baltimore, MD)
*MerA	Merton Annual: studies in culture, spirituality, and social concerns (Decatur, GA)
*Meridians	Meridians: feminism, race, transnationalism (Wesleyan Univ., Middletown, CT)
*Meta	Meta (Univ. of Montreal)
Metamorphoses	Metamorphoses (Amherst, MA)
*MetS	Metaphor and Symbol (Mahwah, NJ)
*MFS	Modern Fiction Studies (Dept of English, Purdue Univ., West Lafayette, IN) (Baltimore, MD)
MichHR	Michigan Historical Review (Central Michigan Univ., Mount Pleasant)
*MichQR	Michigan Quarterly Review (Univ. of Michigan, Ann Arbor)
*MidAmerica	MidAmerica: the yearbook of the Society for the Study of Midwestern Literature (East Lansing, MI)
*MidF	Midwestern Folklore: journal of the Hoosier Folklore Society (Terre Haute, IN)

*MidM Midwestern Miscellany: being a collection of essays and occasional pieces on the Midwest, its writers, and its writing by members of the Society for the Study of Midwestern Literature (East Lansing, MI)
*MidQ Midwest Quarterly: a journal of contemporary thought (Pittsburg State Univ., Pittsburg, KS)
*MiE Mind's Eye: a liberal arts journal (North Adams, MA)
*Misc Miscelánea: a journal of English and American studies (Zaragoza Univ.)
MisR Mississippi Review (Center for Writers, Univ. of Southern Mississippi, Hattiesburg)
*MissQ Mississippi Quarterly: the journal of Southern cultures (Mississippi State Univ., Mississippi State)
*MLN MLN (Baltimore, MD)
*MLQ Modern Language Quarterly: a journal of literary history (Duke Univ., Durham, NC)
*MLR Modern Language Review (Modern Humanities Research Assn) (Leeds)
*ModAge Modern Age: a quarterly review (Intercollegiate Studies Inst., Univ. of Maryland, College Park)
*ModDr Modern Drama (Graduate Centre for Study of Drama, Univ. of Toronto) (Downsview, Ont.)
*Mod/Mod Modernism/Modernity (Baltimore, MD)
ModSch Modern Schoolman (St Louis Univ., St Louis, MO)
Monist Monist: an international quarterly journal of general philosophical inquiry (Chicago / La Salle, IL)
*Montana Montana: the magazine of Western history (Montana Historical Soc., Helena)
*Moreana Moreana (Angers)
*Mosaic Mosaic: a journal for the interdisciplinary study of literature (Univ. of Manitoba, Winnipeg)
*MovIm Moving Image: the journal of the Association of Moving Image Archivists (Minneapolis, MN)
*MP Modern Philology: a journal devoted to research in medieval and modern literature (Chicago, IL)
*MQ Milton Quarterly (Baltimore, MD)
*MR Missouri Review (Univ. of Missouri, Columbia)
*MSAN MSAN: Marlowe Society of America newsletter (South Dakota State Univ., Brookings)
MsM Ms Magazine (New York)
*MSp Moderne Sprachen (Inst. für Anglistik, Univ. of Salzburg)
*MSS Manuscripts (Manuscript Soc., Burbank, CA)
*MStud Milton Studies (Pittsburgh, PA)
MT Machine Translation (Carnegie Mellon Univ., Pittsburgh, PA)
*MTA Mark Twain Annual (Mark Twain Circle of America, Rock Hill, SC)
*MusL Music & Letters (Oxford)
*Mythlore Mythlore: a journal of J. R. R. Tolkien, C. S. Lewis, Charles Williams, and the genres of myth and fantasy studies (Mythopoeic Soc.) (Altadena, CA)
*Mythprint Mythprint: the monthly bulletin of the Mythopoeic Society (San Francisco, CA)
*Nabokovian Nabokovian (Vladimir Nabokov Soc., Univ. of Kansas, Lawrence)
*Narrative Narrative (Soc. for the Study of Narrative Literature, Columbus, OH)
*NCarF North Carolina Folklore Journal (Greenville, NC)
*NCC Nineteenth-Century Contexts: an interdisciplinary journal (Dept of English, Univ. of Notre Dame, IN; Dept of English, Univ. of Lancaster) (Amsterdam)

NCFrS	Nineteenth-Century French Studies (Fredonia, NY)
*NCHR	North Carolina Historical Review (Raleigh, NC)
*NCL	Notes on Contemporary Literature (Carrollton, GA)
*NCLR	North Carolina Literary Review (North Carolina Literary and Historical Assn, Dept of English, East Carolina Univ., Greenville, NC)
*NCP	Nineteenth Century Prose (Dept of Literature and Language, Mesa State College, Grand Junction, CO)
*NCS	Nineteenth Century Studies (Lancaster, PA)
*NCT	Nineteenth Century Theatre and Film (Manchester)
NDH	North Dakota History: journal of the Northern plains (State Historical Soc. of North Dakota, Bismarck)
*NebH	Nebraska History (Nebraska State Historical Soc., Lincoln)
*Neophilologus	Neophilologus: an international journal of modern and mediaeval language and literature (Dordrecht; Boston, MA; London)
*NER	New England Review (Middlebury College, Middlebury, VT)
*NETJ	New England Theatre Journal (Dept of English, Northeastern Univ., Boston, MA)
*NewHR	New Hibernia Review / Irís Éireannach Nua: a quarterly record of Irish studies (Center for Irish Studies / Lárionad an Léinn Éireannaigh, Univ. of St Thomas, St Paul, MN)
NewL	New Leader (American Labor Conference on International Affairs, New York)
*NewLet	New Letters (Univ. of Missouri, Kansas City)
*NHR	Nathaniel Hawthorne Review (Dept of English, Duquesne Univ., Pittsburgh, PA)
NiemR	Nieman Reports (Cambridge, MA)
Nimrod	Nimrod: international journal of prose and poetry (Tulsa, OK)
*NINE	NINE: a journal of baseball history and culture (Univ. of Nebraska, Lincoln)
*NineL	Nineteenth-Century Literature (Berkeley; Los Angeles, CA)
*NLH	New Literary History: a journal of theory and interpretation (Univ. of Virginia, Charlottesville) (Baltimore, MD)
*NM	Neuphilologische Mitteilungen: bulletin de la Société Néophilologique / bulletin of the Modern Language Society (Helsinki)
*Nomina	Nomina: journal of the Society for Name Studies in Britain and Ireland (Glasgow)
NOR	New Orleans Review (Loyola Univ., New Orleans, LA)
*Novel	Novel: a forum on fiction (Brown Univ., Providence, RI)
*Now	Now and Then (East Tennessee State Univ., Johnson City)
*NPDM	Nutmeg Point District Mail (Upper Montclair, NJ)
*NQ	Notes and Queries: for readers and writers, collectors and librarians (Oxford)
NRCLL	New Review of Children's Literature and Librarianship (London)
*NwR	Northwest Review (Univ. of Oregon, Eugene)
*NWSAJ	NWSA Journal: a publication of the National Women's Studies Association (Indiana Univ., Bloomington)
*NYH	New York History (New York State Historical Assn, Cooperstown)
*NYRSF	New York Review of Science Fiction (Pleasantville, NY)
*NYTB	New York Times Book Review
*NYTM	New York Times Magazine (New York)
*Ob3	Obsidian III: literature in the African diaspora (Dept of English, North Carolina State Univ., Raleigh)
OcL	Oceanic Linguistics (Carbondale, IL)

*OEN	Old English Newsletter (Medieval Inst., Western Michigan Univ., Kalamazoo)
OHR	Oral History Review: journal of the Oral History Association (Univ. of Connecticut, Storrs)
OntR	Ontario Review (Princeton, NJ)
OpC	Open City Magazine (New York)
*OpL	OpL | Open Letter: a Canadian journal of writing and theory (London, Ont.)
OurS	Our State: down home in North Carolina (Greensboro, NC)
*OVH	Ohio Valley History: the journal of the Cincinnati Historical Society (Cincinnati, OH)
*OvR	Overland Review (Kansas Folklore Soc., Paola)
OxAm	Oxford American: a magazine from the South (Univ. of Central Arkansas, Conway)
*PAAS	Proceedings of the American Antiquarian Society: a journal of American history and culture through 1876 (Worcester, MA)
*PacHR	Pacific Historical Review (Univ. of California, Los Angeles)
*PacNQ	Pacific Northwest Quarterly: a scholarly journal of Northwest history (Univ. of Washington, Seattle)
*Paideuma	Paideuma: a journal devoted to Ezra Pound scholarship (Univ. of Maine, Orono)
*PAPS	Proceedings of the American Philosophical Society (Philadelphia, PA)
*Para	Paragraph (Oxford)
*Parabola	Parabola (Soc. for the Study of Myth and Tradition, New York)
*Paradoxa	Paradoxa: studies in world literary genres (Vashon Island, WA)
*ParallaxB	Parallax: journal of international perspectives (Boston, MA)
*Parergon	Parergon: journal of the Australian and New Zealand Association for Medieval and Early Modern Studies (Nedlands, W. Australia)
*Parnassus	Parnassus: poetry in review (New York)
*PartA	Partial Answers: journal of literature and the history of ideas (School of Literatures, Hebrew Univ. of Jerusalem)
*PBSA	Papers of the Bibliographical Society of America (New York)
*PCP	Pacific Coast Philology (Pacific Ancient and Modern Language Assn, California State Univ., Northridge)
*PCR	Popular Culture Review: journal of the Far West Popular and American Culture Association (Dept of English, Univ. of Nevada, Las Vegas)
*PE	Peer English: the journal of new critical thinking (Dept of English, Univ. of Leicester)
*PeakeS	Peake Studies (Orzens, Vaud, Switzerland)
*PemM	Pembroke Magazine (Univ. of North Carolina, Pembroke)
*Persuasions	Persuasions (Jane Austen Soc. of North America, New York)
PEW	Philosophy East and West: a quarterly of Asian and comparative thought (Univ. of Hawaii, Honolulu)
*PhilL	Philosophy and Literature (Baltimore, MD)
Philosophy	Philosophy: the journal of the Royal Institute of Philosophy (London)
*PhilR	Philosophy and Rhetoric (University Park, PA)
*PhRS	Philip Roth Studies (Dept of Languages and Communications, Prairie View A & M Univ., Prairie View TX)
PhRSN	Philip Roth Society Newsletter (Dept of Languages and Communications, Prairie View A&M Univ., Prairie View, TX)
*PInt	Poetry International (Dept of English and Comparative Literature, San Diego State Univ., San Diego, CA)

*PJCAC	Phoenix: the journal of the Classics Association of Canada (Trinity College, Toronto)
*PJCL	Prairie Journal of Canadian Literature (Calgary, Alta)
*PLL	Papers on Language & Literature: a quarterly journal for scholars and critics of language and literature (Southern Illinois Univ., Edwardsville)
*PMC	Postmodern Culture: an electronic journal of interdisciplinary criticism (Raleigh, NC) (http://jefferson.village.virginia.edu/pmc/)
*PNRev	PN Review (Manchester)
*PoesiaM	Poesia: mensile internazionale di cultura poetica (Milan)
*Poetry	Poetry (New York; Chicago, IL)
*PowJ	Powys Journal (Powys Soc., Wexham, Bucks.)
PPR	Philosophy and Phenomenological Research (State Univ. of New York, Buffalo)
*PQ	Philological Quarterly (Univ. of Iowa, Iowa City)
*PRev	Poetry Review (London)
*PrH	Printing History: journal of the American Printing History Association (New York)
*Prism(s)	Prism(s): essays in Romanticism (American Conference on Romanticism, Brigham Young Univ., Provo, UT)
Profession	Profession (Modern Language Assn of America, New York)
Proteus	Proteus: a journal of ideas (Shippensburg, PA)
*Proverbium	Proverbium (Ohio State Univ., Columbus)
*PrQ	Print Quarterly (London)
*PrS	Prairie Schooner (Univ. of Nebraska, Lincoln)
*PrSt	Prose Studies: history, theory, criticism (London)
PRv	Philosophical Review (Cornell Univ., Ithaca, NY)
*PS	Post Script: essays in film and the humanities (Commerce, TX)
*PSE	Prague Studies in English (Karlovy Univ., Prague)
*PsyArt	PsyArt: a hyperlink journal for the psychological study of the arts (Dept of English, Univ. of Florida, Gainesville) (http://web.clas.ufl.edu/ipsa/journal/)
*PT	Poetics Today: international journal for theory and analysis of literature and communication (Porter Inst. for Poetics and Semiotics, Tel Aviv Univ.) (Durham, NC)
*PubRQ	Publishing Research Quarterly (New Brunswick, NJ)
*QDLC	Quaderno del Dipartimento di Letterature Comparate (Univ. degli Studi Roma Tre)
QH	Quaker History: the bulletin of Friends Historical Association (Haverford College, Haverford , PA)
*QJS	Quarterly Journal of Speech (Speech Communication Assn, Annandale, VA)
*QPS	Quaderni di Palazzo Serra (Univ. of Genoa)
*QRFV	Quarterly Review of Film and Video (London)
QStud	Québec Studies (Univ. of Vermont, Burlington)
*Quid	Quidditas: JRMMRA, journal of the Rocky Mountain Medieval and Renaissance Association (Provo, UT)
QW	Quarterly West (Univ. of Utah, Salt Lake City)
RAC	Religion and American Culture: a journal of interpretation (Center for the Study of Religion and American Culture) (Berkeley, CA)
*RAEI	Revista alicantina de estudios ingleses (Univ. de Alicante, Alicante)
*RAL	Research in African Literatures (Bloomington, IN)
*Rampike	Rampike (Sault St Marie, Ont.)

*RANAM	Recherches anglaises et nord-américaines (Univ. des Sciences Humaines de Strasbourg)
*Raritan	Raritan: a quarterly review (Rutgers Univ., New Brunswick, NJ)
*RBM	RBM: a journal of rare books, manuscripts, and cultural heritage (Assn of College and Research Libraries, Chicago, IL)
*RCF	Review of Contemporary Fiction (Illinois State Univ., Normal)
*RECTR	Restoration and 18th Century Theatre Research (Loyola Univ., Chicago, IL)
*RelArts	Religion and the Arts: a journal from Boston College (Chestnut Hill, MA)
*ReLit	Religion and Literature (Univ. of Notre Dame, Notre Dame, IN)
*Ren	Renascence: essays on values in literature (Marquette Univ., Milwaukee, WI)
*RenD	Renaissance Drama (Evanston, IL)
*RenP	Renaissance Papers (Southeastern Renaissance Conference) (Columbia, SC)
*Representations	Representations (Univ. of California, Berkeley)
*RES	Review of English Studies: the quarterly journal of English literature and the English language (Oxford)
*REsLA	Revista española de lingüística aplicada (Asociación Española de Lingüística Aplicada, Logroño, La Rioja)
*Restoration	Restoration: studies in English literary culture, 1660–1700 (Tennessee Technological Univ., Cookeville)
*RevR	Revolver Review (Prague)
*RFR	Robert Frost Review (Rock Hill, SC)
*Rhetorica	Rhetorica: a journal for the history of rhetoric (Berkeley, CA)
*RMedS	Reading Medieval Studies (Graduate Centre for Medieval Studies, Univ. of Reading)
*RMER	Rocky Mountain E-Review (Rocky Mountain Modern Language Assn, Pullman, WA) (http://rmmla.wsu.edu/)
*Romanticism	Romanticism (Edinburgh)
*RomNet	Romanticism on the Net (Univ. of Montreal) (http://www.ron.umontreal.ca/)
*Room	Room of One's Own: a feminist journal of literature and criticism (Vancouver)
*RORD	Research Opportunities in Medieval and Renaissance Drama (Univ. of New Orleans, LA)
*RQ	Renaissance Quarterly (Renaissance Soc. of America, New York)
*RSQ	Rhetoric Society Quarterly (Rhetoric Soc. of America, Dept of English, Pennsylvania State Univ., University Park)
*RSV	Rivista di studi vittoriani (Pescara)
RT	Radical Teacher: a Socialist and feminist journal on the theory and practice of teaching (Cambridge, MA)
*SAC	Studies in the Age of Chaucer (New Chaucer Soc., Ohio State Univ., Columbus)
*Sagetrieb	Sagetrieb: a journal devoted to poets in the imagist/objectivist tradition (National Poetry Foundation, Orono, ME)
*SAIL	Studies in American Indian Literatures (Western Washington Univ., Bellingham)
*Salmagundi	Salmagundi: a quarterly of the humanities & social sciences (Skidmore College, Saratoga Springs, NY)
*SAtlR	South Atlantic Review: the journal of the South Atlantic Modern Language Association (Georgia State Univ., Atlanta)
*SBJ	Saul Bellow Journal (West Bloomfield, MI)

*Scintilla	Scintilla (Usk Valley Vaughan Assn, Llantrisant, Usk, Gwent)
*ScLang	Scottish Language (Assn for Scottish Literary Studies, Univ. of Aberdeen)
*SCN	Seventeenth-Century News (Texas A&M Univ., College Station)
*ScopeF	Scope: an online journal of film studies (inst. of Film & Television Studies, Univ. of Nottingham) (http://www.scope.nottingham.ac.uk)
*SCR	South Central Review: the journal of the South Central Modern Language Association (Texas A&M Univ., College Station)
*Scriblerian	Scriblerian and the Kit-Cats (Temple Univ., Philadelphia, PA)
*SCrit	Strumenti critici: rivista quadrimestrale di cultura e critica letteraria (Turin)
*ScSR	Scottish Studies Review (Assn for Scottish Literary Studies, Glasgow)
*SEDERI	SEDERI: yearbook of the Spanish and Portuguese Society for English Renaissance Studies (Univ. of Valladolid)
*SEEJ	Slavic and East European Journal (Univ. of Arizona, Tucson)
*SELit	Studies in English Literature 1500–1900 (Rice Univ., Houston, TX)
*Semicerchio	Semicerchio: rivista di poesia comparata (Florence)
*SevC	Seventeenth Century (Centre for Seventeenth-Century Studies, Univ. of Durham)
*SewR	Sewanee Review (Univ. of the South, Sewanee, TN)
*SFO	Scholar & Feminist Online (Barnard Center for Research on Women, New York)
*SHARP	SHARP News (Macon, GA)
*Shaw	Shaw: the annual of Bernard Shaw studies (University Park, PA)
*ShB	Shakespeare Bulletin: a journal of performance criticism and scholarship (Baltimore, MD)
*SHogg	Studies in Hogg and His World (James Hogg Soc., Univ. of Stirling)
*ShQ	Shakespeare Quarterly (Folger Shakespeare Library, Washington, DC)
*ShS	Shakespeare Survey: an annual survey of Shakespearean studies and production (Cambridge)
*ShSt	Short Story (Columbia, SC)
*SIcon	Studies in Iconography (Kalamazoo, MI)
*SidJ	Sidney Journal (Univ. of Guelph, Ont.)
*Signs	Signs: journal of women in culture and society (Chicago, IL)
*SILTA	Studi italiani di linguistica teorica e applicata (Ospedaletto)
*SixCJ	Sixteenth-Century Journal: the journal of early modern studies (Truman State Univ., Kirksville, MO)
*SJ	Shakespeare Jahrbuch (Deutsche Shakespeare-Gesellschaft, Bochum)
*SJL	Southern Journal of Linguistics (Dept of English, Univ. of North Carolina at Charlotte)- continues SECOL Review
*SlavR	Slavic Review: American quarterly of Soviet and East European studies (Stanford, CA)
*SLI	Studies in the Literary Imagination (Georgia State Univ., Atlanta)
*SmAx	Small Axe (Indiana Univ., Bloomington)
*SNL	Shakespeare Newsletter (Dept of English, Iona College, New Rochelle, NY)
*SoCR	South Carolina Review (Clemson Univ., Clemson, SC)
*SocT	Social Text (Rutgers Univ., New Brunswick, NJ)

*SoCult	Southern Cultures (Center for the Study of the South, Univ. of North Carolina, Chapel Hill)
*Soglie	Soglie: rivista quadrimestrale di poesia e critica letteraria (Badia, Pisa)
*SoLJ	Southern Literary Journal (Dept of English, Univ. of North Carolina, Chapel Hill)
*SondR	Sondheim Review (Milwaukee, WI)
*SoQ	Southern Quarterly (Univ. of Southern Mississippi, Hattiesburg)
*SoR	Southern Review (State Univ. of Louisiana, Baton Rouge)
*SoS	Southern Studies (Northwestern State Univ. of Louisiana, Natchitoches)
*Soundings	Soundings: an interdisciplinary journal (Soc. for Values in Higher Education, Georgetown Univ., Washington, DC; Univ. of Tennessee, Knoxville)
*Southerly	Southerly (English Assn, Sydney)
*SP	Studies in Philology (Chapel Hill, NC)
*SPC	Studies in Popular Culture (Dept of English, Middle Tennessee State Univ., Murfreesboro)
*Spec	Speculum: a journal of medieval studies (Medieval Academy of America, Cambridge, MA)
SpenR	Spenser Review (Macalester College, St Paul, MN)
SPR	Southern Poetry Review (Univ. of North Carolina & Central Piedmont Community College, Charlotte)
*Spring	Spring: the journal of the e. e. cummings Society (Flushing, NY)
*SR	Studies in Romanticism (Boston Univ., Boston, MA)
*SRASP	Shakespeare and Renaissance Association of West Virginia: selected papers (Marshall Univ., Huntington, VA)
*SS	Scandinavian Studies (Lawrence, KS)
*SSE	Sydney Studies in English (Univ. of Sydney)
*SStud	Shakespeare Studies (Madison, NJ)
*SStudT	Shakespeare Studies (Shakespeare Soc. of Japan, Tokyo)
*StAN	Studies in American Naturalism (International Theodore Dreiser Soc.; Univ. of North Carolina, Wilmington)
*StCS	Stephen Crane Studies (Dept of English / Stephen Crane Soc., Virginia Polytechnic Inst. and State Univ., Blacksburg)
*Storytelling	Storytelling: a critical journal of popular narrative (Washington, DC)
*StudCanL	Studies in Canadian Literature / Études en littérature canadienne (Univ. of New Brunswick, Fredericton)
*StudECC	Studies in Eighteenth-Century Culture (American Soc. for Eighteenth-Century Studies) (Baltimore, MD)
*StudN	Studies in the Novel (Univ. of North Texas, Denton)
*Style	Style (Northern Illinois Univ., DeKalb)
*SubStance	SubStance: a review of theory and literary criticism (Univ. of Wisconsin, Madison)
SwJL	Southwest Journal of Linguistics: the journal of the Linguistic Association of the Southwest (Dept of English, Texas Tech Univ., Lubbock)
*SwSt	Swift Studies: annual of the Ehrenpreis Centre for Swift Studies (Münster)
*Symbiosis	Symbiosis: a journal of Anglo-American literary relations (College of St Mark and St John, Plymouth)
Symposium	Symposium: a quarterly journal in modern literatures (Washington, DC)
*Talisman	Talisman: a journal of contemporary poetry and poetics (Jersey City, NJ)
TBR	Texas Books in Review (Stephenville, TX)
*TDR	TDR / The Drama Review: the journal of performance studies (Cambridge, MA)
*Te Reo	Te Reo: journal of the Linguistic Society of New Zealand (Auckland)

TEJ	Tennessee English Journal (Tennessee Tech Univ., Cookeville)
*Tessera	Tessera (Univ. of Quebec)
*TexP	Textual Practice (London)
TexR	Texas Review: humanities in the South (Division of English, Sam Houston State Univ., Huntsville, TX)
*TextC	Textual Cultures: text, contexts, interpretation (Soc. for Textual Scholarship) (Bloomington, IN)
*Textus	Textus: English studies in Italy (Genoa)
*TFSB	Tennessee Folklore Society Bulletin (Middle Tennessee State Univ., Murfreesboro)
Theater	Theater (Yale School of Drama / Yale Repertory Theater, New Haven, CT)
*TheatreS	Theatre Survey: the journal of the American Society for Theatre Research (Dept of Drama, Catholic Univ. of America, Washington, DC)
*THJ	Thomas Hardy Journal (Thomas Hardy Soc., Dorchester)
*THQ	Tennessee Historical Quarterly (Tennessee Historical Soc., Nashville)
*ThSym	Theatre Symposium: a journal of the Southeastern Theatre Conference (Tuscaloosa, AL)
*TJ	Theatre Journal (Assn for Theatre in Higher Education) (Baltimore, MD)
*TLS	Times Literary Supplement (London)
*TMR	The Medieval Review (Univ. of Michigan, Ann Arbor) (http://www.hti.umich.edu/b/bmr/tmr.html)
*TN	Theatre Notebook (Soc. for Theatre Research, London)
*Topia	Topia (McGill Univ., Montreal)
*Transition	Transition (Cambridge, MA)
*TransLit	Translation and Literature (Edinburgh)
*TRB	Tennyson Research Bulletin (Tennyson Soc., Lincoln)
*TRC	Theatre Research in Canada (Univ. of Toronto)
*TRev	Tampa Review: literary journal of the University of Tampa (Tampa, FL)
*TRI	Theatre Research International (Oxford)
*TriQ	TriQuarterly: an international journal of arts, letters, and opinions (Northwestern Univ., Evanston, IL)
*TSB	Thoreau Society Bulletin (Lincoln, MA)
*TSLL	Texas Studies in Literature and Language (Austin, TX)
*TSWL	Tulsa Studies in Women's Literature (Univ. of Tulsa, OK)
*TT	Theatre Topics (Baltimore, MD)
*UC	Upstart Crow: a Shakespeare journal (Dept of English, Clemson Univ., Clemson, SC)
Uncoverings	Uncoverings: the research papers of the American Quilt Society (Lincoln, NE)
*VH	Vermont History (Vermont Historical Soc., Montpelier)
*VIA	VIA: voices in Italian America (Chicago, IL)
*VicR	Victorian Review (Victorian Studies Assn of Western Canada, Univ. of Lethbridge, Alta)
*VIJ	Victorians Institute Journal: Victorian literature, art, and culture (Victorians Inst., Depts of English, Virginia Commonwealth Univ., Richmond, and Univ. of Richmond)
*VLC	Victorian Literature and Culture (New York)
*VLT	Velvet Light Trap (Austin, TX)
*VN	Victorian Newsletter (Western Kentucky Univ., Bowling Green)

*VoicesNY	Voices: journal of the New York Folklore Society (Schenectady, NY)
*VP	Victorian Poetry (Univ. of West Virginia, Morgantown)
*VPR	Victorian Periodicals Review (Niwot, CO)
*VQR	Virginia Quarterly Review: a national journal of literature and discussion (Univ. of Virginia, Charlottesville)
*VS	Victorian Studies: an interdisciplinary journal of social, political, and cultural studies (Univ. of Indiana, Bloomington)
*VWM	Virginia Woolf Miscellany (Southern Connecticut State Univ., New Haven)
*WAL	Western American Literature: quarterly journal of the Western Literature Association (Utah State Univ., Logan)
WCJ	Writing Center Journal (National Writing Centers Assn, Merrimack College, North Andover, MA)
*WCPMN	Willa Cather Pioneer Memorial and Educational Foundation Newsletter and Review (Omaha, NE)
*WCWR	William Carlos Williams Review (Univ. of Texas, Austin)
*WD	Writer's Digest (Cincinnati, OH)
WeBr	West Branch (Bucknell Univ., Lewisburg, PA)
*WebS	Weber Studies: voices and viewpoints of the contemporary West (Ogden, UT)
*Wellsian	Wellsian: the journal of the H. G. Wells Society (Reading)
*WF	Western Folklore (California Folklore Soc., Long Beach)
*WI	Word & Image: a journal of verbal/visual enquiry (London)
*Wildean	Wildean: the journal of the Oscar Wilde Society (Kingston upon Thames)
*WJBS	Western Journal of Black Studies (Washington State Univ., Pullman)
*WL	Women and Language (Fairfax, VA)
*WLA	War, Literature, and the Arts (US Air Force Academy, Colorado Springs, CO)
*WLT	World Literature Today: a literary quarterly of the University of Oklahoma (Norman, OK)
WMH	Wisconsin Magazine of History (State Historical Soc. of Wisconsin, Madison)
*WordsC	Wordsworth Circle (New York Univ.)
*WorldE	World Englishes: journal of English as an international and intranational language (Oxford)
*WRB	Women's Review of Books (Center for Research on Women, Wellesley, MA)
*Writing	Writing (Stamford, CT)
*WS	Women's Studies: an interdisciplinary journal (New York)
*WSA	Woolf Studies Annual (Pace Univ., New York)
*WSJ	Wallace Stevens Journal (Wallace Stevens Soc., Clarkson Univ., Potsdam, NY)
*WVUPP	West Virginia University Philological Papers (Morgantown)
*WWQR	Walt Whitman Quarterly Review (Dept of English, Univ. of Iowa, Iowa City)
*WWr	Women's Writing: the Elizabethan to Victorian period (Wallingford, Oxon.)
*XavR	Xavier Review: a journal of literature and culture (Xavier Univ., New Orleans, LA)
*XCP	XCP: cross-cultural poetics (College of St Catherine, Minneapolis, MN)
*YER	Yeats Eliot Review: an independent journal of scholarship, criticism, and opinion (Little Rock, AR)

*YES	Yearbook of English Studies (Modern Humanities Research Assn) (Leeds)
YJLH	Yale Journal of Law and the Humanities (New Haven, CT)
*YLG	Yale University Library Gazette (New Haven, CT)
YLM	Yale Literary Magazine (New Haven, CT)
*YREAL	REAL: yearbook of research in English and American literature (Tübingen)
ZYZZYVA	ZYZZYVA (San Francisco, CA)

ANNUAL BIBLIOGRAPHY OF ENGLISH LANGUAGE AND LITERATURE

2006

BIBLIOGRAPHY

GENERAL STUDIES

1. Brockman, William S. *Ulysses*: bibliography revisited. *In* (pp. 171–91) **16699**.

2. Cormack, Bradin; Mazzio, Carla. Book use, book theory 1500–1700. Chicago, IL: Univ. of Chicago Library, 2005. pp. xi, 124. (Exhibition catalogue.) Rev. by Jennifer A. Smith in Comitatus (37) 2006, 234–5.

3. Finkelstein, David; McCleery, Alistair. An introduction to book history. (Bibl. 2005, 9.) Rev. by Ann R. Hawkins in SHARP (15:2/3) 2006, 15; by Wallace B. Eberhard in JoH (32:3) 2006, 180.

4. —— —— (eds). The book history reader. (Bibl. 2004, 90018.) London; New York: Routledge, 2006. pp. xiii, 561. (Second ed.: first ed. 2002.)

5. Grieve, Tom. The textual rendition: socio-material criticism reconsidered. PBSA (100:1) 2006, 5–24.

6. Horan, Elizabeth Rosa. Dickinson scholars: Willis Buckingham, discoveries of a bibliographer. *See* **9870**.

7. Howsam, Leslie. Old books and new histories: an orientation to studies in book and print culture. Toronto; Buffalo, NY; London: Toronto UP, 2006. pp. xi, 111. (Studies in book and print culture.)

8. McMullin, B. J. The Book of Common Prayer and the bibliographer. *See* **4782**.

9. Myers, Robin; Harris, Michael; Mandelbrote, Giles (eds). Owners, annotators and the signs of reading. (Bibl. 2005, 19.) Rev. by David McKitterick in TLS, 17 Mar. 2006, 28; by Tom Lockwood in Library (7:3) 2006, 337–9.

10. Newman, Donald J. *The Female Spectator*: a bibliographic essay. *In* (pp. 212–41) **7884**.

11. Pearson, David. Books as history: changing values in a digital age. PBSA (100:4) 2006, 405–24.

12. Sharpe, Richard. Thomas Tanner (1674–1735), the 1697 catalogue, and *Bibliotheca Britannica*. Library (6:4) 2005, 381–421.

BINDING

13. Bennett, Stuart. Trade bookbinding in the British Isles 1660–1800. (Bibl. 2004, 32.) Rev. by Nicholas Pickwoad in Library (6:4) 2005, 464–5; by Joseph Newman in PBSA (99:4) 2005, 623–4; by Thomas E. Kinsella in AJ (16) 2005, 352–4.

14. Boss, Thomas G. Bound to be the best: the Club Bindery: catalogue of an exhibition at the Grolier Club. Boston, MA: Thomas G. Boss Fine Books, 2004. pp. 137. Rev. by Deborah Whiteman in PBSA (100:1) 2006, 134–7.

15. Cohen, Claudia. Book binding ephemera. Seattle, WA: Claudia Cohen, 2005. 1 vol. (unpaginated). (Limited ed. of 30 copies.) Rev. by Robert J. Desmarais in Amphora (143) 2006, 20.

16. Foot, Mirjam M. Bookbinders at work. New Castle, DE: Oak Knoll Press; London: British Library, 2006. pp. viii, 163. Rev. by Anthony Hobson in TLS, 2 June 2006, 30.

17. —— (ed.). Eloquent witnesses: bookbindings and their history. A volume of essays dedicated to the memory of Dr Phiroze Randeria. (Bibl. 2005, 30.) Rev. by Samuel Ellenport in PBSA (99:4) 2005, 634–5; by Margaret M. Smith in JPHS (ns 8) 2005, 60–1.

18. Grossman, Jonathan H. Anne Elliot bound up in Northanger Abbey: the history of the joint publication of Jane Austen's first and last complete novels. *See* **9027**.

19. Krupp, Andrea. Bookcloth in England and America, 1823–50. PBSA (100:1) 2006, 25–87.

20. Lock, Margaret. Bookbinding materials and techniques, 1700–1920. (Bibl. 2005, 34.) Rev. by Karen Osborne in JPHS (ns 8) 2005, 62–3.

21. Pearson, David. English bookbinding styles, 1450–1800: a handbook. (Bibl. 2005, 35.) Rev. by Mirjam Foot in Library (7:2) 2006, 207–8; by Consuela Metzger in SHARP (15:2/3) 2006, 20; by John P. Chalmers in PBSA (100:4) 2006, 475–7.

22. Smith, Helen. 'This one poore blacke gowne lined with white': the clothing of the sixteenth-century English book. *In* (pp. 195–208) **4629**.

23. Socarides, Alexandra. Rethinking the fascicles: Dickinson's writing, copying, and binding practices. *See* **9894**.

BOOK ILLUSTRATION

24. Allingham, Philip V. The illustrations in Dickens's *The Haunted Man and the Ghost's Bargain*: public and private spheres and spaces. *See* **9693**.

25. Bain, Iain. The correspondence of Thomas Bewick. *In* (pp. 23–50) **56**.

26. Barchas, Janine. Apollo, Sappho, and – a grasshopper?! A note on the frontispieces to *The Female Spectator*. *In* (pp. 60–71) **7884**.

27. Barrett, Robert R. How John Carter became Flash Gordon. *See* **14923**.

28. —— Illustrated by J. Allen St John: the Edgar Rice Burroughs, Inc. editions. *See* **14924**.

29. —— An incomplete list of the illustrations of Dorothy Dulin. *See* **14925**.

30. —— *Tarzan and the Madman* and Reed Crandall: thoughts and remembrances. *See* **14926**.

31. Battegazzore, Miguel Angel. A Cubo-Futurist reading of Dickens: Rafael Barradas's 1921 illustrations for *Hard Times*. *See* **9701**.

32. Bredehoft, Thomas A. Comics architecture, multidimensionality, and time: Chris Ware's *Jimmy Corrigan: the Smartest Kid on Earth*. MFS (52:4) 2006, 869–90.

33. Bristow, Joseph. 'The Armytage–Tomson–Watson sequence': poetic illustrations in the periodical press, 1886–96. *See* **11461**.

34. Brown, Gillian. The metamorphic book: children's print culture in the eighteenth century. *See* **7410**.

35. Buchanan-Brown, John. Early Victorian illustrated books: Britain, France, and Germany, 1820–1860. New Castle, DE: Oak Knoll Press, 2005. pp. 304. Rev. by William Vaughan in PrQ (23:3) 2006, 334–5.

36. Cannon, Walter W. From willow cabin to dark house: *Twelfth Night* and the poetics of indoor spaces. *In* (pp. 162–73) **5577**.

37. Chute, Hillary. An interview with Alison Bechdel. MFS (52:4) 2006, 1004–13.

38. Cole, Sarah Rose. The aristocrat in the mirror: male vanity and bourgeois desire in William Makepeace Thackeray's *Vanity Fair*. *See* **11414**.

39. Cooke, Simon. 'The ever-shifting kaleidoscope of the imagination': modern illustrations to the Brontës. *See* **9230**.

40. Cordery, Gareth (ed.). An Edwardian's view of Dickens and his illustrators: Harry Furniss's *Sketch of Boz*. *See* **9722**.

41. Couch, N. C. Christopher; Weiner, Stephen. The Will Eisner companion: the pioneering spirit of the father of the graphic novel. Introd. by Dennis O'Neill. Afterword by Denis Kitchen. New York: DC Comics, 2004. pp. 174.

42. Coughlan, David. Paul Auster's *City of Glass*: the graphic novel. *See* **14513**.

43. Davies, Martin. A tale of two Aesops. *See* **4120**.

44. Davis, Paul Preston (ed.). Howard Pyle: his life, his work: a comprehensive bibliography and pictorial record of Howard Pyle, illustrator, author, teacher, father of American illustration, America's foremost illustrator. Preface by Stephen T. Bruni. Foreword by Howard Pyle Brokaw. *See* **11060**.

45. De Angelis, Valerio Massimo. Super-ambassadors: how comic-book heroes export American values (or do they?). QPS (14) 2006, 353–64.

46. Dietrich, Bryan D. Queen of Pentacles: archetyping Wonder Woman. Extrapolation (47:2) 2006, 207–36.

47. Di Liddo, Annalisa. Paesaggi vittoriani: le due anime di Londra nei romanzi a fumetti di Alan Moore. *In* (pp. 338–48) **7343**.

48. Dixon, Hugh. Thomas Bewick at 250: landmarks in the building of a reputation. *In* (pp. 9–21) **56**.

49. Dong, Lan. Writing Chinese America into words and images: storytelling and retelling of *The Song of Mu Lan*. *See* **17088**.

50. Donlon, Pat. Sophia Rosamond Praeger (1867–1954): a woman of many talents. *In* (pp. 240–55) **648**.

51. Downes, Stephanie. Fashioning Christine de Pizan in Tudor defences of women. *See* **4777**.

52. Drew, Ned; Sternberger, Paul. By its cover: modern American book cover design. *See* **139**.

53. Driver, Martha W. The image in print: book illustration in late medieval England and its sources. (Bibl. 2005, 62.) Rev. by Yu-Chiao Wang in Library (6:4) 2005, 459–60; by Mary C. Olson in SixCJ (37:2) 2006, 475–6; by Sue Powell in JEBS (9) 2006, 175–7; by Judith Collard in Parergon (23:1) 2006, 155–7; by Richard K. Emmerson in Spec (81:3) 2006, 838–40.

54. Emad, Mitra C. Reading Wonder Woman's body: mythologies of gender and nation. *See* **1093**.

55. Gardner, Jared. Archives, collectors, and the new media work of comics. *See* **16804**.

56. Gardner-Medwin, David (ed.). Bewick studies: essays in celebration of the 250th anniversary of the birth of Thomas Bewick 1753–1828. London: British Library for the Bewick Soc., 2003. pp. 160. Rev. by Jane R. Pomeroy in PBSA (99:4) 2005, 625–7.

57. Gerald, Kelly. The world of the cartoons and their importance to O'Connor's fiction. *In* (pp. 26–41) **17825**.

58. Goldman, Paul. Beyond decoration: the illustrations of John Everett Millais. (Bibl. 2005, 75.) Rev. by Stephen Wildman in PrQ (23:1) 2006, 83–4.

59. —— John Everett Millais: illustrator and narrator. With an essay by Tessa Sidey. Aldershot; Burlington, VT: Lund Humphries in assn with Birmingham Museums and Art Gallery, 2004. pp. 71. (Exhibition catalogue.) Rev. by Maroussia Oakley in JPHS (ns 8) 2005, 61–2; by Stephen Wildman in PrQ (23:1) 2006, 83–4; by Julia Thomas in JPRS (15:1) 2006, 98–9.

60. Goldman, Victoria Sears. Evolution of a dream-child: images of Alice and changing conceptions of childhood. *See* **9422**.

61. Graham, Kathryn V. The Devil's own art: topiary in children's fiction. *See* **13668**.

62. Groves, David. 'This class of impostors': Robert Cromek's view of London booksellers and engravers. *See* **9670**.

63. Guignery, Vanessa. The destabilisation of genre in Alain de Botton's iconotexts. *See* **15430**.

64. Hall, Joanne. The wanderer contained: issues of 'inside' and 'outside' in relation to Harold Gray's *Little Orphan Annie* and Marilynne Robinson's *Housekeeping*. *See* **18270**.

65. Hallam, Elizabeth. Speaking to reveal: the body and acts of 'exposure' in early modern popular discourse. *In* (pp. 239–62) **4629**.

66. Hamilton, Margaret. The ABC book of Australian children's illustrators. Sydney: ABC for the Australian Broadcasting Corporation, 2005. pp. 37.

67. Hansen, Thomas S. Classic book jackets: the design legacy of George Salter. Foreword by Milton Glaser. New York: Princeton Architectural Press, 2005. pp. 200. Rev. by Peter Mitham in Amphora (142) 2006, 39–40.

68. Hatfield, Charles. Alternative comics: an emerging literature. (Bibl. 2005, 85.) Rev. by Hillary Chute in MFS (52:4) 2006, 1014–27.

69. —— Comic art, children's literature, and the new comics studies. LU (30:3) 2006, 360–82.

70. HEER, JEET; WORCESTER, KENT (eds). Arguing comics: literary masters on a popular medium. (Bibl. 2005, 87.) Rev. by Louis Phillips in GaR (60:3/4) 2006, 840–3.

71. HOWERTON, PHILLIP. The shrouded mountaintop: intertextuality and the misreading of Thoreau's *Ktaadn*. *See* **11431**.

72. HUGHES, JAMIE A. 'Who watches the watchmen?': ideology and 'real world' superheroes. JPC (39:4) 2006, 546–57.

73. INGERSOLL, EARL G. Doris Lessing's *Playing the Game*. *See* **17125**.

74. JONES, GERARD. Men of tomorrow: geeks, gangsters, and the birth of the comic book. (Bibl. 2005, 91.) Rev. by Laura Hilton in JPC (39:6) 2006, 1096–7; by Nancy Northcott in CLAQ (31:2) 2006, 205–7.

75. JONES, SUSAN. Conrad on the borderlands of Modernism: Maurice Greiffenhagen, Dorothy Richardson and the case of *Typhoon*. *In* (pp. 195–211) **15280**.

76. KNAPP, JAMES A. The bastard art: woodcut illustration in sixteenth-century England. *In* (pp. 151–72) **661**.

77. KOBYASHI, KAZUE. The evolution of the *Arabian Nights* illustrations: an art-historical review. *In* (pp. 171–93) **10714**.

78. LESTER, VALERIE BROWNE. Phiz: the man who drew Dickens. (Bibl. 2005, 97.) Rev. by Anthony Burton in Dickensian (102:1) 2006, 54–6.

79. MCLAUGHLIN, JEFF (ed.). Comics as philosophy. Jackson; London: Mississippi UP, 2005. pp. xix, 246. Rev. by John Shelton Lawrence in JAC (29:4) 2006, 510–12.

80. MALAY, JESSICA L. Isabella Whitney, 'Sister Eldershae', and Cheshire recusancy. *See* **5149**.

81. MARCHANT, JENNIFER. 'Exactly as it was'? H. R. Millar's expansions and subversions of the Psammead trilogy. *In* (pp. 231–53) **17738**.

82. MARTINSON, BARBARA. The journey to school: illustrations from popular American magazines, 1900–1962. *In* (pp. 93–108) **3157**.

83. MAYNARD, JOHN. Two mad-dog Englishmen in the Corfu sun: Lawrence Durrell and Edward Lear. *In* (pp. 255–69) **15631**.

84. MILBURN, COLIN. Nanowarriors: military nanotechnology and comic books. Intertexts (9:1) 2005, 77–103.

85. MILROY, ROLLIN. Emerging from the willows. *See* **16187**.

86. MITCHELL, J. LAWRENCE. Covering Mr Weston. *See* **18132**.

87. MORRIS, FRANKIE. The *Alice* drawings: copies, forgeries, and Tenniel's originals. *See* **9426**.

88. —— Artist of Wonderland: the life, political cartoons, and illustrations of Tenniel. (Bibl. 2005, 103.) Rev. by Richard D. Altick in TLS, 4 Aug. 2006, 22; by Jan Susina in CLAQ (31:2) 2006, 202–5.

89. MORRIS, TOM; MORRIS, MATT (eds). Superheroes and philosophy: truth, justice, and the Socratic way. (Bibl. 2005, 105.) Rev. by John Shelton Lawrence in JAC (29:4) 2006, 510–12.

90. Moscati, Camillo. Giorgio De Gaspari, Italian artist. Trans. by Numeriano Rodenas. *See* **14943**.

91. Nicol, David. The title-page of *The World Tossed at Tennis*: a portrait of a Jacobean playing company? *See* **6369**.

92. Nielsen, Leon; Jørgensen, Jan. Axel Mathiesen: Burroughs' Danish artist. *See* **14946**.

93. O'Brien, Sheila Ruzycki. 'There is no arguing with *pictures*': stretching the canvas of gender in the art portraits, picture-language, and the original illustrations in *Uncle Tom's Cabin*. *See* **11360**.

94. op de Beeck, Nathalie. Suspended animation: picture book storytelling, twentieth-century childhood, and William Nicholson's *Clever Bill*. *See* **17757**.

95. Oropeza, B. J. (ed.). The Gospel according to superheroes: religion and pop culture. New York; Frankfurt: Lang, 2005. pp. xii, 295.

96. Oswald, Emily. Imagining race: illustrating the poems of Paul Laurence Dunbar. *See* **9970**.

97. Pollin, Burton R. When is a Church not a Church? *See* **11041**.

98. Pomeroy, Jane R. Alexander Anderson (1775–1870), wood engraver and illustrator: an annotated bibliography. New Castle, DE: Oak Knoll Press; Worcester, MA: American Antiquarian Soc., 2005. 3 vols. pp. lxxxvi, 2514. Rev. by Laura Wasowicz in Book (68) 2006, 4.

99. —— A new bibliography of the work of wood engraver and illustrator Alexander Anderson. PAAS (115:2) 2005, 317–48.

100. Quinn, Peter. 'Their strongest pine': Thomas Bewick and regional identity in the late nineteenth century. *In* (pp. 111–30) **56**.

101. Reimer, Stephen R. The Urry *Chaucer* and George Vertue. *See* **4342**.

102. Robertson, Mark. From Walton to Gormenghast. *See* **17979**.

103. Romero Jódar, Andrés. The quest for a place in culture: the verbal-iconical production and the evolution of comic-books towards graphic novels. EIUC (14) 2006, 93–110.

104. Ryan, Jennifer D. Black female authorship and the African American graphic novel: historical responsibility in *Icon: a Hero's Welcome*. MFS (52:4) 2006, 918–46.

105. Ryskamp, Charles. The first illustrations to *John Gilpin*. *See* **7681**.

106. Saltman, Judith; Edwards, Gail. Towards a history of design in Canadian children's illustrated books. *See* **13686**.

107. Schroeder, Natalie; Holt, Shari Hodges. The gin epidemic: gin distribution as a means of control and profit in Dickens's early nonfiction and *Oliver Twist*. *See* **9818**.

108. Sears, Victoria. Evolution of a dream-child: images of Alice and changing conceptions of childhood. *See* **9428**.

109. Sironval, Margaret. The image of Sheherazade in French and English editions. *In* (pp. 219–44) **10714**.

110. Soper, Kerry. From swarthy ape to sympathetic everyman and subversive trickster: the development of Irish caricature in American comic strips between 1890 and 1920. JAStud (39:2) 2005, 257–96.

111. Sorensen, Lita. Bryan Talbot. New York: Rosen Central, 2005. pp. 112. (Library of graphic novelists.)

112. Spurlock, J. David (comp.). Grand master of adventure: the drawings of J. Allen St John. Somerset, NJ: Vanguard, 2005. pp. 176. Rev. by Robert R. Barrett in BurB (63) 2005, 28–31.

113. Stern, Jeffrey; Wakeling, Edward. The workwoman's guide to 'the working man's cap'. *See* **9431**.

114. Tattersfield, Nigel. Alexander Anderson, the first American wood engraver: a brief sketch of his early career and his debt to Thomas and John Bewick. *In* (pp. 85–94) **56**.

115. Teorey, Matthew. Escaping the lion's paw: jungle cat imagery and late nineteenth-century political reform. *See* **16053**.

116. Valkeakari, Tuire. Huck, Twain, and the freedman's shackles: struggling with *Huckleberry Finn* today. *See* **11529**.

117. Vegh, Beatriz. Dickens and Barradas in Madrid, 1921: a hospitable meeting. *See* **9833**.

118. Walker, Brian. The comics before 1945. New York: Abrams, 2004. pp. 336.

119. Walsh, Richard. The narrative imagination across media. MFS (52:4) 2006, 855–68.

120. Wiltshire, Irene. *Pickwick* and the pirates. *See* **9839**.

121. Wolf-Meyer, Matthew Joseph. Batman and Robin in the nude; or, Class and its exceptions. Extrapolation (47:2) 2006, 187–206.

122. Wootton, Sarah. Consuming Keats: nineteenth-century representations in art and literature. *See* **10674**.

123. Yamanaka, Yuriko; Nishio, Tetsuo (eds). *The Arabian Nights* and Orientalism: perspectives from East and West. *See* **10714**.

BOOK PRODUCTION, PRINTING, TYPOGRAPHY

124. Anon. Alpenhouse Apparitions' powers of book design. Amphora (144) 2006, 26–31.

125. Baines, Phil. Penguin by design: a cover story, 1935–2005. (Bibl. 2005, 141.) Rev. by Douglas Martin in SHARP (15:1) 2006, 6; by Peter Mitham in Amphora (143) 2006, 21–2.

126. —— Haslam, Andrew. Type and typography. New York: Watson-Guptill, 2005. pp. 224. Rev. by Irene Tichenor in PBSA (100:2) 2006, 281–3.

127. Baker, Peter S. Typing in Old English since 1967: a brief history. OEN (40:1) 2006, 28–37.

128. Berek, Peter. Genres, early modern theatrical title pages, and the authority of print. *In* (pp. 159–75) **4731**.

129. Birdsall, Derek. Notes on book design. New Haven, CT; London: Yale UP, 2004. pp. xii, 236. Rev. by Rollin Milroy in Amphora (142) 2006, 42–4.

130. Bringhurst, Robert. The elements of typographic style. (Bibl. 2000, 250.) Point Roberts, WA: Hartley & Marks, 2004. pp. 382. (Third ed.: first ed. 1992.) Rev. by Jerry Kelly in PBSA (100:1) 2006, 137–8.

131. Calabresi, Bianca F. C. ‘Red incke’: reading the bleeding on the early modern page. *In* (pp. 237–64) **661**.

132. Carlson, David R. A theory of the early English printing firm: jobbing, book publishing, and the problem of productive capacity in Caxton’s work. *In* (pp. 35–68) **4125**.

133. Coldiron, A. E. B. Taking advice from a Frenchwoman: Caxton, Pynson, and Christine de Pizan’s moral proverbs. *In* (pp. 127–66) **4125**.

134. Creesy, Charles. Monticello: the history of a typeface. PrH (25:1) 2006, 3–19.

135. Davies, Martin. A tale of two Aesops. *See* **4120**.

136. Davis, Erin K. Printing at the fair: the printing exhibits at the 1904 Louisiana Purchase International Exposition. PBSA (99:3) 2005, 427–43.

137. Donovan, Stephen K. Research journals: toward uniformity or retaining diversity? *See* **941**.

138. Doubleday, Richard B. Jan Tschichold, designer: the Penguin years. New Castle, DE: Oak Knoll Press; Aldershot: Lund Humphries, 2006. pp. xxi, 218.

139. Drew, Ned; Sternberger, Paul. By its cover: modern American book cover design. New York: Princeton Architectural Press, 2005. pp. 192. Rev. by Rebecca Seltzer in PubRQ (22:3) 2006, 56–7.

140. Egan, Gabriel. ‘As it was, is, or will be played’: title-pages and the theatre industry to 1610. *In* (pp. 92–110) **5334**.

141. Frasca, Ralph. Benjamin Franklin’s printing network: disseminating virtue in early America. Columbia; London: Missouri UP, 2006. pp. ix, 295. Rev. by Charles E. Clark in JAH (93:3) 2006, 839–40; by Julie Hedgepeth Williams in JoH (32:1) 2006, 52–3.

142. Gillespie, Alexandra. ‘Folowynge the trace of mayster Caxton’: some histories of fifteenth-century printed books. *In* (pp. 167–95) **4125**.

143. Gingell, Susan. ‘Always a poem, once a book’: motivations and strategies for print textualizing of Caribbean Canadian dub and performance poetry. *See* **13754**.

144. Green, James N.; Stallybrass, Peter. Benjamin Franklin: writer and printer. *See* **7807**.

145. Gurr, Andrew. Editing Stefano’s book. *See* **6126**.

146. Halkyard, Stella. [Foot]notes toward a supreme fiction: Stevens, Frank Kermode, and the John Rylands University Library. *See* **18637**.

147. Harris, Elizabeth M. Personal impressions: the small printing press in nineteenth-century America. Boston, MA: Godine; London: Merrion Press, 2004. pp. 200. Rev. by Gabriel Rummonds in PBSA (100:3) 2006, 379–82.

148. Henry, Anne. *Quid ais omnium?* Maurice Kyffin’s 1588 *Andria* and the emergence of suspension marks in printed drama. *See* **4895**.

149. Holmes, Heather. Scottish agricultural writers and the creation of their personal identities between 1697 and 1790. *See* **6474**.

150. Holzenberg, Eric; Pena, J. Fernando. Lasting impressions: the Grolier Club Library. (Bibl. 2005, 163.) Rev. by Leslie A. Morris in PBSA (99:4) 2005, 636–8; by William Butts in MSS (58:1) 2006, 57–60.

151. Howard-Hill, T. H. Early modern printers and the standardization of English spelling. *See* **1327**.

152. Hudson, Graham. Artistic printing: a re-evaluation. JPHS (ns 9) 2006, 31–63.

153. Kindel, Eric. Patents progress: the Adjustable Stencil. JPHS (ns 9) 2006, 65–92.

154. Kuskin, William. Introduction: following Caxton's trace. *In* (pp. 1–31) **4125**.

155. —— (ed.). Caxton's trace: studies in the history of English printing. *See* **4125**.

156. Lee, Marshall. Bookmaking: editing/design/production. (Bibl. 2005, 167.) Rev. by Louise Ellis-Barrett in LPub (19:4) 2006, 311–14.

157. Lerer, Seth. Caxton in the nineteenth century. *In* (pp. 325–70) **4125**.

158. Lesser, Zachary. Typographic nostalgia: play-reading, popularity, and the meanings of black-letter. *In* (pp. 99–126) **4731**.

159. Lucas, Peter J. Abraham Wheelock and the presentation of Anglo-Saxon: from manuscript to print. *In* (pp. 383–439) **199**.

160. McMullin, B. J. The eighth edition of Scott's *Lay of the Last Minstrel*. *See* **11147**.

161. —— Some notes on paper and format. BSANZB (28:4) 2004, 92–104.

162. Mannheimer, Katherine. To the letter: the material text as space of adjudication in Pope's *The First Satire of the Second Book of Horace*. *See* **8061**.

163. Maxwell, Julie. A reference to the Ur-*Hamlet* in a compositor's error. *See* **5745**.

164. Milroy, Rollin. The architecture of Charnel House. Amphora (144) 2006, 32–5.

165. Orgel, Stephen. The book of the play. *In* (pp. 13–54) **5334**.

166. Parrish, Paul A. Front matters: Crashaw in the seventeenth century. *See* **6668**.

167. Reid, Robert R. Publications of the Alcuin Society. *See* **854**.

168. Saltman, Judith; Edwards, Gail. Towards a history of design in Canadian children's illustrated books. *See* **13686**.

169. Smith, Helen. 'This one poore blacke gowne lined with white': the clothing of the sixteenth-century English book. *In* (pp. 195–208) **4629**.

170. Smith, Pamela S. Passions in print: private press artistry in New Mexico. *See* **878**.

171. Stoicheff, Peter; Taylor, Andrew (eds). The future of the page. (Bibl. 2005, 183.) Rev. by Germaine Warkentin in Library (6:4) 2005, 472–5; by Liz Jones in ColLit (33:3) 2006, 216–20; by Charlotte C. Morse in JEBS (9) 2006, 200–2; by Alice Gambrell in TextC (1:2) 2006, 177–9.

172. Straznicky, Marta (ed.). The book of the play: playwrights, stationers, and readers in early modern England. *See* **4731**.

173. Suzuki, Toshiyuki. A note on the errata to the 1590 quarto of *The Faerie Queene*. *See* **5121**.

174. Thomson, Ellen Mazur. The graphic forms lectures. PrH (25:1) 2006, 42–55.

175. Vita, Carlo. Sterne e un *ready made* del Settecento: un percorso di lettura. *See* **8183**.

176. Wallace, Andrew. Reading the 1590 *Faerie Queene* with Thomas Nashe. *See* **5125**.

177. Woudhuysen, H. R. A Shelley pamphlet come to light. *See* **11234**.

178. Zurcher, Andrew. Getting it back to front in 1590: Spenser's dedications, Nashe's insinuations, and Ralegh's equivocations. *See* **5131**.

MANUSCRIPTS

179. Alexander, Christine. Arthur Bell Nicholls and the Adamson saga: new discoveries of Brontë memorabilia. *See* **9175**.

180. Alger, Abdullah. Two drypoint etchings in the Exeter Book. NQ (53:2) 2006, 153–4.

181. Barker, Nicolas. To the four winds: what price our literary heritage? TLS, 23 June 2006, 14–15.

182. Bawcutt, Priscilla. *Sir Lamwell* in Scotland. *In* (pp. 83–93) **3972**.

183. Baxter, Katherine Isobel. Fleshing out the bones: two new manuscript leaves of *Falk*. *See* **15244**.

184. —— *The Rescuer* synopsis: a transcription and commentary. *See* **15245**.

185. Berkhout, Carl T. Another late Middle English lyric. *See* **4035**.

186. Boffey, Julia; Edwards, A. S. G. Manuscripts and audience. *In* (pp. 34–50) **4345**.

187. Brantley, Jessica. The visual environment of Carthusian texts: decoration and illustration in Notre Dame 67. *In* (pp. 173–216) **3871**.

188. Bredehoft, Thomas A. Filling the margins of CCCC 41: textual space and a developing archive. RES (57:232) 2006, 721–32.

189. Bryan, Elizabeth J. Amazons and Ursulines. *In* (pp. 21–30) **3896**.

190. Bryan, Eric Shane. Prognostications by thunder in the zodiac: MSS Trinity R.14.52, Sloane 636, and PML M.775. *See* **4083**.

191. Büttner, Frank O. (ed.). The illuminated Psalter: studies in the content, purpose and placement of its images. Turnhout: Brepols, 2004. pp. viii, 616.

192. Casey, Jim. Unfinished business: the termination of Chaucer's Cook's Tale. *See* **4377**.

193. Centerwall, Brandon. *Caracalla*: a new play by George Chapman, in his hand. *See* **6637**.

194. Corradini, Erika. Text and context of a late Old English homily: the Exeter additions to manuscript Cambridge, Corpus Christi College 421. *In* (pp. 77–88) **3407**.

195. Cox, Arthur J. The *Drood* remains revisited: the title-page. *See* **9728**.

196. Crick, Julia; Walsham, Alexandra (eds). The uses of script and print, 1300–1700. (Bibl. 2004, 210.) Rev. by Andrew Cambers in SixCJ (37:1) 2006, 151–3.

197. Deeming, Helen. The songs of St Godric: a neglected context. *See* **4138**.

198. Doane, A. N. The Werden Glossary: structure and sources. *In* (pp. 41–84) **199**.

199. —— Wolf, Kirsten (eds). *Beatus vir*: studies in early English and Norse manuscripts in memory of Phillip Pulsiano. Tempe: Arizona Center for Medieval and Renaissance Studies, 2006. pp. xxix, 549. (Medieval & Renaissance texts & studies, 319.)

200. —— *et al.* (eds). Anglo-Saxon manuscripts in microfiche facsimile: interim index (volumes 1–10). Tempe: Arizona Center for Medieval and Renaissance Studies, 2005. pp. 186. (Medieval & Renaissance texts & studies, 309.)

201. Donoghue, Daniel. A point well taken: manuscript punctuation and Old English poems. *In* (pp. 38–58) **1241**.

202. Doyle, A. I. The copyist of MSS Bodley 283 and Durham Cosin V.ii.15. JEBS (9) 2006, 125–9.

203. Doyle, Kara A. Thisbe out of context: Chaucer's female readers and the Findern Manuscript. *See* **4466**.

204. Easting, Robert. St Patrick's Purgatory: fragments of a second copy of the Middle English stanzaic *Owayne Miles*. *See* **4042**.

205. Eckhardt, Joshua. 'Love-song weeds, and Satyrique thornes': anti-courtly love poetry and Somerset libels. *See* **4834**.

206. Edwards, A. S. G. The contexts of Notre Dame 67. *In* (pp. 107–28) **3871**.

207. Fisher, Celia. Flowers in medieval manuscripts. (Bibl. 2005, 236.) Rev. by Albrecht Classen in TMR, Feb. 2006; by Julie Hotchin in SixCJ (37:2) 2006, 633.

208. Franzen, Christine. On the attribution of additions in Oxford, Bodleian MS Bodley 343 to the Tremulous Hand of Worcester. ANQ (19:1) 2006, 7–8.

209. Fredell, Joel. 'Go litel quaier:' Lydgate's pamphlet poetry. *See* **4214**.

210. Garvey, Ellen Gruber. Anonymity, authorship, and recirculation: a Civil War episode. *See* **8775**.

211. Geddes, Jane. The St Albans Psalter: a book for Christina of Markyate. London: British Library, 2005. pp. 136. Rev. by Jessica Brantley in JEBS (9) 2006, 180–2.

212. Gillespie, Raymond; Refaussé, Raymond (eds). The medieval manuscripts of Christ Church Cathedral, Dublin. Dublin; Portland, OR: Four Courts Press, 2006. pp. 192, (plates) 4.

213. Gillespie, Stuart. A new eighteenth-century Juvenal translator: William Popple's Satires vi and x. *See* **8076**.

214. Gillespie, Vincent. The haunted text: reflections in *A Mirror to Devout People*. *In* (pp. 129–72) **3871**.

215. Gouws, John. Nicholas Oldisworth, Richard Bacon, and the practices of Caroline friendship. *See* **7094**.

216. GRODEN, MICHAEL. Before and after: the manuscripts in textual and genetic criticism of *Ulysses*. *In* (pp. 152–70) **16699**.

217. GROSSI, JOSEPH L., JR. 'Wher ioye is ay lastyng': John Lydgate's *contemptus mundi* in British Library MS Harley 2255. *See* **4217**.

218. GRUND, PETER. A previously unrecorded fragment of the Middle English *Short Metrical Chronicle* in Bibliotheca Philosophica Hermetica M199. *See* **4041**.

219. HALL, DAVID D. Scribal publication in seventeenth-century New England: an introduction and checklist. PAAS (115:1) 2005, 29–80.

220. HALL, J. R. Three studies on the manuscript text of *Beowulf*: lines 47a, 747a, and 2232a. *In* (pp. 441–70) **199**.

221. HALL, MARK F. Manuscript variations of Rudyard Kipling's *Of Swine*. *See* **16907**.

222. HANNA, RALPH. Lambeth Palace Library MS 260 and some aspects of Northern book history. JEBS (9) 2006, 131–40.

223. HAVENS, EARLE. Notes from a literary underground: recusant Catholics, Jesuit priests, and scribal publication in Elizabethan England. *See* **4597**.

224. HILL, JOYCE. Identifying 'texts' in Cotton Julius E.vii: medieval and modern perspectives. *In* (pp. 27–40) **199**.

225. HILMO, MAIDIE. Medieval images, icons, and illustrated English literary texts from the Ruthwell Cross to the Ellesmere Chaucer. (Bibl. 2005, 258.) Rev. by Karla Taylor in SIcon (27) 2006, 223–6; by John C. Hirsh in Spec (81:2) 2006, 532–3.

226. HOROBIN, SIMON. A new fragment of the *Romaunt of the Rose*. *See* **4482**.

227. IOPPOLO, GRACE. Dramatists and their manuscripts in the age of Shakespeare, Jonson, Middleton and Heywood: authorship, authority, and the playhouse. *See* **511**.

228. JACKSON, MACD. P. John Webster, James Shirley, and the Melbourne manuscript. *See* **7181**.

229. KELLER, DEAN H.; GILGENBACH, CARA (comps). A catalogue of the B. George Ulizio Collection in the Kent State University Libraries. *See* **337**.

230. KIERNAN, KEVIN. Odd couples in Ælfric's *Julian and Basilissa* in British Library Cotton MS Otho B.x. *In* (pp. 85–106) **199**.

231. KING, ANDREW. 'Well grounded, finely framed, and strongly trussed up together': the 'medieval' structure of *The Faerie Queene*. *In* (pp. 119–52) **5100**.

232. KNOWLES, JAMES. 'Songs of baser alloy': Jonson's *Gypsies Metamorphosed* and the circulation of manuscript libels. *See* **6880**.

233. LUCAS, PETER J. Abraham Wheelock and the presentation of Anglo-Saxon: from manuscript to print. *In* (pp. 383–439) **199**.

234. MCFADDEN, BRIAN. Sweet odors and interpretative authority in the Exeter Book *Physiologus* and *Phoenix*. *See* **3796**.

235. MCGERR, ROSEMARIE. A statute book and Lancastrian mirror for princes: the Yale Law School manuscript of the *Nova statuta Angliae*. TextC (1:2) 2006, 6–59.

236. McGowan, Joseph P. Elliptical glossing and elliptical compounds in Old English. *In* (pp. 359–81) **199**.

237. McKitterick, David (ed.). The Trinity Apocalypse (Trinity College Cambridge, MS R.16.2). Toronto; Buffalo, NY; London: Toronto UP, 2005. pp. xv, 173, (plates) 24.

238. McRae, Andrew. Reading libels: an introduction. *See* **6431**.

239. Mann, Jill; Nolan, Maura (eds). The text in the community: essays on medieval works, manuscripts, authors, and readers. *See* **3871**.

240. Matsuda, Takami; Linenthal, Richard A.; Scahill, John (eds). The medieval book and a modern collector: essays in honour of Toshiyuki Takamiya. (Bibl. 2005, 286.) Rev. by Susan Powell in Library (7:2) 2006, 203–5; by Simon Horobin in JEBS (9) 2006, 191–3.

241. Mellinkoff, Ruth. Averting demons: the protective power of medieval visual motifs and themes. Los Angeles, CA: Ruth Mellinkoff, 2004. 2 vols. pp. 195; 328. Rev. by Louise Marshall in Spec (81:3) 2006, 891–3.

242. Millman, Jill Seal, *et al.* (eds). Early modern women's manuscript poetry. Introd. by Elizabeth Clarke and Jonathan Gibson. *See* **4760**.

243. Mooney, Linne R. Chaucer's scribe. *See* **4427**.

244. Morgan, Nigel (ed.). Prophecy, apocalypse and the Day of Doom: proceedings of the 2000 Harlaxton Symposium. Stamford: Tyas, 2004. pp. xii, 403, (plates) 91. (Harlaxton medieval studies, 12.) Rev. by John C. Hirsh in MÆ (75:1) 2006, 129–30; by Bryan P. Davis in JEBS (9) 2006, 194–6.

245. Morini, Carla. The Old English *Apollonius* and Wulfstan of York. *See* **3729**.

246. Motion, Andrew. Such attics cleared of me: saving writers' manuscripts for the nation. *See* **356**.

247. Muir, Bernard J. Issues for editors of Anglo-Saxon poetry in manuscript form. *In* (pp. 181–202) **1241**.

248. Nichols, Ann Eljenholm. Pepys Library MS 2125: the *Arma Christi* stubs. JEBS (9) 2006, 117–24.

249. O'Callaghan, Michelle. Performing politics: the circulation of the *Parliament Fart*. *See* **6437**.

250. Orchard, Andy. Computing Cynewulf: the *Judith*-connection. *In* (pp. 75–106) **3871**.

251. Owens, Rebekah. Thomas Kyd and the letters to Puckering. *See* **4894**.

252. Peikola, Matti. Lollard (?) production under the looking glass: the case of Columbia University, Plimpton Add. MS 3. JEBS (9) 2006, 1–23.

253. Pons-Sanz, Sara M. Anglo-Scandinavian trade or paganism? OE *hæðen* in the First Cleopatra Glossary. *See* **1569**.

254. Powell, Kathryn. Meditating on men and monsters: a reconsideration of the thematic unity of the *Beowulf* manuscript. *See* **3756**.

255. Prescott, Andrew. What's in a number? The physical organization of the manuscript collections of the British Library. *In* (pp. 471–525) **199**.

256. Raabe, Wesley. The text of *Eli's Education*: from manuscript to *St Nicholas* magazine. *See* **8969**.

257. RAND, KARI ANNE. A previously unnoticed fragment of John of Burgundy's plague tract and some connected pest regimens. *See* **4086**.

258. RAY, JOAN KLINGEL; WHEELER, RICHARD JAMES. James Stanier Clarke's portrait of Jane Austen. *See* **9065**.

259. REDFORD, PETER. Correspondence in the Burley Manuscript: a conjecture. *See* **6745**.

260. REID-BAXTER, JAMIE. Elizabeth Melville's letters in Edinburgh University Library, Laing III.347. *See* **6653**.

261. REINERT, LAURA. A Middle English text on planting and grafting in Cambridge, Trinity College, O.5.26. *See* **4087**.

262. ROBERTS, JANE. Guide to scripts used in English writings up to 1500. *See* **1335**.

263. RUDOLF, WINFRIED. The source and textual identity of 'homily' Napier XXXI – Ælfric & the *munuccild* of Saint-Maurice d'Agaune. *See* **3718**.

264. RUST, MARTHA. An exposition of women's names in British Library Harley MS 3362. JEBS (9) 2006, 141–8.

265. RUST, MARTHA DANA. 'Le Vostre C': letters and love in Bodleian Library MS Arch. Selden B.24. *In* (pp. 111–38) **4523**.

266. SANDLER, LUCY. The Lichtenthal Psalter and the manuscript patronage of the Bohun family. (Bibl. 2004, 287.) Rev. by Lynda Dennison in Spec (81:3) 2006, 915–18.

267. SAUER, MICHELLE M. Saints Praxedis and Prudentiana in *The Golden Legend* and *The Stacions of Rome*: fragments from Lambeth Palace 72 and MS BL Additional 22283. *See* **4048**.

268. SCOTT-STOKES, CHARITY. Women's books of hours in medieval England: selected texts translated from Latin, Anglo-Norman French and Middle English, with introduction and interpretive essay. Woodbridge, Suffolk; Rochester, NY: Brewer, 2006. pp. xii, 187. (Library of medieval women.)

269. SMITH, EMILY. The local popularity of *The Concealed Fansyes*. *See* **6634**.

270. SMITH, MARTHA NELL. That never told CAN be: May Swenson's manuscript witnesses. *In* (pp. 107–19) **7907**.

271. SMITH, NICHOLAS D. Unpublished poems by Hannah More in Osborn Shelves C.341 and Folger MS M.a.179. *See* **8020**.

272. SOCARIDES, ALEXANDRA. Rethinking the fascicles: Dickinson's writing, copying, and binding practices. *See* **9894**.

273. STANLEY, LIZ. The writing of David Hume's *My Own Life*: the persona of the philosopher *manqué*. *See* **7893**.

274. STEPHENSON, JOSEPH F. On the markings in the manuscript of *Sir John Van Olden Barnavelt*. *See* **6801**.

275. THIJS, CHRISTINE. Levels of learning in Anglo-Saxon Worcester: the evidence re-assessed. *See* **3695**.

276. TREHARNE, ELAINE. Reading from the margins: the uses of Old English homiletic manuscripts in the post-Conquest period. *In* (pp. 329–58) **199**.

277. TWYCROSS, MEG. The *ordo paginarum* revisited, with a digital camera. *In* (pp. 105–31) **3913**.

278. Wakelin, Daniel. The carol in writing: three anthologies from fifteenth-century Norfolk. *See* **4028**.

279. Walmsley, John (ed.). Inside Old English: essays in honour of Bruce Mitchell. *See* **1241**.

280. Watson, Andrew G. Medieval manuscripts in post-medieval England. (Bibl. 2004, 309.) Rev. by Andrew Cambers in SixCJ (37:1) 2006, 110–11.

281. Watts, Cedric. Keats's *Bright Star* and *A Lover's Complaint*. *See* **10670**.

282. Wieland, Gernot R. British Library, MS Royal 15 A.v.: one manuscript or three? *In* (pp. 1–25) **199**.

283. Wilcox, Jonathan. The audience of Ælfric's *Lives of Saints* and the face of Cotton Caligula A.xiv, fols 93–130. *In* (pp. 229–63) **199**.

284. Zapedowska, Magdalena. A lesson in grammar: Dickinson's *Grasped by God* and *Drowning Is Not So Pitiful*. *See* **9898**.

285. Znojemská, Helena. A *scop* among scribes: a reading in the manuscript context of *Widsið*. *See* **3810**.

COLLECTING AND THE LIBRARY

286. Anon. The British Library catalogue of George Bernard Shaw papers. *See* **18487**.

287. —— Documents on Zora Neale Hurston from the Barnard College Archives. *See* **16519**.

288. —— Selected recent acquisitions briefly noted. YLG (80:3/4) 2006, 177–83. (Beinecke Rare Book and Manuscript Library.)

289. Aikin, Jane. Women and intellectual resources: interpreting print culture at the Library of Congress. *In* (pp. 179–207) **690**.

290. Bain, Iain. The correspondence of Thomas Bewick. *In* (pp. 23–50) **56**.

291. Barker, Nicolas. To the four winds: what price our literary heritage? *See* **181**.

292. Barnard, Toby. Libraries and collectors, 1700–1800. *In* (pp. 111–34) **724**.

293. Barrett, Maurie. The great hunt for Governor General's Literary Award winners. Amphora (144) 2006, 14–15.

294. Beedell, A. V.; Harvey, A. D. Bulwer Lytton letters in the National Archives. *See* **10762**.

295. Behrendt, Stephen C. Regency women writers, the archives, and the task(s). *See* **8290**.

296. Bellew, Deborah Fox. Discovering the fiction of Frances Hodgson Burnett. *In* (pp. 205–15) **9300**.

297. Boran, Elizabethanne. Libraries and collectors, 1550–1700. *In* (pp. 91–110) **724**.

298. Bradstock, Margaret. Echoes of Ada Cambridge. *See* **9377**.

299. Butterworth, Richard. The Library goes live! *See* **3029**.

300. Caie, Graham. Bringing the John Murray Archive to the National Library of Scotland. *See* **9328**.

301. Carley, James P. The books of King Henry VIII and his wives. Preface by David Starkey. (Bibl. 2004, 338.) Rev. by Joseph Black in TMR, June 2006;

by Dakota L. Hamilton in SixCJ (37:2) 2006, 473–5; by Alan Bryson in SHARP (15:2/3) 2006, 13; by Sue Powell in JEBS (9) 2006, 171–4; by David M. Head in Historian (68:2) 2006, 378–9.

302. Claghorn, George S. Transcribing a difficult hand: collecting and editing Edwards' letters over thirty-five years. *In* (pp. 217–27) **7762**.

303. Clapinson, Mary. The Bodleian Library and its readers, 1602–1652. BLR (19:1) 2006, 30–46.

304. Cloonan, Michele V. Alice Millard and the gospel of beauty and taste. *In* (pp. 159–78) **690**.

305. Coates, Alan, *et al.* Catalogue of books printed in the fifteenth century now in the Bodleian Library. (Bibl. 2005, 371.) Rev. by Richard A. Linenthal in BLR (19:1) 2006, 21–8.

306. Connor, T. P. Malignant reading: John Squier's Newgate Prison library, 1642–46. Library (7:2) 2006, 154–84.

307. Cotsen, Margit Sperling. The Beatrix Potter collection of Lloyd Cotsen: published on the occasion of his 75th birthday. Introd. and notes by Judy Taylor. Catalogue by Ann Stevenson Hobbs. *See* **18071**.

308. Cotugno, Marianne. Conrad Richter and Karl Goedecker in the archives: the story of an author and a bookseller. *See* **18248**.

309. Danky, James P.; Wiegand, Wayne A. (eds). Women in print: essays on the print culture of American women from the nineteenth and twentieth centuries. Foreword by Elizabeth Long. *See* **690**.

310. Davidson, Paul; Davis, Kristy; Nield, Sophie. The AHRC Mander and Mitchenson Theatre Collection Access for Research Project: conversations with cataloguers. TN (59:3) 2005, 144–64.

311. Davies, Philip John. Viscountess Eccles: an Anglo-American patroness of literature. ContRev (284:1656) 2004, 23–7.

312. Dettmar, Kevin J. H. Bookcases, slipcases, uncut leaves: the anxiety of the gentleman's library. Novel (39:1) 2005, 5–24.

313. Dickinson, Donald C. John Carter: the taste & technique of a bookman. Preface by Sebastian Carter. (Bibl. 2004, 347.) Rev. by Richard W. Clement in PBSA (100:1) 2006, 141–3.

314. Dorney, Kate. Searching for scripts: re-writing the history of British theatre post-1968. *See* **12276**.

315. Ellen, Jane. Cold Wars and culture wars. *See* **11877**.

316. Essick, Robert N. Blake in the marketplace, 2004. *See* **7568**.

317. Feldman, Paula R. Women, literary annuals, and the evidence of inscriptions. *See* **8352**.

318. Fern, Annette. Deconstructing the Goodman: documents of a twentieth-century stage. *See* **12282**.

319. Fisher, Margaret. The music of Ezra Pound. *See* **18083**.

320. Francis, Jane. Changing perspectives in a journey through personal, parochial and schoolmasters' libraries: 1600–1750. *In* (pp. 189–96) **746**.

321. Gardner-Medwin, David. The library of Thomas Bewick. *In* (pp. 51–72) **56**.

322. Gillespie, Raymond. Irish cathedral libraries before 1700. *In* (pp. 176–92) **648**.

323. —— Refaussé, Raymond (eds). The medieval manuscripts of Christ Church Cathedral, Dublin. *See* **212**.

324. Greiner, Donald J. James Dickey's library: a lifetime of poetry and the world of books. *See* **15492**.

325. Halkyard, Stella. [Foot]notes toward a supreme fiction: Stevens, Frank Kermode, and the John Rylands University Library. *See* **18637**.

326. Hammond, Wayne G. Special collections in the service of Tolkien studies. *In* (pp. 331–40) **18804**.

327. Helle, Anita. Lessons from the archive: Sylvia Plath and the politics of memory. *See* **18039**.

328. Hillyard, Brian. David Steuart and Giambattista Bodoni: on the fringes of the British book trade. *In* (pp. 113–25) **746**.

329. Hoare, Peter (gen. ed.). The Cambridge history of libraries in Britain and Ireland: vol. 1, To 1640. Ed. by Elisabeth Leedham-Green and Teresa Webber. Cambridge; New York: CUP, 2006. pp. xx, 688. Rev. by Anthony Hobson in TLS, 8 Dec. 2006, 9–10.

330. —— The Cambridge history of libraries in Britain and Ireland: vol. 2, 1640–1850. Ed. by Giles Mandelbrote and Keith Manley. Cambridge; New York: CUP, 2006. pp. xii, 575. Rev. by Anthony Hobson in TLS, 8 Dec. 2006, 9–10.

331. —— The Cambridge history of libraries in Britain and Ireland: vol. 3, 1850–2000. Ed. by Alistair Black and Peter Hoare. Cambridge; New York: CUP, 2006. pp. xxiv, 737. Rev. by Anthony Hobson in TLS, 8 Dec. 2006, 9–10.

332. Hobson, Anthony. Open shelves. TLS, 8 Dec. 2006, 9–10 (review-article).

333. Hunt, John Dixon. Catalogue. *See* **15864**.

334. Ivory, Yvonne. Oscar Wilde's *The Cardinal of Avignon* and the Oxford definitive edition of his poetry: correspondences and discrepancies. *See* **11609**.

335. Jay, Emma. Queen Caroline's library and its European contexts. BH (9) 2006, 31–55.

336. Jeffrey, Ewan. The outsider: the Michel Saint-Denis Archive: a theatre archive project of the Arts and Humanities Research Council, the University of Sheffield, and the British Library. *See* **12311**.

337. Keller, Dean H.; Gilgenbach, Cara (comps). A catalogue of the B. George Ulizio Collection in the Kent State University Libraries. New Castle, DE: Oak Knoll Press; Kent: Ohio State UP, 2006. pp. xiv, 246.

338. Ker, Neil (ed.). A directory of the parochial libraries of the Church of England and the Church in Wales. Revised by Michael Perkin. London: Bibliographical Soc., 2004. pp. 490. (Revised ed.: first ed. 1959.) Rev. by Joan Williams in BC (54:4) 2005, 611–12.

339. Kerr, Donald Jackson. Amassing treasures for all times: Sir George Grey, colonial bookman and collector. New Castle, DE: Oak Knoll Press; Dunedin: Otago UP, 2006. pp. 351, (plates) 32.

340. Kittredge, Katharine. 'It spoke directly to the heart': discovering the mourning journal of Melesina Trench. *See* **8230**.

341. Knighton, C. S. (ed.). Catalogue of the Pepys Library at Magdalene College, Cambridge: supplementary series: vol. 1. Woodbridge, Suffolk; Rochester, NY: Brewer, 2004. pp. xix, 377.

342. Laroche, Rebecca. Catherine Tollemache's library. NQ (53:2) 2006, 157–8.

343. Lewis, Lucy. Chepman and Myllar: the first printers in Scotland. *In* (pp. 57–69) **746**.

344. —— A newly discovered lyric from Exeter College, Oxford on the theme of 'Know thyself'. *See* **4040**.

345. Lightbourne, Ruth. New Zealand's parliamentary library: its nineteenth-century readers and its book stock. BSANZB (28:4) 2004, 34–48.

346. Lindenbaum, Peter. Dispatches from the archives: the Bates/Williams First Folio and the library it leaves behind. *See* **5194**.

347. Long, Gerald. A twinge of recollection: the National Library in 1904 and thereabouts. Dublin: National Library of Ireland, 2005. pp. 71. (Joyce studies 2004, 18.) Rev. by Edmund L. Epstein in JJLS (20:1) 2006, 10–11.

348. McCarthy, Muriel; Simmons, Ann (eds). The making of Marsh's Library: learning, politics and religion in Ireland, 1650–1750. Dublin; Portland, OR: Four Courts Press, 2004. pp. 288. Rev. by Chris Fauske in ECI (20) 2005, 184–6.

349. MacLeod, Glen. Nathaniel Hawthorne and the Boston Athenaeum. *See* **10386**.

350. Mandelbrote, Giles (ed.). Out of print & into profit: a history of the rare and secondhand book trade in Britain in the 20th century. New Castle, DE: Oak Knoll Press; London: British Library, 2006. pp. 414, (plates) 32.

351. March, Rosemary. Lost: three books from Byron. *See* **9353**.

352. Matsuda, Takami (ed.). *Codices Keionenses*: essays on Western manuscripts and early printed books in Keio University Library. (Bibl. 2005, 430.) Rev. by Carl James Grindley in JEBS (9) 2006, 189–90.

353. Missler, Peter. Gypsy Luke project: preliminary results. *See* **9148**.

354. Monteiro, George. The elder Henry James to a collector: an unpublished letter. *See* **10616**.

355. Mortlock, D. P. Holkham Library: a history and description. Foreword by the Earl of Leicester. [N.p.]: for the Roxburghe Club, 2006. pp. xv, 140.

356. Motion, Andrew. Such attics cleared of me: saving writers' manuscripts for the nation. TLS, 6 Oct. 2006, 14–15.

357. Nelson, Alan H. Calling all (Shakespeare) biographers! Or, A plea for documentary discipline. *In* (pp. 55–67) **5353**.

358. Nicholson, Geoff. Sex collectors. New York: Simon & Schuster, 2006. pp. viii, 274. Rev. by Emily Nussbaum in NYTB, 18 June 2006, 6; by Jonathan Yardley in BkW, 25 June 2006, 2.

359. Ostrowski, Carl. Books, maps and politics: a cultural history of the Library of Congress, 1783–1861. (Bibl. 2004, 8601.) Rev. by Joseph Helminski in AL (78:2) 2006, 413–15.

360. Parks, Stephen, *et al.* (eds). First-line index of English poetry, 1500–1800, in manuscripts of the James M. and Marie-Louise Osborn Collection in the Beinecke Rare Book and Manuscript Library of Yale University. *See* **4764**.

361. Paroissien, David. The Nonesuch Dickens *redux*: a tale of contemporary publishing. *See* **9798**.

362. Pawley, Christine. A 'bouncing babe,' a 'little bastard': women, print, and the Door-Kewaunee Regional Library, 1950–52. *In* (pp. 208–25) **690**.

363. Pollock, Donald. *The Hound of the Baskervilles*, Longman's Colonial Library: a 'new edition'. *See* **9948**.

364. Poole, William. Francis Lodwick's annotations to John Webster's *Academiarum examen* (1654) and John Dury's *Considerations concerning the Present Engagement* (1649). BLR (19:1) 2006, 129–38.

365. Prescott, Andrew. What's in a number? The physical organization of the manuscript collections of the British Library. *In* (pp. 471–525) **199**.

366. Price, John Valdimir. Antiquarian and rare books in London at the beginning of the twenty-first century. RBM (5:1) 2004, 24–37.

367. Roberts, Lewis. Trafficking in literary authority: Mudie's Select Library and the commodification of the Victorian novel. *See* **8710**.

368. Ross, Michael. To sign or to inscribe? *See* **14894**.

369. Rostenberg, Leona; Stern, Madeleine. The changing rare book trade, 1950–2000. RBM (5:1) 2004, 11–23.

370. Severi, Rita. La biblioteca di Oscar Wilde. *See* **11626**.

371. Sherbo, Arthur. From the sale catalogue of the library of William Hazlitt, the essayist. *See* **10417**.

372. Smith, Nicholas D. Hannah More items in the Huntington Library: correspondence and a poem. *See* **8019**.

373. Spevack, Marvin. Isaac D'Israeli's Oxford DCL: romance, speculation, and reality. *See* **9906**.

374. Stalker, Laura. Intramuralia: acquisitions of rare materials, 2004. HLQ (69:2) 2006, 333–52.

375. Stilling, Robert. Between friends: rediscovering the war thoughts of Robert Frost. *See* **16018**.

376. Summit, Jennifer. 'Stable in study': Lydgate's *Fall of Princes* and Duke Humphrey's library. *In* (pp. 207–31) **4231**.

377. Supino, David J. Henry James: a bibliographical catalogue of a collection of editions to 1921. *See* **10607**.

378. Taylor, Dennis. Hardy's copy of Shakespeare's *Othello*. *See* **10335**.

379. Thomas, Jane. 'Forming the literary tastes of the middle and higher classes': Elgin's circulating libraries and their proprietors, 1789–1870. *In* (pp. 91–111) **746**.

380. Thomas, Sylvia. REED and the Record Office: tradition and innovation on the road to access. *In* (pp. 131–9) **3904**.

381. Traue, J. E. Fiction, public libraries and the reading public in colonial New Zealand. BSANZB (28:4) 2004, 84–91.

382. Vancil, David. Some observations about the Samuel Johnson miniature dictionaries in the Cordell Collection. *See* **7959**.

383. Walker, Gregory; Clapinson, Mary; Forbes, Lesley (eds). The Bodleian Library: a subject guide to the collections. (Bibl. 2005, 475.) Rev. by H. R. Woudhuysen in TLS, 3 Feb. 2006, 11.

384. Warkentin, Germaine; Hoare, Peter. Sophisticated Shakespeare: James Toovey and the Morgan Library's 'Sidney' First Folio. *See* **5233**.

385. Wenner, Barbara Britton. Following the trail of Jane Austen's letters. *See* **9090**.

386. Willis, Patricia C. Phillis Wheatley, George Whitefield, and the Countess of Huntingdon in the Beinecke Library. *See* **8249**.

387. Wolf, Edwin, ii; Hayes, Kevin J. The library of Benjamin Franklin. *See* **7813**.

388. Woudhuysen, H. R. Last words from the rhymers. *See* **19451**.

TEXTUAL STUDIES

389. Ackerley, C. J. Obscure locks, simple keys: the annotated *Watt*. Preface by S. E. Gontarski. *See* **14654**.

390. Ackerley, Chris. Samuel Beckett and the geology of the imagination: toward an excavation of *Watt*. *See* **14656**.

391. Alarabi, Nour. *Gondal's Queen* revisited: the importance of Ratchford's edition for interpreting Emily Brontë's religious orientations. *In* (pp. 35–47) **3407**.

392. Altschul, Nadia. The genealogy of scribal versions: a 'fourth way' in medieval editorial theory. TextC (1:2) 2006, 114–36.

393. Angelou, Maya (foreword). *Dust Tracks on a Road*: the restored text established by the Library of America. *See* **16520**.

394. Armand, Louis. From hypertext to vortext: notes on materiality & language. *See* **16649**.

395. —— (ed.). JoyceMedia: James Joyce, hypermedia & textual genetics. *See* **16653**.

396. Atkinson, David. Folk songs in print: text and tradition. *See* **3021**.

397. Baker, Denise N. 'The greatest riddle of the B text' of *Piers Plowman*: why Langland did not scrap the A *Vita*. *In* (pp. 149–63) **3896**.

398. Bammesberger, Alfred. Eight notes on the *Beowulf* text. *In* (pp. 19–37) **1241**.

399. —— Hildeburh's son. *See* **3735**.

400. —— Hrothgar's speech welcoming Beowulf. *See* **3736**.

401. —— A note on *Genesis B*, line 456a. *See* **3776**.

402. —— Old English *guðrinc* in *Beowulf*, 1118b. *See* **3737**.

403. —— Old English *wæteres weorþan* in *Beowulf*, 2791a. *See* **3738**.

404. —— The syntactic analysis of the opening verses in *Beowulf*. *See* **3739**.

405. —— Who does *laþum* refer to at *Beowulf*, line 1257a? *See* **3740**.

406. Barbeau, Jeffrey W. The quest for system: an introduction to Coleridge's lifelong project. *In* (pp. 1–32) **9503**.

407. —— (ed.). Coleridge's assertion of religion: essays on the *Opus Maximum*. *See* **9503**.

408. Barnes, A. W. Editing George Herbert's ejaculations. *See* **6817**.

409. Baxter, Katherine Isobel. Fleshing out the bones: two new manuscript leaves of *Falk*. *See* **15244**.

410. —— *The Rescuer* synopsis: a transcription and commentary. *See* **15245**.

411. Beer, John. Coleridge's *magnum opus* and his *Opus Maximum*. *In* (pp. 281–92) **9503**.

412. Beidler, Peter G. Where's the point? Punctuating Chaucer's *Canterbury Tales*. *In* (pp. 193–203) **4310**.

413. Bell, J. L. Making *Magic*: how L. Frank Baum drafted his penultimate book. *See* **14643**.

414. Berkhout, Carl T. The Old English *Maxims I* 190: *bacum tobreden*. *See* **3785**.

415. Berrie, Phill, *et al.* Authenticating electronic editions. *In* (pp. 269–76) **426**.

416. Bevington, David. One hell of an ending: staging Last Judgment in the Towneley Plays and in *Doctor Faustus* A and B. *In* (pp. 292–310) **3913**.

417. Bigold, Melanie. Elizabeth Rowe's fictional and familiar letters: exemplarity, Enthusiasm, and the production of posthumous meaning. *See* **8124**.

418. Bliss, Jane. The sultan's name in *Generydes* and *Syr Generides*. *See* **1727**.

419. Bloom, Jonathan. The art of revision in the short stories of V. S. Pritchett and William Trevor. *See* **18145**.

420. Bornstein, George. W. E. B. Du Bois and the Jews: ethics, editing, and *The Souls of Black Folk*. *See* **15570**.

421. Bowen, John. Champagne moments. *See* **9577**.

422. Bratman, David. The artistry of omissions and revisions in *The Lord of the Rings*. *In* (pp. 113–38) **18804**.

423. Brown, Cedric C.; Koshi, Tomohiko. Editing the remains of Thomas Traherne. *See* **7146**.

424. Brownlee, Kevin, *et al.* Vernacular literary consciousness *c.*1100–*c.*1500: French, German and English evidence. *In* (pp. 422–71) **3874**.

425. Bryan, Eric Shane. Prognostications by thunder in the zodiac: MSS Trinity R.14.52, Sloane 636, and PML M.775. *See* **4083**.

426. Burnard, Lou; O'Keeffe, Katherine O'Brien; Unsworth, John (eds). Electronic textual editing. New York: Modern Language Assn of America, 2006. pp. vii, 419; 1 CD-ROM.

427. Buzzetti, Dino; McGann, Jerome. Critical editing in a digital horizon. *In* (pp. 53–73) **426**.

428. Case, Mary; Green, David. Rights and permissions in an electronic edition. *In* (pp. 346–57) **426**.

429. Casey, Jim. Unfinished business: the termination of Chaucer's Cook's Tale. *See* **4377**.

430. Cathcart, Charles. John Marston, *The Malcontent*, and the King's Men. *See* **6923**.

431. Centerwall, Brandon. *Caracalla*: a new play by George Chapman, in his hand. *See* **6637**.

432. Centerwall, Brandon S. Who wrote William Basse's *Elegy on Shakespeare*? Rediscovering a poem lost from the Donne canon. *See* **6566**.

433. Chantler, Ashley. Creating an editorial procedure for non-canonical texts. *In* (pp. 49–63) **3407**.

434. Chilcott, Tim. The dating of Clare's *The Shepherd's Calendar*. *See* **9469**.

435. Churchill, Suzanne W. Outing T. S. Eliot. *See* **15680**.

436. Churchwell, Sarah. 'Your sentence was mine too': reading Sylvia Plath in Ted Hughes's *Birthday Letters*. *In* (pp. 260–87) **3405**.

437. Claghorn, George S. Transcribing a difficult hand: collecting and editing Edwards' letters over thirty-five years. *In* (pp. 217–27) **7762**.

438. Cobb, Barbara Mather. Jonson's *Conversations with William Drummond*: a history. *See* **6861**.

439. Cogswell, Thomas. 'The symptomes and vapors of a diseased time': the Earl of Clare and early Stuart manuscript culture. *See* **6839**.

440. Cohen, Edward H. The second series of W. E. Henley's hospital poems. *See* **10428**.

441. Cohen, Milton A. Hemingway's laboratory: the Paris *In Our Time*. *See* **16340**.

442. Corradini, Erika. Text and context of a late Old English homily: the Exeter additions to manuscript Cambridge, Corpus Christi College 421. *In* (pp. 77–88) **3407**.

443. Cox, Arthur J. The *Drood* remains revisited: 'first fancy'. *See* **9727**.

444. —— The *Drood* remains revisited: the title-page. *See* **9728**.

445. Craig, Joanna Hildebrand. Dancing with Hemingway. *See* **16342**.

446. Crane, Greg. Document management and file naming. *In* (pp. 277–90) **426**.

447. Davies, Gwendolyn. Revisiting *Rockbound*: the evolution of a novel. *See* **15429**.

448. Davinroy, Elise. Tomb and womb: reading contexture in Emily Dickinson's *Soft Prison*. *See* **9857**.

449. Deegan, Marilyn. Collection and preservation of an electronic edition. *In* (pp. 358–70) **426**.

450. Deeming, Helen. The songs of St Godric: a neglected context. *See* **4138**.

451. Demers, Patricia. 'Warpe' and 'webb' in the Sidney Psalms: the 'coupled' work of the Countess of Pembroke and Sir Philip Sidney. *In* (pp. 41–58) **3405**.

452. Dille, Catherine. Johnson's *Dictionary* in the nineteenth century: a legacy in transition. *See* **7925**.

453. Doane, A. N.; Wolf, Kirsten (eds). *Beatus vir*: studies in early English and Norse manuscripts in memory of Phillip Pulsiano. *See* **199**.

454. Doll, Dan. 'Like trying to fit a sponge into a matchbox': twentieth-century editing of eighteenth-century journals. *In* (pp. 211–28) **7490**.

455. Donoghue, Daniel. A point well taken: manuscript punctuation and Old English poems. *In* (pp. 38–58) **1241**.

456. Doran, Greg. Sound vision: textual theory and the director. *In* (pp. 43–60) **12336**.

457. Doyle, Brian. A bogey tale. *See* **11288**.

458. Doyno, Victor A. Presentations of violence in *Adventures of Huckleberry Finn*. *See* **11490**.

459. Driscoll, M. J. Levels of transcription. *In* (pp. 254–61) **426**.

460. Durusau, Patrick. Why and how to document your markup choices. *In* (pp. 299–309) **426**.

461. Easting, Robert. St Patrick's Purgatory: fragments of a second copy of the Middle English stanzaic *Owayne Miles*. *See* **4042**.

462. Eaves, Morris. Multimedia body plans: a self-assessment. *In* (pp. 210–23) **426**.

463. Echard, Siân; Partridge, Stephen (eds). The book unbound: editing and reading medieval manuscripts and texts. (Bibl. 2004, 523.) Rev. by Rhiannon Daniels in MLR (101:2) 2006, 500–1; by Greg Waite in ANQ (19:3) 2006, 56–9; by Dario Del Puppo in TextC (1:1) 2006, 96–9.

464. Edwards, A. S. G. The contexts of Notre Dame 67. *In* (pp. 107–28) **3871**.

465. —— Deconstructing Skelton: the texts of the English poems. *See* **5060**.

466. —— F. Scott Fitzgerald, *The Great Gatsby*: 'like an angry diamond'. *See* **15877**.

467. Erwin, Rebecca Schoff. Early editing of Margery Kempe in manuscript and print. *See* **4180**.

468. Eutsey, Dwayne. God's *real* message: *No. 44, The Mysterious Stranger* and the influence of liberal religion on Mark Twain. *See* **11492**.

469. Fenton, Eileen Gifford; Duggan, Hoyt N. Effective methods of producing machine-readable text from manuscript and print sources. *In* (pp. 241–53) **426**.

470. Fisher, Nicholas. The contemporary reception of Rochester's *A Satyr against Mankind*. *See* **7109**.

471. Flanders, Julia. The Women Writers Project: a digital anthology. *In* (pp. 138–49) **426**.

472. Fleming, Robert E. The editing process. *See* **16350**.

473. Fogarty, Anne. Parnellism and the politics of memory: revising *Ivy Day in the Committee Room*. *In* (pp. 104–21) **16695**.

474. Fraistat, Neil; Jones, Steven. The poem and the network: editing poetry electronically. *In* (pp. 105–21) **426**.

475. Francini, Antonella. Mina Loy's prose drafts: the unfinished script of a Modernist. *See* **17286**.

476. Gabler, Hans Walter. Moving a print-based editorial project into electronic form. *In* (pp. 339–45) **426**.

477. Gants, David. Drama case study: *The Cambridge Edition of the Works of Ben Jonson*. *In* (pp. 122–37) **426**.

478. Gillespie, Alexandra. Print culture and the medieval author: Chaucer, Lydgate, and their books, 1473–1557. *See* **4325**.

479. Gillespie, Stuart. A new eighteenth-century Juvenal translator: William Popple's Satires vi and x. *See* **8076**.

480. Goggin, Gerard. Editing Minervas: William Godwin's liminal maneuvers in Mary Wollstonecraft's *Wrongs of Woman*. *In* (pp. 81–99) **3405**.

481. Gonsalves, Joshua David. Problematic figurations of the nation as I-land: a phenomenological report on half-knowledge from 'any isle of Lethe dull'. *See* **10648**.

482. Gooneratne, Yasmine (ed.). *The Village in the Jungle*: revised and annotated in accordance with the original manuscript. *See* **19253**.

483. Gossett, Suzanne. Editing collaborative drama. *See* **5175**.

484. Gouws, John. Nicholas Oldisworth, Richard Bacon, and the practices of Caroline friendship. *See* **7094**.

485. Greenberg, Devorah. Community of the texts: producing the first and second editions of *Acts and Monuments*. *See* **4846**.

486. Groden, Michael. Before and after: the manuscripts in textual and genetic criticism of *Ulysses*. *In* (pp. 152–70) **16699**.

487. —— Problems of annotation in a digital *Ulysses*. *See* **16703**.

488. Grund, Peter. Manuscripts as sources for linguistic research: a methodological case study based on the *Mirror of Lights*. *See* **4085**.

489. —— A previously unrecorded fragment of the Middle English *Short Metrical Chronicle* in Bibliotheca Philosophica Hermetica M199. *See* **4041**.

490. Grylls, David. Gissing's revision of *Thyrza*. *See* **10194**.

491. —— Self and (self-)censorship: Gissing's revision of *The Unclassed*. *See* **10195**.

492. Hagen, Tanya. Thinking outside the Bard: REED, repertory canons, and editing early English drama. *In* (pp. 216–35) **3904**.

493. Hall, J. R. Old English *Exodus* 390b: *witgan larum*. *See* **3773**.

494. —— Three studies on the manuscript text of *Beowulf*: lines 47a, 747a, and 2232a. *In* (pp. 441–70) **199**.

495. Hall, Mark F. Manuscript variations of Rudyard Kipling's *Of Swine*. *See* **16907**.

496. Hanna, Mary. White women's sins; or, Patterns of choice and consequence in the two endings of *Voyage in the Dark*. *See* **18225**.

497. Harding, Jason. 'Eliot without tears'. *See* **15687**.

498. Harmon, William. Tender is *what* night? Surprises in the growth of Fitzgerald's fourth novel. *See* **15879**.

499. Harris, Oliver. Not Burroughs' final fix: materializing *The Yage Letters*. *See* **14955**.

500. Hayman, David. Beckett's *Watt*, the art-historical trace: an archaeological inquest. *See* **14687**.

501. —— How two love letters elicited a singular third person. *In* (pp. 202–12) **14684**.

502. Herman, Luc; Krafft, John M. The evolution of the South-West Africa chapter in Pynchon's *V. See* **18173**.

503. Hessell, Nikki. The opposite of news: rethinking the 1800 *Lyrical Ballads* and the mass media. *See* **11675**.

504. Hickey, Alison. 'The body of my father's writings': Sara Coleridge's genial labor. *In* (pp. 124–47) **3405**.

505. Hill, W. Speed (ed.). New ways of looking at old texts III: papers of the Renaissance English Text Society, 1997–2001. (Bibl. 2005, 587.) Rev. by Gerard Kilroy in RQ (59:2) 2006, 627–8.

506. Holmes, John. Thomas Lodge's *Amours*: the copy-text for imitations of Ronsard in *Phillis*. *See* **4902**.

507. Holmqvist, Ivo. Richard Hughes: an emendation. *See* **16492**.

508. Hopkins, Lisa. A proposed emendation to Ford's *The Broken Heart*. *See* **6802**.

509. Horobin, Simon. A new fragment of the *Romaunt of the Rose*. *See* **4482**.

510. Hughes, Gillian. The Ettrick Shepherd's nephew. *See* **10453**.

511. Ioppolo, Grace. Dramatists and their manuscripts in the age of Shakespeare, Jonson, Middleton and Heywood: authorship, authority, and the playhouse. London; New York: Routledge, 2006. pp. x, 234. (Routledge studies in Renaissance literature and culture, 6.) Rev. by Harold Love in TLS, 19 May 2006, 34; by Tom Lockwood in Library (7:3) 2006, 335–7.

512. Ivory, Yvonne. Oscar Wilde's *The Cardinal of Avignon* and the Oxford definitive edition of his poetry: correspondences and discrepancies. *See* **11609**.

513. Jarvis, Simon. Guides through the park. *See* **9034**.

514. Johnstone, H. Diack. Four lost plays recovered: *The Contrast* and other dramatic works of John Hoadly (1711–1776). *See* **7888**.

515. Johung, Jennifer. Figuring the 'spells' / spelling the figures: Suzan-Lori Parks's 'Scene of Love (?)'. *See* **17964**.

516. Justice, Hilary K. The bones of the others: the Hemingway text from the lost manuscripts to the posthumous novels. *See* **16360**.

517. Kaplan, Carla. Editing an icon. *See* **16527**.

518. Karpovich, Angelina I. The audience as editor: the role of beta readers in online fan-fiction communities. *In* (pp. 171–88) **19868**.

519. Keefer, Michael H. The A and B texts of Marlowe's *Doctor Faustus* revisited. *See* **4928**.

520. Kiernan, Kevin. Digital facsimiles in editing. *In* (pp. 262–8) **426**.

521. —— Odd couples in Ælfric's *Julian and Basilissa* in British Library Cotton MS Otho B.x. *In* (pp. 85–106) **199**.

522. Kimberley, Emma. Textual implications of ekphrasis in contemporary poetry. *In* (pp. 89–99) **3407**.

523. Kinsella, John. Line breaks and back-draft: not a defence of a poem. *See* **16895**.

524. Kirsch, Adam. Good pickings: Elizabeth Bishop's hard-earned mastery. *See* **14791**.

525. Kirschner, Paul. The rancorous coolies in *Typhoon*. *See* **15282**.

526. Klenck, Deborah J. Knuth. Fun and speculation: *Sense and Sensibility* and *Pride and Prejudice* as revisions. *See* **9042**.

527. Knight, Mark. *The Haunted and the Haunters*: Bulwer Lytton's philosophical ghost story. *See* **10767**.

528. Laing, Kathryn. Versions and palimpsests: Rebecca West's *The Sentinel*, *Adela*, and *The Judge*. *In* (pp. 170–85) **19082**.

529. Laubach-Kiani, Philip. 'I close my eyes and try and imagine them': Romantic discourse formations in *Krapp's Last Tape*. *See* **14697**.

530. Lavagnino, John. When not to use TEI. *In* (pp. 334–8) **426**.

531. Lethbridge, J. B. Spenser's last days: Ireland, career, mutability, allegory. *In* (pp. 302–36) **5100**.

532. Levy, Fritz. Behind the back matter: the liminalities of *The Faerie Queene* (1590). *See* **5101**.

533. Lewis, Robert W. The making of *Under Kilimanjaro*. *See* **16368**.

534. Lin, Lidan. From Quigley the writer to Murphy the job seeker: Beckett's evolving vision of characters and plots in *Murphy*. *See* **14698**.

535. Low, Gail. The natural artist: publishing Amos Tutuola's *The Palm-Wine Drinkard* in postwar Britain. *See* **18876**.

536. McCleery, Alistair. The reputation of the 1932 Odyssey Press edition of *Ulysses*. *See* **16723**.

537. McCormack, W. J. Reflections on writing and editing, with reference to National Archives (UK), CO 904/1–3 & HO 161/1–5. *In* (pp. 258–85) **648**.

538. McCue, Jim. Editing Eliot. *See* **15698**.

539. McGavock, Karen. The riddle of his being: an exploration of Peter Pan's perpetually altering state. *In* (pp. 195–215) **14616**.

540. McGinley, Kevin J. The first Edinburgh and London editions of John Home's *Douglas* and the play's early stage history. *See* **7892**.

541. Mandel, Miriam B. Ethics and 'night thoughts': 'truer than the truth'. *See* **16372**.

542. Maner, Martin. The authorship of Jonathan Swift's *A Tale of a Tub* – once more. *See* **8203**.

543. Manseau, Peter. Revising *Night*: Elie Wiesel and the hazards of Holocaust theology. *See* **19147**.

544. Merriam, Thomas. Orthographic changes in *John a Kent* and Hand M of *More*. *See* **4971**.

545. Miller, Linda Patterson. From the 'African book' to *Under Kilimanjaro*: an introduction. *See* **16380**.

546. Moss, Laura. 'Nice audible crying': editions, testimonies, and *Country of My Skull*. *See* **16952**.

547. Muir, Bernard J. Issues for editors of Anglo-Saxon poetry in manuscript form. *In* (pp. 181–202) **1241**.

548. MUNRO, LUCY. Reading printed comedy: Edward Sharpham's *The Fleer*. *In* (pp. 39–58) **4731**.

549. MURRAY, ISOBEL. *The White Bird Passes*: how Jessie Kesson reached the final version. *See* **16850**.

550. NAGLE, CHRISTOPHER. The epistolary passions of sympathy: feeling letters in *Persuasion* and Burney's *The Wanderer*. *See* **9059**.

551. NAVAEI, REZA NAJAFPOUR. *The Lady of Shalott*: a Goethean reading of the text. *In* (pp. 5–12) **3407**.

552. NORRIS, RALPH. Minor sources in Caxton's Roman war. *See* **4128**.

553. NORTON, ANN V. Cordelia and Mrs Crosthwaite: an unpublished chapter of *This Real Night*. *In* (pp. 112–24) **19082**.

554. NORTON, DAVID. A textual history of the King James Bible. *See* **6487**.

555. PACKER, BARBARA. History and form in Emerson's *Fate*. *In* (pp. 432–52) **10064**.

556. PANDA, KEN. *Under Kilimanjaro*: the multicultural Hemingway. *See* **16385**.

557. PARFECT, RALPH. 'God bless my tail!': two unknown fables by Robert Louis Stevenson. *See* **11313**.

558. PAUL, CATHERINE. Marianne Moore: *Observations*. *In* (pp. 422–30) **11788**.

559. PEBWORTH, TED-LARRY. The text of Donne's writings. *In* (pp. 23–34) **6718**.

560. PETERS, MATTHEW. Henry James, American social change, and literary revision. *See* **10590**.

561. PETTITT, THOMAS. Marlowe's texts and oral transmission: towards the *Zielform*. *See* **4936**.

562. PHARAND, MICHEL W. (ed.). Shaw's sex credo. *See* **18500**.

563. PHILLIPS, GEORGE MICAJAH. The Protean text of *Ulysses* and why all editions are equally 'definitive'. *See* **16751**.

564. POOLE, WILLIAM. Marvell's *Ganza's*: an emendation. *See* **6938**.

565. POOLEY, ROGER. Editing *The Pilgrim's Progress*: issues in presenting the early modern text. *In* (pp. 65–76) **3407**.

566. POWERS, LYALL H. (ed.). Henry James at work. By Theodora Bosanquet. With excerpts from her diary and an account of her professional career. *See* **10592**.

567. PRIDMORE, JOSEPH. 'Vindicating the honour of Lancashire': textual variation between editions of James Hanley's *Boy*. *In* (pp. 23–33) **3407**.

568. PRIESTMAN, MARTIN. The progress of society? Darwin's early drafts for *The Temple of Nature*. *In* (pp. 307–19) **7702**.

569. RAABE, WESLEY. The text of *Eli's Education*: from manuscript to *St Nicholas* magazine. *See* **8969**.

570. RAHTZ, SEBASTIAN. Storage, retrieval, and rendering. *In* (pp. 310–33) **426**.

571. RAMSEY, COLIN T. Ann Stephens's *Malaeska*: an unknown early version and some thoughts on dime novels and the gender of readers. *See* **11267**.

572. REFSHAUGE, W. F. Fresh light on A. G. Stephens as editor of Barcroft Boake's works. *See* **9143**.

573. —— *Where the Dead Men Lie. See* **9144**.

574. Reid, S. W. The unpublished typescript version of *A Smile of Fortune. See* **15303**.

575. Richards, Jeffrey. Henry Irving: the actor–manager as *auteur. See* **8593**.

576. Robillard, Douglas. Melville's 'Pale ravener of horrible meat'. *See* **10886**.

577. Robinson, Peter. The *Canterbury Tales* and other medieval texts. *In* (pp. 74–91) **426**.

578. Rogers, Pat. Revisions to Pope's prose works in the *Miscellanies* (1732). *See* **8070**.

579. Roland, Meg. Arthur and the Turks. *See* **4268**.

580. Rossington, Michael. Claire Clairmont's fair copy of Shelley's *Ode to Naples*: a rediscovered manuscript. *See* **11225**.

581. Rowland, Richard. Two plays in one: annotations in the third quarto of *Edward IV. See* **4721**.

582. Ryskamp, Charles. The first illustrations to *John Gilpin. See* **7681**.

583. Sánchez-Martí, Jordi. Reading romance in late medieval England: the case of the Middle English *Ipomedon. See* **3992**.

584. —— Reconstructing the audiences of the Middle English versions of *Ipomedon. See* **3993**.

585. Sauer, Michelle M. Saints Praxedis and Prudentiana in *The Golden Legend* and *The Stacions of Rome*: fragments from Lambeth Palace 72 and MS BL Additional 22283. *See* **4048**.

586. Schachterle, Lance. A long false start: the rejection of chapters of Cooper's *The Bravo* (1831). *See* **9622**.

587. Scull, Christina. What did he know and when did he know it? Planning, inspiration and *The Lord of the Rings. In* (pp. 101–12) **18804**.

588. Shaffer, Elinor. Composing and decomposing the corpus of William Beckford: French and English Beckford. *See* **7546**.

589. Shawcross, John T. Milton in print: a review of some recent editions of *Paradise Lost. See* **7066**.

590. Shillingsburg, Peter. On being textually aware. StAN (1:1/2) 2006, 170–95.

591. —— Publication of Coetzee's *The Humanities in Africa. See* **15225**.

592. Shoptaw, John. Listening to Dickinson. *See* **9893**.

593. Singleton, Antony. The Early English Text Society in the nineteenth century: an organizational history. *See* **3886**.

594. Slater, Michael. 'Invoking' Donne: a grammatical reconstruction of *The Canonization. See* **6752**.

595. Smith, Christopher. Retexts: a review article. *See* **8519**.

596. Smith, Martha Nell. That never told CAN be: May Swenson's manuscript witnesses. *In* (pp. 107–19) **7907**.

597. Smith, Nicholas D. Unpublished poems by Hannah More in Osborn Shelves C.341 and Folger MS M.a.179. *See* **8020**.

598. Smith, Yvonne. In the beginning: David Malouf's *An Imaginary Life*. *See* **17426**.

599. Smyth, Adam. 'Art reflexive': the poetry, sermons, and drama of William Strode (1601?–1645). *See* **7139**.

600. Socarides, Alexandra. Rethinking the fascicles: Dickinson's writing, copying, and binding practices. *See* **9894**.

601. Sotirova, Violeta. Repetition in free indirect style: a dialogue of minds? *See* **17059**.

602. Spencer, Paul. The mystery of *The Red Star of Tarzan*. *See* **14950**.

603. Stamps, Michael W. Peter Whalley: editing Jonson in the eighteenth century. *See* **6905**.

604. Stanley, Liz. The writing of David Hume's *My Own Life*: the persona of the philosopher *manqué*. *See* **7893**.

605. Staples, Joe. 'Discovering' new talent: Charles F. Lummis's conflicted mentorship of Sui Sin Far, Sharlot Hall, and Mary Austin. *See* **17292**.

606. Stauffer, Andrew M. Byronic transmission and the first poem for Caro. *See* **9368**.

607. Steele, Jeremy V. Plato and the love goddess: paganism in two versions of *The Well-Beloved*. *In* (pp. 199–218) **10348**.

608. Steggle, Matthew. *Demoniceacleare* in *The Miseries of Inforst Mariage*. *See* **7193**.

609. —— John Marston's *Entertainment at Ashby* and the 1606 Fleet Conduit eclogue. *See* **6927**.

610. Stone, Marjorie; Thompson, Judith (eds). Literary couplings: writing couples, collaborators, and the construction of authorship. *See* **3405**.

611. Storey, H. Wayne. A question of punctuation and 'ear[s] for dissenting voices': introduction to *Textual Cultures* 1.2. *See* **18051**.

612. Styler, Rebecca. 'What does it matter?': Margaret Oliphant's spiritual autobiography, 1899 and 1990. *In* (pp. 13–22) **3407**.

613. —— Pridmore, Joseph (eds). Textual variations: the impact of textual issues on literary studies. *See* **3407**.

614. Sutherland, Kathryn. On looking into Chapman's *Emma*: how R. W. Chapman's Classicists made Jane Austen a classic. *See* **9078**.

615. Suzuki, Toshiyuki. A note on the errata to the 1590 quarto of *The Faerie Queene*. *See* **5121**.

616. Tadié, Alexis. Perceptions of language in *Lord Jim*. *See* **15318**.

617. Thornton, R. K. R. The raw and the cooked. *See* **9482**.

618. —— What John Clare do we read? *See* **9483**.

619. Trachsler, Richard. How to do things with manuscripts: from Humanist practice to recent textual criticism. TextC (1:1) 2006, 5–28.

620. Turley, Richard Marggraf. Keats, Cornwall and the 'scent of strong-smelling phrases'. *See* **10669**.

621. Vanhoutte, Edward. Prose fiction and modern manuscripts: limitations and possibilities of text encoding for electronic editions. *In* (pp. 161–80) **426**.

622. Van Hulle, Dirk. Authorial translation: Samuel Beckett's *Stirrings Still / Soubresauts*. *In* (pp. 150–60) **426**.

623. Van Kleeck, Justin. Blake's four … *Zoa's*? *See* **7588**.

624. Vitoux, Pierre (trans.). *Constance Chatterley*: la première version de *Lady Chatterley's Lover*. *See* **17062**.

625. Walmsley, John (ed.). Inside Old English: essays in honour of Bruce Mitchell. *See* **1241**.

626. West, William N. Old news: Caxton, de Worde, and the invention of the edition. *In* (pp. 241–74) **4125**.

627. White, Gillian. Awful but cheerful. *See* **14797**.

628. Whittington-Egan, Richard. Living with and annotating Sherlock Holmes. *See* **9955**.

629. Wilkes, G. A. 'Left … to play the ill poet in my own part': the literary relationship of Sidney and Fulke Greville. *See* **5049**.

630. Wittern, Christian. Writing systems and character representation. *In* (pp. 291–8) **426**.

631. Woolley, David. The textual history of *A Tale of a Tub*. *See* **8217**.

632. Zapedowska, Magdalena. A lesson in grammar: Dickinson's *Grasped by God* and *Drowning Is Not So Pitiful*. *See* **9898**.

HISTORY OF PUBLISHING AND BOOKSELLING

633. Adams, David; Armstrong, Adrian (eds). Print and power in France and England, 1500–1800. Aldershot; Burlington, VT: Ashgate, 2006. pp. 157.

634. Adams, Sam. Seren at twenty-five. PNRev (32:5) 2006, 6–8.

635. Adamson, Jane. Talking with oneself and other ostriches. *See* **11269**.

636. Alderson, Brian; de Marez Oyens, Felix. Be merry and wise: origins of children's book publishing in England, 1650–1850. New York: Pierpont Morgan Library for the Bibliographical Soc. of America; New Castle, DE: Oak Knoll Press; London: British Library, 2006. pp. xiv, 318.

637. Amory, Hugh. Bibliography and the book trades: studies in the print culture of early New England. Ed. by David D. Hall. (Bibl. 2005, 754.) Rev. by Sandra M. Gustafson in EAL (41:2) 2006, 347–64.

638. Armstrong, Catherine. 'A just and modest vindication': comparing the responses of the Scottish and English book trades to the Darien Scheme, 1698–1700. *In* (pp. 1–11) **746**.

639. Armstrong, Robert D. 'Impenetrable obscurity': the Comptroller, the Secretary, and Territorial printing. PBSA (99:3) 2005, 411–25.

640. Arnold, John. Fanfrolico frolics. Meanjin (63:3) 2004, 65–74. (Fanfrolico Press.)

641. Bald, Margaret. Literature suppressed on religious grounds. New York: Facts on File, 2006. pp. xxiii, 440. (Facts on File library of world literature) (Banned books.)

642. Barnard, John. First fruits or 'first blights': a new account of the publishing history of Keats's *Poems* (1817). *See* **10633**.

643. Barnard, Toby. Children and books in eighteenth-century Ireland. *In* (pp. 214–38) **648**.

644. —— Print culture, 1700–1800. *In* (pp. 34–58) **724**.

645. Barrett, Robert R. Illustrated by J. Allen St John: the Edgar Rice Burroughs, Inc. editions. *See* **14924**.

646. Bell, Alan. Allen Lane and modern trade publishing. SewR (114:2) 2006, 336–9 (review-article). (Arts and letters.)

647. Bell, Hazel K. Novelist as scholarly editor, mid-twentieth century. *See* **18165**.

648. Benson, Charles; Fitzpatrick, Siobhán (eds). That woman! Studies in Irish bibliography: a Festschrift for Mary 'Paul' Pollard. Dublin: Lilliput Press for the Rare Books Group of the Library Assn of Ireland, 2005. pp. xv, 310. Rev. by David McKitterick in Library (7:2) 2006, 210–11.

649. Berek, Peter. Genres, early modern theatrical title pages, and the authority of print. *In* (pp. 159–75) **4731**.

650. Bergonzi, Bernard. Banville's revenge. *See* **14571**.

651. Blackstock, Allan. Politics and print: a case study. *In* (pp. 234–49) **724**.

652. Borukhov, Boris. *The Phoenix and the Turtle* was published in 1601. *See* **6050**.

653. Bosmajian, Haig A. Burning books. Jefferson, NC; London: McFarland, 2006. pp. 233.

654. Boswell, Jackson Campbell; Holton, Sylvia Wallace. Chaucer's fame in England: *STC* Chauceriana, 1475–1640. *See* **4308**.

655. Bowen, John. Champagne moments. *See* **9577**.

656. Bradshaw, David. Obscenity and censorship. *In* (pp. 103–12) **11788**.

657. Brayman Hackel, Heidi. Reading material in early modern England: print, gender, and literacy. (Bibl. 2005, 780.) Rev. by Tom Lockwood in Library (7:1) 2006, 97–8; by Lissa Beauchamp in SCN (64:1/2) 2006, 50–4; by Joad Raymond in SHARP (15:4) 2006, 13–14; by Fred Schurink in NQ (53:2) 2006, 233–4; by Phyllis R. Brown in RQ (59:1) 2006, 274–5.

658. Brennan, Michael. 'A moment along the way': a venture in publishing Australian poetry. *See* **13707**.

659. Brooks, Douglas A. Inky kin: reading in the age of Gutenberg paternity. *In* (pp. 203–28) **4731**.

660. —— Introduction. *In* (pp. 1–25) **661**.

661. —— (ed.). Printing and parenting in early modern England. Aldershot; Burlington, VT: Ashgate, 2005. pp. xviii, 436. (Women and gender in the early modern world.) Rev. by Juanita Feros Ruys in Parergon (23:2) 2006, 126–8; by David Colclough in JEBS (9) 2006, 168–70; by Phyllis R. Brown in RQ (59:3) 2006, 960–2.

662. Brown, Candy Gunther. The Word in the world: evangelical writing, publishing, and reading in America, 1789–1880. (Bibl. 2004, 762.) Rev. by Renée Bergland in AL (77:4) 2005, 850–2.

663. Brown, Stephen. Scottish Freemasonry and learned printing in the later eighteenth century. *In* (pp. 71–89) **746**.

664. Bruckner, Lynne Dickson. Ben Jonson's branded thumb and the imprint of textual paternity. *In* (pp. 109–30) **661**.

665. Buckridge, Patrick. The age of appreciation: reading and teaching classic literature in Australia in the early twentieth century. ALS (22:3) 2006, 342–56.

666. Buinicki, Martin T. Negotiating copyright: authorship and the discourse of literary property rights in nineteenth-century America. London; New York: Routledge, 2006. pp. xii, 234. (Literary criticism and cultural theory.)

667. Byrne, Paula. Free and easies. *See* **8565**.

668. Caie, Graham. Bringing the John Murray Archive to the National Library of Scotland. *See* **9328**.

669. Calabresi, Bianca F. C. 'Red incke': reading the bleeding on the early modern page. *In* (pp. 237–64) **661**.

670. Capo, Beth Widmaier. 'She is herself a poem': Caresse Crosby, feminine identity, and literary history. *See* **15368**.

671. Carlson, David R. A theory of the early English printing firm: jobbing, book publishing, and the problem of productive capacity in Caxton's work. *In* (pp. 35–68) **4125**.

672. Carpenter, Andrew. Literature in print, 1550–1800. *In* (pp. 301–18) **724**.

673. Carr, Jean Ferguson; Carr, Stephen L.; Schultz, Lucille M. Archives of instruction: nineteenth-century rhetorics, readers, and composition books in the United States. *See* **1881**.

674. Carter, David. 'Some means of learning of the best new books': *All about Books* and the modern reader. *See* **1068**.

675. Cary, Sternick. The Henry Altemus Company: a history and pictorial bibliography. The Woodlands, TX: Sternick, 2005. 1 vol. (various pagings). Rev. by John T. Dizer in DNR (75:1) 2006, 23–4.

676. Cerasulo, Tom. *The Dream Life of Balso Snell* and the vocation of Nathanael West. *See* **19068**.

677. Chilcott, Tim. The dating of Clare's *The Shepherd's Calendar*. *See* **9469**.

678. Chinery, Mary. Wartime fictions: Willa Cather, the Armed Services Editions, and the unspeakable Second World War. *See* **15086**.

679. Christie, Jason. Sampling the culture: 4 notes toward a poetics of plundergraphia and on Kenneth Goldsmith's *Day*. *See* **20239**.

680. Cillerai, Chiara. The eloquence of nature in *Notes on the State of Virginia*. *See* **7905**.

681. Clegg, Cyndia Susan. Checking the father: anxious paternity and Jacobean press censorship. *In* (pp. 291–301) **661**.

682. —— Renaissance play-readers: ordinary and extraordinary. *In* (pp. 23–38) **4731**.

683. Clemens, Jack. Publishing history: birth of the beach book. WD (85:9) 2005, 13.

684. Collins, Billy. My *Howl*. *In* (pp. 100–1) **16122**.

685. COMO, DAVID R. An unattributed pamphlet by William Walwyn: new light on the prehistory of the Leveller movement. *See* **7161**.

686. COONEY, SONDRA MILEY. William Somerville Orr, London publisher and printer: the skeleton in W. & R. Chambers's closet. *In* (pp. 135–47) **746**.

687. COTUGNO, MARIANNE. Conrad Richter and Karl Goedecker in the archives: the story of an author and a bookseller. *See* **18248**.

688. CUNNINGHAM, BERNADETTE. Historical writing, 1660–1750. *In* (pp. 264–81) **724**.

689. CUTTER, MARTHA J. Sui Sin Far's letters to Charles Lummis: contextualizing publication practices for the Asian American subject at the turn of the century. *See* **9980**.

690. DANKY, JAMES P.; WIEGAND, WAYNE A. (eds). Women in print: essays on the print culture of American women from the nineteenth and twentieth centuries. Foreword by Elizabeth Long. Madison; London: Wisconsin UP, 2006. pp. xxi, 308. (Print culture history in modern America.)

691. DARTON, LAWRENCE. The Dartons: an annotated check-list of children's books issued by two publishing houses 1787–1870. Preface and editorial assistance by Brian Alderson. *See* **7413**.

692. DAVIES, MARTIN. A tale of two Aesops. *See* **4120**.

693. DE BELLAIGUE, ERIC (ed.). British book publishing as a business since the 1960s: selected essays. (Bibl. 2005, 809.) Rev. by Ross Alloway in JPHS (ns 9) 2006, 100.

694. DILLE, CATHERINE. Johnson's *Dictionary* in the nineteenth century: a legacy in transition. *See* **7925**.

695. DOUBLEDAY, RICHARD B. Jan Tschichold, designer: the Penguin years. *See* **138**.

696. DREW, NED; STERNBERGER, PAUL. By its cover: modern American book cover design. *See* **139**.

697. DUSSINGER, JOHN A. Fabrications from Samuel Richardson's press. *See* **8093**.

698. —— The negotiations of Sir Charles Grandison. *In* (pp. 32–50) **7255**.

699. EDDY, JACALYN. Bookwomen: creating an empire in children's book publishing, 1919–1939. Madison; London: Wisconsin UP, 2006. pp. x, 211.

700. EGAN, GABRIEL. 'As it was, is, or will be played': title-pages and the theatre industry to 1610. *In* (pp. 92–110) **5334**.

701. ELIAS, A. C., JR. Reissues in the Dublin book trade: the case of George Grierson and William Williamson. *In* (pp. 44–99) **648**.

702. ELIOT, SIMON. What price poetry? Selling Wordsworth, Tennyson, and Longfellow in nineteenth- and early twentieth-century Britain. *See* **11660**.

703. ENGLISH, JAMES F. The economy of prestige: prizes, awards, and the circulation of cultural value. (Bibl. 2005, 819.) Rev. by Elaine Showalter in TLS, 3 Mar. 2006, 12; by Michael North in Mod/Mod (13:3) 2006, 577–8.

704. FEATHER, JOHN. A history of British publishing. (Bibl. 1998, 973.) London; New York: Routledge, 2006. pp. x, 265. (Second ed.: first ed. 1988.)

705. Ferris, Ina. Printing the past: Walter Scott's Bannatyne Club and the antiquarian document. *See* **11138**.

706. Fine, Ruth. The Janus Press, fifty years: *catalogue raisonné* for 1991–2005: indexes for 1995–2005. Burlington: Univ. of Vermont Libraries, 2006. pp. 79. Rev. by Peter Mitham in Amphora (144) 2006, 41–2.

707. Finkelstein, David (ed.). Print culture and the Blackwood tradition, 1805–1930. *See* **1098**.

708. Fleming, Patricia Lockhart; Lamonde, Yvan (gen. eds). History of the book in Canada: vol. 1, Beginnings to 1840. Ed. by Patricia Lockhart Fleming, Giles Gallichan and Yvan Lamonde. (Bibl. 2005, 831.) Rev. by Gregory Klages in CHR (86:3) 2005, 533–5; by Cynthia Sugars in BkCan (34:2) 2005, 14–15; by Kate Eichhorn in Topia (15) 2005, 109–16; by Travis V. Mason in CanL (191) 2006, 155–7.

709. —— —— History of the book in Canada: vol. 2, 1841–1918. Ed. by Yvan Lamonde, Patricia Lockhart Fleming, and Fiona A. Black. (Bibl. 2005, 832.) Rev. by Cynthia Sugars in BkCan (35:8) 2006, 21, 28.

710. Flynn, Philip. Blackwood's *Maga*, Lockhart's *Peter's Letters*, and the politics of publishing. *See* **1102**.

711. Foster, Frances Smith. A narrative of the interesting origins and (somewhat) surprising developments of African American print culture. AmLH (17:4) 2005, 714–40.

712. Frasca, Ralph. Benjamin Franklin's printing network: disseminating virtue in early America. *See* **141**.

713. Gadd, Ian Anders. Were books different? The Stationers' Company in Civil War London, 1640–1645. *In* (pp. 35–58) **728**.

714. Gants, David L. Lists, inventories and catalogues: shifting modes of ordered knowledge in the early modern book trade. *In* (pp. 221–38) **746**.

715. Garnett, Richard. Rupert Hart-Davis Limited: a brief history with a checklist of publications. London: Book Collector; New Castle, DE: Oak Knoll Press, 2004. pp. 93. Rev. by Claire Squires in SHARP (15:1) 2006, 8.

716. Geuder, Ann-Catherine. Chicana/o Literaturbetrieb: Wege in die Öffentlichkeit seit 1965. *See* **11903**.

717. Gillespie, Alexandra. 'Folowynge the trace of mayster Caxton': some histories of fifteenth-century printed books. *In* (pp. 167–95) **4125**.

718. —— Print culture and the medieval author: Chaucer, Lydgate, and their books, 1473–1557. *See* **4325**.

719. Gillespie, Raymond. Print culture, 1550–1700. *In* (pp. 17–33) **724**.

720. —— Reading Ireland: print, reading and social change in early modern Ireland. (Bibl. 2005, 853.) Rev. by Andrew Hadfield in SHARP (15:2/3) 2006, 17.

721. —— Reading print, 1550–1700. *In* (pp. 135–45) **724**.

722. —— Sources for the history of the early modern book in Ireland. *In* (pp. 385–92) **724**.

723. —— Hadfield, Andrew. Introduction: the English-language book in Ireland, *c.*1550–1800. *In* (pp. 1–13) **724**.

724. —— —— (eds). The Irish book in English 1550–1800. Oxford; New York: OUP, 2005. pp. xxi, 477. (Oxford history of the Irish book, 3.) Rev. by S. J. Connolly in SHARP (15:4) 2006, 9–10.

725. Gil Sáenz, Daniel. Reading Diego de San Pedro in Tudor England. *See* **4815**.

726. Going, William T. 'Dr Eliot's five-foot shelf of books': toward a centennial of the Harvard Classics. *See* **3267**.

727. Gokulsing, Tanya. An audience for paper boats: Conrad and the marketing of early Modernism. *See* **15270**.

728. Goldgar, Anne; Frost, Robert I. (eds). Institutional culture in early modern society. Leiden; Boston, MA: Brill, 2004. pp. xxii, 370. (Cultures, beliefs, and traditions, 20.) Rev. by John M. Theilmann in SixCJ (37:1) 2006, 146–8.

729. Grant, Kenneth B. Friendship, finance, and art: Charles Scribner's Sons' relationship with Ernest Hemingway and August Derleth. *See* **16359**.

730. Greco, Albert N., *et al.* The state of scholarly journal publishing: 1981–2000. JSchP (37:3) 2006, 155–214.

731. Grossman, Jonathan H. Anne Elliot bound up in Northanger Abbey: the history of the joint publication of Jane Austen's first and last complete novels. *See* **9027**.

732. Groves, David. 'This class of impostors': Robert Cromek's view of London booksellers and engravers. *See* **9670**.

733. Gump, Steven E. Prestige and the university press. JSchP (37:2) 2006, 69–85.

734. Hadfield, Andrew. Historical writing, 1550–1660. *In* (pp. 250–63) **724**.

735. Hamilton-Emery, Chris. Outtakes and upsurges: starting Salt Publishing. PNRev (32:2) 2005, 8–9.

736. Hammond, Mary. Reading, publishing, and the formation of literary taste in England, 1880–1914. *See* **8382**.

737. Hanna, Robert C. Dickens and plagiarism: part II. *See* **9761**.

738. Hansen, Thomas S. Classic book jackets: the design legacy of George Salter. Foreword by Milton Glaser. *See* **67**.

739. Harms, Dan. Plagiarism, publishing, and the academy. JSchP (38:1) 2006, 1–13.

740. Harris, Elizabeth M. Personal impressions: the small printing press in nineteenth-century America. *See* **147**.

741. Harzewski, Stephanie. Tradition and displacement in the new novel of manners. *In* (pp. 29–46) **19862**.

742. Hess, Scott. Authoring the self: self-representation, authorship, and the print market in British poetry from Pope through Wordsworth. *See* **7129**.

743. Higl, Andrew. Printing power: selling Lydgate, Gower, and Chaucer. *See* **4327**.

744. Hilliard, Chris. The bookmen's dominion: cultural life in New Zealand 1920–1950. *See* **11937**.

745. Hinks, John; Armstrong, Catherine (eds). Printing places: locations of book production & distribution since 1500. (Bibl. 2005, 880.) Rev. by Victoria Gardner in SHARP (15:4) 2006, 10–11.

746. —— —— Worlds of print: diversity in the book trade. New Castle, DE: Oak Knoll Press; London: British Library, 2006. pp. xiii, 240. (Print networks.) Rev. by James Raven in TLS, 20 Oct. 2006, 28.

747. Hoeller, Hildegard. Race, Modernism, and plagiarism: the case of Nella Larsen's *Sanctuary*. *See* **17014**.

748. Holland, Peter; Orgel, Stephen (eds). From performance to print in Shakespeare's England. *See* **5334**.

749. Holmes, Heather. Scottish agricultural writers and the creation of their personal identities between 1697 and 1790. *See* **6474**.

750. Homberger, Eric. New York City and the struggle of the modern. *In* (pp. 314–31) **11776**.

751. Horobin, Simon. A new fragment of the *Romaunt of the Rose*. *See* **4482**.

752. House, Gloria; Weatherston, Rosemary; Ward, Albert M. (eds). A different image: the legacy of Broadside Press: an anthology. *See* **13772**.

753. Howard, June. 'Her very handwriting looks as if she owned the earth': Elizabeth Jordan and editorial power. *In* (pp. 64–76) **690**.

754. Hughes, Gillian. The Ettrick Shepherd's nephew. *See* **10453**.

755. Hunter, Christopher. Reevaluating press freedom in Colonial America. *See* **7809**.

756. Hunter, R. J. John Franckton (d.1620): printer, publisher and bookseller in Dublin. *In* (pp. 2–26) **648**.

757. Jamison, Anne. Collaboration *v.* imitation: authorship and the law. *See* **3286**.

758. Johanningsmeier, Charles. How real American readers originally experienced James's *The Real Thing*. *See* **10570**.

759. Johnson-Woods, Toni. 'Pulp' fiction industry in Australia 1949–1959. *See* **13514**.

760. —— Wonder down under: Australian sci-fi 1948–52. *See* **13515**.

761. Jones, Caroline Viera. A Scottish imprint: George Robertson and *The Australian Encyclopedia*. *In* (pp. 127–33) **746**.

762. Keane, Angela. Richard Carlile's working women: selling books, politics, sex and *The Republican*. *See* **8860**.

763. Kelly, James. Political publishing, 1550–1700. *In* (pp. 194–214) **724**.

764. —— Political publishing, 1700–1800. *In* (pp. 215–33) **724**.

765. Kennedy, Máire. At the Exchange: the eighteenth-century book trade in Cork. *In* (pp. 140–61) **648**.

766. —— Reading print, 1700–1800. *In* (pp. 146–66) **724**.

767. King, Andrew; Plunkett, John (eds). Popular print media, 1820–1900. *See* **8411**.

768. —— —— Victorian print media: a reader. Oxford; New York: OUP, 2005. pp. xiv, 435.

769. Kirsop, Wallace. Cole's Book Arcade: marvellous Melbourne's 'palace of intellect'. *In* (pp. 31–40) **746**.

770. Kitch, Aaron W. Printing bastards: monstrous birth broadsides in early modern England. *In* (pp. 221–36) **661**.

771. Kuskin, William. Introduction: following Caxton's trace. *In* (pp. 1–31) **4125**.

772. —— 'Oncly imagined': vernacular community and the English press. *In* (pp. 199–240) **4125**.

773. —— (ed.). Caxton's trace: studies in the history of English printing. *See* **4125**.

774. Kutzinski, Vera M. Fearful assymetries: Langston Hughes, Nicolás Guillén, and *Cuba libre*. *See* **16485**.

775. Lamb, Karen. Bringing Australia home: Peter Carey, the Booker, and the repatriation of Australian culture. *In* (pp. 17–30) **15021**.

776. Law, Graham. The professional writer and the literary marketplace. *In* (pp. 97–111) **9609**.

777. Lennon, Colm. The print trade, 1550–1700. *In* (pp. 61–73) **724**.

778. —— The print trade, 1700–1800. *In* (pp. 74–87) **724**.

779. Lesser, Zachary. Typographic nostalgia: play-reading, popularity, and the meanings of black-letter. *In* (pp. 99–126) **4731**.

780. Lewis, Jeremy. Penguin special: the life and times of Allen Lane. (Bibl. 2005, 911.) Rev. by Alan Bell in SewR (114:2) 2006, 336–9.

781. Lewis, Lucy. Chepman and Myllar: the first printers in Scotland. *In* (pp. 57–69) **746**.

782. Lewis, Robert W. The making of *Under Kilimanjaro*. *See* **16368**.

783. Lisk, David Thomas. Walt Whitman's attic. *See* **11566**.

784. Loughran, Trish. Disseminating *Common Sense*: Thomas Paine and the problem of the early national bestseller. *See* **8034**.

785. Low, Gail. The natural artist: publishing Amos Tutuola's *The Palm-Wine Drinkard* in postwar Britain. *See* **18876**.

786. McCooey, David. Surviving Australian poetry: the new lyricism. *See* **13804**.

787. McCormack, W. J. Reflections on writing and editing, with reference to National Archives (UK), CO 904/1–3 & HO 161/1–5. *In* (pp. 258–85) **648**.

788. McCue, Jim. Editing Eliot. *See* **15698**.

789. Mace, Nancy A. The history of the grammar patent from 1620 to 1800 and the forms of Lily's Latin grammar. PBSA (100:2) 2006, 177–225.

790. Machan, Tim William. Early Modern Middle English. *In* (pp. 299–322) **4125**.

791. McKay, Barry; Hinks, John; Bell, Maureen (eds). Light on the book trade: essays in honour of Peter Isaac. (Bibl. 2005, 916.) Rev. by Ian Maxted in JPHS (ns 8) 2005, 63–4; by Marja Smolenaars in LibC (41:3) 2006, 409–10.

792. McKitterick, David. A history of Cambridge University Press: vol. 3, New worlds for learning, 1873–1972. (Bibl. 2005, 917.) Rev. by Alan Bell in Library (7:3) 2006, 340–1; by John Feather in JPHS (ns 9) 2006, 104–5.

793. MANDAL, A. A. Making Austen mad: Benjamin Crosby and the non-publication of *Susan*. *See* **9055**.

794. MANDELBROTE, GILES (ed.). Out of print & into profit: a history of the rare and secondhand book trade in Britain in the 20th century. *See* **350**.

795. MARCHITELLO, HOWARD. *Pater patriae*: James I and the imprint of prerogative. *In* (pp. 303–24) **661**.

796. MARSHIK, CELIA. British Modernism and censorship. *See* **12029**.

797. MASLEN, KEITH. Resurrecting Samuel Richardson. *In* (pp. 77–87) **7255**.

798. MASON, JODY. State censorship and Irene Baird's *Waste Heritage*. *See* **14530**.

799. MASTEN, JEFFREY. Editing boys: the performance of genders in print. *In* (pp. 113–34) **5334**.

800. MATTHEWS, NICOLE. Collins and the Commonwealth: publishers' publicity and the twentieth-century circulation of popular fiction titles. *In* (pp. 41–55) **746**.

801. MEYERS, JEFFREY (introd.). Hemingway and Harold Loeb: an unpublished letter. *See* **16379**.

802. MEYERS, TERRY L. The first printings of Swinburne's *Reverse* and *The Turning of the Tide*. *See* **11378**.

803. MICHELSON, BRUCE. Printer's devil: Mark Twain and the American publishing revolution. *See* **11517**.

804. MICKLETHWAIT, DAVID. A curious cross-reference in Webster's *American Dictionary*. *See* **1647**.

805. MILES, GEORGE. The press in the West: a roundup of recent work. PBSA (99:3) 2005, 445–58.

806. MILHOUS, JUDITH; HUME, ROBERT D. Isaac Bickerstaff's copyrights – and a biographical discovery. *See* **7548**.

807. MILLER, LAURA J. Reluctant capitalists: bookselling and the culture of consumption. Chicago, IL; London: Chicago UP, 2006. pp. x, 316. Rev. by Willis G. Regier in JSchP (38:1) 2006, 52–4.

808. MILLER, LINDA PATTERSON. From the 'African book' to *Under Kilimanjaro*: an introduction. *See* **16380**.

809. MONTEIRO, GEORGE. Scudder, Rolfe, and Browning. *See* **9285**.

810. MORASH, CHRISTOPHER. Theatre and print, 1550–1800. *In* (pp. 319–34) **724**.

811. MORGAN, BILL; PETERS, NANCY J. (eds). *Howl* on trial: the battle for free expression. *See* **16112**.

812. MORRISON, ROBERT. William Blackwood and the dynamics of success. *In* (pp. 21–48) **1098**.

813. MORRISSON, MARK. Nationalism and the modern American canon. *In* (pp. 22–35) **11964**.

814. —— Publishing. *In* (pp. 133–42) **11788**.

815. MORTON, JOHN. Tennyson and the 1914–1918 war. *See* **11402**.

816. MOSELEY, MERRITT (ed.). Booker Prize novels, 1969–2005. *See* **13567**.

817. MOSS, LAURA. 'Nice audible crying': editions, testimonies, and *Country of My Skull*. *See* **16952**.

818. MULLIN, KATHERINE. English vice and Irish vigilance: the nationality of obscenity in *Ulysses*. *In* (pp. 68–82) **16695**.

819. MUNRO, CRAIG; SHEAHAN-BRIGHT, ROBYN (eds). Paper empires: a history of the book in Australia 1946–2005. St Lucia: Queensland UP, 2006. pp. xiii, 433, (plates) 24. Rev. by Marilla North in TLS, 20 Oct. 2006, 28–9.

820. MURPHY, PRISCILLA COIT. What a book can do: the publication and reception of *Silent Spring*. *See* **15052**.

821. MURRAY, ISOBEL. *The White Bird Passes*: how Jessie Kesson reached the final version. *See* **16850**.

822. MURRAY, SIMONE. Mixed media: feminist presses and publishing politics. London; Sterling, VA: Pluto Press, 2004. pp. 260. Rev. by Louise Poland in ALS (22:2) 2005, 262–4.

823. MYERS, ROBIN; HARRIS, MICHAEL; MANDELBROTE, GILES (eds). Against the law: crime, sharp practice, and the control of print. (Bibl. 2005, 937.) Rev. by Victoria Gardner in JPHS (ns 9) 2006, 107–8.

824. MYERSON, JOEL. *Leaves of Grass* turns 150. *See* **11575**.

825. NADEL, IRA B. Joyce & his publishers. *See* **16737**.

826. NESTA, FREDERICK. Smith, Elder & Co. and the realities of New Grub Street. *In* (pp. 207–19) **746**.

827. NICKELL, JOE. The case of the missing edition. *See* **7672**.

828. NICOL, DAVID. The title-page of *The World Tossed at Tennis*: a portrait of a Jacobean playing company? *See* **6369**.

829. NORD, DAVID PAUL. Faith in reading: religious publishing and the birth of mass media in America. (Bibl. 2005, 946.) Rev. by Erin A. Smith in AmP (16:1) 2006, 115–17; by Aileen Fyfe in Book (68) 2006, 5–6.

830. NUGENT, ROBERT. The silenced monk. *See* **17493**.

831. O'CONNOR, THOMAS. Religious change, 1550–1800. *In* (pp. 169–93) **724**.

832. ORGEL, STEPHEN. The book of the play. *In* (pp. 13–54) **5334**.

833. OSBOROUGH, W. N. Tribulations of a king's printer: George Grierson II in court. *In* (pp. 28–42) **648**.

834. OWENS, JUDITH. Commercial settings of the 1590 *Faerie Queene*. *See* **5111**.

835. PAROISSIEN, DAVID. The Nonesuch Dickens *redux*: a tale of contemporary publishing. *See* **9798**.

836. PARRISH, PAUL A. Front matters: Crashaw in the seventeenth century. *See* **6668**.

837. PATTEE, AMY. Commodities in literature, literature as commodity: a close look at the Gossip Girl series. *See* **19886**.

838. PEACEY, JASON. Sir Thomas Cotton's consumption of news in 1650s England. *See* **6490**.

839. PELLICER, JUAN CHRISTIAN. Harleian georgic from Tonson's press: the publication of John Philips's *Cyder*, 29 January 1708. *See* **7102**.

840. PINK, EMMA E. Frances Burney's *Camilla*: 'to print my grand work ... by subscription'. *See* **7632**.

841. Poland, Louise. The art of publishing: Violet Teague, Geraldine Rede and the Sign of the Rabbit (1905–09). BSANZB (28:4) 2004, 49–70.

842. Pollock, Donald. *The Hound of the Baskervilles*, Longman's Colonial Library: a 'new edition'. *See* **9948**.

843. Potter, Franz J. The history of gothic publishing, 1800–1835: exhuming the trade. (Bibl. 2005, 965.) Rev. by William St Clair in TLS, 29 Sept. 2006, 27.

844. Powell, David. First publications of John Clare's poems. *See* **9479**.

845. Powell, Michael. *Do the Dead Talk?* The Daisy Bank Printing and Publishing Company of Manchester. *In* (pp. 163–87) **746**.

846. Prendergast, Maria Teresa Micaela. Promiscuous textualities: the Nashe–Harvey controversy and the unnatural productions of print. *In* (pp. 173–95) **661**.

847. Price, John Valdimir. Antiquarian and rare books in London at the beginning of the twenty-first century. *See* **366**.

848. Pridmore, Joseph. 'Vindicating the honour of Lancashire': textual variation between editions of James Hanley's *Boy*. *In* (pp. 23–33) **3407**.

849. Prindle, R. E. Tarzan and the river: part iii. *See* **14948**.

850. Ragaz, Sharon. Maturin, Archibald Constable, and the publication of *Melmoth the Wanderer*. *See* **10808**.

851. Rankin, Deana. Historical writing, 1750–1800. *In* (pp. 282–300) **724**.

852. Rapple, Brendan. Google and access to the world's intellectual heritage. *See* **1027**.

853. Raven, James. Lost libraries: the destruction of great book collections since Antiquity. (Bibl. 2004, 940.) Rev. by Jonathan Bengtson in Library (7:3) 2006, 330–1; by Mark Purcell in PBSA (100:3) 2006, 387–9.

854. Reid, Robert R. Publications of the Alcuin Society. Amphora (140/141) 2005, 5–14.

855. Reimer, Stephen R. The Urry *Chaucer* and George Vertue. *See* **4342**.

856. Roberts, Lewis. Trafficking in literary authority: Mudie's Select Library and the commodification of the Victorian novel. *See* **8710**.

857. Robertson, Randy. Lovelace and the 'barbed Censurers': *Lucasta* and Civil War censorship. *See* **6920**.

858. Rodriguez, Catherine M. The history of a novel's travels abroad: foreign editions of Frances Burney's *Cecilia*. *See* **7634**.

859. Rogal, Samuel J. John Wesley's book stock and the Arminian magazine catalogue of 1789. *See* **8244**.

860. Rosenthal, Bob. A witness. *In* (pp. 44–6) **16122**.

861. Ross, Michael. To sign or to inscribe? *See* **14894**.

862. Rostenberg, Leona; Stern, Madeleine. The changing rare book trade, 1950–2000. *See* **369**.

863. Sabor, Peter. 'A kind of tax on the public': the subscription list to Frances Burney's *Camilla*. *In* (pp. 299–315) **7255**.

864. Saenger, Michael Baird. The birth of advertising. *In* (pp. 197–219) **661**.

865. St Clair, William. But what did we actually read? Literary critics should not lose sight of the sales figures. TLS, 12 May 2006, 13–15.

866. Samek, Toni. Unbossed and unbought: Booklegger Press, the first women-owned American library publisher. *In* (pp. 126–55) **690**.

867. Sanders, Mark. Undesirable publications: J. M. Coetzee on censorship and apartheid. *See* **15224**.

868. Schlicke, Paul. Dickens and the pirates: the case of *The Odd Fellow*. *See* **9816**.

869. Scragg, Leah. The victim of fashion? Rereading the biography of John Lyly. *See* **4906**.

870. Sher, Richard B. The Enlightenment & the book: Scottish authors & their publishers in eighteenth-century Britain, Ireland, & America. *See* **7332**.

871. Sherbo, Arthur. Some more prices of the Second, Third, and Fourth Shakespeare Folios. *See* **5432**.

872. Shillingsburg, Peter. Publication of Coetzee's *The Humanities in Africa*. *See* **15225**.

873. Shohet, Lauren. The masque in/as print. *In* (pp. 176–202) **4731**.

874. Showalter, Elaine. In the age of awards. TLS, 3 Mar. 2006, 12 (review-article).

875. Singleton, Antony. The Early English Text Society in the nineteenth century: an organizational history. *See* **3886**.

876. Sironval, Margaret. The image of Sheherazade in French and English editions. *In* (pp. 219–44) **10714**.

877. Smith, John Saumarez (ed.). The bookshop at 10 Curzon Street: letters between Nancy Mitford and Heywood Hill 1952–73. *See* **17545**.

878. Smith, Pamela S. Passions in print: private press artistry in New Mexico. Santa Fe: Museum of New Mexico Press, 2006. pp. 223.

879. Smyth, Adam. 'Reade in one age and understood i' th' next': recycling satire in the mid-seventeenth century. *See* **6306**.

880. Sova, Dawn B. Literature suppressed on sexual grounds. Preface by Ken Wachsberger. New York: Facts on File, 2006. pp. xviii, 350. (Second ed.: first ed. 1998.)

881. Stape, J. H.; Knowles, Owen. 'In-between man': Conrad–Galsworthy–Pinker. *See* **15314**.

882. Steggle, Matthew. Walter Scot's *True History* and John Taylor the Water-Poet. *See* **7144**.

883. Stilling, Robert. Between friends: rediscovering the war thoughts of Robert Frost. *See* **16018**.

884. Stokes, Claudia. Copyrighting American history: international copyright and the periodization of the nineteenth century. *See* **10759**.

885. Straznicky, Marta. The Red Bull repertory in print, 1605–60. *See* **6389**.

886. —— (ed.). The book of the play: playwrights, stationers, and readers in early modern England. *See* **4731**.

887. Suarez, Michael F.; Zimmerman, Sarah M. John Clare's career, 'Keats's publisher', and the early nineteenth-century English book trade. *See* **9481**.

888. SULLIVAN, CERI. London's early modern creative industrialists. *See* **6313**.

889. SUPINO, DAVID J. Henry James: a bibliographical catalogue of a collection of editions to 1921. *See* **10607**.

890. SUTHERLAND, JOHN. Victorian fiction: writers, publishers, readers. *See* **8718**.

891. TANNENBAUM, ALAN. An American edition of the 1924 Williams bibliography. *See* **9432**.

892. TATTERSFIELD, NIGEL. Alexander Anderson, the first American wood engraver: a brief sketch of his early career and his debt to Thomas and John Bewick. *In* (pp. 85–94) **56**.

893. TAYLOR, GARY. Making meaning marketing Shakespeare 1623. *In* (pp. 55–72) **5334**.

894. THATCHER, SANFORD G. Fair use in theory and practice: reflections on its history and the Google case. JSchP (37:3) 2006, 215–29.

895. THOMAS, FRANCIS-NOËL. Philip Larkin, Barbara Pym, and the accident of literary fame. *See* **17006**.

896. THOMSON, ELLEN MAZUR. The graphic forms lectures. *See* **174**.

897. VAN DER VLIES, ANDREW. 'Hurled by what aim to what tremendous range!': Roy Campbell and the politics of anthologies, 1927–1945. *See* **15011**.

898. VINSON, DUNCAN. 'As far from secular, operatic, rag-time, and jig melodies as is possible': religion and the resurgence of interest in *The Sacred Harp*, 1895–1911. *See* **3091**.

899. WADSWORTH, SARAH. In the company of books: literature and its 'classes' in nineteenth-century America. *See* **8755**.

900. WAITE, NOEL. The Octopus and its silent teachers: a New Zealand response to the British book trade. *In* (pp. 13–30) **746**.

901. WALLER, PHILIP. Writers, readers, and reputations: literary life in Britain, 1870–1918. *See* **8546**.

902. WALTON, SUSAN. Charlotte M. Yonge and the 'historic harem' of Edward Augustus Freeman. *See* **11729**.

903. WARD, SAM. Melodies in the marketplace: John Clare's 100 songs. *See* **9484**.

904. WATRY, MAUREEN (ed.). The Vale Press: Charles Ricketts, a publisher in earnest. (Bibl. 2004, 1001.) Rev. by Paul van Capelleveen in Library (6:4) 2005, 468–70.

905. WHITE, MICHELINE. Women writers and literary–religious circles in the Elizabethan West Country: Anne Dowriche, Anne Lock Prowse, Anne Locke Moyle, Ursula Fulford, and Elizabeth Rous. *See* **4838**.

906. WIGELSWORTH, JEFFREY R. John Toland's economic imperative to print and financing the Harrington edition: a brief assessment. *See* **8226**.

907. WILLIS, PATRICIA C. Phillis Wheatley, George Whitefield, and the Countess of Huntingdon in the Beinecke Library. *See* **8249**.

908. WILPUTTE, EARLA A. 'Too ticklish to meddle with': the silencing of *The Female Spectator*'s political correspondents. *In* (pp. 122–40) **7884**.

909. Wiltshire, Irene. *Pickwick* and the pirates. *See* **9839**.

910. Woolley, David. The textual history of *A Tale of a Tub*. *See* **8217**.

911. Woolley, James. Poor John Harding and Mad Tom: *Harding's Resurrection* (1724). *In* (pp. 102–21) **648**.

912. Worthen, W. B. Print and the poetics of modern drama. *See* **12386**.

913. Wu, Duncan. Hazlitt's unpublished *History of English Philosophy*: the larger context. *See* **10418**.

914. Young, John K. Black writers, White publishers: marketplace politics in twentieth-century African American literature. *See* **12230**.

915. Zboray, Ronald J.; Zboray, Mary Saracino. Literary dollars and social sense: a people's history of the mass market book. London; New York: Routledge, 2005. pp. xxxix, 325. Rev. by Susan S. Williams in JAH (93:1) 2006, 215–16.

916. Zwicker, Steven N. Is there such a thing as Restoration literature? *See* **6321**.

CONTEMPORARY PUBLISHING AND BOOKSELLING

917. Anon. Alpenhouse Apparitions' powers of book design. *See* **124**.

918. Byle, Ann E. (comp.). The making of a Christian bestseller: an insider's guide to Christian publishing. *See* **19482**.

919. Case, Mary; Green, David. Rights and permissions in an electronic edition. *In* (pp. 346–57) **426**.

920. Connor, Tom. The state of the story. *See* **19852**.

921. Dalton, Margaret Stieg. A system destabilized: scholarly books today. JSchP (37:4) 2006, 251–69.

922. Deegan, Marilyn. Collection and preservation of an electronic edition. *In* (pp. 358–70) **426**.

923. Donadio, Rachel. Promotional intelligence. NYTB, 21 May 2006, 31. (Marketing US fiction.)

924. Donovan, Stephen K. The long and the short and the tall. JSchP (38:1) 2006, 36–40. (Reviewing of scholarly books.)

925. Franco Carvalhal, Tania. The future of literary studies: technologies of the image or technologies of writing? *In* (pp. 167–74) **14093**.

926. Goff, Patricia M. Producing Harry Potter: why the medium is still the message. *In* (pp. 27–44) **18355**.

927. Greco, Albert N. Recent trends in scholarly communications: 2001–2005. JSchP (37:4) 2006, 288–306.

928. Lathey, Gillian. The travels of Harry: international marketing and the translation of J. K. Rowling's Harry Potter books. *See* **18347**.

929. Milroy, Rollin. The architecture of Charnel House. *See* **164**.

930. Nel, Philip. Is there a text in this advertising campaign? Literature, marketing, and Harry Potter. *See* **18353**.

931. Pedley, Paul. Digital copyright. *See* **1022**.

932. Powell, Neil. Henry James and cabbages. PNRev (33:1) 2006, 5–6. (Marketing scholarly books.)

933. Taylor, Alasdair. Publishing and electronic piracy. *See* **1039**.

934. Taylor, Kevin. Plagiarism and piracy: a publisher's perspective. LPub (19:4) 2006, 259–66.

935. Updike, John. The end of authorship. NYTB, 25 June 2006, 27.

SCHOLARLY METHOD

936. ANSON, CHRISTOPHER M.; SCHWEGLER, ROBERT A. The Longman handbook for writers and readers. (Bibl. 1997, 1076.) London; New York: Pearson Longman, 2005. pp. xx, 940. (Fourth ed.: first ed. 1997.)

937. BABINGTON, DOUG; LEPAN, DON. The Broadview guide to writing. (Bibl. 2003, 920.) Peterborough, Ont.; Orchard Park, NY: Broadview Press, 2005. pp. 600. (Third ed.: first ed. 1991.)

938. BULLOCK, RICHARD. The Norton field guide to writing. New York; London: Norton, 2006. pp. xxix, 514.

939. BUTCHER, JUDITH; DRAKE, CAROLINE; LEACH, MAUREEN. Butcher's copy-editing: the Cambridge handbook for editors, copy-editors and proofreaders. Cambridge; New York: CUP, 2006. pp. xiv, 543. (Fourth ed.: first ed. 1975.)

940. DAVIDSON, PAUL; DAVIS, KRISTY; NIELD, SOPHIE. The AHRC Mander and Mitchenson Theatre Collection Access for Research Project: conversations with cataloguers. *See* **310**.

941. DONOVAN, STEPHEN K. Research journals: toward uniformity or retaining diversity? JSchP (37:3) 2006, 230–5.

942. DOUGLAS, AUDREY; MACLEAN, SALLY-BETH (eds). REED in review: essays in celebration of the first twenty-five years. *See* **3904**.

943. EINSOHN, AMY. The copyeditor's handbook: a guide for book publishing and corporate communications, with exercises and answer keys. (Bibl. 2000, 1264.) Berkeley; London: California UP, 2006. pp. xiv, 560. (Second ed.: first ed. 2000.)

944. GLENN, CHERYL, *et al.* (eds). The writer's Harbrace handbook. (Bibl. 2001, 881.) Boston, MA: Thomson/Heinle, 2004. pp. xxxii, 896. (Second ed.: first ed. 2001.)

945. GRECO, ALBERT N. Recent trends in scholarly communications: 2001–2005. *See* **927**.

946. GRIFFIN, GABRIELE (ed.). Research methods for English Studies. Edinburgh: Edinburgh UP, 2005. pp. viii, 248.

947. HACKER, DIANA. The Bedford handbook. (Bibl. 1998, 1164.) Basingstoke: Macmillan; Boston, MA: Bedford Books of St Martin's Press, 2006. pp. xlvii, 876, 28. (Seventh ed.: first ed. 1985.) (Orig. pub. as *Rules for Writers.*)

948. KEENE, MICHAEL L.; ADAMS, KATHERINE H. Easy access: the pocket handbook for writers. Boston, MA: McGraw-Hill, 2006. pp. xii, 545.

949. KEERAN, PEGGY; BOWERS, JENNIFER. Literary research and the British Romantic era: strategies and sources. *See* **8408**.

950. KITCHIN, ROB; FULLER, DUNCAN. The academic's guide to publishing. London; Thousand Oaks, CA: Sage, 2005. pp. x, 180.

951. KOHNEN, THOMAS. Variability of form as a methodological problem in historical corpus analysis: the case of modal expressions in directive speech acts. *In* (pp. 220–33) **1227**.

952. LEHR, JOHN. Using REED: a selective bibliography. *In* (pp. 236–60) **3904**.

953. LYNN, STEVEN. Texts and contexts: writing about literature with critical theory. *See* **20099**.

954. ONYSKO, ALEXANDER. Anglicisms in *Der Spiegel*: towards a methodological framework of corpus analysis. *In* (pp. 265–77) **1227**.

955. POLLAK, OLIVER B. The decline and fall of bottom notes, *op. cit.*, *loc. cit.*, and a century of the *Chicago Manual of Style*. JSchP (38:1) 2006, 14–30.

956. RAMAGE, JOHN D.; BEAN, JOHN C.; JOHNSON, JUNE. The Allyn & Bacon guide to writing. (Bibl. 1997, 1106.) London; New York: Pearson Longman, 2006. pp. xlvii, 848. (Fourth ed.: first ed. 1997.)

957. RANSOM, DANIEL J. Annotating Chaucer: some corrections and additions. *In* (pp. 205–15) **4310**.

958. ROBERTS, ROSEMARY, *et al.* (eds). New Hart's rules. (Bibl. 2005, 1089.) Rev. by John Whale in TLS, 10 Feb. 2006, 11.

959. ROSEN, LEONARD J. The academic writer's handbook. London; New York: Pearson Longman, 2006. pp. xii, 562.

960. RUSSELL, IAN. Working *with* tradition: towards a partnership model of fieldwork. *See* **3070**.

961. SHEN, DAN. How stylisticians draw on narratology: approaches, advantages and disadvantages. *See* **14293**.

962. STEVENSON, ANGUS; BROWN, LESLEY (eds). New Oxford dictionary for writers and editors. (Bibl. 2005, 1092.) Rev. by John Whale in TLS, 10 Feb. 2006, 11.

963. THOMAS, SYLVIA. REED and the Record Office: tradition and innovation on the road to access. *In* (pp. 131–9) **3904**.

964. YOUNG, ABIGAIL ANN. 'Practice makes perfect': policies for a cross-disciplinary project. *In* (pp. 52–62) **3904**.

LANGUAGE, LITERATURE, AND THE COMPUTER

965. ANON. Prof. Manfred Markus – bibliography and projects. *In* (pp. 341–58) **1227**.

966. ARMAND, LOUIS (ed.). JoyceMedia: James Joyce, hypermedia & textual genetics. *See* **16653**.

967. BAKER, PAUL. Using corpora in discourse analysis. *See* **1185**.

968. BAKER, PETER S. Typing in Old English since 1967: a brief history. *See* **127**.

969. BERLAND, KEVIN. Formalized curiosity in the electronic age and the uses of on-line text-bases. *See* **7222**.

970. BERRIE, PHILL, *et al.* Authenticating electronic editions. *In* (pp. 269–76) **426**.

971. BIRCHALL, DIANA. The Frances Hodgson Burnett online discussion group: a modern history. *In* (pp. 217–22) **9300**.

972. BUDANITSKY, ALEXANDER; HIRST, GRAEME. Evaluating WordNet-based measures of lexical semantic relatedness. *See* **1473**.

973. BURGHART, ALEX. Web works. TLS, 13 Oct. 2006, 16–17. (Prosopography of Anglo-Saxon England.)

974. BURNARD, LOU; O'KEEFFE, KATHERINE O'BRIEN; UNSWORTH, JOHN (eds). Electronic textual editing. *See* **426**.

975. BUTTERWORTH, RICHARD. The Library goes live! *See* **3029**.

976. BUZZETTI, DINO; MCGANN, JEROME. Critical editing in a digital horizon. *In* (pp. 53–73) **426**.

977. CARSON, CHRISTIE. The evolution of online editing: where will it end? *See* **5161**.

978. CASE, MARY; GREEN, DAVID. Rights and permissions in an electronic edition. *In* (pp. 346–57) **426**.

979. CHRISTIE, EDWARD. *Circolwyrde* 2005: new electronic resources for Anglo-Saxon studies. *See* **3663**.

980. —— *Circolwyrde* 2006: new electronic resources for Anglo-Saxon studies. OEN (40:1) 2006, 59–62.

981. COPPA, FRANCESCA. Writing bodies in space: media fan fiction as theatrical performance. *In* (pp. 225–44) **19868**.

982. COX, JOHN. Scholarly publishing practices: a case of *plus ça change, plus c'est la même chose*? *See* **1076**.

983. CRANE, GREG. Document management and file naming. *In* (pp. 277–90) **426**.

984. CUMMINGS, JAMES. REED and the possibilities of Web technology. *In* (pp. 178–99) **3904**.

985. DEEGAN, MARILYN. Collection and preservation of an electronic edition. *In* (pp. 358–70) **426**.

986. D'HULST, LIEVEN. Can new technologies save the (teaching of) literary history? *In* (pp. 237–46) **14093**.

987. Diller, Hans-Jürgen. The decline of the family of *mōd*: ICAMET and other corpora. *In* (pp. 51–64) **1227**.

988. Dossena, Marina. 19CSC, ICAMET and the diachronic study of specialized discourse in correspondence. *In* (pp. 65–77) **1227**.

989. Driscoll, M. J. Levels of transcription. *In* (pp. 254–61) **426**.

990. Durso, Patricia Keefe. It's just beginning: assessing the impact of the Internet on US multiethnic literature and the 'canon'. *In* (pp. 197–218) **11783**.

991. Durusau, Patrick. Why and how to document your markup choices. *In* (pp. 299–309) **426**.

992. Eaves, Morris. Multimedia body plans: a self-assessment. *In* (pp. 210–23) **426**.

993. Facchinetti, Roberta; Rissanen, Matti (eds). Corpus-based studies of diachronic English. *See* **1209**.

994. Felluga, Dino Franco. The Victorian archive and the disappearance of the book. VS (48:2) 2006, 305–19. (Addressed to the NINES [Networked Infrastructure for Nineteenth-century Electronic Scholarship].)

995. Fenton, Eileen Gifford; Duggan, Hoyt N. Effective methods of producing machine-readable text from manuscript and print sources. *In* (pp. 241–53) **426**.

996. Ferragne, Emmanuel. Quand le Professeur Higgins s'invite sur votre ordinateur: une approche moderne de la dialectologie. *See* **2558**.

997. Flanders, Julia. The Women Writers Project: a digital anthology. *In* (pp. 138–49) **426**.

998. Fraistat, Neil; Jones, Steven. The poem and the network: editing poetry electronically. *In* (pp. 105–21) **426**.

999. Fries, Udo. *'Tis said*, the apostrophe, and the importance of Innsbruck in early English newspapers. *In* (pp. 101–14) **1227**.

1000. Gabler, Hans Walter. Moving a print-based editorial project into electronic form. *In* (pp. 339–45) **426**.

1001. Gants, David. Drama case study: *The Cambridge Edition of the Works of Ben Jonson*. *In* (pp. 122–37) **426**.

1002. Gants, David L. Lists, inventories and catalogues: shifting modes of ordered knowledge in the early modern book trade. *In* (pp. 221–38) **746**.

1003. Greco, Albert N. Recent trends in scholarly communications: 2001–2005. *See* **927**.

1004. Groden, Michael. Problems of annotation in a digital *Ulysses*. *See* **16703**.

1005. Harrison, Brian. Comparative biography and the *DNB*. *See* **19979**.

1006. Hassall, Peter John. Developing an International Corpus of Creative English. *See* **2327**.

1007. Hornero, Ana María; Luzón, María José; Murillo, Silvia (eds). Corpus linguistics: applications for the study of English. *See* **1219**.

1008. Inman, James A.; Hewett, Beth L. (eds). Technology and English Studies: innovative professional paths. Mahwah, NJ; London: Erlbaum, 2006. pp. xv, 250.

1009. Jackson, MacDonald P. The date and authorship of Hand D's contribution to *Sir Thomas More*: evidence from *Literature Online*. *See* **6078**.

1010. —— Shakespeare and the quarrel scene in *Arden of Faversham*. *See* **4684**.

1011. Jordan, Ellen; Craig, Hugh; Antonia, Alexis. The Brontë sisters and the *Christian Remembrancer*: a pilot study in the use of the 'Burrows method' to identify the authorship of unsigned articles in the nineteenth-century periodical press. *See* **9233**.

1012. Kiernan, Kevin. Digital facsimiles in editing. *In* (pp. 262–8) **426**.

1013. —— Odd couples in Ælfric's *Julian and Basilissa* in British Library Cotton MS Otho B.x. *In* (pp. 85–106) **199**.

1014. Kliman, Bernice W. Print and electronic editions inspired by the New Variorum *Hamlet* project. *See* **5736**.

1015. Lavagnino, John. When not to use TEI. *In* (pp. 334–8) **426**.

1016. McGann, Jerome. Culture and technology: the way we live now. What is to be done? NLH (36:1) 2005, 71–82. (Networked Infrastructure for Nineteenth-Century Electronic Scholarship.)

1017. Mahlberg, Michaela. English general nouns: a corpus-theoretical approach. *See* **1494**.

1018. Mair, Christian; Heuberger, Reinhard (eds); Wallmannsberger, Josef (assoc. ed.). Corpora and the history of English: papers dedicated to Manfred Markus on the occasion of his sixty-fifth birthday. *See* **1227**.

1019. Miller, George A.; Hristea, Florentina. WordNet nouns: classes and instances. *See* **1498**.

1020. Nelson, Gerald. The core and periphery of world Englishes: a corpus-based exploration. *See* **2693**.

1021. Pearson, David. Books as history: changing values in a digital age. *See* **11**.

1022. Pedley, Paul. Digital copyright. London: Facet, 2005. pp. 134. (Electronic book.) Rev. by Charles Oppenheim in LPub (19:2) 2006, 156–7.

1023. Pentz, Ed. CrossRef at the crossroads. LPub (19:4) 2006, 250–8.

1024. Price, John Valdimir. Antiquarian and rare books in London at the beginning of the twenty-first century. *See* **366**.

1025. Quah, C. K. Translation and technology. *See* **2916**.

1026. Rahtz, Sebastian. Storage, retrieval, and rendering. *In* (pp. 310–33) **426**.

1027. Rapple, Brendan. Google and access to the world's intellectual heritage. ContRev (286:1673) 2005, 338–43.

1028. Robinson, Peter. The *Canterbury Tales* and other medieval texts. *In* (pp. 74–91) **426**.

1029. Sampson, Geoffrey. Reflections of a dendrographer. *In* (pp. 157–84) **1195**.

1030. Scollon, Ron; Scollon, Suzie Wong. Nexus analysis: discourse and the emerging Internet. *See* **1192**.

1031. Scott, Robert. The Readex Corporation, the American Antiquarian Society, and the brave new world of electronic text: a librarian's perspective. PAAS (115:2) 2005, 295–316.

1032. Simpson-Vlach, Rita C.; Leicher, Sheryl. The MICASE handbook: a resource for users of the Michigan Corpus of Academic Spoken English. *See* **2234**.

1033. Smoot, Jeanne J. Technology: able to assist author and audience. *In* (pp. 219–28) **14093**.

1034. Somerset, Alan. The Blackfriars on tour: provincial analogies. *In* (pp. 80–5) **5577**.

1035. Springer, Robert. On the electronic trail of Blues formulas. *In* (pp. 164–86) **3086**.

1036. Stafanowitsch, Anatol; Gries, Stefan Th. (eds). Corpus-based approaches to metaphor and metonymy. *See* **2141**.

1037. Stephenson, Jenn. Herodotus in the labyrinth: REED and hypertext. *In* (pp. 200–15) **3904**.

1038. Sugawara, Katsuya. Haiku industry: production of literature and the technology of network making. *In* (pp. 213–18) **14093**.

1039. Taylor, Alasdair. Publishing and electronic piracy. LPub (19:3) 2006, 168–74.

1040. Taylor, Kevin. Plagiarism and piracy: a publisher's perspective. *See* **934**.

1041. Thatcher, Sanford G. Fair use in theory and practice: reflections on its history and the Google case. *See* **894**.

1042. Toolan, Michael. Top keyword abridgements of short stories: a corpus-linguistic resource? *See* **16782**.

1043. Turney, Peter D. Similarity of semantic relations. *See* **1781**.

1044. Underberg, Natalie M. Virtual and reciprocal ethnography on the Internet: the East Mims Oral History Project website. JAF (119:473) 2006, 301–11.

1045. Updike, John. The end of authorship. *See* **935**.

1046. Vanhoutte, Edward. Prose fiction and modern manuscripts: limitations and possibilities of text encoding for electronic editions. *In* (pp. 161–80) **426**.

1047. Van Hulle, Dirk. Authorial translation: Samuel Beckett's *Stirrings Still / Soubresauts*. *In* (pp. 150–60) **426**.

1048. Véronis, Jean. Sense tagging: does it make sense? *In* (pp. 273–90) **1195**.

1049. Walker, Janice R.; Taylor, Todd W. The Columbia guide to online style. (Bibl. 1998, 1180.) New York: Columbia UP, 2006. pp. xxi, 288. (Second ed.: first ed. 1998.)

1050. Webster, Jonathan J. (ed.). Computational and quantitative studies. By M. A. K. Halliday. *See* **1193**.

1051. Wittern, Christian. Writing systems and character representation. *In* (pp. 291–8) **426**.

1052. Zughoul, Muhammad Raji; Abu-Alshaar, Awatef Mi'zil. English/Arabic/English machine translation: a historical perspective. *See* **2945**.

NEWSPAPERS AND OTHER PERIODICALS

1053. Adams, Sam. Seren at twenty-five. *See* **634**.

1054. Araujo, Anderson D. *Blast*, Futurism, and the cultural mobility of Modernist (inter)texts. QPS (14) 2006, 427–37.

1055. Ashley, Mike. The age of the storytellers: British popular fiction magazines, 1880–1950. *See* **8611**.

1056. Attebery, Brian. The conquest of Gernsback: Leslie F. Stone and the subversion of science fiction tropes. *In* (pp. 50–66) **13537**.

1057. Bannet, Eve Tavor. Haywood's *Spectator* and the female world. *In* (pp. 82–103) **7884**.

1058. Barrow, Robin. Braddon's haunting memories: rape, class and the Victorian popular press. *See* **9156**.

1059. Bergel, Giles. William Dicey and the networks and places of print culture. *In* (pp. 149–62) **746**.

1060. Bizot, Jean-François. Free press: underground & alternative publications, 1965–1975. Foreword by Barry Miles. New York: Universe, 2006. pp. 255. Rev. by Gary Kamiya in NYTB, 19 Nov. 2006, 19.

1061. Boardman, Kay. 'Charting the golden stream': recent work on Victorian periodicals. VS (48:3) 2006, 505–17 (review-article).

1062. Brake, Laurel. *Maga*, the shilling monthlies, and the New Journalism. *In* (pp. 184–211) **1098**.

1063. —— Codell, Julie F. (eds). Encounters in the Victorian press: editors, authors, readers. (Bibl. 2005, 1160.) Rev. by David Finkelstein in Library (6:4) 2005, 466–8; by Kay Boardman in VS (48:3) 2006, 505–17.

1064. Branson, Susan. Gendered strategies for success in the early nineteenth-century literary marketplace: Mary Carr and the *Ladies' Tea Tray*. JAStud (40:1) 2006, 35–51.

1065. Bristow, Gemma. Brief encounter: Richard Aldington and the *Englishwoman*. *See* **14405**.

1066. Bristow, Joseph. 'The Armytage–Tomson–Watson sequence': poetic illustrations in the periodical press, 1886–96. *See* **11461**.

1067. Campisi, Dale. Little magazines, great divides. Meanjin (63:1) 2004, 159–65.

1068. Carter, David. 'Some means of learning of the best new books': *All about Books* and the modern reader. ALS (22:3) 2006, 329–41.

1069. Casey, Ellen Miller. 'Highly flavoured dishes' and 'highly seasoned garbage': sensation in the *Athenaeum*. *In* (pp. 3–14) **8647**.

1070. Churchill, Suzanne W. The little magazine *Others* and the renovation of modern American poetry. *See* **13722**.

1071. Clarke, Bob. From Grub Street to Fleet Street: an illustrated history of English newspapers to 1899. (Bibl. 2005, 1174.) Rev. by Mark Hampton in JVC (11:2) 2006, 349–56.

1072. COHOON, LORINDA. Festive citizenships: Independence celebrations in New England children's periodicals and series books. CLAQ (31:2) 2006, 132–53.

1073. COHOON, LORINDA B. Serialized citizenships: periodicals, books, and American boys, 1840–1911. Lanham, MD; London: Scarecrow Press, 2006. pp. xxix, 191. Rev. by Ken Parille in CLAQ (31:4) 2006, 385–7.

1074. COLLIER, PATRICK. Modernism on Fleet Street. Aldershot; Burlington, VT: Ashgate, 2006. pp. vii, 257.

1075. COX, J. RANDOLPH. *Dime Novel Roundup* over the years. DNR (75:4) 2006, 105–13.

1076. COX, JOHN. Scholarly publishing practices: a case of *plus ça change, plus c'est la même chose*? LPub (19:4) 2006, 273–6.

1077. CUMMINGS, RALPH F. History of the Happy Hours Brotherhood and the *Dime Novel Roundup*. *See* **13447**.

1078. DAVIDSON, JIM. The second empire. Meanjin (63:1) 2004, 166–71. (Editorship of *Meanjin*.)

1079. DAVIES, LAURENCE. 'A sideways ending to it all': G. W. Steevens, Blackwood, and the *Daily Mail*. *In* (pp. 236–58) **1098**.

1080. DEAN, ANN C. Court culture and political news in London's eighteenth-century newspapers. ELH (73:3) 2006, 631–49.

1081. DE MONTLUZIN, EMILY LORRAINE. Attributions of authorship in the *Gentleman's Magazine*, 1765–1770: a supplement to the *Union List*. NQ (53:2) 2006, 199–209.

1082. —— Identifying 'W.O.' of Marshfield, Gloucestershire: William Oland's contributions to the *Gentleman's Magazine*, 1747–82. *See* **7423**.

1083. —— An 'Ossianic' tribute to the Prince of Wales: Thomas Potts's verses in the *Gentleman's Magazine*, 1762. *See* **8077**.

1084. DONAWERTH, JANE. Illicit reproduction: Clare Winger Harris's *The Fate of the Poseidonia*. *In* (pp. 20–35) **13537**.

1085. DONOVAN, STEPHEN. The muse of *Blackwood's*: Charles Whibley and literary criticism in the world. *In* (pp. 259–86) **1098**.

1086. DONOVAN, STEPHEN K. Research journals: toward uniformity or retaining diversity? *See* **941**.

1087. DOUGHTY, TERRI (ed.). Selections from *The Girl's Own Paper*, 1880–1907. Peterborough, Ont.; Orchard Park, NY: Broadview Press, 2004. pp. 184. (Broadview reprint eds.) Rev. by Amy C. Murphy in VPR (39:1) 2006, 75–7.

1088. DRYDEN, LINDA. At the court of *Blackwood's*: in the Kampong of Hugh Clifford. *In* (pp. 215–35) **1098**.

1089. DUNCAN, IAN. *Blackwood's* and Romantic nationalism. *In* (pp. 70–89) **1098**.

1090. EASLEY, ALEXIS (ed.). RSVP bibliography: 2003–2005. VPR (39:3) 2006, 193–256. (Research Soc. for Victorian Periodicals.)

1091. EASTON, FRASER. Covering sexual disguise: passing women and generic constraint. *See* **7460**.

1092. Ellen, Jane. Cold Wars and culture wars. *See* **11877**.

1093. Emad, Mitra C. Reading Wonder Woman's body: mythologies of gender and nation. JPC (39:6) 2006, 954–84.

1094. Faulkner, Peter. William Morris and the *Scrutiny* tradition. *See* **10940**.

1095. Feldman, Paula R. Women, literary annuals, and the evidence of inscriptions. *See* **8352**.

1096. —— (introd.). *The Keepsake* for 1829. Peterborough, Ont.; Orchard Park, NY: Broadview Press, 2006. pp. 32, vii, 360, (plates) 19. (Broadview encore eds.)

1097. Felsenstein, Frank. Mr Punch at the Great Exhibition: stereotypes of Yankee and Hebrew in 1851. *In* (pp. 17–39) **8523**.

1098. Finkelstein, David (ed.). Print culture and the Blackwood tradition, 1805–1930. Toronto; Buffalo, NY; London: Toronto UP, 2006. pp. 326. (Studies in book and print culture.)

1099. Fisher, Judith L. 'In the present famine of anything substantial': *Fraser's* 'portraits' and the construction of literary celebrity; or, 'Personality, personality is the appetite of the age'. VPR (39:2) 2006, 97–135.

1100. Flynn, Michael J. Novels by literary snobs: the contentious class-coding of Thackerayan parody. *See* **10764**.

1101. Flynn, Philip. Beginning *Blackwood's*: the right mix of *dulce* and *ùtile*. VPR (39:2) 2006, 136–57.

1102. —— Blackwood's *Maga*, Lockhart's *Peter's Letters*, and the politics of publishing. SR (45:1) 2006, 117–31.

1103. Foster, Frances Smith. A narrative of the interesting origins and (somewhat) surprising developments of African American print culture. *See* **711**.

1104. Fries, Udo. *'Tis said*, the apostrophe, and the importance of Innsbruck in early English newspapers. *In* (pp. 101–14) **1227**.

1105. Giordano, Matthew. 'A lesson from' the magazines: Sarah Piatt and the postbellum periodical poet. *See* **11002**.

1106. Goldsmith, Jason N. Hogging the limelight: *The Queen's Wake* and the rise of celebrity authorship. *See* **10441**.

1107. Gontarski, S. E. Beckett and the unnamable voice of (European) Modernism. *See* **14682**.

1108. Gourevitch, Philip (introd.). The *Paris Review* interviews: vol. 1. *See* **11913**.

1109. Grant, Jane. Vultures on every bough. *See* **18736**.

1110. Graves, Nicola. 'Injury for injury'; or, 'The Lady's Revenge': female vengeance in Eliza Haywood's *Female Spectator*. *In* (pp. 157–75) **7884**.

1111. Greco, Albert N., *et al.* The state of scholarly journal publishing: 1981–2000. *See* **730**.

1112. Griffiths, Dennis. Fleet Street: five hundred years of the press. London: British Library, 2006. pp. xvii, 458, (plates) 16. Rev. by Tim Gardam in TLS, 7 July 2006, 19.

1113. Harris, Katherine D. Feminizing the textual body: female readers consuming the literary annual. PBSA (99:4) 2005, 573–622.

1114. Harris, Sharon M.; Garvey, Ellen Gruber (eds). Blue pencils & hidden hands: women editing periodicals, 1830–1910. (Bibl. 2005, 1221.) Rev. by Juliette Berning Schaefer in VPR (39:1) 2006, 83–4.

1115. Henson, Louise, *et al.* (eds). Culture and science in the nineteenth-century media. (Bibl. 2005, 1226.) Rev. by Ashton Nichols in WordsC (36:4) 2005, 175–6.

1116. Hilliard, Chris. The bookmen's dominion: cultural life in New Zealand 1920–1950. *See* **11937**.

1117. Horejsi, Nicole. 'A counterpart to the Ephesian matron': Steele's *Inkle and Yarico* and a feminist critique of the Classics. ECS (39:2) 2006, 201–26.

1118. Howard, June. 'Her very handwriting looks as if she owned the earth': Elizabeth Jordan and editorial power. *In* (pp. 64–76) **690**.

1119. Hughes, Gillian. Duelling scars. TLS, 11 Aug. 2006, 4–5 (review-article). (*Blackwood's Magazine*.)

1120. Ingrassia, Catherine. Eliza Haywood, periodicals, and the function of orality. *In* (pp. 141–56) **7884**.

1121. Jenkins, Henry. 'He's in the closet but he's not gay': male–male desire in *Penthouse* 'letters'. *In* (pp. 133–53) **12592**.

1122. Johanningsmeier, Charles. How real American readers originally experienced James's *The Real Thing*. *See* **10570**.

1123. Johnson, Marilyn. The dead beat: lost souls, lucky stiffs, and the perverse pleasures of obituaries. *See* **3610**.

1124. Johnson, Sammye; Prijatel, Patricia. The magazine from cover to cover. Oxford; New York: OUP, 2006. pp. 416. (Second ed.: first ed. 1999.)

1125. Johnson-Woods, Toni. Story papers in Australia? The curious case of *Once-a-Week* down under. DNR (75:6) 2006, 164–90.

1126. Jordan, Ellen; Craig, Hugh; Antonia, Alexis. The Brontë sisters and the *Christian Remembrancer*: a pilot study in the use of the 'Burrows method' to identify the authorship of unsigned articles in the nineteenth-century periodical press. *See* **9233**.

1127. Joshua, Essaka; Joshua, Eleoma. Thomas Lovell Beddoes and the attribution of articles in the *Wellesley Index* and in the *Oxford Dictionary of National Biography*. *See* **9116**.

1128. Kamrath, Mark L.; Harris, Sharon M. (eds). Periodical literature in eighteenth-century America. (Bibl. 2005, 1244.) Rev. by Elizabeth Hewitt in EAL (41:3) 2006, 574–7; by Charles Johanningsmeier in SHARP (15:2/3) 2006, 18; by Bryan Waterman in AmP (16:2) 2006, 235–8.

1129. King, Andrew. The *London Journal* 1845–83: periodicals, production, and gender. (Bibl. 2005, 1246.) Rev. by Odin Dekkers in VPR (39:1) 2006, 67–9; by Kay Boardman in VS (48:3) 2006, 505–17.

1130. —— Plunkett, John (eds). Popular print media, 1820–1900. *See* **8411**.

1131. —— —— Victorian print media: a reader. *See* **768**.

1132. KING, KATHRYN R. Patriot or opportunist? Eliza Haywood and the politics of *The Female Spectator*. *In* (pp. 104–21) **7884**.

1133. KITCH, CAROLYN. Pages from the past: history and memory in American magazines. (Bibl. 2005, 1247.) Rev. by Joseph P. Bernt in JMCQ (83:2) 2006, 462–3; by Encarna Trinidad in JAStud (40:3) 2006, 670–1.

1134. LARBALESTIER, JUSTINE (ed.). Daughters of earth: feminist science fiction in the twentieth century. *See* **13537**.

1135. LATHAM, ROB. *New Worlds* and the New Wave in fandom: fan culture and the reshaping of science fiction in the sixties. *See* **13539**.

1136. MCLAREN, JOHN. Time to dream. Meanjin (63:1) 2004, 114–18. (Christesen and *Meanjin*.)

1137. MCPHEE, HILARY. Survival struggles. Meanjin (63:1) 2004, 119–25. (Christesen and *Meanjin*.)

1138. MARTÍNEZ LIROLA, MARÍA. A systemic functional analysis of two multimodal covers. *See* **2514**.

1139. MARTINSON, BARBARA. The journey to school: illustrations from popular American magazines, 1900–1962. *In* (pp. 93–108) **3157**.

1140. MERRITT, JULIETTE. Reforming the coquette? Eliza Haywood's vision of a female epistemology. *In* (pp. 176–92) **7884**.

1141. MIGUEL-ALFONSO, RICARDO. Social conservatism, aesthetic education, and the essay genre in Eliza Haywood's *Female Spectator*. *In* (pp. 72–81) **7884**.

1142. MILLIER, BRETT. *Chelsea 8*: political poetry at midcentury. *In* (pp. 94–108) **15599**.

1143. MORRISON, ROBERT. William Blackwood and the dynamics of success. *In* (pp. 21–48) **1098**.

1144. MORRISSON, MARK. Nationalism and the modern American canon. *In* (pp. 22–35) **11964**.

1145. —— Publishing. *In* (pp. 133–42) **11788**.

1146. NEWMAN, DONALD J. *The Female Spectator*: a bibliographic essay. *In* (pp. 212–41) **7884**.

1147. NICHOLAS, DAVID, *et al.* Ideas on creating a consumer market for scholarly journals. LPub (19:4) 2006, 245–9.

1148. NORTH, MICHAEL. Camera works: photography and the twentieth-century word. *See* **12066**.

1149. PATTEN, ROBERT L.; FINKELSTEIN, DAVID. Editing *Blackwood's*; or, What do editors do? *In* (pp. 146–83) **1098**.

1150. PEACEY, JASON. The management of Civil War newspapers: *auteurs*, entrepreneurs and editorial control. *See* **6489**.

1151. PETTIT, ALEXANDER. The Pickering & Chatto *Female Spectator*: nearly four pounds of ephemera, enshrined. *In* (pp. 42–59) **7884**.

1152. PHEGLEY, JENNIFER. Educating the proper woman reader: Victorian family literary magazines and the cultural health of the nation. (Bibl. 2005, 1303.) Rev. by Karen Chase in VIJ (33) 2005, 246–9.

1153. Pitcher, Edward W. R. (comp.). *American Moral & Sentimental Magazine* (New York, 1797–1798): an annotated catalogue. Lewiston, NY; Lampeter: Mellen Press, 2005. pp. 136. (Studies in British and American magazines, 34.)

1154. —— *The Literary Magazine and British Review* (London 1788–1794): an annotated catalogue of the prose and verse. Lewiston, NY; Lampeter: Mellen Press, 2005. 2 vols. pp. 376. (Studies in British and American magazines, 32A/B.)

1155. —— *The Nightingale; or, A mélange de littérature* (Boston, May 10 – July 30, 1796): an annotated catalogue of contents and sources. Lewiston, NY; Lampeter: Mellen Press, 2005. pp. 154. (Studies in British and American magazines, 33.)

1156. —— *The Rural Magazine; or, Vermont Repository* (Rutland, January 1795 – December 1796): an annotated catalogue of the literary contents. Lewiston, NY; Lampeter: Mellen Press, 2005. pp. 270. (Studies in British and American magazines, 37.)

1157. Pollin, Burton R. Kilmer's promotion of Poe. *See* **11038**.

1158. Powell, Neil. The gingko in the garden. PNRev (32:5) 2006, 5–6. (*London Magazine*.)

1159. Puchner, Martin. The aftershocks of *Blast*: manifestos, satire, and the rear-guard of Modernism. *In* (pp. 44–67) **12024**.

1160. Rooks, Noliwe M. Ladies' pages: African American women's magazines and the culture that made them. (Bibl. 2005, 1323.) Rev. by Cynthia A. Callahan in AAR (40:1) 2006, 175–7.

1161. Rosenberg, Leah. Modern romances: the short stories in Una Marson's *The Cosmopolitan* (1928–1931). *See* **17453**.

1162. Ross, John C. The *Forerunner*: an intriguing New Zealand little magazine, 1907–1914. BSANZB (28:4) 2004, 71–83.

1163. Sanders, Mike. 'A jackass load of poetry': the *Northern Star*'s poetry column 1838–1852. *See* **8820**.

1164. Schlicke, Paul. Dickens and the pirates: the case of *The Odd Fellow*. *See* **9816**.

1165. Schoina, Maria. Leigh Hunt's *Letters from Abroad* and the 'Anglo-Italian' discourse of *The Liberal*. *See* **10518**.

1166. Sherbo, Arthur. A forgotten literary give-and-take. NQ (53:3) 2006, 349–50. (*The Egoist: an Individualist Review*.)

1167. Snodgrass, Charles. *Blackwood's* subversive Scottishness. *In* (pp. 90–116) **1098**.

1168. Spedding, Patrick. Measuring the success of Haywood's *Female Spectator* (1744–46). *In* (pp. 193–211) **7884**.

1169. Steinhoff, Eirik. The making of *Chicago Review*: the meteoric years. ChiR (52:2–4) 2006, 292–312.

1170. Strachan, John. 'The mapp'd out skulls of Scotia': *Blackwood's* and the Scottish phrenological controversy. *In* (pp. 49–69) **1098**.

1171. Sturrock, June. Establishing identity: editorial correspondence from the early years of *The Monthly Packet*. *See* **11728**.

1172. Sumpter, Caroline. Innocents and epicures: the child, the fairy tale and avant-garde debate in *fin-de-siècle* little magazines. *See* **16460**.

1173. Szefel, Lisa. Beauty and William Braithwaite. *See* **14844**.

1174. Topliss, Iain. The comic worlds of Peter Arno, William Steig, Charles Addams, and Saul Steinberg. (Bibl. 2005, 1349.) Rev. by Jonathan Greenberg in Mod/Mod (13:2) 2006, 401–3.

1175. VanArsdel, Rosemary T. The *Wellesley Index* forty years later (1966–2006). VPR (39:3) 2006, 257–65.

1176. Warne, Vanessa. Thackeray among the annuals: morality, cultural authority and the literary annual genre. *See* **11419**.

1177. Wild, Jonathan. 'Insects in letters': *John O'London's Weekly* and the new reading public. *See* **13915**.

1178. Wilputte, Earla A. 'Too ticklish to meddle with': the silencing of *The Female Spectator*'s political correspondents. *In* (pp. 122–40) **7884**.

1179. Wiman, Christian. In praise of rareness. Poetry (189:3) 2006, 215–18.

1180. Worden, Daniel. The shameful art: *McSweeney's Quarterly Concern*, comics, and the politics of affect. *See* **18587**.

1181. Wright, Lynn Marie; Newman, Donald J. (eds). Fair philosopher: Eliza Haywood and *The Female Spectator*. *See* **7884**.

1182. Wu, Duncan. The Lamb circle and the *Monthly Repository*. *See* **10707**.

1183. Yaszek, Lisa. From *Ladies Home Journal* to *The Magazine of Fantasy and Science Fiction*: 1950s SF, the offbeat romance story, and the case of Alice Eleanor Jones. *In* (pp. 76–96) **13537**.

THE ENGLISH LANGUAGE

GENERAL STUDIES

1184. AARTS, BAS; MCMAHON, APRIL (eds). The handbook of English linguistics. Oxford; Malden, MA: Blackwell, 2006. pp. xviii, 806. (Blackwell handbooks in linguistics.)

1185. BAKER, PAUL. Using corpora in discourse analysis. London; New York: Continuum, 2006. pp. vii, 198. (Continuum discourse.) Rev. by Alison Duguid in TLS, 17 Nov. 2006, 32.

1186. CURZAN, ANNE; ADAMS, MICHAEL. How English works: a linguistic introduction. London; New York: Pearson Longman, 2006. pp. xxviii, 561. Rev. by Viktor Osinubi in CLAJ (49:3) 2006, 373–7.

1187. GRABES, HERBERT; VIERECK, WOLFGANG (eds). The wider scope of English: papers in English language and literature from the Bamberg Conference of the International Association of University Professors of English. New York; Frankfurt: Lang, 2006. pp. 219. (Univ. of Bamberg studies in English linguistics, 51.)

1188. GRAMLEY, STEPHAN; PAETZOLD, MICHAEL. A survey of Modern English. (Bibl. 1996, 1408.) London; New York: Routledge, 2004. pp. xviii, 397. (Second ed.: first ed. 1992.) Rev. by François Chevillet in EA (59:1) 2006, 101–2.

1189. PINNAVAIA, LAURA. Introduzione alla linguistica inglese. Rome: Carocci, 2006. pp. 112. (Le bussole, 219.)

1190. POSTAL, PAUL M. Skeptical linguistic essays. (Bibl. 2004, 1408.) Rev. by Robert D. Borsley in Lang (82:2) 2006, 442–6.

1191. SANTIPOLO, MATTEO. La varietà dell'inglese contemporaneo. Rome: Carocci, 2006. pp. 127. (Le bussole, 215.)

1192. SCOLLON, RON; SCOLLON, SUZIE WONG. Nexus analysis: discourse and the emerging Internet. London; New York: Routledge, 2004. pp. xvi, 198. Rev. by Jan Blommaert in AppL (26:4) 2005, 600–3.

1193. WEBSTER, JONATHAN J. (ed.). Computational and quantitative studies. By M. A. K. Halliday. London; New York: Continuum, 2005. pp. x, 300. (Collected works of M. A. K. Halliday, 6.) Rev. by Roy Harris in TLS, 17 Nov. 2006, 31.

1194. —— Studies in English language. London; New York: Continuum, 2005. pp. xxx, 353. (Collected works of M. A. K. Halliday, 7.) Rev. by Roy Harris in TLS, 17 Nov. 2006, 31.

1195. WILSON, ANDREW; RAYSON, PAUL; MCENERY, TONY (eds). Corpus linguistics by the Lune: a Festschrift for Geoffrey Leech. New York; Frankfurt: Lang, 2003. pp. 305. (Lódz studies in language, 8.) Rev. by Mario Brdar in Jezikoslovlje (4:2) 2003, 296–303.

HISTORY AND DEVELOPMENT OF ENGLISH

1196. ANON. Prof. Manfred Markus – bibliography and projects. *In* (pp. 341–58) **1227**.

1197. —— (comp.). A bibliography of writings by Bruce Mitchell 1956–2004. *In* (pp. 268–78) **1241**.

1198. ARCHER, DAWN; CULPEPER, JONATHAN. Sociopragmatic annotation: new directions and possibilities in historical linguistics. *In* (pp. 37–58) **1195**.

1199. BEARD, ADRIAN. Language change. London; New York: Routledge, 2004. pp. ix, 114. (Intertext.) Rev. by Paloma Tejada Caller in EIUC (14) 2006, 207–9.

1200. BÖKER, UWE. The recalcitrant corpus of the eighteenth-century canting crew: 'marginal language of marginal people'; or, History from below and within? *In* (pp. 11–34) **1227**.

1201. BROWNLEES, NICHOLAS (ed.). News discourse in early modern Britain: selected papers of CHINED 2004. *See* **4771**.

1202. BURROW, J. A.; TURVILLE-PETRE, THORLAC. A book of Middle English. (Bibl. 1998, 1529.) Oxford; Malden, MA: Blackwell, 2005. pp. viii, 419. (Third ed.: first ed. 1992.)

1203. CRESPO GARCÍA, BEGOÑA. English and Galician in the Middle Ages: a sociohistorical survey. RAEI (17) 2004, 45–63.

1204. DEROLEZ, RENÉ. Byrhtferðus bene docet. *See* **3760**.

1205. DOANE, A. N.; WOLF, KIRSTEN (eds). *Beatus vir*: studies in early English and Norse manuscripts in memory of Phillip Pulsiano. *See* **199**.

1206. DOSSENA, MARINA. 19CSC, ICAMET and the diachronic study of specialized discourse in correspondence. *In* (pp. 65–77) **1227**.

1207. —— 'The cinic Scotomastic'? Johnson, his commentators, Scots, French, and the story of English. *See* **7926**.

1208. ESSER, JÜRGEN. Stylistic change across generations? Conflicting evidence from psycholinguistic and corpuslinguistic data. *In* (pp. 79–100) **1227**.

1209. FACCHINETTI, ROBERTA; RISSANEN, MATTI (eds). Corpus-based studies of diachronic English. New York; Frankfurt: Lang, 2006. pp. 300. (Linguistic insights, 31.)

1210. FREEBORN, DENNIS. From Old English to Standard English: a coursebook in language variation across time. (Bibl. 1999, 1308.) Basingstoke; New York: Palgrave Macmillan, 2006. pp. xxiii, 446. (Studies in English language.) (Third ed.: first ed. 1992.)

1211. GOTTI, MAURIZIO. *Shall* and *will* as third person future auxiliaries in Early Modern English. *In* (pp. 121–39) **1227**.

1212. HAMMOND, WAYNE G.; SCULL, CHRISTINA (eds). *The Lord of the Rings* 1954–2004: scholarship in honor of Richard E. Blackwelder. *See* **18804**.

1213. HERDINA, PHILIP. Mehrsprachigkeit als Problem: eine kritische Betrachtung monolingualer Sprachgeschichtsschreibung am Beispiel des anglonormannischen Einflusses auf das Angelsächsische. MSp (49:1) 2005, 67–122.

1214. HICKEY, RAYMOND. Development and diffusion of Irish English. *In* (pp. 82–117) **2543**.

1215. —— Englishes in Asia and Africa: origin and structure. *In* (pp. 503–35) **2543.**

1216. —— (ed.). Legacies of colonial English: studies in transported dialects. *See* **2543.**

1217. Hogg, Richard; Denison, David (eds). A history of the English language. Cambridge; New York: CUP, 2006. pp. xiii, 495.

1218. Holm, John. Languages in contact: the partial restructuring of vernaculars. (Bibl. 2005, 1397.) Rev. by David J. Sutcliffe in SJL (28:1/2) 2004, 114–22; by Milton M. Azevedo in JPCL (21:1) 2006, 204–8.

1219. Hornero, Ana María; Luzón, María José; Murillo, Silvia (eds). Corpus linguistics: applications for the study of English. New York; Frankfurt: Lang, 2006. pp. 526. (Linguistic insights, 25.)

1220. Jones, Mari C.; Singh, Ishtla. Exploring language change. London; New York: Routledge, 2005. pp. xiv, 213. Rev. by Paloma Tejada Caller in EIUC (14) 2006, 209–11; by Daniel Schreier in JSoc (10:5) 2006, 686–9.

1221. Kay, Christian; Horobin, Simon; Smith, Jeremy (eds). New perspectives on English historical linguistics: selected papers from 12 ICEHL, Glasgow, 21–26 August 2002: 2, Lexis and transmission. (Bibl. 2004, 1444.) Rev. by Richard Dance in NQ (53:4) 2006, 563–5.

1222. Kay, Christian J.; Mackay, Margaret A. (eds). Perspectives on the Older Scottish tongue: a celebration of DOST. *See* **2567.**

1223. Kytö, Merja. The emergence of American English: evidence from seventeenth-century records in New England. *In* (pp. 121–57) **2543.**

1224. McCully, C. B.; Hilles, Sharon. The earliest English: an introduction to Old English language. London; New York: Pearson Longman, 2005. pp. xv, 307. (Learning about language.)

1225. MacDougall, Carl (ed.). Scots: the language of the people. *See* **2576.**

1226. Machan, Tim William. Early Modern Middle English. *In* (pp. 299–322) **4125.**

1227. Mair, Christian; Heuberger, Reinhard (eds); Wallmannsberger, Josef (assoc. ed.). Corpora and the history of English: papers dedicated to Manfred Markus on the occasion of his sixty-fifth birthday. Heidelberg: Winter, 2006. pp. 358. (Anglistische Forschungen, 363.)

1228. Mugglestone, Lynda (ed.). The Oxford history of the English language. Oxford; New York: OUP, 2006. pp. xi, 485.

1229. Nevalainen, Terttu. An introduction to Early Modern English. Oxford; New York: OUP, 2006. pp. 176. Rev. by Jonathan Hope in RES (57:231) 2006, 545–6.

1230. Poplack, Shana; Tagliamonte, Sali. Back to the present: verbal *-s* in the (African American) English diaspora. *In* (pp. 203–23) **2543.**

1231. Raumolin-Brumberg, Helena. Temporal aspects of language change: what can we learn from the CEEC? *In* (pp. 139–56) **1195.**

1232. Rickford, John R. Down for the count? The creole origins hypothesis of AAVE at the hands of the Ottawa Circle, and their supporters. *See* **2642.**

1233. Ringe, Don. A linguistic history of English: vol. 1, From proto Indo-European to proto-Germanic. Oxford; New York: OUP, 2006. pp. vi, 355. (Oxford linguistics.)

1234. Shippey, T. A. History in words: Tolkien's ruling passion. *In* (pp. 25–39) **18804**.

1235. Tani, Akinobu. *Thesaurus of Old English* for Early Middle English: an analysis in light of word pairs in the 'Katherine Group' lives. *In* (pp. 293–303) **1227**.

1236. Treharne, Elaine. Reading from the margins: the uses of Old English homiletic manuscripts in the post-Conquest period. *In* (pp. 329–58) **199**.

1237. Truelove, Alison. Linguistic diversity in the fifteenth-century Stonor Letters. *See* **4082**.

1238. van Gelderen, Elly. A history of the English language. Amsterdam; Philadelphia, PA: Benjamins, 2006. pp. xviii, 334.

1239. van Kemenade, Ans; Los, Bettelou (eds). The handbook of the history of English. Oxford; Malden, MA: Blackwell, 2006. pp. xvi, 655. (Blackwell handbooks in linguistics.)

1240. Walmsley, John. Introduction. *In* (pp. 1–18) **1241**.

1241. —— (ed.). Inside Old English: essays in honour of Bruce Mitchell. Oxford; Malden, MA: Blackwell, 2006. pp. xix, 295.

1242. Zettersten, Arne. The AB language lives. *In* (pp. 13–24) **18804**.

HISTORY OF LINGUISTICS

1243. Anderson, John. Notional grammar. Anglophonia (20) 2006, 9–49.

1244. Apter, Emily. The translation zone: a new comparative literature. *See* **2800**.

1245. Berry, R. M. Language. *In* (pp. 113–22) **11788**.

1246. Böker, Uwe. The recalcitrant corpus of the eighteenth-century canting crew: 'marginal language of marginal people'; or, History from below and within? *In* (pp. 11–34) **1227**.

1247. Burton, T. L.; Ruthven, K. K. *The English Dialect Dictionary* and Dorset usages recorded by *Notes and Queries*. *See* **2548**.

1248. Bygate, Martin. Applied linguistics: a pragmatic discipline, a generic discipline? AppL (26:4) 2005, 568–81.

1249. Coleman, Julie. A history of cant and slang dictionaries: vol. 2, 1785–1858. *See* **1623**.

1250. Cooper, Andrew R. Women's poetry, the 1830s, and monumental problems in the history of language theory. *See* **8766**.

1251. Cormier, Monique C. The reception of Abel Boyer's *Royal Dictionary* in the 18th century. *See* **7605**.

1252. Crystal, David. The fight for English: how language pundits ate, shot, and left. Oxford; New York: OUP, 2006. pp. xi, 239.

1253. Gotti, Maurizio. *Shall* and *will* as third person future auxiliaries in Early Modern English. *In* (pp. 121–39) **1227**.

1254. Iamartino, Giovanni. English flour and Italian bran: Johnson's *Dictionary* and the reformation of Italian lexicography in the early nineteenth century. *See* **7930**.

1255. Jackson, Philip J. B. Mama and papa: the ancestors of modern-day speech science. *In* (pp. 217–36) **7702**.

1256. Knappe, Gabriele. Peter Mark Roget's *Thesaurus of English Words and Phrases*: a mid-nineteenth-century example of the place of phraseology in the history of linguistic theory and practice. *In* (pp. 205–20) **1227**.

1257. Le Prieult, Henri. Délimitations et défenses du territoire: les conditions d'émergence de la linguistique nord-américaine au début du xxe siècle. Anglophonia (19) 2006, 149–59.

1258. Mair, Christian; Heuberger, Reinhard (eds); Wallmannsberger, Josef (assoc. ed.). Corpora and the history of English: papers dedicated to Manfred Markus on the occasion of his sixty-fifth birthday. *See* **1227**.

1259. Pearce, Michael. The Routledge dictionary of English language studies. *See* **1684**.

1260. Pebworth, Ted-Larry; Summers, Claude J. Jonson and his era: overviews of modern research. *See* **6898**.

1261. Rix, Robert W. The Crusonian alphabet: Thomas Spence's *Grand Repository of the English Language*. *See* **8160**.

1262. Rodríguez Juárez, Carolina. A new parameter for the description of subject assignment: the term hierarchy. *See* **1404**.

1263. Schleuter, Paul; Schleuter, June (eds). Francis A. March: selected writings of the first professor of English. Easton, PA: Friends of Skillman Library, Lafayette College, 2005. pp. 279. Rev. by Richard W. Bailey in JEL (34:2) 2006, 153–6.

1264. Senior, Claire. Shades of gray: a diachronic reading of Thomas Hardy's *Neutral Tones*. *See* **10326**.

1265. Stavans, Ilan. Dictionary days: a defining passion. *See* **1657**.

1266. Strand, Amy Dunham. Notes at the intersections of language and literature: the American Dialect Society's early *Dialect Notes*. AS (81:2) 2006, 115–31.

1267. Vicentini, Alessandra. In Johnson's footsteps: Baretti's *English Grammar* and the spread of the English language in Italy during the eighteenth century. *See* **7960**.

1268. Walmsley, John. How the leopard got its spots: English grammatical categories, Latin terms. *In* (pp. 248–67) **1241**.

1269. —— Introduction. *In* (pp. 1–18) **1241**.

1270. Weissbort, Daniel; Ástráður Eysteinsson (eds). Translation: theory and practice: a historical reader. *See* **2939**.

PHONETICS AND PHONOLOGY

HISTORICAL PHONETICS AND PHONOLOGY OF ENGLISH

1271. Balmuth, Miriam. The roots of phonics: a historical introduction. Foreword by Jeanne S. Chall. Austin, TX: Pro-Ed, 2006. pp. 345.

1272. Blevins, Juliette. New perspectives on English sound patterns: 'natural' and 'unnatural' in evolutionary phonology. JEL (34:1) 2006, 6–25.

1273. Boberg, Charles. The Dialect Topography of Montreal. *See* **2599**.

1274. Carroll, Tim; Smith, Emma; White, Martin. Purposeful playing? Purposeful criticism? *In* (pp. 38–60) **5543**.

1275. Chambers, J. K. 'Canadian dainty': the rise and decline of Briticisms in Canada. *In* (pp. 224–41) **2543**.

1276. Essinger, James. Spellbound: the improbable story of English spelling. London: Robson, 2006. pp. xxv, 254.

1277. Fuller, David. Reading Chaucer aloud. *In* (pp. 262–84) **4345**.

1278. Jones, Charles. English pronunciation in the eighteenth and nineteenth centuries. Basingstoke; New York: Palgrave Macmillan, 2006. pp. xi, 402.

1279. Lucas, Peter J. Abraham Wheelock and the presentation of Anglo-Saxon: from manuscript to print. *In* (pp. 383–439) **199**.

1280. Maci, Stefania Maria. The phonetic representation of ME *ī* in some Norfolk works of the late fifteenth century. EngS (87:2) 2006, 148–68.

1281. Miles, Elaine. English words and their spelling: a history of phonological conflicts. *See* **1333**.

1282. Schreier, Daniel. Consonant change in English worldwide: synchrony meets diachrony. (Bibl. 2005, 1447.) Rev. by Stephanie Hackert in JSoc (10:5) 2006, 690–4.

1283. Skouen, Tina. The vocal wit of John Dryden. *See* **6781**.

1284. Trudgill, Peter; Gordon, Elizabeth. Predicting the past: dialect archaeology and Australian English rhoticity. *See* **2707**.

PHONETICS AND PHONOLOGY OF CONTEMPORARY ENGLISH

1285. Atechi, Samuel Ngwa. The phonological influence of English on Awing. EngS (87:2) 2006, 230–48.

1286. Benor, Sarah Bunin; Levy, Roger. The chicken or the egg? A probabilistic account of English binomials. Lang (82:2) 2006, 233–78.

1287. Carr, P.; Brulard, I. Anglo-English influences on Scottish Standard English speakers: *trap/bath/palm/start* and *lot/cloth/thought/north/force*. *See* **2551**.

1288. Childs, Becky; Mallinson, Christine. African American English in Appalachia: dialect accommodation and substrate influence. *See* **2605**.

1289. Dziubalska-Kołaczyk, Katarzyna; Przedlacka, Joanna (eds). English pronunciation models. New York; Frankfurt: Lang, 2005. pp. 476. (Linguistic insights, 21.)

1290. Ferragne, Emmanuel. Quand le Professeur Higgins s'invite sur votre ordinateur: une approche moderne de la dialectologie. *See* **2558**.

1291. Féry, Caroline; Samek-Lodovici, Vieri. Focus projection and prosodic prominence in nested foci. Lang (82:1) 2006, 131–50.

1292. Fridland, Valerie; Bartlett, Kathryn. Correctness, pleasantness, and degree of difference ratings across regions. *See* **2612**.

1293. German, James; Pierrehumbert, Janet; Kaufmann, Stefan. Evidence for phonological constraints on nuclear accent placement. Lang (82:1) 2006, 151–68.

1294. Halliday, M. A. K.; Greaves, William S. Intonation in the grammar of English. Oakville, CT: Equinox, 2006. pp. 256. (Equinox textbooks and surveys in linguistics.)

1295. Hiraga, Masako K. Metaphor and iconicity: a cognitive approach to analyzing texts. *See* **1985**.

1296. Igboanusi, Herbert. A comparative study of the pronunciation features of Igbo English and Yoruba English speakers of Nigeria. *See* **2682**.

1297. Jeffries, Lesley. Discovering language: the structure of Modern English. *See* **1382**.

1298. Keyser, Samuel Jay; Stevens, Kenneth Noble. Enhancement and overlap in the speech chain. Lang (82:1) 2006, 33–63.

1299. Lawler, John M. The data fetishist's guide to rime coherence. Style (40:1/2) 2006, 158–78.

1300. Levon, Erez. Hearing 'gay': prosody, interpretation, and the affective judgments of men's speech. *See* **2217**.

1301. —— Mosaic identity and style: phonological variation among Reform American Jews. *See* **2627**.

1302. Monachino, Teresa. Words fail me. *See* **1499**.

1303. Ngefac, Aloysius; Sala, Bonaventure M. Cameroon Pidgin and Cameroon English at a confluence: a real-time investigation. *See* **2694**.

1304. Olausson, Lena; Sangster, Catherine M. Oxford BBC guide to pronunciation. Oxford; New York: OUP, 2006. pp. xvi, 432.

1305. Roach, Peter; Hartman, James; Setter, Jane (eds). Cambridge English pronouncing dictionary. By Daniel Jones. *See* **1688**.

1306. Roberts, Julie. As old becomes new: glottalization in Vermont. AS (81:3) 2006, 227–49.

1307. Sharbawi, Salbrina Haji. The vowels of Brunei English: an acoustic investigation. *See* **2703**.

1308. Slomanson, Peter; Newman, Michael. Peer group identification and variation in New York Latino English laterals. *See* **2646**.

1309. Starks, Donna; Reffell, Hayley. Reading 'TH': vernacular variables in Pasifika Englishes in South Auckland. *See* **2705**.

1310. Stuart-Smith, Jane; Timmins, Claire; Tweedie, Fiona. Conservation and innovation in a traditional dialect: L-vocalization in Glaswegian. *See* **2591**.

1311. Thomas, Erik R.; Carter, Phillip M. Prosodic rhythm and African American English. *See* **2652**.

1312. Warren, Paul. Oops, I've done a futt: quality and quantity in a New Zealand vowel contrast. Te Reo (49) 2006, 125–43.

1313. Wichmann, Anne; Cauldwell, Richard. *Wh-* questions and attitude: the effect of context. *In* (pp. 291–305) **1195**.

SPELLING, PUNCTUATION, HANDWRITING

1314. Alger, Abdullah. Two drypoint etchings in the Exeter Book. *See* **180**.

1315. Baker, Peter S. Typing in Old English since 1967: a brief history. *See* **127**.

1316. Balmuth, Miriam. The roots of phonics: a historical introduction. Foreword by Jeanne S. Chall. *See* **1271**.

1317. Beason, Larry. Eyes before ease: the unsolved mysteries and secret histories of spelling. Boston, MA: McGraw-Hill, 2006. pp. xii, 276.

1318. Beidler, Peter G. Where's the point? Punctuating Chaucer's *Canterbury Tales*. *In* (pp. 193–203) **4310**.

1319. Claghorn, George S. Transcribing a difficult hand: collecting and editing Edwards' letters over thirty-five years. *In* (pp. 217–27) **7762**.

1320. Donoghue, Daniel. A point well taken: manuscript punctuation and Old English poems. *In* (pp. 38–58) **1241**.

1321. Driscoll, M. J. Levels of transcription. *In* (pp. 254–61) **426**.

1322. Franzen, Christine. On the attribution of additions in Oxford, Bodleian MS Bodley 343 to the Tremulous Hand of Worcester. *See* **208**.

1323. Fries, Udo. *'Tis said*, the apostrophe, and the importance of Innsbruck in early English newspapers. *In* (pp. 101–14) **1227**.

1324. Gillespie, Stuart. A new eighteenth-century Juvenal translator: William Popple's Satires vi and x. *See* **8076**.

1325. Hall, David D. Scribal publication in seventeenth-century New England: an introduction and checklist. *See* **219**.

1326. Henry, Anne. *Quid ais omnium?* Maurice Kyffin's 1588 *Andria* and the emergence of suspension marks in printed drama. *See* **4895**.

1327. Howard-Hill, T. H. Early modern printers and the standardization of English spelling. MLR (101:1) 2006, 16–29.

1328. Jackson, MacD. P. John Webster, James Shirley, and the Melbourne manuscript. *See* **7181**.

1329. Laing, Margaret; Lass, Roger. Early Middle English *knight*: (pseudo)metathesis and lexical specificity. *See* **1579**.

1330. Lotfipour-Saedi, K. Discoursal function of phonological patterns in poetic texts: implications for (UN-)translatability of poetry. *See* **3572**.

1331. McKellar, Jennifer. The poetics of interruption in Mark Twain's *Roughing It*. *See* **11514**.

1332. Merriam, Thomas. Orthographic changes in *John a Kent* and Hand M of *More*. *See* **4971**.

1333. Miles, Elaine. English words and their spelling: a history of phonological conflicts. London; Philadelphia, PA: Whurr, 2005. pp. x, 232.

1334. Rix, Robert W. The Crusonian alphabet: Thomas Spence's *Grand Repository of the English Language*. *See* **8160**.

1335. Roberts, Jane. Guide to scripts used in English writings up to 1500. London: British Library, 2005. pp. xv, 294.

1336. Stanley, E. G. 'God's mercy and kindly thought': the meaning of Old English *myne*, spelt *mine* in the will of Wulfwaru. *See* **1586**.

1337. Storey, H. Wayne. A question of punctuation and 'ear[s] for dissenting voices': introduction to *Textual Cultures* 1.2. *See* **18051**.

1338. Szczepek Reed, Beatrice. Prosodic orientation in English conversation. *See* **2236**.

1339. Terada, Rei. Writing as a child: Lowell's poetic penmanship. *In* (pp. 33–52) **13763**.

1340. Van Kleeck, Justin. Blake's four ... *Zoa's*? *See* **7588**.

1341. Wittern, Christian. Writing systems and character representation. *In* (pp. 291–8) **426**.

1342. Woods, Geraldine. Webster's New World punctuation: simplified and amplified. Chichester; Hoboken, NJ: Wiley, 2006. pp. x, 348.

GRAMMAR

MORPHOLOGY OF CONTEMPORARY ENGLISH

1343. Harris, Alice C. Revisiting anaphoric islands. Lang (82:1) 2006, 114–30. (English and Georgian.)

1344. Hickey, Raymond. Productive lexical processes in present-day English. *In* (pp. 153–68) **1227**.

1345. Mair, Christian. Inflected genitives are spreading in present-day English, but not necessarily to inanimate nouns. *In* (pp. 235–48) **1227**.

1346. Montgomery, Michael. The morphology and syntax of Ulster Scots. *See* **2581**.

1347. Szmrecsanyi, Benedikt. Morphosyntactic persistence in spoken English: a corpus study at the intersection of variationist sociolinguistics, psycholinguistics, and discourse analysis. *See* **2237**.

HISTORICAL MORPHOLOGY OF ENGLISH

1348. Howard-Hill, T. H. Early modern printers and the standardization of English spelling. *See* **1327**.

1349. Miller, D. Gary. Latin suffixal derivatives in English and their Indo-European ancestry. Oxford; New York: OUP, 2006. pp. xxxvi, 386.

SINGLE MORPHEMES

1350. *be-/bi-*] Petré, Peter. The prefix *be-/bi-* as a marker of verbs of deception in Late Old and Early Middle English. BELL (ns 4) 2006, 109–27.

1351. *-cok*] McClure, Peter. The kinship of *Jack*: II, Pet forms of Middle English personal names with the suffixes *-cok* and *-cus*. *See* **1730**.

1352. *-cus*] —— The kinship of *Jack*: II, Pet-forms of Middle English personal names with the suffixes *-cok* and *-cus*. *See* **1730**.

1353. *girly-*] Battistella, Edwin. Girly men and girly girls. AS (81:1) 2006, 100–10.

1354. *-lochy*] King, Jacob. 'Lochy' names and Adomnán's *Nigra dea*. *See* **1706**.

1355. *mōd*] Diller, Hans-Jürgen. The decline of the family of *mōd*: ICAMET and other corpora. *In* (pp. 51–64) **1227**.

1356. *-s*] Agari, Masahiko. Towards the prevalence of the third person singular *-s* in Early Modern English. NM (106:4) 2005, 389–404.

SYNTAX OF CONTEMPORARY ENGLISH

1357. Anderson, John. Notional grammar. *See* **1243**.

1358. Arua, Arua E. Botswana English: some syntactic and lexical features. *See* **2663**.

1359. Austin, Frances. Points of modern English usage lxxxi. EngS (86:3) 2005, 269.

1360. —— Points of modern English usage lxxxii. EngS (87:1) 2006, 99–110.

1361. Benor, Sarah Bunin; Levy, Roger. The chicken or the egg? A probabilistic account of English binomials. *See* **1286**.

1362. Boberg, Charles. The Dialect Topography of Montreal. *See* **2599**.

1363. Bock, Kathryn, *et al.* Number agreement in British and American English: disagreeing to agree collectively. Lang (82:1) 2006, 64–113.

1364. Buregeya, Alfred. Grammatical features of Kenyan English and the extent of their acceptability. *See* **2667**.

1365. Cameron, Deborah. Bad grammar. CritQ (48:2) 2006, 91–4.

1366. Childs, Becky; Mallinson, Christine. African American English in Appalachia: dialect accommodation and substrate influence. *See* **2605**.

1367. Dixon, Robert M. W. A semantic approach to English grammar. Oxford; New York: OUP, 2005. pp. xvi, 543. (Oxford textbooks in linguistics.) (Second ed.: first ed. 1991.) (Orig. pub. as *A New Approach to English Grammar, on Semantic Principles*.)

1368. Dossena, Marina. Scotticisms in grammar and vocabulary: 'Like runes upon a standin' stane'? *See* **2556**.

1369. Duffley, Patrick J. The English gerund–participle: a comparison with the infinitive. New York; Frankfurt: Lang, 2006. pp. ix, 188. (Berkeley insights in linguistics and semiotics, 61.)

1370. Dušková, Libuše. Syntactic constancy of the verb between English and Czech. PSE (24) 2006, 19–44.

1371. Florey, Kitty Burns. Sister Bernadette's barking dog: the quirky history and lost art of diagramming sentences. Hoboken, NJ: Melville House, 2006. pp. 154.

1372. Foley, William. Universal constraints and local conditions in pidginization: case studies from New Guinea. *See* **2736**.

1373. Fukui, Naoki. Theoretical comparative syntax: studies in macro-parameters. London; New York: Routledge, 2006. pp. ix, 422. (Routledge leading linguists, 13.)

1374. Gahl, Susanne; Garnsey, Susan. Knowledge of grammar includes knowledge of syntactic probabilities. Lang (82:2) 2006, 405–10.

1375. German, James; Pierrehumbert, Janet; Kaufmann, Stefan. Evidence for phonological constraints on nuclear accent placement. *See* **1293**.

1376. Giancarli, Pierre-Don. Le futur périphrastique modal français d'"allure extraordinaire' (assertif, interrogatif, impératif) et ses traductions en anglais. Anglophonia (20) 2006, 149–79.

1377. Golato, Andrea. Compliments and compliment responses: grammatical structure and sequential organization. *See* **1805**.

1378. Halliday, M. A. K.; Greaves, William S. Intonation in the grammar of English. *See* **1294**.

1379. Hickey, Raymond. Tracking lexical changes in present-day English. *In* (pp. 93–105) **1195**.

1380. Hollebrandse, Bart; van Hout, Angeliek; Vet, Co (eds). Crosslinguistic views on tense, aspect and modality. Amsterdam; New York: Rodopi, 2005. pp. vii, 259. (Cahiers Chronos, 13.) Rev. by Jimmy Ureel in BELL (ns 4) 2006, 213–16.

1381. Iyeiri, Yoko (ed.). Aspects of English negation. Amsterdam; Philadelphia, PA: Benjamins, 2005. pp. vi, 239.

1382. Jeffries, Lesley. Discovering language: the structure of Modern English. Basingstoke; New York: Palgrave Macmillan, 2006. pp. xvii, 252. (Perspectives on the English language.)

1383. Jonz, Jon. An introduction to English sentence structure: clauses, markers, missing elements. Oakville, CT: Equinox, 2006. pp. 224. (Equinox textbooks and surveys in linguistics.)

1384. Kudrnáčová, Naděžda. Oscillatory corporeal verbs from a semantico-syntactic perspective. *See* **1761**.

1385. Laffut, An. Three-participant constructions in English: a functional–cognitive approach to caused relation. Amsterdam; Philadelphia, PA: Benjamins, 2006. pp. vii, 268. (Studies in language companion series, 79.)

1386. Lakoff, Robin Tolmach. Vulgar Latin: comparative castration (and comparative theories of syntax). Style (40:1/2) 2006, 56–61.

1387. Langendoen, D. Terence. Disjunctive numerals of estimation. Style (40:1/2) 2006, 46–55.

1388. Langlotz, Andreas. Occasional adnominal idiom modification – a cognitive linguistic approach. IJES (6:1) 2006, 85–108.

1389. Levey, Stephen. Tense variation in preadolescent narratives. *See* **2214**.

1390. Lipson, Maxine. Exploring functional grammar. Bologna: CLUEB, 2006. pp. 183.

1391. McCafferty, Kevin. '[T]hunder storms is verry dangese in this contrey they come in less than a minnits notice …': the Northern Subject Rule in Southern Irish English. *See* **2574**.

1392. Mair, Christian. Inflected genitives are spreading in present-day English, but not necessarily to inanimate nouns. *In* (pp. 235–48) **1227**.

1393. Malá, Markéta. Some remarks on participial adverbial clauses from the point of view of functional sentence perspective. PSE (24) 2006, 45–58.

1394. Malinovsky, Milan. Length of sentences and words in Czech and English and in other European languages. MSp (49:2) 2005, 149–57.

1395. Meierkord, Christiane. Syntactic variation in interactions across international Englishes. *See* **2722**.

1396. Merlo, Paola; Ferrer, Eva Esteve. The notion of argument in prepositional phrase attachment. CompLing (32:3) 2006, 341–78.

1397. Mignot, Élise. Les adjectifs: entre déterminant et nom. EA (59:4) 2006, 452–65.

1398. Montgomery, Michael. The morphology and syntax of Ulster Scots. *See* **2581**.

1399. Moya, A. Jesús. On pragmatic functions and their correlation with syntactic functions: a functionalist perspective. Atl (28:1) 2006, 9–28.

1400. Mukerjee, Joybrato; Hoffmann, Sebastian. Describing verb-complementational profiles of new Englishes: a pilot study of Indian English. *See* **2692**.

1401. Nevins, Debbie. The trouble with himorher: winning the battle of the sexes (in pronouns). Writing (29:2) 2006, 7.

1402. Newmeyer, Frederick J. On Gahl and Garnsey on grammar and usage. Lang (82:2) 2006, 399–404.

1403. Postal, Paul M. Remarks on English long-distance anaphora. Style (40:1/2) 2006, 7–19.

1404. Rodríguez Juárez, Carolina. A new parameter for the description of subject assignment: the term hierarchy. Atl (28:1) 2006, 71–88.

1405. Sampson, Geoffrey. Reflections of a dendrographer. *In* (pp. 157–84) **1195**.

1406. Szmrecsanyi, Benedikt. Morphosyntactic persistence in spoken English: a corpus study at the intersection of variationist sociolinguistics, psycholinguistics, and discourse analysis. *See* **2237**.

1407. Tanskanen, Sanna-Kaisa. Collaborating towards coherence: lexical cohesion in English discourse. Amsterdam; Philadelphia, PA: Benjamins, 2006. pp. vii, 192. (Pragmatics & beyond, ns 146.)

1408. Taverniers, Miriam. Grammatical metaphor and lexical metaphor: different perspectives on semantic variation. *See* **2152**.

1409. Thoma, Chrystalla. Combining functional linguistics and skopos theory: a case study of Greek Cypriot and British folktales. New York; Frankfurt: Lang, 2006. pp. 309. (European univ. studies, xxi: Linguistics, 295.)

1410. Trüb, Regina. Nonstandard verbal paradigms in earlier White Southern American English. *See* **2655**.

1411. Van Rooy, Bertus. The extension of the progressive aspect in Black South African English. *See* **2708**.

1412. Velupillai, Viveka. Hawai'i Creole English: a typological analysis of the tense–mood–aspect system. *See* **2748**.

1413. Walker, James A.; Meyerhoff, Miriam. Zero copula in the Eastern Caribbean: evidence from Bequia. *See* **2749**.

1414. Webelhuth, Gert; Dannenberg, Clare J. Southern American English personal datives: the theoretical significance of dialectal variation. *See* **2659**.

1415. Ziegeler, Debra; Lee, Sarah. Causativity reduction in Singaporean English. *See* **2713**.

HISTORICAL SYNTAX OF ENGLISH

1416. Agari, Masahiko. Towards the prevalence of the third person singular *-s* in Early Modern English. *See* **1356**.

1417. Bammesberger, Alfred. The syntactic analysis of the opening verses in *Beowulf*. *See* **3739**.

1418. Expósito González, Mª Cruz. Abstract or concrete nouns: relevant variables in the selection of relative pronouns. REsLA (19) 2006, 103–17.

1419. Garzon, Susan. Social variation and grammatical patterns in 1770s Virginia: evidence from Robert Munford's *The Candidates*. *See* **8022**.

1420. González-Díaz, Victorina. On the nature and distribution of English double periphrastic comparison. RES (57:232) 2006, 623–64.

1421. Hickey, Raymond. English dialect input to the Caribbean. *In* (pp. 326–59) **2543**.

1422. Kohnen, Thomas. Variability of form as a methodological problem in historical corpus analysis: the case of modal expressions in directive speech acts. *In* (pp. 220–33) **1227**.

1423. Martín Arista, Javier; Martín de la Rosa, María Victoria. Old English semantic primes: substantives, determiners and quantifiers. Atl (28:2) 2006, 9–28.

1424. Mitchell, Bruce; Irvine, Susan. A critical bibliography of Old English syntax: supplement 1997–2000 part 1. NM (107:1) 2006, 91–116.

1425. Moessner, Lilo. The subjunctive in Early Modern English adverbial clauses. *In* (pp. 249–63) **1227**.

1426. Montgomery, Michael. Solving Kurath's puzzle: establishing the antecedents of the American Midland dialect region. *In* (pp. 310–25) **2543**.

1427. Pérez-Guerra, Javier. Word order after the loss of the verb-second constraint; or, The importance of Early Modern English in the fixation of syntactic and informative (un-markedness). EngS (86:4) 2005, 342–69.

1428. Suárez Gomez, Cristina. Relativization in early English (950–1250): the position of relative clauses. New York; Frankfurt: Lang, 2006. pp. 149. (Linguistic insights, 49.)

1429. Vicentini, Alessandra. In Johnson's footsteps: Baretti's *English Grammar* and the spread of the English language in Italy during the eighteenth century. *See* **7960**.

1430. Walmsley, John. How the leopard got its spots: English grammatical categories, Latin terms. *In* (pp. 248–67) **1241**.

1431. Wright, Laura. The language of transported Londoners: third person singular present-tense markers in depositions from Virginia and the Bermudas, 1607–1624. *In* (pp. 158–71) **2543**.

1432. Yokota, Yumi. Form and function of demonstratives in the Middle English southern texts and speculation on the origin of *th-* type third person plural pronouns in the north and south. NQ (53:3) 2006, 300–3.

1433. Ziegeler, Debra. Interfaces with English aspect: diachronic and empirical studies. Amsterdam; Philadelphia, PA: Benjamins, 2006. pp. vii, 325. (Studies in language companion series, 82.)

SINGLE SYNTACTICAL ITEMS

1434. *about*] D'Arcy, Alexandra. Lexical replacement and the like(s). *See* **1448**.

1435. *actually*] Ajimer, Karin. Discourse particles in contrast: the case of *in fact* and *actually*. *In* (pp. 23–35) **1195**.

1436. *be + -ing*] Núñez Pertejo, Paloma. Some developments in the semantics of the English progressive from Old English to Early Modern English. RAEI (17) 2004, 211–26.

1437. *be like*] Rollins, Benjamin. The juggernaut among American quotatives: a case study of *be like* in the American South. SJL (30:2) 2006, 70–84.

1438. *bēodan*] López Couso, María José; Méndez Naya, Belén. Complement selection in early English dependent desires: a look at commands and requests. EIUC (14) 2006, 33–53.

1439. *biddan*] —— —— Complement selection in early English dependent desires: a look at commands and requests. *See* **1438**.

1440. *do different*] Shepheard, Richard. Doing different: a word from Norfolk. *See* **9150**.

1441. *even if*] Handley, Simon J.; Feeney, Aidan. Reasoning and pragmatics: the case of *even if*. *In* (pp. 228–53) **1818**.

1442. *fu*] Lefebvre, Claire; Loranger, Virginie. On the properties of Saramaccan *fu*: synchronic and diachronic perspectives. JPCL (21:2) 2006, 275–335.

1443. *have*] Matsumoto, Meiko. The historical development and functional characteristics of composite predicates with *have* and *take* in English. EngS (86:5) 2005, 439–56.

1444. *I believe*] Van Bogaert, Julie. *I guess*, *I suppose* and *I believe* as pragmatic markers: grammaticalization and functions. *See* **1445**.

1445. *I guess*] —— *I guess*, *I suppose* and *I believe* as pragmatic markers: grammaticalization and functions. BELL (ns 4) 2006, 129–49.

1446. *I suppose*] —— *I guess*, *I suppose* and *I believe* as pragmatic markers: grammaticalization and functions. *See* **1445**.

1447. *in fact*] Ajimer, Karin. Discourse particles in contrast: the case of *in fact* and *actually*. *In* (pp. 23–35) **1195**.

1448. *like*] D'Arcy, Alexandra. Lexical replacement and the like(s). AS (81:4) 2006, 339–57.

1449. *ne*] Stein, Gabriele. Unsuppported negative *ne* in Richard Huloet (1552). NQ (53:3) 2006, 305–6.

1450. *no/not*] Merchant, Jason. Why no(t)? Style (40:1/2) 2006, 20–3.

1451. *or*] Chierchia, Gennaro. Semantic and pragmatic competence in children's and adults' comprehension of *or*. *In* (pp. 283–300) **1818**.

1452. *please to*] Gold, David L. A little-noticed English construction: subjectless imperative *please to* + infinitive. Neophilologus (90:1) 2006, 107–17.

1453. *-s*] Poplack, Shana; Tagliamonte, Sali. Back to the present: verbal *-s* in the (African American) English diaspora. *In* (pp. 203–23) **2543**.

1454. *shall*] Gotti, Maurizio. *Shall* and *will* as third person future auxiliaries in Early Modern English. *In* (pp. 121–39) **1227**.

1455. *some*] Baumer, Emmanuel. Étude contrastive de *some* + nom discontinu singulier et de ses traductions en français. Anglophonia (20) 2006, 50–81.

1456. *take*] Matsumoto, Meiko. The historical development and functional characteristics of composite predicates with *have* and *take* in English. *See* **1443**.

1457. *that*] Douay, Catherine. Grammaire et formatage de la réception: les postures allocutives marquées par *this* et *that*. *See* **1461**.

1458. *the*] Sadock, Jerrold M. Getting squishy. Style (40:1/2) 2006, 84–8. (Names of TV shows and use of definite article.)

1459. *they*] Montgomery, Michael. Notes on the development of existential *they*. AS (81:2) 2006, 132–45.

1460. *they*] Tortora, Christina. The case of Appalachian expletive *they*. AS (81:3) 2006, 266–96.

1461. *this*] Douay, Catherine. Grammaire et formatage de la réception: les postures allocutives marquées par *this* et *that*. Anglophonia (20) 2006, 113–31.

1462. *'tis*] Fries, Udo. *'Tis said*, the apostrophe, and the importance of Innsbruck in early English newspapers. *In* (pp. 101–14) **1227**.

1463. *to wit*] Rissanen, Matti. Latin influence on an Old English idiom: *to wit*. *In* (pp. 222–41) **1241**.

1464. *used to*] Binnick, Robert I. *Used to* and habitual aspect in English. Style (40:1/2) 2006, 33–45.

1465. *used to*] Hantson, André. The English perfect and the anti-perfect *used to* viewed from a comparative perspective. EngS (86:3) 2005, 245–68.

1466. *what*] Aarts, Bas, *et al*. *Which* or *what*? A study of interrogative determiners in present-day English. *In* (pp. 9–22) **1195**.

1467. *which*] —— *Which* or *what*? A study of interrogative determiners in present-day English. *In* (pp. 9–22) **1195**.

1468. *will*] Gotti, Maurizio. *Shall* and *will* as third person future auxiliaries in Early Modern English. *In* (pp. 121–39) **1227**.

1469. *you-all*] Hyman, Eric. The *all* of *you-all*. AS (81:3) 2006, 325–31.

VOCABULARY

VOCABULARY OF CONTEMPORARY ENGLISH

1470. Arua, Arua E. Botswana English: some syntactic and lexical features. *See* **2663**.

1471. Benczes, Réka. Creative compounding in English: the semantics of metaphorical and metonymical noun–noun combinations. Amsterdam; Philadelphia, PA: Benjamins, 2006. pp. xiv, 205. (Human cognitive processing, 19.)

1472. Biber, Douglas; Conrad, Susan; Cortes, Viviana. Lexical bundles in speech and writing: an initial taxonomy. *In* (pp. 71–92) **1195**.

1473. Budanitsky, Alexander; Hirst, Graeme. Evaluating WordNet-based measures of lexical semantic relatedness. CompLing (32:1) 2006, 13–47.

1474. Casselman, Bill. Canadian words & sayings. *See* **2603**.

1475. Childs, Becky; Mallinson, Christine. The significance of lexical items in the construction of ethnolinguistic identity: a case study of adolescent spoken and online language. *See* **2759**.

1476. Crosland, Maurice. The language of science: from the vernacular to the technical. Cambridge: Lutterworth Press, 2006. pp. 127. Rev. by Patricia Fara in TLS, 22 & 29 Dec. 2006, 39.

1477. de Klerk, Vivian. Slang and swearing as markers of inclusion and exclusion in adolescence. *In* (pp. 111–27) **2798**.

1478. Dent, Susie. Fanboys and overdogs: the language report. Oxford; New York: OUP, 2005. pp. x, 163.

1479. Dossena, Marina. Scotticisms in grammar and vocabulary: 'Like runes upon a standin' stane'? *See* **2556**.

1480. Glowka, Wayne, *et al.* Among the new words. AS (81:1) 2006, 79–93.

1481. —— Among the new words. AS (81:2) 2006, 180–202.

1482. —— Among the new words. AS (81:3) 2006, 297–313.

1483. —— Among the new words. AS (81:4) 2006, 423–47.

1484. Herrmann, Keith R. The war of words. WLA (18:1/2) 2006, 319–23.

1485. Hicks, Wynford. Quite literally: problem words and how to use them. London; New York: Routledge, 2004. pp. xiv, 251.

1486. Hole, Georgia. The real McCoy: the true stories behind our everyday phrases. Oxford; New York: OUP, 2005. pp. 200.

1487. Hunter, Jenny (ed.). The true blue guide to Australian slang. *See* **2681**.

1488. Jack, Albert. Red herrings and white elephants: the origins of the phrases we use everyday. New York: HarperCollins, 2005. pp. xvi, 256.

1489. Katamba, Francis. English words: structure, history, usage. (Bibl. 1994, 1139.) London; New York: Routledge, 2005. pp. xix, 322. (Second ed.: first ed. 1994.)

1490. Klégr, Aleš; Čermák, Jan. Onomasiological cycle: up the down staircase. PSE (24) 2006, 7–18.

1491. Lillo, Antonio. Exploring rhyming slang in Ireland. *See* **2571**.

1492. MACALISTER, JOHN. Of *weka* and *waiata*: familiarity with borrowings from Te Reo Maori. Te Reo (49) 2006, 101–24.

1493. MCCARTHY, MORTY. Dowtcha boy! An anthology of Cork slang. *See* **2575**.

1494. MAHLBERG, MICHAELA. English general nouns: a corpus-theoretical approach. Amsterdam; Philadelphia, PA: Benjamins, 2005. pp. viii, 206. (Studies in corpus linguistics, 20.)

1495. MALINOVSKY, MILAN. Length of sentences and words in Czech and English and in other European languages. *See* **1394**.

1496. MANN, LEONARD. Green-eyed monsters & Good Samaritans: literary allusions in everyday language. Boston, MA: McGraw-Hill, 2006. pp. xi, 212.

1497. MASI, SILVIA. Lexicographic material under observation: from Johnson's *Dictionary* to a model for a cognition-based dictionary of lexical patterns. *See* **7943**.

1498. MILLER, GEORGE A.; HRISTEA, FLORENTINA. WordNet nouns: classes and instances. CompLing (32:1) 2006, 1–3.

1499. MONACHINO, TERESA. Words fail me. London: Phaidon, 2006. 1 vol. (unpaginated). Rev. by Peter Mitham in Amphora (144) 2006, 42–3.

1500. REES, NIGEL. A man about a dog: euphemisms & other examples of verbal squeamishness. London: Collins, 2006. pp. ix, 417.

1501. SMITH, STEPHANIE A. Household words: *bloomers, sucker, bombshell, scab, nigger, cyber.* Minneapolis; London: Minnesota UP, 2006. pp. xxvi, 207.

1502. TATE, JAMES O. Mind your language! A sea of ruined words. Chronicles (30:2) 2006, 14–16.

1503. TKACHUK, TETYANA. Idioms inside out: money in English idioms. BStE (31) 2005, 63–72.

1504. TULLOCH, ALEXANDER R. Word routes: journeys through etymology. London; Chester Springs, PA: Owen, 2005. pp. 207.

1505. WARREN, BEATRICE. Prolegomena to a study of evaluative words. EngS (87:2) 2006, 210–29.

1506. WILLIAMSON, CHILTON, JR. Manners, morals, language: forsaking the beau ideal. Chronicles (30:2) 2006, 17–19.

1507. WOLF, AARON D. A trip to smart-mouth college: the loss of sacred words. Chronicles (30:2) 2006, 20–1.

1508. YANG, JIAN. Lexical innovations in China English. *See* **2712**.

HISTORICAL VOCABULARY OF ENGLISH

1509. BATELY, JANET. The language of Ohthere's report to King Alfred: some problems and some puzzles for historians and linguists. *In* (pp. 39–53) **3679**.

1510. BERSON, JOEL S. The source for Benjamin Franklin's 'The Drinker's Dictionary' (and was it Mather Byles?). *See* **7805**.

1511. BILLI, MIRELLA. Johnson's beauties: the lexicon of aesthetics in the *Dictionary*. *See* **7916**.

1512. Burridge, Kate. Weeds in the garden of words: further observations on the tangled history of the English language. Cambridge; New York: CUP, 2005. pp. ix, 196.

1513. Cacchiani, Slivia. *Desperately, utterly* and other intensifiers: on their inclusion and definition in Johnson's *Dictionary*. *See* **7920**.

1514. 'Chrysti the Wordsmith'. Verbivore's feast: a banquet of word and phrase origins. Helena, MT: Farcountry Press, 2004. pp. viii, 376.

1515. Diller, Hans-Jürgen. The decline of the family of *mōd*: ICAMET and other corpora. *In* (pp. 51–64) **1227**.

1516. Doane, A. N. The Werden Glossary: structure and sources. *In* (pp. 41–84) **199**.

1517. Donoghue, Daniel. The Tremulous Hand and flying eaglets. *See* **3669**.

1518. Dossena, Marina; Taavitsainen, Irma (eds). Diachronic perspectives on domain-specific English. New York; Frankfurt: Lang, 2006. pp. 280. (Linguistic insights, 40.)

1519. Essinger, James. Spellbound: the improbable story of English spelling. *See* **1276**.

1520. Fairweather, Janet (introd. and trans.). *Liber Eliensis*: a history of the Isle of Ely from the seventh century to the twelfth, compiled by a monk of Ely in the twelfth century. Woodbridge, Suffolk; Rochester, NY: Boydell Press, 2005. pp. xliv, 576. (Includes section on Old English legal terminology.) Rev. by Andy Orchard in NQ (53:4) 2006, 548–9.

1521. Green, Jonathon. Slang by dates. CritQ (48:1) 2006, 99–104.

1522. Gunn, Joshua. Modern occult rhetoric: mass media and the drama of secrecy in the twentieth century. *See* **11918**.

1523. Harbus, Antonina; Poole, Russell (eds). Verbal encounters: Anglo-Saxon and Old Norse studies for Roberta Frank. (Bibl. 2005, 1786.) Rev. by Hanneke Wilson in RES (57:228) 2006, 136–8; by Melanie Heyworth in Parergon (23:1) 2006, 168–71.

1524. Harley, Heidi. English words: a linguistic introduction. Oxford; Malden, MA: Blackwell, 2006. pp. xvii, 296. (Language library.)

1525. Healey, Antonette diPaolo. Straining words and striving voices: polysemy and ambiguity and the importance of context in the disclosure of meaning. *In* (pp. 74–90) **1241**.

1526. Iamartino, Giovanni; DeMaria, Robert, Jr. Samuel Johnson's *Dictionary* and the eighteenth-century world of words: introduction. *See* **7931**.

1527. Kienpointner, Manfred. Emotion terms in the recent history of the English language. *In* (pp. 183–203) **1227**.

1528. Macalister, John. The Maori presence in the New Zealand English lexicon, 1850–2000. *See* **2690**.

1529. McDonald, Nicola (ed.). Medieval obscenities. Woodbridge, Suffolk; Rochester, NY: Boydell Press in assn with the York Medieval Press, 2006. pp. viii, 210. Rev. by Bettina Bildhauer in TLS, 8 Dec. 2006, 27.

1530. McEnery, Tony. Swearing in English: bad language, purity and power from 1586 to the present. London; New York: Routledge, 2006. pp. xv, 276. (Routledge advances in corpus linguistics, 1.)

1531. McGowan, Joseph P. Elliptical glossing and elliptical compounds in Old English. *In* (pp. 359–81) **199**.

1532. Pinnavaia, Laura. Idiomatic expressions regarding food and drink in Johnson's *Dictionary of the English Language* (1755 and 1773). *See* **7948**.

1533. Pireddu, Silvia. The 'landscape of the body': the language of medicine in Johnson's *Dictionary*. *See* **7949**.

1534. Pitts, Brent A.; Furnish, Shearle. The Middle English Apocalypse gloss in British Library MS Additional 18633. NQ (53:3) 2006, 293–5.

1535. Quinion, Michael. Gallimaufry: a hodgepodge of our vanishing vocabulary. Oxford; New York: OUP, 2006. pp. xiii, 272.

1536. Scanlan, J. T. Johnson's *Dictionary* and legal dictionaries. *See* **7954**.

1537. Simes, Gary. Gay slang lexicography: a brief history and a commentary on the first two gay glossaries. *See* **1654**.

1538. Tiffany, Daniel. Flash crib: a genealogy of modern nightlife. DQ (40:4) 2006, 151–64.

1539. Weinstock, Horst. *Vices and Virtues*: ein mittelenglisches Corpus um 1200. *In* (pp. 329–40) **1227**.

SINGLE WORDS AND PHRASES

1540. *afell*] Pons-Sanz, Sara M. The Norse origin of OE *afol* / ME *afell*: is evidence strong enough? *See* **1541**.

1541. *afol*] —— The Norse origin of OE *afol* / ME *afell*: is evidence strong enough? ELN (43:2) 2005, 1–8.

1542. *alleluia*] Morehen, John. *Alleluia*: a question of syllabification, *c*.1550–1625. JDJ (25) 2006, 291–314.

1543. *art*] Burnham, Clint. 13 retro keywords … and why they're worth a second look: *art*. ESCan (30:4) 2004, 5–10.

1544. *back*] Breuer, Horst. Early Modern English *back*: erotic uses. NQ (53:4) 2006, 533–6.

1545. *batshit*] Peters, Mark. A slang word that's spreading like crazy. AS (81:2) 2006, 218–24.

1546. *be like*] Buchstaller, Isabelle. Social stereotypes, personality traits and regional perception displaced: attitudes towards the 'new' quotatives in the UK. JSoc (10:3) 2006, 362–81.

1547. *blue*] Verspoor, Marjolijn H.; de Bie-Kerékjártó, Ágnes. Colorful bits of experience: from *bluestocking* to *blue movie*. EngS (87:1) 2006, 78–98.

1548. *bune*] Breeze, Andrew. *Bune* 'maiden; beloved' in *Ancrene Wisse*. NQ (53:2) 2006, 152–3.

1549. *bunk*] Rawson, Hugh. *Bunk*. AH (57:5) 2006, 16. (History now: why do we say …?)

1550. *careen*] Sayers, William. *Crank* and *careen*. *See* **1556**.

1551. *cat-o'-nine-tails*] MARTIN, RANDALL. *The cat* gets its nine tails. NQ (53:1) 2006, 31–4.

1552. *certain*] KJELLMER, GÖRAN. Certain uncertainties: semantic splits and interpretative strategies. EngS (87:3) 2006, 357–69.

1553. *cocktail*] RAWSON, HUGH. *Cocktail*. AH (57:3) 2006, 21. (History now: why do we say …?)

1554. *community*] MILLER, J. HILLIS. 13 retro keywords … and why they're worth a second look: *community*. ESCan (30:4) 2004, 11–16.

1555. *cool*] PETRUCCI, PETER R.; HEAD, MICHAEL. *Sweet as* is cool for New Zealanders. *See* **1601**.

1556. *crank*] SAYERS, WILLIAM. *Crank* and *careen*. NQ (53:3) 2006, 306–8.

1557. *dialectic*] BURCH, ROBERT. 13 retro keywords … and why they're worth a second look: *dialectic*. ESCan (30:4) 2004, 16–20.

1558. *effect/affect*] EDELMAN, CHARLES. Claudius's 'effects' in *Hamlet*. *See* **5717**.

1559. *embosen*] SCOTT-MACNAB, DAVID. Polysemy in Middle English *embosen* and the hart of *The Book of the Duchess*. *See* **4357**.

1560. *equality*] DAVEY, FRANK. 13 retro keywords … and why they're worth a second look: *equality*. ESCan (30:4) 2004, 21–4.

1561. *experience*] KAMUF, PEGGY. 13 retro keywords … and why they're worth a second look: *experience*. ESCan (30:4) 2004, 24–9.

1562. *fēsen*] PONS-SANZ, S. M. OE *fēs(i)an* / ME *fēsen* revisited. *See* **1563**.

1563. *fēs(i)an*] —— OE *fēs(i)an* / ME *fēsen* revisited. Neophilologus (90:1) 2006, 119–34.

1564. *froten*] WALTER, KATIE LOUISE. The Middle English term *froten*: Absolon and barber-surgery. NQ (53:3) 2006, 303–5.

1565. *G.I.*] RAWSON, HUGH. *G.I.* AH (57:2) 2006, 16. (History now: why do we say …?)

1566. *getryccað*] PONS-SANZ, SARA M. Sharpening, confiding, and OE *getryccað*. NQ (53:2) 2006, 146–50.

1567. *girmit*] MISHRA, SUDESH. Time and *girmit*. *See* **2740**.

1568. *go*] BUCHSTALLER, ISABELLE. Social stereotypes, personality traits and regional perception displaced: attitudes towards the 'new' quotatives in the UK. *See* **1546**.

1569. *hæðen*] PONS-SANZ, SARA M. Anglo-Scandinavian trade or paganism? OE *hæðen* in the First Cleopatra Glossary. MLR (101:3) 2006, 625–37.

1570. *history*] STEVENS, PAUL. 13 retro keywords … and why they're worth a second look: *history*. ESCan (30:4) 2004, 29–33.

1571. *hooker*] RAWSON, HUGH. *Hooker*. AH (57:1) 2006, 16. (History now: why do we say that?)

1572. *hycgan*] BERKHOUT, CARL T. A doubtful Old English gloss in Bede's *Vita sancti Cuthberti*. NQ (53:1) 2006, 10.

1573. *individual*] HERZ, JUDITH SCHERER. 13 retro keywords … and why they're worth a second look: *individual*. ESCan (30:4) 2004, 33–7.

1574. *introductorily*] SHERBO, ARTHUR. *Introductorily* in *OED*. NQ (53:4) 2006, 417.

1575. *jelly*] WALL, WENDY. Shakespearean jell-o: mortality and malleability in the kitchen. Gastronomica (6:1) 2006, 41–50.

1576. *jungle*] GOULDING, CHRISTOPHER. *Jungle*: antedating the entry in *OED*. NQ (53:1) 2006, 30.

1577. *keyword*] PATTERSON, ANNABEL. Keywords: Raymond Williams and others. ESCan (30:4) 2004, 66–80.

1578. *knarre*] BREDEHOFT, THOMAS A. Middle English *knarre*: more porcine imagery in the Miller's portrait. *See* **4371**.

1579. *knight*] LAING, MARGARET; LASS, ROGER. Early Middle English *knight*: (pseudo)metathesis and lexical specificity. NM (106:4) 2005, 405–23.

1580. *lester*] SAYERS, WILLIAM. Exeter Book Riddle 17 and the L-rune: British **lester* 'vessel, oat-straw hive'? *See* **3799**.

1581. *liberation*] GOLDIE, TERRY. 13 retro keywords … and why they're worth a second look: *liberation*. ESCan (30:4) 2004, 37–40.

1582. *literature*] CLARKE, GEORGE ELLIOTT. 13 retro keywords … and why they're worth a second look: *literature*. ESCan (30:4) 2004, 40–6.

1583. *māl*] PONS-SANZ, SARA M. OE *māl* for L *clasma* in Aldhelmian glossaries. NQ (53:4) 2006, 396–8.

1584. *mēnig*] BAMMESBERGER, ALFRED. The Old English adjective *mēnig* 'strong'. NQ (53:2) 2006, 144–6.

1585. *morris dance*] HEANEY, MICHAEL. The earliest reference to the morris dance? FMJ (8:4) 2004, 513–15.

1586. *myne*] STANLEY, E. G. 'God's mercy and kindly thought': the meaning of Old English *myne*, spelt *mine* in the will of Wulfwaru. NQ (53:3) 2006, 287–9.

1587. *neurisn*] MCILWAIN, JAMES T. The condition called *neurisn* in *Leechbook I*. *See* **3786**.

1588. *on*] SLOTE, SAM. On *Worstward Ho*. *See* **14727**.

1589. *orature*] CLARKE, GEORGE ELLIOTT. 13 retro keywords … and why they're worth a second look: *literature*. *See* **1582**.

1590. *organicism*] RAJAN, TILOTTAMA. 13 retro keywords … and why they're worth a second look: *organicism*. ESCan (30:4) 2004, 46–50.

1591. *rooster*] RAWSON, HUGH. *Rooster*. AH (57:4) 2006, 9. (History now: why do we say …?)

1592. *sæstunus*] PORTER, DAVID W. An unrecorded Old English compound. ANQ (19:2) 2006, 3–4.

1593. *smart*] PETERS, HANS. Getting *smart*. *In* (pp. 279–92) **1227**.

1594. *soud*] LEVIN, RICHARD. Petruchio's *soud*. *See* **6111**.

1595. *spend a penny*] EDELMAN, CHARLES. Chapman's *An Humorous Day's Mirth*. Exp (65:1) 2006, 2–4.

1596. *steam*] MEEK, DONALD E. Smoking, drinking, dancing and singing on the high seas: steamships and the uses of *smùid* in Scottish Gaelic. ScLang (25) 2006, 46–70.

1597. *still-vexed*] Hunt, Maurice. Shakespeare's 'still-vexed' *Tempest*. *See* **6130**.

1598. *styccemælum*] Lindström, Bengt. Old English *þreowa* and *styccemælum*. *See* **3801**.

1599. *suveran*] Micklethwait, David. A curious cross-reference in Webster's *American Dictionary*. *See* **1647**.

1600. *sweet*] Carruthers, Mary. 'Sweet Jesus'. *In* (pp. 9–19) **3896**.

1601. *sweet as*] Petrucci, Peter R.; Head, Michael. *Sweet as* is cool for New Zealanders. AS (81:3) 2006, 331–6.

1602. *swurdbora*] Cavill, Paul. The armour-bearer in Abbo's *Passio sancti Eadmundi* and Anglo-Saxon England. *See* **3709**.

1603. *tale of a tub*] Levin, Richard. *A tale of a tub*. NQ (53:4) 2006, 422–5.

1604. *tall poppies*] Peeters, Bert. *Tall poppies* and egalitarianism in Australian discourse: from key word to cultural value. EWW (25:1) 2004, 1–25.

1605. *taste*] Perloff, Marjorie. 13 retro keywords … and why they're worth a second look: *taste*. ESCan (30:4) 2004, 50–5.

1606. *theatricals*] Gold, David L. Dickens, *theatricals* and *Oxford English Dictionary*: a correction. Dickensian (101:3) 2005, 240–1.

1607. *thing*] O'Connor, John. The play's the thing … *See* **5750**.

1608. *þreowa*] Lindström, Bengt. Old English *þreowa* and *styccemælum*. *See* **3801**.

1609. *toilet*] Walls, Kathryn. The unveiling of the dressing table in Pope's *Rape of the Lock*, I.121. *See* **8074**.

1610. *variation*] Edgecombe, Rodney Stenning. An early instance of *variation* meaning *solo dance*. NQ (53:1) 2006, 31.

1611. *wearh*] Robinson, Fred C. Germanic **uargaz* (OE *wearh*) and the Finnish evidence. *In* (pp. 242–7) **1241**.

1612. *windmill*] Hough, Carole. Another note on windmills. NQ (53:4) 2006, 417.

1613. *windmill*] —— An antedating of the *OED* entry for *windmill*. NQ (53:1) 2006, 30–1.

1614. *work*] Watkins, Evan. 13 retro keywords … and why they're worth a second look: *work*. ESCan (30:4) 2004, 57–60.

1615. *wyrd*] Pollack, S. Engendering *wyrd*: notional gender encoded in the Old English poetic and philosophical vocabulary. *See* **3809**.

1616. *y'all*] Parker, David B. *Y'all*: two early examples. AS (81:1) 2006, 110–12.

LEXICOGRAPHY

GENERAL

1617. Billi, Mirella. Johnson's beauties: the lexicon of aesthetics in the *Dictionary*. *See* **7916**.

1618. Böker, Uwe. The recalcitrant corpus of the eighteenth-century canting crew: 'marginal language of marginal people'; or, History from below and within? *In* (pp. 11–34) **1227**.

1619. Burton, T. L.; Ruthven, K. K. *The English Dialect Dictionary* and Dorset usages recorded by *Notes and Queries*. *See* **2548**.

1620. Butler, Susan. Lexicography and world Englishes from Australia to Asia. *See* **2668**.

1621. Cacchiani, Slivia. *Desperately, utterly* and other intensifiers: on their inclusion and definition in Johnson's *Dictionary*. *See* **7920**.

1622. Coleman, Julie. A history of cant and slang dictionaries: vol. 1, 1567–1784. (Bibl. 2005, 1921.) Rev. by François Chevillet in EA (59:2) 2006, 216–18.

1623. —— A history of cant and slang dictionaries: vol. 2, 1785–1858. Oxford; New York: OUP, 2004. pp. 384. Rev. by Paul Dean in TLS, 11 Feb. 2005, 12; by François Chevillet in EA (59:2) 2006, 216–18.

1624. Cooper, Andrew R. Women's poetry, the 1830s, and monumental problems in the history of language theory. *See* **8766**.

1625. DeMaria, Robert, Jr. North and South in Johnson's *Dictionary*. *See* **7924**.

1626. Dierks, Konstantin. Letter writing, stationery supplies, and consumer modernity in the eighteenth-century Atlantic world. *See* **7459**.

1627. Dille, Catherine. Johnson's *Dictionary* in the nineteenth century: a legacy in transition. *See* **7925**.

1628. Dossena, Marina. 'The cinic Scotomastic'? Johnson, his commentators, Scots, French, and the story of English. *See* **7926**.

1629. Gilliver, Peter; Marshall, Jeremy; Weiner, Edmund. The ring of words: Tolkien and the *Oxford English Dictionary*. *See* **18801**.

1630. Gold, David L. Dickens, *theatricals* and *Oxford English Dictionary*: a correction. *See* **1606**.

1631. Green, Jonathon. Slang by dates. *See* **1521**.

1632. Holder, R. W. The dictionary men: their lives and times. Claverton Down: Bath UP, 2004. pp. 294. Rev. by Henry Hitchings in TLS, 28 Jan. 2005, 36.

1633. Hope, Jonathan. Wimping it. TLS, 30 June 2006, 25 (review-article). (Slang dictionaries.)

1634. Hüllen, Werner. A history of *Roget's Thesaurus*: origins, development and design. (Bibl. 2004, 1961.) Rev. by Anne Fabricius in EngS (87:1) 2006, 122–3.

1635. Iamartino, Giovanni. English flour and Italian bran: Johnson's *Dictionary* and the reformation of Italian lexicography in the early nineteenth century. *See* **7930**.

1636. —— DeMaria, Robert, Jr. Samuel Johnson's *Dictionary* and the eighteenth-century world of words: introduction. *See* **7931**.

1637. Josselin-Leray, Amelie; Roberts, Roda P. In search of terms: an empirical approach to lexicography. Meta (50:4:CD-ROM supp.) 2005.

1638. Jung, Sandro. Johnson's *Dictionary* and the language of William Collins's *Odes on Several Descriptive and Allegoric Subjects*. *See* **7932**.

1639. KAY, CHRISTIAN J.; MACKAY, MARGARET A. (eds). Perspectives on the Older Scottish tongue: a celebration of DOST. *See* **2567**.

1640. KERSEY, MEL. 'The wells of English undefiled': Samuel Johnson's Romantic resistance to Britishness. *See* **7935**.

1641. KNAPPE, GABRIELE. Peter Mark Roget's *Thesaurus of English Words and Phrases*: a mid-nineteenth-century example of the place of phraseology in the history of linguistic theory and practice. *In* (pp. 205–20) **1227**.

1642. LERER, SETH. Caxton in the nineteenth century. *In* (pp. 325–70) **4125**.

1643. LYNCH, JACK; MCDERMOTT, ANNE (eds). Anniversary essays on Johnson's dictionary. (Bibl. 2005, 1934.) Rev. by Lynda Mugglestone in NQ (53:4) 2006, 560–3; by Chris P. Pearce in AJ (17) 2006, 341–62.

1644. MCDERMOTT, ANNE. The compilation methods of Johnson's *Dictionary*. *See* **7942**.

1645. MARTIN, KATHERINE CONNOR. Gendered aspects of lexicographer labeling. Dic (26) 2005, 160–73.

1646. MASI, SILVIA. Lexicographic material under observation: from Johnson's *Dictionary* to a model for a cognition-based dictionary of lexical patterns. *See* **7943**.

1647. MICKLETHWAIT, DAVID. A curious cross-reference in Webster's *American Dictionary*. Dic (26) 2005, 194–205.

1648. MUGGLESTONE, LYNDA. Lost for words: the hidden history of the *Oxford English Dictionary*. (Bibl. 2005, 1937.) Rev. by Dorothy Haines in NQ (53:2) 2006, 222–4; by Ron Smith in GaR (60:3/4) 2006, 782–90.

1649. PEARCE, CHRIS P. 'Gleaned as industry should find, or chance should offer it': Johnson's *Dictionary* after 250 years. *See* **7946**.

1650. —— Recovering the 'rigour of interpretative lexicography': border crossings in Johnson's *Dictionary*. *See* **7947**.

1651. PINNAVAIA, LAURA. Idiomatic expressions regarding food and drink in Johnson's *Dictionary of the English Language* (1755 and 1773). *See* **7948**.

1652. PIREDDU, SILVIA. The 'landscape of the body': the language of medicine in Johnson's *Dictionary*. *See* **7949**.

1653. SCANLAN, J. T. Johnson's *Dictionary* and legal dictionaries. *See* **7954**.

1654. SIMES, GARY. Gay slang lexicography: a brief history and a commentary on the first two gay glossaries. Dic (26) 2005, 1–159.

1655. SINGLETON, ANTONY. The Early English Text Society in the nineteenth century: an organizational history. *See* **3886**.

1656. SMITH, RON. Then who *is* the editor of the English language? GaR (60:3/4) 2006, 782–90 (review-article).

1657. STAVANS, ILAN. Dictionary days: a defining passion. Saint Paul, MN: Graywolf Press, 2005. pp. 228. Rev. by Ron Smith in GaR (60:3/4) 2006, 782–90.

1658. TANI, AKINOBU. *Thesaurus of Old English* for Early Middle English: an analysis in light of word pairs in the 'Katherine Group' lives. *In* (pp. 293–303) **1227**.

1659. VANCIL, DAVID. Some observations about the Samuel Johnson miniature dictionaries in the Cordell Collection. *See* **7959**.

1660. VICENTINI, ALESSANDRA. In Johnson's footsteps: Baretti's *English Grammar* and the spread of the English language in Italy during the eighteenth century. *See* **7960**.

DICTIONARIES OF ENGLISH

1661. ANON. Cambridge idioms dictionary. (Bibl. 1998, 2218.) Cambridge; New York: CUP, 2006. pp. xv, 505. (Second ed.: first ed. 1998.) (Orig. pub. as *Cambridge International Dictionary of Idioms*.)

1662. —— The Merriam-Webster thesaurus. Springfield, MA: Merriam-Webster, 2005. pp. 668. (New ed.: first ed. 1978.)

1663. —— (comp.). Oxford dictionary of rhymes. Oxford; New York: OUP, 2006. pp. xxxii, 413.

1664. ALLEN, ROBERT. Allen's dictionary of English phrases. London; New York: Penguin, 2006. pp. xix, 805.

1665. AMMER, CHRISTINE. The Facts on File dictionary of clichés. (Bibl. 2003, 1869.) New York: Facts on File, 2006. pp. x, 534. (Facts on File library of language and literature.) (Second ed.: first ed. 2001.)

1666. AYTO, JOHN; SIMPSON, JOHN A. The Oxford dictionary of modern slang. (Bibl. 2000, 2221.) Oxford; New York: OUP, 2005. pp. 324. (Oxford paperback reference.) (New ed.: first ed. 1992.)

1667. BROOKES, IAN (gen. ed.). The Chambers dictionary. (Bibl. 2003, 38424.) Edinburgh: Chambers Harrap, 2006. pp. xxxi, 1839. (Tenth ed.: first ed. 1901.) (Orig. pub. as *Chambers Twentieth-Century Dictionary*.) Rev. by Eric Korn in TLS, 15 Sept. 2006, 8–9.

1668. CHILDS, PETER; FOWLER, ROGER (eds). The Routledge dictionary of literary terms. (Bibl. 1988, 835.) London; New York: Routledge, 2006. pp. xii, 253. (Routledge dictionaries.) (Third ed.: first ed. 1973.)

1669. CRYER, MAX. The Godzone dictionary of favourite New Zealand words and phrases. Auckland: Exisle, 2006. pp. 191.

1670. DALZELL, TOM; VICTOR, TERRY (eds). The new Partridge dictionary of slang and unconventional English. London; New York: Routledge, 2006. 2 vols. pp. xvii, 2189. Rev. by Jonathan Hope in TLS, 30 June 2006, 25.

1671. DAVIDSON, MARK. Right, wrong, and risky: a dictionary of today's American English usage. New York; London: Norton, 2006. pp. 570.

1672. DEVERSON, TONY; KENNEDY, GRAEME (eds). The New Zealand Oxford dictionary. (Bibl. 2004, 1986.) Rev. by Nelson Wattie in NZBooks (15:3) 2005, 4–5.

1673. DOLAN, TERENCE PATRICK (ed.). A dictionary of Hiberno-English: the Irish use of English. (Bibl. 2002, 1629.) Dublin: Gill & Macmillan, 2004. pp. xxix, 277. (Second ed.: first ed. 1998.) Rev. by Victor Price in TLS, 25 Feb. 2005, 27.

1674. EDWARDS, THORNTON B. Irish! A dictionary of phrases, terms and epithets beginning with the word *Irish*. Douglas Village, Cork: Mercier Press,

2004. pp. 232. Rev. by Fionnuala Carson Williams in FolkL (44) 2005/06, 147–8.

1675. GREEN, JONATHON (ed.). Cassell's dictionary of slang. London: Weidenfeld & Nicolson, 2005. pp. xx, 1565. (Second ed.: first ed. 2000.) Rev. by Jonathan Hope in TLS, 30 June 2006, 25.

1676. HUGHES, GEOFFREY. An encyclopedia of swearing: the social history of oaths, profanity, foul language, and ethnic slurs in the English-speaking world. Armonk, NY: Sharpe, 2005. pp. xxv, 573. Rev. by Henry Hitchings in TLS, 15 Sept. 2006, 9.

1677. KANE, GEORGE. The *Piers Plowman* glossary. *Will's Visions of Do-Well, Do-Better and Do-Best*: a glossary of the English vocabulary of the A, B and C versions as presented in the Athlone Editions. London; New York: Continuum, 2005. pp. xiii, 240.

1678. KENNEDY, X. J.; GIOIA, DANA; BAUERLEIN, MARK. Handbook of literary terms: literature, language, theory. London; New York: Pearson Longman, 2005. pp. viii, 165.

1679. KIPFER, BARBARA ANN (ed.). Roget's 21st-century thesaurus in dictionary form: the essential reference for home, school, or office. (Bibl. 2003, 52642.) New York: Delta Trade Paperbacks, 2005. pp. xii, 962. (Third ed.: first ed. 1992.)

1680. KNOWLES, ELIZABETH M. (ed.). Oxford dictionary of phrase and fable. (Bibl. 2002, 1479.) Oxford; New York: OUP, 2006. pp. 805. (Second ed.: first ed. 2000.)

1681. LATHAM, ALISON (ed.). The Oxford dictionary of musical terms. Oxford; New York: OUP, 2004. 1 vol. (unpaginated). (Oxford paperback reference.) Rev. by Christopher Wintle in MusL (87:2) 2006, 298–300.

1682. MCCUTCHEON, MARC. Descriptionary: a thematic dictionary. (Bibl. 2000, 2257.) New York: Facts on File / Checkmark, 2004. pp. xi, 644. (Facts on File library of language and literature.) (Third ed.: first ed. 1992.)

1683. MAKKAI, ADAM; BOATNER, MAXINE T.; GATES, JOHN E. (eds). Handbook of commonly used American idioms. (Bibl. 1995, 1618.) Hauppage, NY: Barron's, 2004. pp. xiii, 269. (Fourth ed.: first ed. 1966.)

1684. PEARCE, MICHAEL. The Routledge dictionary of English language studies. London; New York: Routledge, 2006. pp. xi, 211.

1685. PRUCHER, JEFFREY. Brave new words: the Oxford dictionary of science fiction. Oxford; New York: OUP, 2006. pp. 384.

1686. QUINN, EDWARD. A dictionary of literary and thematic terms. (Bibl. 2000, 2267.) New York: Facts on File, 2006. pp. vi, 474. (Facts on File library of language and literature.) (Second ed.: first ed. 1999.)

1687. REYNOLDS, RAS DENNIS JABARI (ed.). Jabari authentic Jamaican dictionary of the Jamic language: featuring Jamaican Patwa and Rasta Iyaric, pronunciations and definitions. Waterbury, CT: Around the Way, 2006. pp. 142.

1688. ROACH, PETER; HARTMAN, JAMES; SETTER, JANE (eds). Cambridge English pronouncing dictionary. By Daniel Jones. (Bibl. 2000, 1807.) Cambridge; New York: CUP, 2006. pp. xxi, 599. (Seventeenth ed.: first ed. 1917.)

1689. SOANES, CATHERINE; HAWKER, SARA; ELLIOTT, JULIA (eds). Oxford dictionary of current English. (Bibl. 2001, 1711.) Oxford; New York: OUP, 2006. pp. xvi, 1081. (Fourth ed.: first ed. 2001.)

1690. —— STEVENSON, ANGUS (eds). Concise Oxford English dictionary. (Bibl. 2005, 1970.) Oxford; New York: OUP, 2006. pp. xx, 1708. (Revised eleventh ed.: first ed. 1914.)

1691. SPEARS, RICHARD A. McGraw-Hill's dictionary of American slang and colloquial expressions. (Bibl. 2000, 2276.) Boston, MA: McGraw-Hill, 2006. pp. xxix, 546. (Fourth ed.: first ed. 1989.)

1692. WAITE, MAURICE (ed.). New Oxford spelling dictionary. (Bibl. 2005, 1976.) Rev. by John Whale in TLS, 10 Feb. 2006, 11.

1693. —— Oxford thesaurus of current English. Oxford; New York: OUP, 2006. pp. xii, 987. (Second ed.: first ed. 1997.)

1694. —— *et al.* (eds). Oxford compact thesaurus. Oxford; New York: OUP, 2005. pp. vi, 929. (Third ed.: first ed. 1997.)

1695. WASSERMAN, PAUL; HAUSRATH, DON. Weasel words: the dictionary of American doublespeak. Sterling, VA: Capital, 2006. pp. xiv, 220. (Capital ideas.)

1696. YALLOP, C., *et al.* (eds). Macquarie dictionary. (Bibl. 1996, 2940.) North Ryde, N.S.W.: Macquarie Library, 2005. pp. xx, 1676. (Fourth ed.: first ed. 1981.)

NAMES

GENERAL

1697. BARTON, ANNA JANE. 'What profits me my name?': the aesthetic potential of the commodified name in *Lancelot and Elaine*. *See* **11388**.

1698. BATELY, JANET. The language of Ohthere's report to King Alfred: some problems and some puzzles for historians and linguists. *In* (pp. 39–53) **3679**.

1699. DICKSON, PAUL. Labels for locals: demonyms for folks from the Aaland Islands to Zurich. New York: Collins, 2006. pp. 288.

1700. DONALDSON, SCOTT. A hell of a name for a poet. *See* **18266**.

1701. ENGEL, LEONARD. Identity issues and images in a hard-boiled world: Dashiell Hammett's *Red Harvest* and the mystery/detective genre. *See* **16260**.

1702. HAZELL, DINAH. The plants of Middle-earth: botany and sub-creation. *See* **18805**.

1703. HOUGH, CAROLE. Another note on windmills. *See* **1612**.

1704. —— Bibliography for 2004. Nomina (28) 2005, 175–91.

1705. KENNEDY, ROBERT; ZAMUNER, TANIA. Nicknames and the lexicon of sports. AS (81:4) 2006, 387–422.

1706. KING, JACOB. 'Lochy' names and Adomnán's *Nigra dea*. Nomina (28) 2005, 69–91.

1707. Lipman, Elinor. The writing life. *See* **17232**.

1708. Lopez, Barry (ed.). Home ground: language for an American landscape. *See* **3326**.

1709. Monmonier, Mark. From Squaw Tit to Whorehouse Meadow: how maps name, claim, and inflame. Chicago, IL; London: Chicago UP, 2006. pp. xiv, 215.

1710. Morris, David. The rise of Christian names in the thirteenth century: a case study of the English nobility. Nomina (28) 2005, 43–54.

1711. Pratt, Stella. Summer landscapes: investigating Scottish topographical place-names. Nomina (28) 2005, 93–114.

1712. Reed, John R. Dickens and naming. *See* **9809**.

1713. Rowlands, John; Rowlands, Sheila. The transition from patronymic names to settled surnames in Wales. Nomina (28) 2005, 55–68.

1714. Rust, Martha. An exposition of women's names in British Library Harley MS 3362. *See* **264**.

1715. Salado, Régis. Beckett et Pinget: l'échange des voix. *See* **14722**.

1716. Toolan, Michael. Joke shop names. JLS (34:2) 2005, 165–79.

1717. Viereck, Wolfgang. An atlas of English family names. *In* (pp. 305–28) **1227**.

1718. Vine, Angus. Etymology, names and the search for origins: deriving the past in early modern England. *See* **4823**.

1719. Watts, Victor (ed.); Insley, John (asst ed.). The Cambridge dictionary of English place-names: based on the collections of the English Place-Name Society. (Bibl. 2004, 2059.) Rev. by Graham Jones in Spec (81:2) 2006, 625–7.

SINGLE NAMES

1720. *Afrika*] Debo, Annette. Signifying *Afrika*: Gwendolyn Brooks' later poetry. *See* **14872**.

1721. *Currer Bell*] Harris, Margaret. George Eliot's conversation with Currer Bell. *See* **10026**.

1722. *Dunwich*] Breeze, Andrew. Bede's *civitas Domnoc* and Dunwich, Suffolk. LSE (36) 2005, 1–4.

1723. *Edmund*] Wiltshire, John. The importance of being Edmund: on names in *Mansfield Park*. *In* (pp. 138–47) **8374**.

1724. *Eratostratus*] Ferber, Michael. The curse of the Ephesians: a long footnote to Byron. *See* **9345**.

1725. *Fanny*] Wiltshire, John. The importance of being Edmund: on names in *Mansfield Park*. *In* (pp. 138–47) **8374**.

1726. *Fish*] Grossman, Marshall. The onomastic destiny of Stanley Fish. *In* (pp. 27–52) **7033**.

1727. *Goffore/Goffare*] Bliss, Jane. The sultan's name in *Generydes* and *Syr Generides*. NQ (53:1) 2006, 24–5.

1728. *Goring*] Clausson, Nils. Trivial coincidences or 'pre-planned detonations'? A further note on names in Conan Doyle and Wilde. *See* **11598**.

1729. *Irish*] EDWARDS, THORNTON B. Irish! A dictionary of phrases, terms and epithets beginning with the word *Irish*. *See* **1674**.

1730. *Jack*] MCCLURE, PETER. The kinship of *Jack*: II, Pet-forms of Middle English personal names with the suffixes *-cok* and *-cus*. Nomina (28) 2005, 5–42.

1731. *Lowrence/Lowry*] BREEZE, ANDREW. Henryson's Lowrence the fox. *See* **4158**.

1732. *Magnus*] WALLS, KATHRYN. The 'Magnus effect': names in *The Real Inspector Hound*. *See* **18675**.

1733. *Mercutio*] PALMER, DARYL W. Motion and Mercutio in *Romeo and Juliet*. *See* **6069**.

1734. *Plant*] PLANT, JOHN S. Modern methods and a controversial surname: Plant. Nomina (28) 2005, 115–33.

1735. *Romeo*] JENSEN, MICHAEL P. What's in a name? A real Romeo. SNL (56:1) 2006, 15–16.

1736. *Romeo*] PALMER, DARYL W. Motion and Mercutio in *Romeo and Juliet*. *See* **6069**.

1737. *Shuah*] MELNYK, DAVYD. Interruption: a Shuah thing? *See* **14704**.

1738. *Soutra*] BREEZE, ANDREW. Three Celtic names: *Venicones*, *Tuesis* and *Soutra*. ScLang (25) 2006, 71–9.

1739. *Telamond*] MOORE, ANDREW. An Herculean precedent for Spenser's 'Telamond'. *See* **5106**.

1740. *Windemilnehil*] HOUGH, CAROLE. An antedating of the *OED* entry for *windmill*. *See* **1613**.

MEANING

SEMANTICS

1741. ANDERSON, JOHN. Notional grammar. *See* **1243**.

1742. BARKER, STEPHEN. Renewing meaning: a speech-act theoretic approach. Oxford: Clarendon Press; New York: OUP, 2004. pp. xi, 325. Rev. by Iwona Witczak-Plisiecka in JLS (35:1) 2006, 84–93.

1743. BENCZES, RÉKA. Creative compounding in English: the semantics of metaphorical and metonymical noun–noun combinations. *See* **1471**.

1744. BENOR, SARAH BUNIN; LEVY, ROGER. The chicken or the egg? A probabilistic account of English binomials. *See* **1286**.

1745. BERGLUND, YLVA; MASON, OLIVER. 'But this formula doesn't mean anything ... !?' *In* (pp. 59–69) **1195**.

1746. BIBER, DOUGLAS; CONRAD, SUSAN; CORTES, VIVIANA. Lexical bundles in speech and writing: an initial taxonomy. *In* (pp. 71–92) **1195**.

1747. BUDANITSKY, ALEXANDER; HIRST, GRAEME. Evaluating WordNet-based measures of lexical semantic relatedness. *See* **1473**.

1748. CHIERCHIA, GENNARO. Semantic and pragmatic competence in children's and adults' comprehension of *or*. *In* (pp. 283–300) **1818**.

1749. Clark, Herbert H.; Bangerter, Adrian. Changing ideas about reference. *In* (pp. 25–49) **1818**.

1750. Coulson, Seana. Extemporaneous blending: conceptual integration in humorous discourse from talk radio. *See* **2196**.

1751. Csatár, Péter; Pethő, Gergely; Tóth, Enikő. On possible factors in the aesthetic appreciation of metaphors. JLS (35:1) 2006, 59–71.

1752. Dixon, Robert M. W. A semantic approach to English grammar. *See* **1367**.

1753. Dobrovol'skij, Dmitrij; Piirainen, Elisabeth. Figurative language: cross-cultural and cross-linguistic perspectives. *See* **1926**.

1754. Fraser, Bruce. On the conceptual–procedural distinction. Style (40:1/2) 2006, 24–32.

1755. Healey, Antonette diPaolo. Straining words and striving voices: polysemy and ambiguity and the importance of context in the disclosure of meaning. *In* (pp. 74–90) **1241**.

1756. Hickey, Raymond. Productive lexical processes in present-day English. *In* (pp. 153–68) **1227**.

1757. —— Tracking lexical changes in present-day English. *In* (pp. 93–105) **1195**.

1758. Hollingsworth, Christopher. The force of the entomological Other: insects as instruments of intolerable thought. *In* (pp. 262–77) **3203**.

1759. Kienpointner, Manfred. Emotion terms in the recent history of the English language. *In* (pp. 183–203) **1227**.

1760. Kjellmer, Göran. Certain uncertainties: semantic splits and interpretative strategies. *See* **1552**.

1761. Kudrnáčová, Naděžda. Oscillatory corporeal verbs from a semantico-syntactic perspective. BStE (31) 2005, 35–48.

1762. Lakoff, Robin Tolmach. Vulgar Latin: comparative castration (and comparative theories of syntax). *See* **1386**.

1763. Langendoen, D. Terence. Disjunctive numerals of estimation. *See* **1387**.

1764. Langlotz, Andreas. Idiomatic creativity: a cognitive-linguistic model of idiom-representation and idiom-variation in English. Amsterdam; Philadelphia, PA: Benjamins, 2006. pp. vii, 325. (Human cognitive processing, 17.)

1765. —— Occasional adnominal idiom modification – a cognitive linguistic approach. *See* **1388**.

1766. Lawler, John M. The data fetishist's guide to rime coherence. *See* **1299**.

1767. Martin, J. R.; White, P. R. R. The language of evaluation: appraisal in English. Basingstoke; New York: Palgrave Macmillan, 2005. pp. xii, 278.

1768. Martín Arista, Javier; Martín de la Rosa, María Victoria. Old English semantic primes: substantives, determiners and quantifiers. *See* **1423**.

1769. Nuccorini, Stefania. In search of 'phraseologies': discovering divergences in the use of English and Italian 'true friends'. EJES (10:1) 2006, 33–47.

1770. NÚÑEZ PERTEJO, PALOMA. Some developments in the semantics of the English progressive from Old English to Early Modern English. *See* **1436**.

1771. OLSSON, JOHN. Forensic linguistics: an introduction to language, crime and the law. London; New York: Continuum, 2004. pp. xiii, 269. Rev. by Jeannine Carpenter in AS (81:3) 2006, 320–4.

1772. PARTEE, BARBARA H. Compositionality in formal semantics: selected papers. Oxford; Malden, MA: Blackwell, 2004. pp. xi, 331. (Explorations in semantics.) Rev. by Anna Szabolcsi in Lang (82:1) 2006, 182–5.

1773. PEETERS, BERT. *Tall poppies* and egalitarianism in Australian discourse: from key word to cultural value. *See* **1604**.

1774. PETERS, HANS. Getting *smart*. *In* (pp. 279–92) **1227**.

1775. PETRÉ, PETER. The prefix *be-/bi-* as a marker of verbs of deception in Late Old and Early Middle English. *See* **1350**.

1776. PORTNER, PAUL H. What is meaning? Fundamentals of formal semantics. Oxford; Malden, MA: Blackwell, 2005. pp. ix, 235. (Fundamentals of linguistics.) Rev. by Piotr Stalmaszczyk in JLS (35:1) 2006, 73–8.

1777. ROCKWELL, PATRICIA ANN. Sarcasm and other mixed messages: the ambiguous ways people use language. Lewiston, NY; Lampeter: Mellen Press, 2006. pp. iv, 159.

1778. RODRÍGUEZ JUÁREZ, CAROLINA. A new parameter for the description of subject assignment: the term hierarchy. *See* **1404**.

1779. ROMERO, ESTHER; SORIA, BELÉN. Cognitive metaphor theory revisited. *See* **2109**.

1780. TAVERNIERS, MIRIAM. Grammatical metaphor and lexical metaphor: different perspectives on semantic variation. *See* **2152**.

1781. TURNEY, PETER D. Similarity of semantic relations. CompLing (32:3) 2006, 379–416.

1782. VÉRONIS, JEAN. Sense tagging: does it make sense? *In* (pp. 273–90) **1195**.

1783. VERSPOOR, MARJOLIJN H.; DE BIE-KERÉKJÁRTÓ, ÁGNES. Colorful bits of experience: from *bluestocking* to *blue movie*. *See* **1547**.

1784. WARREN, BEATRICE. Prolegomena to a study of evaluative words. *See* **1505**.

1785. WICHMANN, ANNE; CAULDWELL, RICHARD. *Wh-* questions and attitude: the effect of context. *In* (pp. 291–305) **1195**.

1786. WIERZBICKA, ANNA. English: meaning and culture. Oxford; New York: OUP, 2006. pp. ix, 352.

PRAGMATICS

1787. ARCHER, DAWN; CULPEPER, JONATHAN. Sociopragmatic annotation: new directions and possibilities in historical linguistics. *In* (pp. 37–58) **1195**.

1788. ASAAH, AUGUSTINE H. To speak or not to speak with the whole mouth: textualization of taboo subjects in europhone African literature. *See* **11747**.

1789. BARKER, STEPHEN. Renewing meaning: a speech-act theoretic approach. *See* **1742**.

1790. Bezuidenhout, Anne L.; Morris, Robin K. Implicature, relevance and default pragmatic inference. *In* (pp. 257–82) **1818**.

1791. Black, Elizabeth. Pragmatic stylistics. Edinburgh: Edinburgh UP, 2006. pp. vi, 166. (Edinburgh textbooks in applied linguistics.) Rev. by Jean-Pierre van Noppen in BELL (ns 4) 2006, 205–10.

1792. Bousfield, Derek. The grand debate: where next for politeness research? CLR (3) 2006, 9–15.

1793. Brown, David West. Girls and guys, ghetto and bougie: metapragmatics, ideology and the management of social identities. *See* **2754**.

1794. Chierchia, Gennaro. Semantic and pragmatic competence in children's and adults' comprehension of *or*. *In* (pp. 283–300) **1818**.

1795. Crespo Fernández, Eliecer. La vertiente locutiva e ilocutiva en la manipulación del referente en lengua inglesa. Los procesos mixtos: cuasieufemismo *vs* cuasidisfemismo. EIUC (14) 2006, 71–91.

1796. Díaz Pérez, Francisco Javier. Deixis and verbal politeness in request production in English and Spanish. CLR (3) 2005, 161–76.

1797. Dobrovol'skij, Dmitrij; Piirainen, Elisabeth. Figurative language: cross-cultural and cross-linguistic perspectives. *See* **1926**.

1798. Dontcheva-Navrátilová, Olga. Text typology of resolution. BStE (31) 2005, 19–33.

1799. Eades, Diana. Lexical struggle in court: Aboriginal Australians *versus* the State. *See* **2201**.

1800. Eckstein, Jessica J. Conversion conundrums: listener perceptions of affective influence attempts as mediated by personality and individual differences. ComQ (53:3) 2005, 401–19.

1801. Fridland, Valerie; Bartlett, Kathryn. Correctness, pleasantness, and degree of difference ratings across regions. *See* **2612**.

1802. Furniss, Graham. Orality: the power of the spoken word. *See* **2206**.

1803. García Gómez, Antonio. British and American expressions of politeness in anger-evoking contexts: a cultural-relativistic approach. CLR (3) 2006, 145–59.

1804. Glucksberg, Sam. On the automaticity of pragmatic processes: a modular proposal. *In* (pp. 72–93) **1818**.

1805. Golato, Andrea. Compliments and compliment responses: grammatical structure and sequential organization. Amsterdam; Philadelphia, PA: Benjamins, 2005. pp. x, 248. (Studies in discourse and grammar, 15.)

1806. Handley, Simon J.; Feeney, Aidan. Reasoning and pragmatics: the case of *even if*. *In* (pp. 228–53) **1818**.

1807. Haugh, Michael. Emic perspectives on the positive–negative politeness distinction. CLR (3) 2006, 17–26.

1808. Howarth, Peter. The phraseology of public international English. *See* **2719**.

1809. Kasanga, Luanga A. Requests in a South African variety of English. *See* **2684**.

1810. KELLEY-ROMANO, STEPHANIE. Mythmaking in alien abduction narratives. *See* **3007**.

1811. KOHNEN, THOMAS. Variability of form as a methodological problem in historical corpus analysis: the case of modal expressions in directive speech acts. *In* (pp. 220–33) **1227**.

1812. KRÓLAK, EMILIA; RUDNICKA, KINGA. Selected aspects of directives in Polish. REsLA (19) 2006, 129–42. (Polish and English.)

1813. LEVINE, PHILIP; SCOLLON, RON (eds). Discourse and technology: multimodal discourse analysis. Washington, DC: Georgetown UP, 2004. pp. vi, 229. (Georgetown Univ. Round Table on Languages and Linguistics.) Rev. by Seyyed Abdolhamid Mirhosseini in AppL (26:4) 2005, 597–600.

1814. MERLO, PAOLA; FERRER, EVA ESTEVE. The notion of argument in prepositional phrase attachment. *See* **1396**.

1815. MOYA, A. JESÚS. On pragmatic functions and their correlation with syntactic functions: a functionalist perspective. *See* **1399**.

1816. MUR DUEÑAS, Mª PILAR. A pragmatic approach to the contrastive analysis of a literary work and two of its translations. *See* **10583**.

1817. NOVECK, IRA A. Pragmatic inferences related to logical terms. *In* (pp. 301–21) **1818**.

1818. —— SPERBER, DAN (eds). Experimental pragmatics. Basingstoke; New York: Palgrave Macmillan, 2004. pp. viii, 348. (Palgrave studies in pragmatics, language and cognition.) Rev. by Siobhan Chapman in JLS (35:1) 2006, 79–83.

1819. NUCCORINI, STEFANIA. In search of 'phraseologies': discovering divergences in the use of English and Italian 'true friends'. *See* **1769**.

1820. PATTEMORE, STEPHEN. 'Honourable bigotry'? Relevance theory, conversation analysis and radio talk-backs. *See* **2225**.

1821. PICHLER, PIA. Multifunctional teasing as a resource for identity construction in the talk of British Bangladeshi girls. *See* **2584**.

1822. POVOLNÁ, RENATA. Some notes on interactive discourse items in spoken English. *See* **2228**.

1823. RILEY, DENISE. Impersonal passion: language as affect. Durham, NC; London: Duke UP, 2005. pp. viii, 142. Rev. by Mary Kate McGowan in Hypatia (21:4) 2006, 221–4.

1824. RUBINO, ANTONIA; BETTONI, CAMILLA. Handling complaints cross-culturally: Italians *vs* Anglo-Australians. SILTA (35:2) 2006, 338–58.

1825. SANFORD, A. J.; MOXEY, LINDA M. Exploring quantifiers: pragmatics meets the psychology of comprehension. *In* (pp. 116–37) **1818**.

1826. SANGIORGI, SIMONA. Disney's politeness for profit. CLR (3) 2006, 177–92.

1827. SHEARER-CREMEAN, CHRISTINE; WINKELMANN, CAROL L. (eds). Survivor rhetoric: negotiations and narrativity in abused women's language. *See* **2792**.

1828. TOOLAN, MICHAEL. Joke shop names. *See* **1716**.

1829. Van Bogaert, Julie. *I guess, I suppose* and *I believe* as pragmatic markers: grammaticalization and functions. *See* **1445**.

1830. Weber, Keith; Martin, Matthew M.; Corrigan, Michael. Creating persuasive messages advocating organ donation. *See* **2538**.

1831. Wilamová, Sirma. On the function of hedging devices in negatively polite discourse. BStE (31) 2005, 85–93.

MEDIUM AND REGISTER

RHETORIC AND FIGURES OF SPEECH

1832. Abbott, Don Paul. Splendor and misery: semiotics and the end of rhetoric. Rhetorica (24:3) 2006, 303–23.

1833. Adamson, Sylvia. Deixis and the Renaissance art of self-construction. *See* **5689**.

1834. Airne, David; Benoit, William. Political television advertising in Campaign 2000. ComQ (53:4) 2005, 473–92.

1835. Allis, Michael. Musical reactions to Tennyson: reformulating musical imagery in *The Lotos-Eaters*. *In* (pp. 132–73) **8828**.

1836. Allison, Raphael C. Muriel Rukeyser goes to war: pragmatism, pluralism, and the politics of ekphrasis. *See* **18373**.

1837. Anderson, Judith H. Donne's (im)possible punning. *See* **6698**.

1838. —— Translating investments: metaphor and the dynamic of cultural change in Tudor–Stuart England. (Bibl. 2005, 2210.) Rev. by Michael Householder in Arthuriana (16:1) 2006, 71–3; by Ira Clark in SCN (64:1/2) 2006, 8–11; by Jeff Dolven in RQ (59:2) 2006, 630–1; by David Lee Miller in SidJ (24:1) 2006, 77–80.

1839. Andres, Sophia. Mary Elizabeth Braddon's ambivalent Pre-Raphaelite ekphrasis. *See* **9155**.

1840. Attridge, Derek. Performing metaphors: the singularity of literary figuration. Para (28:2) 2005, 18–34.

1841. Austin, Bill. Robert Frost's use of the arch as figure and symbol. *See* **15998**.

1842. Axcelson, John. The 'dial's moral round': charting Wordsworth's *Evening Walk*. *See* **11646**.

1843. Babcock, Matthew. Bryant's *The Yellow Violet*. *See* **9293**.

1844. Baker, Malcolm. Multiple heads: Pope, the portrait bust, and patterns of repetition. *In* (pp. 224–45) **1894**.

1845. Bamforth, Iain. Pickled essence of Englishman: Thomas Lovell Beddoes. *See* **9113**.

1846. Barker, Simon. 'It's an actor, boss. Unarmed': the rhetoric of *Julius Caesar*. *In* (pp. 227–39) **5805**.

1847. Barot, Rick. Larkin and the apple. *See* **16995**.

1848. Barrett-Graves, Debra. Edmund Spenser's use of the poison-tipped tongue in *The Faerie Queene*. *See* **5072**.

1849. Barton, John. Fluid epiphanies: Margaret Avison's *The Swimmer's Moment*. *See* **14525**.

1850. Baseotto, Paola. Godly sorrow, damnable Despair and *Faerie Queene* I.ix. *See* **5074**.

1851. Batt, Catherine; Renevey, Denis; Whitehead, Christiania. Domesticity and medieval devotional literature. *See* **4057**.

1852. Beall, Emily P. 'As reading as if': Harryette Mullen's 'cognitive similes'. *See* **17671**.

1853. Beer, Francis A.; De Landtsheer, Christ'l. Metaphorical world politics. East Lansing: Michigan State UP, 2004. pp. x, 342. (Rhetoric and public affairs.) Rev. by Jonathan Charteris-Black in MetS (21:2) 2006, 127–32.

1854. Benczes, Réka. Creative compounding in English: the semantics of metaphorical and metonymical noun–noun combinations. *See* **1471**.

1855. Bengels, Barbara. Swift's *A Modest Proposal*. *See* **8184**.

1856. Benson, Sean. 'If I do prove her haggard': Shakespeare's application of hawking tropes to marriage. *See* **6016**.

1857. Berensmeyer, Ingo. Rhetoric, religion, and politics in Sir Thomas Browne's *Religio Medici*. *See* **6601**.

1858. Bidart, Frank. A cross in the void. *In* (pp. 246–54) **16122**.

1859. Binfield, Kevin. Labor and an ethic of variety in *The Farmer's Boy*. *In* (pp. 70–88) **9141**.

1860. Bizzell, Patricia. (Native) American jeremiad: the 'mixedblood' rhetoric of William Apess. *In* (pp. 34–49) **2149**.

1861. Blumenfeld, François. Tropology and rhetoric. ASSA (17) 2006.

1862. Bode, Rita. 'Suckled by the sea': the maternal in *Moby-Dick*. *In* (pp. 181–98) **10897**.

1863. Bollerman, Karen. In the belly, in the bower: divine maternal practice in *Patience*. *In* (pp. 193–218) **3893**.

1864. Booth, Wayne C. The rhetoric of rhetoric: the quest for effective communication. (Bibl. 2005, 2222.) Rev. by Carolyn R. Miller in PhilR (39:3) 2006, 261–3.

1865. Boyarin, Adrienne Williams. Competing biblical and Virgilian allusions in Wyatt's *Who So List to Hounte*. *See* **5150**.

1866. Bredehoft, Thomas A. Middle English *knarre*: more porcine imagery in the Miller's portrait. *See* **4371**.

1867. Brennan, Thomas J. Creating from nothing: Swinburne and Baudelaire in *Ave atque Vale*. *See* **11374**.

1868. Bronstein, Michaela. The half-unravelled web: Keats's intermediate truths. *See* **10638**.

1869. Brooks, Douglas A. (ed.). Printing and parenting in early modern England. *See* **661**.

1870. Brown, Eric C. Performing insects in Shakespeare's *Coriolanus*. *In* (pp. 29–57) **3203**.

1871. Brownlee, Kevin, *et al.* Vernacular literary consciousness *c*.1100–*c*.1500: French, German and English evidence. *In* (pp. 422–71) **3874**.

1872. Bruce, Donald. Spenser's poetic pictures: a vision of beauty. *See* **5077**.

1873. Bruckner, Lynne Dickson. Ben Jonson's branded thumb and the imprint of textual paternity. *In* (pp. 109–30) **661**.

1874. Budd, Malcolm. The characterization of aesthetic qualities by essential metaphors and quasi-metaphors. BJA (46:2) 2006, 133–43.

1875. Burlinson, Christopher. Allegory, space and the material world in the writings of Edmund Spenser. *See* **5079**.

1876. Burton, T. L.; Plummer, John F. (eds). 'Seyd in forme and reverence': essays on Chaucer and Chaucerians in memory of Emerson Brown, Jr. *See* **4310**.

1877. Butler, George F. The fall of Tydeus and the failure of Satan: Statius' *Thebaid*, Dante's *Commedia*, and Milton's *Paradise Lost*. *See* **6977**.

1878. Butler, Todd. Image, rhetoric, and politics in the early Thomas Hobbes. *See* **6838**.

1879. Byatt, A. S. Observe the neurones: between, above and below John Donne. *See* **6705**.

1880. Caers, Eric. When ministers were digging in for a fight .... *See* **13888**.

1881. Carr, Jean Ferguson; Carr, Stephen L.; Schultz, Lucille M. Archives of instruction: nineteenth-century rhetorics, readers, and composition books in the United States. Carbondale: Southern Illinois UP, 2005. pp. xx, 283. (Studies in writing & rhetoric.)

1882. Carruthers, Mary. On affliction and reading, weeping and argument: Chaucer's lachrymose Troilus in context. *See* **4491**.

1883. —— Sweetness. *See* **4037**.

1884. Carruthers, Virginia Kirby-Smith. Durrell's enigmatic Hamlet: mysteries of image and allusion. *See* **15620**.

1885. Carvalho Homem, Rui. Hallucination or lucidity? Vision and time in Ciaran Carson's ekphrastic writing. *See* **15049**.

1886. Centerwall, Brandon S. Who wrote William Basse's *Elegy on Shakespeare*? Rediscovering a poem lost from the Donne canon. *See* **6566**.

1887. Charret-Del Bove, Marion. Les images d'enfermement dans *John Marchmont's Legacy* de Mary Elizabeth Braddon. *See* **9157**.

1888. Chatlos, Jon. Automobility and lyric poetry: the mobile gaze in William Carlos Williams' *The Right of Way*. *See* **19185**.

1889. Cherciu, Lucia. Parody as dialogue and disenchantment: remembering Phoebe Cary. *See* **9438**.

1890. Chickering, Howell. 'And I seyde his opinion was good': how irony works in the Monk's portrait. *In* (pp. 3–18) **4310**.

1891. Chu, Seo-Young Jennie. Dickinson and mathematics. *See* **9855**.

1892. Clark, Ira. The trappings of *All's Well That Ends Well*. *See* **5631**.

1893. Clippinger, David W. Resurrecting the ghost: H.D., Susan Howe, and the haven of poetry. *See* **15527**.

1894. Clymer, Lorna (ed.). Ritual, routine, and regime: repetition in early modern British and European culture. Toronto; Buffalo, NY; London: Toronto

UP in assn with the UCLA Center for Seventeenth- and Eighteenth-Century Studies and the William Andrews Clark Memorial Library, 2006. pp. xi, 258.

1895. Cockcroft, Robert; Cockcroft, Susan (eds). Persuading people: an introduction to rhetoric. (Bibl. 1993, 1450.) Basingstoke; New York: Palgrave Macmillan, 2005. pp. xiii, 258. (Second ed.: first ed. 1992.) Rev. by Raquel Hidalgo Downing in EIUC (14) 2006, 153–66.

1896. Cohen, Joshua. Mermaid-like: the tragedy of Ophelia. *See* **5706**.

1897. Colclough, David. Verse libels and the epideictic tradition in early Stuart England. *See* **6420**.

1898. Colón, Susan. Dickens's *Hard Times* and Dante's *Inferno*. *See* **9721**.

1899. Conti Camaiora, Luisa. Themes and images in John Clare's *Poems Descriptive of Rural Life and Scenery*. *See* **9471**.

1900. Cook, Eleanor. Enigmas and riddles in literature. *See* **3217**.

1901. Copeland, Rita. Chaucer and rhetoric. *In* (pp. 122–43) **4330**.

1902. —— Secular and sacred: the history of rhetoric and religious community in the Middle Ages. *In* (pp. 135–47) **3658**.

1903. Côté, Nicole. Mavis Gallant's shifting poetics of exile: the ironic and the oneiric in two early short stories. *In* (pp. 111–29) **16036**.

1904. Couchman, Jane; Crabb, Ann (eds). Women's letters across Europe, 1400–1700: form and persuasion. *See* **3605**.

1905. Couper, Sarah. Allegory and parody in William Dunbar's *Sen That I Am a Presoneir*. *See* **4133**.

1906. Couture, Barbara; Kent, Thomas (eds). The private, the public, and the published: reconciling private lives and public rhetoric. (Bibl. 2004, 2317.) Rev. by Jeffry Allen Rice in RSQ (38:3) 2006, 343–50.

1907. Cregan-Reid, Vybarr. Bodies, boundaries and queer waters: drowning and prosopopœia in later Dickens. *See* **9729**.

1908. Crippa, Gianni. La descrizione in *Jane Eyre*: tra desiderio del romanzo gotico e principio di realtà. *See* **9181**.

1909. Csatár, Péter; Pethő, Gergely; Tóth, Enikő. On possible factors in the aesthetic appreciation of metaphors. *See* **1751**.

1910. Dabundo, Laura. 'The redemption of the world': the rhetoric of Jane Austen's prayers. *See* **9005**.

1911. Daghlian, Carlos. A ironia como poética na poesia de Emily Dickinson. *See* **9856**.

1912. Davis, Carmel. Words beyond meaning: the language of ascent and the ascent of language in medieval mystical texts. *See* **2289**.

1913. Davis, William. Now, gods, stand up for bastards: the 1603 'Good Quarto' *Hamlet*. *See* **5709**.

1914. Davis, William L. Structural secrets: Shakespeare's complex chiasmus. *See* **5283**.

1915. Daybell, James. Scripting a female voice: women's epistolary rhetoric in sixteenth-century letters of petition. *See* **4774**.

1916. Day-Lindsey, Lisa. Bradstreet's *The Author to Her Book*. *See* **6592**.

1917. De Gooyer, Alan. Surviving *The Tempest*. *See* **6120**.

1918. de Grazia, Margreta. Imprints: Shakespeare, Gutenberg, and Descartes. *In* (pp. 29–58) **661**.

1919. Dennis, Matthew. Red Jacket's rhetoric: postcolonial persuasions on the Native frontiers of the early American Republic. *In* (pp. 16–33) **2149**.

1920. Dennison, Julie. Williams and H.D. figure it out: reconceiving the childbirth metaphor in 'his' *Paterson*, 'her' *Trilogy*. *See* **15532**.

1921. Descargues, Madeleine. The obstetrics of *Tristram Shandy*. *See* **8167**.

1922. Desmet, Christy. Poetry, proof, and pedigree in *The Merchant of Venice*. *See* **5958**.

1923. Devlin, L. Patrick. Analysis of Presidential Primary Campaign commercials of 2004. ComQ (53:4) 2005, 451–71.

1924. Dilworth, Thomas. Keats's *To Autumn*. *See* **10643**.

1925. Dimit, Robert G. 'Why, you … I oughta' …': aposiopesis and the natural language of the passions, 1670–1770. *See* **6237**.

1926. Dobrovol'skij, Dmitrij; Piirainen, Elisabeth. Figurative language: cross-cultural and cross-linguistic perspectives. Oxford: Elsevier, 2005. pp. xii, 419. (Current research in the semantics/pragmatics interface, 13.) Rev. by Zoltán Kövecses in MetS (21:3) 2006, 191–8.

1927. Drout, Michael D. C. The rhetorical evolution of *'Beowulf': the Monsters and the Critics*. *In* (pp. 183–215) **18804**.

1928. DuBois, Andrew. Ashbery's forms of attention. *See* **14454**.

1929. Dubrow, Heather. 'He had the dialect and different skill': authorizers in *Henry V*, *A Lover's Complaint*, and *Othello*. *In* (pp. 121–36) **5913**.

1930. Edgecombe, Rodney Stenning. Paronomasia in a letter by Thomas Hood. *See* **10466**.

1931. Edwards, A. S. G. F. Scott Fitzgerald, *The Great Gatsby*: 'like an angry diamond'. *See* **15877**.

1932. Enterline, Lynn. Rhetoric, discipline, and the theatricality of everyday life in Elizabethan grammar schools. *In* (pp. 173–90) **5334**.

1933. Erickson, Wayne. The poet's power and the rhetoric of humility in Spenser's Dedicatory Sonnets. *See* **5084**.

1934. Erkkilä, Betsy. Phillis Wheatley and the Black American Revolution. *In* (pp. 161–82) **6224**.

1935. Eron, Sarah. Circles and the in-between: shaping time, space, and paradox in Swinburnian verse. *See* **11375**.

1936. Evans, Murray J. Reading 'will' in Coleridge's *Opus Maximum*: the rhetoric of transition and repetition. *In* (pp. 73–95) **9503**.

1937. Everson, William. Eros in *agape*: Rexroth and the sacrality of sex. *See* **18209**.

1938. Fairer, David. 'The year runs round': the poetry of work in eighteenth-century England. *In* (pp. 153–71) **1894**.

1939. Fischer, Barbara K. Museum mediations: reframing ekphrasis in contemporary American poetry. *See* **13743**.

1940. Fishelov, David. *Robinson Crusoe*, 'the Other' and the poetics of surprise. *See* **7714**.

1941. Flaumenhaft, Mera J. Is all the world a stage? Marriage and a metaphor in *As You Like It*. *In* (pp. 71–104) **5394**.

1942. Fleck, Andrew. The ambivalent blush: figural and structural metonymy, modesty, and *Much Ado about Nothing*. *See* **6008**.

1943. —— Imprisoned in the flesh: the return of Petrarch in Nashe's *The Unfortunate Traveler*. *See* **4978**.

1944. Fletcher, Alan J. Reading radical metonymy in *Pearl*. *In* (pp. 47–61) **3658**.

1945. Fletcher, Loraine. Animal rites: a reading of *Venus and Adonis*. *See* **6191**.

1946. Fludernik, Monika. The metaphorics and metonymics of carcerality: reflections on imprisonment as source and target domain in literary texts. *See* **3251**.

1947. Foley, Stephen Merriam. The English Renaissance; or, My last duchess. *See* **4587**.

1948. Fontana, Ernest. Pre-facing simile vehicles in Dante Gabriel Rossetti's sonnets. *See* **11096**.

1949. Frago, Marta. Arte y seudoarte: patrones de ironía en las novelas y guiones de Ruth Prawer Jhabvala. *See* **16598**.

1950. Frank, Roberta. The incomparable wryness of Old English poetry. *In* (pp. 59–73) **1241**.

1951. Franke, William. Linguistic repetition as theological revelation in Christian epic tradition: the case of Joyce's *Finnegans Wake*. *See* **16689**.

1952. Furlani, Andre. Davenport and Sebald's art of excursus. *See* **15416**.

1953. Ganze, Alison L. Dickinson's *'Twas Like a Maelstrom, with a Notch*. *See* **9864**.

1954. Ghasemi, Parvin; Mansooji, Elham. Nature and man in Robert Frost. *See* **16003**.

1955. Gibbons, Reginald. This working against the grain. *See* **16076**.

1956. Gibert, Teresa. Textual, contextual and critical surprises in *Desirée's Baby*. *See* **9459**.

1957. Glaisyer, Natasha. 'A due Circulation in the Veins of the Publick': imagining credit in late seventeenth- and early eighteenth-century England. *See* **6468**.

1958. Glenn, Cheryl; Lyday, Margaret M.; Sharer, Wendy B. (eds). Rhetorical education in America. (Bibl. 2005, 2318.) Rev. by Chris Bell in JMMLA (38:2) 2005, 126–8; by Nancy G. Barron in ANQ (19:2) 2006, 58–61.

1959. Glucksberg, Sam. On the automaticity of pragmatic processes: a modular proposal. *In* (pp. 72–93) **1818**.

1960. Grandjeat, Yves-Charles. L'écriture de la nature chez Barry Lopez: enjeux et stratégies. *See* **17255**.

1961. Greene, Rebekah. Milton's *Comus*. *See* **7010**.

1962. Gregerson, Linda. Rhetorical contract in the lyric poem. *See* **6930**.

1963. Guyer, Sara. Testimony and trope in *Frankenstein*. *See* **11179**.

1964. Hamner, Robert D. Ekphrasis and V. S. Naipaul's *The Enigma of Arrival*. *See* **17722**.

1965. Hannay, Margaret P. Re-revealing the Psalms: the Countess of Pembroke and her early modern readers. *See* **5010**.

1966. Hansen, Tom. Collins's *Japan*. *See* **15239**.

1967. —— Swenson's *The Universe*. *See* **18695**.

1968. Harned, Jon. Rhetoric and perverse desire in Shakespeare's *A Lover's Complaint*. *In* (pp. 149–63) **5913**.

1969. Harol, Corrinne. Virgin idols and verbal devices: Pope's Belinda and the Virgin Mary. *See* **8055**.

1970. Harrell, Willie J., Jr. A call to consciousness and action: mapping the African American jeremiad. *See* **8248**.

1971. Harris, Jonathan Gil. All swell that end swell: dropsy, phantom pregnancy, and the sound of deconception in *All's Well That Ends Well*. *See* **5632**.

1972. Hart, Roderick P.; Daughton, Suzanne M. Modern rhetorical criticism. (Bibl. 1997, 2515.) Boston, MA: Pearson / Allyn & Bacon, 2005. pp. ix, 374. (Third ed.: first ed. 1990.)

1973. Hartwig, Joan. 'Mine honor's pawn': gage-throwing and word-play in Shakespeare's second tetralogy. *See* **5885**.

1974. Haydock, Nicholas. Treasonous founders and pious seducers: Aeneas, Gawain, and aporetic romance. *In* (pp. 82–111) **4550**.

1975. Hearon, Todd. Eric Ormsby's onomatopoetics. *See* **17911**.

1976. Hellwarth, Jennifer Wynne. Afterword. *In* (pp. 395–401) **661**.

1977. Herrero Ruiz, Javier. The role of metaphor, metonymy, and conceptual blending in understanding advertisements: the case of drug-prevention ads. RAEI (19) 2006, 169–90.

1978. Herron, Thomas. Plucking the perrot: *Muiopotmos* and Irish politics. *In* (pp. 80–118) **5100**.

1979. Hickey, Raymond. Productive lexical processes in present-day English. *In* (pp. 153–68) **1227**.

1980. Hill, Jane. 'The river we're all troubled by': David Bottoms and the legacy of James Dickey. *See* **14817**.

1981. Hill, Marylu. 'Eat me, drink me, love me': Eucharist and the erotic body in Christina Rossetti's *Goblin Market*. *See* **11085**.

1982. Hillier, Russell M. 'In a dark parody' of John Bunyan's *The Pilgrim's Progress*: the presence of subversive allegory in Cormac McCarthy's *Outer Dark*. *See* **17301**.

1983. —— Two Patristic sources for John Milton's description of the sun (*Paradise Lost*, III.591–595). *See* **7020**.

1984. Hines, John. 'Aire disguis'd': metaphors of genre and Henry Vaughan's sacred hymns. *See* **7153**.

1985. Hiraga, Masako K. Metaphor and iconicity: a cognitive approach to analyzing texts. Basingstoke; New York: Palgrave Macmillan, 2005. pp. xvi, 261. Rev. by Daniel C. Strack in MetS (21:2) 2006, 121–6.

1986. Hodges, Laura F. Criseyde's 'widewes habit large of samyt broun'. *In* (pp. 37–58) **4523**.

1987. Hodgkins, Hope Howell. The apophatic heart: Graham Greene's negative rhetoric. *See* **16204**.

1988. Höfele, Andreas. *Bestiarium humanum*: Lear's animal kingdom. *In* (pp. 84–98) **5346**.

1989. Hoffmann, A. Robin. Sewing and weaving in *Piers Plowman*. *See* **4195**.

1990. Hofmann, Klaus. Keats's *Ode to a Grecian Urn*. *See* **10650**.

1991. Holden, R. Bradley. Shakespeare's Sonnet 3. *See* **6092**.

1992. Hollingsworth, Christopher. The force of the entomological Other: insects as instruments of intolerable thought. *In* (pp. 262–77) **3203**.

1993. Hopps, Gavin. Beyond embarrassment: a post-secular reading of apostrophe. *See* **8788**.

1994. Houliston, Victor. An apology for Donne's *Pseudo Martyr*. *See* **6722**.

1995. Hovey, Jaime. A thousand words: portraiture, style, and queer Modernism. *See* **11943**.

1996. Howard, Darren. The search for a method: a rhetorical reading of Blake's prophetic symbolism. *See* **7575**.

1997. Howard, W. Scott. Resistance, sacrifice, and historicity in the elegies of Robert Hayden. *In* (pp. 133–52) **13763**.

1998. Hudspeth, Robert N. Later Emerson: 'intellect' and *The Conduct of Life*. *In* (pp. 405–31) **10064**.

1999. Hunt, Maurice. Shakespeare's 'still-vexed' *Tempest*. *See* **6130**.

2000. Hunter, Paul. Seven reasons for rhyme. *In* (pp. 172–98) **1894**.

2001. Hytner, Nicholas; Reinelt, Janelle; Thompson, Ann. Retrospective: Janelle Reinelt. Final session (final thoughts) on heightened language: impasse or interchange? *In* (pp. 161–80) **5543**.

2002. Jackel, Brad. Dante, Doré, and Conrad. *See* **15277**.

2003. Jackson, Kimberley. Vivisected language in H. G. Wells's *The Island of Doctor Moreau*. *See* **19039**.

2004. Jackson-Houlston, Caroline. 'Queen lilies'? The interpenetration of scientific, religious and gender discourses in Victorian representations of plants. *See* **8791**.

2005. Johnson, Andrew. Peter Boyle and the art of poetry. *See* **20189**.

2006. Johnson, Danette Ifert. Feminine style in Presidential debate discourse, 1960–2000. *See* **2211**.

2007. Johnson, Heather. Dangerous skin: bees and female figuration in Maher and Plath. *In* (pp. 129–52) **3203**.

2008. Jones, Susan E. Fragment and focus: Jane Austen and the art of the blazon. *See* **9037**.

2009. Kamuf, Peggy. Composition displacement. *See* **14175**.

2010. Kasrie, Mary Rose. Reading the letters of Judith Sargent Murray: from private correspondence to public voice. *In* (pp. 197–209) **6224**.

2011. Kearns, Michael. Morality and rhetoric in *Moby-Dick*. *In* (pp. 147–64) **10823**.

2012. Keithley, Walter Hank. Swift reading Bacon reading Apollonius. *See* **8199**.

2013. Kennedy, Kathleen E. Hoccleve's dangerous game of draughts. *See* **4163**.

2014. Kewes, Paulina. Acts of remembrance, acts of oblivion: rhetoric, law, and national memory in early Restoration England. *In* (pp. 103–31) **1894**.

2015. Kimberley, Emma. Textual implications of ekphrasis in contemporary poetry. *In* (pp. 89–99) **3407**.

2016. Kinney, Arthur F. The making of a Humanist poetic. *See* **4607**.

2017. Klinge, Markus. The grotesque in *Areopagitica*. *See* **7025**.

2018. Knittel, Janna. Sun dance behind bars: the rhetoric of Leonard Peltier's prison writings. *In* (pp. 110–28) **2149**.

2019. Kolb, Jocelyne. Romantic irony. *In* (pp. 376–92) **8357**.

2020. Koster, Josephine A. The *Vita sancte Alicie Bathoniensis*: transgressions of hagiographic rhetoric in the Wife of Bath's Prologue and Tale. *In* (pp. 35–45) **4310**.

2021. Krysl, Marilyn. Sacred and profane: the sestina as rite. *See* **13792**.

2022. Kuchar, Gary. Andrew Marvell's anamorphic tears. *See* **6932**.

2023. Kumaran, Arul. Robert Greene's Martinist transformation in 1590. *See* **4857**.

2024. Labriola, Albert C. The 'wine of love': viticulture in the poetry of Richard Crashaw. *See* **6665**.

2025. Lakoff, Robin Tolmach. Vulgar Latin: comparative castration (and comparative theories of syntax). *See* **1386**.

2026. Lanone, Catherine. L'explicit(e) dans *The Power and the Glory* de Graham Greene. *See* **16206**.

2027. Lattig, Sharon. The perception of metaphor and the metaphor of perception: the neurodynamics of figuration. Intertexts (9:1) 2005, 23–42.

2028. Lethbridge, J. B. Spenser's last days: Ireland, career, mutability, allegory. *In* (pp. 302–36) **5100**.

2029. Liebler, Naomi Conn. Buying and selling so(u)les: marketing strategies and the politics of performance in *Julius Caesar*. *In* (pp. 165–79) **5805**.

2030. Longaker, Mark Garrett. Idealism and early American rhetoric. *See* **7764**.

2031. McArdle, Andrea. The confluence of law and antebellum Black literature: lawyerly discourse as a rhetoric of empowerment. *See* **11329**.

2032. McAvoy, Liz Herbert. '… the fend set him in my throte': sexuality and the fiendish encounter in Julian of Norwich's *Revelations of Divine Love*. *See* **4175**.

2033. McCarron, Bill. Basilisk puns in *Harry Potter and the Chamber of Secrets*. *See* **18349**.

2034. McCullough, Peter. Donne as preacher. *In* (pp. 167–81) **6718**.

2035. McDowell, Nicholas. Abiezer Coppe, Horace, and the dormouse. *See* **6658**.

2036. McGowan, Tony. Imperfect states: Thoreau, Melville, and 'insectivorous fate'. *In* (pp. 58–86) **3203**.

2037. McKenna, Stephen J. Adam Smith: the rhetoric of propriety. *See* **8145**.

2038. McLoughlin, Kate. Adynaton: a war *topos*. PE (1) 2006, 15–24.

2039. Madden, Etta. 'To make a figure': Benjamin Rush's rhetorical self-construction and scientific authorship. *See* **8130**.

2040. Maddux, H. Clark. Audience and the layered art of method in John Bunyan's *The Life and Death of Mr Badman* and *The Pilgrim's Progress*. *See* **6619**.

2041. Maguire, Laurie. Helen of Troy: representing absolute beauty in language. *See* **5373**.

2042. Maloney, Ian S. Melville's monumental imagination. *See* **10863**.

2043. Manetti, Fabiana. Il linguaggio dell'armonia: studio della similitudine in Percy Bysshe Shelley. *See* **11216**.

2044. Mascuch, Michael. The godly child's 'power and evidence' in the word: orality and literacy in the ministry of Sarah Wright. *In* (pp. 103–26) **6264**.

2045. Mason, David. The seeing 'I'. *See* **13814**.

2046. Mason, Emma. The trouble with comfort: Christina Rossetti, John Ruskin, and leafy emotion. *See* **11088**.

2047. Mason, Oliver; Platt, Rhiannon. Embracing a new creed: lexical patterning and the encoding of ideology. ColLit (33:2) 2006, 154–70. (Bush's State of the Union Address: 2002.)

2048. Matos, Nicole. 'Join, interchangeable phantoms': from metaphor to metonymy in Walcott's *Omeros*. *See* **18928**.

2049. Matteson, John T. 'Deadly voids and unbidden infidelities': death, memory, and the law in *Moby-Dick*. *In* (pp. 117–31) **10823**.

2050. Maus, Katharine Eisaman. A womb of his own: male Renaissance poets in the female body. *In* (pp. 89–108) **661**.

2051. Meek, Richard. Ekphrasis in *The Rape of Lucrece* and *The Winter's Tale*. *See* **6203**.

2052. Mejia-LaPerle, Carol. Domestic rhetors of an early modern family: female persuasions in *A Woman Killed with Kindness*. *In* (pp. 39–54) **3893**.

2053. Mena Martínez, Flor. Occasional phraseological synonymy. *See* **2980**.

2054. Merrett, Robert. Presenting the past: philosophical irony and the rhetoric of double vision from Bishop Butler to T. S. Eliot. *See* **3345**.

2055. Mieder, Wolfgang. 'We are all in the same boat now': proverbial rhetoric in the Churchill–Roosevelt correspondence. *See* **2986**.

2056. Miller, Anthony. Ben Jonson and 'the proper passion of Mettalls'. *See* **6892**.

2057. Miller, Hildy; Bridwell-Bowles, Lillian (eds). Rhetorical women: roles and representations. (Bibl. 2005, 2410.) Rev. by Margaret C. Ervin in ColLit (33:4) 2006, 218–22; by Joanne Craig in RMER (60:1) 2006.

2058. Miller, J. Hillis. Derrida's '*destinerrance*'. *See* **14223**.

2059. Morris, G. S. Blake's *The Fly*. *See* **7581**.

2060. Moschovakis, Nicholas R. Topicality and conceptual blending: *Titus Andronicus* and the case of William Hacket. *See* **6157**.

2061. Mounsey, Chris. Christopher Smart's late religious lyrics: building churches in the air. *In* (pp. 132–50) **1894**.

2062. Mukherji, Subha. False trials in Shakespeare, Massinger, and Ford. *See* **5393**.

2063. Mulryan, John. Milton's *Paradise Regained*. *See* **7043**.

2064. Mulvihill, James. George Campbell's *Philosophy of Rhetoric* and Wordsworth's 'Preface' to *Lyrical Ballads*. *See* **11697**.

2065. —— Upstart talents: rhetoric and the career of reason in English Romantic discourse, 1790–1820. (Bibl. 2004, 2469.) Rev. by Lois Agnew in PrSt (28:1) 2006, 97–100; by H. Lewis Ulman in SR (45:2) 2006, 303–6.

2066. Myers, Benjamin. 'Such is the face of falshood': Spenserian theodicy in Ireland. *See* **5108**.

2067. Nabers, Deak. Victory of law: the Fourteenth Amendment, the Civil War, and American literature, 1852–1867. *See* **8457**.

2068. Naciscione, Anita. Sustainability of phraseological image in discourse. *See* **17048**.

2069. Nassaar, Christopher S. Some remarks on *Parody, Paradox and Play in 'The Importance of Being Earnest'*. *See* **11619**.

2070. Navaei, Reza Najafpour. *The Lady of Shalott*: a Goethean reading of the text. *In* (pp. 5–12) **3407**.

2071. New, Elisa. Variety as religious experience: the poetics of the plain style. *See* **3576**.

2072. Newberry, Paul. Emerging emotion theory: forgiveness and repetition. *In* (pp. 80–99) **1894**.

2073. Nixon, Jude V. 'Vital candle in close heart's vault': energy, optics and Hopkins' spermaceti flame. *See* **10483**.

2074. Olmsted, Wendy. The gentle doctor: Renaissance/Reformation friendship, rhetoric, and emotion in Sidney's *Old Arcadia*. *See* **5042**.

2075. —— Rhetoric: an historical introduction. Oxford; Malden, MA: Blackwell, 2006. pp. xix, 157.

2076. Ower, John. Coleridge's *Rime of the Ancient Mariner*. *See* **9542**.

2077. Patrick, Duncan. Unorthodox theology in two short works by Sterne. *See* **8178**.

2078. Perquin, Jean-Charles. Les stratégies poétiques du refus de vieillir dans *Ulysses* de Tennyson. *See* **11405**.

2079. Perry, Nandra. 'Tis heav'n she speakes': Lady Religion, Saint Teresa, and the politics of ceremony in the poetry of Richard Crashaw. *See* **6669**.

2080. Peterfy, Margit. 'These things astonish me beyond words': wordplay in William Carlos Williams's poetry. *See* **19198**.

2081. Peterson, Calvin M. From doctrine to narrative and back in *The Pilgrim's Progress*. *See* **6620**.

2082. Phillips, Kendall R. Rhetorical maneuvers: subjectivity, power, and resistance. PhilR (39:4) 2006, 310–32.

2083. Pickering, Sam. Painting the wind: poetic art and John Clare. *See* **9478**.

2084. Pilný, Ondřej. Concepts of irony. PSE (24) 2006, 141–56.

2085. Plummer, John F. Fables, *cupiditas*, and vessels of tree: Chaucer's use of the Epistles to Timothy. *In* (pp. 237–45) **4310**.

2086. Pohl, Nicole. 'Perfect reciprocity': salon culture and epistolary conversations. *See* **8011**.

2087. Polletta, Francesca. It was like a fever: storytelling in protest and politics. Chicago, IL; London: Chicago UP, 2006. pp. xiv, 242.

2088. Powell, Malea D. Sarah Winnemucca Hopkins: her wrongs and claims. *In* (pp. 69–94) **2149**.

2089. Praitis, Irena. 'He gathered to himself through the years / Something of everything he knew': metaphor, composites, and multiplicity in the poetry of Alberto Ríos. *See* **18256**.

2090. Prandi, Julie D. Sexual imagery in the verse epistles of Robert Burns and Anna Louise Karsch. *See* **7644**.

2091. Prescott, Anne Lake. Teaching Astrophil's 'coltish gyres': Sidney and the horses of desire. *See* **5043**.

2092. Pruitt, Kristin A. The making of the circle: imagery as pattern in *Paradise Lost*. *See* **7055**.

2093. Quinney, Laura. Escape from repetition: Blake *versus* Locke and Wordsworth. *In* (pp. 63–79) **1894**.

2094. Ragg, Edward. Pragmatic abstraction *vs* metaphor: Stevens' *The Pure Good of Theory* and *Macbeth*. *See* **18651**.

2095. Ramage, John D. Rhetoric: a user's guide. London; New York: Pearson Longman, 2006. pp. xvii, 220.

2096. Rand, Thomas. Shakespeare's *As You Like It*. *See* **5662**.

2097. —— 'Time's eunuch' reconsidered. *See* **10486**.

2098. Ravez, Stéphanie. Beckett l'interrupteur; ou, Des petits textes en prose. *See* **14718**.

2099. Reddy, Srikanth. 'To explain grace requires a curious hand': Marianne Moore's interdisciplinary digressions. *See* **17571**.

2100. Redfield, Karen A. Inside the circle, outside the circle: the continuance of Native American storytelling and the development of rhetorical strategies in English. *In* (pp. 149–64) **2149**.

2101. Reed, J. D. Wilfred Owen's Adonis. *In* (pp. 39–56) **3235**.

2102. Reed, John R. The gentleman in the white waistcoat: Dickens and metonymy. *See* **9810**.

2103. Reid, Christopher. 'Community of mind': quotation and persuasion in the eighteenth-century House of Commons. AJ (17) 2006, 317–40.

2104. Resetarits, C. R. The genomic tropes of Dickinson's *The Veins of Other Flowers*. *See* **9889**.

2105. Reyes-Rodríguez, Antonio. Speeches and declarations: a war of words. *See* **2229**.

2106. Rhatigan, Emma. Knees and elephants: Donne preaches on ceremonial conformity. *See* **6746**.

2107. Riggs, David. The poet in the play: life and art in *Tamburlaine* and *The Jew of Malta*. *In* (pp. 205–24) **5353**.

2108. Rogers, Pat. 'How I want thee, humorous Hogart': the motif of the absent artist in Swift, Fielding and others. *See* **8212**.

2109. Romero, Esther; Soria, Belén. Cognitive metaphor theory revisited. JLS (34:1) 2005, 1–20.

2110. Roof, Judith. In locus parentis. *In* (pp. 371–94) **661**.

2111. Rosenbaum, Susan. Elizabeth Bishop's theater of war. *In* (pp. 53–82) **13763**.

2112. Russell, Corinna. A defence of tautology: repetition and difference in Wordsworth's note to *The Thorn*. *See* **11711**.

2113. Rust, Martha Dana. 'Le Vostre C': letters and love in Bodleian Library MS Arch. Selden B.24. *In* (pp. 111–38) **4523**.

2114. Saenger, Michael Baird. The birth of advertising. *In* (pp. 197–219) **661**.

2115. Sale, Carolyn. Eating air, feeling smells: *Hamlet*'s theory of performance. *See* **5756**.

2116. Sarsfield, Rachel. From the chrysalis to the display case: the butterfly's 'voyage out' in Virginia Woolf. *In* (pp. 87–111) **3203**.

2117. Schmitz, Neil. Doing the Gettysburg Address: Jefferson/Calhoun/Lincoln/King. *See* **10741**.

2118. Scott, Patrick. Clough, bankruptcy, and disbelief: the economic background to *Blank Misgivings*. *See* **9492**.

2119. Seabra Ferreira, Marie-Aline. The passion of the brides: Angela Carter, Marcel Duchamp and Max Ernst. *See* **15063**.

2120. Seeley, Tracy. 'The fair light mystery of images': Alice Meynell's metaphysical turn. *See* **10924**.

2121. Segall, Kreg. Narrative voice, nude women: productive paralysis in *The Faerie Queene*. *See* **5118**.

2122. Share, Don. 'It seems I was reading something': poetic voices in and out of context in Ashbery's *Flow Chart*. *See* **14458**.

2123. Sharifian, Farzad. A cultural-conceptual approach and world Englishes: the case of Aboriginal English. *See* **2704**.

2124. Sharon-Zisser, Shirley. 'True to bondage': the rhetorical forms of female masochism in *A Lover's Complaint*. *In* (pp. 179–90) **5913**.

2125. —— (ed.). Critical essays on Shakespeare's *A Lover's Complaint*: suffering ecstasy. *See* **5913**.

2126. Shaw, Luci. Reversing entropy. *In* (pp. 201–13) **11940**.

2127. Sheen, Erica. 'Why should a dog, a horse, a rat have life, and thou no breath at all?': Shakespeare's animations. *In* (pp. 87–100) **4588**.

2128. Shore, Daniel. 'Fit though few': *Eikonoklastes* and the rhetoric of audience. *See* **7068**.

2129. Simmons, James R., Jr. 'Don't tell me about rears and vices; I have been in the navy all my life': profligacy on the high seas in Jane Austen and Patrick O'Brian. *See* **9071**.

2130. Simpson, James. 'For al my body … weieth nat an unce': empty poets and rhetorical weight in Lydgate's *Churl and Bird*. *In* (pp. 129–46) **4231**.

2131. Singh, Sukhbir. Echoes of Shakespeare's Sonnet 116 in Yeats's *The Indian to His Love*. *See* **19447**.

2132. Sivefors, Per. Ascham and Udall: the unknown language reformer in *Toxophilus*. *See* **4807**.

2133. Sloane, Thomas O. Dr Donne and the image of Christ. *See* **6753**.

2134. Smith, Ali. The armchair, the world: Christine Brooke-Rose and the evocation of self. *See* **14868**.

2135. Smith, Gail K. Art and the body in *Agnes of Sorrento*. *In* (pp. 167–86) **11355**.

2136. Smith, Helen. 'This one poore blacke gowne lined with white': the clothing of the sixteenth-century English book. *In* (pp. 195–208) **4629**.

2137. Smith, Marie Hockenhull. The children will be 'subject to the infamy of their deluded and unfortunate mother': rhetoric of the courtroom, a gothic fantasy and a plain letter to the Lord Chancellor. *See* **11076**.

2138. Sopory, Pradeep. Metaphor and affect. PT (26:3) 2005, 433–58.

2139. Sotirova, Violeta. Repetition in free indirect style: a dialogue of minds? *See* **17059**.

2140. Spangler, Matthew. 'Haunted to the edge of trance': performance and orality in the early poems of W. B. Yeats. *See* **19449**.

2141. Stafanowitsch, Anatol; Gries, Stefan Th. (eds). Corpus-based approaches to metaphor and metonymy. Berlin; New York: Mouton de Gruyter, 2006. pp. 319. (Trends in linguistics: Studies and monographs, 171.)

2142. Starr, G. A. Defoe and biblical memory. *In* (pp. 316–35) **7255**.

2143. Stelmach, Kathryn. From text to tableau: ekphrastic enchantment in *Mrs Dalloway* and *To the Lighthouse*. *See* **19335**.

2144. Stephenson, Jenn. Metatheatre and authentication through metonymic compression in John Mighton's *Possible Worlds*. *See* **17503**.

2145. Stewart, Susan. Some thoughts about Dickinson's *Dont Put Up My Thread & Needle*. *See* **9895**.

2146. Stock, Lorraine Kochanske. 'Peynted … text and [visual] glose': primitivism, ekphrasis, and pictorial intertextuality in the dreamers' bedrooms of *Roman de la Rose* and *Book of the Duchess*. *In* (pp. 97–114) **4310**.

2147. Stojkovic, Tijana. Larkin in the cinema: dynamic visualization in *Show Saturday* and *Here*. *See* **17003**.

2148. Stromberg, Ernest. Resistance and mediation: the rhetoric of irony in Indian boarding-school narratives by Francis La Flesche and Zitkala-Ša. *In* (pp. 95–109) **2149**.

2149. —— (ed.). American Indian rhetorics of survivance: word medicine, word magic. Pittsburgh, PA: Pittsburgh UP, 2006. pp. viii, 286. (Pittsburgh series in composition, literacy, and culture.)

2150. Sugimura, N. K. Changelings and *The Changeling*. *See* **6957**.

2151. Tarr, Rodger L. The tailor's tailor: Thomas Carlyle's Jesus Christ. *See* **9401**.

2152. Taverniers, Miriam. Grammatical metaphor and lexical metaphor: different perspectives on semantic variation. Neophilologus (90:2) 2006, 321–32.

2153. Taylor, Cheryl. The *Cloud*-author's remaking of the pseudo-Dionysius' *Mystical Theology*. *See* **4065**.

2154. Taylor, Jefferey H. Four levels of meaning in the York Cycle of mystery plays: a study in medieval allegory. *See* **3961**.

2155. Teehan, Sheila. The face of Decadence in *The Sacred Fount*. *In* (pp. 109–22) **10568**.

2156. Teichman, Matthew. The germ of a sense. PhilL (30:2) 2006, 567–79.

2157. Thompson, Ann; Thompson, John O. Meaning, 'seeing', printing. *In* (pp. 59–86) **661**.

2158. Thompson, Peggy. 'Why say we no?': the trope of insincere resistance in *The Gentleman Dancing-Master* and *The Plain Dealer*. *See* **7213**.

2159. Tomaiuolo, Saverio. Tennyson and Hopkins from metaphor to metonym: *In Memoriam* and *The Wreck of the Deutschland*. *See* **11409**.

2160. Tseng, Ming-yu. Iconicity in the interplay of the literal and the metaphorical: an example from William Blake's *Jerusalem*. *See* **7587**.

2161. Uzundemir, Özlem. Challenging gender roles through narrative techniques: Virginia Woolf's *To the Lighthouse*. *See* **19341**.

2162. Van Hulle, Dirk. Growth and the grid: organic *vs* constructivist conceptions of poetry. *See* **15720**.

2163. Vickers, Roy. Christian election, Holy Communion and Psalmic language in Ernest Jones's Chartist poetry. *See* **10631**.

2164. Viola, André. A Black Athena in the *Heart of Darkness*; or, Conrad's baffling oxymorons. *See* **15320**.

2165. von Maltzahn, Nicholas. There she blew! *See* **6783**.

2166. Walker, Thomas U. Mounting the soapbox: poetics, rhetoric, and laborlore at the scene of speaking. WF (65:1/2) 2006, 65–98.

2167. Wall, Cynthia Sundberg. The prose of things: transformations of description in the eighteenth century. *See* **7348**.

2168. Watts, Cedric. Fundamental editing: in *A Midsummer Night's Dream*, does 'Bottom' mean *bum*? And how about *arse* and *ass*? *See* **6001**.

2169. Weinroth, Michelle. Engendering consent: the voice of persuasion in *Felix Holt, the Radical*. *See* **10058**.

2170. Westarp, Karl-Heinz. Metaphoric processes in Flannery O'Connor's short fiction. *In* (pp. 111–21) **17825**.

2171. White, Laura Mooneyham. Another response to *'Across the pale parabola of joy': Wodehouse Parodist*. *See* **19243**.

2172. White, Micheline. Power couples and women writers in Elizabethan England: the public voices of Dorcas and Richard Martin and Anne and Hugh Dowriche. *In* (pp. 119–38) **3893**.

2173. Wider, Sarah Ann. Chladni patterns, Lyceum halls, and skillful experimenters: Emerson's new metaphysics for the listening reader. *In* (pp. 86–114) **10064**.

2174. Wilson, Douglas L. Lincoln the persuader. *See* **10742**.

2175. Wolfe, Eric A. Ventriloquizing nation: voice, identity, and radical democracy in Charles Brockden Brown's *Wieland*. *See* **9246**.

2176. Wong, Mitali P. Politics and tropes in Renaissance history plays: understanding a neglected genre. *See* **4747**.

2177. Yamada, Takeo. A Japanese Frost: considerations of synecdoche and sentence sounds. *See* **16020**.

2178. Yarbrough, Stephen R. Inventive intercourse: from rhetorical conflict to the ethical creation of novel truth. Carbondale: Southern Illinois UP, 2006. pp. xvii, 193.

2179. Yates, Julian. Accidental Shakespeare. *See* **6012**.

2180. Youngberg, Quentin. Morphology of Manifest Destiny: the justified violence of John O'Sullivan, Hank Morgan, and George W. Bush. *See* **11532**.

2181. Zagacki, Kenneth S.; Boleyn-Fitzgerald, Patrick A. Rhetoric and anger. PhilR (39:4) 2006, 290–309.

2182. Zapedowska, Magdalena. Longfellow's *The Lighthouse*. *See* **10757**.

2183. Zappen, James Philip (ed.). On persuasion, identification, and dialectical symmetry. By Kenneth Burke. PhilR (39:4) 2006, 333–9.

2184. Ziegeler, Debra; Lee, Sarah. Causativity reduction in Singaporean English. *See* **2713**.

2185. Znojemská, Helena. Sailing the dangerous waters: images of land and sea in *The Seafarer*, *The Panther* and *The Whale*. *See* **3804**.

SPOKEN DISCOURSE

2186. Airne, David; Benoit, William. Political television advertising in Campaign 2000. *See* **1834**.

2187. Ajimer, Karin. Discourse particles in contrast: the case of *in fact* and *actually*. *In* (pp. 23–35) **1195**.

2188. Baxter, Judith (ed.). Speaking out: the female voice in public contexts. *See* **2752**.

2189. Bean, Judith Mattson. Gaining a public voice: a historical perspective on American women's public speaking. *In* (pp. 21–39) **2752**.

2190. Benor, Sarah Bunin; Levy, Roger. The chicken or the egg? A probabilistic account of English binomials. *See* **1286**.

2191. Berger, Lauren; McMakin, Dana; Furman, Wyndol. The language of love: romantic relationships in adolescence. *In* (pp. 129–45) **2798**.

2192. Buchstaller, Isabelle. Social stereotypes, personality traits and regional perception displaced: attitudes towards the 'new' quotatives in the UK. *See* **1546**.

2193. Clark, Herbert H.; Bangerter, Adrian. Changing ideas about reference. *In* (pp. 25–49) **1818**.

2194. Clift, Rebecca. Indexing stance: reported speech as an interactional evidential. JSoc (10:5) 2006, 569–95.

2195. Cody, Cornelia. 'Only in New York City': the New York City personal experience narrative. *See* **2999**.

2196. Coulson, Seana. Extemporaneous blending: conceptual integration in humorous discourse from talk radio. Style (39:2) 2005, 107–22.

2197. Crespo Fernández, Eliecer. La vertiente locutiva e ilocutiva en la manipulación del referente en lengua inglesa. Los procesos mixtos: cuasieufemismo *vs* cuasidisfemismo. *See* **1795**.

2198. de Klerk, Vivian. Slang and swearing as markers of inclusion and exclusion in adolescence. *In* (pp. 111–27) **2798**.

2199. Devlin, L. Patrick. Analysis of Presidential Primary Campaign commercials of 2004. *See* **1923**.

2200. Díaz Pérez, Francisco Javier. Deixis and verbal politeness in request production in English and Spanish. *See* **1796**.

2201. Eades, Diana. Lexical struggle in court: Aboriginal Australians *versus* the State. JSoc (10:2) 2006, 153–80.

2202. Eckert, Penelope. Stylistic practice and the adolescent social order. *In* (pp. 93–110) **2798**.

2203. Eckstein, Jessica J. Conversion conundrums: listener perceptions of affective influence attempts as mediated by personality and individual differences. *See* **1800**.

2204. Erickson, Frederick. Talk and social theory: ecologies of speaking and listening in everyday life. Oxford; Malden, MA: Polity Press in assn with Blackwell, 2004. pp. xi, 228. Rev. by Kanavillil Rajagopalan in JSoc (10:3) 2006, 412–16.

2205. Féry, Caroline; Samek-Lodovici, Vieri. Focus projection and prosodic prominence in nested foci. *See* **1291**.

2206. Furniss, Graham. Orality: the power of the spoken word. Basingstoke; New York: Palgrave Macmillan, 2004. pp. xii, 188. Rev. by Harold Scheub in RAL (37:1) 2006, 128–9.

2207. García Gómez, Antonio. British and American expressions of politeness in anger-evoking contexts: a cultural-relativistic approach. *See* **1803**.

2208. German, James; Pierrehumbert, Janet; Kaufmann, Stefan. Evidence for phonological constraints on nuclear accent placement. *See* **1293**.

2209. Herrmann, Keith R. The war of words. *See* **1484**.

2210. Howarth, Peter. The phraseology of public international English. *See* **2719**.

2211. Johnson, Danette Ifert. Feminine style in Presidential debate discourse, 1960–2000. ComQ (53:1) 2005, 3–20.

2212. Keyser, Samuel Jay; Stevens, Kenneth Noble. Enhancement and overlap in the speech chain. *See* **1298**.

2213. Langendoen, D. Terence. Disjunctive numerals of estimation. *See* **1387**.

2214. Levey, Stephen. Tense variation in preadolescent narratives. JEL (34:2) 2006, 126–52.

2215. —— Visiting London relatives. EWW (27:1) 2006, 45–70. (Relative pronouns in London children's speech.)

2216. LeVine, Philip; Scollon, Ron (eds). Discourse and technology: multimodal discourse analysis. *See* **1813**.

2217. Levon, Erez. Hearing 'gay': prosody, interpretation, and the affective judgments of men's speech. AS (81:1) 2006, 56–78.

2218. —— Mosaic identity and style: phonological variation among Reform American Jews. *See* **2627**.

2219. Litosseliti, Lia. Constructing gender in public arguments: the female voice as emotional voice. *In* (pp. 40–58) **2752**.

2220. Miller, Stephen. Conversation: a history of a declining art. New Haven, CT; London: Yale UP, 2006. pp. xv, 336. Rev. by Alberto Manguel in TLS, 14 July 2006, 3–4.

2221. Moore, Emma. 'You tell all the stories': using a narrative to explore hierarchy within a Community of Practice. *See* **2783**.

2222. Myers, Greg. Applied linguistics and institutions of opinion. AppL (26:4) 2005, 527–44.

2223. —— 'Where are you from?': identifying place. JSoc (10:3) 2006, 320–43.

2224. O'Flynn, Sarah. Ticket to a queer planet? Communication issues affecting lesbian and gay people. *In* (pp. 147–61) **2798**.

2225. Pattemore, Stephen. 'Honourable bigotry'? Relevance theory, conversation analysis and radio talk-backs. RAEI (19) 2006, 299–318.

2226. Pichler, Pia. Multifunctional teasing as a resource for identity construction in the talk of British Bangladeshi girls. *See* **2584**.

2227. Pollack, Mica. Colormute: race talk dilemmas in an American school. *See* **2788**.

2228. Povolná, Renata. Some notes on interactive discourse items in spoken English. BStE (31) 2005, 49–61.

2229. Reyes-Rodríguez, Antonio. Speeches and declarations: a war of words. RAEI (19) 2006, 365–86.

2230. Rockwell, Patricia Ann. Sarcasm and other mixed messages: the ambiguous ways people use language. *See* **1777**.

2231. Sangiorgi, Simona. Disney's politeness for profit. *See* **1826**.

2232. Short, Mick. A corpus-based approach to speech, thought and writing presentation. *In* (pp. 241–71) **1195**.

2233. Simmons, Nancy Craig. Emerson and his audiences: the New England lectures, 1843–1844. *In* (pp. 51–85) **10064**.

2234. Simpson-Vlach, Rita C.; Leicher, Sheryl. The MICASE handbook: a resource for users of the Michigan Corpus of Academic Spoken English. Ann Arbor: Michigan UP, 2006. pp. viii, 318.

2235. Speer, Susan A. Gender talk: feminism, discourse and conversation analysis. *See* **2794**.

2236. Szczepek Reed, Beatrice. Prosodic orientation in English conversation. Basingstoke; New York: Palgrave Macmillan, 2006. pp. xiv, 231.

2237. Szmrecsanyi, Benedikt. Morphosyntactic persistence in spoken English: a corpus study at the intersection of variationist sociolinguistics, psycholinguistics, and discourse analysis. Berlin; New York: Mouton de Gruyter, 2006. pp. xiii, 248. (Trends in linguistics: Studies and monographs, 177.)

2238. Taboada, María Teresa. Building coherence and cohesion: task-oriented dialogue in English and Spanish. (Bibl. 2004, 2676.) Rev. by Tony Berber Sardinha in CompLing (32:2) 2006, 287–9.

2239. Wichmann, Anne; Cauldwell, Richard. *Wh-* questions and attitude: the effect of context. *In* (pp. 291–305) **1195**.

2240. Williams, Angie; Thurlow, Crispin (eds). Talking adolescence: perspectives on communication in the teenage years. *See* **2798**.

2241. Wright, Laura. The language of transported Londoners: third person singular present-tense markers in depositions from Virginia and the Bermudas, 1607–1624. *In* (pp. 158–71) **2543**.

STYLISTICS OF LITERARY TEXTS

2242. Abbott, H. Porter. Samuel Beckett: *Murphy*. *In* (pp. 306–13) **11788**.

2243. Aji, Hélène. 'Writing (as) (and) thinking': Charles Bernstein's work 'in' language. *See* **14761**.

2244. Algoo-Baksh, Stella. Austin C. Clarke's short fiction. *See* **15174**.

2245. Amador Moreno, Carolina P. An analysis of Hiberno-English in the early novels of Patrick MacGill: bilingualism and language shift from Irish to English in County Donegal. *See* **17343**.

2246. Anderson, J. J. Language and imagination in the *Gawain*-poems. *See* **4528**.

2247. Andrews, Corey E. 'Almost the same, but not quite': English poetry by eighteenth-century Scots. *See* **8088**.

2248. Arac, Jonathan. Global and Babel: two perspectives on language in American literature. *See* **3173**.

2249. Armand, Louis. Mind factory: from artifice to intelligence. *See* **16650**.

2250. —— On relativity, synaesthesia and materiality. *See* **16651**.

2251. Armantrout, Rae. Looking for trouble. *See* **9846**.

2252. Baines, Barbara J. 'That ever like is not the same': the vicissitudes of language in *Julius Caesar*. *In* (pp. 139–53) **5805**.

2253. Balcom, John. Translating modern Chinese literature. *In* (pp. 119–34) **3186**.

2254. Ballam, John D. Henry James and a 'sense' of place: the modalities of perception. *See* **10538**.

2255. Balmer, Josephine. What comes next? Reconstructing the Classics. *In* (pp. 184–95) **3186**.

2256. BAMIRO, EDMUND O. The politics of code-switching: English *vs* Nigerian languages. *See* **18563**.

2257. BARRY, ELIZABETH. Beckett and authority: the uses of cliché. *See* **14662**.

2258. BARTELT, GUILLERMO. Hegemonic registers in Momaday's *House Made of Dawn*. *See* **17548**.

2259. BASSNETT, SUSAN; BUSH, PETER (eds). The translator as writer. *See* **3186**.

2260. BATELY, JANET. The language of Ohthere's report to King Alfred: some problems and some puzzles for historians and linguists. *In* (pp. 39–53) **3679**.

2261. BAYLEY, JOHN. Overcoming kitsch: thoughts on linguistic and class resource from Keats to Betjeman. *In* (pp. 225–31) **13735**.

2262. BAYLEY, SALLY. 'I have your head on my wall': Sylvia Plath and the rhetoric of Cold War America. *See* **18028**.

2263. BEEBE, ANN. Dickinson's *Immortal Is an Ample Word*. *See* **9849**.

2264. BIDART, FRANK. A cross in the void. *In* (pp. 246–54) **16122**.

2265. BIGGS, FREDERICK M. Seventeen words of Middle Dutch origin in the Miller's Tale? *See* **4366**.

2266. BLACK, SCOTT. Anachronism and the uses of form in *Joseph Andrews*. *See* **7784**.

2267. BOASE-BEIER, JEAN. Stylistic approaches to translation. Manchester; Northampton, MA: St Jerome, 2006. (Translation practices explained.)

2268. BOOTH, ROY. T. S. Eliot, *Sweeney Agonistes*, and Ben Jonson's *Masque of Queenes*. *See* **15670**.

2269. BORG, RUBEN. Two Ps in a pod: on time in *Finnegans Wake*. *See* **16662**.

2270. BORROFF, MARIE. Narrative artistry in *St Erkenwald* and the *Gawain*-group: the case for common authorship reconsidered. *See* **4529**.

2271. BOTTOMS, PAM. The controversial, subversive 'broken tongue' of Paul Laurence Dunbar. *See* **9961**.

2272. BRATCHER, JAMES T. Coleridge's *Biographia Litteraria*. *See* **9510**.

2273. BREGAZZI, JOSEPHINE. Changing roles: gender marking through syntactic distribution in the Jacobean theater. *In* (pp. 234–49) **5308**.

2274. BRIVIC, SHELDON. Joyce and the invention of language. *In* (pp. 53–69) **16699**.

2275. BRUSTER, DOUGLAS. The politics of Shakespeare's prose. *In* (pp. 95–114) **5421**.

2276. BUTTERFIELD, ARDIS. Chaucer and the detritus of the city. *In* (pp. 3–22) **4312**.

2277. CAIE, GRAHAM D. 'Oh what a lovely plague': the effect of the Black Death on high and low cultures in the English Middle Ages. *See* **3833**.

2278. CAMBONI, MARINA. Resistance to symmetry: Wilson Harris's bridges of language. *In* (pp. 9–20) **16284**.

2279. CANEPARI-LABIB, MICHELA. Fenomeni di '*code-mixing*' e '*code-switching*' nelle opere 'postcoloniali' di Robert Louis Stevenson. *See* **11280**.

2280. —— Writing and translating after the Empire. *See* **17752**.

2281. CANNON, CHRISTOPHER. Chaucer and the language of London. *In* (pp. 79–94) **4312**.

2282. Carruthers, Mary. 'Sweet Jesus'. *In* (pp. 9–19) **3896**.

2283. Cash, Sam. Language in Burroughsland. *See* **14929**.

2284. Cherewatuk, Karen. Malory's Launcelot and the language of sin and confession. *See* **4242**.

2285. Cooper, Carolyn. 'What the backside all you want?': interrogating Rastafari in Derek Walcott's *O Babylon! See* **18922**.

2286. Corbett, John; Findlay, Bill (eds). Serving twa maisters: five classic plays in Scots translation. *See* **12266**.

2287. Cordery, Leona F. A corpus of medieval crusading literature: in search of an identity. *In* (pp. 35–49) **1227**.

2288. Crawford, Robert. Spirit machines: the human and the computational. *In* (pp. 52–68) **13732**.

2289. Davis, Carmel. Words beyond meaning: the language of ascent and the ascent of language in medieval mystical texts. AUMLA (106) 2006, 11–24.

2290. Deen, Rosemary. Dis-covering the words: language and poetry in Josephine Jacobsen. *See* **16574**.

2291. Denny-Brown, Andrea. *Povre* Griselda and the all-consuming *archewyves*. *See* **4387**.

2292. Dente, Carla, *et al.* (eds). Proteus: the language of metamorphosis. *See* **3228**.

2293. Dillon, George L. Corpus, creativity, cliché: where statistics meet aesthetics. JLS (35:2) 2006, 97–103.

2294. Dooley, Patrick K. Stephen Crane's distilled style (and the fine art of swearing). *See* **9652**.

2295. Dray, Colin. The golden fish: on reading J. S. Harry. *See* **16294**.

2296. Dussinger, John A. The negotiations of Sir Charles Grandison. *In* (pp. 32–50) **7255**.

2297. Dvinge, Anne. Complex fate – complex vision: the vernacular and identity in Ralph Ellison's *Juneteenth*. *See* **15737**.

2298. Eckel, Leslie E. Symbols 'mystical and awful': Emerson's and Longfellow's primitive poetics. *See* **10072**.

2299. Emmott, Catherine; Sanford, Anthony J.; Morrow, Lorna I. Capturing the attention of readers? Stylistic and psychological perspectives on the use and effect of text fragmentation in narratives. *See* **13465**.

2300. Ferguson, Christine. Language, science and popular fiction in the Victorian *fin-de-siècle*: the brutal tongue. *See* **8637**.

2301. Findlay, Bill. Motivation in a surrogate translation of Goldoni. *In* (pp. 46–57) **3186**.

2302. Forker, Charles R. John Webster's handbook of model letters: a study in attribution. *See* **7174**.

2303. Forrest-Thomson, Veronica. Swinburne as poet: a reconsideration. *See* **11376**.

2304. Fořt, Bohumil. Are fictional worlds really possible? A short contribution to their semantics. *See* **3252**.

2305. Fromonot, Jacqueline. Le langage de l'hypocrisie chez quelques personnages dickensiens: une rhétorique de l'excès. *See* **9751**.

2306. Galef, David. What's the word? *See* **8140**.

2307. Gane, Gillian. Postcolonial literature and the magic radio: the language of Rushdie's *Midnight's Children*. *See* **18385**.

2308. Garzon, Susan. Social variation and grammatical patterns in 1770s Virginia: evidence from Robert Munford's *The Candidates*. *See* **8022**.

2309. Gąsiorek, Andrzej. Wyndham Lewis: *Tarr*. *In* (pp. 402–10) **11788**.

2310. Gavins, Joanna. (Re)thinking modality: a text-world perspective. *See* **14680**.

2311. Gebhard, Caroline. Inventing a 'Negro literature': race, dialect, and gender in the early work of Paul Laurence Dunbar, James Weldon Johnson, and Alice Dunbar-Nelson. *In* (pp. 162–78) **8435**.

2312. Gelpi, Albert. Poetic language and language poetry: Levertov, Duncan, Creeley. *In* (pp. 180–98) **15599**.

2313. Gilbert, Sandra M. 'The words are purposes'; or, Why dither about diction? *See* **13752**.

2314. Gillespie, Michael Patrick. James Joyce: *Ulysses*. *In* (pp. 384–92) **11788**.

2315. Gilliver, Peter; Marshall, Jeremy; Weiner, Edmund. The ring of words: Tolkien and the *Oxford English Dictionary*. *See* **18801**.

2316. Gladstein, Mimi R. Bilingual wordplay: variations on a theme by Hemingway and Steinbeck. *See* **16357**.

2317. Goatly, Andrew. An analysis of Elizabeth Jennings's *One Flesh*: poem as product and process. *See* **16596**.

2318. Goth, Maik. John Lanchester's *The Debt to Pleasure*: an aesthetics of textual surprise. *See* **16993**.

2319. Graves, Roy Neil. Mezey's *Mercy*. *See* **17500**.

2320. Green, Amy S. Whose voices are these? The arts of language in the plays of Suzan-Lori Parks, Paula Vogel, and Diana Son. *In* (pp. 143–57) **12297**.

2321. Greenwell, Garth. 'The pedagogy of martyrdom': 'witness' in Geoffrey Hill's *The Triumph of Love*. *See* **16420**.

2322. Haldane, Michael. 'Doubling' in Bartholomew Yong's *Diana*. *See* **5152**.

2323. Hammer, Langdon. The crux of the matter: Heather McHugh. *See* **17355**.

2324. Hardman, Malcolm. *Genius loci*: placing place in Gerard Manley Hopkins. *See* **10473**.

2325. Hardman, Phillipa. Lydgate's uneasy syntax. *In* (pp. 12–35) **4231**.

2326. Hardwick, Lorna. 'Murmurs in the cathedral': the impact of translations from Greek poetry and drama on modern work in English by Michael Longley and Seamus Heaney. *See* **17248**.

2327. Hassall, Peter John. Developing an International Corpus of Creative English. WorldE (25:1) 2006, 131–51.

2328. HENRY, ANNE C. 'Explorations in dot-and-dashland': George Meredith's aphasia. *See* **10916**.

2329. HERZ, JUDITH SCHERER. 13 retro keywords ... and why they're worth a second look: *individual*. *See* **1573**.

2330. HILLMAN, BRENDA; PETERSON, KATIE. Hermetic memory: an exchange on Dickinson between two poets. *See* **9868**.

2331. HILTUNEN, RISTO. '*Eala, geferan and gode wyrhtan*': on interjections in Old English. *In* (pp. 91–116) **1241**.

2332. HOGBIN, ELIZABETH; SONG, JAE JUNG. Patterns of relativisation in eighteenth- and twentieth-century written English narrative: a functional–typological perspective. *In* (pp. 182–208) **7255**.

2333. HOLMSTRÖM, LAKSHMI. Let poetry win: the translator as writer – an Indian perspective. *In* (pp. 33–45) **3186**.

2334. HOPKINS, LISA. 'In a little room': Marlowe and *The Allegory of the Tudor Succession*. *See* **4925**.

2335. HOROWITZ, EVAN. *Ulysses*: mired in the universal. *See* **16707**.

2336. HOWE, SUSAN. Experience is the angled road. *See* **9871**.

2337. ILO, ISAIAH. Language in modern African drama. *See* **14363**.

2338. IRVINE, SUSAN. Speaking one's mind in *The Wanderer*. *In* (pp. 117–33) **1241**.

2339. JACKSON, MACD. P. *Anything for a Quiet Life*, IV.ii.1–44: the hazards of collaboration. *See* **6952**.

2340. —— Compound adjectives in *Arden of Faversham*. *See* **4683**.

2341. —— Connectives and the Webster canon. *See* **7180**.

2342. JACKSON, MACDONALD P. Shakespeare and the quarrel scene in *Arden of Faversham*. *See* **4684**.

2343. JARVIS, SIMON. Guides through the park. *See* **9034**.

2344. JASPER, DAVID. 'The wheels of the chariot': religious language in English and German Romanticism. *In* (pp. 95–109) **3415**.

2345. JUNG, SANDRO. Johnson's *Dictionary* and the language of William Collins's *Odes on Several Descriptive and Allegoric Subjects*. *See* **7932**.

2346. KANE, GEORGE. The *Piers Plowman* glossary. *Will's Visions of Do-Well, Do-Better and Do-Best*: a glossary of the English vocabulary of the A, B and C versions as presented in the Athlone Editions. *See* **1677**.

2347. KERSTEN, HOLGER. America's multilingualism and the problem of the literary representation of 'pidgin English'. *See* **8792**.

2348. KEYNES, SIMON; SMYTH, ALFRED P. (eds). Anglo-Saxons: studies presented to Cyril Roy Hart. *See* **3679**.

2349. KIM, HEIDI KATHLEEN. From language to empire: Walt Whitman in the context of nineteenth-century popular Anglo-Saxonism. *See* **11561**.

2350. KINZER, GREG. Excuses and other nonsense: Joan Retallack's *How to Do Things with Words*. *See* **18201**.

2351. KNEPPER, STEVEN. 'Shoot quick, and slow': Southern sporting values, mastery, and language in Faulkner's *Go Down, Moses*. *See* **15817**.

2352. KOHN, ROBERT E. Parody, heteroglossia, and chronotope in Don DeLillo's *Great Jones Street*. *See* **15443**.

2353. KUBOUCHI, TADAO. Wulfstan's Scandinavian loanword usage: an aspect of the linguistic situation in the late Old English Danelaw. *In* (pp. 134–52) **1241**.

2354. LAGAPA, JASON. Something from nothing: the disontological poetics of Leslie Scalapino. *See* **18424**.

2355. LAHEY, ERNESTINE. (Re)thinking world-building: locating the text-worlds of Canadian lyric poetry. *See* **18162**.

2356. LAPIDGE, MICHAEL. An aspect of Old English poetic diction: the postpositioning of prepositions. *In* (pp. 153–80) **1241**.

2357. LARSON, KATHERINE R. From inward conversation to public praise: Mary Sidney Herbert's *Psalmes*. *See* **5012**.

2358. LEE, ANTHONY W. Johnson's symbolic mentors: Addison, Dryden, and *Rambler* 86. *See* **7939**.

2359. LOCK, CHARLES. Powys and the Aether: the Homeric novels. *See* **18124**.

2360. LOXLEY, JAMES. On exegetical duty: historical pragmatics and the grammar of the libel. *See* **6274**.

2361. LÜSCHER-MORATA, DIANE. La souffrance portée au langage dans la prose de Samuel Beckett. *See* **14701**.

2362. LYNCH, PAUL. Not trying to talk alike and succeeding: the authoritative word and internally persuasive word in *Tom Sawyer* and *Huckleberry Finn*. *See* **11513**.

2363. MCCULLY, CHRIS. The word in time: 2, Diplomat and revolutionary. *See* **4332**.

2364. MCDONALD, RUSS. Shakespeare's late style. *See* **5366**.

2365. MACDONALD, SUSAN PECK. Chandler's American style. *See* **15137**.

2366. MCGUIRE, MATT. Dialect(ic) nationalism? The fiction of James Kelman and Roddy Doyle. *See* **16824**.

2367. MCGUIRE, THOMAS. Violence and vernacular in Seamus Heaney's *Beowulf*. *See* **16320**.

2368. MACHAN, TIM WILLIAM. Medieval multilingualism and Gower's literary practice. *See* **4149**.

2369. MCINTYRE, DAN. Logic, reality and mind style in Alan Bennett's *The Lady in the Van*. *See* **14756**.

2370. MCMAHON, GARY. Camp in literature. *See* **3338**.

2371. MCMORRIS, MARK. Discrepant affinities in Caribbean poetry: tradition and demotic Modernism. *See* **13809**.

2372. MCQUADE, MOLLY. Woolf's verb impersonators (and other deviants). *See* **19308**.

2373. MAGNUSSON, LYNNE. Donne's language: the conditions of communication. *In* (pp. 183–200) **6718**.

2374. MARIE-LAVERROU, FLORENCE. Writing the sea in *Weymouth Sands*. *See* **18127**.

2375. Martin, Lydia. Jane Austen's politeness on screen: between ambivalent submission and defiant self-assertion. *See* **9056**.

2376. Masel, Carolyn. 'Keener sounds': Stevens, intimacy, and gender politics. *See* **18644**.

2377. Mehring, Frank. Deutsch, Dutch, double Dutch: authentic and artificial German American dialects. *See* **8952**.

2378. Merriam, Thomas. Low-frequency words, genre, date, and authorship. *See* **5386**.

2379. —— Prosodic symmetry in *King John*. *See* **5849**.

2380. Merriman, Emily Taylor. 'Words, those precious cups of meaning': Augustine's influence on the thought and poetry of Gerard Manley Hopkins, SJ. *In* (pp. 233–54) **3301**.

2381. Messer, H. Collin. Exhausted voices: the inevitable impoverishment of Faulkner's 'garrulous and facile' language. *See* **15826**.

2382. Miethaner, Ulrich. I can look through muddy water: analyzing earlier African American English in Blues lyrics (BLUR). *See* **2632**.

2383. Mignot, Élise. Les adjectifs: entre déterminant et nom. *See* **1397**.

2384. Milesi, Laurent. Joycean choreo-graphies of writing in *Stephen Hero* and *A Portrait of the Artist as a Young Man*. *See* **16730**.

2385. Mira, Alberto. Being Wildean: a dialogue on the importance of style in translation. *In* (pp. 196–207) **3186**.

2386. Monrós Gaspar, Laura. '*Boscovos tromuldo boscovos*': a case study in the translation of William Shakespeare's *All's Well That Ends Well*. *See* **5635**.

2387. Moore, Dafydd. Tennyson, Malory and the Ossianic mode: *The Poems of Ossian* and 'The Death of Arthur'. *See* **11401**.

2388. Morini, Carla. The Old English *Apollonius* and Wulfstan of York. *See* **3729**.

2389. Morini, Massimiliano. Tudor translation in theory and practice. *See* **4619**.

2390. Morris, Daniel. William Carlos Williams: *Paterson*. *In* (pp. 478–85) **11788**.

2391. Moutet, Muriel. Foreign tongues: native and half-caste speech in *Lord Jim*. *See* **15292**.

2392. Munro, Lucy. Richard Brome and *The Book of Bulls*: situating *The New Academy; or, The New Exchange*. *See* **6599**.

2393. Muriungi, Agnes. *Sit Down and Listen*: the invention of (oral) tradition and the imagining of a new nation. *In* (pp. 211–34) **12216**.

2394. Murphy, Richard. Expressionism. *In* (pp. 198–203) **11788**.

2395. Myers, Benjamin. Ashbery's *They Dream Only of America* and *Definition of Blue*. *See* **14456**.

2396. Nydam, Arlen. Numerological tradition in the works of Jupiter Hammon. *See* **7859**.

2397. O'Connor, Laura. Haunted English: the Celtic Fringe, the British Empire, and de-anglicization. *See* **19432**.

2398. Ogawa, Hiroshi. Language and style in two anonymous Old English Easter homilies. *In* (pp. 203–21) **1241**.

2399. O'Leary, Peter. The phosphorescence of thought. *See* **14531**.

2400. Orchard, Andy. Computing Cynewulf: the *Judith*-connection. *In* (pp. 75–106) **3871**.

2401. Ossa-Richardson, Anthony. Ovid and the 'free play with signs' in Thomas Nashe's *The Unfortunate Traveller*. *See* **4983**.

2402. Pandit, Lalita; Hogan, Patrick Colm. Introduction: morsels and modules: on embodying cognition in Shakespeare's plays. *See* **5646**.

2403. Patterson, Annabel. Milton's negativity. *In* (pp. 81–102) **7033**.

2404. Pechey, Graham. 'The scop's twang': adventures of the monosyllable in English verse: 3. *See* **3586**.

2405. Perry, Seamus. Joy perplexed: optimism and complication in Wordsworth, T. H. Green and A. C. Bradley. *See* **11702**.

2406. Pinsky, Robert. No picnic. *In* (pp. 255–9) **16122**.

2407. Pranzatelli, Robert. On Nabokov's definition of art. *See* **17712**.

2408. Prucher, Jeffrey. Brave new words: the Oxford dictionary of science fiction. *See* **1685**.

2409. Putter, Ad. The ways and words of the hunt: notes on *Sir Gawain and the Green Knight*, *The Master of Game*, *Sir Tristrem*, *Pearl*, and *Saint Erkenwald*. *See* **4530**.

2410. Raitt, Suzanne. The rhetoric of efficiency in early Modernism. *See* **19049**.

2411. Regier, Alexander. A brotherhood is broken: Wordsworth, Benjamin, and the fragmentation of language. *See* **11709**.

2412. Richardson, Brian. Bad Joyce: anti-aesthetic practices in *Ulysses*. *See* **16760**.

2413. Riquelme, John Paul. 'Preparatory to anything else': Joyce's styles as forms of memory – the case of 'Eumæus'. *In* (pp. 9–34) **16699**.

2414. Robinson, Ian. T. F. Powys and the renewal of English prose. *See* **18133**.

2415. Rodríguez Guerrero-Strachan, Santiago. Social exiles and language refugees: the case of postcolonial authors. *See* **17755**.

2416. Roldan-Santiago, Serafin. Thematic and structural functions of folklore in Caribbean literature: the case of the 'written' and the 'oral'. *See* **12114**.

2417. Rosen, David. Power, plain English, and the rise of modern poetry. *See* **8818**.

2418. Rutherford, John. Translating fun: *Don Quixote*. *In* (pp. 71–83) **3186**.

2419. Salbayre, Sébastien. Biblical turns of phrase, repetition and circularity in Oscar Wilde's *Salome*. *See* **11622**.

2420. Šaldová, Pavlína. The distribution of finite and participial postmodifiers in fiction and academic prose. PSE (24) 2006, 59–73.

2421. San, Debra. Hiatus of subject and verb in poetic language. Style (39:2) 2005, 137–52.

2422. Schneider, Edgar W.; Wagner, Christian. The variability of literary dialect in Jamaican Creole: Thelwell's *The Harder They Come*. *See* **18738**.

2423. Scott, Matthew. John Keats and the aesthetics of topsy-turvy. *See* **10664**.

2424. Scott, William O. 'A woman's thought runs before her actions': vows as speech acts in *As You Like It*. *See* **5663**.

2425. Semler, L. E. Robert Dallington's *Hypnerotomachia* and the Protestant antiquity of Elizabethan England. *See* **4833**.

2426. Senior, Claire. Shades of gray: a diachronic reading of Thomas Hardy's *Neutral Tones*. *See* **10326**.

2427. Sharkey, E. Joseph. Idling the engine: linguistic skepticism in and around Cortázar, Kafka, and Joyce. *See* **16769**.

2428. Shen, Dan. How stylisticians draw on narratology: approaches, advantages and disadvantages. *See* **14293**.

2429. Shrank, Cathy. A work by John Bale identified? *See* **4766**.

2430. Skouen, Tina. The vocal wit of John Dryden. *See* **6781**.

2431. Slote, Sam. A Eumaean return to style. *See* **16771**.

2432. Smith, Dave. Playing for grace: William Matthews. *See* **17463**.

2433. Sotirova, Violeta. Charting stylistic change: D. H. Lawrence's handling of point of view. *See* **17058**.

2434. Steele, Peter. The master of the sentences: style and Peter Porter. *See* **18070**.

2435. Stigter, Shelley. The dialectics and dialogics of code-switching in the poetry of Gregory Scofield and Louise Halfe. *See* **18435**.

2436. Stojkovic, Tijana. Unnoticed in the casual light of day: Philip Larkin and the plain style. *See* **17004**.

2437. Strauss, Tracy L. Sound and sensibility: Hopkins' word-journey to Hell and back. *See* **10491**.

2438. Sugimori, Masami. Signifying, ordering, and containing the chaos: Whiteness, ideology, and language in *Intruder in the Dust*. *See* **15835**.

2439. Sweeney, Anne. Re-reading the poetry of S. Robert Southwell. *See* **5066**.

2440. Szarmach, Paul E. 'The poetic turn of mind' of the translator of the OE Bede. *In* (pp. 54–68) **3679**.

2441. Tani, Akinobu. *Thesaurus of Old English* for Early Middle English: an analysis in light of word pairs in the 'Katherine Group' lives. *In* (pp. 293–303) **1227**.

2442. Taylor, Chloë. Kristevan themes in Virginia Woolf's *The Waves*. *See* **19338**.

2443. Thijs, Christine. Wærferth's treatment of the miraculous in his Old English translation of Gregory's *Dialogi*. *See* **3696**.

2444. Thornton, R. K. R. What John Clare do we read? *See* **9483**.

2445. Tobin, J. J. M. Shakespeare, Nashe, and *Sir Thomas More*. *See* **6082**.

2446. Toolan, Michael. Top keyword abridgements of short stories: a corpus-linguistic resource? *See* **16782**.

2447. Topia, André. The impossible present: a Flaubertian reading of *Lord Jim*. *See* **15319**.

2448. Tunca, Daria. Paying attention to language, replicas and the role of the artist in Janet Frame's *Living in the Maniototo*. *See* **15984**.

2449. Turley, Richard Marggraf. Keats, Cornwall and the 'scent of strong-smelling phrases'. *See* **10669**.

2450. Turner, Allan. Translation and criticism: the stylistic mirror. *See* **18838**.

2451. Turtle, Will. 'The truth of mere transcript': Browning's *Agamemnon*. *See* **9288**.

2452. Urbanová, Ludmila. Is stylistics a controversial branch of language study? *See* **2536**.

2453. Vauthier, Simone. Framing the passing recalcitrance of *The Wedding Ring*. *In* (pp. 175–205) **16036**.

2454. Vigus, James. 'With his garland and his singing robes about him': the persistence of the literary in *Opus Maximum*. *In* (pp. 97–119) **9503**.

2455. Wall, Cheryl A. Zora Neale Hurston: *Their Eyes Were Watching God*. *In* (pp. 376–83) **11788**.

2456. Wall, Wendy. Shakespearean jell-o: mortality and malleability in the kitchen. *See* **1575**.

2457. Wallach, Jennifer Jensen. Building a bridge of words: the literary autobiography as historical source material. *See* **17717**.

2458. Walmsley, John (ed.). Inside Old English: essays in honour of Bruce Mitchell. *See* **1241**.

2459. Weinstock, Horst. *Vices and Virtues*: ein mittelenglisches Corpus um 1200. *In* (pp. 329–40) **1227**.

2460. West, William N. Mercutio's bad language. *In* (pp. 115–29) **5421**.

2461. Westover, Jeff. Value, commerce, and economy in the poetry of Marianne Moore. *See* **17572**.

2462. Williams, Geoffrey. Biblical resonance: a corpus-driven analysis of collocational resonance in French and English texts. *In* (pp. 255–80) **3341**.

2463. Wilson-Costa, Karyn. The poetry of Robert Burns: 'a melancholy not unallied to mirth'. *See* **7646**.

2464. Wirth-Nesher, Hana. Call it English: the languages of Jewish American literature. *See* **12226**.

2465. Wolosky, Shira. Medical industrial discourses: Muriel Rukeyser's *The Book of the Dead*. *See* **18378**.

2466. Wood, Tahir. Adherence relations in literary and non-literary discourse. *See* **15139**.

2467. Wright, Nancy E. Legal interpretation of defamation in Shakespeare's *Much Ado about Nothing*. *See* **6011**.

2468. Zanotti, Serenella. Joyce in Italy, l'italiano di Joyce. *See* **16794**.

2469. Zapedowska, Magdalena. A lesson in grammar: Dickinson's *Grasped by God* and *Drowning Is Not So Pitiful*. *See* **9898**.

2470. Zapf, Harald. Ethnicity and performance: bilingualism in Spanglish verse culture. *See* **13881**.

STYLISTICS OF NON-LITERARY TEXTS

2471. Alderson, David. Back to the future. *See* **14006**.

2472. Alonso, Pilar. Discourse strategies for global topic construction in complex written texts: evidence from comment articles. RAEI (19) 2006, 9–22.

2473. Bækken, Bjørg. Some aspects of word order in seventeenth-century English. EngS (86:6) 2005, 511–35.

2474. Baxter, Katherine Isobel. Conrad's application to the British Museum: an unpublished letter. *See* **15243**.

2475. Berglund, Ylva; Mason, Oliver. 'But this formula doesn't mean anything … !?' *In* (pp. 59–69) **1195**.

2476. Breuninger, Scott. 'Social gravity' and the *translatio* tradition in early American theories of empire. *See* **7451**.

2477. Briggs, John Channing. Lincoln's speeches reconsidered. *See* **10740**.

2478. Brigley, Zoë. Replication, regeneration or organic birth: the clone in Deryn Rees-Jones' *Quiver* and Donna Haraway's *A Cyborg Manifesto*. *See* **18197**.

2479. Brownlees, Nicholas (ed.). News discourse in early modern Britain: selected papers of CHINED 2004. *See* **4771**.

2480. Collini, Stefan. Smack up: argufying and illumination in the letters of William Empson. *See* **15764**.

2481. Corona Marzol, Isabel. Coming out of the closet 'six feet under': textual silences and the social construction of the family stage in the obituary genres. RAEI (19) 2006, 67–82.

2482. Davies, Carolyn; Maclagan, Margaret. Maori words: read all about it. Testing the presence of 13 Maori words in four New Zealand newspapers from 1997 to 2004. Te Reo (49) 2006, 73–99.

2483. Day, Gary. Beyond management culture: the experience of English. CamQ (34:3) 2005, 213–20.

2484. Dean, Ann C. Court culture and political news in London's eighteenth-century newspapers. *See* **1080**.

2485. de Gregorio Godeo, Eduardo. Critical discourse analysis as an analytical resource for Cultural Studies: exploring the discursive construction of subject positions in British men's magazines' problem pages. RAEI (19) 2006, 83–100.

2486. Dierks, Konstantin. Letter writing, stationery supplies, and consumer modernity in the eighteenth-century Atlantic world. *See* **7459**.

2487. Dirks, Una. Critical discourse analysis of the Iraq conflict in the British and German 'quality' press. RAEI (19) 2006, 101–23.

2488. Dontcheva-Navrátilová, Olga. Text typology of resolution. *See* **1798**.

2489. Dossena, Marina. 19CSC, ICAMET and the diachronic study of specialized discourse in correspondence. *In* (pp. 65–77) **1227**.

2490. —— Taavitsainen, Irma (eds). Diachronic perspectives on domain-specific English. *See* **1518**.

2491. Elliott, Charlene. Considering the connoisseur: probing the language of taste. CRAS (36:2) 2006, 229–36.

2492. Evans, David. High water everywhere: Blues and gospel commentary on the 1927 Mississippi River flood. *In* (pp. 3–75) **3086**.

2493. Fägersten, Kristy Beers. The discursive construction of identity in an Internet Hip Hop community. RAEI (19) 2006, 23–44.

2494. Fries, Udo. *'Tis said*, the apostrophe, and the importance of Innsbruck in early English newspapers. *In* (pp. 101–14) **1227**.

2495. Germano, William. Passive is spoken here. PNRev (31:6) 2005, 10–11.

2496. González Rodríguez, María José. Tracing context in the discourse of the media: features of language-in-use in the British press. RAEI (19) 2006, 149–68.

2497. Goodrich, Amanda. Debating England's aristocracy in the 1790s: pamphlets, polemic, and political ideas. *See* **7613**.

2498. Grigg, Russell. Englishing Lacan. *See* **2840**.

2499. Grund, Peter. Manuscripts as sources for linguistic research: a methodological case study based on the *Mirror of Lights*. *See* **4085**.

2500. Halse, Christine. Writing/reading a life: the rhetorical practice of autobiography. Auto/Biography (14:2) 2006, 95–115.

2501. Herrero Ruiz, Javier. The role of metaphor, metonymy, and conceptual blending in understanding advertisements: the case of drug-prevention ads. *See* **1977**.

2502. Hughes, Ann. *Gangraena* and the struggle for the English Revolution. *See* **6475**.

2503. Imbarrato, Susan Clair. Traveling women: narrative visions of early America. *See* **7468**.

2504. Jeremiah, Milford A. Language and politics: lexical choices observed in discussing Hurricane Katrina. CLAJ (50:1) 2006, 1–19.

2505. Johnson, Marilyn. The dead beat: lost souls, lucky stiffs, and the perverse pleasures of obituaries. *See* **3610**.

2506. Jordan, Ellen; Craig, Hugh; Antonia, Alexis. The Brontë sisters and the *Christian Remembrancer*: a pilot study in the use of the 'Burrows method' to identify the authorship of unsigned articles in the nineteenth-century periodical press. *See* **9233**.

2507. Keeble, David. Interpretive representation: a relevance-theoretic analysis of the opening paragraph of Carlyle's *Chartism*. *See* **9395**.

2508. Kelly-Holmes, Helen. Advertising as multilingual communication. Basingstoke; New York: Palgrave Macmillan, 2005. pp. xiv, 206. Rev. by Ingrid Piller in JSoc (10:2) 2006, 272–7.

2509. Lasky, Melvin J. The language of journalism: vol. 2, Profanity, obscenity and the media. New Brunswick, NJ: Transaction, 2005. pp. xxiv, 339.

2510. Lemarchal, Dominique. Ford's paradoxical development of the personal tone in the writing of propaganda. *In* (pp. 91–7) **15944**.

2511. Lloyd, Sarah. Amour in the shrubbery: reading the detail of English adultery trial publications of the 1780s. *See* **7473**.

2512. Maci, Stefania M. GHD advertising campaign across cultures: a case study. RAEI (19) 2006, 211–23.

2513. Marín Arrese, Juana I.; Núñez Perucha, Begoña. Evaluation and engagement in journalistic commentary and news reportage. RAEI (19) 2006, 225–48.

2514. Martínez Lirola, María. A systemic functional analysis of two multimodal covers. RAEI (19) 2006, 249–60.

2515. Mougnibas, Jean-Claude. Le texte comme simple émanation d'un contexte: étude du manifeste fondateur de la Society for the Protection of Ancient Buildings. *See* **10947**.

2516. Myers, Greg. Applied linguistics and institutions of opinion. *See* **2222**.

2517. Nelson, Ronald J. The writing styles of two war correspondents: Stephen Crane and Ernie Pyle. *See* **9660**.

2518. Nkemleke, Daniel A. Some characteristics of expository writing in Cameroon English. *See* **2695**.

2519. Oha, Obododimma. Well, it is WELL: language and human interest in a virtual community. RAEI (19) 2006, 261–83.

2520. Olsson, John. Forensic linguistics: an introduction to language, crime and the law. *See* **1771**.

2521. Orts Llopis, María Ángeles. The hidden dimension of the language of corporations in America and Spain: perspectives for inter-legal communications. RAEI (19) 2006, 285–98.

2522. Pérez-Paredes, Pascual, *et al.* El ámbito de la oralidad en la investigacíon lingüística anglosajona reciente. REsLA (19) 2006, 163–77.

2523. Perry, Seamus. Joy perplexed: optimism and complication in Wordsworth, T. H. Green and A. C. Bradley. *See* **11702**.

2524. Al-Sa'di, Rami; Hamdan, Jihad M. 'Synchronous online chat' English: computer-mediated communication. WorldE (24:4) 2005, 409–24.

2525. Šaldová, Pavlína. The distribution of finite and participial post-modifiers in fiction and academic prose. *See* **2420**.

2526. Sarat, Austin; Hussain, Nasser. The literary life of clemency: pardon tales in the contemporary United States. *See* **19971**.

2527. Saunders, Max. Critical biography: rhetoric, tone, and autobiography in Ford's critical essays. *In* (pp. 173–88) **15944**.

2528. Schrempp, Gregory. Formulas of conversion: proverbial approaches to technological and scientific exposition. *See* **2991**.

2529. Sell, Jonathan P. A. Rhetoric and wonder in English travel writing, 1560–1613. *See* **4788**.

2530. Short, Mick. A corpus-based approach to speech, thought and writing presentation. *In* (pp. 241–71) **1195**.

2531. Steinlight, Emily. 'ANTI-BLEAK HOUSE': advertising and the Victorian novel. *See* **9823**.

2532. Stiles, Anne. Robert Louis Stevenson's *Jekyll and Hyde* and the double brain. *See* **11323**.

2533. Stuart, Keith. Towards an analysis of academic weblogs. RAEI (19) 2006, 387–404.

2534. Swaminathan, Srividhya. Anthony Benezet's depictions of African oppression: 'that creature of propaganda'. *See* **7481**.

2535. Truelove, Alison. Linguistic diversity in the fifteenth-century Stonor Letters. *See* **4082**.

2536. Urbanová, Ludmila. Is stylistics a controversial branch of language study? BStE (31) 2005, 73–84.

2537. Valdeón, Roberto A. The discursive construction of anti-European sentiment in the *times.co.uk* texts. RAEI (19) 2006, 405–31.

2538. Weber, Keith; Martin, Matthew M.; Corrigan, Michael. Creating persuasive messages advocating organ donation. ComQ (54:1) 2006, 67–87.

2539. Webster, Jonathan J. (ed.). The language of science. By M. A. K. Halliday. London; New York: Continuum, 2004. pp. xxiv, 243. (Collected works of M. A. K. Halliday, 5.) Rev. by Roy Harris in TLS, 17 Nov. 2006, 31.

DIALECTS

GENERAL

2540. Auer, Peter; Hinskens, Frans; Kerswill, Paul (eds). Dialect change: convergence and divergence in European languages. Cambridge; New York: CUP, 2005. pp. xiv, 415. Rev. by Mari C. Jones in JSoc (10:2) 2006, 252–4.

2541. Hickey, Raymond. Dialects of English and their transportation. *In* (pp. 33–58) **2543**.

2542. —— Introduction. *In* (pp. 1–30) **2543**.

2543. —— (ed.). Legacies of colonial English: studies in transported dialects. Cambridge; New York: CUP, 2004. pp. xx, 713. (Studies in English language.) Rev. by Manfred Görlach in EWW (27:1) 2006, 89–101.

2544. Schneider, Edgar Werner, *et al.* (eds). A handbook of varieties of English: a multimedia reference tool. (Bibl. 2005, 2910.) Rev. by Manfred Görlach in EWW (27:1) 2006, 89–101.

2545. Trudgill, Peter. Dialects. (Bibl. 1995, 2364.) London; New York: Routledge, 2004. pp. ix, 78. (Second ed.: first ed. 1994.)

2546. —— New-dialect formation: the inevitability of colonial Englishes. (Bibl. 2005, 2913.) Rev. by Salikoko S. Mufwene in WorldE (25:1) 2006, 177–86.

DIALECTS OF THE BRITISH ISLES

2547. Amador Moreno, Carolina P. An analysis of Hiberno-English in the early novels of Patrick MacGill: bilingualism and language shift from Irish to English in County Donegal. *See* **17343**.

2548. Burton, T. L.; Ruthven, K. K. *The English Dialect Dictionary* and Dorset usages recorded by *Notes and Queries*. NQ (53:4) 2006, 415–17.

2549. Butterfield, Ardis. Chaucer and the detritus of the city. *In* (pp. 3–22) **4312**.

2550. Cannon, Christopher. Chaucer and the language of London. *In* (pp. 79–94) **4312**.

2551. Carr, P.; Brulard, I. Anglo-English influences on Scottish Standard English speakers: *trap/bath/palm/start* and *lot/cloth/thought/north/force*. ScLang (25) 2006, 31–45.

2552. Clarke, Sandra. The legacy of British and Irish English in Newfoundland. *In* (pp. 242–61) **2543**.

2553. Corbett, John; Findlay, Bill (eds). Serving twa maisters: five classic plays in Scots translation. *See* **12266**.

2554. Dolan, Terence Patrick (ed.). A dictionary of Hiberno-English: the Irish use of English. *See* **1673**.

2555. Dossena, Marina. 'The cinic Scotomastic'? Johnson, his commentators, Scots, French, and the story of English. *See* **7926**.

2556. —— Scotticisms in grammar and vocabulary: 'Like runes upon a standin' stane'? Edinburgh: Donald, 2005. pp. ix, 178.

2557. Elmes, Simon. Talking for Britain: a journey through the nation's dialects. (Bibl. 2005, 2925.) Rev. by Lynda Mugglestone in TLS, 31 Mar. 2006, 34.

2558. Ferragne, Emmanuel. Quand le Professeur Higgins s'invite sur votre ordinateur: une approche moderne de la dialectologie. Anglophonia (20) 2006, 133–48.

2559. Findlay, Bill. Motivation in a surrogate translation of Goldoni. *In* (pp. 46–57) **3186**.

2560. —— (ed.). Frae ither tongues: essays on modern translations into Scots. (Bibl. 2005, 2927.) Rev. by Wendy Anderson in ScSR (6:2) 2005, 126–7; by John Corbett in TransLit (14:1) 2005, 116–22.

2561. García Gómez, Antonio. British and American expressions of politeness in anger-evoking contexts: a cultural-relativistic approach. *See* **1803**.

2562. Gordon, Elizabeth; Trudgill, Peter. English input to New Zealand. *In* (pp. 440–55) **2543**.

2563. Hickey, Raymond. Development and diffusion of Irish English. *In* (pp. 82–117) **2543**.

2564. —— English dialect input to the Caribbean. *In* (pp. 326–59) **2543**.

2565. Jones, Christopher. Paul Laurence Dunbar and Robert Burns: vernacular gateways. *See* **9968**.

2566. Kay, Billy. Scots: the mither tongue. (Bibl. 1988, 1153.) Edinburgh: Mainstream, 2006. pp. 224. (Revised ed.: first ed. 1986.)

2567. Kay, Christian J.; Mackay, Margaret A. (eds). Perspectives on the Older Scottish tongue: a celebration of DOST. Edinburgh: Edinburgh UP, 2005. pp. viii, 230. Rev. by Caroline Macafee in ScSR (6:2) 2005, 127–9; by Yuko Yoneyama in ScLang (25) 2006, 94–6.

2568. Kiesling, Scott F. English input to Australia. *In* (pp. 418–39) **2543**.

2569. Kinloch, David. The case of the melodramatic hymen: Lallans and translation. *See* **17317**.

2570. Levey, Stephen. Visiting London relatives. *See* **2215**.

2571. Lillo, Antonio. Exploring rhyming slang in Ireland. EWW (25:2) 2004, 273–85.

2572. Löw-Wiebach, Danielle A. V. Language attitudes and language use in Pitmedden (Aberdeenshire). New York; Frankfurt: Lang, 2006. pp. 376. (VarioLingua, 24.) Rev. by Robert Millar in ScLang (25) 2006, 96–8.

2573. Macafee, Caroline. Scots and Scottish English. *In* (pp. 59–81) **2543**.

2574. McCafferty, Kevin. '[T]hunder storms is verry dangese in this contrey they come in less than a minnits notice …': the Northern Subject Rule in Southern Irish English. EWW (25:1) 2004, 51–79.

2575. McCarthy, Morty. Dowtcha boy! An anthology of Cork slang. Doughcloyne, Wilton, Co. Cork: Collins Press, 2004. pp. 87.

2576. MacDougall, Carl (ed.). Scots: the language of the people. Edinburgh: Black & White, 2006. pp. 272.

2577. McGuire, Matt. Dialect(ic) nationalism? The fiction of James Kelman and Roddy Doyle. *See* **16824**.

2578. McGuire, Thomas. Violence and vernacular in Seamus Heaney's *Beowulf*. *See* **16320**.

2579. Maci, Stefania Maria. The phonetic representation of ME *ī* in some Norfolk works of the late fifteenth century. *See* **1280**.

2580. Meek, Donald E. Smoking, drinking, dancing and singing on the high seas: steamships and the uses of *smùid* in Scottish Gaelic. *See* **1596**.

2581. Montgomery, Michael. The morphology and syntax of Ulster Scots. EWW (27:3) 2006, 295–329.

2582. —— Notes on the development of existential *they*. *See* **1459**.

2583. —— Solving Kurath's puzzle: establishing the antecedents of the American Midland dialect region. *In* (pp. 310–25) **2543**.

2584. Pichler, Pia. Multifunctional teasing as a resource for identity construction in the talk of British Bangladeshi girls. JSoc (10:2) 2006, 225–49.

2585. Romaine, Suzanne. English input to the English-lexicon pidgins and creoles of the Pacific. *In* (pp. 456–99) **2543**.

2586. Sampson, Geoffrey. Reflections of a dendrographer. *In* (pp. 157–84) **1195**.

2587. Schmitt, Holger. The *Ausbau* of present-day Scots. ScLang (25) 2006, 1–30.

2588. Schneider, Edgar W. The English dialect heritage of the Southern United States. *In* (pp. 262–309) **2543**.

2589. Shepheard, Richard. Doing different: a word from Norfolk. *See* **9150**.

2590. Stewart, Bruce. 'To have a father is always big news': theme and structure in *The Engine of Owl-light*. *In* (pp. 37–58) **14627**.

2591. Stuart-Smith, Jane; Timmins, Claire; Tweedie, Fiona. Conservation and innovation in a traditional dialect: L-vocalization in Glaswegian. EWW (27:1) 2006, 71–87.

2592. Treharne, Elaine. Reading from the margins: the uses of Old English homiletic manuscripts in the post-Conquest period. *In* (pp. 329–58) **199**.

2593. Upton, Clive; Widdowson, J. D. A. An atlas of English dialects. (Bibl. 1999, 2581.) London; New York: Routledge, 2006. pp. v, 215. (Second ed.: first ed. 1996.)

2594. Wright, Laura. The language of transported Londoners: third person singular present-tense markers in depositions from Virginia and the Bermudas, 1607–1624. *In* (pp. 158–71) **2543**.

2595. Yokota, Yumi. Form and function of demonstratives in the Middle English southern texts and speculation on the origin of *th-* type third person plural pronouns in the north and south. *See* **1432**.

DIALECTS OF NORTH AMERICA

2596. Alim, H. Samy. Roc the mic right: the language of Hip Hop culture. London; New York: Routledge, 2006. pp. xv, 184.

2597. Bender, Margaret (ed.). Linguistic diversity in the South: changing codes, practices, and ideology. (Bibl. 2004, 3088.) Rev. by Robert Shanafelt in NCarF (53:2) 2006, 64–6.

2598. Berson, Joel S. The source for Benjamin Franklin's 'The Drinker's Dictionary' (and was it Mather Byles?). *See* **7805**.

2599. Boberg, Charles. The Dialect Topography of Montreal. EWW (25:2) 2004, 171–98.

2600. Bock, Kathryn, *et al.* Number agreement in British and American English: disagreeing to agree collectively. *See* **1363**.

2601. Bottoms, Pam. The controversial, subversive 'broken tongue' of Paul Laurence Dunbar. *See* **9961**.

2602. Brown, David West. Girls and guys, ghetto and bougie: metapragmatics, ideology and the management of social identities. *See* **2754**.

2603. Casselman, Bill. Canadian words & sayings. Toronto: McArthur, 2006. pp. xxv, 445.

2604. Chambers, J. K. 'Canadian dainty': the rise and decline of Briticisms in Canada. *In* (pp. 224–41) **2543**.

2605. Childs, Becky; Mallinson, Christine. African American English in Appalachia: dialect accommodation and substrate influence. EWW (25:1) 2004, 27–50.

2606. —— —— The significance of lexical items in the construction of ethnolinguistic identity: a case study of adolescent spoken and online language. *See* **2759**.

2607. Clarke, Sandra. The legacy of British and Irish English in Newfoundland. *In* (pp. 242–61) **2543**.

2608. D'Arcy, Alexandra. Lexical replacement and the like(s). *See* **1448**.

2609. Davidson, Mark. Right, wrong, and risky: a dictionary of today's American English usage. *See* **1671**.

2610. DeBose, Charles. The sociology of African American language: a language planning perspective. Basingstoke; New York: Palgrave Macmillan, 2005. pp. viii, 237.

2611. Epp, Michael H. The traffic in affect: Marietta Holley, suffrage, and late nineteenth-century popular humour. *See* **10456**.

2612. Fridland, Valerie; Bartlett, Kathryn. Correctness, pleasantness, and degree of difference ratings across regions. AS (81:4) 2006, 358–86.

2613. García Gómez, Antonio. British and American expressions of politeness in anger-evoking contexts: a cultural-relativistic approach. *See* **1803**.

2614. Garzon, Susan. Social variation and grammatical patterns in 1770s Virginia: evidence from Robert Munford's *The Candidates*. *See* **8022**.

2615. Glowka, Wayne, *et al.* Among the new words. *See* **1480**.

2616. —— Among the new words. *See* **1481**.

2617. —— Among the new words. *See* **1482**.

2618. —— Among the new words. *See* **1483**.

2619. Gold, David L. A little-noticed English construction: subjectless imperative *please to* + infinitive. *See* **1452**.

2620. —— Panama Canal Zone, the Virgin Islands, and the Cayman Islands! *See* **2674**.

2621. Haugh, Michael. Emic perspectives on the positive–negative politeness distinction. *See* **1807**.

2622. Herrmann, Keith R. The war of words. *See* **1484**.

2623. Jeremiah, Milford A. Linguistic variation in Judge Greg Mathis' courtroom. *See* **2773**.

2624. Johnstone, Barbara; Andrus, Jennifer; Danielson, Andrew E. Mobility, indexicality, and the enregisterment of 'Pittsburghese'. JEL (34:2) 2006, 77–104.

2625. Jones, Christopher. Paul Laurence Dunbar and Robert Burns: vernacular gateways. *See* **9968**.

2626. Kytö, Merja. The emergence of American English: evidence from seventeenth-century records in New England. *In* (pp. 121–57) **2543**.

2627. Levon, Erez. Mosaic identity and style: phonological variation among Reform American Jews. JSoc (10:2) 2006, 181–204.

2628. Lopez, Barry (ed.). Home ground: language for an American landscape. *See* **3326**.

2629. Makkai, Adam; Boatner, Maxine T.; Gates, John E. (eds). Handbook of commonly used American idioms. *See* **1683**.

2630. Mao, LuMing. Reading Chinese fortune cookie: the making of Chinese American rhetoric. Logan: Utah State UP, 2006. pp. xi, 177.

2631. Mehring, Frank. Deutsch, Dutch, double Dutch: authentic and artificial German American dialects. *See* **8952**.

2632. Miethaner, Ulrich. I can look through muddy water: analyzing earlier African American English in Blues lyrics (BLUR). New York; Frankfurt: Lang, 2005. pp. 247. (Regensburger Arbeiten zur Anglistik und Amerikanistik, 47.)

2633. Minnick, Lisa Cohen. Dialect and dichotomy: literary representations of African American speech. (Bibl. 2004, 3140.) Rev. by Milford A. Jeremiah in ANQ (19:2) 2006, 62–4; by Edgar W. Schneider in JPCL (21:2) 2006, 377–80.

2634. Montgomery, Michael. Notes on the development of existential *they*. *See* **1459**.

2635. —— Solving Kurath's puzzle: establishing the antecedents of the American Midland dialect region. *In* (pp. 310–25) **2543**.

2636. Murray, Thomas E.; Simon, Beth Lee (eds). Language variation and change in the American Midland: a new look at 'heartland' English. Amsterdam; Philadelphia, PA: Benjamins, 2006. pp. xii, 319. (Varieties of English around the world: General series, G36.)

2637. Pancake, Ann. Virtual hillbilly: musings on JT LeRoy by a flesh-and-blood West Virginian. *See* **20285**.

2638. Pollack, Mica. Colormute: race talk dilemmas in an American school. *See* **2788**.

2639. Poplack, Shana; Tagliamonte, Sali. Back to the present: verbal *-s* in the (African American) English diaspora. *In* (pp. 203–23) **2543**.

2640. Reyes-Rodríguez, Antonio. Speeches and declarations: a war of words. *See* **2229**.

2641. Richardson, Elaine B. Hiphop literacies. London; New York: Routledge, 2006. pp. xviii, 142. (Literacies.)

2642. Rickford, John R. Down for the count? The creole origins hypothesis of AAVE at the hands of the Ottawa Circle, and their supporters. JPCL (21:1) 2006, 97–155 (review-article).

2643. Roberts, Julie. As old becomes new: glottalization in Vermont. *See* **1306**.

2644. Rollins, Benjamin. The juggernaut among American quotatives: a case study of *be like* in the American South. *See* **1437**.

2645. Schneider, Edgar W. The English dialect heritage of the Southern United States. *In* (pp. 262–309) **2543**.

2646. Slomanson, Peter; Newman, Michael. Peer group identification and variation in New York Latino English laterals. EWW (25:2) 2004, 199–216.

2647. Smith, Katharine Capshaw. The legacy of Paul Laurence Dunbar: dialect and racial configuration in the works of Silas X. Ford and Christina Moody. *See* **9972**.

2648. Smith, Stephanie A. Household words: *bloomers*, *sucker*, *bombshell*, *scab*, *nigger*, *cyber*. *See* **1501**.

2649. Smitherman, Geneva. Word from the mother: language and African Americans. London; New York: Routledge, 2006. pp. xiii, 172.

2650. Spears, Richard A. McGraw-Hill's dictionary of American slang and colloquial expressions. *See* **1691**.

2651. Strand, Amy Dunham. Notes at the intersections of language and literature: the American Dialect Society's early *Dialect Notes*. *See* **1266**.

2652. Thomas, Erik R.; Carter, Phillip M. Prosodic rhythm and African American English. EWW (27:3) 2006, 331–55.

2653. Tortora, Christina. The case of Appalachian expletive *they*. *See* **1460**.

2654. Tricomi, Albert. Dialect and identity in Harriet Jacobs's autobiography and other slave narratives. *See* **10531**.

2655. Trüb, Regina. Nonstandard verbal paradigms in earlier White Southern American English. AS (81:3) 2006, 250–65.

2656. Walker, James A.; Meyerhoff, Miriam. Zero copula in the Eastern Caribbean: evidence from Bequia. *See* **2749**.

2657. Wall, Cheryl A. Zora Neale Hurston: *Their Eyes Were Watching God*. *In* (pp. 376–83) **11788**.

2658. Wasserman, Paul; Hausrath, Don. Weasel words: the dictionary of American doublespeak. *See* **1695**.

2659. Webelhuth, Gert; Dannenberg, Clare J. Southern American English personal datives: the theoretical significance of dialectal variation. AS (81:1) 2006, 31–55.

2660. Wolfram, Walt; Schilling-Estes, Natalie. Remnant dialects in the coastal United States. *In* (pp. 172–202) **2543**.

2661. —— Ward, Ben (eds). American voices: how dialects differ from coast to coast. Oxford; Malden, MA: Blackwell, 2006. pp. xiii, 269.

2662. Wright, Laura. The language of transported Londoners: third person singular present-tense markers in depositions from Virginia and the Bermudas, 1607–1624. *In* (pp. 158–71) **2543**.

DIALECTS OF THE REST OF THE WORLD

2663. Arua, Arua E. Botswana English: some syntactic and lexical features. EWW (25:2) 2004, 255–72.

2664. Bao, Zhiming; Hong, Huaqing. Diglossia and register variation in Singapore English. WorldE (25:1) 2006, 105–14.

2665. Barfield, Steven. 'Jewelinthecrown.co.uk': Orientalism's strange persistence in British South Asian writing. *In* (pp. 111–20) **14238**.

2666. Bieswanger, Markus. German influence on Australian English. Heidelberg: Winter, 2004. pp. viii, 197. (Anglistische Forschungen, 343.)

2667. Buregeya, Alfred. Grammatical features of Kenyan English and the extent of their acceptability. EWW (27:2) 2006, 199–216.

2668. Butler, Susan. Lexicography and world Englishes from Australia to Asia. WorldE (24:4) 2005, 533–46.

2669. Crawford, Robert. Spirit machines: the human and the computational. *In* (pp. 52–68) **13732**.

2670. Cryer, Max. The Godzone dictionary of favourite New Zealand words and phrases. *See* **1669**.

2671. Davies, Carolyn; Maclagan, Margaret. Maori words: read all about it. Testing the presence of 13 Maori words in four New Zealand newspapers from 1997 to 2004. *See* **2482**.

2672. Gane, Gillian. Postcolonial literature and the magic radio: the language of Rushdie's *Midnight's Children*. *See* **18385**.

2673. Gold, David L. A little noticed English construction: subjectless imperative *please to* + infinitive. *See* **1452**.

2674. —— Panama Canal Zone, the Virgin Islands, and the Cayman Islands! RAEI (17) 2004, 117–38.

2675. Gordon, Elizabeth; Trudgill, Peter. English input to New Zealand. *In* (pp. 440–55) **2543**.

2676. Haugh, Michael. Emic perspectives on the positive–negative politeness distinction. *See* **1807**.

2677. Hickey, Raymond. English dialect input to the Caribbean. *In* (pp. 326–59) **2543**.

2678. —— Englishes in Asia and Africa: origin and structure. *In* (pp. 503–35) **2543**.

2679. —— South Asian Englishes. *In* (pp. 536–58) **2543**.

2680. —— South-East Asian Englishes. *In* (pp. 559–85) **2543**.

2681. Hunter, Jenny (ed.). The true blue guide to Australian slang. French's Forest, N.S.W.: New Holland, 2004. pp. 126.

2682. Igboanusi, Herbert. A comparative study of the pronunciation features of Igbo English and Yoruba English speakers of Nigeria. EngS (87:4) 2006, 490–7.

2683. Kachru, Braj B. Asian Englishes: beyond the canon. Hong Kong: Hong Kong UP, 2005. pp. xxii, 333. (Asian Englishes today.) Rev. by Robert D. King in WorldE (24:4) 2005, 547–50.

2684. Kasanga, Luanga A. Requests in a South African variety of English. WorldE (25:1) 2006, 65–89.

2685. Kiesling, Scott F. English input to Australia. *In* (pp. 418–39) **2543**.

2686. Lass, Roger. South African English. *In* (pp. 363–86) **2543**.

2687. Leitner, Gerhard. Australia's many voices: Australian English – the national language. (Bibl. 2005, 3061.) Rev. by Peter Collins in EWW (27:1) 2006, 101–5.

2688. —— Australia's many voices: ethnic Englishes, indigenous and migrant languages: policy and education. Berlin; New York: Mouton de Gruyter, 2004. pp. xiv, 341. (Contributions to the sociology of language, 90:2.) Rev. by Peter Collins in EWW (27:1) 2006, 101–5.

2689. Lim, Lisa (ed.). Singapore English: a grammatical description. (Bibl. 2005, 3062.) Rev. by David Deterding in EWW (27:1) 2006, 106–9.

2690. Macalister, John. The Maori presence in the New Zealand English lexicon, 1850–2000. EWW (27:1) 2006, 1–24.

2691. —— Of *weka* and *waiata*: familiarity with borrowings from Te Reo Maori. *See* **1492**.

2692. Mukerjee, Joybrato; Hoffmann, Sebastian. Describing verb-complementational profiles of new Englishes: a pilot study of Indian English. EWW (27:2) 2006, 147–73.

2693. Nelson, Gerald. The core and periphery of world Englishes: a corpus-based exploration. WorldE (25:1) 2006, 115–29.

2694. Ngefac, Aloysius; Sala, Bonaventure M. Cameroon Pidgin and Cameroon English at a confluence: a real-time investigation. EWW (27:2) 2006, 217–27.

2695. Nkemleke, Daniel A. Some characteristics of expository writing in Cameroon English. EWW (27:1) 2006, 25–44.

2696. Ó Tuathaigh, Gearóid. Language, ideology and national identity. *In* (pp. 42–58) **11829**.

2697. Peeters, Bert. *Tall poppies* and egalitarianism in Australian discourse: from key word to cultural value. *See* **1604**.

2698. Petrucci, Peter R.; Head, Michael. *Sweet as* is cool for New Zealanders. *See* **1601**.

2699. Reynolds, Ras Dennis Jabari (ed.). Jabari authentic Jamaican dictionary of the Jamic language: featuring Jamaican Patwa and Rasta Iyaric, pronunciations and definitions. *See* **1687**.

2700. Rubino, Antonia; Bettoni, Camilla. Handling complaints cross-culturally: Italians *vs* Anglo-Australians. *See* **1824**.

2701. Schreier, Daniel. The backyard as a dialect boundary: individuation, linguistic heterogeneity, and sociolinguistic eccentricity in a small speech community. JEL (34:1) 2006, 26–57.

2702. —— English transported to the South Atlantic Ocean: Tristan da Cunha. *In* (pp. 387–401) **2543**.

2703. Sharbawi, Salbrina Haji. The vowels of Brunei English: an acoustic investigation. EWW (27:3) 2006, 247–64.

2704. Sharifian, Farzad. A cultural-conceptual approach and world Englishes: the case of Aboriginal English. WorldE (25:1) 2006, 11–22.

2705. Starks, Donna; Reffell, Hayley. Reading 'TH': vernacular variables in Pasifika Englishes in South Auckland. JSoc (10:3) 2006, 382–92. (Research note.)

2706. Sudbury, Andrea. English on the Falklands. *In* (pp. 402–17) **2543**.

2707. Trudgill, Peter; Gordon, Elizabeth. Predicting the past: dialect archaeology and Australian English rhoticity. EWW (27:3) 2006, 235–46.

2708. Van Rooy, Bertus. The extension of the progressive aspect in Black South African English. WorldE (25:1) 2006, 37–64.

2709. Warren, Paul. Oops, I've done a futt: quality and quantity in a New Zealand vowel contrast. *See* **1312**.

2710. Wee, Lionel. The semiotics of language ideologies in Singapore. JSoc (10:3) 2006, 344–61.

2711. Yallop, C., *et al.* (eds). Macquarie dictionary. *See* **1696**.

2712. Yang, Jian. Lexical innovations in China English. WorldE (24:4) 2005, 425–36.

2713. Ziegeler, Debra; Lee, Sarah. Causativity reduction in Singaporean English. EWW (27:3) 2006, 265–94.

ENGLISH AS A WORLD LANGUAGE

2714. Aravamudan, Srinivas. Guru English: South Asian religion in a cosmopolitan language. Princeton, NJ; Oxford: Princeton UP, 2006. pp. xiii, 330.

2715. Bacinger, Dunja. Anglicisms in the Croatian press. MSp (48:2) 2004, 7–38.

2716. Canagarajah, A. Suresh. Negotiating the local in English as a *lingua franca*. ARAL (26) 2006, 197–218.

2717. Elder, Catherine; Davies, Alan. Assessing English as a *lingua franca*. ARAL (26) 2006, 282–301.

2718. Gounari, Panayota. Language policy in the United States: uncommon language and the discourse of common sense. BELL (ns 4) 2006, 39–50.

2719. Howarth, Peter. The phraseology of public international English. IJES (6:1) 2006, 109–29.

2720. Kachru, Braj B.; Kachru, Yamuna; Nelson, Cecil L. (eds). The handbook of world Englishes. Oxford; Malden, MA: Blackwell, 2006. pp. 299.

2721. Koeneke, Rodney. Empires of the mind: I. A. Richards and Basic English in China, 1929–1979. *See* **18240**.

2722. Meierkord, Christiane. Syntactic variation in interactions across international Englishes. EWW (25:1) 2004, 109–32.

2723. Pennycook, Alastair. Global Englishes and transcultural flows. London; New York: Routledge, 2006. pp. viii, 189.

2724. Pickering, Lucy. Current research on intelligibility in English as a *lingua franca*. ARAL (26) 2006, 219–33.

2725. Prasad, G. J. V. A minute stretching into centuries: Macaulay, English, and India. *See* **10775**.

2726. Proshina, Zoya G. Intermediary translation from English as a *lingua franca*. WorldE (24:4) 2005, 517–22.

2727. —— Ettkin, Brian P. English–Russian language contacts. WorldE (24:4) 2005, 439–44.

2728. Seidlhofer, Barbara; Breitender, Angelika; Pitzl, Marie-Luise. English as a *lingua franca* in Europe: challenges for applied linguistics. ARAL (26) 2006, 3–34.

2729. Sichyova, Olga N. A note on Russian–English code switching. WorldE (24:4) 2005, 487–94.

2730. Svartvik, Jan; Leech, Geoffrey. English: one tongue, many voices. (Bibl. 2000, 3135.) Basingstoke; New York: Palgrave Macmillan, 2006. pp. xvi, 287. (Revised ed. of *Engelska: öspråk, världsspråk, trendspråk* (1999).)

2731. Ustinova, Irina P.; Bhatia, Tej K. Convergence of English in Russian TV commercials. WorldE (24:4) 2005, 495–508.

2732. Yuzefovich, Natalia G. English in Russian cultural contexts. WorldE (24:4) 2005, 509–16.

PIDGINS AND CREOLES

2733. Avram, Andrei A. Atlantic, Pacific or world wide? Issues in assessing the status of creole features. EWW (25:1) 2004, 81–108.

2734. Cooper, Carolyn. 'What the backside all you want?': interrogating Rastafari in Derek Walcott's *O Babylon! See* **18922**.

2735. Decker, Ken. Moribund English: the case of Gustavia English, St Barthélemy. EWW (25:2) 2006, 217–54.

2736. Foley, William. Universal constraints and local conditions in pidginization: case studies from New Guinea. JPCL (21:1) 2006, 1–44.

2737. Garrett, Paul B. Contact languages as 'endangered' languages: what is there to lose? JPCL (21:1) 2006, 175–90.

2738. Hackert, Stephanie. Urban Bahamian Creole: system and variation. (Bibl. 2004, 3267.) Rev. by Helean McPhee in JPCL (21:2) 2006, 384–9.

2739. Lefebvre, Claire; Loranger, Virginie. On the properties of Saramaccan *fu*: synchronic and diachronic perspectives. *See* **1442**.

2740. Mishra, Sudesh. Time and *girmit*. SocT (82) 2005, 15–36.

2741. Ngefac, Aloysius; Sala, Bonaventure M. Cameroon Pidgin and Cameroon English at a confluence: a real-time investigation. *See* **2694**.

2742. Rickford, John R. Down for the count? The creole origins hypothesis of AAVE at the hands of the Ottawa Circle, and their supporters. *See* **2642**.

2743. Romaine, Suzanne. English input to the English-lexicon pidgins and creoles of the Pacific. *In* (pp. 456–99) **2543**.

2744. Schneider, Edgar W.; Wagner, Christian. The variability of literary dialect in Jamaican Creole: Thelwell's *The Harder They Come*. *See* **18738**.

2745. Sebba, Mark; Dray, Susan. Is it creole, is it English, is it valid? Developing and using a corpus of unstandardised written language. *In* (pp. 223–39) **1195**.

2746. Singler, John Victor. Children and creole genesis. JPCL (21:1) 2006, 157–73.

2747. —— Yes, but not in the Caribbean. JPCL (21:2) 2006, 337–58.

2748. Velupillai, Viveka. Hawai'i Creole English: a typological analysis of the tense–mood–aspect system. EWW (25:2) 2004, 287–99.

2749. Walker, James A.; Meyerhoff, Miriam. Zero copula in the Eastern Caribbean: evidence from Bequia. AS (81:2) 2006, 146–63.

2750. Wolfram, Walt; Ward, Ben (eds). American voices: how dialects differ from coast to coast. *See* **2661**.

SOCIOLINGUISTICS

2751. Archer, Dawn; Culpeper, Jonathan. Sociopragmatic annotation: new directions and possibilities in historical linguistics. *In* (pp. 37–58) **1195**.

2752. Baxter, Judith (ed.). Speaking out: the female voice in public contexts. Basingstoke; New York: Palgrave Macmillan, 2006. pp. xviii, 264. Rev. by Kate Crehan in JSoc (10:5) 2006, 683–6.

2753. Berger, Lauren; McMakin, Dana; Furman, Wyndol. The language of love: romantic relationships in adolescence. *In* (pp. 129–45) **2798**.

2754. Brown, David West. Girls and guys, ghetto and bougie: metapragmatics, ideology and the management of social identities. JSoc (10:5) 2006, 596–610.

2755. Buchstaller, Isabelle. Social stereotypes, personality traits and regional perception displaced: attitudes towards the 'new' quotatives in the UK. *See* **1546**.

2756. Cameron, Deborah. Language, gender, and sexuality: current issues and new directions. AppL (26:4) 2005, 482–502.

2757. Chambers, J. K. 'Canadian dainty': the rise and decline of Briticisms in Canada. *In* (pp. 224–41) **2543**.

2758. Childs, Becky; Mallinson, Christine. African American English in Appalachia: dialect accommodation and substrate influence. *See* **2605**.

2759. —— —— The significance of lexical items in the construction of ethnolinguistic identity: a case study of adolescent spoken and online language. AS (81:1) 2006, 3–30.

2760. Coulmas, Florian. Sociolinguistics: the study of speakers' choices. Cambridge; New York: CUP, 2005. pp. viii, 263. Rev. by Kate Beeching in JSoc (10:2) 2006, 278–82.

2761. Crespo García, Begoña. English and Galician in the Middle Ages: a sociohistorical survey. *See* **1203**.

2762. D'Arcy, Alexandra. Lexical replacement and the like(s). *See* **1448**.

2763. DeBose, Charles. The sociology of African American language: a language planning perspective. *See* **2610**.

2764. Decker, Ken. Moribund English: the case of Gustavia English, St Barthélemy. *See* **2735**.

2765. de Klerk, Vivian. Slang and swearing as markers of inclusion and exclusion in adolescence. *In* (pp. 111–27) **2798**.

2766. Eades, Diana. Lexical struggle in court: Aboriginal Australians *versus* the State. *See* **2201**.

2767. Eckert, Penelope. Stylistic practice and the adolescent social order. *In* (pp. 93–110) **2798**.

2768. Erickson, Frederick. Talk and social theory: ecologies of speaking and listening in everyday life. *See* **2204**.

2769. Esser, Jürgen. Stylistic change across generations? Conflicting evidence from psycholinguistic and corpuslinguistic data. *In* (pp. 79–100) **1227**.

2770. Garrett, Peter; Williams, Angie. Adults' perceptions of communication with younger people. *In* (pp. 35–52) **2798**.

2771. Hawkes, Terence. Nanti everything. *In* (pp. 130–8) **5421**.

2772. Hughes, Geoffrey. An encyclopedia of swearing: the social history of oaths, profanity, foul language, and ethnic slurs in the English-speaking world. *See* **1676**.

2773. Jeremiah, Milford A. Linguistic variation in Judge Greg Mathis' courtroom. SPC (29:1) 2006, 99–119.

2774. Johnson, Danette Ifert. Feminine style in Presidential debate discourse, 1960–2000. *See* **2211**.

2775. Johnstone, Barbara; Andrus, Jennifer; Danielson, Andrew E. Mobility, indexicality, and the enregisterment of 'Pittsburghese'. *See* **2624**.

2776. Kroløkke, Charlotte; Sorensen, Anne Scott. Gender communication theories & analyses: from silence to performance. London; Thousand Oaks, CA: Sage, 2006. pp. xiii, 193. Rev. by Laura C. Prividera in WL (29:1) 2006, 56–7.

2777. Lakoff, Robin Tolmach. Language and woman's place: text and commentaries. Ed. by Mary Bucholtz. (Bibl. 1975, 1247.) Oxford; New York: OUP, 2004. pp. xiv, 309. (Studies in language and gender.) (Second ed.: first ed. 1975.) Rev. by Elizabeth Grace Winkler in AS (81:2) 2006, 203–12.

2778. Levey, Stephen. Tense variation in preadolescent narratives. *See* **2214**.

2779. —— Visiting London relatives. *See* **2215**.

2780. Levon, Erez. Hearing 'gay': prosody, interpretation, and the affective judgments of men's speech. *See* **2217**.

2781. Litosseliti, Lia. Constructing gender in public arguments: the female voice as emotional voice. *In* (pp. 40–58) **2752**.

2782. Martin, Katherine Connor. Gendered aspects of lexicographer labeling. *See* **1645**.

2783. Moore, Emma. 'You tell all the stories': using a narrative to explore hierarchy within a Community of Practice. JSoc (10:5) 2006, 611–40.

2784. Myers, Greg. Applied linguistics and institutions of opinion. *See* **2222**.

2785. —— 'Where are you from?': identifying place. *See* **2223**.

2786. Nevins, Debbie. The trouble with himorher: winning the battle of the sexes (in pronouns). *See* **1401**.

2787. O'Flynn, Sarah. Ticket to a queer planet? Communication issues affecting lesbian and gay people. *In* (pp. 147–61) **2798**.

2788. Pollack, Mica. Colormute: race talk dilemmas in an American school. Princeton, NJ; Oxford: Princeton UP, 2004. pp. xi, 268. Rev. by James Collins in JAR (62:1) 2006, 134–5.

2789. Rampton, Ben. Language in late modernity: interaction in an urban school. Cambridge; New York: CUP, 2006. pp. xviii, 443. (Studies in interactional sociolinguistics, 22.) Rev. by Jean Jacques Weber in BELL (ns 4) 2006, 211–13.

2790. Schmid, Hans-Jörg. Do women and men really live in different cultures? Evidence from the BNC. *In* (pp. 185–221) **1195**.

2791. Schreier, Daniel. The backyard as a dialect boundary: individuation, linguistic heterogeneity, and sociolinguistic eccentricity in a small speech community. *See* **2701**.

2792. Shearer-Cremean, Christine; Winkelmann, Carol L. (eds). Survivor rhetoric: negotiations and narrativity in abused women's language. Toronto; Buffalo, NY; London: Toronto UP, 2004. pp. viii, 241. Rev. by Margaret Baker Graham in NWSAJ (18:2) 2006, 241–4; by Jane Jorgenson in WL (29:2) 2006, 48–9.

2793. Slomanson, Peter; Newman, Michael. Peer group identification and variation in New York Latino English laterals. *See* **2646**.

2794. Speer, Susan A. Gender talk: feminism, discourse and conversation analysis. London; New York: Routledge, 2005. pp. vii, 236. (Women and psychology.) Rev. by Joan Swann in JSoc (10:3) 2006, 407–12.

2795. Szmrecsanyi, Benedikt. Morphosyntactic persistence in spoken English: a corpus study at the intersection of variationist sociolinguistics, psycholinguistics, and discourse analysis. *See* **2237**.

2796. Tuominen, Anne. The endurance of ethnic family rituals. *In* (pp. 17–33) **3157**.

2797. Wichmann, Anne; Cauldwell, Richard. *Wh*- questions and attitude: the effect of context. *In* (pp. 291–305) **1195**.

2798. Williams, Angie; Thurlow, Crispin (eds). Talking adolescence: perspectives on communication in the teenage years. New York; Frankfurt: Lang, 2005. pp. viii, 292. (Language as social action, 3.) Rev. by Joy Koesten in JSoc (10:5) 2006, 694–8.

TRANSLATION AND COMPARATIVE LINGUISTICS

2799. Almquist, Steve. Not quite the gabbling of 'a thing most brutish': Caliban's Kiswahili in Aimé Césaire's *A Tempest*. *See* **6117**.

2800. Apter, Emily. The translation zone: a new comparative literature. Princeton, NJ; Oxford: Princeton UP, 2006. pp. xii, 298. (Translation/transnation.) Rev. by Michelle Slater in MLN (121:4) 2006, 1035–7.

2801. Arrojo, Rosemary. Translation, transference, and the attraction to otherness – Borges, Menard, Whitman. *See* **11545**.

2802. Atechi, Samuel Ngwa. The phonological influence of English on Awing. *See* **1285**.

2803. Bacinger, Dunja. Anglicisms in the Croatian press. *See* **2715**.

2804. Balcom, John. Translating modern Chinese literature. *In* (pp. 119–34) **3186**.

2805. Balmer, Josephine. What comes next? Reconstructing the Classics. *In* (pp. 184–95) **3186**.

2806. Bamiro, Edmund O. The politics of code-switching: English *vs* Nigerian languages. *See* **18563**.

2807. Bassnett, Susan; Bush, Peter (eds). The translator as writer. *See* **3186**.

2808. Baumer, Emmanuel. Étude contrastive de *some* + nom discontinu singulier et de ses traductions en français. *See* **1455**.

2809. Bermann, Sandra; Wood, Michael (eds). Nation, language, and the ethics of translation. *See* **3191**.

2810. Bieswanger, Markus. German influence on Australian English. *See* **2666**.

2811. Biggs, Frederick M. Seventeen words of Middle Dutch origin in the Miller's Tale? *See* **4366**.

2812. Bigliazzi, Silvia. Su alcune varianti traduttive del *Macbeth*. *See* **5922**.

2813. Blevins, Juliette. New perspectives on English sound patterns: 'natural' and 'unnatural' in evolutionary phonology. *See* **1272**.

2814. Boase-Beier, Jean. Stylistic approaches to translation. *See* **2267**.

2815. Breeze, Andrew. *Bune* 'maiden; beloved' in *Ancrene Wisse*. *See* **1548**.

2816. Bueno Alonso, Jorge Luis. Two Spanish renderings of Philip Sidney's 'First Song' from *Astrophil & Stella* (1591): a reappraisal and a new proposal. *See* **5033**.

2817. Caws, Mary Ann. Surprised in translation. *See* **11817**.

2818. Clayton, Hugh. Mussolini and Mr Malakite: further reflections on the Powys brothers in Italian. *See* **18135**.

2819. Coetzee, J. M. Roads to translation. *See* **15199**.

2820. Crespo García, Begoña. English and Galician in the Middle Ages: a sociohistorical survey. *See* **1203**.

2821. Davies, Carolyn; Maclagan, Margaret. Maori words: read all about it. Testing the presence of 13 Maori words in four New Zealand newspapers from 1997 to 2004. *See* **2482**.

2822. Decker, Ken. Moribund English: the case of Gustavia English, St Barthélemy. *See* **2735**.

2823. Derolez, René. Byrhtferðus bene docet. *See* **3760**.

2824. Díaz Pérez, Francisco Javier. Deixis and verbal politeness in request production in English and Spanish. *See* **1796**.

2825. Dobrovol'skij, Dmitrij; Piirainen, Elisabeth. Figurative language: cross-cultural and cross-linguistic perspectives. *See* **1926**.

2826. Dossena, Marina. 'The cinic Scotomastic'? Johnson, his commentators, Scots, French, and the story of English. *See* **7926**.

2827. Drábek, Pavel. František Nevrla's translation of *Hamlet*. *See* **5715**.

2828. Dušková, Libuše. Syntactic constancy of the verb between English and Czech. *See* **1370**.

2829. Eyheragaray, Leticia. *The Strange Gentleman*: Dickens on the Uruguayan stage. *See* **9745**.

2830. Fargione, Daniela. Cynthia Ozick: orthodoxy and irreverence: a critical study. *See* **17948**.

2831. Findlay, Bill. Motivation in a surrogate translation of Goldoni. *In* (pp. 46–57) **3186**.

2832. Foley, William. Universal constraints and local conditions in pidginization: case studies from New Guinea. *See* **2736**.

2833. Freeman, Margaret H.; Takeda, Masako. Art, science, and Ste Emilie's sunsets: a Háj-inspired cognitive approach to translating an Emily Dickinson poem into Japanese. *See* **9862**.

2834. Fukui, Naoki. Theoretical comparative syntax: studies in macroparameters. *See* **1373**.

2835. Ganner, Heidemarie. When a boy is not a boy …: reflections on the deceptive simplicity of the English language. *In* (pp. 115–20) **1227**.

2836. Giancarli, Pierre-Don. Le futur périphrastique modal français d''allure extraordinaire' (assertif, interrogatif, impératif) et ses traductions en anglais. *See* **1376**.

2837. Gladstein, Mimi R. Bilingual wordplay: variations on a theme by Hemingway and Steinbeck. *See* **16357**.

2838. Golato, Andrea. Compliments and compliment responses: grammatical structure and sequential organization. *See* **1805**.

2839. Göske, Daniel. 'There's another rendering now': on translating *Moby-Dick* into German. *In* (pp. 255–73) **10823**.

2840. Grigg, Russell. Englishing Lacan. Meanjin (64:4) 2005, 104–10.

2841. Hahn, Robert. The mockingbird's chops: Charles Wright in Italian. *See* **19358**.

2842. Haldane, Michael. 'Doubling' in Bartholomew Yong's *Diana*. *See* **5152**.

2843. Hantson, André. The English perfect and the anti-perfect *used to* viewed from a comparative perspective. *See* **1465**.

2844. Hardwick, Lorna. 'Murmurs in the cathedral': the impact of translations from Greek poetry and drama on modern work in English by Michael Longley and Seamus Heaney. *See* **17248**.

2845. Harris, Alice C. Revisiting anaphoric islands. *See* **1343**.

2846. Hart, Kevin. Tracking the trace. *See* **3561**.

2847. Haugh, Michael. Emic perspectives on the positive–negative politeness distinction. *See* **1807**.

2848. Herdina, Philip. Mehrsprachigkeit als Problem: eine kritische Betrachtung monolingualer Sprachgeschichtsschreibung am Beispiel des anglonormannischen Einflusses auf das Angelsächsische. *See* **1213**.

2849. Hiraga, Masako K. Metaphor and iconicity: a cognitive approach to analyzing texts. *See* **1985**.

2850. Hirsch, Irene. The Brazilian whale. *In* (pp. 275–88) **10823**.

2851. Hoenselaars, Ton. Between Heaven and Hell: Shakespearian translation, adaptation, and criticism from a historical perspective. *See* **5329**.

2852. Hollebrandse, Bart; van Hout, Angeliek; Vet, Co (eds). Crosslinguistic views on tense, aspect and modality. *See* **1380**.

2853. Holmström, Lakshmi. Let poetry win: the translator as writer – an Indian perspective. *In* (pp. 33–45) **3186**.

2854. Horner, Patrick J. (ed. and trans.). A macaronic sermon collection from late medieval England: Oxford, MS Bodley 649. *See* **4074**.

2855. Jiang, Qiuxia; Guo, Laifu; Jin, Ping. The influence of ideology on translation of foreign literature – a case study of three Chinese versions of *David Copperfield*. *See* **9771**.

2856. Jones, Francis R. 'Geldshark Ares god of war': ideology and time in literary translation. *See* **16290**.

2857. Jones, Mari C.; Singh, Ishtla. Exploring language change. *See* **1220**.

2858. Josek, Jiří. A Czech Shakespeare? *In* (pp. 84–94) **3186**.

2859. Karlin, Daniel. Proust's English. *See* **3297**.

2860. Kelly, Darlene. Lost in translation: the English versions of Gabrielle Roy's early novels. *See* **18366**.

2861. Kelly-Holmes, Helen. Advertising as multilingual communication. *See* **2508**.

2862. Kenda, Jakob J. Rewriting children's literature. *In* (pp. 160–70) **3186**.

2863. Kettemann, Bernhard. Morphologische Integration von und semantische Differenzierung durch Anglizismen im Deutschen. *In* (pp. 169–82) **1227**.

2864. Komem, Aharon. The exit according to Shakespeare. *See* **5657**.

2865. Królak, Emilia; Rudnicka, Kinga. Selected aspects of directives in Polish. *See* **1812**.

2866. Kubouchi, Tadao. Wulfstan's Scandinavian loanword usage: an aspect of the linguistic situation in the late Old English Danelaw. *In* (pp. 134–52) **1241**.

2867. Kutzinski, Vera M. Fearful assymetries: Langston Hughes, Nicolás Guillén, and *Cuba libre*. *See* **16485**.

2868. Lakoff, Robin Tolmach. Vulgar Latin: comparative castration (and comparative theories of syntax). *See* **1386**.

2869. Lautel-Ribstein, Florence. Théories de la traduction au xviiie siècle: entre noblesse et prosaïsme. RANAM (39) 2006, 71–90.

2870. Lefebvre, Claire; Loranger, Virginie. On the properties of Saramaccan *fu*: synchronic and diachronic perspectives. *See* **1442**.

2871. Li, Ruru. '"Who is it that can tell me who I am?" / "Lear's shadow"': a Taiwanese actor's personal response to *King Lear*. *See* **5866**.

2872. Lin, Xavier. Creative translation, translating creatively: a case study on aesthetic coherence in Peter Stambler's Han Shan. *In* (pp. 97–108) **2874**.

2873. Loffredo, Eugenia. Poetry as 'translational form': a trans-generic translation of Jeanne Hyvrard's *Mère la mort* into English. *In* (pp. 158–72) **2874**.

2874. —— Perteghella, Manuela (eds). Translation and creativity: perspectives on creative writing and Translation Studies. London; New York: Continuum, 2006. pp. x, 197.

2875. López Guix, Juan Gabriel. The translator in Aliceland: on translating *Alice in Wonderland* into Spanish. *In* (pp. 95–105) **3186**.

2876. Lorenzo-Modia, María Jesús. Charlotte Lennox's *The Female Quixote* into Spanish: a gender-biased translation. *See* **7972**.

2877. Lotfipour-Saedi, K. Discoursal function of phonological patterns in poetic texts: implications for (UN-)translatability of poetry. *See* **3572**.

2878. Macalister, John. The Maori presence in the New Zealand English lexicon, 1850–2000. *See* **2690**.

2879. —— Of *weka* and *waiata*: familiarity with borrowings from Te Reo Maori. *See* **1492**.

2880. Machan, Tim William. Medieval multilingualism and Gower's literary practice. *See* **4149**.

2881. Maci, Stefania M. GHD advertising campaign across cultures: a case study. *See* **2512**.

2882. Malinovsky, Milan. Length of sentences and words in Czech and English and in other European languages. *See* **1394**.

2883. Mao, LuMing. Reading Chinese fortune cookie: the making of Chinese American rhetoric. *See* **2630**.

2884. Marín Arrese, Juana I.; Núñez Perucha, Begoña. Evaluation and engagement in journalistic commentary and news reportage. *See* **2513**.

2885. Masiello, Francine. Joyce in Buenos Aires (talking sexuality through translation). *See* **16729**.

2886. Meek, Donald E. Smoking, drinking, dancing and singing on the high seas: steamships and the uses of *smùid* in Scottish Gaelic. *See* **1596**.

2887. Merchant, Jason. Why no(t)? *See* **1450**.

2888. Miller, D. Gary. Latin suffixal derivatives in English and their Indo-European ancestry. *See* **1349**.

2889. Mira, Alberto. Being Wildean: a dialogue on the importance of style in translation. *In* (pp. 196–207) **3186**.

2890. Molesini, Andrea. Translating *Omeros*. *See* **18929**.

2891. Monrós Gaspar, Laura. '*Boscovos tromuldo boscovos*': a case study in the translation of William Shakespeare's *All's Well That Ends Well*. *See* **5635**.

2892. Morini, Carla. The Old English *Apollonius* and Wulfstan of York. *See* **3729**.

2893. Morini, Massimiliano. Tudor translation in theory and practice. *See* **4619**.

2894. Morse, Ruth. Reflections in Shakespeare translation. *See* **5390**.

2895. Moul, Victoria. Ben Jonson's *Poetaster*: Classical translation and the location of cultural authority. *See* **6894**.

2896. Mur Dueñas, Mª Pilar. A pragmatic approach to the contrastive analysis of a literary work and two of its translations. *See* **10583**.

2897. Neri, Barbara. *Cobridme de flores*: (un)covering flowers of Portuguese and Spanish poets in *Sonnets from the Portuguese*. *See* **9263**.

2898. Newmark, Peter. The translator as writer. BStE (31) 2005, 95–102.

2899. Nikolaou, Paschalis. Notes on translating the self. *In* (pp. 19–32) **2874**.

2900. Nuccorini, Stefania. In search of 'phraseologies': discovering divergences in the use of English and Italian 'true friends'. *See* **1769**.

2901. O'Donnell, Daniel Paul. Bede's strategy in paraphrasing Cædmon's Hymn. *See* **3765**.

2902. O'Neill, Patrick. Polyglot Joyce: fictions of translation. *See* **16746**.

2903. Onysko, Alexander. Anglicisms in *Der Spiegel*: towards a methodological framework of corpus analysis. *In* (pp. 265–77) **1227**.

2904. Orts Llopis, María Ángeles. The hidden dimension of the language of corporations in America and Spain: perspectives for inter-legal communications. *See* **2521**.

2905. Pánková, Lenka. The for-ever reverberating 'Never more': what do *The Raven's* multiple translations in Czech signify for translation theory? *See* **11036**.

2906. Patton, Simon. The riches of the soul. Meanjin (64:4) 2005, 124–9.

2907. Perteghella, Manuela. Poetry, music and transformation in the Gulf of Naples: a creative voyage of *The Tempest*. *In* (pp. 109–23) **2874**.

2908. Pitts, Brent A.; Furnish, Shearle. The Middle English Apocalypse gloss in British Library MS Additional 18633. *See* **1534**.

2909. Pons-Sanz, Sara M. Anglo-Scandinavian trade or paganism? OE *hæðen* in the First Cleopatra Glossary. *See* **1569**.

2910. —— OE *māl* for L *clasma* in Aldhelmian glossaries. *See* **1583**.

2911. —— Sharpening, confiding, and OE *getryccað*. *See* **1566**.

2912. Prins, Yopie. 'Lady's Greek' (with the accents): a metrical translation of Euripides by A. Mary F. Robinson. *See* **11072**.

2913. —— Metrical translation: nineteenth-century Homers and the hexameter mania. *In* (pp. 229–56) **3191**.

2914. Proshina, Zoya G. Intermediary translation from English as a *lingua franca*. *See* **2726**.

2915. —— Ettkin, Brian P. English–Russian language contacts. *See* **2727**.

2916. Quah, C. K. Translation and technology. Basingstoke; New York: Palgrave Macmillan, 2006. pp. xix, 221. (Palgrave textbooks in translating and interpreting.)

2917. Rabadán, Rosa. Proactive description for useful applications: researching language options for better translation practice. Meta (50:4:CD-ROM supp.) 2005.

2918. Rissanen, Matti. Latin influence on an Old English idiom: *to wit*. *In* (pp. 222–41) **1241**.

2919. Robinson, Fred C. Germanic **uargaz* (OE *wearh*) and the Finnish evidence. *In* (pp. 242–7) **1241**.

2920. Robinson, Peter. Translation and self-accusation: Vittorio Sereni's '*momento psicologico*': translating Ezra Pound. *See* **18106**.

2921. Rubino, Antonia; Bettoni, Camilla. Handling complaints cross-culturally: Italians *vs* Anglo-Australians. *See* **1824**.

2922. Rudd, Niall. Pope's farewell to Horace: *Dialogue* I, 1–22. *See* **8071**.

2923. Rutherford, John. Translating fun: *Don Quixote*. *In* (pp. 71–83) **3186**.

2924. Semler, L. E. Robert Dallington's *Hypnerotomachia* and the Protestant antiquity of Elizabethan England. *See* **4833**.

2925. Sichyova, Olga N. A note on Russian–English code switching. *See* **2729**.

2926. Sowerby, Robin. The Augustan art of poetry: Augustan translation of the Classics. *See* **7435**.

2927. —— The Augustan Lucan. *See* **8126**.

2928. Staten, Henry. Tracking the 'native informant': cultural translation as the horizon of literary translation. *In* (pp. 111–26) **3191**.

2929. Takakuwa, Yoshiko. Another letter from Tokyo. *See* **10333**.

2930. Taylor, Andrew W. Between Surrey and Marot: Nicolas Bourbon and the artful translation of the epigram. *See* **5135**.

2931. THIJS, CHRISTINE. Wærferth's treatment of the miraculous in his Old English translation of Gregory's *Dialogi*. *See* **3696**.

2932. THOMA, CHRYSTALLA. Combining functional linguistics and skopos theory: a case study of Greek Cypriot and British folktales. *See* **1409**.

2933. TROTT, NICOLA. The difficulty of Italy: translation and transmission in George Eliot's *Romola*. *In* (pp. 137–58) **8320**.

2934. TURNER, ALLAN. Translation and criticism: the stylistic mirror. *See* **18838**.

2935. USTINOVA, IRINA P.; BHATIA, TEJ K. Convergence of English in Russian TV commercials. *See* **2731**.

2936. VENUTI, LAWRENCE. Local contingencies: translation and national identities. *In* (pp. 177–202) **3191**.

2937. VERSPOOR, MARJOLIJN H.; DE BIE-KERÉKJÁRTÓ, ÁGNES. Colorful bits of experience: from *bluestocking* to *blue movie*. *See* **1547**.

2938. WEISSBORT, DANIEL. The rewards of translation. PNRev (32:3) 2006, 10–11.

2939. —— ÁSTRÁÐUR EYSTEINSSON (eds). Translation: theory and practice: a historical reader. Oxford; New York: OUP, 2006. pp. xiv, 649.

2940. WILLIAMS, GEOFFREY. Biblical resonance: a corpus-driven analysis of collocational resonance in French and English texts. *In* (pp. 255–80) **3341**.

2941. WILSON, RITA. Eco effects. Meanjin (64:4) 2005, 119–23.

2942. WRIGHT, GILLIAN. Epictetus in eighteenth-century Wales: Timothy Thomas' manuscript translation of the *Enchiridion*. *See* **8222**.

2943. YAMADA, TAKEO. A Japanese Frost: considerations of synecdoche and sentence sounds. *See* **16020**.

2944. YUZEFOVICH, NATALIA G. English in Russian cultural contexts. *See* **2732**.

2945. ZUGHOUL, MUHAMMAD RAJI; ABU-ALSHAAR, AWATEF MI'ZIL. English/Arabic/English machine translation: a historical perspective. Meta (50:3) 2005, 1022–41.

TRADITIONAL CULTURE, FOLKLORE AND FOLKLIFE

GENERAL STUDIES

2946. Anagnostou, Yiorgos. Metaethnography in the age of 'popular folklore'. JAF (119:474) 2006, 381–412.

2947. Baker, Ronald L. Folklore and literary relations: some approaches. IE (28:2) 2006, 6–12.

2948. Bronner, Simon J. 'Gombo' folkloristics: Lafcadio Hearn's creolization and hybridization in the formative period of folklore studies. *See* **10421**.

2949. Chandler, Karen. Paths to freedom: literacy and folk traditions in recent narratives about slavery and emancipation. *See* **16271**.

2950. Chappell, Ben. Bakhtin's barbershop: film as folklorist. *See* **19678**.

2951. de Caro, Frank; Jordan, Rosan Augusta. Re-situating folklore: folk contexts and twentieth-century literature and art. (Bibl. 2005, 3409.) Rev. by James W. Kirkland in WF (65:3) 2006, 349–52.

2952. Harkins, Anthony. Hillbilly: a cultural history of an American icon. (Bibl. 2005, 3412.) Rev. by James N. Gregory in JSH (72:4) 2006, 969–70.

2953. Johnson, Martin L. 'Did the cameraman film you?': finding the folk in H. Lee Waters's movies of local people. WF (64:3/4) 2005, 231–42.

2954. Lake, Frederick C. Folklore and mythology in the Alice books. *See* **9423**.

2955. Mood, Terry Ann. American regional folklore: a sourcebook and research guide. Santa Barbara, CA: ABC-CLIO, 2004. pp. xix, 476. Rev. by Betty J. Belanus in WF (65:3) 2006, 361–3.

2956. Oren, Michel. The enigmatic career of Hernton's *Scarecrow*. *See* **16411**.

2957. Peek, Philip M.; Yankah, Kwesi (eds). African folklore: an encyclopedia. London; New York: Routledge, 2004. pp. xxxii, 593. Rev. by Harriet Lyons and Andrew Lyons in CanJAS (40:3) 2006, 569–72.

2958. Roberts, June E. Reading Erna Brodber: uniting the Black diaspora through folk culture and religion. *See* **14859**.

2959. Underberg, Natalie M. Virtual and reciprocal ethnography on the Internet: the East Mims Oral History Project website. *See* **1044**.

2960. Wakefield, Sarah R. Folklore in British literature: naming and narrating in women's fiction, 1750–1880. *See* **7403**.

2961. Wall, Cheryl A. Zora Neale Hurston: *Their Eyes Were Watching God*. *In* (pp. 376–83) **11788**.

AREA STUDIES AND COLLECTIONS

2962. Birdwell, Michael E.; Dickinson, W. Calvin (eds). Rural life and culture in the Upper Cumberland. Lexington: Kentucky UP, 2004. pp. xi, 369. Rev. by Marie Tedesco in JSH (72:1) 2006, 205–6.

2963. Chandler, Keith. Popular culture in microcosm: the manuscript diaries of Richard Heritage of Marsh Gibbon, Buckinghamshire. FMJ (9:1) 2006, 5–55.

2964. Edwards, Grace Toney; Asbury, JoAnn Aust; Cox, Ricky L. (eds). A handbook to Appalachia: an introduction to the region. *See* **3240**.

2965. Ferraiuolo, Augusto. Boston's north end: negotiating identity in an Italian American neighbourhood. WF (65:3) 2006, 263–302.

2966. Rehder, John B. Appalachian folkways. Baltimore, MD; London: Johns Hopkins UP, 2004. pp. x, 353. (Creating the North American landscape.) Rev. by Melanie Beals Goan in JSH (72:1) 2006, 204–5; by Malcolm Comeaux in MatC (38:2) 2006, 72–4.

2967. Roldan-Santiago, Serafin. Thematic and structural functions of folklore in Caribbean literature: the case of the 'written' and the 'oral'. *See* **12114**.

2968. Stanley, David (ed.). Folklore in Utah: a history and guide to resources. Logan: Utah State UP, 2004. pp. 352. Rev. by Barbara Allen Bogart in WF (64:3/4) 2005, 328–9.

2969. Waide, Blaine. 'Set the house up': celebrating and authorizing cultural experience in Winston-Salem drink houses. NCarF (53:1) 2006, 42–66.

2970. Winkler, Wayne. Walking toward the sunset: the Melungeons of Appalachia. (Bibl. 2005, 3442.) Rev. by Kathryn L. Staley in AppalJ (33:2) 2006, 222–5.

2971. Wishart, David J. (ed.). Encyclopedia of the Great Plains. *See* **3421**.

PROVERBS, PROVERBIAL EXPRESSIONS, RIDDLES, RHYMES, DITES

2972. Arimi, Sailal. Parody: a memory machine of modernizing proverbs. Proverbium (23) 2006, 49–68.

2973. Berger, Arthur Asa. The genius of the Jewish joke. New Brunswick, NJ: Transaction, 2006. pp. xxviii, 184. (Classics in communication and mass culture.)

2974. Bradbury, Nancy Mason. Proverb tradition as a soft source for the *Canterbury Tales*. *See* **4370**.

2975. Hildebrand, Jennifer. 'Dere were no place in heaven for him, an' he were not desired in hell': Igbo cultural beliefs in African American folk expressions. JAAH (91:2) 2006, 127–52.

2976. Langlotz, Andreas. Idiomatic creativity: a cognitive-linguistic model of idiom-representation and idiom-variation in English. *See* **1764**.

2977. Lash, Sarah. Situating puzzles: exploring a neglected genre. MidF (31:2) 2005, 15–38.

2978. Lau, Kimberly J.; Tokofsky, Peter; Winick, Stephen D. (eds). What goes around comes around: the circulation of proverbs in contemporary life. (Bibl. 2004, 3614.) Rev. by Lee-Ellen Marvin in VoicesNY (32:1/2) 2006, 46–7.

2979. Lewis, Paul. Cracking up: American humor in a time of conflict. Chicago, IL; London: Chicago UP, 2006. pp. 240.

2980. Mena Martínez, Flor. Occasional phraseological synonymy. IJES (6:1) 2006, 131–58.

2981. Mieder, Wolfgang. From 'windmills in one's head' to 'tilting at windmills': history and meaning of a proverbial allusion to Cervantes' *Don Quixote*. Proverbium (23) 2006, 343–418.

2982. —— International bibliography of new and reprinted proverb collections. Proverbium (23) 2006, 477–85.

2983. —— International proverb scholarship: an updated bibliography. Proverbium (23) 2006, 487–530.

2984. —— 'The proof of the proverb is in the probing': Alan Dundes as pioneering paremiologist. WF (65:3) 2006, 217–62.

2985. —— Proverbs are the best policy: folk wisdom and American politics. Logan: Utah State UP, 2005. pp. xvi, 323. Rev. by William Westerman in VoicesNY (32:3/4) 2006, 45–6.

2986. —— 'We are all in the same boat now': proverbial rhetoric in the Churchill–Roosevelt correspondence. IJES (6:1) 2006, 1–26.

2987. Monteiro, George. 'Good fences make good neighbors' in the nineteenth century. Proverbium (23) 2006, 419–22.

2988. Polletta, Francesca. It was like a fever: storytelling in protest and politics. *See* **2087**.

2989. Roper, Jonathan. English verbal charms. Helsinki: Suomalainen Tiedeakatemia, Academia Scientiarum Fennica, 2005. pp. 241. (FF communications, 288.) Rev. by Jacqueline Simpson in Folklore (117:3) 2006, 344–5; by Lee Haring in WF (65:3) 2006, 340–3.

2990. —— (ed.). Charms and charming in Europe. Basingstoke; New York: Palgrave Macmillan, 2004. pp. x, 233. Rev. by J. B. Smith in FolkL (44) 2005/06, 143–5; by Jacqueline Simpson in Folklore (117:1) 2006, 106–7; by Lee Haring in WF (65:3) 2006, 340–3.

2991. Schrempp, Gregory. Formulas of conversion: proverbial approaches to technological and scientific exposition. MidF (31:2) 2005, 5–13.

2992. Sobieski, Janet; Mieder, Wolfgang (eds). 'So many heads, so many wits': an anthology of English proverb poetry. Burlington: *Proverbium* in assn with the Dept of German and Russian, Univ. of Vermont, 2005. pp. xiv, 274. (Supplement series of *Proverbium*, 18.)

WRITTEN AND PRINTED MATERIALS, INSCRIPTIONS, EPITAPHS, GRAFFITI

2993. Harvey, A. D. Wall art in England. CritQ (48:1) 2006, 68–79.

NARRATIVE

2994. Beers, Terry (ed.). Gunfight at Mussel Slough: evolution of a Western myth. Santa Clara, CA: Santa Clara Univ.; Berkeley, CA: Heyday, 2004. pp. ix, 309. (California legacy.) Rev. by Lawrence Coates in WAL (41:3) 2006, 354–6.

2995. Bennett, Gillian. Bodies: sex, violence, disease and death in contemporary legend. Jackson; London: Mississippi UP, 2005. pp. xv, 313. Rev. by Jacqueline Simpson in FOAFN (65) 2006.

2996. Berger, Arthur Asa. The genius of the Jewish joke. *See* **2973**.

2997. Bratcher, James T. The Grimalkin story in Baldwin's *Beware the Cat*. *See* **4808**.

2998. Clark, John. Martin and the Green Children. Folklore (117:2) 2006, 207–14.

2999. Cody, Cornelia. 'Only in New York City': the New York City personal experience narrative. JFR (42:2) 2005, 217–44.

3000. Fine, Gary Alan; Campion-Vincent, Véronique; Heath, Chip (eds). Rumor mills: the social impact of rumor and legend. New Brunswick, NJ: Transaction, 2005. pp. xiii, 268. (Social problems and social issues.) Rev. by Gillian Bennett in FOAFN (63) 2005.

3001. Goldstein, Diane E. Once upon a virus: AIDS legends and vernacular risk perception. (Bibl. 2005, 3490.) Rev. by Jan Rosenberg in WF (65:3) 2006, 352–4.

3002. Grenby, M. O. Tame fairies make good teachers: the popularity of early British fairy tales. *See* **7415**.

3003. Griffin, Benjamin. Moving tales: narrative drift in oral culture and scripted theater. *See* **5003**.

3004. Hise, Greg. Sixty stories in search of a city. CH (83:3) 2006, 8–26.

3005. Hobbs, Sandy. Disappearance and denial: a new look at a legend motif on the screen. *See* **12546**.

3006. Keding, Dan; Douglas, Amy (eds). English folktales. Westport, CT: Libraries Unlimited, 2005. pp. xvi, 231, (plates) 8. (World folklore.)

3007. Kelley-Romano, Stephanie. Mythmaking in alien abduction narratives. ComQ (54:3) 2006, 383–406.

3008. Killick, Tim. Truth, imagination and tradition: Allan Cunningham and Scottish short fiction. *See* **9671**.

3009. Lindahl, Carl (ed.). American folktales: from the collections of the Library of Congress. Foreword by Peggy A. Bugler. Armonk, NY: Sharpe, 2004. 2 vols. pp. lxix, 729. Rev. by Linda Ballard in FolkL (44) 2005/06, 149–50; by Cristina Bacchilega in MarvT (20:1) 2006, 105–7.

3010. Miller, D. Quentin. Playing a mean guitar: the legacy of Staggerlee in Baldwin and Morrison. *In* (pp. 121–48) **14546**.

3011. Narváez, Peter. Of corpses: death and humor in folklore and popular culture. (Bibl. 2005, 3508, where title incomplete.) Rev. by Gabe McGuire in FF (35:1/2) 2004, 100–2.

3012. Prezzavento, Paolo. The cowboy as a 'queer conglomerate': Pat Garrett & Billy the Kid. *See* **14961**.

3013. Redfield, Karen A. Inside the circle, outside the circle: the continuance of Native American storytelling and the development of rhetorical strategies in English. *In* (pp. 149–64) **2149**.

3014. Ryan, Patrick. Celticity and storyteller identity: the use and misuse of ethnicity to develop a storyteller's sense of self. Folklore (117:3) 2006, 313–28.

3015. Stimson, Katharine. 'Where Robins hop, and fallen leaves are sere': Keats's robin and the social imagination. *See* **10667**.

3016. Thoma, Chrystalla. Combining functional linguistics and skopos theory: a case study of Greek Cypriot and British folktales. *See* **1409**.

3017. Westwood, Jennifer; Simpson, Jacqueline. The lore of the land: a guide to England's legends, from Spring-Heeled Jack to the Witches of Warboys. (Bibl. 2005, 3525.) Rev. by Linda Ballard in FolkL (44) 2005/06, 145–6; by Tom Shippey in TLS, 3 Mar. 2006, 36.

SONG, MUSIC, BALLAD

3018. Anon. *Polly Vaughan*. EDS (68:3) 2006, 12.

3019. Alim, H. Samy. 'The Natti ain't no punk city': emic views of Hip Hop cultures. Callaloo (29:3) 2006, 969–90.

3020. Askew, Bob. Voices from Hampshire. EDS (68:3) 2006, 6–8. (George Gardiner.)

3021. Atkinson, David. Folk songs in print: text and tradition. FMJ (8:4) 2004, 456–83.

3022. Baker, Ronald L. Baseball and ballads: the soul of culture. IE (28:1) 2005, 21–3.

3023. Bennett, Philip E.; Green, Richard Firth (eds). The singer and the scribe: European ballad traditions and European ballad cultures. Amsterdam; New York: Rodopi, 2004. pp. 223. (Internationale Forschungen zur allgemeinen und vergleichenden Literaturwissenschaft, 75.) Rev. by John D. Niles in NQ (53:1) 2006, 96–7; by David Atkinson in FMJ (9:1) 2006, 113–15.

3024. Berger, Harris M.; Del Negro, Giovanna P. Identity and everyday life: essays in the study of folklore, music, and popular culture. Middletown, CT: Wesleyan UP, 2004. pp. xviii, 185. (Music/culture.) Rev. by Anthony McCann in WF (65:3) 2006, 346–9.

3025. Brackenbury, Alison. *The Water Is Wide*: did English folk song sink? Part 1, Poets. PNRev (31:6) 2005, 43–6.

3026. —— *The Water Is Wide*: did English folk song sink? Part 2, Singers. PNRev (32:1) 2005, 39–41.

3027. Bradtke, Elaine; Yates, Mike; Taylor, Malcolm (eds). Dear companion: Appalachian traditional songs and singers from the Cecil Sharp collection. Preface by Shirley Collins. London: English Folk Dance and Song Soc. in assn with Sharp's Folk Club, 2004. pp. 137. Rev. by Rosaleen Gregory in CFMB (38:4) 2004/05, 20–3; by Jerry Epstein in FMJ (9:1) 2006, 102–5.

3028. Bratcher, James T. Gower's 'Tale of Three Questions' and 'The Clever Peasant Girl' folktale. *See* **4140**.

3029. Butterworth, Richard. The Library goes live! EDS (68:2) 2006, 26–7. (Vaughan Williams Memorial Library online.)

3030. Cherry, Randall. Ethel Waters: 'long, lean, lanky mama'. *In* (pp. 264–82) **3086**.

3031. Cohen, Norm. Folk music: a regional exploration. Westport, CT; London: Greenwood Press, 2005. pp. xliii, 335. (Greenwood guides to American roots music.) Rev. by Gillian A. M. Mitchell in JAStud (40:3) 2006.

3032. Collins, Michael S. Biggie envy and the gangsta sublime. Callaloo (29:3) 2006, 910–38.

3033. Cowley, John. West Indies Blues: an historical overview, 1920s–1950s: Blues and music from the English-speaking West Indies. *In* (pp. 187–263) **3086**.

3034. Diner, Robyn. 'The other white meat': Princess Superstar, irony, sexuality, and Whiteness in Hip Hop. CRAS (36:2) 2006, 195–209.

3035. Duffin, Charles. Echoes of authority: audience and formula in the Scots ballad text. *In* (pp. 135–51) **3023**.

3036. Evans, David. High water everywhere: Blues and gospel commentary on the 1927 Mississippi River flood. *In* (pp. 3–75) **3086**.

3037. Fox, Aaron A. Real country: music and language in working-class culture. Durham, NC; London: Duke UP, 2004. pp. xv, 363. Rev. by Jonathan Silverman in AmQ (58:2) 2006, 545–50.

3038. Freeland, Tom; Smith, Chris. That Dry Creek Eaton clan: a North Mississippi murder ballad of the 1930s. *In* (pp. 126–50) **3086**.

3039. Graves, Michael P.; Fillingim, David (eds). More than precious memories: the rhetoric of Southern gospel music. Macon, GA: Mercer UP, 2004. pp. 310. Rev. by Gavin James Campbell in JSH (72:1) 2006, 217–19.

3040. Green, Richard Firth. F. J. Child and Mikhail Bakhtin. *In* (pp. 123–33) **3023**.

3041. Gregory, E. David. Victorian songhunters: the recovery and editing of English vernacular ballads and folk lyrics, 1820–1883. Lanham, MD; London: Scarecrow Press, 2006. pp. viii, 447.

3042. Grem, Darren E. 'The South got something to say': Atlanta's dirty South and the Southernization of Hip Hop America. SoCult (12:4) 2006, 55–73.

3043. Griffin, Benjamin. Moving tales: narrative drift in oral culture and scripted theater. *See* **5003**.

3044. Gussow, Adam. 'Where is the love?': racial violence, racial healing, and Blues communities. SoCult (12:4) 2006, 33–54.

3045. Heath, R. Scott. True heads: historicizing the Hip_Hop 'nation' in context. Callaloo (29:3) 2006, 846–66.

3046. Herzog, Mary Jean Ronan. Keeping old-time music alive: the contributions of David Holt to Appalachian music and cultures. NCarF (53:1) 2006, 19–25.

3047. Holland-Toll, Linda J. Bridges over and bedrock beneath: the role of ballads in Sharyn McCrumb's Ballad novels. *See* **17312**.

3048. Huber, Patrick. Red necks and red bandanas: Appalachian coal miners and the coloring of union identity, 1912–1936. WF (65:1/2) 2006, 195–210.

3049. Humphreys, Mary; Schofield, Derek. Charlotte Dann. EDS (68:2) 2006, 13–14. (*The Cuckoo and the Nightingale*.)

3050. Jones, Meta DuEwa. An interview with Michael Eric Dyson. *See* **18484**.

3051. Kitts, Lenore. Toni Morrison and 'Sis Joe': the musical heritage of Paul D. *See* **17619**.

3052. Knight, Stephen. Remembering Robin Hood: five centuries of outlaw ideology. EJES (10:2) 2006, 149–61.

3053. Law, Lyn. From Norfolk to Chester *via* Michigan and eBay. EDS (68:2) 2006, 20–1.

3054. McGeachy, Margaret G. Lonesome words: the vocal poetics of the Old English lament and the African American Blues song. *See* **3685**.

3055. McKean, Thomas A. The Stewarts of Fetterangus and literate oral tradition. *In* (pp. 181–207) **3023**.

3056. McNeil, Daniel. American demands, African treasures, mixed possibilities. *See* **18187**.

3057. Mitchell, Gillian A. M. Visions of diversity: cultural pluralism and the nation in the folk music revival movement of the United States and Canada, 1958–65. JAStud (40:3) 2006, 593–614.

3058. Monge, Luigi. Death by fire: African American popular music on the Natchez Rhythm Club fire. *In* (pp. 76–107) **3086**.

3059. Oliver, Paul. *Lookin' for the Bully*: an enquiry into a song and its story. *In* (pp. 108–25) **3086**.

3060. Onderdonk, Julian. Folk songs and hymn tunes. EDS (68:3) 2006, 18–19.

3061. Pavlic, Ed. Rap, soul, and the vortex at 33.3 rpm: Hip Hop's implements and African American modernisms. Callaloo (29:3) 2006, 956–68.

3062. Peterson, James. 'Dead Prezence': money and mortal themes in Hip Hop culture. Callaloo (29:3) 2006, 895–909.

3063. Phillips, Helen (ed.). Robin Hood: medieval and post-medieval. (Bibl. 2005, 3576.) Rev. by Christine Chism in TMR, Sept. 2006.

3064. Ponce, Martin Joseph. Langston Hughes's queer Blues. *See* **16488**.

3065. Porter, Gerald. Century-old folk song manuscript recovered. EDS (68:1) 2006, 28–9.

3066. Punday, Daniel. The Black Arts Movement and the genealogy of multimedia. *See* **14581**.

3067. Quinn, Eithne. Nuthin' but a 'G' thang: the culture and commerce of gangsta rap. New York: Columbia UP, 2005. pp. xiii, 251. (Popular cultures, everyday lives.) Rev. by John White in JAStud (40:1) 2006, 195.

3068. Reith, Sara. The Scottish Travellers' Project. EDS (68:4) 2006, 12–13.

3069. Rosenthal, Debra J. 'Hoods and the woods: rap music as environmental literature. JPC (39:4) 2006, 661–76.

3070. Russell, Ian. Working *with* tradition: towards a partnership model of fieldwork. Folklore (117:1) 2006, 15–32.

3071. —— Atkinson, David (eds). Folk song – tradition, revival and re-creation. (Bibl. 2004, 3750.) Rev. by Sandra Kerr in FMJ (9:1) 2006, 97–9; by C. J. Bearman in WF (65:3) 2006, 368–70.

3072. Scheiber, Andrew. *Jazz* and the future Blues: Toni Morrison's urban folk zone. *See* **17637**.

3073. Schneider, Matthew. Wordsworthian songcatching in America. Anthropoetics (11:2) 2005/06.

3074. Schofield, Derek. The fiddle tunes of John Lock. EDS (68:4) 2006, 10–11.

3075. —— The first week in August: fifty years of the Sidmouth Festival. Matlock: Sidmouth International Festival, 2004. pp. 224. Rev. by Paul Davenport in EDS (66:3) 2004, 28.

3076. —— Jean Orchard and Amy Birch. EDS (68:4) 2006, 8.

3077. —— Sowing the seeds: Cecil Sharp and Charles Marson in Somerset in 1903. FMJ (8:4) 2004, 484–512.

3078. —— *A Wager, a Wager.* EDS (68:4) 2006, 9.

3079. —— Will Atkinson's tune: *Ninety Three Not Out*. EDS (68:1) 2006, 30.

3080. Seal, Graham. A. L. Lloyd in Australia: some conclusions. FMJ (9:1) 2006, 56–71.

3081. Shatwell, Bob. A Pyle of tunes from Hampshire. EDS (68:3) 2006, 14–15. (Richard Pyle of Nether Wallop.)

3082. —— Sartin, Paul (eds). Hampshire dance tunes: country dance tunes from the Pyle family manuscript, 1822. *See* **3110**.

3083. Slagle, Judith Bailey. Ballads and folksongs of Scotland, Ireland and Wales: the collaboration of Joanna Baillie and George Thomson. *See* **9107**.

3084. Spady, James G. The fluoroscope of Brooklyn Hip Hop: Talib Kweli in conversation. Callaloo (29:3) 2006, 993–1011.

3085. Springer, Robert. On the electronic trail of Blues formulas. *In* (pp. 164–86) **3086**.

3086. —— (ed.). Nobody knows where the Blues come from: lyrics and history. Jackson; London: Mississippi UP, 2006. pp. ix, 303. (American made music.)

3087. Spurgeon, Alan L. Waltz the hall: the American play party. Jackson; London: Mississippi UP, 2005. pp. vii, 238. (American made music.) Rev. by Mavis Curtis in Folklore (117:1) 2006, 117–18; by Nancy Cassell McEntire in JSH (72:2) 2006, 496–7.

3088. Stewart, Pete. The day it daws: the Lowland Scots bagpipe and its music 1400 to 1715. Ashby: White House Tune Books, 2005. pp. 98.

3089. Stewart, Susan. The ballad in *Wuthering Heights*. *See* **9222**.

3090. Van Rijn, Guido. Coolidge's Blues: African American Blues songs on Prohibition, migration, unemployment, and Jim Crow. *In* (pp. 151–63) **3086**.

3091. Vinson, Duncan. 'As far from secular, operatic, rag-time, and jig melodies as is possible': religion and the resurgence of interest in *The Sacred Harp*, 1895–1911. JAF (119:474) 2006, 413–43.

3092. Walsh, Robert. An interview with Saul Williams. Callaloo (29:3) 2006, 728–36. (Hip Hop culture.)

3093. White, Shane; White, Graham. The sounds of slavery: discovering African American history through songs, sermons, and speech. Boston, MA: Beacon Press, 2005. pp. xxii, 241. Rev. by Helen Bradley Foster in JAH (92:4) 2006, 1426–7; by Mark M. Smith in JSH (72:3) 2006, 667–9; by James Miller in JAStud (40:3) 2006, 684–5.

3094. Wolfe, Charles K.; Akenson, James E. (eds). Country music goes to war. (Bibl. 2005, 3597.) Rev. by Jolie Jenson in JSH (72:2) 2006, 506–7.

3095. Wood, Peter. John Barleycorn: the evolution of a folk-song family. FMJ (8:4) 2004, 438–55.

3096. Yates, Michael; Roud, Steve. Alice E. Gillington: dweller on the roughs. FMJ (9:1) 2006, 72–94.

3097. Yates, Mike. Why gypsies? Why Travellers? EDS (68:4) 2006, 6–7.

3098. —— Taylor, Malcolm. *The Seeds of Love*. EDS (68:1) 2006, 13.

DANCE AND DRAMA

3099. Cutting, John. History and the morris dance: a look at morris dancing from its earliest days until 1850. Alton, Hants.: Dance Books, 2005. pp. 204. Rev. by Mike Heaney in EDS (68:2) 2006, 40.

3100. Goldgar, Anne; Frost, Robert I. (eds). Institutional culture in early modern society. *See* **728**.

3101. Heaney, Michael. The earliest reference to the morris dance? *See* **1585**.

3102. Law, Lyn. From Norfolk to Chester *via* Michigan and eBay. *See* **3053**.

3103. Marshall, John. Gathering in the name of the outlaw: REED and Robin Hood. *In* (pp. 65–84) **3904**.

3104. Morgan, Victor. A ceremonious society: an aspect of institutional power in early modern Norwich. *In* (pp. 132–63) **728**.

3105. Neal, Lucy. The not quite forgotten Mary Neal. EDS (68:4) 2006, 22–3. (Morris dancing.)

3106. Schofield, Derek. Ceilidh roots. EDS (68:1) 2006, 16–20.

3107. —— The first week in August: fifty years of the Sidmouth Festival. *See* **3075**.

3108. —— Gypsy step-dancing. EDS (68:4) 2006, 16–17.

3109. —— A smaller Pyle of dances from Hampshire. EDS (68:3) 2006, 16. (Richard Pyle of Nether Wallop.)

3110. Shatwell, Bob; Sartin, Paul (eds). Hampshire dance tunes: country dance tunes from the Pyle family manuscript, 1822. Purbrook, Hants.: Hobgoblin, 2006. pp. 64. Rev. by Gavin Atkin in EDS (68:3) 2006, 36–7.

3111. Spurgeon, Alan L. Waltz the hall: the American play party. *See* **3087**.

3112. Wearing, Sally. Morris women not women's morris. EDS (68:4) 2006, 24–5.

CUSTOM AND BELIEF

3113. Allen, David E.; Hatfield, Gabrielle. Medicinal plants in folk tradition: an ethnobotany of Britain & Ireland. Portland, OR; Cambridge: Timber Press, 2004. pp. 431. Rev. by Roy Vickery in FolkL (44) 2005/06, 157.

3114. Bain, Darrell. Life on Santa Claus Lane. *See* **14529**.

3115. Bath, Jo; Newton, John. 'Sensible proof of spirits': ghost belief during the later seventeenth century. Folklore (117:1) 2006, 1–14.

3116. Bowman, Marion. The Holy Thorn ceremony: revival, rivalry and civil religion in Glastonbury. Folklore (117:2) 2006, 123–40.

3117. Buccola, Regina. Fairies, fractious women, and the old faith: fairy lore in early modern British drama and culture. *See* **5992**.

3118. Cashman, Ray. Dying the good death: wake and funeral customs in County Tyrone. NewHR (10:2) 2006, 9–25.

3119. Chamberlain, Mary. Old wives' tales: the history of remedies, charms and spells. Stroud; Charleston, SC: Tempus, 2006. pp. 256. Rev. by Christopher Lawrence in TLS, 1 Dec. 2006, 30–1.

3120. Cohoon, Lorinda. Festive citizenships: Independence celebrations in New England children's periodicals and series books. *See* **1072**.

3121. Coumont, Jean-Pierre. Demonology and witchcraft: an annotated bibliography: with related works on magic, medicine &c. Utrecht: Hes & de Graaf, 2004. pp. x, 585, lxxx. Rev. by Carl Spadoni in PBSA (100:1) 2006, 139–40.

3122. Cruikshank, Julie. Do glaciers listen? Local knowledge, colonial encounters, and social imagination. Vancouver: UBC Press, 2005. pp. xii, 312. (Brenda and David McLean Canadian studies.) Rev. by Jen Hill in CanL (191) 2006, 161–2.

3123. DiGirolamo, Vincent. Newsboy funerals: tales of sorrow and solidarity in urban Amerca. *In* (pp. 156–88) **3157**.

3124. Fischer-Lichte, Erika. Theatre, sacrifice, ritual: exploring forms of political theatre. (Bibl. 2005, 3632.) Rev. by Ramona Mosse in TJ (58:2) 2006, 372–3.

3125. Franks, Benjamin (ed.). The quest for *The Wicker Man*: history, folklore and pagan perspectives. *See* **13126**.

3126. Fudge, Erica. Saying nothing concerning the same: on dominion, purity, and meat in early modern England. *In* (pp. 70–86) **4588**.

3127. Gaudet, Marcia. Ribbon pulls in wedding cakes: tracing a New Orleans tradition. Folklore (117:1) 2006, 87–96.

3128. Gibson, Marion. Retelling Salem stories: gender politics and witches in American culture. *See* **13309**.

3129. Gilbert, Sandra M. Death's door: modern dying and the ways we grieve. *See* **11908**.

3130. Godbeer, Richard. Escaping Salem: the other witch hunt of 1692. New York: OUP, 2005. pp. xiv, 177. (New narratives in American history.) Rev. by Amy M. E. Morris in JAStud (40:3) 2006, 663.

3131. Jackson, Kathy Merlock. Petals and patriarchy: the flower girl in American weddings. *In* (pp. 141–55) **3157**.

3132. Johnstone, Nathan. The Devil and demonism in early modern England. Cambridge; New York: CUP, 2006. pp. x, 334. Rev. by James Sharpe in TLS, 9 June 2006, 6.

3133. Keyworth, G. David. Was the vampire of the eighteenth century a unique type of undead-corpse? Folklore (117:3) 2006, 241–60.

3134. Lamb, Mary Ellen. The popular culture of Shakespeare, Spenser and Jonson. *See* **5095**.

3135. Lewis, Jayne Elizabeth. Spectral currencies in the air of reality: *A Journal of the Plague Year* and the history of apparitions. *See* **7721**.

3136. Lucas, John. Hospitality and the rural tradition: Bloomfield's *May-Day with the Muses*. *In* (pp. 113–41) **9141**.

3137. Miller, April. 'The hair that wasn't there before': demystifying monstrosity and menstruation in *Ginger Snaps* and *Ginger Snaps Unleashed*. *See* **19700**.

3138. Radford, Benjamin; Nickell, Joe. Lake monster mysteries: investigating the world's most elusive creatures. Foreword by Loren Coleman. Lexington: Kentucky UP, 2006. pp. xvii, 190. Rev. by Luke Powers in TFSB (62:1) 2006, 39–40.

3139. Ravalli, Richard. Cotton Mather, levitation, and a case for wonders in history. *See* **6947**.

3140. Roberts, Robin. New Orleans Mardi Gras and gender in three krewes: Rex, the Truck Parades, and Muses. WF (65:3) 2006, 303–28.

3141. Shamas, Laura. 'We three': the mythology of Shakespeare's Weird Sisters. *See* **5944**.

3142. Smith, J. B. Making sweet hay: a West Country custom in its wider context. FolkL (44) 2005/06, 7–29.

3143. Stanfield, Norman. May Day in New Westminster, British Columbia. CFMB (39:4) 2005/06, 1–6.

3144. Stewart, Susan. The ballad in *Wuthering Heights*. *See* **9222**.

3145. Taylor-Blake, Bonnie. Thank God it's not HMS *Friday*. FOAFN (64) 2006.

3146. Ward, David C. The Green Man: Walt Whitman and the Civil War. *See* **11587**.

3147. Wilby, Emma. Cunning folk and familiar spirits: shamanistic visionary traditions in early modern British witchcraft and magic. Brighton; Portland, OR: Sussex Academic Press, 2005. pp. xvi, 317. Rev. by Jacqueline Simpson in Folklore (117:3) 2006, 343–4.

3148. Wood, Juliette. Filming fairies: popular film, audience response and meaning in contemporary fairy lore. *See* **6002**.

MATERIAL CULTURE, TECHNIQUES AND OCCUPATIONS, FOLK ARTS AND CRAFTS

3149. Fenech, Natalino. Lark mirrors: from tools to folk art. FolkL (44) 2005/06, 30–47.

3150. Green, Archie. Perambulating scrapbooks and saloon-sawdust sifters: ghosts along the labor/material culture trail. WF (65:1/2) 2006, 31–46.

3151. Kosut, Mary. An ironic fad: the commodification and consumption of tattoos. JPC (39:6) 2006, 1035–48.

3152. Negus, Tina. Daniel in the den of lions: early medieval carvings and their origins. FolkL (44) 2005/06, 63–77.

3153. Stoneley, Peter. Sewing in Concord. *See* **11452**.

3154. van Keuren, Luise. The American girl at her sampler, *ca* 1630–1850: inspiring a feminine ideal. *In* (pp. 81–92) **3157**.

3155. Weaver, William Woys. The dark side of culinary ephemera: the portrayal of African Americans. Gastronomica (6:3) 2006, 76–81.

CHILDREN'S TRADITIONS

3156. Curtis, Mavis. A sailor went to sea: theme and variations. FMJ (8:4) 2004, 421–37.

3157. Jackson, Kathy Merlock (ed.). Rituals and patterns in children's lives. Madison; London: Wisconsin UP, 2005. pp. x, 285.

3158. McMinn, Jamie; Pickrell, H. Alan. The many faces of childhood: costume and ritualized behavior. *In* (pp. 215–31) **3157**.

3159. Oravec, Jo Ann. From gigapets to Internet: childhood technology rituals as commodities. *In* (pp. 252–68) **3157**.

3160. Roberts, Chris. Heavy words lightly thrown: the reason behind the rhyme. New York: Gotham, 2005. pp. xx, 202. Rev. by Michael Joseph in CLAQ (31:2) 2006, 207–9.

3161. Sugarman, Sally. Playing the game: rituals in children's games. *In* (pp. 124–38) **3157**.

3162. Sumpter, Caroline. Joining the 'crusade against the giants': Keir Hardie's fairy tales and the Socialist child reader. *See* **8881**.

3163. Thomas, Sabrina. The ritual of doll play: implications of understanding children's conceptualization of race. *In* (pp. 111–23) **3157**.

3164. Tuominen, Anne. The endurance of ethnic family rituals. *In* (pp. 17–33) **3157**.

3165. Zirker, Angelika. 'Alice was not surprised': (un)surprises in Lewis Carroll's Alice books. *See* **9435**.

ENGLISH LITERATURE

GENERAL LITERARY STUDIES

GENERAL

3166. Anon. Selected recent acquisitions briefly noted. *See* **288**.

3167. Abbott, John L. (ed.). The selected essays of Donald Greene. (Bibl. 2005, 3688.) Rev. by Robert Murray Davis in EWN (36:1) 2005; by Gloria Sybil Gross in ECS (39:4) 2006, 577–8; by Jack Lynch in AJ (17) 2006, 465–9.

3168. Allen, Brooke. Artistic license: three centuries of good writing and bad behavior. Chicago, IL: Dee, 2004. pp. xi, 244. Rev. by Matt Sturrock in BkCan (34:7) 2005, 27.

3169. Altieri, Charles. The particulars of rapture: an aesthetics of the affects. (Bibl. 2005, 3691.) Rev. by Jeff Westover in Style (39:4) 2005, 489–91; by Rebecca Wanzo in AL (78:3) 2006, 650–2.

3170. Alvarez, Al. The writer's voice. New York; London: Norton, 2005. pp. 128. Rev. by Michael D. Hurley in TLS, 18 Mar. 2005, 25; by Todd Swift in BkCan (34:7) 2005, 31–2; by Lynnell Edwards in GaR (59:4) 2005, 956–60.

3171. Annas, Pamela J.; Rosen, Robert C. Literature and society: an introduction to fiction, poetry, drama, nonfiction. (Bibl. 2000, 3716.) Upper Saddle River, NJ: Pearson / Prentice Hall, 2006. pp. xxx, 1564. (Fourth ed.: first ed. 1990.)

3172. Appelbaum, Robert. Aguecheek's beef, Belch's hiccup, and other gastronomic interjections: literature, culture, and food among the early moderns. Chicago, IL; London: Chicago UP, 2006. pp. xii, 375.

3173. Arac, Jonathan. Global and Babel: two perspectives on language in American literature. ESQ (50:1–3) 2004, 95–119.

3174. Arapoglou, Eleftheria; Kirtunç, Ayse Lahur; Erdem, Murat. Introduction. *In* (pp. 1–11) **3307**.

3175. Attridge, Derek. The singularity of literature. (Bibl. 2004, 3843.) Rev. by Paul J. Hecht in ShB (23:4) 2005, 121–3; by Lucy O'Meara in TexP (19:3) 2005, 379–82; by Wallace Martin in CL (58:3) 2006, 241–55.

3176. Baker, Ronald L. Folklore and literary relations: some approaches. *See* **2947**.

3177. Bald, Margaret. Literature suppressed on religious grounds. *See* **641**.

3178. Balkun, Mary McAleer. The American counterfeit: authenticity and identity in American literature and culture. Tuscaloosa; London: Alabama UP, 2006. pp. xii, 181. (Studies in American literary realism and naturalism.)

3179. Bamforth, Iain. The future of the walk. PNRev (31:5) 2005, 15–17.

3180. —— A lance for hire: four hundred years of *Don Quixote*. PNRev (32:1) 2005, 15–17.

3181. Bancheri, Salvatore; Sayegh, Danièle Yssa (eds). Cross-cultural relations and exile. Ottawa; New York: Legas, 2005. pp. 282.

3182. Barber, Richard. The Holy Grail: imagination and belief. (Bibl. 2005, 3701.) Rev. by Dhira B. Mahoney in Arthuriana (16:4) 2006, 78–80; by Janina P. Traxler in Arthuriana (16:4) 2006, 81–2; by Anne Berthelot in Spec (81:3) 2006, 807–8.

3183. Barnes, Geraldine; Singleton, Gabrielle (eds). Travel and travellers from Bede to Dampier. Newcastle upon Tyne: Cambridge Scholars Press, 2005. pp. vi, 247.

3184. Barnes, Katherine; Jones, Jan Lloyd (eds). Words for their own sake: the pursuit of literature in an economic rationalist world. Melbourne: Australian Scholarly Pubs, 2004. pp. xvii, 152. Rev. by Brigid Rooney in Southerly (65:1) 2005, 168–71.

3185. Basbanes, Nicholas A. Every book its reader: the power of the printed word to stir the world. New York: HarperCollins, 2005. pp. xviii, 360, (plates) 16.

3186. Bassnett, Susan; Bush, Peter (eds). The translator as writer. London; New York: Continuum, 2006. pp. x, 228.

3187. Battaglia, Beatrice. La critica alla cultura occidentale nella letteratura distopica inglese. Ravenna: Longo, 2006. pp. 144. (Il portico: materiali letterari, 136.)

3188. Battersby, James L. Narrativity, self, and self-representation. Narrative (14:1) 2006, 27–44.

3189. Benson, Charles; Fitzpatrick, Siobhán (eds). That woman! Studies in Irish bibliography: a Festschrift for Mary 'Paul' Pollard. *See* **648**.

3190. Berenbaum, May. On the lives of insects in literature. *In* (pp. 3–12) **3203**.

3191. Bermann, Sandra; Wood, Michael (eds). Nation, language, and the ethics of translation. Princeton, NJ; Oxford: Princeton UP, 2005. pp. x, 413. (Translation / transnation.) Rev. by Susan Bernofsky in MLN (120:5) 2005, 1235–9.

3192. Białas, Zbigniew. The body wall: somatics of travelling and discursive practices. New York; Frankfurt: Lang, 2006. pp. 162. (Literary and cultural theory, 24.)

3193. Bigliazzi, Silvia; Wood, Sharon (eds). Collaboration in the arts from the Middle Ages to the present. Aldershot; Burlington, VT: Ashgate, 2006. pp. xi, 221. (Studies in European cultural transition, 35.)

3194. Boehmer, Elleke. Colonial and postcolonial literature: migrant metaphors. (Bibl. 1998, 3613.) Oxford; New York: OUP, 2005. pp. 351. (Second ed.: first ed. 1995.)

3195. Bomarito, Jessica; Hunter, Jeffrey W. (eds). Feminism in literature: a Gale critical companion. Farmington Hills, MI: Thomson/Gale, 2005. 6 vols. pp. 3000.

3196. Bosmajian, Haig A. Burning books. *See* **653**.

3197. Bosworth, David. Conscientious thinking: fundamentalism, nihilism, and the problem of value during the demise of the scientific worldview. GaR (60:3/4) 2006, 712–39.

3198. Bouchet, Claire. Le meurtre de soi: petite histoire du suicide féminin. Cycnos (23:2) 2006, 127–43.

3199. Boucquey, Thierry (gen. ed.). Encyclopedia of world writers. New York: Facts on File, 2005. 3 vols. pp. 1440. (Facts on File library of world literature.)

3200. Brennan, Stephen C. Donald Pizer and the study of American literary Naturalism. StAN (1:1/2) 2006, 3–14.

3201. Brenner, Gerry. Performative criticism: experiments in reader response. (Bibl. 2004, 3859.) Rev. by Ebbe Klitgård in EngS (87:3) 2006, 378.

3202. Brotton, Joyce D. Revising life through literature: dialogical change from the Reformation through postmodernism. Lanham, MD; London: Scarecrow Press, 2006. pp. viii, 187.

3203. Brown, Eric C. (ed.). Insect poetics. Minneapolis; London: Minnesota UP, 2006. pp. xxiii, 382.

3204. Brown, Richard. Joyce's Englishman: 'that het'rogeneous thing' from Stephen's Blake and Dowland to Defoe's 'true-born Englishman'. *In* (pp. 33–49) **16695**.

3205. Brulotte, Gaëtan; Phillips, John (eds). Encyclopedia of erotic literature. London; New York: Routledge, 2006. pp. 1616.

3206. Burger, Mary, *et al.* (eds). Biting the error: writers explore narrative. (Bibl. 2005, 3722.) Rev. by Tracy Whalen in CanL (191) 2006, 143–5.

3207. Burnard, Lou; O'Keeffe, Katherine O'Brien; Unsworth, John (eds). Electronic textual editing. *See* **426**.

3208. Carey, John. What good are the arts? (Bibl. 2005, 3727.) Rev. by Michael Dirda in BkW, 29 Jan. 2006, 15.

3209. Carter, Margaret L. Different blood: the vampire as alien. Winona, MN: Amber Quill Press, 2004. pp. 158. Rev. by Jim Holte in JFA (15:4) 2004, 374–6.

3210. Cartwright, John H.; Baker, Brian. Literature and science: social impact and interaction. Santa Barbara, CA: ABC-CLIO, 2005. pp. xxi, 471. (Science and society.)

3211. Casanova, Pascale. The world republic of letters. Trans. by M. B. DeBevoise. (Bibl. 2005, 3729.) Rev. by Aldon Lynn Nielsen in AmBR (27:4) 2006, 31–2.

3212. Chisholm, Dianne. Queer constellations: subcultural space in the wake of the city. (Bibl. 2005, 3733.) Rev. by Melanie Hawthorne in Mod/Mod (13:4) 2006, 763–5.

3213. Chiwengo, Ngwarsungo. The stepsister and the clan: when the native teaches African American literature. *In* (pp. 154–69) **20098**.

3214. Clay, Cynthia Joyce. Vector theory and the plot structures of literature and drama. North Charleston, SC: Oestara, 2005. pp. 225.

3215. Conley, Tim; Cain, Stephen. Encyclopedia of fictional and fantastic languages. Foreword by Ursula K. Le Guin. Westport, CT; London: Greenwood Press, 2006. pp. xxv, 236.

3216. Conliffe, Mark. On isolation. MidQ (47:2) 2006, 115–30.

3217. Cook, Eleanor. Enigmas and riddles in literature. Cambridge; New York: CUP, 2006. pp. 291. Rev. by Lisa Goldfarb in WSJ (30:2) 2006, 231–3; by Katherine Knight in Folklore (117:3) 2006, 345–6.

3218. Corbella, Walter. Strategies of resistance and the problem of ambiguity in Azar Nafisi's *Reading 'Lolita' in Tehran*. *See* **19960**.

3219. Cottom, Daniel. Unhuman culture. Philadelphia: Pennsylvania UP, 2006. pp. xii, 195. (Misanthropy in literature.)

3220. Couderc, Gilles. 'Faisons un opéra!': les opéras pour enfants de Benjamin Britten. *See* **14497**.

3221. Cox, Stephen. The New Testament and literature: a guide to literary patterns. Chicago, IL: Open Court, 2006. pp. 394.

3222. Crowley, Tony. Wars of words: the politics of language in Ireland, 1537–2004. Oxford; New York: OUP, 2005. pp. viii, 253.

3223. Csicsila, Joseph. Canons by consensus: critical trends and American literature anthologies. Foreword by Tom Quirk. (Bibl. 2005, 3739.) Rev. by Joseph Helminski in AL (78:2) 2006, 413–15.

3224. Daileader, Celia R. Racism, misogyny, and the Othello myth: interracial couples from Shakespeare to Spike Lee. Cambridge; New York: CUP, 2005. pp. ix, 256. Rev. by Ayanna Thompson in ShQ (57:3) 2006, 361–3.

3225. Damrau, Peter. The reception of English Puritan literature in Germany. Leeds: Maney for the Modern Humanities Research Assn, 2006. pp. 214. (MHRA texts and dissertations, 66.) (Bithell series of dissertations, 29.)

3226. Davis, Hugh H. I was a teenage classic: literary adaptation in turn-of-the-millennium teen films. *See* **12465**.

3227. de Asúa, Miguel. Ciencia y literatura: un relato histórico. Buenos Aires: Eudeba, 2004. pp. 206. Rev. by Pablo Brescia in Isis (96:4) 2005, 643–4.

3228. Dente, Carla, *et al.* (eds). Proteus: the language of metamorphosis. Aldershot; Burlington, VT: Ashgate, 2005. pp. xiii, 289. (Studies in European cultural transition.) Rev. by Jeremy Tambling in MLR (101:3) 2006, 816.

3229. de Paulo, Craig J. N.; Messina, Patrick; Stier, Marc (eds). Ambiguity in the Western mind. (Bibl. 2005, 3748.) Rev. by James McGuirk in ACPQ (80:2) 2006, 298–302.

3230. Desblache, Lucile (ed.). Écrire l'animal aujourd'hui. Clermont-Ferrand: Presses Universitaires Blaise-Pascal, 2006. pp. 287. (Cahiers de recherche du CRLMC, Univ. Blaise-Pascal.)

3231. Desmond, John M.; Hawkes, Peter. Adaptation: studying film and literature. *See* **12471**.

3232. Dickerson, Matthew T.; O'Hara, David. From Homer to Harry Potter: a handbook on myth and fantasy. Grand Rapids, MI: Brazos Press, 2006. pp. 272. Rev. by David Bratman in Mythprint (43:8) 2006, 11–13.

3233. Dirda, Michael. Book by book: notes on reading and life. New York: Holt, 2006. pp. xvii, 170. Rev. by Sophie Ratcliffe in TLS, 21 July 2006, 9–10; by Chris Byrd in ANCW (195:12) 2006, 26–7.

3234. Drabble, Margaret (ed.). The Oxford companion to English literature. (Bibl. 2002, 3228.) Oxford; New York: OUP, 2006. pp. viii, 1172. (Sixth ed.: first ed. 1932.)

3235. Dufallo, Basil; McCracken, Peggy (eds). Dead lovers: erotic bonds and the study of premodern Europe. Ann Arbor: Michigan UP, 2006. pp. viii, 172.

3236. Duperray, Max. Londres, promenade sous un ciel couvert. Paris: Houdiard, 2005. pp. 214. (Littérature anglaise.) Rev. by Jean Dobrinsky in EA (59:2) 2006, 245–6.

3237. DuPlessis, Rachel Blau. The pink guitar: writing as feminist practice. (Bibl. 2000, 26382.) Tuscaloosa; London: Alabama UP, 2006. pp. viii, 208. (Modern and contemporary poetics.) (Second ed.: first ed. 1990.)

3238. Durrani, Osman, *et al.* Faust: icon of modern culture. Mountfield: Helm Information, 2004. pp. xii, 444. (Icons of modern culture.) Rev. by Theodore Ziolkowski in MLR (101:1) 2006, 299–300.

3239. Eagleton, Terry. Sweet violence: the idea of the tragic. (Bibl. 2004, 3899.) Rev. by Graham Ward in LitTheol (19:2) 2005, 100–11; by Srila Nayak in Style (39:2) 2005, 226–31.

3240. Edwards, Grace Toney; Asbury, JoAnn Aust; Cox, Ricky L. (eds). A handbook to Appalachia: an introduction to the region. Knoxville: Tennessee UP, 2006. pp. xvi, 279. Rev. by Karina McGill in KenPR (21) 2006, 71–2.

3241. Edwards, Philip. Pilgrimage and literary tradition. (Bibl. 2005, 3759.) Rev. by Tom MacFaul in NQ (53:3) 2006, 367–8.

3242. Eisenhauer, Robert. The fate of translation. New York; Frankfurt: Lang, 2006. pp. xii, 258. (Studies on themes and motifs in literature, 82.)

3243. Elias, Camelia. The fragment: towards a history and poetics of a performative genre. (Bibl. 2005, 3762.) Rev. by Gray Kochhar-Lindgren in SubStance (110) 2006, 172–8; by Polina MacKay in JAStud (40:1) 2006, 170–1.

3244. Ervin, Hazel Arnett. The handbook of African American literature. (Bibl. 2004, 3907.) Rev. by Louis J. Kern in JAStud (40:2) 2006, 426–7.

3245. Eshelman, Raoul. After postmodernism: performatism in literature. *See* **20053**.

3246. Fadiman, Anne (ed.). Rereadings. New York: Farrar, Straus, & Giroux, 2005. pp. xxi, 244. Rev. by Robert Murray Davis in EWN (37:1) 2006; by Nancy Carr in CommRev (4:4) 2006, 55.

3247. Fazzini, Marco (ed.). *Alba literaria*: a history of Scottish literature. Venice: Amos, 2006. pp. xxiii, 825.

3248. Figueredo, D. H. (ed.). Encyclopedia of Caribbean literature. Westport, CT; London: Greenwood Press, 2006. 2 vols. pp. xxix, 1–478; xix, 479–962.

3249. Flanders, Julia. The Women Writers Project: a digital anthology. *In* (pp. 138–49) **426**.

3250. Flora, Joseph M.; Vogel, Amber (eds); Giemza, Bryan (asst ed.). Southern writers: a new biographical dictionary. Baton Rouge: Louisiana State UP, 2006. pp. xxvi, 468. (Southern literary studies.) Rev. by Robert S. Rust in VQR (82:4) 2006, 268–9.

3251. Fludernik, Monika. The metaphorics and metonymics of carcerality: reflections on imprisonment as source and target domain in literary texts. EngS (86:3) 2005, 226–44.

3252. Fořt, Bohumil. Are fictional worlds really possible? A short contribution to their semantics. Style (40:3) 2006, 189–97.

3253. Fowler, Robert (ed.). The Cambridge companion to Homer. Cambridge; New York: CUP, 2004. pp. xvii, 419. (Cambridge companions to literature.) Rev. by David Hopkins in TransLit (15:1) 2006, 97–104.

3254. Fresonke, Kris. Is nature necessary? AmLH (18:1) 2006, 129–43 (review-article).

3255. Frow, John. Genre. London; New York: Routledge, 2006. pp. vi, 171. (New critical idiom.)

3256. Garry, Jane; El-Shamy, Hasan (eds). Archetypes and motifs in folklore. Armonk, NY: Sharpe, 2005. pp. xxxv, 515. Rev. by Ruth B. Bottigheimer in LU (30:2) 2006, 265–7.

3257. Gass, William H. A temple of texts: essays. New York: Knopf, 2006. pp. x, 418. Rev. by Michael Dirda in BkW, 19 Feb. 2006, 15.

3258. Gatta, John. Making nature sacred: literature, religion, and environment in America from the Puritans to the present. (Bibl. 2005, 3780.) Rev. by Andrew Battista in ISLE (12:2) 2005, 269–70; by Charles H. Lippy in CHist (74:4) 2005, 889–91; by Dana Phillips in AL (78:3) 2006, 648–50; by Joy Porter in JAStud (40:2) 2006, 431–2.

3259. Genet, Jacqueline; Fierobe, Claude. La littérature irlandaise. (Bibl. 2005, 3783.) Rev. by Jean Brihault in EA (59:2) 2006, 246–7.

3260. Gibbons, Luke. Gaelic gothic: race, colonization, and Irish culture. Galway: Arlen House, 2004. pp. 96. (Research papers in Irish studies.) Rev. by Conor McCarthy in FDR (1) 2005, 267–8.

3261. Gigante, Denise. Taste: a literary history. (Bibl. 2005, 3784.) Rev. by Jane Stabler in WordsC (36:4) 2005, 155–6; by Jody Greene in ECent (47:1) 2006, 85–9; by Peter Melville in RomNet (44) 2006; by Gillen D'Arcy Wood in ERR (17:5) 2006, 638–40; by Ronald LeBlanc in Gastronomica (6:4) 2006, 110–11.

3262. Gilbar, Steven; Stewart, Dean (eds). Not forgotten: American writers remember the lives of literary mentors, friends & rivals. (Bibl. 2003, 3751.) Boston, MA: Godine, 2006. pp. xii, 227. (Second ed.: first ed. 2002.) (Orig. pub. as *Published & Perished: Memoria, Eulogies and Remembrances of American Writers*.)

3263. Gill, R. B. Why comedy laughs: the shape of laughter and comedy. LitIm (8:2) 2006, 233–50.

3264. Gilman, Sander L.; Zhou, Xun (eds). Smoke: a global history of smoking. London: Reaktion, 2004. pp. 408. Rev. by Keith Miller in TLS, 11 Feb. 2005, 3–4.

3265. Glancy, Diane. In-between places: essays. (Bibl. 2005, 3786.) Rev. by Brewster E. Fitz in GPQ (26:3) 2006, 223.

3266. Goi, Simona; Dolan, Frederick M. (eds). Between terror and freedom: politics, philosophy, and fiction speak of modernity. Lanham, MD: Lexington, 2006. pp. xxvi, 377.

3267. Going, William T. 'Dr Eliot's five-foot shelf of books': toward a centennial of the Harvard Classics. PLL (42:2) 2006, 210–19.

3268. Gonzalez, Alexander G. (ed.). Irish women writers: an A-to-Z guide. Westport, CT; London: Greenwood Press, 2006. pp. xii, 348.

3269. Goodman, Ralph. Privilege, loss and gain in utopian spaces. ESA (48:1) 2005, 19–36.

3270. Grabes, Herbert; Viereck, Wolfgang (eds). The wider scope of English: papers in English language and literature from the Bamberg Conference of the International Association of University Professors of English. *See* **1187**.

3271. Gray, Richard. Writing American literary history. JAStud (40:2) 2006, 399–411 (review-article).

3272. Hadas, Rachel. Notes from the kingdom of illness. LitIm (8:2) 2006, 257–75.

3273. Halperin, David M. The best lover. *In* (pp. 8–21) **3235**.

3274. Hanafin, Patrick; Gearey, Adam; Brooker, Joseph (eds). Law and literature. (Bibl. 2004, 3936.) Rev. by Maria Grahn-Farley in LawL (17:2) 2005, 269–78.

3275. Handley, William R.; Lewis, Nathaniel (eds). True west: authenticity and the American West. (Bibl. 2004, 3938.) Rev. by Lee Clark Mitchell in WAL (40:1) 2005, 88–97; by Luigi Fidanza in JAStud (39:1) 2005, 125.

3276. Harmon, William. A handbook to literature. (Bibl. 1996, 3860.) Upper Saddle River, NJ: Prentice Hall, 2006. pp. ix, 675. (Tenth ed.: first ed. 1960.)

3277. Hart, Jonathan. Interpreting cultures: literature, religion and the human sciences. Basingstoke; New York: Palgrave Macmillan, 2006. pp. xi, 340.

3278. Haskin, Dayton. Donne's afterlife. *In* (pp. 233–46) **6718**.

3279. Hauerwas, Stanley; Wood, Ralph. How the Church became invisible: a Christian reading of American literary tradition. ReLit (38:1) 2006, 61–93.

3280. Helmling, Steven. A martyr to happiness: why Adorno matters. KR (28:4) 2006, 156–72.

3281. Highmore, Ben. Cityscapes: cultural readings in the material and symbolic city. Basingstoke; New York: Palgrave Macmillan, 2005. pp. xiv, 178. Rev. by Peter Kalliney in Mod/Mod (13:4) 2006, 747–54.

3282. Hines, John. Voices in the past: English literature and archaeology. (Bibl. 2004, 3949.) Rev. by Hugh Magennis in EngS (86:5) 2005, 461–3.

3283. Howard, Richard. A lecture on a certain mistrust of the past among young writers. *See* **17486**.

3284. Hutcheon, Linda. A theory of adaptation. London; New York: Routledge, 2006. pp. xviii, 232.

3285. Jahner, Elaine A. Spaces of the mind: narrative and community in the American West. (Bibl. 2005, 3813.) Rev. by Franci Washburn in SAIL (18:2) 2006, 135–8.

3286. Jamison, Anne. Collaboration *v.* imitation: authorship and the law. LawL (18:2) 2006, 199–224.

3287. JANES, REGINA. Losing our heads: beheadings in literature and culture. New York; London: New York UP, 2005. pp. xv, 255. Rev. by Denise Gigante in EC (56:3) 2006, 280–5.

3288. JASPER, DAVID. The sacred desert: religion, literature, art, and culture. (Bibl. 2005, 3815.) Rev. by Elena Volkova in LitTheol (19:2) 2005, 186–7; by Richard Holloway in LitTheol (19:2) 2005, 187–8; by Heather Walton in LitTheol (19:2) 2005, 188–90.

3289. JAVADI, HASAN. Persian literary influence on English literature: with special reference to the nineteenth century. *See* **8401**.

3290. JEFFERS, JENNIFER M. Britain colonized: Hollywood's appropriation of British literature. *See* **12560**.

3291. JOHNSON, PAUL. Creators: from Chaucer and Dürer to Picasso and Disney. New York: HarperCollins, 2006. pp. 310. Rev. by Sara Sklaroff in BkW, 30 Apr. 2006, 8.

3292. JOHNS-PUTRA, ADELINE. The history of the epic. Basingstoke; New York: Palgrave Macmillan, 2006. pp. viii, 259. (Palgrave histories of literature.)

3293. JUSTMAN, STEWART. Literature and human equality. Evanston, IL: Northwestern UP, 2006. pp. 167. (Rethinking theory.)

3294. KAFALENOS, EMMA. Narrative causalities. Columbus: Ohio State UP, 2006. pp. xiii, 247. (Theory and interpretation of narrative.)

3295. KALAGA, WOJCIECH (ed.). The same, the other, the third. Katowice: Silesia UP, 2004. pp. 275. (Prace naukowe Uniwersytetu Ślaskiego w Katowicach, 2231.)

3296. KAMMEN, MICHAEL. A time to every purpose: the four seasons in American culture. (Bibl. 2005, 3822.) Rev. by Jack Flynn in MatC (38:1) 2006, 103–5; by George Conyne in JAStud (40:1) 2006, 179.

3297. KARLIN, DANIEL. Proust's English. Oxford; New York: OUP, 2005. pp. xii, 229.

3298. KATANSKI, AMELIA V. Learning to write 'Indian': the boarding-school experience and American Indian literature. Norman: Oklahoma UP, 2005. pp. xiii, 274. Rev. by Raphael Comprone in AICRJ (30:3) 2005, 154–7; by Gilbert Sakiestewa in JArizH (47:4) 2006, 397–8.

3299. KELLEHER, MARGARET; O'LEARY, PHILIP (eds). The Cambridge history of Irish literature. Cambridge; New York: CUP, 2006. 2 vols. pp. 1286. Rev. by Lucy McDiarmid in TLS, 6 Oct. 2006, 3–4; by Alexandra Poulain in EREA (4:2) 2006.

3300. KELLY, STUART. The book of lost books. (Bibl. 2005, 3824.) Rev. by Joe Queenan in NYTB, 30 Apr. 2006, 12; by Robert N. Matuozzi in SHARP (15:4) 2006, 11; by Phyllis Reeve in Amphora (143) 2006, 20–1.

3301. KENNEDY, ROBERT P.; PAFFENROTH, KIM; DOODY, JOHN (eds). Augustine and literature. Lanham, MD: Lexington, 2006. pp. vi, 414. (Augustine in conversation.)

3302. KHATCHADOURIAN, H. The tragic protagonist and the meaning of suffering. *In* (pp. 97–121) **3394**.

3303. Kiberd, Declan. The Irish writer and the world. (Bibl. 2005, 3826.) Rev. by David Pierce in JJLS (20:1) 2006, 18–19; by Alice Hughes Kersnowski in SewR (114:3) 2006, xlix–li; by Vanina Jobert-Martini in EREA (4:2) 2006.

3304. Kiernan, Brian (ed.). Running wild: essays, fictions and memoirs presented to Michael Wilding. New Delhi: Manohar, 2004. pp. 306. (Sydney studies in society and culture, 22.) Rev. by Brigid Rooney in Southerly (65:1) 2005, 168–71.

3305. Kilfeather, Siobhán. Dublin: a cultural and literary history. Dublin: Liffey Press, 2005. pp. xii, 300.

3306. Kim, Heerak Christian. Key signifier as literary device: its definition and function in literature and media. Lewiston, NY; Lampeter: Mellen Press, 2006. pp. vi, 164.

3307. Kirtunç, Ayse Lahur; Arapoglou, Eleftheria; Erdem, Murat (eds). [City in (culture] in city): proceedings of the Ninth Cultural Studies Symposium, Ege University, Izmir, Turkey. Izmir: Ege Univ., 2005. pp. 244.

3308. Kivy, Peter. The performance of reading: an essay in the philosophy of literature. Oxford; Malden, MA: Blackwell, 2006. pp. xiii, 155. (New directions in aesthetics, 3.)

3309. Knight, Charles A. The literature of satire. (Bibl. 2004, 3972.) Rev. by Leon Guilhamet in ECF (18:2) 2006, 257–9; by David Reid in MLR (101:4) 2006, 1098–9; by Dustin Griffin in AJ (17) 2006, 426–8.

3310. Knight, Stephen. Remembering Robin Hood: five centuries of outlaw ideology. *See* **3052**.

3311. Konkle, Lincoln. Thornton Wilder and the Puritan narrative tradition. *See* **19154**.

3312. Kowalczyk Twarowski, Krzysztof. *Glebae adscripti*: troping place, region, and nature in America. New York; Frankfurt: Lang, 2005. pp. 183. (Literary and cultural theory, 23.)

3313. Kral, Françoise (ed.). Re-presenting otherness: mapping the colonial 'self', mapping the indigenous Other in the literatures of Australia and New Zealand: *actes de la journée d'études organisée à Paris X-Nanterre le 28 juin 2003*. Nanterre: Univ. X-Nanterre, 2005. pp. 202. (Confluences, 25.) Rev. by Lydia Wevers in ALS (22:3) 2006, 397–9.

3314. Kröller, Eva-Marie (ed.). The Cambridge companion to Canadian literature. (Bibl. 2005, 3835.) Rev. by W. J. Keith in BkCan (33:7) 2004, 28–9.

3315. Kuzniar, Alice A. Melancholia's dog. Chicago, IL; London: Chicago UP, 2006. pp. x, 215.

3316. Lacy, Norris J. (ed.). The fortunes of King Arthur. (Bibl. 2005, 3836.) Rev. by Carolyne Larrington in TLS, 26 May 2006, 13.

3317. —— A history of Arthurian scholarship. *See* **3969**.

3318. Larrington, Carolyne. Cuckold and king. TLS, 26 May 2006, 13 (review-article). (King Arthur.)

3319. Lawlor, Clark. Consumption and literature: the making of the Romantic disease. Basingstoke; New York: Palgrave Macmillan, 2006. pp. viii, 243.

3320. Leithart, Peter J. Deep comedy: trinity, tragedy, and hope in Western literature. Moscow, ID: Canon Press, 2004. pp. 159.

3321. Lennon, Joseph. Irish Orientalism: a literary and intellectual history. (Bibl. 2005, 3840.) Rev. by Michael Griffin in FDR (1) 2005, 268–9; by John Marx in VS (48:4) 2006, 718–19.

3322. Lindberg-Wada, Gunilla (ed.). Studying transcultural literary history. Berlin; New York: Mouton de Gruyter, 2006. pp. viii, 316. (Spectrum literature, 10.)

3323. Lingeman, Richard. Double lives: American writers' friendships. New York: Random House, 2006. pp. 255. Rev. by Andrea Harris in StAN (1:1/2) 2006, 202–4.

3324. Livingston, Ira. Between science and literature: an introduction to autopoetics. Foreword by N. Katherine Hayles. Urbana: Illinois UP, 2005. pp. xi, 192.

3325. Long, Lisa A. (ed.). White scholars / African American texts. *See* **20098**.

3326. Lopez, Barry (ed.). Home ground: language for an American landscape. San Antonio, TX: Trinity UP, 2006. pp. xxiv, 449. Rev. by Robert Sullivan in NYTB, 3 Dec. 2006, 72.

3327. Lucking, David. The serpent's part: narrating the self in Canadian literature. (Bibl. 2003, 3807.) Rev. by Julie Mullaney in MLR (101:1) 2006, 239.

3328. Lupack, Alan. The Oxford guide to Arthurian literature. (Bibl. 2005, 3845.) Rev. by Don Hoffman in Arthuriana (16:1) 2006, 77–9; by Rebecca Blustein in Comitatus (37) 2006, 262–3.

3329. Lutz, Tom. Cosmopolitan vistas: American regionalism and literary value. (Bibl. 2004, 3993.) Rev. by Susan Castillo in YES (36:2) 2006, 282–3; by James H. McGuire in ALR (38:3) 2006, 278–9.

3330. McClatchy, J. D. American writers at home. (Bibl. 2005, 3849.) Rev. by Marshall Bruce Gentry in FOR (4) 2006, 152–3.

3331. McDiarmid, Lucy. Field days: Irish literary revivals, ancient and modern. TLS, 6 Oct. 2006, 3–4 (review-article).

3332. McDonald, Beth E. The vampire as numinous experience: spiritual journeys with the undead in British and American literature. (Bibl. 2004, 3998.) Rev. by Reika Lee in PCR (17:2) 2006, 118–19.

3333. MacDougall, Carl (ed.). Scots: the language of the people. *See* **2576**.

3334. Macedo, Gabriela; Esteves da Silva Pereira, Margarida Isabel (eds). Identity and cultural translation: writing across the borders of Englishness: women's writing in English in a European context. New York; Frankfurt: Lang, 2006. pp. 282. (European connections, 15.)

3335. McIntyre, Dan. Point of view in plays: a cognitive stylistic approach to viewpoint in drama and other text-types. *See* **3446**.

3336. McKeon, Michael. The secret history of domesticity: public, private, and the division of knowledge. Baltimore, MD; London: Johns Hopkins UP, 2005. pp. xxv, 873, (plates) 16. Rev. by Brean S. Hammond in TLS, 27 Oct. 2006, 26; by Karen Harvey in ECS (40:1) 2006, 141–4.

3337. McLoughlin, Kate. Adynaton: a war *topos*. *See* **2038**.

3338. McMahon, Gary. Camp in literature. Jefferson, NC; London: McFarland, 2006. pp. vii, 306.

3339. McNamara, Kevin R. Affective democracy and the body (im)politic. *In* (pp. 13–30) **3307**.

3340. Magill, Frank N. (ed.); Irons-Georges, Tracy (assoc. ed.). Cyclopedia of world authors. (Bibl. 1997, 3647.) Pasadena, CA: Salem Press, 2004. pp. clxi, 3432, lxxii. (Fourth revised ed.: first ed. 1958.)

3341. Magrelli, Valerio (ed.). Lezioni di dottorato 2005. Santa Maria Capua Vetere: Spartaco, 2006. pp. 286.

3342. Marret, Sophie; Renaud-Grobras, Pascal (eds). Lectures et écritures du mythe. Rennes: Presses Universitaires de Rennes, 2006. pp. 324. (Interférences.) Rev. by Jacqueline Berben-Masi in EREA (4:2) 2006.

3343. Meddemmen, John. Metamorfosi e '*transmogrification*' in *Harry Potter* e altrove. *See* **18352**.

3344. Mehrotra, Arvind Krishna (ed.). History of Indian literature in English. (Bibl. 2004, 4007.) Rev. by John Oliver Perry in WLT (78:2) 2004, 80–1.

3345. Merrett, Robert. Presenting the past: philosophical irony and the rhetoric of double vision from Bishop Butler to T. S. Eliot. Victoria, B.C.: English Literary Studies, Univ. of Victoria, 2004. pp. 198. (ELS monographs, 91.) Rev. by Matthew Scott in RES (57:232) 2006, 845–6.

3346. Meyer-Dinkgräfe, Daniel (ed.). Consciousness, theatre, literature, and the arts. Newcastle upon Tyne: Cambridge Scholars Press, 2006. pp. xii, 443.

3347. Mikkelsen, Nina. Powerful magic: learning from children's responses to fantasy literature. Foreword by Laurence Yep. (Bibl. 2005, 3863.) Rev. by Ruth Mirtz in LU (30:3) 2006, 419–22.

3348. Miller, Meredith. Historical dictionary of lesbian literature. Lanham, MD; London: Scarecrow Press, 2006. pp. liii, 239. (Historical dictionaries of literature and the arts, 8.)

3349. Mitchell, Marea; Osland, Dianne. Representing women and female desire from *Arcadia* to *Jane Eyre*. (Bibl. 2005, 3865.) Rev. by Susan Lonoff de Cuevas in BrSt (31:3) 2006, 254–6.

3350. Montrose, Louis. The subject of Elizabeth: authority, gender, and representation. Chicago, IL; London: Chicago UP, 2006. pp. xii, 341.

3351. Moretti, Franco; Piazza, Alberto. La letteratura vista da lontano. Turin: Einaudi, 2005. pp. 147. Rev. by Alberto Casadei in Indice (2005:6) 14.

3352. Mortara, Elèna. Letteratura ebraico americana dalle origini alla Shoà: profilo storico letterario e saggi. Rome: Litos, 2006. pp. 346.

3353. Moss, Laura. Playing the monster blind? The practical limitations of updating the Canadian canon. CanL (191) 2006, 7–11.

3354. Mustazza, Leonard. The literary filmography: 6,200 adaptations of books, short stories and other nondramatic works. *See* **12641**.

3355. Myers, Jeffrey. Converging stories: race, ecology, and environmental justice in American literature. (Bibl. 2005, 3870.) Rev. by Steven Rosendale in ANQ (19:4) 2006, 59–62.

3356. Nelson, Emmanuel S. (ed.). The Greenwood encyclopedia of multiethnic American literature. Westport, CT; London: Greenwood Press, 2005. 5 vols. pp. li, 2483.

3357. Newton, Ruth. The stories we tell: composing in a decomposing world. Gainesville: Florida Academic Press, 2006. pp. 137. (New voices.)

3358. Ngai, Sianne. Ugly feelings. (Bibl. 2005, 3872.) Rev. by Jennifer L. Fleissner in Mod/Mod (13:2) 2006, 383–5; by Charles Altieri in ConLit (47:1) 2006, 141–7.

3359. Nicholson, Geoff. Sex collectors. *See* **358**.

3360. Norris, Pamela. Words of love: passionate women from Heloise to Sylvia Plath. London: HarperPress, 2006. pp. 501. Rev. by Gregory Dart in TLS, 15 Sept. 2006, 30.

3361. Orlando, Francesco. Obsolete objects in the literary imagination: ruins, relics, rarities, rubbish, uninhabited places, and hidden treasures. Trans. by Gabriel Pihas and Daniel Seidel. Foreword by David Quint. New Haven, CT; London: Yale UP, 2006. pp. xvii, 500.

3362. Ortiz, Gaye Williams; Joseph, Clara A. B. (eds). Theology and literature: rethinking reader responsibility. Basingstoke; New York: Palgrave Macmillan, 2006. pp. xii, 240.

3363. Ost, François. The law as mirrored in literature. Trans. by Roxanne Lapidus. SubStance (109) 2006, 3–19.

3364. Palmer, Alan. Fictional minds. (Bibl. 2005, 3880.) Rev. by Mary Clayton Coleman in PhilL (30:1) 2006, 299–309.

3365. Panichas, George A. (ed.). On literature, cultures, and religion. By Irving Babbitt. New Brunswick, NJ: Transaction, 2006. pp. liii, 315. (Third ed.: first ed. 1981.) (Orig. pub. as *Irving Babbitt: Representative Writings*.)

3366. Parini, Jay (ed.). British writers: supplement xii. New York: Scribner's Sons, 2006. pp. liv, 456.

3367. Paskow, Alan. The paradoxes of art: a phenomenological investigation. Cambridge; New York: CUP, 2004. pp. xi, 260, (plates) 4. Rev. by Andy Hamilton in BJA (45:4) 2005, 452–4.

3368. Pearn, John. The Antipodes and Erasmus Darwin: the place of Erasmus Darwin in the heritage of Australian literature and biology. *In* (pp. 103–11) **7702**.

3369. Pierce, David. Joyce and company. *See* **16752**.

3370. Pilný, Ondřej. Concepts of irony. *See* **2084**.

3371. Pontuale, Francesco. In their own terms: Italian histories of American literature. QPS (14) 2006, 111–19.

3372. Potolsky, Matthew. Mimesis. London; New York: Routledge, 2006. pp. viii, 176. (New critical idiom.)

3373. Prendergast, Christopher (ed.). Debating world literature. (Bibl. 2004, 4035.) Rev. by John Burt Foster in Comparatist (30) 2006, 137–40; by Arjali Nerlecker in XCP (15/16) 2006, 163–7.

3374. Pye, Gillian. Comedy theory and the postmodern. Humor (19:1) 2006, 53–70.

3375. Quigley, Austin E. Theoretical inquiry: language, linguistics, and literature. (Bibl. 2004, 4038.) Rev. by Jeremy Tambling in MLR (101:2) 2006, 531–2.

3376. Rath, Sura P.; Baral, Kailash C.; Rao, D. Venkat (eds). Reflections on literature, criticism, and theory: essays in honour of Professor Prafulla C. Kar. Delhi: Pencraft International, 2004. pp. 287. Rev. by Amaresh Datta in IndLit (48:3) 2004, 220–4.

3377. Ratmoko, David. On spectrality: fantasies of redemption in the Western canon. New York; Frankfurt: Lang, 2006. pp. 163.

3378. Rayner, Alice. Ghosts: death's double and the phenomena of theater. Minneapolis; London: Minnesota UP, 2006. pp. xxxv, 205.

3379. Reed, Walter L.; Duke, Marshall P. Personalities as *dramatis personae*: an interdisciplinary examination of the self as author. *See* **20126**.

3380. Reilly, John M. Into the workshop: in search of identity and pretexts. MidQ (47:3) 2006, 290–8.

3381. Robinson, David M. Closeted writing and lesbian and gay literature: Classical, early modern, eighteenth-century. Aldershot; Burlington, VT: Ashgate, 2006. pp. xx, 295.

3382. Robinson, Lorraine Hale. Dictionary of North Carolina writers: Hake Talbot to Mary Heaton Vorse. NCLR (15) 2006, 173–92.

3383. Rodríguez García, José María. Literary into cultural translation. Diacritics (34:3/4) 2004, 3–30.

3384. Rood, Tim. The sea! The sea! The shout of the ten thousand in the modern imagination. (Bibl. 2005, 3905.) Rev. by Alexandra Lianeri in TransLit (15:1) 2006, 104–8.

3385. Rooney, Ellen (ed.). The Cambridge companion to feminist literary theory. *See* **14277**.

3386. Royot, Daniel. La littérature américaine. Paris: PUF, 2004. pp. 127. (Que sais-je? 407.) Rev. by Alain Geoffroy in EA (58:2) 2005, 245–6.

3387. Rozelle, Lee. Ecosublime: environmental awe and terror from New World to Oddworld. Tuscaloosa; London: Alabama UP, 2006. pp. viii, 134. Rev. by David M. Grant in ANQ (19:4) 2006, 70–4.

3388. Said, Edward W. On late style: music and literature against the grain. Foreword by Mariam C. Said. Introd. by Michael Wood. New York: Pantheon, 2006. pp. xix, 176. Rev. by Edward Rothstein in NYTB, 16 July 2006, 19; by Gordon McMullan in TLS, 29 Sept. 2006, 30; by Frank Kermode in LRB (28:19) 2006, 7–8.

3389. Sandner, David (ed.). Fantastic literature: a critical reader. (Bibl. 2005, 3913.) Rev. by David Bratman in Mythprint (43:5/6) 2006, 12–13.

3390. Saunders, Corinne J. (ed.). A companion to romance: from Classical to contemporary. (Bibl. 2004, 4053.) Rev. by Joyce Boro in NQ (53:1) 2006, 95.

3391. Sawyer, Andy. Ursula Le Guin and the pastoral mode. *See* **17109**.

3392. Sayre, Gordon M. The Indian chief as tragic hero: native resistance and the literatures of America, from Moctezuma to Tecumseh. (Bibl. 2005, 3915.) Rev. by Jacquelyn Kilpatrick in JAH (93:3) 2006, 853–4; by Maureen Konkle in AICRJ (30:4) 2006, 153–5.

3393. Scholes, Robert; Phelan, James; Kellogg, Robert. The nature of narrative. (Bibl. 1969, 2387.) Oxford; New York: OUP, 2006. pp. xv, 388. (Second ed.: first ed. 1966.)

3394. Schroeder, Chad Matthew (ed.). Cygnifiliana: essays in Classics, comparative literature, and philosophy presented to Professor Roy Arthur Swanson on the occasion of his seventy-fifth birthday. New York; Frankfurt: Lang, 2005. pp. 210.

3395. Schweizer, Bernard (ed.). Approaches to the Anglo and American female epic, 1621–1982. Aldershot; Burlington, VT: Ashgate, 2006. pp. x, 228. Rev. by Cheryl A. Wilson in TSWL (25:2) 2006, 347–8.

3396. Selden, Daniel L. Vergil and the Satanic *cogito*. *See* **7065**.

3397. Seymour, Claire. The operas of Benjamin Britten: expression and evasion. Woodbridge, Suffolk; Rochester, NY: Boydell Press, 2004. pp. x, 358. Rev. by Arnold Whittall in MusL (86:3) 2005, 513–16.

3398. Sinfield, Alan. Cultural politics – queer reading. (Bibl. 1997, 3721.) London; New York: Routledge, 2005. pp. xxi, 104. (Second ed.: first ed. 1994.)

3399. —— On sexuality and power. New York: Columbia UP, 2004. pp. viii, 218. (Between men – between women.) Rev. by Stephen Shapiro in TexP (19:4) 2005, 529–35.

3400. Smoley, Richard. Forbidden faith: the Gnostic legacy from the Gospels to *The Da Vinci Code*. San Francisco, CA: HarperSanFrancisco, 2006. pp. vii, 344. Rev. by Peter Lamborn Wilson in Parabola (31:3) 2006, 105.

3401. Snodgrass, Mary Ellen. Encyclopedia of feminist literature. New York: Facts on File, 2006. pp. xviii, 766. (Facts on File library of world literature.) (Literary movements.)

3402. Sova, Dawn B. Literature suppressed on sexual grounds. Preface by Ken Wachsberger. *See* **880**.

3403. Spargo, R. Clifton. The ethics of mourning: grief and responsibility in elegiac literature. (Bibl. 2005, 3933.) Rev. by Michael Wheeler in YES (36:2) 2006, 269–70.

3404. Steele, Peter. Zones of the imagination. *See* **17250**.

3405. Stone, Marjorie; Thompson, Judith (eds). Literary couplings: writing couples, collaborators, and the construction of authorship. Madison; London: Wisconsin UP, 2006. pp. xiv, 373.

3406. Stow, Simon. Reading our way to democracy? Literature and public ethics. PhilL (30:2) 2006, 410–23.

3407. Styler, Rebecca; Pridmore, Joseph (eds). Textual variations: the impact of textual issues on literary studies. Leicester: Dept of English, Univ. of Leicester, 2006. pp. vi, 99.

3408. Tazón Salces, Juan E.; Carrera Suárez, Isabel (eds). Post/imperial encounters: Anglo-Hispanic cultural relations. Amsterdam; New York: Rodopi, 2005. pp. 239. (Textxet, 45.) Rev. by Christopher Rollason in Atl (28:1) 2006, 133–8.

3409. Teulié, Gilles (ed.). Religious writings & war /Les discours religieux et la guerre. Montpellier: Univ. Paul-Valéry Montpellier III, 2006. pp. 456. (Carnets du CERPANAC, 3.)

3410. Trumble, Angus. A brief history of the smile. New York: Basic Books, 2004. pp. liii, 226.

3411. Tureček, Dalibor. The theory of fictional worlds, aesthetic function, and the future of literary history. Style (40:3) 2006, 221–30.

3412. Vicchio, Stephen J. The image of the biblical Job: a history: vol. 3, Job in the modern world. Eugene, OR: Wipf & Stock, 2006. pp. xix, 247. Rev. by Martin Shuster in MLN (121:5) 2006, 1278–81.

3413. Vida, Vendela (ed.). The Believer book of writers talking to writers. (Bibl. 2005, 3950.) Rev. by Catherine Humble in TLS, 27 Jan. 2006, 32.

3414. Villegas-López, Sonia; Domínguez-García, Beatriz (eds). Literature, gender, space. Huelva: Univ. de Huelva, 2004. pp. 275. (Collectanea / Univ. de Huelva, 74.) Rev. by Sinead McDermott in Atl (27:2) 2005, 221–6.

3415. Visser, Irene; Wilcox, Helen (eds). Transforming holiness: representations of holiness in English and American literary texts. Louvain; Dudley, MA: Peeters, 2006. pp. xx, 217. (Groningen studies in cultural change, 20.)

3416. Wallace, David. Premodern places: Calais to Surinam, Chaucer to Aphra Behn. (Bibl. 2004, 4079.) Rev. by Karen Newman in SStud (34) 2006, 251–7; by Jenna Mead in Parergon (23:1) 2006, 230–4.

3417. Walsh, Jill Paton. *The Poetics* of Aristotle as a practical guide. Introd. by Lisa Sainsbury. *See* **18953**.

3418. Warner, Marina. The word unfleshed: memory in cyberspace. *See* **5768**.

3419. Wells, Marion A. The secret wound: love-melancholy and the early modern romance. Stanford, CA: Stanford UP, 2006. pp. 360. (Figurae.)

3420. Wharton, Thomas. The logogryph: a bibliography of imaginary books. Kentville, N.S.: Gaspereau Press, 2004. pp. 236. Rev. by Phyllis Reeve in Amphora (138) 2005, 27–8.

3421. Wishart, David J. (ed.). Encyclopedia of the Great Plains. Lincoln; London: Nebraska UP, 2004. pp. xviii, 919. Rev. by Brian W. Dippie in WAL (41:3) 2006, 357–8.

3422. Wolf, Werner; Bernhart, Walter (eds). Framing borders in literature and other media. Amsterdam; Atlanta, GA: Rodopi for the Ford Madox Ford Soc., 2006. pp. viii, 482. Rev. by William Nelles in Style (40:4) 2006, 357–60.

3423. Wright, Edmond. Narrative, perception, language, and faith. Basingstoke; New York: Palgrave Macmillan, 2005. pp. xiii, 275.

3424. Yang, Jingjian. In the name of 'father': the motif of 'father on trial' in Western literature. FLS (117) 2006, 159–65. (In Chinese.)

3425. Zajko, Vanda; Leonard, Miriam (eds). Laughing with Medusa: Classical myth and feminist thought. Oxford; New York: OUP, 2006. pp. xiv, 445. (Classical presences.)

DRAMA AND THE THEATRE

3426. Aldgate, Anthony; Robertson, James C. Censorship in theatre and cinema. *See* **12395**.

3427. Allain, Paul; Harvie, Jen (eds). The Routledge companion to theatre and performance. London; New York: Routledge, 2006. pp. xii, 244.

3428. Bloom, Ken. Broadway: its history, people, and places: an encyclopedia. London; New York: Routledge, 2004. pp. xvii, 679.

3429. Bogar, Thomas A. American Presidents attend the theatre: the play-going experiences of each chief executive. Jefferson, NC; London: McFarland, 2006. pp. viii, 433.

3430. Bryer, Jackson R.; Hartig, Mary C. (eds). The Facts on File companion to American drama. (Bibl. 2004, 4103.) Rev. by Lincoln Konkle in NETJ (16) 2005, 143–6.

3431. Chambers, Colin. Inside the Royal Shakespeare Company: creativity and the institution. (Bibl. 2005, 3972.) Rev. by Günter Walch in SJ (142) 2006, 236–40.

3432. Cremona, Vicky Ann, *et al.* (eds). Theatrical events: borders, dynamics, frames. (Bibl. 2005, 3974.) Rev. by Dean Wilcox in TRI (31:1) 2006, 108–9; by Branislav Jakovljevic in TDR (50:1) 2006, 179–83.

3433. Duffy, Meghan; Gerould, Daniel (eds). Comedy: a bibliography of critical studies in English on the theory and practice of comedy in drama, theatre, and performance. New York: Martin E. Segal Theatre Center, 2006. pp. 109.

3434. Dunlap, William. A history of the American theatre from its origins to 1832. Urbana: Illinois UP, 2005. pp. xxiii, 444. Rev. by Jason Shaffer in EAL (41:2) 2006, 383–7.

3435. Erickson, Jon. The ghost of the literary in recent theories of text and performance. TheatreS (47:2) 2006, 245–51.

3436. Felner, Mira; Orenstein, Claudia. The world of theatre. Boston, MA: Pearson / Allyn & Bacon, 2006. pp. xxiii, 458.

3437. Geddes, Jennifer L. Religion and the tragic. *See* **14110**.

3438. Hall, Edith; Macintosh, Fiona. Greek tragedy and the British theatre, 1660–1914. (Bibl. 2005, 3978.) Rev. by Emily Wilson in TLS, 27 Jan. 2006, 24–5; by Keri Walsh in RES (57:230) 2006, 404–6.

3439. —— —— Wrigley, Amanda (eds). Dionysus since 69: Greek tragedy at the dawn of the third millennium. Oxford; New York: OUP, 2004. pp. xviii, 480.

3440. Hischak, Thomas S. American plays and musicals on screen: 650 stage productions and their film and television adaptations. Jefferson, NC; London: McFarland, 2005. pp. vii, 343.

3441. Kattwinkel, Susan (ed.). Audience participation: essays on inclusion in performance. (Bibl. 2003, 3955.) Rev. by Shelley Orr in TJ (58:2) 2006, 369–71.

3442. —— Theatre and travel: tours of the South. Tuscaloosa; London: Alabama UP / Southeastern Theatre Conference, 2005. pp. 128. (Theatre symposium, 13.) Rev. by H. Thorne Compton in JSH (72:4) 2006, 976–7.

3443. Krasner, David; Saltz, David Z. (eds). Staging philosophy: intersections of theater, performance, and philosophy. Ann Arbor: Michigan UP, 2006. pp. 334. (Theater: theory/text/performance.)

3444. Lima, Robert. Stages of evil: occultism in Western theater and drama. Lexington: Kentucky UP, 2005. pp. 329. Rev. by Alastair Sooke in TLS, 15 Dec. 2006, 8; by Dayana Stetco in JFA (16:4) 2006, 374–6.

3445. Luckhurst, Mary; Moody, Jane (eds). Theatre and celebrity in Britain, 1660–2000. (Bibl. 2005, 3985.) Rev. by Tom Mole in TN (60:3) 2006, 184–5.

3446. McIntyre, Dan. Point of view in plays: a cognitive stylistic approach to viewpoint in drama and other text-types. Amsterdam; Philadelphia, PA: Benjamins, 2006. pp. viii, 203. (Linguistic approaches to literature, 3.)

3447. Meyer-Dinkgräfe, Daniel. Theater and consciousness: explanatory scope and future potential. Bristol; Portland, OR: Intellect, 2005. pp. 230. Rev. by Lib Taylor in TRI (31:2) 2006, 211–12.

3448. Mitter, Shomit; Shevtsova, Maria (eds). Fifty key theatre directors. London; New York: Routledge, 2005. pp. xviii, 286. (Routledge key guides.) Rev. by Christa Williford in TT (16:2) 2006, 197–8.

3449. Pizzato, Mark. Ghosts of theatre and cinema in the brain. Basingstoke; New York: Palgrave Macmillan, 2006. pp. 323. (Palgrave studies in theatre and performance history.)

3450. Pritchard, William H. The perfect critic. HR (59:1) 2006, 135–41 (review-article).

3451. Pullen, Kirsten. Actresses and whores: on stage and in society. (Bibl. 2005, 3993.) Rev. by Katie Ahearn in RECTR (19:2) 2004, 44–7; by Naomi Stubbs in TN (59:3) 2005, 174; by Barbara Lewis in TheatreS (47:2) 2006, 321–3.

3452. Reinelt, Janelle G.; Roach, Joseph R. (eds). Critical theory and performance. Ann Arbor: Michigan UP, 2006. pp. 592.

3453. Remshardt, Ralf. Staging the savage God: the grotesque in performance. (Bibl. 2005, 3994.) Rev. by David Robb in ModDr (48:4) 2005, 856–8.

3454. Rollyson, Carl Edmund (ed.). Notable playwrights. Pasadena, CA: Salem Press, 2005. 3 vols. pp. xiv, 1131. (Magill's choice.)

3455. Schneider, Rebecca. Intermediality, infelicity, and scholarship on the slip. *See* **20136**.

3456. Shepherd-Barr, Kirsten. Science on stage: from *Doctor Faustus* to *Copenhagen*. Princeton, NJ; Oxford: Princeton UP, 2006. pp. viii, 271.

3457. Teague, Frances. Shakespeare and the American popular stage. *See* **5441**.

3458. Vaughan, Virginia Mason. Performing Blackness on English stages, 1500–1800. (Bibl. 2005, 3998.) Rev. by Robert C. Evans in CompDr (39:2) 2005, 251–6; by Ian Smith in ShQ (57:2) 2006, 216–18; by Willy Maley in TRI (31:1) 2006, 102–3; by Andrew Duxfield in NQ (53:3) 2006, 381–2; by Ayanna Thompson in RQ (59:3) 2006, 969–70.

3459. Weber, Samuel. Theatricality as medium. (Bibl. 2005, 3999.) Rev. by Branislav Jakovljevic in TDR (50:1) 2006, 179–83.

3460. Wilmer, S. E. (ed.). Writing & rewriting national theatre histories. (Bibl. 2005, 4004.) Rev. by Kimberly M. Jew in JMMLA (38:2) 2005, 129–32.

3461. Wilson, Edwin; Goldfarb, Alvin. Theater: the lively art. (Bibl. 1991, 3139.) Boston, MA: McGraw-Hill, 2005. pp. xxii, 399, (plates) 25. (Fifth ed.: first ed. 1991.)

3462. Wilson, Emily R. Mocked with death: tragic overliving from Socrates to Milton. *See* **5458**.

3463. Zander, Horst. *Julius Caesar* and the critical legacy. *In* (pp. 3–55) **5805**.

3464. Zarilli, Phillip B., *et al.* Theatre histories: an introduction. London; New York: Routledge, 2006. pp. xxxi, 544.

FICTION

3465. Abbott, Carl. Frontiers past and future: science fiction and the American West. Lawrence: Kansas UP, 2006. pp. viii, 230.

3466. Armstrong, Nancy. What feminism did to novel studies. *In* (pp. 99–118) **14277**.

3467. Birch, Dinah. The figure at the window: tales of domestic spirits and the familiar dead. TLS, 22 & 29 Dec. 2006, 25–6 (review-article).

3468. Boyd, Brian. Fiction and theory of mind. *See* **20020**.

3469. Brackett, Mary Virginia. Companion to the British novel: beginnings through the nineteenth century. New York: Facts on File, 2005. pp. xiv, 530.

3470. Brand, Sean. Literary feasts: inspired eating from classic fiction. New York: Atria, 2006. pp. 128.

3471. Brunsdale, Mitzi M. Gumshoes: a dictionary of fictional detectives. Westport, CT; London: Greenwood Press, 2006. pp. xvi, 455.

3472. Chodat, Robert. Naturalism and narrative; or, What computers and human beings can't do. *See* **18117**.

3473. Dalby, Richard (ed.). The Virago book of ghost stories. London: Virago Press, 2006. pp. xvi, 496. Rev. by Dinah Birch in TLS, 22 & 29 Dec. 2006, 25–6.

3474. D'Ammassa, Don. Encyclopedia of fantasy and horror fiction. New York: Facts on File, 2006. pp. viii, 488.

3475. —— Encyclopedia of science fiction. New York: Facts on File, 2004. pp. v, 538.

3476. Davis, J. Madison. The mysterious popularity of the arcane. *See* **9934**.

3477. Derecho, Abigail. Archontic literature: a definition, a history, and several theories of fan fiction. *In* (pp. 61–78) **19868**.

3478. Dinello, Daniel. Technophobia! Science fiction visions of posthuman technology. Austin: Texas UP, 2005. pp. 329. Rev. by Dongshin Yi in SCR (23:3) 2006, 93–5.

3479. Donoghue, Denis. Religion and American fiction. ReLit (38:1) 2006, 31–51.

3480. Eagleton, Terry. The English novel: an introduction. Oxford; Malden, MA: Blackwell, 2005. pp. ix, 365. Rev. by Dominic Rainsford in DickQ (23:2) 2006, 121–5; by Joe Brooker in TexP (19:3) 2006, 404–10; by Rebecca Shapiro in ECN (5) 2006, 339–46.

3481. Fornari, Roberta. 'In tycoons we trust?': reality and fiction of an American icon. QPS (14) 2006, 328–36.

3482. Fuchs, Miriam. The text is myself: women's life writing and catastrophe. (Bibl. 2004, 4158.) Rev. by Brenda Daly in A/B (20:1) 2005, 95–9; by Georgia Johnston in TSWL (25:2) 2006, 354–5.

3483. Gunn, James; Candelaria, Matthew (eds). Speculations on speculation: theories of science fiction. (Bibl. 2005, 4027.) Rev. by Joan Gordon in NYRSF (18:7) 2006, 15–16; by Sherryl Vint in JFA (16:3) 2006, 260–2.

3484. Hale, Dorothy J. (ed.). The novel: an anthology of criticism and theory, 1900–2000. Oxford; Malden, MA: Blackwell, 2006. pp. xiv, 821.

3485. Jameson, Fredric. Archaeologies of the future: the desire called utopia and other science fictions. (Bibl. 2005, 4033.) Rev. by Terry Eagleton in LRB (28:5) 2006, 25–6; by Adam Roberts in NYRSF (18:7) 2006, 21–3; by Michael Saler in TLS, 16 June 2006, 31.

3486. Lazzari, Anna. I testi non finzionali: Dick sulla fantascienza. *In* (pp. 61–9) **15466**.

3487. Luckhurst, Roger. Science fiction. (Bibl. 2005, 4042.) Rev. by Adam Roberts in TexP (19:4) 2005, 536–9.

3488. Madden, David; Bane, Charles; Flory, Sean M. A primer of the novel: for readers and writers. Lanham, MD; London: Scarecrow Press, 2006. pp. xxi, 278.

3489. Maunder, Andrew (ed.). The Facts on File companion to the British short story. New York: Facts on File, 2006. pp. 448.

3490. Mort, John. Read the high country: a guide to western books and films. Westport, CT: Libraries Unlimited, 2006. pp. xviii, 488.

3491. Mullan, John. How novels work. Oxford; New York: OUP, 2006. pp. x, 346.

3492. Neal, Lynn S. Romancing God: evangelical women and inspirational fiction. Chapel Hill; London: North Carolina UP, 2006. pp. xii, 245.

3493. Novy, Marianne. Reading adoption: family and difference in fiction and drama. (Bibl. 2005, 4048.) Rev. by Claudia Nelson in SCR (23:2) 2006, 97–9; by Josephine A. McQuail in CLAQ (31:4) 2006, 395–7.

3494. Parrinder, Patrick. Nation & novel: the English novel from its origins to the present day. Oxford; New York: OUP, 2006. pp. viii, 502. Rev. by John Mullan in TLS, 22 Sept. 2006, 11.

3495. Prucher, Jeffrey. Brave new words: the Oxford dictionary of science fiction. *See* **1685**.

3496. Pulliam, June Michele; Fonseca, Anthony J. Read on – horror fiction. Westport, CT: Libraries Unlimited, 2006. pp. xvii, 182. (Read on.)

3497. Rawlings, Peter. American theorists of the novel: Henry James, Lionel Trilling, Wayne C. Booth. *See* **10595**.

3498. Ricketts, Wendell (ed.). Everything I have is blue: short fiction by working-class men about more-or-less gay life. San Francisco, CA: Suspect Thoughts Press, 2005. pp. 249. Rev. by Gerald Haslam in WAL (40:4) 2006, 478–9.

3499. Ronen, Ruth; Biberman, Efrat. The truth about narrative; or, How does narrative matter? PhilL (30:1) 2006, 118–39.

3500. Rzepka, Charles J. Detective fiction. Oxford; Malden, MA: Polity Press in assn with Blackwell, 2005. pp. vi, 273. (Cultural history of literature.)

3501. Šaldová, Pavlína. The distribution of finite and participial postmodifiers in fiction and academic prose. *See* **2420**.

3502. Sandner, David. Theorizing the fantastic: editing *Fantastic Literature: a Critical Reader* and the six stages of fantasy criticism. JFA (16:4) 2006, 277–301.

3503. Scaggs, John. Crime fiction. (Bibl. 2005, 4055.) Rev. by Sayanti Ganguly in JPC (39:5) 2006, 903–5; by Margaret Kinsman in Clues (24:4) 2006, 74–5.

3504. Scofield, Martin. The Cambridge introduction to the American short story. Cambridge; New York: CUP, 2006. pp. xi, 291. (Cambridge introductions to literature.)

3505. Smiley, Jane. Thirteen ways of looking at the novel. (Bibl. 2005, 4058.) Rev. by Sophie Ratcliffe in TLS, 21 July 2006, 9–10; by Nancy Carr in CommRev (5:2) 2006, 44–7.

3506. Sontag, Susan. At the same time … (the novelist and moral reasoning). ESA (48:1) 2005, 5–17.

3507. Spongberg, Mary; Curthoys, Ann; Caine, Barbara (eds). Companion to women's historical writing. Basingstoke; New York: Palgrave Macmillan, 2005. pp. xvii, 712.

3508. Standish, David. Hollow earth: the long and curious history of imagining strange lands, fantastical creatures, advanced civilizations, and marvelous machines below the earth's surface. New York: Da Capo Press, 2006. pp. 303.

3509. Sutherland, John. How to read a novel: a user's guide. London: Profile, 2006. pp. 263. Rev. by Toby Lichtig in TLS, 10 Nov. 2006, 26; by Maureen Corrigan in BkW, 24 Dec. 2006, 12.

3510. Tibbetts, John C.; Welsh, James Michael. The encyclopedia of novels into film. *See* **12722**.

3511. Travis, Jennifer. Wounded hearts: masculinity, law, and literature in American culture. Chapel Hill; London: North Carolina UP, 2005. pp. x, 222. Rev. by Ryan Schneider in AL (78:4) 2006, 894–7.

3512. Trupe, Alice. Thematic guide to young adult literature. Westport, CT; London: Greenwood Press, 2006. pp. viii, 259.

3513. VANDERMEER, JEFF. Why should I cut your throat? Excursions into the worlds of science-fiction fantasy & horror. Austin, TX: MonkeyBrain, 2004. pp. 336. Rev. by John Langan in Extrapolation (47:2) 2006, 327–32.

3514. VERMEULE, BLAKEY. Gossip and literary narrative. PhilL (30:1) 2006, 102–17.

3515. WALSH, RICHARD. The narrative imagination across media. *See* **119**.

3516. WANG, SONGLIN. The moral choice behind impersonal narrative. FLS (117) 2006, 36–43. (In Chinese.)

3517. WERLOCK, ABBY H. P. (ed.); WERLOCK, JAMES P. (asst ed.). The Facts on File companion to the American novel. New York: Facts on File, 2006. 3 vols. pp. viii, 1519. (Facts on File library of American literature.)

3518. WESTFAHL, GARY. Science fiction and the playing fields of Eaton. Extrapolation (47:1) 2006, 7–15. (J. Lloyd Eaton Conferences on Science Fiction and Fantasy Literature.)

3519. WILAMOVÁ, SIRMA. On expressing negative politeness in English fictional discourse. (Bibl. 2005, 4072.) Rev. by Renata Povolná in ČMF (88:2) 2006, 104–6.

3520. ZUNSHINE, LISA. Why we read fiction: theory of mind and the novel. Columbus: Ohio State UP, 2006. pp. x, 198. Rev. by Beth Lynch in TLS, 16 June 2006, 32; by Brian Boyd in PhilL (30:2) 2006, 590–600.

LITERATURE FOR CHILDREN

3521. ANDERSON, VICKI. The dime novel in children's literature. Jefferson, NC; London: McFarland, 2005. pp. vi, 268. Rev. by J. Randolph Cox in DNR (74:1) 2005, 32–3; by Kent Baxter in LU (30:2) 2006, 268–70; by Bonnie Gaarden in AL (78:3) 2006, 631–3.

3522. CHAPLEAU, SEBASTIEN. New voices in children's literature criticism. (Bibl. 2005, 4080.) Rev. by Lissa Paul in ChildLit (34) 2006, 246–50.

3523. COATS, KAREN. Looking glasses and Neverlands: Lacan, desire, and subjectivity in children's literature. (Bibl. 2004, 4196.) Rev. by Hamida Bosmajian in LU (29:2) 2005, 292–8; by Marah Gubar in ChildLit (33) 2005, 285–8.

3524. DANIEL, CAROLYN. Voracious children: who eats whom in children's literature. London; New York: Routledge, 2006. pp. ix, 265. (Children's literature and culture, 39.)

3525. DEWAN, PAULINE. The house as setting, symbol, and structural motif in children's literature. (Bibl. 2004, 4197.) Rev. by Susan Naramore Maher in LU (29:2) 2005, 286–9.

3526. GLAZER, JOAN I.; GIORGIS, CYNDI. Literature for young children. (Bibl. 2000, 4157.) Upper Saddle River, NJ: Pearson / Prentice Hall, 2005. pp. xii, 346. (Fifth ed.: first ed. 1981.)

3527. GRISWOLD, JEROME. Feeling like a kid: childhood and children's literature. Baltimore, MD; London: Johns Hopkins UP, 2006. pp. 148.

3528. HUNT, PETER (ed.). International companion encyclopedia of children's literature. (Bibl. 2000, 4163.) London; New York: Routledge, 2004. 2 vols. pp. xx, 1374. (Second ed.: first ed. 1996.)

3529. —— Understanding children's literature: key essays from the second edition of the *International Companion Encyclopedia of Children's Literature*. (Bibl. 2003, 4076.) London; New York: Routledge, 2005. pp. ix, 225. (Second ed.: first ed. 1999.)

3530. Jones, Diana Wynne. The tough guide to Fantasyland. New York: Firebird, 2006. pp. 234. (Revised ed.: first ed. 1996.)

3531. Kidd, Kenneth B. Making American boys: boyology and the feral tale. (Bibl. 2004, 4199.) Rev. by Kent Baxter in LU (29:2) 2005, 289–92; by Michael Cobb in Criticism (47:1) 2005, 119–30; by Troy Boone in ChildLit (33) 2005, 237–41.

3532. Lanes, Selma G. Through the looking glass: further adventures & misadventures in the realm of children's literature. Boston, MA: Godine, 2004. pp. viii, 247.

3533. Lathey, Gillian (ed.). The translation of children's literature: a reader. Clevedon; Philadelphia, PA: Multilingual Matters, 2006. pp. viii, 259. (Topics in translation, 31.)

3534. Lupack, Barbara Tepa (ed.). Adapting the Arthurian legends for children: essays on Arthurian juvenilia. (Bibl. 2004, 4203.) Rev. by Gary Schmidt in LU (29:2) 2005, 276–80.

3535. Nikolajeva, Maria. Aesthetic approaches to children's literature. (Bibl. 2005, 4094.) Rev. by Roderick McGillis in LU (30:3) 2006, 413–19.

3536. Norton, Donna E. Multicultural children's literature: through the eyes of many children. (Bibl. 2001, 3602.) Upper Saddle River, NJ: Pearson / Prentice Hall, 2005. pp. viii, 366. (Second ed.: first ed. 2001.)

3537. Salem, Linda C. Children's Literature Studies: cases and discussions. Westport, CT: Libraries Unlimited, 2006. pp. xi, 153.

3538. Stanton, Joseph. The important books: children's picture books as art and literature. (Bibl. 2005, 4098.) Rev. by David L. Russell in LU (30:2) 2006, 280–3.

3539. Zipes, Jack (ed.). The Oxford encyclopedia of children's literature. Oxford; New York: OUP, 2006. 4 vols. pp. xxxiv, 436; 469; 465; 505.

POETRY

3540. Armitage, Simon. Modelling the universe: poetry, science, and the art of metaphor. *In* (pp. 110–22) **13732**.

3541. Baker, David. The pastoral: first and last things. SoR (42:4) 2006, 779–87.

3542. Beer, Gillian. Afterword. *In* (pp. 204–10) **13732**.

3543. Bensimon, Paul, *et al.* (eds). Anthologie bilingue de la poésie anglaise. Preface by Bernard Brugière. Paris: Gallimard, 2005. pp. lxxxii, 2013. (Bibliothèque de la Pléiade, 519.) Rev. by Denis Bonnecase in EA (59:2) 2006, 198–204.

3544. Bernstein, Charles. Hero of the local: Robert Creeley and the persistence of American poetry. *See* **15362**.

3545. Bonnecase, Denis. Installer une présence. EA (59:2) 2006, 198–204 (review-article). (Bilingual ed. of English poetry.)

3546. Bouchard, Gary M. The shape of song in a flood of words: Benedictine education and poetic truth. ABR (57:1) 2006, 3–17.

3547. Bruhn, Mark J. Place deixis and the schematics of imagined space: Milton to Keats. PT (26:3) 2005, 387–432.

3548. Bruns, Gerald L. The material of poetry: sketches for a philosophical poetics. (Bibl. 2005, 4102.) Rev. by Michael Magee in AmBR (27:5) 2006, 8–9.

3549. —— On the anarchy of poetry and philosophy: a guide for the unruly. New York: Fordham UP, 2006. pp. xxix, 274. (Perspectives in Continental philosophy.)

3550. Burnside, John. A science of belonging: poetry as ecology. *In* (pp. 91–106) **13732**.

3551. Červenka, Miroslav. 'Discovering' the fictional worlds of lyric poetry. Style (40:3) 2006, 240–8.

3552. Crawford, Robert (ed.). Contemporary poetry and contemporary science. *See* **13732**.

3553. Dresher, B. Elan; Friedberg, Nila (eds). Formal approaches to poetry: recent developments in metrics. Berlin; New York: Mouton de Gruyter, 2006. pp. viii, 312. (Phonology and phonetics, 11.)

3554. Edwards, David L. Poets and God: Chaucer, Shakespeare, Herbert, Milton, Wordsworth, Coleridge, Blake. (Bibl. 2005, 4106.) Rev. by David Jasper in LitTheol (20:1) 2006, 87–8.

3555. Fraistat, Neil; Jones, Steven. The poem and the network: editing poetry electronically. *In* (pp. 105–21) **426**.

3556. Fry, Stephen. The ode less travelled: unlocking the poet within. London: Hutchinson, 2005. pp. xxv, 357. Rev. by David Orr in NYTB, 1 Oct. 2006, 14.

3557. Gibbons, Reginald. On rhyme. APR (35:6) 2006, 63–9.

3558. Gray, Jeffrey; McCorkle, James; Balkun, Mary McAleer (eds). The Greenwood encyclopedia of American poets and poetry. Westport, CT; London: Greenwood Press, 2006. 5 vols. pp. 1842.

3559. Gundy, Jeff. Where do we discover what we believe? GaR (60:2) 2006, 423–33 (review-article).

3560. Hardy, Barbara. Literary allusion: Hardy and other poets. *In* (pp. 55–77) **10348**.

3561. Hart, Kevin. Tracking the trace. Meanjin (64:4) 2005, 130–8. (Poets translating other poets.)

3562. Heller, Michael. Uncertain poetries: essays on poets, poetry, and poetics. (Bibl. 2005, 4110.) Rev. by Mark Scroggins in Talisman (30/31) 2005/06, 90–5; by Romana Huk in Mod/Mod (13:3) 2006, 599–601; by Roger Mitchell in AmBR (27:5) 2006, 12–13.

3563. Hirsch, Edward. Poet's choice. Orlando, FL: Harcourt, 2006. pp. xv, 432. Rev. by John Savant in ANCW (194:13) 2006, 23–5.

3564. Hoagland, Tony. Real sofistikashun! Essays on poetry and craft. Saint Paul, MN: Graywolf Press, 2006. pp. xiii, 201.

3565. Hooker, Jeremy. Reflections on 'ground'. Scintilla (10) 2006, 34–41.

3566. Howard, Richard. Paper trail: selected prose, 1965–2003. New York: Farrar, Straus, & Giroux, 2004. pp. ix, 434. Rev. by Langdon Hammer in Parnassus (29:1/2) 2006, 97–117.

3567. James, Clive. Listening for the flavor: a notebook. *See* **16580**.

3568. Kenner, Hugh. Rhyme: an unfinished monograph. CK (10:3) 2004, 377–425.

3569. Kumar, Satish. Representing the landscape. PRev (96:3) 2006, 86–7.

3570. Lee, Clarissa. Derek Walcott, human isolation, and traditions of English poetry. *See* **18927**.

3571. Lennard, John. The poetry handbook: a guide to reading poetry for pleasure and practical criticism. (Bibl. 2005, 4119.) Rev. by Caroline Bertonèche in EREA (4:1) 2006.

3572. Lotfipour-Saedi, K. Discoursal function of phonological patterns in poetic texts: implications for (UN-)translatability of poetry. Meta (50:4: CD-ROM supp.) 2005.

3573. Morgan, Edwin. Poetry and virtual realities. *In* (pp. 27–47) **13732**.

3574. Motion, Andrew. Such attics cleared of me: saving writers' manuscripts for the nation. *See* **356**.

3575. Muldoon, Paul. The end of the poem: Oxford lectures on poetry. London; Boston, MA: Faber & Faber, 2006. pp. 406. Rev. by Stephen Burt in TLS, 24 Nov. 2006, 6–8; by Brian Phillips in Poetry (189:3) 2006, 232–4.

3576. New, Elisa. Variety as religious experience: the poetics of the plain style. ReLit (38:1) 2006, 9–25.

3577. Nims, John Frederick; Mason, David. Western wind: an introduction to poetry. Boston, MA: McGraw-Hill, 2006. pp. xl, 646. (Fifth ed.: first ed. 1974.)

3578. O'Donoghue, Bernard. The reality of courtly love. *In* (pp. 7–24) **3836**.

3579. O'Neill, Michael. Criticism as cross-reference. *See* **20110**.

3580. Padel, Ruth. Reading a poem. PNRev (31:5) 2005, 50–7.

3581. Paglia, Camille. Break, blow, burn. (Bibl. 2005, 4127.) Rev. by Kevin Clark in GaR (60:2) 2006, 438–41.

3582. Pankey, Eric. Meditative spaces. SoR (42:4) 2006, 788–93.

3583. Payne, Susan. Essays on British women poets. Ospedaletto Pisa: Pacini, 2006. pp. 136.

3584. Pechey, Graham. 'The scop's twang': adventures of the monosyllable in English verse. PNRev (31:3) 2005, 40–7.

3585. —— 'The scop's twang': adventures of the monosyllable in English verse: 2. PNRev (31:4) 2005, 48–52.

3586. —— 'The scop's twang': adventures of the monosyllable in English verse: 3. PNRev (31:5) 2005, 60–7.

3587. Plumly, Stanley. Pastoral matters. *See* **11580**.

3588. Ryan, Kay. A consideration of poetry. Poetry (188:2) 2006, 148–58.

3589. San, Debra. Hiatus of subject and verb in poetic language. *See* **2421**.

3590. SCHMIDT, MICHAEL. The 2006 StAnza lecture: what, how well, why? *See* **16458**.

3591. SCHNEIDER, MYRA. Repair: writing, poetry and therapy. *See* **7157**.

3592. SCULLY, JAMES. Line break: poetry as social practice. Introd. by Adrienne Rich. Willimantic, CT: Curbstone Press, 2005. pp. xviii, 169. (Second ed.: first ed. 1988.) Rev. by Mark McMorris in AmBR (27:5) 2006, 9–10.

3593. SHAPIRO, KARL; BEUM, ROBERT. The prosody handbook. Mineola, NY: Dover, 2006. pp. ix, 220.

3594. SIMIC, CHARLES. Memory piano. Ann Arbor: Michigan UP, 2006. pp. 237. (Poets on poetry.)

3595. SLAVITT, DAVID R. *Re* verse: essays on poetry and poets. (Bibl. 2005, 4135.) Rev. by Nicholas Birns in HC (43:1) 2006, 19–20.

3596. SOBEL, DAVA. The earth whirls everywhere. Poetry (189:2) 2006, 124–6. (Poetic epigraphs in science books.)

3597. SOBIESKI, JANET; MIEDER, WOLFGANG (eds). 'So many heads, so many wits': an anthology of English proverb poetry. *See* **2992**.

3598. STEWART, SUSAN. Dante and the poetry of meeting. APR (35:4) 2006, 39–42.

3599. TOWNSEND, ANN. Arcadia *redux*. SoR (42:4) 2006, 800–8. (Pastoral.)

3600. WAINWRIGHT, JEFFREY. Poetry: the basics. (Bibl. 2004, 4274.) Rev. by Anthony Radice in PNRev (31:4) 2005, 68; by Tamar Yacobi in PT (26:3) 2005, 557–8.

3601. WARD, JOHN POWELL. The spell of the song: letters, meaning, and English poetry. (Bibl. 2004, 4276.) Rev. by Martha Rust in WordsC (36:4) 2005, 178–9.

3602. WEISSBORT, DANIEL. The rewards of translation. *See* **2938**.

3603. WRIGHT, C. D. Cooling time: an American poetry vigil. *See* **19354**.

PROSE

3604. ATKINS, G. DOUGLAS. Tracing the essay: through experience to truth. (Bibl. 2005, 4139.) Rev. by Ned Stuckey-French in 4thG (8:2) 2006, 157–60.

3605. COUCHMAN, JANE; CRABB, ANN (eds). Women's letters across Europe, 1400–1700: form and persuasion. Aldershot; Burlington, VT: Ashgate, 2005. pp. xv, 336. Rev. by Ellen Moody in RQ (59:3) 2006, 930–2.

3606. DOSSENA, MARINA. 19CSC, ICAMET and the diachronic study of specialized discourse in correspondence. *In* (pp. 65–77) **1227**.

3607. GRIFFITHS, DENNIS. Fleet Street: five hundred years of the press. *See* **1112**.

3608. HOOPER, GLENN; YOUNGS, TIM (eds). Perspectives on travel writing. (Bibl. 2004, 4292.) Rev. by David Seed in MLR (101:4) 2006, 1075–6; by Pere Gifra Adroher in Atl (28:2) 2006, 159–63; by Peter Clark in LitH (15:1) 2006, 77–8.

3609. JEZERNIK, BOÉZIDAR. Wild Europe: the Balkans in the gaze of Western travellers. London: Saqi in assn with the Bosnian Inst., 2004. pp. 320. Rev. by Alex Drace-Francis in Journeys (6:1/2) 2005, 144–5.

3610. JOHNSON, MARILYN. The dead beat: lost souls, lucky stiffs, and the perverse pleasures of obituaries. New York: HarperCollins, 2006. pp. 244, (plates) 8. Rev. by Jane Stern and Michael Stern in NYTB, 12 Mar. 2006, 6; by André Bernard in KR (28:4) 2006, 4–6.

3611. Korhonen, Kuisma. Textual friendship: the essay as impossible encounter, from Plato and Montaigne to Levinas and Derrida. Amherst, NY: Humanity, 2006. pp. 494. (Philosophy and literary theory.)

3612. Landry, Donna. Saddle time. Criticism (46:3) 2004, 441–58. (Travel writing and Orientalism.)

3613. Medina Casado, Carmelo; Ruiz Mas, José (eds). El bisturí inglés: literatura de viajes e hispanismo en lengua inglesa. Jaén: Univ. de Jaén, 2004. pp. 306. (Colección Alonso de Bonilla.) Rev. by José Carlos Redondo Olmedilla in Atl (28:1) 2006, 151–4.

3614. Philippon, Daniel J. Conserving words: how American nature writers shaped the environmental movement. Athens; London: Georgia UP, 2004. pp. xv, 373. Rev. by Timothy Sweet in AL (77:2) 2005, 411–13; by Jim Dwyer in WAL (41:3) 2006, 358–60.

3615. Raumolin-Brumberg, Helena. Temporal aspects of language change: what can we learn from the CEEC? *In* (pp. 139–56) **1195**.

3616. Rigby, Donna. Narrative, creative nonfiction and the personal essay: housing the text. WebS (22:3) 2006, 18–31.

3617. Spongberg, Mary; Curthoys, Ann; Caine, Barbara (eds). Companion to women's historical writing. *See* **3507**.

BIOGRAPHY AND AUTOBIOGRAPHY

3618. Anderson, Linda. Autobiography and the feminist subject. *In* (pp. 119–35) **14277**.

3619. Boelhower, William. Fundamental relations in autobiographical practice. QPS (14) 2006, 174–81.

3620. Boynton, Victoria; Malin, Jo (eds); Nelson, Emmanuel S. (asst ed.). Encyclopedia of women's autobiography. Westport, CT; London: Greenwood Press, 2005. 2 vols. pp. 664. Rev. by Maureen Perkins in Biography (29:2) 2006, 338–41.

3621. Konrád, György. Truth in autobiography. Trans. by Jim Tucker. CK (11:3) 2005, 514–21.

3622. Kunkel, Benjamin. Misery loves memoir. NYTB, 16 July 2006, 27.

3623. Lee, Hermione. Body parts: essays in life-writing. London: Chatto & Windus, 2005. pp. 245. Rev. by Peter Parker in TLS, 4 Feb. 2005, 6; by Sarah Savitt in CamQ (34:4) 2005, 400–3.

3624. —— Virginia Woolf's nose: essays on biography. (Bibl. 2005, 4171.) Rev. by George Fetherling in BkCan (34:5) 2005, 38–9.

3625. Popkin, Jeremy D. History, historians, & autobiography. (Bibl. 2005, 4174.) Rev. by Andrew Hadfield in CLIO (35:3) 2006, 448–53.

3626. Spongberg, Mary; Curthoys, Ann; Caine, Barbara (eds). Companion to women's historical writing. *See* **3507**.

3627. TRIDGELL, SUSAN. Understanding our selves: the dangerous art of biography. (Bibl. 2005, 4178.) Rev. by Roger Averill in A/B (20:2) 2005, 297–300.

3628. WACHTER, PHYLLIS E. Annual bibliography of works about life writing, 2005–2006. Biography (29:4) 2006, 615–725.

3629. WALTER, JAMES. The utility of short lives. Biography (29:2) 2006, 329–37.

RELATED STUDIES

3630. ALTMAN, ROCHELLE. Absent voices: the story of writing systems in the West. New Castle, DE: Oak Knoll Press, 2004. pp. xii, 364. Rev. by Scott Gwara in PBSA (100:1) 2006, 125–34.

3631. ARMSTRONG, KAREN. A short history of myth. Edinburgh: Canongate, 2005. pp. 159. Rev. by Carolyne Larrington in TLS, 18 Nov. 2005, 23; by Laurence Coupe in PNRev (32:4) 2006, 63–4.

3632. BIGSBY, CHRISTOPHER. Introduction: what, then, is the American? *In* (pp. 1–32) **11776**.

3633. BIRCH, DINAH. Land of pure delight. LRB (28:8) 2006, 24–5 (review-article). (Holy Land in English culture.)

3634. BOLAND, EAVAN. From courts and alcoves. PNRev (32:4) 2006, 22–4 (review-article). (Latin poetry by women.)

3635. BONADEI, ROSSANA. Writing radical distance: the Antipodes, from Classical myth to Victorian *mythos*. ConLett (45) 2006, 7–23.

3636. DONNELLY, JAMES S., JR, *et al.* (eds). Encyclopedia of Irish history and culture. (Bibl. 2005, 4184.) Rev. by Francis M. Carroll in NewHR (10:3) 2006, 149–51.

3637. EAGLETON, TERRY. Holy terror. Oxford; New York: OUP, 2005. pp. vii, 148. Rev. by Roger Kershaw in ContRev (288:1681) 2006, 238–9; by Daniel Born in CommRev (4:4) 2006, 56.

3638. FLINT, KATE. Women and reading. Signs (31:2) 2006, 511–36 (review-article).

3639. HALE, JOHN. England and the Italian Renaissance: the growth of interest in its history and art. Introd. by Edward Chaney. (Bibl. 1955–56, 3727.) Oxford; Malden, MA: Blackwell, 2005. pp. xxxv, 178. (Blackwell classic histories of Europe.) (Fourth ed.: first ed. 1954.) Rev. by Keith Miller in TLS, 18 & 25 Aug. 2006, 37.

3640. HILTON, J. A. Anglo-Saxon attitudes: a short introduction to Anglo-Saxonism. Hockwold cum Wilton, Norfolk: Anglo-Saxon Books, 2006. pp. 59. Rev. by Gwendolyn A. Morgan in TMR, Sept. 2006.

3641. LOCKYER, SHARON; PICKERING, MICHAEL (eds). Beyond a joke: the limits of humour. Basingstoke; New York: Palgrave Macmillan, 2005. pp. viii, 212.

3642. LOWRY, ELIZABETH. What literature is made from: fairy tales as the raw stuff of the imagination. TLS, 20 Jan. 2006, 19–20 (review-article).

3643. MOREL, MICHEL. Les affects et la lecture: plaidoyer pour une autre pratique du texte. EtBr (30) 2006, 177–90.

3644. NEMOIANU, VIRGIL. Imperfection and defeat: the role of aesthetic imagination in human society. Budapest; New York: Central European UP, 2006. pp. 150.

3645. ORME, NICHOLAS. Medieval schools: from Roman Britain to Renaissance England. New Haven, CT; London: Yale UP, 2006. pp. xvi, 430. Rev. by Nigel Saul in TLS, 22 Sept. 2006, 24.

3646. ROSS, CATHERINE SHELDRICK; MCKECHNIE, LYNNE E. F.; ROTHBAUER, PAULETTE M. Reading matters: what the research reveals about reading, libraries, and community. Westport, CT: Libraries Unlimited, 2006. pp. x, 277.

3647. STEVENSON, JANE. Women Latin poets: language, gender, and authority from Antiquity to the eighteenth century. Oxford; New York: OUP, 2005. pp. xiv, 659. Rev. by Eavan Boland in PNRev (32:4) 2006, 22–4.

3648. TANNER, MARCUS. The last of the Celts. New Haven, CT; London: Yale UP, 2004. pp. vi, 398, (plates) 16. Rev. by Joanne Craig in RMER (60:2) 2006.

LITERARY THEORY

3649. CHANCE, JANE (ed.). Women medievalists and the academy. *See* **7773**.

3650. CREWE, JONATHAN. Reclaiming character? SStud (34) 2006, 35–40.

3651. GRODEN, MICHAEL; KREISWIRTH, MARTIN; SZEMAN, IMRE (eds). The Johns Hopkins guide to literary theory & criticism. (Bibl. 2000, 26701.) Baltimore, MD; London: Johns Hopkins UP, 2005. pp. xvii, 985. (Second ed.: first ed. 1994.) Rev. by Michael Kramp in RMER (59:2) 2005.

3652. LU, YAODONG. Issues concerning ethical literary criticism. FLS (117) 2006, 32–5. (In Chinese.)

3653. MARTIN, THOMAS L. Poiesis and possible worlds: a study in modality and literary theory. (Bibl. 2005, 4194.) Rev. by David Herman in Style (39:4) 2005, 491–3.

3654. NIE, ZHENZHAO. On ethical literary criticism and moral criticism. *See* **5749**.

3655. PONTUALE, FRANCESCO. Momenti di storia generale: storiografia letteraria americana negli Stati Uniti e in Italia. *In* (pp. 235–54) **3341**.

OLD ENGLISH

GENERAL

3656. Anon. (comp.). A bibliography of writings by Bruce Mitchell 1956–2004. *In* (pp. 268–78) **1241**.

3657. Amodio, Mark C. Writing the oral tradition: oral poetics and literate culture in medieval England. (Bibl. 2005, 4196.) Rev. by Daniel Anlezark in MÆ (75:1) 2006, 144–5; by Thomas A. Bredehoft in Spec (81:2) 2006, 470–1.

3658. Besserman, Lawrence (ed.). Sacred and secular in medieval and early modern cultures. Basingstoke; New York: Palgrave Macmillan, 2006. pp. xviii, 238. (New Middle Ages.)

3659. Bredehoft, Thomas A. Early English metre. Toronto; Buffalo, NY; London: Toronto UP, 2005. pp. viii, 183. (Toronto Old English series.) Rev. by Fritz Kemmler in TMR, Sept. 2006.

3660. —— What are Old English metrical studies for? OEN (39:1) 2005, 25–36.

3661. Burghart, Alex. Web works. *See* **973**.

3662. Cavill, Paul (ed.). The Christian tradition in Anglo-Saxon England: approaches to current scholarship and teaching. (Bibl. 2005, 4202.) Rev. by Chris Jones in EngS (87:1) 2006, 111–12.

3663. Christie, Edward. *Circolwyrde* 2005: new electronic resources for Anglo-Saxon studies. OEN (39:1) 2005, 45–9.

3664. —— *Circolwyrde* 2006: new electronic resources for Anglo-Saxon studies. *See* **980**.

3665. Conde-Silvestre, Juan Camilo; Salvador, Mercedes. Old English studies in Spain: past, present and … future? OEN (40:1) 2006, 38–58.

3666. Doane, A. N.; Wolf, Kirsten (eds). *Beatus vir*: studies in early English and Norse manuscripts in memory of Phillip Pulsiano. *See* **199**.

3667. —— *et al.* (eds). Anglo-Saxon manuscripts in microfiche facsimile: interim index (volumes 1–10). *See* **200**.

3668. Donoghue, Daniel. A point well taken: manuscript punctuation and Old English poems. *In* (pp. 38–58) **1241**.

3669. —— The Tremulous Hand and flying eaglets. ELN (44:1) 2006, 81–6.

3670. Drout, Michael D. C. How tradition works: a meme-based cultural poetics of the Anglo-Saxon tenth century. Tempe: Arizona Center for Medieval and Renaissance Studies, 2006. pp. xvii, 333. (Medieval & Renaissance texts & studies, 306.)

3671. Frank, Roberta. The incomparable wryness of Old English poetry. *In* (pp. 59–73) **1241**.

3672. Griffith, Mark. Whole-verse compound placement in Old English poetry. NQ (53:3) 2006, 253–62.

3673. Hall, Thomas N.; Menzer, Melinda. Old English bibliography 2004. OEN (38:4) 2005, 3–45.

3674. Hiltunen, Risto. *'Eala, geferan and gode wyrhtan'*: on interjections in Old English. *In* (pp. 91–116) **1241**.

3675. Horner, Shari. The language of rape in Old English literature and law: views from the Anglo-Saxon(ist)s. *In* (pp. 149–81) **3692**.

3676. Johnson, David Frame; Treharne, Elaine M. (eds). Readings in medieval texts: interpreting Old and Middle English literature. (Bibl. 2005, 4210.) Rev. by Richard Dance in TMR, Sept. 2006.

3677. Jones, Chris. Strange likeness: the use of Old English in twentieth-century poetry. Oxford; New York: OUP, 2006. pp. viii, 266.

3678. Kabir, Ananya Jahanara. Anglo-Saxon textual attitudes. *In* (pp. 310–23) **3874**.

3679. Keynes, Simon; Smyth, Alfred P. (eds). Anglo-Saxons: studies presented to Cyril Roy Hart. Dublin; Portland, OR: Four Courts Press, 2006. pp. 318. Rev. by Catherine A. M. Clarke in RES (57:231) 2006, 561–2.

3680. Klein, Stacy S. Ruling women: queenship and gender in Anglo-Saxon literature. Notre Dame, IN: Notre Dame UP, 2006. pp. xiii, 282. Rev. by Bettina Bildhauer in TLS, 8 Sept. 2006, 25; by Sharon Rowley in Arthuriana (16:4) 2006, 93–4.

3681. Lapidge, Michael. An aspect of Old English poetic diction: the postpositioning of prepositions. *In* (pp. 153–80) **1241**.

3682. Lavezzo, Kathy. Angels on the edge of the world: geography, literature, and English community, 1000–1534. Ithaca, NY; London: Cornell UP, 2006. pp. xiv, 191, (plates) 4.

3683. Lee, Stuart D.; Solopova, Elizabeth. The keys of Middle-earth: discovering medieval literature through the fiction of J. R. R. Tolkien. *See* **18815**.

3684. Lees, Clare A.; Overing, Gillian R. (eds). A place to believe in: locating medieval landscapes. University Park: Pennsylvania State UP, 2006. pp. x, 272.

3685. McGeachy, Margaret G. Lonesome words: the vocal poetics of the Old English lament and the African American Blues song. Basingstoke; New York: Palgrave Macmillan, 2006. pp. 182. (New Middle Ages.)

3686. Michelet, Fabienne. Creation, migration, and conquest: imaginary geography and sense of space in Old English literature. Oxford; New York: OUP, 2006. pp. xii, 297.

3687. Minnis, Alastair; Johnson, Ian (eds). The Cambridge history of literary criticism: vol. ii, The Middle Ages. *See* **3874**.

3688. Mitchell, Bruce; Irvine, Susan. A critical bibliography of Old English syntax: supplement 1997–2000 part i. *See* **1424**.

3689. Muir, Bernard J. Issues for editors of Anglo-Saxon poetry in manuscript form. *In* (pp. 181–202) **1241**.

3690. Ó Carragáin, Éamonn. Ritual and the Rood: liturgical images and the Old English poems of *The Dream of the Rood* tradition. *See* **3771**.

3691. O'Keeffe, Katherine O'Brien; Orchard, Andy (eds). Latin literature and English lore: studies in Anglo-Saxon literature for Michael Lapidge: vol. i. (Bibl. 2005, 4220.) Rev. by Sara M. Pons-Sanz in TMR, Aug. 2006.

3692. Pasternack, Carol Braun; Weston, Lisa M. C. (eds). Sex and sexuality in Anglo-Saxon England: essays in memory of Daniel Gilmore Calder. Tempe: Arizona Center for Medieval and Renaissance Studies, 2004. pp. xlix, 284. (Medieval & Renaissance texts & studies, 277.) Rev. by Elaine Treharne in RES (57:229) 2006, 262–4.

3693. Phelpstead, Carl. Auden and the Inklings: an alliterative revival. *See* **14509**.

3694. Scheil, Andrew P. The footsteps of Israel: understanding Jews in Anglo-Saxon England. (Bibl. 2005, 4228.) Rev. by Andrew S. Rabin in MP (103:2) 2005, 227–30; by Mary Clayton in TMR, Jan. 2006; by Sybil M. Jack in Parergon (23:1) 2006, 207–9; by Eugene Green in Spec (81:2) 2006, 594–6.

3695. Thijs, Christine. Levels of learning in Anglo-Saxon Worcester: the evidence re-assessed. LSE (36) 2005, 105–31.

3696. —— Wærferth's treatment of the miraculous in his Old English translation of Gregory's *Dialogi*. NQ (53:3) 2006, 272–86.

3697. Walmsley, John. Introduction. *In* (pp. 1–18) **1241**.

3698. —— (ed.). Inside Old English: essays in honour of Bruce Mitchell. *See* **1241**.

3699. Weston, Lisa M. C. *Sanctimoniales cum sanctimoniale*: particular friendships and female community in Anglo-Saxon England. *In* (pp. 35–62) **3692**.

3700. Wickham-Crowley, Kelley M. Living on the *ecg*: the mutable boundaries of land and water in Anglo-Saxon contexts. *In* (pp. 85–110) **3684**.

RELATED STUDIES

3701. Bray, Dorothy. The state of Irish hagiography. HAge (9) 2006.

3702. Dockray-Miller, Mary. Maternal sexuality on the Ruthwell Cross. *In* (pp. 121–46) **3692**.

3703. Lapidge, Michael. The Anglo-Saxon library. Oxford; New York: OUP, 2006. pp. xiv, 407. Rev. by Tom Shippey in LRB (28:11) 2006, 34–5; by Andy Orchard in NQ (53:4) 2006, 544–6.

3704. Shippey, Tom. The most learned man in Europe. LRB (28:11) 2006, 34–5 (review-article). (Libraries and reading in Anglo-Saxon England.)

3705. Thompson, Victoria. Dying and death in later Anglo-Saxon England. Woodbridge, Suffolk; Rochester, NY: Boydell Press, 2004. pp. x, 236. (Anglo-Saxon studies, 4.) Rev. by Daniel Anlezark in MÆ (75:1) 2006, 143; by Martin Welch in Spec (81:2) 2006, 619–20.

3706. Wilson, Katharina M.; Margolis, Nadia (eds). Women in the Middle Ages: an encyclopedia. Westport, CT; London: Greenwood Press, 2004. 2 vols. pp. 997. Rev. by Laura D. Barefield in Arthuriana (16:2) 2006, 109–10.

3707. Wood, Ian. Bede's Jarrow. *In* (pp. 67–84) **3684**.

3708. Wormald, Patrick. The times of Bede: studies in early English Christian society and its historian. Ed. by Stephen Baxter. Oxford; Malden, MA: Blackwell, 2006. pp. xvi, 290.

AUTHORS AND ANONYMOUS WORKS

Ælfric

3709. CAVILL, PAUL. The armour-bearer in Abbo's *Passio sancti Eadmundi* and Anglo-Saxon England. LSE (36) 2005, 47–61.

3710. GRETSCH, MECHTHILD. Ælfric and the cult of saints in late Anglo-Saxon England. Cambridge; New York: CUP, 2005. pp. xi, 263. (Cambridge studies in Anglo-Saxon England, 34.) Rev. by Mary Swan in RES (57:231) 2006, 568–70.

3711. HARE, KENT G. Heroes, saints, and martyrs: holy kingship from Bede to Ælfric. HAge (9) 2006.

3712. HILL, JOYCE. Identifying 'texts' in Cotton Julius E.vii: medieval and modern perspectives. *In* (pp. 27–40) **199**.

3713. KIERNAN, KEVIN. Odd couples in Ælfric's *Julian and Basilissa* in British Library Cotton MS Otho B.x. *In* (pp. 85–106) **199**.

3714. LAVEZZO, KATHY. Gregory's boys: the homoerotic production of English Whiteness. *In* (pp. 63–90) **3692**.

3715. MCFADDEN, BRIAN. 'The books of life': Theotimus as narrator of identity in the Old English lives of St Margaret. *See* **3791**.

3716. PERRELLO, TONY. An undiscovered riddle in Brussels, Bibliothèque Royale MS 1828–1830. *See* **3722**.

3717. ROSSI-REDER, ANDREA. Embodying Christ, embodying nation: Ælfric's accounts of Saints Agatha and Lucy. *In* (pp. 183–202) **3692**.

3718. RUDOLF, WINFRIED. The source and textual identity of 'homily' Napier XXXI – Ælfric & the *munuccild* of Saint-Maurice d'Agaune. RES (57:232) 2006, 607–22.

3719. SZARMACH, PAUL E. 'The poetic turn of mind' of the translator of the OE Bede. *In* (pp. 54–68) **3679**.

3720. WILCOX, JONATHAN. The audience of Ælfric's *Lives of Saints* and the face of Cotton Caligula A.xiv, fols 93–130. *In* (pp. 229–63) **199**.

Saint Aldhelm

3721. PASTERNACK, CAROL BRAUN. The sexual practices of virginity and chastity in Aldhelm's *De virginitate*. *In* (pp. 93–120) **3692**.

3722. PERRELLO, TONY. An undiscovered riddle in Brussels, Bibliothèque Royale MS 1828–1830. ELN (43:2) 2005, 8–14.

3723. PONS-SANZ, SARA M. OE *māl* for L *clasma* in Aldhelmian glossaries. *See* **1583**.

Alfred, King of England (849–899)

3724. DISCENZA, NICOLE. The King's English: strategies of translation in the Old English Boethius. (Bibl. 2005, 4270.) Rev. by Richard Marsden in TMR, Sept. 2006; by Kathryn A. Lowe in TransLit (15:2) 2006, 265–8; by Scott DeGregorio in Spec (81:3) 2006, 835–6.

3725. POLLACK, S. Engendering *wyrd*: notional gender encoded in the Old English poetic and philosophical vocabulary. *See* **3809**.

3726. STANTON, ROBERT. Linguistic fragmentation and redemption before King Alfred. *See* **3775**.

Anglo-Saxon Chronicle

3727. Sheppard, Alice. Families of the king: writing identity in the *Anglo Saxon Chronicle*. Toronto; Buffalo, NY; London: Toronto UP, 2004. pp. x, 266. (Toronto Old English series.) Rev. by Kristen A. Fenton in TMR, Oct. 2006; by Barbara Yorke in LitH (15:2) 2006, 64–5; by Thomas A. Bredehoft in NQ (53:4) 2006, 546–7.

3728. Stafford, Pauline. Chronicle D, 1067 and women: gendering conquest in eleventh-century England. *In* (pp. 208–23) **3679**.

Apollonius of Tyre

3729. Morini, Carla. The Old English *Apollonius* and Wulfstan of York. LSE (36) 2005, 63–104.

The Battle of Maldon

3730. Hall, Mark F. The theory and practice of alliterative verse in the works of J. R. R. Tolkien. *See* **18802**.

3731. Ryner, Bradley D. Exchanging battle: subjective and objective conflicts in *The Battle of Maldon*. EngS (87:3) 2006, 266–76.

Beowulf

3732. Anlezark, Daniel. Grendel and the Book of Wisdom. NQ (53:3) 2006, 262–9.

3733. Bagby, Benjamin. *Beowulf*, the Edda, and the performance of medieval epic: notes from the workshop of a reconstructed 'singer of tales'. *In* (pp. 181–92) **3892**.

3734. Bammesberger, Alfred. Eight notes on the *Beowulf* text. *In* (pp. 19–37) **1241**.

3735. —— Hildeburh's son. NQ (53:1) 2006, 14–17.

3736. —— Hrothgar's speech welcoming Beowulf. NQ (53:3) 2006, 269–72.

3737. —— Old English *guðrinc* in *Beowulf*, 1118b. NM (107:1) 2006, 87–9.

3738. —— Old English *wæteres weorpan* in *Beowulf*, 2791a. ANQ (19:1) 2006, 3–7.

3739. —— The syntactic analysis of the opening verses in *Beowulf*. ANQ (19:4) 2006, 3–7.

3740. —— Who does *laþum* refer to at *Beowulf*, line 1257a? NQ (53:4) 2006, 398–401.

3741. Clark, David. Relaunching the hero: the case of Scyld and Beowulf re-opened. Neophilologus (90:4) 2006, 621–42.

3742. Davidson, Mary Catherine. Speaking of nostalgia in *Beowulf*. MP (103:2) 2005, 143–55.

3743. Drout, Michael D. C. The rhetorical evolution of '*Beowulf*': *the Monsters and the Critics*. *In* (pp. 183–215) **18804**.

3744. Fisher, Matthew A. Working at the crossroads: Tolkien, St Augustine, and the *Beowulf*-poet. *In* (pp. 217–30) **18804**.

3745. Gilsdorf, Ethan. Epic proportions. CommRev (4:4) 2006, 14–21.

3746. Hall, J. R. Three studies on the manuscript text of *Beowulf*: lines 47a, 747a, and 2232a. *In* (pp. 441–70) **199**.

3747. HALL, MARK F. The theory and practice of alliterative verse in the works of J. R. R. Tolkien. *See* **18802**.

3748. JORDAN, JESSICA HOPE. Women refusing the gaze: theorizing Thryth's 'unqueenly custom' in *Beowulf* and the bride's revenge in Quentin Tarantino's *Kill Bill*. HAge (9) 2006.

3749. KIGHTLEY, MICHAEL R. Heorot or Meduseld? Tolkien's use of *Beowulf* in 'The King of the Golden Hall'. *See* **18812**.

3750. LIVINGSTON, MICHAEL; SUTTON, JOHN WILLIAM. Reinventing the hero: Gardner's *Grendel* and the shifting face of *Beowulf* in popular culture. *See* **16049**.

3751. MCGUIRE, THOMAS. Violence and vernacular in Seamus Heaney's *Beowulf*. *See* **16320**.

3752. MICHELET, FABIENNE. Creation, migration, and conquest: imaginary geography and sense of space in Old English literature. *See* **3686**.

3753. OLIVARES MERINO, EUGENIO. The Old English poem *A Vampyre of the Fens*: a bibliographical ghost. Misc (32) 2005, 87–101.

3754. ORCHARD, ANDY. Pride and prodigies: studies in the monsters of the *Beowulf*-manuscript. (Bibl. 1998, 4408.) Rev. by Andrea Schutz in TMR, Jan. 2004; by Antonina Harbus in Parergon (22:2) 2005, 269–70.

3755. ORTON, PETER. Burning idols, burning bridges: Bede, conversion and *Beowulf*. LSE (36) 2005, 5–46.

3756. POWELL, KATHRYN. Meditating on men and monsters: a reconsideration of the thematic unity of the *Beowulf* manuscript. RES (57:228) 2006, 1–15.

3757. STAVER, RUTH JOHNSTON. A companion to *Beowulf*. (Bibl. 2005, 4312.) Rev. by Peter Barry in Eng (55:212) 2006, 213–19; by Daniel Anlezark in MÆ (75:2) 2006, 324–5.

3758. STEELE, FELICIA JEAN. Dreaming of dragons: Tolkien's impact on Heaney's *Beowulf*. *See* **16325**.

3759. TRIPP, RAYMOND P., JR. *Beowulf* 3182b: *lofgeornost*, 'most eager to praise'. NM (106:4) 2005, 425–42.

Byrhtferth

3760. DEROLEZ, RENÉ. Byrhtferðus bene docet. EngS (87:3) 2006, 253–65.

3761. HART, CYRIL (ed. and trans.). Byrhtferth's East Anglian chronicle: a comparative edition and translation of the Latin annals. Lewiston, NY; Lampeter: Mellen Press, 2006. pp. cxxxix, 194. (Early chronicles of England, 3.)

Cædmon's Hymn

3762. CRONAN, DENNIS. Cædmon and Hesiod. EngS (87:4) 2006, 379–401.

3763. MCCULLY, CHRIS. The word in time: 1, 'More like masonry than music'. PNRev (32:4) 2006, 31–2.

3764. NILES, JOHN D. Bede's Cædmon, 'The Man Who Had No Story' (Irish tale-type 2412B). Folklore (117:2) 2006, 141–55.

3765. O'DONNELL, DANIEL PAUL. Bede's strategy in paraphrasing Cædmon's Hymn. JEGP (103:4) 2004, 417–32.

Charms

3766. Roper, Jonathan. English verbal charms. *See* **2989**.

Christ III

3767. Shimomura, Sachi. Odd bodies and visible ends in medieval literature. Basingstoke; New York: Palgrave Macmillan, 2006. pp. ix, 198. (New Middle Ages.)

Cynewulf

3768. Orchard, Andy. Computing Cynewulf: the *Judith*-connection. *In* (pp. 75–106) **3871**.

Daniel

3769. Bugge, John. Virginity and prophecy in the Old English *Daniel*. EngS (87:2) 2006, 127–47.

The Dream of the Rood

3770. Duncan, Thomas G. '*Quid Hinieldus cum Christo?*': the secular expression of the sacred in Old and Middle English lyrics. *In* (pp. 29–46) **3658**.

3771. Ó Carragáin, Éamonn. Ritual and the Rood: liturgical images and the Old English poems of *The Dream of the Rood* tradition. Toronto; Buffalo, NY; London: Toronto UP, 2005. pp. xxxii, 427, (plates) 16. Rev. by Daniel Paul O'Donnell in HAge (9) 2006; by Benjamin de Lee in Comitatus (37) 2006, 272–5.

Exodus

3772. Bammesberger, Alfred. The Old English adjective *mēnig* 'strong'. *See* **1584**.

3773. Hall, J. R. Old English *Exodus* 390b: *witgan larum*. NQ (53:1) 2006, 17–21.

The Fight at Finnsburh

3774. Bammesberger, Alfred. Hildeburh's son. *See* **3735**.

Genesis A

3775. Stanton, Robert. Linguistic fragmentation and redemption before King Alfred. YES (36:1) 2006, 12–26.

Genesis B

3776. Bammesberger, Alfred. A note on *Genesis B*, line 456a. NQ (53:2) 2006, 135–6.

The Grave

3777. Siebert, Eve. A possible source for the addition to *The Grave*. ANQ (19:4) 2006, 8–16.

Homilies

3778. Corradini, Erika. Text and context of a late Old English homily: the Exeter additions to manuscript Cambridge, Corpus Christi College 421. *In* (pp. 77–88) **3407**.

3779. Ogawa, Hiroshi. Language and style in two anonymous Old English Easter homilies. *In* (pp. 203–21) **1241**.

3780. Rudolf, Winfried. The source and textual identity of 'homily' Napier XXXI – Ælfric & the *munuccild* of Saint-Maurice d'Agaune. *See* **3718**.

3781. Treharne, Elaine. Reading from the margins: the uses of Old English homiletic manuscripts in the post-Conquest period. *In* (pp. 329–58) **199**.

Judith

3782. Orchard, Andy. Computing Cynewulf: the *Judith*-connection. *In* (pp. 75–106) **3871**.

3783. Powell, Kathryn. Meditating on men and monsters: a reconsideration of the thematic unity of the *Beowulf* manuscript. *See* **3756**.

Laws

3784. Horner, Shari. The language of rape in Old English literature and law: views from the Anglo-Saxon(ist)s. *In* (pp. 149–81) **3692**.

Maxims I

3785. Berkhout, Carl T. The Old English *Maxims I* 190: *bacum tobreden*. NQ (53:1) 2006, 21–2.

Medical and Scientific Texts

3786. McIlwain, James T. The condition called *neurisn* in *Leechbook I*. NQ (53:2) 2006, 142–4.

Metres of Boethius

3787. Irvine, Susan. Rewriting women in the Old English *Boethius*. *In* (pp. 488–501) **8374**.

Old English Bede

3788. Bredehoft, Thomas A. Filling the margins of CCCC 41: textual space and a developing archive. *See* **188**.

3789. Szarmach, Paul E. 'The poetic turn of mind' of the translator of the OE Bede. *In* (pp. 54–68) **3679**.

3790. Weston, Lisa M. C. *Sanctimoniales cum sanctimoniale*: particular friendships and female community in Anglo-Saxon England. *In* (pp. 35–62) **3692**.

Old English Martyrology

3791. McFadden, Brian. 'The books of life': Theotimus as narrator of identity in the Old English lives of St Margaret. EngS (86:6) 2005, 473–92.

Old English Orosius

3792. Bately, Janet. The language of Ohthere's report to King Alfred: some problems and some puzzles for historians and linguists. *In* (pp. 39–53) **3679**.

Penitentials

3793. Fulk, R. D. Male homoeroticism in the Old English *Canons of Theodore*. *In* (pp. 1–34) **3692**.

The Phoenix

3794. Gorst, E. K. C. Latin sources of the Old English *Phoenix*. NQ (53:2) 2006, 136–42.

3795. McFadden, Brian. Sweet odors and interpretative authority in the Exeter Book *Physiologus* and *Phoenix*. *See* **3796**.

Physiologus

3796. McFadden, Brian. Sweet odors and interpretative authority in the Exeter Book *Physiologus* and *Phoenix*. PLL (42:2) 2006, 181–209.

3797. Znojemská, Helena. Sailing the dangerous waters: images of land and sea in *The Seafarer*, *The Panther* and *The Whale*. *See* **3804**.

Riddles

3798. Murphy, Patrick J. The riders of the celestial wain in Exeter Book Riddle 22. NQ (53:4) 2006, 401–7.

3799. Sayers, William. Exeter Book Riddle 17 and the L-rune: British **lester* 'vessel, oat-straw hive'? ANQ (19:2) 2006, 4–9.

3800. Sorrell, Paul. A bee in my bonnet: solving Riddle 17 of the Exeter Book. *In* (pp. 544–53) **8374**.

Saints' Lives

3801. Lindström, Bengt. Old English *þreowa* and *styccemælum*. NQ (53:1) 2006, 22–3.

3802. Powell, Kathryn. Meditating on men and monsters: a reconsideration of the thematic unity of the *Beowulf* manuscript. *See* **3756**.

The Seafarer

3803. Klein, Stacy S. Gender and the nature of exile in Old English elegies. *In* (pp. 113–31) **3684**.

3804. Znojemská, Helena. Sailing the dangerous waters: images of land and sea in *The Seafarer*, *The Panther* and *The Whale*. PSE (24) 2006, 87–105.

Soul and Body

3805. Siebert, Eve. A possible source for the addition to *The Grave*. *See* **3777**.

The Wanderer

3806. Edsall, Mary Agnes. '*Se þonne þisne wealsteal wise geþohte*': an Augustinian reading of the early English meditation *The Wanderer*. *In* (pp. 37–62) **3301**.

3807. Irvine, Susan. Speaking one's mind in *The Wanderer*. *In* (pp. 117–33) **1241**.

3808. Klein, Stacy S. Gender and the nature of exile in Old English elegies. *In* (pp. 113–31) **3684**.

3809. Pollack, S. Engendering *wyrd*: notional gender encoded in the Old English poetic and philosophical vocabulary. Neophilologus (90:4) 2006, 643–61.

Widsith

3810. Znojemská, Helena. A *scop* among scribes: a reading in the manuscript context of *Widsið*. LittPr (16:31) 2006, 36–64.

The Wife's Lament

3811. Frese, Dolores Warwick. Sexing political tropes of conquest: *The Wife's Lament* and Laȝamon's *Brut*. *In* (pp. 203–33) **3692**.

3812. Kinch, Ashby. The ethical agency of the female lyric voice: *The Wife's Lament* and Catullus 64. SP (103:2) 2006, 121–52.

3813. Klein, Stacy S. Gender and the nature of exile in Old English elegies. *In* (pp. 113–31) **3684**.

Wonders of the East

3814. Powell, Kathryn. Meditating on men and monsters: a reconsideration of the thematic unity of the *Beowulf* manuscript. *See* **3756**.

Wulf and Eadwacer

3815. Daniëlli, Sonja. '*Wulf, min Wulf*': an eclectic analysis of the wolf-man. Neophilologus (90:1) 2006, 135–54.

3816. Klein, Stacy S. Gender and the nature of exile in Old English elegies. *In* (pp. 113–31) **3684**.

Wulfstan

3817. Bately, Janet. The language of Ohthere's report to King Alfred: some problems and some puzzles for historians and linguists. *In* (pp. 39–53) **3679**.

3818. Kubouchi, Tadao. Wulfstan's Scandinavian loanword usage: an aspect of the linguistic situation in the late Old English Danelaw. *In* (pp. 134–52) **1241**.

3819. Morini, Carla. The Old English *Apollonius* and Wulfstan of York. *See* **3729**.

3820. Rudolf, Winfried. The source and textual identity of 'homily' Napier xxxi – Ælfric & the *munuccild* of Saint-Maurice d'Agaune. *See* **3718**.

MIDDLE ENGLISH AND FIFTEENTH CENTURY

GENERAL

3821. Adams, Jenny. Power play: the literature and politics of chess in the late Middle Ages. Philadelphia: Pennsylvania UP, 2006. pp. 252. (Middle Ages.)

3822. Aers, David. Sanctifying signs: making Christian tradition in late medieval England. (Bibl. 2005, 4394.) Rev. by H. L. Spencer in RES (56:223) 2005, 138–40; by Alcuin Blamires in MLR (101:4) 2006, 1085–6; by Joe Ricke in SixCJ (37:1) 2006, 293–5; by David Lawton in Spec (81:3) 2006, 796–7.

3823. Akbari, Suzanne Conklin. Seeing through the veil: optical theory and medieval allegory. (Bibl. 2005, 4395.) Rev. by John V. Fleming in SAC (28) 2006, 271–3; by Peter Brown in Spec (81:2) 2006, 463–4.

3824. Allen, Elizabeth. False fables and exemplary truth in later Middle English literature. (Bibl. 2005, 4396.) Rev. by Edward Wheatley in SAC (28) 2006, 273–6.

3825. Allen, Rosamund (ed.). Eastward bound: travel and travellers, 1050–1550. Manchester; New York: Manchester UP, 2004. pp. xii, 270. Rev. by John Tolan in Spec (81:2) 2006, 466–7.

3826. Bedford, Ronald; Davis, Lloyd; Kelly, Philippa (eds). Early modern autobiography: theories, genres, practices. *See* **4792**.

3827. Besserman, Lawrence (ed.). Sacred and secular in medieval and early modern cultures. *See* **3658**.

3828. Bildhauer, Bettina. Medieval blood. Cardiff: UP of Wales, 2006. pp. x, 245. (Religion and culture in the Middle Ages.)

3829. Børch, Marianne (ed.). Text and voice: the rhetoric of authority in the Middle Ages. (Bibl. 2005, 4408.) Rev. by Michael Foster in TMR, May 2006.

3830. Brantley, Jessica. The visual environment of Carthusian texts: decoration and illustration in Notre Dame 67. *In* (pp. 173–216) **3871**.

3831. Brownlee, Kevin, *et al.* Vernacular literary consciousness *c.*1100–*c.*1500: French, German and English evidence. *In* (pp. 422–71) **3874**.

3832. Burrow, J. A.; Turville-Petre, Thorlac. A book of Middle English. *See* **1202**.

3833. Caie, Graham D. 'Oh what a lovely plague': the effect of the Black Death on high and low cultures in the English Middle Ages. RANAM (39) 2006, 21–31.

3834. Cannon, Christopher. The grounds of English literature. (Bibl. 2005, 4546.) Rev. by Elizabeth M. Tyler in CamQ (34:4) 2005, 408–11; by Nicholas Perkins in TLS, 2 June 2006, 33; by Ralph Hanna in SAC (28) 2006, 281–4; by David Lawton in Spec (81:3) 2006, 820–1.

3835. Chewning, Susannah Mary. Queer desire and heterosexual consummation in the anchoritic mystical tradition. *In* (pp. 68–81) **11883**.

3836. Cooney, Helen (ed.). Writings on love in the English Middle Ages. Basingstoke; New York: Palgrave Macmillan, 2006. pp. xiii, 204. (Studies in Arthurian and courtly cultures.)

3837. Cordery, Leona F. A corpus of medieval crusading literature: in search of an identity. *In* (pp. 35–49) **1227**.

3838. Cornett, Michael. New books across the disciplines. JMEMS (35:3) 2005, 681–705.

3839. —— New books across the disciplines. JMEMS (36:1) 2006, 201–19.

3840. —— New books across the disciplines. JMEMS (36:2) 2006, 455–73.

3841. —— New books across the disciplines. JMEMS (36:3) 2006, 643–66.

3842. Crassons, Kate. Performance anxiety and Watson's vernacular theology. *See* **4171**.

3843. D'Arcens, Louise; Feros Ruys, Juanita (eds). 'Maistresse of my wit': medieval women, modern scholars. (Bibl. 2004, 4630.) Rev. by Natalie Tomas in Parergon (23:1) 2006, 151–3.

3844. D'Arcy, Anne Marie; Fletcher, Alan J. (eds). Studies in late medieval and early Renaissance texts in honour of John Scattergood: 'the key of all good remembrance'. (Bibl. 2005, 4419.) Rev. by Nicholas Perkins in TLS, 24 Mar. 2006, 33; by Jenni Nuttall in RES (57:231) 2006, 575–8.

3845. Davenport, Tony. Medieval narrative: an introduction. (Bibl. 2005, 4420.) Rev. by Siobhain Bly Calkin in TMR, Feb. 2006.

3846. Denny-Brown, Andrea. Rips and slits: the torn garment and the medieval self. *In* (pp. 223–37) **4629**.

3847. Edwards, Robert R. The flight from desire: Augustine and Ovid to Chaucer. Basingstoke; New York: Palgrave Macmillan, 2006. pp. xi, 219. (New Middle Ages.)

3848. Ferster, Judith. The family of origin *versus* the human family: universal love in literature. *In* (pp. 249–61) **3896**.

3849. Finke, Laurie A.; Schichtman, Martin B. King Arthur and the myth of history. (Bibl. 2005, 4805.) Rev. by Anne Berthelot in TMR, Jan. 2006; by Carolyne Larrington in TLS, 26 May 2006, 13; by Rosalind Field in SAC (28) 2006, 290–2; by Glenn Burger in Spec (81:2) 2006, 511–13.

3850. Fissell, Mary E. The politics of reproduction in the English Reformation. Representations (87) 2004, 43–81.

3851. Georgianna, Linda. Vernacular theologies. ELN (44:1) 2006, 87–94.

3852. Goodall, Peter. The author in the study: self-representation as reader and writer in the medieval and early modern periods. *In* (pp. 104–14) **4792**.

3853. Green, Richard Firth; Mooney, Linne R. (eds). Interstices: studies in Middle English and Anglo-Latin texts in honour of A. G. Rigg. (Bibl. 2004, 4641.) Rev. by Michael Calabrese in TMR, Jan. 2006.

3854. Hanna, Ralph. London literature, *c*.1300–1380. (Bibl. 2005, 4436.) Rev. by Tom Shippey in TLS, 31 Mar. 2006, 25; by Alexandra Gillespie in HLQ (69:2) 2006, 315–19; by Simon Horobin in JEBS (9) 2006, 183–5; by Elizabeth Edwards in DalR (86:3) 2006, 475–7; by James Simpson in SAC (28) 2006, 292–5.

3855. Hiatt, Alfred. The making of medieval forgeries: false documents in fifteenth-century England. (Bibl. 2005, 4745.) Rev. by Richard Firth Green in SAC (28) 2006, 298–300; by Paul Strohm in Spec (81:2) 2006, 530–2.

3856. JOHNSON, RICHARD FREEMAN. Saint Michael the Archangel in medieval English legend. (Bibl. 2005, 4441.) Rev. by Sherry L. Reames in Spec (81:4) 2006, 1214–15.

3857. KABIR, ANANYA JAHANARA; WILLIAMS, DEANNE (eds). Postcolonial approaches to the European Middle Ages: translating cultures. (Bibl. 2005, 4442.) Rev. by Robert Costomiris in JCPS (12:1) 2005, 110–12; by Sharon Kinoshita in TMR, May 2006; by Laurie Finke in Arthuriana (16:2) 2006, 105–7; by Jeffrey Jerome Cohen in NQ (53:2) 2006, 221–2; by Lauren Grace Kilroy in Comitatus (37) 2006, 284–6.

3858. KERBY-FULTON, KATHRYN. Books under suspicion: censorship and tolerance of revelatory writing in late medieval England. Notre Dame, IN: Notre Dame UP, 2006. pp. lii, 562.

3859. KUSKIN, WILLIAM. Introduction: following Caxton's trace. *In* (pp. 1–31) **4125**.

3860. —— (ed.). Caxton's trace: studies in the history of English printing. *See* **4125**.

3861. LAVEZZO, KATHY. Angels on the edge of the world: geography, literature, and English community, 1000–1534. *See* **3682**.

3862. —— (ed.). Imagining a medieval English nation. (Bibl. 2005, 4446.) Rev. by Paul Strohm in SAC (27) 2005, 331–4; by John M. Bowers in CLIO (35:2) 2006, 263–70.

3863. LEE, STUART D.; SOLOPOVA, ELIZABETH. The keys of Middle-earth: discovering medieval literature through the fiction of J. R. R. Tolkien. *See* **18815**.

3864. LEES, CLARE A.; OVERING, GILLIAN R. (eds). A place to believe in: locating medieval landscapes. *See* **3684**.

3865. LITTLE, KATHERINE C. Images, texts, and exegetics in Chaucer's Second Nun's Tale. *See* **4421**.

3866. MCAVOY, LIZ HERBERT; HUGHES-EDWARDS, MARI (eds). Anchorites, wombs and tombs: intersections of gender and enclosure in the Middle Ages. Cardiff: UP of Wales, 2005. pp. 240. (Religion and culture in the Middle Ages.) Rev. by Robyn Cadwallader in Parergon (23:1) 2006, 183–5.

3867. MCCARTHY, CONOR. Marriage in medieval England: law, literature, and practice. (Bibl. 2005, 4450.) Rev. by M. Teresa Tavormina in SAC (28) 2006, 303–6.

3868. MCDONALD, NICOLA (ed.). Medieval obscenities. *See* **1529**.

3869. MCDONALD, NICOLA F.; ORMROD, W. M. (eds). Rites of passage: cultures of transition in the fourteenth century. Woodbridge, Suffolk; Rochester, NY: Boydell Press in assn with the York Medieval Press, 2004. pp. vii, 176. Rev. by Charlotte Stanford in TMR, June 2006.

3870. MACHAN, TIM WILLIAM. Early Modern Middle English. *In* (pp. 299–322) **4125**.

3871. MANN, JILL; NOLAN, MAURA (eds). The text in the community: essays on medieval works, manuscripts, authors, and readers. Notre Dame, IN: Notre Dame UP, 2006. Rev. by Ralph Hanna in RES (57:231) 2006, 550–1.

3872. MEALE, CAROL M. Entrapment or empowerment? Women and discourses of love and marriage in the fifteenth century. *In* (pp. 163–78) **3836**.

3873. MEYERSON, MARK D.; THIERY, DANIEL; FRANK, OREN (eds). 'A great effusion of blood'? Interpreting medieval violence. (Bibl. 2005, 4454.) Rev. by Christine M. Rose in Arthuriana (16:4) 2006, 104–7.

3874. MINNIS, ALASTAIR; JOHNSON, IAN (eds). The Cambridge history of literary criticism: vol. II, The Middle Ages. Cambridge; New York: CUP, 2005. pp. xvi, 865. (Cambridge history of literary criticism.) Rev. by Leo Carruthers in EA (59:2) 2006, 218–19; by Kantik Ghosh in RES (57:230) 2006, 403–4; by Suzanne Conklin Akbari in NQ (53:4) 2006, 556–8.

3875. OAKLEY-BROWN, LIZ. Ovid and the cultural politics of translation in early modern England. Aldershot; Burlington, VT: Ashgate, 2006. pp. 222. (Studies in European cultural transition, 34.)

3876. OLSON, LINDA; KERBY-FULTON, KATHRYN (eds). Voices in dialogue: reading women in the Middle Ages. (Bibl. 2005, 4460.) Rev. by Rebecca Krug in TMR, Oct. 2006; by Claire M. Waters in SAC (28) 2006, 313–16.

3877. PERFETTI, LISA. The representation of women's emotions in medieval and early modern culture. (Bibl. 2005, 4463.) Rev. by Elizabeth Allen in TSWL (25:1) 2006, 153–6; by H. L. Spencer in RES (57:229) 2006, 259–60; by Elizabeth Robertson in SAC (28) 2006, 316–19.

3878. POLLARD, A. J. Imagining Robin Hood: the late medieval stories in historical context. (Bibl. 2005, 4468.) Rev. by John Simons in LitH (15:2) 2006, 66–7; by Graham Tulloch in Parergon (23:1) 2006, 190–2.

3879. PURDIE, RHIANNON; ROYAN, NICOLA. Introduction: Tartan Arthur? *In* (pp. 1–7) **3972**.

3880. RAGUIN, VIRGINIA CHIEFFO; STANBURY, SARAH (eds). Women's space: patronage, place, and gender in the medieval Church. Albany: New York State UP, 2005. pp. x, 261. (SUNY series in medieval studies.) Rev. by Catherine Sanok in SAC (28) 2006, 322–5.

3881. ROBERTSON, KELLIE; UEBEL, MICHAEL (eds). The Middle Ages at work: practicing labor in late medieval England. Basingstoke; New York: Palgrave Macmillan, 2004. pp. vi, 267. (New Middle Ages.) Rev. by Stephen Knight in SAC (28) 2006, 325–8.

3882. SAUNDERS, CORINNE; LE SAUX, FRANÇOISE; THOMAS, NEIL (eds). Writing war: medieval literary responses to warfare. (Bibl. 2005, 4478.) Rev. by Daniel E. Thiery in NQ (53:1) 2006, 99–100.

3883. SCATTERGOOD, JOHN. 'The unequal scales of love': love and social class in Andreas Capellanus' *De amore* and some later texts. *In* (pp. 63–79) **3836**.

3884. SCHULTZ, JAMES A. Courtly love, the love of courtliness, and the history of sexuality. Chicago, IL; London: Chicago UP, 2006. pp. xxii, 242.

3885. SHEPARD, ALAN; POWELL, STEPHEN D. (eds). Fantasies of Troy: Classical tales and the social imaginary in medieval and early modern Europe. (Bibl. 2005, 4479.) Rev. by John Watkins in CLIO (35:2) 2006, 270–5.

3886. SINGLETON, ANTONY. The Early English Text Society in the nineteenth century: an organizational history. RES (56:223) 2005, 90–118.

3887. Søndergaard, Leif; Hansen, Rasmus Thorning (eds). Monsters, marvels and miracles: imaginary journeys and landscapes in the Middle Ages. (Bibl. 2005, 4483.) Rev. by Anke Bernau in TMR, Apr. 2006.

3888. Staley, Lynn. Languages of power in the age of Richard II. (Bibl. 2005, 4484.) Rev. by Marion Turner in MÆ (75:1) 2006, 147–8; by Andrew Galloway in SAC (28) 2006, 331–4; by Leo Carruthers in EA (59:4) 2006, 470–1; by William McClellan in Spec (81:4) 2006, 1259–61.

3889. Stein, Robert M.; Prior, Sandra Pierson (eds). Reading medieval culture: essays in honor of Robert W. Hanning. (Bibl. 2005, 4485.) Rev. by Laurie A. Finke in Arthuriana (16:1) 2006, 83–4; by Sarah A. Kelen in TMR, Sept. 2006; by Lisa J. Kiser in SAC (28) 2006, 334–7.

3890. Strohm, Paul. *Politique*: languages of statecraft between Chaucer and Shakespeare. (Bibl. 2005, 4489.) Rev. by Charlotte C. Morse in Spec (81:4) 2006, 1262–4.

3891. Turner, Marion. Greater London. *In* (pp. 25–40) **4312**.

3892. Vitz, Evelyn Birge; Regalado, Nancy Freeman; Lawrence, Marilyn (eds). Performing medieval narrative. Woodbridge, Suffolk; Rochester, NY: Brewer, 2005. pp. xvi, 261. Rev. by Thomas Pettitt in TMR, Nov. 2006; by Peggy McCracken in Arthuriana (16:4) 2006, 114–15; by Elina Gertsman in TheatreS (47:1) 2006, 125–7; by Roger Pensom in MÆ (75:1) 2006, 130–1; by Helen Phillips in Folklore (117:2) 2006, 222–4.

3893. Voaden, Rosalynn; Wolfthal, Diane (eds). Framing the family: narrative and representation in the medieval and early modern periods. Tempe: Arizona Center for Medieval and Renaissance Studies, 2005. pp. xii, 305. (Medieval & Renaissance texts & studies, 280.) Rev. by Holly S. Hurlburt in RQ (59:2) 2006, 570–1.

3894. Watson, Nicholas. Cultural changes. ELN (44:1) 2006, 127–37.

3895. Weinstock, Horst. *Vices and Virtues*: ein mittelenglisches Corpus um 1200. *In* (pp. 329–40) **1227**.

3896. Wheeler, Bonnie (ed.). Mindful spirit in late medieval literature: essays in honor of Elizabeth D. Kirk. Basingstoke; New York: Palgrave Macmillan, 2006. pp. viii, 266. (New Middle Ages.)

3897. Yokota, Yumi. Form and function of demonstratives in the Middle English southern texts and speculation on the origin of *th*- type third person plural pronouns in the north and south. *See* **1432**.

DRAMA

General Studies

3898. Barron, Caroline M. Pageantry on London Bridge in the early fifteenth century. *In* (pp. 91–104) **3913**.

3899. Butterworth, Philip. Magic on the early English stage. (Bibl. 2005, 4496.) Rev. by Max Harris in CompDr (40:1) 2006, 141–4; by Michael Saenger in Comitatus (37) 2006, 225–6; by Henk Gras in TRI (31:3) 2006, 322–3.

3900. Coletti, Theresa. Mary Magdalene and the drama of saints: theater, gender, and religion in late medieval England. (Bibl. 2004, 4693.) Rev. by Claire

Sponsler in MedRen (19) 2006, 336–41; by Ruth Nisse in SAC (28) 2006, 287–90; by Jane Tolmie in Spec (81:3) 2006, 828–9.

3901. Cummings, James. REED and the possibilities of Web technology. *In* (pp. 178–99) **3904**.

3902. Davidson, Clifford. Deliver us from evil: essays on symbolic engagement in early drama. New York: AMS Press, 2004. pp. xiii, 204. (AMS studies in the Middle Ages, 27.) Rev. by Willy Maley in MLR (101:4) 2006, 1090–1.

3903. —— Selected studies in drama & Renaissance literature. New York: AMS Press, 2006. pp. xiv, 275. (AMS studies in the Renaissance, 40.)

3904. Douglas, Audrey; MacLean, Sally-Beth (eds). REED in review: essays in celebration of the first twenty-five years. Toronto; Buffalo, NY; London: Toronto UP, 2006. pp. ix, 271. (Studies in early English drama.)

3905. DuBruck, Edelgard E. The current state of research on late medieval drama, 2004–2005: survey, bibliography, and reviews. FCS (31) 2006, 1–30.

3906. Elliott, John R., *et al.* (eds). Records of early English drama: Oxford. (Bibl. 2004, 4697.) Rev. by Mark C. Pilkinton in CompDr (39:1) 2005, 93–9; by Katherine L. French in SixCJ (36:4) 2005, 1237–8; by Michael Heaney in FMJ (9:1) 2006, 109–11.

3907. Goodland, Katharine. Female mourning and tragedy in medieval and Renaissance English drama: from the raising of Lazarus to *King Lear*. Aldershot; Burlington, VT: Ashgate, 2006. pp. 254. (Studies in performance and early modern drama.)

3908. Grantley, Darryll. English dramatic interludes, 1300–1580: a reference guide. (Bibl. 2005, 4504.) Rev. by Laura Feitzinger Brown in SixCJ (36:3) 2005, 851.

3909. Hagen, Tanya. Thinking outside the Bard: REED, repertory canons, and editing early English drama. *In* (pp. 216–35) **3904**.

3910. Happé, Peter. Cyclic form and the English mystery plays: a comparative study of the English and biblical cycles and their Continental and iconographic counterparts. (Bibl. 2005, 4505.) Rev. by Beatrice Groves in NQ (53:2) 2006, 224–5.

3911. Johnston, Alexandra F. The founding of Records of Early English Drama. *In* (pp. 21–38) **3904**.

3912. Klausner, David N. (ed.). Records of early drama: Wales. Toronto; Buffalo, NY; London: Toronto UP, 2005. pp. clxxviii, 528. (Records of early English drama.) Rev. by Chris Grooms in Arthuriana (16:1) 2006, 75–7; by John J. McGavin in CompDr (40:3) 2006, 365–71.

3913. —— Marsalek, Karen S. (eds). 'Bring furth the pagants': essays in early English drama presented to Alexandra F. Johnston. Toronto; Buffalo, NY; London: Toronto UP, 2006. pp. vi, 329. (Studies in early English drama, 9.)

3914. Lancashire, Anne. Multi-day performance and the London Clerkenwell play. ETh (9:2) 2006, 114–29.

3915. Lehr, John. Using REED: a selective bibliography. *In* (pp. 236–60) **3904**.

3916. MacLean, Sally-Beth. Birthing the concept: the first nine years. *In* (pp. 39–51) **3904**.

3917. —— The southwest entertains: Exeter and local performance patronage. *In* (pp. 58–76) **3913**.

3918. Marsalek, Karen Sawyer. 'Awake your faith': English Resurrection drama and *The Winter's Tale*. *In* (pp. 271–91) **3913**.

3919. Marshall, John. Gathering in the name of the outlaw: REED and Robin Hood. *In* (pp. 65–84) **3904**.

3920. Milling, Jane; Thomson, Peter (eds). The Cambridge history of British theatre: vol. 1, Origins to 1660. (Bibl. 2005, 4510.) Rev. by Robert B. Hornback in SixCJ (37:2) 2006, 488–9.

3921. Murphy, Diane. Medieval mystery plays as popular culture: performing the lives of saints. Lewiston, NY; Lampeter: Mellen Press, 2006. pp. iii, 216.

3922. Normington, Katie. Gender and medieval drama. (Bibl. 2005, 4511.) Rev. by Mark Campbell Chambers in MÆ (75:1) 2006, 152–3; by Elina Gertsman in TheatreS (47:2) 2006, 319–21; by Theresa Coletti in Spec (81:4) 2006, 1240–2.

3923. Owens, Margaret E. Stages of dismemberment: the fragmented body in medieval and early modern drama. (Bibl. 2005, 4512.) Rev. by Kim Solga in TJ (58:3) 2006, 529–31; by D. K. Smith in RQ (59:1) 2006, 288–9.

3924. Ritch, K. Janet. The role of the presenter in medieval drama. *In* (pp. 230–68) **3913**.

3925. Rosser, Gervase. Roles in life: the drama of the medieval guilds. *In* (pp. 140–56) **3904**.

3926. Santana, Richard W. Language and the decline of magic: epistemological shifts in English literature from medieval to Modernist. Lewiston, NY; Lampeter: Mellen Press, 2005. pp. xv, 242.

3927. Scoville, Chester N. Saints and the audience in Middle English biblical drama. (Bibl. 2005, 4514.) Rev. by Heather Hill-Vásquez in Spec (81:4) 2006, 1250–2.

3928. Sponsler, Claire. Ritual imports: performing medieval drama in America. (Bibl. 2005, 4517.) Rev. by Sharon Aronson-Lehavi in TJ (58:2) 2006, 361–2.

3929. Stephenson, Jenn. Herodotus in the labyrinth: REED and hypertext. *In* (pp. 200–15) **3904**.

3930. Stillman, Robert (ed.). Spectacle and public performance in the late Middle Ages and the Renaissance. *See* **4729**.

3931. Sturges, Robert S. 'Wols-hede and outhorne': the ban, bare life, and power in the Passion plays. *In* (pp. 93–108) **3896**.

3932. Thomas, Sylvia. REED and the Record Office: tradition and innovation on the road to access. *In* (pp. 131–9) **3904**.

3933. Twycross, Meg. The *ordo paginarum* revisited, with a digital camera. *In* (pp. 105–31) **3913**.

3934. Walker, Greg. *Fulgens and Lucres* and early Tudor drama. *In* (pp. 23–34) **4734**.

3935. WESTFALL, SUZANNE. What hath REED wrought? REED and patronage. *In* (pp. 85–100) **3904**.

3936. WILLIAMSON, EILA; MCGAVIN, JOHN J. Crossing the border: the provincial records of southeast Scotland. *In* (pp. 157–77) **3904**.

3937. YOUNG, ABIGAIL ANN. 'Practice makes perfect': policies for a cross-disciplinary project. *In* (pp. 52–62) **3904**.

Separate Anonymous Works

Chester Cycle

3938. BUTLER, MICHELLE M. The borrowed expositor. ETh (9:2) 2006, 73–90.

3939. ISHI, MIKIKO. The weeping mothers in *Sumidagawa*, *Curlew River*, and medieval European religious plays. CompDr (39:3/4) 2005/06, 287–305.

3940. MILLS, DAVID. Some theological issues in Chester's plays. *In* (pp. 212–28) **3913**.

Coventry Plays

3941. ALAKAS, BRANDON. Seniority and mastery: the politics of ageism in the Coventry Cycle. ETh (9:1) 2006, 15–36.

3942. DAVIS, LLOYD; SMITH, PETER J.; WALKER, GREG. From revelation to commodity: performing messengers, language and news from the York Cycle to Ben Jonson. *See* **3956**.

Croxton Plays

3943. NISSE, RUTH. Defining acts: drama and the politics of interpretation in late medieval England. (Bibl. 2005, 4524.) Rev. by Gail McMurray Gibson in SAC (28) 2006, 310–13; by Carolyn D. Roark in TheatreS (47:2) 2006, 317–19; by Kathleen Ashley in Spec (81:4) 2006, 1237–9.

Digby Plays

3944. FINDON, JOANNE. Napping in the arbor in the Digby *Mary Magdalene* play. ETh (9:2) 2006, 35–55.

3945. MACI, STEFANIA MARIA. The phonetic representation of ME *ī* in some Norfolk works of the late fifteenth century. *See* **1280**.

3946. SCOVILLE, CHESTER. On bombshells and faulty assumptions: what the Digby *Conversion of Saint Paul* really did with the Acts of the Apostles. *In* (pp. 197–211) **3913**.

Everyman

3947. HARPER, ELIZABETH; MIZE, BRITT. Material economy, spiritual economy, and social critique in *Everyman*. CompDr (40:3) 2006, 263–311.

Mankind

3948. BRANTLEY, JESSICA; FULTON, THOMAS. *Mankind* in a year without kings. JMEMS (36:2) 2006, 321–54.

3949. CHAMBERS, MARK. Weapons of conversion: *Mankind* and medieval stage properties. PQ (83:1) 2004, 1–11.

Towneley Cycle

3950. Bevington, David. One hell of an ending: staging Last Judgment in the Towneley Plays and in *Doctor Faustus* A and B. *In* (pp. 292–310) **3913**.

3951. Edminster, Warren. The preaching fox: festive subversion in the plays of the Wakefield Master. (Bibl. 2005, 4531.) Rev. by Liam Purdon in CompDr (39:1) 2005, 118–25; by Douglas W. Hayes in TMR, Nov. 2006.

3952. Epp, Garrett P. J. Doubting Thomas: 'womans witnes' and the Towneley *Thomas Indie*. *In* (pp. 165–80) **3913**.

3953. Happé, Peter. The Towneley Cycle without the Wakefield Master. RORD (45) 2006, 23–39.

Wisdom

3954. Klausner, David N. The modular structure of *Wisdom*. *In* (pp. 181–96) **3913**.

York Cycle

3955. Davidson, Clifford. York guilds and the Corpus Christi plays: unwilling participants? ETh (9:2) 2006, 11–33.

3956. Davis, Lloyd; Smith, Peter J.; Walker, Greg. From revelation to commodity: performing messengers, language and news from the York Cycle to Ben Jonson. CEl (70) 2006, 1–13.

3957. Donley, Maren L. Mercers, mercantilism, and the maintenance of power: the York *Last Judgment* and the York register. Exemplaria (18:2) 2006, 327–66.

3958. Gusick, Barbara I. Christ's healing of the lame man in the York Cycle's *Entry into Jerusalem*: interpretive challenges for the newly healed. FCS (31) 2006, 80–105.

3959. Kroll, Norma. The failure of emotion and reason in the York Cycle. *In* (pp. 109–20) **3896**.

3960. Rogerson, Margaret. REED *York*: volume 3, 'The revivals'. *In* (pp. 132–61) **3913**.

3961. Taylor, Jefferey H. Four levels of meaning in the York Cycle of mystery plays: a study in medieval allegory. Lewiston, NY; Lampeter: Mellen Press, 2006. pp. ii, 115.

3962. Wiebe, Heather. Benjamin Britten, the 'national faith', and the animation of history in 1950s England. Representations (93) 2006, 76–105.

ROMANCE

General Studies

3963. Bethlehem, Ulrike. Guinevere, a medieval puzzle: images of Arthur's queen in the medieval literature of England and France. Heidelberg: Winter, 2005. pp. vi, 441. (Anglistische Forschungen, 345.)

3964. Børch, Marianne. Writing remembering orality: Geoffrey Chaucer's Sir Thopas. *See* **4369**.

3965. Classen, Albrecht (ed.). Violence in medieval courtly literature: a casebook. London; New York: Routledge, 2004. pp. vi, 352. (Routledge medieval casebooks.) Rev. by Richard W. Kaeuper in TMR, Oct. 2005.

3966. Cooper, Helen. The English romance in time: transforming motifs from Geoffrey of Monmouth to the death of Shakespeare. (Bibl. 2005, 4547.) Rev. by Jordi Sánchez-Martí in Atl (28:1) 2006, 139–44; by Meredith Reynolds in SixCJ (37:1) 2006, 246–8; by Nancy Mason Bradbury in Spec (81:1) 2006, 164–5.

3967. Findon, Joanne. Napping in the arbor in the Digby *Mary Magdalene* play. *See* **3944**.

3968. Keyes, Flo. The literature of hope in the Middle Ages and today: connections in medieval romance, modern fantasy, and science fiction. Jefferson, NC; London: McFarland, 2006. pp. vii, 197.

3969. Lacy, Norris J. (ed.). A history of Arthurian scholarship. Woodbridge, Suffolk; Rochester, NY: Brewer, 2006. pp. xiv, 285. (Arthurian studies.) Rev. by Alan Lupack in Arthuriana (16:4) 2006, 100–2.

3970. Liu, Yin. Middle English romance as prototype genre. ChauR (40:4) 2006, 335–53.

3971. Phillips, Helen. Rites of passage in French and English romances. *In* (pp. 83–107) **3869**.

3972. Purdie, Rhiannon; Royan, Nicola (eds). The Scots and medieval Arthurian legend. Woodbridge, Suffolk; Rochester, NY: Brewer, 2005. pp. viii, 156. (Arthurian studies, 61.) Rev. by Lisabeth C. Buchelt in Arthuriana (16:4) 2006, 107–8; by Janet Hadley Williams in Parergon (23:1) 2006, 197–9; by Simon Horobin in JEBS (9) 2006, 197–9; by Joanna Martin in NQ (53:2) 2006, 220–1.

3973. Reichl, Karl. Turkic bard and medieval entertainer: what a living epic tradition can tell us about oral performance of narrative in the Middle Ages. *In* (pp. 167–78) **3892**.

3974. Rouse, Robert Allen. The idea of Anglo-Saxon England in Middle English romance. (Bibl. 2005, 4554.) Rev. by Bettina Bildhauer in TLS, 6 Jan. 2006, 23; by Sharon Farmer in TMR, Feb. 2006; by Rosalind Field in MÆ (75:1) 2006, 148–9; by H. L. Spencer in RES (57:228) 2006, 128–30; by Emily V. Thornbury in NQ (53:4) 2006, 549–50; by Kathy Lavezzo in Spec (81:3) 2006, 912–13.

3975. Rushton, Cory J. ‘Of an uncouthe stede’: the Scottish knight in Middle English Arthurian romances. *In* (pp. 109–19) **3972**.

3976. Sanders, Arnold. Sir Gareth and the ‘Unfair Unknown’: Malory’s use of the Gawain romances. *See* **4270**.

3977. Saunders, Corinne. Love and loyalty in Middle English romance. *In* (pp. 45–61) **3836**.

3978. —— (ed.). Cultural encounters in the romance of medieval England. (Bibl. 2005, 4555.) Rev. by Judith Jefferson in MÆ (75:2) 2006, 326; by Nicola McDonald in SAC (28) 2006, 328–31; by Glenn Wright in Parergon (23:1) 2006, 201–4.

3979. Shimomura, Sachi. Odd bodies and visible ends in medieval literature. *See* **3767**.

3980. Thompson, Raymond H.; Busby, Keith (eds). Gawain: a casebook. London; New York: Routledge, 2006. pp. viii, 362. (Arthurian characters and themes, 8.) Rev. by Peter H. Goodrich in Arthuriana (16:4) 2006, 111–13.

Separate Anonymous Works

Athelston

3981. Jost, Jean E. Why is Middle English romance so violent? The literary and aesthetic purposes of violence. *In* (pp. 241–67) **3965**.

Charlemagne Romances

3982. Shepherd, Stephen H. A. (ed.). *Turpines Story*: a Middle English translation of the Pseudo-Turpin chronicle. Oxford; New York: OUP for the Early English Text Soc., 2004. pp. lxiii, 105. (EETS, 322.) Rev. by Raluca Radulescu in LSE (36) 2005, 358–60; by Phillipa Hardman in NQ (53:3) 2006, 366–7.

Emare

3983. Inglis, Katherine. Costanza, Constance, Custance and Emaré: Romola's medieval ancestry. *See* **10031**.

Floris and Blauncheflur

3984. Kooper, Erik (ed.). Sentimental and humorous romances: *Floris and Blancheflour*, *Sir Degrevant*, *The Squire of Low Degree*, *The Tournament of Tottenham*, and *The Feast of Tottenham*. Kalamazoo, MI: Medieval Inst., 2006. pp. vii, 221. (Middle English texts.)

Gamelyn

3985. Jost, Jean E. Why is Middle English romance so violent? The literary and aesthetic purposes of violence. *In* (pp. 241–67) **3965**.

Generides

3986. Bliss, Jane. The sultan's name in *Generydes* and *Syr Generides*. *See* **1727**.

3987. Howard, Matthew. 'We are broderen': fraternal bonds and familial loyalty within the fifteenth-century romance of *Generydes*. *In* (pp. 129–42) **4099**.

Golagros and Gawain

3988. Mainer, Sergi. Reinventing Arthur: representations of the Matter of Britain in medieval Scotland and Catalonia. *In* (pp. 135–47) **3972**.

3989. Purdie, Rhiannon. The search for Scottishness in *Golagros and Gawane*. *In* (pp. 95–107) **3972**.

3990. —— Royan, Nicola (eds). The Scots and medieval Arthurian legend. *See* **3972**.

Horn Childe and Maiden Rimnild

3991. Holford, Matthew. History and politics in *Horn Child and Maiden Rimnild*. RES (57:229) 2006, 149–68.

Ipomadon

3992. Sánchez-Martí, Jordi. Reading romance in late medieval England: the case of the Middle English *Ipomedon*. PQ (83:1) 2004, 13–39.

3993. —— Reconstructing the audiences of the Middle English versions of *Ipomedon*. SP (103:2) 2006, 153–77.

King Horn

3994. Holford, Matthew. History and politics in *Horn Child and Maiden Rimnild*. *See* **3991**.

Lancelot of the Laik

3995. Archibald, Elizabeth. *Lancelot of the Laik*: sources, genre, reception. *In* (pp. 71–82) **3972**.

3996. Mainer, Sergi. Reinventing Arthur: representations of the Matter of Britain in medieval Scotland and Catalonia. *In* (pp. 135–47) **3972**.

3997. Purdie, Rhiannon; Royan, Nicola (eds). The Scots and medieval Arthurian legend. *See* **3972**.

Morte Arthure (Alliterative)

3998. Royan, Nicola. The fine art of faint praise in Older Scots historiography. *In* (pp. 43–54) **3972**.

The Siege of Jerusalem

3999. Citrome, Jeremy J. The surgeon in medieval English literature. *See* **4531**.

4000. Livingston, Michael (ed.). Siege of Jerusalem. Kalamazoo, MI: Medieval Inst. in assn with the Univ. of Rochester for TEAMS, 2004. pp. xviii, 397. (Middle English texts.) Rev. by Michael Calabrese in TMR, Aug. 2006.

Sir Bevis of Hampton

4001. Campbell, Kofi. Nation-building colonialist-style in *Bevis of Hampton*. Exemplaria (18:1) 2006, 205–32.

Sir Degarre

4002. Saunders, Corinne. Violent magic in Middle English romance. *In* (pp. 225–40) **3965**.

Sir Degrevant

4003. Kooper, Erik (ed.). Sentimental and humorous romances: *Floris and Blancheflour*, *Sir Degrevant*, *The Squire of Low Degree*, *The Tournament of Tottenham*, and *The Feast of Tottenham*. *See* **3984**.

Sir Eglamour of Artois

4004. Classen, Albrecht (ed.). Discourses on love, marriage, and transgression in medieval and early modern literature. Tempe: Arizona Center for Medieval and Renaissance Studies, 2004. pp. 374. (Medieval & Renaissance texts & studies, 278.) Rev. by Susan S. Morrison in TMR, Feb. 2006.

Sir Lamwell

4005. Bawcutt, Priscilla. *Sir Lamwell* in Scotland. *In* (pp. 83–93) **3972**.

Sir Landeval

4006. Bawcutt, Priscilla. *Sir Lamwell* in Scotland. *In* (pp. 83–93) **3972**.

Sir Launfal

4007. Bawcutt, Priscilla. *Sir Lamwell* in Scotland. *In* (pp. 83–93) **3972**.

4008. Jost, Jean E. Why is Middle English romance so violent? The literary and aesthetic purposes of violence. *In* (pp. 241–67) **3965**.

Sir Orfeo

4009. Saunders, Corinne. Violent magic in Middle English romance. *In* (pp. 225–40) **3965**.

Sir Tristrem

4010. Putter, Ad. The ways and words of the hunt: notes on *Sir Gawain and the Green Knight*, *The Master of Game*, *Sir Tristrem*, *Pearl*, and *Saint Erkenwald*. *See* **4530**.

The Squyr of Lowe Degre

4011. Kooper, Erik (ed.). Sentimental and humorous romances: *Floris and Blancheflour*, *Sir Degrevant*, *The Squire of Low Degree*, *The Tournament of Tottenham*, and *The Feast of Tottenham*. *See* **3984**.

Torrent of Portyngale

4012. Classen, Albrecht (ed.). Discourses on love, marriage, and transgression in medieval and early modern literature. *See* **4004**.

The Weddynge of Sir Gawen and Dame Ragnell

4013. Zaerr, Linda Marie. *The Weddynge of Sir Gawen and Dame Ragnell*: performance and intertextuality in Middle English popular romance. *In* (pp. 193–208) **3892**.

William of Palerne

4014. Cooper, Helen. Love before Troilus. *In* (pp. 25–43) **3836**.

4015. Simons, John. The compositional genetics of *Kingdoms of Elfin* together with a note on tortoises. *In* (pp. 45–60) **18964**.

POETRY

General Studies

4016. Bawcutt, Priscilla. Writing about love in late medieval Scotland. *In* (pp. 179–96) **3836**.

4017. Boffey, Julia; Edwards, A. S. G. A new index of Middle English verse. London: British Library, 2005. pp. xvi, 344. (*Revised version of* bibl. 1943–44, 73.) Rev. by Oliver Pickering in JEBS (9) 2006, 164–7; by E. G. Stanley in NQ (53:3) 2006, 362–4.

4018. Bredehoft, Thomas A. Early English metre. *See* **3659**.

4019. Cooney, Helen. Some new thing: *The Floure and the Leafe* and the cultural shift in the role of the poet in fifteenth century England. *In* (pp. 131–46) **3836**.

4020. Forni, Kathleen (ed.). The Chaucerian apocrypha: a selection. Kalamazoo, MI: Medieval Inst., 2005. pp. vii, 169. (Middle English texts.) Rev. by Richard Osberg in TMR, June 2006.

4021. Hall, Stefan Thomas. The role of medieval Scottish poetry in creating Scottish identity: 'textual nationalism'. Lewiston, NY; Lampeter: Mellen Press, 2006. pp. v, 239.

4022. Hirsh, John C. (ed.). Medieval lyric: Middle English lyrics, ballads, and carols. (Bibl. 2005, 4618.) Rev. by Barbara Newman in LRB (28:10) 2006, 26–7.

4023. Lewis, Lucy. Chepman and Myllar: the first printers in Scotland. *In* (pp. 57–69) **746**.

4024. Newman, Barbara. 'I was such a lovely girl'. LRB (28:10) 2006, 26–7 (review-article).

4025. O'Donoghue, Bernard. The reality of courtly love. *In* (pp. 7–24) **3836**.

4026. Spearing, A. C. Textual subjectivity: the encoding of subjectivity in medieval narratives and lyrics. (Bibl. 2005, 4613.) Rev. by Michael Foster in Style (39:4) 2005, 496–500.

Separate Anonymous Works

The Assembly of Ladies

4027. Meale, Carol M. Entrapment or empowerment? Women and discourses of love and marriage in the fifteenth century. *In* (pp. 163–78) **3836**.

Carols

4028. Wakelin, Daniel. The carol in writing: three anthologies from fifteenth-century Norfolk. JEBS (9) 2006, 25–49.

Charms (ME)

4029. Roper, Jonathan. English verbal charms. *See* **2989**.

Debate Poems

4030. Purdon, Liam O. *Als I Lay in a Winteris Nyt* and the second death. *In* (pp. 45–56) **3896**.

The Feast of Tottenham

4031. Kooper, Erik (ed.). Sentimental and humorous romances: *Floris and Blancheflour, Sir Degrevant, The Squire of Low Degree, The Tournament of Tottenham*, and *The Feast of Tottenham*. *See* **3984**.

The Floure and the Leafe

4032. Cooney, Helen. Some new thing: *The Floure and the Leafe* and the cultural shift in the role of the poet in fifteenth-century England. *In* (pp. 131–46) **3836**.

4033. Meale, Carol M. Entrapment or empowerment? Women and discourses of love and marriage in the fifteenth century. *In* (pp. 163–78) **3836**.

The Infancy of Jesus Christ

4034. Couch, Julie Nelson. Misbehaving God: the case of the Christ Child in MS Laud Misc. 108 *Infancy of Jesus Christ*. *In* (pp. 31–43) **3896**.

Lyrics

4035. Berkhout, Carl T. Another late Middle English lyric. NQ (53:1) 2006, 25–6.

4036. Carruthers, Mary. 'Sweet Jesus'. *In* (pp. 9–19) **3896**.

4037. —— Sweetness. Spec (81:4) 2006, 999–1013.

4038. Duncan, Thomas G. *'Quid Hinieldus cum Christo?'*: the secular expression of the sacred in Old and Middle English lyrics. *In* (pp. 29–46) **3658**.

4039. —— (ed.). A companion to the Middle English lyric. Woodbridge, Suffolk; Rochester, NY: Brewer, 2005. pp. xxv, 302. Rev. by Kathleen Palti in NQ (53:4) 2006, 550–1.

4040. Lewis, Lucy. A newly discovered lyric from Exeter College, Oxford on the theme of 'Know thyself'. MÆ (75:1) 2006, 123–7.

Metrical Chronicle

4041. Grund, Peter. A previously unrecorded fragment of the Middle English *Short Metrical Chronicle* in Bibliotheca Philosophica Hermetica M199. EngS (87:3) 2006, 277–93.

Owayne Miles

4042. Easting, Robert. St Patrick's Purgatory: fragments of a second copy of the Middle English stanzaic *Owayne Miles*. MÆ (75:1) 2006, 84–102.

Physiologus

4043. Wriglesworth, Chad. Myth maker, unicorn maker: C. S. Lewis and the reshaping of medieval thought. *See* **17206**.

Saints' Lives

4044. Scahill, John. Middle English saints' legends. (Bibl. 2005, 4652.) Rev. by Karen Winstead in TMR, Oct. 2006; by Anke Bernau in RES (57:231) 2006, 559–61; by E. G. Stanley in NQ (53:3) 2006, 362–4; by Antonina Harbus in Parergon (23:1) 2006, 205–7.

4045. van Dijk, Mathilde. Being Saint Barbara in England: shifting patterns of holiness in the later Middle Ages. *In* (pp. 1–19) **3415**.

South English Legendary

4046. Ho, Cynthia. The Middle English St Francis: text and context. *In* (pp. 81–91) **3896**.

4047. Thompson, Anne B. Everyday saints and the art of narrative in the *South English Legendary*. (Bibl. 2005, 4655.) Rev. by Rosamund Allen in MLR (101:2) 2006, 511–13; by Lawrence P. Morris in PE (1) 2006, 64–7; by Mary C. Olson in SixCJ (37:1) 2006, 123–4.

The Stacions of Rome

4048. Sauer, Michelle M. Saints Praxedis and Prudentiana in *The Golden Legend* and *The Stacions of Rome*: fragments from Lambeth Palace 72 and MS BL Additional 22283. ANQ (19:2) 2006, 9–16.

The Tale of Beryn

4049. Sturges, Robert S. The Pardoner in Canterbury: class, gender, and urban space in the *Prologue to the Tale of Beryn*. ColLit (33:3) 2006, 52–76.

The Tournament of Tottenham

4050. Kooper, Erik (ed.). Sentimental and humorous romances: *Floris and Blancheflour*, *Sir Degrevant*, *The Squire of Low Degree*, *The Tournament of Tottenham*, and *The Feast of Tottenham*. *See* **3984**.

Wynnere and Wastoure

4051. Coleman, Joyce. The complaint of the makers: *Wynnere and Wastoure* and the 'misperformance topos' in medieval England. *In* (pp. 27–39) **3892**.

4052. Harwood, Britton J. Anxious over peasants: textual disorder in *Winner and Waster.* JMEMS (36:2) 2006, 291–319.

4053. Scattergood, John. London and money: Chaucer's *Complaint to His Purse*. *In* (pp. 162–73) **4312**.

PROSE

General Studies

4054. Edwards, A. S. G. (ed.). A companion to Middle English prose. (Bibl. 2005, 4662.) Rev. by Anne Hudson in MLR (101:4) 2006, 1080–1; by Anthony P. Bale in NQ (53:1) 2006, 97–8.

4055. Expósito González, Mª Cruz. Abstract or concrete nouns: relevant variables in the selection of relative pronouns. *See* **1418**.

4056. Pitts, Brent A.; Furnish, Shearle. The Middle English Apocalypse gloss in British Library MS Additional 18633. *See* **1534**.

Separate Anonymous Works

Ancrene Wisse / Ancrene Riwle

4057. Batt, Catherine; Renevey, Denis; Whitehead, Christiania. Domesticity and medieval devotional literature. LSE (36) 2005, 195–250.

4058. Breeze, Andrew. *Bune* 'maiden; beloved' in *Ancrene Wisse*. *See* **1548**.

4059. Heng, Geraldine. Pleasure, resistance, and a feminist aesthetics of reading. *In* (pp. 53–72) **14277**.

4060. Zettersten, Arne. The AB language lives. *In* (pp. 13–24) **18804**.

The Book of Vices and Virtues

4061. Weinstock, Horst. *Vices and Virtues*: ein mittelenglisches Corpus um 1200. *In* (pp. 329–40) **1227**.

Chronicles

4062. Given-Wilson, Chris. Chronicles: the writing of history in medieval England. (Bibl. 2004, 4873.) Rev. by Sara M. Butler in Spec (81:3) 2006, 852–3.

The Cloud of Unknowing

4063. Davis, Carmel. Words beyond meaning: the language of ascent and the ascent of language in medieval mystical texts. *See* **2289**.

4064. Hirsh, John C. Christianity and the Church. *In* (pp. 241–60) **4345**.

4065. Taylor, Cheryl. The *Cloud*-author's remaking of the pseudo-Dionysius' *Mystical Theology*. MÆ (75:2) 2006, 202–18.

The Craft of Dying

4066. Edwards, A. S. G. The contexts of Notre Dame 67. *In* (pp. 107–28) **3871**.

The Crafte and Knowledge for to Dye Well

4067. Reynolds, Rebecca L. Elaine of Ascolat's death and the *ars moriendi*. *See* **4267**.

Deonise Hid Divinite

4068. Taylor, Cheryl. The *Cloud*-author's remaking of the pseudo-Dionysius' *Mystical Theology*. *See* **4065**.

Devotional Works

4069. Nichols, Ann Eljenholm. Pepys Library MS 2125: the *Arma Christi* stubs. *See* **248**.

The Doctrine of the Hert

4070. Batt, Catherine; Renevey, Denis; Whitehead, Christiania. Domesticity and medieval devotional literature. *See* **4057**.

The Gast of Gy

4071. Sturges, Robert S. Purgatory in the marriage bed: conjugal sodomy in *The Gast of Gy*. *In* (pp. 57–78) **3893**.

Gilte Legende

4072. Sauer, Michelle M. Saints Praxedis and Prudentiana in *The Golden Legend* and *The Stacions of Rome*: fragments from Lambeth Palace 72 and MS BL Additional 22283. *See* **4048**.

Homilies

4073. Hornbeck, J. Patrick, ii. *Lollard* sermons? Soteriology and late medieval dissent. NQ (53:1) 2006, 26–30.

4074. Horner, Patrick J. (ed. and trans.). A macaronic sermon collection from late medieval England: Oxford, MS Bodley 649. Toronto: Pontifical Inst. of Mediaeval Studies, 2006. pp. 544. (Studies and texts, 143.)

4075. Little, Katherine C. 'Bokes ynowe': vernacular theology and fourteenth-century exhaustion. *See* **4199**.

4076. Treharne, Elaine. Reading from the margins: the uses of Old English homiletic manuscripts in the post-Conquest period. *In* (pp. 329–58) **199**.

4077. Waters, Claire M. Angels and earthly creatures: preaching, performance, and gender in the later Middle Ages. (Bibl. 2004, 4886.) Rev. by Katherine Little in SAC (27) 2005, 367–70; by Raymond Clemens in JR (86:2) 2006, 320–2.

Jacob's Well

4078. Fitzgibbons, Moira. *Jacob's Well* and penitential pedagogy. SAC (27) 2005, 213–37.

Katherine Group

4079. Tani, Akinobu. *Thesaurus of Old English* for Early Middle English: an analysis in light of word pairs in the 'Katherine Group' lives. *In* (pp. 293–303) **1227**.

4080. Zettersten, Arne. The AB language lives. *In* (pp. 13–24) **18804**.

Letters

4081. Rust, Martha Dana. 'Le Vostre C': letters and love in Bodleian Library MS Arch. Selden B.24. *In* (pp. 111–38) **4523**.

4082. Truelove, Alison. Linguistic diversity in the fifteenth-century Stonor Letters. RMedS (31) 2005, 77–95.

Medical and Scientific Texts

4083. Bryan, Eric Shane. Prognostications by thunder in the zodiac: MSS Trinity R.14.52, Sloane 636, and PML M.775. ANQ (19:4) 2006, 16–22.

4084. Citrome, Jeremy J. The surgeon in medieval English literature. *See* **4531**.

4085. Grund, Peter. Manuscripts as sources for linguistic research: a methodological case study based on the *Mirror of Lights*. JEL (34:2) 2006, 105–25.

4086. Rand, Kari Anne. A previously unnoticed fragment of John of Burgundy's plague tract and some connected pest regimens. NQ (53:3) 2006, 295–7.

4087. Reinert, Laura. A Middle English text on planting and grafting in Cambridge, Trinity College, O.5.26. ANQ (19:1) 2006, 9–16.

A Mirror to Devout People

4088. Edwards, A. S. G. The contexts of Notre Dame 67. *In* (pp. 107–28) **3871**.

4089. Gillespie, Vincent. The haunted text: reflections in *A Mirror to Devout People*. *In* (pp. 129–72) **3871**.

The Mirroure of the World

4090. Doyle, A. I. The copyist of MSS Bodley 283 and Durham Cosin V.ii.15. *See* **202**.

Prose Brut

4091. Bryan, Elizabeth J. Amazons and Ursulines. *In* (pp. 21–30) **3896**.

4092. Drukker, Tamar S. An eye-witness account or literary historicism? John Page's *Siege of Rouen*. *See* **4284**.

4093. Norris, Ralph. Minor sources in Caxton's Roman war. *See* **4128**.

Saints' Lives

4094. van Dijk, Mathilde. Being Saint Barbara in England: shifting patterns of holiness in the later Middle Ages. *In* (pp. 1–19) **3415**.

RELATED STUDIES

4095. Barolini, Teodolinda (ed.). Medieval constructions in gender and identity: essays in honor of Joan M. Ferrante. Tempe: Arizona Center for Medieval and Renaissance Studies, 2005. pp. xii, 195. (Medieval & Renaissance texts & studies, 293.)

4096. Bejczy, István P. Gerald of Wales on the cardinal virtues: a reappraisal of *De principis instructione*. MÆ (75:2) 2006, 191–201.

4097. Birkholz, Daniel. Mapping medieval utopia: exercises in restraint. JMEMS (36:3) 2006, 585–618.

4098. Clark, James G. A monastic renaissance at St Albans: Thomas Walsingham and his circle, *c*.1350–1440. Oxford: Clarendon Press; New York: OUP, 2004. pp. xi, 316. (Oxford historical monographs.) Rev. by G. H. Martin in Library (7:1) 2006, 90–1.

4099. Davis, Isabel; Müller, Miriam; Jones, Sarah Rees (eds). Love, marriage, and family ties in the later Middle Ages. Turnhout: Brepols, 2003.

pp. xi, 340. (International medieval research, 11.) Rev. by Kathleen Troup in Parergon (23:2) 2006, 131–3.

4100. Day, Mildred Leake (ed. and trans.). Latin Arthurian literature. Woodbridge, Suffolk; Rochester, NY: Brewer, 2005. pp. 284. (Arthurian archives, 9.) Rev. by Thomas H. Crofts in Arthuriana (16:4) 2006, 85–6.

4101. Goering, Joseph. The Virgin and the Grail: origins of a legend. New Haven, CT; London: Yale UP, 2005. pp. xii, 188. Rev. by Lynda Sexon in CHist (75:2) 2006, 416–18.

4102. Kelly, Henry Ansgar. Jews and Saracens in Chaucer's England: a review of the evidence. SAC (27) 2005, 129–69.

4103. King, Andy (ed. and trans.). *Scalacronica* (1272–1363). By Sir Thomas Gray. Woodbridge, Suffolk; Rochester, NY: Boydell Press for the Surtees Soc., 2005. pp. lxiv, 288. (Pubs of the Surtees Soc., 209.) Rev. by Richard J. Moll in TMR, Oct. 2006.

4104. Marks, Richard. Image and devotion in late medieval England. Stroud: Sutton, 2004. pp. viii, 344. Rev. by Kathleen Kamerick in Spec (81:1) 2006, 236–7.

4105. Nickel, Helmut. About the Saxon rebellion and the massacre at Amesbury. Arthuriana (16:1) 2006, 65–70.

4106. Nisse, Ruth. 'Your name will no longer be Aseneth': apocrypha, anti-martyrdom, and Jewish conversion in thirteenth-century England. Spec (81:3) 2006, 734–53.

4107. Over, Kristen Lee. Kingship, conquest, and patria: literary and cultural identities in medieval French and Welsh Arthurian romance. London; New York: Routledge, 2005. pp. xi, 231. (Studies in medieval history and culture.)

4108. Pickens, Rupert T. Arthurian time and space: Chrétien's *Conte del Graal* and Wace's *Brut*. MÆ (75:2) 2006, 219–46.

4109. Ure, John. Pilgrimage: the great adventure of the Middle Ages. London: Constable, 2006. pp. ix, 258, (plates) 8. Rev. by Nicholas Vincent in TLS, 21 July 2006, 24.

4110. Wilson, Katharina M.; Margolis, Nadia (eds). Women in the Middle Ages: an encyclopedia. *See* **3706**.

4111. Wood, Juliette. Where does Britain end? The reception of Geoffrey of Monmouth in Scotland and Wales. *In* (pp. 9–23) **3972**.

AUTHORS

Andrew of Wyntoun

4112. Royan, Nicola. The fine art of faint praise in Older Scots historiography. *In* (pp. 43–54) **3972**.

John Audelay (*fl*.1426)

4113. Citrome, Jeremy J. The surgeon in medieval English literature. *See* **4531**.

John Barbour

4114. ROYAN, NICOLA. The fine art of faint praise in Older Scots historiography. *In* (pp. 43–54) **3972**.

Blind Harry (Henry the Minstrel)

4115. ROYAN, NICOLA. The fine art of faint praise in Older Scots historiography. *In* (pp. 43–54) **3972**.

John Capgrave

4116. JAMES, SARAH. 'Doctryne and studie': female learning and religious debate in Capgrave's *Life of St Katharine*. LSE (36) 2005, 275–302.

William Caxton

4117. AMOS, MARK ADDISON. Violent hierarchies: disciplining women and merchant capitalists in *The Book of the Knyght of the Towre*. *In* (pp. 69–100) **4125**.

4118. CARLSON, DAVID R. A theory of the early English printing firm: jobbing, book publishing, and the problem of productive capacity in Caxton's work. *In* (pp. 35–68) **4125**.

4119. COLDIRON, A. E. B. Taking advice from a Frenchwoman: Caxton, Pynson, and Christine de Pizan's moral proverbs. *In* (pp. 127–66) **4125**.

4120. DAVIES, MARTIN. A tale of two Aesops. Library (7:3) 2006, 257–88.

4121. GILLESPIE, ALEXANDRA. 'Folowynge the trace of mayster Caxton': some histories of fifteenth-century printed books. *In* (pp. 167–95) **4125**.

4122. GOODMAN, JENNIFER R. Caxton's Continent. *In* (pp. 101–23) **4125**.

4123. INGHAM, PATRICIA CLARE. Losing French: vernacularity, nation, and Caxton's English statutes. *In* (pp. 275–98) **4125**.

4124. KUSKIN, WILLIAM. Introduction: following Caxton's trace. *In* (pp. 1–31) **4125**.

4125. —— (ed.). Caxton's trace: studies in the history of English printing. Notre Dame, IN: Notre Dame UP, 2006. pp. xxvii, 394. Rev. by A. S. G. Edwards in TLS, 28 July 2006, 31.

4126. LERER, SETH. Caxton in the nineteenth century. *In* (pp. 325–70) **4125**.

4127. MACHAN, TIM WILLIAM. Early Modern Middle English. *In* (pp. 299–322) **4125**.

4128. NORRIS, RALPH. Minor sources in Caxton's Roman war. SP (103:1) 2006, 68–87.

4129. ROLAND, MEG. Arthur and the Turks. *See* **4268**.

4130. WEST, WILLIAM N. Old news: Caxton, de Worde, and the invention of the edition. *In* (pp. 241–74) **4125**.

Thomas Chestre

4131. BAWCUTT, PRISCILLA. *Sir Lamwell* in Scotland. *In* (pp. 83–93) **3972**.

Sir John Clanvowe

4132. LEACH, ELIZABETH EVA. 'The little pipe sings sweetly while the fowler deceives the bird': Sirens in the later Middle Ages. MusL (87:2) 2006, 187–211.

William Dunbar

4133. COUPER, SARAH. Allegory and parody in William Dunbar's *Sen That I Am a Presoneir.* ScSR (6:2) 2005, 9–20.

4134. MATLOCK, WENDY A. Secrets, gossip and gender in William Dunbar's *The Tretis of the Tua Mariit Wemen and the Wedo*. PQ (83:3) 2004, 209–35.

4135. SCATTERGOOD, JOHN. London and money: Chaucer's *Complaint to His Purse*. *In* (pp. 162–73) **4312**.

Edward of Norwich, Second Duke of York (1373?–1415)

4136. PUTTER, AD. The ways and words of the hunt: notes on *Sir Gawain and the Green Knight*, *The Master of Game*, *Sir Tristrem*, *Pearl*, and *Saint Erkenwald*. *See* **4530**.

4137. SCOTT-MACNAB, DAVID. Polysemy in Middle English *embosen* and the hart of *The Book of the Duchess*. *See* **4357**.

Saint Godric (*c*.1065–1170)

4138. DEEMING, HELEN. The songs of St Godric: a neglected context. MusL (86:2) 2005, 169–85.

John Gower (1325?–1408)

4139. BAKALIAN, ELLEN SHAW. Aspects of love in John Gower's *Confessio Amantis*. (Bibl. 2004, 4985.) Rev. by R. F. Yeager in NQ (53:4) 2006, 553–4.

4140. BRATCHER, JAMES T. Gower's 'Tale of Three Questions' and 'The Clever Peasant Girl' folktale. NQ (53:4) 2006, 409–10.

4141. DAVIS, ISABEL. John Gower's fear of flying: transitional masculinities in the *Confessio Amantis*. *In* (pp. 131–52) **3869**.

4142. DIMMICK, JEREMY. Gower, Chaucer and the art of repentance in Robert Greene's *Vision*. *See* **4851**.

4143. ECHARD, SIÂN (ed.). A companion to Gower. (Bibl. 2004, 4989.) Rev. by Larry Scanlon in SAC (28) 2006, 276–81.

4144. GASSE, ROSANNE. The fierce Achilles in Chaucer, Gower, and the *Gawain*-poet. *In* (pp. 121–34) **4550**.

4145. HIGL, ANDREW. Printing power: selling Lydgate, Gower, and Chaucer. *See* **4327**.

4146. INGLIS, KATHERINE. Costanza, Constance, Custance and Emaré: Romola's medieval ancestry. *See* **10031**.

4147. LITTLE, KATHERINE C. Confession and resistance: defining the self in late medieval England. *See* **4420**.

4148. MCALPINE, MONICA E. 'Cast thy bread upon the waters': a paradigm from Ecclesiastes in Gower's 'Apollonius of Tyre'. *In* (pp. 225–35) **3896**.

4149. MACHAN, TIM WILLIAM. Medieval multilingualism and Gower's literary practice. SP (103:1) 2006, 1–25.

4150. MINNIS, ALASTAIR. 'I speke of folk in seculer estaat': vernacularity and secularity in the age of Chaucer. *See* **4511**.

4151. NICHOLSON, PETER. Love and ethics in Gower's *Confessio Amantis*. Ann Arbor: Michigan UP, 2005. pp. xi, 461. Rev. by Georgiana Donavin in TMR, Mar. 2006; by Diane Watt in RES (57:231) 2006, 546–8.

4152. Nolan, Maura. Lydgate's literary history: Chaucer, Gower, and Canacee. *See* **4225**.

4153. Petrina, Alessandra. 'My maisteris dere': the acknowledgement of authority in *The Kingis Quair*. *See* **4169**.

4154. Yeager, R. F. Gower's French audience: the *Mirour de l'Omme*. ChauR (41:2) 2006, 111–37.

4155. Zaerr, Linda Marie. *The Weddynge of Sir Gawen and Dame Ragnell*: performance and intertextuality in Middle English popular romance. *In* (pp. 193–208) **3892**.

John Hardyng

4156. Cooper, Helen. Lancelot's wives. *See* **4951**.

4157. Ruch, Lisa M. A possible identity for Hugh of Genesis in John Hardyng's *Chronicle*. NQ (53:2) 2006, 150–1.

Robert Henryson

4158. Breeze, Andrew. Henryson's Lowrence the fox. NQ (53:3) 2006, 300.

4159. Rudd, Gillian. Making mention of Aesop: Henryson's fable of the two mice. YES (36:1) 2006, 39–49.

4160. Wetherbee, Winthrop. Cresseid *vs* Troylus in Henryson's *Testament*. *In* (pp. 133–41) **4310**.

4161. —— Criseyde alone. *In* (pp. 299–332) **4523**.

Walter Hilton

4162. Little, Katherine C. Images, texts, and exegetics in Chaucer's Second Nun's Tale. *See* **4421**.

Thomas Hoccleve

4163. Kennedy, Kathleen E. Hoccleve's dangerous game of draughts. NQ (53:4) 2006, 410–14.

4164. Little, Katherine C. Confession and resistance: defining the self in late medieval England. *See* **4420**.

4165. Scattergood, John. London and money: Chaucer's *Complaint to His Purse*. *In* (pp. 162–73) **4312**.

4166. Scott, Anne M. Thomas Hoccleve's selves apart. *In* (pp. 89–103) **4792**.

4167. Smyth, Karen. Reading misreadings in Thomas Hoccleve's *Series*. EngS (87:1) 2006, 3–22.

James I, King of Scotland (1394–1437)

4168. Mooney, Linne R.; Arn, Mary-Jo (eds). *The Kingis Quair* and other prison poems. (Bibl. 2005, 4819.) Rev. by Katie Stevenson in TMR, Oct. 2006.

4169. Petrina, Alessandra. 'My maisteris dere': the acknowledgement of authority in *The Kingis Quair*. ScSR (7:1) 2006, 9–23.

Julian of Norwich

4170. Baker, Denise N. (ed.). *Showings*: authoritative text, contexts, criticism. New York; London: Norton, 2005. pp. xxvii, 213. (Norton critical eds.)

4171. CRASSONS, KATE. Performance anxiety and Watson's vernacular theology. ELN (44:1) 2006, 95–102. (*Responds to* bibl. 1995, 4111.)

4172. DAVIS, CARMEL. Words beyond meaning: the language of ascent and the ascent of language in medieval mystical texts. *See* **2289**.

4173. HIRSH, JOHN C. Christianity and the Church. *In* (pp. 241–60) **4345**.

4174. KERBY-FULTON, KATHRYN. Books under suspicion: censorship and tolerance of revelatory writing in late medieval England. *See* **3858**.

4175. MCAVOY, LIZ HERBERT. '… the fend set him in my throte': sexuality and the fiendish encounter in Julian of Norwich's *Revelations of Divine Love*. RMedS (30) 2004, 33–55.

4176. MAGILL, KEVIN J. Julian of Norwich: mystic or visionary? London; New York: Routledge, 2006. pp. viii, 180.

4177. WATSON, NICHOLAS; JENKINS, JACQUELINE (eds). The writings of Julian of Norwich: *A Vision Showed to a Devout Woman* and *A Revelation of Love*. University Park: Pennsylvania State UP, 2005. pp. xii, 474.

Margery Kempe

4178. ARNOLD, JOHN H.; LEWIS, KATHERINE J. (eds). A companion to *The Book of Margery Kempe*. (Bibl. 2005, 4827.) Rev. by Annie Sutherland in NQ (53:3) 2006, 365–6; by Larry Scanlon in SAC (28) 2006, 276–81.

4179. COLÓN, SUSAN E. 'Gostly labowrys': vocation and profession in *The Book of Margery Kempe*. EngS (86:4) 2005, 283–97.

4180. ERWIN, REBECCA SCHOFF. Early editing of Margery Kempe in manuscript and print. JEBS (9) 2006, 75–94.

4181. KERBY-FULTON, KATHRYN. Books under suspicion: censorship and tolerance of revelatory writing in late medieval England. *See* **3858**.

4182. SANDERS, ARNOLD. Illiterate memory and spiritual experience: Margery Kempe, the liturgy, and the 'woman in the crowd'. *In* (pp. 237–48) **3896**.

4183. WALLACE, DAVID. Periodizing women: Mary Ward (1585–1645) and the premodern canon. *See* **7165**.

4184. WATT, DIANE. Faith in the landscape: overseas pilgrimages in *The Book of Margery Kempe*. *In* (pp. 170–87) **3684**.

4185. YOSHIKAWA, NAOË KUKITA. The Jerusalem pilgrimage: the centre of the structure of the *Book of Margery Kempe*. EngS (86:3) 2005, 193–205.

William Langland

4186. BAKER, DENISE N. 'The greatest riddle of the B text' of *Piers Plowman*: why Langland did not scrap the A *Vita*. *In* (pp. 149–63) **3896**.

4187. BARNEY, STEPHEN A. (ed.). The Penn commentary on *Piers Plowman*: vol. v, C Passus 20–22; B Passus 18–20. Philadelphia: Pennsylvania UP, 2006. pp. xi, 309.

4188. BENSON, C. DAVID. Public *Piers Plowman*: modern scholarship and late medieval English culture. (Bibl. 2005, 4842.) Rev. by Emily Steiner in SAC (27) 2005, 291–4; by Nicolette Zeeman in MÆ (75:1) 2006, 149–51.

4189. —— Salvation theology and poetry in *Piers Plowman*. ELN (44:1) 2006, 103–7. (*Responds to* bibl. 1995, 4111.)

4190. Cannon, Christopher. Chaucer and the language of London. *In* (pp. 79–94) **4312**.

4191. Coleman, Joyce. The complaint of the makers: *Wynnere and Wastoure* and the 'misperformance topos' in medieval England. *In* (pp. 27–39) **3892**.

4192. Fenton, Eileen Gifford; Duggan, Hoyt N. Effective methods of producing machine-readable text from manuscript and print sources. *In* (pp. 241–53) **426**.

4193. Fitzgibbons, Moira. *Jacob's Well* and penitential pedagogy. *See* **4078**.

4194. Galloway, Andrew (ed.). The Penn commentary on *Piers Plowman*: vol. 1, C Prologue – Passus 4; B Prologue – Passus 4; A Prologue – Passus 4. Philadelphia: Pennsylvania UP, 2006. pp. xiii, 491.

4195. Hoffmann, A. Robin. Sewing and weaving in *Piers Plowman*. WS (35:5) 2006, 431–52.

4196. Kane, George. The *Piers Plowman* glossary. *Will's Visions of Do-Well, Do-Better and Do-Best*: a glossary of the English vocabulary of the A, B and C versions as presented in the Athlone Editions. *See* **1677**.

4197. Kerby-Fulton, Kathryn. Books under suspicion: censorship and tolerance of revelatory writing in late medieval England. *See* **3858**.

4198. Lewis, Lucy. A newly discovered lyric from Exeter College, Oxford on the theme of 'Know thyself'. *See* **4040**.

4199. Little, Katherine C. 'Bokes ynowe': vernacular theology and fourteenth-century exhaustion. ELN (44:1) 2006, 109–12.

4200. Mann, Jill. 'He knew nat Catoun': medieval school-texts and Middle English literature. *In* (pp. 41–74) **3871**.

4201. Robertson, Elizabeth. Souls that matter: the gendering of the soul in *Piers Plowman*. *In* (pp. 165–86) **3896**.

4202. Scott, Anne M. *Piers Plowman* and the poor. (Bibl. 2004, 5059.) Rev. by Lawrence Warner in Parergon (23:2) 2006, 165–7.

4203. Steiner, Emily. Radical historiography: Langland, Trevisa, and the *Polychronicon*. *See* **4293**.

4204. Zeeman, Nicolette. *Piers Plowman* and the medieval discourse of desire. Cambridge; New York: CUP, 2006. pp. x, 314. (Cambridge studies in medieval literature, 59.)

Laȝamon

4205. Bryan, Elizabeth J. Amazons and Ursulines. *In* (pp. 21–30) **3896**.

4206. Forest-Hill, Lynn. Giants and enemies of God: the relationship between Caliban and Prospero from the perspective of Insular literary tradition. *See* **6122**.

4207. Frese, Dolores Warwick. Sexing political tropes of conquest: *The Wife's Lament* and Laȝamon's *Brut*. *In* (pp. 203–33) **3692**.

4208. Guilar, Liam. Lawman lived here. PNRev (30:4) 2004, 26–8.

Nicholas Love

4209. Edwards, A. S. G. The contexts of Notre Dame 67. *In* (pp. 107–28) **3871**.

4210. GILLESPIE, VINCENT. The haunted text: reflections in *A Mirror to Devout People*. *In* (pp. 129–72) **3871**.

John Lydgate

4211. BENSON, C. DAVID. Civic Lydgate: the poet and London. *In* (pp. 147–68) **4231**.

4212. DENNY-BROWN, ANDREA. *Povre* Griselda and the all-consuming *archewyves*. *See* **4387**.

4213. EPSTEIN, ROBERT. Eating their words: food and text in the coronation banquet of Henry VI. JMEMS (36:2) 2006, 355–77.

4214. FREDELL, JOEL. 'Go litel quaier:' Lydgate's pamphlet poetry. JEBS (9) 2006, 52–73.

4215. GAYK, SHANNON. Images of pity: the regulatory aesthetics of John Lydgate's religious lyrics. SAC (28) 2006, 175–203.

4216. GILLESPIE, ALEXANDRA. Print culture and the medieval author: Chaucer, Lydgate, and their books, 1473–1557. *See* **4325**.

4217. GROSSI, JOSEPH L., JR. 'Wher ioye is ay lastyng': John Lydgate's *contemptus mundi* in British Library MS Harley 2255. LSE (36) 2005, 303–34.

4218. HARDMAN, PHILLIPA. Lydgate's uneasy syntax. *In* (pp. 12–35) **4231**.

4219. HEYWORTH, GREGORY. Textual identity and the problem of convention: recovering the title of Dresden Oc 66. TextC (1:2) 2006, 143–51. (*Reson and Sensuallyte*.)

4220. HIGL, ANDREW. Printing power: selling Lydgate, Gower, and Chaucer. *See* **4327**.

4221. MEYER-LEE, ROBERT J. Lydgate's laureate pose. *In* (pp. 36–60) **4231**.

4222. MORTIMER, NIGEL. John Lydgate's *Fall of Princes*: narrative tragedy in its literary and political contexts. (Bibl. 2005, 4875.) Rev. by Anthony Bale in MÆ (75:2) 2006, 330–1; by Mary Flannery in NQ (53:2) 2006, 219–20.

4223. NISSE, RUTH. 'Was it not routhe to se?': Lydgate and the styles of martyrdom. *In* (pp. 279–98) **4231**.

4224. NOLAN, MAURA. John Lydgate and the making of public culture. Cambridge; New York: CUP, 2005. pp. ix, 276. (Cambridge studies in medieval literature, 58.) Rev. by Nicholas Perkins in NQ (53:4) 2006, 554–5; by Leo Carruthers in EA (59:4) 2006, 471–2; by Helen Barr in Spec (81:4) 2006, 1239–40; by Emily Runde in Comitatus (37) 2006, 270–2.

4225. —— Lydgate's literary history: Chaucer, Gower, and Canacee. SAC (27) 2005, 59–92.

4226. NOLAN, MAURA B. The performance of the literary: Lydgate's mummings. *In* (pp. 169–206) **4231**.

4227. NORRIS, RALPH. Minor sources in Caxton's Roman war. *See* **4128**.

4228. PETRINA, ALESSANDRA. 'My maisteris dere': the acknowledgement of authority in *The Kingis Quair*. *See* **4169**.

4229. SCANLON, LARRY. Lydgate's poetics: laureation and domesticity in the *Temple of Glass*. *In* (pp. 61–97) **4231**.

4230. —— SIMPSON, JAMES. Introduction. *In* (pp. 1–11) **4231**.

4231. —— —— (eds). John Lydgate: poetry, culture, and Lancastrian England.

Notre Dame, IN: Notre Dame UP, 2006. pp. vi, 314. Rev. by Andrea Denny-Brown in TMR, Nov. 2006.

4232. SIMPSON, JAMES. 'For al my body … weieth nat an unce': empty poets and rhetorical weight in Lydgate's *Churl and Bird*. *In* (pp. 129–46) **4231**.

4233. SOMERSET, FIONA. 'Hard is with seyntis for to make affray': Lydgate the 'poet-propagandist' as hagiographer. *In* (pp. 258–78) **4231**.

4234. STRAKER, SCOTT-MORGAN. Propaganda, intentionality, and the Lancastrian Lydgate. *In* (pp. 98–128) **4231**.

4235. SUMMIT, JENNIFER. 'Stable in study': Lydgate's *Fall of Princes* and Duke Humphrey's library. *In* (pp. 207–31) **4231**.

Richard Maidstone

4236. STALEY, LYNN. The Penitential Psalms and vernacular theology. ELN (44:1) 2006, 113–20.

Sir Thomas Malory

4237. ACKERMAN, FELICIA NIMUE. 'I love nat to be constrayned to love': emotional charity and Malory's world. Arthuriana (16:2) 2006, 21–4.

4238. —— 'I may do no penaunce': spiritual sloth in Malory's *Morte*. Arthuriana (16:1) 2006, 47–53.

4239. ARMSTRONG, DORSEY. The (non-)Christian knight in Malory: a contradiction in terms? Arthuriana (16:2) 2006, 30–4.

4240. —— Postcolonial Palomides: Malory's Saracen knight and the unmaking of Arthurian community. Exemplaria (18:1) 2006, 175–203.

4241. BETHLEHEM, ULRIKE. Guinevere, a medieval puzzle: images of Arthur's queen in the medieval literature of England and France. *See* **3963**.

4242. CHEREWATUK, KAREN. Malory's Launcelot and the language of sin and confession. Arthuriana (16:2) 2006, 68–72.

4243. CLASSEN, ALBRECHT (ed.). Violence in medieval courtly literature: a casebook. *See* **3965**.

4244. COOPER, HELEN. Lancelot's wives. *See* **4951**.

4245. DAVIDSON, ROBERTA. Reading like a woman in Malory's *Morte Darthur*. Arthuriana (16:1) 2006, 21–33.

4246. DOSANJH, KATE. Rest in peace: Launcelot's spiritual journey in *Le Morte Darthur*. Arthuriana (16:2) 2006, 63–7.

4247. FARRELL, THOMAS J. The clash of genres at the Siege of Benwick. Arthuriana (16:2) 2006, 88–93.

4248. FIELD, P. J. C. Malory and Cardiff. Arthuriana (16:2) 2006, 45–8.

4249. GAYLORD, ALAN. Back from the *queste*: Malory's Launcelot enrages Gwenyvere. Arthuriana (16:2) 2006, 78–83.

4250. GOODRICH, PETER H. Saracens and Islamic alterity in Malory's *Le Morte Darthur*. Arthuriana (16:4) 2006, 10–28.

4251. GRIMM, KEVIN T. Sir Thomas Malory's narrative of faith. Arthuriana (16:2) 2006, 16–20.

4252. HARDYMENT, CHRISTINA. Malory: the life and times of King Arthur's chronicler. (Bibl. 2005, 4885.) Rev. by Carolyne Larrington in TLS, 13 Jan. 2006,

11; by Paul Gray in NYTB, 20 Aug. 2006, 12; by Edward Donald Kennedy in Arthuriana (16:4) 2006, 89–91; by K. S. Whetter in MÆ (75:2) 2006, 331–2.

4253. Hodges, Kenneth L. Forging chivalric communities in Malory's *Le Morte d'Arthur.* (Bibl. 2005, 4887.) Rev. by Elaine E. Whitaker in Spec (81:3) 2006, 865.

4254. Hoffman, Donald L. Assimilating Saracens: the aliens in Malory's *Morte Darthur.* Arthuriana (16:4) 2006, 43–64.

4255. Huber, Emily Rebekah. 'Delyver me my dwarff!': Gareth's dwarf and chivalric identity. Arthuriana (16:2) 2006, 49–53.

4256. Jesmok, Janet. 'Alas! Who may truste thys world?': absence of trust in Malory's tale of 'Balin le Sauvage'. Arthuriana (16:2) 2006, 25–9.

4257. Jost, Jean E. Why is Middle English romance so violent? The literary and aesthetic purposes of violence. *In* (pp. 241–67) **3965**.

4258. Keita, Maghan. Saracens and Black knights. Arthuriana (16:4) 2006, 65–77.

4259. King, Andrew. 'Well grounded, finely framed, and strongly trussed up together': the 'medieval' structure of *The Faerie Queene*. *In* (pp. 119–52) **5100**.

4260. Lara Rallo, Carmen. 'Flashing into the crystal mirror': the recurrence of the mirror motif in three Arthurian works. *See* **4544**.

4261. Lynch, Andrew. A tale of 'simple' Malory and the critics. Arthuriana (16:2) 2006, 10–15.

4262. Meale, Carol M. Entrapment or empowerment? Women and discourses of love and marriage in the fifteenth century. *In* (pp. 163–78) **3836**.

4263. Moore, Dafydd. Tennyson, Malory and the Ossianic mode: *The Poems of Ossian* and 'The Death of Arthur'. *See* **11401**.

4264. Norris, Ralph. Minor sources in Caxton's Roman war. *See* **4128**.

4265. Petrina, Alessandra. Forbidden feast, enchanted castle: Arthurian spaces in the Harry Potter novels. *See* **18357**.

4266. Reynolds, Meredith. Malory's use of 'counsel' and 'advyce' in creating a king. Arthuriana (16:2) 2006, 40–4.

4267. Reynolds, Rebecca L. Elaine of Ascolat's death and the *ars moriendi*. Arthuriana (16:2) 2006, 35–9.

4268. Roland, Meg. Arthur and the Turks. Arthuriana (16:4) 2006, 29–42.

4269. Rushton, Cory J. 'Of an uncouthe stede': the Scottish knight in Middle English Arthurian romances. *In* (pp. 109–19) **3972**.

4270. Sanders, Arnold. Sir Gareth and the 'Unfair Unknown': Malory's use of the Gawain romances. Arthuriana (16:1) 2006, 34–46.

4271. Saunders, Corinne. Violent magic in Middle English romance. *In* (pp. 225–40) **3965**.

4272. Sprague, Kurth. The troubled heart of T. H. White: women and *The Once and Future King*. *See* **19120**.

4273. Stuhmiller, Jacqueline. *Iudicium Dei, iudicium fortunae*: trial by combat in Malory's *Le Morte Darthur.* Spec (81:2) 2006, 427–62.

4274. Sweeney, Mickey. Divine love or loving divinely? The ending of Malory's *Morte Darthur*. Arthuriana (16:2) 2006, 73–7.

4275. Thompson, Raymond H.; Busby, Keith (eds). Gawain: a casebook. *See* **3980**.

4276. West, William N. Old news: Caxton, de Worde, and the invention of the edition. *In* (pp. 241–74) **4125**.

4277. Wheeler, Bonnie (ed.). Arthurian studies in honour of P. J. C. Field. (Bibl. 2004, 5131.) Rev. by Sally L. Burch in MÆ (75:1) 2006, 146–7.

4278. Whetter, K. S.; Radulescu, Raluca L. (eds). Re-viewing *Le Morte Darthur*: texts and contexts, characters and themes. (Bibl. 2005, 4895.) Rev. by Karen Cherewatuk in Arthuriana (16:4) 2006, 119–20; by Cheryl Taylor in Parergon (23:1) 2006, 236–8.

'Sir John Mandeville'

4279. Bennett, Michael J. *Mandeville's Travels* and the Anglo-French moment. MÆ (75:2) 2006, 273–92.

4280. Moghaddassi, Fanny. L'ailleurs dans les *Voyages de Mandeville* (xive siècle): entre rêverie populaire et réflexion savante. RANAM (39) 2006, 9–20.

4281. Röhl, Susanne. Der *Livre de Mandeville* im 14. und 15. Jahrhundert: Untersuchungen zur handschriftlichen Überlieferung der kontinentalfranzösischen Version. Munich: Fink, 2004. pp. 276. (Mittelalter-Studien, 6.) Rev. by Martin Gosman in Spec (81:4) 2006, 149–50.

Robert Mannyng

4282. Green, Richard Firth. Morality and immorality. *In* (pp. 199–217) **4345**.

Henry Medwall

4283. Walker, Greg. *Fulgens and Lucres* and early Tudor drama. *In* (pp. 23–34) **4734**.

John Page

4284. Drukker, Tamar S. An eye-witness account or literary historicism? John Page's *Siege of Rouen*. LSE (36) 2005, 251–73.

Paston Family

4285. Castor, Helen. Blood and roses: one family's struggle and triumph during England's tumultuous Wars of the Roses. (Bibl. 2005, 4905.) New York: HarperCollins, 2006. pp. xx, 426, (plates) 8. (Pub. in UK as *Blood & Roses: the Paston Family in the Fifteenth Century*.)

4286. Fulton, Helen. Autobiography and the discourse of urban subjectivity: the Paston Letters. *In* (pp. 191–216) **4792**.

Richard Rolle

4287. Davis, Carmel. Words beyond meaning: the language of ascent and the ascent of language in medieval mystical texts. *See* **2289**.

4288. McIlroy, Claire Elizabeth. The English prose treatises of Richard Rolle. (Bibl. 2005, 4917.) Rev. by Christopher Roman in Spec (81:2) 2006, 560–2.

4289. Shon, Frank. The teleological element in Richard Rolle's *Contra amatores mundi*. MLR (101:1) 2006, 1–15.

Henry Scogan

4290. Pearsall, Derek. The *Canterbury Tales* and London club culture. *In* (pp. 95–108) **4312**.

John Shirley (1366?–1456)

4291. Pearsall, Derek. The *Canterbury Tales* and London club culture. *In* (pp. 95–108) **4312**.

John Trevisa

4292. Minnis, Alastair. 'I speke of folk in seculer estaat': vernacularity and secularity in the age of Chaucer. *See* **4511**.

4293. Steiner, Emily. Radical historiography: Langland, Trevisa, and the *Polychronicon*. SAC (27) 2005, 171–211.

4294. West, William N. Old news: Caxton, de Worde, and the invention of the edition. *In* (pp. 241–74) **4125**.

Thomas Usk

4295. Summers, Joanna. Late medieval prison writing and the politics of autobiography. (Bibl. 2005, 4927.) Rev. by Isabel Davis in TLS, 28 Apr. 2006, 35; by Elizabeth Schirmer in Biography (29:4) 2006, 742–4; by J. A. Burrow in SAC (28) 2006, 337–9; by Kathryn L. Lynch in Spec (81:2) 2006, 608–9.

John Walton

4296. Doyle, A. I. The copyist of MSS Bodley 283 and Durham Cosin V.ii.15. *See* **202**.

John Wyclif

4297. Copeland, Rita. Secular and sacred: the history of rhetoric and religious community in the Middle Ages. *In* (pp. 135–47) **3658**.

4298. Evans, G. R. John Wyclif: myth and reality. Oxford: Lion; Downers Grove, IL: InterVarsity Press, 2005. pp. 320.

4299. —— John Wyclif: the biography of a legend. Auto/Biography (14:1) 2006, 1–20.

4300. Hornbeck, J. Patrick, ii. *Lollard* sermons? Soteriology and late medieval dissent. *See* **4073**.

4301. Little, Katherine C. Confession and resistance: defining the self in late medieval England. *See* **4420**.

4302. —— Images, texts, and exegetics in Chaucer's Second Nun's Tale. *See* **4421**.

4303. Minnis, Alastair. 'I speke of folk in seculer estaat': vernacularity and secularity in the age of Chaucer. *See* **4511**.

4304. —— John Wyclif – all women's friend? *In* (pp. 121–33) **3896**.

GEOFFREY CHAUCER

General Scholarship and Criticism

4305. ANDREW, MALCOLM. The Palgrave literary dictionary of Chaucer. Basingstoke; New York: Palgrave Macmillan, 2006. pp. xvi, 313. (Palgrave literary dictionaries.) Rev. by Elliot Kendall in TLS, 29 Sept. 2006, 33.

4306. BLAMIRES, ALCUIN. Chaucer, ethics, and gender. Oxford; New York: OUP, 2006. pp. 263. Rev. by K. P. Clarke in RES (57:232) 2006, 796–8.

4307. BOFFEY, JULIA; EDWARDS, A. S. G. Manuscripts and audience. *In* (pp. 34–50) **4345**.

4308. BOSWELL, JACKSON CAMPBELL; HOLTON, SYLVIA WALLACE. Chaucer's fame in England: *STC* Chauceriana, 1475–1640. New York: Modern Language Assn of America, 2004. pp. xxvii, 290.

4309. BROWNLEE, KEVIN, *et al.* Vernacular literary consciousness *c.*1100–*c.*1500: French, German and English evidence. *In* (pp. 422–71) **3874**.

4310. BURTON, T. L.; PLUMMER, JOHN F. (eds). 'Seyd in forme and reverence': essays on Chaucer and Chaucerians in memory of Emerson Brown, Jr. Provo, UT: Chaucer Studio Press, 2005. pp. xix, 249.

4311. BUTTERFIELD, ARDIS. Chaucer and the detritus of the city. *In* (pp. 3–22) **4312**.

4312. —— (ed.). Chaucer and the city. Woodbridge, Suffolk; Rochester, NY: Brewer, 2006. pp. xiv, 231. (Chaucer studies, 37.) Rev. by Catherine A. M. Clarke in RES (57:232) 2006, 798–9.

4313. CANNON, CHRISTOPHER. Chaucer and the language of London. *In* (pp. 79–94) **4312**.

4314. —— The lives of Geoffrey Chaucer. *In* (pp. 31–54) **4330**.

4315. CARLSON, DAVID R. Chaucer's jobs. (Bibl. 2005, 4938.) Rev. by Suzanne Conklin Akbari in TMR, Feb. 2006; by Kellie Robertson in SAC (28) 2006, 284–7.

4316. COLETTI, THERESA. 'Paths of long study': reading Chaucer and Christine de Pizan in tandem. SAC (28) 2006, 1–40.

4317. COONEY, HELEN. Some new thing: *The Floure and the Leafe* and the cultural shift in the role of the poet in fifteenth-century England. *In* (pp. 131–46) **3836**.

4318. COX, CATHERINE S. The Judaic Other in Dante, the *Gawain*-poet, and Chaucer. (Bibl. 2005, 4939.) Rev. by Elisa Narin van Court in TMR, Oct. 2006; by Andrew Galloway in RES (57:230) 2006, 401–2; by Shirley Sharon-Zisser in Arthuriana (16:4) 2006, 82–3; by James H. Morey in Spec (81:4) 2006, 1174–6.

4319. DAVIS, PAUL. After the Fire: Chaucer and urban poetics, 1666–1743. *In* (pp. 177–92) **4312**.

4320. ELLIS, STEVE (ed.). Chaucer: an Oxford guide. (Bibl. 2005, 4946.) Rev. by Richard H. Osberg in Arthuriana (16:1) 2006, 73–5.

4321. EVANS, RUTH. The afterword of origins: a response. SAC (28) 2006, 263–70.

4322. FULLER, DAVID. Reading Chaucer aloud. *In* (pp. 262–84) **4345**.

4323. GAYLORD, ALAN T. Reflections on D. W. Robertson, Jr, and 'exegetical criticism'. *See* **14109**.

4324. GILLESPIE, ALEXANDRA. 'Folowynge the trace of mayster Caxton': some histories of fifteenth-century printed books. *In* (pp. 167–95) **4125**.

4325. —— Print culture and the medieval author: Chaucer, Lydgate, and their books, 1473–1557. Oxford; New York: OUP, 2006. pp. xiii, 281. (Oxford English monographs.)

4326. HAMAGUCHI, KEIKO. Non-European women in Chaucer: a postcolonial study. New York; Frankfurt: Lang, 2006. pp. 194. (Studies in English medieval language and literature, 14.)

4327. HIGL, ANDREW. Printing power: selling Lydgate, Gower, and Chaucer. EMS (23) 2006, 57–77.

4328. KERBY-FULTON, KATHRYN. Books under suspicion: censorship and tolerance of revelatory writing in late medieval England. *See* **3858**.

4329. KNAPP, ETHAN. Chaucer criticism and its legacies. *In* (pp. 324–56) **4330**.

4330. LERER, SETH (ed.). The Yale companion to Chaucer. New Haven, CT; London: Yale UP, 2006. pp. ix, 420.

4331. LYNCH, KATHRYN L. (ed.). Geoffrey Chaucer: dream visions and other poems: authoritative texts, contexts, criticism. New York; London: Norton, 2006. pp. xx, 396.

4332. MCCULLY, CHRIS. The word in time: 2, Diplomat and revolutionary. PNRev (32:5) 2006, 45–6.

4333. MCTURK, RORY. Chaucer and the Norse and Celtic worlds. (Bibl. 2005, 4957.) Rev. by Heather O'Donoghue in RES (57:228) 2006, 108–9.

4334. MASI, MICHAEL. Chaucer and gender. New York; Frankfurt: Lang, 2005. pp. 165.

4335. MEYER-LEE, ROBERT J. Lydgate's laureate pose. *In* (pp. 36–60) **4231**.

4336. MITCHELL, JOHN ALLAN. Ethics and exemplary narrative in Chaucer and Gower. (Bibl. 2005, 4958.) Rev. by John C. Hirsh in MÆ (75:1) 2006, 151–2; by Mark Miller in Spec (81:2) 2006, 562–4.

4337. NISSE, RUTH. 'Was it not routhe to se?': Lydgate and the styles of martyrdom. *In* (pp. 279–98) **4231**.

4338. PHILLIPS, HELEN. Chaucer and the nineteenth-century city. *In* (pp. 193–210) **4312**.

4339. PRENDERGAST, THOMAS A. Chaucer's dead body: from corpse to corpus. (Bibl. 2005, 4961.) Rev. by Helen Cooper in SAC (27) 2005, 342–5; by Dosia Reichardt in Parergon (23:1) 2006, 192–4.

4340. PUGH, TISON. Queering medieval genres. Basingstoke; New York: Palgrave Macmillan, 2004. pp. x, 226. (New Middle Ages.) Rev. by Anna Klosowska in SAC (28) 2006, 319–22.

4341. RANSOM, DANIEL J. Annotating Chaucer: some corrections and additions. *In* (pp. 205–15) **4310**.

4342. REIMER, STEPHEN R. The Urry *Chaucer* and George Vertue. ChauR (41:1) 2006, 105–9.

4343. Rossignol, Rosalyn. Critical companion to Chaucer: a literary reference to his life and work. New York: Facts on File, 2006. pp. 560. (Facts on File library of world literature.)

4344. Sadlek, Gregory M. Idleness working: the discourse of love's labor from Ovid through Chaucer and Gower. (Bibl. 2004, 5202.) Rev. by Audrey DeLong in SixCJ (36:4) 2005, 1147–8; by Roger A. Ladd in SixCJ (36:4) 2005, 1148–9; by John C. Ford in TMR, Mar. 2006.

4345. Saunders, Corinne (ed.). A concise companion to Chaucer. Oxford; Malden, MA: Blackwell, 2006. pp. xii, 292. (Blackwell concise companions to literature and culture.)

4346. Simpson, James. Chaucer as a European writer. *In* (pp. 55–86) **4330**.

4347. Smith, D. Vance. Chaucer as an English writer. *In* (pp. 87–121) **4330**.

4348. Trigg, Stephanie. Chaucer's influence and reception. *In* (pp. 297–323) **4330**.

4349. Vaughan, Míċeál F. Personal politics and Thomas Gascoigne's account of Chaucer's death. MÆ (75:1) 2006, 103–22.

4350. Wetherbee, Winthrop, iii. Chaucer and the European tradition. SAC (27) 2005, 3–21. (Presidential address.)

4351. Yeager, R. F. Books and authority. *In* (pp. 51–67) **4345**.

Separate Works

Boece

4352. Machan, Tim William; Minnis, A. J. (eds). Sources of the *Boece*. (Bibl. 2005, 4971.) Rev. by Gregory Heyworth in TextC (1:2) 2006, 170–1; by Ian Johnson in MÆ (75:2) 2006, 329–30.

The Book of the Duchess

4353. Gilbert, Jane. Becoming woman in Chaucer: '*On ne naît pas femme, on le meurt.*' *In* (pp. 109–29) **3869**.

4354. Gross, Karen Elizabeth. Chaucer, Mary Magdalene and the consolation of love. *See* **4469**.

4355. Kensak, Michael. 'My first matere I wil yow telle': losing (and finding) your place in Chaucer's *The Book of the Duchess*. *In* (pp. 83–96) **4310**.

4356. Kruger, Steven F. Dreaming. *In* (pp. 71–89) **4345**.

4357. Scott-Macnab, David. Polysemy in Middle English *embosen* and the hart of *The Book of the Duchess*. LSE (36) 2005, 175–94.

4358. Stock, Lorraine Kochanske. 'Peynted … text and [visual] glose': primitivism, ekphrasis, and pictorial intertextuality in the dreamers' bedrooms of *Roman de la Rose* and *Book of the Duchess*. *In* (pp. 97–114) **4310**.

4359. Williams, Deanne. The dream visions. *In* (pp. 147–78) **4330**.

Canterbury Tales

4360. Aloni, Gila. Extimacy in the Miller's Tale. ChauR (41:2) 2006, 163–84.

4361. Ashe, Laura. Reading like a clerk in the Clerk's Tale. MLR (101:4) 2006, 935–44.

4362. Beechy, Tiffany. Devil take the hindmost: Chaucer, John Gay, and the pecuniary anus. ChauR (41:1) 2005, 71–85.

4363. Beidler, Peter G. New terminology for sources and analogues; or, Let's forget the lost French source for the Miller's Tale. SAC (28) 2006, 225–30.

4364. —— Where's the point? Punctuating Chaucer's *Canterbury Tales*. *In* (pp. 193–203) **4310**.

4365. Benson, C. David. Literary contests and London records in the *Canterbury Tales*. *In* (pp. 129–44) **4312**.

4366. Biggs, Frederick M. Seventeen words of Middle Dutch origin in the Miller's Tale? NQ (53:4) 2006, 407–9.

4367. Blandeau, Agnès. Pasolini, Chaucer and Boccaccio: two medieval texts and their translation into film. Jefferson, NC; London: McFarland, 2006. pp. viii, 210.

4368. Bleeth, Kenneth. The Physician's Tale and remembered texts. SAC (28) 2006, 221–4.

4369. Børch, Marianne. Writing remembering orality: Geoffrey Chaucer's Sir Thopas. EJES (10:2) 2006, 131–48.

4370. Bradbury, Nancy Mason. Proverb tradition as a soft source for the *Canterbury Tales*. SAC (28) 2006, 237–42.

4371. Bredehoft, Thomas A. Middle English *knarre*: more porcine imagery in the Miller's portrait. ELN (43:2) 2005, 14–18.

4372. Buffoni, Franco. Auden critico-poeta in *The Sea and the Mirror*. *In* (pp. 203–33) **3341**.

4373. Bullón-Fernández, María. Private practices in Chaucer's Miller's Tale. SAC (28) 2006, 141–74.

4374. Burton, T. L. Sir Gawain and the green hag: the *real* meaning of the Wife of Bath's Tale. *In* (pp. 75–80) **4310**.

4375. Cartlidge, Neil. Marriage, sexuality, and the family. *In* (pp. 218–40) **4345**.

4376. —— 'Nat that I chalange any thyng of right': love, loyalty, and legality in the Franklin's Tale. *In* (pp. 115–30) **3836**.

4377. Casey, Jim. Unfinished business: the termination of Chaucer's Cook's Tale. ChauR (41:2) 2006, 185–96.

4378. Chickering, Howell. 'And I seyde his opinion was good': how irony works in the Monk's portrait. *In* (pp. 3–18) **4310**.

4379. Collette, Carolyn P. The alchemy of imagination and the labyrinth of meaning: some caveats about the afterlife of sources. SAC (28) 2006, 243–8.

4380. Cooney, Helen (ed.). Writings on love in the English Middle Ages. *See* **3836**.

4381. Cooper, Christine F. 'But algates therby was she understonde': translating Custance in Chaucer's Man of Law's Tale. YES (36:1) 2006, 27–38.

4382. Cooper, Helen. London and Southwark poetic companies: *Si tost c'amis* and the *Canterbury Tales*. *In* (pp. 109–25) **4312**.

4383. —— Love before Troilus. *In* (pp. 25–43) **3836**.

4384. Copeland, Rita. Chaucer and rhetoric. *In* (pp. 122–43) **4330**.

4385. Correale, Robert M. (gen. ed.); Hamel, Mary (assoc. ed.). Sources and analogues of the *Canterbury Tales*: vol. 2. Woodbridge, Suffolk; Rochester, NY: Brewer, 2005. pp. xvi, 824. (Chaucer studies, 35.) Rev. by Simon Horobin in RES (57:230) 2006, 411–12.

4386. Crocker, Holly A. Wifely eye for the manly guy: trading the masculine image in the Shipman's Tale. *In* (pp. 59–73) **4310**.

4387. Denny-Brown, Andrea. *Povre* Griselda and the all-consuming *archewyves*. SAC (28) 2006, 77–115.

4388. Desmond, Marilynn. Ovid's art and the Wife of Bath: the ethics of erotic violence. Ithaca, NY; London: Cornell UP, 2006. pp. xiii, 206.

4389. Dimmick, Jeremy. Gower, Chaucer and the art of repentance in Robert Greene's *Vision*. *See* **4851**.

4390. Dobbs, Elizabeth A. Re-sounding Echo. ChauR (40:3) 2006, 289–310.

4391. Driver, Martha W. Romancing the *Rose*: the readings of Chaucer and Christine. *In* (pp. 147–62) **3836**.

4392. Evans, Ruth. The production of space in Chaucer's London. *In* (pp. 41–56) **4312**.

4393. Eyler, Joshua R.; Sexton, John P. Once more to the grove: a note on symbolic space in the Knight's Tale. ChauR (40:4) 2006, 433–9.

4394. Ferster, Judith. Genre in and of the *Canterbury Tales*. *In* (pp. 177–98) **4345**.

4395. Finlayson, John. Reading Chaucer's Nun's Priest's Tale: mixed genres and multi-layered worlds of illusion. EngS (86:6) 2005, 493–510.

4396. Forest-Hill, Lynn. Giants and enemies of God: the relationship between Caliban and Prospero from the perspective of Insular literary tradition. *See* **6122**.

4397. Frese, Dolores Warwick. The 'buried bodies' of Dante, Boccaccio, and Petrarch: Chaucerian 'sources' for the critical fiction of obedient wives. SAC (28) 2006, 249–56.

4398. Fulton, Helen. The performance of social class: domestic violence in the Griselda story. AUMLA (106) 2006, 25–42.

4399. Gaylord, Alan T. Chaucerian sentences: revisiting a 'crucial passage' from the Nun's Priest's Tale. *In* (pp. 167–80) **4310**.

4400. Gilbert, Jane. Becoming woman in Chaucer: '*On ne naît pas femme, on le meurt.*' *In* (pp. 109–29) **3869**.

4401. Goodwin, Amy W. Chaucer's Clerk's Tale: sources, influences, and allusions. SAC (28) 2006, 231–5.

4402. Green, Richard Firth. Morality and immorality. *In* (pp. 199–217) **4345**.

4403. Gross, Karen Elizabeth. Chaucer, Mary Magdalene and the consolation of love. *See* **4469**.

4404. Hanks, D. Thomas, Jr. Chaucer, *auctoritas*, and the problem of pain. *In* (pp. 219–36) **4310**.

4405. Harwood, Britton. Chaucer on the couch: the Pardoner's performance and the case for psychoanalytic criticism. *In* (pp. 47–57) **4310**.

4406. Harwood, Britton J. Chaucer and the gift (if there is any). SP (103:1) 2006, 26–46.

4407. Hayes, Mary. Privy speech: sacred silence, dirty secrets in the Summoner's Tale. ChauR (40:3) 2006, 263–88.

4408. Heffernan, Carol F. Two 'English fabliaux', Chaucer's Merchant's Tale and Shipman's Tale, and Italian *novelle*. Neophilologus (90:2) 2006, 333–49.

4409. Hirsh, John C. Christianity and the Church. *In* (pp. 241–60) **4345**.

4410. Hodges, Laura F. Chaucer and clothing: clerical and academic costume in the General Prologue to the *Canterbury Tales*. (Bibl. 2005, 5004.) Rev. by Kathleen Tonry in TMR, Aug. 2006; by Andrea Denny-Brown in SAC (28) 2006, 300–3; by Laura L. Howes in Spec (81:4) 2006, 1209–11.

4411. Hume, Cathy. Domestic opportunities: the social comedy of the Shipman's Tale. ChauR (41:2) 2006, 138–62.

4412. Inglis, Katherine. Costanza, Constance, Custance and Emaré: Romola's medieval ancestry. *See* **10031**.

4413. Kendall, Elliot. The great household in the city: the Shipman's Tale. *In* (pp. 145–61) **4312**.

4414. Kendrick, Laura. Lives and works: Chaucer and the compilers of the troubadour songbooks. *In* (pp. 103–15) **4095**.

4415. King, Andrew. 'Well grounded, finely framed, and strongly trussed up together': the 'medieval' structure of *The Faerie Queene*. *In* (pp. 119–52) **5100**.

4416. Koster, Josephine A. The *Vita sancte Alicie Bathoniensis*: transgressions of hagiographic rhetoric in the Wife of Bath's Prologue and Tale. *In* (pp. 35–45) **4310**.

4417. Lampert, Lisa. Gender and Jewish difference from Paul to Shakespeare. (Bibl. 2005, 5011.) Rev. by William Chester Jordan in SAC (27) 2005, 329–31; by Sheila Delany in Spec (81:2) 2006, 551–3.

4418. Lerer, Seth. The *Canterbury Tales*. *In* (pp. 243–94) **4330**.

4419. Lines, Candace. The erotic politics of grief in Surrey's *So Crewel Prison*. *See* **5134**.

4420. Little, Katherine C. Confession and resistance: defining the self in late medieval England. Notre Dame, IN: Notre Dame UP, 2006. pp. vii, 196. Rev. by Stephen Penn in RES (57:232) 2006, 793–5.

4421. —— Images, texts, and exegetics in Chaucer's Second Nun's Tale. JMEMS (36:1) 2006, 103–33.

4422. Mann, Jill. 'He knew nat Catoun': medieval school-texts and Middle English literature. *In* (pp. 41–74) **3871**.

4423. Miller, Mark. Philosophical Chaucer: love, sex, and agency in the *Canterbury Tales*. (Bibl. 2005, 5016.) Rev. by Suzanne Conklin Akbari in NQ (53:4) 2006, 551–3; by Glenn Burger in SAC (28) 2006, 306–9.

4424. Minnis, Alastair. 'I speke of folk in seculer estaat': vernacularity and secularity in the age of Chaucer. *See* **4511**.

4425. —— Purchasing pardon: material and spiritual economies on the Canterbury pilgrimage. *In* (pp. 63–82) **3658**.

4426. —— The wisdom of old women: Alisoun of Bath as *auctrice*. *In* (pp. 99–114) **3836**.

4427. MOONEY, LINNE R. Chaucer's scribe. Spec (81:1) 2006, 97–138.

4428. NOLAN, MAURA. Lydgate's literary history: Chaucer, Gower, and Canacee. *See* **4225**.

4429. NOWLIN, STEELE. Between precedent and possibility: liminality, historicity, and narrative in Chaucer's The Franklin's Tale. SP (103:1) 2006, 47–67.

4430. PALMER, JAMES M. Your malady is no 'sodeyn hap': ophthalmology, Benvenutus Grassus, and January's blindness. ChauR (41:2) 2006, 197–205.

4431. PATTERSON, LEE. The necessity of history: the example of Chaucer's Clerk's Tale. *In* (pp. 187–210) **3896**.

4432. PEARSALL, DEREK. The *Canterbury Tales* and London club culture. *In* (pp. 95–108) **4312**.

4433. PLUMMER, JOHN F. Fables, *cupiditas*, and vessels of tree: Chaucer's use of the Epistles to Timothy. *In* (pp. 237–45) **4310**.

4434. PUGH, TISON. Queering Harry Bailly: gendered carnival, social ideologies, and masculinity under duress in the *Canterbury Tales*. ChauR (41:1) 2006, 39–69.

4435. QUINN, WILLIAM A. The shadow of Chaucer's Jews. Exemplaria (18:2) 2006, 299–325.

4436. REILLY, TERRY. Reading *The Lagoon* and Chaucer's The Knight's Tale through Edward Said's *The World, the Text, and the Critic*. *See* **15304**.

4437. ROBINSON, PETER. The *Canterbury Tales* and other medieval texts. *In* (pp. 74–91) **426**.

4438. ROCK, CATHERINE A. Forsworn and fordone: Arcite as oath-breaker in the Knight's Tale. ChauR (40:4) 2006, 416–32.

4439. ROGERSON, MARGARET. Prime-time drama: *Canterbury Tales* for the small screen. SSE (32) 2006, 45–63.

4440. SANDERS, ARNOLD. Sir Gareth and the 'Unfair Unknown': Malory's use of the Gawain romances. *See* **4270**.

4441. SAUNDERS, CORINNE. Violent magic in Middle English romance. *In* (pp. 225–40) **3965**.

4442. SAYERS, WILLIAM. Gat-toothed Alysoun, gaptoothed Kathleen: sovereignty and dentition. *See* **16766**.

4443. SCANLON, LARRY. Lydgate's poetics: laureation and domesticity in the *Temple of Glass*. *In* (pp. 61–97) **4231**.

4444. SERRANO REYES, JESÚS L.; LEÓN SENDRA, ANTONIO R. (introds and trans). Cuentos de Canterbury. Madrid: Gredos, 2004. pp. 646. (Biblioteca universal Gredos, 24.) Rev. by Jordi Sánchez-Martí in SAC (27) 2005, 350–2.

4445. SHIMOMURA, SACHI. Odd bodies and visible ends in medieval literature. *See* **3767**.

4446. SMITH, NICOLE D. The Parson's predilection for pleasure. SAC (28) 2006, 117–40.

4447. Stanbury, Sarah. Host desecration, Chaucer's Prioress's Tale, and Prague 1389. *In* (pp. 211–24) **3896**.

4448. Sturges, Robert S. The Pardoner in Canterbury: class, gender, and urban space in the *Prologue to the Tale of Beryn*. *See* **4049**.

4449. Thomas, Paul R. Chaucer's Knight's Tale: were Arcite and Emelye really married? Why it matters. *In* (pp. 19–33) **4310**.

4450. Thomas, Susanne Sara. The problem of defining *sovereynetee* in the Wife of Bath's Tale. ChauR (41:1) 2006, 87–97.

4451. Thompson, Kenneth J. Chaucer's warrior bowman: the roles and equipment of the Knight's Yeoman. ChauR (40:4) 2006, 386–415.

4452. Turner, Marion. Greater London. *In* (pp. 25–40) **4312**.

4453. —— Politics and London life. *In* (pp. 13–33) **4345**.

4454. Twomey, Michael W. Reading Chaucer's Latin aloud. *In* (pp. 181–90) **4310**.

4455. Vandeventer Pearman, Tory. Laying siege to female power: Theseus the 'conqueror' and Hippolita the 'asseged' in Chaucer's The Knight's Tale. EMS (23) 2006, 31–40.

4456. Walter, Katie Louise. The Middle English term *froten*: Absolon and barber-surgery. *See* **1564**.

4457. Williams, Tara. "T'assaye in thee thy wommanheede': Griselda chosen, translated, and tried. SAC (27) 2005, 93–127.

4458. Windeatt, Barry. Courtly writing. *In* (pp. 90–109) **4345**.

4459. Wood, Marjorie Elizabeth. The sultaness, Donegild, and fourteenth-century female merchants: intersecting discourses of gender, economy, and Orientalism in Chaucer's Man of Law's Tale. Comitatus (37) 2006, 65–85.

4460. Xiao, Minghan. Plurality and polyphony in the *Canterbury Tales*. FLS (120) 2006, 74–83. (In Chinese.)

4461. Zaerr, Linda Marie. *The Weddynge of Sir Gawen and Dame Ragnell*: performance and intertextuality in Middle English popular romance. *In* (pp. 193–208) **3892**.

The House of Fame

4462. Ferber, Michael. The curse of the Ephesians: a long footnote to Byron. *See* **9345**.

4463. Kruger, Steven F. Dreaming. *In* (pp. 71–89) **4345**.

4464. Scanlon, Larry. Lydgate's poetics: laureation and domesticity in the *Temple of Glass*. *In* (pp. 61–97) **4231**.

4465. Williams, Deanne. The dream visions. *In* (pp. 147–78) **4330**.

The Legend of Good Women

4466. Doyle, Kara A. Thisbe out of context: Chaucer's female readers and the Findern Manuscript. ChauR (40:3) 2006, 231–61.

4467. Driver, Martha W. Romancing the *Rose*: the readings of Chaucer and Christine. *In* (pp. 147–62) **3836**.

4468. Gilbert, Jane. Becoming woman in Chaucer: '*On ne naît pas femme, on le meurt.*' *In* (pp. 109–29) **3869**.

4469. Gross, Karen Elizabeth. Chaucer, Mary Magdalene and the consolation of love. ChauR (41:1) 2006, 1–37.

4470. Hagedorn, Suzanne C. Abandoned women: rewriting the Classics in Dante, Boccaccio, & Chaucer. (Bibl. 2004, 5289.) Rev. by Robert R. Edwards in MP (103:2) 2005, 240–3; by Carolyn P. Collette in SAC (27) 2005, 312–15.

4471. Kruger, Steven F. Dreaming. *In* (pp. 71–89) **4345**.

4472. McCormick, Betsy. A feel for the game: Bourdieu, source study, and the *Legend*. SAC (28) 2006, 257–61.

4473. Nolan, Maura. Lydgate's literary history: Chaucer, Gower, and Canacee. *See* **4225**.

4474. Williams, Deanne. The dream visions. *In* (pp. 147–78) **4330**.

The Parliament of Fowls

4475. Haldane, Michael. *The Soote Season*: Surrey and the amatory elegy. *See* **5133**.

4476. Klassen, Norman. A note on 'hyre' in *Parliament of Fowls*, 284. NQ (53:2) 2006, 154–7.

4477. Kruger, Steven F. Dreaming. *In* (pp. 71–89) **4345**.

4478. Morgan, Gerald. Chaucer's adaptation of Boccaccio's Temple of Venus in *The Parliament of Fowls*. RES (56:223) 2005, 1–36.

4479. Steinberg, Glenn A. Chaucer's mutability in Spenser's *Mutabilitie Cantos*. *See* **5119**.

4480. Williams, Deanne. The dream visions. *In* (pp. 147–78) **4330**.

The Romaunt of the Rose

4481. Driver, Martha W. Romancing the *Rose*: the readings of Chaucer and Christine. *In* (pp. 147–62) **3836**.

4482. Horobin, Simon. A new fragment of the *Romaunt of the Rose*. SAC (28) 2006, 205–15.

4483. Windeatt, Barry. Courtly writing. *In* (pp. 90–109) **4345**.

Short Poems

4484. Cooper, Helen. London and Southwark poetic companies: *Si tost c'amis* and the *Canterbury Tales*. *In* (pp. 109–25) **4312**.

4485. Hill, Thomas D. Adam, 'The firste stocke', and the political context of Chaucer's *Gentilesse*. *In* (pp. 145–50) **4310**.

4486. Holsinger, Bruce. Lyrics and short poems. *In* (pp. 179–212) **4330**.

4487. Scattergood, John. London and money: Chaucer's *Complaint to His Purse*. *In* (pp. 162–73) **4312**.

4488. Yeager, R. F. 'Saving the appearances': ii, Another look at Chaucer's *Complaint to His Empty Purse*. *In* (pp. 151–64) **4310**.

Troilus and Criseyde

4489. Beidler, Peter G. 'That I was born, allas': Criseyde's weary dawn song. *In* (pp. 255–76) **4523**.

4490. Besserman, Lawrence. Chaucer and Dickens use Luke 23.34. ChauR (41:1) 2006, 99–104.

4491. Carruthers, Mary. On affliction and reading, weeping and argument: Chaucer's lachrymose Troilus in context. Representations (93) 2006, 1–21.

4492. Chewning, Susannah. Re-reading/re-teaching Chaucer's Criseyde. *In* (pp. 165–80) **4523**.

4493. Clarke, K. P. Eagles mating with doves: *Troilus and Criseyde*, II.925–931, *Inferno* v and *Purgatorio* IX. NQ (53:3) 2006, 297–9.

4494. Cooney, Helen (ed.). Writings on love in the English Middle Ages. *See* **3836**.

4495. Cooper, Helen. Love before Troilus. *In* (pp. 25–43) **3836**.

4496. Crocker, Holly A. How the woman makes the man: Chaucer's reciprocal fictions in *Troilus and Criseyde*. *In* (pp. 139–64) **4523**.

4497. Dimmick, Jeremy. Gower, Chaucer and the art of repentance in Robert Greene's *Vision*. *See* **4851**.

4498. Doyle, Kara. Criseyde reading, reading Criseyde. *In* (pp. 75–110) **4523**.

4499. Fleming, John V. Criseyde's poem: the anxieties of the Classical tradition. *In* (pp. 277–98) **4523**.

4500. Gasse, Rosanne. The fierce Achilles in Chaucer, Gower, and the *Gawain*-poet. *In* (pp. 121–34) **4550**.

4501. Hill, Thomas Edward. 'She, this in blak': vision, truth, and will in Geoffrey Chaucer's *Troilus and Criseyde*. London; New York: Routledge, 2006. pp. ix, 147. (Studies in medieval history and culture.)

4502. Hodges, Laura F. Criseyde's 'widewes habit large of samyt broun'. *In* (pp. 37–58) **4523**.

4503. Jacobs, Kathryn. Mate or mother: positioning Criseyde among Chaucer's widows. *In* (pp. 59–73) **4523**.

4504. Jost, Jean E. The performative Criseyde: self-conscious dramaturgy. *In* (pp. 207–30) **4523**.

4505. Klassen, Norman. Tragedy and romance in Chaucer's 'litel bok' of *Troilus and Criseyde*. *In* (pp. 156–76) **4345**.

4506. Knapp, Peggy A. Criseyde's beauty: Chaucer and aesthetics. *In* (pp. 231–54) **4523**.

4507. Lombardi, Chiara. Troilo e Criseida nella letteratura occidentale. Rome: Edizioni di Storia e Letteratura, 2005. pp. xiii, 330, (plates) 11. (Temi e testi, 62.) Rev. by Monica Bardi in Indice (2006:3) 17.

4508. Lynch, Andrew. Love in wartime: *Troilus and Criseyde* as Trojan history. *In* (pp. 113–33) **4345**.

4509. Marzec, Marcia Smith; Vitto, Cindy L. Criseyde as codependent: a new approach to an old enigma. *In* (pp. 181–206) **4523**.

4510. Mieszkowski, Gretchen. Medieval go-betweens and Chaucer's Pandarus. Basingstoke; New York: Palgrave Macmillan, 2006. pp. x, 218. (New Middle Ages.)

4511. Minnis, Alastair. 'I speke of folk in seculer estaat': vernacularity and secularity in the age of Chaucer. SAC (27) 2005, 25–58. (Biennial Chaucer Lecture.)

4512. Nair, Sashi. 'O brotel wele of mannes joie unstable!': gender and philosophy in *Troilus and Criseyde*. Parergon (23:2) 2006, 35–56.

4513. Nolan, Barbara. Chaucer's poetics of dwelling in *Troilus and Criseyde*. *In* (pp. 57–75) **4312**.

4514. Petrina, Alessandra. 'My maisteris dere': the acknowledgement of authority in *The Kingis Quair*. *See* **4169**.

4515. Ransom, Daniel J. Apollo's holy laurel: *Troilus and Criseyde* III.542–43. ChauR (41:2) 2006, 206–12.

4516. Rust, Martha Dana. 'Le Vostre C': letters and love in Bodleian Library MS Arch. Selden B.24. *In* (pp. 111–38) **4523**.

4517. Saunders, Corinne. Love and the making of the self: *Troilus and Criseyde*. *In* (pp. 134–55) **4345**.

4518. Stock, Lorraine Kochanske. 'Slydynge' critics: changing critical constructions of Chaucer's Criseyde in the past century. *In* (pp. 11–36) **4523**.

4519. Summit, Jennifer. *Troilus and Criseyde*. *In* (pp. 213–42) **4330**.

4520. Thompson, Diane P. The Trojan War: literature and legends from the Bronze Age to the present. (Bibl. 2004, 5312.) Rev. by Sylvaine Bataille in CEl (68) 2005, 88–91.

4521. Turner, Marion. Greater London. *In* (pp. 25–40) **4312**.

4522. —— Politics and London life. *In* (pp. 13–33) **4345**.

4523. Vitto, Cindy L.; Marzec, Marcia Smith (eds). New perspectives on Criseyde. Asheville, NC: Pegasus Press, 2004. pp. 336. Rev. by George Edmondson in SAC (28) 2006, 340–3.

4524. Wetherbee, Winthrop. Cresseid *vs* Troylus in Henryson's *Testament*. *In* (pp. 133–41) **4310**.

4525. —— Criseyde alone. *In* (pp. 299–332) **4523**.

4526. Windeatt, Barry. *Troilus and Criseyde*: love in a manner of speaking. *In* (pp. 81–97) **3836**.

4527. Wittig, Joseph S. Tereus, Procne, and her sister: Chaucer's representation of Criseyde as victim. *In* (pp. 117–32) **4310**.

GAWAIN-POET

General Scholarship and Criticism

4528. Anderson, J. J. Language and imagination in the *Gawain*-poems. Manchester; New York: Manchester UP, 2005. pp. 247. (Manchester medieval studies.) Rev. by H. L. Spencer in RES (57:228) 2006, 127–8; by Tony Davenport in MÆ (75:2) 2006, 327–8; by Judith A. Jefferson in NQ (53:2) 2006, 218–19; by Antonina Harbus in Parergon (23:2) 2006, 119–21.

4529. Borroff, Marie. Narrative artistry in *St Erkenwald* and the *Gawain*-group: the case for common authorship reconsidered. SAC (28) 2006, 41–76.

4530. Putter, Ad. The ways and words of the hunt: notes on *Sir Gawain and the Green Knight*, *The Master of Game*, *Sir Tristrem*, *Pearl*, and *Saint Erkenwald*. ChauR (40:4) 2006, 354–85.

Separate Works

Cleanness

4531. Citrome, Jeremy J. The surgeon in medieval English literature. Basingstoke; New York: Palgrave Macmillan, 2006. pp. 191. (New Middle Ages.)

Patience

4532. Bollerman, Karen. In the belly, in the bower: divine maternal practice in *Patience*. *In* (pp. 193–218) **3893**.

Pearl

4533. Fletcher, Alan J. Reading radical metonymy in *Pearl*. *In* (pp. 47–61) **3658**.

4534. Maring, Heather. 'Never the less': gift-exchange and the medieval dream-vision *Pearl*. JMMLA (38:2) 2005, 1–15.

St Erkenwald

4535. Borroff, Marie. *St Erkenwald*: narrative and narrative artistry. *In* (pp. 135–48) **3896**.

4536. Schwyzer, Philip. Exhumation and ethnic conflict: from *St Erkenwald* to Spenser in Ireland. Representations (95) 2006, 1–26.

Sir Gawain and the Green Knight

4537. Burton, T. L. Sir Gawain and the green hag: the *real* meaning of the Wife of Bath's Tale. *In* (pp. 75–80) **4310**.

4538. Eldevik, Randi. Mortal hopes: the Trojan framework of *Sir Gawain and the Green Knight* in a doctrinal context. *In* (pp. 49–64) **4550**.

4539. Gasse, Rosanne. The fierce Achilles in Chaucer, Gower, and the *Gawain*-poet. *In* (pp. 121–34) **4550**.

4540. Goodrich, Peter H. Ritual sacrifice and the pre-Christian subtext of Gawain's green girdle. *In* (pp. 65–81) **4550**.

4541. Haydock, Nicholas. Treasonous founders and pious seducers: Aeneas, Gawain, and aporetic romance. *In* (pp. 82–111) **4550**.

4542. Hodapp, William F. Geoffrey of Monmouth and the *Gawain*-poet: remembering Troy. *In* (pp. 17–29) **4550**.

4543. Ingledew, Francis. *Sir Gawain and the Green Knight* and the Order of the Garter. Notre Dame, IN: Notre Dame UP, 2006. pp. xi, 307. Rev. by Carolyne Larrington in TLS, 21 July 2006, 9; by Michael W. Twomey in Arthuriana (16:4) 2006, 91–2; by Gerald Morgan in RES (57:232) 2006, 795–6.

4544. Lara Rallo, Carmen. 'Flashing into the crystal mirror': the recurrence of the mirror motif in three Arthurian works. RAEI (17) 2004, 139–54.

4545. O'Donoghue, Bernard (introd. and trans.). Sir Gawain and the Green Knight. London; New York: Penguin, 2006. pp. xxvi, 94. (Penguin classics.)

4546. Petrina, Alessandra. Forbidden feast, enchanted castle: Arthurian spaces in the Harry Potter novels. *See* **18357**.

4547. Phillips, Bill. 'The taint of a fault': Purgatory, relativism and Humanism in *Sir Gawain and the Green Knight*. RAEI (17) 2004, 227–37.

4548. Pugh, Tison. Queering medieval genres. *See* **4340**.

4549. Risden, E. L. The 'tresounous tulk' in *Sir Gawain and the Green Knight*. *In* (pp. 112–20) **4550**.

4550. —— (ed.). Sir Gawain and the Classical tradition: essays on the ancient antecedents. Jefferson, NC; London: McFarland, 2006. pp. 217.

4551. Rutter, Russell. The treason of Aeneas and the mythographers of Vergil: the Classical tradition in *Sir Gawain and the Green Knight*. *In* (pp. 30–48) **4550**.

4552. Sanders, Arnold. Sir Gareth and the 'Unfair Unknown': Malory's use of the Gawain romances. *See* **4270**.

4553. Saunders, Corinne. Violent magic in Middle English romance. *In* (pp. 225–40) **3965**.

4554. Shimomura, Sachi. Odd bodies and visible ends in medieval literature. *See* **3767**.

4555. Stephens, Carolyn King. The 'pentangle hypothesis': a dating history and resetting of *Sir Gawain and the Green Knight*. FCS (31) 2006, 174–202.

4556. Sweeney, Mickey. *Sir Gawain and the Green Knight*: Classical magic and its function in medieval romance. *In* (pp. 182–210) **4550**.

4557. Thompson, Raymond H.; Busby, Keith (eds). Gawain: a casebook. *See* **3980**.

4558. Thundy, Zacharias P. Classical analogues – Eastern and Western – of *Sir Gawain*. *In* (pp. 135–81) **4550**.

4559. Wells, Sharon. Manners maketh man: living, dining and becoming a man in the later Middle Ages. *In* (pp. 67–81) **3869**.

SIXTEENTH CENTURY

GENERAL

4560. Alexander, Gavin. Writing after Sidney: the literary response to Sir Philip Sidney, 1586–1640. *See* **5030**.

4561. Allen, Rosamund (ed.). Eastward bound: travel and travellers, 1050–1550. *See* **3825**.

4562. Andrea, Bernadette. Travels through Islam in Early Modern English Studies. CLIO (35:2) 2006, 225–43 (review-article).

4563. Baseotto, Paola. Fighting the 'warres of the Lord': incitement to war in Elizabethan devotional writings. *In* (pp. 37–53) **3409**.

4564. Benson, Pamela Joseph; Kirkham, Victoria (eds). Strong voices, weak history: early women writers & canons in England, France, & Italy. (Bibl. 2005, 5094.) Rev. by Patricia Phillippy in RQ (59:1) 2006, 143–5.

4565. Bertram, Benjamin. The time is out of joint: skepticism in Shakespeare's England. (Bibl. 2005, 5096.) Rev. by Jane Pettegree in SixCJ (37:2) 2006, 618–19.

4566. Black, Scott. Of essays and reading in early modern Britain. Basingstoke; New York: Palgrave Macmillan, 2006. pp. ix, 193. (Palgrave studies in the Enlightenment, Romanticism and the cultures of print.)

4567. Bono, Paola. Rewriting the memory of a queen: Dido, Cleopatra, Elizabeth I. EJES (10:2) 2006, 117–30.

4568. Brooks, Douglas A. (ed.). Printing and parenting in early modern England. *See* **661**.

4569. Brown, Georgia. Redefining Elizabethan literature. (Bibl. 2005, 5102.) Rev. by Agnès Lafont in CEl (68) 2005, 87–8; by Lucy Potter in MSAN (26:2) 2006, 3–4.

4570. Campbell, Julie D. Literary circles and gender in early modern Europe: a cross-cultural approach. Aldershot; Burlington, VT: Ashgate, 2006. pp. viii, 221. (Women and gender in the early modern world.)

4571. Carlin, Claire L. (ed.). Imagining contagion in early modern Europe. Basingstoke; New York: Palgrave Macmillan, 2005. pp. xii, 289. Rev. by Matteo Motolese in MLR (101:4) 2006, 1070–1.

4572. Carpenter, Andrew. Literature in print, 1550–1800. *In* (pp. 301–18) **724**.

4573. Castillo, Susan. Colonial encounters in New World writing, 1500–1786: performing America. London; New York: Routledge, 2006. pp. x, 276. Rev. by Amy M. E. Morris in JAStud (40:2) 2006, 422–3.

4574. Cavanagh, Sheila. Romancing the epic: Lady Mary Wroth's *Urania* and literary traditions. *In* (pp. 19–36) **3395**.

4575. Classen, Albrecht (ed.). Discourses on love, marriage, and transgression in medieval and early modern literature. *See* **4004**.

4576. Cornett, Michael. New books across the disciplines. *See* **3838**.

4577. —— New books across the disciplines. *See* **3839**.

4578. —— New books across the disciplines. *See* **3840**.

4579. —— New books across the disciplines. *See* **3841**.

4580. Cotterill, Anne. Digressive voices in early modern English literature. (Bibl. 2004, 5357.) Rev. by Andrew Breeze in MLR (101:4) 2006, 1086–7; by Jameela Lares in HLQ (69:4) 2006, 631–6.

4581. Crawford, Julie. Marvelous Protestantism: monstrous births in post-Reformation England. (Bibl. 2005, 5120.) Rev. by Michael Davies in RES (57:230) 2006, 395–7; by Sarah Covington in RQ (59:2) 2006, 608–10.

4582. Daileader, Celia R. Back door sex: Renaissance gynosodomy, Aretino, and the exotic. *In* (pp. 25–45) **11883**.

4583. Daybell, James (ed.). Women and politics in early modern England, 1450–1700. (Bibl. 2005, 5126.) Rev. by Christina M. Wells in SixCJ (37:1) 2006, 125–6.

4584. Demers, Patricia. Early modern England. (Bibl. 2005, 5127.) Rev. by Janet Clare in RQ (59:2) 2006, 625–6; by Peter Carlson in Comitatus (37) 2006, 235–9.

4585. Dobranski, Stephen B. Readers and authorship in early modern England. (Bibl. 2005, 5128.) Rev. by Joad Raymond in SHARP (15:4) 2006, 13–14; by William H. Sherman in RQ (59:2) 2006, 628–9; by Peter Carlson in Comitatus (37) 2006, 243–6; by Dan Mills in Comitatus (37) 2006, 246–8.

4586. Dobson, Michael. Mushrooms. LRB (28:19) 2006, 9–12 (review-article). (Decadence of court culture and politics.)

4587. Foley, Stephen Merriam. The English Renaissance; or, My last duchess. LitIm (8:1) 2006, 48–62.

4588. Fudge, Erica (ed.). Renaissance beasts: of animals, humans, and other wonderful creatures. Urbana: Illinois UP, 2004. pp. vii, 246. Rev. by Kevin de Ornellas in TLS, 23 July 2004, 33; by Bruce Boehrer in RQ (58:1) 2005, 286–8; by Martin Worthington in SixCJ (36:4) 2005, 1224–6; by Frank Palmeri in CLIO (35:3) 2006, 407–20.

4589. Giese, Loreen L. Malvolio's yellow stockings: coding illicit sexuality in early modern London. *See* **6177**.

4590. Gil, Daniel Juan. Before intimacy: asocial sexuality in early modern England. Minneapolis; London: Minnesota UP, 2006. pp. xvi, 187. Rev. by Gary Waller in SidJ (24:1) 2006, 84–8.

4591. Goodall, Peter. The author in the study: self-representation as reader and writer in the medieval and early modern periods. *In* (pp. 104–14) **4792**.

4592. Grossman, Marshall (ed.). Reading Renaissance ethics. London; New York: Routledge, 2006. pp. 224.

4593. Hager, Alan (gen. ed.). Encyclopedia of British writers: vol. 1, 16th and 17th centuries. New York: Facts on File, 2005. pp. xviii, 478. (Facts on File library of world literature.)

4594. Hamilton, Donna B. (ed.). A concise companion to English Renaissance literature. Oxford; Malden, MA: Blackwell, 2006. pp. ix, 275. (Blackwell concise companions to literature and culture.)

4595. Hamlin, William M. Tragedy and skepticism in Shakespeare's England. (Bibl. 2005, 5143.) Rev. by Brad Greenburg in RQ (59:2) 2006, 638–40; by Robert Ellrodt in EA (59:4) 2006, 474–5.

4596. Hattaway, Michael. Renaissance and reformations: an introduction to early modern English literature. Oxford; Malden, MA: Blackwell, 2005. pp. vii, 253. (Blackwell introductions to literature, 12.) Rev. by Ton Hoenselaars in SEDERI (16) 2006, 189–93.

4597. Havens, Earle. Notes from a literary underground: recusant Catholics, Jesuit priests, and scribal publication in Elizabethan England. PBSA (99:4) 2005, 505–38.

4598. Heitsch, Dorothy; Vallée, Jean-François (eds). Printed voices: the Renaissance culture of dialogue. (Bibl. 2005, 5145.) Rev. by Dosia Reichardt in Parergon (23:1) 2006, 171–3.

4599. Hempfer, Klaus W. (ed.). Poetik des Dialogs: aktuelle Theorie und rinascimentales Selbstverständnis. Stuttgart: Steiner, 2004. pp. 191. (Text und Kontext, 21.) Rev. by Annick Paternoster in MLR (101:3) 2006, 812–13.

4600. Hoenselaars, Ton; Kinney, Arthur F. (eds). Challenging Humanism: essays in honor of Dominic Baker-Smith. Newark: Delaware UP; London: Assoc. UPs, 2005. pp. 335. Rev. by Daniel Wakelin in RQ (59:3) 2006, 957–8; by Peter Happé in BJJ (13) 2006, 226–34.

4601. Höfele, Andreas; von Koppenfels, Werner (eds). Renaissance go-betweens: cultural exchange in early modern Europe. (Bibl. 2005, 5147.) Rev. by Gesa Stedman in RQ (59:2) 2006, 567–8.

4602. Holmes, Jonathan; Streete, Adrian (eds). Refiguring mimesis: representation in early modern literature. Hatfield: UP of Hertfordshire, 2005. pp. xvi, 221. Rev. by Craig Hamilton in TLS, 21 July 2006, 33; by Andrew Hadfield in RES (57:229) 2006, 264–6; by Tom MacFaul in NQ (53:3) 2006, 379–80.

4603. Iyengar, Sujata. Shades of difference: mythologies of skin colour in early modern England. (Bibl. 2005, 5149.) Rev. by Francesca T. Royster in SStud (34) 2006, 187–99; by Jean Feerick in RQ (59:1) 2006, 289–91.

4604. Kelly, Philippa. Dialogues of self-reflection: early modern mirrors. *In* (pp. 62–85) **4792**.

4605. Kendrick, Christopher. Utopia, carnival, and commonwealth in Renaissance England. (Bibl. 2005, 5152.) Rev. by Georgia Brown in SStud (34) 2006, 199–209; by Daniel T. Lochman in SixCJ (37:2) 2006, 634–5; by Anne Lake Prescott in RQ (59:1) 2006, 291–3.

4606. King, John N. Voices of the English Reformation: a sourcebook. (Bibl. 2005, 5155.) Rev. by Frederick Poling in SixCJ (37:1) 2006, 297–8; by J. P. Conlan in LitH (15:1) 2006, 79–80.

4607. Kinney, Arthur F. The making of a Humanist poetic. LitIm (8:1) 2006, 29–43.

4608. Kitzes, Adam H. The politics of melancholy from Spenser to Milton. *See* **6268**.

4609. Knoppers, Laura Lunger; Landes, Joan B. (eds). Monstrous bodies / political monstrosities in early modern Europe. (Bibl. 2005, 5157.) Rev. by Alisa Plant in SixCJ (37:1) 2006, 182–4.

4610. Kumaran, Arul. Robert Greene's Martinist transformation in 1590. *See* **4857**.

4611. Lamb, Mary Ellen. Recent studies in the English Renaissance. SELit (46:1) 2006, 195–252.

4612. Lavezzo, Kathy. Angels on the edge of the world: geography, literature, and English community, 1000–1534. *See* **3682**.

4613. Lockey, Brian C. Law and empire in English Renaissance literature. Cambridge; New York: CUP, 2006. pp. ix, 236.

4614. Maguire, Laurie. Helen of Troy: representing absolute beauty in language. *See* **5373**.

4615. Marotti, Arthur F. Religious ideology and cultural fantasy: Catholic and anti-Catholic discourses in early modern England. Notre Dame, IN: Notre Dame UP, 2005. pp. xii, 307. Rev. by Raymond D. Tumbleson in CathHR (92:3) 2006, 321–2; by Alison Chapman in RQ (59:1) 2006, 267–8.

4616. Maus, Katharine Eisaman. A womb of his own: male Renaissance poets in the female body. *In* (pp. 89–108) **661**.

4617. Ménager, Daniel (ed.). La Renaissance et la nuit. Geneva: Droz, 2005. pp. 270. (Seuils de la modernité, 10.) Rev. by Emily Butterworth in MLR (101:3) 2006, 811–12.

4618. Monta, Susannah Brietz. Martyrdom and literature in early modern England. (Bibl. 2005, 5169.) Rev. by Sarah Covington in RQ (59:1) 2006, 269–70; by Leo Carruthers in EA (59:2) 2006, 219–20.

4619. Morini, Massimiliano. Tudor translation in theory and practice. Aldershot; Burlington, VT: Ashgate, 2006. pp. x, 151.

4620. Oakley-Brown, Liz. Ovid and the cultural politics of translation in early modern England. *See* **3875**.

4621. Orgel, Stephen. Marginal maternity: reading Lady Anne Clifford's *A Mirror for Magistrates*. *In* (pp. 267–89) **661**.

4622. Payne, Paula Harms (ed.). A search for meaning: critical essays on early modern literature. (Bibl. 2004, 5403.) Rev. by Phoebe S. Spinrad in SCN (64:1/2) 2006, 20–2.

4623. Perry, Curtis. Literature and favouritism in early modern England. Cambridge; New York: CUP, 2006. pp. x, 328. Rev. by Michael Dobson in LRB (28:19) 2006, 9–12.

4624. Perry, Kathryn. Unpicking the seam: talking animals and reader pleasure in early modern satire. *In* (pp. 19–36) **4588**.

4625. Pfister, Manfred. *'What's Hecuba to him?'*: vom Nutzen und Nachteil mythischer Geschichten für Shakespeare. *See* **5409**.

4626. Pincombe, Mike (ed.). Travels and translations in the sixteenth century: selected papers from the Second International Conference of the Tudor Symposium (2000). (Bibl. 2005, 5182.) Rev. by Andrew Hadfield in TransLit (14:2) 2005, 249–52.

4627. Quilligan, Maureen. Incest and agency in Elizabeth's England. (Bibl. 2005, 5183.) Rev. by Yael Margalit in CEl (68) 2005, 92–3; by Richard A. McCabe in SStud (34) 2006, 235–47; by Jane Donawerth in RQ (59:2) 2006, 624–5.

4628. Resende, Aimara da Cunha. 'Here's sport, indeed!': interchangeable voices and mass communication in Renaissance England. SEDERI (16) 2006, 71–90.

4629. Richardson, Catherine (ed.). Clothing culture, 1350–1650. Aldershot; Burlington, VT: Ashgate, 2004. pp. xiv, 290. Rev. by Tawny Sherrill in SixCJ (37:1) 2006, 127–8.

4630. Saenger, Michael Baird. The birth of advertising. *In* (pp. 197–219) **661**.

4631. Scott, Alison V. Selfish gifts: the politics of exchange and English courtly literature, 1580–1628. Madison, NJ: Fairleigh Dickinson UP, 2006. pp. 303.

4632. Scott-Warren, Jason. Early modern English literature. (Bibl. 2005, 5194.) Rev. by Adam Smyth in TLS, 5 May 2006, 7–8.

4633. Sheen, Erica; Hutson, Lorna (eds). Literature, politics and law in Renaissance England. (Bibl. 2005, 5196.) Rev. by B. J. Sokol in NQ (53:1) 2006, 105–6; by Gary D. Hamilton in RQ (59:2) 2006, 647–9.

4634. Shrank, Cathy. Writing the nation in Reformation England, 1530–1580. (Bibl. 2005, 5199.) Rev. by Ronald H. Fritze in SixCJ (37:1) 2006, 243–4.

4635. Smith, Helen. 'This one poore blacke gowne lined with white': the clothing of the sixteenth-century English book. *In* (pp. 195–208) **4629**.

4636. Snook, Edith. Women, reading, and the cultural politics of early modern England. (Bibl. 2005, 5201.) Rev. by Gillian Wright in SHARP (15:4) 2006, 14–15; by Sally Parkin in Parergon (23:1) 2006, 213–15.

4637. Spiller, Elizabeth. Science, reading, and Renaissance literature: the art of making knowledge, 1580–1670. (Bibl. 2005, 5202.) Rev. by Cynthia Klestinec in SixCJ (36:4) 2005, 1138–9; by Robin Sowerby in MLR (101:3) 2006, 819–20.

4638. Tiffany, Grace. Love's pilgrimage: the holy journey in English Renaissance literature. Newark: Delaware UP, 2006. pp. 217.

4639. Totaro, Rebecca. Suffering in paradise: the bubonic plague in English literature from More to Milton. (Bibl. 2005, 5206.) Rev. by Paul Slack in MQ (40:1) 2006, 80–1.

4640. Trevor, Douglas. The poetics of melancholy in early modern England. (Bibl. 2005, 5208.) Rev. by Tom MacFaul in NQ (53:2) 2006, 240–1.

4641. Voaden, Rosalynn; Wolfthal, Diane (eds). Framing the family: narrative and representation in the medieval and early modern periods. *See* **3893**.

4642. Walker, Greg. Writing under tyranny: English literature and the Henrician Reformation. (Bibl. 2005, 5211.) Rev. by Andrew Hadfield in TLS, 28 Apr. 2006, 32; by Patrick Collinson in LRB (28:12) 2006, 24–6; by Roderick J. Lyall in CEl (70) 2006, 75–6; by Alessandra Petrina in RQ (59:3) 2006, 941–2; by Tracey A. Sowerby in RES (57:232) 2006, 812–14.

4643. Watson, Robert N. Back to nature: the green and the real in the late Renaissance. Philadelphia: Pennsylvania UP, 2006. pp. viii, 436. Rev. by Gabriel Egan in RES (57:232) 2006, 817–19.

DRAMA AND THE THEATRE

4644. Alakas, Brandon. Seniority and mastery: the politics of ageism in the Coventry Cycle. *See* **3941**.

4645. Anderson, Thomas Page. Performing early modern trauma from Shakespeare to Milton. *See* **6151**.

4646. Ardolino, Frank. The induction of Sly: the influence of *The Spanish Tragedy* on the two *Shrews*. *See* **6104**.

4647. Barbour, Richmond. Before Orientalism: London's theatre of the East 1576–1626. (Bibl. 2005, 5218.) Rev. by Andrew Hiscock in MLR (101:1) 2006, 220–1; by Bernadette Andrea in CLIO (35:2) 2006, 225–43.

4648. Bedford, Ronald. On being a person: Elizabethan acting and the art of self-representation. *In* (pp. 49–61) **4792**.

4649. Berek, Peter. Genres, early modern theatrical title pages, and the authority of print. *In* (pp. 159–75) **4731**.

4650. Bergeron, David M. Textual patronage in English drama, 1570–1640. Aldershot; Burlington, VT: Ashgate, 2006. pp. viii, 247. Rev. by Harold Love in TLS, 29 Sept. 2006, 27; by Jason Scott-Warren in RES (57:232) 2006, 807–9; by Michael G. Brennan in CompDr (40:3) 2006, 377–80.

4651. Berry, Herbert. The Bell Savage Inn and Playhouse in London. MedRen (19) 2006, 121–43.

4652. Borden, Ian. The Blackfriars gladiators: masters of fence, playing a prize, and the Elizabethan and Stuart theatre. *In* (pp. 132–46) **5577**.

4653. Boyd, Brian (ed.). Words that count: essays on early modern authorship in honor of MacDonald P. Jackson. (Bibl. 2005, 5221.) Rev. by Michelle Parkinson in SixCJ (37:2) 2006, 617–18.

4654. Brown, Pamela Allen; Parolin, Peter (eds). Women players in England, 1500–1660: beyond the all-male stage. (Bibl. 2005, 5225.) Rev. by Erika T. Lin in UC (25) 2005, 123–6; by David Kathman in ShB (24:4) 2006, 125–9; by Theodora A. Jankowski in ShQ (57:4) 2006, 478–82; by Sharon Beehler in RQ (59:3) 2006, 967–9; by Sophie Tomlinson in RES (57:232) 2006, 822–4.

4655. Bruster, Douglas. The politics of Shakespeare's prose. *In* (pp. 95–114) **5421**.

4656. Burton, Jonathan. Traffic and turning: Islam and English drama, 1579–1624. (Bibl. 2005, 5227.) Rev. by Richmond Barbour in RQ (59:3) 2006, 971–2.

4657. Butler, Michelle M. The borrowed expositor. *See* **3938**.

4658. Clegg, Cyndia Susan. Renaissance play-readers: ordinary and extraordinary. *In* (pp. 23–38) **4731**.

4659. Cooper, Helen. Guy of Warwick, upstart crows and mounting sparrows. *In* (pp. 119–38) **5353**.

4660. Crane, Mary Thomas. Recent studies in Tudor and Stuart drama. SELit (46:2) 2006, 461–511.

4661. Culhane, Peter. Livy in early Jacobean drama. *See* **7172**.

4662. Cummings, James. REED and the possibilities of Web technology. *In* (pp. 178–99) **3904**.

4663. DAVIDSON, CLIFFORD. Selected studies in drama & Renaissance literature. *See* **3903**.

4664. —— York guilds and the Corpus Christi plays: unwilling participants? *See* **3955**.

4665. DESSEN, ALAN C. Rescripting Shakespeare (and others) in 2005. ShB (23:4) 2005, 7–17.

4666. DIMMOCK, MATTHEW. New Turkes: dramatizing Islam and the Ottomans in early modern England. Aldershot; Burlington, VT: Ashgate, 2005. pp. viii, 243. Rev. by Stephan Schmuck in Eng (55:211) 2006, 102–5; by Daniel Vitkus in RQ (59:1) 2006, 251–3.

4667. DÖRING, TOBIAS. Performances of mourning in Shakespearean theatre and early modern culture. *See* **5289**.

4668. DOUGLAS, AUDREY; MACLEAN, SALLY-BETH (eds). REED in review: essays in celebration of the first twenty-five years. *See* **3904**.

4669. DRAKAKIS, JOHN. Authority and the early modern theatre: representing Robert Weimann. *In* (pp. 139–57) **5421**.

4670. EDELMAN, CHARLES (ed.). The Stukeley plays: *The Battle of Alcazar* by George Peele; *The Famous History of the Life and Death of Captain Thomas Stukeley*. *See* **5001**.

4671. EGAN, GABRIEL. 'As it was, is, or will be played': title-pages and the theatre industry to 1610. *In* (pp. 92–110) **5334**.

4672. FORSE, JAMES H. Getting your name out there: traveling acting companies and royal and aristocratic prestige in Tudor England. Quid (26/27) 2005/06, 90–140.

4673. GIESKES, EDWARD. Representing the professions: administration, law, and theater in early modern England. *See* **5306**.

4674. GOSSETT, SUZANNE. Editing collaborative drama. *See* **5175**.

4675. GURR, ANDREW. London's Blackfriars playhouse and the Chamberlain's Men. *In* (pp. 17–30) **5577**.

4676. —— Playgoing in Shakespeare's London. (Bibl. 1996, 5646.) Cambridge; New York: CUP, 2004. pp. xiv, 344. (Third ed.: first ed. 1987.) Rev. by Elizabeth Klett in TJ (58:3) 2006, 526–7.

4677. HAEKEL, RALF. Die englischen Komödianten in Deutschland: eine Einführung in die Ursprünge des deutschen Berufsschauspiels. Heidelberg: Winter, 2004. pp. 347. (Beiträge zur neueren Literaturgeschichte, 212.) Rev. by Günter Walch in SJ (142) 2006, 236–40.

4678. HILLMAN, DAVID. *Homo clausus* at the theatre. *In* (pp. 161–85) **5421**.

4679. HOLLAND, PETER; ORGEL, STEPHEN (eds). From performance to print in Shakespeare's England. *See* **5334**.

4680. —— —— From script to stage in early modern England. (Bibl. 2005, 5260.) Rev. by Victoria E. Price in MLR (101:4) 2006, 1086–7; by Gabriel Egan in TN (60:1) 2006, 60–2; by Robert Shaughnessy in TRI (31:1) 2006, 106–8; by Peter Hyland in NQ (53:3) 2006, 375–7.

4681. HUTSON, LORNA. Forensic aspects of Renaissance mimesis. *See* **5732**.

4682. Ioppolo, Grace. Dramatists and their manuscripts in the age of Shakespeare, Jonson, Middleton and Heywood: authorship, authority, and the playhouse. *See* **511**.

4683. Jackson, MacD. P. Compound adjectives in *Arden of Faversham*. NQ (53:1) 2006, 51–5.

4684. Jackson, MacDonald P. Shakespeare and the quarrel scene in *Arden of Faversham*. ShQ (57:3) 2006, 249–93.

4685. Johnston, Alexandra F. The founding of Records of Early English Drama. *In* (pp. 21–38) **3904**.

4686. Kalpin, Kathleen. 'As if the end they purpos'd were their own': early modern representations of speech between women. WS (35:8) 2006, 757–77.

4687. Kathman, David. The burial of Thomas Pope. *See* **5549**.

4688. Kermode, Lloyd Edward; Scott-Warren, Jason; van Elk, Martine (eds). Tudor drama before Shakespeare, 1485–1590: new directions for research, criticism, and pedagogy. (Bibl. 2005, 5268.) Rev. by Ineke Murakami in TMR, Mar. 2006; by Robert Shaughnessy in TRI (31:1) 2006, 106–8; by Peter C. Herman in CLIO (36:1) 2006, 107–13; by Kent Cartwright in RQ (59:2) 2006, 631–3.

4689. Kerwin, William. Beyond the body: the boundaries of medicine and early English Renaissance drama. (Bibl. 2005, 5269.) Rev. by Fay Bound Alberti in BHM (80:3) 2006, 582–3; by Stephen Pender in RQ (59:2) 2006, 635–7.

4690. Klausner, David N. (ed.). Records of early drama: Wales. *See* **3912**.

4691. —— Marsalek, Karen S. (eds). 'Bring furth the pagants': essays in early English drama presented to Alexandra F. Johnston. *See* **3913**.

4692. Knutson, Roslyn. What if there wasn't a 'Blackfriars repertory'? *In* (pp. 54–60) **5577**.

4693. Knutson, Roslyn L. Everything's back in play: the impact of REED research on Elizabethan theatre history. *In* (pp. 116–28) **3904**.

4694. —— Theater companies and stages. *In* (pp. 12–22) **4734**.

4695. Kozusko, Matt. Taking liberties. ETh (9:1) 2006, 37–60.

4696. Lehmann, Courtney. Dancing in a (cyber) net: 'Renaissance women', systems theory, and the war of the cinemas. *See* **5562**.

4697. Lehr, John. Using REED: a selective bibliography. *In* (pp. 236–60) **3904**.

4698. Lesser, Zachary. Renaissance drama and the politics of publication: readings in the English book trade. (Bibl. 2005, 5271.) Rev. by Tom Lockwood in Library (6:4) 2005, 460–2; by Mark Bayer in LitH (15:1) 2006, 78–9; by Jeffrey Kahan in MSAN (26:1) 2006, 9–10; by William Proctor Williams in NQ (53:1) 2006, 115–16; by James J. Marino in RQ (59:1) 2006, 272–4.

4699. Lopez, Jeremy. Census of Renaissance drama performance reviews in *Shakespeare Quarterly* and *Shakespeare Survey*, 1948–2005. *See* **5565**.

4700. McCarthy, Jeanne H. The queen's 'unfledged minions': an alternate account of the origins of Blackfriars and of the boy company phenomenon. *In* (pp. 93–117) **5577**.

4701. MacLean, Sally-Beth. Birthing the concept: the first nine years. *In* (pp. 39–51) **3904**.

4702. Mailhol, Jean-Claude. Du poison au poignard: la représentation littéraire et théâtrale d'une héroïne meurtrière, Alice Arden. Cycnos (23:2) 2006, 5–25.

4703. Marsalek, Karen Sawyer. 'Awake your faith': English Resurrection drama and *The Winter's Tale*. *In* (pp. 271–91) **3913**.

4704. Marshall, John. Gathering in the name of the outlaw: REED and Robin Hood. *In* (pp. 65–84) **3904**.

4705. Menon, Madhavi. Wanton words: rhetoric and sexuality in English Renaissance drama. (Bibl. 2005, 5281.) Rev. by Ian Frederick Moulton in SixCJ (36:3) 2005, 947–9.

4706. Menzer, Paul. The actor's inhibition: early modern acting and the rhetoric of restraint. RenD (ns 35) 2006, 83–111.

4707. —— (ed.). Inside Shakespeare: essays on the Blackfriars stage. *See* **5577**.

4708. Meredith, Peter. 'Young men will do it': fun, disorder, and good government in York, 1555: some thoughts on House Book 21. *In* (pp. 41–57) **3913**.

4709. Mills, David. Some theological issues in Chester's plays. *In* (pp. 212–28) **3913**.

4710. Orgel, Stephen. Reading occasions. RenD (ns 34) 2005, 31–45.

4711. Palmer, Barbara D. Star turns or small companies? *In* (pp. 9–40) **3913**.

4712. Panek, Jennifer. Widows and suitors in early modern English comedy. (Bibl. 2004, 5488.) Rev. by Carrie Hintz in LitH (15:2) 2006, 72–3; by Matthew Steggle in NQ (53:1) 2006, 114–15.

4713. Peachman, John. Links between *Mucedorus* and *The Tragical History, Admirable Atchievements and Various Events of Guy Earl of Warwick*. NQ (53:4) 2006, 464–7.

4714. Pfister, Manfred. 'An argument of laughter': cultures of laughter and the theater in early modern England. *In* (pp. 42–67) **5346**.

4715. Polito, Mary. Governmental arts in early Tudor England. (Bibl. 2005, 5287.) Rev. by Michael Anderson in TRI (31:3) 2006, 321–2.

4716. Pollard, Tanya. Drugs and theater in early modern England. (Bibl. 2005, 5288.) Rev. by Barbara Howard Traister in SStud (34) 2006, 232–4; by Kim Solga in RQ (59:1) 2006, 285–6.

4717. Preiss, Richard. Natural authorship. RenD (ns 34) 2005, 69–104.

4718. Reynolds, Bryan (ed.). Transversal enterprises in the drama of Shakespeare and his contemporaries: fugitive explorations. Basingstoke; New York: Palgrave Macmillan, 2006. pp. xi, 271.

4719. —— West, William N. (eds). Rematerializing Shakespeare: authority and representation on the early modern English stage. *See* **5421**.

4720. Ronan, Clifford. Caesar on and off the Renaissance English stage. *In* (pp. 71–89) **5805**.

4721. Rowland, Richard. Two plays in one: annotations in the third quarto of *Edward IV*. TextC (1:1) 2006, 46–63.

4722. Rutter, Tom. Merchants of Venice in *A Knack to Know an Honest Man*. MedRen (19) 2006, 194–209.

4723. SHAPIRO, MICHAEL. The Westminister scholars' *Sapientia Solomonis* as royal gift offering. *In* (pp. 118–22) **5577**.

4724. SIMKIN, STEVIE. Early modern tragedy and the cinema of violence. Basingstoke; New York: Palgrave Macmillan, 2006. pp. viii, 264.

4725. SOMERSET, ALAN. The Blackfriars on tour: provincial analogies. *In* (pp. 80–5) **5577**.

4726. —— Coming home: provincial gentry families: their performers, their great halls, their entertainments, and REED. *In* (pp. 77–90) **3913**.

4727. STEPHENSON, JENN. Herodotus in the labyrinth: REED and hypertext. *In* (pp. 200–15) **3904**.

4728. STERN, TIFFANY. Taking part: actors and audience on the stage at Blackfriars. *In* (pp. 35–53) **5577**.

4729. STILLMAN, ROBERT (ed.). Spectacle and public performance in the late Middle Ages and the Renaissance. Leiden; Boston, MA: Brill, 2006. pp. 257. (Studies in medieval and Reformation traditions, 113.)

4730. STRAZNICKY, MARTA. Reading through the body: women and printed drama. *In* (pp. 59–79) **4731**.

4731. —— (ed.). The book of the play: playwrights, stationers, and readers in early modern England. Amherst: Massachusetts UP, 2006. pp. 237. (Massachusetts studies in early modern culture.)

4732. STRETTER, ROBERT. Cicero on stage: *Damon and Pithias* and the fate of Classical friendship in English Renaissance drama. *See* **4839**.

4733. SULLIVAN, GARRETT A., JR. *Arden of Faversham* and the early modern household. *In* (pp. 73–81) **4734**.

4734. —— CHENEY, PATRICK; HADFIELD, ANDREW (eds). Early modern English drama: a critical companion. Oxford; New York: OUP, 2006. pp. xiii, 338. Rev. by Lisa Hopkins in NQ (53:4) 2006, 572.

4735. THOMAS, SYLVIA. REED and the Record Office: tradition and innovation on the road to access. *In* (pp. 131–9) **3904**.

4736. TINER, ELZA C. Professional players in Stratford-on-Avon, 1587–1602. *In* (pp. 86–92) **5577**.

4737. TURNER, HENRY S. The English Renaissance stage: geometry, poetics, and the practical spatial arts 1580–1630. Oxford; New York: OUP, 2006. pp. xv, 326. Rev. by Sam Thompson in TLS, 17 Nov. 2006, 10; by Andrew Hadfield in ShQ (57:4) 2006, 472–4; by Elizabeth Spiller in RQ (59:3) 2006, 965–7.

4738. TWYCROSS, MEG. The *ordo paginarum* revisited, with a digital camera. *In* (pp. 105–31) **3913**.

4739. WALKER, GREG. *Fulgens and Lucres* and early Tudor drama. *In* (pp. 23–34) **4734**.

4740. WELLS, STANLEY. Shakespeare and Co.: Christopher Marlowe, Thomas Dekker, Ben Jonson, Thomas Middleton, John Fletcher and the other players in his story. *See* **5452**.

4741. WEST, WILLIAM N. Understanding in the Elizabethan theaters. RenD (ns 35) 2006, 113–43.

4742. Westfall, Suzanne. What hath REED wrought? REED and patronage. *In* (pp. 85–100) **3904**.

4743. Williamson, Eila; McGavin, John J. Crossing the border: the provincial records of southeast Scotland. *In* (pp. 157–77) **3904**.

4744. Winkelman, Michael. Marriage relationships in Tudor political drama. (Bibl. 2005, 5308.) Rev. by Kevin De Ornellas in TRI (31:2) 2006, 203–4; by Thomas Fulton in RQ (59:1) 2006, 277–8.

4745. Winston, Jessica. Seneca in early Elizabethan England. *See* **4878**.

4746. Womack, Peter. English Renaissance drama. Oxford; Malden, MA: Blackwell, 2006. pp. vii, 325. (Blackwell guides to literature.)

4747. Wong, Mitali P. Politics and tropes in Renaissance history plays: understanding a neglected genre. Lewiston, NY; Lampeter: Mellen Press, 2006. pp. vii, 167.

4748. Young, Abigail Ann. 'Practice makes perfect': policies for a cross-disciplinary project. *In* (pp. 52–62) **3904**.

FICTION

4749. Martin, Randall (sel. and introd.). Women and murder in early modern news pamphlets and broadside ballads, 1573–1697. *See* **4783**.

4750. Wilson, Katharine. Fictions of authorship in late Elizabethan narratives: Euphues in Arcadia. Oxford; New York: OUP, 2006. pp. 185. Rev. by Paul Salzman in RES (57:232) 2006, 805–7.

POETRY

4751. Bartram, Claire. Social fabric in Thynne's *Debate between Pride and Lowliness*. *In* (pp. 137–49) **4629**.

4752. Blevins, Jacob. Catullan consciousness and the early modern lyric in England: from Wyatt to Donne. (Bibl. 2005, 5311.) Rev. by Eugene D. Hill in SCN (64:1/2) 2006, 74–5.

4753. Cheney, Patrick; Hadfield, Andrew; Sullivan, Garrett A., Jr (eds). Early modern English poetry: a critical companion. Oxford; New York: OUP, 2006. pp. xxiii, 342.

4754. Hadfield, Andrew. Literary contexts: predecessors and contemporaries. *In* (pp. 49–64) **6718**.

4755. Haldane, Michael. *The Soote Season*: Surrey and the amatory elegy. *See* **5133**.

4756. Hamlin, Hannibal. Psalm culture and early modern English literature. (Bibl. 2005, 5317.) Rev. by Kenneth J. E. Graham in SixCJ (36:3) 2005, 862–3; by Richard Todd in MLR (101:3) 2006, 817–18; by Kate Narveson in MP (103:2) 2006, 250–3; by Beth Quitslund in MQ (40:3) 2006, 250–1.

4757. Jack, R. D. S. Music, poetry, and performance at the court of James VI. *See* **6430**.

4758. Kitch, Aaron W. Printing bastards: monstrous birth broadsides in early modern England. *In* (pp. 221–36) **661**.

4759. May, Steven W.; Ringler, William A., Jr. Elizabethan poetry: a bibliography and first-line index of English verse, 1559–1603. (Bibl. 2005, 5321.) Rev. by Brian Vickers in TLS, 10 Feb. 2006, 7–8; by Peter Beal in Library (7:1) 2006, 94–7; by A. E. B. Coldiron in SixCJ (37:1) 2006, 176–9; by Carlo M. Bajetta in NQ (53:1) 2006, 102–5.

4760. Millman, Jill Seal, *et al.* (eds). Early modern women's manuscript poetry. Introd. by Elizabeth Clarke and Jonathan Gibson. Manchester; New York: Manchester UP, 2005. pp. vi, 282.

4761. Montgomery, Will. Susan Howe's Renaissance period: metamorphosis and representation in *Pythagorean Silence* and *Defenestration of Prague*. *See* **16474**.

4762. Mortimer, Anthony (ed.). Petrarch's *Canzoniere* in the English Renaissance. (Bibl. 1979, 4096.) Amsterdam; New York: Rodopi, 2005. pp. 196. (Internationale Forschungen zur allgemeinen und vergleichenden Literaturwissenschaft, 88.) (Second ed.: first ed. 1975.) Rev. by J. G. Nichols in TransLit (15:2) 2006, 268–77.

4763. Owens, Judith. Commercial settings of the 1590 *Faerie Queene*. *See* **5111**.

4764. Parks, Stephen, *et al.* (eds). First-line index of English poetry, 1500–1800, in manuscripts of the James M. and Marie-Louise Osborn Collection in the Beinecke Rare Book and Manuscript Library of Yale University. New Haven, CT: Beinecke Rare Book and Manuscript Library, Yale Univ., 2005. pp. vii, 1190.

4765. Pike, Lionel. Pills to purge melancholy: the evolution of the English ballett. Aldershot; Burlington, VT: Ashgate, 2004. pp. xiv, 361. Rev. by G. Yvonne Kendall in MusL (87:3) 2006, 422–4.

4766. Shrank, Cathy. A work by John Bale identified? NQ (53:4) 2006, 421–2.

4767. Warley, Christopher. Sonnet sequences and social distinction in Renaissance England. (Bibl. 2005, 5326.) Rev. by Andrew Hadfield in TLS, 3 Feb. 2006, 30; by David Hawkes in ShQ (57:2) 2006, 218–20; by Mary Keating in RQ (59:3) 2006, 962–3.

4768. Wilson, Christopher R. Number and music in Campion's measured verse. *See* **4825**.

PROSE

4769. Almond, Philip C. (comp.). Demonic possession and exorcism in early modern England: contemporary texts and their cultural contexts. (Bibl. 2005, 5329.) Rev. by Barbara H. Traister in CLIO (35:3) 2006, 395–406.

4770. Atkinson, Colin B.; Atkinson, Jo (sels and introds). Monument of matrones. Aldershot; Burlington, VT: Ashgate, 2005. 3 vols (various pagings). (Early modern Englishwoman, iii: Essential works for the study of early modern women, 1:4–6.) (Facsimile.)

4771. Brownlees, Nicholas (ed.). News discourse in early modern Britain: selected papers of CHINED 2004. New York; Frankfurt: Lang, 2006. pp. 300. (Linguistic insights, 30.)

4772. Carey, Daniel (ed.). Asian travel in the Renaissance. Preface by Anthony Reid. Oxford; Malden, MA: Blackwell, 2004. pp. x, 234. Rev. by James D. Ryan in RQ (59:1) 2006, 248–9.

4773. Clegg, Cyndia Susan. English Renaissance books on Islam and Shakespeare's *Othello*. *See* **6020**.

4774. Daybell, James. Scripting a female voice: women's epistolary rhetoric in sixteenth-century letters of petition. WWr (13:1) 2006, 3–22.

4775. —— Women letter-writers in Tudor England. Oxford; New York: OUP, 2006. pp. xiii, 328.

4776. Dimmick, Jeremy. Gower, Chaucer and the art of repentance in Robert Greene's *Vision*. *See* **4851**.

4777. Downes, Stephanie. Fashioning Christine de Pizan in Tudor defences of women. Parergon (23:1) 2006, 71–92.

4778. Hadfield, Andrew. Historical writing, 1550–1660. *In* (pp. 250–63) **724**.

4779. Hallam, Elizabeth. Speaking to reveal: the body and acts of 'exposure' in early modern popular discourse. *In* (pp. 239–62) **4629**.

4780. Laroche, Rebecca. Catherine Tollemache's library. *See* **342**.

4781. MacLean, Gerald M. The rise of Oriental travel: English visitors to the Ottoman Empire, 1580–1720. (Bibl. 2004, 5563.) Rev. by Matthew Dimmock in MLR (101:3) 2006, 818–19; by Bernadette Andrea in CLIO (35:2) 2006, 225–43; by Palmira Brummett in MedRen (19) 2006, 295–301.

4782. McMullin, B. J. The Book of Common Prayer and the bibliographer. Library (6:4) 2005, 425–54 (review-article).

4783. Martin, Randall (sel. and introd.). Women and murder in early modern news pamphlets and broadside ballads, 1573–1697. Aldershot; Burlington, VT: Ashgate, 2005. 1 vol. (unpaginated). (Early modern Englishwoman, III: Essential works for the study of early modern women, 1:7.) (Facsimiles.)

4784. Murphy, Kathryn. The date of Edwin Sandys's Paul's Cross sermon '… at what time a maine treason was discouered'. NQ (53:4) 2006, 430–2.

4785. Nevitt, Marcus. An early allusion to *As You Like It*? *See* **5660**.

4786. Schleck, Julia. 'Plain broad narratives of substantial facts': credibility, narrative, and Hakluyt's *Principall Navigations*. *See* **4864**.

4787. Schneider, Gary. The culture of epistolarity: vernacular letters and letter writing in early modern England, 1500–1700. (Bibl. 2005, 5348.) Rev. by Fritz J. Levy in RQ (59:3) 2006, 958–60.

4788. Sell, Jonathan P. A. Rhetoric and wonder in English travel writing, 1560–1613. Aldershot; Burlington, VT: Ashgate, 2006. pp. viii, 215.

4789. Thompson, Torri L. (ed.). Marriage and its dissolution in early modern England: vol. 1. *See* **4876**.

4790. —— Marriage and its dissolution in early modern England: vol. 3. *See* **5140**.

4791. White, Micheline. Power couples and women writers in Elizabethan England: the public voices of Dorcas and Richard Martin and Anne and Hugh Dowriche. *In* (pp. 119–38) **3893**.

BIOGRAPHY AND AUTOBIOGRAPHY

4792. Bedford, Ronald; Davis, Lloyd; Kelly, Philippa (eds). Early modern autobiography: theories, genres, practices. Ann Arbor: Michigan UP, 2006. pp. x, 309.

4793. Botonaki, Effie. Early modern women's diaries and closets: 'chambers of choice mercies and beloved retirement'. *In* (pp. 43–64) **7490**.

4794. Condren, Conal. Specifying the subject in early modern autobiography. *In* (pp. 35–48) **4792**.

4795. Davis, Lloyd. Critical debates and early modern autobiography. *In* (pp. 19–34) **4792**.

4796. Kelly, Philippa. Seeking early modern selves. AUMLA (106) 2006, 1–10.

4797. Prest, Wilfrid. Legal autobiography in early modern England. *In* (pp. 280–94) **4792**.

RELATED STUDIES

4798. Bartels, Emily C. Too many blackamoors: deportation, discrimination, and Elizabeth I. SELit (46:2) 2006, 305–22.

4799. Birkholz, Daniel. Mapping medieval utopia: exercises in restraint. *See* **4097**.

4800. Fissell, Mary E. Vernacular bodies: the politics of reproduction in early modern England. Oxford; New York: OUP, 2004. pp. viii, 283. Rev. by Vern L. Bullough in RQ (59:1) 2006, 283–5.

4801. Habib, Imtiaz. Indians in Shakespeare's England as 'the first-fruits of India': colonial effacement and postcolonial reinscription. JNT (36:1) 2006, 1–19.

4802. Kassell, Lauren. Medicine and magic in Elizabethan England: Simon Forman – astrologer, alchemist, and physician. Oxford: Clarendon Press; New York: OUP, 2005. pp. xviii, 281. (Oxford historical monographs.) Rev. by Nicholas H. Clulee in RQ (59:2) 2006, 606–8.

4803. Sánchez Escribano, Francisco Javier. Portuguese in England in the sixteenth and seventeenth centuries. SEDERI (16) 2006, 109–32.

4804. Stallybrass, Peter. Marginal England: the view from Aleppo. *In* (pp. 27–39) **5401**.

AUTHORS

Thomas Abell (d.1540)

4805. Thompson, Torri L. (ed.). Marriage and its dissolution in early modern England: vol. 1. *See* **4876**.

Roger Ascham

4806. Lezra, Jacques. Nationum origo. *In* (pp. 203–28) **3191**.

4807. Sivefors, Per. Ascham and Udall: the unknown language reformer in *Toxophilus*. NQ (53:1) 2006, 34–5.

William Baldwin

4808. Bratcher, James T. The Grimalkin story in Baldwin's *Beware the Cat*. NQ (53:4) 2006, 428–30.

John Bale

4809. Hadfield, Andrew. Historical writing, 1550–1660. *In* (pp. 250–63) **724**.

4810. Schwyzer, Philip. Literature, nationalism, and memory in early modern England and Wales. (Bibl. 2005, 5383.) Rev. by Mary Floyd-Wilson in SStud (34) 2006, 247–51; by Christopher Ivic in ETh (9:1) 2006, 160–4; by Thomas P. Anderson in SCN (64:1/2) 2006, 31–4; by Tom MacFaul in NQ (53:2) 2006, 225–6; by Jean-Pierre Moreau in EA (59:2) 2006, 220–4.

4811. Sharpe, Richard. Thomas Tanner (1674–1735), the 1697 catalogue, and *Bibliotheca Britannica*. *See* **12**.

4812. Shrank, Cathy. A work by John Bale identified? *See* **4766**.

Thomas Bastard (1565 or 6–1618)

4813. Eckhardt, Joshua. 'Love-song weeds, and Satyrique thornes': anti-courtly love poetry and Somerset libels. *See* **4834**.

Thomas Becon

4814. Baseotto, Paola. Godly sorrow, damnable Despair and *Faerie Queene* I.ix. *See* **5074**.

John Bourchier, Second Baron Berners (1467–1533)

4815. Gil Sáenz, Daniel. Reading Diego de San Pedro in Tudor England. RAEI (17) 2004, 103–15.

Andrew Boorde (1490?–1549)

4816. Hentschell, Roze. A question of nation: foreign clothes on the English subject. *In* (pp. 49–62) **4629**.

Nicholas Breton

4817. Forker, Charles R. John Webster's handbook of model letters: a study in attribution. *See* **7174**.

Lodowick Bryskett

4818. Armstrong, E. A Ciceronian sunburn: a Tudor dialogue on Humanistic rhetoric and civic poetics. Columbia; London: South Carolina UP, 2006. pp. 223. (Studies in rhetoric/communication.) Rev. by Scott Crider in BJJ (13) 2006, 222–6.

George Buchanan (1506–1582)

4819. Crawford, Robert (introd. and trans.). Apollos of the North: selected poems of George Buchanan and Arthur Johnston. Foreword by Edwin Morgan. Edinburgh: Polygon, 2006. pp. liii, 154. Rev. by Sally Mapstone in TLS, 15 Sept. 2006, 27.

4820. Mason, Roger A.; Smith, Martin S. (eds). *A Dialogue on the Law of Kingship among the Scots*: a critical edition and translation of George Buchanan's *De jure regni apud Scotus dialogus*. Aldershot; Burlington, VT: Ashgate, 2004.

pp. lxxv, 228. (St Andrews studies in Reformation history.) Rev. by Maureen M. Meikle in SixCJ (36:3) 2005, 838–40; by Janet Hadley Williams in Parergon (23:1) 2006, 181–3.

4821. SAUER, ELIZABETH. Closet drama and the case of *Tyrannicall-Government Anatomized*. *In* (pp. 80–95) **4731**.

William Byrd (1542 or 3–1623)

4822. KILROY, GERARD. Scribal coincidences: Campion, Byrd, Harington and the Sidney circle. SidJ (22:1/2) 2004, 73–88.

William Camden

4823. VINE, ANGUS. Etymology, names and the search for origins: deriving the past in early modern England. SevC (21:1) 2006, 1–21.

Edmund Campion

4824. KILROY, GERARD. Edmund Campion: memory and transcription. (Bibl. 2005, 5401.) Rev. by John Bossy in TLS, 18 & 25 Aug. 2006, 27.

4825. WILSON, CHRISTOPHER R. Number and music in Campion's measured verse. JDJ (25) 2006, 267–89.

Richard Carew

4826. CHYNOWETH, JOHN (ed.). The survey of Cornwall. Exeter: Devon and Cornwall Record Soc., 2004. 1 vol. (various pagings). (Devon and Cornwall Record Soc., ns 14.) Rev. by J. P. D. Cooper in SixCJ (37:2) 2006, 500–1.

George Cavendish

4827. BRITNELL, RICHARD. Service, loyalty, and betrayal in Cavendish's *The Life and Death of Cardinal Wolsey*. Moreana (42:161) 2005, 3–30.

Henry Chettle

4828. DUNCAN-JONES, KATHERINE. Who was Marlowe's 'brocher of Atheisme'? *See* **4852**.

4829. HYLAND, PETER. Face/off: some speculations on Elizabethan acting. *See* **4968**.

4830. PESTA, DUKE. Articulating skeletons: *Hamlet*, *Hoffman*, and the anatomical graveyard. *See* **5752**.

Miles Coverdale (1488–1568)

4831. OTTENHOFF, JOHN. Translating holiness, the holiness of translation. *In* (pp. 21–39) **3415**.

Robert Crowley

4832. OTTENHOFF, JOHN. Translating holiness, the holiness of translation. *In* (pp. 21–39) **3415**.

Sir Robert Dallington (1561–1637)

4833. SEMLER, L. E. Robert Dallington's *Hypnerotomachia* and the Protestant antiquity of Elizabethan England. SP (103:2) 2006, 208–41.

Sir John Davies (1569–1626)

4834. ECKHARDT, JOSHUA. 'Love-song weeds, and Satyrique thornes': anti-courtly love poetry and Somerset libels. HLQ (69:1) 2006, 47–66.

John Davies of Hereford (1565–1618)

4835. Duncan-Jones, Katherine. A companion for a king? Shakespeare's status anxiety. *See* **6086**.

Thomas Deloney

4836. Carpenter, John. Placing Thomas Deloney. JNT (36:2) 2006, 125–62.

Anne Dowriche (*fl.*1589)

4837. White, Micheline. Power couples and women writers in Elizabethan England: the public voices of Dorcas and Richard Martin and Anne and Hugh Dowriche. *In* (pp. 119–38) **3893**.

4838. —— Women writers and literary–religious circles in the Elizabethan West Country: Anne Dowriche, Anne Lock Prowse, Anne Locke Moyle, Ursula Fulford, and Elizabeth Rous. MP (103:2) 2005, 187–214.

Richard Edwards (1523?–1566)

4839. Stretter, Robert. Cicero on stage: *Damon and Pithias* and the fate of Classical friendship in English Renaissance drama. TSLL (47:4) 2005, 345–65.

Thomas Edwards (*fl.*1595)

4840. Stritmatter, Roger. 'Tilting under Frieries': *Narcissus* (1595) and the affair at Blackfriars. CEl (70) 2006, 39–42.

Elizabeth I, Queen of England (1533–1603)

4841. Leahy, William. Elizabethan triumphal processions. Aldershot; Burlington, VT: Ashgate, 2005. pp. 171. Rev. by Jean Wilson in TLS, 15 July 2005, 29; by Ben Lowe in LitH (15:2) 2006, 67–8; by Elizabeth Zeman in RQ (59:1) 2006, 259–61.

Sir Thomas Elyot

4842. Wallace, Andrew. Virgil and Bacon in the schoolroom. *See* **6560**.

Robert Devereux, Second Earl of Essex

4843. Bowers, Rick. Sir John Harington and the Earl of Essex: the joker as spy. *See* **4866**.

Saint John Fisher (1469–1535)

4844. Staley, Lynn. The Penitential Psalms and vernacular theology. *See* **4236**.

John Foxe (1516–1587)

4845. Escobedo, Andrew. Nationalism and historical loss in Renaissance England: Foxe, Dee, Spenser, Milton. (Bibl. 2005, 5432.) Rev. by Kendrick Prewitt in SixCJ (36:4) 2005, 1153–4.

4846. Greenberg, Devorah. Community of the texts: producing the first and second editions of *Acts and Monuments*. SixCJ (36:3) 2005, 695–715.

4847. Loades, David (ed.). John Foxe at home and abroad. (Bibl. 2005, 5439.) Rev. by Ronald H. Fritze in SixCJ (36:4) 2005, 1108–9.

4848. Netzley, Ryan. The end of reading: the practice and possibility of reading Foxe's *Actes and Monuments*. ELH (73:1) 2006, 187–214.

Arthur Golding

4849. Mann, Jenny C. How to look at a hermaphrodite in early modern England. *See* **7126**.

Robert Greene

4850. Das, Nandini. A new source for Robert Greene's *Planetomachia*. NQ (53:4) 2006, 436–40.

4851. Dimmick, Jeremy. Gower, Chaucer and the art of repentance in Robert Greene's *Vision*. RES (57:231) 2006, 456–73.

4852. Duncan-Jones, Katherine. Who was Marlowe's 'brocher of Atheisme'? NQ (53:4) 2006, 449–52.

4853. Figueredo, Maria Cristina. The shape that matters. *See* **14676**.

4854. Hadfield, Andrew. The Ur-*Hamlet* and the fable of the kid. *See* **5087**.

4855. Hentschell, Roze. A question of nation: foreign clothes on the English subject. *In* (pp. 49–62) **4629**.

4856. Ide, Arata. Robert Greene *Nordovicensis*, the saddler's son. NQ (53:4) 2006, 432–6.

4857. Kumaran, Arul. Robert Greene's Martinist transformation in 1590. SP (103:3) 2006, 243–63.

4858. Melnikoff, Kirk. The 'extremities' of sumptuary law in Robert Greene's *Friar Bacon and Friar Bungay*. MedRen (19) 2006, 227–34.

4859. Mentz, Steve. Romance for sale in early modern England: the rise of prose fiction. Aldershot; Burlington, VT: Ashgate, 2006. pp. x, 261. Rev. by Paul Salzman in RES (57:232) 2006, 805–7.

4860. Reynolds, Bryan; Turner, Henry. Performative transversions: collaborations through and beyond Greene's *Friar Bacon and Friar Bungay*. *In* (pp. 240–50) **4718**.

4861. Spates, William Henry. Proverbs, pox, and the early modern *femme fatale*. *See* **5875**.

4862. Wilson, Katharine. Fictions of authorship in late Elizabethan narratives: Euphues in Arcadia. *See* **4750**.

4863. Wooster, Gerald; Boakes, Janet. Twin dynamics in *The Winter's Tale*. *See* **6210**.

Richard Hakluyt

4864. Schleck, Julia. 'Plain broad narratives of substantial facts': credibility, narrative, and Hakluyt's *Principall Navigations*. RQ (59:3) 2006, 768–94.

Edward Hall

4865. Strohm, Paul. York's paper crown: 'bare life' and Shakespeare's first tragedy. *See* **5841**.

Sir John Harington (1561–1612)

4866. Bowers, Rick. Sir John Harington and the Earl of Essex: the joker as spy. CEl (69) 2006, 13–20.

4867. Kilroy, Gerard. Scribal coincidences: Campion, Byrd, Harington and the Sidney circle. *See* **4822**.

4868. Knapp, James A. The bastard art: woodcut illustration in sixteenth-century England. *In* (pp. 151–72) **661**.

Thomas Harman (*fl.*1567)

4869. Dionne, Craig; Mentz, Steve (eds). Rogues and early modern culture. (Bibl. 2004, 5713.) Rev. by Kevin D. Lindberg in SixCJ (36:4) 2005, 1226–7.

Gabriel Harvey

4870. Prendergast, Maria Teresa Micaela. Promiscuous textualities: the Nashe–Harvey controversy and the unnatural productions of print. *In* (pp. 173–95) **661**.

4871. Schleiner, W. Early modern recovery: Harvey's gendered response to an earthquake in Essex, England, on 7 April 1580. CEl (70) 2006, 15–19.

4872. Steggle, Matthew. Gabriel Harvey, the Sidney circle, and the excellent gentlewoman. SidJ (22:1/2) 2004, 115–29.

4873. Wolfe, Jessica. Humanism, machinery, and Renaissance literature. (Bibl. 2004, 5719.) Rev. by Elizabeth McCutcheon in SixCJ (37:1) 2006, 157–8; by Tom MacFaul in NQ (53:1) 2006, 118–19.

William Haughton

4874. Levin, Richard. A source of Haughton's *Englishmen for My Money.* NQ (53:1) 2006, 57–9.

4875. Stewart, Alan. 'Every soyle to mee is naturall': figuring denization in William Haughton's *English-men for My Money.* RenD (ns 35) 2006, 55–81.

Henry VIII, King of England

4876. Thompson, Torri L. (ed.). Marriage and its dissolution in early modern England: vol. 1. London; Brookfield, VT: Pickering & Chatto, 2005. pp. xxxix, 254. (Facsimiles.) Rev. by Eric Josef Carlson in SixCJ (37:2) 2006, 589–90.

Jasper Heywood

4877. Stapleton, M. L. 'I of old contemptes complayne': Margaret of Anjou and English Seneca. *See* **5840**.

4878. Winston, Jessica. Seneca in early Elizabethan England. RQ (59:1) 2006, 29–58.

Sir Edward Hoby (1560–1617)

4879. Lezra, Jacques. Nationum origo. *In* (pp. 203–28) **3191**.

Sir Thomas Hoby (1530–1566)

4880. Venuti, Lawrence. Local contingencies: translation and national identities. *In* (pp. 177–202) **3191**.

Raphael Holinshed

4881. Djordjevic, Igor. W.P.: the case for William Patten's contribution to Holinshed's *Chronicles* (1587). NQ (53:1) 2006, 40–3.

4882. Forest-Hill, Lynn. Giants and enemies of God: the relationship between Caliban and Prospero from the perspective of Insular literary tradition. *See* **6122**.

4883. Knapp, James A. The bastard art: woodcut illustration in sixteenth-century England. *In* (pp. 151–72) **661**.

4884. Strohm, Paul. York's paper crown: 'bare life' and Shakespeare's first tragedy. *See* **5841**.

Claudius Hollyband (*fl.*1575)

4885. Gil Sáenz, Daniel. Reading Diego de San Pedro in Tudor England. *See* **4815**.

Thomas Hughes (*fl.*1587)

4886. King, Andrew. Dead butchers and fiend-like queens: literary and political history in *The Misfortunes of Arthur* and *Macbeth*. *In* (pp. 121–34) **3972**.

Richard Hyrde

4887. Riddy, Felicity. Fathers and daughters in Holbein's sketch of Thomas More's family. *In* (pp. 19–38) **3893**.

Will Kemp

4888. Howard, Jean E. Stage masculinities, national history, and the making of London theatrical culture. *In* (pp. 199–214) **5401**.

John Knox

4889. Farrow, Kenneth D. John Knox: Reformation rhetoric and the traditions of Scots prose, 1490–1570. (Bibl. 2004, 5736.) Rev. by Daniel Fischlin in RQ (59:3) 2006, 944–6.

Thomas Kyd

4890. Ardolino, Frank. The induction of Sly: the influence of *The Spanish Tragedy* on the two *Shrews*. *See* **6104**.

4891. Colón Semenza, Gregory M. *The Spanish Tragedy* and revenge. *In* (pp. 50–60) **4734**.

4892. Goodland, Katharine. Female mourning and tragedy in medieval and Renaissance English drama: from the raising of Lazarus to *King Lear*. *See* **3907**.

4893. Hadfield, Andrew. The Ur-*Hamlet* and the fable of the kid. *See* **5087**.

4894. Owens, Rebekah. Thomas Kyd and the letters to Puckering. NQ (53:4) 2006, 458–61.

Maurice Kyffin (d.1599)

4895. Henry, Anne. *Quid ais omnium?* Maurice Kyffin's 1588 *Andria* and the emergence of suspension marks in printed drama. RenD (ns 34) 2005, 47–67.

William Lambarde (1536–1601)

4896. Bartram, Claire. Social fabric in Thynne's *Debate between Pride and Lowliness*. *In* (pp. 137–49) **4629**.

Robert Langham (Laneham) (*c.*1535–1579/80)

4897. McCarthy, Penny. Pseudonymous Shakespeare: rioting language in the Sidney circle. *See* **5364**.

Hugh Latimer (1485?–1555)

4898. Thompson, Torri L. (ed.). Marriage and its dissolution in early modern England: vol. 3. *See* **5140**.

John Leland

4899. Sharpe, Richard. Thomas Tanner (1674–1735), the 1697 catalogue, and *Bibliotheca Britannica*. *See* **12**.

4900. Taylor, Andrew W. Between Surrey and Marot: Nicolas Bourbon and the artful translation of the epigram. *See* **5135**.

Anne Vaughan Locke
('A.L.', Anne Prowse, Anne Vaughan Dering) (*c*.1534–1590)

4901. White, Micheline. Women writers and literary–religious circles in the Elizabethan West Country: Anne Dowriche, Anne Lock Prowse, Anne Locke Moyle, Ursula Fulford, and Elizabeth Rous. *See* **4838**.

Thomas Lodge

4902. Holmes, John. Thomas Lodge's *Amours*: the copy-text for imitations of Ronsard in *Phillis*. NQ (53:1) 2006, 55–7.

4903. Mentz, Steve. Romance for sale in early modern England: the rise of prose fiction. *See* **4859**.

John Lyly

4904. Golz, David. The four books of *Doctor Faustus*. *See* **4921**.

4905. Scragg, Leah. Speaking pictures: style and spectacle in Lylian comedy. EngS (86:4) 2005, 298–311.

4906. —— The victim of fashion? Rereading the biography of John Lyly. MedRen (19) 2006, 210–26.

4907. Wilson, Katharine. Fictions of authorship in late Elizabethan narratives: Euphues in Arcadia. *See* **4750**.

Christopher Marlowe

4908. Anderson, Thomas Page. Performing early modern trauma from Shakespeare to Milton. *See* **6151**.

4909. Bevington, David. One hell of an ending: staging Last Judgment in the Towneley Plays and in *Doctor Faustus* A and B. *In* (pp. 292–310) **3913**.

4910. Cheney, Patrick. Biographical representations: Marlowe's life of the author. *In* (pp. 183–204) **5353**.

4911. —— 'Deep-brained sonnets' and 'tragic shows': Shakespeare's late Ovidian art in *A Lover's Complaint*. *In* (pp. 55–77) **5913**.

4912. —— (ed.). The Cambridge companion to Christopher Marlowe. (Bibl. 2005, 5519.) Rev. by Clifford Davidson in CompDr (39:2) 2005, 247–50; by Tobias Döring in SJ (142) 2006, 233–6; by John Lee in MLR (101:4) 2006, 1097–8; by Robert Sawyer in MSAN (26:1) 2006, 7–9; by Adrian Streete in NQ (53:3) 2006, 369–70.

4913. —— Striar, Brian J. (eds). The collected poems of Christopher Marlowe. Oxford; New York: OUP, 2006. pp. xviii, 302. Rev. by Adam Smyth in TLS, 18 & 25 Aug. 2006, 26–7.

4914. Cless, Downing. Ecologically conjuring *Doctor Faustus*. JDTC (20:2) 2006, 145–67.

4915. Cook, Amy; Reynolds, Bryan. Comedic law: protective transversality, deceit conceits, and the conjuring of *Macbeth* and *Doctor Faustus* in Jonson's *The Devil Is an Ass*. *In* (pp. 85–111) **4718**.

4916. Dimmock, Matthew. New Turkes: dramatizing Islam and the Ottomans in early modern England. *See* **4666**.

4917. Dobson, Michael. Moving the audience: Shakespeare, the mob, and the promenade. *See* **5927**.

4918. Duncan-Jones, Katherine. Who was Marlowe's 'brocher of Atheisme'? *See* **4852**.

4919. Gallagher, Lowell. Faustus's blood and the (messianic) question of ethics. ELH (73:1) 2006, 1–29.

4920. Gillies, John. *Tamburlaine* and Renaissance geography. *In* (pp. 35–49) **4734**.

4921. Golz, David. The four books of *Doctor Faustus*. NQ (53:4) 2006, 444–9.

4922. Hiscock, Andrew. The uses of this world: thinking space in Shakespeare, Marlowe, Cary, and Jonson. *See* **5727**.

4923. Honan, Park. Christopher Marlowe: poet & spy. (Bibl. 2005, 5530.) Rev. by Michael Feingold in NYTB, 29 Jan. 2006, 20; by J. P. D. Cooper in TLS, 2 June 2006, 27; by Maurice Charney in SNL (56:1) 2006, 23; by John Bossy in LRB (28:24) 2006, 14; by Lisa Hopkins in MSAN (26:1) 2006, 10–12.

4924. Hopkins, Lisa. A Christopher Marlowe chronology. (Bibl. 2005, 5532.) Rev. by Adam Smyth in TLS, 18 & 25 Aug. 2006, 26–7; by Constance Brown Kuriyama in MSAN (26:2) 2006, 5–6.

4925. —— 'In a little room': Marlowe and *The Allegory of the Tudor Succession*. NQ (53:4) 2006, 442–4. (Attribution of verses accompanying a painting.)

4926. —— Was Marlowe going to Scotland when he died, and does it matter? *In* (pp. 167–82) **5353**.

4927. Ide, Arata. *The Jew of Malta* and the diabolic power of theatrics in the 1580s. SELit (46:2) 2006, 257–79.

4928. Keefer, Michael H. The A and B texts of Marlowe's *Doctor Faustus* revisited. PBSA (100:2) 2006, 227–57.

4929. Keenan, Siobhan. Reading Christopher Marlowe's *Edward II*: the example of John Newdigate in 1601. NQ (53:4) 2006, 452–8.

4930. Kozuka, Takashi; Mulryne, J. R. (eds). Shakespeare, Marlowe, Jonson: new directions in biography. *See* **5353**.

4931. McJannet, Linda. The sultan speaks: dialogue in English plays and histories about the Ottoman Turks. Basingstoke; New York: Palgrave Macmillan, 2006. pp. xi, 243.

4932. Martínez López, Miguel. The philosophy of death in Christopher Marlowe's *Dr Faustus*. *In* (pp. 219–33) **5308**.

4933. Moul, Victoria. Ben Jonson's *Poetaster*: Classical translation and the location of cultural authority. *See* **6894**.

4934. Nicholl, Charles. 'By my onely meanes sett downe': the texts of Marlowe's atheism. *In* (pp. 153–66) **5353**.

4935. Paul, Gavin. Theatrical and national spaces in *Cymbeline*. *See* **5687**.

4936. Pettitt, Thomas. Marlowe's texts and oral transmission: towards the *Zielform*. CompDr (39:2) 2005, 213–42.

4937. Poole, Kristen. The Devil's in the archive: *Doctor Faustus* and Ovidian physics. RenD (ns 35) 2006, 191–219.

4938. —— *Dr Faustus* and Reformation theology. *In* (pp. 96–107) **4734**.

4939. Ray, Sid. Marlow(e)'s Africa: postcolonial queenship in Conrad's *Heart of Darkness* and Marlowe's *Dido, Queen of Carthage*. *See* **15302**.

4940. Reynolds, Bryan; Thompson, Ayanna. Viewing antitheatricality; or, *Tamburlaine*'s post theater. *In* (pp. 168–82) **4718**.

4941. Riggs, David. The poet in the play: life and art in *Tamburlaine* and *The Jew of Malta*. *In* (pp. 205–24) **5353**.

4942. —— The world of Christopher Marlowe. (Bibl. 2004, 5790.) Rev. by Tobias Döring in SJ (142) 2006, 233–6; by Eusebio de Lorenzo in EIUC (14) 2006, 167–87.

4943. Rutkoski, Marie. Breeching the boy in Marlowe's *Edward II*. SELit (46:2) 2006, 281–304.

4944. Stewart, Alan. *Edward II* and male same-sex desire. *In* (pp. 82–95) **4734**.

4945. Sullivan, Garrett A., Jr. Memory and forgetting in English Renaissance drama: Shakespeare, Marlowe, Webster. *See* **5437**.

4946. Vitkus, Daniel. Turks and Jews in *The Jew of Malta*. *In* (pp. 61–72) **4734**.

4947. Wall, Wendy. Dramatic authorship and print. *In* (pp. 1–11) **4734**.

4948. Williams, Deanne. Dido, queen of England. ELH (73:1) 2006, 31–59.

4949. Yan, Xuejun. The ethical dimension of Marlowe's plays of 'desires'. FLS (117) 2006, 61–6. (In Chinese.)

Dorcas (Eccleston) Martin (1537–1599)

4950. White, Micheline. Power couples and women writers in Elizabethan England: the public voices of Dorcas and Richard Martin and Anne and Hugh Dowriche. *In* (pp. 119–38) **3893**.

Christopher Middleton (1560?–1628)

4951. Cooper, Helen. Lancelot's wives. Arthuriana (16:2) 2006, 59–62.

4952. McManus, Clare. *The Roaring Girl* and the London underworld. *In* (pp. 213–24) **4734**.

Sir Thomas More

4953. Beckett, Wendy (introd.). The history of King Richard III. London: Hesperus Press, 2005. pp. xi, 102. (Hesperus classics.) Rev. by Bart van Es in TLS, 10 June 2005, 12.

4954. Boswell, Jackson C. References and allusions to Thomas More: 1641–1700 (part iv). Moreana (42:161) 2005, 31–68.

4955. Curtright, Travis. A 'pre-Machiavellian moment': Thomas More's poetry and *The History of Richard III*. BJJ (13) 2006, 63–82.

4956. Ingham, Patricia Clare. Making all things new: past, progress, and the promise of utopia. JMEMS (36:3) 2006, 479–92.

4957. Lochrie, Karma. Sheer wonder: dreaming utopia in the Middle Ages. JMEMS (36:3) 2006, 493–516.

4958. Majeske, Andrew J. Equity in English Renaissance literature: Thomas More and Edmund Spenser. London; New York: Routledge, 2006. pp. 217. (Literary criticism and cultural theory.)

4959. Marc'hadour, Germain (ed.); Crépin, André (trans.). Poèmes anglais. Angers: Moreanum, 2004. pp. 155. Rev. by Dominique Le Tourneau in Moreana (41:160) 2004, 113–15.

4960. Riddy, Felicity. Fathers and daughters in Holbein's sketch of Thomas More's family. *In* (pp. 19–38) **3893**.

4961. Taillé, Michel (ed.). Histoire, Église et spiritualité: textes et correspondance. Paris: Bayard, 2005. pp. 270. (Essais Bayard.) Rev. by Jean-Pierre Moreau in EA (59:4) 2006, 472–4.

4962. Wegemer, Gerard B.; Smith, Stephen W. (eds). A Thomas More source book. (Bibl. 2004, 5830.) Rev. by Andrew A. Chibi in SixCJ (36:4) 2005, 1145–6; by Alistair Fox in CathHR (92:2) 2006, 279–80.

Henry Parker, Baron Morley (1476–1556)

4963. Attreed, Lorraine; Winkler, Alexandra. Faith and forgiveness: lessons in statecraft for Queen Mary Tudor. SixCJ (36:4) 2005, 971–89.

4964. Taylor, Andrew W. Glass houses: Surrey, Petrarch, and the religious poetics of the 'London' invective. *See* **5136**.

Anne Locke Moyle (1561–1604)

4965. White, Micheline. Women writers and literary–religious circles in the Elizabethan West Country: Anne Dowriche, Anne Lock Prowse, Anne Locke Moyle, Ursula Fulford, and Elizabeth Rous. *See* **4838**.

Anthony Munday

4966. Hamilton, Donna B. Anthony Munday and the Catholics, 1560–1633. (Bibl. 2005, 5579.) Rev. by Arthur F. Marotti in CathHR (92:3) 2006, 323–4; by Thomas Merriam in NQ (53:3) 2006, 374–5; by David M. Bergeron in RQ (59:2) 2006, 633–4.

4967. Hill, Tracey. Anthony Munday and civic culture: theatre, history, and power in early modern London, 1580–1633. (Bibl. 2004, 5834.) Rev. by Greg McNamara in SixCJ (37:2) 2006, 547–9; by David M. Bergeron in RQ (59:1) 2006, 304–5.

4968. Hyland, Peter. Face/off: some speculations on Elizabethan acting. ShB (24:2) 2006, 21–9.

4969. Knight, Stephen. Remembering Robin Hood: five centuries of outlaw ideology. *See* **3052**.

4970. Merriam, Thomas. Munday and the Oxford Shakespeare *More*. *See* **6079**.

4971. —— Orthographic changes in *John a Kent* and Hand M of *More*. NQ (53:4) 2006, 475–8.

4972. Moore, Helen (ed.). Amadis de Gaule. (Bibl. 2004, 5836.) Rev. by Andrew Pettegree in SixCJ (37:1) 2006, 124–5.

4973. Palmer, Daryl W. Metropolitan resurrection in Anthony Munday's Lord Mayor's shows. SELit (46:2) 2006, 371–87.

4974. Phillips, Joshua. Chronicles of wasted time: Anthony Munday, Tudor romance, and literary labor. ELH (73:4) 2006, 781–803.

4975. Wentersdorf, Karl P. On 'momtanish inhumanyty' in *Sir Thomas More*. *See* **6083**.

Thomas Nashe

4976. Couton, Marie. Thomas Nashe lecteur savant, écrivain populaire: le hareng magnifique de *Lenten Stuffe*. RANAM (39) 2006, 41–56.

4977. Duncan-Jones, Katherine. Drayton on Nashe and Shakespeare. *See* **6761**.

4978. Fleck, Andrew. Imprisoned in the flesh: the return of Petrarch in Nashe's *The Unfortunate Traveler*. ELN (43:2) 2005, 22–9.

4979. Hadfield, Andrew. The Ur-*Hamlet* and the fable of the kid. *See* **5087**.

4980. Hillman, Richard. Returning to one's vomit: an intertextual tour of *Eastward Ho*'s Isle of Dogs. *See* **6640**.

4981. Mentz, Steve. Romance for sale in early modern England: the rise of prose fiction. *See* **4859**.

4982. Mohler, Tina. 'What is thy body but a swallowing grave …?': desire underground in *Titus Andronicus*. *See* **6156**.

4983. Ossa-Richardson, Anthony. Ovid and the 'free play with signs' in Thomas Nashe's *The Unfortunate Traveller*. MLR (101:4) 2006, 945–56.

4984. Prendergast, Maria Teresa Micaela. Promiscuous textualities: the Nashe–Harvey controversy and the unnatural productions of print. *In* (pp. 173–95) **661**.

4985. Steggle, Matthew. The *Manipulus florum* in *The Anatomie of Absurditie*. NQ (53:1) 2006, 43–6.

4986. Tobin, J. J. M. Shakespeare, Nashe, and *Sir Thomas More*. *See* **6082**.

4987. Wallace, Andrew. Reading the 1590 *Faerie Queene* with Thomas Nashe. *See* **5125**.

4988. Williams, Deanne. Dido, queen of England. *See* **4948**.

4989. Zurcher, Andrew. Getting it back to front in 1590: Spenser's dedications, Nashe's insinuations, and Ralegh's equivocations. *See* **5131**.

Alexander Neville (1544–1614)

4990. Winston, Jessica. Seneca in early Elizabethan England. *See* **4878**.

Sir Thomas North

4991. Goy-Blanquet, Dominique. La solitude de Coriolan. *See* **5676**.

Edward de Vere, Earl of Oxford

4992. Farina, William. De Vere as Shakespeare: an Oxfordian reading of the canon. Foreword by Felicia Hardison Londré. *See* **5297**.

4993. Pearson, Daphne. Edward de Vere (1550–1604): the crisis and consequences of wardship. Aldershot; Burlington, VT: Ashgate, 2005. pp. 263. Rev. by Eric N. Lindquist in RQ (59:2) 2006, 612–13.

4994. Stritmatter, Roger. 'Tilting under Frieries': *Narcissus* (1595) and the affair at Blackfriars. *See* **4840**.

4995. Whittemore, Hank. The monument. Marshfield Hills, MA: Meadow Geese Press, 2005. pp. lxxv, 843. (Attribution of Shakespeare's sonnets.)

William Painter

4996. Kingsley-Smith, Jane. Sidney, Cinthio, and Painter: a new source for the *Arcadia*. *See* **5039**.

Robert Parry

4997. Evans, G. Blakemore (ed.). The poems of Robert Parry. Tempe: Arizona Center for Medieval and Renaissance Studies for the Renaissance English Text Soc., 2005. pp. x, 380. (Medieval & Renaissance texts & studies, 303.) (Renaissance English Text Soc., 7:30.)

William Patten (1521?–1584)

4998. Djordjevic, Igor. W.P.: the case for William Patten's contribution to Holinshed's *Chronicles* (1587). *See* **4881**.

Thomas Paynell (*fl.*1528–1567)

4999. Thompson, Torri L. (ed.). Marriage and its dissolution in early modern England: vol. 2. London; Brookfield, VT: Pickering & Chatto, 2005. pp. 441. (Facsimile.) Rev. by Eric Josef Carlson in SixCJ (37:2) 2006, 589–90.

George Peele

5000. Dimmock, Matthew. New Turkes: dramatizing Islam and the Ottomans in early modern England. *See* **4666**.

5001. Edelman, Charles (ed.). The Stukeley plays: *The Battle of Alcazar* by George Peele; *The Famous History of the Life and Death of Captain Thomas Stukeley*. Manchester; New York: Manchester UP, 2005. pp. xii, 243. Rev. by William Proctor Williams in NQ (53:4) 2006, 567–8; by Brett D. Hirsch in Parergon (23:1) 2006, 160–3.

5002. Gazzard, Hugh. 'Many a *Herdsman* more disposde to morne': Peele, Campion, and the Portugal expedition of 1589. RES (57:228) 2006, 16–42.

5003. Griffin, Benjamin. Moving tales: narrative drift in oral culture and scripted theater. NLH (37:4) 2006, 725–38.

5004. Odom, Glenn; Reynolds, Bryan. Becomings Roman / comings-to-be villain: pressurized belongings and the coding of ethnicity, religion, and nationality in Peele and Shakespeare's *Titus Andronicus*. *In* (pp. 183–226) **4718**.

Mary Herbert, Countess of Pembroke

5005. Alexander, Gavin. The musical Sidneys. *See* **5029**.

5006. Brennan, Michael. The Sidneys of Penshurst and the monarchy, 1500–1700. *See* **5031**.

5007. Brennan, Michael G. The Sidneys of Penshurst, the earldom of Leicester and the monarchies of England, Spain and France. *See* **5032**.

5008. Demers, Patricia. 'Warpe' and 'webb' in the Sidney Psalms: the 'coupled' work of the Countess of Pembroke and Sir Philip Sidney. *In* (pp. 41–58) **3405**.

5009. Hamlin, Hannibal. 'The highest matter in the noblest forme': the influence of the Sidney Psalms. SidJ (23:1/2) 2005, 133–57.

5010. Hannay, Margaret P. Re-revealing the Psalms: the Countess of Pembroke and her early modern readers. SidJ (23:1/2) 2005, 18–35.

5011. —— Kinnamon, Noel J.; Brennan, Michael G. (eds). Selected works of Mary Sidney Herbert, Countess of Pembroke. Tempe: Arizona Center for Medieval and Renaissance Studies, 2005. pp. xviii, 296. (Medieval & Renaissance texts & studies, 290.) Rev. by Richard Todd in SCN (64:1/2) 2006, 6–8; by Elizabeth Scott-Baumann in NQ (53:4) 2006, 573–4.

5012. Larson, Katherine R. From inward conversation to public praise: Mary Sidney Herbert's *Psalmes*. SidJ (24:1) 2006, 20–44.

5013. Quitslund, Beth. Teaching us how to sing? The peculiarity of the Sidney Psalter. *See* **5044**.

5014. Rienstra, Debra. The Countess of Pembroke and the problem of skill in devotional writing. SidJ (23:1/2) 2005, 37–60.

5015. Sargaser, Elizabeth Harris. Elegiac intimacy: Pembroke's *To the Angell Spirit of the Most Excellent Sir Philip Sidney*. SidJ (23:1/2) 2005, 111–31.

5016. Steggle, Matthew. Gabriel Harvey, the Sidney circle, and the excellent gentlewoman. *See* **4872**.

5017. Williams, Robin P. Sweet swan of Avon: did a woman write Shakespeare? *See* **5457**.

Robert Persons (Parsons) (1546–1610)

5018. Martin, Patrick; Finnis, John. The secret sharers: 'Anthony Rivers' and the Appellant Controversy, 1601–2. HLQ (69:2) 2006, 195–237.

'John Pickering' (Sir John Puckering) (*fl.*1567)

5019. Owens, Rebekah. Thomas Kyd and the letters to Puckering. *See* **4894**.

Sir Walter Ralegh (*c*.1552–1618)

5020. Atkin, Graham. Raleigh, Spenser, and Elizabeth: acts of friendship in *The Faerie Queene* Book iv. *In* (pp. 195–213) **5100**.

5021. Buckman, Ty. Forcing the poet into prose: 'gealous opinions and misconstructions' and Spenser's Letter to Ralegh. *See* **5078**.

5022. Herron, Thomas. Ralegh's gold: placing Spenser's Dedicatory Sonnets. *See* **5091**.

5023. Lorimer, Joyce (ed.). Sir Walter Ralegh's *Discoverie of Guiana*. Aldershot; Burlington, VT: Ashgate, 2006. pp. 380. (Works issued by the Hakluyt Soc., 3:15.)

5024. Zurcher, Andrew. Getting it back to front in 1590: Spenser's dedications, Nashe's insinuations, and Ralegh's equivocations. *See* **5131**.

Thomas Raynalde (*fl.*1540–1551)

5025. Fissell, Mary E. The politics of reproduction in the English Reformation. *See* **3850**.

Elizabeth Cooke Hoby, Lady Russell (*c*.1540–1609)

5026. Malay, Jessica L. Elizabeth Russell's textual performances of self. Comitatus (37) 2006, 146–68.

John Ryckes (*fl.*1525)

5027. Spates, William Henry. Proverbs, pox, and the early modern *femme fatale*. *See* **5875**.

Thomas Sackville, First Earl of Dorset

5028. Malay, Jessica L. Elizabeth Russell's textual performances of self. *See* **5026**.

Sir Philip Sidney

5029. Alexander, Gavin. The musical Sidneys. JDJ (25) 2006, 65–105.

5030. —— Writing after Sidney: the literary response to Sir Philip Sidney, 1586–1640. Oxford; New York: OUP, 2006. pp. xliv, 380.

5031. Brennan, Michael. The Sidneys of Penshurst and the monarchy, 1500–1700. Aldershot; Burlington, VT: Ashgate, 2006. pp. xiv, 188. Rev. by Gavin Alexander in RES (57:232) 2006, 814–17.

5032. Brennan, Michael G. The Sidneys of Penshurst, the earldom of Leicester and the monarchies of England, Spain and France. SidJ (22:1/2) 2004, 25–45.

5033. Bueno Alonso, Jorge Luis. Two Spanish renderings of Philip Sidney's 'First Song' from *Astrophil & Stella* (1591): a reappraisal and a new proposal. SEDERI (16) 2006, 135–51.

5034. Campbell, Julie D. Literary circles and gender in early modern Europe: a cross-cultural approach. *See* **4570**.

5035. Demers, Patricia. 'Warpe' and 'webb' in the Sidney Psalms: the 'coupled' work of the Countess of Pembroke and Sir Philip Sidney. *In* (pp. 41–58) **3405**.

5036. Hadfield, Andrew. *King Lear* and Sidney. *See* **5859**.

5037. Hamlin, Hannibal. 'The highest matter in the noblest forme': the influence of the Sidney Psalms. *See* **5009**.

5038. Kilroy, Gerard. Scribal coincidences: Campion, Byrd, Harington and the Sidney circle. *See* **4822**.

5039. Kingsley-Smith, Jane. Sidney, Cinthio, and Painter: a new source for the *Arcadia*. RES (57:229) 2006, 169–75.

5040. McCarthy, Penny. Pseudonymous Shakespeare: rioting language in the Sidney circle. *See* **5364**.

5041. Mentz, Steve. Romance for sale in early modern England: the rise of prose fiction. *See* **4859**.

5042. Olmsted, Wendy. The gentle doctor: Renaissance/Reformation friendship, rhetoric, and emotion in Sidney's *Old Arcadia*. MP (103:2) 2005, 156–86.

5043. Prescott, Anne Lake. Teaching Astrophil's 'coltish gyres': Sidney and the horses of desire. RenP (2005) 25–42.

5044. Quitslund, Beth. Teaching us how to sing? The peculiarity of the Sidney Psalter. SidJ (23:1/2) 2005, 83–110.

5045. Rienstra, Debra. The Countess of Pembroke and the problem of skill in devotional writing. *See* **5014**.

5046. Sanchez, Melissa E. 'The True Vowed Sacrifice of Unfeigned Love': eros and authority in *The Countess of Pembroke's Arcadia*. SidJ (22:1/2) 2004, 89–104.

5047. Skretkowicz, Victor. *'O pugnam infaustam'*: Sidney's transformations and the last of the Samotheans. SidJ (22:1/2) 2004, 1–24.

5048. Steggle, Matthew. Gabriel Harvey, the Sidney circle, and the excellent gentlewoman. *See* **4872**.

5049. Wilkes, G. A. 'Left … to play the ill poet in my own part': the literary relationship of Sidney and Fulke Greville. RES (57:230) 2006, 291–309.

Robert Sidney, Earl of Leicester

5050. Alexander, Gavin. The musical Sidneys. *See* **5029**.

5051. Brennan, Michael. The Sidneys of Penshurst and the monarchy, 1500–1700. *See* **5031**.

5052. Brennan, Michael G. The Sidneys of Penshurst, the earldom of Leicester and the monarchies of England, Spain and France. *See* **5032**.

5053. Davis, Joel. Robert Sidney's marginal commentary on Tacitus and the English campaigns in the Low Countries. SidJ (24:1) 2006, 1–19.

5054. Hannay, Margaret. 'My daughter Wroth': Lady Mary Wroth in the correspondence of Robert Sidney, Earl of Leicester. SidJ (22:1/2) 2004, 47–72.

5055. Kilroy, Gerard. Scribal coincidences: Campion, Byrd, Harington and the Sidney circle. *See* **4822**.

5056. Steggle, Matthew. Gabriel Harvey, the Sidney circle, and the excellent gentlewoman. *See* **4872**.

5057. Warkentin, Germaine; Hoare, Peter. Sophisticated Shakespeare: James Toovey and the Morgan Library's 'Sidney' First Folio. *See* **5233**.

John Skelton

5058. Baseotto, Paola. Godly sorrow, damnable Despair and *Faerie Queene* i.ix. *See* **5074**.

5059. Cooper, Helen. Skeltonics. LRB (28:24) 2006, 32–4 (review-article).

5060. Edwards, A. S. G. Deconstructing Skelton: the texts of the English poems. LSE (36) 2005, 335–53.

5061. Griffiths, Jane. John Skelton and poetic authority: defining the liberty to speak. Oxford; New York: OUP, 2006. pp. x, 213. (Oxford English monographs.) Rev. by A. S. G. Edwards in TLS, 29 Sept. 2006, 30; by Helen Cooper in LRB (28:24) 2006, 32–4.

5062. Santana, Richard W. Language and the decline of magic: epistemological shifts in English literature from medieval to Modernist. *See* **3926**.

Robert Southwell

5063. LACEY, PAUL A. The vision of the burning babe: Southwell, Levertov, and Duncan. *In* (pp. 161–79) **15599**.

5064. PATTERSON, ANNABEL. Donne's re-formed *La Corona*. *See* **6737**.

5065. SHELL, ALISON. Why didn't Shakespeare write religious verse? *In* (pp. 85–112) **5353**.

5066. SWEENEY, ANNE. Re-reading the poetry of S. Robert Southwell. PNRev (33:1) 2006, 25–8.

5067. SWEENEY, ANNE R. Robert Southwell: snow in Arcadia: redrawing the English lyric landscape, 1586–1595. Manchester; New York: Manchester UP, 2006. pp. x, 314.

Edmund Spenser

5068. ADDISON, CATHERINE. Rhyming against the grain: a new look at the Spenserian stanza. *In* (pp. 337–51) **5100**.

5069. ALPERS, PAUL. 'The Philoctetes problem' and the poetics of pastoral. *See* **5691**.

5070. ARMSTRONG, E. A Ciceronian sunburn: a Tudor dialogue on Humanistic rhetoric and civic poetics. *See* **4818**.

5071. ATKIN, GRAHAM. Raleigh, Spenser, and Elizabeth: acts of friendship in *The Faerie Queene* Book IV. *In* (pp. 195–213) **5100**.

5072. BARRETT-GRAVES, DEBRA. Edmund Spenser's use of the poison-tipped tongue in *The Faerie Queene*. CEACrit (68:1/2) 2005/06, 21–35.

5073. BASEOTTO, PAOLA. Fighting for God, queen and country: Spenser and the morality of violence. Milan: Arcipelago, 2004. pp. 158.

5074. —— Godly sorrow, damnable Despair and *Faerie Queene* I.ix. CEl (69) 2006, 1–11.

5075. BRINK, JEAN R. Precedence and patronage: the ordering of Spenser's Dedicatory Sonnets (1590). SLI (38:2) 2005, 51–72.

5076. BROWN, RICHARD DANSON. MacNeice in fairy land. *In* (pp. 352–69) **5100**.

5077. BRUCE, DONALD. Spenser's poetic pictures: a vision of beauty. ContRev (288:1680) 2006, 73–86.

5078. BUCKMAN, TY. Forcing the poet into prose: 'gealous opinions and misconstructions' and Spenser's Letter to Ralegh. SLI (38:2) 2005, 17–34.

5079. BURLINSON, CHRISTOPHER. Allegory, space and the material world in the writings of Edmund Spenser. Woodbridge, Suffolk; Rochester, NY: Brewer, 2006. pp. xvi, 256. (Studies in Renaissance literature, 17.)

5080. CHAMBERLAIN, RICHARD. Radical Spenser: pastoral, politics and the new aestheticism. Edinburgh: Edinburgh UP, 2005. pp. 161. Rev. by Bart Van Es in TLS, 9 June 2006, 10; by Richard McCabe in RES (57:230) 2006, 399–400; by Tom MacFaul in NQ (53:4) 2006, 566.

5081. CHENEY, PATRICK. 'Deep-brained sonnets' and 'tragic shows': Shakespeare's late Ovidian art in *A Lover's Complaint*. *In* (pp. 55–77) **5913**.

5082. Chishty-Mujahid, Nadya. Character development in Edmund Spenser's *The Faerie Queene*. Lewiston, NY; Lampeter: Mellen Press, 2006. pp. iii, 242.

5083. Demetriou, Tania. 'Essentially Circe': Spenser, Homer, and the Homeric tradition. TransLit (15:2) 2006, 151–76.

5084. Erickson, Wayne. The poet's power and the rhetoric of humility in Spenser's Dedicatory Sonnets. SLI (38:2) 2005, 91–118.

5085. Frontain, Raymond-Jean. Donne, Spenser, and the performative mode of Renaissance poetry. *See* **6715**.

5086. Hadfield, Andrew. Historical writing, 1550–1660. *In* (pp. 250–63) **724**.

5087. —— The Ur-*Hamlet* and the fable of the kid. NQ (53:1) 2006, 46–7.

5088. Hamilton, A. C.; Yamashita, Hiroshi; Suzuki, Toshiyuki (eds). The Faerie Qveene. (Bibl. 2004, 81810.) London; New York: Pearson Longman, 2006. pp. xxi, 787. (Longman annotated English poets.) (Revised second ed.: first ed. 1977.)

5089. Hecht, Paul J. Spenser out of his stanza. Style (39:3) 2005, 316–35.

5090. Herron, Thomas. Plucking the perrot: *Muiopotmos* and Irish politics. *In* (pp. 80–118) **5100**.

5091. —— Ralegh's gold: placing Spenser's Dedicatory Sonnets. SLI (38:2) 2005, 133–47.

5092. Hunt, Maurice. Transforming love's pain in *The Faerie Queene*. ExRC (32:1) 2006, 3–32.

5093. Jung, Sandro. William Collins and the 'zone'. *See* **7668**.

5094. King, Andrew. 'Well grounded, finely framed, and strongly trussed up together': the 'medieval' structure of *The Faerie Queene*. *In* (pp. 119–52) **5100**.

5095. Lamb, Mary Ellen. The popular culture of Shakespeare, Spenser and Jonson. London; New York: Routledge, 2006. pp. x, 271. (Routledge studies in Renaissance literature and culture, 2.)

5096. Landreth, David. At home with Mammon: matter, money, and memory in Book ii of *The Faerie Queene*. ELH (73:1) 2006, 245–74.

5097. Lehnhof, Kent R. Incest and empire in *The Faerie Queene*. ELH (73:1) 2006, 215–43.

5098. Lethbridge, J. B. Recuperating the return to history. *In* (pp. 15–57) **5100**.

5099. —— Spenser's last days: Ireland, career, mutability, allegory. *In* (pp. 302–36) **5100**.

5100. —— (ed.). Edmund Spenser: new and renewed directions. Madison, NJ: Fairleigh Dickinson UP; London: Assoc. UPs, 2006. pp. 385, (plates) 9.

5101. Levy, Fritz. Behind the back matter: the liminalities of *The Faerie Queene* (1590). SLI (38:2) 2005, 73–89.

5102. Majeske, Andrew. Equity in Book v of Spenser's *The Faerie Queene*. LawL (18:1) 2006, 69–99.

5103. Majeske, Andrew J. Equity in English Renaissance literature: Thomas More and Edmund Spenser. *See* **4958**.

5104. Milburn, Colin. Syphilis in Faerie Land: Edmund Spenser and the syphilography of Elizabethan England. Criticism (46:4) 2004, 597–632.

5105. Montgomery, Will. Susan Howe's Renaissance period: metamorphosis and representation in *Pythagorean Silence* and *Defenestration of Prague*. *See* **16474**.

5106. Moore, Andrew. An Herculean precedent for Spenser's 'Telamond'. NQ (53:4) 2006, 461–3.

5107. Moore, John. Pastoral motivation in *The Shepheardes Calender*. *In* (pp. 58–79) **5100**.

5108. Myers, Benjamin. 'Such is the face of falshood': Spenserian theodicy in Ireland. SP (103:4) 2006, 383–416.

5109. Nohrnberg, James. Britomart's gone abroad to Brute-land, Colin Clout's come courting from the salvage Ire-land: exile and the kingdom in some of Spenser's fictions for 'crossing over'. *In* (pp. 214–85) **5100**.

5110. Oram, William A. Introduction: Spenser's paratexts. SLI (38:2) 2005, vii–xviii.

5111. Owens, Judith. Commercial settings of the 1590 *Faerie Queene*. SLI (38:2) 2005, 149–71.

5112. Pirnajmuddin, Hossein. Spenser's *The Faerie Queene*. Exp (64:3) 2006, 131–3.

5113. Potkay, Adam. Spenser, Donne, and the theology of joy. SELit (46:1) 2006, 43–66.

5114. Pugh, Syrithe. Acrasia and bondage: Guyon's perversion of the Ovidian erotic in Book II of *The Faerie Queene*. *In* (pp. 153–94) **5100**.

5115. —— Spenser and Ovid. (Bibl. 2005, 5717.) Rev. by Tom MacFaul in NQ (53:2) 2006, 226–7; by Donald Cheney in RQ (59:1) 2006, 297–9.

5116. Schleiner, W. Early modern recovery: Harvey's gendered response to an earthquake in Essex, England, on 7 April 1580. *See* **4871**.

5117. Schwyzer, Philip. Exhumation and ethnic conflict: from *St Erkenwald* to Spenser in Ireland. *See* **4536**.

5118. Segall, Kreg. Narrative voice, nude women: productive paralysis in *The Faerie Queene*. ExRC (31:2) 2005, 305–39.

5119. Steinberg, Glenn A. Chaucer's mutability in Spenser's *Mutabilitie Cantos*. SELit (46:1) 2006, 27–42.

5120. Suttie, Paul. Self-interpretation in *The Faerie Queene*. Woodbridge, Suffolk; Rochester, NY: Brewer, 2006. pp. x, 227. (Studies in Renaissance literature, 18.)

5121. Suzuki, Toshiyuki. A note on the errata to the 1590 quarto of *The Faerie Queene*. SLI (38:2) 2005, 1–16.

5122. Van Es, Bart. Perils of plants. TLS, 9 June 2006, 10 (review-article). (Ecocriticism and Acrasia's Bower of Bliss.)

5123. —— (ed.). A critical companion to Spenser studies. Basingstoke; New York: Palgrave Macmillan, 2006. pp. xiv, 311. Rev. by Thomas Healy in RES (57:231) 2006, 564–6.

5124. Vine, Angus. Etymology, names and the search for origins: deriving the past in early modern England. *See* **4823**.

5125. Wallace, Andrew. Reading the 1590 *Faerie Queene* with Thomas Nashe. SLI (38:2) 2005, 35–49.

5126. Wareh, Patricia. Humble presents: pastoral and gift-giving in the commendatory verses and Dedicatory Sonnets. SLI (38:2) 2005, 119–32.

5127. Warner, J. Christopher. The Augustinian epic, Petrarch to Milton. (Bibl. 2005, 5725.) Rev. by Tobias Gregory in HLQ (69:2) 2006, 321–31; by Matthew Treherne in MLR (101:4) 2006, 1069–70; by Craig Kallendorf in RQ (59:3) 2006, 839–40.

5128. Watson, E. A. F. Porges. Mutabilitie's debateable land: Spenser's Ireland and the frontiers of Faerie. *In* (pp. 286–301) **5100**.

5129. Williams, Christopher. Hume on the tedium of reading Spenser. BJA (46:1) 2006, 1–16.

5130. Woodcock, Matthew. Fairy in *The Faerie Queene*: Renaissance elf-fashioning and Elizabethan myth-making. (Bibl. 2005, 5730, where title incorrect.) Rev. by Sherron Lux in SixCJ (37:1) 2006, 117–19.

5131. Zurcher, Andrew. Getting it back to front in 1590: Spenser's dedications, Nashe's insinuations, and Ralegh's equivocations. SLI (38:2) 2005, 173–240.

John Stow

5132. Gadd, Ian; Gillespie, Alexandra (eds). John Stow (1525–1605) and the making of the English past. (Bibl. 2005, 5746.) Rev. by Andrew Hadfield in TLS, 14 Apr. 2006, 25; by Lawrence Manley in SStud (34) 2006, 184–7; by Rachel Ramsey in SixCJ (37:2) 2006, 476–8; by Curtis Perry in RQ (59:1) 2006, 296–7; by James Simpson in Spec (81:3) 2006, 849–50.

Henry Howard, Earl of Surrey

5133. Haldane, Michael. *The Soote Season*: Surrey and the amatory elegy. EngS (87:4) 2006, 402–14.

5134. Lines, Candace. The erotic politics of grief in Surrey's *So Crewel Prison*. SELit (46:1) 2006, 1–26.

5135. Taylor, Andrew W. Between Surrey and Marot: Nicolas Bourbon and the artful translation of the epigram. TransLit (15:1) 2006, 1–20.

5136. —— Glass houses: Surrey, Petrarch, and the religious poetics of the 'London' invective. RES (57:231) 2006, 433–55.

Richard Tarleton

5137. Kathman, David. Richard Tarlton and the Haberdashers. NQ (53:4) 2006, 440–2.

Francis Thynne (1545?–1608)

5138. Bartram, Claire. Social fabric in Thynne's *Debate between Pride and Lowliness*. *In* (pp. 137–49) **4629**.

William Tyndale

5139. Rees, Fran. William Tyndale: Bible translator and martyr. Minneapolis, MN: Compass Point, 2006. pp. 112. (Signature lives.)

5140. Thompson, Torri L. (ed.). Marriage and its dissolution in early modern England: vol. 3. London; Brookfield, VT: Pickering & Chatto, 2005. pp. 499. (Facsimiles.) Rev. by Eric Josef Carlson in SixCJ (37:2) 2006, 589–90.

Nicholas Udall

5141. Sivefors, Per. Ascham and Udall: the unknown language reformer in *Toxophilus*. *See* **4807**.

Richard Verstegan (Richard Rowlands)

5142. Arblaster, Paul. Antwerp & the world: Richard Verstegan and the international culture of Catholic reformation. Louvain: Louvain UP, 2004. pp. xiii, 303. (Avisos de Flandes, 9.) Rev. by Alexander S. Wilkinson in SixCJ (37:1) 2006, 221–2.

5143. Lezra, Jacques. Nationum origo. *In* (pp. 203–28) **3191**.

Thomas Watson

5144. Alhiyari, Ibrahim. Thomas Watson: new birth year and privileged ancestry. NQ (53:1) 2006, 35–40.

5145. Duncan-Jones, Katherine. Who was Marlowe's 'brocher of Atheisme'? *See* **4852**.

5146. Mahrt, William Peter. Yonge *versus* Watson and the translation of Italian madrigals. JDJ (25) 2006, 245–66.

Isabella Whitney

5147. Howard, Jean E. Textualizing an urban life: the case of Isabella Whitney. *In* (pp. 217–33) **4792**.

5148. Ingram, Jill Phillips. Idioms of self-interest: credit, identity, and property in English Renaissance literature. *See* **6642**.

5149. Malay, Jessica L. Isabella Whitney, 'Sister Eldershae', and Cheshire recusancy. ELN (43:2) 2005, 18–22.

Sir Thomas Wyatt

5150. Boyarin, Adrienne Williams. Competing biblical and Virgilian allusions in Wyatt's *Who So List to Hounte*. NQ (53:4) 2006, 417–21.

5151. Taylor, Andrew W. Between Surrey and Marot: Nicolas Bourbon and the artful translation of the epigram. *See* **5135**.

Bartholomew Yong

5152. Haldane, Michael. 'Doubling' in Bartholomew Yong's *Diana*. TransLit (14:1) 2005, 1–20.

WILLIAM SHAKESPEARE

Editions and Textual Criticism

5153. Altschuler, Eric Lewin; Jansen, William. The entrances and exits of *Henry VI, Part 2*. *See* **5834**.

5154. Baldwin, Pat; Baldwin, Tom (eds). King Richard III. *See* **5897**.

5155. Bednarz, James P. When did Shakespeare write the choruses of *Henry V*? *See* **5818**.

5156. Berry, Mary; Clamp, Michael (eds). Much ado about nothing. *See* **6005**.

5157. Braunmuller, A. R. On not looking back: sight and sound and text. *In* (pp. 135–51) **5334**.

5158. BRAUNMULLER, ALBERT. A joke and a crux in *Hamlet* Q2. *In* (pp. 200–5) 5577

5159. BRAUN-RAU, ALEXANDRA. William Shakespeares *King Lear* in seinen Fassungen: ein elektronisch-dialogisches Editionsmodell. *See* **5854**.

5160. BROOKS, DOUGLAS A. 'within the book and volume of my brain': *Hamlet* and the crisis of memory – past and present. *See* **5696**.

5161. CARSON, CHRISTIE. The evolution of online editing: where will it end? ShS (59) 2006, 168–81.

5162. CLARY, FRANK NICHOLAS. Having it both ways: reading two early acting editions of *Hamlet*. *See* **5705**.

5163. CORDNER, MICHAEL. 'Are we being theatrical yet?': actors, editors, and the possibilities of dialogue. *In* (pp. 399–414) **5537**.

5164. DAVIS, WILLIAM. Now, gods, stand up for bastards: the 1603 'Good Quarto' *Hamlet*. *See* **5709**.

5165. DAWSON, ANTHONY B. The imaginary text; or, the curse of the Folio. *In* (pp. 141–61) **5537**.

5166. DESSEN, ALAN C. The director as Shakespeare editor. *See* **5498**.

5167. DIPIETRO, CARY. The Shakespeare edition in industrial capitalism. ShS (59) 2006, 147–56. (New Shakespeare.)

5168. DUGAS, DON-JOHN. Marketing the Bard: Shakespeare in performance and print, 1660–1740. *See* **5504**.

5169. ENGLER, BALZ. The editor as translator. ShS (59) 2006, 193–7.

5170. ERNE, LUKAS; KIDNIE, MARGARET JANE (eds). Textual performances: the modern reproduction of Shakespeare's drama. (Bibl. 2005, 5803.) Rev. by Richard Danson Brown in MLR (101:2) 2006, 516–18; by Joachim Frenk in SJ (142) 2006, 255–6; by William Proctor Williams in NQ (53:1) 2006, 110–12.

5171. EVERETT, BARBARA. By the rough seas reft: how the 'badness' of the *Pericles* Quarto may be of Shakespeare's making. *See* **6042**.

5172. GIBSON, REX (ed.). Macbeth. *See* **5930**.

5173. —— The tempest. *See* **6124**.

5174. —— Twelfth Night. *See* **6176**.

5175. GOSSETT, SUZANNE. Editing collaborative drama. ShS (59) 2006, 213–24.

5176. GRAV, PETER. Money changes everything: Quarto and Folio *The Merry Wives of Windsor* and the case for revision. *See* **5985**.

5177. GRIFFIN, BENJAMIN. Emending Caliban's *scamels*. *See* **6125**.

5178. GURR, ANDREW. Editing Stefano's book. *See* **6126**.

5179. HALIO, JAY L. (ed.). The tragedy of King Lear. *See* **5861**.

5180. HENDRICKS, JACQUELYN. A textual crux in *Romeo and Juliet*, v.iii. *See* **6064**.

5181. HODGDON, BARBARA; WORTHEN, W. B. (eds). A companion to Shakespeare and performance. *See* **5537**.

5182. HONIGMANN, E. A. J. Shakespeare's deletions and false starts. RES (56:223) 2005, 37–48.

5183. Howard-Hill, T. H. Early modern printers and the standardization of English spelling. *See* **1327**.

5184. Hunter, Lynette; Lichtenfels, Peter (eds). Shakespeare, language and the stage: The Fifth Wall: approaches to Shakespeare from criticism, performance and theatre studies. *See* **5543**.

5185. Hyman, Eric. Shakespeare's *The Two Gentlemen of Verona* 5.4.83. *See* **6188**.

5186. Hytner, Nicholas; Reinelt, Janelle; Thompson, Ann. Retrospective: Janelle Reinelt. Final session (final thoughts) on heightened language: impasse or interchange? *In* (pp. 161–80) **5543**.

5187. Jackson, MacDonald P. The date and authorship of Hand D's contribution to *Sir Thomas More*: evidence from *Literature Online*. *See* **6078**.

5188. Jenstad, Janelle; Lichtenfels, Peter; Magnusson, Lynne. Text and voice. *In* (pp. 10–37) **5543**.

5189. Jowett, John. Editing Shakespeare's plays in the twentieth century. ShS (59) 2006, 1–19.

5190. —— From print to performance: looking at the masque in *Timon of Athens*. *In* (pp. 73–91) **5334**.

5191. King, Ros (reviser). The comedy of errors. Ed. by T. S. Dorsch. *See* **5669**.

5192. Kliman, Bernice W. Print and electronic editions inspired by the New Variorum *Hamlet* project. *See* **5736**.

5193. Levin, Richard. Petruchio's *soud*. *See* **6111**.

5194. Lindenbaum, Peter. Dispatches from the archives: the Bates/Williams First Folio and the library it leaves behind. TLS, 2 June 2006, 14–15. (Dr Williams's Library.)

5195. Lockwood, Tom. Manuscript, print and the authentic Shakespeare: the Ireland forgeries again. ShS (59) 2006, 108–23.

5196. McEachern, Claire (ed.). Much ado about nothing. *See* **6009**.

5197. McInnis, David. On Cleopatra's 'strange invisible perfume'. *See* **5644**.

5198. McMullan, Gordon. 'The technique of it is mature': inventing the late plays in print and in performance. *In* (pp. 243–60) **5334**.

5199. Maguire, Laurie E. How many children had Alice Walker? *In* (pp. 327–50) **661**.

5200. Marcus, Leah S. (ed.). *The Merchant of Venice*: authoritative text, sources, and contexts, criticism, rewritings, and appropriations. *See* **5971**.

5201. Masten, Jeffrey. Editing boys: the performance of genders in print. *In* (pp. 113–34) **5334**.

5202. Matchett, William H.; Schoenbaum, S. (eds). The life and death of King John; The famous history of the life of Henry VIII. With new and updated critical essays and a revised bibliography. *See* **5848**.

5203. Maxwell, Julie. A reference to the Ur-*Hamlet* in a compositor's error. *See* **5745**.

5204. Menzer, Paul. Dislocating Shakespeare: scene locators and the place of the page. *See* **5904**.

5205. MERRIAM, THOMAS. Some further evidence for Shakespeare's authorship of Hand D in *Sir Thomas More*. *See* **6081**.

5206. MERRIAM, TOM. The identity of Shakespeare in *Henry VIII*. *See* **5845**.

5207. MOWAT, BARBARA A.; WERSTINE, PAUL (eds). All's well that ends well. *See* **5636**.

5208. —— —— Pericles, prince of Tyre. *See* **6046**.

5209. —— —— Shakespeare's sonnets and poems. *See* **6095**.

5210. NEILL, MICHAEL (ed.). Othello, the Moor of Venice. *See* **6033**.

5211. ORGEL, STEPHEN. The book of the play. *In* (pp. 13–54) **5334**.

5212. PARAIZS, JÚLIA. The author, the editor and the translator: William Shakespeare, Alexander Chalmers and Sándor Petőfi; or, The nature of a Romantic edition. ShS (59) 2006, 124–35.

5213. PARKER, PATRICIA. Altering the letter of *Twelfth Night*: 'Some are born great' and the missing signature. *See* **6184**.

5214. PECHTER, EDWARD. Crisis in editing? ShS (59) 2006, 20–38.

5215. PETERSON, KAARA L. *Historica passio*: early modern medicine, *King Lear*, and editorial practice. *See* **5870**.

5216. PUJANTE, ÁNGEL LUIS. Manuel Herrera on Shakespeare: a new Spanish manuscript from the Romantic period. *In* (pp. 21–42) **5308**.

5217. RASMUSSEN, ERIC. The year's contributions to Shakespeare studies: 3, Editions and textual studies. ShS (59) 2006, 375–83.

5218. ROBERTS, JEANNE ADDISON. Women edit Shakespeare. ShS (59) 2006, 136–46.

5219. ROONEY, TOM. 'A thousand Shylocks': Orson Welles and *The Merchant of Venice*. *See* **5975**.

5220. SCHAFER, ELIZABETH. Performance editions, editing and editors. ShS (59) 2006, 198–212.

5221. SEMLER, L. E. A proximate prince: the gooey business of *Hamlet* criticism. *See* **5758**.

5222. SHERBO, ARTHUR. The appendix to Edmond Malone's 1790 *Shakespeare* and the New Variorum *Poems* and *Sonnets*. *See* **6193**.

5223. —— *Introductorily* in *OED*. *See* **1574**.

5224. —— The Longman's Milton and the 1778 Johnson–Steevens *Variorum*. *See* **6098**.

5225. STERN, TIFFANY. Making Shakespeare: from stage to page. (Bibl. 2005, 5831.) Rev. by Martin Coyle in NQ (53:1) 2006, 108–9.

5226. TAYLOR, GARY. Making meaning marketing Shakespeare 1623. *In* (pp. 55–72) **5334**.

5227. TRONCH PÉREZ, JESÚS. Editing (and revering) national authors: Shakespeare and Cervantes. *In* (pp. 43–57) **5308**.

5228. TUMELSON, RONALD A., II. Ferdinand's *wife* and Prospero's *wise*. *See* **6145**.

5229. TURNER, ROBERT KEAN, *et al.* (eds). The winter's tale. *See* **6209**.

5230. VICKERS, BRIAN. By other hands. TLS, 11 Aug. 2006, 10–12 (review-article).

5231. Wall, Wendy. De-generation: editions, offspring, and *Romeo and Juliet*. *In* (pp. 152–70) **5334**.

5232. —— Editors in love? Performing desire in *Romeo and Juliet*. *In* (pp. 197–211) **5537**.

5233. Warkentin, Germaine; Hoare, Peter. Sophisticated Shakespeare: James Toovey and the Morgan Library's 'Sidney' First Folio. PBSA (100:3) 2006, 313–56.

5234. Watts, Cedric. Fundamental editing: in *A Midsummer Night's Dream*, does 'Bottom' mean *bum*? And how about *arse* and *ass*? *See* **6001**.

5235. Wells, Stanley. On being a general editor. ShS (59) 2006, 39–48.

5236. —— Taylor, Gary (gen. eds). The complete works. (Bibl. 2005, 5837.) Rev. by Brian Vickers in TLS, 11 Aug. 2006, 10–12.

5237. Wentersdorf, Karl P. On 'momtanish inhumanyty' in *Sir Thomas More*. *See* **6083**.

5238. —— The Winchester crux in the First Folio's *1 Henry VI*. *See* **5843**.

5239. Williams, William Proctor. Hamlet's pockets: problems with stage directions. *In* (pp. 192–9) **5577**.

5240. Worthen, W. B. Prefixing the author: print, plays, and performance. *In* (pp. 212–30) **5537**.

General Scholarship and Criticism

5241. Ackroyd, Peter. Shakespeare: the biography. (Bibl. 2005, 5840.) Rev. by Andrew Hadfield in Eng (55:211) 2006, 93–101; by Ralph Berry in ContRev (288:1682) 2006, 377–9.

5242. Adams, Byron. 'By season season'd': Shakespeare and Vaughan Williams. JDJ (25) 2006, 183–97.

5243. Alexander, Catherine M. S. (ed.). Shakespeare and language. (Bibl. 2005, 5841.) Rev. by Frank Ardolino in SixCJ (37:1) 2006, 149–51.

5244. Alvis, John E. Liberty in Shakespeare's British plays. *In* (pp. 33–47) **5394**.

5245. Anastaplo, George. Shakespeare's politics revisited. *In* (pp. 197–242) **5394**.

5246. Anderson, Linda. A place in the story: servants and service in Shakespeare's plays. (Bibl. 2005, 5844.) Rev. by Michelle M. Dowd in RQ (59:2) 2006, 643–5.

5247. Anderson, Mark. 'Shakespeare' by another name: the life of Edward de Vere, Earl of Oxford, the man who was Shakespeare. Foreword by Derek Jacobi. (Bibl. 2005, 5846.) Rev. by Alan H. Nelson in TLS, 27 Jan. 2006, 30.

5248. Archer, John Michael. Citizen Shakespeare: freemen, city wives, and aliens in the language of the plays. (Bibl. 2005, 5848.) Rev. by Duncan Salkeld in TLS, 26 May 2006, 33; by Alexander Leggatt in ShQ (57:2) 2006, 222–4; by Chris Fitter in NQ (53:4) 2006, 570–1; by Andrew Majeske in RQ (59:3) 2006, 977–8.

5249. Asquith, Clare. Shadowplay: the hidden beliefs and coded politics of William Shakespeare. (Bibl. 2005, 5850.) Rev. by Andrew Hadfield in Eng (55:211)

2006, 93–101; by Thomas Merriam in NQ (53:2) 2006, 231–2; by Stephen Smith in BJJ (13) 2006, 204–10; by Peter Milward in RelArts (10:1) 2006, 101–8.

5250. Assmann, Aleida. The battle of memories in Shakespeare's histories. *In* (pp. 21–41) **5346**.

5251. Beckwith, Sarah. Shakespeare, crypto-Catholicism, crypto-criticism. MedRen (19) 2006, 259–70 (review-article).

5252. Belsey, Catherine. Shakespeare's little boys: theatrical apprenticeship and the construction of childhood. *In* (pp. 53–72) **5421**.

5253. Berry, Ralph. Shakespeare and the Catholic network. ContRev (286:1671) 2005, 233–8.

5254. Betteridge, Thomas. Shakespearean fantasy and politics. Hatfield: UP of Hertfordshire, 2005. pp. 214. Rev. by Lisa Hopkins in NQ (53:1) 2006, 109–10.

5255. Bevington, David. Shakespeare: the seven ages of human experience. Oxford; Malden, MA: Blackwell, 2005. pp. xi, 264. (Second ed.: first ed. 2002.) Rev. by Park Honan in NQ (53:3) 2006, 373–4.

5256. Bevington, David M. (ed.). The necessary Shakespeare. London; New York: Pearson Longman, 2005. pp. cx, 916, 89, 22. (Second ed.: first ed. 2002.)

5257. Bhatia, Nandi. Acts of authority / acts of resistance: theater and politics in colonial and postcolonial India. Ann Arbor: Michigan UP, 2004. pp. 206. Rev. by Aparna Dharwadker in ModDr (48:2) 2005, 440–4.

5258. Bieito, Calixto; Delgado, Maria M.; Parker, Patricia. Resistant readings, multilingualism and marginality. *In* (pp. 108–37) **5543**.

5259. Bigliazzi, Silvia. Nel prisma del nulla: l'esperienza del non-essere nella drammaturgia shakespeariana. Naples: Liguori, 2005. pp. viii, 168. (Critica letteraria, 68.) Rev. by Sergio Givone in Indice (2006:6) 21.

5260. Blank, Paula. Shakespeare and the mismeasure of Renaissance man. Ithaca, NY; London: Cornell UP, 2006. pp. 214.

5261. Bonetto, Sandra. Coward conscience and bad conscience in Shakespeare and Nietzsche. *See* **5898**.

5262. Bonnefoy, Yves. Shakespeare & the French poet; including an interview with Yves Bonnefoy. Ed. by John Naughton. (Bibl. 2004, 6131.) Rev. by Guillaume Winter in CEl (68) 2005, 83–4; by Ruth Morse in ShQ (57:1) 2006, 110–12; by Michael Edwards in MedRen (19) 2006, 273–8; by Péter Dávidházi in TransLit (15:1) 2006, 122–9.

5263. Bono, Paola. Rewriting the memory of a queen: Dido, Cleopatra, Elizabeth I. *See* **4567**.

5264. Boswell, Jackson C. Two 'new' seventeenth-century portraits of Shakespeare. ShQ (57:3) 2006, 309–17.

5265. Botelho, Keith M. 'Look on this picture, and on this': framing Shakespeare in William Wells Brown's *The Escape*. *See* **9248**.

5266. Boyce, Charles. Critical companion to William Shakespeare: a literary reference to his life and work. (Bibl. 1996, 6240.) New York: Facts on File, 2005. 2 vols. pp. xi, 1066. (Facts on File library of world literature.) (Revised ed.: first ed. 1990.) (Orig. pub. as *Shakespeare A to Z: the Essential Reference to His Plays, His Poems, His Life and Times, and More.*)

5267. Butler, Colin. The practical Shakespeare: the plays in practice and on the page. (Bibl. 2005, 5870.) Rev. by Emma Smith in RES (57:228) 2006, 125–7; by Michael Pringle in RMER (60:1) 2006.

5268. Carvalho Homem, Rui; Hoenselaars, Ton (eds). Translating Shakespeare for the twenty-first century. (Bibl. 2005, 5874.) Rev. by Lukas Erne in SJ (142) 2006, 245–9; by Péter Dávidházi in TransLit (15:1) 2006, 122–9.

5269. Caws, Mary Ann. Surprised in translation. *See* **11817**.

5270. Cefalu, Paul. Revisionist Shakespeare: transitional ideologies in texts and contexts. (Bibl. 2005, 5876.) Rev. by William N. West in ShQ (57:1) 2006, 114–16; by Kevin J. Wetmore, Jr, in TJ (58:3) 2006, 527–9; by Rainer Emig in EREA (4:1) 2006.

5271. Centerwall, Brandon S. Who wrote William Basse's *Elegy on Shakespeare*? Rediscovering a poem lost from the Donne canon. *See* **6566**.

5272. Cerezo, Marta. Critical approaches to Shakespeare: Shakespeare for all time. Madrid: UNED, 2005. pp. 337. Rev. by Juan Antonio Prieto-Pablos in SEDERI (15) 2005, 145–50.

5273. Chandler, David. Catholic Shakespeare: the making of the argument. ELN (44:1) 2006, 29–41.

5274. Charnes, Linda. Hamlet's heirs: Shakespeare and the politics of a new millennium. *See* **5703**.

5275. Cheney, Patrick. Biographical representations: Marlowe's life of the author. *In* (pp. 183–204) **5353**.

5276. Cheney, Patrick Gerard. Shakespeare, national poet-playwright. (Bibl. 2005, 5879.) Rev. by Catherine Belsey in SStud (34) 2006, 170–6; by Jean-Christophe Mayer in CEl (70) 2006, 76–7; by Simon Barker in LitH (15:2) 2006, 68–9.

5277. Clayton, Tom; Brock, Susan; Forés, Vicente (eds). Shakespeare and the Mediterranean: the selected proceedings of the International Shakespeare Association World Congress, Valencia, 2001. (Bibl. 2005, 5881.) Rev. by Herb Weil in ShB (23:1) 2005, 199–203; by Thomas G. Olsen in SixCJ (37:1) 2006, 290–2.

5278. Cohen, Adam Max. Shakespeare and technology: dramatizing early modern technological revolutions. Basingstoke; New York: Palgrave Macmillan, 2006. pp. xiii, 231.

5279. Cooper, Helen. Guy of Warwick, upstart crows and mounting sparrows. *In* (pp. 119–38) **5353**.

5280. Coursen, H. R. Shakespeare translated: derivatives on film and TV. New York; Frankfurt: Lang, 2005. pp. 173. (Studies in Shakespeare, 15.)

5281. Cox, John D. Shakespeare and the French epistemologists. Cithara (45:2) 2006, 23–45.

5282. Crosman, Robert. The world's a stage: Shakespeare and the dramatic view of life. Bethesda, MD: Academica Press, 2005. pp. xiv, 221.

5283. Davis, William L. Structural secrets: Shakespeare's complex chiasmus. Style (39:3) 2005, 237–58.

5284. de Grazia, Margreta. Imprints: Shakespeare, Gutenberg, and Descartes. *In* (pp. 29–58) **661**.

5285. de la Concha, Ángeles (ed.). Shakespeare en la imaginación contemporánea: revisiones y reescrituras de su obra. Madrid: UNED, 2004. pp. 261. Rev. by Celestino Deleyto in Atl (28:2) 2006, 147–51.

5286. Desmet, Christy. The persistence of character. SStud (34) 2006, 46–55.

5287. Díaz-Fernández, José Ramón. Orson Welles's Shakespeare films: an annotated checklist. *See* **13252**.

5288. Donaldson, Ian. Looking sideways: Jonson, Shakespeare and the myths of envy. *In* (pp. 241–57) **5353**.

5289. Döring, Tobias. Performances of mourning in Shakespearean theatre and early modern culture. Basingstoke; New York: Palgrave Macmillan, 2006. pp. viii, 223. (Early modern literature in history.)

5290. Duncan-Jones, Katherine. Drayton on Nashe and Shakespeare. *See* **6761**.

5291. Dutton, Richard. Shakespearean origins. *In* (pp. 69–83) **5353**.

5292. Edwards, Michael. Shakespeare et l'œuvre de la tragédie. Paris: Belin, 2005. pp. 202. Rev. by Pascale Drouet in CEl (69) 2006, 98–100.

5293. Egan, Gabriel. Green Shakespeare: from ecopolitics to ecocriticism. London; New York: Routledge, 2006. pp. xii, 203. (Accents on Shakespeare.) Rev. by David W. Hartwig in CEl (70) 2006, 80–2; by Robert N. Watson in RES (57:232) 2006, 819–22.

5294. —— Shakespeare and Marx. Oxford; New York: OUP, 2004. pp. 168. (Oxford Shakespeare topics.) Rev. by David Hawkes in TLS, 21 Jan. 2005, 28; by Douglas Bruster in ShQ (57:1) 2006, 105–7.

5295. Estok, Simon. An introduction to Shakespeare and ecocriticism: the special cluster. ISLE (12:2) 2005, 109–17.

5296. Falocco, Joe. Is Mark Twain dead? Samuel Clemens and the question of Shakespearean authorship. *See* **11493**.

5297. Farina, William. De Vere as Shakespeare: an Oxfordian reading of the canon. Foreword by Felicia Hardison Londré. Jefferson, NC; London: McFarland, 2006. pp. viii, 271.

5298. Fayard, Nicole. The performance of Shakespeare in France since the Second World War: re-imagining Shakespeare. Lewiston, NY; Lampeter: Mellen Press, 2006. pp. iii, 616.

5299. Fernie, Ewan (ed.). Spiritual Shakespeares. (Bibl. 2005, 5928.) Rev. by Graham Hammill in ShQ (57:2) 2006, 229–32; by Sean Benson in SNL (56:1) 2006, 29, 34; by Christopher Baker in RQ (59:3) 2006, 974–5.

5300. Finnerty, Páraic. Emily Dickinson's Shakespeare. *See* **9859**.

5301. Fitzpatrick, Joan. Shakespeare, Spenser and the contours of Britain: reshaping the Atlantic archipelago. (Bibl. 2005, 5932.) Rev. by Dermot Cavanagh in ETh (9:1) 2006, 135–7.

5302. Fleissner, Robert F. Shakespeare and Africa: the Dark Lady of his sonnets revamped and other Africa-related associations. (Bibl. 2005, 5933.) Rev. by Cecile Williamson Cary in CLAJ (49:3) 2006, 378–80.

5303. Fraser, Russell. Shakespeare and the revolution of the times. SewR (114:4) 2006, 495–511.

5304. Gervais, David. For Shakespeare the European. PNRev (30:4) 2004, 17–22.

5305. Ghezzani, Alessandra. Il mistero Shakespeare secondo Borges. AngP (3:1) 2006, 85–106.

5306. Gieskes, Edward. Representing the professions: administration, law, and theater in early modern England. Newark: Delaware UP, 2006. pp. 365.

5307. González, José Manuel. Shakespearean criticism in contemporary Spain. *In* (pp. 7–16) **5308**.

5308. —— (ed.). Spanish studies in Shakespeare and his contemporaries. Newark: Delaware UP; London: Assoc. UPs, 2006. pp. 327. (International studies in Shakespeare and his contemporaries.) Rev. by Edmund Valentine Campos in ShQ (57:4) 2006, 489–92.

5309. Goodland, Katharine. Female mourning and tragedy in medieval and Renaissance English drama: from the raising of Lazarus to *King Lear*. *See* **3907**.

5310. Goy-Blanquet, Dominique. Shakespeare et l'invention de l'histoire: guide commenté du théâtre historique. (Bibl. 1997, 5625.) Brussels: Le Cri, 2004. pp. 341. (Second ed.: first ed. 1997.) Rev. by Henri Suhamy in EA (59:2) 2006, 233–4.

5311. Greenblatt, Stephen. Will in the world: how Shakespeare became Shakespeare. (Bibl. 2004, 6185.) Rev. by William E. Engel in SewR (113:3) 2005, lvii–lxii; by Enrico Terrinoni in QDLC (1) 2005, 87–9; by Thomas Healy in SJ (142) 2006, 227–33; by Laury Magnus in ColLit (33:4) 2006, 226–8; by Eusebio de Lorenzo in EIUC (14) 2006, 167–87; by Peter Milward in RelArts (10:1) 2006, 101–8.

5312. Greene, Thomas M. Poetry, signs, and magic. (Bibl. 2005, 5946.) Rev. by Patrick Grant in MLR (101:2) 2006, 503–4.

5313. Grundmann, Heike. Shakespeare and European Romanticism. *In* (pp. 29–48) **8357**.

5314. Habicht, Werner. Shakespeare and the founders. *In* (pp. 239–54) **5346**.

5315. Hadfield, Andrew. Shakespeare and Republicanism. Cambridge; New York: CUP, 2005. pp. xiii, 363. Rev. by David Hawkes in TLS, 1 Sept. 2006, 28; by John King in LitH (15:2) 2006, 69–70.

5316. —— Shakespeare, Spenser, and the Matter of Britain. (Bibl. 2004, 6188.) Rev. by Andrew Fleck in SixCJ (37:1) 2006, 248–9; by Naomi McAreavey in MedRen (19) 2006, 282–6.

5317. —— Hammond, Paul (eds). Shakespeare and Renaissance Europe. (Bibl. 2005, 5954.) Rev. by Richard Meek in MLR (101:2) 2006, 520–1.

5318. Haekel, Ralf. Die englischen Komödianten in Deutschland: eine Einführung in die Ursprünge des deutschen Berufsschauspiels. *See* **4677**.

5319. HALE, JOHN. Shakespeare's shoot-outs, with a comparison between *King Lear* and *Hamlet*. *In* (pp. 473–87) **8374**.

5320. HALES, MICK. Shakespeare in the garden: a selection of gardens and an alphabet of plants. New York: Abrams, 2006. pp. 144.

5321. HARDY, BARBARA. The story within the play: fantasy and fable. SJ (142) 2006, 34–46.

5322. HARMON, A. G. Eternal bonds, true contracts: law and nature in Shakespeare's problem plays. (Bibl. 2005, 5959.) Rev. by Andrew Vorder Bruegge in SixCJ (37:1) 2006, 274–5.

5323. HAWKES, TERENCE. Nanti everything. *In* (pp. 130–8) **5421**.

5324. HENDERSON, DIANA E. Collaborations with the past: reshaping Shakespeare across time and media. Ithaca, NY; London: Cornell UP, 2006. pp. xi, 289.

5325. HILLIAM, DAVID. William Shakespeare: England's greatest playwright and poet. New York: Rosen Central, 2005. pp. 112.

5326. HILLMAN, RICHARD. Returning to one's vomit: an intertextual tour of *Eastward Ho*'s Isle of Dogs. *See* **6640**.

5327. HOECKLEY, CHERI L. LARSEN (ed.). Shakespeare's heroines: characteristics of women, moral, political, and historical. *See* **10621**.

5328. HOENSELAARS, A. J. (ed.). Shakespeare's history plays: performance, translation and adaptation in Britain and abroad. Foreword by Dennis Kennedy. (Bibl. 2005, 5970.) Rev. by Kathy Howlett in ShB (23:1) 2005, 208–13; by Manfred Pfister in ShQ (57:1) 2006, 91–4; by Antonella Piazza in CEl (69) 2006, 95–7; by Kevin J. Wetmore, Jr, in TJ (58:3) 2006, 527–9; by Brad Greenburg in SixCJ (37:2) 2006, 486–8; by Deneen Senasi in CompDr (40:2) 2006, 251–5.

5329. HOENSELAARS, TON. Between Heaven and Hell: Shakespearian translation, adaptation, and criticism from a historical perspective. YES (36:1) 2006, 50–64.

5330. —— (ed.). Shakespeare and the language of translation. (Bibl. 2005, 5975.) Rev. by Francis Jones in MLR (101:3) 2006, 821–2; by Jerzy Limon in ShQ (57:1) 2006, 100–2; by Lukas Erne in SJ (142) 2006, 245–9; by Péter Dávidházi in TransLit (15:1) 2006, 122–9.

5331. —— CALVO, CLARA. European Shakespeare: from strength to strength. CEl (70) 2006, 43–5.

5332. HOLBROOK, PETER. Shakespearean immoral individualism: the example of Gide. AUMLA (106) 2006, 149–61.

5333. HOLLAND, PETER. Shakespeare and the *DNB*. *In* (pp. 139–49) **5353**.

5334. —— ORGEL, STEPHEN (eds). From performance to print in Shakespeare's England. Basingstoke; New York: Palgrave Macmillan, 2006. pp. xv, 267. (Redefining British theatre history.)

5335. HOLMES, JONATHAN. 'Sometime a paradox': Shakespeare, Diderot and the problem of character. ShS (59) 2006, 285–97.

5336. HOPKINS, LISA. Shakespeare on the edge: border-crossing in the tragedies and the Henriad. Aldershot; Burlington, VT: Ashgate, 2005. pp. viii, 154. Rev. by

Andrew Hadfield in TLS, 7 Apr. 2006, 33; by Mark Taylor in RQ (59:3) 2006, 975–7.

5337. Houlahan, Mark. Plucking the flower, safety: William Shakespeare and Katherine Mansfield. *In* (pp. 349–58) **8374**.

5338. Hunt, Maurice. Shakespeare's religious allusiveness: its play and tolerance. (Bibl. 2005, 5981.) Rev. by Ralph Berry in RES (56:223) 2005, 141–3; by Anthony Low in ShQ (57:3) 2006, 359–61; by Donald J. Millus in SixCJ (37:2) 2006, 444–5.

5339. Ingram, Jill Phillips. Idioms of self-interest: credit, identity, and property in English Renaissance literature. *See* **6642**.

5340. Ioppolo, Grace. Dramatists and their manuscripts in the age of Shakespeare, Jonson, Middleton and Heywood: authorship, authority, and the playhouse. *See* **511**.

5341. Jackson, Ken. Separate theaters: Bethlem ('Bedlam') Hospital and the Shakespearean stage. (Bibl. 2005, 5985.) Rev. by Kara Molway Russell in CompDr (40:1) 2006, 131–4.

5342. Jackson, MacD. P. Compound adjectives in *Arden of Faversham*. *See* **4683**.

5343. Jackson, MacDonald P. Shakespeare and the quarrel scene in *Arden of Faversham*. *See* **4684**.

5344. James, Brenda; Rubinstein, William D. Truth will out: unmasking the real Shakespeare. (Bibl. 2005, 5987.) Rev. by Andrew Hadfield in Eng (55:211) 2006, 93–101; by Henri Suhamy in EA (59:2) 2006, 224–30.

5345. Jansohn, Christa. The German Shakespeare-Gesellschaft during the Cold War. *In* (pp. 272–91) **5346**.

5346. —— (ed.). German Shakespeare studies at the turn of the twenty-first century. Newark: Delaware UP, 2006. pp. 318. (International studies in Shakespeare and his contemporaries.)

5347. —— In the footsteps of William Shakespeare. Münster: LIT, 2005. pp. vi, 295. (Studien zur englischen Literatur, 20.) Rev. by Paul Menzer in ShQ (57:4) 2006, 492–4.

5348. Josek, Jiří. A Czech Shakespeare? *In* (pp. 84–94) **3186**.

5349. Kermode, Frank. The age of Shakespeare. (Bibl. 2004, 6214.) Rev. by Ralph Berry in ContRev (286:1668) 2005, 49–50; by Peter Milward in RelArts (10:1) 2006, 101–8.

5350. Kinney, Arthur F. Shakespeare and cognition: Aristotle's legacy and Shakespearean drama. London; New York: Routledge, 2006. pp. xvi, 167.

5351. Kliman, Bernice W.; Santos, Rick J. (eds). Latin American Shakespeares. (Bibl. 2005, 5995.) Rev. by Edmund Valentine Campos in ShQ (57:4) 2006, 489–92.

5352. Knowles, Ric. Shakespeare and Canada: essays on production, translation and adaptation. (Bibl. 2005, 5996.) Rev. by Susan Bennett in TRC (25:1/2) 2004, 223–5.

5353. Kozuka, Takashi; Mulryne, J. R. (eds). Shakespeare, Marlowe, Jonson: new directions in biography. Aldershot; Burlington, VT: Ashgate, 2006. pp. x, 321. Rev. by Joost Daalder in Parergon (23:2) 2006, 152–5.

5354. Krims, Marvin Bennett. The mind according to Shakespeare: psychoanalysis in the Bard's writing. Westport, CT; London: Praeger, 2006. pp. xx, 218.

5355. Krippendorff, Ekkehart. Shakespeare politico: drammi storici, drammi romani, tragedie. Rome: Fazi, 2005. pp. 348. (Le terre/pagine, 348.) Rev. by Massimo Bacigalupo in Indice (2006:2) 22.

5356. Lamb, Mary Ellen. The popular culture of Shakespeare, Spenser and Jonson. *See* **5095**.

5357. Lanier, Douglas. Will of the people: recent Shakespeare film parody and the politics of popularization. *In* (pp. 176–96) **5531**.

5358. Leggatt, Alexander. Shakespeare's tragedies: violation and identity. Cambridge; New York: CUP, 2005. pp. ix, 228. Rev. by Jerome de Groot in TLS, 9 Sept. 2005, 26; by Linda Anderson in RQ (59:2) 2006, 640–2.

5359. Li, Yanmei. The buffoon's power and aesthetics: comments on buffoons in Shakespeare's historical plays. FLS (122) 2006, 62–8. (In Chinese.)

5360. Lindley, David. Shakespeare and music. London: Arden Shakespeare, 2006. pp. xii, 284. (Arden critical companions.) Rev. by Skiles Howard in ShQ (57:4) 2006, 474–8.

5361. Lupton, Julia Reinhard. Citizen-saints: Shakespeare and political theology. (Bibl. 2005, 6008.) Rev. by Kristen Poole in ShQ (57:2) 2006, 225–8; by Andrew R. Murphy in JR (86:3) 2006, 513–15; by David Jasper in JAAR (74:4) 2006, 1001–3; by John S. Mebane in RQ (59:1) 2006, 300–2.

5362. —— The religious turn (to theory) in Shakespeare Studies. ELN (44:1) 2006, 145–9.

5363. McAlindon, Tom. Shakespeare minus 'theory'. (Bibl. 2005, 6009.) Rev. by Richard Harp in CompDr (39:1) 2005, 115–17; by Kevin J. Wetmore, Jr, in NETJ (16) 2005, 131–6; by Laetitia Coussement-Boillot in EA (59:3) 2006, 358–9.

5364. McCarthy, Penny. Pseudonymous Shakespeare: rioting language in the Sidney circle. Aldershot; Burlington, VT: Ashgate, 2006. pp. xxiv, 257.

5365. McCrea, Scott. The case for Shakespeare: the end of the authorship question. (Bibl. 2005, 6011.) Rev. by Andrew Hadfield in Eng (55:211) 2006, 93–101.

5366. McDonald, Russ. Shakespeare's late style. Cambridge; New York: CUP, 2006. pp. x, 260. Rev. by Suzanne Gossett in RES (57:232) 2006, 811–12.

5367. —— (ed.). Shakespeare: an anthology of criticism and theory, 1945–2000. (Bibl. 2005, 6012.) Rev. by Sabine Schülting in SJ (142) 2006, 269–70.

5368. McEvoy, Sean. Shakespeare: the basics. (Bibl. 2004, 90076.) London; New York: Routledge, 2006. pp. xiv, 289. (Basics.) (Second ed.: first ed. 2000.)

5369. McGinn, Colin. Shakespeare's philosophy: discovering the meaning behind the plays. London: HarperCollins, 2006. pp. viii, 230.

5370. McLuskie, Kate. Is all well? Shakespeare's play with narratives. SJ (142) 2006, 78–94.

5371. McMullan, Gordon. 'The technique of it is mature': inventing the late plays in print and in performance. *In* (pp. 243–60) **5334**.

5372. McNeely, Trevor. Proteus unmasked: sixteenth-century rhetoric and the art of Shakespeare. (Bibl. 2004, 6233.) Rev. by Dan Mills in SixCJ (36:4) 2005, 1176–8.

5373. Maguire, Laurie. Helen of Troy: representing absolute beauty in language. SEDERI (16) 2006, 31–51.

5374. Maguire, Laurie E. Studying Shakespeare: a guide to the plays. Oxford; Malden, MA: Blackwell, 2004. pp. 241. Rev. by Shannon Murray in ETh (9:1) 2006, 152–3.

5375. Makaryk, Irena R. Shakespeare in the undiscovered bourn: Les Kurbas, Ukrainian Modernism, and early Soviet cultural politics. (Bibl. 2005, 6013.) Rev. by Goran V. Stanivukovic in ShQ (57:1) 2006, 112–14.

5376. —— Price, Joseph G. (eds). Shakespeare in the worlds of Communism and Socialism. Toronto; Buffalo, NY; London: Toronto UP, 2006. pp. xii, 402.

5377. Marrapodi, Michele (ed.). Shakespeare, Italy and intertextuality. (Bibl. 2005, 6019.) Rev. by Sonia Massai in ShQ (57:1) 2006, 97–100; by Andrew Hadfield in Eng (55:211) 2006, 93–101; by Carlo M. Bajetta in NQ (53:2) 2006, 230–1.

5378. Marshall, Louise H. Women and politics in adaptations of Shakespeare's English histories: re-enacting the nation, 1719–1745. BJECS (29:1) 2006, 61–77.

5379. Martindale, Charles; Taylor, A. B. (eds). Shakespeare and the Classics. (Bibl. 2005, 6020.) Rev. by Philip Hardie in TransLit (14:2) 2005, 246–9; by Anne-Julia Zwierlein in SJ (142) 2006, 264–5; by Joanna A. Giuttari in RQ (59:1) 2006, 299–300.

5380. Maslen, R. W. Shakespeare and comedy. London: Arden Shakespeare, 2006. pp. viii, 270. (Arden critical companions.) Rev. by Skiles Howard in ShQ (57:4) 2006, 474–8.

5381. Matei-Chesnoiu, Monica. Shakespeare in the Romanian cultural memory. Foreword by Arthur F. Kinney. Madison, NJ: Fairleigh Dickinson UP, 2006. pp. 272. Rev. by Patricia Lennox in SNL (56:1) 2006, 9–10.

5382. Mayer, Jean-Christophe. Shakespeare's hybrid faith: history, religion and the stage. Basingstoke; New York: Palgrave Macmillan, 2006. pp. ix, 235. (Early modern literature in history.)

5383. Mehl, Dieter. The German Shakespeare-Gesellschaft and '*die Wende*'. *In* (pp. 292–304) **5346**.

5384. Meis, Morgan; Tyree, J. M. Is it okay to read the Coen brothers as literature? *See* **13154**.

5385. Melchiori, Giorgio. Shakespeare all'opera: i drammi nella librettistica italiana. Rome: Bulzoni, 2006. pp. 160. (Piccola biblioteca shakespeariana.)

5386. Merriam, Thomas. Low-frequency words, genre, date, and authorship. NQ (53:4) 2006, 495–8.

5387. Migliarisi, Anna (ed.). Directing and authorship in Western drama. Introd. by Don B. Wilmeth. *See* **12336**.

5388. Milward, Peter. 'The plot thickens': three new books on Shakespeare and religion. RelArts (10:1) 2006, 101–8 (review-article).

5389. —— Shakespeare the Papist. Naples, FL: Sapientia Press of Ave Maria Univ., 2005. pp. xv, 208. Rev. by Thomas Merriam in NQ (53:3) 2006, 370–1.

5390. Morse, Ruth. Reflections in Shakespeare translation. YES (36:1) 2006, 79–89.

5391. —— Shakespeare's ages. ShS (59) 2006, 254–66.

5392. Moyal, Gabriel Louis. Traduire l'Angleterre sous la Restauration: Gibbon et Shakespeare de Guizot. *See* **7826**.

5393. Mukherji, Subha. False trials in Shakespeare, Massinger, and Ford. EC (56:3) 2006, 219–40.

5394. Murley, John A.; Sutton, Sean D. (eds). Perspectives on politics in Shakespeare. Lanham, MD: Lexington, 2006. pp. ix, 265.

5395. Neely, Carol Thomas. Distracted subjects: madness and gender in Shakespeare and early modern culture. (Bibl. 2005, 6039.) Rev. by John Lee in MLR (101:3) 2005, 822–4; by Robert C. Evans in CompDr (39:2) 2005, 251–6; by Ken Jackson in SixCJ (36:4) 2005, 1151–3; by Elisabeth Bronfen in SJ (142) 2006, 257–9; by Deborah Willis in SStud (34) 2006, 212–18; by Katharine Goodland in ETh (9:1) 2006, 154–7; by Kim Solga in TJ (58:3) 2006, 529–31; by Theodora A. Jankowski in MedRen (19) 2006, 317–22.

5396. Nelson, Alan H. Calling all (Shakespeare) biographers! Or, A plea for documentary discipline. *In* (pp. 55–67) **5353**.

5397. Nünning, Ansgar; Sommer, Roy. Die performative Kraft des Erzählens: Formen und Funktionen des Erzählens in Shakespeares Dramen. SJ (142) 2006, 124–41.

5398. Oatley, Keith. Simulation of substance and shadow: inner emotions and outer behavior in Shakespeare's psychology of character. ColLit (33:1) 2006, 15–33.

5399. O'Dair, Sharon. Marx *manqué*: a brief history of Marxist Shakespeare criticism in North America, *ca* 1980–*ca* 2000. *In* (pp. 349–73) **5376**.

5400. Orkin, Martin. Local Shakespeares: proximations and power. (Bibl. 2005, 6043.) Rev. by Kevin J. Wetmore, Jr, in TJ (58:3) 2006, 527–9; by Sophie Tomlinson in ShQ (57:3) 2006, 363–6.

5401. Orlin, Lena Cowen (ed.). Center or margin: revisions of the English Renaissance in honor of Leeds Barroll. Selinsgrove, PA: Susquehanna UP; London: Assoc. UPs, 2006. pp. 318. (Apple–Zimmerman series in early modern culture.)

5402. Palmer, Daryl W. Writing Russia in the age of Shakespeare. (Bibl. 2005, 6045.) Rev. by Jessica Winston in SixCJ (37:2) 2006, 448–50.

5403. Parker, Barbara L. Plato's *Republic* and Shakespeare's Rome: a political study of the Roman works. (Bibl. 2005, 6046.) Rev. by Anne-Julia Zwierlein in SJ (142) 2006, 264–5; by Travis Curtright in SixCJ (37:2) 2006, 620–1.

5404. Partee, Morriss Henry. Childhood in Shakespeare's plays. New York; Frankfurt: Lang, 2006. pp. viii, 139.

5405. Pasquarella, Vincenzo. An interview with Stanley Wells and Stephen Orgel. Foreword by Carla Dente. AngP (3:1) 2006, 131–43.

5406. Paster, Gail Kern. Humoring the body: emotions and the Shakespearean stage. (Bibl. 2005, 6047.) Rev. by Linda Woodbridge in JHM (61:2) 2006, 220–1; by Graham Hammill in SStud (34) 2006, 219–23; by Ros King in MLR (101:4) 2006, 1091–2; by Tanya Pollard in ShQ (57:3) 2006, 356–8; by Shigehisa Kuriyama in CLIO (36:1) 2006, 114–18.

5407. Peachman, John. Links between *Mucedorus* and *The Tragical History, Admirable Atchievements and Various Events of Guy Earl of Warwick*. *See* **4713**.

5408. Pfister, Manfred. 'An argument of laughter': cultures of laughter and the theater in early modern England. *In* (pp. 42–67) **5346**.

5409. —— *'What's Hecuba to him?'*: vom Nutzen und Nachteil mythischer Geschichten für Shakespeare. SJ (142) 2006, 13–33.

5410. Pinciss, Gerald M. Why Shakespeare? An introduction to the playwright's art. London; New York: Continuum, 2005. pp. 192.

5411. Pogue, Kate Emery. Shakespeare's friends. Westport, CT; London: Praeger, 2006. pp. xvii, 183.

5412. Poole, Adrian. Shakespeare and the Victorians. (Bibl. 2005, 6055.) Rev. by Cary M. Mazer in NCT (32:2) 2005, 73–6; by Beátrice Laurent in EREA (4:1) 2006.

5413. Preiss, Richard. Natural authorship. *See* **4717**.

5414. Rackin, Phyllis. Shakespeare and women. (Bibl. 2005, 6059.) Rev. by Rebecca Laroche in ShQ (57:2) 2006, 220–2.

5415. Rampton, David. Plexed artistry: the formal case for Mailer's *Harlot's Ghost*. *See* **17412**.

5416. Ravassat, Mireille. 'The pangs of dispriz'd love' – on some discourses of amorous melancholy in Shakespeare. EREA (4:1) 2006, 51–8.

5417. Ray, Sid. Holy estates: marriage and monarchy in Shakespeare and his contemporaries. (Bibl. 2005, 6061.) Rev. by Amy L. Smith in CompDr (39:1) 2005, 100–3.

5418. Rebholz, Ronald A. Thirty-seven plays by Shakespeare: a sense of the corpus. Lewiston, NY; Lampeter: Mellen Press, 2006. pp. v, 292.

5419. Reid, Robert Lanier. The problem of self-love in Shakespeare's tragedies and in Renaissance and Reformation theology. *In* (pp. 35–56) **5693**.

5420. Reynolds, Bryan (ed.). Transversal enterprises in the drama of Shakespeare and his contemporaries: fugitive explorations. *See* **4718**.

5421. —— West, William N. (eds). Rematerializing Shakespeare: authority and representation on the early modern English stage. Basingstoke; New York: Palgrave Macmillan, 2005. pp. xii, 230.

5422. Rhodes, Neil. Shakespeare and the origins of English. (Bibl. 2005, 6064.) Rev. by Ralph Berry in ContRev (286:1671) 2005, 245–6; by John Lee in MLR (101:3) 2006, 822–4; by Russ McDonald in ShQ (57:3) 2006, 351–3.

5423. Rhu, Lawrence F. Stanley Cavell's American Dream: Shakespeare, philosophy, and Hollywood movies. New York: Fordham UP, 2006. pp. xviii, 248. Rev. by Scott L. Newstok in ShB (24:4) 2006, 57–63.

5424. Romack, Katherine; Fitzmaurice, James (eds). Cavendish and Shakespeare: interconnections. *See* **7092**.

5425. Rosenbaum, Ron. The Shakespeare wars: clashing scholars, public fiascoes, palace coups. New York: Random House, 2006. pp. xvii, 601. Rev. by Walter Kirn in NYTB, 8 Oct. 2006, 22; by Michael Dirda in BkW, 24 Sept. 2006, 15; by Larry Weiss in SNL (56:2) 2006, 47–8, 58, 64.

5426. Rutelli, Romana. Omosessualità in Shakespeare, dal *Romeo and Juliet* (e *Shakespeare in Love*) al *Merchant of Venice*. SCrit (21:2) 2006, 191–206.

5427. Santana, Richard W. Language and the decline of magic: epistemological shifts in English literature from medieval to Modernist. *See* **3926**.

5428. Schurink, Fred. An unnoticed early reference to Shakespeare. NQ (53:1) 2006, 72–5.

5429. Seuntjens, Wolter. Vapours and fumes, damps and qualms: windy passions in the early modern age (1600–1800). EngS (87:1) 2006, 35–52.

5430. Shapiro, James. 1599: a year in the life of William Shakespeare. (Bibl. 2005, 6076.) Rev. by Georgia Brown in UC (25) 2005, 127–9; by John D. Cox in Cithara (45:2) 2006, 54–5.

5431. Shell, Alison. Why didn't Shakespeare write religious verse? *In* (pp. 85–112) **5353**.

5432. Sherbo, Arthur. Some more prices of the Second, Third, and Fourth Shakespeare Folios. NQ (53:1) 2006, 78–9.

5433. Sinfield, Alan. From Bradley to cultural materialism. SStud (34) 2006, 25–34.

5434. —— Shakespeare, authority, sexuality: unfinished business in cultural materialism. London; New York: Routledge, 2006. pp. 225. (Accents on Shakespeare.)

5435. Smith, Peter J. Rome's disgrace: the politics of rape in Shakespeare's *Lucrece*. *See* **6059**.

5436. Sukhanova, Ekaterina. Voicing the distant: Shakespeare and Russian Modernist poetry. (Bibl. 2005, 6089.) Rev. by Péter Dávidházi in TransLit (15:1) 2006, 122–9.

5437. Sullivan, Garrett A., Jr. Memory and forgetting in English Renaissance drama: Shakespeare, Marlowe, Webster. Cambridge; New York: CUP, 2005. pp. vii, 184. Rev. by Kevin De Ornellas in TLS, 13 Oct. 2006, 35; by Zackariah C. Long in ShQ (57:3) 2006, 353–6; by Scott A. Hollifield in MSAN (26:2) 2006, 6–7; by Andrew Stott in RQ (59:3) 2006, 972–4; by Lina Perkins Wilder in SNL (56:2) 2006, 71.

5438. Symington, Rodney. The Nazi appropriation of Shakespeare: cultural politics in the Third Reich. Lewiston, NY; Lampeter: Mellen Press, 2005. pp. ix, 310.

5439. Takada, Yasunari. A Shakespearean distance: Europe, modernity and traditional values. SStudT (43) 2005, 1–36.

5440. Taylor, Michael. The year's contributions to Shakespeare studies: 1, Critical studies. ShS (59) 2006, 347–68.

5441. Teague, Frances. Shakespeare and the American popular stage. Cambridge; New York: CUP, 2006. pp. ix, 221.

5442. Thompson, Ann; Thompson, John O. Meaning, 'seeing', printing. *In* (pp. 59–86) **661**.

5443. Velz, John W. Shakespeare and the Geneva Bible: the circumstances. *In* (pp. 113–18) **5353**.

5444. Vickers, Brian. The face of the Bard? TLS, 18 & 25 Aug. 2006, 16–17.

5445. von Ledebur, Ruth Freifrau. 'The country that gave birth to you a second time': an essay about the political history of the German Shakespeare Society 1918–1945. *In* (pp. 255–71) **5346**.

5446. Waage, Frederick O. Shakespeare unearth'd. ISLE (12:2) 2005, 139–64.

5447. Wall, Wendy. Shakespearean jell-o: mortality and malleability in the kitchen. *See* **1575**.

5448. Wang, Zhongxiang. Constructing an ethical utopia: the aesthetic significance of Shakespeare's plays. FLS (118) 2006, 18–31. (In Chinese.)

5449. Weil, Judith. Service and dependency in Shakespeare's plays. (Bibl. 2005, 6107.) Rev. by Melissa Walter in RQ (59:3) 2006, 979–80.

5450. Wells, Robin Headlam. Shakespeare's Humanism. Cambridge; New York: CUP, 2005. pp. x, 278. Rev. by Jeffrey Kahan in Cithara (46:1) 2006, 53–5.

5451. Wells, Stanley. Looking for sex in Shakespeare. (Bibl. 2005, 6109.) Rev. by Richard Danson Brown in MLR (101:2) 2006, 516–18; by Tibor Fabiny in SixCJ (37:2) 2006, 490–1; by Louis Crompton in JHo (51:3) 2006, 267–70.

5452. —— Shakespeare and Co.: Christopher Marlowe, Thomas Dekker, Ben Jonson, Thomas Middleton, John Fletcher and the other players in his story. London; New York: Allen Lane, 2006. pp. xv, 285. Rev. by Peter Wentworth in TLS, 3 Nov. 2006, 8.

5453. Wharton, Robin. 'There are no mothers-in-law in ballet': 'doing' Shakespeare in dance. ShB (23:3) 2005, 7–22.

5454. White, R. S. Where is Shakespeare's autobiography? *In* (pp. 174–88) **4792**.

5455. Wilcox, Helen. 'Who is it that can tell me who I am?': Shakespeare and the representation of individual identity. AUMLA (106) 2006, 61–70.

5456. Williams, George Walton. Shakespeare's twins: choric juxtaposition. RenP (2005) 43–50.

5457. Williams, Robin P. Sweet swan of Avon: did a woman write Shakespeare? Berkeley, CA: Wilton Circle Press, 2006. pp. xxviii, 291. Rev. by Gary Waller in SidJ (24:1) 2006, 81–3.

5458. Wilson, Emily R. Mocked with death: tragic overliving from Socrates to Milton. Baltimore, MD; London: Johns Hopkins UP, 2004. pp. 289. Rev. by

Raphael Lyne in TLS, 2 Sept. 2005, 20; by William E. Engel in ShY (15) 2005, 453–8; by Jeremy Tambling in MLR (100:4) 2005, 1074–5; by Margaret J. Arnold in RQ (58:4) 2005, 1445–6; by Deborah Steiner in LRB (28:4) 2006, 29–30.

5459. Wilson, Richard. Secret Shakespeare: studies in theatre, religion and resistance. (Bibl. 2004, 6307.) Rev. by Thomas Healy in SJ (142) 2006, 227–33; by R. V. Young in RQ (59:2) 2006, 642–3.

5460. Xiao, Sixin. The meaning of human existence: different views in Shakespeare's dramas and Christianity. FLS (117) 2006, 143–51. (In Chinese.)

5461. Zhang, Jing. Shakespeare and world literature: the historical significance and modern interpretation – an interview with Professor Wang Zhongxiang. FLS (120) 2006, 1–9. (In Chinese.)

5462. Zimmerman, Susan. The early modern corpse in Shakespeare's theatre. (Bibl. 2005, 6124.) Rev. by Sam Thompson in TLS, 10 Mar. 2006, 28; by Elizabeth D. Harvey in RQ (59:2) 2006, 637–8.

Productions

5463. Abbate, Alessandro. 'There is no such thing as …' a forest: criticism of Thatcherite Britain in Christine Edzard's *As You Like It*. *See* **5652**.

5464. Aebischer, Pascale. Shakespeare, sex, and violence: negotiating masculinities in Branagh's *Henry V* and Taymor's *Titus*. *In* (pp. 112–32) **5531**.

5465. —— Shakespeare's violated bodies: stage and screen performance. (Bibl. 2005, 6126.) Rev. by Michelle Parkinson in SixCJ (36:4) 2005, 1143–4; by Emma French in TN (59:2) 2005, 115; by Anja Müller-Wood in SJ (142) 2006, 259–61.

5466. Albanese, Denise. School for scandal? New-media *Hamlet*, Olivier and camp connoisseurship. *See* **5690**.

5467. Altschuler, Eric Lewin; Jansen, William. The entrances and exits of *Henry VI, Part 2*. *See* **5834**.

5468. Anderegg, Michael. Cinematic Shakespeare. (Bibl. 2005, 6128.) Rev. by Annalisa Castaldo in ShB (23:3) 2005, 81–3.

5469. —— Orson Welles and after: *Julius Caesar* and twentieth-century totalitarianism. *In* (pp. 295–305) **5805**.

5470. Arden, Annabel; Hendricks, Margo; Hunter, Lynette. Gesture, language and the body. *In* (pp. 61–88) **5543**.

5471. Armstrong, Alan. Arthur's fall. *See* **5847**.

5472. Aune, M. G. The uses of *Richard III*: from Robert Cecil to Richard Nixon. *See* **5896**.

5473. Bartoshevitch, Alexey. The Forest of Arden in Stalin's Russia: Shakespeare's comedies in the Soviet theatre of the thirties. *In* (pp. 104–13) **5376**.

5474. Bates, Laura Raidonis. Shakespeare and the working man: Communist applications during nationalist periods in Latvia. *In* (pp. 38–55) **5376**.

5475. Belsey, Catherine. Shakespeare's little boys: theatrical apprenticeship and the construction of childhood. *In* (pp. 53–72) **5421**.

5476. Bennett, Susan. Shakespeare on vacation. *In* (pp. 494–508) **5537**.

5477. Bevington, David; Welsh, Anne Marie; Greenwald, Michael L. Shakespeare: script, stage, screen. London; New York: Pearson Longman, 2006. pp. vii, 931.

5478. Bogart, Anne; Escolme, Bridget; Worthen, W. B. Making things difficult. *In* (pp. 138–60) **5543**.

5479. Bosman, Anston. History between theaters. *In* (pp. 191–207) **5334**.

5480. Bradby, David; Doran, Greg; Jackson, Russell. Gestures that speak: spectators who listen. *In* (pp. 89–107) **5543**.

5481. Braunmuller, A. R. On not looking back: sight and sound and text. *In* (pp. 135–51) **5334**.

5482. Brown, John Russell. *Hamlet. See* **5697**.

5483. —— Shakespeare dancing: a theatrical study of the plays. (Bibl. 2005, 6138.) Rev. by Terence Zeeman in TT (16:1) 2006, 107–9; by Stephen J. Phillips in NQ (53:1) 2006, 112–14.

5484. Brusberg-Kiermeier, Stefani; Helbig, Jörg (eds). Shakespeare in the media: from the Globe Theatre to the World Wide Web. (Bibl. 2004, 6329.) Rev. by Eckart Voigts-Virchow in SJ (142) 2006, 268–9.

5485. Bulman, James C. Queering the audience: all-male casts in recent Shakespeare performances. *In* (pp. 564–87) **5537**.

5486. Burnett, Mark Thornton. Figuring the global/historical in filmic Shakespeare tragedy. *In* (pp. 133–54) **5531**.

5487. Burt, Richard. SShockspeare: (Nazi) Shakespeare goes Heil-lywood. *In* (pp. 437–56) **5537**.

5488. Cannon, Walter W. From willow cabin to dark house: *Twelfth Night* and the poetics of indoor spaces. *In* (pp. 162–73) **5577**.

5489. Carroll, Tim; Smith, Emma; White, Martin. Purposeful playing? Purposeful criticism? *In* (pp. 38–60) **5543**.

5490. Cartwright, Kent. Staging the 'lock-out' scene in the Folio *Comedy of Errors. See* **5667**.

5491. Conkie, Rob. The Globe Theatre project: Shakespeare and authenticity. Lewiston, NY; Lampeter: Mellen Press, 2006. pp. ii, 283.

5492. Copsey, Doug. With our good Will: 30 years of Shakespeare in Idaho. Caldwell, ID: Caxton Press, 2006. pp. 249.

5493. Cordner, Michael. 'Are we being theatrical yet?': actors, editors, and the possibilities of dialogue. *In* (pp. 399–414) **5537**.

5494. Crystal, David. Pronouncing Shakespeare: the Globe experiment. (Bibl. 2005, 6152.) Rev. by Andrew Hadfield in Eng (55:211) 2006, 93–101; by Robert Shaughnessy in TRI (31:1) 2006, 106–8.

5495. Dawson, Anthony B. The imaginary text; or, the curse of the Folio. *In* (pp. 141–61) **5537**.

5496. de Grazia, Margreta. Hamlet's smile. *In* (pp. 231–42) **5334**.

5497. Delgado, Maria M. Journeys of cultural transference: Calixto Bieito's multilingual Shakespeares. MLR (101:1) 2006, 106–50.

5498. Dessen, Alan C. The director as Shakespeare editor. ShS (59) 2006, 182–92.

5499. —— Rescripting Shakespeare (and others) in 2005. *See* **4665**.

5500. DiPietro, Cary. Shakespeare and Modernism. Cambridge; New York: CUP, 2006. pp. viii, 234. Rev. by Marie-Dominique Garnier in EA (59:4) 2006, 475–7; by Douglas Bruster in RES (57:232) 2006, 824–6.

5501. Dobson, Michael. Moving the audience: Shakespeare, the mob, and the promenade. *See* **5927**.

5502. —— Shakespeare performances in England, 2005. ShS (59) 2006, 298–337.

5503. Donaldson, Peter S. Hamlet among the pixelvisionaries: video art, authenticity, and 'wisdom' in Almereyda's *Hamlet*. *In* (pp. 216–37) **5531**.

5504. Dugas, Don-John. Marketing the Bard: Shakespeare in performance and print, 1660–1740. Columbia; London: Missouri UP, 2006. pp. xiv, 271.

5505. Escolme, Bridget. Talking to the audience: Shakespeare, performance, self. (Bibl. 2005, 6158.) Rev. by Pascale Aebischer in ShQ (57:2) 2006, 232–4; by Robert Shaughnessy in TRI (31:1) 2006, 106–8.

5506. Ewert, Kevin. *Henry V*. *See* **5822**.

5507. Ford, John R. Changeable taffeta: re-dressing the bears in *Twelfth Night*. *In* (pp. 174–91) **5577**.

5508. —— 'Methinks you are glass': looking for *The Comedy of Errors* in performance. *See* **5668**.

5509. Freeman, Jane. Unexpected rainfall: working in the wings on Robert Lepage's *Macbeth*. *In* (pp. 285–306) **12336**.

5510. French, Emma. Selling Shakespeare to Hollywood: the marketing of filmed Shakespeare adaptations from 1989 into the new millennium. Hatfield: UP of Hertfordshire, 2006. pp. x, 223. Rev. by Helen Hull in ShB (24:3) 2006, 67–70.

5511. Gaines, Barry. The single performance of *Hamlet* that changed theatre history. *In* (pp. 206–15) **5577**.

5512. Galery, Maria Clara Versiani. Caliban/cannibal/carnival: Cuban articulations of Shakespeare's *The Tempest*. *In* (pp. 307–27) **5376**.

5513. Gilbert, Miriam. Performance as deflection. *In* (pp. 319–34) **5537**.

5514. Gillies, John. Stanislavski, *Othello*, and the motives of eloquence. *In* (pp. 267–84) **5537**.

5515. Goltz, Thomas. Assassinating Shakespeare: the true confessions of a bard in the bush. London; San Francisco, CA: Saqi, 2006. pp. 253, (plates) 8. Rev. by Tom Chesshyre in TLS, 14 July 2006, 30; by Alan Riding in NYTB, 3 Dec. 2006, 73.

5516. Gossett, Suzanne. 'Tell thy story': Mary Zimmerman's *Pericles*. *See* **6043**.

5517. Greenwald, Michael L. Multicultural and regendered Romans: *Julius Caesar* in North America, 1969–2000. *In* (pp. 319–32) **5805**.

5518. Gregor, Keith. *Julius Caesar* and the Spanish transition. *In* (pp. 205–16) **5308**.

5519. Guneratne, Anthony R. 'Thou dost usurp authority': Beerbohm Tree, Reinhardt, Olivier, Welles, and the politics of adapting Shakespeare. *In* (pp. 31–53) **5531**.

5520. Guntner, Lawrence. In search of a Socialist Shakespeare: *Hamlet* on East German stages. *In* (pp. 177–204) **5376**.

5521. Gurr, Andrew. London's Blackfriars playhouse and the Chamberlain's Men. *In* (pp. 17–30) **5577**.

5522. —— The Shakespeare Company, 1594–1642. (Bibl. 2005, 6170.) Rev. by Yael Margalit in CEl (68) 2005, 91–2; by Günter Walch in SJ (142) 2006, 236–40; by Elizabeth Klett in TJ (58:3) 2006, 526–7; by Gabriel Egan in SixCJ (37:1) 2006, 155–7; by Derek Peat in Parergon (23:2) 2006, 139–41.

5523. Habicht, Werner. Shakespeare and the Berlin Wall. *In* (pp. 157–76) **5376**.

5524. Hamburger, Maik. Shakespeare the politicizer: two notable stagings in East Germany. *In* (pp. 205–9) **5376**.

5525. Hampton-Reeves, Stuart. Shakespeare, *Henry VI* and the Festival of Britain. *In* (pp. 285–96) **5537**.

5526. Hatchuel, Sarah. Shakespeare: from stage to screen. (Bibl. 2005, 6174.) Rev. by John L. Simons in ShB (23:1) 2005, 213–15.

5527. —— Vienne-Guerrin, Nathalie (eds). Shakespeare on screen: *A Midsummer Night's Dream*: proceedings of the conference organized at the Université de Rouen, 5–6 December 2003 by the ERAC, Équipe de Recherche sur les Aires Culturelles, CETAS, Centre d'Études Transdisciplinaires Anglo-saxonnes. *See* **5995**.

5528. —— —— Shakespeare on screen: *Richard III*: proceedings of the conference organised at the Université de Rouen, 4–5 March 2005. *See* **5900**.

5529. Henderson, Diana E. Learning from Campbell Scott's *Hamlet*. *In* (pp. 77–95) **5531**.

5530. —— Performing history: *Henry IV*, money, and the fashion of the times. *In* (pp. 376–96) **5537**.

5531. —— (ed.). A concise companion to Shakespeare on screen. Afterword by Kathleen McLuskie. Oxford; Malden, MA: Blackwell for the *Sociological Review*, 2006. pp. xxiv, 264. (Blackwell concise companions to literature and culture.) Rev. by Brian Willis in CEl (70) 2006, 77–8; by Jorge Luis Bueno Alonso in SEDERI (16) 2006, 179–88.

5532. Hendricks, Margo. Vision of color: spectacle, spectators, and the performance of race. *In* (pp. 511–26) **5537**.

5533. Hilský, Martin. Translations of politics / politics of translation: Czech experience. *In* (pp. 215–27) **5376**.

5534. Hobgood, Allison P. *Twelfth Night*'s 'notorious abuse' of Malvolio: shame, humorality, and early modern spectatorship. *See* **6178**.

5535. Hodgdon, Barbara. Inoculating the old stock: Shakespearean chorographies. RenD (ns 34) 2005, 3–29.

5536. —— Spectacular bodies: acting + cinema + Shakespeare. *In* (pp. 96–111) **5531**.

5537. —— Worthen, W. B. (eds). A companion to Shakespeare and performance. Oxford; Malden, MA: Blackwell, 2005. pp. xvi, 688. (Blackwell companions to literature and culture.) Rev. by Jeremy Lopez in ShQ (57:3) 2006, 366–71.

5538. Holland, Peter. Shakespeare's two bodies. *In* (pp. 36–56) **5537**.

5539. Holmes, Jonathan. Merely players? Actors' accounts of performing Shakespeare. (Bibl. 2005, 6178.) Rev. by Cynthia Lewis in ShB (23:2) 2005, 115–18; by Günter Walch in SJ (142) 2006, 236–40.

5540. Homan, Sidney. Directing Shakespeare: a scholar onstage. (Bibl. 2004, 6372.) Rev. by Julia Matthews in SixCJ (36:4) 2005, 1183–4.

5541. Hoskins, Jim. The dances of Shakespeare. London; New York: Routledge, 2005. pp. xxv, 135.

5542. Huang, Alexander. Shakespeare, performance, and autobiographical interventions. *See* **5863**.

5543. Hunter, Lynette; Lichtenfels, Peter (eds). Shakespeare, language and the stage: The Fifth Wall: approaches to Shakespeare from criticism, performance and theatre studies. London: Arden Shakespeare, 2005. pp. xviii, 190. (Shakespeare and language.) Rev. by Ric Knowles in ShQ (57:2) 2006, 235–7.

5544. Hytner, Nicholas; Reinelt, Janelle; Thompson, Ann. Retrospective: Janelle Reinelt. Final session (final thoughts) on heightened language: impasse or interchange? *In* (pp. 161–80) **5543**.

5545. Ichikawa, Mariko. Were the doors open or closed? The use of stage doors in the Shakespearean theatre. TN (60:1) 2006, 5–29.

5546. Jenstad, Janelle; Lichtenfels, Peter; Magnusson, Lynne. Text and voice. *In* (pp. 10–37) **5543**.

5547. Jones, Nicholas. A bogus hero: Welles's *Othello* and the construction of race. *See* **6028**.

5548. Jowett, John. From print to performance: looking at the masque in *Timon of Athens*. *In* (pp. 73–91) **5334**.

5549. Kathman, David. The burial of Thomas Pope. NQ (53:1) 2006, 79–80.

5550. Kelly, Veronica. Australia's Lily Brayton: performer and theatre artist. NCT (33:1) 2006, 39–59.

5551. Kidnie, Margaret Jane. *The Taming of the Shrew*. *See* **6110**.

5552. Klett, Elizabeth. Many bodies, many voices: performing androgyny in Fiona Shaw and Deborah Warner's *Richard II*. *See* **5890**.

5553. —— 'O, how this mother swells up toward my heart': performing mother and father in Helena Kaut-Howson's cross-gender *King Lear*. *See* **5864**.

5554. Knowles, Ric. Encoding/decoding Shakespeare: *Richard III* at the 2002 Stratford Festival. *In* (pp. 297–318) **5537**.

5555. Knutson, Roslyn. What if there wasn't a 'Blackfriars repertory'? *In* (pp. 54–60) **5577**.

5556. Knutson, Roslyn L. Everything's back in play: the impact of REED research on Elizabethan theatre history. *In* (pp. 116–28) **3904**.

5557. Ko, Yu Jin. 'The Mousetrap' and remembrance in Michael Almereyda's *Hamlet*. *See* **5737**.

5558. Kossak, Saskia. 'Frame my face to all occasions': Shakespeare's *Richard III* on screen. *See* **5903**.

5559. Kujawińska Courtney, Krystyna. Krystyna Skuszanka's Shakespeare of political allusions and metaphors in Communist Poland. *In* (pp. 228–45) **5376**.

5560. Lake, James H. Effects of primacy and recency upon audience response to two film versions of *Othello*. *See* **6029**.

5561. Lanier, Douglas. Shakespeare on the record. *In* (pp. 415–36) **5537**.

5562. Lehmann, Courtney. Dancing in a (cyber) net: 'Renaissance women', systems theory, and the war of the cinemas. RenD (ns 34) 2005, 121–61.

5563. —— A thousand Shakespeares: from cinematic saga to feminist geography; or, The escape from Iceland. *In* (pp. 588–609) **5537**.

5564. Loomba, Ania. Shakespeare and the possibilities of postcolonial performance. *In* (pp. 121–37) **5537**.

5565. Lopez, Jeremy. Census of Renaissance drama performance reviews in *Shakespeare Quarterly* and *Shakespeare Survey*, 1948–2005. RORD (45) 2006, 41–104.

5566. McDonald, Russ. Look to the lady: Sarah Siddons, Ellen Terry, and Judi Dench on the Shakespearean stage. (Bibl. 2005, 6195.) Rev. by Barbara Mackey in TJ (58:4) 2006, 722–4.

5567. McLuskie, Kathleen. Shakespeare goes slumming: Harlem '37 and Birmingham '97. *In* (pp. 249–66) **5537**.

5568. McMullan, Gordon. 'The technique of it is mature': inventing the late plays in print and in performance. *In* (pp. 243–60) **5334**.

5569. McNamee, Eugene. Once more unto the breach: Branagh's *Henry V*, Blair's war and the UK constitution. *In* (pp. 17–29) **12636**.

5570. Makaryk, Irena R. Performance and ideology: Shakespeare in 1920s Ukraine. *In* (pp. 15–37) **5376**.

5571. —— Wartime *Hamlet*. *In* (pp. 119–35) **5376**.

5572. Márkus, Zoltán. War, lechery, and goulash Communism: *Troilus and Cressida* in Socialist Hungary. *In* (pp. 246–69) **5376**.

5573. Massai, Sonia (ed.). World-wide Shakespeares: local appropriations in film and performance. London; New York: Routledge, 2005. pp. xii, 199.

5574. Matheson, Tom. Royal *Caesar*. *In* (pp. 307–18) **5805**.

5575. Mazer, Cary M. Not not Shakespeare: directorial adaptation, authorship, and ownership. *See* **6067**.

5576. Menzer, Paul. The tragedians of the city? Q1 *Hamlet* and the settlements of the 1590s. *See* **5746**.

5577. —— (ed.). Inside Shakespeare: essays on the Blackfriars stage. Selinsgrove, PA: Susquehanna UP; London: Assoc. UPs, 2006. pp. 244. (Apple–Zimmerman series in early modern culture.)

5578. Momose, Isumi. Japanese studies in Shakespeare: interpreting English drama through the Noh and *theatrum mundi*. Lewiston, NY; Lampeter: Mellen Press, 2006. pp. ix, 173.

5579. Osborne, Laurie E. Shakespearean screen/play. *In* (pp. 163–78) **5537**.

5580. Ostrovsky, Arkady. Shakespeare as founding father of Socialist realism: the Soviet affair with Shakespeare. *In* (pp. 56–83) **5376**.

5581. Palfrey, Simon; Stern, Tiffany. What does the cued part cue? Parts and cues in *Romeo and Juliet*. *In* (pp. 179–96) **5537**.

5582. Pemble, John. Shakespeare goes to Paris: how the Bard conquered France. (Bibl. 2005, 6210.) Rev. by Richard Schoch in ShQ (57:2) 2006, 237–9.

5583. Phelan, Peggy. Reconstructing love: *King Lear* and theatre architecture. *In* (pp. 13–35) **5537**.

5584. Preiss, Richard. Robert Armin do the Police in different voices. *In* (pp. 208–27) **5334**.

5585. Prescott, Paul. Inheriting the Globe: the reception of Shakespearean space and audience in contemporary reviewing. *In* (pp. 359–75) **5537**.

5586. —— *Richard III. See* **5905**.

5587. Richman, David. Smelling their way to Dover: a blind director's take on blind Gloucester. *In* (pp. 156–61) **5577**.

5588. Richmond, Michael L. Kenneth Branagh's *Henry V* (1989). *In* (pp. 501–14) **12712**.

5589. Riga, Frank P. 'Where is that worthless dreamer?': Bottom's fantastic redemption in Hoffman's *A Midsummer Night's Dream*. *See* **5999**.

5590. Rigney, James. Stage worlds of *Julius Caesar*: theatrical features and their history. *In* (pp. 287–93) **5805**.

5591. Rutter, Carol Chillington. Maverick Shakespeare. *In* (pp. 335–58) **5537**.

5592. Sale, Carolyn. Eating air, feeling smells: *Hamlet*'s theory of performance. *See* **5756**.

5593. Sanders, Eve Rachele. The body of the actor in *Coriolanus*. *See* **5680**.

5594. Schafer, Elizabeth. Performance editions, editing and editors. *See* **5220**.

5595. —— Reconciliation Shakespeare? Aboriginal presence in Australian Shakespeare production. *In* (pp. 63–78) **12360**.

5596. Schoch, Richard W. Reforming Shakespeare. RenD (ns 34) 2005, 105–19.

5597. —— Shakespeare the Victorian. *In* (pp. 232–48) **5537**.

5598. Senelick, Laurence. A five-year plan for *The Taming of the Shrew*. *In* (pp. 84–103) **5376**.

5599. —— 'Thus conscience doth make cowards of us all': new documentation on the Okhlopkov *Hamlet*. *In* (pp. 136–56) **5376**.

5600. Shand, G. B. Guying the guys and girling the *Shrew*: (post)feminist fun and Shakespeare's Globe. *In* (pp. 550–63) **5537**.

5601. Shapiro, Michael. *The Merchant of Venice* after the Holocaust; or, Shakespearean romantic comedy meets Auschwitz. *See* **5979**.

5602. Shaughnessy, Robert. On location. *In* (pp. 79–100) **5537**.

5603. —— Stage, screen, and nation: *Hamlet* and the space of history. *In* (pp. 55–76) **5531**.

5604. Shim, Jung-Soon. Translating emotions for the local audience. *See* **6072**.

5605. Sillars, Stuart. Painting Shakespeare: the artist as critic, 1720–1820. Cambridge; New York: CUP, 2006. pp. xviii, 337, (plates) 16. Rev. by Jay L. Halio in SNL (56:2) 2006, 53.

5606. Smallwood, Robert (ed.). Players of Shakespeare: 6, Essays in the performance of Shakespeare's history plays. (Bibl. 2004, 6425.) Rev. by Günter Walch in SJ (142) 2006, 236–40; by Charles Whitworth in CEl (70) 2006, 78–80.

5607. Smith, Bruce R. Ragging *Twelfth Night*: 1602, 1996, 2002–3. *In* (pp. 57–78) **5537**.

5608. Smith, Emma. The year's contributions to Shakespeare studies: 2, Shakespeare in performance. ShS (59) 2006, 368–75.

5609. Smith-Howard, Alycia. Studio Shakespeare: the Royal Shakespeare Company at the Other Place. Aldershot; Burlington, VT: Ashgate, 2006. pp. 210.

5610. Staines, Christopher. Third time lucky: playing all the suitors in *The Merchant of Venice*. *See* **5980**.

5611. Stern, Tiffany. Taking part: actors and audience on the stage at Blackfriars. *In* (pp. 35–53) **5577**.

5612. Sturgess, Kim C. Shakespeare and the American nation. (Bibl. 2005, 6232.) Rev. by Richard Burt in ShQ (57:1) 2006, 102–5; by Thomas Cartelli in CLIO (35:2) 2006, 275–80; by Donald J. Millus in SixCJ (37:1) 2006, 166–7; by Katherine West Scheil in TheatreS (47:1) 2006, 131–3; by Keith Mears in JAStud (40:1) 2006, 201–2.

5613. Thompson, Ayanna (ed.). Colorblind Shakespeare: new perspectives on race and performance. London; New York: Routledge, 2006. pp. xvii, 262.

5614. Tiner, Elza C. Professional players in Stratford-on-Avon, 1587–1602. *In* (pp. 86–92) **5577**.

5615. Tompkins, Joanne. Conflicting fields of vision: performing self and Other in two intercultural Shakespeare productions. *In* (pp. 610–24) **5537**.

5616. Tulloch, John. Shakespeare and Chekhov in production and reception: theatrical events and their audiences. (Bibl. 2005, 6237.) Rev. by Stuart Young in ModDr (49:1) 2006, 127–9; by Gretchen E. Minton in CompDr (40:3) 2006, 383–6.

5617. Walker, Elsie. Getting back to Shakespeare: whose film is it anyway? *In* (pp. 8–30) **5531**.

5618. Wall, Wendy. De-generation: editions, offspring, and *Romeo and Juliet*. *In* (pp. 152–70) **5334**.

5619. —— Editors in love? Performing desire in *Romeo and Juliet*. *In* (pp. 197–211) **5537**.

5620. Wang, Shuhua. From Maoism to (post)modernism: *Hamlet* in Communist China. *In* (pp. 283–302) **5376**.

5621. Weimann, Robert. Ideology and performance in East German versions of Shakespeare. *In* (pp. 328–48) **5376**.

5622. Wells, Stanley. Boys should be girls. FLS (117) 2006, 10–15.

5623. Werstine, Paul. Margins to the centre: REED and Shakespeare. *In* (pp. 101–15) **3904**.

5624. Williams, William Proctor. Hamlet's pockets: problems with stage directions. *In* (pp. 192–9) **5577**.

5625. Wood, Juliette. Filming fairies: popular film, audience response and meaning in contemporary fairy lore. *See* **6002**.

5626. Worthen, W. B. Prefixing the author: print, plays, and performance. *In* (pp. 212–30) **5537**.

5627. Yong, Li Lan. Shakespeare and the fiction of the intercultural. *In* (pp. 527–49) **5537**.

5628. Young, Alan R. Henry Irving's Hamlet: some visual sources. *See* **5773**.

5629. Zander, Horst (ed.). *Julius Caesar*: new critical essays. *See* **5805**.

5630. Zhang, Xiao Yang. The Chinese vision of Shakespeare (from 1950 to 1990): Marxism and Socialism. *In* (pp. 270–82) **5376**.

Separate Works

All's Well That Ends Well

5631. Clark, Ira. The trappings of *All's Well That Ends Well*. Style (39:3) 2005, 277–98.

5632. Harris, Jonathan Gil. All swell that end swell: dropsy, phantom pregnancy, and the sound of deconception in *All's Well That Ends Well*. RenD (ns 35) 2006, 169–89.

5633. Howard, Jean E. Female agency in *All's Well That Ends Well*. AUMLA (106) 2006, 43–60.

5634. Levin, Richard A. Did Helena have a Renaissance? EngS (87:1) 2006, 23–34.

5635. Monrós Gaspar, Laura. '*Boscovos tromuldo boscovos*': a case study in the translation of William Shakespeare's *All's Well That Ends Well*. SEDERI (16) 2006, 53–70.

5636. Mowat, Barbara A.; Werstine, Paul (eds). All's well that ends well. New York: Washington Square Press, 2006. pp. liv, 282. (New Folger Library Shakespeare.)

5637. Mukherji, Subha. Jonson's *The New Inn* and a revisiting of the 'amorous jurisdiction'. *See* **6895**.

Antony and Cleopatra

5638. Bosman, Anston. 'Best play with Mardian': eunuch and blackamoor as imperial culturegram. SStud (34) 2006, 123–57.

5639. Dañobeitia Fernández, María Luisa. Cleopatra's role-taking: a study of *Antony and Cleopatra*. *In* (pp. 171–95) **5308**.

5640. Davis, Lloyd; Smith, Peter J.; Walker, Greg. From revelation to commodity: performing messengers, language and news from the York Cycle to Ben Jonson. *See* **3956**.

5641. Deats, Sara Munson (ed.). *Antony and Cleopatra*: new critical essays. London; New York: Routledge, 2005. pp. x, 341. (Shakespeare criticism, 30.) Rev. by Helen Smith in CamQ (35:1) 2006, 89–94.

5642. Escolme, Bridget. *Antony and Cleopatra*. Basingstoke; New York: Palgrave Macmillan, 2006. pp. ix, 180. (Shakespeare handbooks.)

5643. Hiscock, Andrew. The uses of this world: thinking space in Shakespeare, Marlowe, Cary, and Jonson. *See* **5727**.

5644. McInnis, David. On Cleopatra's 'strange invisible perfume'. CEl (69) 2006, 51.

5645. Nuyts-Giornal, Josée. 'Who fears a sentence or an old man's saw shall by a painted cloth be kept in awe': genre print and early modern English literature. CEl (70) 2006, 21–31.

5646. Pandit, Lalita; Hogan, Patrick Colm. Introduction: morsels and modules: on embodying cognition in Shakespeare's plays. ColLit (33:1) 2006, 1–13.

5647. Parker, Barbara L. From monarchy to tyranny: *Julius Caesar* among Shakespeare's Roman works. *In* (pp. 111–26) **5805**.

5648. Parker, Patricia. Barbers, infidels, and renegades: *Antony and Cleopatra*. *In* (pp. 65–87) **5401**.

5649. Rosenberg, Marvin. The masks of Antony and Cleopatra. Ed. by Mary Rosenberg. Newark: Delaware UP, 2006. pp. 605. Rev. by Robert A. Logan in CompDr (40:3) 2006, 374–7.

5650. Valentini, Maria. Marc'Antonio e la necessità del tempo. Rome: Bulzoni, 2005. pp. 144. (Piccola biblioteca shakespeariana, 38.)

5651. von Koppenfels, Werner. *Laesa imaginatio*; or, Imagination infected by passion in Shakespeare's love tragedies. *In* (pp. 68–83) **5346**.

As You Like It

5652. Abbate, Alessandro. 'There is no such thing as …' a forest: criticism of Thatcherite Britain in Christine Edzard's *As You Like It*. ShB (23:4) 2005, 33–45.

5653. Detmer-Goebel, Emily. Agency and the threat of cuckoldry in *As You Like It* and *The Merchant of Venice*. KenPR (20) 2005, 14–19.

5654. Dubrow, Heather. Fringe benefits: Rosalind and the purlieux of the forest. NQ (53:1) 2006, 67–9.

5655. Flaumenhaft, Mera J. Is all the world a stage? Marriage and a metaphor in *As You Like It*. *In* (pp. 71–104) **5394**.

5656. Freeman, Franklin. Images of affection (*storge*) in *As You Like It* and *King Lear*. *See* **17184**.

5657. Komem, Aharon. The exit according to Shakespeare. PNRev (32:4) 2006, 10. (Translations of 'All the world's a stage'.)

5658. Lehmann, Courtney. A thousand Shakespeares: from cinematic saga to feminist geography; or, The escape from Iceland. *In* (pp. 588–609) **5537**.

5659. Marshall, Cynthia (ed.). As you like it. (Bibl. 2004, 6476.) Rev. by Katherine West Scheil in ShB (23:1) 2005, 203–7; by Juliet Dusinberre in ShQ (57:3) 2006, 344–6.

5660. Nevitt, Marcus. An early allusion to *As You Like It*? NQ (53:4) 2006, 484–6.

5661. Nichols, David K. The domestic politics of Shakespeare's comedies. *In* (pp. 49–69) **5394**.

5662. Rand, Thomas. Shakespeare's *As You Like It*. Exp (64:3) 2006, 141–4.

5663. Scott, William O. 'A woman's thought runs before her actions': vows as speech acts in *As You Like It*. PhilL (30:2) 2006, 528–39.

5664. Sherbo, Arthur. *Introductorily* in *OED*. *See* **1574**.

5665. Soule, Lesley Wade. *As You Like It*. (Bibl. 2005, 6277.) Rev. by Douglas King in ShB (24:3) 2006, 125–31.

The Comedy of Errors

5666. Callaghan, Dympna. Do characters have souls? SStud (34) 2006, 41–5.

5667. Cartwright, Kent. Staging the 'lock-out' scene in the Folio *Comedy of Errors*. ShB (24:4) 2006, 1–12.

5668. Ford, John R. 'Methinks you are glass': looking for *The Comedy of Errors* in performance. ShB (24:1) 2006, 11–28.

5669. King, Ros (reviser). The comedy of errors. Ed. by T. S. Dorsch. (Bibl. 1990, 3726.) Cambridge; New York: CUP, 2004. pp. xiii, 131. (New Cambridge Shakespeare.) (New ed.: first ed. 1989.) Rev. by Thomas G. Olsen in SixCJ (37:2) 2006, 482–3.

5670. Pandit, Lalita. Emotion, perception and anagnorisis in *The Comedy of Errors*: a cognitive perspective. ColLit (33:1) 2006, 94–126.

Coriolanus

5671. Banerjee, Rita. The common good and the necessity of war: emergent republican ideals in Shakespeare's *Henry V* and *Coriolanus*. *See* **5817**.

5672. Blits, Jan H. Spirit, soul, and city: Shakespeare's *Coriolanus*. Lanham, MD: Lexington, 2006. pp. ix, 243.

5673. Brown, Eric C. Performing insects in Shakespeare's *Coriolanus*. *In* (pp. 29–57) **3203**.

5674. Cavalli, Luciano. *Giulio Cesare*, *Coriolano* e il teatro della Repubblica: una lettura politica di Shakespeare. *See* **5780**.

5675. George, David (ed.). Coriolanus. (Bibl. 2004, 6497.) Rev. by Andrew Hadfield in Eng (55:211) 2006, 93–101.

5676. Goy-Blanquet, Dominique. La solitude de Coriolan. EA (59:4) 2006, 387–400.

5677. Kaufman, Peter Iver. English Calvinism and the crowd: *Coriolanus* and the history of religious reform. CHist (75:2) 2006, 314–42.

5678. Parker, Barbara L. From monarchy to tyranny: *Julius Caesar* among Shakespeare's Roman works. *In* (pp. 111–26) **5805**.

5679. Paterson, Margot. 'But where am I?': *Coriolan* by J. M. R. Lenz. RECTR (20:1/2) 2005, 34–44.

5680. Sanders, Eve Rachele. The body of the actor in *Coriolanus.* ShQ (57:4) 2006, 387–412.

5681. Steible, Mary. *Coriolanus*: a guide to the play. (Bibl. 2005, 6286.) Rev. by Andrew Hadfield in Eng (55:211) 2006, 93–101.

Cymbeline

5682. Alvis, John E. Liberty in Shakespeare's British plays. *In* (pp. 33–47) **5394**.

5683. Buccola, Regina. Fairies, fractious women, and the old faith: fairy lore in early modern British drama and culture. *See* **5992**.

5684. Edgecombe, Rodney Stenning. Shakespeare's *Cymbeline* and Gibbon's *The History of the Decline and Fall of the Roman Empire*. Exp (64:4) 2006, 204–6.

5685. King, Ros. *Cymbeline*: constructions of Britain. Aldershot; Burlington, VT: Ashgate, 2005. pp. xiv, 197. Rev. by Peter Holbrook in TLS, 28 Oct. 2005, 20; by David J. Baker in ShQ (57:2) 2006, 228–9; by Jenna Stook in MedRen (19) 2006, 279–82; by Mark Taylor in RQ (59:1) 2006, 302–4.

5686. Novy, Marianne. Adopted children and constructions of heredity, nurture, and parenthood in Shakespeare's romances. *In* (pp. 55–74) **6264**.

5687. Paul, Gavin. Theatrical and national spaces in *Cymbeline*. Comitatus (37) 2006, 169–92.

5688. Ragg, Edward. Love, wine, desire: Stevens' *Montrachet-le-Jardin* and Shakespeare's *Cymbeline*. *See* **18650**.

Hamlet

5689. Adamson, Sylvia. Deixis and the Renaissance art of self-construction. SEDERI (16) 2006, 5–29.

5690. Albanese, Denise. School for scandal? New-media *Hamlet*, Olivier and camp connoisseurship. RenD (ns 34) 2005, 185–208.

5691. Alpers, Paul. 'The Philoctetes problem' and the poetics of pastoral. Representations (86) 2004, 4–19.

5692. Appelbaum, Robert. Aguecheek's beef, Belch's hiccup, and other gastronomic interjections: literature, culture, and food among the early moderns. *See* **3172**.

5693. Batson, Beatrice (ed.). Shakespeare's Christianity: the Protestant and Catholic poetics of *Julius Caesar, Macbeth*, and *Hamlet*. Waco, TX: Baylor Univ., 2006. pp. xvii, 178.

5694. Botelho, Keith M. 'Look on this picture, and on this': framing Shakespeare in William Wells Brown's *The Escape*. *See* **9248**.

5695. Braunmuller, Albert. A joke and a crux in *Hamlet* Q2. *In* (pp. 200–5) **5577**.

5696. Brooks, Douglas A. 'within the book and volume of my brain': *Hamlet* and the crisis of memory – past and present. FLS (117) 2006, 24–31.

5697. Brown, John Russell. *Hamlet*. Basingstoke; New York: Palgrave Macmillan, 2006. pp. viii, 180. (Shakespeare handbooks.)

5698. Bruster, Douglas. The politics of Shakespeare's prose. *In* (pp. 95–114) **5421**.

5699. Burnett, Mark Thornton. Figuring the global/historical in filmic Shakespeare tragedy. *In* (pp. 133–54) **5531**.

5700. Cantor, Paul A. Shakespeare, *Hamlet*. (Bibl. 2005, 6307.) Rev. by Andrew Hadfield in Eng (55:211) 2006, 93–101.

5701. Carruthers, Virginia Kirby-Smith. Durrell's enigmatic Hamlet: mysteries of image and allusion. *See* **15620**.

5702. Cathcart, Charles. John Marston, *The Malcontent*, and the King's Men. *See* **6923**.

5703. Charnes, Linda. Hamlet's heirs: Shakespeare and the politics of a new millennium. London; New York: Routledge, 2006. pp. xi, 152. (Accents on Shakespeare.)

5704. Cieślak, Magdalena. Łukasz Barczyk's *Hamlet* (2004), a 'pearl of the millennium' for a new millennium audience. ShB (24:1) 2006, 47–55.

5705. Clary, Frank Nicholas. Having it both ways: reading two early acting editions of *Hamlet*. SNL (56:1) 2006, 7–8, 28–30.

5706. Cohen, Joshua. Mermaid-like: the tragedy of Ophelia. SNL (56:2) 2006, 57.

5707. Cook, Amy. Staging nothing: *Hamlet* and cognitive science. SubStance (110) 2006, 83–99.

5708. Curran, John E., Jr. Hamlet, Protestantism, and the mourning of contingency: not to be. Aldershot; Burlington, VT: Ashgate, 2006. pp. xxix, 246.

5709. Davis, William. Now, gods, stand up for bastards: the 1603 'Good Quarto' *Hamlet*. TextC (1:2) 2006, 60–89.

5710. de Grazia, Margreta. Hamlet's smile. *In* (pp. 231–42) **5334**.

5711. Deitchman, Elizabeth A. Shakespeare Stiles style: Shakespeare, Julia Stiles, and American girl culture. *In* (pp. 478–94) **5537**.

5712. Doloff, Steven. Hamlet's progress of dust: a parody of Pythagoras' metempsychosis? NQ (53:1) 2006, 69–70.

5713. Donaldson, Peter S. Hamlet among the pixelvisionaries: video art, authenticity, and 'wisdom' in Almereyda's *Hamlet*. *In* (pp. 216–37) **5531**.

5714. Donoghue, Denis. The not-quite said. *See* **10016**.

5715. Drábek, Pavel. František Nevrla's translation of *Hamlet*. BStE (31) 2005, 119–27.

5716. Duncan-Jones, Katherine. A companion for a king? Shakespeare's status anxiety. *See* **6086**.

5717. Edelman, Charles. Claudius's 'effects' in *Hamlet*. NQ (53:1) 2006, 70–1.

5718. Emig, Rainer. Competing melancholies: (en-)gendering discourses of selfhood in early modern English literature. *See* **7206**.

5719. GAINES, BARRY. The single performance of *Hamlet* that changed theatre history. *In* (pp. 206–15) **5577**.

5720. GOODHUE, ELIZABETH K. When Yorick takes his tea; or, The commerce of consumptive passions in the case of Laurence Sterne. *See* **8172**.

5721. GUNTNER, LAWRENCE. In search of a Socialist Shakespeare: *Hamlet* on East German stages. *In* (pp. 177–204) **5376**.

5722. HADFIELD, ANDREW. The Ur-*Hamlet* and the fable of the kid. *See* **5087**.

5723. HALE, JOHN. Shakespeare's shoot-outs, with a comparison between *King Lear* and *Hamlet*. *In* (pp. 473–87) **8374**.

5724. HAMBURGER, MAIK. Shakespeare the politicizer: two notable stagings in East Germany. *In* (pp. 205–9) **5376**.

5725. HAVERKAMP, ANSELM. The ghost of history: *Hamlet* and the politics of paternity. LawL (18:2) 2006, 171–97.

5726. HENDERSON, DIANA E. Learning from Campbell Scott's *Hamlet*. *In* (pp. 77–95) **5531**.

5727. HISCOCK, ANDREW. The uses of this world: thinking space in Shakespeare, Marlowe, Cary, and Jonson. Cardiff: UP of Wales, 2004. pp. x, 249.

5728. HODGDON, BARBARA. Inoculating the old stock: Shakespearean chorographies. *See* **5535**.

5729. HOGAN, PATRICK COLM. Narrative universals, heroic tragi-comedy, and Shakespeare's political ambivalence. *See* **5829**.

5730. HUNT, CAROLINE. Hamlet, Tiberius, and the elephants' graveyard. ShB (23:3) 2005, 43–51.

5731. HUSAIN, ADRIAN A. Politics and genre in *Hamlet*. Foreword by John Bayley. (Bibl. 2005, 6334.) Rev. by Martin Coyle in NQ (53:2) 2006, 227–9.

5732. HUTSON, LORNA. Forensic aspects of Renaissance mimesis. Representations (94) 2006, 80–109.

5733. JORDAN-FINNEGAN, RYDER. Individuation and the power of evil on the nature of the human psyche: studies in C. G. Jung, Arthur Miller, and Shakespeare. Lewiston, NY; Lampeter: Mellen Press, 2006. pp. v, 272.

5734. KEYWORTH, G. DAVID. Was the vampire of the eighteenth century a unique type of undead-corpse? *See* **3133**.

5735. KIDNIE, MARGARET JANE. Where is *Hamlet*? Text, performance, and adaptation. *In* (pp. 101–20) **5537**.

5736. KLIMAN, BERNICE W. Print and electronic editions inspired by the New Variorum *Hamlet* project. ShS (59) 2006, 157–67.

5737. KO, YU JIN. 'The Mousetrap' and remembrance in Michael Almereyda's *Hamlet*. ShB (23:4) 2005, 19–32.

5738. KRÄTZER, JÜRGEN (ed.). Hamlet und kein Ende: Les-Arten, Spiel-Räume & Kunst-Stücke. Bremerhaven: Wirtschaftsverlag NW, 2004. pp. 284. (Die Horen, 213.) Rev. by Tobias Döring in SJ (141) 2005, 256–7.

5739. KUBIAK, ANTHONY; REYNOLDS, BRYAN. The delusion of critique: subjunctive space, transversality, and the conceit of deceit in *Hamlet*. *In* (pp. 207–25) **5421**.

5740. KUMAMOTO, CHIKAKO. Shakespeare's *Hamlet*. Exp (64:4) 2006, 201–4.

5741. MA, YUANLONG. A tragedy of desire: a Lacanian interpretation of *Hamlet*. FLS (121) 2006, 93–6. (In Chinese.)

5742. MCEVOY, SEAN (ed.). William Shakespeare's *Hamlet*: a sourcebook. London; New York: Routledge, 2006. pp. xiii, 183. (Routledge guides to literature.)

5743. MAKARYK, IRENA R. Wartime *Hamlet*. *In* (pp. 119–35) **5376**.

5744. MANFERLOTTI, STEFANO. Amleto in parodia. Rome: Bulzoni, 2005. pp. 140. (Piccola biblioteca shakespeariana, 36.) Rev. by Franco Marenco in Indice (2005:7/8) 18.

5745. MAXWELL, JULIE. A reference to the Ur-*Hamlet* in a compositor's error. NQ (53:4) 2006, 463–4.

5746. MENZER, PAUL. The tragedians of the city? Q1 *Hamlet* and the settlements of the 1590s. ShQ (57:2) 2006, 162–82.

5747. MILWARD, PETER. Meta-drama in *Hamlet* and *Macbeth*. *In* (pp. 1–18) **5693**.

5748. MONTGOMERY, WILL. Susan Howe's Renaissance period: metamorphosis and representation in *Pythagorean Silence* and *Defenestration of Prague*. *See* **16474**.

5749. NIE, ZHENZHAO. On ethical literary criticism and moral criticism. FLS (118) 2006, 8–17. (In Chinese.)

5750. O'CONNOR, JOHN. The play's the thing … SNL (55:4) 2005/06, 113.

5751. PALMER, DARYL W. Hamlet's Northern lineage: masculinity, climate, and the mechanician in early modern Britain. RenD (ns 35) 2006, 3–25.

5752. PESTA, DUKE. Articulating skeletons: *Hamlet*, *Hoffman*, and the anatomical graveyard. CEl (69) 2006, 21–39.

5753. PLUMER, ERIC. 'There's a divinity that shapes our ends': an Augustinian reading of *Hamlet*. *In* (pp. 63–93) **3301**.

5754. RHODES, NEIL. *Hamlet* and Humanism. *In* (pp. 120–9) **4734**.

5755. ROE, JOHN. Unfinished business: *A Lover's Complaint* and *Hamlet*, *Romeo and Juliet* and *The Rape of Lucrece*. *In* (pp. 109–20) **5913**.

5756. SALE, CAROLYN. Eating air, feeling smells: *Hamlet*'s theory of performance. RenD (ns 35) 2006, 145–68.

5757. SCHOENFELDT, MICHAEL. 'Give sorrow words': emotional loss and the articulation of temperament in early modern England. *In* (pp. 143–64) **3235**.

5758. SEMLER, L. E. A proximate prince: the gooey business of *Hamlet* criticism. SSE (32) 2006, 97–122.

5759. SENELICK, LAURENCE. 'Thus conscience doth make cowards of us all': new documentation on the Okhlopkov *Hamlet*. *In* (pp. 136–56) **5376**.

5760. SHAUGHNESSY, ROBERT. Stage, screen, and nation: *Hamlet* and the space of history. *In* (pp. 55–76) **5531**.

5761. SHEEN, ERICA. 'Why should a dog, a horse, a rat have life, and thou no breath at all?': Shakespeare's animations. *In* (pp. 87–100) **4588**.

5762. SMITH, BRUCE R. Mona Lisa takes a mountain hike, Hamlet goes for an ocean dip. *In* (pp. 238–53) **5401**.

5763. Soncini, Sara. *'The very age and body of the time'*: l'*Amleto* di Federico Tiezzi e i problemi della traduzione diacronica. AngP (3:1) 2006, 107–30.
5764. Taylor, Dennis. Hardy and *Hamlet*. *In* (pp. 38–54) **10348**.
5765. Taylor, Mark. Shakespeare's *Hamlet*. Exp (65:1) 2006, 4–7.
5766. Wall, Wendy. Dramatic authorship and print. *In* (pp. 1–11) **4734**.
5767. Wang, Shuhua. From Maoism to (post)modernism: *Hamlet* in Communist China. *In* (pp. 283–302) **5376**.
5768. Warner, Marina. The word unfleshed: memory in cyberspace. Raritan (26:1) 2006, 1–13.
5769. Wehrs, Donald R. Moral physiology, ethical prototypes, and denaturing of sense in Shakespearean tragedy. ColLit (33:1) 2006, 67–92.
5770. Williams, William Proctor. Hamlet's pockets: problems with stage directions. *In* (pp. 192–9) **5577**.
5771. Yang, Huilin. Space for interpretation and imagination: Shakespeare and *Hamlet* in the history of criticism. FLS (122) 2006, 53–61. (In Chinese.)
5772. Yang, Lingui. Cognition and recognition: Hamlet's power of knowledge. FLS (117) 2006, 16–23.
5773. Young, Alan R. Henry Irving's Hamlet: some visual sources. NCT (32:2) 2005, 3–19.

Julius Caesar

5774. Anderegg, Michael. Orson Welles and after: *Julius Caesar* and twentieth-century totalitarianism. *In* (pp. 295–305) **5805**.
5775. Baines, Barbara J. 'That ever like is not the same': the vicissitudes of language in *Julius Caesar*. *In* (pp. 139–53) **5805**.
5776. Barker, Simon. 'It's an actor, boss. Unarmed': the rhetoric of *Julius Caesar*. *In* (pp. 227–39) **5805**.
5777. Bates, Laura Raidonis. Shakespeare and the working man: Communist applications during nationalist periods in Latvia. *In* (pp. 38–55) **5376**.
5778. Batson, Beatrice (ed.). Shakespeare's Christianity: the Protestant and Catholic poetics of *Julius Caesar*, *Macbeth*, and *Hamlet*. *See* **5693**.
5779. Candido, Joseph. 'Time … come round': plot construction in *Julius Caesar*. *In* (pp. 127–38) **5805**.
5780. Cavalli, Luciano. *Giulio Cesare*, *Coriolano* e il teatro della Repubblica: una lettura politica di Shakespeare. Soveria Mannelli: Rubbettino, 2006. pp. 175. (Saggi.)
5781. Greenwald, Michael L. Multicultural and regendered Romans: *Julius Caesar* in North America, 1969–2000. *In* (pp. 319–32) **5805**.
5782. Gregor, Keith. *Julius Caesar* and the Spanish transition. *In* (pp. 205–16) **5308**.
5783. Hawkes, David. Shakespeare's *Julius Caesar*: Marxist and post-Marxist approaches. *In* (pp. 199–212) **5805**.
5784. Hogan, Patrick Colm. Narrative universals, heroic tragi-comedy, and Shakespeare's political ambivalence. *See* **5829**.
5785. Holderness, Graham; Nevitt, Marcus. Major among the minors: a cultural materialist reading of *Julius Caesar*. *In* (pp. 257–69) **5805**.

5786. Hopkins, D. J. Performance and urban space in Shakespeare's Rome; or, 'S.P.Q.L.' *In* (pp. 35–52) **5121**.

5787. Jehne, Martin. History's alternative Caesars: *Julius Caesar* and current historiography. *In* (pp. 59–70) **5805**.

5788. Kahn, Coppélia. 'Passions of some difference': friendship and emulation in *Julius Caesar*. *In* (pp. 271–83) **5805**.

5789. Kezar, Dennis. *Julius Caesar*'s analogue clock and the accents of history. *In* (pp. 241–55) **5805**.

5790. Liebler, Naomi Conn. Buying and selling so(u)les: marketing strategies and the politics of performance in *Julius Caesar*. *In* (pp. 165–79) **5805**.

5791. Mahler, Andreas. 'There is restitution, no end of restitution, only not for us': experimental tragedy and the early modern subject in *Julius Caesar*. *In* (pp. 181–95) **5805**.

5792. Mahon, John W. Providence in *Julius Caesar*. *In* (pp. 91–110) **5693**.

5793. Matheson, Tom. Royal *Caesar*. *In* (pp. 307–18) **5805**.

5794. Parker, Barbara L. From monarchy to tyranny: *Julius Caesar* among Shakespeare's Roman works. *In* (pp. 111–26) **5805**.

5795. Raffel, Burton (introd. and notes). *Julius Caesar*. With an essay by Harold Bloom. New Haven, CT; London: Yale UP, 2006. pp. xxxi, 159. (Annotated Shakespeare.)

5796. Rigney, James. Stage worlds of *Julius Caesar*: theatrical features and their history. *In* (pp. 287–93) **5805**.

5797. Ronan, Clifford. Caesar on and off the Renaissance English stage. *In* (pp. 71–89) **5805**.

5798. Simmons, J. L. From theatre to Globe: the construction of character in *Julius Caesar*. *In* (pp. 155–63) **5805**.

5799. Smith, Suzanne. Shakespeare and the politics of honor: purpose and performance in *Julius Caesar*. IJPP (33:3) 2006, 243–80.

5800. Tempera, Mariangela. Political Caesar: *Julius Caesar* on the Italian stage. *In* (pp. 333–43) **5805**.

5801. Thomas, Vivian. Shakespeare's sources: translations, transformations, and intertextuality in *Julius Caesar*. *In* (pp. 91–110) **5805**.

5802. Weihrs, Donald R. Moral physiology, ethical prototypes, and denaturing of sense in Shakespearean tragedy. *See* **5769**.

5803. Willbern, David. Constructing Caesar: a psychoanalytic reading. *In* (pp. 213–26) **5805**.

5804. Zander, Horst. *Julius Caesar* and the critical legacy. *In* (pp. 3–55) **5805**.

5805. —— (ed.). *Julius Caesar*: new critical essays. London; New York: Routledge, 2005. pp. x, 360. (Shakespeare criticism, 29.)

King Edward III

5806. Edelman, Charles. Morose's fights at sea in *Epicœne*. *See* **6867**.

King Henry IV

5807. Cobb, Barbara Mather. 'Suppose that you have seen the well-appointed king': imagining succession in the Henriad. CEl (70) 2006, 33–8.

5808. Cohen, Derek. The play of cynicism in *Henry IV, Part Two.* AUMLA (106) 2006, 87–103.

5809. Falco, Raphael. Charisma and institution-building in Shakespeare's second tetralogy. *In* (pp. 215–37) **5401**.

5810. Harris, Jonathan Gil. Rematerializing Shakespeare's intertheatricality: the Occidental/Oriental palimpsest. *In* (pp. 75–94) **5421**.

5811. Hartwig, Joan. 'Mine honor's pawn': gage-throwing and word-play in Shakespeare's second tetralogy. *See* **5885**.

5812. Henderson, Diana E. Performing history: *Henry IV*, money, and the fashion of the times. *In* (pp. 376–96) **5537**.

5813. Hoffman, Dean A. 'Bypaths and indirect crooked ways': *mise-en-scène* in Orson Welles's *Chimes at Midnight. See* **12817**.

5814. Laird, David. Falstaff's vocation: a response to Arthur F. Kinney. Connotations (13:1/2) 2003/04, 23–31.

5815. Nuyts-Giornal, Josée. 'Who fears a sentence or an old man's saw shall by a painted cloth be kept in awe': genre print and early modern English literature. *See* **5645**.

King Henry V

5816. Aebischer, Pascale. Shakespeare, sex, and violence: negotiating masculinities in Branagh's *Henry V* and Taymor's *Titus*. *In* (pp. 112–32) **5531**.

5817. Banerjee, Rita. The common good and the necessity of war: emergent republican ideals in Shakespeare's *Henry V* and *Coriolanus*. CompDr (40:1) 2006, 29–49.

5818. Bednarz, James P. When did Shakespeare write the choruses of *Henry V*? NQ (53:4) 2006, 486–9.

5819. Cantor, Paul A. Shakespeare's *Henry V*: from the medieval to the modern world. *In* (pp. 11–31) **5394**.

5820. Cobb, Barbara Mather. 'Suppose that you have seen the well-appointed king': imagining succession in the Henriad. *See* **5807**.

5821. Dubrow, Heather. 'He had the dialect and different skill': authorizers in *Henry V*, *A Lover's Complaint*, and *Othello*. *In* (pp. 121–36) **5913**.

5822. Ewert, Kevin. *Henry V*. Basingstoke; New York: Palgrave Macmillan, 2006. pp. vii, 166. (Shakespeare handbooks.)

5823. Falco, Raphael. Charisma and institution-building in Shakespeare's second tetralogy. *In* (pp. 215–37) **5401**.

5824. Guneratne, Anthony R. 'Thou dost usurp authority': Beerbohm Tree, Reinhardt, Olivier, Welles, and the politics of adapting Shakespeare. *In* (pp. 31–53) **5531**.

5825. Harrington, Maura Grace. The disappearance of MacMorris: Shakespeare's doomed attempt at portraying British unity. SNL (55:4) 2005/06, 99, 102, 110.

5826. Harris, Jonathan Gil. Rematerializing Shakespeare's intertheatricality: the Occidental/Oriental palimpsest. *In* (pp. 75–94) **5421**.

5827. Hartwig, Joan. 'Mine honor's pawn': gage-throwing and word-play in Shakespeare's second tetralogy. *See* **5885**.

5828. HOFFMAN, DEAN A. 'Bypaths and indirect crooked ways': *mise-en-scène* in Orson Welles's *Chimes at Midnight. See* **12817**.

5829. HOGAN, PATRICK COLM. Narrative universals, heroic tragi-comedy, and Shakespeare's political ambivalence. ColLit (33:1) 2006, 34–66.

5830. JORDAN, CONSTANCE. *Henry V* and the Tudor monarchy. *In* (pp. 108–19) **4734**.

5831. MCNAMEE, EUGENE. Once more unto the breach: Branagh's *Henry V*, Blair's war and the UK constitution. *In* (pp. 17–29) **12636**.

5832. RICHMOND, MICHAEL L. Kenneth Branagh's *Henry V* (1989). *In* (pp. 501–14) **12712**.

5833. SHEPHERD, ROBERT K. Shakespeare's *Henry V*: person and persona. *In* (pp. 196–204) **5308**.

King Henry VI

5834. ALTSCHULER, ERIC LEWIN; JANSEN, WILLIAM. The entrances and exits of *Henry VI, Part 2*. NQ (53:4) 2006, 467–70.

5835. CHARTIER, ROGER. Jack Cade, the skin of a dead lamb, and the hatred for writing. SStud (34) 2006, 77–89.

5836. EDELMAN, CHARLES. Morose's fights at sea in *Epicœne*. *See* **6867**.

5837. HAMPTON-REEVES, STUART. Shakespeare, *Henry VI* and the Festival of Britain. *In* (pp. 285–96) **5537**.

5838. HOWARD, JEAN E. Stage masculinities, national history, and the making of London theatrical culture. *In* (pp. 199–214) **5401**.

5839. LAROQUE, FRANÇOIS. '*Blue-apron culture*': la culture populaire dans *2 Henry VI* de Shakespeare et *The Shoemaker's Holiday* de Thomas Dekker. RANAM (39) 2006, 57–70.

5840. STAPLETON, M. L. 'I of old contemptes complayne': Margaret of Anjou and English Seneca. CLS (43:1/2) 2006, 100–33.

5841. STROHM, PAUL. York's paper crown: 'bare life' and Shakespeare's first tragedy. JMEMS (36:1) 2006, 75–101.

5842. WALTONEN, KARMA. *Saint Joan*: from Renaissance witch to New Woman. *See* **18503**.

5843. WENTERSDORF, KARL P. The Winchester crux in the First Folio's *1 Henry VI*. ShQ (57:4) 2006, 443–9.

King Henry VIII

5844. MATCHETT, WILLIAM H.; SCHOENBAUM, S. (eds). The life and death of King John; The famous history of the life of Henry VIII. With new and updated critical essays and a revised bibliography. *See* **5848**.

5845. MERRIAM, TOM. The identity of Shakespeare in *Henry VIII*. Tokyo: Renaissance Inst., Sophia Univ., 2005. pp. 167. (Renaissance monographs, 32.) Rev. by Ralph Berry in NQ (53:2) 2006, 229–30.

5846. ZAIDI, ALI SHEHZAD. Self-contradiction in *Henry VIII* and *La cisma de Inglaterra*. SP (103:3) 2006, 329–44.

King John

5847. ARMSTRONG, ALAN. Arthur's fall. ShB (24:1) 2006, 1–10.

5848. Matchett, William H.; Schoenbaum, S. (eds). The life and death of King John; The famous history of the life of Henry VIII. With new and updated critical essays and a revised bibliography. New York: Signet Classics, 2004. pp. lxi, 444. (Signet Classics Shakespeare.) (Second ed.: first ed. 1986.)

5849. Merriam, Thomas. Prosodic symmetry in *King John*. NQ (53:1) 2006, 62–5.

5850. Pandit, Lalita; Hogan, Patrick Colm. Introduction: morsels and modules: on embodying cognition in Shakespeare's plays. *See* **5646**.

King Lear

5851. Aldama, Frederick Luis. Race, cognition, and emotion: Shakespeare on film. *See* **6013**.

5852. Alvis, John E. Liberty in Shakespeare's British plays. *In* (pp. 33–47) **5394**.

5853. Bouchard, Larry D. Playing nothing for someone: *Lear*, Bottom, and kenotic integrity. LitTheol (19:2) 2005, 159–80.

5854. Braun-Rau, Alexandra. William Shakespeares *King Lear* in seinen Fassungen: ein elektronisch-dialogisches Editionsmodell. Tübingen: Niemeyer, 2004. pp. xii, 173. (Beihefte zu *editio*, 20.) Rev. by Dieter Mehl in PBSA (99:4) 2005, 627–8.

5855. Dawson, Anthony. Reading Kurosawa reading Shakespeare. *In* (pp. 155–75) **5531**.

5856. Du, Wenwei. Shakespeare in Chinese *xiqu* forms: its implications in directing and authorship. *In* (pp. 193–212) **12336**.

5857. Ellrodt, Robert. Self-consistency in the characters in Shakespeare's *King Lear*. BJJ (13) 2006, 139–47.

5858. Freeman, Franklin. Images of affection (*storge*) in *As You Like It* and *King Lear*. *See* **17184**.

5859. Hadfield, Andrew. *King Lear* and Sidney. NQ (53:4) 2006, 489–90.

5860. Hale, John. Shakespeare's shoot-outs, with a comparison between *King Lear* and *Hamlet*. *In* (pp. 473–87) **8374**.

5861. Halio, Jay L. (ed.). The tragedy of King Lear. (Bibl. 1996, 6152.) Cambridge; New York: CUP, 2005. pp. xix, 314. (New Cambridge Shakespeare.) (Revised ed.: first ed. 1992.)

5862. Höfele, Andreas. *Bestiarium humanum*: Lear's animal kingdom. *In* (pp. 84–98) **5346**.

5863. Huang, Alexander. Shakespeare, performance, and autobiographical interventions. ShB (24:2) 2006, 31–47.

5864. Klett, Elizabeth. 'O, how this mother swells up toward my heart': performing mother and father in Helena Kaut-Howson's cross-gender *King Lear*. ShB (23:3) 2005, 53–73.

5865. Lehmann, Courtney. A thousand Shakespeares: from cinematic saga to feminist geography; or, The escape from Iceland. *In* (pp. 588–609) **5537**.

5866. Li, Ruru. '"Who is it that can tell me who I am?" / "Lear's shadow"': a Taiwanese actor's personal response to *King Lear*. ShQ (57:2) 2006, 195–215.

5867. LINTON, JOAN PONG. Kurosawa's *Ran* (1985) and *King Lear*: towards a conversation on historical responsibility. QRFV (23:4) 2006, 341–51.

5868. MENZER, PAUL. Dislocating Shakespeare: scene locators and the place of the page. *See* **5904**.

5869. MOORE, PETER R. The nature of *King Lear.* EngS (87:2) 2006, 169–90.

5870. PETERSON, KAARA L. *Historica passio*: early modern medicine, *King Lear*, and editorial practice. ShQ (57:1) 2006, 1–22.

5871. PHELAN, PEGGY. Reconstructing love: *King Lear* and theatre architecture. *In* (pp. 13–35) **5537**.

5872. RICHMAN, DAVID. Smelling their way to Dover: a blind director's take on blind Gloucester. *In* (pp. 156–61) **5577**.

5873. SCOLNICOV, HANNA. 'Who is it that can tell me who I am?': individual, subject and self in *King Lear.* SJ (142) 2006, 142–56.

5874. SHEEN, ERICA. 'Why should a dog, a horse, a rat have life, and thou no breath at all?': Shakespeare's animations. *In* (pp. 87–100) **4588**.

5875. SPATES, WILLIAM HENRY. Proverbs, pox, and the early modern *femme fatale*. NQ (53:1) 2006, 47–51.

5876. TINK, JAMES. 'Expose thyself to what [*sic*] wretches feel': the figure of bare life in *King Lear* and *Timon of Athens*. SStudT (43) 2005, 37–61.

5877. TOMPKINS, JOANNE. Conflicting fields of vision: performing self and Other in two intercultural Shakespeare productions. *In* (pp. 610–24) **5537**.

5878. WOOD, MICHAEL. The languages of cinema. *In* (pp. 79–88) **3191**.

5879. WOOLLEY, JAMES. Poor John Harding and Mad Tom: *Harding's Resurrection* (1724). *In* (pp. 102–21) **648**.

King Richard II

5880. ANDERSON, THOMAS PAGE. Performing early modern trauma from Shakespeare to Milton. *See* **6151**.

5881. ARMSTRONG, ALAN. 'What is become of Bushy? Where is Green?': metadramatic reference to doubling actors in *Richard II*. *In* (pp. 149–55) **5577**.

5882. BATSON, BEATRICE (ed.). Shakespeare's second historical tetralogy: some Christian features. (Bibl. 2005, 6484.) Rev. by John W. Mahon in SNL (55:4) 2005/06, 93–4.

5883. COBB, BARBARA MATHER. 'Suppose that you have seen the well-appointed king': imagining succession in the Henriad. *See* **5807**.

5884. FALCO, RAPHAEL. Charisma and institution-building in Shakespeare's second tetralogy. *In* (pp. 215–37) **5401**.

5885. HARTWIG, JOAN. 'Mine honor's pawn': gage-throwing and word-play in Shakespeare's second tetralogy. CEACrit (68:1/2) 2005/06, 3–11.

5886. HAVERKAMP, ANSELM. *Richard II*, Bracton, and the end of political theology. LawL (16:3) 2004, 313–26.

5887. HODGDON, BARBARA. Inoculating the old stock: Shakespearean chorographies. *See* **5535**.

5888. HOGAN, PATRICK COLM. Narrative universals, heroic tragi-comedy, and Shakespeare's political ambivalence. *See* **5829**.

5889. Jones, Gordon P. 'That dismall day in the morning'. NQ (53:4) 2006, 499–505. (Essex Rebellion.)

5890. Klett, Elizabeth. Many bodies, many voices: performing androgyny in Fiona Shaw and Deborah Warner's *Richard II*. TJ (58:2) 2006, 175–94.

5891. Kuchar, Gary. Andrew Marvell's anamorphic tears. *See* **6932**.

5892. Lemon, Rebecca. Treason by words: literature, law, and rebellion in Shakespeare's England. *See* **6816**.

5893. Worden, Blair. Shakespeare in life and art: biography and *Richard II*. *In* (pp. 23–42) **5353**.

King Richard III

5894. Aldama, Frederick Luis. Race, cognition, and emotion: Shakespeare on film. *See* **6013**.

5895. Aune, M. G. Star power: Al Pacino, *Looking for Richard* and the cultural capital of Shakespeare on film. *See* **12950**.

5896. —— The uses of *Richard III*: from Robert Cecil to Richard Nixon. ShB (24:3) 2006, 23–47.

5897. Baldwin, Pat; Baldwin, Tom (eds). King Richard III. (Bibl. 2001, 5101.) Cambridge; New York: CUP, 2005. pp. xii, 260. (Cambridge school Shakespeare.) (Second ed.: first ed. 2000.)

5898. Bonetto, Sandra. Coward conscience and bad conscience in Shakespeare and Nietzsche. PhilL (30:2) 2006, 512–27.

5899. Burns, Edward. *Richard III*. Tavistock: Northcote House in assn with the British Council, 2006. pp. viii, 120. (Writers and their work.)

5900. Hatchuel, Sarah; Vienne-Guerrin, Nathalie (eds). Shakespeare on screen: *Richard III*: proceedings of the conference organised at the Université de Rouen, 4–5 March 2005. Mont-Saint-Aignan: Pubs de l'Univ. de Rouen, 2005. pp. 333. (Pubs de l'Univ. de Rouen, 375.) Rev. by Thomas A. Pendleton in SNL (55:4) 2005/06, 89–90, 96; by Frédéric Delord in CEl (69) 2006, 100–2; by Ton Hoenselaars in SEDERI (16) 2006, 195–8.

5901. Howard, Jean E. Stage masculinities, national history, and the making of London theatrical culture. *In* (pp. 199–214) **5401**.

5902. Knowles, Ric. Encoding/decoding Shakespeare: *Richard III* at the 2002 Stratford Festival. *In* (pp. 297–318) **5537**.

5903. Kossak, Saskia. 'Frame my face to all occasions': Shakespeare's *Richard III* on screen. Vienna: Braumüller, 2005. pp. x, 243. (Austrian studies in English, 92.) Rev. by Kenneth S. Rothwell in MSp (50:2) 2006, 147–9.

5904. Menzer, Paul. Dislocating Shakespeare: scene locators and the place of the page. ShB (24:2) 2006, 1–19.

5905. Prescott, Paul. *Richard III*. Basingstoke; New York: Palgrave Macmillan, 2006. pp. x, 185. (Shakespeare handbooks.)

A Lover's Complaint

5906. Bell, Ilona. Shakespeare's exculpatory complaint. *In* (pp. 91–107) **5913**.

5907. Cheney, Patrick. 'Deep-brained sonnets' and 'tragic shows': Shakespeare's late Ovidian art in *A Lover's Complaint*. *In* (pp. 55–77) **5913**.

5908. Dubrow, Heather. 'He had the dialect and different skill': authorizers in *Henry V, A Lover's Complaint*, and *Othello*. *In* (pp. 121–36) **5913**.

5909. Harned, Jon. Rhetoric and perverse desire in Shakespeare's *A Lover's Complaint*. *In* (pp. 149–63) **5913**.

5910. Roe, John. Unfinished business: *A Lover's Complaint* and *Hamlet, Romeo and Juliet* and *The Rape of Lucrece*. *In* (pp. 109–20) **5913**.

5911. Schiffer, James. 'Honey words': *A Lover's Complaint* and the fine art of seduction. *In* (pp. 137–48) **5913**.

5912. Sharon-Zisser, Shirley. 'True to bondage': the rhetorical forms of female masochism in *A Lover's Complaint*. *In* (pp. 179–90) **5913**.

5913. —— (ed.). Critical essays on Shakespeare's *A Lover's Complaint*: suffering ecstasy. Aldershot; Burlington, VT: Ashgate, 2006. pp. x, 203.

5914. —— Whitworth, Stephen. Introduction: generating dialogue on Shakespeare's *A Lover's Complaint*. *In* (pp. 1–53) **5913**.

5915. Sherbo, Arthur. The Longman's Milton and the 1778 Johnson–Steevens *Variorum*. *See* **6098**.

5916. Stegner, Paul. A reconciled maid: *A Lover's Complaint* and confessional practices in early modern England. *In* (pp. 79–90) **5913**.

5917. Watts, Cedric. Keats's *Bright Star* and *A Lover's Complaint*. *See* **10670**.

5918. Whitworth, Stephen. 'Where excess begs all': Shakespeare, Freud, and the diacritics of melancholy. *In* (pp. 165–77) **5913**.

Love's Labour's Lost

5919. Hilský, Martin. Translations of politics / politics of translation: Czech experience. *In* (pp. 215–27) **5376**.

Macbeth

5920. Barcus, Patrick. The rules of the game: fact in fiction. *See* **18306**.

5921. Batson, Beatrice (ed.). Shakespeare's Christianity: the Protestant and Catholic poetics of *Julius Caesar, Macbeth*, and *Hamlet*. *See* **5693**.

5922. Bigliazzi, Silvia. Su alcune varianti traduttive del *Macbeth*. ConLett (43) 2005, 357–74.

5923. Brown, John Russell. *Macbeth*. Basingstoke; New York: Palgrave Macmillan, 2005. pp. xiii, 172. (Shakespeare handbooks.) Rev. by Douglas King in ShB (24:3) 2006, 125–31.

5924. Burnett, Mark Thornton. Figuring the global/historical in filmic Shakespeare tragedy. *In* (pp. 133–54) **5531**.

5925. Cook, Amy; Reynolds, Bryan. Comedic law: protective transversality, deceit conceits, and the conjuring of *Macbeth* and *Doctor Faustus* in Jonson's *The Devil Is an Ass*. *In* (pp. 85–111) **4718**.

5926. Dawson, Anthony. Reading Kurosawa reading Shakespeare. *In* (pp. 155–75) **5531**.

5927. Dobson, Michael. Moving the audience: Shakespeare, the mob, and the promenade. ShB (23:2) 2005, 19–27.

5928. Floyd-Wilson, Mary. English epicures and Scottish witches. ShQ (57:2) 2006, 131–61.

5929. Freeman, Jane. Unexpected rainfall: working in the wings on Robert Lepage's *Macbeth*. *In* (pp. 285–306) **12336**.

5930. Gibson, Rex (ed.). Macbeth. (Bibl. 1993, 3883.) Cambridge; New York: CUP, 2005. pp. xii, 180. (Cambridge school Shakespeare.) (Second ed.: first ed. 1993.)

5931. Hamburger, Maik. Shakespeare the politicizer: two notable stagings in East Germany. *In* (pp. 205–9) **5376**.

5932. Hateley, Erica. Lady Macbeth in detective fiction: criminalizing the female reader. Clues (24:4) 2006, 31–46.

5933. Hunt, Maurice. Reformation/Counter-Reformation *Macbeth*. EngS (86:5) 2005, 379–98.

5934. King, Andrew. Dead butchers and fiend-like queens: literary and political history in *The Misfortunes of Arthur* and *Macbeth*. *In* (pp. 121–34) **3972**.

5935. Leggatt, Alexander (ed.). William Shakespeare's *Macbeth*: a sourcebook. London; New York: Routledge, 2006. pp. xv, 197. (Routledge guides to literature.) Rev. by Ralph Berry in NQ (53:4) 2006, 569–70.

5936. Lemon, Rebecca. Treason by words: literature, law, and rebellion in Shakespeare's England. *See* **6816**.

5937. Lucking, David. Imperfect speakers: Macbeth and the name of king. EngS (87:4) 2006, 415–25.

5938. McFall, E. K. *Macbeth* and Dante's *Inferno*. NQ (53:4) 2006, 490–4.

5939. McLuskie, Kathleen. Shakespeare goes slumming: Harlem '37 and Birmingham '97. *In* (pp. 249–66) **5537**.

5940. Maley, Willy; Murphy, Andrew (eds). Shakespeare and Scotland. (Bibl. 2005, 6561.) Rev. by Ronald J. Boling in ShQ (57:1) 2006, 88–91; by Katherine McClune in NQ (53:3) 2006, 371–3.

5941. Milward, Peter. Meta-drama in *Hamlet* and *Macbeth*. *In* (pp. 1–18) **5693**.

5942. Miola, Robert S. 'I could not say "Amen"': prayer and Providence in *Macbeth*. *In* (pp. 57–71) **5693**.

5943. Ragg, Edward. Pragmatic abstraction *vs* metaphor: Stevens' *The Pure Good of Theory* and *Macbeth*. *See* **18651**.

5944. Shamas, Laura. 'We three': the mythology of Shakespeare's Weird Sisters. New York; Frankfurt: Lang, 2006. pp. viii, 140.

5945. Taylor, David. 'A vacant space, an empty stage': *Prometheus Unbound*, *The Last Man*, and the problem of dramatic (re)form. *See* **11231**.

5946. Tompkins, Joanne. Conflicting fields of vision: performing self and Other in two intercultural Shakespeare productions. *In* (pp. 610–24) **5537**.

5947. Tredell, Nicolas (ed.). *Macbeth*. Basingstoke; New York: Palgrave Macmillan, 2006. pp. xi, 177. (Readers' guides to essential criticism.)

5948. Wilders, John (ed.). Macbeth. (Bibl. 2004, 6783.) Rev. by Katherine Rowe in ShQ (57:3) 2006, 346–8.

5949. Williams, William Proctor (ed.). *Macbeth*. Naperville, IL: MediaFusion, 2006. pp. xx, 312. (Sourcebooks Shakespeare.)

Measure for Measure

5950. Hunt, Maurice. Being precise in *Measure for Measure*. Ren (58:4) 2006, 243–67.

5951. Jensen, Pamela K. Vienna vice: invisible leadership and deep politics in Shakespeare's *Measure for Measure*. *In* (pp. 105–54) **5394**.

5952. Lorenz, Philip. Notes on the 'religious turn': mystery, metaphor, medium. ELN (44:1) 2006, 163–72.

5953. Mukherji, Subha. Jonson's *The New Inn* and a revisiting of the 'amorous jurisdiction'. *See* **6895**.

The Merchant of Venice

5954. Bayerdörfer, Hans-Peter. Shylock on the German stage in the post-Shoa period. *In* (pp. 205–23) **5346**.

5955. Berry, Philippa. Incising Venice: the violence of cultural incorporation in *The Merchant of Venice*. *In* (pp. 40–53) **5401**.

5956. Bildhauer, Bettina. Medieval blood. *See* **3828**.

5957. Chernaik, Warren. *The Merchant of Venice*. Plymouth: Northcote House in assn with the British Council, 2005. pp. 128. (Writers and their work.) Rev. by Andrew Hadfield in Eng (55:211) 2006, 93–101.

5958. Desmet, Christy. Poetry, proof, and pedigree in *The Merchant of Venice*. Cithara (46:1) 2006, 39–51.

5959. Detmer-Goebel, Emily. Agency and the threat of cuckoldry in *As You Like It* and *The Merchant of Venice*. *See* **5653**.

5960. Fowler, Elizabeth. Shylock's virtual injuries. SStud (34) 2006, 56–64.

5961. Gross, Kenneth. Shylock is Shakespeare. Chicago, IL; London: Chicago UP, 2006. pp. xi, 202.

5962. Heschel, Susannah. From Jesus to Shylock: Christian supersessionism and *The Merchant of Venice*. HTR (99:4) 2006, 407–31.

5963. Hirsch, Brett D. 'A gentle and no Jew': the difference marriage makes in *The Merchant of Venice*. Parergon (23:1) 2006, 119–29.

5964. Hirschfeld, Heather. 'We all expect a gentle answer, Jew': *The Merchant of Venice* and the psychotheology of conversion. ELH (73:1) 2006, 61–81.

5965. Jackson, Kenneth S. 'More other than you desire' in *The Merchant of Venice*. ELN (44:1) 2006, 151–6.

5966. Jorgens, Elise Bickford. A rhetoric of dissonance: music in *The Merchant of Venice*. JDJ (25) 2006, 107–28.

5967. Kruse, Horst H. Allusions to *The Merchant of Venice* and the New Testament in *God Rest You Merry, Gentlemen*: Hemingway's anti-Semitism reconsidered. *See* **16367**.

5968. Lewin, Judith. Jewish heritage and secular inheritance in Walter Scott's *Ivanhoe*. *See* **11145**.

5969. McCullough, Christopher. *The Merchant of Venice.* (Bibl. 2005, 6605.) Rev. by Douglas King in ShB (24:3) 2006, 125–31.

5970. Mahler, Andreas. Point of reference or semantic space? Functions of Venice in early modern English drama. *In* (pp. 161–79) **5346**.

5971. Marcus, Leah S. (ed.). *The Merchant of Venice*: authoritative text, sources, and contexts, criticism, rewritings, and appropriations. New York; London: Norton, 2006. pp. xiii, 347. (Norton critical eds.)

5972. Nichols, David K. The domestic politics of Shakespeare's comedies. *In* (pp. 49–69) **5394**.

5973. Pressler, Mirjam. 'If you prick us, do we not bleed?': Shylock as a theatrical figure, as a human being, and as a father. *In* (pp. 224–36) **5346**.

5974. Raffel, Burton (introd. and notes). *The Merchant of Venice.* With an essay by Harold Bloom. New Haven, CT; London: Yale UP, 2006. pp. xxxvi, 167. (Annotated Shakespeare.)

5975. Rooney, Tom. 'A thousand Shylocks': Orson Welles and *The Merchant of Venice.* ShS (59) 2006, 63–8.

5976. Roston, Murray. Sacred and secular in *The Merchant of Venice. In* (pp. 83–98) **3658**.

5977. Rutter, Tom. Merchants of Venice in *A Knack to Know an Honest Man. See* **4722**.

5978. Schwartz, Regina M. The price of justice and love in *The Merchant of Venice.* TriQ (124) 2006, 225–41.

5979. Shapiro, Michael. *The Merchant of Venice* after the Holocaust; or, Shakespearean romantic comedy meets Auschwitz. Cithara (46:1) 2006, 3–23.

5980. Staines, Christopher. Third time lucky: playing all the suitors in *The Merchant of Venice.* ShB (24:4) 2006, 33–56.

5981. Stewart, Stanley. Shylock and Jacob, the patriarch. Cithara (46:1) 2006, 24–38.

5982. Tiffany, Grace. Law and self-interest in *The Merchant of Venice.* PLL (42:4) 2006, 384–400.

5983. Turner, Henry S. The problem of the more-than-one: friendship, calculation, and political association in *The Merchant of Venice.* ShQ (57:4) 2006, 413–42.

The Merry Wives of Windsor

5984. Buccola, Regina. Fairies, fractious women, and the old faith: fairy lore in early modern British drama and culture. *See* **5992**.

5985. Grav, Peter. Money changes everything: Quarto and Folio *The Merry Wives of Windsor* and the case for revision. CompDr (40:2) 2006, 217–40.

5986. Holland, Peter. *The Merry Wives of Windsor*: the performance of community. ShB (23:2) 2005, 5–18.

5987. Nichols, David K. The domestic politics of Shakespeare's comedies. *In* (pp. 49–69) **5394**.

5988. Rackin, Phyllis. Our canon, ourselves. *In* (pp. 91–113) **5401**.

A Midsummer Night's Dream

5989. Booth, Stephen. A discourse on the witty partition of *A Midsummer Night's Dream*. *In* (pp. 216–22) **5577**.

5990. Bouchard, Larry D. Playing nothing for someone: *Lear*, Bottom, and kenotic integrity. *See* **5853**.

5991. Bourus, Terri A. (ed.). A Midsummer Night's dream. Naperville, IL: MediaFusion, 2006. pp. xviii, 268. (Sourcebooks Shakespeare.)

5992. Buccola, Regina. Fairies, fractious women, and the old faith: fairy lore in early modern British drama and culture. Selinsgrove, PA: Susquehanna UP; London: Assoc. UPs, 2006. pp. 293. (Apple–Zimmerman series in early modern culture.)

5993. Coatalen, Guillaume. *A Midsummer Night's Dream*, ii.i.128–129 and *Georgics*, iii.274–277. NQ (53:1) 2006, 66.

5994. Guneratne, Anthony R. 'Thou dost usurp authority': Beerbohm Tree, Reinhardt, Olivier, Welles, and the politics of adapting Shakespeare. *In* (pp. 31–53) **5531**.

5995. Hatchuel, Sarah; Vienne-Guerrin, Nathalie (eds). Shakespeare on screen: *A Midsummer Night's Dream*: proceedings of the conference organized at the Université de Rouen, 5–6 December 2003 by the ERAC, Équipe de Recherche sur les Aires Culturelles, CETAS, Centre d'Études Transdisciplinaires Anglo-saxonnes. Mont-Saint-Aignan: Pubs de l'Univ. de Rouen, 2004. pp. 273. (Pubs de l'Univ. de Rouen, 351.) Rev. by Laurie E. Osborne in ShQ (57:1) 2006, 117–19.

5996. Newstok, Scott L. (introd.). Why *A Midsummer Night's Dream*? By Kenneth Burke. ShQ (57:3) 2006, 297–308.

5997. Nichols, David K. The domestic politics of Shakespeare's comedies. *In* (pp. 49–69) **5394**.

5998. Raffel, Burton (introd. and notes). *A Midsummer Night's Dream*. With an essay by Harold Bloom. New Haven, CT; London: Yale UP, 2005. pp. 173. (Annotated Shakespeare.) Rev. by Patricia Lennox in SNL (55:2) 2005, 41–2.

5999. Riga, Frank P. 'Where is that worthless dreamer?': Bottom's fantastic redemption in Hoffman's *A Midsummer Night's Dream*. Mythlore (25:1/2) 2006, 197–211.

6000. Walsh, William. Shakespeare's lion and Ha Jin's tiger: the interplay of imagination and reality. *See* **16599**.

6001. Watts, Cedric. Fundamental editing: in *A Midsummer Night's Dream*, does 'Bottom' mean *bum*? And how about *arse* and *ass*? AngP (3:1) 2006, 213–22.

6002. Wood, Juliette. Filming fairies: popular film, audience response and meaning in contemporary fairy lore. Folklore (117:3) 2006, 279–95.

6003. Yang, Zhengrun. The interpretation of dreams in Shakespeare's plays. *See* **6147**.

Much Ado about Nothing

6004. Anyó, Joaquim. *Tirante il Bianco* and *Much Ado about Nothing*. NQ (53:4) 2006, 482–4.

6005. Berry, Mary; Clamp, Michael (eds). Much ado about nothing.

Cambridge; New York: CUP, 2005. pp. xii, 196. (Cambridge school Shakespeare.)

6006. Cassal, Steve. Shakespeare's *Much Ado about Nothing.* Exp (64:3) 2006, 138–40.

6007. Collington, Philip D. 'Stuffed with all honourable virtues': *Much Ado about Nothing* and *The Book of the Courtier.* SP (103:3) 2006, 281–312.

6008. Fleck, Andrew. The ambivalent blush: figural and structural metonymy, modesty, and *Much Ado about Nothing.* ANQ (19:1) 2006, 16–23.

6009. McEachern, Claire (ed.). Much ado about nothing. London: Arden Shakespeare, 2006. pp. xix, 345. (Arden Shakespeare: third series.) Rev. by Pamela Allen Brown in ShQ (57:4) 2006, 466–9.

6010. Nichols, David K. The domestic politics of Shakespeare's comedies. *In* (pp. 49–69) **5394**.

6011. Wright, Nancy E. Legal interpretation of defamation in Shakespeare's *Much Ado about Nothing.* BJJ (13) 2006, 93–108.

6012. Yates, Julian. Accidental Shakespeare. SStud (34) 2006, 90–122.

Othello

6013. Aldama, Frederick Luis. Race, cognition, and emotion: Shakespeare on film. ColLit (33:1) 2006, 197–213.

6014. Ardolino, Frank. Pinter's *Betrayal* and Shakespeare's *Othello. See* **18015**.

6015. Bartels, Emily C. *Othello* and the Moor. *In* (pp. 140–51) **4734**.

6016. Benson, Sean. 'If I do prove her haggard': Shakespeare's application of hawking tropes to marriage. SP (103:2) 2006, 186–207.

6017. Berger, Harry, Jr. Artificial couples: the apprehensive household in Dutch pendants and *Othello. In* (pp. 114–57) **5401**.

6018. Calvo, Clara. Deforeignizing Shakespeare: *Otelo* in Romantic Spain. *In* (pp. 117–29) **5308**.

6019. Chamberlain, Stephanie. Resolving clandestine disputes: narrative strategy and competing juridical authority in *Othello.* ExRC (31:2) 2005, 259–78.

6020. Clegg, Cyndia Susan. English Renaissance books on Islam and Shakespeare's *Othello.* PCP (41) 2006, 1–12.

6021. Daileader, Celia R. Racism, misogyny, and the Othello myth: inter-racial couples from Shakespeare to Spike Lee. *See* **3224**.

6022. Dubrow, Heather. 'He had the dialect and different skill': authorizers in *Henry V, A Lover's Complaint*, and *Othello. In* (pp. 121–36) **5913**.

6023. Erickson, Peter; Hunt, Maurice (eds). Approaches to teaching Shakespeare's *Othello.* (Bibl. 2005, 6646.) Rev. by William C. Johnson in Style (39:3) 2005, 373–5; by Robert C. Evans in CompDr (40:1) 2006, 138–41.

6024. Fei, Faye Chunfang; Sun, William Huizhu. *Othello* and Beijing Opera: appropriation as a two-way street. TDR (50:1) 2006, 120–33.

6025. Gillies, John. Stanislavski, *Othello*, and the motives of eloquence. *In* (pp. 267–84) **5537**.

6026. Guneratne, Anthony R. 'Thou dost usurp authority': Beerbohm

Tree, Reinhardt, Olivier, Welles, and the politics of adapting Shakespeare. *In* (pp. 31–53) **5531**.

6027. HUNT, MAURICE. Anthony Trollope's *Lady Anna* and Shakespeare's *Othello*. *See* **11470**.

6028. JONES, NICHOLAS. A bogus hero: Welles's *Othello* and the construction of race. ShB (23:1) 2005, 9–28.

6029. LAKE, JAMES H. Effects of primacy and recency upon audience response to two film versions of *Othello*. SNL (56:2) 2006, 45–6.

6030. MACAULAY, MARCIA. When chaos is come again: narrative and narrative analysis in *Othello*. Style (39:3) 2005, 259–76.

6031. MAHLER, ANDREAS. Point of reference or semantic space? Functions of Venice in early modern English drama. *In* (pp. 161–79) **5346**.

6032. MANZANAS, ANA MARÍA. The making and unmaking of a colonial subject: *Othello*. *In* (pp. 130–47) **5308**.

6033. NEILL, MICHAEL (ed.). Othello, the Moor of Venice. Oxford; New York: OUP, 2006. pp. x, 491. (Oxford Shakespeare.) Rev. by Duncan Salkeld in TLS, 18 & 25 Aug. 2006, 26.

6034. NEWSTOK, SCOTT L. *Touch* of Shakespeare: Welles unmoors Othello. ShB (23:1) 2005, 29–86.

6035. SCHWARTZ, REGINA M. Tragedy and the Mass. LitTheol (19:2) 2005, 139–58.

6036. SMITH, EMMA. *Othello*. Plymouth: Northcote House in assn with the British Council, 2005. pp. viii, 104. (Writers and their work.) Rev. by Andrew Hadfield in Eng (55:211) 2006, 93–101.

6037. STRICKLER, BREYAN. Sex in the city: an ecocritical perspective on the place of gender and race in *Othello*. ISLE (12:2) 2005, 119–37.

6038. TAYLOR, DENNIS. Hardy's copy of Shakespeare's *Othello*. *See* **10335**.

6039. VAUGHAN, VIRGINIA MASON. Blacking-up at the Blackfriars Theatre. *In* (pp. 123–31) **5577**.

6040. VON KOPPENFELS, WERNER. *Laesa imaginatio*; or, Imagination infected by passion in Shakespeare's love tragedies. *In* (pp. 68–83) **5346**.

Pericles

6041. DOBSON, MICHAEL. Moving the audience: Shakespeare, the mob, and the promenade. *See* **5927**.

6042. EVERETT, BARBARA. By the rough seas reft: how the 'badness' of the *Pericles* Quarto may be of Shakespeare's making. TLS, 11 Aug. 2006, 13–16.

6043. GOSSETT, SUZANNE. 'Tell thy story': Mary Zimmerman's *Pericles*. ShQ (57:2) 2006, 183–94. (Shakespeare performed.)

6044. —— (ed.). Pericles. (Bibl. 2005, 6671.) Rev. by Gordon McMullan in SJ (142) 2006, 252–5.

6045. LEVIN, RICHARD. The 'herb woman' in *Pericles*. SNL (56:1) 2006, 3, 6.

6046. MOWAT, BARBARA A.; WERSTINE, PAUL (eds). Pericles, prince of Tyre. New York: Washington Square Press, 2005. pp. lvii, 245. (New Folger Library Shakespeare.)

6047. Novy, Marianne. Adopted children and constructions of heredity, nurture, and parenthood in Shakespeare's romances. *In* (pp. 55–74) **6264**.

The Phoenix and the Turtle

6048. Benoit, Raymond. Dickinson's *I Died for Beauty* and Shakespeare's *The Phoenix and the Turtle*. *See* **9850**.

6049. Bishop, Tom. Personal fowl: *The Phoenix and the Turtle* and the question of character. SStud (34) 2006, 65–74.

6050. Borukhov, Boris. *The Phoenix and the Turtle* was published in 1601. NQ (53:1) 2006, 71–2.

The Rape of Lucrece

6051. Greenstadt, Amy. 'Read it in me': the author's will in *Lucrece*. ShQ (57:1) 2006, 45–70.

6052. Jackson, MacDonald P. Shakespeare and the quarrel scene in *Arden of Faversham*. *See* **4684**.

6053. Meek, Richard. Ekphrasis in *The Rape of Lucrece* and *The Winter's Tale*. *See* **6203**.

6054. Parker, Barbara L. From monarchy to tyranny: *Julius Caesar* among Shakespeare's Roman works. *In* (pp. 111–26) **5805**.

6055. Pellicer, Juan Christian. 'The food of my delighted fancy': another echo of *Lucrece* in Keats. *See* **10657**.

6056. Roe, John. Unfinished business: *A Lover's Complaint* and *Hamlet*, *Romeo and Juliet* and *The Rape of Lucrece*. *In* (pp. 109–20) **5913**.

6057. Sherbo, Arthur. The appendix to Edmond Malone's 1790 *Shakespeare* and the New Variorum *Poems* and *Sonnets*. *See* **6193**.

6058. —— The Longman's Milton and the 1778 Johnson–Steevens *Variorum*. *See* **6098**.

6059. Smith, Peter J. Rome's disgrace: the politics of rape in Shakespeare's *Lucrece*. CritS (17:3) 2005, 15–26.

Romeo and Juliet

6060. Attridge, Derek. Performing metaphors: the singularity of literary figuration. *See* **1840**.

6061. Benson, Sean. 'If I do prove her haggard': Shakespeare's application of hawking tropes to marriage. *See* **6016**.

6062. Edgecombe, Rodney Stenning. Trans-formal translation: plays into ballets, with special reference to Kenneth MacMillan's *Romeo and Juliet*. YES (36:1) 2006, 65–78.

6063. García-Mainar, Luis. Shakespeare's *Romeo and Juliet* and male melodrama. *In* (pp. 148–70) **5308**.

6064. Hendricks, Jacquelyn. A textual crux in *Romeo and Juliet*, v.iii. NQ (53:4) 2006, 479–82.

6065. Low, Jennifer A. 'Bodied forth': spectator, stage, and actor in the early modern theater. *See* **6644**.

6066. McKim, William M. Romeo's 'death-markt' imagination and its tragic consequences. KenPR (20) 2005, 38–45.

6067. Mazer, Cary M. Not not Shakespeare: directorial adaptation, authorship, and ownership. ShB (23:2) 2005, 28–42.

6068. Palfrey, Simon; Stern, Tiffany. What does the cued part cue? Parts and cues in *Romeo and Juliet*. *In* (pp. 179–96) **5537**.

6069. Palmer, Daryl W. Motion and Mercutio in *Romeo and Juliet*. PhilL (30:2) 2006, 540–54.

6070. Reynolds, Bryan; Segal, James. Fugitive explorations in *Romeo and Juliet*: searching for transversality inside the goldmine of *R&J*space. *In* (pp. 124–67) **4718**.

6071. Roe, John. Unfinished business: *A Lover's Complaint* and *Hamlet*, *Romeo and Juliet* and *The Rape of Lucrece*. *In* (pp. 109–20) **5913**.

6072. Shim, Jung-Soon. Translating emotions for the local audience. ADS (49) 2006, 3–5.

6073. von Koppenfels, Werner. *Laesa imaginatio*; or, Imagination infected by passion in Shakespeare's love tragedies. *In* (pp. 68–83) **5346**.

6074. Wall, Wendy. De-generation: editions, offspring, and *Romeo and Juliet*. *In* (pp. 152–70) **5334**.

6075. —— Editors in love? Performing desire in *Romeo and Juliet*. *In* (pp. 197–211) **5537**.

6076. West, William N. Mercutio's bad language. *In* (pp. 115–29) **5421**.

6077. White, R. S. *Solomon & Gaenor*: a Welsh Jewish *Romeo and Juliet*. *See* **13069**.

Sir Thomas More

6078. Jackson, MacDonald P. The date and authorship of Hand D's contribution to *Sir Thomas More*: evidence from *Literature Online*. ShS (59) 2006, 69–78.

6079. Merriam, Thomas. Munday and the Oxford Shakespeare *More*. NQ (53:4) 2006, 470–4.

6080. —— Orthographic changes in *John a Kent* and Hand M of *More*. *See* **4971**.

6081. —— Some further evidence for Shakespeare's authorship of Hand D in *Sir Thomas More*. NQ (53:1) 2006, 65–6.

6082. Tobin, J. J. M. Shakespeare, Nashe, and *Sir Thomas More*. NQ (53:1) 2006, 59–62.

6083. Wentersdorf, Karl P. On 'momtanish inhumanyty' in *Sir Thomas More*. SP (103:2) 2006, 178–85.

Sonnets

6084. Batchelor, John. Alfred Tennyson: problems of biography. *See* **11389**.

6085. Crews, Brian. Rewriting/deconstructing Shakespeare: outlining possibilities, sometimes humorous, for Sonnet 18. *In* (pp. 61–72) **5308**.

6086. Duncan-Jones, Katherine. A companion for a king? Shakespeare's status anxiety. TLS, 14 Apr. 2006, 14–15.

6087. Edmondson, Paul; Wells, Stanley. Shakespeare's sonnets. (Bibl. 2005, 6714.) Rev. by Elizabeth Holtze in RMER (60:1) 2006; by Katherine Duncan-Jones in NQ (53:1) 2006, 107–8.

6088. Frank, Bernhard. Shakespeare's Sonnet 29. Exp (64:3) 2006, 136–7.

6089. Fuchs, Dieter. Mythopoetisch-polyphones Erzählen in Shakespeares Sonetten 153/154. SJ (142) 2006, 95–104.

6090. Gray, Ronald. Will in the universe: Shakespeare's sonnets, Plato's *Symposium*, alchemy and Renaissance Neoplatonism. ShS (59) 2006, 225–38.

6091. Gregerson, Linda. Rhetorical contract in the lyric poem. *See* **6930**.

6092. Holden, R. Bradley. Shakespeare's Sonnet 3. Exp (64:4) 2006, 194–7.

6093. Kinsella, Thomas. Readings in poetry. Dublin: Dedalus, 2006. pp. 48. (Peppercanister, 25.) Rev. by Floyd Skloot in SewR (114:3) 2006, lv–lvii.

6094. Marshall, Gail. Elizabeth Barrett Browning and Shakespeare: translating the language of intimacy. *See* **9262**.

6095. Mowat, Barbara A.; Werstine, Paul (eds). Shakespeare's sonnets and poems. New York: Washington Square Press, 2006. pp. xix, 684. (New Folger Library Shakespeare.)

6096. Sharon-Zisser, Shirley; Whitworth, Stephen. Introduction: generating dialogue on Shakespeare's *A Lover's Complaint*. *In* (pp. 1–53) **5913**.

6097. Sherbo, Arthur. The appendix to Edmond Malone's 1790 *Shakespeare* and the New Variorum *Poems* and *Sonnets*. *See* **6193**.

6098. —— The Longman's Milton and the 1778 Johnson–Steevens *Variorum*. NQ (53:1) 2006, 75–8.

6099. Singh, Sukhbir. Echoes of Shakespeare's Sonnet 116 in Yeats's *The Indian to His Love*. *See* **19447**.

6100. Tsur, Reuven. Delivery style and listener response in the rhythmical performance of Shakespeare's sonnets. ColLit (33:1) 2006, 170–96.

6101. Wei, Yeo Wei. *Monna Innominata* and Christina Rossetti's audible unhappiness. *In* (pp. 174–93) **8828**.

6102. Whittemore, Hank. The monument. *See* **4995**.

6103. Wu, Xueping. An analysis of *The Portrait of Mr W.H. See* **11634**.

The Taming of the Shrew

6104. Ardolino, Frank. The induction of Sly: the influence of *The Spanish Tragedy* on the two *Shrews*. ExRC (31:2) 2005, 165–87.

6105. Bates, Laura Raidonis. Shakespeare and the working man: Communist applications during nationalist periods in Latvia. *In* (pp. 38–55) **5376**.

6106. Benson, Sean. 'If I do prove her haggard': Shakespeare's application of hawking tropes to marriage. *See* **6016**.

6107. Bruster, Douglas. The politics of Shakespeare's prose. *In* (pp. 95–114) **5421**.

6108. Deitchman, Elizabeth A. Shakespeare Stiles style: Shakespeare, Julia Stiles, and American girl culture. *In* (pp. 478–94) **5537**.

6109. Gilbert, Miriam. Performance as deflection. *In* (pp. 319–34) **5537**.

6110. Kidnie, Margaret Jane. *The Taming of the Shrew*. Basingstoke; New York: Palgrave Macmillan, 2006. pp. x, 171. (Shakespeare handbooks.)

6111. Levin, Richard. Petruchio's *soud*. NQ (53:4) 2006, 478–9.

6112. O'Connor, Kelly Newman. What do Petruchio and Katherina wear to Bianca's wedding? SNL (55:4) 2005/06, 113.

6113. Rackin, Phyllis. Our canon, ourselves. *In* (pp. 91–113) **5401**.

6114. Schafer, Carol. David Auburn's *Proof*: taming Cinderella. *See* **14493**.

6115. Senelick, Laurence. A five-year plan for *The Taming of the Shrew*. *In* (pp. 84–103) **5376**.

6116. Shand, G. B. Guying the guys and girling the *Shrew*: (post)feminist fun and Shakespeare's Globe. *In* (pp. 550–63) **5537**.

The Tempest

6117. Almquist, Steve. Not quite the gabbling of 'a thing most brutish': Caliban's Kiswahili in Aimé Césaire's *A Tempest*. Callaloo (29:2) 2006, 587–607.

6118. Beard, Pauline. 'Something harder': the discovery of the self through Greece, fable, and fairy tale. *In* (pp. 203–14) **15631**.

6119. Boltz, Ingeborg. Remythologisierung als Aneignungsstrategie: zu zwei Shakespeare-Szenen in der bildenen Kunst. SJ (142) 2006, 105–23.

6120. De Gooyer, Alan. Surviving *The Tempest*. Raritan (26:2) 2006, 148–68.

6121. Feerick, Jean. 'Divided in soyle': plantation and degeneracy in *The Tempest* and *The Sea Voyage*. RenD (ns 35) 2006, 27–54.

6122. Forest-Hill, Lynn. Giants and enemies of God: the relationship between Caliban and Prospero from the perspective of Insular literary tradition. ShS (59) 2006, 239–53.

6123. Galery, Maria Clara Versiani. Caliban/cannibal/carnival: Cuban articulations of Shakespeare's *The Tempest*. *In* (pp. 307–27) **5376**.

6124. Gibson, Rex (ed.). The tempest. (Bibl. 2003, 38406.) Cambridge; New York: CUP, 2005. pp. xii, 180. (Cambridge school Shakespeare.) (Second ed.: first ed. 2001.)

6125. Griffin, Benjamin. Emending Caliban's *scamels*. NQ (53:4) 2006, 494–5.

6126. Gurr, Andrew. Editing Stefano's book. ShS (59) 2006, 91–107.

6127. Hoenselaars, Ton. Between Heaven and Hell: Shakespearian translation, adaptation, and criticism from a historical perspective. *See* **5329**.

6128. Hogan, Patrick Colm. Narrative universals, heroic tragi-comedy, and Shakespeare's political ambivalence. *See* **5829**.

6129. Horowitz, Arthur. Prospero's 'true preservers': Peter Brook, Yukio Ninagawa, and Giorgio Strehler – twentieth-century directors approach Shakespeare's *The Tempest*. (Bibl. 2004, 6998.) Rev. by Marianne Szlyk in ShB (24:3) 2006, 134–7.

6130. Hunt, Maurice. Shakespeare's 'still-vexed' *Tempest*. Style (39:3) 2005, 299–315.

6131. Kelsey, Lin. 'Many sorts of music': musical genre in *Twelfth Night* and *The Tempest*. *See* **6180**.

6132. La Grand, Virginia; Mattson, Craig T. Brave new performance space: castaway pedagogy in the age of Caliban. *See* **14847**.

6133. Lobsien, Verena Olejniczak. Narrating Caliban: structural skepticism and the invention of the Other in early modern English literature. *In* (pp. 101–27) **5346**.

6134. Lupton, Julia Reinhard. The minority of Caliban: thinking with Shakespeare and Locke. YREAL (22) 2006, 1–35.

6135. Mooneeram, Roshni. Language politics in Dev Virahsawmy's *Toufann*, a postcolonial rewriting of *The Tempest*. JCL (41:3) 2006, 67–81.

6136. Moore, Mary. Wonder, imagination, and the matter of theatre in *The Tempest*. PhilL (30:2) 2006, 496–511.

6137. Mulrooney, Jonathan. Rough magic: *In America*. *See* **19704**.

6138. O'Dair, Sharon. *The Tempest* as *Tempest*: does Paul Mazursky 'green' William Shakespeare? ISLE (12:2) 2005, 165–78.

6139. Perteghella, Manuela. Poetry, music and transformation in the Gulf of Naples: a creative voyage of *The Tempest*. *In* (pp. 109–23) **2874**.

6140. Piazza, Antonella. *'Prospero's sea-sorrows'*: l'odissea di Prospero. *In* (pp. 251–59) **11824**.

6141. Raffel, Burton (ed.). *The Tempest*. With an essay by Harold Bloom. New Haven, CT; London: Yale UP, 2006. pp. xxxiv, 157. (Annotated Shakespeare.)

6142. Romero Jódar, Andrés. 'A stranger in a strange land': an existentialist reading of Frederick Clegg in *The Collector* by John Fowles. *See* **15976**.

6143. Tribble, Evelyn B. 'The dark backward and abysm of time': *The Tempest* and memory. ColLit (33:1) 2006, 151–68.

6144. Trüstedt, Katrin. Secondary satire and the sea-change of romance: reading William Shakespeare's *The Tempest*. LawL (17:3) 2005, 345–64.

6145. Tumelson, Ronald A., ii. Ferdinand's *wife* and Prospero's *wise*. ShS (59) 2006, 79–90.

6146. Van den Berg, Sara. Rhetoric and intimacy in *The Tempest*. RenP (2005) 51–60.

6147. Yang, Zhengrun. The interpretation of dreams in Shakespeare's plays. FLS (122) 2006, 45–52. (In Chinese.)

Timon of Athens

6148. Jowett, John. From print to performance: looking at the masque in *Timon of Athens*. *In* (pp. 73–91) **5334**.

6149. —— (ed.). The life of Timon of Athens. (Bibl. 2004, 7032.) Rev. by Gordon McMullan in SJ (142) 2006, 252–5.

6150. Tink, James. 'Expose thyself to what [*sic*] wretches feel': the figure of bare life in *King Lear* and *Timon of Athens*. *See* **5876**.

Titus Andronicus

6151. Anderson, Thomas Page. Performing early modern trauma from Shakespeare to Milton. Aldershot; Burlington, VT: Ashgate, 2006. pp. 225. Rev. by Heather Hirschfeld in ShQ (57:4) 2006, 487–9; by Catherine Silverstone in RES (57:232) 2006, 801–3; by Andrew Escobedo in CompDr (40:3) 2006, 386–9.

6152. Cartelli, Thomas. Taymor's *Titus* in time and space: surrogation and interpolation. *See* **13102**.

6153. Cordner, Michael. 'Are we being theatrical yet?': actors, editors, and the possibilities of dialogue. *In* (pp. 399–414) **5537**.

6154. Culhane, Peter. Livy and *Titus Andronicus*. Eng (55:211) 2006, 1–13.

6155. Donaldson, Peter S. Game space / tragic space: Julie Taymor's *Titus*. *In* (pp. 457–77) **5537**.

6156. Mohler, Tina. 'What is thy body but a swallowing grave …?': desire underground in *Titus Andronicus*. ShQ (57:1) 2006, 23–44.

6157. Moschovakis, Nicholas R. Topicality and conceptual blending: *Titus Andronicus* and the case of William Hacket. ColLit (33:1) 2006, 127–50.

6158. Odom, Glenn; Reynolds, Bryan. Becomings Roman / comings-to-be villain: pressurized belongings and the coding of ethnicity, religion, and nationality in Peele and Shakespeare's *Titus Andronicus*. *In* (pp. 183–226) **4718**.

6159. Parker, Barbara L. From monarchy to tyranny: *Julius Caesar* among Shakespeare's Roman works. *In* (pp. 111–26) **5805**.

6160. Solga, Kim. Rape's metatheatrical return: rehearsing sexual violence among the early moderns. TJ (58:1) 2006, 53–72.

6161. Williams, William Proctor. Hamlet's pockets: problems with stage directions. *In* (pp. 192–9) **5577**.

6162. Yates, Julian. Accidental Shakespeare. *See* **6012**.

Troilus and Cressida

6163. Apfelbaum, Roger. Shakespeare's *Troilus and Cressida*: textual problems and performance solutions. (Bibl. 2004, 7057.) Rev. by Paul J. Hecht in ShB (23:2) 2005, 119–22; by Tara J. Hayes in SixCJ (37:2) 2006, 615–16.

6164. de Alvarez, Leo Paul S. What is a man? A reading of *Troilus and Cressida*. *In* (pp. 155–95) **5394**.

6165. Lombardi, Chiara. Troilo e Criseida nella letteratura occidentale. *See* **4507**.

6166. Márkus, Zoltán. War, lechery, and goulash Communism: *Troilus and Cressida* in Socialist Hungary. *In* (pp. 246–69) **5376**.

6167. Shirley, Frances A. (ed.). *Troilus and Cressida*. (Bibl. 2005, 6797.) Rev. by Daniel Juan Gil in ShQ (57:3) 2006, 349–51.

6168. von Koppenfels, Werner. *Laesa imaginatio*; or, Imagination infected by passion in Shakespeare's love tragedies. *In* (pp. 68–83) **5346**.

6169. Wilcher, Robert. Suckling's fruition poems and Shakespeare's *Troilus and Cressida*. *See* **7140**.

Twelfth Night

6170. Appelbaum, Robert. Aguecheek's beef, Belch's hiccup, and other gastronomic interjections: literature, culture, and food among the early moderns. *See* **3172**.

6171. Cannon, Walter W. From willow cabin to dark house: *Twelfth Night* and the poetics of indoor spaces. *In* (pp. 162–73) **5577**.

6172. Carroll, Tim; Smith, Emma; White, Martin. Purposeful playing? Purposeful criticism? *In* (pp. 38–60) **5543**.

6173. Edmondson, Paul. *Twelfth Night*. (Bibl. 2005, 6801.) Rev. by Michael Modarelli in ShB (24:4) 2006, 133–5.

6174. Ford, John R. Changeable taffeta: re-dressing the bears in *Twelfth Night*. *In* (pp. 174–91) **5577**.

6175. —— *Twelfth Night*: a guide to the play. Westport, CT; London: Greenwood Press, 2006. pp. xiv, 200. (Greenwood guides to Shakespeare.) Rev. by Marguerite A. Tassi in ShB (24:3) 2006, 131–4.

6176. Gibson, Rex (ed.). Twelfth Night. (Bibl. 1993, 3884.) Cambridge; New York: CUP, 2005. pp. xii, 180. (Cambridge school Shakespeare.) (Second ed.: first ed. 1993.)

6177. Giese, Loreen L. Malvolio's yellow stockings: coding illicit sexuality in early modern London. MedRen (19) 2006, 235–46.

6178. Hobgood, Allison P. *Twelfth Night*'s 'notorious abuse' of Malvolio: shame, humorality, and early modern spectatorship. ShB (24:3) 2006, 1–22.

6179. Josipovici, Gabriel. The singer on the shore: essays, 1991–2004. Manchester: Carcanet Press in assn with the European Jewish Publication Soc., 2006. pp. x, 347, (plates) 8. Rev. by Jeff Bursey in BkCan (35:8) 2006, 15.

6180. Kelsey, Lin. 'Many sorts of music': musical genre in *Twelfth Night* and *The Tempest*. JDJ (25) 2006, 129–81.

6181. Maslen, R. W. *Twelfth Night*, gender, and comedy. *In* (pp. 130–9) **4734**.

6182. Masten, Jeffrey. Editing boys: the performance of genders in print. *In* (pp. 113–34) **5334**.

6183. Menzer, Paul. Dislocating Shakespeare: scene locators and the place of the page. *See* **5904**.

6184. Parker, Patricia. Altering the letter of *Twelfth Night*: 'Some are born great' and the missing signature. ShS (59) 2006, 49–62.

6185. Smith, Bruce R. Ragging *Twelfth Night*: 1602, 1996, 2002–3. *In* (pp. 57–78) **5537**.

6186. Tragelehn, C. M.; Tragelehn, B. K. (eds). Zwölfte Nacht; oder, Was ihr wollt. Frankfurt: Stroemfeld, 2004. pp. 234. (Alt englisches Theater neu, 3.) Rev. by Anika Bárdos in SJ (142) 2006, 249–52.

The Two Gentlemen of Verona

6187. Boltz, Ingeborg. Remythologisierung als Aneignungsstrategie: zu zwei Shakespeare-Szenen in der bildenen Kunst. *See* **6119**.

6188. Hyman, Eric. Shakespeare's *The Two Gentlemen of Verona* 5.4.83. Exp (64:4) 2006, 198–201.

The Two Noble Kinsmen

6189. Rasmussen, Eric; Proudfoot, G. R. (eds). The two noble kinsmen. (Bibl. 2005, 6817.) Rev. by Emma Smith in TLS, 19 May 2006, 33.

Venus and Adonis

6190. Enterline, Lynn. Rhetoric, discipline, and the theatricality of everyday life in Elizabethan grammar schools. *In* (pp. 173–90) **5334**.

6191. Fletcher, Loraine. Animal rites: a reading of *Venus and Adonis*. CritS (17:3) 2005, 1–14.

6192. Kuchar, Gary. Andrew Marvell's anamorphic tears. *See* **6932**.

6193. Sherbo, Arthur. The appendix to Edmond Malone's 1790 *Shakespeare* and the New Variorum *Poems* and *Sonnets*. PBSA (100:1) 2006, 119–23.

6194. —— The Longman's Milton and the 1778 Johnson–Steevens *Variorum*. *See* **6098**.

The Winter's Tale

6195. Diehl, Huston. 'Strike all that look upon with marvel': theatrical and theological wonder in *The Winter's Tale*. *In* (pp. 19–34) **5421**.

6196. Kelley, Sharon A. Shakespeare's *The Winter's Tale*. Exp (64:3) 2006, 140–1.

6197. Laqué, Stephan. '*Lawful as eating*' – Mythos und Regeneration in *The Winter's Tale*. SJ (142) 2006, 60–77.

6198. Lorenz, Philip. Notes on the 'religious turn': mystery, metaphor, medium. *See* **5952**.

6199. Lyne, Raphael. English Guarini: recognition and reception. *See* **6676**.

6200. McMullan, Gordon. 'The technique of it is mature': inventing the late plays in print and in performance. *In* (pp. 243–60) **5334**.

6201. Maillet, Gregory. 'Fidelity to the word': Lonerganian conversion through Shakespeare's *The Winter's Tale* and Dante's *Purgatorio*. RelArts (10:2) 2006, 219–43.

6202. Marsalek, Karen Sawyer. 'Awake your faith': English Resurrection drama and *The Winter's Tale*. *In* (pp. 271–91) **3913**.

6203. Meek, Richard. Ekphrasis in *The Rape of Lucrece* and *The Winter's Tale*. SELit (46:2) 2006, 389–414.

6204. Merriam, Tom. The identity of Shakespeare in *Henry VIII*. *See* **5845**.

6205. Merten, Kai. *Broadside ballads* und *old wives' tales*: zur Intermedialität des Erzählens in Shakespeares *The Winter's Tale*. SJ (142) 2006, 47–59.

6206. Novy, Marianne. Adopted children and constructions of heredity, nurture, and parenthood in Shakespeare's romances. *In* (pp. 55–74) **6264**.

6207. Přidalová, Jana. Symbolic images of mimesis, *trompe l'œil* and a veil in Shakespeare's *The Winter's Tale*. BStE (31) 2005, 175–83.

6208. Schoenfeldt, Michael. 'Give sorrow words': emotional loss and the articulation of temperament in early modern England. *In* (pp. 143–64) **3235**.

6209. Turner, Robert Kean, *et al*. (eds). The winter's tale. New York: Modern Language Assn of America, 2004. pp. xxvii, 974. (New variorum ed. of Shakespeare.)

6210. Wooster, Gerald; Boakes, Janet. Twin dynamics in *The Winter's Tale*. SStudT (43) 2005, 62–90.

SEVENTEENTH CENTURY

GENERAL

6211. ANON. (comp.). Recent articles. *See* **7214**.

6212. ALEXANDER, GAVIN. Writing after Sidney: the literary response to Sir Philip Sidney, 1586–1640. *See* **5030**.

6213. ANDREA, BERNADETTE. Travels through Islam in Early Modern English Studies. *See* **4562**.

6214. BAKER, JENNIFER J. Securing the commonwealth: debt, speculation, and writing in the making of early America. (Bibl. 2005, 6842.) Rev. by Stephen Mihm in Book (70) 2006, 2–3.

6215. BALLASTER, ROS. Fabulous Orients: fictions of the East in England, 1662–1785. Oxford; New York: OUP, 2005. pp. xiii, 408. Rev. by Robert L. Mack in RES (57:230) 2006, 420–3.

6216. —— (ed.). Fables of the East: selected tales, 1662–1785. (Bibl. 2005, 6843.) Rev. by Tom Keymer in TLS, 24 Mar. 2006, 24–5; by Robert L. Mack in RES (57:230) 2006, 420–3.

6217. BLACK, SCOTT. Of essays and reading in early modern Britain. *See* **4566**.

6218. BOSWELL, JACKSON C. References and allusions to Thomas More: 1641–1700 (part IV). *See* **4954**.

6219. BOWERBANK, SYLVIA. Speaking for nature: women and ecologies of early modern England. (Bibl. 2005, 6849.) Rev. by Shana Cohen in Isis (97:3) 2006, 554–5; by Bridget Keegan in 1650–1850 (13) 2006, 332–6.

6220. BRANCH, MICHAEL P. (ed.). Reading the roots: American nature writing before *Walden*. (Bibl. 2004, 7131.) Rev. by Kris Fresonke in AmLH (18:1) 2006, 129–43.

6221. BROOKS, DOUGLAS A. (ed.). Printing and parenting in early modern England. *See* **661**.

6222. BURNHAM, MICHELLE. Land, labor, and colonial economics in Thomas Morton's *New English Canaan*. *See* **7088**.

6223. CARPENTER, ANDREW. Literature in print, 1550–1800. *In* (pp. 301–18) **724**.

6224. CARRUTH, MARY C. (ed.). Feminist interventions in Early American Studies. Tuscaloosa; London: Alabama UP, 2006. pp. xxii, 328.

6225. CASTILLO, SUSAN. Colonial encounters in New World writing, 1500–1786: performing America. *See* **4573**.

6226. —— SCHWEITZER, IVY (eds). A companion to the literatures of Colonial America. Oxford; Malden, MA: Blackwell, 2005. pp. xv, 608. (Blackwell companions to literature and culture.)

6227. CHAKRAVARTY, PRASANTA. Like parchment in the fire: literature and Radicalism in the English Civil War. *See* **6982**.

6228. CHALMERS, HERO. Royalist women writers, 1650–1689. (Bibl. 2005, 7236.) Rev. by Paul Hartle in MLR (101:4) 2006, 1092–4.

6229. CLYMER, LORNA (ed.). Ritual, routine, and regime: repetition in early modern British and European culture. *See* **1894**.

6230. Colacurcio, Michael J. Godly letters: the literature of the American Puritans. Notre Dame, IN: Notre Dame UP, 2006. pp. 640.

6231. Cornett, Michael. New books across the disciplines. *See* **3838**.

6232. —— New books across the disciplines. *See* **3839**.

6233. —— New books across the disciplines. *See* **3840**.

6234. —— New books across the disciplines. *See* **3841**.

6235. Daemen-de Gelder, Katrien. Recitations of nationhood: Sir Robert Ayton (1570–1638) and the canon of early modern Scottish literature. *See* **6537**.

6236. Davidson, Jenny. Hypocrisy and the politics of politeness: manners and morals from Locke to Austen. (Bibl. 2004, 7150.) Rev. by Vera Nünning in MLQ (66:4) 2005, 551–4.

6237. Dimit, Robert G. 'Why, you … I oughta' …': aposiopesis and the natural language of the passions, 1670–1770. StudECC (35) 2006, 161–76.

6238. Dobson, Michael. Mushrooms. *See* **4586**.

6239. Doerksen, Daniel W.; Hodgkins, Christopher (eds). Centered on the Word: literature, Scripture, and the Tudor–Stuart middle way. (Bibl. 2005, 6872.) Rev. by Christopher Baker in SixCJ (37:1) 2006, 288–90; by R. V. Young in BJJ (13) 2006, 217–21.

6240. Elias, A. C., Jr. Reissues in the Dublin book trade: the case of George Grierson and William Williamson. *In* (pp. 44–99) **648**.

6241. Faith, Melanie. Correcting the date of the 'conceited *Newes*'. *See* **6917**.

6242. Faller, Lincoln. 'A dance to which one's feet can still respond'. ECent (46:3) 2005, 207–16 (review-article). (Tribute to J. Douglas Canfield.)

6243. Fudge, Erica. Saying nothing concerning the same: on dominion, purity, and meat in early modern England. *In* (pp. 70–86) **4588**.

6244. —— (ed.). Renaissance beasts: of animals, humans, and other wonderful creatures. *See* **4588**.

6245. Gil, Daniel Juan. Before intimacy: asocial sexuality in early modern England. *See* **4590**.

6246. Gill, Catie. Women in the seventeenth-century Quaker community: a literary study of political identities, 1650–1700. (Bibl. 2005, 6878.) Rev. by Sally Parkin in Parergon (23:1) 2006, 166–7; by Judith Kegan Gardiner in RQ (59:3) 2006, 950–2.

6247. Gillespie, Stuart; Hopkins, David (eds). The Oxford history of literary translation in English: vol. 3, 1660–1790. Oxford; New York: OUP, 2005. pp. vii, 572. Rev. by John Style in EJES (10:2) 2006, 207–9.

6248. Goodall, Peter. The author in the study: self-representation as reader and writer in the medieval and early modern periods. *In* (pp. 104–14) **4792**.

6249. Greene, Jody. The trouble with ownership: literary property and authorial liability in England, 1660–1730. (Bibl. 2005, 6881.) Rev. by Christopher Flint in 1650–1850 (13) 2006, 346–50.

6250. Gribben, C. R. A. The literary cultures of the Scottish Reformation. RES (57:228) 2006, 64–82.

6251. Grossman, Marshall (ed.). Reading Renaissance ethics. *See* **4592**.

6252. Gustafson, Sandra M. (comp.). Historicizing race in Early American Studies: a roundtable with Joanna Brooks, Philip Gould, and David Kazanjian. *See* **20076**.

6253. Hager, Alan (ed.). The age of Milton: an encyclopedia of major 17th-century British and American authors. (Bibl. 2005, 6883.) Rev. by Peter Barry in Eng (55:212) 2006, 213–19.

6254. —— (gen. ed.). Encyclopedia of British writers: vol. 1, 16th and 17th centuries. *See* **4593**.

6255. Hall, David D. Scribal publication in seventeenth-century New England: an introduction and checklist. *See* **219**.

6256. Hamilton, Donna B. (ed.). A concise companion to English Renaissance literature. *See* **4594**.

6257. Harris, Sharon M. Feminist theories and Early American Studies. *In* (pp. 3–10) **6224**.

6258. Harvey, A. D. The Roman ideal of rural retirement in seventeenth- and eighteenth-century England. *See* **8078**.

6259. Hattaway, Michael. Renaissance and reformations: an introduction to early modern English literature. *See* **4596**.

6260. Hempfer, Klaus W. (ed.). Poetik des Dialogs: aktuelle Theorie und rinascimentales Selbstverständnis. *See* **4599**.

6261. Hoenselaars, Ton; Kinney, Arthur F. (eds). Challenging Humanism: essays in honor of Dominic Baker-Smith. *See* **4600**.

6262. Holmes, Jonathan; Streete, Adrian (eds). Refiguring mimesis: representation in early modern literature. *See* **4602**.

6263. Hume, Robert D. The economics of culture in London, 1660–1740. HLQ (69:4) 2006, 487–533.

6264. Immel, Andrea; Witmore, Michael (eds). Childhood and children's books in early modern Europe, 1550–1800. London; New York: Routledge, 2006. pp. viii, 341. (Children's literature and culture, 38.) Rev. by Aileen Fyfe in TLS, 22 & 29 Dec. 2006, 41; by Ruth Carver Capasso in CLAQ (31:4) 2006, 387–9.

6265. Kahn, Victoria. Wayward contracts: the crisis of political obligation in England, 1640–1674. (Bibl. 2005, 6894.) Rev. by Joad Raymond in MQ (40:3) 2006, 246–9.

6266. Kelly, Philippa. Dialogues of self-reflection: early modern mirrors. *In* (pp. 62–85) **4792**.

6267. King, Thomas A. The castrato's castration. *See* **7752**.

6268. Kitzes, Adam H. The politics of melancholy from Spenser to Milton. London; New York: Routledge, 2006. pp. ix, 260. (Literary criticism and cultural theory.)

6269. Krueger, Misty. Some current publications. Restoration (30:1) 2006, 43–67.

6270. Lamb, Mary Ellen. Recent studies in the English Renaissance. *See* **4611**.

6271. Lewis, Rhodri. Of 'Origenian Platonisme': Joseph Glanvill on the pre-existence of souls. *See* **6809**.

6272. Lockey, Brian C. Law and empire in English Renaissance literature. *See* **4613**.

6273. Longfellow, Erica. Women and religious writing in early modern England. (Bibl. 2005, 6903.) Rev. by Erin E. Kelly in SixCJ (37:2) 2006, 485–6; by Jennifer Waldron in JR (86:3) 2006, 477–9; by Victoria E. Burke in NQ (53:2) 2006, 234–5; by Guyonne Leduc in EA (59:1) 2006, 104–6.

6274. Loxley, James. On exegetical duty: historical pragmatics and the grammar of the libel. HLQ (69:1) 2006, 83–103.

6275. Mackie, Erin. Boys will be boys: masculinity, criminality, and the Restoration rake. ECent (46:2) 2005, 129–49.

6276. McRae, Andrew. Literature, satire, and the early Stuart State. (Bibl. 2005, 6910.) Rev. by David Reid in MLR (101:2) 2006, 515–16.

6277. McWilliams, John. New England's crises and cultural memory: literature, politics, history, religion, 1620–1860. (Bibl. 2005, 6911.) Rev. by Jennifer Bernstein in EAL (41:3) 2006, 569–74.

6278. Markley, Robert. The Far East and the English imagination, 1600–1730. Cambridge; New York: CUP, 2006. pp. viii, 316. Rev. by Jerome de Groot in TLS, 14 July 2006, 31.

6279. Marotti, Arthur F. Religious ideology and cultural fantasy: Catholic and anti-Catholic discourses in early modern England. *See* **4615**.

6280. Maus, Katharine Eisaman. A womb of his own: male Renaissance poets in the female body. *In* (pp. 89–108) **661**.

6281. Ménager, Daniel (ed.). La Renaissance et la nuit. *See* **4617**.

6282. Meyers, Karen. Colonialism and the Revolutionary period: beginnings to 1800. New York: Facts on File, 2006. pp. 96. (Backgrounds to American literature.)

6283. Mowry, Melissa M. The bawdy politic in Stuart England, 1660–1714: political pornography and prostitution. (Bibl. 2005, 6915.) Rev. by Mara I. Amster in SixCJ (37:2) 2006, 438–9.

6284. Paster, Gail Kern; Rowe, Katherine; Floyd-Wilson, Mary (eds). Reading the early modern passions: essays in the cultural history of emotion. (Bibl. 2005, 6919.) Rev. by Mary Thomas Crane in ColLit (33:1) 2006, 239–42; by Kristine Steenbergh in CEl (69) 2006, 97–8; by Diana E. Henderson in SStud (34) 2006, 224–31; by Helen Wilcox in MLR (101:4) 2006, 1089–90; by Kate Frost in BJJ (13) 2006, 234–8.

6285. Perry, Curtis. Literature and favouritism in early modern England. *See* **4623**.

6286. Perry, Kathryn. Unpicking the seam: talking animals and reader pleasure in early modern satire. *In* (pp. 19–36) **4588**.

6287. Persels, Jeff; Ganim, Russell (eds). Fecal matters in early modern literature and art: studies in scatology. (Bibl. 2005, 6923.) Rev. by Albrecht Classen in SixCJ (36:4) 2005, 1105–6.

6288. Pohl, Nicole. Women, space, and utopia, 1600–1800. Aldershot; Burlington, VT: Ashgate, 2006. pp. 200. (Women and gender in the early modern world.)

6289. Poole, William. *Nuncius inanimatus*: seventeenth-century telegraphy: the schemes of Francis Godwin and Henry Reynolds. *See* **6811**.

6290. Prescott, Anne Lake. Refusing translation: the Gregorian Calendar and early modern English writers. *See* **6744**.

6291. Purkiss, Diane. Literature, gender and politics during the English Civil War. Cambridge; New York: CUP, 2005. pp. vi, 300. Rev. by R. C. Richardson in LitH (15:2) 2006, 70–2; by James Loxley in RQ (59:3) 2006, 982–3.

6292. Rankin, Deana. Between Spenser and Swift: English writing in seventeenth-century Ireland. (Bibl. 2005, 6927.) Rev. by Thomas Healy in TLS, 21 July 2006, 11; by Richard A. McCabe in RES (57:229) 2006, 270–1; by Clare Carroll in RQ (59:3) 2006, 980–2.

6293. Reichardt, Dosia. The constitution of narrative identity in seventeenth-century prison writing. *In* (pp. 115–29) **4792**.

6294. Resende, Aimara da Cunha. 'Here's sport, indeed!': interchangeable voices and mass communication in Renaissance England. *See* **4628**.

6295. Ribeiro, Aileen. Fashion and fiction: dress in art and literature in Stuart England. (Bibl. 2005, 6929.) Rev. by Kevin Sharpe in TLS, 12 May 2006, 24.

6296. Richardson, Catherine (ed.). Clothing culture, 1350–1650. *See* **4629**.

6297. Richetti, John. The Cambridge history of English literature, 1660–1780. (Bibl. 2005, 6931.) Rev. by Jennifer Golightly in RECTR (20:1/2) 2005, 100–4; by Claude Rawson in TLS, 10 Mar. 2006, 3–5; by Philip Smallwood in AJ (17) 2006, 363–9.

6298. Salzman, Paul. Reading early modern women's writing. Oxford; New York: OUP, 2006. pp. 247.

6299. Sauer, Elizabeth. 'Paper-contestations' and textual communities in England, 1640–1675. (Bibl. 2005, 6934.) Rev. by Maureen Bell in TLS, 21 Apr. 2006, 31; by Joad Raymond in SHARP (15:4) 2006, 13–14.

6300. Scott, Alison V. Selfish gifts: the politics of exchange and English courtly literature, 1580–1628. *See* **4631**.

6301. Seelig, Sharon Cadman. Autobiography and gender in early modern literature. Cambridge; New York: CUP, 2006. pp. ix, 214. (Reading women's lives, 1600–1680.) Rev. by Elizabeth Scott-Baumann in TLS, 8 Sept. 2006, 25.

6302. Seuntjens, Wolter. Vapours and fumes, damps and qualms: windy passions in the early modern age (1600–1800). *See* **5429**.

6303. Sharpe, Kevin. A patch on the left. TLS, 12 May 2006, 24–5 (review-article). (Fashion in Stuart culture.)

6304. Smallwood, Philip. Literary histories old and new. AJ (17) 2006, 363–9 (review-article).

6305. Smyth, Adam. 'Profit and delight': printed miscellanies in England, 1640–1682. (Bibl. 2005, 6941.) Rev. by Timothy Raylor in MP (103:2) 2005, 263–7; by John Vance in Scriblerian (38:2) 2006, 325–6.

6306. —— 'Reade in one age and understood i' th' next': recycling satire in the mid-seventeenth century. HLQ (69:1) 2006, 67–82.

6307. —— (ed.). A pleasing sinne: drink and conviviality in seventeenth-century England. (Bibl. 2005, 6942.) Rev. by Beat Kümin in SixCJ (37:1) 2006, 128–30; by Bryan N. S. Gooch in SCN (64:1/2) 2006, 22–6.

6308. Spencer, Jane. Literary relations: kinship and the canon 1660–1830. (Bibl. 2005, 6944.) Rev. by Richard Terry in RES (57:230) 2006, 406–7.

6309. Staub, Susan C. Nature's cruel stepdames: murderous women in the street literature of seventeenth-century England. (Bibl. 2005, 6945.) Rev. by Viviana Comensoli in RQ (59:1) 2006, 279–81.

6310. Staves, Susan. A literary history of women's writing in Britain, 1660–1789. Cambridge; New York: CUP, 2006. pp. xi, 536.

6311. Stephanson, Raymond. The yard of wit: male creativity and sexuality, 1650–1750. (Bibl. 2005, 6946.) Rev. by Laura Rosenthal in 1650–1850 (11) 2005, 551–4.

6312. Stevens, Laura M. The poor Indians: British missionaries, Native Americans, and Colonial sensibility. (Bibl. 2005, 6947.) Rev. by Phillip H. Round in EAL (41:1) 2006, 145–8; by Beth Barton Schweiger in LitH (15:2) 2006, 76–7.

6313. Sullivan, Ceri. London's early modern creative industrialists. SP (103:3) 2006, 313–28.

6314. Tiffany, Grace. Love's pilgrimage: the holy journey in English Renaissance literature. *See* **4638**.

6315. Wall, Cynthia. Recent studies in the Restoration and eighteenth century. SELit (46:3) 2006, 657–724.

6316. Watson, Robert N. Back to nature: the green and the real in the late Renaissance. *See* **4643**.

6317. White, Ed. The backcountry and the city: colonization and conflict in early America. Minneapolis; London: Minnesota UP, 2005. pp. xix, 236. Rev. by Andrew Newman in EAL (41:3) 2006, 592–600.

6318. Wiseman, S. J. Hairy on the inside: metamorphosis and civility in English werewolf texts. *In* (pp. 50–69) **4588**.

6319. Wiseman, Susan. Conspiracy and virtue: women, writing, and politics in seventeenth-century England. Oxford; New York: OUP, 2006. pp. 384.

6320. Wright, Nancy E.; Ferguson, Margaret W.; Buck, A. R. (eds). Women, property, and the letters of the law in early modern England. (Bibl. 2005, 6964.) Rev. by Constance Jordan in SStud (34) 2006, 268–74.

6321. Zwicker, Steven N. Is there such a thing as Restoration literature? HLQ (69:3) 2006, 425–49.

DRAMA AND THE THEATRE

6322. Anderson, Thomas Page. Performing early modern trauma from Shakespeare to Milton. *See* **6151**.

6323. Astington, John H. Playing the man: acting at the Red Bull and the Fortune. ETh (9:2) 2006, 130–43.

6324. Berek, Peter. Genres, early modern theatrical title pages, and the authority of print. *In* (pp. 159–75) **4731**.

6325. Bergeron, David M. Textual patronage in English drama, 1570–1640. *See* **4650**.

6326. Borden, Ian. The Blackfriars gladiators: masters of fence, playing a prize, and the Elizabethan and Stuart theatre. *In* (pp. 132–46) **5577**.

6327. Bosman, Anston. History between theaters. *In* (pp. 191–207) **5334**.

6328. Bregazzi, Josephine. Changing roles: gender marking through syntactic distribution in the Jacobean theater. *In* (pp. 234–49) **5308**.

6329. Britland, Karen. Drama at the courts of Queen Henrietta Maria. Cambridge; New York: CUP, 2006. pp. ix, 294.

6330. Bush-Bailey, Gilli. Treading the bawds: actresses and playwrights on the late Stuart stage. Manchester; New York: Manchester UP, 2006. pp. 226. (Women, theatre and performance.)

6331. Centerwall, Brandon. A greatly exaggerated demise: the remaking of the Children of Paul's as the Duke of York's Men (1608). ETh (9:1) 2006, 85–107.

6332. Clegg, Cyndia Susan. Renaissance play-readers: ordinary and extraordinary. *In* (pp. 23–38) **4731**.

6333. Crane, Mary Thomas. Recent studies in Tudor and Stuart drama. *See* **4660**.

6334. Dawson, Mark S. Gentility and the comic theatre of late Stuart London. (Bibl. 2005, 6985.) Rev. by R. C. Richardson in LitH (15:2) 2006, 74–5; by David Roberts in NQ (53:4) 2006, 575–7; by Ira Clark in RQ (59:2) 2006, 654–5.

6335. Dessen, Alan C. Rescripting Shakespeare (and others) in 2005. *See* **4665**.

6336. Dimmock, Matthew. New Turkes: dramatizing Islam and the Ottomans in early modern England. *See* **4666**.

6337. Donohue, Joseph (ed.). The Cambridge history of British theatre: vol. 2, 1660 to 1895. (Bibl. 2005, 6988.) Rev. by Jennifer Golightly in RECTR (20:1/2) 2005, 100–4.

6338. Egan, Gabriel. 'As it was, is, or will be played': title-pages and the theatre industry to 1610. *In* (pp. 92–110) **5334**.

6339. Eis, Joel D.; Earnest, Stephen. The actor as archeologist: aspects of the dramaturgy of the Restoration stage rediscovered in performance. *See* **7211**.

6340. Gieskes, Edward. Representing the professions: administration, law, and theater in early modern England. *See* **5306**.

6341. Gossett, Suzanne. Editing collaborative drama. *See* **5175**.

6342. Gurr, Andrew. London's Blackfriars playhouse and the Chamberlain's Men. *In* (pp. 17–30) **5577**.

6343. —— Playgoing in Shakespeare's London. *See* **4676**.

6344. Haekel, Ralf. Die englischen Komödianten in Deutschland: eine Einfuhrung in die Ursprunge des deutschen Berufsschauspiels. *See* **4677**.

6345. Holland, Peter; Orgel, Stephen (eds). From performance to print in Shakespeare's England. *See* **5334**.

6346. Hughes, Derek. Rape on the Restoration stage. ECent (46:3) 2005, 225–36.

6347. Hutson, Lorna. Forensic aspects of Renaissance mimesis. *See* **5732**.

6348. Ichikawa, Mariko. Were the doors open or closed? The use of stage doors in the Shakespearean theatre. *See* **5545**.

6349. Ioppolo, Grace. Dramatists and their manuscripts in the age of Shakespeare, Jonson, Middleton and Heywood: authorship, authority, and the playhouse. *See* **511**.

6350. Isaac, Megan Lynn. Legitimizing magic in *The Birth of Merlin*. *See* **7121**.

6351. Jackson, MacD. P. Connectives and the Webster canon. *See* **7180**.

6352. Johnson, Odai. Absence and memory in Colonial American theatre: Fiorelli's plaster. Basingstoke; New York: Palgrave Macmillan, 2006. pp. x, 322. (Palgrave studies in theatre and performance history.)

6353. Kathman, David. The burial of Thomas Pope. *See* **5549**.

6354. Knowles, James. 'Can ye not tell a man from a marmoset?': apes and others on the early modern stage. *In* (pp. 138–63) **4588**.

6355. —— 'Songs of baser alloy': Jonson's *Gypsies Metamorphosed* and the circulation of manuscript libels. *See* **6880**.

6356. Knutson, Roslyn. What if there wasn't a 'Blackfriars repertory'? *In* (pp. 54–60) **5577**.

6357. Knutson, Roslyn L. Theater companies and stages. *In* (pp. 12–22) **4734**.

6358. Lehmann, Courtney. Dancing in a (cyber) net: 'Renaissance women', systems theory, and the war of the cinemas. *See* **5562**.

6359. Lopez, Jeremy. Census of Renaissance drama performance reviews in *Shakespeare Quarterly* and *Shakespeare Survey*, 1948–2005. *See* **5565**.

6360. McCarthy, Jeanne H. The queen's 'unfledged minions': an alternate account of the origins of Blackfriars and of the boy company phenomenon. *In* (pp. 93–117) **5577**.

6361. McLuskie, Kathleen. Figuring the consumer for early modern drama. *In* (pp. 186–206) **5421**.

6362. Marsden, Jean I. Fatal desire: women, sexuality, and the English stage, 1660–1720. Ithaca, NY; London: Cornell UP, 2006. pp. viii, 216.

6363. Mehl, Dieter; Stock, Angela; Zwierlein, Anne-Julia (eds). Plotting early modern London: new essays on Jacobean city comedy. (Bibl. 2005, 7026.) Rev. by Enno Ruge in SJ (142) 2006, 261–3; by W. David Kay in MLR (101:4) 2006, 1088–9.

6364. Menzer, Paul (ed.). Inside Shakespeare: essays on the Blackfriars stage. *See* **5577**.

6365. Morash, Christopher. Theatre and print, 1550–1800. *In* (pp. 319–34) **724**.

6366. Munro, Lucy. Children of the Queen's Revels: a Jacobean theatre repertory. (Bibl. 2005, 7030.) Rev. by Roslyn Knutson in TLS, 10 Feb. 2006, 20; by Jeremy Lopez in RES (57:229) 2006, 268–70.

6367. Nicol, David. 'My little what shall I call thee': reinventing rape tragedy in William Rowley's *All's Lost by Lust*. *See* **7123**.

6368. —— The repertory of Prince Charles's (I) Company, 1608–1625. ETh (9.2) 2006, 57–72.

6369. —— The title-page of *The World Tossed at Tennis*: a portrait of a Jacobean playing company? NQ (53:2) 2006, 158–9.

6370. Nunn, Hilary M. Staging anatomies: dissection and spectacle in early Stuart tragedy. Aldershot; Burlington, VT: Ashgate, 2005. pp. viii, 231. (Literary and scientific cultures of early modernity.) Rev. by Clifford Armion in CEl (68) 2005, 93–4; by Matthew Greenfield in RQ (59:1) 2006, 286–7.

6371. Nussbaum, Felicity. 'More than a woman': early memoirs of British actresses. *In* (pp. 225–42) **7255**.

6372. O'Neill, John. Rambler and cully: Rochester's satire and the self-presentation of the Restoration rake. *See* **7115**.

6373. Orgel, Stephen. Reading occasions. *See* **4710**.

6374. Peachman, John. Links between *Mucedorus* and *The Tragical History, Admirable Atchievements and Various Events of Guy Earl of Warwick*. *See* **4713**.

6375. Quiring, Björn. A consuming dish: supplementing Raffield. LawL (17:3) 2005, 397–404.

6376. Raffield, Paul. A discredited priesthood: the failings of common lawyers and their representation in seventeenth-century satirical drama. *See* **7107**.

6377. Ravelhofer, Barbara. The early Stuart masque: dance, costume, and music. Oxford; New York: OUP, 2006. pp. xvi, 317. Rev. by Karen Britland in RES (57:232) 2006, 800–1.

6378. Reynolds, Bryan (ed.). Transversal enterprises in the drama of Shakespeare and his contemporaries: fugitive explorations. *See* **4718**.

6379. Ronan, Clifford. Caesar on and off the Renaissance English stage. *In* (pp. 71–89) **5805**.

6380. Shapiro, Michael. The Westminister scholars' *Sapientia Solomonis* as royal gift offering. *In* (pp. 118–22) **5577**.

6381. Shohet, Lauren. The masque in/as print. *In* (pp. 176–202) **4731**.

6382. Simkin, Stevie. Early modern tragedy and the cinema of violence. *See* **4724**.

6383. Solomon, Diana. Anne Bracegirdle's breaches. 1650–1850 (11) 2005, 229–49.

6384. Steggle, Matthew. Players at the Maidenhead Inn, Islington, 1618. *See* **7143**.

6385. Stern, Tiffany. Taking part: actors and audience on the stage at Blackfriars. *In* (pp. 35–53) **5577**.

6386. Stillman, Robert (ed.). Spectacle and public performance in the late Middle Ages and the Renaissance. *See* **4729**.

6387. Straznicky, Marta. Privacy, playreading, and women's closet drama, 1550–1700. (Bibl. 2004, 7311.) Rev. by Alison Findlay in MedRen (19) 2006, 334–6; by Alexandra G. Bennett in NQ (53:3) 2006, 377–8; by Carol Blessing in RQ (59:1) 2006, 275–7; by Guyonne Leduc in EA (59:1) 2006, 106–8.

6388. —— Reading through the body: women and printed drama. *In* (pp. 59–79) **4731**.

6389. —— The Red Bull repertory in print, 1605–60. ETh (9:2) 2006, 144–56.

6390. —— (ed.). The book of the play: playwrights, stationers, and readers in early modern England. *See* **4731**.

6391. Sullivan, Garrett A., Jr; Cheney, Patrick; Hadfield, Andrew (eds). Early modern English drama: a critical companion. *See* **4734**.

6392. Thompson, James. J. Douglas Canfield and Restoration drama. ECent (46:3) 2005, 201–6.

6393. Thomson, Peter. The Cambridge introduction to English theatre, 1660–1900. Cambridge; New York: CUP, 2006. pp. xiv, 310.

6394. Tiner, Elza C. Professional players in Stratford-on-Avon, 1587–1602. *In* (pp. 86–92) **5577**.

6395. Tomlinson, Sophie. Women on stage in Stuart drama. Cambridge; New York: CUP, 2005. pp. xiv, 294.

6396. Turner, Henry S. The English Renaissance stage: geometry, poetics, and the practical spatial arts 1580–1630. *See* **4737**.

6397. Vaughan, Virginia Mason. Blacking-up at the Blackfriars Theatre. *In* (pp. 123–31) **5577**.

6398. Webster, Jeremy W. Performing libertinism in Charles II's court: politics, drama, sexuality. (Bibl. 2005, 7049.) Rev. by David Roberts in NQ (53:4) 2006, 575–7.

6399. Wells, Stanley. Shakespeare and Co.: Christopher Marlowe, Thomas Dekker, Ben Jonson, Thomas Middleton, John Fletcher and the other players in his story. *See* **5452**.

6400. Womack, Peter. English Renaissance drama. *See* **4746**.

6401. Wong, Mitali P. Politics and tropes in Renaissance history plays: understanding a neglected genre. *See* **4747**.

6402. Zucker, Adam; Farmer, Alan B. (eds). Localizing Caroline drama: politics and economics of the early modern English stage, 1625–1642. Basingstoke; New York: Palgrave Macmillan, 2006. pp. xvi, 259.

FICTION

6403. Brink, Jean R. Theorizing attribution and authorship: *Rivall Friendship*, an anonymous seventeenth-century romance. SidJ (22:1/2) 2004, 105–13.

6404. Carnell, Rachel. Partisan politics, narrative realism, and the rise of the British novel. Basingstoke; New York: Palgrave Macmillan, 2006. pp. x, 226.

6405. Haldane, Michael. The date of Thomas Combe's *Fortunatus* and its relation to Thomas Dekker's *Old Fortunatus*. MLR (101:2) 2006, 313–24.

6406. Hammond, Brean; Regan, Shaun. Making the novel: fiction and society in Britain, 1660–1789. Basingstoke; New York: Palgrave Macmillan, 2006. pp. xii, 268. Rev. by Henry Power in RES (57:231) 2006, 573–5.

6407. Henriksen, Erin; Polydorou, Desma (sels and introds). Fiction of unknown or questionable attribution: 1, *Diotrephe* and *The Amorous Abbess*.

Aldershot; Burlington, VT: Ashgate, 2006. pp. xxvi, 192, 140. (Early modern Englishwoman, II: Printed writings, 1641–1700, 3:9.) (Facsimiles.)

6408. —— —— Fiction of unknown or questionable attribution: 2, *Peppa* and *Alcander and Philocrates*. Aldershot; Burlington, VT: Ashgate, 2006. pp. xxvi, 130, 132. (Early modern Englishwoman, II: Printed writings, 1641–1700, 3:10.) (Facsimiles.)

6409. LOEBER, ROLF; LOEBER, MAGDA; BURNHAM, ANNE MULLIN. A guide to Irish fiction, 1650–1900. Dublin; Portland, OR: Four Courts Press, 2006. pp. cxv, 1489, (plates) 64.

6410. MARTIN, RANDALL (sel. and introd.). Women and murder in early modern news pamphlets and broadside ballads, 1573–1697. *See* **4783**.

LITERATURE FOR CHILDREN

6411. ALDERSON, BRIAN; DE MAREZ OYENS, FELIX. Be merry and wise: origins of children's book publishing in England, 1650–1850. *See* **636**.

6412. FUDGE, ERICA. Learning to laugh: children and being human in early modern thought. *In* (pp. 19–39) **6264**.

6413. LERER, SETH. 'Thy life to mend, this book attend': reading and healing in the arc of children's literature. NLH (37:3) 2006, 631–42.

POETRY

6414. BELLANY, ALASTAIR. Singing libel in early Stuart England: the case of the Staines fiddlers, 1627. HLQ (69:1) 2006, 177–93.

6415. BRADY, ANDREA. English funerary elegy in the seventeenth century: laws in mourning. Basingstoke; New York: Palgrave Macmillan, 2006. pp. x, 265. (Early modern literature in history.)

6416. CALDWELL, TANYA M. Restoration parodies of Virgil and English literary values. HLQ (69:3) 2006, 383–401.

6417. CARPENTER, ANDREW. Two early printed verse squibs from Cork. *In* (pp. 164–74) **648**.

6418. CHENEY, PATRICK; HADFIELD, ANDREW; SULLIVAN, GARRETT A., JR (eds). Early modern English poetry: a critical companion. *See* **4753**.

6419. CLARKE, ELIZABETH. Re-reading the Exclusion Crisis. *See* **6460**.

6420. COLCLOUGH, DAVID. Verse libels and the epideictic tradition in early Stuart England. HLQ (69:1) 2006, 15–30.

6421. CRAIG, BARRY L. St Augustine and the Metaphysical poets. *In* (pp. 97–116) **3301**.

6422. DAVIDSON, CLIFFORD. Selected studies in drama & Renaissance literature. *See* **3903**.

6423. DOELMAN, JAMES. Epigrams and political satire in early Stuart England. HLQ (69:1) 2006, 31–45.

6424. DRAGSTRA, HENK. Politics of holiness: royalty for the masses in *The Wandering Jew's Chronicle*. *In* (pp. 61–80) **3415**.

6425. FISHER, NICHOLAS. The contemporary reception of Rochester's *A Satyr against Mankind*. *See* **7109**.

6426. —— Rochester's contemporary reception: the evidence of the memorial verses. *See* **7110**.

6427. HADFIELD, ANDREW. Literary contexts: predecessors and contemporaries. *In* (pp. 49–64) **6718**.

6428. HAMMOND, PAUL. The making of Restoration poetry. Woodbridge, Suffolk; Rochester, NY: Brewer, 2006. pp. xxiii, 230. (Studies in Renaissance literature, 16.)

6429. HUNTER, PAUL. Seven reasons for rhyme. *In* (pp. 172–98) **1894**.

6430. JACK, R. D. S. Music, poetry, and performance at the court of James VI. JDJ (25) 2006, 37–63.

6431. MCRAE, ANDREW. Reading libels: an introduction. HLQ (69:1) 2006, 1–13.

6432. MILLMAN, JILL SEAL, *et al.* (eds). Early modern women's manuscript poetry. Introd. by Elizabeth Clarke and Jonathan Gibson. *See* **4760**.

6433. MONTGOMERY, WILL. Susan Howe's Renaissance period: metamorphosis and representation in *Pythagorean Silence* and *Defenestration of Prague*. *See* **16474**.

6434. MORRIS, AMY M. E. Popular measures: poetry and church order in seventeenth-century Massachusetts. (Bibl. 2005, 7075.) Rev. by William J. Scheick in SCN (64:1/2) 2006, 57–9; by Philip Gould in AL (78:4) 2006, 869–72.

6435. MORTIMER, ANTHONY (ed.). Petrarch's *Canzoniere* in the English Renaissance. *See* **4762**.

6436. NELSON, NICOLAS H. The pleasure of poetry: reading and enjoying British poetry from Donne to Burns. Westport, CT; London: Praeger, 2006. pp. x, 267.

6437. O'CALLAGHAN, MICHELLE. Performing politics: the circulation of the *Parliament Fart*. HLQ (69:1) 2006, 121–38.

6438. PARKS, STEPHEN, *et al.* (eds). First-line index of English poetry, 1500–1800, in manuscripts of the James M. and Marie-Louise Osborn Collection in the Beinecke Rare Book and Manuscript Library of Yale University. *See* **4764**.

6439. PATTERSON, ANNABEL. Donne's re-formed *La Corona*. *See* **6737**.

6440. PERRYMAN, JOHN. Back to *The Bay Psalm Book*: T. S. Eliot's identity crisis and *Sweeney Erect*. *See* **15709**.

6441. PIKE, LIONEL. Pills to purge melancholy: the evolution of the English ballett. *See* **4765**.

6442. PURSGLOVE, GLYN. 'Storms turn to music' (*The Rain-bow*). *See* **7156**.

6443. RUMRICH, JOHN P.; CHAPLIN, GREGORY (eds). Seventeenth-century British poetry, 1603–1660: authoritative texts, criticism. New York; London: Norton, 2006. pp. xxii, 999. (Norton critical eds.)

6444. SCHURINK, FRED. An unnoticed early reference to Shakespeare. *See* **5428**.

6445. SEELEY, TRACY. 'The fair light mystery of images': Alice Meynell's metaphysical turn. *See* **10924**.

6446. SHARGEL, RAPHAEL. Damned by excessive praise: *Jonsonus Virbius* and the foibles of reputation. *See* **6903**.

6447. Smith, Emily. The local popularity of *The Concealed Fansyes*. *See* **6634**.

6448. Soubrenie, Élisabeth. L'art de la conversion au siècle de la poésie métaphysique anglaise. Paris: Belles Lettres, 2004. pp. 456. Rev. by Jean-Marie Maguin in EA (59:1) 2006, 108–10.

6449. Williams, Abigail. Poetry and the creation of a Whig literary culture, 1681–1714. (Bibl. 2005, 7083.) Rev. by David Hopkins in NQ (53:2) 2006, 242–5.

PROSE

6450. Armstrong, Catherine. 'A just and modest vindication': comparing the responses of the Scottish and English book trades to the Darien Scheme, 1698–1700. *In* (pp. 1–11) **746**.

6451. Babb, Valerie. Of harlots and hags: feminine embodiments of early American Whiteness. *In* (pp. 97–111) **6224**.

6452. Bækken, Bjørg. Some aspects of word order in seventeenth-century English. *See* **2473**.

6453. Bannet, Eve Tavor. Empire of letters: letter manuals and transatlantic correspondence, 1680–1820. (Bibl. 2005, 7089.) Rev. by John D. Baird in TLS, 19 May 2006, 29; by Melanie Bigold in NQ (53:4) 2006, 579–80; by Konstantin Dierks in RES (57:232) 2006, 826–7.

6454. Bath, Jo; Newton, John. 'Sensible proof of spirits': ghost belief during the later seventeenth century. *See* **3115**.

6455. Bernet, Claus. Jerusalemvorstellungen in radikalpietistischen und radikalpuritanischen Siedlungen Nordamerikas. Amst (51:2) 2006, 141–66.

6456. Brennan, Michael G. (ed.). The origins of the Grand Tour: the travels of Robert Montagu, Lord Mandeville (1649–1654), William Hammond (1655–1658), and Banaster Maynard (1660–1663). London: Hakluyt Soc., 2004. pp. xvii, 331. (Works issued by the Hakluyt Soc., 3:14.) Rev. by Jeremy Black in NQ (53:1) 2006, 121–2; by David Stymeist in RQ (59:1) 2006, 250–1.

6457. Brownlees, Nicholas (ed.). News discourse in early modern Britain: selected papers of CHINED 2004. *See* **4771**.

6458. Carey, Daniel (ed.). Asian travel in the Renaissance. Preface by Anthony Reid. *See* **4772**.

6459. Ceppi, Elisabeth. Invisible labor: Puritan servitude and the demonic possession of Elizabeth Knapp. AL (78:2) 2006, 263–92.

6460. Clarke, Elizabeth. Re-reading the Exclusion Crisis. SevC (21:1) 2006, 141–59.

6461. Connolly, Ruth. A manuscript treatise by Viscountess Ranelagh (1614–1691). NQ (53:2) 2006, 170–2.

6462. Connor, T. P. Malignant reading: John Squier's Newgate Prison library, 1642–46. *See* **306**.

6463. Cunningham, Bernadette. Historical writing, 1660–1750. *In* (pp. 264–81) **724**.

6464. Dunan-Page, Anne. John Bunyan's *A Confession of My Faith* and Restoration Anabaptism. *See* **6612**.

6465. Farmer, Alan B. Play-reading, news-reading, and Ben Jonson's *The Staple of News*. *In* (pp. 127–58) **4731**.

6466. Feroli, Teresa. Political speaking justified: women prophets and the English Revolution. Newark: Delaware UP, 2006. pp. 270.

6467. Franklin, Colleen. Northern gothic: *The Strange and Dangerous Voyage of Captaine Thomas James*. *In* (pp. 147–54) **13541**.

6468. Glaisyer, Natasha. 'A due Circulation in the Veins of the Publick': imagining credit in late seventeenth- and early eighteenth-century England. ECent (46:3) 2005, 277–97.

6469. Guard, Pippa. A defence of the first English actress. *See* **7158**.

6470. Hadfield, Andrew. Historical writing, 1550–1660. *In* (pp. 250–63) **724**.

6471. Hallam, Elizabeth. Speaking to reveal: the body and acts of 'exposure' in early modern popular discourse. *In* (pp. 239–62) **4629**.

6472. Heaton, Gabriel. *The Poor Man's Petition*: Anthony Atkinson and the politics of libel. HLQ (69:1) 2006, 105–20.

6473. Hodgson, Elizabeth. The domestic 'fruite of Eves transgression' in Stuart funeral sermons. PrSt (28:1) 2006, 1–18.

6474. Holmes, Heather. Scottish agricultural writers and the creation of their personal identities between 1697 and 1790. FolkL (44) 2005/06, 87–109.

6475. Hughes, Ann. *Gangraena* and the struggle for the English Revolution. Oxford; New York: OUP, 2004. pp. vii, 482. Rev. by Philip Baker in SHARP (14:4) 2005, 15; by Sharon Achinstein in RES (57:230) 2006, 407–9; by Nicholas McDowell in NQ (53:2) 2006, 235–7; by Michael Mendle in RQ (59:2) 2006, 649–50.

6476. Keck, Karen Rae. Catherine, not Elizabeth: the misattribution of the letters in Edinburgh University Library Laing.III.347. *See* **6652**.

6477. Kewes, Paulina. Acts of remembrance, acts of oblivion: rhetoric, law, and national memory in early Restoration England. *In* (pp. 103–31) **1894**.

6478. Keyworth, G. David. Was the vampire of the eighteenth century a unique type of undead-corpse? *See* **3133**.

6479. Kietzman, Mary Jo. The self-fashioning of an early modern Englishwoman: Mary Carleton's lives. (Bibl. 2005, 7127.) Rev. by Lisa McClain in SixCJ (37:1) 2006, 121–2.

6480. Knights, Mark. Representation and misrespresentation in later Stuart Britain: partisanship and political culture. (Bibl. 2005, 7128.) Rev. by Kevin Sharpe in TLS, 20 Jan. 2006, 26; by Jeremy Black in NQ (53:1) 2006, 122–3.

6481. Lewis, Jayne Elizabeth. Spectral currencies in the air of reality: *A Journal of the Plague Year* and the history of apparitions. *See* **7721**.

6482. McJannet, Linda. The sultan speaks: dialogue in English plays and histories about the Ottoman Turks. *See* **4931**.

6483. Martin, Randall (sel. and introd.). Women and murder in early modern news pamphlets and broadside ballads, 1573–1697. *See* **4783**.

6484. Mascuch, Michael. The godly child's 'power and evidence' in the word: orality and literacy in the ministry of Sarah Wright. *In* (pp. 103–26) **6264**.

6485. Morrissey, Mary; Wright, Gillian. Piety and sociability in early modern women's letters. WWr (13:1) 2006, 44–59.

6486. Nevitt, Marcus Andrew. Women and the pamphlet culture of Revolutionary England, 1640–1660. Aldershot; Burlington, VT: Ashgate, 2006. pp. xii, 218. (Women and gender in the early modern world.) Rev. by Joad Raymond in TLS, 8 Sept. 2006, 28–9.

6487. Norton, David. A textual history of the King James Bible. Cambridge; New York: CUP, 2005. pp. ix, 387. Rev. by B. J. McMullin in Library (7:1) 2006, 99–100.

6488. O'Driscoll, Sally. Reading through desire: interpretive practices for eighteenth-century popular culture. BJECS (29:2) 2006, 237–51.

6489. Peacey, Jason. The management of Civil War newspapers: *auteurs*, entrepreneurs and editorial control. SevC (21:1) 2006, 99–127.

6490. —— Sir Thomas Cotton's consumption of news in 1650s England. Library (7:1) 2006, 3–24.

6491. Peters, Kate. Print culture and the early Quakers. (Bibl. 2005, 7142.) Rev. by Evan Haefeli in HLQ (69:3) 2006, 469–76; by Susanna Calkins in SCN (64:1/2) 2006, 54–6; by Betty Hagglund in SHARP (15:2/3) 2006, 20–1; by Thomas D. Hamm in Historian (68:4) 2006, 889–90; by Alexandra Halasz in RQ (59:1) 2006, 271–2.

6492. Poole, William. Francis Lodwick's annotations to John Webster's *Academiarum examen* (1654) and John Dury's *Considerations concerning the Present Engagement* (1649). *See* **364**.

6493. Rivett, Sarah. 'Keepers of the covenant': submissive captives and maternal redeemers in Colonial New England (1660–1680). *In* (pp. 45–59) **6224**.

6494. Sell, Jonathan P. A. Rhetoric and wonder in English travel writing, 1560–1613. *See* **4788**.

6495. Semler, Liam E. Designs on the self: Inigo Jones, marginal writing, and Renaissance self-assembly. *In* (pp. 252–67) **4792**.

6496. Smith, Emily. The local popularity of *The Concealed Fansyes*. *See* **6631**.

6497. Steggle, Matthew. 'Greene's Baboone': Thomas Greene, ape impersonator? TN (60:2) 2006, 72–5.

6498. Sullivan, Vickie B. Machiavelli, Hobbes, and the formation of a liberal republicanism in England. (Bibl. 2005, 7185.) Rev. by Conal Condren in SixCJ (36:4) 2005, 1130–1.

6499. Suzuki, Mihoko (sel. and introd.). Mary Carleton. *See* **6630**.

6500. Thompson, Torri L. (ed.). Marriage and its dissolution in early modern England: vol. 3. *See* **5140**.

6501. —— Marriage and its dissolution in early modern England: vol. 4. *See* **7191**.

6502. Thorne, Alison. Women's petitionary letters and early seventeenth-century treason trials. WWr (13:1) 2006, 23–43.

6503. Urban, Marsha. Seventeenth-century mothers' advice books. Basingstoke; New York: Palgrave Macmillan, 2006. pp. 206.

6504. Warburton, Rachel. 'The Lord hath joined us together, and wo be to them that should part us': Katharine Evans and Sarah Cheevers as traveling friends. TSLL (47:4) 2005, 402–24.

BIOGRAPHY AND AUTOBIOGRAPHY

6505. Bedford, Ronald; Davis, Lloyd; Kelly, Philippa (eds). Early modern autobiography: theories, genres, practices. *See* **4792**.

6506. Botonaki, Effie. Early modern women's diaries and closets: 'chambers of choice mercies and beloved retirement'. *In* (pp. 43–64) **7490**.

6507. Bunker, Nancy Mohrlock. Feminine and fashionable: regendering the iconologies of Mary Frith's 'notorious reputation'. *See* **6950**.

6508. Condren, Conal. Specifying the subject in early modern autobiography. *In* (pp. 35–48) **4792**.

6509. Davis, Lloyd. Critical debates and early modern autobiography. *In* (pp. 19–34) **4792**.

6510. Davis, Paul. After the Fire: Chaucer and urban poetics, 1666–1743. *In* (pp. 177–92) **4312**.

6511. Doll, Dan; Munns, Jessica (eds). Recording and reordering: essays on the seventeenth- and eighteenth-century diary and journal. *See* **7490**.

6512. Kouffman, Avra. Women's diaries of late Stuart England: an overview. *In* (pp. 65–101) **7490**.

6513. Mitchell, Adrian. William Dampier's unaccepted life. *In* (pp. 268–79) **4792**.

6514. Munns, Jessica. Accounting for Providence: contemporary descriptions of the Restoration of Charles II. *In* (pp. 102–21) **7490**.

6515. Nussbaum, Felicity. 'More than a woman': early memoirs of British actresses. *In* (pp. 225–42) **7255**.

6516. Prest, Wilfrid. Legal autobiography in early modern England. *In* (pp. 280–94) **4792**.

6517. Pritchard, Allan. English biography in the seventeenth century: a critical survey. (Bibl. 2005, 7171.) Rev. by David Hawkes in TLS, 28 Apr. 2006, 32; by Peter McCullough in Biography (29:4) 2006, 745–7; by Kate Bennett in RES (57:232) 2006, 803–5.

6518. Ridley, Glynis. Sacred and secular places: an Atlantic divide. *In* (pp. 22–42) **7490**.

6519. Wilcox, Helen. Selves in strange lands: autobiography and exile in the mid-seventeenth century. *In* (pp. 131–57) **4792**.

RELATED STUDIES

6520. Cranmer, David. English music in the library of King João IV of Portugal. SEDERI (16) 2006, 153–60.

6521. Dekoninck, Ralph, *et al.* *Emblemata sacra*: emblem books from the Marits Sabbe Library, Katholieke Universiteit Leuven. Philadelphia, PA: Saint Joseph's UP, 2006. pp. xiii, 101. (Exhibition catalogue.)

6522. Ellis, Markman. The coffee-house: a cultural history. London: Weidenfeld & Nicolson, 2004. pp. xiv, 304, (plates) 8. Rev. by Norma Clarke in TLS, 26 Nov. 2004, 11.

6523. Fissell, Mary E. Vernacular bodies: the politics of reproduction in early modern England. *See* **4800**.

6524. Handa, Rumiko. Authorship of *The Most Notable Antiquity* (1655): Inigo Jones and early printed books. PBSA (100:3) 2006, 357–78.

6525. Irwin, Raymond D. Books on early American history and culture, 1951–1960: an annotated bibliography. Westport, CT; London: Praeger, 2006. pp. xii, 298. (Bibliographies and indexes in American history, 50.)

6526. Monaghan, E. Jennifer. Learning to read and write in Colonial America. Amherst: Massachusetts UP for the American Antiquarian Soc., 2005. pp. xiii, 491. (Studies in print culture and the history of the book.) Rev. by Pat Crain in Book (68) 2006, 3.

6527. Sánchez Escribano, Francisco Javier. Portuguese in England in the sixteenth and seventeenth centuries. *See* **4803**.

6528. Suter, Keith. The rise and fall of English coffee houses. ContRev (286:1669) 2005, 107–10.

LITERARY THEORY

6529. Cannan, Paul D. Emergence of dramatic criticism in England: from Jonson to Pope. Basingstoke; New York: Palgrave Macmillan, 2006. pp. x, 225.

AUTHORS

Lancelot Andrewes

6530. Duffy, Eamon. Hew their bones in sunder. LRB (28:15) 2006, 30–2 (review-article). (Sermons and lectures.)

6531. McCullough, Peter (ed.). Lancelot Andrewes: selected sermons and lectures. Oxford; New York: OUP, 2005. pp. lx, 491. Rev. by Eamon Duffy in LRB (28:15) 2006, 30–2.

6532. Rhatigan, Emma. Knees and elephants: Donne preaches on ceremonial conformity. *See* **6746**.

6533. Stegner, Paul. A reconciled maid: *A Lover's Complaint* and confessional practices in early modern England. *In* (pp. 79–90) **5913**.

Robert Armin

6534. Preiss, Richard. Robert Armin do the Police in different voices. *In* (pp. 208–27) **5334**.

Mary Astell

6535. Bennett, Joan S. Mary Astell, Lucy Hutchinson, John Milton, and feminist liberation theology. *In* (pp. 139–66) **7033**.

6536. Taylor, E. Derek; New, Melvyn (eds). Mary Astell and John Norris: letters concerning the love of God. (Bibl. 2005, 7197.) Rev. by Whitney Vitale in Scriblerian (38:2) 2006, 323–4; by Guyonne Leduc in EA (59:4) 2006, 477–9.

Sir Robert Ayton (1570–1638)

6537. Daemen-de Gelder, Katrien. Recitations of nationhood: Sir Robert Ayton (1570–1638) and the canon of early modern Scottish literature. EngS (87:4) 2006, 426–41.

Francis Bacon (1561–1626)

6538. Ash, Eric H. Power, knowledge, and expertise in Elizabethan England. (Bibl. 2005, 7201.) Rev. by Rudolph P. Almasy in SixCJ (37:2) 2006, 536–7; by Stephen Johnston in Isis (97:2) 2006, 348–9.

6539. Barbour, Reid. Bacon, atomism, and imposture: the true and the useful in history, myth, and theory. *In* (pp. 17–43) **6558**.

6540. Briggs, John C. 'The very idea!': Francis Bacon and E. O. Wilson on the rehabilitation of *eidos*. *In* (pp. 89–108) **6558**.

6541. Butler, Todd. Bacon and the politics of the prudential imagination. SELit (46:1) 2006, 93–111.

6542. Ciglioni, Guido. The hidden life of matter: techniques for prolonging life in the writings of Francis Bacon. *In* (pp. 129–44) **6558**.

6543. Dzelzainis, Martin. 'The Feminine part of every Rebellion': Francis Bacon on sedition and libel, and the beginning of ideology. HLQ (69:1) 2006, 139–52.

6544. Falocco, Joe. Is Mark Twain dead? Samuel Clemens and the question of Shakespearean authorship. *See* **11493**.

6545. Houston, Chloë. 'An idea for a principality'? Encountering the East in Bacon's *New Atlantis*. SevC (21:1) 2006, 22–32.

6546. Ingram, Jill Phillips. Idioms of self-interest: credit, identity, and property in English Renaissance literature. *See* **6642**.

6547. Keithley, Walter Hank. Swift reading Bacon reading Apollonius. *See* **8199**.

6548. Korhonen, Kuisma. Textual friendship: the essay as impossible encounter, from Plato and Montaigne to Levinas and Derrida. *See* **3611**.

6549. Levy, Fritz. Francis Bacon, *The Advancement of Learning*, and historical thought. *In* (pp. 203–21) **6558**.

6550. Lynch, William T. A society of Baconians? The collective development of Bacon's method in the Royal Society of London. *In* (pp. 173–202) **6558**.

6551. McCanles, Michael. The New Science and the *via negativa*: a mystical source for Baconian empiricism. *In* (pp. 45–68) **6558**.

6552. McKnight, Stephen A. The religious foundations of Francis Bacon's thought. Columbia; London: Missouri UP, 2006. pp. 193. (Eric Voegelin Inst. series in political philosophy.)

6553. Martin, Catherine Gimelli. The feminine birth of the mind: regendering the empirical subject in Bacon and his followers. *In* (pp. 69–88) **6558**.

6554. Mukherji, Subha. False trials in Shakespeare, Massinger, and Ford. *See* **5393**.

6555. Olmsted, Wendy. Rhetoric: an historical introduction. *See* **2075**.

6556. Reiss, Timothy J. 'Seated between the old world and the new': geopolitics, natural philosophy, and proficient method. *In* (pp. 223–46) **6558**.

6557. Rodríguez García, José María. Patterns of conversion in Francis Bacon's *New Atlantis*. LIT (17:2) 2006, 179–211.

6558. Solomon, Julie Robin; Martin, Catherine Gimelli (eds). Francis Bacon and the refiguring of early modern thought: essays to commemorate *The Advancement of Learning* (1605–2005). Aldershot; Burlington, VT: Ashgate, 2005. pp. ix, 257. (Literary and scientific cultures of early modernity.) Rev. by Alan H. Nelson in TLS, 7 July 2006, 33; by Rose-Mary Sargent in Isis (97:4) 2006, 758–9; by Pete Langman in RQ (59:3) 2006, 939–41.

6559. Valentini, Maria. Jonathan Swift e la filosofia di Francis Bacon. *In* (pp. 31–47) **3341**.

6560. Wallace, Andrew. Virgil and Bacon in the schoolroom. ELH (73:1) 2006, 161–85.

6561. Weinberger, Jerry. Francis Bacon and the unity of knowledge: reason and revelation. *In* (pp. 109–27) **6558**.

John Banks

6562. De Pando Mena, Paula. Emasculated subjects and subjugated wives: discourses of domination in John Banks's *Vertue Betray'd* (1682). SEDERI (16) 2006, 161–75.

Jane Barker

6563. Kvande, Marta. Jane Barker and Delarivière Manley: public women against the public sphere. ECN (5) 2006, 143–74.

Clement Barksdale (1609–1687)

6564. Williams, George Walton. Clement Barksdale's translations of Richard Crashaw's epigrams. *See* **6672**.

Lording Barry

6565. Griffin, Andrew. *Ram Alley* and female spectatorship. ETh (9:2) 2006, 91–7.

William Basse

6566. Centerwall, Brandon S. Who wrote William Basse's *Elegy on Shakespeare*? Rediscovering a poem lost from the Donne canon. ShS (59) 2006, 267–84.

Richard Baxter

6567. Lim, Paul Chang-Ha. In pursuit of purity, unity, and liberty: Richard Baxter's Puritan ecclesiology in its seventeenth-century context. (Bibl. 2005, 7222.) Rev. by Hans Boersma in SixCJ (37:1) 2006, 134–6.

6568. West, Philip. Nathaniel Wanley and George Herbert: the dis-engaged and *The Temple*. *See* **6824**.

Francis Beaumont (1584–1616)

6569. Busse, Claire M. 'Pretty fictions' and 'little stories': child actors on the early modern stage. *In* (pp. 75–101) **6264**.

6570. Mann, Jenny C. How to look at a hermaphrodite in early modern England. *See* **7126**.

6571. Munro, Lucy. *The Knight of the Burning Pestle* and generic experimentation. *In* (pp. 189–99) **4734**.

6572. Thomson, Leslie. Who's in, who's out? *The Knight of the Burning Pestle* on the Blackfriars stage. *In* (pp. 61–71) **5577**.

Sir John Beaumont (1583–1627)

6573. Eckhardt, Joshua. 'Love-song weeds, and Satyrique thornes': anti-courtly love poetry and Somerset libels. *See* **4834**.

6574. Prescott, Anne Lake. Refusing translation: the Gregorian Calendar and early modern English writers. *See* **6744**.

Beaumont and Fletcher

6575. Lyne, Raphael. English Guarini: recognition and reception. *See* **6676**.

Aphra Behn

6576. Copeland, Nancy. Staging gender in Behn and Centlivre: women's comedy and the theatre. (Bibl. 2005, 7237.) Rev. by Lisa A. Freeman in Scriblerian (38:2) 2006, 319–20.

6577. Dugaw, Dianne; Powell, Amanda. Sapphic self-fashioning in the baroque era: women's Petrarchan parody in English and Spanish. *See* **7096**.

6578. Ellison, Katherine E. Fatal news: reading and information overload in early eighteenth-century literature. London; New York: Routledge, 2006. pp. x, 158. (Literary criticism and cultural theory.)

6579. Frangos, Jennifer. Aphra Behn's cunning stunts: *To the Fair Clarinda*. ECent (45:1) 2004, 21–40.

6580. Hayden, Judy. Of privileges and masculine parts: the learned lady in Aphra Behn's *Sir Patient Fancy*. PLL (42:3) 2006, 317–31.

6581. Iwanisziw, Susan B. (ed.). *Oroonoko*: adaptations and offshoots. Aldershot; Burlington, VT: Ashgate, 2006. pp. xxii, 369. (Early modern Englishwoman, 1500–1750: Contemporary eds.) Rev. by Michael Caines in TLS, 22 Sept. 2006, 33.

6582. —— Troping *Oroonoko* from Behn to Bandele. (Bibl. 2004, 7504.) Rev. by Alison Conway in Scriblerian (38:2) 2006, 313–14.

6583. Lobsien, Verena Olejniczak. Narrating Caliban: structural skepticism and the invention of the Other in early modern English literature. *In* (pp. 101–27) **5346**.

6584. Martin, Judith E. Luise Mühlbach's *Aphra Behn* (1849): auto/biography of a woman artist. Neophilologus (90:4) 2006, 585–600.

6585. Mason, Matthew. Slavery, servitude, and British representations of Colonial North America. *See* **7966**.

6586. Stapleton, M. L. Admired and understood: the poetry of Aphra Behn. (Bibl. 2004, 7511.) Rev. by Gillian Manning in 1650–1850 (13) 2006, 329–31.

6587. Starr, G. Gabrielle. Cavendish, aesthetics, and the anti-Platonic line. *See* **7093**.

6588. Wilcox, Helen. 'Forgive, O Lord, forgive our trespasses': the failure of holiness in seventeenth-century English lyric poetry. *In* (pp. 41–59) **3415**.

Thomas Betterton

6589. Conway, Alison. Known fact or urban legend? Nell Gwynn's Oxford pronouncement. *See* **8146**.

Roger Boyle, First Earl of Orrery

6590. Keenan, Tim. Boyle's *Guzman* at Lincoln's Inn Fields 1669. TN (60:2) 2006, 76–93.

William Bradford

6591. Read, David. New World, known world: shaping knowledge in early Anglo-American writing. *See* **7138**.

Anne Bradstreet

6592. Day-Lindsey, Lisa. Bradstreet's *The Author to Her Book*. Exp (64:2) 2006, 66–9.

6593. Harvey, Tamara. 'My goods are true': tenth Muses in the New World market. *In* (pp. 13–26) **6224**.

6594. Hellwarth, Jennifer Wynne. Afterword. *In* (pp. 395–401) **661**.

Richard Brathwait

6595. Raffield, Paul. A discredited priesthood: the failings of common lawyers and their representation in seventeenth-century satirical drama. *See* **7107**.

Richard Brome

6596. Brooks, Douglas A. Inky kin: reading in the age of Gutenberg paternity. *In* (pp. 203–28) **4731**.

6597. Hirsch, Brett D. Thomas Heywood and the werewolves: sources for *The Witches of Lancashire*. *See* **6831**.

6598. —— Werewolves and severed hands: Webster's *The Duchess of Malfi* and Heywood and Brome's *The Witches of Lancashire*. *See* **7178**.

6599. Munro, Lucy. Richard Brome and *The Book of Bulls*: situating *The New Academy; or, The New Exchange*. BJJ (13) 2006, 125–38.

6600. Steggle, Matthew. Richard Brome: place and politics on the Caroline stage. (Bibl. 2005, 7268.) Rev. by Matthew C. Hansen in CompDr (39:1) 2005, 112–14; by William Proctor Williams in NQ (53:3) 2006, 378–9.

Sir Thomas Browne (1605–1682)

6601. Berensmeyer, Ingo. Rhetoric, religion, and politics in Sir Thomas Browne's *Religio Medici*. SELit (46:1) 2006, 113–32.

6602. Edwards, Karen. Milton's reformed animals: an early modern bestiary: introduction. *See* **6995**.

6603. Preston, Claire. Thomas Browne and the writing of early modern science. (Bibl. 2005, 7275.) Rev. by Deborah E. Harkness in BHM (80:3) 2006, 584–6; by Michael Hunter in Isis (97:3) 2006, 557–8; by William C. Johnson in NQ (53:1) 2006, 119–21; by Peter Maber in SevC (21:1) 2006, 184–8.

Sir George Buck (d.1623)

6604. Stephenson, Joseph F. On the markings in the manuscript of *Sir John Van Olden Barnavelt*. *See* **6801**.

John Bunyan

6605. Bertsch, Janet. Storytelling in the works of Bunyan, Grimmelshausen, Defoe, and Schnabel. (Bibl. 2005, 7280.) Rev. by Peter Skrine in MLR (101:3) 2006, 929–30; by Linde Katritzky in Scriblerian (38:2) 2006, 318–19.

6606. Blackford, Holly. Vital signs at play: objects as vessels of mother–daughter discourse in Louisa May Alcott's *Little Women*. *See* **8961**.

6607. Branch, Lori. Rituals of spontaneity: sentiment and secularism from free prayer to Wordsworth. Waco, TX: Baylor Univ., 2006. pp. xiii, 348.

6608. Burke, Mary. 'Of that rank that is meanest and most despised of all': Victorian Romany studies and the recovery of John Bunyan's 'gypsy' origins. 1650–1850 (13) 2006, 245–63.

6609. Ciocca, Rossella. Metafisica del viaggiare: pellegrinaggi. *In* (pp. 97–107) **11824**.

6610. Collmer, Robert G. Roman Catholic versions of *The Pilgrim's Progress*. 1650–1850 (13) 2006, 225–43.

6611. Damrau, Peter. The reception of English Puritan literature in Germany. *See* **3225**.

6612. Dunan-Page, Anne. John Bunyan's *A Confession of My Faith* and Restoration Anabaptism. PrSt (28:1) 2006, 19–40.

6613. Ellison, Katherine E. Fatal news: reading and information overload in early eighteenth-century literature. *See* **6578**.

6614. Greig, James C. G. John Buchan, Calvinism, Bunyan and the Classics. *See* **14887**.

6615. Hillier, Russell M. 'In a dark parody' of John Bunyan's *The Pilgrim's Progress*: the presence of subversive allegory in Cormac McCarthy's *Outer Dark*. *See* **17301**.

6616. Hofmeyr, Isabel. *The Pilgrim's Progress* as world literature: John Bunyan and George Simeon Mwase in Nyasaland. 1650–1850 (13) 2006, 175–99.

6617. —— The portable Bunyan: a transnational history of *The Pilgrim's Progress*. (Bibl. 2004, 7534.) Rev. by N. H. Keeble in TransLit (14:2) 2005, 252–5.

6618. Lynch, Beth. John Bunyan and the language of conviction. (Bibl. 2005, 7284.) Rev. by Andrew Sutton-Jones in LitTheol (19:3) 2005, 280–2; by David Hawkes in TLS, 12 May 2006, 30; by Christopher E. Garrett in SCN (64:1/2) 2006, 34–7.

6619. Maddux, H. Clark. Audience and the layered art of method in John Bunyan's *The Life and Death of Mr Badman* and *The Pilgrim's Progress*. 1650–1850 (13) 2006, 265–86.

6620. Peterson, Calvin M. From doctrine to narrative and back in *The Pilgrim's Progress*. 1650–1850 (13) 2006, 287–311.

6621. Pooley, Roger. Editing *The Pilgrim's Progress*: issues in presenting the early modern text. *In* (pp. 65–76) **3407**.

6622. Zinck, Arlette; Brown, Sylvia. *The Pilgrim's Progress* among aboriginal Canadians: missionary translations of Bunyan into Cree and Inuktitut. 1650–1850 (13) 2006, 201–23.

Robert Burton

6623. Dimakopoulou, Stamatina. Remapping the affinities between the baroque and the postmodern: the folds of melancholy & the melancholy of the fold. EREA (4:1) 2006, 75–82.

6624. Lund, Mary Ann. Robert Burton the spiritual physician: religion and medicine in *The Anatomy of Melancholy*. RES (57:232) 2006, 665–83.

Samuel Butler (1612–1680)

6625. Terry, Richard. Mock-heroic from Butler to Cowper: an English genre and discourse. Aldershot; Burlington, VT: Ashgate, 2005. pp. 216. (Studies in early modern English literature.) Rev. by Kirk Combe in NQ (53:3) 2006, 382–3; by Robert Phiddian in AJ (17) 2006, 423–6.

Thomas Campion

6626. Gazzard, Hugh. 'Many a *Herdsman* more disposde to morne': Peele, Campion, and the Portugal expedition of 1589. *See* **5002**.

6627. Kilroy, Gerard. Scribal coincidences: Campion, Byrd, Harington and the Sidney circle. *See* **4822**.

Thomas Carew

6628. Doelman, James. The statues in Carew's *To G.N., from Wrest*: other possibilities. ELN (43:2) 2005, 47–50.

6629. Smith, Peter J. Rome's disgrace: the politics of rape in Shakespeare's *Lucrece*. *See* **6059**.

Mary Carleton (1642?–1673)

6630. Suzuki, Mihoko (sel. and introd.). Mary Carleton. Aldershot; Burlington, VT: Ashgate, 2006. 1 vol. (various pagings). (Early modern Englishwoman, II: Printed writings, 1641–1700, 3:6.) (Facsimile.)

Elizabeth Cary, Viscountess Falkland

6631. Clarke, Danielle. *The Tragedy of Mariam* and the politics of marriage. *In* (pp. 248–59) **4734**.

6632. Hiscock, Andrew. The uses of this world: thinking space in Shakespeare, Marlowe, Cary, and Jonson. *See* **5727**.

Mary Cary

6633. Loewenstein, David. Scriptural exegesis, female prophecy, and radical politics in Mary Cary. SELit (46:1) 2006, 133–53.

Lady Jane Cavendish

6634. Smith, Emily. The local popularity of *The Concealed Fansyes*. NQ (53:2) 2006, 189–93.

Robert Chamberlain

6635. Munro, Lucy. Richard Brome and *The Book of Bulls*: situating *The New Academy; or, The New Exchange*. *See* **6599**.

George Chapman

6636. Bassnett, Susan. Writing and translating. *In* (pp. 173–83) **3186**.

6637. Centerwall, Brandon. *Caracalla*: a new play by George Chapman, in his hand. TLS, 31 Mar. 2006, 14–15.

6638. Edelman, Charles. Chapman's *An Humorous Day's Mirth*. *See* **1595**.

6639. Florby, Gunilla. Echoing texts: George Chapman's *Conspiracy and Tragedy of Charles, Duke of Byron*. Lund: Lund UP, 2004. pp. 181. (Lund studies in English, 109.) Rev. by John Huntington in RQ (59:1) 2006, 305–7.

6640. Hillman, Richard. Returning to one's vomit: an intertextual tour of *Eastward Ho*'s Isle of Dogs. NQ (53:4) 2006, 508–14.

6641. Hyland, Peter. Face/off: some speculations on Elizabethan acting. *See* **4968**.

6642. Ingram, Jill Phillips. Idioms of self-interest: credit, identity, and property in English Renaissance literature. London; New York: Routledge, 2006. pp. xi, 182. (Literary criticism and cultural theory.)

6643. Lautel-Ribstein, Florence. Théories de la traduction au xviie siècle: entre noblesse et prosaïsme. *See* **2869**.

6644. Low, Jennifer A. 'Bodied forth': spectator, stage, and actor in the early modern theater. CompDr (39:1) 2005, 1–29.

6645. Wheeler, Martin. 'The obiect whereto all his actions tend': George Chapman's *Ouids Banquet of Sence* and the thrill of the chase. MLR (101:2) 2006, 325–46.

Charles I, King of England

6646. Daems, Jim; Nelson, Holly Faith (eds). *Eikon Basilike: the Portraiture of His Sacred Majesty in His Solitudes and Sufferings*, with selections from *Eikonoklastes*. Peterborough, Ont.; Orchard Park, NY: Broadview Press, 2006. pp. 334. Rev. by Neil Forsyth in TLS, 4 Aug. 2006, 23; by Anthony Low in BJJ (13) 2006, 211–14.

6647. Poynting, Sarah. Deciphering the king: Charles I's letters to Jane Whorwood. SevC (21:1) 2006, 128–40.

Robert Chester

6648. Borukhov, Boris. *The Phoenix and the Turtle* was published in 1601. *See* **6050**.

Anne Clifford,
Countess of Dorset, Pembroke and Montgomery

6649. Myers, Anne M. Construction sites: the architecture of Anne Clifford's diaries. ELH (73:3) 2006, 581–600.

6650. Orgel, Stephen. Marginal maternity: reading Lady Anne Clifford's *A Mirror for Magistrates*. *In* (pp. 267–89) **661**.

6651. Wright, Nancy E. Accounting for a life: the household accounts of Lady Anne Clifford. *In* (pp. 234–51) **4792**.

Elizabeth Colville, Lady Colville of Culross (Elizabeth Melville)

6652. KECK, KAREN RAE. Catherine, not Elizabeth: the misattribution of the letters in Edinburgh University Library Laing.III.347. NQ (53:1) 2006, 90–1.

6653. REID-BAXTER, JAMIE. Elizabeth Melville's letters in Edinburgh University Library, Laing III.347. NQ (53:4) 2006, 525–8.

William Congreve

6654. CZENNIA, BÄRBEL. The taming of the rake: Congreve's *The Way of the World* on the German eighteenth-century stage. 1650–1850 (11) 2005, 265–99.

6655. MARTIN, RANDALL. *The cat* gets its nine tails. *See* **1551**.

Anne Conway (1631–1679)

6656. HUTTON, SARAH. Anne Conway: a woman philosopher. Cambridge; New York: CUP, 2004. pp. viii, 271. Rev. by Karol K. Weaver in SCN (64:1/2) 2006, 41–2.

John Cooke (d. *c*.1614)

6657. STEGGLE, MATTHEW. 'Greene's Baboone': Thomas Greene, ape impersonator? *See* **6497**.

Abiezer Coppe (1619–1672)

6658. MCDOWELL, NICHOLAS. Abiezer Coppe, Horace, and the dormouse. NQ (53:2) 2006, 166–8.

Charles Cotton

6659. WHITEHEAD, ANGUS. 'A various complicated *ill*': echoes of Cotton and Cowley in *Evelina*. *See* **7636**.

Abraham Cowley

6660. BEDFORD, RONALD. Milton's military Heaven revisited. *See* **6965**.

6661. BENET, DIANA TREVIÑO. Milton's toad; or, Satan's dream. *See* **6966**.

6662. HAMMOND, PAUL. The date of Marvell's *The Mower against Gardens*. *See* **6931**.

6663. WALLACE, ANDREW. Virgil and Bacon in the schoolroom. *See* **6560**.

6664. WHITEHEAD, ANGUS. 'A various complicated *ill*': echoes of Cotton and Cowley in *Evelina*. *See* **7636**.

Richard Crashaw

6665. LABRIOLA, ALBERT C. The 'wine of love': viticulture in the poetry of Richard Crashaw. JDJ (24) 2005, 335–51.

6666. MCDOWELL, SEAN. From 'lively' art to 'glitt'ring expressions': Crashaw's initial reception reconsidered. JDJ (24) 2005, 229–62.

6667. NEWTON, FRANCIS. Silius Italicus, Daniel Heinsius, and Richard Crashaw: the genesis of Crashaw's Latin poem *Bulla* ('The Bubble'), with a new edition of the text. JDJ (24) 2005, 263–95.

6668. PARRISH, PAUL A. Front matters: Crashaw in the seventeenth century. JDJ (24) 2005, 303–34.

6669. Perry, Nandra. 'Tis heav'n she speakes': Lady Religion, Saint Teresa, and the politics of ceremony in the poetry of Richard Crashaw. ReLit (38:2) 2006, 1–23.

6670. Roberts, John R. Richard Crashaw: an annotated bibliography of criticism, 1981–2002. JDJ (24) 2005, 1–228.

6671. Roberts, Lorraine. Representing a forsaken woman: Crashaw's *Alexias*. JDJ (23) 2004, 347–62.

6672. Williams, George Walton. Clement Barksdale's translations of Richard Crashaw's epigrams. JDJ (24) 2005, 353–7.

Samuel Daniel

6673. Alt, Christina. Directed readings: paratext in *A Game at Chess* and *The Tragedie of Philotas*. *See* **6949**.

6674. Brink, Jean R. Precedence and patronage: the ordering of Spenser's Dedicatory Sonnets (1590). *See* **5075**.

6675. Cheney, Patrick. 'Deep-brained sonnets' and 'tragic shows': Shakespeare's late Ovidian art in *A Lover's Complaint*. *In* (pp. 55–77) **5913**.

6676. Lyne, Raphael. English Guarini: recognition and reception. YES (36:1) 2006, 90–102.

6677. Quinn, Kelly A. Fulke Greville's friendly patronage. *See* **6812**.

Sir William Davenant

6678. Hoenselaars, Ton. Between Heaven and Hell: Shakespearian translation, adaptation, and criticism from a historical perspective. *See* **5329**.

John Day

6679. Hyland, Peter. Face/off: some speculations on Elizabethan acting. *See* **4968**.

Thomas Dekker

6680. Bunker, Nancy Mohrlock. Feminine and fashionable: regendering the iconologies of Mary Frith's 'notorious reputation'. *See* **6950**.

6681. Calabresi, Bianca F. C. 'Red incke': reading the bleeding on the early modern page. *In* (pp. 237–64) **661**.

6682. Cañadas, Ivan. A new source for the title and themes of *The Scarlet Letter*. *See* **10368**.

6683. Degenhardt, Jane Hwang. Catholic martyrdom in Dekker and Massinger's *The Virgin Martir* and the early modern threat of 'turning Turk'. ELH (73:1) 2006, 83–117.

6684. Fleck, Andrew. Marking difference and national identity in Dekker's *The Shoemaker's Holiday*. SELit (46:2) 2006, 349–70.

6685. Fulton, Helen. The performance of social class: domestic violence in the Griselda story. *See* **4398**.

6686. Haldane, Michael. The date of Thomas Combe's *Fortunatus* and its relation to Thomas Dekker's *Old Fortunatus*. *See* **6405**.

6687. —— From Plato to Pullman – the circle of invisibility and parallel worlds: *Fortunatus*, Mercury, and the Wishing-Hat: part II. Folklore (117:3) 2006, 261–78.

6688. —— The translation of the unseen self: *Fortunatus*, Mercury and the Wishing-Hat. Folklore (117:2) 2006, 171–89.

6689. HENTSCHELL, ROZE. A question of nation: foreign clothes on the English subject. *In* (pp. 49–62) **4629**.

6690. LAROQUE, FRANÇOIS. '*Blue-apron culture*': la culture populaire dans *2 Henry VI* de Shakespeare et *The Shoemaker's Holiday* de Thomas Dekker. *See* **5839**.

6691. LESSER, ZACHARY. Typographic nostalgia: play-reading, popularity, and the meanings of black-letter. *In* (pp. 99–126) **4731**.

6692. MCMANUS, CLARE. *The Roaring Girl* and the London underworld. *In* (pp. 213–24) **4734**.

6693. SCOTT, SARAH. 'Sell[ing] your selues away': pathologizing and gendering the socio-economic in *The Honest Whore, Part 1*. *See* **6956**.

6694. VELLA BONAVITA, HELEN. Maids, wives and widows: multiple meaning and marriage in *The Witch of Edmonton*. *See* **7125**.

6695. WALSH, BRIAN. Performing historicity in Dekker's *The Shoemaker's Holiday*. SELit (46:2) 2006, 323–48.

Sir John Denham

6696. LAUTEL-RIBSTEIN, FLORENCE. Théories de la traduction au XVIIe siècle: entre noblesse et prosaïsme. *See* **2869**.

John Donne (1572–1631)

6697. ADAMSON, SYLVIA. Deixis and the Renaissance art of self-construction. *See* **5689**.

6698. ANDERSON, JUDITH H. Donne's (im)possible punning. JDJ (23) 2004, 59–68.

6699. AUSTERN, LINDA PHYLLIS. Words on music: the case of early modern England. JDJ (25) 2006, 199–244.

6700. BAUMLIN, JAMES S. Reading Donne's *Communitie*. ExRC (32:1) 2006, 50–75.

6701. BELL, ILONA. Gender matters: the women in Donne's poems. *In* (pp. 201–16) **6718**.

6702. BLACKLEY, BRIAN. Reading the genres of *Metempsychosis*. CEACrit (68:1/2) 2005/06, 12–20.

6703. BURROW, COLIN. Recribrations. LRB (28:19) 2006, 3–6 (review-article). (Biography of Donne.)

6704. BYATT, A. S. Feeling thought: Donne and the embodied mind. *In* (pp. 247–57) **6718**.

6705. —— Observe the neurones: between, above and below John Donne. TLS, 22 Sept. 2006, 13–15.

6706. CAIN, TOM. Donne's political world. *In* (pp. 83–99) **6718**.

6707. —— Elegy and autobiography: *The Bracelet* and the death of Henry Donne. JDJ (23) 2004, 25–57.

6708. CAREY, JOHN. Is the author dead? Or, The mermaids and the robot. *In* (pp. 43–54) **5353**.

6709. Centerwall, Brandon S. Who wrote William Basse's *Elegy on Shakespeare*? Rediscovering a poem lost from the Donne canon. *See* **6566**.

6710. Craig, Barry L. St Augustine and the Metaphysical poets. *In* (pp. 97–116) **3301**.

6711. De Gooyer, Alan. Surviving *The Tempest*. *See* **6120**.

6712. DiPasquale, Theresa. The feminine Trinity in *Upon the Annuntiation and Passion*. JDJ (23) 2004, 117–38.

6713. Duncan-Jones, Katherine. Live with me: obstacles and opportunities in the latest biography of John Donne. TLS, 22 Sept. 2006, 3–4 (review-article).

6714. Eckhardt, Joshua. 'Love-song weeds, and Satyrique thornes': anti-courtly love poetry and Somerset libels. *See* **4834**.

6715. Frontain, Raymond-Jean. Donne, Spenser, and the performative mode of Renaissance poetry. ExRC (32:1) 2006, 76–102.

6716. Furey, Constance. 'The selfe undone': individualism and relationality in John Donne and Aemilia Lanyer. HTR (99:4) 2006, 469–86.

6717. Guibbory, Achsah. Erotic poetry. *In* (pp. 133–47) **6718**.

6718. —— (ed.). The Cambridge companion to John Donne. Cambridge; New York: CUP, 2006. pp. xviii, 288. (Cambridge companions to literature.) Rev. by Robert C. Evans in BJJ (13) 2006, 196–204.

6719. Hadfield, Andrew. Literary contexts: predecessors and contemporaries. *In* (pp. 49–64) **6718**.

6720. Haskin, Dayton. Donne's afterlife. *In* (pp. 233–46) **6718**.

6721. Herz, Judith Scherer. Reading and rereading Donne's poetry. *In* (pp. 101–15) **6718**.

6722. Houliston, Victor. An apology for Donne's *Pseudo-Martyr*. RES (57:231) 2006, 474–86.

6723. Hurley, Ann Hollinshead. John Donne's poetry and early modern visual culture. Selinsgrove, PA: Susquehanna UP; London: Assoc. UPs, 2005. pp. 248. (Apple–Zimmerman series in early modern culture.)

6724. Johnson, Jeffrey. Consecrating Lincoln's Inn Chapel. JDJ (23) 2004, 139–60.

6725. Lein, Clayton D. Donne, Thomas Myriell, and the musicians of St Paul's. JDJ (23) 2004, 215–47.

6726. Lemon, Rebecca. Treason by words: literature, law, and rebellion in Shakespeare's England. *See* **6816**.

6727. Low, Anthony. Absence in Donne's *Holy Sonnets*: between Catholic and Calvinist. JDJ (23) 2004, 95–115.

6728. McCullough, Peter. Donne as preacher. *In* (pp. 167–81) **6718**.

6729. McDowell, Sean. *W;t*, Donne's *Holy Sonnets*, and the problem of pain. JDJ (23) 2004, 161–83.

6730. Magnusson, Lynne. Donne's language: the conditions of communication. *In* (pp. 183–200) **6718**.

6731. Mansour, Wisam. Donne's *The Flea*. Exp (65:1) 2006, 7–9.

6732. Marotti, Arthur F. The social context and nature of Donne's writing: occasional verse and letters. *In* (pp. 35–48) **6718**.

6733. Moses, John (ed.). One equall light: an anthology of the writings of John Donne. Foreword by Rowan Williams. Grand Rapids, MI; Cambridge: Eerdmans, 2004. pp. xvi, 352. Rev. by William E. Engel in SewR (113:3) 2005, lxii–lxvi.

6734. Nelson, Holly Faith. 'Make all things new! And without end!': the eschatological vision of Henry Vaughan. *See* **7155**.

6735. Nuyts-Giornal, Josée. 'Who fears a sentence or an old man's saw shall by a painted cloth be kept in awe': genre print and early modern English literature. *See* **5645**.

6736. Pando Cantelli, María J. John Donne, Francisco de Quevedo, and the construction of subjectivity in early modern poetry. *In* (pp. 89–113) **5308**.

6737. Patterson, Annabel. Donne's re-formed *La Corona*. JDJ (23) 2004, 69–93.

6738. —— Donne's sermons back in fashion? JDJ (23) 2004, 363–70 (review-article).

6739. —— Satirical writing: Donne in shadows. *In* (pp. 117–31) **6718**.

6740. Pebworth, Ted-Larry. The text of Donne's writings. *In* (pp. 23–34) **6718**.

6741. Post, Jonathan F. S. Donne's life: a sketch. *In* (pp. 1–22) **6718**.

6742. Potkay, Adam. Spenser, Donne, and the theology of joy. *See* **5113**.

6743. Prescott, Anne Lake. 'Forms of joy and art': Donne, David, and the power of music. JDJ (25) 2006, 3–36.

6744. —— Refusing translation: the Gregorian Calendar and early modern English writers. YES (36:1) 2006, 1–11.

6745. Redford, Peter. Correspondence in the Burley Manuscript: a conjecture. JDJ (23) 2004, 249–56.

6746. Rhatigan, Emma. Knees and elephants: Donne preaches on ceremonial conformity. JDJ (23) 2004, 185–213.

6747. Roberts, John R. John Donne, never done: a reassessment of modern criticism. JDJ (23) 2004, 1–24.

6748. Saunders, Ben. Desiring Donne: poetry, sexuality, interpretation. Cambridge, MA; London: Harvard UP, 2006. pp. viii, 248.

6749. Semler, L. E. Select bibliography. *In* (pp. 259–77) **6718**.

6750. Shami, Jeanne. John Donne and conformity in crisis in the late Jacobean pulpit. (Bibl. 2005, 7393.) Rev. by Annabel Patterson in JDJ (23) 2004, 363–70; by Richard Todd in MLR (101:1) 2006, 223–4.

6751. Shell, Alison; Hunt, Arnold. Donne's religious world. *In* (pp. 65–82) **6718**.

6752. Slater, Michael. 'Invoking' Donne: a grammatical reconstruction of *The Canonization*. NQ (53:2) 2006, 159–64.

6753. Sloane, Thomas O. Dr Donne and the image of Christ. Rhetorica (24:2) 2006, 187–216.

6754. Stringer, Gary A. (gen. ed.). The variorum edition of the poetry of John Donne: vol. 7:1, The *Holy Sonnets*. Ed. by Gary A. Stringer, Dennis A. Flynn and Ted-Larry Pebworth. Bloomington: Indiana UP, 2005. pp. cvii, 606. Rev. by Albert C. Labriola in SCN (64:1/2) 2006, 1–3.

6755. Stubbs, John. Donne: the reformed soul. London: Viking, 2006. pp. xxvi, 565. Rev. by Katherine Duncan-Jones in TLS, 22 Sept. 2006, 3–4; by Colin Burrow in LRB (28:19) 2006, 3–6.

6756. Targoff, Ramie. Facing death. *In* (pp. 217–31) **6718**.

6757. Wall, John N. John Donne practices law: the case of the Brentwood School. JDJ (23) 2004, 257–319.

6758. —— 'That holy roome': John Donne and the conduct of worship at St Paul's Cathedral. RenP (2005) 61–84.

6759. Wilcox, Helen. Devotional writing. *In* (pp. 149–66) **6718**.

Michael Drayton

6760. Brink, Jean R. Precedence and patronage: the ordering of Spenser's Dedicatory Sonnets (1590). *See* **5075**.

6761. Duncan-Jones, Katherine. Drayton on Nashe and Shakespeare. NQ (53:4) 2006, 524–5.

6762. Fox, Bradley A. Verbal allusions in Milton's *Samson Agonistes* to his *History of Britain* and to Drayton's *Poly-Olbion*. *See* **7007**.

6763. Vine, Angus. Etymology, names and the search for origins: deriving the past in early modern England. *See* **4823**.

William Drummond of Hawthornden (1585–1649)

6764. Cobb, Barbara Mather. Jonson's *Conversations with William Drummond*: a history. *See* **6861**.

John Dryden

6765. Berensmeyer, Ingo. The art of oblivion: politics of remembering and forgetting in Restoration England. *See* **7149**.

6766. Brady, Jennifer. Dryden on *Epicœne*'s 'malicious pleasure': the case of the Otters. RenP (2005) 103–20.

6767. —— Wish-fulfillment fantasies in Dryden's *Aureng-Zebe*. PQ (83:1) 2004, 41–60.

6768. Davis, Paul. After the Fire: Chaucer and urban poetics, 1666–1743. *In* (pp. 177–92) **4312**.

6769. Hoenselaars, Ton. Between Heaven and Hell: Shakespearian translation, adaptation, and criticism from a historical perspective. *See* **5329**.

6770. Hopkins, David. Fiddling while Rome burns? Dryden criticism at the tercentenary. AJ (17) 2006, 371–7 (review-article).

6771. —— An uncollected translation from Voiture by John Dryden. TransLit (14:1) 2005, 64–70.

6772. Lautel-Ribstein, Florence. Théories de la traduction au xviie siècle: entre noblesse et prosaïsme. *See* **2869**.

6773. Lee, Anthony W. Johnson's symbolic mentors: Addison, Dryden, and *Rambler* 86. *See* **7939**.

6774. Lewis, Jayne; Novak, Maximillian E. (eds). Enchanted ground: reimagining John Dryden. (Bibl. 2005, 7418.) Rev. by Kirk Combe in NQ (53:2)

2006, 241–2; by Taylor Corse in Scriblerian (38:2) 2006, 306–7; by David Hopkins in AJ (17) 2006, 371–7.

6775. Maurer, Shawn Lisa. Fathers, sons, and lovers: the transformation of masculine authority in Dryden's *Aureng-Zebe*. ECent (46:2) 2005, 151–73.

6776. Pritchard, William H. Dryden rules. HR (58:4) 2006, 541–67.

6777. Rawson, Claude; Santesso, Aaron (eds). John Dryden (1631–1700): his politics, his plays, and his poets. A tercentenary celebration held at Yale University 6–7 October, 2000. (Bibl. 2005, 7422.) Rev. by Adam Rounce in RES (57:230) 2006, 425–6; by James A. Winn in 1650–1850 (13) 2006, 324–8; by David Hopkins in AJ (17) 2006, 371–7.

6778. Reverand, Cedric D., ii. John Dryden: personal concerns of the impersonal poet. 1650–1850 (13) 2006, 3–21.

6779. Roper, Alan. Johnson, Dryden, and an allusion to Horace. *See* **7953**.

6780. Saslow, Edward L. 'Stopp'd in other hands': the payment of Dryden's pension for 1668–1670. Restoration (30:1) 2006, 31–42.

6781. Skouen, Tina. The vocal wit of John Dryden. Rhetorica (24:4) 2006, 371–401.

6782. Visconsi, Elliott. The First Amendment and the poetics of Church and State. Raritan (26:2) 2006, 114–36.

6783. von Maltzahn, Nicholas. There she blew! TLS, 3 Feb. 2006, 13. (Whale imagery.)

6784. Young, Heather. Satire as a virus: generic inhabitation and transformation in Swift's *Tale*. *See* **8219**.

6785. Zwicker, Steven N. (ed.). The Cambridge companion to John Dryden. (Bibl. 2005, 7429.) Rev. by Anna Battigelli in 1650–1850 (13) 2006, 317–24; by Robert Blattès in EA (59:1) 2006, 110–12; by David Hopkins in AJ (17) 2006, 371–7.

Elizabeth Evelinge (Sister Magdalen Augustine) (*fl.*1622–1635)

6786. Walker, Claire (sel. and introd.). Elizabeth Evelinge iii. Aldershot; Burlington, VT: Ashgate, 2006. 1 vol. (various pagings). (Early modern Englishwoman: Printed writings, 1500–1640, 4:1.)

John Evelyn

6787. Campbell-Culver, Maggie. A passion for trees: the legacy of John Evelyn. London: Eden Project, 2006. pp. 282.

6788. Darley, Gillian. John Evelyn: living for ingenuity. New Haven, CT; London: Yale UP, 2006. pp. xiv, 382, (plates) 16.

6789. Scurr, Ruth. First fruit. TLS, 18 & 25 Aug. 2006, 7 (review-article). (Evelyn's diaries.)

6790. Strong, Roy (sel. and introd.). The diary of John Evelyn. Ed. by E. S. de Beer. London: Everyman, 2006. pp. lxx, 1013. Rev. by Ruth Scurr in TLS, 18 & 25 Aug. 2006, 7.

Edward Fairfax

6791. Jung, Sandro. 'O think in what sweet lays, how sweetly strong / Our Fairfax warbles Tasso's forcefull song': William Collins and Edward Fairfax. *See* **7667**.

Thomas Fairfax, Third Baron Fairfax

6792. Major, Philip. Jumping Josaphat. TLS, 28 July 2006, 15. (Fairfax's translation of *Barlaam and Josaphat*.)

Sir Richard Fanshawe

6793. del Río, Eduardo R. The context of translation: Richard Fanshawe and Spanish verse. RAEI (17) 2004, 65–80.

Nicholas Ferrar

6794. Barnes, A. W. Editing George Herbert's ejaculations. *See* **6817**.

Payne Fisher (1616–1693)

6795. Bedford, Ronald. Milton's military Heaven revisited. *See* **6965**.

John Fletcher (1579–1625)

6796. Chalmers, Hero; Sanders, Julie; Tomlinson, Sophie (eds). Three seventeenth-century plays on women and performance. Manchester; New York: Manchester UP, 2006. pp. xv, 332. (Revels plays companion library.) (*The Wild-Goose Chase*; *The Bird in a Cage*; *The Convent of Pleasure*.)

6797. Feerick, Jean. 'Divided in soyle': plantation and degeneracy in *The Tempest* and *The Sea Voyage*. *See* **6121**.

6798. Jowitt, Claire. *The Island Princess* and race. *In* (pp. 287–97) **4734**.

6799. Lyne, Raphael. English Guarini: recognition and reception. *See* **6676**.

6800. Merriam, Thomas. Low-frequency words, genre, date, and authorship. *See* **5386**.

6801. Stephenson, Joseph F. On the markings in the manuscript of *Sir John Van Olden Barnavelt*. NQ (53:4) 2006, 522–4.

John Ford (1586–*c*.1640)

6802. Hopkins, Lisa. A proposed emendation to Ford's *The Broken Heart*. NQ (53:1) 2006, 91–2.

6803. Low, Jennifer A. 'Bodied forth': spectator, stage, and actor in the early modern theater. *See* **6644**.

6804. McCabe, Richard A. *'Tis Pity She's a Whore* and incest. *In* (pp. 309–20) **4734**.

6805. Mukherji, Subha. False trials in Shakespeare, Massinger, and Ford. *See* **5393**.

6806. Shawcross, John. Remarks for a discussion of *Intentionality and the New Traditionalism*: some liminal means to literary revisionism. *See* **20139**.

6807. Vella Bonavita, Helen. Maids, wives and widows: multiple meaning and marriage in *The Witch of Edmonton*. *See* **7125**.

Ursula Bampfield Fulford (*c*.1566–1639)

6808. White, Micheline. Women writers and literary religious circles in the Elizabethan West Country: Anne Dowriche, Anne Lock Prowse, Anne Locke Moyle, Ursula Fulford, and Elizabeth Rous. *See* **4838**.

Joseph Glanvill (1636–1680)

6809. Lewis, Rhodri. Of 'Origenian Platonisme': Joseph Glanvill on the pre-existence of souls. HLQ (69:2) 2006, 267–300.

Francis Godwin ('Domingo Gonzales')

6810. Poole, William. Marvell's *Ganza's*: an emendation. *See* **6938**.

6811. —— *Nuncius inanimatus*: seventeenth-century telegraphy: the schemes of Francis Godwin and Henry Reynolds. SevC (21:1) 2006, 45–72.

Fulke Greville, Lord Brooke (1554–1628)

6812. Quinn, Kelly A. Fulke Greville's friendly patronage. SP (103:4) 2006, 417–35.

6813. Wilkes, G. A. 'Left … to play the ill poet in my own part': the literary relationship of Sidney and Fulke Greville. *See* **5049**.

James Harrington (1611–1677)

6814. Wigelsworth, Jeffrey R. John Toland's economic imperative to print and financing the Harrington edition: a brief assessment. *See* **8226**.

Peter Hausted (d.1645)

6815. Marlow, Christopher. Friendship, misogyny and anti-theatrical prejudice: the difference of *The Rivall Friends*. PE (1) 2006, 25–33.

Sir John Hayward

6816. Lemon, Rebecca. Treason by words: literature, law, and rebellion in Shakespeare's England. Ithaca, NY; London: Cornell UP, 2006. pp. ix, 234.

George Herbert

6817. Barnes, A. W. Editing George Herbert's ejaculations. TextC (1:2) 2006, 90–113.

6818. Brand, Clinton A. Analogies of sovereignty in Herbert's *To All Angels and Saints*. JDJ (23) 2004, 321–46.

6819. Craig, Barry L. St Augustine and the Metaphysical poets. *In* (pp. 97–116) **3301**.

6820. de la Mare, Ben. Measure and meaning in George Herbert's *Discipline*. SevC (21:1) 2006, 33–44.

6821. Gaston, Paul L. George Herbert, the 'hymn menders', and the Anglican hymn tradition. JDJ (25) 2006, 315–32.

6822. Malpezzi, Frances M. Herbertian intentionality: *Man* and the spiritualizing of genre. ExRC (32:1) 2006, 118–27.

6823. Miller-Blaise, Anne-Marie. Beauté et iconicité dans *The Temple* de George Herbert: '*If I but lift mine eyes*'. EA (59:2) 2006, 131–44.

6824. West, Philip. Nathaniel Wanley and George Herbert: the dis-engaged and *The Temple*. RES (57:230) 2006, 337–58.

6825. Wilcox, Helen. 'Forgive, O Lord, forgive our trespasses': the failure of holiness in seventeenth-century English lyric poetry. *In* (pp. 41–59) **3415**.

Robert Herrick (1591–1674)

6826. Hammons, Pamela. Robert Herrick's gift trouble: male subjects 'trans-shifting' into objects. Criticism (47:1) 2005, 31–64.

6827. Pugh, Syrithe. Ovidian exile in the *Hesperides*: Herrick's politics of intertextuality. RES (57:232) 2006, 733–65.

Thomas Heywood

6828. Bosman, Anston. 'Best play with Mardian': eunuch and blackamoor as imperial culturegram. *See* **5638**.

6829. Culhane, Peter. Livy in early Jacobean drama. *See* **7172**.

6830. Guard, Pippa. A defence of the first English actress. *See* **7158**.

6831. Hirsch, Brett D. Thomas Heywood and the werewolves: sources for *The Witches of Lancashire*. NQ (53:4) 2006, 531–3.

6832. Jankowski, Theodora A. Class categorization, capitalism, and the problem of 'gentle' identity in *The Royall King and the Loyall Subject* and *Eastward Ho!* MedRen (19) 2006, 144–74.

6833. Lindberg, Kevin. Thomas Heywood's *The Royall King, and the Loyall Subject* and the fall of Robert Devereux, Second Earl of Essex. CompDr (39:1) 2005, 31–53.

6834. Mejia-LaPerle, Carol. Domestic rhetors of an early modern family: female persuasions in *A Woman Killed with Kindness*. *In* (pp. 39–54) **3893**.

6835. Orgel, Stephen. Marginal maternity: reading Lady Anne Clifford's *A Mirror for Magistrates*. *In* (pp. 267–89) **661**.

6836. Rowland, Richard. Two plays in one: annotations in the third quarto of *Edward IV*. *See* **4721**.

6837. —— (ed.). The first and second parts of King Edward IV. (Bibl. 2005, 7511.) Rev. by Paul Dean in EngS (87:3) 2006, 370–3; by Tracey Hill in CamQ (35:1) 2006, 94–7.

Thomas Hobbes (1588–1679)

6838. Butler, Todd. Image, rhetoric, and politics in the early Thomas Hobbes. JHI (67:3) 2006, 465–87.

John Holles, Earl of Clare (*c*.1565–[1637)

6839. Cogswell, Thomas. 'The symptomes and vapors of a diseased time': the Earl of Clare and early Stuart manuscript culture. RES (57:230) 2006, 310–36.

Sir Robert Howard (1626–1698)

6840. Burke, Helen. Teague and the ethnicization of labor in early modern British culture. ECent (46:3) 2005, 237–44.

Anne Hutchinson

6841. Smith, Cheryl C. Out of her place: Anne Hutchinson and the dislocation of power in New World politics. JAC (29:4) 2006, 437–53.

Lucy Hutchinson

6842. Bennett, Joan S. Mary Astell, Lucy Hutchinson, John Milton, and feminist liberation theology. *In* (pp. 139–66) **7033**.

6843. Berry, Boyd. Conversation in Hutchinson's *Order and Disorder* and Milton's *Paradise Lost*. RenP (2005) 85–102.

6844. Goldberg, Jonathan. Lucy Hutchinson writing matter. ELH (73:1) 2006, 275–301.

6845. Hammons, Pamela. Polluted palaces: gender, sexuality and property in Lucy Hutchinson's *Elegies*. WWr (13:3) 2006, 392–415.

Elinor James (*c*.1649–1719)

6846. McDowell, Paula (sel. and introd.). Elinor James. (Bibl. 2005, 7522.) Rev. by Dosia Reichardt in Parergon (23:1) 2006, 186–7.

James I and VI, King of England and Scotland (1566–1625)

6847. Marchitello, Howard. *Pater patriae*: James I and the imprint of prerogative. *In* (pp. 303–24) **661**.

6848. Shamas, Laura. 'We three': the mythology of Shakespeare's Weird Sisters. *See* **5944**.

Richard Johnson (1573–1659?)

6849. Davis, Alex. Savagery, civility, and popular literature: Richard Johnson's *Tom a Lincolne*. SP (103:3) 2006, 264–80.

Ben Jonson

6850. Aaron, Melissa D. 'Beware at what hands thou receiv'st thy commodity': *The Alchemist* and the King's Men fleece the customers, 1610. *In* (pp. 72–9) **5577**.

6851. Baker, Christopher; Harp, Richard. Jonson's *Volpone* and Dante. CompDr (39:1) 2005, 55–74.

6852. Booth, Roy. T. S. Eliot, *Sweeney Agonistes*, and Ben Jonson's *Masque of Queenes*. *See* **15670**.

6853. Borukhov, Boris. Was the 5th Earl of Rutland Ben Jonson's friend? NQ (53:4) 2006, 515–16.

6854. Brady, Jennifer. Dryden on *Epicœne*'s 'malicious pleasure': the case of the Otters. *See* **6766**.

6855. Bruckner, Lynne Dickson. Ben Jonson's branded thumb and the imprint of textual paternity. *In* (pp. 109–30) **661**.

6856. Buccola, Regina. Fairies, fractious women, and the old faith: fairy lore in early modern British drama and culture. *See* **5992**.

6857. Busse, Claire M. 'Pretty fictions' and 'little stories': child actors on the early modern stage. *In* (pp. 75–101) **6264**.

6858. Butler, Martin. *The Masque of Blackness* and Stuart court culture. *In* (pp. 152–63) **4734**.

6859. Cañadas, Ivan. The influence of Ben Jonson's *Volpone* on Mary Wollstonecraft's *Maria; or, The Wrongs of Woman*. *See* **8257**.

6860. Cheney, Patrick. Biographical representations: Marlowe's life of the author. *In* (pp. 183–204) **5353**.

6861. Cobb, Barbara Mather. Jonson's *Conversations with William Drummond*: a history. BJJ (13) 2006, 29–42.

6862. Cook, Amy; Reynolds, Bryan. Comedic law: protective transversality, deceit conceits, and the conjuring of *Macbeth* and *Doctor Faustus* in Jonson's *The Devil Is an Ass*. *In* (pp. 85–111) **4718**.

6863. Creaser, John. Jonson's *Bartholomew Fair* and Bancroft's *Dangerous Positions*. RES (57:229) 2006, 176–84.

6864. Davis, Lloyd. The love life of Ben Jonson. *In* (pp. 227–40) **5353**.

6865. —— Smith, Peter J.; Walker, Greg. From revelation to commodity: performing messengers, language and news from the York Cycle to Ben Jonson. *See* **3956**.

6866. Donaldson, Ian. Looking sideways: Jonson, Shakespeare and the myths of envy. *In* (pp. 241–57) **5353**.

6867. Edelman, Charles. Morose's fights at sea in *Epicœne*. NQ (53:4) 2006, 516–19.

6868. Eggert, Katherine. *The Alchemist* and science. *In* (pp. 200–12) **4734**.

6869. Farmer, Alan B. Play-reading, news-reading, and Ben Jonson's *The Staple of News*. *In* (pp. 127–58) **4731**.

6870. Frost, Kate Gartner. 'All come in': Penshurst as David's Tabernacle. ExRC (32:1) 2006, 103–17.

6871. Gants, David. Drama case study: *The Cambridge Edition of the Works of Ben Jonson*. *In* (pp. 122–37) **426**.

6872. González, José Manuel. The court drama of Ben Jonson and Calderón. *In* (pp. 250–61) **5308**.

6873. —— (ed.). Spanish studies in Shakespeare and his contemporaries. *See* **5308**.

6874. Griffin, Andrew R. Sexuality, speech, and narcissism in Jonson's *Epicœne*. BJJ (13) 2006, 83–92.

6875. Hentschell, Roze. A question of nation: foreign clothes on the English subject. *In* (pp. 49–62) **4629**.

6876. Hillman, Richard. Returning to one's vomit: an intertextual tour of *Eastward Ho*'s Isle of Dogs. *See* **6640**.

6877. Hiscock, Andrew. The uses of this world: thinking space in Shakespeare, Marlowe, Cary, and Jonson. *See* **5727**.

6878. Hyland, Peter. Jonson's *Epigram 89, To Edward Alleyn*. Exp (64:4) 2006, 206–7.

6879. Knowles, James. Jonson in Scotland: Jonson's mid-Jacobean crisis. *In* (pp. 259–77) **5353**.

6880. —— 'Songs of baser alloy': Jonson's *Gypsies Metamorphosed* and the circulation of manuscript libels. HLQ (69:1) 2006, 153–76.

6881. Koslow, Julian. Humanist schooling and Ben Jonson's *Poetaster*. ELH (73:1) 2006, 119–59.

6882. Kozuka, Takashi; Mulryne, J. R. (eds). Shakespeare, Marlowe, Jonson: new directions in biography. *See* **5353**.

6883. Lamb, Mary Ellen. The popular culture of Shakespeare, Spenser and Jonson. *See* **5095**.

6884. Lemon, Rebecca. Treason by words: literature, law, and rebellion in Shakespeare's England. *See* **6816**.

6885. Levin, Richard. *A tale of a tub. See* **1603**.

6886. Lockwood, Tom. Ben Jonson in the Romantic age. (Bibl. 2005, 7562.) Rev. by Michael W. Stamps in BJJ (13) 2006, 189–96.

6887. Lyne, Raphael. English Guarini: recognition and reception. *See* **6676**.

6888. —— *Volpone* and the Classics. *In* (pp. 177–88) **4734**.

6889. McAdam, Ian. The Puritan dialectic of law and grace in *Bartholomew Fair*. SELit (46:2) 2006, 415–33.

6890. McDermott, Kristen. Jonson's gossips and the Stuart family drama. ETh (9:1) 2006, 61–83.

6891. Mahler, Andreas. Point of reference or semantic space? Functions of Venice in early modern English drama. *In* (pp. 161–79) **5346**.

6892. Miller, Anthony. Ben Jonson and 'the proper passion of Mettalls'. Parergon (23:2) 2006, 57–72.

6893. Miller, David Lee. All father: Ben Jonson and the psychodynamics of authorship. *In* (pp. 131–47) **661**.

6894. Moul, Victoria. Ben Jonson's *Poetaster*: Classical translation and the location of cultural authority. TransLit (15:1) 2006, 21–46.

6895. Mukherji, Subha. Jonson's *The New Inn* and a revisiting of the 'amorous jurisdiction'. LawL (18:2) 2006, 149–69.

6896. Over, William. Alterity and assimilation in Jonson's Masques of *Blackness* and *Beauty*: 'I, with so much strength / Of argument resisted'. CLR (1) 2004, 43–54.

6897. Paster, Gail Kern. *Bartholomew Fair* and the humoral body. *In* (pp. 260–71) **4734**.

6898. Pebworth, Ted-Larry; Summers, Claude J. Jonson and his era: overviews of modern research. BJJ (13) 2006, 149–71 (review-article).

6899. Phillips, Patrick. 'You need not fear the house': the absence of plague in *The Alchemist*. BJJ (13) 2006, 43–62.

6900. Ribes, Purificación. Spanish adaptations of Ben Jonson's *Volpone*. *In* (pp. 262–98) **5308**.

6901. Sanchez, Reuben. 'Things like truths, well feigned': mimesis and secrecy in Jonson's *Epicœne*. CompDr (40:3) 2006, 313–36.

6902. Sanders, Julie. Jonson's Caroline coteries. *In* (pp. 279–94) **5353**.

6903. Shargel, Raphael. Damned by excessive praise: *Jonsonus Virbius* and the foibles of reputation. CEl (69) 2006, 41–9.

6904. —— The devolution of *The Alchemist*: Garrick, Gentleman, and 'genteel comedy'. RECTR (19:2) 2004, 1–21.

6905. Stamps, Michael W. Peter Whalley: editing Jonson in the eighteenth century. BJJ (13) 2006, 1–28.

6906. Trüstedt, Katrin. Secondary satire and the sea-change of romance: reading William Shakespeare's *The Tempest*. *See* **6144**.

6907. Wall, Wendy. Dramatic authorship and print. *In* (pp. 1–11) **4734**.

6908. Weineck, Silke-Maria. Dead children: Ben Jonson's epitaph *On My First Sonne*. *In* (pp. 128–42) **3235**.

6909. Yearling, Rebecca. John Marston's *What You Will* and the war of the theaters. *See* **6928**.

Henry King (1592–1669)

6910. Wilcher, Robert. Suckling's fruition poems and Shakespeare's *Troilus and Cressida*. *See* **7140**.

Aemilia Lanyer

6911. Furey, Constance. 'The selfe undone': individualism and relationality in John Donne and Aemilia Lanyer. *See* **6716**.

6912. Furey, Constance M. Utopia of desire: the real and ideal in Aemilia Lanyer's *Salve Deus Rex Judaeorum*. JMEMS (36:3) 2006, 561–84.

6913. Ingram, Jill Phillips. Idioms of self-interest: credit, identity, and property in English Renaissance literature. *See* **6642**.

6914. Leonard, John. Aemilia Lanyer's 'many worlds'. Cithara (45:2) 2006, 46–52.

6915. Wallace, David. Periodizing women: Mary Ward (1585–1645) and the premodern canon. *See* **7165**.

Thomas Lessey (1650–1724)

6916. Fisher, Nicholas. The contemporary reception of Rochester's *A Satyr against Mankind*. *See* **7109**.

Laurence Lisle (*fl.*1614)

6917. Faith, Melanie. Correcting the date of the 'conceited *Newes*'. NQ (53:4) 2006, 505–8.

William Lithgow

6918. Bosworth, Clifford Edmund. An intrepid Scot: William Lithgow of Lanark's travels in the Ottoman lands, North Africa and Central Europe, 1609–21. Aldershot; Burlington, VT: Ashgate, 2006. pp. xviii, 193. Rev. by Katharine Craik in TLS, 4 Aug. 2006, 30.

John Locke (1632–1704)

6919. Quinney, Laura. Escape from repetition: Blake *versus* Locke and Wordsworth. *In* (pp. 63–79) **1894**.

Richard Lovelace

6920. Robertson, Randy. Lovelace and the 'barbed Censurers': *Lucasta* and Civil War censorship. SP (103:4) 2006, 465–98.

Thomas Manley (1628–1690)

6921. Bedford, Ronald. Milton's military Heaven revisited. *See* **6965**.

Gervase Markham

6922. GRAHAM, ELSPETH. Reading, writing, and riding horses in early modern England: James Shirley's *Hyde Park* (1632) and Gervase Markham's *Cavelarice* (1607). *In* (pp. 116–37) **4588**.

John Marston (1575?–1634)

6923. CATHCART, CHARLES. John Marston, *The Malcontent*, and the King's Men. RES (57:228) 2006, 43–63.

6924. CULHANE, PETER. Livy in early Jacobean drama. *See* **7172**.

6925. HILLMAN, RICHARD. Returning to one's vomit: an intertextual tour of *Eastward Ho*'s Isle of Dogs. *See* **6640**.

6926. SPINRAD, PHOEBE S. The sacralization of revenge in *Antonio's Revenge*. CompDr (39:2) 2005, 169–85.

6927. STEGGLE, MATTHEW. John Marston's *Entertainment at Ashby* and the 1606 Fleet Conduit eclogue. MedRen (19) 2006, 249–55.

6928. YEARLING, REBECCA. John Marston's *What You Will* and the war of the theaters. BJJ (13) 2006, 109–23.

Andrew Marvell

6929. EDMUNDSON, MELISSA. 'Try what depth the centre draws': Classicism and Neoclassicism in Andrew Marvell's *A Dialogue between the Resolved Soul, and Created Pleasure*. EngS (87:3) 2006, 294–302.

6930. GREGERSON, LINDA. Rhetorical contract in the lyric poem. KR (28:2) 2006, 161–78.

6931. HAMMOND, PAUL. The date of Marvell's *The Mower against Gardens*. NQ (53:2) 2006, 178–81.

6932. KUCHAR, GARY. Andrew Marvell's anamorphic tears. SP (103:3) 2006, 345–81.

6933. LEWIS, RHODRI. An unpublished letter from Andrew Marvell to William Petty. NQ (53:2) 2006, 181–3.

6934. LUCAS, JOHN. Scholar poets and history. *See* **17273**.

6935. MCWILLIAMS, JOHN. Marvell and Milton's literary friendship reconsidered. SELit (46:1) 2006, 155–77.

6936. MARSHALL, ASHLEY. 'I saw him dead': Marvell's elegy for Cromwell. SP (103:4) 2006, 499–521.

6937. PARKER, IAN C. Marvell's use of Sylvester's *Du Bartas*, II.iv.4. NQ (53:2) 2006, 172–8.

6938. POOLE, WILLIAM. Marvell's *Ganza's*: an emendation. NQ (53:2) 2006, 183–4.

6939. REICHARDT, DOSIA. Marvell's 'interior paramour': Clora meets the cavaliers in *The Gallery*. Parergon (23:2) 2006, 97–118.

6940. ROBERTSON, RANDY. Lovelace and the 'barbed Censurers': *Lucasta* and Civil War censorship. *See* **6920**.

6941. VON MALTZAHN, NICHOLAS. An Andrew Marvell chronology. (Bibl. 2005, 7634.) Rev. by Thomas Healy in TLS, 3 Feb. 2006, 28; by David Norbrook in NQ (53:4) 2006, 574–5.

Philip Massinger

6942. Bosman, Anston. 'Best play with Mardian': eunuch and blackamoor as imperial culturegram. *See* **5638**.

6943. Degenhardt, Jane Hwang. Catholic martyrdom in Dekker and Massinger's *The Virgin Martir* and the early modern threat of 'turning Turk'. *See* **6683**.

6944. Feerick, Jean. 'Divided in soyle': plantation and degeneracy in *The Tempest* and *The Sea Voyage*. *See* **6121**.

6945. Mukherji, Subha. False trials in Shakespeare, Massinger, and Ford. *See* **5393**.

6946. Stephenson, Joseph F. On the markings in the manuscript of *Sir John Van Olden Barnavelt*. *See* **6801**.

Cotton Mather

6947. Ravalli, Richard. Cotton Mather, levitation, and a case for wonders in history. CSR (35:2) 2006, 193–204.

Increase Mather

6948. Carruth, Mary C. Between abjection and redemption: Mary Rowlandson's subversive corporeality. *In* (pp. 60–79) **6224**.

Thomas Middleton

6949. Alt, Christina. Directed readings: paratext in *A Game at Chess* and *The Tragedie of Philotas*. PQ (83:2) 2004, 127–44.

6950. Bunker, Nancy Mohrlock. Feminine and fashionable: regendering the iconologies of Mary Frith's 'notorious reputation'. ExRC (31:2) 2005, 211–57.

6951. Hirsch, Brett D. Werewolves and severed hands: Webster's *The Duchess of Malfi* and Heywood and Brome's *The Witches of Lancashire*. *See* **7178**.

6952. Jackson, MacD. P. *Anything for a Quiet Life*, iv.ii.1–44: the hazards of collaboration. NQ (53:1) 2006, 87–90.

6953. Kalpin, Kathleen. 'As if the end they purpos'd were their own': early modern representations of speech between women. *See* **4686**.

6954. Neill, Michael. Death and *The Revenger's Tragedy*. *In* (pp. 164–76) **4734**.

6955. Newman, Karen. *A Chaste Maid in Cheapside* and London. *In* (pp. 237–47) **4734**.

6956. Scott, Sarah. 'Sell[ing] your selues away': pathologizing and gendering the socio-economic in *The Honest Whore, Part* i. RORD (45) 2006, 1–22.

6957. Sugimura, N. K. Changelings and *The Changeling*. EC (56:3) 2006, 241–63.

Middleton and Rowley

6958. Burnett, Mark Thornton. *The Changeling* and masters and servants. *In* (pp. 298–308) **4734**.

6959. Calbi, Maurizio. Approximate bodies: gender and power in early modern drama and anatomy. (Bibl. 2005, 7651.) Rev. by Katharine Craik in TLS, 20 Jan. 2006, 28.

6960. HEDRICK, DONALD; REYNOLDS, BRYAN. I might like you better if we slept together: the historical drift of place in *The Changeling*. *In* (pp. 112–23) **4718**.

John Milton (1608–1674)

6961. ACOSTA, ANA M. Reading Genesis in the long eighteenth century: from Milton to Mary Shelley. Aldershot; Burlington, VT: Ashgate, 2006. pp. vi, 207.

6962. ADNEY, KARLEY. It's not a matter of messenger but of message: Hardy's support for Miltonic principles in *Jude the Obscure*. *See* **10248**.

6963. ARNOLD, RICHARD. Logic of the Fall: right reason and (im)pure reason in Milton's *Paradise Lost*. New York; Frankfurt: Lang, 2006. pp. xii, 115.

6964. BATES, BRIAN. *Welcome Joy, and Welcome Sorrow*: fancy, imagination, and Keats's re-visioning of *L'Allegro* and *Il Penseroso*. *See* **10636**.

6965. BEDFORD, RONALD. Milton's military Heaven revisited. AUMLA (106) 2006, 123–48.

6966. BENET, DIANA TREVIÑO. Milton's toad; or, Satan's dream. MStud (45) 2006, 38–52.

6967. BENNETT, JOAN S. Mary Astell, Lucy Hutchinson, John Milton, and feminist liberation theology. *In* (pp. 139–66) **7033**.

6968. BERENSMEYER, INGO. The art of oblivion: politics of remembering and forgetting in Restoration England. *See* **7149**.

6969. BERRY, BOYD. Conversation in Hutchinson's *Order and Disorder* and Milton's *Paradise Lost*. *See* **6843**.

6970. BLEVINS, JACOB. Influence, anxiety, and the symbolic: a Lacanian rereading of Bloom. *See* **14023**.

6971. BLYTHE, JOAN. Milton's Mary and Eve and garlands of roses in seventeenth-century art and handbooks of devotion. CEACrit (68:1/2) 2005/06, 85–96.

6972. BRADBURN, ELIZABETH. Theatrical wonder, amazement, and the construction of spiritual agency in *Paradise Lost*. CompDr (40:1) 2006, 77–98.

6973. BRADY, MAURA. Galileo in action: the 'telescope' in *Paradise Lost*. MStud (44) 2005, 129–52.

6974. BRYSON, MICHAEL. The tyranny of Heaven: Milton's rejection of God as king. (Bibl. 2005, 7660.) Rev. by Louis Schwartz in MQ (40:3) 2006, 239–45.

6975. BUHLER, STEPHEN M. 'Soft *Lydian* Airs' meet 'Anthems clear': intelligibility in Milton, Handel, and Mark Morris. JDJ (25) 2006, 333–53.

6976. BURBERY, TIMOTHY J. From orthodoxy to heresy: a theological analysis of Sonnets XIV and XVIII. MStud (45) 2006, 1–20.

6977. BUTLER, GEORGE F. The fall of Tydeus and the failure of Satan: Statius' *Thebaid*, Dante's *Commedia*, and Milton's *Paradise Lost*. CLS (43:1/2) 2006, 134–52.

6978. —— Milton's meeting with Galileo: a reconsideration. MQ (39:3) 2005, 132–9.

6979. —— Milton's Pandora: Eve, sin, and the mythographic tradition. MStud (44) 2005, 153–78.

6980. CAMPBELL, MARY BAINE. Busy bees: utopia, dystopia, and the very small. JMEMS (36:3) 2006, 619–42.

6981. Carey, John (ed.). Complete shorter poems. (Bibl. 2000, 7361.) London; New York: Pearson Longman, 2006. pp. xxvi, 523. (Longman annotated English poets.) (Revised second ed.: first ed. 1971.)

6982. Chakravarty, Prasanta. Like parchment in the fire: literature and Radicalism in the English Civil War. London; New York: Routledge, 2006. pp. x, 212. (Literary criticism and cultural theory.)

6983. Conley, Tim. Darius in Milton's Pandemonium. NQ (53:2) 2006, 184–5.

6984. Connolly, Joy. The aesthetics of the collective in Vergil and Milton. LitIm (8:3) 2006, 477–92.

6985. Connor, John T. Milton's *Art of Logic* and the force of conviction. MStud (45) 2006, 187–209.

6986. Conti, Brooke. 'That really too anxious protestation': crisis and autobiography in Milton's prose. MStud (45) 2006, 149–86.

6987. Corthell, Ronald. Go ask Alice: daughter, patron, and poet in *A Mask Presented at Ludlow Castle*. MStud (44) 2005, 111–28.

6988. Crossley, Robert. H. G. Wells, visionary telescopes, and the 'Matter of Mars'. *See* **19034**.

6989. Daems, Jim; Nelson, Holly Faith (eds). *Eikon Basilike: the Portraiture of His Sacred Majesty in His Solitudes and Sufferings*, with selections from *Eikonoklastes*. *See* **6646**.

6990. Dawson, Hugh J. The afterlife of the widower's dream: rereading Milton's final sonnet. MStud (45) 2006, 21–37.

6991. Dietrich, Bryan D. Queen of Pentacles: archetyping Wonder Woman. *See* **46**.

6992. Dowling, Paul M. Civil liberty and philosophic liberty in John Milton's *Areopagitica*. IJPP (33:3) 2006, 281–94.

6993. Dubrow, Heather. The masquing of genre in *Comus*. MStud (44) 2005, 62–83.

6994. Durham, Charles W. 'Suffering for truth's sake': the conflict between Abdiel and Satan in *Paradise Lost*. CEACrit (68:1/2) 2005/06, 60–6.

6995. Edwards, Karen. Milton's reformed animals: an early modern bestiary: introduction. MQ (39:3) 2005, 121–31.

6996. —— Milton's reformed animals: an early modern bestiary, A–C. MQ (39:4) 2005, 183–292.

6997. —— Milton's reformed animals: an early modern bestiary, D–F. MQ (40:2) 2006, 99–187.

6998. Esterhammer, Angela (ed.). Northrop Frye on Milton and Blake. *See* **14084**.

6999. Fenton, Mary C. Milton's places of hope: spiritual and political connections of hope with land. Aldershot; Burlington, VT: Ashgate, 2006. pp. viii, 225.

7000. —— Milton's view of Ireland: reform, reduction, and nationalist polity. MStud (44) 2005, 203–29.

7001. —— Satan's hope abounding in *Paradise Lost*. CEACrit (68:1/2) 2005/06, 47–59.

7002. Festa, Thomas. Place, source, and voice in *Paradise Lost*. ELN (44:1) 2006, 57–66.

7003. Fish, Stanley. Dregs, anyone? CEACrit (68:1/2) 2005/06, 43–6.

7004. —— 'There is nothing he cannot ask': Milton, liberalism, and terrorism. *In* (pp. 243–64) **7033**.

7005. —— Why Milton matters; or, Against historicism. MStud (44) 2005, 1–12.

7006. Fowler, Alastair (ed.). Paradise lost. (Bibl. 2002, 6555.) Harlow; New York: Longman, 2006. (Longman annotated English poets.) (Revised ed.: first ed. 1971.)

7007. Fox, Bradley A. Verbal allusions in Milton's *Samson Agonistes* to his *History of Britain* and to Drayton's *Poly-Olbion*. NQ (53:2) 2006, 188–9.

7008. Gervais, David. The poetry of the novel. *See* **9023**.

7009. Gorbunov, Andrey N. Christ's temptations in the wilderness (Milton and Dostoyevsky). LitTheol (20:1) 2006, 46–62.

7010. Greene, Rebekah. Milton's *Comus*. Exp (64:4) 2006, 208–10.

7011. Gregory, Tobias. From many gods to one: divine action in Renaissance epic. Chicago, IL; London: Chicago UP, 2006. pp. x, 247.

7012. Grey, Robin (ed.). Melville and Milton: an edition and analysis of Melville's annotations on Milton. (Bibl. 2004, 8021.) Rev. by Clark Davis in MQ (39:3) 2005, 155–8; by Robert Wilcher in MLR (101:2) 2006, 523–4.

7013. Grossman, Marshall. The onomastic destiny of Stanley Fish. *In* (pp. 27–52) **7033**.

7014. Hale, John. Milton as multilingual: selected essays. Ed. by Lisa Marr and Chris Ackerley. Introd. by Beverley Sherry. Dunedin: English Dept, Univ. of Otago, 2005. pp. xviii, 282. (Otago studies in English, 8.) Rev. by Richard J. DuRocher in MQ (40:1) 2006, 63–9; by Alastair Fowler in TransLit (15:2) 2006, 277–81.

7015. Hale, John K. Milton's Cambridge Latin: performing in the genres, 1625–1632. (Bibl. 2005, 7685.) Rev. by Robert Cummings in RES (57:231) 2006, 562–4.

7016. Hawkes, David (ed.). Paradise lost. New York: Fine Creative Media, 2004. pp. 496. (Barnes & Noble classics.) Rev. by John T. Shawcross in MQ (40:3) 2006, 220–34.

7017. Herman, Peter C. Destabilizing Milton: *Paradise Lost* and the poetics of incertitude. (Bibl. 2005, 7692.) Rev. by Šárka Kühnová in NQ (53:2) 2006, 238–40; by Bill Goldstein in RQ (59:2) 2006, 650–2.

7018. Herz, Judith Scherer. 13 retro keywords … and why they're worth a second look: *individual*. *See* **1573**.

7019. Hillier, Russell M. Grotius's *Christus patiens* and Milton's *Samson Agonistes*. Exp (65:1) 2006, 9–13.

7020. —— Two Patristic sources for John Milton's description of the sun (*Paradise Lost*, III.591–595). NQ (53:2) 2006, 185–7.

7021. Himy, Armand. John Milton (1608–1674). (Bibl. 2004, 8028.) Rev. by Jean-Marie Maguin in CEl (68) 2005, 84–6.

7022. Johnson, Eugene. The failed jeremiad in *Samson Agonistes*. SELit (46:1) 2006, 179–94.

7023. Kastan, David Scott (ed.). Paradise lost. Indianapolis, IN: Hackett, 2005. pp. lxxix, 427. Rev. by John T. Shawcross in MQ (40:3) 2006, 220–34.

7024. Kean, Margaret (ed.). John Milton's *Paradise Lost*: a sourcebook. (Bibl. 2005, 7697.) Rev. by Thomas H. Luxon in MQ (40:3) 2006, 252–5.

7025. Klinge, Markus. The grotesque in *Areopagitica*. MStud (45) 2006, 82–128.

7026. Knoppers, Laura Lunger; Colón Semenza, Gregory M. (eds). Milton in popular culture. Basingstoke; New York: Palgrave Macmillan, 2006. pp. 260.

7027. Kranidas, Thomas. Milton and the rhetoric of zeal. (Bibl. 2005, 7705.) Rev. in SRASP (29) 2006, 93; by James S. Baumlin in ColLit (33:2) 2006, 194–8; by Nicholas von Maltzahn in MQ (40:1) 2006, 60–2; by Michael Delahoyde in RMER (60:2) 2006; by Anthony Low in BJJ (13) 2006, 211–14.

7028. Labriola, Albert C. The Son as an angel in *Paradise Lost*. *In* (pp. 105–18) **7033**.

7029. Lewalski, Barbara K. Barbara K. Lewalski on why Milton matters. MStud (44) 2005, 13–21.

7030. —— Milton's idea of authorship. *In* (pp. 53–79) **7033**.

7031. Lieb, Michael. Returning the Gorgon Medusa's gaze: terror and annihilation in Milton. *In* (pp. 229–42) **7033**.

7032. —— Theological Milton: deity, discourse, and heresy in the Miltonic canon. Pittsburgh, PA: Duquesne UP, 2006. pp. xi, 348. (Medieval & Renaissance literary studies.) Rev. by Susanne Woods in BJJ (13) 2006, 214–17.

7033. —— Labriola, Albert C. (eds). Milton in the age of Fish: essays on authorship, text, and terrorism. Pittsburgh, PA: Duquesne UP, 2006. pp. xi, 320. (Medieval & Renaissance literary studies.)

7034. Loewenstein, David. *Samson Agonistes* and the culture of religious terror. *In* (pp. 203–28) **7033**.

7035. Luxon, Thomas H. Single imperfection: Milton, marriage, and friendship. (Bibl. 2005, 7712.) Rev. by John Mulryan in Cithara (45:2) 2006, 56–7; by Margaret J. Arnold in RQ (59:3) 2006, 983–5.

7036. McLoone, George H. Composing the uneasy station: confession and absence in *Paradise Regain'd*. MStud (45) 2006, 53–81.

7037. McWilliams, John. Marvell and Milton's literary friendship reconsidered. *See* **6935**.

7038. Malpezzi, Frances M. Emerson's allusive art: a Transcendental angel in Miltonic myrtle beds. *See* **10087**.

7039. Martin, Catherine Gimelli (ed.). Milton and gender. (Bibl. 2005, 7717.) Rev. by Paula Loscocco in RQ (59:1) 2006, 307–9.

7040. Maus, Katharine Eisaman. A womb of his own: male Renaissance poets in the female body. *In* (pp. 89–108) **661**.

7041. Mayer, Joseph G. Between two pillars: the hero's plight in *Samson Agonistes* and *Paradise Regained*. (Bibl. 2005, 7722.) Rev. by Stephen B. Dobranski in MQ (40:1) 2006, 70–5.

7042. Miner, Earl (ed.); Moeck, William; Jablonski, Steven Edward (asst eds). *Paradise Lost*, 1668–1968: three centuries of commentary. (Bibl. 2005, 7726.) Rev. by John Leonard in MQ (39:3) 2005, 151–4.

7043. Mulryan, John. Milton's *Paradise Regained*. Exp (64:4) 2006, 211.

7044. Myers, Benjamin. Milton's theology of freedom. Berlin; New York: Mouton de Gruyter, 2006. pp. xiv, 209. (Arbeiten zur Kirchesgeschichte, 98.)

7045. —— Prevenient grace and conversion in *Paradise Lost*. MQ (40:1) 2006, 20–36.

7046. Odell, D. W. Pope's *The Dunciad* 4.425–30. *See* **8063**.

7047. Oldman, Elizabeth. 'Against such hellish mischief fit to oppose': a Grotian reading of Milton's war in Heaven. WLA (18:1/2) 2006, 143–66.

7048. Olmsted, Wendy. Rhetoric: an historical introduction. *See* **2075**.

7049. Ortiz, Joseph M. 'The reforming of reformation': theatrical, Ovidian, and musical figuration in Milton's *Mask*. MStud (44) 2005, 84–110.

7050. Patterson, Annabel. Milton's negativity. *In* (pp. 81–102) **7033**.

7051. Pellicer, Juan Christian. Virgil's *Georgics* II in *Paradise Lost*. TransLit (14:2) 2005, 129–47.

7052. Pierce, Robert B. Reading *Paradise Regained* ethically. PhilL (30:1) 2006, 208–22.

7053. Poole, William. Milton and the idea of the Fall. (Bibl. 2005, 7736.) Rev. by Neil Forsyth in TLS, 10 Mar. 2006, 5; by the same in MQ (40:1) 2006, 48–59; by James Egan in SCN (64:1/2) 2006, 29–31; by Šárka Kühnová in NQ (53:2) 2006, 237–8; by Amy Dunham Stackhouse in RQ (59:2) 2006, 652–4.

7054. Post, Jonathan F. S. Footloose in Paradise: Masaccio, Milton, and Renaissance realism. HLQ (69:3) 2006, 403–23.

7055. Pruitt, Kristin A. The making of the circle: imagery as pattern in *Paradise Lost*. CEACrit (68:1/2) 2005/06, 67–75.

7056. Pullman, Philip (introd.). Paradise lost. Oxford; New York: OUP, 2005. pp. 374. Rev. by John T. Shawcross in MQ (40:3) 2006, 220–34.

7057. Putnam, Michael C. J. The *Aeneid* and *Paradise Lost*: ends and conclusions. LitIm (8:3) 2006, 387–410.

7058. Rampton, David. Plexed artistry: the formal case for Mailer's *Harlot's Ghost*. *See* **17412**.

7059. Revard, Stella P. Milton and Henry More: the chariot of paternal deity in *Paradise Lost*, Book VI. *In* (pp. 119–37) **7033**.

7060. Sauer, Elizabeth. Closet drama and the case of *Tyrannicall-Government Anatomized*. *In* (pp. 80–95) **4731**.

7061. —— Milton's *Of True Religion*, Protestant nationhood, and the negotiation of liberty. MQ (40:1) 2006, 1–19.

7062. —— Tolerationism, the Irish crisis, and Milton's *On the Late Massacre in Piemont*. MStud (44) 2005, 40–61.

7063. Savoie, John. Justifying the ways of God and man: theodicy in Augustine and Milton. *In* (pp. 139–54) **3301**.

7064. Sedley, David L. Sublimity and skepticism in Montaigne and Milton. Ann Arbor: Michigan UP, 2005. pp. vi, 208. Rev. by Elaine Limbrick in RQ (59:3) 2006, 893–5.

7065. Selden, Daniel L. Vergil and the Satanic *cogito*. LitIm (8:3) 2006, 345–85.

7066. Shawcross, John T. Milton in print: a review of some recent editions of *Paradise Lost*. MQ (40:3) 2006, 220–34 (review-article).

7067. —— Rethinking Milton Studies: time present and time past. (Bibl. 2005, 7753.) Rev. by Joseph Wittreich in MQ (39:3) 2005, 140–2; by Anthony Low in BJJ (13) 2006, 211–14.

7068. Shore, Daniel. 'Fit though few': *Eikonoklastes* and the rhetoric of audience. MStud (45) 2006, 129–48.

7069. Silver, Victoria. 'Unequal proceedings' and equitable interpretations in the seventeenth century. YREAL (22) 2006, 37–71.

7070. Stoll, Abraham. Discontinuous wound: Milton and Deism. MStud (44) 2005, 179–202.

7071. Tanner, John S.; Collings, Justin. How Adams and Jefferson read Milton and Milton read them. MQ (40:3) 2006, 207–19.

7072. Teskey, Gordon. Delirious Milton: the fate of the poet in modernity. Cambridge, MA; London: Harvard UP, 2006. pp. vi, 214.

7073. —— (ed.). *Paradise Lost*: authoritative text, sources and backgrounds, criticism. New York; London: Norton, 2005. pp. xxx, 591. (Norton critical eds.) Rev. by John T. Shawcross in MQ (40:3) 2006, 220–34.

7074. Thomas, Arvind. Milton and table manners. MQ (40:1) 2006, 37–47.

7075. Thomas, Catherine. Chaste bodies and poisonous desires in Milton's *Mask*. SELit (46:2) 2006, 435–59.

7076. von Maltzahn, Nicholas. There she blew! *See* **6783**.

7077. Walker, William. Resemblance and reference in recent criticism on *Paradise Lost*. MQ (40:3) 2006, 189–206.

7078. Wilcox, Helen. 'Forgive, O Lord, forgive our trespasses': the failure of holiness in seventeenth-century English lyric poetry. *In* (pp. 41–59) **3415**.

7079. Williams, Carolyn D. Bestiality in eighteenth-century English literature: 'the Dev'l himself is in that *Mare*'. *See* **7440**.

7080. Wilson, Emily R. Mocked with death: tragic overliving from Socrates to Milton. *See* **5458**.

7081. Wilson, Penelope. Homer and English epic. *In* (pp. 272–86) **3253**.

7082. Wittreich, Joseph. Joseph Wittreich on why Milton matters. MStud (44) 2005, 22–39.

7083. —— Protocols and provocations: Milton's gestures of rebellion. CEACrit (68:1/2) 2005/06, 76–84.

7084. —— 'The ramifications of those ramifications': compounding contexts for *Samson Agonistes*. *In* (pp. 167–99) **7033**.

7085. —— Why Milton matters: a new preface to his writings. Basingstoke; New York: Palgrave Macmillan, 2006. pp. xxv, 253.

7086. WOODS, SUSANNE. Abdiel centers freedom. *In* (pp. 279–90) **5401**.

Henry More

7087. REVARD, STELLA P. Milton and Henry More: the chariot of paternal deity in *Paradise Lost*, Book VI. *In* (pp. 119–37) **7033**.

Thomas Morton (1575–1646)

7088. BURNHAM, MICHELLE. Land, labor, and colonial economics in Thomas Morton's *New English Canaan*. EAL (41:3) 2006, 405–28.

7089. READ, DAVID. New World, known world: shaping knowledge in early Anglo-American writing. *See* **7138**.

Walter Mountfort (*fl*.1615–1634)

7090. PANGALLO, MATTEO A. A new source for a speech in *The Launching of the Mary*. NQ (53:4) 2006, 528–31.

Margaret Cavendish, Duchess of Newcastle

7091. CHALMERS, HERO; SANDERS, JULIE; TOMLINSON, SOPHIE (eds). Three seventeenth-century plays on women and performance. *See* **6796**.

7092. ROMACK, KATHERINE; FITZMAURICE, JAMES (eds). Cavendish and Shakespeare: interconnections. Aldershot; Burlington, VT: Ashgate, 2006. pp. xii, 217.

7093. STARR, G. GABRIELLE. Cavendish, aesthetics, and the anti-Platonic line. ECS (39:3) 2006, 295–308.

Nicholas Oldisworth (1611–1645)

7094. GOUWS, JOHN. Nicholas Oldisworth, Richard Bacon, and the practices of Caroline friendship. TSLL (47:4) 2005, 366–401.

'Orinda' (Katherine Philips)

7095. ANDREADIS, HARRIETTE. Re-configuring early modern friendship: Katherine Philips and homoerotic desire. SELit (46:3) 2006, 523–42.

7096. DUGAW, DIANNE; POWELL, AMANDA. Sapphic self-fashioning in the baroque era: women's Petrarchan parody in English and Spanish. StudECC (35) 2006, 127–60.

Thomas Otway

7097. MAHLER, ANDREAS. Point of reference or semantic space? Functions of Venice in early modern English drama. *In* (pp. 161–79) **5346**.

Sir Thomas Overbury

7098. FAITH, MELANIE. Correcting the date of the 'conceited *Newes*'. *See* **6917**.

William Penn

7099. BERNET, CLAUS. Jerusalemvorstellungen in radikalpietistischen und radikalpuritanischen Siedlungen Nordamerikas. *See* **6455**.

7100. MEHRING, FRANK. Deutsch, Dutch, double Dutch: authentic and artificial German American dialects. *See* **8952**.

William Percy (1575–1648)

7101. Dimmock, Matthew (ed.). William Percy's *Mahomet and His Heaven*: a critical edition. Aldershot; Burlington, VT: Ashgate, 2006. pp. 259.

John Philips (1676–1709)

7102. Pellicer, Juan Christian. Harleian georgic from Tonson's press: the publication of John Philips's *Cyder*, 29 January 1708. Library (7:2) 2006, 185–98.

7103. Rogers, Pat. John Philips, Pope, and political georgic. MLQ (66:4) 2005, 411–42.

Edward Pococke (1648–1727)

7104. Fisher, Nicholas. The contemporary reception of Rochester's *A Satyr against Mankind*. *See* **7109**.

William Prynne

7105. Hentschell, Roze. A question of nation: foreign clothes on the English subject. *In* (pp. 49–62) **4629**.

Samuel Purchas

7106. Campbell, Mary Baine. Busy bees: utopia, dystopia, and the very small. *See* **6980**.

Edward Ravenscroft (1654?–1707)

7107. Raffield, Paul. A discredited priesthood: the failings of common lawyers and their representation in seventeenth-century satirical drama. LawL (17:3) 2005, 365–95.

Henry Reynolds (*fl.*1627–1632)

7108. Poole, William. *Nuncius inanimatus*: seventeenth-century telegraphy: the schemes of Francis Godwin and Henry Reynolds. *See* **6811**.

John Wilmot, Earl of Rochester

7109. Fisher, Nicholas. The contemporary reception of Rochester's *A Satyr against Mankind*. RES (57:229) 2006, 185–220.

7110. —— Rochester's contemporary reception: the evidence of the memorial verses. Restoration (30:1) 2006, 1–14.

7111. Johnson, James William. A profane wit: the life of John Wilmot, Earl of Rochester. (Bibl. 2005, 7828.) Rev. by Moyra Haslett in Eng (54:210) 2005, 229–32; by Kirk Combe in NQ (53:1) 2006, 123–4; by Larry Carver in Scriblerian (38:2) 2006, 308–9.

7112. Lautel-Ribstein, Florence. Théories de la traduction au xviie siècle: entre noblesse et prosaïsme. *See* **2869**.

7113. Mackie, Erin. Boys will be boys: masculinity, criminality, and the Restoration rake. *See* **6275**.

7114. Miller, Eric. Epicurean gardens in William Temple and John Wilmot. *See* **7145**.

7115. O'Neill, John. Rambler and cully: Rochester's satire and the self-presentation of the Restoration rake. 1650–1850 (11) 2005, 189–209.

7116. WILCOX, HELEN. 'Forgive, O Lord, forgive our trespasses': the failure of holiness in seventeenth-century English lyric poetry. *In* (pp. 41–59) **3415**.

Mary Rowlandson

7117. CARRUTH, MARY C. Between abjection and redemption: Mary Rowlandson's subversive corporeality. *In* (pp. 60–79) **6224**.

7118. RIVETT, SARAH. 'Keepers of the covenant': submissive captives and maternal redeemers in Colonial New England (1660–1680). *In* (pp. 45–59) **6224**.

William Rowley

7119. CENTERWALL, BRANDON. A greatly exaggerated demise: the remaking of the Children of Paul's as the Duke of York's Men (1608). *See* **6331**.

7120. DARBY, TRUDI L. The date of William Rowley's *A Shoemaker, a Gentleman*. NQ (53:1) 2006, 83–4.

7121. ISAAC, MEGAN LYNN. Legitimizing magic in *The Birth of Merlin*. ETh (9:1) 2006, 109–21.

7122. KARPINSKA, MONIKA. Bawdily manipulations: spheres of female power in *The Birth of Merlin*. ETh (9:1) 2006, 123–9.

7123. NICOL, DAVID. 'My little what shall I call thee': reinventing rape tragedy in William Rowley's *All's Lost by Lust*. MedRen (19) 2006, 175–93.

7124. —— The title-page of *The World Tossed at Tennis*: a portrait of a Jacobean playing company? *See* **6369**.

7125. VELLA BONAVITA, HELEN. Maids, wives and widows: multiple meaning and marriage in *The Witch of Edmonton*. Parergon (23:2) 2006, 73–95.

George Sandys

7126. MANN, JENNY C. How to look at a hermaphrodite in early modern England. SELit (46:1) 2006, 67–91.

Walter Scot (1614?–1694?)

7127. STEGGLE, MATTHEW. Walter Scot's *True History* and John Taylor the Water-Poet. *See* **7144**.

Elkanah Settle

7128. DALPORTO, JEANNIE. The Succession Crisis and Elkanah Settle's *The Conquest of China by the Tartars*. ECent (45:2) 2004, 131–46.

Samuel Sewall (1652–1730)

7129. SWEET, TIMOTHY. 'What concernment hath America in these things!': local and global in Samuel Sewall's Plum Island passage. EAL (41:2) 2006, 213–40.

Thomas Shadwell

7130. CANFIELD, J. DOUGLAS. Late Shadwell and early bourgeois comedy. ECent (46:2) 2005, 105–28.

Edward Sharpham (1576–1608)

7131. MUNRO, LUCY. Reading printed comedy: Edward Sharpham's *The Fleer*. *In* (pp. 39–58) **4731**.

James Shirley

7132. Chalmers, Hero; Sanders, Julie; Tomlinson, Sophie (eds). Three seventeenth-century plays on women and performance. *See* **6796**.

7133. Görtschacher, Wolfgang. Drama adaptation: James Shirley, David Garrick and *The Gamester(s)*. MSp (50:2) 2006, 89–100.

7134. Graham, Elspeth. Reading, writing, and riding horses in early modern England: James Shirley's *Hyde Park* (1632) and Gervase Markham's *Cavelarice* (1607). *In* (pp. 116–37) **4588**.

7135. Jackson, MacD. P. John Webster, James Shirley, and the Melbourne manuscript. *See* **7181**.

7136. Munro, Lucy. Richard Brome and *The Book of Bulls*: situating *The New Academy; or, The New Exchange*. *See* **6599**.

Captain John Smith (1580–1631)

7137. Carson, James Taylor. When is an ocean not an ocean? Geographies of the Atlantic world. SoQ (43:4) 2006, 16–45.

7138. Read, David. New World, known world: shaping knowledge in early Anglo-American writing. Columbia; London: Missouri UP, 2005. pp. x, 177. Rev. by Philip Gould in AL (78:4) 2006, 869–72.

William Strode

7139. Smyth, Adam. 'Art reflexive': the poetry, sermons, and drama of William Strode (1601?–1645). SP (103:4) 2006, 436–64.

Sir John Suckling

7140. Wilcher, Robert. Suckling's fruition poems and Shakespeare's *Troilus and Cressida*. NQ (53:2) 2006, 164–6.

Josuah Sylvester (1563–1618)

7141. Jackson, MacDonald. A new author for an old epitaph: *Qualis vita* and Joshua Sylvester. NQ (53:1) 2006, 80–3.

7142. Parker, Ian C. Marvell's use of Sylvester's *Du Bartas*, II.iv.4. *See* **6937**.

John Taylor (1580–1653)

7143. Steggle, Matthew. Players at the Maidenhead Inn, Islington, 1618. NQ (53:4) 2006, 519–21.

7144. —— Walter Scot's *True History* and John Taylor the Water-Poet. ELN (43:2) 2005, 30–4.

Sir William Temple

7145. Miller, Eric. Epicurean gardens in William Temple and John Wilmot. DalR (86:3) 2006, 329–44.

Thomas Traherne

7146. Brown, Cedric C.; Koshi, Tomohiko. Editing the remains of Thomas Traherne. RES (57:232) 2006, 766–82.

7147. Ross, Jan (ed.). The works of Thomas Traherne: vol. 1, *Inducements to Retiredness*; *A Sober View of Dr Twisses His Considerations*; *Seeds of Eternity; or,*

The Nature of the Soul; *The Kingdom of God*. Woodbridge, Suffolk; Rochester, NY: Brewer, 2005. pp. xxiv, 571. Rev. by Jacob Blevins in SCN (64:1/2) 2006, 3–6; by Alison Kershaw in Parergon (23:1) 2006, 228–30.

7148. Ward, John Powell. Traherne's cosmic consciousness. Scintilla (10) 2006, 9–21.

Sir Samuel Tuke (d.1674)

7149. Berensmeyer, Ingo. The art of oblivion: politics of remembering and forgetting in Restoration England. EJES (10:1) 2006, 81–96.

7150. Vander Motten, J. P.; Daemen-de Gelder, Katrien. Sir Samuel Tuke (*c*.1615–1674) at the 'little court' of Mary Stuart (1631–1660). NQ (53:2) 2006, 168–70.

Sir John Vanbrugh

7151. Hammond, Brean. Joseph Addison's opera *Rosamond*: Britishness in the early eighteenth century. *See* **7527**.

7152. Rampton, David. Plexed artistry: the formal case for Mailer's *Harlot's Ghost*. *See* **17412**.

Henry Vaughan

7153. Hines, John. 'Aire disguis'd': metaphors of genre and Henry Vaughan's sacred hymns. Scintilla (10) 2006, 164–82.

7154. Nauman, Jonathan; Thomas, Peter. Sir Charles Egerton of Newborough. Scintilla (10) 2006, 196–207.

7155. Nelson, Holly Faith. 'Make all things new! And without end!': the eschatological vision of Henry Vaughan. Scintilla (10) 2006, 222–35.

7156. Pursglove, Glyn. 'Storms turn to music' (*The Rain-bow*). Scintilla (10) 2006, 54–75.

7157. Schneider, Myra. Repair: writing, poetry and therapy. Scintilla (10) 2006, 82–92.

Richard Walden (*fl*.1662)

7158. Guard, Pippa. A defence of the first English actress. LitH (15:2) 2006, 1–19.

Ellis Walker (*fl*.1692)

7159. Wright, Gillian. Epictetus in eighteenth-century Wales: Timothy Thomas' manuscript translation of the *Enchiridion*. *See* **8222**.

Edmund Waller

7160. Raylor, Timothy. The early poetic career of Edmund Waller. HLQ (69:2) 2006, 239–65.

William Walwyn (1600–1681)

7161. Como, David R. An unattributed pamphlet by William Walwyn: new light on the prehistory of the Leveller movement. HLQ (69:3) 2006, 353–82.

Nathaniel Wanley (1634–1680)

7162. Cuda, Anthony J. T. S. Eliot's forgotten 'poet of lines', Nathaniel Wanley. *See* **15682**.

7163. Ferber, Michael. The curse of the Ephesians: a long footnote to Byron. *See* **9345**.

7164. West, Philip. Nathaniel Wanley and George Herbert: the dis-engaged and *The Temple*. *See* **6824**.

Mary Ward (1585–1645)

7165. Wallace, David. Periodizing women: Mary Ward (1585–1645) and the premodern canon. JMEMS (36:2) 2006, 397–453.

Anna Weamys

7166. Campbell, Julie D. Literary circles and gender in early modern Europe: a cross-cultural approach. *See* **4570**.

7167. Mitchell, Marea (sel. and introd.). Anna Weamys. Aldershot; Burlington, VT: Ashgate, 2005. pp. xvi, 199. (Early modern Englishwoman, II: Printed writings, 1641–1700, 3:7.)

John Webster

7168. Bregazzi, Josephine. Changing roles: gender marking through syntactic distribution in the Jacobean theater. *In* (pp. 234–49) **5308**.

7169. Callaghan, Dympna. *The Duchess of Malfi* and early modern widows. *In* (pp. 272–86) **4734**.

7170. Cañadas, Ivan. A new source for the title and themes of *The Scarlet Letter*. *See* **10368**.

7171. Cathcart, Charles. John Marston, *The Malcontent*, and the King's Men. *See* **6923**.

7172. Culhane, Peter. Livy in early Jacobean drama. TransLit (14:1) 2005, 21–44.

7173. Ellis, Anthony. The Machiavel and the virago: uses of Italian types in Webster's *The White Devil*. JDTC (20:2) 2006, 49–74.

7174. Forker, Charles R. John Webster's handbook of model letters: a study in attribution. MedRen (19) 2006, 45–118.

7175. García, Luciano. *The Duchess of Malfi* and *El mayordomo de la duquesa de Amalfi* revisited: some differences in literary convention and cultural horizon. *In* (pp. 299–310) **5308**.

7176. González, José Manuel (ed.). Spanish studies in Shakespeare and his contemporaries. *See* **5308**.

7177. Goodland, Katharine. Female mourning and tragedy in medieval and Renaissance English drama: from the raising of Lazarus to *King Lear*. *See* **3907**.

7178. Hirsch, Brett D. Werewolves and severed hands: Webster's *The Duchess of Malfi* and Heywood and Brome's *The Witches of Lancashire*. NQ (53:1) 2006, 92–4.

7179. Jackson, MacD. P. *Anything for a Quiet Life*, IV.ii.1–44: the hazards of collaboration. *See* **6952**.

7180. —— Connectives and the Webster canon. NQ (53:1) 2006, 85–7.

7181. —— John Webster, James Shirley, and the Melbourne manuscript. MedRen (19) 2006, 21–44.

7182. Jackson, MacDonald. A new author for an old epitaph: *Qualis vita* and Joshua Sylvester. *See* **7141**.

7183. Lehmann, Courtney; Reynolds, Bryan. Awakening the werewolf within: self-help, vanishing mediation, and transversality in *The Duchess of Malfi*. *In* (pp. 227–39) **4718**.

7184. Lindley, Arthur. Uncrowning carnival: the laughter of subversion and the subversion of laughter in *The Duchess of Malfi*. AUMLA (106) 2006, 105–21.

7185. Mukherji, Subha. Jonson's *The New Inn* and a revisiting of the 'amorous jurisdiction'. *See* **6895**.

7186. Smith, Peter J. Rome's disgrace: the politics of rape in Shakespeare's *Lucrece*. *See* **6059**.

7187. Sullivan, Garrett A., Jr. Memory and forgetting in English Renaissance drama: Shakespeare, Marlowe, Webster. *See* **5437**.

7188. Wilson, Luke. *The White Devil* and the law. *In* (pp. 225–36) **4734**.

Thomas Wharton (1648–1715)

7189. Clark, J. Kent. Whig's progress: Tom Wharton between revolutions. Madison, NJ: Fairleigh Dickinson UP; London: Assoc. UPs, 2004. pp. 318. Rev. by Evan Haefeli in HLQ (69:3) 2006, 469–76.

William Whately (1583–1639)

7190. Clegg, Cyndia Susan. Checking the father: anxious paternity and Jacobean press censorship. *In* (pp. 291–301) **661**.

7191. Thompson, Torri L. (ed.). Marriage and its dissolution in early modern England: vol. 4. London; Brookfield, VT: Pickering & Chatto, 2005. pp. 506. (Facsimiles.) Rev. by Eric Josef Carlson in SixCJ (37:2) 2006, 589–90.

Sir George Wheler (1650–1723)

7192. Mitsi, Efterpi. Travel, memory and authorship: George Wheler's *A Journey into Greece* (1682). Restoration (30:1) 2006, 15–29.

George Wilkins

7193. Steggle, Matthew. *Demoniceacleare* in *The Miseries of Inforst Mariage*. NQ (53:4) 2006, 514–15.

Roger Williams (1604?–1683)

7194. Glover, Jeffrey. *Wunnaumwáyean*: Roger Williams, English credibility, and the Colonial land market. EAL (41:3) 2006, 429–53.

7195. Read, David. New World, known world: shaping knowledge in early Anglo-American writing. *See* **7138**.

Gerrard Winstanley

7196. Chakravarty, Prasanta. Like parchment in the fire: literature and Radicalism in the English Civil War. *See* **6982**.

John Winthrop the Elder (1588–1649)

7197. Schweitzer, Ivy. Perfecting friendship: politics and affiliation in early American literature. Chapel Hill; London: North Carolina UP, 2006. pp. xi, 276.

George Wither

7198. Edwards, Karen. Milton's reformed animals: an early modern bestiary: introduction. *See* **6995**.

7199. Goodrich, Peter. *Lex laetans*: three theses on the unbearable lightness of legal critique. LawL (17:3) 2005, 293–319.

Anthony Wood

7200. Goldgar, Anne; Frost, Robert I. (eds). Institutional culture in early modern society. *See* **728**.

7201. Haugen, Kristine. Imagined universities: public insult and the *terrae filius* in early modern Oxford. *In* (pp. 317–43) **728**.

Thomas Worthington (1549–1627)

7202. Patterson, Annabel. Donne's re-formed *La Corona*. *See* **6737**.

Lady Mary Wroth

7203. Alexander, Gavin. The musical Sidneys. *See* **5029**.

7204. Campbell, Julie D. Literary circles and gender in early modern Europe: a cross-cultural approach. *See* **4570**.

7205. Cavanagh, Sheila. Romancing the epic: Lady Mary Wroth's *Urania* and literary traditions. *In* (pp. 19–36) **3395**.

7206. Emig, Rainer. Competing melancholies: (en-)gendering discourses of selfhood in early modern English literature. EREA (4:1) 2006, 59–65.

7207. Hannay, Margaret. 'My daughter Wroth': Lady Mary Wroth in the correspondence of Robert Sidney, Earl of Leicester. *See* **5054**.

7208. Payne, Susan. Essays on British women poets. *See* **3583**.

7209. Towers, Heide. Politics and female agency in Lady Mary Wroth's *Love's Victorie*. WWr (13:3) 2006, 432–47.

7210. Zimbalist, Barbara. Critical perspectives on Lady Mary Wroth's *The Countess of Montgomery's Urania*: an annotated bibliography. SidJ (24:1) 2006, 45–74.

William Wycherley

7211. Eis, Joel D.; Earnest, Stephen. The actor as archeologist: aspects of the dramaturgy of the Restoration stage rediscovered in performance. RECTR (19:2) 2004, 22–38.

7212. Ribes, Purificación. Country wives and country girls in eighteenth-century England: a history of theatrical rewriting. *See* **7819**.

7213. Thompson, Peggy. 'Why say we no?': the trope of insincere resistance in *The Gentleman Dancing-Master* and *The Plain Dealer*. PLL (42:4) 2006, 420–39.

EIGHTEENTH CENTURY

GENERAL

7214. Anon. (comp.). Recent articles. Scriblerian (38:2) 2006, 213–90.

7215. Agorni, Mirella. A marginal(ized) perspective on translation history: women and translation in the eighteenth century. Meta (50:3) 2005, 817–30.

7216. Alvarez Faedo, María José. A bio-bibliography of eighteenth-century religious women in England and Spain. Lewiston, NY; Lampeter: Mellen Press, 2005. pp. viii, 131. (Studies in women and religion, 44.)

7217. Andrea, Bernadette. Travels through Islam in Early Modern English Studies. *See* **4562**.

7218. Ballaster, Ros. Fabulous Orients: fictions of the East in England, 1662–1785. *See* **6215**.

7219. Bannet, Eve Tavor. The Bluestocking sisters: women's patronage, Millenium Hall, and 'the visible providence of a Country'. *See* **8131**.

7220. Batchelor, Jennie. Dress, distress and desire: clothing and the female body in eighteenth-century literature. (Bibl. 2005, 7935.) Rev. by Audrey Bilger in TSWL (25:1) 2006, 158–60; by Sarah Prescott in NQ (53:4) 2006, 577–8.

7221. —— Kaplan, Cora (eds). British women's writing in the long eighteenth century: authorship, politics, and history. (Bibl. 2005, 7936.) Rev. by Betty A. Schellenberg in ECS (40:1) 2006, 132–5.

7222. Berland, Kevin. Formalized curiosity in the electronic age and the uses of on-line text-bases. AJ (17) 2006, 391–414.

7223. Birch, Dinah. Eager to please: make sure to read the children – but sceptically. TLS, 10 Feb. 2006, 3–4 (review-article).

7224. Böker, Uwe. The recalcitrant corpus of the eighteenth-century canting crew: 'marginal language of marginal people'; or, History from below and within? *In* (pp. 11–34) **1227**.

7225. Bolton, Linda. Facing the Other: ethical disruption and the American mind. (Bibl. 2004, 8839.) Rev. by Philip Joseph in AL (77:3) 2005, 639–41.

7226. Braida, Antonella. Dante and the Romantics. *See* **8303**.

7227. Brewer, David A. The afterlife of character, 1726–1825. (Bibl. 2005, 7945.) Rev. by Andrew Piper in SHARP (15:1) 2006, 6–7; by George Justice in 1650–1850 (13) 2006, 350–4.

7228. Brodey, Inger S. B. On pre-Romanticism or sensibility: defining ambivalences. *In* (pp. 10–28) **8357**.

7229. Butte, George. I know that you know that I know: narrating subjects from Moll Flanders to Marnie. (Bibl. 2005, 7948.) Rev. by David Herman in MFS (52:3) 2006, 753–6.

7230. Carpenter, Andrew. Literature in print, 1550–1800. *In* (pp. 301–18) **724**.

7231. Carruth, Mary C. (ed.). Feminist interventions in Early American Studies. *See* **6224**.

7232. Carter, Sophie. Purchasing power: representing prostitution in eighteenth-century English popular print culture. (Bibl. 2005, 7953.) Rev. by Betty Hagglund in JPHS (ns 8) 2005, 59–60.

7233. Cass, Jeffrey. Interrogating Orientalism: theories and practices. *In* (pp. 25–45) **8395**.

7234. Castillo, Susan. Colonial encounters in New World writing, 1500–1786: performing America. *See* **4573**.

7235. —— Schweitzer, Ivy (eds). A companion to the literatures of Colonial America. *See* **6226**.

7236. Chico, Tita. Designing women: the dressing room in eighteenth-century English literature and culture. (Bibl. 2005, 7958.) Rev. by Katie Ahearn in RECTR (19:2) 2004, 44–7; by Karen Harvey in ECS (40:1) 2006, 141–4.

7237. Clarke, Norma. The rise and fall of the woman of letters. (Bibl. 2004, 8298.) Rev. by Jennie Batchelor in ECS (39:3) 2006, 391–3.

7238. Clery, E. J. The feminization debate in eighteenth-century England: literature, commerce and luxury. (Bibl. 2005, 7961.) Rev. by Thomas K. Meier in AJ (17) 2006, 464–5.

7239. Clymer, Lorna (ed.). Ritual, routine, and regime: repetition in early modern British and European culture. *See* **1894**.

7240. Colacurcio, Michael J. Godly letters: the literature of the American Puritans. *See* **6230**.

7241. Craciun, Adriana. British women writers and the French Revolution: citizens of the world. (Bibl. 2005, 7964.) Rev. by Simon Bainbridge in BJ (34:1) 2006, 80–1.

7242. de Montluzin, Emily Lorraine. Attributions of authorship in the *Gentleman's Magazine*, 1765–1770: a supplement to the *Union List*. *See* **1081**.

7243. Dimit, Robert G. 'Why, you … I oughta' …': aposiopesis and the natural language of the passions, 1670–1770. *See* **6237**.

7244. Douthwaite, Julia V.; Vidal, Mary (eds). The interdisciplinary century: tensions and convergences in eighteenth-century art, history and literature. Oxford: Voltaire Foundation, 2005. pp. xxxiv, 312. (Studies in Voltaire and the eighteenth century.) Rev. by Ed Lilley in MLR (101:2) 2006, 537–8.

7245. Edwards, Gavin. Narrative order, 1789–1819: life and story in an age of revolution. Basingstoke; New York: Palgrave Macmillan, 2006. pp. viii, 207.

7246. Elias, A. C., Jr. Reissues in the Dublin book trade: the case of George Grierson and William Williamson. *In* (pp. 44–99) **648**.

7247. Erkkilä, Betsy. Mixed bloods and other crosses: rethinking American literature from the Revolution to the Culture Wars. (Bibl. 2005, 7976.) Rev. by Susan Castillo in EAL (41:2) 2006, 339–45.

7248. Faller, Lincoln. 'A dance to which one's feet can still respond'. *See* **6242**.

7249. Ferber, Michael. The Romantic system of the arts. *In* (pp. 552–70) **8357**.

7250. —— (ed.). A companion to European Romanticism. *See* **8357**.

7251. Foster, Frances Smith. Creative collaboration: as African American as sweet potato pie. *In* (pp. 17–33) **8435**.

7252. France, Peter; Haynes, Kenneth (eds). The Oxford history of literary translation: vol. 4, 1790–1900. Oxford; New York: OUP, 2006. pp. xv, 595. Rev. by Alain Jumeau in EA (59:4) 2006, 469–70.

7253. Fulford, Tim. Romantic Indians: Native Americans, British literature, and transatlantic culture, 1765–1830. Oxford; New York: OUP, 2006. pp. x, 318.

7254. Gatrell, Vic. City of laughter: sex and satire in eighteenth-century London. London: Atlantic, 2006. pp. xxiii, 696. Rev. by Kenneth Baker in TLS, 1 Sept. 2006, 27.

7255. Gibson, Colin; Marr, Lisa (eds). New windows on a woman's world: essays for Jocelyn Harris: vol. 1. Dunedin: English Dept, Univ. of Otago, 2005. pp. xiv, 373. (Otago studies in English, 9.)

7256. —— —— New windows on a woman's world: essays for Jocelyn Harris: vol. 2. *See* **8374**.

7257. Gillespie, Stuart; Hopkins, David (eds). The Oxford history of literary translation in English: vol. 3, 1660–1790. *See* **6247**.

7258. Gilroy, Amanda (ed.). Green and pleasant land: English culture and the Romantic countryside. *See* **8377**.

7259. Goodman, Kevis. Georgic modernity and British Romanticism: poetry and the mediation of history. (Bibl. 2005, 8318.) Rev. by Sarah Jordan in 1650–1850 (13) 2006, 388–91; by Ashley Chantler in BJ (34:2) 2006, 192–4.

7260. Gordon, Scott Paul. A new latitude in the culture wars. 1650–1850 (12) 2006, 3–20.

7261. Goring, Paul. The rhetoric of sensibility in eighteenth-century culture. (Bibl. 2005, 7985.) Rev. by Lorri Nandrea in Novel (38:2/3) 2005, 291–4; by Gillian Skinner in Eng (54:210) 2005, 232–7; by John Mullan in TLS, 17 Mar. 2006, 29; by Odai Johnson in TJ (58:3) 2006, 523–4; by Anne H. Stevens in ECN (5) 2006, 380–4.

7262. Gustafson, Sandra M. (comp.). Historicizing race in Early American Studies: a roundtable with Joanna Brooks, Philip Gould, and David Kazanjian. *See* **20076**.

7263. Hall, Wade (ed.). The Kentucky anthology: two hundred years of writing in the Bluegrass State. Lexington: Kentucky UP, 2005. pp. xv, 880. Rev. by Mark Burgh in ArkR (37:2) 2006, 131.

7264. Harris, Sharon M. Executing race: early American women's narratives of race, society, and the law. (Bibl. 2005, 7992.) Rev. by Susan K. Harris in AL (78:1) 2006, 185–7; by Angela Vietto in EAL (41:3) 2006, 555–67; by Joanna Brooks in Legacy (23:2) 2006, 199–200.

7265. —— Feminist theories and Early American Studies. *In* (pp. 3–10) **6224**.

7266. Harvey, A. D. The Roman ideal of rural retirement in seventeenth- and eighteenth-century England. *See* **8078**.

7267. Harvey, Karen. Reading sex in the eighteenth century: bodies and gender in English erotic culture. (Bibl. 2005, 7994.) Rev. by Tim Hitchcock in JHS (15:1) 2006, 139–43; by Jeremy Gregory in LitH (15:2) 2006, 75–6; by Caroline Breashears in Scriblerian (38:2) 2006, 331–2.

7268. HAYWOOD, IAN. The revolution in popular literature: print, politics, and the people, 1790–1860. (Bibl. 2005, 7998.) Rev. by Michael Scrivener in WordsC (36:4) 2005, 185–6; by Joanne Shattock in Romanticism (12:1) 2006, 62–3; by Kelly Mays in VS (49:1) 2006, 149–51.

7269. HENKE, CHRISTOPH. 'The old solid *English* standard of common sense' – British common sense discourse in the eighteenth century. *See* **8194**.

7270. HEWITT, ELIZABETH. Correspondence and American literature, 1770–1865. Cambridge; New York: CUP, 2004. pp. x, 230. (Cambridge studies in American literature and culture, 146.) Rev. by Barbara L. Hussey in JAC (29:3) 2006, 370–1; by Elizabeth Delaney in JAStud (40:2) 2006, 434–5.

7271. HOEVELER, DIANE LONG. The female captivity narrative: blood, water, and Orientalism. *In* (pp. 46–71) **8395**.

7272. —— CASS, JEFFREY (eds). Interrogating Orientalism: contextual approaches and pedagogical perspectives. *See* **8395**.

7273. HORSMAN, ALAN. 'A bite medicinally': Leslie Stephen and Virginia Woolf's eighteenth-century essays. *In* (pp. 226–34) **8374**.

7274. HOTZ, JEFFREY. Divergent visions: the early United States through the lens of travel. London; New York: Routledge, 2006. pp. x, 318.

7275. HUBER, WERNER (ed.). The Corvey Library and Anglo-German cultural exchanges, 1770–1837: essays to honour Rainer Schöwerling. Munich: Fink, 2004. pp. xiv, 199. (Corvey-Studien, 8.) Rev. by Hilary Brown in MLR (101:4) 2006, 1076–7.

7276. HUME, ROBERT D. The economics of culture in London, 1660–1740. *See* **6263**.

7277. HURLEY, ALISON E. A conversation of their own: watering-place correspondence among the Bluestockings. ECS (40:1) 2006, 1–21.

7278. IMMEL, ANDREA; WITMORE, MICHAEL (eds). Childhood and children's books in early modern Europe, 1550–1800. *See* **6264**.

7279. INGRAM, ALLAN. Steering toward sanity: the compass points of madness in eighteenth-century Britain. 1650–1850 (11) 2005, 3–20.

7280. —— FAUBERT, MICHELLE. Cultural constructions of madness in eighteenth-century writing: representing the insane. Basingstoke; New York: Palgrave Macmillan, 2005. pp. x, 245. Rev. by Andrew Elfenbein in WordsC (36:4) 2005, 158–9; by Rebecca Rees in RES (57:229) 2006, 266–8.

7281. IWANISZIW, SUSAN B. (ed.). *Oroonoko*: adaptations and offshoots. *See* **6581**.

7282. JEFFARES, A. NORMAN; VAN DE KAMP, PETER (eds). Irish literature in the eighteenth century: an annotated anthology. Dublin; Portland, OR: Irish Academic Press, 2006. pp. xx, 402. Rev. by Lucy McDiarmid in TLS, 6 Oct. 2006, 3–4.

7283. JOSEPH, BETTY. Reading the East India Company, 1720–1840: colonial currencies of gender. (Bibl. 2005, 8010.) Rev. by Thomas M. Curley in AJ (16) 2005, 340–2; by Leah Reade Rosenberg in Scriblerian (38:2) 2006, 328–9.

7284. KATRITZKY, LINDE. Johnson and the Earl of Shelburne's circle. *See* **7934**.

7285. Keen, Paul. The 'balloonomania': science and spectacle in 1780s England. ECS (39:4) 2006, 507–35.

7286. Keeran, Peggy; Bowers, Jennifer. Literary research and the British Romantic era: strategies and sources. *See* **8408**.

7287. Kerrison, Catherine. Claiming the pen: women and intellectual life in the early American South. Ithaca, NY; London: Cornell UP, 2006. pp. xiii, 265. Rev. by Angela Vietto in EAL (41:3) 2006, 555–67; by Lorri Glover in JAH (93:3) 2006, 861–2.

7288. Keymer, Thomas; Mee, Jon (eds). The Cambridge companion to English literature 1740–1830. (Bibl. 2005, 8014.) Rev. by A. F. T. Lurcock in NQ (53:4) 2006, 580–1.

7289. Killeen, Jarlath. Gothic Ireland: horror and the Irish Anglican imagination in the long eighteenth century. Dublin; Portland, OR: Four Courts Press, 2005. pp. 240. Rev. by Elizabeth Tilley in CJIS (31:2) 2005, 72–3.

7290. King, Thomas A. The castrato's castration. *See* **7752**.

7291. Knott, Sarah; Taylor, Barbara (eds). Women, gender and Enlightenment. (Bibl. 2005, 8016.) Rev. by Paula Marantz Cohen in TLS, 3 Feb. 2006, 10.

7292. Leitz, Robert C., iii; Cope, Kevin L. Imagining the sciences: expressions of new knowledge in the 'long' eighteenth century. (Bibl. 2005, 8019.) Rev. by Kenneth W. Graham in MLR (101:3) 2006, 827–8.

7293. Lindop, Grevel. Self deceptions. *See* **8427**.

7294. Lund, Roger D. Augustan burlesque and the genesis of *Joseph Andrews*. *See* **7788**.

7295. McIlvanney, Liam; Ryan, Ray (eds). Ireland and Scotland: culture and society, 1700–2000. (Bibl. 2005, 8023.) Rev. by Michael Brown in ECI (20) 2005, 173–7.

7296. Markley, Robert. The Far East and the English imagination, 1600–1730. *See* **6278**.

7297. Meyers, Karen. Colonialism and the Revolutionary period: beginnings to 1800. *See* **6282**.

7298. Moore, Seán. The culture of paper credit: the new economic criticism and the postcolonial eighteenth century. *See* **14228**.

7299. Morton, Timothy. Food studies in the Romantic period: (s)mashing history. *See* **8451**.

7300. —— (ed.). Cultures of taste / theories of appetite: eating Romanticism. *See* **8452**.

7301. Moskal, Jeanne; Wooden, Shannon R. (eds). Teaching British women writers, 1750–1900. (Bibl. 2005, 8032.) Rev. by Theresa A. Dougal in VS (48:3) 2006, 528–30.

7302. O'Gorman, Francis; Turner, Katherine (eds). The Victorians and the eighteenth century: reassessing the tradition. (Bibl. 2004, 8368.) Rev. by William R. McKelvy in VIJ (33) 2005, 249–51; by Monika Fludernik in DickQ (23:3) 2006, 196–9.

7303. O'Neill, Michael; Sandy, Mark (eds). Romanticism: critical concepts in literary and cultural studies. *See* **8465**.

7304. Oueijan, Naji. Sexualizing the Orient. *See* **8469**.

7305. Palmeri, Frank (ed.). Humans and other animals in eighteenth-century British culture: representation, hybridity, ethics. Aldershot; Burlington, VT: Ashgate, 2006. pp. 240.

7306. Peer, Larry H. The year's work in Romanticism Studies. *See* **8471**.

7307. —— Hoeveler, Diane Long (eds). Romanticism: comparative discourses. Aldershot; Burlington, VT: Ashgate, 2006. pp. xiii, 208. (Nineteenth century.)

7308. Perry, Ruth. Deserted villages, kindly landlords, and overdetermined marriages in eighteenth-century England. *In* (pp. 243–57) **7255**.

7309. —— Novel relations: the transformation of kinship in English literature and culture, 1748–1818. (Bibl. 2005, 8044.) Rev. by Anya Taylor in WordsC (36:4) 2005, 188–9; by Heidi Hutner in TSWL (25:1) 2006, 156–7; by Wendy Jones Nakanishi in EngS (87:3) 2006, 374–5; by Jennie Batchelor in NQ (53:1) 2006, 124–5; by Paula R. Backscheider in Scriblerian (38:2) 2006, 315–17; by James Cruise in AJ (17) 2006, 454–7.

7310. Pitcher, Edward W. R. (comp.). *American Moral & Sentimental Magazine* (New York, 1797–1798): an annotated catalogue. *See* **1153**.

7311. —— *The Literary Magazine and British Review* (London 1788–1794): an annotated catalogue of the prose and verse. *See* **1154**.

7312. —— *The Nightingale; or, A mélange de littérature* (Boston, May 10 – July 30, 1796): an annotated catalogue of contents and sources. *See* **1155**.

7313. —— *The Rural Magazine; or, Vermont Repository* (Rutland, January 1795 – December 1796): an annotated catalogue of the literary contents. *See* **1156**.

7314. Poetzsch, Markus. 'Visionary dreariness': readings in Romanticism's quotidian sublime. *See* **8480**.

7315. Pohl, Nicole. Women, space, and utopia, 1600–1800. *See* **6288**.

7316. Price, Fiona. 'Myself creating what I saw': the morality of the spectator in eighteenth-century gothic. GothS (8:2) 2006, 1–17.

7317. Quéma, Anne. The gothic and the fantastic in the age of digital reproduction. ESCan (30:4) 2004, 81–119.

7318. Rapple, Brendan. Google and access to the world's intellectual heritage. *See* **1027**.

7319. Richardson, Alan; Lee, Debbie (eds). Early Black British writing: Olaudah Equiano, Mary Prince, and others: selected texts with introduction, critical essays. Boston, MA: Houghton Mifflin, 2004. pp. ix, 443. (New Riverside eds.) Rev. by Kit Kincade in ECN (5) 2006, 378–80.

7320. Richardson, John. Slavery and Augustan literature: Swift, Pope, Gay. (Bibl. 2004, 9312.) Rev. by Paul Baines in MLR (101:2) 2006, 521–2.

7321. Robertson, Ben P. (comp.). Annual bibliography for 2004. *See* **8494**.

7322. —— Annual bibliography for 2005. *See* **8495**.

7323. Rogers, Pat. 'How I want thee, humorous Hogart': the motif of the absent artist in Swift, Fielding and others. *See* **8212**.

7324. —— Revisions to Pope's prose works in the *Miscellanies* (1732). *See* **8070**.

7325. Rovee, Christopher Kent. Imagining the gallery: the social body of British Romanticism. *See* **8499**.

7326. Russett, Margaret. Fictions and fakes: forging Romantic authenticity, 1760–1845. *See* **8501**.

7327. Salusinszky, Imre (ed.). Northrop Frye's writings on the eighteenth and nineteenth centuries. *See* **14280**.

7328. Scanlan, J. T. A celebration. 1650–1850 (12) 2006, 35–45. (State of Eighteenth-Century Studies.)

7329. Schellenberg, Betty A. The professionalization of women writers in eighteenth-century Britain. (Bibl. 2005, 8066.) Rev. by Fiona Ritchie in TLS, 3 Feb. 2006, 29; by Melanie B. Bigold in RES (57:228) 2006, 106–7; by Jennie Batchelor in ECS (39:3) 2006, 391–3; by Peter Knox-Shaw in SHARP (15:2/3) 2006, 24–5; by Michael Wells in CanL (191) 2006, 127–8.

7330. Schenk, H. G. The revolt against the eighteenth century. *See* **8509**.

7331. Seuntjens, Wolter. Vapours and fumes, damps and qualms: windy passions in the early modern age (1600–1800). *See* **5429**.

7332. Sher, Richard B. The Enlightenment & the book: Scottish authors & their publishers in eighteenth-century Britain, Ireland, & America. Chicago, IL; London: Chicago UP, 2006. pp. xxvi, 815.

7333. Skipp, Jenny. Masculinity and social stratification in eighteenth-century erotic literature, 1700–1821. BJECS (29:2) 2006, 253–69.

7334. Smallwood, Philip. Literary histories old and new. *See* **6304**.

7335. Spector, Sheila A. Jewish translations of British Romantic literature (1753–1858): a preliminary bibliography. *In* (pp. 195–210) **8523**.

7336. —— (ed.). The Jews and British Romanticism: politics, religion, culture. *See* **8523**.

7337. Staves, Susan. A literary history of women's writing in Britain, 1660–1789. *See* **6310**.

7338. Taylor, Barbara. Feminists *versus* gallants: manners and morals in Enlightenment Britain. *See* **8272**.

7339. Thomas, Jane. 'Forming the literary tastes of the middle and higher classes': Elgin's circulating libraries and their proprietors, 1789–1870. *In* (pp. 91–111) **746**.

7340. Tobin, Beth Fowkes. Colonizing nature: the tropics in British arts and letters, 1760–1820. (Bibl. 2005, 8077.) Rev. by Janet Sorensen in CLIO (35:3) 2006, 426–30; by Ann Shteir in ECS (40:1) 2006, 120–3; by Noah Heringman in 1650–1850 (13) 2006, 340–5.

7341. Treadwell, James. Autobiographical writing and British literature, 1783–1834. (Bibl. 2005, 8079.) Rev. by Mark Schoenfield in SR (45:1) 2006, 136–42; by Julian North in Biography (29:2) 2006, 341–4.

7342. Trulli, Maristella. La crescita della 'città mostruosa': tradizione e trasformazione nella Londra augustea. *In* (pp. 65–89) **7343**.

7343. —— Pontrandolfo, Luisa (eds). Londra tra memoria letteraria e modernità: dal Seicento ai nostri giorni. Venice: Marsilio, 2006. pp. xxxvi, 406. (Ricerche.)

7344. Vicinus, Martha. Intimate friends: women who loved women, 1778–1928. (Bibl. 2005, 8083.) Rev. by Judith Halberstam in VS (48:2) 2006, 373–4; by Dianne Chisholm in Mod/Mod (13:4) 2006, 760–3.

7345. Vietto, Angela. Daughters of the tenth Muse: new histories of women and writing in early America. EAL (41:3) 2006, 555–67 (review-article).

7346. —— Women and authorship in Revolutionary America. Aldershot; Burlington, VT: Ashgate, 2005. pp. ix, 147. (Women and gender in the early modern world.)

7347. Wall, Cynthia. Recent studies in the Restoration and eighteenth century. *See* **6315**.

7348. Wall, Cynthia Sundberg. The prose of things: transformations of description in the eighteenth century. Chicago, IL; London: Chicago UP, 2006. pp. xiii, 316.

7349. Wertheimer, Eric. Underwriting: the poetics of insurance in America, 1722–1872. Stanford, CA: Stanford UP, 2006. pp. xviii, 187.

7350. White, Ed. The backcountry and the city: colonization and conflict in early America. *See* **6317**.

7351. Wright, Julia M. 'All the fire-side circle': Irish women writers and the Sheridan–Lefanu coterie. KSJ (55) 2006, 63–72.

7352. Wroth, Celestina. 'To root the old woman out of our minds': women educationalists and plebeian culture in late eighteenth-century Britain. ECL (30:2) 2006, 48–73.

7353. Yadav, Alok. Before the empire of English: literature, provinciality, and nationalism in eighteenth-century Britain. (Bibl. 2004, 8426.) Rev. by David H. Radcliffe in 1650–1850 (13) 2006, 373–6.

DRAMA AND THE THEATRE

7354. Barbieri, M. Chiara. La pagina e la scena: l'attore inglese nella trattatistica del '700. Florence: Le Lettere, 2006. pp. 352. (Storia dello spettacolo: Fonti, 7.)

7355. Burke, Helen M. Riotous performances: the struggle for hegemony in the Irish theatre, 1712–1784. (Bibl. 2004, 8435.) Rev. by Seán Patrick Donlan in ECI (20) 2005, 198–200.

7356. Bush-Bailey, Gilli. Treading the bawds: actresses and playwrights on the late Stuart stage. *See* **6330**.

7357. Byrne, Paula. Free and easies. *See* **8565**.

7358. Findlay, Bill. Motivation in a surrogate translation of Goldoni. *In* (pp. 46–57) **3186**.

7359. Frank, Frederick S. (ed.). The origins of the modern study of gothic drama, together with a re-edition of *Gothic Drama from Walpole to Shelley* (1947) by Bertrand Evans. Lewiston, NY; Lampeter: Mellen Press, 2006. pp. iv, 315.

7360. Hanley, Ryan Patrick. From Geneva to Glasgow: Rousseau and Adam Smith on the theater and commercial society. StudECC (35) 2006, 177–202.

7361. Jian, Changhuai. Ethical examination of 18th-century English drama. FLS (121) 2006, 71–6. (In Chinese.)

7362. Johnson, Odai. Absence and memory in Colonial American theatre: Fiorelli's plaster. *See* **6352**.

7363. Maginnes, F. Arant. Thomas Abthorpe Cooper: father of the American stage 1775–1849. (Bibl. 2004, 8447.) Rev. by Odai Johnson in TheatreS (47:2) 2006, 327–9.

7364. Marsden, Jean I. Fatal desire: women, sexuality, and the English stage, 1660–1720. *See* **6362**.

7365. Marshall, Louise H. Women and politics in adaptations of Shakespeare's English histories: re-enacting the nation, 1719–1745. *See* **5378**.

7366. Morash, Christopher. Irish theatre. *In* (pp. 322–38) **11829**.

7367. —— Theatre and print, 1550–1800. *In* (pp. 319–34) **724**.

7368. Nussbaum, Felicity. 'More than a woman': early memoirs of British actresses. *In* (pp. 225–42) **7255**.

7369. Ragussis, Michael. Passing for a Jew, on stage and off: stage Jews and cross-dressing Gentiles in Georgian England. *In* (pp. 41–60) **8523**.

7370. Richards, Jeffrey H. Drama, theatre, and identity in the American New Republic. Cambridge; New York: CUP, 2005. pp. xi, 392. (Cambridge studies in American theatre and drama, 22.) Rev. by Matthew H. Wikander in RES (57:230) 2006, 423–5.

7371. Thomson, Peter. The Cambridge introduction to English theatre, 1660–1900. *See* **6393**.

7372. Worrall, David. Theatric revolution: drama, censorship and Romantic period subcultures, 1773–1832. *See* **8607**.

FICTION

7373. Armstrong, Nancy. How novels think: the limits of British individualism from 1719–1900. *See* **8610**.

7374. Austin, Michael. 'Jesting with the truth': *figura*, trace, and the boundaries of fiction in *Robinson Crusoe* and its sequels. *See* **7708**.

7375. Barrio-Vilar, Laura. Getting a taste of the Other: the eighteenth-century British novel as the epitome of masquerade. CLR (1) 2004, 55–67.

7376. Bony, Alain. Leonora, Lydia et les autres: étude sur le (nouveau) roman anglais du xviiie siècle. (Bibl. 2005, 8124.) Rev. by Anne Bandry in Scriblerian (38:2) 2006, 298–9.

7377. Brown, Marshall. The gothic text. (Bibl. 2005, 8125.) Rev. by Lawrence Lipking in SR (45:2) 2006, 312–17; by Peter Garrett in ECent (47:1) 2006, 81–4; by Jerrold E. Hogle in ERR (17:5) 2006, 629–33.

7378. Carnell, Rachel. Partisan politics, narrative realism, and the rise of the British novel. *See* **6404**.

7379. Chiu, Frances A. Faulty towers: reform, Radicalism and the gothic castle, 1760–1800. *See* **8232**.

7380. CHOI, JULIE. The metropolis and mental life in the novel. NLH (37:4) 2006, 707–24.

7381. CORMAN, BRIAN. Clara Reeve's *The Progress of Romance* and the canon of the novel in 1785. *In* (pp. 126–40) **7255**.

7382. DAVIDSON, CATHY N. Revolution and the word: the rise of the novel in America. (Bibl. 2005, 8127.) Rev. by Sandra M. Gustafson in EAL (41:2) 2006, 347–64; by Emory Elliott in AL (78:3) 2006, 615–17; by Anna Mae Duane in ECN (5) 2006, 370–3.

7383. FESTA, LYNN. Sentimental figures of empire in eighteenth-century Britain and France. Baltimore, MD; London: Johns Hopkins UP, 2006. pp. viii, 300.

7384. FREEMAN, ARTHUR. New Goldsmith? *See* **7846**.

7385. HAMMOND, BREAN; REGAN, SHAUN. Making the novel: fiction and society in Britain, 1660–1789. *See* **6406**.

7386. HOGBIN, ELIZABETH; SONG, JAE JUNG. Patterns of relativisation in eighteenth- and twentieth-century written English narrative: a functional–typological perspective. *In* (pp. 182–208) **7255**.

7387. JOHNSON, NANCY E. The English Jacobin novel on rights, property, and the law: critiquing the contract. (Bibl. 2005, 8137.) Rev. by Michael Gamer in WordsC (36:4) 2005, 186–7; by Malcolm Kelsall in BJ (33:1) 2005, 61–4.

7388. JOHNSTON, ELIZABETH. How women really are: disturbing parallels between reality television and 18th-century fiction. *In* (pp. 115–32) **19992**.

7389. KNIGHT, MARK; WOODMAN, THOMAS (eds). Biblical religion and the novel, 1700–2000. Aldershot; Burlington, VT: Ashgate, 2006. pp. viii, 170.

7390. LEVITT, MORTON P. The rhetoric of Modernist fiction from a new point of view. *See* **13542**.

7391. LOEBER, ROLF; LOEBER, MAGDA; BURNHAM, ANNE MULLIN. A guide to Irish fiction, 1650–1900. *See* **6409**.

7392. LOGAN, LISA M. Columbia's daughters in drag; or, Cross-dressing, collaboration, and authorship in early American novels. *In* (pp. 240–52) **6224**.

7393. MCMASTER, JULIET. Reading the body in the eighteenth-century novel. (Bibl. 2005, 8142.) Rev. by Janice Hewlett Koelb in WordsC (36:4) 2005, 152–3.

7394. MANDAL, A. A. Making Austen mad: Benjamin Crosby and the non-publication of *Susan*. *See* **9055**.

7395. MEE, JON. Anti-Jacobin novels: representation and revolution. HLQ (69:4) 2006, 649–53 (review-article).

7396. NOVÁKOVÁ, SOŇA. Women and the city: representing London in eighteenth-century British literature. PSE (24) 2006, 119–27.

7397. RIGGS, PÁDRAIGÍN; VANCE, NORMAN. Irish prose fiction. *In* (pp. 245–66) **11829**.

7398. SPACKS, PATRICIA ANN MEYER. Novel beginnings: experiments in eighteenth-century English fiction. New Haven, CT; London: Yale UP, 2006. pp. ix, 309. (Yale guides to English literature.)

7399. STARR, G. GABRIELLE. Lyric generations: poetry and the novel in the long eighteenth century. (Bibl. 2005, 8155.) Rev. by Tiffany Potter in 1650–1850

(11) 2005, 567–71; by Paul Baines in MLR (101:2) 2006, 522–3; by Sophie Gee in ECF (18:2) 2006, 262–4.

7400. Tougaw, Jason Daniel. Strange cases: the medical case history and the British novel. London; New York: Routledge, 2006. pp. x, 244. (Literary criticism and cultural theory.)

7401. Verhoeven, W. M. (gen. ed.). Anti-Jacobin novels: vol. 6, Anon., *Berkeley Hall; or, The Pupil of Experience* (1796). Ed. by W. M. Verhoeven. London; Brookfield, VT: Pickering & Chatto, 2005. pp. xxxvi, 528. Rev. by Jon Mee in HLQ (69:4) 2006, 649–53.

7402. Vietto, Angela. Inscribing manhood and enacting womanhood in the Early Republic. *In* (pp. 253–66) **6224**.

7403. Wakefield, Sarah R. Folklore in British literature: naming and narrating in women's fiction, 1750–1880. New York; Frankfurt: Lang, 2006. pp. viii, 176. (Studies on themes and motifs in literature, 80.)

7404. Weyler, Karen A. Intricate relations: sexual and economic desire in American fiction, 1789–1814. (Bibl. 2005, 8161.) Rev. by Lisa M. Vetere in Legacy (23:2) 2006, 200–1.

7405. Yoshioka, Chiharu. Dialectic of enlightenment in the 1960s gothic: Angela Carter's *Heroes and Villains*. *See* **15065**.

7406. Zunshine, Lisa. Bastards and foundlings: illegitimacy in eighteenth-century England. (Bibl. 2005, 8164.) Rev. by John O'Brien in 1650–1850 (13) 2006, 358–61.

7407. Zuroski, Eugenia. Disenchanting China: Orientalism and the aesthetics of reason in the English novel. Novel (38:2/3) 2005, 254–71.

LITERATURE FOR CHILDREN

7408. Alderson, Brian; de Marez Oyens, Felix. Be merry and wise: origins of children's book publishing in England, 1650–1850. *See* **636**.

7409. Barnard, Toby. Children and books in eighteenth-century Ireland. *In* (pp. 214–38) **648**.

7410. Brown, Gillian. The metamorphic book: children's print culture in the eighteenth century. ECS (39:3) 2006, 351–62.

7411. Cosslett, Tess. Talking animals in British children's fiction, 1786–1914. *See* **8739**.

7412. Crain, Patricia. Spectral literacy: the case of *Goody Two-Shoes*. *In* (pp. 213–42) **6264**.

7413. Darton, Lawrence. The Dartons: an annotated check-list of children's books issued by two publishing houses 1787–1870. Preface and editorial assistance by Brian Alderson. New Castle, DE: Oak Knoll Press; London: British Library, 2004. pp. lx, 729, (plates) 8. Rev. by Andrea Immel in TLS, 2 June 2006, 30; by Edmund M. B. King in Library (7:1) 2006, 103–4; by Leslie McGrath in PBSA (100:2) 2006, 283–5; by M. O. Grenby in SHARP (15:2/3) 2006, 14.

7414. Fergus, Jan. Solace in books: reading trifling adventures at Rugby School. *In* (pp. 243–59) **6264**.

7415. Grenby, M. O. Tame fairies make good teachers: the popularity of early British fairy tales. LU (30:1) 2006, 1–24.

7416. Lerer, Seth. 'Thy life to mend, this book attend': reading and healing in the arc of children's literature. *See* **6413**.

7417. Ruwe, Donelle (ed.). Culturing the child, 1690–1914: essays in memory of Mitzi Myers. (Bibl. 2005, 8171.) Rev. by Anne Lundin in LU (30:3) 2006, 405–9; by Naomi Wood in ChildLit (34) 2006, 218–21; by Kimberley Reynolds in VS (48:3) 2006, 564–6.

7418. Shefrin, Jill. 'Governesses to their children': royal and aristocratic mothers educating daughters in the reign of George III. *In* (pp. 181–211) **6264**.

7419. Wroth, Celestina. 'To root the old woman out of our minds': women educationalists and plebeian culture in late eighteenth-century Britain. *See* **7352**.

POETRY

7420. Andrews, Corey E. 'Almost the same, but not quite': English poetry by eighteenth-century Scots. *See* **8088**.

7421. Backscheider, Paula R. Eighteenth-century women poets and their poetry: inventing agency, inventing genre. (Bibl. 2005, 8173.) Rev. by Helen Deutsch in LRB (28:18) 2006, 25–6; by Betty A. Schellenberg in ECS (40:1) 2006, 132–5.

7422. Caldwell, Tanya M. Restoration parodies of Virgil and English literary values. *See* **6416**.

7423. de Montluzin, Emily Lorraine. Identifying 'W.O.' of Marshfield, Gloucestershire: William Oland's contributions to the *Gentleman's Magazine*, 1747–82. ANQ (19:2) 2006, 21–31.

7424. Deutsch, Helen. Had I been born a hero. LRB (28:18) 2006, 25–6 (review-article). (Women poets.)

7425. Dragstra, Henk. Politics of holiness: royalty for the masses in *The Wandering Jew's Chronicle*. *In* (pp. 61–80) **3415**.

7426. Fairer, David. 'The year runs round': the poetry of work in eighteenth-century England. *In* (pp. 153–71) **1894**.

7427. Furst, Lilian R. Lighting up the night. *In* (pp. 505–21) **8357**.

7428. Gerrard, Christine (ed.). A companion to eighteenth-century poetry. Oxford; Malden, MA: Blackwell, 2006. pp. xiv, 605. (Blackwell companions to literature and culture, 44.)

7429. Hess, Scott. Authoring the self: self-representation, authorship, and the print market in British poetry from Pope through Wordsworth. London; New York: Routledge, 2005. pp. viii, 395. (Literary criticism and cultural theory.) Rev. by Mark Schoenfield in SR (45:1) 2006, 136–42.

7430. Hopps, Gavin; Stabler, Jane (eds). Romanticism and religion from William Cowper to Wallace Stevens. *See* **8789**.

7431. Hunter, Paul. Seven reasons for rhyme. *In* (pp. 172–98) **1894**.

7432. Nelson, Nicolas H. The pleasure of poetry: reading and enjoying British poetry from Donne to Burns. *See* **6436**.

7433. PARKS, STEPHEN, *et al.* (eds). First-line index of English poetry, 1500–1800, in manuscripts of the James M. and Marie-Louise Osborn Collection in the Beinecke Rare Book and Manuscript Library of Yale University. *See* **1764**.

7434. RABIN, DANA. The Jew Bill of 1753: masculinity, virility, and the nation. *See* **7478**.

7435. SOWERBY, ROBIN. The Augustan art of poetry: Augustan translation of the Classics. Oxford; New York: OUP, 2006. pp. viii, 368. Rev. by John Talbot in EC (56:3) 2006, 285–93.

7436. STABILE, SUSAN M. Memory's daughters: the material culture of remembrance in eighteenth-century America. (Bibl. 2005, 8203.) Rev. by Susan Kurjiaka in AL (77:3) 2005, 637–9.

7437. STIMSON, KATHARINE. 'Where Robins hop, and fallen leaves are sere': Keats's robin and the social imagination. *See* **10667**.

7438. TERRY, RICHARD. Mock-heroic from Butler to Cowper: an English genre and discourse. *See* **6625**.

7439. WHITE, SIMON; GOODRIDGE, JOHN; KEEGAN, BRIDGET (eds). Robert Bloomfield: lyric, class, and the Romantic canon. *See* **9141**.

7440. WILLIAMS, CAROLYN D. Bestiality in eighteenth-century English literature: 'the Dev'l himself is in that *Mare*'. BJECS (29:2) 2006, 271–84.

7441. WOLFSON, SUSAN J. Borderlines: the shiftings of gender in British Romanticism. *See* **8832**.

7442. WOOLLEY, JAMES. Poor John Harding and Mad Tom: *Harding's Resurrection* (1724). *In* (pp. 102–21) **648**.

7443. ZIMBARDO, ROSE A. Reading and writing the landscape. HLQ (69:4) 2006, 637–48 (review-article).

PROSE

7444. BABB, VALERIE. Of harlots and hags: feminine embodiments of early American Whiteness. *In* (pp. 97–111) **6224**.

7445. BENDING, STEPHEN. 'Miserable reflections on the sorrows of my life': letters, loneliness, and gardening in the 1760s. TSWL (25:1) 2006, 31–47.

7446. BERG, TEMMA F. The lives and letters of an eighteenth-century circle of acquaintance. Aldershot; Burlington, VT: Ashgate, 2006. pp. x, 295.

7447. BOHLS, ELIZABETH A.; DUNCAN, IAN (eds). Travel writing 1700–1830: an anthology. Oxford; New York: OUP, 2005. pp. xl, 520. (Oxford world's classics.) Rev. by Katherine Turner in EJES (10:2) 2006, 205–7.

7448. BRANT, CLARE. Eighteenth-century letters and British culture. Basingstoke; New York: Palgrave Macmillan, 2006. pp. x, 431.

7449. —— Murder she wrote? The real and imagined letters of Mary Blandy. WWr (13:2) 2006, 60–72.

7450. BRENNAN, MICHAEL G. (ed.). The origins of the Grand Tour: the travels of Robert Montagu, Lord Mandeville (1649–1654), William Hammond (1655–1658), and Banaster Maynard (1660–1663). *See* **6456**.

7451. BREUNINGER, SCOTT. 'Social gravity' and the *translatio* tradition in early American theories of empire. SoQ (43:4) 2006, 70–108.

7452. Brown, Stephen. Scottish Freemasonry and learned printing in the later eighteenth century. *In* (pp. 71–89) **746**.

7453. Burl, Aubrey; Mortimer, Neil (eds). Stukeley's *Stonehenge*: an unpublished manuscript, 1721–1724. New Haven, CT; London: Yale UP, 2005. pp. viii, 164, (plates) 8. Rev. by Lee Morrissey in AJ (17) 2006, 469–70.

7454. Chen, Jeng-Guo S. The British view of Chinese civilization and the emergence of class consciousness. *See* **8842**.

7455. Coleman, Deirdre. Entertaining entomology: insects and insect performers in the eighteenth century. ECL (30:3) 2006, 107–34.

7456. Cox, John D. Traveling south: travel narratives and the construction of American identity. (Bibl. 2005, 8225.) Rev. by Edlie L. Wong in Biography (29:4) 2006, 736–9; by Kevin E. O'Donnell in JSH (72:4) 2006, 920–1.

7457. Cunningham, Bernadette. Historical writing, 1660–1750. *In* (pp. 264–81) **724**.

7458. Dean, Ann C. Court culture and political news in London's eighteenth-century newspapers. *See* **1080**.

7459. Dierks, Konstantin. Letter writing, stationery supplies, and consumer modernity in the eighteenth-century Atlantic world. EAL (41:3) 2006, 473–94.

7460. Easton, Fraser. Covering sexual disguise: passing women and generic constraint. StudECC (35) 2006, 95–125.

7461. Ernest, John. Liberation historiography: African American writers and the challenge of history, 1794–1861. Chapel Hill; London: North Carolina UP, 2004. pp. xiv, 426. Rev. by Xiomara Santamarina in AmQ (58:1) 2006, 245–53; by Stephen Knadler in AL (78:4) 2006, 880–2; by P. Sterling Stuckey in JAAH (91:1) 2006, 88–90.

7462. Eslinger, Ellen (ed.). Running mad for Kentucky: frontier travel accounts. Lexington: Kentucky UP, 2004. pp. xi, 288. Rev. by Katherine Ledford in AppH (34:2) 2006, 96–9.

7463. Faller, Lincoln. Tales of a poisoning female parricide and a prostitute treated 'in a manner too shocking to mention': two criminal cases and 'the *Clarissa* effect'. *See* **8095**.

7464. Glaisyer, Natasha. 'A due Circulation in the Veins of the Publick': imagining credit in late seventeenth- and early eighteenth-century England. *See* **6468**.

7465. Grathwol, Kathleen B. Maria Edgeworth and the 'true use of books' for eighteenth-century girls. *In* (pp. 73–91) **9999**.

7466. Holmes, Heather. Scottish agricultural writers and the creation of their personal identities between 1697 and 1790. *See* **6474**.

7467. Howe, John R. Language and political meaning in Revolutionary America. (Bibl. 2005, 8230.) Rev. by David McKay in AJ (17) 2006, 457–61.

7468. Imbarrato, Susan Clair. Traveling women: narrative visions of early America. Athens: Ohio UP, 2006. pp. xiii, 254.

7469. Juengel, Scott J. Mungo Park's artificial skin; or, The year the White man passed. ECent (47:1) 2006, 19–38.

7470. Kelley, Anne. 'Her zeal for the publick good': the political agenda in Elizabeth Burnet's *A Method of Devotion* (1708). WWr (13:3) 2006, 448–74.

7471. Konuk, Kader. Ethnomasquerade in Ottoman–European encounters: reenacting Lady Mary Wortley Montagu. *See* **8015**.

7472. Lewis, Jayne Elizabeth. Spectral currencies in the air of reality: *A Journal of the Plague Year* and the history of apparitions. *See* **7721**.

7473. Lloyd, Sarah. Amour in the shrubbery: reading the detail of English adultery trial publications of the 1780s. ECS (39:4) 2006, 421–42.

7474. O'Driscoll, Sally. Reading through desire: interpretive practices for eighteenth-century popular culture. *See* **6488**.

7475. Palmeri, Frank. Conjectural history and satire: narrative as historical argument from Mandeville to Malthus (and Foucault). *See* **7999**.

7476. Percy, Carol. Writing from the asylum: Martha Shakespear Lloyd at the linguistic limits of eighteenth-century femininity. WWr (13:1) 2006, 98–120.

7477. Potter, Tiffany. Circular taxonomies: regulating European and American women through representations of North American Indian women. EAL (41:2) 2006, 183–211.

7478. Rabin, Dana. The Jew Bill of 1753: masculinity, virility, and the nation. ECS (39:2) 2006, 157–71.

7479. Rankin, Deana. Historical writing, 1750–1800. *In* (pp. 282–300) **724**.

7480. Straub, Kristina. 'In the posture of children': eighteenth-century British servants and children. *In* (pp. 127–51) **6264**.

7481. Swaminathan, Srividhya. Anthony Benezet's depictions of African oppression: 'that creature of propaganda'. BJECS (29:1) 2006, 115–30.

7482. van Tilburg, Marja. Domesticating holiness: holiness, gender, and education in conduct literature, 1780–1890. *In* (pp. 111–26) **3415**.

7483. Vietto, Angela. Inscribing manhood and enacting womanhood in the Early Republic. *In* (pp. 253–66) **6224**.

7484. Walker, Robert G. A source for 'waxen tables' in *Martinus Scriblerus*. NQ (53:2) 2006, 197.

7485. Weyler, Karen A. An actor in the drama of revolution: Deborah Sampson, print, and performance in the creation of celebrity. *In* (pp. 183–93) **6224**.

7486. Whelan, Timothy. Politics, religion, and romance: letters of Eliza Gould Flower, 1794–1802. WordsC (36:3) 2005, 85–109.

7487. Wu, Duncan. The journalism of William Hazlitt (1737–1820) in Boston (1784–5): a critical and bibliographical survey. RES (57:229) 2006, 221–46. (The Reverend William Hazlitt, father of the essayist.)

BIOGRAPHY AND AUTOBIOGRAPHY

7488. Bannet, Eve Tavor. Trading routes and eighteenth-century migrations: reframing Janet Schaw. *In* (pp. 137–57) **7490**.

7489. Doll, Dan. 'Like trying to fit a sponge into a matchbox': twentieth-century editing of eighteenth-century journals. *In* (pp. 211–28) **7490**.

7490. —— Munns, Jessica (eds). Recording and reordering: essays on the seventeenth- and eighteenth-century diary and journal. Lewisburg, PA: Bucknell UP; London: Assoc. UPs, 2006. pp. 248. (Bucknell studies in eighteenth-century literature and culture.)

7491. Harding, Anthony John. 'Domestick privacies': biography and the sanctifying of privacy, from Johnson to Martineau. *See* **7927**.

7492. Hindmarsh, D. Bruce. The Evangelical conversion narrative: spiritual autobiography in early modern England. (Bibl. 2005, 8264.) Rev. by John Whale in TLS, 17 Feb. 2006, 32; by David Ceri Jones in BJECS (29:2) 2006, 289–91; by Elspeth Jajdelska in RES (57:230) 2006, 426–8.

7493. Hudson, Angela Pulley. Imagining Mary Musgrove: 'Georgia's Creek Indian Princess' and Southern identity. *In* (pp. 112–25) **6224**.

7494. Kelly, James. Bordering on fact in early eighteenth-century sea journals. *In* (pp. 158–84) **7490**.

7495. McKenzie, Andrea. The real Macheath: social satire, appropriation, and eighteenth-century criminal biography. *See* **7823**.

7496. Marr, Lisa. 'All Dressed in Green': a woman's account of the 1798 Rebellion. *In* (pp. 249–58) **8374**.

7497. Nussbaum, Felicity. 'More than a woman': early memoirs of British actresses. *In* (pp. 225–42) **7255**.

7498. Parker, Peter. Naked portraits: the lives of their times: how the art of biography evolved. TLS, 5 May 2006, 3–4 (review-article).

7499. Ridley, Glynis. Sacred and secular places: an Atlantic divide. *In* (pp. 22–42) **7490**.

7500. Spradlin, Derrick. Westward expansion, Indian subjugation, and the frontier gazes of Jackson Johonnet, Zebulon Montgomery Pike, and James Kirk Paulding. *See* **10989**.

7501. Woodfine, Philip. 'Nothing but dust & the most minute particles': historians and the evidence of journals and diaries. *In* (pp. 185–210) **7490**.

RELATED STUDIES

7502. Carpenter, Andrew. Some reflections on the first twenty years of the Eighteenth-Century Ireland Society and its journal *Eighteenth-Century Ireland / Iris an dá chultúr*. ECI (20) 2005, 11–16.

7503. Coleman, Deirdre. Romantic colonization and British anti-slavery. Cambridge; New York: CUP, 2005. pp. xv, 273. (Cambridge studies in Romanticism, 61.) Rev. by Vincent Carretta in SR (45:1) 2006, 133–6; by Michael J. Franklin in BJ (34:1) 2006, 82–3.

7504. Ellis, Markman. The coffee-house: a cultural history. *See* **6522**.

7505. Hilton, Lisa. Mistress Peachum's pleasure. London: Weidenfeld & Nicolson, 2005. pp. xix, 204, (plates) 16. (Biography of Lavinia Fenton, the original Polly Peachum.)

7506. Irwin, Raymond D. Books on early American history and culture, 1951–1960: an annotated bibliography. *See* **6525**.

7507. Monaghan, E. Jennifer. Learning to read and write in Colonial America. *See* **6526**.

7508. O'Halloran, Clare. Golden Ages and barbarous nations: antiquarian debate and cultural politics in Ireland, *c*.1750–1800. Cork: Cork UP in assn with Field Day, 2004. pp. viii, 271. (Critical conditions.) Rev. by Jacqueline Hill in ECI (20) 2005, 178–80.

7509. Prescott, Sarah. 'What Foes more dang'rous than too strong Allies?': Anglo-Welsh relations in eighteenth-century London. HLQ (69:4) 2006, 535–54.

7510. Rajan, Tilottama; Plotnitsky, Arkady (eds). Idealism without absolutes: philosophy and Romantic culture. *See* **8928**.

7511. Robertson, John. The case for the Enlightenment: Scotland and Naples, 1680–1760. Cambridge; New York: CUP, 2005. pp. xii, 453, (plates) 8. (Ideas in context, 73.) Rev. by James A. Harris in TLS, 24 Mar. 2006, 12.

7512. Schoina, Maria. Cities of the mind: Venice and London in late eighteenth-century *capriccio* paintings. *In* (pp. 149–68) **3307**.

7513. Sparks, Randy J. The Southern way of death: the meaning of death in antebellum White evangelical culture. *See* **8934**.

7514. Suter, Keith. The rise and fall of English coffee houses. *See* **6528**.

7515. Wahrman, Dror. The making of the modern self: identity and culture in eighteenth-century England. New Haven, CT; London: Yale UP, 2004. pp. xviii, 414. Rev. by Karol Berger, Jill Campbell and Don Herzog in ECS (40:1) 2006, 149–56.

LITERARY THEORY

7516. Barbieri, M. Chiara. La pagina e la scena: l'attore inglese nella trattatistica del '700. *See* **7354**.

7517. Cannan, Paul D. Emergence of dramatic criticism in England: from Jonson to Pope. *See* **6529**.

7518. Jung, Sandro. An unpublished letter by Percival Stockdale. ANQ (19:3) 2006, 11–13.

7519. London, April. Isaac D'Israeli and literary history: opinion, anecdote, and secret history in the early nineteenth century. *See* **8949**.

AUTHORS

Hannah Adams (1755–1831)

7520. Zettsu, Tomoyuki. Cannibal connections: a Buddhist reading of *The Encantadas*. *See* **10914**.

John Adams (1704–1740)

7521. Di Loreto, Sonia. Pirates and ambassadors: John Adams and Thomas Jefferson in Europe. QPS (14) 2006, 201–6.

Joseph Addison

7522. Bannet, Eve Tavor. Haywood's *Spectator* and the female world. *In* (pp. 82–103) **7884**.

7523. Bending, Stephen. 'Miserable reflections on the sorrows of my life': letters, loneliness, and gardening in the 1760s. *See* **7445**.

7524. Bony, Alain (introd. and notes). Essais de critique et d'esthétique. Pau: Univ. de Pau, 2004. pp. 264. Rev. by Robert Ellrodt in EA (59:2) 2006, 236–7.

7525. Briggs, Peter M. Joseph Addison and the art of listening: birdsong, Italian opera and the music of the English tongue. AJ (16) 2005, 157–76.

7526. Haan, Estelle. *Vergilius redivivus*: studies in Joseph Addison's Latin poetry. (Bibl. 2005, 8320.) Rev. by J. W. Binns in MLR (101:2) 2006, 504–5.

7527. Hammond, Brean. Joseph Addison's opera *Rosamond*: Britishness in the early eighteenth century. ELH (73:3) 2006, 601–29.

7528. Lee, Anthony W. Johnson's symbolic mentors: Addison, Dryden, and *Rambler* 86. *See* **7939**.

7529. Lubey, Kathleen. Eliza Haywood's amatory aesthetic. *See* **7873**.

7530. Wiebe, Heather. Benjamin Britten, the 'national faith', and the animation of history in 1950s England. *See* **3962**.

7531. Wright, Lynn Marie; Newman, Donald J. (eds). Fair philosopher: Eliza Haywood and *The Female Spectator*. *See* **7884**.

7532. Zuroski, Eugenia. Disenchanting China: Orientalism and the aesthetics of reason in the English novel. *See* **7407**.

Mark Akenside

7533. Dix, Robin. The literary career of Mark Akenside, including an edition of his non-medical prose. Madison, NJ: Fairleigh Dickinson UP, 2006. pp. 410.

James Arbuckle

7534. Karian, Stephen. Swift, Arbuckle, and *The Beasts' Confession to the Priest*. *See* **8198**.

John Arbuthnot

7535. Ross, Angus (ed.). The correspondence of Dr John Arbuthnot. Munich: Fink, 2006. pp. 547. (Monographs on eighteenth-century English literature and culture.) Rev. by Chris Mounsey in BJECS (29:2) 2006, 296–7.

Mrs (Anna Letitia) Barbauld (1743–1825)

7536. Heinowitz, Rebecca Cole. 'Thy world, Columbus, shall be free': British Romantic deviance and Spanish American revolution. ERR (17:2) 2006, 151–9.

7537. Janowitz, Anne. Women Romantic poets: Anna Barbauld and Mary Robinson. Tavistock: Northcote House in assn with the British Council, 2004. pp. xii, 124. Rev. by Simon Bainbridge in BJ (34:1) 2006, 80–1.

7538. Keymer, Thomas. Lady Echlin: Richardson's window on eighteenth-century Ireland. *In* (pp. 62–76) **7255**.

7539. McCarthy, William. Performance, pedagogy, and politics: Mrs Thrale, Mrs Barbauld, Monsieur Itard. *In* (pp. 261–76) **6264**.

7540. Rohrbach, Emily. Anna Barbauld's history of the future: a deviant way to poetic agency. ERR (17:2) 2006, 179–87.

James Beattie

7541. Santesso, Aaron. A careful longing: the poetics and problems of nostalgia. *See* **7856**.

William Beckford

7542. Alexander, Boyd (ed.). Life at Fonthill, 1807–1822: from the correspondence of William Beckford. Stroud: Nonsuch, 2006. pp. 315, (plates) 8.

7543. Cass, Jeffrey. Homoerotics and Orientalism in William Beckford's *Vathek*: Liberalism and the problem of pederasty. *In* (pp. 107–20) **8395**.

7544. Graham, Kenneth W.; Berland, Kevin (eds). William Beckford and the new millennium. (Bibl. 2004, 8664.) Rev. by Karen Junod in AJ (17) 2006, 443–8.

7545. Junod, Karen. Artists' lives in eighteenth-century Britain: the strange case of William Beckford. AJ (16) 2005, 237–57.

7546. Shaffer, Elinor. Composing and decomposing the corpus of William Beckford: French and English Beckford. CompCrit (25) 2004, 255–65 (review-article).

George Berkeley

7547. Ross, Ian Campbell. Was Berkeley a Jacobite? *Passive Obedience* revisited. ECI (20) 2005, 17–30.

Isaac Bickerstaff

7548. Milhous, Judith; Hume, Robert D. Isaac Bickerstaff's copyrights – and a biographical discovery. PQ (83:3) 2004, 259–73.

Robert Bisset (1759–1805)

7549. Verhoeven, W. M. (gen. ed.). Anti-Jacobin novels: vol. 4, Robert Bisset, *Douglas; or, The Highlander* (1800), volumes i and ii. Ed. by Richard Cronin. London; Brookfield, VT: Pickering & Chatto, 2005. pp. xxvii, 282. Rev. by Robert Morrison in WordsC (36:4) 2005, 189–91; by Jon Mee in HLQ (69:4) 2006, 649–53.

7550. —— Anti-Jacobin novels: vol. 5, Robert Bisset, *Douglas; or, The Highlander* (1800), volumes iii and iv. Ed. by Richard Cronin. London; Brookfield, VT: Pickering & Chatto, 2005. pp. v, 282. Rev. by Jon Mee in HLQ (69:4) 2006, 649–53.

Hugh Blair

7551. Curley, Thomas M. Samuel Johnson and truth: the first systematic detection of literary deception in James Macpherson's *Ossian*. With a response by Nick Groom. *See* **7921**.

7552. Probyn, Clive. Referencing the real: Hugh Blair, Joshua Reynolds, Samuel Johnson, and the limits of representation. *In* (pp. 258–75) **7255**.

Robert Blair

7553. Bentley, E. B. *Grave* indignities: greed, hucksterism, and oblivion: Blake's watercolors for Blair's *Grave*. Blake (40:2) 2006, 66–71.

William Blake (1757–1827)

7554. Ackland, Michael. Breeding 'reptiles of the mind': Blake's dialectics of vision and Stead's critique of Pollitry in *The Man Who Loved Children*. *See* **18594**.

7555. Ankarsjö, Magnus. William Blake and gender. Jefferson, NC; London: McFarland, 2006. pp. ix, 210.

7556. Antonielli, Arianna. Trapassare la superficie fenomenica: il sostrato cristiano e cabalistico nell'opus blakiano. ConLett (42) 2004, 391–414.

7557. Barr, Mark L. Prophecy, the law of insanity, and *The [First] Book of Urizen*. SELit (46:4) 2006, 739–62.

7558. Beer, John. William Blake: a literary life. (Bibl. 2005, 8360.) Rev. by Morton D. Paley in WordsC (36:4) 2005, 156–8.

7559. Bentley, E. B. *Grave* indignities: greed, hucksterism, and oblivion: Blake's watercolors for Blair's *Grave*. *See* **7553**.

7560. Bentley, G. E., Jr. William Blake and his circle: a checklist of publications and discoveries in 2004. Blake (39:1) 2005, 4–37.

7561. —— William Blake and his circle: a checklist of publications and discoveries in 2005. Blake (40:1) 2006, 4–41.

7562. Castellani, Aldo. Montale e Blake: il caso dell' *Angelo nero*. SCrit (21:3) 2006, 447–52.

7563. Castellano, Katey. 'The road of excess leads to the palace of wisdom': alternative economies of excess in Blake's Continental prophecies. PLL (42:1) 2006, 3–24.

7564. Clark, Steve; Suzuki, Masashi (eds). The reception of Blake in the Orient. London; New York: Continuum, 2006. pp. xii, 348. (Continuum reception studies.)

7565. —— Worrall, David (eds). Blake, nation, and empire. Basingstoke; New York: Palgrave Macmillan, 2006. pp. xii, 263.

7566. Dumitrescu, Alexandra. Bootstrapping *Finnegans Wake*. *See* **16681**.

7567. Eaves, Morris. Multimedia body plans: a self-assessment. *In* (pp. 210–23) **426**.

7568. Essick, Robert N. Blake in the marketplace, 2004. Blake (38:4) 2005, 124–50.

7569. Esterhammer, Angela (ed.). Northrop Frye on Milton and Blake. *See* **14084**.

7570. Farrell, Michael. John Locke's ideology of education and William Blake's 'Proverbs of Hell'. NQ (53:3) 2006, 310–11.

7571. Green, Matthew J. A. Visionary materialism in the early works of William Blake: the intersection of Enthusiasm and empiricism. (Bibl. 2005, 8364.) Rev. by Marcel O'Gorman in Romanticism (12:2) 2006, 160–2.

7572. Groves, David. 'Great and singular genius': further references to Blake (and Cromek) in the *Scots Magazine*. Blake (39:1) 2005, 47–9.

7573. —— 'This class of impostors': Robert Cromek's view of London booksellers and engravers. *See* **9670**.

7574. Holmes, Richard (ed.). Gilchrist on Blake: *Life of William Blake, Pictor Ignotus*. New York: HarperPerennial, 2005. pp. xlii, 437. (Classic biographies.) Rev. by Peter Parker in TLS, 5 May 2006, 3–4.

7575. Howard, Darren. The search for a method: a rhetorical reading of Blake's prophetic symbolism. ERR (17:5) 2006, 559–74.

7576. Hughes, John. Music and inspiration in Blake's poetry. *In* (pp. 85–106) **8828**.

7577. Ishizuka, Hisao. Enlightening the fibre-woven body: William Blake and eighteenth-century fibre medicine. LitMed (25:1) 2006, 72–92.

7578. Larrissy, Edward. Blake and modern literature. Basingstoke; New York: Palgrave Macmillan, 2006. pp. vi, 188.

7579. Michael, Jennifer Davis. Blake and the city. Lewisburg, PA: Bucknell UP, 2006. pp. 235.

7580. Miner, Paul. Blake and the sinful arts of forgiveness. EngS (86:5) 2005, 399–423.

7581. Morris, G. S. Blake's *The Fly*. Exp (65:1) 2006, 16–18.

7582. Quinney, Laura. Escape from repetition: Blake *versus* Locke and Wordsworth. *In* (pp. 63–79) **1894**.

7583. —— Swerving Neo-Platonists. *See* **11707**.

7584. Schuchard, Marsha Keith. William Blake and the Jewish Swedenborgians. *In* (pp. 61–86) **8523**.

7585. Stevenson, W. H. Blake's Advent birthday. Blake (40:1) 2006, 45. (Dating *The Marriage of Heaven and Hell*.)

7586. Tearle, Oliver. Blake's *London* in *A Tale of Two Cities*. *See* **9829**.

7587. Tseng, Ming-yu. Iconicity in the interplay of the literal and the metaphorical: an example from William Blake's *Jerusalem*. JLS (35:1) 2006, 31–57.

7588. Van Kleeck, Justin. Blake's four … *Zoa's*? Blake (39:1) 2005, 38–43.

7589. —— 'Tenderness & love not uninspired': Blake's re-vision of Sentimentalism in *The Four Zoas*. Blake (39:2) 2005, 60–77.

7590. Wallace, Christina. Intersecting Blake: rereading *The Marriage of Heaven and Hell*. *In* (pp. 225–38) **11781**.

7591. White, Harry. Cruel holiness and honest virtue in the works of William Blake. Blake (40:2) 2006, 52–65.

7592. Whitehead, Angus. A quotation from Lord Byron's *The Two Foscari* in William Blake's *The Ghost of Abel*. *See* **9373**.

7593. —— William Blake's subsidiary design of a dog in his *Heads of the Poets* tempera of William Cowper (*c*.1800–1803): an identification. NQ (53:3) 2006, 316–20.

7594. Williams, Nicholas M. (ed.). Palgrave advances in William Blake studies. Basingstoke; New York: Palgrave Macmillan, 2006. pp. xii, 283. (Palgrave advances.)

7595. Wright, Julia M. Blake, nationalism, and the politics of alienation. (Bibl. 2005, 8398.) Rev. by Harriet Kramer Linkin in CLIO (35:2) 2006, 281–7.

7596. Yoder, R. Paul. Blake and the Book of Numbers: Joshua the giant killer and the tears of Balaam. *In* (pp. 87–102) **8523**.

James Boswell

7597. Aurthur, Tim; Calt, Steven. Opium and Samuel Johnson. *See* **7915**.

7598. Boulton, James T.; McLoughlin, T. O. (eds). An account of Corsica, the journal of a tour to that island, and memoirs of Pascal Paoli. Oxford; New York: OUP, 2006. pp. lii, 250. Rev. by Michael Lister in TLS, 19 May 2006, 33.

7599. Bundock, Michael. Johnson and women in Boswell's *Life of Johnson*. *See* **7918**.

7600. Katritzky, Linde. Johnson and the Earl of Shelburne's circle. *See* **7934**.

7601. Lee, Anthony W. Allegories of mentoring: Johnson and Frances Burney's *Cecilia*. *See* **7627**.

7602. McDermott, Anne. The compilation methods of Johnson's *Dictionary*. *See* **7942**.

7603. Radner, John B. Constructing an adventure and negotiating for narrative control: Johnson and Boswell in the Hebrides. *In* (pp. 59–78) **3405**.

7604. Rogers, Pat. The second Mrs Wymondesold: the widow, the divorcee, Johnson, and Reynolds. HLQ (69:4) 2006, 607–16.

Abel Boyer (1667–1729)

7605. Cormier, Monique C. The reception of Abel Boyer's *Royal Dictionary* in the 18th century. Dic (26) 2005, 174–93.

Hugh Henry Brackenridge

7606. Shaffer, Jason. Making 'an excellent die': death, mourning, and patriotism in the propaganda plays of the American Revolution. EAL (41:1) 2006, 1–27.

Frances Brooke

7607. Drummond, John. Frances Brooke's *Rosina*: a lesson in morality. *In* (pp. 141–52) **7255**.

7608. Little, Ann M. Cloistered bodies: convents in the Anglo-American imagination in the British conquest of Canada. ECS (39:2) 2006, 187–200.

Edmund Burke (1729–1797)

7609. Balfour, Ian. Torso: (the) sublime sex, beautiful bodies, and the matter of the text. *See* **9500**.

7610. Colombino, Laura. '*We are horribly sensitive*': Thomas Hardy e la psicofisica del sublime. *See* **10260**.

7611. Dickson, Leigh Wetherall. Authority and legitimacy: the cultural context of Lady Caroline Lamb's novels. *See* **10692**.

7612. Dwan, David. Abstract hatred: Yeats and the counter-revolutionary paradigm. *See* **19416**.

7613. Goodrich, Amanda. Debating England's aristocracy in the 1790s: pamphlets, polemic, and political ideas. Woodbridge, Suffolk; Rochester, NY:

Boydell Press, 2005. pp. x, 213. (Royal Historical Soc. studies in history.) Rev. by Wilfrid Prest in Parergon (23:2) 2006, 137–9.

7614. Himmelfarb, Gertrude. The moral imagination: from Edmund Burke to Lionel Trilling. *See* **8392**.

7615. Lee, Yoon Sun. Nationalism and irony: Burke, Scott, Carlyle. (Bibl. 2004, 8753.) Rev. by Harry E. Shaw in VS (48:3) 2006, 549–51.

7616. Lock, F. P. Edmund Burke: vol. 2, 1784–1797. Oxford: Clarendon Press; New York: OUP, 2006. pp. 660, (plates) 24.

7617. Nelson, Dale J. Haggard's *She*: Burke's sublime in a popular romance. *See* **10238**.

7618. O'Donnell, Katherine. 'Dear Dicky', 'Dear Dick', 'Dear Friend', 'Dear Shackleton': Edmund Burke's love for Richard Shackleton. SELit (46:3) 2006, 619–40.

7619. Peters, Julie Stone. Theatricality, legalism, and the scenography of suffering: the trial of Warren Hastings and Richard Brinsley Sheridan's *Pizarro*. *See* **8142**.

7620. Price, Fiona. Resisting 'the spirit of innovation': the other historical novel and Jane Porter. *See* **11059**.

7621. Shusterman, Richard. Somaesthetics and Burke's sublime. BJA (45:4) 2005, 323–41.

Fanny Burney (Mme d'Arblay)

7622. Abbott, John L. 'This long & cruel perplexity': Frances Burney in love, 1784–86. AJ (17) 2006, 261–96.

7623. Brock, Claire. The feminization of fame, 1750–1830. *See* **7981**.

7624. Gilbert, Elizabeth Deirdre. Desires and history: historical representation in Frances Burney's *Edwy and Elgiva* and Joanna Baillie's *Ethwald*. ERR (17:3) 2006, 327–34.

7625. Kraft, Elizabeth. Female heroic action in Frances Burney's *Camilla*. *In* (pp. 37–54) **3395**.

7626. Kuypers, Aziza. Tomaso Gerachi, clothes, and class in Frances Burney's *Camilla*. NQ (53:2) 2006, 212–14.

7627. Lee, Anthony W. Allegories of mentoring: Johnson and Frances Burney's *Cecilia*. ECN (5) 2006, 249–76.

7628. McMaster, Juliet. The suicide scene in *Cecilia*: Frances Burney and the realistic gothic. *In* (pp. 209–24) **7255**.

7629. Moss, Sarah. Spilling the beans: food and authorship in Frances Burney's early journals. WWr (13:3) 2006, 416–31.

7630. Nagle, Christopher. The epistolary passions of sympathy: feeling letters in *Persuasion* and Burney's *The Wanderer*. *See* **9059**.

7631. Park, Julie. Pains and pleasures of the automaton: Frances Burney's mechanics of coming out. ECS (40:1) 2006, 23–49.

7632. Pink, Emma E. Frances Burney's *Camilla*: 'to print my grand work … by subscription'. ECS (40:1) 2006, 51–68.

7633. Rennhak, Katharina. Tropes of exile in the 1790s: English women writers and French emigrants. ERR (17:5) 2006, 575–92.

7634. Rodriguez, Catherine M. The history of a novel's travels abroad: foreign editions of Frances Burney's *Cecilia*. PBSA (99:4) 2005, 539–71.

7635. Sabor, Peter. 'A kind of tax on the public': the subscription list to Frances Burney's *Camilla*. *In* (pp. 299–315) **7255**.

7636. Whitehead, Angus. 'A various complicated *ill*': echoes of Cotton and Cowley in *Evelina*. NQ (53:3) 2006, 309–10.

7637. Wiltshire, John. Pathography? Medical progress and medical experience from the viewpoint of the patient. *See* **7962**.

7638. Zunshine, Lisa. Caught unawares by a benefactor: embodying the deserving object of charity in the eighteenth-century novel. *See* **7796**.

Robert Burns

7639. Andrews, Corey E. 'Almost the same, but not quite': English poetry by eighteenth-century Scots. *See* **8088**.

7640. Gorji, Mina. Burying Bloomfield: poetical remains and 'the unlettered muse'. *In* (pp. 232–52) **9141**.

7641. Harding, Anthony John. 'Domestick privacies': biography and the sanctifying of privacy, from Johnson to Martineau. *See* **7927**.

7642. Jones, Christopher. Paul Laurence Dunbar and Robert Burns: vernacular gateways. *See* **9968**.

7643. Langan, Celeste. Scotch drink & Irish harps: mediations of the national air. *In* (pp. 25–49) **8828**.

7644. Prandi, Julie D. Sexual imagery in the verse epistles of Robert Burns and Anna Louise Karsch. CLS (43:1/2) 2006, 153–70.

7645. Tholoniat, Yann. '*Doing nothing*': Robert Burns et l'ambiguïté de la *skholê*. RANAM (39) 2006, 91–103.

7646. Wilson-Costa, Karyn. The poetry of Robert Burns: 'a melancholy not unallied to mirth'. EREA (4:1) 2006, 10–15.

Lady Sophia Burrell (1750?–1802)

7647. Johns-Putra, Adeline. Gendering Telemachus: Anna Seward and the epic rewriting of Fénelon's *Télémaque*. *In* (pp. 85–97) **3395**.

Joseph Butler (1692–1752)

7648. Newberry, Paul. Emerging emotion theory: forgiveness and repetition. *In* (pp. 80–99) **1894**.

Mather Byles

7649. Berson, Joel S. The source for Benjamin Franklin's 'The Drinker's Dictionary' (and was it Mather Byles?). *See* **7805**.

George Campbell

7650. Mulvihill, James. George Campbell's *Philosophy of Rhetoric* and Wordsworth's 'Preface' to *Lyrical Ballads*. *See* **11697**.

John Campbell (1708–1775)

7651. Rogers, Shef. Alternatives to the novel: romance, alchemy, and *The Travels and Adventures of Edward Brown, Esq.* (1739). *In* (pp. 288–98) **7255**.

Charlotte Charke

7652. Shevelow, Kathryn. Charlotte: being a true account of an actress's flamboyant adventures in eighteenth-century London's wild and wicked theatrical world. (Bibl. 2005, 8465.) Rev. by Michael Caines in TLS, 1 Dec. 2006, 31.

Thomas Chatterton

7653. Axcelson, John. Saving Chatterton: imagining historical transmission in Coleridge. *See* **9498**.

7654. Heys, Alistair (ed.). From gothic to Romantic: Thomas Chatterton's Bristol. Bristol: Redcliffe, 2005. pp. 144. Rev. by Sharon Ruston in TLS, 16 June 2006, 33; by Jonathon Shears in BJ (34:2) 2006, 196–7.

Charles Churchill

7655. Rounce, Adam. 'A clamour too loud to be distinct': William Warburton's literary squabbles. *See* **8238**.

Colley Cibber

7656. Hardy, John. The wit to realise dulness. *In* (pp. 166–81) **7255**.

John Cleland

7657. Donato, Clorinda. Public and private negotiations of gender in eighteenth-century England and Italy: Lady Mary Wortley Montagu and the case of Catterina Vizzani. *See* **8014**.

7658. Gladfelder, Hal (ed.). Memoirs of a coxcomb. Peterborough, Ont.; Orchard Park, NY: Broadview Press, 2005. pp. 284. (Broadview eds.) Rev. by Michael Caines in TLS, 17 June 2005, 26.

7659. Rosenthal, Laura J. Infamous commerce: prostitution in eighteenth-century British literature and culture. Ithaca, NY; London: Cornell UP, 2006. pp. x, 270.

James Cobb (1756–1818)

7660. Bhattacharya, Nandini. Slavery, colonialism, and connoisseurship: gender and eighteenth-century literary transnationalism. *See* **7670**.

Catharine Cockburn (Catharine Trotter)

7661. Kelley, Anne (sel. and introd.). Catharine Trotter's *The Adventures of a Young Lady* and other works. Aldershot; Burlington, VT: Ashgate, 2006. pp. xiii, 289. Rev. by Robin Kirschbaum in BJECS (29:2) 2006, 301–2.

Jane Collier

7662. Craik, Katharine A. (ed.). An essay on the art of ingeniously tormenting. Oxford; New York: OUP, 2006. pp. xlv, 111. (Oxford world's classics.)

7663. Woodward, Carolyn. Jane Collier, Sarah Fielding, and the motif of tormenting. AJ (16) 2005, 259–73.

William Collins (1721–1759)

7664. Fry, Paul H. Progresses of poetry. *See* **11665**.

7665. Jung, Sandro. Hermogenes as a possible source for William Collins's 'sweetness'. ANQ (19:3) 2006, 3–6.

7666. —— Johnson's *Dictionary* and the language of William Collins's *Odes on Several Descriptive and Allegoric Subjects. See* **7932**.

7667. —— 'O think in what sweet lays, how sweetly strong / Our Fairfax warbles Tasso's forcefull song': William Collins and Edward Fairfax. ELN (43:2) 2005, 59–68.

7668. —— William Collins and the 'zone'. ANQ (19:2) 2006, 16–21.

George Colman the Elder (1732–1794)

7669. Mounsey, Chris. Persona, elegy, and desire. *See* **8005**.

George Colman the Younger (1762–1836)

7670. Bhattacharya, Nandini. Slavery, colonialism, and connoisseurship: gender and eighteenth-century literary transnationalism. Aldershot; Burlington, VT: Ashgate, 2006. pp. viii, 201.

7671. Horejsi, Nicole. 'A counterpart to the Ephesian matron': Steele's *Inkle and Yarico* and a feminist critique of the Classics. *See* **1117**.

Ebenezer Cooke (*c*.1667–*c*.1732)

7672. Nickell, Joe. The case of the missing edition. CEACrit (68:1/2) 2005/06, 111–16. (*Sotweed Redivivus.*)

John Gilbert Cooper

7673. Jung, Sandro. William Collins and the 'zone'. *See* **7668**.

Hannah Cowley

7674. Arons, Wendy. Performance, mobility, and the domestication of female desire in *The Belle's Stratagem*. 1650–1850 (11) 2005, 251–64.

7675. Cox, Jeffrey N. Cowley's bold stroke for comedy. ERR (17:3) 2006, 361–75.

7676. DeRochi, Jack. Re-ordering a formative hierarchy: Hannah Cowley's comedies of manners. RECTR (20:1/2) 2005, 1–15.

7677. Escott, Angela. The imperial project: resistance and revolution in Hannah Cowley's Oriental musical comedy. RECTR (20:1/2) 2005, 80–96.

7678. Gay, Penny. What happened to Hannah Cowley? *In* (pp. 153–65) **7255**.

William Cowper

7679. Brunström, Conrad. 'Leaving the herd': how queer was Cowper? BJECS (29:2) 2006, 157–67.

7680. —— William Cowper: religion, satire, society. (Bibl. 2004, 8830.) Rev. by Adam Rounce in AJ (17) 2006, 428–31.

7681. Ryskamp, Charles. The first illustrations to *John Gilpin*. NQ (53:2) 2006, 210–12.

7682. Santesso, Aaron. A careful longing: the poetics and problems of nostalgia. *See* **7856**.

7683. Seeley, Tracy. 'The fair light mystery of images': Alice Meynell's metaphysical turn. *See* **10924**.

7684. Terry, Richard. Mock-heroic from Butler to Cowper: an English genre and discourse. *See* **6625**.

7685. Underhill, Hugh. 'Domestic happiness, thou only bliss': common and divided ground in William Cowper and Robert Bloomfield. *In* (pp 267–87) **9141**.

7686. Whitehead, Angus. William Blake's subsidiary design of a dog in his *Heads of the Poets* tempera of William Cowper (*c*.1800–1803): an identification. *See* **7593**.

George Crabbe

7687. Connolly, Joy. The aesthetics of the collective in Vergil and Milton. *See* **6984**.

7688. Powell, Neil. George Crabbe: an English life, 1754–1832. (Bibl. 2004, 8836.) Rev. by Norman Scarfe in PNRev (31:3) 2005, 90–1.

7689. Santesso, Aaron. A careful longing: the poetics and problems of nostalgia. *See* **7856**.

'J. Hector St John de Crèvecœur' (Michel-Guillaume Jean de Crèvecœur)

7690. Myles, Anne G. Elegiac patriarchs: Crèvecœur and the war of masculinities. *In* (pp. 147–60) **6224**.

Samuel Croxall ('Nestor Ironside') (1688/9–1752)

7691. Jung, Sandro. A possible source for Horace Walpole's *Otranto*. *See* **8235**.

Richard Cumberland

7692. Cox, Jeffrey N. Cowley's bold stroke for comedy. *See* **7675**.

Edmund Curll

7693. Maner, Martin. The authorship of Jonathan Swift's *A Tale of a Tub* – once more. *See* **8203**.

Erasmus Darwin

7694. Elliott, Paul. The Derbyshire 'Darwinians': the persistence of Erasmus Darwin's influence on a British provincial literary and scientific community, *c*.1780–1850. *In* (pp. 179–92) **7702**.

7695. Harris, Stuart. The poet as pathologist: myth and medicine in Erasmus Darwin's epic. *In* (pp. 321–35) **7702**.

7696. Heringman, Noah. Romantic rocks, aesthetic geology. (Bibl. 2004, 8846.) Rev. by Rose A. Zimbardo in HLQ (69:4) 2006, 637–48.

7697. Jackson, Philip J. B. Mama and papa: the ancestors of modern-day speech science. *In* (pp. 217–36) **7702**.

7698. Jackson-Houlston, Caroline. 'Queen lilies'? The interpenetration of scientific, religious and gender discourses in Victorian representations of plants. *See* **8791**.

7699. King-Hele, Desmond. Catching up with Erasmus Darwin in the new century. *In* (pp. 13–29) **7702**.

7700. Pearn, John. The Antipodes and Erasmus Darwin: the place of Erasmus Darwin in the heritage of Australian literature and biology. *In* (pp. 103–11) **7702**.

7701. Priestman, Martin. The progress of society? Darwin's early drafts for *The Temple of Nature*. *In* (pp. 307–19) **7702**.

7702. Smith, C. U. M.; Arnott, Robert (eds). The genius of Erasmus Darwin. Aldershot; Burlington, VT: Ashgate, 2004. pp. xvii, 417. (Science, technology, and culture, 1700–1945.)

7703. Tange, Andrea Kaston. Constance Naden and the erotics of evolution: mating the woman of letters with the man of science. *See* **10959**.

7704. Uglow, Jenny. But what about the women? The Lunar Society's attitude to women and science, and to the education of girls. *In* (pp. 163–77) **7702**.

7705. Valsania, Maurizio. 'Another and the same': nature and human beings in Erasmus Darwin's doctrine of love and imagination. *In* (pp. 337–55) **7702**.

Mary Davys

7706. Glover, Susan Paterson. Engendering legitimacy: law, property, and early eighteenth-century fiction. Lewisburg, PA: Bucknell UP; London: Assoc. UPs, 2006. pp. 231. (Bucknell studies in eighteenth-century literature and culture.)

Daniel Defoe

7707. Appelbaum, Robert. Aguecheek's beef, Belch's hiccup, and other gastronomic interjections: literature, culture, and food among the early moderns. *See* **3172**.

7708. Austin, Michael. 'Jesting with the truth': *figura*, trace, and the boundaries of fiction in *Robinson Crusoe* and its sequels. ECN (5) 2006, 1–36.

7709. Barchas, Janine. Crusoe's struggles with sexuality. ECN (5) 2006, 93–116.

7710. —— 'Kits, cats, sacks, and wives': the female multitude on Robinson Crusoe's island. *In* (pp. 103–25) **7255**.

7711. Barrio-Vilar, Laura. Getting a taste of the Other: the eighteenth-century British novel as the epitome of masquerade. *See* **7375**.

7712. Conliffe, Mark. On isolation. *See* **3216**.

7713. Ellison, Katherine E. Fatal news: reading and information overload in early eighteenth-century literature. *See* **6578**.

7714. Fishelov, David. *Robinson Crusoe*, 'the Other' and the poetics of surprise. Connotations (14:1–3) 2004/05, 1–18.

7715. Free, Melissa. Un-erasing Crusoe: *Farther Adventures* in the nineteenth century. BH (9) 2006, 89–130.

7716. Furbank, P. N.; Owens, W. R. A political biography of Daniel Defoe. London; Brookfield, VT: Pickering & Chatto, 2006. pp. viii, 277. (Eighteenth-century political biographies, 1.) Rev. by John Mullan in LRB (28:14) 2006, 26–8; by John Raven in TLS, 18 & 25 Aug. 2006, 6–7; by Paula R. Backscheider in ECS (40:1) 2006, 116–20.

7717. Glover, Susan Paterson. Engendering legitimacy: law, property, and early eighteenth-century fiction. *See* **7706**.

7718. Hinnant, Charles Haskell. *Moll Flanders*, *Roxana*, and the French tradition of the pseudo-memoir. AJ (17) 2006, 203–31.

7719. Kersey, Mel. 'The wells of English undefiled': Samuel Johnson's Romantic resistance to Britishness. *See* **7935**.

7720. Knapp, John. An early holograph poem by Defoe and his *Hymn to Peace*. NQ (53:2) 2006, 193–5.

7721. Lewis, Jayne Elizabeth. Spectral currencies in the air of reality: *A Journal of the Plague Year* and the history of apparitions. Representations (87) 2004, 82–101.

7722. McKim, Anne. Defoe in Scotland: a spy among us. Edinburgh: Scottish Cultural Press, 2005. pp. 128. Rev. by Michael Lister in TLS, 29 Sept. 2006, 32.

7723. Marbais, Peter Christian. Roxana and 'my woman, Amy': failure of mutual recognition in Defoe's *Roxana*. ECN (5) 2006, 117–42.

7724. Marroni, Michela. *The Moonstone* di Wilkie Collins: *Robinson Crusoe* come percorso intertestuale. *See* **9598**.

7725. Mason, Matthew. Slavery, servitude, and British representations of Colonial North America. *See* **7966**.

7726. May, Jill P. James Barrie's pirates: *Peter Pan*'s place in pirate history and lore. *In* (pp. 69–78) **14616**.

7727. Merrett, Robert. Daniel Defoe and Islam. Lumen (24) 2005, 19–34.

7728. Mullan, John. Restless Daniel. LRB (28:14) 2006, 26–8 (review-article). (Biographies of Defoe.)

7729. Novak, Maximillian E.; Fisher, Carl (eds). Approaches to teaching Defoe's *Robinson Crusoe*. (Bibl. 2005, 8537.) Rev. by Nina Chordas in RMER (60:1) 2006.

7730. Oliver, Kathleen M. Defoe's poetic reformation: from poem to novel, from pillory to penitentiary. CLIO (35:2) 2006, 157–78.

7731. Owens, W. R.; Furbank, P. N. (gen. eds). Religious and didactic writings of Daniel Defoe: vol. 1, *The Family Instructor*, volume I (1715). Ed. by P. N. Furbank. London; Brookfield, VT: Pickering & Chatto, 2006. pp. 336. (Pickering masters.) Rev. by Paula R. Backscheider in ECS (40:1) 2006, 116–20.

7732. —— —— Religious and didactic writings of Daniel Defoe: vol. 2, *The Family Instructor*, volume II (1718). Ed. by P. N. Furbank. London; Brookfield, VT: Pickering & Chatto, 2006. pp. 336. (Pickering masters.) Rev. by Paula R. Backscheider in ECS (40:1) 2006, 116–20.

7733. —— —— Religious and didactic writings of Daniel Defoe: vol. 3, *A New Family Instructor* (1727). Ed. by W. R. Owens. London; Brookfield, VT: Pickering & Chatto, 2006. pp. 326. (Pickering masters.) Rev. by Paula R. Backscheider in ECS (40:1) 2006, 116–20.

7734. —— —— Religious and didactic writings of Daniel Defoe: vol. 4, *Religious Courtship* (1722). Ed. by G. A. Starr. London; Brookfield, VT: Pickering & Chatto, 2006. pp. 301. (Pickering masters.) Rev. by Paula R. Backscheider in ECS (40:1) 2006, 116–20.

7735. —— —— Religious and didactic writings of Daniel Defoe: vol. 5, *Conjugal Lewdness* (1727). Ed. by Liz Bellamy. London; Brookfield, VT: Pickering & Chatto, 2006. pp. 284. (Pickering masters.) Rev. by Paula R. Backscheider in ECS (40:1) 2006, 116–20.

7736. —— —— Satire, fantasy, and writings on the supernatural: vol. 1, *The True-Born Englishman* and other poems. Ed. by W. R. Owens. London; Brookfield, VT: Pickering & Chatto, 2003. pp. vi, 536. (Pickering masters.) Rev. by Stephen H. Gregg in Eng (55:211) 2006, 105–8.

7737. —— —— Satire, fantasy, and writings on the supernatural: vol. 2, *Jure Divino.* Ed. by P. N. Furbank. London; Brookfield, VT: Pickering & Chatto, 2003. pp. vi, 388. (Pickering masters.) Rev. by Stephen H. Gregg in Eng (55:211) 2006, 105–8.

7738. —— —— Satire, fantasy, and writings on the supernatural: vol. 3, *The Consolidator* (1705); *Memoirs of Count Tariff, &c.* (1713); *The Quarrel of the School-boys at Athens.* Ed. by Geoffrey Sill. London; Brookfield, VT: Pickering & Chatto, 2003. pp. 264. (Pickering masters.) Rev. by Stephen H. Gregg in Eng (55:211) 2006, 105–8.

7739. —— —— Satire, fantasy, and writings on the supernatural: vol. 4, *Minutes of the Negotiations of Monsr Mesnager* (1717); *Secret Memoirs of a Treasonable Conference at S— House* (1717); *The Old Whig and Modern Whig Revived.* Ed. by P. N. Furbank. London; Brookfield, VT: Pickering & Chatto, 2003. pp. 215. (Pickering masters.) Rev. by Stephen H. Gregg in Eng (55:211) 2006, 105–8.

7740. —— —— Satire, fantasy, and writings on the supernatural: vol. 5, *The Conduct of Christians Made the Sport of Infidels* (1717); *A Continuation of Letters Written by a Turkish Spy at Paris* (1718). Ed. by David Blewett. London; Brookfield, VT: Pickering & Chatto, 2005. pp. 215. (Pickering masters.) Rev. by Stephen H. Gregg in Eng (55:211) 2006, 105–8.

7741. —— —— Satire, fantasy, and writings on the supernatural: vol. 6, *The Political History of the Devil* (1726). Ed. by John Mullan. London; Brookfield, VT: Pickering & Chatto, 2005. pp. 326. (Pickering masters.) Rev. by Stephen H. Gregg in Eng (55:211) 2006, 105–8.

7742. —— —— Satire, fantasy, and writings on the supernatural: vol. 7, *A System of Magick* (1727). Ed. by Peter Elmer. London; Brookfield, VT: Pickering & Chatto, 2005. pp. 313. (Pickering masters.) Rev. by Stephen H. Gregg in Eng (55:211) 2006, 105–8.

7743. —— —— Satire, fantasy, and writings on the supernatural: vol. 8, *An Essay on the History and Reality of Apparitions* (1727). Ed. by G. A. Starr. London; Brookfield, VT: Pickering & Chatto, 2005. pp. 416. (Pickering masters.) Rev. by Stephen H. Gregg in Eng (55:211) 2006, 105–8.

7744. Parkin-Gounelas, Ruth. The insistence of the object – and its sublimations. *See* **13575**.

7745. Rampaul, Giselle A. Black Crusoe, White Friday: carnivalesque reversals in Samuel Selvon's *Moses Ascending* and Derek Walcott's *Pantomime.* *See* **18450**.

7746. Raven, James. Set apart. TLS, 18 & 25 Aug. 2006, 6–7 (review-article). (Defoe's politics.)

7747. Richetti, John J. The life of Daniel Defoe. (Bibl. 2005, 8539.) Rev. by John Mullan in LRB (28:14) 2006, 26–8; by James Raven in TLS, 18 & 25 Aug. 2006, 6–7; by Paula R. Backscheider in ECS (40:1) 2006, 116–20.

7748. Rosenthal, Laura J. Infamous commerce: prostitution in eighteenth-century British literature and culture. *See* **7659.**

7749. Solinger, Jason. Jane Austen and the gentrification of commerce. *See* **9073.**

7750. Starr, G. A. Defoe and biblical memory. *In* (pp. 316–35) **7255.**

7751. Wehner, David Z. To live this life intensely and well: the rebirth of Milkman Dead in Toni Morrison's *Song of Solomon*. *In* (pp. 71–93) **17642.**

John Dennis

7752. King, Thomas A. The castrato's castration. SELit (46:3) 2006, 563–84.

Georgiana Spencer Cavendish, Duchess of Devonshire (1757–1806)

7753. Gross, Jonathan David (ed.). Emma; or, The unfortunate attachment: a sentimental novel. (Bibl. 2004, 8893.) Rev. by Margot Strickland in BJ (33:1) 2005, 64–5; by Susan Allen Ford in ERR (17:5) 2006, 640–5.

John Dyer

7754. Edgecombe, Rodney Stenning. An allusion to Dyer in a letter by Hood. *See* **10463.**

Bryan Edwards (1743–1800)

7755. Davidson, Michael. The dream of a public language: modernity, manifesto, and the citizen subject. *See* **7777.**

Jonathan Edwards (1703–1758)

7756. Bailey, Richard A. Driven by passion: Jonathan Edwards and the art of preaching. *In* (pp. 64–78) **7762.**

7757. Claghorn, George S. Transcribing a difficult hand: collecting and editing Edwards' letters over thirty five years. *In* (pp. 217–27) **7762.**

7758. Danaher, William J., Jr. The Trinitarian ethics of Jonathan Edwards. Louisville, KY: Westminster John Knox Press, 2004. pp. xi, 324. (Columbia series in Reformed theology.) Rev. by William J. Wainwright in CHist (74:2) 2005, 386–8.

7759. Dyrness, William A. Reformed theology and visual culture: the Protestant imagination from Calvin to Edwards. (Bibl. 2005, 8563.) Rev. by Maria Crăciun in SixCJ (37:1) 2006, 153–4.

7760. Hambrick-Stowe, Charles. The 'inward sweet sense' of Christ in Jonathan Edwards. *In* (pp. 79–95) **7762.**

7761. Hart, D. G. Jonathan Edwards and the origins of experimental Calvinism. *In* (pp. 161–80) **7762.**

7762. —— Lucas, Sean Michael; Nichols, Stephen J. (eds). The legacy of Jonathan Edwards: American religion and the Evangelical tradition. Grand Rapids, MI: Baker Academic, 2003. pp. 255. Rev. by Robert E. Brown in SixCJ (35:4) 2004, 1129–30.

7763. Leader, Jennifer L. 'In love with the image': transitive being and typological desire in Jonathan Edwards. EAL (41:2) 2006, 153–81.

7764. Longaker, Mark Garrett. Idealism and early American rhetoric. RSQ (36:3) 2006, 281–308.

7765. LUCAS, SEAN MICHAEL. Jonathan Edwards between Church and academy: a bibliographic essay. *In* (pp. 228–47) **7762**.

7766. McDERMOTT, GERALD R. Jonathan Edwards and the national covenant: was he right? *In* (pp. 147–57) **7762**.

7767. NEW, ELISA. Confession, Reformation, and Counter-Reformation in the career of Robert Lowell. *In* (pp. 13–32) **13763**.

7768. NICHOLS, STEPHEN J. Last of the Mohican missionaries: Jonathan Edwards at Stockbridge. *In* (pp. 47–63) **7762**.

7769. OLIPHANT, K. SCOTT. Jonathan Edwards on apologetics: reason and the noetic effects of sin. *In* (pp. 131–46) **7762**.

7770. PHILLIPS, SIOBHAN. 'Loved philology': Emily Dickinson's Trinitarian world. *See* **9887**.

7771. SCHWEITZER, IVY. Imaginative conjunctions on the imperial 'frontier': Catharine Sedgwick reads Mungo Park. *In* (pp. 126–43) **6224**.

7772. STOUT, HARRY S. Jonathan Edwards' tri-world vision. *In* (pp. 27–46) **7762**.

Elizabeth Elstob

7773. CHANCE, JANE (ed.). Women medievalists and the academy. Madison; London: Wisconsin UP, 2005. pp. xlvi, 1073. Rev. by Monica Green in TMR, June 2006; by Jacqueline de Weever in Arthuriana (16:2) 2006, 98–100.

7774. WAITE, GREG. The Saxon nymph and her illustrious women: Elizabeth Elstob's notebook (Oxford Bodleian Library Manuscript Ballard 64). *In* (pp. 351–73) **7255**.

Olaudah Equiano

7775. CARRETTA, VINCENT. Equiano, the African: biography of a self-made man. Athens; London: Georgia UP, 2005. pp. xxiv, 436. Rev. by John Bugg in ECS (39:4) 2006, 571–3; by John Saillant in EAL (41:3) 2006, 600–3.

7776. COLLINS, JANELLE. Passage to slavery, passage to freedom: Olaudah Equiano and the sea. MidQ (47:3) 2006, 209–23.

7777. DAVIDSON, MICHAEL. The dream of a public language: modernity, manifesto, and the citizen subject. FLS (122) 2006, 13–27.

7778. RICHARDSON, ALAN; LEE, DEBBIE (eds). Early Black British writing: Olaudah Equiano, Mary Prince, and others: selected texts with introduction, critical essays. *See* **7319**.

Edmund John Eyre (1767–1816)

7779. NIELSEN, WENDY C. Edmund Eyre's *The Maid of Normandy*; or, Charlotte Corday in Anglo-Irish docudrama. CompDr (40:2) 2006, 169–90.

Elizabeth Graeme Fergusson (1737–1801)

7780. OUSTERHOUT, ANNE M. The most learned woman in America: a life of Elizabeth Graeme Fergusson. (Bibl. 2005, 8599.) Rev. by Angela Vietto in EAL (41:3) 2006, 555–67.

Robert Fergusson

7781. Andrews, Corey E. 'Almost the same, but not quite': English poetry by eighteenth-century Scots. *See* **8088**.

7782. Brown, Rhona. The city poetry of Robert Fergusson and Robert Hogg. SHogg (16) 2005, 36–51.

Henry Fielding

7783. Ackroyd, Peter (foreword). The life of Mr Jonathan Wild the great. London: Hesperus Press, 2004. pp. ix, 189. (Hesperus classics.) Rev. by Melvyn New in Scriblerian (38:2) 2006, 302–3.

7784. Black, Scott. Anachronism and the uses of form in *Joseph Andrews*. Novel (38:2/3) 2005, 147–64.

7785. Grimm, Reinhold. Fielding's *Tom Jones* and the European novel since Antiquity: Fielding's *Tom Jones* as a final joinder. (Bibl. 2005, 8609.) Rev. by Sanford J. Smoller in PemM (38) 2006, 317–33.

7786. Kelleher, Paul. 'The glorious lust of doing good': *Tom Jones* and the virtues of sexuality. Novel (38:2/3) 2005, 165–92.

7787. Lockwood, Thomas F. (ed.). Plays: vol. 1, 1728–1731. Oxford: Clarendon Press; New York: OUP, 2004. pp. x, 808. (Wesleyan ed. of the works of Henry Fielding.) Rev. by David Roberts in NQ (52:4) 2005, 546–7; by Brian McCrea in Scriblerian (37:2 / 38:1) 2005, 93–6; by Tom Keymer in MLR (101:3) 2006, 825–7.

7788. Lund, Roger D. Augustan burlesque and the genesis of *Joseph Andrews*. SP (103:1) 2006, 88–119.

7789. Parker, G. F. 'Talking Scripture out of Church': Parson Adams and the practicality of translation. TransLit (14:2) 2005, 179–95.

7790. Pettit, Alexander. The Pickering & Chatto *Female Spectator*: nearly four pounds of ephemera, enshrined. *In* (pp. 42–59) **7884**.

7791. Rogers, Pat. 'How I want thee, humorous Hogart': the motif of the absent artist in Swift, Fielding and others. *See* **8212**.

7792. Rosenthal, Laura J. Infamous commerce: prostitution in eighteenth-century British literature and culture. *See* **7659**.

7793. Smoller, Sanford J. Due credit. PemM (38) 2006, 317–33 (review-article). (*Tom Jones*.)

7794. Wilputte, Earla A. 'Too ticklish to meddle with': the silencing of *The Female Spectator*'s political correspondents. *In* (pp. 122–40) **7884**.

7795. Yahav-Brown, Amit. Gypsies, nomadism, and the limits of realism. *See* **10062**.

7796. Zunshine, Lisa. Caught unawares by a benefactor: embodying the deserving object of charity in the eighteenth-century novel. ECN (5) 2006, 37–65.

Sarah Fielding

7797. Woodward, Carolyn. Jane Collier, Sarah Fielding, and the motif of tormenting. *See* **7663**.

7798. ZUNSHINE, LISA. Caught unawares by a benefactor: embodying the deserving object of charity in the eighteenth-century novel. *See* **7796**.

Samuel Foote

7799. KINSERVIK, MATTHEW J. The politics and poetics of sodomy in the age of George III. *See* **7903**.

James Fordyce (1720–1796)

7800. VORACHEK, LAURA. Intertextuality and ideology: Jane Austen's *Pride and Prejudice* and James Fordyce's *Sermons to Young Women*. *In* (pp. 129–37) **8374**.

Hannah Webster Foster

7801. HIBBARD, ANDREA L.; PARRY, JOHN T. Law, seduction, and the Sentimental heroine: the case of Amelia Norman. AL (78:2) 2006, 325–55.

7802. KOROBKIN, LAURA H. 'Can your volatile daughter ever acquire your wisdom?': luxury and false ideals in *The Coquette*. EAL (41:1) 2006, 79–107.

7803. SCHWEITZER, IVY. Perfecting friendship: politics and affiliation in early American literature. *See* **7197**.

Benjamin Franklin

7804. ANDERSON, DOUGLAS. Benjamin Franklin and his readers. EAL (41:3) 2006, 535–53 (review-article).

7805. BERSON, JOEL S. The source for Benjamin Franklin's 'The Drinker's Dictionary' (and was it Mather Byles?) AS (81:2) 2006, 164–79.

7806. FRASCA, RALPH. Benjamin Franklin's printing network: disseminating virtue in early America. *See* **141**.

7807. GREEN, JAMES N.; STALLYBRASS, PETER. Benjamin Franklin: writer and printer. New Castle, DE: Oak Knoll Press; London: British Library, 2006. pp. x, 179. Rev. by J. A. Leo Lemay in Book (69) 2006, 7–9.

7808. HUANG, NIAN-SHENG. From the 'fur cap' to Poor Richard: the Chinese connection. PAPS (150:2) 2006, 205–40.

7809. HUNTER, CHRISTOPHER. Reevaluating press freedom in Colonial America. YREAL (22) 2006, 73–96.

7810. LEMAY, J. A. LEO. The life of Benjamin Franklin. Philadelphia: Pennsylvania UP, 2006. 2 vols. pp. xiv, 549; xiv, 647. Rev. by Douglas Anderson in EAL (41:3) 2006, 535–53; by Kerry S. Walters in JAH (93:3) 2006, 838–9.

7811. OLSON, LESTER C. Benjamin Franklin's vision of American community: a study in rhetorical iconology. (Bibl. 2005, 8638.) Rev. by Douglas Anderson in EAL (41:3) 2006, 535–53.

7812. WESLING, MEG. The opacity of everyday life: segregation and the iconicity of uplift in *The Street*. *See* **18000**.

7813. WOLF, EDWIN, II; HAYES, KEVIN J. The library of Benjamin Franklin. Philadelphia, PA: American Philosophical Soc., 2006. pp. xiv, 966. (Memoirs of the American Philosophical Soc., 257.)

7814. WOOD, GORDON S. The Americanization of Benjamin Franklin. (Bibl. 2004, 8955.) Rev. by Douglas Anderson in EAL (41:3) 2006, 535–53.

David Garrick (1717–1779)

7815. GÖRTSCHACHER, WOLFGANG. Drama adaptation: James Shirley, David Garrick and *The Gamester(s)*. *See* **7133**.

7816. HOLMES, JONATHAN. 'Sometime a paradox': Shakespeare, Diderot and the problem of character. *See* **5335**.

7817. JUNG, SANDRO. David Mallet and David Garrick. *See* **7995**.

7818. LOCK, F. P. New Garrick letters. TN (60:2) 2006, 94–7.

7819. RIBES, PURIFICACIÓN. Country wives and country girls in eighteenth-century England: a history of theatrical rewriting. SEDERI (16) 2006, 91–108.

7820. SHARGEL, RAPHAEL. The devolution of *The Alchemist*: Garrick, Gentleman, and 'genteel comedy'. *See* **6904**.

John Gay

7821. BEECHY, TIFFANY. Devil take the hindmost: Chaucer, John Gay, and the pecuniary anus. *See* **4362**.

7822. HALL, DEWEY W. Beggars can be choosers: from Gay to Inchbald. *See* **7898**.

7823. MCKENZIE, ANDREA. The real Macheath: social satire, appropriation, and eighteenth-century criminal biography. HLQ (69:4) 2006, 581–605.

Edward Gibbon

7824. CHEEKE, STEPHEN. 'What so many have told, who would tell again?': Romanticism and the commonplaces of Rome. ERR (17:5) 2006, 521–41.

7825. EDGECOMBE, RODNEY STENNING. Shakespeare's *Cymbeline* and Gibbon's *The History of the Decline and Fall of the Roman Empire*. *See* **5684**.

7826. MOYAL, GABRIEL LOUIS. Traduire l'Angleterre sous la Restauration: Gibbon et Shakespeare de Guizot. Meta (50:3) 2005, 881–905.

William Gilpin

7827. BROWN, JULIA PREWITT. Taking off from *The Art of Memory*. *In* (pp. 3–8) **8374**.

7828. BURKE, TIM. Colonial spaces and national identities in *The Banks of Wye*: Bloomfield and the Wye after Wordsworth. *In* (pp. 89–112) **9141**.

7829. JOHNSON, NICHOLAS. *'Kennst du das Land?'*: learning the language of landscape in *Little Women*. *See* **8965**.

7830. MIALL, DAVID S. Representing the picturesque: William Gilpin and the laws of nature. ISLE (12:2) 2005, 75–93.

William Godwin ('Edward Baldwin') (1756–1836)

7831. BREWER, WILLIAM D. (ed.). St Leon: a tale of the sixteenth century. Peterborough, Ont.; Orchard Park, NY: Broadview Press, 2006. pp. 507. (Broadview eds.) Rev. by Nora Crook in TLS, 9 June 2006, 36.

7832. CLEMIT, PAMELA. Self-analysis as social critique: the autobiographical writings of Godwin and Rousseau. Romanticism (11:2) 2005, 161–80.

7833. GAROFALO, DANIELA. 'A left-handed way': modern masters in William Godwin's *Caleb Williams*. ERR (17:2) 2006, 237–44.

7834. GOGGIN, GERARD. Editing Minervas: William Godwin's liminal maneuvers in Mary Wollstonecraft's *Wrongs of Woman*. *In* (pp. 81–99) **3405**.

7835. Hindle, Maurice. Victim of romance: the life and death of Fanny Godwin. *See* **8263**.

7836. Holmes, Richard (ed.). Godwin on Wollstonecraft: memoirs of the author of *The Rights of Woman*. New York: HarperPerennial, 2005. pp. xxxvii, 106. (Classic biographies.) Rev. by Peter Parker in TLS, 5 May 2006, 3–4.

7837. Mandell, Laura. Producing hate in 'private' letters: Horace Walpole, Mary Hays. *See* **8236**.

7838. Markley, A. A. Aristocrats behaving badly: gambling and dueling in the 1790s novel of reform. ERR (17:2) 2006, 161–8.

7839. O'Shaugnessy, David. St Dunstan and *De occulta philosophia*: an inspiration for Godwin's *St Leon*. NQ (53:3) 2006, 314–15.

7840. Pfau, Thomas. Romantic moods: paranoia, trauma, and melancholy, 1790–1840. (Bibl. 2005, 8677.) Rev. by Grevel Lindop in TLS, 9 June 2006, 8–9.

7841. Robinson, Terry F. 'A mere skeleton of history': reading relics in Jane Austen's *Northanger Abbey*. *See* **9067**.

7842. Todd, Janet. Suicide and biography. *See* **8273**.

7843. Ward, Ian. A man of feelings: William Godwin's Romantic embrace. LawL (17:1) 2005, 21–46.

7844. Weiss, Deborah. Suffering, sentiment, and civilization: pain and politics in Mary Wollstonecraft's *Short Residence*. *See* **8275**.

Oliver Goldsmith (1730?–1774)

7845. Branch, Lori. Rituals of spontaneity: sentiment and secularism from free prayer to Wordsworth. *See* **6607**.

7846. Freeman, Arthur. New Goldsmith? TLS, 15 Dec. 2006, 15. (*Memoirs of Lady Harriot Butler*.)

7847. Mack, Robert L. Oliver Goldsmith's *The Vicar of Wakefield*, spiritual Sentimentalism, and the lost polar expedition of Sir John Franklin. ELN (44:1) 2006, 43–56.

7848. Mitchell, Sebastian. Oliver Goldsmith's *The Deserted Village*: past, present, and future. Eng (55:212) 2006, 123–39.

7849. Perry, Ruth. Deserted villages, kindly landlords, and overdetermined marriages in eighteenth-century England. *In* (pp. 243–57) **7255**.

7850. Santesso, Aaron. A careful longing: the poetics and problems of nostalgia. *See* **7856**.

7851. Watt, James. Goldsmith's cosmopolitanism. ECL (30:1) 2006, 56–75.

George Granville, Baron Lansdowne

7852. Stewart, Stanley. Shylock and Jacob, the patriarch. *See* **5981**.

Thomas Gray (1716–1771)

7853. Gorji, Mina. Burying Bloomfield: poetical remains and 'the unlettered muse'. *In* (pp. 232–52) **9141**.

7854. Haggerty, George. Horace Walpole's epistolary friendships. *See* **8233**.

7855. Mounsey, Chris. Persona, elegy, and desire. *See* **8005**.

7856. Santesso, Aaron. A careful longing: the poetics and problems of nostalgia. Newark: Delaware UP, 2006. pp. 221.

Elizabeth Hamilton (1758–1816)

7857. Grogan, Claire. Identifying foreign bodies: New Philosophers and Hottentots in Elizabeth Hamilton's *Memoirs of Modern Philosophers*. ECF (18:3) 2006, 305–27.

Jupiter Hammon

7858. Harrell, Willie J., Jr. A call to consciousness and action: mapping the African American jeremiad. *See* **8248**.

7859. Nydam, Arlen. Numerological tradition in the works of Jupiter Hammon. AAR (40:2) 2006, 207–20.

William Hatchett (*fl*.1730–1741)

7860. Spedding, Patrick. A bibliography of Eliza Haywood. *See* **7881**.

Mary Hays

7861. Brooks, Marilyn L. (ed.). The correspondence (1779–1843) of Mary Hays, British novelist. (Bibl. 2004, 9004, where title incorrect.) Rev. by Nicole Pohl in WWr (13:1) 2006, 166–70.

7862. Fisk, Nicole Plyler. 'A wild, wick slip she was': the passionate female in *Wuthering Heights* and the *Memoirs of Emma Courtney*. *See* **9213**.

7863. Mandell, Laura. Producing hate in 'private' letters: Horace Walpole, Mary Hays. *See* **8236**.

7864. Walker, Gina Luria. Mary Hays (1759–1843): the growth of a woman's mind. Aldershot; Burlington, VT: Ashgate, 2006. pp. viii, 287.

7865. Wallace, Miriam L. (ed.). *The Memoirs of Emma Courtney* by Mary Hays; and *Adeline Mowbray; or, The Mother and the Daughter*, by Amelia Alderson Opie. Glen Allen, VA: College Publishing, 2004. pp. xiii, 645. (Eighteenth-century literature.)

Eliza Haywood

7866. Bannet, Eve Tavor. Haywood's *Spectator* and the female world. *In* (pp. 82–103) **7884**.

7867. Barchas, Janine. Apollo, Sappho, and – a grasshopper?! A note on the frontispieces to *The Female Spectator*. *In* (pp. 60–71) **7884**.

7868. Glover, Susan Paterson. Engendering legitimacy: law, property, and early eighteenth-century fiction. *See* **7706**.

7869. Graves, Nicola. 'Injury for injury'; or, 'The Lady's Revenge': female vengeance in Eliza Haywood's *Female Spectator*. *In* (pp. 157–75) **7884**.

7870. Harzewski, Stephanie. The *Fantomina* phenomenon: Eliza Haywood and the formation of a heroine. ECN (5) 2006, 175–96.

7871. Ingrassia, Catherine. Eliza Haywood, periodicals, and the function of orality. *In* (pp. 141–56) **7884**.

7872. King, Kathryn R. Patriot or opportunist? Eliza Haywood and the politics of *The Female Spectator*. *In* (pp. 104–21) **7884**.

7873. Lubey, Kathleen. Eliza Haywood's amatory aesthetic. ECS (39:3) 2006, 309–22.

7874. McGuire, Kelly. Mourning and material culture in Eliza Haywood's *The History of Miss Betsy Thoughtless*. ECF (18:3) 2006, 281–304.

7875. MacKenzie, Niall. Eliza Haywood in a 'scrutinising age'. AJ (16) 2005, 177–97.

7876. Merritt, Juliette. Reforming the coquette? Eliza Haywood's vision of a female epistemology. *In* (pp. 176–92) **7884**.

7877. Miguel-Alfonso, Ricardo. Social conservatism, aesthetic education, and the essay genre in Eliza Haywood's *Female Spectator*. *In* (pp. 72–81) **7884**.

7878. Newman, Donald J. *The Female Spectator*: a bibliographic essay. *In* (pp. 212–41) **7884**.

7879. Pettit, Alexander. The Pickering & Chatto *Female Spectator*: nearly four pounds of ephemera, enshrined. *In* (pp. 42–59) **7884**.

7880. Rivero, Albert J. Doubling Eliza: Austen's remembrance of Richardson (and perhaps Haywood) in *Sense and Sensibility*. *In* (pp. 93–103) **8374**.

7881. Spedding, Patrick. A bibliography of Eliza Haywood. London; Brookfield, VT: Pickering & Chatto, 2004. pp. 848. (Includes bibliography of William Hatchett.) Rev. by Kevin L. Cope in 1650–1850 (11) 2005, 620–4; by Niall MacKenzie in AJ (17) 2006, 437–43.

7882. —— Measuring the success of Haywood's *Female Spectator* (1744–46). *In* (pp. 193–211) **7884**.

7883. Wilputte, Earla A. 'Too ticklish to meddle with': the silencing of *The Female Spectator*'s political correspondents. *In* (pp. 122–40) **7884**.

7884. Wright, Lynn Marie; Newman, Donald J. (eds). Fair philosopher: Eliza Haywood and *The Female Spectator*. Lewisburg, PA: Bucknell UP; London: Assoc. UPs, 2006. pp. 252. (Bucknell studies in eighteenth-century literature and culture.)

Elizabeth Helme (d.1814?)

7885. Salih, Sara. The silence of Miss Lambe: *Sanditon* and fictions of 'race' in the Abolition era. *See* **9068**.

John Hervey, Baron Hervey (1696–1743)

7886. Morris, Marilyn. Transgendered perspectives on premodern sexualities. *See* **8016**.

Benjamin Hoadly

7887. Johnstone, H. Diack. Four lost plays recovered: *The Contrast* and other dramatic works of John Hoadly (1711–1776). *See* **7888**.

John Hoadly

7888. Johnstone, H. Diack. Four lost plays recovered: *The Contrast* and other dramatic works of John Hoadly (1711–1776). RES (57:231) 2006, 487–506.

Thomas Holcroft

7889. Zunshine, Lisa. Caught unawares by a benefactor: embodying the deserving object of charity in the eighteenth-century novel. *See* **7796**.

John Home (1722–1808)

7890. Jung, Sandro. Lady Randolph, the 'monument of woe': love and loss in John Home's *Douglas*. RECTR (20:1/2) 2005, 16–27.

7891. Lopez, John-David. Recovered voices: the sources of *The Siege of Valencia*. *See* **10424**.

7892. McGinley, Kevin J. The first Edinburgh and London editions of John Home's *Douglas* and the play's early stage history. TN (60:3) 2006, 134–46.

David Hume (1711–1776)

7893. Stanley, Liz. The writing of David Hume's *My Own Life*: the persona of the philosopher *manqué*. Auto/Biography (14:4) 2006, 320–38.

Francis Hutcheson

7894. Carey, Daniel. Locke, Shaftesbury, and Hutcheson: contesting diversity in the Enlightenment and beyond. *See* **8135**.

7895. Guerrini, Anita. Alexander Monro *primus* and the moral theatre of anatomy. ECent (47:1) 2006, 1–18.

Gilbert Imlay

7896. Richards, Cynthia D. Romancing the sublime: why Mary Wollstonecraft fell in love with that cad, Gilbert Imlay. *See* **8269**.

7897. Todd, Janet. Suicide and biography. *See* **8273**.

Elizabeth Inchbald

7898. Hall, Dewey W. Beggars can be choosers: from Gay to Inchbald. ERR (17:3) 2006, 341–50.

7899. Nielsen, Wendy C. A tragic farce: Revolutionary women in Elizabeth Inchbald's *The Massacre* and European drama. ERR (17:3) 2005, 275–88.

7900. Tucker, Kathryn. Joanna Baillie's and Elizabeth Inchbald's moral aesthetics: humanizing actors and madmen. *See* **9109**.

7901. Wilcox, Lance. Idols and idolaters in *A Simple Story*. AJ (17) 2006, 297–316.

William Henry Ireland

7902. Lockwood, Tom. Manuscript, print and the authentic Shakespeare: the Ireland forgeries again. *See* **5195**.

William Jackson

7903. Kinservik, Matthew J. The politics and poetics of sodomy in the age of George III. BJECS (29:2) 2006, 219–36.

Thomas Jefferson

7904. Allen, Brooke. Jefferson the skeptic. HR (59:2) 2006, 193–217.

7905. Cillerai, Chiara. The eloquence of nature in *Notes on the State of Virginia*. EAL (41:1) 2006, 59–78.

7906. Creesy, Charles. Monticello: the history of a typeface. *See* **134**.

7907. Crumbley, Paul; Gantt, Patricia M. (eds). Body my house: May Swenson's work and life. Logan: Utah State UP, 2006. pp. 254.

7908. Di Loreto, Sonia. Pirates and ambassadors: John Adams and Thomas Jefferson in Europe. *See* **7521**.

7909. McArdle, Andrea. The confluence of law and antebellum Black literature: lawyerly discourse as a rhetoric of empowerment. *See* **11329**.

7910. Rebok, Sandra. Two exponents of the Enlightenment: transatlantic communication by Thomas Jefferson and Alexander von Humboldt. SoQ (43:4) 2006, 126–52.

7911. Schmitz, Neil. Doing the Gettysburg Address: Jefferson/Calhoun/ Lincoln/King. *See* **10741**.

7912. Spencer, Suzette. Historical memory, romantic narrative, and Sally Hemings. *See* **15141**.

7913. Tanner, John S.; Collings, Justin. How Adams and Jefferson read Milton and Milton read them. *See* **7071**.

Mr (Edward) Jerningham (1737?–1812)

7914. Lopez, John-David. Recovered voices: the sources of *The Siege of Valencia*. *See* **10424**.

Dr Samuel Johnson (1709–1784)

7915. Aurthur, Tim; Calt, Steven. Opium and Samuel Johnson. AJ (17) 2006, 85–99.

7916. Billi, Mirella. Johnson's beauties: the lexicon of aesthetics in the *Dictionary*. Textus (19:1) 2006, 131–49.

7917. Brack, O. M., Jr (ed.). A commentary on Mr Pope's principles of morality, or *Essay on Man*: a translation from the French. (Bibl. 2005, 8749.) Rev. by Steven Shankman in AJ (17) 2006, 415–16.

7918. Bundock, Michael. Johnson and women in Boswell's *Life of Johnson*. AJ (16) 2005, 81–109.

7919. Bush, Jamie. Courtship and private character in Johnson's *Rambler* essays on marriage. ELN (43:2) 2005, 50–9.

7920. Cacchiani, Slivia. *Desperately*, *utterly* and other intensifiers: on their inclusion and definition in Johnson's *Dictionary*. Textus (19:1) 2006, 217–36.

7921. Curley, Thomas M. Samuel Johnson and truth: the first systematic detection of literary deception in James Macpherson's *Ossian*. With a response by Nick Groom. AJ (17) 2006, 119–201.

7922. Davies, Philip John. Viscountess Eccles: an Anglo-American patroness of literature. *See* **311**.

7923. Davis, Matthew M. 'Ask for the old paths': Johnson and the usages controversy. AJ (17) 2006, 17–68.

7924. DeMaria, Robert, Jr. North and South in Johnson's *Dictionary*. Textus (19:1) 2006, 11–31.

7925. Dille, Catherine. Johnson's *Dictionary* in the nineteenth century: a legacy in transition. AJ (16) 2005, 21–37.

7926. Dossena, Marina. 'The cinic Scotomastic'? Johnson, his commentators, Scots, French, and the story of English. Textus (19:1) 2006, 51–67.

7927. Harding, Anthony John. 'Domestick privacies': biography and the sanctifying of privacy, from Johnson to Martineau. DalR (85:3) 2005, 371–89.

7928. Hitchings, Henry. Dr Johnson's *Dictionary*: the extraordinary story of the book that defined the world. (Bibl. 2005, 8758.) Rev. by Ron Smith in GaR (60:3/4) 2006, 782–90; by Freya Johnston in AJ (17) 2006, 417–18.

7929. Holder, R. W. The dictionary men: their lives and times. *See* **1632**.

7930. Iamartino, Giovanni. English flour and Italian bran: Johnson's *Dictionary* and the reformation of Italian lexicography in the early nineteenth century. Textus (19:1) 2006, 203–16.

7931. —— DeMaria, Robert, Jr. Samuel Johnson's *Dictionary* and the eighteenth-century world of words: introduction. Textus (19:1) 2006, 5–10.

7932. Jung, Sandro. Johnson's *Dictionary* and the language of William Collins's *Odes on Several Descriptive and Allegoric Subjects*. Textus (19:1) 2006, 69–85.

7933. Karounos, Michael. *Rasselas* and the riddle of the caves: setting eternity in the hearts of men. AJ (16) 2005, 39–58.

7934. Katritzky, Linde. Johnson and the Earl of Shelburne's circle. AJ (17) 2006, 101–18.

7935. Kersey, Mel. 'The wells of English undefiled': Samuel Johnson's Romantic resistance to Britishness. AJ (17) 2006, 69–84.

7936. Kinsella, Thomas E. The pride of literature: Arthur Murphy's *Essay on Johnson*. *See* **8024**.

7937. Larsen, Lyle. Joseph Baretti's feud with Hester Thrale. *See* **8042**.

7938. Lee, Anthony W. Allegories of mentoring: Johnson and Frances Burney's *Cecilia*. *See* **7627**.

7939. —— Johnson's symbolic mentors: Addison, Dryden, and *Rambler* 86. AJ (16) 2005, 59–79.

7940. —— Mentoring relationships in the life and writings of Samuel Johnson: a study in the dynamics of eighteenth-century literary mentoring. (Bibl. 2005, 8768.) Rev. by Scott D. Vander Ploeg in KenPR (21) 2006, 73–4.

7941. Lonsdale, Roger (ed.). The lives of the most eminent English poets, with critical observations on their works. Oxford: Clarendon Press; New York: OUP, 2006. 4 vols. pp. xvii, 440; xv, 425; xv, 467; xv, 649. Rev. by H. J. Jackson in TLS, 28 Apr. 2006, 33; by Claude Rawson in ECS (40:1) 2006, 109–15.

7942. McDermott, Anne. The compilation methods of Johnson's *Dictionary*. AJ (16) 2005, 1–20.

7943. Masi, Silvia. Lexicographic material under observation: from Johnson's *Dictionary* to a model for a cognition-based dictionary of lexical patterns. Textus (19:1) 2006, 237–57.

7944. Mayhew, Robert J. Landscape, literature, and English religious culture, 1660–1800: Samuel Johnson and languages of natural description. (Bibl. 2005, 8771.) Rev. by Rose A. Zimbardo in HLQ (69:4) 2006, 637–48.

7945. Parker, Peter. Naked portraits: the lives of their times: how the art of biography evolved. *See* **7498**.

7946. Pearce, Chris P. 'Gleaned as industry should find, or chance should offer it': Johnson's *Dictionary* after 250 years. AJ (17) 2006, 341–62 (review-article).

7947. —— Recovering the 'rigour of interpretative lexicography': border crossings in Johnson's *Dictionary*. Textus (19:1) 2006, 33–50.

7948. Pinnavaia, Laura. Idiomatic expressions regarding food and drink in Johnson's *Dictionary of the English Language* (1755 and 1773). Textus (19:1) 2006, 151–65.

7949. Pireddu, Silvia. The 'landscape of the body': the language of medicine in Johnson's *Dictionary*. Textus (19:1) 2006, 107–29.

7950. Probyn, Clive. Referencing the real: Hugh Blair, Joshua Reynolds, Samuel Johnson, and the limits of representation. *In* (pp. 258–75) **7255**.

7951. Radner, John B. Constructing an adventure and negotiating for narrative control: Johnson and Boswell in the Hebrides. *In* (pp. 59–78) **3405**.

7952. Rizzo, Betty. Lyttelton's ghosts: an impassioned indecision. AJ (16) 2005, 219–35.

7953. Roper, Alan. Johnson, Dryden, and an allusion to Horace. NQ (53:2) 2006, 198–9.

7954. Scanlan, J. T. Johnson's *Dictionary* and legal dictionaries. Textus (19:1) 2006, 87–106.

7955. Scherwatzky, Steven. Samuel Johnson's Augustinianism revisited. AJ (17) 2006, 1–16.

7956. Smith, Ron. Then who *is* the editor of the English language? *See* **1656**.

7957. Sudan, Rajani. Mud, mortar, and other technologies of empire. ECent (45:2) 2004, 147–69.

7958. Tankard, Paul. Johnson and the hot potato: scholarship and the 'science of fables'. *In* (pp. 336–50) **7255**.

7959. Vancil, David. Some observations about the Samuel Johnson miniature dictionaries in the Cordell Collection. Textus (19:1) 2006, 167–78.

7960. Vicentini, Alessandra. In Johnson's footsteps: Baretti's *English Grammar* and the spread of the English language in Italy during the eighteenth century. Textus (19:1) 2006, 179–202.

7961. Weinbrot, Howard D. Aspects of Samuel Johnson: essays on his arts, mind, afterlife, and politics. Newark: Delaware UP, 2005. pp. 417. Rev. by Nicholas Hudson in CLIO (36:1) 2006, 135–9.

7962. Wiltshire, John. Pathography? Medical progress and medical experience from the viewpoint of the patient. Southerly (66:1) 2006, 22–36.

7963. Zuroski, Eugenia. Disenchanting China: Orientalism and the aesthetics of reason in the English novel. *See* **7407**.

The Rev. Samuel Johnson (1696–1772)

7964. Longaker, Mark Garrett. Idealism and early American rhetoric. *See* **7764**.

Charles Johnstone

7965. Blackwell, Mark. The people things make: Locke's *Essay Concerning Human Understanding* and the properties of the self. *See* **8185**.

Edward Kimber (1719–1769)

7966. Mason, Matthew. Slavery, servitude, and British representations of Colonial North America. SoQ (43:4) 2006, 109–25.

John Langhorne (1735–1779)

7967. Lucas, John. Hospitality and the rural tradition: Bloomfield's *May-Day with the Muses*. *In* (pp. 113–41) **9141**.

William Law (1686–1761)

7968. Joling-van der Sar, Gerda J. The controversy between William Law and John Wesley. *See* **8243**.

John Leacock

7969. Shaffer, Jason. Making 'an excellent die': death, mourning, and patriotism in the propaganda plays of the American Revolution. *See* **7606**.

John Lee (d.1781)

7970. Ribes, Purificación. Country wives and country girls in eighteenth-century England: a history of theatrical rewriting. *See* **7819**.

Charlotte Lennox

7971. Berg, Temma F. The lives and letters of an eighteenth-century circle of acquaintance. *See* **7446**.

7972. Lorenzo-Modia, María Jesús. Charlotte Lennox's *The Female Quixote* into Spanish: a gender-biased translation. YES (36:1) 2006, 103–14.

7973. Mack, Ruth. Quixotic ethnography: Charlotte Lennox and the dilemma of cultural observation. Novel (38:2/3) 2005, 193–213.

7974. Palo, Sharon Smith. The good effects of a whimsical study: romance and women's learning in Charlotte Lennox's *The Female Quixote*. ECF (18:2) 2005/06, 203–28.

M. G. Lewis

7975. Cooper, L. Andrew. Gothic threats: the role of danger in the critical evaluation of *The Monk* and *The Mysteries of Udolpho*. GothS (8:2) 2006, 18–34.

7976. Fincher, Max. The gothic as camp: queer aesthetics in *The Monk*. RomNet (44) 2006.

7977. Malenas, Ellen. Reform ideology and generic structure in Matthew Lewis's *Journal of a West India Proprietor*. StudECC (35) 2006, 27–51.

7978. Pu, Ruoqian. The moral principles in gothic novels: an ethical study of *The Monk*. FLS (118) 2006, 41–9. (In Chinese.)

George Lillo

7979. Johnstone, H. Diack. Four lost plays recovered: *The Contrast* and other dramatic works of John Hoadly (1711–1776). *See* **7888**.

Robert Lloyd (1733–1764)

7980. Mounsey, Chris. Persona, elegy, and desire. *See* **8005**.

Catharine Macaulay (1731–1791)

7981. Brock, Claire. The feminization of fame, 1750–1830. Basingstoke; New York: Palgrave Macmillan, 2006. pp. ix, 242. (Palgrave studies in the Enlightenment, Romanticism and the cultures of print.)

7982. Davies, Kate. Revolutionary correspondence: reading Catharine Macaulay and Mercy Otis Warren. WWr (13:1) 2006, 73–97.

7983. Gunther-Canada, Wendy. Catharine Macaulay on the paradox of paternal authority in Hobbesian politics. Hypatia (21:2) 2006, 150–73.

'Murtagh McDermot' (Francis Gentleman) (1728–1784)

7984. Shargel, Raphael. The devolution of *The Alchemist*: Garrick, Gentleman, and 'genteel comedy'. *See* **6904**.

Henry Mackenzie

7985. Mandell, Laura (ed.). *The Castle of Otranto* and *The Man of Feeling*. *See* **8237**.

James Macpherson (1736–1796)

7986. Connell, Philip. British identities and the politics of ancient poetry in later eighteenth-century England. *See* **8037**.

7987. Curley, Thomas M. Samuel Johnson and truth: the first systematic detection of literary deception in James Macpherson's *Ossian*. With a response by Nick Groom. *See* **7921**.

7988. de Montluzin, Emily Lorraine. An 'Ossianic' tribute to the Prince of Wales: Thomas Potts's verses in the *Gentleman's Magazine*, 1762. *See* **8077**.

7989. Dentith, Simon. Epic and empire in nineteenth-century Britain. *See* **8335**.

7990. Gaskill, Howard (ed.). The reception of 'Ossian' in Europe. (Bibl. 2005, 8808.) Rev. by Lesa Ní Mhunghaile in ECI (20) 2005, 169–72; by Sebastian Mitchell in TransLit (14:2) 2005, 255–62; by Landeg White in TLS, 14 Apr. 2006, 24; by Murray G. H. Pittock in MLR (101:4) 2006, 1078.

7991. Hlobil, Tomáš. Ossianism in the Bohemian lands. MLR (101:3) 2006, 789–97.

7992. Moore, Dafydd. Enlightenment and romance in James Macpherson's *The Poems of Ossian*: myth, genre and cultural change. (Bibl. 2004, 9086.) Rev. by Lesa Ní Mhunghaile in ECI (20) 2005, 169–72; by Susan Manning in ScSR (6:2) 2005, 129–31.

7993. —— James Macpherson and 'Celtic Whiggism'. ECL (30:1) 2006, 1–24.

7994. —— Tennyson, Malory and the Ossianic mode: *The Poems of Ossian* and 'The Death of Arthur'. *See* **11401**.

David Mallet

7995. Jung, Sandro. David Mallet and David Garrick. ANQ (19:1) 2006, 25–7.

7996. —— David Mallet and Thomas Percy. ANQ (19:1) 2006, 23–5.

7997. —— Mallet's version of St Kilda in *Amyntor and Theodora; or, The Hermit* (1747). ScSR (6:2) 2005, 21–31.

Edmond Malone

7998. Sherbo, Arthur. The appendix to Edmond Malone's 1790 *Shakespeare* and the New Variorum *Poems* and *Sonnets*. *See* **6193**.

Bernard Mandeville

7999. Palmeri, Frank. Conjectural history and satire: narrative as historical argument from Mandeville to Malthus (and Foucault). Narrative (14:1) 2006, 64–84.

8000. Rosenthal, Laura J. Infamous commerce: prostitution in eighteenth-century British literature and culture. *See* **7659**.

8001. Summerfield, Henry. Virtues and Christian virtues, vices and gross vices: some accusations against Bernard Mandeville reconsidered. ELN (43:2) 2005, 35–46.

Mary de la Rivière Manley

8002. Hodgson-Wright, Stephanie (sel. and introd.). Delarivier Manley. Aldershot; Burlington, VT: Ashgate, 2006. 1 vol. (various pagings). (Early modern Englishwoman, ii: Printed writings, 1641–1700, 3:12.) (Facsimiles.)

8003. Kvande, Marta. Jane Barker and Delarivière Manley: public women against the public sphere. *See* **6563**.

8004. Spedding, Patrick. Measuring the success of Haywood's *Female Spectator* (1744–46). *In* (pp. 193–211) **7884**.

William Mason

8005. Mounsey, Chris. Persona, elegy, and desire. SELit (46:3) 2006, 601–18.

James Miller (1706–1744)

8006. Heinowitz, Rebecca Cole. 'Thy world, Columbus, shall be free': British Romantic deviance and Spanish American revolution. *See* **7536**.

8007. Johnstone, H. Diack. Four lost plays recovered: *The Contrast* and other dramatic works of John Hoadly (1711–1776). *See* **7888**.

Elizabeth Montagu

8008. Bannet, Eve Tavor. The Bluestocking sisters: women's patronage, Millenium Hall, and 'the visible providence of a Country'. *See* **8131**.

8009. —— Lives, letters, and tales in Sarah Scott's *Journey through Every Stage of Life*. *See* **8132**.

8010. Bending, Stephen. Mrs Montagu's contemplative bench: Bluestocking gardens and female retirement. HLQ (69:4) 2006, 555–80.

8011. Pohl, Nicole. 'Perfect reciprocity': salon culture and epistolary conversations. WWr (13:1) 2006, 139–59.

Lady Mary Wortley Montagu

8012. Bannet, Eve Tavor. Haywood's *Spectator* and the female world. *In* (pp. 82–103) **7884**.

8013. Brophy, Sarah. Women, aging, and gossip in Lady Mary Wortley Montagu's letters of the 1720s. ECent (45:1) 2004, 1–20.

8014. Donato, Clorinda. Public and private negotiations of gender in eighteenth-century England and Italy: Lady Mary Wortley Montagu and the case of Catterina Vizzani. BJECS (29:2) 2006, 169–89.

8015. Konuk, Kader. Ethnomasquerade in Ottoman–European encounters: reenacting Lady Mary Wortley Montagu. Criticism (46:3) 2004, 393–414.

8016. Morris, Marilyn. Transgendered perspectives on premodern sexualities. SELit (46:3) 2006, 585–600.

8017. Weise, Wendy S. Seeing and the difference it makes: ocularity, gender, and space in Swift's and Montagu's 'Dressing Room' satires. *See* **8216**.

Hannah More ('Z')

8018. PAGE, JUDITH W. Reforming honeysuckles: Hannah More's *Cœlebs in Search of a Wife* and the politics of women's gardens. KSJ (55) 2006, 111–36.

8019. SMITH, NICHOLAS D. Hannah More items in the Huntington Library: correspondence and a poem. HLQ (69:4) 2006, 617–29.

8020. —— Unpublished poems by Hannah More in Osborn Shelves C.341 and Folger MS M.a.179. RES (57:232) 2006, 581–606.

8021. WEBB, SAMANTHA. One man's trash is another man's dinner: food and the poetics of scarcity in the Cheap Repository Tracts. ERR (17:4) 2006, 419–36.

Robert Munford (d.1784)

8022. GARZON, SUSAN. Social variation and grammatical patterns in 1770s Virginia: evidence from Robert Munford's *The Candidates*. JMMLA (38:2) 2005, 16–30.

Arthur Murphy

8023. HANNA, ROBERT C. Dickens and plagiarism: part II. *See* **9761**.

8024. KINSELLA, THOMAS E. The pride of literature: Arthur Murphy's *Essay on Johnson*. AJ (16) 2005, 129–56.

Judith Sargent Murray

8025. BAKER, JENNIFER J. Judith Sargent Murray's medium between calculation and feeling. *In* (pp. 210–24) **6224**.

8026. KASRIE, MARY ROSE. Reading the letters of Judith Sargent Murray: from private correspondence to public voice. *In* (pp. 197–209) **6224**.

John Newton (1725–1807)

8027. YENIKA-AGBAW, VIVIAN. Capitalism and the culture of hate in Granfield's *Amazing Grace: the Story of the Hymn*. JBlaS (36:3) 2006, 353–61.

Samson Occom (1723–1792)

8028. LOPENZINA, DREW. 'The whole wilderness shall blossom as the rose': Samson Occom, Joseph Johnson, and the question of native settlement on Cooper's frontier. *See* **9620**.

Mr (John) Oldmixon (1673–1742)

8029. ROGERS, PAT (ed.). The letters, life, and works of John Oldmixon. (Bibl. 2005, 8851.) Rev. by Chris Fauske in Scriblerian (38:2) 2006, 324–5.

James Orr (1770–1816)

8030. DORNAN, STEPHEN. Beyond the Milesian pale: the poetry of James Orr. ECI (20) 2005, 140–55.

Thomas Paine (1737–1809)

8031. GOODRICH, AMANDA. Debating England's aristocracy in the 1790s: pamphlets, polemic, and political ideas. *See* **7613**.

8032. HITCHENS, CHRISTOPHER. Thomas Paine's *Rights of Man*: a biography. Crows Nest, N.S.W.: Allen & Unwin; Vancouver: Douglas & McIntyre, 2006. pp. 158. (10 books that shook the world.) Rev. by John Barrell in LRB (28:23) 2006, 14–15.

8033. Larkin, Edward. Thomas Paine and the literature of revolution. Cambridge; New York: CUP, 2005. pp. x, 205. Rev. by Matthew Rainbow Hale in JAH (93:2) 2006, 504–5.

8034. Loughran, Trish. Disseminating *Common Sense*: Thomas Paine and the problem of the early national bestseller. AL (78:1) 2006, 1–28.

8035. Nelson, Craig. Thomas Paine: enlightenment, revolution, and the birth of modern nations. New York: Viking, 2006. pp. 396, (plates) 16.

8036. Webb, Joe. Echoes of Paine: tracing *The Age of Reason* through the writings of Emerson. *See* **10116**.

Thomas Percy

8037. Connell, Philip. British identities and the politics of ancient poetry in later eighteenth-century England. HistJ (49:1) 2006, 161–92.

8038. Jung, Sandro. David Mallet and Thomas Percy. *See* **7996**.

8039. McDermott, Anne. The compilation methods of Johnson's *Dictionary*. *See* **7942**.

8040. Schneider, Matthew. Wordsworthian songcatching in America. *See* **3073**.

Hester Lynch Piozzi (Mrs Thrale)

8041. Knapp, Oswald G. (ed.). The intimate letters of Piozzi and Pennington. Stroud: Nonsuch, 2005. pp. 284. Rev. by Michael Caines in TLS, 13 Oct. 2006, 34.

8042. Larsen, Lyle. Joseph Baretti's feud with Hester Thrale. AJ (16) 2005, 111–27.

8043. McCarthy, William. Performance, pedagogy, and politics: Mrs Thrale, Mrs Barbauld, Monsieur Itard. *In* (pp. 261–76) **6264**.

8044. Stabler, Jane. Devotion and diversion: early nineteenth-century British women travellers in Italy and the Catholic Church. *In* (pp. 15–34) **8320**.

Alexander Pope

8045. Ackroyd, Peter (foreword). *The Rape of the Lock: a Heroicomical Poem in Five Cantos* and *A Key to the Lock*. London: Hesperus Press, 2004. pp. ix, 85. (Hesperus poetry.) Rev. by Melvyn New in Scriblerian (38:2) 2006, 302–3.

8046. Baker, Malcolm. Multiple heads: Pope, the portrait bust, and patterns of repetition. *In* (pp. 224–45) **1894**.

8047. Brown, Iain Gordon. Water, windows, and women: the significance of Venice for Scots in the age of the Grand Tour. ECL (30:3) 2006, 1–50.

8048. Conti Camaiora, Luisa. Alexander Pope's *Epistle to Dr Arbuthnot*. Milan: ISU Univ. Cattolica, 2006. pp. 88.

8049. Davis, Paul. After the Fire: Chaucer and urban poetics, 1666–1743. *In* (pp. 177–92) **4312**.

8050. Domingo, Darryl P. 'The various modes of Nature's *least* admirable workes'; or, The collected *Dunciad*. Lumen (23) 2004, 91–114.

8051. Emig, Rainer. Competing melancholies: (en-)gendering discourses of selfhood in early modern English literature. *See* **7206**.

8052. Goldgar, Anne; Frost, Robert I. (eds). Institutional culture in early modern society. *See* **728**.

8053. Hammond, Brean. Pope amongst the satirists, 1660–1750. Plymouth: Northcote House in assn with the British Council, 2005. pp. xv, 107. (Writers and their work.) Rev. by Chris Fauske in Scriblerian (38:2) 2006, 299–301.

8054. Hardy, John. The wit to realise dulness. *In* (pp. 166–81) **7255**.

8055. Harol, Corrinne. Virgin idols and verbal devices: Pope's Belinda and the Virgin Mary. ECent (45:1) 2004, 41–59.

8056. Haugen, Kristine. Imagined universities: public insult and the *terrae filius* in early modern Oxford. *In* (pp. 317–43) **728**.

8057. Ingram, Allan; Faubert, Michelle. Cultural constructions of madness in eighteenth-century writing: representing the insane. *See* **7280**.

8058. Jones, Tom. Pope and Berkeley: the language of poetry and philosophy. (Bibl. 2005, 8891.) Rev. by Peter Walmsley in RES (57:232) 2006, 828–9.

8059. Latimer, Bonnie. Alchemies of satire: a history of the sylphs in *The Rape of the Lock*. RES (57:232) 2006, 684–700.

8060. Ma, Xian. Harmony: ethics in Pope's *Windsor-Forest*. FLS (117) 2006, 77–81. (In Chinese.)

8061. Mannheimer, Katherine. To the letter: the material text as space of adjudication in Pope's *The First Satire of the Second Book of Horace*. CLS (43:1/2) 2006, 1–18.

8062. Manning, Susan. Characterless women and representative men: a transatlantic perspective. *See* **10579**.

8063. Odell, D. W. Pope's *The Dunciad* 4.425–30. Exp (64:2) 2006, 71–3.

8064. O'Gorman, Francis. Oscar Wilde and Pope. *See* **11620**.

8065. Parker, G. F. 'Talking Scripture out of Church': Parson Adams and the practicality of translation. *See* **7789**.

8066. Rogers, Pat. The Alexander Pope encyclopedia. (Bibl. 2004, 9146.) Rev. by Peter Barry in Eng (55:212) 2006, 213–19; by Robin Dix in Scriblerian (38:2) 2006, 301–2.

8067. —— John Philips, Pope, and political georgic. *See* **7103**.

8068. —— The last days of Lord Peterborough: the earl, the opera singer, and a new letter by Pope. PQ (83:3) 2004, 237–57.

8069. —— The memory of Henrietta Tempest: Pope's *Winter* and the great storm. *In* (pp. 276–87) **7255**.

8070. —— Revisions to Pope's prose works in the *Miscellanies* (1732). RES (57:232) 2006, 701–6.

8071. Rudd, Niall. Pope's farewell to Horace: *Dialogue* I, 1–22. TransLit (14:2) 2005, 240–5.

8072. Sudan, Rajani. Mud, mortar, and other technologies of empire. *See* **7957**.

8073. Vendler, Helen. Poets thinking: Pope, Whitman, Dickinson, Yeats. (Bibl. 2005, 8914.) Rev. by Tamar Yacobi in PT (26:3) 2005, 554–6; by Lynnell Edwards in GaR (59:4) 2005, 956–60; by Nicolas de Warren in EC (56:1) 2006, 102–10; by Jennifer Leader in EDJ (15:1) 2006, 83–94.

8074. Walls, Kathryn. The unveiling of the dressing table in Pope's *Rape of the Lock*, i.121. NQ (53:2) 2006, 196–7.

8075. Wilson, Penelope. Homer and English epic. *In* (pp. 272–86) **3253**.

William Popple (1700/1701–1764)

8076. Gillespie, Stuart. A new eighteenth-century Juvenal translator: William Popple's Satires vi and x. TransLit (15:1) 2006, 47–96.

Thomas Potts (*fl.*1762)

8077. de Montluzin, Emily Lorraine. An 'Ossianic' tribute to the Prince of Wales: Thomas Potts's verses in the *Gentleman's Magazine*, 1762. ANQ (19:4) 2006, 22–5.

Matthew Prior

8078. Harvey, A. D. The Roman ideal of rural retirement in seventeenth- and eighteenth-century England. ContRev (288:1682) 2006, 357–66.

George Psalmanazar

8079. Keevak, Michael. The pretended Asian: George Psalmanazar's eighteenth-century Formosan hoax. (Bibl. 2005, 8917.) Rev. by Paul Tankard in AJ (16) 2005, 310–15.

8080. Lynch, Jack. Forgery as performance art: the strange case of George Psalmanazar. 1650–1850 (11) 2005, 21–35.

Henry James Pye

8081. Verhoeven, W. M. (gen. ed.). Anti-Jacobin novels: vol. 1, General introduction; Henry James Pye, *The Democrat* (2nd edn, 1796); Henry James Pye, *The Aristocrat* (1799). Ed. by W. M. Verhoeven. London; Brookfield, VT: Pickering & Chatto, 2005. pp. cxiii, 332. Rev. by Robert Morrison in WordsC (36:4) 2005, 189–91; by Jon Mee in HLQ (69:4) 2006, 649–53.

Ann Radcliffe

8082. Brewer, William D. The French Revolution as a romance: Mary Robinson's *Hubert de Sevrac*. *See* **8117**.

8083. Chandler, Anne. Ann Radcliffe and natural theology. StudN (38:2) 2006, 133–53.

8084. Cooper, L. Andrew. Gothic threats: the role of danger in the critical evaluation of *The Monk* and *The Mysteries of Udolpho*. *See* **7975**.

8085. Dekker, George G. The fictions of Romantic tourism: Radcliffe, Scott, and Mary Shelley. Stanford, CA: Stanford UP, 2005. pp. x, 314. Rev. by Esther Schor in TLS, 25 Nov. 2005, 10–11; by Nigel Leask in KSJ (55) 2006, 278–80.

8086. Lansdown, Richard. 'Rare in burlesque': *Northanger Abbey*. *See* **9045**.

8087. Lewis, Jayne. 'No colour of language': Radcliffe's aesthetic unbound. ECS (39:3) 2006, 377–90.

Allan Ramsay (1686–1758)

8088. Andrews, Corey E. 'Almost the same, but not quite': English poetry by eighteenth-century Scots. ECent (47:1) 2006, 59–79.

Clara Reeve

8089. Corman, Brian. Clara Reeve's *The Progress of Romance* and the canon of the novel in 1785. *In* (pp. 126–40) **7255**.

8090. Wiltshire, John. The importance of being Edmund: on names in *Mansfield Park*. *In* (pp. 138–47) **8374**.

Samuel Richardson

8091. Batsaki, Yota. *Clarissa*; or, Rake *versus* usurer. Representations (93) 2006, 22–48.

8092. Doody, Margaret Anne. Hidden histories of decline: autopsy, George II's heart attack, and the dying condition in *Clarissa* and *Tristram Shandy*. *In* (pp. 3–31) **7255**.

8093. Dussinger, John A. Fabrications from Samuel Richardson's press. PBSA (100:2) 2006, 259–79.

8094. —— The negotiations of Sir Charles Grandison. *In* (pp. 32–50) **7255**.

8095. Faller, Lincoln. Tales of a poisoning female parricide and a prostitute treated 'in a manner too shocking to mention': two criminal cases and 'the *Clarissa* effect'. ECN (5) 2006, 197–247.

8096. Gibson, Colin; Marr, Lisa (eds). New windows on a woman's world: essays for Jocelyn Harris: vol. 1. *See* **7255**.

8097. Greenup, Sylvia. The undesigning scribbler, the well-read lady and the aristocratic cad: Richardson's art of literary allusion in *Clarissa*. AngP (3:1) 2006, 145–63.

8098. Hannah, Robert. Calendar styles in Richardson's *Sir Charles Grandison*. *In* (pp. 51–61) **7255**.

8099. Hughes, Clair. Dressed in fiction. *See* **8651**.

8100. Jones, Wendy. Consensual fictions: women, liberalism, and the English novel. *See* **8656**.

8101. Keymer, Thomas. Lady Echlin: Richardson's window on eighteenth-century Ireland. *In* (pp. 62–76) **7255**.

8102. —— Sabor, Peter. *Pamela* in the marketplace: literary controversy and print culture in eighteenth-century Britain and Ireland. (Bibl. 2005, 8944.) Rev. by Fred Parker in TLS, 17 Feb. 2006, 35.

8103. Li, Hui; Zhong, Ming. On the uncertainty of interpretation: a case study of *Clarissa*. FLS (118) 2006, 99–104. (In Chinese.)

8104. Mallinson, Jonathan. What's in a name? Reflections on Voltaire's *Paméla*. ECF (18:2) 2005/06, 157–68.

8105. Maslen, Keith. Resurrecting Samuel Richardson. *In* (pp. 77–87) **7255**.

8106. Rivero, Albert J. Doubling Eliza: Austen's remembrance of Richardson (and perhaps Haywood) in *Sense and Sensibility*. *In* (pp. 93–103) **8374**.

8107. Rosenthal, Laura J. Infamous commerce: prostitution in eighteenth-century British literature and culture. *See* **7659**.

8108. —— Pamela's work. ECent (46:3) 2005, 245–53.

8109. Yahav-Brown, Amit. Reasonableness and domestic fiction. ELH (73:4) 2006, 805–30.

8110. Zhu, Weihong. Virginity, virtue and reward: the view of virginity of *Pamela*. FLS (120) 2006, 84–9. (In Chinese.)

8111. Zunshine, Lisa. Can we teach the 'deep intersubjectivity' of Richardson's *Clarissa*? *In* (pp. 88–99) **7255**.

8112. —— Harris, Jocelyn (eds). Approaches to teaching the novels of Samuel Richardson. New York: Modern Language Assn of America, 2006. pp. xiii, 216. (Approaches to teaching world literature, 87.)

Joseph Ritson

8113. Morton, Timothy. Joseph Ritson, Percy Shelley and the making of Romantic vegetarianism. *See* **11218**.

James Robertson (*fl.*1768–1788)

8114. Jung, Sandro. Hermogenes as a possible source for William Collins's 'sweetness'. *See* **7665**.

Mary Robinson (1758–1800)

8115. Allen, Emily. Loss incommensurable: economics of imbalance in Mary Robinson's *Walsingham*. ECN (5) 2006, 67–92.

8116. Binhammer, Katherine. Female homosociality and the exchange of men: Mary Robinson's *Walsingham*. WS (35:3) 2006, 221–40.

8117. Brewer, William D. The French Revolution as a romance: Mary Robinson's *Hubert de Sevrac*. PLL (42:2) 2006, 115–49.

8118. —— Mary Robinson as dramatist: the *Nobody* catastrophe. ERR (17:3) 2006, 265–73.

8119. Brock, Claire. The feminization of fame, 1750–1830. *See* **7981**.

8120. Fay, Elizabeth. Mary Robinson: on trial in the public court. SR (45:3) 2006, 397–423.

8121. Janowitz, Anne. Women Romantic poets: Anna Barbauld and Mary Robinson. *See* **7537**.

8122. Markley, A. A. Aristocrats behaving badly: gambling and dueling in the 1790s novel of reform. *See* **7838**.

8123. Rooney, Morgan. 'Belonging to no/body': Mary Robinson, *The Natural Daughter*, and rewriting feminine identity. ECF (18:3) 2006, 355–72.

Elizabeth Singer Rowe

8124. Bigold, Melanie. Elizabeth Rowe's fictional and familiar letters: exemplarity, Enthusiasm, and the production of posthumous meaning. BJECS (29:1) 2006, 1–14.

Nicholas Rowe

8125. Sennett, Herbert. Nicholas Rowe and the beginnings of feminism on the London stage. Bethesda, MD: Academica Press, 2005. pp. 217.

8126. Sowerby, Robin. The Augustan Lucan. TransLit (14:2) 2005, 148–78.

8127. Williams, William Proctor. Hamlet's pockets: problems with stage directions. *In* (pp. 192–9) **5577**.

Susanna Rowson

8128. Hibbard, Andrea L.; Parry, John T. Law, seduction, and the Sentimental heroine: the case of Amelia Norman. *See* **7801**.

8129. Rust, Marion. 'Daughters of America', *Slaves in Algiers*: activism and abnegation off Rowson's Barbary Coast. *In* (pp. 227–39) **6224**.

Benjamin Rush

8130. Madden, Etta. 'To make a figure': Benjamin Rush's rhetorical self-construction and scientific authorship. EAL (41:2) 2006, 241–72.

Sarah Scott

8131. Bannet, Eve Tavor. The Bluestocking sisters: women's patronage, Millenium Hall, and 'the visible providence of a Country'. ECL (30:1) 2006, 25–55.

8132. —— Lives, letters, and tales in Sarah Scott's *Journey through Every Stage of Life*. AJ (17) 2006, 233–59.

Anna Seward

8133. Johns-Putra, Adeline. Gendering Telemachus: Anna Seward and the epic rewriting of Fénelon's *Télémaque*. *In* (pp. 85–97) **3395**.

Anthony Ashley Cooper, Third Earl of Shaftesbury

8134. Branch, Lori. Rituals of spontaneity: sentiment and secularism from free prayer to Wordsworth. *See* **6607**.

8135. Carey, Daniel. Locke, Shaftesbury, and Hutcheson: contesting diversity in the Enlightenment and beyond. Cambridge; New York: CUP, 2006. pp. x, 260. (Ideas in context, 74.)

8136. Newberry, Paul. Emerging emotion theory: forgiveness and repetition. *In* (pp. 80–99) **1894**.

8137. Potolsky, Matthew. Hardy, Shaftesbury, and aesthetic education. *See* **10314**.

William Shenstone

8138. Hunt, John Dixon. Catalogue. *See* **15864**.

Richard Brinsley Sheridan

8139. Bhattacharya, Nandini. Slavery, colonialism, and connoisseurship: gender and eighteenth-century literary transnationalism. *See* **7670**.

8140. Galef, David. What's the word? NQ (53:3) 2006, 308–9. (Malapropism.)

8141. Heinowitz, Rebecca Cole. 'Thy world, Columbus, shall be free': British Romantic deviance and Spanish American revolution. *See* **7536**.

8142. Peters, Julie Stone. Theatricality, legalism, and the scenography of suffering: the trial of Warren Hastings and Richard Brinsley Sheridan's *Pizarro*. LawL (18:1) 2006, 15–45.

Christopher Smart

8143. Branch, Lori. Rituals of spontaneity: sentiment and secularism from free prayer to Wordsworth. *See* **6607**.

8144. Mounsey, Chris. Christopher Smart's late religious lyrics: building churches in the air. *In* (pp. 132–50) **1894**.

Adam Smith (1723–1790)

8145. McKenna, Stephen J. Adam Smith: the rhetoric of propriety. Albany: New York State UP, 2006. pp. 184. Rev. by John D. Schaeffer in Style (40:4) 2006, 368–74.

Alexander Smith (*fl.*1714–1726)

8146. Conway, Alison. Known fact or urban legend? Nell Gwynn's Oxford pronouncement. NQ (53:2) 2006, 209–10.

Charlotte Smith

8147. Harries, Elizabeth Wanning. 'Unfinish'd sentences': the Romantic fragment. *In* (pp. 360–75) **8357**.

8148. Joshua, Essaka. Charlotte Smith's *Desmond*: romance and the man of principle in the domestic and public spheres. ECN (5) 2006, 277–319.

8149. Knowles, Claire. Female poetic tradition in the Regency period: Susan Evance and the evolution of sentimentality. *See* **10119**.

8150. Rennhak, Katharina. Tropes of exile in the 1790s: English women writers and French emigrants. *See* **7633**.

8151. Wiley, Michael. The geography of displacement and replacement in Charlotte Smith's *The Emigrants*. ERR (17:1) 2006, 55–68.

Tobias Smollett

8152. Dryden, Robert G. 'Luck be a lady tonight': Jane Austen's precarious idealization of naval heroes in *Persuasion*. *See* **9012**.

8153. Gibson, William. Art and money in the writings of Tobias Smollett. Lewisburg, PA: Bucknell UP; London: Assoc. UPs, 2006. pp. 232. (Bucknell studies in eighteenth-century literature and culture.)

8154. —— Smelfungus's strumpet: Smollett's iconoclastic reading of the Medici Venus in *Travels through France and Italy*. 1650–1850 (13) 2006, 53–69.

8155. McMorran, Will. From Quixote to Caractacus: influence, intertextuality, and *Chitty Chitty Bang Bang*. *See* **12820**.

8156. Pym, Anthony. The translator as author: two Quixotes. TransLit (14:1) 2005, 71–81 (review-article).

8157. Rogers, Pat. 'How I want thee, humorous Hogart': the motif of the absent artist in Swift, Fielding and others. *See* **8212**.

8158. Shields, Juliet. Smollett's Scots and sodomites: British masculinity in *Roderick Random*. ECent (46:2) 2005, 175–88.

8159. Wallace, Tara Ghoshal. 'About savages and the awfulness of America': colonial corruptions in *Humphry Clinker*. ECF (18:2) 2006, 229–50.

Thomas Spence

8160. Rix, Robert W. The Crusonian alphabet: Thomas Spence's *Grand Repository of the English Language*. ELN (43:2) 2005, 69–92.

Mariana Starke (1762?–1838)

8161. Mellor, Anne K. Embodied cosmopolitanism and the British Romantic woman writer. ERR (17:3) 2006, 289–300.

Sir Richard Steele

8162. Horejsi, Nicole. 'A counterpart to the Ephesian matron': Steele's *Inkle and Yarico* and a feminist critique of the Classics. *See* **1117**.

8163. Mackie, Erin. Boys will be boys: masculinity, criminality, and the Restoration rake. *See* **6275**.

George Steevens (1736–1800)

8164. Sherbo, Arthur. *Introductorily* in *OED*. *See* **1574**.

Laurence Sterne

8165. Bobker, Danielle. Carriages, conversation, and *A Sentimental Journey*. StudECC (35) 2006, 243–66.

8166. Chico, Tita. Minute particulars: microscopy and eighteenth-century narrative. Mosaic (39:2) 2006, 143–61.

8167. Descargues, Madeleine. The obstetrics of *Tristram Shandy*. EA (59:4) 2006, 401–13.

8168. de Voogd, Peter; Neubauer, John (eds). The reception of Laurence Sterne in Europe. (Bibl. 2005, 9031.) Rev. by David Nokes in TLS, 3 Mar. 2006, 26; by Melvyn New in Scriblerian (38:2) 2006, 295–8.

8169. Doody, Margaret Anne. Hidden histories of decline: autopsy, George II's heart attack, and the dying condition in *Clarissa* and *Tristram Shandy*. *In* (pp. 3–31) **7255**.

8170. Folkenflik, Robert (introd. and notes). The life and opinions of Tristram Shandy, gentleman. New York: Modern Library, 2004. pp. xxxviii, 665. (Modern Library classics.) Rev. by W. B. Gerard in Scriblerian (38:2) 2006, 309–10.

8171. Gibson, William. Smelfungus's strumpet: Smollett's iconoclastic reading of the Medici Venus in *Travels through France and Italy*. *See* **8154**.

8172. Goodhue, Elizabeth K. When Yorick takes his tea; or, The commerce of consumptive passions in the case of Laurence Sterne. JEMCS (6:1) 2006, 51–83.

8173. Henke, Christoph. 'The old solid *English* standard of common sense' – British common sense discourse in the eighteenth century. *See* **8194**.

8174. Josipovici, Gabriel. The singer on the shore: essays, 1991–2004. *See* **6179**.

8175. Keymer, Thomas (ed.). Laurence Sterne's *Tristram Shandy*: a casebook. Oxford; New York: OUP, 2006. pp. x, 264. (Casebooks in criticism.)

8176. McMorran, Will. From Quixote to Caractacus: influence, intertextuality, and *Chitty Chitty Bang Bang*. *See* **12820**.

8177. Nokes, David. Continental views. TLS, 3 Mar. 2006, 26 (review-article).

8178. Patrick, Duncan. Unorthodox theology in two short works by Sterne. RES (56:223) 2005, 49–58.

8179. Pierce, David. Joyce and company. *See* **16752**.

8180. Porton, Richard. In praise of folly: an interview with Michael Winterbottom. *See* **19692**.

8181. STERNBERG, MEIR. Telling in time (III): chronology, estrangement, and stories of literary history. PT (27:1) 2006, 125–235.

8182. TOKER, LEONA. Narrative enthymeme: the examples of Laurence Sterne and James Joyce. PartA (4:2) 2006, 163–74.

8183. VITA, CARLO. Sterne e un *ready made* del Settecento: un percorso di lettura. LProv (126/127) 2006, 29–47.

Jonathan Swift

8184. BENGELS, BARBARA. Swift's *A Modest Proposal*. Exp (65:1) 2006, 13–15.

8185. BLACKWELL, MARK. The people things make: Locke's *Essay Concerning Human Understanding* and the properties of the self. StudECC (35) 2006, 77–94.

8186. CRITCHLEY, SIMON. *Satura resartus*: living in the woods with bears. LawL (17:3) 2005, 433–41.

8187. DEGATEGNO, PAUL J.; STUBBLEFIELD, R. JAY. Critical companion to Jonathan Swift: a literary reference to his life and works. New York: Facts on File, 2006. pp. vi, 474. (Facts on File library of world literature.)

8188. DÜRING, MICHAEL. From gunpowder to Krakatit: notes on a Swiftian motif in Karel Čapek's novel *Krakatit: an Atomic Phantasy*. SwSt (21) 2006, 121–4.

8189. ELLISON, KATHERINE E. Fatal news: reading and information overload in early eighteenth-century literature. *See* **6578**.

8190. FARRELL, JOHN. Paranoia and modernity: Cervantes to Rousseau. Ithaca, NY; London: Cornell UP, 2006. pp. 341.

8191. FRANK, STEVEN. Upside-down chairs: a celebration of satire. Writing (29:2) 2006, 18–19.

8192. GLOVER, SUSAN PATERSON. Engendering legitimacy: law, property, and early eighteenth-century fiction. *See* **7706**.

8193. HAWES, CLEMENT (ed.). *Gulliver's Travels* and other writings: complete text with introduction, historical context, critical essays. With a note on the texts by Robert J. Griffin. Boston, MA: Houghton Mifflin, 2004. pp. xi, 550. (New Riverside eds.) Rev. by Kenneth Craven in Scriblerian (38:2) 2006, 303–5.

8194. HENKE, CHRISTOPH. 'The old solid *English* standard of common sense' – British common sense discourse in the eighteenth century. BELL (ns 4) 2006, 51–65.

8195. INGRAM, ALLAN; FAUBERT, MICHELLE. Cultural constructions of madness in eighteenth-century writing: representing the insane. *See* **7280**.

8196. JOHNSON, CHRISTOPHER D. The nature of fallen things: another look at Lucretius and *A Tale of a Tub*. SwSt (21) 2006, 39–47.

8197. JUST, MELANIE MARIA (ed.). Jonathan Swift's *On Poetry – a Rapsody*: a critical edition, with a historical introduction and commentary. New York; Frankfurt: Lang, 2004. pp. 315. (Münster monographs on English literature, 29.) Rev. by Andrew Carpenter in ECI (20) 2005, 188–90; by William Kupersmith in Scriblerian (38:2) 2006, 290–2.

8198. KARIAN, STEPHEN. Swift, Arbuckle, and *The Beasts' Confession to the Priest*. SwSt (21) 2006, 87–106.

8199. Keithley, Walter Hank. Swift reading Bacon reading Apollonius. SwSt (21) 2006, 118–20.

8200. Kelly, Ann Cline. Written in stone: Swift's use of St Patrick's Cathedral as a text. SwSt (21) 2006, 107–17.

8201. Levin, Richard. *A tale of a tub. See* **1603**.

8202. Lund, Roger D. (ed.). Jonathan Swift's *Gulliver's Travels*: a sourcebook. London; New York: Routledge, 2006. pp. xvii, 197. (Routledge guides to literature.)

8203. Maner, Martin. The authorship of Jonathan Swift's *A Tale of a Tub* – once more. SwSt (21) 2006, 27–38.

8204. Monsman, Gerald. Satiric models for Charles Lamb's *A Dissertation upon Roast Pig. See* **10703**.

8205. Nokes, David. Continental views. *See* **8177**.

8206. Panagopoulos, Nic. Gulliver and the horse: an enquiry into equine ethics. SwSt (21) 2006, 56–75.

8207. Percival, W. Keith. Some aspects of Jonathan Swift's perspective on language. 1650–1850 (11) 2005, 47–9.

8208. Rabb, Melinda. The secret memoirs of Lemuel Gulliver: satire, secrecy, and Swift. ELH (73:2) 2006, 325–54.

8209. Real, Hermann J. Swift's non-reading. *In* (pp. 124–38) **648**.

8210. —— (ed.). The reception of Jonathan Swift in Europe. (Bibl. 2005, 9084.) Rev. by David Nokes in TLS, 3 Mar. 2006, 26; by Adam Rounce in SHARP (15:2/3) 2006, 22.

8211. Robinson, Elaine L. Gulliver as slave trader: racism reviled by Jonathan Swift. Jefferson, NC; London: McFarland, 2006. pp. ix, 241.

8212. Rogers, Pat. 'How I want thee, humorous Hogart': the motif of the absent artist in Swift, Fielding and others. PLL (42:1) 2006, 25–45.

8213. Steele, Peter. Zones of the imagination. *See* **17250**.

8214. Valentini, Maria. Jonathan Swift e la filosofia di Francis Bacon. *In* (pp. 31–47) **3341**.

8215. Ward, James. Which crisis? The politics of distress in *A Modest Proposal*. SwSt (21) 2006, 76–86.

8216. Weise, Wendy S. Seeing and the difference it makes: ocularity, gender, and space in Swift's and Montagu's 'Dressing Room' satires. WS (35:8) 2006, 707–38.

8217. Woolley, David. The textual history of *A Tale of a Tub*. SwSt (21) 2006, 7–26.

8218. Woolley, James. Poor John Harding and Mad Tom: *Harding's Resurrection* (1724). *In* (pp. 102–21) **648**.

8219. Young, Heather. Satire as a virus: generic inhabitation and transformation in Swift's *Tale*. SwSt (21) 2006, 48–55.

Thomas Swift (1664 or 5–1752)

8220. Maner, Martin. The authorship of Jonathan Swift's *A Tale of a Tub* – once more. *See* **8203**.

John Thelwall ('John Beaufort') (1764–1834)

8221. Felsenstein, Frank. Liberty men. John Thelwall and the end of slavery. TLS, 8 Sept. 2006, 12.

Timothy Thomas (1693 or 4–1751)

8222. Wright, Gillian. Epictetus in eighteenth-century Wales: Timothy Thomas' manuscript translation of the *Enchiridion*. TransLit (14:1) 2005, 45–63.

James Thomson (1700–1748)

8223. Hillyard, Brian. David Steuart and Giambattista Bodoni: on the fringes of the British book trade. *In* (pp. 113–25) **746**.

8224. Stevenson, Louise L. The transatlantic travels of James Thomson's *The Seasons* and its baggage of material culture, 1730–1870. PAAS (116:1) 2006, 121–65.

John Toland (1670–1722)

8225. Stoll, Abraham. Discontinuous wound: Milton and Deism. *See* **7070**.

8226. Wigelsworth, Jeffrey R. John Toland's economic imperative to print and financing the Harrington edition: a brief assessment. JPHS (ns 9) 2006, 5–12.

Jacob Tonson the Elder (1656–1736)

8227. Pellicer, Juan Christian. Harleian georgic from Tonson's press: the publication of John Philips's *Cyder*, 29 January 1708. *See* **7102**.

John Horne Tooke

8228. Cooper, Andrew R. Women's poetry, the 1830s, and monumental problems in the history of language theory. *See* **8766**.

8229. Wilson, Ross. Coleridge and the life of language. *See* **9565**.

Melesina (Chenevix) St George Trench (1768–1827)

8230. Kittredge, Katharine. 'It spoke directly to the heart': discovering the mourning journal of Melesina Trench. TSWL (25:2) 2006, 335–45.

Horace Walpole

8231. Chaplin, Sue. 'Written in the black letter': the gothic and/in the rule of law. LawL (17:1) 2005, 47–68.

8232. Chiu, Frances A. Faulty towers: reform, Radicalism and the gothic castle, 1760–1800. RomNet (44) 2006.

8233. Haggerty, George. Horace Walpole's epistolary friendships. BJECS (29:2) 2006, 201–18.

8234. Haggerty, George E. Queering Horace Walpole. SELit (46:3) 2006, 543–62.

8235. Jung, Sandro. A possible source for Horace Walpole's *Otranto*. ANQ (19:2) 2006, 31–3.

8236. Mandell, Laura. Producing hate in 'private' letters: Horace Walpole, Mary Hays. ERR (17:2) 2006, 169–77.

8237. —— (ed.). *The Castle of Otranto* and *The Man of Feeling*. London; New York: Pearson Longman, 2006. pp. xxvi, 292. (Longman cultural eds.)

William Warburton

8238. ROUNCE, ADAM. 'A clamour too loud to be distinct': William Warburton's literary squabbles. AJ (16) 2005, 199–217.

Mercy Otis Warren

8239. DAVIES, KATE. Revolutionary correspondence: reading Catharine Macaulay and Mercy Otis Warren. *See* **7982**.

8240. SHAFFER, JASON. Making 'an excellent die': death, mourning, and patriotism in the propaganda plays of the American Revolution. *See* **7606**.

Thomas Warton the Younger (1728–1790)

8241. CONNELL, PHILIP. British identities and the politics of ancient poetry in later eighteenth-century England. *See* **8037**.

Isaac Watts

8242. SHOPTAW, JOHN. Listening to Dickinson. *See* **9893**.

John Wesley

8243. JOLING-VAN DER SAR, GERDA J. The controversy between William Law and John Wesley. EngS (87:4) 2006, 442–65.

8244. ROGAL, SAMUEL J. John Wesley's book stock and the Arminian magazine catalogue of 1789. Lewiston, NY; Lampeter: Mellen Press, 2006. pp. 177.

The Wesleys

8245. WATSON, J. R. The presentation of holiness and the concept of Christian perfection in the sermons and hymns of the Wesleys, 1730–1780. *In* (pp. 81–94) **3415**.

Phillis Wheatley

8246. BHATTACHARYA, NANDINI. Slavery, colonialism, and connoisseurship: gender and eighteenth-century literary transnationalism. *See* **7670**.

8247. ERKKILÄ, BETSY. Phillis Wheatley and the Black American Revolution. *In* (pp. 161–82) **6224**.

8248. HARRELL, WILLIE J., JR. A call to consciousness and action: mapping the African American jeremiad. CRAS (36:2) 2006, 149–80.

8249. WILLIS, PATRICIA C. Phillis Wheatley, George Whitefield, and the Countess of Huntingdon in the Beinecke Library. YLG (80:3/4) 2006, 161–76.

George Whitefield (1714–1770)

8250. WILLIS, PATRICIA C. Phillis Wheatley, George Whitefield, and the Countess of Huntingdon in the Beinecke Library. *See* **8249**.

Laurence Whyte (*c*.1683–1753)

8251. HUNTER, DAVID. Inviting Handel to Ireland: Laurence Whyte and the challenge of poetic evidence. ECI (20) 2005, 156–68.

John Wilkes

8252. SAINSBURY, JOHN. John Wilkes: the lives of a libertine. Aldershot; Burlington, VT: Ashgate, 2006. pp. xxiv, 282. Rev. by David Nokes in TLS, 24 Nov. 2006, 29.

Edward Williams ('Iolo Morganwg') (1746–1826)

8253. Jenkins, Geraint H. (ed.). A rattleskull genius: the many faces of Iolo Morganwg. Cardiff: UP of Wales, 2005. pp. xviii, 515. (Iolo Morganwg and the Romantic tradition in Wales.) Rev. by Richard Gravil in Romanticism (12:1) 2006, 65–7.

Anne Finch, Countess of Winchilsea

8254. Emig, Rainer. Competing melancholies: (en-)gendering discourses of selfhood in early modern English literature. *See* **7206**.

8255. Jordan, Nicolle. 'Where Power is absolute': Royalist politics and the improved landscape in a poem by Anne Finch, Countess of Winchilsea. ECent (46:3) 2005, 255–75.

Mary Wollstonecraft

8256. Acosta, Ana M. Reading Genesis in the long eighteenth century: from Milton to Mary Shelley. *See* **6961**.

8257. Cañadas, Ivan. The influence of Ben Jonson's *Volpone* on Mary Wollstonecraft's *Maria; or, The Wrongs of Woman*. ANQ (19:3) 2006, 6–10.

8258. Comitini, Patricia. Vocational philanthropy and British women's writing, 1790–1810: Wollstonecraft, More, Edgeworth, Wordsworth. (Bibl. 2005, 9134.) Rev. by Amy Harris in ECS (40:1) 2006, 135–41.

8259. Franklin, Caroline. Mary Wollstonecraft: a literary life. (Bibl. 2004, 9362.) Rev. by Julian North in BJ (33:1) 2005, 65–7; by Fiona Price in MLR (101:3) 2006, 828–9.

8260. Goggin, Gerard. Editing Minervas: William Godwin's liminal maneuvers in Mary Wollstonecraft's *Wrongs of Woman*. *In* (pp. 81–99) **3405**.

8261. Gordon, Lyndall. Mary Wollstonecraft: a new genus. London; Boston, MA: Little, Brown, 2005. pp. x, 562, (plates) 16. Rev. by Esther Schor in TLS, 11 Feb. 2005, 4–5.

8262. —— Vindication: a life of Mary Wollstonecraft. (Bibl. 2005, 9137.) Rev. by Alan Helms in GLRW (13:5) 2006, 37–8.

8263. Hindle, Maurice. Victim of romance: the life and death of Fanny Godwin. WWr (13:3) 2006, 331–47.

8264. Holmes, Richard (ed.). Godwin on Wollstonecraft: memoirs of the author of *The Rights of Woman*. *See* **7836**.

8265. Howard, Carol. Wollstonecraft's thoughts on slavery and corruption. ECent (45:1) 2004, 61–86.

8266. Joshua, Essaka. Charlotte Smith's *Desmond*: romance and the man of principle in the domestic and public spheres. *See* **8148**.

8267. Jump, Harriet Devine. 'One cry for justice': Virginia Woolf reads Mary Wollstonecraft. *In* (pp. 41–60) **13735**.

8268. Khalip, Jacques. A disappearance in the world: Wollstonecraft and melancholy skepticism. Criticism (47:1) 2005, 85–106.

8269. Richards, Cynthia D. Romancing the sublime: why Mary Wollstonecraft fell in love with that cad, Gilbert Imlay. TSWL (25:1) 2006, 71–91.

8270. SWIFT, SIMON. Mary Wollstonecraft and the 'reserve of reason'. SR (45:1) 2006, 3–24.

8271. —— Romanticism, literature and philosophy: expressive rationality in Rousseau, Kant, Wollstonecraft and contemporary theory. London; New York: Continuum, 2006. pp. 181. (Continuum literary studies.)

8272. TAYLOR, BARBARA. Feminists *versus* gallants: manners and morals in Enlightenment Britain. Representations (87) 2004, 125–48.

8273. TODD, JANET. Suicide and biography. CompCrit (25) 2006, 57–66.

8274. VAN KLEECK, JUSTIN. 'Tenderness & love not uninspired': Blake's revision of Sentimentalism in *The Four Zoas*. *See* **7589**.

8275. WEISS, DEBORAH. Suffering, sentiment, and civilization: pain and politics in Mary Wollstonecraft's *Short Residence*. SR (45:2) 2006, 199–221.

Ann Yearsley

8276. LANDRY, DONNA. Georgic ecology. *In* (pp. 253–66) **9141**.

Arthur Young

8277. REILLY, TERRY. Arthur Young's *Travels in France*: historicity and the use of literary forms. *In* (pp. 122–36) **7490**.

NINETEENTH CENTURY

GENERAL

8278. Abrams, Robert E. Landscape and ideology in American renaissance literature: topographies of skepticism. (Bibl. 2005, 9159.) Rev. by James McIntosh in MLQ (66:4) 2005, 559–61; by David Greenham in JAStud (39:3) 2005, 545–6.

8279. Alexander, Christine; McMaster, Juliet (eds). The child writer from Austen to Woolf. (Bibl. 2005, 9164.) Rev. by Robert Barnard in BrSt (31:1) 2006, 87–8; by Valerie Sanders in JVC (11:2) 2006, 381–5; by Patsy Stoneman in RES (57:230) 2006, 393–5; by Lisa Brocklebank in VicR (32:1) 2006, 86–8; by Judith Plotz in VS (49:1) 2006, 118–20.

8280. Allen, John. Homelessness in American literature: romanticism, realism, and testimony. London; New York: Routledge, 2004. pp. vii, 195. (American popular literature and culture.)

8281. Ambrosini, Richard; Dury, Richard (eds). Robert Louis Stevenson: writer of boundaries. *See* **11272**.

8282. Arac, Jonathan. The emergence of American literary narrative, 1820–1860. (Bibl. 2005, 9169.) Rev. by John McWilliams in NineL (61:2) 2006, 249–52.

8283. Armstrong, Jeannette. Keynote address: the aesthetic qualities of aboriginal writing. StudCanL (31:1) 2006, 20–30.

8284. Atwood, Margaret. Moving targets: selected critical prose, 1982–2004. *See* **11751**.

8285. Avallone, Charlene. Women reading Melville / Melville reading women. *In* (pp. 41–59) **10897**.

8286. Bainbridge, Simon. Napoleon and European Romanticism. *In* (pp. 450–66) **8357**.

8287. Baker, Anne. Heartless immensity: literature, culture, and geography in antebellum America. Ann Arbor: Michigan UP, 2006. pp. 173.

8288. Barolini, Helen. Their other side: six American women and the lure of Italy. New York: Fordham UP, 2006. pp. xxix, 309.

8289. Beaumont, Matthew. Cacotopianism, the Paris Commune, and England's anti-Communist imaginary, 1870–1900. ELH (73:2) 2006, 465–87.

8290. Behrendt, Stephen C. Regency women writers, the archives, and the task(s). KSJ (55) 2006, 48–53.

8291. Belluscio, Steven J. To be suddenly White: literary realism and racial passing. Columbia; London: Missouri UP, 2006. pp. xi, 288.

8292. Bennett, Michael. Democratic discourses: the radical Abolition movement and antebellum American literature. (Bibl. 2005, 9187.) Rev. by Australia Tarver in ColLit (33:3) 2006, 198–203.

8293. Bergland, Renée. The Native American nineteenth century: rewriting the American renaissance. ESQ (52:1/2) 2006, 141–54.

8294. Bigazzi, Carlo (ed.). Studi Irlandesi. Rome: Yorick, 2004. pp. 160. Rev. by Simona Vannini in EtIr (30:1) 2005, 225–6.

8295. Birch, Dinah. Eager to please: make sure to read the children – but sceptically. *See* **7223**.

8296. Bivona, Dan; Henkle, Roger B. The imagination of class: masculinity and the Victorian urban poor. Columbus: Ohio State UP, 2006. pp. xvi, 208.

8297. Blair, Jennifer, *et al.* (eds). ReCalling early Canada: reading the political in literary and cultural production. (Bibl. 2005, 9191.) Rev. by George Melnyk in CHR (87:3) 2006, 530–1; by Heather Milne in Topia (15) 2006, 142–5.

8298. Boardman, Kay; Jones, Shirley (eds). Popular Victorian women writers. Manchester; New York: Manchester UP, 2004. pp. 245. Rev. by Nickianne Moody in WWr (13:2) 2006, 321–6.

8299. Bohata, Kirsti. Postcolonialism revisited. *See* **11780**.

8300. Boone, Troy. Youth of darkest England: working-class children at the heart of Victorian empire. (Bibl. 2005, 9194.) Rev. by Elizabeth Gargano in CLAQ (31:1) 2006, 99–102.

8301. Boudreau, Kristin. The spectacle of death: populist literary responses to American capital cases. Amherst, NY: Prometheus, 2006. pp. 292.

8302. Boyd, Anne E. Writing for immortality: women and the emergence of high literary culture in America. (Bibl. 2005, 9197.) Rev. by Renée Bergland in AL (77:4) 2005, 850–2; by Annamaria Formichella Elsden in JMMLA (38:2) 2005, 132–4; by Claire Brock in JAStud (40:1) 2006, 164–5.

8303. Braida, Antonella. Dante and the Romantics. Basingstoke; New York: Palgrave Macmillan, 2004. pp. x, 241. Rev. by Jeremy Tambling in YES (36:2) 2006, 270–1.

8304. Branson, Susan. Gendered strategies for success in the early nineteenth-century literary marketplace: Mary Carr and the *Ladies' Tea Tray*. *See* **1064**.

8305. Brickhouse, Anna. Transamerican literary relations and the nineteenth-century public sphere. (Bibl. 2005, 9201.) Rev. by Claudia Sadowski-Smith in AL (78:3) 2006, 624–7; by Ashley Hales in JAStud (40:1) 2006, 167.

8306. Browner, Stephanie P. Profound science and elegant literature: imagining doctors in nineteenth-century America. Philadelphia: Pennsylvania UP, 2005. pp. 304. Rev. by Linda Simon in LitMed (25:1) 2006, 175–8; by Lisa A. Long in JAH (93:1) 2006, 225–6; by Bernice L. Hausman in AL (78:3) 2006, 659–62; by James Emmett Ryan in SAtlR (71:1) 2006, 168–73.

8307. Bryden, Inga. Reinventing King Arthur: the Arthurian legends in Victorian culture. (Bibl. 2005, 9206.) Rev. by Asa Briggs in LitH (15:2) 2006, 79; by Linda K. Hughes in VS (48:3) 2006, 559–60.

8308. Buell, Lawrence. Religion and the environmental imagination in American literature. *In* (pp. 216–38) **8429**.

8309. Burlingham, Russell; Billis, Roger (eds). Reformed characters: the Reform Club in history and literature: an anthology with commentary. Foreword by Edward Pearce. London: Reform Club, 2005. pp. xvi, 279, (plates) 16. Rev. by Jonathan Parry in TLS, 7 July 2006, 33.

8310. Carino, Peter. Why baseball has a literature: family, community, home. IE (28:1) 2005, 7–20.

8311. Carroll, Joseph. Literary Darwinism: evolution, human nature, and literature. (Bibl. 2005, 9212.) Rev. by Jonathan Smith in VS (48:3) 2006, 573–4.
8312. Carruth, Mary C. (ed.). Feminist interventions in Early American Studies. *See* **6224**.
8313. Cass, Jeffrey. Interrogating Orientalism: theories and practices. *In* (pp. 25–45) **8395**.
8314. Castronovo, Russ. American literature *internationale*. ESQ (50:1–3) 2004, 59–93.
8315. Cavaliero, Roderick. *Italia Romantica*: English Romantics and Italian freedom. (Bibl. 2005, 9215.) Rev. by Peter Cochran and Anne Fleming in BJ (34:1) 2006, 85–90.
8316. Chai, Leon. Romantic theory: forms of reflexivity in the Revolutionary era. Baltimore, MD; London: Johns Hopkins UP, 2006. pp. xx, 283.
8317. Chamberlin, J. Edward. The worthy and the worthless: books and people in late Victorian England. *See* **11597**.
8318. Chandler, James; Gilmartin, Kevin (eds). Romantic metropolis: the urban scene of British culture, 1780–1840. (Bibl. 2005, 9217.) Rev. by Gregory Dart in TLS, 17 Feb. 2006, 35; by Ashley Chantler in BJ (34:2) 2006, 192–4.
8319. Chapman, Alison; Stabler, Jane. Introduction. *In* (pp. 1–14) **8320**.
8320. —— —— (eds). Unfolding the South: nineteenth-century British women writers and artists in Italy. Manchester; New York: Manchester UP, 2003. pp. ix, 246. Rev. by Nanora Sweet in NineL (58:4) 2004, 555–9; by Maria Schoina in WordsC (36:4) 2005, 168–71; by Antonella Braida in MLR (100:1) 2005, 276–7; by Pauline Nestor in VS (48:2) 2006, 348–50.
8321. Chialant, Maria Teresa (ed.). Viaggio e letteratura. *See* **11824**.
8322. Cleary, Joe; Connolly, Claire (eds). The Cambridge companion to modern Irish culture. *See* **11829**.
8323. Cleere, Eileen. Avuncularism: capitalism, patriarchy, and nineteenth-century English culture. (Bibl. 2004, 10005.) Rev. by Tara McGann in StudN (38:3) 2006, 372–4; by Eileen Gillooly in VS (48:3) 2006, 547–9.
8324. Coates, Peter. Eastenders go west: English sparrows, immigrants, and the nature of fear. *See* **14837**.
8325. Cognard-Black, Jennifer; Walls, Elizabeth MacLeod (eds). Kindred hands: letters on writing by British and American women authors, 1865–1935. Iowa City: Iowa UP, 2006. pp. vi, 247. Rev. by Lucy Carlyle in TLS, 4 Aug. 2006, 26.
8326. Collier, Patrick. Modernism on Fleet Street. *See* **1074**.
8327. Cullingford, Elizabeth Butler. 'Our nuns are *not* a nation': politicizing the convent in Irish literature and film. EI (41:1/2) 2006, 9–39.
8328. Daly, Nicholas. Literature, technology, and modernity, 1860–2000. (Bibl. 2005, 9228.) Rev. by Christoph Lindner in Eng (54:210) 2005, 244–8; by John Xiros Cooper in Mod/Mod (13:1) 2006, 202–4; by John Marx in Novel (39:2) 2006, 291–4; by Jean-Pierre Naugrette in EA (59:1) 2006, 118–19.
8329. Danahay, Martin A. Gender at work in Victorian culture: literature, art and masculinity. (Bibl. 2005, 9230.) Rev. in GissJ (42:1) 2006, 35–7; by Chris

Louttit in DickQ (23:3) 2006, 199–202; by Annie Escuret in CVE (63) 2006, 502–3; by Laurent Bury in EA (59:4) 2006, 487–8.

8330. DAVIS, LEITH; DUNCAN, IAN; SORENSEN, JANET (eds). Scotland and the borders of Romanticism. (Bibl. 2005, 9231.) Rev. by Jonathan V. Farina in WordsC (36:4) 2005, 165–6.

8331. DAWSON, GOWAN. Literature and science under the microscope. JVC (11:2) 2006, 301–15.

8332. DAWSON, MELANIE. Laboring to play: home entertainment and the spectacle of middle-class cultural life, 1850–1920. Tuscaloosa; London: Alabama UP, 2005. pp. x, 257. Rev. by Lori Merish in Legacy (23:2) 2006, 210–12.

8333. DELANO, STERLING F. Brook Farm: the dark side of utopia. (Bibl. 2005, 9233.) Rev. by Carol Farley Kessler in AL (77:4) 2005, 852–4.

8334. DEMOOR, MARYSA (ed.). Marketing the author: authorial personae, narrative selves, and self-fashioning, 1880–1930. (Bibl. 2005, 9235.) Rev. by Nickianne Moody in WWr (13:2) 2006, 321–6.

8335. DENTITH, SIMON. Epic and empire in nineteenth-century Britain. Cambridge; New York: CUP, 2006. pp. vii, 245. (Cambridge studies in nineteenth-century literature and culture, 52.)

8336. DESPOTOPOULOU, ANNA. '*La maladie fin de siècle*': the symbols of Aestheticism and the aesthetics of Symbolism. Dia-keimena (7) 2005, 267–84.

8337. DIMOCK, WAI CHEE. Through other continents: American literature across deep time. Princeton, NJ; Oxford: Princeton UP, 2006. pp. 243.

8338. DIX, ANDREW; TAYLOR, JONATHAN (eds). Figures of heresy: radical theology in English and American writing, 1800–2000. Brighton; Portland, OR: Sussex Academic Press, 2005. pp. xii, 212.

8339. DONOGHUE, DENIS. The American classics: a personal essay. (Bibl. 2005, 9239.) Rev. by Joseph M. Hassett in ILS (26:1) 2006, 27.

8340. DONOVAN, STEPHEN. Stevenson and popular entertainment. *In* (pp. 70–82) **11272**.

8341. DUCILLE, ANN. On canons: anxious history and the rise of Black feminist literary studies. *In* (pp. 29–52) **14277**.

8342. EASLEY, ALEXIS. First person anonymous: women writers and Victorian print media, 1830–70. (Bibl. 2004, 9442.) Rev. by Emma Mason in TLS, 20 Jan. 2006, 29; by Janice Schroeder in VPR (39:1) 2006, 85–6.

8343. EBBATSON, ROGER. Heidegger's bicycle: interfering with Victorian texts. Brighton; Portland, OR: Sussex Academic Press, 2006. pp. viii, 172. (Critical inventions.)

8344. —— An imaginary England: nation, landscape and literature, 1840–1920. Ed. by Ann Donahue. (Bibl. 2005, 9241.) Rev. by Valerie Purton in TRB (8:5) 2006, 398–401.

8345. EDWARDS, GAVIN. Narrative order, 1789–1819: life and story in an age of revolution. *See* **7245**.

8346. EDWARDS, JUSTIN D. Gothic Canada: reading the spectre of a national literature. (Bibl. 2005, 9242.) Rev. by Marlene Goldman in CanL (191) 2006, 114–15.

8347. Elliott, Emory (introd.). A forum on Joanna Brooks, *American Lazarus: Religion and the Rise of African American and Native American Literatures*. With a response by Joanna Brooks. ELN (44:1) 2006, 259–82.

8348. Evans, Brad. Before cultures: the ethnographic imagination in American literature, 1865–1920. (Bibl. 2005, 9249.) Rev. by Ralph E. Rodriguez in Novel (39:2) 2006, 284–7; by Susan Hegeman in AnthQ (79:1) 2006, 183–5.

8349. Faflak, Joel; Wright, Julia M. (eds). Nervous reactions: Victorian recollections of Romanticism. (Bibl. 2004, 9449.) Rev. by Mark Sandy in BJ (33:1) 2005, 68–70; by Robert Morrison in VPR (39:2) 2006, 183–4; by Kenneth Daley in VS (48:3) 2006, 551–3.

8350. Fantina, Richard (ed.). Straight writ queer: non-normative expressions of heterosexuality in literature. Foreword by Calvin Thomas. *See* **11883**.

8351. Fazzini, Marco (ed.). Resisting alterities: Wilson Harris and other avatars of otherness. *See* **16284**.

8352. Feldman, Paula R. Women, literary annuals, and the evidence of inscriptions. KSJ (55) 2006, 54–62.

8353. —— (introd.). *The Keepsake* for 1829. *See* **1096**.

8354. Felluga, Dino Franco. The Victorian archive and the disappearance of the book. *See* **994**.

8355. Felton, R. Todd. A journey into the Transcendentalists' New England. Berkeley, CA: Roaring Forties Press, 2006. pp. 179. (ArtPlace.)

8356. Ferber, Michael. The Romantic system of the arts. *In* (pp. 552–70) **8357**.

8357. —— (ed.). A companion to European Romanticism. Oxford; Malden, MA: Blackwell, 2005. pp. xiii, 586. (Blackwell companions to literature and culture, 38.) Rev. by Diane Long Hoeveler in ERR (17:4) 2006, 508–11.

8358. Fisher, Judith L. 'In the present famine of anything substantial': *Fraser's* 'portraits' and the construction of literary celebrity; or, 'Personality, personality is the appetite of the age.' *See* **1099**.

8359. Floyd, Janet; Forster, Laurel (eds). The recipe reader: narrative, contexts, traditions. (Bibl. 2005, 9257.) Rev. by Teresa Mangum in TSWL (25:1) 2006, 172–6.

8360. Floyd, Phylis. Orientalism *redux*. NCS (19) 2005, 151–8.

8361. Flynn, Philip. Beginning *Blackwood's*: the right mix of *dulce* and *ùtile*. *See* **1101**.

8362. —— Blackwood's *Maga*, Lockhart's *Peter's Letters*, and the politics of publishing. *See* **1102**.

8363. Foster, Frances Smith. Creative collaboration: as African American as sweet potato pie. *In* (pp. 17–33) **8435**.

8364. —— A narrative of the interesting origins and (somewhat) surprising developments of African American print culture. *See* **711**.

8365. France, Peter; Haynes, Kenneth (eds). The Oxford history of literary translation: vol. 4, 1790–1900. *See* **7252**.

8366. Frawley, Maria H. Invalidism and identity in nineteenth-century Britain. (Bibl. 2005, 9259.) Rev. by Lennard J. Davis in VS (48:2) 2006, 362–4.

8367. Fulford, Tim. Romantic Indians and their inventors. ERR (17:2) 2006, 139–50.

8368. —— Romantic Indians: Native Americans, British literature, and transatlantic culture, 1765–1830. *See* **7253**.

8369. —— Lee, Debbie; Kitson, Peter J. Literature, science and exploration in the Romantic era: bodies of knowledge. (Bibl. 2005, 9262.) Rev. by Timothy Morton in Romanticism (11:2) 2005, 256–8; by Trevor H. Levere in WordsC (36:4) 2005, 172–4; by Robert Fraser in MLR (101:3) 2006, 831–2; by Robert Mitchell in KSJ (55) 2006, 275–8.

8370. Gálik, Marián (ed.). *Fin de siècle* (Decadence) in Sino-Western literary confrontation: selected papers read at the international symposium, Vienna University, June 9, 1999. Bratislava: Inst. of Oriental and African Studies, Slovak Academy of Sciences, 2005. pp. 151.

8371. Gardner, Sarah E. Blood & irony: Southern White women's narratives of the Civil War, 1861–1937. (Bibl. 2005, 9265.) Rev. by Laura F. Edwards in NCHR (82:1) 2005, 113–14; by Paul Christian Jones in SoS (ns 12:3/4) 2005, 167–70; by Lauren Coats in AL (78:3) 2006, 617–19.

8372. Gerzina, Gretchen Holbrook (ed.). Black Victorians / Black Victoriana. (Bibl. 2004, 9461.) Rev. by Keith Hughes in MLR (101:1) 2006, 230–1.

8373. Gezari, Janet. Sandra M. Gilbert and Susan Gubar's *The Madwoman in the Attic*. EC (56:3) 2006, 264–79. (New impressions, 12.) (*Discusses* bibl. 1979, 6437.)

8374. Gibson, Colin; Marr, Lisa (eds). New windows on a woman's world: essays for Jocelyn Harris: vol. 2. Dunedin: English Dept, Univ. of Otago, 2005. pp. vii, 559. (Otago studies in English, 9.)

8375. Gilbert, Sandra M. Death's door: modern dying and the ways we grieve. *See* **11908**.

8376. Gilmore, Michael T. A plot against America: free speech and the American renaissance. Raritan (26:2) 2006, 90–113.

8377. Gilroy, Amanda (ed.). Green and pleasant land: English culture and the Romantic countryside. Louvain; Dudley, MA: Peeters, 2004. pp. xvi, 201. (Groningen studies in cultural change, 8.)

8378. González, Gilbert G. Culture of empire: American writers, Mexico, and Mexican immigrants, 1880–1930. (Bibl. 2005, 9272.) Rev. by Manuel G. Gonzales in CH (83:2) 2005, 72–3; by Eric V. Meeks in PacHR (75:3) 2006, 512–14.

8379. Greven, David. Men beyond desire: manhood, sex, and violation in American literature. (Bibl. 2005, 9277.) Rev. by Samuel Chase Coale in NHR (32:2) 2006, 42–5.

8380. Haggerty, George E. Queer gothic. *See* **11920**.

8381. Hall, Wade (ed.). The Kentucky anthology: two hundred years of writing in the Bluegrass State. *See* **7263**.

8382. Hammond, Mary. Reading, publishing, and the formation of literary taste in England, 1880 1914. Aldershot; Burlington, VT: Ashgate, 2006. pp. xii, 209. (Nineteenth century.)

8383. Hanson, Gillian Mary. Riverbank and seashore in nineteenth- and twentieth-century British literature. Jefferson, NC; London: McFarland, 2006. pp. 180.

8384. Harrell, Willie J., Jr. A call to consciousness and action: mapping the African American jeremiad. *See* **8248**.

8385. Harris, Katherine D. Feminizing the textual body: female readers consuming the literary annual. *See* **1113**.

8386. Harris, Sharon M. Feminist theories and Early American Studies. *In* (pp. 3–10) **6224**.

8387. Harris, W. C. *E pluribus unum*: nineteenth-century American literature and the Constitutional paradox. (Bibl. 2005, 9285.) Rev. by John Shelton Lawrence in JAC (29:2) 2006, 235–8.

8388. Haslam, Jason; Wright, Julia M. (eds). Captivating subjects: writing confinement, citizenship, and nationhood in the nineteenth century. Toronto; Buffalo, NY; London: Toronto UP, 2005. pp. viii, 270. Rev. by Sean Grass in VS (48:2) 2006, 364–6.

8389. Helsinger, Elizabeth. Recent studies in the nineteenth century. SELit (46:4) 2006, 901–56.

8390. Hetherington, Carol; Petersson, Irmtraud (comps). Annual bibliography of studies in Australian literature: 2005. ALS (22:3) 2006, 375–89.

8391. Hewitt, Elizabeth. Correspondence and American literature, 1770–1865. *See* **7270**.

8392. Himmelfarb, Gertrude. The moral imagination: from Edmund Burke to Lionel Trilling. Chicago, IL: Dee, 2006. pp. xii, 259. Rev. by Kathryn Sutherland in TLS, 16 June 2006, 30; by Peter Heinegg in ANCW (194:15) 2006, 23–4.

8393. Hoagwood, Terence Allan; Ledbetter, Kathryn. 'Colour'd shadows': contexts in publishing, printing, and reading nineteenth-century British women writers. (Bibl. 2005, 9292.) Rev. by Katherine D. Harris in WordsC (36:4) 2005, 180–1.

8394. Hoeveler, Diane Long. The female captivity narrative: blood, water, and Orientalism. *In* (pp. 46–71) **8395**.

8395. —— Cass, Jeffrey (eds). Interrogating Orientalism: contextual approaches and pedagogical perspectives. Columbus: Ohio State UP, 2006. pp. vii, 277.

8396. Holmes, Martha Stoddard. Fictions of affliction: physical disability in Victorian culture. (Bibl. 2005, 9294.) Rev. by Meegan Kennedy in LitMed (25:1) 2006, 172–5; by Ross G. Forman in JVC (11:2) 2006, 360–4; by Julia Miele Rodas in VLC (34:1) 2006, 371–84.

8397. Hotz, Jeffrey. Divergent visions: the early United States through the lens of travel. *See* **7274**.

8398. Huber, Werner (ed.). The Corvey Library and Anglo-German cultural exchanges, 1770–1837: essays to honour Rainer Schöwerling. *See* **7275**.

8399. Hurst, Isobel. Victorian women writers and the Classics: the feminine of Homer. Oxford; New York: OUP, 2006. pp. 253. (Classical presences.)

8400. Jarvis, Robin. The Romantic period: the intellectual and cultural context of English literature, 1789–1830. (Bibl. 2005, 9303.) Rev. by Megan Hiatt in YES (36:2) 2006, 271–2.

8401. Javadi, Hasan. Persian literary influence on English literature: with special reference to the nineteenth century. Costa Mesa, CA: Mazda, 2005. pp. xiii, 254. (Bibliotheca Iranica: Literature series, 8.) (New ed.: first ed. 1983.)

8402. Jay, Elisabeth. Charlotte Mary Yonge and Tractarian aesthetics. *See* **11727**.

8403. —— 'In her father's steps she trod': Anne Thackeray Ritchie imagining Paris. *See* **11069**.

8404. Jeffares, A. Norman; van de Kamp, Peter (eds). Irish literature in the nineteenth century: an annotated anthology: vol. 1. Dublin; Portland, OR: Irish Academic Press, 2006. pp. xxii, 399. Rev. by Lucy McDiarmid in TLS, 6 Oct. 2006, 3–4.

8405. Kalaidjian, Walter (ed.). The Cambridge companion to American Modernism. *See* **11964**.

8406. Kaplan, Harold. Democratic humanism & American literature. New Brunswick, NJ: Transaction, 2005. pp. xxxiii, 297.

8407. Keach, William. Arbitrary power: Romanticism, language, politics. (Bibl. 2005, 9310.) Rev. by Simon Bainbridge in CamQ (34:4) 2005, 397–400; by William Galperin in ERR (16:4) 2005, 515–18; by Malcolm Kelsall in BJ (33:1) 2005, 61–4; by Eliza Richards in EC (56:1) 2006, 94–102; by Kevin Gilmartin in SR (45:2) 2006, 299–303; by Spencer Hall in KSJ (55) 2006, 259–60.

8408. Keeran, Peggy; Bowers, Jennifer. Literary research and the British Romantic era: strategies and sources. Lanham, MD; London: Scarecrow Press, 2005. pp. xi, 257. (Literary research, 1.)

8409. Kern, Stephen. When did the Victorian period end? Relativity, sexuality, narrative. JVC (11:2) 2006, 326–38.

8410. Killeen, Jarlath. Gothic Ireland: horror and the Irish Anglican imagination in the long eighteenth century. *See* **7289**.

8411. King, Andrew; Plunkett, John (eds). Popular print media, 1820–1900. London; New York: Routledge, 2004. 3 vols. pp. 1736.

8412. —— —— Victorian print media: a reader. *See* **768**.

8413. Klimasmith, Betsy. At home in the city: urban domesticity in American literature and culture, 1850–1930. (Bibl. 2005, 9317.) Rev. by Cara Elana Erdheim in StAN (1:1/2) 2006, 204–7.

8414. Köhler, Angelika. Ambivalent desires: the New Woman between social modernization and modern writing. *See* **11980**.

8415. Kolb, Jocelyne. Romantic irony. *In* (pp. 376–92) **8357**.

8416. Kucich, John J. Ghostly communion: cross-cultural Spiritualism in nineteenth-century American literature. (Bibl. 2005, 9318.) Rev. by Robert S. Cox in JAH (93:1) 2006, 215.

8417. Lane, Christopher. Hatred & civility: the antisocial life in Victorian England. (Bibl. 2005, 9320.) Rev. by Caroline Reitz in Novel (39:1) 2005, 126–8.

8418. Langford, Rachel (ed.). Depicting desire: gender, sexuality and the family in nineteenth-century Europe: literary and artistic perspectives. New York; Frankfurt: Lang, 2005. pp. 277. (European connections, 21.)

8419. Larkin, Edward. Thomas Paine and the literature of revolution. *See* **8033**.

8420. Lathbury, Roger. Realism and regionalism: 1860–1910. New York: Facts on File, 2006. pp. 96. (Backgrounds to American literature.)

8421. Law, Graham. The professional writer and the literary marketplace. *In* (pp. 97–111) **9609**.

8422. Law, John E.; Østermark-Johansen, Lene (eds). Victorian and Edwardian responses to the Italian Renaissance. Aldershot; Burlington, VT: Ashgate, 2005. pp. xxi, 300. Rev. by Stefano Evangelista in VS (48:4) 2006, 729–31; by Annie Escuret in CVE (63) 2006, 504.

8423. Lawlor, Clark. Consumption and literature: the making of the Romantic disease. *See* **3319**.

8424. Leader, Jennifer. Fitting in: Dickinson among others. *See* **9876**.

8425. Lee, Maurice S. Slavery, philosophy, and American literature, 1830–1860. (Bibl. 2005, 9325.) Rev. by Saranne Weller in JAStud (40:3) 2006, 671; by Albert J. von Frank in NineL (61:3) 2006, 375–8.

8426. Lewis, Clay. Butcher's bill. *See* **15820**.

8427. Lindop, Grevel. Self deceptions. TLS, 9 June 2006, 8–9 (review-article).

8428. Lokke, Kari. Woman and fame: Germaine de Staël and Regency women writers. KSJ (55) 2006, 73–9.

8429. Lundin, Roger (ed.). There before us: religion, literature, and culture from Emerson to Wendell Berry. Afterword by Andrew Delbanco. Grand Rapids, MI; Cambridge: Eerdmans, 2006. pp. xxii, 250.

8430. Lussier, Mark. Colonial counterflow: from Orientalism to Buddhism. *In* (pp. 90–106) **8395**.

8431. Lutes, Jean Marie. Front-page girls: women journalists in American culture and fiction, 1880–1930. *See* **12000**.

8432. Lye, Colleen. America's Asia: racial form and American literature, 1893–1945. (Bibl. 2005, 9332.) Rev. by Crystal Parikh in AL (78:1) 2006, 192–4; by Naoko Shibushawa in PacHR (75:3) 2006, 504–6; by Daniel Y. Kim in Novel (39:2) 2006, 276–9.

8433. Lyons, Paul. American Pacificism: Oceania in the US imagination. London; New York: Routledge, 2006. pp. xii, 271. (Postcolonial literatures.) Rev. by Paloma Fresno Calleja in Atl (28:2) 2006, 165–70.

8434. McCann, A. L. The literature of extinction. *See* **19372**.

8435. McCaskill, Barbara; Gebhard, Caroline (eds). Post-bellum, pre-Harlem: African American literature and culture, 1877–1919. New York; London: New York UP, 2006. pp. xiv, 298.

8436. McCaw, Neil (ed.). Writing Irishness in nineteenth-century British culture. (Bibl. 2005, 9334.) Rev. by Edward Larrissy in WordsC (36:4) 2005, 167–8.

8437. McGann, Jerome. Culture and technology: the way we live now. What is to be done? *See* **1016**.

8438. Mackenthun, Gesa. Fictions of the Black Atlantic in American foundational literature. (Bibl. 2004, 9515.) Rev. by Rachel van Duyvenbode in JAStud (39:3) 2005, 565–6.

8439. Maltz, Diana. British Aestheticism and the urban working classes, 1870–1900: beauty for the people. Basingstoke; New York: Palgrave Macmillan, 2006. pp. x, 290. (Palgrave studies in nineteenth-century writing and culture.) Rev. by Pierre Coustillas in GissJ (42:2) 2006, 31–4; by Talia Schaffer in NineL (61:2) 2006, 260–3.

8440. Marias, Javier. Written lives. Trans. by Margaret Jull Costa. *See* **12026**.

8441. Markovits, Stefanie. The crisis of action in nineteenth-century English literature. Columbus: Ohio State UP, 2006. pp. ix, 258.

8442. Marshall, Megan. The Peabody sisters: three women who ignited American Romanticism. *See* **10794**.

8443. Martin, Ronald E. The languages of difference: American writers and anthropologists reconfigure the primitive, 1878–1940. (Bibl. 2005, 9345.) Rev. by James Dawes in AL (78:2) 2006, 393–4.

8444. Marucci, Franco. Storia della letteratura inglese: 4, Dal 1870 al 1921. Florence: Le Lettere, 2006. pp. 1230. (Lettere universitá, 22.)

8445. Mason, Jennifer. Civilized creatures: urban animals, Sentimental culture, and American literature, 1850–1900. (Bibl. 2005, 9347.) Rev. by Lara Langer Cohen in Legacy (23:2) 2006, 209–10.

8446. Maunder, Andrew; Moore, Grace (eds). Victorian crime, madness and sensation. (Bibl. 2004, 9524.) Rev. by Marlene Tromp in VS (48:3) 2006, 536–8.

8447. Mellor, Anne K. What's different about 'Regency' women writers? KSJ (55) 2006, 42–7.

8448. Melman, Billie. The culture of history: English uses of the past, 1800–1953. Oxford; New York: OUP, 2006. pp. xii, 363.

8449. Mitchell, Lee Clark. Authenticity, the West, and literature. WAL (40:1) 2005, 88–97 (review-article).

8450. Mortensen, Peter. British Romanticism and Continental influences: writing in an age of europhobia. (Bibl. 2005, 9356.) Rev. by Richard Gravil in WordsC (36:4) 2005, 164–5.

8451. Morton, Timothy. Food studies in the Romantic period: (s)mashing history. Romanticism (12:1) 2006, 1–4.

8452. —— (ed.). Cultures of taste / theories of appetite: eating Romanticism. Basingstoke; New York: Palgrave Macmillan, 2004. pp. xxi, 287. Rev. by Christine Roth in NCS (19) 2005, 135–8; by Gillen D'Arcy Wood in WordsC (36:4) 2005, 153–4; by Richard Marggraf Turley in BJ (33:1) 2005, 60–1.

8453. Mount, Nick. When Canadian literature moved to New York. (Bibl. 2005, 9359.) Rev. by W. J. Keith in BkCan (34:7) 2005, 18.

8454. Mullen, Alexandra. The lost Romantic. *See* **10516**.

8455. Murphy, Gretchen. Hemispheric imaginings: the Monroe Doctrine and narratives of US empire. Durham, NC; London: Duke UP, 2005. pp. xi, 195. (New Americanists.) Rev. by Claudia Sadowski-Smith in AL (78:3) 2006, 624–7.

8456. Murray, Christopher John (gen. ed.). Encyclopedia of the Romantic era, 1760–1850. (Bibl. 2004, 9531.) Rev. by Diane Long Hoeveler in ERR (17:4) 2006, 508–11.

8457. Nabers, Deak. Victory of law: the Fourteenth Amendment, the Civil War, and American literature, 1852–1867. Baltimore, MD; London: Johns Hopkins UP, 2006. pp. xii, 239.

8458. Nemoianu, Virgil. Sacrality and the aesthetic in the early nineteenth century. *In* (pp. 393–412) **8357**.

8459. Nord, Deborah Epstein. Gypsies & the British imagination, 1807–1930. New York: Columbia UP, 2006. pp. xii, 221.

8460. Nori, Giuseppe. Tipologie eroiche del rinascimento americano. *In* (pp. 91–137) **3341**.

8461. Nudelman, Franny. John Brown's body: slavery, violence & the culture of war. (Bibl. 2004, 9535.) Rev. by S.-M. Grant in JAStud (39:1) 2005, 131–3; by Jane E. Schultz in JAH (92:4) 2006, 1435–6; by Eric Solomon in AL (78:3) 2006, 657–9.

8462. Nwankwo, Ifeoma Kiddoe. Black cosmopolitanism: racial consciousness and transnational identity in the nineteenth-century Americas. Philadelphia: Pennsylvania UP, 2005. pp. viii, 291. (Rethinking the Americas.) Rev. by Michelle Stephens in AL (78:3) 2006, 638–40.

8463. O'Callaghan, Evelyn. Women writing the West Indies, 1804–1939: 'a hot place, belonging to us'. London; New York: Routledge, 2004. pp. x, 224. Rev. by Caryl Phillips in TLS, 21 May 2004, 29; by Alison Donnell in JWIL (15:1/2) 2006, 209–12.

8464. O'Gorman, Francis. Partly autonomous? Literary–historical reflections on Richard Price, *British Society 1680–1880*. JVC (11:1) 2006, 160–7.

8465. O'Neill, Michael; Sandy, Mark (eds). Romanticism: critical concepts in literary and cultural studies. London; New York: Routledge, 2006. 4 vols. pp. 1592.

8466. O'Rourke, James. Sex, lies, and autobiography: the ethics of confession. Charlottesville; London: Virginia UP, 2006. pp. xii, 215.

8467. Ortemann, Marie-Jeanne. Of some mind-travellers and … prize neurotics: a reading of English Romanticism. *In* (pp. 383–98) **11824**.

8468. O'Toole, Tina (ed.). Dictionary of Munster women writers 1800–2000 / Scríbhneoirí ban na Mumhan, 1800–2000. Foreword by Patricia Coughlan and Éibhear Walshe. Cork: Cork UP, 2005. pp. xlvi, 330.

8469. Oueijan, Naji. Sexualizing the Orient. Prism(s) (14) 2006, 7–25.

8470. Page, Judith W. Imperfect sympathies: Jews and Judaism in British Romantic literature and culture. (Bibl. 2005, 9371.) Rev. by Michael Scrivener in ERR (16:4) 2005, 511–15.

8471. Peer, Larry H. The year's work in Romanticism Studies. Prism(s) (14) 2006, 119–25.

8472. —— Hoeveler, Diane Long (eds). Romanticism: comparative discourses. *See* **7307**.

8473. Pennell, Melissa McFarland. Masterpieces of American Romantic literature. Westport, CT; London: Greenwood Press, 2006. pp. x, 202. (Greenwood introduces literary masterpieces.)

8474. Perry, Imani. Occupying the universal, embodying the subject: African American literary jurisprudence. LawL (17:1) 2005, 97–129.

8475. Phillips, Jerry. Romanticism and Transcendentalism: 1800–1860. New York: Facts on File, 2006. pp. 96. (Backgrounds to American literature.)

8476. Piepmeier, Alison. Out in public: configurations of women's bodies in nineteenth-century America. Chapel Hill; London: North Carolina UP, 2004. pp. xi, 278. Rev. by Susan K. Harris in AL (78:1) 2006, 185–7.

8477. Pike, David L. Subterranean cities: the world beneath Paris and London, 1800–1945. Ithaca, NY; London: Cornell UP, 2005. pp. xviii, 355. Rev. by David Ashford in Mod/Mod (13:4) 2006, 755–7.

8478. Pionke, Albert D. Plots of opportunity: representing conspiracy in Victorian England. (Bibl. 2005, 9384.) Rev. by Tamara S. Wagner in VIJ (33) 2005, 229–32; by Andrea Kaston Tange in VPR (39:1) 2006, 86–8.

8479. Pizer, Donald. Late nineteenth-century American literary Naturalism: a re-introduction. ALR (38:3) 2006, 189–202.

8480. Poetzsch, Markus. 'Visionary dreariness': readings in Romanticism's quotidian sublime. London; New York: Routledge, 2006. pp. ix, 227. (Literary criticism and cultural theory.)

8481. Pollin, Burton R. Poe's seductive influence on great writers. *See* **11040**.

8482. Poovey, Mary. Discriminating reading. VicR (31:2) 2005, 10–35.

8483. —— Mediums, media, mediation: response. *See* **20118**.

8484. Pratt, Lynda (ed.). Robert Southey and the contexts of English Romanticism. *See* **11250**.

8485. Preis-Smith, Agata; Paryż, Marek (eds). The poetics of America: explorations in the literature and culture of the United States. (Bibl. 2005, 9385.) Rev. by John Armstrong in JAStud (40:1) 2006, 193–4.

8486. Proehl, Kristen. Transforming the 'madman into a saint': the cultural memory site of John Brown's raid on Harper's Ferry in antislavery literature and history. *In* (pp. 107–20) **8537**.

8487. PURCHASE, SEAN. Key concepts in Victorian literature. Basingstoke; New York: Palgrave Macmillan, 2006. pp. xxi, 282. (Palgrave key concepts.)

8488. PUSTIANAZ, MARCO; VILLA, LUISA (eds). Maschilità decadenti: la lunga *fin de siècle*. Bergamo: Bergamo UP / Sestante, 2004. pp. 368. (Le zebre, 6.) Rev. by Giulio Iacoli in Indice (2005:7/8) 16.

8489. PUTZI, JENNIFER. Identifying marks: race, gender, and the marked body in nineteenth-century America. Athens; London: Georgia UP, 2006. pp. xii, 195.

8490. QUÉMA, ANNE. The gothic and the fantastic in the age of digital reproduction. *See* **7317**.

8491. QUIRK, TOM; SCHARNHORST, GARY (eds). American history through literature, 1870–1920. Detroit, MI: Scribner's Sons / Thomson Gale, 2006. 3 vols. pp. xx, 1339.

8492. RISS, ARTHUR. Race, slavery, and liberalism in nineteenth-century American literature. Cambridge; New York: CUP, 2006. pp. viii, 238. (Cambridge studies in American literature and culture.)

8493. ROBBINS, SARAH. Managing literacy, mothering America: women's narratives on reading and writing in the nineteenth century. (Bibl. 2004, 9568.) Rev. by Carolyn Sorisio in AL (78:1) 2006, 182–5; by Lucille M. Schultz in Legacy (23:2) 2006, 203–4.

8494. ROBERTSON, BEN P. (comp.). Annual bibliography for 2004. KSJ (55) 2006, 284–324.

8495. —— Annual bibliography for 2005. KSJ (55) 2006, 325–54.

8496. ROBINSON, ALAN. Imagining London, 1770–1900. (Bibl. 2005, 8061.) Rev. by Lucy Munro in TLS, 6 Jan. 2006, 22; by Michael Wheeler in MLR (101:2) 2006, 524–5; by Jeffrey Hill in LitH (15:2) 2006, 80; by Richard Maxwell in VS (48:3) 2006, 538–41.

8497. ROCHE, ANTHONY (ed.). The UCD aesthetic: celebrating 150 years of UCD writers. Dublin: New Island, 2005. pp. 298. (University College Dublin.)

8498. RODAS, JULIA MIELE. Mainstreaming Disability Studies? VLC (34:1) 2006, 371–84 (review-article).

8499. ROVEE, CHRISTOPHER KENT. Imagining the gallery: the social body of British Romanticism. Stanford, CA: Stanford UP, 2006. pp. xii, 251.

8500. RUBIN, LOUIS D., JR. Where the Southern cross the Yellow Dog: on writers and writing. Columbia; London: Missouri UP, 2005. pp. xiii, 144. Rev. by Larry D. Griffin in ArkR (37:2) 2006, 133–4.

8501. RUSSETT, MARGARET. Fictions and fakes: forging Romantic authenticity, 1760–1845. Cambridge; New York: CUP, 2006. pp. xiii, 258. (Cambridge studies in Romanticism, 64.) Rev. by Grevel Lindop in TLS, 9 June 2006, 8–9.

8502. SAGLIA, DIEGO. Orientalism. *In* (pp. 467–85) **8357**.

8503. ST CLAIR, WILLIAM. The reading nation in the Romantic period. (Bibl. 2004, 9577.) Rev. by Robert D. Hume in PQ (83:3) 2004, 321–31; by Richard Cronin in MLR (101:3) 2006, 830–1; by Leslie Howsam in PBSA (100:1) 2006, 152–4; by Michelle Levy in HLQ (69:3) 2006, 477–86; by Mary Ellen Brown in JFR (43:1) 2006, 82–4; by Christine Kenyon Jones in Romanticism (12:2) 2006,

150–2; by Doucet Devin Fischer in KSJ (55) 2006, 251–4; by Maureen Bell in JPHS (ns 9) 2006, 111–13.

8504. Salusinszky, Imre (ed.). Northrop Frye's writings on the eighteenth and nineteenth centuries. *See* **14280**.

8505. Samuels, Shirley. Facing America: iconography and the Civil War. (Bibl. 2004, 9579.) Rev. by Philip Joseph in AL (77:3) 2005, 639–41; by Timothy Sweet in ALR (38:3) 2006, 281–2.

8506. Sánchez-Eppler, Karen. Dependent states: the child's part in nineteenth-century American culture. Chicago, IL; London: Chicago UP, 2005. pp. xxviii, 260. Rev. by Jane F. Thrailkill in Legacy (23:2) 2006, 201–3.

8507. Sanders, Lise Shapiro. Consuming fantasies: labor, leisure, and the London shopgirl, 1880–1920. Columbus: Ohio State UP, 2006. pp. xi, 279. Rev. by Judith Flanders in TLS, 7 July 2006, 32; by Maria Teresa Chialant in VS (49:1) 2006, 143–4.

8508. Sayre, Robert; Löwy, Michael. Romanticism and capitalism. *In* (pp. 433–49) **8357**.

8509. Schenk, H. G. The revolt against the eighteenth century. Prism(s) (14) 2006, 73–118.

8510. Schocket, Eric. Vanishing moments: class and American literature. Ann Arbor: Michigan UP, 2006. pp. xv, 300. (Class: culture.)

8511. Schoolfield, George C. A Baedeker of Decadence: charting a literary fashion, 1884–1927. (Bibl. 2004, 9582.) Rev. by Jeremy Tambling in MLR (101:1) 2006, 214–16.

8512. Schweighauser, Philipp. The noises of American literature, 1890–1985: toward a history of literary acoustics. Gainesville: Florida UP, 2006. pp. viii, 262.

8513. Shamir, Milette. Inexpressible privacy: the interior life of antebellum American literature. Philadelphia: Pennsylvania UP, 2006. pp. 282.

8514. Siegel, Jonah. Haunted museum: longing, travel, and the art–romance tradition. (Bibl. 2005, 9414.) Rev. by Laurent Bury in EA (59:4) 2006, 482–3.

8515. Silver, Andrew. Minstrelsy and murder: the crisis of Southern humor, 1835–1925. Baton Rouge: Louisiana State UP, 2006. pp. xii, 222. (Southern literary studies.)

8516. Simpson, Mark. Trafficking subjects: the politics of mobility in nineteenth-century America. Minneapolis; London: Minnesota UP, 2005. pp. xxxi, 193. Rev. by John M. Freiermuth in AL (78:2) 2006, 389–91.

8517. Skipp, Jenny. Masculinity and social stratification in eighteenth-century erotic literature, 1700–1821. *See* **7333**.

8518. Sloan, John. Quarrels and coteries in the 1890s. YES (36:2) 2006, 245–58.

8519. Smith, Christopher. Retexts: a review article. YES (36:2) 2006, 259–63 (review-article).

8520. Spears, Timothy B. Chicago dreaming: Midwesterners and the city, 1871–1919. Chicago, IL; London: Chicago UP, 2005. pp. xxiii, 322. Rev. by James Guthrie in DreiS (36:2) 2005, 50–2; by Reginald Dyck in AL (78:3) 2006, 620–2.

8521. Specq, Francois. Transcendence: seekers and seers in the age of Thoreau. *See* **11450**.

8522. Spector, Sheila A. Jewish translations of British Romantic literature (1753–1858): a preliminary bibliography. *In* (pp. 195–210) **8523**.

8523. —— (ed.). The Jews and British Romanticism: politics, religion, culture. Basingstoke; New York: Palgrave Macmillan, 2005. pp. xiv, 334. Rev. by Emily A. Bernhard Jackson in WordsC (36:4) 2005, 163–4.

8524. Spooner, Catherine. Fashioning gothic bodies. Manchester; New York: Manchester UP, 2004. pp. 224. Rev. by Lisa Hopkins in GothS (8:2) 2006, 148–9.

8525. Stafford, Fiona. Scottish Romanticism and Scotland in Romanticism. *In* (pp. 49–66) **8357**.

8526. Stafford, Jane; Williams, Mark. Maoriland: New Zealand literature, 1872–1914. Wellington, New Zealand: Victoria UP, 2006. pp. 350. Rev. by Kirstine Moffat in JNZL (24:1) 2006, 148–54.

8527. Stauffer, Andrew M. Anger, revolution, and Romanticism. (Bibl. 2005, 9419.) Rev. by Sharon Ruston in TLS, 3 Mar. 2006, 33; by Alan Rawes in Romanticism (12:2) 2006, 158–60; by Richard Marggraf Turley in BJ (34:1) 2006, 74–6.

8528. Stauffer, John; Trodd, Zoe. Meteor of war: the John Brown cycle. *In* (pp. 121–44) **8537**.

8529. Stetz, Margaret D. 'Ballads in prose': genre crossing in late Victorian women's writing. *See* **18879**.

8530. Stokes, Claudia. Copyrighting American history: international copyright and the periodization of the nineteenth century. *See* **10759**.

8531. Stowe, William W. Writing Mount Auburn: language, landscape, and place. PAPS (150:2) 2006, 296–317.

8532. Strange, Julie-Marie. Death, grief and poverty in Britain, 1870–1914. Cambridge; New York: CUP, 2005. pp. x, 294. (Cambridge social and cultural histories, 6.) Rev. by Allan Kellehear in VS (48:4) 2006, 751–2.

8533. Stromberg, Ernest (ed.). American Indian rhetorics of survivance: word medicine, word magic. *See* **2149**.

8534. Sumpter, Caroline. Innocents and epicures: the child, the fairy tale and avant-garde debate in *fin-de-siècle* little magazines. *See* **16460**.

8535. Sundquist, Eric J. Empire and slavery in American literature, 1820–1865. Jackson; London: Mississippi UP, 2006. pp. 254.

8536. Tarver, Australia. Reading race and intertextuality from the Abolitionist era to the Harlem renaissance. ColLit (33:3) 2006, 198–203 (review-article).

8537. Taylor, Andrew; Herrington, Eldrid (eds). The afterlife of John Brown. Basingstoke; New York: Palgrave Macmillan, 2005. pp. xii, 243.

8538. Thomas, David Wayne. Cultivating Victorians: liberal culture and the aesthetic. (Bibl. 2005, 9427.) Rev. by Anne Humpherys in JVC (11:2) 2006, 373–6; by Christopher Kent in NCC (28:3) 2006, 260–3; by Peter O'Neill in JPRS (15:1) 2006, 104–7.

8539. Thomas, Jane. 'Forming the literary tastes of the middle and higher classes': Elgin's circulating libraries and their proprietors, 1789–1870. *In* (pp. 91–111) **746**.

8540. —— Revising the late Victorian and early Modernist canon: a review article. YES (36:2) 2006, 264–8 (review-article).

8541. Thompson, Helen (ed.). The current debate about the Irish literary canon: essays reassessing *The Field Day Anthology of Irish Writing*. *See* **12189**.

8542. Trachtenberg, Alan. Shades of Hiawatha: staging Indians, making Americans, 1880–1930. (Bibl. 2005, 9432.) Rev. by Jean Chothia in JAStud (40:1) 2006, 202–3; by Bruce E. Johansen in AICRJ (30:2) 2006, 173–4.

8543. Trulli, Maristella; Pontrandolfo, Luisa (eds). Londra tra memoria letteraria e modernità: dal Seicento ai nostri giorni. *See* **7343**.

8544. Villa, Luisa. 'Desisting resistance': the representation of Schopenhauerian pessimism in late nineteenth-century Britain. *In* (pp. 115–31) **16284**.

8545. Vogel, Todd. Rewriting White: race, class, and cultural capital in nineteenth-century America. (Bibl. 2005, 9441.) Rev. by Jeffory A. Clymer in AL (78:3) 2006, 622–4; by Rachel van Duyvenbode in JAStud (40:2) 2006, 457–8.

8546. Waller, Philip. Writers, readers, and reputations: literary life in Britain, 1870–1918. Oxford; New York: OUP, 2006. pp. x, 1181. Rev. by Dinah Birch in TLS, 1 Sept. 2006, 3–4.

8547. Wayne, Tiffany K. Encyclopedia of Transcendentalism. New York: Facts on File, 2006. pp. x, 374. (Facts on File library of American literature.) (Literary movements.)

8548. Webb, Timothy. Homer and the Romantics. *In* (pp. 287–310) **3253**.

8549. Weinstein, Cindy. Family, kinship, and sympathy in nineteenth-century American literature. (Bibl. 2005, 9444.) Rev. by Elizabeth Stockton in Legacy (23:1) 2006, 94–5.

8550. Wertheimer, Eric. Underwriting: the poetics of insurance in America, 1722–1872. *See* **7349**.

8551. Wheeler, Michael. The old enemies: Catholic and Protestant in nineteenth-century English culture. Cambridge; New York: CUP, 2006. pp. xv, 352.

8552. White, Edmund. Arts and letters. San Francisco, CA: Cleis Press, 2004. pp. x, 360. Rev. by Michael Dirda in BkW, 14 Nov. 2004, 15; by Thomas March in AmBR (26:6) 2005, 20.

8553. Wilczynski, Marek. American culture wars, 1803–1861. ATQ (20:3) 2006, 505–11.

8554. Wild, Jonathan. The rise of the office clerk in literary culture, 1880–1939. Basingstoke; New York: Palgrave Macmillan, 2006. pp. ix, 211. Rev. by Paul Duguid in TLS, 1 Sept. 2006, 28.

8555. Willburn, Sarah A. Possessed Victorians: extra spheres in nineteenth-century mystical writings. Aldershot; Burlington, VT: Ashgate, 2006. pp. xi, 182. (Nineteenth century.)

8556. Williams, Susan S. Reclaiming authorship: literary women in America, 1850–1900. Philadelphia: Pennsylvania UP, 2006. pp. 255.

8557. Willis, Lloyd. Henry Wadsworth Longfellow, United States national literature, and the canonical erasure of material nature. *See* **10756**.

8558. Wootton, Sarah. Consuming Keats: nineteenth-century representations in art and literature. *See* **10674**.

8559. Wright, Julia M. 'All the fire-side circle': Irish women writers and the Sheridan–Lefanu coterie. *See* **7351**.

8560. Zhou, Xiaojing; Najmi, Samina (eds). Form and transformation in Asian American literature. (Bibl. 2005, 9454.) Rev. by María Isabel Seguro Gómez in Atl (28:2) 2006, 171–6; by Bella Adams in JAStud (40:3) 2006, 688–9.

8561. Zwierlein, Anne-Julia (ed.). Unmapped countries: biological visions in nineteenth-century literature and culture. London: Anthem Press, 2005. pp. xv, 282. (Anthem nineteenth-century studies.) Rev. by Annie Escuret in CVE (62) 2005, 219–21; by Bernard Lightman in VS (48:2) 2006, 358–60.

DRAMA AND THE THEATRE

8562. Andrews, Malcolm. Charles Dickens and his performing selves: Dickens and the public readings. *See* **9695**.

8563. Booth, Michael R. The acting of Henry Irving. TN (59:3) 2005, 122–42.

8564. Brooks, Daphne A. Bodies in dissent: spectacular performances of race and freedom, 1850–1910. Durham, NC; London: Duke UP, 2006. pp. xii, 475.

8565. Byrne, Paula. Free and easies. TLS, 27 Oct. 2006, 20 (review-article). (Romantic-era theatre.)

8566. Christiansen, Richard. A theater of our own: a history and a memoir of 1,001 nights in Chicago. Foreword by Brian Dennehy. Evanston, IL: Northwestern UP, 2004. pp. xvii, 317. Rev. by Reginald Dyck in AL (78:3) 2006, 620–2.

8567. Croft, Susan. 'A new untravelled region in herself': women's school plays in late nineteenth- and early twentieth-century Australia. *In* (pp. 29–42) **12360**.

8568. Danahay, Martin A.; Chisholm, Alexander (eds). Jekyll and Hyde dramatized: the 1887 Richard Mansfield script and the evolution of the story on stage. *See* **11284**.

8569. Davidson, Paul; Davis, Kristy; Nield, Sophie. The AHRC Mander and Mitchenson Theatre Collection Access for Research Project: conversations with cataloguers. *See* **310**.

8570. Davis, Jim. Collins and the theatre. *In* (pp. 168–80) **9609**.

8571. Denisoff, Dennis. Theater, burlesque, and performance in the nineteenth century. NCS (19) 2005, 159–63.

8572. Erdman, Andrew L. Blue vaudeville: sex, morals and the mass marketing of amusement, 1895–1915. (Bibl. 2005, 9473.) Rev. by Monica Stufft in TJ (58:2) 2006, 380–1; by Michael Peterson in TRI (31:2) 2006, 208–9; by John W. Frick in NCT (33:1) 2006, 92–4.

8573. Findlay, Bill. Motivation in a surrogate translation of Goldoni. *In* (pp. 46–57) **3186**.

8574. Ford, Sarah. Liberty contained: Sarah Pogson's *The Young Carolinians; or, Americans in Algiers*. EAL (41:1) 2006, 109–28.

8575. Frank, Frederick S. (ed.). The origins of the modern study of gothic drama, together with a re-edition of *Gothic Drama from Walpole to Shelley* (1947) by Bertrand Evans. *See* **7359**.

8576. Frisken, Amanda. Victoria Woodhull's sexual revolution: political theatre and the popular press in nineteenth-century America. (Bibl. 2005, 9477.) Rev. by B. Bennett in JAStud (39:2) 2005, 316; by Faye E. Dudden in AmP (16:1) 2006, 117–19; by Robert Avery in QJS (92:4) 2006, 432–4.

8577. Furneaux, Holly. 'Worrying to death' – reinterpreting Dickens's critique of the new Poor Law in *Oliver Twist* and contemporary adaptations. *See* **9753**.

8578. Greenwald, Michael L. (comp.). The Longman anthology of modern and contemporary drama: a global perspective. London; New York: Pearson Longman, 2004. pp. xiii, 1008.

8579. Guest, Kristen. Culture, class, and colonialism: the struggle for an English national theatre, 1879–1913. JVC (11:2) 2006, 281–300.

8580. Hardee, Lewis J., Jr. The Lambs theatre club. Jefferson, NC; London: McFarland, 2006. pp. xi, 276.

8581. Kahan, Jeffrey. The cult of Kean. Aldershot; Burlington, VT: Ashgate, 2006. pp. 206.

8582. Lindfors, Bernth. Ira Aldridge's London debut. *See* **8975**.

8583. López Rodríguez, Miriam; Narbona Carrión, Maria Dolores. Women's contribution to nineteenth-century American theatre. (Bibl. 2005, 9490.) Rev. by Karl M. Kippola in TheatreS (47:1) 2006, 136–8.

8584. Luckhurst, Mary (ed.). A companion to modern British and Irish drama, 1880–2005. *See* **12324**.

8585. Maunder, Andrew. 'I will not live in poverty and neglect': *East Lynne* on the East End stage. *In* (pp. 173–87) **8647**.

8586. Mayer, David. *Why Girls Leave Home*: Victorian and Edwardian 'bad-girl' melodrama parodied in early film. TJ (58:4) 2006, 575–93.

8587. Morash, Christopher. Irish theatre. *In* (pp. 322–38) **11829**.

8588. Newey, Katherine. Women's theatre writing in Victorian Britain. Basingstoke; New York: Palgrave Macmillan, 2005. pp. ix, 269.

8589. Newman, Judie. The afterlife of *Dred* on the British stage. *In* (pp. 208–24) **11355**.

8590. O'Connor, Marion. William Poel's letters on tour in Yorkshire, 1877/8. TN (59:2) 2005, 62–90.

8591. Powell, Kerry (ed.). The Cambridge companion to Victorian and Edwardian theatre. (Bibl. 2005, 9498.) Rev. by Jane Moody in ModDr (48:3) 2005, 621–3; by Katherine Newey in VS (49:1) 2006, 129–31.

8592. Radavich, David. Twain, Howells, and the origins of Midwestern drama. *See* **11521**.

8593. Richards, Jeffrey. Henry Irving: the actor-manager as *auteur*. NCT (32:2) 2005, 20–35.

8594. —— Sir Henry Irving: a Victorian actor and his world. London; New York: Hambledon & London, 2005. pp. xi, 508, (plates) 16. Rev. by John Stokes in TLS, 14 Apr. 2006, 7; by Michael R. Booth in TN (60:2) 2006, 123–4.

8595. Roy, Donald. A theatre for all seasons: the Queen's Theatre, Hull, 1846–1869. TN (60:3) 2006, 147–74.

8596. Schafer, Elizabeth; Smith, Susan Bradley (eds). Playing Australia: Australian theatre and the international stage. *See* **12360**.

8597. Shellard, Dominic; Nicholson, Steve; Handley, Miriam. The Lord Chamberlain regrets: a history of British theatre censorship. London: British Library, 2004. pp. x, 197. Rev. by Peter Davison in Library (6:4) 2005, 470–2.

8598. Stetz, Margaret D. Gender and the London theatre, 1880–1920. (Bibl. 2005, 9503.) Rev. by Katherine Newey in VS (49:1) 2006, 129–31.

8599. Stokes, John. The French actress and her English audience. (Bibl. 2005, 9504.) Rev. by Patrick O'Connor in TLS, 7 Apr. 2006, 20.

8600. Sutcliffe, Allan. Pepper's Ghost and *A Christmas Carol*. *See* **9827**.

8601. Thomson, Peter. The Cambridge introduction to English theatre, 1660–1900. *See* **6393**.

8602. Tunbridge, Laura. From count to chimney sweep: Byron's *Manfred* in London theatres. *See* **9372**.

8603. Vandevelde, Karen. The alternative dramatic revival in Ireland, 1897–1913. Dublin; Bethesda, MD: Maunsel, 2005. pp. xii, 394.

8604. Voskuil, Lynn M. Acting naturally: Victorian theatricality and authenticity. (Bibl. 2005, 9507.) Rev. by Richard W. Schoch in NCT (32:2) 2005, 76–7.

8605. Watt, Stephen. Modern American drama. *In* (pp. 102–26) **11964**.

8606. Wheeler, Leigh Ann. Against obscenity: reform and the politics of womanhood, 1873–1935. Baltimore, MD; London: Johns Hopkins UP, 2004. pp. xiii, 251. (Refiguring American political history.) Rev. by Encarna Trinidad in JAStud (40:3) 2006, 683–4.

8607. Worrall, David. Theatric revolution: drama, censorship and Romantic period subcultures, 1773–1832. Oxford; New York: OUP, 2006. pp. viii, 407. Rev. by Paula Byrne in TLS, 27 Oct. 2006, 20.

FICTION

8608. Andres, Sophia. The Pre-Raphaelite art of the Victorian novel: narrative challenges to visual gendered boundaries. (Bibl. 2005, 9510.) Rev. by Susan Jaret McKinstry in JPRS (15:1) 2006, 108–11; by Elizabeth Helsinger in VS (48:4) 2006, 727–9.

8609. Annesley, James. Fictions of globalization. *See* **13411**.

8610. Armstrong, Nancy. How novels think: the limits of British individualism from 1719–1900. New York: Columbia UP, 2005. pp. x, 191. Rev. by John Kucich in NineL (61:3) 2006, 368–72.

8611. Ashley, Mike. The age of the storytellers: British popular fiction magazines, 1880–1950. New Castle, DE: Oak Knoll Press; London: British Library, 2006. pp. ix, 308.

8612. Barrish, Phillip. White liberal identity, literary pedagogy, and classic American realism. Columbus: Ohio State UP, 2005. pp. ix, 168.

8613. Beers, Terry (ed.). Gunfight at Mussel Slough: evolution of a Western myth. *See* **2994**.

8614. Beran, Zdeněk. *Teleny* and the question of *fin de siècle* sexuality. PSE (24) 2006, 129–39. (*Extended version of* bibl. 2005, 12366.)

8615. Bergman, Jill; Bernardi, Debra (eds). Our sisters' keepers: nineteenth-century benevolence literature by American women. (Bibl. 2005, 9513.) Rev. by Bernadette H. Hyner in RMER (60:1) 2006; by Gregory Eiselein in Legacy (23:2) 2006, 204–5.

8616. Bredesen, Dagni. Conformist subversion: ambivalent agency in *Revelations of a Lady Detective*. *See* **10408**.

8617. Brocklebank, Lisa. Psychic reading. *See* **10956**.

8618. Brooks, Peter. Realist vision. (Bibl. 2005, 9519.) Rev. by Francis O'Gorman in DickQ (23:1) 2006, 47–9; by Rebecca N. Mitchell in GER (37) 2006, 59–60.

8619. Brown, Harry J. Injun Joe's ghost: the Indian mixed-blood in American writing. (Bibl. 2004, 9696.) Rev. by Frederick Luis Aldama in AL (77:2) 2005, 418–21; by Susan Castillo in EAL (41:2) 2006, 339–45.

8620. Buell, Lawrence. Downwardly mobile for conscience's sake: voluntary simplicity from Thoreau to Lily Bart. *See* **11426**.

8621. Bulson, Eric. Novels, maps, modernity: the spatial imagination, 1850–2000. London; New York: Routledge, 2006. pp. xi, 176. (Literary criticism and cultural theory.)

8622. Buzard, James. Disorienting fiction: the autoethnographic work of nineteenth-century British novels. (Bibl. 2005, 9525.) Rev. by Kathy Alexis Psomiades in Novel (39:1) 2005, 119–22; by Catherine Gallagher in VS (49:1) 2006, 109–11.

8623. Caldwell, Janis McLarren. Literature and medicine in nineteenth-century Britain: from Mary Shelley to George Eliot. (Bibl. 2005, 9526.) Rev. by Gowan Dawson in BJ (33:1) 2005, 67–8; by Miriam Bailin in VS (48:2) 2006, 360–2; by Marcia K. Farrell in JHM (61:2) 2006, 225–6; by Michael Davis in GER (37) 2006, 61–2.

8624. Callanan, Laura. Deciphering race: White anxiety, racial conflict, and the turn to fiction in mid-Victorian English prose. Columbus: Ohio State UP, 2006. pp. viii, 185.

8625. Carens, Timothy L. Outlandish English subjects in the Victorian domestic novel. (Bibl. 2005, 9527.) Rev. by Luke Spencer in BrSt (31:3) 2006, 264–5.

8626. Carlisle, Janice. Common scents: comparative encounters in high Victorian fiction. (Bibl. 2005, 9528.) Rev. by Barbara T. Gates in VLC (34:1) 2006, 385–7; by Sylvère Monod in EA (59:2) 2006, 239–40.

8627. Casey, Ellen Miller. 'Highly flavoured dishes' and 'highly seasoned garbage': sensation in the *Athenaeum*. *In* (pp. 3–14) **8647**.

8628. Chakravarty, Gautam. The Indian Mutiny and the British imagination. (Bibl. 2005, 9529.) Rev. by Ann-Barbara Graff in CLIO (35:3) 2006, 444–8.

8629. Christensen, Allan Conrad. Nineteenth-century narratives of contagion: our feverish contact. (Bibl. 2005, 9530.) Rev. by Stephanie Cross in TLS, 17 Feb. 2006, 36; by Sylvère Monod in EA (59:3) 2006, 365–6; by Jill L. Matus in VS (49:1) 2006, 167–9.

8630. Deardorff, Donald Lee, II. Hero and anti-hero in the American foot-ball novel: changing conceptions of masculinity from the nineteenth century to the twenty-first century. Lewiston, NY; Lampeter: Mellen Press, 2006. pp. iii, 141.

8631. Dellamora, Richard. Friendship's bonds: democracy and the novel in Victorian England. (Bibl. 2005, 9540.) Rev. by Valerie Sanders in YES (36:2) 2006, 273–4; by Kate Thomas in GLQ (12:1) 2006, 161–3; by Asa Briggs in LitH (15:2) 2006, 81; by Michael Ragussis in VS (48:3) 2006, 543–5.

8632. Demirtürk, E. Lâle. Charting the terrain of Black urban subjects: the African American great migration novel. *In* (pp. 97–106) **3307**.

8633. Diamond, Michael. Lesser breeds: racial attitudes in popular British fiction, 1890–1940. London: Anthem Press, 2006. pp. 229, (plates) 12.

8634. Dolin, Tim. First steps toward a history of the mid-Victorian novel in colonial Australia. *See* **9735**.

8635. Dubberke, Ray. Who wrote *The Welfleet Mystery*? *See* **9738**.

8636. Escuret, Annie. Excès et sacré dans la littérature victorienne et édouardienne. *See* **9743**.

8637. Ferguson, Christine. Language, science and popular fiction in the Victorian *fin-de-siècle*: the brutal tongue. Aldershot; Burlington, VT: Ashgate, 2006. pp. x, 180. (Nineteenth century.) Rev. by Christine Devine in RES (57:231) 2006, 556–8.

8638. Forbes, Shannon. Women's transition from Victorian to contemporary identity as portrayed in the modern novel. *See* **13476**.

8639. Free, Melissa. Un-erasing Crusoe: *Farther Adventures* in the nineteenth century. *See* **7715**.

8640. Freedgood, Elaine. The ideas in things: fugitive meaning in the Victorian novel. Chicago, IL; London: Chicago UP, 2006. pp. x, 196.

8641. Fulton, DoVeanna S. Speaking power: Black feminist orality in women's narratives of slavery. *See* **8850**.

8642. Gallagher, Catherine. The body economic: life, death, and sensation in political economy and the Victorian novel. Princeton, NJ; Oxford:

Princeton UP, 2006. pp. 209. Rev. by Elaine Freedgood in Novel (39:1) 2006, 123–5; by Mary Poovey in VS (49:1) 2006, 107–9; by Rosemarie Bodenheimer in NineL (61:1) 2006, 103–7.

8643. Gray, Robert; Keep, Christopher. 'An uninterrupted current': homoeroticism and collaborative authorship in *Teleny*. *In* (pp. 193–208) **3405**.

8644. Grylls, David. Smoke signals: the sexual semiotics of smoking in Victorian fiction. Eng (55:211) 2006, 15–35.

8645. Hack, Daniel. The material interests of the Victorian novel. (Bibl. 2005, 9557.) Rev. by Jonathan H. Grossman in Novel (39:1) 2005, 135–7; by Christina Crosby in VS (48:3) 2006, 541–3; by Francis O'Gorman in RES (57:232) 2006, 843–5; by Irene Tucker in NineL (61:3) 2006, 385–91.

8646. Haggerty, George E. 'Dung, guts and blood': sodomy, abjection and gothic fiction in the early nineteenth century. *See* **11180**.

8647. Harrison, Kimberly; Fantina, Richard (eds). Victorian sensations: essays on a scandalous genre. Columbus: Ohio State UP, 2006. pp. xxiii, 278.

8648. Heller, Deborah. Literary sisterhoods: imagining women artists. Montreal; Buffalo, NY; London: McGill-Queen's UP, 2005. pp. 182. Rev. by A. Mary Murphy in CanL (191) 2006, 173–4.

8649. Hervouet-Farrar, Isabelle. *'And that criminal a woman and a mother'*: femmes meurtrières et roman à sensation en Grande-Bretagne à la fin du 19ème siècle. Cycnos (23:2) 2006, 77–93.

8650. Hibbard, Andrea L.; Parry, John T. Law, seduction, and the Sentimental heroine: the case of Amelia Norman. *See* **7801**.

8651. Hughes, Clair. Dressed in fiction. Oxford; New York: Berg, 2006. pp. ix, 214. Rev. by Christine Bayles Kortsch in TSWL (25:2) 2006, 348–50.

8652. James, Louis. The Victorian novel. Oxford; Malden, MA: Blackwell, 2006. pp. xii, 249. (Blackwell guides to literature.) Rev. by Matthew Beaumont in TLS, 16 June 2006, 30.

8653. Jin, Qiong. The characterization of priests and their cultural connotations in the novels of the Victorian women writers. FLS (122) 2006, 94–100. (In Chinese.)

8654. Johnson, Claudia Durst. Labor and workplace issues in literature. Westport, CT; London: Greenwood Press, 2006. pp. xix, 183. (Exploring social issues through literature.)

8655. Johnson-Woods, Toni. Story papers in Australia? The curious case of *Once-a-Week* down under. *See* **1125**.

8656. Jones, Wendy. Consensual fictions: women, liberalism, and the English novel. Toronto; Buffalo, NY; London: Toronto UP, 2005. pp. x, 255. Rev. by Pam Morris in Novel (38:2/3) 2005, 304–7; by David Wayne Thomas in VS (48:4) 2006, 762–4.

8657. Jordan-Lake, Joy. Whitewashing *Uncle Tom's Cabin*: nineteenth-century women novelists respond to Stowe. *See* **11354**.

8658. Kaser, James A. The Washington DC of fiction: a research guide. Lanham, MD; London: Scarecrow Press, 2006. pp. xiii, 351.

8659. Kickham, Lisbet. Protestant women novelists and Irish society 1879–1922. (Bibl. 2005, 9577.) Rev. by Sinéad Mooney in MLR (101:4) 2006, 1099–1100.

8660. Killick, Tim. Truth, imagination and tradition: Allan Cunningham and Scottish short fiction. *See* **9671**.

8661. Knight, Mark; Woodman, Thomas (eds). Biblical religion and the novel, 1700–2000. *See* **7389**.

8662. Kreilkamp, Ivan. Voice and the Victorian storyteller. Cambridge; New York: CUP, 2005. pp. viii, 252. (Cambridge studies in nineteenth-century literature and culture, 49.) Rev. by James Buzard in Novel (39:1) 2005, 129–32; by Jakob Lothe in RES (57:230) 2006, 430–1; by Matthew Reynolds in VS (49:1) 2006, 116–18.

8663. Kungl, Carla T. Creating the fictional female detective: the sleuth heroines of British women writers, 1890–1940. *See* **13535**.

8664. LeBlanc, Edward T. The LeBlanc bibliography listings. DNR (75:2) 2006, 44–6.

8665. Lehan, Richard. Realism and Naturalism: the novel in an age of transition. (Bibl. 2005, 9584.) Rev. by Donna M. Campbell in DreiS (36:2) 2005, 57–9; by Victoria Stewart in LitH (15:2) 2006, 88.

8666. LeMenager, Stephanie. Manifest and other destinies: territorial fictions of the nineteenth-century United States. (Bibl. 2005, 9585.) Rev. by Gretchen Murphy in AL (78:1) 2006, 180–2; by Bethany Schneider in GPQ (26:3) 2006, 219; by Nicole Tonkovich in WAL (41:2) 2006, 212–13.

8667. Lesjak, Carolyn. Working fictions: a genealogy of the Victorian novel. Durham, NC; London: Duke UP, 2006. pp. x, 270. (Post-contemporary interventions.)

8668. Letissier, Georges. Le texte victorien à l'âge postmoderne: jouvence ou sénescence? *Fingersmith* de Sarah Waters et le mélodrame victorien. *See* **20352**.

8669. Levitt, Morton P. The rhetoric of Modernist fiction from a new point of view. *See* **13542**.

8670. Loeber, Rolf; Loeber, Magda; Burnham, Anne Mullin. A guide to Irish fiction, 1650–1900. *See* **6409**.

8671. Logan, Lisa M. Columbia's daughters in drag; or, Cross-dressing, collaboration, and authorship in early American novels. *In* (pp. 240–52) **6224**.

8672. Lutz, Deborah. The dangerous lover: gothic villains, Byronism, and the nineteenth-century narrative. *See* **9350**.

8673. McLaughlin, Kevin. Paperwork: fiction and mass mediacy in the paper age. (Bibl. 2005, 9591.) Rev. by Margaret F. Nichols in SHARP (15:2/3) 2006, 19–20; by Daniel Hack in VS (48:4) 2006, 760–2; by Paul Ellis in HarSJ (2:1) 2006, 65–6; by Ross F. Collins in JoH (32:1) 2006, 53.

8674. MacLeod, Kirsten. Fictions of British Decadence: high art, popular culture, and the *fin de siècle*. Basingstoke; New York: Palgrave Macmillan, 2006. pp. ix, 222. (Palgrave studies in nineteenth-century writing and culture.)

8675. Malcolm, Cheryl Alexander; Malcolm, David (eds). British and Irish short-fiction writers, 1945–2000. Farmington Hills, MI: Thomson/Gale, 2006. pp. xx, 372. (Dictionary of literary biography, 319.)

8676. Mandal, A. A. Making Austen mad: Benjamin Crosby and the non-publication of *Susan*. *See* **9055**.

8677. Mangham, Andrew. The detective fiction of female adolescent violence. *See* **10134**.

8678. Manning, Susan. Characterless women and representative men: a transatlantic perspective. *See* **10579**.

8679. —— That exhumation scene again: transatlantic Hogg. *See* **10448**.

8680. Mansfield-Kelley, Deane; Marchino, Lois A. (eds). The Longman anthology of detective fiction. London; New York: Pearson Longman, 2005. pp. xiii, 482.

8681. Maunder, Andrew (gen. ed.). Sensationalism and the sensation debate. Ed. by Andrew Maunder. London; Brookfield, VT: Pickering & Chatto, 2004. pp. xlviii, 400. (Varieties of women's sensation fiction 1855–1890, 1.) Rev. by Anthea Trodd in VicR (31:2) 2005, 132–4.

8682. Moore, Lewis D. Cracking the hard-boiled detective: a critical history from the 1920s to the present. *See* **13565**.

8683. Morgan, William M. Questionable charity: gender, humanitarianism, and complicity in US literary realism. (Bibl. 2005, 9596.) Rev. by Morgan Sweeney in AL (77:4) 2005, 864–7.

8684. Morris, Pam. Imagining inclusive society in nineteenth-century novels: the code of sincerity in the public sphere. (Bibl. 2005, 9597.) Rev. by Malcolm Hardman in MLR (101:3) 2006, 832–3; by John Bowen in NineL (61:1) 2006, 113–16.

8685. Nemesvari, Richard. 'Judged by a purely literary standard': sensation fiction, horizons of expectation, and the generic construction of Victorian realism. *In* (pp. 15–28) **8647**.

8686. Nevins, Jess. The encyclopedia of fantastic Victoriana. Austin, TX: MonkeyBrain, 2005. pp. 1009. Rev. by Kelly Searsmith in JFA (16:4) 2006, 369–73.

8687. Newitz, Annalee. Pretend we're dead: capitalist monsters in American pop culture. *See* **13570**.

8688. Norquay, Glenda. Trading texts: negotiations of the professional and the popular in the case of *Treasure Island*. *In* (pp. 60–9) **11272**.

8689. O'Connell, Helen. Ireland and the fiction of improvement. Oxford; New York: OUP, 2006. pp. 228.

8690. Ofek, Galia. Sensational hair: gender, genre, and fetishism in the sensational decade. *In* (pp. 102–14) **8647**.

8691. O'Gorman, Francis (ed.). A concise companion to the Victorian novel. Oxford; Malden, MA: Blackwell, 2005. pp. xxiii, 277. (Blackwell concise companions to literature and culture.)

8692. Ostrowski, Carl. Slavery, labor reform, and intertextuality in antebellum print culture: the slave narrative and the city-mysteries novel. *See* **9919**.

8693. Pal-Lapinski, Piya. The exotic woman in nineteenth-century British fiction and culture: a reconsideration. (Bibl. 2005, 9600.) Rev. by Eleanor J. Harrington-Austin in VS (48:4) 2006, 715–17.

8694. Panek, LeRoy Lad. The origins of the American detective story. Jefferson, NC; London: McFarland, 2006. pp. vii, 227.

8695. Patterson, Martha H. Beyond the Gibson Girl: reimagining the American New Woman, 1895–1915. (Bibl. 2005, 9604.) Rev. by Jennifer L. Lawhorn in JPC (39:5) 2006, 909–10; by Carolyn Kitch in JoH (32:1) 2006, 54–5.

8696. Pedlar, Valerie. 'The most dreadful visitation': male madness in Victorian fiction. Liverpool: Liverpool UP, 2006. pp. 182. (Liverpool English texts and studies, 46.)

8697. Pettitt, Clare. Patent inventions: intellectual property and the Victorian novel. (Bibl. 2005, 9606.) Rev. by Daniel Hack in Novel (39:1) 2005, 146–9.

8698. Petty, Leslie. Romancing the vote: feminist activism in American fiction, 1870–1920. Athens; London: Georgia UP, 2006. pp. viii, 231.

8699. Polcini, Valentina. La formazione negata: parabole liminali di infanzia e negazione nel *Bildungsroman* vittoriano. RSV (18/19) 2004/05, 205–28.

8700. Price, Leah; Thurschwell, Pamela (eds). Literary secretaries / secretarial culture. Aldershot; Burlington, VT: Ashgate, 2005. pp. viii, 168. Rev. by Jenny Diski in LRB (27:15) 2005, 29–32; by Christopher Keep in VS (49:1) 2006, 113–16.

8701. Pykett, Lyn. Collins and the sensation novel. *In* (pp. 50–64) **9609**.

8702. Raimon, Eve Allegra. The 'tragic mulatta' revisited: race and nationalism in nineteenth-century antislavery fiction. (Bibl. 2005, 9611.) Rev. by Cherene Sherrard-Johnson in Legacy (23:2) 2006, 206–7; by Jené Schoenfeld in AL (78:4) 2006, 887–9.

8703. Rainone, Joseph (ed.). The Five Cent Wide Awake Library featuring all Frank Reade (Jr) appearances. Baldwin, NY: Almond Press, 2005. pp. iv, 56. (Art & history of American popular fiction, 1a.) Rev. by J. Randolph Cox in DNR (74:2) 2005, 66–7.

8704. Reid, Margaret. Cultural secrets as narrative form: storytelling in nineteenth-century America. (Bibl. 2004, 9765.) Rev. by Joseph Helminski in AL (78:2) 2006, 413–15.

8705. Reitz, Caroline. Detecting the nation: fictions of detection and the imperial venture. (Bibl. 2004, 8982.) Rev. by Nicholas Daly in Novel (39:1) 2005, 133–4.

8706. Richardson, LeeAnne M. New Woman and colonial adventure fiction in Victorian Britain: gender, genre, and empire. Gainesville: Florida UP, 2006. pp. 181. Rev. by Lucy Carlyle in TLS, 17 Nov. 2006, 32–3.

8707. Riggs, Pádraigín; Vance, Norman. Irish prose fiction. *In* (pp. 245–66) **11829**.

8708. Rivers, Bronwyn. Women at work in the Victorian novel: the question of middle-class women's employment. Lewiston, NY; Lampeter: Mellen Press, 2005. pp. xv, 234.

8709. Roberts, Adam. Science fiction. *See* **13592**.

8710. Roberts, Lewis. Trafficking in literary authority: Mudie's Select Library and the commodification of the Victorian novel. VLC (34:1) 2006, 1–25.

8711. Rosenthal, Debra J. Race mixture in nineteenth-century US and Spanish American fictions: gender, culture, and nation building. (Bibl. 2004, 9769.) Rev. by Claudia Sadowski-Smith in AL (78:3) 2006, 624–7.

8712. Roy, Anindyo. Civility and empire: literature and culture in British India, 1822–1922. London; New York: Routledge, 2005. pp. viii, 216. (Routledge research in postcolonial literatures, 7.)

8713. Schuman, Lydia C. The Edward T. LeBlanc bibliography of story papers, dime novels, and libraries. DNR (75:2) 2006, 35–43.

8714. Simpson, Hyacinth M. Bibliography of anglophone West Indian short stories. JWIL (12:1/2) 2004, 204–13.

8715. Smith, Eric D. A voyage to future pasts: the vengeance of other time in Ronald Wright's *A Scientific Romance*. *See* **19388**.

8716. Stripling, Mahala Yates. Bioethics and medical issues in literature. Westport, CT; London: Greenwood Press, 2005. pp. xxviii, 224. (Exploring social issues through literature.)

8717. Surridge, Lisa Anne. Bleak houses: marital violence in Victorian fiction. (Bibl. 2005, 9620.) Rev. by Lydia Murdoch in CLIO (36:1) 2006, 139–44; by Ann L. Ardis in NineL (61:3) 2006, 381–4.

8718. Sutherland, John. Victorian fiction: writers, publishers, readers. (Bibl. 2000, 25576.) Basingstoke; New York: Palgrave Macmillan, 2006. pp. xxv, 198. (Second ed.: first ed. 1995.)

8719. Swenson, Kristine. Medical women and Victorian fiction. (Bibl. 2005, 9621.) Rev. by Beth Torgerson in JMMLA (38:2) 2005, 135–7; by Maria Frawley in TSWL (25:1) 2006, 162–5; by Nadine Cooper in ELT (49:1) 2006, 118–19.

8720. Talairach-Vielmas, Laurence. Victorian sensational shoppers: representing transgressive femininity in Wilkie Collins's *No Name*. *See* **9607**.

8721. Tawil, Ezra. The making of racial sentiment: slavery and the birth of the frontier romance. Cambridge; New York: CUP, 2006. pp. ix, 244. (Cambridge studies in American literature and culture, 151.)

8722. Thomas, Ronald R. *The Moonstone*, detective fiction and forensic science. *In* (pp. 65–78) **9609**.

8723. Tougaw, Jason Daniel. Strange cases: the medical case history and the British novel. *See* **7400**.

8724. Traue, J. E. Fiction, public libraries and the reading public in colonial New Zealand. *See* **381**.

8725. Tremper, Ellen. I'm no angel: the blonde in fiction and film. Charlottesville; London: Virginia UP, 2006. pp. xiv, 288. (Cultural frames, framing culture.)

8726. Vietto, Angela. Inscribing manhood and enacting womanhood in the Early Republic. *In* (pp. 253–66) **6221**.

8727. Wagner, Tamara S. 'A strange chronicle of the olden time': revisions of the Regency in the construction of Victorian domestic fiction. *See* **9087**.

8728. Wakefield, Sarah R. Folklore in British literature: naming and narrating in women's fiction, 1750–1880. *See* **7403**.

8729. Weliver, Phyllis. The musical crowd in English fiction, 1840–1910: class, culture and nation. Basingstoke; New York: Palgrave Macmillan, 2006. pp. ix, 245. (Palgrave studies in nineteenth-century writing and culture.)

8730. Wetherell, Rodney. Subtopia or Sunnyside? *See* **19898**.

8731. Whyte, Iain Boyd. Anglo-German conflict in popular fiction, 1870–1914. *In* (pp. 43–99) **11790**.

8732. Williams, Carolyn. Genre matters: response. VS (48:2) 2006, 295–304.

8733. Wiltshire, Irene. *Pickwick* and the pirates. *See* **9839**.

8734. Yoshioka, Chiharu. Dialectic of enlightenment in the 1960s gothic: Angela Carter's *Heroes and Villains*. *See* **15065**.

8735. Zimmerman, David Andrew. Panic! Markets, crises & crowds in American fiction. Chapel Hill; London: North Carolina UP, 2006. pp. xii, 294. (Cultural studies of the US.)

8736. Zou, Huiling. On the Indian images in the White canons of 19th-century America. FLS (121) 2006, 45–51. (In Chinese.)

LITERATURE FOR CHILDREN

8737. Alderson, Brian; de Marez Oyens, Felix. Be merry and wise: origins of children's book publishing in England, 1650–1850. *See* **636**.

8738. Cohoon, Lorinda B. Serialized citizenships: periodicals, books, and American boys, 1840–1911. *See* **1073**.

8739. Cosslett, Tess. Talking animals in British children's fiction, 1786–1914. Aldershot; Burlington, VT: Ashgate, 2006. pp. 205. (Nineteenth century.)

8740. Darton, Lawrence. The Dartons: an annotated check-list of children's books issued by two publishing houses 1787–1870. Preface and editorial assistance by Brian Alderson. *See* **7413**.

8741. Dizer, John T. American children's literature, 1890–1940: heroic tales that shaped adult lives. *See* **13661**.

8742. Dobrin, Sidney I.; Kidd, Kenneth B. (eds). Wild things: children's culture and ecocriticism. (Bibl. 2004, 9783.) Rev. by Nathalie op de Beeck in ChildLit (33) 2005, 280–4.

8743. Doughty, Terri (ed.). Selections from *The Girl's Own Paper*, 1880–1907. *See* **1087**.

8744. Dowker, Ann. *Five Children and It*: some parallels with the nineteenth-century moral tale. *In* (pp. 169–83) **17738**.

8745. Fowler, James. The golden harp: Mary de Morgan's centrality in Victorian fairy-tale literature. *See* **9684**.

8746. Grenby, M. O. Tame fairies make good teachers: the popularity of early British fairy tales. *See* **7415**.

8747. Hoffman, Tyler. John Brown and children's literature. *In* (pp. 187–202) **8537**.

8748. Martin, Michelle H. Brown gold: milestones of African American children's picture books, 1845–2002. (Bibl. 2004, 9791.) Rev. by Philip Nel in ChildLit (33) 2005, 242–51; by Violet J. Harris in LU (30:2) 2006, 274–9.

8749. Pomeroy, Jane R. A new bibliography of the work of wood engraver and illustrator Alexander Anderson. *See* **99**.

8750. Singh, Rashna B. Goodly is our heritage: children's literature, empire, and the certitude of character. (Bibl. 2005, 9658.) Rev. by M. Daphne Kutzer in LU (30:1) 2006, 151–4.

8751. Sorby, Angela. Schoolroom poets: childhood and the place of American poetry, 1865–1917. (Bibl. 2005, 9659.) Rev. by Gary D. Schmidt in LU (30:3) 2006, 410–13; by Richard Flynn in ChildLit (34) 2006, 222–6; by Lynnell Edwards in GaR (60:2) 2006, 449–50.

8752. Stoneley, Peter. Consumerism and American girls' literature, 1860–1940. (Bibl. 2005, 9660.) Rev. by Sue Currell in MLR (101:1) 2006, 234–5.

8753. Thompson, Mary Shine; Keenan, Celia (eds). Treasure islands: studies in children's literature. Dublin; Portland, OR: Four Courts Press, 2006. pp. 219. Rev. by Margaret Mackey in CLAQ (31:3) 2006, 302–4.

8754. Tosi, Laura. Quando il giardino incantato non è un paese delle meraviglie; ovvero, L'ambiguo confine tra utopia e distopia nella letteratura per ragazzi. RSV (18/19) 2004/05, 95–108.

8755. Wadsworth, Sarah. In the company of books: literature and its 'classes' in nineteenth-century America. Amherst: Massachusetts UP, 2006. pp. xiii, 278. (Studies in print culture and the history of the book.)

POETRY

8756. Barrett, Faith. Civil War poetry in Southern newspapers and magazines. Book (70) 2006, 7.

8757. Bercovitch, Sacvan (gen. ed.). The Cambridge history of American literature: vol. 4, Nineteenth-century poetry. Cambridge; New York: CUP, 2004. pp. x, 562. Rev. by Richard Gray in JAStud (40:2) 2006, 399–411.

8758. Blair, Kirstie. Swinburne's spasms: *Poems and Ballads* and the 'Spasmodic School'. *See* **11373**.

8759. —— Victorian poetry and the culture of the heart. Oxford; New York: OUP, 2006. pp. vi, 273. (Oxford English monographs.) Rev. by John Holmes in RES (57:232) 2006, 840–1.

8760. Boudreau, Kristin. Elegies for the Haymarket anarchists. AL (77:2) 2005, 319–47.

8761. Bradstock, Margaret. Echoes of Ada Cambridge. *See* **9377**.

8762. Bristow, Joseph (ed.). The *fin-de-siècle* poem: English literary culture and the 1890s. (Bibl. 2005, 9675.) Rev. by Regenia Gagnier in VS (48:4) 2006, 771–3; by Talia Schaffer in JPRS (15:2) 2006, 93–6.

8763. Clarke, George Elliott. Anna Minerva Henderson: an Afro New Brunswick response to Canadian (Modernist) poetry. *See* **16404**.

8764. Clausson, Nils. 'Perpetuating the language': Romantic tradition, the genre function, and the origins of the trench lyric. *See* **13728**.

8765. Comet, Noah. Letitia Landon and Romantic Hellenism. *See* **10708**.

8766. Cooper, Andrew R. Women's poetry, the 1830s, and monumental problems in the history of language theory. WS (35:7) 2006, 621–55.

8767. Corballis, Richard. Zealandia among the poets: a sesquicentennial tribute. *In* (pp. 331–48) **8374**.

8768. Davies, Damian Walford; Turley, Richard Marggraf (eds). The monstrous debt: modalities of Romantic influence in twentieth-century literature. Foreword by Lucy Newlyn. *See* **13735**.

8769. Drew, John M. L. (ed.). The pride of mankind. Oswestry, Salop.: Hedge Sparrow Press, 2006. pp. xii, 46. Rev. by Duane DeVries in DickQ (23:3) 2006, 202–4.

8770. Echeruo, Michael J. Nineteenth-century Anglo-Nigerian poetry. *In* (pp. 15–41) **11860**.

8771. Fisher, Benjamin F. Guide to the year's work: the poets of the nineties. VP (44:3) 2006, 361–4.

8772. Fontana, Ernest. Too late: the Pre-Raphaelites, Tennyson, and Browning. *See* **11392**.

8773. Fontana, Ernest L. Victorian doors. *See* **11082**.

8774. Furst, Lilian R. Lighting up the night. *In* (pp. 505–21) **8357**.

8775. Garvey, Ellen Gruber. Anonymity, authorship, and recirculation: a Civil War episode. BH (9) 2006, 159–78.

8776. Gaull, Marilyn. Revisiting 1970: Carl Woodring and *Politics in English Romantic Poetry*. *See* **14107**.

8777. Gioia, Dana; Yost, Chryss; Hicks, Jack (eds). California poetry: from the Gold Rush to the present. Santa Clara, CA: Santa Clara Univ.; Berkeley, CA: Heyday, 2004. pp. xxix, 376. (California legacy.) Rev. by Jacqueline Marcus in PInt (10) 2006, 170–1.

8778. Gray, Erik. The poetry of indifference: from the Romantics to the *Rubáiyát*. Amherst: Massachusetts UP, 2005. pp. 151. Rev. by Christopher Decker in EC (56:3) 2006, 293–302; by Richard Cronin in KSJ (55) 2006, 257–8.

8779. Gray, F. Elizabeth. 'Syren strains': Victorian women's devotional poetry and John Keble's *The Christian Year*. *See* **10677**.

8780. Gray, Janet. Race and time: American women's poetics from antislavery to racial modernity. (Bibl. 2005, 9686.) Rev. by Susan Kurjiaka in AL (77:3) 2005, 637–9.

8781. Gregory, E. David. Victorian songhunters: the recovery and editing of English vernacular ballads and folk lyrics, 1820–1883. *See* **3041**.

8782. Greiner, Donald J. (ed.). Classes on modern poetry and the art of poetry. Foreword by Pat Conroy. *See* **13757**.

8783. Gwynn, R. S. Haunted palaces, trembling strings. *See* **11018**.

8784. Hall, Susan Grove. From voice to persona: Amelia Welby's lyric tradition in Sarah M. B. Piatt's early poetry. *See* **11003**.

8785. Hamilton, John. The revival of the ode. *In* (pp. 345–59) **8357**.

8786. Hess, Scott. Authoring the self: self-representation, authorship, and the print market in British poetry from Pope through Wordsworth. *See* **7429**.

8787. Hinds, Michael; Matterson, Stephen (eds). Rebound: the American poetry book. *See* **13770**.

8788. Hopps, Gavin. Beyond embarrassment: a post-secular reading of apostrophe. Romanticism (11:2) 2005, 224–41.

8789. —— Stabler, Jane (eds). Romanticism and religion from William Cowper to Wallace Stevens. Aldershot; Burlington, VT: Ashgate, 2006. pp. viii, 262. (Nineteenth century.)

8790. Hughes, Linda K. Daughters of Danaus and Daphne: women poets and the marriage question. VLC (34:2) 2006, 481–93.

8791. Jackson-Houlston, Caroline. 'Queen lilies'? The interpenetration of scientific, religious and gender discourses in Victorian representations of plants. JVC (11:1) 2006, 84–110.

8792. Kersten, Holger. America's multilingualism and the problem of the literary representation of 'pidgin English'. Amst (51:1) 2006, 75–91.

8793. LaPorte, Charles. Atheist prophecy: Mathilde Blind, Constance Naden, and the Victorian poetess. *See* **9130**.

8794. Lau, Beth. Home, exile, and *Wanderlust* in Austen and the Romantic poets. *See* **9046**.

8795. Leonard, Keith D. Fettered genius: the African American bardic poet from slavery to Civil Rights. Charlottesville; London: Virginia UP, 2006. pp. ix, 283.

8796. Lockard, Joe. 'Earth feels the time of prophet-song': John Brown and public poetry. *In* (pp. 69–87) **8537**.

8797. —— Jacksonian mobs, free speech, and the rise of American antislavery poetry. YREAL (22) 2006, 117–44.

8798. Loeffelholz, Mary. From school to salon: reading nineteenth-century American women's poetry. (Bibl. 2005, 9701.) Rev. by Carolyn Sorisio in AL (78:1) 2006, 182–5.

8799. Low, Dennis. The literary protégées of the Lake Poets. *See* **11239**.

8800. Lyu, Claire Chi-ah. A sun within a sun: the power and elegance of poetry. Pittsburgh, PA: Pittsburgh UP, 2006. pp. xiii, 222.

8801. Mason, Emma. Women poets of the nineteenth century. Plymouth: Northcote House, 2006. pp. xi, 148. (Writers and their work.)

8802. Matthews, Samantha. Poetical remains: poets' graves, bodies, and books in the nineteenth century. (Bibl. 2004, 9826.) Rev. by Scott Hess in WordsC (36:4) 2005, 150–2; by Roger Evans in TRB (8:5) 2006, 401–4; by William Hughes in SHARP (15:1) 2006, 10; by Charles LaPorte in VS (48:3) 2006, 555–7; by David E. Latané, Jr, in SAtlR (71:1) 2006, 150–4.

8803. O'Brien, Peggy. Writing Lough Derg: from William Carleton to Seamus Heaney. Syracuse, NY: Syracuse UP, 2006. pp. xxiii, 312. (Irish studies.)

8804. O'Donoghue, Bernard. Poetry in Ireland. *In* (pp. 173–89) **11829**.

8805. O'Gorman, Francis (ed.). Victorian poetry: an annotated anthology. (Bibl. 2004, 9830.) Rev. by Marcus Waithe in MLR (101:3) 2006, 833–4.

8806. O'NEILL, MICHAEL. 'The all-sustaining air': Yeats, Stevens, Rich, Bishop – responses to Romantic poetry. *In* (pp. 143–62) **13735**.

8807. —— 'The burden of ourselves': Arnold as a post-Romantic poet. *See* **8987**.

8808. PAREJO VADILLO, ANA. Women poets and urban Aestheticism: passengers of modernity. Basingstoke; New York: Palgrave Macmillan, 2005. pp. xi, 266. (Palgrave studies in nineteenth-century writing and culture.) Rev. by Cynthia Scheinberg in NineL (61:1) 2006, 120–4.

8809. PARR, KATHERINE. Integrating women's writing into the canon: women poets of Young Ireland. *In* (pp. 235–65) **12189**.

8810. PASCOE, JUDITH. The hummingbird cabinet: a rare and curious history of Romantic collectors. Ithaca, NY; London: Cornell UP, 2006. pp. xiii, 222. Rev. by Andrew Bennett in NineL (61:3) 2006, 372–5.

8811. PHELAN, JOE. From pit and willage. TLS, 3 Nov. 2006, 9–10 (review-article). (Working-class poets.)

8812. PHELAN, JOSEPH P. The nineteenth-century sonnet. Basingstoke; New York: Palgrave Macmillan, 2006. pp. vii, 192. Rev. by Clive Wilmer in TLS, 29 Sept. 2006, 31; by John Holmes in RES (57:231) 2006, 558–9.

8813. PHILLIPS, HELEN. Chaucer and the nineteenth-century city. *In* (pp. 193–210) **4312**.

8814. REGAN, STEPHEN. The Victorian sonnet, from George Meredith to Gerard Manley Hopkins. *See* **10918**.

8815. RIEDE, DAVID G. Allegories of one's own mind: melancholy in Victorian poetry. (Bibl. 2005, 9714.) Rev. by Charles LaPorte in NineL (61:2) 2006, 252–5.

8816. ROBINSON, ERIC. *Married at Last*: a new source for Clare's *Don Juan*. *See* **9480**.

8817. ROBINSON, JEFFREY C. Unfettered poetry: fancy in British Romanticism. Basingstoke; New York: Palgrave Macmillan, 2006. pp. x, 301.

8818. ROSEN, DAVID. Power, plain English, and the rise of modern poetry. New Haven, CT; London: Yale UP, 2006. pp. x, 212.

8819. ROSENBERG, JOHN D. Elegy for an age: the presence of the past in Victorian literature. (Bibl. 2005, 9715.) Rev. by Adrian Poole in RES (57:229) 2006, 261–2; by Linda M. Austin in VS (48:3) 2006, 557–9; by Richard D. Altick in JPRS (15:1) 2006, 95–6.

8820. SANDERS, MIKE. 'A jackass load of poetry': the *Northern Star*'s poetry column 1838–1852. VPR (39:1) 2006, 46–66.

8821. SCHMITZ, NEIL. Doing the Gettysburg Address: Jefferson/Calhoun/Lincoln/King. *See* **10741**.

8822. STAUFFER, ANDREW M. Guide to the year's work: general materials. VP (44:3) 2006, 311–16.

8823. STIMSON, KATHARINE. 'Where Robins hop, and fallen leaves are sere': Keats's robin and the social imagination. *See* **10667**.

8824. SUTTON, EMMA. 'The music spoke for us': music and sexuality in *fin-de-siècle* poetry. *In* (pp. 213–29) **8828**.

8825. Turley, Richard Marggraf. The politics of language in Romantic literature. (Bibl. 2005, 143190.) Rev. by Dan Kline in PrSt (28:1) 2006, 103–7.

8826. Verdonck, Joris. 'Those colours saved for better days': history and myth in the poetry on the Battle of Isandlwana, Zululand, 1879: a New Historicist reading. BELL (ns 4) 2006, 93–108.

8827. Watson, J. R. Ancient or modern, *Ancient and Modern*: the Victorian hymn and the nineteenth century. YES (36:2) 2006, 1–16.

8828. Weliver, Phyllis (ed.). The figure of music in nineteenth-century British poetry. Aldershot; Burlington, VT: Ashgate, 2005. pp. xiii, 266. (Music in nineteenth-century Britain.) Rev. by Robert Terrell Bledsoe in VS (48:3) 2006, 553–5.

8829. White, Simon; Goodridge, John; Keegan, Bridget (eds). Robert Bloomfield: lyric, class, and the Romantic canon. *See* **9141**.

8830. Wilmer, Clive. Captured in time. TLS, 29 Sept. 2006, 31 (review-article). (Sonnets.)

8831. Wilson, Charles Reagan. 'Just a little talk with Jesus': Elvis Presley, religious music, and Southern spirituality. SoCult (12:4) 2006, 74–91.

8832. Wolfson, Susan J. Borderlines: the shiftings of gender in British Romanticism. Stanford, CA: Stanford UP, 2006. pp. xxii, 430.

8833. Woolford, John. The critique of Romantic solipsism in Tennyson's *The Palace of Art*. *See* **11411**.

8834. Zimbardo, Rose A. Reading and writing the landscape. *See* **7443**.

PROSE

8835. Allen, Thomas. Clockwork nation: modern time, moral perfectionism and American identity in Catharine Beecher and Henry Thoreau. *See* **11422**.

8836. Anderson, Monica. Women and the politics of travel, 1870–1914. Madison, NJ: Fairleigh Dickinson UP, 2006. pp. 287. Rev. by Barbara T. Gates in Biography (29:4) 2006, 733–5.

8837. Bercovitch, Sacvan (gen. ed.). The Cambridge history of American literature: vol. 3, Prose writing, 1860–1920. Cambridge; New York: CUP, 2005. pp. xi, 813. Rev. by Richard Gray in JAStud (40:2) 2006, 399–411.

8838. Binfield, Kevin (ed.). Writings of the Luddites. Baltimore, MD; London: Johns Hopkins UP, 2004. pp. xxviii, 279. Rev. by Malcolm Hardman in MLR (101:3) 2006, 829–30; by Ben P. Robertson in KSJ (55) 2006, 265–8.

8839. Bohls, Elizabeth A.; Duncan, Ian (eds). Travel writing 1700–1830: an anthology. *See* **7447**.

8840. Callanan, Laura. Deciphering race: White anxiety, racial conflict, and the turn to fiction in mid-Victorian English prose. *See* **8624**.

8841. Carr, Jean Ferguson; Carr, Stephen L.; Schultz, Lucille M. Archives of instruction: nineteenth-century rhetorics, readers, and composition books in the United States. *See* **1881**.

8842. Chen, Jeng-Guo S. The British view of Chinese civilization and the emergence of class consciousness. ECent (45:2) 2004, 193–205.

8843. DAVIES, LAURENCE. 'A sideways ending to it all': G. W. Steevens, Blackwood, and the *Daily Mail*. *In* (pp. 236–58) **1098**.

8844. DONOVAN, STEPHEN. The muse of *Blackwood's*: Charles Whibley and literary criticism in the world. *In* (pp. 259–86) **1098**.

8845. ELSDEN, ANNAMARIA FORMICHELLA. Watery angels: Sophia Peabody Hawthorne's artistic argument in *Notes in England and Italy*. *In* (pp. 129–45) **10790**.

8846. ERNEST, JOHN. Liberation historiography: African American writers and the challenge of history, 1794–1861. *See* **7461**.

8847. FICHTELBERG, JOSEPH. The Devil designs a career: Aaron Burr and the shaping of enterprise. EAL (41:3) 2006, 495–513.

8848. FISH, CHERYL J. Black and White women's travel narratives: antebellum explorations. (Bibl. 2005, 9749.) Rev. by John M. Freiermuth in AL (78:2) 2006, 389–91; by Kristin Waters in JAC (29:2) 2006, 229–30; by Lisa M. Logan in Legacy (23:1) 2006, 95–6.

8849. FORBES, CURDELLA. Selling that Caribbean woman down the river: diasporic travel narratives and the global economy. *See* **11160**.

8850. FULTON, DOVEANNA S. Speaking power: Black feminist orality in women's narratives of slavery. Albany: New York State UP, 2006. pp. xvi, 164.

8851. HADDAD, EMILY A. 'Better than the reality': the Egyptian market in nineteenth-century British travel writing. *In* (pp. 72–89) **8395**.

8852. HALL, JULIE E. At the crisis of our fate: Sophia Peabody Hawthorne's Civil War correspondence. *In* (pp. 61–76) **10790**.

8853. HAMMOND, ANDREW. Imagined colonialism: Victorian travellers in South-East Europe. *See* **10719**.

8854. IMBARRATO, SUSAN CLAIR. Traveling women: narrative visions of early America. *See* **7468**.

8855. JARKA, HORST; JARKA, LOIS (eds). The others' Austria: impressions of American and British travellers: vol. 1, 1814–1914. Riverside, CA: Ariadne Press, 2005. pp. 435. (Studies in Austrian literature, culture, and thought.)

8856. JOHNSON, CLAUDIA DURST. Labor and workplace issues in literature. *See* **8654**.

8857. JOHNSTON, ANNA. Missionary writing and empire, 1800–1860. (Bibl. 2005, 9763.) Rev. by Angela Smith in MLR (101:1) 2006, 231–2.

8858. JOSHUA, ESSAKA; JOSHUA, ELEOMA. Thomas Lovell Beddoes and the attribution of articles in the *Wellesley Index* and in the *Oxford Dictionary of National Biography*. *See* **9116**.

8859. JUN, HELEN H. Black Orientalism: nineteenth-century narratives of race and US citizenship. *See* **9915**.

8860. KEANE, ANGELA. Richard Carlile's working women: selling books, politics, sex and *The Republican*. LitH (15:2) 2006, 20–33.

8861. KONUK, KADER. Ethnomasquerade in Ottoman–European encounters: reenacting Lady Mary Wortley Montagu. *See* **8015**.

8862. LARRABEE, MARY JEANNE. 'I know what a slave knows': Mary Prince's epistemology of resistance. WS (35:5) 2006, 453–73.

8863. Lawrence, Deborah. Writing the trail: five women's frontier narratives. Iowa City: Iowa UP, 2006. pp. 158.

8864. Lee, Pamela. Queen of all I surveyed: Sarah Peabody Hawthorne's 'Cuba Journal' and the imperial gaze. *In* (pp. 163–79) **10790**.

8865. McArdle, Andrea. The confluence of law and antebellum Black literature: lawyerly discourse as a rhetoric of empowerment. *See* **11329**.

8866. McLeod, Mona Kedslie (ed.). From Charlotte Square to Fingal's Cave: reminiscences of a journey through Scotland 1820–1824. East Linton, E. Lothian: Tuckwell Press, 2004. pp. 244. Rev. by John Harries in ScSR (6:2) 2005, 136–8.

8867. Makino, Arimichi. Commodore Perry as white phantom: *Moby-Dick* in the context of the modern age. *See* **10862**.

8868. Matus, Jill. Collaboration and collusion: two Victorian writing couples and their Orientalist texts. *In* (pp. 175–92) **3405**.

8869. Nash, Geoffrey P. From empire to Orient: travellers to the Middle East 1830–1926. London; New York: Tauris, 2005. pp. 252. Rev. by Tim Mackintosh-Smith in TLS, 15 Sept. 2006, 12.

8870. Nixon, Jude V. 'Eternity in the vesture of time': Carlyle, thermodynamic discourse, and apocalyptic anxieties. *See* **9398**.

8871. O'Donnell, Kevin E.; Hollingsworth, Helen. Seekers of scenery: travel writing from southern Appalachia, 1840–1900. (Bibl. 2005, 9776.) Rev. by Anne E. Rowe in NCHR (82:4) 2005, 527–8; by Katherine Ledford in AppH (34:2) 2006, 99–100; by C. Brenden Martin in JSH (72:2) 2006, 467–8; by Durwood Dunn in THQ (65:2) 2006, 188–9.

8872. Ostrowski, Carl. Slavery, labor reform, and intertextuality in antebellum print culture: the slave narrative and the city-mysteries novel. *See* **9919**.

8873. Powell, Michael. *Do the Dead Talk?* The Daisy Bank Printing and Publishing Company of Manchester. *In* (pp. 163–87) **746**.

8874. Robbins, Sarah. *Woman's Work for Woman*: gendered print culture in American mission movement narratives. *In* (pp. 251–80) **690**.

8875. Sanborn, Geoffrey. Whence come you, Queequeg? *See* **10893**.

8876. Schmeller, Erik S. Perceptions of race and nation in English and American travel writers, 1833–1914. New York; Frankfurt: Lang, 2004. pp. x, 117. (Travel writing across the disciplines, 5.)

8877. Schor, Esther. Acts of union: Theodosia Garrow Trollope and Frances Power Cobbe on the Kingdom of Italy. *In* (pp. 90–109) **8320**.

8878. Scott, Grant F. (ed.). Joseph Severn: letters and memoirs. Aldershot; Burlington, VT: Ashgate, 2005. pp. xxxv, 716. Rev. by Nicholas Roe in KSR (19) 2005, 161–3; by John Whale in WordsC (36:4) 2005, 195–6; by Caroline Bertonèche in KSJ (55) 2006, 244–6; by Jonathon Shears in BJ (34:1) 2006, 77–80.

8879. Stabler, Jane. Devotion and diversion: early nineteenth-century British women travellers in Italy and the Catholic Church. *In* (pp. 15–34) **8320**.

8880. Steinlight, Emily. 'ANTI-BLEAK HOUSE': advertising and the Victorian novel. *See* **9823**.

8881. Sumpter, Caroline. Joining the 'crusade against the giants': Keir Hardie's fairy tales and the Socialist child reader. LitH (15:2) 2006, 34–49.

8882. Tinnemeyer, Andrea. Identity politics of the captivity narrative after 1848. Lincoln; London: Nebraska UP, 2006. pp. xxii, 157.

8883. Tricomi, Albert. Dialect and identity in Harriet Jacobs's autobiography and other slave narratives. *See* **10531**.

8884. van Tilburg, Marja. Domesticating holiness: holiness, gender, and education in conduct literature, 1780–1890. *In* (pp. 111–26) **3415**.

8885. Vietto, Angela. Inscribing manhood and enacting womanhood in the Early Republic. *In* (pp. 253–66) **6224**.

8886. Voeller, Carey R. 'I have not told half we suffered': Overland Trail women's narratives and the genre of suppressed textual mourning. Legacy (23:2) 2006, 148–62.

8887. Walton, Susan. Charlotte M. Yonge and the 'historic harem' of Edward Augustus Freeman. *See* **11729**.

8888. Warrior, Robert. The people and the word: reading Native nonfiction. (Bibl. 2005, 9792.) Rev. by Frederick Luis Aldama in MELUS (31:1) 2006, 152–5.

8889. Whelan, Timothy. Politics, religion, and romance: letters of Eliza Gould Flower, 1794–1802. *See* **7486**.

8890. White, Shane; White, Graham. The sounds of slavery: discovering African American history through songs, sermons, and speech. *See* **3093**.

BIOGRAPHY AND AUTOBIOGRAPHY

8891. Amigoni, David (ed.). Life writing and Victorian culture. Aldershot; Burlington, VT: Ashgate, 2006. pp. xi, 236. (Nineteenth century.) Rev. by Matthew Rubery in RES (57:232) 2006, 841–3.

8892. Anderson, Eric Gary. Indian agency: *Life of Black Hawk* and the countercolonial provocations of early Native American writing. ESQ (52:1/2) 2006, 75–104.

8893. Auerbach, Emily. Searching for Jane Austen: restoring the 'fleas' and 'bad breath'. *See* **8997**.

8894. Booth, Alison. How to make it as a woman: collective biographical history from Victoria to the present. (Bibl. 2005, 9803.) Rev. by Janice Carlisle in A/B (20:1) 2005, 90–4; by Mary Ellis Gibson in Biography (29:2) 2006, 344–9; by Jessica Cox in MLR (101:4) 2006, 1072–3; by Jessica Berman in VWM (70) 2006, 38–9; by Sally Mitchell in NineL (61:3) 2006, 378–81.

8895. Carlson, David J. Sovereign selves: American Indian autobiography and the law. Urbana: Illinois UP, 2006. pp. viii, 217. Rev. by Laura L. Mielke in Biography (29:4) 2006, 740–2.

8896. Cox, Arthur J. The *Drood* remains revisited: 'first fancy'. *See* **9727**.

8897. Davis, Rocío G. Begin here: a critical introduction to the Asian American childhood. *In* (pp. 161–80) **11995**.

8898. Evans, G. R. John Wyclif: the biography of a legend. *See* **4299**.

8899. Goldman, Lawrence. A monument to the Victorian age? Continuity and discontinuity in the Dictionaries of National Biography 1882–2004. JVC (11:1) 2006, 111–32. (Focus on the Oxford *DNB*, 2.)

8900. HABICH, ROBERT D. Holmes, Cabot, and Edward Emerson and the challenges of writing Emerson's biography in the 1880s. *In* (pp. 3–32) **10064**.

8901. HARDING, ANTHONY JOHN. 'Domestick privacies': biography and the sanctifying of privacy, from Johnson to Martineau. *See* **7927**.

8902. HEIDT, SARAH J. 'The materials for a "Life"': collaboration, publication, and the Carlyles' afterlives. *See* **9410**.

8903. HIGGINS, ANDREW C. Reconstructing rebellion: the politics of narrative in the Confederate memoir. MissQ (58:1/2) 2004/05, 119–39.

8904. HOLLAND, PETER. Shakespeare and the *DNB*. *In* (pp. 139–49) **5353**.

8905. HOLMES, RICHARD (ed.). Gilchrist on Blake: *Life of William Blake, Pictor Ignotus*. *See* **7574**.

8906. HSU, HSUAN L. Personality, race, and geopolitics in Joseph Heco's *Narrative of a Japanese*. Biography (29:2) 2006, 273–306.

8907. KAPLAN, CATHERINE. Theft and counter-theft: Joseph Plumb Martin's Revolutionary war. EAL (41:3) 2006, 515–34.

8908. LAI, SHU-FANG. Dickens's representation of childhood trauma. *See* **9777**.

8909. MCPHERSON, SUSAN. On being 'tempted to knit': writing, reviewing and reading biography. NCC (28:1) 2006, 49–65.

8910. MURPHY, PATRICIA. In science's shadow: literary constructions of late Victorian women. *See* **10304**.

8911. PARKER, PETER. Naked portraits: the lives of their times: how the art of biography evolved. *See* **7498**.

8912. PIERCE, YOLANDA. Hell without fires: slavery, Christianity, and the antebellum spiritual narrative. Foreword by Stephen W. Angell and Anthony B. Pinn. (Bibl. 2005, 9820.) Rev. by Nancy A. Hardesty in JSH (72:3) 2006, 666–7.

8913. POWELL, MALEA D. Sarah Winnemucca Hopkins: her wrongs and claims. *In* (pp. 69–94) **2149**.

8914. SCHMIDGALL, GARY (ed.). Conserving Walt Whitman's fame: selections from Horace Traubel's *Conservator*, 1890–1919. *See* **11584**.

8915. SPRADLIN, DERRICK. Westward expansion, Indian subjugation, and the frontier gazes of Jackson Johonnet, Zebulon Montgomery Pike, and James Kirk Paulding. *See* **10989**.

8916. STROMBERG, ERNEST. Resistance and mediation: the rhetoric of irony in Indian boarding-school narratives by Francis La Flesche and Zitkala-Ša. *In* (pp. 95–109) **2149**.

RELATED STUDIES

8917. BARRINGER, TIM. Men at work: art and labour in Victorian Britain. New Haven, CT; London: Yale UP for the Paul Mellon Centre for Studies in British Art, 2005. pp. xi, 379. Rev. by Laurent Bury in EA (59:4) 2006, 486–7.

8918. DESLANDES, PAUL R. Oxbridge men: British masculinity and the undergraduate experience, 1850–1920. Bloomington: Indiana UP, 2005. pp. xviii, 319. Rev. by Sheldon Rothblatt in VS (49:1) 2006, 163–4.

8919. Donaldson, Susan V. Masters, slaves, and the 'mind of the South'. MissQ (58:1/2) 2004/05, 193–204.

8920. Faulk, Barry J. Music hall & modernity: the late Victorian discovery of popular culture. (Bibl. 2005, 9841.) Rev. by Richard Duvall in VPR (39:2) 2006, 181–2; by Peter Bailey in JVC (11:1) 2006, 180–4.

8921. Featherstone, Simon. Vestal flirtations: the performance of the feminine in late nineteenth-century British music hall. NCS (19) 2005, 99–112.

8922. Flanders, Judith. Consuming passions: leisure and pleasure in Victorian Britain. London: HarperPress, 2006. pp. xvii, 604, (plates) 24. Rev. by Rosemary Ashton in TLS, 22 Sept. 2006, 36.

8923. Frost, Linda. Never one nation: freaks, savages and Whiteness in US popular culture, 1850–1877. Minneapolis; London: Minnesota UP, 2005. pp. xix, 241. Rev. by Jeff Berglund in AmP (16:2) 2006, 229–33; by Kenneth Salzer in Legacy (23:2) 2006, 207–9.

8924. Geary, Laurence M.; Kelleher, Margaret (eds). Nineteenth-century Ireland: a guide to recent research. Dublin: University College Dublin Press, 2005. pp. xii, 340. Rev. by Timothy G. McMahon in VS (48:2) 2006, 344–6.

8925. Grusin, Richard. Culture, technology, and the creation of America's national parks. Cambridge; New York: CUP, 2004. pp. xx, 212. (Cambridge studies in American literature and culture, 137.) Rev. by Brooke Ann Smith in WAL (40:2) 2005, 224–6.

8926. Heilmann, Ann; Beetham, Margaret (eds). New Woman hybridities: femininity, feminism, and international consumer culture, 1880–1930. London; New York: Routledge, 2004. pp. xv, 279. (Routledge transatlantic perspectives on American literature, 1.) Rev. by Avril Horner in JAStud (39:2) 2005, 321–2; by Stephanie Spencer in LitH (15:2) 2006, 84–5.

8927. Leaney, Enda. Phrenology in nineteenth-century Ireland. NewHR (10:3) 2006, 24–42.

8928. Rajan, Tilottama; Plotnitsky, Arkady (eds). Idealism without absolutes: philosophy and Romantic culture. Albany: New York State UP, 2004. pp. vii, 262. (SUNY series: Intersections – philosophy and critical theory.) Rev. by Richard Eldridge in ERR (17:4) 2006, 511–20.

8929. Robertson, John. The case for the Enlightenment: Scotland and Naples, 1680–1760. *See* **7511**.

8930. Rowland, Herbert. More than meets the eye: Hans Christian Andersen and nineteenth-century American criticism. Madison, NJ: Fairleigh Dickinson UP, 2006. pp. 274.

8931. Schad, John. Queer fish: Christian unreason from Darwin to Derrida. Brighton; Portland, OR: Sussex Academic Press, 2004. pp. viii, 177. Rev. by Marcus Waithe in TRB (8:5) 2006, 404–6; by Lori Branch in VS (48:4) 2006, 754–6.

8932. Sicherman, Barbara. Connecting lives: women and reading, then and now. *In* (pp. 3–24) **690**.

8933. Snyder, Laura J. Reforming philosophy: a Victorian debate on science and society. Chicago, IL; London: Chicago UP, 2006. pp. x, 386. Rev. by John North in TLS, 20 Oct. 2006, 4–5.

8934. Sparks, Randy J. The Southern way of death: the meaning of death in antebellum White evangelical culture. SoQ (44:1) 2006, 32–50.

8935. Stowe, Steven M. Irony and Southern authorship. MissQ (58:1/2) 2004/05, 175–82.

8936. Sutcliffe, Allan. From Devonshire House to the Bull Ring, Birmingham: a Dickensian contribution to the music hall. Dickensian (102:1) 2006, 21–3.

8937. Suter, Keith. The rise and fall of English coffee houses. *See* **6528**.

8938. Tholoniat, Richard. *Summer schools, Scottish reels* et *MacBrayne Steamers*: regards français sur les cultures écossaises 1850–1914. RANAM (39) 2006, 119–31.

8939. Trafton, Scott. Egypt land: race and nineteenth-century American Egyptomania. Durham, NC; London: Duke UP, 2004. pp. xix, 348. (New Americanists.) Rev. by Gretchen Murphy in AL (78:1) 2006, 180–2.

8940. Tribble, Evelyn. The 'conscientious discharge of their duties': women in the Dunedin Shakespeare Club, 1877–1898. *In* (pp. 554–9) **8374**.

8941. Watson, Harry L. Think about the South: Michael O'Brien, *Conjectures of Order: Intellectual Life and the American South, 1810–1860*. MissQ (58:1/2) 2004/05, 183–91.

8942. Watson, Nicola J. The literary tourist: readers and places in Romantic and Victorian Britain. Basingstoke; New York: Palgrave Macmillan, 2006. pp. viii, 244.

8943. Webby, Elizabeth. Not reading the nation: Australian readers of the 1890s. ALS (22:3) 2006, 308–18.

8944. Wyatt-Brown, Bertram. Comment on Michael O'Brien's *Conjectures of Order*. MissQ (58:1/2) 2004/05, 161–73.

8945. Zboray, Ronald J.; Zboray, Mary Saracino. Everyday ideas: socioliterary experience among antebellum New Englanders. Knoxville: Tennessee UP, 2006. pp. xxv, 430.

LITERARY THEORY

8946. Atherton, Carol. Defining literary criticism: scholarship, authority, and the possession of literary knowledge, 1880–2002. (Bibl. 2005, 9862.) Rev. by Gary Day in TLS, 13 Jan. 2006, 28.

8947. Camlot, Jason. The Victorian critic as naturalizing agent. ELH (73:2) 2006, 489–518.

8948. Donovan, Stephen. The muse of *Blackwood's*: Charles Whibley and literary criticism in the world. *In* (pp. 259–86) **1098**.

8949. London, April. Isaac D'Israeli and literary history: opinion, anecdote, and secret history in the early nineteenth century. PT (26:3) 2005, 351–86.

8950. Porter, James I. Homer: the history of an idea. *In* (pp. 324–43) **3253**.

8951. Stokes, Claudia. Writers in retrospect: the rise of American literary history, 1875–1910. Chapel Hill; London: North Carolina UP, 2006. pp. xi, 241.

AUTHORS

Charles Follen Adams (1842–1918)

8952. Mehring, Frank. Deutsch, Dutch, double Dutch: authentic and artificial German American dialects. Amst (51:1) 2006, 93–113.

Henry Adams

8953. O'Brien, Michael. Henry Adams and the Southern Question. Athens; London: Georgia UP, 2005. pp. xiv, 201. (Mercer Univ. Lamar Memorial Lectures, 47.) Rev. by J. C. Levenson in NCHR (82:3) 2005, 409–11; by James Turner in JAH (93:1) 2006, 223–4.

8954. Wills, Garry. Henry Adams and the making of America. (Bibl. 2005, 9897.) Rev. by Michael O'Brien in TLS, 20 Jan. 2006, 8.

John Quincy Adams (1767–1848)

8955. Murphy, Gretchen. Hemispheric imaginings: the Monroe Doctrine and narratives of US empire. *See* **8455**.

Jane Addams

8956. Brown, Victoria Bissell. The education of Jane Addams. (Bibl. 2005, 9898.) Rev. by Kathleen Weiler in NWSAJ (18:2) 2006, 230–4.

8957. Hamington, Maurice. Embodied care: Jane Addams, Maurice Merleau-Ponty, and feminist ethics. Urbana: Illinois UP, 2004. pp. 181. Rev. by Grace Clement in NWSAJ (18:1) 2006, 224–6; by Peta Bowden in Hypatia (21:3) 2006, 210–14.

Grace Aguilar

8958. Page, Judith W. Anglo-Jewish identity and the politics of cultivation in Hazlitt, Aguilar, and Disraeli. *In* (pp. 149–64) **8523**.

Bronson Alcott

8959. Schreiner, Samuel A., Jr. The Concord quartet: Alcott, Emerson, Hawthorne, Thoreau, and the friendship that freed the American mind. Chichester; Hoboken, NJ: Wiley, 2006. pp. ix, 246.

Louisa M. Alcott

8960. Abate, Michelle Ann. Topsy and topsy-turvy Jo: Harriet Beecher Stowe's *Uncle Tom's Cabin* and/in Louisa May Alcott's *Little Women*. ChildLit (34) 2006, 59–82.

8961. Blackford, Holly. Vital signs at play: objects as vessels of mother–daughter discourse in Louisa May Alcott's *Little Women*. ChildLit (34) 2006, 1–36.

8962. Cheever, Susan. American Bloomsbury: Louisa May Alcott, Ralph Waldo Emerson, Margaret Fuller, Nathaniel Hawthorne, and Henry David Thoreau: their lives, their loves, their work. New York: Simon & Schuster, 2006. pp. xvi, 223, (plates) 8.

8963. Clark, Beverly Lyon (ed.). Louisa May Alcott: the contemporary reviews. (Bibl. 2004, 9969.) Rev. by Mary Lamb Shelden in ChildLit (34) 2006, 209–13.

8964. Eiselein, Gregory. Modernity and Louisa May Alcott's *Jo's Boys*. ChildLit (34) 2006, 83–108.

8965. Johnson, Nicholas. '*Kennst du das Land?*': learning the language of landscape in *Little Women*. ChildLit (34) 2006, 37–58.

8966. Keyser, Elizabeth Lennox. 'Things change, Jo': reflections on twenty years in children's literature. ChildLit (34) 2006, 193–207. (2003 Francelia Butler Lecture.)

8967. McElaney, Hugh. Alcott's freaking of boyhood: the perplex of gender and disability in *Under the Lilacs*. ChildLit (34) 2006, 139–60.

8968. Mills, Claudia. 'The canary and the nightingale': performance and virtue in *Eight Cousins* and *Rose in Bloom*. ChildLit (34) 2006, 109–38.

8969. Raabe, Wesley. The text of *Eli's Education*: from manuscript to *St Nicholas* magazine. ChildLit (34) 2006, 161–85.

8970. Shealy, Daniel (ed.). Alcott in her own time: a biographical chronicle of her life, drawn from recollections, interviews, and memoirs by family, friends, and associates. (Bibl. 2005, 9913.) Rev. by Mary Lamb Shelden in ChildLit (34) 2006, 209–13.

8971. Showalter, Elaine (ed.). Little women; Little men; Jo's boys. (Bibl. 2005, 9914.) Rev. by Mary Lamb Shelden in ChildLit (34) 2006, 209–13.

8972. Speicher, Allison. When it all goes South: re-imagining Alcott's Little Women in *The Sheltered Life*. *See* **16132**.

8973. Stadler, Gustavus. Troubling minds: the cultural politics of genius in the United States, 1840–1890. Minneapolis; London: Minnesota UP, 2006. pp. xxxii, 217.

8974. Stoneley, Peter. Sewing in Concord. *See* **11452**.

Ira Frederick Aldridge (1807–1867)

8975. Lindfors, Bernth. Ira Aldridge's London debut. TN (60:1) 2006, 30–44.

Horatio Alger, Jr

8976. Shaheen, Aaron. Endless frontiers and emancipation from history: Horatio Alger's reconstruction of place and time in *Ragged Dick*. ChildLit (33) 2005, 20–40.

Grant Allen ('Cecil Power', 'Olive Pratt Rayner')

8977. Morton, Peter. The busiest man in England: Grant Allen and the writing trade, 1875–1900. (Bibl. 2005, 9921.) Rev. by Pierre Coustillas in GissJ (42:1) 2006, 29–35; by David Finkelstein in VPR (39:3) 2006, 298–300; by Nicholas Daly in NineL (61:1) 2006, 124–7.

Washington Allston

8978. Paley, Morton D. Coleridge and Washington Allston's *The Sisters*. *See* **9543**.

William Apess (b.1798)

8979. Bayers, Peter L. William Apess's manhood and native resistance in Jacksonian America. MELUS (31:1) 2006, 123–46.

8980. Bizzell, Patricia. (Native) American jeremiad: the 'mixedblood' rhetoric of William Apess. *In* (pp. 34–49) **2149**.

8981. Carlson, David J. Sovereign selves: American Indian autobiography and the law. *See* **8895**.

William Archer

8982. Maunder, Andrew. 'I will not live in poverty and neglect': *East Lynne* on the East End stage. *In* (pp. 173–87) **8647**.

Matthew Arnold

8983. Camlot, Jason. The Victorian critic as naturalizing agent. *See* **8947**.

8984. Guest, Kristen. Culture, class, and colonialism: the struggle for an English national theatre, 1879–1913. *See* **8579**.

8985. Leerssen, Joep. Englishness, ethnicity and Matthew Arnold. EJES (10:1) 2006, 63–79.

8986. Machann, Clinton. Guide to the year's work: Matthew Arnold. VP (44:3) 2006, 316–21.

8987. O'Neill, Michael. 'The burden of ourselves': Arnold as a post-Romantic poet. YES (36:2) 2006, 109–24.

8988. Perry, Seamus. Joy perplexed: optimism and complication in Wordsworth, T. H. Green and A. C. Bradley. *See* **11702**.

8989. Phelan, Joseph. Clough, Arnold, Béranger, and the legacy of 1848. *See* **9491**.

8990. Prins, Yopie. Metrical translation: nineteenth-century Homers and the hexameter mania. *In* (pp. 229–56) **3191**.

8991. Stone, Donald. Arnold's Chinese remnant. FLS (119) 2006, 11–22.

8992. Walker, Richard J. Pious works: aesthetics, ethics, and the modern individual in Robert Louis Stevenson's *Strange Case of Dr Jekyll and Mr Hyde*. *In* (pp. 265–74) **11272**.

Thomas Arnold (1795–1842)

8993. Olsen, Flemming. Thomas Arnold the teacher. Copenhagen: Danish Univ. of Education, 2004. pp. 141. Rev. by Ebbe Klitgård in EngS (86:5) 2005, 466–7.

Jane Austen

8994. Alexander, Christine; Owen, David. *Lady Susan*: a re-evaluation of Jane Austen's epistolary novel. Persuasions (27) 2005, 54–68.

8995. Anderson, Kathleen. The Jane Austen diet: the weight of women in Austen's letters. Persuasions (27) 2005, 75–87.

8996. Aroutian, Joanna. The sexual family in *Mansfield Park*. ERR (17:2) 2006, 229–35.

8997. Auerbach, Emily. Searching for Jane Austen: restoring the 'fleas' and 'bad breath'. Persuasions (27) 2005, 31–8.

8998. Bander, Elaine. Jane Austen's letters: facts and fictions. Persuasions (27) 2005, 119–29.

8999. Basson, Mary. Mr Darcy's letter – a figure in the dance. Persuasions (27) 2005, 152–62.

9000. Brown, Julia Prewitt. Taking off from *The Art of Memory*. *In* (pp. 3–8) **8374**.

9001. Brückmann, Patricia C. 'Such days as these': books, readers, and libraries in *Persuasion*. *In* (pp. 9–28) **8374**.

9002. Cho, Sonjeong. An ethics of becoming: configurations of feminine subjectivity in Jane Austen, Charlotte Brontë, and George Eliot. London; New York: Routledge, 2006. pp. viii, 254. (Literary criticism and cultural theory.)

9003. Cronin, Richard; McMillan, Dorothy (eds). Emma. (Bibl. 2005, 9970.) Rev. by Simon Jarvis in TLS, 10 Feb. 2006, 4–6; by Kathryn Sutherland in RES (57:232) 2006, 833–8.

9004. Cummins, Nicola. Affectionate, indulgent, dyslexic? Reassessing Mr Woodhouse. *In* (pp. 29–39) **8374**.

9005. Dabundo, Laura. 'The redemption of the world': the rhetoric of Jane Austen's prayers. Persuasions (27) 2006, 242–52.

9006. Dadlez, E. M. Dense insensibility: Humean vices and virtues in the work of Jane Austen. 1650–1850 (12) 2006, 147–74.

9007. Deresiewicz, William. Jane Austen and the Romantic poets. (Bibl. 2005, 9973.) Rev. by William Galperin in WordsC (36:4) 2005, 144–8.

9008. Despotopoulou, Anna. Girls on film: postmodern renderings of Jane Austen and Henry James. YES (36:1) 2006, 115–30.

9009. Deutsch, Helen. Had I been born a hero. *See* **7424**.

9010. Devine, Jodi A. Letters and their role in revealing class and personal identity in *Pride and Prejudice*. Persuasions (27) 2005, 99–111.

9011. Downie, J. A. Who says she's a bourgeois writer? Reconsidering the social and political contexts of Jane Austen's novels. ECS (40:1) 2006, 69–84.

9012. Dryden, Robert G. 'Luck be a lady tonight': Jane Austen's precarious idealization of naval heroes in *Persuasion*. 1650–1850 (13) 2006, 91–115.

9013. —— Reading and teaching our way out of Jane Austen novels (naval options). Persuasions (27) 2005, 208–18.

9014. Emsley, Sarah Baxter. Jane Austen's philosophy of the virtues. (Bibl. 2005, 9978.) Rev. by Lorrie Clark in DalR (86:3) 2006, 477–8; by Peter Knox-Shaw in NineL (61:2) 2006, 245–9.

9015. Fergus, Jan. The comedy of gendered whining in *Persuasion* and *Emma*. *In* (pp. 40–55) **8374**.

9016. —— 'The whinnying of Harpies?': humor in Jane Austen's letters. Persuasions (27) 2005, 13–30.

9017. Ferriss, Suzanne. Narrative and cinematic doubleness: *Pride and Prejudice* and *Bridget Jones's Diary*. *In* (pp. 71–84) **19862**.

9018. Francus, Marilyn. Calamity Jane? Austen and Owen Wister's *The Virginian*. *See* **19238**.

9019. Frey, Anne. A nation without nationalism: the reorganization of feeling in Austen's *Persuasion*. Novel (38:2/3) 2005, 214–34.

9020. Fulford, Sarah. 'Nation and narration': the English novel and Englishness. *In* (pp. 157–65) **14238**.

9021. Fullerton, Susannah. Jane Austen and crime. Madison, WI: Jones, 2006. pp. xiii, 248.

9022. Galperin, William. 'Describing what never happened': Jane Austen and the history of missed opportunities. ELH (73:2) 2006, 355–82.

9023. Gervais, David. The poetry of the novel. PNRev (31:5) 2005, 43–7.

9024. Gibson, Colin; Marr, Lisa (eds). New windows on a woman's world: essays for Jocelyn Harris: vol. 2. *See* **8374**.

9025. Greenfield, Susan C. The absent-minded heroine; or, Elizabeth Bennet has a thought. ECS (39:3) 2006, 337–50.

9026. Greenham, David. The concept of irony: Jane Austen's *Emma* and Philip Roth's *Sabbath's Theater*. *See* **18314**.

9027. Grossman, Jonathan H. Anne Elliot bound up in Northanger Abbey: the history of the joint publication of Jane Austen's first and last complete novels. Persuasions (27) 2005, 195–207.

9028. Himes, Amanda E. Fanny Price and the (dis)comforts of home. Persuasions (27) 2005, 253–9.

9029. Holzwarth, Elsie G. Austen and the admiral: commemorating the bicentenary of the Battle of Trafalgar, 21 October 1805. Persuasions (27) 2005, 163–72.

9030. Hong, Mary. 'A great talker upon little matters': trivializing the everyday in *Emma*. Novel (38:2/3) 2005, 235–53.

9031. Hudelet, Ariane. Chorégraphies implicites et explicites: la danse dans *Pride and Prejudice*, du texte à l'écran. EA (59:4) 2006, 414–26.

9032. Hurley, Alison E. A conversation of their own: watering-place correspondence among the Bluestockings. *See* **7277**.

9033. Jackson, H. J. Raising the unread: Mary Brunton and Jane Austen. *See* **9291**.

9034. Jarvis, Simon. Guides through the park. TLS, 10 Feb. 2006, 4–6 (review-article). (Austen's style and the textual history of her works.)

9035. Jenkins, Joyce L. The puzzle of Fanny Price. PhilL (30:2) 2006, 346–60.

9036. Jones, Christine A. On fairy tales, their sensitive characters, and the sensible readers they create. TSWL (25:1) 2006, 13–30.

9037. Jones, Susan E. Fragment and focus: Jane Austen and the art of the blazon. Persuasions (27) 2005, 69–74.

9038. Jones, Vivien. Austen's nieces: case studies in women and writing. *In* (pp. 56–68) **8374**.

9039. —— (ed.). Selected letters. (Bibl. 2005, 9997.) Rev. by Gillian Wright in WWr (13:1) 2006, 170–2.

9040. Kagawa, P. Keiro. Jane Austen, the architect: (re)building spaces at *Mansfield Park*. WS (35:2) 2006, 125–43.

9041. Kenney, Theresa. 'Slyness seems the fashion': dexterous revelations in *Pride and Prejudice*. Persuasions (27) 2005, 263–9.

9042. Klenck, Deborah J. Knuth. Fun and speculation: *Sense and Sensibility* and *Pride and Prejudice* as revisions. Persuasions (27) 2005, 39–53.

9043. Knox-Shaw, Peter. Jane Austen and the Enlightenment. (Bibl. 2004, 10035.) Rev. by Adela Pinch in Romanticism (11:2) 2005, 258–60; by William Galperin in WordsC (36:4) 2005, 144–8; by Rodney Farnsworth in ERR (17:1) 2006, 122–8; by Kathryn Sutherland in RES (57:228) 2006, 116–20; by Colin Jager in 1650–1850 (13) 2006, 379–84; by Pierre Goubert in EA (59:1) 2006, 112–13; by Christopher Olaf Blum in ModAge (48:3) 2006, 277–80.

9044. Kroeber, Karl. Jane Austen criticism, 1951–2004. StudN (38:1) 2006, 108–16 (review-article).

9045. Lansdown, Richard. 'Rare in burlesque': *Northanger Abbey*. PQ (83:1) 2004, 61–81.

9046. Lau, Beth. Home, exile, and *Wanderlust* in Austen and the Romantic poets. PCP (41) 2006, 91–107.

9047. —— Jane Austen and John Keats: negative capability, romance and reality. KSJ (55) 2006, 81–110.

9048. Le Faye, Deirdre. A chronology of Jane Austen and her family. Cambridge; New York: CUP, 2006. pp. xv, 776. Rev. by Claire Harman in TLS, 14 July 2006, 32.

9049. —— Jane Austen: a family record. By William Austen-Leigh and Richard Arthur Austen-Leigh. (Bibl. 2004, 10039.) Rev. by Linda V. Troost in ECS (39:3) 2006, 397–405.

9050. Leithart, Peter J. Miniatures and morals: the Christian novels of Jane Austen. Moscow, ID: Canon Press, 2004. pp. 197.

9051. Looser, Devoney. Another Jane: Jane Porter, Austen's contemporary. *In* (pp. 235–48) **8374**.

9052. Losano, Antonia. 'A great passion for taking likenesses': the woman painter in *Emma*. Persuasions (27) 2005, 185–94.

9053. Lott, Anna. Staging a lesson: the theatricals and proper conduct in *Mansfield Park*. StudN (38:3) 2006, 275–87.

9054. McFarlane, Brian. Saying what other people mean. Meanjin (64:4) 2005, 152–9. (Film adaptation.)

9055. Mandal, A. A. Making Austen mad: Benjamin Crosby and the non-publication of *Susan*. RES (57:231) 2006, 507–25.

9056. Martin, Lydia. Jane Austen's politeness on screen: between ambivalent submission and defiant self-assertion. CLR (3) 2006, 193–208.

9057. Massei, Marie-Laure. L'excès dans le premier volume des *Juvenilia* de Jane Austen. CVE (63) 2006, 137–48.

9058. Monaghan, David. 'A cheerful confidence in futurity': the movement motif in Austen's novel and Dear/Michell's film adaptation of *Persuasion*. *In* (pp. 69–92) **8374**.

9059. Nagle, Christopher. The epistolary passions of sympathy: feeling letters in *Persuasion* and Burney's *The Wanderer*. Persuasions (27) 2005, 88–98.

9060. Nelles, William. Omniscience for atheists; or, Jane Austen's infallible narrator. Narrative (14:2) 2006, 118–31.

9061. O'Farrell, Mary Ann. Missing Jane Austen: Henry James considers the old maid. *See* **10585**.

9062. Olmsted, Wendy. Rhetoric: an historical introduction. *See* **2075**.

9063. Olsen, Kirstin. All things Austen: an encyclopedia of Austen's world. (Bibl. 2005, 10030.) Rev. by Peter Barry in Eng (55:212) 2006, 213–19.

9064. Ray, Joan Klingel. The truth about Jane Austen and Tom Lefroy. NQ (53:3) 2006, 311–14.

9065. —— Wheeler, Richard James. James Stanier Clarke's portrait of Jane Austen. Persuasions (27) 2005, 112–18.

9066. Rivero, Albert J. Doubling Eliza: Austen's remembrance of Richardson (and perhaps Haywood) in *Sense and Sensibility*. *In* (pp. 93–103) **8374**.

9067. Robinson, Terry F. 'A mere skeleton of history': reading relics in Jane Austen's *Northanger Abbey*. ERR (17:2) 2006, 215–27.

9068. Salih, Sara. The silence of Miss Lambe: *Sanditon* and fictions of 'race' in the Abolition era. ECF (18:3) 2006, 329–53.

9069. Searle, Alison. The moral imagination: biblical imperatives, narrative and hermeneutics in *Pride and Prejudice*. Ren (59:1) 2006, 17–32.

9070. Sette, Miriam. Jane Austen, *Persuasion* and the roots of modernity. RSV (18/19) 2004/05, 81–94.

9071. Simmons, James R., Jr. 'Don't tell me about rears and vices; I have been in the navy all my life': profligacy on the high seas in Jane Austen and Patrick O'Brian. ELN (43:2) 2005, 93–102.

9072. Smith, Kenneth. The probable location of 'Longbourn' in Jane Austen's *Pride and Prejudice*. Persuasions (27) 2005, 234–41.

9073. Solinger, Jason. Jane Austen and the gentrification of commerce. Novel (38:2/3) 2005, 272–90.

9074. Stafford, Fiona (ed.). Jane Austen's *Emma*: a casebook. Oxford; New York: OUP, 2006. pp. 432. (Casebooks in criticism.)

9075. Stohr, Karen. Practical wisdom and moral imagination in *Sense and Sensibility*. PhilL (30:2) 2006, 378–94.

9076. Stovel, Bruce. The new Emma in *Emma*. *In* (pp. 104–15) **8374**.

9077. Sutherland, Kathryn. Jane Austen's textual lives: from Aeschylus to Bollywood. (Bibl. 2005, 10057.) Rev. by Simon Jarvis in TLS, 10 Feb. 2006, 4–6; by Peter Shillingsburg in RES (57:230) 2006, 397–9; by Peter Knox-Shaw in SHARP (15:2/3) 2006, 24–5.

9078. —— On looking into Chapman's *Emma*: how R. W. Chapman's Classicists made Jane Austen a classic. TLS, 13 Jan. 2006, 12–13.

9079. —— Why Jane Austen is not Charlotte Brontë. *In* (pp. 116–28) **8374**.

9080. Takei, Akiko. Jane Austen and 'a society of sickness'. Persuasions (27) 2005, 142–51.

9081. TAUCHERT, ASHLEY. Romancing Jane Austen: narrative, realism, and the possibility of a happy ending. Basingstoke; New York: Palgrave Macmillan, 2005. pp. xv, 192. (Language, discourse, society.) Rev. by Michael Caines in TLS, 8 Sept. 2006, 28.

9082. TODD, JANET. The Cambridge introduction to Jane Austen. Cambridge; New York: CUP, 2006. pp. xi, 152. (Cambridge introductions to literature.)

9083. —— (ed.). Jane Austen in context. (Bibl. 2005, 10060.) Rev. by Simon Jarvis in TLS, 10 Feb. 2006, 4–6; by Fiona Stafford in RES (57:232) 2006, 829–31.

9084. TOKER, LEONA. Love, that four-letter word: a response to Amanpal Garcha. Connotations (13:1/2) 2003/04, 105–10.

9085. TROOST, LINDA V. The importance of being Austen. ECS (39:3) 2006, 397–405 (review-article).

9086. VORACHEK, LAURA. Intertextuality and ideology: Jane Austen's *Pride and Prejudice* and James Fordyce's *Sermons to Young Women*. *In* (pp. 129–37) **8374**.

9087. WAGNER, TAMARA S. 'A strange chronicle of the olden time': revisions of the Regency in the construction of Victorian domestic fiction. MLQ (66:4) 2005, 443–75.

9088. WEISSER, SUSAN OSTROV. Charlotte Brontë, Jane Austen, and the meaning of love. *See* **9205**.

9089. WELLS, JULIETTE. Mothers of chick lit? Women writers, readers, and literary history. *In* (pp. 47–70) **19862**.

9090. WENNER, BARBARA BRITTON. Following the trail of Jane Austen's letters. Persuasions (27) 2005, 130–41.

9091. —— Prospect and refuge in the landscape of Jane Austen. Aldershot; Burlington, VT: Ashgate, 2006. pp. xiv, 124.

9092. WHITE, GABRIELLE D. V. Jane Austen in the context of Abolition: 'a fling at the slave trade'. Basingstoke; New York: Palgrave Macmillan, 2006. pp. ix, 231.

9093. WI, WING-CHI. Jane Austen and the dialectic of misrecognition. New York; Frankfurt: Lang, 2005. pp. 343. (Anglo-amerikanische Studien, 27.)

9094. WILKES, JOANNE. 'Clever women': Anne Mozley, Jane Austen, and Charlotte Brontë. *In* (pp. 297–308) **8374**.

9095. WILSON, CHERYL A. *Bride and Prejudice*: a Bollywood comedy of manners. *See* **19680**.

9096. WILTSHIRE, JOHN. The importance of being Edmund: on names in *Mansfield Park*. *In* (pp. 138–47) **8374**.

9097. —— Jane Austen: introductions and interventions. Basingstoke; New York: Palgrave Macmillan, 2006. pp. x, 232. (Second ed.: first ed. 2003.)

9098. —— (ed.). Mansfield Park. (Bibl. 2005, 10070.) Rev. by Simon Jarvis in TLS, 10 Feb. 2006, 4–6; by Kathryn Sutherland in RES (57:232) 2006, 833–8.

9099. WINBORN, COLIN. The literary economy of Jane Austen and George Crabbe. (Bibl. 2004, 10092.) Rev. by Rodney Farnsworth in ERR (17:1) 2006, 122–8; by Kathryn Sutherland in RES (57:228) 2006, 116–20.

9100. Wyvill, Carol. Sauce for the gander: gender and morality in three Jane Austen novels. *In* (pp. 148–54) **8374**.

9101. Zuroski, Eugenia. Disenchanting China: Orientalism and the aesthetics of reason in the English novel. *See* **7407**.

Walter Bagehot

9102. Houston, Gail Turley. From Dickens to *Dracula*: gothic, economics, and Victorian fiction. Cambridge; New York: CUP, 2005. pp. xv, 165. (Cambridge studies in nineteenth-century literature and culture, 48.) Rev. by Robert Mighall in TLS, 5 Aug. 2005, 28; by Nadine Cooper in ELT (49:1) 2006, 118–19; by Gill Ballinger in DickQ (23:1) 2006, 44–7; by Sylvère Monod in EA (59:3) 2006, 364–5.

Joanna Baillie

9103. Gilbert, Deirdre. That homo-geneous thing, an Englishman. RECTR (20:1/2) 2005, 57–63.

9104. Gilbert, Elizabeth Deirdre. Desires and history: historical representation in Frances Burney's *Edwy and Elgiva* and Joanna Baillie's *Ethwald*. *See* **7624**.

9105. Hewitt, Regina. Symbolic interactions: social problems and literary interventions in the works of Baillie, Scott, and Landor. Lewisburg, PA: Bucknell UP; London: Assoc. UPs, 2006. pp. 280. (Bucknell studies in eighteenth-century literature and culture.)

9106. Judson, Barbara. 'Sympathetic curiosity': the theater of Joanna Baillie. TSWL (25:1) 2006, 49–70.

9107. Slagle, Judith Bailey. Ballads and folksongs of Scotland, Ireland and Wales: the collaboration of Joanna Baillie and George Thomson. KSJ (55) 2006, 137–57.

9108. —— Joanna Baillie's religious ideology: the dichotomy of fundamentalism and liberalism in *The Martyr* and *A View of the General Tenour of the New Testament Regarding the Nature and Dignity of Jesus Christ*. ERR (17:3) 2006, 301–14.

9109. Tucker, Kathryn. Joanna Baillie's and Elizabeth Inchbald's moral aesthetics: humanizing actors and madmen. ERR (17:3) 2006, 335–40.

P. T. (Phineas Taylor) Barnum (1810–1891)

9110. Runzo, Sandra. Emily Dickinson's American Museum. *See* **9891**.

Katharine Lee Bates (b.1859)

9111. Leopold, Ellen. 'My soul is among lions': Katharine Lee Bates's account of the illness and death of Katharine Coman. Legacy (23:1) 2006, 60–73.

'Louis Becke' (George Lewis Becke)

9112. Bradshaw, Ann Lane. Joseph Conrad and Louis Becke. *See* **15249**.

Thomas Lovell Beddoes

9113. Bamforth, Iain. Pickled essence of Englishman: Thomas Lovell Beddoes. JTLBS (12) 2006, 14–19.

9114. Baulch, David M. The 'deserted home' of the psyche: madness and the medical subject of Romantic science in Thomas Lovell Beddoes's *The Brides' Tragedy*. JTLBS (12) 2006, 9–13.

9115. Grinnell, George C. Thomas Beddoes and the physiology of Romantic medicine. SR (45:2) 2006, 223–50.

9116. Joshua, Essaka; Joshua, Eleoma. Thomas Lovell Beddoes and the attribution of articles in the *Wellesley Index* and in the *Oxford Dictionary of National Biography*. JTLBS (12) 2006, 3–8.

9117. Karlin, Daniel. On being second-rate: the skeleton art of Thomas Lovell Beddoes. YES (36:2) 2006, 35–50.

9118. Webb, Samantha. 'Not so pleasant to the taste': Coleridge in Bristol during the mixed bread campaign of 1795. *See* **9560**.

Henry Ward Beecher

9119. Applegate, Debby. The most famous man in America: the biography of Henry Ward Beecher. New York: Doubleday, 2006. pp. 527. Rev. by Michael Kazin in NYTB, 16 July 2006, 1, 10.

9120. Garvey, T. Gregory. Creating the culture of reform in antebellum America. *See* **16221**.

John Bell (*fl*.1899)

9121. Jones, Lawrence. Three 'bush' novels and the colonial myth. *In* (pp. 359–84) **8374**.

Edward Bellamy

9122. Beaumont, Matthew. Shopping in utopia: *Looking Backward*, the department store, and the dreamscape of consumption. NCC (28:3) 2006, 191–209.

9123. Wagner, Vivian. Unsettling Oz: technological anxieties in the novels of L. Frank Baum. *See* **14648**.

Matilda Betham-Edwards (1836–1919)

9124. Rees, Joan. Matilda Betham-Edwards: novelist, travel writer and francophile. Hastings: Hastings Press, 2006. pp. 140.

Ambrose Bierce ('Dod Grile')

9125. Blume, Donald T. Ambrose Bierce's civilians and soldiers in context: a critical study. (Bibl. 2004, 10137.) Rev. by Keith Mears in JAStud (39:2) 2005, 310–11; by Will Kaufman in JAStud (39:2) 2005, 311–12.

9126. —— (ed.). Tales of soldiers and civilians. Kent: Ohio State UP, 2004. pp. xxxii, 222. Rev. by Keith Mears in JAStud (39:2) 2006, 310–11.

9127. Owens, David M. The Devil's topographer: Ambrose Bierce and the American war story. Knoxville: Tennessee UP, 2006. pp. xii, 166.

Mathilde Blind (1841–1896)

9128. Diedrick, James. 'The hectic beauty of decay': positivist Decadence in Mathilde Blind's late poetry. VLC (34:2) 2006, 631–48.

9129. FLETCHER, ROBERT P. 'Heir of all the universe': evolutionary epistemology in Mathilde Blind's *Birds of Passage: Songs of the Orient and Occident*. VP (43:4) 2005, 435–53.

9130. LAPORTE, CHARLES. Atheist prophecy: Mathilde Blind, Constance Naden, and the Victorian poetess. VLC (34:2) 2006, 427–41.

9131. RUDY, JASON R. Rapturous forms: Mathilde Blind's Darwinian poetics. VLC (34:2) 2006, 443–59.

Robert Bloomfield

9132. BINFIELD, KEVIN. Labor and an ethic of variety in *The Farmer's Boy*. *In* (pp. 70–88) **9141**.

9133. BURKE, TIM. Colonial spaces and national identities in *The Banks of Wye*: Bloomfield and the Wye after Wordsworth. *In* (pp. 89–112) **9141**.

9134. CHRISTMAS, WILLIAM J. *The Farmer's Boy* and contemporary politics. *In* (pp. 27–48) **9141**.

9135. GORJI, MINA. Burying Bloomfield: poetical remains and 'the unlettered muse'. *In* (pp. 232–52) **9141**.

9136. KEEGAN, BRIDGET. Science, superstition, and song: varieties of religious experience in the poetry of Robert Bloomfield. *In* (pp. 195–212) **9141**.

9137. LUCAS, JOHN. Hospitality and the rural tradition: Bloomfield's *May-Day with the Muses*. *In* (pp. 113–41) **9141**.

9138. MCEATHRON, SCOTT. An infant poem of war: Bloomfield's *On Seeing the Launch of the 'Boyne'*. *In* (pp. 213–31) **9141**.

9139. UNDERHILL, HUGH. 'Domestic happiness, thou only bliss': common and divided ground in William Cowper and Robert Bloomfield. *In* (pp. 267–87) **9141**.

9140. WHITE, SIMON. A lyric for the artisan poet: *To My Old Oak Table*. *In* (pp. 178–94) **9141**.

9141. —— GOODRIDGE, JOHN; KEEGAN, BRIDGET (eds). Robert Bloomfield: lyric, class, and the Romantic canon. Lewisburg, PA: Bucknell UP, 2006. pp. 315.

Wilfrid Scawen Blunt

9142. VILLA, LUISA. A footnote to cultural history: Modernism, imperialism, and Wilfrid Scawen Blunt. *In* (pp. 263–77) **12076**.

Barcroft Boake (1866–1892)

9143. REFSHAUGE, W. F. Fresh light on A. G. Stephens as editor of Barcroft Boake's works. ALS (22:3) 2006, 368–71.

9144. —— *Where the Dead Men Lie*. ALS (22:3) 2006, 372–4.

'Rolf Boldrewood' (Thomas Alexander Browne) (1826–1915)

9145. WEVERS, LYDIA. Becoming native: Australian novelists and the New Zealand Wars. ALS (22:3) 2006, 319–28.

George Borrow

9146. CHANDLER, DAVID. Borrow's tailless foxes and his myth of independence. GBB (32) 2006, 7–19.

9147. MENCHER, BARRIE. George Borrow: novelist. GBB (32) 2006, 20–32.

9148. Missler, Peter. Gypsy Luke project: preliminary results. GBB (32) 2006, 32–48.

9149. Ridler, Ann M.; Murphy, Martin. Borrow and the South-Sea Islanders, with an additional note on 'far Iolchos and Spain'. GBB (32) 2006, 68–72.

9150. Shepheard, Richard. Doing different: a word from Norfolk. GBB (32) 2006, 82–7.

Dion Boucicault

9151. Harrison, Kimberly. Political persuasion in Mary Braddon's *The Octoroon; or, The Lily of Louisiana*. *In* (pp. 212–24) **8647**.

9152. Mullenix, Elizabeth Reitz. Yankee doodle Dixie: performing nationhood on the eve of war. JADT (18:3) 2006, 33–54.

9153. Wood, Sarah F. Refusing to RIP; or, Return of the dispossessed: the transatlantic revivals of Irving's *Rip Van Winkle*. *See* **10524**.

George Bourne (1780–1845)

9154. Bruce, Dickson D., Jr. *Lorette*: anti-Catholicism and religious freedom in antebellum America. YREAL (22) 2006, 97–115.

Mary Elizabeth Braddon (Mrs Maxwell)

9155. Andres, Sophia. Mary Elizabeth Braddon's ambivalent Pre-Raphaelite ekphrasis. VN (108) 2005, 1–6.

9156. Barrow, Robin. Braddon's haunting memories: rape, class and the Victorian popular press. WWr (13:3) 2006, 348–68.

9157. Charret-Del Bove, Marion. Les images d'enfermement dans *John Marchmont's Legacy* de Mary Elizabeth Braddon. CVE (63) 2006, 375–85.

9158. Dorré, Gina M. Victorian fiction and the cult of the horse. *See* **9736**.

9159. Golden, Catherine J. Censoring her sensationalism: Mary Elizabeth Braddon and *The Doctor's Wife*. *In* (pp. 29–40) **8647**.

9160. Gravatt, Denise Hunter. 'A rod of flexible steel in that little hand': female dominance and male masochism in Mary Elizabeth Braddon's *Aurora Floyd*. *In* (pp. 109–23) **11883**.

9161. Harrison, Kimberly. Political persuasion in Mary Braddon's *The Octoroon; or, The Lily of Louisiana*. *In* (pp. 212–24) **8647**.

9162. Henderson, Ian. Looking at Lady Audley: Symbolism, the stage, and the Antipodes. NCT (33:1) 2006, 3–25.

9163. —— Mid-Victorian reading and the Antipodes. ALS (22:3) 2006, 294–307.

9164. Nayder, Lillian. 'The threshold of an open window': transparency, opacity, and social boundaries in *Aurora Floyd*. *In* (pp. 188–99) **8647**.

9165. Schroeder, Natalie; Schroeder, Ronald A. From sensation to society: representations of marriage in the fiction of Mary Elizabeth Braddon, 1862–1866. Newark: Delaware UP, 2006. pp. 290.

9166. Sears, Albert C. Mary Elizabeth Braddon and the 'combination novel'. *In* (pp. 41–52) **8647**.

9167. Tatum, Karen F. Explaining the depiction of violence against women in Victorian literature: applying Julia Kristeva's theory of abjection to Dickens,

Brontë, and Braddon. Lewiston, NY; Lampeter: Mellen Press, 2005. pp. ii, 199. (Studies in British literature, 100.)

9168. Wagner, Tamara S. 'Magnetic' clues to the past: reinvestigating the Victorians' regency in *Eleanor's Victory*. Clues (25:1) 2006, 81–95.

9169. Wagner, Tamara Silvia. The miser's new notes and the Victorian sensation novel: plotting the magic of paper money. VicR (31:2) 2005, 79–98.

Anne Brontë

9170. Colón, Christine. Framing the texts: power and subversion in Anne Brontë's *The Tenant of Wildfell Hall* and Wilkie Collins's *The Woman in White*. *In* (pp. 223–37) **8418**.

9171. Hale, Elizabeth. Long-suffering professional females: the case of nanny lit. *In* (pp. 103–18) **19862**.

9172. Poole, Russell. Seeing 'a little more of the world' (and not being able to change it) in *Agnes Grey*. *In* (pp. 259–76) **8374**.

Branwell Brontë

9173. Cheney, Phyllis. Branwell revisited. BrSt (31:3) 2006, 230–9.

9174. FitzGerald, Sally. *Painful Life*, *Azrael*, *The Weary*, and *Dr Wheelhouse*: the diverse legacy of Branwell Brontë. BrSt (31:2) 2006, 113–19.

Charlotte Brontë

9175. Alexander, Christine. Arthur Bell Nicholls and the Adamson saga: new discoveries of Brontë memorabilia. BrSt (31:3) 2006, 194–209.

9176. Berman, Carolyn Vellenga. Creole crossings: domestic fiction and the reform of colonial slavery. *See* **9988**.

9177. Bertrandias, Bernadette. Charlotte Brontë's *Jane Eyre*: la parole orpheline. Paris: Ellipses, 2004. pp. 119. (Littérature anglo-saxonne.) Rev. by Bénédicte Coste in CVE (61) 2005, 341–6; by Joan Bellamy in BrSt (31:2) 2006, 167–8.

9178. —— De *Shirley* à *Villette*: comment Jane Eyre peut-elle vieillir? CVE (63) 2006, 209–21.

9179. Betsinger, Sue Ann. *The Professor*: the third participant. BrSt (31:2) 2006, 101–11.

9180. Cho, Sonjeong. An ethics of becoming: configurations of feminine subjectivity in Jane Austen, Charlotte Brontë, and George Eliot. *See* **9002**.

9181. Crippa, Gianni. La descrizione in *Jane Eyre*: tra desiderio del romanzo gotico e principio di realtà. ConLett (46) 2006, 293–314.

9182. Emberson, Ian M. Pilgrims from loneliness: an interpretation of Charlotte Brontë's *Jane Eyre* and *Villette*. Haworth, W. Yorks.: Brontë Soc., 2005. pp. 150. Rev. by Yukari Oda in BrSt (31:3) 2006, 256–7.

9183. Gass, Joanne. *The Autobiography of My Mother*: Jamaica Kincaid's revision of *Jane Eyre* and *Wide Sargasso Sea*. *In* (pp. 63–78) **16864**.

9184. Griswold, Jerry. The meanings of *Beauty and the Beast*. *See* **12786**.

9185. Hansen, Astrid. The book she never wrote: Charlotte and the Chartists. BrSt (31:2) 2006, 157–8.

9186. Harris, Margaret. George Eliot's conversation with Currer Bell. *See* **10026**.

9187. Heiniger, Abigail. The faery and the beast. BrSt (31:1) 2006, 23–9. (*Jane Eyre*.)

9188. Henderson, Diana E. Collaborations with the past: reshaping Shakespeare across time and media. *See* **5324**.

9189. Houston, Gail Turley. From Dickens to *Dracula*: gothic, economics, and Victorian fiction. *See* **9102**.

9190. Jones, Jason B. Lost causes: historical consciousness in Victorian literature. *See* **9394**.

9191. Longmuir, Anne. Anne Lister and lesbian desire in Charlotte Brontë's *Shirley*. BrSt (31:2) 2006, 145–55.

9192. Malane, Rachel. Sex in mind: the gendered brain in nineteenth-century literature and mental sciences. New York; Frankfurt: Lang, 2005. pp. xiv, 229. (Studies in nineteenth-century British literature, 22.)

9193. Marutollo, Anna. The many faces of Frances. BrSt (31:3) 2006, 210–19.

9194. Michie, Elsie B. (ed.). Charlotte Brontë's *Jane Eyre*: a casebook. Oxford; New York: OUP, 2006. pp. viii, 212.

9195. Mignot, Élise. Les adjectifs: entre déterminant et nom. *See* **1397**.

9196. Palmer, Sally B. Projecting the gaze: the magic lantern, cultural discipline, and *Villette*. VicR (32:1) 2006, 18–40.

9197. Peschier, Diana. Nineteenth-century anti-Catholic discourses: the case of Charlotte Brontë. (Bibl. 2005, 10175.) Rev. by Lewis Burton in BrSt (31:1) 2006, 88–91; by Maria LaMonaca in VS (49:1) 2006, 120–2; by Maureen Moran in NineL (61:1) 2006, 107–10.

9198. Polcini, Valentina. *'As if silence spoke'*: voci, silenzi ed echi visivi nella rappresentazione della natura e degli archetipi femminili in *Shirley*. RSV (18/19) 2004/05, 169–94.

9199. Quarm, Joan. Pink silk and purple gray: Charlotte Brontë's wish-fulfillment in *Villette*. BrSt (31:1) 2006, 1–6.

9200. Ruth, Jennifer. Novel professions: interested disinterest and the making of the professional in the Victorian novel. Columbus: Ohio State UP, 2006. pp. viii, 151. (Victorian critical interventions.) Rev. by Carolyn Lesjak in Novel (39:1) 2005, 138–41; by Barry J. Faulk in VS (49:1) 2006, 111–13.

9201. Shockley, Evie. The horrors of homelessness: gothic doubling in Kincaid's *Lucy* and Brontë's *Villette*. *In* (pp. 45–62) **16864**.

9202. Stone, Laurie. Why Charlotte dissed Emily. LitR (49:3) 2006, 63–70.

9203. Sutherland, Kathryn. Why Jane Austen is not Charlotte Brontë. *In* (pp. 116–28) **8374**.

9204. Tatum, Karen F. Explaining the depiction of violence against women in Victorian literature: applying Julia Kristeva's theory of abjection to Dickens, Brontë, and Braddon. *See* **9167**.

9205. Weisser, Susan Ostrov. Charlotte Brontë, Jane Austen, and the meaning of love. BrSt (31:2) 2006, 93–100.

9206. Wells, Juliette. Mothers of chick lit? Women writers, readers, and literary history. *In* (pp. 47–70) **19862**.

9207. Wilkes, Joanne. 'Clever women': Anne Mozley, Jane Austen, and Charlotte Brontë. *In* (pp. 297–308) **8374**.

9208. Yin, Qiping. *Shirley*: the narrative of 'progress' deconstructed and the image of the Babel constructed. FLS (118) 2006, 78–86. (In Chinese.)

Emily Brontë

9209. Alarabi, Nour. *Gondal's Queen* revisited: the importance of Ratchford's edition for interpreting Emily Brontë's religious orientations. *In* (pp. 35–47) **3407**.

9210. Arnedillo, Oscar. That wind from the west. BrSt (31:3) 2006, 240–7.

9211. Beauvais, Jennifer. Domesticity and the female demon in Charlotte Dacre's *Zofloya* and Emily Brontë's *Wuthering Heights*. RomNet (44) 2006.

9212. Dunmore, Helen (foreword). Poems of solitude. London: Hesperus Press, 2004. pp. 83. Rev. by James McGrath in PNRev (31:6) 2005, 72.

9213. Fisk, Nicole Plyler. 'A wild, wick slip she was': the passionate female in *Wuthering Heights* and the *Memoirs of Emma Courtney*. BrSt (31:2) 2006, 133–43.

9214. Flintoff, Everard. The geography of *Wuthering Heights*. BrSt (31:1) 2006, 37–52.

9215. Harpham, Geoffrey Galt. On the grotesque: strategies of contradiction in art and literature. (Bibl. 1986, 7260.) Aurora, CO: Davies, 2006. pp. 292. (Critical studies in the humanities.) (Second ed.: first ed. 1982.)

9216. Khair, Tabish. 'Let me in – let me in!' Why does terror come from elsewhere? JPW (42:2) 2006, 155–63.

9217. Lonoff, Sue; Hasseler, Terri A. (eds). Approaches to teaching Emily Brontë's *Wuthering Heights*. New York: Modern Language Assn of America, 2006. pp. vii, 195. (Approaches to teaching world literature.)

9218. Marsden, Simon. Imagination, materiality and the act of writing in Emily Brontë's diary papers. NCC (28:1) 2006, 35–47.

9219. Piciucco, Pier Paolo. *Wuthering Heights* as a childlike fairy tale. BrSt (31:3) 2006, 220–9.

9220. Raymond, Claire. The posthumous voice in women's writing from Mary Shelley to Sylvia Plath. *See* **11192**.

9221. Reeves, Amy Carol. Emily Brontë's pedagogy of desire in *Wuthering Heights*. VN (109) 2006, 16–21.

9222. Stewart, Susan. The ballad in *Wuthering Heights*. Representations (86) 2004, 175–97.

9223. Stone, Laurie. Why Charlotte dissed Emily. *See* **9202**.

9224. Stoneman, Patsy. Addresses from the land of the dead: Emily Brontë and Shelley. BrSt (31:2) 2006, 121–31.

9225. Swamy, Vinay. Traversing the Atlantic: from Brontë's *Wuthering Heights* to Condé's *La Migration des cœurs*. JCarL (4:2) 2006, 61–74.

9226. Tytler, Graeme. 'Nelly, I am Heathcliff!': the problem of 'identification' in *Wuthering Heights*. MidQ (47:2) 2006, 167–81.

The Rev. Patrick Brontë

9227. GLEN, HEATHER. A solitary man. TLS, 21 Apr. 2006, 24 (review-article).

9228. GREEN, DUDLEY. 'Always at my post': the letters of the Revd Patrick Brontë. BrSt (31:3) 2006, 179–93.

9229. —— (ed.). The letters of the Reverend Patrick Brontë. Foreword by Asa Briggs. (Bibl. 2005, 10210.) Rev. by Joan Bellamy in BrSt (31:1) 2006, 83–7; by Heather Glen in TLS, 21 Apr. 2006, 24.

The Brontës

9230. COOKE, SIMON. 'The ever-shifting kaleidoscope of the imagination': modern illustrations to the Brontës. BrSt (31:1) 2006, 7–22.

9231. EAGLETON, TERRY. Myths of power: a Marxist study of the Brontës. (Bibl. 2005, 10217.) Rev. by Patsy Stoneman in BrSt (31:3) 2006, 252–4.

9232. INGHAM, PATRICIA. The Brontës. Oxford; New York: OUP, 2006. pp. xix, 273. (Oxford world's classics.) (Authors in context.) Rev. by Charmian Knight in BrSt (31:3) 2006, 248–50.

9233. JORDAN, ELLEN; CRAIG, HUGH; ANTONIA, ALEXIS. The Brontë sisters and the *Christian Remembrancer*: a pilot study in the use of the 'Burrows method' to identify the authorship of unsigned articles in the nineteenth-century periodical press. VPR (39:1) 2006, 21–45.

9234. SOLINAS DONGHI, BEATRICE. Un anno decisivo per i Brontë: luglio 1845 – agosto 1846. LProv (126/127) 2006, 49–63.

9235. TORGERSON, BETH. Reading the Brontë body: disease, desire, and the constraints of culture. (Bibl. 2005, 10226.) Rev. by Sara L. Pearson in BrSt (31:2) 2006, 172–4; by Athena Vrettos in VS (48:3) 2006, 530–2.

Maria Gowen Brooks (1794 or 5–1845)

9236. LOW, DENNIS. The literary protégées of the Lake Poets. *See* **11239**.

Rhoda Broughton

9237. FABER, LINDSEY. One sister's surrender: rivalry and resistance in Rhoda Broughton's *Cometh Up as a Flower*. *In* (pp. 149–59) **8647**.

9238. HELLER, TAMAR. 'That muddy, polluted flood of earthly love': ambivalence about the body in Rhoda Broughton's *Not Wisely but Too Well*. *In* (pp. 87–101) **8647**.

9239. MAUNDER, ANDREW (gen. ed.). Sensation with a purpose: Felicia Skene, *Hidden Depths* (1866). Ed. by Lillian Nayder. Erotic sensationalism: Rhoda Broughton, *Cometh Up as a Flower* (1867). Ed. by Tamar Heller. *See* **11238**.

Charles Brockden Brown

9240. DOOLEN, ANDY. Fugitive empire: locating early American imperialism. *See* **9619**.

9241. KAFER, PETER. Charles Brockden Brown's Revolution and the birth of American gothic. (Bibl. 2005, 10237.) Rev. by Elizabeth Jane Wall Hinds in ECF (18:3) 2006, 383–5.

9242. LAM, BETHANY L. Brown's *Wieland; or, The Transformation: an American Tale*. Exp (64:2) 2006, 78–81.

9243. McNutt, Donald J. Urban revelations: images of ruin in the American city, 1790–1860. London; New York: Routledge, 2006. pp. xi, 198. (Literary criticism and cultural theory.)

9244. Slawinski, Scott. Validating bachelorhood: audience, patriarchy, and Charles Brockden Brown's editorship of the *Monthly Magazine* and *American Review.* (Bibl. 2005, 10241.) Rev. by Mark L. Kamrath in EAL (41:3) 2006, 577–83.

9245. Sutherland, Helen. Varieties of Protestant experience: religion and the *Doppelgänger* in Hogg, Brown, and Hawthorne. *See* **10450**.

9246. Wolfe, Eric A. Ventriloquizing nation: voice, identity, and radical democracy in Charles Brockden Brown's *Wieland*. AL (78:3) 2006, 431–57.

Henry Box Brown (b.1816)

9247. Brooks, Daphne A. Bodies in dissent: spectacular performances of race and freedom, 1850–1910. *See* **8564**.

William Wells Brown (1815–1884)

9248. Botelho, Keith M. 'Look on this picture, and on this': framing Shakespeare in William Wells Brown's *The Escape*. CompDr (39:2) 2005, 187–212.

9249. Stadler, Gustavus. Troubling minds: the cultural politics of genius in the United States, 1840–1890. *See* **8973**.

Elizabeth Barrett Browning

9250. Armstrong, Isobel. *Casa Guidi Windows*: spectacle and politics in 1851. *In* (pp. 51–69) **8320**.

9251. Avery, Simon. Telling it slant: Promethean, Whig, and Dissenting politics in Elizabeth Barrett's poetry of the 1830s. VP (44:4) 2006, 405–24.

9252. Bailey, Peggy Dunn. 'Hear the voice of the [female] bard': *Aurora Leigh* as a Romantic female epic. *In* (pp. 117–37) **3395**.

9253. Chapman, Alison. *Risorgimenti*: Spiritualism, politics and Elizabeth Barrett Browning. *In* (pp. 70–89) **8320**.

9254. Cronin, Richard. *Casa Guidi Windows*: Elizabeth Barrett Browning, Italy and the poetry of citizenship. *In* (pp. 35–50) **8320**.

9255. Dalley, Lana L. 'The least "angelical" poem in the language': political economy, gender, and the heritage of *Aurora Leigh*. VP (44:4) 2006, 525–42.

9256. Davies, Corinne. Two of Elizabeth Barrett Browning's Pan poems and their after-life in Robert Browning's *Pan and Luna*. VP (44:4) 2006, 561–9.

9257. Fish, Laura. *Strange Music*: engaging imaginatively with the family of Elizabeth Barrett Browning from a creole and Black woman's perspective. VP (44:4) 2006, 507–24. (Fish's novel in progress, *Strange Music*.)

9258. Hurst, Isobel. 'The feminine of Homer': Elizabeth Barrett Browning's *Casa Guidi Windows*. *In* (pp. 181–95) **8418**.

9259. Johnson, Stephanie L. *Aurora Leigh*'s radical youth: Derridean *parergon* and the narrative frame in *A Vision of Poets*. VP (44:4) 2006, 425–44.

9260. Keirstead, Christopher M. A 'bad patriot'? Elizabeth Barrett Browning and cosmopolitanism. VIJ (33) 2005, 69–95.

9261. LEVINE, CAROLINE. Strategic formalism: toward a new method in Cultural Studies. VS (48:4) 2006, 625–57.

9262. MARSHALL, GAIL. Elizabeth Barrett Browning and Shakespeare: translating the language of intimacy. VP (44:4) 2006, 467–86.

9263. NERI, BARBARA. *Cobridme de flores*: (un)covering flowers of Portuguese and Spanish poets in *Sonnets from the Portuguese*. VP (44:4) 2006, 571–83.

9264. SAUNDERS, CLARE BROOME. 'Judge no more what ladies do': Elizabeth Barrett Browning's active medievalism, the female troubadour, and Joan of Arc. VP (44:4) 2006, 585–97.

9265. STONE, MARJORIE. Guide to the year's work: Elizabeth Barrett Browning. VP (44:3) 2006, 322–31.

9266. —— TAYLOR, BEVERLY. 'Confirm my voice': 'my sisters', poetic audiences, and the published voices of E.B.B. VP (44:4) 2006, 391–403.

9267. TAYLOR, OLIVIA GATTI. Written in blood: the art of mothering epic in the poetry of Elizabeth Barrett Browning. VP (44:2) 2006, 153–64.

9268. TUCKER, HERBERT F. An EBBigrammar of motives; or, Ba for short. VP (44:4) 2006, 445–65.

9269. —— Tactical formalism: a response to Caroline Levine. VS (49:1) 2006, 85–95.

9270. VAN REMOORTEL, MARIANNE. (Re)gendering Petrarch: Elizabeth Barrett Browning's *Sonnets from the Portuguese*. TSWL (25:2) 2006, 247–66.

9271. WOODWORTH, ELIZABETH. Elizabeth Barrett Browning, Coventry Patmore, and Alfred Tennyson on Napoleon III: the hero-poet and Carlylean heroics. VP (44:4) 2006, 543–60.

Robert Browning

9272. BERBEGLIA, SIMONETTA. Robert Browning at Vieusseux's. RSV (18/19) 2004/05, 67–80.

9273. BOHM, ARND. Increasing suspicion about Browning's grammarian. VP (44:2) 2006, 165–82.

9274. DAVIES, CORINNE. Two of Elizabeth Barrett Browning's Pan poems and their after-life in Robert Browning's *Pan and Luna*. *See* **9256**.

9275. DAVISON-PÉGON, CLAIRE. 'Untext me here' – what exactly constitutes the text of a radio play? *See* **17385**.

9276. FONTANA, ERNEST. Gender and sexual anxiety in Browning's *Waring* and *The Guardian-Angel*. VP (44:2) 2006, 183–9.

9277. —— Too late: the Pre-Raphaelites, Tennyson, and Browning. *See* **11392**.

9278. GARDNER, KEVIN J. John Betjeman's *Bristol and Clifton*: echoes of Robert Browning's *My Last Duchess*. *See* **14773**.

9279. KEIRSTEAD, CHRISTOPHER M. Stranded at the border: Browning, France, and the challenge of cosmopolitanism in *Red Cotton Night-Cap Country*. VP (43:4) 2005, 411–34.

9280. KREILKAMP, IVAN. 'One more picture': Robert Browning's optical unconscious. ELH (73:2) 2006, 409–35.

9281. LERNER, LAURENCE. Browning's painters. YES (36:2) 2006, 96–108.

9282. Loucks, James F.; Stauffer, Andrew M. (eds). Robert Browning's poetry: authoritative texts, criticism. New York; London: Norton, 2006. pp. x, 689. (Norton critical eds.) (Second ed.: first ed. 1979.)

9283. Marks, Thomas. 'A sort of magic': enchantment and disenchantment in the work of Tennyson and his contemporaries. *See* **11399**.

9284. Martens, Britta. Guide to the year's work: Robert Browning. VP (44:3) 2006, 332–40.

9285. Monteiro, George. Scudder, Rolfe, and Browning. ANQ (19:3) 2006, 14–16.

9286. Starzyk, Lawrence J. Browning's *Childe Roland*: the visionary poetic. VN (108) 2005, 14–21.

9287. Tholoniat, Yann. Les préliminaires textuels de Robert Browning. CVE (63) 2006, 463–79.

9288. Turtle, Will. 'The truth of mere transcript': Browning's *Agamemnon*. TransLit (14:2) 2005, 196–211.

9289. Xu, Shufang. The women enclosed: Robert Browning's four dramatic monologues. FLS (117) 2006, 104–10. (*My Last Duchess*; *Andrea del Sarto*; *Porphyria's Lover*; *Gold Hair*.) (In Chinese.)

The Brownings

9290. Davies, Corinne; Stone, Marjorie. 'Singing song for song': the Brownings 'in the poetic relation'. *In* (pp. 151–74) **3405**.

Mary Brunton

9291. Jackson, H. J. Raising the unread: Mary Brunton and Jane Austen. TLS, 7 Apr. 2006, 14–15.

9292. Sutherland, Kathryn. Why Jane Austen is not Charlotte Brontë. *In* (pp. 116–28) **8374**.

William Cullen Bryant

9293. Babcock, Matthew. Bryant's *The Yellow Violet*. Exp (65:1) 2006, 21–6.

9294. Barrucand, Michel. L'espace en poésie – poésie de l'espace: les Fireside Poets. Anglophonia (19) 2006, 33–43.

Laura Curtis Bullard

9295. Joseph, Maia. Mass appeal(s): representations of women's public speech in suffrage literature. CRAS (36:1) 2006, 67–91.

Mrs Bullock (*fl.*1801)

9296. Verhoeven, W. M. (gen. ed.). Anti-Jacobin novels: vol. 3, Mrs Bullock, *Dorothea; or, A Ray of the New Light* (1801). Ed. by M. O. Grenby. London; Brookfield, VT: Pickering & Chatto, 2005. pp. xxxi, 210. Rev. by Robert Morrison in WordsC (36:4) 2005, 189–91; by Jon Mee in HLQ (69:4) 2006, 649–53.

Frances Hodgson Burnett

9297. Bellew, Deborah Fox. Discovering the fiction of Frances Hodgson Burnett. *In* (pp. 205–15) **9300**.

9298. Birchall, Diana. The Frances Hodgson Burnett online discussion group: a modern history. *In* (pp. 217–22) **9300**.

9299. Carpenter, Angelica Shirley. Lady of the manor. *In* (pp. 93–112) **9300**.

9300. —— (ed.). In the garden: essays in honor of Frances Hodgson Burnett. Syracuse, NY: Syracuse UP, 2006. pp. xvi, 261.

9301. Druley, Deborah. The changing mothering roles in *Little Lord Fauntleroy, A Little Princess*, and *The Secret Garden*. *In* (pp. 51–66) **9300**.

9302. Dunbar, Carole. Rats in black holes and corners: an examination of Frances Hodgson Burnett's portrayal of the urban poor. *In* (pp. 67–77) **9300**.

9303. Frobose, Paul H. Film adaptations of Frances Hodgson Burnett's stories. *In* (pp. 131–46) **9300**.

9304. —— A filmography of motion picture adaptations of Frances Hodgson Burnett's stories. *In* (pp. 231–42) **9300**.

9305. Gerzina, Gretchen Holbrook. Keeper of the keys: Gretchen Holbrook Gerzina interviews Penny Deupree. *In* (pp. 223–30) **9300**.

9306. Griswold, Jerry. Snugness: the robin in its nest. *In* (pp. 147–52) **9300**.

9307. Kawabata, Ariko. Rereading *Little Lord Fauntleroy*: deconstructing the innocent child. *In* (pp. 33–49) **9300**.

9308. Lurie, Alison. *The Making of a Marchioness*. *In* (pp. 79–92) **9300**.

9309. Maier, Barbara Jo. 'A delicate invisible hand': Frances Hodgson Burnett's contributions to theatre for youth. *In* (pp. 113–29) **9300**.

9310. Stokes, Sally Sims. Painting the garden: Noel Streatfeild, the garden as restorative, and pre-1950 dramatizations of *The Secret Garden*. *In* (pp. 169–87) **9300**.

9311. Thwaite, Ann. A biographer looks back. *In* (pp. 17–31) **9300**.

9312. Weldy, Lance. Dreams, imaginations, and shattered illusions: overlooked realism in Carol Wiseman's film adaptation of Burnett's *A Little Princess*. *In* (pp. 189–203) **9300**.

John Burroughs

9313. Sumner, David Thomas. 'That could happen': nature writing, the nature fakers, and a rhetoric of ascent. ISLE (12:2) 2005, 31–53.

9314. Warren, James Perrin. John Burroughs and the place of nature. Athens; London: Georgia UP, 2006. pp. xiii, 266.

Sir Richard Burton

9315. Jasanoff, Maya. Let in the djinns. LRB (28:5) 2006, 34–5 (review-article).

9316. Kennedy, Dane. The highly civilized man: Richard Burton and the Victorian world. (Bibl. 2005, 10279.) Rev. by Maya Jasanoff in LRB (28:5) 2006, 34–5; by Eitan Bar-Yosef in VS (48:4) 2006, 706–8.

9317. Matus, Jill. Collaboration and collusion: two Victorian writing couples and their Orientalist texts. *In* (pp. 175–92) **3405**.

9318. Sironval, Margaret. The image of Sheherazade in French and English editions. *In* (pp. 219–44) **10714**.

9319. Yamanaka, Yuriko; Nishio, Tetsuo (eds). *The Arabian Nights* and Orientalism: perspectives from East and West. *See* **10714**.

Samuel Butler (1835–1902)

9320. Verzella, Massimo. Darwinism and its consequences: machines taking over man in Samuel Butler's absurd tableau. RSV (18/19) 2004/05, 151–68.

George Gordon Noel, Lord Byron

9321. Agosti, Annamaria. Frammenti del sublime romantico: Byron, Shelley, Wordsworth. ConLett (42) 2004, 435–56.

9322. Bainbridge, Simon. Lord Ruthven's power: Polidori's *The Vampyre*, doubles and the Byronic imagination. *See* **11055**.

9323. Beckett, John. Byron and Rochdale. BJ (33:1) 2005, 13–24.

9324. Beevers, Robert. The Byronic image: the poet portrayed. Abingdon: Olivia Press, 2005. pp. 163. Rev. by Michael Edson in KSJ (55) 2006, 235–8; by Margot Strickland in BJ (34:2) 2006, 191–2.

9325. Bone, Drummond (ed.). The Cambridge companion to Byron. (Bibl. 2005, 10289.) Rev. by J. Andrew Hubbell in SR (45:1) 2006, 142–51; by Matthew Bevis in CamQ (35:1) 2006, 97–101; by Fiona Wilson in KSJ (55) 2006, 233–5; by Ashley Chantler in BJ (34:1) 2006, 68–70.

9326. Brown, Iain Gordon. Water, windows, and women: the significance of Venice for Scots in the age of the Grand Tour. *See* **8047**.

9327. Brückmann, Patricia C. 'Such days as these': books, readers, and libraries in *Persuasion*. *In* (pp. 9–28) **8374**.

9328. Caie, Graham. Bringing the John Murray Archive to the National Library of Scotland. BJ (34:1) 2006, 49–55.

9329. Caldwell, Roger. Byron, Auden, and the poetry of disenchantment. PNRev (32:2) 2005, 46–8.

9330. Cardwell, Richard (ed.). The reception of Byron in Europe: vol. 1, Southern Europe, France and Romania. (Bibl. 2005, 10292.) Rev. by David Nokes in TLS, 3 Mar. 2006, 26.

9331. —— The reception of Byron in Europe: vol. 2, Northern, Central, and Eastern Europe. (Bibl. 2005, 10293.) Rev. by David Nokes in TLS, 3 Mar. 2006, 26.

9332. Cass, Jeffrey. Irish girls gone wild: *Glenarvon*, Regency hypocrisy, and Spartan virtue. *See* **10691**.

9333. Cheeke, Stephen. 'What so many have told, who would tell again?': Romanticism and the commonplaces of Rome. *See* **7824**.

9334. Clubbe, John. Byron, Sully, and the power of portraiture. (Bibl. 2005, 10296.) Rev. by Peter W. Graham in WordsC (36:4) 2005, 149–50; by Michael Edson in KSJ (55) 2006, 235–8; by Malcolm Kelsall in BJ (34:1) 2006, 63–4.

9335. —— Thomas Sully's portrait of Lord Byron. BJ (33:1) 2005, 1–12.

9336. Cochran, Peter. Byron's influence on European Romanticism. *In* (pp. 67–85) **8357**.

9337. —— (ed.); Rees, Michael (trans.). Lord Byron's life in Italy. By Teresa Guiccioli. (Bibl. 2005, 10299.) Rev. by Frances Wilson in TLS, 15 Sept. 2006, 29; by Ian Gilmour in KSR (20) 2006, 156–9; by Andrew Nicholson in BJ (34:1) 2006, 64–8.

9338. Dennis, Ian. ''Twas nature gnaw'd them to this resolution': Byron's poetry and mimetic desire. Contagion (12/13) 2006, 115–32.

9339. Dickson, Leigh Wetherall. Authority and legitimacy: the cultural context of Lady Caroline Lamb's novels. *See* **10692**.

9340. Dingley, Robert. Byron and the Coliseum: the art of recycling. BJ (33:1) 2005, 25–35.

9341. Douglass, Paul. Lady Caroline Lamb before Byron: the Godfrey Vassal Webster affair. *See* **10694**.

9342. —— Paradise decomposed: Byron's decadence and Wordsworthian nature in *Childe Harold* iii and iv. BJ (34:1) 2006, 9–19.

9343. —— An unpublished letter from Lord Byron to Lady Caroline Lamb. NQ (53:3) 2006, 322–3.

9344. Felluga, Dino Franco. The perversity of poetry: Romantic ideology and the popular male poet of genius. (Bibl. 2005, 10307.) Rev. by Richard Cronin in Romanticism (11:2) 2005, 254–6; by Matthew Rowlinson in VS (48:2) 2006, 366–8.

9345. Ferber, Michael. The curse of the Ephesians: a long footnote to Byron. BJ (33:1) 2005, 43–51.

9346. Goldsmith, Jason N. The promiscuity of print: John Clare's *Don Juan* and the culture of Romantic celebrity. *See* **9473**.

9347. Harries, Elizabeth Wanning. 'Unfinish'd sentences': the Romantic fragment. *In* (pp. 360–75) **8357**.

9348. Hughes, Gillian. 'Native energy': Byron and Hogg as Scottish poets. BJ (34:2) 2006, 133–42.

9349. Kersey, Mel. Inherited forms and the burden of time in *Childe Harold's Pilgrimage*. *In* (pp. 502–14) **8374**.

9350. Lutz, Deborah. The dangerous lover: gothic villains, Byronism, and the nineteenth-century narrative. Columbus: Ohio State UP, 2006. pp. xii, 117.

9351. Mahler, Andreas. Point of reference or semantic space? Functions of Venice in early modern English drama. *In* (pp. 161–79) **5346**.

9352. Marandi, Seyed Mohammed. Byron's infidel and the Muslim fisherman. KSR (20) 2006, 133–55.

9353. March, Rosemary. Lost: three books from Byron. NQ (53:3) 2006, 323–5.

9354. Mellor, David. Was Byron's terminal illness a form of neurosyphilis? BJ (34:2) 2006, 127–32.

9355. Minta, Stephen. Lord Byron and Mavrokordatos. Romanticism (12:2) 2006, 126–42.

9356. Mole, Tom. 'Nourished by that abstinence': consumption and control in *The Corsair*. Romanticism (12:1) 2006, 26–34.

9357. Montanari, Anna. 'Fanny of Rimini': Byron traduttore nel v dell'*Inferno*. ConLett (43) 2005, 143–61.

9358. Morrison, Steven. 'My native land, goodnight': Joyce and Byron. *In* (pp. 50–67) **16695**.

9359. Nicholson, Andrew. Byron's introduction to the Prince Regent in 1812. BJ (34:2) 2006, 147–54.

9360. Nokes, David. Continental views. *See* **8177**.

9361. O'Neill, Michael. 'A magic voice and verse': Byron's approaches to the ode, 1814–16. BJ (34:2) 2006, 101–14.

9362. Parker, Fred. Between Satan and Mephistopheles: Byron and the Devil. CamQ (35:1) 2006, 1–29.

9363. Peterfreund, Stuart. Juan the memorious: the Feinaiglian narrative dynamics of *Don Juan*. ERR (17:4) 2006, 403–18.

9364. Potter, Gordon. Byron's numerology revisited: *Don Juan*. BJ (34:2) 2006, 115–25.

9365. Sharkey, Michael. Byron's 'Deluge': *Heaven and Earth*. BJ (34:1) 2006, 35–48.

9366. Shears, Jonathon. 'A tale untold': the search for a story in Byron's *Lara*. BJ (34:1) 2006, 1–8.

9367. Stabler, Jane. Thomas Campbell and Lord Byron: a note on the evidence of asterisks. BJ (33:1) 2005, 37–42.

9368. Stauffer, Andrew M. Byronic transmission and the first poem for Caro. BJ (34:2) 2006, 143–5.

9369. Stein, Atara. The Byronic hero in film, fiction, and television. (Bibl. 2005, 10337.) Rev. by Brian C. Cooney in BJ (33:1) 2005, 58–9; by Wendy C. Nielsen in KSJ (55) 2006, 238–41; by Lorrie Palmer in JPFT (34:3) 2006, 140–1.

9370. Stewart-Smith, Elizabeth. Hours of idleness. BJ (34:2) 2006, 155–64. (Elizabeth Pigot's friendship with Byron.)

9371. Strathman, Christopher A. Romantic poetry and the fragmentary imperative: Schlegel, Byron, Joyce, Blanchot. Albany: New York State UP, 2006. pp. xi, 204. Rev. by Mark Sandy in BJ (34:2) 2006, 195–6.

9372. Tunbridge, Laura. From count to chimney sweep: Byron's *Manfred* in London theatres. MusL (87:2) 2006, 212–36.

9373. Whitehead, Angus. A quotation from Lord Byron's *The Two Foscari* in William Blake's *The Ghost of Abel*. NQ (53:3) 2006, 325–6.

9374. Yu, Jie-Ae. Heredity and free choice in Byron's *Werner*. KSR (20) 2006, 119–32.

George Washington Cable

9375. Gillman, Susan. Adaptation and Americas Studies. *See* **10525**.

9376. Payne, James Robert. George Washington Cable's *John March* and *Gideon's Band*: a (White) boy is being beaten. ALR (38:3) 2006, 239–48.

Ada Cambridge

9377. Bradstock, Margaret. Echoes of Ada Cambridge. Southerly (65:3) 2005, 170–81.

Bartley Campbell

9378. Grabes, Herbert. Melodrama against the revival of racism? Bartley Campbell's *The White Slave* (1882). YREAL (22) 2006, 259–67.

Thomas Campbell

9379. Stabler, Jane. Thomas Campbell and Lord Byron: a note on the evidence of asterisks. *See* **9367**.

Jane Welsh Carlyle

9380. Fielding, Kenneth J.; Sorensen, David R. (eds). Jane Carlyle: newly selected letters. (Bibl. 2005, 10360.) Rev. by Helen Sutherland in WWr (13:1) 2006, 172–4.

Thomas Carlyle

9381. Álvarez Fernández, Elisa. Goethe: Carlyle's spiritual guide. LitB (25:1/2) 2005, 88–101.

9382. apRoberts, Ruth. Carlyle's religion: the new evangel. LitB (25:1/2) 2005, 102–20.

9383. Breton, Rob. Gospels and grit: work and labour in Carlyle, Conrad and Orwell. Toronto; Buffalo, NY; London: Toronto UP, 2005. pp. 246.

9384. Campbell, Ian. Carlyle and Divinity Hall. LitB (25:1/2) 2005, 1–23.

9385. Cordery, Lindsey. Dickens in Latin America: Borrioboola-Gha revisited. *See* **9723**.

9386. Critchley, Simon. *Satura resartus*: living in the woods with bears. *See* **8186**.

9387. Dugger, Julie M. Black Ireland's race: Thomas Carlyle and the Young Ireland Movement. VS (48:3) 2006, 461–85.

9388. Evans, James. God-intoxicated men: religion and drunkenness in Carlyle's works. LitB (25:1/2) 2005, 318–35.

9389. Frame, Frances. Anxious allusions: the Bible in Thomas Carlyle's correspondence. LitB (25:1/2) 2005, 336–78.

9390. Frye, Lowell T. 'Vocables, still vocables': linguistic and religious despair in Thomas Carlyle's *Latter-Day Pamphlets*. LitB (25:1/2) 2005, 196–216.

9391. Gardner, Peter. The seductive politics of *Mary Barton*. *See* **10151**.

9392. Hill, Marylu. 'History is a real prophetic manuscript': reason and revelation in Thomas Carlyle's historical essays. LitB (25:1/2) 2005, 122–38.

9393. Jessop, Ralph. Carlyle's agnosticism: an altar to the unknown and unknowable God. LitB (25:1/2) 2005, 380–433.

9394. Jones, Jason B. Lost causes: historical consciousness in Victorian literature. Columbus: Ohio State UP, 2006. pp. xii, 134. (Victorian critical interventions.)

9395. Keeble, David. Interpretive representation: a relevance-theoretic analysis of the opening paragraph of Carlyle's *Chartism*. JLS (34:1) 2005, 41–59.

9396. McCracken-Flesher, Caroline. Carlyle, Irving, and the problematics of prophecy. LitB (25:1/2) 2005, 24–52.

9397. Morrow, John. Thomas Carlyle. London; New York: Hambledon/ Continuum, 2006. pp. xvi, 301, (plates) 8.

9398. Nixon, Jude V. 'Eternity in the vesture of time': Carlyle, thermodynamic discourse, and apocalyptic anxieties. LitB (25:1/2) 2005, 164–95.

9399. Pionke, Albert D. Beyond 'the hero as prophet': a survey of images of Islam in Carlyle's works. LitB (25:1/2) 2005, 496–511.

9400. Sorensen, David R. 'A tragical position': Carlyle, Turgenev, and the religion of revolution in the nineteenth century. LitB (25:1/2) 2005, 290–316.

9401. Tarr, Rodger L. The tailor's tailor: Thomas Carlyle's Jesus Christ. LitB (25:1/2) 2005, 140–63.

9402. Ulrich, John M. Thomas Carlyle, Edward Irving, and millennialist discourse. LitB (25:1/2) 2005, 54–87.

9403. —— Thomas Carlyle, Richard Owen, and the paleontological articulation of the past. JVC (11:1) 2006, 30–58.

9404. Vanden Bossche, Chris R.; Brattin, Joel J.; Trela, D. J. (eds). Past and present. Berkeley; London: California UP, 2005. pp. ciii, 843, (plates) 17. (Norman and Charlotte Strouse ed. of the works of Thomas Carlyle, 4.)

9405. Walls, Laura Dassow. 'If body can sing': Emerson and Victorian science. *In* (pp. 334–66) **10064**.

9406. Wiesenfarth, Joseph. Carlyle and the prelude to *Middlemarch*. *See* **10059**.

9407. Willis, Mark. Charles Dickens and fictions of the crowd. *See* **9838**.

9408. Woodworth, Elizabeth. Elizabeth Barrett Browning, Coventry Patmore, and Alfred Tennyson on Napoleon III: the hero-poet and Carlylean heroics. *See* **9271**.

The Carlyles

9409. Campbell, Ian, *et al.* (eds). The collected letters of Thomas and Jane Welsh Carlyle: vol. 33, August 1857 – June 1858. Durham, NC; London: Duke UP, 2006. pp. xxxvii, 308. Rev. by Rosemary Ashton in TLS, 21 Apr. 2006, 25.

9410. Heidt, Sarah J. 'The materials for a "Life"': collaboration, publication, and the Carlyles' afterlives. NCC (28:1) 2006, 21–33.

9411. Sorensen, David R. 'Unfold your self': Kenneth J. Fielding and Carlyle Studies, 1988–2004. LitB (25:1/2) 2005, 512–32.

Edward Carpenter (1844–1929)

9412. Copley, Antony. A spiritual Bloomsbury: Hinduism and homosexuality in the lives and writings of Edward Carpenter, E. M. Forster, and Christopher Isherwood. Lanham, MD: Lexington, 2006. pp. xi, 397.

'Lewis Carroll' (Charles Lutwidge Dodgson)

9413. Amor, Anne Clark; O'Connor, Michael. Second marriages: second thoughts: Charles Dodgson's leaflet *Marriage Service: Till Death Us Do Part, July 22, 1877*. Carrollian (15) 2005, 34–48.

9414. Brooker, Will. Alice's adventures: Lewis Carroll in popular culture. (Bibl. 2004, 10374.) Rev. by Joel D. Chaston in CLAQ (31:3) 2006, 304–6.

9415. Brown, Gillian. The metamorphic book: children's print culture in the eighteenth century. *See* **7410**.

9416. Cohen, Morton N. Catherine Sinclair and Lewis Carroll: the changing landscape of children's literature. KnLet (77) 2006, 1–6.

9417. Demakos, Matthew. Accountably and unaccountably shy – part 2. Carrollian (15) 2005, 18–33.

9418. Fetherston, Sonia. Shoscombe through the looking-glass. *See* **9936**.

9419. Foulkes, Richard. Lewis Carroll and the Victorian stage: theatricals in a quiet life. (Bibl. 2005, 10400, where title incorrect.) Rev. by Sos Eltis in RES (57:228) 2006, 122–4; by Michael Irwin in TN (60:1) 2006, 63–5; by Michael Heyman in CLAQ (31:4) 2006, 392–5; by Annie Escuret in CVE (63) 2006, 498–9; by Anne Varty in TRI (31:3) 2006, 323–4; by Hugues Lebailly in VS (49:1) 2006, 127–9.

9420. Gardner, Martin. A Gardner's nosegay: further annotations. KnLet (76) 2006, 1–3.

9421. —— (ed.). The annotated *Hunting of the Snark*: the full text of Lewis Carroll's great nonsense epic *The Hunting of the Snark*. Introd. by Adam Gopnik. New York; London: Norton, 2006. pp. xli, 152.

9422. Goldman, Victoria Sears. Evolution of a dream-child: images of Alice and changing conceptions of childhood. KnLet (77) 2006, 17–22.

9423. Lake, Frederick C. Folklore and mythology in the Alice books. KnLet (76) 2006, 8–12.

9424. López Guix, Juan Gabriel. The translator in Aliceland: on translating *Alice in Wonderland* into Spanish. *In* (pp. 95–105) **3186**.

9425. Mason, John. C. L. Dodgson's childhood playmate and lifelong friend: Thomas Vere Bayne. Carrollian (15) 2005, 3–14.

9426. Morris, Frankie. The *Alice* drawings: copies, forgeries, and Tenniel's originals. KnLet (77) 2006, 12–16.

9427. Ransom, Jenifer. An archetype of transformation. KnLet (76) 2006, 30–2.

9428. Sears, Victoria. Evolution of a dream-child: images of Alice and changing conceptions of childhood. KnLet (76) 2006, 19–23.

9429. Smith, William Jay. Lewis Carroll, the poet. GetR (19:4) 2006, 557–67.

9430. Steele, Stephen. Van Caulaert au pays de Lewis Carroll: *Sylvie and Bruno* recommencé. ConLett (42) 2004, 527–38.

9431. Stern, Jeffrey; Wakeling, Edward. The workwoman's guide to 'the working man's cap'. Carrollian (15) 2005, 15–17.

9432. Tannenbaum, Alan. An American edition of the 1924 Williams bibliography. Carrollian (15) 2005, 56–7.

9433. Vallone, Lynne. Reading girlhood in Victorian photography. LU (29:2) 2005, 190–210.

9434. Wakeling, Edward. C. L. Dodgson meets a famous American architect. KnLet (77) 2006, 27. (Richard Morris Hunt.)

9435. Zirker, Angelika. 'Alice was not surprised': (un)surprises in Lewis Carroll's Alice books. Connotations (14:1–3) 2004/05, 19–37.

Alice Cary

9436. Cherciu, Lucia. Parody as dialogue and disenchantment: remembering Phoebe Cary. *See* **9438**.

9437. Schultz, Elizabeth. *Bartleby, the Scrivener* and *Uncle Christopher's*: sites of wage slavery and domestic abuse. *In* (pp. 82–97) **10897**.

Phoebe Cary

9438. Cherciu, Lucia. Parody as dialogue and disenchantment: remembering Phoebe Cary. ATQ (20:1) 2006, 325–41.

Sir Roger Casement (1864–1916)

9439. McCormack, W. J. Reflections on writing and editing, with reference to National Archives (UK), CO 904/1–3 & HO 161/1–5. *In* (pp. 258–85) **648**.

9440. Moran, James. *The Field Day Anthology* and the impossibility of Roger Casement. *In* (pp. 219–33) **12189**.

Alexander Chalmers

9441. Paraizs, Júlia. The author, the editor and the translator: William Shakespeare, Alexander Chalmers and Sándor Petőfi; or, The nature of a Romantic edition. *See* **5212**.

Charles Haddon Spurgeon Chambers (1860–1921)

9442. Schafer, Elizabeth. A tale of two Australians: Haddon Chambers, Gilbert Murray and the imperial London stage. *In* (pp. 108–25) **12360**.

Charles W. Chesnutt

9443. Baker, Barbara A. Jamming with Julius: Charles Chesnutt and the post-bellum, pre-Harlem Blues. *In* (pp. 133–45) **8435**.

9444. Bentley, Nancy. The strange career of love and slavery: Chesnutt, Engels, Masoch. AmLH (17:3) 2005, 460–85.

9445. Mohr, Janet. Charles Chesnutt's women. CLAJ (49:4) 2006, 423–45.

9446. Peterson, Carla L. Commemorative ceremonies and invented traditions: history, memory, and modernity in the 'New Negro' novel of the nadir. *In* (pp. 34–56) **8435**.

9447. Simmons, Ryan. Chesnutt and realism: a study of the novels. Tuscaloosa; London: Alabama UP, 2006. pp. viii, 198. (Studies in American literary realism and naturalism.)

9448. Wilson, Matthew. Reading *The Human Stain* through Charles W. Chesnutt: the genre of the passing novel. *See* **18335**.

9449. —— Whiteness in the novels of Charles W. Chesnutt. (Bibl. 2004, 10416.) Rev. by Stephen K. Knadler in MFS (52:1) 2006, 213–17; by Joseph R. McElrath, Jr, in ALR (39:1) 2006, 89–91.

9450. Wonham, Henry B. Playing the races: ethnic caricature and American literary realism. (Bibl. 2005, 10423.) Rev. by Habiba Ibrahim in AL (78:4) 2006, 882–4.

Nora Chesson (Nora Hopper) (1871–1906)

9451. Stetz, Margaret D. 'Ballads in prose': genre crossing in late Victorian women's writing. *See* **18879**.

Lydia Maria Child

9452. Husband, Julie. Anticipating Progressive Era reformers: Lydia Maria Child and the mothering State. ESQ (50:4) 2004, 283–314.

9453. Mills, Bruce. Poe, Fuller, and the mesmeric arts: transition states in the American renaissance. *See* **10146**.

9454. Murphy, Gretchen. Hemispheric imaginings: the Monroe Doctrine and narratives of US empire. *See* **8455**.

9455. Sederholm, Carl H. Dividing religion from theology in Lydia Maria Child's *Hobomok*. ATQ (20:3) 2006, 553–64.

Kate Chopin

9456. Beer, Janet; Nolan, Elizabeth (eds). Kate Chopin's *The Awakening*: a sourcebook. London; New York: Routledge, 2004. pp. xviii, 163. (Routledge guides to literature.) Rev. by Elke Kinkel in EJES (10:1) 2006, 102–4.

9457. Church, Joseph. An abuse of art in Chopin's *The Awakening*. ALR (39:1) 2006, 20–3.

9458. Davis, Doris. The enigma at the keyboard: Chopin's Mademoiselle Reisz. MissQ (58:1/2) 2004/05, 89–104.

9459. Gibert, Teresa. Textual, contextual and critical surprises in *Desirée's Baby*. Connotations (14:1–3) 2004/05, 38–67.

9460. Heuston, Sean. Chopin's *The Awakening*. Exp (64:4) 2006, 220–3.

9461. Howard, Hugh. Writers of the American South: their literary landscapes. *See* **11945**.

9462. Nigro, Kathleen. Mr Emerson comes to St Louis: *Inspiration* and Kate Chopin. ConS (ns 14) 2006, 91–103.

9463. Parmiter, Tara K. Taking the waters: the summer place and women's health in Kate Chopin's *The Awakening*. ALR (39:1) 2006, 1–19.

9464. Stein, Allen F. Women and autonomy in Kate Chopin's short fiction. (Bibl. 2005, 10429.) Rev. by Carmen Birkle in Amst (51:3) 2006, 444–6.

Clara Mary Jane Clairmont (1798–1879)

9465. Leslie, Lisa. The fact that is in fiction: autobiography in Claire Clairmont's *The Pole*. KSR (20) 2006, 69–88.

9466. Rossington, Michael. Claire Clairmont's fair copy of Shelley's *Ode to Naples*: a rediscovered manuscript. *See* **11225**.

John Clare

9467. Blythe, Ronald. John Clare and the gypsies. JCSJ (25) 2006, 78–85.

9468. Cantú, Vera (ed.). Poems descriptive of rural life and scenery. Introd. by Carlo M. Bajetta. Milan: ISU Univ. Cattolica, 2006. pp. 180.

9469. Chilcott, Tim. The dating of Clare's *The Shepherd's Calendar*. JCSJ (25) 2006, 65–77.

9470. Chirico, Paul. 'Bounds of place and time': the future of Clare's past. JCSJ (25) 2006, 7–10.

9471. Conti Camaiora, Luisa. Themes and images in John Clare's *Poems Descriptive of Rural Life and Scenery*. Milan: Europrint, 2006. pp. 146.

9472. Fritzsche, Peter. Stranded in the present: modern time and the melancholy of history. Cambridge, MA; London: Harvard UP, 2004. pp. 268. Rev. by Emily Rohrbach in SR (45:3) 2006, 486–90.

9473. Goldsmith, Jason N. The promiscuity of print: John Clare's *Don Juan* and the culture of Romantic celebrity. SELit (46:4) 2006, 803–32.

9474. Gorji, Mina. Burying Bloomfield: poetical remains and 'the unlettered muse'. *In* (pp. 232–52) **9141**.

9475. Houghton, Sarah. The 'community' of John Clare's Helpston. SELit (46:4) 2006, 781–802.

9476. Jacobus, Mary. Cloud studies: the visible invisible. Gramma (16) 2006, 219–47.

9477. Landry, Donna. Georgic ecology. *In* (pp. 253–66) **9141**.

9478. Pickering, Sam. Painting the wind: poetic art and John Clare. SewR (113:3) 2005, 468–77 (review-article). (Arts and letters.)

9479. Powell, David. First publications of John Clare's poems. Baltimore, MD: John Clare Soc. of North America, 2004. pp. xvi, 88. (Research papers on John Clare, 1.) Rev. by Greg Crossan in JCSJ (25) 2006, 86–90.

9480. Robinson, Eric. *Married at Last*: a new source for Clare's *Don Juan*. WordsC (37:2) 2006, 92.

9481. Suarez, Michael F.; Zimmerman, Sarah M. John Clare's career, 'Keats's publisher', and the early nineteenth-century English book trade. SR (45:3) 2006, 377–96.

9482. Thornton, R. K. R. The raw and the cooked. JCSJ (24) 2005, 78–86. (Editions of Clare.)

9483. —— What John Clare do we read? PNRev (31:4) 2005, 54–6.

9484. Ward, Sam. Melodies in the marketplace: John Clare's 100 songs JCSJ (25) 2006, 11–30.

M. (Mary) Clarke (Mary Clarke Carr)

9485. Branson, Susan. Gendered strategies for success in the early nineteenth-century literary marketplace: Mary Carr and the *Ladies' Tea Tray*. *See* **1064**.

Marcus Clarke

9486. Boehm, Beth A. Nostalgia to amnesia: Charles Dickens, Marcus Clarke and narratives of Australia's convict origins. *See* **9705**.

9487. McCann, Andrew. Marcus Clarke's bohemia: literature and modernity in colonial Melbourne. Carlton South, Vic.: Melbourne UP, 2004. pp. vii, 254. Rev. by Nicholas Birns in ALS (22:3) 2006, 390–1.

Arthur Hugh Clough

9488. Birch, Dinah. Little was expected of Annie. LRB (28:20) 2006, 26 (review-article). (Annie Clough.)

9489. Kenny, Anthony. Arthur Hugh Clough: a poet's life. (Bibl. 2005, 10453.) Rev. by Daniel Karlin in TLS, 13 Jan. 2006, 3–4; by Simone Lavabre in EA (59:4) 2006, 485–6.

9490. O'Gorman, Francis. Clough's difficulties. YES (36:2) 2006, 125–38.

9491. Phelan, Joseph. Clough, Arnold, Béranger, and the legacy of 1848. SELit (46:4) 2006, 833–48.

9492. Scott, Patrick. Clough, bankruptcy, and disbelief: the economic background to *Blank Misgivings*. VP (44:2) 2006, 123–34.

9493. Sutherland, Gillian. Faith, duty and the power of mind: the Cloughs and their circle, 1820–1960. Cambridge; New York: CUP, 2006. pp. x, 262. Rev. by Anthony Kenny in TLS, 16 June 2006, 27; by Dinah Birch in LRB (28:20) 2006, 26.

Frances Power Cobbe (1822–1904)

9494. Mitchell, Sally. Frances Power Cobbe: Victorian feminist, journalist, reformer. (Bibl. 2004, 10458.) Rev. by Nancy LoPatin-Lummis in VPR (39:1) 2006, 72–3.

9495. Schor, Esther. Acts of union: Theodosia Garrow Trollope and Frances Power Cobbe on the Kingdom of Italy. *In* (pp. 90–109) **8320**.

William Cobbett

9496. Fritzsche, Peter. Stranded in the present: modern time and the melancholy of history. *See* **9472**.

Mary Elizabeth Coleridge

9497. Stanford, Donald E. A critical study of the works of four British writers: Margaret Louisa Woods (1856–1945), Mary Coleridge (1861–1907), Sir Henry Newbolt (1862–1938), R. C. Trevelyan (1872–1951). Ed. by R. W. Crump. Lewiston, NY; Lampeter: Mellen Press, 2006. pp. xxxii, 318.

Samuel Taylor Coleridge

9498. Axcelson, John. Saving Chatterton: imagining historical transmission in Coleridge. WordsC (36:3) 2005, 126–33.

9499. —— Timing the apocalypse: the career of *Religious Musings*. ERR (16:4) 2005, 439–54.

9500. Balfour, Ian. Torso: (the) sublime sex, beautiful bodies, and the matter of the text. ECS (39:3) 2006, 323–36.

9501. Barbeau, Jeffrey W. The quest for system: an introduction to Coleridge's lifelong project. *In* (pp. 1–32) **9503**.

9502. —— Science and the depersonalization of the divine: Pantheism, Utilitarianism, and the limits of natural theology. *In* (pp. 163–85) **9503**.

9503. —— (ed.). Coleridge's assertion of religion: essays on the *Opus Maximum*. Louvain; Dudley, MA: Peeters, 2006. pp. xvi, 312. (Studies in philosophical theology, 33.)

9504. Beavers, Katy. Poetical, political and personal epistolary thoughts of Charles Lamb and Samuel Taylor Coleridge. *See* **10700**.

9505. Beer, John. Coleridge's *magnum opus* and his *Opus Maximum*. *In* (pp. 281–92) **9503**.

9506. —— Coleridge, Ted Hughes, and Sylvia Plath: mythology and identity. *In* (pp. 123–41) **13735**.

9507. Berkeley, Richard. The providential wreck: Coleridge and Spinoza's metaphysics. ERR (17:4) 2006, 457–75.

9508. Bernstein, Susan. On music framed: the Eolian harp in Romantic writing. *In* (pp. 70–84) **8828**.

9509. Blaxland-de Lange, Simon. Owen Barfield: Romanticism come of age: a biography. Foreword by Andrew Welburn. *See* **14583**.

9510. Bratcher, James T. Coleridge's *Biographia Litteraria*. Exp (64:2) 2006, 76–8.

9511. Burwick, Frederick. Mendelssohn and Coleridge on words, thoughts, and things. *In* (pp. 245–73) **8523**.

9512. Cheshire, Paul. '*In Cælibe Toro meo*': Coleridge's 'old sofa, half bed' at Greta Hall. ColB (ns 27) 2006, 65–6.

9513. Christie, William. Samuel Taylor Coleridge: a literary life. Basingstoke; New York: Palgrave Macmillan, 2006. pp. xviii, 250. (Literary lives.)

9514. Davidson, Graham. Duty and power: conflicts of the will in Coleridge's creation of the self. *In* (pp. 121–44) **9503**.

9515. Davies, Lloyd Guy. Standing at Mont Blanc: Coleridge and Midrash. *In* (pp. 275–97) **8523**.

9516. Edwards, Pamela. The statesman's science: history, nature, and law in the political thought of Samuel Taylor Coleridge. (Bibl. 2004, 10476.) Rev. by David P. Haney in WordsC (36:4) 2005, 176–8; by James Vigus in ColB (ns 27) 2006, 67–71; by Anya Taylor in ERR (17:3) 2006, 397–401; by Graham Davidson in RES (57:230) 2006, 418–20; by David M. Craig in JMH (78:3) 2006, 706–8.

9517. Evans, Murray J. Reading 'will' in Coleridge's *Opus Maximum*: the rhetoric of transition and repetition. *In* (pp. 73–95) **9503**.

9518. Fried, Daniel. The politics of the Coleridgean symbol. SELit (46:4) 2006, 763–79.

9519. Gregory, Alan P. R. 'That I may be here': human persons and divine personeity in the *Opus Maximum*. *In* (pp. 187–211) **9503**.

9520. Guyer, Sara. Testimony and trope in *Frankenstein*. *See* **11179**.

9521. Hampton, Alexander J. B. The struggle for reason: early development of triadic self-consciousness in the *Opus Maximum*. ColB (ns 27) 2006, 45–55.

9522. Hardy, Daniel W. Harmony and mutual implication in the *Opus Maximum*. *In* (pp. 33–52) **9503**.

9523. Hedley, Douglas. *Philosophia Trinitatis*: Coleridge, Pantheism, and a Christian Cabbala. *In* (pp. 213–31) **9503**.

9524. Hessell, Nikki. The opposite of news: rethinking the 1800 *Lyrical Ballads* and the mass media. *See* **11675**.

9525. Hickey, Alison. 'The body of my father's writings': Sara Coleridge's genial labor. *In* (pp. 124–47) **3405**.

9526. Jasper, David. 'The wheels of the chariot': religious language in English and German Romanticism. *In* (pp. 95–109) **3415**.

9527. Jay, Mike. The fruitful matrix of ghosts: Samuel Taylor Coleridge's psychic investigations. TLS, 5 May 2006, 14–15.

9528. Keanie, Andrew. *Coleridge, the Damaged Archangel*. EC (56:1) 2006, 72–93. (New impressions, 11.) (*Discusses* bibl. 1971, 7025.)

9529. Keil, Katherine. O'Connor's *A Good Man Is Hard to Find*. *See* **17828**.

9530. Koelzer, Robert. Abrams among the nightingales: revisiting the greater Romantic lyric. *See* **14184**.

9531. KOOY, MICHAEL JOHN. Coleridge and melancholy: the case of the Wedding-Guest. EREA (4:1) 2006, 1–9.

9532. LEADER, ZACHARY. Writers' blocks. *See* **11689**.

9533. MCCULLY, CHRIS. The word in time: 4, Under the influence: *Lyrical Ballads*. PNRev (33:1) 2006, 51–3.

9534. MCKUSICK, JAMES C. Nature. *In* (pp. 413–32) **8357**.

9535. MCLEAN, KAREN. Individuality, utility, and distinction: Plotinian concepts in the *Opus Maximum*. *In* (pp. 233–53) **9503**.

9536. MASSON, SCOTT. Repeating the act of the infinite in the finite: theological anthropology in Coleridge's *Opus Maximum*. *In* (pp. 145–62) **9503**.

9537. MAYBERRY, TOM; DAVIDSON, GRAHAM. Coleridge's Bristol. ColB (ns 27) 2006, 1–16.

9538. MERITT, MARK D. De Quincey's Coleridge and the dismantling of Romantic authority. *See* **9688**.

9539. MILLER, CHRISTOPHER R. The invention of evening: perception and time in Romantic poetry. Cambridge; New York: CUP, 2006. pp. ix, 262. (Cambridge studies in Romanticism, 66.)

9540. MORRISON, RONALD D. Coleridge's mad ox: the English, animals, and the French Revolution. KenPR (20) 2005, 46–51.

9541. NORTH, JOHN. Master classes. TLS, 20 Oct. 2006, 4–5 (review-article). (Science and Utilitarianism.)

9542. OWER, JOHN. Coleridge's *Rime of the Ancient Mariner*. Exp (65:1) 2006, 19–21.

9543. PALEY, MORTON D. Coleridge and Washington Allston's *The Sisters*. WordsC (36:3) 2005, 113–16.

9544. PERRY, SEAMUS. Self-management. *See* **11248**.

9545. RAJAN, TILOTTAMA. 13 retro keywords ... and why they're worth a second look: *organicism*. *See* **1590**.

9546. REID, NICHOLAS. Coleridge, form and symbol; or, The ascertaining vision. Aldershot; Burlington, VT: Ashgate, 2006. pp. ix, 189. (Nineteenth century.)

9547. —— The *logosophia*: how the *logos* acts as unifying principle in Coleridge's thought. *In* (pp. 255–80) **9503**.

9548. SCOTT, MATTHEW. John Keats and the aesthetics of topsy-turvy. *See* **10664**.

9549. SIMONS, THOMAS R. Coleridge beyond Kant and Hegel: transcendent aesthetics and the dialectic pentad. SR (45:3) 2006, 465–81.

9550. SISMAN, ADAM. The friendship: Wordsworth and Coleridge. *See* **11715**.

9551. SONOI, CHINE. Coleridge and the British slave trade. ColB (ns 27) 2006, 27–37.

9552. SPECTOR, STANLEY J. Coleridge's misreading of Spinoza. *In* (pp. 233–44) **8523**.

9553. STILLINGER, JACK. Romantic complexity: Keats, Coleridge, and Wordsworth. *See* **10666**.

9554. TAYLOR, ANYA. Erotic Coleridge: women, love, and the law against divorce. Basingstoke; New York: Palgrave Macmillan, 2005. pp. x, 219.

9555. —— Massaging *Erotic Coleridge*. WordsC (37:2) 2006, 85–91.

9556. Toor, Kiran. 'O yes! but I can!' – Coleridge's chemical others. ColB (ns 27) 2006, 17–26.

9557. Tsur, Reuven. *Kubla Khan* – poetic structure, hypnotic quality, and cognitive style: a study in mental, vocal, and critical performance. Amsterdam; Philadelphia, PA: Benjamins, 2006. pp. 252. (Human cognitive processing, 16.) Rev. by Patrick Colm Hogan in Style (40:4) 2006, 374–9.

9558. Ulmer, William A. The alienation of the elect in Coleridge's Unitarian prophecies. RES (57:231) 2006, 526–44.

9559. Vigus, James. 'With his garland and his singing robes about him': the persistence of the literary in *Opus Maximum*. *In* (pp. 97–119) **9503**.

9560. Webb, Samantha. 'Not so pleasant to the taste': Coleridge in Bristol during the mixed bread campaign of 1795. Romanticism (12:1) 2006, 5–14.

9561. Whelan, Timothy. Coleridge, the *Morning Post*, and female '*illustrissimae*': an unpublished autograph. ERR (17:1) 2006, 21–38.

9562. Wilczynski, Marek. *Lumen obscurum*: Coleridge and the conservative Romantic theology in New England. ATQ (20:4) 2006, 599–610.

9563. Wilson, Eric G. Coleridge's melancholia: an anatomy of Limbo. (Bibl. 2005, 10535.) Rev. by Eric Gidal in WordsC (36:4) 2005, 159–61; by John L. Mahoney in ERR (17:4) 2006, 495–9.

9564. —— Matter and spirit in the age of animal magnetism. PhilL (30:2) 2006, 329–45.

9565. Wilson, Ross. Coleridge and the life of language. ColB (ns 27) 2006, 38–44.

9566. Wright, Luke S. H. *On the Divine Ideas*: the systematic theology of Samuel Taylor Coleridge. *In* (pp. 53–72) **9503**.

Sara Coleridge

9567. Hickey, Alison. 'The body of my father's writings': Sara Coleridge's genial labor. *In* (pp. 124–47) **3405**.

9568. Low, Dennis. The literary protégées of the Lake Poets. *See* **11239**.

John Payne Collier (1789–1883)

9569. Freeman, Arthur; Freeman, Janet Ing. John Payne Collier: scholarship and forgery in the nineteenth century. (Bibl. 2005, 10538.) Rev. by Bernice W. Kliman in ShQ (57:1) 2006, 109–10.

Wilkie Collins (1824–1889)

9570. Allan, Janice M. A lock without a key: language and detection in Collins's *The Law and the Lady*. Clues (25:1) 2006, 45–57.

9571. Bachman, Maria K. Scandalous sensations: *The Woman in White* on the Victorian stage. VN (109) 2006, 1–9.

9572. Baker, William. Wilkie Collins's diary for 1868: nine months in the life of an author. VIJ (33) 2005, 197–227.

9573. —— (ed.). The public face of Wilkie Collins: the collected letters: vol. 1, Letters 1831–1864. (Bibl. 2005, 10541.) Rev. by John Bowen in TLS, 3 Feb. 2006, 4–5.

9574. —— The public face of Wilkie Collins: the collected letters: vol. 2, Letters 1865–1873. (Bibl. 2005, 10542.) Rev. by John Bowen in TLS, 3 Feb. 2006, 4–5.

9575. —— The public face of Wilkie Collins: the collected letters: vol. 3, Letters 1874–1883. (Bibl. 2005, 10543.) Rev. by John Bowen in TLS, 3 Feb. 2006, 4–5.

9576. —— The public face of Wilkie Collins: the collected letters: vol. 4, Letters 1884–1889. (Bibl. 2005, 10544.) Rev. by John Bowen in TLS, 3 Feb. 2006, 4–5.

9577. Bowen, John. Champagne moments. TLS, 3 Feb. 2006, 4–5 (review-article). (Letters.)

9578. —— Collins's shorter fiction. *In* (pp. 37–49) **9609**.

9579. Colón, Christine. Framing the texts: power and subversion in Anne Brontë's *The Tenant of Wildfell Hall* and Wilkie Collins's *The Woman in White*. *In* (pp. 223–37) **8418**.

9580. Cox, Jessica. Representations of illegitimacy in Wilkie Collins's early novels. PQ (83:2) 2004, 147–69.

9581. Daly, Suzanne. Indiscreet jewels: *The Eustace Diamonds*. *See* **11467**.

9582. Davis, Jim. Collins and the theatre. *In* (pp. 168–80) **9609**.

9583. Dever, Carolyn. The marriage plot and its alternatives. *In* (pp. 112–24) **9609**.

9584. Dolin, Tim. Collins's career and the visual arts. *In* (pp. 17–22) **9609**.

9585. Dupeyron-Lafay, Françoise. L'excès dans la fiction de Wilkie Collins. CVE (63) 2006, 49–61.

9586. Flint, Kate. Disability and difference. *In* (pp. 153–67) **9609**.

9587. Hack, Daniel. Revenge stories of modern life. *See* **10024**.

9588. Harrington, Ellen Burton. From the lady and the law to the lady detective: gender and voice in Collins and Dickens. *See* **9762**.

9589. Hervouet-Farrar, Isabelle. Images du vieillir chez Wilkie Collins. CVE (63) 2006, 261–75.

9590. Hollington, Michael. *The Perils of Certain English Prisoners*: Dickens, Collins, Morley and Central America. *See* **9765**.

9591. Kreisel, Deanna K. Wolf children and automata: bestiality and boredom at home and abroad. *See* **11301**.

9592. Kucich, John. Collins and Victorian masculinity. *In* (pp. 125–38) **9609**.

9593. Law, Graham. The professional writer and the literary marketplace. *In* (pp. 97–111) **9609**.

9594. Lewis, Paul. Burning: the evidence. *See* **9779**.

9595. Malane, Rachel. Sex in mind: the gendered brain in nineteenth-century literature and mental sciences. *See* **9192**.

9596. Malik, Rachel. The afterlife of Wilkie Collins. *In* (pp. 181–93) **9609**.

9597. Mangham, Andrew. 'What could I do?': nineteenth-century psychology and the horrors of masculinity in *The Woman in White*. *In* (pp. 115–25) **8647**.

9598. Marroni, Michela. *The Moonstone* di Wilkie Collins: *Robinson Crusoe* come percorso intertestuale. ConLett (43) 2005, 193–209.

9599. Murphy, Patricia. In science's shadow: literary constructions of late Victorian women. *See* **10304**.

9600. Nayder, Lillian. Collins and empire. *In* (pp. 139–52) **9609**.

9601. NEMESVARI, RICHARD. The mark of the brotherhood: homosexual panic and the foreign Other in Wilkie Collins's *The Woman in White*. *In* (pp. 95–108) **11883**.

9602. PYKETT, LYN. Collins and the sensation novel. *In* (pp. 50–64) **9609**.

9603. —— Wilkie Collins. (Bibl. 2005, 10552.) Rev. by Stephen Wade in ContRev (288:1681) 2006, 243–5.

9604. SALOTTO, ELEANOR. Gothic returns in Collins, Dickens, Zola, and Hitchcock. Basingstoke; New York: Palgrave Macmillan, 2006. pp. 198.

9605. SWARTZ, JENNIFER A. 'Personal property at her disposal': inheritance law, the single woman, and *The Moonstone*. *In* (pp. 160–9) **8647**.

9606. TALAIRACH-VIELMAS, LAURENCE. La loi du silence: écrire le crime dans *Man and Wife* de Wilkie Collins. Cycnos (23:2) 2006, 63–76.

9607. —— Victorian sensational shoppers: representing transgressive femininity in Wilkie Collins's *No Name*. VicR (31:2) 2005, 56–78.

9608. TAYLOR, JENNY BOURNE. The later novels. *In* (pp. 79–96) **9609**.

9609. —— (ed.). The Cambridge companion to Wilkie Collins. Cambridge; New York: CUP, 2006. pp. xix, 207. (Cambridge companions to literature.)

9610. THOMAS, RONALD R. *The Moonstone*, detective fiction and forensic science. *In* (pp. 65–78) **9609**.

9611. TRODD, ANTHEA. The early writing. *In* (pp. 23–36) **9609**.

9612. WAGNER, TAMARA S. Sensationalizing Victorian suburbia: Wilkie Collins's *Basil*. *In* (pp. 200–11) **8647**.

9613. WILLEY, VICKI CORKRAN. Wilkie Collins's 'secret dictate': *The Moonstone* as a response to imperialist panic. *In* (pp. 225–33) **8647**.

9614. YOUNG-ZOOK, MONICA M. Wilkie Collins's Gwilty conscience: gender and colonialism in *Armadale*. *In* (pp. 234–45) **8647**.

9615. ZIGAROVICH, JOLENE. Wilkie Collins, narrativity, and epitaph. DSA (36) 2006, 229–64.

James Collinson (1825–1881)

9616. CONTRERAS, JORGE. James Collinson, the *campo santo*, and the birth of the Pre-Raphaelite Brotherhood. JPRS (15:1) 2006, 5–18.

J. Fenimore Cooper

9617. BOTTALICO, MICHELE. Visioni d'oltreoceano: Irving e Cooper su Londra. *In* (pp. 133–48) **7343**.

9618. BUINICKI, MARTIN T. Negotiating copyright: authorship and the discourse of literary property rights in nineteenth century America. *See* **666**.

9619. DOOLEN, ANDY. Fugitive empire: locating early American imperialism. Minneapolis; London: Minnesota UP, 2005. pp. xxvii, 254. Rev. by Andrew Newman in EAL (41:3) 2006, 592–600.

9620. LOPENZINA, DREW. 'The whole wilderness shall blossom as the rose': Samson Occom, Joseph Johnson, and the question of native settlement on Cooper's frontier. AmQ (58:4) 2006, 1119–45.

9621. NEMOIANU, VIRGIL. The triumph of imperfection: the Silver Age of sociocultural moderation in Europe, 1815–1848. Columbia; London: South

Carolina UP, 2006. pp. xi, 258. Rev. by Mihai I. Spariosu in MLN (121:5) 2006, 1272–4.

9622. Schachterle, Lance. A long false start: the rejection of chapters of Cooper's *The Bravo* (1831). PAAS (115:1) 2005, 81–126.

9623. Schweitzer, Ivy. Imaginative conjunctions on the imperial 'frontier': Catharine Sedgwick reads Mungo Park. *In* (pp. 126–43) **6224**.

9624. —— Perfecting friendship: politics and affiliation in early American literature. *See* **7197**.

9625. Sloan, Karen S. The nineteenth-century church music controversy: a possible referent for Cooper's 'manifestly impossible' singing-master in *The Last of the Mohicans*. ANQ (19:1) 2006, 33–42.

9626. —— Reterritorializing Cooper's marginalia in *The Last of the Mohicans*: authorial commentary as rhetorical borderland. ANQ (19:2) 2006, 33–9.

9627. Smith, Lindsey Claire. Cross-cultural hybridity in James Fenimore Cooper's *The Last of the Mohicans*. ATQ (20:3) 2006, 527–52.

9628. Tawil, Ezra. The making of racial sentiment: slavery and the birth of the frontier romance. *See* **8721**.

9629. Wegener, Signe O. James Fenimore Cooper *versus* the cult of domesticity: progressive themes of femininity and family in the novels. Jefferson, NC; London: McFarland, 2005. pp. v, 191.

9630. White, Craig. Student companion to James Fenimore Cooper. Westport, CT; London: Greenwood Press, 2006. pp. xiii, 209. (Student companions to classic writers.)

9631. White, Jenny L. The landscapes of Susan Howe's *Thorow*. *See* **16477**.

9632. Zou, Huiling. On the Indian images in the White canons of 19th-century America. *See* **8736**.

George Copway (1818–1863?)

9633. Rex, Cathy. Survivance and fluidity: George Copway's *The Life, History, and Travels of Kah-ge-ga-gah-bowh*. SAIL (18:2) 2006, 1–33.

'Marie Corelli' (Mary Mackay)

9634. Fisher, Benjamin F. Marie Corelli's *Barabbas*, *The Sorrows of Satan* and generic transition. WWr (13:2) 2006, 304–20.

9635. Guest, Kristen. Rewriting Faust: Marie Corelli's female tragedy. VIJ (33) 2005, 149–77.

9636. Hallim, Robyn. Marie Corelli's best-selling electric creed. WWr (13:2) 2006, 267–83.

9637. Hartnell, Elaine M. Morals and metaphysics: Marie Corelli, religion and the gothic. WWr (13:2) 2006, 284–303.

9638. Hipsky, Martin. The Corellian romance *contra* modernity: *The Treasure of Heaven* and *Innocent*. WWr (13:2) 2006, 206–24.

9639. Kuehn, Julia. *'Je t'aime … moi non plus'*: deconstructing love in *Open Confession to a Man from a Woman*. WWr (13:2) 2006, 225–45.

9640. MacLeod, Kirsten (ed.). Wormwood: a drama of Paris. Peterborough, Ont.; Orchard Park, NY: Broadview Press, 2004. pp. 407. (Broadview eds.) Rev. by Elaine M. Hartnell in WWr (13:2) 2006, 327–9.

9641. Moody, Nickianne. Moral uncertainty and the afterlife: explaining the popularity of Marie Corelli's early novels. WWr (13:2) 2006, 188–205.

9642. Siebers, Alisha. The genius in *Ardath: the Story of a Dead Self.* WWr (13:2) 2006, 246–66.

9643. Talairach-Vielmas, Laurence. Portrait de l'artiste en jeune femme: *Wormwood* (1890) de Marie Corelli. CVE (63) 2006, 447–62.

'Barry Cornwall' (Bryan Waller Procter)

9644. Turley, Richard Marggraf. Keats, Cornwall and the 'scent of strong-smelling phrases'. *See* **10669**.

Hannah Crafts

9645. Ballinger, Gill; Lustig, Tim; Townshend, Dale. Missing intertexts: Hannah Crafts's *The Bondwoman's Narrative* and African American literary history. JAStud (39:2) 2005, 207–37.

9646. Bernier, Celeste-Marie; Newman, Judie. *The Bondwoman's Narrative*: text, paratext, intertext and hypertext. JAStud (39:2) 2005, 147–65.

9647. Gates, Henry Louis, Jr; Robbins, Hollis (eds). In search of Hannah Crafts: critical essays on *The Bondwoman's Narrative*. (Bibl. 2005, 10575.) Rev. by Cynthia S. Hamilton in JAStud (39:2) 2005, 305–8; by Lauren Hauptman in AAR (40:2) 2006, 389–91.

Stephen Crane

9648. Alonzo, Juan. From derision to desire: the 'greaser' in Stephen Crane's Mexican stories and D. W. Griffith's early westerns. WAL (38:4) 2004, 374–401.

9649. Campbell, Donna. Reflections on Stephen Crane. StCS (15:1) 2006, 13–16.

9650. Church, Joseph. Uncanny moments in the work of Stephen Crane. StCS (15:1) 2006, 20–7.

9651. Colvert, James B. Stephen Crane: notions of an aged reader. StCS (15:1) 2006, 6–8.

9652. Dooley, Patrick K. Stephen Crane's distilled style (and the fine art of swearing). StCS (15:1) 2006, 28–31.

9653. Eisenhauer, Robert. Parables of disfiguration: reason and excess from Romanticism to the avant-garde. *See* **11208**.

9654. Hiro, Molly. How it feels to be without a face: race and the reorientation of sympathy in the 1890s. Novel (39:2) 2006, 179–203.

9655. Kuga, Shunji. Momentous sounds and silences in Stephen Crane. StCS (15:1) 2006, 17–19.

9656. Link, Eric Carl. Bitter questions: six Crane moments. StCS (15:1) 2006, 3–5.

9657. Meacham, Meredith. Contemplating sand and trees in *The Open Boat* and the *Odyssey.* Humanist (66:3) 2006, 43–4.

9658. NAGEL, JAMES. Donald Pizer, American Naturalism, and Stephen Crane. StAN (1:1/2) 2006, 30–5.

9659. —— Limitations of perspective in the fiction of Stephen Crane. StCS (15:1) 2006, 9–12.

9660. NELSON, RONALD J. The writing styles of two war correspondents: Stephen Crane and Ernie Pyle. WVUPP (51) 2004, 36–42.

9661. PASCHKE-JOHANNES, J. EDWIN. Existential moments in Stephen Crane's poems. StCS (15:1) 2006, 32–6.

9662. SCHAEFER, MICHAEL. 'Heroes have no shame in their lives': manhood, heroics, and compassion in *The Red Badge of Courage* and *A Mystery of Heroism*. WLA (18:1/2) 2006, 104–13.

9663. SORRENTINO, PAUL (ed.). Stephen Crane remembered. Tuscaloosa; London: Alabama UP, 2006. pp. xiii, 385. (Studies in American literary realism and naturalism.)

9664. SORRENTINO, PAUL M. Student companion to Stephen Crane. Westport, CT; London: Greenwood Press, 2006. pp. viii, 171. (Student companions to classic writers.) Rev. by Peter Barry in Eng (55:212) 2006, 213–19.

Isabella Valancy Crawford

9665. HULAN, SHELLEY. Isabella Valancy Crawford's *Hugh and Ion*: crafting a Samsonian hero. CanP (58) 2006, 10–35.

9666. PETERMAN, MICHAEL. Writing for the illustrated story papers in the 1870s: individuality and conformity in Isabella Valancy Crawford's stories and serialized fiction. ShSt (13:1) 2005, 73–87.

Thomas Crofton Croker (1798–1854)

9667. MARKEY, ANNE. The discovery of Irish folklore. NewHR (10:4) 2006, 21–43.

Robert Hartley Cromek

9668. BENTLEY, E. B. *Grave* indignities: greed, hucksterism, and oblivion: Blake's watercolors for Blair's *Grave*. *See* **7553**.

9669. GROVES, DAVID. 'Great and singular genius': further references to Blake (and Cromek) in the *Scots Magazine*. *See* **7572**.

9670. —— 'This class of impostors': Robert Cromek's view of London booksellers and engravers. Blake (40:1) 2006, 45.

Allan Cunningham

9671. KILLICK, TIM. Truth, imagination and tradition: Allan Cunningham and Scottish short fiction. ScSR (6:2) 2005, 49–59.

Robert Curzon

9672. BOWERS, TERENCE. Robert Curzon, Orientalism, and the *ars peregrinationis*. VIJ (33) 2005, 117–47. (*Visits to Monasteries in the Levant*.)

Richard Henry Dana, Sr (1787–1879)

9673. KEETLEY, DAWN. Homicidal envy: the case of Richard Henry Dana, Sr's *Paul Felton*. EAL (41:2) 2006, 273–304.

Charles Darwin (1809–1882)

9674. Ridley, Mark. How to read Darwin. London: Granta, 2005. pp. viii, 119. Rev. by Andrew Harvey in TLS, 25 Mar. 2005, 30.

John Davidson

9675. Hynd, Hazel. A sense of place: landscape and location in the poetry of John Davidson. VP (43:4) 2005, 497–512.

9676. Morgan, Edwin. Poetry and virtual realities. *In* (pp. 27–47) **13732**.

Lucretia Maria Davidson (1808–1825)

9677. Ashworth, Suzanne. Invalid insurrections: intellect and appetite in Catharine Maria Sedgwick's biography of Lucretia Maria Davidson. ATQ (20:2) 2006, 419–47.

Richard Harding Davis

9678. Murphy, Gretchen. Hemispheric imaginings: the Monroe Doctrine and narratives of US empire. *See* **8455**.

Thomas Davis (1814–1845)

9679. Paterson, Adrian. 'An imagined music': Yeats, music and the Irish tradition. *In* (pp. 135–69) **12189**.

J. W. De Forest

9680. Buinicki, Martin T. John W. De Forest's *Miss Ravenel's Conversion* and the limits of Sentimental citizenship. ALR (39:1) 2006, 48–63.

9681. Thompson, Todd. Reconstructive realism: satire in *Miss Ravenel's Conversion from Secession to Loyalty*. JAC (29:4) 2006, 425–36.

Alonzo Delano (1806–1874)

9682. Witschi, Nicolas S. Alonzo 'Old Block' Delano. Boise, ID: Boise State Univ., 2006. pp. 52. (Boise State Univ. Western writers, 169.)

Martin R. Delany

9683. Levine, Robert. Twelve years with Martin Delany: a confession. *In* (pp. 173–85) **20098**.

Mary de Morgan (1850–1907)

9684. Fowler, James. The golden harp: Mary de Morgan's centrality in Victorian fairy-tale literature. ChildLit (33) 2005, 224–36.

Thomas De Quincey

9685. Bridgwater, Patrick. De Quincey's gothic masquerade. Amsterdam; New York: Rodopi, 2004. pp. 183. (Internationale Forschungen zur allgemeinen und vergleichenden Literaturwissenschaft, 80.) Rev. by Marcus Waithe in YES (36:2) 2006, 277–8.

9686. Dillon, Sarah. Reinscribing De Quincey's palimpsest: the significance of the palimpsest in contemporary literary and cultural studies. TexP (19:3) 2005, 243–63.

9687. Krishnan, Sanjay. Opium and empire: the transports of Thomas De Quincey. B2 (33:2) 2006, 203–34.

9688. Meritt, Mark D. De Quincey's Coleridge and the dismantling of Romantic authority. A/B (20:2) 2005, 195–229.

9689. Slote, Sam. A Eumaean return to style. *See* **16771**.

Thomas Frognall Dibdin (1776–1847)

9690. Lerer, Seth. Caxton in the nineteenth century. *In* (pp. 325–70) **4125**.

Charles Dickens

9691. Aikens, Kristina. The daughter's desire in *Dombey and Son*. CritS (17:2) 2005, 77–91.

9692. Allan, Janice M. (ed.). Charles Dickens's *Bleak House*: a sourcebook. (Bibl. 2005, 10638.) Rev. by Robert Tracy in DickQ (23:1) 2006, 39–41.

9693. Allingham, Philip V. The illustrations in Dickens's *The Haunted Man and the Ghost's Bargain*: public and private spheres and spaces. DSA (36) 2006, 75–123.

9694. Alter, Robert. Imagined cities: urban experience and the language of the novel. (Bibl. 2005, 10639.) Rev. by Olga Stein in BkCan (34:5) 2005, 15–16; by Arnold Weinstein in LitIm (8:1) 2006, 159–66; by Jeremy Tambling in DickQ (23:2) 2006, 125–7; by Peter Kalliney in Mod/Mod (13:4) 2006, 747–54; by Arnold Weinstein in LitIm (8:1) 2006, 159–66; by Martha Kuhlman in Comparatist (30) 2006, 144–5; by Richard Maxwell in VS (48:3) 2006, 538–41.

9695. Andrews, Malcolm. Charles Dickens and his performing selves: Dickens and the public readings. Oxford; New York: OUP, 2006. pp. xiv, 331.

9696. Antinucci, Raffaella. Alfonso Cuarón's 'late experimentations': Dickens and post-modernism. *In* (pp. 293–317) **9791**.

9697. Archibald, Diana C. 'Of all the horrors … the foulest and most cruel': sensation and Dickens's *Oliver Twist*. *In* (pp. 53–63) **8647**.

9698. Ballinger, Gill; Lustig, Tim; Townshend, Dale. Missing intertexts: Hannah Crafts's *The Bondwoman's Narrative* and African American literary history. *See* **9645**.

9699. Barnabé, Jean-Philippe. Borges as a reader of Dickens. DSA (36) 2006, 285–97.

9700. Bar-Yosef, Eitan. 'It's the old story': David and Uriah in II Samuel and *David Copperfield*. MLR (101:4) 2006, 957–65.

9701. Battegazzore, Miguel Angel. A Cubo-Futurist reading of Dickens: Rafael Barradas's 1921 illustrations for *Hard Times*. DSA (36) 2006, 299–306.

9702. Berard, Jane H. Dickens and landscape discourse. New York; Frankfurt: Lang, 2006. pp. x, 188. (Studies in nineteenth-century British literature, 16.)

9703. Besserman, Lawrence. Chaucer and Dickens use Luke 23.34. *See* **4490**.

9704. Bodenheimer, Rosemarie. Dickens, fascinated. VS (48:2) 2006, 268–76.

9705. Boehm, Beth A. Nostalgia to amnesia: Charles Dickens, Marcus Clarke and narratives of Australia's convict origins. VN (109) 2006, 9–14.

9706. Bowen, John; Patten, Robert L. (eds). Palgrave advances in Charles Dickens studies. Basingstoke; New York: Palgrave Macmillan, 2006. pp. x, 334.

(Palgrave advances.) Rev. by Nicola Bradbury in Dickensian (102:2) 2006, 160–2.

9707. Bown, Nicola; Burdett, Carolyn; Thurschwell, Pamela (eds). The Victorian supernatural. (Bibl. 2005, 10645.) Rev. by Vybarr Cregan-Reid in TexP (19:3) 2005, 390–5.

9708. Bridgham, Elizabeth. The *Dickens Quarterly* checklist. DickQ (23:1) 2006, 55–9.

9709. —— The *Dickens Quarterly* checklist. DickQ (23:2) 2006, 138–41.

9710. —— The *Dickens Quarterly* checklist. DickQ (23:3) 2006, 209–13.

9711. Camus, Marianne. Dickens et Gaskell; ou, Les difficultés mid-victoriennes à dire le vieillir. CVE (63) 2006, 223–33.

9712. —— Gender and madness in the novels of Charles Dickens. (Bibl. 2005, 10654.) Rev. by Natalie McKnight in Dickensian (101:3) 2005, 243–5.

9713. Casotti, Francesco M. *Great Expectations*: l'inizio e la fine di una storia. *In* (pp. 61–93) **9791**.

9714. Chialant, Maria Teresa. *'This grey, monstrous London of ours'*: squarci ottocenteschi. *In* (pp. 151–63) **7343**.

9715. Christensen, Allan C. Authors at work in *Great Expectations* and *A Strange Story*. *In* (pp. 29–50) **9791**.

9716. Claybaugh, Amanda. Toward a new transatlanticism: Dickens in the United States. VS (48:3) 2006, 439–60.

9717. Cohen, William A. Interiors: sex and the body in Dickens. CritS (17:2) 2005, 5–19.

9718. Cole, Nathalie Bell. Travel, the road and the city in adaptations of *Great Expectations*. *In* (pp. 265–92) **9791**.

9719. Coleman, Rosemary. Nell and Sophronia – Catherine, Mary, and Georgina: solving the female puzzle and the gender conundrum in *The Old Curiosity Shop*. DSA (36) 2006, 33–55.

9720. Colledge, Gary L. *The Life of Our Lord* revisited. DSA (36) 2006, 125–51.

9721. Colón, Susan. Dickens's *Hard Times* and Dante's *Inferno*. Exp (65:1) 2006, 31–3.

9722. Cordery, Gareth (ed.). An Edwardian's view of Dickens and his illustrators: Harry Furniss's *Sketch of Boz*. Greensboro, NC: ELT Press, 2005. pp. xii, 116. (1880–1920 British authors, 20.) Rev. by M. Y. A[ndrews] in Dickensian (102:1) 2006, 58–60.

9723. Cordery, Lindsey. Dickens in Latin America: Borrioboola-Gha revisited. DSA (36) 2006, 355–61.

9724. Coste, Marie-Amélie. L'usure et la défiguration chez Dickens. CVE (63) 2006, 249–60.

9725. Courtemanche, Eleanor. 'Naked truth is the best eloquence': Martineau, Dickens, and the moral science of realism. *See* **10799**.

9726. Coustillas, Pierre (ed.). Collected works of George Gissing on Charles Dickens: vol. 1, Essays, introductions and reviews. Afterword by Alan S. Watts. *See* **10186**.

9727. Cox, Arthur J. The *Drood* remains revisited: 'first fancy'. DickQ (23:2) 2006, 108–20.

9728. —— The *Drood* remains revisited: the title-page. DickQ (23:1) 2006, 14–28.

9729. Cregan-Reid, Vybarr. Bodies, boundaries and queer waters: drowning and prosopopœia in later Dickens. CritS (17:2) 2005, 20–33.

9730. Dalmagro, María Cristina. The reversal of innocence: Somers, Dickens, and a 'shared Oliver'. DSA (36) 2006, 319–30.

9731. D'Auria, Verónica. Spectacle and estrangement in Dickens. DSA (36) 2006, 349–54.

9732. Del Grosso, Simone. Strategie narrative e metodologie del montaggio dell'*incipit* da Charles Dickens a Martin Scorsese: Jump Cut su Lean, Cuarón e la BBC. *In* (pp. 319–340) **9791**.

9733. de Mattos, Tomás. A Borgesian clue to Dickens's characterization in *Pickwick Papers*. DSA (36) 2006, 273–83.

9734. DeVine, Christine (ed.). Collected works of George Gissing on Charles Dickens: vol. 3, Forster's life of Dickens, abridged and revised by George Gissing. Afterword by James A. Davies. *See* **10190**.

9735. Dolin, Tim. First steps toward a history of the mid-Victorian novel in colonial Australia. ALS (22:3) 2006, 273–93.

9736. Dorré, Gina M. Victorian fiction and the cult of the horse. Aldershot; Burlington, VT: Ashgate, 2006. pp. 179.

9737. Drew, John M. L. (ed.). The pride of mankind. *See* **8769**.

9738. Dubberke, Ray. Who wrote *The Welfleet Mystery*? Dickensian (100:3) 2004, 247–8.

9739. Easson, Angus; Brown, Margaret (eds). The letters of Charles Dickens: supplement iv. Dickensian (100:3) 2004, 226–38.

9740. —— —— The letters of Charles Dickens: supplement vi. Dickensian (102:2) 2006, 117–30.

9741. Eaton, Michael. *The Dickensian* goes to the cinematograph. Dickensian (101:3) 2005, 233–9.

9742. Edgecombe, Rodney Stenning. Dickens and Hood's *Ode to Rae Wilson, Esq.*: two points of contact. Dickensian (101:3) 2005, 211–12.

9743. Escuret, Annie. Excès et sacré dans la littérature victorienne et édouardienne. CVE (63) 2006, 63–83.

9744. Evangelista, Paola. La nave e il fiume: prigionia e libertà in *Great Expectations*. *In* (pp. 147–64) **9791**.

9745. Eyheragaray, Leticia. *The Strange Gentleman*: Dickens on the Uruguayan stage. DSA (36) 2006, 341–8.

9746. Eysell, Joanne. A medical companion to Dickens's fiction. (Bibl. 2005, 10679.) Rev. by John Cosnett in Dickensian (102:1) 2006, 50–2.

9747. Falzon, Alex R. All's well, that begins well? True starts and false endings in *Great Expectations*. *In* (pp. 51–60) **9791**.

9748. Ferster, Judith. The family of origin *versus* the human family: universal love in literature. *In* (pp. 249–61) **3896**.

9749. Flynn, Michael J. Novels by literary snobs: the contentious class-coding of Thackerayan parody. *See* **10764**.

9750. Fontana, Ernest. Metaphoric mules: Dickens's Tom Gradgrind and Dante's Vanni Fucci. VN (109) 2006, 24–5.

9751. Fromonot, Jacqueline. Le langage de l'hypocrisie chez quelques personnages dickensiens: une rhétorique de l'excès. CVE (63) 2006, 85–95.

9752. Furneaux, Holly. 'It is impossible to be gentler': the homoerotics of male nursing in Dickens's fiction. CritS (17:2) 2005, 34–47.

9753. —— 'Worrying to death' – reinterpreting Dickens's critique of the new Poor Law in *Oliver Twist* and contemporary adaptations. Dickensian (101:3) 2005, 213–24.

9754. Garnett, Robert R. The crisis of 1863. DickQ (23:3) 2006, 181–91. (Ellen Ternan's pregnancy.)

9755. Gervais, David. Dostoevsky and the English novel: Dickens, John Cowper Powys and D. H. Lawrence. CamQ (35:1) 2006, 49–71.

9756. —— The poetry of the novel. *See* **9023**.

9757. Ginsburg, Michal Peled. House and home in *Dombey and Son*. DSA (36) 2006, 57–73.

9758. Glancy, Ruth (ed.). Charles Dickens's *A Tale of Two Cities*: a sourcebook. London; New York: Routledge, 2006. pp. xiii, 174. (Routledge guides to literature.)

9759. Gold, David L. Dickens, *theatricals* and *Oxford English Dictionary*: a correction. *See* **1606**.

9760. Hager, Kelly. Jasper Packlemerton, Victorian freak. VLC (34:1) 2006, 209–32.

9761. Hanna, Robert C. Dickens and plagiarism: part II. Dickensian (100:3) 2004, 209–14.

9762. Harrington, Ellen Burton. From the lady and the law to the lady detective: gender and voice in Collins and Dickens. Storytelling (6:1) 2006, 19–31.

9763. Harris, Wilson. Resistances to alterity. *In* (pp. 3–7) **16284**.

9764. Hartley, Jenny. Undertexts and intertexts: the women of Urania Cottage, secrets and *Little Dorrit*. CritS (17:2) 2005, 63–76.

9765. Hollington, Michael. *The Perils of Certain English Prisoners*: Dickens, Collins, Morley and Central America. Dickensian (101:3) 2005, 197–210.

9766. Hori, Masahiro. Investigating Dickens' style: a collocational analysis. (Bibl. 2005, 10697.) Rev. by Roger D. Sell in Dickensian (101:3) 2005, 245–7.

9767. Houston, Gail Turley. From Dickens to *Dracula*: gothic, economics, and Victorian fiction. *See* **9102**.

9768. Huguet, Christine. 'There's not a doubt of the dress': changing clothes in Dickens's fiction. Dickensian (102:1) 2006, 24–31.

9769. Jaeck, Nathalie. Dickens: entre système organique et hémorragie textuelle. CVE (63) 2006, 403–18.

9770. James, Elizabeth. Charles Dickens. (Bibl. 2005, 10701.) Rev. by Michael Slater in Dickensian (102:1) 2006, 52–3.

9771. JIANG, QIUXIA; GUO, LAIFU; JIN, PING. The influence of ideology on translation of foreign literature – a case study of three Chinese versions of *David Copperfield*. FLS (120) 2006, 166–75. (In Chinese.)

9772. JOHN, JULIET. Charles Dickens's *Oliver Twist*: a sourcebook. London; New York: Routledge, 2006. pp. xix, 195. (Routledge guides to literature.)

9773. JOHNSON, CLAUDIA DURST. Labor and workplace issues in literature. *See* **8654**.

9774. KANE, MARY PATRICIA. Haunted expectations: spectral apparitions and the self-made man. *In* (pp. 95–112) **9791**.

9775. KEIRSTEAD, CHRISTOPHER M. In search of the 'great human family': tourism, mass culture, and the knowable community of Dickens' *American Notes*. NCP (33:1) 2006, 117–32.

9776. KLIMASZEWSKI, MELISA. Examining the wet nurse: breasts, power, and penetration in Victorian England. WS (35:4) 2006, 323–46.

9777. LAI, SHU-FANG. Dickens's representation of childhood trauma. FLS (119) 2006, 38–46.

9778. LAURI-LUCENTE, GLORIA. David Lean's *Great Expectations*: transfiguration or transformation? *In* (pp. 243–63) **9791**.

9779. LEWIS, PAUL. Burning: the evidence. Dickensian (100:3) 2004, 197–208. (Dickens's letters.)

9780. LI, ZENG. Ethical analyses of the morality of different classes in *Bleak House*. FLS (118) 2006, 32–40. (In Chinese.)

9781. LOUGY, ROBERT E. Inaugural wounds: the shaping of desire in five nineteenth-century English narratives. (Bibl. 2004, 10708.) Rev. by Laurie Langbauer in VS (48:2) 2006, 370–2.

9782. MAACK, ANNEGRET. Peter Carey's *Jack Maggs*: an Aussie story? *In* (pp. 229–43) **15024**.

9783. MACDONALD, TARA. 'red-headed animal': race, sexuality and Dickens's Uriah Heep. CritS (17:2) 2005, 48–62.

9784. MCKNIGHT, NATALIE. Dickens and Darwin: a rhetoric of pets. Dickensian (102:2) 2006, 131–43.

9785. MCMORRAN, WILL. From Quixote to Caractacus: influence, intertextuality, and *Chitty Chitty Bang Bang*. *See* **12820**.

9786. MAGNI, CHIARA. Mani che parlano: isotopie gestuali in *Great Expectations*. *In* (pp. 195–212) **9791**.

9787. MARCHBANKS, PAUL. From caricature to character: the intellectually disabled in Dickens's novels (part one). DickQ (23:1) 2006, 3–13. (*Nicholas Nickleby*.)

9788. —— From caricature to character: the intellectually disabled in Dickens's novels (part two). DickQ (23:2) 2006, 67–84. (*Barnaby Rudge*.)

9789. —— From caricature to character: the intellectually disabled in Dickens's novels (part three). DickQ (23:3) 2006, 169–80. (*David Copperfield*; *Little Dorrit*; *Our Mutual Friend*.)

9790. MARRONI, FRANCESCO. Melancholy as narratorial paradigm in *Great Expectations*. *In* (pp. 9–28) **9791**.

9791. —— (ed.). *Great Expectations*: nel laboratorio di Charles Dickens. Rome: Aracne, 2004. pp. 348. (Studi di anglistica, 4.)

9792. Moore, Grace. Dickens and empire: discourses of class, race, and colonialism in the works of Charles Dickens. (Bibl. 2005, 10717.) Rev. by Lillian Nayder in VS (48:2) 2006, 331–3; by Anthony Chennells in CLIO (35:3) 2006, 437–43; by Rod Edmond in Dickensian (102:1) 2006, 48–50.

9793. Murphy, Terence Patrick. The uncertainties of conversational exchange: dialogue monitoring as a function of the narrative voice. Style (39:4) 2005, 396–411.

9794. Newey, Vincent. The scriptures of Charles Dickens: novels of ideology, novels of the self. (Bibl. 2005, 10722.) Rev. by Nicola Bradbury in MLR (101:1) 2006, 229–30.

9795. O'Gorman, Francis. Dickens and Yeats's *The Municipal Gallery Revisited*. *See* **19434**.

9796. Pagetti, Carlo. *'Entering the world of a novel'*: Londra, l'enigma della città. *In* (pp. 3–17) **7343**.

9797. Parker, David. Christmas and Charles Dickens. New York: AMS Press, 2005. pp. xv, 355. (AMS studies in the nineteenth century, 34.) Rev. by Patrick J. McCarthy in DickQ (23:3) 2006, 192–5.

9798. Paroissien, David. The Nonesuch Dickens *redux*: a tale of contemporary publishing. DickQ (23:1) 2006, 50–2.

9799. —— The romantic and the familiar: third-person narration in chapter 11 of *Bleak House*. VN (110) 2006, 23–7.

9800. Partenza, Paola. *Great Expectations* e l'avventura interiore. *In* (pp. 125–45) **9791**.

9801. Payne, David. The reenchantment of nineteenth-century fiction: Dickens, Thackeray, George Eliot, and serialization. (Bibl. 2005, 10730.) Rev. by Daniel Novak in Novel (39:1) 2005, 142–5; by Deborah Wynne in VS (48:4) 2006, 756–8; by Mark Turner in GER (37) 2006, 57–8.

9802. Polcini, Valentina. Tutoring in *Great Expectations*: Mr Jaggers and the rhetoric of direction. *In* (pp. 213–22) **9791**.

9803. Pontrandolfo, Luisa. Londra 1851: trasparenze e ombre del Crystal Palace in Mayhew e Dickens. *In* (pp. 165–84) **7343**.

9804. Powell, Neil. Mr Boythorn's canary. PNRev (32:4) 2006, 5–6.

9805. Purchase, Sean. 'The less said about it the better': slavery and silence in Dickens. Dickensian (102:2) 2006, 144–58.

9806. —— 'Speaking of them as a body': Dickens, slavery and *Martin Chuzzlewit*. CritS (18:1) 2006, 1–16.

9807. Purton, Valerie. Dickens, Robert Lytton and a newly discovered letter. Dickensian (102:2) 2006, 101–16.

9808. Quiring, Björn. A consuming dish: supplementing Raffield. *See* **6375**.

9809. Reed, John R. Dickens and naming. DSA (36) 2006, 183–97.

9810. —— The gentleman in the white waistcoat: Dickens and metonymy. Style (39:4) 2005, 412–26.

9811. —— The riches of redundancy: *Our Mutual Friend*. StudN (38:1) 2006, 15–35.

9812. Ruth, Jennifer. Novel professions: interested disinterest and the making of the professional in the Victorian novel. *See* **9200**.

9813. Salotto, Eleanor. Gothic returns in Collins, Dickens, Zola, and Hitchcock. *See* **9604**.

9814. Sanders, Andrew. Dickens and the idea of the comic novel. YES (36:2) 2006, 51–64.

9815. Sasso, Eleonora. Charles Dickens's heart of darkness: anthropophagy and lycanthropy in *Great Expectations*. *In* (pp. 185–94) **9791**.

9816. Schlicke, Paul. Dickens and the pirates: the case of *The Odd Fellow*. Dickensian (100:3) 2004, 224–5.

9817. Schmidt-Haberkamp, Barbara. The writing-back paradigm revisited: Peter Carey, *Jack Maggs*, and Charles Dickens, *Great Expectations*. *In* (pp. 245–62) **15024**.

9818. Schroeder, Natalie; Holt, Shari Hodges. The gin epidemic: gin distribution as a means of control and profit in Dickens's early nonfiction and *Oliver Twist*. DSA (36) 2006, 1–32.

9819. Schwan, Anne. The limitations of a somatics of resistance: sexual performativity and gender dissidence in Dickens's *Dombey and Son*. CritS (17:2) 2005, 92–106.

9820. Smith, Andrew. Dickens' ghosts: invisible economies and Christmas. VicR (31:2) 2005, 36–55.

9821. Smith, Karl. Honeythunder, Exeter Hall and the Jamaican uprising. Dickensian (102:1) 2006, 5–19.

9822. Soccio, Anna Enrichetta. The (im)perfect ladies: modelli di femminilità in *Great Expectations*. *In* (pp. 113–24) **9791**.

9823. Steinlight, Emily. 'ANTI-BLEAK HOUSE': advertising and the Victorian novel. Narrative (14:2) 2006, 132–62.

9824. Stevens, Jason W. Insurrection and Depression-era politics in Selznick's *A Tale of Two Cities* (1935). *See* **13088**.

9825. Stuchebrukhov, Olga. *Bleak House* as an allegory of a middle-class nation. DickQ (23:3) 2006, 147–68.

9826. Susina, Jan. Textual building blocks: Charles Dickens and E. Nesbit's literary borrowings in *Five Children and It*. *In* (pp. 151–68) **17738**.

9827. Sutcliffe, Allan. Pepper's Ghost and *A Christmas Carol*. Dickensian (101:3) 2005, 225–32.

9828. Tatum, Karen F. Explaining the depiction of violence against women in Victorian literature: applying Julia Kristeva's theory of abjection to Dickens, Brontë, and Braddon. *See* **9167**.

9829. Tearle, Oliver. Blake's *London* in *A Tale of Two Cities*. NQ (53:3) 2006, 335–6.

9830. Tomaiuolo, Saverio. Dickens to postmodernity and back. *In* (pp. 223–42) **9791**.

9831. Torres, Alicia. Dickens's Oliver and Somers's orphan: a traffic in identities. DSA (36) 2006, 331–40.

9832. Tracy, Robert. Jasper's plot: inventing *The Mystery of Edwin Drood*. DickQ (23:1) 2006, 29–38.

9833. Vegh, Beatriz. Dickens and Barradas in Madrid, 1921: a hospitable meeting. DSA (36) 2006, 307–13.

9834. —— (ed.). Charles Dickens en América Latina: reflexiones desde Montevideo. Montevideo: Linardi & Risso, 2005. pp. 269. (Monteviseana, 1.) Rev. by Christine Huguet in DickQ (23:3) 2006, 205–7.

9835. Verzella, Massimo. La caratterizzazione del *villain* in *Great Expectations*: fisiognomica, patognomica e atavismo. *In* (pp. 165–84) **9791**.

9836. Wheeler, William A. (reviser). The Dickens dictionary. By Gilbert A. Pierce. (Bibl. 1924, 1522.) Mineola, NY: Dover, 2006. pp. viii, 594. (Dover books on literature and drama.) (Rev. ed.: first ed. 1872.)

9837. Wilkes, David M. 'This most Protean sitter': the factory worker and triangular desire in *Hard Times*. DSA (36) 2006, 153–81.

9838. Willis, Mark. Charles Dickens and fictions of the crowd. DickQ (23:2) 2006, 85–107.

9839. Wiltshire, Irene. *Pickwick* and the pirates. Dickensian (102:1) 2006, 32–44.

9840. Wolfreys, Julian. The old story, with a difference: Pickwick's vision. Columbus: Ohio State UP, 2006. pp. ix, 122. (Victorian critical interventions.) Rev. by Stephen Jarvis in Dickensian (102:1) 2006, 60–1.

9841. Woodcock, Bruce. Unsettling illusions: Carey and capital in *Jack Maggs*. *In* (pp. 263–73) **15024**.

9842. Zangen, Britta. Our daughters must be wives: marriageable young women in the novels of Dickens, Eliot, and Hardy. (Bibl. 2005, 10765.) Rev. by Natalie McKnight in DickQ (23:2) 2006, 127–9.

Anna E. (Anna Elizabeth) Dickinson (1842–1932)

9843. Gallman, J. Matthew. America's Joan of Arc: the life of Anna Elizabeth Dickinson. Oxford; New York: OUP, 2006. pp. viii, 262. Rev. by Christine Bold in TLS, 22 & 29 Dec. 2006, 11.

Emily Dickinson

9844. Anon. (ed.). Emily Dickinson's herbarium. Cambridge, MA; London: Belknap Press of Harvard UP, 2006. pp. 207. (Facsimile with interpretative essays.)

9845. Anikeeva, Tatiana. Emily Dickinson's voice in Russia. EDJ (15:1) 2006, 79–82.

9846. Armantrout, Rae. Looking for trouble. EDJ (15:2) 2006, 4–5. (*I Had Not Minded — Walls.*)

9847. Bang, Mary Jo. I.E., on Emily & influence. EDJ (15:2) 2006, 66–8.

9848. Bednarowski, Mary Farrell. Intimations of bodily holiness in selected poems by Walt Whitman, Emily Dickinson, and Wallace Stevens. *In* (pp. 147–60) **3415**.

9849. Beebe, Ann. Dickinson's *Immortal Is an Ample Word*. Exp (65:1) 2006, 36–9.

9850. Benoit, Raymond. Dickinson's *I Died for Beauty* and Shakespeare's *The Phoenix and the Turtle*. ANQ (19:4) 2006, 31–3.

9851. Bianchi, Martha Dickinson (introd.). The single hound: poems of a lifetime. London: Hesperus Press, 2005. pp. xvii, 170. (Hesperus poetry.) Rev. by Jane Yeh in PNRev (32:4) 2006, 54.

9852. Boruch, Marianne. Heavy lifting. *See* **16302**.

9853. Brantley, Richard E. Experience and faith: the late Romantic imagination of Emily Dickinson. (Bibl. 2005, 10769.) Rev. by Robert M. Ryan in WordsC (36:4) 2005, 162; by Jane Donahue Eberwein in EDJ (15:1) 2006, 96–100; by Joel Pace in Symbiosis (10:1) 2006, 87–90.

9854. Brown, Marshall. Negative poetics: on skepticism and the lyric voice. *See* **11653**.

9855. Chu, Seo-Young Jennie. Dickinson and mathematics. EDJ (15:1) 2006, 35–55.

9856. Daghlian, Carlos. A ironia como poética na poesia de Emily Dickinson. GavB (24/25) 2003/04, 59–74.

9857. Davinroy, Elise. Tomb and womb: reading contexture in Emily Dickinson's *Soft Prison*. Legacy (23:1) 2006, 1–13.

9858. Everson, Landis. Poet to poet: sharing poetry. *See* **15792**.

9859. Finnerty, Páraic. Emily Dickinson's Shakespeare. Amherst: Massachusetts UP, 2006. pp. viii, 267. Rev. by Steven Gould Axelrod in EDJ (15:2) 2006, 119–22.

9860. Fontana, Ernest L. Victorian doors. *See* **11082**.

9861. Frank, Bernhard. Dickinson's *The Soul Selects Her Own Society*. Exp (65:1) 2006, 34–5.

9862. Freeman, Margaret H.; Takeda, Masako. Art, science, and Ste Emilie's sunsets: a Háj-inspired cognitive approach to translating an Emily Dickinson poem into Japanese. Style (40:1/2) 2006, 109–27.

9863. Fuss, Diana. The sense of an interior: four writers and the rooms that shaped them. (Bibl. 2004, 10767.) Rev. by Jennifer Leader in EDJ (15:1) 2006, 83–94.

9864. Ganze, Alison L. Dickinson's *'Twas Like a Maelstrom, with a Notch*. Exp (64:2) 2006, 86–9.

9865. Gardner, Thomas. A door ajar: contemporary writers and Emily Dickinson. Oxford; New York: OUP, 2006. pp. ix, 257. Rev. by Logan Esdale in EDJ (15:2) 2006, 115–19.

9866. Gerhardt, Christine. 'Often seen — but seldom felt': Emily Dickinson's reluctant ecology of place. EDJ (15:1) 2006, 56–78.

9867. Gilbert, Sandra M. Dickinson in the kitchen. *See* **16082**.

9868. Hillman, Brenda; Peterson, Katie. Hermetic memory: an exchange on Dickinson between two poets. EDJ (15:2) 2006, 47–53.

9869. Hogue, Cynthia. 'lives — like Dollars': Dickinson and the poetics of witness. EDJ (15:2) 2006, 40–6.

9870. Horan, Elizabeth Rosa. Dickinson scholars: Willis Buckingham, discoveries of a bibliographer. EDISB (18:1) 2006, 8–11.

9871. Howe, Susan. Experience is the angled road. EDJ (15:2) 2006, 34–7.

9872. Jackson, Virginia. Dickinson's misery: a theory of lyric reading. (Bibl. 2005, 10790.) Rev. by Faith Barrett in EDJ (15:1) 2006, 100–3.

9873. Kelly, Barbara. Selected bibliography. EDISB (18:1) 2006, 15–16.

9874. Kirk, Connie Ann. Emily Dickinson: a biography. (Bibl. 2004, 10773.) Rev. by Stephanie Munro in JAStud (39:2) 2005, 327; by Peter Barry in Eng (55:212) 2006, 213–19; by Françoise Delphy in EA (59:1) 2006, 113–14.

9875. Ladin, Jay. Meeting her maker: Emily Dickinson's God. CC (56:3) 2006, 338–46.

9876. Leader, Jennifer. Fitting in: Dickinson among others. EDJ (15:1) 2006, 83–94 (review-article).

9877. Lundin, Roger. Nimble believing: Dickinson and the conflict of interpretations. *In* (pp. 80–109) **8429**.

9878. Malroux, Claire. Chambre avec vue sur l'éternité: Emily Dickinson. Paris: Gallimard, 2005. pp. 290. Rev. by Alfred Corn in EDJ (15:1) 2006, 95–6; by Anne Mellenthin in EDISB (18:1) 2006, 15.

9879. —— The interior atlas. EDJ (15:2) 2006, 10–13.

9880. Manheim, Daniel L. The signifying spinster: how Emily Dickinson found her voice. ESQ (51:4) 2005, 213–49.

9881. Mayer, Nancy. The American Romantics and religion in the present tense. *See* **11438**.

9882. Mitchell, Domhnall. Ardent spirits: temperance in Emily Dickinson's writing. EDJ (15:2) 2006, 95–112.

9883. —— Measures of possibility: Emily Dickinson's manuscripts. (Bibl. 2005, 10797.) Rev. by Melanie Hubbard in EDJ (15:1) 2006, 103–6.

9884. Nepveu, Pierre. A little toil of love: l'Amérique and Quebec's Emily Dickinson. Trans. by David Palmieri. EDJ (15:1) 2006, 1–15.

9885. Padel, Ruth. The journey or the dance? On syllables belonging to each other. PRev (96:2) 2006, 77–88.

9886. Perelman, Bob. So. EDJ (15:2) 2006, 22–33. (Influence on American Modernism.)

9887. Phillips, Siobhan. 'Loved philology': Emily Dickinson's Trinitarian world. ESQ (51:4) 2005, 251–75.

9888. Raymond, Claire. The posthumous voice in women's writing from Mary Shelley to Sylvia Plath. *See* **11192**.

9889. Resetarits, C. R. The genomic tropes of Dickinson's *The Veins of Other Flowers*. KR (28:1) 2006, 79–85.

9890. Rudden, Patricia S. Blindness never brewed: a Dickinson analogue of Nyro's *Sweet Blindness*. EDISB (18:1) 2006, 3–5.

9891. Runzo, Sandra. Emily Dickinson's American Museum. ESQ (51:4) 2005, 277–305.

9892. Ryan, Michael. My favorite poet. EDJ (15:2) 2006, 38–9.

9893. Shoptaw, John. Listening to Dickinson. Representations (86) 2004, 20–52.

9894. Socarides, Alexandra. Rethinking the fascicles: Dickinson's writing, copying, and binding practices. EDJ (15:2) 2006, 69–94.

9895. Stewart, Susan. Some thoughts about Dickinson's *Dont Put Up My Thread & Needle*. EDJ (15:2) 2006, 58–65.

9896. von der Heydt, Jim. The writer's occupation: Dickinson and Emerson out of doors. ESQ (51:4) 2005, 307–39.

9897. Wolosky, Shira. Emily Dickinson: reclusion against itself. CK (12:3) 2006, 443–59.

9898. Zapedowska, Magdalena. A lesson in grammar: Dickinson's *Grasped by God* and *Drowning Is Not So Pitiful*. EDJ (15:1) 2006, 16–34.

9899. —— Wrestling with silence: Emily Dickinson's Calvinist God. ATQ (20:1) 2006, 379–98.

Benjamin Disraeli

9900. Flavin, Michael. Benjamin Disraeli: the novel as political discourse. Brighton; Portland, OR: Sussex Academic Press, 2005. pp. vii, 221. Rev. by Robert O'Kell in VS (49:1) 2006, 157–9.

9901. Hibbert, Christopher. Disraeli: a personal history. (Bibl. 2005, 10805.) Rev. by H. G. R. Erben in Auto/Biography (14:4) 2006, 393–6.

9902. Kuhn, William. Sexual ambiguity in the life of Disraeli. GLRW (13:4) 2006, 16–18.

9903. Page, Judith W. Anglo-Jewish identity and the politics of cultivation in Hazlitt, Aguilar, and Disraeli. *In* (pp. 149–64) **8523**.

9904. Spector, Sheila A. Orientalism in Disraeli's *Alroy*. *In* (pp. 121–36) **8395**.

Isaac D'Israeli (1766–1848)

9905. Peterfreund, Stuart. Identity, diaspora, and the secular voice in the works of Isaac D'Israeli. *In* (pp. 127–47) **8523**.

9906. Spevack, Marvin. Isaac D'Israeli's Oxford DCL: romance, speculation, and reality. BLR (19:1) 2006, 139–42.

9907. Verhoeven, W. M. (gen. ed.). Anti-Jacobin novels: vol. 8, Isaac D'Israeli, *Vaurien; or, Sketches of the Times* (1797). Ed. by Nicola Trott. London; Brookfield, VT: Pickering & Chatto, 2005. pp. xxxiv, 306. Rev. by Jon Mee in HLQ (69:4) 2006, 649–53.

Ella Hepworth Dixon

9908. Fehlbaum, Valerie. Ella Hepworth Dixon: the story of a modern woman. (Bibl. 2005, 10817.) Rev. by Margaret D. Stetz in VS (49:1) 2006, 126–7.

Richard Watson Dixon

9909. Hurley, Michael D. Darkening the subject of Hopkins' prosody. *See* **10475**.

Digby Mackworth Dolben

9910. Dau, Duc. Perfect chastity: celibacy and virgin marriage in Tractarian poetry. *See* **10960**.

Alfred Domett (1811–1887)

9911. Fontana, Ernest. Gender and sexual anxiety in Browning's *Waring* and *The Guardian-Angel*. *See* **9276**.

Frederick Douglass

9912. Abdur-Rahman, Aliyyah I. 'The strangest freaks of despotism': queer sexuality in antebellum African American slave narratives. AAR (40:2) 2006, 223–37.

9913. Archuleta, Micki. Life, liberty and the pursuit of happiness: a fugitive slave on individual rights and community responsibilities. NCS (19) 2005, 35–45.

9914. Garvey, T. Gregory. Creating the culture of reform in antebellum America. *See* **16221**.

9915. Jun, Helen H. Black Orientalism: nineteenth-century narratives of race and US citizenship. AmQ (58:4) 2006, 1047–66.

9916. Levine, Robert. Twelve years with Martin Delany: a confession. *In* (pp. 173–85) **20098**.

9917. Luria, Sarah. Capital speculations: writing and building Washington, DC. *See* **11567**.

9918. Newtown, George. From bottom to top: Frederick Douglass glimpses male identity from the closet. A/B (20:2) 2005, 246–67.

9919. Ostrowski, Carl. Slavery, labor reform, and intertextuality in antebellum print culture: the slave narrative and the city-mysteries novel. AAR (40:3) 2006, 493–506.

9920. Stadler, Gustavus. Troubling minds: the cultural politics of genius in the United States, 1840–1890. *See* **8973**.

9921. Tang, Edward. Rebirth of a nation: Frederick Douglass as postwar founder in *Life and Times*. JAStud (39:1) 2005, 19–39.

Edward Dowden

9922. Moon, Michael. Solitude, singularity, seriality: Whitman *vis-à-vis* Fourier. *See* **11573**.

Ernest Dowson

9923. Grafe, Adrian. Dowson's excesses and poetics. CVE (63) 2006, 97–109.

Sir Arthur Conan Doyle

9924. Abrams, Jerold J. From Sherlock Holmes to the hard-boiled detective in *film noir*. *In* (pp. 69–88) **12452**.

9925. Acton, Tom. Ved Dzabqu qd vnh Urod. *See* **14886**.

9926. Barloon, Jim. The case for identity: Sherlock Holmes and the singular find. Clues (25:1) 2006, 33–44. (*A Case of Identity*.)

9927. Billings, Harold. The *materia medica* of Sherlock Holmes. BSJ (56:3) 2006, 37–46.

9928. Cawelti, John G. Sherlock Holmes: the case of the perpetual detective. Storytelling (6:1) 2006, 7–17.

9929. Clausson, Nils. The simple art of stealing: the case of Raymond Chandler's purloined 'rats behind the wainscoting'. *See* **15132**.

9930. —— Trivial coincidences or 'pre-planned detonations'? A further note on names in Conan Doyle and Wilde. *See* **11598**.

9931. Cooper, Barbara Roisman. *Sherlock Holmes: the Final Adventure*: the playwright and two actors. *See* **15503**.

9932. Curtis, Donald E. *The Lion's Mane*: a topical review. BSJ (56:4) 2006, 15–19.

9933. Dahlinger, S. E. Some observations upon the segregation of the Bea (*sic*). BSJ (56:3) 2006, 6–18. (*The Adventure of Shoscombe Old Place.*)

9934. Davis, J. Madison. The mysterious popularity of the arcane. WLT (80:3) 2006, 28–30.

9935. Ferguson, Christine. Footnotes on *Trilby*: the human foot as evolutionary icon in late Victorian culture. *See* **9957**.

9936. Fetherston, Sonia. Shoscombe through the looking-glass. BSJ (56:1) 2006, 41–50. (*The Adventure of Shoscombe Old Place.*)

9937. Gelly, Christophe. *Le Chien des Baskerville*: poétique du roman policier chez Conan Doyle. Lyons: Presses Universitaires de Lyon, 2005. pp. 205. (Champ anglophone.) Rev. by Jean-Pierre Naugrette in EA (59:4) 2006, 488–90.

9938. Harris, Bruce. The golden barrier explained. BSJ (56:3) 2006, 23–4.

9939. —— Two peas in a pod: Sherlock Holmes and Abraham Lincoln. BSJ (56:4) 2006, 37–40.

9940. Herman, Deborah. Arthur Conan Doyle, the handsome sailor. BSJ (56:2) 2006, 33–6.

9941. Jaffee, Walter W. Sir Arthur Conan Doyle, whaler. BSJ (56:2) 2006, 37–40. (*The Adventure of Black Peter.*)

9942. Jumeau, Alain (trans. and notes). *Étoile d'argent* et autres aventures de Sherlock Holmes. Paris: Gallimard, 2005. pp. 335. (FolioBilingue.) Rev. by Agnès Botz in CVE (63) 2006, 489–90.

9943. Klinger, Leslie S. (ed.). The new annotated Sherlock Holmes. With additional research by Patricia J. Chui. Introd. by John le Carré. (Bibl. 2005, 10859.) Rev. by Richard Whittington-Egan in ContRev (286:1669) 2005, 95–101.

9944. Machinal, Hélène. Conan Doyle: de Sherlock Holmes au Professeur Challenger. Rennes: Presses Universitaires de Rennes, 2004. pp. 368. (Interférences.) Rev. by Max Duperray in EREA (4:1) 2006.

9945. Musto, David F. Holmes and heredity. BSJ (56:2) 2006, 25–7.

9946. Panek, LeRoy L. Thoughts about the beginning of the detective story in America. *See* **13573**.

9947. Pollak, Michael. A kind word for Sebastian Moran. BSJ (56:3) 2006, 19–22. (*The Adventure of the Empty House.*)

9948. Pollock, Donald. *The Hound of the Baskervilles*, Longman's Colonial Library: a 'new edition'. BSJ (56:2) 2006, 57–9.

9949. Press, Charles. When did Arthur Conan Doyle meet Jean Leckie? BSJ (56:2) 2006, 41–52.

9950. Randall, Warren. A study in stanzas: Arthurs, authors, and poetry. BSJ (56:4) 2006, 28–36. (Doyle and Guiterman on Poe.)

9951. Rennison, Nick. Sherlock Holmes: the unauthorized biography. London: Atlantic, 2005. pp. xvii, 280. Rev. by Robert Mighall in TLS, 11 Nov. 2005, 26.

9952. Shreffler, Philip A. Watson's weird tales: horror in the Sherlockian canon. BSJ (56:2) 2006, 6–16.

9953. Siddiqi, Yumna. The cesspool of empire: Sherlock Holmes and the return of the repressed. VLC (34:1) 2006, 233–47.

9954. Silverstein, Albert; Ventura, Marie. The search for forbidden knowledge: Holmes, Moriarty, and the Faust legend. BSJ (56:1) 2006, 29–40.

9955. Whittington-Egan, Richard. Living with and annotating Sherlock Holmes. ContRev (286:1669) 2005, 95–101 (review-article).

Edward Du Bois (1774–1850)

9956. Verhoeven, W. M. (gen. ed.). Anti-Jacobin novels: vol. 9, Sophia King, *Waldorf; or, The Dangers of Philosophy* (1798) Ed. by Adriana Craciun. Edward Dubois, *St Godwin: a Tale of the Sixteenth, Seventeenth, and Eighteenth Centuries* (2nd edn, 1800). Ed. by Robert Miles. London; Brookfield, VT: Pickering & Chatto, 2005. pp. lii, 246. Rev. by Jon Mee in HLQ (69:4) 2006, 649–53.

George du Maurier (1834–1896)

9957. Ferguson, Christine. Footnotes on *Trilby*: the human foot as evolutionary icon in late Victorian culture. NCC (28:2) 2006, 127–44.

Paul Laurence Dunbar

9958. Aldrich, Abigail J. The Hamilton family and the trials of Job: the clash of faith and fate in Paul Laurence Dunbar's *The Sport of the Gods*. CLAJ (50:2) 2006, 219–37.

9959. Bearss, Linda. Dunbar's fiction: transgressing the limits of realism to breach the horizon of Modernism. MidM (34) 2006, 69–77.

9960. Bennett, Paula Bernat. Rewriting Dunbar: realism, Black women poets, and the genteel. *In* (pp. 146–61) **8435**.

9961. Bottoms, Pam. The controversial, subversive 'broken tongue' of Paul Laurence Dunbar. MidM (34) 2006, 6–26.

9962. Davidson, Adenike Marie. Marginal spaces, marginal texts: Alice Dunbar-Nelson and the African American prose poem. *See* **9974**.

9963. Denney, Sheena. 'The province of the poet': biographical themes in Paul Laurence Dunbar's *Herrick*. MidM (34) 2006, 53–60.

9964. Fishkin, Shelley Fisher. Race and the politics of memory: Mark Twain and Paul Laurence Dunbar. *See* **11496**.

9965. Gebhard, Caroline. Inventing a 'Negro literature': race, dialect, and gender in the early work of Paul Laurence Dunbar, James Weldon Johnson, and Alice Dunbar-Nelson. *In* (pp. 162–78) **8435**.

9966. Holder, Stephen C. A man of his times: the fiction of Paul Laurence Dunbar. MidM (34) 2006, 61–8.

9967. Jarrett, Gene Andrew; Morgan, Thomas Lewis (eds). The complete stories of Paul Laurence Dunbar. Foreword by Shelley Fisher Fishkin. Athens: Ohio UP, 2005. pp. xlv, 542.

9968. Jones, Christopher. Paul Laurence Dunbar and Robert Burns: vernacular gateways. MidM (34) 2006, 27–35.

9969. Mink, Joanna Stephens; Luker, Patrice Kahler. Some connections between Hardy's blinded bird and Dunbar's caged bird. *See* **10298**.

9970. Oswald, Emily. Imagining race: illustrating the poems of Paul Laurence Dunbar. BH (9) 2006, 213–33.

9971. Roman, Camille. The caged bird's song and its (dis)contents. PCP (41) 2006, 32–8.

9972. Smith, Katharine Capshaw. The legacy of Paul Laurence Dunbar: dialect and racial configuration in the works of Silas X. Ford and Christina Moody. MidM (34) 2006, 36–52.

Alice Dunbar-Nelson

9973. Brown, Nikki L. War work, social work, community work: Alice Dunbar-Nelson, federal war work agencies, and Southern African American women. *In* (pp. 197–209) **8435**.

9974. Davidson, Adenike Marie. Marginal spaces, marginal texts: Alice Dunbar-Nelson and the African American prose poem. SoQ (44:1) 2006, 51–64.

9975. Gebhard, Caroline. Inventing a 'Negro literature': race, dialect, and gender in the early work of Paul Laurence Dunbar, James Weldon Johnson, and Alice Dunbar-Nelson. *In* (pp. 162–78) **8435**.

9976. Mitchell, Koritha A. Antilynching plays: Angelina Weld Grimké, Alice Dunbar-Nelson, and the evolution of African American drama. *In* (pp. 210–30) **8435**.

Toru Dutt

9977. Lootens, Tricia. Bengal, Britain, France: the locations and translations of Toru Dutt. VLC (34:2) 2006, 573–90.

George Dyer

9978. Wu, Duncan. The Lamb circle and the *Monthly Repository*. *See* **10707**.

Edith Eaton ('Sui Sin Far')

9979. Birkle, Carmen. Orientalisms in *fin-de-siècle* America. *See* **9983**.

9980. Cutter, Martha J. Sui Sin Far's letters to Charles Lummis: contextualizing publication practices for the Asian American subject at the turn of the century. ALR (38:3) 2006, 259–75.

9981. Lee, James Kyung-Jin. Asian Americans. *In* (pp. 174–93) **11776**.

9982. Staples, Joe. 'Discovering' new talent: Charles F. Lummis's conflicted mentorship of Sui Sin Far, Sharlot Hall, and Mary Austin. *See* **17292**.

Winnifred Babcock Eaton ('Onoto Watanna')

9983. Birkle, Carmen. Orientalisms in *fin-de-siècle* America. Amst (51:3) 2006, 323–42.

Emily Eden

9984. O'CINNEIDE, MUIREANN. The Victorian suburb as imperial stage: Emily Eden and the theatrics of empire. Journeys (7:1) 2006, 51–65.

9985. WAGNER, TAMARA S. 'A strange chronicle of the olden time': revisions of the Regency in the construction of Victorian domestic fiction. *See* **9087**.

Maria Edgeworth

9986. BANNET, EVE TAVOR. Maria and Rachel: transatlantic identities and the epistolary assimilation of difference. *In* (pp. 31–56) **9999**.

9987. BEESEMYER, IRENE BASEY. 'I thought I never set my eyes on a finer figure of a man': Maria Edgeworth scrutinizes masculinity in *Castle Rackrent*, *Ennui*, and *The Absentee*. *In* (pp. 109–29) **9999**.

9988. BERMAN, CAROLYN VELLENGA. Creole crossings: domestic fiction and the reform of colonial slavery. Ithaca, NY; London: Cornell UP, 2006. pp. xi, 240. Rev. by Janet C. Myers in VS (49:1) 2006, 139–41.

9989. BOTKIN, FRANCES R. Finding her own voice or 'being on her own bottom': a community of women in Maria Edgeworth's *Helen*. *In* (pp. 93–108) **9999**.

9990. CORDON, JOANNE. Revising stereotypes of nationality and gender: why Maria Edgeworth did not write *Castle Belinda*. *In* (pp. 131–60) **9999**.

9991. DABUNDO, LAURA. Maria Edgeworth and the Irish 'thin places'. *In* (pp. 193–8) **9999**.

9992. GRATHWOL, KATHLEEN B. Maria Edgeworth and the 'true use of books' for eighteenth-century girls. *In* (pp. 73–91) **9999**.

9993. HARVEY, ALISON. West Indian Obeah and English 'obee': race, femininity, and questions of colonial consolidation in Maria Edgeworth's *Belinda*. *In* (pp. 1–29) **9999**.

9994. KAUFMAN, HEIDI; FAUSKE, CHRIS (eds). An uncomfortable authority: Maria Edgeworth and her contexts. (Bibl. 2004, 10871.) Rev. by Clíona Ó Gallchoir in NineL (61:1) 2006, 99–103.

9995. MARKLEY, A. A. Aristocrats behaving badly: gambling and dueling in the 1790s novel of reform. *See* **7838**.

9996. MURPHY, SHARON. Maria Edgeworth and romance. (Bibl. 2005, 10899.) Rev. by Nicola Trott in TLS, 6 Jan. 2006, 23.

9997. NARAIN, MONA. Not the angel in the house: intersections of the public and private in Maria Edgeworth's *Moral Tales* and *Practical Education*. *In* (pp. 57–71) **9999**.

9998. NASH, JULIE. 'Standing in distress between tragedy and comedy': servants in Maria Edgeworth's *Belinda*. *In* (pp. 161–74) **9999**.

9999. —— (ed.). New essays on Maria Edgeworth. Aldershot; Burlington, VT: Ashgate, 2006. pp. xvii,203. (Nineteenth century.)

10000. Ó GALLCHOIR, CLÍONA. Maria Edgeworth: women, Enlightenment and nation. (Bibl. 2005, 10900.) Rev. by Nicola Trott in TLS, 6 Jan. 2006, 23; by Michael Brown in ILS (26:1) 2006, 19.

10001. —— *Uncle Tom's Cabin* and the Irish national tale. *In* (pp. 24–45) **11355**.

10002. RYAN, KARA M. Justice, citizenship, and the question of feminine subjectivity: reading *The Absentee* as a historical novel. *In* (pp. 175–92) **9999**.

10003. SMITH, JAMES M. Two Irish national tales: complete texts with introduction, historical contexts, critical essays. Introd. by Vera Kreilkamp. Boston, MA: Houghton Mifflin, 2005. pp. viii, 447. (New Riverside eds.) (*Castle Rackrent*; *The Wild Irish Girl*.) Rev. by Kathryn Strong in ECN (5) 2006, 392–4.

'George Egerton' (Mary Chavelita Dunne Bright)

10004. MAIER, SARAH E. Symbolist Salomés and the dance of Dionysus. *See* **11614**.

'George Eliot' (Mary Ann Evans)

10005. ALBRECHT, THOMAS. Sympathy and telepathy: the problem of ethics in George Eliot's *The Lifted Veil*. ELH (73:2) 2006, 437–63.

10006. ASHTON, ROSEMARY. A blackguard and his —: the scandal that surrounded George Eliot and G. H. Lewes on their trip to Weimar. TLS, 27 Oct. 2006, 14–15.

10007. BOWLBY, RACHEL. Family realisms: Freud and Greek tragedy. EC (56:2) 2006, 111–38. (F. W. Bateson Memorial Lecture.)

10008. BROOKES, BARBARA; PAGE, DOROTHY. The red-headed heroine. *In* (pp. 157–65) **8374**.

10009. BURSTEIN, MIRIAM ELIZABETH. Narrating women's history in Britain, 1770–1902. Aldershot; Burlington, VT: Ashgate, 2004. pp. 220. (Nineteenth century.) Rev. by Rosemary Mitchell in CLIO (35:2) 2006, 298–303; by Rohan Maitzen in JVC (11:1) 2006, 199–203.

10010. CHASE, KAREN (ed.). *Middlemarch* in the twenty-first century. Oxford; New York: OUP, 2006. pp. xi, 208. Rev. by Matthew Beaumont in TLS, 18 & 25 Aug. 2006, 37.

10011. CHO, SONJEONG. An ethics of becoming: configurations of feminine subjectivity in Jane Austen, Charlotte Brontë, and George Eliot. *See* **9002**.

10012. COTUGNO, CLARE. Stowe, Eliot, and the reform aesthetic. *In* (pp. 111–30) **11355**.

10013. DAVIS, MICHAEL. George Eliot and nineteenth-century psychology: exploring the unmapped country. Aldershot; Burlington, VT: Ashgate, 2006. pp. 210. (Nineteenth century.)

10014. DEL SAPIO GARBERO, MARIA. Mappe e fantasmi: resoconti dall'Impero di Kipling, Hardy e altri. *In* (pp. 157–78) **11824**.

10015. DOLIN, TIM. George Eliot. (Bibl. 2005, 10917.) Rev. by Stephen Wade in ContRev (288:1681) 2006, 243–5; by Alain Jumeau in EA (59:4) 2006, 483–4.

10016. DONOGHUE, DENIS. The not-quite said. Salmagundi (152) 2006, 71–87. (Tragic sense and its inexpressibility.)

10017. FERSTER, JUDITH. The family of origin *versus* the human family: universal love in literature. *In* (pp. 249–61) **3896**.

10018. FRAGOSO, MARGAUX. Imagination, morality, and the spectre of Sade in George Eliot's *Romola* and *Daniel Deronda*. GER (37) 2006, 25–35.

10019. FREED, MARK M. Problems of community and freedom in George Eliot's *Daniel Deronda*. JMMLA (38:2) 2005, 59–77.

10020. Frome, Susan. The sage of unbelief: George Eliot and unorthodox choices. Humanist (66:4) 2006, 27–30.

10021. Galvan, Jill. The narrator as medium in George Eliot's *The Lifted Veil*. VS (48:2) 2006, 240–8.

10022. Gettelman, Debra. Reading ahead in George Eliot. Novel (39:1) 2005, 25–47.

10023. Goslee, David. R. H. Hutton's novel theology. *See* **10520**.

10024. Hack, Daniel. Revenge stories of modern life. VS (48:2) 2006, 277–86.

10025. Hardy, Barbara. Writing a critic's biography. GEGHLS (50/51) 2006, 110–24.

10026. Harris, Margaret. George Eliot's conversation with Currer Bell. GEGHLS (50/51) 2006, 130–42.

10027. Hennelly, Mark M., Jr. 'The secrets of good brewing, the folly of stinginess': *Adam Bede*'s carnival. VLC (34:1) 2006, 47–69.

10028. Hollander, Elizabeth. Ariadne and the rippled nose: portrait likenesses in *Middlemarch*. VLC (34:1) 2006, 167–87.

10029. Horowitz, Evan. George Eliot: the conservative. VS (49:1) 2006, 7–32.

10030. Hunt, Aeron. Calculations and concealments: infanticide in mid-nineteenth-century Britain. VLC (34:1) 2006, 71–94.

10031. Inglis, Katherine. Costanza, Constance, Custance and Emaré: Romola's medieval ancestry. GER (37) 2006, 17–23.

10032. Jenkins, R. J. Laughing with George Eliot. GER (37) 2006, 36–45.

10033. Johnston, Judith. George Eliot and the discourses of medievalism. Turnhout: Brepols, 2006. pp. viii, 210. (Making the Middle Ages, 6.) Rev. by Clare A. Simmons in TMR, Nov. 2006; by Rosemary Greentree in Parergon (23:2) 2006, 145–7.

10034. Jones, Jason B. Lost causes: historical consciousness in Victorian literature. *See* **9394**.

10035. Jougan, Sylvie. Excès et pénurie dans *Middlemarch*: le cas de Mr Casaubon. CVE (63) 2006, 123–35.

10036. Jusová, Iveta; Reyes, Dan. Edward Said, *Reuben Sachs*, and Victorian Zionism. SocT (87) 2006, 35–46.

10037. Kehler, Grace. *Armgart*'s voice problems. VLC (34:1) 2006, 147–66.

10038. Leighton, Angela. Resurrections of the body: women writers and the idea of the Renaissance. *In* (pp. 222–38) **8320**.

10039. McCormack, Kathleen. George Eliot's English travels: composite characters and coded communications. (Bibl. 2005, 10936.) Rev. by Rosemary Ashton in TLS, 31 Mar. 2006, 32; by Ruth M. Harris in GER (37) 2006, 51–3.

10040. Maitzen, Rohan. Martha Nussbaum and the moral life of *Middlemarch*. PhilL (30:1) 2006, 190–207.

10041. Monod, Sylvère (ed. and trans.). Middlemarch. Preface by Virginia Woolf. Paris: Gallimard, 2006. pp. 1152. Rev. by Alain Jumeau in EA (59:3) 2006, 363–4.

10042. Mueller, Monika. George Eliot US: transatlantic literary and cultural perspectives. (Bibl. 2005, 10942.) Rev. by Rainer Emig in Amst (51:3) 2006, 443–4.

10043. Murphy, Margueritte. The ethic of the gift in George Eliot's *Daniel Deronda*. VLC (34:1) 2006, 189–207.

10044. Oestreich, Kate. Deviant celibacy: renouncing Dinah's little fetish in *Adam Bede*. *In* (pp. 82–93) **11883**.

10045. Palmer, Alan. Intermental thought in the novel: the Middlemarch mind. Style (39:4) 2005, 427–39.

10046. Rees, Joan. Christmas in Ryde. GEGHLS (50/51) 2006, 128–9.

10047. Rignall, John. George Eliot and the idea of travel. YES (36:2) 2006, 139–52.

10048. —— George Eliot and Weimar: 'an affinity for what the world calls "dull places"'. GER (37) 2006, 7–16.

10049. Röder-Bolton, Gerlinde. George Eliot in Germany, 1854–55: 'cherished memories'. Aldershot; Burlington, VT: Ashgate, 2006. pp. x, 180. (Nineteenth century.) Rev. by Rosemary Ashton in TLS, 15 Sept. 2006, 31.

10050. Shillock, Larry T. Hoarding motherhood in *Silas Marner*. WVUPP (52) 2005, 33–44.

10051. Siegel, Daniel. Preacher's vigil, landlord's watch: charity by the clock in *Adam Bede*. Novel (39:1) 2005, 48–74.

10052. Smith, Karl. Honeythunder, Exeter Hall and the Jamaican uprising. *See* **9821**.

10053. Solie, Ruth A. 'Music their larger soul': George Eliot's *The Legend of Jubal* and Victorian musicality. *In* (pp. 107–31) **8828**.

10054. Stimpson, Catharine R. Do these deaths surpass understanding? The literary figure of the mother who murders. *See* **17643**.

10055. Tague, Gregory. Character and consciousness: George Eliot, Thomas Hardy, E. M. Forster, D. H. Lawrence: phenomenological, ecological, and ethical readings. Bethesda, MD: Academica Press, 2005. pp. xvi, 281.

10056. Trott, Nicola. The difficulty of Italy: translation and transmission in George Eliot's *Romola*. *In* (pp. 137–58) **8320**.

10057. Waldron, Mary (ed.). Adam Bede. Peterborough, Ont.; Orchard Park, NY: Broadview Press, 2005. pp. 642. (Broadview eds.) Rev. by Graham Handley in GER (37) 2006, 46–7.

10058. Weinroth, Michelle. Engendering consent: the voice of persuasion in *Felix Holt, the Radical*. VIJ (33) 2005, 7–44.

10059. Wiesenfarth, Joseph. Carlyle and the prelude to *Middlemarch*. GEGHLS (50/51) 2006, 143–6.

10060. Willburn, Sarah. Possessed individualism in George Eliot's *Daniel Deronda*. VLC (34:1) 2006, 271–89.

10061. Wolfit, Margaret. Aesop's *Fables* and George Eliot's Brother and Sister sonnets. GER (37) 2006, 65–6.

10062. Yahav-Brown, Amit. Gypsies, nomadism, and the limits of realism. MLN (121:5) 2006, 1124–47.

Ralph Waldo Emerson

10063. Bosco, Ronald A.; Myerson, Joel. The Emerson brothers: a fraternal biography in letters. Oxford; New York: OUP, 2006. pp. xxv, 416.

10064. —— —— (eds). Emerson: bicentennial essays. Boston: Massachusetts Historical Soc., 2006. pp. xx, 473. (Massachusetts Historical Soc. studies in American history and culture, 10.)

10065. —— —— The selected lectures of Ralph Waldo Emerson. Athens; London: Georgia UP, 2005. pp. xxxvi, 379.

10066. Bradbury, Nicola. *De cette triste plume tâtonnante*: Henry James and *The Task of the Translator*. *See* **10541**.

10067. Buell, Lawrence. Saving Emerson for posterity. *In* (pp. 33–47) **10064**.

10068. Burkholder, Robert E. (Re)visiting *The Adirondacs*: Emerson's confrontation with wild nature. *In* (pp. 247–69) **10064**.

10069. Cavell, Stanley. Reflections on Wallace Stevens at Mount Holyoke. *In* (pp. 61–79, 84–8) **11769**.

10070. Cheever, Susan. American Bloomsbury: Louisa May Alcott, Ralph Waldo Emerson, Margaret Fuller, Nathaniel Hawthorne, and Henry David Thoreau: their lives, their loves, their work. *See* **8962**.

10071. Cole, Phyllis. The new movement's tide: Emerson and women's rights. *In* (pp. 117–52) **10064**.

10072. Eckel, Leslie E. Symbols 'mystical and awful': Emerson's and Longfellow's primitive poetics. ESQ (52:1/2) 2006, 45–74.

10073. Finseth, Ian. Evolution, cosmopolitanism, and Emerson's antislavery politics. AL (77:4) 2005, 729–60.

10074. Fuller, Randall. Errand into the wilderness: Perry Miller as American scholar. AmLH (18:1) 2006, 102–28.

10075. Garvey, T. Gregory. Creating the culture of reform in antebellum America. *See* **16221**.

10076. —— Emerson, Garrison, and the anti-slavery society. *In* (pp. 153–82) **10064**.

10077. Glucksman, Fredrica B. Concord comes to Cold Mountain: Emersonian elements in Charles Frazier's *Cold Mountain*. *See* **15992**.

10078. Gougeon, Len. Emerson and the British: challenging the limits of liberty. YREAL (22) 2006, 179–213.

10079. —— Emerson, Whitman, and eros. *See* **11556**.

10080. —— The legacy of reform: Emersonian idealism, Moorfield Storey, and the Civil Rights Movement. *In* (pp. 183–210) **10064**.

10081. Habich, Robert D. Holmes, Cabot, and Edward Emerson and the challenges of writing Emerson's biography in the 1880s. *In* (pp. 3–32) **10064**.

10082. Hudspeth, Robert N. Later Emerson: 'intellect' and *The Conduct of Life*. *In* (pp. 405–31) **10064**.

10083. Korhonen, Kuisma. Textual friendship: the essay as impossible encounter, from Plato and Montaigne to Levinas and Derrida. *See* **3611**.

10084. Larson, Kerry. Illiberal Emerson. NCP (33:1) 2006, 28–72.

10085. McClelland, James. Losing grip: Emerson, Leroux and the work of identity. JAStud (39:2) 2005, 239–55.

10086. Magee, Michael. male north. (Bibl. 2004, 10971.) Rev. by Raphael Allison in AL (78:1) 2006, 190–2.

10087. Malpezzi, Frances M. Emerson's allusive art: a Transcendental angel in Miltonic myrtle beds. Connotations (14:1–3) 2004/05, 162–72.

10088. Mayer, Nancy. The American Romantics and religion in the present tense. *See* **11438**.

10089. Meehan, Sean Ross. Emerson's photographic thinking. AQ (62:2) 2006, 27–58.

10090. Mott, Wesley T. 'The power of recurring to the sublime at pleasure': Emerson and feeling. *In* (pp. 367–90) **10064**.

10091. Nigro, Kathleen. Mr Emerson comes to St Louis: *Inspiration* and Kate Chopin. *See* **9462**.

10092. Nowatzki, Robert C. 'Our only truly national poets': blackface minstrelsy and cultural nationalism. ATQ (20:1) 2006, 361–78.

10093. Obuchowski, Peter A. Emerson and science: Goethe, monism, and the search for unity. Great Barrington, MA: SteinerBooks, 2005. pp. xvii, 121.

10094. Packer, Barbara. History and form in Emerson's *Fate*. *In* (pp. 432–52) **10064**.

10095. —— Signing off: religious indifference in America. *In* (pp. 1–22) **8429**.

10096. Paryż, Marek. Beyond the traveler's testimony: Emerson's *English Traits* and the construction of postcolonial counter-discourse. ATQ (20:3) 2006, 565–90.

10097. Quinn, Gerard. The crooked straightness of Frost and Emerson. *See* **16012**.

10098. Richardson, Joan. Recombinant A.N.W.: appetites of words. *See* **10618**.

10099. Roberson, Susan L. Emerson, Columbus, and the geography of self-reliance: the example of the sermons. *In* (pp. 273–88) **10064**.

10100. Robinson, David M. Experience, instinct, and Emerson's philosophical reorientation. *In* (pp. 391–404) **10064**.

10101. —— (ed.). The political Emerson: essential writings on politics and social reform. Boston, MA: Beacon Press, 2004. pp. 212. Rev. by Robert N. Hudspeth in MaHR (7) 2005, 120–31.

10102. Rochelle, Warren G. The Emersonian choice: connections between dragons and humans in Le Guin's Earthsea cycle. *See* **17108**.

10103. Ronan, John. Thoreau's declaration of independence from Emerson in *Walden*. *See* **11445**.

10104. Schreiner, Samuel A., Jr. The Concord quartet: Alcott, Emerson, Hawthorne, Thoreau, and the friendship that freed the American mind. *See* **8959**.

10105. Schwetman, John D. Romanticism and the cortical stack: cyberpunk subjectivity in the Takeshi Kovacs novels of Richard K. Morgan. *See* **20305**.

10106. SIMMONS, NANCY CRAIG. Emerson and his audiences: the New England lectures, 1843–1844. *In* (pp. 51–85) **10064**.

10107. SMITH, CALEB. Emerson and incarceration. AL (78:2) 2006, 207–34.

10108. SPECQ, FRANCOIS. Transcendence: seekers and seers in the age of Thoreau. *See* **11450**.

10109. STADLER, GUSTAVUS. Troubling minds: the cultural politics of genius in the United States, 1840–1890. *See* **8973**.

10110. THOMAS, JOSEPH M. Poverty and power: revisiting Emerson's poetics. *In* (pp. 213–46) **10064**.

10111. VAN CROMPHOUT, GUSTAAF. Emerson on language as action. *In* (pp. 315–33) **10064**.

10112. VON DER HEYDT, JIM. The writer's occupation: Dickinson and Emerson out of doors. *See* **9896**.

10113. VON FRANK, ALBERT J. Emerson and Gnosticism. *In* (pp. 289–314) **10064**.

10114. WALLS, LAURA DASSOW. 'If body can sing': Emerson and Victorian science. *In* (pp. 334–66) **10064**.

10115. WARDROP, DANEEN. Li-Young Lee's *The Cleaving* and the figure of the father. *See* **17092**.

10116. WEBB, JOE. Echoes of Paine: tracing *The Age of Reason* through the writings of Emerson. ATQ (20:3) 2006, 513–25.

10117. WIDER, SARAH ANN. Chladni patterns, Lyceum halls, and skillful experimenters: Emerson's new metaphysics for the listening reader. *In* (pp. 86–114) **10064**.

10118. WILSON, LESLIE PERRIN. 'The tenant is more than the house': selected Emerson portraits in the Concord Free Public Library. NCP (33:1) 2006, 73–116.

S. Evance (*fl*.1808–1818)

10119. KNOWLES, CLAIRE. Female poetic tradition in the Regency period: Susan Evance and the evolution of sentimentality. KSJ (55) 2006, 199–225.

Frederick William Faber

10120. BLAIR, KIRSTIE. Breaking loose: Frederick Faber and the failure of reserve. VP (44:1) 2006, 25–41.

'Martha Farquharson' (Martha Finley)

10121. HARRIS, MARLA. 'A history not then taught in history books': (re)writing Reconstruction in historical fiction for children and young adults. LU (30:1) 2006, 94–116.

Edward Douglas Fawcett (b.1866)

10122. KENNEDY, GERRY. Apocalypse then. *See* **16137**.

Sir Samuel Ferguson

10123. PATERSON, ADRIAN. 'An imagined music': Yeats, music and the Irish tradition. *In* (pp. 135–69) **12189**.

'Fanny Fern' (Sara Payson (Willis) Parton)

10124. Harris, Jennifer. Marketplace transactions and Sentimental currencies in Fanny Fern's *Ruth Hall*. ATQ (20:1) 2006, 343–59.

Kate Field (1838–1896)

10125. Scharnhorst, Gary. Kate Field and Anthony Trollope: the gaps in the record. *See* **11477**.

'Michael Field' (Katharine Bradley and Edith Cooper)

10126. Bashant, Wendy. Aesthetes and queens: Michael Field, John Ruskin, and *Bellerophôn*. JPRS (15:1) 2006, 74–94.

10127. Dever, Carolyn. Strategic Aestheticism: a response to Caroline Levine. VS (49:1) 2006, 94–9.

10128. Fraser, Hilary. A visual field: Michael Field and the gaze. VLC (34:2) 2006, 553–71.

10129. O'Gorman, Francis. Michael Field and Sapphic fame: 'My dark-leaved laurels will endure'. VLC (34:2) 2006, 649–61.

10130. York, Lorraine. Crowding the garret: women's collaborative writing and the problematics of space. *In* (pp. 288–307) **3405**.

Mary Hallock Foote

10131. Gruber, Laura Katherine. 'The naturalistic impulse': limitations of gender and landscape in Mary Hallock Foote's Idaho stories. WAL (38:4) 2004, 352–73.

10132. Shein, Debra. When geography matters: Mary Hallock Foote's *Maverick* and the mystery of the Snake River lava beds. ALR (38:3) 2006, 249–58.

Sophia (King) Fortnum (1781/2–*c*.1805)

10133. Verhoeven, W. M. (gen. ed.). Anti-Jacobin novels: vol. 9, Sophia King, *Waldorf; or, The Dangers of Philosophy* (1798) Ed. by Adriana Craciun. Edward Dubois, *St Godwin: a Tale of the Sixteenth, Seventeenth, and Eighteenth Centuries* (2nd edn, 1800). Ed. by Robert Miles. *See* **9956**.

Mary Fortune

10134. Mangham, Andrew. The detective fiction of female adolescent violence. Clues (25:1) 2006, 70–80.

Harold Frederic

10135. Urbanczyk, Aaron. A 'study of church in America': Catholicism as exotic Other in *The Damnation of Theron Ware*. RelArts (10:1) 2006, 39–58.

Mary E. Wilkins Freeman

10136. Campbell, Donna. 'Where are the ladies?': Wharton, Glasgow, and American women Naturalists. StAN (1:1/2) 2006, 152–69.

10137. Campbell, Donna M. Howells' untrustworthy realist: Mary Wilkins Freeman. ALR (38:2) 2006, 115–31.

10138. Carter, James Bucky. Princes, beasts, or royal pains: men and masculinity in the revisionist fairy tales of Mary E. Wilkins Freeman. MarvT (20:1) 2006, 30–46.

10139. Tritt, Michael. Selling a birthright for pottage: Mary Freeman's allusion to Genesis in *A New England Nun*. ANQ (19:4) 2006, 34–41.

James Anthony Froude

10140. Cook, Daniel. Froude's post-Christian apostate and the uneven development of unbelief. ReLit (38:2) 2006, 49–71.

10141. Heidt, Sarah J. 'The materials for a "Life"': collaboration, publication, and the Carlyles' afterlives. *See* **9410**.

Margaret Fuller

10142. Avallone, Charlene. Elizabeth Palmer Peabody and the 'art' of conversation. *In* (pp. 23–44) **10790**.

10143. Cheever, Susan. American Bloomsbury: Louisa May Alcott, Ralph Waldo Emerson, Margaret Fuller, Nathaniel Hawthorne, and Henry David Thoreau: their lives, their loves, their work. *See* **8962**.

10144. Cole, Phyllis. The new movement's tide: Emerson and women's rights. *In* (pp. 117–52) **10064**.

10145. Dimock, Wai Chee. The planetary dead: Margaret Fuller, Ancient Egypt, Italian revolution. ESQ (50:1–3) 2004, 23–57.

10146. Mills, Bruce. Poe, Fuller, and the mesmeric arts: transition states in the American renaissance. Columbia; London: Missouri UP, 2006. pp. xx, 202.

10147. Stadler, Gustavus. Troubling minds: the cultural politics of genius in the United States, 1840–1890. *See* **8973**.

Frederick J. Furnivall

10148. Singleton, Antony. The Early English Text Society in the nineteenth century: an organizational history. *See* **3886**.

Elizabeth Gaskell

10149. Camus, Marianne. Dickens et Gaskell; ou, Les difficultés mid-victoriennes à dire le vieillir. *See* **9711**.

10150. Colón, Susan E. Professional frontiers in Elizabeth Gaskell's *My Lady Ludlow*. WWr (13:3) 2006, 475–94.

10151. Gardner, Peter. The seductive politics of *Mary Barton*. VIJ (33) 2005, 45–67.

10152. Glen, Heather. Of many hearts: Elizabeth Gaskell's observant art. TLS, 10 Nov. 2006, 3–4 (review-article).

10153. Harris, Margaret. Taking bearings: Elizabeth Gaskell's *North and South* televised. SSE (32) 2006, 65–82.

10154. Horton, Richard. Mr Thornton's experiments: literary transformations in culture and health. TLS, 10 Feb. 2006, 14–15.

10155. Kelly, David. In its own light: a view of the BBC's *North & South*. SSE (32) 2006, 83–96.

10156. Kemaloglu, Azer Banu. 'Male north' *versus* 'female south' in Gaskell's *North and South*. *In* (pp. 81–96) **3307**.

10157. Meir, Natalie Kapetanios. 'Household forms and ceremonies': narrating routines in Elizabeth Gaskell's *Cranford*. StudN (38:1) 2006, 1–14.

10158. Ohno, Tatsuhiro. Chronology and statistics: objective understanding of authorial meaning. *See* **14244**.

10159. Ouyang, Meihe; Zhou, Xianghua. *Mary Barton*: the ambivalent consciousness in the Victorian cultural context. FLS (118) 2006, 87–92. (In Chinese.)

10160. Palmer, Sean. Macaulay's revolution: New Historicism, the working classes, and Elizabeth Gaskell's *North and South*. *See* **10774**.

10161. Shattock, Joanne (gen. ed.). The works of Elizabeth Gaskell: vol. 1, Journalism, early fiction and personal writings. Ed. by Joanne Shattock. London; Brookfield, VT: Pickering & Chatto, 2005. pp. xliii, 477. (Pickering masters.) Rev. by Heather Glen in TLS, 10 Nov. 2006, 3–4.

10162. —— The works of Elizabeth Gaskell: vol. 2, Novellas and shorter fiction: I, *The Moorland Cottage*, *Cranford* and related writings. Ed. by Alan Shelston. London; Brookfield, VT: Pickering & Chatto, 2005. pp. xxvi, 368. (Pickering masters.) Rev. by Heather Glen in TLS, 10 Nov. 2006, 3–4.

10163. —— The works of Elizabeth Gaskell: vol. 3, Novellas and shorter fiction: II, *Round the Sofa* and tales from *Household Words* (1852–9). Ed. by Charlotte Mitchell. London; Brookfield, VT: Pickering & Chatto, 2005. pp. xxv, 490. (Pickering masters.) Rev. by Heather Glen in TLS, 10 Nov. 2006, 3–4.

10164. —— The works of Elizabeth Gaskell: vol. 4, Novellas and shorter fiction: III, *Cousin Phillis* and other tales from *All the Year Round* and *The Cornhill Magazine* (1859–64). Ed. by Linda Hughes. London; Brookfield, VT: Pickering & Chatto, 2006. pp. xxx, 577. (Pickering masters.) Rev. by Heather Glen in TLS, 10 Nov. 2006, 3–4.

10165. —— The works of Elizabeth Gaskell: vol. 5, *Mary Barton: a Tale of Manchester Life* (1848); and William Gaskell, *Two Lectures on the Lancashire Dialect*. Ed. by Joanne Wilkes. London; Brookfield, VT: Pickering & Chatto, 2005. pp. xxiii, 398. (Pickering masters.) Rev. by Heather Glen in TLS, 10 Nov. 2006, 3–4.

10166. —— The works of Elizabeth Gaskell: vol. 6, *Ruth* (1853). Ed. by Deirdre d'Albertis. London; Brookfield, VT: Pickering & Chatto, 2006. pp. xxv, 351. (Pickering masters.) Rev. by Heather Glen in TLS, 10 Nov. 2006, 3–4.

10167. —— The works of Elizabeth Gaskell: vol. 7, *North and South* (1855). Ed. by Elisabeth Jay. London; Brookfield, VT: Pickering & Chatto, 2005. pp. xxix, 456. (Pickering masters.) Rev. by Heather Glen in TLS, 10 Nov. 2006, 3–4.

10168. —— The works of Elizabeth Gaskell: vol. 8, *The Life of Charlotte Brontë*. Ed. by Linda H. Peterson. London; Brookfield, VT: Pickering & Chatto, 2006. pp. xxxii, 530. (Pickering masters.) Rev. by Heather Glen in TLS, 10 Nov. 2006, 3–4.

10169. —— The works of Elizabeth Gaskell: vol. 9, *Sylvia's Lovers*. Ed. by Marion Shaw. London; Brookfield, VT: Pickering & Chatto, 2006. pp. xxvi, 479. (Pickering masters.) Rev. by Heather Glen in TLS, 10 Nov. 2006, 3–4.

10170. —— The works of Elizabeth Gaskell: vol. 10, *Wives and Daughters*. Ed. by Josie Billington. London; Brookfield, VT: Pickering & Chatto, 2006. pp. xxix, 590. (Pickering masters.) Rev. by Heather Glen in TLS, 10 Nov. 2006, 3–4.

10171. Smith, Whitney Womack. Stowe, Gaskell, and the woman reformer. *In* (pp. 89–110) **11355**.

William Gaskell

10172. Shattock, Joanne (gen. ed.). The works of Elizabeth Gaskell: vol. 5, *Mary Barton: a Tale of Manchester Life* (1848); and William Gaskell, *Two Lectures on the Lancashire Dialect*. Ed. by Joanne Wilkes. *See* **10165**.

W. S. (William Schwenck) Gilbert (1836–1911)

10173. Davidson, Jim. Dominion culture. Meanjin (63:3) 2004, 75–84.

10174. May, Jill P. James Barrie's pirates: *Peter Pan*'s place in pirate history and lore. *In* (pp. 69–78) **14616**.

Anne Gilchrist

10175. Marsden, Steve. *A Woman Waits for Me*: Anne Gilchrist's reading of *Leaves of Grass*. *See* **11568**.

Caroline Howard Gilman (1794–1888)

10176. Kenny, Gale L. Mastering childhood: paternalism, slavery, and the Southern domestic in Caroline Howard Gilman's antebellum children's literature. SoQ (44:1) 2006, 65–87.

George Gissing

10177. Badolato, Francesco. George Gissing: romanziere del tardo periodo vittoriano. Introd. by Pierre Coustillas. Afterword by Andrea Sciffo. Soveria Mannelli, Catanzaro: Rubbettino, 2005. pp. 300. (Il colibri.) Rev. by R. Price in GissJ (42:2) 2006, 38–41.

10178. Bell, Hazel K. The index to the papers of Henry Ryecroft. GissJ (42:3) 2006, 14–22.

10179. Chialant, Maria Teresa. *Eve's Ransom*: narrative strategies and politics of gender. RSV (17) 2004, 91–108.

10180. —— (ed. and trans.). Il riscatto di Eva. Naples: Liguori, 2005. pp. lii, 410. Rev. by Michael Cronin in GissJ (42:3) 2006, 42–4.

10181. Clarke, Meaghan. New Woman on Grub Street: art in the city. *In* (pp. 31–40) **10220**.

10182. Coustillas, Pierre. George Gissing: the definitive bibliography. (Bibl. 2005, 11069.) Rev. by John Spiers in ELT (49:1) 2006, 109–14; by Paul W. Nash in Library (7:2) 2006, 213–14.

10183. —— Gissing: a life in death – a cavalcade of Gissing criticism in the last hundred years. *In* (pp. 212–25) **10220**.

10184. —— *Human Odds and Ends*: a historical, structural and aesthetic approach to Gissing's 'twenty sketches'. RSV (17) 2004, 13–30.

10185. —— Where 'Affable Hawk' stepped in; or, How Desmond MacCarthy roamed on Gissing's trail for over three decades. GissJ (42:2) 2006, 12–24.

10186. —— (ed.). Collected works of George Gissing on Charles Dickens: vol. 1, Essays, introductions and reviews. Afterword by Alan S. Watts. Grayswood, Surrey: Grayswood Press, 2004. pp. xi, 261. Rev. by D. J. Taylor in TLS, 9 Apr. 2004, 3–4; by Bouwe Postmus in GissJ (40:2) 2004, 33–5; by Peter Hunt in ChesR (30:1/2) 2004, 97–102; by Christine Huguet in CVE (61) 2005, 335–7; by David Paroissien in DickQ (23:2) 2006, 129–33.

10187. —— (introd.). *The Muse of the Halls*. GissJ (42:3) 2006, 1–14.

10188. Dennis, Richard. Buildings, residences, and mansions: George Gissing's 'prejudice against flats'. *In* (pp. 41–62) **10220**.

10189. DeVine, Christine. Class in turn-of-the-century novels of Gissing, James, Hardy, and Wells. (Bibl. 2005, 11072.) Rev. by Pierre Coustillas in GissJ (42:3) 2006, 38–42; by Guy Cuthbertson in RES (57:231) 2006, 551–3; by Rosemarie Morgan in THJ (22) 2006, 266–73.

10190. —— (ed.). Collected works of George Gissing on Charles Dickens: vol. 3, Forster's life of Dickens, abridged and revised by George Gissing. Afterword by James A. Davies. Grayswood, Surrey: Grayswood Press, 2005. pp. xi, 291. Rev. by Bouwe Postmus in GissJ (41:3) 2005, 32–5; by David Paroissien in DickQ (23:2) 2006, 129–33; by Christine Huguet in CVE (63) 2006, 491–4.

10191. Ettorre, Emanuela. *The Nether World* and the abysmal topography of human negativity. RSV (17) 2004, 49–68.

10192. —— Coustillas, Pierre. Introduction. RSV (17) 2004, 9–12.

10193. Evans, Elizabeth F. 'Counter-jumpers' and 'queens of the street': the shop girl of Gissing and his contemporaries. *In* (pp. 109–17) **10220**.

10194. Grylls, David. Gissing's revision of *Thyrza*. GissJ (42:1) 2006, 1–17.

10195. —— Self and (self-)censorship: Gissing's revision of *The Unclassed*. RSV (17) 2004, 31–48.

10196. Halperin, John. Gissing's urban neurasthenia. *In* (pp. 180–8) **10220**.

10197. Hammond, Mary. 'Amid the dear old horrors': memory, London, and literary labour in *The Private Papers of Henry Ryecroft*. *In* (pp. 171–9) **10220**.

10198. Huguet, Christine. Art et histoire: l'excès dans *Demos* de George Gissing. CVE (63) 2006, 111–22.

10199. —— 'Muddy depths': the Thames in Gissing's fiction. *In* (pp. 162–70) **10220**.

10200. James, Simon J. In public: George Gissing, newspapers and the city. *In* (pp. 189–98) **10220**.

10201. —— (ed.). Collected works of George Gissing on Charles Dickens: vol. 2, *Charles Dickens: a Critical Study*. Afterword by David Parker. (Bibl. 2005, 11076.) Rev. by David Paroissien in DickQ (23:2) 2006, 129–33.

10202. Liggins, Emma. 'Citizens of London?': working women, leisure, and urban space in Gissing's 1880s fiction. *In* (pp. 100–8) **10220**.

10203. —— George Gissing, the working woman, and urban culture. Aldershot; Burlington, VT: Ashgate, 2006. pp. xxxii, 193. Rev. by Pierre Coustillas in GissJ (42:4) 2006, 37–40.

10204. McCracken, Scott. Between dreamworlds and real worlds: Gissing's London. *In* (pp. 86–99) **10220**.

10205. McQuail, Josephine A. 'Woman as an invader': travel and travail in George Gissing's *The Odd Women*. *In* (pp. 139–51) **10220**.

10206. Marroni, Francesco. *Born in Exile*: George Gissing's construction of Godwin Peak as an *'exul immeritus'*. RSV (17) 2004, 69–90.

10207. Mitchell, Margaret E. 'Children of the street': reconfiguring gender in Gissing's London. *In* (pp. 129–38) **10220**.

10208. Neacey, Markus. 'A crazy idea ... All gone off in smoke': George Gissing and Miss Curtis: part one, Gissing in Eastbourne *anno* 1888. GissJ (42:4) 2006, 1–14.

10209. —— Gissing's literal revenge and Jordan's collected silences in *The Prize Lodger*. GissJ (42:1) 2006, 19–28.

10210. Nesta, Frederick. Smith, Elder & Co. and the realities of New Grub Street. *In* (pp. 207–19) **746**.

10211. Petyt, Anthony (introd.). George Gissing: *Walks about Ilkley*. GissJ (42:4) 2006, 14–28.

10212. Postmus, Bouwe. George Gissing's *Scrapbook*: a storehouse of 'elements of drama to be fused and minted in his brain'. *In* (pp. 199–211) **10220**.

10213. Radford, Andrew. Unmanned by marriage and the metropolis in Gissing's *The Whirlpool*. VN (110) 2006, 10–18.

10214. Robinson, Alan. Crystal Palace, Crouch End and Camberwell: John Ruskin and George Gissing on mass culture in late Victorian London. *In* (pp. 203–20) **7343**.

10215. Ryle, Martin; Taylor, Jenny Bourne (eds). George Gissing: voices of the unclassed. Aldershot; Burlington, VT: Ashgate, 2005. pp. viii, 163. (Nineteenth century.) Rev. by Pierre Coustillas in GissJ (42:2) 2006, 28–31.

10216. Sanders, Lise Shapiro. Consuming fantasies: labor, leisure, and the London shopgirl, 1880–1920. *See* **8507**.

10217. Selig, Robert L. Escape from marriage: a Gissing theme. GissJ (42:2) 2006, 1–11.

10218. Sjöholm, Christina (trans. and introd.); Coustillas, Pierre; Coustillas, Hélène (notes). Vid joniska havet: anteckningar från en resa i Syditalien. (By the Ionian Sea: notes of a ramble in southern Italy.) Stockholm: Atlantis, 2004. pp. 160. Rev. by Annika Juuso Savary in GissJ (40:4) 2004, 38–41.

10219. Sloan, John. Gissing, literary bohemia, and the metropolitan circle. *In* (pp. 75–85) **10220**.

10220. Spiers, John (ed.). Gissing and the city: cultural crisis and the making of books in late Victorian England. Basingstoke; New York: Palgrave Macmillan, 2006. pp. xiv, 225. Rev. by William Greenslade in GissJ (42:3) 2006, 33–8; by Diana Maltz in VS (49:1) 2006, 141–3.

10221. Villa, Luisa. Gissing's *Saturnalia*: urban crowds, carnivalesque subversion and the crisis of paternal authority. *In* (pp. 63–74) **10220**.

10222. Vorachek, Laura. Rebellion in the metropolis: George Gissing's New Woman musician. *In* (pp. 118–28) **10220**.

10223. Whelan, Lara Baker. The clash of space and culture: Gissing and the rise of the 'new' suburban. *In* (pp. 152–61) **10220**.

10224. Young, Arlene. Character and the modern city: George Gissing's urban negotiations. ELT (49:1) 2006, 49–62.

William Ewart Gladstone

10225. Windscheffel, Ruth Clayton. Politics, religion and text: W. E. Gladstone and Spiritualism. JVC (11:1) 2006, 1–29.

William Golder (1810–1876)

10226. Opie, Brian. *The New Zealand Minstrelsy* (1852): William Golder and the beginnings of a national literature in New Zealand. VP (44:3) 2006, 273–92.

10227. —— William Golder's *The New Zealand Survey* (1867): the relation between poetry and photography as media of representation. JNZL (24:1) 2006, 36–57.

'Sarah Grand' (Frances Elizabeth Clarke)

10228. Heilmann, Ann. New Woman strategies: Sarah Grand, Olive Schreiner, Mona Caird. (Bibl. 2005, 11092.) Rev. by Nickianne Moody in WWr (13:2) 2006, 321–6.

George Griffith

10229. Kennedy, Gerry. Apocalypse then. *See* **16137**.

Sutton E. Griggs

10230. Karafilis, Maria. Oratory, embodiment, and US citizenship in Sutton E. Griggs's *Imperium in Imperio*. AAR (40:1) 2006, 125–43.

George Grossmith (1847–1912)
and Weedon Grossmith (1852–1919)

10231. Morton, Peter. 'The funniest book in the world': Waugh and *The Diary of a Nobody*. *See* **18996**.

Sir Henry Rider Haggard

10232. Aguirre, Robert D. Informal empire: Mexico and Central America in Victorian culture. Minneapolis; London: Minnesota UP, 2005. pp. xxix, 198. Rev. by Ruth Hoberman in CLIO (35:3) 2006, 431–7; by Brian Gasser in RES (57:228) 2006, 114–16.

10233. Cantor, Paul A.; Hufnagel, Peter. The empire of the future: imperialism and modernism in H. G. Wells. *See* **19031**.

10234. Ferguson, Christine. Footnotes on *Trilby*: the human foot as evolutionary icon in late Victorian culture. *See* **9957**.

10235. Frank, Catherine O. Of testaments and tattoos: the Wills Act of 1837 and Rider Haggard's *Mr Meeson's Will* (1888). LawL (18:3) 2006, 323–41.

10236. Garzillo, Pietro. 'Esibizionismi' vittoriani ed edoardiani: l'Africa imperiale vista da Londra. *In* (pp. 179–91) **11824**.

10237. Nelson, Dale. Little-known books (and a little-known story) in Lewis' background: a fifth selection. *See* **17195**.

10238. Nelson, Dale J. Haggard's *She*: Burke's sublime in a popular romance. Mythlore (24:3/4) 2006, 111–17.

10239. WEVERS, LYDIA. Becoming native: Australian novelists and the New Zealand Wars. *See* **9145**.

10240. YOUNG, SHANNON. Myths of castration: Freud's 'eternal feminine' and Rider Haggard's *She*. VN (108) 2005, 21–30.

10241. —— *She*: Rider Haggard's queer adventures. *In* (pp. 134–44) **11883**.

Thomas Chandler Haliburton

10242. DAVIES, RICHARD A. Inventing Sam Slick: a biography of Thomas Chandler Haliburton. Toronto; Buffalo, NY; London: Toronto UP, 2005. pp. xi, 316, (plates) 24. Rev. by David Staines in CanL (191) 2006, 117–18.

10243. LYNCH, GERALD. The attractive repulsive American: Thomas Chandler Haliburton's Sam Slick. ShSt (13:1) 2005, 61–72.

Arthur Henry Hallam

10244. BATCHELOR, JOHN. Alfred Tennyson: problems of biography. *See* **11389**.

Sir William Rowan Hamilton (1805–1865)

10245. HEWITT, RACHEL. Wordsworth and the Ordnance Survey in Ireland: 'dreaming o'er the map of things'. *See* **11676**.

Thomas Hardy

10246. ANON. Filmography: film and television adaptations of Thomas Hardy. *In* (pp. 196–201) **10349**.

10247. ABRAVANEL, GENEVIEVE. Hardy's transatlantic Wessex: constructing the local in *The Mayor of Casterbridge*. Novel (39:1) 2005, 97–117.

10248. ADNEY, KARLEY. It's not a matter of messenger but of message: Hardy's support for Miltonic principles in *Jude the Obscure*. HarSJ (2:2) 2006, 35–43.

10249. AL-AJMI, NADA. Women in Thomas Hardy's *On the Western Circuit*. HarSJ (2:2) 2006, 44–51.

10250. ALEXANDER, MICHAEL. The Thomas Hardy Birthday Lecture 2005, delivered at the Thomas Hardy Society in Dorchester, June 2005. PNRev (32:2) 2005, 23–8.

10251. ALLINGHAM, PHILIP. Screening the flashback: three ways of opening *The Mayor of Casterbridge*. *In* (pp. 124–39) **10349**.

10252. ASQUITH, MARK. Thomas Hardy, metaphysics and music. (Bibl. 2005, 11111.) Rev. in HarSJ (2:2) 2006, 77–81.

10253. BATE, JONATHAN. Wheels within: different roads into the life of Thomas Hardy. TLS, 8 Dec. 2006, 3–4 (review-article).

10254. BEER, GILLIAN. The senses in musical settings of Hardy's poems. THJ (22) 2006, 7–14.

10255. BINDING, PAUL. Built to last: creative connections between Ibsen and Hardy. TLS, 4 Aug. 2006, 12–13.

10256. BOYLAN, REBECCA WARBURTON. Phantom photographs: the camera's pursuit and disruption of consciousness in *Jude the Obscure*. THJ (22) 2006, 72–84.

10257. CARDWELL, SARAH. Working the land: representations of rural England in adaptations of Thomas Hardy's novels. *In* (pp. 19–34) **12506**.

10258. Clammer, David. The Corsican mischief. HarSJ (2:1) 2006, 43–51. (*The Trumpet-Major* and the Napoleonic Wars.)

10259. Clapp-Itnyre, Alisa. The contentious 'figure' of music in the poetry of Thomas Hardy. HarSJ (2:2) 2006, 26–34.

10260. Colombino, Laura. '*We are horribly sensitive*': Thomas Hardy e la psicofisica del sublime. RSV (18/19) 2004/05, 121–50.

10261. Dalziel, Pamela. Faith, doubt, and loving-kindness: a sermon. HarSJ (2:1) 2006, 55–8.

10262. —— The gospel according to Hardy. *In* (pp. 3–19) **10348**.

10263. —— Strange sermon: the gospel according to Thomas Hardy. TLS, 17 Mar. 2006, 12–13.

10264. Del Sapio Garbero, Maria. Mappe e fantasmi: resoconti dall'Impero di Kipling, Hardy e altri. *In* (pp. 157–78) **11824**.

10265. Escuret, Annie. Excès et sacré dans la littérature victorienne et édouardienne. *See* **9743**.

10266. Falkenberg, Betty. A letter from Charlotte Mew. *See* **17498**.

10267. Fincham, Anthony. Emma Hardy: the (mad) woman in the attic? THJ (22) 2006, 105–15.

10268. Frizzell, Robert Alan. Corroded life: Emma Lavinia Hardy, 1840–1912: a retrospective diagnosis of syphilis. TLS, 8 Dec. 2006, 12–13.

10269. Garson, Marjorie. Written in stone: Hardy's grotesque sublime. *In* (pp. 96–117) **10348**.

10270. Gatrell, Simon. Dress, body and psyche in *The Romantic Adventures of a Milkmaid*: *Tess of the d'Urbervilles* and *The Mayor of Casterbridge*. THJ (22) 2006, 143–58.

10271. —— The erotics of dress in *A Pair of Blue Eyes*. *In* (pp. 118–35) **10348**.

10272. —— Wessex on film. *In* (pp. 37–49) **10349**.

10273. Grindle, Juliet; Gatrell, Simon (eds). Tess of the d'Urbervilles. Introd. by Penny Boumelha. Notes by Nancy Barrineau. (Bibl. 1988, 5148.) Oxford; New York: OUP, 2005. pp. l, 443. (Oxford world's classics.) (New ed.: first ed. 1988.) Rev. by Michael Irwin in HarSJ (2:1) 2006, 67–9.

10274. Hardy, Barbara. Literary allusion: Hardy and other poets. *In* (pp. 55–77) **10348**.

10275. Heath, Kay. In the eye of the beholder: Victorian age construction and the specular self. *See* **11469**.

10276. Herbert, Michael. Hardy and Lawrence – and their mothers. THJ (22) 2006, 116–28.

10277. Hynes, Samuel. Hardy and the battle god. *In* (pp. 245–61) **10348**.

10278. Johnson, Trevor. Hardy, Betjeman and 'honest doubt'. THJ (22) 2006, 186–95.

10279. —— *How I Built Myself a House*: Hardy's first venture into fiction, 1865. HarSJ (2:1) 2006, 16–20.

10280. Katz, Alison. *Jude the Obscure*: the (en)graven image. THJ (22) 2006, 85–104.

10281. Keith, W. J. Thomas Hardy and the Powyses. *In* (pp. 270–85) **10348**.

10282. Kendall, Tim. Modern English war poetry. *See* **13788**.

10283. King, Jeannette. Whatever happened to 'good little Thomas Hardy'? Re-writing Hardy and his fiction in P. B. Parris's *His Arms Are Full of Broken Things* and Emma Tennant's *Tess*. HarSJ (2:1) 2006, 21–9.

10284. Knoepflmacher, U. C. Hardy's subterranean child. *In* (pp. 78–95) **10348**.

10285. Knowles, Ronald. Thomas Hardy: elements of the tragic. THJ (22) 2006, 223–34.

10286. Kramer, Dale. *The Woodlanders*: the conflicting visions of Phil Agland and Thomas Hardy. *In* (pp. 140–52) **10349**.

10287. —— (ed.). The woodlanders. Introd. by Penny Boumelha. Oxford; New York: OUP, 2005. pp. lii, 360. (Oxford world's classics.) (New ed.: first ed. 2000.) Rev. by Michael Irwin in HarSJ (2:1) 2006, 67–9.

10288. Kramer, Kathryn. An agnostic cliffhanger: anxiety and belief in Hardy's *A Pair of Blue Eyes* and Leslie Stephen's *A Bad Five Minutes in the Alps*. THJ (22) 2006, 196–207.

10289. Levine, George. *The Woodlanders* and the Darwinian grotesque. *In* (pp. 174–98) **10348**.

10290. Levinson, Marjorie. Object-loss and object-bondage: economies of representation in Hardy's poetry. ELH (73:2) 2006, 549–80.

10291. Lorentzen, Eric G. Reading Hodge: preserving rural epistemologies in Hardy's *Far from the Madding Crowd*. VN (110) 2006, 1–9.

10292. Malane, Rachel. Sex in mind: the gendered brain in nineteenth-century literature and mental sciences. *See* **9192**.

10293. Manford, Alan (ed.). A pair of blue eyes. Introd. by Tim Dolin. (Bibl. 1988, 5158.) Oxford; New York: OUP, 2005. pp. lviii, 374. (Oxford world's classics.) (New ed.: first ed. 1985.) Rev. by Michael Irwin in HarSJ (2:1) 2006, 67–9.

10294. Matz, Aaron. Terminal satire and *Jude the Obscure*. ELH (73:2) 2006, 519–47.

10295. Miller, J. Hillis. Individual and community in *The Return of the Native*: a reappraisal. *In* (pp. 154–73) **10348**.

10296. Millgate, Michael. Thomas Hardy: a biography revisited. (Bibl. 2004, 11132.) Rev. by Michael Thorpe in EngS (87:4) 2006, 498–9; by Stanley Weintraub in ELT (49:1) 2006, 69–73; by Phillip Mallett in HarSJ (2:2) 2006, 71–4.

10297. Mink, JoAnna Stephens. A possible connection to *The Mayor of Casterbridge*: Lucetta and Lillie. THJ (22) 2006, 159–72.

10298. —— Luker, Patrice Kahler. Some connections between Hardy's blinded bird and Dunbar's caged bird. HarSJ (2:1) 2006, 30–6.

10299. Mitchell, Judith. All fall down: Hardy's heroes on the 1990s cinema screen. *In* (pp. 76–95) **10349**.

10300. Monti, Silvia. La formidabile ala della passione: le donne e l'amore nella narrativa di Thomas Hardy. ConLett (46) 2006, 333–52.

10301. Morgan, Rosemarie. Guide to the year's work: Thomas Hardy. VP (44:3) 2006, 341–56.

10302. —— Staging the *Native*: aspects of screening *The Return of the Native*. *In* (pp. 108–23) **10349**.

10303. Morgan, William W. Aesthetics and thematics in Hardy's volumes of verse: the example of *Time's Laughingstocks*. *In* (pp. 219–44) **10348**.

10304. Murphy, Patricia. In science's shadow: literary constructions of late Victorian women. Columbia; London: Missouri UP, 2006. pp. ix, 239.

10305. Musselwhite, David. Social transformation in Hardy's tragic novels: megamachines and phantasms. (Bibl. 2004, 11134.) Rev. by Tim Armstrong in MLR (101:1) 2006, 235–6; by Arthur Efron in HarSJ (2:2) 2006, 16–25.

10306. Natarajan, Uttara. Pater and the genealogy of Hardy's modernity. SELit (46:4) 2006, 849–61.

10307. Neill, Edward. The secret life of Thomas Hardy: 'retaliatory fiction'. (Bibl. 2004, 11136.) Rev. by Michael Thorpe in EngS (86:5) 2005, 465–6; by John Hughes in THJ (22) 2006, 260–3.

10308. Nemesvari, Richard. Romancing the text: genre, indeterminacy, and televising *Tess of the d'Urbervilles*. *In* (pp. 170–82) **10349**.

10309. Norman, Andrew. Thomas Hardy: behind the inscrutable smile. Tiverton, Devon: Halsgrove, 2004. pp. 160. Rev. by Michael Thorpe in EngS (86:5) 2005, 465–6; in HarSJ (2:2) 2006, 75–6.

10310. Page, Norman. Opening time: Hardy's poetic thresholds. *In* (pp. 262–9) **10348**.

10311. Pawlikowska, Michalina. Letter from Poland. HarSJ (2:2) 2006, 64–7. (Polish translations.)

10312. Pierce-Jones, Roy. Screening the short stories: from the 1950s to the 1990s. *In* (pp. 63–75) **10349**.

10313. Pite, Ralph. Thomas Hardy: the guarded life. London: Picador, 2006. pp. vii, 522, (plates) 16. Rev. by Jonathan Bate in TLS, 8 Dec. 2006, 3–4; by Michael Irwin in THJ (22) 2006, 258–60.

10314. Potolsky, Matthew. Hardy, Shaftesbury, and aesthetic education. SELit (46:4) 2006, 863–78.

10315. Ray, Martin. The collected letters of Thomas Hardy: some additional notes. THJ (22) 2006, 48–71.

10316. —— Thomas Hardy's *Geographical Knowledge*. NQ (53:3) 2006, 343–4.

10317. —— Thomas Hardy's letter to Charles Hiatt. NQ (53:3) 2006, 338.

10318. —— (ed.). Thomas Hardy remembered. Aldershot; Burlington, VT: Ashgate, 2005. pp. 350. (Nineteenth century.)

10319. Reel, Edmèe; Reel, Jerome V., Jr. Thomas Hardy, Rutland Boughton, and *The Queen of Cornwall*. Arthuriana (16:1) 2006, 54–60.

10320. Rimmer, Mary. 'My scripture manner': reading Hardy's biblical and liturgical allusion. *In* (pp. 20–37) **10348**.

10321. Riquelme, John Paul. Dissonance, simulacra, and the grain of the voice in Roman Polanski's *Tess*. *In* (pp. 153–69) **10349**.

10322. Roberts, Beth Ellen. One voice and many: modern poets in dialogue. *See* **13848**.

10323. Rode, Scott. Reading and mapping Hardy's roads. London; New York: Routledge, 2006. pp. vii, 146. (Studies in major literary authors.)

10324. Schwarz, Daniel R. Reading the modern British and Irish novel, 1890–1930. Oxford; Malden, MA: Blackwell, 2005. pp. ix, 297. (Reading the novel, 1.)

10325. Schweik, Robert. Adapting Hardy's *Jude the Obscure* for the screen: a study in contrasts. *In* (pp. 183–95) **10349**.

10326. Senior, Claire. Shades of gray: a diachronic reading of Thomas Hardy's *Neutral Tones*. VP (44:2) 2006, 213–33.

10327. Seymour, Claire. 'A song outlasts a dynasty': Gerald Finzi's settings of Thomas Hardy's poetry. THJ (22) 2006, 15–32.

10328. Shires, Linda M. (ed.). *Tess of the d'Urbervilles*: complete text with introduction, historical contexts, critical essays. Boston, MA: Houghton Mifflin, 2005. pp. viii, 527. (New Riverside eds.) Rev. by Michael Irwin in HarSJ (2:1) 2006, 67–9.

10329. Steele, Jeremy V. Plato and the love goddess: paganism in two versions of *The Well-Beloved*. *In* (pp. 199–218) **10348**.

10330. Strong, Jeremy. *Tess*, *Jude*, and the problem of adapting Hardy. LitFQ (34:3) 2006, 195–203.

10331. Swann, Furse. Hardy, Jude, Cambridge and the Moules. THJ (22) 2006, 173–85.

10332. Tague, Gregory. Character and consciousness: George Eliot, Thomas Hardy, E. M. Forster, D. H. Lawrence: phenomenological, ecological, and ethical readings. *See* **10055**.

10333. Takakuwa, Yoshiko. Another letter from Tokyo. HarSJ (2:2) 2006, 68–70. (Japanese translations.)

10334. Taylor, Dennis. Hardy and *Hamlet*. *In* (pp. 38–54) **10348**.

10335. —— Hardy's copy of Shakespeare's *Othello*. THJ (22) 2006, 33–47.

10336. Teece, Philip. Adventures under the dome: astronomers in literature. Descant (37:2) 2006, 38–45.

10337. Thomas, Jane. Thomas Hardy and desire: from Sappho to The Stranglers. THJ (22) 2006, 129–42.

10338. Tiefer, Hillary. The natural and the cultivated in the novels of Thomas Hardy. THJ (22) 2006, 208–22.

10339. Tolfree, Patrick. Dorchester Prison and Thomas Hardy. HarSJ (2:1) 2006, 59–61.

10340. Tomalin, Claire. Thomas Hardy: the time-torn man. London: Viking, 2006. pp. xxv, 486, (plates) 16. Rev. by Jonathan Bate in TLS, 8 Dec. 2006, 3–4.

10341. Toobe, Ben. Music in *The Mayor of Casterbridge*. HarSJ (2:2) 2006, 52–4.

10342. Topia, André. Le supplément et la perte; ou, Le recyclage manqué (Thomas Hardy, *An Imaginative Woman*). EA (59:3) 2006, 279–91.

10343. Webster, Roger. From painting to cinema: visual elements in Hardy's fiction. *In* (pp. 20–36) **10349**.

10344. Wetzsteon, Rachel. Influential ghosts: a study of Auden's sources. *See* **14511**.

10345. Widdowson, Peter. The silent era: Thomas Hardy goes way down east. *In* (pp. 50–62) **10349**.

10346. Wilson, Keith. *Far from the Madding Crowd* in the cinema: the problem of textual fidelity. *In* (pp. 96–107) **10349**.

10347. —— 'We thank you … most of all, perhaps, for *The Dynasts*': Hardy's epic drama re-evaluated. THJ (22) 2006, 235–54.

10348. —— (ed.). Thomas Hardy reappraised: essays in honour of Michael Millgate. Toronto; Buffalo, NY; London: Toronto UP, 2006. pp. xxiii, 304.

10349. Wright, T. R. (ed.). Thomas Hardy on screen. Cambridge; New York: CUP, 2005. pp. xiv, 216. Rev. by Anthony Cummins in TLS, 2 June 2006, 33; by Roger Ebbatson in THJ (22) 2006, 263–5; by Christoph Lindner in Style (40:4) 2006, 379–81; by Tim Dolin in NineL (61:3) 2006, 397–402.

10350. Wright, Terry. 'Hardy as a cinematic novelist': three aspects of narrative technique. *In* (pp. 8–19) **10349**.

10351. Wu, Weihua. Incestuous love: exploration of narrative motif of *Jude the Obscure*. FLS (118) 2006, 105–12. (In Chinese.)

10352. Yeazell, Ruth Bernard. Hardy's rural painting of the Dutch school. *In* (pp. 136–53) **10348**.

Frances Ellen Watkins Harper

10353. Bassard, Katherine Clay. Private interpretations: the defense of slavery, nineteenth-century hermeneutics, and the poetry of Frances E. W. Harper. *In* (pp. 110–40) **8429**.

George Washington Harris

10354. Hitchcock, Bert. Well, maybe just this once: Erskine Caldwell, Old Southwest humor, and funny ha-ha. *In* (pp. 27–45) **15001**.

Bret Harte

10355. Scharnhorst, Gary. Bret Harte's Naturalism. StAN (1:1/2) 2006, 144–51.

10356. —— Nabokov and Bret Harte: an overlooked allusion in *Lolita*. *See* **17715**.

10357. Watson, Matthew A. The Argonauts of '49: class, gender, and partnership in Bret Harte's West. WAL (40:1) 2005, 33–53.

May Laffan Hartley (1849–1916)

10358. Kahn, Helena Kelleher. Late nineteenth-century Ireland's political and religious controversies in the fiction of May Laffan Hartley. Greensboro, NC: ELT Press, 2005. pp. ix, 276. (1880–1920 British authors, 19.) Rev. by Jill Brady Hampton in VS (48:4) 2006, 720–1.

Julian Hawthorne

10359. Bird, Otto A.; Bird, Katharine. From witchery to sanctity: the religious vicissitudes of the Hawthornes. *See* **10365**.

Nathaniel Hawthorne

10360. Adams, Fred C. Blood vengeance in *The Scarlet Letter*. NHR (32:2) 2006, 1–12.

10361. Balestrini, Nassim Winnie. From fiction to libretto: Irving, Hawthorne, and James as opera. *See* **10521**.

10362. Barton, John Cyril. The anti-gallows movement in antebellum America. *See* **10816**.

10363. Benziman, Galia. Challenging the biological: the fantasy of male birth as nineteenth-century narrative of ethical failure. *See* **11174**.

10364. Berri, Barbara. Nathaniel Hawthorne: dal sublime al trascendentale. Milan: Arcipelago, 2005. pp. 360. Rev. by Mara Logaldo in ConLett (46) 2006, 458–9.

10365. Bird, Otto A.; Bird, Katharine. From witchery to sanctity: the religious vicissitudes of the Hawthornes. South Bend, IN: St Augustine's Press, 2004. pp. 164.

10366. Bonnet, Michèle. Consuming tragedy and 'the little cannibal' in *The House of the Seven Gables*. ATQ (20:2) 2006, 481–97.

10367. Budick, Emily Miller. Hawthorne, Pearl, and the primal sin of culture. JAStud (39:2) 2005, 167–85.

10368. Cañadas, Ivan. A new source for the title and themes of *The Scarlet Letter*. NHR (32:1) 2006, 43–51.

10369. Cheever, Susan. American Bloomsbury: Louisa May Alcott, Ralph Waldo Emerson, Margaret Fuller, Nathaniel Hawthorne, and Henry David Thoreau: their lives, their loves, their work. *See* **8962**.

10370. Church, Joseph. A problem of conception and creation in Hawthorne's *The Artist of the Beautiful*. NHR (32:2) 2006, 13–22.

10371. Davis, Clark. Hawthorne's shyness: ethics, politics, and the question of engagement. (Bibl. 2005, 11194.) Rev. by T. J. Lustig in JAStud (40:3) 2006, 655; by John Dolis in NHR (32:2) 2006, 45–50.

10372. De Biasio, Anna. Romanzi e musei: Nathaniel Hawthorne, Henry James e il rapporto con l'arte. Venice: Istituto Veneto di Scienze, Lettere ed Arti, 2006. pp. viii, 209. (Memorie: classe di scienze morali, lettere ed arti, 111.)

10373. de Rocher, Cecile Anne (ed.). Elizabeth Manning Hawthorne: a life in letters. Tuscaloosa; London: Alabama UP, 2006. pp. xiv, 211. Rev. by David B. Kesterson in NHR (32:2) 2006, 50–5.

10374. Elbert, Monika M.; Hall, Julie E.; Rodier, Katharine (eds). Reinventing the Peabody sisters. *See* **10790**.

10375. Gengarelly, Tony. Nathaniel Hawthorne as art critic: the Italian experience and *The Marble Faun*. MiE, Spring 2006, 40–56.

10376. Herbert, T. Walter. Different from himself: Hawthorne and the masks of masculinity. ESQ (50:4) 2004, 269–82.

10377. Hoople, Robin. Great stone faces: Henry James, Theodore Roosevelt, and the quest for American authenticity. *See* **10562**.

10378. Jay, Elisabeth. 'Who are you gentle reader?': John Updike – *A Month of Sundays* (1975). *See* **18883**.

10379. Jones, Wanda Faye. Scopolamine poisoning and the death of Dimmesdale in *The Scarlet Letter*. NHR (32:1) 2006, 52–62.

10380. Ketterer, David. 'Another dimension of space': Canadian science fiction and fantasy and Atwood's *Blind Assassin*. *In* (pp. 7–34) **13541**.

10381. Kevorkian, Martin. Reading the bloody 'face of nature': the persecution of religion in Hawthorne's *The Marble Faun*. Contagion (12/13) 2006, 133–45.

10382. Kleitz, Dorsey. Herman Melville, Matthew Perry, and the *Narrative of the Expedition of an American Squadron to the China Seas and Japan*. *See* **10855**.

10383. Kolin, Philip C. Parks's *In the Blood*. *See* **17965**.

10384. Lanati, Barbara. Ottocento e dintorni: E. A. Poe, W. Whitman, H. Melville, N. Hawthorne. *See* **11027**.

10385. Lee, Jee Yoon. 'The rude contact of some actual circumstance': Hawthorne and Salem's East India marine museum. ELH (73:4) 2006, 949–73.

10386. MacLeod, Glen. Nathaniel Hawthorne and the Boston Athenaeum. NHR (32:1) 2006, 1–29. (*A Virtuoso's Collection*.)

10387. Meltzer, Milton. Nathaniel Hawthorne: a biography. Minneapolis, MN: Lerner, 2006. pp. 160.

10388. Milder, Robert. Exiled royalties: Melville and the life we imagine. *See* **10870**.

10389. Neary, John. Shadows and illuminations: spiritual journeys to the dark side in *Young Goodman Brown* and *Eyes Wide Shut*. RelArts (10:2) 2006, 244–70.

10390. O'Gorman, Farrell. White, Black, and Brown: reading O'Connor after Richard Rodriguez. *See* **17839**.

10391. Peters, Matthew. Hawthorne's Tennyson. TLS, 21 July 2006, 15.

10392. Sayers, William. Gardens of horror and delight: Hawthorne's *Rappaccini's Daughter* and Boccaccio's *Decameron*. NHR (32:1) 2006, 30–42.

10393. Schreiner, Samuel A., Jr. The Concord quartet: Alcott, Emerson, Hawthorne, Thoreau, and the friendship that freed the American mind. *See* **8959**.

10394. Stoneley, Peter. Sewing in Concord. *See* **11452**.

10395. Sutherland, Helen. Varieties of Protestant experience: religion and the *Doppelgänger* in Hogg, Brown, and Hawthorne. *See* **10450**.

10396. Thompson, Corey Evan. Melville's *Monody*: possibly for Malcolm? *See* **10904**.

10397. Toal, Catherine. 'Some things which should never have happened': fiction, identification, and *Benito Cereno*. *See* **10906**.

10398. Ullén, Magnus. The half-vanished structure: Hawthorne's allegorical dialectics. (Bibl. 2004, 11226.) Rev. by Samuel Chase Coale in NHR (32:2) 2006, 39–42.

10399. —— Reading with 'the eye of faith': the structural principle of Hawthorne's romances. TSLL (48:1) 2006, 1–36.

10400. Valenti, Patricia Dunlavy. Sophia Peabody Hawthorne: a life: vol. 1, 1809–1847. Columbia; London: Missouri UP, 2004. pp. 312. Rev. by Larry J. Reynolds in NHR (32:2) 2006, 37–9.

10401. Visser, Irene. Of women, slaves and cannibals: dynamics of holiness in three American novels of the mid-nineteenth century. *In* (pp. 127–45) **3415**.

10402. Werner, Marta; Lawrence, Nicholas. This is his – this is my mystery: the common journal of Nathaniel and Sophia Hawthorne, 1842–1843. *In* (pp. 3–22) **10790**.

10403. Williamson, Richard J. The impact of Franklin Pierce on Nathaniel Hawthorne: friendship, politics, and the literary imagination. Lewiston, NY; Lampeter: Mellen Press, 2006. pp. vi, 164.

10404. Wright, Sarah Bird. Critical companion to Nathaniel Hawthorne: a literary reference to his life and work. New York: Facts on File, 2006. pp. 352.

10405. Ben-Zvi, Yael. Clinging to one spot: Hawthorne's native-born settlers. ESQ (52:1/2) 2006, 17–44.

Mary Cecil Hay (1840?–1886)

10406. Maunder, Andrew (gen. ed.). Sensation and detection: Mary Cecil Hay, *Old Myddelton's Money* (1874). Ed. by Mark Knight. London; Brookfield, VT: Pickering & Chatto, 2004. pp. xxvi, 333. (Varieties of women's sensation fiction 1855–1890, 5.) Rev. by Anthea Trodd in VicR (31:2) 2005, 132–4.

Benjamin Robert Haydon

10407. Higgins, David Minden. Romantic genius and the literary magazine: biography, celebrity, and politics. (Bibl. 2005, 11227.) Rev. by Barton Swaim in TLS, 20 Oct. 2006, 27; by Malcolm Kelsall in BJ (34:2) 2006, 190–1.

William Stephens Hayward

10408. Bredesen, Dagni. Conformist subversion: ambivalent agency in *Revelations of a Lady Detective*. Clues (25:1) 2006, 20–32.

William Hazlitt

10409. Brock, Claire. The feminization of fame, 1750–1830. *See* **7981**.

10410. Cheeke, Stephen. 'What so many have told, who would tell again?': Romanticism and the commonplaces of Rome. *See* **7824**.

10411. Dart, Gregory (ed.). Metropolitan writings. Manchester: Carcanet Press, 2005. pp. xix, 199. (Fyfield.) Rev. by Laura Keynes in TLS, 18 Feb. 2005, 30.

10412. Ford, Peter B. Writing the 'love letter' from the lack: the economy of absence in Hazlitt's *Liber Amoris*. EREA (4:1) 2006, 16–21.

10413. Gillingham, Lauren. The novel of fashion redressed: Bulwer-Lytton's *Pelham* in a 19th-century context. *See* **10765**.

10414. Khalip, Jacques. Virtual conduct: disinterested agency in Hazlitt and Keats. ELH (73:4) 2006, 885–912.

10415. Newlyn, Lucy. Hazlitt and Edward Thomas on walking. EC (56:2) 2006, 163–87.

10416. Page, Judith W. Anglo-Jewish identity and the politics of cultivation in Hazlitt, Aguilar, and Disraeli. *In* (pp. 149–64) **8523**.

10417. Sherbo, Arthur. From the sale catalogue of the library of William Hazlitt, the essayist. ANQ (19:3) 2006, 17–26.

10418. Wu, Duncan. Hazlitt's unpublished *History of English Philosophy*: the larger context. Library (7:1) 2006, 25–64.

10419. —— The journalism of William Hazlitt (1737–1820) in Boston (1784–5): a critical and bibliographical survey. *See* **7487**.

10420. —— The Lamb circle and the *Monthly Repository*. *See* **10707**.

Lafcadio Hearn ('Koizumi Yakumo')

10421. Bronner, Simon J. 'Gombo' folkloristics: Lafcadio Hearn's creolization and hybridization in the formative period of folklore studies. JFR (42:2) 2005, 141–84.

Felicia Dorothea Hemans

10422. Cass, Jeffrey. 'The race of the Cid': blood, darkness, and the captivity narrative in Felicia Hemans's *The Siege of Valencia*. ERR (17:3) 2006, 315–26.

10423. Forbes, Aileen. Besieged vision: *The Siege of Valencia* and Felicia Hemans's theater of sacrifice. KSJ (55) 2006, 158–78.

10424. Lopez, John-David. Recovered voices: the sources of *The Siege of Valencia*. ERR (17:1) 2006, 69–87.

10425. Mason, Emma. 'Love's the burning boy': Hemans's critical legacy. *In* (pp. 205–24) **13735**.

10426. Vincent, Patrick. A continent of Corinnes: the Romantic poetess and the diffusion of liberal culture in Europe, 1815–50. *In* (pp. 486–504) **8357**.

W. E. Henley

10427. Cohen, Edward H. The epigraph to Henley's *In Hospital*. VN (109) 2006, 14–16.

10428. —— The second series of W. E. Henley's hospital poems. YLG (78:3/4) 2004, 128–50.

G. A. Henty

10429. Erll, Astrid. Re-writing as re-visioning: modes of representing the 'Indian Mutiny' in British novels, 1857 to 2000. EJES (10:2) 2006, 163–85.

10430. Worsfold, Brian. The Victorian ethic of self-help and its implications for contemporary ageing. *See* **10769**.

James A. Herne

10431. Anderson, Donald. Grounded perceptions: land and value in two plays of the New England decline. AmDr (15:2) 2006, 1–29.

Thomas Wentworth Higginson

10432. Beebe, Ann. Dickinson's *Immortal Is an Ample Word*. *See* **9849**.

10433. Kopacz, Paula. Walking through the minefield of American literature: the case of Higginson's *Army Life in a Black Regiment*. KenPR (20) 2005, 25–30.

Charles Howard Hinton (1853–1907)

10434. Franza, Mariateresa. Viaggio nella quarta dimensione: i '*scientific romances*' di Charles H. Hinton. *In* (pp. 423–35) **11824**.

John Cam Hobhouse

10435. Cheeke, Stephen. 'What so many have told, who would tell again?': Romanticism and the commonplaces of Rome. *See* **7824**.

Barbara Hofland

10436. Frey, Anne. Barbara Hofland's profession: questioning the calling. WordsC (36:3) 2005, 110–12.

James Hogg (1770–1835)

10437. Ballantyne, John. Hogg's role in *The Scotch Gentleman*. SHogg (16) 2005, 131–3.

10438. Barcus, James E. (ed.). Mador of the moor. Edinburgh: Edinburgh UP, 2005. pp. lvii, 130. (Stirling / South Carolina research ed. of the collected works of James Hogg.) Rev. by Caroline McCracken-Flesher in SHogg (16) 2005, 161–3.

10439. de Groot, H. B. Musical notation in the *Highland Journeys*: did Hogg have perfect pitch? SHogg (16) 2005, 127–30.

10440. Fielding, Penny. Burial letters: death and dreaming in Hogg's *Cousin Mattie*. SHogg (16) 2005, 5–19.

10441. Goldsmith, Jason N. Hogging the limelight: *The Queen's Wake* and the rise of celebrity authorship. SHogg (16) 2005, 52–60.

10442. Haggerty, George E. 'Dung, guts and blood': sodomy, abjection and gothic fiction in the early nineteenth century. *See* **11180**.

10443. Hughes, Gillian. 'Native energy': Byron and Hogg as Scottish poets. *See* **9348**.

10444. —— *et al.* (eds). The collected letters of James Hogg: vol. 1, 1800–1819. Edinburgh: Edinburgh UP, 2004. pp. lviii, 490. (Stirling/South Carolina research ed. of the collected works of James Hogg, 15.) Rev. by Silvia Mergenthal in ScSR (6:2) 2005, 134–6.

10445. —— The collected letters of James Hogg: vol. 2, 1820–1831. Edinburgh: Edinburgh UP, 2006. pp. liii, 538. (Stirling/South Carolina research ed. of the collected works of James Hogg, 18.)

10446. Jackson, Richard D. James Hogg's 'Kilmeny' and the road to Duneira. SHogg (16) 2005, 62–70.

10447. Mack, Douglas (ed.). The queen's wake. (Bibl. 2005, 11283.) Rev. by Linda Stewart in SHogg (16) 2005, 165–7.

10448. Manning, Susan. That exhumation scene again: transatlantic Hogg. SHogg (16) 2005, 86–111. (Hugh McNaughtan Memorial Lecture for 2004.)

10449. Miller, Karl. Who wrote James Hogg? Aspects of authorship in the *Confessions*. SHogg (16) 2005, 112–26. (Hugh McNaughtan Memorial Lecture for 2005.)

10450. Sutherland, Helen. Varieties of Protestant experience: religion and the *Doppelgänger* in Hogg, Brown, and Hawthorne. SHogg (16) 2005, 71–85.

10451. Velasco, Ismael. Paradoxical readings: reason, religion and tradition in James Hogg's *Private Memoirs and Confessions of a Justified Sinner*. ScSR (7:1) 2006, 38–52.

Robert Hogg (1802–1834)

10452. BROWN, RHONA. The city poetry of Robert Fergusson and Robert Hogg. *See* **7782**.

10453. HUGHES, GILLIAN. The Ettrick Shepherd's nephew. SHogg (16) 2005, 20–35.

10454. —— (ed.). By other Hoggs. *See* **10455**.

William Hogg (1767–1847)

10455. HUGHES, GILLIAN (ed.). By other Hoggs. SHogg (16) 2005, 134–60.

Marietta Holley

10456. EPP, MICHAEL H. The traffic in affect: Marietta Holley, suffrage, and late nineteenth-century popular humour. CRAS (36:1) 2006, 93–115.

Oliver Wendell Holmes

10457. DOWLING, WILLIAM C. Oliver Wendell Holmes in Paris: medicine, theology, and the autocrat of the breakfast table. Hanover, NH; London: UP of New England; Durham: New Hampshire UP, 2006. pp. xviii, 179. (Becoming modern.) Rev. by Renée Tursi in TLS, 24 Nov. 2006, 29.

10458. GOUGEON, LEN. Emerson, Whitman, and eros. *See* **11556**.

10459. —— The legacy of reform: Emersonian idealism, Moorfield Storey, and the Civil Rights Movement. *In* (pp. 183–210) **10064**.

10460. HABICH, ROBERT D. Holmes, Cabot, and Edward Emerson and the challenges of writing Emerson's biography in the 1880s. *In* (pp. 3–32) **10064**.

10461. WEINSTEIN, MICHAEL A. The imaginative prose of Oliver Wendell Holmes. Columbia; London: Missouri UP, 2006. pp. ix, 203.

May Holt (Mrs Reginald Fairbairn)

10462. NEWEY, KATHERINE. When is an Australian playwright not an Australian playwright? The case of May Holt. *In* (pp. 93–107) **12360**.

Thomas Hood

10463. EDGECOMBE, RODNEY STENNING. An allusion to Dyer in a letter by Hood. NQ (53:3) 2006, 326.

10464. —— Dickens and Hood's *Ode to Rae Wilson, Esq.*: two points of contact. *See* **9742**.

10465. —— A faulty musical allusion in a Hood letter. NQ (53:3) 2006, 326–7.

10466. —— Paronomasia in a letter by Thomas Hood. ANQ (19:4) 2006, 26.

10467. RIVERS, BRYAN. 'Tenderly' and 'with care': Thomas Hood's *The Bridge of Sighs* and the suicide of Harriet Shelley. NQ (53:3) 2006, 327–9.

'Anthony Hope' (Sir Anthony Hope Hawkins) (1863–1933)

10468. DOLININ, ALEXANDER. Ods Bod(t)kins! *See* **17696**.

Gerard Manley Hopkins (1844–1889)

10469. ADDISON, CATHERINE. Stress felt, stroke dealt: the spondee, the text, and the reader. Style (39:2) 2005, 153–74.

10470. ALPERS, PAUL. 'The Philoctetes problem' and the poetics of pastoral. *See* **5691**.

10471. Dau, Duc. Perfect chastity: celibacy and virgin marriage in Tractarian poetry. *See* **10960**.

10472. Groves, Peter. Hopkins and Tractarianism. VP (44:1) 2006, 105–12.

10473. Hardman, Malcolm. *Genius loci*: placing place in Gerard Manley Hopkins. MLR (101:1) 2006, 30–47.

10474. Humphries, Simon. A eunuch for God: Gerard Manley Hopkins, SJ, Catullus and castration. TLS, 22 & 29 Dec. 2006, 18–19.

10475. Hurley, Michael D. Darkening the subject of Hopkins' prosody. VP (43:4) 2005, 485–96.

10476. Jenkins, Alice (ed.). The poems of Gerard Manley Hopkins: a sourcebook. London; New York: Routledge, 2006. pp. xvi, 174. (Routledge guides to literature.)

10477. Loomis, Jeffrey B. Guide to the year's work: Hopkins. VP (44:3) 2006, 357–61.

10478. Merriman, Emily Taylor. Corresponding grace: Hopkins' theory and use of rhyme. HopQ (32:3/4) 2005, 85–111.

10479. —— 'Words, those precious cups of meaning': Augustine's influence on the thought and poetry of Gerard Manley Hopkins, SJ. *In* (pp. 233–54) **3301**.

10480. Muller, Jill. Gerard Manley Hopkins and Victorian Catholicism: a heart in hiding. (Bibl. 2003, 10604.) Rev. by James Finn Cotter in VS (48:2) 2006, 340–2.

10481. Nixon, Jude V. Fathering graces at Hampstead: Manley Hopkins' *The Old Trees* and Gerard Manley Hopkins' *Binsey Poplars*. VP (44:2) 2006, 191–211.

10482. —— 'Goldengrove unleaving': Hopkins' *Spring and Fall*, Christina Rossetti's *Mirrors of Life and Death*, and the politics of inclusion. VP (43:4) 2005, 473–84.

10483. —— 'Vital candle in close heart's vault': energy, optics and Hopkins' spermaceti flame. HopQ (32:3/4) 2005, 65.

10484. Palmer, Pamela. A Hopkins bibliography 1998–2002. HopQ (32:1/2) 2005, 15–44.

10485. Phillips, Catherine L.; Thornton, R. K. R. Two unpublished letters of Gerard Manley Hopkins. HopQ (32:1/2) 2005, 8–14.

10486. Rand, Thomas. 'Time's eunuch' reconsidered. HopQ (32:1/2) 2005, 3–7.

10487. Regan, Stephen. The Victorian sonnet, from George Meredith to Gerard Manley Hopkins. *See* **10918**.

10488. Schlatter, Fredric W. George Teeling: mutual friend of Newman and Hopkins. HopQ (32:3/4) 2005, 112–28.

10489. —— Hopkins and Baillie. SP (103:4) 2006, 522–42. (Alexander William Mowbray Baillie.)

10490. Sobolev, Dennis. Being and contemplation in the poetry of Gerard Manley Hopkins. Eng (55:211) 2006, 37–63.

10491. Strauss, Tracy L. Sound and sensibility: Hopkins' word-journey to Hell and back. HopQ (32:3/4) 2005, 129–38.

10492. Tomaiuolo, Saverio. Tennyson and Hopkins from metaphor to metonym: *In Memoriam* and *The Wreck of the Deutschland*. *See* **11409**.

10493. Tracy, D. H. Bad ideas. *See* **15356**.

10494. Wardi, Eynel. Hopkins the Romantic? The question of empathy in *Spring and Fall*. VP (44:3) 2006, 237–50.

Pauline Elizabeth Hopkins

10495. Brooks, Daphne A. Bodies in dissent: spectacular performances of race and freedom, 1850–1910. *See* **8564**.

10496. Cordell, Sigrid Anderson. 'The case was very black against' her: Pauline Hopkins and the politics of racial ambiguity at the *Colored American Magazine*. AmP (16:1) 2006, 52–73.

10497. Peterson, Carla L. Commemorative ceremonies and invented traditions: history, memory, and modernity in the 'New Negro' novel of the nadir. *In* (pp. 34–56) **8435**.

10498. Wallinger, Hanna. Pauline E. Hopkins: a literary biography. (Bibl. 2005, 11328.) Rev. by Jill Bergman in Legacy (23:1) 2006, 98–9.

W. D. Howells

10499. Budd, Louis J. W. D. Howells and Mark Twain judge each other 'aright'. ALR (38:2) 2006, 97–114.

10500. Campbell, Donna M. Howells' untrustworthy realist: Mary Wilkins Freeman. *See* **10137**.

10501. Cutler, Edward S. Literary modernity and the problem of a national literature: understanding William Dean Howells' critique of Walt Whitman. ALR (38:2) 2006, 132–44.

10502. Kohler, Michelle. Realism and the perception of romance in *The Rise of Silas Lapham*. ALR (38:3) 2006, 223–38.

10503. Murillo, Cindy. 'I do not pretend to illustrate any great truths': two newly recovered interviews with W. D. Howells. ALR (39:1) 2006, 74–86.

10504. Murphy, John J. William to Willa, courtesy of Sarah: Cather, Jewett, and Howellsian principles. *See* **15105**.

10505. Nettels, Elsa. Howells and Wharton. ALR (38:2) 2006, 160–73.

10506. Newlin, Keith. 'I am as ever your disciple': the friendship of Hamlin Garland and W. D. Howells. *See* **16051**.

10507. Puskar, Jason. William Dean Howells and the insurance of the real. AmLH (18:1) 2006, 29–58.

10508. Radavich, David. Twain, Howells, and the origins of Midwestern drama. *See* **11521**.

10509. Roman, Camille. The caged bird's song and its (dis)contents. *See* **9971**.

John Howison

10510. McMullen, Bonnie Shannon. 'A wrong port': colonial Havana under Northern eyes. Journeys (7:1) 2006, 67–80.

Catherine Hubback

10511. Sutherland, Kathryn. Why Jane Austen is not Charlotte Brontë. *In* (pp. 116–28) **8374**.

10512. Wagner, Tamara S. 'A strange chronicle of the olden time': revisions of the Regency in the construction of Victorian domestic fiction. *See* **9087**.

Thomas Hughes (1822–1896)

10513. Knutsen, Torbjørn L. Dumbledore's pedagogy: knowledge and virtue at Hogwarts. *In* (pp. 197–212) **18355**.

Leigh Hunt

10514. Fermanis, Porscha. *Isabella*, *Lamia*, and 'Merry Old England'. *See* **10644**.

10515. Holden, Anthony. The wit in the dungeon: a life of Leigh Hunt. London; Boston, MA: Little, Brown, 2005. pp. xvii, 430. Rev. by Grevel Lindop in TLS, 8 Apr. 2005, 24–5; by John Jones in LRB (27:18) 2005, 32–3; by Megan Marshall in NYTB, 1 Jan. 2006, 13; by Alexandra Mullen in HR (59:2) 2006, 327–34; by Kathryn Chittick in DickQ (23:1) 2006, 41–4.

10516. Mullen, Alexandra. The lost Romantic. HR (59:2) 2006, 327–34 (review-article).

10517. Roe, Nicholas. Fiery heart: the first life of Leigh Hunt. (Bibl. 2005, 11361.) Rev. by Kathryn Chittick in DickQ (23:1) 2006, 41–4.

10518. Schoina, Maria. Leigh Hunt's *Letters from Abroad* and the 'Anglo-Italian' discourse of *The Liberal*. Romanticism (12:2) 2006, 115–25.

10519. Stimson, Katharine. 'Where Robins hop, and fallen leaves are sere': Keats's robin and the social imagination. *See* **10667**.

Richard Holt Hutton

10520. Goslee, David. R. H. Hutton's novel theology. ReLit (38:2) 2006, 25–47.

Washington Irving

10521. Balestrini, Nassim Winnie. From fiction to libretto: Irving, Hawthorne, and James as opera. New York; Frankfurt: Lang, 2005. pp. xii, 582. (Mainzer Studien zur Amerikanistik, 51.) Rev. by John L. Idol in NHR (32:2) 2006, 55–9.

10522. Bottalico, Michele. Visioni d'oltreoceano: Irving e Cooper su Londra. *In* (pp. 133–48) **7343**.

10523. Mullenix, Elizabeth Reitz. Yankee doodle Dixie: performing nationhood on the eve of war. *See* **9152**.

10524. Wood, Sarah F. Refusing to RIP; or, Return of the dispossessed: the transatlantic revivals of Irving's *Rip Van Winkle*. Symbiosis (10:1) 2006, 3–19.

Helen Hunt Jackson

10525. Gillman, Susan. Adaptation and Americas Studies. Genre (38:4) 2005, 413–41.

10526. Ramirez, Karen E. Reading Helen Hunt Jackson's *Ramona*. Boise, ID: Boise State Univ., 2006. pp. 56. (Boise State Univ. Western writers, 171.)

Harriet Jacobs

10527. Abdur-Rahman, Aliyyah I. 'The strangest freaks of despotism': queer sexuality in antebellum African American slave narratives. *See* **9912**.

10528. Berman, Carolyn Vellenga. Creole crossings: domestic fiction and the reform of colonial slavery. *See* **9988**.

10529. Larson, Jennifer. Converting passive womanhood to active sisterhood: agency, power, and subversion in Harriet Jacobs's *Incidents in the Life of a Slave Girl*. WS (35:8) 2006, 739–56.

10530. Li, Stephanie. Motherhood as resistance in Harriet Jacobs's *Incidents in the Life of a Slave Girl*. Legacy (23:1) 2006, 14–29.

10531. Tricomi, Albert. Dialect and identity in Harriet Jacobs's autobiography and other slave narratives. Callaloo (29:2) 2006, 619–33.

Henry James (1843–1916)

10532. Anesko, Michael. O O O O that Ja-hame-sian rag / It's so elegant / So intelligent: tracing appropriations of the Master's aura in Modernist critical discourse. HJR (27:3) 2006, 264–74.

10533. Arapoglou, Eleftheria. 'New York revisited': Henry James's urban quest. *In* (pp. 121–36) **3307**.

10534. Ascari, Maurizio. 'The Master in the middle distance': Max Beerbohm, Henry James and literary forgery. *In* (pp. 87–96) **10568**.

10535. Austin-Smith, Brenda. Sex and the maiden: authenticity and the erotic adaptation of *The Wings of the Dove*. *See* **13127**.

10536. Babbage, Frances. The play of surface: theater and *The Turn of the Screw*. CompDr (39:2) 2005, 131–56.

10537. Balestrini, Nassim Winnie. From fiction to libretto: Irving, Hawthorne, and James as opera. *See* **10521**.

10538. Ballam, John D. Henry James and a 'sense' of place: the modalities of perception. HJEJ (8) 2004.

10539. Bauer, Dale M. The shape of Baym's career. *See* **14018**.

10540. Bersani, Leo. The it in the I: Patrice Leconte, Henry James, and analytic love. HJR (27:3) 2006, 202–14.

10541. Bradbury, Nicola. *De cette triste plume tâtonnante*: Henry James and *The Task of the Translator*. YES (36:1) 2006, 138–44.

10542. Brazzelli, Nicoletta. Giochi d'ombra e di luce: gli spazi narrativi in *What Maisie Knew*. Culture (18) 2004, 213–32.

10543. Budick, Emily Miller. Hawthorne, Pearl, and the primal sin of culture. *See* **10367**.

10544. Cabus-Coldwell, Andrea. Figuring the princess: *The Princess Casamassima* and Pater's *Mona Lisa*. *In* (pp. 123–33) **10568**.

10545. Cagidemetrio, Alide. *The Wings of the Dove*: tracing the phantom of the palace. HJR (27:3) 2006, 215–27.

10546. Charon, Rita. Narrative lights on clinical acts: what we, like Maisie, know. PartA (4:2) 2006, 41–58.

10547. Combs, Robert. The importance of being Henry James: what the Master learned from Oscar Wilde. *In* (pp. 186–200) **10568**.

10548. Conroy, Mark. On not representing Milly Theale: sacrificing for art in *The Wings of the Dove*. *In* (pp. 134–56) **10568**.

10549. Cousineau, Thomas J. Ritual unbound: reading sacrifice in Modernist fiction. (Bibl. 2005, 11392.) Rev. by William A. Johnsen in ANQ (19:1) 2006, 66–9; by Andrew Mozina in StudN (38:2) 2006, 263–5; by Philippe Birgy in Anglophonia (19) 2006, 321–2; by Jesse Matz in Mod/Mod (13:4) 2006, 779–81; by Marlene Briggs in VWM (70) 2006, 41; by Mia L. McIver in WSA (12) 2006, 258–64.

10550. Cutting, Andrew. Death in Henry James. (Bibl. 2005, 11393.) Rev. by Nicola Bradbury in TLS, 20 Jan. 2006, 28; by Fiona Macdonald in RES (57:231) 2006, 566–8.

10551. Da Silva, Stephen. Papa, postcards, perfume, phallic keys: James, Symonds, and late Victorian fictions of homosexuality. *In* (pp. 201–38) **10568**.

10552. Davidson, Rob. The Master and the Dean: the literary criticism of Henry James and William Dean Howells. (Bibl. 2005, 11395.) Rev. by Bev Hogue in MFS (52:3) 2006, 735–7.

10553. De Biasio, Anna. Romanzi e musei: Nathaniel Hawthorne, Henry James e il rapporto con l'arte. *See* **10372**.

10554. Despotopoulou, Anna. Girls on film: postmodern renderings of Jane Austen and Henry James. *See* **9008**.

10555. Donoghue, Denis. The not-quite said. *See* **10016**.

10556. Eaton, Mark A. Miramax, Merchant–Ivory, and the new nobrow culture: niche marketing *The Wings of the Dove* and *The Golden Bowl*. *See* **13128**.

10557. Fisher, James. On the ladder of social observation: images of Decadence and morality in James's *Washington Square* and Wilde's *An Ideal Husband*. *In* (pp. 167–85) **10568**.

10558. Fogel, Daniel Mark. Creating scholarly community: a thirty year view of the *HJR* and the Henry James Society. HJR (27:3) 2006, 285–92.

10559. Foote, Stephanie. Henry James and the parvenus: reading taste in *The Spoils of Poynton*. HJR (27:1) 2006, 42–60.

10560. Gunn, Giles. The moral relevance of America's greatest travel book in an age of terror. *In* (pp. 39–50) **11824**.

10561. Hoagwood, Terence. 'Postmodern mirrors'. *See* **12897**.

10562. Hoople, Robin. Great stone faces: Henry James, Theodore Roosevelt, and the quest for American authenticity. CRAS (36:3) 2006, 345–62.

10563. Horne, Philip. Henry James and 'the forces of violence': on the track of 'big game' in *The Jolly Corner*. HJR (27:3) 2006, 237–47.

10564. Horowitz, Floyd R. (ed.). The uncollected Henry James: newly discovered stories. London: Duckworth, 2004. pp. xv, 319. Rev. by Nicola Bradbury in TLS, 21 Jan. 2005, 29; by Bernard Richards in EC (55:4) 2005, 374–81.

10565. Hutchison, Hazel. Seeing and believing: Henry James and the spiritual world. Basingstoke; New York: Palgrave Macmillan, 2006. pp. xxi, 202.

10566. Intonti, Vittoria. Henry James: una Londra di parole. *In* (pp. 237–53) **7343**.

10567. Izzo, David Garrett. The Henry James revival of the 1930s. *In* (pp. 13–34) **10568**.

10568. —— O'Hara, Daniel T. (eds). Henry James against the Aesthetic Movement: essays on the middle and late fiction. Jefferson, NC; London: McFarland, 2006. pp. x, 246.

10569. Izzo, Donatella. Killing mothers: Decadent women in James's literary tales. *In* (pp. 55–86) **10568**.

10570. Johanningsmeier, Charles. How real American readers originally experienced James's *The Real Thing*. HJR (27:1) 2006, 75–99.

10571. Jöttkandt, Sigi. Acting beautifully: Henry James and the ethical aesthetic. (Bibl. 2005, 11414.) Rev. by Greg W. Zacharias in HJEJ (10) 2006.

10572. —— Hate's rebate, or love's largesse: back to back on *The Bench of Desolation*. HJEJ (9) 2006.

10573. Klein, Marcus. What to make of *Maisie*. NER (27:4) 2006, 134–57.

10574. Kovács, Ágnes Zsófia. The function of the imagination in the writings of Henry James: the production of a civilized experience. Lewiston, NY; Lampeter: Mellen Press, 2006. pp. iv, 261.

10575. Lapoujade, David. Henry James: perspective et géométrie. EA (59:3) 2006, 319–28.

10576. Lodge, David. The year of Henry James; or, Timing is all: the story of a novel. With other essays on the genesis, composition and reception of literary fiction. *See* **17239**.

10577. McMillan, Gloria. The invisible friends: the lost worlds of Henry James and H. G. Wells. Extrapolation (47:1) 2006, 134–47.

10578. Maitzen, Rohan. Martha Nussbaum and the moral life of *Middlemarch*. *See* **10040**.

10579. Manning, Susan. Characterless women and representative men: a transatlantic perspective. Symbiosis (10:1) 2006, 21–45.

10580. Meeuwis, Michael. Living the dream: Benjamin's *Arcades Project* and *The Golden Bowl*. HJR (27:1) 2006, 61–74.

10581. Michie, Elsie. The odd couple: Anthony Trollope and Henry James. HJR (27:1) 2006, 10–23.

10582. Miller, J. Hillis. Literature as conduct: speech acts in Henry James. (Bibl. 2005, 11433.) Rev. by Henry Sussman in Atl (28:2) 2006, 135–9; by Henry Sussman in MLN (121:5) 2006, 1262–7.

10583. Mur Dueñas, Mª Pilar. A pragmatic approach to the contrastive analysis of a literary work and two of its translations. RAEI (17) 2004, 189–200.

10584. Newell, Kate. *Washington Square*'s 'virus of suggestion': source texts, intertexts, and adaptations. *See* **13122**.

10585. O'Farrell, Mary Ann. Missing Jane Austen: Henry James considers the old maid. HJR (27:1) 2006, 1–9.

10586. OTTEN, THOMAS J. A superficial reading of Henry James: preoccupations with the material world. Columbus: Ohio State UP, 2006. pp. xxiv, 197. Rev. by Miranda El-Rayess in TLS, 8 Sept. 2006, 28.

10587. PAGAN, NICHOLAS O. Henry James's children and the gift of friendship. PQ (83:3) 2004, 275–96.

10588. PALMER, S. R. The elusive correlation: dialogic medical politics in *The Wings of the Dove*. NCS (19) 2005, 113–33.

10589. PEASE, DONALD E. The extraterritoriality of the literature for our planet. *See* **20114**.

10590. PETERS, MATTHEW. Henry James, American social change, and literary revision. CamQ (34:4) 2005, 323–51.

10591. PIGEON, ELAINE. (Homo)sexuality and Impressionism in Henry James's *The Ambassadors*. *In* (pp. 121–32) **8418**.

10592. POWERS, LYALL H. (ed.). Henry James at work. By Theodora Bosanquet. With excerpts from her diary and an account of her professional career. Ann Arbor: Michigan UP, 2006. pp. ix, 142.

10593. RAITT, SUZANNE. The rhetoric of efficiency in early Modernism. *See* **19049**.

10594. RAW, LAURENCE. Adapting Henry James to the screen: gender, fiction, and film. Lanham, MD; London: Scarecrow Press, 2006. pp. vii, 297, (plates) 12.

10595. RAWLINGS, PETER. American theorists of the novel: Henry James, Lionel Trilling, Wayne C. Booth. London; New York: Routledge, 2006. pp. xii, 171. (Routledge critical thinkers.)

10596. REED, KIMBERLY C.; BEIDLER, PETER G. (eds). Approaches to teaching Henry James's *Daisy Miller* and *The Turn of the Screw*. New York: Modern Language Assn of America, 2005. pp. vii, 221. (Approaches to teaching world literature.) Rev. by Nadine Cooper in ELT (49:1) 2006, 118–19; by Robert M. Hogge in RMER (60:1) 2006.

10597. RIGHTER, WILLIAM. American memory in Henry James: void and value. (Bibl. 2005, 11447.) Rev. by Denis Flannery in MLR (101:2) 2006, 526–7.

10598. ROBINSON, SOLVEIG C. 'At all times conspicuous as art': Henry James, Margaret Oliphant, and resistance to Decadence. *In* (pp. 97–108) **10568**.

10599. ROSENBAUM, EMILY. 'The stuff of poetry and tragedy and art': Henry James, the theater, and audience. ALR (38:3) 2006, 203–22.

10600. ROSENBERG, JOSEPH ELKANAH. Tangible objects: grasping *The Aspern Papers*. HJR (27:3) 2006, 256–63.

10601. ROWE, JOHN CARLOS. Henry James and the United States. HJR (27:3) 2006, 228–36.

10602. RUBERY, MATTHEW. Unspoken intimacy in Henry James's *The Papers*. NineL (61:3) 2006, 343–67.

10603. SAVOY, ERIC. Subjunctive biography. HJR (27:3) 2006, 248–55.

10604. SINGLETON, JANE. Henry James – Aristotle's ally, an exclusive pact? PhilL (30:1) 2006, 61–78.

10605. Snediker, Michael. Stasis & verve: Henry James and the fictions of patience. HJR (27:1) 2006, 24–41.

10606. Stuart, Christopher. Henry James's *The Ambassadors* and the Christian redemption myth: 'How neatly extremes may sometimes meet.' LitB (24:1/2) 2004, 157–73.

10607. Supino, David J. Henry James: a bibliographical catalogue of a collection of editions to 1921. Liverpool: Liverpool UP, 2006. pp. xxiv, 515, (plates) 32. Rev. by Oliver Herford in TLS, 4 Aug. 2006, 27.

10608. Teehan, Sheila. The face of Decadence in *The Sacred Fount*. *In* (pp. 109–22) **10568**.

10609. Tóibín, Colm. Henry James for Venice. *See* **18772**.

10610. —— (sel. and introd.). The New York stories of Henry James. New York: New York Review, 2006. pp. xxviii, 557. (New York Review Books classics.)

10611. Underwood, Ben. Purely Platonic relations with Isabel: Henry James's *The Portrait of a Lady* and Plato's allegory of the cave. ANQ (19:2) 2006, 46–51.

10612. Walhout, M. D. The Liberal saint: American Liberalism and the problem of character. *In* (pp. 172–93) **8429**.

10613. Walshe, Éibhear. The vanishing homoerotic: Colm Tóibín's gay fictions. *See* **18773**.

10614. Wrenn, Angus. Henry, Hueffer, Holbein, history and representation. *In* (pp. 163–71) **15944**.

10615. Yacobi, Tamar. *The Beldonald Holbein*: the artist's power and its dangers as narrative center. HJR (27:3) 2006, 275–84.

Henry James, Sr (1811–1882)

10616. Monteiro, George. The elder Henry James to a collector: an unpublished letter. ANQ (19:4) 2006, 30–1.

William James (1842–1910)

10617. Dooley, Patrick K. Jack London's *South of the Slot* and William James's *The Divided Self and the Process of its Unification*. *See* **17242**.

10618. Richardson, Joan. Recombinant A.N.W.: appetites of words. Configurations (13:1) 2005, 117–33. (Alfred North Whitehead.)

10619. Walhout, M. D. The Liberal saint: American Liberalism and the problem of character. *In* (pp. 172–93) **8429**.

Anna Jameson

10620. Chance, Jane (ed.). Women medievalists and the academy. *See* **7773**.

10621. Hoeckley, Cheri L. Larsen (ed.). Shakespeare's heroines: characteristics of women, moral, political, and historical. Peterborough, Ont.; Orchard Park, NY: Broadview Press, 2005. pp. 464. (Broadview eds.)

Joseph Jefferson (1829–1905)

10622. Mullenix, Elizabeth Reitz. Yankee doodle Dixie: performing nationhood on the eve of war. *See* **9152**.

10623. Wood, Sarah F. Refusing to RIP; or, Return of the dispossessed: the transatlantic revivals of Irving's *Rip Van Winkle*. *See* **10524**.

Sarah Orne Jewett

10624. Foster, Travis M. Matthiessen's public privates: homosexual expression and the aesthetics of sexual inversion. AL (78:2) 2006, 235–62.

10625. Murphy, John J. William to Willa, courtesy of Sarah: Cather, Jewett, and Howellsian principles. *See* **15105**.

10626. Smith, Gayle. 'My river ... leads to the sea': Sarah Orne Jewett's *Country By-Ways* as Thoreauvian travel narrative. ConS (ns 14) 2006, 37–59.

Geraldine Jewsbury

10627. Heidt, Sarah J. 'The materials for a "Life"': collaboration, publication, and the Carlyles' afterlives. *See* **9410**.

Maria Jane Jewsbury (Mrs Fletcher)

10628. Low, Dennis. The literary protégées of the Lake Poets. *See* **11239**.

Lionel Johnson

10629. Monteiro, George. The presence of Lionel Johnson in Frost's poetry. *See* **16009**.

Mary F. Johnson

10630. Jones, Gwendolyn. Virginia writers in the New South: Thomas Nelson Page, Ellen Glasgow, and Mary Johnson. *See* **16129**.

Ernest Charles Jones (1819–1869)

10631. Vickers, Roy. Christian election, Holy Communion and Psalmic language in Ernest Jones's Chartist poetry. JVC (11:1) 2006, 59–83.

Edward Zane Carroll Judson ('Ned Buntline')

10632. Pepper, R. D. Ned Buntline and Joseph Pulitzer's *New York World*. DNR (75:3) 2006, 81–8.

John Keats

10633. Barnard, John. First fruits or 'first blights': a new account of the publishing history of Keats's *Poems* (1817). Romanticism (12:2) 2006, 71–101.

10634. Barth, J. Robert. Keats's way of salvation. SR (45:2) 2006, 285–97.

10635. Bassnett, Susan. Writing and translating. *In* (pp. 173–83) **3186**.

10636. Bates, Brian. *Welcome Joy, and Welcome Sorrow*: fancy, imagination, and Keats's re-visioning of *L'Allegro* and *Il Penseroso*. CEACrit (67:3) 2005, 15–27.

10637. Bayley, John. Overcoming kitsch: thoughts on linguistic and class resource from Keats to Betjeman. *In* (pp. 225–31) **13735**.

10638. Bronstein, Michaela. The half-unravelled web: Keats's intermediate truths. KSR (20) 2006, 44–51.

10639. Brown, Sally, *et al.* Keats and Italy: a history of the Keats–Shelley house in Rome. Rome: Il Labirinto, 2005. pp. 120. Rev. by Roderick Cavaliero in KSR (19) 2005, 159–61.

10640. Caws, Mary Ann. Surprised in translation. *See* **11817**.

10641. Conti Camaiora, Luisa. John Keats's *La Belle Dame sans Merci*: narration and narrators. Milan: Europrint, 2006. pp. 170.

10642. Deen, Rosemary. Dis-covering the words: language and poetry in Josephine Jacobsen. *See* **16574**.

10643. Dilworth, Thomas. Keats's *To Autumn*. Exp (65:1) 2006, 26–8.

10644. Fermanis, Porscha. *Isabella*, *Lamia*, and 'Merry Old England'. EC (56:2) 2006, 139–62.

10645. Ferris, Erin. Owing to Psyche. ERR (16:4) 2005, 399–415.

10646. Folkmann, Mads Nygaard. The transfigurative mode of Romantic discourse: poetic models in Novalis, Keats, and Stagnelius. Prism(s) (14) 2006, 27–56.

10647. Gallant, Christine. Keats and Romantic Celticism. Basingstoke; New York: Palgrave Macmillan, 2005. pp. vi, 174. Rev. by Stephen Knight in Folklore (117:2) 2006, 226–8; by Meiko O'Halloran in KSJ (55) 2006, 270–3.

10648. Gonsalves, Joshua David. Problematic figurations of the nation as I-land: a phenomenological report on half-knowledge from 'any isle of Lethe dull'. SR (45:3) 2006, 425–64.

10649. Haldane, Michael. From Plato to Pullman – the circle of invisibility and parallel worlds: *Fortunatus*, Mercury, and the Wishing-Hat: part ii. *See* **6687**.

10650. Hofmann, Klaus. Keats's *Ode to a Grecian Urn*. SR (45:2) 2006, 251–84.

10651. Khalip, Jacques. Virtual conduct: disinterested agency in Hazlitt and Keats. *See* **10414**.

10652. Koelzer, Robert. Abrams among the nightingales: revisiting the greater Romantic lyric. *See* **14184**.

10653. La Cassagnère, Christian. Keats's gleaming melancholy: a reading of *Endymion*. EREA (4:1) 2006, 43–50.

10654. Lau, Beth. Jane Austen and John Keats: negative capability, romance and reality. *See* **9047**.

10655. Miller, Christopher R. The invention of evening: perception and time in Romantic poetry. *See* **9539**.

10656. Okada, Akiko. Keats and English Romanticism in Japan. New York; Frankfurt: Lang, 2006. pp. 230.

10657. Pellicer, Juan Christian. 'The food of my delighted fancy': another echo of *Lucrece* in Keats. ANQ (19:3) 2006, 13–14.

10658. Peterfreund, Stuart. Earl Wasserman: a critical (re)-reading. *See* **14257**.

10659. Plumly, Stanley. Pastoral matters. *See* **11580**.

10660. Robinson, Polly. 'Physician to all men'? – the influence of Keats's medical training. KSR (20) 2006, 32–43.

10661. Sandy, Mark. Poetics of self and form in Keats and Shelley: Nietzschean subjectivity and genre. Aldershot; Burlington, VT: Ashgate, 2005. pp. xvii, 142. (Nineteenth century.) Rev. by Jonathon Shears in BJ (34:1) 2006, 77–80.

10662. Sasso, Gianpaolo. Il segreto di Keats: il fantasma della *Belle Dame sans Merci*. Bologna: Pendragon, 2006. pp. 260. (Le sfere.)

10663. Scott, Grant F. (ed.). Joseph Severn: letters and memoirs. *See* **8878**.

10664. Scott, Matthew. John Keats and the aesthetics of topsy-turvy. ERR (17:2) 2006, 245–54.

10665. Sell, Jonathan P. A. Allusion and ambiguity in Seamus Heaney's *Blackberry-Picking*. *See* **16323**.

10666. Stillinger, Jack. Romantic complexity: Keats, Coleridge, and Wordsworth. Urbana: Illinois UP, 2006. pp. xii, 264.

10667. Stimson, Katharine. 'Where Robins hop, and fallen leaves are sere': Keats's robin and the social imagination. KSR (20) 2006, 58–68.

10668. Turley, Richard Marggraf. 'Johnny's in the basement': Keats, Bob Dylan, and the end of influence. *In* (pp. 181–204) **13735**.

10669. —— Keats, Cornwall and the 'scent of strong-smelling phrases'. Romanticism (12:2) 2006, 102–14.

10670. Watts, Cedric. Keats's *Bright Star* and *A Lover's Complaint*. NQ (53:3) 2006, 320–2.

10671. Weaver, Russell. Questioning Keats: an introduction to applied hermeneutics. New York; Frankfurt: Lang, 2006. pp. xvi, 253. (Studies in nineteenth-century British literature, 23.)

10672. Whale, John. John Keats. (Bibl. 2005, 11539.) Rev. by Jonathon Shears in BJ (34:1) 2006, 77–80.

10673. —— John Keats and Tony Harrison: the burden of history. *In* (pp. 163–80) **13735**.

10674. Wootton, Sarah. Consuming Keats: nineteenth-century representations in art and literature. Basingstoke; New York: Palgrave Macmillan, 2006. pp. xi, 215. Rev. by Richard Marggraf Turley in BJ (34:2) 2006, 197–8.

John Keble

10675. Blair, Kirstie (ed.). John Keble in context. (Bibl. 2004, 11497.) Rev. by Carol Marie Engelhardt in VIJ (33) 2005, 252–5; by Francis L. Fennell in VS (48:3) 2006, 524–6.

10676. Gelpi, Barbara Charlesworth. John Keble and Hurrell Froude in pastoral dialogue. VP (44:1) 2006, 7–24.

10677. Gray, F. Elizabeth. 'Syren strains': Victorian women's devotional poetry and John Keble's *The Christian Year*. VP (44:1) 2006, 61–76.

10678. Jay, Elisabeth. Charlotte Mary Yonge and Tractarian aesthetics. *See* **11727**.

Emma Dunham Kelley-Hawkins (1863–1938)

10679. Bauer, Dale M. Master thoughts. *In* (pp. 186–97) **20098**.

10680. Harris, Jennifer. Black like? The strange case of Emma Dunham Kelley-Hawkins. AAR (40:3) 2006, 401–19.

Fanny Kemble

10681. Burroughs, Catherine. 'If the informing spirit be mine': Frances Anne Kemble and theory in rehearsal. RECTR (20:1/2) 2005, 28–33.

John Kerr (*fl.*1814–1834)

10682. Wood, Sarah F. Refusing to RIP; or, Return of the dispossessed: the transatlantic revivals of Irving's *Rip Van Winkle. See* **10524**.

Hannah Tapfield King (b.1808)

10683. Jalowitz, Alan C. The daughters of Penelope: tradition and innovation in American epics by women. *In* (pp. 141–58) **3395**.

Charles Kingsley

10684. Fontana, Ernest L. Kingsley's *Ode to the North-East Wind* and Frost's *To the Thawing Wind. See* **16001**.

10685. Klaver, J. M. I. The apostle of the flesh: a critical life of Charles Kingsley. Leiden; Boston, MA: Brill, 2006. pp. xv, 680. (Brill's studies in intellectual history, 140.)

Caroline M. Kirkland ('Mrs Mary Clavers')

10686. Obuchowski, Mary DeJong. 'Murdered Banquos of the forest': Caroline Kirkland's environmentalism. MidM (33) 2005, 73–9.

10687. Smith, Laura. Reconfiguring frontier architecture in Caroline Kirkland's Western sketches. WS (35:2) 2006, 171–202.

F. (Francis) Kirkpatrick (*fl.*1804)

10688. Blackstock, Allan. Politics and print: a case study. *In* (pp. 234–49) **724**.

Charles Knight

10689. Gray, Valerie. Charles Knight: educator, publisher, writer. Aldershot; Burlington, VT: Ashgate, 2006. pp. xvii, 233. (Nineteenth century.)

Lady Caroline Lamb

10690. Bainbridge, Simon. Lord Ruthven's power: Polidori's *The Vampyre*, doubles and the Byronic imagination. *See* **11055**.

10691. Cass, Jeffrey. Irish girls gone wild: *Glenarvon*, Regency hypocrisy, and Spartan virtue. CEACrit (68:1/2) 2005/06, 126–37.

10692. Dickson, Leigh Wetherall. Authority and legitimacy: the cultural context of Lady Caroline Lamb's novels. WWr (13:3) 2006, 369–91.

10693. Douglass, Paul. Lady Caroline Lamb: a biography. (Bibl. 2004, 11514.) Rev. by Peter W. Graham in BJ (33:1) 2005, 53–5; by Constance M. Fulmer in PCP (41) 2006, 143–5.

10694. —— Lady Caroline Lamb before Byron: the Godfrey Vassal Webster affair. WordsC (36:3) 2005, 117–24.

10695. —— That 'vital spark of genius': Lady Caroline Lamb's writing before Byron. PCP (41) 2006, 43–62.

10696. —— An unpublished letter from Lord Byron to Lady Caroline Lamb. *See* **9343**.

10697. —— (comp.). The whole disgraceful truth: selected letters of Lady Caroline Lamb. Basingstoke; New York: Palgrave Macmillan, 2006. pp. xii, 250. Rev. by Claire Harman in TLS, 3 Nov. 2006, 10.

10698. March, Rosemary. Lost: three books from Byron. *See* **9353**.

10699. Stauffer, Andrew M. Byronic transmission and the first poem for Caro. *See* **9368**.

Charles Lamb

10700. Beavers, Katy. Poetical, political and personal epistolary thoughts of Charles Lamb and Samuel Taylor Coleridge. ColB (ns 27) 2006, 56–64.

10701. Chang, Elizabeth H. 'Eyes of the proper almond shape': blue-and-white china in the British imaginary, 1823–1888. NCS (19) 2005, 17–34.

10702. Hall, Edith. No man's lands: modern myths of the Cyclops. TLS, 26 May 2006, 14–15.

10703. Monsman, Gerald. Satiric models for Charles Lamb's *A Dissertation upon Roast Pig*. NCP (33:1) 2006, 1–27.

10704. Saloman, Randi. 'Charles Lamb is dead': Arnold Bennett's *Journalism for Women* and *A Room of One's Own*. *See* **19327**.

Mary Lamb

10705. Straight, Julie. Women, religion, and insanity in Mary Lamb's *The Young Mahometan*. ERR (16:4) 2005, 417–38.

10706. Watson, Kathy. The Devil kissed her: the story of Mary Lamb. London: Bloomsbury; New York: Tarcher/Penguin, 2004. pp. 245. Rev. by Felicity James in CamQ (34:4) 2005, 387–91.

The Lambs

10707. Wu, Duncan. The Lamb circle and the *Monthly Repository*. Romanticism (12:2) 2006, 143–9.

Letitia Elizabeth Landon (L.E.L.)

10708. Comet, Noah. Letitia Landon and Romantic Hellenism. WordsC (37:2) 2006, 76–80.

10709. Vincent, Patrick. A continent of Corinnes: the Romantic poetess and the diffusion of liberal culture in Europe, 1815–50. *In* (pp. 486–504) **8357**.

Walter Savage Landor

10710. Hewitt, Regina. Symbolic interactions: social problems and literary interventions in the works of Baillie, Scott, and Landor. *See* **9105**.

10711. Slote, Sam. A Eumaean return to style. *See* **16771**.

Edward William Lane

10712. Kobyashi, Kazue. The evolution of the *Arabian Nights* illustrations: an art-historical review. *In* (pp. 171–93) **10714**.

10713. Matus, Jill. Collaboration and collusion: two Victorian writing couples and their Orientalist texts. *In* (pp. 175–92) **3405**.

10714. Yamanaka, Yuriko; Nishio, Tetsuo (eds). *The Arabian Nights* and Orientalism: perspectives from East and West. London; New York: Tauris, 2006. pp. xvii, 269. Rev. by Marina Warner in TLS, 3 Nov. 2006, 7–8.

Andrew Lang

10715. Leighton, Mary Elizabeth. Andrew Lang and the 1885 Merton Professorship of English Language and Literature at Oxford. NQ (53:3) 2006, 336–8.

Emily Lawless

10716. Maume, Patrick. Emily Lawless's *Maelcho* and the crisis of the imperial romance. EI (41:3/4) 2006, 245–66.

Emma Lazarus

10717. Cavitch, Max. Emma Lazarus and the golem of liberty. AmLH (18:1) 2006, 1–28.

10718. Schor, Esther. Emma Lazarus. New York: Schocken, 2006. pp. xiii, 347. (Jewish encounters.) Rev. by Caleb Crain in NYTB, 31 Dec. 2006, 18.

Edward Lear

10719. Hammond, Andrew. Imagined colonialism: Victorian travellers in South-East Europe. NCC (28:2) 2006, 87–104.

10720. Maynard, John. Two mad-dog Englishmen in the Corfu sun: Lawrence Durrell and Edward Lear. *In* (pp. 255–69) **15631**.

'Vernon Lee' (Violet Paget)

10721. Bristow, Joseph. Vernon Lee's art of feeling. TSWL (25:1) 2006, 117–39.

10722. Burton, Nick; Fraser, Hilary. Mirror visions and dissolving views: Vernon Lee and the museological experiments of Patrick Geddes. NCC (28:2) 2006, 145–60.

10723. Fluhr, Nicole. Empathy and identity in Vernon Lee's *Hauntings*. VS (48:2) 2006, 287–94.

10724. Harrington, Emily. The strain of sympathy: A. Mary F. Robinson, *The New Arcadia*, and Vernon Lee. *See* **11071**.

10725. Kane, Mary Patricia. The uncanny mother in Vernon Lee's *Prince Alberic and the Snake Lady*. VicR (32:1) 2006, 41–62.

10726. Leighton, Angela. Resurrections of the body: women writers and the idea of the Renaissance. *In* (pp. 222–38) **8320**.

10727. Marcus, Laura. 'A new form of true beauty': aesthetics and early film criticism. Mod/Mod (13:2) 2006, 267–89.

10728. Maxwell, Catherine. Vernon Lee and the ghosts of Italy. *In* (pp. 201–21) **8320**.

10729. Towheed, Shafquat. The creative evolution of scientific paradigms: Vernon Lee and the debate over the hereditary transmission of acquired characters. VS (49:1) 2006, 33–61.

Sheridan Le Fanu

10730. Welter, Nancy. Women alone: Le Fanu's *Carmilla* and Rossetti's *Goblin Market*. *In* (pp. 138–48) **8647**.

10731. Zuber, Devin P. Swedenborg and the disintegration of language in Sheridan Le Fanu's sensation fiction. *In* (pp. 74–84) **8647**.

Anna Austen Lefroy (1793–1872)

10732. Jones, Vivien. Austen's nieces: case studies in women and writing. *In* (pp. 56–68) **8374**.

Charles Lever

10733. Sutherland, John. Lever's columns: a novelist who contributed to great fiction without becoming great. TLS, 15 Dec. 2006, 14.

Amy Levy

10734. Goody, Alex. Murder in Mile End: Amy Levy, Jewishness, and the city. VLC (34:2) 2006, 461–79.

10735. Jusová, Iveta; Reyes, Dan. Edward Said, *Reuben Sachs*, and Victorian Zionism. *See* **10036**.

G. H. Lewes

10736. Ashton, Rosemary. A blackguard and his —: the scandal that surrounded George Eliot and G. H. Lewes on their trip to Weimar. *See* **10006**.

10737. Rees, Joan. Christmas in Ryde. *See* **10046**.

Isabella Lickbarrow

10738. Parrish, Constance (ed.). Collected poems. (Bibl. 2005, 11603.) Rev. by Duncan Wu in PNRev (31:3) 2005, 91–2.

10739. Payne, Susan. Essays on British women poets. *See* **3583**.

Abraham Lincoln (1809–1865)

10740. Briggs, John Channing. Lincoln's speeches reconsidered. Baltimore, MD; London: Johns Hopkins UP, 2005. pp. xi, 370. Rev. by Linda Simon in PrSt (28:1) 2006, 107–9.

10741. Schmitz, Neil. Doing the Gettysburg Address: Jefferson/Calhoun/Lincoln/King. AQ (62:2) 2006, 145–52.

10742. Wilson, Douglas L. Lincoln the persuader. ASch (75:4) 2006, 31–43.

Elizabeth Lynn Linton

10743. Henry, Peaches. A revised approach to relationality in women's autobiography: the case of Eliza Linton's *The Autobiography of Christopher Kirkland*. A/B (20:1) 2005, 18–37.

Charles Lloyd (1775–1839)

10744. Verhoeven, W. M. (gen. ed.). Anti-Jacobin novels: vol. 2, Charles Lloyd, *Edmund Oliver* (1798). Ed. by Philip Cox. London; Brookfield, VT: Pickering & Chatto, 2005. pp. xxxiv, 228. Rev. by Robert Morrison in WordsC (36:4) 2005, 189–91; by Jon Mee in HLQ (69:4) 2006, 649–53.

John Gibson Lockhart (1794–1854)

10745. Duncan, Ian. *Blackwood's* and Romantic nationalism. *In* (pp. 70–89) **1098**.

10746. Flynn, Philip. Blackwood's *Maga*, Lockhart's *Peter's Letters*, and the politics of publishing. *See* **1102**.

10747. MacCarthy, Anne. J. G. Lockhart's *The Penitence of Don Roderick* as a source for J. C. Mangan's *The Penance of Don Rodrigo*. NQ (53:3) 2006, 330–2.

10748. Swaim, Barton. 'What is Scott?'. John Gibson Lockhart's professional amateurism. VPR (39:3) 2006, 280–97.

Henry Wadsworth Longfellow

10749. Barrucand, Michel. L'espace en poésie – poésie de l'espace: les Fireside Poets. *See* **9294**.

10750. Cavitch, Max. Emma Lazarus and the golem of liberty. *See* **10717**.

10751. Eckel, Leslie E. Symbols 'mystical and awful': Emerson's and Longfellow's primitive poetics. *See* **10072**.

10752. Eliot, Simon. What price poetry? Selling Wordsworth, Tennyson, and Longfellow in nineteenth- and early twentieth-century Britain. *See* **11660**.

10753. Irmscher, Christoph. Longfellow *redux*. Urbana: Illinois UP, 2006. pp. xvi, 350.

10754. McNally, Michael D. The Indian passion play: contesting the real Indian in *Song of Hiawatha* pageants, 1901–1965. AmQ (58:1) 2006, 105–36.

10755. Salska, Agnieszka. From national to supranational conception of literature: the case of Henry Wadsworth Longfellow. ATQ (20:4) 2006, 611–28.

10756. Willis, Lloyd. Henry Wadsworth Longfellow, United States national literature, and the canonical erasure of material nature. ATQ (20:4) 2006, 629–46.

10757. Zapedowska, Magdalena. Longfellow's *The Lighthouse*. Exp (65:1) 2006, 28–31.

James Russell Lowell

10758. Cutler, Edward S. Literary modernity and the problem of a national literature: understanding William Dean Howells' critique of Walt Whitman. *See* **10501**.

10759. Stokes, Claudia. Copyrighting American history: international copyright and the periodization of the nineteenth century. AL (77:2) 2005, 291–317.

Charles Lucas (1769–1854)

10760. Verhoeven, W. M. (gen. ed.). Anti-Jacobin novels: vol. 10, Charles Lucas, *The Infernal Quixote: a Tale of the Day* (1801). Ed. by Mary Peace. London; Brookfield, VT: Pickering & Chatto, 2005. pp. xxvii, 438. Rev. by Jon Mee in HLQ (69:4) 2006, 649–53.

Emma Lyon (1788–1870)

10761. Scrivener, Michael. Following the muse: inspiration, prophecy, and difference in the poetry of Emma Lyon (1788–1870), Anglo-Jewish poet. *In* (pp. 105–26) **8523**.

Edward Bulwer Lytton, Baron Lytton (1803–1873)

10762. Beedell, A. V.; Harvey, A. D. Bulwer Lytton letters in the National Archives. NQ (53:3) 2006, 332–5.

10763. Christensen, Allan Conrad (ed.). The subverting vision of Bulwer Lytton: bicentenary reflections. (Bibl. 2004, 11575.) Rev. by Richard Salmon in VS (48:3) 2006, 566–8.

10764. Flynn, Michael J. Novels by literary snobs: the contentious class-coding of Thackerayan parody. DSA (36) 2006, 199–228.

10765. GILLINGHAM, LAUREN. The novel of fashion redressed: Bulwer-Lytton's *Pelham* in a 19th-century context. VicR (32:1) 2006, 63–85.

10766. HENDERSON, IAN. Mid-Victorian reading and the Antipodes. *See* **9163**.

10767. KNIGHT, MARK. *The Haunted and the Haunters*: Bulwer Lytton's philosophical ghost story. NCC (28:3) 2006, 245–55.

10768. MARKS, THOMAS. 'A sort of magic': enchantment and disenchantment in the work of Tennyson and his contemporaries. *See* **11399**.

10769. WORSFOLD, BRIAN. The Victorian ethic of self-help and its implications for contemporary ageing. CVE (63) 2006, 189–208.

Thomas Babington, Lord Macaulay

10770. ADAMS, EDWARD. Macaulay's *History of England* and the dilemmas of Liberal epic. NCP (33:2) 2006, 149–74.

10771. CREGAN-REID, VYBARR. Macaulay and the historical sublime; or, Forgetting the past and the future. NCP (33:2) 2006, 225–51.

10772. EDWARDS, OWEN DUDLEY. The ranks of Tuscany: Macaulay on Ranke's *Die römischen Päpste*. NCP (33:2) 2006, 49–81.

10773. HANSON, DAVID C. Precocity and sibling relations: Goethe and Macaulay family life writing. NCP (33:2) 2006, 18–48.

10774. PALMER, SEAN. Macaulay's revolution: New Historicism, the working classes, and Elizabeth Gaskell's *North and South*. NCP (33:2) 2006, 197–224.

10775. PRASAD, G. J. V. A minute stretching into centuries: Macaulay, English, and India. NCP (33:2) 2006, 175–96.

10776. TUCKER, IRENE. Macaulay's paranoid Parliament: queer theory, Victorian medicine, and *The History of England*. NCP (33:2) 2006, 82–123.

George MacDonald

10777. GAARDEN, BONNIE. *The Golden Key*: a double reading. Mythlore (24:3/4) 2006, 35–52.

10778. MCCULLOCH, FIONA. 'A strange race of beings': undermining innocence in *The Princess and the Goblin*. ScSR (7:1) 2006, 53–67.

10779. NELSON, DALE. Little-known books (and a little-known story) in Lewis' background: a fifth selection. *See* **17195**.

10780. PERSYN, CATHERINE. 'In my end is my beginning': the fin-negans motif in George MacDonald's *At the Back of the North Wind*. Mythlore (24:3/4) 2006, 53–69.

10781. TOUSSAINT THIRIET, BENJAMINE. *'For the childlike is the divine'*: la quête de la jeunesse éternelle dans les contes et *romances* de George MacDonald. CVE (63) 2006, 323–34.

Agnes Maule Machar ('Fidelis')

10782. JANES, DANIELA. Brainworkers: the middle-class labour reformer and the late Victorian Canadian industrial novel. CanL (191) 2006, 70–84.

John McPherson (1817–1845)

10783. SCHNEIDER, MATTHEW. Wordsworthian songcatching in America. *See* **3073**.

James Clarence Mangan

10784. HASLAM, RICHARD. 'Broad farce and thrilling tragedy': Mangan's fiction and Irish gothic. EI (41:3/4) 2006, 215–44.

10785. MACCARTHY, ANNE. J. G. Lockhart's *The Penitence of Don Roderick* as a source for J. C. Mangan's *The Penance of Don Rodrigo*. *See* **10747**.

10786. PATERSON, ADRIAN. 'An imagined music': Yeats, music and the Irish tradition. *In* (pp. 135–69) **12189**.

10787. WURTZ, JAMES F. Scarce more than a corpse: Famine memory and representations of the gothic in *Ulysses*. *See* **16790**.

Mary Peabody Mann

10788. ARD, PATRICIA M. Transcendentalism for children: Mary Peabody Mann's *The Flower People*. *In* (pp. 216–31) **10790**.

10789. COOPER, MICHAELA B. Should not those things be known? Mary Mann's *Juanita* and the limits of domesticity. *In* (pp. 146–62) **10790**.

10790. ELBERT, MONIKA M.; HALL, JULIE E.; RODIER, KATHARINE (eds). Reinventing the Peabody sisters. Iowa City: Iowa UP, 2006. pp. xxi, 271.

10791. LAZO, RODRIGO. Against the Cuba guide: the 'Cuba Journal,' *Juanita*, and travel writing. *In* (pp. 180–95) **10790**.

10792. LOTT, DESHAE E. Like one happy family: Mary Peabody Mann's method for influencing reform. *In* (pp. 91–107) **10790**.

10793. MARSHALL, MEGAN. The Peabody sisters as sisters. *In* (pp. 248–58) **10790**.

10794. —— The Peabody sisters: three women who ignited American Romanticism. Boston, MA: Houghton Mifflin, 2005. pp. xx, 602. Rev. by Julie E. Hall in NHR (32:1) 2006, 74–80; by Marilyn S. Blackwell in VH (74:1) 2006, 75–7; by Rebecca Steinitz in WRB (23:1) 2006, 22–3.

10795. RODIER, KATHARINE. Authorizing Sarah Winnemucca? Elizabeth Peabody and Mary Peabody Mann. *In* (pp. 108–25) **10790**.

10796. VASQUEZ, MARK. Declaration and defence: Elizabeth Palmer Peabody, Mary Peabody Mann, and the complex rhetoric of mediation. *In* (pp. 45–58) **10790**.

Florence Marryat

10797. MAUNDER, ANDREW (gen. ed.). Domestic sensationalism: Florence Marryat, *Love's Conflict* (1865). Ed. by Andrew Maunder. London; Brookfield, VT: Pickering & Chatto, 2004. pp. liii, 447. (Varieties of women's sensation fiction 1855–1890, 2.) Rev. by Anthea Trodd in VicR (31:2) 2005, 132–4.

Harriet Martineau

10798. COLELLA, SILVANA. The liberty of fiction: Harriet Martineau's *Illustrations of Political Economy*. RSV (18/19) 2004/05, 33–66.

10799. COURTEMANCHE, ELEANOR. 'Naked truth is the best eloquence': Martineau, Dickens, and the moral science of realism. ELH (73:2) 2006, 383–407.

10800. EASLEY, ALEXIS. The woman of letters at home: Harriet Martineau and the Lake District. VLC (34:1) 2006, 291–310.

10801. Granata, Silvia. Anatomists and public opinion: literary representations of a troubled relationship. *See* **11178**.

10802. Logan, Deborah (ed.). Harriet Martineau's writing on the British Empire. Preface by Patrick Brantlinger. London; Brookfield, VT: Pickering & Chatto, 2004. 5 vols. pp. xlix, 248; xxvii, 298; 270; xi, 236; xvi, 415. (Pickering masters.) Rev. by Maria Frawley in VPR (39:1) 2006, 69–72.

10803. Romeo, Marcella. Ologrammi e stereotipi coloniali nell'opera di Harriet Martineau. Pescare: Tracce, 2006. pp. 276. (Armorica saggi.)

10804. —— (ed. and trans.). L'isola dell'Aurora. Palermo: Quattrosoli, 2006. pp. 158.

10805. Van, Annette. Realism, speculation, and the gold standard in Harriet Martineau's *Illustrations of Political Economy*. VLC (34:1) 2006, 115–29.

Mary Ann Bryan Mason (1802–1881)

10806. York, Maurice C. Mary Ann Bryan Mason's literary milestone: *A Wreath from the Woods of Carolina*. NCLR (15) 2006, 18–23.

C. R. Maturin

10807. Connolly, Claire. Theatre and nation in Irish Romanticism: the tragic dramas of Charles Robert Maturin and Richard Lalor Sheil. EI (41:3/4) 2006, 185–214.

10808. Ragaz, Sharon. Maturin, Archibald Constable, and the publication of *Melmoth the Wanderer*. RES (57:230) 2006, 359–73.

James Clerk Maxwell (1831–1879)

10809. Beer, Gillian. Afterword. *In* (pp. 204–10) **13732**.

E. J. (Emily Juliana) May

10810. Gargano, Elizabeth. Death by learning: zymosis and the perils of school in E. J. May's *Dashwood Priory*. ChildLit (33) 2005, 1–19.

Henry Mayhew

10811. Pontrandolfo, Luisa. Londra 1851: trasparenze e ombre del Crystal Palace in Mayhew e Dickens. *In* (pp. 165–84) **7343**.

L. T. Meade

10812. Miller, Elizabeth Carolyn. 'Shrewd women of business': Madame Rachel, Victorian consumerism, and L. T. Meade's *The Sorceress of the Strand*. VLC (34:1) 2006, 311–32.

Herman Melville

10813. Avallone, Charlene. Women reading Melville / Melville reading women. *In* (pp. 41–59) **10897**.

10814. Baker, Anne. Mapping and measurement in *Moby-Dick*. *In* (pp. 182–96) **10823**.

10815. Balaam, Peter. 'Piazza to the north': Melville reading Sedgwick. *In* (pp. 60–81) **10897**.

10816. Barton, John Cyril. The anti-gallows movement in antebellum America. YREAL (22) 2006, 145–78.

10817. Blair, Ruth M. Enchanted isles: a response to Robert C. Suggs on *Typee*. ESQ (51:1–3) 2006, 87–92.

10818. Blumenthal, Rachel. Melville's *The Encantadas*. Exp (64:4) 2006, 218–20.

10819. Bode, Rita. 'Suckled by the sea': the maternal in *Moby-Dick*. *In* (pp. 181–98) **10897**.

10820. Bonanno, Danilo. *A chartless voyage*: presenze leopardiane nell'opera di Herman Melville. Pisa: ETS, 2006. pp. 306. (Poesis e critica mitica, 35.)

10821. Bryant, John. Melville essays the romance: comedy and being in *Frankenstein*, *The Big Bear of Arkansas*, and *Moby-Dick*. NineL (61:3) 2006, 277–310.

10822. —— Taipi, Tipii, *Typee*: place, memory, and text: a response to Robert C. Suggs. ESQ (51:1–3) 2005, 137–67.

10823. —— Edwards, Mary K. Bercaw; Marr, Timothy (eds). Ungraspable phantom: essays on *Moby-Dick*. Kent, OH; London: Kent State UP, 2006. pp. xvii, 373.

10824. Burns, Mark K. 'In this simple savage old rules would not apply': cetology and the subject of race in *Moby-Dick*. *In* (pp. 199–208) **10823**.

10825. Calder, Alex. Mapping *Typee*: space and the genres of truth. ESQ (51:1–3) 2005, 115–20.

10826. Chauche, Catherine. Bartleby, the caller of conscience: melancholy in Melville's *Bartleby*: a phenomenological approach. EREA (4:1) 2006, 104–10.

10827. Clymer, Jeffory A. Property and selfhood in Herman Melville's *Pierre*. NineL (61:2) 2006, 171–99.

10828. Coffler, Gail H. (comp.). Melville's allusions to religion: a comprehensive index and glossary. (Bibl. 2004, 11629.) Rev. by Kathleen E. Kier in Leviathan (8:3) 2006, 72–5.

10829. Colacurcio, Michael. Charity and its discontents: pity and politics in Melville's fiction. *In* (pp. 49–79) **8429**.

10830. Colatrella, Carol. *Moby-Dick*'s lessons; or, How reading might save one's life. *In* (pp. 165–81) **10823**.

10831. Cooper, William. Melville's *Poor Man's Pudding and Rich Man's Crumbs*. Exp (64:3) 2006, 144–6.

10832. Delbanco, Andrew. Melville: his world and work. (Bibl. 2005, 11675.) Rev. by Karl Miller in TLS, 6 Jan. 2006, 11; by André Bernard in KR (28:4) 2006, 1–3; by James O. Tate in Chronicles (30:1) 2006, 33–4.

10833. Diorio, Mary Ann L. A student's guide to Herman Melville. Berkeley Heights, NJ: Enslow, 2006. pp. 160. (Understanding literature.)

10834. Dryden, Edgar A. Monumental Melville: the formation of a literary career. (Bibl. 2005, 11679.) Rev. by Michael Robertson in AL (77:2) 2005, 416–18; by John Wenke in Leviathan (8:1) 2006, 91–5.

10835. Ellis, Juniper. Island queens: women and power in Melville's South Pacific. *In* (pp. 163–80) **10897**.

10836. Evans, David H. 'That great Leviathan … which is but an artifical man': *Moby-Dick* and the Lowell factory system. ESQ (50:4) 2004, 315–50.

10837. EVELEV, JOHN. Tolerable entertainment: Herman Melville and professionalism in antebellum New York. Amherst: Massachusetts UP, 2006. pp. xii, 232.

10838. FANNING, SUSAN GARBARINI. 'Kings of the upside-down world': challenging White hegemony in *Moby-Dick*. *In* (pp. 209–23) **10823**.

10839. FLORY, WENDY STALLARD. Melville and Isabel: the author and the woman within in the 'inside narrative' of *Pierre*. *In* (pp. 121–40) **10897**.

10840. —— Melville, *Moby-Dick* and the depressive mind: Queequeg, Starbuck, Stubb, and Flask as symbolic characters. *In* (pp. 81–99) **10823**.

10841. GENTRY, APRIL. Critical companion to Herman Melville: a literary reference to his life and work. New York: Facts on File, 2006. pp. 400.

10842. GÖSKE, DANIEL. 'There's another rendering now': on translating *Moby-Dick* into German. *In* (pp. 255–73) **10823**.

10843. GUNN, GILES B. (ed.). A historical guide to Herman Melville. (Bibl. 2005, 11685.) Rev. by Gale Temple in Leviathan (8:3) 2006, 67–71.

10844. HERBERT, T. WALTER. Facts, fictions, and wisdom in Melville's *Typee*. ESQ (51:1–3) 2005, 93–103.

10845. HERMAN, DEBORAH. Arthur Conan Doyle, the handsome sailor. *See* **9940**.

10846. HIRSCH, IRENE. The Brazilian whale. *In* (pp. 275–88) **10823**.

10847. HOWARD, LORI N. 'Ungainly gambols' and circumnavigating the truth: breaking the narrative of *Moby-Dick*. *In* (pp. 25–36) **10823**.

10848. HUME, BEVERLY A. Of cuttle-fish and women: Melville's Goneril in *The Confidence-Man*. *In* (pp. 199–212) **10897**.

10849. JACOBSON, KAREN F. Obsessive–compulsive disorder in *Moby-Dick*, *L'Assommoir*, and *Buddenbrooks*: interpreting literary texts through psychological categories. Lewiston, NY; Lampeter: Mellen Press, 2005. pp. iv, 321. (Studies in comparative literature, 66.)

10850. KATO, YUJI. Herman Melville and modern Japan: a speculative reinterpretation of the critical history. Leviathan (8:3) 2006, 11–18.

10851. KEARNS, MICHAEL. Morality and rhetoric in *Moby-Dick*. *In* (pp. 147–64) **10823**.

10852. KELLEY, WYN. 'Lying in various attitudes': staging Melville's Pip in digital media. *In* (pp. 337–53) **10823**.

10853. —— 'Tender kinswoman': Gail Hamilton and gendered justice in *Billy Budd*. *In* (pp. 98–117) **10897**.

10854. —— (ed.). A companion to Herman Melville. Oxford; Malden, MA: Blackwell, 2006. pp. xxvii, 582. (Blackwell companions to literature and culture, 41.)

10855. KLEITZ, DORSEY. Herman Melville, Matthew Perry, and the *Narrative of the Expedition of an American Squadron to the China Seas and Japan*. Leviathan (8:3) 2006, 25–32.

10856. LANATI, BARBARA. Ottocento e dintorni: E. A. Poe, W. Whitman, H. Melville, N. Hawthorne. *See* **11027**.

10857. LAZO, RODRIGO J. 'So Spanishly poetic': *Moby-Dick*'s doubloon and Latin America. *In* (pp. 224–37) **10823**.

10858. LOMBARDO, GIUSEPPE. Herman Melville's transatlantic negotiations: Israel Potter as an expatriate prototype. QPS (14) 2006, 207–13.

10859. LÓPEZ LIQUETE, MARIA FELISA. When silence speaks: the Chola widow. *In* (pp. 213–28) **10897**.

10860. MCGOWAN, TONY. Imperfect states: Thoreau, Melville, and 'insectivorous fate'. *In* (pp. 58–86) **3203**.

10861. MCNUTT, DONALD J. Urban revelations: images of ruin in the American city, 1790–1860. *See* **9243**.

10862. MAKINO, ARIMICHI. Commodore Perry as white phantom: *Moby-Dick* in the context of the modern age. Leviathan (8:3) 2006, 19–24.

10863. MALONEY, IAN S. Melville's monumental imagination. London; New York: Routledge, 2006. pp. x,166. (Studies in major literary authors.)

10864. MARIANI, GIORGIO. 'Chiefly known by his rod': the Book of Jonah, Mapples' sermon, and scapegoating. *In* (pp. 37–57) **10823**.

10865. MAROVITZ, SANFORD E. Correspondences: paranoiac lexicographers and the Melvillean heroes. *In* (pp. 100–13) **10823**.

10866. MARR, TIMOTHY. Circassian longings: Melville's Orientalization of Eden. *In* (pp. 229–51) **10897**.

10867. MARSH, CLAYTON. Stealing time: Poe's confidence men and the '*rush* of the age'. *See* **11032**.

10868. MATTESON, JOHN T. 'Deadly voids and unbidden infidelities': death, memory, and the law in *Moby-Dick*. *In* (pp. 117–31) **10823**.

10869. MEYER, JOSEPH MATTHEW. Melville's *Bartleby, the Scrivener.* Exp (64:2) 2006, 84–6.

10870. MILDER, ROBERT. Exiled royalties: Melville and the life we imagine. Oxford; New York: OUP, 2006. pp. xx, 290.

10871. MILLER, KARL. A little like a whale. TLS, 6 Jan. 2006, 11 (review-article).

10872. MITCHELL, DAVID T.; SNYDER, SHARON L. Masquerades of impairment: charity as a confidence game. Leviathan (8:1) 2006, 35–60.

10873. MUDGETT, KATHRYN. 'I stand alone here upon the open sea': Starbuck and the limits of positive law. *In* (pp. 132–44) **10823**.

10874. NOWATZKI, ROBERT C. 'Our only truly national poets': blackface minstrelsy and cultural nationalism. *See* **10092**.

10875. OSBORNE, RICHARD. 'Blackface' minstrelsy from Melville to Moby. CritQ (48:1) 2006, 14–25.

10876. OSHIMA, YUKIKO. Dreaming a dream of interracial bonds: from *Hope Leslie* to *Moby-Dick*. *In* (pp. 238–51) **10823**.

10877. —— Native America in *The Confidence-Man*: quite an original satire and scene. Leviathan (8:3) 2006, 51–60.

10878. OTTER, SAMUEL. Leviathanic revelations: Laurie Anderson's, Rinde Eckert's, and John Barrymore's *Moby-Dicks*. *In* (pp. 291–304) **10823**.

10879. —— *Typee*: 'an almost incredible book'. ESQ (51:1–3) 2005, 169–85.

10880. Pease, Donald E. The extraterritoriality of the literature for our planet. *See* **20114**.

10881. Peters, Matthew. A new source for *The Waste Land*. *See* **15710**.

10882. Porter, Burton. The head & the heart: philosophy in literature. Amherst, NY: Humanity, 2006. pp. 177.

10883. Quinby, Lee. True places: the mapped and the unmappable in *Typee*. ESQ (51:1–3) 2005, 121–7.

10884. Ricca, Brad J. 'Strange imperious instantaneousness': mysteries of space/time in *Pierre; or, The Ambiguities*. Leviathan (8:2) 2006, 3–16.

10885. Robertson-Lorant, Laurie. Melville and the women in his life. *In* (pp. 15–37) **10897**.

10886. Robillard, Douglas. Melville's 'Pale ravener of horrible meat'. Leviathan (8:2) 2006, 85.

10887. —— (ed.). John Marr and other sailors, with some sea-pieces. Kent, OH; London: Kent State UP, 2006. pp. ix, 235. (Facsimile.)

10888. Ryan, James Emmett. Ishmael's recovery: injury, illness, and convalescence in *Moby-Dick*. Leviathan (8:1) 2006, 17–34.

10889. Ryan, Steven T. Cicero's head in Melville's *Bartleby the Scrivener*. ELN (43:2) 2005, 116–33.

10890. Saiki, Ikuno. A shadow of the Far East: Fedallah, or a Japanese sea drifter. Leviathan (8:3) 2006, 33–42.

10891. Samuels, Ellen. From Melville to Eddie Murphy: the disability con in American literature and film. Leviathan (8:1) 2006, 61–82.

10892. Sanborn, Geoffrey. Purple haze: making sense of uncertainty (and uncertainty of sense) in *Typee*. ESQ (51:1–3) 2005, 129–35.

10893. —— Whence come you, Queequeg? AL (77:2) 2005, 227–57.

10894. Schiavini, Cinzia. My city of ruins: American topographies and European heritage in Herman Melville and Edgar Allan Poe's urban landscape. QPS (14) 2006, 240–6.

10895. Schultz, Elizabeth. *Bartleby, the Scrivener* and *Uncle Christopher's*: sites of wage slavery and domestic abuse. *In* (pp. 82–97) **10897**.

10896. —— Feminizing *Moby-Dick*: contemporary women perform the whale. *In* (pp. 305–20) **10823**.

10897. —— Springer, Haskell (eds). Melville & women. Kent, OH: Kent State UP, 2006. pp. viii, 287, (plates) 8.

10898. Smith, Vanessa. Crossing the beach at Taipivai: the psychogeography of islands. ESQ (51:1–3) 2005, 105–13.

10899. Specq, Francois. Transcendence: seekers and seers in the age of Thoreau. *See* **11450**.

10900. Stratman, Jacob. Melville's *Frenzy in the Wake*. Exp (64:3) 2006, 146–9.

10901. Suggs, Robert C. Accuracy, actuality, and interpretation: the question of *Typee*: a rejoinder to critics. ESQ (51:1–3) 2005, 187–208.

10902. —— Melville's flight to Taipi: topographical, archaeological, and historical considerations. ESQ (51:1–3) 2005, 47–86.

10903. Tawil, Ezra F. Captain Babo's cabin: Stowe, race and misreading in *Benito Cereno*. Leviathan (8:2) 2006, 37–51.

10904. Thompson, Corey Evan. Melville's *Monody*: possibly for Malcolm? ANQ (19:2) 2006, 39–44.

10905. Thompson, G. R. Being there: Melville and the romance of real-life adventure. ESQ (51:1–3) 2005, 1–46.

10906. Toal, Catherine. 'Some things which should never have happened': fiction, identification, and *Benito Cereno*. NineL (61:1) 2006, 32–65.

10907. Urbanczyk, Aaron. 'In me, many worthies recline, and converse': the role of philosophers in Melville's fiction. EArtsS (34:1) 2005, 75–90.

10908. Visser, Irene. Of women, slaves and cannibals: dynamics of holiness in three American novels of the mid-nineteenth century. *In* (pp. 127–45) **3415**.

10909. Wallace, Robert K. Douglass and Melville: anchored together in a neighborly style. (Bibl. 2005, 11711.) Rev. by Milton Reigelman in KenPR (20) 2005, 72–3.

10910. —— Fusing with the muse: Eckert's *Great Whales* as homage and prophecy. *In* (pp. 321–36) **10823**.

10911. Weinauer, Ellen. Women, ownership, and gothic manhood in *Pierre*. *In* (pp. 141–60) **10897**.

10912. Williams, Dennis. Filling the void: a Lacanian angle of vision on *Moby-Dick*. *In* (pp. 61–80) **10823**.

10913. Winter, Aaron. Seeds of discontent: the expanding satiric range of Melville's transatlantic diptychs. Leviathan (8:2) 2006, 17–35.

10914. Zettsu, Tomoyuki. Cannibal connections: a Buddhist reading of *The Encantadas*. Leviathan (8:3) 2006, 43–50.

10915. Zou, Huiling. On the Indian images in the White canons of 19th-century America. *See* **8736**.

George Meredith

10916. Henry, Anne C. 'Explorations in dot-and-dashland': George Meredith's aphasia. NineL (61:3) 2006, 311–42.

10917. Jenkins, Melissa Shields. 'Was ever hero in this fashion won?': alternative sexualities in the novels of George Meredith. *In* (pp. 124–33) **11883**.

10918. Regan, Stephen. The Victorian sonnet, from George Meredith to Gerard Manley Hopkins. YES (36:2) 2006, 17–34.

10919. Soccio, Anna Enrichetta. Secrecy and revelation in George Meredith's *Lord Ormont and His Aminta*. RSV (18/19) 2004/05, 109–20.

'Owen Meredith' (Edward Robert Bulwer Lytton, First Earl of Lytton) (1831–1891)

10920. Purton, Valerie. Dickens, Robert Lytton and a newly discovered letter. *See* **9807**.

10921. Woodworth, Elizabeth. Elizabeth Barrett Browning, Coventry Patmore, and Alfred Tennyson on Napoleon III: the hero-poet and Carlylean heroics. *See* **9271**.

Alice Meynell

10922. Austin, Linda M. Self against childhood: the contributions of Alice Meynell to a psycho-physiology of memory. VLC (34:1) 2006, 249–68.

10923. Peterson, Linda H. Alice Meynell's *Preludes*; or, Preludes to what future poetry? VLC (34:2) 2006, 405–26.

10924. Seeley, Tracy. 'The fair light mystery of images': Alice Meynell's metaphysical turn. VLC (34:2) 2006, 663–84.

John Stuart Mill

10925. Capaldi, Nicholas. John Stuart Mill: a biography. (Bibl. 2005, 11722.) Rev. by Linda C. Raeder in ANQ (19:1) 2006, 62–6.

W. T. (William Thomas) Moncrieff (1794–1857)

10926. Bolton, Betsy. Saving the rajah's daughter: spectacular logic in Moncrieff's *Cataract of the Ganges*. ERR (17:4) 2006, 477–93.

10927. Wiltshire, Irene. *Pickwick* and the pirates. *See* **9839**.

Thomas Moore (1779–1852)

10928. Langan, Celeste. Scotch drink & Irish harps: mediations of the national air. *In* (pp. 25–49) **8828**.

10929. Ward, Sam. Melodies in the marketplace: John Clare's 100 songs. *See* **9484**.

Lady Morgan (Sydney Owenson)

10930. Dornan, Stephen. Beyond the Milesian pale: the poetry of James Orr. *See* **8030**.

10931. Franklin, Michael J. 'Passion's empire': Sydney Owenson's 'Indian venture', Phoenicianism, Orientalism, and binarism. SR (45:2) 2006, 181–97.

10932. Ó Gallchoir, Clíona. *Uncle Tom's Cabin* and the Irish national tale. *In* (pp. 24–45) **11355**.

10933. Smith, James M. Two Irish national tales: complete texts with introduction, historical contexts, critical essays. Introd. by Vera Kreilkamp. *See* **10003**.

James Morier

10934. Manning, Peter J. The Persian Wordsworth. *See* **11693**.

William Morris (1834–1896)

10935. Amison, Anne. An unexpected guest. *See* **18775**.

10936. Arata, Stephen. Stevenson, Morris, and the value of idleness. *In* (pp. 3–12) **11272**.

10937. Beaumont, Matthew. Shopping in utopia: *Looking Backward*, the department store, and the dreamscape of consumption. *See* **9122**.

10938. Boos, Florence S. Guide to the year's work: the Pre-Raphaelites. *See* **11106**.

10939. Cloonan, Michele V. Alice Millard and the gospel of beauty and taste. *In* (pp. 159–78) **690**.

10940. Faulkner, Peter. William Morris and the *Scrutiny* tradition. JWMS (16:4) 2006, 27–46.

10941. Gadoin, Isabelle, *et al.* (eds). News from nowhere. Paris: Ellipses, 2004. pp. 230. (CAPES agrégation anglais.) Rev. by Trevor Harris in JWMS (16:2/3) 2005, 105–7.

10942. Kawabata, Yasuo. Kenji Ohtsuki and the Tokyo centenary of the birth of William Morris. JWMS (16:4) 2006, 5–26.

10943. Latham, David; Latham, Sheila. William Morris: an annotated bibliography 2002–2003. JWMS (16:4) 2006, 49–76.

10944. Leighton, Angela. Buried deep: the wandering ghosts behind Dante Gabriel Rossetti's words. *See* **11101**.

10945. LeMire, Eugene D. A bibliography of William Morris. New Castle, DE: Oak Knoll Press; London: British Library, 2006. pp. lxvi, 386. Rev. by Robert Coupe in JWMS (16:4) 2006, 77–81.

10946. Mezzetti Radaelli, Monia. Considerazioni su un toponimo: *No-where* o *Now-here*? RSV (18/19) 2004/05, 195–204.

10947. Mougnibas, Jean-Claude. Le texte comme simple émanation d'un contexte: étude du manifeste fondateur de la Society for the Protection of Ancient Buildings. CVE (63) 2006, 419–32.

10948. Pinkney, Tony (ed.). We met Morris: interviews with William Morris, 1885–96. (Bibl. 2005, 11751.) Rev. by Martin Delveaux in JWMS (16:4) 2006, 81–6.

10949. Stetz, Margaret. 'Caught in the trap': William Morris, machinery, and popular film from Charlie Chaplin to Nick Park. JPRS (15:1) 2006, 61–73.

10950. Waithe, Marcus. The laws of hospitality: liberty, generosity, and the limits of dissent in William Morris's *The Tables Turned* and *News from Nowhere*. YES (36:2) 2006, 212–29.

10951. —— William Morris's utopia of strangers: Victorian medievalism and the ideal of hospitality. Woodbridge, Suffolk; Rochester, NY: Brewer, 2006. pp. xv, 218. (English Assn studies.)

Anna Cora Mowatt

10952. Macki, Adrienne. Challenging gendered spaces: Anna Cora Mowatt's courageous story. NETJ (16) 2005, 1–20.

Anne Mozley (1809–1891)

10953. Wilkes, Joanne. 'Clever women': Anne Mozley, Jane Austen, and Charlotte Brontë. *In* (pp. 297–308) **8374**.

John Muir (1838–1914)

10954. Gifford, Terry. Reconnecting with John Muir: essays in post-pastoral practice. Athens; London: Georgia UP, 2006. pp. x, 201.

Mary Noailles Murfree ('Charles Egbert Craddock')

10955. Satterwhite, Emily. Reading Craddock, reading Murfree: local color, authenticity, and geographies of reception. AL (78:1) 2006, 59–88.

Frederic W. H. Myers

10956. Brocklebank, Lisa. Psychic reading. VS (48:2) 2006, 233–9.

Constance Naden

10957. LAPORTE, CHARLES. Atheist prophecy: Mathilde Blind, Constance Naden, and the Victorian poetess. *See* **9130**.

10958. MURPHY, PATRICIA. In science's shadow: literary constructions of late Victorian women. *See* **10304**.

10959. TANGE, ANDREA KASTON. Constance Naden and the erotics of evolution: mating the woman of letters with the man of science. NineL (61:2) 2006, 200–40.

John Henry Newman

10960. DAU, DUC. Perfect chastity: celibacy and virgin marriage in Tractarian poetry. VP (44:1) 2006, 77–92.

10961. KENNY, ANTHONY. The long goodbye. TLS, 15 Dec. 2006, 12–13 (review-article). (Newman's letters and diaries.)

10962. MCGRATH, FRANCIS J. (ed.). The letters and diaries of John Henry Newman: vol. 10, The final step, 1 November 1843 – 6 October 1845. Oxford; New York: OUP, 2006. pp. 1010. Rev. by Anthony Kenny in TLS, 15 Dec. 2006, 12–13.

10963. —— (ed.); TRACEY, GERARD (asst ed.). The letters and diaries of John Henry Newman: vol. 9, Littlemore and the parting of friends, May 1842 – October 1843. Oxford; New York: OUP, 2006. pp. xxxix, 833. Rev. by Ian Ker in TLS, 27 Oct. 2006, 30.

10964. SCHLATTER, FREDRIC W. George Teeling: mutual friend of Newman and Hopkins. *See* **10488**.

Hume Nisbet (1849–1921?)

10965. WEVERS, LYDIA. Becoming native: Australian novelists and the New Zealand Wars. *See* **9145**.

Mrs (Margaret) Oliphant (1828–1897)

10966. JONES, WENDY. Consensual fictions: women, liberalism, and the English novel. *See* **8656**.

10967. O'GORMAN, FRANCIS. 'Amiable but determined autocracy': Margaret Oliphant, Venice, and the inheritance of Ruskin. *In* (pp. 183–200) **8320**.

10968. ROBINSON, SOLVEIG C. 'At all times conspicuous as art': Henry James, Margaret Oliphant, and resistance to Decadence. *In* (pp. 97–108) **10568**.

10969. STYLER, REBECCA. 'What does it matter?': Margaret Oliphant's spiritual autobiography, 1899 and 1990. *In* (pp. 13–22) **3407**.

Amelia Opie

10970. SALIH, SARA. The silence of Miss Lambe: *Sanditon* and fictions of 'race' in the Abolition era. *See* **9068**.

10971. WALLACE, MIRIAM L. (ed.). *The Memoirs of Emma Courtney* by Mary Hays; and *Adeline Mowbray; or, The Mother and the Daughter*, by Amelia Alderson Opie. *See* **7865**.

Lloyd Osbourne

10972. HIRSCH, GORDON. Tontines, tontine insurance, and commercial culture: Stevenson and Osbourne's *The Wrong Box*. *In* (pp. 83–94) **11272**.

Thomas Nelson Page

10973. Jones, Gwendolyn. Virginia writers in the New South: Thomas Nelson Page, Ellen Glasgow, and Mary Johnson. *See* **16129**.

Francis Turner Palgrave

10974. Fontana, Ernest L. Kingsley's *Ode to the North-East Wind* and Frost's *To the Thawing Wind*. *See* **16001**.

Walter Pater

10975. Cabus-Coldwell, Andrea. Figuring the princess: *The Princess Casamassima* and Pater's *Mona Lisa*. *In* (pp. 123–33) **10568**.

10976. Camlot, Jason. The Victorian critic as naturalizing agent. *See* **8947**.

10977. Coates, John. The hidden laughter of women: an aspect of Pater's sensibility. NCP (33:1) 2006, 166–95.

10978. Evangelista, Stefano. 'Lovers and philosophers at once': aesthetic Platonism in the Victorian *fin de siècle*. YES (36:2) 2006, 230–44.

10979. Gillard-Estrada, Anne-Florence. Les dialogues de Walter Pater avec Platon le philosophe et l'amoureux. CVE (63) 2006, 387–402.

10980. Lambert-Charbonnier, Martine. Walter Pater et les 'portraits imaginaires': images de la culture et images de soi. Paris: L'Harmattan, 2004. pp. 300. (Critiques littéraires.) Rev. by Gilbert Pham-Thanh in CVE (62) 2005, 211–14; by Alain Jumeau in EA (59:3) 2006, 366–8.

10981. Leighton, Angela. Resurrections of the body: women writers and the idea of the Renaissance. *In* (pp. 222–38) **8320**.

10982. Love, Heather K. Forced exile: Walter Pater's queer modernism. *In* (pp. 19–43) **12024**.

10983. Natarajan, Uttara. Pater and the genealogy of Hardy's modernity. *See* **10306**.

10984. Pigeon, Elaine. (Homo)sexuality and Impressionism in Henry James's *The Ambassadors*. *In* (pp. 121–32) **8418**.

10985. Rosenfeld, Natania. Less light: the end(s) of Aestheticism in Pater, Ondaatje, and Sebald. Mod/Mod (13:2) 2006, 349–66.

Coventry Patmore

10986. Heiniger, Abigail. The faery and the beast. *See* **9187**.

10987. Hurley, Michael D. Darkening the subject of Hopkins' prosody. *See* **10475**.

10988. Woodworth, Elizabeth. Elizabeth Barrett Browning, Coventry Patmore, and Alfred Tennyson on Napoleon III: the hero-poet and Carlylean heroics. *See* **9271**.

James Kirke Paulding

10989. Spradlin, Derrick. Westward expansion, Indian subjugation, and the frontier gazes of Jackson Johonnet, Zebulon Montgomery Pike, and James Kirk Paulding. EArtsS (34:1) 2005, 39–50.

Elizabeth Palmer Peabody

10990. Avallone, Charlene. Elizabeth Palmer Peabody and the 'art' of conversation. *In* (pp. 23–44) **10790**.

10991. Earhart, Amy. Elizabeth Peabody on the 'temperament of the colored classes': African Americans, progressive history, and education in a democratic system. *In* (pp. 77–90) **10790**.

10992. Elbert, Monika M. Elizabeth Palmer Peabody's problematic feminism and the feminization of Transcendentalism. *In* (pp. 199–215) **10790**.

10993. —— Hall, Julie E.; Rodier, Katharine (eds). Reinventing the Peabody sisters. *See* **10790**.

10994. Marshall, Megan. Elizabeth Palmer Peabody: the first Transcendentalist? MaHR (8) 2006, 1–15.

10995. —— The Peabody sisters as sisters. *In* (pp. 248–58) **10790**.

10996. —— The Peabody sisters: three women who ignited American Romanticism. *See* **10794**.

10997. Rodier, Katharine. Authorizing Sarah Winnemucca? Elizabeth Peabody and Mary Peabody Mann. *In* (pp. 108–25) **10790**.

10998. Ronda, Bruce A. Elizabeth Peabody and the fate of Transcendentalism. *In* (pp. 232–47) **10790**.

10999. Vasquez, Mark. Declaration and defence: Elizabeth Palmer Peabody, Mary Peabody Mann, and the complex rhetoric of mediation. *In* (pp. 45–58) **10790**.

George W. Peck

11000. Stinson, Emmett. Dark pleasures. Meanjin (65:2) 2006, 181–6.

Watts Phillips (1825–1874)

11001. Tetens, Kristan. Commemorating the French Revolution on the Victorian stage: Henry Irving's *The Dead Heart*. *See* **11057**.

Sarah Morgan Piatt (Sarah Morgan Bryan)

11002. Giordano, Matthew. 'A lesson from' the magazines: Sarah Piatt and the postbellum periodical poet. AmP (16:1) 2006, 23–51.

11003. Hall, Susan Grove. From voice to persona: Amelia Welby's lyric tradition in Sarah M. B. Piatt's early poetry. TSWL (25:2) 2006, 223–46.

11004. Wearn, Mary McCartin. Subjection and subversion in Sarah Piatt's maternal poetics. Legacy (23:2) 2006, 163–77.

Edgar Allan Poe

11005. Acton, Tom. Ved Dzabqu qd vnh Urod. *See* **14886**.

11006. Cagliero, Roberto (ed.). Fantastico Poe. (Bibl. 2004, 11813.) Rev. by Maria Truglio in EAPR (6:1) 2005, 57–9.

11007. Chu, Seo-Young Jennie. Hypnotic ratiocination. EAPR (6:1) 2005, 5–19.

11008. Church, Joseph. 'To make Venus vanish': misogyny as motive in Poe's *Murders in the Rue Morgue*. ATQ (20:2) 2006, 407–18.

11009. Doctorow, E. L. Our Edgar. VQR (82:4) 2006, 241–7. (Lawrence on Poe.)

11010. Drain, Kim. Poe's death-watches and the architecture of doubt. NER (27:2) 2006, 169–77. (Revaluations.)

11011. Ehrlich, Heyward. Poe in cyberspace. EAPR (6:2) 2005, 56–64.

11012. Faherty, Duncan. 'A certain unity of design': Edgar Allan Poe's *Tales of the Grotesque and Arabesque* and the terrors of Jacksonian democracy. EAPR (6:2) 2005, 4–21.

11013. Fargione, Daniela. Giardini e labirinti: l'America di Edgar Allan Poe. Turin: CELID, 2005. pp. 94. (Letteratura.)

11014. Fisher, Benjamin F. (ed.). The essential tales and poems of Edgar Allan Poe. New York: Barnes & Noble, 2004. pp. xlv, 642. Rev. by Peter Norberg in EAPR (6:1) 2005, 51–2.

11015. Gold, Joshua Robert. The dwarf in the machine: a theological figure and its sources. MLN (121:5) 2006, 1220–36.

11016. Grimstad, Paul. C. Auguste Dupin and Charles S. Peirce: an abductive affinity. EAPR (6:2) 2005, 22–30.

11017. Gruesser, John C. Madmen and moonbeams: the narrator in *The Fall of the House of Usher.* EAPR (5:1) 2004, 80–90.

11018. Gwynn, R. S. Haunted palaces, trembling strings. SewR (114:4) 2006, 578–87. (State of letters.)

11019. Harpham, Geoffrey Galt. On the grotesque: strategies of contradiction in art and literature. *See* **9215**.

11020. Harrington, Maura Grace. 'My narrative': the story of the non-disinterested narrator in Poe's *Hop-Frog.* EAPR (5:1) 2004, 91–9.

11021. Hecker, William F. (ed.). Private Perry and Mister Poe: the West Point poems, 1831. (Bibl. 2005, 11814.) Rev. by Benjamin F. Fisher in EAPR (6:2) 2005, 47–9; by Jeffrey C. Alfier in WLA (18:1/2) 2006, 348–9.

11022. Hoffman, Daniel. Returns from the grave: the spirit of Poe in contemporary fiction. EAPR (5:1) 2004, 6–15.

11023. Hughes, James. Those who passed through: unusual visits to unlikely places – Edgar Allen Poe. NYH (87:2) 2006, 249–53.

11024. Hutchisson, James M. Poe. (Bibl. 2005, 11815.) Rev. by Kevin J. Hayes in EAPR (6:2) 2005, 43–6; by H. A. Scott Trask in Chronicles (30:3) 2006, 29–30; by Mary Weaks-Baxter in JSH (72:4) 2006, 937–8.

11025. Kennedy, J. Gerald. Poe, Fitzgerald, and the American Nightmare. EAPR (5:2) 2004, 4–14.

11026. Kimball, A. Samuel. D-ciphering Dupin's fac-simile signature: the infanticidal implications of a '*dessein si funeste*'. EAPR (6:1) 2005, 20–36.

11027. Lanati, Barbara. Ottocento e dintorni: E. A. Poe, W. Whitman, H. Melville, N. Hawthorne. Turin: CELID, 2006. pp. 152. (Letteratura.)

11028. Levine, Stuart; Levine, Susan F. (eds). Eureka. (Bibl. 2004, 11835.) Rev. by Barbara Cantalupo in EAPR (6:1) 2005, 53–4.

11029. Lindner, April. Interview with Dana Gioia. EAPR (6:1) 2005, 37–46.

11030. McArthur, Debra. A student's guide to Edgar Allan Poe. Berkeley Heights, NJ: Enslow, 2006. pp. 160. (Understanding literature.)

11031. McNutt, Donald J. Urban revelations: images of ruin in the American city, 1790–1860. *See* **9243**.

11032. Marsh, Clayton. Stealing time: Poe's confidence men and the '*rush* of the age'. AL (77:2) 2005, 259–89.

11033. Mills, Bruce. Poe, Fuller, and the mesmeric arts: transition states in the American renaissance. *See* **10146**.

11034. Minato, Keiji. Poe and the position of the poet in contemporary Japan. EAPR (5:1) 2004, 29–46.

11035. Osipova, Elvira. The reception of *Eureka* in Russia. EAPR (5:1) 2004, 16–28.

11036. Pánková, Lenka. The for-ever reverberating 'Never more': what do *The Raven's* multiple translations in Czech signify for translation theory? EAPR (5:1) 2004, 100–8.

11037. Peeples, Scott. The afterlife of Edgar Allan Poe. (Bibl. 2005, 11819.) Rev. by Nina Baym in AL (77:2) 2005, 414–16; by Alexander Hammond in EAPR (6:2) 2005, 39–42.

11038. Pollin, Burton R. Kilmer's promotion of Poe. SoQ (44:1) 2006, 120–50.

11039. —— Poe and Ray Bradbury: a persistent influence and interest. EAPR (6:2) 2005, 31–8.

11040. —— Poe's seductive influence on great writers. New York: IUniverse, 2004. pp. x, 262. Rev. by Heyward Ehrlich in EAPR (5:2) 2004, 48–53.

11041. —— When is a Church not a Church? EAPR (5:1) 2004, 47–56. (Illustrator Frederick Stuart Church and painter Frederic Edwin Church.)

11042. Ralickas, Vivian. The abject sublime in Poe. *In* (pp. 41–58) **8418**.

11043. Randall, Warren. A study in stanzas: Arthurs, authors, and poetry. *See* **9950**.

11044. Richards, Eliza. Gender and the poetics of reception in Poe's circle. (Bibl. 2005, 11823.) Rev. by Mary F. Brewer in JAStud (40:1) 2006, 196.

11045. Rohy, Valerie. Ahistorical. GLQ (12:1) 2006, 61–83. (*Ligeia*.)

11046. Savoye, Jeffrey A. Two biographical digressions: Poe's wandering trunk and Dr Carter's mysterious sword cane. EAPR (5:2) 2004, 14–42.

11047. Scharnhorst, Gary. The history of a letter: Edgar Allan Poe to Joseph M. Field in 1846. ANQ (19:4) 2006, 26–9.

11048. Schiavini, Cinzia. My city of ruins: American topographies and European heritage in Herman Melville and Edgar Allan Poe's urban landscape. *See* **10894**.

11049. Shear, Walter. Poe's fiction: the hypnotic magic of the senses. MidQ (47:3) 2006, 276–89.

11050. Stashower, Daniel. Edgar Allan Poe and the murder of Mary Rogers. Banbury, Oxon.: Oneworld, 2006. pp. 326.

11051. Thompson, G. R. (ed.). The selected writings of Edgar Allan Poe: authoritative texts, backgrounds and contexts, criticism. (Bibl. 2004, 11864.) Rev. by Kent P. Ljungquist in EAPR (6:1) 2005, 47–50.

11052. Walters, C. T. *The Philosophy of Furniture* and Poe's aesthetics of fictional design. EAPR (5:1) 2004, 57–79.

11053. Willis, Martin. Mesmerists, monsters, and machines: science fiction and the cultures of science in the nineteenth century. *See* **11200**.

11054. Woolf, Paul. Prostitutes, Paris, and Poe: the sexual economy of Edgar Allan Poe's *The Murders in the Rue Morgue*. Clues (25:1) 2006, 6–19.

John Polidori

11055. Bainbridge, Simon. Lord Ruthven's power: Polidori's *The Vampyre*, doubles and the Byronic imagination. BJ (34:1) 2006, 21–34.

11056. Bishop, Franklin Charles (ed.). *The Vampyre* and other writings. (Bibl. 2005, 11828.) Rev. by Max Fincher in TLS, 17 Feb. 2006, 37.

Walter Herries Pollock (1850–1926)

11057. Tetens, Kristan. Commemorating the French Revolution on the Victorian stage: Henry Irving's *The Dead Heart*. NCT (32:2) 2005, 36–69.

Jane Porter

11058. Looser, Devoney. Another Jane: Jane Porter, Austen's contemporary. *In* (pp. 235–48) **8374**.

11059. Price, Fiona. Resisting 'the spirit of innovation': the other historical novel and Jane Porter. MLR (101:3) 2006, 638–51.

Howard Pyle

11060. Davis, Paul Preston (ed.). Howard Pyle: his life, his work: a comprehensive bibliography and pictorial record of Howard Pyle, illustrator, author, teacher, father of American illustration, America's foremost illustrator. Preface by Stephen T. Bruni. Foreword by Howard Pyle Brokaw. New Castle, DE: Oak Knoll Press, 2004. pp. xiii, 872. Rev. by S. L. Harrison in SHARP (15:2/3) 2006, 14–15.

11061. May, Jill P. James Barrie's pirates: *Peter Pan*'s place in pirate history and lore. *In* (pp. 69–78) **14616**.

Dollie Radford

11062. Livesey, Ruth. Dollie Radford and the ethical aesthetics of *fin-de-siècle* poetry. VLC (34:2) 2006, 495–517.

Charles Reade

11063. Bury, Laurent. Jusqu'où faut-il aller trop loin: Charles Reade, une esthétique de l'excès. CVE (63) 2006, 33–47.

11064. Fantina, Richard. 'Chafing at the social cobwebs': gender and transgender in the work of Charles Reade. *In* (pp. 126–37) **8647**.

11065. Murphy, Patricia. In science's shadow: literary constructions of late Victorian women. *See* **10304**.

11066. Vitanza, Diana. Naturalism in Charles Reade's experimental novel *Griffith Gaunt*. *In* (pp. 64–73) **8647**.

Frederic Mansel Reynolds (d.1850)

11067. Feldman, Paula R. (introd.). *The Keepsake* for 1829. *See* **1096**.

John Rollin Ridge (Yellow Bird) (1827–1867)

11068. WHITLEY, EDWARD. 'The first white aboriginal': Walt Whitman and John Rollin Ridge. *See* **11588**.

Anne Thackeray Ritchie

11069. JAY, ELISABETH. 'In her father's steps she trod': Anne Thackeray Ritchie imagining Paris. YES (36:2) 2006, 197–211.

Sir Charles G. D. Roberts

11070. WHALEN, TERRY (ed.). Selected animal stories: a critical edition. Ottawa: Tecumseh Press, 2005. pp. vii, 327.

A. Mary F. (Agnes Mary Frances) Robinson (Mary Duclaux) (1857–1944)

11071. HARRINGTON, EMILY. The strain of sympathy: A. Mary F. Robinson, *The New Arcadia*, and Vernon Lee. NineL (61:1) 2006, 66–98.

11072. PRINS, YOPIE. 'Lady's Greek' (with the accents): a metrical translation of Euripides by A. Mary F. Robinson. VLC (34:2) 2006, 591–618.

Henry Crabb Robinson

11073. WU, DUNCAN. The Lamb circle and the *Monthly Repository*. *See* **10707**.

'Rosa Matilda' (Charlotte Dacre)

11074. BEAUVAIS, JENNIFER. Domesticity and the female demon in Charlotte Dacre's *Zofloya* and Emily Brontë's *Wuthering Heights*. *See* **9211**.

11075. HOEVELER, DIANE LONG. Charlotte Dacre's Zofloya: the gothic demonization of the Jew. *In* (pp. 165–78) **8523**.

11076. SMITH, MARIE HOCKENHULL. The children will be 'subject to the infamy of their deluded and unfortunate mother': rhetoric of the courtroom, a gothic fantasy and a plain letter to the Lord Chancellor. LawL (18:3) 2006, 403–30. (*Zofloya*.)

Christina Rossetti

11077. ARSENEAU, MARY. Recovering Christina Rossetti: female community and Incarnational poetics. (Bibl. 2004, 11899.) Rev. by Linda E. Marshall in JPRS (15:2) 2006, 77–9.

11078. D'AMICO, DIANE. Christina Rossetti's breast cancer: 'another matter, painful to dwell upon'. JPRS (15:2) 2006, 29–50.

11079. —— KENT, DAVID A. Rossetti and the Tractarians. VP (44:1) 2006, 93–103.

11080. DIELEMAN, KAREN. Christina Rossetti, the communion of saints and *Verses*. JPRS (15:1) 2006, 27–49.

11081. FABB, NIGEL; HALLE, MORRIS. Metrical complexity in Christina Rossetti's verse. ColLit (33:2) 2006, 91–114.

11082. FONTANA, ERNEST L. Victorian doors. PhilL (30:1) 2006, 277–88.

11083. HARRISON, ANTONY H. (ed.). The letters of Christina Rossetti: vol. 4, 1887–1894. (Bibl. 2005, 11859.) Rev. by Linda E. Marshall in JPRS (15:2) 2006, 72–7.

11084. Hassett, Constance W. Christina Rossetti: the patience of style. Charlottesville; London: Virginia UP, 2005. pp. xiii, 276. (Victorian literature and culture.) Rev. by Roderick McGillis in CLAQ (31:2) 2006, 211–16; by Linda E. Marshall in JPRS (15:2) 2006, 79–81; by Julie Melnyk in VS (49:1) 2006, 122–4; by Lorraine Janzen Kooistra in NineL (61:1) 2006, 117–20.

11085. Hill, Marylu. 'Eat me, drink me, love me': Eucharist and the erotic body in Christina Rossetti's *Goblin Market*. VP (43:4) 2005, 455–72.

11086. Ives, Maura. The letters of Christina Rossetti: two new letters. JPRS (15:1) 2006, 19–26.

11087. Leighton, Angela. Buried deep: the wandering ghosts behind Dante Gabriel Rossetti's words. *See* **11101**.

11088. Mason, Emma. The trouble with comfort: Christina Rossetti, John Ruskin, and leafy emotion. YES (36:2) 2006, 169–79.

11089. Mendoza, Victor Roman. 'Come buy': the crossing of sexual and consumer desire in Christina Rossetti's *Goblin Market*. ELH (73:4) 2006, 913–47.

11090. Morrison, Kevin A. Gabriele Rossetti's life and studies: a source for Christina Rossetti's *Winter: My Secret*? ELN (43:2) 2005, 159–66.

11091. Nixon, Jude V. 'Goldengrove unleaving': Hopkins' *Spring and Fall*, Christina Rossetti's *Mirrors of Life and Death*, and the politics of inclusion. *See* **10482**.

11092. Raymond, Claire. The posthumous voice in women's writing from Mary Shelley to Sylvia Plath. *See* **11192**.

11093. Roe, Dinah. Christina Rossetti's faithful imagination: the devotional poetry and prose. Basingstoke; New York: Palgrave Macmillan, 2006. pp. xi, 220.

11094. Wei, Yeo Wei. *Monna Innominata* and Christina Rossetti's audible unhappiness. *In* (pp. 174–93) **8828**.

11095. Welter, Nancy. Women alone: Le Fanu's *Carmilla* and Rossetti's *Goblin Market*. *In* (pp. 138–48) **8647**.

Dante Gabriel Rossetti

11096. Fontana, Ernest. Pre-facing simile vehicles in Dante Gabriel Rossetti's sonnets. Style (39:4) 2005, 440–7.

11097. Fredeman, William E. (ed.). The correspondence of Dante Gabriel Rossetti: the Chelsea years, 1863–1872: vol. 4, Prelude to crisis: 1868–1870. Woodbridge, Suffolk; Rochester, NY: Brewer, 2004. pp. xxxiv, 573. Rev. by David G. Riede in VP (43:2) 2005, 263–6; by Angela Leighton in TLS, 18 & 25 Aug. 2006, 3–4; by Peter Faulkner in JWMS (16:4) 2006, 96–8.

11098. —— The correspondence of Dante Gabriel Rossetti: the Chelsea years, 1863–1872: vol. 5, Prelude to crisis: 1871–1872. Completed by Roger C. Lewis, *et al*. Woodbridge, Suffolk; Rochester, NY: Brewer, 2005. pp. xxxiv, 676. Rev. by Angela Leighton in TLS, 18 & 25 Aug. 2006, 3–4; by Peter Faulkner in JWMS (16:4) 2006, 96–8.

11099. —— The correspondence of Dante Gabriel Rossetti: the last decade, 1873–1882: vol. 6, Kelmscott to Birchington, 1873–1874. Completed by

Roger C. Lewis, *et al.* Woodbridge, Suffolk; Rochester, NY: Brewer in assn with the Modern Humanities Research Assn, 2006. pp. 436.

11100. Holmes, John. Dante Gabriel Rossetti and the late Victorian sonnet sequence: sexuality, belief and the self. (Bibl. 2005, 11870.) Rev. by Joe Phelan in TLS, 3 Mar. 2006, 32–3; by Natalie M. Houston in RES (57:231) 2006, 553–4; by Annie Escuret in CVE (63) 2006, 500–1; by David E. Riede in JPRS (15:2) 2006, 85–8.

11101. Leighton, Angela. Buried deep: the wandering ghosts behind Dante Gabriel Rossetti's words. TLS, 18 & 25 Aug. 2006, 3–4 (review-article).

11102. Ormond, Leonée. Dante Gabriel Rossetti and the Old Masters. YES (36:2) 2006, 153–68.

11103. Rivers, Bryan. The 'fiery serpent': typological topography in Dante Rossetti's *Jenny*. JPRS (15:2) 2006, 5–13.

11104. Roussillon-Constanty, Laurence. Texte, trame, signe: les ficelles de l'art selon Dante Gabriel Rossetti. CVE (63) 2006, 433–45.

11105. Weliver, Phyllis. The 'silent song' of D. G. Rossetti's *The House of Life*. *In* (pp. 194–212) **8828**.

The Rossettis

11106. Boos, Florence S. Guide to the year's work: the Pre-Raphaelites. VP (44:3) 2006, 364–75.

María Amparo Ruiz de Burton (1832–1895)

11107. Deines, Timothy. Interrogating the moral contract in Ruiz de Burton's *The Squatter and the Don*. YREAL (22) 2006, 269–91.

11108. de la Luz Montes, Amelia María; Goldman, Anne Elizabeth (eds). María Amparo Ruiz de Burton: critical and pedagogical perspectives. (Bibl. 2005, 11885.) Rev. by María C. González in WAL (41:2) 2006, 220–2.

11109. Gillman, Susan. Adaptation and Americas Studies. *See* **10525**.

John Ruskin

11110. Bashant, Wendy. Aesthetes and queens: Michael Field, John Ruskin, and *Bellerophôn*. *See* **10126**.

11111. Birch, Dinah. 'Who wants authority?': Ruskin as a Dissenter. YES (36:2) 2006, 65–77.

11112. —— (ed.). Selected writings. Oxford; New York: OUP, 2004. pp. xxxviii, 324. (Oxford world's classics.) Rev. by Marcus Waithe in MLR (101:3) 2006, 834–5.

11113. Casaliggi, C. The physicality and metaphysicality of water in Ruskin's *Modern Painters* I. Acme (59:1) 2006, 171–88.

11114. Cloonan, Michele V. Alice Millard and the gospel of beauty and taste. *In* (pp. 159–78) **690**.

11115. Coyle, John. Ruskin, Proust and the art of failure. EC (56:1) 2006, 28–49.

11116. Craig, David Melville. John Ruskin and the ethics of consumption. Charlottesville; London: Virginia UP, 2006. pp. x, 422. (Studies in religion and culture.)

11117. DETTMAR, KEVIN J. H. Bookcases, slipcases, uncut leaves: the anxiety of the gentleman's library. *See* **312**.

11118. LENG, ANDREW. Recontextualizing 'The Two Boyhoods': Ruskin, Thornbury and the double lives of Turner. PrSt (28:1) 2006, 54–73.

11119. MASON, EMMA. The trouble with comfort: Christina Rossetti, John Ruskin, and leafy emotion. *See* **11088**.

11120. MOUGNIBAS, JEAN-CLAUDE. Le texte comme simple émanation d'un contexte: étude du manifeste fondateur de la Society for the Protection of Ancient Buildings. *See* **10947**.

11121. O'GORMAN, FRANCIS. 'Amiable but determined autocracy': Margaret Oliphant, Venice, and the inheritance of Ruskin. *In* (pp. 183–200) **8320**.

11122. —— Ruskin, Venice, and the endurance of authorship. NCS (19) 2005, 83–97.

11123. QUINN, PETER. 'Their strongest pine': Thomas Bewick and regional identity in the late nineteenth century. *In* (pp. 111–30) **56**.

11124. ROBINSON, ALAN. Crystal Palace, Crouch End and Camberwell: John Ruskin and George Gissing on mass culture in late Victorian London. *In* (pp. 203–20) **7343**.

11125. ROSENFELD, NATANIA. Less light: the end(s) of Aestheticism in Pater, Ondaatje, and Sebald. *See* **10985**.

11126. SOCCIO, ANNA ENRICHETTA. The (im)perfect ladies: modelli di femminilità in *Great Expectations*. *In* (pp. 113–24) **9791**.

11127. WARDI, EYNEL. Hopkins the Romantic? The question of empathy in *Spring and Fall*. *See* **10494**.

Dora Russell (1830–1905)

11128. MAUNDER, ANDREW (gen. ed.). Newspaper sensationalism: Dora Russell, *Beneath the Wave* (1878). Ed. by Graham Law. London; Brookfield, VT: Pickering & Chatto, 2004. pp. xliv, 347. (Varieties of women's sensation fiction 1855–1890, 6.) Rev. by Anthea Trodd in VicR (31:2) 2005, 132–4.

Abram Joseph Ryan (1836–1886)

11129. O'CONNELL, DAVID. Furl that banner: the life of Abram J. Ryan, poet–priest of the South. Macon, GA: Mercer UP, 2006. pp. xvii, 251.

Robert H. Scott (*fl.*1895)

11130. WEVERS, LYDIA. Becoming native: Australian novelists and the New Zealand Wars. *See* **9145**.

Sir Walter Scott

11131. BURSTEIN, MIRIAM ELIZABETH. Narrating women's history in Britain, 1770–1902. *See* **10009**.

11132. CALDER, JENNI. Figures in a landscape: Scott, Stevenson, and routes to the past. *In* (pp. 121–32) **11272**.

11133. DAHLINGER, S. E. Some observations upon the segregation of the Bea (*sic*). *See* **9933**.

11134. Dawson, Terence. The effective protagonist in the nineteenth-century British novel: Scott, Brontë, Eliot, Wilde. (Bibl. 2005, 11912.) Rev. by Marcus Waithe in YES (36:2) 2006, 274–5.

11135. Dekker, George G. The fictions of Romantic tourism: Radcliffe, Scott, and Mary Shelley. *See* **8085**.

11136. Elbert, Monika. Nature, magic, and history in Stowe and Scott. *In* (pp. 46–64) **11355**.

11137. Ferguson, Stuart. The imaginative construction of historical character: what Georg Lukács and Walter Scott could tell contemporary novelists. ScSR (6:2) 2005, 32–48.

11138. Ferris, Ina. Printing the past: Walter Scott's Bannatyne Club and the antiquarian document. Romanticism (11:2) 2005, 143–60.

11139. Fulford, Tim. Romantic Indians and their inventors. *See* **8367**.

11140. Henderson, Diana E. Collaborations with the past: reshaping Shakespeare across time and media. *See* **5324**.

11141. Hewitt, David; Lumsden, Alison (eds). The heart of Mid-lothian. Edinburgh: Edinburgh UP, 2004. pp. xvi, 770. (Edinburgh ed. of the Waverley novels.) Rev. by Meiko O'Halloran in SHogg (16) 2005, 175–7.

11142. Hewitt, Regina. Symbolic interactions: social problems and literary interventions in the works of Baillie, Scott, and Landor. *See* **9105**.

11143. Knight, Stephen. Remembering Robin Hood: five centuries of outlaw ideology. *See* **3052**.

11144. Krull, Andrew D. Spectacles of disaffection: politics, ethics, and sentiment in Walter Scott's *Old Mortality*. ELH (73:3) 2006, 695–727.

11145. Lewin, Judith. Jewish heritage and secular inheritance in Walter Scott's *Ivanhoe*. ANQ (19:1) 2006, 27–33.

11146. McCracken-Flesher, Caroline. Possible Scotlands: Walter Scott and the story of tomorrow. Oxford; New York: OUP, 2005. pp. viii, 225. Rev. by Barton Swaim in TLS, 14 Apr. 2006, 26; by Judith Wilt in SR (45:3) 2006, 483–6.

11147. McMullin, B. J. The eighth edition of Scott's *Lay of the Last Minstrel*. PBSA (100:4) 2006, 447–61.

11148. Maxwell, Richard. A game of yes and no: childhood and apocalypse in *Porius*. *See* **18128**.

11149. Miller, Gavin. National confessions: queer theory meets Scottish literature. ScSR (6:2) 2005, 60–71.

11150. Parrott, Jennifer. 'Slaves of the imagination': Sir Walter Scott in the works of Virginia Woolf. *See* **19316**.

11151. Price, Fiona. Resisting 'the spirit of innovation': the other historical novel and Jane Porter. *See* **11059**.

11152. St Clair, William. But what did we actually read? Literary critics should not lose sight of the sales figures. *See* **865**.

11153. Simons, John. The compositional genetics of *Kingdoms of Elfin* together with a note on tortoises. *In* (pp. 45–60) **18964**.

11154. Simpson, Michael. Wavering on Europe: Walter Scott and the equilibrium of the empires. Romanticism (11:2) 2005, 127–42.

11155. SOUBIGOU, GILLES. French portraits of Sir Walter Scott: images of the great unknown. ScSR (7:1) 2006, 24–37.

11156. STEWART, SUSAN. The ballad in *Wuthering Heights*. *See* **9222**.

11157. SWAIM, BARTON. 'What is Scott?': John Gibson Lockhart's professional amateurism. *See* **10748**.

11158. YAHAV-BROWN, AMIT. Gypsies, nomadism, and the limits of realism. *See* **10062**.

Mary Seacole (1805–1881)

11159. FLUHR, NICOLE. 'Their calling me "mother" was not, I think, altogether unmeaning': Mary Seacole's maternal personae. VLC (34:1) 2006, 95–113.

11160. FORBES, CURDELLA. Selling that Caribbean woman down the river: diasporic travel narratives and the global economy. JWIL (13:1/2) 2005, 1–27.

11161. SALIH, SARA. 'A gallant heart to the empire': autoethnography and imperial identity in Mary Seacole's *Wonderful Adventures*. PQ (83:2) 2004, 171–95.

Catharine Maria Sedgwick

11162. ASHWORTH, SUZANNE. Invalid insurrections: intellect and appetite in Catharine Maria Sedgwick's biography of Lucretia Maria Davidson. *See* **9677**.

11163. AVALLONE, CHARLENE. Catharine Sedgwick and the circles of New York. Legacy (23:2) 2006, 115–31.

11164. BALAAM, PETER. 'Piazza to the north': Melville reading Sedgwick. *In* (pp. 60–81) **10897**.

11165. Ó GALLCHOIR, CLÍONA. *Uncle Tom's Cabin* and the Irish national tale. *In* (pp. 24–45) **11355**.

11166. OSHIMA, YUKIKO. Dreaming a dream of interracial bonds: from *Hope Leslie* to *Moby-Dick*. *In* (pp. 238–51) **10823**.

11167. OUSLEY, LAURIE. The business of housekeeping: the mistress, the domestic worker, and the construction of class. Legacy (23:2) 2006, 132–47.

11168. SCHWEITZER, IVY. Imaginative conjunctions on the imperial 'frontier': Catharine Sedgwick reads Mungo Park. *In* (pp. 126–43) **6224**.

11169. —— Perfecting friendship: politics and affiliation in early American literature. *See* **7197**.

Anna Sewell

11170. DORRÉ, GINA M. Victorian fiction and the cult of the horse. *See* **9736**.

Richard Lalor Sheil (1791–1851)

11171. CONNOLLY, CLAIRE. Theatre and nation in Irish Romanticism: the tragic dramas of Charles Robert Maturin and Richard Lalor Sheil. *See* **10807**.

11172. SAGLIA, DIEGO. 'The illegitimate assistance of political allusion': politics and the hybridization of Romantic tragedy in the drama of Richard Lalor Sheil. TJ (58:2) 2006, 249–67.

Mary Shelley

11173. ACOSTA, ANA M. Reading Genesis in the long eighteenth century: from Milton to Mary Shelley. *See* **6961**.

11174. Benziman, Galia. Challenging the biological: the fantasy of male birth as nineteenth-century narrative of ethical failure. WS (35:4) 2006, 375–95.

11175. Bryant, John. Melville essays the romance: comedy and being in *Frankenstein*, *The Big Bear of Arkansas*, and *Moby-Dick*. *See* **10821**.

11176. Comitini, Patricia. The limits of discourse and the ideology of form in Mary Shelley's *Frankenstein*. KSJ (55) 2006, 179–98.

11177. Dekker, George G. The fictions of Romantic tourism: Radcliffe, Scott, and Mary Shelley. *See* **8085**.

11178. Granata, Silvia. Anatomists and public opinion: literary representations of a troubled relationship. ConLett (45) 2006, 97–115.

11179. Guyer, Sara. Testimony and trope in *Frankenstein*. SR (45:1) 2006, 77–115.

11180. Haggerty, George E. 'Dung, guts and blood': sodomy, abjection and gothic fiction in the early nineteenth century. GothS (8:2) 2006, 35–51.

11181. Hindle, Maurice. Victim of romance: the life and death of Fanny Godwin. *See* **8263**.

11182. Hoobler, Dorothy; Hoobler, Thomas. The monsters: Mary Shelley and the curse of Frankenstein. London; Boston, MA: Little, Brown, 2006. pp. 375. Rev. by Alice K. Turner in BkW, 16 July 2006, 9.

11183. Jones, Jonathan. Hidden voices: language and ideology in philosophy of language of the long eighteenth century and Mary Shelley's *Frankenstein*. TexP (19:3) 2005, 265–87.

11184. Khalip, Jacques. A disappearance in the world: Wollstonecraft and melancholy skepticism. *See* **8268**.

11185. Law, Jules. Being there: gothic violence and virtuality in *Frankenstein*, *Dracula*, and *Strange Days*. ELH (73:4) 2006, 975–96.

11186. Leslie, Lisa. The fact that is in fiction: autobiography in Claire Clairmont's *The Pole*. *See* **9465**.

11187. Lokke, Kari E. Tracing women's Romanticism: gender, history and transcendence. (Bibl. 2005, 11979.) Rev. by Linda M. Lewis in RomNet (44) 2006; by Sura P. Rath in RMER (60:2) 2006.

11188. Macfarlane, Robert. Monstrosity, fakery, and authorship in *My Life as a Fake*. *In* (pp. 335–48) **15024**.

11189. Morgan, Monique R. *Frankenstein*'s singular events: inductive reasoning, narrative technique, and generic classification. RomNet (44) 2006.

11190. Petillo, Mariacristina. Sulle strade degli Shelley. *See* **11221**.

11191. Phillips, Bill. *Frankenstein* and Mary Shelley's 'wet ungenial summer'. Atl (28:2) 2006, 59–68.

11192. Raymond, Claire. The posthumous voice in women's writing from Mary Shelley to Sylvia Plath. Aldershot; Burlington, VT: Ashgate, 2006. pp. 262.

11193. Reese, Diana. A troubled legacy: Mary Shelley's *Frankenstein* and the inheritance of human rights. Representations (96) 2006, 48–72.

11194. Sánchez-Palencia Carazo, Carolina; Almagro Jiménez, Manuel. Gathering the limbs of the text in Shelley Jackson's *Patchwork Girl*. *See* **16571**.

11195. Schwetman, John D. Romanticism and the cortical stack: cyberpunk subjectivity in the Takeshi Kovacs novels of Richard K. Morgan. *See* **20305**.

11196. Stabler, Jane. Devotion and diversion: early nineteenth-century British women travellers in Italy and the Catholic Church. *In* (pp. 15–34) **8320**.

11197. Taylor, David. 'A vacant space, an empty stage': *Prometheus Unbound*, *The Last Man*, and the problem of dramatic (re)form. *See* **11231**.

11198. Thompson, Terry W. Shelley's *Frankenstein*. Exp (64:2) 2006, 81–4.

11199. Vine, Steve. Mary Shelley's sublime bodies: *Frankenstein*, *Matilda*, *The Last Man*. Eng (55:212) 2006, 141–56.

11200. Willis, Martin. Mesmerists, monsters, and machines: science fiction and the cultures of science in the nineteenth century. Kent, OH; London: Kent State UP, 2006. pp. viii, 272.

Percy Bysshe Shelley

11201. Agosti, Annamaria. Frammenti del sublime romantico: Byron, Shelley, Wordsworth. *See* **9321**.

11202. Bernstein, Susan. On music framed: the Eolian harp in Romantic writing. *In* (pp. 70–84) **8828**.

11203. Bieri, James. Percy Bysshe Shelley: a biography: exile of unfulfilled reknown, 1816–1822. (Bibl. 2005, 11997.) Rev. by Michael O'Neill in KSJ (55) 2006, 228–31; by Ian Gilmour in BJ (34:1) 2006, 70–2.

11204. —— Percy Bysshe Shelley: a biography: youth's unextinguished fire, 1792–1816. (Bibl. 2005, 11998.) Rev. by Michael O'Neill in KSJ (55) 2006, 228–31.

11205. Brown, Sally, *et al.* Keats and Italy: a history of the Keats–Shelley house in Rome. *See* **10639**.

11206. Colbert, Benjamin. Shelley's eye: travel writing and aesthetic vision. (Bibl. 2005, 12001.) Rev. by William A. Ulmer in WordsC (36:4) 2005, 171–2; by Lisa Vargo in KSR (20) 2006, 163–6; by Cian Duffy in Romanticism (12:2) 2006, 156–8; by Nicholas Birns in SR (45:3) 2006, 490–5; by Arthur Bradley in BJ (34:1) 2006, 73–4.

11207. Duffy, Cian. Shelley and the revolutionary sublime. (Bibl. 2005, 12005.) Rev. by Sharon Ruston in TLS, 31 Mar. 2006, 32–3; by Richard Marggraf Turley in RES (57:232) 2006, 831–3.

11208. Eisenhauer, Robert. Parables of disfiguration: reason and excess from Romanticism to the avant-garde. New York; Frankfurt: Lang, 2005. pp. xii, 404. (Studies on themes and motifs in literature, 79.)

11209. Fraistat, Neil; Jones, Steven. The poem and the network: editing poetry electronically. *In* (pp. 105–21) **426**.

11210. Goulding, Christopher. Shelley's cosmological sublime: William Herschel, James Lind and 'the multitudinous orb'. RES (57:232) 2006, 783–92.

11211. Guyer, Sara. Testimony and trope in *Frankenstein*. *See* **11179**.

11212. Harries, Elizabeth Wanning. 'Unfinish'd sentences': the Romantic fragment. *In* (pp. 360–75) **8357**.

11213. Jung, Sandro. Overcoming tyranny: love, truth and meaning in Shelley's *Prometheus Unbound*. KSR (20) 2006, 89–101.

11214. LESLIE, LISA. The fact that is in fiction: autobiography in Claire Clairmont's *The Pole*. *See* **9465**.

11215. LOWE, PETER. Christian Romanticism: T. S. Eliot's response to Percy Shelley. *See* **15697**.

11216. MANETTI, FABIANA. Il linguaggio dell'armonia: studio della similitudine in Percy Bysshe Shelley. Venice: Supernova, 2006. pp. 64. (Saggi.)

11217. MILLER, CHRISTOPHER R. The invention of evening: perception and time in Romantic poetry. *See* **9539**.

11218. MORTON, TIMOTHY. Joseph Ritson, Percy Shelley and the making of Romantic vegetarianism. Romanticism (12:1) 2006, 52–61.

11219. OGAWA, KIMIYO. 'Suspended' sense in *Alastor*: Shelley's musical trope and eighteenth-century medical discourse. *In* (pp. 50–69) **8828**.

11220. PETERFREUND, STUART. Earl Wasserman: a critical (re)-reading. *See* **14257**.

11221. PETILLO, MARIACRISTINA. Sulle strade degli Shelley. Rome: Aracne, 2006. pp. 224.

11222. REIMAN, DONALD H.; FRAISTAT, NEIL (eds). The complete poetry of Percy Bysshe Shelley: vol. 2. Baltimore, MD; London: Johns Hopkins UP, 2004. pp. xlvii, 862. Rev. by Jeffery Vail in WordsC (36:4) 2005, 194–5; by Nancy Goslee in KSJ (55) 2006, 226–8.

11223. RIVERS, BRYAN. 'Tenderly' and 'with care': Thomas Hood's *The Bridge of Sighs* and the suicide of Harriet Shelley. *See* **10467**.

11224. RIZO-PATRÓN, EILEEN. Bachelard's subversive hermeneutics: a reading of lightning in Shelley's *Prometheus Unbound*. RelArts (10:3) 2006, 355–73.

11225. ROSSINGTON, MICHAEL. Claire Clairmont's fair copy of Shelley's *Ode to Naples*: a rediscovered manuscript. RES (56:223) 2005, 59–89.

11226. RUSTON, SHARON. Shelley and vitality. (Bibl. 2005, 12029.) Rev. by Sharrona Pearl in Isis (97:2) 2006, 373; by Robert Mitchell in KSJ (55) 2006, 275–8.

11227. SACHS, JONATHAN. 'Yet the Capital of the World': Rome, repetition, and history in Shelley's later writings. NCC (28:2) 2006, 105–26.

11228. SANDY, MARK. Poetics of self and form in Keats and Shelley: Nietzschean subjectivity and genre. *See* **10661**.

11229. SCHILLE, CANDY. Orsino's 'solemn comedy' and Shelley's 'tragedy' *The Cenci*. RECTR (20:1/2) 2005, 64–79.

11230. STONEMAN, PATSY. Addresses from the land of the dead: Emily Brontë and Shelley. *See* **9224**.

11231. TAYLOR, DAVID. 'A vacant space, an empty stage': *Prometheus Unbound*, *The Last Man*, and the problem of dramatic (re)form. KSR (20) 2006, 18–31.

11232. TOPIA, ANDRÉ. Le supplément et la perte; ou, Le recyclage manqué (Thomas Hardy, *An Imaginative Woman*). *See* **10342**.

11233. WEINBERG, ALAN. 'All things are sold': the degrading intrusiveness of commerce, with reference to Shelley's *Queen Mab* v. KSR (20) 2006, 102–18.

11234. WOUDHUYSEN, H. R. A Shelley pamphlet come to light. TLS, 14 July 2006, 12.

John Sheppard (1785–1879)

11235. Whelan, Timothy. Thomas Poole's 'intimations of immortality' in a letter to John Sheppard, February 1837. Romanticism (11:2) 2005, 199–223.

Mary Martha Sherwood

11236. Lewis, Lisa. Of Kim and Little Henry. *See* **16915**.

Catherine Sinclair

11237. Cohen, Morton N. Catherine Sinclair and Lewis Carroll: the changing landscape of children's literature. *See* **9416**.

Felicia Skene

11238. Maunder, Andrew (gen. ed.). Sensation with a purpose: Felicia Skene, *Hidden Depths* (1866). Ed. by Lillian Nayder. Erotic sensationalism: Rhoda Broughton, *Cometh Up as a Flower* (1867). Ed. by Tamar Heller. London; Brookfield, VT: Pickering & Chatto, 2004. pp. lx, 532. (Varieties of women's sensation fiction 1855–1890, 4.) Rev. by Anthea Trodd in VicR (31:2) 2005, 132–4.

Caroline Bowles Southey (1786–1854)

11239. Low, Dennis. The literary protégées of the Lake Poets. Aldershot; Burlington, VT: Ashgate, 2006. pp. 202. (Nineteenth century.)

Robert Southey

11240. Hickey, Alison. 'The body of my father's writings': Sara Coleridge's genial labor. *In* (pp. 124–47) **3405**.

11241. Holmes, Richard (ed.). Southey on Nelson: *The Life of Nelson*. New York: HarperPerennial, 2004. pp. 301. (Classic biographies.) Rev. by Peter Parker in TLS, 5 May 2006, 3–4.

11242. Holzwarth, Elsie G. Austen and the admiral: commemorating the bicentenary of the Battle of Trafalgar, 21 October 1805. *See* **9029**.

11243. Jones, Christine Kenyon. 'Nor in my conscience, nor my stomach, rise': food and eating in Southey's verse. Romanticism (12:1) 2006, 15–25.

11244. Mayberry, Tom; Davidson, Graham. Coleridge's Bristol. *See* **9537**.

11245. Nemoianu, Virgil. The triumph of imperfection: the Silver Age of sociocultural moderation in Europe, 1815–1848. *See* **9621**.

11246. Parker, Fred. Between Satan and Mephistopheles: Byron and the Devil. *See* **9362**.

11247. Perry, Seamus. Never failing. TLS, 22 & 29 Dec. 2006, 29 (review-article).

11248. —— Self-management. LRB (28:2) 2006, 18–21 (review-article).

11249. Phillips, Joshua. Chronicles of wasted time: Anthony Munday, Tudor romance, and literary labor. *See* **4974**.

11250. Pratt, Lynda (ed.). Robert Southey and the contexts of English Romanticism. Aldershot; Burlington, VT: Ashgate, 2006. pp. xxix, 267. (Nineteenth century.)

11251. —— (gen. ed.). Robert Southey: poetical works 1793–1810: vol. 1, *Joan of Arc*. Ed. by Lynda Pratt. (Bibl. 2005, 12053.) Rev. by Michael Wiley in WordsC

(36:4) 2005, 192–4; by Seamus Perry in LRB (28:2) 2006, 18–21; by Jean Raimond in EA (59:2) 2006, 205–15.

11252. —— Robert Southey: poetical works 1793–1810: vol. 2, *Madoc*. Ed. by Lynda Pratt with the assistance of Carol Bolton and Paul Jarman. (Bibl. 2005, 12054.) Rev. by Michael Wiley in WordsC (36:4) 2005, 192–4; by Seamus Perry in LRB (28:2) 2006, 18–21; by Jean Raimond in EA (59:2) 2006, 205–15.

11253. —— Robert Southey: poetical works 1793–1810: vol. 3, *Thalaba the Destroyer*. Ed. by Tim Fulford with the assistance of Daniel E. White and Carol Bolton. (Bibl. 2005, 12055.) Rev. by Michael Wiley in WordsC (36:4) 2005, 192–4; by Seamus Perry in LRB (28:2) 2006, 18–21; by Jean Raimond in EA (59:2) 2006, 205–15.

11254. —— Robert Southey: poetical works 1793–1810: vol. 4, *The Curse of Kehama*. Ed. by Daniel Sanjiv Roberts. (Bibl. 2005, 12056.) Rev. by Michael Wiley in WordsC (36:4) 2005, 192–4; by Seamus Perry in LRB (28:2) 2006, 18–21; by Jean Raimond in EA (59:2) 2006, 205–15.

11255. —— Robert Southey: poetical works 1793–1810: vol. 5, Selected shorter poems *c*.1793–1810. Ed. by Lynda Pratt. (Bibl. 2005, 12057.) Rev. by Michael Wiley in WordsC (36:4) 2005, 192–4; by Seamus Perry in LRB (28:2) 2006, 18–21; by Jean Raimond in EA (59:2) 2006, 205–15.

11256. Raimond, Jean. Robert Southey: le retour. EA (59:2) 2006, 205–15 (review-article).

11257. Speck, W. A. Robert Southey: entire man of letters. New Haven, CT; London: Yale UP, 2006. pp. xx, 305, (plates) 16. Rev. by Seamus Perry in TLS, 22 & 29 Dec. 2006, 29.

E. D. E. N. Southworth

11258. Abate, Michelle Ann. Launching a gender b(l)acklash: E. D. E. N. Southworth's *The Hidden Hand* and the emergence of (racialized) White tomboyism. CLAQ (31:1) 2006, 40–64.

11259. Landry, H. Jordan. Of tricks, tropes, and trollops: revisions to the seduction novel in E. D. E. N. Southworth's *The Hidden Hand*. JMMLA (38:2) 2005, 31–44.

11260. Naranjo-Huebl, Linda. The road to perdition: E. D. E. N. Southworth and the critics. AmP (16:2) 2006, 123–50.

Harriet Prescott Spofford

11261. Bode, Rita. Narrative revelations: Harriet Prescott Spofford's *Amber Gods* revisited. ESQ (50:4) 2004, 233–67.

11262. Ellis, R. J. 'Latent color' and 'exaggerated snow': Whiteness and race in Harriet Prescott Spofford's *The Amber Gods*. JAStud (40:2) 2006, 257–82.

Sir Leslie Stephen

11263. de Gay, Jane. Virginia Woolf's novels and the literary past. *See* **19275**.

11264. Farr, Liz. Stevenson and the unfamiliar: the aesthetics of late nineteenth-century biography. *In* (pp. 36–47) **11272**.

11265. Horsman, Alan. 'A bite medicinally': Leslie Stephen and Virginia Woolf's eighteenth-century essays. *In* (pp. 226–34) **8374**.

11266. Kramer, Kathryn. An agnostic cliffhanger: anxiety and belief in Hardy's *A Pair of Blue Eyes* and Leslie Stephen's *A Bad Five Minutes in the Alps*. *See* **10288**.

Ann S. Stephens

11267. Ramsey, Colin T. Ann Stephens's *Malaeska*: an unknown early version and some thoughts on dime novels and the gender of readers. DNR (75:3) 2006, 67–76.

Robert Louis Stevenson

11268. Abrahamson, R. L. Living in a book: RLS as an engaged reader. *In* (pp. 13–22) **11272**.

11269. Adamson, Jane. Talking with oneself and other ostriches. Meanjin (63:4) 2004, 103–14. (*Dr Jekyll and Mr Hyde*.)

11270. Alliata, Michela Vanon. *Markheim* and the shadow of the Other. *In* (pp. 299–311) **11272**.

11271. Ambrosini, Richard. The four boundary-crossings of R. L. Stevenson, novelist and anthropologist. *In* (pp. 23–35) **11272**.

11272. —— Dury, Richard (eds). Robert Louis Stevenson: writer of boundaries. Madison; London: Wisconsin UP, 2006. pp. xxx, 377. Rev. by Anne Stiles in NineL (61:3) 2006, 403–6.

11273. Arata, Stephen. Stevenson, Morris, and the value of idleness. *In* (pp. 3–12) **11272**.

11274. Balderston, Daniel. Murder by suggestion: *El sueño de los héroes* and *The Master of Ballantrae*. *In* (pp. 348–58) **11272**.

11275. Ballarin, Charles, *et al.* (eds). *Le Maître de Ballantrae* et autres romans. Paris: Gallimard, 2005. pp. xxxix, 1389. (Bibliothèque de la Pléiade, 513.) Rev. by Annie Escuret in CVE (62) 2005, 216–19.

11276. Benziman, Galia. Challenging the biological: the fantasy of male birth as nineteenth-century narrative of ethical failure. *See* **11174**.

11277. Buckton, Oliver S. Cruising with Robert Louis Stevenson: the South Seas from journal to fiction. *In* (pp. 199–212) **11272**.

11278. Butler, Lisa. 'that damned old business of the war in the members': the discourse of (in)temperance in Robert Louis Stevenson's *The Strange Case of Dr Jekyll and Mr Hyde*. RomNet (44) 2006.

11279. Calder, Jenni. Figures in a landscape: Scott, Stevenson, and routes to the past. *In* (pp. 121–32) **11272**.

11280. Canepari-Labib, Michela. Fenomeni di '*code-mixing*' e '*code-switching*' nelle opere 'postcoloniali' di Robert Louis Stevenson. ConLett (43) 2005, 211–31.

11281. Castricano, Jodey. Much ado about handwriting: countersigning with the other hand in Stevenson's *The Strange Case of Dr Jekyll and Mr Hyde*. RomNet (44) 2006.

11282. Colley, Ann C. Light, darkness, and shadow: Stevenson in the South Seas. *In* (pp. 181–9) **11272**.

11283. —— Robert Louis Stevenson and the colonial imagination. (Bibl. 2004, 12117.) Rev. by Stephen Arata in VS (48:3) 2006, 568–71.

11284. Danahay, Martin A.; Chisholm, Alexander (eds). Jekyll and Hyde dramatized: the 1887 Richard Mansfield script and the evolution of the story on stage. Jefferson, NC; London: McFarland, 2005. pp. x, 230.

11285. Davis, Michael. Incongruous compounds: re-reading *Jekyll and Hyde* and late Victorian psychology. JVC (11:2) 2006, 207–25.

11286. Denisoff, Dennis. Consumerism and Stevenson's misfit masculinities. *In* (pp. 286–98) **11272**.

11287. Donovan, Stephen. Stevenson and popular entertainment. *In* (pp. 70–82) **11272**.

11288. Doyle, Brian. A bogey tale. ASch (75:3) 2006, 144. (*Dr Jekyll and Mr Hyde*.)

11289. Dryden, Linda. 'City of dreadful night': Stevenson's gothic London. *In* (pp. 252–64) **11272**.

11290. Dury, Richard. Crossing the bounds of single identity: *Dr Jekyll and Mr Hyde* and a paper in a French scientific journal. *In* (pp. 237–51) **11272**.

11291. Eagleton, Mary. Rewriting the master: Emma Tennant and Robert Louis Stevenson. LIT (17:3/4) 2006, 223–41.

11292. Farr, Liz. Stevenson and the unfamiliar: the aesthetics of late nineteenth century biography. *In* (pp. 36–47) **11272**.

11293. Goh, Robbie B. H. Stevenson and the property of language: narrative, value, modernity. *In* (pp. 169–80) **11272**.

11294. Gray, William. Robert Louis Stevenson: a literary life. (Bibl. 2004, 12123.) Rev. by Stephen Arata in VS (48:3) 2006, 568–71.

11295. Harman, Claire. Myself and the other fellow: a life of Robert Louis Stevenson. (Bibl. 2005, 12069.) Rev. by Andrew O'Hagan in LRB (27:4) 2005, 10–12; by Matthew Sturgis in TLS, 11 Mar. 2005, 8; by George Fetherling in BkCan (34:5) 2005, 38; by John Crowley in BkW, 22 Jan. 2006, 13.

11296. Hirsch, Gordon. Tontines, tontine insurance, and commercial culture: Stevenson and Osbourne's *The Wrong Box*. *In* (pp. 83–94) **11272**.

11297. Horvath, Gabriela. Initiation and symbol in Robert Louis Stevenson: *Treasure Island* revisited. ConLett (44) 2005, 473–83.

11298. Houston, Gail Turley. From Dickens to *Dracula*: gothic, economics, and Victorian fiction. *See* **9102**.

11299. Jaeck, Nathalie. The greenhouse *vs* the glasshouse: Stevenson's stories as textual matrices. *In* (pp. 48–59) **11272**.

11300. Katz, Wendy R. Whitman and Thoreau as literary stowaways in Stevenson's American writings. *In* (pp. 327–37) **11272**.

11301. Kreisel, Deanna K. Wolf children and automata: bestiality and boredom at home and abroad. Representations (96) 2006, 21–47.

11302. Letissier, Georges. Hyphologie et pharologie dans *Lighthousekeeping* de Jeanette Winterson. *See* **19232**.

11303. Lucas, Ann Lawson. The pirate chief in Salgari, Stevenson, and Calvino. *In* (pp. 338–47) **11272**.

11304. McCracken-Flesher, Caroline. Burking the Scottish body: Robert Louis Stevenson and the resurrection men. *In* (pp. 133–44) **11272**.

11305. MacDuffie, Allen. Irreversible transformations: Robert Louis Stevenson's *Dr Jekyll and Mr Hyde* and Scottish energy science. Representations (96) 2006, 1–20.

11306. MacLachlan, Christopher (ed.). *Travels with a Donkey in the Cévennes* and *The Amateur Emigrant*. London; New York: Penguin, 2004. pp. xlii, 269. (Penguin classics.)

11307. Malzhan, Manfred. Voices of the Scottish empire. *In* (pp. 158–68) **11272**.

11308. May, Jill P. James Barrie's pirates: *Peter Pan*'s place in pirate history and lore. *In* (pp. 69–78) **14616**.

11309. Menikoff, Barry. Narrating Scotland: the imagination of Robert Louis Stevenson. Columbia; London: South Carolina UP, 2005. pp. xii, 233. Rev. by Jenni Calder in ScSR (7:1) 2006, 124–5.

11310. Miller, Renata Kobetts. Recent reinterpretations of Stevenson's *Dr Jekyll and Mr Hyde*: why and how this novel continues to affect us. Lewiston, NY; Lampeter: Mellen Press, 2005. pp. v, 249. (Studies in British literature, 101.)

11311. Naugrette, Jean-Pierre. *The Master of Ballantrae*; or, The writing of frost and stone. *In* (pp. 97–108) **11272**.

11312. Norquay, Glenda. Trading texts: negotiations of the professional and the popular in the case of *Treasure Island*. *In* (pp. 60–9) **11272**.

11313. Parfect, Ralph. 'God bless my tail!': two unknown fables by Robert Louis Stevenson. TLS, 20 Jan. 2006, 11–13.

11314. —— Violence in the South Seas: Stevenson, the eye, and desire. *In* (pp. 190–8) **11272**.

11315. Parkes, Christopher. *Treasure Island* and the romance of the British civil service. CLAQ (31:4) 2006, 332–45.

11316. Rago, Jane V. *Dr Jekyll and Mr Hyde*: a 'men's narrative' of hysteria and containment. *In* (pp. 275–85) **11272**.

11317. Reed, Thomas L., Jr. The transforming draught: *Jekyll and Hyde*, Robert Louis Stevenson and the Victorian alcohol debate. Jefferson, NC; London: McFarland, 2006. pp. x, 258.

11318. Rees, Ellen. Holy witch and wanton saint: gothic precursors for Isak Dinesen's *The Dreamers*. *See* **15508**.

11319. Reid, Julia. Robert Louis Stevenson, science, and the *fin de siècle*. Basingstoke; New York: Palgrave Macmillan, 2006. pp. xiii, 241. (Palgrave studies in nineteenth-century writing and culture.)

11320. —— Stevenson, romance, and evolutionary psychology. *In* (pp. 215–27) **11272**.

11321. Sandison, Alan. Masters of the hovering life: Robert Musil and R. L. Stevenson. *In* (pp. 315–26) **11272**.

11322. Silverstein, Albert; Ventura, Marie. The search for forbidden knowledge: Holmes, Moriarty, and the Faust legend. *See* **9954**.

11323. Stiles, Anne. Robert Louis Stevenson's *Jekyll and Hyde* and the double brain. SELit (46:4) 2006, 879–900.

11324. Turnbull, Olena M. Robert Louis Stevenson and nineteenth-century theories of evolution: crossing the boundaries between ideas and art. *In* (pp. 228–36) **11272**.

11325. Villa, Luisa. Quarreling with the father. *In* (pp. 109–20) **11272**.

11326. Walker, Richard J. Pious works: aesthetics, ethics, and the modern individual in Robert Louis Stevenson's *Strange Case of Dr Jekyll and Mr Hyde*. *In* (pp. 265–74) **11272**.

11327. Wright, Louise E. Jack London's knowledge of Thoreau. *See* **17245**.

Maria W. Stewart (1803–1879)

11328. Bean, Judith Mattson. Gaining a public voice: a historical perspective on American women's public speaking. *In* (pp. 21–39) **2752**.

11329. McArdle, Andrea. The confluence of law and antebellum Black literature: lawyerly discourse as a rhetoric of empowerment. LawL (17:2) 2005, 183–223.

Elizabeth Drew Barstow Stoddard

11330. Çelikkol, Ayşe. *The Morgesons*, aesthetic predicaments, and the competitive logic of the market economy. AL (78:1) 2006, 29–57.

11331. Hager, Christopher. Hunger for the literal: writing and industrial change in Elizabeth Stoddard's *The Morgesons*. AL (77:4) 2005, 699–728.

Bram Stoker

11332. Boyd, A. Gustav Meyrink and the evolution of the literary vampire: from feared bloodsucker to esoteric phenomenon. Neophilologus (90:4) 2006, 601–20.

11333. Cain, Jimmie E., Jr. Bram Stoker and russophobia: evidence of the British fear of Russia in *Dracula* and *The Lady of the Shroud*. Jefferson, NC; London: McFarland, 2006. pp. xi, 203.

11334. Hoeveler, Diane Long. Objectifying anxieties: scientific ideologies in Bram Stoker's *Dracula* and *The Lair of the White Worm*. RomNet (44) 2006.

11335. Houston, Gail Turley. From Dickens to *Dracula*: gothic, economics, and Victorian fiction. *See* **9102**.

11336. Joslin, Lyndon W. Count Dracula goes to the movies: Stoker's novel adapted, 1922–2003. *See* **12563**.

11337. Law, Jules. Being there: gothic violence and virtuality in *Frankenstein*, *Dracula*, and *Strange Days*. *See* **11185**.

11338. Menegaldo, Gilles; Sipière, Dominique (eds). *Dracula*: l'œuvre de Bram Stoker et le film de Francis F. Coppola. Paris: Ellipses, 2005. pp. 379. Rev. by Annie Escuret in CVE (63) 2006, 481–5.

11339. Miller, Elizabeth. *Coitus interruptus*: sex, Bram Stoker, and *Dracula*. RomNet (44) 2006.

11340. Murray, Paul. From the shadow of Dracula: a life of Bram Stoker. (Bibl. 2005, 12098.) Rev. by Stephen Wade in ContRev (286:1669) 2005, 114–15.

11341. Paquet-Deyris, Anne-Marie; Menegaldo, Gilles. *Dracula*. Neuilly: Atlande, 2006. pp. 192. (Clefs concours: anglais-littérature.) Rev. by Annie Escuret in CVE (63) 2006, 486–8.

11342. Sellers, Jason. Dracula's band of the hand: suppressed male onanism. ELN (43:2) 2005, 148–59.

11343. Walton, James. Crystal music in Hoffmann and Stoker. ELN (43:2) 2005, 133–48.

Harriet Beecher Stowe

11344. Abate, Michelle Ann. Topsy and topsy-turvy Jo: Harriet Beecher Stowe's *Uncle Tom's Cabin* and/in Louisa May Alcott's *Little Women*. *See* **8960**.

11345. Bennett, Bridget. Spirited away: the death of Little Eva and the farewell performances of 'Katie King'. JAStud (40:1) 2006, 1–16.

11346. Berman, Carolyn Vellenga. Creole crossings: domestic fiction and the reform of colonial slavery. *See* **9988**.

11347. Best, Stephen M. The fugitive's properties: law and the poetics of possession. (Bibl. 2004, 12152.) Rev. by Philip Joseph in AL (77:3) 2005, 639–41.

11348. Buinicki, Martin T. Negotiating copyright: authorship and the discourse of literary property rights in nineteenth-century America. *See* **666**.

11349. Cotugno, Clare. Stowe, Eliot, and the reform aesthetic. *In* (pp. 111–30) **11355**.

11350. Elbert, Monika. Nature, magic, and history in Stowe and Scott. *In* (pp. 46–64) **11355**.

11351. Foster, Shirley. The construction of self in *Sunny Memories*. *In* (pp. 149–66) **11355**.

11352. Franklin, Caroline. Stowe and the Byronic heroine. *In* (pp. 3–23) **11355**.

11353. Gates, Henry Louis, Jr. Cabin fever. NYTB, 22 Oct. 2006, 31. (*Uncle Tom's Cabin* and its influence.)

11354. Jordan-Lake, Joy. Whitewashing *Uncle Tom's Cabin*: nineteenth-century women novelists respond to Stowe. Nashville, TN: Vanderbilt UP, 2005. pp. xxvi, 204. Rev. by Barbara Hochman in JAH (93:2) 2006, 528.

11355. Kohn, Denise; Meer, Sarah; Todd, Emily B. (eds). Transatlantic Stowe: Harriet Beecher Stowe and European culture. Iowa City: Iowa UP, 2006. pp. xxxi, 258.

11356. Levine, Robert. Twelve years with Martin Delany: a confession. *In* (pp. 173–85) **20098**.

11357. Mackay, John. The first years of *Uncle Tom's Cabin* in Russia. *In* (pp. 67–88) **11355**.

11358. Meer, Sarah. Uncle Tom mania: slavery, minstrelsy, and transatlantic culture in the 1850s. (Bibl. 2005, 12110.) Rev. by Robert Nowatzki in JSH (72:4) 2006, 939–40; by Debra J. Rosenthal in Legacy (23:1) 2006, 96–8; by Michelle

Stephens in AL (78:3) 2006, 638–40; by Martin Crawford in JAAH (91:4) 2006, 471–3.

11359. Newman, Judie. The afterlife of *Dred* on the British stage. *In* (pp. 208–24) **11355**.

11360. O'Brien, Sheila Ruzycki. 'There is no arguing with *pictures*': stretching the canvas of gender in the art portraits, picture-language, and the original illustrations in *Uncle Tom's Cabin*. ATQ (20:2) 2006, 448–80.

11361. Ó Gallchoir, Clíona. *Uncle Tom's Cabin* and the Irish national tale. *In* (pp. 24–45) **11355**.

11362. Parille, Ken. 'The medicine of sympathy': mothers, sons, and affective pedagogy in antebellum America. TSWL (25:1) 2006, 93–115.

11363. Richards, Jason. Imitation nation: blackface minstrelsy and the making of African American selfhood in *Uncle Tom's Cabin*. Novel (39:2) 2006, 204–20.

11364. Rineer, Carla. Stowe and religious iconography. *In* (pp. 187–207) **11355**.

11365. Ross, Donald. *Sunny Memories* and serious proposals. *In* (pp. 131–46) **11355**.

11366. Smith, Gail K. Art and the body in *Agnes of Sorrento*. *In* (pp. 167–86) **11355**.

11367. Smith, Whitney Womack. Stowe, Gaskell, and the woman reformer. *In* (pp. 89–110) **11355**.

11368. Stoneley, Peter. Sewing in Concord. *See* **11452**.

11369. Tawil, Ezra. The making of racial sentiment: slavery and the birth of the frontier romance. *See* **8721**.

11370. Tawil, Ezra F. Captain Babo's cabin: Stowe, race and misreading in *Benito Cereno*. *See* **10903**.

11371. Visser, Irene. Of women, slaves and cannibals: dynamics of holiness in three American novels of the mid-nineteenth century. *In* (pp. 127–45) **3415**.

John Strachan (1778–1867)

11372. Wood, Sarah F. Refusing to RIP; or, Return of the dispossessed: the transatlantic revivals of Irving's *Rip Van Winkle*. *See* **10524**.

Algernon Charles Swinburne

11373. Blair, Kirstie. Swinburne's spasms: *Poems and Ballads* and the 'Spasmodic School'. YES (36:2) 2006, 180–96.

11374. Brennan, Thomas J. Creating from nothing: Swinburne and Baudelaire in *Ave atque Vale*. VP (44:3) 2006, 251–71.

11375. Eron, Sarah. Circles and the in-between: shaping time, space, and paradox in Swinburnian verse. VP (44:3) 2006, 293–309.

11376. Forrest-Thomson, Veronica. Swinburne as poet: a reconsideration. JPRS (15:2) 2006, 51–71.

11377. Levin, Yisrael; Louis, Margot K. Guide to the year's work: Swinburne. VP (44:3) 2006, 375–80.

11378. Meyers, Terry L. The first printings of Swinburne's *Reverse* and *The Turning of the Tide*. NQ (53:3) 2006, 342–3.

11379. —— (ed.). Uncollected letters of Algernon Charles Swinburne. London; Brookfield, VT: Pickering & Chatto, 2004/05. 3 vols. pp. xxvi, 1264. Rev. by Rikky Rooksby in VP (43:2) 2005, 266–74; by Richard Frith in JWMS (16:2/3) 2005, 144–8; by Margot K. Louis in JPRS (14:2) 2005, 115–18; by Catherine Maxwell in YES (36:2) 2006, 275–7.

11380. Poster, Carol. 'If thou art God, avenge thyself!': Sade and Swinburne as Christian atheists. *In* (pp. 244–57) **11883**.

11381. Schwab, Arnold T. Wilde and Swinburne: part 1. *See* **11625**.

John Addington Symonds

11382. Da Silva, Stephen. Papa, postcards, perfume, phallic keys: James, Symonds, and late Victorian fictions of homosexuality. *In* (pp. 201–38) **10568**.

Arthur Symons

11383. Despotopoulou, Anna. *'La maladie fin de siècle'*: the symbols of Aestheticism and the aesthetics of Symbolism. *See* **8336**.

11384. Pointner, Petra. A prelude to Modernism: studies on the urban and erotic poetry of Arthur Symons. Heidelberg: Winter, 2004. pp. 255. (Anglistische Forschungen, 339.)

11385. Prins, Yopie. Sappho recomposed: a song cycle by Granville and Helen Bantock. *In* (pp. 230–58) **8828**.

Alfred, Lord Tennyson

11386. Allis, Michael. Musical reactions to Tennyson: reformulating musical imagery in *The Lotos-Eaters*. *In* (pp. 132–73) **8828**.

11387. Ball, Martin. Pro patria mori. *See* **13700**.

11388. Barton, Anna Jane. 'What profits me my name?': the aesthetic potential of the commodified name in *Lancelot and Elaine*. VP (44:2) 2006, 135–52.

11389. Batchelor, John. Alfred Tennyson: problems of biography. YES (36:2) 2006, 78–95.

11390. Eliot, Simon. What price poetry? Selling Wordsworth, Tennyson, and Longfellow in nineteenth- and early twentieth-century Britain. *See* **11660**.

11391. Fisher, Devon. 'And so we are kept going': collective memory and the romance. MidQ (47:4) 2006, 336–49.

11392. Fontana, Ernest. Too late: the Pre-Raphaelites, Tennyson, and Browning. JPRS (15:1) 2006, 50–60.

11393. Gray, Erik (ed.). *In Memoriam*: authoritative text; criticism. New York; London: Norton, 2004. pp. xxvii, 252. (Norton critical eds.) (Second ed.: first ed. 1973.)

11394. Harris, Kurt. Mourning at the mother's breast: death and weaning in Tennyson's *In Memoriam*. PsyArt (10) 2006.

11395. Hixon, Martha. *The Lady of Shalott* as paradigm in Patricia McKillip's *The Tower at Stony Wood*. *See* **17365**.

11396. Hughes, Linda K. Guide to the year's work: Tennyson. VP (44:3) 2006, 381–7.

11397. Lara Rallo, Carmen. 'Flashing into the crystal mirror': the recurrence of the mirror motif in three Arthurian works. *See* **4544**.

11398. Markley, A. A. Stateliest measures: Tennyson and the literature of Greece and Rome. (Bibl. 2005, 12153.) Rev. by Matthew Reynolds in RES (57:228) 2006, 124–5.

11399. Marks, Thomas. 'A sort of magic': enchantment and disenchantment in the work of Tennyson and his contemporaries. TRB (8:5) 2006, 331–52.

11400. Millgate, Michael (ed.). Table-rapping with Tennyson: Ella Coltman: *Visit to Freshwater.* LitIm (8:1) 2006, 1–17.

11401. Moore, Dafydd. Tennyson, Malory and the Ossianic mode: *The Poems of Ossian* and 'The Death of Arthur'. RES (57:230) 2006, 374–91.

11402. Morton, John. Tennyson and the 1914–1918 war. TRB (8:5) 2006, 353–67.

11403. Navaei, Reza Najafpour. *The Lady of Shalott*: a Goethean reading of the text. *In* (pp. 5–12) **3407**.

11404. O'Neill, Michael. 'So lightly, beautifully built': Tennyson's palaces of art. TRB (8:5) 2006, 319–30.

11405. Perquin, Jean-Charles. Les stratégies poétiques du refus de vieillir dans *Ulysses* de Tennyson. CVE (63) 2006, 295–307.

11406. Perry, Seamus. Alfred Tennyson. (Bibl. 2005, 12157.) Rev. by Matthew Campbell in TRB (8:5) 2006, 407–9; by Herbert Tucker in NineL (61:1) 2006, 110–13.

11407. Peters, Matthew. Hawthorne's Tennyson. *See* **10391**.

11408. Scott, Patrick. Tennyson's *In Memoriam*, section 123, and the submarine forest on the Lincolnshire coast. VN (110) 2006, 28–30.

11409. Tomaiuolo, Saverio. Tennyson and Hopkins from metaphor to metonym: *In Memoriam* and *The Wreck of the Deutschland*. TRB (8:5) 2006, 368–87.

11410. Woodworth, Elizabeth. Elizabeth Barrett Browning, Coventry Patmore, and Alfred Tennyson on Napoleon III: the hero-poet and Carlylean heroics. *See* **9271**.

11411. Woolford, John. The critique of Romantic solipsism in Tennyson's *The Palace of Art*. RES (57:232) 2006, 707–20.

William Makepeace Thackeray

11412. Bronzini, Stefano. A passeggio con Amelia e Becky: una commedia umana londinese: *Vanity Fair* di W. M. Thackeray. *In* (pp. 185–201) **7343**.

11413. Burstein, Miriam Elizabeth. Narrating women's history in Britain, 1770–1902. *See* **10009**.

11414. Cole, Sarah Rose. The aristocrat in the mirror: male vanity and bourgeois desire in William Makepeace Thackeray's *Vanity Fair.* NineL (61:2) 2006, 137–70.

11415. Flynn, Michael J. Novels by literary snobs: the contentious class-coding of Thackerayan parody. *See* **10764**.

11416. JAY, ELISABETH. 'In her father's steps she trod': Anne Thackeray Ritchie imagining Paris. *See* **11069**.

11417. KURNICK, DAVID. Empty houses: Thackeray's theater of interiority. VS (48:2) 2006, 257–67.

11418. SUTHERLAND, JOHN. Lever's columns: a novelist who contributed to great fiction without becoming great. *See* **10733**.

11419. WARNE, VANESSA. Thackeray among the annuals: morality, cultural authority and the literary annual genre. VPR (39:2) 2006, 158–78.

11420. WILTSE, ED. 'The shout of the beef-eating British': nation and genre in *Vanity Fair*. CEACrit (67:3) 2005, 41–64.

Henry David Thoreau

11421. ALCORIZA, JAVIER; LASTRA, ANTONIO (eds and trans). Walden. Madrid: Cátedra, 2005. pp. 357. (Letras universales.) Rev. by Antonio Casado da Rocha in Atl (27:2) 2005, 191–5.

11422. ALLEN, THOMAS. Clockwork nation: modern time, moral perfectionism and American identity in Catharine Beecher and Henry Thoreau. JAStud (39:1) 2005, 65–86.

11423. BAMFORTH, IAIN. The future of the walk. *See* **3179**.

11424. BARBOUR, JOHN D. The value of solitude: the ethics and spirituality of aloneness in autobiography. (Bibl. 2005, 12179.) Rev. by Kevin Lewis in A/B (20:1) 2005, 112–15.

11425. BRADBURY, NICOLA. *De cette triste plume tâtonnante*: Henry James and *The Task of the Translator*. *See* **10541**.

11426. BUELL, LAWRENCE. Downwardly mobile for conscience's sake: voluntary simplicity from Thoreau to Lily Bart. AmLH (17:4) 2005, 653–65.

11427. CAVELL, STANLEY. Reflections on Wallace Stevens at Mount Holyoke. *In* (pp. 61–79, 84–8) **11769**.

11428. CHEEVER, SUSAN. American Bloomsbury: Louisa May Alcott, Ralph Waldo Emerson, Margaret Fuller, Nathaniel Hawthorne, and Henry David Thoreau: their lives, their loves, their work. *See* **8962**.

11429. DERAIL-IMBERT, AGNÈS. La philosophie à la plage. EA (59:3) 2006, 304–18.

11430. HOWERTON, PHIL. A possible source for *Walden*. TSB (254) 2006, 7.

11431. HOWERTON, PHILLIP. The shrouded mountaintop: intertextuality and the misreading of Thoreau's *Ktaadn*. ConS (ns 14) 2006, 23–35.

11432. HUDSPETH, ROBERT N. Additions to the Thoreau bibliography. TSB (255) 2006, 13–15.

11433. KATZ, WENDY R. Whitman and Thoreau as literary stowaways in Stevenson's American writings. *In* (pp. 327–37) **11272**.

11434. KERTING, VERENA. Henry David Thoreau's aesthetics: a modern approach to the world. New York; Frankfurt: Lang, 2006. pp. ix, 189. (European univ. studies, XIV: Anglo-Saxon language and literature, 425.)

11435. LINEBAUGH, DONALD W. The man who found Thoreau: Roland W. Robbins and the rise of historical archaeology in America. Durham:

New Hampshire UP, 2005. pp. xii, 294. Rev. by Charles E. Orser, Jr, in JAH (92:4) 2006, 1499.

11436. Ljungquist, Kent P. 'A strange, wild land, permeated by sea and wind': Esther Forbes in Thoreau's tracks through Cape Cod. *See* **15915**.

11437. McGowan, Tony. Imperfect states: Thoreau, Melville, and 'insectivorous fate'. *In* (pp. 58–86) **3203**.

11438. Mayer, Nancy. The American Romantics and religion in the present tense. MidQ (47:4) 2006, 350–61.

11439. Maynard, W. Barksdale. Walden Pond: a history. (Bibl. 2004, 12255.) Rev. by Robert Jackson in ISLE (12:2) 2005, 290.

11440. Newman, Lance. Our common dwelling: Henry Thoreau, Transcendentalism, and the class politics of nature. (Bibl. 2005, 12206.) Rev. by Donald McNutt in Blueline (27) 2006, 156–7.

11441. Olson, Steven P. Henry David Thoreau: American Naturalist, writer, and Transcendentalist. New York: Rosen Central, 2006. pp. 112. (Library of American thinkers.)

11442. Packer, Barbara. Signing off: religious indifference in America. *In* (pp. 1–22) **8429**.

11443. Peck, H. Daniel. Unlikely kindred spirits: a new vision of landscape in the works of Henry David Thoreau and Asher B. Durand. AmLH (17:4) 2005, 687–713.

11444. Robinson, David M. Natural life: Thoreau's worldly Transcendentalism. (Bibl. 2004, 12266.) Rev. by Donna Mendelson in ISLE (12:2) 2005, 293–4; by Dana Phillips in AL (78:3) 2006, 648–50.

11445. Ronan, John. Thoreau's declaration of independence from Emerson in *Walden*. NCP (33:1) 2006, 133–65.

11446. Schofield, Edmund A. 'Grisly Steven': Thoreau's dog-day afternoon in Walden Woods. TSB (254) 2006, 1–5.

11447. Schreiner, Samuel A., Jr. The Concord quartet: Alcott, Emerson, Hawthorne, Thoreau, and the friendship that freed the American mind. *See* **8959**.

11448. Schulenberg, Ulf. Books, rocks, and sentimental education – self-culture and the desire for the really real in Henry David Thoreau. Amst (51:2) 2006, 167–91.

11449. Smith, Gayle. 'My river … leads to the sea': Sarah Orne Jewett's *Country By-Ways* as Thoreauvian travel narrative. *See* **10626**.

11450. Specq, François. Transcendence: seekers and seers in the age of Thoreau. Higganum, CT: Higganum Hill, 2006. pp. ix, 229. (Directions 21.)

11451. Stewart, Shawn. Transcendental romance meets the ministry of pain: the Thoreau brothers, Ellen Sewall, and her father. ConS (ns 14) 2006, 5–21.

11452. Stoneley, Peter. Sewing in Concord. WS (35:4) 2006, 397–412.

11453. Taylor, Andrew. Consenting to violence: Henry David Thoreau, John Brown, and the Transcendent intellectual. *In* (pp. 89–105) **8537**.

11454. Tyree, J. M. Thoreau, Whitman, and the matter of New York. NER (27:1) 2006, 61–75. (Literary lives.)

11455. Wright, Louise E. Jack London's knowledge of Thoreau. *See* **17245**.

11456. Zárate, Tara Houlihan. *'I want, I want!'*: Transcendental epiphanies in Saul Bellow's *Henderson, the Rain King*. *See* **14753**.

Thomas Bangs Thorpe

11457. Bryant, John. Melville essays the romance: comedy and being in *Frankenstein*, *The Big Bear of Arkansas*, and *Moby-Dick*. *See* **10821**.

Mary Tighe

11458. Chakravarti, Debnita. The female epic and the journey toward self-definition in Mary Tighe's *Psyche*. *In* (pp. 99–116) **3395**.

11459. Linkin, Harriet Kramer (ed.). The collected poems and journals of Mary Tighe. (Bibl. 2005, 12216.) Rev. by Averill Buchanan in ECI (20) 2005, 196–7; by Diego Saglia in WordsC (36:4) 2005, 183–4; by Elisa E. Beshero-Bondar in 1650–1850 (13) 2006, 400–4.

11460. Taylor, Henry. The virtually unknown poetry of Harcourt Mountain. *See* **17659**.

'Graham R. Tomson' (Rosamund Marriott Watson)

11461. Bristow, Joseph. 'The Armytage–Tomson–Watson sequence': poetic illustrations in the periodical press, 1886–96. VLC (34:2) 2006, 519–51.

11462. Hughes, Linda K. Graham R.: Rosamund Marriott Watson, woman of letters. Athens: Ohio UP, 2005. pp. xxv, 397. Rev. by Celeste Pottier in Biography (29:2) 2006, 349–51; by Linda H. Peterson in VPR (39:3) 2006, 300–2.

Albion W. Tourgée

11463. Elliott, Mark Emory. Color-blind justice: Albion Tourgée and the quest for racial equality from the Civil War to *Plessy v. Ferguson*. Oxford; New York: OUP, 2006. pp. viii, 388.

11464. Karcher, Carolyn L. *Bricks without Straw*: Albion W. Tourgée's 'Black Reconstruction'. YREAL (22) 2006, 241–58.

Anthony Trollope

11465. Bredesen, Dagni. 'What's a woman to do?': managing money and manipulating fictions in Trollope's *Can You Forgive Her?* and *The Eustace Diamonds*. VicR (31:2) 2005, 99–122.

11466. Colella, Silvana. Sweet money: cultural and economic value in Trollope's *Autobiography*. NCC (28:1) 2006, 5–20.

11467. Daly, Suzanne. Indiscreet jewels: *The Eustace Diamonds*. NCS (19) 2005, 69–81.

11468. Earle, Bo. Policing and performing Liberal individuality in Anthony Trollope's *The Warden*. NineL (61:1) 2006, 1–31.

11469. Heath, Kay. In the eye of the beholder: Victorian age construction and the specular self. VLC (34:1) 2006, 27–45.

11470. Hunt, Maurice. Anthony Trollope's *Lady Anna* and Shakespeare's *Othello*. VN (110) 2006, 18–23.

11471. Michie, Elsie. The odd couple: Anthony Trollope and Henry James. *See* **10581**.

11472. Newlin, George (ed.). Everyone and everything in Trollope. Armonk, NY: Sharp, 2005. 4 vols. pp. 3911.

11473. Picton, Hervé. De Newman à Colenso: Trollope et l'Église d'Angleterre. EA (59:2) 2006, 145–55.

11474. —— Église et scandales: Trollope ou la condamnation de l'excès. CVE (63) 2006, 161–72.

11475. Ruth, Jennifer. Novel professions: interested disinterest and the making of the professional in the Victorian novel. *See* **9200**.

11476. Scannell, James M. History or quickie history: elections in Anthony Trollope and Ford Madox Ford. *In* (pp. 147–54) **15944**.

11477. Scharnhorst, Gary. Kate Field and Anthony Trollope: the gaps in the record. VN (109) 2006, 21–3.

11478. Swafford, Kevin R. Performance anxiety; or, The production of class in Anthony Trollope's *The Claverings*. JMMLA (38:2) 2005, 45–58.

11479. Van, Annette. Ambivalent speculations: America as England's future in *The Way We Live Now*. Novel (39:1) 2005, 75–96.

11480. Ziegenhagen, Timothy. Trollope's professional gentleman: medical training and medical practice in *Doctor Thorne* and *The Warden*. StudN (38:2) 2006, 154–71.

Frances Trollope

11481. Van, Annette. Ambivalent speculations: America as England's future in *The Way We Live Now*. *See* **11479**.

Sojourner Truth

11482. Ernest, John. The floating icon and the fluid text: rereading the *Narrative of Sojourner Truth*. AL (78:3) 2006, 459–86.

11483. Zackodnik, Teresa C. 'I don't know how you will feel when I get through': racial difference, woman's rights, and Sojourner Truth. FemSt (30:1) 2004, 49–73.

'Mark Twain' (Samuel L. Clemens)

11484. Arac, Jonathan. Revisiting Huck: idol and target. MTA (3) 2005, 9–12.

11485. Asayama, Ryuichi. Mutual influences: Mark Twain's and Charles Dudley Warner's views of children in their early works. MTA (2) 2004, 51–63.

11486. Budd, Louis J. W. D. Howells and Mark Twain judge each other 'aright'. *See* **10499**.

11487. Buinicki, Martin T. Negotiating copyright: authorship and the discourse of literary property rights in nineteenth-century America. *See* **666**.

11488. Bush, Harold K., Jr. Mark Twain's Lincoln as 'man of the border': religion, free thinking, and the Civil War. *In* (pp. 141–71) **8429**.

11489. Clack, Randall A. 'The widow's son': Masonic parody in *Adventures of Huckleberry Finn*. MTA (2) 2004, 65–74.

11490. Doyno, Victor A. Presentations of violence in *Adventures of Huckleberry Finn*. MTA (2) 2004, 75–93.

11491. Driscoll, Kerry. 'Man factories' and the 'White Indians' of Camelot: re-reading the Native subtext of *A Connecticut Yankee in King Arthur's Court*. MTA (2) 2004, 7–23.

11492. Eutsey, Dwayne. God's *real* message: *No. 44, The Mysterious Stranger* and the influence of liberal religion on Mark Twain. MTA (3) 2005, 53–66.

11493. Falocco, Joe. Is Mark Twain dead? Samuel Clemens and the question of Shakespearean authorship. MTA (2) 2004, 25–40.

11494. Ferrer, Hugh. Notes on the *Connecticut Yankee*. IowaR (36:2) 2006, 168–75.

11495. Fisher, Leona W. *The Adventures of Tom Sawyer* and *The Great Brain*: liminality, ritual, and race in the construction of the 'real American boy'. *In* (pp. 191–214) **3157**.

11496. Fishkin, Shelley Fisher. Race and the politics of memory: Mark Twain and Paul Laurence Dunbar. JAStud (40:2) 2006, 283–309.

11497. Fulton, Joe B. The Reverend Mark Twain: theological burlesque, form, and content. Kent: Ohio State UP, 2006. pp. 228.

11498. Gair, Christopher. Whitewashed exteriors: Mark Twain's imitation Whites. JAStud (39:2) 2005, 187–205.

11499. Harrington, Paula. Dawson's Landing: on the disappearance of domesticity in a slaveholding town. MTA (3) 2005, 91–7.

11500. Henrickson, Gary P. The missing landscapes of Mark Twain. MTA (2) 2004, 41–9.

11501. Higgins, Andrew C. Reconstructing rebellion: the politics of narrative in the Confederate memoir. *See* **8903**.

11502. Hitchcock, Bert. Well, maybe just this once: Erskine Caldwell, Old Southwest humor, and funny ha-ha. *In* (pp. 27–45) **15001**.

11503. Hoffmann, Donald. Mark Twain in paradise: his voyages to Bermuda. Columbia; London: Missouri UP, 2006. pp. x, 185. (Mark Twain and his circle.)

11504. Hooker, Rebecca. Additions to the Mark Twain library. ALR (38:3) 2006, 276–7.

11505. Jackson, Robert. Seeking the region in American literature and culture: modernity, dissidence, innovation. (Bibl. 2005, 12247.) Rev. by Jane Atteridge Rose in FOR (4) 2006, 154–6; by Judith Richardson in JAH (93:3) 2006, 907–8.

11506. Jenn, Ronald. From American frontier to European borders: publishing French translations of Mark Twain's novels *Tom Sawyer* and *Huckleberry Finn* (1884–1963). BH (9) 2006, 235–60.

11507. Johnson, Claudia Durst. Youth gangs in literature. *See* **13513**.

11508. Justus, James H. Fetching the Old Southwest: humorous writing from Longstreet to Twain. (Bibl. 2005, 12248.) Rev. by Michael Allen in JSH (72:1) 2006, 167–8; by Benjamin F. Fisher in ArkR (37:3) 2006, 199–201; by Gregg Camfield in SoQ (44:1) 2006, 188–90.

11509. Kirk, Connie Ann. Mark Twain: a biography. (Bibl. 2004, 12324.) Rev. by Peter Barry in Eng (55:212) 2006, 213–19; by Iain Borrowman in JAStud (40:2) 2006, 436–7.

11510. Kiskis, Michael J. Critical humbug: Samuel Clemens' *Adventures of Huckleberry Finn*. MTA (3) 2005, 13–22.

11511. Knoeller, Christian. 'A profession older than writing': echoes of *Huckleberry Finn* in Steinbeck's *Travels with Charley: in Search of America*. *See* **18618**.

11512. Kruse, Horst. The old mamsell and the mysterious stranger: Mark Twain's encounter with German literature and the writing of *No. 44, The Mysterious Stranger*. ALR (39:1) 2006, 64–73.

11513. Lynch, Paul. Not trying to talk alike and succeeding: the authoritative word and internally persuasive word in *Tom Sawyer* and *Huckleberry Finn*. StudN (38:2) 2006, 172–86.

11514. McKellar, Jennifer. The poetics of interruption in Mark Twain's *Roughing It*. Style (39:3) 2005, 336–47.

11515. McLennan, Rachael. Unpacking 'something dark': narrating Southern female adolescence in Jill McCorkle's *The Cheer Leader*, Sylvia Wilkinson's *Bone of My Bones* and Thulani Davis's *1959*. *See* **17309**.

11516. Messent, Peter; Budd, Louis J. (eds). A companion to Mark Twain. Oxford; Malden, MA: Blackwell, 2005. pp. xviii, 568. (Blackwell companions to literature and culture, 38.)

11517. Michelson, Bruce. Printer's devil: Mark Twain and the American publishing revolution. Berkeley; London: California UP, 2006. pp. xiii, 299.

11518. Morris, Linda A. The eloquent silence in *Hellfire Hotchkiss*. MTA (3) 2005, 43–51.

11519. Powers, Ron. Mark Twain: a life. (Bibl. 2005, 12266.) Rev. by Christopher Benfey in TLS, 17 Mar. 2006, 4–5; by Robert Middlekauff in JAH (93:2) 2006, 544.

11520. Pratt, J. Michael. A fossil guide to Mark Twain's essay *Was the World Made for Man?* MTA (3) 2005, 81–9.

11521. Radavich, David. Twain, Howells, and the origins of Midwestern drama. MidAmerica (31) 2004, 25–42.

11522. Railton, Stephen. Mark Twain tries to get the last laugh: Hadleyburg and other performances. MTA (3) 2005, 23–36.

11523. Rasmussen, R. Kent. Critical companion to Mark Twain: a literary reference to his life and work. (Bibl. 1996, 12605.) New York: Facts on File, 2006. 2 vols. pp. xlviii, 1120. (Second ed.: first ed. 1995.) (Orig. pub. as *Mark Twain A to Z: the Essential Reference to His Life and Writings*.)

11524. Rohman, Chad. A great dark: Mark Twain's continuing voyage into uncertainty. MTA (3) 2005, 67–80.

11525. Scharnhorst, Gary. A recovered Mark Twain letter to Henry M. Whitney in 1895. ALR (39:1) 2006, 87–8.

11526. —— (ed.). Mark Twain: the complete interviews. Tuscaloosa; London: Alabama UP, 2006. pp. xii, 719. (Studies in American literary realism and naturalism.)

11527. SEGUIN, ROBERT. Cultural revolution, the discourse of intellectuals, and other folk tales. *In* (pp. 95–115) **14159**.

11528. SZUBERLA, GUY. Local color, local news, and *The Man That Corrupted Hadleyburg*. MidAmerica (31) 2004, 43–56.

11529. VALKEAKARI, TUIRE. Huck, Twain, and the freedman's shackles: struggling with *Huckleberry Finn* today. Atl (28:2) 2006, 29–43.

11530. VOGEL, DAN. Mark Twain's Jews. Jersey City, NJ: KTAV, 2006. pp. xiv, 146.

11531. WILSON, CHARLES E., JR. Race and racism in literature. *See* **13644**.

11532. YOUNGBERG, QUENTIN. Morphology of Manifest Destiny: the justified violence of John O'Sullivan, Hank Morgan, and George W. Bush. CRAS (35:3) 2005, 315–33.

11533. ZIFF, LARZER. Mark Twain. (Bibl. 2005, 12276.) Rev. by David B. Kesterson in MissQ (57:4) 2004, 685–91.

11534. ZOU, HUILING. On the Indian images in the White canons of 19th-century America. *See* **8736**.

Lois Waisbrooker (1826–1909)

11535. PASSET, JOANNE E. Power through print: Lois Waisbrooker and grassroots feminism. *In* (pp. 229–50) **690**.

'Robert Walters' (George Roberts) (b.1832)

11536. HENDERSON, IAN. Looking at Lady Audley: Symbolism, the stage, and the Antipodes. *See* **9162**.

Mrs Humphry Ward (Mary Augusta Arnold)

11537. WILT, JUDITH. Behind her times: transition England in the novels of Mary Arnold Ward. (Bibl. 2005, 12282.) Rev. by Stephen Prickett in ReLit (38:1) 2006, 135–7; by Gisela Argyle in VS (48:4) 2006, 765–6; by Beth Sutton-Ramspeck in NineL (61:2) 2006, 263–7.

Charles Dudley Warner

11538. ASAYAMA, RYUICHI. Mutual influences: Mark Twain's and Charles Dudley Warner's views of children in their early works. *See* **11485**.

Susan Warner

11539. HARRIS, MARLA. 'A history not then taught in history books': (re)writing Reconstruction in historical fiction for children and young adults. *See* **10121**.

Mrs Amelia Ball (Coppuck) Welby (1819–1852)

11540. HALL, SUSAN GROVE. From voice to persona: Amelia Welby's lyric tradition in Sarah M. B. Piatt's early poetry. *See* **11003**.

Mrs (Jane) West (1758–1852)

11541. VERHOEVEN, W. M. (gen. ed.). Anti-Jacobin novels: vol. 7, Jane West, *A Tale of the Times* (1799). Ed. by Amanda Gilroy. London; Brookfield, VT: Pickering & Chatto, 2005. pp. xxxiv, 398. Rev. by Jon Mee in HLQ (69:4) 2006, 649–53.

Matthew West (d.1814)

11542. NIELSEN, WENDY C. Edmund Eyre's *The Maid of Normandy*; or, Charlotte Corday in Anglo-Irish docudrama. *See* **7779**.

Joseph Blanco White

11543. ALMEIDA, JOSELYN. Blanco White and the making of Anglo-Hispanic Romanticism. ERR (17:4) 2006, 437–56.

William Hale White ('Mark Rutherford')

11544. IVARD, JEAN-MICHEL. De la crainte de la damnation éternelle aux prémisses de l'angoisse existentielle contemporaine: inquiétudes sotériologiques et eschatologiques chez William Hale White ('Mark Rutherford'). CVE (63) 2006, 359–72.

Walt Whitman

11545. ARROJO, ROSEMARY. Translation, transference, and the attraction to otherness – Borges, Menard, Whitman. Diacritics (34:3/4) 2004, 31–53.

11546. ASPIZ, HAROLD. So long! Walt Whitman's poetry of death. (Bibl. 2005, 12292.) Rev. by Michael Robertson in AL (77:2) 2005, 416–18.

11547. BARTON, JOHN CYRIL. The anti-gallows movement in antebellum America. *See* **10816**.

11548. BEDNAROWSKI, MARY FARRELL. Intimations of bodily holiness in selected poems by Walt Whitman, Emily Dickinson, and Wallace Stevens. *In* (pp. 147–60) **3415**.

11549. BOHAN, RUTH L. Looking into Walt Whitman: American art, 1850–1920. University Park: Pennsylvania State UP, 2006. pp. xiv, 261.

11550. BRADBURY, NICOLA. *De cette triste plume tâtonnante*: Henry James and *The Task of the Translator*. *See* **10541**.

11551. BUINICKI, MARTIN T. Negotiating copyright: authorship and the discourse of literary property rights in nineteenth-century America. *See* **666**.

11552. COUNDOURIOTIS, ELENI. Rethinking cosmopolitanism in Nadine Gordimer's *The Conservationist*. *See* **16158**.

11553. CUTLER, EDWARD S. Literary modernity and the problem of a national literature: understanding William Dean Howells' critique of Walt Whitman. *See* **10501**.

11554. EISENHAUER, ROBERT. Parables of disfiguration: reason and excess from Romanticism to the avant-garde. *See* **11208**.

11555. FOLSOM, ED; PRICE, KENNETH M. Re-scripting Walt Whitman: an introduction to his life and work. (Bibl. 2005, 12315.) Rev. by Michael Robertson in WWQR (23:3/4) 2005/06, 147–8.

11556. GOUGEON, LEN. Emerson, Whitman, and eros. WWQR (23:3/4) 2005/06, 126–46.

11557. Greenspan, Ezra. Walt Whitman's *Song of Myself*: a sourcebook and critical edition. London; New York: Routledge, 2005. pp. xiii, 210. (Routledge guides to literature.) Rev. by Luke Mancuso in WWQR (23:3/4) 2005/06, 148–51.

11558. Hawlin, Stefan. Ivor Gurney's creative reading of Walt Whitman: thinking of Paumanok. *See* **16239**.

11559. Katz, Wendy R. Whitman and Thoreau as literary stowaways in Stevenson's American writings. *In* (pp. 327–37) **11272**.

11560. Killingsworth, M. Jimmie. Walt Whitman and the earth: a study in ecopoetics. (Bibl. 2005, 12326.) Rev. by Anne Baker in ISLE (12:2) 2005, 268–9.

11561. Kim, Heidi Kathleen. From language to empire: Walt Whitman in the context of nineteenth-century popular Anglo-Saxonism. WWQR (24:1) 2006, 1–19.

11562. Kummings, Donald D. (ed.). A companion to Walt Whitman. Oxford; Malden, MA: Blackwell, 2006. pp. xiii, 607. (Blackwell companions to literature and culture, 40.)

11563. Lanati, Barbara. Ottocento e dintorni: E. A. Poe, W. Whitman, H. Melville, N. Hawthorne. *See* **11027**.

11564. Lawson, Andrew. Walt Whitman and the class struggle. Iowa City: Iowa UP, 2006. pp. xxiv, 157. (Iowa Whitman.) Rev. by William Pannapacker in WWQR (24:1) 2006, 39–41; by M. Wynn Thomas in NineL (61:3) 2006, 391–3.

11565. Lepenies, Wolf. The closing of the Met: German Romanticism, American democracy, and a touch of irony. TLS, 24 Mar. 2006, 13–15.

11566. Lisk, David Thomas. Walt Whitman's attic. MassR (47:1) 2006, 154–67.

11567. Luria, Sarah. Capital speculations: writing and building Washington, DC. Durham: New Hampshire UP, 2006. pp. xxxi, 196. (Becoming modern.)

11568. Marsden, Steve. *A Woman Waits for Me*: Anne Gilchrist's reading of *Leaves of Grass*. WWQR (23:3/4) 2005/06, 95–125.

11569. Mayer, Nancy. The American Romantics and religion in the present tense. *See* **11438**.

11570. Mazur, Krystyna. Poetry and repetition: Walt Whitman, Wallace Stevens, John Ashbery. (Bibl. 2005, 12334.) Rev. by Nick Halpern in WSJ (30:2) 2006, 238–40.

11571. Mills, Bruce. Poe, Fuller, and the mesmeric arts: transition states in the American renaissance. *See* **10146**.

11572. Monteiro, George. Peaches and penumbras: Ginsberg's *Supermarket in California*. *See* **16109**.

11573. Moon, Michael. Solitude, singularity, seriality: Whitman *vis-à-vis* Fourier. ELH (73:2) 2006, 303–23.

11574. Moores, D. J. Mystical discourse in Wordsworth and Whitman: a transatlantic bridge. *See* **11696**.

11575. Myerson, Joel. *Leaves of Grass* turns 150. MSS (58:1) 2006, 5–18.

11576. —— Walt Whitman and the Trimbales: New Zealand, the first concordance of *Leaves of Grass*, and the Dunedin Public Library. WWQR (24:1) 2006, 20–32.

11577. NEPVEU, PIERRE. A little toil of love: l'Amérique and Quebec's Emily Dickinson. Trans. by David Palmieri. *See* **9884**.

11578. OLIVER, CHARLES M. Critical companion to Walt Whitman: a literary reference to his life and work. New York: Facts on File, 2006. pp. viii, 408.

11579. OSTRIKER, ALICIA. May Swenson, Whitman's daughter. *In* (pp. 40–54) **7907**.

11580. PLUMLY, STANLEY. Pastoral matters. SoR (42:4) 2006, 794–9.

11581. PRICE, KENNETH M. To Walt Whitman, America. (Bibl. 2004, 12403.) Rev. by Michael Robertson in AL (77:2) 2005, 416–18; by W. Reginald Rampone, Jr, in SCR (23:3) 2006, 100–3; by George Conyne in JAStud (40:1) 2006, 194.

11582. REYNOLDS, DAVID S. (ed.). Leaves of grass. Oxford; New York: OUP, 2005. pp. xvi, 167. Rev. by Gregory Woods in PNRev (32:3) 2006, 92–3.

11583. RUBINSTEIN, RACHEL. Going native, becoming modern: American Indians, Walt Whitman, and the Yiddish poet. AmQ (58:2) 2006, 431–53.

11584. SCHMIDGALL, GARY (ed.). Conserving Walt Whitman's fame: selections from Horace Traubel's *Conservator*, 1890–1919. Iowa City: Iowa UP, 2006. pp. lviii, 418. (Iowa Whitman.)

11585. SOWDER, MICHAEL. Whitman's ecstatic union: conversion and ideology in *Leaves of Grass*. London; New York: Routledge, 2005. pp. ix, 172. (Studies in major literary authors.)

11586. TYREE, J. M. Thoreau, Whitman, and the matter of New York. *See* **11454**.

11587. WARD, DAVID C. The Green Man: Walt Whitman and the Civil War. PNRev (32:5) 2006, 38–42.

11588. WHITLEY, EDWARD. 'The first white aboriginal': Walt Whitman and John Rollin Ridge. ESQ (52:1/2) 2006, 105–39.

John Greenleaf Whittier

11589. BARRUCAND, MICHEL. L'espace en poésie – poésie de l'espace: les Fireside Poets. *See* **9294**.

11590. WINEAPPLE, BRENDA (ed.). Selected poems. New York: Library of America, 2004. pp. 187. (American poets project.) Rev. by Daniel Hoffman in SewR (113:3) 2005, lxviii–lxxi.

Robert P. (Robert Percy) Whitworth (1831–1901)

11591. WEVERS, LYDIA. Becoming native: Australian novelists and the New Zealand Wars. *See* **9145**.

Lady Wilde (1826–1896)

11592. PARR, KATHERINE. Integrating women's writing into the canon: women poets of Young Ireland. *In* (pp. 235–65) **12189**.

Oscar Wilde

11593. ALDERSON, DAVID. 'Not everyone knows fuck all about Foucault': Will Self's *Dorian* and post-gay culture. *See* **18446**.

11594. Allen, James Sloan. Nietzsche and Wilde: an ethics of style. SewR (114:3) 2006, 386–402.

11595. Beran, Zdeněk. *Teleny* and the question of *fin de siècle* sexuality. *See* **8614**.

11596. Chadwick, Peter. Wilde's creative strategies. Wildean (29) 2006, 28–39.

11597. Chamberlin, J. Edward. The worthy and the worthless: books and people in late Victorian England. JWIL (15:1/2) 2006, 164–86.

11598. Clausson, Nils. Trivial coincidences or 'pre-planned detonations'? A further note on names in Conan Doyle and Wilde. Wildean (29) 2006, 89–90.

11599. Combs, Robert. The importance of being Henry James: what the Master learned from Oscar Wilde. *In* (pp. 186–200) **10568**.

11600. Dibb, Geoff. Oscar Wilde's lecture tours of the United Kingdom, 1883–85. Wildean (29) 2006, 2–11.

11601. Elfenbein, Andrew (ed.). Oscar Wilde's *The Picture of Dorian Gray*. London; New York: Pearson Longman, 2006. pp. xxxv, 310. (Longman cultural eds.)

11602. Evangelista, Stefano. 'Lovers and philosophers at once': aesthetic Platonism in the Victorian *fin de siècle*. *See* **10978**.

11603. Fisher, James. On the ladder of social observation: images of Decadence and morality in James's *Washington Square* and Wilde's *An Ideal Husband*. *In* (pp. 167–85) **10568**.

11604. Fox, Paul. The time of his life: Peter Pan and the Decadent nineties. *In* (pp. 23–45) **14616**.

11605. Gillespie, Michael Patrick (ed.). *The Importance of Being Earnest*: authoritative texts, backgrounds, criticism. New York; London: Norton, 2006. pp. xii, 209. (Norton critical eds.)

11606. Heath, Kay. In the eye of the beholder: Victorian age construction and the specular self. *See* **11469**.

11607. Heller, Janet Ruth. Oscar Wilde's problem play: *A Woman of No Importance*. Wildean (29) 2006, 47–60.

11608. Hovey, Jaime. A thousand words: portraiture, style, and queer Modernism. *See* **11943**.

11609. Ivory, Yvonne. Oscar Wilde's *The Cardinal of Avignon* and the Oxford definitive edition of his poetry: correspondences and discrepancies. NQ (53:3) 2006, 338–41.

11610. Kaplan, Morris. Sodom on the Thames: sex, love, and scandal in Wilde times. (Bibl. 2005, 12398.) Rev. by Iain Ross in TLS, 13 Jan. 2006, 24; by Charles Upchurch in VS (48:4) 2006, 769–71.

11611. Killeen, Jarlath. The faiths of Oscar Wilde: Catholicism, folklore and Ireland. Basingstoke; New York: Palgrave Macmillan, 2005. pp. xi, 228. (Palgrave studies in nineteenth-century writing and culture.) Rev. by D. C. Rose in ILS (26:1) 2006, 26.

11612. Lalonde, Jeremy. A 'revolutionary outrage': *The Importance of Being Earnest* as social criticism. ModDr (48:4) 2005, 659–76.

11613. McFarlane, Brian. Saying what other people mean. *See* **9054**.

11614. Maier, Sarah E. Symbolist Salomés and the dance of Dionysus. NCC (28:3) 2006, 211–23.

11615. Mayer, Sandra. 'A conspiracy of silence'? The reception of Wilde's literary work in early twentieth-century Britain. Wildean (29) 2006, 61–9.

11616. Mira, Alberto. Being Wildean: a dialogue on the importance of style in translation. *In* (pp. 196–207) **3186**.

11617. Moran, Leslie J. On realism and the law film: the case of Oscar Wilde. *In* (pp. 77–93) **12636**.

11618. Morgan, Margery M. Shaw and the sex reformers. *See* **18496**.

11619. Nassaar, Christopher S. Some remarks on *Parody, Paradox and Play in 'The Importance of Being Earnest'*. Connotations (14:1–3) 2004/05, 173–6. (*Response to* bibl. 2005, 12405.)

11620. O'Gorman, Francis. Oscar Wilde and Pope. NQ (53:3) 2006, 341–2.

11621. Rose, D. C. Oscar Wilde, poète anglais / Oscar Wilde, écrivain français. Wildean (29) 2006, 81–8.

11622. Salbayre, Sébastien. Biblical turns of phrase, repetition and circularity in Oscar Wilde's *Salome*. CVE (63) 2006, 175–86.

11623. Schnitzer, Carol. A husband's tragedy: the relationship between art and life in Oscar Wilde's *An Ideal Husband*. VN (109) 2006, 25–9.

11624. Schroeder, Horst. *Earnest* in a German court. Wildean (29) 2006, 70–5.

11625. Schwab, Arnold T. Wilde and Swinburne: part 1. Wildean (29) 2006, 12–27.

11626. Severi, Rita. La biblioteca di Oscar Wilde. Palermo: Novecento, 2004. pp. 200.

11627. Silvani, Giovanna; Strukelj, Vanja. The legend of Salome in nineteenth-century literature and art. *In* (pp. 105–19) **8418**.

11628. Small, Ian (gen. ed.). The complete works of Oscar Wilde: vol. 2, *De Profundis*; *Epistola: in Carcere et Vinculis*. Ed. by Ian Small. Oxford; New York: OUP, 2005. pp. 345. Rev. by Peter Hollindale in RES (57:228) 2006, 130–4.

11629. —— The complete works of Oscar Wilde: vol. 3, *The Picture of Dorian Gray*: the 1890 and 1891 texts. Ed. by Joseph Bristow. (Bibl. 2005, 12424.) Rev. by Peter Hollindale in RES (57:228) 2006, 130–4; by John G. Peters in TextC (1:2) 2006, 157–8.

11630. Stetz, Margaret D. 'Ballads in prose': genre crossing in late Victorian women's writing. *See* **18879**.

11631. —— Rebecca West, Aestheticism, and the legacy of Oscar Wilde. *In* (pp. 157–69) **19082**.

11632. Wan, Marco. From the rack to the press: representation of the Oscar Wilde trials in the French newspaper *Le Temps*. LawL (18:1) 2006, 47–67.

11633. Whittington-Egan, Richard. Oscar Wilde in the twentieth century. ContRev (288:1680) 2006, 89–100.

11634. Wu, Xueping. An analysis of *The Portrait of Mr W.H.* FLS (121) 2006, 81–5. (In Chinese.)

Cynric R. Williams (*fl.*1826)

11635. Nordius, Janina. Racism and Radicalism in Jamaican gothic: Cynric R. Williams's *Hamel: the Obeah Man*. ELH (73:3) 2006, 673–93.

Mrs Henry Wood

11636. Maunder, Andrew. 'I will not live in poverty and neglect': *East Lynne* on the East End stage. *In* (pp. 173–87) **8647**.

11637. —— (gen. ed.). Gothic sensationalism: Ellen Wood, *St Martin's Eve* (1866). Ed. by Lyn Pykett. London; Brookfield, VT: Pickering & Chatto, 2004. pp. xxxiv, 446. (Varieties of women's sensation fiction 1855–1890, 3.) Rev. by Anthea Trodd in VicR (31:2) 2005, 132–4.

Constance Fenimore Woolson

11638. Conroy, Mark. On not representing Milly Theale: sacrificing for art in *The Wings of the Dove*. *In* (pp. 134–56) **10568**.

Dorothy Wordsworth

11639. Hubbell, Andrew. How Wordsworth invented picnicking and saved British culture. *See* **11681**.

11640. McKusick, James C. Nature. *In* (pp. 413–32) **8357**.

11641. Stabler, Jane. Devotion and diversion: early nineteenth-century British women travellers in Italy and the Catholic Church. *In* (pp. 15–34) **8320**.

11642. Wallace, Anne D. Home at Grasmere again: revising the family in Dove Cottage. *In* (pp. 101–23) **3405**.

William Wordsworth

11643. Anon. (comp.). Geoffrey Hartman: a bibliography, 1954–2005. WordsC (37:1) 2006, 39–42.

11644. Agosti, Annamaria. Frammenti del sublime romantico: Byron, Shelley, Wordsworth. *See* **9321**.

11645. Allen, Stuart; Roberts, Jonathan. Wordsworth and the thought of affection: *Michael*, *The Force of Prayer*, *Song at the Feast of Brougham Castle*. ERR (16:4) 2005, 455–70.

11646. Axcelson, John. The 'dial's moral round': charting Wordsworth's *Evening Walk*. ELH (73:3) 2006, 651–71.

11647. Baker, John Haydn. Browning and Wordsworth. (Bibl. 2004, 12485.) Rev. by Laura Dabundo in WordsC (36:4) 2005, 197.

11648. Balfour, Ian. Responding to the call: Hartman between Wordsworth and Hegel. WordsC (37:1) 2006, 15–16.

11649. Bohm, Arnd. Toys of wrath: *The Prelude* 10:363–74 and *Aeneid* 7:374–84. WordsC (36:3) 2005, 124–6.

11650. —— Wordsworth's *Nutting* and the Ovidian *Nux*. SR (45:1) 2006, 25–48.

11651. Branch, Lori. Rituals of spontaneity: sentiment and secularism from free prayer to Wordsworth. *See* **6607**.

11652. Bratcher, James T. Coleridge's *Biographia Litteraria*. *See* **9510**.

11653. Brown, Marshall. Negative poetics: on skepticism and the lyric voice. Representations (86) 2004, 120–40.

11654. Bruhn, Mark J. Cognition and representation in Wordsworth's London. SR (45:2) 2006, 157–80.

11655. Burke, Tim. Colonial spaces and national identities in *The Banks of Wye*: Bloomfield and the Wye after Wordsworth. *In* (pp. 89–112) **9141**.

11656. Cavone, Vito. *London's 'hubbub'*: la città come opposizione all'ordine naturale nel *Prelude* di William Wordsworth. *In* (pp. 117–32) **7343**.

11657. Clarke, Edward. Ariel among the second selves: Stevens and Wordsworth in creative conversation. *See* **18629**.

11658. Deshmane, Chetan. Wordsworth's *A Slumber*. Exp (64:4) 2006, 214–18.

11659. Douglass, Paul. Paradise decomposed: Byron's decadence and Wordsworthian nature in *Childe Harold* III and IV. *See* **9342**.

11660. Eliot, Simon. What price poetry? Selling Wordsworth, Tennyson, and Longfellow in nineteenth- and early twentieth-century Britain. PBSA (100:4) 2006, 425–45.

11661. Ferreccio, Giuliana. Paesaggi della coscienza: la formazione poetica di William Wordsworth. Turin: Stampatori, 2006. pp. 198.

11662. Fosso, Kurt. Buried communities: Wordsworth and the bonds of mourning. (Bibl. 2005, 12478.) Rev. by Scott Hess in WordsC (36:4) 2005, 150–2.

11663. François, Anne-Lise. 'Hum-men': in place of further development. WordsC (37:1) 2006, 19–22.

11664. —— 'O happy living things': Frankenfoods and the bounds of Wordsworthian natural piety. *In* (pp. 249–89) **3266**.

11665. Fry, Paul H. Progresses of poetry. WordsC (37:1) 2006, 22–7.

11666. Gelpi, Barbara Charlesworth. John Keble and Hurrell Froude in pastoral dialogue. *See* **10676**.

11667. Gibson, Andrew. 'A dim and undetermined sense of unknown modes of being': Wordsworth, *The Prelude* and the beginnings of modernity. EA (59:3) 2006, 263–78.

11668. Gill, Stephen (ed.). William Wordsworth's *The Prelude*: a casebook. Oxford; New York: OUP, 2006. pp. viii, 406. (Casebooks in criticism.)

11669. Goodman, Kevis. On Geoffrey Hartman's psycho-aesthetics. WordsC (37:1) 2006, 17–19.

11670. Haldane, Michael. From Plato to Pullman – the circle of invisibility and parallel worlds: *Fortunatus*, Mercury, and the Wishing-Hat: part II. *See* **6687**.

11671. Harding, Anthony John. 'Domestick privacies': biography and the sanctifying of privacy, from Johnson to Martineau. *See* **7927**.

11672. Hartman, Geoffrey. The psycho-aesthetics of Romantic moonshine: Wordsworth's profane illumination. WordsC (37:1) 2006, 8–14.

11673. Haughton, Hugh. Power and hiding places: Wordsworth and Seamus Heaney. *In* (pp. 61–100) **13735**.

11674. Hess, Scott. Wordsworth's 'system', the critical reviews, and the reconstruction of literary authority. ERR (16:4) 2005, 471–97.

11675. Hessell, Nikki. The opposite of news: rethinking the 1800 *Lyrical Ballads* and the mass media. SR (45:3) 2006, 331–55.

11676. Hewitt, Rachel. Wordsworth and the Ordnance Survey in Ireland: 'dreaming o'er the map of things'. WordsC (37:2) 2006, 80–5.

11677. Hickey, Alison. 'The body of my father's writings': Sara Coleridge's genial labor. *In* (pp. 124–47) **3405**.

11678. Hill, Alan G. The triumphs of memory: Petrarch, Augustine, and Wordsworth's ascent of Snowdon. RES (57:229) 2006, 247–58.

11679. —— Wordsworth prepares to move from Grasmere (1810): an unpublished letter. ELN (43:2) 2005, 96–102.

11680. Houghton, Sarah. The 'community' of John Clare's Helpston. *See* **9475**.

11681. Hubbell, Andrew. How Wordsworth invented picnicking and saved British culture. Romanticism (12:1) 2006, 44–51.

11682. Hughes, Felicity. William Wordsworth and Wonderful Walker. Seathwaite, Cumbria: Duddon Valley Local History Group, 2004. pp. 108. Rev. by Graham Tulloch in SHogg (15) 2004, 182–4.

11683. Ishikura, Waka. The reception and translation of Wordsworth in Japan. CLCWeb (8:2) 2006.

11684. Jones, J. Jennifer. Absorbing hesitation: Wordsworth and the theory of the panorama. SR (45:3) 2006, 357–75.

11685. Joshua, Essaka. Wordsworth among the Aristotelians. JHI (67:3) 2006, 511–22.

11686. Kim, Benjamin. Generating a national sublime: Wordsworth's *The River Duddon* and *The Guide to the Lakes*. SR (45:1) 2006, 49–75.

11687. Lattig, Sharon. The perception of metaphor and the metaphor of perception: the neurodynamics of figuration. *See* **2027**.

11688. Laubach-Kiani, Philip. 'I close my eyes and try and imagine them': Romantic discourse formations in *Krapp's Last Tape*. *See* **14697**.

11689. Leader, Zachary. Writers' blocks. TLS, 3 Nov. 2006, 11 (review-article). (Wordsworth and Coleridge's friendship.)

11690. McCully, Chris. The word in time: 4, Under the influence: *Lyrical Ballads*. *See* **9533**.

11691. MacKay, John. Inscription and modernity: from Wordsworth to Mandelstam. Bloomington: Indiana UP, 2006. pp. x, 303.

11692. McKusick, James C. Nature. *In* (pp. 413–32) **8357**.

11693. Manning, Peter J. The Persian Wordsworth. ERR (17:2) 2006, 189–96.

11694. Miller, Christopher R. The invention of evening: perception and time in Romantic poetry. *See* **9539**.

11695. Mook, Lorne. The everyday and the teleological: time-conflict, progression, and affect in Books 1 and 2 of *The Prelude*. ERR (17:5) 2006, 593–605.

11696. Moores, D. J. Mystical discourse in Wordsworth and Whitman: a transatlantic bridge. Louvain; Dudley, MA: Peeters, 2006. pp. 248. (Studies in spirituality: supplements, 11.)

11697. Mulvihill, James. George Campbell's *Philosophy of Rhetoric* and Wordsworth's 'Preface' to *Lyrical Ballads*. NQ (53:3) 2006, 315–16.

11698. Natarajan, Uttara. Pater and the genealogy of Hardy's modernity. *See* **10306**.

11699. Norris, Cara. The suspension of Habeas Corpus and narrative proliferation in Wordsworth's *The Borderers*. ERR (17:2) 2006, 197–203.

11700. Orel, Harold (ed.). William Wordsworth: interviews and recollections. (Bibl. 2005, 12507.) Rev. by Grevel Lindop in TLS, 9 June 2006, 8–9; by John Williams in BJ (34:2) 2006, 198–200.

11701. Pace, Joel; Scott, Matthew E. (eds). Wordsworth in American literary culture. (Bibl. 2005, 12508.) Rev. by Fiona Robertson in Romanticism (12:1) 2006, 63–5; by Angela Sorby in ERR (17:4) 2006, 502–7.

11702. Perry, Seamus. Joy perplexed: optimism and complication in Wordsworth, T. H. Green and A. C. Bradley. TLS, 14 July 2006, 13–15.

11703. Peterfreund, Stuart. Juan the memorious: the Feinaiglian narrative dynamics of *Don Juan*. *See* **9363**.

11704. Peterson, Linda H. Alice Meynell's *Preludes*; or, Preludes to what future poetry? *See* **10923**.

11705. Pritchard, William H. Possibilities for Wordsworth. HR (59:2) 2006, 309–16 (review-article).

11706. Quinney, Laura. Escape from repetition: Blake *versus* Locke and Wordsworth. *In* (pp. 63–79) **1894**.

11707. —— Swerving Neo-Platonists. WordsC (37:1) 2006, 31–8.

11708. Redfield, Marc. Geoffrey Hartman: a deviant homage. *See* **14268**.

11709. Regier, Alexander. A brotherhood is broken: Wordsworth, Benjamin, and the fragmentation of language. ERR (17:5) 2006, 607–28.

11710. Reid, Ian. Wordsworth and the formation of English Studies. (Bibl. 2004, 12547.) Rev. by Sally Bushell in BJ (33:1) 2005, 70–1.

11711. Russell, Corinna. A defence of tautology: repetition and difference in Wordsworth's note to *The Thorn*. Para (28:2) 2005, 104–18.

11712. Schneider, Matthew. Wordsworthian songcatching in America. *See* **3073**.

11713. Sell, Jonathan P. A. Allusion and ambiguity in Seamus Heaney's *Blackberry-Picking*. *See* **16323**.

11714. Shengold, Leonard. A brief psychoanalytic note on Wordsworth, poetic creativity, and love. APR (33:1) 2004, 27–9.

11715. Sisman, Adam. The friendship: Wordsworth and Coleridge. London: HarperCollins, 2006. pp. xxv, 480, (plates) 8. Rev. by Zachary Leader in TLS, 3 Nov. 2006, 11.

11716. Steinman, Lisa M. 'Beauty, resonance, integrity': creative readings of Wordsworth in twentieth-century American poetry. *In* (pp. 101–22) **13735**.

11717. Stillinger, Jack. Romantic complexity: Keats, Coleridge, and Wordsworth. *See* **10666**.

11718. Stimpson, Catharine R. Do these deaths surpass understanding? The literary figure of the mother who murders. *See* **17643**.

11719. Swift, Simon. Mary Wollstonecraft and the 'reserve of reason'. *See* **8270**.

11720. Tong, Joanne C. 'A spirit in the woods': Hegelian aesthetics and Wordsworth's *Nutting*. ELN (43:2) 2005, 102–15.

11721. Walker, Richard J. Pious works: aesthetics, ethics, and the modern individual in Robert Louis Stevenson's *Strange Case of Dr Jekyll and Mr Hyde*. *In* (pp. 265–74) **11272**.

11722. Wallace, Anne D. Home at Grasmere again: revising the family in Dove Cottage. *In* (pp. 101–23) **3405**.

11723. Williams, John. Britain's Nelson and Wordsworth's *Happy Warrior*: a case of cautious dissent. Romanticism (11:2) 2005, 181–98.

11724. Wilner, Joshua. 'Self-displacing vision': Snowdon and the dialectic of the senses. WordsC (37:1) 2006, 27–30.

11725. Yousef, Nancy. Wordsworth, Sentimentalism, and the defiance of sympathy. ERR (17:2) 2006, 205–13.

Frances Wright

11726. Bederman, Gail. Revisiting Nashoba: slavery, utopia, and Frances Wright in America, 1818–1826. AmLH (17:3) 2005, 438–59.

Charlotte M. Yonge

11727. Jay, Elisabeth. Charlotte Mary Yonge and Tractarian aesthetics. VP (44:1) 2006, 43–59.

11728. Sturrock, June. Establishing identity: editorial correspondence from the early years of *The Monthly Packet*. VPR (39:3) 2006, 266–79.

11729. Walton, Susan. Charlotte M. Yonge and the 'historic harem' of Edward Augustus Freeman. JVC (11:2) 2006, 226–55.

TWENTIETH CENTURY

GENERAL

11730. ANON. Notable Latino writers. Pasadena, CA: Salem Press, 2006. 3 vols. pp. xxii, 1000. (Magill's choice.)

11731. —— (ed.). Women's Studies Association (N.Z.) conference proceedings 2005. Wellington, New Zealand: Women's Studies Association (N.Z.), 2005. pp. 221.

11732. ABOUL-ELA, HOSAM. Global South, local South: the new postnationalism in US Southern Studies. AL (78:4) 2006, 847–58 (review-article).

11733. ADAMOWICZ, ELZA (ed.). Surrealism: crossings/frontiers. New York; Frankfurt: Lang, 2006. pp. 222, (plates) 16. (European connections, 18.)

11734. ALAM, FAKRUL (ed.). South Asian writers in English. Detroit, MI: Gale Research, 2006. pp. xxiii, 490. (Dictionary of literary biography, 323.)

11735. ALCOBIA-MURPHY, SHANE. 'Not forgotten or passed over at the proper time': the representation of violent events in contemporary culture. *See* **16416**.

11736. ALDAMA, FREDERICK LUIS. Brown on brown: Chicano/a representations of gender, sexuality, and ethnicity. (Bibl. 2005, 12540.) Rev. by Jesse Alemán in MELUS (31:1) 2006, 162–4.

11737. —— Spilling the beans in Chicanolandia: conversations with writers and artists. Austin: Texas UP, 2006. pp. vii, 294.

11738. ALEXANDER, NEAL; MURPHY, SHANE; OAKMAN, ANNE (eds). To the other shore: crosscurrents in Irish and Scottish literature. Belfast: Cló Ollscoil na Banríona, 2004. Rev. by Bernard Escarbelt in EtIr (30:1) 2005, 227–8.

11739. ALLEN, JOHN. Homelessness in American literature: romanticism, realism, and testimony. *See* **8280**.

11740. ALLMENDINGER, BLAKE. Imagining the African American West. (Bibl. 2005, 12544.) Rev. by Michael K. Johnson in WAL (41:3) 2006, 336–44; by Matthew C. Whitaker in JArizH (47:4) 2006, 389–90.

11741. APTER, EMILY. The translation zone: a new comparative literature. *See* **2800**.

11742. ARAUJO, ANDERSON D. *Blast*, Futurism, and the cultural mobility of Modernist (inter)texts. *See* **1054**.

11743. ARBINOWITZ, PAULA. Social representations within American Modernism. *In* (pp. 261–83) **11964**.

11744. ARMSTRONG, JEANNETTE. Keynote address: the aesthetic qualities of aboriginal writing. *See* **8283**.

11745. ARMSTRONG, TIM. Modernism: a cultural history. Oxford; Malden, MA: Polity Press in assn with Blackwell, 2005. pp. x, 176. (Themes in twentieth-century literature and culture.) Rev. by Katherine Baxter in NQ (53:4) 2006, 581–2; by Edwin J. Barton in AL (78:4) 2006, 874–6.

11746. ARNOLD, JOHN. Fanfrolico frolics. *See* **640**.

11747. ASAAH, AUGUSTINE H. To speak or not to speak with the whole mouth: textualization of taboo subjects in europhone African literature. JBlaS (36:4) 2006, 497–514.

11748. Ashcroft, Bill; Griffiths, Gareth; Tiffin, Helen (eds). The Post-Colonial Studies reader. (Bibl. 1997, 11877.) London; New York: Routledge, 2006. pp. xxviii, 587. (Second ed.: first ed. 1995.)

11749. Atkinson, William. The perils of world literature. WLT (80:5) 2006, 43–7.

11750. Attwell, David. Rewriting modernity: studies in Black South African literary history. Scottsville: KwaZulu-Natal UP, 2005; Athens: Ohio UP, 2006. pp. x, 236.

11751. Atwood, Margaret. Moving targets: selected critical prose, 1982–2004. Concord, Ont.: House of Anansi Press, 2004. pp. 422. Rev. by Sally Chivers in CanL (190) 2006, 141–3.

11752. —— Writing with intent: essays, reviews, personal prose, 1983–2005. New York: Carroll & Graf, 2005. pp. xvii, 427.

11753. Avalos, Hector. Strangers in our own land: religion in contemporary Latina/o literature. Nashville, TN: Abingdon Press, 2005. pp. xxi, 229.

11754. Badia, Janet; Phegley, Jennifer (eds). Reading women: literary figures and cultural icons from the Victorian age to the present. (Bibl. 2005, 12549.) Rev. by Nicola Humble in TLS, 6 Oct. 2006, 30; by Patrocinio Schweickart in VS (48:4) 2006, 732–3.

11755. Baker, Barbara (ed.). The way we write: interviews with award-winning writers. London; New York: Continuum, 2006. pp. xv, 234.

11756. Baldick, Chris. The modern movement: 1910–1940. (Bibl. 2005, 12551.) Rev. by David Ayers in Eng (54:210) 2005, 242–4; by Jason Harding in CamQ (34:4) 2005, 416–19; by Lachlan Mackinnon in TLS, 21 July 2006, 6–7.

11757. Ballinger, Gill; Lustig, Tim; Townshend, Dale. Missing intertexts: Hannah Crafts's *The Bondwoman's Narrative* and African American literary history. *See* **9645**.

11758. Banerjee, A. (ed.). Humanistic interpretations of modern British and American writers: essays in literary criticism. *See* **20011**.

11759. Barillas, William. The Midwestern pastoral: place and landscape in literature of the American heartland. Athens: Ohio UP, 2006. pp. xviii, 258. Rev. by Todd Davis in Style (40:4) 2006, 381–3.

11760. Baringer, Sandra. The metanarrative of suspicion in late twentieth-century America. London; New York: Routledge, 2004. pp. vii, 176. (Literary criticism and cultural theory.)

11761. Barolini, Helen. Their other side: six American women and the lure of Italy. *See* **8288**.

11762. Barone, Dennis. 'We've always been different': Louisa Ermelino's Spring Street trilogy and Italian American women's writing. *See* **20227**.

11763. Baronti Marchiò, Roberto. Avanguardia e modernismo: il vorticismo inglese. *In* (pp. 161–201) **3341**.

11764. Bassard, Katherine Clay. The race for faith: justice, mercy, and the sign of the Cross in African American literature. ReLit (38:1) 2006, 95–114.

11765. Bataille, Gretchen M. Native American women writers. PemM (38) 2006, 92–6.

11766. Baugh, Eddie. Literary theory and the Caribbean: theory, belief and desire; or, Designing theory. *See* **14019**.

11767. Beaulieu, Elizabeth Ann (ed.). Writing African American women: an encyclopedia of literature by and about women of colour. Westport, CT; London: Greenwood Press, 2006. pp. xxiv, 991.

11768. Belluscio, Steven J. To be suddenly White: literary realism and racial passing. *See* **8291**.

11769. Benfey, Christopher; Remmler, Karen (eds). Artists, intellectuals, and World War II: the Pontigny encounters at Mount Holyoke College, 1942–1944. Amherst: Massachusetts UP, 2006. pp. xiii, 294.

11770. Bennett, Bruce. Homing in: essays on Australian literature and selfhood. Perth, W. Australia: API Network, 2006. pp. vi, 297. Rev. by Pradeep Trikha in Antipodes (20:2) 2006, 211–12.

11771. —— In the shadows: the spy in Australian literary history and culture. Antipodes (20:1) 2006, 28–37.

11772. Berger, Alan L.; Cronin, Gloria L. (eds). Jewish American and Holocaust literature: representation in the postmodern world. (Bibl. 2004, 12602.) Rev. by Helene Meyers in PhRS (1:2) 2005, 179–80.

11773. Bergman, David. The violet hour: the Violet Quill and the making of gay culture. (Bibl. 2005, 12562.) Rev. by Arthur L. Little, Jr, in AL (77:3) 2005, 648–51.

11774. Berry, R. M. Language. *In* (pp. 113–22) **11788**.

11775. Bigazzi, Carlo (ed.). Studi irlandesi. *See* **8294**.

11776. Bigsby, Christopher (ed.). The Cambridge companion to modern American culture. Cambridge; New York: CUP, 2006. pp. xv, 496.

11777. Birgy, Philippe. Une terrible beauté: les modernistes anglais à l'épreuve de la critique girardienne. (Bibl. 2005, 12565.) Rev. by Adolphe Haberer in EA (59:2) 2006, 244–5.

11778. Bloch, Avital H.; Umansky, Lauri (eds). Impossible to hold: women and culture in the 1960s. (Bibl. 2005, 12566.) Rev. by Sarah Graham in JAStud (40:2) 2006, 418–19.

11779. Boehmer, Elleke. Stories of women: gender and narrative in the postcolonial nation. Manchester; New York: Manchester UP, 2005. pp. x, 239.

11780. Bohata, Kirsti. Postcolonialism revisited. Cardiff: UP of Wales, 2004. pp. xii, 209. (Writing Wales in English.) (CREW series of critical and scholarly studies.) Rev. by Sinéad Sturgeon in MLR (101:3) 2006, 835–6.

11781. Boldt-Irons, Leslie; Federici, Corrado; Virgulti, Ernesto (eds). Images and imagery: frames, borders, limits – interdisciplinary perspectives. New York; Frankfurt: Lang, 2005. pp. xv, 293. (Studies on themes and motifs in literature, 74.)

11782. Bolton, Jonathan. Mid-term autobiography and the Second World War. JML (30:1) 2006, 155–72.

11783. Bona, Mary Jo; Maini, Irma (eds). Multiethnic literature and canon debates. Albany: New York State UP, 2006. pp. xiv, 242.

11784. Borshuk, Michael. Swinging the vernacular: jazz and African American Modernist literature. London; New York: Routledge, 2006. pp. xi, 252. (Studies in African American history and culture.)

11785. Boudreau, Kristin. The spectacle of death: populist literary responses to American capital cases. *See* **8301**.

11786. Bourke, Roger. Prisoners of the Japanese: literary imagination and the prisoner-of-war experience. St Lucia: Queensland UP, 2006. pp. 208.

11787. Bradshaw, David. Obscenity and censorship. *In* (pp. 103–12) **11788**.

11788. —— Dettmar, Kevin J. H. (eds). A companion to Modernist literature and culture. Oxford; Malden, MA: Blackwell, 2006. pp. xxi, 592. (Blackwell companions to literature and culture, 39.)

11789. Breaux, Quo Vadis Gex. Tom Dent's role in the organizational mentoring of African American Southern writers: a memoir. *See* **15452**.

11790. Bridgham, Fred (ed.). The First World War as a clash of cultures. Rochester, NY: Camden House, 2006. pp. vi, 336. (Studies in German literature, linguistics, and culture.)

11791. Brooker, Peter. Bohemia in London: the social scene of early Modernism. (Bibl. 2005, 12580.) Rev. by Jeremy Tambling in MLR (101:1) 2006, 214–16.

11792. —— Thacker, Andrew (eds). Geographies of Modernism: literatures, cultures, spaces. (Bibl. 2005, 12581.) Rev. by Peter Kalliney in Mod/Mod (13:4) 2006, 747–54; by Michael H. Whitworth in RES (57:232) 2006, 851–2; by Peter Childs in JPW (42:1) 2006, 117–19.

11793. Brown, Lois. The encyclopedia of the Harlem literary renaissance. New York: Facts on File, 2005. pp. ix, 612.

11794. Brown, Nicholas. Utopian generations: the political horizon of twentieth-century literature. (Bibl. 2005, 12583.) Rev. by Loren Glass in ConLit (47:3) 2006, 491–6.

11795. Brown-Guillory, Elizabeth (ed.). Middle passages and the healing place of history: migration and identity in Black women's literature. Columbus: Ohio State UP, 2006. pp. xiii, 201.

11796. Bucher, Katherine; Manning, M. Lee. Young adult literature: exploration, evaluation, and appreciation. Upper Saddle River, NJ: Pearson / Prentice Hall, 2006. pp. xix, 395.

11797. Bucknor, Michael A.; Coleman, Daniel. Introduction: rooting and routing Caribbean Canadian writing. JWIL (14:1/2) 2005, i–xliii.

11798. Buell, Lawrence. Religion and the environmental imagination in American literature. *In* (pp. 216–38) **8429**.

11799. Burlingham, Russell; Billis, Roger (eds). Reformed characters: the Reform Club in history and literature: an anthology with commentary. Foreword by Edward Pearce. *See* **8309**.

11800. Burstein, Janet. Telling the little secrets: American Jewish writing since the 1980s. Madison; London: Wisconsin UP, 2006. pp. xv, 264.

11801. Bush, Ronald. Imagist poetics and the cultural politics of Modernism. QPS (14) 2006, 419–27.

11802. Buzelin, Hélène. A socio-historical perspective on French translations of West Indian fiction. *See* **17719**.

11803. Calder, Alison; Wardhaugh, Robert (eds). History, literature, and the writing of the Canadian prairies. (Bibl. 2005, 12587.) Rev. by W. A. Waiser in CHR (87:2) 2006, 340–1; by Janice Fiamengo in CanL (191) 2006, 113–14.

11804. Calderón, Héctor. Narratives of Greater Mexico: essays on Chicano literary history, genre, and borders. (Bibl. 2004, 12634.) Rev. by Rafael Pérez-Torres in AL (78:4) 2006, 892–4.

11805. Campisi, Dale. Little magazines, great divides. *See* **1067**.

11806. Capo, Beth Widmaier. 'She is herself a poem': Caresse Crosby, feminine identity, and literary history. *See* **15368**.

11807. Carino, Peter. Why baseball has a literature: family, community, home. *See* **8310**.

11808. Carosso, Andrea; Concilio, Carmen (eds). *Real cities*: rappresentazioni della città negli Stati Uniti e in Canada. Turin: Otto, 2006. pp. 160. (Nova americana.)

11809. Carpenter, Faedra Chatard. An interview with Gwendolyn D. Pough. Callaloo (29:3) 2006, 808–14.

11810. Carroll, Anne Elizabeth. Word, image, and the New Negro: representation and identity in the Harlem renaissance. (Bibl. 2005, 12592.) Rev. by Stephanie Brown in AmP (16:1) 2006, 119–21; by Australia Tarver in ColLit (33:3) 2006, 198–203; by George Bornstein in MichQR (45:4) 2006, 713–21; by Kenneth W. Warren in JAH (93:2) 2006, 569–70.

11811. Cart, Michael; Jenkins, Christine A. The heart has its reasons: young adult literature with gay/lesbian/queer content, 1969–2004. Lanham, MD; London: Scarecrow Press, 2006. pp. xxi, 207. (Scarecrow studies in young adult literature, 18.) Rev. by B. Aaron Talbot in CLAQ (31:4) 2006, 390–2.

11812. Carter, David. 'Some means of learning of the best new books': *All about Books* and the modern reader. *See* **1068**.

11813. Caruth, Cathy. Confronting political trauma. ConnR (28:1) 2006, 179–82.

11814. Castro, Brian. Making oneself foreign. *See* **13090**.

11815. Castronovo, David. Beyond the gray flannel suit: books from the 1950s that made American culture. (Bibl. 2005, 12594.) Rev. by Judie Newman in MLR (101:4) 2006, 1103–4; by Robert Donahoo in FOR (4) 2006, 157–9.

11816. Cawelti, John G. Mystery, violence, and popular culture: essays. (Bibl. 2005, 12596.) Rev. by Greg Forter in AL (78:4) 2006, 897–9.

11817. Caws, Mary Ann. Surprised in translation. Chicago, IL; London: Chicago UP, 2006. pp. xi, 145.

11818. Celiker, Mehmet Ali. Stuck in the middle of cultures: post-colonial metropolitans. *In* (pp. 55–66) **3307**.

11819. Chen, Aimin. Chinese American literature from the perspective of Orientalism. FLS (122) 2006, 112–18. (In Chinese.)

11820. Cheng, Vincent J. Inauthentic: the anxiety over culture and identity. (Bibl. 2004, 12647.) Rev. by Ben Schreier in PhRS (2:2) 2006, 168–71.

11821. Cherolis, Stephanie. When language fails: witnessing Holocaust testimony. ConnR (28:1) 2006, 93–101.

11822. Cheyfitz, Eric. The (post)colonial construction of Indian country: US American Indian literatures and federal Indian law. *In* (pp. 3–124) **11823**.

11823. —— (ed.). The Columbia guide to American Indian literatures of the United States since 1945. New York: Columbia UP, 2006. pp. x, 438. (Columbia guides to literature since 1945.)

11824. Chialant, Maria Teresa (ed.). Viaggio e letteratura. Venice: Marsilio, 2006. pp. 461. (Ricerche.)

11825. Chinitz, David. The new Harlem renaissance studies. Mod/Mod (13:2) 2006, 375–82 (review-article).

11826. Chlebek, Diana (comp.). Annual bibliography of Commonwealth literature 2005: Canada. *See* **19487**.

11827. Clarke, George Elliott. Does (Afro-)Caribbean Canadian literature exist? In the Caribbean? JWIL (14:1/2) 2005, 260–302.

11828. Clay, Catherine. British women writers, 1914–1945: professional work and friendship. Aldershot; Burlington, VT: Ashgate, 2006. pp. vi, 184. Rev. by Melissa Sullivan in TSWL (25:2) 2006, 352–4; by Diana Wallace in RES (57:232) 2006, 856–8.

11829. Cleary, Joe; Connolly, Claire (eds). The Cambridge companion to modern Irish culture. Cambridge; New York: CUP, 2005. pp. xvi, 363. Rev. by Kate Costello-Sullivan in ILS (25:1) 2005, 26; by Clare Hutton in TLS, 18 Feb. 2005, 30; by Donna Schuster in JJLS (20:2) 2006, 15.

11830. Coffman, Christine E. Insane passions: lesbianism and psychosis in literature and film. Middletown, CT: Wesleyan UP, 2006. pp. viii, 288.

11831. Cognard-Black, Jennifer; Walls, Elizabeth MacLeod (eds). Kindred hands: letters on writing by British and American women authors, 1865–1935. *See* **8325**.

11832. Collier, Patrick. Modernism on Fleet Street. *See* **1074**.

11833. Collini, Stefan. Absent minds: intellectuals in Britain. Oxford; New York: OUP, 2006. pp. viii, 526. Rev. by Michael Karwowski in ContRev (288:1682) 2006, 339–44.

11834. Collins, Lisa Gail. Activists who yearn for art that transforms: parallels in the Black Arts and Feminist Art Movements in the United States. Signs (31:3) 2006, 717–52.

11835. Comentale, Edward P. Modernism, cultural production, and the British avant-garde. (Bibl. 2005, 12616.) Rev. by Christoph Lindner in Eng (54:210) 2005, 244–8.

11836. —— Gąsiorek, Andrzej (eds). T. E. Hulme and the question of Modernism. *See* **16516**.

11837. Connor, Steven (ed.). The Cambridge companion to postmodernism. (Bibl. 2005, 12617.) Rev. by Catherine Bernard in EA (59:1) 2006, 121–2.

11838. Cooper, John Xiros. Modernism and the culture of market society. (Bibl. 2005, 12619.) Rev. by Janine Utell in JMMLA (38:2) 2005, 155–61; by Meg

Albrinck in VWM (68) 2005/06, 19–20; by Catherine Bernard in EA (59:1) 2006, 116–18.

11839. Corey, Stephen (commentary). 'Into the hectic unknown': correspondence from the archives of *The Georgia Review*, 1947–76. GaR (60:3/4) 2006, 606–700.

11840. Cotta Ramusino, Elena. Riflessioni su guerra e letteratura. ConLett (45) 2006, 133–46.

11841. Crouch, Stanley. The artificial White man: essays on authenticity. New York: Basic Civitas, 2004. pp. 244. Rev. by Edward Margolies in AAR (40:3) 2006, 601–3.

11842. Cuddy-Keane, Melba. Global Modernism. *In* (pp. 558–64) **11788**.

11843. Culler, Jonathan. The problem of Modernism. QPS (14) 2006, 414–17.

11844. Cullingford, Elizabeth Butler. 'Our nuns are *not* a nation': politicizing the convent in Irish literature and film. *See* **8327**.

11845. Curtis, Anthony. Virginia Woolf: Bloomsbury & beyond. *See* **19272**.

11846. Cutter, Martha J. Lost and found in translation: contemporary ethnic American writing and the politics of language diversity. Chapel Hill; London: North Carolina UP, 2005. pp. viii, 326.

11847. Czarnecki, Kristin. 'A house made with stones / full of stories': anthologizing Native American literature. *In* (pp. 61–82) **11783**.

11848. Das, Santanu. Touch and intimacy in First World War literature. Cambridge; New York: CUP, 2005. pp. xiii, 269. Rev. by Mark Bostridge in TLS, 16 June 2006, 4–5; by Sandra M. Gilbert in RES (57:232) 2006, 849–51.

11849. Davis, Rocío G.; Lee, Sue-Im (eds). Literary gestures: the aesthetic in Asian American writing. Philadelphia, PA: Temple UP, 2006. pp. vi, 239.

11850. Davis, Todd F.; Womack, Kenneth. Postmodern humanism in contemporary literature and culture: reconciling the void. Basingstoke; New York: Palgrave Macmillan, 2006. pp. xxv, 198.

11851. Dawson, Melanie. Laboring to play: home entertainment and the spectacle of middle-class cultural life, 1850–1920. *See* **8332**.

11852. Decker, Jeffrey Louis. Saint Oprah. MFS (52:1) 2006, 169–78 (review-article).

11853. de la Concha, Ángeles (ed.). Shakespeare en la imaginación contemporánea: revisiones y reescrituras de su obra. *See* **5285**.

11854. DeLoughrey, Elizabeth M.; Handley, George B.; Gosson, Renée K. (eds). Caribbean literature and the environment: between nature and culture. (Bibl. 2005, 12632.) Rev. by Martin Munro in RAL (37:3) 2006, 217–18.

11855. del Río-Álvaro, Constanza; García-Mainar, Luis Miguel (eds). Memory, imagination and desire in contemporary Anglo-American literature and film. (Bibl. 2004, 12672.) Rev. by Silvia Martínez Falquina in Misc (32) 2005, 135–41.

11856. DelRosso, Jeana. Writing Catholic women: contemporary international Catholic girlhood narratives. (Bibl. 2005, 12633.) Rev. by Nancy Lusignan Schultz in TSWL (25:2) 2006, 357–9.

11857. DeShazer, Mary K. Fractured borders: reading women's cancer literature. Ann Arbor: Michigan UP, 2005. pp. vii, 301.

11858. DeSoto, Aureliano Maria. On the trail of the Chicana/o subject: literary texts and contexts in the formulation of Chicana/o Studies. *In* (pp. 41–60) **11783**.

11859. Devlin, Rachel. Relative intimacy: fathers, adolescent daughters, and postwar American culture. Chapel Hill; London: North Carolina UP, 2005. pp. ix, 254. (Gender and American culture.) Rev. by Rachael McLennan in JAStud (40:3) 2006, 656–7.

11860. Diala, Isidore (ed.). The responsible critic: essays on African literature in honor of Professor Ben Obumselu. Trenton, NJ: Africa World Press, 2006. pp. xxiii, 310.

11861. Dickstein, Morris. The mirror in the roadway: literature and the real world. (Bibl. 2005, 12635.) Rev. by Michael Gorra in TLS, 6 Jan. 2006, 22; by Jay Martin in AR (64:2) 2006, 379; by William Kerrigan in Raritan (26:1) 2006, 163–70; by Irving Malin in HC (43:3) 2006, 20–2.

11862. Dimock, Wai Chee. Through other continents: American literature across deep time. *See* **8337**.

11863. DiPietro, Cary. Shakespeare and Modernism. *See* **5500**.

11864. Dix, Andrew; Taylor, Jonathan (eds). Figures of heresy: radical theology in English and American writing, 1800–2000. *See* **8338**.

11865. Doan, Laura; Garrity, Jane. Modernism queered. *In* (pp. 542–50) **11788**.

11866. Donnell, Alison. Twentieth-century Caribbean literature: critical moments in anglophone literary history. London; New York: Routledge, 2006. pp. x, 278.

11867. Dotson, Daniel. Portrayal of mathematicians in fictional works. CLCWeb (8:4) 2006.

11868. Duncan, Patti. Tell this silence: Asian American women writers and the politics of speech. (Bibl. 2004, 12688.) Rev. by Yoonmee Chang in AL (77:4) 2005, 858–61.

11869. Duncan, Russell; Juncker, Clara (eds). Transnational America: contours of modern US culture. Copenhagen: Museum Tusculanum Press, 2004. pp. 276. Rev. by Johan Callens in EngS (87:3) 2006, 375–7.

11870. Duvall, John N. Regionalism in American Modernism. *In* (pp. 242–60) **11964**.

11871. Dwyer, June. Canon-openers, book clubs, and middlebrow culture. *In* (pp. 167–82) **11783**.

11872. Eckstein, Barbara. Sustaining New Orleans: literature, local memory, and the fate of a city. London; New York: Routledge, 2006. pp. xvi, 280.

11873. Edwards, Brian T. Morocco bound: disorienting America's Maghreb, from Casablanca to the Marrakech Express. Durham, NC; London: Duke UP,

2005. pp. xv, 366. (New Americanists.) Rev. by Ali Behdad in CL (58:2) 2006, 180–2.

11874. Edwards, Nadi. Edward Baugh: the critic as mediator. *See* **14638**.

11875. Eigenbrod, Renate. Travelling knowledges: positioning the im/migrant reader of aboriginal literatures in Canada. Winnipeg: Manitoba UP, 2005. pp. xvi, 280. Rev. by Rob Appleford in GPQ (26:4) 2006, 292–3; by Margery Fee in CanL (191) 2006, 196–8.

11876. Elam, Harry J., Jr; Jackson, Kennell (eds). Black cultural traffic: crossroads in global performance and popular culture. Ann Arbor: Michigan UP, 2005. pp. x, 404.

11877. Ellen, Jane. Cold Wars and culture wars. Meanjin (63:1) 2004, 142–6. ('*Meanjin* Archive'.)

11878. Elliott, Emory (introd.). A forum on Joanna Brooks, *American Lazarus: Religion and the Rise of African American and Native American Literatures*. With a response by Joanna Brooks. *See* **8347**.

11879. Emenyonu, Ernest N., *et al.* (eds). New women's writing in African literature: a review. Oxford: Currey; Portsmouth, NH: Heinemann, 2004. pp. 224. (African literature today, 24.) Rev. by Ezenwa-Ohaeto in RAL (37:1) 2006, 139–42.

11880. English, Daylanne K. Unnatural selections: eugenics in American Modernism and the Harlem renaissance. (Bibl. 2005, 12657.) Rev. by David Chinitz in Mod/Mod (13:2) 2006, 375–82; by Riché Richardson in AL (78:3) 2006, 627–9.

11881. Esty, Joshua. A shrinking island: Modernism and national culture in England. (Bibl. 2005, 12663.) Rev. by Ryan Trimm in Novel (39:2) 2006, 273–5.

11882. Evans, Patrick. 'Pakeha-style biculturalism' and the Maori writer. JNZL (24:1) 2006, 11–35.

11883. Fantina, Richard (ed.). Straight writ queer: non-normative expressions of heterosexuality in literature. Foreword by Calvin Thomas. Jefferson, NC; London: McFarland, 2006. pp. vii, 266.

11884. Farrell, Frank B. Why does literature matter? (Bibl. 2005, 12670.) Rev. by Andrew J. Taggart in ColLit (33:4) 2006, 204–16.

11885. Fazzini, Marco (ed.). Resisting alterities: Wilson Harris and other avatars of otherness. *See* **16284**.

11886. Ferguson, Roderick A. Aberrations in black: toward a queer theory of color critique. (Bibl. 2004, 12703.) Rev. by Arthur L. Little, Jr, in AL (77:3) 2005, 648–51.

11887. —— African American masculinity and the study of social formations. AmQ (58:1) 2006, 213–19 (review article).

11888. Ferraro, Thomas J. Feeling Italian: the art of ethnicity in America. New York; London: New York UP, 2005. pp. xv, 256. (Nation of newcomers.) Rev. by Jeffrey Louis Decker in AmQ (58:4) 2006, 1239–47; by Fred Gardaphé in AmBR (27:5) 2006, 18.

11889. Field, Douglas (ed.). American Cold War culture. Edinburgh: Edinburgh UP, 2005. pp. ix, 214. Rev. by Susan L. Carruthers in Mod/Mod (13:1) 2006, 210–12.

11890. Field, Edward. The man who would marry Susan Sontag; and other intimate portraits of the Bohemian Era. Madison; London: Wisconsin UP, 2005. pp. xv, 284. (Living out.) Rev. by Andrew Rosenheim in TLS, 4 Aug. 2006, 26.

11891. Findlay, John M. Something in the soil? Literature and regional identity in the 20th-century Pacific Northwest. PacNQ (97:4) 2006, 179–89.

11892. Flannery, Eóin. Morning yet on *Field Day*? Ireland, *Field Day* and postcolonialism. *In* (pp. 41–62) **12189**.

11893. Flannery, Kathryn Thoms. Feminist literacies, 1968–75. (Bibl. 2005, 12676.) Rev. by Sharon J. Kirsch in WL (29:1) 2006, 55–6.

11894. Franco, Dean J. Ethnic American literature: comparing Chicano, Jewish, and African American writing. Charlottesville; London: Virginia UP, 2006. pp. x, 219.

11895. Friedman, Susan Stanford. Periodizing Modernism: postcolonial modernities and the space/time borders of Modernist Studies. Mod/Mod (13:3) 2006, 425–43.

11896. Froula, Christine. On French and British freedoms: early Bloomsbury and the brothels of Modernism. CVE (62) 2005, 137–56.

11897. Frykholm, Amy Johnson. Rapture culture: Left Behind in Evangelical America. (Bibl. 2005, 12684.) Rev. by Martin L. Johnson in WF (65:3) 2006, 357–9.

11898. Fusco, Serena. *Blurring the lines*: dal nazionalismo culturale alla diaspora. *In* (pp. 94–124) **11954**.

11899. Gadsby, Meredith M. Sucking salt: Caribbean women writers, migration, and survival. Columbia; London: Missouri UP, 2006. pp. xii, 225.

11900. Gardaphé, Fred L. From wiseguys to wise men: the gangster and Italian American masculinities. London; New York: Routledge, 2006. pp. xix, 244.

11901. —— Leaving Little Italy: essaying Italian American culture. (Bibl. 2004, 12723.) Rev. by Steven J. Belluscio in MFS (52:1) 2006, 228–31.

11902. Gerster, Robin. No man is a naked island: the Australian POW story. Southerly (65:2) 2005, 44–59.

11903. Geuder, Ann-Catherine. Chicana/o Literaturbetrieb: Wege in die Öffentlichkeit seit 1965. Heidelberg: Winter, 2004. pp. 408. (American studies, 121.)

11904. Gibbons, Reginald. Fortunately, the marks on the page are alien. APR (35:4) 2006, 49–52.

11905. Gibson, Colin; Marr, Lisa (eds). New windows on a woman's world: essays for Jocelyn Harris: vol. 2. *See* **8374**.

11906. Gikandi, Simon. Preface: Modernism in the world. Mod/Mod (13:3) 2006, 419–24.

11907. Gilbert, Geoff. Before Modernism was: modern history and the constituency of writing. (Bibl. 2005, 12694.) Rev. by Tim Armstrong in TexP (19:4) 2005, 551–4.

11908. Gilbert, Sandra M. Death's door: modern dying and the ways we grieve. New York; London: Norton, 2006. pp. xxv, 580.

11909. Glajar, Valentina; Radulescu, Domnica (eds). Vampirettes, wretches, and Amazons: Western representations of East European women. (Bibl. 2005, 12697.) Rev. by Ulrike Rainer in SlavR (65:3) 2006, 571–2; by Olga Mesropova in SEEJ (50:2) 2006, 356–8.

11910. Glass, Loren. Authors Inc.: literary celebrity in the modern United States, 1880–1980. (Bibl. 2005, 12698.) Rev. by Steven Fink in ALR (38:3) 2006, 279–81; by Kinohi Nishikawa in AL (78:3) 2006, 652–4.

11911. Goebel, Walter; Schabio, Saskia (eds). Beyond the Black Atlantic: relocating modernization and technology. London; New York: Routledge, 2006. pp. ix, 210.

11912. Goldsmith, Kenneth. Paragraphs on conceptual writing. OpL (twelfth series) (7) 2005, 98–101.

11913. Gourevitch, Philip (introd.). The *Paris Review* interviews: vol. 1. New York: Picador USA, 2006. pp. xviii, 510.

11914. Gräbe, Ina. Theory and technology in contemporary South African writing: from self-conscious exploration to contextual appropriation. *In* (pp. 203–12) **14093**.

11915. Gray, Stephen (ed.). Indaba: interviews with African writers. Pretoria: Protea Book House, 2005. pp. 223. Rev. by M. J. Daymond in RAL (37:3) 2006, 205–8.

11916. Griesinger, Emily; Eaton, Mark (eds). The gift of story: narrating hope in a postmodern world. Waco, TX: Baylor Univ., 2006. pp. xii, 391.

11917. Gruesser, John Cullen. Confluences: postcolonialism, African American literary studies, and the Black Atlantic. (Bibl. 2005, 12709.) Rev. by Eric Keenaghan in JML (29:3) 2006, 176–90; by Jonathan Eburne in MFS (52:3) 2006, 748–52; by Michelle Stephens in AL (78:3) 2006, 638–40.

11918. Gunn, Joshua. Modern occult rhetoric: mass media and the drama of secrecy in the twentieth century. Tuscaloosa; London: Alabama UP, 2005. pp. xxix, 340. (Rhetoric, culture, and social critique.) Rev. by John Shelton Lawrence in JAC (29:4) 2006, 502–3.

11919. Gunnars, Kristjana. Stranger at the door: writers and the act of writing. Waterloo, Ont.: Wilfrid Laurier UP, 2004. pp. xiii, 121. Rev. by Norbert Schürer in WLT (80:1) 2006, 59–60.

11920. Haggerty, George E. Queer gothic. Urbana: Illinois UP, 2006. pp. x, 231.

11921. Hakutani, Yoshinobu. Cross-cultural visions in African American Modernism: from spatial narrative to jazz haiku. Columbus: Ohio State UP, 2006. pp. ix, 251.

11922. Hall, Edith. No man's lands: modern myths of the Cyclops. *See* **10702**.

11923. Hamilton, Stephen (comp.). Annual bibliography of Commonwealth literature 2005: New Zealand. *See* **19503**.

11924. Hammill, Faye; Miskimmin, Esme; Sponenberg, Ashlie (eds). Encyclopedia of British women's writing, 1900–1950. Basingstoke; New York: Palgrave Macmillan, 2006. pp. xi, 343.

11925. Hammond, Andrew. The Balkans and the West: constructing the European Other, 1945–2003. (Bibl. 2005, 12717.) Rev. by Andi Mihalache in Journeys (6:1/2) 2005, 140–3.

11926. —— (ed.). Cold War literature: writing the global conflict. London; New York: Routledge, 2006. pp. x, 272. (Routledge studies in twentieth-century literature, 3.)

11927. Hammond, Mary. Reading, publishing, and the formation of literary taste in England, 1880–1914. *See* **8382**.

11928. Hanson, Gillian Mary. Riverbank and seashore in nineteenth- and twentieth-century British literature. *See* **8383**.

11929. Hardwick, Lorna. 'Shards and suckers': contemporary reception of Homer. *In* (pp. 344–62) **3253**.

11930. Harman, Mark. A Gaelic blackbird in the shadow of language. SewR (114:3) 2006, 442–8. (State of letters.)

11931. Hendin, Josephine G. Heartbreakers: women and violence in contemporary culture and literature. Basingstoke; New York: Palgrave Macmillan, 2004. pp. viii, 312. Rev. by Mary Jo Bona in NWSAJ (18:2) 2006, 248–50; by Greg Forter in AL (78:4) 2006, 897–9.

11932. Henneberg, Sylvia B. Of creative crones and poetry: developing Age Studies through literature. *See* **18413**.

11933. Herring, Scott. Lines on the land: writers, art, and the national parks. (Bibl. 2004, 12764.) Rev. by Brooke Ann Smith in WAL (40:2) 2005, 224–6.

11934. Hetherington, Carol; Petersson, Irmtraud (comps). Annual bibliography of studies in Australian literature: 2005. *See* **8390**.

11935. Heywood, Christopher. A history of South African literature. (Bibl. 2005, 12727.) Rev. by Antoine J. Bullier in EA (59:1) 2006, 122–3; by Peter Ayers in CanJAS (40:3) 2006, 565–7.

11936. Higgins, Hannah. Border crossings: three transnationalisms of Fluxus. *In* (pp. 265–85) **12305**.

11937. Hilliard, Chris. The bookmen's dominion: cultural life in New Zealand 1920–1950. Auckland: Auckland UP, 2006. pp. viii, 136. (AUP studies in cultural and social history, 3.) Rev. by Ken Arvidson in JNZL (24:1) 2006, 160–5.

11938. Hilliard, Christopher. To exercise our talents: the democratization of writing in Britain. Cambridge, MA; London: Harvard UP, 2006. pp. 390. (Harvard historical studies, 150.) Rev. by Jonathan Rose in TLS, 20 Oct. 2006, 25–6.

11939. Himmelfarb, Gertrude. The moral imagination: from Edmund Burke to Lionel Trilling. *See* **8392**.

11940. Holberg, Jennifer L. (ed.). Shouts and whispers: twenty-one writers speak about their writing and their faith. Grand Rapids, MI; Cambridge: Eerdmans, 2006. pp. xiv, 255.

11941. Homberger, Eric. New York City and the struggle of the modern. *In* (pp. 314–31) **11776**.

11942. Hornung, Alfred. 'Unstoppable' creolization: the evolution of the South into a transnational cultural space. AL (78:4) 2006, 859–67 (review-article).

11943. Hovey, Jaime. A thousand words: portraiture, style, and queer Modernism. Columbus: Ohio State UP, 2006. pp. ix, 136.

11944. Howard, Ben. Audacious Ireland. *See* **15045**.

11945. Howard, Hugh. Writers of the American South: their literary landscapes. New York: Rizzoli, 2005. pp. 285. Rev. by Marshall Bruce Gentry in FOR (4) 2006, 152–3.

11946. Howells, Coral Ann (ed.). Where are the voices coming from? Canadian culture and the legacies of history. Amsterdam; New York: Rodopi, 2004. pp. xxiii, 266. (Cross/cultures: readings in the post-colonial literatures in English, 73.) Rev. by Rocío G. Davis in CanL (189) 2006, 147.

11947. Huang, Guiyou (ed.). The Columbia guide to Asian American literature since 1945. New York: Columbia UP, 2006. pp. 256. (Columbia guides to literature since 1945.)

11948. Huang, Su-ching. Mobile homes: spatial and cultural negotiation in Asian American literature. London; New York: Routledge, 2006. pp. xi, 128. (Studies in Asian Americans.)

11949. Hutchinson, George. In search of Nella Larsen: a biography of the color line. *See* **17015**.

11950. Ikin, Van; Jorgensen, Darren (comps). Annual bibliography of Commonwealth literature 2005: Australia. *See* **19506**.

11951. Irele, F. Abiola; Gikandi, Simon (eds). The Cambridge history of African and Caribbean literature. (Bibl. 2005, 12738.) Rev. by Gloria Nne Onyeoziri in CanJAS (40:3) 2006, 536–45.

11952. Irvine, Dean (ed.). Canadian Modernists meet. (Bibl. 2005, 12739.) Rev. by Zailig Pollock in CanP (58) 2006, 115–22.

11953. Irwin, Amanda L. La identidad hispana en la literatura de los Estados Unidos. Chasqui (33:2) 2004, 144–50 (review-article).

11954. Izzo, Donatella (ed.). Suzie Wong non abita più qui: la letteratura delle minoranze asiatiche negli Stati Uniti. Milan: Shake, 2006. pp. 318. (I libri di Àcoma, 5.)

11955. —— Spandri, Elena (eds). 'Contact zones': rewriting genre across the East–West border. Naples: Liguori, 2003. pp. 247.

11956. Jaffe, Aaron. Modernism and the culture of celebrity. (Bibl. 2005, 12741.) Rev. by Christoph Lindner in Eng (54:210) 2005, 244–8; by Faye Hammill in Mod/Mod (13:2) 2006, 389–90; by Sean Latham in JJLS (20:1) 2006, 6–7.

11957. Jamal, Ashraf. Predicaments of culture in South Africa. Pretoria: Unisa Press, 2005. pp. xiii, 171. (Imagined South Africa.)

11958. Jameson, W. C. (ed.). Hot coffee and cold truth: living and writing the West. Albuquerque: New Mexico UP, 2006. pp. xii, 206.

11959. Jarraway, David R. Sublime objects and mystic subjects: some Lacanian speculations about Canadian fantasy literature *via* Barbara Gowdy's *The White Bone*. *In* (pp. 81–94) **13541**.

11960. Johnson, Michael K. 'The like of which is found nowhere else in all the world': placing and imagining an African American West. WAL (41:3) 2006, 336–44 (review-article).

11961. Johnson, Rob. The lost years of William S. Burroughs: Beats in South Texas. *See* **14958**.

11962. Johnson, Sarah Anne. The very telling: conversations with American writers. Hanover, NH; London: UP of New England, 2006. pp. xii, 206.

11963. Jondot, Jacqueline. Du rêve à la réalité: l'espace américain des écrivains d'expression anglaise du Proche-Orient arabe. Anglophonia (19) 2006, 171–82.

11964. Kalaidjian, Walter (ed.). The Cambridge companion to American Modernism. Cambridge; New York: CUP, 2005. pp. xix, 333. (Cambridge companions to literature.) Rev. by Denise Ginfray in EREA (4:2) 2006; by Lionel Kelly in RES (57:228) 2006, 120–2.

11965. Kalliney, Peter. Reading maps, writing cities. Mod/Mod (13:4) 2006, 747–54 (review-article).

11966. Karem, Jeff. The romance of authenticity: the cultural politics of regional and ethnic literatures. (Bibl. 2004, 12797.) Rev. by David A. Allred in WAL (40:3) 2005, 360–1; by Nicholas Sloboda in StudN (38:1) 2006, 128–9; by Victoria Ramirez in AL (78:3) 2006, 633–5.

11967. Karwowski, Michael. Do we need intellectuals? ContRev (288:1682) 2006, 339–44 (review-article).

11968. Katrak, Ketu H. Politics of the female body: postcolonial women writers of the Third World. New Brunswick, NJ; London: Rutgers UP, 2006. pp. xxix, 291.

11969. Katz, Steven T.; Rosen, Alan (eds). Obliged by memory: literature, religion, ethics: a collection of essays honoring Elie Wiesel's seventieth birthday. Syracuse, NY: Syracuse UP, 2006. pp. xviii, 188. (Religion, theology, and the Holocaust.)

11970. Kavalski, Emilian. 'All o' we is one': imaginary federation or the federation of the imagination of the West Indies. JWIL (13:1/2) 2005, 28–56.

11971. Kavka, Misha; Lawn, Jennifer; Paul, Mary (eds). Gothic N.Z.: the darker side of Kiwi culture. Dunedin: Otago UP, 2006. pp. 175.

11972. Kearney, Richard. Navigations: collected Irish essays, 1976–2006. Dublin: Lilliput Press, 2006. pp. xix, 453.

11973. Kercher, Stephen E. Revel with a cause: liberal satire in postwar America. Chicago, IL; London: Chicago UP, 2006. pp. 575.

11974. Kern, Stephen. When did the Victorian period end? Relativity, sexuality, narrative. *See* **8409**.

11975. King, Bruce. The internationalization of English literature. (Bibl. 2005, 12761.) Rev. by Julie Mullaney in PNRev (31:3) 2005, 82–3; by Bill Schwarz in MLR (101:2) 2006, 529–30; by Lachlan Mackinnon in TLS, 21 July 2006, 6–7; by Xavier Pons in EREA (4:2) 2006; by Philip Tew in JPW (42:1) 2006, 121–2.

11976. —— To be or not to be diasporic: Alas, poor India! I knew her. JPW (42:2) 2006, 139–54.

11977. King, Richard H. The regions and regionalism. *In* (pp. 53–72) **11776**.

11978. Klaus, H. Gustav; Knight, Stephen (eds). 'To hell with culture': anarchism in twentieth-century British literature. (Bibl. 2005, 12765.) Rev. by Carolyn Perry in LitH (15:2) 2006, 89–90.

11979. Knudsen, Eva Rask. The circle & the spiral: a study of Australian Aboriginal and New Zealand Māori literature. Amsterdam; New York: Rodopi, 2004. pp. xiv, 360. (Cross/cultures: readings in the post-colonial literatures in English, 68.) Rev. by Dieter Riemenschneider in JPW (42:1) 2006, 106–8.

11980. Köhler, Angelika. Ambivalent desires: the New Woman between social modernization and modern writing. Heidelberg: Winter, 2004. pp. 331. (American studies, 113.) Rev. by Maureen Reed in Amst (51:2) 2006, 242–4.

11981. Koval, Ramona (ed.). Tasting life twice: conversations with remarkable writers. (Bibl. 2005, 12767.) Rev. by Stephanie Green in TLS, 13 Jan. 2006, 28.

11982. Krumrey, Diane. Displacing the nation: contemporary literature by and about immigrants. Anglophonia (19) 2006, 243–52.

11983. Lang, John (ed.). Appalachia and beyond: conversations with writers from the Mountain South. Knoxville: Tennessee UP, 2006. pp. xviii, 362.

11984. Lanone, Catherine. Art and the 'second darkness'. *See* **19301**.

11985. Larrissy, Edward. Blake and modern literature. *See* **7578**.

11986. Lathbury, Roger. American Modernism: 1910–1945. New York: Facts on File, 2006. pp. 96. (Backgrounds to American literature.)

11987. —— Realism and regionalism: 1860–1910. *See* **8420**.

11988. Law, John E.; Østermark-Johansen, Lene (eds). Victorian and Edwardian responses to the Italian Renaissance. *See* **8422**.

11989. Lawrence, Keith; Cheung, Floyd (eds). Recovered legacies: authority and identity in early Asian American literature. (Bibl. 2005, 12775.) Rev. by Rocío G. Davis in JAAS (9:3) 2006, 329–32.

11990. Leader, Jennifer. Fitting in: Dickinson among others. *See* **9876**.

11991. Leak, Jeffrey B. Racial myths and masculinity in African American literature. (Bibl. 2005, 12776.) Rev. by Priscilla R. Ramsey in JAAH (91:3) 2006, 352–4; by Janelle Collins in ArkR (37:1) 2006, 67–8.

11992. Lee, James Kyung-Jin. Urban triage: race and the fictions of multiculturalism. (Bibl. 2005, 12777.) Rev. by Alex Feerst in AL (78:2) 2006, 408–9; by Viet Thanh Nguyen in AmerJ (32:1) 2006, 136–8.

11993. Leonard, Frances; Cearley, Ramona (eds). Conversations with Texas writers. Introd. by Joe Holley. (Bibl. 2005, 12779.) Rev. by Don B. Graham in GPQ (26:1) 2006, 45–6.

11994. Lewis, Clay. Butcher's bill. *See* **15820**.

11995. Lim, Shirley Geok-lin, *et al.* (eds). Transnational Asian American literature: sites and transits. Philadelphia, PA: Temple UP, 2006. pp. xii, 306.

11996. Looker, Benjamin. Point from which creation begins: the Black Artists' Group of St Louis. Columbia; London: Missouri UP, 2004. pp. xxvii, 316. Rev. by Julius E. Thompson in JAH (92:4) 2006, 1514–15; by Debi Hamlin in JAAH (91:2) 2006, 238–40.

11997. Loomba, Ania, *et al.* (eds). Postcolonial Studies and beyond. (Bibl. 2005, 12789.) Rev. by Bruce Avery in SStud (34) 2006, 209–12.

11998. Luangphinith, Seri. Homeward bound: settler aesthetics in Hawai'i's literature. *See* **19396**.

11999. Lundin, Roger (ed.). There before us: religion, literature, and culture from Emerson to Wendell Berry. Afterword by Andrew Delbanco. *See* **8429**.

12000. Lutes, Jean Marie. Front-page girls: women journalists in American culture and fiction, 1880–1930. Ithaca, NY; London: Cornell UP, 2006. pp. xi, 226.

12001. Lyon, Janet. Gender and sexuality. *In* (pp. 221–41) **11964**.

12002. Lyons, Paul. American Pacificism: Oceania in the US imagination. *See* **8433**.

12003. McBride, Dwight A. Why I hate Abercrombie & Fitch: essays on race and sexuality. New York; London: New York UP, 2005. pp. xiv, 251. (Sexual cultures.) Rev. by Tyler Bradway in ColLit (33:4) 2006, 223–5; by Rinaldo Walcott in GLQ (12:3) 2006, 510–13.

12004. McCann, A. L. The literature of extinction. *See* **19372**.

12005. McCann, Sean. Therapy for a wounded nation. *See* **12778**.

12006. McCaskill, Barbara; Gebhard, Caroline (eds). Post-bellum, pre-Harlem: African American literature and culture, 1877–1919. *See* **8435**.

12007. McCormack, W. J. Reflections on writing and editing, with reference to National Archives (UK), CO 904/1–3 & HO 161/1–5. *In* (pp. 258–85) **648**.

12008. McCulloch, Margery Palmer (ed.). Modernism and nationalism: literature and society in Scotland, 1918–1939: source documents for the Scottish renaissance. (Bibl. 2004, 12827.) Rev. by Alan Freeman in ScSR (6:2) 2005, 113–18; by Nancy K. Gish in Mod/Mod (13:1) 2006, 196–9; by Carla Rodríguez González in Atl (28:2) 2006, 185–90.

12009. McDonald, Gail. American literature and culture, 1900–1960. Oxford; Malden, MA: Blackwell, 2006. pp. 224. (Blackwell introductions to literature.)

12010. McElroy, Colleen J. (ed.). Page to page: retrospectives of writers from *The Seattle Review*. Seattle; London: Washington UP, 2006. pp. xviii, 397.

12011. McGraw, Eliza R. L. Two covenants: representations of Southern Jewishness. (Bibl. 2005, 12797.) Rev. by Derek Parker Royal in JSH (72:3) 2006, 727–8; by Guy Lancaster in ArkR (37:1) 2006, 74–5; by Jules Chametzky in AL (78:4) 2006, 878–9.

12012. McGruder, Kevin. To be heard in print: Black gay writers in 1980s New York. Ob3 (6:1) 2005, 49–65.

12013. McGuinness, Patrick. Imagism. *In* (pp. 183–8) **11788**.

12014. McInerny, Ralph. Some Catholic writers. South Bend, IN: St Augustine's Press, 2006. pp. 176.

12015. MacKay, Marina. 'Doing business with totalitaria': British late Modernism and the politics of reputation. ELH (73:3) 2006, 729–53.

12016. Mackean, Ian (ed.). The essentials of literature in English, post-1914. London: Hodder Arnold, 2005. pp. xiv, 391. Rev. by K. J. Gilchrist in EWN (36:3) 2006.

12017. McKee, Kathryn; Trefzer, Annette (introds). The US South in global contexts: a collection of position statements. AL (78:4) 2006, 691–739.

12018. McLaren, John. Time to dream. *See* **1136**.

12019. McLeod, John. Postcolonial London: rewriting the metropolis. (Bibl. 2005, 12800.) Rev. by Matthew Mead in JPW (42:1) 2006, 119–21.

12020. McMahon, Elizabeth. Encapsulated space: the paradise-prison of Australia's island imaginary. *See* **16193**.

12021. McPhee, Hilary. Survival struggles. *See* **1137**.

12022. McRuer, Robert. Queer America. *In* (pp. 215–34) **11776**.

12023. Maeder, Beverly (ed.). The seeming and the seen: essays in modern visual and literary culture. New York; Frankfurt: Lang, 2006. pp. 373. (Transatlantic aesthetics and culture, 1.)

12024. Mao, Douglas; Walkowitz, Rebecca L. (eds). Bad modernisms. Durham, NC; London: Duke UP, 2006. pp. 365.

12025. Marcus, Laura; Nicholls, Peter (eds). The Cambridge history of twentieth-century English literature. (Bibl. 2004, 12838.) Rev. by Jeff Wallace in Eng (55:211) 2006, 118–21; by Kevin J. H. Dettmar in Mod/Mod (13:4) 2006, 783–4; by Jean-Pierre Naugrette in EA (59:3) 2006, 368–70.

12026. Marias, Javier. Written lives. Trans. by Margaret Jull Costa. New York: New Directions, 2006. pp. 200. Rev. by Christopher Benfey in NYTB, 12 Mar. 2006, 11; by Peter Parker in TLS, 5 May 2006, 3–4.

12027. Marie, Caroline. The fountainpen and the metronome: Bloomsbury dancing, or not. CVE (62) 2005, 121–35.

12028. Marino, John B. The Grail legend in modern literature. (Bibl. 2005, 12806.) Rev. by Carolyne Larrington in TLS, 26 May 2006, 13; by Andrew E. Mathis in Arthuriana (16:1) 2006, 79–80; by Andrew Breeze in MLR (101:4) 2006, 1082–4.

12029. Marshik, Celia. British Modernism and censorship. Cambridge; New York: CUP, 2006. pp. xii, 257. Rev. by Matthew Creasy in TLS, 3 Nov. 2006, 29.

12030. Marucci, Franco. Storia della letteratura inglese: 4, Dal 1870 al 1921. *See* **8444**.

12031. Meaney, Geraldine. The sons of Cuchulainn: violence, the family, and the Irish canon. EI (41:1/2) 2006, 242–61.

12032. Mellard, James M. Beyond Lacan. Albany: New York State UP, 2006. pp. xi, 288. (SUNY series in psychoanalysis and culture.)

12033. Melman, Billie. The culture of history: English uses of the past, 1800–1953. *See* **8448**.

12034. Meyer, Sabine. Faulty analogies: queer White critics teaching African American texts. *In* (pp. 123–33) **20098**.

12035. Michaels, Walter Benn. The shape of the signifier: 1967 to the end of history. (Bibl. 2005, 12818.) Rev. by Wallace Martin in CL (58:3) 2006, 241–55.

12036. Miller, Danny L.; Hatfield, Sharon; Norman, Gurney (eds). An American vein: critical readings in Appalachian literature. (Bibl. 2005, 12822.) Rev. by Judith Hatchett in KenPR (20) 2005, 71–2; by Edwina Pendarvis in Now (22:2) 2006, 57–8.

12037. Miller, Jane. Reading into old age. Raritan (26:1) 2006, 14–30.

12038. Miller, Marlowe A. Masterpieces of British Modernism. Westport, CT; London: Greenwood Press, 2006. pp. x, 200. (Greenwood introduces literary masterpieces.)

12039. Mitchell, Lee Clark. Authenticity, the West, and literature. *See* **8449**.

12040. Montes, Rafael Miguel. Generational traumas in contemporary Cuban American literature: making places = *haciendo lugares*. Lewiston, NY; Lampeter: Mellen Press, 2006. pp. iii, 168.

12041. Moody, Nickianne. Feminism and popular culture. *In* (pp. 172–91) **14277**.

12042. Moore-Gilbert, Bart. Postcolonial Modernism. *In* (pp. 551–7) **11788**.

12043. Morgan, Stacy I. Rethinking social realism: African American art and literature, 1930–1953. (Bibl. 2005, 12827.) Rev. by James Smethurst in MFS (52:3) 2006, 725–7; by Riché Richardson in AL (78:3) 2006, 627–9.

12044. Morrisson, Mark. Nationalism and the modern American canon. *In* (pp. 22–35) **11964**.

12045. —— Publishing. *In* (pp. 133–42) **11788**.

12046. Moses, Wilson J. Segregation nostalgia and Black authenticity. AmLH (17:3) 2005, 621–42 (review-article).

12047. Moses, Wilson Jeremiah. Creative conflict in African American thought: Frederick Douglass, Alexander Crummell, Booker T. Washington, W. E. B. Du Bois, and Marcus Garvey. (Bibl. 2005, 10831.) Rev. by Ira Dworkin in AL (77:2) 2005, 421–4; by Andrew Radford in JAStud (40:1) 2006, 189–90.

12048. Mulkerns, Val. 'Did you once see Shelley plain?': Dublin, *The Bell*, the fifties. NewHR (10:3) 2006, 9–23.

12049. Mullen, Bill V. Afro-Orientalism. Minneapolis; London: Minnesota UP, 2004. pp. xliv, 240. Rev. by George Uba in AL (78:2) 2006, 405–7.

12050. Mullin, Katherine. Modernisms and feminisms. *In* (pp. 136–52) **14277**.

12051. Muponde, Robert; Primorac, Ranka (eds). Versions of Zimbabwe: new approaches to literature and culture. Harare: Weaver Press, 2005. pp. xxii, 262. Rev. by Flora Veit-Wild in RAL (37:3) 2006, 193–204.

12052. Mura, David. Asia and Japanese Americans in the postwar era: the White gaze and the silenced sexual subject. AmLH (17:3) 2005, 604–20 (review-article).

12053. Murphy, Neil. Political fantasies: Irish writing and the problem of reading strategies. *In* (pp. 63–88) **12189**.

12054. Murphy, Richard. Expressionism. *In* (pp. 198–203) **11788**.

12055. Musila, Grace (comp.). Annual bibliography of Commonwealth literature 2005: Central and East Africa. *See* **19516**.

12056. Nadell, Martha Jane. Enter the New Negroes: images of race in American culture. (Bibl. 2005, 12831.) Rev. by George Bornstein in MichQR (45:4) 2006, 713–21; by Habiba Ibrahim in AL (78:4) 2006, 882–4; by Kate Dossett in JAStud (40:1) 2006, 191–2.

12057. —— Modernism and race. *In* (pp. 527–34) **11788**.

12058. Narayan, Shyamala A. (comp.). Annual bibliography of Commonwealth literature 2005: India. *See* **19517**.

12059. Nash, Ilana. American sweethearts: teenage girls in twentieth-century popular culture. Bloomington: Indiana UP, 2006. pp. viii, 264. Rev. by Kathy O'Shaughnessy in TLS, 6 Oct. 2006, 30–1; by Deidre Johnson in DNR (75:5) 2006, 150–1.

12060. Newell, Stephanie. West African literatures: ways of reading. Oxford; New York: OUP, 2006. pp. ix, 259. (Oxford studies in postcolonial literatures in English.)

12061. Newton, Pauline T. Transcultural women of late twentieth-century US American literature: first-generation migrants from islands and peninsulas. Aldershot; Burlington, VT: Ashgate, 2005. pp. xiii, 233.

12062. Nicol, Bran. Postmodernism. *In* (pp. 565–70) **11788**.

12063. Nielsen, Aldon Lynn. Integral music: languages of African American innovation. (Bibl. 2005, 12838.) Rev. by Tony Bolden in ANQ (19:3) 2006, 59–62; by Andrew Levy in AmBR (27:5) 2006, 4–5.

12064. Nolan, Emer. Modernism and the Irish Revival. *In* (pp. 157–72) **11829**.

12065. Nord, Deborah Epstein. Gypsies & the British imagination, 1807–1930. *See* **8459**.

12066. North, Michael. Camera works: photography and the twentieth-century word. Oxford; New York: OUP, 2005. pp. ix, 255. Rev. by Marianna Torgovnick in AL (78:3) 2006, 629–31.

12067. O'Callaghan, Evelyn. Women writing the West Indies, 1804–1939: 'a hot place, belonging to us'. *See* **8463**.

12068. Ogude, James, *et al.* (eds). Es'kia continued: literary appreciation, education, African humanism & culture, social consciousness. Johannesburg: Stainbank, 2004. pp. xxvii, 438. Rev. by Abdul Samed Bemath in RAL (37:3) 2006, 210–12.

12069. Olson, Liesl. Sex and sexuality. *In* (pp. 143–51) **11788**.

12070. Ording, Dominic. Portraits of the American heartland at the crossroads of the counterculture. MidAmerica (31) 2004, 104–14.

12071. Ortega, Mariana. Being lovingly, knowingly ignorant: White feminism and women of color. *See* **17261**.

12072. O'Toole, Tina (ed.). Dictionary of Munster women writers 1800–2000 / Scríbhneoirí ban na Mumhan, 1800–2000. Foreword by Patricia Coughlan and Éibhear Walshe. *See* **8468**.

12073. Ozick, Cynthia. The din in the head: essays. Boston, MA: Houghton Mifflin, 2006. pp. x, 243. Rev. by Walter Kirn in NYTB, 2 July 2006, 8.

12074. Padley, Steve. Key concepts in contemporary literature. *See* **19518**.

12075. Patey, Caroline. In the mood for Provence, in the heart of the modern: Bloomsbury and Southern France. *In* (pp. 83–98) **12076**.

12076. —— Cianci, Giovanni; Cuojati, Francesca (eds). Anglo-American modernity and the Mediterranean. Milan: Cisalpino, 2006. pp. 399. (Quaderni di Acme.)

12077. Paulhan, Claire. Henry Church and the literary magazine *Mesures*: 'the American resource'. *In* (pp. 89–100) **11769**.

12078. Pearce, Joseph. Literary giants, literary Catholics. London: HarperCollins; San Francisco, CA: Ignatius Press, 2005. pp. 425. Rev. by John W. Osborne in EWN (36:3) 2006.

12079. Pelan, Rebecca. Literally loose cannon or loosening the literary canon. *In* (pp. 89–109) **12189**.

12080. Perera, S. W. Annual bibliography of Commonwealth literature 2005: Sri Lanka. *See* **19519**.

12081. Pérez, Vincent. Remembering the hacienda: history and memory in the Mexican American Southwest. College Station: Texas A&M UP, 2006. pp. xi, 251. (Rio Grande / Río Bravo, 11.)

12082. Perry, Imani. Occupying the universal, embodying the subject: African American literary jurisprudence. *See* **8474**.

12083. Pfister, Joel. Individuality incorporated: Indians and the multicultural modern. Durham, NC; London: Duke UP, 2004. pp. xiv, 304. (New Americanists.) Rev. by Linda Lizut Helstern in WAL (41:3) 2006, 362–3; by Lincoln Geraghty in JAStud (40:3) 2006, 673–4.

12084. Philipson, Robert. The Harlem renaissance as postcolonial phenomenon. AAR (40:1) 2006, 145–60.

12085. Phillips, Kathy J. Manipulating masculinity: war and gender in modern British and American literature. Basingstoke; New York: Palgrave Macmillan, 2006. pp. 227.

12086. Pierce, David. Light, freedom and song: a cultural history of modern Irish writing. New Haven, CT; London: Yale UP, 2005. pp. x, 350. (Cultural history of modern Irish writing.) Rev. by Andrew Haggerty in JJLS (20:2) 2006, 9.

12087. Pike, David L. Subterranean cities: the world beneath Paris and London, 1800–1945. *See* **8477**.

12088. Poddar, Prem; Johnson, David (eds). A historical companion to postcolonial literatures in English. Edinburgh: Edinburgh UP, 2005. pp. xxvii, 574. Rev. by Simon During in ALS (22:3) 2006, 393–6; by Graham MacPhee in ColLit (33:3) 2006, 220–2.

12089. Pollin, Burton R. Poe's seductive influence on great writers. *See* **11040**.

12090. Port, Cynthia. 'Ages are the stuff': the traffic in ages in interwar Britain. *See* **17294**.

12091. Porter, Joy; Roemer, Kenneth M. (eds). The Cambridge companion to Native American literature. (Bibl. 2005, 12863.) Rev. by James MacKay in JAStud (40:3) 2006, 674–5; by Jace Weaver in AICRJ (30:3) 2006, 132–4.

12092. Poteet, William Mark. Gay men in modern Southern literature: ritual, initiation, & the construction of masculinity. New York; Frankfurt: Lang, 2006. pp. 225.

12093. Potter, Jane. Boys in khaki, girls in print: women's literary responses to the Great War, 1914–1918. Oxford: Clarendon Press; New York: OUP, 2005. pp. xiii, 257. (Oxford English monographs.) Rev. by David Finkelstein in SHARP (15:4) 2006, 12.

12094. Potter, Rachel. Modernism and democracy: literary culture, 1900–1930. Oxford; New York: OUP, 2006. pp. x, 198.

12095. Priest, Ann-Marie. Great writers, great loves: the reinvention of love in the twentieth century. Melbourne: Black, 2006. pp. 298.

12096. Proietti, Salvatore. The Middle Passage and the remaking of the world: Du Bois and after. *See* **15580**.

12097. Punday, Daniel. The Black Arts Movement and the genealogy of multimedia. *See* **14581**.

12098. Pustianaz, Marco; Villa, Luisa (eds). Maschilità decadenti: la lunga *fin de siècle*. *See* **8488**.

12099. Pyle, Robert Michael. Out-of-doors in America: seven contemporary looks at the more-than-human. WAL (38:4) 2004, 418–34 (review-article).

12100. Quantic, Diane D. Seven ways of looking at the Great Plains literary landscape. HGP (39:2) 2006, 23–41.

12101. Quashie, Kevin Everod. Black women, identity, and cultural theory (un)becoming the subject. (Bibl. 2004, 12902.) Rev. by Jennifer Williams in AL (77:2) 2005, 430–2.

12102. Quirk, Tom; Scharnhorst, Gary (eds). American history through literature, 1870–1920. *See* **8491**.

12103. Rainey, Lawrence (ed.). Modernism: an anthology. (Bibl. 2005, 12874.) Rev. by Jason Harding in Mod/Mod (13:1) 2006, 171–8.

12104. Ramazani, Jahan. Modernist bricolage, postcolonial hybridity. Mod/Mod (13:3) 2006, 445–63.

12105. Rangno, Erik V. R. Contemporary American literature: 1945–present. New York: Facts on File, 2005. pp. 96. (Backgrounds to American literature.)

12106. Raphael-Hernandez, Heike (ed.). Blackening Europe: the African American presence. Foreword by Paul Gilroy. (Bibl. 2005, 12875.) Rev. by John Wharton Lowe in AAR (40:3) 2006, 591–3.

12107. Rasula, Jed. Jazz and American Modernism. *In* (pp. 157–76) **11964**.

12108. —— Jazzbandism. GaR (60:1) 2006, 61–124. (Modernist aesthetics.)

12109. REBOLLEDO, TEY DIANA. The chronicles of Panchita Villa and other guerrilleras: essays on Chicana/Latina literature and criticism. Austin: Texas UP, 2005. pp. x, 270. (Chicana matters.)

12110. RICHARDS, PHILLIP. Black heart: the moral life of recent African American letters. New York; Frankfurt: Lang, 2006. pp. xxxii, 252. (Intersections in communications and culture, 12.)

12111. RICKETTS, WENDELL. 'We almost killed ourselves with rage': working-class lives in recent American writing. WAL (40:4) 2006, 449–61.

12112. RIGAL-CELLARD, BERNADETTE. Le mythe et la plume: la littérature indienne contemporaine en Amérique du Nord. Monaco: Du Rocher, 2004. pp. 417. (Nuage rouge.) Rev. by Françoise Besson in Anglophonia (17) 2005, 483–5.

12113. ROCHE, ANTHONY (ed.). The UCD aesthetic: celebrating 150 years of UCD writers. *See* **8497**.

12114. ROLDAN-SANTIAGO, SERAFIN. Thematic and structural functions of folklore in Caribbean literature: the case of the 'written' and the 'oral'. JCarL (4:1) 2005, 1–9.

12115. ROSEN, ALAN. Sounds of defiance: the Holocaust, multilingualism, and the problem of English. (Bibl. 2005, 12887.) Rev. by Natania Rosenfeld in Biography (29:3) 2006, 490–3.

12116. ROSS, MARLON B. Manning the race: reforming Black men in the Jim Crow era. New York; London: New York UP, 2004. pp. xii, 463. Rev. by Roderick A. Ferguson in AmQ (58:1) 2006, 213–19.

12117. ROSTAN, KIMBERLY. Reading traumatically and representing the real in collective suffering. ColLit (33:2) 2006, 172–83 (review-article).

12118. RUBIN, DEREK (ed.). Who we are: on being (and not being) a Jewish American writer. (Bibl. 2005, 12893.) Rev. by Bonnie Lyons in PhRS (1:2) 2005, 183–4.

12119. RUBIN, LOUIS D., JR. Where the Southern cross the Yellow Dog: on writers and writing. *See* **8500**.

12120. RUEDA ESQUIBEL, CATRIÓNA. With her machete in her hand: reading Chicana lesbians. Austin: Texas UP, 2006. pp. xvi, 245. (Chicana matters.) Rev. by Sara E. Cooper and Rosa A. Martinez in JLesS (10:3/4) 2006, 197–201.

12121. RYAN, JUDITH; WALLACE-CRABBE, CHRIS (eds). Imagining Australia: literature and culture in the new New World. (Bibl. 2005, 12898.) Rev. by Robert Clarke in ALS (22:3) 2006, 391–3.

12122. RYAN, JUDYLYN S. Spirituality as ideology in Black women's film and literature. (Bibl. 2005, 12899.) Rev. by William B. Covey in MFS (52:3) 2006, 705–15.

12123. SAMMELLS, NEIL (ed.). Beyond borders: IASIL essays on modern Irish writing. (Bibl. 2004, 12930.) Rev. by Seán Kennedy in CJIS (31:2) 2005, 75–6.

12124. SAMUELS, ELLEN. From Melville to Eddie Murphy: the disability con in American literature and film. *See* **10891**.

12125. SAMUELS, SELINA (ed.). Australian writers, 1950–1975. (Bibl. 2004, 12931.) Rev. by Carole Ferrier in ALS (22:2) 2005, 258–60.

12126. —— Australian writers, 1975–2000. Detroit, MI: Gale Research, 2006. pp. xix, 484. (Dictionary of literary biography, 325.)

12127. Sánchez, Marta Ester. 'Shakin' up' race and gender: intercultural connections in Puerto Rican, African American, and Chicano narratives and culture (1965–1995). Austin: Texas UP, 2005. pp. xvi, 202. (Chicana matters.)

12128. Sanders, Lise Shapiro. Consuming fantasies: labor, leisure, and the London shopgirl, 1880–1920. *See* **8507**.

12129. Sanders, Mark A. American Modernism and the New Negro renaissance. *In* (pp. 129–56) **11964**.

12130. Sarker, Sonita. Afterword: Modernisms in our image … always, partially. Mod/Mod (13:3) 2006, 561–6.

12131. Satterfield, Terre; Slovic, Scott (eds). What's nature worth? Narrative expressions of environmental values. (Bibl. 2004, 12933.) Rev. by Jim Dwyer in WAL (41:3) 2006, 358–60.

12132. Saunders, Max. Literary Impressionism. *In* (pp. 204–11) **11788**.

12133. Sawaya, Francesca. Modern women, modern work: domesticity, professionalism, and American writing, 1890–1950. (Bibl. 2005, 12906.) Rev. by Christopher Newfield in AL (78:2) 2006, 415–18.

12134. Scafe, Suzanne (comp.). Annual bibliography of Commonwealth literature 2005: the Caribbean. *See* **19526**.

12135. Schlote, Christiane. Interpreters of transnationalism: South Asian American women writers. Amst (51:3) 2006, 387–409.

12136. Schocket, Eric. Vanishing moments: class and American literature. *See* **8510**.

12137. Scholes, Robert. Paradoxy of Modernism. New Haven, CT; London: Yale UP, 2006. pp. xiv, 295. Rev. by Alan Blackstock in RMER (60:2) 2006.

12138. Schweighauser, Philipp. The noises of American literature, 1890–1985: toward a history of literary acoustics. *See* **8512**.

12139. Scott, Bonnie Kime. Modernism and gender. *In* (pp. 535–41) **11788**.

12140. Scott, Helen. Caribbean women writers and globalization: fictions of independence. Aldershot; Burlington, VT: Ashgate, 2006. pp. 193.

12141. Seaman, Donna. Writers on the air: conversations about books. (Bibl. 2005, 12911.) Rev. by Savannah Schroll in CrN (28) 2006, 155–7.

12142. Shamsie, Muneeza. Annual bibliography of Commonwealth literature 2005: Pakistan. *See* **19529**.

12143. Sherbo, Arthur. A forgotten literary give-and-take. *See* **1166**.

12144. Sherry, Vincent B. (ed.). The Cambridge companion to the literature of the First World War. (Bibl. 2005, 12919.) Rev. by Hilda D. Spear in Eng (54:210) 2005, 238–42; by Geneviève Brassard in YES (36:2) 2006, 280–1.

12145. Shiach, Morag. Modernism, labour, and selfhood in British literature and culture, 1890–1930. (Bibl. 2005, 12920.) Rev. by Tim Armstrong in TexP (19:4) 2005, 551–4; by Michael Bell in MLR (101:3) 2006, 836–7.

12146. Short, Robert. Dada. *In* (pp. 163–8) **11788**.

12147. Siegel, Lee. Falling upwards: essays in defense of the imagination. New York: Basic Books, 2006. pp. xxii, 337. Rev. by Michael Wood in NYTB, 29 Oct. 2006, 24.

12148. Silver, Andrew. Minstrelsy and murder: the crisis of Southern humor, 1835–1925. *See* **8515**.

12149. Silvers, Robert B.; Epstein, Barbara (eds). The company they kept: writers on unforgettable friendships. New York: New York Review, 2006. pp. 298.

12150. Skerl, Jennie (ed.). Reconstructing the Beats. (Bibl. 2005, 12924.) Rev. by Jaap Van Der Bent in EngS (86:6) 2005, 561–2.

12151. Slocombe, Will. Nihilism and the sublime postmodern: the (hi)story of a difficult relationship from Romanticism to postmodernism. London; New York: Routledge, 2006. pp. xiv, 210. (Literary criticism and cultural theory.)

12152. Smith, Angela K. Suffrage discourse in Britain during the First World War. Aldershot; Burlington, VT: Ashgate, 2005. pp. 153. Rev. by Jane Potter in SHARP (15:2/3) 2006, 23.

12153. Smith, John; Cohn, Deborah (eds). Look away! The US South in New World Studies. (Bibl. 2005, 12928.) Rev. by Hosam Aboul-Ela in AL (78:4) 2006, 847–58; by Faith Pullin in JAStud (40:3) 2006, 679–80.

12154. Smith, Judith E. Visions of belonging: family stories, popular culture, and postwar democracy, 1940–1960. New York: Columbia UP, 2004. pp. xiv, 444. (Popular cultures, everyday lives.) Rev. by Elspeth H. Brown in CRAS (35:3) 2005, 335–44; by Catherine Jurca in AmQ (58:1) 2006, 221–7; by W. J. Rorabaugh in PacHR (75:4) 2006, 681–3.

12155. Sollors, Werner. African Americans since 1900. *In* (pp. 153–73) **11776**.

12156. Soto, Michael. The Modernist nation: generation, renaissance, and twentieth-century American literature. (Bibl. 2004, 12958.) Rev. by Judie Newman in MLR (101:3) 2006, 837–8.

12157. Spears, Timothy B. Chicago dreaming: Midwesterners and the city, 1871–1919. *See* **8520**.

12158. Sperati, Elisa. The Harlem renaissance e Nella Larsen: nuovi orizzonti in campo letterario e una nuova voce alla letteratura di colore. *See* **17018**.

12159. Srikanth, Rajini. The world next door: South Asian American literature and the idea of America. (Bibl. 2004, 12960.) Rev. by Helena Grice in JAStud (39:2) 2005, 346–7.

12160. Stafford, Jane; Williams, Mark. Maoriland: New Zealand literature, 1872–1914. *See* **8526**.

12161. Stauffer, John; Trodd, Zoe. Meteor of war: the John Brown cycle. *In* (pp. 121–44) **8537**.

12162. Steinhoff, Eirik. The making of *Chicago Review*: the meteoric years. *See* **1169**.

12163. Stevenson, Randall. The last of England? Oxford; New York: OUP, 2004. pp. xiv, 624. (Oxford English literary history, 12.) Rev. by James Wood in LRB (26:10) 2004, 11–12; by Lachlan Mackinnon in TLS, 21 July 2006, 6–7; by Armelle Parey in EREA (4:2) 2006.

12164. Stewart, Victoria. Narratives of memory: British writing of the 1940s. Basingstoke; New York: Palgrave Macmillan, 2006. pp. vi, 218.

12165. Stockton, Sharon. The economics of fantasy: rape in twentieth-century literature. Columbus: Ohio State UP, 2006. pp. vii, 235.

12166. Stoppard, Tom, *et al.* Writers. WLT (80:2) 2006, 19–21.

12167. Stosuy, Brandon (ed.). Up is up, but so is down: New York's downtown literary scene, 1974–1992. Afterword by Dennis Cooper and Eileen Myles. New York; London: New York UP, 2006. pp. 510. Rev. by Meghan O'Rourke in NYTB, 19 Nov. 2006, 22.

12168. Strange, Julie-Marie. Death, grief and poverty in Britain, 1870–1914. *See* **8532**.

12169. Stromberg, Ernest (ed.). American Indian rhetorics of survivance: word medicine, word magic. *See* **2149**.

12170. Sullivan, Rebecca. Visual habits: nuns, feminism, and American postwar popular culture. Toronto; Buffalo, NY; London: Toronto UP, 2005. pp. xi, 255. Rev. by Nancy Lusignan Schultz in TSWL (25:2) 2006, 357–9.

12171. Summers, Martin. Manliness and its discontents: the Black middle class and the transformation of masculinity, 1900–1930. Chapel Hill; London: North Carolina UP, 2004. pp. xii, 380. (Gender and American culture.) Rev. by Roderick A. Ferguson in AmQ (58:1) 2006, 213–19; by W. Lawrence Hogue in Mod/Mod (13:1) 2006, 200–2; by Mick Weems in WF (65:3) 2006, 355–6.

12172. Sumpter, Caroline. Innocents and epicures: the child, the fairy tale and avant-garde debate in *fin-de-siècle* little magazines. *See* **16460**.

12173. Sun, Hong. The evolution of pre- and post-Stonewall gay literature in America. *See* **18902**.

12174. Sundquist, Eric J. Strangers in the land: Blacks, Jews, post-Holocaust America. Cambridge, MA; London: Belknap Press of Harvard UP, 2005. pp. 662. Rev. by Lauren J. Gantz in PhRS (2:2) 2006, 166–8; by Jules Chametzky in AL (78:4) 2006, 878–9.

12175. Sutherland-Addy, Esi; Diaw, Aminata (eds). Women writing Africa: West Africa and the Sahel. New York: Feminist Press at the City Univ. of New York, 2005. pp. xxxi, 480. (Women Writing Africa project, 2.) Rev. by E. Frances White in WRB (23:2) 2006, 6–7.

12176. Szefel, Lisa. Beauty and William Braithwaite. *See* **14844**.

12177. Talib, Ismail S. (comp.). Annual bibliography of Commonwealth literature 2005: Malaysia and Singapore. *See* **19531**.

12178. Tanner, Laura E. Lost bodies: inhabiting the borders of life and death. Ithaca, NY; London: Cornell UP, 2006. pp. xiii, 264.

12179. Tarver, Australia. Reading race and intertextuality from the Abolitionist era to the Harlem renaissance. *See* **8536**.

12180. —— Barnes, Paula C. (eds). New voices on the Harlem renaissance: essays on race, gender, and literary discourse. Madison, NJ: Fairleigh Dickinson UP, 2006. pp. 300.

12181. Tatum, Charles M. Chicano and Chicana literature: *otra voz del pueblo*. Tucson: Arizona UP, 2006. pp. vii, 219. (Mexican American experience.)

12182. Taylor, Andrew; Herrington, Eldrid (eds). The afterlife of John Brown. *See* **8537**.

12183. Temple, Christel N. Literary Pan-Africanism: history, contexts, and criticism. (Bibl. 2005, 12942.) Rev. by Mark Christian in JBlaS (36:3) 2006, 456–9.

12184. —— Rescuing the literary in Black Studies. JBlaS (36:5) 2006, 764–85.

12185. Teuton, Sean. A question of relationship: internationalism and assimilation in recent American Indian Studies. AmLH (18:1) 2006, 152–74 (review-article).

12186. Thomas, Jane. Revising the late Victorian and early Modernist canon: a review article. *See* **8540**.

12187. Thompson, Carlyle Van. Eating the Black body: miscegenation as sexual consumption in African American literature and culture. New York; Frankfurt: Lang, 2006. pp. xiii, 231. (African American literature and culture, 10.)

12188. Thompson, Graham. The business of America: the cultural production of a post-war nation. (Bibl. 2005, 14677.) Rev. by Christopher Newfield in AL (78:2) 2006, 415–18.

12189. Thompson, Helen (ed.). The current debate about the Irish literary canon: essays reassessing *The Field Day Anthology of Irish Writing*. Lewiston, NY; Lampeter: Mellen Press, 2006. pp. vi, 360.

12190. Tiffin, Helen. A tale of three places. JWIL (15:1/2) 2006, 187–95.

12191. Tighe, Carl. Writing and responsibility. (Bibl. 2005, 12947.) Rev. by David Watson in LitH (15:1) 2006, 74–5.

12192. Torgovnick, Marianna. The war complex: World War II in our time. Chicago, IL; London: Chicago UP, 2005. pp. xxi, 209. Rev. by Eric Solomon in AL (78:3) 2006, 657–9.

12193. Treglown, Jeremy. Our secret harmonies: the *TLS* life of Anthony Powell – with Maclaren-Ross, Pryce-Jones and Orwell. *See* **18115**.

12194. Trulli, Maristella; Pontrandolfo, Luisa (eds). Londra tra memoria letteraria e modernità: dal Seicento ai nostri giorni. *See* **7343**.

12195. Turner, Joyce Moore. Caribbean crusaders and the Harlem renaissance. Introd. by Franklin W. Knight. (Bibl. 2005, 12950.) Rev. by Mark I. Helbling in JAH (93:2) 2006, 568–9.

12196. TuSmith, Bonnie; Byerman, Keith E. (eds). Critical essays on John Edgar Wideman. *See* **19144**.

12197. Ty, Eleanor. The politics of the visible in Asian North American narratives. (Bibl. 2004, 12984.) Rev. by Benzi Zhang in ESCan (30:4) 2004, 231–5; by Crystal Parikh in AL (78:1) 2006, 192–4.

12198. —— Goellnicht, Donald (eds). Asian North American identities: beyond the hyphen. (Bibl. 2004, 12985.) Rev. by Christine Kim in CanL (189) 2006, 174–5.

12199. TYLEE, CLAIRE M. (ed.). 'In the open': Jewish women writers and British culture. Newark: Delaware UP, 2006. pp. 272.

12200. UNDERWOOD, THOMAS A. A visit with Walker Percy: an interview and a recollection. *See* **17988**.

12201. VASSANJI, M. G. Am I a Canadian writer? *See* **18894**.

12202. VEIT-WILD, FLORA. De-silencing the past – challenging 'patriotic history': new books on Zimbabwean literature. RAL (37:3) 2006, 193–204 (review-article).

12203. VILLA, LUISA. A footnote to cultural history: Modernism, imperialism, and Wilfrid Scawen Blunt. *In* (pp. 263–77) **12076**.

12204. VISCUSI, ROBERT. Buried Caesars, and other secrets of Italian American writing. Albany: New York State UP, 2006. pp. xxii, 272. (SUNY series in Italian/American culture.)

12205. WACHHOLZ, MICHAEL. Entgrenzung der Geschichte: eine Untersuchung zum geschichtlichen Denken der amerikanischen Postmoderne. Heidelberg: Winter, 2005. pp. 234. (American studies, 122.)

12206. WALKOWITZ, REBECCA L. The location of literature: the transnational book and the migrant writer. *See* **18009**.

12207. WALLER, PHILIP. Writers, readers, and reputations: literary life in Britain, 1870–1918. *See* **8546**.

12208. WALTERS, WENDY W. At home in diaspora: Black international writing. (Bibl. 2005, 12957.) Rev. by Cynthia Tolentino in Novel (39:2) 2006, 295–8.

12209. WANG, HAIYAN. The past and future of American Vietnam War literature studies in China. FLS (117) 2006, 166–72. (In Chinese.)

12210. WARREN, CRYSTAL (introd.). Annual bibliography of Commonwealth literature 2005: South Africa. *See* **19535**.

12211. WATKIN, WILLIAM. On mourning: theories of loss in modern literature. Edinburgh: Edinburgh UP, 2004. pp. vi, 245. Rev. by Patricia Rae in Mod/Mod (13:2) 2006, 405–7.

12212. WEAKS-BAXTER, MARY. Reclaiming the American farmer: the reinvention of a regional mythology in twentieth-century Southern writing. Baton Rouge: Louisiana State UP, 2006. pp. xi, 191. (Southern literary studies.) Rev. by William Conlogue in SoQ (44:1) 2006, 191–3.

12213. WEAVER, JACE; WOMACK, CRAIG S.; WARRIOR, ROBERT. American Indian literary nationalism. Foreword by Simon J. Ortiz. Afterword by Lisa Brooks. Albuquerque: New Mexico UP, 2006. pp. xxii, 272.

12214. WEBER, DONALD. Haunted in the New World: Jewish American culture from Cahan to *The Goldbergs*. Bloomington: Indiana UP, 2005. pp. xiii, 250. (Jewish literature and culture.) Rev. by Jeffrey Shandler in AJH (92:3) 2004, 395–6.

12215. WEINGARTEN, MARC. The gang that wouldn't write straight: Wolfe, Thompson, Didion, and the New Journalism revolution. *See* **15501**.

12216. WEISS, BETTINA (ed.). The end of unheard narratives: contemporary perspectives on Southern African literatures. Heidelberg: Kalliope, 2004.

pp. 260. Rev. by Flora Veit-Wild in RAL (37:3) 2006, 193–204; by M. J. Daymond in RAL (37:3) 2006, 205–8.

12217. WHALEY, PRESTON, JR. Blows like a horn: Beat writing, jazz, style, and markets in the transformation of US culture. (Bibl. 2004, 13002.) Rev. by Scott Saul in AL (77:4) 2005, 862–4.

12218. WHITE, EDMUND. Arts and letters. *See* **8552**.

12219. WILCOX, CRAIG. Edwardian excursion. Meanjin (63:3) 2004, 23–32. (Australian expatriate writers.)

12220. WILD, JONATHAN. The rise of the office clerk in literary culture, 1880–1939. *See* **8554**.

12221. WILLIAMS, JENNIFER HARDY. Modernism's religious other. ELN (44:1) 2006, 67–74.

12222. WILLIAMS, MARK (ed.). Writing at the edge of the universe: essays from the 'Creative Writing in New Zealand' conference, University of Canterbury, August 2003. (Bibl. 2005, 12967.) Rev. by Stuart Murray in JPW (42:1) 2006, 109–10.

12223. WILLIAMSON, ALAN. Westernness: a meditation. Charlottesville; London: Virginia UP, 2006. pp. xi, 182. (Under the sign of nature.)

12224. WILLS, CLAIR. Women writers and the death of rural Ireland: realism and nostalgia in the 1940s. EI (41:1/2) 2006, 192–212.

12225. WINCHELL, MARK ROYDEN. Reinventing the South: versions of a literary region. Columbia; London: Missouri UP, 2006. pp. xiv, 253.

12226. WIRTH-NESHER, HANA. Call it English: the languages of Jewish American literature. Princeton, NJ; Oxford: Princeton UP, 2006. pp. xv, 224. Rev. by Jules Chametzky in AL (78:4) 2006, 878–9.

12227. WURTZ, JAMES F. 'Liberation and oppression are inextricably bound': sports, narrative, and the colonial experience. IE (28:1) 2005, 25–34.

12228. YAEGER, PATRICIA. *Circum*-Atlantic superabundance: milk as world-making in Alice Randall and Kara Walker. *See* **18186**.

12229. YAFFE, DAVID. Fascinating rhythm: reading jazz in American writing. Princeton, NJ; Oxford: Princeton UP, 2006. pp. ix, 230. Rev. by Ed Pavlic in ConLit (47:2) 2006, 304–15.

12230. YOUNG, JOHN K. Black writers, White publishers: marketplace politics in twentieth-century African American literature. Jackson; London: Mississippi UP, 2006. pp. ix, 230.

12231. ZIOLKOWSKI, THEODORE. Ovid and the moderns. Ithaca, NY; London: Cornell UP, 2005. pp. xvi, 262. Rev. by Duncan F. Kennedy in MLR (101:3) 2006, 928–9; by Philip Hardie in TransLit (15:2) 2006, 261–5.

THEATRE

12232. ABBOTSON, SUSAN C. W. Masterpieces of 20th-century American drama. (Bibl. 2005, 12980.) Rev. by Peter Barry in Eng (55:212) 2006, 213–19.

12233. ACKERMAN, ALAN. Liberalism, democracy, and the twentieth-century American theater. AmLH (17:4) 2005, 765–80 (review-article).

12234. Ackerman, Alan; Puchner, Martin (eds). Against theatre: creative destructions on the modernist stage. Basingstoke; New York: Palgrave Macmillan, 2006. pp. xii, 259. (Performance interventions.)

12235. Albee, Edward. The beginnings of Off-Broadway. Dramatist (8:6) 2006, 14–21.

12236. Appleford, Rob (ed.). Aboriginal drama and theatre. Toronto: Playwrights Canada Press, 2005. pp. xv, 187. (Critical perspectives on Canadian theatre in English, 1.) Rev. by Erin Elliott in CanTR (128) 2006, 139.

12237. Aston, Elaine; Harris, Geraldine (eds). Feminist futures? Theatre, performance, theory. *See* **19538**.

12238. Babbage, Frances. The play of surface: theater and *The Turn of the Screw*. *See* **10536**.

12239. Barfield, Steven. 'Jewelinthecrown.co.uk': Orientalism's strange persistence in British South Asian writing. *In* (pp. 111–20) **14238**.

12240. Barranger, Milly S. Margaret Webster: a life in the theater. (Bibl. 2005, 12985.) Rev. by Barbara Mackey in TJ (58:1) 2006, 158–60; by Lesley Broder in RMER (60:1) 2006; by Cindy Rosenthal in TDR (50:2) 2006, 164–5.

12241. Bennett, Stuart (ed.). Theatre for children and young people: 50 years of professional theatre in the UK. Foreword by Wolfgang Schneider. London: Aurora Metro Press, 2005. pp. 244. Rev. by Emma McEvoy in TN (60:2) 2006, 122–3.

12242. Bennett, Susan. Theatre audiences *redux*. TheatreS (47:2) 2006, 225–30.

12243. —— (ed.). Feminist theatre and performance. Toronto: Playwrights Canada Press, 2006. pp. xvii, 161. (Critical perspectives on Canadian theatre in English, 4.)

12244. Berghaus, Gunter. Theatre, performance, and the historical avant-garde. Basingstoke; New York: Palgrave Macmillan, 2005. pp. xxii, 374. (Palgrave studies in theatre and performance history.)

12245. Bernstein, Robin (ed.). Cast out: queer lives in theater. Foreword by Jill Dolan. Ann Arbor: Michigan UP, 2006. pp. xii, 233. (Triangulations.)

12246. Bial, Henry. Acting Jewish: negotiating ethnicity on the American stage & screen. (Bibl. 2005, 12990.) Rev. by Jeff Wax in TJ (58:4) 2006, 716–17.

12247. Billington, Michael. Cricket and theatre: Australians observed. *In* (pp. 144–58) **12360**.

12248. Blackadder, Neil. Performing opposition: modern theater and the scandalized audience. (Bibl. 2004, 13037.) Rev. by Brian Singleton in ModDr (48:4) 2005, 844–6; by Shelley Orr in TJ (58:2) 2006, 369–71.

12249. Boon, Richard; Plastow, Jane (eds). Theatre and empowerment: community drama on the world stage. (Bibl. 2005, 12995.) Rev. by Lois Sherlow in CanJAS (40:3) 2006, 556–8.

12250. Bottoms, Stephen J. Playing underground: a critical history of the 1960s off-off-Broadway movement. (Bibl. 2005, 12996.) Rev. by Arnold Aronson in ModDr (48:3) 2005, 611–13; by Stephen Petrus in NYH (87:2) 2006, 254–7.

12251. Brewer, Mary F. Staging Whiteness. (Bibl. 2005, 12999.) Rev. by Emily Colborn-Roxworthy in ModDr (49:1) 2006, 120–2; by James M. Cherry in TJ (58:4) 2006, 725–6.

12252. Brisbane, Katherine. Not wrong – just different: observations on the rise of contemporary Australian theatre. Strawberry Hills, N.S.W.: Currency Press, 2005. pp. ix, 370. Rev. by Julian Meyrick in ADS (49) 2006, 117–20; by Bill Dunstone in TRI (31:3) 2006, 318–19.

12253. Brooks, Daphne A. Bodies in dissent: spectacular performances of race and freedom, 1850–1910. *See* **8564**.

12254. Brown, Kevin. 'Tis pity she's a whore: the revision of Mary Magdalene in contemporary fiction. PLL (42:3) 2006, 291–316.

12255. Brown-Guillory, Elizabeth. 'Feet don't fail me now!': place and displacement in Black women's plays from the United States, South Africa, and England. CLAJ (49:4) 2006, 383–405.

12256. Bryer, Jackson R.; Davison, Richard A. (eds). The art of the American musical: conversations with the creators. New Brunswick, NJ; London: Rutgers UP, 2005. pp. xvi, 308. Rev. by Greg White in TheatreS (47:2) 2006, 353–5.

12257. Canning, Charlotte; Swain, Elizabeth. Social change, artistic ferment. *In* (pp. 17–44) **12297**.

12258. Cardullo, Bert (ed.). The drama is coming now: the theater criticism of Richard Gilman. New Haven, CT; London: Yale UP, 2005. pp. xviii, 351.

12259. Chambers, Jonathan L. Messiah of the new technique: John Howard Lawson, Communism, and American theatre, 1923–1937. *See* **17071**.

12260. Chansky, Dorothy. Composing ourselves: the Little Theatre movement and the American audience. (Bibl. 2005, 13005.) Rev. by Rosemarie K. Bank in ModDr (49:1) 2006, 130–5.

12261. Christiansen, Richard. A theater of our own: a history and a memoir of 1,001 nights in Chicago. Foreword by Brian Dennehy. *See* **8566**.

12262. Cohen-Cruz, Jan. Local acts: community-based performance in the United States. (Bibl. 2005, 13007.) Rev. by Terry Brino-Dean in TJ (58:2) 2006, 367–9; by Bruce McConachie in TheatreS (47:1) 2006, 140–2.

12263. Cole, Catherine M. African performance and the postcolony. TheatreS (47:2) 2006, 199–207.

12264. Coleman, Cy. Fighting honestly. *In* (pp. 24–37) **12375**.

12265. Conteh-Morgan, John; Olaniyan, Tejumola (eds). African drama and performance. (Bibl. 2005, 13009.) Rev. by Awam Amkpa in TheatreS (47:1) 2006, 123–5.

12266. Corbett, John; Findlay, Bill (eds). Serving twa maisters: five classic plays in Scots translation. Glasgow: Assn for Scottish Literary Studies, 2005. pp. xxxvii, 376. (Assn for Scottish Literary Studies, 34.) Rev. by Adrienne Scullion in ScSR (6:2) 2005, 124–6; by Robert Cummings in TransLit (15:1) 2006, 142–9.

12267. Coursen, H. R. Shakespeare translated: derivatives on film and TV. *See* **5280**.

12268. Croft, Susan. 'A new untravelled region in herself': women's school plays in late nineteenth- and early twentieth-century Australia. *In* (pp. 29–42) **12360**.

12269. Cummings, Scott T. Remaking American theatre: Charles Mee, Anne Bogart, and the SITI Company. Cambridge; New York: CUP, 2006. pp. xxi, 318. (Cambridge studies in American theatre and drama, 25.)

12270. Dean, Joan Fitzpatrick. Riot and great anger: stage censorship in twentieth-century Ireland. (Bibl. 2005, 13015.) Rev. by Jerome Joseph Day in NewHR (10:3) 2006, 145–7; by Karin Maresh in TheatreS (47:1) 2006, 144–6.

12271. Denkert, Darcie. A fine romance. (Bibl. 2005, 13017.) Rev. by John Olson in SondR (12:3) 2006, 39.

12272. Devine, Harriet, *et al.* Looking back: playwrights at the Royal Court, 1956–2006. London; Boston, MA: Faber & Faber, 2006. pp. 334. (Interviews.) Rev. by John Stokes in TLS, 4 Aug. 2006, 18.

12273. Dickinson, Peter. Going west: queer theatre in British Columbia. *In* (pp. 203–17) **12353**.

12274. Dike, Fatima, *et al.* Beyond the USA, beyond the UK. *In* (pp. 199–218) **12297**.

12275. Dolan, Jill. Utopia in performance: finding hope at the theater. Ann Arbor: Michigan UP, 2005. pp. ix, 233. Rev. by Susan Bennett in TJ (58:4) 2006, 728–30.

12276. Dorney, Kate. Searching for scripts: re-writing the history of British theatre post-1968. TN (59:2) 2005, 102–12.

12277. Doughty, Annie A. Folktales retold: a critical overview of stories updated for children. *See* **13663**.

12278. Durang, Christopher. Off-Broadway: of thee I sink. Dramatist (8:6) 2006, 12–13.

12279. Elam, Harry J. The *TDR* Black theatre issue: refiguring the avant-garde. *In* (pp. 41–66) **12305**.

12280. Falkenberg, Peter. Why devise, why now? Why New Zealand? TT (15:1) 2005, 39–40. (Stage adaptations of non-dramatic texts.)

12281. Fensham, Rachel, *et al.* The dolls' revolution: Australian theatre and cultural imagination. Melbourne: Australian Scholarly Pubs, 2005. pp. ix, 415, (plates) 30. Rev. by Peta Tait in ADS (49) 2006, 114–17; by Helena Grehan in TRI (31:3) 2006, 319–20.

12282. Fern, Annette. Deconstructing the Goodman: documents of a twentieth-century stage. TheatreS (47:1) 2006, 93–105. (*Re:* sources.)

12283. Fiebach, Joachim. Avant-garde and performance cultures in Africa. *In* (pp. 67–91) **12305**.

12284. Filewod, Alan. Theatrical nationhood in radical mobility: *The Farm Show* futures and the Banner / Ground Zero collaborations. *See* **16309**.

12285. Fletcher, Anne. A closed shop? Max Gorelik and The Provincetown. EOR (28) 2006, 80–100.

12286. Fowler, Jim; Gray, Jonathan. Unleashing Britain: theatre gets real 1955–64. London: V&A, 2005. pp. 128. Rev. by John Stokes in TLS, 4 Aug. 2006, 18.

12287. Frayling, Christopher. Mad, bad and dangerous? The scientist and the cinema. (Bibl. 2005, 13024.) Rev. by Roz Kaveney in TLS, 19 May 2006, 20.

12288. Freeman, Sara. Writing the history of an alternative-theatre company: mythology and the last years of Joint Stock. TheatreS (47:1) 2006, 51–72.

12289. Furnish, Ben. Nostalgia in Jewish American theatre and film, 1979–2004. New York; Frankfurt: Lang, 2005. pp. 188. (Twentieth-century American Jewish writers, 11.)

12290. Gale, Maggie B.; Gardner, Viv (eds). Auto/biography and identity: women, theatre, and performance. (Bibl. 2005, 13027.) Rev. by Maria DiCenzo in ModDr (49:1) 2006, 122–4; by Susan Bennett in Biography (29:3) 2006, 495–7.

12291. Giannachi, Gabriella. Virtual theatres: an introduction. (Bibl. 2004, 13079.) Rev. by David Z. Saltz in ModDr (48:3) 2005, 629–31; by Jason Farman in TJ (58:2) 2006, 364–5; by Mick Wallis in TRI (31:3) 2006, 325–6.

12292. Gibson, Melissa Dana. 1979 and all that: periodization in postwar British theatre history. TheatreS (47:1) 2006, 33–50.

12293. Giles, Freda Scott. From *Raisin in the Sun* to *Venus*: embodiment of and re/union with the lost home. NETJ (16) 2005, 97–115.

12294. Godiwala, Dimple (ed.). Alternatives within the mainstream: British Black and Asian theatres. Newcastle upon Tyne: Cambridge Scholars Press, 2006. pp. xi, 415. Rev. by Steven Barfield in TN (60:2) 2006, 119–21.

12295. Grant, Mark N. The rise and fall of the Broadway musical. Boston, MA: Northeastern UP, 2004. pp. x, 365, (plates) 12. Rev. by Laurie Schmeling in TT (16:2) 2006, 193–4; by Stacy Wolf in TJ (58:3) 2006, 513–14.

12296. Greene, Alexis. Women and war: the plays of Emily Mann, Lavonne Mueller, Shirley Lauro, Naomi Wallace, Shirley Gee, and Anne Devlin. *In* (pp. 82–92) **12297**.

12297. —— (ed.). Women writing plays: three decades of the Susan Smith Blackburn Prize. Foreword by Emilie S. Kilgore. Introd. by Marsha Norman. Austin: Texas UP, 2006. pp. xv, 302. (Louann Atkins Temple women and culture series, 13.)

12298. Greenfield, Mandy. First-person singular: female writers embrace the one-person play. *In* (pp. 158–69) **12297**.

12299. Greenwald, Michael L. (comp.). The Longman anthology of modern and contemporary drama: a global perspective. *See* **8578**.

12300. Guest, Kristen. Culture, class, and colonialism: the struggle for an English national theatre, 1879–1913. *See* **8579**.

12301. Haney, William S., ii. Postmodern theater and the void of conceptions. Newcastle upon Tyne: Cambridge Scholars Press, 2006. pp. viii, 160.

12302. Hardee, Lewis J., Jr. The Lambs theatre club. *See* **8580**.

12303. Harding, James M. From cutting edge to rough edge: on the transnational foundations of avant-garde performance. *In* (pp. 18–40) **12305**.

12304. —— Rosenthal, Cindy (eds). Restaging the sixties: radical theaters and their legacies. Ann Arbor: Michigan UP, 2006. pp. viii, 452.

12305. —— Rouse, John (eds). Not the other avant-garde: transnational foundations of avant-garde performance. Ann Arbor: Michigan UP, 2006. pp. viii, 304. (Theater: theory/text/performance.)

12306. Harvie, Jen. Staging the UK. Manchester; New York: Manchester UP, 2005. pp. ix, 246. Rev. by Aleks Sierz in TRI (31:2) 2006, 205–6; by Steven Barfield in TN (60:3) 2006, 182–4; by Joanne Zerdy in TheatreS (47:2) 2006, 349–51.

12307. Herrington, Joan. Building the base. TheatreS (47:2) 2006, 231–7. (US community theatre.)

12308. Hischak, Thomas S. Enter the playmakers: directors and choreographers on the New York stage. Lanham, MD; London: Scarecrow Press, 2006. pp. xi, 141.

12309. Huhndorf, Shari. American Indian drama and the politics of performance. *In* (pp. 288–318) **11823.**

12310. Illidge, Paul. Glass cage: the Crest Theatre story. Toronto: McArthur, 2004. pp. 348. Rev. by Graham Harley in LRC (13:7) 2005, 16–17.

12311. Jeffrey, Ewan. The outsider: the Michel Saint-Denis Archive: a theatre archive project of the Arts and Humanities Research Council, the University of Sheffield, and the British Library. TN (60:1) 2006, 45–51.

12312. Jordan, Eamonn (ed.). Theatre stuff: critical essays on contemporary Irish theatre. (Bibl. 2005, 117295.) Rev. by Patrick Longergan in FDR (1) 2005, 257–62.

12313. Kirle, Bruce. Unfinished show business: Broadway musicals as works-in-process. Carbondale: Southern Illinois UP, 2005. pp. xxv, 252, (plates) 26. (Theater in the Americas.) Rev. by Mary Jo Lodge in TJ (58:3) 2006, 514–16.

12314. Knapp, Raymond. The American musical and the formation of national identity. Princeton, NJ; Oxford: Princeton UP, 2005. pp. xxi, 361. Rev. by Michael Friedman in LRB (27:7) 2005, 25; by Andrea Most in JAH (92:3) 2005, 1049–50; by Mary Jo Lodge in TJ (58:3) 2006, 514–16; by Alisa Clapp-Itnyre in Historian (68:2) 2006, 349–50.

12315. Knopf, Robert (ed.). Theater and film: a comparative anthology. (Bibl. 2005, 13058.) Rev. by Sunny Statler in TRI (31:2) 2006, 204–5; by Michelle Mills Smith in TJ (58:4) 2006, 709–10.

12316. Knowles, Richard Paul. Reading the material theatre. (Bibl. 2005, 13060.) Rev. by Willmar Sauter in ModDr (48:2) 2005, 461–3.

12317. Krasner, David. American drama 1945–2000. Oxford; Malden, MA: Blackwell, 2006. pp. vii, 216. (Blackwell introductions to literature, 14.)

12318. —— *et al.* African American theatre. TheatreS (47:2) 2006, 191–7.

12319. Kruger, Loren. Geographical acts: place, performance, and pedagogy. AmLH (17:4) 2005, 781–93 (review-article).

12320. Kuppers, Petra. Disability and contemporary performance: bodies on edge. (Bibl. 2005, 13064.) Rev. by Sheila C. Moeschen in ModDr (48:2) 2005, 463–5; by Olivia Whitmer in TJ (58:2) 2006, 378–9.

12321. Kustow, Michael. Peter Brook: a biography. (Bibl. 2005, 13065.) Rev. by Steven Barfield in TN (59:3) 2005, 175–6.

12322. LeRoy, Zoaunne. Theatre Saint Paul: that theatre on Holly Street. Rochester, WA: LeRoy Log, 2005. pp. 72.

12323. Luckhurst, Mary. Dramaturgy: a revolution in theatre. Cambridge; New York: CUP, 2006. pp. xiii, 297. (Cambridge studies in modern theatre.) Rev. by Laura Baggaley in TLS, 17 Mar. 2006, 28; by Ros King in RES (57:231) 2006, 554–6; by Colin Chambers in TN (60:3) 2006, 185–6.

12324. —— (ed.). A companion to modern British and Irish drama, 1880–2005. Oxford; Malden, MA: Blackwell, 2006. pp. xvii, 584. (Blackwell companions to literature and culture, 43.)

12325. MacDonald, Gwynn. Engaging social issues, expressing a political outlook. *In* (pp. 104–14) **12297**.

12326. McMillin, Scott. The musical as drama: a study of the principles and conventions behind musical shows from Kern to Sondheim. Princeton, NJ; Oxford: Princeton UP, 2006. pp. xvi, 230.

12327. McNally, Michael D. The Indian passion play: contesting the real Indian in *Song of Hiawatha* pageants, 1901–1965. *See* **10754**.

12328. McNally, Terrence. A blueprint for the house. *In* (pp. 38–47) **12375**.

12329. Magelssen, Scott. Making history in the second person: post-touristic considerations for living historical interpretation. *See* **17966**.

12330. Malik, Rachel. The afterlife of Wilkie Collins. *In* (pp. 181–93) **9609**.

12331. Martin, Bradford D. The theater is in the street: politics and performance in sixties America. (Bibl. 2005, 13072.) Rev. by Nina Hein in TJ (58:2) 2006, 371–2.

12332. Maufort, Marc. 'Listen to them cry out from their dreaming': Blak Inside and the search for an Aboriginal stage aesthetic. Antipodes (20:1) 2006, 56–62.

12333. Mayer, David. *Why Girls Leave Home*: Victorian and Edwardian 'bad-girl' melodrama parodied in early film. *See* **8586**.

12334. Merwin, Ted. In their own image: New York Jews in Jazz Age popular culture. New Brunswick, NJ; London: Rutgers UP, 2006. pp. xiii, 215.

12335. Meyrick, Julian. Sightlines and bloodlines: the influence of British theatre on Australia in the post-1945 era. *In* (pp. 43–62) **12360**.

12336. Migliarisi, Anna (ed.). Directing and authorship in Western drama. Introd. by Don B. Wilmeth. Ottawa; New York: Legas, 2006. pp. 312. (Studies in drama and theatre, 5.)

12337. Moraga, Cherríe L. And Frida looks back: the art of Latina/o queer heroics. *In* (pp. 79–90) **12245**.

12338. Moran, James. Staging the Easter Rising: 1916 as theatre. Cork: Cork UP, 2005. pp. 116. Rev. by Aaron Krall in TJ (58:4) 2006, 718–19.

12339. Morash, Christopher. Irish theatre. *In* (pp. 322–38) **11829**.

12340. Most, Andrea. Making Americans: Jews and the Broadway musical. (Bibl. 2005, 13080.) Rev. by Ann Pellegrini in AJH (92:2) 2004, 253–5; by Susana Araújo in JAStud (39:3) 2005, 568; by Daniel Stein in Amst (51:1) 2006, 127–9.

12341. Moynagh, Maureen. Can I get a witness? Performing community in African Nova Scotian theatre. *See* **14833**.

12342. —— (ed.). African Canadian theatre. Toronto: Playwrights Canada Press, 2005. pp. xxxii, 130. (Critical perspectives on Canadian theatre in English, 2.) Rev. by Erin Elliott in CanTR (128) 2006, 139–40.

12343. Murphy, Brenda. The Provincetown Players and the culture of modernity. Cambridge; New York: CUP, 2005. pp. xix, 282. (Cambridge studies in American theatre and drama, 23.) Rev. by Cheryl Black in CompDr (40:3) 2006, 380–3.

12344. —— Theatre. *In* (pp. 411–29) **11776**.

12345. Ng, Wing Chung. Chinatown theatre as transnational business: new evidence from Vancouver during the exclusion era. BCS (148) 2005/06, 25–54.

12346. Nicholson, Steve. The censorship of British drama, 1900–1968: vol. 2, 1933–1952. Exeter: Exeter UP, 2005. pp. vi, 431. (Exeter performance studies.) Rev. by William C. Boles in CompDr (40:2) 2006, 244–7.

12347. O'Farrell, Ciara. Louis D'Alton and the Abbey Theatre. Dublin; Portland, OR: Four Courts Press, 2004. pp. 240, (plates) 16. Rev. by Christopher Baugh in TN (59:3) 2005, 176–7; by Christopher Grignard in CJIS (31:2) 2005, 74–5.

12348. O'Reilly, Anne F. Sacred play: soul-journeys in contemporary Irish theatre. (Bibl. 2005, 13088.) Rev. by Kay Martinovich in NewHR (10:1) 2006, 155–6.

12349. Ostrow, Stuart. Present at the creation, leaping in the dark, and going against the grain: *1776*, *Pippin*, *M. Butterfly*, *La Bête*, & other Broadway adventures. New York: Applause, 2006. pp. xvii, 166.

12350. Ozieblo Rajkowska, Bárbara; Narbona-Carrión, María Dolores (eds). Codifying the national self: spectators, actors, and the American dramatic text. New York; Frankfurt: Lang, 2006. pp. 299. (Dramaturgies, 17.)

12351. Pilný, Ondřej. Irony and identity in modern Irish drama. Prague: Litteraria Pragensia, 2006. pp. 186.

12352. Platt, Len. Musical comedy on the West End stage, 1890 1939. (Bibl. 2004, 13160.) Rev. by Peter Bailey in JVC (11:1) 2006, 180–4.

12353. Ratsoy, Ginny (ed.). Theatre in British Columbia. Toronto: Playwrights Canada Press, 2006. pp. xxiv, 228. (Critical perspectives on Canadian theatre in English, 6.)

12354. Rogerson, Margaret. REED *York*: volume 3, 'The revivals'. *In* (pp. 132–61) **3913**.

12355. Román, David. Performance in America: contemporary US culture and the performing arts. Durham, NC; London: Duke UP, 2005. pp. xx, 353.

12356. Rosenthal, Cindy. Ellen Stewart: La Mama of us all. TDR (50:2) 2006, 12–51. (La Mama Experimental Theatre Club.)

12357. Rossi, Umberto. Ambiguous spokespersons: the DJ and talk-radio host in US fiction, cinema and drama. *See* **15484**.

12358. Salter, Denis. Change the world, one play at a time: Teesri Duniya Theatre and the aesthetics of social action. *See* **18892**.

12359. SAVRAN, DAVID. The search for America's soul: theatre in the Jazz Age. TJ (58:3) 2006, 459–76.

12360. SCHAFER, ELIZABETH; SMITH, SUSAN BRADLEY (eds). Playing Australia: Australian theatre and the international stage. Amsterdam; Atlanta, GA: Rodopi, 2003. pp. ix, 230. (Australian playwrights, 9.) Rev. by Helena Grehan in ADS (45) 2004, 198–201; by Alan Filewod in ModDr (47:3) 2004, 546–9; by Martin Orkin in ALS (22:1) 2005, 123–6; by Marc Maufort in Antipodes (20:1) 2006, 103–4.

12361. SELL, MIKE. Avant-garde performance and the limits of criticism: approaching the Living Theatre, happenings/Fluxus, and the Black Arts Movement. Ann Arbor: Michigan UP, 2005. pp. vi, 327. (Theater: theory/text/performance.)

12362. SHELLARD, DOMINIC; NICHOLSON, STEVE; HANDLEY, MIRIAM. The Lord Chamberlain regrets: a history of British theatre censorship. *See* **8597**.

12363. SIBLEY, BRIAN. *Mary Poppins*: 'practically perfect in every way': the musical. *See* **18862**.

12364. SIMON, JOHN IVAN. John Simon on theater: criticism, 1974–2003. Introd. by Jack O'Brien. (Bibl. 2005, 13110.) Rev. by William H. Pritchard in HR (59:1) 2006, 135–41.

12365. SMITH, SUSAN BRADLEY. Inez Bensusan, suffrage theatre's nice colonial girl. *In* (pp. 126–41) **12360**.

12366. —— Rhetoric, reconciliation and other national pastimes: showcasing contemporary Australian theatre in London. *In* (pp. 195–211) **12360**.

12367. STARCK, KATHLEEN. 'I believe in the power of theatre': British women's drama of the 1980s and 1990s. Trier: WVT, 2005. pp. 269. (Contemporary drama in English, 12.) Rev. by Susan Croft in TRI (31:2) 2006, 202–3.

12368. STERNFELD, JESSICA. The megamusical. Bloomington: Indiana UP, 2006. pp. xi, 441. (Profiles in popular music.)

12369. STERNLICHT, SANFORD. Masterpieces of modern British and Irish drama. (Bibl. 2005, 13114.) Rev. by Peter Barry in Eng (55:212) 2006, 213–19.

12370. STOESSER, PAUL J. Authorship and the implications of design in Roy Mitchell's art of directing. *In* (pp. 135–51) **12336**.

12371. TAVES, BRIAN. P. G. Wodehouse and Hollywood: screenwriting, satires, and adaptations. Foreword by Richard Briers. *See* **19242**.

12372. TUCKER, BETSY RUDELICH. Politics in the spotlight: doing feminist theatre. Iris (48) 2004, 26–9.

12373. VANDEVELDE, KAREN. The alternative dramatic revival in Ireland, 1897–1913. *See* **8603**.

12374. —— 'What's all the stir about?': Gerald MacNamara, Synge, and the early Abbey Theatre. *See* **17383**.

12375. VIAGAS, ROBERT (ed.). The alchemy of theatre: the divine science: essays on theatre & the art of collaboration. New York: Applause, 2006. pp. 284.

12376. WALKER, JULIA A. Expressionism and Modernism in the American theatre: bodies, voices, words. (Bibl. 2005, 13125.) Rev. by Jonathan Chambers in TJ (58:2) 2006, 365–6; by Edmund Lingan in TheatreS (47:2) 2006, 331–4.

12377. WALLACE, CLARE. Suspect cultures: narrative, identity and citation in 1990s new drama. Prague: Litteraria Pragensia, 2006. pp. 308.

12378. WASSERSTEIN, WENDY. Generosity. *In* (pp. 8–16) **12375**.

12379. WATT, STEPHEN. Drama. *In* (pp. 237–43) **11788**.

12380. —— Modern American drama. *In* (pp. 102–26) **11964**.

12381. WEBER, MYLES. Reflections of Peter Brook. NER (27:1) 2006, 149–52 (review-article).

12382. WERTHEIM, ALBERT. Staging the war: American drama and World War II. (Bibl. 2005, 13131.) Rev. by Alan Ackerman in AmLH (17:4) 2005, 765–80; by J. Chris Westgate in NETJ (16) 2005, 141–3.

12383. WHEELER, LEIGH ANN. Against obscenity: reform and the politics of womanhood, 1873–1935. *See* **8606**.

12384. WILLIAMS, PETER. Strange affinities: representation and affect in Australian POW drama. *See* **12807**.

12385. WILLIAMS-WITHERSPOON, KIMMIKA. The secret messages in African American theater: hidden meanings embedded in public discourse. Lewiston, NY; Lampeter: Mellen Press, 2006. pp. ix, 315.

12386. WORTHEN, W. B. Print and the poetics of modern drama. Cambridge; New York: CUP, 2005. pp. xi, 209. Rev. by David Krasner in TJ (58:3) 2006, 524–6; by Paul Menzer in RES (57:232) 2006, 809–10.

CINEMA

General

12387. ANON. Filmography: film and television adaptations of Thomas Hardy. *In* (pp. 196–201) **10349**.

12388. AARON, MICHELE (ed.). New queer cinema: a critical reader. (Bibl. 2004, 13209.) Rev. by James Morrison in GLQ (12:1) 2006, 135–46; by Kyle Stevens in FilCr (31:1/2) 2006, 173–6.

12389. ABBOTT, CARL. Frontiers past and future: science fiction and the American West. *See* **3465**.

12390. ABEL, MARCO. Own your lack! New Lacanian film theory encounters the real in contemporary cinema. SAtlR (71:1) 2006, 132–40 (review-article).

12391. ABEL, RICHARD (ed.). Encyclopedia of early cinema. (Bibl. 2005, 13134.) Rev. by J. B. Kaufman in NCT (33:1) 2006, 90–1.

12392. ABRAMS, JEROLD J. The epistemology of James Bond: the logic of abduction. *In* (pp. 157–71) **15903**.

12393. —— From Sherlock Holmes to the hard-boiled detective in *film noir*. *In* (pp. 69–88) **12452**.

12394. ALDAMA, FREDERICK LUIS. Race, cognition, and emotion: Shakespeare on film. *See* **6013**.

12395. ALDGATE, ANTHONY; ROBERTSON, JAMES C. Censorship in theatre and cinema. Edinburgh: Edinburgh UP, 2005. pp. 195. Rev. by Rebecca Hewett in TJ (58:4) 2006, 710–11.

12396. ALSAYYAD, NEZAR. Cinematic urbanism: a history of the modern from reel to real. London; New York: Routledge, 2006. pp. xiii, 256.

12397. Andrew, Geoff. Film directors A–Z: a concise guide to the art of 250 great film-makers. London: Carlton, 2005. pp. 252. (Revised ed.: first ed. 1999.) (Orig. pub. as *Directors A–Z*.)

12398. Andrews, David. Soft in the middle: the contemporary softcore feature in its contexts. *See* **19575**.

12399. Aoki, Keith. Is Chan still missing? An essay about the film *Snow Falling on Cedars* (1999) and representations of Asian Americans in US films. *In* (pp. 679–99) **12712**.

12400. Aronstein, Susan. Hollywood knights: Arthurian cinema and the politics of nostalgia. (Bibl. 2005, 13139.) Rev. by Tison Pugh in Arthuriana (16:2) 2006, 97–8; by MaryLynn Saul in JPC (39:4) 2006, 697–9; by Arthur Lindley in TMR, Oct. 2006.

12401. Arp, Robert; Decker, Kevin S. 'That fatal kiss': objectification and women. *In* (pp. 201–13) **15903**.

12402. Auerbach, Jonathan. American Studies and film, blindness and insight. AmQ (58:1) 2006, 31–50.

12403. Badley, Linda; Palmer, R. Barton; Schneider, Steven Jay (eds). Traditions in world cinema. New Brunswick, NJ; London: Rutgers UP, 2006. pp. xxi, 266.

12404. Baron, Lawrence. Projecting the Holocaust into the present: the changing focus of contemporary Holocaust cinema. (Bibl. 2005, 13146.) Rev. by Frank Manchel in JPFT (34:1) 2006, 47; by Deborah Carmichael in FilmH (36:2) 2006, 59–60.

12405. Bartov, Omer. The 'Jew' in cinema: from *The Golem* to *Don't Touch My Holocaust*. (Bibl. 2005, 13150.) Rev. by David Biale in Mod/Mod (13:2) 2006, 399–401; by David Desser in SlavR (65:1) 2006, 175–6.

12406. Baugh, Lloyd. Martin Scorsese's *The Last Temptation of Christ*: a critical reassessment of its sources, its theological problems, and its impact on the public. *In* (pp. 173–92) **12933**.

12407. Beck, Jerry. The animated movie guide. Chicago, IL: Chicago Review Press, 2005. pp. xx, 348.

12408. Bellin, Joshua David. Framing monsters: fantasy film and social alienation. (Bibl. 2005, 13153.) Rev. by Lorrie Palmer in JFA (16:4) 2006, 380–4.

12409. Belton, John. American cinema, American culture. (Bibl. 1994, 9979.) Boston, MA: McGraw-Hill, 2005. pp. xxviii, 452. (Second ed.: first ed. 1994.)

12410. Benshoff, Harry M.; Griffin, Sean. America on film: representing race, class, gender, and sexuality at the movies. Oxford; Malden, MA: Blackwell, 2004. pp. xvi, 371.

12411. —— —— Queer images: a history of gay and lesbian film in America. Lanham, MD; Oxford: Rowman & Littlefield, 2006. pp. viii, 321. (Genre and beyond.) Rev. by Ron Briley in FilmH (36:2) 2006, 62–3.

12412. —— —— (eds). Queer cinema: the film reader. (Bibl. 2004, 13231.) Rev. by James Morrison in GLQ (12:1) 2006, 135–46.

12413. Bernardi, Daniel. Interracial joysticks: pornography's web of racial attractions. *In* (pp. 220–43) **12592**.

12414. Bernstein, Matthew. Movies and the reassessment of America. *In* (pp. 22–47) **12481**.

12415. Berry, Torriano; Berry, Venise T. Historical dictionary of African American cinema. London; New York: Routledge, 2006. pp. 448.

12416. Beuka, Robert. SuburbiaNation: reading suburban landscape in twentieth-century American fiction and film. (Bibl. 2004, 13234.) Rev. by Patrick Meanor in MFS (52:3) 2006, 728–31; by Wanja von der Goltz in Amst (51:3) 2006, 453–4.

12417. Biesen, Sheri Chinen. Blackout: World War II and the origins of *film noir*. (Bibl. 2005, 13155.) Rev. by Philip French in TLS, 5 May 2006, 10–11; by Charles Maland in Cineaste (31:3) 2006, 82–3.

12418. Bilton, Alan. Buster Keaton and the South: the first things and the last. JAStud (40:3) 2006, 487–502.

12419. Bodnar, John. Blue-collar Hollywood: liberalism, democracy, and working people in American film. (Bibl. 2005, 13159.) Rev. by Elspeth H. Brown in CRAS (35:3) 2005, 335–44.

12420. Bogle, Donald. Bright boulevards, bold dreams: the story of Black Hollywood. (Bibl. 2005, 13160.) Rev. by James Shade in XavR (25:2) 2005, 78–84.

12421. Boland, Michaela; Bodey, Michael. Aussiewood: Australia's leading directors and actors tell how they conquered Hollywood. Crows Nest, N.S.W.: Allen & Unwin, 2004. pp. 294, (plates) 16.

12422. Boldt-Irons, Leslie; Federici, Corrado; Virgulti, Ernesto (eds). Images and imagery: frames, borders, limits – interdisciplinary perspectives. *See* **11781**.

12423. Bondanella, Peter. Hollywood Italians: dagos, palookas, Romeos, wise guys, and Sopranos. (Bibl. 2005, 13163.) Rev. by Ronald Wilson in FilmQ (60:1) 2006, 67–8.

12424. Booker, M. Keith. Alternate Americas: science fiction film and American culture. Westport, CT; London: Praeger, 2006. pp. viii, 274, (plates) 14.

12425. Bordwell, David. The way Hollywood tells it: story and style in modern movies. Berkeley; London: California UP, 2006. pp. x, 298. Rev. by Paula Marantz Cohen in TLS, 5 May 2006, 11–12.

12426. Boyd, David; Palmer, R. Barton (eds). After Hitchcock: influence, imitation, and intertextuality. *See* **13181**.

12427. Brégent-Heald, Dominique. Dark limbo: *film noir* and the North American borders. JAC (29:2) 2006, 125–38.

12428. Brereton, Pat. Hollywood utopia: ecology in contemporary American cinema. Bristol; Portland, OR: Intellect, 2005. pp. 270. Rev. by Harri Kilpi in ScopeF (6) 2006.

12429. Britton, Wesley Alan. Onscreen and undercover: the ultimate book of movie espionage. Westport, CT; London: Praeger, 2006. pp. vii, 208, (plates) 13.

12430. Brodie, Ian. A journey through New Zealand film. Auckland: HarperCollins, 2006. pp. 144.

12431. Bronfen, Elisabeth. Home in Hollywood: the imaginary geography of cinema. (Bibl. 2005, 13171, where scholar details incorrect.) Rev. by David Seed in JAStud (39:3) 2005, 546–7.

12432. Bruhm, Steven. Nightmare on Sesame Street; or, The self-possessed child. GothS (8:2) 2006, 98–113.

12433. Buhle, Paul. Popular culture. *In* (pp. 392–410) **11776**.

12434. Butterfield, Beth. Being-toward-death and taking pleasure in beauty: James Bond and existentialism. *In* (pp. 3–15) **15903**.

12435. Cahir, Linda Costanzo. Literature into film: theory and practical approaches. Foreword by James M. Welsh. Jefferson, NC; London: McFarland, 2006. pp. vii, 307.

12436. Campbell, Russell. Marked women: prostitutes and prostitution in the cinema. Madison; London: Wisconsin UP, 2006. pp. xiv, 450. (Wisconsin film studies.)

12437. Cardwell, Sarah. Working the land: representations of rural England in adaptations of Thomas Hardy's novels. *In* (pp. 19–34) **12506**.

12438. Carmichael, Deborah A. (ed.). The landscape of Hollywood westerns: ecocriticism in an American film genre. Salt Lake City: Utah UP, 2006. pp. vi, 248.

12439. Carr, Steven Alan. Mass murder, modernity, and the alienated gaze. *In* (pp. 57–73) **12661**.

12440. Carroll, Noël; Choi, Jinhee (eds). Philosophy of film and motion pictures: an anthology. Oxford; Malden, MA: Blackwell, 2006. pp. ix, 430. (Blackwell philosophy anthologies.)

12441. Cashill, Robert. All things Kong-sidered. *See* **12924**.

12442. Casillo, Robert. Reflections on Italian American cinema. VIA (17:1) 2006, 1–27.

12443. Chennault, Ronald E. Hollywood films about schools: where race, politics, and education intersect. Basingstoke; New York: Palgrave Macmillan, 2006. pp. 192.

12444. Child, Abigail. This is called moving: a critical poetics of film. Tuscaloosa; London: Alabama UP, 2005. pp. xxv, 290. (Modern and contemporary poetics.) Rev. by Scott M. Tomberlin in RMER (60:1) 2006.

12445. Chopra-Gant, Mike. Hollywood genres and postwar America: masculinity, family and nation in popular movies and *film noir*. London; New York: Tauris, 2006. pp. x, 219. (Cinema and society.)

12446. Chung, Hye Seung. Hollywood Asian: Philip Ahn and the politics of cross-ethnic performance. Philadelphia, PA: Temple UP, 2006. pp. xxii, 232.

12447. Codell, Julie F. (ed.). Genre, gender, race, and world cinema. Oxford; Malden, MA: Blackwell, 2006. pp. ix, 474.

12448. Coffman, Christine E. Insane passions: lesbianism and psychosis in literature and film. *See* **11830**.

12449. COHAN, STEVEN. Incongruous entertainment: camp, cultural value, and the MGM musical. Durham, NC; London: Duke UP, 2005. pp. viii, 368. Rev. by Leah Perry in JPC (39:4) 2006, 692–4.

12450. COLEMAN, CYNTHIA-LOU. Framing cinematic Indians within the social construction of place. AmS (46:3/4) 2005, 275–93.

12451. COLLINS, BILL. The secret English passions of 'Mr Movies'. Meanjin (63:3) 2004, 108–16 (review-article). (Australian reception of British film.)

12452. CONARD, MARK T. (ed.). The philosophy of *film noir*. Foreword by Robert Porfirio. Lexington: Kentucky UP, 2006. pp. xv, 248. Rev. by Travis J. Rodgers in Intertexts (9:2) 2005, 180–3.

12453. CONLEY, TOM. Film hieroglyphs: ruptures in classical cinema. Minneapolis; London: Minnesota UP, 2006. pp. xlvi, 252.

12454. CONNOR, RACHEL. H.D. and the image. *See* **15529**.

12455. COOK, PAM. Screening the past: memory and nostalgia in cinema. (Bibl. 2005, 13192.) Rev. by Paul Grainge in ScopeF (5) 2006.

12456. COPPA, FRANCESCA. A brief history of media fandom. *In* (pp. 41–59) **19868**.

12457. CORKIN, STANLEY. Cowboys as cold warriors: the western and US history. (Bibl. 2005, 13193.) Rev. by Barton Keeton in AL (78:2) 2006, 395–7; by Richard Slotkin in FilmQ (59:4) 2006, 54–5.

12458. CORNES, JUDY. Alcohol in the movies, 1898–1962: a critical history. Jefferson, NC; London: McFarland, 2006. pp. xi, 251.

12459. COURTNEY, SUSAN. Hollywood fantasies of miscegenation: spectacular narratives of gender and race. (Bibl. 2005, 13194.) Rev. by Krin Gabbard in FilmQ (60:1) 2006, 66–7.

12460. CYRINO, MONICA SILVEIRA. Big screen Rome. Oxford; Malden, MA: Blackwell, 2005. pp. ix, 274.

12461. DALLE VACCHE, ANGELA (ed.). The visual turn: classical film theory and art history. (Bibl. 2005, 13199.) Rev. by Jennifer Wild in SubStance (111) 2006, 149–52.

12462. DALTON, MARY M. The Hollywood curriculum: teachers in the movies. (Bibl. 1999, 13226.) New York; Frankfurt: Lang, 2004. pp. 173. (Counterpoints, 256.) (Second ed.: first ed. 1999.)

12463. DANKS, ADRIAN. The global art of found-footage cinema. *In* (pp. 241–53) **12403**.

12464. DAVE, PAUL. Visions of England: class and culture in contemporary cinema. Oxford; New York: Berg, 2006. pp. xv, 205. (Talking images.) Rev. by David Archibald in Cineaste (32:1) 2006, 78–9.

12465. DAVIS, HUGH H. I was a teenage classic: literary adaptation in turn-of-the-millennium teen films. JAC (29:1) 2006, 52–60.

12466. DAVIS, ROBERT; DE LOS RIOS, RICCARDO. From Hollywood to Tokyo: resolving a tension in contemporary narrative cinema. FilCr (31:1/2) 2006, 157–72.

12467. DE ANGELIS, VALERIO MASSIMO; ROSSI, UMBERTO (eds). Trasmigrazioni: i mondi di Philip K. Dick. *See* **15466**.

12468. DECHERNEY, PETER. Hollywood and the culture elite: how the movies became American. New York: Columbia UP, 2005. pp. x, 269. (Film and culture.) Rev. by Hiroshi Kitamura in AmQ (58:4) 2006, 1263–73; by Heidi Kenaga in MovIm (6:2) 2006, 138–41.

12469. DENNIS, JEFFERY P. Queering teen culture: all-American boys and same-sex desire in film and television. New York: Harrington Park Press, 2006. pp. xii, 221.

12470. DESILET, GREGORY E. Our faith in evil: melodrama and the effects of entertainment violence. Jefferson, NC; London: McFarland, 2006. pp. x, 346.

12471. DESMOND, JOHN M.; HAWKES, PETER. Adaptation: studying film and literature. Boston, MA: McGraw-Hill, 2006. pp. xii, 266.

12472. DESPOTOPOULOU, ANNA. Girls on film: postmodern renderings of Jane Austen and Henry James. *See* **9008**.

12473. DESSER, DAVID; FRIEDMAN, LESTER D. American Jewish filmmakers. (Bibl. 2004, 13271.) Rev. by Mikel J. Koven in ScopeF (5) 2006.

12474. DICKENSON, BEN. Hollywood's new radicalism: war, globalisation and the movies from Reagan to George W. Bush. London; New York: Tauris, 2006. pp. xvi, 216. (Cinema and society.)

12475. DI FATE, VINCENT. Where do little green men come from? A speculative look at the origins of a pop culture idol. *In* (pp. 69–93) **12548**.

12476. DILLON, STEVEN. The Solaris effect: art & artifice in contemporary American film. *See* **19594**.

12477. DIMENDBERG, EDWARD. *Film noir* and the spaces of modernity. (Bibl. 2005, 13214.) Rev. by Philip French in TLS, 5 May 2006, 10–11.

12478. DIXON, WHEELER WINSTON. The endless embrace of hell: hopelessness and betrayal in *film noir*. *In* (pp. 38–56) **12661**.

12479. —— Movies and postwar recovery. *In* (pp. 162–81) **12481**.

12480. —— Visions of Paradise: images of Eden in the cinema. New Brunswick, NJ; London: Rutgers UP, 2006. pp. ix, 220. Rev. by Antoinette F. Winstead in FilmH (36:2) 2006, 65–6.

12481. —— (ed.). American cinema of the 1940s: themes and variations. New Brunswick, NJ; London: Rutgers UP, 2006. pp. xiv, 283. (Screen decades.)

12482. DONALSON, MELVIN. Masculinity in the interracial buddy film. Jefferson, NC; London: McFarland, 2006. pp. vi, 201.

12483. DORSKY, NATHANIEL. Devotional cinema. Berkeley, CA: Tuumba Press, 2005. pp. 54. (Second ed.: first ed. 2003.) Rev. by Anton Karl Kozlovic in ScopeF (5) 2006.

12484. DOTSON, DANIEL. Portrayal of mathematicians in fictional works. *See* **11867**.

12485. DRESNER, LISA M. The female investigator in literature, film, and popular culture. *See* **13459**.

12486. DUFFLEY, SEAN P. (ed.). Oz under scrutiny. *See* **14644**.

12487. DURRANI, OSMAN, *et al.* Faust: icon of modern culture. *See* **3238**.

12488. DVORAK, MARTA. Blurring bodies / blurring borders: a cinematic aesthetics of the grotesque. *See* **13159**.

12489. EARLY, GERALD. Jungle fever: Ian Fleming's James Bond novels, the Cold War, and Jamaica. *See* **15898**.

12490. EBERWEIN, ROBERT (ed.). The war film. (Bibl. 2005, 13226.) Rev. by Michael S. Shull in FilmH (36:2) 2006, 63–5.

12491. EDWARDS, EMILY D. Metaphysical media: the occult experience in popular culture. Carbondale: Southern Illinois UP, 2005. pp. xiii, 248. Rev. by Roddy Knowles in JPC (39:6) 2006, 1099–1101.

12492. ELDRED, LAURA G. Francie Pig *vs* the Fat Green Blob from Outer Space: horror films and *The Butcher Boy*. *See* **17295**.

12493. EMMONS, MARK. Film and television: a guide to the reference literature. Westport, CT: Libraries Unlimited, 2006. pp. xvi, 366. (Reference sources in the humanities.)

12494. EXUM, J. CHERYL (ed.). The Bible in film – the Bible and film. Leiden; Boston, MA: Brill, 2006. pp. 190.

12495. EZRA, ELIZABETH; ROWDEN, TERRY (eds). Transnational cinema. London; New York: Routledge, 2006. pp. viii, 213. (In focus – Routledge film readers.)

12496. FABE, MARILYN. Closely watched films: an introduction to the art of narrative film technique. (Bibl. 2004, 13284.) Rev. by Donald F. Larsson in FilmQ (59:4) 2006, 53–4.

12497. FEENEY, MARK. Nixon at the movies: a book about belief. (Bibl. 2005, 13230.) Rev. by Alan Nadel in FilmQ (59:4) 2006, 62–4.

12498. FEIL, KEN. Dying for a laugh: disaster movies and the camp imagination. Middletown, CT: Wesleyan UP, 2005. pp. xxix, 233. Rev. by Erin Foster in FilCr (30:3) 2006, 72–4.

12499. FELLEMAN, SUSAN. Art in the cinematic imagination. Austin: Texas UP, 2006. pp. xi, 199.

12500. FISCHER, LUCY. 'The shock of the new:' electrification, illumination, urbanization, and the cinema. *In* (pp. 19–37) **12661**.

12501. FISHER, CELESTE A. Black on Black: urban youth films and the multicultural audience. Lanham, MD; London: Scarecrow Press, 2006. pp. xxviii, 123.

12502. FISHER, JAMES. On the ladder of social observation: images of Decadence and morality in James's *Washington Square* and Wilde's *An Ideal Husband*. *In* (pp. 167–85) **10568**.

12503. FORSTER, GREG. 'Just a stupid policeman': Bond and the rule of law. *In* (pp. 121–37) **15903**.

12504. FOSTER, GWENDOLYN AUDREY. Performing modernity and gender in the 1930s. *In* (pp. 93–109) **12661**.

12505. FOURNIER, GINA. *Thelma & Louise* and women in Hollywood. *See* **13096**.

12506. FOWLER, CATHERINE; HELFIELD, GILLIAN (eds). Representing the rural: space, place, and identity in films about the land. Detroit, MI: Wayne State UP, 2006. pp. ix, 369. (Contemporary approaches to film and television.)

12507. Franklin, Daniel P. Politics and film: the political culture of film in the United States. Lanham, MD; Oxford: Rowman & Littlefield, 2006. pp. 222.

12508. French, Philip. Westerns: aspects of a movie genre. Manchester: Carcanet Press, 2005. pp. xii, 247. (Carcanet film.) Rev. by Tom Yarwood in TLS, 10 Mar. 2006, 28.

12509. Fridlund, Bert. The spaghetti western: a thematic analysis. Jefferson, NC; London: McFarland, 2006. pp. vii, 296.

12510. Furnish, Ben. Nostalgia in Jewish American theatre and film, 1979–2004. *See* **12289**.

12511. Fury, David. Maureen O'Sullivan: 'no average Jane'. *See* **14931**.

12512. Gabbard, Krin. Black magic: White Hollywood and African American culture. (Bibl. 2005, 13234.) Rev. by Toru Kiuchi in AAR (40:1) 2006, 183–5.

12513. Gallagher, Mark. Action figures: men, action films, and contemporary adventure narratives. Basingstoke; New York: Palgrave Macmillan, 2006. pp. vi, 234.

12514. Gardaphé, Fred L. From wiseguys to wise men: the gangster and Italian American masculinities. *See* **11900**.

12515. Gates, Philippa. Detecting men: masculinity and the Hollywood detective film. Albany: New York State UP, 2006. pp. x, 346. (SUNY series: Cultural studies in cinema/video.)

12516. Gehring, Wes D. Mr Deeds goes to Yankee Stadium: baseball films in the Capra tradition. Forewords by Carl Erskine and Steve Bell. (Bibl. 2004, 13300.) Rev. by Chris Lamb in NINE (14:1) 2005, 194–6.

12517. Geiger, Jeffrey; Rutsky, R. L. (eds). Film analysis: a Norton reader. New York; London: Norton, 2005. pp. 960.

12518. Getachew, Mahlete-Tsigé. How to live (and how to die). *In* (pp. 17–33) **15903**.

12519. Giannetti, Louis; Eyman, Scott. Flashback: a brief history of film. (Bibl. 1996, 13713.) Upper Saddle River, NJ: Pearson/Prentice Hall, 2006. pp. xi, 612. (Fifth ed.: first ed. 1986.)

12520. Gibbons, Luke. Projecting the nation: cinema and culture. *In* (pp. 206–24) **11829**.

12521. Gibbs, John; Pye, Douglas (eds). Style and meaning: studies in the detailed analysis of film. (Bibl. 2005, 13241.) Rev. by James Walters in ScopeF (6) 2006.

12522. Gibson, Marion. Retelling Salem stories: gender politics and witches in American culture. *See* **13309**.

12523. Giglio, Ernest D. Here's looking at you: Hollywood, film & politics. (Bibl. 2000, 12955.) New York; Frankfurt: Lang, 2005. pp. xvii, 327. (Politics, media, & popular culture, 11.) (Second ed.: first ed. 2000.)

12524. Gilmore, Richard A. Doing philosophy at the movies. Albany: New York State UP, 2005. pp. xi, 183. Rev. by Tom Paulus in ScopeF (6) 2006.

12525. Gormley, Paul. The new-brutality film: race and affect in contemporary Hollywood culture. *See* **19606**.

12526. Graves, Mark A.; Engle, F. Bruce. A reference guide to film genres. Westport, CT; London: Greenwood Press, 2006. pp. xv, 344.

12527. Griesinger, Emily; Eaton, Mark (eds). The gift of story: narrating hope in a postmodern world. *See* **11916**.

12528. Grieveson, Lee. Policing cinema: movies and censorship in early twentieth-century America. Berkeley; London: California UP, 2004. pp. xiii, 348. Rev. by Francis G. Couvares in FilmQ (59:4) 2006, 65–6.

12529. Griffiths, Robin (ed.). British queer cinema. London; New York: Routledge, 2006. pp. xi, 248. (British popular cinema.)

12530. Grindley, Carl James. Arms and the man: the curious inaccuracy of medieval arms and armor in contemporary film. FilmH (36:1) 2006, 14–19.

12531. Gunning, Tom. Modernity and cinema: a culture of shocks and flows. *In* (pp. 297–315) **12661**.

12532. Guynn, William. Writing history in film. London; New York: Routledge, 2006. pp. ix, 225.

12533. Harris, Keith M. Boys, boyz, bois: an ethics of Black masculinity in film and popular media. London; New York: Routledge, 2006. pp. xi, 156. (Studies in African American history and culture.)

12534. Hayward, Susan. Cinema Studies: the key concepts. (Bibl. 2000, 13008.) London; New York: Routledge, 2006. pp. xv, 586. (Third ed.: first ed. 1996.) (Orig. pub. as *Key Concepts in Cinema Studies*.)

12535. Heffernan, Kevin. Ghouls, gimmicks, and gold: horror films and the American movie business, 1953–1968. (Bibl. 2005, 13254.) Rev. by Susan Allen Ford in GothS (8:2) 2006, 141–2.

12536. Heins, Marjorie. Sex and the law: a tale of shifting boundaries. *In* (pp. 168–88) **12592**.

12537. Held, Jacob M. 'Don't you men know any other way?': punishment beyond retributivism and deterrence. *In* (pp. 139–53) **15903**.

12538. —— South, James B. (eds). James Bond and philosophy: questions are forever. *See* **15903**.

12539. Hendin, Josephine G. Heartbreakers: women and violence in contemporary culture and literature. *See* **11931**.

12540. Hentges, Sarah. Pictures of girlhood: modern female adolescence on film. Jefferson, NC; London: McFarland, 2006. pp. vii, 258. Rev. by Carol-Ann Farkas in JPC (39:4) 2006, 680–2.

12541. Higson, Andrew. A green and pleasant land: rural spaces and British cinema. *In* (pp. 240–65) **12506**.

12542. Hirsch, Joshua. Afterimage: film, trauma, and the Holocaust. Philadelphia, PA: Temple UP, 2004. pp. xvi, 213. (Emerging media.) Rev. by Janet Walker in FilmQ (60:1) 2006, 58–9.

12543. —— *Film gris* reconsidered. JPFT (34:2) 2006, 82–93.

12544. Hischak, Thomas S. American plays and musicals on screen: 650 stage productions and their film and television adaptations. *See* **3440**.

12545. —— Through the screen door: what happened to the Broadway musical when it went to Hollywood. (Bibl. 2005, 13260.) Rev. by Diana Calderazzo in TJ (58:4) 2006, 715–16.

12546. Hobbs, Sandy. Disappearance and denial: a new look at a legend motif on the screen. FOAFN (65) 2006.

12547. Hodgdon, Barbara; Worthen, W. B. (eds). A companion to Shakespeare and performance. *See* **5537**.

12548. Hogan, David J. (ed.). Science fiction America: essays on SF cinema. Jefferson, NC; London: McFarland, 2006. pp. viii, 280.

12549. Hogan, Ron; Bogdanovich, Peter. The stewardess is flying the plane! American films of the 1970s. New York: Bullfinch Press, 2005. pp. 271.

12550. Horowitz, Josh. The mind of the modern moviemaker: 20 conversations with the new generation of filmmakers. New York: Plume, 2006. pp. xvii, 302.

12551. Horsley, Jake. Dogville *vs* Hollywood. London: Boyars, 2005. pp. 379. Rev. by Adam Nayman in Cineaste (31:4) 2006, 94–5.

12552. Howells, Coral Ann (ed.). Where are the voices coming from? Canadian culture and the legacies of history. *See* **11946**.

12553. Humphries, Reynold. The Hollywood horror film, 1931–1941: madness in a social landscape. Lanham, MD; London: Scarecrow Press, 2006. pp. xvi, 283.

12554. Humphries-Brooks, Stephenson. Cinematic Savior: Hollywood's making of the American Christ. Westport, CT; London: Praeger, 2006. pp. x, 159. Rev. by Tom Aitken in TLS, 6 Oct. 2006, 31.

12555. Indick, William. Psycho thrillers: cinematic explorations of the mysteries of the mind. Jefferson, NC; London: McFarland, 2006. pp. vii, 187.

12556. Ingram, David. Green screen: environmentalism and Hollywood cinema. Exeter: Exeter UP, 2004. pp. 240. (Representing American culture.) Rev. by Terry Gifford in JAStud (40:1) 2006, 176–7.

12557. Irwin, John T. Unless the threat of death is behind them: hard-boiled fiction and *film noir*. *See* **13509**.

12558. James, Annie Morgan. Enchanted places, land and sea, and wilderness: Scottish Highland landscape and identity in cinema. *In* (pp. 185–201) **12506**.

12559. James, David. The most typical avant-garde: history and geography of minor cinemas in Los Angeles. Berkeley; London: California UP, 2005. pp. xiv, 548. Rev. by Federico Caprotti in JCG (24:1) 2006, 116–17.

12560. Jeffers, Jennifer M. Britain colonized: Hollywood's appropriation of British literature. Basingstoke; New York: Palgrave Macmillan, 2006. pp. xii, 282.

12561. Jenkins, Henry. 'He's in the closet but he's not gay': male–male desire in *Penthouse* 'letters'. *In* (pp. 133–53) **12592**.

12562. Johnston, Robert K. Reel spirituality: theology and film in dialogue. (Bibl. 2002, 11461.) Grand Rapids, MI: Baker Academic, 2006. pp. 351. (Engaging culture.) (Second ed.: first ed. 2000.)

12563. JOSLIN, LYNDON W. Count Dracula goes to the movies: Stoker's novel adapted, 1922–2003. (Bibl. 1999, 12141.) Jefferson, NC; London: McFarland, 2006. pp. viii, 272. (Second ed.: first ed. 1999.)

12564. JUHASZ, ALEXANDER; LERNER, JESSE (eds). F is for phony: fake documentary and truth's undoing. Minneapolis; London: Minnesota UP, 2006. pp. 255. (Visible evidence, 17.)

12565. KAMIR, ORIT. Framed: women in law and film. Durham, NC; London: Duke UP, 2006. pp. xix, 324.

12566. KANE, TIM. The changing vampire of film and television: a critical study of the growth of a genre. Jefferson, NC; London: McFarland, 2006. pp. 240.

12567. KARLIN, WAYNE. War movies: journeys to Vietnam: scenes and outtakes. Willimantic, CT: Curbstone Press, 2005. pp. 216.

12568. KARLSON, KRISTINE BUTLER. Movies and the march home. *In* (pp. 140–61) **12481**.

12569. KAVENEY, ROZ. From *Alien* to *The Matrix*: reading science fiction film. London; New York: Tauris, 2005. pp. 208. Rev. by Matthew Wilhelm Kapell in Extrapolation (47:2) 2006, 324–7.

12570. KEATHLEY, CHRISTIAN. Cinephilia and history; or, The wind in the trees. Bloomington: Indiana UP, 2006. pp. xiv, 212.

12571. KEIL, CHARLIE; STAMP, SHELLEY (eds). American cinema's transitional era: audiences, institutions, practices. (Bibl. 2004, 13333.) Rev. by Rob King in NCT (32:2) 2005, 78–85.

12572. KELLER, ALEXANDRA. From Stella Dallas to Lila Lipscomb: reading real motherhood through reel motherhood. WVUPP (52) 2005, 1–16.

12573. KELLER, JAMES R.; STRATYNER, LESLIE (eds). Almost Shakespeare: reinventing his works for cinema and television. (Bibl. 2005, 13273.) Rev. by Nicholas Jones in ShB (24:3) 2006, 71–3.

12574. KIBBEY, ANN. Theory of the image: capitalism, contemporary film, and women. Bloomington: Indiana UP, 2005. pp. x, 240.

12575. KING, C. RICHARD; LEONARD, DAVID J. (eds). Visual economies of/in motion: sport and film. New York; Frankfurt: Lang, 2006. pp. x, 274. (Cultural critique, 6.)

12576. KITSES, JIM. Horizons west: directing the western from John Ford to Clint Eastwood. (Bibl. 2005, 13280.) Rev. by Joanna Hearne in GPQ (26:1) 2006, 49–50; by Leonard Engel in WAL (41:1) 2006, 82–3.

12577. KLEIN, MARTY. Pornography: what men see when they watch. *In* (pp. 244–57) **12592**.

12578. KNEPPER, MARTY S.; LAWRENCE, JOHN S. World War II and Iowa: Hollywood's pastoral myth for the nation. *In* (pp. 323–39) **12506**.

12579. KOLKER, ROBERT. Film, form, and culture. Boston, MA: McGraw-Hill, 2006. pp. x, 326; 1 CD-ROM. (Third ed.: first ed. 1999.)

12580. KOWALSKI, DEAN A. The new millennium Bond and *yin–yang* Chinese cosmology. *In* (pp. 215–27) **15903**.

12581. KOZLOFF, SARAH. Movies on the edge of war. *In* (pp. 48–73) **12481**.

12582. Kruger, Loren. Filming the edgy city: cinematic narrative and urban form in postapartheid Johannesburg. RAL (37:2) 2006, 141–63.

12583. Lagayette, Pierre. From *Scarface* to *Bugsy*: gangsters as enduring icons of the American Dream. QPS (14) 2006, 337–44.

12584. Landy, Marcia. Movies and the fate of genre. *In* (pp. 222–43) **12481**.

12585. Langford, Barry. Film genre: Hollywood and beyond. Edinburgh: Edinburgh UP, 2005. pp. x, 310. (Film genres.) Rev. by Elaine Lennon in ScopeF (6) 2006.

12586. Lanier, Douglas. Will of the people: recent Shakespeare film parody and the politics of popularization. *In* (pp. 176–96) **5531**.

12587. Lawrence, John Shelton. A filmography of western films with ecocritical and environmental representations. *In* (pp. 229–33) **12438**.

12588. —— Western ecological films: the subgenre with no name. *In* (pp. 19–50) **12438**.

12589. Lebow, Alisa. Faking what? Making a mockery of documentary. *In* (pp. 223–37) **12564**.

12590. Lefebvre, Martin (ed.). Landscape and film. London; New York: Routledge, 2006. pp. xxxi, 361. (AFI film readers.)

12591. Lehman, Christopher P. American animated cartoons of the Vietnam era: a study of social commentary in films and television programs, 1961–1973. Jefferson, NC; London: McFarland, 2006. pp. viii, 223.

12592. Lehman, Peter (ed.). Pornography: film and culture. New Brunswick, NJ; London: Rutgers UP, 2006. pp. viii, 272. (Rutgers depth of field series.)

12593. Lehmann, Courtney. Dancing in a (cyber) net: 'Renaissance women', systems theory, and the war of the cinemas. *See* **5562**.

12594. Leonard, David J. Screens fade to black: contemporary African American cinema. *See* **19623**.

12595. Leonard, Richard. Movies that matter: reading film through the lens of faith. Chicago, IL: Loyola Press, 2006. pp. xxv, 172.

12596. Leskosky, Richard J. Size matters: big bugs on the big screen. *In* (pp. 319–41) **3203**.

12597. Lichtenfeld, Eric. Action speaks louder: violence, spectacle, and the American action movie. Foreword by Richard Slotkin. Westport, CT; London: Praeger, 2004. pp. xxi, 313.

12598. Lopate, Phillip (ed.). American movie critics: an anthology from the silents until now. New York: Library of America, 2006. pp. xxvii, 720. Rev. by Clive James in NYTB, 4 June 2006, 36–9; by Robert Sklar in Cineaste (31:4) 2006, 89–90.

12599. Lorence, James J. Screening America: United States history through film since 1900. London; New York: Pearson Longman, 2006. pp. xii, 212.

12600. Lott, M. Ray. Police on screen: Hollywood cops, detectives, marshals, and rangers. Jefferson, NC; London: McFarland, 2006. pp. vii, 214.

12601. Loy, R. Philip. Westerns in a changing America, 1955–2000. (Bibl. 2005, 13296.) Rev. by Deborah Allison in JPFT (33:4) 2006, 213; by Edward Buscombe in GPQ (26:3) 2006, 223–4.

12602. McCreadie, Marsha. Women screenwriters today: their lives and words. Westport, CT; London: Praeger, 2006. pp. xxiv, 176. Rev. by Jean O'Reilly in FllCr (31:1/2) 2006, 176–9.

12603. MacDonald, Scott (ed.). Art in Cinema: documents toward a history of the film society. Philadelphia, PA: Temple UP, 2006. pp. xi, 307. (Wide angle.)

12604. McFarlane, Brian. The heart of things. *See* **19632**.

12605. —— Mothers: some kids do 'ave 'em. *See* **19717**.

12606. McGilligan, Patrick (ed.). Backstory 4: interviews with screenwriters of the 1970s and 1980s. Berkeley; London: California UP, 2006. pp. x, 424.

12607. McGinn, Colin. The power of movies: how screen and mind interact. (Bibl. 2005, 13306.) Rev. by Wyatt Mason in NYTB, 22 Jan. 2006, 4.

12608. McGowan, Todd; Kunkle, Sheila (eds). Lacan and contemporary film. (Bibl. 2004, 13361.) Rev. by Marco Abel in SAtlR (71:1) 2006, 132–40.

12609. McKinney, William J. James Bond and the philosophy of technology: it's more than just the gadgets of Q Branch. *In* (pp. 187–97) **15903**.

12610. McLaughlin, Robert L.; Parry, Sally E. We'll always have the movies: American cinema during World War II. Lexington: Kentucky UP, 2006. pp. ix, 357. Rev. by Robert Fyne in FilmH (36:2) 2006, 60–1.

12611. Mahar, Karen Ward. Women filmmakers in early Hollywood. Baltimore, MD; London: Johns Hopkins UP, 2006. pp. x, 291, (plates) 16.

12612. Malik, Rachel. The afterlife of Wilkie Collins. *In* (pp. 181–93) **9609**.

12613. Maltby, Richard; Stokes, Melvyn (eds). Hollywood abroad: audiences and cultural exchange. London: British Film Inst., 2004. pp. v, 183. Rev. by Martin Barker in ScopeF (4) 2006.

12614. Marciniak, Katarzyna. Alienhood: citizenship, exile, and the logic of difference. Minneapolis; London: Minnesota UP, 2006. pp. xx, 197.

12615. Marcus, Greil. The shape of things to come: prophecy and the American voice. *See* **18319**.

12616. Marcus, Laura. Film. *In* (pp. 250–7) **11788**.

12617. Marez, Curtis. Pancho Villa meets Sun Yat-sen: Third World revolution and the history of Hollywood cinema. *See* **13121**.

12618. Marroni, Francesco (ed.). *Great Expectations*: nel laboratorio di Charles Dickens. *See* **9791**.

12619. Martin, Adrian. Empathy connection. *See* **19711**.

12620. Martin, Lydia. Jane Austen's politeness on screen: between ambivalent submission and defiant self assertion. *See* **9056**.

12621. Martin, Nina K. Never laugh at a man with his pants down: the affective dynamics of comedy and porn. *In* (pp. 189–205) **12592**.

12622. Marubbio, M. Elise. Killing the Indian maiden: images of Native American women in film. Lexington: Kentucky UP, 2006. pp. xiii, 298.

12623. Mast, Gerald; Kawin, Bruce F. A short history of the movies. London; New York: Pearson Longman, 2006. pp. xii, 772. (Ninth ed.: first ed. 1971.)

12624. Menand, Louis. Do movies have rights? *In* (pp. 183–202) **15511**.

12625. Merlock, Ray. Growing up with westerns. *In* (pp. 235–51) **3157**.

12626. Metz, Walter. Engaging film criticism: film history and contemporary American cinema. (Bibl. 2004, 13379.) Rev. by David T. Johnson in LitFQ (34:4) 2006, 332–3.

12627. —— Hollywood cinema. *In* (pp. 374–91) **11776**.

12628. Middleton, Darren J. N. (ed.). Scandalizing Jesus: Kazantzakis's *The Last Temptation of Christ* fifty years on. *See* **12933**.

12629. Mills, Katie. The road story and the rebel: moving through film, fiction, and television. Carbondale: Southern Illinois UP, 2006. pp. xiii, 270.

12630. Milutis, Joe. Ether: the nothing that connects everything. Minneapolis; London: Minnesota UP, 2006. pp. xxiii, 208. Rev. by Sherryl Vint in Extrapolation (47:3) 2006, 509–13.

12631. Mitchell, Charles P. Filmography of social issues: a reference guide. Westport, CT; London: Greenwood Press, 2004. pp. x, 318. Rev. by John Saddington in ScopeF (4) 2006.

12632. Mizejewski, Linda. Hardboiled & high heeled: the woman detective in popular culture. (Bibl. 2004, 13383.) Rev. by Adrienne L. McLean in FilmQ (59:4) 2006, 58–9; by Heidi Slettedahl MacPherson in JAStud (40:2) 2006, 443–4.

12633. Moran, Albert; Vieth, Errol. Film in Australia: an introduction. Cambridge; New York: CUP, 2006. pp. xii, 219.

12634. —— —— Historical dictionary of Australian and New Zealand cinema. Lanham, MD; London: Scarecrow Press, 2005. pp. xiii, 414. (Historical dictionaries of literature and the arts, 6.)

12635. Moran, Leslie J. On realism and the law film: the case of Oscar Wilde. *In* (pp. 77–93) **12636**.

12636. —— *et al.* (eds). Law's moving image. London: Cavendish, 2004. pp. xviii, 255. Rev. by Edward Mussawir in LawL (17:1) 2005, 131–52.

12637. Morrison, James. Still new, still queer, still cinema? GLQ (12:1) 2006, 135–46 (review-article).

12638. Mort, John. Read the high country: a guide to western books and films. *See* **3490**.

12639. Most, Marshall G.; Rudd, Robert. Stars, stripes and diamonds: American culture and the baseball film. Jefferson, NC; London: McFarland, 2006. pp. ix, 190.

12640. Muir, John Kenneth. The encyclopedia of superheroes on film and television. Jefferson, NC; London: McFarland, 2004. pp. x, 621. Rev. by P. Andrew Miller in JFA (15:2) 2004, 171–2.

12641. Mustazza, Leonard. The literary filmography: 6,200 adaptations of books, short stories and other nondramatic works. Jefferson, NC; London: McFarland, 2006. 2 vols. pp. vii, 725.

12642. Nemerov, Alexander. Icons of grief: Val Lewton's home front pictures. Berkeley; London: California UP, 2005. pp. xii, 213. Rev. by Robert Fyne in FilmH (36:1) 2006, 82.

12643. Neroni, Hilary. The violent woman: femininity, narrative, and violence in contemporary American cinema. (Bibl. 2005, 13323.) Rev. by Elizabeth

Nathanson in FJCM (47:1) 2006, 126–8; by William B. Covey in MFS (52:3) 2006, 705–15.

12644. Newitz, Annalee. Pretend we're dead: capitalist monsters in American pop culture. *See* **13570**.

12645. Niemi, Robert. History in the media: film and television. Santa Barbara, CA: ABC-CLIO, 2006. pp. xxiii, 501.

12646. Oishi, Eve. Screen memories: fakeness in Asian American media practice. *In* (pp. 196–219) **12564**.

12647. —— Visual perversions: race, sex, and cinematic pleasure. *See* **14553**.

12648. Ording, Dominic. Portraits of the American heartland at the crossroads of the counterculture. *See* **12070**.

12649. Ostherr, Kirsten. Cinematic prophylaxis: globalization and contagion in the discourse of world health. Durham, NC; London: Duke UP, 2005. pp. xii, 275.

12650. Overstreet, Deborah Wilson. Not your mother's vampire: vampires in young adult fiction. *See* **13684**.

12651. Paietta, Ann C. Saints, clergy, and other religious figures on film and television, 1895–2003. Jefferson, NC; London: McFarland, 2005. pp. vii, 192. Rev. by Erin Hill-Parks in FilmH (36:2) 2006, 68–9.

12652. Palmer, R. Barton. The British New Wave: a modernist cinema. *In* (pp. 52–64) **12403**.

12653. Parish, James Robert. Fiasco: a history of Hollywood's iconic flops. Chichester; Hoboken, NJ: Wiley, 2006. pp. viii, 359.

12654. Perry, Ted (ed.). Masterpieces of modernist cinema. Bloomington: Indiana UP, 2006. pp. 341.

12655. Petro, Patrice. Legacies of Weimar cinema. *In* (pp. 235–52) **12661**.

12656. Phillips, John. Transgender on screen. Basingstoke; New York: Palgrave Macmillan, 2006. pp. viii, 196.

12657. Phillips, Kendall R. Projected fears: horror films and American culture. (Bibl. 2005, 13336.) Rev. by John Armstrong in JAStud (40:2) 2006, 445–6.

12658. Picart, Caroline Joan (Kay) S.; Frank, David A. Frames of evil: the Holocaust as horror in American film. Foreword by Dominick LaCapra. Introd. by Edward J. Ingebretsen. Carbondale: Southern Illinois UP, 2006. pp. xxi, 186.

12659. Pizzato, Mark. Ghosts of theatre and cinema in the brain. *See* **3449**.

12660. Pomerance, Murray. The dramaturgy of action and involvement in sports film. QRFV (23:4) 2006, 311–29.

12661. —— (ed.). Cinema and modernity. New Brunswick, NJ: Rutgers UP, 2006. pp. ix, 373.

12662. Powell, Anna. Deleuze and horror film. Edinburgh: Edinburgh UP, 2005. pp. vii, 232. Rev. by Patricia Allmer in ScopeF (6) 2006.

12663. Powrie, Phil; Davies, Ann; Babington, Bruce (eds). The trouble with men: masculinities in European and Hollywood cinema. London;

New York: Wallflower Press, 2004. pp. x, 253. Rev. by Angelo Restivo in SAtlR (70:4) 2005, 160–6.

12664. Pramaggiore, Maria; Wallis, Tom. Film: a critical introduction. Boston, MA: Pearson / Allyn & Bacon, 2006. pp. xv, 432.

12665. Prats, Armando José. Last stand at the Ia Drang Valley: memory, mission, and the shape of victory in *We Were Soldiers*. *See* **19765**.

12666. Preston, Catherine L. Movies and national identity. *In* (pp. 94–116) **12481**.

12667. Prince, Stephen (ed.). The horror film. (Bibl. 2004, 13409.) Rev. by Maria Pramaggiore in FilmQ (59:3) 2006, 76–7; by Steffen Hantke in Paradoxa (20) 2006, 312–14.

12668. Pritchard, William H. The perfect critic. *See* **3450**.

12669. Rancière, Jacques. Film fables. Trans. by Emiliano Battista. Oxford; New York: Berg, 2006. pp. viii, 196. (Talking images.)

12670. Rapf, Joanna. Movies and the family. *In* (pp. 200–21) **12481**.

12671. Raw, Laurence. Adapting Henry James to the screen: gender, fiction, and film. *See* **10594**.

12672. Rayner, Alice. Ghosts: death's double and the phenomena of theater. *See* **3378**.

12673. Restuccia, Frances L. Amorous acts: Lacanian ethics in Modernism, film, and queer theory. Stanford, CA: Stanford UP, 2006. pp. xvi, 175.

12674. Rhu, Lawrence F. Stanley Cavell's American Dream: Shakespeare, philosophy, and Hollywood movies. *See* **5423**.

12675. Richardson, Michael. Surrealism and cinema. Oxford; New York: Berg, 2006. pp. 202.

12676. Riley, Michael O. L. Frank Baum and the early motion picture industry. *See* **14647**.

12677. Rollins, Peter C.; O'Connor, John E. (eds). Hollywood's West: the American frontier in film, television, and history. (Bibl. 2005, 13358.) Rev. by Robert Fyne in FilmH (36:1) 2006, 76–7.

12678. Rosenbaum, Jonathan. Essential cinema: on the necessity of film canons. Baltimore, MD; London: Johns Hopkins UP, 2004. pp. xxi, 445.

12679. Rosenstone, Robert A. History on film / film and history. London; New York: Pearson Longman, 2006. pp. xii, 182. (History: concepts, theories and practice.)

12680. Rossi, Umberto. Ambiguous spokespersons: the DJ and talk-radio host in US fiction, cinema and drama. *See* **15484**.

12681. Rothman, William. Film, modernity, Cavell. *In* (pp. 316–32) **12661**.

12682. Royer, Carl; Royer, Diana. The spectacle of isolation in horror films: dark parades. New York; London: Haworth Press, 2005. pp. xvii, 120.

12683. Rutelli, Romana. Dal libro allo schermo: sulle traduzioni intersemiotiche dal testo verbale al cinema. Pisa: ETS, 2004. pp. 160. (Piazza universale, 1.) Rev. by Elvira La Torre in TFr (32:1) 2005, 213–19.

12684. Sachleben, Mark; Yenerall, Kevan M. Seeing the bigger picture: understanding politics through film & television. New York; Frankfurt: Lang, 2004. pp. xiii, 337. (Politics, media, & popular culture, 9.)

12685. Samuels, Ellen. From Melville to Eddie Murphy: the disability con in American literature and film. *See* **10891**.

12686. Sanders, Steven M. *Film noir* and the meaning of life. *In* (pp. 91–105) **12452**.

12687. Sapre, Erin E. Wartime propaganda: enemies defined by race. WVUPP (51) 2004, 91–103.

12688. Schmid, David. Natural born celebrities: serial killers in American culture. Chicago, IL; London: Chicago UP, 2005. pp. viii, 327. Rev. by Jean Murley in JPC (39:5) 2006, 912–14.

12689. Schneider, Steven Jay. Movies and the march to war. *In* (pp. 74–93) **12481**.

12690. —— (ed.). Horror film and psychoanalysis: Freud's worst nightmare. (Bibl. 2005, 13372.) Rev. by Maria Pramaggiore in FilmQ (59:3) 2006, 76–7.

12691. Schuchardt, Read Mercer. *Cherchez la femme fatale*: the mother of *film noir*. *In* (pp. 49–68) **12452**.

12692. Semmerling, Tim Jon. 'Evil' Arabs in American popular film: Orientalist fear. Austin: Texas UP, 2006. pp. viii, 303.

12693. Shaki, Femi Okiremuete. Modernity and the African cinema. Trenton, NJ: Africa World Press, 2004. pp. 453. Rev. by Sheila Petty in AfSR (49:1) 2006, 169–70.

12694. Sheckels, Theodore F. The difficulties of translating Peter Carey's postmodern fiction into popular film. *In* (pp. 83–100) **15024**.

12695. Sheridan, Earl. Conservative implications of the irrelevance of racism in contemporary African American cinema. *See* **19654**.

12696. Short, Sue. Misfit sisters: screen horror as female rites of passage. Basingstoke; New York: Palgrave Macmillan, 2006. pp. xi, 196.

12697. Simkin, Stevie. Early modern tragedy and the cinema of violence. *See* **4724**.

12698. Simon, John. John Simon on film: criticism, 1982–2001. Introd. by Bruce Beresford. New York: Applause, 2005. pp. 662. Rev. by William H. Pritchard in HR (59:1) 2006, 135–41.

12699. Simpson, Paul; Roddis, Helen; Bushell, Michaela (eds). The Rough Guide to cult movies. London: Haymarket, 2004. pp. 480. (Rough Guides reference guides.)

12700. Sison, Antonio D. Screening Schillebeeckx: theology and Third Cinema in dialogue. Foreword by Robert J. Schreiter. Basingstoke; New York: Palgrave Macmillan, 2006. pp. xii, 231.

12701. Skoble, Aeon J. Moral clarity and practical reason in *film noir*. *In* (pp. 41–8) **12452**.

12702. Slocum, J. David (ed.). Hollywood and war: the film reader. London; New York: Routledge, 2006. pp. ix, 372. (In focus – Routledge film readers.)

12703. Smith, Judith E. Visions of belonging: family stories, popular culture, and postwar democracy, 1940–1960. *See* **12154**.
12704. Smyth, J. E. Reconstructing American historical cinema: from *Cimarron* to *Citizen Kane*. Lexington: Kentucky UP, 2006. pp. xiii, 447.
12705. Sobchack, Vivian. Carnal thoughts: embodiment and moving image culture. (Bibl. 2005, 13394.) Rev. by Gaylyn Studlar in FilmQ (60:1) 2006, 62–3.
12706. Spencer, Nicholas. Movies and the renegotiation of genre. *In* (pp. 117–39) **12481**.
12707. Stanfield, Peter. Body and soul: jazz and Blues in American film, 1927–1963. Urbana: Illinois UP, 2005. pp. x, 213. Rev. by David Segal in Cineaste (31:3) 2006, 79–81.
12708. Stetz, Margaret. 'Caught in the trap': William Morris, machinery, and popular film from Charlie Chaplin to Nick Park. *See* **10949**.
12709. Stevens, George, Jr (ed.). Conversations with the great moviemakers of Hollywood's golden age at the American Film Institute. New York: Knopf, 2006. pp. xx, 710.
12710. Stewart, Jacqueline Najuma. Migrating to the movies: cinema and Black urban modernity. Berkeley; London: California UP, 2005. pp. xxiii, 343. Rev. by Laura Quinn in FilCr (29:3) 2005, 73–8.
12711. Stoehr, Kevin L. Nihilism in film and television: a critical overview, *Citizen Kane* to *The Sopranos*. Jefferson, NC; London: McFarland, 2006. pp. 216.
12712. Strickland, Rennard; Foster, Teree; Banks, Taunya (eds). Screening justice – the cinema of law: significant films of law, order and social justice. Buffalo, NY: Hein, 2006. pp. xxxiii, 743.
12713. Sullivan, Rebecca. Visual habits: nuns, feminism, and American postwar popular culture. *See* **12170**.
12714. Sweet, Matthew. Shepperton Babylon: the lost worlds of British cinema. (Bibl. 2005, 13406.) Rev. by Aubrey Anne D'Arminio in MovIm (6:1) 2006, 131–4.
12715. Tallaferro, Charles; Le Gall, Michel. Bond as chivalric, comic hero. *In* (pp. 95–108) **15903**.
12716. Tasker, Yvonne (ed.). Action and adventure cinema. London; New York: Routledge, 2004. pp. xv, 414.
12717. Tatar, Maria. Secrets beyond the door: the story of Bluebeard and his wives. (Bibl. 2005, 13407.) Rev. by Gary Schmidt in LU (30:1) 2006, 143–7; by Rosan Augusta Jordan in MarvT (20:1) 2006, 119–22.
12718. Tedesco, Matthew. The moral status of the double-0 agent: thinking about the license to kill. *In* (pp. 111–20) **15903**.
12719. Telotte, J. P. Lost in space: television as science fiction icon. JPFT (33:4) 2006, 178–86.
12720. Thompson, Raymond H.; Busby, Keith (eds). Gawain: a casebook. *See* **3980**.
12721. Thomson, David. The new biographical dictionary of film. (Bibl. 2003, 12854.) New York: Knopf, 2004. pp. 989. (Revised ed.: first ed. 1975.)

12722. Tibbetts, John C.; Welsh, James Michael. The encyclopedia of novels into film. (Bibl. 2000, 4133.) New York: Facts on File, 2005. pp. xxii, 586. (Facts on File film reference library.) (Second ed.: first ed. 1997.)

12723. Tolchin, Karen R. Part blood, part ketchup: coming of age in American literature and film. *See* **13629**.

12724. Tremper, Ellen. I'm no angel: the blonde in fiction and film. *See* **8725**.

12725. Valantin, Jean-Michel. Hollywood, the Pentagon and Washington: the movies and national security from World War II to the present day. London: Anthem Press, 2005. pp. xii, 159. Rev. by Charles Wukasch in FilmH (36:2) 2006, 66–7.

12726. Vaughn, Stephen. Freedom and entertainment: rating the movies in an age of new media. Cambridge; New York: CUP, 2006. pp. xvi, 336. Rev. by Hiroshi Kitamura in AmQ (58:4) 2006, 1263–73.

12727. Vineberg, Steve. High comedy in American movies: class and humor from the 1920s to the present. Lanham, MD; Oxford: Rowman & Littlefield, 2005. pp. x, 209. (Genre and beyond.) Rev. by Maria DiBattista in Cineaste (31:1) 2005, 73–5.

12728. Waddell, Calum. Minds of fear. Baltimore, MD: Midnight Marquee Press, 2005. pp. 279. (Horror film.)

12729. Wager, Jans B. Dames in the driver's seat: rereading *film noir*. (Bibl. 2005, 13417.) Rev. by Deborah Allison in FilCr (30:2) 2006, 76–9; by William B. Covey in PS (26:1) 2006, 62–5.

12730. Walker, Janet. Trauma cinema: documenting incest and the Holocaust. (Bibl. 2005, 13418.) Rev. by Tom Conley in Biography (29:3) 2006, 493–5.

12731. Wartenberg, Thomas E.; Curran, Angela (eds). The philosophy of film: introductory text and readings. (Bibl. 2005, 13422.) Rev. by Katherine Thomson-Jones in BJA (46:2) 2006, 210–12.

12732. Wasson, Haidee. Museum movies: the Museum of Modern Art and the birth of art cinema. Berkeley; London: California UP, 2005. pp. xiii, 314. Rev. by Barbara Selznick in MovIm (6:2) 2006, 136–8.

12733. Wayne, Mike (ed.). Understanding film: Marxist perspectives. London; Sterling, VA: Pluto Press, 2005. pp. 253.

12734. Wee, Valerie. Resurrecting and updating the teen slasher: the case of *Scream*. *See* **13045**.

12735. Wendland, Albert. The universe in a frame: the domestic sublime in *Adam Strange* and fifties SF. *See* **13637**.

12736. Wexman, Virginia Wright. A history of film. (Bibl. 2003, 12634.) Boston, MA: Pearson / Allyn & Bacon, 2006. pp. x, 494. (Sixth ed.: first ed. 1979.)

12737. Wheeler, Leigh Ann. Against obscenity: reform and the politics of womanhood, 1873–1935. *See* **8606**.

12738. Whitfield, Stephen J. The culture of the Cold War. *In* (pp. 256–74) **11776**.

12739. Williams, Linda (ed.). Porn studies: proliferating pornographies on/screen: an introduction. Durham, NC; London: Duke UP, 2004. pp. 516. Rev. by Carla Freccero in GLQ (11:3) 2005, 469–71; by Todd Morrison in JHo (50:4) 2005, 211–15.

12740. Williams, Linda Ruth. The erotic thriller in contemporary cinema. Bloomington: Indiana UP, 2005. pp. xiii, 466. Rev. by David Andrews in JPC (39:4) 2006, 677–8.

12741. Williams, Tony. Movies and the 'enemy' within. *In* (pp. 182–99) **12481**.

12742. Wilmsen, Carl. Cinematic conquest: breaking the Mexican American connection to the land in the movies. *In* (pp. 182–211) **12438**.

12743. Wilson, Eric G. Secret cinema: gnostic vision in film. London; New York: Continuum, 2006. pp. 174.

12744. Wolf, Werner; Bernhart, Walter (eds). Framing borders in literature and other media. *See* **3422**.

12745. Wood, Jason. 100 American independent films. London: British Film Inst., 2004. pp. xiii, 263. (BFI screen guides.) Rev. by Glen Jones in ScopeF (4) 2006.

12746. Wood, Juliette. Filming fairies: popular film, audience response and meaning in contemporary fairy lore. *See* **6002**.

12747. Wood, Robin. Personal views: explorations in film. Detroit, MI: Wayne State UP, 2006. pp. xiv, 423. (Contemporary approaches to film and television.)

12748. Wright, T. R. (ed.). Thomas Hardy on screen. *See* **10349**.

12749. Young, Paul. The cinema dreams its rivals: media fantasy films from radio to the Internet. Minneapolis; London: Minnesota UP, 2006. pp. xxxv, 311. Rev. by Noah Arceneaux in JPC (39:5) 2006, 897–8.

12750. Zani, Steven. James Bond and Q: Heidegger's technology; or, 'You're not a sportsman, Mr Bond.' *In* (pp. 173–86) **15903**.

Individual Films

***10 Things I Hate about You* (1999)**

12751. Deitchman, Elizabeth A. Shakespeare Stiles style: Shakespeare, Julia Stiles, and American girl culture. *In* (pp. 478–94) **5537**.

***2001: a Space Odyssey* (1968)**

12752. Gilbert, James. Auteur with an A. *In* (pp. 29–41) **12754**.

12753. Grant, Barry Keith. Of men and monoliths: science fiction, gender, and *2001: a Space Odyssey*. *In* (pp. 69–86) **12754**.

12754. Kolker, Robert (ed.). Stanley Kubrick's *2001: a Space Odyssey*: new essays. Oxford; New York: OUP, 2006. pp. viii, 189, (plates) 18.

12755. Landy, Marcia. The cinematic brain in *2001: a Space Odyssey*. *In* (pp. 87–104) **12754**.

12756. Mamber, Stephen. Kubrick in space. *In* (pp. 55–68) **12754**.

12757. Mateas, Michael. Reading HAL: representation and artificial intelligence. *In* (pp. 105–25) **12754**.

12758. Miller, Mark Crispin. *2001:* a cold descent. *In* (pp. 122–45) **13202**.

12759. Palmer, R. Barton. *2001*: the critical reception and the generation gap. *In* (pp. 13–27) **12754**.

12760. Telotte, J. P. The gravity of *2001: a Space Odyssey*. *In* (pp. 43–53) **12754**.

12761. Toles, George. Double minds and double binds in Stanley Kubrick's fairy tale. *In* (pp. 147–76) **12754**.

The 27th Day **(1957)**

12762. Joslin, Lyndon W. The Cold War in orbit: two films of aliens, arsenals, and interventions. *In* (pp. 151–65) **12548**.

The Accused **(1949)**

12763. Palmer, R. Barton. Moral man in the dark city: *film noir*, the postwar religious revival, and *The Accused*. *In* (pp. 187–206) **12452**.

Adam's Rib **(1949)**

12764. Papke, David Ray. Genre, gender, and jurisprudence in *Adam's Rib* (1949). *In* (pp. 69–79) **12712**.

Air Force One **(1997)**

12765. Ventura, Patricia. A new 'Marshall' plan: terrorism, globalization, blockbusters, and *Air Force One*. Genre (38:4) 2005, 327–52.

The Alamo **(1960)**

12766. Thompson, Frank. Reprinting the legend: the Alamo on film. *See* **19675**.

Alien Films **(1979–1997)**

12767. Clark, Mark. Pets or meat: *Alien*, *Aliens*, and the indifference of the gods. *In* (pp. 233–45) **12548**.

12768. Gallardo C., Ximena; Smith, C. Jason. Alien woman: the making of Lt Ellen Ripley. (Bibl. 2005, 13441.) Rev. by Lorrie Palmer in JFA (16:4) 2006, 385–9.

12769. Melzer, Patricia. Alien constructions: science fiction and feminist thought. *See* **13561**.

All about Eve **(1950)**

12770. Rotolo, Steven J. Motherhood, fertility, and creativity in Mankiewitz's *All about Eve*. WVUPP (52) 2005, 70–6.

All Quiet on the Western Front **(1930)**

12771. Chambers, John Whiteclay, II. The movies and the antiwar debate in America, 1930–1941. FilmH (36:1) 2006, 44–57.

American Beauty **(1999)**

12772. Erickson, Leslie Goss. Re-visioning of the heroic journey in postmodern literature: Toni Morrison, Julia Alvarez, Arthur Miller, and *American Beauty*. *See* **17598**.

12773. Johnston, Robert K. Beyond futility: *American Beauty* and the Book of Ecclesiastes. *In* (pp. 85–96) **11916**.

12774. Laytham, D. Brent. Time for hope: *The Sixth Sense*, *American Beauty*, *Memento*, and *Twelve Monkeys*. *In* (pp. 69–83) **11916**.

***American History X* (1998)**

12775. Roth, LuAnne. Beyond *communitas*: cinematic food events and the negotiation of power, belonging, and exclusion. WF (64:3/4) 2005, 163–87.

***Amistad* (1997)**

12776. Stoddard, Jeremy D.; Marcus, Alan S. The burden of historical representation: race, freedom, and the 'educational' Hollywood film. *See* **12880**.

***Annie Hall* (1977)**

12777. Steed, J. P. The subversion of the Jews: post-World War II anxiety, humor, and identity in Woody Allen and Philip Roth. *See* **18332**.

***Apocalypse Now* (1979)**

12778. McCann, Sean. Therapy for a wounded nation. CommRev (4:3) 2006, 30–6.

***The Apprenticeship of Duddy Kravitz* (1974)**

12779. Henderson, Scott. Ted Kotcheff: *The Apprenticeship of Duddy Kravitz*. *In* (pp. 247–57) **11946**.

***The Atomic City* (1952)**

12780. Hogan, David J. *Atomic City*, atomic world. *In* (pp. 57–68) **12548**.

***The Atomic Kid* (1954)**

12781. Okuda, Ted. *The Atomic Kid*: radioactivity finds Andy Hardy. *In* (pp. 120–9) **12548**.

***Attack* (1956)**

12782. Brown, Kathleen A. 'Vestments of civil life' in *Caine Mutiny* and *Attack*. *See* **12811**.

***Bamboozled* (2000)**

12783. Elam, Harry J., Jr. Spike Lee's *Bamboozled*. *In* (pp. 346–62) **11876**.

***Barry Lyndon* (1975)**

12784. Wickre, Bille. Pictures, plurality, and puns: a visual approach to *Barry Lyndon*. *In* (pp. 165–84) **13202**.

***Beautiful Thing* (1996)**

12785. Nowlan, Bob. The politics of love in three recent US and UK films of young gay romance: a symptomatic reading of *Beautiful Thing*, *Get Real*, and *Edge of Seventeen*. *See* **12851**.

***Beauty and the Beast* (1991)**

12786. Griswold, Jerry. The meanings of *Beauty and the Beast*. Peterborough, Ont.; Orchard Park, NY: Broadview Press, 2004. pp. 258, (plates) 24. Rev. by Martha Hixon in ChildLit (34) 2006, 214–17.

beDevil **(1993)**

12787. Olubas, Brigitta. Image, affect and memory: relations of looking in Tracey Moffatt's *beDevil!* Southerly (65:1) 2005, 81–90.

The Best Years of Our Lives **(1946)**

12788. Friedlander, Benjamin. The best years of our lives: Randall Jarrell's war poetry. *In* (pp. 83–111) **13763**.

The Big Sleep **(1946)**

12789. Knight, Deborah. On reason and passion in *The Maltese Falcon*. *In* (pp. 207–21) **12452**.

Billy Elliot **(2000)**

12790. Kidd, Kerry. The child in the cinema: representations of a rural dystopia in *Billy Elliot* and *The Color of Paradise*. *In* (pp. 213–23) **12506**.

12791. Lancioni, Judith. Cinderella dances *Swan Lake*: reading *Billy Elliot* as fairytale. JPC (39:5) 2006, 709–28.

12792. Wayne, Mike. The performing Northern working class in British cinema: cultural representation and its political economy. *See* **12875**.

The Black Hole **(1979)**

12793. Rhodes, Gary D. Entropy in B-flat; or, Disordered thoughts on *The Black Hole*. *In* (pp. 225–32) **12548**.

Blade **(1998)**

12794. Carroll, Hamilton. Vampire capitalism: globalization, race, and the postnational body in *Blade*. Genre (38:4) 2005, 371–88.

Blade Runner **(1982)**

12795. La Polla, Franco. Da Philip K. Dick a Hollywood: ovvero, La quadratura del cerchio. *In* (pp. 275–81) **15466**.

The Blair Witch Project **(1999)**

12796. Harrison, Matthew B. Making strange impressions: the unsettling craft of self-critical cinema. QRFV (23:5) 2006, 423–36.

Blonde Venus **(1932)**

12797. Ngai, Sianne. Black Venus, *Blonde Venus*. *In* (pp. 145–78) **12024**.

Blow Out **(1981)**

12798. Verevis, Constantine. For ever Hitchcock: *Psycho* and its remakes. *In* (pp. 15–29) **13181**.

Blow-Up **(1966)**

12799. Tomasulo, Frank P. 'You're tellin' me you didn't see': Hitchcock's *Rear Window* and Antonioni's *Blow-Up*. *In* (pp. 145–72) **13181**.

Body Double **(1984)**

12800. Verevis, Constantine. For ever Hitchcock: *Psycho* and its remakes. *In* (pp. 15–29) **13181**.

Bonnie and Clyde **(1967)**

12801. Leggett, B. J. Convergence and divergence in the movie review: *Bonnie and Clyde*. FilCr (30:2) 2006, 1–23.

12802. Slocum, J. David. Rethinking regulation: violence and 1967 Hollywood. *In* (pp. 173–86) **12636**.

Bordertown (1935)

12803. Bender, Steven W. Savage *fronteras* and tribal boundaries: chasing success in Hollywood's *Bordertown* (1935). *In* (pp. 13–24) **12712**.

Boyz N the Hood (1991)

12804. Harrison, Keith. From boyz (n the hood) to men: cultural perceptions of African American 'ballers' and 'scholar ballers' in higher education. *In* (pp. 85–102) **12575**.

Bram Stoker's Dracula (1992)

12805. Menegaldo, Gilles; Sipière, Dominique (eds). *Dracula*: l'œuvre de Bram Stoker et le film de Francis F. Coppola. *See* **11338**.

Brassed Off (1996)

12806. Wayne, Mike. The performing Northern working class in British cinema: cultural representation and its political economy. *See* **12875**.

'Breaker' Morant (1980)

12807. Williams, Peter. Strange affinities: representation and affect in Australian POW drama. Southerly (65:2) 2005, 71–85.

Brighton Rock (1947)

12808. Chibnall, Steve. *Brighton Rock*. (Bibl. 2005, 13494.) Rev. by James Leggott in ScopeF (4) 2006.

The Brother from Another Planet (1984)

12809. Bould, Mark. The false salvation of the here and now: aliens, images, and the commodification of desire in *The Brother from Another Planet*. *In* (pp. 79–102) **13232**.

Cabin in the Sky (1943)

12810. Gerstner, David A. Manly arts: masculinity and nation in early American cinema. *See* **13220**.

The Caine Mutiny (1954)

12811. Brown, Kathleen A. 'Vestments of civil life' in *Caine Mutiny* and *Attack*. FilmH (36:2) 2006, 30–7.

Caravaggio (1986)

12812. Richardson, Niall. Queering a gay cliché: the rough trade / sugar daddy relationship in Derek Jarman's *Caravaggio*. Para (28:3) 2005, 36–53.

Casablanca (1942)

12813. Chanter, Tina. Abjection and the constitutive nature of difference: class mourning in *Margaret's Museum* and legitimating myths of innocence in *Casablanca*. Hypatia (21:3) 2006, 86–106.

Casino (1995)

12814. Casillo, Robert. Il sacro e il profano in *Casino* di Martin Scorsese. *In* (pp. 61–83) **11808**.

The Castle (1997)

12815. MacNeil, William P. 'It's the vibe!': the common law imaginary down under. *In* (pp. 31–44) **12636**.

Cat People (1942)

12816. Nochimson, Martha P. Val Lewton at RKO: the social dimensions of horror. Cineaste (31:4) 2006, 9–17.

Chimes at Midnight (1965)

12817. Hoffman, Dean A. 'Bypaths and indirect crooked ways': *mise-en-scène* in Orson Welles's *Chimes at Midnight*. ShB (23:1) 2005, 87–112.

The China Syndrome (1979)

12818. Wills, John. Celluloid chain reactions: *The China Syndrome* and Three Mile Island. EurJAC (25:2) 2006, 109–22.

Chinatown (1974)

12819. Holt, Jason. A darker shade: realism in neo-*noir*. *In* (pp. 23–40) **12452**.

Chitty Chitty Bang Bang (1968)

12820. McMorran, Will. From Quixote to Caractacus: influence, intertextuality, and *Chitty Chitty Bang Bang*. JPC (39:5) 2006, 756–79.

Citizen Kane (1941)

12821. Brill, Lesley. Crowds, power, and transformation in cinema. Detroit, MI: Wayne State UP, 2006. pp. x, 279.

12822. Ebrahimian, Babak A. The cinematic theater. *See* **19549**.

12823. Jackson, Kathy Merlock. Leaving Rosebud, leaving the valley: vestiges of childhood in two classic films from 1941. JAC (29:3) 2006, 296–306.

12824. Salmon, Paul. 'What will people think … what I tell them to think': Orson Welles and the trailer for *Citizen Kane*. CanJFS (15:2) 2006, 96–113.

City of Hope (1991)

12825. Smith, Greg M. Passersby and politics: *City of Hope* and the multiple-protagonist film. *In* (pp. 117–33) **13232**.

The Claim (2000)

12826. Allingham, Philip. Screening the flashback: three ways of opening *The Mayor of Casterbridge*. *In* (pp. 124–39) **10349**.

12827. Gatrell, Simon. Wessex on film. *In* (pp. 37–49) **10349**.

12828. Mitchell, Judith. All fall down: Hardy's heroes on the 1990s cinema screen. *In* (pp. 76–95) **10349**.

A Clockwork Orange (1971)

12829. Gehrke, Pat J. Deviant subjects in Foucault and *A Clockwork Orange*: criminological constructions of subjectivity. *In* (pp. 146–64) **13202**.

The Conversation (1974)

12830. Palmer, R. Barton. The Hitchcockian romance and the '70s paranoid thriller. *In* (pp. 85–108) **13181**.

The Crying Game (1992)

12831. Seligsohn, Andrew J. 'The stirring-up of passion': must we fear an aesthetic politics? *In* (pp. 87–117) **3266**.

The D.I. (1957)

12832. Miller, Pat. From paradigm to parody: war and the shifting sands of American manhood. *See* **12873**.

Dancing on the Moon (1935)

12833. Kohl, Leonard J. Cartoons and technocracy: Disney's *The Mad Doctor* and Fleischer's *Dancing on the Moon*. *In* (pp. 24–39) **12548**.

Dark City (1998)

12834. Fitting, Peter. Il mondo che sta dietro tutto questo: l'eredità di Philip K. Dick. *In* (pp. 263–74) **15466**.

12835. Wilson, Eric G. Gnostic paranoia in Proyas's *Dark City*. LitFQ (34:3) 2006, 232–9.

The Day the Earth Stood Still (1951)

12836. Haspell, Paul. Future shock on the National Mall: Washington, DC, as disputed ideological space in Robert Wise's *The Day the Earth Stood Still*. JPFT (34:2) 2006, 62–71.

Days of Heaven (1978)

12837. Pinard, Mary. Haunted by waters: the river in American films of the West. *In* (pp. 127–40) **12438**.

Dead Again (1991)

12838. Hark, Ina Rae. Psycho or psychic? Hitchcock, *Dead Again*, and the paranormal. *In* (pp. 65–82) **13181**.

Death Race 2000 (1975)

12839. Senn, Bryan. The sport of violence: *Death Race 2000* and *Rollerball*. *In* (pp. 207–16) **12548**.

Decline and Fall ... of a Birdwatcher (1968)

12840. Davis, Robert Murray. Up to a point, Mr Foxwell: the adaptation of *Decline and Fall*. *See* **18990**.

The Deer Hunter (1978)

12841. McCann, Sean. Therapy for a wounded nation. *See* **12778**.

12842. Pothier, Jacques. *The Deer Hunter*: essai de topologie imaginaire américaine. Anglophonia (19) 2006, 23–32.

Detour (1945)

12843. Cantor, Paul A. *Film noir* and the Frankfurt School: America as wasteland in Edgar Ulmer's *Detour*. *In* (pp. 139–61) **12452**.

Disorder in the Court (1936)

12844. Coyne, Randall. *Disorder in the Court* (1936): images of lawyers and the Three Stooges. *In* (pp. 25–33) **12712**.

***Dr Jekyll and Mr Hyde* (1931)**

12845. Senn, Bryan. *Dr Jekyll and Mr Hyde* (1931): science, society, and sexuality. *In* (pp. 17–23) **12548**.

***Dr Strangelove* (1964)**

12846. Sperb, Jason. The magic of words: voice-overs and storytelling in Kubrick's *Dr Strangelove*. Storytelling (5:4) 2006, 261–71.

***Do the Right Thing* (1989)**

12847. Harrison, Jeffrey L.; O'Connell, Stephen C.; Wilson, Sarah E. Law and rage in *Do the Right Thing* (1989). *In* (pp. 487–99) **12712**.

***Double Indemnity* (1944)**

12848. Dussere, Erik. Out of the past, into the supermarket: consuming *film noir*. FilmQ (60:1) 2006, 16–27.

***Dressed to Kill* (1980)**

12849. Verevis, Constantine. For ever Hitchcock: *Psycho* and its remakes. *In* (pp. 15–29) **13181**.

***Easy Rider* (1969)**

12850. Bapis, Elaine M. *Easy Rider* (1969): landscaping the modern western. *In* (pp. 157–81) **12438**.

***Edge of Seventeen* (1998)**

12851. Nowlan, Bob. The politics of love in three recent US and UK films of young gay romance: a symptomatic reading of *Beautiful Thing*, *Get Real*, and *Edge of Seventeen*. JHo (50:4) 2005, 141–84.

***Elizabeth* (1998)**

12852. Moss, David Grant. A queen for whose time? Elizabeth I as icon for the twentieth century. JPC (39:5) 2006, 796–816.

***The Emperor Jones* (1933)**

12853. Alsen, Eberhard. Racism and the film version of Eugene O'Neill's *The Emperor Jones*. *See* **17886**.

***eXistenZ* (1999)**

12854. Den Tandt, Christophe. The realist underground: referential practices at the turn of the twenty-first century. BELL (ns 4) 2006, 67–79.

***Eyes Wide Shut* (1999)**

12855. Deleyto, Celestino. 1999, a closet odyssey: sexual discourses in *Eyes Wide Shut*. Atl (28:1) 2006, 29–43.

12856. Kreider, Tim. Introducing sociology. *In* (pp. 280–97) **13202**.

12857. Loewenberg, Peter. Freud, Schnitzler, and *Eyes Wide Shut*. *In* (pp. 255–79) **13202**.

12858. Neary, John. Shadows and illuminations: spiritual journeys to the dark side in *Young Goodman Brown* and *Eyes Wide Shut*. *See* **10389**.

12859. Raphael, Frederic. The pumpkinification of Stanley K. *In* (pp. 62–73) **13202**.

12860. ROSENBAUM, JONATHAN. In dreams begin responsibilities. *In* (pp. 245–54) **13202**.

Far from the Madding Crowd (1967)

12861. WILSON, KEITH. *Far from the Madding Crowd* in the cinema: the problem of textual fidelity. *In* (pp. 96–107) **10349**.

Fargo (1996)

12862. CARRIERE, JEANNE L. Cold comfort: law and community in Ethan and Joel Coen's *Fargo* (1996). *In* (pp. 633–56) **12712**.

12863. LUHR, WILLIAM G. (ed.). The Coen brothers' *Fargo*. (Bibl. 2005, 13565.) Rev. by Kristen Grant in VLT (57) 2006, 98–100.

The Fifth Element (1997)

12864. CHAN, EDWARD K. On returning: 'America' in *The Fifth Element* and *Kal Ho Naa Ho*. Genre (38:4) 2005, 389–412.

Fight Club (1999)

12865. BISHOP, KYLE. Artistic schizophrenia: how *Fight Club*'s message is subverted by its own nature. SPC (29:1) 2006, 41–56.

12866. DUSSERE, ERIK. Out of the past, into the supermarket: consuming *film noir*. *See* **12848**.

12867. TA, LYNN M. Hurt so good: *Fight Club*, masculine violence, and the crisis of capitalism. JAC (29:3) 2006, 265–77.

The Fisher King (1991)

12868. HERZOG, MICHAEL B. Attunement and healing: *The Fisher King*. *In* (pp. 263–77) **11916**.

Flash Gordon Films (1936–1940)

12869. KOHL, LEONARD J. Flash Gordon conquers the Great Depression and World War too! The *Flash Gordon* serial trilogy. *In* (pp. 40–56) **12548**.

The Fountainhead (1949)

12870. JOHNSON, DONALD LESLIE. The fountainheads: Wright, Rand, the FBI and Hollywood. *See* **18184**.

Frenzy (1972)

12871. SKLAR, ROBERT. Death at work: Hitchcock's violence and spectator identification. *In* (pp. 217–34) **13181**.

Full Metal Jacket (1987)

12872. MCCANN, SEAN. Therapy for a wounded nation. *See* **12778**.

12873. MILLER, PAT. From paradigm to parody: war and the shifting sands of American manhood. WVUPP (51) 2004, 117–24.

12874. WILLOQUET-MARICONDI, PAULA. Full-Metal-Jacketing; or, Masculinity in the making. *In* (pp. 218–41) **13202**.

The Full Monty (1997)

12875. WAYNE, MIKE. The performing Northern working class in British cinema: cultural representation and its political economy. QRFV (23:4) 2006, 287–97.

Get Real (1998)

12876. Nowlan, Bob. The politics of love in three recent US and UK films of young gay romance: a symptomatic reading of *Beautiful Thing*, *Get Real*, and *Edge of Seventeen*. *See* **12851**.

Girl, Interrupted (1999)

12877. Marshall, Elizabeth. Borderline girlhoods: mental illness, adolescence, and femininity in *Girl, Interrupted*. *See* **13951**.

Gladiator (2000)

12878. Winkler, Martin M. (ed.). *Gladiator*: film and history. (Bibl. 2004, 13641.) Rev. by Michael J. Carter in PJCAC (60:1/2) 2006, 183–5; by Mikel J. Koven in ScopeF (5) 2006.

Glamour (1934)

12879. Hoagwood, Terence. 'Postmodern mirrors'. *See* **12897**.

Glory (1989)

12880. Stoddard, Jeremy D.; Marcus, Alan S. The burden of historical representation: race, freedom, and the 'educational' Hollywood film. FilmH (36:1) 2006, 26–35.

The Godfather (1972–1990)

12881. Poon, Phoebe. The Corleone chronicles: revisiting the *Godfather* films as trilogy. JPFT (33:4) 2006, 187–95.

The Golden Bowl (2000)

12882. Eaton, Mark A. Miramax, Merchant–Ivory, and the new nobrow culture: niche marketing *The Wings of the Dove* and *The Golden Bowl*. *See* **13128**.

Gone with the Wind (1939)

12883. Antolini, Katharine Lane. Scarlett O'Hara as Confederate woman. WVUPP (51) 2004, 23–35.

Gorillas in the Mist (1988)

12884. Kanner, Melinda. Going on instinct: gendering primatology in film. *See* **12911**.

Grand Canyon (1991)

12885. Hsu, Hsuan L. Racial privacy, the L.A. ensemble film, and Paul Haggis's *Crash*. *See* **19693**.

The Grapes of Wrath (1940)

12886. Sickels, Robert C. Landscapes of failure in John Ford's *The Grapes of Wrath* (1939). *In* (pp. 61–80) **12438**.

The Great Dictator (1940)

12887. Karetnikova, Inga. Seven masterpieces of 1940s cinema. Oxford; Portsmouth, NH: Heinemann, 2006. pp. 208.

Great Expectations (1946)

12888. Cole, Nathalie Bell. Travel, the road and the city in adaptations of *Great Expectations*. *In* (pp. 265–92) **9791**.

12889. Del Grosso, Simone. Strategie narrative e metodologie del montaggio dell'*incipit* da Charles Dickens a Martin Scorsese: Jump Cut su Lean, Cuarón e la BBC. *In* (pp. 319–340) **9791**.

12890. Lauri-Lucente, Gloria. David Lean's *Great Expectations*: transfiguration or transformation? *In* (pp. 243–63) **9791**.

***Great Expectations* (1998)**

12891. Antinucci, Raffaella. Alfonso Cuarón's 'late experimentations': Dickens and post-modernism. *In* (pp. 293–317) **9791**.

12892. Del Grosso, Simone. Strategie narrative e metodologie del montaggio dell'*incipit* da Charles Dickens a Martin Scorsese: Jump Cut su Lean, Cuarón e la BBC. *In* (pp. 319–340) **9791**.

***The Grey Fox* (1982)**

12893. Hutchinson, David. Phillip Borsos: *The Grey Fox*. *In* (pp. 167–75) **11946**.

***A Guy Named Joe* (1943)**

12894. Christie, Ian. Heavenly justice. *In* (pp. 3–16) **12636**.

***The Harder They Come* (1972)**

12895. Younger, Prakash. Historical experience in *The Harder They Come*: Jamaica in the cultural world system. SocT (82) 2005, 43–63.

***Heartland* (1979)**

12896. Embry, Jessie L. Nature and *Heartland* (1979). *In* (pp. 141–56) **12438**.

***The Heiress* (1949)**

12897. Hoagwood, Terence. 'Postmodern mirrors'. LitFQ (34:4) 2006, 267–73.

12898. Newell, Kate. *Washington Square*'s 'virus of suggestion': source texts, intertexts, and adaptations. *See* **13122**.

***Hellraiser Films* (1987–)**

12899. Kane, Paul. The Hellraiser films and their legacy. Foreword by Doug Bradley. Jefferson, NC; London: McFarland, 2006. pp. vii, 247.

***High Treason* (1930)**

12900. Soister, John T. *High Treason*: great expectations. *In* (pp. 7–16) **12548**.

***The Hill* (1965)**

12901. Claydon, E. Anna. The representation of masculinity in British cinema of the 1960s: *Lawrence of Arabia*, *The Loneliness of the Long Distance Runner*, and *The Hill*. *See* **12934**.

***Hitler – Beast of Berlin* (1939)**

12902. Miller, Cynthia J. The 'B' movie goes to war in *Hitler, Beast of Berlin* (1939). FilmH (36:1) 2006, 58–64.

***A Hole in the Head* (1959)**

12903. Russo, John Paul. Ethnic rebel: Frank Capra's Italian American film. VIA (17:1) 2006, 28–58.

Hoosiers **(1986)**

12904. LEONARD, DAVID J. 'Is this heaven?': White sporting masculinities and the Hollywood imagination. *In* (pp. 165–94) **12575**.

Household Saints **(1993)**

12905. KUHN, REBECCA. Italian/American women: the home, religion, and theology in Nancy Savoca's *Household Saints*. VIA (16:2) 2005, 31–44.

How Green Was My Valley **(1941)**

12906. JACKSON, KATHY MERLOCK. Leaving Rosebud, leaving the valley: vestiges of childhood in two classic films from 1941. *See* **12823**.

Hud **(1963)**

12907. BARRA, ALLEN. Larry McMurtry: writing westerns from *Hud* to *Brokeback Mountain*. *See* **17381**.

I Married a Monster from Outer Space **(1958)**

12908. CLARK, MARY. Scenes from a marriage: the sexual politics of *I Married a Monster from Outer Space*. *In* (pp. 166–75) **12548**.

If ... **(1968)**

12909. SUTTON, PAUL. *If ...* London; New York: Tauris, 2005. pp. 114. (Turner classic movies: British film guides.)

Innerspace **(1987)**

12910. GERAGHTY, LINCOLN. Love's fantastic voyage: crossing between science fiction and romantic comedy in *Innerspace*. Extrapolation (47:1) 2006, 123–33.

Instinct **(1999)**

12911. KANNER, MELINDA. Going on instinct: gendering primatology in film. JPFT (33:4) 2006, 206–12.

In This Our Life **(1942)**

12912. BINGGELI, ELIZABETH. Burbanking bigger and Bette the bitch. *See* **19374**.

Invasion of the Saucer Men **(1957)**

12913. JOSLIN, LYNDON W. Cosmic frames and cover-ups: *Invasion of the Saucer Men* and the UFO conspiracy of silence. *In* (pp. 138–50) **12548**.

The Iron Giant **(1999)**

12914. ARCHER, JACQUE DAY. *The Iron Giant*: a gun with a soul. *In* (pp. 256–68) **12548**.

It Came from Outer Space **(1953)**

12915. YAMAMOTO, JERRY. In them we trust? Fear, faith, and *It Came from Outer Space*. *In* (pp. 94–103) **12548**.

It's a Wonderful Life **(1946)**

12916. KARETNIKOVA, INGA. Seven masterpieces of 1940s cinema. *See* **12887**.

The Jazz Singer **(1927)**

12917. MARCUS, LAURA. 'A new form of true beauty': aesthetics and early film criticism. *See* **10727**.

Jude (1996)

12918. MITCHELL, JUDITH. All fall down: Hardy's heroes on the 1990s cinema screen. *In* (pp. 76–95) **10349**.

12919. SCHWEIK, ROBERT. Adapting Hardy's *Jude the Obscure* for the screen: a study in contrasts. *In* (pp. 183–95) **10349**.

12920. STRONG, JEREMY. *Tess*, *Jude*, and the problem of adapting Hardy. *See* **10330**.

Killer of Sheep (1977)

12921. BRILL, LESLEY. Crowds, power, and transformation in cinema. *See* **12821**.

The Killers (1946)

12922. JARVIE, IAN. Knowledge, morality, and tragedy in *The Killers* and *Out of the Past*. *In* (pp. 163–85) **12452**.

The King Is Alive (2000)

12923. BOUCHARD, LARRY D. Playing nothing for someone: *Lear*, Bottom, and kenotic integrity. *See* **5853**.

King Kong (1933)

12924. CASHILL, ROBERT. All things Kong-sidered. Cineaste (31:2) 2006, 39–43.

Kiss Me Deadly (1955)

12925. WOOLFOLK, ALAN. The horizon of disenchantment: *film noir*, Camus, and the vicissitudes of descent. *In* (pp. 107–23) **12452**.

Lady in the Lake (1946)

12926. GERNALZICK, NADJA. To act or to perform: distinguishing filmic autobiography. Biography (29:1) 2006, 1–13.

Lady Sings the Blues (1972)

12927. HAWKINS, ALFONSO W., JR. A nonnegotiable Blues catharsis in character: Billie Holiday in *Lady Sings the Blues* and Ursa Corregidora in *Corregidora*. *See* **16634**.

The Last Days of Chez Nous (1992)

12928. HOLCOMBE, VANESSA. Writing place: Helen Garner's *The Last Days of Chez Nous*. *See* **16056**.

The Last Seduction (1994)

12929. HOLT, JASON. A darker shade: realism in neo-*noir*. *In* (pp. 23–40) **12452**.

The Last September (1999)

12930. FRANKS, JILL. Sex, guns, and death: Deborah Warner's adaptation of *The Last September*. *See* **14821**.

The Last Temptation of Christ (1988)

12931. BAUGH, LLOYD. Martin Scorsese's *The Last Temptation of Christ*: a critical reassessment of its sources, its theological problems, and its impact on the public. *In* (pp. 173–92) **12933**.

12932. Brown, Kevin. 'Tis pity she's a whore: the revision of Mary Magdalene in contemporary fiction. *See* **12254**.

12933. Middleton, Darren J. N. (ed.). Scandalizing Jesus: Kazantzakis's *The Last Temptation of Christ* fifty years on. London; New York: Continuum, 2005. pp. xxi, 265.

Lawrence of Arabia (1962)

12934. Claydon, E. Anna. The representation of masculinity in British cinema of the 1960s: *Lawrence of Arabia*, *The Loneliness of the Long Distance Runner*, and *The Hill*. Lewiston, NY; Lampeter: Mellen Press, 2005. pp. v, 331. (Studies in the history and criticism of film, 12.)

The Life of Brian (1979)

12935. Auxier, Randall E. A very naughty boy: getting right with Brian. *In* (pp. 65–81) **13316**.

12936. Croskery, Patrick. Monty Python and the search for the meaning of life. *In* (pp. 161–72) **13316**.

12937. Faison, Stephen. God forgive us. *In* (pp. 125–39) **13316**.

12938. Hardcastle, Gary L.; Reisch, George A. (eds). Monty Python and philosophy: nudge nudge, think think! *See* **13316**.

12939. Schilbrack, Kevin. 'Life's a piece of shit': heresy, humanism, and heroism in *Monty Python's Life of Brian*. *In* (pp. 13–23) **13316**.

12940. Slowik, Edward. Existentialism in Monty Python: Kafka, Camus, Nietzsche, and Sartre. *In* (pp. 173–85) **13316**.

Limbo (1999)

12941. Barrett, Laura. The space of ambiguity: representations of nature in *Limbo*. *In* (pp. 238–60) **13232**.

Little Voice (1998)

12942. Wayne, Mike. The performing Northern working class in British cinema: cultural representation and its political economy. *See* **12875**.

Logan's Run (1976)

12943. Tinnell, Robert. *Logan's Run* to relevance. *In* (pp. 217–24) **12548**.

Lone Star (1996)

12944. Felleman, Susan. Oedipus edits (*Lone Star*). *In* (pp. 158–73) **13232**.

12945. Gordon, Rebecca M. Psychic borders and legacies left hanging in *Lone Star* and *Men with Guns*. *In* (pp. 215–37) **13232**.

The Loneliness of the Long Distance Runner (1962)

12946. Claydon, E. Anna. The representation of masculinity in British cinema of the 1960s: *Lawrence of Arabia*, *The Loneliness of the Long Distance Runner*, and *The Hill*. *See* **12934**.

The Long Goodbye (1973)

12947. Dussere, Erik. Out of the past, into the supermarket: consuming *film noir*. *See* **12848**.

The Long Voyage Home (1940)

12948. Brietzke, Zander. *The Long Voyage Home*: a vicious cycle at sea. *See* **17892**.

The Longest Day (1962)

12949. Toplin, Robert Brent. Hollywood's D-Day from the perspective of the 1960s and 1990s: *The Longest Day* and *Saving Private Ryan*. *See* **13043**.

Looking for Richard (1996)

12950. Aune, M. G. Star power: Al Pacino, *Looking for Richard* and the cultural capital of Shakespeare on film. QRFV (23:4) 2006, 353–67.

Lost Book Found (1996)

12951. op de Beeck, Nathalie. Found objects (Jem Cohen, Ben Katchor, Walter Benjamin). MFS (52:4) 2006, 807–31.

M. Butterfly (1993)

12952. Vota, Alessandra. Constructing and de-constructing Butterfly: from Loti's *Madame Chrysanthème* to Cronenberg's *M. Butterfly*. *In* (pp. 83–106) **11955**.

The Mad Doctor (1933)

12953. Kohl, Leonard J. Cartoons and technocracy: Disney's *The Mad Doctor* and Fleischer's *Dancing on the Moon*. *In* (pp. 24–39) **12548**.

The Maltese Falcon (1941)

12954. Knight, Deborah. On reason and passion in *The Maltese Falcon*. *In* (pp. 207–21) **12452**

The Manchurian Candidate (1962)

12955. Bell, Matt. 'Your worst fears made flesh': *The Manchurian Candidate*'s paranoid delusion and Gay Liberation. GLQ (12:1) 2006, 85–116.

12956. Jacobson, Matthew Frye; González, Gaspar. What have they built you to do? *The Manchurian Candidate* and Cold War America. Minneapolis; London: Minnesota UP, 2006. pp. xv, 234.

Mansfield Park (1999)

12957. Fulford, Sarah. 'Nation and narration': the English novel and Englishness. *In* (pp. 157–65) **14238**.

Map of the Human Heart (1993)

12958. Henderson, Scott. Vincent Ward: *Map of the Human Heart*. *In* (pp. 217–28) **11946**.

Margaret's Museum (1995)

12959. Chanter, Tina. Abjection and the constitutive nature of difference: class mourning in *Margaret's Museum* and legitimating myths of innocence in *Casablanca*. *See* **12813**.

12960. Henderson, Scott. Mort Ransen: *Margaret's Museum*. *In* (pp. 179–89) **11946**.

Matewan (1987)

12961. Norden, Martin F. The theo-political landscape of *Matewan*. *In* (pp. 103–16) **13232**.

12962. Rieser, Klaus. Men in context: gender in *Matewan* and *Men with Guns*. *In* (pp. 174–93) **13232**.

The Matrix (1999–)

12963. Fitting, Peter. Il mondo che sta dietro tutto questo: l'eredità di Philip K. Dick. *In* (pp. 263–74) **15466**.

12964. Kapell, Matthew; Doty, William G. (eds). Jacking in to the *Matrix* franchise: cultural reception and interpretation. (Bibl. 2004, 13733.) Rev. by Tim McCarthy in Extrapolation (47:1) 2006, 154–60; by Mindy Hutchings in PCR (17:2) 2006, 119–20.

12965. Melzer, Patricia. Alien constructions: science fiction and feminist thought. *See* **13561**.

12966. Schwetman, John D. Romanticism and the cortical stack: cyberpunk subjectivity in the Takeshi Kovacs novels of Richard K. Morgan. *See* **20305**.

A Matter of Life and Death (1946)

12967. Christie, Ian. Heavenly justice. *In* (pp. 3–16) **12636**.

The Meaning of Life (1983)

12968. Asma, Stephen T. Against Transcendentalism: *Monty Python's 'The Meaning of Life'* and Buddhism. *In* (pp. 93–110) **13316**.

12969. Carroll, Noël. What Mr Creosote knows about laughter. *In* (pp. 25–35) **13316**.

12970. Croskery, Patrick. Monty Python and the search for the meaning of life. *In* (pp. 161–72) **13316**.

12971. Erickson, Stephen A. Is there life after *Monty Python's 'The Meaning of Life'*? *In* (pp. 111–21) **13316**.

12972. Faison, Stephen. God forgive us. *In* (pp. 125–39) **13316**.

12973. Hardcastle, Gary L.; Reisch, George A. (eds). Monty Python and philosophy: nudge nudge, think think! *See* **13316**.

12974. Housel, Rebecca. *Monty Python and the Holy Grail*: philosophy, gender, and society. *In* (pp. 83–92) **13316**.

12975. Huss, John. Monty Python and David Hume on religion. *In* (pp. 141–51) **13316**.

12976. Slowik, Edward. Existentialism in Monty Python: Kafka, Camus, Nietzsche, and Sartre. *In* (pp. 173–85) **13316**.

Memento (2000)

12977. Laytham, D. Brent. Time for hope: *The Sixth Sense*, *American Beauty*, *Memento*, and *Twelve Monkeys*. *In* (pp. 69–83) **11916**.

12978. Panek, Elliot. The poet and the detective: defining the psychological puzzle film. FilCr (31:1/2) 2006, 62–88.

12979. Seligsohn, Andrew J. 'The stirring-up of passion': must we fear an aesthetic politics? *In* (pp. 87–117) **3266**.

Men with Guns (1997)

12980. Carroll, Hamilton. Tourism and territory: constructing the nation in *Men with Guns* (*Hombres armados*). *In* (pp. 194–214) **13232**.

12981. Gordon, Rebecca M. Psychic borders and legacies left hanging in *Lone Star* and *Men with Guns*. *In* (pp. 215–37) **13232**.

12982. Rieser, Klaus. Men in context: gender in *Matewan* and *Men with Guns*. *In* (pp. 174–93) **13232**.

Miss Mary (1986)

12983. Gatto, Katherine Gyékényesi. The spacialization of motherhood: *estancia*, nation, and gendered space in María Luisa Bemberg's *Miss Mary*. WVUPP (52) 2005, 109–14.

Monty Python and the Holy Grail (1975)

12984. Croskery, Patrick. Monty Python and the search for the meaning of life. *In* (pp. 161–72) **13316**.

12985. Faison, Stephen. God forgive us. *In* (pp. 125–39) **13316**.

12986. Hardcastle, Gary L. Themes in contemporary analytic philosophy as reflected in the work of Monty Python. *In* (pp. 265–75) **13316**.

12987. —— Reisch, George A. (eds). Monty Python and philosophy: nudge nudge, think think! *See* **13316**.

12988. Housel, Rebecca. *Monty Python and the Holy Grail*: philosophy, gender, and society. *In* (pp. 83–92) **13316**.

Mulan (1998)

12989. Dong, Lan. Writing Chinese America into words and images: storytelling and retelling of *The Song of Mu Lan*. *See* **17088**.

The Navigator: a Mediaeval Odyssey (1988)

12990. Hale, Elizabeth. Underworlds down under: *Under the Mountain* and *The Navigator*. *In* (pp. 101–10) **11971**.

The Night of the Hunter (1955)

12991. Pinard, Mary. Haunted by waters: the river in American films of the West. *In* (pp. 127–40) **12438**.

Night of the Living Dead (1968)

12992. Bishop, Kyle. Raising the dead: unearthing the nonliterary origins of zombie cinema. JPFT (33:4) 2006, 196–205.

Nightjohn (1996)

12993. Chandler, Karen. Paths to freedom: literacy and folk traditions in recent narratives about slavery and emancipation. *See* **16271**.

North by Northwest (1959)

12994. Brill, Lesley. Crowds, power, and transformation in cinema. *See* **12821**.

12995. Palmer, R. Barton. The Hitchcockian romance and the '70s paranoid thriller. *In* (pp. 85–108) **13181**.

Northwest Passage (1940)

12996. GLOVER, SUSAN PATERSON. East goes west: the technicolor environment of *Northwest Passage* (1940). *In* (pp. 111–26) **12438**.

Notorious (1946)

12997. KARETNIKOVA, INGA. Seven masterpieces of 1940s cinema. *See* **12887**.

Nude on the Moon (1961)

12998. WINSTEAD, CHASE. Two faces of voyeurism: *Nude on the Moon* and *X – the Man with the X-Ray Eyes*. *In* (pp. 176–87) **12548**.

The Omega Man (1971)

12999. BAKER, RYAN. 'Conclusion of all our yesterdays': the Jungian text of *The Omega Man*. *In* (pp. 196–206) **12548**.

Out of the Past (1947)

13000. JARVIE, IAN. Knowledge, morality, and tragedy in *The Killers* and *Out of the Past*. *In* (pp. 163–85) **12452**.

13001. WOOLFOLK, ALAN. The horizon of disenchantment: *film noir*, Camus, and the vicissitudes of descent. *In* (pp. 107–23) **12452**.

Pale Rider (1985)

13002. HUEMANN, JOE; MURRAY, ROBIN. Hydraulic mining then and now: the case of *Pale Rider* (1985). *In* (pp. 94–110) **12438**.

Paradise Road (1997)

13003. WILLIAMS, PETER. Strange affinities: representation and affect in Australian POW drama. *See* **12807**.

The Parallax View (1974)

13004. PALMER, R. BARTON. The Hitchcockian romance and the '70s paranoid thriller. *In* (pp. 85–108) **13181**.

Passion Fish (1992)

13005. NEWMAN, MICHAEL Z. Character and complexity in American independent cinema: *21 Grams* and *Passion Fish*. FilCr (31:1/2) 2006, 89–106.

Performance (1970)

13006. FREY, MATTIAS. London *à la mode*: fashion, genre, and historical space in *Performance*. QRFV (23:4) 2006, 369–75.

Persuasion (1995)

13007. MONAGHAN, DAVID. 'A cheerful confidence in futurity': the movement motif in Austen's novel and Dear/Michell's film adaptation of *Persuasion*. *In* (pp. 69–92) **8374**.

The Piano (1993)

13008. SIMMONS, ROCHELLE. The postmodern *Piano*. *In* (pp. 402–17) **8374**.

Pinocchio (1940)

13009. HONEYMAN, SUSAN. Manufactured agency and the playthings who dream it for us. *See* **13673**.

Platoon **(1986)**

13010. McCann, Sean. Therapy for a wounded nation. *See* **12778**.

Pleasantville **(1998)**

13011. Fitting, Peter. Il mondo che sta dietro tutto questo: l'eredità di Philip K. Dick. *In* (pp. 263–74) **15466**.

The Postman Always Rings Twice

13012. Conard, Mark T. Nietzsche and the meaning and definition of *noir*. *In* (pp. 7–22) **12452**.

The President Vanishes **(1934)**

13013. Chambers, John Whiteclay, ii. The movies and the antiwar debate in America, 1930–1941. *See* **12771**.

Pride and Prejudice **(1940)**

13014. Hudelet, Ariane. Chorégraphies implicites et explicites: la danse dans *Pride and Prejudice*, du texte à l'écran. *See* **9031**.

The Private Lives of Elizabeth and Essex **(1939)**

13015. Moss, David Grant. A queen for whose time? Elizabeth I as icon for the twentieth century. *See* **12852**.

The Producers **(1968)**

13016. Symons, Alex. An audience for Mel Brooks's *The Producers*: the avant-garde of the masses. JPFT (34:1) 2006, 24–32.

Psycho **(1960)**

13017. Brill, Lesley. Hitchcockian silence: *Psycho* and Jonathan Demme's *The Silence of the Lambs*. *In* (pp. 31–46) **13181**.

13018. Sklar, Robert. Death at work: Hitchcock's violence and spectator identification. *In* (pp. 217–34) **13181**.

13019. Verevis, Constantine. For ever Hitchcock: *Psycho* and its remakes. *In* (pp. 15–29) **13181**.

Psycho **(1998)**

13020. —— For ever Hitchcock: *Psycho* and its remakes. *In* (pp. 15–29) **13181**.

Pulp Fiction **(1994)**

13021. Conard, Mark T. Symbolism, meaning, and nihilism in Quentin Tarantino's *Pulp Fiction*. *In* (pp. 125–38) **12452**.

The Quiet American **(1958)**

13022. Bushnell, William S. Paying for the damage: *The Quiet American* revisited. FilmH (36:2) 2006, 38–44.

13023. Kerr, Douglas. *The Quiet American* and the novel. *See* **16205**.

The Quiet Man **(1952)**

13024. Moran, Albert. Migrancy, tourism, settlement, and rural cinema. *In* (pp. 224–39) **12506**.

A Raisin in the Sun **(1961)**

13025. May, Theresa J. 'Consequences unforeseen …' in *Raisin in the Sun* and *Caroline; or, Change*. *See* **20102**.

Rear Window (1954)

13026. Blazer, Seth M. Rear window ethics: domestic privacy *versus* public responsibility in the evolution of voyeurism. MidQ (47:4) 2006, 379–92.

13027. Palmer, R. Barton. The Hitchcockian romance and the '70s paranoid thriller. *In* (pp. 85–108) **13181**.

13028. Tomasulo, Frank P. 'You're tellin' me you didn't see': Hitchcock's *Rear Window* and Antonioni's *Blow-Up*. *In* (pp. 145–72) **13181**.

A Reasonable Man (1999)

13029. Lenta, Patrick. The *tikoloshe* and the reasonable man. *See* **16161**.

Rebel without a Cause (1955)

13030. Frascella, Lawrence; Weisel, Al. Live fast, die young: the wild ride of making *Rebel without a Cause*. (Bibl. 2005, 13729.) Rev. by Stephanie Zacharek in NYTB, 8 Jan. 2006, 26.

13031. Loizidou, Elena. Rebel without a cause? *In* (pp. 45–59) **12636**.

The Red Shoes (1948)

13032. Connelly, Mark. *The Red Shoes*. London; New York: Tauris, 2005. pp. 96. (Turner classic movies: British film guides.)

The Return of Dracula (1958)

13033. Knee, Adam. Shadows of *Shadow of a Doubt*. *In* (pp. 49–64) **13181**.

Ride the Pink Horse (1947)

13034. Silver, Alain. *Ride the Pink Horse*: money, mischance, murder, and the monads of *film noir*. *In* (pp. 223–37) **12452**.

Rio Bravo (1959)

13035. Arnold, David L. G. My rifle, my pony, and feathers: music and the making of men in Howard Hawks' *Rio Bravo*. QRFV (23:3) 2006, 267–79.

A River Runs through It (1992)

13036. Pinard, Mary. Haunted by waters: the river in American films of the West. *In* (pp. 127–40) **12438**.

Rollerball (1975)

13037. Senn, Bryan. The sport of violence: *Death Race 2000* and *Rollerball*. *In* (pp. 207–16) **12548**.

The Rose Tattoo (1955)

13038. McDaniel, L. Bailey. Reel Italian: melodrama, Magnani, and alternative subjects in *The Rose Tattoo*. *See* **19175**.

Rudy (1993)

13039. Leonard, David J. 'Is this heaven?': White sporting masculinities and the Hollywood imagination. *In* (pp. 165–94) **12575**.

Ruggles of Red Gap (1935)

13040. O'Reilly, Jean. A case study: *Ruggles of Red Gap*, Leo McCarey and Charles Laughton. QRFV (23:5) 2006, 407–22.

Samson and Delilah (1949)

13041. Kozlovic, Anton Karl. The old Story Teller as a John the Baptist figure in DeMille's *Samson and Delilah*. CLCWeb (8:3) 2006.

The Satan Bug (1965)

13042. Lester, Alan Dirk. *The Satan Bug*: some nightmares are quite inescapable. *In* (pp. 188–95) **12548**.

Saving Private Ryan (1998)

13043. Toplin, Robert Brent. Hollywood's D-Day from the perspective of the 1960s and 1990s: *The Longest Day* and *Saving Private Ryan*. FilmH (36:2) 2006, 25–9.

Schindler's List (1993)

13044. Mandel, Naomi. Against the unspeakable: complicity, the Holocaust, and slavery in America. Charlottesville; London: Virginia UP, 2006. pp. xi, 278. (Cultural frames, framing culture.)

Scream (1996–)

13045. Wee, Valerie. Resurrecting and updating the teen slasher: the case of *Scream*. JPFT (34:2) 2006, 50–61.

Screamers (1995)

13046. La Polla, Franco. Da Philip K. Dick a Hollywood: ovvero, La quadratura del cerchio. *In* (pp. 275–81) **15466**.

The Search (1948)

13047. Etheridge, Brian C. In search of Germans: contested Germany in the production of *The Search*. JPFT (34:1) 2006, 34–45.

The Searchers (1956)

13048. Eckstein, Arthur M.; Lehman, Peter (eds). *The Searchers*: essays and reflections on John Ford's classic western. (Bibl. 2004, 13840.) Rev. by John Belton in TSLL (47:3) 2005, 80–2; by the same in FilmQ (59:3) 2006, 80–2.

13049. McFarlane, Brian. Brokeback and Outback. Meanjin (65:1) 2006, 65–71.

13050. Sharrett, Christopher. Through a door darkly: a reappraisal of John Ford's *The Searchers*. Cineaste (31:4) 2006, 4–8.

The Secret of Roan Inish (1994)

13051. Turim, Maureen; Turim-Nygren, Mika. Of spectral mothers and lost children: war, folklore, and psychoanalysis in *The Secret of Roan Inish*. *In* (pp. 134–57) **13232**.

Set It Off (1996)

13052. Brody, Jennifer DeVere. Moving violations: performing globalization and feminism in *Set It Off*. *In* (pp. 363–78) **11876**.

Shadow of a Doubt (1943)

13053. Knee, Adam. Shadows of *Shadow of a Doubt*. *In* (pp. 49–64) **13181**.

Shakespeare in Love (1998)

13054. WALL, WENDY. Editors in love? Performing desire in *Romeo and Juliet*. *In* (pp. 197–211) **5537**.

The Shining (1980)

13055. COCKS, GEOFFREY. Death by typewriter: Stanley Kubrick, the Holocaust, and *The Shining*. *In* (pp. 185–217) **13202**.

13056. JOHNSON, DIANE. Writing *The Shining*. *In* (pp. 55–61) **13202**.

Shock Corridor (1963)

13057. STERRITT, DAVID. Fuller, Foucault, and forgetting: the eye of power in *Shock Corridor*. *In* (pp. 194–210) **12661**.

Short Cuts (1993)

13058. HSU, HSUAN L. Racial privacy, the L.A. ensemble film, and Paul Haggis's *Crash*. *See* **19693**.

13059. MAR AZCONA, M. Making sense of a multi-protagonist film: audience-response research and Robert Altman's *Short Cuts* (1993). Misc (32) 2005, 11–22.

Showgirls (1995)

13060. SALVATO, NICK. Tramp sensibility and the afterlife of *Showgirls*. TJ (58:4) 2006, 633–48.

The Silence of the Lambs (1991)

13061. BRILL, LESLEY. Crowds, power, and transformation in cinema. *See* **12821**.

13062. —— Hitchcockian silence: *Psycho* and Jonathan Demme's *The Silence of the Lambs*. *In* (pp. 31–46) **13181**.

Silent Tongue (1994)

13063. WYNANDS, SANDRA. Sam Shepard's anti-western *Silent Tongue* as cultural critique. CRAS (35:3) 2005, 299–313.

Singin' in the Rain (1952)

13064. EWING, MARILYN M. 'Gotta dance!': structure, corruption, and syphilis in *Singin' in the Rain*. JPFT (34:1) 2006, 12–23.

The Sixth Sense (1999)

13065. LAYTHAM, D. BRENT. Time for hope: *The Sixth Sense*, *American Beauty*, *Memento*, and *Twelve Monkeys*. *In* (pp. 69–83) **11916**.

13066. SEYMOUR, DAVID M. Film and law: in search of a critical method. *In* (pp. 107–19) **12636**.

Smoke Signals (1998)

13067. HEARNE, JOANNA. John Wayne's teeth: speech, sound and representation in *Smoke Signals* and *Imagining Indians*. WF (64:3/4) 2005, 189–208.

Snow Falling on Cedars (1999)

13068. AOKI, KEITH. Is Chan still missing? An essay about the film *Snow Falling on Cedars* (1999) and representations of Asian Americans in US films. *In* (pp. 679–99) **12712**.

***Solomon & Gaenor* (1999)**

13069. WHITE, R. S. *Solomon & Gaenor*: a Welsh Jewish *Romeo and Juliet*. AUMLA (106) 2006, 71–85.

***The Space Children* (1958)**

13070. JOSLIN, LYNDON W. The Cold War in orbit: two films of aliens, arsenals, and interventions. *In* (pp. 151–65) **12548**.

***Stagecoach* (1939)**

13071. CARMICHAEL, DEBORAH A. The living presence of Monument Valley in John Ford's *Stagecoach* (1939). *In* (pp. 212–28) **12438**.

13072. ERISMAN, FRED. *Stagecoach* in space: the legacy of *Firefly*. *See* **19789**.

***A Star Is Born* (1937)**

13073. HOAGWOOD, TERENCE. 'Postmodern mirrors'. *See* **12897**.

***Star Maps* (1997)**

13074. FOJAS, CAMILLA. Schizopolis: border cinema and the global city (of angels). Aztlan (31:1) 2006, 7–31.

***Starship Troopers* (1997)**

13075. WEISS, KEN. The brave new world of *Starship Troopers*. *In* (pp. 246–55) **12548**.

***Star Trek* (1986–)**

13076. BRODERICK, JAMES F. The literary galaxy of *Star Trek*: an analysis of references and themes in the television series and films. *See* **13276**.

***Stella* (1990)**

13077. PARCHESKY, JENNIFER. Adapting *Stella Dallas*: class boundaries, consumerism, and hierarchies of taste. *See* **18148**.

***Stella Dallas* (1937)**

13078. PARCHESKY, JENNIFER. Adapting *Stella Dallas*: class boundaries, consumerism, and hierarchies of taste. *See* **18148**.

***Step Down to Terror* (1958)**

13079. KNEE, ADAM. Shadows of *Shadow of a Doubt*. *In* (pp. 49–64) **13181**.

***The Stepfather* (1987)**

13080. HARRIS, MARTIN. Hammett's Flitcraft parable, *The Stepfather*, and the significance of falling beams. LitFQ (34:3) 2006, 240–8.

***The Story of Temple Drake* (1933)**

13081. BARKER, DEBORAH. Moonshine and magnolias: *The Story of Temple Drake* and *The Birth of a Nation*. FJ (22:1/2) 2006, 140–75.

***The Straight Story* (1999)**

13082. COLE, KEVIN L. Geographies of hope: Kathleen Norris and David Lynch. *In* (pp. 247–62) **11916**.

***Strange Days* (1995)**

13083. LAW, JULES. Being there: gothic violence and virtuality in *Frankenstein*, *Dracula*, and *Strange Days*. *See* **11185**.

Strictly Ballroom **(1992)**

13084. Seco Salvador, Olga. *Strictly Ballroom* (1992): departure from traditional Anglo-Australian discourses or veiled confirmation of old national-encouragement mechanisms? Misc (32) 2005, 103–14.

Sunset Boulevard **(1950)**

13085. Chivers, Sally. Baby Jane grew up: the dramatic intersection of age with disability. *See* **13124**.

Superman Films **(1978–)**

13086. Skelton, Stephen. The Gospel according to the world's greatest superhero. Eugene, OR: Harvest House, 2006. pp. 171.

The Sweet Hereafter **(1997)**

13087. Hutchinson, David. Atom Egoyan: *The Sweet Hereafter*. *In* (pp. 137–48) **11946**.

A Tale of Two Cities **(1935)**

13088. Stevens, Jason W. Insurrection and Depression-era politics in Selznick's *A Tale of Two Cities* (1935). LitFQ (34:3) 2006, 176–93.

A Taste of Honey **(1961)**

13089. Palmer, R. Barton. The British New Wave: a modernist cinema. *In* (pp. 52–64) **12403**.

Taxi Driver **(1976)**

13090. Castro, Brian. Making oneself foreign. Meanjin (64:4) 2005, 4–14. (Insularity of Australian culture.)

Tempest **(1982)**

13091. O'Dair, Sharon. *The Tempest* as *Tempest*: does Paul Mazursky 'green' William Shakespeare? *See* **6138**.

Tender Mercies **(1983)**

13092. Wood, Gerald C. Loving Mac, Beth, and John: grace in the plays and films of Horton Foote. *See* **15913**.

Tess **(1979)**

13093. Riquelme, John Paul. Dissonance, simulacra, and the grain of the voice in Roman Polanski's *Tess*. *In* (pp. 153–69) **10349**.

13094. Strong, Jeremy. *Tess*, *Jude*, and the problem of adapting Hardy. *See* **10330**.

13095. Wright, Terry. 'Hardy as a cinematic novelist': three aspects of narrative technique. *In* (pp. 8–19) **10349**.

Thelma & Louise **(1991)**

13096. Fournier, Gina. *Thelma & Louise* and women in Hollywood. Jefferson, NC; London: McFarland, 2006. pp. 256.

13097. Wiegand, Shirley A. Deception and artifice: *Thelma & Louise* (1991) and the legal hermeneutic. *In* (pp. 581–606) **12712**.

The Thirteenth Warrior (1999)

13098. Bihlmeyer, Jaime. Novel, script, image: a case study of the phallic (m)other in mainstream culture. *In* (pp. 153–64) **11781**.

A Thousand Acres (1997)

13099. Lehmann, Courtney. A thousand Shakespeares: from cinematic saga to feminist geography; or, The escape from Iceland. *In* (pp. 588–609) **5537**.

Thunder Rock (1943)

13100. Christie, Ian. Heavenly justice. *In* (pp. 3–16) **12636**.

Titus (1999)

13101. Aebischer, Pascale. Shakespeare, sex, and violence: negotiating masculinities in Branagh's *Henry V* and Taymor's *Titus*. *In* (pp. 112–32) **5531**.

13102. Cartelli, Thomas. Taymor's *Titus* in time and space: surrogation and interpolation. RenD (ns 34) 2005, 163–84.

13103. Donaldson, Peter S. Game space / tragic space: Julie Taymor's *Titus*. *In* (pp. 457–77) **5537**.

13104. Escoda Agustí, Clara. Julie Taymor's *Titus* (1999): framing violence and activating responsibility. Atl (28:1) 2006, 57–70.

Total Recall (1990)

13105. La Polla, Franco. Da Philip K. Dick a Hollywood: ovvero, La quadratura del cerchio. *In* (pp. 275–81) **15466**.

Touch of Evil (1958)

13106. Newstok, Scott L. *Touch* of Shakespeare: Welles unmoors Othello. *See* **6034**.

13107. Ryan, Cheyney. 'Across the border – again?': the labyrinth of law in Orson Welles's *Touch of Evil* (1958). *In* (pp. 197–207) **12712**.

Toy Story (1995–)

13108. Botting, Fred; Wilson, Scott. Toy law, toy joy, *Toy Story 2*. *In* (pp. 61–73) **12636**.

13109. Lury, Celia. A more developed sign: the legal mediation of things. *In* (pp. 209–23) **12636**.

13110. Rose, Sarah. Traditional western values in Disney & Pixar's *Toy Story* and *Toy Story 2*. KenPR (20) 2005, 63–7.

Trainspotting (1996)

13111. Ezra, Elizabeth (ed.). European cinema. Oxford; New York: OUP, 2004. pp. x, 344. Rev. by Stephen Woollock in ScopeF (5) 2006.

13112. Lury, Celia. A more developed sign: the legal mediation of things. *In* (pp. 209–23) **12636**.

True Lies (1994)

13113. Metz, Walter. Exposing the lies of Hitchcock's truth. *In* (pp. 109–24) **13181**.

The Truman Show (1998)

13114. Fitting, Peter. Il mondo che sta dietro tutto questo: l'eredità di Philip K. Dick. *In* (pp. 263–74) **15466**.

Tulsa (1949)

13115. Rollins, Peter C. *Tulsa* (1949) as an oil-field film: a study in ecological ambivalence. ChronOkla (82:3) 2004, 352–67.

Twelve Monkeys (1995)

13116. Laytham, D. Brent. Time for hope: *The Sixth Sense*, *American Beauty*, *Memento*, and *Twelve Monkeys*. *In* (pp. 69–83) **11916**.

Vertigo (1958)

13117. Hark, Ina Rae. Psycho or psychic? Hitchcock, *Dead Again*, and the paranormal. *In* (pp. 65–82) **13181**.

13118. Palmer, R. Barton. The Hitchcockian romance and the '70s paranoid thriller. *In* (pp. 85–108) **13181**.

Videodrome (1983)

13119. Genosko, Gary. Phatic (dys)functions: the shifting contour of the TV screen. *In* (pp. 13–24) **11781**.

13120. Panek, Elliot. The poet and the detective: defining the psychological puzzle film. *See* **12978**.

Viva Villa! (1934)

13121. Marez, Curtis. Pancho Villa meets Sun Yat-sen: Third World revolution and the history of Hollywood cinema. AmLH (17:3) 2005, 486–505.

Washington Square (1997)

13122. Newell, Kate. *Washington Square*'s 'virus of suggestion': source texts, intertexts, and adaptations. LitFQ (34:3) 2006, 204–11.

The Watermelon Woman (1995)

13123. Reid-Pharr, Robert F. Makes me feel mighty real: *The Watermelon Woman* and the critique of Black visuality. *In* (pp. 130–40) **12564**.

What Ever Happened to Baby Jane? (1962)

13124. Chivers, Sally. Baby Jane grew up: the dramatic intersection of age with disability. CRAS (36:2) 2006, 211–27.

White Christmas (1954)

13125. Rhodes, John David. *White Christmas*; or, Modernism. Mod/Mod (13:2) 2006, 291–308.

The Wicker Man (1973)

13126. Franks, Benjamin (ed.). The quest for *The Wicker Man*: history, folklore and pagan perspectives. Edinburgh: Luath Press, 2006. pp. 187, (plates) 8.

The Wings of the Dove (1997)

13127. Austin-Smith, Brenda. Sex and the maiden: authenticity and the erotic adaptation of *The Wings of the Dove*. CRAS (36:3) 2006, 331–44.

13128. Eaton, Mark A. Miramax, Merchant–Ivory, and the new nobrow culture: niche marketing *The Wings of the Dove* and *The Golden Bowl*. LitFQ (34:4) 2006, 257–66.

The Winslow Boy **(1999)**

13129. Morra, Irene. Performing the Edwardian ideal: David Mamet and *The Winslow Boy*. ModDr (48:4) 2005, 744–57.

Witness for the Prosecution **(1957)**

13130. Wesling, Wayne T. Trial as theater: *Witness for the Prosecution* (1957). *In* (pp. 131–47) **12712**.

The Woman in the Window **(1945)**

13131. Palmer, R. Barton. Moral man in the dark city: *film noir*, the postwar religious revival, and *The Accused*. *In* (pp. 187–206) **12452**.

The Woodlanders **(1997)**

13132. Kramer, Dale. *The Woodlanders*: the conflicting visions of Phil Agland and Thomas Hardy. *In* (pp. 140–52) **10349**.

X **(1963)**

13133. Winstead, Chase. Two faces of voyeurism: *Nude on the Moon* and *X – the Man with the X-Ray Eyes*. *In* (pp. 176–87) **12548**.

Zoot Suit **(1981)**

13134. Ledwon, Lenora. *Zoot Suit* (1981): realism, romance and the anti-musical – film as social justice. *In* (pp. 425–43) **12712**.

Directors

'Woody Allen' (Allen Stewart Konigsberg)

13135. Blake, Richard A. Street smart: the New York of Lumet, Allen, Scorsese, and Lee. (Bibl. 2005, 13852.) Rev. by James F. Scott in ANQ (19:4) 2006, 66–70; by George W. Hunt in ANCW (194:7) 2006, 24–5.

13136. Kapsis, Robert E.; Coblentz, Kathie (eds). Woody Allen: interviews. Jackson; London: Mississippi UP, 2006. pp. lv, 200. (Conversations with filmmakers.)

13137. Lauder, Robert E. Woody's world: the presence of God's absence. ANCW (194:18) 2006, 24–5.

13138. Silet, Charles L. P. (ed.). The films of Woody Allen: critical essays. Lanham, MD; London: Scarecrow Press, 2006. pp. xviii, 339.

Robert Altman

13139. Kolker, Robert. The 'new' American cinema. *In* (pp. 231–40) **12403**.

William Beaudine, Sr (1892–1970)

13140. Marshall, Wendy L. William Beaudine: from silents to television. (Bibl. 2005, 13854.) Rev. by Richard Harrison in ScopeF (5) 2006.

Frank Borzage

13141. Dumont, Hervé. Frank Borzage: the life and films of a Hollywood romantic. Trans. by Jonathan Kaplansky. Foreword by Martin Scorsese. Jefferson, NC; London: McFarland, 2006. pp. vii, 420.

Stan Brakhage

13142. SITNEY, P. ADAMS. Brakhage and Modernism. *In* (pp. 159–78) **12651**.

Kenneth Branagh

13143. CROWL, SAMUEL. The films of Kenneth Branagh. Westport, CT; London: Praeger, 2006. pp. xi, 204. Rev. by Shannon Blake Skelton in TJ (58:4) 2006, 714–15.

13144. WHITE, MARK. Kenneth Branagh. London; Boston, MA: Faber & Faber, 2005. pp. xi, 323, (plates) 8.

Tod Browning

13145. BOMBACI, NANCY. Freaks in late Modernist American culture: Nathanael West, Djuna Barnes, Tod Browning, and Carson McCullers. *See* **19067**.

13146. MANON, HUGH S. Seeing through seeing through: the *trompe l'œil* effect and bodily difference in the cinema of Tod Browning. FJCM (47:1) 2006, 60–82.

Tim Burton

13147. McMAHAN, ALISON. The films of Tim Burton: animating live action in contemporary Hollywood. (Bibl. 2005, 13857.) Rev. by Rahul Hamid in Cineaste (31:4) 2006, 92–4.

13148. SALISBURY, MARK (ed.). Burton on Burton. Foreword by Johnny Depp. London; Boston, MA: Faber & Faber, 2006. pp. xxi, 289. (Revised ed.: first ed. 2000.)

James Cameron

13149. KELLER, ALEXANDRA. James Cameron. London; New York: Routledge, 2006. pp. ix, 193. (Routledge film guidebooks.)

Frank Capra

13150. SMOODIN, ERIC LOREN. Regarding Frank Capra: audience, celebrity, and American film studies, 1930–1960. Durham, NC; London: Duke UP, 2004. pp. xii, 301. Rev. by Ian Scott in JAStud (40:2) 2006, 451–2.

John Carpenter

13151. CONRICH, IAN; WOODS, DAVID (eds). The cinema of John Carpenter: the technique of terror. (Bibl. 2005, 13859.) Rev. by Philip L. Simpson in Paradoxa (20) 2006, 334–9.

Charlie Chaplin

13152. SCHICKEL, RICHARD (ed.). The essential Chaplin: perspectives on the life and art of the great comedian. Chicago, IL: Dee, 2006. pp. 315. Rev. by Robert Jackson in VQR (82:4) 2006, 270.

Joel and Ethan Coen

13153. ALLEN, WILLIAM RODNEY (ed.). The Coen brothers: interviews. Jackson; London: Mississippi UP, 2006. pp. xxxii, 208. (Conversations with filmmakers.)

13154. MEIS, MORGAN; TYREE, J. M. Is it okay to read the Coen brothers as literature? GetR (19:1) 2006, 61–73.

Merian C. Cooper

13155. VAZ, MARK COTTA. Living dangerously: the adventures of Merian C. Cooper, creator of *King Kong*. (Bibl. 2005, 13865.) Rev. by Camille McCutcheon in JPC (39:4) 2006, 687–8.

Francis Ford Coppola

13156. KOLKER, ROBERT. The 'new' American cinema. *In* (pp. 231–40) **12403**.

13157. PHILLIPS, GENE D. Godfather: the intimate Francis Ford Coppola. (Bibl. 2004, 13966.) Rev. by Vincent Lobrutto in FilmQ (59:4) 2006, 57–8.

David Cronenberg

13158. BEARD, WILLIAM. The artist as monster: the cinema of David Cronenberg. (Bibl. 2005, 125478.) Toronto; Buffalo, NY; London: Toronto UP, 2006. pp. xii, 568. (Revised ed.: first ed. 2001.)

13159. DVORAK, MARTA. Blurring bodies / blurring borders: a cinematic aesthetics of the grotesque. EtCan (57) 2004, 73–83.

Cecil B. DeMille

13160. BIRCHARD, ROBERT S. Cecil B. DeMille's Hollywood. Foreword by Kevin Thomas. Lexington: Kentucky UP, 2004. pp. xvi, 430. Rev. by Andrew Dawson in JAStud (39:1) 2005, 113–14; by Scott Simmon in FilmQ (59:4) 2006, 51–2.

Brian De Palma

13161. LEITCH, THOMAS M. How to steal from Hitchcock. *In* (pp. 251–70) **13181**.

Walt Disney

13162. BRODE, DOUGLAS. Multiculturalism and the Mouse: race and sex in Disney entertainment. Austin: Texas UP, 2005. pp. 292, (plates) 8.

13163. GABLER, NEAL. Walt Disney: the triumph of the American imagination. New York: Knopf, 2006. pp. xx, 851. Rev. by Bruce Handy in NYTB, 3 Dec. 2006, 36–7; by Michael Dirda in BkW, 3 Dec. 2006, 15.

13164. JACKSON, KATHY MERLOCK (ed.). Walt Disney: conversations. Jackson; London: Mississippi UP, 2006. pp. xxvii, 143. (Conversations with comic artists.) Rev. by Carol-Ann Farkas in JPC (39:6) 2006, 1094–6; by Paula T. Connolly in CLAQ (31:2) 2006, 209–11.

13165. SAMMOND, NICHOLAS. Babes in Tomorrowland: Walt Disney and the making of the American child, 1930–1960. Durham, NC; London: Duke UP, 2005. pp. 472. Rev. by Chris McGee in LU (30:3) 2006, 401–4; by Erika Doss in JAH (93:1) 2006, 281–2; by Julia L. Mickenberg in AmQ (58:4) 2006, 1217–27.

Thomas Dixon (1864–1946)

13166. GAINES, JANE M. Thomas Dixon and race melodrama. *In* (pp. 151–63) **15511**.

13167. LINK, WILLIAM A. Epilogue: the enduring worlds of Thomas Dixon. *In* (pp. 203–10) **15511**.

13168. SLIDE, ANTHONY. American racist: the life and films of Thomas Dixon. (Bibl. 2005, 13874.) Rev. by Jené Schoenfeld in AL (78:2) 2006, 391–3.

Bill Douglas

13169. BAREFOOT, GUY. Autobiography and the autobiographical in the Bill Douglas trilogy. Biography (29:1) 2006, 14–29.

Terence Fisher

13170. SPICER, ANDREW. Creativity and the 'B' feature: Terence Fisher's crime films. FilCr (30:2) 2006, 24–42.

John Ford (b.1894)

13171. COWIE, PETER. John Ford and the American West. (Bibl. 2005, 13875.) Rev. by Susan Forsyth in JAStud (40:1) 2006, 168.

Peter Greenaway

13172. KARASTATHI, SYLVIA. Filming the Dutch still life: Peter Greenaway's objects. Gramma (14) 2006, 199–218.

13173. KEESEY, DOUGLAS. The films of Peter Greenaway: sex, death, and provocation. Jefferson, NC; London: McFarland, 2006. pp. vii, 231.

D. W. Griffith

13174. ALONZO, JUAN. From derision to desire: the 'greaser' in Stephen Crane's Mexican stories and D. W. Griffith's early westerns. *See* **9648**.

13175. REGESTER, CHARLENE. The cinematic representation of race in *The Birth of a Nation*: a Black horror film. *In* (pp. 164–82) **15511**.

Howard Hawks

13176. BREIVOLD, SCOTT (ed.). Howard Hawks: interviews. Jackson; London: Mississippi UP, 2006. pp. xli, 215. (Conversations with filmmakers.)

13177. WOOD, ROBIN. Howard Hawks. Detroit, MI: Wayne State UP, 2006. pp. xxv, 210. (Contemporary approaches to film and television.) (Third ed.: first ed. 1968.)

Sir Alfred Hitchcock

13178. ACEVEDO-MUÑOZ, ERNESTO R. Melo-thriller: Hitchcock, genre, and nationalism in Pedro Almodóvar's *Women on the Verge of a Nervous Breakdown*. *In* (pp. 173–94) **13181**.

13179. BADE, JAMES N. Murnau's *The Last Laugh* and Hitchcock's subjective camera. QRFV (23:3) 2006, 257–66.

13180. BELTON, JOHN. Hitchcock and the classical paradigm. *In* (pp. 235–47) **13181**.

13181. BOYD, DAVID; PALMER, R. BARTON (eds). After Hitchcock: influence, imitation, and intertextuality. Austin: Texas UP, 2006. pp. 282.

13182. CHANDLER, CHARLOTTE. It's only a movie: Alfred Hitchcock, a personal biography. New York: Simon & Schuster, 2005. pp. xvi, 349.

13183. COHEN, TOM. Hitchcock's cryptonymies: vol. 1, Secret agents. Minneapolis; London: Minnesota UP, 2005. pp. xxiv, 284. Rev. by Christopher D. Morris in FilCr (30:1) 2005, 72–8; by Paul Gordon in CL (58:2) 2006, 183–5.

13184. —— Hitchcock's cryptonymies: vol. 2, War machines. Minneapolis; London: Minnesota UP, 2005. pp. xvi, 300. Rev. by Christopher D. Morris in FilCr (30:1) 2005, 72–8; by Paul Gordon in CL (58:2) 2006, 183–5.

13185. Flower, Dean. Some refrigerator talk about Alfred Hitchcock. HR (58:4) 2006, 681–8 (review-article).

13186. Leitch, Thomas M. How to steal from Hitchcock. *In* (pp. 251–70) **13181**.

13187. McElhaney, Joe. The death of classical cinema: Hitchcock, Lang, Minnelli. Albany: New York State UP, 2006. pp. xiv, 255. (SUNY series: Horizons of cinema.)

13188. Met, Philippe. 'Knowing too much' about Hitchcock: the genesis of the Italian *giallo*. *In* (pp. 195–214) **13181**.

13189. Metz, Walter. Exposing the lies of Hitchcock's truth. *In* (pp. 109–24) **13181**.

13190. —— Modernity and the crisis in truth: Alfred Hitchcock and Fritz Lang. *In* (pp. 74–89) **12661**.

13191. Neupert, Richard. Red blood on white bread: Hitchcock, Chabrol, and French cinema. *In* (pp. 127–43) **13181**.

13192. Pomerance, Murray. An eye for Hitchcock. (Bibl. 2005, 13886.) Rev. by Marcia Landy in QRFV (23:2) 2006, 174–8.

13193. Salotto, Eleanor. Gothic returns in Collins, Dickens, Zola, and Hitchcock. *See* **9604**.

13194. Singer, Irving. Three philosophical filmmakers: Hitchcock, Welles, Renoir. (Bibl. 2005, 13887.) Rev. by Christian W. Denker in BJA (45:3) 2005, 308–9.

13195. Walker, Michael. Hitchcock's motifs. Amsterdam: Amsterdam UP, 2005. pp. 490. (Film culture in transition.)

13196. Yanal, Robert J. Hitchcock as philosopher. (Bibl. 2005, 13889.) Rev. by Douglas Macleod in FilmH (36:1) 2006, 83.

Gavin Hood

13197. Archibald, David. Violence and redemption: an interview with Gavin Hood. Cineaste (31:2) 2006, 44–7.

James Ivory

13198. Long, Robert Emmet (ed.). James Ivory in conversation: how Merchant Ivory makes its movies. Foreword by Janet Maslin. (Bibl. 2005, 13890.) Rev. by Myles Weber in SewR (113:4) 2005, cxi–cxiii.

Peter Jackson (b.1961)

13199. Sibley, Brian. Peter Jackson: a film-maker's journey. Sydney: HarperCollins, 2006. pp. xiv, 578, (plates) 16.

Derek Jarman

13200. Dillon, Steven. Derek Jarman and lyric film: the mirror and the sea. (Bibl. 2005, 13892.) Rev. by Wheeler Winston Dixon in FilmQ (59:3) 2006, 70–1.

Elia Kazan

13201. Schickel, Richard. Elia Kazan: a biography. (Bibl. 2005, 13895.) Rev. by Dan Georgakas in Cineaste (31:2) 2006, 73–4.

Stanley Kubrick

13202. COCKS, GEOFFREY; DIEDRICK, JAMES; PERUSEK, GLENN (eds). Depth of field: Stanley Kubrick, film, and the uses of history. Madison; London: Wisconsin UP, 2006. pp. ix, 330. (Wisconsin film studies.)

13203. GEHRKE, PAT J.; ERCOLINI, G. L. Subjected wills: the antihumanism of Kubrick's later films. *In* (pp. 101–21) **13202**.

13204. LOBRUTTO, VINCENT. The written word and the very visual Stanley Kubrick. *In* (pp. 31–54) **13202**.

13205. NAREMORE, JAMES. Stanley Kubrick and the aesthetics of the grotesque. FilmQ (60:1) 2006, 4–14.

13206. PERUSEK, GLENN. Kubrick's armies: strategy, hierarchy, and motive in the war films of Stanley Kubrick. *In* (pp. 77–100) **13202**.

13207. SPERB, JASON. The Kubrick façade: faces and voices in the films of Stanley Kubrick. Lanham, MD; London: Scarecrow Press, 2006. pp. x, 187.

13208. WHITE, SUSAN. Kubrick's obscene shadows. *In* (pp. 127–46) **12754**.

Fritz Lang

13209. MCELHANEY, JOE. The death of classical cinema: Hitchcock, Lang, Minnelli. *See* **13187**.

13210. METZ, WALTER. Modernity and the crisis in truth: Alfred Hitchcock and Fritz Lang. *In* (pp. 74–89) **12661**.

David Lean

13211. PHILLIPS, GENE D. Beyond the epic: the life & films of David Lean. Lexington: Kentucky UP, 2006. pp. xvii, 545, (plates) 24. Rev. by Jonathan Yardley in BkW, 19 Nov. 2006, 2.

D. Ross Lederman

13212. DIXON, WHEELER WINSTON. A cinema of violence: the films of D. Ross Lederman. FilCr (30:3) 2006, 38–65.

Mike Leigh

13213. WATSON, GARRY. The cinema of Mike Leigh: a sense of the real. London: Wallflower, 2004. pp. x, 207. (Directors' cuts.) Rev. by Richard Armstrong in FilmQ (59:2) 2006, 62–3.

Richard Linklater

13214. ESTHER, JOHN. The transparency of things: an interview with Richard Linklater. Cineaste (31:4) 2006, 64–5.

Sidney Lumet

13215. GEORGAKAS, DAN. Still 'making movies': an interview with Sidney Lumet. Cineaste (31:2) 2006, 6–13.

13216. RAPF, JOANNA E. (ed.). Sidney Lumet: interviews. Jackson; London: Mississippi UP, 2006. pp. xlvii, 200. (Conversations with filmmakers.) Rev. by Ken Dvorak in FilmH (36:2) 2006, 69.

David Lynch

13217. BAQUÉ, ZACHARY. *Twin Peaks*; ou, L'exploration de l'espace américain. *See* **13267**.

13218. HOLT, JASON. A darker shade: realism in neo-*noir*. *In* (pp. 23–40) **12452**.

13219. VASS, MICHAEL. Cinematic meaning in the works of David Lynch: revisiting *Twin Peaks: Fire Walk with Me*, *Lost Highway*, and *Mulholland Drive*. Cineaction (67) 2005, 12–25.

Oscar Micheaux

13220. GERSTNER, DAVID A. Manly arts: masculinity and nation in early American cinema. Durham, NC; London: Duke UP, 2006. pp. xiii, 316.

13221. GREEN, J. RONALD. With a crooked stick: the films of Oscar Micheaux. Bloomington: Indiana UP, 2004. pp. 314. Rev. by Brigid Maher in JFV (57:4) 2005, 49–50; by Jacqueline Stewart in FilmQ (59:4) 2006, 67–70.

13222. STEWART, JACQUELINE NAJUMA. Migrating to the movies: cinema and Black urban modernity. *See* **12710**.

Vincente Minnelli

13223. MCELHANEY, JOE. The death of classical cinema: Hitchcock, Lang, Minnelli. *See* **13187**.

Dudley Murphy

13224. DELSON, SUSAN. Dudley Murphy, Hollywood wild card. Minneapolis; London: Minnesota UP, 2006. pp. xiii, 251, (plates) 32.

Mira Nair

13225. MUIR, JOHN KENNETH. Mercy in her eyes: the films of Mira Nair. New York: Applause, 2006. pp. 290, (plates) 16.

Max Ophüls

13226. METZ, WALTER C. 'Who am I in this story?': on the film adaptations of Max Ophüls. LitFQ (34:4) 2006, 285–93.

Michael Powell

13227. MOOR, ANDREW. Powell & Pressburger: a cinema of magic spaces. (Bibl. 2005, 13928.) Rev. by Philip Gillett in ScopeF (6) 2006.

Carol Reed

13228. EVANS, PETER WILLIAM. Carol Reed. Manchester; New York: Manchester UP, 2005. pp. ix, 198. (British film makers.)

George A. Romero

13229. PAFFENROTH, KIM. Gospel of the living dead: George Romero's visions of hell on earth. Waco, TX: Baylor Univ., 2006. pp. ix, 195.

Nancy Savoca

13230. HOSTERT, ANNA CAMAITI. Filming on the hyphen: gender and ethnicity in Italian/American cinema. VIA (17:1) 2006, 59–68.

John Sayles

13231. BARON, CYNTHIA. Sayles between the systems: bucking 'industry policy' and indie apolitical chic. *In* (pp. 16–50) **13232**.

13232. CARSON, DIANE; KENAGA, HEIDI (eds). Sayles talk: new perspectives on independent filmmaker John Sayles. Detroit, MI: Wayne State UP, 2006. pp. viii, 285. (Contemporary approaches to film and television series.)

13233. WOLOCH, ALEX. Breakups and reunions: late realism in early Sayles. *In* (pp. 51–78) **13232**.

John Schlesinger

13234. BURUMA, IAN. Conversations with John Schlesinger. New York: Random House, 2006. pp. xxvi, 177, (plates) 8.

Martin Scorsese

13235. KOLKER, ROBERT. The 'new' American cinema. *In* (pp. 231–40) **12403**.

13236. RAYMOND, MARC. The multiplicity of generic discourses and the meaning and pleasure of *Mean Streets*. CanJFS (15:2) 2006, 62–80.

Ridley Scott

13237. D'ANGELO, MIKE. Ridley *v.* Tony. Esquire (146:5) 2006, 58–60.

Tony Scott

13238. D'ANGELO, MIKE. Ridley *v.* Tony. *See* **13237**.

Steven Spielberg

13239. BUCKLAND, WARREN. Directed by Steven Spielberg: poetics of the contemporary Hollywood blockbuster. London; New York: Continuum, 2006. pp. xiii, 242.

13240. FRIEDMAN, LESTER D. Citizen Spielberg. Urbana: Illinois UP, 2006. pp. 361.

George Stevens

13241. MOSS, MARILYN ANN. Giant: George Stevens, a life on film. (Bibl. 2005, 13941.) Rev. by Bernard F. Dick in FilmQ (59:4) 2006, 55–6.

Preston Sturges

13242. BRILL, LESLEY. Crowds, power, and transformation in cinema. *See* **12821**.

13243. MCELHANEY, JOE. Fast talk: Preston Sturges and the speed of language. *In* (pp. 273–94) **12661**.

13244. RAPFOGEL, JARED. The screwball social studies of Preston Sturges. Cineaste (31:3) 2006, 6–12.

Quentin Tarantino

13245. BERG, CHARLES RAMIREZ. A taxonomy of alternative plots in recent films: classifying the 'Tarantino effect'. *See* **19579**.

13246. CROUCH, STANLEY. The artificial White man: essays on authenticity. *See* **11841**.

13247. HOLT, JASON. A darker shade: realism in neo-*noir*. *In* (pp. 23–40) **12452**

Marylou Tibaldo-Bongiorno

13248. HOSTERT, ANNA CAMAITI. Filming on the hyphen: gender and ethnicity in Italian/American cinema. *See* **13230**.

John Waters

13249. LEV, LEORA. Against the grain: John Waters on Dennis Cooper (interview). *In* (pp. 131–48) **15336**.

Orson Welles (1915–1985)

13250. Benamou, Catherine L. The artifice of realism and the lure of the 'real' in Orson Welles's *F for Fake* and other t(r)eas(u)er(e)s. *In* (pp. 143–70) **12564**.

13251. Callow, Simon. Orson Welles: hello Americans. London: Cape, 2006. pp. xviii, 506, (plates) 24. Rev. by Edmund Fawcett in TLS, 21 July 2006, 36; by Gary Giddins in NYTB, 3 Sept. 2006, 12–13; by Jonathan Rosenbaum in Cineaste (31:4) 2006, 88–9.

13252. Díaz-Fernández, José Ramón. Orson Welles's Shakespeare films: an annotated checklist. ShB (23:1) 2005, 113–36.

13253. Garis, Robert. The films of Orson Welles. (Bibl. 2005, 13945.) Rev. by Edward Gallafent in Mod/Mod (13:1) 2006, 204–5.

13254. Heylin, Clinton. Despite the system: Orson Welles *versus* the Hollywood studios. Chicago, IL: Chicago Review Press, 2005. pp. xiii, 402. Rev. by Peter Lambert in TLS, 1 Apr. 2005, 20.

13255. McBride, Joseph. What ever happened to Orson Welles? A portrait of an independent career. Lexington: Kentucky UP, 2006. pp. xviii, 344.

13256. McGonigal, Jane. SuperGaming: ubiquitous play and performance for massively scaled community. *See* **19043**.

13257. Rasmussen, Randy Loren. Orson Welles: six films analyzed, scene by scene. Jefferson, NC; London: McFarland, 2006. pp. viii, 268. (*Citizen Kane*; *The Magnificent Ambersons*; *The Lady from Shanghai*; *Touch of Evil*; *The Trial*; *Chimes at Midnight*.)

Elmo Williams

13258. Williams, Elmo. Elmo Williams: a Hollywood memoir. Jefferson, NC; London: McFarland, 2006. pp. vii, 272.

Frederick Wiseman

13259. Grant, Barry Keith (ed.). Five films by Frederick Wiseman. Foreword by Frederick Wiseman. Berkeley; London: California UP, 2006. pp. xiii, 432.

RADIO, TELEVISION, INTERACTIVE MEDIA

13260. Anon. Filmography: film and television adaptations of Thomas Hardy. *In* (pp. 196–201) **10349**.

13261. Abbott, Jon. Irwin Allen television productions, 1964–1970: a critical history of *Voyage to the Bottom of the Sea*, *Lost in Space*, *The Time Tunnel*, and *Land of the Giants*. Jefferson, NC; London: McFarland, 2006. pp. v, 346.

13262. Adare, Sierra S. 'Indian' stereotypes in TV science fiction: First Nations' voices speak out. (Bibl. 2005, 13953.) Rev. by Nicolas G. Rosenthal in Montana (56:2) 2006, 80–1; by Stephanie Norton Joynes in AICRJ (30:1) 2006, 151–3.

13263. Akass, Kim. Throwing the baby out with the bath water: Miranda and the myth of maternal instinct on *Sex and the City*. SFO (3:1) 2004.

13264. —— McCabe, Janet (eds). Reading *Sex and the City*. (Bibl. 2005, 13954.) Rev. by Marcia Landy in QRFV (23:1) 2006, 83–7.

13265. —— —— Reading *The L Word*: outing contemporary television. Introd. by Sarah Warn. *See* **19770**.

13266. Allingham, Philip. Screening the flashback: three ways of opening *The Mayor of Casterbridge*. *In* (pp. 124–39) **10349**.

13267. Baqué, Zachary. *Twin Peaks*; ou, L'exploration de l'espace américain. Anglophonia (19) 2006, 79–86.

13268. Barrett, Robert R. The anomaly of *Tarzan and the Forbidden City*. *See* **14921**.

13269. Battis, Jes. Blood relations: chosen families in *Buffy the Vampire Slayer* and *Angel*. (Bibl. 2005, 13958.) Rev. by Mary Kirby-Diaz in JPC (39:5) 2006, 907–8.

13270. Becker, Ron. Gay TV and straight America. New Brunswick, NJ; London: Rutgers UP, 2006. pp. x, 283.

13271. Bender, Jack; Bender, Carole. Warner Brothers' Tarzan TV series. *See* **14927**.

13272. Bertonneau, Thomas; Paffenroth, Kim. The truth is out there: Christian faith and the classics of TV science fiction. Grand Rapids, MI: Brazos Press, 2006. pp. 272.

13273. Block, Mitchell W. The truth about *No Lies* (if you can believe it). *In* (pp. 187–95) **12564**.

13274. Booker, M. Keith. Drawn to television: primetime animation from *The Flintstones* to *Family Guy*. Westport, CT; London: Praeger, 2006. pp. xii, 191. (Praeger television collection.)

13275. Brighouse, Harry. Why is an argument clinic less silly than an abuse clinic or a contradiction clinic? *In* (pp. 53–63) **13316**.

13276. Broderick, James F. The literary galaxy of *Star Trek*: an analysis of references and themes in the television series and films. Jefferson, NC; London: McFarland, 2006. pp. 233.

13277. Bubel, Claudia M.; Spitz, Alice. 'One of the last vestiges of gender bias': the characterization of women through the telling of dirty jokes in *Ally McBeal*. Humor (19:1) 2006, 71–104.

13278. Carey, Rosalind. 'My brain hurts!' *In* (pp. 187–99) **13316**.

13279. Cartmel, Andrew. Through time: an unauthorised and unofficial history of *Doctor Who*. London; New York: Continuum, 2005. pp. xiii, 226.

13280. Chapman, James. Inside the Tardis: the worlds of *Dr Who*: a cultural history. London; New York: Tauris, 2006. pp. viii, 262. Rev. by Jon Barnes in TLS, 23 June 2006, 33.

13281. Cole, Nathalie Bell. Travel, the road and the city in adaptations of *Great Expectations*. *In* (pp. 265–92) **9791**.

13282. Conway, Richard J. A trip to the queer circus: reimagined masculinities in *Will & Grace*. *In* (pp. 75–84) **13336**.

13283. Cook, John R.; Wright, Peter (eds). British science fiction television: a hitchhiker's guide. London; New York: Tauris, 2006. pp. viii, 296 (Popular television genres.)

13284. Coppa, Francesca. A brief history of media fandom. *In* (pp. 41–59) **19868**.

13285. —— Writing bodies in space: media fan fiction as theatrical performance. *In* (pp. 225–44) **19868**.

13286. Coursen, H. R. Shakespeare translated: derivatives on film and TV. *See* **5280**.

13287. Courtis, Brian. Arresting developments. Meanjin (63:3) 2004, 216–22. (*Neighbours* and *The Bill*.)

13288. Cox, Jim. The daytime serials of television, 1946–1960. Jefferson, NC; London: McFarland, 2006. pp. x, 236.

13289. —— Historical dictionary of American radio soap operas. Lanham, MD; London: Scarecrow Press, 2005. pp. xix, 292, (plates) 8. (Historical dictionaries of literature and the arts, 3.)

13290. Cragin, Becca. Lesbians and serial TV: *Ellen* finds her inner adult. *In* (pp. 193–208) **13336**.

13291. Crawley, Melissa. Mr Sorkin goes to Washington: shaping the President on television's *The West Wing*. Jefferson, NC; London: McFarland, 2006. pp. viii, 224.

13292. Croskery, Patrick. Monty Python and the search for the meaning of life. *In* (pp. 161–72) **13316**.

13293. Davis, Glyn; Dickinson, Kay (eds). Teen TV: genre, consumption, identity. London: British Film Inst., 2004. pp. viii, 197. Rev. by Ewan Kirkland in ScopeF (5) 2006.

13294. Davison-Pégon, Claire. 'Untext me here' – what exactly constitutes the text of a radio play? *See* **17385**.

13295. Del Grosso, Simone. Strategie narrative e metodologie del montaggio dell'*incipit* da Charles Dickens a Martin Scorsese: Jump Cut su Lean, Cuarón e la BBC. *In* (pp. 319–340) **9791**.

13296. Dennis, Jeffery P. Queering teen culture: all-American boys and same-sex desire in film and television. *See* **12469**.

13297. Donaldson, Peter S. Game space / tragic space: Julie Taymor's *Titus*. *In* (pp. 457–77) **5537**.

13298. Dunleavy, Trisha. Ourselves in primetime: a history of New Zealand television drama. Auckland: Auckland UP, 2005. pp. x, 340.

13299. Edgerton, Gary R.; Rose, Brian G. (eds). Thinking outside the box: a contemporary television genre reader. Lexington: Kentucky UP, 2005. pp. vi, 368.

13300. Edwards, Emily D. Metaphysical media: the occult experience in popular culture. *See* **12491**.

13301. Emmons, Mark. Film and television: a guide to the reference literature. *See* **12493**.

13302. Falzone, P. J. The final frontier is queer: aberrancy, archetype and audience-generated folklore in K/S slashfiction. WF (64:3/4) 2005, 243–61.

13303. Fearn-Banks, Kathleen. Historical dictionary of African American television. Lanham, MD; London: Scarecrow Press, 2006. pp. xli, 526, (plates) 16. (Historical dictionaries of literature and the arts, 7.)

13304. Feasey, Rebecca. Watching *Charmed*: why teen television appeals to women. JPFT (34:1) 2006, 2–9.

13305. Fitzpatrick, Kathleen. The anxiety of obsolescence: the American novel in the age of television. *See* **13473**.

13306. Gatrell, Simon. Wessex on film. *In* (pp. 37–49) **10349**.

13307. Genosko, Gary. Phatic (dys)functions: the shifting contour of the TV screen. *In* (pp. 13–24) **11781**.

13308. Geraghty, Lincoln. A network of support: coping with trauma through *Star Trek* fan letters. JPC (39:6) 2006, 1002–24.

13309. Gibson, Marion. Retelling Salem stories: gender politics and witches in American culture. EurJAC (25:2) 2006, 85–107.

13310. Gray, Herman. Where have all the Black shows gone? *In* (pp. 311–25) **11876**.

13311. Green, Paul. A history of television's *The Virginian*, 1962–1971. Foreword by Frank Price. *See* **19239**.

13312. Hand, Richard J. Escape with Joseph Conrad! The adaptation of Joseph Conrad's fiction on American old-time radio. *See* **15273**.

13313. —— Terror on the air! Horror radio in America, 1931–1952. Foreword by David Kogan. Jefferson, NC; London: McFarland, 2006. pp. 184.

13314. Hardcastle, Gary L. My years with Monty Python; or, What's so funny about language, truth, and analyticity? *In* (pp. 253–64) **13316**.

13315. —— Themes in contemporary analytic philosophy as reflected in the work of Monty Python. *In* (pp. 265–75) **13316**.

13316. —— Reisch, George A. (eds). Monty Python and philosophy: nudge nudge, think think! Chicago, IL: Open Court, 2006. pp. xi, 291. (Popular culture and philosophy, 19.)

13317. Harzewski, Stephanie. The limits of defamiliarization: *Sex and the City* as late heterosexuality. SFO (3:1) 2004.

13318. Hawkes, Terence. Nanti everything. *In* (pp. 130–8) **5421**.

13319. Hellekson, Karen; Busse, Kristina (eds). Fan fiction and fan communities in the age of the Internet: new essays. *See* **19868**.

13320. Henderson, Carol E. Layed bare: the filmic representation of *Go Tell It on the Mountain*. *In* (pp. 139–46) **14544**.

13321. Highfield, Jonathan. Suckling from the crocodile's tit: wildlife and nation formation in Australian narratives. *See* **15026**.

13322. Hight, Craig; Roscoe, Jane. *Forgotten Silver*: a New Zealand television hoax and its audience. *In* (pp. 171–86) **12564**.

13323. Hilliard, Robert L.; Keith, Michael C. The quieted voice: the rise and demise of localism in American radio. Carbondale: Southern Illinois UP, 2005. pp. xiv, 242. Rev. by Erika Engstrom in PCR (17:1) 2006, 95–6.

13324. Hipsky, Martin. Post-Cold War paranoia in *The Corrections* and *The Sopranos*. *See* **15988**.

13325. Hischak, Thomas S. American plays and musicals on screen: 650 stage productions and their film and television adaptations. *See* **3440**.

13326. Hogan, David J. Secret identity, fragile identity: TV's Superman in *Superman on Earth*, *The Stolen Costume*, *The Face and the Voice*, and *Panic in the Sky*. *In* (pp. 104–19) **12548**.

13327. Hudelet, Ariane. Chorégraphies implicites et explicites: la danse dans *Pride and Prejudice*, du texte à l'écran. *See* **9031**.

13328. Hurd, Robert. Taking *Seinfeld* seriously: modernism in popular culture. NLH (37:4) 2006, 761–76.

13329. Huss, John. Monty Python and David Hume on religion. *In* (pp. 141–51) **13316**.

13330. Johnson, Lisa. The stripper as resisting reader: stripper iconography and sex-worker feminism on *The Sopranos*. SFO (3:1) 2004.

13331. Johnson-Smith, Jan. American science fiction TV: *Star Trek*, *Stargate* and beyond. (Bibl. 2005, 14006.) Rev. by Joseph Milicia in NYRSF (18:5) 2006, 17–18.

13332. Jowett, Lorna. Sex and the slayer: a Gender Studies primer for the *Buffy* fan. (Bibl. 2005, 14007.) Rev. by Terri A. Fredrick in NWSAJ (18:2) 2006, 239–40.

13333. Juhasz, Alexander; Lerner, Jesse (eds). F is for phony: fake documentary and truth's undoing. *See* **12564**.

13334. Juul, Jesper. Half-real: video games between real rules and fictional worlds. Cambridge, MA; London: MIT Press, 2005. pp. ix, 233. Rev. by Stuart Moulthrop in AmBR (27:5) 2006, 22–3.

13335. Kane, Tim. The changing vampire of film and television: a critical study of the growth of a genre. *See* **12566**.

13336. Keller, James R.; Stratyner, Leslie (eds). The new queer aesthetic on television: essays on recent programming. Jefferson, NC; London: McFarland, 2006. pp. vi, 216.

13337. Kessler, Kelly. Politics of the sitcom formula: *Friends*, *Mad about You*, and the Sapphic second banana. *In* (pp. 130–46) **13336**.

13338. Kiernan, Anna. No satisfaction: *Sex and the City*, *Run Catch Kiss*, and the conflict of desires in chick lit's new heroines. *In* (pp. 207–18) **19862**.

13339. Kingwell, Mark. Crayon in the brain: machining happiness in the time of Homer. Descant (37:2) 2006, 68–87.

13340. Knox, Simone. Reading the ungraspable double-codedness of *The Simpsons*. JPFT (34:2) 2006, 72–81.

13341. Larsen, Svend-Erik. Fiction and virtual reality. *In* (pp. 255–68) **14093**.

13342. Lee, Katherine Hyunmi. The ghost of Gary Cooper: masculinity, homosocial bonding, and *The Sopranos*. SFO (3:1) 2004.

13343. Lotz, Amanda D. Redesigning women: television after the network era. Urbana: Illinois UP, 2006. pp. x, 224. (Feminist studies and media culture.) Rev. by Naeemah Clark in JoH (32:3) 2006, 182–3.

13344. Lury, Celia. A more developed sign: the legal mediation of things. *In* (pp. 209–23) **12636**.

13345. Lury, Karen. Interpreting television. London: Hodder Arnold, 2005. pp. vii, 198.

13346. Mabry, A. Rochelle. About a girl: female subjectivity and sexuality in contemporary 'chick' culture. *In* (pp. 191–206) **19862**.

13347. McAllister, Ken S. Game work: language, power and computer game culture. Tuscaloosa; London: Alabama UP, 2004. pp. xiv, 232. (Rhetoric, culture, and social critique.) Rev. by Jacob S. Turner in QJS (92:1) 2006, 109–12.

13348. McGonigal, Jane. SuperGaming: ubiquitous play and performance for massively scaled community. *See* **19043**.

13349. McLeod, Elizabeth. The original *Amos 'n' Andy*: Freeman Gosden, Charles Correll, and the 1928–1943 radio serial. Jefferson, NC; London: McFarland, 2005. pp. vii, 215.

13350. Magoulick, Mary. Frustrating female heroism: mixed messages in *Xena*, *Nikita*, and *Buffy*. JPC (39:5) 2006, 729–55.

13351. Malik, Rachel. The afterlife of Wilkie Collins. *In* (pp. 181–93) **9609**.

13352. Marcus, Greil. The shape of things to come: prophecy and the American voice. *See* **18319**.

13353. Marroni, Francesco (ed.). *Great Expectations*: nel laboratorio di Charles Dickens. *See* **9791**.

13354. Martinez-Sierra, Juan José. Using Bourdieu to approach the concept of television as an instrument of social reproduction in the US: the paradox of *The Simpsons*. ASSA (18) 2006.

13355. Merlock, Ray. Growing up with westerns. *In* (pp. 235–51) **3157**.

13356. Midwinter, Eric. The people's jesters: British comedians in the 20th century. London: Third Age Press, 2006. pp. 229.

13357. Miller, Margo. Masculinity and male intimacy in nineties sitcoms: *Seinfeld* and the ironic dismissal. *In* (pp. 147–59) **13336**.

13358. Miller, Pat. From paradigm to parody: war and the shifting sands of American manhood. *See* **12873**.

13359. Mills, Katie. The road story and the rebel: moving through film, fiction, and television. *See* **12629**.

13360. Montemurro, Beth. Charlotte chooses her choice: liberal feminism on *Sex and the City*. SFO (3:1) 2004.

13361. Moore, Barbara; Bensman, Marvin R.; Van Dyke, Jim. Prime-time television: a concise history. Westport, CT; London: Praeger, 2006. pp. x, 305. Rev. by Matthew J. Bosisio in AmJ (23:4) 2006, 126–7.

13362. Morgan, Rosemarie. Staging the *Native*: aspects of screening *The Return of the Native*. *In* (pp. 108–23) **10349**.

13363. Moss, David Grant. A queen for whose time? Elizabeth I as icon for the twentieth century. *See* **12852**.

13364. Mustazza, Leonard. The literary filmography: 6,200 adaptations of books, short stories and other nondramatic works. *See* **12641**.

13365. Nadel, Alan. Television in Black-and-White America: race and national identity. (Bibl. 2005, 14025.) Rev. by Steven D. Classen in JAH (93:2) 2006, 588–9.

13366. NEMESVARI, RICHARD. Romancing the text: genre, indeterminacy, and televising *Tess of the d'Urbervilles*. *In* (pp. 170–82) **10349**.

13367. NEWMAN, KIM. *Doctor Who*. London: British Film Inst., 2005. pp. vi, 138. (BFI TV classics.) Rev. by Jenny Turner in LRB (28:12) 2006, 8–10.

13368. NIEMI, ROBERT. History in the media: film and television. *See* **12645**.

13369. ORAVEC, JO ANN. From gigapets to Internet: childhood technology rituals as commodities. *In* (pp. 252–68) **3157**.

13370. PAIETTA, ANN C. Saints, clergy, and other religious figures on film and television, 1895–2003. *See* **12651**.

13371. PAOLUCCI, PAUL; RICHARDSON, MARGARET. Dramaturgy, humor, and criticism: how Goffman reveals *Seinfeld*'s critique of American culture. Humor (19:1) 2006, 27–52.

13372. PARRY-GILES, TREVOR; PARRY-GILES, SHAWN J. The prime-time Presidency: *The West Wing* and US nationalism. Urbana: Illinois UP, 2006. pp. x, 231.

13373. PATEMAN, MATTHEW. The aesthetics of culture in *Buffy the Vampire Slayer*. Jefferson, NC; London: McFarland, 2006. pp. xi, 276.

13374. PIERCE-JONES, ROY. Screening the short stories: from the 1950s to the 1990s. *In* (pp. 63–75) **10349**.

13375. REISCH, GEORGE A. Monty Python's utterly devastating critique of ordinary language philosophy. *In* (pp. 231–42) **13316**.

13376. RELKE, DIANA M. A. Drones, clones, and alpha babes: retro-fitting *Star Trek*'s humanism, post-9/11. Calgary, Alta: Calgary UP, 2006. pp. xx, 168.

13377. RICHARDSON, ALAN. Tractatus comedo-philosophicus. *In* (pp. 217–29) **13316**.

13378. ROGERSON, MARGARET. Prime-time drama: *Canterbury Tales* for the small screen. *See* **4439**.

13379. ROLINSON, DAVE. Alan Clarke. Manchester; New York: Manchester UP, 2005. pp. x, 197. (Television series.)

13380. ROMAN, JAMES W. From daytime to primetime: the history of American television programs. Westport, CT; London: Greenwood Press, 2005. pp. xxvii, 345. Rev. by Mike Chopra-Gant in JAStud (40:2) 2006, 446–7.

13381. RYAN, MARIE-LAURE. Avatars of story. Minneapolis; London: Minnesota UP, 2006. pp. xxiv, 275. (Electronic mediations, 17.)

13382. SACHLEBEN, MARK; YENERALL, KEVAN M. Seeing the bigger picture: understanding politics through film & television. *See* **12684**.

13383. SADOCK, JERROLD M. Getting squishy. *See* **1458**.

13384. SCHARNHORST, GARY. Nabokov and Bret Harte: an overlooked allusion in *Lolita*. *See* **17715**.

13385. SCHMID, DAVID. Natural born celebrities: serial killers in American culture. *See* **12688**.

13386. SHEEHAN, HELENA. The continuing story of Irish television drama: tracking the tiger. Dublin; Portland, OR: Four Courts Press, 2004. pp. x, 178; 1 CD-ROM. (Broadcasting and Irish society, 3.) Rev. by Rob Savage in FDR (1) 2005, 275.

13387. Short, Sue. Misfit sisters: screen horror as female rites of passage. *See* **12696**.

13388. Siourbas, Helen. More than just survival: the successful quest for voice in Guy Gavriel Kay's *Tigana* and Randy Bradshaw's *The Song Spinner*. *In* (pp. 73–80) **13541**.

13389. Slowik, Edward. Existentialism in Monty Python: Kafka, Camus, Nietzsche, and Sartre. *In* (pp. 173–85) **13316**.

13390. Smith, Kurt. The limits of Horatio's philosophy. *In* (pp. 37–51) **13316**.

13391. Snauffer, Douglas. Crime television. Westport, CT; London: Praeger, 2006. pp. x, 260. (Praeger television collection.)

13392. Spinelli, Michelle. Madness in *Monty Python's Flying Circus*. *In* (pp. 153–60) **13316**.

13393. Stoehr, Kevin L. Nihilism in film and television: a critical overview, *Citizen Kane* to *The Sopranos*. *See* **12711**.

13394. Szasz, Ferenc Morton. A new Mexican 'Davy Crockett': Walt Disney's version of the life and legend of Elfego Baca. JSwest (48:3) 2006, 261–74.

13395. Taves, Brian. P. G. Wodehouse and Hollywood: screenwriting, satires, and adaptations. Foreword by Richard Briers. *See* **19242**.

13396. Taylor, James. Why is a philosopher like a Python? How philosophical examples work. *In* (pp. 201–13) **13316**.

13397. Treglown, Jeremy. Make use of me. *See* **17437**.

13398. Tropp, Laura. 'Faking a sonogram': representations of motherhood on *Sex and the City*. JPC (39:5) 2006, 861–77.

13399. Turner, Cristy. Fabulousness as fetish: queer politics in *Sex and the City*. SFO (3:1) 2004.

13400. Turner, Jenny. Across the tellyverse. LRB (28:12) 2006, 8–10 (review-article). (*Dr Who*.)

13401. Vaughn, Stephen. Freedom and entertainment: rating the movies in an age of new media. *See* **12726**.

13402. Watson, Elwood (ed.). Searching the soul of *Ally McBeal*: critical essays. Jefferson, NC; London: McFarland, 2006. pp. viii, 246.

13403. Weldy, Lance. Dreams, imaginations, and shattered illusions: overlooked realism in Carol Wiseman's film adaptation of Burnett's *A Little Princess*. *In* (pp. 189–203) **9300**.

13404. Wright, T. R. (ed.). Thomas Hardy on screen. *See* **10349**.

13405. Wyn, Johanna. Youth in the media: adult stereotypes of younger people. *In* (pp. 23–34) **2798**.

13406. Young, Paul. The cinema dreams its rivals: media fantasy films from radio to the Internet. *See* **12749**.

FICTION

13407. Aarons, Victoria. What happened to Abraham? Reinventing the covenant in American Jewish fiction. (Bibl. 2005, 14070.) Rev. by Susan Jacobowitz in PhRS (1:2) 2005, 181–3.

13408. Abell, Stephen. Hold the hooptedoodle: Mack's rules for writing westerns. *See* **17114**.

13409. Acheson, James; Ross, Sarah C. E. (eds). The contemporary British novel. Edinburgh: Edinburgh UP, 2005. pp. iv, 250.

13410. Anderson, Douglas A. The mainstreaming of fantasy and the legacy of *The Lord of the Rings*. *In* (pp. 301–15) **18804**.

13411. Annesley, James. Fictions of globalization. London; New York: Continuum, 2006. pp. vi, 202. (Continuum literary studies.)

13412. Ashley, Mike. The age of the storytellers: British popular fiction magazines, 1880–1950. *See* **8611**.

13413. Ball, John Clement. Imagining London: postcolonial fiction and the transnational metropolis. (Bibl. 2004, 14185.) Rev. by Joseph McLaughlin in MFS (52:1) 2006, 238–42; by Matthew Mead in JPW (42:1) 2006, 119–21.

13414. Barnard, Rita. Modern American fiction. *In* (pp. 39–67) **11964**.

13415. Barrish, Phillip. White liberal identity, literary pedagogy, and classic American realism. *See* **8612**.

13416. Bechtel, Greg. 'There and back again': progress in the discourse of Todorovian, Tolkienian and mystic fantasy theory. *See* **18778**.

13417. Beers, Terry (ed.). Gunfight at Mussel Slough: evolution of a Western myth. *See* **2994**.

13418. Bell, Bernard W. The contemporary African American novel: its folk roots and modern literary branches. (Bibl. 2005, 14082.) Rev. by Stephen Knadler in AL (78:4) 2006, 880–2.

13419. Bender, Bert. Evolution and 'the sex problem': American narratives during the eclipse of Darwinism. (Bibl. 2005, 14083.) Rev. by Chris L. Massey in DreiS (36:2) 2005, 48–50; by David Depew in JAH (92:4) 2006, 1465–6; by Richard Bellon in Isis (97:2) 2006, 359–60; by Bernice L. Hausman in AL (78:3) 2006, 659–62; by Tom Quirk in ALR (39:1) 2006, 91–3; by Helen Sutherland in JAStud (40:2) 2006, 417.

13420. Berglund, Jeff. Cannibal fictions: American explorations of colonialism, race, gender and sexuality. Madison; London: Wisconsin UP, 2006. pp. xv, 233.

13421. Berndt, Katrin. Female identity in contemporary Zimbabwean fiction. Bayreuth: Breitinger, 2005. pp. 285. (Bayreuth African studies, 23.) Rev. by Flora Veit-Wild in RAL (37:3) 2006, 193–204; by Ann Elizabeth Willey in RAL (37:3) 2006, 212–13.

13422. Bernheimer, Kate. This rapturous form. MarvT (20:1) 2006, 67–83.

13423. Berry, R. M. R. M. Berry answers Joseph Tabbi. *See* **14764**.

13424. Betz, Phyllis M. Lesbian detective fiction: woman as author, subject, and reader. Jefferson, NC; London: McFarland, 2006. pp. ix, 197.

13425. Bharat, Meenakshi (ed.). Desert in bloom: contemporary Indian women's fiction in English. Delhi: Pencraft International, 2004. pp. 240. Rev. by Frederick Luis Aldama in WLT (79:1) 2005, 87.

13426. Bigge, Ryan. The new geographers. Descant (35:2) 2004, 81–7.

13427. BIRBALSINGH, FRANK. The Indo-Caribbean short story. JWIL (12:1/2) 2004, 118–34.

13428. BOGEN, ANNA. Compton Mackenzie, liberal education, and the Oxford novel: 'sympathy for the normal'. *See* **17364**.

13429. BONE, MARTYN. The postsouthern sense of place in contemporary fiction. (Bibl. 2005, 14087.) Rev. by Leigh Anne Duck in ConLit (47:2) 2006, 299–303.

13430. BOUTROS, FATIM. Revision als Illusion? Die Aufarbeitung der Sklaverei in neueren Romanen der anglophonen Karibik. Würzburg: Königshausen & Neumann, 2004. pp. 177. (Studien zur 'Neuen Welt', 10.) Rev. by Carmen Birkle in Amst (51:2) 2006, 247–9.

13431. BREU, CHRISTOPHER. Hard-boiled masculinities. Minneapolis; London: Minnesota UP, 2005. pp. 245. Rev. by Ryan Schneider in AL (78:4) 2006, 894–7.

13432. BRIGANTI, CHIARA; MEZEI, KATHY. Domestic Modernism, the interwar novel, and E. H. Young. Aldershot; Burlington, VT: Ashgate, 2006. pp. viii, 211. Rev. by Christina Hardyment in TLS, 8 Sept. 2006, 27.

13433. BROWN, JOANNE; ST CLAIR, NANCY. The distant mirror: reflections on young adult historical fiction. Lanham, MD; London: Scarecrow Press, 2006. pp. ix, 210. (Scarecrow studies in young adult literature, 21.)

13434. BRUHM, STEVEN. Nightmare on Sesame Street; or, The self-possessed child. *See* **12432**.

13435. BULSON, ERIC. Novels, maps, modernity: the spatial imagination, 1850–2000. *See* **8621**.

13436. BURROWS, VICTORIA. Whiteness and trauma: the mother–daughter knot in the fiction of Jean Rhys, Jamaica Kincaid, and Toni Morrison. (Bibl. 2004, 19199.) Rev. by Patricia Moran in TSWL (25:1) 2006, 165–70.

13437. BYERMAN, KEITH. Remembering the past in contemporary African American fiction. (Bibl. 2005, 14100.) Rev. by William R. Nash in AAR (40:1) 2006, 190–2.

13438. CASSUTO, LEONARD. *The Maltese Falcon* and the hard-boiled sentimental. *See* **16259**.

13439. CHRISTIAN, B. MARIE. Belief in dialogue: US Latina writers confront their religious heritage. New York: Other Press, 2005. pp. xxix, 253.

13440. COALE, SAMUEL CHASE. Paradigms of paranoia: the culture of conspiracy in contemporary American fiction. (Bibl. 2005, 14109.) Rev. by Douglas Keesey in PLL (42:2) 2006, 220–3; by Rosalie Murphy Baum in RMER (60:2) 2006; by Peter Knight in JAStud (40:3) 2006, 651–2.

13441. COLE, CATHY. Private dicks and feisty chicks: an interrogation of crime fiction. Fremantle, W. Australia: Curtin Univ., 2004. pp. 271. Rev. by Susan Rowland in Clues (24:4) 2006, 73.

13442. COLEMAN, JAMES W. Faithful vision: treatments of the sacred, spiritual, and supernatural in twentieth-century African American fiction. Baton Rouge: Louisiana State UP, 2006. pp. 252. (Southern literary studies.) Rev. by Isiah Lavender, III, in ArkR (37:2) 2006, 138–9.

13443. Conroy, Mark. Muse in the machine: American fiction and mass publicity. (Bibl. 2005, 14112.) Rev. by Kinohi Nishikawa in AL (78:3) 2006, 652–4.

13444. Cowart, David. Trailing clouds: immigrant fiction in contemporary America. Ithaca, NY; London: Cornell UP, 2006. pp. xii, 249. (Cornell paperbacks.)

13445. Cox, J. Randolph. *Dime Novel Roundup* over the years. *See* **1075**.

13446. Cox, James H. Muting white noise: Native American and European American novel traditions. Norman: Oklahoma UP, 2006. pp. xi, 338. (American Indian literature and critical studies, 51.)

13447. Cummings, Ralph F. History of the Happy Hours Brotherhood and the *Dime Novel Roundup*. DNR (75:4) 2006, 100–4.

13448. Dale, Judith. Re-reading war stories. *In* (pp. 63–70) **11731**.

13449. Dandridge, Rita B. Black women's activism: reading African American women's historical romances. (Bibl. 2004, 14217.) Rev. by Heike Raphael-Hernandez in Amst (51:2) 2006, 246–7.

13450. Davin, Eric Leif. Partners in wonder: women and the birth of science fiction, 1926–1965. Lanham, MD: Lexington, 2006. pp. xiv, 429.

13451. Davis, J. Madison. The murderous women writers of Oz. WLT (80:1) 2006, 9–10.

13452. Deardorff, Donald Lee, II. Hero and anti-hero in the American football novel: changing conceptions of masculinity from the nineteenth century to the twenty-first century. *See* **8630**.

13453. Debus, Allen A. Dinosaurs in fantastic fiction: a thematic survey. Forewords by Donald F. Glut and Mark F. Berry. Jefferson, NC; London: McFarland, 2006. pp. ix, 220.

13454. DeGraw, Sharon. The subject of race in American science fiction. London; New York: Routledge, 2006. pp. 192.

13455. Demirtürk, E. Lâle. Charting the terrain of Black urban subjects: the African American great migration novel. *In* (pp. 97–106) **3307**.

13456. Deonandan, Raywat. A scientist's relationship with science fiction. *In* (pp. 131–8) **13541**.

13457. Diamond, Michael. Lesser breeds: racial attitudes in popular British fiction, 1890–1940. *See* **8633**.

13458. Donahue, Peter; Trombold, John (eds). Reading Seattle: the city in prose. Seattle; London: Washington UP, 2004. pp. xvi, 320. Rev. by Peter Heldrich in PacNQ (96:2) 2005, 105–6; by O. Alan Weltzien in WAL (41:1) 2006, 85–6.

13459. Dresner, Lisa M. The female investigator in literature, film, and popular culture. Jefferson, NC; London: McFarland, 2006. pp. 240.

13460. Driscoll, Catherine. One true pairing: the romance of pornography, and the pornography of romance. *In* (pp. 79–96) **19868**.

13461. Dudley, John. A man's game: masculinity and the anti-aesthetics of American literary Naturalism. (Bibl. 2005, 14128.) Rev. by Hildegard Hoeller in AL (78:1) 2006, 187–9; by Peter F. Murphy in SAtlR (71:1) 2006, 160–2.

13462. Eagleton, Mary. Figuring the woman author in contemporary fiction. Basingstoke; New York: Palgrave Macmillan, 2005. pp. viii, 193.

13463. Eagleton, Terry. Making a break. LRB (28:5) 2006, 25–6 (review-article). (Jameson on utopianism.)

13464. Elliott, Emory. Society and the novel in twentieth-century America. *In* (pp. 430–49) **11776**.

13465. Emmott, Catherine; Sanford, Anthony J.; Morrow, Lorna I. Capturing the attention of readers? Stylistic and psychological perspectives on the use and effect of text fragmentation in narratives. JLS (35:1) 2006, 1–30.

13466. English, James F. (ed.). A concise companion to contemporary British fiction. Oxford; Malden, MA: Blackwell, 2006. pp. xi, 281. (Blackwell concise companions to literature and culture.) Rev. by Claire Squires in RES (57:230) 2006, 414–16.

13467. Fahy, Thomas. Freak shows and the modern American imagination: constructing the damaged body from Willa Cather to Truman Capote. Basingstoke; New York: Palgrave Macmillan, 2006. pp. x, 192. (American literature readings in the 21st century.)

13468. Falzone, P. J. The final frontier is queer: aberrancy, archetype and audience-generated folklore in K/S slashfiction. *See* **13302**.

13469. Faris, Wendy B. Ordinary enchantments: magical realism and the remystification of narrative. (Bibl. 2004, 14231.) Rev. by Seymour Menton in WLT (79:2) 2005, 110–11.

13470. Farr, Cecilia Konchar. Reading Oprah: how Oprah's Book Club changed the way America reads. (Bibl. 2005, 14132.) Rev. by Jeffrey Louis Decker in MFS (52:1) 2006, 169–78; by Kinohi Nishikawa in AL (78:3) 2006, 652–4.

13471. Finder, Joseph. Where have all the strivers gone? NYTB, 9 Apr. 2006, 35.

13472. Finney, Brian. English fiction since 1984: narrating a nation. Basingstoke; New York: Palgrave Macmillan, 2006. pp. vii, 233.

13473. Fitzpatrick, Kathleen. The anxiety of obsolescence: the American novel in the age of television. Nashville, TN: Vanderbilt UP, 2006. pp. x, 268.

13474. Fleissner, Jennifer. Women, compulsion, modernity: the moment of American Naturalism. (Bibl. 2004, 14237.) Rev. by Hildegard Hoeller in AL (78:1) 2006, 187–9.

13475. Folks, Jeffrey Jay. Damaged lives: Southern & Caribbean narrative from Faulkner to Naipaul. New York; Frankfurt: Lang, 2005. pp. 137.

13476. Forbes, Shannon. Women's transition from Victorian to contemporary identity as portrayed in the modern novel. Lewiston, NY; Lampeter: Mellen Press, 2006. pp. iv, 176.

13477. Forrest, Katherine V. (ed.). Lesbian pulp fiction: the sexually intrepid world of lesbian paperback novels, 1950–1965. (Bibl. 2005, 14137.) Rev. by Carol Seajay in WRB (23:1) 2006, 18–19.

13478. Foster, Thomas. The souls of cyberfolk: posthumanism as vernacular theory. Minneapolis; London: Minnesota UP, 2005. pp. xxix, 312. (Electronic mediations, 13.)

13479. Fulton, DoVeanna S. Speaking power: Black feminist orality in women's narratives of slavery. *See* **8850**.

13480. Gable, Craig (ed.). Ebony rising: short fiction of the greater Harlem renaissance era. Bloomington: Indiana UP, 2004. pp. xlii, 552. Rev. by David Chinitz in Mod/Mod (13:2) 2006, 375–82.

13481. Gannon, Charles E. Rumors of war and infernal machines: technomilitary agenda-setting in American and British speculative fiction. (Bibl. 2005, 14142.) Rev. by Lincoln Geraghty in JAStud (39:1) 2005, 121–2.

13482. Giles, James R. The spaces of violence. Tuscaloosa; London: Alabama UP, 2006. pp. xv, 209. Rev. by James Schiff in AmBR (28:1) 2006, 13–14.

13483. Glotfelty, Cheryll. The riddle of ghost towns in the environmental imagination. WAL (41:3) 2006, 244–65.

13484. Goodheart, Eugene. Pieces of resistance. Cambridge; New York: CUP, 2005. pp. 200. (US fiction and criticism.)

13485. Gordon, Neta. Charted territory: Canadian literature by women, the genealogical plot, and SKY Lee's *Disappearing Moon Café*. *See* **17096**.

13486. Grabolle, Harro. Verdun and the Somme. Budapest: Akadémiai Kiadó, 2004. pp. 236. (Philosophiae doctores.) Rev. by Hilda D. Spear in Eng (54:210) 2005, 238–42.

13487. Greaney, Michael. Contemporary fiction and the uses of theory: the novel from structuralism to postmodernism. Basingstoke; New York: Palgrave Macmillan, 2006. pp. vii, 183.

13488. Green, Jeremy. Late postmodernism: American fiction at the millennium. (Bibl. 2005, 14150.) Rev. by Stephen J. Burn in MFS (52:1) 2006, 231–4.

13489. Gregson, Ian. Character and satire in postwar fiction. London; New York: Continuum, 2006. pp. 181. (Continuum literary studies.)

13490. Gunn, James. Inside science fiction. (Bibl. 1995, 13119.) Lanham, MD; London: Scarecrow Press, 2006. pp. viii, 251. (Second ed.: first ed. 1992.)

13491. Gunnars, Kristjana. On writing short books. WLT (78:2) 2004, 21–5.

13492. Hallissy, Margaret. Reading Irish American fiction: the hyphenated self. Basingstoke; New York: Palgrave Macmillan, 2006. pp. 211.

13493. Halliwell, Martin. Images of idiocy: the idiot figure in modern fiction and film. (Bibl. 2004, 14257.) Rev. by Susana Araújo in JAStud (39:3) 2005, 557–8.

13494. Hanna, Mary. L'écriture des anglophones blanches, de Jean Rhys à Pauline Melville. *See* **17472**.

13495. Hateley, Erica. Lady Macbeth in detective fiction: criminalizing the female reader. *See* **5932**.

13496. Hellekson, Karen; Busse, Kristina (eds). Fan fiction and fan communities in the age of the Internet: new essays. *See* **19868**.

13497. Heller, Deborah. Literary sisterhoods: imagining women artists. *See* **8648**.

13498. Hepburn, Allan. Intrigue: espionage and culture. (Bibl. 2005, 14164.) Rev. by William J. Palmer in ConLit (47:3) 2006, 497–501.

13499. —— Reading Venice. Descant (36:1) 2005, 112–22.

13500. Herald, Diana Tixier. Genreflecting: a guide to popular reading interests. Ed. by Wayne A. Wiegand. Westport, CT: Libraries Unlimited, 2006. pp. xix, 562. (Genreflecting advisory series.) (Sixth ed.: first ed. 1982.)

13501. Ho, Jennifer Ann. Consumption and identity in Asian American coming-of-age novels. (Bibl. 2005, 14168.) Rev. by Katarzyna Cwiertka in Gastronomica (6:2) 2006, 106; by George Uba in AL (78:2) 2006, 405–7.

13502. Hochman, Baruch. Character: under erasure? PartA (4:2) 2006, 91–101.

13503. Hoffman, Daniel. Returns from the grave: the spirit of Poe in contemporary fiction. *See* **11022**.

13504. Hogbin, Elizabeth; Song, Jae Jung. Patterns of relativisation in eighteenth- and twentieth-century written English narrative: a functional–typological perspective. *In* (pp. 182–208) **7255**.

13505. Honeyman, Susan. Elusive childhood: impossible representations in modern fiction. (Bibl. 2005, 14172.) Rev. by Suzanna E. Henshon in LU (30:2) 2006, 283–5; by Karen Coats in CLAQ (31:1) 2006, 87–90.

13506. Howard, June. 'Her very handwriting looks as if she owned the earth': Elizabeth Jordan and editorial power. *In* (pp. 64–76) **690**.

13507. Humphries, David T. Different dispatches: journalism in American Modernist prose. London; New York: Routledge, 2006. pp. ix, 247. (Literary criticism and cultural theory.) Rev. by Lisa Mullikin Parcell in AmJ (23:3) 2006, 118–19.

13508. Ingman, Heather. Women's spirituality in the twentieth century: an exploration through fiction. (Bibl. 2004, 14276.) Rev. by Birgit Breninger in Amst (51:3) 2006, 449–51.

13509. Irwin, John T. Unless the threat of death is behind them: hard-boiled fiction and *film noir*. Baltimore, MD; London: Johns Hopkins UP, 2006. pp. xii, 290.

13510. Joella, Ethan. In breach of story: breaking the shackles of traditional fiction. IFR (33:1/2) 2006, 38–51.

13511. Johnsen, Rosemary Erickson. Contemporary feminist historical crime fiction. Basingstoke; New York: Palgrave Macmillan, 2006. pp. xvii, 173.

13512. Johnson, Claudia Durst. Labor and workplace issues in literature. *See* **8654**.

13513. —— Youth gangs in literature. Westport, CT; London: Greenwood Press, 2004. pp. 230. (Exploring social issues through literature.) Rev. by Rachael McLennan in JAStud (39:2) 2006, 325–6.

13514. Johnson-Woods, Toni. 'Pulp' fiction industry in Australia 1949–1959. Antipodes (20:1) 2006, 63–7.

13515. —— Wonder down under: Australian sci-fi 1948–52. Extrapolation (47:1) 2006, 112–22.

13516. Jones, Suzanne W. Race mixing: Southern fiction since the sixties. (Bibl. 2004, 14283.) Rev. by Victoria Ramirez in AL (78:3) 2006, 633–5; by W. Lawrence Hogue in SoQ (44:1) 2006, 194–7.

13517. Joseph, Maia. Mass appeal(s): representations of women's public speech in suffrage literature. *See* **9295**.

13518. Kaplan, Deborah. Construction of fan fiction: character through narrative. *In* (pp. 134–53) **19868**.

13519. Kaser, James A. The Washington DC of fiction: a research guide. *See* **8658**.

13520. Kaveney, Roz. In the tradition ... *In* (pp. 162–75) **18793**.

13521. Kendrick, Christopher. Tendencies of utopia: reflections on recent work in the modern utopian tradition. CulL (9) 2006.

13522. Ketterer, David. 'Another dimension of space': Canadian science fiction and fantasy and Atwood's *Blind Assassin*. *In* (pp. 7–34) **13541**.

13523. Kevane, Bridget. Latino gospel and cultural renewal in Chicana fiction. *See* **15167**.

13524. Keyes, Flo. The literature of hope in the Middle Ages and today: connections in medieval romance, modern fantasy, and science fiction. *See* **3968**.

13525. King, Jeannette. The Victorian Woman Question in contemporary feminist fiction. (Bibl. 2005, 14192.) Rev. by Cheryl A. Wilson in TSWL (25:1) 2006, 176–7.

13526. King, Rosemary A. Border confluences: borderland narratives from the Mexican War to the present. (Bibl. 2005, 14193.) Rev. by Jeanne Campbell Reesman in AL (77:3) 2005, 644–6.

13527. Kirk, John. Figuring the landscape: writing the topographies of community and place. *See* **17045**.

13528. Knight, Mark; Woodman, Thomas (eds). Biblical religion and the novel, 1700–2000. *See* **7389**.

13529. Knight, Stephen. A hundred years of fiction. Cardiff: UP of Wales, 2004. pp. xviii, 217. (Writing Wales in English.) (CREW series of critical and scholarly studies.) Rev. by Jane Aaron in MLR (101:3) 2006, 839–40.

13530. Koloze, Jeff. An ethical analysis of the portrayal of abortion in American fiction: Dreiser, Hemingway, Faulkner, Dos Passos, Brautigan, and Irving. Lewiston, NY; Lampeter: Mellen Press, 2005. pp. vi, 375. (Studies in American literature, 78.)

13531. Kort, Wesley A. Place and space in modern fiction. (Bibl. 2005, 14194.) Rev. by Lynn Poland in JAAR (74:1) 2006, 251–3; by Peter Kalliney in Mod/Mod (13:4) 2006, 747–54.

13532. Koshy, Susan. Sexual naturalization: Asian Americans and miscegenation. (Bibl. 2005, 14195.) Rev. by George Uba in AL (78:2) 2006, 405–7.

13533. Krouse, Tonya. Freedom as effacement in *The Golden Notebook*: theorizing pleasure, subjectivity, and authority. *See* **17127**.

13534. Krupat, Arnold; Elliott, Michael A. American Indian fiction and anticolonial resistance. *In* (pp. 127–82) **11823**.

13535. Kungl, Carla T. Creating the fictional female detective: the sleuth heroines of British women writers, 1890–1940. Jefferson, NC; London: McFarland, 2006. pp. vii, 207.

13536. Lane, Richard J. The postcolonial novel. Oxford; Malden, MA: Polity Press in assn with Blackwell, 2006. pp. 146.

13537. Larbalestier, Justine (ed.). Daughters of earth: feminist science fic-tion in the twentieth century. Middletown, CT: Wesleyan UP, 2006. pp. xix, 397.

13538. Larsen, Svend-Erik. Fiction and virtual reality. *In* (pp. 255–68) **14093**.

13539. Latham, Rob. *New Worlds* and the New Wave in fandom: fan culture and the reshaping of science fiction in the sixties. Extrapolation (47:2) 2006, 296–315.

13540. LeBlanc, Edward T. The LeBlanc bibliography listings. *See* **8664**.

13541. Leroux, Jean-François; La Bossière, Camille R. (eds). Worlds of wonder: readings in Canadian science fiction and fantasy literature. Ottawa: Ottawa UP, 2004. pp. vi, 202. (Re appraisals: Canadian writers, 26.)

13542. Levitt, Morton P. The rhetoric of Modernist fiction from a new point of view. Hanover, NH; London: UP of New England, 2006. pp. xv, 200. Rev. by David Gillota in JJLS (20:2) 2006, 17.

13543. Little, Judith A. (ed.). Feminist philosophy and science fiction: utopias and dystopias. Amherst, NY: Prometheus, 2006. pp. 370.

13544. Lodge, David. The year of Henry James; or, Timing is all: the story of a novel. With other essays on the genesis, composition and reception of literary fiction. *See* **17239**.

13545. López Ropero, Mª Lourdes. Anglo-Caribbean migration novel: writing from the diaspora. Alicante: Univ. de Alicante, 2004. pp. 215. (Monografías, Univ. de Alicante.) Rev. by Bárbara Arizti in Misc (32) 2005, 129–33.

13546. McCleery, Alistair. Tauchnitz and Albatross: a 'community of interests' in English-language paperback publishing, 1934–51. Library (7:3) 2006, 297–316.

13547. MacDonald, Marianne. Harry Potter and the fan-fiction phenomenon. *See* **18350**.

13548. MacDougall, Robert. The wire devils: pulp thrillers, the telephone, and action at a distance in the wiring of a nation. *See* **17773**.

13549. McGann, Jerome. 'The grand heretics of modern fiction': Laura Riding, John Cowper Powys, and the subjective correlative. *See* **18250**.

13550. McGill, Robert. Everybody knows: community and the Canadian short story. Descant (35:2) 2004, 141–4.

13551. McHale, Brian. Cognition *en abyme*: models, manuals, maps. *See* **18561**.

13552. Madden, David. Touching the web of Southern novelists. Knoxville: Tennessee UP, 2006. pp. xii, 258.

13553. MALIK, RACHEL. The afterlife of Wilkie Collins. *In* (pp. 181–93) **9609**.

13554. MANDEL, NAOMI. Against the unspeakable: complicity, the Holocaust, and slavery in America. *See* **13044**.

13555. MANISCALCO BASILE, GIOVANNI; SUVIN, DARKO (eds). Nuovissime mappe dell'inferno: distopia oggi. (Bibl. 2004, 14325.) Rev. by Francesco Guglieri in Indice (2006:7/8), 17.

13556. MANSFIELD-KELLEY, DEANE; MARCHINO, LOIS A. (eds). The Longman anthology of detective fiction. *See* **8680**.

13557. MARKLEY, ROBERT. Dying planet: Mars in science and the imagination. (Bibl. 2005, 14219.) Rev. by Gregory Benford in NYRSF (18:7) 2006, 8–9.

13558. MARSHALL, CARMEN ROSE. Black professional women in recent American fiction. Jefferson, NC; London: McFarland, 2004. pp. viii, 219.

13559. MARTZ, JESSE. The novel. *In* (pp. 215–26) **11788**.

13560. MATTHEWS, NICOLE. Collins and the Commonwealth: publishers' publicity and the twentieth-century circulation of popular fiction titles. *In* (pp. 41–55) **746**.

13561. MELZER, PATRICIA. Alien constructions: science fiction and feminist thought. Austin: Texas UP, 2006. pp. x, 325.

13562. MILLS, KATIE. The road story and the rebel: moving through film, fiction, and television. *See* **12629**.

13563. MOHR, DUNJA M. Worlds apart: dualism and transgression in contemporary female dystopias. (Bibl. 2005, 14229.) Rev. by Sherryl Vint in JFA (16:3) 2006, 257–9.

13564. MONK, PATRICIA. Alien theory: the alien as archetype in the science fiction short story. Lanham, MD; London: Scarecrow Press, 2006. pp. xxxv, 387.

13565. MOORE, LEWIS D. Cracking the hard-boiled detective: a critical history from the 1920s to the present. Jefferson, NC; London: McFarland, 2006. pp. viii, 298.

13566. MORGAN, GWENDOLYN A. The intervention of false medieval authorities as a literary device in popular fiction: from Tolkien to *The Da Vinci Code*. Lewiston, NY; Lampeter: Mellen Press, 2006. pp. vii, 120.

13567. MOSELEY, MERRITT (ed.). Booker Prize novels, 1969–2005. Detroit, MI: Gale Research, 2006. pp. xx, 467. (Dictionary of literary biography, 326.)

13568. NAGY-ZEKMI, SILVIA (ed.). Paradoxical citizenship: Edward Said. *See* **14238**.

13569. NAJITA, SUSAN Y. Decolonizing cultures in the Pacific: reading history and trauma in contemporary fiction. London; New York: Routledge, 2006. pp. xviii, 236. (Routledge research in postcolonial literatures, 14.)

13570. NEWITZ, ANNALEE. Pretend we're dead: capitalist monsters in American pop culture. Durham, NC; London: Duke UP, 2006. pp. viii, 223. Rev. by Roz Kaveney in TLS, 21 July 2006, 33.

13571. PAES DE BARROS, DEBORAH. Fast cars and bad girls: nomadic subjects and women's road stories. (Bibl. 2005, 14243.) Rev. by Stephanie LeMenager in WAL (41:2) 2006, 216–17; by Maureen Reed in Amst (51:2) 2006, 244–6.

13572. Palmer, Christopher. Big Dumb Objects in science fiction: sublimity, banality, and modernity. Extrapolation (47:1) 2006, 95–111.

13573. Panek, LeRoy L. Thoughts about the beginning of the detective story in America. BSJ (56:2) 2006, 17–24.

13574. Panek, LeRoy Lad. The origins of the American detective story. *See* **8694**.

13575. Parkin-Gounelas, Ruth. The insistence of the object – and its sublimations. Gramma (14) 2006, 141–59.

13576. Pepper, Andrew. State power matters: power, the State and political struggle in the post-war American novel. *See* **14960**.

13577. Petty, Leslie. Romancing the vote: feminist activism in American fiction, 1870–1920. *See* **8698**.

13578. Phelan, James. Living to tell about it: a rhetoric and ethics of character narration. (Bibl. 2005, 14253.) Rev. by Janis McLarren Caldwell in StudN (38:3) 2006, 377–9.

13579. Philips, Deborah. Women's fiction 1945–2005: writing romance. London; New York: Continuum, 2006. pp. 162. (Continuum literary studies.) Rev. by Lucy Carlyle in TLS, 11 Aug. 2006, 31.

13580. Phillips, Lawrence. London narratives: post-war fiction and the city. London; New York: Continuum, 2006. pp. 174. (Continuum literary studies.)

13581. Pollock, Mary S.; Rainwater, Catherine (eds). Figuring animals: essays on animal images in art, literature, philosophy, and popular culture. (Bibl. 2005, 14258.) Rev. by Frank Palmeri in CLIO (35:3) 2006, 407–20.

13582. Posman, Sarah. A Bakhtinian perspective on lesbian crime writing. *See* **15950**.

13583. Price, Leah; Thurschwell, Pamela (eds). Literary secretaries/ secretarial culture. *See* **8700**.

13584. Primorac, Ranka. The place of tears: the novel and politics in modern Zimbabwe. London; New York: Tauris Academic Studies, 2006. pp. viii, 241.

13585. Randolph, Ladette (ed.). A different plain: contemporary Nebraska fiction writers. Introd. by Mary Pipher. Lincoln; London: Nebraska UP, 2004. pp. xv, 398. Rev. by Becky Faber in WAL (41:1) 2006, 84.

13586. Reeds, Kenneth. Magical realism: a problem of definition. Neophilologus (90:2) 2006, 175–96.

13587. Richards, Gary. Lovers and beloveds: sexual otherness in Southern fiction, 1936–1961. (Bibl. 2005, 14262.) Rev. by Martyn Bone in SoLJ (39:1) 2006, 119–27.

13588. Richardson, Brian. Unnatural voices: extreme narration in modern and contemporary fiction. Columbus: Ohio State UP, 2006. pp. xiii, 166.

13589. Richler, Noah. This is my country, what's yours? A literary atlas of Canada. Toronto: McClelland & Stewart, 2006. pp. 476. Rev. by Clara Thomas in BkCan (35:9) 2006, 8–9.

13590. Riggs, Pádraigín; Vance, Norman. Irish prose fiction. *In* (pp. 245–66) **11829**.

13591. Rio, David. Nevada's non-Anglo European immigrants and their interpreters in contemporary American fiction. Anglophonia (19) 2006, 45–54.

13592. Roberts, Adam. Science fiction. (Bibl. 2001, 8196.) London; New York: Routledge, 2006. pp. vi, 159. (New critical idiom.) (Second ed.: first ed. 2000.)

13593. Rogers, Jane, *et al.* (eds). Good fiction guide. Oxford; New York: OUP, 2005. pp. 520. (Second ed.: first ed. 2001.)

13594. Rosenberg, Leah. Modern romances: the short stories in Una Marson's *The Cosmopolitan* (1928–1931). *See* **17453**.

13595. Saguaro, Shelley. Garden plots: the politics and poetics of gardens. Aldershot; Burlington, VT: Ashgate, 2006. pp. xiii, 249.

13596. Scambray, Kenneth. Queen Calafia's paradise: California and the Italian American novel. Madison, NJ: Fairleigh Dickinson UP, 2006. pp. 211.

13597. Scatasta, Gino. Where was Jack the Ripper? Urban space in the British [true (crime] novel). *In* (pp. 137–48) **3307**.

13598. Schuman, Lydia C. The Edward T. LeBlanc bibliography of story papers, dime novels, and libraries. *See* **8713**.

13599. Scott, A. O. In search of the best: what is the best work of American fiction published in the past 25 years? NYTB, 21 May 2006, 16–19.

13600. Seed, David. Brainwashing: the fictions of mind control: a study of novels and films since World War II. (Bibl. 2005, 14273.) Rev. by Peter Knight in JAStud (40:2) 2006, 449–50.

13601. Seshagiri, Urmila. Modernist ashes, postcolonial phoenix: Jean Rhys and the evolution of the English novel in the twentieth century. *See* **18229**.

13602. Shaffer, Brian W. Reading the novel in English, 1950–2000. Oxford; Malden, MA: Blackwell, 2006. pp. x, 264. (Reading the novel.)

13603. —— (ed.). A companion to the British and Irish novel 1945–2000. Oxford; Malden, MA: Blackwell, 2005. pp. xix, 583. (Blackwell companions to literature and culture, 28.) Rev. by Bharat Tandon in TLS, 25 Feb. 2005, 30.

13604. Showalter, Elaine. Faculty towers: the academic novel and its discontents. (Bibl. 2005, 14275.) Rev. by Vivienne M. Anderson in ColLit (33:3) 2006, 205–7; by Alan T. McKenzie in MFS (52:3) 2006, 757–9; by Stephen Wade in ContRev (288:1682) 2006, 376–7.

13605. Shupak, Greg. *Decline and Fall* as a critique of Marxism. EWN (36:2) 2005.

13606. Sicher, Efraim (ed.). Holocaust novelists. (Bibl. 2004, 14379.) Rev. by Lucie Benchouiha in MLR (101:2) 2006, 509–10.

13607. —— Skradol, Natalia. A world neither brave nor new: reading dystopian fiction after 9/11. PartA (4:1) 2006, 151–79.

13608. Simpson, Hyacinth M. Bibliography of anglophone West Indian short stories. *See* **8714**.

13609. —— Patterns and periods: oral aesthetics and a century of Jamaican short story writing. JWIL (12:1/2) 2004, 1–30.

13610. Simpson, Paul. The Rough Guide to cult fiction. London: Haymarket, 2005. pp. 363. (Rough Guides.) Rev. by Chris Tayler in TLS, 8 Apr. 2005, 33.

13611. Smith, Eric D. A voyage to future pasts: the vengeance of other time in Ronald Wright's *A Scientific Romance*. *See* **19388**.

13612. Spaulding, A. Timothy. Re-forming the past: history, the fantastic, and the postmodern slave narrative. (Bibl. 2005, 14280.) Rev. by Sherryl Vint in Extrapolation (47:2) 2006, 316–21.

13613. Spencer, Nicholas. After utopia: the rise of critical space in twentieth-century American fiction. Lincoln; London: Nebraska UP, 2006. pp. 271.

13614. Spurgeon, Sara L. Exploding the western: myths of empire on the postmodern frontier. (Bibl. 2005, 14281.) Rev. by Blake Allmendinger in PacHR (75:2) 2006, 328–9.

13615. Spurlock, J. David (comp.). Grand master of adventure: the drawings of J. Allen St John. *See* **112**.

13616. Squier, Susan Merrill. Liminal lives: imagining the human at the frontiers of biomedicine. (Bibl. 2005, 14282.) Rev. by Bernice L. Hausman in AL (78:3) 2006, 659–62.

13617. Stasi, Mafalda. The toy soldiers from Leeds: the slash palimpsest. *In* (pp. 115–33) **19868**.

13618. Staunton, Irene (ed.). Writing now: more stories from Zimbabwe. Harare: Weaver Press, 2005. pp. 306. Rev. by James Gibbs in WLT (80:6) 2006, 70.

13619. Stein, Mark. Black British literature: novels of transformation. (Bibl. 2005, 14286.) Rev. by Matthew Mead in JPW (42:1) 2006, 119–21.

13620. Storey, Michael L. Representing the Troubles in Irish short fiction. (Bibl. 2004, 14389.) Rev. by William F. Martin in NewHR (10:3) 2006, 156–7.

13621. Stripling, Mahala Yates. Bioethics and medical issues in literature. *See* **8716**.

13622. Su, John J. Ethics and nostalgia in the contemporary novel. Cambridge; New York: CUP, 2005. pp. vii, 226. Rev. by Jennifer Delisle in DalR (86:3) 2006, 474–5.

13623. Sullivan, C. W., iii. Robert A. Heinlein: reinventing series SF in the 1950s. *See* **16329**.

13624. Sullivan, Joanna. Redefining the novel in Africa. RAL (37:4) 2006, 177–88.

13625. Sundquist, Eric. Dry bones. *In* (pp. 217–30) **15746**.

13626. Tatsumi, Takayuki. Full metal Apache: transactions between cyberpunk Japan and avant-pop America. Durham, NC; London: Duke UP, 2006. pp. xxvi, 241. Rev. by Ryan Smith in AmBR (28:1) 2006, 10–11.

13627. Tew, Philip. The contemporary British novel. (Bibl. 2004, 14396.) Rev. by Adriana Neagu in Eng (55:212) 2006, 229–32.

13628. Thielmann, Pia. Hotbeds: Black–White love in novels from the United States, Africa, and the Caribbean. Zomba, Malawi: Kachere, 2004. pp. 384. (Kachere monographs, 19.) Rev. by Katrin Berndt in RAL (37:1) 2006, 157–8.

13629. Tolchin, Karen R. Part blood, part ketchup: coming of age in American literature and film. Lanham, MD: Lexington, 2006. pp. xi, 127.

13630. Trayiannoudi, Litsa. London, New Haven, Gloucester: aggregations of diversity / dispersed centers. *In* (pp. 31–44) **3307**.

13631. Vambe, Maurice Taonezvi. African oral story-telling tradition and the Zimbabwean novel in English. Pretoria: Unisa Press, 2004. pp. vii, 130. Rev. by Flora Veit-Wild in RAL (37:3) 2006, 193–204.

13632. Walkowitz, Rebecca L. Cosmopolitan style: Modernism beyond the nation. New York: Columbia UP, 2006. pp. xiii, 231.

13633. Wall, Cheryl A. Worrying the line: Black women writers, lineage, and literary tradition. (Bibl. 2005, 14297.) Rev. by Kathryne V. Lindberg in JAH (92:4) 2006, 1515–16; by Carol E. Henderson in MFS (52:1) 2006, 217–21; by Susan Belasco in AL (78:3) 2006, 640–2.

13634. Weinstein, Philip. Unknowing: the work of Modernist fiction. (Bibl. 2005, 14305.) Rev. by Edwin J. Barton in AL (78:4) 2006, 874–6; by Maria DiBattista in Novel (39:2) 2006, 280–3.

13635. Weiss, Allan. The Canadian apocalypse. *In* (pp. 35–45) **13541**.

13636. Weliver, Phyllis. The musical crowd in English fiction, 1840–1910: class, culture and nation. *See* **8729**.

13637. Wendland, Albert. The universe in a frame: the domestic sublime in *Adam Strange* and fifties SF. Extrapolation (47:2) 2006, 237–48.

13638. Wetherell, Rodney. Subtopia or Sunnyside? *See* **19898**.

13639. Whelehan, Imelda. The feminist bestseller: from *Sex and the Single Girl* to *Sex and the City*. Basingstoke; New York: Palgrave Macmillan, 2005. pp. viii, 236.

13640. Whyte, Iain Boyd. Anglo-German conflict in popular fiction, 1870–1914. *In* (pp. 43–99) **11790**.

13641. Wilhelmus, Tom. Ah, England. HR (59:2) 2006, 345–51. (Contemporary fiction.)

13642. Williams, Peter. Strange affinities: representation and affect in Australian POW drama. *See* **12807**.

13643. Willis, Elizabeth. English detective fiction and the 'People's War'. FMLS (42:1) 2006, 13–21.

13644. Wilson, Charles E., Jr. Race and racism in literature. Westport, CT; London: Greenwood Press, 2005. pp. xviii, 154. (Exploring social issues through literature.)

13645. Winthrop-Young, Geoffrey. The Third Reich in alternate history: aspects of a genre-specific depiction of Nazi culture. JPC (39:5) 2006, 878–96.

13646. Woledge, Elizabeth. Intimatopia: genre intersections between slash and the mainstream. *In* (pp. 97–114) **19868**.

13647. Wolff, Ellen M. An anarchy in the mind and in the heart: narrating Anglo-Ireland. Lewisburg, PA: Bucknell UP, 2005. pp. 236.

13648. Wollaeger, Mark. Modernism, media, and propaganda: British narrative from 1900 to 1945. Princeton, NJ; Oxford: Princeton UP, 2006. pp. xxv, 335.

13649. Wong, Mitali P.; Hasan, Zia. The fiction of South Asians in North America and the Caribbean: a critical study of English-language works since 1950. (Bibl. 2005, 14314.) Rev. by Crystal Parikh in AL (78:1) 2006, 192–4.

13650. Wyatt, Jean. Risking difference: identification, race, and community in contemporary fiction and feminism. (Bibl. 2005, 14316.) Rev. by Jennifer Williams in AL (77:2) 2005, 430–2.

13651. Yaszek, Lisa. From *Ladies Home Journal* to *The Magazine of Fantasy and Science Fiction*: 1950s SF, the offbeat romance story, and the case of Alice Eleanor Jones. *In* (pp. 76–96) **13537**.

13652. Young, Hershini Bhana. Haunting capital: memory, text and the Black diasporic body. Hanover, NH; London: UP of New England, 2005. pp. ix, 235. (Reencounters with colonialism: new perspectives on the Americas.)

13653. Yuen, Wong Kin; Westfahl, Gary; Chan, Amy Kit-Sze (eds). World weavers: globalization, science fiction, and the cybernetic revolution. Hong Kong: Hong Kong UP, 2005. pp. xi, 307. Rev. by Donald M. Hassler in Extrapolation (47:1) 2006, 168–70.

13654. Zackodnik, Teresa C. The mulatta and the politics of race. (Bibl. 2005, 14321.) Rev. by Cherene Sherrard-Johnson in Legacy (23:2) 2006, 206–7; by Jené Schoenfeld in AL (78:4) 2006, 887–9.

13655. Zimmerman, David Andrew. Panic! Markets, crises & crowds in American fiction. *See* **8735**.

13656. Zucker, David J. Women rabbis: a novel idea. JudQ (55:1/2) 2006, 109–16.

LITERATURE FOR CHILDREN

13657. Clark, Dorothy G. Hyperread: children's literature, CD-ROMs, and the new literacy. *See* **19779**.

13658. Cohoon, Lorinda B. Serialized citizenships: periodicals, books, and American boys, 1840–1911. *See* **1073**.

13659. Cosslett, Tess. Talking animals in British children's fiction, 1786–1914. *See* **8739**.

13660. de Manuel, Dolores; Davis, Rocío G. Editors' introduction: critical perspectives on Asian American children's literature. LU (30:2) 2006, v–xv.

13661. Dizer, John T. American children's literature, 1890–1940: heroic tales that shaped adult lives. Lewiston, NY; Lampeter: Mellen Press, 2005. pp. xxi, 260, (plates) 20. Rev. by J. Randolph Cox in DNR (75:5) 2006, 151–2.

13662. Donelson, Kenneth L.; Nilsen, Alleen Pace. Literature for today's young adults. *See* **19905**.

13663. Doughty, Annie A. Folktales retold: a critical overview of stories updated for children. Jefferson, NC; London: McFarland, 2006. pp. xiii, 205. Rev. by Susan Louise Stewart in CLAQ (31:3) 2006, 307–9.

13664. Doughty, Terri (ed.). Selections from *The Girl's Own Paper*, 1880–1907. *See* **1087**.

13665. Eddy, Jacalyn. Bookwomen: creating an empire in children's book publishing, 1919–1939. *See* **699**.

13666. Erisman, Fred. Boys' books, boys' dreams, and the mystique of flight. Fort Worth: Texas Christian UP, 2006. pp. xx, 346.

13667. Gebel, Doris (ed.). Crossing boundaries with children's books. Lanham, MD; London: Scarecrow Press, 2006. pp. xiv, 431.

13668. Graham, Kathryn V. The Devil's own art: topiary in children's fiction. ChildLit (33) 2005, 94–114.

13669. Hamilton, Margaret. The ABC book of Australian children's illustrators. *See* **66**.

13670. Hatfield, Charles. Comic art, children's literature, and the new comics studies. *See* **69**.

13671. Hoffman, A. Robin. Socialization and saying 'Cheese!': School Picture Day in children's books. CLAQ (31:4) 2006, 313–31.

13672. Hoffman, Tyler. John Brown and children's literature. *In* (pp. 187–202) **8537**.

13673. Honeyman, Susan. Manufactured agency and the playthings who dream it for us. CLAQ (31:2) 2006, 109–31.

13674. Johnson, Joanna Webb. Chick Lit Jr: more than glitz and glamour for teens and tweens. *In* (pp. 141–57) **19862**.

13675. Jones, Katharine. Getting rid of children's literature. LU (30:3) 2006, 287–315.

13676. Kidd, Kenneth. 'A' is for Auschwitz: psychoanalysis, trauma theory, and the 'children's literature of atrocity'. ChildLit (33) 2005, 120–49.

13677. Kokkola, Lydia. Representing the Holocaust in children's literature. (Bibl. 2003, 14204.) Rev. by Naomi Sokoloff in LU (30:1) 2006, 139–43.

13678. Latrobe, Kathy Howard. Ten English authors for young adults. WLT (79:1) 2005, 69–72.

13679. Leeper, Angela. Poetry in literature for youth. Lanham, MD; London: Scarecrow Press, 2006. pp. xi, 303. (Literature for youth, 8.)

13680. MacCann, Donnarae. The sturdy fabric of cultural imperialism: tracing its patterns in contemporary children's novels. *See* **20231**.

13681. McMinn, Jamie; Pickrell, H. Alan. The many faces of childhood: costume and ritualized behavior. *In* (pp. 215–31) **3157**.

13682. Mickenberg, Julia L. Learning from the Left: children's literature, the Cold War, and radical politics in the United States. Oxford; New York: OUP, 2006. pp. xi, 389. Rev. by Gary D. Schmidt in LU (30:3) 2006, 422–6.

13683. Nelson, Claudia. Writing the reader: the literary child in and beyond the book. CLAQ (31:3) 2006, 222–36.

13684. Overstreet, Deborah Wilson. Not your mother's vampire: vampires in young adult fiction. Lanham, MD; London: Scarecrow Press, 2006. pp. 163.

13685. Saltman, Judith. The ordinary and the fabulous: Canadian fantasy literature for children. *In* (pp. 189–200) **13541**.

13686. —— Edwards, Gail. Towards a history of design in Canadian children's illustrated books. Amphora (142) 2006, 4–14.

13687. Seale, Doris; Slapin, Beverly (eds). A broken flute: the Native experience in books for children. Walnut Creek, CA: AltaMira Press; Berkeley,

CA: Oyate, 2005. pp. x, 463. (Contemporary Native American communities, 14.) Rev. by Jaye T. Darby in AICRJ (30:2) 2006, 145–8.

13688. SMITH, KATHARINE CAPSHAW. Children's literature of the Harlem renaissance. (Bibl. 2005, 14354.) Rev. by Fern Kory in ChildLit (33) 2005, 258–62; by Michelle H. Martin in JAAH (91:3) 2006, 348–50; by the same in CLAQ (31:1) 2006, 102–5.

13689. SOLOMON, DEBORAH. The stuff of fiction. NYTM, 9 Apr. 2006, 17.

13690. THOMPSON, MARY SHINE; KEENAN, CELIA (eds). Treasure islands: studies in children's literature. *See* **8753**.

13691. THONGTHIRAJ, RAHPEE. Negotiated identities and female personal space in Thai American adolescent literature. LU (30:2) 2006, 234–49.

POETRY

13692. ADAMS, SAM. Letter from Wales. PNRev (31:6) 2005, 8–9.

13693. —— Seren at twenty-five. *See* **634**.

13694. ADAMS, TERRI M.; FULLER, DOUGLAS B. The words have changed but the ideology remains the same: misogynistic lyrics in rap music. JBlaS (36:6) 2006, 938–57.

13695. ALTIERI, CHARLES. The art of twentieth-century American poetry: Modernism and after. Oxford; Malden, MA: Blackwell, 2006. pp. xi, 245. (Blackwell introductions to literature.)

13696. ASHTON, JENNIFER. From Modernism to postmodernism: American poetry and theory in the twentieth century. Cambridge; New York: CUP, 2005. pp. x, 201. (Cambridge studies in American literature and culture, 149.)

13697. AXELROD, STEVEN GOULD; ROMAN, CAMILLE; TRAVISANO, THOMAS (eds). The new anthology of American poetry: vol. 2, Modernisms, 1900–1950. New Brunswick, NJ; London: Rutgers UP, 2005. pp. xxxv, 819. Rev. by Cheri Colby Langdell in PCP (41) 2006, 150–3.

13698. BAER, WILLIAM. Fourteen on form: conversations with poets. (Bibl. 2004, 14496.) Rev. by Jeff Gundy in GaR (60:1) 2006, 243–7.

13699. BAKER, ROBERT. The extravagant: crossings of modern poetry and modern philosophy. (Bibl. 2005, 14364.) Rev. by Jeff Gundy in GaR (60:2) 2006, 423–33.

13700. BALL, MARTIN. Pro patria mori. Meanjin (63:3) 2004, 3–12.

13701. BANG, MARY JO. I.E., on Emily & influence. *See* **9847**.

13702. BARR, JOHN. American poetry in the new century. *See* **19915**.

13703. BELLARSI, FRANCA. 'Poetry of suburbia where art thou?' EtCan (60) 2006, 119–37.

13704. BERTRAM, VICKI. Gendering poetry: contemporary women and men poets. London: Pandora, 2005. pp. ix, 246. Rev. by Kate Clanchy in PNRev (32:1) 2005, 43–5.

13705. BLAESER, KIMBERLY M. Canons and canonization: American Indian poetics through autonomy, colonization, nationalism, and decolonization. *In* (pp. 183–287) **11823**.

13706. Boruch, Marianne. In the blue pharmacy: essays on poetry and other transformations. (Bibl. 2005, 14369.) Rev. by Ashley Brown in WLT (80:3) 2006, 76–7; by Claire Keyes in GaR (60:1) 2006, 255–6.

13707. Brennan, Michael. 'A moment along the way': a venture in publishing Australian poetry. Southerly (65:1) 2005, 105–14.

13708. Bridges, James. The Georgians and their England. IGSJ (10) 2004, 49–68.

13709. Brinton, Ian. Black Mountain in England: 1. *See* **16994**.

13710. —— Black Mountain in England: 2. *See* **18857**.

13711. —— Black Mountain in England: 3. *See* **18847**.

13712. —— Black Mountain in England: 4. *See* **15371**.

13713. Brooks, David. The Australian line. Agenda (41:1/2) 2005, 11–21.

13714. Broom, Sarah. Contemporary British and Irish poetry: an introduction. Basingstoke; New York: Palgrave Macmillan, 2006. pp. x, 278. Rev. by Barry Wood in PNRev (33:1) 2006, 75–6.

13715. Buckley, Christopher. The poet on the poem. *See* **14897**.

13716. Buffington, Robert. Campaigning for poetry. *See* **18727**.

13717. Burnell, Jocelyn Bell. Astronomy and poetry. *In* (pp. 125–40) **13732**.

13718. Burnside, John. Mind the gap: on reading American poetry. PRev (96:3) 2006, 56–67.

13719. Butling, Pauline; Rudy, Susan. Writing in our time: Canada's radical poetries in English (1957–2003). (Bibl. 2005, 14374.) Rev. by Danielle Fournier in Topia (15) 2006, 150–2; by Kit Dobson in CanL (190) 2006, 117–18.

13720. —— —— (eds). Poets talk: conversations with Robert Kroetsch, Daphne Marlatt, Erin Mouré, Dionne Brand, Marie Annharte Baker, Jeff Derksen, and Fred Wah. Edmonton: Alberta UP, 2005. pp. xvii, 197. Rev. by Tanis MacDonald in CanL (190) 2006, 110–11; by Alison Calder in GPQ (26:3) 2006, 221–2.

13721. Caplan, David. Questions of possibility: contemporary poetry and poetic form. (Bibl. 2005, 14379.) Rev. by Willard Spiegelman in Mod/Mod (13:3) 2006, 597–9.

13722. Churchill, Suzanne W. The little magazine *Others* and the renovation of modern American poetry. Aldershot; Burlington, VT: Ashgate, 2006. pp. xii, 290.

13723. Clanchy, Kate. Gendering poetry. PNRev (32:1) 2005, 43–5 (review-article).

13724. Clark, Heather. The Ulster renaissance: poetry in Belfast, 1962–1972. Oxford; New York: OUP, 2006. pp. viii, 245.

13725. Clark, Jim. 'Unto all generations of the faithful heart': Donald Davidson, the Vanderbilt Agrarians, and Appalachian poetry. *See* **15420**.

13726. Clark, Steve; Ford, Mark (eds). Something we have that they don't: British and American poetic relations since 1925. (Bibl. 2005, 14381.) Rev. by David C. Ward in PNRev (31:3) 2005, 52–5.

13727. Clarke, George Elliott. Anna Minerva Henderson: an Afro New Brunswick response to Canadian (Modernist) poetry. *See* **16404**.

13728. Clausson, Nils. 'Perpetuating the language': Romantic tradition, the genre function, and the origins of the trench lyric. JML (30:1) 2006, 104–28.

13729. Clippinger, David. The mind's landscape: William Bronk and twentieth-century American poetry. *See* **14865**.

13730. Corballis, Richard. Zealandia among the poets: a sesquicentennial tribute. *In* (pp. 331–48) **8374**.

13731. Cowan, T. L. Punk rock clit lit: reading toward a punk poetics in *Bent on Writing: Contemporary Queer Tales*. *See* **19923**.

13732. Crawford, Robert (ed.). Contemporary poetry and contemporary science. Oxford; New York: OUP, 2006. pp. xvi, 234.

13733. Critchley, Simon. Surfaciality: some poems by Fernando Pessoa, one by Wallace Stevens, and the brief sketch of a poetic ontology. *See* **18631**.

13734. Davidson, Michael. Guys like us: citing masculinity in Cold War poetics. (Bibl. 2004, 14518.) Rev. by Eric Schocket in AL (77:2) 2005, 424–6.

13735. Davies, Damian Walford; Turley, Richard Marggraf (eds). The monstrous debt: modalities of Romantic influence in twentieth-century literature. Foreword by Lucy Newlyn. Detroit, MI: Wayne State UP, 2006. pp. xv, 247.

13736. Del Mercato, Barbara. La poesia tra comunità e istituzione: il caso di Toronto. *In* (pp. 137–58) **11808**.

13737. Dennis, Oliver. City limits. Meanjin (65:2) 2006, 87–91. (Australian poetry.)

13738. Donoghue, Denis. Contemporary poetry: keeping the conversation going. PNRev (31:6) 2005, 16–21.

13739. DuPlessis, Rachel Blau. Blue studios: poetry and its cultural work. Tuscaloosa; London: Alabama UP, 2006. pp. x, 302. (Modern and contemporary poetics.)

13740. Emeny, Richard (sel. and introd.). Edward Thomas on the Georgians. *See* **18746**.

13741. Entwistle, Alice. Plath and contemporary British poetry. *In* (pp. 63–70) **18038**.

13742. Epstein, Andrew. Beautiful enemies: friendship and postwar American poetry. Oxford; New York: OUP, 2006. pp. xvi, 359.

13743. Fischer, Barbara K. Museum mediations: reframing ekphrasis in contemporary American poetry. London; New York: Routledge, 2006. pp. xiv, 228. (Literary criticism and cultural theory.)

13744. Fletcher, Angus. A new theory for American poetry: democracy, the environment, and the future of imagination. (Bibl. 2005, 14394.) Rev. by Victoria N. Alexander in Style (39:4) 2005, 501–5; by Stephen Yenser in AmLH (17:4) 2005, 856–68.

13745. Ford, Mark. A driftwood altar: essays and reviews. Introd. by Nick Everett. London; Baltimore, MD: Waywiser, 2005. pp. 304. Rev. by Michael Peverett in PNRev (32:5) 2006, 77–8.

13746. —— WINKFIELD, TREVOR (eds). The New York Poets II: an anthology. Manchester: Carcanet Press, 2006. pp. xvi, 216. Rev. by John Redmond in TLS, 8 Sept. 2006, 22–3.

13747. FRIEDLANDER, BENJAMIN. Simulcast: four experiments in criticism. (Bibl. 2004, 14535.) Rev. by V. Nicholas LoLordo in AmBR (27:5) 2006, 7–8.

13748. FROST, ELISABETH A.; HOGUE, CYNTHIA (eds). Innovative women poets: an anthology of contemporary poetry and interviews. Iowa City: Iowa UP, 2006. pp. xv, 424.

13749. GABBIN, JOANNE V. (ed.). Furious flower: African American poetry from the Black Arts Movement to the present. Charlottesville; London: Virginia UP, 2004. pp. 318. Rev. by Jan Wesley in PInt (10) 2006, 167–70.

13750. GIBBONS, REGINALD. This working against the grain. *See* **16076**.

13751. GILBERT, ALAN. Another future: poetry and art in a postmodern twilight. Middletown, CT: Wesleyan UP, 2006. pp. vi, 263. Rev. by Elisabeth A. Frost in AmBR (28:1) 2006, 14–15.

13752. GILBERT, SANDRA M. 'The words are purposes'; or, Why dither about diction? MichQR (45:2) 2006, 307–15.

13753. GILLIS, ALAN A. Irish poetry of the 1930s. Oxford; New York: OUP, 2005. pp. viii, 228. Rev. by Dillon Johnston in ILS (26:1) 2006, 14.

13754. GINGELL, SUSAN. 'Always a poem, once a book': motivations and strategies for print textualizing of Caribbean Canadian dub and performance poetry. JWIL (14:1/2) 2005, 220–59.

13755. GIOIA, DANA; YOST, CHRYSS; HICKS, JACK (eds). California poetry: from the Gold Rush to the present. *See* **8777**.

13756. GRAY, JEFFREY. Mastery's end: travel and postwar American poetry. (Bibl. 2005, 14401.) Rev. by Juliana Spahr in AL (78:2) 2006, 397–8; by Ann Keniston in ConLit (47:3) 2006, 483–90.

13757. GREINER, DONALD J. (ed.). Classes on modern poetry and the art of poetry. Foreword by Pat Conroy. Columbia; London: South Carolina UP, 2004. pp. xxxv, 310. Rev. by Susan Meyers in SoCR (38:1) 2005, 251–3.

13758. GRIFFITHS, JANE. Alice and Freda. TLS, 19 May 2006, 5 (review-article). (Women poets.)

13759. GUBAR, SUSAN. The importance of canonization: a response to Jay Ladin. MichQR (45:2) 2006, 316–21.

13760. GUINNESS, SELINA (ed.). The new Irish poets. *See* **19929**.

13761. GUNDY, JEFF. Form and range. GaR (60:1) 2006, 243–7 (review-article).

13762. GWYNN, R. S. Haunted palaces, trembling strings. *See* **11018**.

13763. HARALSON, ERIC (ed.). Reading the Middle Generation anew: culture, community, and form in twentieth-century American poetry. Iowa City: Iowa UP, 2006. pp. viii, 264.

13764. HART, JONATHAN. Poetry in the age of theory and technology. *In* (pp. 175–88) **14093**.

13765. HARTMAN, STEPHANIE. Reading the scar in breast cancer poetry. FemSt (30:1) 2004, 155–77.

13766. Hass, Robert Bernard. (Re) reading Bergson: Frost, Pound and the legacy of modern poetry. *See* **16005**.

13767. Heiss, Anita. Black poetics. Meanjin (65:1) 2006, 180–91. (Australian Aboriginal poetry and politics.)

13768. Herbert, W. N. Testament and confessions of an informationist. *In* (pp. 72–87) **13732**.

13769. Hill, Jane. Fucked Ivanhoes in the deep obsession of memory: Andrew Hudgins, David Bottoms, and the legacy of war in Southern poetry. *See* **16478**.

13770. Hinds, Michael; Matterson, Stephen (eds). Rebound: the American poetry book. Amsterdam: New York: Rodopi, 2004. pp. 208. (Textxet, 44.)

13771. Hopps, Gavin; Stabler, Jane (eds). Romanticism and religion from William Cowper to Wallace Stevens. *See* **8789**.

13772. House, Gloria; Weatherston, Rosemary; Ward, Albert M. (eds). A different image: the legacy of Broadside Press: an anthology. Detroit, MI: Univ. of Detroit Mercy Press / Broadside Press, 2004. pp. 285; 1 CD-ROM. Rev. by George Bornstein in MichQR (45:4) 2006, 713–21.

13773. Howarth, Peter. The battle for centre ground. *See* **17970**.

13774. —— British poetry in the age of Modernism. Cambridge; New York: CUP, 2005. pp. ix, 224. Rev. by Steven Matthews in RES (57:231) 2006, 548–9.

13775. Hu, Shaohua. Wen Yiduo's poems and modern British and American poems. FLS (119) 2006, 149–55. (In Chinese.)

13776. Huber, Patrick. 'A blessing to people': Dorsey Dixon and his sacred mission of song. SoCult (12:4) 2006, 111–31.

13777. Hummer, T. R. The muse in the machine: essays on poetry and the anatomy of the body politic. Athens; London: Georgia UP, 2006. pp. viii, 214. (Life of poetry.)

13778. Hunter, Aislinn. Get the poem outdoors. Arc (54) 2005, 18–23.

13779. Izenberg, Oren. Oppen's silence, Crusoe's silence, and the silence of other minds. *See* **17906**.

13780. Jackson, Bruce. Get your ass in the water and swim like me: African American narrative poetry from oral tradition. London; New York: Routledge, 2004. pp. xvi, 244; 1 audio CD. Rev. by Valerie F. Kinloch in JAAH (91:2) 2006, 236–8.

13781. Jenkins, Lee M. The language of Caribbean poetry: boundaries of expression. (Bibl. 2005, 14423.) Rev. by Mark McMorris in ConLit (47:3) 2006, 505–22.

13782. Jenness, David; Velsey, Don. Classic American popular song: the second half-century, 1950–2000. London; New York: Routledge, 2006. pp. xx, 385. Rev. by Andrew Milner in SondR (12:3) 2006, 40; by Robert W. Miles in SewR (114:4) 2006, lxxix–lxxxi.

13783. Kalaidjian, Walter. The edge of Modernism: American poetry and the traumatic past. Baltimore, MD; London: Johns Hopkins UP, 2006. pp. x, 239.

13784. Kane, Daniel (ed.). Don't ever get famous: essays on New York writing after the New York School. Normal, IL: Dalkey Archive Press, 2006. pp. xix, 399.

13785. Keery, James. *The Burning Baby* and the bathwater: 1, 'Black magic bubblings'; 2, 'The second death'; 3, 'Thomas's malign influence'; 4, 'Legislating for the millennium'; 5, 'The new bible of Belsen'; 6, 'Punch-drunk "romantic" scribblers'. *See* **18743**.

13786. —— The *Burning Baby* and the bathwater: 9, 'Muddying inclusivity'. PNRev (30:4) 2004, 40–2.

13787. —— The *Burning Baby* and the bathwater: 12, 'The originating hand'. *See* **15326**.

13788. Kendall, Tim. Modern English war poetry. Oxford; New York: OUP, 2006. pp. 276.

13789. Kent, Alan M. (ed.). The dreamt sea: an anthology of Anglo-Cornish poetry, 1928–2004. Foreword by John Hurst. London: Boutle, 2004. pp. 218. Rev. by John Greening in TLS, 25 Feb. 2005, 30.

13790. Kimberley, Emma. Textual implications of ekphrasis in contemporary poetry. *In* (pp. 89–99) **3407**.

13791. Kirsch, Adam, *et al.* Ambition and greatness: an exchange. Poetry (185:6) 2005, 445–53.

13792. Krysl, Marilyn. Sacred and profane: the sestina as rite. APR (33:2) 2004, 7–12.

13793. Kvidera, Peter. Resonant presence: legal narratives and literary space in the poetry of early Chinese immigrants. AL (77:3) 2005, 511–39.

13794. Ladin, Jay. 'After the end of the world': poetry and the Holocaust. MichQR (45:2) 2006, 284–306.

13795. Lent, John. Wilfred Watson and the shift from modern to postmodern forms in Canadian poetry. *See* **18988**.

13796. Leonard, Keith D. Fettered genius: the African American bardic poet from slavery to Civil Rights. *See* **8795**.

13797. Levin, Dana. The heroics of style: a study in three parts. *See* **19938**.

13798. Loffredo, Eugenia; Perteghella, Manuela (eds). Translation and creativity: perspectives on creative writing and Translation Studies. *See* **2874**.

13799. Longley, Edna. Remember again: how Edward Thomas haunts his fellow poets. *See* **18748**.

13800. Lowney, John. History, memory, and the literary Left: modern American poetry, 1935–1968. Iowa City: Iowa UP, 2006. pp. xii, 287. (Contemporary North American poetry.)

13801. —— William Carlos Williams and modern poetry: from Modernism to modernisms. *See* **19193**.

13802. Lyu, Claire Chi-ah. A sun within a sun: the power and elegance of poetry. *See* **8800**.

13803. McCabe, Susan. Cinematic Modernism: Modernist poetry and film. (Bibl. 2005, 14444.) Rev. by David Trotter in Mod/Mod (13:2) 2006, 394–6; by David Seed in TexP (19:4) 2006, 540–3.

13804. McCooey, David. Surviving Australian poetry: the new lyricism. Agenda (41:1/2) 2005, 22–36.

13805. McDonald, Peter. Difficulty, democracy, and modern poetry: a lecture delivered at the University of Edinburgh, 14 November 2003. *See* **15700**.

13806. McFee, Michael. The napkin manuscripts: selected essays and an interview. Foreword by Doris Betts. *See* **17338**.

13807. —— Seven questions about Southern poetry. MissQ (58:1/2) 2004/05, 217–53.

13808. MacGowan, Christopher. Twentieth-century American poetry. (Bibl. 2004, 14594.) Rev. by David C. Ward in PNRev (31:3) 2005, 52–5.

13809. McMorris, Mark. Discrepant affinities in Caribbean poetry: tradition and demotic Modernism. ConLit (47:3) 2006, 505–22 (review-article).

13810. Maio, Samuel. Creating another self: voice in modern American personal poetry. (Bibl. 1995, 13601.) Kirksville, MO: Truman State UP, 2005. pp. x, 375. (Second ed.: first ed. 1995.)

13811. Manhire, Bill. Letter from Wellington. PRev (96:2) 2006, 117–19. (New Zealand poetry.)

13812. Marshall, Ian; Simpson, Megan. Deconstructing haiku: a dialogue. ColLit (33:3) 2006, 117–34.

13813. Marx, Edward. The idea of a colony: cross-culturalism in modern poetry. (Bibl. 2005, 14452.) Rev. by Ruth A. Grogan in ESCan (30:4) 2004, 226–31; by Hugh Davis in Soundings (88:1/2) 2005, 427–33; by Ian F. A. Bell in MLR (101:2) 2006, 527–8; by Eric Keenaghan in JML (29:3) 2006, 176–90.

13814. Mason, David. The seeing 'I'. SewR (114:4) 2006, 640–5 (review-article). (Arts and letters.)

13815. Miller, Chris. The Mandelstam syndrome and the 'old heroic bang'. PNRev (31:4) 2006, 14–22.

13816. Mitchell, Margaretta K. The face of poetry: portraits. Ed. by Zack Rogow. Foreword by Robert Hass. Berkeley; London: California UP, 2005. pp. xxxii, 354.

13817. Moramarco, Fred; Zolynas, Al (eds). The poetry of men's lives: an international anthology. Athens; London: Georgia UP, 2005. pp. xxv, 417. Rev. by Jacqueline Marcus in PInt (10) 2006, 206–7; by Charles Harper Webb in PInt (10) 2006, 208.

13818. Narbeshuber, Lisa. Relearning Denise Levertov's *Alphabet*: war, flesh, and the intimacy of otherness. *See* **17162**.

13819. Nelson, Barney. Dana Gioia is wrong about cowboy poetry. *See* **16125**.

13820. Nelson, Cary. Modern American poetry. *In* (pp. 68–101) **11964**.

13821. Newcomb, John Timberman. Would poetry disappear? American verse and the crisis of modernity. (Bibl. 2004, 14610.) Rev. by Mike Chasar in JMMLA (38:2) 2005, 147–9.

13822. Nielsen, Aldon Lynn; Ramey, Lauri (eds). Every goodbye ain't gone: an anthology of innovative poetry by African Americans. Tuscaloosa;

London: Alabama UP, 2006. pp. 305. (Modern and contemporary poetics.) Rev. by Howard Rambsy, II, in AAR (40:1) 2006, 187–90.

13823. O'Brien, Peggy. Writing Lough Derg: from William Carleton to Seamus Heaney. *See* **8803**.

13824. O'Donoghue, Bernard. Poetry in Ireland. *In* (pp. 173–89) **11829**.

13825. —— 'Where are the war poets': poetry and hope – the case of C. Day Lewis. *See* **17171**.

13826. Orr, David. A toast to the happy couplet. NYTB, 4 June 2006, 47. (Epithalamion.)

13827. Ostriker, Alicia. Holocaust poetry: another view. MichQR (45:2) 2006, 326–35.

13828. Owen, Catherine, *et al.* Inviting the incubus, kissing the succubi: the muse in Canadian women's poetry, 2005. *See* **19948**.

13829. Painter, Kirsten Blythe. Flint on a bright stone: a revolution of precision and restraint in American, Russian, and German Modernism. Stanford, CA: Stanford UP, 2006. pp. xx, 306. (Verbal art.) Rev. by Edwin J. Barton in AL (78:4) 2006, 874–6.

13830. Parisi, Joseph; Young, Stephen (eds). Between the lines: a history of poetry in letters. Chicago, IL: Dee, 2006. pp. xviii, 426.

13831. Park, Josephine Nock-hee. 'A loose horse': Asian American poetry and the aesthetics of the ideogram. *In* (pp. 123–36) **11849**.

13832. Parkes, Adam. Poetry. *In* (pp. 227–36) **11788**.

13833. Paterson, Don; Simic, Charles (eds). New British poetry. (Bibl. 2004, 14612.) Rev. by John O'Donoghue in PNRev (31:4) 2005, 64–6.

13834. Patke, Rajeev S. Postcolonial poetry in English. Oxford; New York: OUP, 2006. pp. xii, 267. (Oxford studies in postcolonial liteatures in English.)

13835. Patton, Christopher. Sensuous analysis: the art of reading poetry. BkCan (34:6) 2005, 31–2.

13836. Perelman, Bob. So. *See* **9886**.

13837. Perloff, Marjorie. Avant-garde community and the individual talent: the case of language poetry. FLS (120) 2006, 20–37.

13838. —— The avant-garde phase of American Modernism. *In* (pp. 195–217) **11964**.

13839. —— Can a contemporary poet write about the Holocaust? MichQR (45:2) 2006, 336–40.

13840. —— Differentials: poetry, poetics, pedagogy. (Bibl. 2004, 14618.) Rev. by Bob Perelman in AL (77:4) 2005, 867–9; by Glenn J. Freeman in JMMLA (38:2) 2005, 164–6; by Thomas Docherty in MLR (101:4) 2006, 1102–3.

13841. Pugh, Christina. Humor anxiety. Poetry (189:3) 2006, 228–31.

13842. Raitt, Suzanne. The rhetoric of efficiency in early Modernism. *See* **19049**.

13843. Rampersad, Arnold (ed.); Herbold, Hilary (assoc. ed.). The Oxford anthology of African American poetry. Oxford; New York: OUP, 2006. pp. xxix, 424. Rev. by Melba Joyce Boyd in BSch (36:2/3) 2006, 63–5.

13844. Rasula, Jed. Syncopations: the stress of innovation in contemporary American poetry. (Bibl. 2004, 14626.) Rev. by Brooke Horvath in AL (78:2) 2006, 402–4; by Pierre Joris in AmBR (27:5) 2006, 3–4.

13845. Redmond, John. Picture these. TLS, 8 Sept. 2006, 22–3 (review-article). (New York Poets.)

13846. Rees-Jones, Deryn (ed.). Consorting with angels: essays on modern women poets. (Bibl. 2005, 14478.) Rev. by Jane Griffiths in TLS, 19 May 2006, 5.

13847. —— Modern women poets. Newcastle upon Tyne: Bloodaxe, 2005. pp. 416. Rev. by Jane Griffiths in TLS, 19 May 2006, 5.

13848. Roberts, Beth Ellen. One voice and many: modern poets in dialogue. Newark: Delaware UP, 2006. pp. 202.

13849. Robinson, Peter. Twentieth-century poetry: selves and situations. (Bibl. 2005, 14482.) Rev. by Emily Taylor Merriman in EC (56:2) 2006, 209–17.

13850. Rogoff, Jay. Shocking, surprising Snodgrass. *See* **18546**.

13851. Rosen, David. Power, plain English, and the rise of modern poetry. *See* **8818**.

13852. Rubinstein, Rachel. Going native, becoming modern: American Indians, Walt Whitman, and the Yiddish poet. *See* **11583**.

13853. Schaefer, Judy (ed.). The poetry of nursing: poems and commentaries of leading nurse-poets. Kent: Ohio State UP, 2006. pp. ix, 208. (Literature and medicine, 7.)

13854. Schultz, Susan M. A poetics of impasse in modern and contemporary American poetry. (Bibl. 2005, 14487.) Rev. by Claudia A. Becker in RMER (60:1) 2006; by Elizabeth Robinson in AmBR (27:5) 2006, 10–11; by Thomas Fink in Talisman (32/33) 2006, 249–51.

13855. Sheldon, Glenn. South of our selves: Mexico in the poems of Williams, Kerouac, Corso, Ginsberg, Levertov, and Hayden. (Bibl. 2004, 14637.) Rev. by Jeanne Campbell Reesman in AL (77:3) 2005, 644–6.

13856. Sheppard, Robert. The poetry of saying: British poetry and its discontents 1950–2000. Liverpool: Liverpool UP, 2005. pp. viii, 274. Rev. by David Kennedy in PNRev (32:4) 2006, 62–3.

13857. Smith, Dave. Hunting men: reflections on a life in American poetry. *See* **18540**.

13858. Smith, Stan. Irish poetry and the construction of modern identity: Ireland between fantasy and history. (Bibl. 2005, 14492.) Rev. by Michael Murphy in Eng (55:212) 2006, 225–9.

13859. Spiegelman, Willard. How poets see the world: the art of description in contemporary poetry. (Bibl. 2005, 14495.) Rev. by Rachel Hadas in Mod/Mod (13:3) 2006, 595–7; by Bonnie Costello in LitIm (8:2) 2006, 225–8; by David Mason in SewR (114:4) 2006, 640–5; by Ann Keniston in ConLit (47:3) 2006, 483–90.

13860. Stein, Julia. The New West in contemporary Western working-class poetry, 1990–2005. WAL (40:4) 2006, 462–74 (review-article).

13861. Steiner, Wendy. On the unspeakability argument. MichQR (45:2) 2006, 341–7. (Holocaust poetry.)

13862. Stout, Janis P. Coming out of war: poetry, grieving, and the culture of the World Wars. (Bibl. 2005, 14497.) Rev. by Teresa Knudsen in RMER (60:1) 2006.

13863. Sugawara, Katsuya. Haiku industry: production of literature and the technology of network making. *In* (pp. 213–18) **14093**.

13864. Tillinghast, Richard. Poetry and what is real. (Bibl. 2005, 14504.) Rev. by Jeff Gundy in GaR (60:2) 2006, 423–33.

13865. Turner, Daniel Cross. New Fugitives: contemporary poets of countermemory and the futures of Southern poetry. *See* **15398**.

13866. Van der Vlies, Andrew. 'Hurled by what aim to what tremendous range!': Roy Campbell and the politics of anthologies, 1927–1945. *See* **15011**.

13867. Vickery, John B. The modern elegiac temper. Baton Rouge: Louisiana State UP, 2006. pp. ix, 251.

13868. Wagner-Martin, Linda. Plath and contemporary American poetry. *In* (pp. 52–62) **18038**.

13869. Waldrop, Rosmarie. Dissonance (if you are interested). (Bibl. 2005, 14508.) Rev. by Michael Peverett in PNRev (32:5) 2006, 77–8; by Daniel Gustav Anderson in RMER (60:1) 2006; by Mark McMorris in AmBR (27:5) 2006, 9–10.

13870. Walter, George (ed.). In Flanders fields: poetry of the First World War. London; New York: Allen Lane, 2004. pp. xviii, 382. Rev. by R. K. R. Thornton in PNRev (31:6) 2005, 62–3.

13871. Ward, David C. Criticism makes nothing happen. PNRev (31:3) 2005, 52–5 (review-article).

13872. Westover, Jeffrey W. The colonial moment: discoveries and settlements in modern American poetry. (Bibl. 2005, 14511.) Rev. by Susan Rosenbaum in SAtlR (71:1) 2006, 166–8.

13873. Whyte, Christopher. Modern Scottish poetry. (Bibl. 2004, 14653.) Rev. by Nancy K. Gish in Mod/Mod (13:1) 2006, 196–9.

13874. Wilmer, Clive. Donald Davie's arguments with Modernism. *See* **15422**.

13875. Wilson, Charles Reagan. 'Just a little talk with Jesus': Elvis Presley, religious music, and Southern spirituality. *See* **8831**.

13876. Wiman, Christian. Ambition and survival: essays. Omaha, NB: Zoo Press, 2004. pp. 225.

13877. —— In praise of rareness. *See* **1179**.

13878. Woods, Tim. 'Preferring the wrong way': mapping the ethical diversity of US twentieth-century poetry. *In* (pp. 450–68) **11776**.

13879. Wootten, William. In the circus. *See* **16940**.

13880. Young, David. Six Modernist moments in poetry. Iowa City: Iowa UP, 2006. pp. xiv, 175. Rev. by Chris Beyers in WSJ (30:2) 2006, 241–2.

13881. Zapf, Harald. Ethnicity and performance: bilingualism in Spanglish verse culture. Amst (51:1) 2006, 13–27.

13882. Zhang, Benzi. Of nonlimited locality/identity: Chinese diaspora poetry in America. JAStud (40:1) 2006, 133–53.

PROSE

13883. Anderson, Monica. Women and the politics of travel, 1870–1914. *See* **8836**.

13884. Ball, Martin. Pro patria mori. *See* **13700**.

13885. Bercovitch, Sacvan (gen. ed.). The Cambridge history of American literature: vol. 3, Prose writing, 1860–1920. *See* **8837**.

13886. Brennan, Bernadette. Kim Mahood's *Craft for a Dry Lake*: a work in progress. Southerly (66:1) 2006, 91–105.

13887. Brigley, Zoë. Replication, regeneration or organic birth: the clone in Deryn Rees-Jones' *Quiver* and Donna Haraway's *A Cyborg Manifesto*. *See* **18197**.

13888. Caers, Eric. When ministers were digging in for a fight ... BELL (ns 4) 2006, 5–20.

13889. Callus, Ivan. (Auto)thanatography or (auto)thanatology? Mark C. Taylor, Simon Critchley and the writing of the dead. FMLS (41:4) 2005, 428–38.

13890. de Gregorio Godeo, Eduardo. Critical discourse analysis as an analytical resource for Cultural Studies: exploring the discursive construction of subject positions in British men's magazines' problem pages. *See* **2485**.

13891. Donahue, Peter; Trombold, John (eds). Reading Seattle: the city in prose. *See* **13458**.

13892. Evans, David. High water everywhere: Blues and gospel commentary on the 1927 Mississippi River flood. *In* (pp. 3–75) **3086**.

13893. Germano, William. Passive is spoken here. *See* **2495**.

13894. Glotfelty, Cheryll. The riddle of ghost towns in the environmental imagination. *See* **13483**.

13895. Halse, Christine. Writing/reading a life: the rhetorical practice of autobiography. *See* **2500**.

13896. Jarka, Horst; Jarka, Lois (eds). The others' Austria: impressions of American and British travellers: vol. 1, 1814–1914. *See* **8855**.

13897. Johnson, Amanda. Passage to Indonesia. *See* **19967**.

13898. Kaplan, Brett Ashley. Anatole Broyard's *Human Stain*: performing postracial consciousness. *See* **18316**.

13899. Konuk, Kader. Ethnomasquerade in Ottoman–European encounters: reenacting Lady Mary Wortley Montagu. *See* **8015**.

13900. Koo, Halia. (Wo)men travellers: physical and narrative boudaries. Mosaic (39:2) 2006, 19–36.

13901. Lancaster, Jane (introd. and notes). By motor to the Golden Gate. Jefferson, NC; London: McFarland, 2004. pp. x, 267. Rev. by Mari A. Firkatian in JPC (39:4) 2006, 682–3.

13902. Mieder, Wolfgang. 'We are all in the same boat now': proverbial rhetoric in the Churchill–Roosevelt correspondence. *See* **2986**.

13903. Murray, David. Sovereignty and the struggle for representation in American Indian nonfiction. *In* (pp. 319–56) **11823**.

13904. Nash, Geoffrey P. From empire to Orient: travellers to the Middle East 1830–1926. *See* **8869**.

13905. Nelson, Ronald J. The writing styles of two war correspondents: Stephen Crane and Ernie Pyle. *See* **9660**.

13906. Noriega, Chon A.; Belcher, Wendy (eds). I am Aztlán: the personal essay in Chicano Studies. Los Angeles, CA: UCLA Chicano Studies Research Center, 2004. pp. xi, 265. Rev. by Carlos Gallego in Biography (29:2) 2006, 360–2.

13907. Oldfield, Sybil (ed.). Afterwords: letters on the death of Virginia Woolf. (Bibl. 2005, 14542.) Rev. by Stuart N. Clarke in VWM (68) 2005/06, 22.

13908. Price, John. Not just any land: a personal and literary journey into the American grasslands. (Bibl. 2005, 14546.) Rev. by Jennifer Henderson in ISLE (12:2) 2005, 281–2; by Matthew J. C. Cella in WAL (40:3) 2005, 354–5.

13909. Robbins, Sarah. *Woman's Work for Woman*: gendered print culture in American mission movement narratives. *In* (pp. 251–80) **690**.

13910. Russo Bullaro, Grace. Frances Mayes' *Bella Tuscany* and the reconfiguration of self and home. EArtsS (34:1) 2005, 7–19.

13911. Schmeller, Erik S. Perceptions of race and nation in English and American travel writers, 1833–1914. *See* **8876**.

13912. Sobel, Dava. The earth whirls everywhere. *See* **3596**.

13913. Stewart, Lucretia (ed.). Travelling hopefully: a golden age of travel writing. London: Theniju, 2006. pp. 306. Rev. by Matthew Bell in TLS, 23 June 2006, 34.

13914. Westerman, Molly. 'Of skulls or spirits': the haunting space between fictional(ized) history and historical note. *See* **14489**.

13915. Wild, Jonathan. 'Insects in letters': *John O'London's Weekly* and the new reading public. LitH (15:2) 2006, 50–62.

13916. Williams, Lisa. Letters to Virginia Woolf. *See* **19349**.

BIOGRAPHY AND AUTOBIOGRAPHY

13917. Armitage, Susan. Western women's biographies. WAL (41:1) 2006, 66–72 (review-article).

13918. Baumgartner, Holly L. Re-assimilation as the need to tell: Native American writers, Bakhtin, and autobiography. *In* (pp. 131–48) **2149**.

13919. Bidinger, Elizabeth. The ethics of working-class autobiography: representation of family by four American authors. *See* **19129**.

13920. Boardman, Kathleen A.; Woods, Gioia (eds). Western subjects: autobiographical writing in the North American West. (Bibl. 2005, 14569.) Rev. by Larry Ellis in GPQ (26:3) 2006, 220–1.

13921. Bowker, Gordon. Nuts about St Cyps: lessons and quarrels in the lives of George Orwell. *See* **17916**.

13922. Carlson, David J. Sovereign selves: American Indian autobiography and the law. *See* **8895**.

13923. CHERNEKOFF, JANICE. Resistance literature at home: rereading women's autobiographies from the Civil Rights and Black Power movements. A/B (20:1) 2005, 38–58.

13924. CONNOR, KIMBERLY RAE. Truth and talent in interpreting ethnic American autobiography: from White to Black and beyond. *In* (pp. 209–22) **20098**.

13925. COULLIE, JUDITH LÜTGE. Closest of strangers: South African women's life writing. Johannesburg: Witwatersrand UP, 2004. pp. 386. Rev. by Sam Raditlhalo in Biography (29:2) 2006, 367–74.

13926. COUSER, G. THOMAS. Vulnerable subjects: ethics and life writing. (Bibl. 2005, 14582.) Rev. by Tanya Y. Kam in A/B (20:1) 2005, 100–7; by David B. Eubanks in PrSt (28:1) 2006, 100–3.

13927. DAVIS, ROCÍO G. Asian American autobiography for children: critical paradigms and creative practice. LU (30:2) 2006, 185–201.

13928. —— Begin here: a critical introduction to the Asian American childhood. *In* (pp. 161–80) **11995**.

13929. —— National and ethnic affiliation in internment autobiographies of childhood by Jeanne Wakatsuki Houston and George Takei. Amst (51:3) 2006, 355–68.

13930. DICKINSON, HILARY; ERBEN, MICHAEL. Nostalgia and autobiography: the past in the present. Auto/Biography (14:3) 2006, 223–44.

13931. EAKIN, PAUL JOHN (ed.). The ethics of life writing. (Bibl. 2004, 14719.) Rev. by Leona Toker in PartA (4:1) 2006, 205–8.

13932. EATON, GALE. Well-dressed role models: the portrayal of women in biographies for children. Lanham, MD; London: Scarecrow Press, 2006. pp. 277.

13933. EVANS, G. R. John Wyclif: the biography of a legend. *See* **4299**.

13934. FITZGERALD, STEPHANIE. Intimate geographies: reclaiming citizenship and community in *The Autobiography of Delfina Cuero* and Bonita Nuñez's *Diaries*. AICRJ (30:1) 2006, 109–29.

13935. FRASER, RUSSELL. Shakespeare and the revolution of the times. *See* **5303**.

13936. GIGLIO, ERNEST D. Here's looking at you: Hollywood, film & politics. *See* **12523**.

13937. GOLDMAN, LAWRENCE. A monument to the Victorian age? Continuity and discontinuity in the Dictionaries of National Biography 1882–2004. *See* **8899**.

13938. GONE, JOSEPH. 'As if reviewing his life': Bull Lodge's narrative and the mediation of self-representation. AICRJ (30:1) 2006, 67–86.

13939. GRUBGELD, ELIZABETH. Castleleslie.com: autobiography, heritage tourism, and digital design. NewHR (10:1) 2006, 46–64.

13940. HALVERSON, CATHRYN. Home on the fringe: 'Western' autobiography, 1936–1937. WAL (41:1) 2006, 23–48.

13941. —— Maverick autobiographies: women writers and the American West, 1900–1940. (Bibl. 2004, 14726.) Rev. by Jennifer Dawes Adkison in WAL (41:2)

2006, 225–6; by Jenny Emery Davidson in TSWL (25:2) 2006, 350–2; by Victoria Lamont in Legacy (23:2) 2006, 212–13.

13942. HOLLAND, PETER. Shakespeare and the *DNB*. *In* (pp. 139–49) **5353**.

13943. JOHNSON, KENDALL. Imagining self and community in American Indian autobiography. *In* (pp. 357–409) **11823**.

13944. KNITTEL, JANNA. Sun dance behind bars: the rhetoric of Leonard Peltier's prison writings. *In* (pp. 110–28) **2149**.

13945. KOZUKA, TAKASHI; MULRYNE, J. R. (eds). Shakespeare, Marlowe, Jonson: new directions in biography. *See* **5353**.

13946. LEWIS, REINA. Rethinking Orientalism: women, travel, and the Ottoman harem. New Brunswick, NJ; London: Rutgers UP, 2004. pp. xv, 297. Rev. by Gillian Whitlock in Biography (29:2) 2006, 383–5.

13947. MCENTYRE, MARILYN CHANDLER. Hope in hard times: moments of epiphany in illness narratives. *In* (pp. 229–45) **11916**.

13948. MCPHERSON, SUSAN. On being 'tempted to knit': writing, reviewing and reading biography. *See* **8909**.

13949. MADSEN, DEBORAH L. Chinese American writers of the real and the fake: authenticity and the twin traditions of life writing. CRAS (36:3) 2006, 257–71.

13950. —— The Oriental/Occidental dynamic in Chinese American life writing: Pardee Lowe and Jade Snow Wong. Amst (51:3) 2006, 343–53.

13951. MARSHALL, ELIZABETH. Borderline girlhoods: mental illness, adolescence, and femininity in *Girl, Interrupted*. LU (30:1) 2006, 117–33.

13952. MEYERS, JEFFREY. Arthur Miller's outtakes. *See* **17526**.

13953. MOORE-GILBERT, BART. The *Confessions* of Saint Augustine: roots and routes of postcolonial life writing. A/B (20:2) 2005, 155–69.

13954. NELSON, ALAN H. Calling all (Shakespeare) biographers! Or, A plea for documentary discipline. *In* (pp. 55–67) **5353**.

13955. NYE, MARY JO. Scientific biography: history of science by another means? Isis (97:2) 2006, 322–9.

13956. ORFORD, MARGIE. Transition, trauma, and triumph: contemporary Namibian women's literature. *In* (pp. 159–73) **12216**.

13957. PRYS-WILLIAMS, BARBARA. Twentieth-century autobiography. (Bibl. 2005, 14627.) Rev. by Jane Aaron in MLR (101:4) 2006, 1101–2.

13958. RAHEJA, MICHELLE H. 'I leave it with the people of the United States to say': autobiographical disruption in the personal narratives of Black Hawk and Ely S. Parker. AICRJ (30:1) 2006, 87–108.

13959. SAVOY, ERIC. Subjunctive biography. *See* **10603**.

13960. SCHLATTER, FREDRIC W. George Teeling: mutual friend of Newman and Hopkins. *See* **10488**.

13961. SCOTT, CATHERINE. Time out of joint: the narcotic effect of prolepsis in Christopher Reeve's *Still Me*. Biography (29:2) 2006, 307–28.

13962. TERRALL, MARY. Biography as cultural history of science. Isis (97:2) 2006, 306–13.

13963. THWAITE, ANN. A biographer looks back. *In* (pp. 17–31) **9300**.

13964. Tridgell, Susan. Communicative clashes in Australian culture and autobiography. Auto/Biography (14:4) 2006, 285–301.

13965. Van Dyne, Susan R. The problem of biography. *In* (pp. 3–20) **18038**.

13966. Whittington-Egan, Richard. Oscar Wilde in the twentieth century. *See* **11633**.

13967. Williams, Piper Kendrix. The impossibility of return: Black women's migrations to Africa. *See* **14399**.

13968. Wiltshire, John. Pathography? Medical progress and medical experience from the viewpoint of the patient. *See* **7962**.

13969. York, Lorraine. Biography/autobiography. *In* (pp. 28–42) **14478**.

13970. Zhao, Shankui. Biographical ethics and its modern turn. FLS (117) 2006, 53–60. (In Chinese.)

RELATED STUDIES

13971. Barker, Paul. Medium rare: with Big Brother bestriding the global village, a chance to read what McLuhan really wrote. TLS, 17 Mar. 2006, 3–4 (review-article).

13972. Becker, Patti Clayton. Books and libraries in American society during World War II: weapons in the war of ideas. London; New York: Routledge, 2005. pp. vii, 294. (Studies in American popular history and culture.) Rev. by Carl Ostrowski in SHARP (14:4) 2005, 11.

13973. Chidester, David. Authentic fakes: religion and American popular culture. Berkeley; London: California UP, 2005. pp. xii, 294. Rev. by Lynn Schofield Clark in AmQ (58:2) 2006, 523–33; by Benjamin Hedin in GaR (60:2) 2006, 411–22.

13974. Cianci, Giovanni. The primitives are upon us: Jane Harrison's Dionysian Mediterranean. *In* (pp. 247–62) **12076**.

13975. Coltelli, Laura (ed.). Uomini sulla luna. Urbino: QuattroVenti, 2006. pp. 225.

13976. Deslandes, Paul R. Oxbridge men: British masculinity and the undergraduate experience, 1850–1920. *See* **8918**.

13977. Gonick, Marnina. Between 'Girl Power' and 'Reviving Ophelia': constituting the neoliberal girl subject. NWSAJ (18:2) 2006, 1–23.

13978. Graves, James Bau. Cultural democracy: the arts, community, and the public purpose. Urbana: Illinois UP, 2005. pp. xi, 256. Rev. by Lisa S. Higgins and Teresa Hollingsworth in WF (64:3/4) 2005, 332–4.

13979. Gumbrecht, Hans Ulrich. Slow and brilliant: reactions to Geoffrey Galt Harpham's diagnosis of the humanities today. *See* **19995**.

13980. Haag, Michael. Alexandria: city of memory. New Haven, CT; London: Yale UP, 2004. pp. 368. Rev. by Roger Bowen in DeusL (ns 9) 2003–2005, 141–4; by John Rodenbeck in TLS, 7 Jan. 2005, 9.

13981. Hedin, Benjamin. The religion of now. GaR (60:2) 2006, 411–22 (review-article). (American popular culture.)

13982. Heilmann, Ann; Beetham, Margaret (eds). New Woman hybridities: femininity, feminism, and international consumer culture, 1880–1930. *See* **8926**.

13983. Labarre, Nicolas. Les États-Unis à l'heure du changement de paradigme: *Mass Culture* 1957. RANAM (39) 2006, 147–57.

13984. McCormick, John. On taste. SewR (113:4) 2005, 628–33. (State of letters.)

13985. North, Michael. Visual culture. *In* (pp. 177–94) **11964**.

13986. O'Connor, Laura. Between two languages. SewR (114:3) 2006, 433–42. (State of letters.) (Gaelic poetry.)

13987. Ó Giolláin, Diarmuid. Folk culture. *In* (pp. 225–44) **11829**.

13988. Ó Gráda, Cormac. Jewish Ireland in the age of Joyce: a socioeconomic history. Princeton, NJ; Oxford: Princeton UP, 2006. pp. xii, 300.

13989. Pospíšil, Tomáš. Spies, bombers, liberators and lovers: images of Americans in Czech film. BStE (31) 2005, 147–54.

13990. Ragazzi, Franco (ed.). Marinetti: futurismo in Liguria. Genoa: De Ferrari, 2006. pp. 238.

13991. Rooney, Kathleen. Reading with Oprah: the book club that changed America. Fayetteville: Arkansas UP, 2005. pp. xiv, 234. Rev. by Trysh Travis in SHARP (14:4) 2005, 13; by Beth Luey in PubRQ (21:4) 2005, 102–3; by Jeffrey Louis Decker in MFS (52:1) 2006, 169–78; by Benjamin Hedin in GaR (60:2) 2006, 411–22.

13992. Schad, John. Queer fish: Christian unreason from Darwin to Derrida. *See* **8931**.

13993. Scott, David. 'To be liberated from the obscurity of themselves': an interview with Rex Nettleford. SmAx (10:2) 2006, 97–246.

13994. Sicherman, Barbara. Connecting lives: women and reading, then and now. *In* (pp. 3–24) **690**.

13995. Specht, Mary Helen. The emerging critical power of cool. MichQR (45:4) 2006, 598–609.

13996. Steiner, George. A new literacy. PNRev (32:5) 2006, 14–19. (Athenæum Lecture: 2005.)

13997. Stewart, Susan. Thoughts on the role of the humanities in contemporary life. With a response by Geoffrey Galt Harpham. *See* **20002**.

13998. Terzo, Leonardo. Sul concetto di '*trash*'. ConLett (46) 2006, 365–84.

13999. Tholoniat, Richard. *Summer schools*, *Scottish reels* et *MacBrayne Steamers*: regards français sur les cultures écossaises 1850–1914. *See* **8938**.

14000. van Elteren, Mel. Imperial gestures in portrayals of US culture as a 'universal culture'. Amst (51:2) 2006, 207–38.

14001. Williams, William Proctor. Inclusive ignorance: the anthology, English Studies, and higher education in the United States. NQ (53:4) 2006, 536–42.

LITERARY THEORY

14002. Anon. (comp.). Geoffrey Hartman: a bibliography, 1954–2005. *See* **11643**.

14003. Aboul-Ela, Hosam. Global South, local South: the new post-nationalism in US Southern Studies. *See* **11732**.

14004. Ackerman, Alan. Liberalism, democracy, and the twentieth-century American theater. *See* **12233**.

14005. Adamson, Joseph; Wilson, Jean (eds). *The Secular Scripture* and other writings on critical theory, 1976–1991. Toronto; Buffalo, NY; London: Toronto UP, 2006. pp. xliii, 588. (Collected works of Northrop Frye, 18.)

14006. Alderson, David. Back to the future. ESCan (30:4) 2004, 167–87 (review-article).

14007. Allington, Daniel. First steps towards a rhetorical psychology of literary interpretation. *See* **15242**.

14008. Anderson, Linda. Autobiography and the feminist subject. *In* (pp. 119–35) **14277**.

14009. Anesko, Michael. O O O O that Ja-hame-sian rag / It's so elegant / So intelligent: tracing appropriations of the Master's aura in Modernist critical discourse. *See* **10532**.

14010. Arac, Jonathan. Global and Babel: two perspectives on language in American literature. *See* **3173**.

14011. —— Revisiting Huck: idol and target. *See* **11484**.

14012. Armstrong, Nancy. What feminism did to novel studies. *In* (pp. 99–118) **14277**.

14013. Asante, Molefi Kete; Mazama, Ama (eds). Encyclopedia of Black Studies. London; Thousand Oaks, CA: Sage, 2005. pp. xxxii, 531. Rev. by Kwame Botwe-Asamoah in JBlaS (36:4) 2006, 635–6.

14014. Ashton, Jennifer. From Modernism to postmodernism: American poetry and theory in the twentieth century. *See* **13696**.

14015. Atkinson, William. The perils of world literature. *See* **11749**.

14016. Auerbach, Jonathan. American Studies and film, blindness and insight. *See* **12402**.

14017. Balfour, Ian. Responding to the call: Hartman between Wordsworth and Hegel. *See* **11648**.

14018. Bauer, Dale M. The shape of Baym's career. AmLH (17:4) 2005, 646–52.

14019. Baugh, Eddie. Literary theory and the Caribbean: theory, belief and desire; or, Designing theory. JWIL (15:1/2) 2006, 3–14.

14020. Belsey, Catherine. Culture and the real: theorizing cultural criticism. *See* **20015**.

14021. Bessière, Jean. Autorité, légitimité de la littérature, communication, et paradigmes critiques. *In* (pp. 33–44) **14093**.

14022. —— The facticity of the literary work. Trans. by Yves Gilonne. Para (28:2) 2005, 41–56.

14023. Blevins, Jacob. Influence, anxiety, and the symbolic: a Lacanian rereading of Bloom. Intertexts (9:2) 2005, 123–38.

14024. Boer, Roland. A level playing field? Metacommentary and Marxism. *In* (pp. 51–69) **14159**.

14025. Boyd, Brian. Theory is dead – like a zombie. PhilL (30:1) 2006, 289–98 (review-article).

14026. Breen, Margaret Sönser; Blumenfeld, Warren J. (eds). Butler matters: Judith Butler's impact on feminist and queer studies. Aldershot; Burlington, VT: Ashgate, 2005. pp. x, 222.

14027. Brennan, Stephen C. Donald Pizer and the study of American literary Naturalism. *See* **3200**.

14028. Brooks, Joanna. Working definitions: race, ethnic studies, and early American literature. EAL (41:2) 2006, 313–20.

14029. Buchanan, Ian. National allegory today: a return to Jameson. *In* (pp. 173–88) **14159**.

14030. Burger, Patrick R. *Red Shadows* through the lens of Northrop Frye's archetypal criticism. *See* **16466**.

14031. Callaghan, Dympna. Do characters have souls? *See* **5666**.

14032. Campbell, Jan. Hysteria, mimesis and the phenomenological imaginary. TexP (19:3) 2005, 331–51.

14033. Canepari-Labib, Michela. Writing and translating after the Empire. *See* **17752**.

14034. Cao, Li. The ethico-political agenda of postcolonial criticism: a case study of Spivak. FLS (119) 2006, 23–31. (In Chinese.)

14035. Cao, Shunqing. The construction of a new paradigm of Comparative Literature Studies. FLS (118) 2006, 150–60. (In Chinese.)

14036. Carey, John. Is the author dead? Or, The mermaids and the robot. *In* (pp. 43–54) **5353**.

14037. Carruth, Mary C. (ed.). Feminist interventions in Early American Studies. *See* **6224**.

14038. Cass, Jeffrey. Interrogating Orientalism: theories and practices. *In* (pp. 25–45) **8395**.

14039. Castle, Gregory. Literary theory. Oxford; Malden, MA: Blackwell, 2006. pp. 256. (Blackwell guides to literature.)

14040. Castronovo, Russ. American literature *internationale*. *See* **8314**.

14041. Caws, Mary Ann. Surrealism. *In* (pp. 189–97) **11788**.

14042. Červenka, Miroslav. 'Discovering' the fictional worlds of lyric poetry. *See* **3551**.

14043. Chaudhuri, Shohini. Feminist film theorists: Laura Mulvey, Kaja Silverman, Teresa de Lauretis, Barbara Creed. London; New York: Routledge, 2006. pp. x, 148.

14044. Chen, Aimin. Chinese American literature from the perspective of Orientalism. *See* **11819**.

14045. Chernetsky, Vitaly. Postmodernism, or the cultural logic of postcommunism? The cultures of the former Soviet bloc encounter Jameson. *In* (pp. 143–70) **14159**.

14046. Chiang, Mark. Autonomy and representation: aesthetics and the crisis of Asian American cultural politics in the controversy over *Blu's Hanging*. *In* (pp. 17–34) **11849**.

14047. Chow, Rey. Poststructuralism: theory as critical self-consciousness. *In* (pp. 195–210) **14277**.

14048. Clarke, George Elliott. 13 retro keywords … and why they're worth a second look: *literature*. *See* **1582**.

14049. Cleghorn, Angus. Affirming theatrical distances: Stevens over seas. *See* **18630**.

14050. Cobley, Evelyn. Hard going after theory. ESCan (30:4) 2004, 188–204 (review-article).

14051. Cohen, Debra Rae. Sheepish Modernism: Rebecca West, the Adam brothers, and the taxonomies of criticism. *In* (pp. 143–56) **19082**.

14052. Cole, Catherine M. African performance and the postcolony. *See* **12263**.

14053. Crassons, Kate. Performance anxiety and Watson's vernacular theology. *See* **4171**.

14054. Crick, Brian. Love confounded: revaluing the Great Tradition. (Bibl. 2004, 14858.) Rev. by Michael John DiSanto in VicR (31:2) 2005, 126–8.

14055. Crivelli, Renzo S. Rolando Anzilotti e la nascita degli studi americani in Italia. QPS (14) 2006, 81–90.

14056. Cuddy-Keane, Melba. Global Modernism. *In* (pp. 558–64) **11788**.

14057. Curreli, Mario. I dubbi del traduttore giovane, con due lettere inedite di F. R. Leavis. AngP (3:1) 2006, 195–211.

14058. Davey, Frank. 13 retro keywords … and why they're worth a second look: *equality*. *See* **1560**.

14059. Davies, Paul. Strange weather: Beckett from the perspective of ecocriticism. *In* (pp. 66–78) **14684**.

14060. Davis-Undiano, Robert Con. *World Literature Today* goes back to the future. WLT (79:1) 2005, 3–4.

14061. Day, Iyko. Interventing innocence: race, 'resistance,' and the Asian North American avant-garde. *In* (pp. 35–51) **11849**.

14062. Deane, Seamus. Edward Said (1935–2003): a late style of humanism. FDR (1) 2005, 189–202.

14063. de Bellaigue, Christopher. Where Said was wrong. TLS, 19 May 2006, 6–7 (review-article).

14064. Denham, Robert D. Northrop Frye: religious visionary and architect of the spiritual world. (Bibl. 2005, 14751.) Rev. by Scott Dransfield in ReLit (38:1) 2006, 143–5; by Robert James Merrett in CanL (190) 2006, 153–5.

14065. DeRosa, Robin. Critical tricksters: race, theory, and *Old Indian Legends*. *In* (pp. 167–95) **2149**.

14066. Desmet, Christy. The persistence of character. *See* **5286**.

14067. DeSoto, Aureliano Maria. On the trail of the Chicana/o subject: literary texts and contexts in the formulation of Chicana/o Studies. *In* (pp. 41–60) **11783**.

14068. Diala, Isidore. Ben Obumselu and the dialectic of cultures. *In* (pp. 271–93) **11860**.

14069. —— (ed.). The responsible critic: essays on African literature in honor of Professor Ben Obumselu. *See* **11860**.

14070. Dillon, Sarah. Reinscribing De Quincey's palimpsest: the significance of the palimpsest in contemporary literary and cultural studies. *See* **9686**.

14071. Doan, Laura; Garrity, Jane. Modernism queered. *In* (pp. 542–50) **11788**.

14072. Docherty, Thomas. Aesthetic democracy. *See* **20045**.

14073. Dolzani, Michael (ed.). Northrop Frye's notebooks on romance. Toronto; Buffalo, NY; London: Toronto UP, 2004. pp. lxii, 503. (Collected works of Northrop Frye, 15.) Rev. by Graham N. Forst in CanL (190) 2006, 161–2.

14074. Domínguez, César; Wiersma, Mark D. Literary emergence as a case study of theory in comparative literature. Trans. by Carla Dechant. *See* **20046**.

14075. Donadio, Rachel. Keeper of the canon. NYTB, 8 Jan. 2006, 27.

14076. Donaldson, Jeffery; Mendelson, Alan (eds). Frye and the Word: religious contexts in the writings of Northrop Frye. (Bibl. 2004, 14884.) Rev. by Barbara Pell in CanL (189) 2006, 172–3.

14077. Drakakis, John. Authority and the early modern theatre: representing Robert Weimann. *In* (pp. 139–57) **5421**.

14078. duCille, Ann. On canons: anxious history and the rise of Black feminist literary studies. *In* (pp. 29–52) **14277**.

14079. Eagleton, Terry. A response. LitTheol (19:2) 2005, 132–8.

14080. Eeckhout, Bart. Why would the spatial be so special? A critical analysis of the spatial turn in American Studies. QPS (14) 2006, 19–37.

14081. Egan, Gabriel. Green Shakespeare: from ecopolitics to ecocriticism. *See* **5293**.

14082. Eoyang, Eugene. An 'erotics' of theory: technological paradigms for comparative literature. *In* (pp. 53–63) **14093**.

14083. Erickson, Jon. The ghost of the literary in recent theories of text and performance. *See* **3435**.

14084. Esterhammer, Angela (ed.). Northrop Frye on Milton and Blake. Toronto; Buffalo, NY; London: Toronto UP, 2005. pp. xxxiv, 490. (Collected works of Northrop Frye, 16.)

14085. Estok, Simon. An introduction to Shakespeare and ecocriticism: the special cluster. *See* **5295**.

14086. Evans, Margaret Carpenter. Rosemond Tuve: a life of the mind. (Bibl. 2005, 14775.) Rev. by Margaret Thickstun in MQ (40:3) 2006, 256–7.

14087. Evans, Ruth. The afterword of origins: a response. *See* **4321**.

14088. Faller, Lincoln. 'A dance to which one's feet can still respond'. *See* **6242**.

14089. Faulkner, Peter. William Morris and the *Scrutiny* tradition. *See* **10940**.

14090. Ferguson, Roderick A. African American masculinity and the study of social formations. *See* **11887**.

14091. Ficociello, Robert. Fish(ing) for colonial counter narratives in the short fiction of Paul Bowles. *In* (pp. 167–73) **14238**.

14092. Figueira, Dorothy M. Going global and marketing multiculturalism. *In* (pp. 97–110) **14093**.

14093. —— (ed.). Cybernetic ghosts: literature in the age of theory and technology. Provo, UT: International Comparative Literature Assn, Brigham Young Univ., 2004. pp. iii, 274.

14094. Fish, Stanley. Why Milton matters; or, Against historicism. *See* **7005**.

14095. Fogel, Daniel Mark. Creating scholarly community: a thirty-year view of the *HJR* and the Henry James Society. *See* **10558**.

14096. Fokkema, Douwe. Aesthetics of rewriting. *In* (pp. 121–34) **14093**.

14097. Fořt, Bohumil. How many (different) kinds of fictional worlds are there? Style (40:3) 2006, 272–83.

14098. Foster, Travis M. Matthiessen's public privates: homosexual expression and the aesthetics of sexual inversion. *See* **10624**.

14099. François, Anne-Lise. 'Hum-men': in place of further development. *See* **11663**.

14100. Frank, Adam. Some avenues for feeling. Criticism (46:3) 2004, 511–24 (review-article).

14101. Freedman, Carl. About Delany writing: an anatomical meditation. *See* **15434**.

14102. Friedman, Susan Stanford. Periodizing Modernism: postcolonial modernities and the space/time borders of Modernist Studies. *See* **11895**.

14103. Fry, Paul H. Progresses of poetry. *See* **11665**.

14104. Fulford, Sarah. 'Nation and narration': the English novel and Englishness. *In* (pp. 157–65) **14238**.

14105. Garrard, Greg. Ecocriticism. (Bibl. 2004, 14933.) Rev. by Ursula K. Heise in ConLit (47:2) 2006, 289–98.

14106. Garren, Samuel B. The honeysuckle and the camellia: a reader-response theory of literary interpretation. *See* **17122**.

14107. Gaull, Marilyn. Revisiting 1970: Carl Woodring and *Politics in English Romantic Poetry*. WordsC (37:2) 2006, 71–2.

14108. Gaylord, Alan T. Chaucerian sentences: revisiting a 'crucial passage' from the Nun's Priest's Tale. *In* (pp. 167–80) **4310**.

14109. —— Reflections on D. W. Robertson, Jr, and 'exegetical criticism'. ChauR (40:3) 2006, 311–33.

14110. Geddes, Jennifer L. Religion and the tragic. LitTheol (19:2) 2005, 97–9.

14111. George, Rosemary Marangoly. Feminists theorize colonial/postcolonial. *In* (pp. 211–31) **14277**.

14112. Gervais, David. 'English' and criticism. CamQ (34:3) 2005, 243–50.

14113. Gezari, Janet. Sandra M. Gilbert and Susan Gubar's *The Madwoman in the Attic*. *See* **8373**.

14114. Ghosh, Ranjan. The wor(l)d, the text and the (in)fusionist. *In* (pp. 57–66) **14238**.

14115. Gibson, Melissa Dana. 1979 and all that: periodization in postwar British theatre history. *See* **12292**.

14116. Gidley, Mick. Marcus Cunliffe writes America. JAStud (39:3) 2005, 371–82.

14117. Gikandi, Simon. Postcolonial theory and the specter of nationalism. CLIO (36:1) 2006, 69–84 (review-article).

14118. Gillespie, Gerald. The conflict between synthetic globalism and the desire for cultural identity. *In* (pp. 45–52) **14093**.

14119. Gillespie, Michael Patrick. The aesthetics of chaos: nonlinear thinking and contemporary literary criticism. (Bibl. 2004, 14941.) Rev. by Patrick A. McCarthy in ELT (49:1) 2006, 92–5.

14120. —— Fargnoli, A. Nicholas (eds). *Ulysses* in critical perspective. Foreword by Sebastian D. G. Knowles. *See* **16699**.

14121. Gilroy, Paul. Postcolonial melancholia. New York: Columbia UP, 2005. pp. xvi, 170. (Wellek Library lectures in critical theory.) Rev. by Charlie Samuya Veric in AmQ (58:1) 2006, 255–64.

14122. Giordano, Fedora. Elémire Zolla americanista. QPS (14) 2006, 98–110.

14123. Gitlin, Todd. The necessity of public intellectuals. Raritan (26:1) 2006, 123–36.

14124. Goldie, Terry. 13 retro keywords … and why they're worth a second look: *liberation*. *See* **1581**.

14125. Gooder, R. D. What English was. CamQ (34:3) 2005, 297–311.

14126. Goodheart, Eugene. Pieces of resistance. *See* **13484**.

14127. Goodman, Kevis. On Geoffrey Hartman's psycho-aesthetics. *See* **11669**.

14128. Gordon, Scott Paul. A new latitude in the culture wars. *See* **7260**.

14129. Gould, Philip. What we mean when we say 'race'. *See* **20072**.

14130. Gourgouris, Stathis. *Orientalism* and the open horizon of secular criticism. SocT (87) 2006, 11–20.

14131. Gray, Richard. Writing American literary history. *See* **3271**.

14132. Greaney, Michael. Contemporary fiction and the uses of theory: the novel from structuralism to postmodernism. *See* **13487**.

14133. Griesinger, Emily. Narrating hope in a postmodern world. *In* (pp. 1–23) **11916**.

14134. Grossman, Marshall. The onomastic destiny of Stanley Fish. *In* (pp. 27–52) **7033**.

14135. Guerin, Wilfred L., *et al.* A handbook of critical approaches to literature. (Bibl. 1999, 3927.) Oxford; New York: OUP, 2005. pp. xvi, 424. (Fifth ed.: first ed. 1966.)

14136. Gustafson, Sandra M. (comp.). Historicizing race in Early American Studies: a roundtable with Joanna Brooks, Philip Gould, and David Kazanjian. *See* **20076**.

14137. Hale, Dorothy J. (ed.). The novel: an anthology of criticism and theory, 1900–2000. *See* **3484**.

14138. Halkyard, Stella. [Foot]notes toward a supreme fiction: Stevens, Frank Kermode, and the John Rylands University Library. *See* **18637**.

14139. Harpham, Geoffrey Galt. The character of criticism. London; New York: Routledge, 2006. pp. 195.

14140. Harris, Sharon M. Feminist theories and Early American Studies. *In* (pp. 3–10) **6224**.

14141. Harrison, Nicholas. Who needs an idea of the literary? Para (28:2) 2005, 1–17.

14142. Hart, Jonathan. Poetry in the age of theory and technology. *In* (pp. 175–88) **14093**.

14143. Hartman, Geoffrey; O'Hara, Daniel T. (eds). The Geoffrey Hartman reader. (Bibl. 2005, 14824.) Rev. by Julian Wolfreys in CamQ (34:4) 2005, 404–8; by John Coyle in EJES (10:2) 2006, 199–203.

14144. Harwood, Britton. Chaucer on the couch: the Pardoner's performance and the case for psychoanalytic criticism. *In* (pp. 47–57) **4310**.

14145. Hawkes, David. Shakespeare's *Julius Caesar*: Marxist and post-Marxist approaches. *In* (pp. 199–212) **5805**.

14146. Hawley, John C. Edward Said, John Berger, Jean Mohr: seeking an other optic. *In* (pp. 203–10) **14238**.

14147. Hegeman, Susan. Culture, patriotism, and the habitus of a discipline; or, What happens to American Studies in a moment of globalization? Genre (38:4) 2005, 443–66.

14148. Hendricks, Randy. The 'whatness' of the thing: David Madden as critic. *In* (pp. 21–34) **17397**.

14149. Heng, Geraldine. Pleasure, resistance, and a feminist aesthetics of reading. *In* (pp. 53–72) **14277**.

14150. Herman, David; Jahn, Manfred; Ryan, Marie-Laure (eds). Routledge encyclopedia of narrative theory. (Bibl. 2005, 14834.) Rev. by Sylvie Patron in Style (39:4) 2005, 479–88.

14151. Herz, Judith Scherer. 13 retro keywords ... and why they're worth a second look: *individual*. *See* **1573**.

14152. Hill, Jane. 'The river we're all troubled by': David Bottoms and the legacy of James Dickey. *See* **14817**.

14153. Himmelfarb, Gertrude. The moral imagination: from Edmund Burke to Lionel Trilling. *See* **8392**.

14154. Homer, Sean. Narratives of history, narratives of time. *In* (pp. 71–91) **14159**.

14155. Hoy, David Couzens. Critical resistance: from poststructuralism to post-critique. Cambridge, MA; London: MIT Press, 2004. pp. viii, 274. Rev. by Brett Parker in SubStance (111) 2006, 153–7.

14156. Huang, Yunte. Was Ezra Pound a New Historicist? Poetry and poetics in the age of globalization. *See* **18090**.

14157. Huddart, David. Homi K. Bhabha. London; New York: Routledge, 2005. pp. xiii, 202. (Routledge critical thinkers.)

14158. Irr, Caren. The American grounds of globalization: Jameson's return to Hegel. *In* (pp. 213–39) **14159**.

14159. —— Buchanan, Ian (eds). On Jameson: from postmodernism to globalization. Albany: New York State UP, 2006. pp. 290.

14160. Irwin, Robert. For lust of knowing: the Orientalists and their enemies. London; New York: Allen Lane, 2006. pp. 409. Rev. by Christopher de Bellaigue in TLS, 19 May 2006, 6–7; by Maya Jasanoff in LRB (28:11) 2006, 14–15; by Robert L. Mack in RES (57:230) 2006, 420–3.

14161. Iser, Wolfgang. How to do theory. Oxford; Malden, MA: Blackwell, 2006. pp. x, 211. (How to study literature.)

14162. Izzo, David Garrett; O'Hara, Daniel T. (eds). Henry James against the Aesthetic Movement: essays on the middle and late fiction. *See* **10568**.

14163. Izzo, Donatella. Introduzione: alla scoperta dell'Asian America. *In* (pp. 7–35) **11954**.

14164. Jackson, Kenneth S. 'More other than you desire' in *The Merchant of Venice*. *See* **5965**.

14165. Jackson, Tony E. Explanation, interpretation, and close reading: the progress of cognitive poetics. PT (26:3) 2005, 519–33 (review-article).

14166. Jacobus, Mary. The poetics of psychoanalysis: in the wake of Klein. Oxford; New York: OUP, 2005. pp. 303.

14167. Jasanoff, Maya. Before and after Said. LRB (28:11) 2006, 14–15 (review-article).

14168. Jay, Paul. Locating disciplinary change: the afterlives of area and international studies in the age of globalization. AmLH (18:1) 2006, 175–89 (review-article).

14169. Johnson, Christopher. Derrida: the machine and the animal. Para (28:3) 2005, 102–20.

14170. Jones, Katharine. Getting rid of children's literature. *See* **13675**.

14171. Jost, Walter (ed.). The essential Wayne Booth. Chicago, IL; London: Chicago UP, 2006. pp. vi, 375.

14172. Joubert, Claire. Saussure rereads Derrida: language and critique. EJES (10:1) 2006, 49–62.

14173. Jusová, Iveta; Reyes, Dan. Edward Said, *Reuben Sachs*, and Victorian Zionism. *See* **10036**.

14174. Kamuf, Peggy. 13 retro keywords … and why they're worth a second look: *experience*. *See* **1561**.

14175. —— Composition displacement. MLN (121:4) 2006, 872–92.

14176. Kawamoto, Koji. Orectic or anorectic: literary theory from an Eastern perspective. *In* (pp. 11–20) **14093**.

14177. Kazanjian, David. 'When they come here they feal so free': race and Early American Studies. *See* **20089**.

14178. Keanie, Andrew. *Coleridge, the Damaged Archangel. See* **9528**.

14179. Keery, James. The *Burning Baby* and the bathwater: 9, 'Muddying inclusivity'. *See* **13786**.

14180. Kermode, Frank. Going against. LRB (28:19) 2006, 7–8 (review-article). (Said's theory of 'late style'.)

14181. Kirsch, Adam. Starving hysterical naked. *See* **16105**.

14182. Knapp, Ethan. Chaucer criticism and its legacies. *In* (pp. 324–56) **4330**.

14183. Kocela, Christopher. Resighting gender theory: Butler's lesbian phallus in Acker's *Pussy. See* **14371**.

14184. Koelzer, Robert. Abrams among the nightingales: revisiting the greater Romantic lyric. WordsC (37:2) 2006, 67–71.

14185. Korang, Kwaku Larbi. Where is Africa? When is the West's Other? Literary postcoloniality in a comparative anthropology. *See* **18567**.

14186. LaCapra, Dominick. History in transit: experience, identity, critical theory. (Bibl. 2005, 14872.) Rev. by Michael Jardine in LitH (15:2) 2006, 63–4.

14187. Lane, Richard J. Fifty key literary theorists. London; New York: Routledge, 2006. pp. viii, 268. (Routledge key guides.)

14188. Lattig, Sharon. The perception of metaphor and the metaphor of perception: the neurodynamics of figuration. *See* **2027**.

14189. Lawson-Peebles, Robert. An uncommon pursuit. CamQ (34:3) 2005, 269–79.

14190. Lee, Taek-Gwang. Realism without Lukács. PE (1) 2006, 4–14.

14191. Lehan, Richard. Naturalism and the realms of the text: the problem restated. *See* **15562**.

14192. Lesjak, Carolyn. History, narrative, and realism: Jameson's search for a method. *In* (pp. 27–50) **14159**.

14193. Levin, Richard Louis. Looking for an argument: critical encounters with the new approaches to the criticism of Shakespeare and his contemporaries. (Bibl. 2003, 14897.) Rev. by Brian Boyd in PhilL (30:1) 2006, 289–98.

14194. Levine, Caroline. Scaled up, writ small: a response to Carolyn Dever and Herbert F. Tucker. VS (49:1) 2006, 100–5.

14195. —— Strategic formalism: toward a new method in Cultural Studies. *See* **9261**.

14196. Levine, Robert. Twelve years with Martin Delany: a confession. *In* (pp. 173–85) **20098**.

14197. Lewalski, Barbara K. Barbara K. Lewalski on why Milton matters. *See* **7029**.

14198. Li, Dingqing. Borrowing, integration, creation: the localization of Western literary criticism and the construction of Chinese literary criticism: an interview with Professor Hu Yamin. *See* **20093**.

14199. —— Ethical literary criticism and the construction of humanistic spirit. FLS (117) 2006, 44–52. (In Chinese.)

14200. Lieb, Michael; Labriola, Albert C. (eds). Milton in the age of Fish: essays on authorship, text, and terrorism. *See* **7033**.

14201. LIU, LIDAN. The legacy and the future of *Orientalism*. *In* (pp. 129–43) **14238**.

14202. LONG, LISA A. (ed.). White scholars / African American texts. *See* **20098**.

14203. LUCAS, JOHN. Peter Porter: the metropolitan voice. *See* **18069**.

14204. LUNSFORD, ANDREA A.; OUZGANE, LAHOUCINE (eds). Crossing borderlands: composition and postcolonial studies. (Bibl. 2004, 15054.) Rev. by Taryn L. Okuma in ColLit (33:2) 2006, 188–91.

14205. LUO, JIEYING. Harold Bloom studies in China in the last 15 years. FLS (119) 2006, 163–7 (review-article). (In Chinese.)

14206. MCCABE, SUSAN. Whither sexuality and gender? 'What that sign signifies' and the rise of queer historicism. *See* **20100**.

14207. MCCRACKEN, SCOTT. Between dreamworlds and real worlds: Gissing's London. *In* (pp. 86–99) **10220**.

14208. MACKINNON, LACHLAN. Where's Steptoe? TLS, 21 July 2006, 6–7 (review-article). (Surveys of twentieth-century English culture.)

14209. MACLACHLAN, IAN (ed.). Jacques Derrida: critical thought. (Bibl. 2005, 14901.) Rev. by Thomas Docherty in MLR (101:3) 2006, 813–14.

14210. MACRAE, ALASDAIR. Professor Derry Jeffares: an appreciation. PNRev (32:3) 2006, 7.

14211. MAGNUS, KATHY DOW. The unaccountable subject: Judith Butler and the social conditions of intersubjective agency. Hypatia (21:2) 2006, 81–103.

14212. MAGOME, KIYOKO. Edward Said's counterpoint. *In* (pp. 67–74) **14238**.

14213. MAGUIRE, LAURIE E. How many children had Alice Walker? *In* (pp. 327–50) **661**.

14214. MAKOWSKY, VERONICA. From the road not taken to the multi-lane highway: *MELUS*, the journal. *In* (pp. 23–39) **11783**.

14215. MAO, DOUGLAS. Modern American literary criticism. *In* (pp. 284–307) **11964**.

14216. MATZ, JESSE. Cultures of impression. *In* (pp. 298–330) **12024**.

14217. MENKIS, RICHARD; RAVVIN, NORMAN (eds). The Canadian Jewish Studies reader. Calgary, Alta: Red Deer Press, 2004. pp. 493. Rev. by Melina Baum Singer in CanL (191) 2006, 110–13.

14218. MEYER, SABINE. Faulty analogies: queer White critics teaching African American texts. *In* (pp. 123–33) **20098**.

14219. MIALL, DAVID S. Literary reading: empirical & theoretical studies. New York; Frankfurt: Lang, 2006. pp. 234.

14220. MIDTTUN, BIRGITTE HUITFELDT. Crossing the borders: an interview with Julia Kristeva. Hypatia (21:4) 2006, 164–77.

14221. MIKKONEN, KAI. Can fiction become fact? The fiction-to-fact transition in recent theories of fiction. Style (40:4) 2006, 291–313.

14222. MILLER, J. HILLIS. 13 retro keywords … and why they're worth a second look: *community*. *See* **1554**.

14223. —— Derrida's '*destinerrance*'. MLN (121:4) 2006, 893–910.

14224. MILLER, TYRUS. Futurism. *In* (pp. 169–75) **11788**.

14225. Milne, Heather. The elliptical subject: citation and reciprocity in critical readings of *Ana Historic*. *See* **17448**.

14226. Mohan, Chandra. Lines of globalization and the threat to literary studies. *In* (pp. 111–20) **14093**.

14227. Moody, Nickianne. Feminism and popular culture. *In* (pp. 172–91) **14277**.

14228. Moore, Seán. The culture of paper credit: the new economic criticism and the postcolonial eighteenth century. ECent (45:1) 2004, 87–108.

14229. Moretti, Franco. Graphs, maps, trees: abstract models for a literary history. (Bibl. 2005, 14926.) Rev. by Germaine Warkentin in Library (7:3) 2006, 342–4.

14230. Morisco, Gabriella. Glauco Cambon's craft of reading. QPS (14) 2006, 91–7.

14231. Morrisson, Mark. Nationalism and the modern American canon. *In* (pp. 22–35) **11964**.

14232. Moss, John; Morra, Linda M. (eds). At the speed of light there is only illumination: a reappraisal of Marshall McLuhan. Ottawa: Ottawa UP, 2004. pp. 261. (Re-appraisals: Canadian writers, 27.) Rev. by L. B. Kuffert in CHR (87:2) 2006, 351–3.

14233. Mullin, Katherine. Modernisms and feminisms. *In* (pp. 136–52) **14277**.

14234. Munton, Alan. Vorticism. *In* (pp. 176–82) **11788**.

14235. Nadal-Melsió, Sara. Georg Lukács: *magus realismus*? Diacritics (34:2) 2004, 62–84.

14236. Nadel, Ira B. Historicizing *Ulysses*. *In* (pp. 135–51) **16699**.

14237. Nagel, James. Donald Pizer, American Naturalism, and Stephen Crane. *See* **9658**.

14238. Nagy-Zekmi, Silvia (ed.). Paradoxical citizenship: Edward Said. Lanham, MD: Lexington, 2006. pp. xxxix, 252.

14239. Nicol, Bran. Postmodernism. *In* (pp. 565–70) **11788**.

14240. Nikolchina, Miglena. Matricide in language: writing theory in Kristeva and Woolf. (Bibl. 2004, 15109.) Rev. by Janet Sayers in NWSAJ (18:2) 2006, 226–8; by Jeanette McVicker in VWM (69) 2006, 16–17; by Kristin Czarnecki in WSA (12) 2006, 254–8.

14241. Ochoa, John. Said's Foucault; or, The places of the critic. *In* (pp. 49–56) **14238**.

14242. O'Connor, Alan. Raymond Williams. Lanham, MD; Oxford: Rowman & Littlefield, 2006. pp. x, 127. (Critical media studies.)

14243. O'Dair, Sharon. Marx *manqué*: a brief history of Marxist Shakespeare criticism in North America, *ca* 1980–*ca* 2000. *In* (pp. 349–73) **5376**.

14244. Ohno, Tatsuhiro. Chronology and statistics: objective understanding of authorial meaning. EngS (87:3) 2006, 327–56.

14245. Olds, Marshall C. Literary Symbolism. *In* (pp. 155–62) **11788**.

14246. Olmsted, Wendy. Rhetoric: an historical introduction. *See* **2075**.

14247. Onufer, Petr. An interview with Terry Eagleton. RevR (62) 2006, 167–78.

14248. Orlando, Valérie. Knowledge, power, and fear: Edward Said and the 'mainstreaming' of postcolonial literary theory. *In* (pp. 3–14) **14238**.

14249. Page, Ruth E. Literary and linguistic approaches to feminist narratology. Basingstoke; New York: Palgrave Macmillan, 2006. pp. xi, 209.

14250. Pala, Maurizio. *City, country and theory*: Londra in *The Country and the City* di Raymond Williams. *In* (pp. 301–23) **7343**.

14251. Palmer, Sean. Macaulay's revolution: New Historicism, the working classes, and Elizabeth Gaskell's *North and South*. *See* **10774**.

14252. Pan, Zhengwen. The 'retrogression' and 'progression' of the concept of 'world literature' in China. FLS (122) 2006, 159–68.

14253. Parkin-Gounelas, Ruth. The insistence of the object – and its sublimations. *See* **13575**.

14254. Patai, Daphne; Corral, Will (eds). Theory's empire: an anthology of dissent. (Bibl. 2005, 14957.) Rev. by Simon Jarvis in TLS, 13 Jan. 2006, 23; by Brian Boyd in PhilL (30:1) 2006, 289–98; by Mark Jarman in HR (59:1) 2006, 153–60; by Brian J. Reilly in MLN (121:4) 2006, 911–28; by Michael Bérubé in CommRev (4:3) 2006, 42–5.

14255. Patterson, Annabel. Keywords: Raymond Williams and others. *See* **1577**.

14256. Perry, Seamus. Joy perplexed: optimism and complication in Wordsworth, T. H. Green and A. C. Bradley. *See* **11702**.

14257. Peterfreund, Stuart. Earl Wasserman: a critical (re)-reading. WordsC (37:2) 2006, 64–7.

14258. Piccinato, Stefania. The beginning of African American Studies in Italy. QPS (14) 2006, 52–61.

14259. Pontuale, Francesco. In their own terms: Italian histories of American literature. *See* **3371**.

14260. Pritchard, William H. Possibilities for Wordsworth. *See* **11705**.

14261. Pulitano, Elvira. Toward a Native American critical theory. (Bibl. 2005, 14973.) Rev. by Susan Bernardin in WLT (79:1) 2005, 111; by Gregory Wright in WAL (41:3) 2006, 352–3; by Sean Teuton in AmLH (18:1) 2006, 152–74.

14262. Quéma, Anne. The gothic and the fantastic in the age of digital reproduction. *See* **7317**.

14263. Ramzy, Rasha I. Historiography as a means for power: 'otherization' and imperialism through the writings of Edward Said. *In* (pp. 85–93) **14238**.

14264. Rath, Sura P. What would Said say? Some reflections on tradition, imperialism, and globalism. *In* (pp. 95–110) **14238**.

14265. Rawlings, Peter. American theorists of the novel: Henry James, Lionel Trilling, Wayne C. Booth. *See* **10595**.

14266. Reading, Amy. Vulgarity's ironist: New Criticism, midcult, and Nabokov's *Pale Fire*. *See* **17713**.

14267. Rebolledo, Tey Diana. The chronicles of Panchita Villa and other guerrilleras: essays on Chicana/Latina literature and criticism. *See* **12109**.

14268. Redfield, Marc. Geoffrey Hartman: a deviant homage. WordsC (37:1) 2006, 3–8.

14269. Reilly, Brian J. Hopkins impromptu: following Jacques Derrida through *Theory's Empire*. MLN (121:4) 2006, 911–28 (review-article).

14270. Reilly, Terry. Reading *The Lagoon* and Chaucer's The Knight's Tale through Edward Said's *The World, the Text, and the Critic*. *See* **15304**.

14271. Reinelt, Janelle G.; Roach, Joseph R. (eds). Critical theory and performance. *See* **3452**.

14272. Restuccia, Frances L. Amorous acts: Lacanian ethics in Modernism, film, and queer theory. *See* **12673**.

14273. Rhu, Lawrence F. Stanley Cavell's American Dream: Shakespeare, philosophy, and Hollywood movies. *See* **5423**.

14274. Roberts, John R. John Donne, never done: a reassessment of modern criticism. *See* **6747**.

14275. Rodden, John. Remembering Irving Howe. Salmagundi (148/149) 2005/06, 243–57.

14276. Rooney, Ellen. The literary politics of feminist theory. *In* (pp. 73–95) **14277**.

14277. —— (ed.). The Cambridge companion to feminist literary theory. Cambridge; New York: CUP, 2006. pp. ix, 309. (Cambridge companions to literature.)

14278. Roraback, Erik. Para-baroque conceptual intersections & interventions: *Finnegans Wake*, *Gravity's Rainbow* and *The Writing of the Disaster*. *See* **16763**.

14279. Rothberg, Michael. Construction work: theory, migration, and labor in an age of globalization. *In* (pp. 117–41) **14159**.

14280. Salusinszky, Imre (ed.). Northrop Frye's writings on the eighteenth and nineteenth centuries. Toronto; Buffalo, NY; London: Toronto UP, 2005. pp. xli, 415. (Collected works of Northrop Frye, 17.)

14281. Sandner, David. Theorizing the fantastic: editing *Fantastic Literature: a Critical Reader* and the six stages of fantasy criticism. *See* **3502**.

14282. Savoy, Eric. Subjunctive biography. *See* **10603**.

14283. Sayre, Robert; Löwy, Michael. Romanticism and capitalism. *In* (pp. 433–49) **8357**.

14284. Scanlan, J. T. A celebration. *See* **7328**.

14285. Schmeling, Manfred. Le romancier comparatiste: pour une théorie esthétique de la production interculturelle. *In* (pp. 135–46) **14093**.

14286. Schneider, Rebecca. Intermediality, infelicity, and scholarship on the slip. *See* **20136**.

14287. Schoene, Berthold. Queer politics, queer theory, and the future of 'identity': spiralling out of culture. *In* (pp. 293–302) **14277**.

14288. Schweizer, Bernard. Rebecca West's philosophy of history and the critique of postmodernism. *In* (pp. 223–44) **19082**.

14289. Searle, Leroy. Literature departments and the practice of theory. MLN (121:5) 2006, 1237–61.

14290. Sedlmayr, Gerold. Investigating the relation between original and interpretation: deconstruction and the ethical reading of literature. MSp (50:2) 2006, 75–88.

14291. Seguin, Robert. Cultural revolution, the discourse of intellectuals, and other folk tales. *In* (pp. 95–115) **14159**.

14292. Semler, L. E. A proximate prince: the gooey business of *Hamlet* criticism. *See* **5758**.

14293. Shen, Dan. How stylisticians draw on narratology: approaches, advantages and disadvantages. Style (39:4) 2005, 381–95.

14294. Sheng, Anfeng. A call for literary studies: an interview with J. Hillis Miller. FLS (122) 2006, 1–12.

14295. Shiu, Anthony Sze-Fai. On loss: anticipating a future for Asian American Studies. MELUS (31:1) 2006, 3–33.

14296. Shusterman, Ronald. Philosophy through pictures: ideas and iconotexts from I. A. Richards to Alain de Botton. *See* **15431**.

14297. Silver, Victoria. 'Unequal proceedings' and equitable interpretations in the seventeenth century. *See* **7069**.

14298. Sinfield, Alan. From Bradley to cultural materialism. *See* **5433**.

14299. Singh, Amritjit; Johnson, Bruce G. (eds). Interviews with Edward W. Said. Jackson; London: Mississippi UP, 2004. pp. xxxiii, 253. (Conversations with public intellectuals.) Rev. by Tej N. Dhar in MELUS (31:1) 2006, 165–8; by Anna Bernard in JPW (42:1) 2006, 114–16.

14300. Slocombe, Will. Littered with meaning: the problem of sign pollution in postmodern, post-structuralist and ecocritical thought. TexP (19:4) 2005, 493–508.

14301. Smith, Jad. Custom, association, and the mixed mode: Locke's early theory of cultural reproduction. ELH (73:4) 2006, 831–53.

14302. Sorensen, David R. 'Unfold your self': Kenneth J. Fielding and Carlyle Studies, 1988–2004. *See* **9411**.

14303. Spiridon, Monica. Literature is dead, long live literature: a challenge to literary theories. *In* (pp. 79–86) **14093**.

14304. Stevens, Paul. 13 retro keywords … and why they're worth a second look: *history*. *See* **1570**.

14305. Stock, Lorraine Kochanske. 'Slydynge' critics: changing critical constructions of Chaucer's Criseyde in the past century. *In* (pp. 11–36) **4523**.

14306. Stokes, Claudia. Writers in retrospect: the rise of American literary history, 1875–1910. *See* **8951**.

14307. Stone, Marjorie; Thompson, Judith. Taking joint stock: a critical survey of scholarship on literary couples and collaboration. *In* (pp. 309–33) **3405**.

14308. Su, Hui. The ways and methods of Comparative Literature Studies: an interview with Professor Kwok-kan Tam (Tan Guogen). FLS (120) 2006, 10–19. (In Chinese.)

14309. Surin, Kenneth. Theology and Marxism: the tragic and tragi-comic. LitTheol (19:2) 2005, 112–31.

14310. Sutherland, Kathryn. On looking into Chapman's *Emma*: how R. W. Chapman's Classicists made Jane Austen a classic. *See* **9078**.

14311. Suvin, Darko. Exile as mass outrage and intellectual mission: miseries and splendours of forced displacement. *In* (pp. 69–95) **11824**.

14312. Suzuki, Erin. Consuming desires: melancholia and consumption in *Blu's Hanging*. *See* **19398**.

14313. Suzuki, Mihoko; Dufault, Roseanna (eds). Diversifying the discourse: the Florence Howe Award for Outstanding Feminist Scholarship, 1990–2004. New York: Modern Language Assn of America, 2006. pp. xxvii, 342.

14314. Szegedy-Maszák, Mihály. The concept of canon: masterpiece and evolution in literary history. *In* (pp. 65–78) **14093**.

14315. Szeman, Imre. Who's afraid of national allegory? Jameson, literary criticism, globalization. *In* (pp. 189–211) **14159**.

14316. Taggart, Andrew J. The function and value of literature and literary studies reconsidered. ColLit (33:4) 2006, 204–16 (review-article).

14317. Takada, Yasunari. A Shakespearean distance: Europe, modernity and traditional values. *See* **5439**.

14318. Thomas, Michael. The reception of Derrida: translation and transformation. Basingstoke; New York: Palgrave Macmillan, 2006. pp. xv, 190.

14319. Thompson, James. J. Douglas Canfield and Restoration drama. *See* **6392**.

14320. Thompson, Mark. Versions of pluralism: William Empson, Isaiah Berlin, and the Cold War. LitIm (8:1) 2006, 65–87.

14321. Tucker, Irene. Macaulay's paranoid Parliament: queer theory, Victorian medicine, and *The History of England*. *See* **10776**.

14322. Tureček, Dalibor. The theory of fictional worlds, aesthetic function, and the future of literary history. *See* **3411**.

14323. Tyson, Lois. Critical theory today: a user-friendly guide. *See* **20155**.

14324. Valente, Joseph. *Ulysses* and queer theory: a continuing history. *In* (pp. 88–113) **16699**.

14325. Van Es, Bart. Perils of plants. *See* **5122**.

14326. Vannini, Simona. The second coming of the author. SCrit (21:1) 2006, 1–16.

14327. Varma, Rashmi. On common ground? Feminist theory and critical race studies. *In* (pp. 232–60) **14277**.

14328. Veric, Charlie Samuya. On the potential of failure. *See* **20161**.

14329. Wagner, Tamara Silvia. Occidentalism: Edward Said's legacy for the Occidentalist imaginary and its critique. *In* (pp. 145–53) **14238**.

14330. Wake, Paul; Malpas, Simon (eds). The Routledge companion to critical theory. London; New York: Routledge, 2006. pp. xiii, 296.

14331. Walker, Eric C. The long revolution of Raymond Williams: *Culture and Society* fifty years on. WordsC (37:2) 2006, 60–3.

14332. Walker, William. Resemblance and reference in recent criticism on *Paradise Lost*. *See* **7077**.

14333. Wallace, Emily Mitchell. 'Hares and hounds': critical guides to Williams. *See* **19206**.

14334. Wang, Haiyan. The past and future of American Vietnam War literature studies in China. *See* **12209**.

14335. Ward, Graham. Steiner and Eagleton: the practice of hope and the idea of the tragic. LitTheol (19:2) 2005, 100–11 (review-article).

14336. Watkins, Evan. Generally historicizing. *In* (pp. 15–25) **14159**.

14337. Watson, Jay. Introduction: situating Whiteness in Faulkner Studies, situating Faulkner in Whiteness Studies. *See* **15839**.

14338. Watson, Nicholas. Cultural changes. *See* **3894**.

14339. Waugh, Patricia (ed.). Literary theory and criticism: an Oxford guide. Oxford; New York: OUP, 2006. pp. xx, 598.

14340. Weed, Elizabeth. Feminist psychoanalytic literary criticism. *In* (pp. 261–82) **14277**.

14341. Wegner, Phillip E. Periodizing Jameson; or, Notes toward a cultural logic of globalization. *In* (pp. 241–79) **14159**.

14342. Westfahl, Gary. Science fiction and the playing fields of Eaton. *See* **3518**.

14343. Wihl, Gary. Modernist critical prose. *In* (pp. 516–23) **11788**.

14344. Williams, Adebayo. The missing scholar as icon: Ben Obumselu and the crisis of intellectual modernity in Africa. *In* (pp. 1–14) **11860**.

14345. Williams, Jennifer Hardy. Modernism's religious other. *See* **12221**.

14346. Williams, R. John. 'Doing history': Nuruddin Farah's *Sweet and Sour Milk*, Subaltern Studies, and the postcolonial trajectory of silence. *See* **15793**.

14347. Wilner, Joshua. 'Self-displacing vision': Snowdon and the dialectic of the senses. *See* **11724**.

14348. Wittreich, Joseph. 'The ramifications of those ramifications': compounding contexts for *Samson Agonistes*. *In* (pp. 167–99) **7033**.

14349. Wolfreys, Julian (ed.). The J. Hillis Miller reader. Edinburgh: Edinburgh UP, 2005. pp. x, 454. Rev. by John Coyle in EJES (10:2) 2006, 199–203.

14350. Xu, Jing. An interview with Professor Harold Bloom. FLS (121) 2006, 1–6.

14351. Yang, Huilin. Space for interpretation and imagination: Shakespeare and *Hamlet* in the history of criticism. *See* **5771**.

14352. Yates, Julian. Accidental Shakespeare. *See* **6012**.

14353. Yuan, Xianlai. Christian culture and the history of Western literature: an interview with Prof. Liu Jian-jun. FLS (119) 2006, 1–10. (In Chinese.)

14354. Zhang, Jing. Shakespeare and world literature: the historical significance and modern interpretation – an interview with Professor Wang Zhongxiang. *See* **5461**.

AUTHORS

Edward Abbey

14355. Dooley, Patrick K. The inhuman metaphysics of Edward Abbey and Robinson Jeffers: 'to travel down the strange falling scale'. ISLE (12:2) 2005, 11–30.

14356. Kennedy, Joy. Artistry of hunger: desire and appetite in *Desert Solitaire*. WAL (38:4) 2004, 402–16.

14357. Petersen, David (ed.). Postcards from Ed: dispatches and salvos from an American iconoclast. Minneapolis, MN: Milkweed, 2006. pp. xv, 296, (plates) 16. Rev. by Jonathan Miles in NYTB, 19 Nov. 2006, 23.

14358. Pozza, David M. Bedrock and paradox: the literary landscape of Edward Abbey. New York; Frankfurt: Lang, 2006. pp. viii, 99.

Chinua Achebe

14359. Bamiro, Edmund O. The politics of code-switching: English *vs* Nigerian languages. *See* **18563**.

14360. Erritouni, Ali. Contradictions and alternatives in Chinua Achebe's *Anthills of the Savannah*. JML (29:2) 2006, 50–74.

14361. George, Olakunle. Achebe's *Arrow of God*. CLS (42:4) 2005, 344–62.

14362. Huang, Yonglin; Sang, Jun. Cultural conflicts and the collapse of folk culture: a folkloric perspective to *Things Fall Apart*. FLS (121) 2006, 32–9. (In Chinese.)

14363. Ilo, Isaiah. Language in modern African drama. CLCWeb (8:4) 2006.

14364. Irele, F. Abiola. Ezeulu as world-historical figure: preliminary notes on Chinua Achebe's *Arrow of God*. *In* (pp. 97–111) **11860**.

14365. Maduka, Chidi T. Chinua Achebe and military dictatorship in Nigeria: a study of *Anthills of the Savannah*. *In* (pp. 213–25) **11860**.

14366. Mulengela, Bwendo. Structured silences: a study of Nabokov, Conrad, Ngũgĩ, and Achebe. *In* (pp. 147–70) **11860**.

14367. Nwachukwu-Agbada, J. O. J. Behind the irony curtain: Chinua Achebe and femality revisited. *In* (pp. 79–96) **11860**.

14368. Okonkwo, Chris. 'It was like meeting an old friend': an interview with John Edgar Wideman. *See* **19137**.

14369. Olufunwa, Harry. Achebe's spatial temporalities: literary chronotopes in *Things Fall Apart* and *Arrow of God*. CritS (17:3) 2005, 49–65.

Kathy Acker

14370. Indiana, Gary. Ackerville. LRB (28:24) 2006, 24–5 (review-article).

14371. Kocela, Christopher. Resighting gender theory: Butler's lesbian phallus in Acker's *Pussy*. LIT (17:1) 2006, 77–104.

14372. Scholder, Amy; Harryman, Carla; Ronell, Avital (eds). Lust for life: on the writings of Kathy Acker. London; New York: Verso, 2006. pp. viii, 120. Rev. by Roz Kaveney in TLS, 6 Oct. 2006, 31; by Gary Indiana in LRB (28:24) 2006, 24–5.

14373. TOMAIUOLO, SAVERIO. Dickens to postmodernity and back. *In* (pp. 223–42) **9791**.

Valentine Ackland

14374. BINGHAM, FRANCES. The practice of the presence of Valentine: Ackland in Warner's work. *In* (pp. 29–44) **18964**.

Peter Ackroyd

14375. NEAGU, ADRIANA. Peter Ackroyd's Englishness: a Continental view. ContRev (288:1681) 2006, 217–36.

14376. TEECE, PHILIP. Adventures under the dome: astronomers in literature. *See* **10336**.

Milton Acorn

14377. LAHEY, ERNESTINE. (Re)thinking world-building: locating the text-worlds of Canadian lyric poetry. *See* **18162**.

Harold Mario Mitchell Acton (b.1904)

14378. GE, GUILU. Western spiritual crisis and Oriental cultural support: themes concerning China in Harold Acton's novels. FLS (117) 2006, 133–42. (In Chinese.)

Douglas Adams

14379. HANLON, MICHAEL. The science of *The Hitchhiker's Guide to the Galaxy*. Basingstoke: Macmillan; New York: St Martin's Press, 2005. pp. vii, 195.

14380. KENDA, JAKOB J. Rewriting children's literature. *In* (pp. 160–70) **3186**.

Gerry Adams (b.1948)

14381. WHALEN, LACHLAN. 'Our barbed wire ivory tower': the prison writings of Gerry Adams. NewHR (10:2) 2006, 123–39.

Robert Adamson

14382. KINSELLA, JOHN. Line breaks and back-draft: not a defence of a poem. *See* **16895**.

14383. KNOTTENBELT, ELIZABETH. 'If there were world enough and time'. Agenda (41:1/2) 2005, 196–9 (review-article).

James Agee

14384. ASHDOWN, PAUL (ed.). Selected journalism. Knoxville: Tennessee UP, 2005. pp. xlvii, 166. (Second ed.: first ed. 1985.) Rev. by Stephen Henighan in TLS, 4 Aug. 2006, 10–11; by Bonnie Bressers in JoH (32:2) 2006, 114.

14385. BROMWICH, DAVID. Neutered Valentines. LRB (28:17) 2006, 11–14 (review-article).

14386. FOLKS, JEFFREY J. Madden, Agee, and Knoxville. *In* (pp. 35–45) **17397**.

14387. FRICKE, TOM. Mystery and manners: a conversation with Robert Coles. MichQR (45:1) 2006, 7–26.

14388. HENIGHAN, STEPHEN. Knoxville, campsites and cruise holidays. TLS, 4 Aug. 2006, 10–11 (review-article).

14389. HUMPHRIES, DAVID T. Different dispatches: journalism in American Modernist prose. *See* **13507**.

14390. Jacobs, Tom. Poeticizing the political image: Caldwell, Bourke-White, and the recasting of phototextual expression. *In* (pp. 92–113) **15001**.

14391. Lofaro, Michael A.; Davis, Hugh (eds). James Agee rediscovered: the journals of *Let Us Now Praise Famous Men* and other new manuscripts. (Bibl. 2005, 15087.) Rev. by Steve Goodson in AlaR (59:3) 2006, 214–15.

14392. Sragow, Michael (ed.). Film writing and selected journalism. New York: Library of America, 2005. pp. 748. (Library of America, 160.) Rev. by Stephen Henighan in TLS, 4 Aug. 2006, 10–11.

14393. —— *Let Us Now Praise Famous Men, A Death in the Family,* & shorter fiction. (Bibl. 2005, 15091.) Rev. by Stephen Henighan in TLS, 4 Aug. 2006, 10–11.

Agha Shahid Ali (b.1949)

14394. Islam, Maimuna Dali. A way in the world of an Asian American existence: Agha Shahid Ali's transimmigrant spacing of North America and India and Kashmir. *In* (pp. 257–73) **11995**.

14395. Newman, Amy. 'Separation's geography': Agha Shahid Ali's scholarship of evanescence. HC (43:2) 2006, 1–14.

Rukhsana Ahmad

14396. Greene, Alexis. New voices: Moira Buffini, Sarah Ruhl, and Rukhsana Ahmad. *In* (pp. 219–40) **12297**.

14397. Menon, Jisha. Unimaginable fine communities: identities in traffic in Rukhsana Ahmad's *Black Shalwar.* ModDr (48:2) 2005, 407–27.

Ama Ata Aidoo

14398. Bryan, Violet Harrington. Conflicting identities in the women of Ama Ata Aidoo's drama and fiction. *In* (pp. 15–31) **11795**.

14399. Williams, Piper Kendrix. The impossibility of return: Black women's migrations to Africa. Frontiers (27:2) 2006, 54–86.

Edward Albee

14400. Albee, Edward. The beginnings of Off-Broadway. *See* **12235**.

14401. Bailin, Deborah. Our kind: Albee's animals in *Seascape* and *The Goat; or, Who Is Sylvia?* JADT (18:1) 2006, 5–23.

14402. Bernstein, Robin. Edward Albee: a playwright who happens to be gay: an interview. *In* (pp. 185–90) **12245**.

14403. Ehrhardt, Michael. Back on the beach: Edward Albee. GLRW (13:1) 2006, 31–2. (Interview.)

14404. Jenckes, Norma. Structure of feeling in Tennessee Williams's *The Night of the Iguana* and Edward Albee's *A Delicate Balance. See* **19170**.

Richard Aldington

14405. Bristow, Gemma. Brief encounter: Richard Aldington and the *Englishwoman.* ELT (49:1) 2006, 3–13.

14406. MacCarthy, Anne. Irene Rathbone's annotations to Brigit Patmore's memoir. *See* **18190**.

Meena Alexander

14407. MAXEY, RUTH. An interview with Meena Alexander. KR (28:1) 2006, 187–94.

Sherman Alexie

14408. ELLIOTT, MICHAEL A. Indian patriots on Last Stand Hill. AmQ (58:4) 2006, 987–1015.

14409. HOMANS, MARGARET. Adoption narratives, trauma, and origins. *See* **17612**.

14410. LEIBMAN, LAURA ARNOLD. A bridge of difference: Sherman Alexie and the politics of mourning. AL (77:3) 2006, 541–61.

14411. TELLEFSEN, BLYTHE. America is a Diet Pepsi: Sherman Alexie's *Reservation Blues*. WAL (40:2) 2005, 125–47.

André Alexis (b.1957)

14412. CHARIANDY, DAVID. Haunted diasporas: the second-generation stories of André Alexis. JWIL (12:1/2) 2004, 79–89.

Judith Alguire

14413. ALGUIRE, JUDITH. My mother's diary. PJCL (45) 2005/06, 15–17.

Zaynab Alkali

14414. EDWIN, SHIRIN. We belong here too: accommodating African Muslim feminism in African feminist theory *via* Zaynab Alkali's *The Virtuous Woman* and *'The Cobwebs' and Other Stories*. Frontiers (27:3) 2006, 140–56.

Pamela Allen

14415. PARSONS, ELIZABETH. Identity territory: Pamela Allen's picture books in the Australian psyche. Antipodes (20:1) 2006, 50–5.

Dorothy Allison

14416. DI PRETE, LAURA. 'Foreign bodies': trauma, corporeality, and textuality in contemporary American culture. London; New York: Routledge, 2006. pp. x, 146. (Literary criticism and cultural theory.)

David Almond (b.1951)

14417. LATHAM, DON. David Almond: memory and magic. Lanham, MD; London: Scarecrow Press, 2006. pp. x, 151. (Scarecrow studies in young adult literature.)

Julia Cooley Altrocchi (b.1893)

14418. JALOWITZ, ALAN C. The daughters of Penelope: tradition and innovation in American epics by women. *In* (pp. 141–58) **3395**.

Julia Alvarez

14419. ERICKSON, LESLIE GOSS. Re-visioning of the heroic journey in postmodern literature: Toni Morrison, Julia Alvarez, Arthur Miller, and *American Beauty*. *See* **17598**.

14420. HICKMAN, TRENTON. Hagiographic commemorafiction in Julia Alvarez's *In the Time of the Butterflies* and *In the Name of Salomé*. MELUS (31:1) 2006, 99–121.

14421. KIRSCHNER, LUZ ANGÉLICA. His/tory and its vicissitudes in Alvarez's *In the Time of the Butterflies* and Atwood's *The Handmaid's Tale*. CLCWeb (8:4) 2006.

14422. ORTIZ, LISA M. 'Becoming a butterfly': Julia Alvarez's *In the Time of the Butterflies* as autoethnography. A/B (20:2) 2005, 230–45.

14423. PATTERSON, RICHARD F. Resurrecting Rafael: fictional incarnations of a Dominican dictator. Callaloo (29:1) 2006, 223–37.

Kingsley Amis ('Robert Markham', 'William Tanner')

14424. COLLINI, STEFAN. Do you think he didn't know? LRB (28:24) 2006, 28–31 (review-article). (Biography of Amis.)

14425. LEADER, ZACHARY. The life of Kingsley Amis. London: Cape; New York: Vintage, 2006. pp. xii, 996, (plates) 32. Rev. by Stefan Collini in LRB (28:24) 2006, 28–31.

Martin Amis

14426. BROOKER, JOSEPH. Satire bust: the wagers of *Money*. LawL (17:3) 2005, 321–44.

14427. GŁAZ, ADAM. The self in time: reversing the irreversible in Martin Amis's *Time's Arrow*. JLS (35:2) 2006, 105–22.

14428. KEULKS, GAVIN (ed.). Martin Amis: postmodernism and beyond. Basingstoke; New York: Palgrave Macmillan, 2006. pp. xii, 241.

A. R. Ammons

14429. CASTELLITTO, GEORGE P. A. R. Ammons and Arthur Miller: unexpected metaphysical connections. *See* **17514**.

14430. LEHMAN, DAVID. A. R. Ammons: 'God is the sense the world makes without God'. APR (35:3) 2006, 19–21.

14431. OLSON, TED. Reconciliation and return: A. R. Ammons's poetry as autobiography. NCLR (15) 2006, 93–112.

Mulk Raj Anand

14432. BERMAN, JESSICA. Comparative colonialisms: Joyce, Anand, and the question of engagement. *See* **16661**.

Rudolfo Anaya

14433. HUNT, ALEX. In search of Anaya's carp: mapping ecological consciousness and Chicano myth. ISLE (12:2) 2005, 179–206.

M. T. (Matthew Tobin) Anderson (b.1968)

14434. LEVY, MICHAEL. 'The sublimation of real life': malls, shopping, and advertising in recent young adult SF. NYRSF (18:7) 2006, 10–12.

Sherwood Anderson

14435. BASSETT, JOHN E. Sherwood Anderson: an American career. Selinsgrove, PA: Susquehanna UP, 2006. pp. 146.

14436. DUNNE, ROBERT. A new book of the grotesques: contemporary approaches to Sherwood Anderson's early fiction. (Bibl. 2005, 15161.) Rev. by Margaret Boe Birns in StAN (1:1/2) 2006, 199–201.

14437. Merva, Michael. An illusion of understanding: listeners and tellers in Sherwood Anderson's *Winesburg, Ohio* and Carson McCullers' *The Heart Is a Lonely Hunter.* MidM (33) 2005, 36–47.

14438. Rachels, David. Erskine Caldwell's short stories: teetering on the edge of the canon. *In* (pp. 11–26) **15001**.

14439. Rideout, Walter B. Sherwood Anderson: a writer in America: vol. 1. Introd. by Charles E. Modlin. Madison; London: Wisconsin UP, 2006. pp. 833. Rev. by William H. Pritchard in TLS, 14 July 2006, 32.

Maya Angelou

14440. Agins, Donna Brown. Maya Angelou: 'diversity makes for a rich tapestry'. Berkeley Heights, NJ: Enslow, 2006. pp. 128. (African American biography library.)

14441. Bosničová, Nina. Changing perspectives on religion in African American women's autobiographies. BStE (31) 2005, 111–18.

Marion Angus (1866–1946)

14442. Gordon, Katherine (ed.). Voices from their ain countrie: the poems of Marion Angus and Violet Jacob. Glasgow: Assn for Scottish Literary Studies, 2006. pp. xii, 402. (Assn for Scottish Literary Studies, 36.)

Donald Antrim

14443. Antrim, Donald. The afterlife. New York: Farrar, Straus, & Giroux, 2006. pp. 195. (Memoirs.)

Gloria Anzaldúa

14444. Bowery, Anne-Marie. Voices from within: Gloria Anzaldúa, bell hooks, and Roberta Bondi. *In* (pp. 51–68) **11916**.

Jean Arasanayagam

14445. Ho, Elaine Y. L.; Rambukwella, Harshana. A question of belonging: reading Jean Arasanayagam through nationalist discourse. JCL (41:2) 2006, 61–81.

Ayi Kwei Armah

14446. Ogwude, Sophia O. Of hounds and quarry: the African human condition on canvas. *In* (pp. 237–51) **11860**.

Simon Armitage

14447. Armitage, Simon. Modelling the universe: poetry, science, and the art of metaphor. *In* (pp. 110–22) **13732**.

14448. Murray, Stuart. Autism and the contemporary sentimental: fiction and the narrative fascination of the present. *See* **16455**.

14449. Van Hulle, Dirk. Growth and the grid: organic *vs* constructivist conceptions of poetry. *See* **15720**.

Jeannette Armstrong

14450. Haladay, Jane. The grandmother language: writing community process in Jeannette Armstrong's *whispering in shadows*. StudCanL (31:1) 2006, 32–48.

Harriette Arnow

14451. Ballard, Sandra L.; Chung, Haeja K. (eds). The collected short stories of Harriette Simpson Arnow. East Lansing: Michigan State UP, 2005. pp. 259. Rev. by Martha Billips in AppalJ (33:3/4) 2006, 363–6.

Molefi K. Asante (b.1942)

14452. McNeil, Daniel. American demands, African treasures, mixed possibilities. *See* **18187**.

Oscar Asche (1871–1936)

14453. Singleton, Brian. Oscar Asche, Orientalism, and British musical comedy. (Bibl. 2005, 15191.) Rev. by Jacky Bratton in ModDr (48:3) 2005, 619–21; by Maggie B. Gale in TRI (31:2) 2006, 209–10.

John Ashbery

14454. DuBois, Andrew. Ashbery's forms of attention. Tuscaloosa; London: Alabama UP, 2006. pp. xxiv, 161. (Modern and contemporary poetics.)

14455. Jacobs, J. L.; Schleifer, Ronald. The plainsong of *The Double Dream of Spring*: John Ashbery, Olivier Messiaen, and rituals of the sacred. PQ (83:3) 2004, 297–320.

14456. Myers, Benjamin. Ashbery's *They Dream Only of America* and *Definition of Blue*. Exp (65:1) 2006, 47–50.

14457. Richie, Eugene (ed.). Selected prose. (Bibl. 2005, 15196.) Rev. by Bonnie Costello in Mod/Mod (13:1) 2006, 206–8.

14458. Share, Don. 'It seems I was reading something': poetic voices in and out of context in Ashbery's *Flow Chart*. PNRev (32:1) 2005, 31–5.

14459. Steinman, Lisa M. 'Beauty, resonance, integrity': creative readings of Wordsworth in twentieth-century American poetry. *In* (pp. 101–22) **13735**.

Isaac Asimov

14460. Asimov, Janet Jeppson. Notes for a memoir: on Isaac Asimov, life, and writing. Amherst, NY: Prometheus, 2006. pp. 207, (plates) 4. Rev. by Jennifer Bardi in Humanist (66:6) 2006, 44–5.

14461. Freedman, Carl (ed.). Conversations with Isaac Asimov. Jackson; London: Mississippi UP, 2005. pp. xxvi, 170. (Literary conversations.) Rev. by Donald M. Hassler in Extrapolation (47:1) 2006, 168–70.

14462. Ramraj, Ruby S. Robots and artificial intelligence in Asimov's *The Caves of Steel* and Sawyer's *Golden Fleece*. *In* (pp. 139–46) **13541**.

Kate Atkinson

14463. McDermott, Sinead. Kate Atkinson's family romance: missing mothers and hidden histories in *Behind the Scenes at the Museum*. CritS (18:2) 2006, 67–78.

Margaret Atwood

14464. Atwood, Margaret. Moving targets: selected critical prose, 1982–2004. *See* **11751**.

14465. —— Writing with intent: essays, reviews, personal prose, 1983–2005. *See* **11752**.

14466. BARZILAI, SHULI. A case of negative *mise en abyme*: Margaret Atwood and the Grimm brothers. PartA (4:2) 2006, 191–204.

14467. COOKE, NATHALIE. Margaret Atwood: a critical companion. Westport, CT; London: Greenwood Press, 2004. pp. xi, 175. (Critical companions to popular contemporary writers.) Rev. by Peter Barry in Eng (55:212) 2006, 213–19.

14468. DAVEY, FRANK. Class and power in Margaret Atwood's suburbs and edge cities. EtCan (60) 2006, 97–108.

14469. DAVIES, MADELEINE. Margaret Atwood's female bodies. *In* (pp. 58–71) **14478**.

14470. DVORAK, MARTA. Margaret Atwood's humor. *In* (pp. 114–29) **14478**.

14471. FANG, HONG. *Oryx and Crake*: a postmodernist science fiction. FLS (121) 2006, 105–12. (In Chinese.)

14472. GORJUP, BRANKO. Margaret Atwood's poetry and poetics. *In* (pp. 130–44) **14478**.

14473. GUO, GUOLIANG; ZHAO, JIE. Blindness and insight: an interpretation of existentialist engagement in *The Blind Assassin*. FLS (121) 2006, 113–20. (In Chinese.)

14474. HENGEN, SHANNON. Margaret Atwood and environmentalism. *In* (pp. 72–85) **14478**.

14475. HOWELLS, CORAL ANN. Five ways of looking at *The Penelopiad*. SSE (32) 2006, 5–18.

14476. —— Margaret Atwood: *Alias Grace*. *In* (pp. 29–37) **11946**.

14477. —— Margaret Atwood's dystopian visions: *The Handmaid's Tale* and *Oryx and Crake*. *In* (pp. 161–75) **14478**.

14478. —— (ed.). The Cambridge companion to Margaret Atwood. Cambridge; New York: CUP, 2006. pp. xvi, 200. (Cambridge companions to literature.)

14479. KETTERER, DAVID. 'Another dimension of space': Canadian science fiction and fantasy and Atwood's *Blind Assassin*. *In* (pp. 7–34) **13541**.

14480. KIRSCHNER, LUZ ANGÉLICA. His/tory and its vicissitudes in Alvarez's *In the Time of the Butterflies* and Atwood's *The Handmaid's Tale*. *See* **14421**.

14481. LAWN, JENNIFER. The word as remnant: Margaret Atwood and Janet Frame. *In* (pp. 385–401) **8374**.

14482. NISCHIK, REINGARD M. Margaret Atwood's short stories and shorter fictions. *In* (pp. 145–60) **14478**.

14483. RAO, ELEONORA. Home and nation in Margaret Atwood's later fiction. *In* (pp. 100–13) **14478**.

14484. ROBINSON, ALAN. *Alias Laura*: representations of the past in Margaret Atwood's *The Blind Assassin*. MLR (101:2) 2006, 347–59.

14485. SELIGSOHN, ANDREW J. 'The stirring-up of passion': must we fear an aesthetic politics? *In* (pp. 87–117) **3266**.

14486. SOMACARRERA, PILAR. Power politics: power and identity. *In* (pp. 43–57) **14478**.

14487. STAINES, DAVID. Margaret Atwood in her Canadian context. *In* (pp. 12–27) **14478**.

14488. VEVAINA, COOMI S. Margaret Atwood and history. *In* (pp. 86–99) **14478**.

14489. Westerman, Molly. 'Of skulls or spirits': the haunting space between fictional(ized) history and historical note. CLIO (35:3) 2006, 369–93.

14490. Wilson, Sharon R. Blindness and survival in Margaret Atwood's major novels. *In* (pp. 176–90) **14478**.

14491. Wolbert, Alexandra. Re membering: the treatment of time in Margaret Atwood's *The Edible Woman* and *Cat's Eye*. EtCan (59) 2005, 171–81.

14492. York, Lorraine. Biography/autobiography. *In* (pp. 28–42) **14478**.

David Auburn

14493. Schafer, Carol. David Auburn's *Proof*: taming Cinderella. AmDr (15:1) 2006, 1–16.

W. H. Auden

14494. Buffoni, Franco. Auden critico-poeta in *The Sea and the Mirror*. *In* (pp. 203–33) **3341**.

14495. Burt, Stephen; Brooks-Motl, Hannah (eds). Randall Jarrell on W. H. Auden. (Bibl. 2005, 15234.) Rev. by Peter Robinson in PNRev (32:2) 2005, 61; by Mark Ford in TLS, 20 Jan. 2006, 24; by Guy Cuthbertson in RES (57:228) 2006, 111–12.

14496. Caldwell, Roger. Byron, Auden, and the poetry of disenchantment. *See* **9329**.

14497. Couderc, Gilles. 'Faisons un opéra!': les opéras pour enfants de Benjamin Britten. RANAM (39) 2006, 159–76.

14498. Duggett, Tom. In solitude, for company: the city in W. H. Auden's *Horae Canonicae*. Eng (54:210) 2005, 195–208.

14499. Ford, Mark. A lover's complaints. *See* **16584**.

14500. Hamilton, Craig. The imagined cities in W. H. Auden's *Memorial for the City*. ELN (43:2) 2005, 170–9.

14501. Hickman, Trenton. Theodore Roethke and the poetics of place. *In* (pp. 183–202) **13763**.

14502. Izzo, David Garrett. Then and now: W. H. Auden, Christopher Isherwood, Tony Kushner, and Fascist creep. *In* (pp. 56–97) **16962**.

14503. Jones, Chris. Strange likeness: the use of Old English in twentieth-century poetry. *See* **3677**.

14504. La Grand, Virginia; Mattson, Craig T. Brave new performance space: castaway pedagogy in the age of Caliban. *See* **14847**.

14505. Mao, Douglas. A shaman in common: Lewis, Auden, and the queerness of Liberalism. *In* (pp. 206–37) **12024**.

14506. Marchetti, Paola. 'The pallid children': Auden and the Mediterranean. *In* (pp. 295–312) **12076**.

14507. Matthews, Steven. W. H. Auden: *Look, Stranger! In* (pp. 287–96) **11788**.

14508. Mukherji, Subha. Jonson's *The New Inn* and a revisiting of the 'amorous jurisdiction'. *See* **6895**.

14509. Phelpstead, Carl. Auden and the Inklings: an alliterative revival. JEGP (103:4) 2004, 433–57.

14510. Roberts, Beth Ellen. One voice and many: modern poets in dialogue. *See* **13848**.

14511. Wetzsteon, Rachel. Influential ghosts: a study of Auden's sources. London; New York: Routledge, 2006. pp. xiv, 128. (Studies in major literary authors.)

Paul Auster

14512. Canci, Saniye. Urban space and identity in Paul Auster's *City of Glass*. *In* (pp. 45–54) **3307**.

14513. Coughlan, David. Paul Auster's *City of Glass*: the graphic novel. MFS (52:4) 2006, 832–54.

14514. Dimovitz, Scott A. Public personae and the private I: de-compositional ontology in Paul Auster's *The New York Trilogy*. MFS (52:3) 2006, 613–33.

14515. Donovan, Christopher. Postmodern counternarratives: irony and audience in the novels of Paul Auster, Don DeLillo, Charles Johnson and Tim O'Brien. London; New York: Routledge, 2005. pp. x, 249. (Literary criticism and cultural theory.) Rev. by Anna Marie Focà in TexP (19:3) 2005, 383–6.

14516. Hyvärinen, Matti. Acting, thinking, and telling: Anna Blume's dilemma in Paul Auster's *In the Country of Last Things*. PartA (4:2) 2006, 59–77.

14517. Milne, W. S. The poetry of Paul Auster. Agenda (41:3/4) 2005, 100–11.

14518. Peacock, James. Signs of grace: Paul Auster's *Oracle Night*. Eng (55:211) 2006, 65–78.

14519. Peacock, Jim. Carrying the burden of representation: Paul Auster's *The Book of Illusions*. JAStud (40:1) 2006, 53–69.

14520. Worthington, Marjorie. Auster's *City of Glass*. Exp (64:3) 2006, 179–82.

Mary Austin

14521. Blackbird, Chelsea; Nelson, Barney (eds). Mary Austin's Southwest: an anthology of her literary criticism. (Bibl. 2005, 15257.) Rev. by Gwen Sullivan in RMER (60:1) 2006.

14522. Reed, Maureen E. A woman's place: women writing New Mexico. (Bibl. 2005, 15261.) Rev. by Mary Greenfield in Montana (56:1) 2006, 80–2; by Tey Diana Rebolledo in PacHR (75:3) 2006, 497–8.

14523. Schaefer, Heike. Mary Austin's regionalism: reflections on gender, genre, and geography. (Bibl. 2005, 15263.) Rev. by Elizabeth J. Wright in ISLE (12:2) 2005, 304–5; by Shelley Armitage in TSWL (25:1) 2006, 170–2.

14524. Staples, Joe. 'Discovering' new talent: Charles F. Lummis's conflicted mentorship of Sui Sin Far, Sharlot Hall, and Mary Austin. *See* **17292**.

Margaret Avison

14525. Barton, John. Fluid epiphanies: Margaret Avison's *The Swimmer's Moment*. Arc (56) 2006, 60–5.

Marilou Awiakta (b.1936)

14526. WATKINS, JAMES H. The double-weave of self and other: ethnographic acts and autobiographical occasions in Marilou Awiakta's *Selu: Seeking the Corn-Mother's Wisdom*. AICRJ (30:1) 2006, 5–16.

Jimmy Santiago Baca

14527. STAPLETON, LARA. An interview with Jimmy Santiago Baca. InR (28:1) 2006, 49–53.

Sally-Ann Bagita (Sally-Ann Pipi)

14528. CAVALLARO, DANIELA. Reading across cultures: two stories from Papua New Guinea on arranged marriages. Misc (32) 2005, 57–67.

Darrell Bain (b.1939)

14529. BAIN, DARRELL. Life on Santa Claus Lane. Kingsport, TN: Twilight Times, 2004. pp. 117.

Irene Baird (1901–1981)

14530. MASON, JODY. State censorship and Irene Baird's *Waste Heritage*. CanL (191) 2006, 192–5.

J. A. (John Alec) Baker (b.1926)

14531. O'LEARY, PETER. The phosphorescence of thought. ELN (44:1) 2006, 215–18.

Marie Annharte Baker

14532. GRAUER, LALLY. 'A weasel pops in and out of old tunes': exchanging words. StudCanL (31:1) 2006, 116–27. (Interview.)

John Balaban

14533. CLIFFORD, EMILY CLARE. 'Before I was domesticated': delivering the Vietnam moment in the fatherhood poetry of Bruce Weigl and John Balaban. *See* **19005**.

14534. SMOOT, JEANNE J. Technology: able to assist author and audience. *In* (pp. 219–28) **14093**.

James Baldwin

14535. BELIELE, KELVIN. The prophetic burden: James Baldwin as a latter-day Jeremiah. *In* (pp. 187–206) **11916**.

14536. BRIM, MATT. Papas' baby: impossible paternity in *Going to Meet the Man*. JML (30:1) 2006, 173–98.

14537. BUSH, HAROLD K., JR. A passion for the impossible: Richard Rorty, John Okada, and James Baldwin. *In* (pp. 171–86) **11916**.

14538. BYERMAN, KEITH. Secular word: sacred flesh: preachers in the fiction of Baldwin and Morrison. *In* (pp. 187–204) **14546**.

14539. COBB, MICHAEL L. Racial blasphemies: religious irreverence and race in American literature. London; New York: Routledge, 2005. pp. ix, 145.

14540. GATES, HENRY LOUIS, JR. Cabin fever. *See* **11353**.

14541. HARRIS, TRUDIER. Watchers watching watchers: positioning characters and readers in Baldwin's *Sonny's Blues* and Morrison's *Recitatif*. *In* (pp. 103–20) **14546**.

14542. Henderson, Carol E. Layed bare: the filmic representation of *Go Tell It on the Mountain*. *In* (pp. 139–46) **14544**.

14543. —— Refiguring the flesh: the word, the body, and the rituals of being in *Beloved* and *Go Tell It on the Mountain*. *In* (pp. 149–65) **14546**.

14544. —— (ed.). James Baldwin's *Go Tell It on the Mountain*: historical and critical essays. New York; Frankfurt: Lang, 2006. pp. xv, 162. (Modern American literature: new approaches, 49.)

14545. Kérchy, Anna. Narrating the beat of the heart, jazzing the text of desire: a comparative interface of James Baldwin's *Another Country* and Toni Morrison's *Jazz*. *In* (pp. 37–62) **14546**.

14546. King, Lovalerie; Scott, Lynn Orilla (eds). James Baldwin and Toni Morrison: comparative critical and theoretical essays. Basingstoke; New York: Palgrave Macmillan, 2006. pp. ix, 300.

14547. Lewis, Leslie W. *Philadelphia Fire* and *The Fire Next Time*: Wideman responds to Baldwin. *In* (pp. 145–59) **19144**.

14548. M'Baye, Babacar. Resistance against racial, sexual, and social oppression in *Go Tell It on the Mountain* and *Beloved*. *In* (pp. 167–86) **14546**.

14549. Miller, D. Quentin. Playing a mean guitar: the legacy of Staggerlee in Baldwin and Morrison. *In* (pp. 121–48) **14546**.

14550. Mirin, Jonathan. The art of Whiteness in the nonfiction of James Baldwin and Toni Morrison. *In* (pp. 223–38) **14546**.

14551. Mitchell, Keith. Femininity, abjection, and (Black) masculinity in James Baldwin's *Giovanni's Room* and Toni Morrison's *Beloved*. *In* (pp. 261–86) **14546**.

14552. Norman, Brian. Crossing identitarian lines: Women's Liberation and James Baldwin's early essays. WS (35:3) 2006, 241–64.

14553. Oishi, Eve. Visual perversions: race, sex, and cinematic pleasure. Signs (31:3) 2006, 641–74.

14554. Omry, Keren. Baldwin's bop 'n' Morrison's mood: bebop and race in James Baldwin's *Another Country* and Toni Morrison's *Jazz*. *In* (pp. 11–35) **14546**.

14555. Phillips, Michelle H. Revising revision: methodologies of love, desire, and resistance in *Beloved* and *If Beale Street Could Talk*. *In* (pp. 63–81) **14546**.

14556. Powers, Peter Kerry. The treacherous body: isolation, confession, and community in James Baldwin. AL (77:4) 2005, 787–813.

14557. Relyea, Sarah. Outsider citizens: the remaking of postwar identity in Wright, Beauvoir, and Baldwin. London; New York: Routledge, 2006. pp. 204. (Literary criticism and cultural theory.)

14558. Schur, Richard. Unseen or unspeakable? Racial evidence in Baldwin's and Morrison's nonfiction. *In* (pp. 205–21) **14546**.

14559. Scott, Lynn Orilla. Revising the incest story: Toni Morrison's *The Bluest Eye* and James Baldwin's *Just above My Head*. *In* (pp. 83–102) **14546**.

14560. Tan, Huijuan. James Baldwin's literary patricide and African American literature turn. FLS (122) 2006, 130–8. (In Chinese.)

J. G. Ballard

14561. Gąsiorek, Andrzej. J. G. Ballard. Manchester; New York: Manchester UP, 2005. pp. 228. (Contemporary British novelists.)

14562. Kraitsowits, Stephan. *The Unlimited Dream Company*, roman surréaliste? Une mise en regard transtextuelle. EtBr (30) 2006, 115–29.

Toni Cade Bambara

14563. Goodwin, John. Márquez's *A Very Old Man with Enormous Wings* and Bambara's *The Lesson*. Exp (64:2) 2006, 118–21.

Lynne Reid Banks (b.1929)

14564. Liberman, Sherri. Lynne Reid Banks. New York: Rosen Central, 2006. pp. 112. (Library of author biographies.)

Russell Banks

14565. Connor, Kimberly Rae. More heat than light: the legacy of John Brown in Russell Banks's *Cloudsplitter*. *In* (pp. 203–24) **8537**.

14566. Hutchinson, David. Atom Egoyan: *The Sweet Hereafter*. *In* (pp. 137–48) **11946**.

14567. Matthews, Sebastian (introd.). Peripheral pleasures: letters to Russell Banks, Daniel Halpern, and Stanley Plumly. *See* **17462**.

14568. Weber, Alexander. *From postmodernism to neorealism*: ästhetische Illusion und Identitätskonstruktion in den Romanen von Russell Banks. Trier: WVT, 2004. pp. 337. (SALS: Studien zur anglistischen Literatur- und Sprachwissenschaft, 21.) Rev. by Julia Breitbach in Amst (51:3) 2006, 446–9.

Helen F. (Helen Francesca) Bantock (1868–1961)

14569. Prins, Yopie. Sappho recomposed: a song cycle by Granville and Helen Bantock. *In* (pp. 230–58) **8828**.

John Banville

14570. Berensmeyer, Ingo. Between the canons: John Banville's reception in national and international contexts. *In* (pp. 291–309) **12189**.

14571. Bergonzi, Bernard. Banville's revenge. PNRev (31:4) 2005, 9–10. (Guinness Peat Aviation Co. Prize, 1989.)

14572. D'hoker, Elke. Confession and atonement in contemporary fiction: J. M. Coetzee, John Banville, and Ian McEwan. *See* **15201**.

14573. —— Visions of alterity: representation in the works of John Banville. (Bibl. 2005, 15287.) Rev. by Kersti Tarien Powell in EJES (10:1) 2006, 108–10.

14574. Franks, Jill. Sex, guns, and death: Deborah Warner's adaptation of *The Last September*. *See* **14821**.

14575. McNamee, Brendan. Dancing the grave dance: science, art and religion in John Banville's *Kepler*. EngS (86:5) 2005, 424–38.

14576. —— The human moment: self, other and suspension in John Banville's *Ghosts*. Misc (32) 2005, 69–85.

14577. —— The quest for God in the novels of John Banville, 1973–2005: a postmodern spirituality. Lewiston, NY; Lampeter: Mellen Press, 2006. pp. v, 286.

Amiri Baraka (LeRoi Jones)

14578. Baraka, Amiri. *Howl* and hail. *In* (pp. 19–23) **16122**.

14579. Fouché, Rayvon. Say it loud, I'm Black and I'm proud: African Americans, American artifactual culture, and Black vernacular technological creativity. AmQ (58:3) 2006, 639–61.

14580. Matlin, Daniel. 'Lift up yr self!': reinterpreting Amiri Baraka (LeRoi Jones), Black Power, and the uplift tradition. JAH (93:1) 2006, 91–116.

14581. Punday, Daniel. The Black Arts Movement and the genealogy of multimedia. NLH (37:4) 2006, 777–94.

Gopal Baratham (b.1935)

14582. Holden, Philip. Writing conspiracy: race and rights in two Singapore novels. JPW (42:1) 2006, 58–70.

Owen Barfield

14583. Blaxland-de Lange, Simon. Owen Barfield: Romanticism come of age: a biography. Foreword by Andrew Welburn. Forest Row, E. Sussex: Temple Lodge, 2006. pp. xii, 356.

14584. Tennyson, G. B. (ed.). Owen Barfield on C. S. Lewis. *See* **17203**.

Maurice Baring

14585. Coates, John. Baring's moral exploration in *Cat's Cradle*. Ren (59:1) 2006, 33–52.

Howard Barker

14586. Barker, Howard. Death, the one and the art of theatre. (Bibl. 2005, 15295.) Rev. by Adrian Curtin in TJ (58:1) 2006, 166–7; by John Bull in TRI (31:1) 2006, 112–13.

14587. Gritzner, Karoline; Rabey, David Ian (eds). Theatre of catastrophe: new essays on Howard Barker. London: Oberon, 2006. pp. 240.

14588. Lamb, Charles. The theatre of Howard Barker. London; New York: Routledge, 2005. pp. 228. Rev. by John Bull in TRI (31:1) 2006, 112–13.

Pat Barker

14589. Shaddock, Jennifer. Dreams of Melanesia: masculinity and the exorcism of war in Pat Barker's *The Ghost Road*. MFS (52:3) 2006, 656–74.

14590. Westerman, Molly. 'Of skulls or spirits': the haunting space between fictional(ized) history and historical note. *See* **14489**.

Sebastian Barker

14591. Lindop, Grevel. Sebastian Barker in conversation. PNRev (32:4) 2006, 51–3.

Djuna Barnes

14592. Bombaci, Nancy. Freaks in late Modernist American culture: Nathanael West, Djuna Barnes, Tod Browning, and Carson McCullers. *See* **19067**.

14593. Hardie, Melissa Jane. Repulsive Modernism: Djuna Barnes' *The Book of Repulsive Women*. JML (29:1) 2005, 118–32.

14594. Herring, Phillip F.; Stutman, Osias (eds). The collected poems; with notes toward the memoirs. (Bibl. 2005, 15325.) Rev. by Irene Gammel in LitR (49:4) 2006, 156–9; by Brian Phillips in Poetry (189:3) 2006, 241–3.

14595. Loncraine, Rebecca. Djuna Barnes: *Nightwood*. *In* (pp. 297–305) **11788**.

14596. Rupprecht, Caroline. Subject to delusions: narcissism, Modernism, gender. Evanston, IL: Northwestern UP, 2006. pp. xi, 203. (Avant-garde & Modernism studies.)

Julian Barnes ('Dan Kavanagh')

14597. Guignery, Vanessa. The fiction of Julian Barnes. Basingstoke; New York: Palgrave Macmillan, 2006. pp. viii, 168. (Readers' guides to essential criticism.)

14598. Tollance, Pascale. Écriture et silence: texte-écran et texte-énigme dans *Evermore* de Julian Barnes. EtBr (30) 2006, 131–44.

14599. Wilson, Keith. 'Why aren't the books enough?': authorial pursuit in Julian Barnes's *Flaubert's Parrot* and *A History of the World in 10½ Chapters*. CritW (47:4) 2006, 362–74.

Helen Barolini

14600. Barolini, Helen. A circular journey. New York: Fordham UP, 2006. pp. ix, 210.

Edward F. Barrett (1869–1936)

14601. Phelan, Sheila. Edward F. Barrett (1869–1936), Abbey playwright. NewHR (10:1) 2006, 139–46.

J. M. Barrie

14602. Clark, Emily. The female figure in J. M. Barrie's *Peter Pan*: the small and the mighty. *In* (pp. 303–19) **14616**.

14603. Coats, Karen. Child-hating: *Peter Pan* in the context of Victorian hatred. *In* (pp. 3–22) **14616**.

14604. Fox, Paul. The time of his life: Peter Pan and the Decadent nineties. *In* (pp. 23–45) **14616**.

14605. Hsiao, Irene. The pang of stone words. *In* (pp. 155–71) **14616**.

14606. McGavock, Karen. The riddle of his being: an exploration of Peter Pan's perpetually altering state. *In* (pp. 195–215) **14616**.

14607. Martin, Cathlena; Taylor, Laurie. Playing in Neverland: *Peter Pan* video-game revisions. *In* (pp. 173–93) **14616**.

14608. May, Jill P. James Barrie's pirates: *Peter Pan*'s place in pirate history and lore. *In* (pp. 69–78) **14616**.

14609. Morse, M. Jay. The kiss: female sexuality and power in J. M. Barrie's *Peter Pan*. *In* (pp. 281–302) **14616**.

14610. Pennington, John. Peter Pan, Pullman, and Potter: anxieties of growing up. *In* (pp. 237–62) **14616**.

14611. Roth, Christine. Babes in boy-land: J. M. Barrie and the Edwardian girl. *In* (pp. 47–67) **14616**.

14612. Rudd, David. The blot of Peter Pan. *In* (pp. 263–78) **14616**.

14613. Smith, Clay Kinchen. Problematizing piccaninnies; or, How J. M. Barrie uses graphemes to counter racism in *Peter Pan*. *In* (pp. 107–25) **14616**.

14614. Walker, Rosanna West. The birth of a Lost Boy: traces of J. M. Barrie's *Peter Pan* in Willa Cather's *The Professor's House*. *In* (pp. 127–52) **14616**.

14615. Wasinger, Carrie. Getting Peter's goat: hybridity, androgyny, and terror in *Peter Pan*. *In* (pp. 217–36) **14616**.

14616. White, Donna R.; Tarr, C. Anita (eds). J. M. Barrie's *Peter Pan* in and out of time: a children's classic at 100. Lanham, MD; London: Scarecrow Press, 2006. pp. xxvi,339. (Children's Literature Assn centennial studies, 4.) Rev. by J. J. Purdon in TLS, 22 & 29 Dec. 2006, 38–9.

14617. Wiggins, Kayla McKinney. More darkly down the left arm: the duplicity of fairyland in the plays of J. M. Barrie. *In* (pp. 79–104) **14616**.

Lynda Barry (b.1956)

14618. Tensuan, Theresa M. Comic visions and revisions in the work of Lynda Barry and Marjane Satrapi. MFS (52:4) 2006, 947–64.

Sebastian Barry

14619. Cregan, David. 'Everyman's story is the whisper of God': sacred and secular in Barry's dramaturgy. *In* (pp. 61–79) **14627**.

14620. Cullingford, Elizabeth Butler. Colonial policing: *The Steward of Christendom* and *The Whereabouts of Eneas McNulty*. *In* (pp. 121–44) **14627**.

14621. Denman, Peter. From rhetoric to narrative: the poems of Sebastian Barry. *In* (pp. 9–23) **14627**.

14622. Foster, John Wilson. 'All the long traditions': loyalty and service in Barry and Ishiguro. *In* (pp. 99–119) **14627**.

14623. Foster, Roy. 'Something of us will remain': Sebastian Barry and Irish history. *In* (pp. 183–97) **14627**.

14624. Gleitman, Claire. 'In the dark margin of things:' *Whistling Psyche* and the illness of the Empire. *In* (pp. 209–27) **14627**.

14625. Grene, Nicholas. Out of history: from *The Steward of Christendom* to *Annie Dunne*. *In* (pp. 167–82) **14627**.

14626. Mahony, Christina Hunt. Children of the light amid the 'risky dancers': Barry's naïfs and the poetry of humanism. *In* (pp. 83–98) **14627**.

14627. —— (ed.). Out of history: essays on the writings of Sebastian Barry. Washington, DC: Catholic Univ. of America Press; Dublin: Carysfort Press, 2006. pp. viii, 262.

14628. Ní Dhuibhne, Éilís. Transcending genre: Sebastian Barry's juvenile fiction. *In* (pp. 25–36) **14627**.

14629. Roche, Anthony. Redressing the Irish theatrical landscape: Sebastian Barry's *The Only True History of Lizzie Finn*. *In* (pp. 147–65) **14627**.

14630. Stewart, Bruce. 'To have a father is always big news': theme and structure in *The Engine of Owl-light*. *In* (pp. 37–58) **14627**.

14631. Tóibín, Colm. *Hinterland*: the public becomes private. *In* (pp. 199–208) **14627**.

John Barth

14632. Clavier, Berndt. John Barth and postmodernism: spatiality, travel, montage. New York; Frankfurt: Lang, 2006. pp. 328. (Studies on themes and motifs in literature, 83.)

14633. Lin, Yuzhen. A Barthesian interpretation of funhouse: the deconstructive features of *Lost in the Funhouse*. FLS (120) 2006, 67–73. (In Chinese.)

14634. Punday, Daniel. John Barth's occasional writing: the institutional construction of postmodernism in *The Friday Book*. AL (77:3) 2005, 591–619.

Donald Barthelme

14635. Cao, Shanke. Reflection of another spirit in *Snow White*: the changing morality in post-modernist literature. FLS (117) 2006, 67–76. (In Chinese.)

Edward Baugh (b.1936)

14636. Baugh, Eddie. Confessions of a critic. JWIL (15:1/2) 2006, 15–28.

14637. Breiner, Laurence A. Responsibility and craft in the poetry of Edward Baugh. JWIL (15:1/2) 2006, 60–73.

14638. Edwards, Nadi. Edward Baugh: the critic as mediator. JWIL (15:1/2) 2006, 33–54.

14639. Forbes, Curdella. 'Fractured epiphanies': memory, mourning and loss in Edward Baugh's *It Was the Singing*. JWIL (15:1/2) 2006, 74–91.

14640. Griffith, Glyne. Edward Baugh's literary and cultural criticism. JWIL (15:1/2) 2006, 102–9.

Frank Baum

14641. Adams, David A. Baum, Burroughs, and the Theosophy connection. *See* **14914**.

14642. Barrett, Laura. From Wonderland to wasteland: *The Wonderful Wizard of Oz*, *The Great Gatsby*, and the new American fairy tale. PLL (42:2) 2006, 150–80.

14643. Bell, J. L. Making *Magic*: how L. Frank Baum drafted his penultimate book. BaumB (50:1) 2006, 30–42.

14644. Duffley, Sean P. (ed.). Oz under scrutiny. BaumB (49:3) 2005, 25–32.

14645. Erisman, Fred. Why *The Flying Girl* crashed. BaumB (50:1) 2006, 20–6.

14646. McQuade, Molly. In the land of Baum. LitIm (8:1) 2006, 129–53.

14647. Riley, Michael O. L. Frank Baum and the early motion picture industry. BaumB (49:3) 2005, 13–24.

14648. Wagner, Vivian. Unsettling Oz: technological anxieties in the novels of L. Frank Baum. LU (30:1) 2006, 25–53.

Nina Bawden

14649. Wilkie-Stibbs, Christine. Borderland children: reflection on narratives of abjection. *See* **15860**.

Paul Beatty

14650. Grassian, Daniel. Passing into post-ethnicity: a study of Danzy Senna's *Caucasia*. *See* **20332**.

Robin Becker (b.1951)

14651. Krysl, Marilyn. Sacred and profane: the sestina as rite. *See* **13792**.

Samuel Beckett

14652. Anon. (comp.). Bibliographie 1975–2005. EA (59:1) 2006, 91–9.

14653. Abbott, H. Porter. Samuel Beckett: *Murphy*. *In* (pp. 306–13) **11788**.

14654. Ackerley, C. J. Obscure locks, simple keys: the annotated *Watt*. Preface by S. E. Gontarski. JBecS (14:1/2) 2005, 4–292.

14655. —— Samuel Beckett and Max Nordau: degeneration, sausage poisoning, the bloodied rafflesia, coenaesthesis, and the not-I. *In* (pp. 167–76) **14684**.

14656. Ackerley, Chris. Samuel Beckett and the geology of the imagination: toward an excavation of *Watt*. JBecS (13:2) 2004, 150–63.

14657. Albrecht, Klaus. Günter Albrecht – Samuel Beckett – Axel Kaun. JBecS (13:2) 2004, 24–38.

14658. Alfano, Gianfranco; Cortellessa, Andrea (eds). Tegole dal cielo: 1, L'effetto Beckett nella cultura italiana. Rome: EdUP, 2006. pp. 299. (Antalia, 1.)

14659. Auster, Paul (ed.). Samuel Beckett: the Grove centenary edition: vol. 2, Novels. Introd. by Salman Rushdie. New York: Grove Press, 2006. pp. xiv, 521.

14660. —— Samuel Beckett: the Grove centenary edition: vol. 4, Poems, short fiction, criticism. Introd. by J. M. Coetzee. New York: Grove Press, 2006. pp. xiv, 569.

14661. Barker, Stephen. *Qu'est-ce que c'est d'après* in Beckettian time. *In* (pp. 98–115) **14684**.

14662. Barry, Elizabeth. Beckett and authority: the uses of cliché. Basingstoke; New York: Palgrave Macmillan, 2006. pp. x, 232.

14663. Beplate, Justin. Now and then again. TLS, 21 Apr. 2006, 11–12 (review-article). (Interviews with Beckett; influence on him of Joyce.)

14664. —— Who speaks? Grammar, memory, and identity in Beckett's *Company*. JML (29:1) 2005, 153–65.

14665. Blau, Herbert. 'The *commodius vicus*' of Beckett: vicissitudes of the arts in the science of affliction. *In* (pp. 22–38) **14684**.

14666. Bonafous-Murat, Carle. Et pour quleques *pennies* de plus: du bon usage de Ticklepenny dans *Murphy*. EA (59:1) 2006, 60–74.

14667. Brater, Enoch. Beckett and a way of thinking. BecC (29:2) 2006, 13.

14668. Breuer, Horst. Samuel Beckett and experimental psychology. EngS (87:3) 2006, 303–18.

14669. Clément, Bruno. What the philosophers do with Samuel Beckett. Trans. by Anthony Uhlmann. *In* (pp. 116–37) **14684**.

14670. Connor, Steven. Beckett's atmospheres. *In* (pp. 52–65) **14684**.

14671. Croall, Jonathan. The coming of Godot: a short history of a masterpiece. London: Oberon, 2005. pp. 155.

14672. Davies, Paul. Strange weather: Beckett from the perspective of ecocriticism. *In* (pp. 66–78) **14684**.

14673. DIMOCK, WAI CHEE. Weird conjunction: 'Dante and the lobster'. *In* (pp. 197–201) **14684**.

14674. DIMOVITZ, SCOTT A. Public personae and the private I: de-compositional ontology in Paul Auster's *The New York Trilogy*. *See* **14514**.

14675. FELDMAN, MATTHEW. Beckett's poss and the dog's dinner: an empirical survey of the 1930s 'Psychology' and 'Philosophy Notes'. JBecS (13:2) 2004, 69–94.

14676. FIGUEREDO, MARIA CRISTINA. The shape that matters. BecC (28:2) 2005, 10.

14677. FISCHER-SEIDEL, THERESE; FRIES-DIECKMANN, MARION (eds). Der unbekannte Beckett: Samuel Beckett und die deutsche Kultur. Frankfurt: Suhrkamp, 2005. pp. 357. (Suhrkamp Taschenbuch, 3674.) Rev. by Ulrika Maude in Mod/Mod (13:3) 2006, 591–3.

14678. FRIEDMAN, ALAN WARREN. Beckett's musicals. EA (59:1) 2006, 47–59.

14679. GARFORTH, JULIAN A. Samuel Beckett, Fritz Mauthner, and the *Whoroscope* notebook: Beckett's *Beiträge zu einer Kritik der Sprache*. JBecS (13:2) 2004, 49–68.

14680. GAVINS, JOANNA. (Re)thinking modality: a text-world perspective. JLS (34:2) 2005, 79–93. (First-person narration in *Molloy*.)

14681. GERMONI, KARINE. From Joyce to Beckett: the Beckettian dramatic interior monologue. JBecS (13:2) 2004, 137–49.

14682. GONTARSKI, S. E. Beckett and the unnamable voice of (European) Modernism. JBecS (13:2) 2004, 177–87.

14683. —— Greying the canon: Beckett in performance. *In* (pp. 141–57) **14684**.

14684. —— UHLMANN, ANTHONY (eds). Beckett after Beckett. Gainesville: Florida UP, 2006. pp. 227. (Crosscurrents.)

14685. GOODALL, JANE R. Lucky's energy. *In* (pp. 187–96) **14684**.

14686. GUNN, DAN. Until the gag is chewed: Samuel Beckett's letters: eloquence and 'near speechlessness'. TLS, 21 Apr. 2006, 13–15.

14687. HAYMAN, DAVID. Beckett's *Watt*, the art-historical trace: an archaeological inquest. JBecS (13:2) 2004, 95–109.

14688. —— How two love letters elicited a singular third person. *In* (pp. 202–12) **14684**.

14689. HODGDON, BARBARA. Inoculating the old stock: Shakespearean chorographies. *See* **5535**.

14690. HOUPPERMANS, SJEF. Samuel Beckett and the French tradition. JBecS (13:2) 2004, 164–76.

14691. IRIGARAY, LUCE. The path toward the Other. *In* (pp. 39–51) **14684**.

14692. ISER, WOLFGANG. Erasing narration: Samuel Beckett's *Malone Dies* and *Texts for Nothing*. PartA (4:2) 2006, 1–18.

14693. JAURRETCHE, COLLEEN (ed.). Beckett, Joyce and the art of the negative. *See* **16709**.

14694. KATZ, DANIEL. Beckett's absent Paris: *Malone Dies*, Céline, and the Modernist city. EA (59:1) 2006, 7–17.

14695. King, John. Reading for the plotless: the difficult characters of Samuel Beckett's *A Dream of Fair to Middling Women*. JML (29:1) 2005, 133–52.

14696. Knowlson, James; Knowlson, Elizabeth (eds). Beckett remembering, remembering Beckett: a centenary celebration. New York: Arcade, 2006. pp. xx, 313. Rev. by Justin Beplate in TLS, 21 Apr. 2006, 11–12; by Ed Minus in SewR (114:3) 2006, lviii–lix.

14697. Laubach-Kiani, Philip. 'I close my eyes and try and imagine them': Romantic discourse formations in *Krapp's Last Tape*. JBecS (13:2) 2004, 125–36.

14698. Lin, Lidan. From Quigley the writer to Murphy the job seeker: Beckett's evolving vision of characters and plots in *Murphy*. EngS (87:3) 2006, 319–26.

14699. Lloyd, David. Republics of difference: Yeats, MacGreevy, Beckett. *See* **19405**.

14700. Love, Damian. Doing him into the eye: Samuel Beckett's Rimbaud. MLQ (66:4) 2005, 477–503.

14701. Lüscher-Morata, Diane. La souffrance portée au langage dans la prose de Samuel Beckett. Amsterdam; New York: Rodopi, 2005. pp. 312. (Faux titre, 266.)

14702. Mahon, Derek. Watt is the word: the 'brief scattered lights' of Beckett's poems. TLS, 3 Nov. 2006, 12–13. (Commentary.)

14703. Malone, Christopher. 'If I go on long enough calling that my life I'll end up by believing it': Samuel Beckett and contemporary Irish memoir. *In* (pp. 195–216) **12189**.

14704. Melnyk, Davyd. Interruption: a Shuah thing? JBecS (13:2) 2004, 110–24.

14705. Migernier, Eric. Beckett and French theory: the narration of transgression. New York; Frankfurt: Lang, 2006. pp. 144. (Francophone cultures and literatures, 50.)

14706. Milutinović, Zoran. The death of representation and the representation of death: Ionesco, Beckett, and Stoppard. *See* **18673**.

14707. Montalto, Sandro. Beckett e Keaton: il comico e l'angoscia di esistere. Alessandria: dell'Orso, 2006. pp. viii, 192. (Studi e ricerche, 52.)

14708. Moorjani, Angela. Beckett's second skins. BecC (29:1) 2006, 6–7.

14709. Murphy, Neil. Political fantasies: Irish writing and the problem of reading strategies. *In* (pp. 63–88) **12189**.

14710. Nixon, Mark. Writing 'I': Samuel Beckett's German diaries. JBecS (13:2) 2004, 10–23.

14711. O'Beirne, Emer. Dying for silence: language and its absence in the late work of Nathalie Sarraute and Samuel Beckett. FMLS (41:4) 2005, 396–406.

14712. Oppenheim, Lois (ed.). Palgrave advances in Samuel Beckett studies. (Bibl. 2005, 15409.) Rev. by Chris Ackerley in JJLS (20:1) 2006, 19–20.

14713. Pasqualicchio, Nicola. Il sarto gnostico: temi e figure del teatro di Beckett. Verona: Ombre Corte, 2006. pp. 140.

14714. Pilling, John. Beckett and Mauthner revisited. *In* (pp. 158–66) **14684**.

14715. —— Dates and difficulties in Beckett's *Whoroscope* notebook. JBecS (13.2) 2004, 39–48.

14716. Rathjen, Friedhelm. Samuel Beckett. Reinbek: Rowohlt Taschenbuch Verlag, 2006. pp. 155. (Rowohlts Monographien, 50678.)

14717. —— Weder noch: Aufsätze zu Samuel Beckett. Scheessel, Germany: ReJoyce, 2005. pp. 166. (ReJoyce, 7.)

14718. Ravez, Stéphanie. Beckett l'interrupteur; ou, Des petits textes en prose. EA (59:1) 2006, 18–30.

14719. Ross, Ciaran. Aux frontières du vide: Beckett: une écriture sans mémoire ni désir. Amsterdam; New York: Rodopi, 2004. pp. 310. (Faux titre, 249.)

14720. —— 'Where do we come in?': responding to otherness in *Waiting for Godot*. EA (59:1) 2006, 75–90.

14721. Russell, Richard. Talking with ghosts of Irish playwrights past: Marina Carr's *By the Bog of Cats* ... *See* **15046**.

14722. Salado, Régis. Beckett et Pinget: l'échange des voix. EA (59:1) 2006, 31–46.

14723. Salmon-Bitton, Nirit. 'Himself he devises too for company': self-making in Samuel Beckett's *Company*. LitMed (25:1) 2006, 142–55.

14724. Schwab, Gabriele. Writing against memory and forgetting. LitMed (25:1) 2006, 95–121.

14725. Sheehan, Paul. Births for nothing: Beckett's ontology of parturition. *In* (pp. 177–86) **14684**.

14726. Slade, Andrew. Lyotard, Beckett, Duras, and the postmodern sublime. New York; Frankfurt: Lang, 2006. pp. vi, 150. (Currents in comparative Romance languages and literatures, 146.)

14727. Slote, Sam. On *Worstward Ho*. JBecS (13:2) 2004, 188–205.

14728. Tagliaferri, Aldo. La via dell'impossibile: le prose brevi di Beckett. Rome: EdUP, 2006. pp. 141. (Antalia, 3.)

14729. Uhlmann, Anthony. Samuel Beckett and the occluded image. *In* (pp. 79–97) **14684**.

14730. Van Hulle, Dirk. Authorial translation: Samuel Beckett's *Stirrings Still/Soubresauts*. *In* (pp. 150–60) **426**.

14731. Weller, Shane. Beckett, literature, and the ethics of alterity. Basingstoke; New York: Palgrave Macmillan, 2006. pp. ix, 218.

14732. Ben-Zvi, Linda (ed.). Drawing on Beckett: portraits, performances, and cultural contexts. (Bibl. 2004, 15698.) Rev. by Natka Bianchini in TJ (58:1) 2006, 157–8.

George Randolph Bedford (1868–1941)

14733. Gilbert, Helen. Millennial blues; racism, nationalism, and the legacy of empire. *In* (pp. 12–28) **12360**.

Sir Max Beerbohm

14734. Ascari, Maurizio. 'The Master in the middle distance': Max Beerbohm, Henry James and literary forgery. *In* (pp. 87–96) **10568**.

14735. Davison, Sarah. Catching Mrs Brown: Max Beerbohm's influence on Virginia Woolf's *Mr Bennett and Mrs Brown*. *See* **19274**.

14736. Owston, John. Cervantes' *Don Quixote*, volume 1, part 1, chapters 12, 13, and 14, as a narrative source for Sir Max Beerbohm's *Zuleika Dobson*. NQ (53:3) 2006, 344–6.

14737. Pham-Thanh, Gilbert. Figures de l'excès dans *Zuleika Dobson* de Max Beerbohm: de la difficulté d'être dandy. CVE (63) 2006, 149–59.

Brendan Behan

14738. Lotringer, Sylvère. The thin man: an interview with Brendan Behan. FDR (1) 2005, 3–27.

Florence Eveleen Eleanore Olliffe, Lady Bell (1851–1930)

14739. Stewart, Eleanor. Infanticide et émancipation féminine dans *Alan's Wife* d'Elizabeth Robins et de Florence Bell. *See* **18264**.

Madison Smartt Bell

14740. Gyssels, Kathleen. La révolution haïtienne vue par un Américain. CritP (62:711/712) 2006, 665–74.

Marvin Bell

14741. Bunge, Nancy. Influencing each other through the mail: William Stafford's and Marvin Bell's *Segues* and Jim Harrison's and Ted Kooser's *Braided Creek*. *See* **18588**.

Saul Bellow

14742. Assadi, Jamal. Acting, rhetoric, & interpretation in selected novels by F. Scott Fitzgerald & Saul Bellow. *See* **15868**.

14743. Birindelli, Roberto. Individuo e società in *Herzog* di Saul Bellow. Naples: Liguori, 2005. pp. viii, 206. (Critica letteraria, 65.)

14744. Cardon, Lauren. *Herzog* as 'survival literature'. SBJ (20:2) 2004, 85–108.

14745. Cohen, Mark. Body language: spoken *vs* silent communication in *Herzog*. SBJ (20:2) 2004, 3–17.

14746. Cronin, Gloria L.; Means, Robert S. (comps). Selected annotated bibliography: 2001–2002. SBJ (20:2) 2004, 117–31.

14747. Liu, Wensong. Saul Bellow's fiction: power relations and female representation. Xiamen: Xiamen UP, 2004. pp. iii, 290. Rev. by Keith Lawrence in SBJ (20:2) 2004, 109–16.

14748. Manea, Norman. Some thoughts on Saul Bellow. Salmagundi (148/149) 2005/06, 258–70.

14749. Muhlestein, Dan. Presence, absence, and commodity fetish in *Ravelstein*. SBJ (20:2) 2004, 65–84.

14750. Royal, Derek Parker, *et al*. Looking at Saul Bellow (1915–2005). PhRS (1:2) 2005, 115–24.

14751. Shy, Todd. The prospect of too much freedom: Saul Bellow's management of abundance. SBJ (20:2) 2004, 51–64.

14752. Witteveld, Peter. Tamkin the trickster: laughter and trembling before the immanence of the essential in Saul Bellow's *Seize the Day*. SBJ (20:2) 2004, 19–40.

14753. Zárate, Tara Houlihan. '*I want, I want!*': Transcendental epiphanies in Saul Bellow's *Henderson, the Rain King*. SBJ (20:2) 2004, 41–50.

Alan Bennett

14754. Bennett, Alan. Untold stories. (Bibl. 2005, 15463.) Rev. by Charles McGrath in NYTB, 9 Apr. 2006, 28; by Michael Dirda in BkW, 9 Apr. 2006, 15.

14755. Conliffe, Mark. On isolation. *See* **3216**.

14756. McIntyre, Dan. Logic, reality and mind style in Alan Bennett's *The Lady in the Van*. JLS (34:1) 2005, 21–40.

Arnold Bennett

14757. Saloman, Randi. 'Charles Lamb is dead': Arnold Bennett's *Journalism for Women* and *A Room of One's Own*. *See* **19327**.

John Berger

14758. Hawley, John C. Edward Said, John Berger, Jean Mohr: seeking an other optic. *In* (pp. 203–10) **14238**.

Thomas Berger

14759. Thompson, Raymond H.; Busby, Keith (eds). Gawain: a casebook. *See* **3980**.

Steven Berkoff

14760. Cross, Robert. Steven Berkoff and the theatre of self-performance. (Bibl. 2004, 15732.) Rev. by Annette Pankratz in ModDr (48:2) 2005, 459–61.

Charles Bernstein

14761. Aji, Hélène. 'Writing (as) (and) thinking': Charles Bernstein's work 'in' language. EA (59:3) 2006, 341–55.

Ted Berrigan

14762. Keelan, Claudia; Notley, Alice. A conversation: September 2002 – December 2003. *See* **17778**.

14763. Notley, Alice (ed.); Berrigan, Anselm; Berrigan, Edmund (asst eds). The collected poems of Ted Berrigan. Berkeley; London: California UP, 2005. pp. ix, 749. Rev. by Daniel Kane in PNRev (32:5) 2006, 82–3; by Jordan Davis in ChiR (52:2–4) 2006, 353–60; by Michael Leddy in WLT (80:6) 2006, 70–1.

R. M. (Ralph Marion) Berry (b.1947)

14764. Berry, R. M. R. M. Berry answers Joseph Tabbi. AmBR (27:5) 2006, 37–8. (Response to Tabbi's review of Berry's novel *Frank*.)

14765. Tabbi, Joseph. Joseph Tabbi answers R. M. Berry. AmBR (27:5) 2006, 38.

Wendell Berry

14766. Dalton, Katherine. Rendering us again in affection: an interview with Wendell Berry. Chronicles (30:7) 2006, 31–6.

John Berryman

14767. Berryman, John. A visit to Ezra Pound in St Elizabeth's Hospital, 1948. *See* **18078**.

14768. Boruch, Marianne. Heavy lifting. *See* **16302**.

14769. Burt, Stephen. My name is Henri: contemporary poets discover John Berryman. *In* (pp. 233–51) **13763**.

14770. Thomas, Harry. Berryman and Pound. MichQR (45:4) 2006, 613–16.

Ursula Bethell

14771. Whiteford, Peter (ed.). Vibrant with words: the letters of Ursula Bethell. (Bibl. 2005, 15479.) Rev. by Jane Stafford in JNZL (24:1) 2006, 155–9.

Sir John Betjeman

14772. Bayley, John. Overcoming kitsch: thoughts on linguistic and class resource from Keats to Betjeman. *In* (pp. 225–31) **13735**.

14773. Gardner, Kevin J. John Betjeman's *Bristol and Clifton*: echoes of Robert Browning's *My Last Duchess*. ANQ (19:3) 2006, 35–8.

14774. Guilding, Ruth. The shared vision of John Piper and John Betjeman: how to like everything. TLS, 4 Aug. 2006, 16–17.

14775. Johnson, Trevor. Hardy, Betjeman and 'honest doubt'. *See* **10278**.

14776. Manwaring, Randle. John Betjeman – a centenary view. ContRev (288:1681) 2006, 209–11.

14777. Wilson, A. N. Betjeman. London: Hutchinson, 2006. pp. 375. Rev. by Timothy Mowl in TLS, 15 Sept. 2006, 36; by Charles McGrath in NYTB, 3 Dec. 2006, 28–9.

Doris Betts

14778. Betts, Doris. Whispering hope. *In* (pp. 35–42) **11940**.

14779. Eads, Martha Greene. Prosaic grace: Doris Betts's *Souls Raised from the Dead*. *In* (pp. 103–16) **11916**.

Jean Betts (b.1955)

14780. Dike, Fatima, *et al.* Beyond the USA, beyond the UK. *In* (pp. 199–218) **12297**.

Frank Bidart

14781. Bidart, Frank. A cross in the void. *In* (pp. 246–54) **16122**.

14782. Greenwell, Garth. Frank Bidart, lyric poet. Parnassus (29:1/2) 2006, 330–47.

14783. Keniston, Ann. Overheard voices: address and subjectivity in postmodern American poetry. *See* **18042**.

14784. Longenbach, James. The very rich hours of Frank Bidart. Salmagundi (148/149) 2005/06, 271–83.

14785. Polito, Robert. Holy the Fifth International. *In* (pp. 226–42) **16122**.

Carmel Bird (b.1940)

14786. Rodríguez Salas, Gerardo. 'Time and tide': an interview with Carmel Bird. Atl (28:2) 2006, 125–32.

Elizabeth Bishop

14787. Abeni, Damiano; Duranti, Riccardo; Fatica, Ottavio (eds and trans). Miracolo a colazione. Milan: Adelphi, 2006. pp. 288. (Biblioteca Adelphi, 487.) Rev. by Francesco Rognoni in Indice (2006:4) 17; by Massimo Bacigalupo in Semicerchio (34) 2006, 94–5.

14788. Ellis, Jonathan. Art and memory in the work of Elizabeth Bishop. Aldershot; Burlington, VT: Ashgate, 2006. pp. 226.

14789. Hickman, Trenton. Theodore Roethke and the poetics of place. *In* (pp. 183–202) **13763**.

14790. Hoff, Amy K. Bishop, the autobiographical pact, and poetic pedagogy. CEAF (35:2) 2006.

14791. Kirsch, Adam. Good pickings: Elizabeth Bishop's hard-earned mastery. TLS, 28 Apr. 2006, 3–4 (review-article).

14792. Mason, Emma. 'Love's the burning boy': Hemans's critical legacy. *In* (pp. 205–24) **13735**.

14793. O'Neill, Michael. 'The all-sustaining air': Yeats, Stevens, Rich, Bishop – responses to Romantic poetry. *In* (pp. 143–62) **13735**.

14794. Quinn, Alice (ed.). *Edgar Allan Poe & the Juke-Box*: uncollected poems, drafts, and fragments. New York: Farrar, Straus, & Giroux, 2006. pp. xx, 367. Rev. by John Palattella in BosR (31:3) 2006, 45–6; by Gillian White in LRB (28:10) 2006, 8–10; by Adam Kirsch in TLS, 28 Apr. 2006, 3–4.

14795. Rosenbaum, Susan. Elizabeth Bishop's theater of war. *In* (pp. 53–82) **13763**.

14796. Saunders, Judith P. Tomlinson's *In Oklahoma*: Bishop's *The Armadillo* as literary source. *See* **18850**.

14797. White, Gillian. Awful but cheerful. LRB (28:10) 2006, 8–10 (review-article). (Bishop's drafts.)

14798. Zona, Kirstin Hotelling. May Swenson and Elizabeth Bishop. *In* (pp. 55–80) **7907**.

Alexander Blackburn (b.1929)

14799. Nizalowski, John. Embracing the West: an interview with Alexander Blackburn. BRev (26:4) 2006, 5, 25.

Algernon Blackwood

14800. Thompson, Terry W. 'He used to wear a veil': pursuing the Other in Algernon Blackwood's *The Listener*. PLL (42:1) 2006, 95–110.

Clark Blaise

14801. Davis, Rocío G. Performing dialogic subjectivities: the aesthetic project of autobiographical collaboration in *Days and Nights in Calcutta*. *In* (pp. 159–72) **11849**.

William J. (William James) Blake (1894–1968)

14802. Rowley, Hazel. Her darling boy. TLS, 6 Jan. 2006, 10 (review-article). (Correspondence of Stead and Blake.)

Robin Blaser

14803. NICHOLS, MIRIAM (ed.). The fire: collected essays of Robin Blaser. Berkeley; London: California UP, 2006. pp. xvii, 516, (plates) 6.

Mary Clearman Blew

14804. FUNDA, EVELYN I. Mary Clearman Blew. Boise, ID: Boise State Univ., 2006. pp. 51. (Boise State Univ. Western writers, 172.)

Francesca Lia Block

14805. KAPLAN, DEBORAH; RABINOWITZ, REBECCA. 'Beautiful, or thick, or right, or complicated': queer heterosexuality in the young adult works of Francesca Lia Block and Cynthia Voigt. *In* (pp. 196–207) **11883**.

Robert Bly

14806. PICHASKE, DAVID. Where now 'Midwestern literature'? *See* **19520**.

14807. VAN NESS, GORDON. 'The fiercest hearts are in love with a wild perfection': the James Dickey / James Wright correspondence. *See* **15496**.

Louise Bogan

14808. GREGERSON, LINDA. Rhetorical contract in the lyric poem. *See* **6930**.

14809. KINZIE, MARY (ed.). A poet's prose: selected writings of Louise Bogan; with the uncollected poems. (Bibl. 2005, 15518.) Rev. by Jeffrey Meyers in GaR (60:3/4) 2006, 775–81; by Carol Bere in WRB (23:5) 2006, 33–4.

14810. MEYERS, JEFFREY. Confronting the demons. *See* **15495**.

Eric Bogosian

14811. BOGOSIAN, ERIC. Eric Bogosian on character. Dramatist (8:4) 2006, 28–9.

Eavan Boland

14812. LOJEK, HELEN. Man, woman, soldier: Heaney's *In Memoriam Francis Ledwidge* and Boland's *Heroic*. *See* **16319**.

14813. LOJO RODRÍGUEZ, LAURA M[A]. Female iconography and subjectivity in Eavan Boland's *In Her Own Image*. Atl (28:1) 2006, 89–100.

14814. VILLAR, PILAR. 'The text of it': a conversation with Eavan Boland. NewHR (10:2) 2006, 52–67.

Kate Bornstein (b.1948)

14815. BERNSTEIN, ROBIN. Kate Bornstein and Barbara Carrellas: queer theater, musicals to masturbation, a conversation with Too Tall Blondes. *In* (pp. 103–11) **12245**.

David Bottoms

14816. HILL, JANE. Fucked Ivanhoes in the deep obsession of memory: Andrew Hudgins, David Bottoms, and the legacy of war in Southern poetry. *See* **16478**.

14817. —— 'The river we're all troubled by': David Bottoms and the legacy of James Dickey. JDN (22:2) 2006, 23–40.

14818. WALSH, WILLIAM. David Bottoms: an interview. FiveP (10:1/2) 2006, 269–87.

Andrew Bovell (b.1962)

14819. Pulford, Donald. The history wars and *Holy Day (the Red Sea)*: Andrew Bovell's dramatic black armband. Antipodes (20:2) 2006, 150–4.

Elizabeth Bowen

14820. Corcoran, Neil. Elizabeth Bowen: the enforced return. (Bibl. 2005, 15534.) Rev. by Melissa Fegan in Mod/Mod (13:2) 2006, 403–5; by Susan Osborn in MFS (52:1) 2006, 187–97.

14821. Franks, Jill. Sex, guns, and death: Deborah Warner's adaptation of *The Last September*. NewHR (10:3) 2006, 122–36.

14822. Gunby, Ingrid. 'There is no ghost in this house': home and history in Elizabeth Bowen. *In* (pp. 213–25) **8374**.

14823. Ingman, Heather. Translating between cultures: a Kristevan reading of the theme of the foreigner in some twentieth-century novels by Irish women. *See* **17803**.

14824. Landon, Lana Hartman; Smith, Laurel. Early works by modern women writers: Woolf, Bowen, Mansfield, Cather, and Stein. *See* **19300**.

14825. Osborn, Susan. Reconsidering Elizabeth Bowen. MFS (52:1) 2006, 187–97 (review-article).

14826. Palusci, Oriana. '*The London Blitz*': uno sguardo di genere. *In* (pp. 281–97) **7343**.

14827. Rumbarger, Lee. Housekeeping: women Modernists' writings on war and home. *See* **19326**.

Jane Bowles

14828. Tinkler, Alan. Jane Bowles. RCF (26:2) 2006, 66–87.

Paul Bowles

14829. D'Amico, Maria Vittoria. '*Baptism of solitude*': Paul Bowles e l'aura del deserto. *In* (pp. 223–34) **11824**.

14830. Edwards, Brian T. Sheltering screens: Paul Bowles and foreign relations. AmLH (17:2) 2005, 307–34.

14831. Ficociello, Robert. Fish(ing) for colonial counter-narratives in the short fiction of Paul Bowles. *In* (pp. 167–73) **14238**.

14832. Ortells Montón, Elena. 'Viajero en tierra extraña': Paul Bowles y la retórica de la interculturalidad. CLR (1) 2004, 89–95.

George Elroy Boyd (b.1952)

14833. Moynagh, Maureen. Can I get a witness? Performing community in African Nova Scotian theatre. CanTR (125) 2006, 41–6.

Thomas Boyd

14834. Bruce, Brian. Thomas Boyd: lost author of the 'Lost Generation'. Akron, OH: Akron UP, 2006. pp. xv, 188. (Series on Ohio history and culture.) Rev. by Sarah Domet in OVH (6:4) 2006, 80–1.

William Boyd

14835. ELICES, JUAN F. The satiric worlds of William Boyd: a case-study. New York; Frankfurt: Lang, 2006. pp. 259. (European univ. studies, XIV: Anglo-Saxon language and literature, 412.)

Kay Boyle

14836. REYNES, ANNE. L'imaginaire de l'exil chez Kay Boyle. Anglophonia (19) 2006, 271–8.

T. Coraghessan Boyle

14837. COATES, PETER. Eastenders go west: English sparrows, immigrants, and the nature of fear. JAStud (39:3) 2005, 431–62.

14838. ROSE, DANIEL ASA. In conversation with T. Coraghessan Boyle. BkW, 16 July 2006, 3.

Ray Bradbury

14839. BLEDIG, JOAN D. Of Burroughs … and Bradbury. *See* **14928**.

14840. POLLIN, BURTON R. Poe and Ray Bradbury: a persistent influence and interest. *See* **11039**.

14841. TIBBETTS, JOHN C. Ray Bradbury's EPCOT adventure. Storytelling (6:1) 2006, 57–63. (Experimental Prototype Community of Tomorrow.)

Barbara Taylor Bradford

14842. DUDGEON, PIERS. The woman of substance: the life and works of Barbara Taylor Bradford. London: HarperCollins, 2005. pp. xvi, 347, (plates) 32. Rev. by Sophie Harrison in NYTB, 12 Nov. 2006, 61.

Charles A. (Charles Andrew) Brady (1912–1995)

14843. LOVERING, JOSEPH P. The well-made historical novels of American regionalist Charles A. Brady, 1912–1995: defender of the moral fabric of local cultures. Lewiston, NY; Lampeter: Mellen Press, 2006. pp. vi, 176.

William Stanley Beaumont Braithwaite

14844. SZEFEL, LISA. Beauty and William Braithwaite. Callaloo (29:2) 2006, 560–86.

Mona Brand

14845. GILBERT, HELEN. Millennial blues; racism, nationalism, and the legacy of empire. *In* (pp. 12–28) **12360**.

Di Brandt

14846. MACDONALD, TANIS. Reparative strategies: an interview with Di Brandt. Arc (57) 2006, 36–48.

Edward Kamau Brathwaite

14847. LA GRAND, VIRGINIA; MATTSON, CRAIG T. Brave new performance space: castaway pedagogy in the age of Caliban. CSR (35:4) 2006, 471–91.

14848. RODRÍGUEZ GUERRERO-STRACHAN, SANTIAGO. Social exiles and language refugees: the case of postcolonial authors. *See* **17755**.

Richard Brautigan

14849. McDermott, James Dishon. Austere style in twentieth-century literature: literary minimalism. Lewiston, NY; Lampeter: Mellen Press, 2006. pp. iii, 153.

Christopher Brennan (1870–1932)

14850. Barnes, Katherine. The higher self in Christopher Brennan's poems: esotericism, Romanticism, symbolism. Leiden; Boston, MA: Brill, 2006. pp. xii, 317. (Aries, 2.)

Maeve Brennan

14851. Bourke, Angela. Maeve Brennan: homesick at *The New Yorker*. (Bibl. 2005, 15564.) Rev. by Anne Fogarty in FDR (1) 2005, 253–5.

Breyten Breytenbach

14852. Coullie, Judith Lütge; Jacobs, J. U. (eds). A.k.a. Breyten Breytenbach: critical approaches to his writings and paintings. (Bibl. 2005, 15566.) Rev. by Mark Sanders in RAL (37:3) 2006, 209–10.

Robert Bridges

14853. Hurley, Michael D. Darkening the subject of Hopkins' prosody. *See* **10475**.

14854. Schlatter, Fredric W. Hopkins and Baillie. *See* **10489**.

André Brink

14855. Diala, Isidore. André Brink and Malraux. ConLit (47:1) 2006, 91–113.

14856. Gräbe, Ina. Theory and technology in contemporary South African writing: from self-conscious exploration to contextual appropriation. *In* (pp. 203–12) **14093**.

Erna Brodber

14857. Dance, Daryl Cumber. Who was Cock Robin? A new reading of Erna Brodber's *Jane and Louisa Will Soon Come Home*. CLAJ (50:1) 2006, 20–36.

14858. Page, Kezia. 'Two places can make children': Erna Brodber's *Louisiana*. JWIL (13:1/2) 2005, 57–79.

14859. Roberts, June E. Reading Erna Brodber: uniting the Black diaspora through folk culture and religion. Westport, CT; London: Praeger, 2006. pp. xiv, 275. (Contributions in Afro-American and African studies, 210.)

Joseph Brodsky (b.1940)

14860. Haven, Cynthia L. Uncle Grisha was right. KR (28:3) 2006, 159–68 (review-article).

14861. Shtern, Ludmila. Brodsky: a personal memoir. (Bibl. 2005, 15573.) Rev. by Cynthia L. Haven in KR (28:3) 2006, 159–68.

14862. Steele, Peter. Zones of the imagination. *See* **17250**.

14863. Weissbort, Daniel. From Russian with love: Joseph Brodsky in English: pages from a journal, 1996–97. (Bibl. 2005, 15575.) Rev. by Cynthia L. Haven in KR (28:3) 2006, 159–68.

Louis Bromfield

14864. WATERMAN, JAYNE. Suburban self-alienation: Louis Bromfield's *Mr Smith*. MidAmerica (32) 2005, 61–6.

William Bronk

14865. CLIPPINGER, DAVID. The mind's landscape: William Bronk and twentieth-century American poetry. Newark: Delaware UP, 2006. pp. 288. Rev. by Jon Curley in AmBR (28:1) 2006, 17.

14866. GILMORE, LYMAN. The force of desire: a life of William Bronk. Jersey City, NJ: Talisman House, 2006. pp. xxix, 348. Rev. by Jon Curley in AmBR (28:1) 2006, 17; by Harry Smith in Confrontation (94/95) 2006, 337–8.

Rupert Brooke

14867. VANCE, NORMAN. Classics and the Dardanelles campaign. NQ (53:3) 2006, 347–9.

Christine Brooke-Rose

14868. SMITH, ALI. The armchair, the world: Christine Brooke-Rose and the evocation of self. TLS, 24 Mar. 2006, 21–2 (review-article).

Anita Brookner

14869. PETIT, LAURENCE. Romance of a family or inverted 'family romance': familial gaze or narratorial look in Anita Brookner's *Family and Friends*. LIT (17:3/4) 2006, 379–97.

Gwendolyn Brooks

14870. ALEXANDER, ELIZABETH (ed.). The essential Gwendolyn Brooks. New York: Library of America, 2005. pp. xxvi, 148. (American poets project, 19.) Rev. by Danielle Chapman in Poetry (189:1) 2006, 54–63.

14871. CHAPMAN, DANIELLE. Sweet bombs. Poetry (189:1) 2006, 54–63 (review-article). (Influence of Eliot on Brooks.)

14872. DEBO, ANNETTE. Signifying *Afrika*: Gwendolyn Brooks' later poetry. Callaloo (29:1) 2006, 168–81.

14873. GILMORE, SUSAN. 'It had the beat inevitable': Gwendolyn Brooks's report from the fifties. Sagetrieb (19:3) 2006, 105–40.

14874. GOODMAN, JENNY. Revisionary postwar heroism in Gwendolyn Brooks's *Annie Allen*. *In* (pp. 159–80) **3395**.

14875. MALEWITZ, RAYMOND. 'My newish voice': rethinking Black power in Gwendolyn Brooks's whirlwind. Callaloo (29:2) 2006, 531–44.

14876. SULLIVAN, JAMES D. Writing about Gwendolyn Brooks anyway. *In* (pp. 198–208) **20098**.

Catharine Savage Brosman (b.1934)

14877. MIDDLETON, DAVID. Gatherings: four American poets. SewR (113:3) 2005, 485–99 (review-article). (Arts and letters.)

Alice Brown (1857–1948)

14878. ANDERSON, DONALD. Grounded perceptions: land and value in two plays of the New England decline. *See* **10431**.

George Mackay Brown (b.1921)

14879. Bevan, Archie; Murray, Brian (eds). The collected poems of George Mackay Brown. London: Murray, 2005. pp. xxiv, 547.

14880. Dunn, Douglas. An island voice: memories and myths of George Mackay Brown. TLS, 11 Aug. 2006, 3–4 (review-article).

14881. Fergusson, Maggie. George Mackay Brown: the life. London: Murray, 2006. pp. xiv, 363, (plates) 8. Rev. by Douglas Dunn in TLS, 11 Aug. 2006, 3–4.

Rita Mae Brown

14882. Sun, Hong. The evolution of pre- and post-Stonewall gay literature in America. *See* **18902**.

Dennis Brutus

14883. Karim, Aisha; Sustar, Lee (eds). Poetry & protest: a Dennis Brutus reader. Chicago, IL: Haymarket, 2006. pp. 414.

Winifred Bryher (Annie Winifred Ellerman, 'Bryher') (b.1894)

14884. McCabe, Susan. Whither sexuality and gender? 'What that sign signifies' and the rise of queer historicism. *See* **20100**.

14885. —— (introd.). Visa for Avalon: a novel. (Bibl. 2005, 15598.) Rev. by Charlotte Mandel in ELT (49:1) 2006, 114–17.

John Buchan (1875–1940)

14886. Acton, Tom. Ved Dzabqu qd vnh Urod. JBJ (34) 2006, 40–5. (Scudder's code in *The Thirty-Nine Steps*.)

14887. Greig, James C. G. John Buchan, Calvinism, Bunyan and the Classics. JBJ (35) 2006, 5–11.

14888. Haldane, John. Fiction's enigma innovations: the art of the thriller. JBJ (35) 2006, 12–14.

14889. Henshaw, Peter. John Buchan and the invention of Canada, 1902–1940. JBJ (34) 2006, 18–29.

14890. —— A 'murky and distorted genius': John Buchan on Cecil Rhodes, 1901–1940. JBJ (35) 2006, 21–30.

14891. Lownie, Andrew. John Buchan: Conservative politician. JBJ (35) 2006, 31–4.

14892. Macdonald, Kate. The translations of John Buchan's wartime histories. JBJ (34) 2006, 30–5.

14893. Redley, Michael (introd.). Buchan's speech to the Empire Club. JBJ (34) 2006, 2–10.

14894. Ross, Michael. To sign or to inscribe? JBJ (34) 2006, 11–17. (Signed copies of Buchan's books.)

Pearl S. Buck

14895. Leong, Karen J. The China mystique: Pearl S. Buck, Anna May Wong, Mayling Soong, and the transformation of American Orientalism. Berkeley; London: California UP, 2005. pp. x, 236, (plates) 14. Rev. by Christina Klein in JAH (93:1) 2006, 261–2; by Robert Shaffer in PacHR (75:4) 2006, 695–6; by Mina Shin in JAAS (9:3) 2006, 319–27.

14896. MEYER, MIKE. Pearl of the Orient. NYTB, 5 Mar. 2006, 23.

Christopher Buckley

14897. BUCKLEY, CHRISTOPHER. The poet on the poem. APR (35:3) 2006, 47.

14898. —— Sleepwalk: California dreamin' and a last dance with the '60s. Spokane: Eastern Washington UP, 2006. pp. 160. (Memoirs.)

Charles Bukowski

14899. MARTIN, JOHN (ed.). Come on in! New poems. New York: Ecco, 2006. pp. 279.

14900. MILES, BARRY. Charles Bukowski. Charlottesville; London: Virginia UP, 2005. pp. 314. Rev. by Ron Powers in NYTB, 19 Nov. 2006, 24.

Carlos Bulosan

14901. MILLER, JOSHUA L. The gorgeous laughter of Filipino modernity: Carlos Bulosan's *The Laughter of My Father*. *In* (pp. 238–68) **12024**.

Basil Bunting

14902. DI PIERO, W. S. Brag, sweet tenor bull. Poetry (185:6) 2005, 454–62 (review-article).

14903. TOMLINSON, CHARLES. Objectivism: William Carlos Williams and Basil Bunting. *In* (pp. 133–45) **16284**.

Eugene Burdick

14904. FERRER, HUGH. Notes on the *Connecticut Yankee*. *See* **11494**.

Anthony Burgess

14905. BISWELL, ANDREW. The real life of Anthony Burgess. (Bibl. 2005, 15619.) Rev. by Colin Burrow in LRB (28:3) 2006, 19–20; by Anthony Radice in ContRev (288:1682) 2006, 380–2.

14906. BROWN, KEVIN. 'Tis pity she's a whore: the revision of Mary Magdalene in contemporary fiction. *See* **12254**.

14907. BURROW, COLIN. Not quite nasty. LRB (28:3) 2006, 19–20 (review-article). (Burgess's unfashionableness.)

14908. GEHRKE, PAT J. Deviant subjects in Foucault and *A Clockwork Orange*: criminological constructions of subjectivity. *In* (pp. 146–64) **13202**.

Mebane Holoman Burgwyn (1914–1992)

14909. DAVIS, SARAH W. '[Her] destiny lay in the land': an overview of the literature of Mebane Holoman Burgwyn. NCLR (15) 2006, 24–31.

James Lee Burke (b.1936)

14910. BOGUE, BARBARA. James Lee Burke and the soul of Dave Robicheaux: a critical study of the crime fiction series. Jefferson, NC; London: McFarland, 2006. pp. x, 209.

Kenneth Burke (b.1897)

14911. NEWSTOK, SCOTT L. (introd.). Why *A Midsummer Night's Dream*? By Kenneth Burke. *See* **5996**.

John Burnside

14912. Burnside, John. A lie about my father. London: Cape, 2006. pp. 323. (Memoirs.)

14913. —— A science of belonging: poetry as ecology. *In* (pp. 91–106) **13732.**

Edgar Rice Burroughs

14914. Adams, David A. Baum, Burroughs, and the Theosophy connection. BurB (58) 2004, 24–6.

14915. —— A folklorist reading of *Tarzan and the Forbidden City.* BurB (62) 2005, 3–12.

14916. —— *Llana of Gathol*: a Jungian interpretation. BurB (68) 2006, 3–12.

14917. —— *The Resurrection of Jimber-Jaw*: the cave man in American society. BurB (60) 2004, 3–4.

14918. —— Some remarks on Edgar Rice Burroughs' *Tarzan the Magnificent.* BurB (59) 2004, 3–8.

14919. —— A study of *Land of Terror.* BurB (64) 2005, 3–10.

14920. Adams, David Arthur. *Escape on Venus*: E.R.B.'s alchemy at bay. BurB (67) 2006, 3–9.

14921. Barrett, Robert R. The anomaly of *Tarzan and the Forbidden City.* BurB (62) 2005, 13–17.

14922. —— Edgar Rice Burroughs and the mystery woman. BurB (64) 2005, 25–9.

14923. —— How John Carter became Flash Gordon. BurB (60) 2004, 19–26.

14924. —— Illustrated by J. Allen St John: the Edgar Rice Burroughs, Inc. editions. BurB (58) 2004, 7–23.

14925. —— An incomplete list of the illustrations of Dorothy Dulin. BurB (66) 2006, 22–3.

14926. —— *Tarzan and the Madman* and Reed Crandall: thoughts and remembrances. BurB (66) 2006, 3–9.

14927. Bender, Jack; Bender, Carole. Warner Brothers' Tarzan TV series. BurB (63) 2005, 32–3.

14928. Bledig, Joan D. Of Burroughs … and Bradbury. BurB (67) 2006, 28–33.

14929. Cash, Sam. Language in Burroughsland. BurB (67) 2006, 17–25.

14930. Decuyper, Michel. The French translations of Edgar Rice Burroughs, 1926–1950. Trans. by Elaine Casella. BurB (62) 2005, 31–3.

14931. Fury, David. Maureen O'Sullivan: 'no average Jane'. BurB (65) 2006, 9–11.

14932. Gaitonde, Vishwas R. Magic men. BurB (59) 2004, 28–31. (Quacks in the Tarzan books.)

14933. Galloway, Stan. Alienation in *Tarzan's First Love.* BurB (62) 2005, 19–23.

14934. Hanson, Alan. Tarzan and the hideous hunter: *The Death of Tarzan.* BurB (67) 2006, 11–16.

14935. Harwood, John; Starr, H. W. Comedy of errors: a refutation of the 'errors' charged against the Burroughs stories. BurB (64) 2005, 11–22.

14936. McWhorter, George T. Addendum: memos from Morbus. BurB (63) 2005, 6–8.

14937. —— Castaway notes. BurB (65) 2006, 3–5.

14938. —— Madman and baboon boy. BurB (66) 2006, 11.

14939. —— Maltu Mephis! A study of *Carson of Venus*. BurB (61) 2005, 3–5.

14940. —— Quest for the fountain of youth. BurB (57) 2004, 3–5.

14941. —— Stone Age recollections. BurB (58) 2004, 3–5.

14942. Minyard, Applewhite. Cloning men and story ideas. BurB (63) 2005, 3–5.

14943. Moscati, Camillo. Giorgio De Gaspari, Italian artist. Trans. by Numeriano Rodenas. BurB (65) 2006, 7–8.

14944. Nielsen, Leon. From Tarzan to Conan: notes on the possible influence of Edgar Rice Burroughs on the writings of Robert E. Howard. *See* **16470**.

14945. —— Numa – lord of the beasts. BurB (68) 2006, 13–17.

14946. —— Jørgensen, Jan. Axel Mathiesen: Burroughs' Danish artist. BurB (57) 2004, 7–10.

14947. Prindle, R. E. It hurts me, too: Emma and the *anima*. BurB (59) 2004, 17–25.

14948. —— Tarzan and the river: part III. BurB (57) 2004, 11–19.

14949. Puncer, Frank. 'Consider yourself kissed': E.R.B.'s World War II letters to Caryl Lee. BurB (65) 2006, 23–32.

14950. Spencer, Paul. The mystery of *The Red Star of Tarzan*. BurB (62) 2005, 24–30.

14951. Tucapskey, Vladimir. Tarzan beaten, changed, or silenced. BurB (61) 2005, 29–33.

14952. Warbaby, Dugald. Edgar Rice Burroughs: the early married years. BurB (60) 2004, 27–32.

William Burroughs

14953. Burroughs, William. Notes on *Frisk*. *In* (pp. 80–2) **15336**.

14954. Eisenhauer, Robert. Parables of disfiguration: reason and excess from Romanticism to the avant-garde. *See* **11208**.

14955. Harris, Oliver. Not Burroughs' final fix: materializing *The Yage Letters*. PMC (16:2) 2006.

14956. —— (ed.). The Yage letters *redux*. *See* **16102**.

14957. Houen, Alex. William S. Burroughs's *Cities of the Red Night* trilogy: writing outer space. JAStud (40:3) 2006, 523–49.

14958. Johnson, Rob. The lost years of William S. Burroughs: Beats in South Texas. College Station: Texas A&M UP, 2006. pp. 200, (plates) 8.

14959. Ohle, David (comp.). Cursed from birth: the short, unhappy life of William S. Burroughs, Jr. New York: Soft Skull Press, 2006. pp. 210.

14960. Pepper, Andrew. State power matters: power, the State and political struggle in the post-war American novel. TexP (19:4) 2005, 467–91.

14961. Prezzavento, Paolo. The cowboy as a 'queer conglomerate': Pat Garrett & Billy the Kid. QPS (14) 2006, 309–17.

14962. SCHNEIDERMAN, DAVIS; WALSH, PHILIP (eds). Retaking the universe: William S. Burroughs in the age of globalization. (Bibl. 2004, 15901.) Rev. by Katie Stewart in JAStud (39:2) 2005, 343–4; by David Banash in PMC (16:2) 2006.

Catherine Bush

14963. MACKINNON, JOHN E. Risk and resilience in Catherine Bush's *Minus Time*. JCL (41:2) 2006, 101–20.

Agnes Bushell (b.1949)

14964. FERSTER, JUDITH. The family of origin *versus* the human family: universal love in literature. *In* (pp. 249–61) **3896**.

Candace Bushnell

14965. FERRISS, SUZANNE; YOUNG, MALLORY (eds). Chick lit: the new woman's fiction. *See* **19862**.

14966. KIERNAN, ANNA. No satisfaction: *Sex and the City, Run Catch Kiss*, and the conflict of desires in chick lit's new heroines. *In* (pp. 207–18) **19862**.

14967. MABRY, A. ROCHELLE. About a girl: female subjectivity and sexuality in contemporary 'chick' culture. *In* (pp. 191–206) **19862**.

Octavia Butler

14968. ANDERSON, CRYSTAL S. 'The girl isn't white': new racial dimensions in Octavia Butler's *Survivor*. Extrapolation (47:1) 2006, 35–50.

14969. GOVAN, SANDRA Y. Going to see the woman: a visit with Octavia E. Butler. Ob3 (6:2/7:1) 2005/06, 14–39.

14970. HAIRSTON, ANDREA. Octavia Butler – praise song to a prophetic artist. *In* (pp. 287–304) **13537**.

14971. HAMPTON, GREGORY. *Kindred*: history, revision, and (re)memory of bodies. Ob3 (6:2/7:1) 2005/06, 105–17.

14972. JENKINS, ALICE. Knowing and geography in Octavia Butler, Ursula K. Le Guin and Maureen McHugh. JFA (16:4) 2006, 320–34.

14973. RICHARD, THELMA SHINN. Defining kindred: Octavia Butler's postcolonial perspective. Ob3 (6:2/7:1) 2005/06, 118–34.

14974. RUFFIN, KIMBERLY J. Parable of a 21st-century religion: Octavia Butler's Afrofuturistic bridge between science and religion. Ob3 (6:2/7:1) 2005/06, 87–104.

14975. WANZO, REBECCA. Apocalyptic empathy: a *Parable* of postmodern sentimentality. Ob3 (6:2/7:1) 2005/06, 72–86.

14976. WARFIELD, ANGELA. Reassessing the utopian novel: Octavia Butler, Jacques Derrida, and the impossible future of utopia. Ob3 (6:2/7:1) 2005/06, 61–71.

Mary Butts

14977. RADFORD, ANDREW. Defending nature's holy shrine: Mary Butts, Englishness, and the Persephone myth. JML (29:3) 2006, 126–49.

A. S. Byatt

14978. Bourdarot, Émilie. Les mondes parallèles dans *The Virgin in the Garden*, *Babel Tower* et *A Whistling Woman* de A. S. Byatt. EtBr (30) 2006, 95–104.

14979. Franková, Milada. The postmodern bravura of A. S. Byatt. AtlCR (3:1) 2005, 108–19.

14980. Gauthier, Tim S. Narrative desire and historical reparations: A. S. Byatt, Ian McEwan, Salman Rushdie. London; New York: Routledge, 2006. pp. ix, 211. (Literary criticism and cultural theory.)

14981. Gorski, Hedwig. The riddle of correspondences in A. S. Byatt's *Possession: a Romance* with H.D.'s *Trilogy*. Storytelling (5:4) 2006, 223–34.

14982. Hidalgo, Pilar. Doris Lessing and A. S. Byatt: writing *The Golden Notebook* in the 1990s. *See* **17124**.

14983. O'Neill, John. Adam's novel? The *Omphalos* and the ending of *Possession*. CritW (47:4) 2006, 331–44.

14984. Petit, Laurence. Textual and pictorial distortions: sublimity and abjection in A. S. Byatt's *The Chinese Lobster*. EtBr (31) 2006, 117–26.

14985. —— 'Truth in framing': Medusa's defeat; or, The triumph of the 'framed' self in A. S. Byatt's *Medusa's Ankles*. *In* (pp. 117–36) **11781**.

14986. Tiffin, Jessica. Ice, glass, snow: fairy tale as art and metafiction in the writing of A. S. Byatt. MarvT (20:1) 2006, 47–66.

14987. Walker, Jonathan. An interview with A. S. Byatt and Lawrence Norfolk. ConLit (47:3) 2006, 318–42.

John Cage

14988. Armand, Louis. Writing after: Joyce, Cage. *See* **16652**.

14989. Joseph, Brandon W. Andy Warhol's *Sleep*: the play of repetition. *In* (pp. 179–207) **12654**.

14990. McCaffery, Steve. Transcoherence and deletion: the mesostic writings of John Cage. EA (59:3) 2006, 329–40.

14991. Perloff, Marjorie. 'Moving information': on Kenneth Goldsmith's *The Weather*. *See* **20243**.

James M. Cain

14992. Whiting, Frederick. Playing against type: statistical personhood, depth narrative, and the business of genre in James M. Cain's *Double Indemnity*. JNT (36:2) 2006, 190–227.

Erskine Caldwell

14993. Arnold, Edwin T. Erskine Caldwell and Judge Lynch: Caldwell's role in the anti-lynching campaigns of the 1930s. *In* (pp. 183–202) **15001**.

14994. Cook, Sylvia J. Erskine Caldwell: Modernism from the bottom up. *In* (pp. 58–76) **15001**.

14995. Duck, Leigh Anne. The nation's region: Southern Modernism, segregation, and US nationalism. Athens; London: Georgia UP, 2006. pp. x, 340. (New Southern studies.)

14996. Dyen, Jonathan. 'Ripe for revolution': ideological struggle in *God's Little Acre*. *In* (pp. 150–64) **15001**.

14997. Hitchcock, Bert. Well, maybe just this once: Erskine Caldwell, Old Southwest humor, and funny ha-ha. *In* (pp. 27–45) **15001**.

14998. Jacobs, Tom. Poeticizing the political image: Caldwell, Bourke-White, and the recasting of phototextual expression. *In* (pp. 92–113) **15001**.

14999. Leiter, Andrew B. Sexual degeneracy and the anti-lynching tradition in Erskine Caldwell's *Trouble in July*. *In* (pp. 203–22) **15001**.

15000. McDonald, Robert L. Selected bibliography of works on Erskine Caldwell: 1982–2005. *In* (pp. 223–30) **15001**.

15001. —— (ed.). Reading Erskine Caldwell: new essays. Jefferson, NC; London: McFarland, 2006. pp. viii, 239.

15002. Metress, Christopher. Repetition as radical critique in Erskine Caldwell's *God's Little Acre*. *In* (pp. 165–82) **15001**.

15003. Palmer, Louis. Bourgeois Blues: class, Whiteness, and Southern gothic in early Faulkner and Caldwell. *See* **15828**.

15004. Rachels, David. Erskine Caldwell's short stories: teetering on the edge of the canon. *In* (pp. 11–26) **15001**.

15005. Rieger, Christopher B. Silent spring on Tobacco Road: the degradation of the environment in Erskine Caldwell's fiction. *In* (pp. 131–49) **15001**.

15006. Ruppersburg, Hugh. Comedy and satire in Erskine Caldwell's *The Sure Hand of God*. *In* (pp. 46–57) **15001**.

15007. Smith, Joyce Caldwell. Cubist strategies: from Williams's *Red Wheelbarrow* to Caldwell's *Yellow Girl*. *In* (pp. 77–91) **15001**.

15008. Wilson, Natalie. Social injustice embodied: Caldwell and the grotesque. *In* (pp. 114–30) **15001**.

Camara Laye

15009. Ogwude, Sophia O. Of hounds and quarry: the African human condition on canvas. *In* (pp. 237–51) **11860**.

Roy Campbell

15010. Connolly, Cressida. The rare and the beautiful: the art, loves, and lives of the Garman sisters. New York: Ecco, 2004. pp. xiv, 320. Rev. by Jeremy Treglown in TLS, 10 Sept. 2004, 32.

15011. Van der Vlies, Andrew. 'Hurled by what aim to what tremendous range!': Roy Campbell and the politics of anthologies, 1927–1945. ESA (48:1) 2005, 64–85.

Will D. Campbell

15012. Campbell, Will. Writing as subversion. *In* (pp. 85–94) **11940**.

Norma Elia Cantú (b.1947)

15013. Kraver, Jeraldine R. Norma Elia Cantú's fictional autobioethnography: not-quite-true stories about real life on La Frontera. A/B (20:1) 2005, 76–89.

Thomas Caplan

15014. Cardi, Luciana. Angela Carter's postmodern rewriting of Japan: the metamorphosis of Lady Murasaki and of the Oriental fox. *In* (pp. 61–81) **11955**.

Truman Capote

15015. Gentry, Marshall Bruce. He would have been a good man: compassion and meanness in Truman Capote and Flannery O'Connor. *In* (pp. 42–55) **17825**.

Mary Caraker

15016. Di Fiore, Elisa. Of witches and wives: fictional roles in Mary Caraker's *Women of the Kalevala*. *In* (pp. 45–60) **11955**.

Peter Carey

15017. Ashcroft, Bill. Simulation, resistance and transformation: *The Unusual Life of Tristan Smith*. *In* (pp. 199–214) **15024**.

15018. Birns, Nicholas. 'A dazzled eye': *Kristu-Du* and the architecture of tyranny. *In* (pp. 101–14) **15024**.

15019. Bliss, Carolyn. Lies and silences: cultural masterplots and existential authenticity in Peter Carey's *True History of the Kelly Gang*. *In* (pp. 275–300) **15024**.

15020. Eustace, John. Going bush: performing the pastoral in Peter Carey's *Bliss*. Antipodes (20:2) 2006, 108–16.

15021. Gaile, Andreas. Bibliography. *In* (pp. 349–408) **15024**.

15022. —— The 'contrarian streak': an interview with Peter Carey (conducted on 26 March 2004 in Manhattan). *In* (pp. 3–16) **15024**.

15023. —— Towards an alphabet of Australian culture. *In* (pp. 33–51) **15024**.

15024. —— (ed.). Fabulating beauty: perspectives on the fiction of Peter Carey. Amsterdam; New York: Rodopi, 2004. pp. xxxv, 438. (Cross/cultures: readings in the post-colonial literatures in English, 78.) Rev. by Jean-François Vernay in ALS (22:3) 2006, 399–401.

15025. Hassall, Anthony J. A wildly distorted account? Peter Carey's *30 Days in Sydney*. *In* (pp. 319–33) **15024**.

15026. Highfield, Jonathan. Suckling from the crocodile's tit: wildlife and nation formation in Australian narratives. Antipodes (20:2) 2006, 127–40.

15027. Jose, Nicholas. *Bliss* and damnation: Peter Carey in Australia. *In* (pp. 137–47) **15024**.

15028. Lamb, Karen. Bringing Australia home: Peter Carey, the Booker, and the repatriation of Australian culture. *In* (pp. 17–30) **15024**.

15029. Larsson, Christer. Cross references: allusions to Christian tradition in Peter Carey's fiction. *In* (pp. 53–70) **15024**.

15030. Maack, Annegret. Peter Carey's *Jack Maggs*: an Aussie story? *In* (pp. 229–43) **15024**.

15031. McCredden, Lyn. Sacred exchange: Peter Carey's *Oscar and Lucinda* religion. *In* (pp. 171–8) **15024**.

15032. MACFARLANE, ROBERT. Monstrosity, fakery, and authorship in *My Life as a Fake*. *In* (pp. 335–48) **15024**.

15033. MACINTYRE, PAM. Regarding *The Big Bazoohley*. *In* (pp. 215–28) **15024**.

15034. O'REILLY, NATHANAEL. Rejecting and perpetuating the anti-suburban tradition: representations of the suburbs in *The Tax Inspector*, *Johnno*, and *Cloudstreet*. Antipodes (20:1) 2006, 20–5.

15035. PAGETTI, CARLO. *'Entering the world of a novel'*: Londra, l'enigma della città. *In* (pp. 3–17) **7343**.

15036. RAUWERDA, ANTJE. Multi-nationality and layers of mouse in Peter Carey's *The Unusual Life of Tristan Smith*. Antipodes (20:2) 2006, 117–23.

15037. SCHMIDT-HABERKAMP, BARBARA. The writing-back paradigm revisited: Peter Carey, *Jack Maggs*, and Charles Dickens, *Great Expectations*. *In* (pp. 245–62) **15024**.

15038. SCHWALM, TANJA. 'Relax and enjoy the show': circensian animal spaces in Australian and Latin American magical realist fiction. JCL (41:3) 2006, 83–102.

15039. SHECKELS, THEODORE F. The difficulties of translating Peter Carey's postmodern fiction into popular film. *In* (pp. 83–100) **15024**.

15040. SQUEO, ALESSANDRA. Madri e matrigne: la 'metropoli' vittoriana di Peter Carey. *In* (pp. 325–38) **7343**.

15041. TOMAIUOLO, SAVERIO. Dickens to postmodernity and back. *In* (pp. 223–42) **9791**.

15042. WOODCOCK, BRUCE. Unsettling illusions: Carey and capital in *Jack Maggs*. *In* (pp. 263–73) **15024**.

A. R. (Albert Richardson) Carman (1865–1939)

15043. JANES, DANIELA. Brainworkers: the middle-class labour reformer and the late Victorian Canadian industrial novel. *See* **10782**.

Marina Carr

15044. DOYLE, MARIA. Dead center: tragedy and the reanimated body in Marina Carr's *The Mai* and *Portia Coughlan*. ModDr (49:1) 2006, 41–59.

15045. HOWARD, BEN. Audacious Ireland. SewR (114:3) 2006, 403–18.

15046. RUSSELL, RICHARD. Talking with ghosts of Irish playwrights past: Marina Carr's *By the Bog of Cats …* CompDr (40:2) 2006, 149–68.

James Carroll

15047. GRAY, TIMOTHY. 'A world without gravity': the urban pastoral spirituality of Jim Carroll and Kathleen Norris. *See* **17777**.

Hayden Carruth

15048. HAMILL, SAM (ed.). Toward the distant islands: new & selected poems. Port Townsend, WA: Copper Canyon Press, 2006. pp. xiv, 181. Rev. by Brian Henry in NYTB, 10 Sept. 2006, 32.

Ciaran Carson

15049. CARVALHO HOMEM, RUI. Hallucination or lucidity? Vision and time in Ciaran Carson's ekphrastic writing. EtBr (31) 2006, 127–41.

15050. Cone, Temple. Knowing the street map by foot: Ciaran Carson's *Belfast Confetti*. NewHR (10:3) 2006, 68–86.

15051. Malone, Christopher. 'If I go on long enough calling that my life I'll end up by believing it': Samuel Beckett and contemporary Irish memoir. *In* (pp. 195–216) **12189**.

Rachel Carson

15052. Murphy, Priscilla Coit. What a book can do: the publication and reception of *Silent Spring*. Amherst: Massachusetts UP, 2005. pp. xvi, 254. (Studies in print culture and the history of the book.) Rev. by Steven Jackson in AmJ (23:1) 2006, 134–5.

15053. Rieger, Christopher B. Silent spring on Tobacco Road: the degradation of the environment in Erskine Caldwell's fiction. *In* (pp. 131–49) **15001**.

15054. Zhu, Xinfu. Sylvia Plath: writing in the silent spring. *See* **18056**.

Angela Carter

15055. Cardi, Luciana. Angela Carter's postmodern rewriting of Japan: the metamorphosis of Lady Murasaki and of the Oriental fox. *In* (pp. 61–81) **11955**.

15056. Gamble, Sarah. Angela Carter: a literary life. Basingstoke; New York: Palgrave Macmillan, 2006. pp. viii, 239. (Literary lives.)

15057. —— 'There's no place like home': Angela Carter's rewriting of the domestic. LIT (17:3/4) 2006, 277–300.

15058. Griswold, Jerry. The meanings of *Beauty and the Beast*. *See* **12786**.

15059. Lowry, Elizabeth. What literature is made from: fairy tales as the raw stuff of the imagination. *See* **3642**.

15060. Monson-Rosen, Madeleine. 'The most primeval of passions': incest in the service of women in Angela Carter's *The Magic Toyshop*. *In* (pp. 232–43) **11883**.

15061. Munford, Rebecca (ed.). Re-visiting Angela Carter: texts, contexts, intertexts. Basingstoke; New York: Palgrave Macmillan, 2006. pp. xiv, 207.

15062. Parkin-Gounelas, Ruth. The insistence of the object – and its sublimations. *See* **13575**.

15063. Seabra Ferreira, Marie-Aline. The passion of the brides: Angela Carter, Marcel Duchamp and Max Ernst. EtBr (31) 2006, 83–103.

15064. Tonkin, Maggie. Musing on Baudelaire: Angela Carter's *Black Venus* and the poet as dead beloved. LIT (17:3/4) 2006, 301–23.

15065. Yoshioka, Chiharu. Dialectic of enlightenment in the 1960s gothic: Angela Carter's *Heroes and Villains*. GothS (8:2) 2006, 68–79.

Betty Smartt Carter (b.1965)

15066. Carter, Betty Smartt. Tired of victory, bored by defeat: restoring proper sadness to Christian art. *In* (pp. 172–82) **11940**.

Martin Carter

15067. Dalleo, Raphael. Authority and the occasion for speaking in the Caribbean literary field: Martin Carter and George Lamming. SmAx (10:2) 2006, 19–39.

Justin Cartwright (b.1945)

15068. Marais, Mike. Race, reading, and tolerance in three postapartheid novels. *In* (pp. 253–69) **11860**.

Raymond Carver

15069. Carver, Maryann Burk. What it used to be like: a portrait of my marriage to Raymond Carver. New York: St Martin's Press, 2006. pp. xi, 356. Rev. by Joyce Johnson in NYTB, 24 Sept. 2006, 18.

15070. McDermott, James Dishon. Austere style in twentieth-century literature: literary minimalism. *See* **14849**.

15071. Schweizer, Harold. On waiting in Raymond Carver's *A Small, Good Thing*. JSSE (46) 2006, 139–45.

15072. Siebert, Hilary. Houses of identity: inhabiting and emerging from despair. JSSE (46) 2006, 129–38.

15073. Verley, Claudine. *Errand*; or, Raymond Carver's realism in a champagne cork. JSSE (46) 2006, 147–63.

15074. Zhou, Jingqiong. Raymond Carver's short fiction in the history of black humor. New York; Frankfurt: Lang, 2006. pp. x, 142.

Joyce Cary

15075. Eustace, John C. Who can resist? The radical ambivalence of Joyce Cary's *Aissa Saved*. EngS (87:1) 2006, 62–77.

15076. Lock, Charles. Indirect rule and the continuities of Nigerian fiction. *In* (pp. 181–96) **11860**.

Neal Cassady

15077. Carden, Mary Paniccia. 'Adventures in auto-eroticism': economies of travelling masculinity in autobiographical texts by Jack Kerouac and Neal Cassady. *See* **16841**.

15078. Sandison, David; Vickers, Graham. Neal Cassady: the fast life of a Beat hero. Chicago, IL: Chicago Review Press, 2006. pp. xi, 340, (plates) 16. Rev. by James Campbell in NYTB, 19 Nov. 2006, 11.

Ana Castillo

15079. Michael, Magali Cornier. New visions of community in contemporary American fiction: Tan, Kingsolver, Castillo, Morrison. *See* **18722**.

Brian Castro

15080. Gunew, Sneja. Between auto/biography and theory: can 'ethnic abjects' write theory? CLS (42:4) 2005, 363–78.

15081. Ma, Lili. Identity and creativity: reading Brian Castro's *After China*. FLS (120) 2006, 97–102. (In Chinese.)

Willa Cather

15082. Adkison, Jennifer Dawes. 'These is my words' … or are they? *See* **20346**.

15083. Bennett, Nichole. In pursuit of the outland engine: a fictional source for *The Professor's House*. WCPMN (49:3) 2006, 71–3.

15084. BESTON, JOHN. Willa Cather and Patrick White. *See* **19117**.

15085. CARUSO, ISABELLA. *Vissi d'arte*: the female artist in Cather and Colette. WCPMN (50:2) 2006, 35–7.

15086. CHINERY, MARY. Wartime fictions: Willa Cather, the Armed Services Editions, and the unspeakable Second World War. CathS (6) 2006, 285–96.

15087. COHEN, DEBRA RAE. Culture and the 'cathedral': tourism as potlatch in *One of Ours*. CathS (6) 2006, 184–204.

15088. DAVIS-GEORGE, JOSIE B. Reflections of Jenny Lind within *The Song of the Lark*. WCPMN (49:3) 2006, 57–60.

15089. DE ROCHE, LINDA. Student companion to Willa Cather. Westport, CT; London: Greenwood Press, 2006. pp. x, 218. (Student companions to classic writers.)

15090. FUISZ, LISBETH STRIMPLE. Willa Cather and Myra Kelly in *McClure's Magazine*. WCPMN (50:2) 2006, 39–42.

15091. AL-GHALITH, ASAD. Willa Cather's use of inner light. IFR (32:1/2) 2005, 32–7.

15092. GORMAN, MICHAEL. Jim Burden and the White man's burden: *My Ántonia* and empire. CathS (6) 2006, 28–57.

15093. HAYTOCK, JENNIFER. Looking at agony: World War I in *The Professor's House*. CathS (6) 2006, 228–43.

15094. HERRING, SCOTT. Catherian friendship; or, How not to do the history of homosexuality. MFS (52:1) 2006, 66–91.

15095. HUNTSINGER, JAMIE. Discovering images of an American wasteland: a study of Willa Cather's Midwestern landscapes. HGP (39:2) 2006, 5–22.

15096. JAMES, PEARL. The 'Enid problem': dangerous modernity in *One of Ours*. CathS (6) 2006, 92–128.

15097. JONES, ANDY. War in Nebraska: Willa Cather's *One of Ours*. WCPMN (50:1) 2006, 3–6.

15098. KINGSBURY, CELIA M. 'Squeezed into an unnatural shape': Bayliss Wheeler and the element of control in *One of Ours*. CathS (6) 2006, 129–44.

15099. LANDON, LANA HARTMAN; SMITH, LAUREL. Early works by modern women writers: Woolf, Bowen, Mansfield, Cather, and Stein. *See* **19300**.

15100. LINDEMANN, MARILEE (ed.). The Cambridge companion to Willa Cather. (Bibl. 2005, 15733.) Rev. by Mary R. Ryder in GPQ (26:4) 2006, 288–9.

15101. LINK, FREDERICK M. (ed.). Shadows on the rock. With a historical essay and notes by John J. Murphy and David Stouck. Lincoln; London: Nebraska UP, 2005. pp. xii, 382, (plates) 24. (Willa Cather scholarly eds.) Rev. by Steven Trout in GPQ (26:4) 2006, 288.

15102. —— RONNING, KARI A. (eds). One of ours. With a historical essay and explanatory notes by Richard C. Harris. Lincoln; London: Nebraska UP, 2006. pp. xii, 866, (plates) 28. (Willa Cather scholarly eds.)

15103. MEYER, SUSAN. Coughing girls in *The Song of the Lark*: Willa Cather, breathing, and the health of the artist. WCPMN (50:2) 2006, 27–30.

15104. —— On the front and at home: Wharton, Cather, the Jews, and the First World War. CathS (6) 2006, 205–27.

15105. Murphy, John J. William to Willa, courtesy of Sarah: Cather, Jewett, and Howellsian principles. ALR (38:2) 2006, 145–59.

15106. Noe, Mark D. Cather's *O Pioneers!* Exp (64:3) 2006, 149–51.

15107. O'Connor, Margaret Anne. The not-so-great war: Cather family letters and the Spanish–American War. CathS (6) 2006, 58–69.

15108. Park, Haein. A quest for memory in Willa Cather's *Death Comes for the Archbishop*. WCPMN (50:1) 2006, 13–17.

15109. Perriman, Wendy K. Cather's literary choreography: the 'glittering idea' of scientific warfare in *The Professor's House*. CathS (6) 2006, 244–70.

15110. Quantic, Diane D. Seven ways of looking at the Great Plains literary landscape. *See* **12100**.

15111. Robison, Mark A. Recreation in World War I and the practice of play in *One of Ours*. CathS (6) 2006, 160–83.

15112. Romines, Ann. Willa Cather's Civil War: a very long engagement. CathS (6) 2006, 1–27.

15113. Ross, Patricia A. The spell cast by remains: the myth of wilderness in modern American literature. *See* **16387**.

15114. Russell, Danielle. Between the angle and the curve: mapping gender, race, space, and identity in Willa Cather and Toni Morrison. London; New York: Routledge, 2006. pp. x, 226. (Literary criticism and cultural theory.)

15115. Ryder, Mary R. 'As green as their money': the doughboy naïfs in *One of Ours*. CathS (6) 2006, 145–59.

15116. —— That d—d mob of women performers: women artists as rivals in Cather's fiction. WCPMN (50:2) 2006, 31–4.

15117. Seaton, James. Religion and literature in Sinclair Lewis and Willa Cather. MidAmerica (32) 2005, 31–7.

15118. Stich, Klaus P. Cather's 'Midi Romanesque': missionaries, myth, and the Grail in *Death Comes for the Archbishop*. StudN (38:1) 2006, 57–73.

15119. Stout, Janis P. Between two wars in a breaking world: Willa Cather and the persistence of war consciousness. CathS (6) 2006, 70–91.

15120. —— (ed.). Willa Cather and material culture: real-world writing, writing the real world. (Bibl. 2005, 15749.) Rev. by Duncan White in JAStud (39:3) 2005, 573–4; by Mary Paniccia Carden in MFS (52:1) 2006, 203–7; by Michelle Abate in HC (43:4) 2006, 17–18; by Francesca Sawaya in Legacy (23:1) 2006, 99–100.

15121. Swenson, Jeffrey. Art and the immigrant: the Other as muse in Cather's *My Ántonia* and Rølvaag's *Boat of Longing*. MidAmerica (32) 2005, 16–30.

15122. Trout, Steven. Rebuilding the Outland engine: a new source for *The Professor's House*. CathS (6) 2006, 271–84.

15123. Walker, Rosanna West. The birth of a Lost Boy: traces of J. M. Barrie's *Peter Pan* in Willa Cather's *The Professor's House*. *In* (pp. 127–52) **14616**.

Theresa Hak Kyung Cha

15124. Fusco, Serena. 'You see only her traces': Theresa Hak Kyung Cha's *Dictée*; or, The performance of a voice. *In* (pp. 175–96) **11955**.

15125. Hayot, Eric. Immigrating fictions: unfailing mediation in *Dictée* and *Becoming Madame Mao*. ConLit (47:4) 2006, 601–35.

15126. Lee, Kun Jong. Rewriting Hesiod, revisioning Korea: Theresa Hak Kyung Cha's *Dictée* as a subversive Hesiodic *Catalogue of Women*. ColLit (33:3) 2006, 77–99.

15127. Lionnet, Françoise. Translating grief. *In* (pp. 315–35) **3191**.

15128. Mukherjee, Srimati. Nation, immigrant, text: Theresa Hak Kyung Cha's *Dictée*. *In* (pp. 197–215) **11995**.

15129. Takada, Mayumi. Annihilating possibilities: witnessing and testimony through cinematic love in Theresa Hak Kyung Cha's *Dictée*. LIT (17:1) 2006, 23–48.

Michael Chabon

15130. Cawelti, John G. Sherlock Holmes: the case of the perpetual detective. *See* **9928**.

Aidan Chambers

15131. Greenway, Betty. Aidan Chambers: master literary choreographer. Lanham, MD; London: Scarecrow Press, 2006. pp. xvii, 133. (Scarecrow studies in young adult literature, 25.)

Raymond Chandler

15132. Clausson, Nils. The simple art of stealing: the case of Raymond Chandler's purloined 'rats behind the wainscoting'. ANQ (19:3) 2006, 32–4.

15133. Everett, Barbara. A lethal fall. *See* **16999**.

15134. Gernalzick, Nadja. To act or to perform: distinguishing filmic autobiography. *See* **12926**.

15135. Howe, Alexander N. The detective and the analyst: truth, knowledge, and psychoanalysis in the hard-boiled fiction of Raymond Chandler. Clues (24:4) 2006, 15–29.

15136. Knight, Deborah. On reason and passion in *The Maltese Falcon*. *In* (pp. 207–21) **12452**.

15137. MacDonald, Susan Peck. Chandler's American style. Style (39:4) 2005, 448–68.

15138. Tani, Stefano (ed.). Romanzi e racconti: vol. 1, 1933–1942. Milan: Mondadori, 2005. pp. clxxx, 1654. (I Meridiani.) Rev. by Fulvio Gianaria and Alberto Mittone in Indice (2005:3) 21.

15139. Wood, Tahir. Adherence relations in literary and non-literary discourse. JLS (35:2) 2006, 165–80.

Fred Chappell

15140. Middleton, David. Gatherings: four American poets. *See* **14877**.

Barbara Chase-Riboud

15141. Spencer, Suzette. Historical memory, romantic narrative, and Sally Hemings. AAR (40:3) 2006, 507–31.

Bruce Chatwin

15142. Lindsay, Claire. Luis Sepúlveda, Bruce Chatwin and the global travel writing circuit. CLS (43:1/2) 2006, 57–78.

Amit Chaudhuri (b.1962)

15143. Chaudhuri, Amit. Interlude. JPW (42:2) 2006, 213–22. (Memoir.)

Denise Chávez

15144. Wright, Elizabeth J. 'She and I are molecules': the disabled body in Denise Chávez's *The Last of the Menu Girls.* WAL (41:1) 2006, 5–22.

Kelly Cherry

15145. Chappell, Fred. Kelly Cherry in her poetry: the subject as object. MissQ (58:1/2) 2004/05, 255–76.

G. K. Chesterton

15146. Barnabé, Jean-Philippe. Borges as a reader of Dickens. *See* **9699**.

15147. Coffman, Frank. Robert E. Howard and poetic narrative: the bardic tradition and 'popular modernities'. *See* **16468**.

15148. Knight, Mark. Chesterton and evil. (Bibl. 2004, 16055.) Rev. by Bernard Bergonzi in YES (36:2) 2006, 279–80.

15149. Robbins, Harold. The last of the realists: G. K. Chesterton, his life & his work. Norfolk, VA: IHS Press, 2004. pp. 160.

15150. Schwartz, Adam. The third spring: G. K. Chesterton, Graham Greene, Christopher Dawson, and David Jones. (Bibl. 2005, 15778.) Rev. by Clark M. Brittain in CHist (74:4) 2005, 862–4; by Stratford Caldecott in ModAge (48:3) 2006, 273–6.

15151. Williams, Donald T. Mere humanity: G. K. Chesterton, C. S. Lewis, and J. R. R. Tolkien on the human condition. Nashville, TN: Broadman & Holman, 2006. pp. 212. Rev. by Ruby Dunlap in Mythprint (43:5/6) 2006, 13–14.

Tracy Chevalier

15152. Safit, Ilan. Animating vision: visual adaptation in *Girl with a Pearl Earring. See* **19701**.

Frank Chin

15153. Madsen, Deborah L. Chinese American writers of the real and the fake: authenticity and the twin traditions of life writing. *See* **13949**.

Shimmer Chinodya

15154. Attree, Lizzy. Reshaping communities: the representation of HIV/AIDS in literature from South Africa and Zimbabwe. *In* (pp. 61–79) **12216**.

C. B. (Clement Byrne) Christesen (b.1911)

15155. Campisi, Dale. Little magazines, great divides. *See* **1067**.

15156. Davidson, Jim. The second empire. *See* **1078**.

15157. Ellen, Jane. Cold Wars and culture wars. *See* **11877**.

15158. Excell, Patricia. Fine-spun song. Meanjin (63:1) 2004, 149–51. (Lyric poems.)

15159. Grant, Jane. Vultures on every bough. *See* **18736**.

15160. Heseltine, Harry. Only connect. Meanjin (63:1) 2004, 152–8. (Short stories.)

15161. McLaren, John. Time to dream. *See* **1136**.

15162. McPhee, Hilary. Survival struggles. *See* **1137**.

Agatha Christie ('Mary Westmacott')

15163. Makinen, Merja. Agatha Christie: investigating femininity. Basingstoke; New York: Palgrave Macmillan, 2006. pp. xiii, 205. (Crime files.)

Caryl Churchill

15164. Wang, Lan. The artificiality in the definition of identity and gender: an interpretation of *Cloud Nine*. FLS (119) 2006, 32–7. (In Chinese.)

Sir Winston Churchill (1874–1965)

15165. Mieder, Wolfgang. 'We are all in the same boat now': proverbial rhetoric in the Churchill–Roosevelt correspondence. *See* **2986**.

Sandra Cisneros

15166. Groover, Kristina K. Reconstructing the sacred: Latina feminist theology in Sandra Cisneros's *Woman Hollering Creek*. ELN (44:1) 2006, 191–7.

15167. Kevane, Bridget. Latino gospel and cultural renewal in Chicana fiction. ELN (44:1) 2006, 177–82.

Amy Clampitt

15168. Kitchen, Judith. The letter of the life. *See* **17272**.

15169. Spiegelman, Willard (ed.). Love, Amy: the selected letters of Amy Clampitt. (Bibl. 2005, 15799.) Rev. by Judith Kitchen in GaR (60:3/4) 2006, 760–74.

15170. Whale, John. John Keats and Tony Harrison: the burden of history. *In* (pp. 163–80) **13735**.

Joan Clark (b.1934)

15171. Fuller, Danielle. Riding a rolling wave: a conversation with Joan Clark. CanL (189) 2006, 121–33.

Robert Clark (b.1952)

15172. Vránová, Martina. Intertextuality in *Love among the Ruins*. BStE (31) 2005, 185–96.

J. P. Clark-Bekederemo (John Pepper Clark)

15173. Nwahunanya, Chinyere. Tragedy in African literary drama. *In* (pp. 197–211) **11860**.

Austin C. Clarke (b.1934)

15174. Algoo-Baksh, Stella. Austin C. Clarke's short fiction. JWIL (12:1/2) 2004, 90–103.

15175. Bucknor, Michael A. 'Voices under the window' of representation: Austin Clarke's poetics of (body)-memory in *The Meeting Point*. JWIL (13:1/2) 2005, 141–75.

15176. Casteel, Sarah Phillips. Experiences of arrival: Jewishness and Caribbean Canadian identity in Austin Clarke's *The Meeting Point*. JWIL (14:1/2) 2005, 113–40.

15177. Chariandy, David. 'That's what you want, isn't it?': Austin Clarke and the new politics of recognition. JWIL (14:1/2) 2005, 141–65.

George Elliott Clarke

15178. Larson, Katherine. Resistance from the margins in George Elliott Clarke's *Beatrice Chancy.* CanL (189) 2006, 103–18.

15179. Moynagh, Maureen. Can I get a witness? Performing community in African Nova Scotian theatre. *See* **14833**.

Helen Clarkson

15180. Schwartz, Richard A. Family, gender, and society in 1950s American fiction of nuclear apocalypse: *Shadow on the Hearth*, *Tomorrow!*, *The Last Day*, and *Alas, Babylon*. *See* **19391**.

Pearl Cleage

15181. Macdonald, Sharman; Miller, Susan; Cleage, Pearl. Our bodies, ourselves. *In* (pp. 93–103) **12297**.

Beverly Cleary

15182. Sweeney, Meghan M. Checking out America: libraries as agents of acculturation in three mid-century girls' books. *See* **17266**.

Michelle Cliff

15183. Bloyd, Rebekah. Sounds and silences in the Jamaican household: Michelle Cliff's *Columba*. BStE (31) 2005, 103–10.

15184. Dagbovie, Sika Alaine. Fading to White, fading away: biracial bodies in Michelle Cliff's *Abeng* and Danzy Senna's *Caucasia*. AAR (40:1) 2006, 93–109.

15185. Gourdine, Angeletta K. M. Caribbean *tabula rasa*: textual touristing as carnival in contemporary Caribbean women's writing. *See* **16861**.

15186. Van Nyhuis, Alison. Moving beyond black and white issues: Jewishness and symbols of womanhood in *Abeng.* JWIL (13:1/2) 2005, 176–95.

Sir Hugh Clifford

15187. Dryden, Linda. At the court of *Blackwood's*: in the Kampong of Hugh Clifford. *In* (pp. 215–35) **1098**.

Charmian Clift

15188. Brown, Max. Charmian and George: the marriage of George Johnston and Charmian Clift. Dural, N.S.W.: Rosenberg, 2004. pp. 255. Rev. by Susan Carson in ALS (22:2) 2005, 256–8.

Lucille Clifton

15189. Holladay, Hilary. Wild blessings: the poetry of Lucille Clifton. (Bibl. 2005, 15809.) Rev. by Deborah Hooker in SoLJ (39:1) 2006, 128–32.

15190. Lupton, Mary Jane. Lucille Clifton: her life and letters. Westport, CT; London: Praeger, 2006. pp. xiii, 172. (Women writers of color.)

Andrei Codrescu

15191. Codrescu, Andrei. *Howl* in Transylvania. *In* (pp. 47–56) **16122**.

15192. Olson, Kirby. Andrei Codrescu and the myth of America. (Bibl. 2005, 15815.) Rev. by Paul Keyes in AmBR (26:2) 2006, 26–7.

Liza Cody

15193. Schaffer, Rachel. Unreliable narration in Liza Cody's Eva Wylie series. Storytelling (6:1) 2006, 33–41.

J. M. Coetzee

15194. Artwell, David. The life and times of Elizabeth Costello: J. M. Coetzee and the public sphere. *In* (pp. 25–41) **15223**.

15195. Attridge, Derek. J. M. Coetzee and the ethics of reading: literature in the event. (Bibl. 2005, 15820.) Rev. by Lucy Graham in RAL (37:4) 2006, 240.

15196. Bell, Michael. What is it like to be a nonracist? Elizabeth Costello and J. M. Coetzee on the lives of animals and men. *In* (pp. 172–92) **15223**.

15197. Benson, Stephen. Literary music: writing music in contemporary fiction. *See* **17420**.

15198. Buikema, Rosemarie. Literature and the production of ambiguous memory: confession and double thoughts in Coetzee's *Disgrace*. EJES (10:2) 2006, 187–97.

15199. Coetzee, J. M. Roads to translation. Meanjin (64:4) 2005, 141–51.

15200. Cooppan, Vilashini. National literature in transnational times: writing transition in the 'new' South Africa. *In* (pp. 346–69) **3191**.

15201. D'hoker, Elke. Confession and atonement in contemporary fiction: J. M. Coetzee, John Banville, and Ian McEwan. CritW (48:1) 2006, 31–43.

15202. Dimock, Wai Chee. Genre as world system: epic and novel on four continents. Narrative (14:1) 2006, 85–101. (Dialogue.)

15203. Dragunoiu, Dana. J. M. Coetzee's *Life & Times of Michael K* and the thin theory of the good. JCL (41:1) 2006, 69–92.

15204. Durrant, Sam. J. M. Coetzee, Elizabeth Costello, and the limits of the sympathetic imagination. *In* (pp. 118–34) **15223**.

15205. —— Postcolonial narrative and the work of mourning: J. M. Coetzee, Wilson Harris, and Toni Morrison. (Bibl. 2005, 15824.) Rev. by Pranav Jani in Callaloo (29:2) 2006, 682–8; by James Graham in JPW (42:1) 2006, 111–13.

15206. Fiorella, Lucia. Figure del male nella narrativa di J. M. Coetzee. Pisa: ETS, 2006. pp. 250. (Anglistica.)

15207. Geertsema, Johan. White natives? Dan Roodt, Afrikaner identity and the politics of the sublime. JCL (41:3) 2006, 103–20.

15208. Gräbe, Ina. Theory and technology in contemporary South African writing: from self-conscious exploration to contextual appropriation. *In* (pp. 203–12) **14093**.

15209. Graham, Lucy. Textual transvestism: the female voices of J. M. Coetzee. *In* (pp. 217–35) **15223**.

15210. Hayes, Patrick. 'An author I have not read': Coetzee's *Foe*, Dostoevsky's *Crime and Punishment*, and the problem of the novel. RES (57:230) 2006, 273–90.

15211. Head, Dominic. A belief in frogs: J. M. Coetzee's enduring faith in fiction. *In* (pp. 100–17) **15223**.

15212. Jacobs, Johan. Writing reconciliation: South African fiction after apartheid. *In* (pp. 177–95) **16284**.

15213. Jolly, Rosemary. Going to the dogs: humanity in J. M. Coetzee's *Disgrace*, *The Lives of Animals*, and South Africa's Truth and Reconciliation Commission. *In* (pp. 148–71) **15223**.

15214. Lenta, Patrick. 'Legal illegality': *Waiting for the Barbarians* after September 11. JPW (42:1) 2006, 71–83.

15215. MacLeod, Lewis. 'Do we of necessity become puppets in a story?'; or, Narrating the world: on speech, silence, and discourse in J. M. Coetzee's *Foe*. MFS (52:1) 2006, 1–18.

15216. Marais, Michael. Death and the space of the response to the Other in J. M. Coetzee's *The Master of Petersburg*. *In* (pp. 83–99) **15223**.

15217. Marais, Mike. J. M. Coetzee's *Disgrace* and the task of the imagination. JML (29:2) 2006, 75–93.

15218. —— Race, reading, and tolerance in three postapartheid novels. *In* (pp. 253–69) **11860**.

15219. Medin, Daniel L. Trials and errors at the turn of the millennium: on *The Human Stain* and J. M. Coetzee's *Disgrace*. *See* **18321**.

15220. Neill, Michael. 'The language of the heart': confession, metaphor, and grace in J. M. Coetzee's *Age of Iron*. *In* (pp. 515–43) **8374**.

15221. Nicora, Flaminia. *Foe* e la violenza della parola: teorizzare il personaggio postmoderno e postcoloniale. ConLett (43) 2005, 339–55.

15222. Poyner, Jane. J. M. Coetzee in conversation with Jane Poyner. *In* (pp. 21–4) **15223**.

15223. —— (ed.). J. M. Coetzee and the idea of the public intellectual. Athens: Ohio UP, 2006. pp. vii, 246.

15224. Sanders, Mark. Undesirable publications: J. M. Coetzee on censorship and apartheid. LawL (18:1) 2006, 101–14.

15225. Shillingsburg, Peter. Publication of Coetzee's *The Humanities in Africa*. BSANZB (28:4) 2004, 105–12.

15226. Sikorska, Liliana (ed.). A universe of (hi)stories: essays on J. M. Coetzee. New York; Frankfurt: Lang, 2006. pp. 150. (Polish studies in English language and literature, 15.)

15227. Stanton, Katherine. Cosmopolitan fictions: ethics, politics, and global change in the works of Kazuo Ishiguro, Michael Ondaatje, Jamaica Kincaid, and J. M. Coetzee. *See* **16566**.

15228. Van Vuuren, Marijke. Beyond words: silence in William Golding's *Darkness Visible* and J. M. Coetzee's *Life and Times of Michael K*. *See* **16150**.

15229. Wang, Jinghui. Contrast of two empires: reading Coetzee's allegorical *Waiting for the Barbarians*. FLS (122) 2006, 153–8. (In Chinese.)

15230. Wright, Laura. Writing 'out of all the camps': J. M. Coetzee's narratives of displacement. London; New York: Routledge, 2006. pp. x, 154. (Studies in major literary authors.)

Leonard Cohen

15231. Rogers, Shelagh. A conversation with Leonard Cohen. Brick (77) 2006, 20–30.

Henri Cole (b.1956)

15232. Hennessy, Christopher. Henri Cole: an interview. APR (33:3) 2004, 43–6.

Cy Coleman

15233. Coleman, Cy. Fighting honestly. *In* (pp. 24–37) **12375**.

Helena Coleman (1860–1953)

15234. Chambers, Jennifer. 'You woman-hearted, poet-brained wonder worker!': the poetic dialogue of love between Ethelwyn Wetherald and Helena Coleman. *See* **19086**.

Wanda Coleman

15235. Schmidt, Tyler T. 'Womanish' and 'wily': the poetry of Wanda Coleman. Ob3 (6:1) 2005, 128–43.

James Lincoln Collier (b.1928)

15236. Sonneborn, Liz. James Lincoln Collier. New York: Rosen Central, 2006. pp. 112. (Library of author biographies.)

R. G. Collingwood

15237. Wallach, Jennifer Jensen. Building a bridge of words: the literary autobiography as historical source material. *See* **17717**.

Billy Collins (b.1941)

15238. Collins, Billy. My *Howl*. *In* (pp. 100–1) **16122**.

15239. Hansen, Tom. Collins's *Japan*. Exp (64:2) 2006, 124–6.

Merle Collins

15240. Meehan, Kevin. Romance and revolution: reading women's narratives of Caribbean decolonization. TSWL (25:2) 2006, 291–306.

Frank A. Collymore (1893–1980)

15241. Dalleo, Raphael. Shadows, funerals, and the terrified consciousness in Frank Collymore's short fiction. JWIL (12:1/2) 2004, 184–95.

Joseph Conrad

15242. Allington, Daniel. First steps towards a rhetorical psychology of literary interpretation. JLS (35:2) 2006, 123–44. (*Heart of Darkness*.)

15243. Baxter, Katherine Isobel. Conrad's application to the British Museum: an unpublished letter. Conradian (31:2) 2006, 79–84.

15244. —— Fleshing out the bones: two new manuscript leaves of *Falk*. Conradian (31:2) 2006, 103–13.

15245. —— *The Rescuer* synopsis: a transcription and commentary. Conradian (31:1) 2006, 117–27.

15246. Bock, Martin. Joseph Conrad and germ theory: why Captain Allistoun smiles thoughtfully. Conradian (31:2) 2006, 1–14.

15247. Bonney, William W. Suspended. *In* (pp. 175–93) **15280**.

15248. Bowers, Terence. Conrad's *Aeneid*: *Heart of Darkness* and the Classical epic. Conradiana (38.2) 2006, 115–42.

15249. Bradshaw, Ann Lane. Joseph Conrad and Louis Becke. EngS (86:3) 2005, 206–25.

15250. Breton, Rob. Gospels and grit: work and labour in Carlyle, Conrad and Orwell. *See* **9383**.

15251. Britzolakis, Christina. Pathologies of the imperial metropolis: Impressionism as traumatic afterimage in Conrad and Ford. JML (29:1) 2005, 1–20.

15252. Cantor, Paul A.; Hufnagel, Peter. The empire of the future: imperialism and modernism in H. G. Wells. *See* **19031**.

15253. Chialant, Maria Teresa. '*Dead calm*': il viaggio per mare in *The Shadow-Line* di Joseph Conrad. *In* (pp. 193–221) **11824**.

15254. Collits, Terry. Postcolonial Conrad: paradoxes of empire. London; New York: Routledge, 2005. pp. xiii, 226. (Routledge research in postcolonial literatures, 12.)

15255. Daleski, H. M. The *sjuzhet* as a Conradian mode of thinking. PartA (4:2) 2006, 151–61.

15256. Damrosch, David (ed.). Joseph Conrad and Rudyard Kipling, *Heart of Darkness, The Man Who Would Be King* and other works on empire. New York: Columbia UP, 2006. pp. xxv, 273.

15257. Davies, Laurence. 'The thing which was not' and the thing that is also: Conrad's ironic shadowing. *In* (pp. 223–37) **15280**.

15258. —— Stape, J. H. (eds). The collected letters of Joseph Conrad: vol. 7, 1920–1922. Cambridge; New York: CUP, 2005. pp. lxv, 656, (plates) 8. Rev. by Sylvère Monod in Conradian (31:1) 2006, 130–40; by Tanya Gokulsing in NQ (53:2) 2006, 247–8.

15259. Del Sapio Garbero, Maria. Mappe e fantasmi: resoconti dall'Impero di Kipling, Hardy e altri. *In* (pp. 157–78) **11824**.

15260. Deng, Yingling. Exploration of time in *The Secret Agent*. FLS (118) 2006, 93–8. (In Chinese.)

15261. Devlin, Kimberly J. The scopic drive and visual projection in *Heart of Darkness*. MFS (52:1) 2006, 19–41.

15262. Donovan, Stephen. Conrad in Swedish: the first translation. Conradian (31:2) 2006, 114–35.

15263. —— Joseph Conrad and popular culture. Basingstoke; New York: Palgrave Macmillan, 2005. pp. xiii, 236. Rev. by Chris GoGwilt in VS (49:1) 2006, 124–6.

15264. Erdinast-Vulcan, Daphna. Some millennial footnotes on *Heart of Darkness*. *In* (pp. 55–65) **15280**.

15265. Escuret, Annie. Excès et sacré dans la littérature victorienne et édouardienne. *See* **9743**.

15266. Fothergill, Anthony. Connoisseurs of terror and the political aesthetics of anarchism: *Nostromo* and *A Set of Six*. *In* (pp. 137–54) **15280**.

15267. Fraser, Jennifer Margaret. 'A matter of tears': grieving in *Under Western Eyes*. *In* (pp. 251–65) **15280**.

15268. Galván, Fernando; Santiago Fernández, José (eds). El corazón de las tinieblas. Madrid: Cátedra, 2005. pp. 251. (Letras universales, 380.) Rev. by Jesús Varela Zapata in Atl (28:1) 2006, 145–9.

15269. GoGwilt, Christopher. Opera and the passage of literature: Joseph Conrad, Pramoedya Ananta Toer, and the cultural dialectic of abysmal taste. *In* (pp. 101–19) **15280**.

15270. Gokulsing, Tanya. An audience for paper boats: Conrad and the marketing of early Modernism. Conradiana (38:1) 2006, 59–78.

15271. Hampson, Robert. Conrad's heterotopic fiction: composite maps, superimposed sites, and impossible spaces. *In* (pp. 121–35) **15280**.

15272. Hampson, Robert G. Spatial stories: Conrad and Iain Sinclair. Conradian (31:1) 2006, 52–71.

15273. Hand, Richard J. Escape with Joseph Conrad! The adaptation of Joseph Conrad's fiction on American old-time radio. Conradiana (38:1) 2006, 17–58.

15274. Harpham, Geoffrey Galt. Beyond mastery: the future of Conrad's beginnings. *In* (pp. 17–38) **15280**.

15275. —— On the grotesque: strategies of contradiction in art and literature. *See* **9215**.

15276. Harrison, Nicholas. Who needs an idea of the literary? *See* **14141**.

15277. Jackel, Brad. Dante, Doré, and Conrad. Conradiana (38:2) 2006, 103–14.

15278. Jones, Susan. Conrad on the borderlands of Modernism: Maurice Greiffenhagen, Dorothy Richardson and the case of *Typhoon*. *In* (pp. 195–211) **15280**.

15279. Kaplan, Carola M. Beyond gender: deconstructions of masculinity and femininity from *Karain* to *Under Western Eyes*. *In* (pp. 267–79) **15280**.

15280. —— Mallios, Peter; White, Andrea (eds). Conrad in the twenty-first century: contemporary approaches and perspectives. London; New York: Routledge, 2005. pp. xxii, 326.

15281. Kil, Hye Ryoung. Conrad's 'undying hope' of the Polish nation: Western ideal and Eastern reality. Mosaic (39:2) 2006, 1–17.

15282. Kirschner, Paul. The rancorous coolies in *Typhoon*. NQ (53:3) 2006, 343.

15283. Knowles, Owen; Stape, J. H. Conrad and Hamlin Garland: a correspondence recovered. Conradian (31:2) 2006, 62–78.

15284. Lock, Charles. Indirect rule and the continuities of Nigerian fiction. *In* (pp. 181–96) **11860**.

15285. Mallios, Peter. An interview with Edward Said. *In* (pp. 283–303) **15280**.

15286. Mallios, Peter Lancelot. Reading *The Secret Agent* now: the press, the police, the premonition of simulation. *In* (pp. 155–72) **15280**.

15287. Middleton, Tim. Joseph Conrad. London; New York: Routledge, 2006. pp. xv, 201. (Routledge guides to literature.)

15288. Miller, David. A nasty smell of cooking: Lilian Hallowes, Joseph Conrad's 'typewriter young lady'. TLS, 28 Apr. 2006, 16–17.

15289. —— The unenchanted garden: children, childhood, and Conrad. Conradian (31:2) 2006, 28–47.

15290. Mongia, Padmini. Between men: Conrad in the fiction of two contemporary Indian writers. *In* (pp. 85–99) **15280**.

15291. Monod, Sylvère. Heemskirk, the Dutch lieutenant. Conradian (31:2) 2006, 85–91.

15292. Moutet, Muriel. Foreign tongues: native and half-caste speech in *Lord Jim*. Conradian (31:1) 2006, 1–15.

15293. Mulengela, Bwendo. Structured silences: a study of Nabokov, Conrad, Ngũgĩ, and Achebe. *In* (pp. 147–70) **11860**.

15294. Nelson, Ronald J. The writing styles of two war correspondents: Stephen Crane and Ernie Pyle. *See* **9660**.

15295. Paccaud-Huguet, Josiane. 'One of those trifles that awaken ideas': the Conradian moment. Conradian (31:1) 2006, 72–85.

15296. Paris, Bernard J. Conrad's Charlie Marlow: a new approach to *Heart of Darkness* and *Lord Jim*. Basingstoke; New York: Palgrave Macmillan, 2005. pp. x, 173.

15297. Parry, Benita. The moment and afterlife of *Heart of Darkness*. *In* (pp. 39–53) **15280**.

15298. Pedot, Richard. *A tangle of unrelated things*: l'étrangeté du texte dans *The Secret Sharer* (Joseph Conrad). EtBr (30) 2006, 1–11.

15299. Peters, John Gerard. The Cambridge introduction to Joseph Conrad. Cambridge; New York: CUP, 2006. pp. x, 146. (Cambridge introductions to literature.)

15300. Rafalski, Kazimierz. Kipling and Conrad. *See* **16928**.

15301. Raschke, Debrah. Modernism, metaphysics, and sexuality. Selinsgrove, PA: Susquehanna UP, 2006. pp. 240.

15302. Ray, Sid. Marlow(e)'s Africa: postcolonial queenship in Conrad's *Heart of Darkness* and Marlowe's *Dido, Queen of Carthage*. Conradiana (38:2) 2006, 143–61.

15303. Reid, S. W. The unpublished typescript version of *A Smile of Fortune*. Conradian (31:2) 2006, 92–102.

15304. Reilly, Terry. Reading *The Lagoon* and Chaucer's The Knight's Tale through Edward Said's *The World, the Text, and the Critic*. Conradiana (38:2) 2006, 175–82.

15305. Richardson, Brian. Conrad and posthumanist narration: fabricating class and consciousness onboard the *Narcissus*. *In* (pp. 213–22) **15280**.

15306. Ross, Stephen. Conrad and empire. (Bibl. 2005, 15917.) Rev. by Jennifer L. French in MFS (52:3) 2006, 745–8.

15307. Rygiel, Mary Ann. Belgian settings and colonialism in Conrad and Malouf. *See* **17424**.

15308. ŠAVLE, MAJDA. Conrad in Slovenia: translations and critical reception. Conradian (31:2) 2006, 136–41.

15309. SCHWARZ, DANIEL R. Reading the modern British and Irish novel, 1890–1930. *See* **10324**.

15310. SEWLALL, HARRY. Postcolonial/postmodern spatiality in *Almayer's Folly* and *An Outcast of the Islands*. Conradiana (38:1) 2006, 79–93.

15311. SHAFFER, BRIAN W. Joseph Conrad: *Heart of Darkness*. *In* (pp. 314–23) **11788**.

15312. SIMMONS, ALLAN H. Joseph Conrad. Basingstoke; New York: Palgrave Macmillan, 2006. pp. xi, 239. (Critical issues.)

15313. STAPE, J. H. (ed.); BUSZA, ANDREW (asst ed.). Notes on life and letters. (Bibl. 2004, 16209.) Rev. by Wallace Watson in StudN (38:1) 2006, 121–3; by Dirk Van Hulle in Conradian (31:2) 2006, 142–7; by Tanya Gokulsing in NQ (53:2) 2006, 247–8.

15314. —— KNOWLES, OWEN. 'In-between man': Conrad–Galsworthy–Pinker. Conradian (31:2) 2006, 48–61.

15315. —— —— Marlow's audience in *Youth* and *Heart of Darkness*: a historical note. Conradian (31:1) 2006, 104–16.

15316. STEVENS, HAROLD RAY. Conrad, geopolitics, and *The Future of Constantinople*. Conradian (31:2) 2006, 15–27.

15317. STOCKDALE, MARK. Conrad's sea: invisibility and the death of a symbol. Conradiana (38:1) 2006, 1–16.

15318. TADIÉ, ALEXIS. Perceptions of language in *Lord Jim*. Conradian (31:1) 2006, 16–36.

15319. TOPIA, ANDRÉ. The impossible present: a Flaubertian reading of *Lord Jim*. Conradian (31:1) 2006, 37–51.

15320. VIOLA, ANDRÉ. A Black Athena in the *Heart of Darkness*; or, Conrad's baffling oxymorons. Conradiana (38:2) 2006, 163–73.

15321. WHITE, ANDREA. Writing from within: autobiography and immigrant subjectivity in *The Mirror of the Sea*. *In* (pp. 241–9) **15280**.

15322. WILSON, JOHN HOWARD. A question of influence and experience: a response to Edward Lobb. *See* **19002**.

15323. WOLLAEGER, MARK. Conrad's darkness revisited: mediated warfare and Modern(ist) propaganda in *Heart of Darkness* and *The Unlighted Coast*. *In* (pp. 67–82) **15280**.

George Cram Cook (1873–1924)

15324. BEN-ZVI, LINDA (ed.). The road to the temple: a biography of George Cram Cook. *See* **16136**.

Hugh Cook (b.1942)

15325. LUX, ELAINE. Narrative bones: Amy Tan's *Bonesetter's Daughter* and Hugh Cook's *Homecoming Man*. *In* (pp. 117–32) **11916**.

Dorian Cooke (1916–2005)

15326. KEERY, JAMES. The *Burning Baby* and the bathwater: 12, 'The originating hand'. PNRev (31:6) 2005, 57–61.

15327. Riley, Peter. Dorian Cooke. PNRev (32:4) 2006, 9–10.

Bernard Cooper

15328. Cooper, Bernard. The bill from my father: a memoir. New York: Simon & Schuster, 2006. pp. viii, 240.

Dennis Cooper

15329. Annesley, James. Contextualizing Cooper. *In* (pp. 68–79) **15336**.

15330. Burroughs, William. Notes on *Frisk*. *In* (pp. 80–2) **15336**.

15331. Glück, Robert. Dennis Cooper (interviewed). *In* (pp. 241–59) **15336**.

15332. Jackson, Earl, Jr. Killer looks: Dennis Cooper's tough Platonic love. *In* (pp. 83–93) **15336**.

15333. Killian, Kevin. Guide to trust #2. *In* (pp. 105–16) **15336**.

15334. Lev, Leora. Against the grain: John Waters on Dennis Cooper (interview). *In* (pp. 131–48) **15336**.

15335. —— Sacred disorder of the mind: sublimity, desire police, and Dennis Cooper's hallucination of words. *In* (pp. 200–24) **15336**.

15336. —— (ed.). Enter at your own risk: the dangerous art of Dennis Cooper. Madison, NJ: Fairleigh Dickinson UP, 2006. pp. 278, (plates) 12.

15337. Stosuy, Brandon; Brose, Lawrence. Notes toward *Caught*. *In* (pp. 117–30) **15336**.

15338. Taylor, Marvin. 'A Dorian Gray type of thing': male–male desire and the crisis of representation in Dennis Cooper's *Closer*. *In* (pp. 175–99) **15336**.

Susan Cooper (b.1935)

15339. Butler, Charles. Four British fantasists: place and culture in the children's fantasies of Penelope Lively, Alan Garner, Diana Wynne Jones, and Susan Cooper. *See* **17234**.

'William Cooper' (Harry S. Hoff)

15340. Taylor, D. J. Behind the scenes: William Cooper reappraised. TLS, 9 June 2006, 15–17. (Commentary.)

Robert Coover

15341. Briasco, Luca. The American baseball hero: an unstable icon. QPS (14) 2006, 345–52.

Wendy Cope

15342. Payne, Susan. Essays on British women poets. *See* **3583**.

Daniel Corkery

15343. Delaney, Paul. 'Nobody now knows which …': transition and piety in Daniel Corkery's short fiction. NewHR (10:1) 2006, 100–10.

Robert Cormier

15344. Campbell, Patty. Robert Cormier: daring to disturb the universe. New York: Delacorte Press, 2006. pp. 287.

Jayne Cortez

15345. Anderson, T. J., iii. Notes to make the sound come right: four innovators of jazz poetry. (Bibl. 2004, 16232.) Rev. by Scott Saul in AL (77:4) 2005, 862–4.

Douglas Coupland

15346. HOLLINGER, VERONICA. Notes on the contemporary apocalyptic imagination: William Gibson's *Neuromancer* and Douglas Coupland's *Girlfriend in a Coma*. *In* (pp. 47–56) **13541**.

15347. MILLER, D. QUENTIN. Deeper Blues; or, The posthuman Prometheus: cybernetic renewal and the late twentieth-century American novel. *See* **18884**.

Sir Noël Coward (1899–1973)

15348. DAY, BARRY. Coward on film: the cinema of Noël Coward. Foreword by Sir John Mills. (Bibl. 2005, 15951.) Rev. by Philip Gillett in ScopeF (6) 2006.

15349. FARFAN, PENNY. Noël Coward and sexual modernism: *Private Lives* as queer comedy. ModDr (48:4) 2005, 677–88.

Hart Crane

15350. ACKER, PAUL. Hart Crane's 1931 postcard from the Torreón de Los Remedios. ANQ (19:4) 2006, 43–7.

15351. ADDISON, CATHERINE. Stress felt, stroke dealt: the spondee, the text, and the reader. *See* **10469**.

15352. GUY-BRAY, STEPHEN. The really broken tower. ANQ (19:4) 2006, 41–3.

15353. HAMMER, LANGDON (ed.). Complete poems and selected letters. New York: Library of America, 2006. pp. xiii, 849. (Library of America, 168.)

15354. REED, BRIAN M. Hart Crane: after his lights. Tuscaloosa; London: Alabama UP, 2006. pp. viii, 295. (Modern and contemporary poetics.) Rev. by Jim Nawrocki in GLRW (13:6) 2006, 49.

15355. TAPPER, GORDON A. The machine that sings: Modernism, Hart Crane, and the culture of the body. London; New York: Routledge, 2006. pp. x, 221. (Studies in major literary authors.)

15356. TRACY, D. H. Bad ideas. Poetry (189:2) 2006, 135–45. (Error in poetry.)

15357. WARGACKI, JOHN. The 'logic of metaphor' at work: Hart Crane's Marian metaphor in *The Bridge*. RelArts (10:3) 2006, 329–54.

Nathalia Crane (b.1913)

15358. JALOWITZ, ALAN C. The daughters of Penelope: tradition and innovation in American epics by women. *In* (pp. 141–58) **3395**.

Robert Crawford

15359. CRAWFORD, ROBERT. Spirit machines: the human and the computational. *In* (pp. 52–68) **13732**.

Sharon Creech

15360. MCGINTY, ALICE B. Sharon Creech. New York: Rosen Central, 2006. pp. 112. (Library of author biographies.)

15361. TIGHE, MARY ANN. Sharon Creech: the words we choose to say. Lanham, MD; London: Scarecrow Press, 2006. pp. xv, 123. (Scarecrow studies in young adult literature, 22.)

Robert Creeley

15362. Bernstein, Charles. Hero of the local: Robert Creeley and the persistence of American poetry. TexP (19:3) 2005, 373–7.

15363. Gelpi, Albert. Poetic language and language poetry: Levertov, Duncan, Creeley. *In* (pp. 180–98) **15599**.

Michael Crichton

15364. Bihlmeyer, Jaime. Novel, script, image: a case study of the phallic (m)other in mainstream culture. *In* (pp. 153–64) **11781**.

Alison Croggon (b.1962)

15365. McCarthy, Patricia. Conjugating ourselves: three Australian women poets: Katherine Gallagher, Alison Croggon and M. T. C. Cronin. *See* **15366**.

M. T. C. Cronin (b.1963)

15366. McCarthy, Patricia. Conjugating ourselves: three Australian women poets: Katherine Gallagher, Alison Croggon and M. T. C. Cronin. Agenda (41:1/2) 2005, 179–95 (review-article).

Lynn Crosbie (b.1963)

15367. Shearer, Karis. The poetics of autobiography: reading Lynn Crosbie's *Alphabet City*. OpL (twelfth series) (5) 2005, 71–83.

Caresse Crosby (Mary Phelps Jacob) (1892–1970)

15368. Capo, Beth Widmaier. 'She is herself a poem': Caresse Crosby, feminine identity, and literary history. Legacy (23:1) 2006, 30–43.

'Amanda Cross' (Carolyn G. Heilbrun)

15369. Caws, Mary Ann. Walking (even now) with Carolyn. *See* **19974**.

Aleister Crowley

15370. Gunn, Joshua. Modern occult rhetoric: mass media and the drama of secrecy in the twentieth century. *See* **11918**.

Andrew Crozier (b.1943)

15371. Brinton, Ian. Black Mountain in England: 4. PNRev (32:5) 2006, 50–3.

Countee Cullen

15372. Jarraway, David. No heaven in Harlem: Countee Cullen and his diasporic doubles. *In* (pp. 214–37) **12180**.

Patrick Cullinan

15373. Cullinan, Patrick (comp.). Imaginative trespasser: letters between Bessie Head and Patrick and Wendy Cullinan, 1963–1977. *See* **16304**.

e. e. cummings

15374. Demarcq, Jacques. Translated from the Cummings. Spring (ns 13) 2004, 104–10.

15375. Grumman, Bob. The importance of technical innovation in the poetic maturation of Cummings. Spring (ns 13) 2004, 74–89.

15376. Headrick, Paul. The pragmatism of *anyone*. Spring (ns 13) 2004, 49–57.

15377. Hunt, B. J. Cummings's *Anyone Lived in a Pretty How Town*. Exp (64:4) 2006, 226–8.

15378. Kidd, Millie. Cummings the performer. Spring (ns 13) 2004, 18–26.

15379. MacLeod, Glen. E. E. Cummings and Wallace Stevens: kinship and rivalry. Spring (ns 13) 2004, 36–48.

15380. Martin, W. Todd. *The Enormous Room* as spiritual autobiography: a Puritan context for the text. Spring (ns 13) 2004, 27–35.

15381. Sawyer-Lauçanno, Christopher. E. E. Cummings: a biography. (Bibl. 2004, 16266.) Rev. by Iain Landles in Spring (ns 13) 2004, 143–6; by Michael Webster in Spring (ns 13) 2004, 147–53.

15382. Terblanche, Étienne. E. E. Cummings' fluid 'objectivity': a deep ecological response to Michael Webster's *New Nature Poetry and the Old*. Spring (ns 13) 2004, 128–42. (*Response to* bibl. 2001, 13917.)

15383. —— Holons and the poetry of T. S. Eliot and E. E. Cummings. *See* **15718**.

15384. Webster, Michael. Cummings' sinister dexterity: exercises in meaning and unmeaning. Spring (ns 13) 2004, 90–103.

Nancy Cunard

15385. Lucas, John (ed.). Poems of Nancy Cunard: from the Bodleian Library. Nottingham: Trent, 2005. pp. 96. Rev. by Vicki Bertram in PNRev (32:5) 2006, 71.

15386. Morresi, Renata. Negotiating identity: Nancy Cunard's otherness. *In* (pp. 147–58) **16284**.

15387. Strachan, Walter. Portraits of four poets. Ed. by Geoffrey Strachan. *See* **18972**.

15388. Winkiel, Laura. Nancy Cunard's *Negro* and the transnational politics of race. Mod/Mod (13:3) 2006, 507–30.

Michael Cunningham (b.1952)

15389. Alley, Henry. *Mrs Dalloway* and three of its contemporary children. *See* **19257**.

Christopher Paul Curtis

15390. Levin, Judy. Christopher Paul Curtis. New York: Rosen Central, 2006. pp. 112. (Library of author biographies.)

Roald Dahl

15391. Gelletly, LeeAnne. Gift of imagination: the story of Roald Dahl. Greensboro, NC: Morgan Reynolds, 2006. pp. 160.

15392. Treglown, Jeremy (ed.). Collected stories. New York: Knopf, 2006. pp. xxxvii, 850. (Everyman's library, 300.) Rev. by Erica Wagner in NYTB, 3 Dec. 2006, 84.

James Dalziel (b.1876)

15393. Forman, Ross G. Projecting from Possession Point: Hong Kong, hybridity, and the shifting grounds of imperialism in James Dalziel's turn-of-the-century fiction. Criticism (46:4) 2004, 533–74.

Tsitsi Dangarembga

15394. STONE, E. KIM. In the bedroom: the formation of single women's performative space in Tsitsi Dangarembga's *Nervous Conditions*. JCL (41:1) 2006, 111–26.

Achmat Dangor

15395. COOPPAN, VILASHINI. National literature in transnational times: writing transition in the 'new' South Africa. *In* (pp. 346–69) **3191**.

Mark Z. Danielewski

15396. COX, KATHARINE. What has made me? Locating mother in the textual labyrinth of Mark Z. Danielewski's *House of Leaves*. CritS (18:2) 2006, 4–15.

15397. MURPHET, JULIAN. Behind the scenes: production, animation, and postmodern value. *See* **18949**.

Kate Daniels (b.1953)

15398. TURNER, DANIEL CROSS. New Fugitives: contemporary poets of countermemory and the futures of Southern poetry. MissQ (58:1/2) 2004/05, 315–45.

Richard Dankleff (b.1925)

15399. MULLER, ERIK. Oregon poet: Richard Dankleff. NwR (44:3) 2006, 135–53.

Jack Dann

15400. SCHWEITZER, DARRELL. An interview with Jack Dann. NYRSF (18:8) 2006, 13–18.

Edwidge Danticat

15401. CALLAHAN, SARAH. Passageways of remembrance. Ob3 (6:2 / 7:1) 2005/06, 240–9.

15402. CONWELL, JOAN. Papa's masks: roles of the father in Danticat's *The Dew Breaker*. Ob3 (6:2 / 7:1) 2005/06, 221–39.

15403. DHAR, NANDINI. Memory, gender, race and class: Edwidge Danticat's *The Farming of Bones*. Ob3 (6:2/7:1) 2005/06, 185–202.

15404. GOURDINE, ANGELETTA K. M. Caribbean *tabula rasa*: textual touristing as carnival in contemporary Caribbean women's writing. *See* **16861**.

15405. JOHNSON, NEWTONA. Challenging internal colonialism: Edwidge Danticat's feminist emancipatory enterprise. Ob3 (6:2/7:1) 2005/06, 147–66.

15406. PATTERSON, RICHARD F. Resurrecting Rafael: fictional incarnations of a Dominican dictator. *See* **14423**.

15407. ROSSI, JENNIFER C. 'Let the words bring wings to our feet': negotiating exile and trauma through narrative in Danticat's *Breath, Eyes, Memory*. Ob3 (6:2/7:1) 2005/06, 203–20.

15408. VEGA-GONZÁLEZ, SUSANA. Sites of memory, sites of mourning and history: Danticat's insights into the past. RAEI (17) 2004, 297–304.

15409. WEIR-SOLEY, DONNA. Voudoun symbolism in *The Farming of Bones*. Ob3 (6:2/7:1) 2005/06, 167–84.

Paula Danziger

15410. Reed, Jennifer Bond. Paula Danziger: voice of teen troubles. Berkeley Heights, NJ: Enslow, 2006. pp. 104. (Authors teens love.)

Olive Tilford Dargan ('Fielding Burke')

15411. Ackerman, Kathy Cantley. The heart of revolution: the radical life and novels of Olive Dargan. (Bibl. 2005, 15999.) Rev. by Robert Weldon Whalen in NCHR (81:4) 2004, 482–3.

15412. Mantooth, Wes. 'You factory folks who sing this song will surely understand': culture, ideology, and action in the Gastonia novels of Myra Page, Grace Lumpkin, and Olive Dargan. London; New York: Routledge, 2006. pp. vii, 235. (Literary criticism and cultural theory.)

Amma Darko (b.1956)

15413. Higgins, MaryEllen (Ellie). Transnational, transcultural feminisms? Amma Darko's response in *Beyond the Horizon*. TSWL (25:2) 2006, 307–22.

Helen Darville ('Helen Demidenko') (b.1971)

15414. Ozick, Cynthia. The rights of history and the rights of imagination. *In* (pp. 3–18) **11969**.

Guy Davenport

15415. Bamberger, W. C. (ed.). Guy Davenport and James Laughlin: selected letters. *See* **17019**.

15416. Furlani, Andre. Davenport and Sebald's art of excursus. LitIm (8:2) 2006, 319–30.

15417. Haynes, Kenneth. An overview of the stories. LitIm (8:2) 2006, 307–12.

15418. Sturgeon, Stephen. Our truest kin: a reading of Guy Davenport's *On Some Lines of Virgil*. LitIm (8:2) 2006, 313–18.

Avram Davidson

15419. Wessells, Henry. Avram Davidson in the skin magazines; or, The thankless labor of the bibliographer. NPDM (11:1) 2006.

Donald Davidson

15420. Clark, Jim. 'Unto all generations of the faithful heart': Donald Davidson, the Vanderbilt Agrarians, and Appalachian poetry. MissQ (58:1/2) 2004/05, 299–313.

Donald Davie

15421. Gibbons, Reginald. This working against the grain. *See* **16076**.

15422. Wilmer, Clive. Donald Davie's arguments with Modernism. PNRev (30:4) 2004, 31–4.

Andrew Davies

15423. Cardwell, Sarah. Andrew Davies. Manchester; New York: Manchester UP, 2005. pp. xii, 227. (Television series.)

Hugh Sykes Davies (b.1909)

15424. Remy, Michel. British Surrealist writing and painting: re-marking the margin. *In* (pp. 171–81) **11733**.

Donald D. Davis (b.1944)

15425. Davis, Donald. Mama learns to drive. Little Rock, AK: August House, 2005. pp. 120. (Memoir.)

Margaret Thomson Davis (b.1926)

15426. Davis, Margaret Thomson. Write from the heart: the extraordinary real-life story of Glasgow's favourite novelist, Margaret Thomson Davis. Edinburgh: Black & White, 2006. pp. vi, 250, (plates) 8.

Thulani Davis (b.1948)

15427. McLennan, Rachael. Unpacking 'something dark': narrating Southern female adolescence in Jill McCorkle's *The Cheer Leader*, Sylvia Wilkinson's *Bone of My Bones* and Thulani Davis's *1959*. *See* **17309**.

Christopher Dawson

15428. Drollinger, Frank. C. S. Lewis & Christopher Dawson: on history and historicism. *See* **17180**.

Frank Parker Day

15429. Davies, Gwendolyn. Revisiting *Rockbound*: the evolution of a novel. CanL (189) 2006, 15–30.

Alain de Botton

15430. Guignery, Vanessa. The destabilisation of genre in Alain de Botton's iconotexts. EtBr (31) 2006, 143–57.

15431. Shusterman, Ronald. Philosophy through pictures: ideas and iconotexts from I. A. Richards to Alain de Botton. EtBr (31) 2006, 158–75.

Ingrid de Kok (b.1951)

15432. Penberthy, Jenny. Cartography of one's own country: an interview with Ingrid de Kok. CapR (second series) (46) 2005, 5–18.

Samuel R. Delany

15433. Delany, Samuel R. About writing: seven essays, four letters, and five interviews. Middletown, CT: Wesleyan UP, 2005. pp. xii, 419.

15434. Freedman, Carl. About Delany writing: an anatomical meditation. Extrapolation (47:1) 2006, 16–29.

15435. Tucker, Jeffrey Allen. A sense of wonder: Samuel R. Delany, race, identity and difference. (Bibl. 2005, 16021.) Rev. by Ikechukwu Okafor-Newsum in RAL (37:1) 2006, 153–4; by Molefi Kete Asante in AAR (40:1) 2006, 196–7.

Don DeLillo

15436. DePietro, Thomas (ed.). Conversations with Don DeLillo. (Bibl. 2005, 16029.) Rev. by Marni Gauthier in Mod/Mod (13:2) 2006, 410–12.

15437. Dewey, Joseph. Beyond grief and nothing: a reading of Don DeLillo. Columbia; London: South Carolina UP, 2006. pp. 172.

15438. Di Prete, Laura. ‘Foreign bodies’: trauma, corporeality, and textuality in contemporary American culture. *See* **14416**.

15439. Donovan, Christopher. Postmodern counternarratives: irony and audience in the novels of Paul Auster, Don DeLillo, Charles Johnson and Tim O’Brien. *See* **14515**.

15440. Eaton, Mark. Inventing hope: the question of belief in Don DeLillo’s novels. *In* (pp. 31–49) **11916**.

15441. Engles, Tim; Duvall, John N. (eds). Approaches to teaching DeLillo’s *White Noise*. New York: Modern Language Assn of America, 2006. pp. vi, 240. (Approaches to teaching world literature, 85.)

15442. Hungerford, Amy. Don DeLillo’s Latin Mass. ConLit (47:3) 2006, 343–80.

15443. Kohn, Robert E. Parody, heteroglossia, and chronotope in Don DeLillo’s *Great Jones Street*. Style (39:2) 2005, 206–16.

15444. Morley, Catherine. Don DeLillo’s transatlantic dialogue with Sergei Eisenstein. JAStud (40:1) 2006, 17–34.

15445. Radford, Andrew. Confronting the chaos theory of history in DeLillo’s *Libra*. MidQ (47:3) 2006, 224–43.

15446. Rosen, Elizabeth. Lenny Bruce and his nuclear shadow Marvin Lundy: Don DeLillo’s apocalyptists extraordinaires. JAStud (40:1) 2006, 97–112.

15447. Russo, John Paul. The future without a past: the humanities in a technological society. (Bibl. 2005, 16045.) Rev. by Diana Kichuk in SHARP (15:1) 2006, 11.

15448. Wilcox, Leonard. Terrorism and art: Don DeLillo’s *Mao II* and Jean Baudrillard’s *The Spirit of Terrorism*. Mosaic (39:2) 2006, 89–105.

15449. Zhang, Jie; Kong, Yan. Symbolization of life: a dialogical interpretation of *White Noise*. FLS (121) 2006, 40–4. (In Chinese.)

Charles de Lint (b.1951)

15450. Steven, Laurence. Welwyn Wilton Katz and Charles de Lint: new fantasy as a Canadian postcolonial genre. *In* (pp. 57–72) **13541**.

Ella Deloria

15451. Goodspeed-Chadwick, Julie. The heteroglot voice in Ella Deloria’s *Waterlily*. PemM (38) 2006, 87–91.

Thomas C. Dent

15452. Breaux, Quo Vadis Gex. Tom Dent’s role in the organizational mentoring of African American Southern writers: a memoir. AAR (40:2) 2006, 339–43.

15453. Thomas, Lorenzo. The need to speak: Tom Dent and the shaping of a Black aesthetic. AAR (40:2) 2006, 325–38.

15454. Ward, Jerry W., Jr. The art of Tom Dent: notes on early evidence. AAR (40:2) 2006, 319–24.

August Derleth (‘Stephen Grendon’) (1909–1971)

15455. Grant, Kenneth B. August Derleth’s self-promotion. MidAmerica (32) 2005, 46–52.

15456. —— Friendship, finance, and art: Charles Scribner's Sons' relationship with Ernest Hemingway and August Derleth. *See* **16359**.

Anita Desai

15457. Khan, Nyla Ali. The fiction of nationality in an era of transnationalism. (Bibl. 2005, 16057.) Rev. by Sunanda Mongia in JCPS (12:1) 2005, 115–17.

Sarah Dessen

15458. Holsten, Anthony James. 'About this girl': an interview with Sarah Dessen. NCLR (15) 2006, 46–52.

15459. Tedesco, Laureen. Sarah Dessen's cautiously optimistic realism: decades beyond the teen problem novel. NCLR (15) 2006, 53–63.

Anne Devlin

15460. Manista, Frank. Any Irish in you? The crises of Irishness in contemporary Irish drama. *In* (pp. 267–90) **12189**.

Polly Devlin

15461. Ingman, Heather. Translating between cultures: a Kristevan reading of the theme of the foreigner in some twentieth-century novels by Irish women. *See* **17803**.

Philip K. Dick ('Richard Phillips') (1928–1982)

15462. Barone, Adriano. *Il sognatore d'armi*: il labirinto come gioco del ratto. *In* (pp. 195–203) **15466**.

15463. Briasco, Luca. *'Early in the bright sun-yellowed morning'*: *Cronache del dopobomba* tra *mainstream* e genere. *In* (pp. 188–94) **15466**.

15464. Carratello, Mattia. Piccole città, piccoli uomini e un futuro possibile: i romanzi *mainstream* di Philip K. Dick. *In* (pp. 156–67) **15466**.

15465. De Angelis, Valerio Massimo. Storiografie multiple in *L'uomo nell'alto castello*. *In* (pp. 168–77) **15466**.

15466. —— Rossi, Umberto (eds). Trasmigrazioni: i mondi di Philip K. Dick. Florence: Le Monnier, 2006. pp. 298. (Cartografie dell'immaginario: Saggi di letterature comparate.)

15467. Dillon, Grace L. L'impulso divinatorio di Philip K. Dick: il ragno e l'ape. *In* (pp. 52–60) **15466**.

15468. Fitting, Peter. Il mondo che sta dietro tutto questo: l'eredità di Philip K. Dick. *In* (pp. 263–74) **15466**.

15469. Formenti, Carlo. La Gnosi in Philip K. Dick. *In* (pp. 35–47) **15466**.

15470. Frasca, Gabriele. Come rimanere rimasti: *La trasmigrazione di Timothy Archer*. *In* (pp. 237–60) **15466**.

15471. Gallo, Domenico. La lotteria del sistema solare. *In* (pp. 115–22) **15466**.

15472. Gnocchini, Antonio. Los Angeles: un'opera di Philip K. Dick. *In* (pp. 48–51) **15466**.

15473. Holliday, Valerie. Masculinity in the novels of Philip K. Dick. Extrapolation (47:2) 2006, 280–95.

15474. Jameson, Fredric. Storia e salvezza in Philip K. Dick. *In* (pp. 15–34) **15466**.

15475. La Polla, Franco. Da Philip K. Dick a Hollywood: ovvero, La quadratura del cerchio. *In* (pp. 275–81) **15466**.

15476. Lazzari, Anna. I testi non finzionali: Dick sulla fantascienza. *In* (pp. 61–9) **15466**.

15477. Mckee, Gabriel. Pink beams of light from the god in the gutter: the science-fictional religion of Philip K. Dick. Lanham, MD; London: UP of America, 2004. pp. xii, 84. Rev. by Everett L. Hamner in JFA (16:3) 2006, 249–52.

15478. Nati, Maurizio. Paura del diverso: fobie d'oltre oceano in *Occhio nel cielo*. *In* (pp. 131–41) **15466**.

15479. Pagetti, Carlo. Introduzione: Philip K. Dick, la critica e il *gubble* di Manfred Steiner. *In* (pp. 5–11) **15466**.

15480. Portelli, Alessandro. Da che parte stai? Il conflitto cosmico in *La città sostituita*. *In* (pp. 123–30) **15466**.

15481. Prezzavento, Paolo. *Allegoricus semper interpres delirat*: un oscuro scrutare tra teologia e paranoia. *In* (pp. 225–36) **15466**.

15482. Proietti, Salvatore. Vuoti di potere e resistenza umana: Dick, *Ubik* e l'epica americana. *In* (pp. 204–16) **15466**.

15483. Rispoli, Francesca. *Scorrete lacrime, disse il poliziotto*: la nascita di un essere umano autentico. *In* (pp. 217–24) **15466**.

15484. Rossi, Umberto. Ambiguous spokespersons: the DJ and talk-radio host in US fiction, cinema and drama. QPS (14) 2006, 318–27.

15485. —— Il gioco del ratto: avvisaglie *avantpop* in *I giocatori di Titano*. *In* (pp. 142–55) **15466**.

15486. Sutin, Lawrence. Divine invasions: a life of Philip K. Dick. New York: Carroll & Graf, 2005. pp. xiii, 352, (plates) 8.

15487. Suvin, Darko. Arrivederci e salve: differenziazioni nell'ultimo Philip K. Dick. *In* (pp. 83–112) **15466**.

15488. Vallorani, Nicoletta. Con gli occhi di un bambino: lo sguardo di Manfred su una società psicotica. *In* (pp. 178–87) **15466**.

15489. Wolk, Tony. La danza delle tartarughe: il gioco degli androidi nella narrativa di Philip K. Dick. *In* (pp. 70–82) **15466**.

James Dickey

15490. Copestake, Ian D. Jeffers and the inhumanism of James Dickey's *To the White Sea*. JDN (23:1) 2006, 42–9.

15491. Flannagan, Beckie. In defense of the authentic: James Dickey's critical poetics. JDN (22:2) 2006, 17–22.

15492. Greiner, Donald J. James Dickey's library: a lifetime of poetry and the world of books. JDN (22:2) 2006, 1–9.

15493. —— Making the truth: James Dickey's last major interview. JDN (23:1) 2006, 1–26.

15494. Hill, Jane. 'The river we're all troubled by': David Bottoms and the legacy of James Dickey. *See* **14817**.

15495. Meyers, Jeffrey. Confronting the demons. GaR (60:3/4) 2006, 775–81 (review-article).

15496. Van Ness, Gordon. 'The fiercest hearts are in love with a wild perfection': the James Dickey / James Wright correspondence. JDN (22:2) 2006, 10–16.

15497. Welling, Bart H. 'A peculiar kind of intimacy': men, nature, and the unnatural in *The Sheep Child* and *Deliverance*. JDN (23:1) 2006, 27–41.

Joan Didion

15498. Didion, Joan. The year of magical thinking. (Bibl. 2005, 16093.) Rev. by Gaby Weiner in Auto/Biography (14:4) 2006, 398–400.

15499. Pulitano, Elvira. From Joan Didion to Roland Barthes: travels in mixedblood metaphors and mixed messages, remembering Louis Owens. *See* **17944**.

15500. Wang, Haimeng. The meaningless simulation age: the void in Didion's *Play It as It Lays*. FLS (119) 2006, 115–22. (In Chinese.)

15501. Weingarten, Marc. The gang that wouldn't write straight: Wolfe, Thompson, Didion, and the New Journalism revolution. New York: Crown, 2006. pp. 225. Rev. by Nick Ravo in JPC (39:6) 2006, 1106–7.

Pietro di Donato

15502. Shiffman, Dan. Pietro di Donato's *Christ in Concrete* and Catholic social thought. VIA (16:2) 2005, 57–72.

Steven Dietz

15503. Cooper, Barbara Roisman. *Sherlock Holmes: the Final Adventure*: the playwright and two actors. BSJ (56:4) 2006, 24–7.

Fatima Dike

15504. Dike, Fatima, *et al.* Beyond the USA, beyond the UK. *In* (pp. 199–218) **12297**.

Annie Dillard

15505. Cochoy, Nathalie. Le réalisme infime d'Annie Dillard dans *Teaching a Stone to Talk*. Anglophonia (19) 2006, 291–8.

'Isak Dinesen' (Karen Blixen)

15506. Jensen, Finn. Karen Blixen and Lawrence Durrell: two aspects of Modernism. *See* **15626**.

15507. Mullins, Maire. The gift of grace: Isak Dinesen's *Babette's Feast*. *In* (pp. 279–96) **11916**.

15508. Rees, Ellen. Holy witch and wanton saint: gothic precursors for Isak Dinesen's *The Dreamers*. SS (78:3) 2006, 333–48.

Melvin Dixon

15509. Joyce, Justin A.; McBride, Dwight A. (eds). A Melvin Dixon critical reader. Jackson; London: Mississippi UP, 2006. pp. xxx, 159.

Thomas Dixon (1864–1946)

15510. Brundage, W. Fitzhugh. Thomas Dixon: American Proteus. *In* (pp. 23–45) **15511**.

15511. Gillespie, Michele K.; Hall, Randal L. (eds). Thomas Dixon, Jr, and the birth of modern America. Baton Rouge: Louisiana State UP, 2006.

pp. viii, 224, (plates) 6. (Making the modern South.) Rev. by Sylvia Cook in SPC (29:2) 2006, 130–1.

15512. LINK, WILLIAM A. Epilogue: the enduring worlds of Thomas Dixon. *In* (pp. 203–10) **15511**.

15513. LYERLY, CYNTHIA LYNN. Gender and race in Dixon's religious ideology. *In* (pp. 80–104) **15511**.

15514. MENAND, LOUIS. Do movies have rights? *In* (pp. 183–202) **15511**.

15515. REGESTER, CHARLENE. The cinematic representation of race in *The Birth of a Nation*: a Black horror film. *In* (pp. 164–82) **15511**.

15516. ROMINE, SCOTT. Thomas Dixon and the literary production of Whiteness. *In* (pp. 124–50) **15511**.

15517. SMITH, JOHN DAVID. 'My books are hard reading for a Negro': Tom Dixon and his African American critics, 1905–1939. *In* (pp. 46–79) **15511**.

15518. STRICKLIN, DAVID. 'Ours is a century of light': Dixon's strange consistency. *In* (pp. 105–23) **15511**.

15519. WEISENBURGER, STEVEN (introd.). The sins of the father: a romance of the South. Lexington: Kentucky UP, 2004. pp. xxx, 316. Rev. by Jené Schoenfeld in AL (78:2) 2006, 391–3.

Kildare Dobbs (b.1923)

15520. DOBBS, KILDARE. Running the rapids: a writer's life. Dublin: Lilliput Press, 2005. pp. 240.

E. L. Doctorow

15521. BANKER, PAUL V. Doctorow's *Billy Bathgate* and Sophocles's *Oedipus Rex*. Exp (64:3) 2006, 171–4.

15522. PEPPER, ANDREW. State power matters: power, the State and political struggle in the post-war American novel. *See* **14960**.

15523. WILDE, LAWRENCE. The search for reconciliation in E. L. Doctorow's *City of God*. RelArts (10:3) 2006, 391–405.

Ivan Doig

15524. DOIG, IVAN. Heart earth. (Bibl. 1999, 15836.) Orlando, FL: Harcourt, 2006. pp. 160. (Second ed.: first ed. 1993.)

Emma Donoghue (b.1969)

15525. WIGSTON, NANCY. Interview with Emma Donoghue. BkCan (34:5) 2005, 11–13.

Hilda Doolittle ('H.D.')

15526. CAMBONI, MARINA (ed.). H.D.'s poetry: 'the meanings that words hide'. (Bibl. 2003, 16309.) Rev. by Helen Sword in Paideuma (33:2/3) 2004, 275–8; by Victoria Bazin in MLR (101:1) 2006, 236–7.

15527. CLIPPINGER, DAVID W. Resurrecting the ghost: H.D., Susan Howe, and the haven of poetry. Sagetrieb (19:3) 2006, 141–72.

15528. COLLECOTT, DIANA. The poetry of H.D. *In* (pp. 358–66) **11788**.

15529. CONNOR, RACHEL. H.D. and the image. Manchester; New York: Manchester UP, 2004. pp. vii, 152. Rev. by Ian F. A. Bell in JAStud (39:3) 2005, 549–50.

15530. CURRY, RENÉE R. H.D., Dove, Glück, and Levin: the poetry of Afroasiatic and White Greece. Sagetrieb (19:3) 2006, 173–200.

15531. DEBO, ANNETTE. Whiteness and the Black/White border in H.D. Paideuma (33:2/3) 2004, 155–75.

15532. DENNISON, JULIE. Williams and H.D. figure it out: reconceiving the childbirth metaphor in 'his' *Paterson*, 'her' *Trilogy*. Paideuma (33:2/3) 2004, 223–45.

15533. EMMITT, HELEN V. Forgotten memories and unheard rhythms: H.D.'s poetics as a response to male Modernism. Paideuma (33:2/3) 2004, 131–53.

15534. FAUBION, S. RENÉE. 'This is no rune nor symbol': the sensual in H.D.'s feminized sublime. Paideuma (33:2/3) 2004, 111–30.

15535. GORSKI, HEDWIG. The riddle of correspondences in A. S. Byatt's *Possession: a Romance* with H.D.'s *Trilogy*. *See* **14981**.

15536. HICKMAN, MIRANDA B. The geometry of Modernism: the Vorticist idiom in Lewis, Pound, H.D., and Yeats. *See* **17215**.

15537. HOLLENBERG, DONNA KROLIK. 'Within the world of your perceptions': the letters of Denise Levertov and H.D. Paideuma (33:2/3) 2004, 247–71.

15538. KEELING, BRET L. Modernist anonymity and H.D.'s *Pygmalion*: whose story is this? Paideuma (33:2/3) 2004, 177–202.

15539. MCCABE, SUSAN. Whither sexuality and gender? 'What that sign signifies' and the rise of queer historicism. *See* **20100**.

15540. MCDONALD, GAIL. A homemade heaven: Modernist poetry and the Social Gospel. *In* (pp. 194–215) **8429**.

15541. PEARSON, JOANNE. H.D.: dancing with variable feet. Paideuma (33:1) 2004, 17–31.

15542. SANTESSO, AARON. *Responsibilities*: H.D. and Yeats. Paideuma (33:2/3) 2004, 203–21.

15543. WILLIS, ELIZABETH. A public history of the dividing line: H.D., the Bomb, and the roots of the postmodern. FLS (120) 2006, 38–54.

Edward Dorn

15544. BRINTON, IAN. Black Mountain in England: 5. PNRev (33:1) 2006, 45–8.

Michael Dorris

15545. CANNON, SARITA. Rayona Taylor and Michael Dorris as tricksters in crime. PemM (38) 2006, 64–79.

John Dos Passos

15546. LUDINGTON, TOWNSEND. Explaining Dos Passos's naturalism. StAN (1:1/2) 2006, 36–41.

15547. STOLZ, CLAUDIA MATHERLY. Dos Passos's *Three Soldiers*: a case study. WVUPP (51) 2004, 77–84.

Mark Doty

15548. Doty, Mark. Human seraphim: *Howl*, sex, and holiness. *In* (pp. 11–18) **16122**.

15549. —— The poet on the poem. APR (35:6) 2006, 17. (*Theory of the Sublime.*)

Sharon Doubiago

15550. Downes, Jeremy M. 'Against the fathers' amnesia': Sharon Doubiago, *Hard Country*, and women's epic. *In* (pp. 181–209) **3395**.

Norman Douglas

15551. Russo, John Paul. In the footsteps of Norman Douglas and Edward Hutton. *In* (pp. 349–65) **11824**.

Rita Dove

15552. Curry, Renée R. H.D., Dove, Glück, and Levin: the poetry of Afroasiatic and White Greece. *See* **15530**.

15553. Ingersoll, Earl G. (ed.). Conversations with Rita Dove. (Bibl. 2003, 16337.) Rev. by Adele Newson-Horst in WLT (79:1) 2005, 92–3.

15554. Righelato, Pat. Understanding Rita Dove. Columbia; London: South Carolina UP, 2006. pp. 249. (Understanding contemporary American literature.)

Brian Doyle

15555. Anon. Brian Doyle. WLT (80:3) 2006, 6–8. (Interview.)

Roddy Doyle

15556. McGuire, Matt. Dialect(ic) nationalism? The fiction of James Kelman and Roddy Doyle. *See* **16824**.

15557. Wurtz, James F. 'Liberation and oppression are inextricably bound': sports, narrative, and the colonial experience. *See* **12227**.

Margaret Drabble

15558. Phinn, Gordon. Chronicler of life in contemporary Britain: interview with Margaret Drabble. BkCan (34:3) 2005, 12–14.

Theodore Dreiser

15559. Cassuto, Leonard; Eby, Clare Virginia (eds). The Cambridge companion to Theodore Dreiser. (Bibl. 2004, 16445.) Rev. by Nancy Warner Barrineau in ALR (38:2) 2006, 185–6.

15560. Huang, Kaihong. On 'American Dream' in the transitional society: *Sister Carrie*'s moral tendency. FLS (119) 2006, 143–8. (In Chinese.)

15561. Juras, Uwe. Pleasing to the 'I': the culture of personality and its representations in Theodore Dreiser and F. Scott Fitzgerald. (Bibl. 2005, 16142.) Rev. by Renate von Bardeleben in StAN (1:1/2) 2006, 207–10.

15562. Lehan, Richard. Naturalism and the realms of the text: the problem restated. StAN (1:1/2) 2006, 15–29.

15563. Lindquist, Barbara. Theodore Dreiser, thermodynamics, and the 'manly man': an analysis of gender relations in the Cowperwood trilogy. MidAmerica (31) 2004, 57–68.

15564. Loving, Jerome. The last Titan: a life of Theodore Dreiser. (Bibl. 2005, 16144.) Rev. by Kathleen Drowne in JAH (92:4) 2006, 1463–4; by Vincent Fitzpatrick in AL (78:1) 2006, 189–90; by Leonard Cassuto in AmQ (58:4) 2006, 1249–61.

15565. Riggio, Thomas P. Dreiser and Kirah Markham: the play's the thing. StAN (1:1/2) 2006, 109–27.

15566. Rusch, Frederic E.; Pizer, Donald (eds). Theodore Dreiser: interviews. (Bibl. 2005, 16148.) Rev. by Robert M. Dowling in ALR (38:2) 2006, 186–8.

15567. Totten, Gary. 'American seen': the road and the look of American culture in Dreiser's *A Hoosier Holiday.* ALR (39:1) 2006, 24–47.

15568. Zhu, Zhenwu. *Sister Carrie*: a city immigrant in crisis of ecological ethics. FLS (119) 2006, 137–42. (In Chinese.)

W. E. B. Du Bois

15569. Andrade, Heather Russell. Revising critical judgments of *The Autobiography of an Ex-Colored Man. See* **16611**.

15570. Bornstein, George. W. E. B. Du Bois and the Jews: ethics, editing, and *The Souls of Black Folk.* TextC (1:1) 2006, 64–74.

15571. Connor, Kimberly Rae. More heat than light: the legacy of John Brown in Russell Banks's *Cloudsplitter.* *In* (pp. 203–24) **8537**.

15572. Farland, Maria. W. E. B. Du Bois, anthropometric science, and the limits of racial uplift. AmQ (58:4) 2006, 1017–45.

15573. Gougeon, Len. The legacy of reform: Emersonian idealism, Moorfield Storey, and the Civil Rights Movement. *In* (pp. 183–210) **10064**.

15574. Hicks, Scott. W. E. B. Du Bois, Booker T. Washington, and Richard Wright: toward an ecocriticism of color. Callaloo (29:1) 2006, 202–22.

15575. Hiro, Molly. How it feels to be without a face: race and the reorientation of sympathy in the 1890s. *See* **9654**.

15576. Husband, Julie. W. E. B. Du Bois's *John Brown*: placing racial justice at the center of a Socialist politics. *In* (pp. 159–71) **8537**.

15577. Jahn, Karen F. Will the circle be unbroken? Jazzing story in *Hoop Roots.* *In* (pp. 57–70) **19144**.

15578. Melamed, Jodi. W. E. B. Du Bois's unAmerican end. AAR (40:3) 2006, 533–50.

15579. Miller, Monica L. The Black dandy as bad Modernist. *In* (pp. 179–205) **12024**.

15580. Proietti, Salvatore. The Middle Passage and the remaking of the world: Du Bois and after. QPS (14) 2006, 232–9.

15581. Rabaka, Reiland. The souls of Black radical folk: W. E. B. Du Bois, critical social theory, and the state of Africana Studies. JBlaS (36:5) 2006, 732–63.

15582. Scheiber, Andrew J. The folk, the school, and the marketplace: locations of culture in *The Souls of Black Folk.* *In* (pp. 250–67) **8435**.

15583. Smith, John David. 'My books are hard reading for a Negro': Tom Dixon and his African American critics, 1905–1939. *In* (pp. 46–79) **15511**.

15584. Smith, Shawn Michelle. Photography on the color line: W. E. B. Du Bois, race, and visual culture. Durham, NC; London: Duke UP, 2004. pp. xviii, 225, (plates) 24. Rev. by Ira Dworkin in AL (77:2) 2005, 421–4; by Mark Whalan in JAStud (39:3) 2005, 572–3.

15585. Velikova, Roumiana. Replacing the father: W. E. B. Du Bois's reflections on George Washington's birthday. Callaloo (29:2) 2006, 658–79.

Alan Duff (b.1950)

15586. Wilson, Janet. Suffering and survival: body and voice in recent Maori writing. *In* (pp. 425–38) **8374**.

Laurie Duggan

15587. McCooey, David. Local elegies: Laurie Duggan and the world. Agenda (41:1/2) 2005, 162–8.

Denise Duhamel

15588. DiMarco, Danette. 'Misfortune's monsters / the human … race': Mina Loy's American lineage and an urban poetry of economic deprivation. *See* **17284**.

K. Sello Duiker

15589. Odhiambo, Tom. Socio-sexual experiences of Black South African men in K. Sello Duiker's *Thirteen Cents* and *The Quiet Violence of Dreams*. *In* (pp. 83–97) **12216**.

David James Duncan

15590. Duncan, David James. The collision of faith and fiction: cleaning up the wreckage. *In* (pp. 183–93) **11940**.

Robert Duncan

15591. Bertholf, Robert J. Decision at the apogee: Duncan's anarchist critique of Denise Levertov. *In* (pp. 1–17) **15599**.

15592. —— Gelpi, Albert (eds). The letters of Robert Duncan and Denise Levertov. (Bibl. 2005, 16174.) Rev. by Eavan Boland in PNRev (30:4) 2004, 12–15.

15593. Boland, Eavan. A broken connection. PNRev (30:4) 2004, 12–15 (review-article). (Duncan and Levertov.)

15594. Capinha, Graça. Robert Duncan and the question of law: Ernst Kantorowicz and the poet's two bodies. *In* (pp. 18–31) **15599**.

15595. Dewey, Anne. Poetic authority and the public sphere of politics in the activist 1960s: the Duncan–Levertov debate. *In* (pp. 109–25) **15599**.

15596. Felstiner, John. The Hasid and the kabbalist. *In* (pp. 81–9) **15599**.

15597. —— The Hasid and the kabbalist. *See* **17153**.

15598. Gelpi, Albert. Poetic language and language poetry: Levertov, Duncan, Creeley. *In* (pp. 180–98) **15599**.

15599. —— Bertholf, Robert J. (eds). Robert Duncan and Denise Levertov: the poetry of politics, the politics of poetry. Stanford, CA: Stanford UP, 2006. pp. xiv, 209.

15600. Hollenberg, Donna Krolik. Visions of the field in poetry and painting: Denise Levertov, Robert Duncan, and John Button. *In* (pp. 43–59) **15599**.

15601. Johnston, Devin. Better to stumble to it: the start of Duncan's *Letters: Poems, 1953–1956*. *In* (pp. 32–42) **15599**.

15602. Lacey, Paul A. The vision of the burning babe: Southwell, Levertov, and Duncan. *In* (pp. 161–79) **15599**.

15603. Millier, Brett. *Chelsea 8*: political poetry at midcentury. *In* (pp. 94–108) **15599**.

15604. O'Leary, Peter. The phosphorescence of thought. *See* **14531**.

15605. —— Prophetic frustrations: Robert Duncan's *Tribunals*. *In* (pp. 126–47) **15599**.

15606. Rodriguez Herrera, Jose. Revolution or death? Levertov's poetry in time of war. *In* (pp. 148–60) **15599**.

15607. Shurin, Aaron. The People's P***k: a dialectical tale. *In* (pp. 71–80) **15599**.

15608. Tallman, Ellen. My stories with Robert Duncan. *In* (pp. 63–70) **15599**.

Helen Dunmore (b.1952)

15609. Adolph, Andrea. The reader's body: reader response and the consuming body in Helen Dunmore's *Talking to the Dead*. LIT (17:3/4) 2006, 353–77.

Nell Dunn (b.1936)

15610. Minogue, Sally; Palmer, Andrew. Confronting the abject: women and dead babies in modern English fiction. *See* **18524**.

Stephen Dunn

15611. Dunn, Stephen. One summer: musings about avoidance, temperament, and the poem becoming a poem. GaR (59:4) 2005, 817–21.

Edward John Plunkett, Lord Dunsany

15612. Carlson, David J. Lord Dunsany and the Great War: *Don Rodriguez* and the rebirth of romance. Mythlore (25:1/2) 2006, 93–104.

Christopher Durang

15613. Durang, Christopher. Off-Broadway: of thee I sink. *See* **12278**.

15614. —— *et al.* Joking aside: a conversation about comedy with Christopher Durang, Gina Gionfriddo, Sarah Ruhl, and Wendy Wasserstein. *In* (pp. 181–90) **12297**.

Lawrence Durrell

15615. Alexandre-Garner, Corinne. Coming to Medusa: from desire to fear, and from love to disgust: glosses on Durrell's discourse on modern love. *In* (pp. 191–202) **15631**.

15616. Battaglia, Beatrice. An introduction to myth and dystopia in Lawrence Durrell's works. DeusL (ns 9) 2003–2005, 69–81.

15617. Beard, Pauline. 'Something harder': the discovery of the self through Greece, fable, and fairy tale. *In* (pp. 203–14) **15631**.

15618. Calonne, David Stephen. The discovery of yourself: Lawrence Durrell and Gostan Zarian in Greece. *In* (pp. 62–75) **15631**.

15619. Calotychos, Vangelis. 'Lawrence Durrell, the bitterest lemon?': Cyps and Brits loving each other to death in Cyprus, 1953–57. *In* (pp. 169–87) **15631**.

15620. Carruthers, Virginia Kirby-Smith. Durrell's enigmatic Hamlet: mysteries of image and allusion. DeusL (ns 9) 2003–2005, 25–33.

15621. Diboll, Mike. The secret history of Lawrence Durrell's *The Alexandria Quartet*: the Mountolive–Hosnani affair, Britain, and the Wafd. *In* (pp. 79–105) **15631**.

15622. Durrell, Margaret; MacNiven, Susan; MacNiven, Ian. Margaret Durrell remembers …: a dialogue on Corfu. *In* (pp. 36–45) **15631**.

15623. Escobar, Matthew. Fictional universe and the self in Lawrence Durrell's *Monsieur; or, The Prince of Darkness*. DeusL (ns 9) 2003–2005, 52–68.

15624. Hirst, Anthony. 'The old poet of the city': Cavafy in Darley's Alexandria. *In* (pp. 106–19) **15631**.

15625. Hope, Penelope Durrell. Corfu 2000. *In* (pp. 33–5) **15631**.

15626. Jensen, Finn. Karen Blixen and Lawrence Durrell: two aspects of Modernism. DeusL (ns 9) 2003–2005, 161–8.

15627. Karagiorgos, Panos. An unpublished letter of Durrell to Marie Aspioti. *In* (pp. 57–61) **15631**.

15628. Keller, Jane Eblen. Durrell's ode to the olive. *In* (pp. 298–307) **15631**.

15629. Leatham, John. Durrell on Rhodes. *In* (pp. 145–50) **15631**.

15630. Lillios, Anna. The Alexandrian mirages of Durrell and Cavafy. *In* (pp. 120–8) **15631**.

15631. —— (ed.). Lawrence Durrell and the Greek world. Selinsgrove, PA: Susquehanna UP; London: Assoc. UPs, 2004. pp. 336.

15632. McKenna, Bernard. The myth of Other: Darley's representations of female homosexuality in *Balthazar*. DeusL (ns 9) 2003–2005, 3–24.

15633. Maynard, John. Two mad-dog Englishmen in the Corfu sun: Lawrence Durrell and Edward Lear. *In* (pp. 255–69) **15631**.

15634. Parker, Allison Cay. Lawrence Durrell and Paul Cézanne: a personal landscape of art and fiction. DeusL (ns 9) 2003–2005, 153–7.

15635. Plo Alastrué, Ramón. Foregrounding process: postmodernist traits in *The Avignon Quintet*. DeusL (ns 9) 2003–2005, 34–51.

15636. Quinn, Patrick. 'More than a fascination wiith the Divine Marquis': John Fowles's *The Magus* and Lawrence Durrell's *The Alexandria Quartet*. *In* (pp. 270–81) **15631**.

15637. Raizis, Marios Byron. Lawrence Durrell and the Greek poets: a contribution to cultural history. *In* (pp. 241–54) **15631**.

15638. Rose, John M. Multiple truths and multiple narratives: Nietzsche's perspectivism and the narrative structure of *The Alexandria Quartet*. *In* (pp. 215–38) **15631**.

15639. SEIGNEURIE, KEN. Sweeping *The Alexandria Quartet* out of a dusty corner. DeusL (ns 9) 2003–2005, 82–110.

15640. STEWART, JACK. Soundscapes, smellscapes, and cityscapes in *The Alexandria Quartet*. *In* (pp. 129–42) **15631**.

15641. STONEBACK, H. R. *Prospero's Cell*: a meditation on place. *In* (pp. 285–97) **15631**.

15642. TOURNAY, PETRA. Colonial encounters: Lawrence Durrell's *Bitter Lemons of Cyprus*. *In* (pp. 158–68) **15631**.

15643. TREMAYNE, PENELOPE. Memories of Durrell. *In* (pp. 153–7) **15631**.

15644. VALAORITIS, NANOS. Remembering the poets: translating Seferis with Durrell and Bernard Spencer. *In* (pp. 46–53) **15631**.

15645. ZAHLAN, ANNE R. The Negro as icon: transformation and the Black body in Lawrence Durrell's *The Avignon Quintet*. SAtlR (71:1) 2006, 74–88.

Eva Emery Dye (1855–1947)

15646. BROWNE, SHERI BARTLETT. Eva Emery Dye: romance with the West. (Bibl. 2005, 16193.) Rev. by Susan Armitage in WAL (41:1) 2006, 66–72.

Geoff Dyer

15647. KELLMAN, STEVEN G. Ghosting the Lost Generation: Geoff Dyer's *Paris Trance*. IFR (33:1/2) 2006, 9–17.

'Bob Dylan' (Robert Zimmerman)

15648. DYLAN, BOB. Chronicles: vol. 1. (Bibl. 2005, 16212.) Rev. by Michael Karwowski in ContRev (286:1669) 2005, 113–14; by Adrian Grafe in EA (59:4) 2006, 490–3.

15649. GRAY, MICHAEL. The Bob Dylan encyclopedia. London; New York: Continuum, 2006. pp. xix, 736; 1 CD-ROM. Rev. by Mark Kidel in TLS, 10 Nov. 2006, 22.

15650. HISHMEH, RICHARD E. Marketing genius: the friendship of Allen Ginsberg and Bob Dylan. *See* **16103**.

15651. KIDEL, MARK. From R to B. TLS, 10 Nov. 2006, 22 (review-article). (Dylan encyclopaedia.)

15652. MARCUS, GREIL. Like a rolling stone: Bob Dylan at the crossroads. New York: PublicAffairs, 2005. pp. xiv, 283. Rev. by Jeff Wiederkehr in AmBR (27:4) 2006, 26–7.

15653. POLITO, ROBERT. Holy the Fifth International. *In* (pp. 226–42) **16122**.

15654. POLIZZOTTI, MARK. Bob Dylan: *Highway 61 Revisited*. London; New York: Continuum, 2006. pp. 161.

15655. TURLEY, RICHARD MARGGRAF. 'Johnny's in the basement': Keats, Bob Dylan, and the end of influence. *In* (pp. 181–204) **13735**.

15656. VERNEZZE, PETER; PORTER, CARL J. (eds). Bob Dylan and philosophy: it's alright, ma (I'm only thinking). Chicago, IL: Open Court, 2006. pp. xvii, 205. (Popular culture and philosophy, 17.)

Ketaki Kushari Dyson (b.1940)

15657. Barat, Urbashi. From resistance to regeneration: Ketaki Kushari Dyson's *Night's Sunlight* and Dina Mehta's *Getting Away with Murder*. *In* (pp. 3–10) **11731**.

Edward McMaken Eager (1911–1964)

15658. Richey, Esther Gilman. Only half magic: Edward Eager's revision of Nesbit's Psammead trilogy. *In* (pp. 255–69) **17738**.

William Eastlake

15659. Malphrus, P. Ellen. 'Dancing past the ultimate arrow': an overview of William Eastlake's life and works. RCF (26:2) 2006, 7–35.

Fred Ebb

15660. Striff, Erin. Mimicry and murder: female impersonation in *Chicago*. JADT (18:3) 2006, 77–89.

Mignon Good Eberhart (b.1899)

15661. Cypert, Rick. America's Agatha Christie: Mignon Good Eberhart, her life and works. (Bibl. 2005, 16230.) Rev. by LeRoy L. Panek in GPQ (26:4) 2006, 290.

Randolph Edmonds (1900–1983)

15662. Krasner, David. The theatre of Sheppard Randolph Edmonds. NETJ (16) 2005, 21–41.

Margaret Edson (b.1961)

15663. McDowell, Sean. *W;t*, Donne's *Holy Sonnets*, and the problem of pain. *See* **6729**.

15664. Rimmon-Kenan, Shlomith. Margaret Edson's *Wit* and the art of analogy. Style (40:4) 2006, 346–56.

Greg Egan (b.1961)

15665. Hayles, N. Katherine. My mother was a computer: digital subjects and literary texts. *See* **18622**.

W. D. Ehrhart

15666. Clifford, Emily Clare. 'Before I was domesticated': delivering the Vietnam moment in the fatherhood poetry of Bruce Weigl and John Balaban. *See* **19005**.

T. S. Eliot

15667. Abbott, Ruth. T. S. Eliot's ghostly footfalls: the versification of *Four Quartets*. CamQ (34:4) 2005, 365–85. (Prize essay.)

15668. Badenhausen, Richard. T. S. Eliot and the art of collaboration. (Bibl. 2005, 16240.) Rev. by Jeremy Noel-Tod in TLS, 26 May 2006, 11–12; by Ronald Bush in RES (57:231) 2006, 570–1; by John Young in TextC (1:2) 2006, 152–4.

15669. Bennett, Benjamin. All theater is revolutionary theater. (Bibl. 2005, 16244.) Rev. by Stanton B. Garner, Jr, in ModDr (48:4) 2005, 842–4; by Andrew Sofer in TheatreS (47:2) 2006, 341–2.

15670. Booth, Roy. T. S. Eliot, *Sweeney Agonistes*, and Ben Jonson's *Masque of Queenes*. NQ (53:3) 2006, 351–2.

15671. Boruch, Marianne. Heavy lifting. *See* **16302**.

15672. Brazeal, Gregory. The alleged Pragmatism of T. S. Eliot. PhilL (30:1) 2006, 248–64.

15673. Brooker, Jewel Spears (ed.). T. S. Eliot: the contemporary reviews. (Bibl. 2005, 16248.) Rev. by Jan Gorak in ELN (43:2) 2005, 200–3; by Victor Strandberg in SewR (113:3) 2005, lxxvi–lxxix; by Frank J. Kearful in PartA (4:1) 2006, 197–201.

15674. Brown, Joyce Compton. Rising out of the wasteland: images of death, decay, and rebirth in the Ballad novels of Sharyn McCrumb. *See* **17311**.

15675. Candeloro, Antonio. *Journey of the Magi* di T. S. Eliot e *La adoración de los magos* di Luis Cernuda: ri-scritture poetiche. AngP (3:1) 2006, 164–93.

15676. Carey, John. Is the author dead? Or, The mermaids and the robot. *In* (pp. 43–54) **5353**.

15677. Chao, Shun-liang. 'To form a new compound': Eliot, Bergson, and Cubism. EtBr (31) 2006, 55–67.

15678. Chapman, Danielle. Sweet bombs. *See* **14871**.

15679. Chinitz, David. T. S. Eliot: *The Waste Land*. *In* (pp. 324–32) **11788**.

15680. Churchill, Suzanne W. Outing T. S. Eliot. Criticism (47:1) 2005, 7–30.

15681. Collecott, Diana. The poetry of H.D. *In* (pp. 358–66) **11788**.

15682. Cuda, Anthony J. T. S. Eliot's forgotten 'poet of lines', Nathaniel Wanley. ANQ (19:2) 2006, 52–8.

15683. Däumer, Elisabeth. Blood and witness: the reception of *Murder in the Cathedral* in postwar Germany. CLS (43:1/2) 2006, 79–99.

15684. Daunt, Ricardo. T. S. Eliot e Fernando Pessoa: diálogos de New Haven: ensaios. São Paulo: Landy, 2004. pp. 223. Rev. by George Monteiro in GavB (26/27) 2005/06, 242–4.

15685. Ford, Mark. Hyacinth boy. LRB (28:18) 2006, 32–4 (review-article). (Sexuality and *The Waste Land*.)

15686. Galloway, Stan. Alienation in *Tarzan's First Love*. *See* **14933**.

15687. Harding, Jason. 'Eliot without tears'. Mod/Mod (13:1) 2006, 171–8 (review article).

15688. Hargrove, Nancy D. T. S. Eliot's year abroad, 1910–1911: the visual arts. SAtlR (71:1) 2006, 89–131.

15689. Hart, Jeffrey. Robert Frost and T. S. Eliot: Modernisms. *See* **16004**.

15690. Hochman, Baruch. Character: under erasure? *See* **13502**.

15691. Hume, Amy. Listening for the 'sound of water over a rock': heroism and the role of the reader in *The Waste Land*. YER (23:3/4) 2006, 2–13.

15692. Jacobs, Struan. T. S. Eliot and Michael Polanyi on tradition in literature and in science. DalR (86:3) 2006, 373–88.

15693. Kaplan, Harold. Poetry, politics, and culture: argument in the work of Eliot, Pound, Stevens, and Williams. New Brunswick, NJ: Transaction, 2006. pp. xi, 279. Rev. by Alan Filreis in WSJ (30:2) 2006, 235–6.

15694. Kinsella, Thomas. Readings in poetry. *See* **6093**.

15695. Laity, Cassandra; Gish, Nancy K. (eds). Gender, desire, and sexuality in Eliot. (Bibl. 2004, 16545.) Rev. by Leonard Diepeveen in ELT (49:1) 2005, 103–6.

15696. Livorni, Ernesto. Montale traduttore di Eliot: una questione di '*belief*'. *In* (pp. 139–60) **3341**.

15697. Lowe, Peter. Christian Romanticism: T. S. Eliot's response to Percy Shelley. Youngstown, NY: Cambria Press, 2006. pp. xii, 285.

15698. McCue, Jim. Editing Eliot. EC (56:1) 2006, 1–27. (Critical opinion.)

15699. McDonald, Gail. A homemade heaven: Modernist poetry and the Social Gospel. *In* (pp. 194–215) **8429**.

15700. McDonald, Peter. Difficulty, democracy, and modern poetry: a lecture delivered at the University of Edinburgh, 14 November 2003. PNRev (31:3) 2005, 19–24.

15701. McGann, Jerome. 'The grand heretics of modern fiction': Laura Riding, John Cowper Powys, and the subjective correlative. *See* **18250**.

15702. McMorris, Mark. Discrepant affinities in Caribbean poetry: tradition and demotic Modernism. *See* **13809**.

15703. Mason, Emma. 'Love's the burning boy': Hemans's critical legacy. *In* (pp. 205–24) **13735**.

15704. Miller, James E., Jr. T. S. Eliot: the making of an American poet, 1888–1922. (Bibl. 2005, 16287.) Rev. by Jeremy Noel-Tod in TLS, 26 May 2006, 11–12; by Mark Ford in LRB (28:18) 2006, 32–4.

15705. Noel-Tod, Jeremy. Frank conversations. TLS, 26 May 2006, 11–12 (review-article).

15706. Obumselu, Ben. Christopher Okigbo: a poet's identity. *In* (pp. 57–78) **11860**.

15707. Patea, Viorica (ed. and trans.). La tierra baldía. Madrid: Cátedra, 2005. pp. 328. (Letras universales, 381.) Rev. by Paul Scott Derrick in Atl (28:2) 2006, 141–5.

15708. Peddie, Ian. Thomas McGrath, T. S. Eliot, and the commissars of culture. *See* **17347**.

15709. Perryman, John. Back to *The Bay Psalm Book*: T. S. Eliot's identity crisis and *Sweeney Erect*. MidQ (47:3) 2006, 244–61.

15710. Peters, Matthew. A new source for *The Waste Land*. NQ (53:3) 2006, 352–3. (Melville's journals.)

15711. Pollard, Charles W. New World Modernisms: T. S. Eliot, Derek Walcott, and Kamau Brathwaite. (Bibl. 2005, 16293.) Rev. by Neil ten Kortenaar in RAL (37:1) 2006, 162–3; by Eric Keenaghan in JML (29:3) 2006, 176–90; by J. Dillon Brown in JWIL (15:1/2) 2006, 218–22.

15712. Raine, Craig. T. S. Eliot. Oxford; New York: OUP, 2006. pp. xxi, 202. (Lives and legacies.)

15713. Rainey, Lawrence. Revisiting *The Waste Land*. (Bibl. 2005, 16297.) Rev. by Hugh Graham in BkCan (34:9) 2005, 23; by Jeremy Noel-Tod in TLS, 26 May 2006, 11–12; by Jason Harding in Mod/Mod (13:1) 2006, 171–8; by Mark Ford in LRB (28:18) 2006, 32–4.

15714. —— (ed.). The annotated *Waste Land*, with T. S. Eliot's contemporary prose. (Bibl. 2005, 16298.) Rev. by Jeremy Noel-Tod in TLS, 26 May 2006, 11–12; by Jason Harding in Mod/Mod (13:1) 2006, 171–8; by Mark Ford in LRB (28:18) 2006, 32–4.

15715. RANKIN, WALTER. Subverting literary allusions in Eliot and Özdamar. CLCWeb (8:3) 2006.

15716. SAEKI, KEIKO. Return to the ordinary world: from *The Family Reunion* to *The Cocktail Party*. YER (23:3/4) 2006, 27–39.

15717. STANLAKE, CHRISTY. JudyLee Oliva's *The Fire and the Rose* and the modeling of platial theories in Native American dramaturgy. *See* **20316**.

15718. TERBLANCHE, ÉTIENNE. Holons and the poetry of T. S. Eliot and E. E. Cummings. AUMLA (105) 2006, 85–108.

15719. TROTTER, DAVID. T. S. Eliot and cinema. Mod/Mod (13:2) 2006, 237–65.

15720. VAN HULLE, DIRK. Growth and the grid: organic *vs* constructivist conceptions of poetry. Neophilologus (90:3) 2006, 491–507.

15721. WIHL, GARY. Modernist critical prose. *In* (pp. 516–23) **11788**.

15722. WILSON, JAMES MATTHEW. Thomas MacGreevy reads T. S. Eliot and Jack B. Yeats: making Modernism Catholic. YER (23:3/4) 2006, 14–26.

15723. WILSON, JOHN HOWARD. A question of influence and experience: a response to Edward Lobb. *See* **19002**.

15724. ZAJKO, VANDA. Homer and *Ulysses*. *In* (pp. 311–23) **3253**.

15725. ZILCOSKY, JOHN. Modern monuments: T. S. Eliot, Nietzsche, and the problem of history. JML (29:1) 2005, 21–33.

Stanley Elkin

15726. DOUGHERTY, DAVID C. (introd.). Prospects of recovery: two unpublished sketches by Stanley Elkin. NER (27:4) 2006, 41–56.

15727. TRISTMAN, RICHARD. Tragic soliloquy, stand-up spiel. NER (27:4) 2006, 36–40.

Bret Easton Ellis

15728. DALLMANN, ANTJE. ConspiraCities and creative paranoia: Ellis's *Glamorama*, Hustvedt's *The Blindfold*, and Whitehead's *The Intuitionist*. Anglophonia (19) 2006, 67–78.

15729. VINCENT-ARNAUD, NATHALIE. Cartographie du vide: les 'non-lieux' de l'espace américain dans *The Informers* de Bret Easton Ellis. Anglophonia (19) 2006, 107–16.

Harlan Ellison

15730. DI FILIPO, PAUL. Stripped down naked: the short stories of Harlan Ellison. NYRSF (18:5) 2006, 1, 8–14.

Ralph Ellison

15731. ANDERSON, PAUL ALLEN. Ralph Ellison on lyricism and swing. AmLH (17:2) 2005, 280–306.

15732. —— Ralph Ellison's music lessons. *In* (pp. 82–103) **15746**.

15733. Blair, Sara. Ellison, photography, and the origins of invisibility. *In* (pp. 56–81) **15746**.

15734. Bourassa, Alan. Affect, history, and race and Ellison's *Invisible Man*. CLCWeb (8:2) 2006.

15735. Cheng, Anne Anlin. Ralph Ellison and the politics of melancholia. *In* (pp. 121–36) **15746**.

15736. Crane, Gregg. Ralph Ellison's constitutional faith. *In* (pp. 104–20) **15746**.

15737. Dvinge, Anne. Complex fate – complex vision: the vernacular and identity in Ralph Ellison's *Juneteenth*. Amst (51:2) 2006, 193–206.

15738. Eversley, Shelly. Female iconography in *Invisible Man*. *In* (pp. 172–87) **15746**.

15739. Jackson, Lawrence. Ralph Ellison's invented life: a meeting with the ancestors. *In* (pp. 11–34) **15746**.

15740. Kim, Daniel Y. Writing manhood in black and yellow: Ralph Ellison, Frank Chin, and the literary politics of identity. (Bibl. 2005, 16336.) Rev. by Ryan Schneider in AL (78:4) 2006, 894–7.

15741. Lee, Julie Sun-Joo. Knucklebones and knocking-bones: the accidental trickster in Ellison's *Invisible Man*. AAR (40:3) 2006, 461–73.

15742. Morel, Lucas E. (ed.). Ralph Ellison and the raft of hope: a political companion to *Invisible Man*. (Bibl. 2004, 16593.) Rev. by Sara Blair in Mod/Mod (13:4) 2006, 781–3.

15743. Parrish, Tim. Invisible Ellison: the fight to be a Negro leader. *In* (pp. 137–56) **15746**.

15744. Posnock, Ross. Introduction: Ellison's joking. *In* (pp. 1–10) **15746**.

15745. —— Ralph Ellison, Hannah Arendt and the meaning of politics. *In* (pp. 201–16) **15746**.

15746. —— (ed.). The Cambridge companion to Ralph Ellison. Cambridge; New York: CUP, 2005. pp. xiv, 237. (Cambridge companions to literature.)

15747. Rankine, Patrice D. Ulysses in black: Ralph Ellison, Classicism, and African American literature. Madison; London: Wisconsin UP, 2006. pp. 254. (Wisconsin studies in Classics.)

15748. Rodriguez, Denise. Homewood's 'music of invisibility': John Edgar Wideman's *Sent for You Yesterday* and the Black urban tradition. *In* (pp. 127–44) **19144**.

15749. Saunders, Laura. Ellison and the Black Church: the gospel according to Ralph. *In* (pp. 35–55) **15746**.

15750. Shiffman, Mark. Confessional ethics in Augustine and Ralph Ellison. *In* (pp. 343–62) **3301**.

15751. Sundquist, Eric. Dry bones. *In* (pp. 217–30) **15746**.

15752. Thomas, J. D. Ellison's *Invisible Man*. Exp (65:1) 2006, 42–4.

15753. Tracy, Steven Carl (ed.). A historical guide to Ralph Ellison. (Bibl. 2004, 16601.) Rev. by Edward Margolies in AAR (40:1) 2006, 192–4.

15754. Warren, Kenneth W. Chaos not quite controlled: Ellison's uncompleted transit to *Juneteenth*. *In* (pp. 188–200) **15746**.

15755. Wittreich, Joseph. 'The ramifications of those ramifications': compounding contexts for *Samson Agonistes*. *In* (pp. 167–99) **7033**.

15756. Wright, John S. Ellison's experimental attitude and the technologies of illumination. *In* (pp. 157–71) **15746**.

15757. —— Shadowing Ralph Ellison. Jackson, London: Mississippi UP, 2006. pp. xxiv, 269. (Margaret Walker Anderson series in African American studies.)

15758. Yaffe, David. Fascinating rhythm: reading jazz in American writing. *See* **12229**.

James Ellroy

15759. Mancall, Jim. 'You're a watcher, lad': detective fiction, pornography, and Ellroy's L.A. Quartet. Clues (24:4) 2006, 3–14.

Buchi Emecheta

15760. Friedli-Clapié, Lisa. Undercurrents of Mammy Wata symbolism in Buchi Emecheta's *The Joys of Motherhood*. WVUPP (52) 2005, 83–90.

15761. McLeod, John. Postcolonial fictions of adoption. *See* **18449**.

15762. Muoneke, Romanus. Migration, transformation, and identity in Buchi Emecheta's *In the Ditch* and *Kehinde*. *In* (pp. 52–75) **11795**.

Anne Emery (b.1907)

15763. Litton, Joyce. Dinny Gordon: proto-feminist. JAC (29:1) 2006, 43–51.

William Empson (1906–1984)

15764. Collini, Stefan. Smack up: argufying and illumination in the letters of William Empson. TLS, 7 July 2006, 3–5 (review-article).

15765. Haffenden, John. Three's company: William Empson and *The Wife Is Praised*. TLS, 1 Dec. 2006, 14–15.

15766. —— William Empson: among the mandarins. (Bibl. 2005, 16345.) Rev. by Mark Thompson in PNRev (32:2) 2005, 31–3; by Martin Dodsworth in EC (56:2) 2006, 199–209; by Stephen Burt in NYTB, 10 Sept. 2006, 28; by David Fuller in RES (57:228) 2006, 112–14; by John Shusterman in EREA (4:1) 2006.

15767. —— William Empson: vol. II, Against the Christians. Oxford; New York: OUP, 2006. pp. xxii, 797, (plates) 16. Rev. by Frank Kermode in LRB (28:22) 2006, 12–14.

15768. —— (ed.). Selected letters of William Empson. Oxford; New York: OUP, 2006. pp. lxi, 729. Rev. by Stefan Collini in TLS, 7 July 2006, 3–5; by Adam Phillips in LRB (28:15) 2006, 26–7; by Stephen Burt in NYTB, 10 Sept. 2006, 28; by John Lyon in PNRev (33:1) 2006, 20–2.

15769. Kermode, Frank. 'Disgusting'. LRB (28:22) 2006, 12–14 (review-article). (Biography of Empson.)

15770. Lyon, John. Empson's letters. PNRev (33:1) 2006, 20–2 (review-article).

15771. Phillips, Adam. No reason for not asking. LRB (28:15) 2006, 26–7 (review-article). (Empson's letters.)

15772. POLLOTT, RICHARD. The poet's repose: William Empson and the faces of Buddha. PNRev (32:3) 2006, 54–6.

15773. THOMPSON, MARK. Hugging an exotic kind of goat. PNRev (32:2) 2005, 31–3 (review-article). (Biography of Empson.)

Marian Engel

15774. VERDUYN, CHRISTL; GARAY, KATHLEEN (eds). Marian Engel: life in letters. (Bibl. 2005, 16347.) Rev. by George Fetherling in BkCan (33:9) 2004, 19–20; by Laura M. Robinson in CanL (189) 2006, 145–6.

Eve Ensler (b.1953)

15775. KAVENY, M. CATHLEEN. The perfect storm: *The Vagina Monologues* and Catholic higher education. ANCW (194:16) 2006, 14–19.

Louise Erdrich

15776. AUSTENFELD, THOMAS. German heritage and culture in Louise Erdrich's *The Master Butchers Singing Club*. GPQ (26:1) 2006, 3–11.

15777. FRITSCH, ESTHER. *Reading gossip*: Funktionen von Klatsch in Romanen ethnischer amerikanischer Autorinnen. Trier: WVT, 2004. pp. 221. (Mosaic, 23.) Rev. by Carmen Birkle in Amst (51:3) 2006, 451–3.

15778. GARGANO, ELIZABETH. Oral narrative and Ojibwa story cycles in Louise Erdrich's *The Birchback House* and *The Game of Silence*. CLAQ (31:1) 2006, 27–39.

15779. KEENAN, DEIRDRE. Unrestricted territory: gender, two spirits, and Louise Erdrich's *The Last Report on the Miracles at Little No Horse*. AICRJ (30:2) 2006, 1–15.

15780. KNOELLER, CHRISTIAN P. A 'Hopi basket full of photographs': interpreting visual art in multi-genre works by contemporary Native American writers. *See* **17549**.

15781. LISCHKE, UTE; MCNAB, DAVID T. Storytelling and cultural identity: Louise Erdrich's exploration of the German/American connection in *The Master Butchers Singing Club*. EurJAC (25:3) 2006, 189–203.

15782. MCNAB, DAVID T. The significance of place and indigenous knowledge in Louise Erdrich's *Books and Islands in Ojibwe Country* (2003). EurJAC (25:3) 2006, 205–19.

15783. PURDY, JOHN. Moving stories: visualization, *mise-en-scène*, and Native American fiction. *See* **17388**.

15784. SARRIS, GREG; JACOBS, CONNIE A.; GILES, JAMES R. (eds). Approaches to teaching the works of Louise Erdrich. (Bibl. 2005, 16372.) Rev. by Julie Barak in GPQ (26:3) 2006, 223.

Martín Espada

15785. MURILLO, JOHN. The republic of Espada. BRev (26:6) 2006, 7, 31.

Marc Estrin (b.1939)

15786. COPELAND, MARION W. Voices of the least loved: cockroaches in the contemporary American novel. *In* (pp. 153–75) **3203**.

Jeffrey Eugenides

15787. Consonni, Stefania. Come nasce un premio Pulitzer: *Middlesex* di Jeffrey Eugenides. Àcoma (32) 2006, 144–59.

15788. Schiff, James. A conversation with Jeffrey Eugenides. MR (29:3) 2006, 100–19.

15789. Sifuentes, Zachary. Strange anatomy, strange sexuality: the queer body in Jeffrey Eugenides' *Middlesex*. *In* (pp. 145–57) **11883**.

Mari Evans (b.1923)

15790. Evans, Mari. Clarity as concept: a poet's perspective: a collection of essays. Chicago, IL: Third World Press, 2006. pp. xvii, 192.

Bernardine Evaristo (b.1959)

15791. Hooper, Karen. On the road: Bernardine Evaristo interviewed. JCL (41:1) 2006, 3–16.

Landis Everson (b.1926)

15792. Everson, Landis. Poet to poet: sharing poetry. EDISB (18:1) 2006, 6–7.

Nuruddin Farah

15793. Williams, R. John. 'Doing history': Nuruddin Farah's *Sweet and Sour Milk*, Subaltern Studies, and the postcolonial trajectory of silence. RAL (37:4) 2006, 161–76.

Richard Fariña

15794. Davis, Robert Murray. Whatever happened to Richard Fariña? WLT (80:3) 2006, 39–41.

J. G. (James Gordon) Farrell (b.1935)

15795. Erll, Astrid. Re-writing as re-visioning: modes of representing the 'Indian Mutiny' in British novels, 1857 to 2000. *See* **10429**.

William Faulkner

15796. Abdur-Rahman, Aliyyah I. White disavowal, Black enfranchisement, and the homoerotic in William Faulkner's *Light in August*. FJ (22:1/2) 2006, 176–92.

15797. Aboul-Ela, Hosam. The poetics of peripheralization: Faulkner and the question of the postcolonial. AL (77:3) 2005, 483–509.

15798. Ali, Seemee. Faulkner's Augustinian sense of time. *In* (pp. 287–300) **3301**.

15799. Anderson, Nancy Grisham (ed.). Reading Faulkner: introductions to the first thirteen novels. Knoxville: Tennessee UP, 2006. pp. xx, 200.

15800. Atkinson, Ted. Faulkner and the Great Depression: aesthetics, ideology, and cultural politics. (Bibl. 2005, 16391.) Rev. by Terrell L. Tebbetts in ArkR (37:2) 2006, 134–5.

15801. Barker, Deborah. Moonshine and magnolias: *The Story of Temple Drake* and *The Birth of a Nation*. *See* **13081**.

15802. Brister, J. G. *Absalom, Absalom!* and the semiotic Other. FJ (22:1/2) 2006, 39–53.

15803. Cobb, Michael L. Racial blasphemies: religious irreverence and race in American literature. *See* **14539**.

15804. Duck, Leigh Anne. The nation's region: Southern Modernism, segregation, and US nationalism. *See* **14995**.

15805. Duvall, John N. 'A strange nigger': Faulkner and the minstrel performance of Whiteness. FJ (22:1/2) 2006, 106–19.

15806. Eddy, Charmaine. Labor, economy, and desire: rethinking American nationhood through Yoknapatawpha. MissQ (57:4) 2004, 569–92.

15807. Entzminger, Betina. Passing as miscegenation: Whiteness and homoeroticism in Faulkner's *Absalom, Absaolm!* FJ (22:1/2) 2006, 90–105.

15808. Fruscione, Joseph. 'One tale, one telling': parallelism, influence, and exchange between Faulkner's *The Unvanquished* and Hemingway's *For Whom the Bell Tolls*. WLA (18:1/2) 2006, 279–300.

15809. Fulton, Lorie Watkins. William Faulkner reprised: isolation in Toni Morrison's *Song of Solomon*. *See* **17606**.

15810. Fury, Frank. Designs of identity and images of American boxing tradition in Faulkner's *Absalom, Absalom!* SPC (29:2) 2006, 69–86.

15811. Hagood, Taylor. Negotiating the marble bonds of Whiteness: hybridity and imperial impulse in Faulkner. FJ (22:1/2) 2006, 24–38.

15812. Hannon, Charles. Faulkner and the discourses of culture. (Bibl. 2005, 16416.) Rev. by Paula Elyseu Mesquita in AL (78:4) 2006, 876–7.

15813. He, Chang; Chen, Jiao'e. The story behind 'absences': a study of the historical consciousness in *A Rose for Emily*. FLS (121) 2006, 57–64. (In Chinese.)

15814. Hickman, Lisa C. William Faulkner and Joan Williams: the romance of two writers. Foreword by Richard Bausch. Jefferson, NC; London: McFarland, 2006. pp. ix, 218.

15815. Jackson, Chuck. American emergencies: Whiteness, the National Guard, and *Light in August*. FJ (22:1/2) 2006, 193–208.

15816. Jarrett, Gene Andrew. 'For endless generations': myth, dynasty, and Frank Yerby's *The Foxes of Harrow*. *See* **19455**.

15817. Knepper, Steven. 'Shoot quick, and slow': Southern sporting values, mastery, and language in Faulkner's *Go Down, Moses*. SPC (29:2) 2006, 87–106.

15818. Kodat, Catherine Gunther. Posting Yoknapatawpha. MissQ (57:4) 2004, 593–618.

15819. Labatt, Blair. Faulkner the storyteller. (Bibl. 2005, 16424.) Rev. by Taylor Hagood in StudN (38:2) 2006, 267–9.

15820. Lewis, Clay. Butcher's bill. SewR (114:2) 2006, 324–32 (review-article). (Arts and letters.)

15821. Liang, Xiaodong. Frenzy, violence and death: on the ruling metaphors in Faulkner's *Dry September*. FLS (117) 2006, 111–18. (In Chinese.)

15822. López, Alfred J. Queering Whiteness, queering Faulkner: Hightower's 'wild bulges'. FJ (22:1/2) 2006, 74–89.

15823. Lurie, Peter. Vision's immanence: Faulkner, film, and the popular imagination. (Bibl. 2004, 16673.) Rev. by Paula Elyseu Mesquita in AL (78:4) 2006, 876–7.

15824. McHaney, Thomas L. First is Jefferson: Faulkner shapes his domain. MissQ (57:4) 2004, 511–34.

15825. Meriwether, James B. (ed.). Essays, speeches, & public letters; updated, with material never before collected in one volume. (Bibl. 2005, 16431.) Rev. by Michael Millgate in MissQ (57:4) 2004, 657–9.

15826. Messer, H. Collin. Exhausted voices: the inevitable impoverishment of Faulkner's 'garrulous and facile' language. SoLJ (39:1) 2006, 1–15.

15827. Metz, Walter. Woody's Melindas and Todd's stories: complex film narratives in the light of literary Modernism. *See* **19713**.

15828. Palmer, Louis. Bourgeois Blues: class, Whiteness, and Southern gothic in early Faulkner and Caldwell. FJ (22:1/2) 2006, 120–39.

15829. Parini, Jay. One matchless time: a life of William Faulkner. (Bibl. 2004, 16679.) Rev. by Hugh Graham in BkCan (34:5) 2005, 25–6.

15830. Peek, Charles A.; Hamblin, Robert W. (eds). A companion to Faulkner studies. (Bibl. 2004, 16682.) Rev. by Owen Robinson in JAStud (39:2) 2005, 338; by Peter Barry in Eng (55:212) 2006, 213–19.

15831. Pitt, Kristin E. National conflict and narrative possibility in Faulkner and Garro. CLCWeb (8:2) 2006.

15832. Ross, Patricia A. The spell cast by remains: the myth of wilderness in modern American literature. *See* **16387**.

15833. Sivils, Matthew Wynn. Reading trees in Southern literature. SoQ (44:1) 2006, 88–102.

15834. Spillers, Hortense J. Topographical topics: Faulknerian space. MissQ (57:4) 2004, 535–68.

15835. Sugimori, Masami. Signifying, ordering, and containing the chaos: Whiteness, ideology, and language in *Intruder in the Dust*. FJ (22:1/2) 2006, 54–73.

15836. Towner, Theresa M.; Carothers, James B. Collected stories: glossary and commentary. Jackson; London: Mississippi UP, 2006. pp. xiv, 501. (Reading Faulkner.)

15837. Urgo, Joseph R. The Yoknapatawpha project: the map of a deeper existence. MissQ (57:4) 2004, 639–55.

15838. —— Abadie, Ann J. (eds). Faulkner and his contemporaries: Faulkner and Yoknapatawpha, 2002. (Bibl. 2005, 16452.) Rev. by Erik Dussere in SAtlR (70:4) 2005, 146–9.

15839. Watson, Jay. Introduction: situating Whiteness in Faulkner Studies, situating Faulkner in Whiteness Studies. FJ (22:1/2) 2006, 3–23.

15840. Weinstein, Arnold. Recovering your story: Proust, Joyce, Woolf, Faulkner, Morrison. *See* **16787**.

15841. Xu, Zhiqiang. Translation and interpretation of *Sanctuary* as a title. FLS (120) 2006, 62–6. (In Chinese.)

15842. ZEITLIN, MICHAEL. The uncanny and the opaque in Yoknapatawpha and beyond. MissQ (57:4) 2004, 619–37.

15843. ZENDER, KARL F. William Faulkner: *The Sound and the Fury*. *In* (pp. 333–41) **11788**.

Jessie Fauset

15844. BARNES, PAULA C. Dorothy West: Harlem renaissance writer? *In* (pp. 99–124) **12180**.

15845. RANSOM, PORTIA BOULWARE. Black love and the Harlem renaissance: an essay in African American literary criticism. *See* **17017**.

15846. TARVER, AUSTRALIA. *My House and a Glimpse of My Life Therein*: migrating lives in the short fiction of Jessie Fauset. *In* (pp. 125–50) **12180**.

Elaine Feinstein

15847. ANON. Close to the bone: Elaine Feinstein talks about beginning. PRev (96:2) 2006, 57–62. (Interview.)

15848. CRAIK, ROGER. 'High and dry and dead': a source for Ted Hughes's *Pike*. *See* **16498**.

Edna Ferber

15849. HOAGWOOD, TERENCE. 'Postmodern mirrors'. *See* **12897**.

Lawrence Ferlinghetti

15850. BACIGALUPO, MASSIMO (ed. and trans.). Il lume non spento. Novara: Interlinea, 2006. pp. 90. (Lyra, 26.)

15851. STEFANELLI, MARIA ANITA. Lawrence Ferlinghetti's 'surreal migrations'. QPS (14) 2006, 289–300.

Helen Fielding (b.1958)

15852. FERRISS, SUZANNE. Narrative and cinematic doubleness: *Pride and Prejudice* and *Bridget Jones's Diary*. *In* (pp. 71–84) **19862**.

15853. —— YOUNG, MALLORY (eds). Chick lit: the new woman's fiction. *See* **19862**.

15854. GUERRERO, LISA A. 'Sistahs are doin' it for themselves': chick lit in black and white. *In* (pp. 87–101) **19862**.

15855. MABRY, A. ROCHELLE. About a girl: female subjectivity and sexuality in contemporary 'chick' culture. *In* (pp. 191–206) **19862**.

15856. MAZZA, CRIS. Who's laughing now? A short history of chick lit and the perversion of a genre. *In* (pp. 17–28) **19862**.

15857. SÉLLEI, NÓRA. Bridget Jones and Hungarian chick lit. *In* (pp. 173–88) **19862**.

15858. UMMINGER, ALISON. Supersizing Bridget Jones: what's really eating the women in chick lit. *In* (pp. 239–52) **19862**.

Timothy Findley

15859. WALDREP, SHELTON. *Nom de guerre*: homosociality in Timothy Findley's *The Wars*. *In* (pp. 209–18) **11883**.

Anne Fine

15860. Wilkie-Stibbs, Christine. Borderland children: reflection on narratives of abjection. LU (30:3) 2006, 316–36.

Ian Hamilton Finlay

15861. Baridon, Michel. Nature and the politics of hope: Ermenonville and Little Sparta. WI (21:4) 2005, 288–93.

15862. Follo, Valentina. 'The Roman world has been empty since the Romans'. WI (21:4) 2005, 274–87.

15863. Gilonis, Harry. Where time becomes space – Ian Hamilton Finlay's garden in Provence. WI (21:4) 2005, 308–22.

15864. Hunt, John Dixon. Catalogue. WI (21:4) 2005, 323–65. (Exhibition at Univ. of Philadelphia: 2005.)

15865. —— Ian Hamilton Finlay and the commonplace – book to garden and back. WI (21:4) 2005, 294–307.

Jack Finney

15866. Seabrook, Jack. Stealing through time: on the writings of Jack Finney. Jefferson, NC; London: McFarland, 2006. pp. 220.

Ronald Firbank

15867. Hollinghurst, Alan. Saved by art: the shy, steely, original Ronald Firbank. TLS, 17 Nov. 2006, 12–15.

F. Scott Fitzgerald

15868. Assadi, Jamal. Acting, rhetoric, & interpretation in selected novels by F. Scott Fitzgerald & Saul Bellow. New York; Frankfurt: Lang, 2006. pp. viii, 188.

15869. Bardet, Pascal. '*One hundred false starts*': l'espace fitzgéraldien; ou, La quête d'un ailleurs impossible. Anglophonia (19) 2006, 253–60.

15870. Barrett, Laura. From Wonderland to wasteland: *The Wonderful Wizard of Oz*, *The Great Gatsby*, and the new American fairy tale. *See* **14642**.

15871. Berman, Ronald. Modernity and progress: Fitzgerald, Hemingway, Orwell. (Bibl. 2005, 16484.) Rev. by Ruth Prigozy in HemR (25:2) 2006, 150–3; by Erin Clair in RMER (60:1) 2006.

15872. Canterbery, E. Ray; Birch, Thomas. F. Scott Fitzgerald: under the influence. Saint Paul, MN: Paragon House, 2006. pp. xix, 396.

15873. Christie, Stuart. Margin and center: positioning F. Scott Fitzgerald. FLS (121) 2006, 22–31.

15874. Curnutt, Kirk. Of Mussolini and macaroni: Hemingway, Fitzgerald, and expatriate 'Italianicity'. *In* (pp. 75–89) **16388**.

15875. —— (ed.). A historical guide to F. Scott Fitzgerald. (Bibl. 2004, 16742.) Rev. by Kathleen Drowne in JMMLA (38:2) 2005, 162–4; by Michael Nowlin in StudN (38:3) 2006, 374–7.

15876. D'Arcy, Julian Meldon. 'Glory, glory to the black and orange!': Princeton, the Ivy League football hero, and the fiction of F. Scott Fitzgerald. Aethlon (23:2) 2006, 59–73.

15877. Edwards, A. S. G. F. Scott Fitzgerald, *The Great Gatsby*: 'like an angry diamond'. ANQ (19:2) 2006, 51–2.

15878. Forter, Greg. F. Scott Fitzgerald, Modernist studies, and the *fin-de-siècle* crisis in masculinity. AL (78:2) 2006, 293–323.

15879. Harmon, William. Tender is *what* night? Surprises in the growth of Fitzgerald's fourth novel. Connotations (14:1–3) 2004/05, 109–18.

15880. Hays, Peter L. Fitzgerald and Fragonard. ANQ (19:3) 2006, 27–30.

15881. Kennedy, J. Gerald. Poe, Fitzgerald, and the American Nightmare. *See* **11025**.

15882. Kirby, Lisa A. Shades of passing: teaching and interrogating identity in Roth's *The Human Stain* and Fitzgerald's *The Great Gatsby*. *See* **18317**.

15883. Kraus, Joe. De-centering the canon: understanding *The Great Gatsby* as an ethnic novel. *In* (pp. 127–44) **11783**.

15884. Maffi, Mario. Untender is the night in the Garden of Eden: Fitzgerald, Hemingway, and the Mediterranean. *In* (pp. 99–117) **12076**.

15885. Prigozy, Ruth. F. Scott Fitzgerald: *The Great Gatsby*. *In* (pp. 342–9) **11788**.

15886. Rielly, Edward J. F. Scott Fitzgerald: a biography. (Bibl. 2005, 16499.) Rev. by Peter Barry in Eng (55:212) 2006, 213–19.

15887. Wixson, Christopher. Ragged edges: the curious case of F. Scott Fitzgerald's *The Vegetable*. AmDr (15:2) 2006, 48–60.

15888. Wright, John S. Ellison's experimental attitude and the technologies of illumination. *In* (pp. 157–71) **15746**.

15889. Younger, Prakash. Historical experience in *The Harder They Come*: Jamaica in the cultural world system. *See* **12895**.

John Dennis Fitzgerald (b.1907)

15890. Fisher, Leona W. *The Adventures of Tom Sawyer* and *The Great Brain*: liminality, ritual, and race in the construction of the 'real American boy'. *In* (pp. 191–214) **3157**.

Penelope Fitzgerald

15891. Stonebridge, Lyndsey. Hearing them speak: voices in Wilfred Bion, Muriel Spark and Penelope Fitzgerald. *See* **18574**.

Zelda Fitzgerald

15892. Wagner-Martin, Linda. Zelda Sayre Fitzgerald: an American woman's life. (Bibl. 2005, 16505.) Rev. by Michael Nowlin in StudN (38:3) 2006, 374–7; by Michael S. McCreedy in AlaR (59:2) 2006, 159–60.

George Fitzmaurice

15893. Brennan, Fiona. George Fitzmaurice: 'wild in his own way': biography of an Abbey playwright. Foreword by Fintan O'Toole. Dublin: Carysfort Press, 2005. pp. xxix, 211.

Richard Flanagan (b.1961)

15894. Polack, Fiona. Taking the waters: abjection and homecoming in *The Shipping News* and *Death of a River Guide*. *See* **18147**.

15895. Schwalm, Tanja. 'Relax and enjoy the show': circensian animal spaces in Australian and Latin American magical realist fiction. *See* **15038**.

Thomas Flanagan ('James Bonner')

15896. Marr, Lisa. 'All Dressed in Green': a woman's account of the 1798 Rebellion. *In* (pp. 249–58) **8374**.

Ian Fleming

15897. Butterfield, Beth. Being-toward-death and taking pleasure in beauty: James Bond and existentialism. *In* (pp. 3–15) **15903**.

15898. Early, Gerald. Jungle fever: Ian Fleming's James Bond novels, the Cold War, and Jamaica. NewLet (72:1) 2005/06, 172–98.

15899. Forster, Greg. 'Just a stupid policeman': Bond and the rule of law. *In* (pp. 121–37) **15903**.

15900. Getachew, Mahlete-Tsigé. How to live (and how to die). *In* (pp. 17–33) **15903**.

15901. Gibson, Suzie. Bond and phenomenology: shaken, not stirred. *In* (pp. 49–62) **15903**.

15902. Held, Jacob M. 'Don't you men know any other way?': punishment beyond retributivism and deterrence. *In* (pp. 139–53) **15903**.

15903. —— South, James B. (eds). James Bond and philosophy: questions are forever. Chicago, IL: Open Court, 2006. pp. xv, 244. (Popular culture and philosophy, 23.)

15904. Landa, Ishay. James Bond: a Nietzschean for the Cold War. *In* (pp. 79–93) **15903**.

15905. Matheson, Sue. He who eats meat wins: appetite, power, and Nietzsche in the novels of Ian Fleming. *In* (pp. 63–77) **15903**.

15906. South, James B. Six to four against: James Bond and the hope for a meaningful life. *In* (pp. 35–46) **15903**.

15907. Tallaferro, Charles; Le Gall, Michel. Bond as chivalric, comic hero. *In* (pp. 95–108) **15903**.

15908. Tedesco, Matthew. The moral status of the double-0 agent: thinking about the license to kill. *In* (pp. 111–20) **15903**.

15909. Vinen, Richard. Out of Jamaica. TLS, 2 June 2006, 36 (review-article).

15910. Winder, Simon. The man who saved Britain. London: Picador, 2006. pp. 263. Rev. by Richard Vinen in TLS, 2 June 2006, 36.

Horton Foote

15911. Avery, Laurence G. Horton Foote and the American theater. MissQ (58:1/2) 2004/05, 387–95 (review-article).

15912. Haynes, Robert. The Kidders and the Disappointment Club: a critical theme in Horton Foote's *The Young Man from Atlanta*. JADT (18:1) 2006, 24–33.

15913. Wood, Gerald C. Loving Mac, Beth, and John: grace in the plays and films of Horton Foote. RelArts (10:3) 2006, 374–90.

Esther Forbes

15914. Higonnet, Margaret R. Time out: trauma and play in *Johnny Tremain* and *Alan and Naomi*. ChildLit (33) 2005, 150–70.

15915. LJUNGQUIST, KENT P. 'A strange, wild land, permeated by sea and wind': Esther Forbes in Thoreau's tracks through Cape Cod. ConS (ns 14) 2006, 75–89.

15916. TRIBUNELLA, ERIC L. Narrative loss and the melancholic reader of *Johnny Tremain*. LU (30:1) 2006, 76–93.

Carolyn Forché

15917. GRIEVE-CARLSON, GARY. 'Where is your god?': theophany and *The Angel of History*. Ren (58:4) 2006, 289–303.

'Ford Madox Ford' (Ford Madox Hueffer)

15918. BOULTER, JONATHAN. 'After … Armageddon': trauma and history in Ford Madox Ford's *No Enemy*. *In* (pp. 77–90) **15944**.

15919. BRITZOLAKIS, CHRISTINA. Pathologies of the imperial metropolis: Impressionism as traumatic afterimage in Conrad and Ford. *See* **15251**.

15920. CHANTLER, ASHLEY. Creating an editorial procedure for non-canonical texts. *In* (pp. 49–63) **3407**.

15921. CHRISTENSEN, PETER G. Contrasting 'Condition of the Country' novels: Ford Madox Ford's *Parade's End* and Boris Pasternak's *Doctor Zhivago*. *In* (pp. 19–29) **15944**.

15922. COLOMBINO, LAURA. Negotiating with Gauguin's 'solar myth': art, economy and ideology in Ford Madox Ford's Provence. *In* (pp. 51–64) **12076**.

15923. COOPER, HARRIET Y. The duality of Ford's historical imagination. *In* (pp. 189–99) **15944**.

15924. DELBANCO, NICHOLAS. An old man mad about writing. *In* (pp. 219–31) **15944**.

15925. FLANAGAN, ANNE MARIE. Poised 'between anger and irony': Ford's representation of Lady Mary. *In* (pp. 31–9) **15944**.

15926. FORTUNATI, VITA. The impact of the First World War on private lives: a comparison of European and American writers (Ford, Hemingway, and Remarque). *In* (pp. 53–64) **15944**.

15927. GAŞIOREK, ANDRZEJ. 'In the mirror of the arts': Ford's Modernism and the reconstruction of post-war literary culture. *In* (pp. 201–17) **15944**.

15928. HARDING, JASON. The swan song of historical romance: *The First Queen* trilogy. *In* (pp. 111–20) **15944**.

15929. HASLAM, SARA. Ford Madox Ford: *The Good Soldier*. *In* (pp. 350–7) **11788**.

15930. —— *The Rash Act* and *Henry for Hugh*: a Fordian history of self-construction; or, Where is [m]other? *In* (pp. 121–33) **15944**.

15931. —— (ed.). Ford Madox Ford and the city. (Bibl. 2005, 16541.) Rev. by Gregory Dart in TLS, 10 Feb. 2006, 32; by Martin Stannard in RES (57:230) 2006, 428–30.

15932. JUDD, ALAN. Using Ford in fiction. *In* (pp. 135–45) **15944**.

15933. LAMBERTI, ELENA. Writing history: Ford and the debate on objective truth in the late 20th century. *In* (pp. 99–110) **15944**.

15934. LEMARCHAL, DOMINIQUE. Ford's paradoxical development of the personal tone in the writing of propaganda. *In* (pp. 91–7) **15944**.

15935. McDonough, Robert E. *Mister Bosphorus and the Muses*: history and representation in Ford Madox Ford's poem. *In* (pp. 155–62) **15944**.

15936. Mickalites, Carey J. *The Good Soldier* and capital's interiority complex. StudN (38:3) 2006, 288–303.

15937. Monta, Anthony P. *Parade's End* in the context of national efficiency. *In* (pp. 41–51) **15944**.

15938. Parrinder, Patrick. 'All that is solid melts into air': Ford and the spirit of Edwardian England. *In* (pp. 5–17) **15944**.

15939. Saunders, Max. Critical biography: rhetoric, tone, and autobiography in Ford's critical essays. *In* (pp. 173–88) **15944**.

15940. Scannell, James M. History or quickie history: elections in Anthony Trollope and Ford Madox Ford. *In* (pp. 147–54) **15944**.

15941. Skinner, Paul. The painful process of reconstruction: history in *No Enemy* and *Last Post*. *In* (pp. 65–75) **15944**.

15942. Wiesenfarth, Joseph. Ford Madox Ford and the regiment of women: Violet Hunt, Jean Rhys, Stella Bowen, Janice Biala. (Bibl. 2005, 16547.) Rev. by Max Saunders in Biography (29:4) 2006, 726–33; by Victoria Stewart in LitH (15:2) 2006, 83–4; by Christine Reynier in CVE (63) 2006, 495–7.

15943. —— An interview with Alan Judd. *See* **16795**.

15944. —— (ed.). History and representation in Ford Madox Ford's writings. Amsterdam; Atlanta, GA: Rodopi for the Ford Madox Ford Soc., 2004. pp. xi, 241. (International Ford Madox Ford studies, 3.) Rev. by Terry Caesar in ELT (49:1) 2006, 79–81; by Victoria Stewart in LitH (15:2) 2006, 83–4.

15945. Wrenn, Angus. Henry, Hueffer, Holbein, history and representation. *In* (pp. 163–71) **15944**.

Mark Ford

15946. Ford, Mark. A driftwood altar: essays and reviews. Introd. by Nick Everett. *See* **13745**.

Richard Ford (b.1944)

15947. Dobozy, Tamas. How not to be a 'dickhead': partisan politics in Richard Ford's *Independence Day*. CritS (18:1) 2006, 40–59.

Silas X. Ford (*fl.*1902)

15948. Smith, Katharine Capshaw. The legacy of Paul Laurence Dunbar: dialect and racial configuration in the works of Silas X. Ford and Christina Moody. *See* **9972**.

Richard Foreman

15949. Kalb, Jonathan. In conversation with Richard Foreman. Dramatist (8:6) 2006, 6–11.

Katherine V. Forrest (b.1939)

15950. Posman, Sarah. A Bakhtinian perspective on lesbian crime writing. CLCWeb (8:3) 2006.

Veronica Forrest-Thomson

15951. Milne, Drew. The art of wit and the Cambridge Science Park. *In* (pp. 170–87) **13732**.

E. M. Forster

15952. Chander, Harish. The politics of exclusion in *A Passage to India* and *Native Son*. CLAJ (49:3) 2006, 366–72.

15953. Christensen, Timothy. Bearing the White man's burden: misrecognition and cultural difference in E. M. Forster's *A Passage to India*. Novel (39:2) 2006, 155–78.

15954. Christie, Stuart. Worlding Forster: the passage from pastoral. London; New York: Routledge, 2005. pp. xiv, 208. (Studies in major literary authors, 37.)

15955. Copley, Antony. A spiritual Bloomsbury: Hinduism and homosexuality in the lives and writings of Edward Carpenter, E. M. Forster, and Christopher Isherwood. *See* **9412**.

15956. Dettmar, Kevin J. H. Bookcases, slipcases, uncut leaves: the anxiety of the gentleman's library. *See* **312**.

15957. Erll, Astrid. Re-writing as re-visioning: modes of representing the 'Indian Mutiny' in British novels, 1857 to 2000. *See* **10429**.

15958. Gualtieri, Elena. From *A Room with a View* to the Fascist spectacle: Bloomsbury in Italy. CVE (62) 2005, 93–107.

15959. Hollington, Michael. Forster, Alexandria, Modernism: the Mediterranean 'at a slight angle'. *In* (pp. 279–93) **12076**.

15960. Jackson, Tony E. The de-composition of writing in *A Passage to India*. JML (29:3) 2006, 1–18.

15961. Jeffreys, Peter. Eastern questions: Hellenism and Orientalism in the writings of E. M. Forster and C. P. Cavafy. Greensboro, NC: ELT Press, 2005. pp. ix, 212. (1880–1920 British authors, 18.) Rev. by J. H. Stape in ELT (49:1) 2006, 73–6.

15962. Kreisel, Deanna K. Wolf children and automata: bestiality and boredom at home and abroad. *See* **11301**.

15963. Lanone, Catherine. Art and the 'second darkness'. *See* **19301**.

15964. Lucas, John. E. M. Forster: an enabling modesty. EREA (4:2) 2006, 34–44.

15965. Panda, Ram Narayan. Forster's *A Passage to India*. Exp (64:4) 2006, 228–31.

15966. Pirbhai, Mariam. Against the Oriental(ist) current: homosexuality and empire in E. M. Forster's *The Other Boat*. DalR (86:3) 2006, 345–58.

15967. Raschke, Debrah. Modernism, metaphysics, and sexuality. *See* **15301**.

15968. Roy, Anindyo. Civility and empire: literature and culture in British India, 1822–1922. *See* **8712**.

15969. Shaheen, Mohammad. E. M. Forster and the politics of imperialism. (Bibl. 2005, 16566.) Rev. by Tony Webster in LitH (15:1) 2006, 85–6.

15970. Tague, Gregory. Character and consciousness: George Eliot, Thomas Hardy, E. M. Forster, D. H. Lawrence: phenomenological, ecological, and ethical readings. *See* **10055**.

15971. Williams, Melanie. Only connect: *Howards End* and theories of justice. LawL (18:2) 2006, 253–80.

Connie May Fowler

15972. Terry, Laura. Concealing and revealing: painting the Southern literary landscape. *See* **20273**.

Karen Joy Fowler (b.1950)

15973. Duchamp, L. Timmel. Something rich and strange: Karen Joy Fowler's *What I Didn't See*. *In* (pp. 356–80) **13537**.

John Fowles

15974. Jensen, Hal. All endeavour useless. TLS, 31 Mar. 2006, 20 (review-article). (Journals.)

15975. Quinn, Patrick. 'More than a fascination wiith the Divine Marquis': John Fowles's *The Magus* and Lawrence Durrell's *The Alexandria Quartet*. *In* (pp. 270–81) **15631**.

15976. Romero Jódar, Andrés. 'A stranger in a strange land': an existentialist reading of Frederick Clegg in *The Collector* by John Fowles. Atl (28:1) 2006, 45–55.

John Fox, Jr (1863–1919)

15977. Smith, Jimmie Dean, *et al.* 'I wouldn't dirty my hands on trash like you': ethnic determinism in John Fox, Jr and Loretta Lynn. KenPR (20) 2005, 57–62.

Janet Frame

15978. Bazin, Claire. 'From the rim of the farthest circle'. JNZL (24:1) 2006, 115–29.

15979. Delrez, Marc. The missing chapter in Janet Frame's *Living in the Maniototo*. JNZL (24:1) 2006, 73–93.

15980. Gordon, Pamela; Harold, Denis; Manhire, Bill (eds). The goose bath: poems. Auckland: Random House, 2006. pp. 221.

15981. Hogue, Bev. Naming the bones: bodies of knowledge in contemporary fiction. *See* **17611**.

15982. Lawn, Jennifer. The word as remnant: Margaret Atwood and Janet Frame. *In* (pp. 385–401) **8374**.

15983. Mortelette, Ivane. 'A proof that I did exist': Janet Frame and photography. JNZL (24:1) 2006, 94–114.

15984. Tunca, Daria. Paying attention to language, replicas and the role of the artist in Janet Frame's *Living in the Maniototo*. JPW (42:1) 2006, 32–43.

Pat Frank

15985. Schwartz, Richard A. Family, gender, and society in 1950s American fiction of nuclear apocalypse: *Shadow on the Hearth*, *Tomorrow!*, *The Last Day*, and *Alas, Babylon*. *See* **19391**.

Jonathan Franzen

15986. ANNESLEY, JAMES. Market corrections: Jonathan Franzen and the 'novel of globalization'. JML (29:2) 2006, 111–28.

15987. FRANZEN, JONATHAN. The discomfort zone: a personal history. New York: Farrar, Straus, & Giroux, 2006. pp. 195. Rev. by Stephen Burn in TLS, 20 Oct. 2006, 26.

15988. HIPSKY, MARTIN. Post-Cold War paranoia in *The Corrections* and *The Sopranos*. PMC (16:2) 2006.

Kathleen Fraser

15989. DRISCOLL, KERRY. Gendered poetics. *See* **19189**.

Michael Frayn

15990. MOSELEY, MERRITT. Understanding Michael Frayn. Columbia; London: South Carolina UP, 2006. pp. xii, 209. (Understanding contemporary British literature.)

15991. STEWART, VICTORIA. 'The big war outside and the little war at home': anamnesis and the Second World War in recent British fiction. Eng (54:210) 2005, 209–24.

Charles Frazier (b.1950)

15992. GLUCKSMAN, FREDRICA B. Concord comes to Cold Mountain: Emersonian elements in Charles Frazier's *Cold Mountain*. ConS (ns 14) 2006, 105–19.

Marilyn French

15993. ELLIOTT, JANE. Time of death: the end of the 1960s and the problem of feminist futurity in *The Women's Room* and *Vida*. MFS (52:1) 2006, 143–68.

Brian Friel

15994. MANISTA, FRANK. Any Irish in you? The crises of Irishness in contemporary Irish drama. *In* (pp. 267–90) **12189**.

15995. RUSSELL, RICHARD RANKIN. The liberating fictional truth of community in Brian Friel's *The Freedom of the City*. SAtlR (71:1) 2006, 42–73.

15996. —— 'Something is being eroded': the Agrarian epistemology of Brian Friel's *Translations*. NewHR (10:2) 2006, 106–22.

Robert Frost

15997. AMANO, KYOKO. Frost's *Acquainted with the Night*. Exp (65:1) 2006, 39–42.

15998. AUSTIN, BILL. Robert Frost's use of the arch as figure and symbol. RFR (15) 2005, 67–81.

15999. BUXTON, RACHEL. Robert Frost and Northern Irish poetry. (Bibl. 2004, 16843.) Rev. by Michael Mays in RFR (15) 2005, 121–3.

16000. FAGGEN, ROBERT (ed.). The notebooks of Robert Frost. Cambridge, MA; London: Belknap Press of Harvard UP, 2006. pp. xxxii, 809.

16001. FONTANA, ERNEST L. Kingsley's *Ode to the North-East Wind* and Frost's *To the Thawing Wind*. RFR (15) 2005, 94–100.

16002. Freeman, Donald C. Burning gold: for John Robert Ross. Style (40:1/2) 2006, 128–32. (*Nothing Gold Can Stay.*)

16003. Ghasemi, Parvin; Mansooji, Elham. Nature and man in Robert Frost. CLAJ (49:4) 2006, 462–81.

16004. Hart, Jeffrey. Robert Frost and T. S. Eliot: Modernisms. SewR (114:4) 2006, 551–77. (Poe's influence.) (State of letters.)

16005. Hass, Robert Bernard. (Re) reading Bergson: Frost, Pound and the legacy of modern poetry. JML (29:1) 2005, 55–75.

16006. Kirk, Connie Ann. A student's guide to Robert Frost. Berkeley Heights, NJ: Enslow, 2006. pp. 160. (Understanding literature.)

16007. Lespi, Jeremy. 'Is it the neighbor?': a close reading of Robert Frost's *The Housekeeper*. RFR (15) 2005, 50–66.

16008. Maxwell, Glyn. Dead on a side track: on Frost's *War Thoughts at Home*. VQR (82:4) 2006, 120–33.

16009. Monteiro, George. The presence of Lionel Johnson in Frost's poetry. RFR (15) 2005, 101–12.

16010. Morlan, Anna. Frost and Shade, and questions of design. *See* **17707**.

16011. O'Connell, Mike. Frost's *After Apple-Picking*. Exp (64:2) 2006, 91–3.

16012. Quinn, Gerard. The crooked straightness of Frost and Emerson. RFR (15) 2005, 113–19. (*Corrected reprint of* bibl. 2005, 16611.)

16013. Roberts, Beth Ellen. One voice and many: modern poets in dialogue. *See* **13848**.

16014. Rotella, Guy. Frost and invitation. RFR (15) 2005, 35–49.

16015. Rudolf, Anthony (ed.). Robert Frost in his own words. By Claude Vigée. PNRev (32:1) 2005, 19–23.

16016. Seale, Lisa. Robert Frost at the University of Detroit, 1962. RFR (15) 2005, 9–34.

16017. Sell, Jonathan P. A. Allusion and ambiguity in Seamus Heaney's *Blackberry-Picking*. *See* **16323**.

16018. Stilling, Robert. Between friends: rediscovering the war thoughts of Robert Frost. VQR (82:4) 2006, 113–19.

16019. Walters, Kristin. Bibliography of Frost scholarship 2004–2005. RFR (15) 2005, 124–6.

16020. Yamada, Takeo. A Japanese Frost: considerations of synecdoche and sentence sounds. RFR (15) 2005, 82–93.

Athol Fugard

16021. Correia, José. *Exits and Entrances*: Fugard on theatre in South Africa and the other apartheid. EIUC (14) 2006, 111–21.

16022. Graham, Shane. Private trauma, public drama: Fugard, Kani, and Ntshona's *The Island* and Maponya's *Gangsters*. ESA (48:1) 2005, 107–23.

16023. Nwahunanya, Chinyere. Tragedy in African literary drama. *In* (pp. 197–211) **11860**.

William Gaddis

16024. KOHN, ROBERT E. Postmodernist Manichaean allegory in William Gaddis's *Carpenter's Gothic*. Style (40:4) 2006, 334–45.

Ernest J. Gaines

16025. BROWN, ANNE GRAY. The scribe of River Lake Plantation: a conversation with Ernest J. Gaines. SoQ (44:1) 2006, 9–31.

16026. CLARK, KEITH. Que(e)rying the prison-house of Black male desire: homosociality in Ernest Gaines's *Three Men*. AAR (40:2) 2006, 239–55.

Lorena Gale

16027. GALE, LORENA. A servant in Mecca: one playwright's experience of New York. CanTR (125) 2006, 47–55.

16028. TOMPKINS, JOANNE. Remember the nation: Lorena Gale's *Je me souviens*. CanTR (125) 2006, 56–61.

Zona Gale

16029. TOMLINSON, SUSAN. 'Curiously without body': the hidden language of Zona Gale's *Faint Perfume*. MFS (52:3) 2006, 570–87.

Damon Galgut (b.1963)

16030. MILLER, ANDIE. Ambiguous territory: Damon Galgut. JCL (41:2) 2006, 139–45.

Katherine Gallagher (b.1935)

16031. MCCARTHY, PATRICIA. Conjugating ourselves: three Australian women poets: Katherine Gallagher, Alison Croggon and M. T. C. Cronin. *See* **15366**.

Tess Gallagher

16032. SETOUCHI, JUKUCH. Distant rain. Spokane: Eastern Washington UP, 2006. pp. 36. (Interviews.)

Mavis Gallant

16033. BESNER, NEIL. Re-reading *The Moslem Wife*: fugitive irony in the light of imagination. *In* (pp. 163–73) **16036**.

16034. BRANDT, DI. Fascists, mothers and provisional others in Mavis Gallant's *The Pegnitz Junction*. *In* (pp. 29–49) **16036**.

16035. CÔTÉ, NICOLE. Mavis Gallant's shifting poetics of exile: the ironic and the oneiric in two early short stories. *In* (pp. 111–29) **16036**.

16036. GUNNARS, KRISTJANA (ed.). Transient questions: new essays on Mavis Gallant. Amsterdam; New York: Rodopi, 2004. pp. xi, 209. (Cross/cultures: readings in the post-colonial literatures in English, 74.) Rev. by Laurie Kruk in CanL (189) 2006, 149–50.

16037. LENT, JOHN. Transitory closure in Mavis Gallant's *In Transit*: a writer's view of the transition from modern to postmodern poetics in short fiction. *In* (pp. 51–69) **16036**.

16038. LYNCH, GERALD. An intangible cure for death by homesickness: Mavis Gallant's Canadian short story cycle 'Linnet Muir'. *In* (pp. 1–27) **16036**.

16039. NG, MARIA NOËLLE. Women out of Fleeting Place: hotel living in Mavis Gallant's short stories. *In* (pp. 93–110) **16036**.

16040. STEVENS, PETER. An 'I' for an evanescent eye: the personal and the private – autobiography, essay and story. *In* (pp. 71–91) **16036**.

16041. VAUTHIER, SIMONE. Framing the passing recalcitrance of *The Wedding Ring*. *In* (pp. 175–205) **16036**.

16042. WINTHER, PER. The volatile eye of the beholder: voice, epiphany and grace in the short fiction of Mavis Gallant. *In* (pp. 131–62) **16036**.

16043. ZICHY, FRANCIS. Gallant's *The Remission*. Exp (64:3) 2006, 168–71.

John Galsworthy

16044. FURST, LILIAN R. 'The ironic little dark chasms of life': narrative strategies in John Galsworthy's *Forsyte Saga* and Thomas Mann's *Buddenbrooks*. LIT (17:2) 2006, 157–77.

16045. STAPE, J. H.; KNOWLES, OWEN. 'In-between man': Conrad–Galsworthy–Pinker. *See* **15314**.

James Galvin

16046. TREDINNICK, MARK. The land's wild music: encounters with Barry Lopez, Peter Matthiessen, Terry Tempest Williams, & James Galvin. (Bibl. 2005, 16637.) Rev. by Deborah Straw in GaR (60:3/4) 2006, 844–5.

Cristina Garcia

16047. KANDIYOTI, DALIA. Consuming nostalgia: nostalgia and the marketplace in Cristina García and Ana Menéndez. MELUS (31:1) 2006, 81–97.

16048. YU, SU-LIN. Sisterhood as cultural difference in Amy Tan's *The Hundred Secret Senses* and Cristina Garcia's *The Agüero Sisters*. *See* **18724**.

John Gardner (b.1933)

16049. LIVINGSTON, MICHAEL; SUTTON, JOHN WILLIAM. Reinventing the hero: Gardner's *Grendel* and the shifting face of *Beowulf* in popular culture. SPC (29:1) 2006, 1–16.

Hamlin Garland

16050. KNOWLES, OWEN; STAPE, J. H. Conrad and Hamlin Garland: a correspondence recovered. *See* **15283**.

16051. NEWLIN, KEITH. 'I am as ever your disciple': the friendship of Hamlin Garland and W. D. Howells. PLL (42:3) 2006, 264–90.

16052. —— Why Hamlin Garland left the main traveled road. StAN (1:1/2) 2006, 70–89.

16053. TEOREY, MATTHEW. Escaping the lion's paw: jungle cat imagery and late nineteenth-century political reform. ANQ (19:1) 2006, 42–7.

Alan Garner

16054. BUTLER, CHARLES. Four British fantasists: place and culture in the children's fantasies of Penelope Lively, Alan Garner, Diana Wynne Jones, and Susan Cooper. *See* **17234**.

Helen Garner

16055. EGGINS, SUZANNE. Real stories: ethics and narrative in Helen Garner's *Joe Cinque's Consolation*. Southerly (65:1) 2005, 122–32.

16056. Holcombe, Vanessa. Writing place: Helen Garner's *The Last Days of Chez Nous*. Southerly (65:1) 2005, 143–54.

David Garnett

16057. Jolly, Margaretta. A word is a bridge: death and epistolary form in the correspondence of Sylvia Townsend Warner and David Garnett. *In* (pp. 11–28) **18964**.

George Garrett

16058. Clabough, Casey. 'The primary story': an interview with George Garrett. ChattR (26:4) 2006, 104–13.

16059. Pridmore, Joseph. Mass violence and the crowd: the perception of proletarian community in working-class writers of the 1930s. EREA (4:2) 2006, 45–55.

William Gass

16060. Gass, William H. A temple of texts: essays. *See* **3257**.

16061. Gervais, Bertrand. Reading as a close encounter of the third kind: an experiment with Gass's *Order of Insects*. *In* (pp. 179–99) **3203**.

William Allen Gaston (b.1953)

16062. Ruthig, Ingrid. Coming along for the ride: interview with Bill Gaston. BkCan (33:8) 2004, 9–10.

Tim Gautreaux

16063. Hebert-Leiter, Maria. An interview with Tim Gautreaux. CaroQ (57:2) 2005, 66–74.

Maurice Gee

16064. Hale, Elizabeth. Underworlds down under: *Under the Mountain* and *The Navigator*. *In* (pp. 101–10) **11971**.

Hanay Geiogamah (b.1945)

16065. De Wagter, Caroline. Performing the American multi-ethnic 'Other' in Hwang's *Bondage* and Geiogamah's *Foghorn*. *See* **16546**.

Martha Gellhorn

16066. Meyers, Jeffrey. The title of Martha Gellhorn's *The Heart of Another*. NCL (36:2) 2006, 10–11.

16067. Moorehead, Caroline (ed.). The collected letters of Martha Gellhorn. New York: Holt, 2006. pp. 531. Rev. by Kate McLoughlin in TLS, 23 June 2006, 4–6; by Francine du Plessix Gray in NYTB, 27 Aug. 2006, 16; by Marc Weingarten in BkW, 20 Aug. 2006, 15.

16068. —— Selected letters of Martha Gellhorn. New York: Holt, 2006. pp. x, 531. Rev. by Lorna Scott Fox in ColJR (45:2) 2006, 56–8.

16069. Moreira, Peter. Hemingway on the China front: his WWII spy mission with Martha Gellhorn. *See* **16381**.

Amitav Ghosh

16070. Black, Shameem. Cosmopolitanism at home: Amitav Ghosh's *The Shadow Lines*. JCL (41:3) 2006, 45–65.

16071. Chambers, Claire. Representations of the oil encounter in Amitav Ghosh's *The Circle of Reason*. JCL (41:1) 2006, 33–50.

16072. Ghosh, Amitav. Incendiary circumstances: a chronicle of the turmoil of our times. Boston, MA: Houghton Mifflin, 2005. pp. x, 305.

16073. Gupta, R. K. 'That which a man takes for himself no one can deny him': Amitav Ghosh's *The Glass Palace* and the colonial experience. IFR (33:1/2) 2006, 18–26.

16074. Mongia, Padmini. Between men: Conrad in the fiction of two contemporary Indian writers. *In* (pp. 85–99) **15280**.

16075. Spyra, Ania. Is cosmopolitanism not for women? Migration in Qurratulain Hyder's *Sita Betrayed* and Amitav Ghosh's *The Shadow Lines*. Frontiers (27:2) 2006, 1–26.

Reginald Gibbons

16076. Gibbons, Reginald. This working against the grain. APR (35:2) 2006, 15–21.

William Gibson

16077. Hollinger, Veronica. Notes on the contemporary apocalyptic imagination: William Gibson's *Neuromancer* and Douglas Coupland's *Girlfriend in a Coma*. *In* (pp. 47–56) **13541**.

16078. McHale, Brian. Cognition *en abyme*: models, manuals, maps. *See* **18561**.

16079. Murphet, Julian. Behind the scenes: production, animation, and postmodern value. *See* **18949**.

16080. Rapatzikou, Tatiani G. Gothic motifs and the fiction of William Gibson. Amsterdam; New York: Rodopi, 2004. pp. xxiv, 253, (plates) 16. (Postmodern studies, 36.) Rev. by Stacy Gillis in GothS (8:2) 2006, 146–8.

16081. Schwetman, John D. Romanticism and the cortical stack: cyberpunk subjectivity in the Takeshi Kovacs novels of Richard K. Morgan. *See* **20305**.

Sandra M. Gilbert

16082. Gilbert, Sandra M. Dickinson in the kitchen. EDJ (15:2) 2006, 1–3.

Charlotte Perkins Gilman (Mrs Stetson)

16083. Duneer, Anita. On the verge of a breakthrough: projections of escape from the attic and the thwarted tower in Charlotte Perkins Gilman's *The Yellow Wallpaper* and Susan Glaspell's *The Verge*. JADT (18:1) 2006, 34–53.

16084. Golden, Catherine J. (ed.). Charlotte Perkins Gilman's *The Yellow Wall-Paper*: a sourcebook and critical edition. (Bibl. 2005, 16686.) Rev. by Elke Kinkel in EJES (10:1) 2006, 102–4.

16085. Knight, Denise D. 'I could paint still life as well as any one on earth': Charlotte Perkins Gilman and the world of art. WS (35:5) 2006, 475–92.

16086. Nadkarni, Asha. Eugenic feminism: Asian reproduction in the US national imaginary. Novel (39:2) 2006, 221–44.

16087. Quawas, Rula. A New Woman's journey into insanity: descent and return in *The Yellow Wallpaper*. AUMLA (105) 2006, 35–53.

16088. St Jean, Shawn (ed.). *The Yellow Wall-Paper* by Charlotte Perkins Gilman: a dual-text critical edition. Athens: Ohio UP, 2006. pp. xxiv, 120.

16089. Tomlinson, Susan. 'Curiously without body': the hidden language of Zona Gale's *Faint Perfume*. *See* **16029**.

Rebecca Claire Gilman

16090. Stacks, Geoffrey. Simon wasn't there: the Sambo strategy, consumable theater, and Rebecca Gilman's *Spinning into Butter.* AAR (40:2) 2006, 285–97.

Mary Gilmore

16091. Strauss, Jennifer (ed.). Collected verse of Mary Gilmore: vol. 1, 1887–1929. St Lucia: Queensland UP, 2004. pp. 741. (Academy eds of Australian literature.) Rev. by Paul Hetherington in TLS, 3 Mar. 2006, 33.

Allen Ginsberg

16092. Ball, Gordon. Wopbopgooglemop: *Howl* and its influences. *In* (pp. 92–9) **16122**.

16093. Baraka, Amiri. *Howl* and hail. *In* (pp. 19–23) **16122**.

16094. Bidart, Frank. A cross in the void. *In* (pp. 246–54) **16122**.

16095. Birkerts, Sven. Not then, not now. *In* (pp. 73–83) **16122**.

16096. Brown, Kurt. A thirteen-year-old cadet. *In* (pp. 124–30) **16122**.

16097. Codrescu, Andrei. *Howl* in Transylvania. *In* (pp. 47–56) **16122**.

16098. Collins, Billy. My *Howl*. *In* (pp. 100–1) **16122**.

16099. Doty, Mark. Human seraphim: *Howl*, sex, and holiness. *In* (pp. 11–18) **16122**.

16100. Gates, David. Welcoming *Howl* into the canon. *In* (pp. 159–64) **16122**.

16101. Gornick, Vivian. Wild at heart. *In* (pp. 3–10) **16122**.

16102. Harris, Oliver (ed.). The Yage letters *redux*. (Bibl. 1965, 8061.) San Francisco, CA: City Lights, 2006. pp. 127. (Fourth ed.: first ed. 1963.) Rev. by Davis Schneiderman in AmBR (28:1) 2006, 22–3.

16103. Hishmeh, Richard E. Marketing genius: the friendship of Allen Ginsberg and Bob Dylan. JAC (29:4) 2006, 395–405.

16104. Katz, Eliot. Radical eyes: political poetics and *Howl*. *In* (pp. 183–211) **16122**.

16105. Kirsch, Adam. Starving hysterical naked. Poetry (188:5) 2006, 442–8 (review-article).

16106. Kramer, Jane. The best mind. *In* (pp. 148–58) **16122**.

16107. Lieberman-Plimpton, Juanita; Morgan, Bill (eds). The book of martyrdom and artifice: first journals and poems, 1937–1952. New York: Da Capo Press, 2006. pp. xviii, 523.

16108. Lopate, Phillip. *Howl* and me. *In* (pp. 131–9) **16122**.

16109. Monteiro, George. Peaches and penumbras: Ginsberg's *Supermarket in California*. NCL (36:2) 2006, 4–5.

16110. Moody, Rick. On the granite steps of the madhouse with shaven heads. *In* (pp. 59–72) **16122**.

16111. Morgan, Bill. I celebrate myself: the somewhat private life of Allen Ginsberg. New York: Viking, 2006. pp. xv, 702. Rev. by Walter Kirn in NYTB, 19 Nov. 2006, 14–15, 25; by Anthony Cuda in BkW, 26 Nov. 2006, 13.

16112. —— Peters, Nancy J. (eds). *Howl* on trial: the battle for free expression. San Francisco, CA: City Lights, 2006. pp. xiv, 224. Rev. by Fred Moramarco in Humanist (66:6) 2006, 42–3.

16113. Muske-Dukes, Carol. *Howl* in and out of prison. *In* (pp. 243–5) **16122**.

16114. Myles, Eileen. Repeating Allen. *In* (pp. 84–91) **16122**.

16115. Perloff, Marjorie. 'A lost battalion of Platonic conversationalists': *Howl* and the language of Modernism. *In* (pp. 24–43) **16122**.

16116. Piercy, Marge. The best bones for soup have meat on them. *In* (pp. 212–13) **16122**.

16117. Pinsky, Robert. No picnic. *In* (pp. 255–9) **16122**.

16118. —— Peace, poetry and negation. *See* **19440**.

16119. Polito, Robert. Holy the Fifth International. *In* (pp. 226–42) **16122**.

16120. Rosenthal, Bob. A witness. *In* (pp. 44–6) **16122**.

16121. Sante, Luc. The ballot of eternity. *In* (pp. 219–25) **16122**.

16122. Shinder, Jason (ed.). The poem that changed America: *Howl* fifty years later. New York: Farrar, Straus, & Giroux, 2006. pp. xlii, 290. Rev. by Eric Miles Williamson in BkW, 16 Apr. 2006, 4–5; by Michael Piafsky in MR (29:2) 2006, 165–7; by Adam Kirsch in Poetry (188:5) 2006, 442–8.

16123. Waldman, Anne. Premises of consciousness. *In* (pp. 260–71) **16122**.

Dana Gioia

16124. Lindner, April. Interview with Dana Gioia. *See* **11029**.

16125. Nelson, Barney. Dana Gioia is wrong about cowboy poetry. WAL (40:4) 2006, 404–22.

Githa Hariharan

16126. Navarro Tejero, Antonia. Gender and caste in the anglophone Indian novels of Arundhati Roy and Githa Hariharan: feminist issues in cross-cultural perspectives. *See* **18365**.

Ellen Glasgow

16127. Binggeli, Elizabeth. Burbanking bigger and Bette the bitch. *See* **19374**.

16128. Campbell, Donna. 'Where are the ladies?': Wharton, Glasgow, and American women Naturalists. *See* **10136**.

16129. Jones, Gwendolyn. Virginia writers in the New South: Thomas Nelson Page, Ellen Glasgow, and Mary Johnson. EGN (57) 2006, 3–6, 10.

16130. MacDonald, Edgar. Character and place: Ellen Glasgow's Edmonia Bredalbane. EGN (56) 2006, 3–4, 8–14.

16131. Niewiadomska-Flis, Urszula. Pretty is as pretty does? The issue of female beauty in Ellen Glasgow's fiction. EGN (57) 2006, 9–13.

16132. Speicher, Allison. When it all goes South: re-imagining Alcott's Little Women in *The Sheltered Life*. EGN (57) 2006, 7–8.

Susan Glaspell

16133. Duneer, Anita. On the verge of a breakthrough: projections of escape from the attic and the thwarted tower in Charlotte Perkins Gilman's *The Yellow Wallpaper* and Susan Glaspell's *The Verge*. *See* **16083**.

16134. Hinz-Bode, Kristina. Susan Glaspell and the anxiety of expression: language and isolation in the plays. Jefferson, NC; London: McFarland, 2006. pp. ix, 292.

16135. Ben-Zvi, Linda. Susan Glaspell: a life. (Bibl. 2005, 16715.) Rev. by Cheryl Black in TJ (58:1) 2006, 151–3; by Kurt Eisen in EOR (28) 2006, 184–6; by Lisa MacFarlane in AL (78:4) 2006, 872–3.

16136. —— (ed.). The road to the temple: a biography of George Cram Cook. Jefferson, NC; London: McFarland, 2005. pp. viii, 356. Rev. by Robert K. Sarlós in EOR (28) 2006, 166–8.

George Glendon (*fl.*1910)

16137. Kennedy, Gerry. Apocalypse then. TLS, 8 Sept. 2006, 13.

Molly Gloss

16138. Adkison, Jennifer Dawes. 'These is my words' … or are they? *See* **20346**.

Douglas H. Glover

16139. Beardsworth, Adam. Romancing the 'mysterious bonds of syntax': allegory and the ethics of desire in Douglas Glover's *My Romance* and *Iglaf and Swan*. StudCanL (30:2) 2005, 161–80.

16140. —— Writing from the sidelines: peripheral critique in Glover's *State of the Nation*. ShSt (13:1) 2005, 35–45.

16141. Dobozy, Tamas; Harrison, Brady. Interview with Douglas Glover. ShSt (13:1) 2005, 107–13.

16142. Novack, Sandra. Structural unity in fiction. Descant (37:2) 2006, 131–45.

Louise Glück

16143. Curry, Renée R. H.D., Dove, Glück, and Levin: the poetry of Afroasiatic and White Greece. *See* **15530**.

16144. Diehl, Joanne Feit (ed.). On Louise Glück: change what you see. (Bibl. 2005, 16724.) Rev. by Nicole Devarenne in Mod/Mod (13:2) 2006, 409–10.

16145. Keniston, Ann. Overheard voices: address and subjectivity in postmodern American poetry. *See* **18042**.

16146. Morris, Daniel. The poetry of Louise Glück: a thematic introduction. Columbia; London: Missouri UP, 2006. pp. xi, 274.

16147. Sewell, Lisa. 'In the end, the one who has nothing wins': Louise Glück and the poetics of anorexia. LIT (17:1) 2006, 49–76.

Gail Godwin

16148. Neufeld, Rob (ed.). The making of a writer: journals, 1961–1963. New York: Random House, 2006. pp. xii, 333. Rev. by Liesl Schillinger in NYTB, 5 Mar. 2006, 8.

Poh Seng Goh

16149. Goh, Robbie B. H. Imagining the nation: the role of Singapore poetry in English in 'emergent nationalism'. *See* **18765**.

William Golding

16150. Van Vuuren, Marijke. Beyond words: silence in William Golding's *Darkness Visible* and J. M. Coetzee's *Life and Times of Michael K*. ESA (48:1) 2005, 93–106.

Rebecca Goldstein

16151. Goldstein, Rebecca. The fiction of the self and the self of fiction. MassR (47:2) 2006, 293–309.

Guillermo Gómez-Peña

16152. De Chiara, Marina. Fusco and Gómez-Peña: *The Couple in the Cage*. QPS (14) 2006, 189–94.

Maud Gonne

16153. Bobotis, Andrea. Rival maternities: Maud Gonne, Queen Victoria, and the reign of the political mother. VS (49:1) 2006, 63–83.

Ray González

16154. Lemon, Alex. An interview with Ray González. InR (28:1) 2006, 121–7.

Allegra Goodman

16155. Meyers, Helene. Jewish gender trouble: women writing men of valor. TSWL (25:2) 2006, 323–34.

16156. Solomon, Deborah. Writer's laboratory. NYTM, 15 Jan. 2006, 15. (Interview.)

Nadine Gordimer

16157. Attwell, David. Tribute to Nadine Gordimer. ESA (48:1) 2005, 1–3.

16158. Coundouriotis, Eleni. Rethinking cosmopolitanism in Nadine Gordimer's *The Conservationist*. ColLit (33:3) 2006, 1–28.

16159. Erritouni, Ali. Apartheid inequality and postapartheid utopia in Nadine Gordimer's *July's People*. RAL (37:4) 2006, 68–84.

16160. Johnson, R. W. Old fires: Gordimer, Lessing and Daphne Rooke. *See* **18281**.

16161. Lenta, Patrick. The *tikoloshe* and the reasonable man. LawL (16:3) 2004, 353–79.

16162. Levy, Judith. Narrative as a way of being: Nadine Gordimer's *The Conservationist*. PartA (4:2) 2006, 103–14.

16163. Ogede, Ode S. The liberal tradition in South African literature: still a curse? Nadine Gordimer's *A Guest of Honour* revisited. IFR (33:1/2) 2006, 1–8.

16164. ZULLI, TANIA. Nadine Gordimer: strategie narrative di una transizione politica. Naples: Liguori, 2005. pp. viii, 196. (Domini: monografie del Dipartimento di Scienze Linguistiche e Letterarie, Univ. degli Studi G. D'Annunzio, 9.)

Mary Gordon (b.1949)

16165. GORDON, MARY. My mother's body. ASch (75:4) 2006, 63–78.

Phyllis Gotlieb (b.1926)

16166. GRACE, DOMINICK M. Mind matters: intellect and identity in the works of Phyllis Gotlieb. *In* (pp. 105–17) **13541**.

Barbara Gowdy

16167. CRAWFORD, CHERYL COWDY. 'The bomb is only a metaphor now': Barbara Gowdy's *Falling Angels*. Descant (37:1) 2006, 64–71.

16168. GORDON, NETA. Barbara Gowdy and the sanctity of love. Descant (37:1) 2006, 72–81.

16169. HAYWARD, SALLY. Going into the family closet: difference and disability in Barbara Gowdy's *Mr Sandman*. Descant (37:1) 2006, 82–9.

16170. HEIGHTON, STEVEN. Points of faith: an interview with Barbara Gowdy. Descant (37:1) 2006, 17–37.

16171. JARRAWAY, DAVID R. Sublime objects and mystic subjects: some Lacanian speculations about Canadian fantasy literature *via* Barbara Gowdy's *The White Bone*. *In* (pp. 81–94) **13541**.

16172. MARTENS, DEBRA. Keeping body and soul together. Descant (37:1) 2006, 59–61.

16173. MAYS, JOHN BENTLEY. Gowdy's Toronto: a note. Descant (37:1) 2006, 42–5.

16174. NEWBERRY, MARY. Filming Gowdy. Descant (37:1) 2006, 109–23.

16175. RIGELHOF, T. F. Gravel, grass and gut: the fiction of Barbara Gowdy. Descant (37:1) 2006, 99–106.

16176. RYMHS, DEENA. In search of the missing link: finding the narrator in Barbara Gowdy's *The White Bone*. Descant (37:1) 2006, 90–8.

Patricia Grace

16177. BARKER, CLARE. From narrative prosthesis to disability counter-narrative: reading the politics of difference in *Potiki* and *the bone people*. JNZL (24:1) 2006, 130–47.

16178. BATTISTA, JON. Magic fire women: balance and imbalance in the depiction of Maori women in Maori literature in English. *In* (pp. 16–24) **11731**.

16179. DALE, JUDITH. Re-reading war stories. *In* (pp. 63–70) **11731**.

16180. GANNER, HEIDEMARIE. When a boy is not a boy ...: reflections on the deceptive simplicity of the English language. *In* (pp. 115–20) **1227**.

16181. WILSON, JANET. Suffering and survival: body and voice in recent Maori writing. *In* (pp. 425–38) **8374**.

Jorie Graham

16182. GARDNER, THOMAS. A door ajar: contemporary writers and Emily Dickinson. *See* **9865**.

16183. MORRIS, ADALAIDE. The act of the mind: thought experiments in the poetry of Jorie Graham and Leslie Scalapino. *In* (pp. 146–66) **13732**.

W. S. (William Sydney) Graham (b.1918)

16184. PITE, RALPH; JONES, HESTER (eds). W. S. Graham: speaking towards you. (Bibl. 2005, 16793.) Rev. by Alan Baker in CritS (18:1) 2006, 136–9.

16185. SNOW, MARGARET. W. S. Graham and 'terrible times': conversations with Nessie Graham. PNRev (32:4) 2006, 46–9.

Kenneth Grahame

16186. LUO, LIANGGONG. *The Wind in the Willows*: a utopia of home. FLS (120) 2006, 90–6. (In Chinese.)

16187. MILROY, ROLLIN. Emerging from the willows. Amphora (143) 2006, 12–17.

Harley Granville-Barker

16188. STILES, ANNE. Granville-Barker's effeminate heterosexuals: the new drama's new men. *In* (pp. 219–31) **11883**.

Robert Graves

16189. CARDER, RICHARD. Gurney's journeys to Graves. *See* **16238**.

16190. MCKINLEY, JAMES. Subject: Robert Graves: random notes of a biographer. NewLet (72:1) 2005/06, 274–97.

16191. QUINN, PATRICK. 'More than a fascination wiith the Divine Marquis': John Fowles's *The Magus* and Lawrence Durrell's *The Alexandria Quartet*. *In* (pp. 270–81) **15631**.

16192. VOGEL, AMBER. Not Elizabeth to his Raleigh: Laura Riding, Robert Graves, and origins of *The White Goddess*. *In* (pp. 229–39) **3405**.

Robert Gray (b.1945)

16193. MCMAHON, ELIZABETH. Encapsulated space: the paradise-prison of Australia's island imaginary. Southerly (65:1) 2005, 20–30.

Simon Gray

16194. GRAY, SIMON. The year of the jouncer. London: Granta, 2006. pp. 282. (Memoirs.)

'Henry Green' (Henry Vincent Yorke)

16195. WOOD, JAMES. A plausible magic: Henry Green, the last English Modernist. TLS, 6 Jan. 2006, 12–13.

Graham Greene

16196. BERGONZI, BERNARD. Banville's revenge. *See* **14571**.

16197. —— A study in Greene: Graham Greene and the art of the novel. Oxford; New York: OUP, 2006. pp. ix, 197. Rev. by Eric Ormsby in TLS, 15 Dec. 2006, 6.

16198. BOSCO, MARK. Graham Greene's Catholic imagination. (Bibl. 2005, 16813.) Rev. by Robert Murray Davis in EWN (36:2) 2005; by John C. Waldmeir in JR (86:2) 2006, 356–8; by Adam Schwartz in ReLit (38:1) 2006, 139–42; by Andrew M. Greeley in ANCW (194:5) 2006, 25–6.

16199. Bushnell, William S. Paying for the damage: *The Quiet American* revisited. *See* **13022**.

16200. Ferrer, Hugh. Notes on the *Connecticut Yankee*. *See* **11494**.

16201. Fluet, Lisa. Hit-man Modernism. *In* (pp. 269–97) **12024**.

16202. Gale, Robert L. Characters and plots in the fiction of Graham Greene. Jefferson, NC; London: McFarland, 2006. pp. ix, 353.

16203. Ganteau, Jean-Michel. 'A conflict between an image and a man': the visual diction of romance in Graham Greene's *The End of the Affair*. EtBr (31) 2006, 69–81.

16204. Hodgkins, Hope Howell. The apophatic heart: Graham Greene's negative rhetoric. Ren (59:1) 2006, 53–75.

16205. Kerr, Douglas. *The Quiet American* and the novel. StudN (38:1) 2006, 95–107.

16206. Lanone, Catherine. L'explicit(e) dans *The Power and the Glory* de Graham Greene. EA (59:4) 2006, 427–40.

16207. McClymond, Kathryn. Ritual and power in *Monsignor Quixote*: a ritual studies approach. JRS (20:1) 2006, 11–20.

16208. Miyano, Shoko. Innocence in Graham Greene's novels. New York; Frankfurt: Lang, 2006. pp. 122.

16209. Roston, Murray. Graham Greene's narrative strategies: a study of the major novels. Basingstoke; New York: Palgrave Macmillan, 2006. pp. vi, 168.

16210. Thomson, Ian. Our man in Tallinn: Graham Greene's chance encounter with a model spy. TLS, 3 Mar. 2006, 14–15.

16211. —— Troubled but faithful: Graham Greene's relationship with *The Tablet*. TLS, 18 & 25 Aug. 2006, 14–16.

16212. —— (ed.). Articles of faith: the collected *Tablet* journalism of Graham Greene. Oxford: Signal in assn with *The Tablet*, 2006. pp. xxvi, 183. Rev. by Eric Ormsby in TLS, 15 Dec. 2006, 6.

16213. Whitfield, Stephen J. The culture of the Cold War. *In* (pp. 256–74) **11776**.

Lavinia Greenlaw (b.1962)

16214. Milne, Drew. The art of wit and the Cambridge Science Park. *In* (pp. 170–87) **13732**.

Augusta, Lady Gregory

16215. Hill, Judith. Lady Gregory: an Irish life. (Bibl. 2005, 16823.) Rev. by Declan Kiberd in TLS, 3 Mar. 2006, 6–7.

16216. Kiberd, Declan. A woman's roles. TLS, 3 Mar. 2006, 6–7 (review-article).

16217. McDiarmid, Lucy. The Irish art of controversy. (Bibl. 2005, 16824.) Rev. by Julian Hanna in Mod/Mod (13:3) 2006, 580–2; by Catherine E. Paul in SoCR (39:1) 2006, 216–18.

Eamon Grennan

16218. Walsh, William. When language fails: an interview with Eamon Grennan. KR (28:3) 2006, 125–39.

Kate Grenville

16219. Wang, Liping. Reflection of Kate Grenville's radical feminism: an interpretation of *Dark Places* and *The Idea of Perfection*. FLS (120) 2006, 103–7. (In Chinese.)

Zane Grey

16220. Pauly, Thomas H. Zane Grey: his life, his adventures, his women. (Bibl. 2005, 16827.) Rev. by Jonathan Miles in NYTB, 1 Jan. 2006, 8–9; by Steve Cox in JArizH (47:4) 2006, 400–1.

Angelina Weld Grimké

16221. Garvey, T. Gregory. Creating the culture of reform in antebellum America. Athens; London: Georgia UP, 2006. pp. xii, 263. Rev. by Alex Nagy in AmJ (23:2) 2006, 171–2.

16222. Mitchell, Koritha A. Antilynching plays: Angelina Weld Grimké, Alice Dunbar-Nelson, and the evolution of African American drama. *In* (pp. 210–30) **8435**.

John Grisham

16223. Swirski, Peter. Briefcases for hire: American hardboiled to legal fiction. *See* **16263**.

Allen Grossman

16224. Morris, Daniel (ed.). Poetry's poet: essays on the poetry, pedagogy, and poetics of Allen Grossman. Orono, ME: National Poetry Foundation, 2004. pp. vii, 278.

Edith Searle Grossmann

16225. Jones, Lawrence. Three 'bush' novels and the colonial myth. *In* (pp. 359–84) **8374**.

John Guare

16226. Guare, John. John Guare on dialogue. Dramatist (8:4) 2006, 13–15.

Susan Gubar (b.1944)

16227. Gubar, Susan. Reading in the waiting room. SFO (4:2) 2006.

Arthur Guiterman (1871–1943)

16228. Randall, Warren. A study in stanzas: Arthurs, authors, and poetry. *See* **9950**.

'Bill Gulick' (Grover Cleveland Gulick) (b.1916)

16229. Gulick, Bill. Sixty-four years as a writer. Caldwell, ID: Caxton Press, 2006. pp. 344.

Thom Gunn

16230. Michelucci, Stefania. La maschera, il corpo e l'anima: saggio sulla poesia di Thom Gunn. Milan: Unicopli, 2006. pp. 318. (Biblioteca di anglistica.)

16231. Miller, Karl. Cambridge men. Raritan (26:2) 2006, 137–45.

16232. Wilmer, Clive. Remembering Thom Gunn. PNRev (32:3) 2006, 32–4.

Abdulrazak Gurnah (b.1948)

16233. Gurnah, Abdulrazak. Writing & place. WLT (78:2) 2004, 26–8.

Ivor Gurney

16234. Banfield, Stephen. Gurney and Housman. IGSJ (10) 2004, 33–48.

16235. Barham, Peter. Forgotten lunatics of the Great War. New Haven, CT; London: Yale UP, 2004. pp. viii, 451, (plates) 8. Rev. by Hilary Thornton in IGSJ (10) 2004, 101–4.

16236. Blevins, Pamela. Ivor Gurney's friends: Ethel Voynich – 'E.L.V.': revolutionary, novelist, translator, composer. *See* **18916**.

16237. —— *et al.* Bibliographical update. IGSJ (10) 2004, 85–92.

16238. Carder, Richard. Gurney's journeys to Graves. IGSJ (10) 2004, 73–84.

16239. Hawlin, Stefan. Ivor Gurney's creative reading of Walt Whitman: thinking of Paumanok. ELT (49:1) 2006, 31–48.

16240. Kavanagh, P. J. (ed.). Collected poems. (Bibl. 1983, 11516.) Manchester: Carcanet Press, 2004. pp. xlvii, 410. (Fyfield.) (Revised ed.: first ed. 1982.) Rev. by Robert J. Yates in IGSJ (10) 2004, 122–5; by R. K. R. Thornton in PNRev (31:6) 2005, 49–50.

16241. Thornton, R. K. R. Blessed rage for order. PNRev (31:6) 2005, 49–50 (review-article). (Gurney's *Collected Poems.*)

Woody Guthrie

16242. Briley, Ronald. 'Woody Sez': Woody Guthrie, the *People's Daily World*, and indigenous radicalism. CH (84:1) 2006, 30–43.

Brion Gysin

16243. Geiger, John. Nothing is true, everything is permitted: the life of Brion Gysin. New York: Disinformation, 2005. pp. 336, (plates) 16. Rev. by George Fetherling in BkCan (35:1) 2006, 37–8; by Davis Schneiderman in AmBR (27:5) 2006, 30.

Marilyn Hacker

16244. Biggs, Mary. 'Present, infinitesimal, infinite': the political vision and 'femin' poetics of Marilyn Hacker. Frontiers (27:1) 2006, 1–20.

Jessica Hagedorn

16245. Fritsch, Esther. *Reading gossip*: Funktionen von Klatsch in Romanen ethnischer amerikanischer Autorinnen. *See* **15777**.

16246. Mendoza, Victor. A queer nomadology of Jessica Hagedorn's *Dogeaters*. AL (77:4) 2005, 815–45.

16247. Twelbeck, Kirsten. Beyond a postmodern denial of reference: forms of resistance in Jessica Hagedorn's *Dogeaters*. Amst (51:3) 2006, 425–37.

Kimiko Hahn (b.1955)

16248. Grotjohn, Robert. Kimiko Hahn's 'interlingual poetics' in *Mosquito and Art*. *In* (pp. 219–34) **11995**.

Louise Halfe (b.1953)

16249. Stigter, Shelley. The dialectics and dialogics of code-switching in the poetry of Gregory Scofield and Louise Halfe. *See* **18435**.

Martin Hall (b.1952)

16250. Petzold, Jochen. Children's literature after apartheid: examining 'hidden histories' of South Africa's past. *See* **18139**.

Radclyffe Hall

16251. Thompson, Dawn. Prussic acid with a twist: *The Well of Loneliness*, M. E. Kerr, and young adult readers. CLAQ (31:3) 2006, 282–99.

Sharlot Mabridth Hall (1870–1943)

16252. Staples, Joe. 'Discovering' new talent: Charles F. Lummis's conflicted mentorship of Sui Sin Far, Sharlot Hall, and Mary Austin. *See* **17292**.

Mark Halliday (b.1949)

16253. Williamson, Alan. Cynicism. APR (35:3) 2006, 39–43.

Daniel Halpern (b.1945)

16254. Matthews, Sebastian (introd.). Peripheral pleasures: letters to Russell Banks, Daniel Halpern, and Stanley Plumly. *See* **17462**.

Edmond Hamilton (b.1904)

16255. Nelson, Dale. Is Lewis' Ransom Trilogy indebted to Yank magazine science fiction? *See* **17194**.

Hugo Hamilton

16256. Hamilton, Hugo. The harbor boys: a memoir. London: HarperCollins, 2006. pp. 263.

16257. —— The sailor in the wardrobe. London; New York: Fourth Estate, 2006. pp. 263. (Memoirs.)

Patrick Hamilton

16258. Goulding, Simon. Patrick Hamilton's *Hangover Square* and the landscapes of Fascism. EREA (4:2) 2006, 56–61.

Dashiell Hammett

16259. Cassuto, Leonard. *The Maltese Falcon* and the hard-boiled sentimental. Clues (23:2) 2005, 32–49.

16260. Engel, Leonard. Identity issues and images in a hard-boiled world: Dashiell Hammett's *Red Harvest* and the mystery/detective genre. EArtsS (34:1) 2005, 51–60.

16261. Harris, Martin. Hammett's Flitcraft parable, *The Stepfather*, and the significance of falling beams. *See* **13080**.

16262. Knight, Deborah. On reason and passion in *The Maltese Falcon*. *In* (pp. 207–21) **12452**.

16263. Swirski, Peter. Briefcases for hire: American hardboiled to legal fiction. JAC (29:3) 2006, 307–20.

Patricia Hampl (b.1946)

16264. Hampl, Patricia. Blue arabesque: a search for the sublime. Orlando, FL: Harcourt, 2006. pp. 215. Rev. by Kathryn Harrison in NYTB, 29 Oct. 2006, 16.

James Hanley

16265. Gokulsing, Tanya. An audience for paper boats: Conrad and the marketing of early Modernism. *See* **15270**.

16266. Pridmore, Joseph. Mass violence and the crowd: the perception of proletarian community in working-class writers of the 1930s. *See* **16059**.

16267. —— 'Vindicating the honour of Lancashire': textual variation between editions of James Hanley's *Boy*. *In* (pp. 23–33) **3407**.

Barry Hannah

16268. Kachuba, John B. Breadcrumb trails and spider webs: form in *Yonder Stands Your Orphan*. MissQ (58:1/2) 2004/05, 75–87.

Lorraine Hansberry

16269. Mafe, Diana Adesola. Black women on Broadway: the duality of Lorraine Hansberry's *A Raisin in the Sun* and Ntozake Shange's *for colored girls*. AmDr (15:2) 2006, 30–47.

16270. Radavich, David. African American drama from the Midwest. *See* **16489**.

Joyce Hansen (b.1942)

16271. Chandler, Karen. Paths to freedom: literacy and folk traditions in recent narratives about slavery and emancipation. CLAQ (31:1) 2006, 3–26.

Ron Hansen (b.1947)

16272. Hansen, Ron. Faith and fiction. *In* (pp. 105–12) **11940**.

David Hare

16273. Alley, Henry. *Mrs Dalloway* and three of its contemporary children. *See* **19257**.

16274. Defraeye, Piet. Authorship regained and retained? David Hare's *Via Dolorosa*. *In* (pp. 61–72) **12336**.

16275. Schafer, Elizabeth. Playing Australia in the theatre: an interview with Cate Blanchett. *In* (pp. 212–18) **12360**.

Donald Harington

16276. Copeland, Marion W. Voices of the least loved: cockroaches in the contemporary American novel. *In* (pp. 153–75) **3203**.

William Harmon (b.1938)

16277. Benthall, Al. Worlds of eye and ear in the poems of William Harmon. MissQ (58:1/2) 2004/05, 277–98.

Claire Harris (b.1937)

16278. Blumenthal, Anna S. Claire Harris's *She*: the MPD metaphor and the postcolonial Caribbean woman. DalR (86:3) 2006, 259–71.

Clare Winger Harris (b.1891)

16279. DONAWERTH, JANE. Illicit reproduction: Clare Winger Harris's *The Fate of the Poseidonia*. *In* (pp. 20–35) **13537**.

Frank Harris

16280. PHARAND, MICHEL W. (ed.). Shaw's sex credo. *See* **18500**.

Jana Harris

16281. HARRIS, JANA. *The Laundress by the Lake, 1892*. TriQ (124) 2006, 97–125.

Wilson Harris

16282. CAMBONI, MARINA. Resistance to symmetry: Wilson Harris's bridges of language. *In* (pp. 9–20) **16284**.

16283. —— FAZZINI, MARCO. An interview with Wilson Harris in Macerata. Ed. by Hena Maes-Jelinek. *In* (pp. 53–64) **16284**.

16284. FAZZINI, MARCO (ed.). Resisting alterities: Wilson Harris and other avatars of otherness. Amsterdam; New York: Rodopi, 2004. pp. xiv, 255. (Cross/cultures: readings in the post-colonial literatures in English, 71.) Rev. by Anuradha Dingwaney Needham in RAL (37:1) 2006, 155–7.

16285. HARRIS, WILSON. Resistances to alterity. *In* (pp. 3–7) **16284**.

16286. MAES-JELINEK, HENA. 'Otherness' in Wilson Harris's fiction: *The Dark Jester*. *In* (pp. 41–52) **16284**.

16287. POZZI, MONICA. When the Other is Wilson Harris. *In* (pp. 21–40) **16284**.

Jim Harrison

16288. BUNGE, NANCY. Influencing each other through the mail: William Stafford's and Marvin Bell's *Segues* and Jim Harrison's and Ted Kooser's *Braided Creek*. *See* **18588**.

M. John Harrison

16289. BOULD, MARK; REID, MICHELLE (eds). Parietal games: critical writings by and on M. John Harrison. Reading: Science Fiction Foundation, 2005. pp. 357. Rev. by David Moyle in Extrapolation (47:1) 2006, 160–4.

Tony Harrison

16290. JONES, FRANCIS R. 'Geldshark Ares god of war': ideology and time in literary translation. YES (36:1) 2006, 191–203. (*Agamemnon*.)

16291. OSTERWALDER, HANS. 'Eros/Thanatos a pair': the dialectic of life and death in Tony Harrison's *Laureate's Block*. CritS (17:3) 2005, 85–99.

16292. ROWLAND, ANTONY. Holocaust poetry: awkward poetics in the work of Sylvia Plath, Geoffrey Hill, Tony Harrison and Ted Hughes. *See* **18050**.

16293. WHALE, JOHN. John Keats and Tony Harrison: the burden of history. *In* (pp. 163–80) **13735**.

J. S. Harry

16294. DRAY, COLIN. The golden fish: on reading J. S. Harry. ALS (22:2) 2005, 192–204.

Josephine Hart

16295. Kimball, A. Samuel. 'And her substance would be mine': envy, hate, and ontological evacuation in Josephine Hart's *Sin*. Contagion (12/13) 2006, 239–58.

Moss Hart

16296. Brown, Jared. Moss Hart: a prince of the theatre: a biography in three acts. New York: Back Stage, 2006. pp. ix, 452. Rev. by Charles Marowitz in AmBR (28:1) 2006, 21–2.

Kenneth J. Harvey

16297. Stein, Olga. Inside Kenneth J. Harvey. BkCan (35:6) 2006, 9–10. (Interview.)

Gwen Harwood
('Francis Geyer', 'T. F. Kline', 'Walter Lehmann', 'Miriam Stone')

16298. King, Richard. A symphony complete. Meanjin (63:1) 2004, 185–90 (review-article).

16299. Kratzmann, Gregory. Who was Alan Carvosso? Meanjin (63:1) 2004, 177–84.

16300. Lucas, Rose. 'Lines of confusion, stones of emptiness': the place of mourning in Gwen Harwood's *Herongate*. Southerly (65:3) 2005, 146–55.

Sara Henderson Hay (1906–1987)

16301. Smith, Ellen McGrath. A stepmother for *Transformations*: Sara Henderson Hay's *Story Hour.* Sagetrieb (19:3) 2006, 41–75.

Robert Hayden

16302. Boruch, Marianne. Heavy lifting. APR (35:5) 2006, 51–7. (Tragic themes.)

16303. Howard, W. Scott. Resistance, sacrifice, and historicity in the elegies of Robert Hayden. *In* (pp. 133–52) **13763**.

Bessie Head

16304. Cullinan, Patrick (comp.). Imaginative trespasser: letters between Bessie Head and Patrick and Wendy Cullinan, 1963–1977. Johannesburg: Witwatersrand UP; Trenton, NJ: Africa World Press, 2005. pp. xi, 268, (plates) 8.

16305. Gagiano, Annie. Entering the oppressor's mind: a strategy of writing in Bessie Head's *A Question of Power,* Yvonne Vera's *The Stone Virgins* and Unity Dow's *The Screaming of the Innocent*. JCL (41:2) 2006, 43–60.

16306. LeSeur, Geta. Head, Schwarz-Bart, and Kincaid: refashioning alternative landscapes. CLAJ (50:2) 2006, 207–18.

16307. Nazareth, Peter. Path of thunder: meeting Bessie Head. RAL (37:4) 2006, 211–29.

16308. Weiss, Bettina. An approach to homoerotic female desire in *Three Moments in a Marriage*, *The Purple Violet of Oshaantu*, and *A Question of Power. In* (pp. 117–44) **12216**.

Michael Healey

16309. FILEWOD, ALAN. Theatrical nationhood in radical mobility: *The Farm Show* futures and the Banner / Ground Zero collaborations. CanTR (125) 2006, 9–15.

16310. NICHOLS, GLEN. Playing together: a collaborative approach to theatre translation. *In* (pp. 73–90) **12336**.

Seamus Heaney

16311. BASSNETT, SUSAN. Writing and translating. *In* (pp. 173–83) **3186**.

16312. BROWN, RICHARD DANSON. MacNeice in fairy land. *In* (pp. 352–69) **5100**.

16313. GATTO, MARISTELLA. Traduzioni e metamorfosi londinesi: la metropolitana come inferno in Seamus Heaney. *In* (pp. 373–83) **7343**.

16314. HARDWICK, LORNA. 'Murmurs in the cathedral': the impact of translations from Greek poetry and drama on modern work in English by Michael Longley and Seamus Heaney. *See* **17248**.

16315. HART, HENRY. Seamus Heaney: circling back. SewR (114:3) 2006, 456–62 (review-article). (Arts and letters.)

16316. HAUGHTON, HUGH. Power and hiding places: Wordsworth and Seamus Heaney. *In* (pp. 61–100) **13735**.

16317. JONES, CHRIS. Strange likeness: the use of Old English in twentieth-century poetry. *See* **3677**.

16318. KENNEDY-ANDREWS, ELMER. John Montague: global regionalist? *See* **17550**.

16319. LOJEK, HELEN. Man, woman, soldier: Heaney's *In Memoriam Francis Ledwidge* and Boland's *Heroic*. NewHR (10:1) 2006, 123–38.

16320. MCGUIRE, THOMAS. Violence and vernacular in Seamus Heaney's *Beowulf*. NewHR (10:1) 2006, 79–99.

16321. NIKOLAOU, PASCHALIS. Notes on translating the self. *In* (pp. 19–32) **2874**.

16322. O'BRIEN, EUGENE. Rereading the canon: towards a literary redefinition of Irishness. *In* (pp. 113–33) **12189**.

16323. SELL, JONATHAN P. A. Allusion and ambiguity in Seamus Heaney's *Blackberry-Picking*. RAEI (17) 2004, 261–82.

16324. SLOAN, BARRY. The redress of imagination: Bernard Mac Laverty's *Grace Notes*. *In* (pp. 303–15) **11916**.

16325. STEELE, FELICIA JEAN. Dreaming of dragons: Tolkien's impact on Heaney's *Beowulf*. Mythlore (25:1/2) 2006, 137–46.

16326. TWIDDY, IAIN. Seamus Heaney's versions of pastoral. EC (56:1) 2006, 50–71.

Anthony Hecht

16327. HOY, PHILIP. Anthony Hecht in conversation. (Bibl. 2002, 14887.) London: Between the Lines, 2004. pp. 168. (Third ed.: first ed. 1999.)

Steven Heighton (b.1961)

16328. ROBINS, ELLIOT. No ghosts here: Steven Heighton interviewed. BkCan (35:8) 2006, 7–8.

Robert A. Heinlein

16329. Sullivan, C. W., iii. Robert A. Heinlein: reinventing series SF in the 1950s. Extrapolation (47:1) 2006, 66–76.

Lyn Hejinian

16330. Edmond, Jacob. Lyn Hejinian and Russian estrangement. PT (27:1) 2006, 97–124.

16331. Sadoff, Ira. On the margins: part two. APR (35:2) 2006, 51–5. (Prose poems.)

Lillian Hellman

16332. Martinson, Deborah. Lillian Hellman: a life with foxes and scoundrels. (Bibl. 2005, 16960.) Rev. by Louis Bayard in BkW, 8 Jan. 2006, 9.

David Helwig

16333. Helwig, David. The names of things: a memoir. Erin, Ont.: Porcupine's Quill, 2006. pp. 299.

Ernest Hemingway

16334. Balbert, Peter. Courage at the border-line: Balder, Hemingway, and Lawrence's *The Captain's Doll*. *See* **17030**.

16335. Bittner, John Robert; Flora, Joseph M. Anti-Fascist symbols and subtexts in *A Farewell to Arms*: Hemingway, Mussolini, and journalism in the 1920s. *In* (pp. 100–7) **16388**.

16336. Boese, Gil K. *Under Kilimanjaro*: the other Hemingway. HemR (25:2) 2006, 114–18.

16337. Bradley, Jacqueline. Hemingway's *The Sun Also Rises*. Exp (64:4) 2006, 231–4.

16338. Bruccoli, Matthew J.; Baughman, Judith S. (eds). Hemingway and the mechanism of fame: statements, public letters, introductions, forewords, prefaces, blurbs, reviews, and endorsements. Columbia; London: South Carolina UP, 2006. pp. xxxi, 145. Rev. by David M. Earle in HemR (25:2) 2006, 146–9.

16339. Cirino, Mark. 'A bicycle is a splendid thing': Hemingway's source for Bartolomeo Aymo in *A Farewell to Arms*. HemR (26:1) 2006, 106–14.

16340. Cohen, Milton A. Hemingway's laboratory: the Paris *In Our Time*. Tuscaloosa; London: Alabama UP, 2005. pp. xiv, 267. Rev. by Jim Barloon in HemR (26:1) 2006, 121–3.

16341. Comley, Nancy R. The Italian education of Ernest Hemingway. *In* (pp. 41–50) **16388**.

16342. Craig, Joanna Hildebrand. Dancing with Hemingway. HemR (25:2) 2006, 82–6. (Copyediting *Under Kilimanjaro*.)

16343. Curnutt, Kirk. Of Mussolini and macaroni: Hemingway, Fitzgerald, and expatriate 'Italianicity'. *In* (pp. 75–89) **16388**.

16344. Cutchins, Dennis. *All the Pretty Horses*: Cormac McCarthy's reading of *For Whom the Bell Tolls*. *See* **17297**.

16345. DeFazio, Albert J., iii (ed.). Dear Papa, Dear Hotch: the correspondence of Ernest Hemingway and A. E. Hotchner. Preface by A. E. Hotchner. (Bibl. 2005, 16974.) Rev. by Robert Trogdon in HemR (25:2) 2006, 140–2.

16346. Eby, Carl P. Wake up alone and like it! Dorothy Hollis, Marjorie Hillis, and *To Have and Have Not*. HemR (26:1) 2006, 96–105.

16347. Fantina, Richard. Ernest Hemingway: machismo and masochism. (Bibl. 2005, 16978.) Rev. by Jamie Ebersole in HemR (25:2) 2006, 143–6.

16348. —— Pegging Ernest Hemingway: masochism, sodomy, and the dominant woman. *In* (pp. 46–67) **11883**.

16349. Field, Allyson Nadia. Expatriate lifestyle as tourist destination: *The Sun Also Rises* and experiential travelogues of the twenties. HemR (25:2) 2006, 29–43.

16350. Fleming, Robert E. The editing process. HemR (25:2) 2006, 91–4.

16351. —— Ettore Moretti: Hemingway's 'legitimate war hero'? *In* (pp. 167–73) **16388**.

16352. Flora, Joseph M. Nick Adams in Italy. *In* (pp. 185–200) **16388**.

16353. Florczyk, Steven. A captain in Hemingway's court? The story of Ernest Hemingway, *A Farewell to Arms*, and the unpublished papers of Robert W. Bates. *In* (pp. 62–72) **16388**.

16354. Fortunati, Vita. Hemingway, the embodiment of the American myth, and Italian Leftist writers. *In* (pp. 225–31) **16388**.

16355. —— The impact of the First World War on private lives: a comparison of European and American writers (Ford, Hemingway, and Remarque). *In* (pp. 53–64) **15944**.

16356. Fruscione, Joseph. 'One tale, one telling': parallelism, influence, and exchange between Faulkner's *The Unvanquished* and Hemingway's *For Whom the Bell Tolls*. *See* **15808**.

16357. Gladstein, Mimi R. Bilingual wordplay: variations on a theme by Hemingway and Steinbeck. HemR (26:1) 2006, 81–95.

16358. Godfrey, Laura Gruber. Hemingway and cultural geography: the landscape of logging in *The End of Something*. HemR (26:1) 2006, 47–62.

16359. Grant, Kenneth B. Friendship, finance, and art: Charles Scribner's Sons' relationship with Ernest Hemingway and August Derleth. MidM (33) 2005, 29–41.

16360. Justice, Hilary K. The bones of the others: the Hemingway text from the lost manuscripts to the posthumous novels. Kent, OH; London: Kent State UP, 2006. pp. 192.

16361. Kaye, Jeremy. The 'whine' of Jewish manhood: re-reading Hemingway's anti-Semitism, reimagining Robert Cohn. HemR (25:2) 2006, 44–60.

16362. Kellman, Steven G. Ghosting the Lost Generation: Geoff Dyer's *Paris Trance*. *See* **15647**.

16363. Kennedy, J. Gerald. Angling for affection: absent fathers, fatherhood, and fishing in *A Farewell to Arms*. *In* (pp. 119–30) **16388**.

16364. Kitunda, Jeremiah M. Ernest Hemingway's African book: an appraisal. HemR (25:2) 2006, 107–13.

16365. Knodt, Ellen Andrews. 'Suddenly and unreasonably': shooting the sergeant in *A Farewell to Arms*. *In* (pp. 149–57) **16388**.

16366. Koch, Stephen. The breaking point: Hemingway, Dos Passos, and the murder of José Robles. (Bibl. 2005, 16982.) Rev. by Martin Tucker in Confrontation (92/93) 2005/06, 303–4.

16367. Kruse, Horst H. Allusions to *The Merchant of Venice* and the New Testament in *God Rest You Merry, Gentlemen*: Hemingway's anti-Semitism reconsidered. HemR (25:2) 2006, 61–75.

16368. Lewis, Robert W. The making of *Under Kilimanjaro*. HemR (25:2) 2006, 87–90.

16369. Li, Luchen. A heart enshrouded in the landscape: an impressionist reading of *Big Two-Hearted River*. MidAmerica (31) 2004, 17–24.

16370. Maffi, Mario. Untender is the night in the Garden of Eden: Fitzgerald, Hemingway, and the Mediterranean. *In* (pp. 99–117) **12076**.

16371. Maier, Kevin. Hemingway's hunting: an ecological reconsideration. HemR (25:2) 2006, 119–22.

16372. Mandel, Miriam B. Ethics and 'night thoughts': 'truer than the truth'. HemR (25:2) 2006, 95–100.

16373. —— Internal structures: the conservatism of *A Farewell to Arms*. *In* (pp. 174–84) **16388**.

16374. —— (ed.). A companion to Hemingway's *Death in the Afternoon*. (Bibl. 2005, 16984.) Rev. by Micaela Muñoz Calvo in Misc (32) 2005, 117–27.

16375. Martin, Lawrence H. *The Revolutionist*: historical context and political ideology. *In* (pp. 90–9) **16388**.

16376. —— Safari in the age of Kenyatta. HemR (25:2) 2006, 101–6.

16377. Melling, Philip. Cultural imperialism, Afro-Cuban religion, and Santiago's failure in Hemingway's *The Old Man and the Sea*. HemR (26:1) 2006, 6–24.

16378. Meyers, Jeffrey. Picasso and Hemingway: a dud poem and a live grenade. MichQR (45:3) 2006, 422–32.

16379. —— (introd.). Hemingway and Harold Loeb: an unpublished letter. MichQR (45:3) 2006, 433–8.

16380. Miller, Linda Patterson. From the 'African book' to *Under Kilimanjaro*: an introduction. HemR (25:2) 2006, 78–81.

16381. Moreira, Peter. Hemingway on the China front: his WWII spy mission with Martha Gellhorn. Washington, DC: Potomac, 2006. pp. xviii, 245, (plates) 8. Rev. by Kaimei Zheng in HemR (26:1) 2006, 115–21.

16382. Moreland, Kim. Bringing 'Italianicity' home: Hemingway returns to Oak Park. *In* (pp. 51–61) **16388**.

16383. Narbeshuber, Lisa. Hemingway's *In Our Time*: Cubism, conservation, and the suspension of identification. HemR (25:2) 2006, 9–28.

16384. O'Shaughnessey, Margaret. Painters and paintings in *Across the River and into the Trees*. *In* (pp. 201–11) **16388**.

16385. Panda, Ken. *Under Kilimanjaro*: the multicultural Hemingway. HemR (25:2) 2006, 128–31.

16386. Putnam, Ann. The last good country. HemR (25:2) 2006, 132–5.

16387. ROSS, PATRICIA A. The spell cast by remains: the myth of wilderness in modern American literature. London; New York: Routledge, 2006. pp. ix, 174. (Literary criticism and cultural theory.)

16388. SANDERSON, RENA (ed.). Hemingway's Italy: new perspectives. Baton Rouge: Louisiana State UP, 2006. pp. viii, 252.

16389. SAVOLA, DAVID. 'A very sinister book': *The Sun Also Rises* as critique of pastoral. HemR (26:1) 2006, 25–46.

16390. SCHWARZ, JEFFREY A. Who's the foreigner now? Rethinking 1920s American prejudice in *A Farewell to Arms*. *In* (pp. 108–16) **16388**.

16391. STEWART, MATTHEW C. Ernest Hemingway's *How Death Sought Out the Town Major of Roncade*: observations on the development of a writer. LitIm (8:2) 2006, 211–19.

16392. STOLTZFUS, BEN. Sartre, *nada*, and Hemingway's African stories. CLS (42:3) 2005, 205–28.

16393. STONEBACK, H. R. Hemingway's Stresa – getting it right: actual and symbolic landscape, deep structure, and the Borromean subtext. *In* (pp. 131–9) **16388**.

16394. —— *Under Kilimanjaro* – truthiness at late light; or, Would Oprah kick Hemingway out of her Book Club? HemR (25:2) 2006, 123–7.

16395. SU, SHUNQIANG. The essence of Hemingway's 'code hero'. FLS (119) 2006, 123–9. (In Chinese.)

16396. TANNER, STEPHEN L. Wrath and agony in *Across the River and into the Trees*. *In* (pp. 212–21) **16388**.

16397. TAYLOR, BEVERLY. 'Arms and the man': an Italian lineage for the wedding of love and war in *A Farewell to Arms*. *In* (pp. 140–8) **16388**.

16398. TILTON, MARGARET. Why we need Hemingway: Whiteness in a multicultural age. ConnR (28:2) 2006, 153–61.

16399. TYLER, LISA. 'Dangerous families' and 'intimate harm' in Hemingway's *Indian Camp*. TSLL (48:1) 2006, 37–53.

16400. VERNON, ALEX. Soldiers once and still: Ernest Hemingway, James Salter & Tim O'Brien. (Bibl. 2004, 17253.) Rev. by John Whalen-Bridge in AL (77:4) 2005, 854–6.

16401. WAGNER-MARTIN, LINDA. At the heart of *A Farewell to Arms*. *In* (pp. 158–66) **16388**.

16402. WILHELM, RANDALL S. Objects on the table: anxiety and still life in Hemingway's *A Farewell to Arms*. HemR (26:1) 2006, 63–80.

16403. YANG, RENJING. Ernest Hemingway in China. Xiamen: Xiamen UP, 2006. pp. xx, 332, (plates) 8. Rev. (in Chinese) by Wang Zhongxiang in FLS (122) 2006, 169–71.

Anna Minerva Henderson (1887–1987)

16404. CLARKE, GEORGE ELLIOTT. Anna Minerva Henderson: an Afro New Brunswick response to Canadian (Modernist) poetry. CanL (189) 2006, 32–48.

Beth Henley

16405. Andreach, Robert J. Understanding Beth Henley. Columbia; London: South Carolina UP, 2006. pp. 192. (Understanding contemporary American literature.)

16406. Gussow, Mel. Entering the mainstream: the plays of Beth Henley, Marsha Norman, and Wendy Wasserstein. *In* (pp. 45–53) **12297**.

16407. Plunka, Gene A. Freudian psychology and Beth Henley's popular culture satire: *Signature*. JPC (39:4) 2006, 639–60.

Sir A. P. (Alan Patrick) Herbert (1890–1971)

16408. Lurcock, Tony. Evelyn Waugh, A. P. Herbert and divorce reform. *See* **18994**.

James Herbert

16409. Freeman, Nick. 'A decadent appetite for the lurid'? James Herbert, *The Spear* and 'Nazi gothic'. GothS (8:2) 2006, 80–97.

W. N. Herbert (b.1961)

16410. Herbert, W. N. Testament and confessions of an informationist. *In* (pp. 72–87) **13732**.

Calvin C. Hernton (1933–2001)

16411. Oren, Michel. The enigmatic career of Hernton's *Scarecrow*. Callaloo (29:2) 2006, 608–18.

Karen Hesse

16412. Clarke, Nzingha. Karen Hesse. New York: Rosen Central, 2006. pp. 112. (Library of author biographies.)

John Hewitt (1907–1987)

16413. Heaney, Liam. John Hewitt: a poet of the Antrim Glens. ContRev (286:1673) 2005, 344–50.

Susan Hicks-Beach (Mrs William Hicks-Beach) (b.1878)

16414. Viviani, Aglaia. La donna cancellata: *The Memoirs of the Nameless Mother of the Cardinal Ippolito de' Medici* di Mrs Hicks Beach. LProv (126/127) 2006, 93–7.

Tomson Highway

16415. Howells, Coral Ann. Tomson Highway: *Kiss of the Fur Queen*. *In* (pp. 83–92) **11946**.

Geoffrey Hill

16416. Alcobia-Murphy, Shane. 'Not forgotten or passed over at the proper time': the representation of violent events in contemporary culture. CLR (2) 2005, 19–40.

16417. Buxton, Rachel. Transaction and transcendence: Geoffrey Hill's vision of *Canaan*. CamQ (34:4) 2005, 353–63.

16418. Ciompi, Fausto. *Mundus furiosus*: *Speech! Speech!* di Geoffrey Hill. Soglie (8:1) 2006, 28–55.

16419. Day, Thomas. You read me too well. TLS, 2 June 2006, 9 (review-article).

16420. Greenwell, Garth. 'The pedagogy of martyrdom': 'witness' in Geoffrey Hill's *The Triumph of Love*. LitIm (8:1) 2006, 91–108.

16421. James, Stephen. 'A conflict of opposites': Robert Lowell and Geoffrey Hill. *See* **17270**.

16422. Roberts, Andrew Michael. Geoffrey Hill. Plymouth: Northcote House in assn with the British Council, 2004. pp. xv, 126. (Writers and their work.) Rev. by Martin Dodsworth in Eng (55:211) 2006, 108–14.

16423. Rowland, Antony. Holocaust poetry: awkward poetics in the work of Sylvia Plath, Geoffrey Hill, Tony Harrison and Ted Hughes. *See* **18050**.

16424. Wainwright, Jeffrey. Acceptable words: essays on the poetry of Geoffrey Hill. Manchester; New York: Manchester UP, 2005. pp. xi, 155. Rev. by Thomas Day in TLS, 2 June 2006, 9; by Andrew Michael Roberts in RES (57:232) 2006, 854–6.

Reginald Hill
('Dick Morland', 'Patrick Ruell', 'Charles Underhill')

16425. Ling, Peter J. Identity, allusions, and agency in Reginald Hill's *Good Morning, Midnight*. Clues (24:4) 2006, 59–71.

Susan Hill

16426. Quéma, Anne. Family and symbolic violence in *The Mist in the Mirror*. GothS (8:2) 2006, 114–35.

Brenda Hillman

16427. Hillman, Brenda; Peterson, Katie. Hermetic memory: an exchange on Dickinson between two poets. *See* **9868**.

16428. McCabe, Susan. *Platonic Oxygen*: on Brenda Hillman's *Pieces of Air in the Epic*. DQ (41:2) 2006, 65–71.

Jack Hilton (b.1900)

16429. Pridmore, Joseph. Mass violence and the crowd: the perception of proletarian community in working-class writers of the 1930s. *See* **16059**.

Chester Himes

16430. Crawford, Norlisha. Good, bad, and beautiful: Chester Himes's *Femmes in Harlem*. NWSAJ (18:2) 2006, 193–217.

16431. Story, Ralph D. The dissonant chord: Chester Himes' *Lonely Crusade*. CLAJ (49:3) 2006, 283–304.

Barry Hines

16432. Kirk, John. Figuring the landscape: writing the topographies of community and place. *See* **17045**.

Rolando Hinojosa

16433. Martinez, Manuel Luis. An interview with Rolando Hinojosa-Smith. InR (28:1) 2006, 7–10.

16434. Pollock, Mary Sanders. Crime and community in the Rafe Buenrostro mysteries. Clues (24:3) 2006, 7–14.

Edward Hirsch

16435. HIRSCH, EDWARD; ZAGAJEWSKI, ADAM. Edward Hirsch and Adam Zagajewski: a conversation. FiveP (10:1/2) 2006, 33–44.

Jane Hirshfield (b.1953)

16436. ERWIN, SHEILA. From the interior outward: a talk with poet Jane Hirshfield. BRev (26:3) 2006, 5.

Ndeutala Selma Hishongwa (b.1952)

16437. ORFORD, MARGIE. Transition, trauma, and triumph: contemporary Namibian women's literature. *In* (pp. 159–73) **12216**.

Kaleni Hiyalwa

16438. ORFORD, MARGIE. Transition, trauma, and triumph: contemporary Namibian women's literature. *In* (pp. 159–73) **12216**.

Edward Hoagland

16439. HOAGLAND, EDWARD. Miles from nowhere. ASch (75:3) 2006, 48–63. (British Columbia.)

Will Hobbs

16440. JOHANSON, PAULA. Will Hobbs. New York: Rosen Central, 2006. pp. 112. (Library of author biographies.)

Merle Hodge

16441. MEEHAN, KEVIN. Romance and revolution: reading women's narratives of Caribbean decolonization. *See* **15240**.

16442. ZONANA, JOYCE. 'Tee', 'Cyn-Cyn', 'Cynthia', 'Dou-dou': remembering and forgetting the 'true-true name' in Merle Hodge's *Crick Crack, Monkey*. *In* (pp. 139–54) **11795**.

Philip Hodgins (b.1959)

16443. KANE, PAUL. Philip Hodgins: a note on the life of the work. Agenda (41:1/2) 2005, 144–6.

Daniel Hoffman

16444. GWYNN, R. S. Haunted palaces, trembling strings. *See* **11018**.

Linda Hogan

16445. CASSON, CHRISTINE. 'A forest dreaming': landscape and displacement in the Native American Indian poetry of Linda Hogan. Agenda (41:3/4) 2005, 113–24.

16446. FIANDT, JULIE. Autobiographical activism in the Americas: narratives of personal and cultural healing by Aurora Levins Morales and Linda Hogan. WS (35:6) 2006, 567–84.

Alan Hollinghurst

16447. GRIMSHAW, TAMMY. Hollinghurst's *The Swimming-Pool Library*. Exp (64:4) 2006, 242–5.

Jeremy Hooker (b.1941)

16448. HOOKER, JEREMY. Reflections on 'ground'. *See* **3565**.

Bell Hooks

16449. Bowery, Anne-Marie. Voices from within: Gloria Anzaldúa, bell hooks, and Roberta Bondi. *In* (pp. 51–68) **11916**.

A. D. (Alec Derwent) Hope (b.1907)

16450. James, Clive. An errant oracle: rhymes and rhizomes of Australia in the life of A. D. Hope. TLS, 19 May 2006, 3–4 (review-article).

16451. McCulloch, Ann. Dance of the nomad: a study of the selected notebooks of A. D. Hope. Canberra: Pandanus, Research School of Pacific and Asian Studies, Australian National Univ., in assn with Pacific Linguists, 2005. pp. xxxi, 366. Rev. by Clive James in TLS, 19 May 2006, 3–4.

16452. Milne, W. S. Defending the intellect: A. D. Hope's poetry and criticism. Agenda (41:1/2) 2005, 147–54.

Nalo Hopkinson

16453. Anatol, Giselle Liza. Maternal discourses in Nalo Hopkinson's *Midnight Robber*. AAR (40:1) 2006, 111–24.

16454. Simpson, Hyacinth M. Fantastic alternatives: journeys into the imagination: a conversation with Nalo Hopkinson. JWIL (14:1/2) 2005, 96–112.

Nick Hornby

16455. Murray, Stuart. Autism and the contemporary sentimental: fiction and the narrative fascination of the present. LitMed (25:1) 2006, 24–45.

A. E. Housman

16456. Banfield, Stephen. Gurney and Housman. *See* **16234**.

16457. Behrman, E. J. Housman in Paris. ANQ (19:3) 2006, 30–2.

16458. Schmidt, Michael. The 2006 StAnza lecture: what, how well, why? PRev (96:2) 2006, 65–76. (Canons of taste; poets as critics.)

16459. Woudhuysen, H. R. (ed.). A.E.H.–A.W.P.: a Classical friendship. Tunbridge Wells: Foundling Press, 2006. pp. 68. Rev. by Michael Caines in TLS, 19 May 2006, 33.

Laurence Housman

16460. Sumpter, Caroline. Innocents and epicures: the child, the fairy tale and avant-garde debate in *fin-de-siècle* little magazines. NCC (28:3) 2006, 225–44.

Velina Houston

16461. Jew, Kimberly M. Dismantling the realist character in Velina Hasu Houston's *Tea* and David Henry Hwang's *FOB*. *In* (pp. 187–202) **11849**.

Chenjerai Hove

16462. Berndt, Katrin. Eloquent silence as a mode of identity construction in Chenjerai Hove's novel *Bones*. *In* (pp. 147–58) **12216**.

Richard Howard

16463. Coles, Katharine. Among so many others: dazzling instructions. KR (28:2) 2006, 118–37.

16464. HAMMER, LANGDON. Hall of voices: Richard Howard. Parnassus (29:1/2) 2006, 97–117 (review-article).

16465. HOWARD, RICHARD. Paper trail: selected prose, 1965–2003. *See* **3566**.

Robert E. Howard (1906–1936)

16466. BURGER, PATRICK R. *Red Shadows* through the lens of Northrop Frye's archetypal criticism. DarkM (2:1/2) 2005, 38–55.

16467. BURKE, RUSTY. Robert E. Howard: New Deal heroic fantasist. DarkM (2:1/2) 2005, 18–26.

16468. COFFMAN, FRANK. Robert E. Howard and poetic narrative: the bardic tradition and 'popular modernities'. DarkM (2:1/2) 2005, 4–17.

16469. HALL, MARK. Crash go the civilizations: some notes on Robert E. Howard's use of history and anthropology. DarkM (2:1/2) 2005, 27–37.

16470. NIELSEN, LEON. From Tarzan to Conan: notes on the possible influence of Edgar Rice Burroughs on the writings of Robert E. Howard. BurB (63) 2005, 23–6, 33.

Susan Howe

16471. CLIPPINGER, DAVID W. Resurrecting the ghost: H.D., Susan Howe, and the haven of poetry. *See* **15527**.

16472. GARDNER, THOMAS. A door ajar: contemporary writers and Emily Dickinson. *See* **9865**.

16473. HARRIS, KAPLAN P. Susan Howe's art and poetry, 1968–1974. ConLit (47:3) 2006, 440–71.

16474. MONTGOMERY, WILL. Susan Howe's Renaissance period: metamorphosis and representation in *Pythagorean Silence* and *Defenestration of Prague*. JAStud (40:3) 2006, 615–33.

16475. SAVAGE, ELIZABETH. Love, the lyric, and history in Lorine Niedecker and Susan Howe. *See* **17761**.

16476. SELBY, NICK. 'Created space': mapping America as poem in Gary Snyder's *Mountains and Rivers without End* and Susan Howe's *Secret History of the Dividing Line*. *See* **18550**.

16477. WHITE, JENNY L. The landscapes of Susan Howe's *Thorow*. ConLit (47:2) 2006, 236–60.

Andrew Hudgins

16478. HILL, JANE. Fucked Ivanhoes in the deep obsession of memory: Andrew Hudgins, David Bottoms, and the legacy of war in Southern poetry. WVUPP (51) 2004, 130–9.

W. H. Hudson ('Henry Harford')

16479. SCHMITT, CANNON. Darwin's savage mnemonics. Representations (88) 2004, 55–80.

16480. SHRUBSALL, DENNIS (ed.). The unpublished letters of W. H. Hudson, the first literary environmentalist, 1841–1922. Lewiston, NY; Lampeter: Mellen Press, 2006. 2 vols. pp. vi, 853.

Langston Hughes

16481. Brunner, Edward. Langston Hughes: *Fine Clothes to the Jew*. *In* (pp. 367–75) **11788**.

16482. Castronovo, Russ. Theme for African American literature B. *In* (pp. 29–39) **20098**.

16483. De Santis, Christopher C. (ed.). Langston Hughes: a documentary volume. (Bibl. 2005, 17093.) Rev. by David Chioni Moore in RAL (37:1) 2006, 154–5.

16484. Evans, Nicholas M. Wandering aesthetic, wandering consciousness: diasporic impulses and 'vagrant' desires in Langston Hughes's early poetry. *In* (pp. 151–93) **12180**.

16485. Kutzinski, Vera M. Fearful assymetries: Langston Hughes, Nicolás Guillén, and *Cuba libre*. Diacritics (34:3/4) 2004, 112–42.

16486. Leach, Laurie F. Langston Hughes: a biography. (Bibl. 2004, 17369.) Rev. by Robert Butler in AAR (40:2) 2006, 386–7.

16487. Nardi, Steven A. 'By the pale dull pallor of an old gas light': technology and vision in Langston Hughes's *The Weary Blues*. *In* (pp. 253–68) **12180**.

16488. Ponce, Martin Joseph. Langston Hughes's queer Blues. MLQ (66:4) 2005, 505–37.

16489. Radavich, David. African American drama from the Midwest. MidAmerica (32) 2005, 95–119.

16490. Scott, Jonathan. Advanced, repressed, and popular: Langston Hughes during the Cold War. ColLit (33:2) 2006, 30–51.

16491. —— Socialist joy in the writing of Langston Hughes. Columbia; London: Missouri UP, 2006. pp. xiv, 248.

Richard Hughes

16492. Holmqvist, Ivo. Richard Hughes: an emendation. NQ (53:3) 2006, 356–7.

Ted Hughes

16493. Archer, Jacque Day. *The Iron Giant*: a gun with a soul. *In* (pp. 256–68) **12548**.

16494. Bassnett, Susan. Writing and translating. *In* (pp. 173–83) **3186**.

16495. Beer, John. Coleridge, Ted Hughes, and Sylvia Plath: mythology and identity. *In* (pp. 123–41) **13735**.

16496. Churchwell, Sarah. 'Your sentence was mine too': reading Sylvia Plath in Ted Hughes's *Birthday Letters*. *In* (pp. 260–87) **3405**.

16497. Clanchy, Kate. Gendering poetry. *See* **13723**.

16498. Craik, Roger. 'High and dry and dead': a source for Ted Hughes's *Pike*. ANQ (19:1) 2006, 59–62.

16499. Gardini, Nicola. Il poeta importante: come fare un ritratto di Ted Hughes. PoesiaM (210) 2006, 39–44.

16500. Koren, Yehuda; Negev, Eilat. A lover of unreason: the life and tragic death of Assia Wevill. London: Robson, 2006. pp. xviii, 280, (plates) 24.

16501. Middlebrook, Diane. The poetry of Sylvia Plath and Ted Hughes: call and response. *In* (pp. 156–71) **18038**.

16502. —— Stevens in the marriage of Sylvia Plath and Ted Hughes. *See* **18647**.

16503. Miller, Karl. Cambridge men. *See* **16231**.

16504. Osborne, Thomas. Polarities of Englishness: Larkin, Hughes and national culture. *See* **17000**.

16505. Ou, Hong. The Taoist tendency in Ted Hughes's poetry. FLS (118) 2006, 70–7. (In Chinese.)

16506. Peel, Robin. From *Dogs* to *Crow*: Ted Hughes and a 'world lost' 1956–1970. Eng (55:212) 2006, 157–80.

16507. Raine, Craig. Ordinary, sacred things: Ted Hughes and the visionary's double vision. TLS, 24 Nov. 2006, 11–13.

16508. Roberts, Neil. Ted Hughes: a literary life. Basingstoke; New York: Palgrave Macmillan, 2006. pp. x, 254. (Literary lives.)

16509. Rowland, Antony. Holocaust poetry: awkward poetics in the work of Sylvia Plath, Geoffrey Hill, Tony Harrison and Ted Hughes. *See* **18050**.

16510. Storey, H. Wayne. A question of punctuation and 'ear[s] for dissenting voices': introduction to *Textual Cultures* 1.2. *See* **18051**.

16511. Weissbort, Daniel. The troubled mechanic: Ted Hughes and translation. PNRev (32:4) 2006, 11.

E. M. (Edith Maude) Hull

16512. Frost, Laura. The romance of cliché: E. M. Hull, D. H. Lawrence, and interwar erotic fiction. *In* (pp. 94–118) **12024**.

Keri Hulme

16513. Barker, Clare. From narrative prosthesis to disability counternarrative: reading the politics of difference in *Potiki* and *the bone people*. *See* **16177**.

16514. Battista, Jon. Magic fire women: balance and imbalance in the depiction of Maori women in Maori literature in English. *In* (pp. 16–24) **11731**.

16515. Wilson, Janet. Suffering and survival: body and voice in recent Maori writing. *In* (pp. 425–38) **8374**.

T. E. Hulme

16516. Comentale, Edward P.; Gąsiorek, Andrzej (eds). T. E. Hulme and the question of Modernism. Aldershot; Burlington, VT: Ashgate, 2006. pp. viii, 248.

Josephine Humphreys

16517. Locklear, Erica Abrams. 'What are you?': exploring racial categorization in *Nowhere Else on Earth*. SoLJ (39:1) 2006, 33–53.

T. A. G. (Thomas Arthur Guy) Hungerford (b.1915)

16518. Crouch, Michael. The literary larrikin: a critical biography of T. A. G. Hungerford. Crawley: Western Australia UP, 2005. pp. xix, 260, (plates) 8.

Zora Neale Hurston

16519. Anon. Documents on Zora Neale Hurston from the Barnard College Archives. SFO (3:2) 2005.

16520. Angelou, Maya (foreword). *Dust Tracks on a Road*: the restored text established by the Library of America. New York: HarperPerennial, 2006. pp. xii, 308, (plates) 16.

16521. Bosničová, Nina. Changing perspectives on religion in African American women's autobiographies. *See* **14441**.

16522. Cartwright, Keith. 'To walk with the storm': Oya as the transformative 'I' of Zora Neale Hurston's Afro-Atlantic callings. AL (78:4) 2006, 741–67.

16523. duCille, Ann. The mark of Zora: reading between the lines of legend and legacy. SFO (3:2) 2005.

16524. Duck, Leigh Anne. The nation's region: Southern Modernism, segregation, and US nationalism. *See* **14995**.

16525. Hoeller, Hildegard. Racial currency: Zora Neale Hurston's *The Gilded Six-Bits* and the gold-standard debate. AL (77:4) 2005, 761–85.

16526. Jirousek, Lori. Ethnics and ethnographers: Zora Neale Hurston and Anzia Yezierska. JML (29:2) 2006, 19–32.

16527. Kaplan, Carla. Editing an icon. SFO (3:2) 2005.

16528. Kraut, Anthea. Everybody's fire dance: Zora Neale Hurston and American dance history. SFO (3:2) 2005.

16529. Patterson, Tiffany Ruby. Zora Neale Hurston and a history of Southern life. (Bibl. 2005, 17137.) Rev. by Harry A. Reed in JAH (93:1) 2006, 262–3; by Lori Robison in JSH (72:4) 2006, 977–8; by Nathan Grant in AAR (40:3) 2006, 593–5; by Rachel Farebrother in JAStud (40:3) 2006, 672–3.

16530. Ransom, Portia Boulware. Black love and the Harlem renaissance: an essay in African American literary criticism. *See* **17017**.

16531. Seguin, Robert. Cultural revolution, the discourse of intellectuals, and other folk tales. *In* (pp. 95–115) **14159**.

16532. Sivils, Matthew Wynn. Reading trees in Southern literature. *See* **15833**.

16533. Spencer, Stephen. Racial politics and the literary reception of Zora Neale Hurston's *Their Eyes Were Watching God*. *In* (pp. 111–26) **11783**.

16534. Wall, Cheryl A. Zora Neale Hurston: *Their Eyes Were Watching God*. *In* (pp. 376–83) **11788**.

16535. —— Zora Neale Hurston's essays: on *Art and Such*. SFO (3:2) 2005.

16536. Warnes, Andrew. Guantánamo, Eatonville, Accompong: barbecue and the diaspora in the writings of Zora Neale Hurston. JAStud (40:2) 2006, 367–89.

16537. West, M. Genevieve. Zora Neale Hurston and American literary culture. (Bibl. 2005, 17142.) Rev. by Deborah Hooker in SoLJ (39:1) 2006, 128–32.

Aldous Huxley

16538. Birnbaum, Milton. Aldous Huxley: a quest for values. (Bibl. 1973, 12167.) New Brunswick, NJ: Transaction, 2006. pp. xxii, 230. (Second ed.: first ed. 1971.)

16539. Meyers, Jeffrey. Domenichino and Huxley's *Antic Hay*. NCL (36:3) 2006, 10–12.

16540. Minogue, Sally; Palmer, Andrew. Confronting the abject: women and dead babies in modern English fiction. *See* **18524**.

16541. Prindle, R. E. Tarzan and the river: part iii. *See* **14948**.

Elspeth Huxley

16542. Lassner, Phyllis. Colonial strangers: women writing at the end of the British Empire. (Bibl. 2005, 17153.) Rev. by Jason Mezey in MFS (52:3) 2006, 738–41; by Faye Hammill in YES (36:2) 2006, 281–2.

David Henry Hwang

16543. Bak, John S. *Vestis virum reddit*: the gender politics of drag in Williams's *A Streetcar Named Desire* and Hwang's *M. Butterfly*. *See* **19165**.

16544. Bavaro, Vincenzo. Politiche di gender e soggettivazione nazionale nell'America asiatica. *In* (pp. 60–93) **11954**.

16545. —— Lo sciopero in scena: *story-telling* e mascolinità in *The Dance and the Railroad* di David H. Hwang. *In* (pp. 193–216) **11954**.

16546. De Wagter, Caroline. Performing the American multi-ethnic 'Other' in Hwang's *Bondage* and Geiogamah's *Foghorn*. BELL (ns 4) 2006, 81–92.

16547. Jew, Kimberly M. Dismantling the realist character in Velina Hasu Houston's *Tea* and David Henry Hwang's *FOB*. *In* (pp. 187–202) **11849**.

Witi Ihimaera

16548. Battista, Jon. Magic fire women: balance and imbalance in the depiction of Maori women in Maori literature in English. *In* (pp. 16–24) **11731**.

16549. Fox, Alistair. The symbolic function of the operatic allusions in Witi Ihimaera's *The Dream Swimmer*. JPW (42:1) 2006, 4–17.

Chukwuemeka Ike

16550. Onuekwusi, Jasper A. Realism as the great quest of the novel in Chukwuemeka Ike's *Our Children Are Coming*. *In* (pp. 227–36) **11860**.

Lawson Fusao Inada

16551. Holliday, Shawn. Lawson Fusao Inada, Charles Mingus, and *The Great Bassist*. NCL (36:4) 2006, 11–12.

William Inge

16552. Johnson, Jeff. Kushner, Inge and *Little Sheba*: strange bedfellows. *In* (pp. 28–40) **16962**.

16553. Voss, Ralph F. Tennessee Williams's *Sweet Bird of Youth* and William Inge's *Bus Riley's Back in Town*: coincidences from a friendship. *See* **19182**.

Esiaba Irobi

16554. Diala, Isidore. Violent obsessions: Esiaba Irobi's drama and the discourse of terrorism. ModDr (49:1) 2006, 60–75.

John Irving (b.1942)

16555. Eisenstein, Paul. On the ethics of sanctified sacrifice: John Irving's *A Prayer for Owen Meany.* LIT (17:1) 2006, 1–21.

Christopher Isherwood

16556. Carr, Jamie M. Queer times: Christopher Isherwood's modernity. London; New York: Routledge, 2006. pp. ix, 178. (Studies in major literary authors.)

16557. Copley, Antony. A spiritual Bloomsbury: Hinduism and homosexuality in the lives and writings of Edward Carpenter, E. M. Forster, and Christopher Isherwood. *See* **9412**.

16558. Izzo, David Garrett. Then and now: W. H. Auden, Christopher Isherwood, Tony Kushner, and Fascist creep. *In* (pp. 56–97) **16962**.

Kazuo Ishiguro

16559. Ackerley, Chris. 'What precisely is this "greatness"?': Kazuo Ishiguro's *The Remains of the Day* and the well-made play. *In* (pp. 461–72) **8374**.

16560. Chong, Kevin. Interview with Kazuo Ishiguro. BkCan (34:5) 2005, 17–19.

16561. Ekelund, Bo G. Misrecognizing history: complicitous genres in Kazuo Ishiguro's *The Remains of the Day*. IFR (32:1/2) 2005, 70–90.

16562. Forsythe, Ruth. Cultural displacement and the mother–daughter relationship in Kazuo Ishiguro's *A Pale View of Hills*. WVUPP (52) 2005, 99–108.

16563. Foster, John Wilson. 'All the long traditions': loyalty and service in Barry and Ishiguro. *In* (pp. 99–119) **14627**.

16564. Marcus, Amit. Kazuo Ishiguro's *The Remains of the Day*: the discourse of self-deception. PartA (4:1) 2006, 129–50.

16565. Sim, Wai-chew. Globalization and dislocation in the novels of Kazuo Ishiguro. Lewiston, NY; Lampeter: Mellen Press, 2006. pp. xiii, 305.

16566. Stanton, Katherine. Cosmopolitan fictions: ethics, politics, and global change in the works of Kazuo Ishiguro, Michael Ondaatje, Jamaica Kincaid, and J. M. Coetzee. London; New York: Routledge, 2006. pp. vii, 103. (Literary criticism and cultural theory.)

Arturo Islas

16567. Aldama, Frederick Luis (ed.). Critical mappings of Arturo Islas's fictions. Tempe, AZ: Bilingual Press/Editorial Bilingue, 2004. pp. 300.

David Ives

16568. Ives, David. The exploding rose: David Ives on the one-act play. Dramatist (8:4) 2006, 22–3.

Charles Jackson

16569. Crowley, John W. Charles Jackson's *Fall of Valor* revaluated. SewR (114:2) 2006, 259–77.

Shelley Jackson (b.1963)

16570. HAYLES, N. KATHERINE. My mother was a computer: digital subjects and literary texts. *See* **18622**.

16571. SÁNCHEZ-PALENCIA CARAZO, CAROLINA; ALMAGRO JIMÉNEZ, MANUEL. Gathering the limbs of the text in Shelley Jackson's *Patchwork Girl*. Atl (28:1) 2006, 115–29.

Shirley Jackson

16572. MURPHY, BERNICE M. (ed.). Shirley Jackson: essays on the literary legacy. (Bibl. 2005, 17181.) Rev. by Laura Dabundo in GothS (8:2) 2006, 144–6.

Violet Jacob (1863–1946)

16573. GORDON, KATHERINE (ed.). Voices from their ain countrie: the poems of Marion Angus and Violet Jacob. *See* **14442**.

Josephine Jacobsen

16574. DEEN, ROSEMARY. Dis-covering the words: language and poetry in Josephine Jacobsen. LitIm (8:2) 2006, 285–302.

C. L. R. (Cyril Lionel Robert) James (1901–1989)

16575. GAIR, CHRISTOPHER (ed.). Beyond boundaries: C. L. R. James and postnational studies. London; Ann Arbor, MI: Pluto Press, 2006. pp. 202. Rev. by Paul Giles in JAStud (40:3) 2006, 662–3.

16576. MEEHAN, KEVIN. Romance and revolution: reading women's narratives of Caribbean decolonization. *See* **15240**.

16577. STEPHENS, MICHELLE ANN. Black empire: the masculine global imaginary of Caribbean intellectuals in the United States, 1914–1962. Durham, NC; London: Duke UP, 2005. pp. xii, 366. (New Americanists.) Rev. by Charlie Samuya Veric in AmQ (58:1) 2006, 255–64.

16578. WEBB, CONSTANCE (ed.). The Nobbie stories for children and adults. Foreword by Anna Grimshaw. Lincoln; London: Nebraska UP, 2006. pp. xxi, 119.

16579. WURTZ, JAMES F. 'Liberation and oppression are inextricably bound': sports, narrative, and the colonial experience. *See* **12227**.

Clive James (b.1939)

16580. JAMES, CLIVE. Listening for the flavor: a notebook. Poetry (189:3) 2006, 219–27.

P. D. James

16581. CINGAL, DELPHINE. Rupture du contrat social: les meurtrières dans l'œuvre de P. D. James. Cycnos (23:2) 2006, 95–108.

Storm Jameson

16582. BIRKETT, JENNIFER. Margaret Storm Jameson and the London PEN Centre: mobilising commitment. EREA (4:2) 2006, 81–9.

16583. MURAT, JEAN-CHRISTOPHE. L'anglaise et le Continent: la seconde guerre mondiale mise en textes dans les 'Novels of the Crisis' de Margaret Storm Jameson. EtBr (30) 2006, 55–69.

Randall Jarrell

16584. Ford, Mark. A lover's complaints. TLS, 20 Jan. 2006, 24 (review article).

16585. Friedlander, Benjamin. The best years of our lives: Randall Jarrell's war poetry. *In* (pp. 83–111) **13763**.

16586. Kennedy, X. J. Greensboro and the riddles of Randall Jarrell. SewR (113:3) 2005, 440–9. (State of letters.)

16587. Knoepflmacher, U. C. The Hansel and Gretel syndrome: survivorship fantasies and parental desertion. *See* **16913**.

16588. Meyers, Jeffrey. Allusions in Jarrell's *Pictures from an Institution*. NCL (36:2) 2006, 5–8.

16589. Oostdijk, Diederik. Randall Jarrell and the age of consumer culture. *In* (pp. 113–32) **13763**.

16590. Pritchard, William H. Randall Jarrell's poetry. LitIm (8:2) 2006, 175–93.

Robinson Jeffers

16591. Copestake, Ian D. Jeffers and the inhumanism of James Dickey's *To the White Sea*. *See* **15490**.

16592. Dooley, Patrick K. The inhuman metaphysics of Edward Abbey and Robinson Jeffers: 'to travel down the strange falling scale'. *See* **14355**.

'Gish Jen' (Lillian Gen)

16593. Byers, Michele. Material bodies and performative identities: Mona, Neil, and the Promised Land. *See* **18307**.

Jerry B. Jenkins

16594. Mleynek, Sherryll. The rhetoric of the 'Jewish problem' in the Left Behind novels. *See* **16982**.

16595. Morgan, David T. The new Brothers Grimm and their Left Behind fairy tales. *See* **16983**.

Elizabeth Jennings

16596. Goatly, Andrew. An analysis of Elizabeth Jennings's *One Flesh*: poem as product and process. JLS (34:2) 2005, 139–63.

Humphrey Jennings

16597. Remy, Michel. British Surrealist writing and painting: re-marking the margin. *In* (pp. 171–81) **11733**.

Ruth Prawer Jhabvala

16598. Frago, Marta. Arte y seudoarte: patrones de ironía en las novelas y guiones de Ruth Prawer Jhabvala. Atl (28:2) 2006, 109–22.

Ha Jin (b.1956)

16599. Walsh, William. Shakespeare's lion and Ha Jin's tiger: the interplay of imagination and reality. PLL (42:4) 2006, 339–59.

16600. Zhou, Xiaojing. Writing otherwise than as a 'native informant': Ha Jin's poetry. *In* (pp. 274–94) **11995**.

Rita Joe

16601. McKegney, Sam. 'I was at war – but it was a gentle war': the power of the positive in Rita Joe's autobiography. AICRJ (30:1) 2006, 33–52.

Angela Johnson (b.1961)

16602. Hinton, KaaVonia. Angela Johnson: poetic prose. Lanham, MD; London: Scarecrow Press, 2006. pp. xv, 107.

Charles Johnson (b.1948)

16603. Byrd, Rudolph P. Charles Johnson's novels: writing the American palimpsest. Bloomington: Indiana UP, 2005. pp. xi, 215.

16604. Donovan, Christopher. Postmodern counternarratives: irony and audience in the novels of Paul Auster, Don DeLillo, Charles Johnson and Tim O'Brien. *See* **14515**.

16605. Keizer, Arlene R. Black subjects: identity formation in the contemporary narrative of slavery. (Bibl. 2005, 17207.) Rev. by Susan L. Blake in AAR (40:3) 2006, 587–8; by Susan Belasco in AL (78:3) 2006, 640–2.

16606. Storhoff, Gary. Understanding Charles Johnson. (Bibl. 2005, 17209.) Rev. by Marc Steinberg in AAR (40:1) 2006, 194–6.

Colin Johnson (Mudrooroo Narogin)

16607. Archer-Lean, Clare. Cross-cultural analysis of the writings of Thomas King and Colin Johnson (Mudrooroo). *See* **16877**.

16608. Clark, Maureen. Terror as White female in Mudrooroo's vampire trilogy. JCL (41:2) 2006, 121–38.

Diane Johnson

16609. Johnson, Diane. Writing *The Shining*. *In* (pp. 55–61) **13202**.

George Clayton Johnson (b.1929)

16610. Tinnell, Robert. *Logan's Run* to relevance. *In* (pp. 217–24) **12548**.

James Weldon Johnson

16611. Andrade, Heather Russell. Revising critical judgments of *The Autobiography of an Ex-Colored Man*. AAR (40:2) 2006, 257–70.

16612. Barnhart, Bruce. Chronopolitics and race, rag-time and symphonic time in *The Autobiography of an Ex-Colored Man*. AAR (40:3) 2006, 551–69.

16613. Biers, Katherine. Syncope fever: James Weldon Johnson and the Black phonographic voice. Representations (96) 2006, 99–125.

16614. Dowling, Robert M. A marginal man in Black bohemia: James Weldon Johnson in the New York Tenderloin. *In* (pp. 117–32) **8435**.

16615. Gebhard, Caroline. Inventing a 'Negro literature': race, dialect, and gender in the early work of Paul Laurence Dunbar, James Weldon Johnson, and Alice Dunbar-Nelson. *In* (pp. 162–78) **8435**.

Linton Kwesi Johnson

16616. Dawson, Ashley. Linton Kwesi Johnson's dub poetry and the political aesthetics of carnival in Britain. SmAx (11:1) 2006, 54–69.

Maggie Pogue Johnson (*fl.*1910)

16617. Bennett, Paula Bernat. Rewriting Dunbar: realism, Black women poets, and the genteel. *In* (pp. 146–61) **8435**.

George Johnston ('Shane Martin') (1912–1970)

16618. Brown, Max. Charmian and George: the marriage of George Johnston and Charmian Clift. *See* **15188**.

Jennifer Johnston

16619. Cardin, Bertrand. Reflections in Jennifer Johnston's *This Is Not a Novel*. CJIS (31:2) 2005, 34–41.

16620. Yang, Jincai. Three metaphors in Jennifer Johnston's *The Railway Station Man*. FLS (117) 2006, 82–9. (In Chinese.)

Wayne Johnston

16621. MacLeod, Alexander. History *versus* geography in Wayne Johnston's *The Colony of Unrequited Dreams*. CanL (189) 2006, 69–83.

Elizabeth Jolley

16622. Lindsay, Elaine. 'As one whom his mother comforteth, so will I comfort you': Elizabeth Jolley's catalogue of consolation. Southerly (66:1) 2006, 52–65.

16623. Lurie, Caroline (sel. and introd.). Learning to dance: Elizabeth Jolley: her life and work. Camberwell, Vic.; New York: Viking, 2006. pp. 305.

Alice Eleanor Jones

16624. Yaszek, Lisa. From *Ladies Home Journal* to *The Magazine of Fantasy and Science Fiction*: 1950s SF, the offbeat romance story, and the case of Alice Eleanor Jones. *In* (pp. 76–96) **13537**.

Diana Wynne Jones

16625. Butler, Charles. Four British fantasists: place and culture in the children's fantasies of Penelope Lively, Alan Garner, Diana Wynne Jones, and Susan Cooper. *See* **17234**.

16626. Mendlesohn, Farah. Diana Wynne Jones: children's literature and the fantastic tradition. (Bibl. 2005, 17224.) Rev. by David Bratman in Mythprint (43:1/2) 2006, 12–13; by Michael Levy in JFA (16:3) 2006, 253–6; by Mike Cadden in CLAQ (31:1) 2006, 97–9.

Edward P. Jones

16627. McCarron, Bill. 'Most lost' in Edward P. Jones's *Lost in the City*. NCL (36:2) 2006, 11–12.

Gayl Jones

16628. Chandra, Sarika. Interruptions: tradition, borders, and narrative in Gayl Jones's *Mosquito*. *In* (pp. 137–53) **16637**.

16629. Clabough, Casey. 'Toward an all-inclusive structure': the early fiction of Gayl Jones. Callaloo (29:2) 2006, 634–57.

16630. Epes, Heather E. Identity and conceptual limitation in Gayl Jones's *The Healing*: from turtle to human being. *In* (pp. 11–39) **16637**.

16631. Fahy, Thomas. Unsilencing lesbianism in the early fiction of Gayl Jones. *In* (pp. 203–20) **16637**.

16632. Gordon, Nickesia S. On the couch with Dr Fraud: insidious trauma and distorted female community in Gayl Jones' *Eva's Man*. Ob3 (6:1) 2005, 66–89.

16633. Griffiths, Jennifer. Uncanny spaces: trauma, cultural memory, and the female body in Gayl Jones's *Corregidora* and Maxine Hong Kingston's *The Woman Warrior*. StudN (38:3) 2006, 353–70.

16634. Hawkins, Alfonso W., Jr. A nonnegotiable Blues catharsis in character: Billie Holiday in *Lady Sings the Blues* and Ursa Corregidora in *Corregidora*. CLAJ (50:1) 2006, 37–63.

16635. Li, Stephanie. Love and the trauma of resistance in Gayl Jones's *Corregidora*. Callaloo (29:1) 2006, 131–50.

16636. Mills, Fiona. Telling the untold tale: Afro-Latino/a identifications in the work of Gayl Jones. *In* (pp. 91–115) **16637**.

16637. —— (ed.); Mitchell, Keith (asst ed.). After the pain: essays on Gayl Jones. New York; Frankfurt: Lang, 2006. pp. xvi, 266. (African American literature and culture, 8.)

16638. Mitchell, Keith B. 'Trouble in mind': (re)visioning myth, sexuality, and race in Gayl Jones's *Corregidora*. *In* (pp. 155–71) **16637**.

16639. Rambsy, Howard, II. Things deserving echoes: Gayl Jones's liberating poetry. *In* (pp. 221–39) **16637**.

16640. Stallings, L. H. From mules to turtle and unicorn women: the gender-folk revolution and the legacy of the Obeah in Gayl Jones's *The Healing*. *In* (pp. 65–89) **16637**.

16641. Terry, Jill. 'reads kinda like jazz in they rhythm': Gayl Jones's recent jazz conversations. *In* (pp. 117–36) **16637**.

16642. Venugopal, Shubha. Textual transformations and female metamorphosis: reading Gayl Jones's *The Healing*. *In* (pp. 31–63) **16637**.

Gwyneth Jones ('Ann Halam')

16643. Hollinger, Veronica. 'Prefutural tension': Gwyneth Jones's gradual apocalypse. *In* (pp. 326–39) **13537**.

Madison Jones

16644. Gretlund, Jan Nordby. Madison Jones' garden of innocence. Odense: UP of Southern Denmark, 2005. pp. 207. Rev. by Jeffrey J. Folks in SAtlR (70:4) 2005, 149–52.

Erica Jong

16645. Jong, Erica. Seducing the demon: writing for my life. New York: Tarcher/Putnam, 2006. pp. 279.

June Jordan

16646. Kinloch, Valerie. June Jordan: her life and letters. Westport, CT; London: Praeger, 2006. pp. xv, 200. (Women writers of color.)

Gabriel Josipovici

16647. Josipovici, Gabriel. The singer on the shore: essays, 1991–2004. *See* **6179**.

James Joyce

16648. Anyfanti, Alexandra. Time, space, and consciousness in James Joyce's *Ulysses*. HJS (4:2) 2003/04.

16649. Armand, Louis. From hypertext to vortext: notes on materiality & language. HJS (4:2) 2003/04.

16650. —— Mind factory: from artifice to intelligence. HJS (6:1) 2005.

16651. —— On relativity, synaesthesia and materiality. HJS (7:1) 2006.

16652. —— Writing after: Joyce, Cage. HJS (5:1) 2004.

16653. —— (ed.). JoyceMedia: James Joyce, hypermedia & textual genetics. Prague: Litteraria Pragensia, 2004. pp. xii, 175. Rev. by Ben Leubner in JJLS (20:2) 2006, 4–5.

16654. Attridge, Derek (ed.). The Cambridge companion to James Joyce. (Bibl. 2005, 17244.) Rev. by Janine Utell in JMMLA (38:2) 2005, 155–61.

16655. —— James Joyce's *Ulysses*: a casebook. (Bibl. 2005, 17245.) Rev. by John Nash in RES (56:223) 2005, 164–6; by Finn Fordham in Mod/Mod (13:2) 2006, 367–73.

16656. Balsamo, Gian. Joyce's messianism: Dante, negative existence, and the messianic self. (Bibl. 2005, 17246.) Rev. by Gerald Gillespie in JJLS (20:1) 2006, 12–13.

16657. Baumann, Andrew E. 'The river ever runs, & Anna calls': a Joyce–Deleuzian *billet deux*. HJS (5:2) 2005.

16658. Bénéjam, Valérie. Parallax opoponax. HJS (7:1) 2006.

16659. —— The reprocessing of trash in *Ulysses*: recycling and (post)creation. HJS (5:1) 2004.

16660. Beplate, Justin. Now and then again. *See* **14663**.

16661. Berman, Jessica. Comparative colonialisms: Joyce, Anand, and the question of engagement. Mod/Mod (13:3) 2006, 465–85.

16662. Borg, Ruben. Two Ps in a pod: on time in *Finnegans Wake*. JML (29:1) 2005, 76–93.

16663. Brivic, Sheldon. Joyce and the invention of language. *In* (pp. 53–69) **16699**.

16664. —— Joyce's reverse advertisement for himself in *Finnegans Wake*. HJS (5:2) 2005.

16665. Brockman, William S. *Ulysses*: bibliography revisited. *In* (pp. 171–91) **16699**.

16666. Brooker, Joseph. Joyce's critics: transitions in reading and culture. (Bibl. 2004, 17569.) Rev. by Joseph Kelly in JJLS (20:2) 2006, 13.

16667. Brown, Richard. Joyce's Englishman: 'that het'rogeneous thing' from Stephen's Blake and Dowland to Defoe's 'true-born Englishman'. *In* (pp. 33–49) **16695**.

16668. Bulson, Eric. The Cambridge introduction to James Joyce. Cambridge; New York: CUP, 2006. pp. xii, 139. (Cambridge introductions to literature.)

16669. CEIA, CARLOS. Modernism, Joyce, and Portuguese literature. CLCWeb (8:1) 2006.

16670. CHAPMAN, WAYNE K. Joyce and Yeats: Easter 1916 and the Great War. NewHR (10:4) 2006, 137–51.

16671. CHENG, VINCENT J. Nation without borders: Joyce, cosmopolitanism, and the inauthentic Irishman. *In* (pp. 212–33) **16695**.

16672. CHERTOFF, DANIEL S. Joyce's *Ulysses* and the Book of Esther. Exp (64:3) 2006, 151–3.

16673. CHEUSE, ALAN. Rereading *A Portrait of the Artist as a Young Man*. SewR (114:3) 2006, 448–55. (State of letters.)

16674. CRIVELLI, RENZO S. Joyce as university teacher and the 'south Slav question'. *In* (pp. 121–32) **12076**.

16675. CULLETON, CLAIRE A. Joyce and the G-men: J. Edgar Hoover's manipulation of Modernism. (Bibl. 2004, 17576.) Rev. by Zack Bowen in JJLS (20:1) 2006, 17.

16676. DETTMAR, KEVIN J. H. Bookcases, slipcases, uncut leaves: the anxiety of the gentleman's library. *See* **312**.

16677. DEVLIN, KIMBERLY J. En-gendered choice and agency in *Ulysses*. *In* (pp. 70–87) **16699**.

16678. —— Taste and consumption in *Ulysses*. Dublin: National Library of Ireland, 2004. pp. 31. (Joyce studies 2004, 9.) Rev. by Timothy J. Sutton in JJLS (20:1) 2006, 8–9.

16679. DIBATTISTA, MARIA. This is not a movie: *Ulysses* and cinema. Mod/Mod (13:2) 2006, 219–35.

16680. DOWNING, GREGORY M. Joycean pop culture: fragments toward an institutional history and futurology. *In* (pp. 117–34) **16699**.

16681. DUMITRESCU, ALEXANDRA. Bootstrapping *Finnegans Wake*. HJS (7:1) 2006.

16682. EMIG, RAINER (ed.). *Ulysses*: James Joyce. (Bibl. 2004, 17584.) Rev. by Finn Fordham in Mod/Mod (13:2) 2006, 367–73.

16683. FARGNOLI, A. NICHOLAS. James Joyce's Catholic moments. Dublin: National Library of Ireland, 2004. pp. 23. (Joyce studies 2004, 10.) Rev. by Timothy J. Sutton in JJLS (20:1) 2006, 8–9.

16684. —— GILLESPIE, MICHAEL PATRICK. Critical companion to James Joyce. New York: Facts on File, 2006. pp. xiv, 450. (Facts on File library of world literature.)

16685. FOGARTY, ANNE. Parnellism and the politics of memory: revising *Ivy Day in the Committee Room*. *In* (pp. 104–21) **16695**.

16686. —— MARTIN, TIMOTHY (eds). Joyce on the threshold. (Bibl. 2005, 17274.) Rev. by Kevin J. H. Dettmar in JJLS (20:2) 2006, 12.

16687. FORDHAM, FINN. Spooky Joyce. Mod/Mod (13:2) 2006, 367–73 (review-article).

16688. —— The universalization of *Finnegans Wake* and the real HCE. *In* (pp. 198–211) **16695**.

16689. Franke, William. Linguistic repetition as theological revelation in Christian epic tradition: the case of Joyce's *Finnegans Wake*. Neophilologus (90:1) 2006, 155–72.

16690. Freedman, Ariela. Did it flow? Bridging aesthetics and history in Joyce's *Ulysses*. Mod/Mod (13:1) 2006, 107–22.

16691. Gabler, Hans Walter. The rocky road to *Ulysses*. Dublin: National Library of Ireland, 2004. pp. 47. (Joyce studies 2004, 15.) Rev. by Edmund L. Epstein in JJLS (20:1) 2006, 10–11.

16692. Germoni, Karine. From Joyce to Beckett: the Beckettian dramatic interior monologue. *See* **14681**.

16693. Gibbons, Luke. Spaces of time through times of space: Joyce, Ireland and colonial modernity. FDR (1) 2005, 71–85.

16694. Gibson, Andrew. 'That stubborn Irish thing': *A Portrait of the Artist* and history: chapter 1. *In* (pp. 85–103) **16695**.

16695. —— Platt, Len (eds). Joyce, Ireland, Britain. Foreword by Sebastian D. G. Knowles. Gainesville: Florida UP, 2006. pp. viii, 243. (Florida James Joyce.)

16696. Gibson, George Cinclair. Wake rites: the ancient Irish rituals of *Finnegans Wake*. Gainesville: Florida UP, 2005. pp. xiv, 277. (Florida James Joyce.) Rev. by Catherine Simpson Kalish in JJLS (20:2) 2006, 14.

16697. Gillespie, Michael Patrick. Edna O'Brien and the lives of James Joyce. *In* (pp. 78–91) **17794**.

16698. —— James Joyce: *Ulysses*. *In* (pp. 384–92) **11788**.

16699. —— Fargnoli, A. Nicholas (eds). *Ulysses* in critical perspective. Foreword by Sebastian D. G. Knowles. Gainesville: Florida UP, 2006. pp. x, 225. (Florida James Joyce.) Rev. by Stacey Herbert in JJLS (20:2) 2006, 10–11.

16700. Gordon, John. Joyce and reality: the empirical strikes back. (Bibl. 2004, 17594.) Rev. by Sebastian Knowles in JJLS (20:2) 2006, 6–7.

16701. —— The m'intosh murder mystery. JML (29:1) 2005, 94–101.

16702. Groden, Michael. Before and after: the manuscripts in textual and genetic criticism of *Ulysses*. *In* (pp. 152–70) **16699**.

16703. —— Problems of annotation in a digital *Ulysses*. HJS (4:2) 2003/04.

16704. Gunn, Ian; Wright, Mark. Visualising Joyce. HJS (7:1) 2006.

16705. Harrington, Judith. James Joyce: suburban tenor. Dublin: National Library of Ireland, 2005. pp. 43, (plates) 3. (Joyce studies 2004, 16.) Rev. by Edmund L. Epstein in JJLS (20:1) 2006, 10–11.

16706. Herr, Cheryl Temple. Joyce and the art of shaving. Dublin: National Library of Ireland, 2004. pp. 27. (Joyce studies 2004, 11.) Rev. by Timothy J. Sutton in JJLS (20:1) 2006, 8–9.

16707. Horowitz, Evan. *Ulysses*: mired in the universal. Mod/Mod (13:1) 2006, 123–41.

16708. Hutton, Clare. Joyce, the 'Library' episode, and the institution of revivalism. *In* (pp. 122–38) **16695**.

16709. Jaurretche, Colleen (ed.). Beckett, Joyce and the art of the negative. Amsterdam; New York: Rodopi, 2005. pp. 246. (European Joyce studies, 16.) Rev. by Patrick Bixby in JJLS (20:2) 2006, 8–9.

16710. Jones, Ellen Carol; Beja, Morris (eds). Twenty-first Joyce. (Bibl. 2004, 17608.) Rev. by Eric D. Smith in SAtlR (71:1) 2006, 173–6.

16711. Kim, Sharon. Edith Wharton and epiphany. *See* **19101**.

16712. Knowles, Sebastian D. G. Humor detection in *Ulysses*. Dublin: National Library of Ireland, 2004. pp. 35. (Joyce studies 2004, 12.) Rev. by Timothy J. Sutton in JJLS (20:1) 2006, 8–9.

16713. Latham, Sean. Joyce's Modernism. Dublin: National Library of Ireland, 2005. pp. 55. (Joyce studies 2004, 17.) Rev. by Edmund L. Epstein in JJLS (20:1) 2006, 10–11.

16714. LeBlanc, Jim. Being-for-others in *Two Gallants*: sycophancy and symbiosis. HJS (7:1) 2006.

16715. Lent, John. Transitory closure in Mavis Gallant's *In Transit*: a writer's view of the transition from modern to postmodern poetics in short fiction. *In* (pp. 51–69) **16036**.

16716. Lernout, Geert. James Joyce, reader. Dublin: National Library of Ireland, 2004. pp. 39. (Joyce studies 2004, 13.) Rev. by Timothy J. Sutton in JJLS (20:1) 2006, 8–9.

16717. Lewty, Jane. *Finnegans Wake*: losing control in Book iii.iii. HJS (5:1) 2004.

16718. Lewty, Jane A. Aurality and adaptation: radioplay in *Ulysses*. HJS (6:1) 2005.

16719. Long, Gerald. A twinge of recollection: the National Library in 1904 and thereabouts. *See* **347**.

16720. McCaffery, Steve. Transcoherence and deletion: the mesostic writings of John Cage. *See* **14990**.

16721. McCarthy, Patrick A. Joyce, family, *Finnegans Wake*. Dublin: National Library of Ireland, 2005. pp. 35. (Joyce studies 2004, 19.) Rev. by Edmund L. Epstein in JJLS (20:1) 2006, 10–11.

16722. McCarthy, Tom. Letting rip: the primal scene, the veil and excreta in Joyce and Freud. HJS (5:1) 2004.

16723. McCleery, Alistair. The reputation of the 1932 Odyssey Press edition of *Ulysses*. PBSA (100:1) 2006, 89–103.

16724. McGann, Jerome. 'The grand heretics of modern fiction': Laura Riding, John Cowper Powys, and the subjective correlative. *See* **18250**.

16725. McHugh, Roland. Annotations to *Finnegans Wake*. (Bibl. 1995, 17211.) Baltimore, MD; London: Johns Hopkins UP, 2006. pp. xx, 628. (Third ed.: first ed. 1980.) Rev. by Wim Van Mierlo in JJLS (20:2) 2006, 7.

16726. Maddox, Brenda. Roots of Bloom: James Joyce in 'Judapest'. TLS, 30 June 2006, 14. (Twentieth International James Joyce Symposium in Budapest.)

16727. Manista, Francis C. Voice, boundary, and identity in the works of James Joyce. Lewiston, NY; Lampeter: Mellen Press, 2006. pp. ix, 222.

16728. Marvin, John. *Finnegans Wake* iii.3 and the third millennium: the ghost of Modernisms yet to come. HJS (6:1) 2005.

16729. Masiello, Francine. Joyce in Buenos Aires (talking sexuality through translation). Diacritics (34:3/4) 2004, 55–72.

16730. Milesi, Laurent. Joycean choreo-graphies of writing in *Stephen Hero* and *A Portrait of the Artist as a Young Man*. HJS (7:1) 2006.

16731. Mitchell, Andrew. Excremental self-creation in *Finnegans Wake*. HJS (5:1) 2004.

16732. Morrison, Steven. 'My native land, goodnight': Joyce and Byron. *In* (pp. 50–67) **16695**.

16733. Mullin, Katherine. English vice and Irish vigilance: the nationality of obscenity in *Ulysses*. *In* (pp. 68–82) **16695**.

16734. Murphy, Neil. Political fantasies: Irish writing and the problem of reading strategies. *In* (pp. 63–88) **12189**.

16735. Murphy, Terence Patrick. Interpreting marked order narration: the case of James Joyce's *Eveline*. JLS (34:2) 2005, 107–24.

16736. Nadel, Ira B. Historicizing *Ulysses*. *In* (pp. 135–51) **16699**.

16737. —— Joyce & his publishers. Dublin: National Library of Ireland, 2005. pp. 59. (Joyce studies 2004, 20.) Rev. by Edmund L. Epstein in JJLS (20:1) 2006, 10–11.

16738. Nash, John. Irish audiences and English readers: the cultural politics of Shane Leslie's *Ulysses* reviews. *In* (pp. 139–52) **16695**.

16739. Nolan, Emer. Modernism and the Irish Revival. *In* (pp. 157–72) **11829**.

16740. Norris, Andrew. Joyce and the post-epiphanic. HJS (5:2) 2005.

16741. Norris, Margot. Fact, fiction, and anti-Semitism in the 'Cyclops' episode of Joyce's *Ulysses*. JNT (36:2) 2006, 163–89.

16742. —— Narratology and *Ulysses*. *In* (pp. 35–50) **16699**.

16743. Nunes, Mark. Semiotic perturbations: what the frog's eye tells us about *Finnegans Wake*. HJS (5:1) 2004.

16744. O'Brien, Eugene. Rereading the canon: towards a literary redefinition of Irishness. *In* (pp. 113–33) **12189**.

16745. Oeler, Karla. A collective interior monologue: Sergei Parajanov and Eisenstein's Joyce-inspired vision of cinema. MLR (101:2) 2006, 472–87.

16746. O'Neill, Patrick. Polyglot Joyce: fictions of translation. Toronto; Buffalo, NY; London: Toronto UP, 2005. pp. x, 301. Rev. by Vike Martina Plock in Mod/Mod (13:3) 2006, 582–3.

16747. O'Rourke, Fran. Joyce's quotation from Aristotle: 'alwisest Stagyrite'. Dublin: National Library of Ireland, 2005. pp. 59, (plates) 3. (Joyce studies 2004, 21.) Rev. by Edmund L. Epstein in JJLS (20:1) 2006, 10–11.

16748. Parascandola, Louis; McGarrity, Maria. 'I'm a … naughty girl': prostitution and outsider women in James Joyce's *The Boarding House* and Eric Walrond's *The Palm Porch*. CLAJ (50:2) 2006, 141–61.

16749. Pedot, Richard. Reading events in James Joyce's *An Encounter*. FMLS (42:1) 2006, 1–12.

16750. Pelaschiar, Laura. 'Making geography a romance': Joyce's Mediterranean feminine. *In* (pp. 209–26) **12076**.

16751. Phillips, George Micajah. The Protean text of *Ulysses* and why all editions are equally 'definitive'. HJS (4:2) 2003/04.

16752. Pierce, David. Joyce and company. London; New York: Continuum, 2006. pp. 180.

16753. Pilling, John. Beckett and Mauthner revisited. *In* (pp. 158–66) **14684**.

16754. Platt, Len. 'No such race': the *Wake* and Aryanism. *In* (pp. 155–77) **16695**.

16755. Plock, Vike Martina. A feat of strength in 'Ithaca': Eugen Sandow and physical culture in Joyce's *Ulysses*. JML (30:1) 2006, 129–39.

16756. Rabaté, Jean-Michel. Aspace of Dumbillsilly: when Joyce translates Lacan. CritQ (48:1) 2006, 26–42.

16757. Rademacher, Jörg W. James Joyce. Munich: Deutscher Taschenbuch Verlag, 2004. pp. 357. (DTV Premium.) Rev. by Katharina Hagena in JJLS (20:1) 2006, 14.

16758. Rathjen, Friedhelm. James Joyce. Reinbek: Rowohlt Taschenbuch Verlag, 2004. pp. 155. (Rowohlts Monographien, 50591.) Rev. by Kerstin Stranz in JJLS (20:1) 2006, 16.

16759. Restivo, Giuseppina. From *Exiles* to *Ulysses*: the influence of three Italian authors on Joyce – Giacosa, Praga, Oriani. *In* (pp. 133–51) **12076**.

16760. Richardson, Brian. Bad Joyce: anti-aesthetic practices in *Ulysses*. HJS (7:1) 2006.

16761. Riquelme, John Paul. 'Preparatory to anything else': Joyce's styles as forms of memory – the case of 'Eumæus'. *In* (pp. 9–34) **16699**.

16762. Roncacci, Francesco. 'Hades' in Zurich: a note on Joyce's *Ulysses*. ConLett (42) 2004, 475–6.

16763. Roraback, Erik. Para-baroque conceptual intersections & interventions: *Finnegans Wake*, *Gravity's Rainbow* and *The Writing of the Disaster*. HJS (5:2) 2005.

16764. Roughley, Alan R. Feigning Dublin: Joyce's repositionings of his readers. HJS (7:1) 2006.

16765. Santana, Richard W. Language and the decline of magic: epistemological shifts in English literature from medieval to Modernist. *See* **3926**.

16766. Sayers, William. Gat-toothed Alysoun, gaptoothed Kathleen: sovereignty and dentition. HJS (6:1) 2005.

16767. Schork, R. J. Joycean permutations on a Roman Pope Peter. *In* (pp. 147–54) **3394**.

16768. Schwarz, Daniel R. Reading the modern British and Irish novel, 1890–1930. *See* **10324**.

16769. Sharkey, E. Joseph. Idling the engine: linguistic skepticism in and around Cortázar, Kafka, and Joyce. Washington, DC: Catholic Univ. of America Press, 2006. pp. xvi, 283.

16770. Shelton, Jen. Joyce and the narrative structure of incest. Foreword by Sebastian D. G. Knowles. Gainesville: Florida UP, 2006. pp. xii, 157. (Florida James Joyce.)

16771. Slote, Sam. A Eumaean return to style. HJS (6:1) 2005.

16772. Stanzel, Franz K. Österreich(isches) in James Joyces *Ulysses*. MSp (48:2) 2004, 1–6.

16773. Strathman, Christopher A. Romantic poetry and the fragmentary imperative: Schlegel, Byron, Joyce, Blanchot. *See* **9371**.

16774. Streit, Wolfgang. Joyce/Foucault: sexual confessions. (Bibl. 2005, 17342.) Rev. by Vike Martina Plock in Mod/Mod (13:1) 2006, 191–2.

16775. Sullam, Sara. Ulysse francophone: poetiche francesi in *Ulysses* tra prosa e poesia. Acme (59:1) 2006, 213–41.

16776. Thacker, Andrew (ed.). *Dubliners*: James Joyce. Basingstoke; New York: Palgrave Macmillan, 2006. pp. ix, 229. (New casebooks.)

16777. Theall, Donald F. Transformations of the book in Joyce's dream vision of digiculture. HJS (4:2) 2003/04.

16778. Thiher, Allen. Fiction refracts science: Modernist writers from Proust to Borges. (Bibl. 2005, 17344.) Rev. by Linda Simon in Isis (97:2) 2006, 374.

16779. Thompson, Helen. Hysterical hooliganism: O'Brien, Freud, Joyce. *In* (pp. 31–57) **17794**.

16780. Thurston, Luke. James Joyce and the problem of psychoanalysis. (Bibl. 2004, 17690.) Rev. by David G. Wright in ELT (49:1) 2006, 95–9; by Peter de Voogd in EngS (87:1) 2006, 119–21; by Craig Monk in MLR (101:4) 2006, 1100–1.

16781. Toker, Leona. Narrative enthymeme: the examples of Laurence Sterne and James Joyce. *See* **8182**.

16782. Toolan, Michael. Top keyword abridgements of short stories: a corpus-linguistic resource? JLS (35:2) 2006, 181–94.

16783. Tully, Nola (ed.). Yes I said yes I will yes: a celebration of James Joyce, *Ulysses*, and 100 years of Bloomsday. Foreword by Frank McCourt. Introd. by Isaiah Sheffer. (Bibl. 2004, 17695.) Rev. by Michael J. O'Shea in JJLS (20:1) 2006, 15.

16784. Valente, Joseph. *Ulysses* and queer theory: a continuing history. *In* (pp. 88–113) **16699**.

16785. Van Hulle, Dirk. Textual awareness: a genetic study of late manuscripts by Joyce, Proust, and Mann. (Bibl. 2005, 17350.) Rev. by Sam Slote in TextC (1:1) 2006, 106–8; by Wim Van Mierlo in Mod/Mod (13:4) 2006, 777–9; by Finn Fordham in JJLS (20:1) 2006, 4–5.

16786. Van Mierlo, Wim. The greater Ireland beyond the sea: James Joyce, exile, and Irish emigration. *In* (pp. 178–97) **16695**.

16787. Weinstein, Arnold. Recovering your story: Proust, Joyce, Woolf, Faulkner, Morrison. New York: Random House, 2006. pp. xii, 496.

16788. Wollaeger, Mark. His master's voice: a portrait of the artist as propagandist. HJS (7:1) 2006.

16789. Wondrich, Roberta Gefter. 'All the seas of the world': Joycean thresholds of the unknown. A reading of the marine and watery element from *Dubliners* to *Ulysses*. *In* (pp. 229–43) **12076**.

16790. Wurtz, James F. Scarce more than a corpse: Famine memory and representations of the gothic in *Ulysses*. JML (29:1) 2005, 102–17.

16791. Yang, Jian. Joyce's views of the canon. FLS (122) 2006, 86–93. (In Chinese.)

16792. Yoshida, Hiromi. Joyce & Jung: the 'four stages of eroticism' in *A Portrait of the Artist as a Young Man*. New York; Frankfurt: Lang, 2004. pp. xxi, 170.

16793. Zajko, Vanda. Homer and *Ulysses*. *In* (pp. 311–23) **3253**.

16794. Zanotti, Serenella. Joyce in Italy, l'italiano di Joyce. Rome: Aracne, 2004. pp. 194. (Scienze dell'antichità, filologico-letterarie e storico-artistiche, 98.)

'Alan Judd' (Alan Edwin Petty) (b.1946)

16795. Wiesenfarth, Joseph. An interview with Alan Judd. ConLit (47:1) 2006, 1–29.

Cynthia Kadohata

16796. Woo, Celestine. Bicultural world creation: Laurence Yep, Cynthia Kadohata, and Asian American fantasy. *In* (pp. 173–86) **11849**.

Chester Kallman (b.1921)

16797. Marchetti, Paola. 'The pallid children': Auden and the Mediterranean. *In* (pp. 295–312) **12076**.

Sarah Kane

16798. Bond, Edward. The mark of Kane. CLR (2) 2005, 7–17.

16799. Wixson, Christopher. 'In better places': space, identity, and alienation in Sarah Kane's *Blasted*. CompDr (39:1) 2005, 75–91.

John Kani

16800. Graham, Shane. Private trauma, public drama: Fugard, Kani, and Ntshona's *The Island* and Maponya's *Gangsters*. *See* **16022**.

16801. Nwahunanya, Chinyere. Tragedy in African literary drama. *In* (pp. 197–211) **11860**.

Jan Karon (b.1937)

16802. Karon, Jan. The miracle and the myth. *In* (pp. 120–9) **11940**.

Kapka Kassabova

16803. Fresno Calleja, Paloma. 'If pain were a country': migration, travel and identity in Kapka Kassabova's *Reconnaissance*. JPW (42:1) 2006, 18–31.

Ben Katchor

16804. Gardner, Jared. Archives, collectors, and the new media work of comics. MFS (52:4) 2006, 787–806.

16805. op de Beeck, Nathalie. Found objects (Jem Cohen, Ben Katchor, Walter Benjamin). *See* **12951**.

Welwyn Wilton Katz

16806. Steven, Laurence. Welwyn Wilton Katz and Charles de Lint: new fantasy as a Canadian postcolonial genre. *In* (pp. 57–72) **13541**.

Stanley Kauffmann

16807. Johnson, Jeff. Kushner, Inge and *Little Sheba*: strange bedfellows. *In* (pp. 28–40) **16962**.

Moises Kaufman

16808. Brown, Rich. Moisés Kaufman: the copulation of form and content. TT (15:1) 2005, 51–67.

16809. Charles, Casey. Panic in *The Project*: critical Queer Studies and the Matthew Shepard murder. LawL (18:2) 2006, 225–52.

Shirley Kaufman

16810. Felstiner, John. 'the tree making us / look again': Shirley Kaufman's roots in the air. ISLE (12:2) 2005, 1–10.

'Anna Kavan' (Helen Woods Edmonds)

16811. Crees, Mark. To the frozen future: the thwarted fiction of Anna Kavan. TLS, 24 Nov. 2006, 19 (review-article).

16812. Reed, Jeremy. A stranger on earth: the life and work of Anna Kavan. London; Chester Springs, PA: Owen, 2006. pp. 207, (plates) 16. Rev. by Mark Crees in TLS, 24 Nov. 2006, 19.

Guy Gavriel Kay

16813. Siourbas, Helen. More than just survival: the successful quest for voice in Guy Gavriel Kay's *Tigana* and Randy Bradshaw's *The Song Spinner*. *In* (pp. 73–80) **13541**.

Jackie Kay (b.1961)

16814. McClellan, Sarah. The nation of mother and child in the work of Jackie Kay. Ob3 (6:1) 2005, 114–27.

Elia Kazan

16815. Murphy, Brenda. Uneasy collaboration: Miller, Kazan, and *After the Fall*. *See* **17527**.

Molly Keane ('M. J. Farrell')

16816. Walshe, Éibhear; Young, Gwenda (eds). Molly Keane: essays in contemporary criticism. Dublin; Portland, OR: Four Courts Press, 2006. pp. 224.

Weldon Kees

16817. Reidel, James (introd.). To Weldon Kees. *See* **18212**.

16818. Turco, Lewis. Vern Rutsala's surreal world. *See* **18393**.

16819. Wormser, Baron. Weldon's song. SewR (114:4) 2006, 534–50.

Garrison Keillor

16820. Heller, Janet Ruth. The nature of learning in Garrison Keillor's *Drowning 1954* and *After a Fall*. MidAmerica (32) 2005, 53–60.

Edith Summers Kelley

16821. Campbell, Donna. 'Where are the ladies?': Wharton, Glasgow, and American women Naturalists. *See* **10136**.

Myra Kelly

16822. Fuisz, Lisbeth Strimple. Willa Cather and Myra Kelly in *McClure's Magazine*. *See* **15090**.

James Kelman

16823. Klaus, H. Gustav. James Kelman. (Bibl. 2005, 17384.) Rev. by Simon Kővesi in TLS, 13 Jan. 2006, 28.

16824. McGuire, Matt. Dialect(ic) nationalism? The fiction of James Kelman and Roddy Doyle. ScSR (7:1) 2006, 80–94.

16825. Pittin-Hédon, Marie-Odile. '*Translated accounts*': James Kelman et l'impossible médiation. EtBr (30) 2006, 145–56.

Randall Kenan

16826. Cornett, Sheryl. Smitten by Victoriana: Randall Kenan's down East boyhood with books, storytelling, and the power of language. NCLR (15) 2006, 11–17.

A. L. (Alison Louise) Kennedy (b.1965)

16827. Neagu, Adriana. No half measures, all for the writing: a conversation with A. L. Kennedy. ScSR (7:1) 2006, 110–23.

Adrienne Kennedy (b.1931)

16828. Kolin, Philip C. The fission of Tennessee Williams's plays into Adrienne Kennedy's. *See* **19171**.

16829. —— *Milena's Wedding*, 'paragraphs [and] passages', and the formation of Adrienne Kennedy's canon. CLAJ (50:1) 2006, 64–83.

16830. —— Parks's *In the Blood*. *See* **17965**.

16831. —— Understanding Adrienne Kennedy. (Bibl. 2005, 17392.) Rev. by James Fisher in TheatreS (47:1) 2006, 114–16; by Felicia Hardison Londré in CompDr (40:2) 2006, 256–8.

16832. Radavich, David. African American drama from the Midwest. *See* **16489**.

16833. Vorlicky, Robert. Blood relations: Adrienne Kennedy and Tony Kushner. *In* (pp. 41–55) **16962**.

X. J. Kennedy

16834. Kennedy, X. J. Greensboro and the riddles of Randall Jarrell. *See* **16586**.

Brendan Kennelly

16835. Sedlmayr, Gerold. Brendan Kennelly's literary works: the developing art of an Irish writer, 1959–2000. Lewiston, NY; Lampeter: Mellen Press, 2005. pp. xvii, 399. (Studies in Irish literature, 15.)

Maurice Kenny

16836. Sweeney, Chad. An interview with Maurice Kenny. WLT (79:2) 2005, 66–9.

Jane Kenyon

16837. Hall, Donald. The best day the worst day: life with Jane Kenyon. (Bibl. 2005, 17400.) Rev. by Keith Taylor in MichQR (45:4) 2006, 702–12.

16838. Peseroff, Joyce (ed.). Simply lasting: writers on Jane Kenyon. (Bibl. 2005, 17404.) Rev. by Keith Taylor in MichQR (45:4) 2006, 702–12.

16839. Pride, Mike. The abiding presence of Jane Kenyon. SewR (113:3) 2005, 458–62. (State of letters.)

16840. Taylor, Keith. The presence of Jane Kenyon. MichQR (45:4) 2006, 702–12 (review-article).

Jack Kerouac

16841. Carden, Mary Paniccia. 'Adventures in auto-eroticism': economies of travelling masculinity in autobiographical texts by Jack Kerouac and Neal Cassady. Journeys (7:1) 2006, 1–25.

16842. Condo, George (introd.). Book of sketches, 1952–53. London; New York: Penguin, 2006. pp. xii, 413. (Penguin poets.)

16843. Dittman, Michael J. Jack Kerouac: a biography. (Bibl. 2004, 17763.) Rev. by Katie Stewart in JAStud (39:3) 2005, 553–4; by Peter Barry in Eng (55:212) 2006, 213–19.

16844. Eisenhauer, Robert. Parables of disfiguration: reason and excess from Romanticism to the avant-garde. *See* **11208**.

16845. Hrebeniak, Michael. Action writing: Jack Kerouac's wild form. Carbondale: Southern Illinois UP, 2006. pp. xi, 301.

16846. Maher, Paul, Jr (ed.). Empty phantoms: interviews and encounters with Jack Kerouac. New York: Thunder's Mouth Press; London: Orion, 2005. pp. xxii, 503.

M. E. Kerr (Marijane Meaker, 'Ann Aldrich', 'Vin Parker')

16847. Spring, Albert. M. E. Kerr. New York: Rosen Central, 2006. pp. 112. (Library of author biographies.)

16848. Thompson, Dawn. Prussic acid with a twist: *The Well of Loneliness*, M. E. Kerr, and young adult readers. *See* **16251**.

Ken Kesey

16849. Pepper, Andrew. State power matters: power, the State and political struggle in the post-war American novel. *See* **14960**.

Jessie Kesson

16850. Murray, Isobel. *The White Bird Passes*: how Jessie Kesson reached the final version. ScSR (7:1) 2006, 68–79.

John Oliver Killens

16851. Van Thompson, Carlyle. Miscegenation as sexual consumption: the enduring legacy of America's White supremacist culture of violence in John Oliver Killens' *Youngblood*. CLAJ (50:2) 2006, 174–206.

Joyce Kilmer (1886–1918)

16852. Pollin, Burton R. Kilmer's promotion of Poe. *See* **11038**.

16853. —— Kilmer's *Trees* and Asselineau's *Trees*. Exp (64:3) 2006, 156–9.

Myung-Mi Kim (b.1957)

16854. Park, Josephine Nock-Hee. 'Composed of many lengths of bone': Myung-Mi Kim's reimagination of image and epic. *In* (pp. 235–56) **11995**.

Jamaica Kincaid

16855. BRAZIEL, JANA EVANS. 'Another line was born ...': Genesis, genealogy, and genre in Jamaica Kincaid's *Mr Potter*. *In* (pp. 127–50) **16864**.

16856. COVI, GIOVANNA. Alterity: Jamaica Kincaid's resistance. *In* (pp. 197–208) **16284**.

16857. DONATIEN-YSSA, PATRICIA. Tuer pour survivre, tragédies assassines caraïbes. Cycnos (23:2) 2006, 109–25.

16858. EWERT, JEANNE C. 'Great plant appropriators': and acquisitive gardeners: Jamaica Kincaid's ambivalent *Garden (Book)*. *In* (pp. 113–26) **16864**.

16859. FORBES, CURDELLA. Selling that Caribbean woman down the river: diasporic travel narratives and the global economy. *See* **11160**.

16860. GASS, JOANNE. *The Autobiography of My Mother*: Jamaica Kincaid's revision of *Jane Eyre* and *Wide Sargasso Sea*. *In* (pp. 63–78) **16864**.

16861. GOURDINE, ANGELETTA K. M. Caribbean *tabula rasa*: textual touristing as carnival in contemporary Caribbean women's writing. SmAx (10:2) 2006, 80–96.

16862. JAY, JULIA DE FOOR. 'What a history you have': ancestral memory, cultural history, migration patterns, and the quest for autonomy in the fiction of Jamaica Kincaid. *In* (pp. 117–38) **11795**.

16863. LANG-PERALTA, LINDA. 'Smiling with my mouth turned down': ambivalence in Jamaica Kincaid's *Lucy* and *My Garden (Book)*: *In* (pp. 33–44) **16864**.

16864. —— (ed.). Jamaica Kincaid and Caribbean double crossings. Newark: Delaware UP, 2006. pp. 171.

16865. LESEUR, GETA. Head, Schwarz-Bart, and Kincaid: refashioning alternative landscapes. *See* **16306**.

16866. PAGE, KEZIA. 'What if he did not have a sister [who lived in the United States]?': Jamaica Kincaid's *My Brother* as remittance text. SmAx (11:1) 2006, 37–53.

16867. RAHIM, JENNIFER. 'No place to go': homosexual space and the discourse of 'unspeakable' contents in *My Brother* and *Black Fauns*. JWIL (13:1/2) 2005, 119–40.

16868. —— The operations of the closet and the discourse of unspeakable contents in *Black Fauns* and *My Brother*. *See* **17480**.

16869. SHEEHAN, THOMAS W. Caribbean impossibility: the lack of Jamaica Kincaid. *In* (pp. 79–95) **16864**.

16870. SHOCKLEY, EVIE. The horrors of homelessness: gothic doubling in Kincaid's *Lucy* and Brontë's *Villette*. *In* (pp. 45–62) **16864**.

16871. SMITH, DERIK; BEUMEL, CLIFF. My Other: imperialism and subjectivity in Jamaica Kincaid's *My Brother*. *In* (pp. 96–112) **16864**.

16872. STANTON, KATHERINE. Cosmopolitan fictions: ethics, politics, and global change in the works of Kazuo Ishiguro, Michael Ondaatje, Jamaica Kincaid, and J. M. Coetzee. *See* **16566**.

Stephen King ('Richard Bachman')

16873. JOHNSON, DIANE. Writing *The Shining*. *In* (pp. 55–61) **13202**.

16874. STRENGELL, HEIDI. Dissecting Stephen King: from the gothic to literary Naturalism. (Bibl. 2005, 17433.) Rev. by Jon Barnes in TLS, 14 July 2006, 30–1.

16875. WHITELAW, NANCY. Dark dreams: the story of Stephen King. Greensboro, NC: Morgan Reynolds, 2006. pp. 128.

16876. WIATER, STAN; GOLDEN, CHRISTOPHER; WAGNER, HANK. The complete Stephen King universe: a guide to the worlds of Stephen King. London: Orbit; New York: St Martin's Griffin, 2006. pp. xxxii, 512.

Thomas King

16877. ARCHER-LEAN, CLARE. Cross-cultural analysis of the writings of Thomas King and Colin Johnson (Mudrooroo). Lewiston, NY; Lampeter: Mellen Press, 2006. pp. 359.

16878. ROBINSON, JACK. The aesthetics of talk in Thomas King's *Medicine River*. StudCanL (31:1) 2006, 75–94.

Barbara Kingsolver

16879. AUSTENFELD, ANNE MARIE. The revelatory narrative circle in Barbara Kingsolver's *The Poisonwood Bible*. JNT (36:2) 2006, 293–305.

16880. HOMANS, MARGARET. Adoption narratives, trauma, and origins. *See* **17612**.

16881. JONES, SUZANNE W. The Southern family farm as endangered species: possibilities for survival in Barbara Kingsolver's *Prodigal Summer*. SoLJ (39:1) 2006, 83–97.

16882. MEILLON, BÉNÉDICTE. Barbara Kingsolver's *'Homeland' and Other Stories* about another America. Anglophonia (19) 2006, 261–9.

16883. MICHAEL, MAGALI CORNIER. New visions of community in contemporary American fiction: Tan, Kingsolver, Castillo, Morrison. *See* **18722**.

16884. THOMAS, P. L. Reading, learning, teaching Barbara Kingsolver. New York; Frankfurt: Lang, 2005. pp. viii, 154. (Confronting the text, confronting the world, 1.)

Maxine Hong Kingston

16885. BANERJEE, MITA. The Asian American in a turtleneck: fusing the aesthetic and the didactic in Maxine Hong Kingston's *Tripmaster Monkey*. *In* (pp. 55–69) **11849**.

16886. BAVARO, VINCENZO. Politiche di gender e soggettivazione nazionale nell'America asiatica. *In* (pp. 60–93) **11954**.

16887. DONG, LAN. Writing Chinese America into words and images: storytelling and retelling of *The Song of Mu Lan*. *See* **17088**.

16888. GRIFFITHS, JENNIFER. Uncanny spaces: trauma, cultural memory, and the female body in Gayl Jones's *Corregidora* and Maxine Hong Kingston's *The Woman Warrior*. *See* **16633**.

16889. MADSEN, DEBORAH L. Chinese American writers of the real and the fake: authenticity and the twin traditions of life writing. *See* **13949**.

16890. Sabine, Maureen Alice. Maxine Hong Kingston's broken book of life: an intertextual study of *The Woman Warrior* and *China Men*. (Bibl. 2005, 17452.) Rev. by Wendy Ho in MFS (52:1) 2006, 221–5.

16891. Vastolo, Manuela. '*The real and the fake*': autobiografia, fiction e rappresentatività. *In* (pp. 36–59) **11954**.

16892. —— 'Tavoli e chimere': testualità e metatestualità in *Tripmaster Monkey: His Fake Book*. *In* (pp. 217–58) **11954**.

David P. Kinloch

16893. Kinloch, David. The case of the melodramatic hymen: Lallans and translation. *See* **17317**.

John Kinsella (b.1963)

16894. Kinsella, John. Fast, loose beginnings: a memoir of intoxications. Carlton South, Vic.: Melbourne UP, 2006. pp. vii, 243.

16895. —— Line breaks and back-draft: not a defence of a poem. PRev (95:4) 2005/06, 70–8.

W. P. Kinsella

16896. MacDonald, Christine Urban. Circles in the corn: Native American spirituality in Kinsella's *Shoeless Joe*. Aethlon (23:2) 2006, 103–21.

Rudyard Kipling

16897. Adams, Jad. Kipling. London: Haus, 2005. pp. 218. Rev. by Lisa Lewis in KJ (80:318) 2006, 51–2.

16898. Bennett, Nichole. In pursuit of the outland engine: a fictional source for *The Professor's House*. *See* **15083**.

16899. Berry, Mark. How did the elephant get its trunk? What or who inspired the setting for Kipling's *The Elephant's Child*. KJ (79:315) 2005, 28–9.

16900. Budoyan, Diana. The symbolism of the animal world in Kipling's *The Jungle Book*. KJ (80:319) 2006, 27–32.

16901. Damrosch, David (ed.). Joseph Conrad and Rudyard Kipling, *Heart of Darkness*, *The Man Who Would Be King* and other works on empire. *See* **15256**.

16902. Del Sapio Garbero, Maria. Mappe e fantasmi: resoconti dall'Impero di Kipling, Hardy e altri. *In* (pp. 157–78) **11824**.

16903. Dentith, Simon. Epic and empire in nineteenth-century Britain. *See* **8335**.

16904. Dillingham, William B. Rudyard Kipling: hell and heroism. (Bibl. 2005, 17467.) Rev. by Sam Pickering in SewR (114:2) 2006, 332–6; by David Page in KJ (80:317) 2006, 54–5.

16905. Erll, Astrid. Re-writing as re-visioning: modes of representing the 'Indian Mutiny' in British novels, 1857 to 2000. *See* **10429**.

16906. Goethals, Helen. Poetry and power: Rudyard Kipling and the war in South Africa 1899–1902. KJ (79:316) 2005, 8–23.

16907. Hall, Mark F. Manuscript variations of Rudyard Kipling's *Of Swine*. ANQ (19:2) 2006, 44–6.

16908. Hooper, Teresa. Playing by the rules: Kipling's 'Great Game' *vs* 'the great dance' in C. S. Lewis's space trilogy. *See* **17188**.

16909. Hunt, Robert R. Tracking *The Explorer*: Kipling's adventure poem and the Pacific Northwest. KJ (80:319) 2006, 33–44.

16910. Imlah, Mick. Cold days for Elsie: what Kipling chose not to leave behind. TLS, 7 Apr. 2006, 3–4 (review-article). (Letters.)

16911. Jarman, Francis. Kipling's 'rather unpleasant story'. KJ (80:318) 2006, 15–23.

16912. Johnson, Jay. Rudyard Kipling's 1907 cross-Canada speaking tour: imperialism and nationalism in postcolonial Canada. KJ (80:317) 2006, 19–31.

16913. Knoepflmacher, U. C. The Hansel and Gretel syndrome: survivorship fantasies and parental desertion. ChildLit (33) 2005, 171–84.

16914. Kreisel, Deanna K. Wolf children and automata: bestiality and boredom at home and abroad. *See* **11301**.

16915. Lewis, Lisa. Of Kim and Little Henry. KJ (80:319) 2006, 53–5.

16916. Lock, Charles. Indirect rule and the continuities of Nigerian fiction. *In* (pp. 181–96) **11860**.

16917. MacFie, Alexander Lyon. Kipling and Orientalism. KJ (80:317) 2006, 46–53.

16918. Moran, Neil K. Kipling and Afghanistan: a study of the young author as journalist writing on the Afghan Border Crisis of 1884–1885. (Bibl. 2005, 17481.) Rev. by David Page in KJ (80:317) 2006, 57–8.

16919. Nicholls, Mark. Cormell Price's prophesy. KJ (80:318) 2006, 47–50.

16920. —— Stalky's image. KJ (80:319) 2006, 48–50.

16921. Norwich, John Julius. Rudyard Kipling (1865–1936). KJ (79:315) 2005, 11–27.

16922. Park, Clara Claiborne. Wiser and more temperate: John Lockwood Kipling and his son. KJ (80:319) 2006, 9–21.

16923. Pickering, Sam. Kipling then and now. SewR (114:2) 2006, 332–6 (review-article). (Arts and letters.)

16924. Pinney, Thomas (ed.). Interviews with Rudyard Kipling: i. KJ (79:316) 2005, 24–37.

16925. —— Interviews with Rudyard Kipling: ii, At home with Rudyard Kipling. KJ (80:317) 2006, 32–45.

16926. —— Interviews with Rudyard Kipling: iii, A visit to Rudyard Kipling. KJ (80:318) 2006, 26–34.

16927. Prindle, R. E. Tarzan and the river: part iii. *See* **14948**.

16928. Rafalski, Kazimierz. Kipling and Conrad. KJ (80:319) 2006, 51–2.

16929. —— Kipling interest in Poland. KJ (80:318) 2006, 24–5.

16930. Roake, A. D. (ed.). Rudyard Kipling's religious verse. London: Serendipity, 2005. pp. 176. Rev. by R. C. Ayers in KJ (80:317) 2006, 55–6.

16931. Saum, Lewis O. Rudyard Kipling and the Pacific Northwest. PacNQ (97:3) 2006, 126–9. (Lost poem *The Explorer* (1898).)

16932. Slade, Roy. Promoting Rudyard Kipling. KJ (79:315) 2005, 30–9.

16933. Welch, Brenda. Rudyard Kipling's jungle: the casting out and the letting in. KJ (80:317) 2006, 8–18.

16934. Williams, Patrick. Not looking for a new (Labour) England: Billy Bragg, Kipling, and *ressentiment*. *In* (pp. 93–110) **16284**.

16935. Williams, Rowan. The address at the service of commemoration, Burwash. KJ (80:318) 2006, 10–13.

16936. Wilson, Alastair. The New Readers' Guide: compiling notes for *The Day's Work*. KJ (80:319) 2006, 56–8.

August Kleinzahler

16937. Cochrane, Mark. Very particular noise: an interview with August Kleinzahler. CapR (42) 2004, 5–35.

Irena Klepfisz

16938. Ladin, Jay. 'After the end of the world': poetry and the Holocaust. *See* **13794**.

William Kloefkorn

16939. Kloefkorn, William. At home on this moveable earth. Lincoln; London: Nebraska UP, 2006. pp. 217. (Memoirs.) Rev. by David R. Pichaske in GPQ (26:4) 2006, 295–6.

Kenneth Koch

16940. Wootten, William. In the circus. LRB (28:15) 2006, 36–7 (review-article). (Koch and New York Poets.)

Arthur Koestler

16941. Walker, Robert G. A critical preface to Koestler's *Scum of the Earth*. SewR (114:2) 2006, 278–91.

Joy Kogawa

16942. Baron, Henry. Joy Kogawa: an interview. *In* (pp. 162–71) **11940**.

16943. McGonegal, Julie. The future of racial memory: forgiveness, reconciliation, and redress in Joy Kogawa's *Obasan* and *Itsuka*. StudCanL (30:2) 2005, 55–78.

Andrew Koh

16944. Yeoh, Paul. Writing Singapore gay identities: queering the nation in Johann S. Lee's *Peculiar Chris* and Andrew Koh's *Glass Cathedral*. *See* **17089**.

Yusef Komunyakaa

16945. Dargan, Kyle G. 'Excursions': a conversation with Yusef Komunyakaa. Callaloo (29:3) 2006, 741–50.

16946. Francini, Antonella. Yusef Komunyakaa: i *totem* della poesia. PoesiaM (210) 2006, 24–35.

16947. Marvin, Tom. Komunyakaa's *Tu Do Street*. Exp (64:4) 2006, 248–51.

E. L. Konigsburg

16948. Ambrosek, Renee. E. L. Konigsburg. New York: Rosen Central, 2006. pp. 112. (Library of author biographies.)

Dean Koontz

16949. Milroy, Rollin. The architecture of Charnel House. *See* **164**.

Ted Kooser

16950. Bunge, Nancy. Influencing each other through the mail: William Stafford's and Marvin Bell's *Segues* and Jim Harrison's and Ted Kooser's *Braided Creek*. *See* **18588**.

Robert Kroetsch

16951. Clarke, Bronagh. Canadian citizens as postcolonial subjects? Reading Robert Kroetsch's *The Lovely Treachery of Words*. CritS (18:3) 2006, 5–18.

Antjie Krog

16952. Moss, Laura. 'Nice audible crying': editions, testimonies, and *Country of My Skull*. RAL (37:4) 2006, 85–104.

Maxine Kumin

16953. Kumin, Maxine. Writing in multiple genres. PrS (79:4) 2005, 5–8.

Stanley Kunitz

16954. Lentine, Genine. A curious gladness: a garden conversation. APR (35:3) 2006, 11–13.

Hanif Kureishi

16955. Gilman, Sander L. The fanatic: Philip Roth and Hanif Kureishi confront success. *See* **18310**.

16956. Martino, Pierpaolo. *'There was a sound that London had'*: la Londra di Hanif Kureishi. *In* (pp. 349–61) **7343**.

16957. Maxey, Ruth. 'Life in the diaspora is often held in a strange suspension': first-generation self-fashioning in Hanif Kureishi's narratives of home and return. JCL (41:3) 2006, 5–25.

16958. Vitali, Chiara. Il valore sociopolitico di *Borderline* di Hanif Kureishi. Culture (18) 2004, 275–83.

Tony Kushner

16959. Alekson, Paula T. When worlds collide: the Kushner–Lamos *A Dybbuk* at Hartford Stage. *In* (pp. 149–71) **16962**.

16960. Fisher, James. 'Angels of fructification': Tennessee Williams, Tony Kushner, and images of homosexuality on the American stage. *In* (pp. 5–27) **16962**.

16961. —— 'Succumbing to luxury': history, language, and hope in *Homebody/Kabul*. *In* (pp. 190–200) **16962**.

16962. —— (ed.). Tony Kushner: new essays on the art and politics of the plays. Jefferson, NC; London: McFarland, 2006. pp. viii, 225.

16963. Fujita, Atsushi. Queer politics to fabulous politics in *Angels in America*: pinklisting and forgiving Roy Cohn. *In* (pp. 112–26) **16962**.

16964. Izzo, David Garrett. Then and now: W. H. Auden, Christopher Isherwood, Tony Kushner, and Fascist creep. *In* (pp. 56–97) **16962**.

16965. Johnson, Jeff. Kushner, Inge and *Little Sheba*: strange bedfellows. *In* (pp. 28–40) **16962**.

16966. Juntunen, Jacob. Repairing reality: the media and *Homebody/Kabul* in New York, 2001. *In* (pp. 172–89) **16962**.

16967. Knoepflmacher, U. C. The Hansel and Gretel syndrome: survivorship fantasies and parental desertion. *See* **16913**.

16968. Krasner, David. Stonewall, 'constant historical progress', and *Angels in America*. *In* (pp. 98–111) **16962**.

16969. Londré, Felicia Hardison. Two illusions: cultural borrowings and transcendence. *In* (pp. 127–34) **16962**.

16970. May, Theresa J. 'Consequences unforeseen …' in *Raisin in the Sun* and *Caroline; or, Change*. *See* **20102**.

16971. Mihaylova, Stefka. Reading Corneille with Brecht: *The Comedy of Illusion* and the illusions of citizenship. *In* (pp. 135–48) **16962**.

16972. Minton, Gretchen E.; Schultz, Ray. *Angels in America*: adapting to a new medium in a new millennium. AmDr (15:1) 2006, 17–42.

16973. Powers, W. Douglas. Lifted above Tennessee Williams's *Hot Tin Roof*: Tony Kushner's *Angels in America* as Midrash. *See* **19177**.

16974. Stern, Bert. The therapy of desire. *In* (pp. 201–14) **16962**.

16975. Stevenson, Catherine. 'Seek for something new': mothers, change, and creativity in Tony Kushner's *Angels in America*, *Homebody/Kabul*, and *Caroline; or, Change*. ModDr (48:4) 2005, 758–76.

16976. Thompson, David M. The transcendent dimensions of private places: personhood and the law in *Lawrence v. Texas* and *Angels in America*. TriQ (124) 2006, 242–56.

16977. Vorlicky, Robert. Blood relations: Adrienne Kennedy and Tony Kushner. *In* (pp. 41–55) **16962**.

16978. Wisner, Buell. 'Waiting in the angel's wings': Marxist fantasia in Naomi Wallace's *Slaughter City*. *See* **18950**.

Ellen Kuzwayo

16979. Muriungi, Agnes. *Sit Down and Listen*: the invention of (oral) tradition and the imagining of a new nation. *In* (pp. 211–34) **12216**.

Winona LaDuke

16980. Salaita, Steven. The Holy Land in transit: colonialism and the quest for Canaan. Foreword by Peter Gran. Syracuse, NY: Syracuse UP, 2006. pp. ix, 234. (Middle East studies beyond dominant paradigms.)

Alex La Guma

16981. Wanyama, Mzenga. Cohesion in the novels of Alex La Guma: a dialogic analysis. ColLit (33:2) 2006, 115–34.

Tim F. LaHaye

16982. Mleynek, Sherryll. The rhetoric of the 'Jewish problem' in the Left Behind novels. LitTheol (19:4) 2005, 367–83.

16983. Morgan, David T. The new Brothers Grimm and their Left Behind fairy tales. Macon, GA: Mercer UP, 2006. pp. xi, 222.

Jhumpa Lahiri

16984. MALANDRINO, RAFFAELLA. Immaginare l'India attraverso la diaspora: *A Real Durwan* e *The Treatment of Bibi Haldar* di Jhumpa Lahiri. *In* (pp. 285–317) **11954**.

16985. MITRA, MADHUPARNA. Lahiri's *Mrs Sen's*. Exp (64:3) 2006, 185–9.

16986. RAJAN, GITA. Ethical responsibility in intersubjective spaces: reading Jhumpa Lahiri's *Interpreter of Maladies* and *A Temporary Matter*. *In* (pp. 123–41) **11995**.

16987. —— Poignant pleasures: feminist ethics as aesthetics in Jhumpa Lahiri and Anita Rau Badami. *In* (pp. 104–20) **11849**.

George Lamming

16988. BROWN, J. DILLON. Exile and cunning: the tactical difficulties of George Lamming. ConLit (47:4) 2006, 669–94.

16989. DALLEO, RAPHAEL. Authority and the occasion for speaking in the Caribbean literary field: Martin Carter and George Lamming. *See* **15067**.

16990. GAINES, KEVIN. E. Franklin Frazier's revenge: anticolonialism, nonalignment, and Black intellectuals' critiques of Western culture. AmLH (17:3) 2005, 506–29.

16991. RODRÍGUEZ GUERRERO-STRACHAN, SANTIAGO. Social exiles and language refugees: the case of postcolonial authors. *See* **17755**.

Anne Lamott

16992. BUTURIAN, LINDA. Anne Lamott: an interview. *In* (pp. 194–200) **11940**.

John Lanchester

16993. GOTH, MAIK. John Lanchester's *The Debt to Pleasure*: an aesthetics of textual surprise. Connotations (14:1–3) 2004/05, 135–61.

R. F. Langley (b.1938)

16994. BRINTON, IAN. Black Mountain in England: 1. PNRev (31:3) 2005, 65–8.

Philip Larkin

16995. BAROT, RICK. Larkin and the apple. GetR (19:3) 2006, 490–7.

16996. BORUCH, MARIANNE. Heavy lifting. *See* **16302**.

16997. BRADFORD, RICHARD. First boredom, then fear: the life of Philip Larkin. London; Chester Springs, PA: Owen, 2005. pp. 272, (plates) 16. Rev. by David C. Ward in SewR (114:4) 2006, 623–8.

16998. COOPER, STEPHEN. Philip Larkin: subversive writer. (Bibl. 2005, 17572.) Rev. by Neil Powell in PNRev (32:3) 2006, 65–72.

16999. EVERETT, BARBARA. A lethal fall. LRB (28:9) 2006, 13–16.

17000. OSBORNE, THOMAS. Polarities of Englishness: Larkin, Hughes and national culture. CritQ (48:1) 2006, 43–67.

17001. PALMER, RICHARD; WHITE, JOHN (eds). Jazz writings: essays and reviews 1940–84. London; New York: Continuum, 2004. pp. xxxv, 180. (Continuum impacts.) Rev. by Neil Powell in PNRev (32:3) 2006, 65–72.

17002. POWELL, NEIL. Playing snooker with dice: Philip Larkin's juvenilia and jazz. PNRev (32:3) 2006, 65–72 (review-article).

17003. STOJKOVIC, TIJANA. Larkin in the cinema: dynamic visualization in *Show Saturday* and *Here*. EngS (86:4) 2005, 312–24.

17004. —— Unnoticed in the casual light of day: Philip Larkin and the plain style. London; New York: Routledge, 2006. pp. ix, 235. (Studies in major literary authors.)

17005. STOREY, MARK. Larkin's *Going, Going*. Exp (64:4) 2006, 236–9.

17006. THOMAS, FRANCIS-NOËL. Philip Larkin, Barbara Pym, and the accident of literary fame. NER (27:2) 2006, 8–26. (Literary lives.)

17007. TOLLEY, A. T. (ed.). Early poems and juvenilia. London; Boston, MA: Faber & Faber, 2005. pp. xxv, 382. Rev. by Adam Kirsch in TLS, 13 May 2005, 9–10; by Neil Powell in PNRev (32:3) 2006, 65–72.

17008. TRENGOVE-JONES, TIMOTHY. Philip Larkin's *Wedding-Wind*. ESA (48:1) 2005, 87–91.

17009. WARD, DAVID C. Something like nothing: Larkin again. SewR (114:4) 2006, 623–8 (review-article). (Arts and letters.)

Nella Larsen

17010. ANDERSON, MICHAEL. Passing strange. TLS, 6 Oct. 2006, 26 (review-article). (Biography of Larsen.)

17011. CAMPBELL, JAMES. White lies. LRB (28:19) 2006, 21–2 (review-article). (Biography of Larsen.)

17012. DOYLE, LAURA. Transnational history at our backs: a long view of Larsen, Woolf, and queer racial subjectivity in Atlantic Modernism. Mod/Mod (13:3) 2006, 531–59.

17013. HAMPTON, GREGORY J. Beauty and the exotic: writing Black bodies in Nella Larsen's *Quicksand*. CLAJ (50:2) 2006, 162–73.

17014. HOELLER, HILDEGARD. Race, Modernism, and plagiarism: the case of Nella Larsen's *Sanctuary*. AAR (40:3) 2006, 421–37.

17015. HUTCHINSON, GEORGE. In search of Nella Larsen: a biography of the color line. Cambridge, MA; London: Belknap Press of Harvard UP, 2006. pp. x, 611. Rev. by Evelyn C. White in BkW, 21 May 2006, 14; by James Campbell in LRB (28:19) 2006, 21–2; by Michael Anderson in TLS, 6 Oct. 2006, 26.

17016. LANDRY, H. JORDAN. Seeing Black women anew through lesbian desire in Nella Larsen's *Passing*. RMER (60:1) 2006.

17017. RANSOM, PORTIA BOULWARE. Black love and the Harlem renaissance: an essay in African American literary criticism. Lewiston, NY; Lampeter: Mellen Press, 2005. pp. v, 181.

17018. SPERATI, ELISA. The Harlem renaissance e Nella Larsen: nuovi orizzonti in campo letterario e una nuova voce alla letteratura di colore. ConLett (42) 2004, 477–500.

James Laughlin

17019. BAMBERGER, W. C. (ed.). Guy Davenport and James Laughlin: selected letters. New York; London: Norton, 2006. pp. 256. Rev. by Michael Dirda in BkW, 17 Dec. 2006, 15.

17020. Epler, Barbara; Javitch, Daniel (eds). The way it wasn't: from the files of James Laughlin. New York: New Directions, 2006. pp. 342. Rev. by Michael Dirda in BkW, 17 Dec. 2006, 15.

Margaret Laurence

17021. Beckman-Long, Brenda. Female subjectivity and confession in Margaret Laurence's *A Jest of God*. Tessera (37/38) 2005, 11–23.

17022. Comeau, Paul. Margaret Laurence's epic imagination. Edmonton: Alberta UP, 2005. pp. xviii, 186. Rev. by David Stouck in GPQ (26:4) 2006, 283–5.

17023. Powers, Lyall H. Alien heart: the life and work of Margaret Laurence. (Bibl. 2003, 17838.) Rev. by Frances W. Kaye in GPQ (26:1) 2006, 43–4.

17024. Socken, Paul G. (ed.). Intimate strangers: the letters of Margaret Laurence & Gabrielle Roy. Winnipeg: Manitoba UP, 2004. pp. xvi, 104. Rev. by Clara Thomas in BkCan (34:8) 2005, 26–7; by David Stouck in GPQ (26:4) 2006, 283–5.

17025. Stouck, David. The making of Margaret Laurence's epic voice. GPQ (26:4) 2006, 283–5 (review-article).

17026. Xiques, Donez. Margaret Laurence: the making of a writer. Toronto: Dundurn, 2005. pp. 408, (plates) 8. Rev. by Clara Thomas in BkCan (34:8) 2005, 26–7; by David Stouck in GPQ (26:4) 2006, 283–5.

Ann Lauterbach

17027. Lauterbach, Ann. The night sky: writings on the poetics of experience. (Bibl. 2005, 17598.) Rev. by Jeff Gundy in GaR (60:2) 2006, 423–33.

D. H. Lawrence

17028. Arnold, John. Fanfrolico frolics. *See* **640**.

17029. Bachrach, Arthur J. D. H. Lawrence in New Mexico: 'the time is different there'. Santa Fe: Museum of New Mexico Press, 2006. pp. xv, 120.

17030. Balbert, Peter. Courage at the border-line: Balder, Hemingway, and Lawrence's *The Captain's Doll*. PLL (42:3) 2006, 227–63.

17031. —— Freud, Frazer, and Lawrence's palimpsestic novella: dreams and the heaviness of male destiny in *The Fox*. StudN (38:2) 2006, 211–33.

17032. Banerjee, A. The ever-elusive D. H. Lawrence. SewR (114:4) 2006, 619–22 (review-article). (Arts and letters.)

17033. Boulton, James T. (ed.). Late essays and articles. (Bibl. 2004, 17928.) Rev. by Andrew Harrison in StudN (38:2) 2006, 250–60.

17034. Chen, Hong. Romantic morality in D. H. Lawrence's animal poems. FLS (119) 2006, 47–55. (In Chinese.)

17035. Cuny, Noëlle. Atrabile, vagrancy and latency in the post-war novels of D. H. Lawrence. EREA (4:1) 2006, 22–7.

17036. Doctorow, E. L. Our Edgar. *See* **11009**.

17037. Ellis, David (ed.). D. H. Lawrence's *Women in Love*: a casebook. Oxford; New York: OUP, 2006. pp. viii, 282. (Casebooks in criticism.)

17038. Franks, Jill. Islands and the Modernists: the allure of isolation in art, literature, and science. *See* **18708**.

17039. Frost, Laura. The romance of cliché: E. M. Hull, D. H. Lawrence, and interwar erotic fiction. *In* (pp. 94–118) **12024**.

17040. Gervais, David. Dostoevsky and the English novel: Dickens, John Cowper Powys and D. H. Lawrence. *See* **9755**.

17041. Goodheart, Eugene. D. H. Lawrence: the utopian vision. New Brunswick, NJ: Transaction, 2006. pp. xix, 190.

17042. Grmelová, Anna. Encounters with otherness in D. H. Lawrence's *St Mawr*. LittPr (16:31) 2006, 78–82.

17043. Hancock, Tim. 'You couldn't make it up': the love of bare facts in Mina Loy's Italian poems. *See* **17287**.

17044. Herbert, Michael. Hardy and Lawrence – and their mothers. *See* **10276**.

17045. Kirk, John. Figuring the landscape: writing the topographies of community and place. LitH (15:1) 2006, 1–17.

17046. Lackey, Michael. The literary Modernist assault on philosophy. PhilL (30:1) 2006, 50–60.

17047. Meyers, Jeffrey. D. H. Lawrence, comedian. Salmagundi (152) 2006, 205–22.

17048. Naciscione, Anita. Sustainability of phraseological image in discourse. IJES (6:1) 2006, 43–56.

17049. Pender, Anne. 'Phrases between us': the poetry of Anna Wickham. *See* **19122**.

17050. Ragg-Kirkby, Helena. Perversion and pestilence: D. H. Lawrence and the Germans. *In* (pp. 101–15) **11790**.

17051. Raschke, Debrah. Modernism, metaphysics, and sexuality. *See* **15301**.

17052. Reeve, N. H.; Worthen, John (eds). Introductions and reviews. (Bibl. 2004, 17948.) Rev. by Andrew Harrison in StudN (38:2) 2006, 250–60; by John Lyon in RES (57:230) 2006, 412–14.

17053. Roberts, Neil. D. H. Lawrence, travel and cultural difference. (Bibl. 2005, 17627.) Rev. by Andrew Harrison in StudN (38:2) 2006, 250–60; by Mara Kalnins in NQ (53:2) 2006, 245–6.

17054. Ryu, Doo-Sun. D. H. Lawrence's *The Rainbow* and *Women in Love*: a critical study. New York; Frankfurt: Lang, 2005. pp. xii, 166.

17055. Scherr, Barry J. D. H. Lawrence today: literature, culture, politics. (Bibl. 2005, 17631.) Rev. by Andrew Harrison in StudN (38:2) 2006, 250–60.

17056. Schwarz, Daniel R. Reading the modern British and Irish novel, 1890–1930. *See* **10324**.

17057. Son, Youngjoo. Here and now: the politics of social space in D. H. Lawrence and Virginia Woolf. London; New York: Routledge, 2006. pp. ix, 252. (Studies in major literary authors.)

17058. Sotirova, Violeta. Charting stylistic change: D. H. Lawrence's handling of point of view. EngS (87:4) 2006, 466–89.

17059. —— Repetition in free indirect style: a dialogue of minds? Style (39:2) 2005, 123–36.

17060. Steele, Bruce (ed.). *Psychoanalysis and the Unconscious* and *Fantasia of the Unconscious*. (Bibl. 2005, 17634.) Rev. by Andrew Harrison in StudN (38:2) 2006, 250–60; by Garry Watson in ELT (49:1) 2006, 106–9.

17061. Tague, Gregory. Character and consciousness: George Eliot, Thomas Hardy, E. M. Forster, D. H. Lawrence: phenomenological, ecological, and ethical readings. *See* **10055**.

17062. Vitoux, Pierre (trans.). *Constance Chatterley*: la première version de *Lady Chatterley's Lover*. Paris: Autrement, 2005. pp. 333. Rev. by Joseph Dobrinsky in CVE (62) 2005, 214–15; by Ginette Roy in EA (59:2) 2006, 242–3.

17063. Wexler, Joyce Piell. D. H. Lawrence: *Women in Love*. *In* (pp. 393–401) **11788**.

17064. Worthen, John. D. H. Lawrence: the life of an outsider. London; New York: Allen Lane, 2005. pp. xxvi, 517, (plates) 16. Rev. by Mark Crees in TLS, 18 Mar. 2005, 11; by A. Banerjee in SewR (114:4) 2006, 619–22.

17065. Wright, Terry R. Holiness in the modern world: Durkheim, Otto, Bataille, and Lawrence. *In* (pp. 161–79) **3415**.

17066. Yahav-Brown, Amit. Gypsies, nomadism, and the limits of realism. *See* **10062**.

17067. Zhang, Jianjia. Sex ethics in Lawrence's fiction. FLS (117) 2006, 90–6. (In Chinese.)

T. E. Lawrence

17068. Brown, Malcolm (ed.). T. E. Lawrence in war and peace: an anthology of the military writings of Lawrence of Arabia. (Bibl. 2005, 17639.) Rev. by Ian Beckett in TLS, 13 Jan. 2006, 28.

17069. Meyers, Jeffrey. T. E. Lawrence and *The English Patient*. NCL (36:3) 2006, 2–4.

Henry Lawson

17070. Lee, Christopher. City bushman: Henry Lawson and the Australian imagination. Fremantle, W. Australia: Curtin Univ., 2004. pp. 272. Rev. by Lucy Frost in ALS (22:2) 2005, 253–4; by Nathanael O'Reilly in Biography (29:2) 2006, 380–3.

John Howard Lawson (1894–1977)

17071. Chambers, Jonathan L. Messiah of the new technique: John Howard Lawson, Communism, and American theatre, 1923–1937. Carbondale: Southern Illinois UP, 2006. pp. xv, 268, (plates) 12. (Theater in the Americas.)

17072. Horne, Gerald. The final victim of the blacklist: John Howard Lawson, dean of the Hollywood Ten. Berkeley; London: California UP, 2006. pp. xxiii, 360. Rev. by Larry Ceplair in Cineaste (32:1) 2006, 74–5.

Robert Lax

17073. Harford, James. Merton and friends: a joint biography of Thomas Merton, Robert Lax, and Edward Rice. *See* **17490**.

Stephen Leacock

17074. Bowker, Alan (ed.). On the front line of life: Stephen Leacock: memories and reflections, 1935–1944. Toronto: Dundurn, 2004. pp. 264. Rev. by George Fetherling in BkCan (34:4) 2005, 35; by Michiel Horn in CHR (87:1) 2006, 144–6.

17075. Staines, David; Nimmo, Barbara (eds). The letters of Stephen Leacock. Oxford; Don Mills, Ont.: OUP, 2006. pp. xi, 564, (plates) 16. Rev. by George Fetherling in BkCan (35:8) 2006, 24–5.

'John le Carré' (David John Cornwell)

17076. Ford, E. H. Sources for le Carré's Pyms. NCL (36:3) 2006, 8–10.

17077. Whitfield, Stephen J. The culture of the Cold War. *In* (pp. 256–74) **11776**.

William J. Lederer (b.1912)

17078. Ferrer, Hugh. Notes on the *Connecticut Yankee*. *See* **11494**.

Chang-rae Lee

17079. Cheng, Anne Anlin. Passing, natural selection, and love's failure: ethics of survival from Chang-rae Lee to Jacques Lacan. AmLH (17:3) 2005, 553–74.

17080. Huang, Betsy. Citizen Kwang: Chang-rae Lee's *Native Speaker* and the politics of consent. JAAS (9:3) 2006, 243–69.

17081. Russell, Keith A. Colonial naming and renaming in *A Gesture Life* by Chang-rae Lee. NCL (36:4) 2006, 7–9.

Dennis Lee

17082. Lecker, Robert. The cadence of *Civil Elegies*. Toronto: Cormorant, 2006. pp. vii, 87.

Easton Lee (b.1931)

17083. Fish, Laura. *Strange Music*: engaging imaginatively with the family of Elizabeth Barrett Browning from a creole and Black woman's perspective. *See* **9257**.

Harper Lee

17084. Hitchcock, Bert. Climbing into and walking around in someone else's skin. AlaR (59:4) 2006, 285–90 (review-article).

17085. Liu, Guozhi. On the bi-circular structure in *To Kill a Mockingbird*. FLS (119) 2006, 130–6. (In Chinese.)

17086. Rui, Yuping; Fan, Yi. A moral criticism on the growing-up theme in *To Kill a Mockingbird*. FLS (122) 2006, 119–29. (In Chinese.)

17087. Shields, Charles J. Mockingbird: a portrait of Harper Lee. New York: Holt, 2006. pp. 337. Rev. by Garrison Keillor in NYTB, 11 June 2006, 11; by Meghan O'Rourke in BkW, 23 July 2006, 15; by Bert Hitchcock in AlaR (59:4) 2006, 285–90.

Jeanne M. Lee

17088. Dong, Lan. Writing Chinese America into words and images: storytelling and retelling of *The Song of Mu Lan*. LU (30:2) 2006, 218–33.

Johann S. Lee (b.1971)

17089. Yeoh, Paul. Writing Singapore gay identities: queering the nation in Johann S. Lee's *Peculiar Chris* and Andrew Koh's *Glass Cathedral*. JCL (41:3) 2006, 121 35.

Li-Young Lee (b.1957)

17090. Ingersoll, Earl G. (ed.). Breaking the alabaster jar: conversations with Li-Young Lee. Rochester, NY: BOA, 2006. pp. 191. (American readers, 7.)

17091. Malandra, Marc. 'Little candle in the pulpit': the sacred legacy of memory and genealogy in Li-Young Lee's *Book of My Nights*. ELN (44:1) 2006, 19–27.

17092. Wardrop, Daneen. Li-Young Lee's *The Cleaving* and the figure of the father. AmerJ (32:2) 2006, 49–65.

17093. Xu, Wenying. An exile's will to canon and its tension with ethnicity: Li-Young Lee. *In* (pp. 145–64) **11783**.

17094. —— Transcendentalism, ethnicity, and food in the work of Li-Young Lee. B2 (33:2) 2006, 129–57.

Marie G. Lee (b.1964)

17095. Chiu, Monica. The cultural production of Asian American young adults in the novels of Marie G. Lee, An Na, and Doris (*sic*) Jones Yang. LU (30:2) 2006, 168–84.

Sky Lee

17096. Gordon, Neta. Charted territory: Canadian literature by women, the genealogical plot, and SKY Lee's *Disappearing Moon Café*. Narrative (14:2) 2006, 163–79.

Tanith Lee

17097. Griswold, Jerry. The meanings of *Beauty and the Beast*. *See* **12786**.

Tzu Pheng Lee

17098. Goh, Robbie B. H. Imagining the nation: the role of Singapore poetry in English in 'emergent nationalism'. *See* **18765**.

Ursula K. Le Guin

17099. Bernardo, Susan M.; Murphy, Graham J. Ursula K. Le Guin: a critical companion. Westport, CT; London: Greenwood Press, 2006. pp. xi, 198. (Critical companions to popular contemporary writers.)

17100. Cadden, Mike. Taking different roads to the city: the development of Ursula K. Le Guin's young adult novels. Extrapolation (47:3) 2006, 427–44.

17101. —— Ursula K. Le Guin beyond genre: fiction for children and adults. (Bibl. 2005, 17656.) Rev. by Brian Attebery in CLAQ (31:2) 2006, 199–202.

17102. Cheyne, Ria. Ursula K. Le Guin and translation. Extrapolation (47:3) 2006, 457–70.

17103. Erlich, Richard D. Le Guin and God: quarreling with the One, critiquing pure reason. Extrapolation (47:3) 2006, 351–79.

17104. Fritzsche, Sonja. Publishing Ursula K. Le Guin in East Germany. Extrapolation (47:3) 2006, 471–87.

17105. JENKINS, ALICE. Knowing and geography in Octavia Butler, Ursula K. Le Guin and Maureen McHugh. *See* **14972**.

17106. LINDOW, SANDRA J. Wild gifts: anger management and moral development in the fiction of Ursula K. Le Guin and Maurice Sendak. Extrapolation (47:3) 2006, 445–56.

17107. LOTHIAN, ALEXIS. Grinding axes and balancing oppositions: the transformation of feminism in Ursula K. Le Guin's science fiction. Extrapolation (47:3) 2006, 380–95.

17108. ROCHELLE, WARREN G. The Emersonian choice: connections between dragons and humans in Le Guin's Earthsea cycle. Extrapolation (47:3) 2006, 417–26.

17109. SAWYER, ANDY. Ursula Le Guin and the pastoral mode. Extrapolation (47:3) 2006, 396–416.

17110. SUVIN, DARKO. On U. K. Le Guin's 'second Earthsea trilogy' and its cognitions: a commentary. Extrapolation (47:3) 2006, 488–504.

Alan Lelchuk

17111. MORTARA, ELÈNA. The last transatlantic ambassador of American literature? Philip Roth (un)masked as Ziff by Alan Lelchuk. QPS (14) 2006, 220–31.

Madeleine L'Engle

17112. L'ENGLE, MADELEINE. The cosmic questions. *In* (pp. 214–24) **11940**.

17113. ROSENBERG, AARON. Madeleine L'Engle. New York: Rosen Central, 2006. pp. 112. (Library of author biographies.)

Elmore Leonard

17114. ABELL, STEPHEN. Hold the hooptedoodle: Mack's rules for writing westerns. TLS, 23 June 2006, 21–2 (review-article).

William Le Queux (1864–1927)

17115. HAMMOND, ANDREW. Imagined colonialism: Victorian travellers in South-East Europe. *See* **10719**.

Shane Leslie

17116. NASH, JOHN. Irish audiences and English readers: the cultural politics of Shane Leslie's *Ulysses* reviews. *In* (pp. 139–52) **16695**.

Doris Lessing ('Jane Somers')

17117. BROOKES, BARBARA; PAGE, DOROTHY. The red-headed heroine. *In* (pp. 157–65) **8374**.

17118. BROWN, BYRON K. 'Aspects of each other': Lessing, Laing, and the question of authority. DLS (25:1) 2005, 12–16.

17119. CHOWN, LINDA E. Revisiting reliable narration and the politics of perspective. DLS (25:1) 2005, 16–19.

17120. DE MUL, SARAH. The politics of the Zimbabwean everyday in Doris Lessing's *African Laughter: Four Visits to Zimbabwe* (1992). DLS (25:2) 2006, 10–14.

17121. GARDINER, JUDITH KEGAN. Historicizing homophobia in *The Golden Notebook* and *The Day Stalin Died*. DLS (25:2) 2006, 14–18.

17122. GARREN, SAMUEL B. The honeysuckle and the camellia: a reader-response theory of literary interpretation. DLS (25:1) 2005, 19–22.

17123. GRAY, BILLY. A conversation with Doris Lessing: 'Lucky the culture where the old can talk to the young and the young can talk to the old.' DLS (24:1/2) 2004, 1, 23–30.

17124. HIDALGO, PILAR. Doris Lessing and A. S. Byatt: writing *The Golden Notebook* in the 1990s. DLS (25:1) 2005, 22–5.

17125. INGERSOLL, EARL G. Doris Lessing's *Playing the Game*. DLS (25:1) 2005, 5–8.

17126. JOHNSON, R. W. Old fires: Gordimer, Lessing and Daphne Rooke. *See* **18281**.

17127. KROUSE, TONYA. Freedom as effacement in *The Golden Notebook*: theorizing pleasure, subjectivity, and authority. JML (29:3) 2006, 39–56.

17128. LACEY, LAUREN. Genealogy and becoming in the *Canopus in Argos: Archives* series. DLS (25:2) 2006, 18–23.

17129. LEE, AMY. *The Summer before the Dark*: the void of motherhood. DLS (24:1/2) 2004, 15–18.

17130. LEONARD, SUZANNE. Playing in the shadows: aging and female invisibility in *The Summer before the Dark*. DLS (24:1/2) 2004, 11–15.

17131. MARSHALL, LENI. Changing bodies, changing minds: *The Diaries of Jane Somers*. DLS (24:1/2) 2004, 19–22.

17132. PALUSCI, ORIANA. '*The London Blitz*': uno sguardo di genere. *In* (pp. 281–97) **7343**.

17133. PERRAKIS, PHYLLIS STERNBERG. Journeys of the spirit: the older woman in Doris Lessing's works. DLS (24:1/2) 2004, 39–43.

17134. PEZZULICH, EVELYN. Coming of age: the emergence of the aging female protagonist in literature. DLS (24:1/2) 2004, 7–10.

17135. PORT, CYNTHIA. 'None of it adds up': economies of aging in *The Diary of a Good Neighbour*. DLS (24:1/2) 2004, 30–5.

17136. REGE, JOSNA. The child is mother of the woman: exchanges between age and youth in Doris Lessing. DLS (24:1/2) 2004, 3–7.

17137. SAXTON, RUTH. Sex over sixty? From *Love, Again* to *The Sweetest Dream*. DLS (24:1/2) 2004, 44–7.

17138. SIZEMORE, CHRISTINE W. Patterns of aging in the ninth stage of life: *The Diary of a Good Neighbour*. DLS (24:1/2) 2004, 36–9.

17139. TIGER, VIRGINIA. 'Our chroniclers tell us': Lessing's sequel to *Mara and Dann*. DLS (25:2) 2006, 23–5.

17140. WATERMAN, DAVID. Identity in Doris Lessing's space fiction. Youngstown, NY: Cambria Press, 2006. pp. xxiv, 140.

17141. WATKINS, SUSAN. '*Grande dame*' or 'New Woman': Doris Lessing and the palimpsest. LIT (17:3/4) 2006, 243–62.

17142. —— Writing in a minor key. DLS (25:2) 2006, 6–10.

Meridel Le Sueur

17143. Alaimo, Stacy. 'Comrades of surge': Meridel Le Sueur, Cultural Studies, and the corporeal turn. ISLE (12:2) 2005, 55–74.

17144. Kosiba, Sara. The strength of the Midwestern proletariat: Meridel Le Sueur and the ideal proletarian literature. MidAmerica (31) 2004, 80–90.

Jonathan Lethem

17145. Schiff, James. A conversation with Jonathan Lethem. MR (29:1) 2006, 116–34.

Ho Hon Leung (b.1961)

17146. Park, Josephine Nock-hee. 'A loose horse': Asian American poetry and the aesthetics of the ideogram. *In* (pp. 123–36) **11849**.

Denise Levertov

17147. Bertholf, Robert J. Decision at the apogee: Duncan's anarchist critique of Denise Levertov. *In* (pp. 1–17) **15599**.

17148. Boland, Eavan. A broken connection. *See* **15593**.

17149. Dewey, Anne. Poetic authority and the public sphere of politics in the activist 1960s: the Duncan–Levertov debate. *In* (pp. 109–25) **15599**.

17150. Dougherty, James. Presence, silence and the holy in Denise Levertov's poems. Ren (58:4) 2006, 305–26.

17151. Driscoll, Kerry. Gendered poetics. *See* **19189**.

17152. Felstiner, John. The Hasid and the kabbalist. *In* (pp. 81–9) **15599**.

17153. —— The Hasid and the kabbalist. NwR (44:1) 2006, 140–7.

17154. Gelpi, Albert. Poetic language and language poetry: Levertov, Duncan, Creeley. *In* (pp. 180–98) **15599**.

17155. —— Bertholf, Robert J. (eds). Robert Duncan and Denise Levertov: the poetry of politics, the politics of poetry. *See* **15599**.

17156. Hollenberg, Donna Krolik. Visions of the field in poetry and painting: Denise Levertov, Robert Duncan, and John Button. *In* (pp. 43–59) **15599**.

17157. —— 'Within the world of your perceptions': the letters of Denise Levertov and H.D. *See* **15537**.

17158. Johnston, Devin. Better to stumble to it: the start of Duncan's *Letters: Poems, 1953–1956*. *In* (pp. 32–42) **15599**.

17159. Lacey, Paul A. The vision of the burning babe: Southwell, Levertov, and Duncan. *In* (pp. 161–79) **15599**.

17160. MacGowan, Christopher. Poet to poet: four books of correspondence. *See* **19194**.

17161. Millier, Brett. *Chelsea 8*: political poetry at midcentury. *In* (pp. 94–108) **15599**.

17162. Narbeshuber, Lisa. Relearning Denise Levertov's *Alphabet*: war, flesh, and the intimacy of otherness. CRAS (36:2) 2006, 131–48.

17163. Rodriguez Herrera, Jose. Revolution or death? Levertov's poetry in time of war. *In* (pp. 148–60) **15599**.

17164. Rosenbaum, Susan. Elizabeth Bishop's theater of war. *In* (pp. 53–82) **13763**.

17165. Shurin, Aaron. The People's P***k: a dialectical tale. *In* (pp. 71–80) **15599**.

Phillis Levin (b.1954)

17166. Curry, Renée R. H.D., Dove, Glück, and Levin: the poetry of Afroasiatic and White Greece. *See* **15530**.

Philip Levine

17167. Bethea, Arthur F. Philip Levine's *Magpiety* and his literary debt to Czeslaw Milosz. ColLit (33:3) 2006, 100–16.

Aurora Levins Morales (b.1954)

17168. Fiandt, Julie. Autobiographical activism in the Americas: narratives of personal and cultural healing by Aurora Levins Morales and Linda Hogan. *See* **16446**.

Myron Levoy (b.1930)

17169. Higonnet, Margaret R. Time out: trauma and play in *Johnny Tremain* and *Alan and Naomi*. *See* **15914**.

Andrea Levy (b.1956)

17170. McLeod, John. Postcolonial fictions of adoption. *See* **18449**.

C. Day Lewis ('Nicholas Blake')

17171. O'Donoghue, Bernard. 'Where are the war poets': poetry and hope – the case of C. Day Lewis. PNRev (31:3) 2005, 57–61.

C. S. (Clive Staples) Lewis ('N. W. Clerk') (1898–1963)

17172. Barkman, Adam. C. S. Lewis and the enduring relevance of the monarchy. CSL (37:4) 2006, 1–15, 21–4.

17173. Bassham, Gregory; Walls, Jerry L. (eds). *The Chronicles of Narnia* and philosophy: the lion, the witch, and the worldview. (Bibl. 2005, 17720.) Rev. by Adam Barkman in CSR (35:4) 2006, 537–40.

17174. Blaxland-de Lange, Simon. Owen Barfield: Romanticism come of age: a biography. Foreword by Andrew Welburn. *See* **14583**.

17175. Camery-Hoggatt, Jerry. God in the plot: storytelling and the many-sided truth of the Christian faith. CSR (35:4) 2006, 451–70.

17176. Caughey, Shanna (ed.). Revisiting Narnia: fantasy, myth, and religion in C. S. Lewis's *Chronicles*. (Bibl. 2005, 17727.) Rev. by Andrew White in LU (30:3) 2006, 427–30.

17177. Christopher, Joe R. Narnia guides. Mythprint (43:5/6) 2006, 4–7 (review-article).

17178. Dorsett, Lyle. Seeking the secret place: the spiritual formation of C. S. Lewis. (Bibl. 2005, 17733.) Rev. by Joe R. Christopher in Mythprint (43:7) 2006, 4–5.

17179. Downing, David C. Into the wardrobe: C. S. Lewis and the Narnia chronicles. (Bibl. 2005, 17735.) Rev. by Andrew White in LU (30:3) 2006, 427–30.

17180. Drollinger, Frank. C. S. Lewis & Christopher Dawson: on history and historicism. CSL (37:6) 2006, 1–9.

17181. DUPUY, KENNETH. Science and Scientism in C. S. Lewis: some misunderstandings. CSL (37:6) 2006, 10–15, 19.

17182. DURIEZ, COLIN. A field guide to Narnia. (Bibl. 2004, 18030.) Rev. by Joe R. Christopher in Mythprint (43:5/6) 2006, 4–7.

17183. FIFE, ERNELLE. Wise warriors in Tolkien, Lewis, and Rowling. *See* **18794**.

17184. FREEMAN, FRANKLIN. Images of affection (*storge*) in *As You Like It* and *King Lear.* CSL (37:5) 2006, 9–11, 20.

17185. GILCHRIST, K. J. A morning after war: C. S. Lewis and WWI. (Bibl. 2005, 17745.) Rev. by Dale Nelson in CSL (37:1) 2006, 18.

17186. GRIESINGER, EMILY. The search for 'deeper magic': J. K. Rowling and C. S. Lewis. *In* (pp. 317–31) **11916**.

17187. GRIFFIN, WILLIAM. C. S. Lewis: the authentic voice. (Bibl. 1998, 17448.) Oxford: Lion, 2005. pp. 440. (New ed.: first ed. 1988.)

17188. HOOPER, TERESA. Playing by the rules: Kipling's 'Great Game' *vs* 'the great dance' in C. S. Lewis's space trilogy. Mythlore (25:1/2) 2006, 105–26.

17189. HOOPER, WALTER (ed.). Collected letters: vol. 3, Narnia, Cambridge, and Joy, 1950–1963. London: HarperCollins, 2006. pp. xx, 1810.

17190. JACOBS, ALAN. The Narnian: the life and imagination of C. S. Lewis. (Bibl. 2005, 17749.) Rev. by Joe R. Christopher in Mythprint (43:3) 2006, 11–12; by Clara Sarrocco in CSL (37:6) 2006, 20.

17191. JANES, BURTON K. Beyond Aslan: essays on C. S. Lewis. Gainesville, FL: Bridge-Logos, 2006. pp. xvii, 232. Rev. by Clara Sarrocco in CSL (37:6) 2006, 20.

17192. KHODDAM, SALWA. The enclosed garden in C. S. Lewis's *The Chronicles of Narnia*. CSL (37:1) 2006, 1–10.

17193. MCCLAIN, WILLIAM J. C. S. Lewis and the reflective Christian. CSL (37:3) 2006, 1–9.

17194. NELSON, DALE. Is Lewis' Ransom Trilogy indebted to Yank magazine science fiction? CSL (37:4) 2006, 18–19.

17195. —— Little-known books (and a little-known story) in Lewis' background: a fifth selection. CSL (37:2) 2006, 8–15.

17196. —— A 'scientifiction' source for Lewis' *The Great Divorce*. CSL (37:3) 2006, 18.

17197. NIEDBALA, AMANDA M. From Hades to Heaven: Greek mythological influences in C. S. Lewis's *The Silver Chair*. Mythlore (24:3/4) 2006, 71–93.

17198. O'DONOGHUE, BERNARD. The reality of courtly love. *In* (pp. 7–24) **3836**.

17199. PHELPSTEAD, CARL. Auden and the Inklings: an alliterative revival. *See* **14509**.

17200. POE, HARRY LEE; POE, REBECCA WHITTEN (eds). C. S. Lewis remembered: collected reflections of students, friends & colleagues. Grand Rapids, MI: Zondervan, 2006. pp. 270.

17201. ROGERS, JONATHAN. The world according to Narnia: Christian meaning in C. S. Lewis's beloved *Chronicles*. (Bibl. 2005, 17783.) Rev. by Joe R. Christopher in Mythprint (43:5/6) 2006, 4–7.

17202. Schakel, Peter J. The way into Narnia: a reader's guide. (Bibl. 2005, 17787.) Rev. by Joe R. Christopher in Mythprint (43:5/6) 2006, 4–7.

17203. Tennyson, G. B. (ed.). Owen Barfield on C. S. Lewis. (Bibl. 1991, 14051.) San Rafael, CA: Barfield Press, 2006. pp. 196. (Second ed.: first ed. 1989.)

17204. White, Michael. C. S. Lewis: the boy who chronicled Narnia. London: Abacus, 2005. pp. xi, 268, (plates) 8.

17205. Williams, Donald T. Mere humanity: G. K. Chesterton, C. S. Lewis, and J. R. R. Tolkien on the human condition. *See* **15151**.

17206. Wriglesworth, Chad. Myth maker, unicorn maker: C. S. Lewis and the reshaping of medieval thought. Mythlore (25:1/2) 2006, 29–40.

Janet Lewis (b.1899)

17207. Middleton, David. Gatherings: four American poets. *See* **14877**.

Sinclair Lewis

17208. Bucco, Martin. Sinclair Lewis as reader and critic. (Bibl. 2004, 18062.) Rev. by Sanford E. Marovitz in WAL (41:2) 2006, 217–18.

17209. McGuire, David. An empty vision: the American Dream on *Main Street*. MidM (33) 2005, 55–72.

17210. Rogal, Samuel J. (comp.). A guide to the characters in the novels, short stories, and plays of Sinclair Lewis. Lewiston, NY; Lampeter: Mellen Press, 2006. 3 vols. pp. 494; 493; 471.

17211. Seaton, James. Religion and literature in Sinclair Lewis and Willa Cather. *See* **15117**.

Wyndham Lewis

17212. Comentale, Edward P.; Gąsiorek, Andrzej (eds). T. E. Hulme and the question of Modernism. *See* **16516**.

17213. Gąsiorek, Andrzej. Wyndham Lewis and Modernism. Plymouth: Northcote House in assn with the British Council, 2004. pp. xii, 175. (Writers and their work.) Rev. by Michael H. Whitworth in RES (57:230) 2006, 409–11.

17214. —— Wyndham Lewis: *Tarr*. *In* (pp. 402–10) **11788**.

17215. Hickman, Miranda B. The geometry of Modernism: the Vorticist idiom in Lewis, Pound, H.D., and Yeats. Austin: Texas UP, 2005. pp. xix, 332. (Literary Modernism.)

17216. Mao, Douglas. A shaman in common: Lewis, Auden, and the queerness of Liberalism. *In* (pp. 206–37) **12024**.

17217. Munton, Alan. Vorticism. *In* (pp. 176–82) **11788**.

17218. —— Wyndham Lewis: from Proudhon to Hitler (and back): the strange political journey of Wyndham Lewis. EREA (4:2) 2006, 27–33.

17219. Neilson, Brett. Wyndham Lewis in Morocco: spatial philosophy and the politics of race. *In* (pp. 313–26) **12076**.

17220. Ophir, Ella Zohar. Toward a pitiless fiction: abstraction, comedy, and Modernist antihumanism. MFS (52:1) 2006, 92–120.

17221. Pfannkuchen, Antje. From vortex to Vorticism: Ezra Pound's art and science. *See* **18104**.

17222. Puchner, Martin. The aftershocks of *Blast*: manifestos, satire, and the rear-guard of Modernism. *In* (pp. 44–67) **12024**.

Shirley Lim

17223. Lim, Shirley Geok-lin. Not an academic memoir. SFO (4:2) 2006.

17224. Ng, Andrew Hock-Soon. Malaysian gothic: the motif of haunting in K. S. Maniam's *Haunting the Tiger* and Shirley Lim's *Haunting*. *See* **17434**.

17225. Tay, Eddie. Hegemony, national allegory, exile: the poetry of Shirley Lim. TexP (19:3) 2005, 289–308.

Su-chen Christine Lim (b.1948)

17226. Quayum, Mohammad A. Keeper of the creative flame: Su-chen Christine Lim interviewed. JCL (41:3) 2006, 145–58.

Anne Morrow Lindbergh

17227. Winters, Kathleen C. Anne Morrow Lindbergh: first lady of the air. Basingstoke; New York: Palgrave Macmillan, 2006. pp. xiv, 241.

Jack Lindsay

17228. Arnold, John. Fanfrolico frolics. *See* **640**.

Vachel Lindsay (1879–1931)

17229. Rogal, Samuel J. The call of the road: the geographical journey of Vachel Lindsay. Bethesda, MD: Academica Press, 2006. pp. 257.

R. Zamora Linmark

17230. Bavaro, Vincenzo. '*Les enfants du paradis*': sopravvivenza e performance in *Rolling the R's* di R. Zamora Linmark. *In* (pp. 259–84) **11954**.

Gillian Linscott

17231. Talburt, Nancy Ellen; Young, Juana. Targeting change: the Nell Bray novels by Gillian Linscott. Clues (24:4) 2006, 49–58.

Elinor Lipman

17232. Lipman, Elinor. The writing life. BkW, 21 May 2006, 8.

Robin Lippincott

17233. Alley, Henry. *Mrs Dalloway* and three of its contemporary children. *See* **19257**.

Penelope Lively

17234. Butler, Charles. Four British fantasists: place and culture in the children's fantasies of Penelope Lively, Alan Garner, Diana Wynne Jones, and Susan Cooper. Lanham, MD; London: Scarecrow Press, 2006. pp. viii, 311.

Margot Livesey

17235. Ellis, Sherry. Memories that reach back into consciousness: an interview with Lan Samantha Chang. IowaR (36:2) 2006, 157–67.

Douglas Lochhead

17236. Wills, Deborah. 'The flesh continuing': pain, poetry and the therapeutic landscape. Arc (54) 2005, 47–54.

Liz Lochhead

17237. Woddis, Carole. Women's imaginations: experimenting with theatrical form. *In* (pp. 170–80) **12297**.

David Lodge

17238. Ciocca, Rossella. Metafisica del viaggiare: pellegrinaggi. *In* (pp. 97–107) **11824**.

17239. Lodge, David. The year of Henry James; or, Timing is all: the story of a novel. With other essays on the genesis, composition and reception of literary fiction. London: Harvill Press, 2006. pp. xiii, 332. Rev. by Henry Hitchings in TLS, 9 June 2006, 40.

Christopher Logue

17240. Nikolaou, Paschalis. Notes on translating the self. *In* (pp. 19–32) **2874**.

Jack London

17241. DePastino, Todd (ed.). The road. New Brunswick, NJ; London: Rutgers UP, 2006. pp. xlix, 168. (Subterranean lives.)

17242. Dooley, Patrick K. Jack London's *South of the Slot* and William James's *The Divided Self and the Process of its Unification*. WAL (41:1) 2006, 50–64.

17243. Reesman, Jeanne Campbell. Rough justice in Jack London's *Mauki*. StAN (1:1/2) 2006, 42–69.

17244. Swafford, Kevin R. Resounding the abyss: the politics of narration in Jack London's *The People of the Abyss*. JPC (39:5) 2006, 838–60.

17245. Wright, Louise E. Jack London's knowledge of Thoreau. ConS (ns 14) 2006, 51–72.

Michael Longley

17246. Alcobia-Murphy, Shane. 'Not forgotten or passed over at the proper time': the representation of violent events in contemporary culture. *See* **16416**.

17247. Brearton, Fran. Reading Michael Longley. Newcastle upon Tyne: Bloodaxe, 2006. pp. 285.

17248. Hardwick, Lorna. 'Murmurs in the cathedral': the impact of translations from Greek poetry and drama on modern work in English by Michael Longley and Seamus Heaney. YES (36:1) 2006, 204–15.

17249. Pillonca, Giovanni. Michael Longley: le 'stazioni segrete'. PoesiaM (207) 2006, 42–9.

17250. Steele, Peter. Zones of the imagination. Meanjin (63:2) 2004, 4–11. (Journey symbolism.)

Lucas Longo (1919–1992)

17251. Michaud, Marie-Christine. The alienation of Italian American immigrants: the case of *The Family on Vendetta Street* by Lucas Longo. VIA (16:2) 2005, 45–56.

Anita Loos

17252. Hammill, Faye. 'One of the few books that doesn't stink': the intellectuals, the masses and *Gentlemen Prefer Blondes*. CritS (17:3) 2005, 27–48.

Phillip Lopate (b.1943)

17253. Lopate, Phillip. *Howl* and me. *In* (pp. 131–9) **16122**.

17254. Taylor, Anita Darcel. Interview with Phillip Lopate. 4thG (8:1) 2006, 125–37.

Barry Lopez

17255. Grandjeat, Yves-Charles. L'écriture de la nature chez Barry Lopez: enjeux et stratégies. Anglophonia (19) 2006, 279–89.

17256. Martin, Christian. On resistance: an interview with Barry Lopez. GaR (60:1) 2006, 13–30.

17257. Tydeman, William. Interview with Barry Lopez. NwR (44:2) 2006, 96–116.

17258. Warner, Diane. An annotated bibliography of selected works by Barry Lopez. NwR (44:2) 2006, 117–37.

Audre Lorde (Gamba Adisa)

17259. Driver, Susan. Between theories and life-writings: feminist daughters communicating desires across generational differences. WS (35:4) 2006, 347–74.

17260. Hall, Joan Wylie (ed.). Conversations with Audre Lorde. (Bibl. 2004, 18105.) Rev. by Andrea Shaw in WLT (80:1) 2006, 60.

17261. Ortega, Mariana. Being lovingly, knowingly ignorant: White feminism and women of color. Hypatia (21:3) 2006, 56–74.

Bret Lott

17262. Lott, Bret. Why have we given up the ghost? Notes on reclaiming literary fiction. *In* (pp. 43–60) **11940**.

H. P. Lovecraft

17263. Schoell, William. H. P. Lovecraft: master of weird fiction. Greensboro, NC: Morgan Reynolds, 2004. pp. 128. (World writers.)

17264. Sederholm, Carl. What screams are made of: representing cosmic fear in H. P. Lovecraft's *Pickman's Model*. JFA (16:4) 2006, 335–49.

17265. Waugh, Robert H. The monster in the mirror: looking for H. P. Lovecraft. New York: Hippocampus Press, 2006. pp. 302. Rev. by Tim Evans in Extrapolation (47:1) 2006, 164–6.

Maud Hart Lovelace

17266. Sweeney, Meghan M. Checking out America: libraries as agents of acculturation in three mid-century girls' books. ChildLit (33) 2005, 41–65.

Robert Lowell (1917–1977)

17267. Gowrie, Grey. Robert Lowell: a memoir. Agenda (41:3/4) 2005, 60–74.

17268. Hahn, Robert. Lowell in perspective. SewR (113:3) 2005, 478–85 (review-article). (Arts and letters.)

17269. Hamilton, Saskia (ed.). The letters of Robert Lowell. (Bibl. 2005, 17873.) Rev. by Dennis O'Driscoll in Agenda (41:3/4) 2005, 182–4; by Valerie

Duff-Strautmann in PNRev (32:4) 2006, 55–6; by Judith Kitchen in GaR (60:3/4) 2006, 760–74.

17270. James, Stephen. 'A conflict of opposites': Robert Lowell and Geoffrey Hill. Symbiosis (10:1) 2006, 63–85.

17271. Jamison, Kay Redfield. Contemporary psychology and contemporary poetry: perspectives on mood disorders. *In* (pp. 191–203) **13732**.

17272. Kitchen, Judith. The letter of the life. GaR (60:3/4) 2006, 760–74 (review-article).

17273. Lucas, John. Scholar poets and history. PNRev (31:4) 2005, 25–7.

17274. Meyers, Jeffrey. Robert Lowell's *Beyond the Alps*. NCL (36:1) 2006, 4–6.

17275. New, Elisa. Confession, Reformation, and Counter-Reformation in the career of Robert Lowell. *In* (pp. 13–32) **13763**.

17276. Pinsky, Robert. Peace, poetry and negation. *See* **19440**.

17277. Polito, Robert. Holy the Fifth International. *In* (pp. 226–42) **16122**.

17278. Saunders, Judith P. Tomlinson's *In Oklahoma*: Bishop's *The Armadillo* as literary source. *See* **18850**.

17279. Terada, Rei. Writing as a child: Lowell's poetic penmanship. *In* (pp. 33–52) **13763**.

Malcolm Lowry

17280. Rourke, Brian. Malcolm Lowry's memory machine: an eclectic systemë. JML (29:3) 2006, 19–38.

Pat Lowther

17281. Wiesenthal, Christine. The half-lives of Pat Lowther. Toronto; Buffalo, NY; London: Toronto UP, 2005. pp. xii, 489, (plates) 8. Rev. by Mervyn Nicholson in CanL (191) 2006, 132–4.

Mina Loy

17282. Churchill, Suzanne W. The little magazine *Others* and the renovation of modern American poetry. *See* **13722**.

17283. Davidson, Michael. The dream of a public language: modernity, manifesto, and the citizen subject. *See* **7777**.

17284. DiMarco, Danette. 'Misfortune's monsters / the human … race': Mina Loy's American lineage and an urban poetry of economic deprivation. Sagetrieb (19:3) 2006, 77–104.

17285. Driscoll, Kerry. Gendered poetics. *See* **19189**.

17286. Francini, Antonella. Mina Loy's prose drafts: the unfinished script of a Modernist. QPS (14) 2006, 438–44.

17287. Hancock, Tim. 'You couldn't make it up': the love of bare facts in Mina Loy's Italian poems. Eng (54:210) 2005, 175–94.

17288. Lauro, Sarah Juliet. The fruits of their labors: the childbirth poetry of Plath, Sexton, and Loy. *See* **18044**.

17289. Thurston, Michael. Mina Loy: *Lunar Baedecker*. *In* (pp. 411–21) **11788**.

Craig Lucas (b.1951)

17290. Lucas, Craig. Making a fresh start. *In* (pp. 215–24) **12245**.

Charles F. Lummis

17291. Cutter, Martha J. Sui Sin Far's letters to Charles Lummis: contextualizing publication practices for the Asian American subject at the turn of the century. *See* **9980**.

17292. Staples, Joe. 'Discovering' new talent: Charles F. Lummis's conflicted mentorship of Sui Sin Far, Sharlot Hall, and Mary Austin. WAL (40:2) 2005, 175–205.

Grace Lumpkin

17293. Mantooth, Wes. 'You factory folks who sing this song will surely understand': culture, ideology, and action in the Gastonia novels of Myra Page, Grace Lumpkin, and Olive Dargan. *See* **15412**.

Rose Macaulay

17294. Port, Cynthia. 'Ages are the stuff': the traffic in ages in interwar Britain. NWSAJ (18:1) 2006, 138–61.

Patrick McCabe

17295. Eldred, Laura G. Francie Pig *vs* the Fat Green Blob from Outer Space: horror films and *The Butcher Boy*. NewHR (10:3) 2006, 53–67.

Colum McCann (b.1965)

17296. Mara, Miriam. The geography of body: borders in Edna O'Brien's *Down by the River* & Colum McCann's *Sisters*. *In* (pp. 311–30) **12189**.

Cormac McCarthy

17297. Cutchins, Dennis. *All the Pretty Horses*: Cormac McCarthy's reading of *For Whom the Bell Tolls*. WAL (41:3) 2006, 267–99.

17298. Ellis, Jay. No place for home: spatial constraint and character flight in the novels of Cormac McCarthy. London; New York: Routledge, 2006. pp. ix, 356.

17299. —— 'What happens to country' in *Blood Meridian*. RMER (60:1) 2006.

17300. Guillemin, Georg. The pastoral vision of Cormac McCarthy. (Bibl. 2004, 18170.) Rev. by Robert Sickels in ISLE (12:2) 2005, 299–300.

17301. Hillier, Russell M. 'In a dark parody' of John Bunyan's *The Pilgrim's Progress*: the presence of subversive allegory in Cormac McCarthy's *Outer Dark*. ANQ (19:4) 2006, 52–9.

17302. Potts, James. McCarthy, Mac Airt and mythology: *Suttree* and the Irish High King. MissQ (58:1/2) 2004/05, 25–39.

17303. Sanborn, Wallis R., iii. Animals in the fiction of Cormac McCarthy. Jefferson, NC; London: McFarland, 2006. pp. 190.

17304. Zheng, Jianqing. A note on horses in *All the Pretty Horses*. NCL (36:2) 2006, 8–9.

Mary McCarthy

17305. Goi, Simona. Arendt's heroes and McCarthy's group: the politics of the social. *In* (pp. 291–318) **3266**.

Adam McCay (1874–1947)

17306. Nelson, Penelope. Under the influence? Adam McCay: journalist, poet, letter writer and influential friend. ALS (22:2) 2005, 245–52.

Harry K. (Harry Kirby) McClintock (1882–1957)

17307. Moon, Michael. Solitude, singularity, seriality: Whitman *vis-à-vis* Fourier. *See* **11573**.

Jill McCorkle

17308. Bennett, Barbara. Gender understanding in young adult literature: reading Jill McCorkle's *Ferris Beach*. NCLR (15) 2006, 64–72.

17309. McLennan, Rachael. Unpacking 'something dark': narrating Southern female adolescence in Jill McCorkle's *The Cheer Leader*, Sylvia Wilkinson's *Bone of My Bones* and Thulani Davis's *1959*. EurJAC (25:2) 2006, 139–52.

Sharyn McCrumb (b.1948)

17310. Anon. A Sharyn McCrumb bibliography. IMR (22) 2006, 35–6.

17311. Brown, Joyce Compton. Rising out of the wasteland: images of death, decay, and rebirth in the Ballad novels of Sharyn McCrumb. IMR (22) 2006, 15–23.

17312. Holland-Toll, Linda J. Bridges over and bedrock beneath: the role of ballads in Sharyn McCrumb's Ballad novels. JAC (29:3) 2006, 337–44.

17313. Holloway, Kimberley M. Keeping the legends: Celtic mythology in the Ballad novels of Sharyn McCrumb. IMR (22) 2006, 8–14.

Carson McCullers

17314. Bombaci, Nancy. Freaks in late Modernist American culture: Nathanael West, Djuna Barnes, Tod Browning, and Carson McCullers. *See* **19067**.

17315. Merva, Michael. An illusion of understanding: listeners and tellers in Sherwood Anderson's *Winesburg, Ohio* and Carson McCullers' *The Heart Is a Lonely Hunter. See* **14437**.

'Hugh MacDiarmid' (C. M. Grieve)

17316. Herbert, W. N. Testament and confessions of an informationist. *In* (pp. 72–87) **13732**.

17317. Kinloch, David. The case of the melodramatic hymen: Lallans and translation. PNRev (33:1) 2006, 41–3.

17318. Morgan, Edwin. Poetry and virtual realities. *In* (pp. 27–47) **13732**.

17319. O'Connor, Laura. Haunted English: the Celtic Fringe, the British Empire, and de-anglicization. *See* **19432**.

17320. Schmidt, Michael. Wallace Stevens: arranging, deepening, enchanting Britain. *See* **18656**.

Martin McDonagh

17321. O'Brien, Karen. 'Ireland mustn't be such a bad place so': mapping the 'real' terrain of the Aran Islands. JDTC (20:2) 2006, 169–83.

Thomas MacDonagh

17322. Booth, Michael. Thomas MacDonagh as literary theorist: song-verse and speech-verse. *In* (pp. 173–94) **12189**.

Ann-Marie MacDonald

17323. Howells, Coral Ann. Ann-Marie Macdonald: *Fall on Your Knees*. *In* (pp. 53–60) **11946**.

Betty MacDonald

17324. Kraig, Beth. It's about time somebody out here wrote the truth: Betty Bard MacDonald and North/Western regionalism. WAL (40:3) 2005, 237–71.

Dwight Macdonald

17325. Rodden, John; Rossi, John. Dethroning the lords of kitsch: Dwight Macdonald and the making of a journalist. CommRev (4:3) 2006, 12–20.

Sharman Macdonald

17326. Macdonald, Sharman; Miller, Susan; Cleage, Pearl. Our bodies, ourselves. *In* (pp. 93–103) **12297**.

Walter McDonald

17327. Maxson, Helen F. New fences on the dust: photography and Wallace Stevens's 'rage for order' in Walt McDonald's *Whatever the Wind Delivers*. *See* **18645**.

Jo McDougall

17328. McDougall, Jo. In the land of onion sets: a poet pays tribute to the influence of Flannery O'Connor. *See* **17833**.

Ian McEwan

17329. Benson, Stephen. Literary music: writing music in contemporary fiction. *See* **17420**.

17330. Boylan, Roger. Ian McEwan's family values. BosR (31:1) 2006, 41–4.

17331. Childs, Peter (ed.). The fiction of Ian McEwan. Basingstoke; New York: Palgrave Macmillan, 2006. pp. xiii, 166. (Readers' guides to essential criticism.)

17332. D'hoker, Elke. Confession and atonement in contemporary fiction: J. M. Coetzee, John Banville, and Ian McEwan. *See* **15201**.

17333. Gauthier, Tim S. Narrative desire and historical reparations: A. S. Byatt, Ian McEwan, Salman Rushdie. *See* **14980**.

17334. McEwan, Ian. Ian McEwan & Antony Gormley: a conversation about art and nature. KR (28:1) 2006, 104–12.

17335. Stewart, Victoria. 'The big war outside and the little war at home': anamnesis and the Second World War in recent British fiction. *See* **15991**.

Gwendolyn MacEwen

17336. Reid, Mary. 'This is the world as we have made it': Gwendolyn MacEwen's poetics of history. CanP (58) 2006, 36–54.

Leslie McFarlane (b.1902)

17337. Greenwald, Marilyn S. The secret of the Hardy Boys: Leslie McFarlane and the Stratemeyer Syndicate. (Bibl. 2005, 17974.) Rev. by T. Randolph Cox in DNR (75:3) 2006, 90–1; by Benjamin Lefebvre in ChildLit (34) 2006, 239–45; by Bonnie Gaarden in AL (78:3) 2006, 631–3.

Michael McFee

17338. McFee, Michael. The napkin manuscripts: selected essays and an interview. Foreword by Doris Betts. Knoxville: Tennessee UP, 2006. pp. xvi, 207.

Andrew McGahan

17339. Potter, Emily. Andrew McGahan's *The White Earth* and the ecological poetics of memory. Antipodes (20:2) 2006, 177–82.

John McGahern

17340. McGahern, John. All will be well: a memoir. London: Faber & Faber, 2005; New York: Knopf, 2006. pp. 289. Rev. by Jonathan Yardley in BkW, 12 Mar. 2006, 2; by Richard Rankin Russell in NewHR (10:4) 2006, 156–9; by Ed Minus in SewR (114:3) 2006, liii–lv.

17341. Russell, Richard Rankin. Reading John McGahern's *The Barracks* through Yeats's *Down by the Salley Gardens*. NCL (36:1) 2006, 3–4.

Peter McGehee (1955–1991)

17342. Frontain, Raymond-Jean. 'Nobody smart stays': Peter McGehee and Arkansas. ArkR (37:3) 2006, 148–66.

Patrick MacGill (b.1890)

17343. Amador Moreno, Carolina P. An analysis of Hiberno-English in the early novels of Patrick MacGill: bilingualism and language shift from Irish to English in County Donegal. Lewiston, NY; Lampeter: Mellen Press, 2006. pp. viii, 350.

Roger McGough

17344. Wright, Ben. The poetry of Roger McGough: the Liverpool renaissance. Lewiston, NY; Lampeter: Mellen Press, 2006. pp. v, 328.

John McGrath

17345. Bradby, David; Capon, Susanna. Freedom's pioneer: John McGrath's work in theatre, film and television. Exeter: Exeter UP, 2005. pp. xxii, 250. (Exeter performance studies.) Rev. by Bill McDonnell in TRI (31:2) 2006, 214–15.

Thomas McGrath

17346. Boehnlein, James M. Embracing contraries: the competing narratives of Tom McGrath's *Letter to an Imaginary Friend: Part One*. MidAmerica (32) 2005, 38–45.

17347. Peddie, Ian. Thomas McGrath, T. S. Eliot, and the commissars of culture. WAL (40:3) 2006, 423–48.

Thomas MacGreevy

17348. Lloyd, David. Republics of difference: Yeats, MacGreevy, Beckett. *See* **19405**.

17349. Wilson, James Matthew. Thomas MacGreevy reads T. S. Eliot and Jack B. Yeats: making Modernism Catholic. *See* **15722**.

Thomas McGuane

17350. Grant, J. Kerry. Apocryphal America: Thomas McGuane's troubled republic. CritW (48:1) 2006, 103–11.

Medbh McGuckian

17351. Alcobia-Murphy, Shane. 'Not forgotten or passed over at the proper time': the representation of violent events in contemporary culture. *See* **16416**.

17352. Mitchell, Erin C. Slippage at the threshold: postmodern hospitality in Medbh McGuckian's poetry. LIT (17:2) 2006, 137–55.

Arthur Machen

17353. Fox, Paul. Eureka in yellow: the art of detection in Arthur Machen's Keynote mysteries. Clues (25:1) 2006, 58–69.

Heather McHugh

17354. Giusti, Francesco. Heather McHugh: la poesia dell'occhio. PoesiaM (202) 2006, 65–76.

17355. Hammer, Langdon. The crux of the matter: Heather McHugh. ASch (75:3) 2006, 41–2.

17356. Ladin, Jay. Heather McHugh and the schooling of American poetry. Parnassus (29:1/2) 2006, 120–37 (review-article).

Maureen F. McHugh

17357. Jenkins, Alice. Knowing and geography in Octavia Butler, Ursula K. Le Guin and Maureen McHugh. *See* **14972**.

Ralph M. McInerny
('Harry Austin', 'Edward Mackin', 'Monica Quill')

17358. McInerny, Ralph M. I alone have escaped to tell you: my life and pastimes. Notre Dame, IN: Notre Dame UP, 2006. pp. 167.

Tom Mac Intyre (b.1931)

17359. Manista, Frank. Any Irish in you? The crises of Irishness in contemporary Irish drama. *In* (pp. 267–90) **12189**.

Claude McKay

17360. Gosciak, Josh. The shadowed country: Claude McKay and the romance of the Victorians. New Brunswick, NJ; London: Rutgers UP, 2006. pp. x, 205.

17361. Maxwell, William J. (ed.). Complete poems. (Bibl. 2004, 18229.) Rev. by Gary E. Holcomb in AAR (40:2) 2006, 383–5.

17362. Ramesh, Kotti Sree; Rani, Kandula Nirupa. Claude McKay: the literary identity from Jamaica to Harlem and beyond. Jefferson, NC; London: McFarland, 2006. pp. vii, 208.

17363. Stephens, Michelle Ann. Black empire: the masculine global imaginary of Caribbean intellectuals in the United States, 1914–1962. *See* **16577**.

Sir Compton Mackenzie

17364. Bogen, Anna. Compton Mackenzie, liberal education, and the Oxford novel: 'sympathy for the normal'. ELT (49:1) 2006, 14–30.

Patricia McKillip

17365. Hixon, Martha. *The Lady of Shalott* as paradigm in Patricia McKillip's *The Tower at Stony Wood*. JFA (16:3) 2006, 191–205.

17366. Kelso, Sylvia. The king and the enchanter: gender, power and authority in Patricia McKillip's fantasy novels. NYRSF (18:6) 2006, 1, 8–12.

17367. Le Lievre, Kerrie. 'I will play no games with you': riddlery, narrative and ethics in *The Riddle-Master's Game*. JFA (16:3) 2006, 233–45.

17368. Mains, Christine. For love or for money: the concept of loyalty in the works of Patricia McKillip. JFA (16:3) 2006, 219–32.

17369. Ringel, Faye. The art of Patricia McKillip: music and magic. JFA (16:3) 2006, 178–90.

E. A. (Ewart Alan) Mackintosh (1893–1917)

17370. Campbell, Colin; Green, Rosalind. Can't shoot a man with a cold: Lt E. Alan Mackintosh, 1893–1917, poet of the Highland Division. Glendaruel: Argyll, 2004. pp. 221. Rev. by R. K. R. Thornton in PNRev (31:6) 2005, 62–3.

Patricia McKissack (b.1944)

17371. Chandler, Karen. Paths to freedom: literacy and folk traditions in recent narratives about slavery and emancipation. *See* **16271**.

Reginald McKnight

17372. Nicholas, Xavier. A conversation with Reginald McKnight. Callaloo (29:2) 2006, 304–21.

Cecily Mackworth (1911–2006)

17373. Strachan, Walter. Portraits of four poets. Ed. by Geoffrey Strachan. *See* **18972**.

Julian Maclaren-Ross

17374. Treglown, Jeremy. Our secret harmonies: the *TLS* life of Anthony Powell – with Maclaren-Ross, Pryce-Jones and Orwell. *See* **18115**.

Bernard Mac Laverty

17375. Benson, Stephen. Literary music: writing music in contemporary fiction. *See* **17420**.

17376. Russell, Richard Rankin. An interview with Bernard Mac Laverty. ILS (26:1) 2006, 21–2.

17377. Sloan, Barry. The redress of imagination: Bernard Mac Laverty's *Grace Notes*. *In* (pp. 303–15) **11916**.

Alistair MacLeod

17378. Jirgens, Karl. Time and place: interview with Alistair MacLeod. Rampike (14:2) 2006, 10–19.

17379. Omhovère, Claire. Roots and routes in a selection of stories by Alistair MacLeod. CanL (189) 2006, 50–67.

Terry McMillan

17380. Guerrero, Lisa A. 'Sistahs are doin' it for themselves': chick lit in black and white. *In* (pp. 87–101) **19862**.

Larry McMurtry

17381. Barra, Allen. Larry McMurtry: writing westerns from *Hud* to *Brokeback Mountain*. AH (57:2) 2006, 18.

Terrence McNally

17382. McNally, Terrence. A blueprint for the house. *In* (pp. 38–47) **12375**.

Gerald MacNamara

17383. Vandevelde, Karen. 'What's all the stir about?': Gerald MacNamara, Synge, and the early Abbey Theatre. NewHR (10:3) 2006, 108–21.

Louis MacNeice

17384. Brown, Richard Danson. MacNeice in fairy land. *In* (pp. 352–69) **5100**.

17385. Davison-Pégon, Claire. 'Untext me here' – what exactly constitutes the text of a radio play? EtBr (30) 2006, 73–82.

17386. Roberts, Beth Ellen. One voice and many: modern poets in dialogue. *See* **13848**.

17387. Wilson, James Matthew. Louis MacNeice's struggle with Aristotelian ethics. NewHR (10:4) 2006, 53–70.

D'Arcy McNickle

17388. Purdy, John. Moving stories: visualization, *mise-en-scène*, and Native American fiction. WAL (41:2) 2006, 177–200.

Conor McPherson (b.1971)

17389. Kerrane, Kevin. The structural elegance of Conor McPherson's *The Weir*. NewHR (10:4) 2006, 105–21.

17390. Wallace, Clare. A micronarrative imperative: Conor McPherson's monologue dramas. ISR (14:1) 2006, 1–10.

James Alan McPherson (b.1943)

17391. Beavers, Herman. Postmodern heroics, misreading and irony in the fictions of James Alan McPherson and Toni Morrison. *See* **17588**.

David Madden

17392. Berger, Aimee. 'One would have almost thought her body thought': embodiment and consciousness in *The Suicide's Wife*. *In* (pp. 79–102) **17397**.

17393. Folks, Jeffrey J. Madden, Agee, and Knoxville. *In* (pp. 35–45) **17397**.

17394. Garrett, George. You play your mask: some notes on the poems of David Madden. *In* (pp. 1–6) **17397**.

17395. Hendricks, Randy. The 'whatness' of the thing: David Madden as critic. *In* (pp. 21–34) **17397**.

17396. —— Perkins, James A. David Madden on his work: an interview. *In* (pp. 117–48) **17397**.

17397. —— —— (eds). David Madden: a writer for all genres. Knoxville: Tennessee UP, 2006. pp. xiv, 177.

17398. Justus, James H. Realism singing: David Madden as playwright. *In* (pp. 7–20) **17397**.

17399. Perkins, James A. David Madden's short fiction. *In* (pp. 47–60) **17397**.

17400. Schafer, William J. David Madden's early novels. *In* (pp. 61–77) **17397**.

17401. Wier, Allen. *Sharpshooter*: David Madden's verbal sketchbook of the Civil War. *In* (pp. 103–15) **17397**.

Naomi Cornelia Long Madgett (b.1923)

17402. Madgett, Naomi Long. Pilgrim journey: autobiography. Detroit, MI: Lotus Press, 2006. pp. 492.

Haki Madhubuti ('Don L. Lee')

17403. Andrade, Heather Russell. Poetry, prose, and politics: perspectives on works by Haki Madhubuti. AL (78:1) 2006, 169–78 (review-article).

Sindiwe Magona

17404. Attree, Lizzy. Reshaping communities: the representation of HIV/AIDS in literature from South Africa and Zimbabwe. *In* (pp. 61–79) **12216**.

17405. Jacobs, Johan. Writing reconciliation: South African fiction after apartheid. *In* (pp. 177–95) **16284**.

Rabindranath Maharaj (b.1955)

17406. Ruthig, Ingrid. The potencies of chaos: Ingrid Ruthig interviews novelist Rabindranath Maharaj. BkCan (34:6) 2005, 11–12.

Norman Mailer

17407. Duguid, Scott. The addiction of masculinity: Norman Mailer's *Tough Guys Don't Dance* and the cultural politics of Reaganism. JML (30:1) 2006, 23–30.

17408. Howley, Ashton. Mailer again: heterophobia in *Tough Guys Don't Dance*. JML (30:1) 2006, 31–46.

17409. Lennon, J. Michael. Norman Mailer: novelist, journalist, or historian? JML (30:1) 2006, 91–103.

17410. McDonald, Brian. Post-Holocaust theodicy, American imperialism, and the 'very Jewish Jesus' of Norman Mailer's *The Gospel According to the Son*. JML (30:1) 2006, 78–90.

17411. Partridge, Jeffrey F. L. *The Gospel According to the Son* and Christian belief. JML (30:1) 2006, 64–77.

17412. Rampton, David. Plexed artistry: the formal case for Mailer's *Harlot's Ghost*. JML (30:1) 2006, 47–63.

17413. Ryan, James Emmett. 'Insatiable as good old America': *Tough Guys Don't Dance* and popular criminality. JML (30:1) 2006, 17–22.

17414. Weingarten, Marc. The gang that wouldn't write straight: Wolfe, Thompson, Didion, and the New Journalism revolution. *See* **15501**.

17415. Whalen-Bridge, John. The karma of words: Mailer since *Executioner's Song*. JML (30:1) 2006, 1–16. (Interview.)

Sara Maitland

17416. WORKMAN, NANCY. Creating a new saint: Incarnational theology and Sara Maitland's *Ancestral Truths*. LitTheol (19:4) 2005, 355–66.

Bernard Malamud

17417. BRIASCO, LUCA. The American baseball hero: an unstable icon. *See* **15341**.

17418. SMITH, JANNA MALAMUD. My father is a book: a memoir of Bernard Malamud. Boston, MA: Houghton Mifflin, 2006. pp. xi, 292. Rev. by Jonathan Yardley in BkW, 19 Mar. 2006, 2.

Thomas Mallon

17419. TEECE, PHILIP. Adventures under the dome: astronomers in literature. *See* **10336**.

David Malouf

17420. BENSON, STEPHEN. Literary music: writing music in contemporary fiction. Aldershot; Burlington, VT: Ashgate, 2006. pp. 178.

17421. O'REILLY, NATHANAEL. Rejecting and perpetuating the anti-suburban tradition: representations of the suburbs in *The Tax Inspector*, *Johnno*, and *Cloudstreet*. *See* **15034**.

17422. RABALAIS, KEVIN. Interview with David Malouf. GT (59) 2006, 163–73.

17423. RANDALL, DON. 'Some further being': engaging with the Other in David Malouf's *An Imaginary Life*. JCL (41:1) 2006, 17–32.

17424. RYGIEL, MARY ANN. Belgian settings and colonialism in Conrad and Malouf. Antipodes (20:2) 2006, 169–73.

17425. SEGER, NATALIE. Imagining transcendence: the poetry of David Malouf. ALS (22:2) 2005, 146–59.

17426. SMITH, YVONNE. In the beginning: David Malouf's *An Imaginary Life*. ALS (22:2) 2005, 160–74.

David Mamet

17427. BARTON, BRUCE. Imagination in transition: Mamet's move to film. (Bibl. 2005, 18068.) Rev. by Johan Callens in BELL (ns 4) 2006, 195–203.

17428. BIGSBY, CHRISTOPHER (ed.). The Cambridge companion to David Mamet. (Bibl. 2005, 18069.) Rev. by Jeanne-Andrée Nelson in ModDr (48:2) 2005, 452–4; by Andrew Radford in JAStud (40:1) 2006, 160–1.

17429. MCDERMOTT, JAMES DISHON. Austere style in twentieth-century literature: literary minimalism. *See* **14849**.

17430. MORRA, IRENE. Performing the Edwardian ideal: David Mamet and *The Winslow Boy*. *See* **13129**.

17431. ROHRKEMPER, JOHN. Stiffed: David Mamet's men. MidAmerica (31) 2004, 69–79.

Bill Manhire

17432. ROBINSON, PETER. Have you no homes? PNRev (31:3) 2005, 49–50. (Manhire's alcoholic father.)

17433. Wootten, William. On Bill Manhire. PNRev (32:5) 2006, 54–7.

K. S. Maniam

17434. Ng, Andrew Hock-Soon. Malaysian gothic: the motif of haunting in K. S. Maniam's *Haunting the Tiger* and Shirley Lim's *Haunting*. Mosaic (39:2) 2006, 75–87.

Emily Mann

17435. Mann, Emily. The female gaze. *In* (pp. 75–81) **12297**.

Olivia Manning

17436. Braybrooke, Neville; Braybrooke, June. Olivia Manning: a life. Ed. by Francis King. (Bibl. 2005, 18078.) Rev. by Jeremy Treglown in LRB (28:3) 2006, 21–2.

17437. Treglown, Jeremy. Make use of me. LRB (28:3) 2006, 21–2 (review-article). (Autobiographical fiction.)

'Katherine Mansfield' (Kathleen Mansfield Beauchamp, 'Julian Mark')

17438. Atkinson, William. Mrs Sheridan's masterstroke: liminality in Katherine Mansfield's *The Garden-Party*. EngS (87:1) 2006, 53–61.

17439. Brock, Richard. Disapprobation, disobedience and the nation in Katherine Mansfield's New Zealand stories. JNZL (24:1) 2006, 58–72.

17440. Houlahan, Mark. Plucking the flower, safety: William Shakespeare and Katherine Mansfield. *In* (pp. 349–58) **8374**.

17441. Landon, Lana Hartman; Smith, Laurel. Early works by modern women writers: Woolf, Bowen, Mansfield, Cather, and Stein. *See* **19300**.

17442. Rodríguez Salas, Gerardo. An annotated bibliography on Katherine Mansfield. RAEI (17) 2004, 307–32.

17443. Sarti Evans, Antonella. Katherine Mansfield: il viaggio. LProv (126/127) 2006, 81–92.

17444. Shen, Dan. Subverting surface and doubling irony: subtexts of Mansfield's *Revelations* and others. EngS (87:2) 2006, 191–209.

Maishe Maponya

17445. Graham, Shane. Private trauma, public drama: Fugard, Kani, and Ntshona's *The Island* and Maponya's *Gangsters*. *See* **16022**.

Dambudzo Marechera

17446. Muponde, Robert. 'The eyes of a buck': figuring the child in the Zimbabwean short story in English. *In* (pp. 99–116) **12216**.

Donald Margulies

17447. Margulies, Donald. The gilded dream: Donald Margulies on the problem of writing autobiographically. Dramatist (8:4) 2006, 30–1.

Daphne Marlatt

17448. Milne, Heather. The elliptical subject: citation and reciprocity in critical readings of *Ana Historic*. CanP (57) 2005, 86–102.

17449. York, Lorraine. Crowding the garret: women's collaborative writing and the problematics of space. *In* (pp. 288–307) **3405**.

Debra K. Marquart

17450. Marquart, Debra K. The horizontal world: growing up wild in the middle of nowhere. New York: Counterpoint, 2006. pp. xxiii, 270.

Paule Marshall

17451. Cobb, Michael L. Racial blasphemies: religious irreverence and race in American literature. *See* **14539**.

17452. Gnage, Marie Foster. Reconfiguring self: a matter of place in selected novels by Paule Marshall. *In* (pp. 96–116) **11795**.

Una Marson

17453. Rosenberg, Leah. Modern romances: the short stories in Una Marson's *The Cosmopolitan* (1928–1931). JWIL (12:1/2) 2004, 170–83.

Demetria Martínez (b.1960)

17454. Kevane, Bridget. Latino gospel and cultural renewal in Chicana fiction. *See* **15167**.

17455. Lomas, Laura. 'The war cut out my tongue': domestic violence, foreign wars, and translation in Demetria Martínez. AL (78:2) 2006, 357–87.

17456. Romero, Channette. Embodying Latina salvation: Demetria Martínez's *Mother Tongue*. ELN (44:1) 2006, 183–9.

John Masefield

17457. Errington, Philip W. John Masefield, the 'Great Auk' of English literature: a bibliography. (Bibl. 2005, 18118.) Rev. by Steven Escar Smith in PBSA (99:4) 2005, 631–4; by Marian Ka in LibC (41:3) 2006, 410–12.

17458. —— (ed.). Sea-fever: selected poems. Manchester: Carcanet Press, 2005. pp. xxv, 259. (Fyfield.) Rev. by Neil Powell in TLS, 3 June 2005, 7; by James Bridges in IGSJ (11) 2005, 136–7.

Bobbie Ann Mason

17459. Bidinger, Elizabeth. The ethics of working-class autobiography: representation of family by four American authors. *See* **19129**.

17460. Collado-Rodríguez, Francisco. Minimalism, post-humanism, and the recovery of history in Bobbie Ann Mason's *Zigzagging down a Wild Trail*. SoLJ (39:1) 2006, 98–118.

William Matthews

17461. Brown, Kurt; Kearney, Meg; Weiner, Estha (eds). Blues for Bill: a tribute to William Matthews. Akron, OH: Akron UP, 2005. pp. xviii, 134. (Akron series in poetry.)

17462. Matthews, Sebastian (introd.). Peripheral pleasures: letters to Russell Banks, Daniel Halpern, and Stanley Plumly. GaR (60:3/4) 2006, 534–49.

17463. Smith, Dave. Playing for grace: William Matthews. GaR (59:4) 2005, 777–93.

17464. Wojahn, David; Harms, James. An interview with William Matthews. *In* (pp. 85–117) **17461**.

Mustapha Matura

17465. Gough, Kathleen M. Polymorphous *Playboys*: Irish–Caribbean dancing. *See* **18709**.

W. Somerset Maugham

17466. Meyers, Jeffrey. Somerset Maugham: a life. (Bibl. 2004, 18333.) Rev. by Tracy Lee Simmons in SewR (113:4) 2005, cxiii–cxv.

Zakes Mda

17467. Gräbe, Ina. Theory and technology in contemporary South African writing: from self-conscious exploration to contextual appropriation. *In* (pp. 203–12) **14093**.

Matthew Mead (b.1924)

17468. Riley, Peter. Matthew Mead: a note. PNRev (32:3) 2006, 8–10.

Pablo Medina (b.1948)

17469. Medina, Pablo. A Cuban poet in New York. InR (28:1) 2006, 149–55.

Dina Mehta

17470. Barat, Urbashi. From resistance to regeneration: Ketaki Kushari Dyson's *Night's Sunlight* and Dina Mehta's *Getting Away with Murder*. *In* (pp. 3–10) **11731**.

Askold Melnyczuk

17471. Pierce, William. Interview with Askold Melnyczuk. GT (54) 2005, 221–38.

Pauline Melville

17472. Hanna, Mary. L'écriture des anglophones blanches, de Jean Rhys à Pauline Melville. CritP (62:711/712) 2006, 720–6.

17473. Shemak, April. Alter/natives: myth, translation and the native informant in Pauline Melville's *The Ventriloquist's Tale*. TexP (19:3) 2005, 353–72.

Samuel Menashe

17474. Brown, Kurt. Neglected. BosR (31:2) 2006, 43–4.

17475. Ricks, Christopher (ed.). New and selected poems. (Bibl. 2005, 18165.) Rev. by David Orr in NYTB, 19 Mar. 2006, 14.

H. L. Mencken

17476. Hamilton, Sharon. The Jews on Mencken's block and Guy Vanderhaeghe's *The Englishman's Boy*. *See* **18889**.

17477. Lesser, Wendy. Haute booboisie. LRB (28:13) 2006, 21–2 (review-article). (Biography of Mencken.)

17478. Rodgers, Marion Elizabeth. Mencken: the American iconoclast. (Bibl. 2005, 18183.) Rev. by Frederick Betz in DreiS (36:2) 2005, 45–8; by Wendy Lesser in LRB (28:13) 2006, 21–2; by Thomas Frank in BkW, 5 Feb. 2006, 2; by Joseph Scotchie in Chronicles (30:5) 2006, 29–30; by Charles A. Fecher in Menckeniana (177) 2006, 12–13.

Alfred H. Mendes

17479. Rahim, Jennifer. 'No place to go': homosexual space and the discourse of 'unspeakable' contents in *My Brother* and *Black Fauns*. *See* **16867**.

17480. —— The operations of the closet and the discourse of unspeakable contents in *Black Fauns* and *My Brother*. SmAx (10:2) 2006, 1–18.

Christopher Meredith (b.1954)

17481. Kirk, John. Figuring the landscape: writing the topographies of community and place. *See* **17045**.

William Meredith

17482. Gregerson, Linda. Rhetorical contract in the lyric poem. *See* **6930**.

Louise Meriwether

17483. Demirtürk, E. Lâle. Writing the urban discourse into the Black ghetto imaginary: Louise Meriwether's *Daddy Was a Number Runner*. SoLJ (39:1) 2006, 71–82.

Judith Merril (Judith Grossman (b.1923), 'Ernest Hamilton', 'Rose Sharon', 'Eric Thorstein', 'Judy Zissman')

17484. Schwartz, Richard A. Family, gender, and society in 1950s American fiction of nuclear apocalypse: *Shadow on the Hearth*, *Tomorrow!*, *The Last Day*, and *Alas, Babylon*. *See* **19391**.

James Merrill

17485. Apter, Emily. Translation with no original: scandals of textual reproduction. *In* (pp. 159–74) **3191**.

17486. Howard, Richard. A lecture on a certain mistrust of the past among young writers. Salmagundi (152) 2006, 3–10.

17487. Keniston, Ann. Overheard voices: address and subjectivity in postmodern American poetry. *See* **18042**.

17488. Materer, Timothy. James Merrill's polyphonic muse. ConLit (47:2) 2006, 207–35.

17489. Tracy, D. H. Bad ideas. *See* **15356**.

Thomas Merton

17490. Harford, James. Merton and friends: a joint biography of Thomas Merton, Robert Lax, and Edward Rice. London; New York: Continuum, 2006. pp. 320, (plates) 20. Rev. by James Martin in ANCW (195:20) 2006, 25–7.

17491. Kreyling, Michael. A good monk is hard to find: Thomas Merton, Flannery O'Connor, the American Catholic writer, and the Cold War. *In* (pp. 1–17) **17825**.

17492. McDonald, Joan C. Tom Merton: a personal biography. Milwaukee, WI: Marquette UP, 2006. pp. 468.

17493. Nugent, Robert. The silenced monk. ANCW (194:17) 2006, 8–12.

17494. Szabo, Lynn R. (ed.). In the dark before dawn: new selected poems of Thomas Merton. Preface by Kathleen Norris. (Bibl. 2005, 18203.) Rev. by Victor A. Kramer in MerA (18) 2005, 349–52.

17495. Tattoni, Igina. Thomas Merton: a mediator 'in a time of crisis'. QPS (14) 2006, 247–56.

Grace Metalious

17496. Gault, Cinda. Grace Metalious' *Peyton Place*: sentimental storm-trooper or popular throw-back? JPC (39:6) 2006, 985–1001.

Charlotte Mew

17497. Falkenberg, Betty. Charlotte Mew in America. PNRev (32:2) 2005, 36–9.

17498. —— A letter from Charlotte Mew. PNRev (32:3) 2006, 8.

17499. King, Jeannette. Whatever happened to 'good little Thomas Hardy'? Re-writing Hardy and his fiction in P. B. Parris's *His Arms Are Full of Broken Things* and Emma Tennant's *Tess*. *See* **10283**.

Robert Mezey (b.1935)

17500. Graves, Roy Neil. Mezey's *Mercy*. Exp (65:1) 2006, 56–61.

Anne Michaels (b.1958)

17501. Howells, Coral Ann. Anne Michaels: *Fugitive Pieces*. *In* (pp. 107–17) **11946**.

John Mighton (b.1957)

17502. Klaver, Elizabeth. Possible worlds, mathematics, and John Mighton's *Possible Worlds*. Narrative (14:1) 2006, 45–63.

17503. Stephenson, Jenn. Metatheatre and authentication through metonymic compression in John Mighton's *Possible Worlds*. TJ (58:1) 2006, 73–93.

17504. Young, David. An interview with John Mighton. Brick (78) 2006, 127–38.

Edna St Vincent Millay ('Nancy Boyd')

17505. Furr, Derek. Listening to Millay. JML (29:2) 2006, 94–110.

Alice Duer Miller (1874–1942)

17506. Chapman, Mary. 'Are women people?': Alice Duer Miller's poetry and politics. AmLH (18:1) 2006, 59–85.

Arthur Miller

17507. Abbotson, Susan C. The dangers of memory in Arthur Miller's *I Can't Remember Anything*. JADT (18:2) 2006, 27–39.

17508. Bigsby, Christopher. Arthur Miller: a critical study. (Bibl. 2005, 18230.) Rev. by Geoffrey Heptonstall in ContRev (286:1673) 2005, 374–5; by Jeffrey D. Mason in ModDr (48:3) 2005, 609–11; by Richard K. Tharp in TJ (58:3) 2006, 534–5; by Alan Ackerman in TheatreS (47:2) 2006, 336–7.

17509. —— Arthur Miller: un-American. ArMJ (1:1) 2006, 2–17.

17510. —— A final conversation with Arthur Miller. ArMJ (1:1) 2006, 61–77.

17511. —— (ed.). Remembering Arthur Miller. (Bibl. 2005, 18231.) Rev. by Nick Tanner in TLS, 17 Mar. 2006, 28; by George P. Castellitto in ArMJ (1:1) 2006, 79–80.

17512. BRATER, ENOCH. Arthur Miller: a playwright's life and works. London; New York: Thames & Hudson, 2005. pp. 143. Rev. by George P. Castellitto in ArMJ (1:1) 2006, 80–1.

17513. —— (ed.). Arthur Miller's America: theater & culture in a time of change. (Bibl. 2005, 18234.) Rev. by Brenda Murphy in ModDr (49:1) 2006, 135–7; by Alan Ackerman in TJ (58:3) 2006, 535–6; by Jeffrey D. Mason in TheatreS (47:1) 2006, 116–18.

17514. CASTELLITTO, GEORGE P. A. R. Ammons and Arthur Miller: unexpected metaphysical connections. AmDr (15:1) 2006, 74–84.

17515. CENTOLA, STEVEN R. 'Pattern born amid formlessness': the law of chaos in the plays of Arthur Miller. ArMJ (1:1) 2006, 19–29.

17516. —— CIRULLI, MICHELLE (eds). The critical response to Arthur Miller. Westport, CT; London: Praeger, 2006. pp. xvii, 562.

17517. EGERTON, KATHERINE. A funny thing happened on the way to the Cross: Arthur Miller's *Resurrection Blues*. JADT (18:2) 2006, 9–26.

17518. ERICKSON, LESLIE GOSS. Re-visioning of the heroic journey in postmodern literature: Toni Morrison, Julia Alvarez, Arthur Miller, and *American Beauty*. *See* **17598**.

17519. ESPEJO ROMERO, RAMÓN. Some notes about Arthur Miller's drama in Francoist Spain: towards a European history of Miller. JAStud (39:3) 2005, 485–509.

17520. GIBSON, MARION. Retelling Salem stories: gender politics and witches in American culture. *See* **13309**.

17521. HARRINGTON, GARY. Galloping ghosts in *Death of a Salesman*. ANQ (19:1) 2006, 58–9.

17522. JORDAN-FINNEGAN, RYDER. Individuation and the power of evil on the nature of the human psyche: studies in C. G. Jung, Arthur Miller, and Shakespeare. *See* **5733**.

17523. KUSHNER, TONY (ed.). Collected plays, 1944–1961. New York: Library of America, 2006. pp. x, 774. (Library of America, 163.) Rev. by George P. Castellitto in ArMJ (1:1) 2006, 81–2.

17524. LIMA, ROBERT. Stages of evil: occultism in Western theater and drama. *See* **3444**.

17525. MASON, JEFFREY. Arthur Miller's staging of the threshold of violence. ArMJ (1:1) 2006, 31–48.

17526. MEYERS, JEFFREY. Arthur Miller's outtakes. AmDr (15:1) 2006, 85–8. (Playwright's forum.)

17527. MURPHY, BRENDA. Uneasy collaboration: Miller, Kazan, and *After the Fall*. ArMJ (1:1) 2006, 49–59.

17528. STERNLICHT, SANFORD. Willy Loman: Arthur Miller's crypto-Jew. ERec (57:1) 2006, 46–56.

Heather Ross Miller (b.1939)

17529. ZUBER, ISABEL. Heather's introduction. PemM (38) 2006, 202–3.

Henry Miller

17530. Monti, Silvia. Fisicità e amore nella narrativa di Henry Miller e Jeanette Winterson. ConLett (44) 2005, 555–77.

Susan Miller (b.1944)

17531. Macdonald, Sharman; Miller, Susan; Cleage, Pearl. Our bodies, ourselves. *In* (pp. 93–103) **12297**.

Steven Millhauser

17532. Alexander, Danielle. Cohabitation: on *Revenge* by Steven Millhauser. RCF (26:1) 2006, 77–89.

17533. —— Ponce, Pedro; Rodríguez, Alicita. Steven Millhauser. RCF (26:1) 2006, 7–76.

17534. Ponce, Pedro. 'a game we no longer understood': theatrical audiences in the fiction of Steven Millhauser. RCF (26:1) 2006, 90–109.

17535. Rodríguez, Alicita. Architecture and structure in Steven Millhauser's *Martin Dressler: the Tale of an American Dreamer.* RCF (26:1) 2006, 110–26.

Anchee Min (b.1957)

17536. Hayot, Eric. Immigrating fictions: unfailing mediation in *Dictée* and *Becoming Madame Mao. See* **15125**.

Robert Minhinnick

17537. Gregson, Ian. The Baghdad moon, the Pepsi globe: Robert Minhinnick. PNRev (31:6) 2005, 52–5.

Rohinton Mistry

17538. Fisher, Susan. Teaching Rohinton Mistry's *A Fine Balance*: two cheers for universalism. CanL (190) 2006, 180–7.

17539. Malieckal, Bindu. Parsis, emigration, and immigration in Rohinton Mistry's *'Swimming Lessons' and Other Stories from Firozsha Baag.* PLL (42:4) 2006, 360–83.

17540. Morey, Peter. Rohinton Mistry. Manchester; New York: Manchester UP, 2004. pp. xiii, 209. (Contemporary world writers.)

17541. Tokaryk, Tyler. Keynes, storytelling, and realism: literary and economic discourse in Rohinton Mistry's *A Fine Balance.* StudCanL (30:2) 2005, 1–31.

Margaret Mitchell

17542. Antolini, Katharine Lane. Scarlett O'Hara as Confederate woman. *See* **12883**.

W. O. (William Ormond) Mitchell (b.1914)

17543. Mitchell, Barbara; Mitchell, Ormond. Mitchell: the life of W. O. Mitchell: the years of fame, 1948–1998. Toronto: McClelland & Stewart, 2005. pp. x, 477. Rev. by Dick Harrison in LRC (14:1) 2006, 25–7.

Naomi Mitchison

17544. Murray, Isobel. 'Clemency Ealasaid July 1940': the turning point in a poet's war. ScSR (6:2) 2005, 72–83.

Nancy Mitford

17545. SMITH, JOHN SAUMAREZ (ed.). The bookshop at 10 Curzon Street: letters between Nancy Mitford and Heywood Hill 1952–73. London: Lincoln, 2004. pp. 191, (plates) 8. Rev. by Lucy Dallas in TLS, 18 Feb. 2005, 30–1.

Nicholasa Mohr

17546. BELLVER SÁEZ, PILAR. *Nilda* de Nicholasa Mohr: el *Bildungsroman* y la aparición de un espacio puetorriqueño en la literatura de los EEUU. Atl (28:1) 2006, 101–13.

Monique Mojica

17547. MOJICA, MONIQUE. Of borders, identity, and cultural icons: a rant. CanTR (125) 2006, 35–40.

N. Scott Momaday

17548. BARTELT, GUILLERMO. Hegemonic registers in Momaday's *House Made of Dawn*. Style (39:4) 2005, 469–78.

17549. KNOELLER, CHRISTIAN P. A 'Hopi basket full of photographs': interpreting visual art in multi-genre works by contemporary Native American writers. IE (28:2) 2006, 13–16.

John Montague

17550. KENNEDY-ANDREWS, ELMER. John Montague: global regionalist? CamQ (35:1) 2006, 31–48.

L. M. Montgomery

17551. DEVEREUX, CECILY (ed.). Anne of Green Gables. Peterborough, Ont.; Orchard Park, NY: Broadview Press, 2004. pp. 400. (Broadview eds.) Rev. by Benjamin Lefebvre in CanL (189) 2006, 158–60.

17552. FREVER, TRINNA S. Anne Shirley, storyteller: orality and *Anne of Green Gables*. StudCanL (30:2) 2005, 115–41.

17553. GAMMEL, IRENE (ed.). The intimate life of L. M. Montgomery. (Bibl. 2005, 18288.) Rev. by Heidi MacDonald in CHR (87:1) 2006, 141–3; by Benjamin Lefebvre in CanL (189) 2006, 158–60.

17554. HAMMILL, FAYE. 'A new and exceedingly brilliant star': L. M. Montgomery, *Anne of Green Gables*, and Mary Miles Minter. MLR (101:3) 2006, 652–70.

Anne Moody

17555. HUDSON, ANGELA PULLEY. Mississippi lost and found: Anne Moody's autobiograph(ies) and racial melancholia. A/B (20:2) 2005, 282–96.

Christina Moody (*fl.*1910)

17556. SMITH, KATHARINE CAPSHAW. The legacy of Paul Laurence Dunbar: dialect and racial configuration in the works of Silas X. Ford and Christina Moody. *See* **9972**.

Rick Moody

17557. MILLARD, KENNETH. Rick Moody's *Purple America*: gothic resuscitation in the nuclear age. TSLL (47:3) 2005, 253–68.

17558. Moody, Rick. On the granite steps of the madhouse with shaven heads. *In* (pp. 59–72) **16122**.

Michael Moorcock

17559. Papke, Mary E. A space of her own: Pamela Zoline's *The Heat Death of the Universe*. *In* (pp. 144–59) **13537**.

C. L. (Catherine Lucille) Moore ('Lawrence O'Donnell', 'Lewis Padgett') (1911–1987)

17560. Wymer, Thomas L. Feminism, technology, and art in C. L. Moore's *No Woman Born*. Extrapolation (47:1) 2006, 51–65.

George Moore

17561. Dorré, Gina M. Victorian fiction and the cult of the horse. *See* **9736**.

Lorrie Moore

17562. Fagan, Monica. Choirs and split voices: female identity construction in Lorrie Moore's *Who Will Run the Frog Hospital?* ColLit (33:2) 2006, 52–69.

Marianne Moore

17563. Anderson, David. Marianne Moore's 'fertile procedure': fusing scientific method and organic form through syllabic technique. Paideuma (33:2/3) 2004, 83–108.

17564. Churchill, Suzanne W. The little magazine *Others* and the renovation of modern American poetry. *See* **13722**.

17565. Cull, Ryan E. 'Complexities which will remain complexities': the environmentalist epistemology of Marianne Moore's *An Octopus*. Paideuma (33:2/3) 2004, 3–27.

17566. Falkenberg, Betty. Charlotte Mew in America. *See* **17497**.

17567. Miller, Cristanne. Cultures of Modernism: Marianne Moore, Mina Loy, & Elsa Lasker-Schüler: gender and literary community in New York and Berlin. (Bibl. 2005, 18318.) Rev. by Janet Lyon in Mod/Mod (13:3) 2006, 585–7.

17568. Nardi, Paola A. Marianne Moore: ambiguous Modernism. QPS (14) 2006, 445–54.

17569. O'Connor, Laura. Haunted English: the Celtic Fringe, the British Empire, and de-anglicization. *See* **19432**.

17570. Paul, Catherine. Marianne Moore: *Observations*. *In* (pp. 422–30) **11788**.

17571. Reddy, Srikanth. 'To explain grace requires a curious hand': Marianne Moore's interdisciplinary digressions. AL (77:3) 2005, 451–81.

17572. Westover, Jeff. Value, commerce, and economy in the poetry of Marianne Moore. Paideuma (33:2/3) 2004, 29–52.

17573. Wheeler, Lesley; Gavaler, Chris. Impostors and chameleons: Marianne Moore and the Carlisle Indian School. Paideuma (33:2/3) 2004, 53–82.

Lizelia Augusta Jenkins Moorer (*fl.*1907)

17574. Bennett, Paula Bernat. Rewriting Dunbar: realism, Black women poets, and the genteel. *In* (pp. 146–61) **8435**.

Shani Mootoo

17575. Corr, John. Queer nostalgia and unnatural disgust in Shani Mootoo's *Cereus Blooms at Night*. JWIL (14:1/2) 2005, 67–95.

17576. Donatien-Yssa, Patricia. Tuer pour survivre, tragédies assassines caraïbes. *See* **16857**.

17577. May, Vivian M. Trauma in paradise: willful and strategic ignorance in *Cereus Blooms at Night*. Hypatia (21:3) 2006, 107–35.

Cherríe Moraga

17578. Moraga, Cherríe L. And Frida looks back: the art of Latina/o queer heroics. *In* (pp. 79–90) **12245**.

Edwin Morgan

17579. Fazzini, Marco. Alterities from outer space: Edwin Morgan's science fiction poems. *In* (pp. 225–41) **16284**.

17580. Jones, Chris. Strange likeness: the use of Old English in twentieth-century poetry. *See* **3677**.

17581. Morgan, Edwin. Poetry and virtual realities. *In* (pp. 27–47) **13732**.

Sally Morgan

17582. Prentice, Chris. From liminality to reconciliation: the politics of Aboriginal women's life-narratives. *In* (pp. 277–96) **8374**.

Kenneth Morris (1879–1937)

17583. Sullivan, C. W., iii. Kenneth Morris: the milestone in Welsh Celtic fantasy fiction. JFA (16:2) 2005, 142–51.

Tracie Morris

17584. Hume, Christine. Improvisational insurrection: the sound poetry of Tracie Morris. ConLit (47:3) 2006, 415–39.

Willie Morris (1934–1999)

17585. Bales, Jack. Willie Morris: an exhaustive annotated bibliography and a biography. Foreword by Rick Bragg. Jefferson, NC; London: McFarland, 2006. pp. ix, 393. Rev. by Michael P. Spikes in ArkR (37:3) 2006, 201–2.

17586. King, Larry L. In search of Willie Morris: the mercurial life of a legendary writer and editor. New York: Public Affairs, 2006. pp. xxix, 353. Rev. by Will Blythe in NYTB, 26 Mar. 2006, 16; by Jonathan Yardley in BkW, 2 Apr. 2006, 2; by Michael P. Spikes in ArkR (37:2) 2006, 136–8.

Toni Morrison

17587. Bate, Nancy Berkowitz. Toni Morrison's *Beloved*: psalm and sacrament. *In* (pp. 26–70) **17642**.

17588. Beavers, Herman. Postmodern heroics, misreading and irony in the fictions of James Alan McPherson and Toni Morrison. FLS (121) 2006, 13–21.

17589. Benedrix, Beth. Intimate fatality: *Song of Solomon* and the journey home. *In* (pp. 94–115) **17642**.

17590. Burr, Benjamin. Mythopoetic syncretism in *Paradise* and the deconstruction of hospitality in *Love*. *In* (pp. 159–74) **17642**.

17591. Byerman, Keith. Secular word: sacred flesh: preachers in the fiction of Baldwin and Morrison. *In* (pp. 187–204) **14546**.

17592. Cheng, Anne Anlin. Love and the wounded subject. PCP (41) 2006, 16–19.

17593. Crayton, Lisa A. A student's guide to Toni Morrison. Berkeley Heights, NJ: Enslow, 2006. pp. 160. (Understanding literature.)

17594. Degler, Rebecca. Rituals and 'other' religions in *The Bluest Eye*. *In* (pp. 232–55) **17642**.

17595. Di Prete, Laura. 'Foreign bodies': trauma, corporeality, and textuality in contemporary American culture. *See* **14416**.

17596. Douglas, Christopher. What *The Bluest Eye* knows about them: culture, race, identity. AL (78:1) 2006, 141–68.

17597. Eckstein, Lars. A love supreme: jazzthetic strategies in Toni Morrison's *Beloved*. AAR (40:2) 2006, 271–83.

17598. Erickson, Leslie Goss. Re-visioning of the heroic journey in postmodern literature: Toni Morrison, Julia Alvarez, Arthur Miller, and *American Beauty*. Lewiston, NY; Lampeter: Mellen Press, 2006. pp. iii, 246.

17599. Fallon, Robert. Music and the allegory of memory in *Margaret Garner*. MFS (52:2) 2006, 524–41.

17600. Fletcher, Judith. Signifying Circe in Toni Morrison's *Song of Solomon*. CW (99:4) 2006, 405–18.

17601. Flint, Holly. Toni Morrison's *Paradise*: Black cultural citizenship in the American Empire. AL (78:3) 2006, 585–612.

17602. Foulks, Beverly. Trial by fire: the theodicy of Toni Morrison in *Sula*. *In* (pp. 8–25) **17642**.

17603. Franco, Dean. What we talk about when we talk about *Beloved*. MFS (52:2) 2006, 415–39.

17604. Fritsch, Esther. *Reading gossip*: Funktionen von Klatsch in Romanen ethnischer amerikanischer Autorinnen. *See* **15777**.

17605. Fulton, Lorie Watkins. 'A direction of one's own': alienation in *Mrs Dalloway* and *Sula*. *See* **19283**.

17606. —— William Faulkner reprised: isolation in Toni Morrison's *Song of Solomon*. MissQ (58:1/2) 2004/05, 7–24.

17607. Goyal, Yogita. The gender of diaspora in Toni Morrison's *Tar Baby*. MFS (52:2) 2006, 393–414.

17608. Harris, Trudier. Watchers watching watchers: positioning characters and readers in Baldwin's *Sonny's Blues* and Morrison's *Recitatif*. *In* (pp. 103–20) **14546**.

17609. Henderson, Carol E. Refiguring the flesh: the word, the body, and the rituals of being in *Beloved* and *Go Tell It on the Mountain*. *In* (pp. 149–65) **14546**.

17610. Hilfrich, Carola. Anti-Exodus: countermemory, gender, race, and everyday life in Toni Morrison's *Paradise*. MFS (52:2) 2006, 321–49.

17611. Hogue, Bev. Naming the bones: bodies of knowledge in contemporary fiction. MFS (52:1) 2006, 121–42.

17612. Homans, Margaret. Adoption narratives, trauma, and origins. Narrative (14:1) 2006, 4–26.

17613. Jackson, Chuck. A 'headless display': *Sula*, soldiers, and lynching. MFS (52:2) 2006, 374–92.

17614. Jenkins, Candice M. Pure black: class, color, and intraracial politics in Toni Morrison's *Paradise*. MFS (52:2) 2006, 270–96.

17615. Jessee, Sharon. The 'female revealer' in *Beloved*, *Jazz* and *Paradise*: syncretic spirituality in Toni Morrison's trilogy. *In* (pp. 129–58) **17642**.

17616. —— 'Git way inside us, keep us strong': Toni Morrison and the art of critical production. MFS (52:1) 2006, 179–86 (review-article).

17617. Kérchy, Anna. Narrating the beat of the heart, jazzing the text of desire: a comparative interface of James Baldwin's *Another Country* and Toni Morrison's *Jazz*. *In* (pp. 37–62) **14546**.

17618. King, Lovalerie; Scott, Lynn Orilla (eds). James Baldwin and Toni Morrison: comparative critical and theoretical essays. *See* **14546**.

17619. Kitts, Lenore. Toni Morrison and 'Sis Joe': the musical heritage of Paul D. MFS (52:2) 2006, 495–523.

17620. Lilienfeld, Jane. 'To have the reader work *with* the author': the circulation of knowledge in Virginia Woolf's *To the Lighthouse* and Toni Morrison's *Jazz*. *See* **19303**.

17621. Mandel, Naomi. Against the unspeakable: complicity, the Holocaust, and slavery in America. *See* **13044**.

17622. M'Baye, Babacar. Resistance against racial, sexual, and social oppression in *Go Tell It on the Mountain* and *Beloved*. *In* (pp. 167–86) **14546**.

17623. Michael, Magali Cornier. New visions of community in contemporary American fiction: Tan, Kingsolver, Castillo, Morrison. *See* **18722**.

17624. Michlin, Monica. Narrative as empowerment: *Push* and the *signifying* on prior African American novels on incest. *See* **18409**.

17625. Miller, D. Quentin. Playing a mean guitar: the legacy of Staggerlee in Baldwin and Morrison. *In* (pp. 121–48) **14546**.

17626. Mirin, Jonathan. The art of Whiteness in the nonfiction of James Baldwin and Toni Morrison. *In* (pp. 223–38) **14546**.

17627. Mitchell, Keith. Femininity, abjection, and (Black) masculinity in James Baldwin's *Giovanni's Room* and Toni Morrison's *Beloved*. *In* (pp. 261–86) **14546**.

17628. Omry, Keren. Baldwin's bop 'n' Morrison's mood: bebop and race in James Baldwin's *Another Country* and Toni Morrison's *Jazz*. *In* (pp. 11–35) **14546**.

17629. O'Reilly, Andrea. Toni Morrison and motherhood: a politics of the heart. (Bibl. 2005, 18368.) Rev. by Aoi Mori in AAR (40:1) 2006, 177–80; by Sharon Jessee in MFS (52:1) 2006, 179–86.

17630. Peterson, Christopher. Beloved's claim. MFS (52:3) 2006, 548–69.

17631. Peterson, Nancy J. Introduction: on incendiary art, the moral imagination, and Toni Morrison. MFS (52:2) 2006, 261–8.

17632. Phillips, Michelle H. Revising revision: methodologies of love, desire, and resistance in *Beloved* and *If Beale Street Could Talk*. *In* (pp. 63–81) **14546.**

17633. Pocock, Judy. 'Through a glass darkly': typology in Toni Morrison's *Song of Solomon*. CRAS (35:3) 2005, 281–98.

17634. Robolin, Stéphane. Loose memory in Toni Morrison's *Paradise* and Zoë Wicomb's *David's Story*. MFS (52:2) 2006, 297–320.

17635. Russell, Danielle. Between the angle and the curve: mapping gender, race, space, and identity in Willa Cather and Toni Morrison. *See* **15114.**

17636. Sathyaraj, V.; Neelakantan, G. Family and parenting in Toni Morrison's *Love*. NCL (36:4) 2006, 9–10.

17637. Scheiber, Andrew. *Jazz* and the future Blues: Toni Morrison's urban folk zone. MFS (52:2) 2006, 470–94.

17638. Schur, Richard. Dream or nightmare? Roth, Morrison, and America. *See* **18330.**

17639. —— Unseen or unspeakable? Racial evidence in Baldwin's and Morrison's nonfiction. *In* (pp. 205–21) **14546.**

17640. Scott, Lynn Orilla. Revising the incest story: Toni Morrison's *The Bluest Eye* and James Baldwin's *Just above My Head*. *In* (pp. 83–102) **14546.**

17641. Stave, Shirley A. The master's tools: Morrison's *Paradise* and the problem of Christianity. *In* (pp. 215–31) **17642.**

17642. —— (ed.). Toni Morrison and the Bible: contested intertextualities. New York; Frankfurt: Lang, 2006. pp. vi, 258. (African American literature and culture, 12.)

17643. Stimpson, Catharine R. Do these deaths surpass understanding? The literary figure of the mother who murders. TriQ (124) 2006, 45–62.

17644. Surányi, Ágnes. The Bible as intertext in Toni Morrison's novels. *In* (pp. 116–28) **17642.**

17645. Sweeney, Megan. 'Something rogue': commensurability, commodification, crime, and justice in Toni Morrison's later fiction. MFS (52:2) 2006, 440–69.

17646. Tang, Hongmei. The image of the ghost and the politics of body inscription: on the image of the revived ghost in Morrison's *Beloved*. FLS (117) 2006, 119–26. (In Chinese.)

17647. Terry, Jennifer. A new world religion? Creolisation and Candomblé in Toni Morrison's *Paradise*. *In* (pp. 192–214) **17642.**

17648. Wardi, Anissa Janine. Jazz funerals and mourning songs: Toni Morrison's call to the ancestors in *Sula*. *In* (pp. 175–91) **17642.**

17649. Watson, Reginald. Derogatory images of sex: the Black woman and her plight in Toni Morrison's *Beloved*. CLAJ (49:3) 2006, 313–35.

17650. Wehner, David Z. To live this life intensely and well: the rebirth of Milkman Dead in Toni Morrison's *Song of Solomon*. *In* (pp. 71–93) **17642.**

17651. Weinstein, Arnold. Recovering your story: Proust, Joyce, Woolf, Faulkner, Morrison. *See* **16787.**

17652. Wittreich, Joseph. 'The ramifications of those ramifications': compounding contexts for *Samson Agonistes*. *In* (pp. 167–99) **7033**.

17653. Yeldho, Joe V.; Neelakantan, G. Toni Morrison's depiction of the city in *Jazz*. NCL (36:1) 2006, 14–16.

17654. Yoon, Seongbo. Home for the outdoored: geographies of exclusion, gendered space, and postethnicity in Toni Morrison's *Paradise*. CEACrit (67:3) 2005, 65–80.

John Mortimer

17655. Lord, Graham. John Mortimer: the devil's advocate: the unauthorised biography. London: Orion, 2005; New York: Dunne, 2006. pp. x, 326, (plates) 16. (Pub. in US as *John Mortimer: the Secret Lives of Rumpole's Creator.*)

Beatrice Mosionier (Beatrice Culleton) (b.1949)

17656. Smulders, Sharon. 'A double assault': the victimization of aboriginal women and children in *In Search of April Raintree*. Mosaic (39:2) 2006, 37–55.

Nicholas Mosley

17657. Rahbaran, Shiva. The paradox of freedom: a study of Nicholas Mosley's intellectual development in his novels and other writings. Normal, IL: Dalkey Archive Press, 2006. pp. xvi, 312.

Andrew Motion

17658. Motion, Andrew. In the blood: a memoir of my childhood. London; Boston, MA: Faber & Faber, 2006. pp. 326. Rev. by Frank Kermode in LRB (28:17) 2006, 18; by Adam Thorpe in TLS, 29 Sept. 2006, 6–7.

Harcourt Mountain (1890–1969)

17659. Taylor, Henry. The virtually unknown poetry of Harcourt Mountain. HC (43:3) 2006, 1–15.

Mourning Dove (Humishuma, Christine Quintasket)

17660. Lamont, Victoria. Native American oral practice and the popular novel; or, Why Mourning Dove wrote a western. WAL (39:4) 2005, 368–93.

Es'kia Mphahlele

17661. Ogude, James, *et al.* (eds). Es'kia continued: literary appreciation, education, African humanism & culture, social consciousness. *See* **12068**.

Lisel Mueller

17662. Foster, Linda Nemec. Transformation of the world: the metaphor of fairy tale in the poetry of Lisel Mueller. MidAmerica (32) 2005, 78–87.

17663. Heller, Janet Ruth. The theme of isolation in recent poems by Lisel Mueller. MidM (33) 2005, 43–54.

Bharati Mukherjee

17664. Davis, Rocío G. Performing dialogic subjectivities: the aesthetic project of autobiographical collaboration in *Days and Nights in Calcutta*. *In* (pp. 159–72) **11849**.

Paul Muldoon

17665. Burt, Stephen. Connection charge. TLS, 24 Nov. 2006, 6–8 (review-article). (Muldoon's Oxford lectures on poetry.)

17666. Jamison, Kay Redfield. Contemporary psychology and contemporary poetry: perspectives on mood disorders. *In* (pp. 191–203) **13732**.

17667. Muldoon, Paul. The end of the poem: Oxford lectures on poetry. *See* **3575**.

17668. Phillips, Brian. Eight takes. Poetry (189:3) 2006, 232–4 (review-article). (Muldoon's criticism.)

17669. Russell, Richard Rankin. The Yeatsian refrain in Paul Muldoon's *Moy Sand and Gravel*. ANQ (19:3) 2006, 50–6.

17670. Twiddy, Iain. Grief brought to numbers: Paul Muldoon's circular elegies. Eng (55:212) 2006, 181–99.

Harryette Mullen

17671. Beall, Emily P. 'As reading as if': Harryette Mullen's 'cognitive similes'. JLS (34:2) 2005, 125–37.

17672. Turner, Daniel Cross. New Fugitives: contemporary poets of countermemory and the futures of Southern poetry. *See* **15398**.

Talbot Mundy

17673. Taves, Brian. Talbot Mundy, philosopher of adventure: a critical biography. Jefferson, NC; London: McFarland, 2006. pp. vii, 302. Rev. by Jeff Evans in JPC (39:6) 2006, 1093–4.

John Munonye

17674. Ebeogu, Afam. Theme and setting in the novels of John Munonye. *In* (pp. 113–31) **11860**.

17675. Ogwude, Sophia O. Of hounds and quarry: the African human condition on canvas. *In* (pp. 237–51) **11860**.

Alice Munro

17676. Charman, Caitlin J. There's got to be some wrenching and slashing: horror and retrospection in Alice Munro's *Fits*. CanL (191) 2006, 13–30.

17677. Henighan, Stephen. The sense of an ending: Alice Munro's 'lovely tricks' of storytelling. TLS, 27 Oct. 2006, 21–2 (review-article).

17678. Howells, Coral Ann. Alice Munro's heritage narratives. *In* (pp. 5–14) **11946**.

17679. Phelan, James. Judgment, progression, and ethics in portrait narratives: the case of Alice Munro's *Prue*. PartA (4:2) 2006, 115–29.

17680. Thacker, Robert. Alice Munro: writing her lives. Toronto: McClelland & Stewart, 2005. pp. 603, (plates) 32. Rev. by Magdalene Redekop in LRC (14:4) 2006, 6–7; by Héliane Ventura in CanL (191) 2006, 128–30.

Iris Murdoch

17681. Bok, Sissela. Simone Weil and Iris Murdoch: the possibility of dialogue. GenI (22:4) 2005, 71 8.

17682. Nicol, Bran. Iris Murdoch's aesthetics of masochism. JML (29:2) 2006, 148–65.

Pat Murphy (b.1955)

17683. Haran, Joan. Simians, cyborgs, and women in *Rachel in Love*. *In* (pp. 244–64) **13537**.

Thomas Murphy (b.1935)

17684. Poulain, Alexandra. Playing out the rising: Sean O'Casey's *The Plough and the Stars* and Tom Murphy's *The Patriot Game*. *See* **17810**.

Gilbert Murray

17685. Schafer, Elizabeth. A tale of two Australians: Haddon Chambers, Gilbert Murray and the imperial London stage. *In* (pp. 108–25) **12360**.

Les A. Murray

17686. Cone, Temple. Murray's *Presence: Translations from the Natural World*. Exp (64:2) 2006, 121–4.

T. C. Murray

17687. Phelan, Sheila. Edward F. Barrett (1869–1936), Abbey playwright. *See* **14601**.

Walter Dean Myers

17688. Snodgrass, Mary Ellen. Walter Dean Myers: a literary companion. Jefferson, NC; London: McFarland, 2006. pp. vii, 309. (McFarland literary companions, 4.)

Vladimir Nabokov

17689. Balestrini, Nassim W. *Britva* and abstract art. Nabokovian (56) 2006, 31–8.

17690. Belletto, Steven. The Zemblan who came in from the cold; or, Nabokov's *Pale Fire*, chance, and the Cold War. ELH (73:3) 2006, 755–80.

17691. Bouchet, Marie. De Dolores, CO à Lolita, TX: détours et retours à travers '*the crazy quilt of forty-eight states*'. Anglophonia (19) 2006, 9–22.

17692. Boyd, Brian. Annotations to *Ada*: 26, Part I chapter 26. Nabokovian (56) 2006, 64–74.

17693. Cai, Lili. *Lolita*: the eternal tragedy of being lost in desire and time. FLS (118) 2006, 129–34. (In Chinese.)

17694. de la Durantaye, Leland. Eichmann, empathy, and *Lolita*. PhilL (30:2) 2006, 311–28.

17695. de Vries, Gerard; Johnson, D. Barton. Vladimir Nabokov and the art of painting. With an essay by Liana Ashenden. Amsterdam: Amsterdam UP, 2006. pp. 223. Rev. by Thomas Seifrid in SEEJ (50:4) 2006, 741–2.

17696. Dolinin, Alexander. Ods Bod(t)kins! Nabokovian (56) 2006, 27–8.

17697. Eylon, Yuval. Understand all, forgive nothing: the self-indictment of Humbert Humbert. PhilL (30:1) 2006, 158–73.

17698. Fet, Victor. Adakisme, Dolikisme; the Kirkaldy connection. Nabokovian (56) 2006, 14–19. (Entomological allusions in *Ada*.)

17699. Hamrit, Jacqueline. The silence of madness in *Signs and Symbols* by Vladimir Nabokov. PsyArt (10) 2006.

17700. Jacobs, Karen. Optical miniatures in text and image: detail and totality in Nabokov's *Speak, Memory* and Sebald's *The Emigrants*. EtBr (31) 2006, 105–15.

17701. Jedličková, Alice. From otherworldliness and a two-world scheme to 'heterocosmica': a visit to a museum with Cortázar and Nabokov. Style (40:3) 2006, 258–71.

17702. Luxemburg, Alexander M. The mystery of Vladimir Nabokov's sources: some new ideas on *Lolita*'s intertextual links. Connotations (14:1–3) 2004/05, 119–34.

17703. McCarthy, Penny. *Lolita*: wellsprings and influences. Nabokovian (56) 2006, 38–48.

17704. Maguire, James. Duality and harmony: the critical role of the variants in *Pale Fire*. Nabokovian (56) 2006, 6–14.

17705. Marcus, Amit. The self-deceptive and the other-deceptive narrating character: the case of *Lolita*. Style (39:2) 2005, 187–205.

17706. Meyers, Jeffrey. Notes on *Lolita*. NCL (36:5) 2006, 2–4.

17707. Morlan, Anna. Frost and Shade, and questions of design. Nabokovian (56) 2006, 19–27.

17708. Mulengela, Bwendo. Structured silences: a study of Nabokov, Conrad, Ngũgĩ, and Achebe. *In* (pp. 147–70) **11860**.

17709. Neumann, Claus-Peter. Consciousness as creative force and prison cell in Nabokov's *Mademoiselle O*. RAEI (17) 2004, 201–9.

17710. O'Rourke, James. Sex, lies, and autobiography: the ethics of confession. *See* **8466**.

17711. Parker, Stephen Jan; Knickmeier, Kelly. 2004 Nabokov bibliography. Nabokovian (56) 2006, 75–90.

17712. Pranzatelli, Robert. On Nabokov's definition of art. Nabokovian (56) 2006, 29–31.

17713. Reading, Amy. Vulgarity's ironist: New Criticism, midcult, and Nabokov's *Pale Fire*. AQ (62:2) 2006, 77–98.

17714. Ross, Charles Stanley. Nabokov and world literature. CLCWeb (8:2) 2006.

17715. Scharnhorst, Gary. Nabokov and Bret Harte: an overlooked allusion in *Lolita*. Nabokovian (56) 2006, 5–6.

17716. Sklyarenko, Alexey. Russian poets and potentates as Scots and Scandinavians in *Ada*; three 'Tartar' poets: part one. Nabokovian (56) 2006, 49–63.

17717. Wallach, Jennifer Jensen. Building a bridge of words: the literary autobiography as historical source material. Biography (29:3) 2006, 446–61.

V. S. (Vidiadhar Surajprasad) Naipaul (b.1932)

17718. Bhattacharya, Baidik. Naipaul's New World: postcolonial modernity and the enigma of belated space. Novel (39:2) 2006, 245–67.

17719. Buzelin, Hélène. A socio-historical perspective on French translations of West Indian fiction. JWIL (13:1/2) 2005, 80–118.

17720. Deb, Siddhartha. Naipaul, Rushdie, Seth. *See* **18457**.

17721. Dooley, Gillian. V. S. Naipaul, man and writer. Columbia; London: South Carolina UP, 2006. pp. 164.

17722. Hamner, Robert D. Ekphrasis and V. S. Naipaul's *The Enigma of Arrival*. Comparatist (30) 2006, 37–51.

17723. Laferl, Christopher F. Two novels featuring popular music: V. S. Naipaul's *Miguel Street* and Guillermo Cabrera Infante's *Tres tristes tigres*. MSp (50:2) 2006, 53–73.

17724. Malak, Amin. Naipaul's travelogues and the 'clash of civilizations' complex. CC (56:2) 2006, 261–8.

17725. Pagetti, Carlo. *'Entering the world of a novel'*: Londra, l'enigma della città. *In* (pp. 3–17) **7343**.

17726. Wilson, Gregory A. 'His own portion of the earth': the rhetoric of alienation and separation in Naipaul's *A House for Mr Biswas*. PE (1) 2006, 34–44.

R. K. Narayan

17727. Chaudhuri, Rosinka. The reality of Malgudi: R. K. Narayan's peculiarly Indian style. TLS, 4 Aug. 2006, 19–20 (review-article).

Marcia Nardi

17728. MacGowan, Christopher. Poet to poet: four books of correspondence. *See* **19194**.

Ogden Nash

17729. Parker, Douglas M. Ogden Nash: the life and work of America's laureate of light verse. Foreword by Dana Gioia. (Bibl. 2005, 18487.) Rev. by Louis Phillips in GaR (59:4) 2005, 961–3.

Sena Jeter Naslund

17730. Cawelti, John G. Sherlock Holmes: the case of the perpetual detective. *See* **9928**.

Gloria Naylor

17731. Fritsch, Esther. *Reading gossip*: Funktionen von Klatsch in Romanen ethnischer amerikanischer Autorinnen. *See* **15777**.

17732. Paterson, Kathryn M. Gloria Naylor's North/South dichotomy and the reversal of the Middle Passage: juxtaposed migrations within *Mama Day*. *In* (pp. 76–95) **11795**.

Peter Nazareth

17733. Nazareth, Peter. Path of thunder: meeting Bessie Head. *See* **16307**.

John G. Neihardt

17734. Neihardt, Hilda Martinsen. The broidered garment: the love story of Mona Martinsen and John G. Neihardt. Lincoln; London: Nebraska UP, 2006. pp. x, 303.

E. (Edith) Nesbit (1858–1924)

17735. Briggs, Julia. *The Amulet* and other stories of time. *In* (pp. 215–30) **17738**.

17736. Dowker, Ann. *Five Children and It*: some parallels with the nineteenth-century moral tale. *In* (pp. 169–83) **17738**.

17737. Flegel, Monica. A momentary hunger: Fabianism and didacticism in E. Nesbit's writing for children. *In* (pp. 17–38) **17738**.

17738. Jones, Raymond E. (ed.). E. Nesbit's Psammead trilogy: a children's classic at 100. Lanham, MD; London: Scarecrow Press for the Children's Literature Assn, 2006. pp. xxv, 273. (Children's Literature Assn centennial studies, 3.)

17739. Marchant, Jennifer. 'Exactly as it was'? H. R. Millar's expansions and subversions of the Psammead trilogy. *In* (pp. 231–53) **17738**.

17740. Nelson, Claudia. The 'It' girl (and boy): ideologies of gender in the Psammead trilogy. *In* (pp. 1–15) **17738**.

17741. Rahn, Suzanne. News from E. Nesbit: *The Story of the Amulet* and the Socialist utopia. *In* (pp. 185–213) **17738**.

17742. Reimer, Mavis. The beginning of the end: writing empire in E. Nesbit's Psammead books. *In* (pp. 39–62) **17738**.

17743. Richey, Esther Gilman. Only half magic: Edward Eager's revision of Nesbit's Psammead trilogy. *In* (pp. 255–69) **17738**.

17744. Rosenberg, Teya. Generic manipulation and mutation: E. Nesbit's Psammead series as early magical realism. *In* (pp. 63–88) **17738**.

17745. Rudd, David. Where It was, there shall five children be: staging desire in *Five Children and It*. *In* (pp. 135–49) **17738**.

17746. Susina, Jan. Textual building blocks: Charles Dickens and E. Nesbit's literary borrowings in *Five Children and It*. *In* (pp. 151–68) **17738**.

17747. White, Donna R. Communicating humor in E. Nesbit's fantasy trilogy. *In* (pp. 111–33) **17738**.

17748. Wood, Naomi. Materiality, the wish, and the marvelous: E. Nesbit's comic spirituality in the Psammead trilogy. *In* (pp. 89–110) **17738**.

Sir Henry Newbolt

17749. Stanford, Donald E. A critical study of the works of four British writers: Margaret Louisa Woods (1856–1945), Mary Coleridge (1861–1907), Sir Henry Newbolt (1862–1938), R. C. Trevelyan (1872–1951). Ed. by R. W. Crump. *See* **9497**.

Amy (Amy Lynn) Newman

17750. Loreto, Paola. In the Modernist grain: Amy Newman and the poetics of impermanence. QPS (14) 2006, 455–66.

Fae Myenne Ng (b.1956)

17751. Izzo, Donatella. 'A new rule for the imagination': rewriting Modernism in *Bone*. *In* (pp. 137–55) **11849**.

Ngũgĩ wa Thiong'o

17752. Canepari-Labib, Michela. Writing and translating after the Empire. Culture (18) 2004, 233–58.

17753. Ilo, Isaiah. Language in modern African drama. *See* **14363**.

17754. MULENGELA, BWENDO. Structured silences: a study of Nabokov, Conrad, Ngũgĩ, and Achebe. *In* (pp. 147–70) **11860**.

17755. RODRÍGUEZ GUERRERO-STRACHAN, SANTIAGO. Social exiles and language refugees: the case of postcolonial authors. JCarL (4:1) 2005, 75–84.

Beverley Nichols

17756. BOGEN, ANNA. Compton Mackenzie, liberal education, and the Oxford novel: 'sympathy for the normal'. *See* **17364**.

William Nicholson

17757. OP DE BEECK, NATHALIE. Suspended animation: picture book storytelling, twentieth-century childhood, and William Nicholson's *Clever Bill*. LU (30:1) 2006, 54–75.

Mike Nicol (b.1951)

17758. TITLESTAD, MICHAEL; KISSACK, MIKE. The secularization of South Africa's Truth and Reconciliation Commission in Mike Nicol's *The Ibis Tapestry*. RAL (37:4) 2006, 48–67.

Lorine Niedecker

17759. BERRY, ELEANOR. Paradoxes of form in the poetry of Lorine Niedecker. *In* (pp. 203–32) **13763**.

17760. GOLSTON, MICHAEL. Petalbent devils: Louis Zukofsky, Lorine Niedecker, and the Surrealist praying mantis. *See* **19469**.

17761. SAVAGE, ELIZABETH. Love, the lyric, and history in Lorine Niedecker and Susan Howe. Sagetrieb (19:3) 2006, 11–40.

Lewis Nkosi

17762. STIEBEL, LINDY; GUNNER, LIZ (eds). Still beating the drum: critical perspectives on Lewis Nkosi. Amsterdam; New York: Rodopi, 2005. pp. xxxv, 375. (Cross/cultures: readings in the post-colonial literatures in English, 81.) Rev. by Michael Janis in AfSR (49:3) 2006, 129–31.

William F. Nolan (b.1928)

17763. TINNELL, ROBERT. *Logan's Run* to relevance. *In* (pp. 217–24) **12548**.

Lewis Nordan

17764. FARCA, PAULA ANCA. Whistling the Blues and washing the language in Lewis Nordan's *Wolf Whistle*. NCL (36:5) 2006, 4–5.

Lawrence Norfolk (b.1963)

17765. WALKER, JONATHAN. An interview with A. S. Byatt and Lawrence Norfolk. *See* **14987**.

Marsha Norman

17766. GUSSOW, MEL. Entering the mainstream: the plays of Beth Henley, Marsha Norman, and Wendy Wasserstein. *In* (pp. 45–53) **12297**.

Frank Norris

17767. CLAYBAUGH, AMANDA. He could not cable. LRB (28:14) 2006, 31–2 (review-article). (Biography of Norris.)

17768. Cruz, Denise. Reconsidering *McTeague*'s 'Mark' and 'Mac': intersections of US Naturalism, imperial masculinities, and desire between men. AL (78:3) 2006, 487–517.

17769. Eperjesi, John R. The imperialist imaginary: visions of Asia and the Pacific in American culture. Foreword by Donald E. Pease. (Bibl. 2005, 18518.) Rev. by Jon Davidann in JAH (92:4) 2006, 1461; by Krystyn Moon in PacHR (75:2) 2006, 330–2.

17770. Fleissner, Jennifer L. The biological clock: Edith Wharton, Naturalism, and the temporality of womanhood. *See* **19095**.

17771. Link, Eric Carl. The theodicy problem in the works of Frank Norris. StAN (1:1/2) 2006, 90–108.

17772. Long, Denise Howard. A dentist no more: the destruction of masculinity in *McTeague*. MidAmerica (32) 2005, 67–77.

17773. MacDougall, Robert. The wire devils: pulp thrillers, the telephone, and action at a distance in the wiring of a nation. AmQ (58:3) 2006, 715–41.

17774. McElrath, Joseph R., Jr; Crisler, Jesse S. Frank Norris: a life. (Bibl. 2005, 18520.) Rev. by Keith Newlin in DreiS (36:2) 2005, 54–7; by Victor Davis Hanson in NYTB, 1 Jan. 2006, 12; by Amanda Claybaugh in LRB (28:14) 2006, 31–2; by Leonard Cassuto in AmQ (58:4) 2006, 1249–61.

Kathleen Norris (b.1947)

17775. Buturian, Linda. Kathleen Norris: an interview. *In* (pp. 61–71) **11940**.

17776. Cole, Kevin L. Geographies of hope: Kathleen Norris and David Lynch. *In* (pp. 247–62) **11916**.

17777. Gray, Timothy. 'A world without gravity': the urban pastoral spirituality of Jim Carroll and Kathleen Norris. TSLL (47:3) 2005, 213–52.

Alice Notley (b.1945)

17778. Keelan, Claudia; Notley, Alice. A conversation: September 2002 – December 2003. APR (33:3) 2004, 15–19.

17779. Robbins, Amy. Alice Notley's post-confessional I: toward a poetics of postmodern witness. PCP (41) 2006, 76–90.

Alden Nowlan

17780. Lahey, Ernestine. (Re)thinking world-building: locating the text-worlds of Canadian lyric poetry. *See* **18162**.

Mpho 'M'atsepo Nthunya (b.1930)

17781. Weiss, Bettina. An approach to homoerotic female desire in *Three Moments in a Marriage*, *The Purple Violet of Oshaantu*, and *A Question of Power*. *In* (pp. 117–44) **12216**.

Winston Ntshona

17782. Graham, Shane. Private trauma, public drama: Fugard, Kani, and Ntshona's *The Island* and Maponya's *Gangsters*. *See* **16022**.

17783. Nwahunanya, Chinyere. Tragedy in African literary drama. *In* (pp. 197–211) **11860**.

Bruce Nugent (1906–1987)

17784. Schmidt, Tyler T. 'in the glad flesh of my fear': corporeal inscriptions in Richard Bruce Nugent's *Geisha Man*. AAR (40:1) 2006, 161–73.

Flora Nwapa

17785. Nwankwo, Chimalum. African literature and the woman: the imagined reality as a strategy of dissidence. Meridians (6:2) 2006, 195–208.

Joyce Carol Oates

17786. Araújo, Susana. Joyce Carol Oates reread: overview and interview with the author. CritS (18:3) 2006, 92–105.

17787. Jirgens, Karl. Talking with Joyce Carol Oates. Rampike (14:2) 2006, 4–8.

17788. Johnson, Greg. Fictions of the new millennium: an interview with Joyce Carol Oates. MichQR (45:2) 2006, 387–400.

17789. —— (ed.). Joyce Carol Oates: conversations, 1970–2006. Princeton, NJ: Ontario Review Press, 2006. pp. ix, 249, (plates) 12.

17790. Sutton, Brian. An unconscious obsession: the influence of Flannery O'Connor's novels on Joyce Carol Oates's *Where Are You Going, Where Have You Been? See* **17848**.

Patrick O'Brian

17791. Brown, Anthony Gary. The Patrick O'Brian muster book: persons, animals, ships and cannon in the Aubrey–Maturin sea novels. Foreword by Colin White. (Bibl. 2000, 19157.) Jefferson, NC; London: McFarland, 2006. pp. ix, 395. (Second ed.: first ed. 1999.)

17792. Simmons, James R., Jr. 'Don't tell me about rears and vices; I have been in the navy all my life': profligacy on the high seas in Jane Austen and Patrick O'Brian. *See* **9071**.

Edna O'Brien

17793. Balzano, Wanda. Godot land and its ghosts: the uncanny genre and gender of Edna O'Brien's *Sister Imelda*. *In* (pp. 92–109) **17794**.

17794. Colletta, Lisa; O'Connor, Maureen (eds). Wild colonial girl: essays on Edna O'Brien. Madison; London: Wisconsin UP, 2006. pp. viii, 175. (Irish studies in literature and culture.)

17795. Farquharson, Danine; Schrank, Bernice. Blurring boundaries, intersecting lives: history, gender, and violence in Edna O'Brien's *House of Splendid Isolation*. *In* (pp. 110–42) **17794**.

17796. Gillespie, Michael Patrick. Edna O'Brien and the lives of James Joyce. *In* (pp. 78–91) **17794**.

17797. Harris, Michael. Outside history: Edna O'Brien's *House of Splendid Isolation*. NewHR (10:1) 2006, 111–22.

17798. Laing, Kathryn; Mooney, Sinéad; O'Connor, Maureen (eds). Edna O'Brien: new critical perspectives. Dublin: Carysfort Press, 2006. pp. viii, 252.

17799. Mara, Miriam. The geography of body: borders in Edna O'Brien's *Down by the River* & Colum McCann's *Sisters*. *In* (pp. 311–30) **12189**.

17800. Pelan, Rebecca. Edna O'Brien's 'love objects'. *In* (pp. 58–77) **17794**.

17801. Thompson, Helen. Hysterical hooliganism: O'Brien, Freud, Joyce. *In* (pp. 31–57) **17794**.

'Flann O'Brien' (Brian O'Nolan, 'Myles na gCopaleen')

17802. Maslen, R. W. Flann O'Brien's bombshells: *At Swim-Two-Birds* and *The Third Policeman*. NewHR (10:4) 2006, 84–104.

Kate O'Brien

17803. Ingman, Heather. Translating between cultures: a Kristevan reading of the theme of the foreigner in some twentieth-century novels by Irish women. YES (36:1) 2006, 177–90.

17804. Walshe, Éibhear. Kate O'Brien: a writing life. Dublin; Portland, OR: Irish Academic Press, 2006. pp. xii, 194, (plates) 8. Rev. by Donna Decker Schuster in NewHR (10:3) 2006, 154–5.

Tim O'Brien

17805. Donovan, Christopher. Postmodern counternarratives: irony and audience in the novels of Paul Auster, Don DeLillo, Charles Johnson and Tim O'Brien. *See* **14515**.

17806. Stocks, Claire. Acts of cultural identification: Tim O'Brien's *July, July*. EurJAC (25:3) 2006, 173–88.

17807. Young, William. Missing in action: Vietnam and sadism in Tim O'Brien's *In the Lake of the Woods*. MidQ (47:2) 2006, 131–43.

Sean O'Casey

17808. Ayling, Ronald. Sean O'Casey's theatre of war. Vernon, B.C.: Kalamalka Press, 2004. pp. xxiii, 76. (Mackie lecture and reading series, 1.) Rev. by Paul O'Brien in ILS (26:1) 2006, 25.

17809. Moran, James. Staging the Easter Rising: 1916 as theatre. *See* **12338**.

17810. Poulain, Alexandra. Playing out the rising: Sean O'Casey's *The Plough and the Stars* and Tom Murphy's *The Patriot Game*. EA (59:2) 2006, 156–69.

Flannery O'Connor

17811. Ashley, Jack Dillard. 'The very heart of mystery': theophany in O'Connor's stories. *In* (pp. 102–10) **17825**.

17812. Baldwin, Debra Romanick. Augustinian physicality and the rhetoric of the grotesque in the art of Flannery O'Connor. *In* (pp. 301–25) **3301**.

17813. Behling, Laura L. The necessity of disability in *Good Country People* and *The Lame Shall Enter First*. FOR (4) 2006, 88–98.

17814. Bethea, Arthur F. O'Connor's *A Good Man Is Hard to Find*. Exp (64:4) 2006, 239–42.

17815. Brinkmeyer, Robert H., Jr. Taking it to the streets: Flannery O'Connor, prophecy, and the Civil Rights Movement. FOR (4) 2006, 99–109.

17816. Cash, Jean W. Flannery O'Connor as communicant: a constant devotion. *In* (pp. 149–61) **17825**.

17817. Cobb, Michael L. Racial blasphemies: religious irreverence and race in American literature. *See* **14539**.

17818. Daniel, Scott. Gender-bending innuendo and mystical theology in O'Connor's *Wise Blood*. FOR (4) 2006, 110–21.

17819. Darretta, John Lawrence. Before the sun has set: retribution in the fiction of Flannery O'Connor. New York; Frankfurt: Lang, 2006. pp. 147. (Studies on themes and motifs in literature, 84.)

17820. Doriza, Garifallia. The rise of the I–It world in Flannery O'Connor's monologic community. LitTheol (19:4) 2005, 311–26.

17821. Esposito, Scott. Well-crafted transformations: an interview with Edward Falco. *See* **20229**.

17822. Gentry, Marshall Bruce. He would have been a good man: compassion and meanness in Truman Capote and Flannery O'Connor. *In* (pp. 42–55) **17825**.

17823. Gerald, Kelly. The world of the cartoons and their importance to O'Connor's fiction. *In* (pp. 26–41) **17825**.

17824. Gordon, Sarah. Seeking beauty in darkness: Flannery O'Connor and the French Catholic renaissance. *In* (pp. 68–84) **17825**.

17825. Gretlund, Jan Nordby; Westarp, Karl-Heinz (eds). Flannery O'Connor's radical reality. Columbia; London: South Carolina UP, 2006. pp. xvii, 196.

17826. Hewitt, Avis. 'Someone to shoot her every minute of her life': maternity and violent death in Helena María Viramontes and Flannery O'Connor. FOR (4) 2006, 12–26.

17827. Karnes, Rebecca S. 'On earth as in heaven': the potential, peril, and paradox of community in Flannery O'Connor's *The Life You Save May Be Your Own*. FOR (4) 2006, 122–30.

17828. Keil, Katherine. O'Connor's *A Good Man Is Hard to Find*. Exp (65:1) 2006, 44–7.

17829. Kevane, Bridget; Viramontes, Helena María. Viramontes on O'Connor. FOR (4) 2006, 5–11. (Interview.)

17830. Kreyling, Michael. A good monk is hard to find: Thomas Merton, Flannery O'Connor, the American Catholic writer, and the Cold War. *In* (pp. 1–17) **17825**.

17831. Lake, Christina Bieber. The incarnational art of Flannery O'Connor. (Bibl. 2005, 18565.) Rev. by Ralph C. Wood in FOR (4) 2006, 143–6.

17832. Lott, Bret. Why have we given up the ghost? Notes on reclaiming literary fiction. *In* (pp. 43–60) **11940**.

17833. McDougall, Jo. In the land of onion sets: a poet pays tribute to the influence of Flannery O'Connor. FOR (4) 2006, 69–87.

17834. Meeks, Lila N. Flannery O'Connor's art: a gesture of grace. *In* (pp. 18–25) **17825**.

17835. Montgomery, Marion. Fiction's echo of revelation: Flannery O'Connor's challenge as Thomistic maker. *In* (pp. 122–37) **17825**.

17836. —— Hillbilly Thomist: Flannery O'Connor, St Thomas, and the limits of art. Jefferson, NC; London: McFarland, 2006. 2 vols. pp. viii, 692.

17837. NESTER, NANCY L. O'Connor's *A Good Man Is Hard To Find*. Exp (64:2) 2006, 115–18.

17838. O'GORMAN, FARRELL. Peculiar crossroads: Flannery O'Connor, Walker Percy, and Catholic vision in postwar Southern fiction. (Bibl. 2005, 18573.) Rev. by Ralph C. Wood in MissQ (57:4) 2004, 661–5; by Thomas Bonner, Jr, in XavR (25:2) 2005, 84–6; by Bertram Wyatt-Brown in CHist (74:3) 2005, 658–60; by Bryan Giemza in SoLJ (39:1) 2006, 133–6.

17839. —— White, Black, and Brown: reading O'Connor after Richard Rodriguez. FOR (4) 2006, 32–49.

17840. —— RODRIGUEZ, RICHARD. 'A twenty-first century writer': Richard Rodriguez on Flannery O'Connor. FOR (4) 2006, 27–31. (Interview.)

17841. PASTOOR, CHARLES. Moments of grace in James Wilcox's *Modern Baptists*. *See* **19150**.

17842. ROBILLARD, DOUGLAS, JR (ed.). The critical response to Flannery O'Connor. (Bibl. 2005, 18577.) Rev. by Carla L. Verderame in FOR (4) 2006, 147–9.

17843. SAMWAY, PATRICK. Toward discerning how Flannery O'Connor's fiction can be considered 'Roman Catholic'. *In* (pp. 162–75) **17825**.

17844. SESSIONS, W. A. 'Then I discovered the Germans': O'Connor's encounter with Guardini and German thinkers of the interwar period. *In* (pp. 56–67) **17825**.

17845. SIMPSON, MELISSA. Flannery O'Connor: a biography. (Bibl. 2005, 18578.) Rev. by Virginia Wray in FOR (4) 2006, 150–1.

17846. SKEI, HANS H. O'Connor's *Everything That Rises Must Converge* and theories of the short story sequence. *In* (pp. 138–48) **17825**.

17847. SRIGLEY, SUSAN. Flannery O'Connor's sacramental art. (Bibl. 2005, 18579.) Rev. by Doris Betts in CHist (75:2) 2006, 461–2; by Bryan Giemza in SoLJ (39:1) 2006, 133–6; by W. A. Sessions in FOR (4) 2006, 137–42.

17848. SUTTON, BRIAN. An unconscious obsession: the influence of Flannery O'Connor's novels on Joyce Carol Oates's *Where Are You Going, Where Have You Been?* FOR (4) 2006, 54–68.

17849. THÖRNQVIST, INGER. The church-historical origin of O'Connor's blood symbolism. *In* (pp. 85–101) **17825**.

17850. WESTARP, KARL-HEINZ. Metaphoric processes in Flannery O'Connor's short fiction. *In* (pp. 111–21) **17825**.

17851. WHITT, MARGARET EARLEY. An O'Connor redemption in Tommy Lee Jones's *The Three Burials of Melquiades Estrada*. FOR (4) 2006, 134–6.

17852. WOOD, RALPH C. Flannery O'Connor and the Christ-haunted South. (Bibl. 2004, 18759.) Rev. by Thomas F. Haddox in MissQ (58:1/2) 2004/05, 418–22; by Lindsay M. Sullivan in LitTheol (19:2) 2005, 181–4; by David C. Alexander in CHist (74:1) 2005, 199–201; by Helen R. Andretta in StudN (38:3) 2006, 382–3.

Scott O'Dell

17853. PAYMENT, SIMONE. Scott O'Dell. New York: Rosen Central, 2006. pp. 112. (Library of author biographies.)

Clifford Odets

17854. Cardullo, Robert. Odets's *Awake and Sing!* Exp (64:4) 2006, 234–6.

Nuala O'Faolain

17855. Malone, Christopher. 'If I go on long enough calling that my life I'll end up by believing it': Samuel Beckett and contemporary Irish memoir. *In* (pp. 195–216) **12189**.

Liam O'Flaherty

17856. Marchbanks, Paul. Lessons in lunacy: mental illness in Liam O'Flaherty's *Famine*. NewHR (10:2) 2006, 92–105.

Howard O'Hagan

17857. Hingston, Kylee-Anne. The declension of a story: narrative structure in Howard O'Hagan's *Tay John*. StudCanL (30:2) 2005, 181–90.

Frank O'Hara

17858. Esposito, Scott. Well-crafted transformations: an interview with Edward Falco. *See* **20229**.

17859. Sadoff, Ira. Frank O'Hara's intimate fictions. APR (35:6) 2006, 49–52.

17860. Ware, Karen. Frank O'Hara's oranges: the relations between poetry, painting, and painters. *In* (pp. 93–104) **11781**.

John O'Hara

17861. Bruccoli, Matthew J. (ed.). John O'Hara: a documentary volume. Detroit, MI: Gale Research, 2006. pp. xxxvii, 444. (Dictionary of literary biography, 324.)

John Okada

17862. Bush, Harold K., Jr. A passion for the impossible: Richard Rorty, John Okada, and James Baldwin. *In* (pp. 171–86) **11916**.

17863. Kim, Daniel Y. Once more, with feeling: Cold War masculinity and the sentiment of patriotism in John Okada's *No-No Boy*. Criticism (47:1) 2005, 65–83.

17864. Lee, James Kyung-Jin. Asian Americans. *In* (pp. 174–93) **11776**.

Donal O'Kelly (b.1958)

17865. Manista, Frank. Any Irish in you? The crises of Irishness in contemporary Irish drama. *In* (pp. 267–90) **12189**.

Christopher Okigbo

17866. Obumselu, Ben. Christopher Okigbo: a poet's identity. *In* (pp. 57–78) **11860**.

Ben Okri

17867. Ogwude, Sophia O. Of hounds and quarry: the African human condition on canvas. *In* (pp. 237–51) **11860**.

Douglas Oliver

17868. Keelan, Claudia; Notley, Alice. A conversation: September 2002 – December 2003. *See* **17778**.

17869. Oliver, Douglas. Whisper 'Louise'. Hastings: Reality Street, 2005. pp. 438. (Memoir of Oliver and of Louise Michel.) Rev. by John Muckle in PNRev (32:5) 2006, 78–9.

Mary Oliver

17870. Gordon, Sarah. Entomophagy: representations of insect eating in literature and mass media. *In* (pp. 342–62) **3203**.

Tillie Olsen

17871. Biagiotti, Cinzia. Silenzi infranti: la scrittura di Tillie Olsen. Urbino: QuattroVenti, 2005. pp. 269. (Crossroads.)

Charles Olson

17872. Brinton, Ian. Black Mountain in England: 1. *See* **16994**.

17873. —— Black Mountain in England: 2. *See* **18857**.

17874. —— Black Mountain in England: 3. *See* **18847**.

17875. Joyce, Michael. On the OlsonNow Forum. AmBR (27:3) 2006, 13.

17876. Narbeshuber, Lisa. Relearning Denise Levertov's *Alphabet*: war, flesh, and the intimacy of otherness. *See* **17162**.

Stewart O'Nan (b.1961)

17877. Collins, Marty. An interview with Stewart O'Nan. ConnR (28:2) 2006, 128–39.

Michael Ondaatje

17878. Chu, Patricia P. 'A flame against a sleeping lake of petrol': form and the sympathetic witness in Selvadurai's *Funny Boy* and Ondaatje's *Anil's Ghost*. *In* (pp. 86–103) **11849**.

17879. Gin, Pascal. Dire le monde: discours argumentatif et mondialisme dans *Anil's Ghost* de Michael Ondaatje. StudCanL (30:2) 2005, 32–54.

17880. Lundgren, Jodi. 'Colour disrobed itself from the body': the racialized aesthetics of liberation in Michael Ondaatje's *In the Skin of a Lion*. CanL (190) 2006, 15–29.

17881. Meyers, Jeffrey. T. E. Lawrence and *The English Patient*. *See* **17069**.

17882. Rosenfeld, Natania. Less light: the end(s) of Aestheticism in Pater, Ondaatje, and Sebald. *See* **10985**.

17883. Stanton, Katherine. Cosmopolitan fictions: ethics, politics, and global change in the works of Kazuo Ishiguro, Michael Ondaatje, Jamaica Kincaid, and J. M. Coetzee. *See* **16566**.

17884. Westerman, Molly. 'Of skulls or spirits': the haunting space between fictional(ized) history and historical note. *See* **14489**.

Eugene O'Neill

17885. Alexander, Doris. Eugene O'Neill's last plays: separating art from autobiography. (Bibl. 2005, 18636.) Rev. by J. Chris Westgate in TJ (58:3) 2006, 532–3; by Thomas F. Connolly in EOR (28) 2006, 188–91.

17886. Alsen, Eberhard. Racism and the film version of Eugene O'Neill's *The Emperor Jones*. CLAJ (49:4) 2006, 406–22.

17887. Berger, Jason. Refiguring O'Neill's early sea plays: maritime labor enters the age of modernity. EOR (28) 2006, 13–31.

17888. Bernstein, Samuel J. Making it, madness, and motherhood: the deep structure of *All God's Chillun Got Wings*. EOR (28) 2006, 50–61.

17889. Black, Stephen A. Hints of the tragic in *Fog* and other early O'Neill plays. EOR (28) 2006, 7–12.

17890. —— Tragic anagnorisis in *The Iceman Cometh*. EOR (28) 2006, 147–64.

17891. Brietzke, Zander. The gift of Ric Burns. EOR (28) 2006, 113–30.

17892. —— *The Long Voyage Home*: a vicious cycle at sea. EOR (28) 2006, 32–49.

17893. Gelb, Arthur; Gelb, Barbara. Behind the scenes of O'Neill's elephant *opus*. EOR (28) 2006, 101–12.

17894. Ki, Wing-chi. The s(ub)lime symptom and O'Neill's *Long Day's Journey into Night*. JDTC (20:2) 2006, 5–23.

17895. Koutsoudaki, Mary. The Greek plays of Eugene O'Neill. Athens: Parousia, 2004. pp. 223. Rev. by Robert Simpson McLean in EOR (28) 2006, 178–80.

17896. Lima, Robert. Stages of evil: occultism in Western theater and drama. *See* **3444**.

17897. Monks, Aoife. 'Genuine negroes and real bloodhounds': cross-dressing, Eugene O'Neill, the Wooster Group, and *The Emperor Jones*. ModDr (48:3) 2005, 540–64.

17898. Porter, Laurin. Musical and literary allusions in O'Neill's final plays. EOR (28) 2006, 131–46.

17899. Törnqvist, Egil. Eugene O'Neill: a playwright's theatre. Jefferson, NC; London: McFarland, 2004. pp. vi, 262. Rev. by Laurin Porter in EOR (28) 2006, 174–6.

17900. Westgate, J. Chris. Staging the 'poor, wicked lot': O'Neill's rebuttal to fallen women plays. EOR (28) 2006, 62–79.

Han Ong

17901. Hsu, Hsuan L. Mimicry, spatial captation, and Feng Shui in Han Ong's *Fixer Chao*. MFS (52:3) 2006, 675–704.

Tess Akaeke Onwueme

17902. Bartlett-Pack, Juluette. Recovering the past: transatlantic migration, hybrid identities, and healing in Tess Onwueme's *The Missing Face*. *In* (pp. 171–82) **11795**.

17903. Uko, Iniobong I. Gender and identity in the works of Osonye Tess Onwueme. Trenton, NJ: Africa World Press, 2005. pp. xxii, 306.

George Oppen

17904. Barzilai, Lyn Graham. George Oppen: a critical study. Jefferson, NC; London: McFarland, 2006. pp. vii, 223.

17905. Finkelstein, Norman. The sacred and the real in *The Tablets* of Armand Schwerner. *See* **18432**.

17906. Izenberg, Oren. Oppen's silence, Crusoe's silence, and the silence of other minds. Mod/Mod (13:1) 2006, 41–65.

17907. Nicholls, Peter. George Oppen in exile: Mexico and Maritain. JAStud (39:1) 2005, 1–18.

17908. Vescia, Monique Claire. Depression glass: documentary photography and the medium of the camera-eye in Charles Reznikoff, Geoerge Oppen, and William Carlos Williams. London; New York: Routledge, 2006. pp. xx, 154. (Literary criticism and cultural theory.)

E. Phillips (Edward Phillips) Oppenheim ('Anthony Partridge') (1866–1946)

17909. Haldane, John. Fiction's enigma innovations: the art of the thriller. *See* **14888**.

Dael Orlandersmith

17910. Carpenter, Bridget, *et al.* Crossing borders: a conversation with Bridget Carpenter, Lynn Nottage, Dael Orlandersmith, and Diana Son. *In* (pp. 115–26) **12297**.

Eric Ormsby (b.1941)

17911. Hearon, Todd. Eric Ormsby's onomatopoetics. Parnassus (29:1/2) 2006, 244–67 (review-article).

Gregory Orr

17912. Orr, Gregory. Praxiteles and the shapes of grief. NLH (37:3) 2006, 673–80.

Simon Ortiz

17913. Coltelli, Laura. Postfazione: scrivere la voce: la narrativa breve di Simon Ortiz. *In* (pp. 201–25) **13975**.

'George Orwell' (Eric Blair)

17914. Anderson, Paul (ed.). Orwell in *Tribune*: *As I Please* and other writings, 1943–7. London: Politico's, 2006. pp. ix, 401. Rev. by Kate McLoughlin in TLS, 3 Nov. 2006, 28.

17915. Bluemel, Kristin. George Orwell and the radical eccentrics: intermodernism in literary London. (Bibl. 2004, 18859.) Rev. by Nick Hubble in TexP (19:4) 2005, 555–9; by Lisa Colletta in Mod/Mod (13:1) 2006, 192–4; by Annette Gilson in MFS (52:1) 2006, 242–5; by Janine Utell in ColLit (33:4) 2006, 198–203.

17916. Bowker, Gordon. Nuts about St Cyps: lessons and quarrels in the lives of George Orwell. TLS, 15 Sept. 2006, 13–15. (Commentary.)

17917. Breton, Rob. Gospels and grit: work and labour in Carlyle, Conrad and Orwell. *See* **9383**.

17918. Clarke, Ben. Orwell and Englishness. RES (57:228) 2006, 83–105.

17919. Gleason, Abbott; Goldsmith, Jack; Nussbaum, Martha C. (eds). On *Nineteen Eighty-Four*: Orwell and our future. (Bibl. 2005, 18680.) Rev. by Janine Utell in ColLit (33:4) 2006, 198–203.

17920. INGLE, STEPHEN. The social and political thought of George Orwell: a reassessment. London; New York: Routledge, 2005. pp. 225. (Routledge studies in social and political thought, 45.)

17921. MEYERS, JEFFREY. Orwell's satiric humor. CommRev (5:1) 2006, 34–41.

17922. RODDEN, JOHN. Every intellectual's big brother: George Orwell's literary siblings. Austin: Texas UP, 2006. pp. xiii, 263. (Literary Modernism.)

17923. —— Fellow contrarians? Christopher Hitchens and George Orwell. KR (28:1) 2006, 142–65.

17924. —— Remembering Irving Howe. *See* **14275**.

17925. TREGLOWN, JEREMY. Our secret harmonies: the *TLS* life of Anthony Powell – with Maclaren-Ross, Pryce-Jones and Orwell. *See* **18115**.

17926. UTELL, JANINE. Why we (still) read Orwell. ColLit (33:4) 2006, 198–203 (review-article).

John Osborne

17927. EDGAR, DAVID. Stalking out. LRB (28:14) 2006, 8–10 (review-article).

17928. HEILPERN, JOHN. John Osborne: a patriot for us. London: Chatto & Windus, 2006. pp. xv, 528, (plates) 16. Rev. by John Stokes in TLS, 23 June 2006, 3; by David Edgar in LRB (28:14) 2006, 8–10.

Femi Osofisan ('Okinba Launko')

17929. OYEDELE, WALE. Femi Osofisan's postmodern performance. *In* (pp. 171–80) **11860**.

Wilfred Owen

17930. CLAUSSON, NILS. Owen's antiphonal response to tradition: etymology and genre in *Anthem for Doomed Youth*. ELN (43:2) 2005, 166–9.

17931. GARTH, JOHN. Frodo and the Great War. *In* (pp. 41–56) **18804**.

17932. HIPP, DANIEL. The poetry of shell shock: wartime trauma and healing in Wilfred Owen, Ivor Gurney and Siegfried Sassoon. (Bibl. 2005, 18709.) Rev. by Heather Lusty in JML (30:1) 2006, 199–209; by Jeffrey C. Alfier in WLA (18:1/2) 2006, 344–7.

17933. HUGHES, JOHN. Owen's *Dulce et Decorum Est*. Exp (64:3) 2006, 160–2.

17934. MORTON, JOHN. Tennyson and the 1914–1918 war. *See* **11402**.

17935. REED, J. D. Wilfred Owen's Adonis. *In* (pp. 39–56) **3235**.

17936. WHALE, JOHN. John Keats and Tony Harrison: the burden of history. *In* (pp. 163–80) **13735**.

Louis Owens

17937. BENSON, MELANIE R. 'Carrying our people's bones': Louis Owens, south by southwest. PemM (38) 2006, 43–54.

17938. CHRISTIE, STUART. Crossing the frontier: hollow men, modernist militias, and mixedblood mimesis in Louis Owens' *Dark River*. WAL (40:1) 2005, 5–31.

17939. COLONNESE, TOM. Louis Owens: the last word. PemM (38) 2006, 9–11.

17940. Helstern, Linda Lizut. Louis Owens. Boise, ID: Boise State Univ., 2005. pp. 55. (Boise State Univ. Western writers, 168.)

17941. Kilpatrick, Jacquelyn (ed.). Louis Owens: literary reflections on his life and work. (Bibl. 2005, 18711.) Rev. by David Mogen in WAL (40:2) 2005, 209–10; by Carrie Louise Sheffield in MFS (52:1) 2006, 225–8.

17942. LaLonde, Chris. The prick of Pine Mountain. PemM (38) 2006, 30–42.

17943. Peters, Jesse. Rivers and shadows. PemM (38) 2006, 28–9.

17944. Pulitano, Elvira. From Joan Didion to Roland Barthes: travels in mixedblood metaphors and mixed messages, remembering Louis Owens. PemM (38) 2006, 17–27.

17945. Purdy, John. Moving stories: visualization, *mise-en-scène*, and Native American fiction. *See* **17388**.

17946. —— Ripples: conferences, correspondence, and correlations. PemM (38) 2006, 12–16.

Rochelle Owens

17947. Bossler, Gregory. Writers and their work: Rochelle Owens. Dramatist (8:6) 2006, 28–31.

Cynthia Ozick

17948. Fargione, Daniela. Cynthia Ozick: orthodoxy and irreverence: a critical study. Rome: Aracne, 2005. pp. xii, 265. (A10, 131.)

17949. Levine, Michael G. The belated witness: literature, testimony, and the question of Holocaust survival. *See* **18581**.

17950. Ozick, Cynthia. The din in the head: essays. *See* **12073**.

17951. —— A youthful intoxication. NYTB, 10 Dec. 2006, 35. (Influence of Leo Baeck.)

17952. Sinclair, Clive. The scholar and the pagan: Cynthia Ozick's house of judgement. TLS, 3 Nov. 2006, 19–20 (review-article).

Myra Page

17953. Mantooth, Wes. 'You factory folks who sing this song will surely understand': culture, ideology, and action in the Gastonia novels of Myra Page, Grace Lumpkin, and Olive Dargan. *See* **15412**.

Chuck Palahniuk

17954. Bishop, Kyle. Artistic schizophrenia: how *Fight Club*'s message is subverted by its own nature. *See* **12865**.

Grace Paley

17955. Accardo, Annalucia. Grace Paley: 'passings' between African American and Jewish cultural paradigms. QPS (14) 2006, 480–7.

17956. —— 'Mi baciò con cattiveria, da spaccarmi praticamente il labbro': le rappresentazioni della violenza nell'opera di Grace Paley. Àcoma (32) 2006, 39–51.

Américo Paredes

17957. López Morín, José R. The legacy of Américo Paredes. College Station: Texas A&M UP, 2006. pp. xviii, 169, (plates) 6. (Rio Grande / Río Bravo, 10.)

17958. Saldívar, Ramón. The borderlands of culture: Américo Paredes and the transnational imaginary. Durham, NC; London: Duke UP, 2006. pp. x, 525. (New Americanists.)

Dorothy Parker

17959. Fitzpatrick, Kevin C. A journey into Dorothy Parker's New York. Foreword by Marion Mead. Berkeley, CA: Roaring Forties Press, 2005. pp. 147. (ArtPlace.)

Robert B. Parker

17960. Schmid, Georg. Profiling the American detective: Parker's prose on the coded game of sleuth and rogue, and the tradition of the crime story. (Bibl. 2005, 18740.) Rev. by Carmen Birkle in Amst (51:2) 2006, 240–2.

Stewart Parker

17961. Russell, Richard Rankin. Exorcising the ghosts of conflict in Northern Ireland: Stewart Parker's *The Iceberg* and *Pentecost*. EI (41:3/4) 2006, 42–58.

Suzan-Lori Parks

17962. Green, Amy S. Whose voices are these? The arts of language in the plays of Suzan-Lori Parks, Paula Vogel, and Diana Son. *In* (pp. 143–57) **12297**.

17963. Hogue, Bev. Naming the bones: bodies of knowledge in contemporary fiction. *See* **17611**.

17964. Johung, Jennifer. Figuring the 'spells' / spelling the figures: Suzan-Lori Parks's 'Scene of Love (?)'. TJ (58:1) 2006, 39–52.

17965. Kolin, Philip C. Parks's *In the Blood*. Exp (64:4) 2006, 245–8.

17966. Magelssen, Scott. Making history in the second person: post-touristic considerations for living historical interpretation. TJ (58:2) 2006, 291–312.

Peter Parnell

17967. Parnell, Peter. 'The first time …': doing a stage biography. Dramatist (8:4) 2006, 24–7.

P. B. Parris

17968. King, Jeannette. Whatever happened to 'good little Thomas Hardy'? Re-writing Hardy and his fiction in P. B. Parris's *His Arms Are Full of Broken Things* and Emma Tennant's *Tess*. *See* **10283**.

Ann Patchett

17969. Patchett, Ann. Truth & beauty: a friendship. New York: HarperCollins, 2004. pp. 257. Rev. by Mary Cappello in WRB (22:1) 2004, 4–5.

Don Paterson (b.1963)

17970. Howarth, Peter. The battle for centre ground. PNRev (32:2) 2005, 43–4.

Isabel Paterson (1886–1960)

17971. Cox, Stephen. Representing Isabel Paterson. AmLH (17:2) 2005, 244–58.

Katherine Paterson

17972. Paterson, Katherine. Image and imagination. *In* (pp. 13–28) **11940**.

17973. —— Making meaning. *In* (pp. 240–55) **11940**.

Tom Paulin

17974. Nikolaou, Paschalis. Notes on translating the self. *In* (pp. 19–32) **2874**.

17975. Raphael, Frederic. Context and con/text. PNRev (32:4) 2006, 16–20. (*Crusoe's Secret*.)

17976. —— Paulin: a biopsy: annotations on *Crusoe's Secret*. PNRev (32:5) 2006, 30–3.

Gary Paulsen

17977. Chandler, Karen. Paths to freedom: literacy and folk traditions in recent narratives about slavery and emancipation. *See* **16271**.

Mervyn Peake

17978. Mills, Alice. Stuckness in the fiction of Mervyn Peake. Amsterdam; New York: Rodopi, 2005. pp. 239. (Costerus, ns 157.) Rev. by Pierre François in PeakeS (10:1) 2005, 46–50.

17979. Robertson, Mark. From Walton to Gormenghast. PeakeS (9:4) 2006, 23–9.

17980. Winnington, G. Peter. The voice of the heart: the working of Mervyn Peake's imagination. Liverpool: Liverpool UP, 2006. pp. xiii, 290. (Liverpool English texts and studies, 48.)

Philippa Pearce

17981. Paruolo, Elena. *Tom's Midnight Garden*: la '*time fantasy*' di Philippa Pearce. *In* (pp. 437–54) **11824**.

Walker Percy

17982. Desmond, John F. Resurrecting the body: Walker Percy and the sensuous-erotic spirit. Ren (58:3) 2006, 195–210.

17983. —— Walker Percy and writing the Holocaust. ReLit (38:2) 2006, 101–16.

17984. —— Walker Percy's search for community. (Bibl. 2004, 18936.) Rev. by Douglas Mitchell in MissQ (58:1/2) 2004/05, 413–15; by Doreen Fowler in FOR (4) 2006, 160–1.

17985. Harwell, David Horace (ed.). Walker Percy remembered: a portrait in the words of those who knew him. Chapel Hill; London: North Carolina UP, 2006. pp. x, 187.

17986. Montgomery, Marion. Eudora Welty and Walker Percy: the concept of home in their lives and literature. Jefferson, NC; London: McFarland, 2004. pp. v, 214. Rev. by Patrick J. Walsh in ModAge (48:2) 2006, 166–9.

17987. —— Fiction's echo of revelation: Flannery O'Connor's challenge as Thomistic maker. *In* (pp. 122–37) **17825**.

17988. UNDERWOOD, THOMAS A. A visit with Walker Percy: an interview and a recollection. MissQ (58:1/2) 2004/05, 141–59.

Maxwell Perkins

17989. BRUCCOLI, MATTHEW J.; BAUGHMAN, JUDITH S. (eds). The sons of Maxwell Perkins: letters of F. Scott Fitzgerald, Ernest Hemingway, Thomas Wolfe, and their editor. (Bibl. 2004, 18941.) Rev. by Thomas K. Meier in StudN (38:2) 2006, 262–3.

Penny Perkins (b.1962)

17990. COPELAND, MARION W. Voices of the least loved: cockroaches in the contemporary American novel. *In* (pp. 153–75) **3203**.

Elliot Perlman

17991. MACK, MICHAEL. Market economy and the abolition of singularity in Elliot Perlman's *Seven Types of Ambiguity*. Antipodes (20:2) 2006, 183–91.

Fernando Pessoa (Antonio Nogueira, 'Alexander Search')

17992. CRITCHLEY, SIMON. Surfaciality: some poems by Fernando Pessoa, one by Wallace Stevens, and the brief sketch of a poetic ontology. *See* **18631**.

17993. DAUNT, RICARDO. T. S. Eliot e Fernando Pessoa: diálogos de New Haven: ensaios. *See* **15684**.

Julia Mood Peterkin

17994. KREIDLER, JAN. Reviving Julia Peterkin as a trickster writer. JAC (29:4) 2006, 468–74.

Ann Petry

17995. BINGGELI, ELIZABETH. Burbanking bigger and Bette the bitch. *See* **19374**.

17996. ERVIN, HAZEL ARNETT. The critical response to Ann Petry. (Bibl. 2005, 18777.) Rev. by Rita B. Dandridge in CLAJ (50:1) 2006, 115–17.

17997. PETRY, ELISABETH (ed.). Can anything beat White? A Black family's letters. Jackson; London: Mississippi UP, 2005. pp. xxx, 190.

17998. SCOTT, WILLIAM. Material resistance and the agency of the body in Ann Petry's *The Street*. AL (78:1) 2006, 89–116.

17999. SHOCKLEY, EVIE. Buried alive: gothic homelessness, Black women's sexuality, and (living) death in Ann Petry's *The Street*. AAR (40:3) 2006, 439–60.

18000. WESLING, MEG. The opacity of everyday life: segregation and the iconicity of uplift in *The Street*. AL (78:1) 2006, 117–40.

Jim Phelan (1895–1966)

18001. PRIDMORE, JOSEPH. Mass violence and the crowd: the perception of proletarian community in working-class writers of the 1930s. *See* **16059**.

Marlene NourbeSe Philip (b.1947)

18002. FORBES, CURDELLA. Selling that Caribbean woman down the river: diasporic travel narratives and the global economy. *See* **11160**.

18003. MAHLIS, KRISTEN. M. NourbeSe Philip: language, place, and exile. JWIL (14:1/2) 2005, 166–201.

18004. SAUNDERS, PATRICIA. Trying tongues, e-raced identities, and the possibilities of be/longing: conversations with NourbeSe Philip. JWIL (14:1/2) 2005, 202–19.

Carl Phillips (b.1959)

18005. HAMMER, LANGDON. The leaves rush, greening, back: Carl Phillips. ASch (75:4) 2006, 58–9.

Caryl Phillips

18006. CALBI, MAURIZIO. Atlantic sounds: home, memory, and belonging in Caryl Phillips's travel writing. *In* (pp. 51–66) **11824**.

18007. HALLORAN, VIVIAN NUN. Race, creole, and national identities in Rhys's *Wide Sargasso Sea* and Phillips's *Cambridge*. *See* **18223**.

18008. MCLEOD, JOHN. Postcolonial fictions of adoption. *See* **18449**.

18009. WALKOWITZ, REBECCA L. The location of literature: the transnational book and the migrant writer. ConLit (47:4) 2006, 527–45.

Marge Piercy

18010. ELLIOTT, JANE. Time of death: the end of the 1960s and the problem of feminist futurity in *The Women's Room* and *Vida*. *See* **15993**.

18011. PIERCY, MARGE. The best bones for soup have meat on them. *In* (pp. 212–13) **16122**.

Josephine Pinckney (1895–1957)

18012. BELLOWS, BARBARA L. A talent for living: Josephine Pinckney and the Charleston literary tradition. Baton Rouge: Louisiana State UP, 2006. pp. xvi, 301, (plates) 14. (Southern literary studies.)

Winsome Pinnock (b.1961)

18013. MARZETTE, DELINDA. Coming to voice: navigating the interstices in plays by Winsome Pinnock. *In* (pp. 32–51) **11795**.

Robert Pinsky

18014. PINSKY, ROBERT. No picnic. *In* (pp. 255–9) **16122**.

Harold Pinter

18015. ARDOLINO, FRANK. Pinter's *Betrayal* and Shakespeare's *Othello*. Exp (65:1) 2006, 50–3.

18016. BAKER, WILLIAM; ROSS, JOHN C. Harold Pinter: a bibliographical history. New Castle, DE: Oak Knoll Press, 2005. pp. xl, 323. Rev. by Carl Spadoni in SHARP (15:2/3) 2006, 10.

18017. BEGLEY, VARUN. Harold Pinter and the twilight of Modernism. Toronto; Buffalo, NY; London: Toronto UP, 2005. pp. vi, 207. Rev. by David Krasner in TJ (58:3) 2006, 524–6; by Hugh Graham in BkCan (35:3) 2006, 22.

18018. CANZIANI, ROBERTO; CAPITTA, GIANFRANCO. Harold Pinter: scena e potere. Milan: Garzanti, 2005. pp. 252.

18019. INAN, DILEK. The city beneath, beyond, and above: Harold Pinter's London. *In* (pp. 67–80) **3307**.

18020. MACAULAY, ALASTAIR. Did you see Kim and the kids? Pinter's women and the trauma of imagined experience. TLS, 14 Apr. 2006, 18–19.

18021. Pinter, Harold. Art, truth, and politics. Dramatist (8:4) 2006, 6–12.

18022. Weales, Gerald. Harold Pinter and the Nobel Prize. SewR (114:4) 2006, 603–9. (State of letters.)

Robert M. Pirsig

18023. Granger, David A. John Dewey, Robert Pirsig, and the art of living: revisioning aesthetic education. Basingstoke; New York: Palgrave Macmillan, 2006. pp. xii, 307.

Sol T. Plaatje

18024. Green, Michael. Generic instability and the national project: history, nation, and form in Sol T. Plaatje's *Mhudi*. RAL (37:4) 2006, 34–47.

Sylvia Plath

18025. Axelrod, Steven Gould. The poetry of Sylvia Plath. *In* (pp. 73–89) **18038**.

18026. Badia, Janet. *The Bell Jar* and other prose. *In* (pp. 124–38) **18038**.

18027. Bassnett, Susan. Sylvia Plath: an introduction to the poetry. (Bibl. 1987, 12205.) Basingstoke; New York: Palgrave Macmillan, 2005. pp. 172. (Second ed.: first ed. 1987.)

18028. Bayley, Sally. 'I have your head on my wall': Sylvia Plath and the rhetoric of Cold War America. EurJAC (25:3) 2006, 155–71.

18029. Beer, John. Coleridge, Ted Hughes, and Sylvia Plath: mythology and identity. *In* (pp. 123–41) **13735**.

18030. Brain, Tracy. Sylvia Plath's letters and journals. *In* (pp. 139–55) **18038**.

18031. Britzolakis, Christina. *Ariel* and other poems. *In* (pp. 107–23) **18038**.

18032. Bundtzen, Lynda K. Plath and psychoanalysis: uncertain truths. *In* (pp. 36–51) **18038**.

18033. Churchwell, Sarah. 'Your sentence was mine too': reading Sylvia Plath in Ted Hughes's *Birthday Letters*. *In* (pp. 260–87) **3405**.

18034. Clanchy, Kate. Gendering poetry. *See* **13723**.

18035. Curtis, Diana. Plath's *Tulips*. Exp (64:3) 2006, 177–9.

18036. Entwistle, Alice. Plath and contemporary British poetry. *In* (pp. 63–70) **18038**.

18037. Gill, Jo. *The Colossus* and *Crossing the Water*. *In* (pp. 90–106) **18038**.

18038. —— (ed.). The Cambridge companion to Sylvia Plath. Cambridge; New York: CUP, 2006. pp. xxi, 182. (Cambridge companions to literature.) Rev. by Sally Bayley in RES (57:232) 2006, 853–4.

18039. Helle, Anita. Lessons from the archive: Sylvia Plath and the politics of memory. FemSt (31:3) 2005, 631–52.

18040. Jamison, Kay Redfield. Contemporary psychology and contemporary poetry: perspectives on mood disorders. *In* (pp. 191–203) **13732**.

18041. Johnson, Heather. Dangerous skin: bees and female figuration in Maher and Plath. *In* (pp. 129–52) **3203**.

18042. Keniston, Ann. Overheard voices: address and subjectivity in postmodern American poetry. London; New York: Routledge, 2006. pp. xi, 171. (Literary criticism and cultural theory.)

18043. LADIN, JAY. 'After the end of the world': poetry and the Holocaust. *See* **13794**.

18044. LAURO, SARAH JULIET. The fruits of their labors: the childbirth poetry of Plath, Sexton, and Loy. NwR (44:2) 2006, 149–64.

18045. MIDDLEBROOK, DIANE. The poetry of Sylvia Plath and Ted Hughes: call and response. *In* (pp. 156–71) **18038**.

18046. —— Stevens in the marriage of Sylvia Plath and Ted Hughes. *See* **18647**.

18047. NELSON, DEBORAH. Plath, history and politics. *In* (pp. 21–35) **18038**.

18048. PEEL, ROBIN. Body, word, and photograph: Sylvia Plath's Cold War collage and the thalidomide scandal. JAStud (40:1) 2006, 71–95.

18049. RAYMOND, CLAIRE. The posthumous voice in women's writing from Mary Shelley to Sylvia Plath. *See* **11192**.

18050. ROWLAND, ANTONY. Holocaust poetry: awkward poetics in the work of Sylvia Plath, Geoffrey Hill, Tony Harrison and Ted Hughes. Edinburgh: Edinburgh UP, 2005. pp. vii, 192. Rev. by Christine Berberich in Mod/Mod (13:3) 2006, 567–75.

18051. STOREY, H. WAYNE. A question of punctuation and 'ear[s] for dissenting voices': introduction to *Textual Cultures* 1.2. TextC (1:2) 2006, 1–5.

18052. TRINIDAD, DAVID. 'Two sweet ladies': Sexton and Plath's friendship and mutual influence. *See* **18480**.

18053. VAN DYNE, SUSAN R. The problem of biography. *In* (pp. 3–20) **18038**.

18054. VAN HULLE, DIRK. Growth and the grid: organic *vs* constructivist conceptions of poetry. *See* **15720**.

18055. WAGNER-MARTIN, LINDA. Plath and contemporary American poetry. *In* (pp. 52–62) **18038**.

18056. ZHU, XINFU. Sylvia Plath: writing in the silent spring. FLS (119) 2006, 108–14. (In Chinese.)

William Plomer

18057. KISSACK, MIKE; TITLESTAD, MICHAEL. Vision, doubt, anguish and retreat: the fraught Liberal context of William Plomer's *Turbott Wolfe*. ESA (48:1) 2005, 37–61.

Stanley Plumly

18058. CAVALIERI, GRACE. The poet and the poem from the Library of Congress. PemM (38) 2006, 251–67. (Interview.)

18059. MATTHEWS, SEBASTIAN (introd.). Peripheral pleasures: letters to Russell Banks, Daniel Halpern, and Stanley Plumly. *See* **17462**.

Frederik Pohl ('Jordan Park')

18060. HASSLER, DONALD M. A platinum moment for Frederik Pohl: from golden pulp to steely. Extrapolation (47:1) 2006, 148–52.

Sharon Pollock

18061. NORTHOF, ANNE. Postcolonial tragedy in the Crowsnest Pass: two rearview reflections by Sharon Pollock and John Murrell. GPQ (26:4) 2006, 235–44.

Cole Porter

18062. KIMBALL, ROBERT (ed.). Selected lyrics. New York: Library of America, 2006. pp. xxii, 178. (American poets project, 21.) Rev. by David Barber in NYTB, 9 July 2006, 8.

Katherine Anne Porter

18063. TITUS, MARY. The ambivalent art of Katherine Anne Porter. (Bibl. 2005, 18848.) Rev. by Janis P. Stout in StudN (38:3) 2006, 379–81.

18064. UNRUE, DARLENE HARBOUR. Antonieta Rivas Mercado: Katherine Anne Porter's horror and inspiration. JSwest (47:4) 2005, 615–35.

18065. —— Katherine Anne Porter: the life of an artist. (Bibl. 2005, 18849.) Rev. by Paul Gray in NYTB, 1 Jan. 2006, 11; by Janis P. Stout in StudN (38:3) 2006, 379–81.

Peter Porter

18066. BENNETT, BRUCE. The poet as biographer: Peter Porter. CritS (18:1) 2006, 66–77.

18067. CAESAR, ADRIAN. 'The lying art': Peter Porter's modest proposals. CritS (18:1) 2006, 123–31.

18068. JAMES, CLIVE. The simple excellence of Peter Porter. CritS (18:1) 2006, 78–92.

18069. LUCAS, JOHN. Peter Porter: the metropolitan voice. CritS (18:1) 2006, 109–22.

18070. STEELE, PETER. The master of the sentences: style and Peter Porter. CritS (18:1) 2006, 93–108.

Beatrix Potter

18071. COTSEN, MARGIT SPERLING. The Beatrix Potter collection of Lloyd Cotsen: published on the occasion of his 75th birthday. Introd. and notes by Judy Taylor. Catalogue by Ann Stevenson Hobbs. Los Angeles, CA: Cotsen Occasional Press, 2004. pp. xvi, 190. Rev. by Robin Greer in PBSA (100:4) 2006, 471–2.

Dennis Potter

18072. ALLINGHAM, PHILIP. Screening the flashback: three ways of opening *The Mayor of Casterbridge*. *In* (pp. 124–39) **10349**.

Ezra Pound

18073. AJI, HÉLÈNE. Melancholy in lieu of recantation: Ezra Pound's 'Drafts and Fragments'. EREA (4:1) 2006, 37–42.

18074. BACIGALUPO, MASSIMO. 'Forth on the godly sea': the Mediterranean in Pound, Yeats and Stevens. *In* (pp. 31–49) **12076**.

18075. —— Pound/Izzo. QPS (14) 2006, 63–80.

18076. —— Rapallo fra futurismo e vorticismo: Marinetti e Ezra Pound. *In* (pp. 193–203) **13990**.

18077. BELL, IAN F. A.; LLAND, MERIEL. Silence and solidity in early Anglo-American Modernism: Nietzsche, the fourth dimension, and Ezra Pound: part one. Symbiosis (10:1) 2006, 47–61.

18078. Berryman, John. A visit to Ezra Pound in St Elizabeth's Hospital, 1948. MichQR (45:4) 2006, 617–20.

18079. Campbell, Timothy C. Wireless writing in the age of Marconi. Minneapolis; London: Minnesota UP, 2006. pp. xviii, 222. (Electronic mediations, 16.)

18080. Cesari, Luca (ed.). Carte italiane 1930–1944: letteratura e arte. Milan: Archinto, 2005. pp. 422. Rev. by Carlo Vita in Indice (2006:4) 16.

18081. Coyle, Michael. Ezra Pound: *Hugh Selwyn Mauberley*. *In* (pp. 431–9) **11788**.

18082. Eastham, Scott. In Pound's China – the stone books speak. Paideuma (33:1) 2004, 89–117.

18083. Fisher, Margaret. The music of Ezra Pound. YLG (80:3/4) 2006, 139–60.

18084. Grieve, Tom. The textual rendition: socio-material criticism reconsidered. *See* **5**.

18085. Harmon, William. 'A few pages brought down from the forked hill unsullied'. SewR (114:4) 2006, 610–18 (review-article). (Arts and letters.)

18086. Hass, Robert Bernard. (Re) reading Bergson: Frost, Pound and the legacy of modern poetry. *See* **16005**.

18087. Hayot, Eric. Chinese dreams: Pound, Brecht, Tel Quel. (Bibl. 2004, 19030.) Rev. by Alexander C. Y. Huang in CLS (43:1/2) 2006, 187–90.

18088. Hickman, Miranda B. The geometry of Modernism: the Vorticist idiom in Lewis, Pound, H.D., and Yeats. *See* **17215**.

18089. Hinojosa, Lynne Walhout. The modern artist as historian, courtier, and saint: typology and art history from Vasari to Pound. CLIO (35:2) 2006, 201–24.

18090. Huang, Yunte. Was Ezra Pound a New Historicist? Poetry and poetics in the age of globalization. FLS (122) 2006, 28–44.

18091. Jarman, Mark. Your anonymous correspondent: Ezra Pound and *The Hudson Review*. HR (59:3) 2006, 359–75.

18092. Jones, Chris. Strange likeness: the use of Old English in twentieth-century poetry. *See* **3677**.

18093. Judge, Elizabeth F. Make it Pound: translation, professionalism and the right to Propertian discourse in *Homage to Sextus Propertius*. Paideuma (33:1) 2004, 127–63.

18094. Kaplan, Harold. Poetry, politics, and culture: argument in the work of Eliot, Pound, Stevens, and Williams. *See* **15693**.

18095. Kite, Stephen. Architecture as *technê*: Adrian Stokes, Ezra Pound and the art of the machine. Paideuma (33:1) 2004, 33–55.

18096. Levin, Dana. The heroics of style: a study in three parts. *See* **19938**.

18097. McDonald, Gail. A homemade heaven: Modernist poetry and the Social Gospel. *In* (pp. 194–215) **8429**.

18098. MacGowan, Christopher. Poet to poet: four books of correspondence. *See* **19194**.

18099. Makin, Peter (ed.). Ezra Pound's *Cantos*: a casebook. Oxford; New York: OUP, 2006. pp. xvi, 264. (Casebooks in criticism.)

18100. Nadel, Ira B. Ezra Pound: a literary life. (Bibl. 2005, 18881.) Rev. by Tim Redman in Mod/Mod (13:1) 2006, 189–90.

18101. —— (ed.). Early writings. London; New York: Penguin, 2005. pp. xxxviii, 408.

18102. Park, Josephine Nock-Hee. 'Composed of many lengths of bone': Myung-Mi Kim's reimagination of image and epic. *In* (pp. 235–56) **11995**.

18103. —— 'A loose horse': Asian American poetry and the aesthetics of the ideogram. *In* (pp. 123–36) **11849**.

18104. Pfannkuchen, Antje. From vortex to Vorticism: Ezra Pound's art and science. Intertexts (9:1) 2005, 61–76.

18105. Ricciardi, Caterina. Ezra Pound, ghiande di luce. Rimini: Raffaelli, 2006. pp. 182. (Quaderni poundiani, 4.)

18106. Robinson, Peter. Translation and self-accusation: Vittorio Sereni's '*momento psicologico*': translating Ezra Pound. Agenda (41:3/4) 2005, 125–34.

18107. Rossa, Jesse. Ezra Pound in his time and beyond: the influence of Ezra Pound on twentieth-century poetry: a catalog of an exhibition, Special Collections Department, Hugh M. Morris Library. Newark: Univ. of Delaware Library, 2006. pp. xv, 37.

18108. Sitney, P. Adams. Brakhage and Modernism. *In* (pp. 159–78) **12654**.

18109. Thomas, Harry. Berryman and Pound. *See* **14770**.

18110. Trotter, David. T. S. Eliot and cinema. *See* **15719**.

18111. Zajko, Vanda. Homer and *Ulysses*. *In* (pp. 311–23) **3253**.

18112. Zheng, Jianqing. Ezra Pound's employment of Chinese images. Paideuma (33:1) 2004, 119–25.

Anthony Powell

18113. Barber, Michael. Anthony Powell: a life. (Bibl. 2005, 18906.) Rev. by Christine Berberich in EWN (35:3) 2005.

18114. Birns, Nicholas. Understanding Anthony Powell. (Bibl. 2005, 18907.) Rev. by Christine Berberich in EWN (35:3) 2005.

18115. Treglown, Jeremy. Our secret harmonies: the *TLS* life of Anthony Powell – with Maclaren-Ross, Pryce-Jones and Orwell. TLS, 27 Jan. 2006, 13–15.

Patricia Powell

18116. Davis, Andrea. Translating narratives of masculinity across borders: a Jamaican case study. *See* **18254**.

Richard Powers

18117. Chodat, Robert. Naturalism and narrative; or, What computers and human beings can't do. NLH (37:4) 2006, 685–706.

18118. Eckstein, Lars; Reinfandt, Christoph. The parody of *Parody as Cultural Memory in Richard Powers's 'Galatea 2.2'*: a response to Anca Rosu. Connotations (13:1/2) 2003/04, 93–102.

18119. Miller, D. Quentin. Deeper Blues; or, The posthuman Prometheus: cybernetic renewal and the late twentieth-century American novel. *See* **18884**.

18120. Pellegrin, Jean-Yves. La vulgarisation dans *The Gold Bug Variations* de Richard Powers; ou, La mise en cultures de la connaissance. RANAM (39) 2006, 229–39.

18121. Thomas, J. T. Deciphering the code in Richard Powers's *The Gold Bug Variations*. NCL (36:5) 2006, 9–10.

18122. Wald, Carol Ann. Reflexivity, reproduction, and evolution: from von Neumann to Powers. Mosaic (39:2) 2006, 163–79.

John Cowper Powys (1872–1963)

18123. Gervais, David. Dostoevsky and the English novel: Dickens, John Cowper Powys and D. H. Lawrence. *See* **9755**.

18124. Lock, Charles. Powys and the Aether: the Homeric novels. PowJ (16) 2006, 10–33.

18125. McGann, Jerome. 'The grand heretics of modern fiction': Laura Riding, John Cowper Powys, and the subjective correlative. *See* **18250**.

18126. Marie-Laverrou, Florence. John Cowper Powys dans le contexte moderniste: le hors-texte au cœur du texte. EtBr (30) 2006, 41–53.

18127. —— Writing the sea in *Weymouth Sands*. PowJ (16) 2006, 49–65.

18128. Maxwell, Richard. A game of yes and no: childhood and apocalypse in *Porius*. PowJ (16) 2006, 84–102.

18129. Rands, Susan. Dr R. D. Reid and John Cowper Powys. PowJ (16) 2006, 115–20.

Llewelyn Powys (1884–1939)

18130. Schmidt, Michael. Wallace Stevens: arranging, deepening, enchanting Britain. *See* **18656**.

T. F. Powys (1875–1953)

18131. Mencher, Elaine (afterword). *Blind Bartimæus*. PowJ (16) 2006, 121–78.

18132. Mitchell, J. Lawrence. Covering Mr Weston. PowJ (16) 2006, 80–3.

18133. Robinson, Ian. T. F. Powys and the renewal of English prose. PowJ (16) 2006, 34–48.

18134. Tomlinson, Geoffrey. Black bryony and the acceptability of death. PowJ (16) 2006, 103–14.

The Powys Brothers

18135. Clayton, Hugh. Mussolini and Mr Malakite: further reflections on the Powys brothers in Italian. PowJ (16) 2006, 66–80.

18136. Keith, W. J. Thomas Hardy and the Powyses. *In* (pp. 270–85) **10348**.

Sophia Rosamond Praeger (1867–1954)

18137. Donlon, Pat. Sophia Rosamond Praeger (1867–1954): a woman of many talents. *In* (pp. 240–55) **648**.

Terry Pratchett

18138. Cockrell, Amanda. Where the falling angel meets the rising ape: Terry Pratchett's Discworld. HC (43:1) 2006, 1–15.

Karen Press

18139. Petzold, Jochen. Children's literature after apartheid: examining 'hidden histories' of South Africa's past. CLAQ (30:2) 2005, 140–51.

Reynolds Price

18140. McEntyre, Marilyn Chandler. Hope in hard times: moments of epiphany in illness narratives. *In* (pp. 229–45) **11916**.

Christopher Priest

18141. Butler, Andrew M. (ed.). Christopher Priest: the interaction. (Bibl. 2005, 18932.) Rev. by John Clute in NYRSF (18:8) 2006, 1, 4–5; by David Moyle in Extrapolation (47:1) 2006, 160–4.

18142. Stewart, Victoria. 'The big war outside and the little war at home': anamnesis and the Second World War in recent British fiction. *See* **15991**.

F. T. Prince

18143. Kirkham, Michael. The finer grain: the art of F. T. Prince. Agenda (41:3/4) 2005, 75–88.

18144. —— (introd.). Letters from F. T. Prince: 1986–1991. Agenda (41:3/4) 2005, 90–9.

V. S. Pritchett

18145. Bloom, Jonathan. The art of revision in the short stories of V. S. Pritchett and William Trevor. Basingstoke; New York: Palgrave Macmillan, 2006. pp. xvii, 252.

E. Annie Proulx

18146. Bavaro, Vincenzo. Il *closet* e la finestra; ovvero, '*What's love got to do with it?*': note su *Brokeback Mountain*. Àcoma (32) 2006, 28–38.

18147. Polack, Fiona. Taking the waters: abjection and homecoming in *The Shipping News* and *Death of a River Guide*. JCL (41:1) 2006, 93–109.

Olive Higgins Prouty

18148. Parchesky, Jennifer. Adapting *Stella Dallas*: class boundaries, consumerism, and hierarchies of taste. Legacy (23:2) 2006, 178–98.

J. H. Prynne

18149. Brinton, Ian. Black Mountain in England: 5. *See* **15544**.

18150. Milne, Drew. The art of wit and the Cambridge Science Park. *In* (pp. 170–87) **13732**.

18151. Padel, Ruth. The journey or the dance? On syllables belonging to each other. *See* **9885**.

Philip Pullman (b.1946)

18152. Colás, Santiago. Telling true stories; or, The immanent ethics of material spirit (and spiritual matter) in Philip Pullman's *His Dark Materials*. Discourse (27:1) 2005, 34–66.

18153. HALDANE, MICHAEL. From Plato to Pullman – the circle of invisibility and parallel worlds: *Fortunatus*, Mercury, and the Wishing Hat: part II. *See* **6687**.

18154. KENDA, JAKOB J. Rewriting children's literature. *In* (pp. 160–70) **3186**.

18155. KING, SHELLEY. 'All wound up': Pullman's marvelous/uncanny *Clockwork*. ChildLit (33) 2005, 66–93.

18156. LENZ, MILLICENT; SCOTT, CAROLE (eds). *His Dark Materials* illuminated: critical essays on Philip Pullman's trilogy. (Bibl. 2005, 18952.) Rev. by Naomi Wood in CLAQ (31:1) 2006, 90–3.

18157. PENNINGTON, JOHN. Peter Pan, Pullman, and Potter: anxieties of growing up. *In* (pp. 237–62) **14616**.

18158. SQUIRES, CLAIRE. Philip Pullman, master storyteller: a guide to the worlds of *His Dark Materials*. London; New York: Continuum, 2006. pp. x, 214.

18159. WATKINS, TONY. Dark matter: shedding light on Philip Pullman's trilogy *His Dark Materials*. Downers Grove, IL: InterVarsity Press, 2006. pp. 221.

18160. WITTREICH, JOSEPH. 'The ramifications of those ramifications': compounding contexts for *Samson Agonistes*. *In* (pp. 167–99) **7033**.

Al Purdy

18161. BUDDE, ROBERT (sel. and introd.). The more easily kept illusions: the poetry of Al Purdy. Afterword by Russell Morton Brown. Waterloo, Ont.: Wilfrid Laurier UP, 2006. pp. xvi, 80. Rev. by Jeremy Lalonde in BkCan (35:8) 2006, 26–7.

18162. LAHEY, ERNESTINE. (Re)thinking world-building: locating the text-worlds of Canadian lyric poetry. JLS (35:2) 2006, 145–64.

18163. SOLECKI, SAM (ed.). Yours, Al: the collected letters of Al Purdy. (Bibl. 2005, 18976.) Rev. by Jeremy Lalonde in BkCan (33:9) 2004, 14; by John Lennox in Arc (55) 2005, 84–90; by Paul Denham in CanL (189) 2006, 175–7; by Tracy Ware in CanP (58) 2006, 123–7.

James Purdy

18164. O'HARA, DANIEL T. Bringing out the terror: James Purdy and the culture of vision. B2 (33:2) 2006, 75–90.

Barbara Pym

18165. BELL, HAZEL K. Novelist as scholarly editor, mid-twentieth century. JSchP (37:2) 2006, 119–30.

18166. DONATO, DEBORAH. Reading Barbara Pym. Madison, NJ: Fairleigh Dickinson UP; London: Assoc. UPs, 2005. pp. 124.

18167. RAZ, ORNA. Dandies, acolytes and teddy boys: ambiguous treatment of male sexuality in Barbara Pym's novels of the 1950s. PartA (4:1) 2006, 107–28.

18168. THOMAS, FRANCIS-NOËL. Philip Larkin, Barbara Pym, and the accident of literary fame. *See* **17006**.

18169. TINCKNELL, ESTELLA. Jane or Prudence? Barbara Pym's single women, female fulfilment and career choices in the 'age of marriages'. CritS (18:2) 2006, 31–44.

Thomas Pynchon

18170. Baringer, Sandra. The metanarrative of suspicion in late twentieth-century America. *See* **11760**.

18171. Davidson, Michael. The dream of a public language: modernity, manifesto, and the citizen subject. *See* **7777**.

18172. Elhefnaway, Nader. A critical clue: the life and times of Pynchon's Shale Schoenmaker. NCL (36:3) 2006, 4–6.

18173. Herman, Luc; Krafft, John M. The evolution of the South-West Africa chapter in Pynchon's *V.* ConLit (47:2) 2006, 261–88.

18174. Hinds, Elizabeth Jane Wall (ed.). The multiple worlds of Pynchon's *Mason & Dixon*: eighteenth-century contexts, postmodern observations. (Bibl. 2005, 18986.) Rev. by Celia Wallhead in Atl (28:2) 2006, 153–8.

18175. Kopp, Manfred. Triangulating Thomas Pynchon's eighteenth-century world: theory, structure & paranoia in *Mason & Dixon*. Essen: Blaue Eule, 2004. pp. 300. (Arbeiten zur Amerikanistik, 37.) Rev. by Sascha Pöhlmann in Amst (51:1) 2006, 129–31.

18176. Roraback, Erik. Para-baroque conceptual intersections & interventions: *Finnegans Wake*, *Gravity's Rainbow* and *The Writing of the Disaster*. *See* **16763**.

18177. Rossi, Umberto. Ambiguous spokespersons: the DJ and talk-radio host in US fiction, cinema and drama. *See* **15484**.

18178. Sun, Wanjun. Dissipating subject and realizing humanity: an analysis of Pynchon's postmodernist characters. FLS (121) 2006, 65–70. (In Chinese.)

18179. Weisenburger, Steven. A *Gravity's Rainbow* companion: sources and contexts for Pynchon's novel. (Bibl. 1991, 15103.) Athens; London: Georgia UP, 2006. pp. xii, 412. (Second ed.: first ed. 1988.)

18180. Witzling, David. The sensibility of postmodern Whiteness in *V*; or, Thomas Pynchon's identity problem. ConLit (47:3) 2006, 381–414.

Peter Quartermain (b.1934)

18181. Klobucar, Andrew. Slow learner: an interview with Peter Quartermain. CapR (second series) (44) 2004, 5–25.

Santha Rama Rau

18182. Burton, Antoinette. The ugly Americans: gender, geopolitics and the career of postcolonial cosmopolitanism in the novels of Santha Rama Rau. JCL (41:2) 2006, 5–19.

Ayn Rand

18183. Hunt, Lester H. Thus spake Howard Roark: Nietzschean ideas in *The Fountainhead*. PhilL (30:1) 2006, 79–101.

18184. Johnson, Donald Leslie. The fountainheads: Wright, Rand, the FBI and Hollywood. Jefferson, NC; London: McFarland, 2005. pp. xii, 231. Rev. by David Dunn in ScopeF (6) 2006.

18185. Smith, Tara. Ayn Rand's normative ethics: the virtuous egoist. Cambridge; New York: CUP, 2006. pp. x, 318.

Alice Randall

18186. Yaeger, Patricia. *Circum*-Atlantic superabundance: milk as world-making in Alice Randall and Kara Walker. AL (78:4) 2006, 769–98.

Dudley Randall (b.1914)

18187. McNeil, Daniel. American demands, African treasures, mixed possibilities. CRAS (36:2) 2006, 181–93.

Claudia Rankine (b.1963)

18188. Sadoff, Ira. On the margins: part two. *See* **16331**.

Frederic Raphael

18189. Raphael, Frederic. The pumpkinification of Stanley K. *In* (pp. 62–73) **13202**.

Irene Rathbone (1892–1980)

18190. MacCarthy, Anne. Irene Rathbone's annotations to Brigit Patmore's memoir. ANQ (19:3) 2006, 38–44.

Terence Rattigan

18191. Morra, Irene. Performing the Edwardian ideal: David Mamet and *The Winslow Boy*. *See* **13129**.

Tom Raworth

18192. Reed, Brian M. Carry on, England: Tom Raworth's *West Wind*, intuition, and neo-avant-garde poetics. ConLit (47:2) 2006, 170–206.

Herbert Read

18193. Antliff, Mark; Antliff, Allan (introds). To George Woodcock. *See* **18202**.

18194. —— —— To Herbert Read. *See* **18203**.

Ishmael Reed

18195. Carpio, Glenda R. Conjuring the mysteries of slavery: voodoo, fetishism, and stereotype in Ishmael Reed's *Flight to Canada*. AL (77:3) 2005, 563–89.

18196. Strombeck, Andrew. The conspiracy of masculinity in Ishmael Reed. AAR (40:2) 2006, 299–311.

Deryn Rees-Jones

18197. Brigley, Zoë. Replication, regeneration or organic birth: the clone in Deryn Rees-Jones' *Quiver* and Donna Haraway's *A Cyborg Manifesto*. CritS (18:2) 2006, 16–30.

'Robert Reginald' (Michael Burgess) (b.1948)

18198. Reginald, R. Trilobite dreams; or, The autodidact's tale. Riverside, CA: Ariadne Press, 2006. pp. 128.

Frederick Reiken (b.1966)

18199. Wasserman, Eric. Interview with Frederick Reiken. GT (56) 2005, 61–85.

Ruth Rendell ('Barbara Vine')

18200. KYZLINKOVÁ, LIDIA. Rendell/Vine: the historical universality of degradation between nations and genders. BStE (31) 2005, 139–46.

Joan Retallack

18201. KINZER, GREG. Excuses and other nonsense: Joan Retallack's *How to Do Things with Words*. ConLit (47:1) 2006, 62–90.

Kenneth Rexroth

18202. ANTLIFF, MARK; ANTLIFF, ALLAN (introds). To George Woodcock. ChiR (52:2–4) 2006, 84–8.

18203. —— —— To Herbert Read. ChiR (52:2–4) 2006, 89–93.

18204. APTER, EMILY. Translation with no original: scandals of textual reproduction. *In* (pp. 159–74) **3191**.

18205. BEER, JOHN (introd.). Three letters. ChiR (52:2–4) 2006, 41–8.

18206. —— To Jonathan Williams. ChiR (52:2–4) 2006, 94–9.

18207. BLECHMAN, MAX (introd.). To D. S. Savage. ChiR (52:2–4) 2006, 63–83.

18208. BLY, ROBERT. Remembering Kenneth Rexroth. ChiR (52:2–4) 2006, 117–20.

18209. EVERSON, WILLIAM. Eros in *agape*: Rexroth and the sacrality of sex. ChiR (52:2–4) 2006, 111–16.

18210. KNABB, KEN. Rexroth's San Francisco journalism. ChiR (52:2–4) 2006, 137–44.

18211. MORROW, BRADFORD. An afternoon with Kenneth. ChiR (52:2–4) 2006, 177–89.

18212. REIDEL, JAMES (introd.). To Weldon Kees. ChiR (52:2–4) 2006, 49–62.

18213. ROSEMONT, FRANKLIN. Rexroth's Chicago, Chicago's Rexroth: Wobblies, Dil Picklers, and Windy City Dada. ChiR (52:2–4) 2006, 151–63.

18214. SCROGGINS, MARK (introd.). To Louis Zukofsky. ChiR (52:2–4) 2006, 17–40.

18215. WOODCOCK, GEORGE. Realms beyond the mountains: notes on Kenneth Rexroth. ChiR (52:2–4) 2006, 121–30.

18216. ZHENG, YANHONG. On the influences of Chinese classical poetry upon Kenneth Rexroth's poems. FLS (120) 2006, 160–5. (In Chinese.)

Clay Reynolds (b.1949)

18217. ROTHFORK, JOHN. The theater and small town Texas in Clay Reynolds's *The Tentmaker*. CritW (48:1) 2006, 90–101.

Charles Reznikoff

18218. COONEY, SEAMUS (ed.). The poems of Charles Reznikoff: 1918–1975. (Bibl. 2005, 19043.) Rev. by Joshua Clover in NYTB, 22 Jan. 2006, 13.

18219. MARINACCIO, ROCCO. 'The sight to see and the will to do': Charles Reznikoff and the poetics of exposure. LIT (17:2) 2006, 105–35.

18220. VESCIA, MONIQUE CLAIRE. Depression glass: documentary photography and the medium of the camera-eye in Charles Reznikoff, Geoerge Oppen, and William Carlos Williams. *See* **17908**.

Jean Rhys

18221. Berman, Carolyn Vellenga. Creole crossings: domestic fiction and the reform of colonial slavery. *See* **9988**.

18222. Gass, Joanne. *The Autobiography of My Mother*: Jamaica Kincaid's revision of *Jane Eyre* and *Wide Sargasso Sea*. *In* (pp. 63–78) **16864**.

18223. Halloran, Vivian Nun. Race, creole, and national identities in Rhys's *Wide Sargasso Sea* and Phillips's *Cambridge*. SmAx (11:1) 2006, 87–104.

18224. Hanna, Mary. L'écriture des anglophones blanches, de Jean Rhys à Pauline Melville. *See* **17472**.

18225. —— White women's sins; or, Patterns of choice and consequence in the two endings of *Voyage in the Dark*. JWIL (15:1/2) 2006, 132–63.

18226. Johnson, Erica L. Auto-ghostwriting *Smile, Please: an Unfinished Autobiography*. Biography (29:4) 2006, 563–83.

18227. Minogue, Sally; Palmer, Andrew. Confronting the abject: women and dead babies in modern English fiction. *See* **18524**.

18228. Nardin, Jane. 'As soon as I sober up I start again': alcohol and the will in Jean Rhys's pre-war novels. PLL (42:1) 2006, 46–72.

18229. Seshagiri, Urmila. Modernist ashes, postcolonial phoenix: Jean Rhys and the evolution of the English novel in the twentieth century. Mod/Mod (13:3) 2006, 487–505.

18230. Simpson, Anne B. Territories of the psyche: the fiction of Jean Rhys. (Bibl. 2005, 19055.) Rev. by Patricia Moran in TSWL (25:1) 2006, 165–70.

18231. Zhang, Deming. Canon rewriting and identity narrating: on *Wide Sargasso Sea*. FLS (119) 2006, 77–83. (In Chinese.)

Anne Rice ('Anne Rampling', 'A. N. Roquelaure')

18232. Holmes, Trevor. Becoming-other: (dis)embodiments of race in Anne Rice's *Tale of the Body Thief*. RomNet (44) 2006.

Adrienne Rich

18233. Bermann, Sandra. Translating history. *In* (pp. 257–73) **3191**.

18234. Henneberg, Sylvia B. Of creative crones and poetry: developing Age Studies through literature. *See* **18413**.

18235. Langdell, Cheri Colby. Adrienne Rich: the moment of change. Westport, CT; London: Praeger, 2004. pp. xviii, 277. (Contributions in women's studies, 198.) Rev. by Maire Mullins in PCP (41) 2006, 146–8.

18236. O'Neill, Michael. 'The all-sustaining air': Yeats, Stevens, Rich, Bishop – responses to Romantic poetry. *In* (pp. 143–62) **13735**.

18237. Sheridan, Susan. Adrienne Rich and the Women's Liberation Movement: a politics of reception. WS (35:1) 2006, 17–45.

18238. Steinman, Lisa M. 'Beauty, resonance, integrity': creative readings of Wordsworth in twentieth-century American poetry. *In* (pp. 101–22) **13735**.

18239. Stimpson, Catharine R. Do these deaths surpass understanding? The literary figure of the mother who murders. *See* **17643**.

I. A. (Ivor Armstrong) Richards (b.1893)

18240. KOENEKE, RODNEY. Empires of the mind: I. A. Richards and Basic English in China, 1929–1979. Stanford, CA: Stanford UP, 2004. pp. 256. Rev. by Howard Malchow in Albion (36:4) 2005, 780–2.

Dorothy Miller Richardson (1873–1957)

18241. JONES, SUSAN. Conrad on the borderlands of Modernism: Maurice Greiffenhagen, Dorothy Richardson and the case of *Typhoon*. *In* (pp. 195–211) **15280**.

18242. MARCUS, LAURA. Dorothy Richardson: *Pilgrimage*. *In* (pp. 440–9) **11788**.

18243. MARIE-LAVERROU, FLORENCE. John Cowper Powys dans le contexte moderniste: le hors-texte au cœur du texte. *See* **18126**.

18244. NYMAN, MICKI. Dorothy M. Richardson's 1948 letter to Lita Hornick. ANQ (19:1) 2006, 47–58.

18245. RAITT, SUZANNE. The rhetoric of efficiency in early Modernism. *See* **19049**.

'Henry Handel Richardson' (Ethel Florence Lindesay Robertson)

18246. LINDSEY, DUNYA. 'Composing the self': metaphors of creativity in Henry Handel Richardson's *Myself When Young*. ALS (22:2) 2005, 205–16.

Mordecai Richler

18247. HENDERSON, SCOTT. Ted Kotcheff: *The Apprenticeship of Duddy Kravitz*. *In* (pp. 247–57) **11946**.

Conrad Richter

18248. COTUGNO, MARIANNE. Conrad Richter and Karl Goedecker in the archives: the story of an author and a bookseller. PBSA (100:1) 2006, 105–17.

Laura Riding (Laura (Riding) Jackson)

18249. FRIEDMANN, ELIZABETH. A mannered grace: the life of Laura (Riding) Jackson. (Bibl. 2005, 19076.) Rev. by Mark Jacobs in Eng (54:210) 2005, 248–52.

18250. MCGANN, JEROME. 'The grand heretics of modern fiction': Laura Riding, John Cowper Powys, and the subjective correlative. Mod/Mod (13:2) 2006, 309–23.

18251. OPHIR, ELLA ZOHAR. Toward a pitiless fiction: abstraction, comedy, and Modernist antihumanism. *See* **17220**.

18252. VOGEL, AMBER. Not Elizabeth to his Raleigh: Laura Riding, Robert Graves, and origins of *The White Goddess*. *In* (pp. 229–39) **3405**.

Lynn Riggs

18253. ROACH, JOSEPH. World Bank drama. ESQ (50:1–3) 2004, 157–76. (*Green Grow the Lilacs*.)

Joan Riley

18254. DAVIS, ANDREA. Translating narratives of masculinity across borders: a Jamaican case study. CarQ (52:2/3) 2006, 22–38.

Peter Riley (b.1940)

18255. Greaves, Sara R. The coconstitution of text and context: eco-phenomenology in Peter Riley's *Excavations*. EtBr (30) 2006, 105–14.

Alberto Ríos

18256. Praitis, Irena. 'He gathered to himself through the years / Something of everything he knew': metaphor, composites, and multiplicity in the poetry of Alberto Ríos. CLR (1) 2004, 81–8.

Dale Ritterbusch (b.1946)

18257. McGuire, Thomas. The flow of war and time measured in the river-run of Dale Ritterbusch's lyric poetry. WLA (18:1/2) 2006, 96–103.

Amélie Rives

18258. Lucey, Donna M. Archie and Amélie: love and madness in the Gilded Age. New York: Harmony, 2006. pp. vii, 339, (plates) 8.

Kenneth Roberts

18259. Glover, Susan Paterson. East goes west: the technicolor environment of *Northwest Passage* (1940). *In* (pp. 111–26) **12438**.

Lynette Roberts

18260. McGuinness, Patrick. The poetry of Lynette Roberts. PNRev (32:2) 2005, 52–9.

Michèle Roberts

18261. Parker, Emma. Sex changes: the politics of pleasure in the novels of Michèle Roberts. LIT (17:3/4) 2006, 325–51.

Elizabeth Robins ('C. E. Raimond')

18262. Farfan, Penny. Women, Modernism, and performance. (Bibl. 2005, 19091.) Rev. by Ann Wilson in ModDr (48:4) 2005, 847–50; by Kate Egerton in JMMLA (38:2) 2005, 153–5; by Dorothy Chansky in TJ (58:1) 2006, 155–7; by Margaret F. Savilonis in TheatreS (47:1) 2006, 142–4; by Steven Putzel in VWM (69) 2006, 15–16; by Season Ellison in WS (35:8) 2006, 779–82; by Kathleen Worley in WSA (12) 2006, 246–9.

18263. Joseph, Maia. Mass appeal(s): representations of women's public speech in suffrage literature. *See* **9295**.

18264. Stewart, Eleanor. Infanticide et émancipation féminine dans *Alan's Wife* d'Elizabeth Robins et de Florence Bell. Cycnos (23:2) 2006, 45–60.

Edwin Arlington Robinson

18265. Alpers, Paul. 'The Philoctetes problem' and the poetics of pastoral. *See* **5691**.

18266. Donaldson, Scott. A hell of a name for a poet. SewR (113:4) 2005, 633–41. (State of letters.)

18267. Gale, Robert L. An Edwin Arlington Robinson encyclopedia. Jefferson, NC; London: McFarland, 2006. pp. vi, 271.

18268. Turco, Lewis. Robinson and the democracy of form. SewR (114:4) 2006, 587–94. (State of letters.)

Marilynne Robinson

18269. Gardner, Thomas. A door ajar: contemporary writers and Emily Dickinson. *See* **9865**.

18270. Hall, Joanne. The wanderer contained: issues of 'inside' and 'outside' in relation to Harold Gray's *Little Orphan Annie* and Marilynne Robinson's *Housekeeping*. CritS (18:3) 2006, 37–50.

Richard Rodriguez

18271. O'Gorman, Farrell. White, Black, and Brown: reading O'Connor after Richard Rodriguez. *See* **17839**.

18272. —— Rodriguez, Richard. 'A twenty-first century writer': Richard Rodriguez on Flannery O'Connor. *See* **17840**.

Theodore Roethke

18273. Dorset, Phyllis F. Roethke remembered. SewR (113:3) 2005, 450–7. (State of letters.)

18274. Hickman, Trenton. Theodore Roethke and the poetics of place. *In* (pp. 183–202) **13763**.

18275. Hirsch, Edward (ed.). Selected poems. (Bibl. 2005, 19106.) Rev. by Jeffrey Meyers in PNRev (32:4) 2006, 54–5.

18276. Rampton, David. Plexed artistry: the formal case for Mailer's *Harlot's Ghost*. *See* **17412**.

18277. Sell, Jonathan P. A. Allusion and ambiguity in Seamus Heaney's *Blackberry-Picking*. *See* **16323**.

Jane Rogers (b.1952)

18278. Franková, Milada. Jane Rogers's novel explorations. BStE (31) 2005, 129–37.

Edwin Rolfe

18279. Finnegan, Jim. Edwin Rolfe's historical witness to the spectacle of McCarthyism. ColLit (33:3) 2006, 135–47.

John Romeril

18280. Williams, Peter. Strange affinities: representation and affect in Australian POW drama. *See* **12807**.

Daphne Rooke

18281. Johnson, R. W. Old fires: Gordimer, Lessing and Daphne Rooke. TLS, 7 July 2006, 14–15.

Leon Rooke

18282. Dobozy, Tamas; Harrison, Brady. Interview with Leon Rooke. ShSt (13:1) 2005, 115–18.

18283. Gorjup, Branko (ed.). White gloves of the doorman: the works of Leon Rooke. Toronto: Exile, 2004. pp. xxi, 441; 1 DVD. Rev. by Michael Harris in BkCan (34:2) 2005, 13–14.

Isaac Rosenberg

18284. Arditi, Neil. The remains of Isaac Rosenberg. Parnassus (29:1/2) 2006, 372–86 (review-article).

18285. Liddiard, Jean (ed.). Selected poems and letters. (Bibl. 2003, 19386.) Rev. by Neil Arditi in Parnassus (29:1/2) 2006, 372–86.

18286. Noakes, Vivien (ed.). The poems and plays of Isaac Rosenberg. (Bibl. 2005, 19123.) Rev. by Neil Arditi in Parnassus (29:1/2) 2006, 372–86.

Joe Rosenblatt (b.1933)

18287. Berry, David. Getting to know Joe. *In* (pp. 89–94) **18296**.

18288. Donati, Ada. Canadian *I Ching*. *In* (pp. 83–8) **18296**.

18289. Drache, Sharon Abron. Phantasmagoric visions of fish and bees: the Hebraic and proletarian roots of Joe Rosenblatt's *œuvre*: poetry, prose and drawings. *In* (pp. 63–70) **18296**.

18290. Evangelisti, Italo. The body of Rosenblatt's poetry. *In* (pp. 139–50) **18296**.

18291. Keating, Diane. The larval clothes of Joe Rosenblatt. *In* (pp. 18–26) **18296**.

18292. Owen, Catherine. Joe Rosenblatt: Dionysian Taoist. *In* (pp. 120–30) **18296**.

18293. Rizzardi, Alfredo. Poet in the water maze. *In* (pp. 71–82) **18296**.

18294. Rogers, Linda. Cuppa Joe. *In* (pp. 52–60) **18296**.

18295. —— Paradigm lost: the occult compass of Joe Rosenblatt. *In* (pp. 7–13) **18296**.

18296. —— (ed.). Joe Rosenblatt: essays on his works. Toronto; Buffalo, NY; Lancaster: Guernica, 2006. pp. 157. (Writers series, 15.)

18297. Safarik, Allan. Joe. *In* (pp. 32–51) **18296**.

18298. Smith, Faye. From python to parrot. *In* (pp. 103–8) **18296**.

Alan Ross (b.1922)

18299. Hughes, David (sel. and introd.). Poems. (Bibl. 2005, 19125.) Rev. by John Lucas in TLS, 3 Mar. 2006, 27.

18300. Lucas, John. From Sussex to everywhere. TLS, 3 Mar. 2006, 27 (review-article). (Ross's melancholia.)

18301. Powell, Neil. The gingko in the garden. *See* **1158**.

Fran Ross (1935–1985)

18302. Leverette, Tru. Traveling identities: mixed-race quests and Fran Ross's *Oreo*. AAR (40:1) 2006, 79–91.

Sinclair Ross

18303. Stouck, David. As for Sinclair Ross. (Bibl. 2005, 19128.) Rev. by Andrew Lesk in BkCan (34:6) 2005, 21–2; by Peter Dickinson in GPQ (26:4) 2006, 290–1; by Robert Thacker in CanL (191) 2006, 108–10.

Henry Roth

18304. Kellman, Steven G. Redemption: the life of Henry Roth. (Bibl. 2005, 19132.) Rev. by Toby Lichtig in TLS, 10 Mar. 2006, 8; by Christopher Tayler in LRB (28:6) 2006, 19–22; by Myles Weber in MichQR (45:3) 2006, 560–7; by Alan Gibbs in JAStud (40:3) 2006, 667–8.

18305. Tayler, Christopher. You wanna play bad? LRB (28:6) 2006, 19–22 (review-article). (*Call It Sleep*.)

Philip Roth

18306. Barcus, Patrick. The rules of the game: fact in fiction. IE (28:2) 2006, 22–6.

18307. Byers, Michele. Material bodies and performative identities: Mona, Neil, and the Promised Land. PhRS (2:2) 2006, 102–20.

18308. Dobozy, Tamas. The Holocaust as fiction: Derrida's *Demeure* and the Demjanjuk trial in Philip Roth's *Operation Shylock*. PhRS (1:1) 2005, 37–52.

18309. Faisst, Julia. 'Delusionary thinking, whether white or black or in between': fictions of race in Philip Roth's *The Human Stain*. PhRS (2:2) 2006, 121–37.

18310. Gilman, Sander L. The fanatic: Philip Roth and Hanif Kureishi confront success. CL (58:2) 2006, 153–69.

18311. Goldblatt, Roy. The whitening of the Jews and the changing face of Newark. PhRS (2:2) 2006, 86–101.

18312. Gooblar, David. 'Oh Freud, do I know!': Philip Roth, Freud, and narrative therapy. PhRS (1:1) 2005, 67–81.

18313. Gordon, Andrew. Philip Roth's *Patrimony* and Art Spiegelman's *Maus*: Jewish sons remembering their fathers. PhRS (1:1) 2005, 53–66.

18314. Greenham, David. The concept of irony: Jane Austen's *Emma* and Philip Roth's *Sabbath's Theater*. PhRS (1:2) 2005, 163–74.

18315. Halio, Jay L.; Siegel, Ben (eds). Turning up the flame: Philip Roth's later novels. (Bibl. 2005, 19149.) Rev. by Willis Salomon in PhRS (1:2) 2005, 175–7.

18316. Kaplan, Brett Ashley. Anatole Broyard's *Human Stain*: performing postracial consciousness. PhRS (1:2) 2005, 125–44.

18317. Kirby, Lisa A. Shades of passing: teaching and interrogating identity in Roth's *The Human Stain* and Fitzgerald's *The Great Gatsby*. PhRS (2:2) 2006, 151–60.

18318. McQuade, Molly. A fan's index to *Portnoy's Complaint*. TriQ (126) 2006, 150–61.

18319. Marcus, Greil. The shape of things to come: prophecy and the American voice. New York: Farrar, Straus, & Giroux, 2006. pp. 320.

18320. Mayné, Gilles. Transgression de l'espace et espace de la transgression dans *The Human Stain* de Philip Roth. Anglophonia (19) 2006, 197–209.

18321. Medin, Daniel L. Trials and errors at the turn of the millennium: on *The Human Stain* and J. M. Coetzee's *Disgrace*. PhRS (1:1) 2005, 82–92.

18322. Mortara, Elèna. The last transatlantic ambassador of American literature? Philip Roth (un)masked as Ziff by Alan Lelchuk. *See* **17111**.

18323. Posnock, Ross. Philip Roth's rude truth: the art of immaturity. Princeton, NJ; Oxford: Princeton UP, 2006. pp. xx, 301.

18324. Royal, Derek Parker. Annual bibliography: Philip Roth criticism and resources – 2004. PhRS (1:2) 2005, 185–9.

18325. —— Annual bibliography: Philip Roth criticism and resources – 2005. PhRS (2:2) 2006, 172–6.

18326. —— Plotting the frames of subjectivity: identity, death, and narrative in Philip Roth's *The Human Stain*. ConLit (47:1) 2006, 114–40.

18327. —— (ed.). Philip Roth: new perspectives on an American author. Foreword by Daniel Walden. (Bibl. 2005, 19173.) Rev. by Steven G. Kellman in PhRS (1:2) 2005, 177–9; by David Gooblar in TLS, 7 Apr. 2006, 33; by Catherine Morley in JAStud (40:3) 2006, 676–7; by Paul Hollander in Cithara (46:1) 2006, 60–1.

18328. —— *et al.* Looking at Saul Bellow (1915–2005). *See* **14750**.

18329. Safer, Elaine B. Mocking the age: the later novels of Philip Roth. Albany: New York State UP, 2006. pp. x, 219. (SUNY series in modern Jewish literature and culture.)

18330. Schur, Richard. Dream or nightmare? Roth, Morrison, and America. PhRS (1:1) 2005, 19–36.

18331. Shostak, Debra. Philip Roth: countertexts, counterlives. (Bibl. 2005, 19179.) Rev. by David Brauner in PhRS (1:1) 2005, 105–7; by Jay Martin in HC (43:3) 2006, 18–19.

18332. Steed, J. P. The subversion of the Jews: post-World War II anxiety, humor, and identity in Woody Allen and Philip Roth. PhRS (1:2) 2005, 145–62.

18333. Steinberg, Gillian. Philip Roth's *Defender of the Faith*: a modern Midrash. PhRS (1:1) 2005, 7–18.

18334. Stow, Simon. Written and unwritten America: Roth on reading, politics, and theory. *In* (pp. 361–73) **3266**.

18335. Wilson, Matthew. Reading *The Human Stain* through Charles W. Chesnutt: the genre of the passing novel. PhRS (2:2) 2006, 138–50.

J. K. Rowling

18336. Beahm, George. Fact, fiction, and folklore in Harry Potter's world: an unofficial guide. Charlottesville, VA: Hampton Roads, 2005. pp. xix, 256.

18337. Cockrell, Amanda. Harry Potter and the witch hunters: a social context for the attacks on *Harry Potter*. JAC (29:1) 2006, 24–30.

18338. Fife, Ernelle. Wise warriors in Tolkien, Lewis, and Rowling. *See* **18794**.

18339. Gemmill, Maia A.; Nexon, Daniel H. Children's crusade: the religious politics of Harry Potter. *In* (pp. 79–100) **18355**.

18340. Goff, Patricia M. Producing Harry Potter: why the medium is still the message. *In* (pp. 27–44) **18355**.

18341. Griesinger, Emily. The search for 'deeper magic': J. K. Rowling and C. S. Lewis. *In* (pp. 317–31) **11916**.

18342. Hall, Martin. The fantasy of realism; or, Mythology as methodology. *In* (pp. 177–94) **18355**.

18343. Jackson, Patrick Thaddeus; Mandaville, Peter. Global hero: Harry Potter abroad. *In* (pp. 45–59) **18355**.

18344. Kenda, Jakob J. Rewriting children's literature. *In* (pp. 160–70) **3186**.

18345. Kirk, Connie Ann. The J. K. Rowling encyclopedia. Westport, CT; London: Greenwood Press, 2006. pp. xlvi, 374.

18346. Knutsen, Torbjørn L. Dumbledore's pedagogy: knowledge and virtue at Hogwarts. *In* (pp. 197–212) **18355**.

18347. Lathey, Gillian. The travels of Harry: international marketing and the translation of J. K. Rowling's Harry Potter books. LU (29:2) 2005, 141–51.

18348. Long, David. Quidditch, imperialism, and the sport–war intertext. *In* (pp. 127–54) **18355**.

18349. McCarron, Bill. Basilisk puns in *Harry Potter and the Chamber of Secrets*. NCL (36:1) 2006, 2.

18350. MacDonald, Marianne. Harry Potter and the fan-fiction phenomenon. GLRW (13:1) 2006, 28–30.

18351. Mayes-Elma, Ruthann. Females and Harry Potter: not all that empowering. Lanham, MD; Oxford: Rowman & Littlefield, 2006. pp. vii, 155. (Reverberations.)

18352. Meddemmen, John. Metamorfosi e '*transmogrification*' in *Harry Potter* e altrove. ConLett (46) 2006, 431–43.

18353. Nel, Philip. Is there a text in this advertising campaign? Literature, marketing, and Harry Potter. LU (29:2) 2005, 236–67.

18354. Neumann, Iver B. Naturalizing geography: Harry Potter and the realms of Muggles, magic folks, and giants. *In* (pp. 157–75) **18355**.

18355. Nexon, Daniel H.; Neumann, Iver B. (eds). Harry Potter and international relations. Lanham, MD; Oxford: Rowman & Littlefield, 2006. pp. vii, 245.

18356. Pennington, John. Peter Pan, Pullman, and Potter: anxieties of growing up. *In* (pp. 237–62) **14616**.

18357. Petrina, Alessandra. Forbidden feast, enchanted castle: Arthurian spaces in the Harry Potter novels. Mythlore (24:3/4) 2006, 95–110.

18358. Pugh, Tison; Wallace, David L. Heteronormative heroism and queering the school story in J. K. Rowling's *Harry Potter* series. CLAQ (31:3) 2006, 260–81.

18359. Sexton, Colleen A. J. K. Rowling. Minneapolis, MN: Twenty-first Century, 2006. pp. 112. (Biography.)

18360. Sterling-Folker, Jennifer; Folker, Brian. Conflict and the nation-state: magical mirrors of Muggles and refracted images. *In* (pp. 103–26) **18355**.

18361. Towns, Ann; Rumelili, Bahar. Foreign yet familiar: international politics and the reception of Potter in Turkey and Sweden. *In* (pp. 61–77) **18355**.

18362. Willis, Ika. Keeping promises to queer children: making space (for Mary Sue) at Hogwarts. *In* (pp. 153–70) **19868**.

Arundhati Roy

18363. Anand, Divya. Inhabiting the space of literature: an ecocritical study of Arundhati Roy's *God of Small Things* and O. V. Vijayan's *The Legends of Khasak*. ISLE (12:2) 2005, 95–108.

18364. Mongia, Padmini. Between men: Conrad in the fiction of two contemporary Indian writers. *In* (pp. 85–99) **15280**.

18365. Navarro Tejero, Antonia. Gender and caste in the anglophone Indian novels of Arundhati Roy and Githa Hariharan: feminist issues in cross cultural perspectives. Lewiston, NY; Lampeter: Mellen Press, 2005. pp. iv, 172. (Women's studies, 45.)

Gabrielle Roy

18366. Kelly, Darlene. Lost in translation: the English versions of Gabrielle Roy's early novels. StudCanL (30:2) 2005, 96–114.

18367. Morency, Jean. Journalisme et littérarité: *Peuples du Canada* de Gabrielle Roy. EtCan (56) 2004, 73–81.

18368. Socken, Paul. Gabrielle Roy and William Arthur Deacon. EtCan (59) 2005, 145–55.

18369. Socken, Paul G. (ed.). Intimate strangers: the letters of Margaret Laurence & Gabrielle Roy. *See* **17024**.

18370. Stouck, David. The making of Margaret Laurence's epic voice. *See* **17025**.

Robert Chester Ruark (1915–1965)

18371. Almquist, Steve. Not quite the gabbling of 'a thing most brutish': Caliban's Kiswahili in Aimé Césaire's *A Tempest*. *See* **6117**.

Bernice Rubens

18372. Hu, Lei. Imprisonment and madness: scapegoat motif in Bernice Rubens' works. FLS (119) 2006, 56–61. (In Chinese.)

Muriel Rukeyser

18373. Allison, Raphael C. Muriel Rukeyser goes to war: pragmatism, pluralism, and the politics of ekphrasis. ColLit (33:2) 2006, 1–29.

18374. Burt, Stephen. Head of dream. TLS, 24 Mar. 2006, 26 (review-article). (*Collected Poems*.)

18375. Goodman, Jenny. 'Presumption' and 'unlearning': reading Muriel Rukeyser's *The Book of the Dead* as a woman's American epic. TSWL (25:2) 2006, 267–89.

18376. Kaufman, Janet E.; Herzog, Anne F.; Levi, Jan Heller (eds). The collected poems of Muriel Rukeyser. (Bibl. 2005, 19253.) Rev. by Stephen Burt in TLS, 24 Mar. 2006, 26; by Michele S. Ware in ColLit (33:2) 2006, 199–201; by Suzanne Gardinier in WRB (23:4) 2006, 10–11.

18377. Ronda, Bruce A. 'I see your mouth calling / before the words arrive': Muriel Rukeyser's *The Soul and Body of John Brown* and 1930s America. *In* (pp. 173–85) **8537**.

18378. Wolosky, Shira. Medical–industrial discourses: Muriel Rukeyser's *The Book of the Dead*. LitMed (25:1) 2006, 156–71.

Salman Rushdie

18379. Barfield, Steven. 'Jewelinthecrown.co.uk': Orientalism's strange persistence in British South Asian writing. *In* (pp. 111–20) **14238**.

18380. Canepari-Labib, Michela. Writing and translating after the Empire. *See* **17752**.

18381. Cormack, Alistair. Migration and the politics of narrative form: realism and the postcolonial subject in *Brick Lane*. *See* **20173**.

18382. Deb, Siddhartha. Naipaul, Rushdie, Seth. *See* **18457**.

18383. Deszcz, Justyna. Rushdie in Wonderland: fairytaleness in Salman Rushdie's fiction. (Bibl. 2004, 19321.) Rev. by Stephen Benson in MarvT (20:1) 2006, 122–4.

18384. Fetherling, George. Salmon Rushdie interviewed. BkCan (34:8) 2005, 9–10.

18385. Gane, Gillian. Postcolonial literature and the magic radio: the language of Rushdie's *Midnight's Children*. PT (27:3) 2006, 569–96.

18386. Gauthier, Tim S. Narrative desire and historical reparations: A. S. Byatt, Ian McEwan, Salman Rushdie. *See* **14980**.

18387. Konig, Eva. Between cultural imperialism and the *fatwa*: colonial echoes and postcolonial dialogue in Salman Rushdie's *Haroun and the Sea of Stories*. IFR (33:1/2) 2006, 52–62.

18388. Kunow, Rüdiger. Architect of the cosmopolitan dream: Salman Rushdie. Amst (51:3) 2006, 369–85.

18389. Parkin-Gounelas, Ruth. The insistence of the object – and its sublimations. *See* **13575**.

18390. Volná, Lída. Myth in the Indian novel in English: *Midnight's Children*'s call for plurality and tolerance. ParallaxB (3:1) 2006, 91–101.

Joanna Russ

18391. Salvini, Laura. Quartetto di 'J' per autrice e lettrice: *Female Man* di Joanna Russ. Àcoma (32) 2006, 52–60.

Charles M. Russell

18392. Cristy, Raphael James. Charles M. Russell: the storyteller's art. (Bibl. 2005, 19282.) Rev. by Jim Hoy in GPQ (26:1) 2006, 41–2.

Vern Rutsala (b.1934)

18393. Turco, Lewis. Vern Rutsala's surreal world. HC (43:4) 2006, 1–14.

Michael Ryan

18394. Ryan, Michael. My favorite poet. *See* **9892**.

George Ryga

18395. Doran, Greg. Sound vision: textual theory and the director. *In* (pp. 43–60) **12336**.

Louis Sachar (b.1954)

18396. Wilkie-Stibbs, Christine. Borderland children: reflection on narratives of abjection. *See* **15860**.

V. Sackville-West

18397. Utell, Janine. Leaving her father's house: Sackville-West's *Saint Joan of Arc* and Woolf's *Three Guineas*. VWM (69) 2006, 7–8.

Kerri Sakamoto

18398. Cuder-Domínguez, Pilar. Surviving history: Kerri Sakamoto interviewed. JCL (41:3) 2006, 137–43.

J. D. Salinger

18399. Salinger, Wendy. Listen: a memoir. New York: Bloomsbury, 2005. pp. 243.

18400. Sommers, Michael A. J. D. Salinger. New York: Rosen Central, 2006. pp. 112. (Library of author biographies.)

18401. Weber, Myles. Consuming silences: how we read authors who don't publish. (Bibl. 2005, 19297.) Rev. by Steven G. Kellman in GaR (59:4) 2005, 964–5; by Claire Harman in TLS, 17 Feb. 2006, 34.

Mary Jo Salter

18402. Stewart, Robert. Order & disorder: an interview with Mary Jo Salter. NewLet (72:3/4) 2006, 112–27.

Mary Ann Samyn (b.1970)

18403. McGuire, Amanda. Interest in interiors: an interview with Mary Ann Samyn. LauR (40:2) 2006, 58–68.

Carl Sandburg

18404. Berman, Paul. This here phizzog: faces and places in the work of Carl Sandburg. TLS, 29 Sept. 2006, 13–15. (Commentary.)

Scott R. (Scott Russell) Sanders (b.1945)

18405. Sanders, Scott Russell. A private history of awe. New York: North Point Press, 2006. pp. 322.

Andrew Sant (b.1950)

18406. Knottenbelt, Elizabeth. 'If there were world enough and time'. *See* **14383**.

George Santayana

18407. Jarraway, David R. 'Both sides and neither': Stevens, Santayana, and the aestheticism of androgyny. *See* **18639**.

18408. Willis, Lloyd. Henry Wadsworth Longfellow, United States national literature, and the canonical erasure of material nature. *See* **10756**.

Sapphire (b.1950)

18409. Michlin, Monica. Narrative as empowerment: *Push* and the *signifying* on prior African American novels on incest. EA (59:2) 2006, 170–85.

Frank Sargeson

18410. Gwynne, Joel. Frank Sargeson: the secular visionary. JPW (42:1) 2006, 44–57.

Ken Saro-Wiwa

18411. Caminero-Santangelo, Byron. Of freedom and oil: nation, globalization, and civil liberties in the writing of Ken Saro-Wiwa. YREAL (22) 2006, 293–308.

18412. Lock, Charles. Indirect rule and the continuities of Nigerian fiction. *In* (pp. 181–96) **11860**.

May Sarton

18413. HENNEBERG, SYLVIA B. Of creative crones and poetry: developing Age Studies through literature. NWSAJ (18:1) 2006, 106–25.

Siegfried Sassoon

18414. EGREMONT, MAX. Siegfried Sassoon: a biography. (Bibl. 2005, 19320.) Rev. by Daniel Swift in NYTB, 1 Jan. 2006, 5.

18415. MORTON, JOHN. Tennyson and the 1914–1918 war. *See* **11402**.

William Satchell

18416. JONES, LAWRENCE. Three 'bush' novels and the colonial myth. *In* (pp. 359–84) **8374**.

D. S. (Derek S.) Savage (b.1917)

18417. BLECHMAN, MAX (introd.). To D. S. Savage. *See* **18207**.

Robert J. Sawyer

18418. RAMRAJ, RUBY S. Robots and artificial intelligence in Asimov's *The Caves of Steel* and Sawyer's *Golden Fleece*. *In* (pp. 139–46) **13541**.

18419. VINT, SHERRYL. Coding of race in science fiction: what's wrong with the obvious? *In* (pp. 119–30) **13541**.

Robert Saxton (b.1952)

18420. SIMS, CLARE. An interview with Robert Saxton. PNRev (32:1) 2005, 51–2.

Dorothy L. Sayers

18421. ACTON, TOM. Ved Dzabqu qd vnh Urod. *See* **14886**.

18422. CHANCE, JANE (ed.). Women medievalists and the academy. *See* **7773**.

18423. DEAN, CHRISTOPHER (ed.). Further studies in Sayers: essays presented to Dr Barbara Reynolds on her 90th birthday, 13th June, 2004. Hurstpierpoint, W. Sussex: Dorothy L. Sayers Soc., 2004. pp. 85. Rev. by Laura K. Simmons in SEVEN (21) 2004, 112–14.

Leslie Scalapino

18424. LAGAPA, JASON. Something from nothing: the disontological poetics of Leslie Scalapino. ConLit (47:1) 2006, 30–61.

18425. MORRIS, ADALAIDE. The act of the mind: thought experiments in the poetry of Jorie Graham and Leslie Scalapino. *In* (pp. 146–66) **13732**.

Wendy Scarfe (b.1933)

18426. BODE, KATHERINE. Reading (in/and) *Miranda*. ALS (22:3) 2006, 357–67.

James C. Schaap (b.1948)

18427. SCHAAP, JAMES CALVIN. Writing and knowing. *In* (pp. 130–51) **11940**.

Paul Schrader (b.1946)

18428. WILLS, GARRY. Paul Schrader: an interview. *In* (pp. 113–19) **11940**.

Grace Schulman (b.1935)

18429. MASON, DAVID. Grace Schulman's song of praise. SewR (113:3) 2005, 407–21.

George Schuyler

18430. Ferguson, Jeffrey B. The sage of Sugar Hill: George S. Schuyler and the Harlem renaissance. (Bibl. 2005, 19336.) Rev. by Anne Elizabeth Carroll in JAH (93:2) 2006, 567–8.

Delmore Schwartz

18431. Keller, Jim. Delmore Schwartz's strange times. *In* (pp. 153–81) **13763**.

Armand Schwerner

18432. Finkelstein, Norman. The sacred and the real in *The Tablets* of Armand Schwerner. AmLH (17:2) 2005, 259–79.

Gregory A. Scofield (b.1966)

18433. Jamieson, Sara. *Âyahkwêw* songs: AIDS and mourning in Gregory Scofield's *Urban Rez* poems. CanP (57) 2005, 52–64.

18434. Scudeler, June. 'The song I am singing': Gregory Scofield's interweavings of Métis, gay, and Jewish selfhoods. StudCanL (31:1) 2006, 129–45.

18435. Stigter, Shelley. The dialectics and dialogics of code-switching in the poetry of Gregory Scofield and Louise Halfe. AIQ (30:1/2) 2006, 49–60.

Mrs Evelyn Scott

18436. Collins, Roger. Intersecting lives and intertwining works: Owen Merton and Evelyn Scott. *In* (pp. 311–30) **8374**.

18437. Jenkins, Andrea Powell. 'The last […] thing one needed to know': Kristeva's 'herethics' in Evelyn Scott's *Escapade* and *The Narrow House*. JML (29:3) 2006, 78–102.

Kim Scott (b.1957)

18438. Slater, Lisa. *Benang*, this 'most local of histories': annexing colonial records into a world without end. JCL (41:1) 2006, 51–68.

18439. —— Kim Scott's *Benang*: monstrous (textual) bodies. Southerly (65:1) 2005, 63–73.

Margaret Scott (b.1934)

18440. Blair, Ruth. Finding home: the poetry of Margaret Scott. ALS (22:2) 2005, 133–45.

18441. Scott, Margaret. A little more: celebrating a life of letters. Hobart, Tas.: Summerhill, 2005. pp. xiii, 157.

Paul Scott

18442. Mezey, Jason Howard. Mourning the death of the Raj? Melancholia as historical engagement in Paul Scott's *Raj Quartet*. StudN (38:3) 2006, 327–52.

Djanet Sears

18443. Brown-Guillory, Elizabeth. Place and displacement in Djanet Sears's *Harlem Duet* and *The Adventures of a Black Girl in Search of God*. *In* (pp. 155–70) **11795**.

Eve Kosofsky Sedgwick

18444. Sedgwick, Eve Kosofsky. Teaching/depression. SFO (4:2) 2006.

Tim Seibles

18445. Rowell, Charles Henry. Permission to sing ... that's what made me love it': an interview with Tim Seibles. Callaloo (29:1) 2006, 62–75.

Will Self

18446. Alderson, David. 'Not everyone knows fuck all about Foucault': Will Self's *Dorian* and post-gay culture. TexP (19:3) 2005, 309–29.

Shyam Selvadurai (b.1965)

18447. Chu, Patricia P. 'A flame against a sleeping lake of petrol': form and the sympathetic witness in Selvadurai's *Funny Boy* and Ondaatje's *Anil's Ghost*. *In* (pp. 86–103) **11849**.

18448. Lesk, Andrew. Ambivalence at the site of authority: desire and difference in *Funny Boy*. CanL (190) 2006, 31–46.

Samuel Selvon

18449. McLeod, John. Postcolonial fictions of adoption. CritS (18:2) 2006, 45–55.

18450. Rampaul, Giselle A. Black Crusoe, White Friday: carnivalesque reversals in Samuel Selvon's *Moses Ascending* and Derek Walcott's *Pantomime*. CLR (1) 2004, 69–80.

Maurice Sendak

18451. Knoepflmacher, U. C. The Hansel and Gretel syndrome: survivorship fantasies and parental desertion. *See* **16913**.

18452. Lindow, Sandra J. Wild gifts: anger management and moral development in the fiction of Ursula K. Le Guin and Maurice Sendak. *See* **17106**.

Olive Senior

18453. Senior, Olive. The poem as gardening, the story as su-su: finding a literary voice. JWIL (14:1/2) 2005, 35–50.

18454. Stouck, Jordan. Towards a Caribbean Canadian post-national: Olive Senior and *Gardening in the Tropics*. JWIL (14:1/2) 2005, 13–34.

Robert Service

18455. Baetz, Joel. Robert Service's war correspondence and poetry. CanP (58) 2006, 55–78.

Vikram Seth (b.1952)

18456. Benson, Stephen. Literary music: writing music in contemporary fiction. *See* **17420**.

18457. Deb, Siddhartha. Naipaul, Rushdie, Seth. JPW (42:2) 2006, 238–50 (review-article).

18458. —— Strands of family. TLS, 20 Jan. 2006, 23 (review-article).

18459. Seth, Vikram. Two lives. (Bibl. 2005, 19361.) Rev. by Siddhartha Deb in JPW (42:2) 2006, 238–50.

18460. Wachtel, Eleanor. An interview with Vikram Seth. Brick (78) 2006, 36–48.

Mary Lee Settle

18461. Brosi, George. Mary Lee Settle: a biographical overview: the life of a literary freedom seeker. AppH (34:1) 2006, 16–25.

18462. Bruccoli, Matthew J. Mary Lee Settle interviews: the *Paris Review* years. AppH (34:1) 2006, 90–5.

18463. Delaney, Janice. The first lady of PEN Faulkner: celebrating American writers. AppH (34:1) 2006, 60–2.

18464. Douglass, Thomas E. *The Scapegoat*: establishing a genre. AppH (34:1) 2006, 78–82.

18465. Hill, Jane. Mary Lee Settle: an interview. FiveP (10:1/2) 2006, 185–203.

18466. Joyner, Nancy Carol. *All the Brave Promises*: Settle's first memoir. AppH (34:1) 2006, 70–2.

18467. Lawrence, Starling. Remembrances of Mary Lee Settle: in the literary trenches with Mary Lee. AppH (34:1) 2006, 36–40.

18468. Long, Kate. Mary Lee Settle interviews: 'Roger Mary Lee Williams'. AppH (34:1) 2006, 83–9.

18469. Maillard, Keith. Mary Lee Settle's literary legacy: a powerful shock of recognition. AppH (34:1) 2006, 63–9.

18470. Moore, Phyllis Wilson. Tribute to Mary Lee Settle: the Mother Jones of West Virginia literature. AppH (34:1) 2006, 11–14.

18471. Neville, Katherine. Remembrances of Mary Lee Settle: 'I simply know things.' AppH (34:1) 2006, 28–31.

18472. Simmons, Gordon. A Mary Lee Settle bibliography. AppH (34:1) 2006, 98–102.

18473. Willis, Meredith Sue. *The Clam Shell*: opening to life with resolute passion. AppH (34:1) 2006, 73–7.

'Dr Seuss' (Theodor Seuss Geisel)

18474. Nel, Philip. Dr Seuss: American icon. (Bibl. 2004, 19405.) Rev. by Richard Flynn in ChildLit (33) 2005, 263–7.

18475. Peterson, Todd. Theodor Seuss Geisel, author and illustrator. New York: Ferguson, 2006. pp. 160.

Anne Sexton

18476. Knoepflmacher, U. C. The Hansel and Gretel syndrome: survivorship fantasies and parental desertion. *See* **16913**.

18477. Lauro, Sarah Juliet. The fruits of their labors: the childbirth poetry of Plath, Sexton, and Loy. *See* **18044**.

18478. Puglisi, Floriana. Transgressing boundaries: a geography of Anne Sexton's spirituality. Turin: Otto, 2006. pp. viii, 145. (Nova americana.)

18479. Smith, Ellen McGrath. A stepmother for *Transformations*: Sara Henderson Hay's *Story Hour*. *See* **16301**.

18480. Trinidad, David. 'Two sweet ladies': Sexton and Plath's friendship and mutual influence. APR (35:6) 2006, 21–9.

18481. Van Ness, Gordon. ‘The fiercest hearts are in love with a wild perfection’: the James Dickey / James Wright correspondence. *See* **15496**.

Anthony Shaffer

18482. Franks, Benjamin (ed.). The quest for *The Wicker Man*: history, folklore and pagan perspectives. *See* **13126**.

Tupac Shakur (b.1971)

18483. Brown, Timothy J. Reaffirming African American cultural values: Tupac Shakur’s *Greatest Hits* as a musical autobiography. WJBS (29:1) 2005, 558–73.

18484. Jones, Meta DuEwa. An interview with Michael Eric Dyson. Callaloo (29:3) 2006, 786–802.

Ntozake Shange

18485. Mafe, Diana Adesola. Black women on Broadway: the duality of Lorraine Hansberry’s *A Raisin in the Sun* and Ntozake Shange’s *for colored girls*. *See* **16269**.

Karl Shapiro

18486. Oostdijk, Diederik. The wartime success of Karl Shapiro’s *V-Letter*. Neophilologus (90:3) 2006, 445–62.

George Bernard Shaw

18487. Anon. The British Library catalogue of George Bernard Shaw papers. London: British Library, 2005. pp. xvii, 321. Rev. by Arthur Searle in Library (7:3) 2006, 341–2.

18488. Carter, Patricia M. ‘Until it was historical’: a letter and an interview. Shaw (24) 2004, 11–37. (Shaw’s relationship with Molly Tompkins.)

18489. Conolly, L. W. *Mrs Warren’s Profession* and the Lord Chamberlain. Shaw (24) 2004, 46–95.

18490. Dukore, Bernard F. Sex and salvation. Shaw (24) 2004, 112–18.

18491. Gahan, Peter. *Jitta’s Atonement*: the birth of psychoanalysis and ‘the fetters of the feminine psyche’. Shaw (24) 2004, 128–65.

18492. Gibbs, A. M. Bernard Shaw: a life. Gainesville: Florida UP, 2005. pp. xiii, 554. (Florida Bernard Shaw.) Rev. by Roy Foster in TLS, 21 July 2006, 13; by David Edgar in LRB (28:18) 2006, 11–12; by T. F. Evans in IndS (44:1/2) 2006, 14–16.

18493. Grioni, John S. A lifetime friendship. IndS (44:1/2) 2006, 4–13. (Paul Troubetzskoy.)

18494. Holroyd, Michael. Dionysos, do the right thing: why Shaw is the writer for our times. TLS, 21 July 2006, 14–15.

18495. Laurence, Dan H. Victorians unveiled: some thoughts on *Mrs Warren’s Profession*. Shaw (24) 2004, 38–45.

18496. Morgan, Margery M. Shaw and the sex reformers. Shaw (24) 2004, 96–111.

18497. Pagliaro, Harold. Truncated love in *Candida* and *Heartbreak House*. Shaw (24) 2004, 204–14.

18498. Pfeiffer, John R. A continuing checklist of Shaviana. Shaw (24) 2004, 264–92.

18499. Pharand, Michel W. A selected bibliography of writings by and about Bernard Shaw concerning love, sex, marriage, women, and related topics. Shaw (24) 2004, 221–35.

18500. —— (ed.). Shaw's sex credo. Shaw (24) 2004, 215–20. (Letter to Frank Harris.)

18501. Sherbo, Arthur. Further matters Shavian. PBSA (100:4) 2006, 463–9.

18502. Stafford, Tony. 'The end of the hearth and the home': the deconstructing fireplace in Shaw's early plays. IndS (44:1/2) 2006, 17–30.

18503. Waltonen, Karma. *Saint Joan*: from Renaissance witch to New Woman. Shaw (24) 2004, 186–203.

18504. Weintraub, Rodelle. What makes Johnny run? Shaw's *Man and Superman* as a pre-Freudian dream play. Shaw (24) 2004, 119–27.

Luci Shaw (b.1928)

18505. Shaw, Luci. Reversing entropy. *In* (pp. 201–13) **11940**.

Patrick Shaw-Stewart (1888–1917)

18506. Vance, Norman. Classics and the Dardanelles campaign. *See* **14867**.

Sam Shepard

18507. Hishmeh, Richard E. Marketing genius: the friendship of Allen Ginsberg and Bob Dylan. *See* **16103**.

18508. Rosen, Carol. Sam Shepard: a 'poetic rodeo'. (Bibl. 2005, 19427.) Rev. by Johan Callens in BELL (ns 4) 2006, 195–203; by the same in TRI (31:2) 2006, 213–14.

18509. Saddik, Annette J. 'You just forged ahead': image, authenticity, and freedom in the plays of Tennessee Williams and Sam Shepard. *See* **19179**.

18510. Tarancón, Juan A. Visions of the true West: Sam Shepard, identity and myth. RAEI (17) 2004, 283.

18511. Westgate, J. Chris. Negotiating the American West in Sam Shepard's family plays. ModDr (48:4) 2005, 726–43.

Delia Sherman

18512. Tighe, Heidi. Fragmented roles: Delia Sherman's *The Porcelain Dove* as metafictive text. NYRSF (18:5) 2006, 1, 4–7.

Carol Shields

18513. Roberts, Gillian. Sameness and difference: border crossings in *The Stone Diaries* and *Larry's Party*. CanL (191) 2006, 86–102.

18514. Wachtel, Eleanor. Scrapbook of Carol. Room (29:2) 2006, 7–21.

18515. Wasmeier, Marie-Louise. Fictional fossils: life and death writing in Carol Shields's *The Stone Diaries*. FMLS (41:4) 2005, 439–48.

18516. Weese, Katherine. The 'invisible' woman: narrative strategies in *The Stone Diaries*. JNT (36:1) 2006, 90–120.

Leslie Marmon Silko

18517. Arnold, Ellen L. The word made visible: Leslie Marmon Silko's *Almanac of the Dead*. *In* (pp. 214–37) **2149**.

18518. Baringer, Sandra. The metanarrative of suspicion in late twentieth-century America. *See* **11760**.

18519. Ferguson, Suzanne. Europe and the quest for home in James Welch's *The Heartsong of Charging Elk* and Leslie Marmon Silko's *Gardens in the Dunes*. *See* **19008**.

18520. Fitz, Brewster E. Silko: writing storyteller and medicine woman. (Bibl. 2004, 19469.) Rev. by Joshua Dolezal in WAL (41:3) 2006, 346–7; by James J. Donahue in MELUS (31:1) 2006, 156–8; by Delilah Orr in AICRJ (30:1) 2006, 173–5.

18521. Knoeller, Christian P. A 'Hopi basket full of photographs': interpreting visual art in multi-genre works by contemporary Native American writers. *See* **17549**.

18522. Olsen, Erica. Silko's *Ceremony*. Exp (64:3) 2006, 182–5.

18523. Purdy, John. Moving stories: visualization, *mise-en-scène*, and Native American fiction. *See* **17388**.

Alan Sillitoe

18524. Minogue, Sally; Palmer, Andrew. Confronting the abject: women and dead babies in modern English fiction. JML (29:3) 2006, 103–25.

Charles Simic

18525. Molesini, Andrea. On that invisible line: five lectures. Venice: Cafoscarina, 2006. pp. 64. (Saggi.)

18526. Simic, Charles. Memory piano. *See* **3594**.

Neil Simon

18527. McNally, Terrence. *Barefoot in the Park*. Dramatist (8:5) 2006, 32–43. (From the archives.)

Louis Simpson

18528. Lucas, John. Scholar poets and history. *See* **17273**.

18529. Perloff, Marjorie. 'A lost battalion of Platonic conversationalists': *Howl* and the language of Modernism. *In* (pp. 24–43) **16122**.

Iain Sinclair

18530. Hampson, Robert G. Spatial stories: Conrad and Iain Sinclair. *See* **15272**.

May Sinclair

18531. Kunka, Andrew J.; Troy, Michele K. (eds). May Sinclair: moving towards the modern. Aldershot; Burlington, VT: Ashgate, 2006. pp. xiii, 262.

Upton Sinclair

18532. Arthur, Anthony. Radical innocent: Upton Sinclair. New York: Random House, 2006. pp. xiv, 380. Rev. by David Thomson in NYTB, 2 July 2006, 10; by Julia M. Klein in ColJR (45:2) 2006, 58–60.

18533. Coodley, Lauren (ed.). The land of orange groves and jails: Upton Sinclair's California. By Upton Sinclair. (Bibl. 2005, 19464.) Rev. by Charles Wollenberg in CH (83:2) 2005, 69–70; by Lawrence Coates in WAL (41:3) 2006, 354–6.

18534. Galloway, Stan. Alienation in *Tarzan's First Love*. *See* **14933**.

18535. Mattson, Kevin. Upton Sinclair and the other American century. Chichester; Hoboken, NJ: Wiley, 2006. pp. x, 294. Rev. by David Thomson in NYTB, 2 July 2006, 10; by Julia M. Klein in ColJR (45:2) 2006, 58–60.

Burns Singer

18536. McGuinness, Patrick. Burns Singer. PNRev (32:4) 2006, 41–3.

Sacheverell Sitwell

18537. Scuriatti, Laura. Walking the tightrope: Sacheverell Sitwell's rewriting of the Mediterranean in *Southern Baroque Art*. *In* (pp. 327–40) **12076**.

Elizabeth Smart

18538. Echlin, Kim. Elizabeth Smart: a fugue essay on women and creativity. Toronto: Women's Press, 2004. pp. vii, 237. (Women who rock.) Rev. by Clara Thomas in BkCan (33:7) 2004, 23.

Jane Smiley

18539. Lehmann, Courtney. A thousand Shakespeares: from cinematic saga to feminist geography; or, The escape from Iceland. *In* (pp. 588–609) **5537**.

Dave Smith ('Smith Cornwell')

18540. Smith, Dave. Hunting men: reflections on a life in American poetry. Baton Rouge: Louisiana State UP, 2006. pp. 299.

Iain Crichton Smith

18541. Wickman, Matthew. Gaelic poetry's province of stone: Iain Crichton Smith and the Hebridean echoes of Paul de Man's late work. ScSR (6:2) 2005, 99–112.

Pauline Smith

18542. Hooper, Myrtle. Textual surprise in Pauline Smith's *The Sinner*. Connotations (14:1–3) 2004/05, 68–86.

Stevie Smith

18543. Strachan, Walter. Portraits of four poets. Ed. by Geoffrey Strachan. *See* **18972**.

Zadie Smith

18544. Erll, Astrid. Re-writing as re-visioning: modes of representing the 'Indian Mutiny' in British novels, 1857 to 2000. *See* **10429**.

18545. Sell, Jonathan P. A. Chance and gesture in Zadie Smith's *White Teeth* and *The Autograph Man*: a model for multicultural identity. JCL (41:3) 2006, 27–44.

W. D. Snodgrass

18546. Rogoff, Jay. Shocking, surprising Snodgrass. SoR (42:4) 2006, 885–92.

Gary Snyder

18547. Gray, Timothy. Gary Snyder and the Pacific Rim: creating countercultural community. Iowa City: Iowa UP, 2006. pp. xx, 352. (Contemporary North American poetry.)

18548. Hunt, Anthony. Genesis, structure, and meaning in Gary Snyder's *Mountains and Rivers without End*. Reno: Nevada UP, 2004. pp. viii, 316. (Western literature.) Rev. by David Landis Barnhill in WAL (40:2) 2005, 226–7.

18549. Martin, Julia. Seeing a corner of the sky in Gary Snyder's *Mountains and Rivers without End*. WAL (40:1) 2005, 55–87.

18550. Selby, Nick. 'Created space': mapping America as poem in Gary Snyder's *Mountains and Rivers without End* and Susan Howe's *Secret History of the Dividing Line*. JAStud (39:1) 2005, 41–64.

'Somerville and Ross'
(Edith Somerville and Violet Martin)

18551. York, Lorraine. Crowding the garret: women's collaborative writing and the problematics of space. *In* (pp. 288–307) **3405**.

Stephen Sondheim

18552. Calderazzo, Diana. Stephen Sondheim's *Assassins* and the wartime political climate. ThSym (14) 2006, 138–51.

18553. Orloff, Rich. The musicals of Stephen Sondheim and John Weidman. Dramatist (8:3) 2006, 32–40.

18554. Swayne, Steve. How Sondheim found his sound. Ann Arbor: Michigan UP, 2005. pp. xvi, 315. Rev. by Andrew J. Milner in SondR (12:2) 2005, 49.

Susan Sontag

18555. Brintnall, Kent L. Regarding the pain of Christ: Susan Sontag at the foot of the Cross. Discourse (27:1) 2005, 119–40.

18556. Brothers, Caroline. Educating the heart. Meanjin (63:1) 2004, 73–86. (Interview.)

18557. De Cusatis, Felice. Two acts of the same play: fiction and reality in Susan Sontag's *In America: a Novel*. QPS (14) 2006, 195–200.

18558. Heller, Dana. Desperately seeking Susan. CommRev (5:1) 2006, 10–16.

18559. Platizky, Roger. Sontag's *The Way We Live Now*. Exp (65:1) 2006, 53–6.

Aaron Sorkin (b.1961)

18560. Crawley, Melissa. Mr Sorkin goes to Washington: shaping the President on television's *The West Wing*. *See* **13291**.

Gilbert Sorrentino

18561. McHale, Brian. Cognition *en abyme*: models, manuals, maps. PartA (4:2) 2006, 175–89.

Ahdaf Soueif

18562. Wynne, Catherine. Navigating the *mezzaterra*: home, harem and the hybrid family in Ahdaf Soueif's *The Map of Love*. CritS (18:2) 2006, 56–66.

Wole Soyinka

18563. Bamiro, Edmund O. The politics of code-switching: English *vs* Nigerian languages. WorldE (25:1) 2006, 23–35.

18564. Buikema, Rosemarie. Literature and the production of ambiguous memory: confession and double thoughts in Coetzee's *Disgrace*. *See* **15198**.

18565. Izevbaye, Dan. From Ogun to Mandela: the Nigerian myth of the pan-African hero. *In* (pp. 133–46) **11860**.

18566. Jeyifo, Biodun. Wole Soyinka: politics, poetics and postcolonialism. (Bibl. 2005, 19544.) Rev. by Esiaba Irobi in TJ (58:1) 2006, 149–50.

18567. Korang, Kwaku Larbi. Where is Africa? When is the West's Other? Literary postcoloniality in a comparative anthropology. Diacritics (34:2) 2004, 38–61.

18568. Nwahunanya, Chinyere. Tragedy in African literary drama. *In* (pp. 197–211) **11860**.

18569. Ogwude, Sophia O. Of hounds and quarry: the African human condition on canvas. *In* (pp. 237–51) **11860**.

18570. Soyinka, Wole. You must set forth at dawn: a memoir. New York: Random House, 2006. pp. xx, 499. Rev. by Norman Rush in NYTB, 23 Apr. 2006, 12–13; by Keith B. Richburg in BkW, 21 May 2006, 7.

Muriel Spark

18571. Brown, Peter Robert. 'There's something about Mary': narrative and ethics in *The Prime of Miss Jean Brodie*. JNT (36:2) 2006, 228–53.

18572. Labay-Morère, Julie. 'Voices at play' in Muriel Spark's *The Comforters* and Evelyn Waugh's *The Ordeal of Gilbert Pinfold*. EtBr (30) 2006, 83–93.

18573. Miller, Gavin. National confessions: queer theory meets Scottish literature. *See* **11149**.

18574. Stonebridge, Lyndsey. Hearing them speak: voices in Wilfred Bion, Muriel Spark and Penelope Fitzgerald. TexP (19:4) 2005, 445–65.

Frank H. (Frank Hamilton) Spearman (1859–1937)

18575. White, Tom. From McCook to *Whispering Smith*. NebH (87:3) 2006, 98–119.

Bernard Spencer

18576. Valaoritis, Nanos. Remembering the poets: translating Seferis with Durrell and Bernard Spencer. *In* (pp. 46–53) **15631**.

Stephen Spender

18577. Brett, Michael (ed.). New collected poems. (Bibl. 2004, 19562.) Rev. by Roger Caldwell in PNRev (31:4) 2005, 68–70.

18578. Callahan, David. Stephen Spender, the 1930s, and Spanish writing. Misc (32) 2005, 39–56.

18579. Sutherland, John. Stephen Spender: a literary life. London: Viking, 2004; Oxford; New York: OUP, 2005. pp. 627. Rev. by Nicholas Jenkins in TLS, 13 Aug. 2004, 3–6; by Stefan Collini in LRB (26:14) 2004, 6–10; by Richard Danson Brown in MLR (100:3) 2005, 799–801; by Michael Dirda in BkW, 23 Jan. 2005, 15; by Joan Bridgman in ContRev (286:1668) 2005, 51–2.

Art Spiegelman

18580. Gordon, Andrew. Philip Roth's *Patrimony* and Art Spiegelman's *Maus*: Jewish sons remembering their fathers. *See* **18313**.

18581. Levine, Michael G. The belated witness: literature, testimony, and the question of Holocaust survival. Stanford, CA: Stanford UP, 2006. pp. xii, 236. (Cultural memory in the present.)

18582. Loman, Andrew. 'Well intended liberal slop': allegories of race in Spiegelman's *Maus*. JAStud (40:3) 2006, 551–71.

18583. Mandel, Naomi. Against the unspeakable: complicity, the Holocaust, and slavery in America. *See* **13044**.

18584. Marelli, Cristina. *Maus* di Art Spiegelman e l'incomunicabilità dell'esperienza. ConLett (46) 2006, 393–408.

18585. Versluys, Kristiaan. Art Spiegelman's *In the Shadow of No Towers*: 9/11 and the representation of trauma. MFS (52:4) 2006, 980–1003.

18586. Whitlock, Gillian. Autographics: the seeing 'I' of the comics. MFS (52:4) 2006, 965–79.

18587. Worden, Daniel. The shameful art: *McSweeney's Quarterly Concern*, comics, and the politics of affect. MFS (52:4) 2006, 891–917.

William Stafford

18588. Bunge, Nancy. Influencing each other through the mail: William Stafford's and Marvin Bell's *Segues* and Jim Harrison's and Ted Kooser's *Braided Creek*. MidM (33) 2005, 48–56.

Laurence Stallings (1894–1968)

18589. Garrett, George. His one and only novel: Laurence Stallings's *Plumes*. SewR (114:2) 2006, 244–58.

Peter Stambler (b.1944)

18590. Lin, Xavier. Creative translation, translating creatively: a case study on aesthetic coherence in Peter Stambler's Han Shan. *In* (pp. 97–108) **2874**.

'Burt L. Standish' (Gilbert Patten) (1866–1945)

18591. Peterson, Scott. The Penobscot and the dime novelist: Louis Sockalexis as the source of Gilbert Patten's Frank Merriwell. DNR (75:2) 2006, 47–56.

Donald E. Stanford (b.1913)

18592. Middleton, David. Gatherings: four American poets. *See* **14877**.

Olaf Stapledon

18593. Burbank, Richard D. Musical fusion in the works of Olaf Stapledon: a matrix of storms and stars. JFA (16:4) 2006, 350–68.

Christina Stead (b.1902)

18594. Ackland, Michael. Breeding 'reptiles of the mind': Blake's dialectics of vision and Stead's critique of Pollitry in *The Man Who Loved Children*. StudN (38:2) 2006, 234–49.

18595. Adie, Mathilda. Female quest in Christina Stead's *For Love Alone*. Lund: Dept of English, Lund Univ., 2004. pp. 221. (Lund studies in English, 107.) Rev. by Laurence Chamlou in EA (59:4) 2006, 494–6.

18596. Harris, Margaret (ed.). Dearest Munx: the letters of Christina Stead and William J. Blake. (Bibl. 2005, 19570.) Rev. by Hazel Rowley in TLS, 6 Jan. 2006, 10.

18597. Rowley, Hazel. Her darling boy. *See* **14802**.

Flora Annie Steel

18598. Cowasjee, Saros (ed.). A Raj collection. (Bibl. 2005, 19571.) Rev. by Guy Cuthbertson in ELT (49:1) 2006, 76–9.

Gertrude Stein

18599. Bell, John. Gertrude Stein's *Identity*: puppet Modernism in the US. TDR (50:1) 2006, 87–99.

18600. Cope, Karin. Passionate collaborations: learning to live with Gertrude Stein. Victoria, B.C.: English Literary Studies, Univ. of Victoria, 2005. pp. 343. (ELS eds, 93.)

18601. DeKoven, Marianne (ed.). *Three Lives*; and *QED.*: authoritative texts, contexts, criticism. New York; London: Norton, 2006. pp. xi, 542. (Norton critical eds.)

18602. Giroud, Vincent. Picasso and Gertrude Stein. New York: Metropolitan Museum of Art; New Haven, CT: Yale UP, 2006. pp. 55.

18603. Hilder, Jamie. 'After all one must know more than one sees and one does not see a cube in its entirety': Gertrude Stein and *Picasso* and Cubism. CritS (17:3) 2005, 66–84.

18604. Hovey, Jaime. Gertrude Stein: *Three Lives*. *In* (pp. 450–8) **11788**.

18605. Kinsella, John. Line breaks and back-draft: not a defence of a poem. *See* **16895**.

18606. Landon, Lana Hartman; Smith, Laurel. Early works by modern women writers: Woolf, Bowen, Mansfield, Cather, and Stein. *See* **19300**.

18607. Meyers, Jeffrey. Picasso and Hemingway: a dud poem and a live grenade. *See* **16378**.

18608. Mills, Jean. Gertrude on the block: writing, love, and fame in *Stanzas in Meditation*. PQ (83:2) 2004, 197–210.

18609. Mitrano, G. F. Gertrude Stein: woman without qualities. (Bibl. 2005, 19593.) Rev. by Clive Bush in RES (57:232) 2006, 847–9.

18610. Morgan, Lynn M. Strange anatomy: Gertrude Stein and the avant-garde embryo. Hypatia (21:1) 2006, 15–34.

18611. Sitney, P. Adams. Brakhage and Modernism. *In* (pp. 159–78) **12654**.

18612. Watson, Dana Cairns. Gertrude Stein and the essence of what happens. (Bibl. 2005, 19598.) Rev. by Barbara Will in MFS (52:3) 2006, 721–4; by Kate McLoughlin in JAStud (40:2) 2006, 460.

18613. Wilson, Mary. Stein's *The Gentle Lena*. Exp (64:2) 2006, 89–91.

John Steinbeck

18614. Barcus, Patrick. The rules of the game: fact in fiction. *See* **18306**.

18615. Clemente, Vince. John Steinbeck's Sag Harbor: that place for the heart to rest. SoCR (39:1) 2006, 142–55.

18616. Gambino, Richard. Coming home to John Steinbeck's 'Italian American' novel. ItalA (24:1) 2006, 6–8.

18617. Gladstein, Mimi R. Bilingual wordplay: variations on a theme by Hemingway and Steinbeck. *See* **16357**.

18618. Knoeller, Christian. 'A profession older than writing': echoes of *Huckleberry Finn* in Steinbeck's *Travels with Charley: in Search of America*. MidM (33) 2005, 22–35.

18619. Railsback, Brian; Meyer, Michael J. (eds). A John Steinbeck encyclopedia. Westport, CT; London: Greenwood Press, 2006. pp. lviii, 482.

18620. Schultz, Jeffrey; Li, Luchen. Critical companion to John Steinbeck: a literary reference to his life and work. New York: Facts on File, 2005. pp. ix, 406. (Facts on File library of American literature.)

18621. Sickels, Robert C. Landscapes of failure in John Ford's *The Grapes of Wrath* (1939). *In* (pp. 61–80) **12438**.

Neal Stephenson

18622. Hayles, N. Katherine. My mother was a computer: digital subjects and literary texts. Chicago, IL; London: Chicago UP, 2005. pp. x, 290. Rev. by Stuart Moulthrop in AmBR (27:5) 2006, 22–3; by Mara Mills in WRB (23:4) 2006, 26–8.

Wallace Stevens

18623. Bacigalupo, Massimo. 'Forth on the godly sea': the Mediterranean in Pound, Yeats and Stevens. *In* (pp. 31–49) **12076**.

18624. Bednarowski, Mary Farrell. Intimations of bodily holiness in selected poems by Walt Whitman, Emily Dickinson, and Wallace Stevens. *In* (pp. 147–60) **3415**.

18625. Benfey, Christopher; Remmler, Karen (eds). Artists, intellectuals, and World War II: the Pontigny encounters at Mount Holyoke College, 1942–1944. *See* **11769**.

18626. Berger, Charles. Angels in Florida: Stevens and sublimation. WSJ (30:2) 2006, 171–82.

18627. Blount, J. Donald (ed.). The contemplated spouse: the letters of Wallace Stevens to Elsie. Columbia; London: South Carolina UP, 2006. pp. xi, 430. Rev. by George S. Lensing in WSJ (30:1) 2006, 116–19.

18628. Cavell, Stanley. Reflections on Wallace Stevens at Mount Holyoke. *In* (pp. 61–79, 84–8) **11769**.

18629. Clarke, Edward. Ariel among the second selves: Stevens and Wordsworth in creative conversation. WSJ (30:1) 2006, 30–44.

18630. Cleghorn, Angus. Affirming theatrical distances: Stevens over seas. PNRev (32:5) 2006, 64–6.

18631. Critchley, Simon. Surfaciality: some poems by Fernando Pessoa, one by Wallace Stevens, and the brief sketch of a poetic ontology. Gramma (14) 2006, 107–29.

18632. Davis, William V. Wallace Stevens and R. S. Thomas: influence *sans* anxiety. WSJ (30:1) 2006, 86–97.

18633. Dechand, Thomas. 'Like a new knowledge of reality': on Stevens and Peirce. MLN (121:5) 2006, 1107–23.

18634. Dolan, Frederick M. Wallace Stevens and the terrors of modernity. *In* (pp. 3–14) **3266**.

18635. Goldfarb, Lisa. Erotics of sound in Wallace Stevens. WSJ (30:2) 2006, 138–58.

18636. Haglund, David. Stevens, Duchamp, and the American 'ism', 1915–1919. PNRev (32:5) 2006, 59–64.

18637. Halkyard, Stella. [Foot]notes toward a supreme fiction: Stevens, Frank Kermode, and the John Rylands University Library. WSJ (30:1) 2006, 104–10.

18638. Helgeson, Karen. Current bibliography. WSJ (30:1) 2006, 120–4.

18639. Jarraway, David R. 'Both sides and neither': Stevens, Santayana, and the aestheticism of androgyny. WSJ (30:2) 2006, 210–25.

18640. Kaplan, Harold. Poetry, politics, and culture: argument in the work of Eliot, Pound, Stevens, and Williams. *See* **15693**.

18641. Leggett, B. J. Late Stevens: the final fiction. (Bibl. 2005, 19672.) Rev. by Thomas Dechand in MLN (121:5) 2006, 1270–2.

18642. Levin, Jonathan. Wallace Stevens: *Harmonium*. *In* (pp. 457–68) **11788**.

18643. MacLeod, Glen. E. E. Cummings and Wallace Stevens: kinship and rivalry. *See* **15379**.

18644. Masel, Carolyn. 'Keener sounds': Stevens, intimacy, and gender politics. WSJ (30:2) 2006, 159–70.

18645. Maxson, Helen F. New fences on the dust: photography and Wallace Stevens's 'rage for order' in Walt McDonald's *Whatever the Wind Delivers*. WAL (39:4) 2005, 420–43.

18646. Mehlman, Jeffrey. Thoughts on Wallace Stevens's contribution at Pontigny-en-Amérique. *In* (pp. 80–3) **11769**.

18647. Middlebrook, Diane. Stevens in the marriage of Sylvia Plath and Ted Hughes. WSJ (30:1) 2006, 45–51.

18648. Morris, Tim. Wallace Stevens: poetry and criticism. Cambridge: Salt, 2006. pp. xxvi, 209. Rev. by Stephen Burt in WSJ (30:2) 2006, 233–5.

18649. O'Neill, Michael. 'The all-sustaining air': Yeats, Stevens, Rich, Bishop – responses to Romantic poetry. *In* (pp. 143–62) **13735**.

18650. Ragg, Edward. Love, wine, desire: Stevens' *Montrachet-le-Jardin* and Shakespeare's *Cymbeline*. WSJ (30:2) 2006, 183–209.

18651. —— Pragmatic abstraction *vs* metaphor: Stevens' *The Pure Good of Theory* and *Macbeth*. WSJ (30:1) 2006, 5–29.

18652. Reeves, Gareth. A Modernist dialectic: Stevens and Williams in the poetry of Charles Tomlinson. WSJ (30:1) 2006, 57–85.

18653. Rehder, Robert. Wallace Stevens's imaginary Europe. PNRev (32:5) 2006, 67–9.

18654. Richardson, Joan. Recombinant A.N.W.: appetites of words. *See* **10618**.

18655. Rudd, Andrew. 'Not to the Bible but to Wallace Stevens' – what R. S. Thomas found there. PNRev (30:4) 2004, 49–51.

18656. Schmidt, Michael. Wallace Stevens: arranging, deepening, enchanting Britain. WSJ (30:1) 2006, 52–6.

18657. Steinman, Lisa M. 'Beauty, resonance, integrity': creative readings of Wordsworth in twentieth-century American poetry. *In* (pp. 101–22) **13735**.

18658. Welton, Matthew. Unnecessary angels: Patrick Mackie, Jeremy Over, and their use of Wallace Stevens. WSJ (30:1) 2006, 98–103.

Anne Stevenson

18659. Caldwell, Roger. Commonsense marvels. TLS, 20 Jan. 2006, 25 (review-article).

Elinore Pruitt Stewart

18660. Adkison, Jennifer Dawes. 'These is my words' … or are they? *See* **20346**.

18661. Embry, Jessie L. Nature and *Heartland* (1979). *In* (pp. 141–56) **12438**.

George R. Stewart, Jr

18662. Wagge, Fred. The crucial role of the environment in the writings of George Stewart (1895–1980): a life of America's literary ecologist. Lewiston, NY; Lampeter: Mellen Press, 2006. pp. viii, 580.

Sean Stewart (b.1965)

18663. Howey, Ann F. 'Half in and half out of things': boundaries in Sean Stewart's *The Night Watch*. *In* (pp. 95–103) **13541**.

Adrian Stokes

18664. Cuojati, Francesca. 'A tale of two shores': the Adriatic and its modernisms: on Ivan Meštrović, Andrian Stokes and the cultural imagination. *In* (pp. 153–208) **12076**.

18665. Kite, Stephen. Architecture as *technê*: Adrian Stokes, Ezra Pound and the art of the machine. *See* **18095**.

John Stone (b.1936)

18666. Monteiro, George. John Stone's twice-told secrets of a heart: *Cadaver* and *An Infected Heart*. NCL (36:4) 2006, 4–6.

Leslie F. Stone

18667. Attebery, Brian. The conquest of Gernsback: Leslie F. Stone and the subversion of science fiction tropes. *In* (pp. 50–66) **13537**.

Ruth Stone

18668. Wasserman, Rosanne. Ruth Stone: a gift from the universe. APR (35:3) 2006, 49–54.

Tom Stoppard

18669. Barker, Roberta. The circle game: gender, time, and 'revolution' in Tom Stoppard's *The Coast of Utopia*. ModDr (48:4) 2005, 706–25.

18670. Brater, Enoch. Playing for time (and playing with time) in Tom Stoppard's *Arcadia*. CompDr (39:2) 2005, 157–68.

18671. Chung, Moonyoung. Stage as hyperspace: theatricality of Stoppard. ModDr (48:4) 2005, 689–705.

18672. Crews, Brian. Rewriting/deconstructing Shakespeare: outlining possibilities, sometimes humorous, for Sonnet 18. *In* (pp. 61–72) **5308**.

18673. Milutinović, Zoran. The death of representation and the representation of death: Ionesco, Beckett, and Stoppard. CompDr (40:3) 2006, 337–64.

18674. Niederhoff, Burkhard. Who shot the hare in Stoppard's *Arcadia*? A reply to Anja Müller-Muth. Connotations (13:1/2) 2003/04, 170–8.

18675. Walls, Kathryn. The 'Magnus effect': names in *The Real Inspector Hound*. ELN (43:2) 2005, 180–92.

Lytton Strachey

18676. Caine, Barbara. Bombay to Bloomsbury: a biography of the Strachey family. (Bibl. 2005, 19706.) Rev. by Trev Broughton in CamQ (34:4) 2005, 392–7.

18677. Levy, Paul (ed.); Marcus, Penelope (asst ed.). The letters of Lytton Strachey. (Bibl. 2005, 19709.) Rev. by Todd Avery in Mod/Mod (13:1) 2006, 188–9; by Michael Dirda in BkW, 8 Jan. 2006, 15; by Christine Froula in VWM (70) 2006, 39–40.

18678. Villa, Luisa. A footnote to cultural history: Modernism, imperialism, and Wilfrid Scawen Blunt. *In* (pp. 263–77) **12076**.

Mark Strand

18679. Lucas, Dave. I am not what I am: the poetry of Mark Strand. VQR (82:4) 2006, 248–59 (review-article).

18680. Stewart, Robert. The scrupulous attention: an interview with Mark Strand. NewLet (72:2) 2006, 80–94.

The Stratemeyer Syndicate

18681. Erisman, Fred. Flying to the rescue: origin and sources of the Ted Scott flying stories. DNR (75:1) 2006, 3–11.

18682. Rehak, Melanie. Girl sleuth: Nancy Drew and the women who created her. (Bibl. 2005, 19715.) Rev. by Deidre A. Johnson in DNR (75:3) 2006, 89–90; by Nancy Northcott in CLAQ (31:2) 2006, 205–7; by Nan Cinnater in WRB (23:2) 2006, 24–5.

Noel Streatfeild

18683. Stokes, Sally Sims. Painting the garden: Noel Streatfeild, the garden as restorative, and pre-1950 dramatizations of *The Secret Garden*. *In* (pp. 169–87) **9300**.

J. M. (John Moray) Stuart-Young (b.1881)

18684. Newell, Stephanie. The forger's tale: the search for Odeziaku. Athens: Ohio UP, 2006. pp. xii, 233. (New African histories.)

J. C. (Jacqueline Cecilia) Sturm (b.1927)

18685. Duppé, Claudia. Seeking home: J. C. Sturm carves a space between. EngAot (60) 2006, 78–86.

William Styron

18686. Dovi, Suzanne. *Sophie's Choice*: letting chance decide. PhilL (30:1) 2006, 174–89.

18687. Ozick, Cynthia. The rights of history and the rights of imagination. *In* (pp. 3–18) **11969**.

Ronald Sukenick

18688. Katz, Adam. Narrative thinking and experiential knowledge: the example of Ronald Sukenick. TSLL (47:3) 2005, 189–212.

18689. Kohn, Robert E. Sukenick's *Out*. Exp (64:3) 2006, 174–7.

Walter Sullivan (b.1924)

18690. Sullivan, Walter. Nothing gold can stay: a memoir. Columbia; London: Missouri UP, 2006. pp. x, 196. Rev. by Sam Pickering in SewR (113:4) 2005, xciii–c.

'Sekou Sundiata' (Robert Feaster) (b.1948)

18691. Feinstein, Sascha. Fronting the band: an interview with Sekou Sundiata. BrC (10:2) 2006, 47, 56–72.

May Swenson

18692. Crumbley, Paul. May Swenson and other animals: her poetics of natural selection. *In* (pp. 138–56) **7907**.

18693. Geffen, Alice (comp.). Bibliography of the works of May Swenson. Ed. by Maure Lyn Smith. *In* (pp. 205–38) **7907**.

18694. Grabher, Gudrun M. De-Cartesianizing the universe: May Swenson's design of wor(l)ds. *In* (pp. 81–106) **7907**.

18695. Hansen, Tom. Swenson's *The Universe*. Exp (64:3) 2006, 166–8.

18696. Hogue, Cynthia. Material girl: May Swenson's logopoetic materialism. *In* (pp. 120–37) **7907**.

18697. Juhasz, Suzanne. The queer poetics of May Swenson. *In* (pp. 181–94) **7907**.

18698. Ostriker, Alicia. May Swenson, Whitman's daughter. *In* (pp. 40–54) **7907**.

18699. Smith, Martha Nell. That never told CAN be: May Swenson's manuscript witnesses. *In* (pp. 107–19) **7907**.

18700. Soty, Mark. *Questions* and more questions: two shells for May Swenson. *In* (pp. 191–204) **7907**.

18701. Spooner, Michael. How everything happens: notes on May Swenson's theory of writing. *In* (pp. 157–80) **7907**.

18702. Swenson, Paul. A figure in the tapestry: the poet's feeling runs ahead of her imagination (Greenwich Village, 1949–50). *In* (pp. 27–39) **7907**.

18703. Zona, Kirstin Hotelling. May Swenson and Elizabeth Bishop. *In* (pp. 55–80) **7907**.

Graham Swift

18704. Berlatsky, Eric. ‘The swamps of myth … and empirical fishing lines’: historiography, narrativity, and the ‘here and now’ in Graham Swift’s *Waterland.* JNT (36:2) 2006, 254–92.

18705. MacLeod, Lewis. ‘Our lost, discredited souls’: narrating the masculine interior in Graham Swift’s *Shuttlecock* and *Ever After.* CritW (47:4) 2006, 375–88.

18706. Widdowson, Peter. Graham Swift. Plymouth: Northcote House in assn with the British Council, 2006. pp. xi, 123. (Writers and their work.)

J. M. Synge

18707. Deitz, Paula. The springtime of local life: the plays of J. M. Synge. SewR (114:3) 2006, 478–80. (Arts and letters.)

18708. Franks, Jill. Islands and the Modernists: the allure of isolation in art, literature, and science. Jefferson, NC; London: McFarland, 2006. pp. vii, 206.

18709. Gough, Kathleen M. Polymorphous *Playboys*: Irish–Caribbean dancing. ModDr (48:4) 2005, 777–99.

18710. Markey, Anne. The discovery of Irish folklore. *See* **9667**.

18711. Roche, Anthony. Redressing the Irish theatrical landscape: Sebastian Barry’s *The Only True History of Lizzie Finn.* *In* (pp. 147–65) **14627**.

18712. Russell, Richard. Talking with ghosts of Irish playwrights past: Marina Carr’s *By the Bog of Cats …* *See* **15046**.

18713. Vandevelde, Karen. ‘What’s all the stir about?’: Gerald MacNamara, Synge, and the early Abbey Theatre. *See* **17383**.

Rabindranath Tagore

18714. Chaudhuri, Amit. Two giant brothers. LRB (28:8) 2006, 27–30 (review-article). (Tagore’s poems.)

18715. Chaudhuri, Sukanta (ed.). Selected poems. (Bibl. 2005, 19745.) Rev. by Amit Chaudhuri in LRB (28:8) 2006, 27–30.

18716. Majumdar, Nivedita. Nationalizing the woman: nation and gender in Tagore’s *The Home and the World.* JCPS (12:1) 2005, 24–41.

‘Kathrine Talbot’ (Ilse Eva Barker) (1921–2006)

18717. Oldham, Alison. Noël Welch and Kathrine Talbot. *See* **19021**.

Gay Talese (b.1932)

18718. Talese, Gay. A writer’s life. New York: Knopf, 2006. pp. 429. Rev. by Trevor Butterworth in BkW, 7 May 2006, 5.

Raymond Tallis (b.1946)

18719. Tredell, Nicolas. Raymond Tallis in conversation. PNRev (31:4) 2005, 41–6.

Amy Tan

18720. Adams, Bella. Amy Tan. Manchester; New York: Manchester UP, 2005. pp. xi, 220. (Contemporary world writers.)

18721. Lux, Elaine. Narrative bones: Amy Tan’s *Bonesetter’s Daughter* and Hugh Cook’s *Homecoming Man.* *In* (pp. 117–32) **11916**.

18722. Michael, Magali Cornier. New visions of community in contemporary American fiction: Tan, Kingsolver, Castillo, Morrison. Iowa City: Iowa UP, 2006. pp. viii, 246.

18723. Rosinsky, Natalie M. Amy Tan: author and storyteller. Minneapolis, MN: Compass Point, 2006. pp. 112. (Signature lives.)

18724. Yu, Su-lin. Sisterhood as cultural difference in Amy Tan's *The Hundred Secret Senses* and Cristina Garcia's *The Agüero Sisters*. CritW (47:4) 2006, 345–61.

18725. Zou, Jianjun. The mystical Orient in Amy Tan's novels: a case study of *The Bonesetter's Daughter*. FLS (122) 2006, 101–11. (In Chinese.)

Miriam Tane (b.1916)

18726. Marsh, John. The *Justice* poetry of Miriam Tane. Legacy (23:1) 2006, 44–59.

Allen Tate

18727. Buffington, Robert. Campaigning for poetry. SewR (113:3) 2005, 345–64.

Elizabeth Taylor (1912–1975)

18728. Broughton, Trev. The smell of lavender water: Elizabeth Taylor's relentless Englishness. TLS, 9 June 2006, 23–4.

Mildred D. Taylor

18729. Davis-Undiano, Robert Con. Mildred D. Taylor and the art of making a difference. WLT (78:2) 2004, 11–13.

18730. Harris, Marla. 'A history not then taught in history books': (re)writing Reconstruction in historical fiction for children and young adults. *See* **10121**.

18731. Taylor, Mildred D. My life as a writer. WLT (78:2) 2004, 7–10.

Sydney Taylor (b.1904)

18732. Sweeney, Meghan M. Checking out America: libraries as agents of acculturation in three mid-century girls' books. *See* **17266**.

Emma Tennant ('Catherine Aydy')

18733. Eagleton, Mary. Rewriting the master: Emma Tennant and Robert Louis Stevenson. *See* **11291**.

18734. King, Jeannette. Whatever happened to 'good little Thomas Hardy'? Re-writing Hardy and his fiction in P. B. Parris's *His Arms Are Full of Broken Things* and Emma Tennant's *Tess*. *See* **10283**.

Kylie Tennant

18735. Grant, Jane. Kylie Tennant: a life. Canberra: National Library of Australia, 2006. pp. vii, 156. (Australian life.)

18736. —— Vultures on every bough. Meanjin (63:1) 2004, 126–32. (Correspondence between Tennant and Christesen.)

Hallam Tennyson (1921–2005)

18737. Shaw, Marion. Hallam Tennyson (1921–2005). TRB (8:5) 2006, 390–2.

Ekwueme Michael Thelwell (b.1935)

18738. SCHNEIDER, EDGAR W.; WAGNER, CHRISTIAN. The variability of literary dialect in Jamaican Creole: Thelwell's *The Harder They Come*. JPCL (21:1) 2006, 45–96.

Paul Theroux

18739. FERRER, HUGH. Notes on the *Connecticut Yankee*. *See* **11494**.

Madeleine Thien (b.1974)

18740. CHONG, KEVIN. From short stories to a novel: Thien's journey. BkCan (35:4) 2006, 11–13. (Interview.)

Abigail Thomas

18741. THOMAS, ABIGAIL. A three dog life. Orlando, FL: Harcourt, 2006. pp. 182.

Bertha Thomas

18742. BOHATA, KIRSTI. Bertha Thomas: the New Woman and 'Anglo-Welsh' hybridity. *In* (pp. 17–34) **8926**.

Dylan Thomas

18743. KEERY, JAMES. *The Burning Baby* and the bathwater: 1, 'Black magic bubblings'; 2, 'The second death'; 3, 'Thomas's malign influence'; 4, 'Legislating for the millennium'; 5, 'The new bible of Belsen'; 6, 'Punch-drunk "romantic" scribblers'. PNRev (33:1) 2006, 56–62.

18744. LYCETT, ANDREW. Dylan Thomas: a new life. (Bibl. 2004, 19788.) Rev. by Michael Kinsella in PNRev (31:4) 2005, 70–1.

18745. MAHON, DEREK (sel.). Poems. London; Boston, MA: Faber & Faber, 2004. pp. 77. Rev. by Michael Kinsella in PNRev (31:4) 2005, 70–1.

Edward Thomas (1878–1917)

18746. EMENY, RICHARD (sel. and introd.). Edward Thomas on the Georgians. Cheltenham: Cyder Press, 2004. pp. 214. Rev. by Lynn Parker in IGSJ (10) 2004, 97–8.

18747. KENDALL, JUDY. The dating of Edward Thomas's mature verse. NQ (53:3) 2006, 346–7.

18748. LONGLEY, EDNA. Remember again: how Edward Thomas haunts his fellow poets. TLS, 17 Feb. 2006, 16–17.

18749. NEWLYN, LUCY. Hazlitt and Edward Thomas on walking. *See* **10415**.

18750. STILLING, ROBERT. Between friends: rediscovering the war thoughts of Robert Frost. *See* **16018**.

18751. THOMAS, R. GEORGE (ed.). The collected poems and war diary, 1917. Introd. by Peter Sacks. (Bibl. 2005, 19778.) Rev. by Judy Kendall in PNRev (31:6) 2005, 62.

Lorenzo Thomas (b.1944)

18752. GERY, JOHN. Lorenzo Thomas (1944–2005). Callaloo (29:1) 2006, 2–7.

R. S. (Ronald Stuart) Thomas (1913–2000)

18753. DAVIS, WILLIAM V. Wallace Stevens and R. S. Thomas: influence *sans* anxiety. *See* **18632**.

18754. Morgan, Barry. Strangely orthodox: R. S. Thomas and his poetry of faith. Foreword by Rowan Williams. Llandysul: Gomer Press, 2006. pp. 64.

18755. Rogers, Byron. The man who went into the west: the life of R. S. Thomas. London: Aurum, 2006. pp. x, 326. Rev. by Alan Brownjohn in TLS, 22 Sept. 2006, 33.

18756. Rudd, Andrew. 'Not to the Bible but to Wallace Stevens' – what R. S. Thomas found there. *See* **18655**.

Clara Ann Thompson (1869–1949)

18757. Bennett, Paula Bernat. Rewriting Dunbar: realism, Black women poets, and the genteel. *In* (pp. 146–61) **8435**.

Hunter S. Thompson

18758. Steadman, Ralph. The joke's over: bruised memories: Gonzo, Hunter S. Thompson and me. Orlando, FL: Harcourt, 2006. pp. xviii, 396. Rev. by Mark Kamine in TLS, 10 Nov. 2006, 26–7; by Will Blythe in NYTB, 19 Nov. 2006, 12.

18759. Weingarten, Marc. The gang that wouldn't write straight: Wolfe, Thompson, Didion, and the New Journalism revolution. *See* **15501**.

Judith Thompson

18760. Dike, Fatima, *et al.* Beyond the USA, beyond the UK. *In* (pp. 199–218) **12297**.

18761. Knowles, Ric (ed.). Judith Thompson. Toronto: Playwrights Canada Press, 2005. pp. xv, 156. (Critical perspectives on Canadian theatre in English, 3.) Rev. by Erin Elliott in CanTR (128) 2006, 140–1.

18762. McKinnie, Michael. The state of the nation. CanTR (125) 2006, 5–8.

Priscilla Jane Thompson (1871–1942)

18763. Bennett, Paula Bernat. Rewriting Dunbar: realism, Black women poets, and the genteel. *In* (pp. 146–61) **8435**.

Rupert Thomson

18764. Hynes, James. The dreamlife of Rupert Thomson. BosR (31:2) 2006, 39–42.

Edwin Thumboo

18765. Goh, Robbie B. H. Imagining the nation: the role of Singapore poetry in English in 'emergent nationalism'. JCL (41:2) 2006, 21–41.

Wallace Thurman

18766. Ganter, Granville. Decadence, sexuality, and the bohemian vision of Wallace Thurman. *In* (pp. 194–213) **12180**.

'James Tiptree, Jr' (Alice Sheldon, 'Raccoona Sheldon')

18767. Duchamp, L. Timmel. Something rich and strange: Karen Joy Fowler's *What I Didn't See*. *In* (pp. 356–80) **13537**.

18768. Pearson, Wendy. (Re)reading James Tiptree, Jr's *And I Awoke and Found Me Here on the Cold Hill Side*. *In* (pp. 168–89) **13537**.

18769. Phillips, Julie. James Tiptree, Jr: the double life of Alice B. Sheldon. New York: St Martin's Press, 2006. pp. vi, 469, (plates) 16. Rev. by Dave Itzkoff in NYTB, 20 Aug. 2006, 1, 8; by Martin Morse Wooster in BkW, 6 Aug. 2006, 4; by Michael Saler in TLS, 13 Oct. 2006, 27; by Susanna J. Sturgis in WRB (23:6) 2006, 3–4.

18770. Saler, Michael. A lady's man and his pen. TLS, 13 Oct. 2006, 27 (review-article).

Colm Tóibín (b.1955)

18771. Lodge, David. The year of Henry James; or, Timing is all: the story of a novel. With other essays on the genesis, composition and reception of literary fiction. *See* **17239**.

18772. Tóibín, Colm. Henry James for Venice. HJR (27:3) 2006, 192–201. (James's influence on Tóibín.)

18773. Walshe, Éibhear. The vanishing homoerotic: Colm Tóibín's gay fictions. NewHR (10:4) 2006, 122–36.

J. R. R. Tolkien

18774. Albero Poveda, Jaume. Villains and the representation of evil in J. R. R. Tolkien's fiction of Middle-earth. BStE (31) 2005, 155–74.

18775. Amison, Anne. An unexpected guest. Mythlore (25:1/2) 2006, 127–36.

18776. Anderson, Douglas A. The mainstreaming of fantasy and the legacy of *The Lord of the Rings*. *In* (pp. 301–15) **18804**.

18777. Atkins, Barry. Games. *In* (pp. 151–61) **18793**.

18778. Bechtel, Greg. 'There and back again': progress in the discourse of Todorovian, Tolkienian and mystic fantasy theory. ESCan (30:4) 2004, 139–66.

18779. Bossert, A. R. 'Surely you don't disbelieve': Tolkien and Pius X: anti-Modernism in Middle-earth. Mythlore (25:1/2) 2006, 53–76.

18780. Bratman, David. The artistry of omissions and revisions in *The Lord of the Rings*. *In* (pp. 113–38) **18804**.

18781. Brown, Devin. From isolation to community: Frodo's incomplete personal quest in *The Lord of the Rings*. Mythlore (25:1/2) 2006, 163–73.

18782. Burns, Marjorie. King and hobbit: the exalted and lowly in Tolkien's created worlds. *In* (pp. 139–51) **18804**.

18783. —— Perilous realms: Celtic and Norse in Tolkien's Middle-earth. Toronto; Buffalo, NY; London: Toronto UP, 2005. pp. xii, 225. Rev. by Kathryn Stelmach in Comitatus (37) 2006, 223–5.

18784. Caesar, Judith. Tolkien's *The Lord of the Rings* and Dante's *Inferno*. Exp (64:3) 2006, 162–6.

18785. Chance, Jane. Subversive fantasist: Tolkien on class difference. *In* (pp. 153–68) **18804**.

18786. —— (ed.). Tolkien and the invention of myth: a reader. (Bibl. 2005, 19802.) Rev. by Wulfstan Clough in Historian (67:4) 2005, 814–15; by Chad Engbers in LU (30:1) 2006, 134–8; by Anthony B. Buccitelli in WF (65:3) 2006, 343–5.

18787. Crocker, Holly A. Masculinity. *In* (pp. 111–23) **18793**.

18788. Dickerson, Matthew; Evans, Jonathan. Ents, elves, and Eriador: the environmental vision of J. R. R. Tolkien. Lexington: Kentucky UP, 2006. pp. xxvi, 316. (Culture of the land: a series in the New Agrarianism.)

18789. Drout, Michael D. C. The rhetorical evolution of *'Beowulf': the Monsters and the Critics*. *In* (pp. 183–215) **18804**.

18790. —— Towards a better Tolkien criticism. *In* (pp. 15–28) **18793**.

18791. —— (ed.). J. R. R. Tolkien encyclopedia: scholarship and critical assessment. London; New York: Routledge, 2006. pp. 808. Rev. by John Garth in TLS, 22 & 29 Dec. 2006, 34.

18792. Eaglestone, Robert. Invisibility. *In* (pp. 73–84) **18793**.

18793. —— (ed.). Reading *The Lord of the Rings*: new writings on Tolkien's trilogy. London; New York: Continuum, 2005. pp. vi, 214. Rev. by David Bratman in Mythprint (43:10/11) 2006, 10–12.

18794. Fife, Ernelle. Wise warriors in Tolkien, Lewis, and Rowling. Mythlore (25:1/2) 2006, 147–62.

18795. Fimi, Dimitra. 'Mad' elves and 'elusive beauty': some Celtic strands of Tolkien's mythology. Folklore (117:2) 2006, 156–70.

18796. Fisher, Matthew A. Working at the crossroads: Tolkien, St Augustine, and the *Beowulf*-poet. *In* (pp. 217–30) **18804**.

18797. Flieger, Verlyn. Tolkien and the idea of the book. *In* (pp. 283–99) **18804**.

18798. —— (ed.). Smith of Wootton Major. (Bibl. 2005, 19811.) Rev. by David Bratman in Mythprint (43:3) 2006, 14.

18799. Garth, John. Frodo and the Great War. *In* (pp. 41–56) **18804**.

18800. —— Tolkien and the Great War: the threshold of Middle-earth. (Bibl. 2005, 19814.) Rev. by Janet Brennan Croft in WLT (79:1) 2005, 93.

18801. Gilliver, Peter; Marshall, Jeremy; Weiner, Edmund. The ring of words: Tolkien and the *Oxford English Dictionary.* Oxford; New York: OUP, 2006. pp. xvi, 234. Rev. by John Garth in TLS, 23 June 2006, 28.

18802. Hall, Mark F. The theory and practice of alliterative verse in the works of J. R. R. Tolkien. Mythlore (25:1/2) 2006, 41–52.

18803. Hammond, Wayne G. Special collections in the service of Tolkien studies. *In* (pp. 331–40) **18804**.

18804. —— Scull, Christina (eds). *The Lord of the Rings* 1954–2004: scholarship in honor of Richard E. Blackwelder. Milwaukee, WI: Marquette UP, 2006. pp. 387.

18805. Hazell, Dinah. The plants of Middle-earth: botany and sub-creation. Kent, OH; London: Kent State UP, 2006. pp. 136.

18806. Hill, Paul. The Anglo-Saxons. Stroud; Charleston, SC: Tempus, 2006. pp. 223, (plates) 16.

18807. Hostetter, Carl F. 'Elvish as she is spoke'. *In* (pp. 231–55) **18804**.

18808. Hunnewell, Sumner G. Naysayers in the works of Tolkien. *In* (pp. 169–81) **18804**.

18809. Hunter, John C. The evidence of things not seen: critical mythology and *The Lord of the Rings*. JML (29:2) 2006, 129–47.

18810. Jorgensen, Estelle Ruth. Myth, song, and music education: the case of Tolkien's *The Lord of the Rings* and Swann's *The Road Goes Ever On*. JAE (40:3) 2006, 1–21.

18811. Kaveney, Roz. In the tradition …. *In* (pp. 162–75) **18793**.

18812. Kightley, Michael R. Heorot or Meduseld? Tolkien's use of *Beowulf* in 'The King of the Golden Hall'. Mythlore (24:3/4) 2006, 119–34.

18813. Kleinman, Scott. Service. *In* (pp. 138–48) **18793**.

18814. Langford, Barry. Time. *In* (pp. 29–46) **18793**.

18815. Lee, Stuart D.; Solopova, Elizabeth. The keys of Middle-earth: discovering medieval literature through the fiction of J. R. R. Tolkien. Basingstoke; New York: Palgrave Macmillan, 2005. pp. xii, 284. Rev. by Michael D. C. Drout in NQ (53:4) 2006, 555–6.

18816. Livingston, Michael. The shell-shocked hobbit: the First World War and Tolkien's trauma of the ring. Mythlore (25:1/2) 2006, 77–92.

18817. Malpas, Simon. Home. *In* (pp. 85–98) **18793**.

18818. Neville, Jennifer. Women. *In* (pp. 101–10) **18793**.

18819. Ortenberg, Veronica. In search of the Holy Grail: the quest for the Middle Ages. London; New York: Hambledon/Continuum, 2006. pp. xv, 336, (plates) 8.

18820. Phelpstead, Carl. Auden and the Inklings: an alliterative revival. *See* **14509**.

18821. Rateliff, John D. 'And all the days of her life are forgotten': *The Lord of the Rings* as mythic prehistory. *In* (pp. 67–100) **18804**.

18822. Roberts, Adam. The one ring. *In* (pp. 59–70) **18793**.

18823. Rutledge, Fleming. The battle for Middle-earth: Tolkien's divine design in *Lord of the Rings*. (Bibl. 2004, 19892.) Rev. by Brian Murdoch in LitTheol (19:2) 2005, 192–5.

18824. Saxey, Esther. Homoeroticism. *In* (pp. 124–37) **18793**.

18825. Scull, Christina. What did he know and when did he know it? Planning, inspiration and *The Lord of the Rings*. *In* (pp. 101–12) **18804**.

18826. —— Hammond, Wayne G. The J. R. R. Tolkien companion & guide. Boston, MA: Houghton Mifflin, 2006. 2 vols. pp. 2300.

18827. —— —— The J. R. R. Tolkien companion: vol. 1, Chronology. London: HarperCollins, 2006. pp. 1019. Rev. by John Garth in TLS, 22 & 29 Dec. 2006, 34.

18828. —— —— The J. R. R. Tolkien companion: vol. 2, Reader's guide. London: HarperCollins, 2006. pp. 1279. Rev. by John Garth in TLS, 22 & 29 Dec. 2006, 34.

18829. Shieff, Sarah. Well-laundered elves: purity and degeneration in *The Lord of the Rings*. *In* (pp. 111–19) **11971**.

18830. Shippey, T. A. History in words: Tolkien's ruling passion. *In* (pp. 25–39) **18804**.

18831. Smith, Arden R. Tolkienian Gothic. *In* (pp. 267–81) **18804**.

18832. Smith, Thomas W. Tolkien's Catholic imagination: meditation and tradition. ReLit (38:2) 2006, 73–100.

18833. Steele, Felicia Jean. Dreaming of dragons: Tolkien's impact on Heaney's *Beowulf*. *See* **16325**.

18834. Sturgis, Amy H. Re-imagining Rose: portrayals of Tolkien's Rosie Cotton in twenty-first-century fan fiction. Mythlore (24:3/4) 2006, 165–87.

18835. Swazo, Norman K. Bereshith and Ainulindalë: allegoresis and exegesis in tension. JFA (16:4) 2006, 302–19.

18836. Thomas, Paul Edmund. Towards quite unforeseen goals. *In* (pp. 57–65) **18804**.

18837. Treschow, Michael; Duckworth, Mark. Bombadil's role in *The Lord of the Rings*. Mythlore (25:1/2) 2006, 175–96.

18838. Turner, Allan. Translation and criticism: the stylistic mirror. YES (36:1) 2006, 158–76.

18839. Ware, Jim. Finding God in *The Hobbit*. Carol Stream, IL: Salt River/ Tyndale House, 2006. pp. xxiv, 177.

18840. West, Richard C. 'Her choice was made and her doom appointed': tragedy and divine comedy in the tale of Aragorn and Arwen. *In* (pp. 317–29) **18804**.

18841. Whetter, K. S.; McDonald, R. Andrew. 'In the hilt is fame': resonances of medieval swords and sword-lore in J. R. R. Tolkien's *The Hobbit* and *The Lord of the Rings*. Mythlore (25:1/2) 2006, 5–28.

18842. Williams, Donald T. Mere humanity: G. K. Chesterton, C. S. Lewis, and J. R. R. Tolkien on the human condition. *See* **15151**.

18843. Wood, Ralph C. J. R. R. Tolkien: postmodern visionary of hope. *In* (pp. 333–55) **11916**.

18844. Zemmour, Corinne. Tolkien in the land of Arthur: the Old Forest episode from *The Lord of the Rings*. Mythlore (24:3/4) 2006, 135–63.

18845. Zettersten, Arne. The AB language lives. *In* (pp. 13–24) **18804**.

18846. Zlosnik, Sue. Gothic echoes. *In* (pp. 47–58) **18793**.

Charles Tomlinson

18847. Brinton, Ian. Black Mountain in England: 3. PNRev (32:3) 2006, 76–80.

18848. MacGowan, Christopher. Poet to poet: four books of correspondence. *See* **19194**.

18849. Reeves, Gareth. A Modernist dialectic: Stevens and Williams in the poetry of Charles Tomlinson. *See* **18652**.

18850. Saunders, Judith P. Tomlinson's *In Oklahoma*: Bishop's *The Armadillo* as literary source. ANQ (19:3) 2006, 44–50.

John Kennedy Toole

18851. Collins, Kevin. Toole's *A Confederacy of Dunces* chapter 14: psychological bankruptcy? NCL (36:2) 2006, 2–4.

Jean Toomer

18852. Farebrother, Rachel. 'Adventuring through the pieces of a still unorganized mosaic': reading Jean Toomer's collage aesthetic in *Cane*. JAStud (40:3) 2006, 503–21.

18853. FORD, KAREN JACKSON. Split-gut song: Jean Toomer and the poetics of modernity. (Bibl. 2005, 19863.) Rev. by Mark Whalan in MELUS (31:1) 2006, 159–61.

18854. GRANT, NATHAN. Masculinist impulses: Toomer, Hurston, Black writing, and modernity. (Bibl. 2005, 19864.) Rev. by David Chinitz in Mod/Mod (13:2) 2006, 375–82; by Alicia Casey Baum and Dwonna Naomi Goldstone in JAAH (91:2) 2006, 219–21; by Geta LeSeur in CLAJ (49:4) 2006, 485–9.

18855. THOMPSON-CAGER, CHEZIA B. Teaching Jean Toomer's 1923 *Cane*. New York; Frankfurt: Lang, 2006. pp. xxiv, 156. (Studies in African and African American literature, 9.)

18856. WHALAN, MARK (ed.). The letters of Jean Toomer, 1919–1924. Foreword by Barbara Foley. Knoxville: Tennessee UP, 2006. pp. xliv, 249.

Chris Torrance (b.1941)

18857. BRINTON, IAN. Black Mountain in England: 2. PNRev (31:5) 2005, 74–7.

Lola Lemire Tostevin

18858. MARTIN-DEMOOR, LISA. 'You must give death a name …': (re)reading Lola Lemire Tostevin's *Small Amulets* and *A Portrait*. OpL (twelfth series) (5) 2005, 52–66.

John Tranter

18859. ROBINSON, PETER. John Tranter and tradition. Agenda (41:1/2) 2005, 155–61.

'B. Traven' (Albert Otto Max Feige, Ret Marut)

18860. GIFFORD, BARRY. B. Traven: the man who never forgot. Brick (78) 2006, 8–12.

P. L. Travers

18861. LAWSON, VALERIE. Mary Poppins, she wrote: the life of P. L. Travers. London: Aurum, 2005. pp. xviii, 380, (plates) 16. Rev. by Chelsea Cain in NYTB, 22 Oct. 2006, 25.

18862. SIBLEY, BRIAN. *Mary Poppins*: 'practically perfect in every way': the musical. New York: Disney, 2006. pp. 160.

Sophie Treadwell

18863. DICKEY, JERRY; LÓPEZ-RODRÍGUEZ, MIRIAM (eds). Broadway's bravest woman: selected writings of Sophie Treadwell. Carbondale: Southern Illinois UP, 2006. pp. xv, 271, (plates) 6. Rev. by Lucy Carlyle in TLS, 1 Dec. 2006, 31.

R. C. (Robert Calverley) Trevelyan (1872–1951)

18864. STANFORD, DONALD E. A critical study of the works of four British writers: Margaret Louisa Woods (1856–1945), Mary Coleridge (1861–1907), Sir Henry Newbolt (1862–1938), R. C. Trevelyan (1872–1951). Ed. by R. W. Crump. *See* **9497**.

William Trevor

18865. BLOOM, JONATHAN. The art of revision in the short stories of V. S. Pritchett and William Trevor. *See* **18145**.

18866. Ormsby-Lennon, Hugh. Fools of fiction: reading William Trevor's stories. Dublin; Bethesda, MD: Maunsel, 2005. pp. xvi, 378.

18867. Russell, Richard Rankin. The tragedy of Imelda's terminal silence in William Trevor's *Fools of Fortune*. PLL (42:1) 2006, 73–94.

T. Minh-Ha (Thi Minh-Ha) Trinh (b.1952)

18868. Driver, Susan. Between theories and life-writings: feminist daughters communicating desires across generational differences. *See* **17259**.

Christos Tsiolkas (b.1965)

18869. Vernay, Jean-François. An interview with Christos Tsiolkas. Antipodes (20:1) 2006, 38–40.

18870. —— Only disconnect – canonizing homonormative values: representation and the paradox of gayness in Christos Tsiolkas's *Loaded*. Antipodes (20:1) 2006, 41–5.

Scott Turow

18871. MacDonald, Andrew F.; MacDonald, Gina. Scott Turow: a critical companion. Westport, CT; London: Greenwood Press, 2005. pp. 224. (Critical companions to popular contemporary writers.) Rev. by Peter Barry in Eng (55:212) 2006, 213–19.

Joseph Tusiani (b.1924)

18872. Siani, Cosma. Due mondi e quattro lingue: la poesia di Joseph Tusiani. PoesiaM (206) 2006, 15–23.

Lisa Tuttle (b.1952)

18873. Hawkins, Cathy. The universal wife: exploring 1970s feminism with Lisa Tuttle's *Wives*. *In* (pp. 199–216) **13537**.

Amos Tutuola

18874. Dunton, Chris. Pupils, witch doctor, vengeance: Amos Tutuola as playwright. RAL (37:4) 2006, 1–14.

18875. Lock, Charles. Indirect rule and the continuities of Nigerian fiction. *In* (pp. 181–96) **11860**.

18876. Low, Gail. The natural artist: publishing Amos Tutuola's *The Palm-Wine Drinkard* in postwar Britain. RAL (37:4) 2006, 15–33.

Anne Tyler

18877. Adams, Susan S. Loss and decline in the novels of Anne Tyler: the 'slipping-down' life. Lewiston, NY; Lampeter: Mellen Press, 2006. pp. iii, 220.

Katharine Tynan

18878. Fogarty, Anne. Parnellism and the politics of memory: revising *Ivy Day in the Committee Room*. *In* (pp. 104–21) **16695**.

18879. Stetz, Margaret D. 'Ballads in prose': genre crossing in late Victorian women's writing. VLC (34:2) 2006, 619–29.

Yoshiko Uchida

18880. Chen, Fu-Jen; Yu, Su-Lin. Reclaiming the Southwest: a traumatic space in the Japanese American internment narrative. *See* **20266**.

Barry Unsworth (b.1930)

18881. Russell, Richard Rankin. The dramatic conversion of Nicholas Barber in Barry Unsworth's *Morality Play*. Ren (58:3) 2006, 221–39.

John Updike

18882. Bailey, Peter J. Rabbit (un)redeemed: the drama of belief in John Updike's fiction. Madison, NJ: Fairleigh Dickinson UP, 2006. pp. 295.

18883. Jay, Elisabeth. 'Who are you gentle reader?': John Updike – *A Month of Sundays* (1975). LitTheol (19:4) 2005, 346–54.

18884. Miller, D. Quentin. Deeper Blues; or, The posthuman Prometheus: cybernetic renewal and the late twentieth-century American novel. AL (77:2) 2005, 379–407.

18885. Zhu, Xuefeng. Faith and terror: on John Updike's latest novel *Terrorist*. FLS (121) 2006, 52–6. (In Chinese.)

Jane Urquhart

18886. Lepaludier, Laurent; Colvile, Georgiana. An interview with Jane Urquhart. EtCan (59) 2005, 203–11.

Luis Valdez

18887. Ledwon, Lenora. *Zoot Suit* (1981): realism, romance and the anti-musical – film as social justice. *In* (pp. 425–43) **12712**.

Jean Valentine

18888. Cleary, Suzanne. Be still and know: silence in the poetry of Jean Valentine. LauR (40:2) 2006, 13–22.

Guy Vanderhaeghe

18889. Hamilton, Sharon. The Jews on Mencken's block and Guy Vanderhaeghe's *The Englishman's Boy*. StudCanL (30:2) 2005, 142–60.

18890. Sorenson, Sue. Don't hanker to be no prophet: Guy Vanderhaeghe and the Bible. CanL (191) 2006, 32–46.

Carl Van Vechten

18891. Brunner, Edward. Langston Hughes: *Fine Clothes to the Jew*. *In* (pp. 367–75) **11788**.

Rahul Varma

18892. Salter, Denis. Change the world, one play at a time: Teesri Duniya Theatre and the aesthetics of social action. CanTR (125) 2006, 69–74.

M. G. Vassanji

18893. Fisher, Susan. History, memory, home: an exchange with M. G. Vassanji. CanL (190) 2006, 49–61.

18894. Vassanji, M. G. Am I a Canadian writer? CanL (190) 2006, 7–13.

Iris Vaughan (1890–1977)

18895. Alexander, Peter F. Who is Iris Vaughan? New light on a remarkable colonial child autobiographer. AUMLA (105) 2006, 17–34.

Elizabeth Dewberry Vaughn

18896. DEWBERRY, ELIZABETH. Writing as an act of worship. *In* (pp. 95–104) **11940**.

Yvonne Vera

18897. DRIVER, DOROTHY; SAMUELSON, MEG. History's intimate invasions: Yvonne Vera's *The Stone Virgins*. *In* (pp. 175–208) **12216**.

18898. GAGIANO, ANNIE. Entering the oppressor's mind: a strategy of writing in Bessie Head's *A Question of Power*, Yvonne Vera's *The Stone Virgins* and Unity Dow's *The Screaming of the Innocent*. *See* **16305**.

18899. HEMMINGS, JESSICA. 'How all life is lived, in patches': quilting metaphors in the fiction of Yvonne Vera. *In* (pp. 235–50) **12216**.

18900. PFUKWA, CHARLES. The imagery and potential power of *mbira* and *kwela* rhythms in Yvonne Vera's *Without a Name* and *Butterfly Burning*. *In* (pp. 251–60) **12216**.

Gore Vidal

18901. ALTMAN, DENNIS. Gore Vidal's America. Oxford; Malden, MA: Polity Press in assn with Blackwell, 2005. pp. x, 216. Rev. by James Polchin in GLRW (13:6) 2006, 34–5.

18902. SUN, HONG. The evolution of pre- and post-Stonewall gay literature in America. FLS (118) 2006, 122–8. (In Chinese.)

18903. VIDAL, GORE. Point to point navigation: a memoir, 1964 to 2006. New York: Doubleday, 2006. pp. 277. Rev. by Christopher Hitchens in NYTB, 26 Nov. 2006, 12.

Helena María Viramontes

18904. HEWITT, AVIS. 'Someone to shoot her every minute of her life': maternity and violent death in Helena María Viramontes and Flannery O'Connor. *See* **17826**.

18905. KEVANE, BRIDGET; VIRAMONTES, HELENA MARÍA. Viramontes on O'Connor. *See* **17829**.

Gerald Vizenor

18906. SALAITA, STEVEN. The Holy Land in transit: colonialism and the quest for Canaan. Foreword by Peter Gran. *See* **16980**.

18907. VIZENOR, GERALD. World Literature Association Achievement Award Lecture, October 20, 2005, Los Angeles, California. PemM (38) 2006, 97–100.

Ivan Vladislavic (b.1957)

18908. MARAIS, MIKE. Race, reading, and tolerance in three postapartheid novels. *In* (pp. 253–69) **11860**.

Paula Vogel

18909. CUMMINS, AMY ELIZABETH. 'Driving in the reverse gear': alienation and non-linear chronology in Paula Vogel's *How I Learned to Drive*. NCL (36:1) 2006, 12–14.

18910. GREEN, AMY S. Whose voices are these? The arts of language in the plays of Suzan-Lori Parks, Paula Vogel, and Diana Son. *In* (pp. 143–57) **12297**.

Cynthia Voigt

18911. Kaplan, Deborah; Rabinowitz, Rebecca. 'Beautiful, or thick, or right, or complicated': queer heterosexuality in the young adult works of Francesca Lia Block and Cynthia Voigt. *In* (pp. 196–207) **11883**.

Ellen Bryant Voigt (b.1943)

18912. Chappell, Fred. Ellen Bryant Voigt and the art of distance. SewR (113:3) 2005, 422–39.

Kurt Vonnegut, Jr

18913. Davis, Todd F. Kurt Vonnegut's crusade; or, How a postmodern harlequin preached a new kind of humanism. Albany: New York State UP, 2006. pp. ix, 166. (SUNY series in postmodern culture.)

18914. Klinkowitz, Jerome. The Vonnegut effect. (Bibl. 2005, 19918.) Rev. by Donald E. Morse in MFS (52:3) 2006, 718–21.

18915. Thomas, Paul Lee. Reading, learning, teaching Kurt Vonnegut. New York; Frankfurt: Lang, 2006. pp. viii, 172. (Confronting the text, confronting the world, 2.)

E. L. (Ethel Lillian) Voynich (1864–1960)

18916. Blevins, Pamela. Ivor Gurney's friends: Ethel Voynich – 'E.L.V.': revolutionary, novelist, translator, composer. IGSJ (10) 2004, 13–30.

Helen Waddell

18917. Chance, Jane (ed.). Women medievalists and the academy. *See* **7773**.

Fred Wah

18918. Day, Iyko. Interventing innocence: race, 'resistance,' and the Asian North American avant-garde. *In* (pp. 35–51) **11849**.

18919. Farr, Roger. Surprise, unpredictability, and improvisation: an interview with Fred Wah. CapR (48) 2006, 5–25.

Arthur Edward Waite

18920. McLaren, Scott. Hermeticism and the metaphysics of goodness in the novels of Charles Williams. *See* **19159**.

Derek Walcott

18921. Baugh, Edward. Derek Walcott. Cambridge; New York: CUP, 2006. pp. xiv, 254. (Cambridge studies in African and Caribbean literature, 10.)

18922. Cooper, Carolyn. 'What the backside all you want?': interrogating Rastafari in Derek Walcott's *O Babylon!* JWIL (15:1/2) 2006, 196–201.

18923. Fumagalli, Maria Cristina; Patrick, Peter L. Two healing narratives: suffering, reintegration, and the struggle of language. SmAx (10:2) 2006, 61–79.

18924. Giannopoulou, Zina. Intertextualizing Polyphemus: politics and ideology in Walcott's *Odyssey*. CompDr (40:1) 2006, 1–28.

18925. Irvine, Alexander. 'Betray them both, or give back what they give?': Derek Walcott's deterritorialization of Western myth. JCarL (4:1) 2005, 123–32.

18926. Jay, Paul. Fated to unoriginality: the politics of mimicry in Derek Walcott's *Omeros*. Callaloo (29:2) 2006, 545–59.

18927. Lee, Clarissa. Derek Walcott, human isolation, and traditions of English poetry. JCarL (4:1) 2005, 109–22.

18928. Matos, Nicole. 'Join, interchangeable phantoms': from metaphor to metonymy in Walcott's *Omeros*. SmAx (10:2) 2006, 40–60.

18929. Molesini, Andrea. Translating *Omeros*. QPS (14) 2006, 467–71.

18930. —— (ed. and trans.). Il levriero di Tiepolo. Milan: Adelphi, 2004. pp. 339. Rev. by Massimo Bacigalupo in Indice (2006:6) 20.

18931. Oloruntoba-Oju, Omotayo. The redness of Blackness: revisiting Derek Walcott's mulatto aesthetics. CarQ (52:1) 2006, 12–25.

18932. Rampaul, Giselle A. Black Crusoe, White Friday: carnivalesque reversals in Samuel Selvon's *Moses Ascending* and Derek Walcott's *Pantomime*. *See* **18450**.

18933. Rodríguez Guerrero-Strachan, Santiago. Social exiles and language refugees: the case of postcolonial authors. *See* **17755**.

Anne Waldman (b.1945)

18934. Sadoff, Ira. On the margins: part two. *See* **16331**.

18935. Waldman, Anne. Premises of consciousness. *In* (pp. 260–71) **16122**.

Alice Walker

18936. Bates, Gerri. Alice Walker: a critical companion. (Bibl. 2005, 19959.) Rev. by Peter Barry in Eng (55:212) 2006, 213–19.

18937. Michlin, Monica. Narrative as empowerment: *Push* and the *signifying* on prior African American novels on incest. *See* **18409**.

18938. Sikorski, Grace. Stepping into the same river twice: the tragic sexual mulatto and subversion of the inside/outside dialectic in the novels of E. Lynn Harris and Alice Walker. *In* (pp. 183–95) **11883**.

18939. Šimčíková, Karla. Life and its survival: Walker's new religion in *Now Is the Time to Open Your Heart*. CLIN (9:1/2) 2006, 37–46.

18940. —— To live fully, here and now: the healing vision in the works of Alice Walker. Lanham, MD: Lexington, 2006. pp. xiii, 179.

18941. Wang, Chengyu. On the deviation of conversation in *The Temple of My Familiar*. FLS (118) 2006, 135–41. (In Chinese.)

18942. Wang, Xiaoying. A literary text of Blues: Alice Walker's short story *1955*. FLS (117) 2006, 127–32. (In Chinese.)

George F. Walker (b.1947)

18943. Lane, Harry (ed.). George F. Walker. Toronto: Playwrights Canada Press, 2006. pp. xv, 205. (Critical perspectives on Canadian theatre in English, 5.)

18944. McCoy, Amanda. Equal before and under the law: rethinking the marginality in *This Is Wonderland*. *In* (pp. 187–95) **18943**.

18945. Maufort, Marc. 'Some kind of transition place between heaven and hell': George Walker's aesthetics of hybridity in *Heaven*. *In* (pp. 177–86) **18943**.

18946. Mombourquette, Mary Pat. Walker's women in the East End plays: *Love and Anger*. *In* (pp. 61–74) **18943**.

Kath Walker (Oodgeroo Noonuccal)

18947. Gallagher, Katherine. Towards reconciliation: inspiration and leadership – Oodgeroo of the Tribe Noonuccal (1920–1993) and Judith Wright (1915–2000). *See* **19371**.

Margaret Walker

18948. Scott, William. Belonging to history: Margaret Walker's *For My People*. MLN (121:5) 2006, 1083–1106.

David Foster Wallace

18949. Murphet, Julian. Behind the scenes: production, animation, and postmodern value. SSE (32) 2006, 143–65.

Naomi Wallace

18950. Wisner, Buell. 'Waiting in the angel's wings': Marxist fantasia in Naomi Wallace's *Slaughter City*. JADT (18:1) 2006, 54–70.

Sir Hugh Walpole (1884–1941)

18951. Steele, Elizabeth. Sir Hugh Walpole and the United States: a novelist's view of 1919–1936 America. Lewiston, NY; Lampeter: Mellen Press, 2006. pp. xv, 215.

Eric Walrond (1898–1966)

18952. Parascandola, Louis; McGarrity, Maria. 'I'm a … naughty girl': prostitution and outsider women in James Joyce's *The Boarding House* and Eric Walrond's *The Palm Porch*. *See* **16748**.

Jill Paton Walsh

18953. Walsh, Jill Paton. *The Poetics* of Aristotle as a practical guide. Introd. by Lisa Sainsbury. LU (29:2) 2005, 211–21.

Donald Wandrei (b.1908)

18954. Nelson, Dale. A 'scientifiction' source for Lewis' *The Great Divorce*. *See* **17196**.

Ping Wang (b.1957)

18955. Zhou, Xiaojing. Writing otherwise than as a 'native informant': Ha Jin's poetry. *In* (pp. 274–94) **11995**.

Walter Wangerin

18956. Matthis, Chris. Walter Wangerin's unfinished gospel. Cresset (70:2) 2006, 37–40.

18957. Wangerin, Walter, Jr. Glory into glory. *In* (pp. 72–84) **11940**.

Andy Warhol

18958. Greenberg, Jan; Jordan, Sandra. Andy Warhol: prince of pop. New York: Delacorte Press, 2004. pp. 193, (plates) 32. Rev. by Joe Lowmiller in JAAL (49:1) 2005, 75–6.

18959. Hoberman, J. You've got three minutes. LRB (28:14) 2006, 29–30 (review-article). (Warhol's films.)

18960. JOSEPH, BRANDON W. Andy Warhol's *Sleep*: the play of repetition. *In* (pp. 179–207) **12654**.

Betsy Warland

18961. YORK, LORRAINE. Crowding the garret: women's collaborative writing and the problematics of space. *In* (pp. 288–307) **3405**.

Alan Warner

18962. SCHOENE, BERTHOLD. The walking cure: *Heimat*, masculinity and mobile narration in Alan Warner's *The Man Who Walks*. ScSR (7:1) 2006, 95–109.

Sylvia Townsend Warner

18963. BINGHAM, FRANCES. The practice of the presence of Valentine: Ackland in Warner's work. *In* (pp. 29–44) **18964**.

18964. DAVIES, GILL; MALCOLM, DAVID; SIMONS, JOHN (eds). Critical essays on Sylvia Townsend Warner, English novelist 1893–1978. Lewiston, NY; Lampeter: Mellen Press, 2006. pp. vi, 164.

18965. HINNOV, EMILY M. A counter-reading to conquest: 'Primitivism' and utopian longing in Sylvia Townsend Warner's *Mr Fortune's Maggot*. *In* (pp. 83–102) **18964**.

18966. HOPKINS, CHRIS. Sylvia Townsend Warner and the historical novel 1936–1948. *In* (pp. 117–43) **18964**.

18967. JACOBS, MARY. Sylvia Townsend Warner and the politics of the English pastoral 1925–1934. *In* (pp. 61–82) **18964**.

18968. JOLLY, MARGARETTA. A word is a bridge: death and epistolary form in the correspondence of Sylvia Townsend Warner and David Garnett. *In* (pp. 11–28) **18964**.

18969. LECERCLE, JEAN-JACQUES. De Jane Austen au *Manifeste communiste*: Sylvia Townsend Warner et la révolution de 1848. EA (59:3) 2006, 292–303.

18970. MALCOLM, DAVID. *The Flint Anchor* and the conventions of historical fiction. *In* (pp. 145–62) **18964**.

18971. SIMONS, JOHN. The compositional genetics of *Kingdoms of Elfin* together with a note on tortoises. *In* (pp. 45–60) **18964**.

18972. STRACHAN, WALTER. Portraits of four poets. Ed. by Geoffrey Strachan. PNRev (31:6) 2005, 30–40.

18973. SYKES, ROSEMARY. 'This was a lesson in history': Sylvia Townsend Warner, George Townsend Warner and the matter of history. *In* (pp. 103–15) **18964**.

Robert Penn Warren

18974. BECK, CHARLOTTE H. Robert Penn Warren, critic. Knoxville: Tennessee UP, 2006. pp. x, 192.

18975. CRONIN, GLORIA L.; SIEGEL, BEN (eds). Conversations with Robert Penn Warren. Jackson; London: Mississippi UP, 2005. pp. xxi, 231. (Literary conversations.) Rev. by Jonathan S. Cullick in JSH (72:3) 2006, 706–7.

18976. HEUSTON, SEAN. Anybody raised down home – down South: *Brother to Dragons* and Warren's Southern ethnography. MissQ (58:1/2) 2004/05, 347–72.

18977. MacKethan, Lucinda. ‘Trying to make contact’: *Mortmain* as pre-text for Robert Penn Warren’s *Portrait of a Father*. MissQ (58:1/2) 2004/05, 373–86.

18978. Runyon, Randolph Paul. Ghostly parallels: Robert Penn Warren and the lyric poetic sequence. Knoxville: Tennessee UP, 2006. pp. 233.

Booker T. Washington

18979. Hicks, Scott. W. E. B. Du Bois, Booker T. Washington, and Richard Wright: toward an ecocriticism of color. *See* **15574**.

18980. Kowalski, Philip J. No excuses for our dirt: Booker T. Washington and the ‘New Negro’ middle class. *In* (pp. 181–96) **8435**.

Wendy Wasserstein

18981. Durang, Christopher, *et al.* Joking aside: a conversation about comedy with Christopher Durang, Gina Gionfriddo, Sarah Ruhl, and Wendy Wasserstein. *In* (pp. 181–90) **12297**.

18982. Gussow, Mel. Entering the mainstream: the plays of Beth Henley, Marsha Norman, and Wendy Wasserstein. *In* (pp. 45–53) **12297**.

18983. McLaughlin, Buzz. Conversation with Wendy Wasserstein. Dramatist (8:4) 2006, 36–45. (From the archives.)

18984. Wasserstein, Wendy. Generosity. *In* (pp. 8–16) **12375**.

Roger Waters (b.1943)

18985. Sacido Romero, Jorge; Varela Cabo, Luis Miguel. Roger Waters’ poetry of the absent father: British identity in Pink Floyd’s *The Wall*. Atl (28:2) 2006, 45–58.

Maurine Dallas Watkins (1896–1969)

18986. Striff, Erin. Mimicry and murder: female impersonation in *Chicago*. *See* **15660**.

Sheila Watson

18987. Flahiff, F. T. Always someone to kill the doves: a life of Sheila Watson. (Bibl. 2005, 20008.) Rev. by George Melnyk in CanL (190) 2006, 106–8.

Wilfred Watson

18988. Lent, John. Wilfred Watson and the shift from modern to postmodern forms in Canadian poetry. CapR (second series) (45) 2004, 103–20.

Evelyn Waugh

18989. Coffey, Laura. Evelyn Waugh’s country house trinity: memory, history and Catholicism in *Brideshead Revisited*. LitH (15:1) 2006, 59–73.

18990. Davis, Robert Murray. Up to a point, Mr Foxwell: the adaptation of *Decline and Fall*. EWN (36:2) 2005.

18991. Easter, Kathryn S. Something so different. EWN (37:1) 2006.

18992. Fiala, Nathan. Strange bedfellows: reading Evelyn Waugh and Frantz Fanon. EWN (35:3) 2005.

18993. Labay-Morère, Julie. ‘Voices at play’ in Muriel Spark’s *The Comforters* and Evelyn Waugh’s *The Ordeal of Gilbert Pinfold*. *See* **18572**.

18994. Lurcock, Tony. Evelyn Waugh, A. P. Herbert and divorce reform. EWN (35:2) 2004.

18995. McCartney, George. Evelyn Waugh and the Modernist tradition. (Bibl. 2004, 20045.) Rev. by Jonathan Pitcher in EWN (35:2) 2004.

18996. Morton, Peter. 'The funniest book in the world': Waugh and *The Diary of a Nobody*. EWN (36:1) 2005.

18997. Platon, Mircea. Drama, architecture, art, and grace: Evelyn Waugh's Roman Catholicism. EWN (34:3) 2004.

18998. Ramsay, Allan. The green baize door: social identity in Wodehouse: part two. *See* **19241**.

18999. Stannard, Martin. In search of a city: civilization, humanism and English gothic in *A Handful of Dust*. Connotations (14:1–3) 2004/05, 183–204. (*Response to* bibl. 2005, 20013.)

19000. White, Laura. The rejection of beauty in Waugh's *Brideshead Revisited*. Ren (58:3) 2006, 181–94.

19001. Whitechapel, Simon. *Brideshead* revista'd: Bacchus, Beelzebub and 'the Botanical Gardens'. EWN (36:3) 2006.

19002. Wilson, John Howard. A question of influence and experience: a response to Edward Lobb. Connotations (14:1–3) 2004/05, 205–12. (*Response to* bibl. 2005, 20013.)

The Waughs

19003. Waugh, Alexander. Fathers and sons: the autobiography of a family. (Bibl. 2004, 20048.) Rev. by Robert Murray Davis in EWN (35:3) 2005; by Douglas Lane Patey in EWN (35:3) 2005.

John Weidman (b.1946)

19004. Orloff, Rich. The musicals of Stephen Sondheim and John Weidman. *See* **18553**.

Bruce Weigl

19005. Clifford, Emily Clare. 'Before I was domesticated': delivering the Vietnam moment in the fatherhood poetry of Bruce Weigl and John Balaban. WLA (18:1/2) 2006, 53–65.

Daniel Evan Weiss (b.1953)

19006. Copeland, Marion W. Voices of the least loved: cockroaches in the contemporary American novel. *In* (pp. 153–75) **3203**.

James Welch

19007. Donahue, James J. 'A world away from his people': James Welch's *The Heartsong of Charging Elk* and the Indian historical novel. SAIL (18:2) 2006, 54–82.

19008. Ferguson, Suzanne. Europe and the quest for home in James Welch's *The Heartsong of Charging Elk* and Leslie Marmon Silko's *Gardens in the Dunes*. SAIL (18:2) 2006, 34–53.

19009. Hollrah, Patrice. The strength of Native women in James Welch's *Winter in the Blood*. SAIL (18:3) 2006, 58–66.

19010. Lemberg, Jennifer. Transmitted trauma and 'absent memory' in James Welch's *The Death of Jim Loney*. SAIL (18:3) 2006, 67–81.

19011. Mariani, Giorgio. Reversing the captivity narrative: James Welch's *The Heartsong of Charging Elk*. QPS (14) 2006, 214–19.

19012. Murphy, Anthony G. Communicating history: James Welch's *Killing Custer* and the cultural translation of the Battle of the Little Bighorn. *In* (pp. 196–213) **2119**.

19013. Nelson, Christopher. Embodying the Indian: rethinking blood, culture, and identity in James Welch's *Winter in the Blood* and *The Death of Jim Loney*. WAL (41:3) 2006, 301–34.

19014. Opitz, Andrea. 'The primitive has escaped control': narrating the nation in *The Heartsong of Charging Elk*. SAIL (18:3) 2006, 98–106.

19015. Orton, Thomas. Keening Woman and Today: James Welch's early unpublished novel. SAIL (18:3) 2006, 52–7.

19016. Round, Phillip H. *There Is a Right Way*. SAIL (18:3) 2006, 82–9.

19017. Shanley, Kathryn W. Circling back, closing in: remembering James Welch. SAIL (18:3) 2006, 3–13.

19018. Tremblay, Gail. Remembering James Welch's poetry. SAIL (18:3) 2006, 49–51.

19019. Vest, James Hansford C. The hero's journey in James Welch's *Fools Crow* and traditional Pikuni sacred geography. CanJNS (25:1) 2005, 337–53.

19020. Weidman, Bette. Closure in James Welch's *Fools Crow*. SAIL (18:3) 2006, 90–7.

Noël Welch

19021. Oldham, Alison. Noël Welch and Kathrine Talbot. PNRev (31:3) 2005, 8–12.

Fay Weldon

19022. Russell, Lorena. Latent lesbians and heterosexual narrative: tracing a queer poetics in Fay Weldon's fiction. *In* (pp. 170–82) **11883**.

Orson Welles (1915–1985)

19023. Anderegg, Michael. Orson Welles and after: *Julius Caesar* and twentieth-century totalitarianism. *In* (pp. 295–305) **5805**.

19024. Callow, Simon. Orson Welles: hello Americans. *See* **13251**.

19025. Hand, Richard J. Escape with Joseph Conrad! The adaptation of Joseph Conrad's fiction on American old-time radio. *See* **15273**.

19026. Rooney, Tom. 'A thousand Shylocks': Orson Welles and *The Merchant of Venice*. *See* **5975**.

Dorothy Wellesley (1889–1956)

19027. Harper, Lisa. Courting the muse: Dorothy Wellesley and W. B. Yeats. *In* (pp. 211–28) **3405**.

Paul Iselin Wellman (1898–1966)

19028. Masters, Hilary. In rooms of memory. PrS (79:4) 2005, 13–20.

H. G. Wells

19029. Anon. (comp.). New books and articles on H. G. Wells. Wellsian (29) 2006, 63–8.

19030. Benziman, Galia. Challenging the biological: the fantasy of male birth as nineteenth-century narrative of ethical failure. *See* **11174**.

19031. Cantor, Paul A.; Hufnagel, Peter. The empire of the future: imperialism and modernism in H. G. Wells. StudN (38:1) 2006, 36–56.

19032. Chialant, Maria Teresa. *'This grey, monstrous London of ours'*: squarci ottocenteschi. *In* (pp. 151–63) **7343**.

19033. Christensen, Timothy. The 'bestial mark' of race in *The Island of Dr Moreau*. Criticism (46:4) 2004, 575–95.

19034. Crossley, Robert. H. G. Wells, visionary telescopes, and the 'Matter of Mars'. PQ (83:1) 2004, 83–114.

19035. Feir, Gordon D. H. G. Wells at the end of his tether: his social and political adventures. Lincoln, NE: iUniverse, 2005. pp. xii, 234. Rev. by John S. Partington in Wellsian (29) 2006, 56–62.

19036. Ferguson, Christine. Language, science and popular fiction in the Victorian *fin-de-siècle*: the brutal tongue. *See* **8637**.

19037. Gangale, Thomas; Dudley-Rowley, Marilyn. When was the War of the Worlds? Wellsian (29) 2006, 2–20.

19038. Haldane, Michael. From Plato to Pullman – the circle of invisibility and parallel worlds: *Fortunatus*, Mercury, and the Wishing-Hat: part ii. *See* **6687**.

19039. Jackson, Kimberley. Vivisected language in H. G. Wells's *The Island of Doctor Moreau*. Wellsian (29) 2006, 20–36.

19040. Lázaro Lafuente, Luis Alberto. H. G. Wells en España: estudio de los expedientes de censura (1939–1978). Madrid: Verbum, 2004. pp. 250. (Verbum ensayo.) Rev. by Juan Francisco Elices Agudo in Atl (27:1) 2005, 93–8.

19041. Luxemburg, Alexander M. The mystery of Vladimir Nabokov's sources: some new ideas on *Lolita*'s intertextual links. *See* **17702**.

19042. McCarthy, Penny. *Lolita*: wellsprings and influences. *See* **17703**.

19043. McGonigal, Jane. SuperGaming: ubiquitous play and performance for massively scaled community. ModDr (48:3) 2005, 471–91.

19044. MacKenzie, Norman. The man who invented tomorrow. Meanjin (63:1) 2004, 4–13.

19045. McMillan, Gloria. The invisible friends: the lost worlds of Henry James and H. G. Wells. *See* **10577**.

19046. Pagetti, Carlo. *'Entering the world of a novel'*: Londra, l'enigma della città. *In* (pp. 3–17) **7343**.

19047. Parrinder, Patrick; Partington, John S. (eds). The reception of H. G. Wells in Europe. (Bibl. 2005, 20055.) Rev. by Annie Escuret in CVE (62) 2005, 215–16.

19048. Prindle, R. E. Tarzan and the river: part iii. *See* **14948**.

19049. Raitt, Suzanne. The rhetoric of efficiency in early Modernism. Mod/Mod (13:1) 2006, 89–105.

19050. So, Hiroshi. *The Wheels of Chance* and the discourse of improvement of health. Wellsian (29) 2006, 37–47.

19051. Willis, Martin. Mesmerists, monsters, and machines: science fiction and the cultures of science in the nineteenth century. *See* **11200**.

19052. Yeffeth, Glenn (ed.). *The War of the Worlds*: fresh perspectives on the H. G. Wells classic. Dallas, TX: BenBella, 2005. pp. vi, 292. Rev. by John S. Partington in Wellsian (29) 2006, 51–6.

Rebecca Wells

19053. Boyd, Elizabeth B. Ya yas, grits, and sweet potato queens: contemporary Southern belles and the prescriptions that guide them. *In* (pp. 159–72) **19862**.

Irvine Welsh

19054. Kelly, Aaron. Irvine Welsh. Manchester; New York: Manchester UP, 2005. pp. viii, 240. (Contemporary British novelists.) Rev. by Niall O'Gallagher in ScSR (7:1) 2006, 131–3.

19055. Kirk, John. Figuring the landscape: writing the topographies of community and place. *See* **17045**.

Eudora Welty

19056. Folks, Jeffrey J. The fierce humanity of Morgana: Welty's *The Golden Apples*. SoLJ (39:1) 2006, 16–32.

19057. Marrs, Suzanne. Eudora Welty: a biography. (Bibl. 2005, 20086.) Rev. by Marvin J. LaHood in WLT (80:5) 2006, 76–7; by John Givner in BkCan (35:1) 2006, 18–19; by Trish Crapo in WRB (23:1) 2006, 9–10.

19058. Montgomery, Marion. Eudora Welty and Walker Percy: the concept of home in their lives and literature. *See* **17986**.

19059. Sivils, Matthew Wynn. Reading trees in Southern literature. *See* **15833**.

Darren S. Wershler-Henry (b.1966)

19060. Drucker, Johanna. Un-visual and conceptual. OpL (twelfth series) (7) 2005, 117–30.

Timberlake Wertenbaker

19061. Wertenbaker, Timberlake. Prescription for a playwriting life: Dear Emily: on being a playwright. *In* (pp. 241–6) **12297**.

19062. —— Stafford-Clark, Max; Billington, Michael. A conversation: Timberlake Wertenbaker, Max Stafford-Clark, and Michael Billington. *In* (pp. 54–68) **12297**.

Dorothy West

19063. Barnes, Paula C. Dorothy West: Harlem renaissance writer? *In* (pp. 99–124) **12180**.

19064. Duboin, Corinne. Poétique de l'espace insulaire dans *The Wedding* de Dorothy West. Anglophonia (19) 2006, 97–105.

Mae West

19065. Bak, John S. 'May I have a drag … ?': Mae West, Tennessee Williams, and the politics of a gay identity. *See* **19164**.

19066. Louvish, Simon. Mae West: it ain't no sin. London; Boston, MA: Faber & Faber, 2005. pp. xvii, 491.

'Nathanael West' (Nathan Wallenstein Weinstein)

19067. Bombaci, Nancy. Freaks in late Modernist American culture: Nathanael West, Djuna Barnes, Tod Browning, and Carson McCullers. New York; Frankfurt: Lang, 2006. pp. 175. (Modern American literature, 47.)

19068. Cerasulo, Tom. *The Dream Life of Balso Snell* and the vocation of Nathanael West. AQ (62:2) 2006, 59–75.

19069. Greenberg, Jonathan. Nathanael West and the mystery of feeling. MFS (52:3) 2006, 588–612.

19070. Martin, Jay. Nathanael West: *Miss Lonleyhearts*. *In* (pp. 469–77) **11788**.

'Rebecca West' (Mrs H. M. Andrews)

19071. Christensen, Peter G. The Azev affair and *The Birds Fall Down*: a true story on a parallel universe? *In* (pp. 80–96) **19082**.

19072. Cohen, Debra Rae. Sheepish Modernism: Rebecca West, the Adam brothers, and the taxonomies of criticism. *In* (pp. 143–56) **19082**.

19073. Frigerio, Francesca. Music and the feminine art of detail in Rebecca West's *Harriet Hume*. *In* (pp. 125–39) **19082**.

19074. Golubov, Nattie. Rebecca West's *Strange Necessity*: literature, love, and the good. *In* (pp. 206–21) **19082**.

19075. Laing, Kathryn. Versions and palimpsests: Rebecca West's *The Sentinel*, *Adela*, and *The Judge*. *In* (pp. 170–85) **19082**.

19076. Lassner, Phyllis. Rebecca West's shadowy Other. *In* (pp. 43–63) **19082**.

19077. Norton, Ann V. Cordelia and Mrs Crosthwaite: an unpublished chapter of *This Real Night*. *In* (pp. 112–24) **19082**.

19078. Paxton, Nancy L. Renegotiating the public and private divide: reconsidering Rebecca West's *The Judge*. *In* (pp. 189–205) **19082**.

19079. Schofield, Mary Anne. Marking the frontiers of World War II with 'stabilized disorder': Rebecca West reads St Augustine. *In* (pp. 327–42) **3301**.

19080. Schweizer, Bernard. Epic form and (re)vision in Rebecca West's *Black Lamb and Grey Falcon*. *In* (pp. 69–81) **3395**.

19081. —— Rebecca West's philosophy of history and the critique of postmodernism. *In* (pp. 223–44) **19082**.

19082. —— (ed.). Rebecca West today: contemporary critical approaches. Newark: Delaware UP, 2006. pp. 334.

19083. Stec, Loretta. Rebecca West in South Africa: the limits of Liberalism. *In* (pp. 64–79) **19082**.

19084. Stetz, Margaret D. Rebecca West, Aestheticism, and the legacy of Oscar Wilde. *In* (pp. 157–69) **19082**.

19085. Wilson, Cheryl A. Performing women in *The Fountain Overflows*. *In* (pp. 99–111) **19082**.

A. Ethelwyn Wetherald

19086. Chambers, Jennifer. 'You woman-hearted, poet-brained wonder worker!': the poetic dialogue of love between Ethelwyn Wetherald and Helena Coleman. CanP (57) 2005, 65–85.

Edith Wharton

19087. Abureesh, Ali H. Dr. C. G. Jung visits *The House of Mirth*. PsyArt (10) 2006.

19088. Bourosa, Alan. Wharton's aesthetics and the ethics of affect. CLAJ (50:1) 2006, 84–106.

19089. Bruni, John. Becoming American: evolution and performance in Edith Wharton's *The Custom of the Country*. Intertexts (9:1) 2005, 43–59.

19090. Buell, Lawrence. Downwardly mobile for conscience's sake: voluntary simplicity from Thoreau to Lily Bart. *See* **11426**.

19091. Campbell, Donna. 'Where are the ladies?': Wharton, Glasgow, and American women Naturalists. *See* **10136**.

19092. Daalder, Joost. Frustrated emancipation in Edith Wharton's *The Age of Innocence*. *In* (pp. 166–79) **8374**.

19093. Farwell, Tricia M. Love and death in Edith Wharton's fiction. New York; Frankfurt: Lang, 2006. pp. 162. (Modern American literature: new approaches, 48.)

19094. Ferruggia, Gabriella. Edith Wharton's *Motor-Flight through France*. *In* (pp. 65–81) **12076**.

19095. Fleissner, Jennifer L. The biological clock: Edith Wharton, Naturalism, and the temporality of womanhood. AL (78:3) 2006, 519–48.

19096. Fournier, Suzanne J. Edith Wharton's *Ethan Frome*: a reference guide. Westport, CT; London: Praeger, 2006. pp. xiv, 157.

19097. Griffith, Jean C. 'Lita is – jazz': the Harlem renaissance, cabaret culture, and racial amalgamation in Edith Wharton's *Twilight Sleep*. StudN (38:1) 2006, 74–94.

19098. Harden, Edgar F. An Edith Wharton chronology. Basingstoke; New York: Palgrave Macmillan, 2005. pp. xi, 146. (Author chronologies.)

19099. Hochman, Barbara. The good, the bad, and the literary: Edith Wharton's *Bunner Sisters* and the social context of reading. StAN (1:1/2) 2006, 128–43.

19100. Hughes, Clair. Dressed in fiction. *See* **8651**.

19101. Kim, Sharon. Edith Wharton and epiphany. JML (29:3) 2006, 150–75.

19102. —— Lamarckism and the construction of transcendence in *The House of Mirth*. StudN (38:2) 2006, 187–210.

19103. Leighton, Angela. Resurrections of the body: women writers and the idea of the Renaissance. *In* (pp. 222–38) **8320**.

19104. Meyer, Susan. On the front and at home: Wharton, Cather, the Jews, and the First World War. *See* **15104**.

19105. Nettels, Elsa. Howells and Wharton. *See* **10505**.

19106. Ohler, Paul. Edith Wharton's evolutionary conception: Darwinian allegory in her major novels. London; New York: Routledge, 2006. pp. xviii, 212. (Studies in major literary authors.)

19107. Olin-Ammentorp, Julie. Edith Wharton's writings from the Great War. (Bibl. 2005, 20124.) Rev. by Jill M. Kress in MFS (52:1) 2006, 207–10.

19108. Rives, Darcie D. Haunted by violence: Edith Wharton's *The Decoration of Houses* and her gothic fiction. EWR (22:1) 2006, 8–15.

19109. Thomas, J. D. Tribal culture, pantomime, and the communicative face in Edith Wharton's *The Age of Innocence*. EWR (22:1) 2006, 1–5.

19110. Thompson, Terry W. Old Testament sourcing in Edith Wharton's *All Souls*. ANQ (19:4) 2006, 47–52.

19111. Wells, Juliette. Mothers of chick lit? Women writers, readers, and literary history. *In* (pp. 47–70) **19862**.

E. B. (Elwyn Brooks) White (1899–1985)

19112. Guth, Dorothy Lobrano (ed.); White, Martha (reviser). Letters of E. B. White. Foreword by John Updike. New York: HarperCollins, 2006. pp. 736. (Revised ed.: first ed. 1976.)

Edmund White (b.1940)

19113. White, Edmund. Lost in the funhouse: *My Lives* and my autobiographical novels. TLS, 19 May 2006, 14–15. (Commentary.)

19114. —— My lives. (Bibl. 2005, 20146.) Rev. by Thom Nickels in GLRW (13:3) 2006, 35–6.

Kenneth White

19115. Bowd, Gavin; Forsdick, Charles; Bissell, Norman (eds). Grounding a world: essays on the work of Kenneth White: the St Andrews Symposium organised by Gavin Bowd and Charles Forsdick at the University of St Andrews, 10–11 October 2003. Glasgow: Alba, 2005. pp. 226.

Patrick White

19116. Beston, John. Why are epiphanies so prominent in Patrick White's novels? AUMLA (105) 2006, 109–21.

19117. —— Willa Cather and Patrick White. Antipodes (20:2) 2006, 164–8.

19118. Hubber, Brian; Smith, Vivian. Patrick White: a bibliography. (Bibl. 2005, 20150.) Rev. by Greg Clarke in Southerly (65:1) 2005, 160–2.

T. H. (Terence Hanbury) White ('James Aston') (1906–1964)

19119. Nelson, Dale. Little-known books (and a little-known story) in Lewis' background: a fifth selection. *See* **17195**.

19120. Sprague, Kurth. The troubled heart of T. H. White: women and *The Once and Future King*. Arthuriana (16:3) 2006, 1–197.

John Robert Whiting (1917–1963)

19121. Lima, Robert. Stages of evil: occultism in Western theater and drama. *See* **3444**.

'Anna Wickham' (Edith Mary Alice Hepburn)

19122. Pender, Anne. 'Phrases between us': the poetry of Anna Wickham. ALS (22:2) 2005, 229–44.

Zoë Wicomb

19123. Lenta, Patrick. The *tikoloshe* and the reasonable man. *See* **16161**.

19124. Robolin, Stéphane. Loose memory in Toni Morrison's *Paradise* and Zoë Wicomb's *David's Story*. *See* **17634**.

John Edgar Wideman

19125. Andrade, Heather Russell. Race, representation, and intersubjectivity in the works of John Edgar Wideman. *In* (pp. 43–56) **19144**.

19126. Bergevin, Gerald W. 'Traveling here below': John Edgar Wideman's *The Island Martinique* and the strategy of melancholy. *In* (pp. 71–89) **19144**.

19127. Berben-Masi, Jacqueline. Of basketball and beads: following the thread of one's origins. *In* (pp. 31–41) **19144**.

19128. Berry, Stacey L. The individual and the collective: threatening Blackness in Wideman's *Philadelphia Fire*. *In* (pp. 161–73) **19144**.

19129. Bidinger, Elizabeth. The ethics of working-class autobiography: representation of family by four American authors. Jefferson, NC; London: McFarland, 2006. pp. ix, 202.

19130. Byerman, Keith E. Queering Blackness: race and sexual identity in *A Glance Away* and *Hurry Home*. *In* (pp. 93–105) **19144**.

19131. Casmier, Stephen. The funky novels of John Edgar Wideman: odor and ideology in *Reuben*, *Philadelphia Fire*, and *The Cattle Killing*. *In* (pp. 191–204) **19144**.

19132. Douglas, Jennifer D. 'Ill seen ill said': tropes of vision and the articulation of race relations in *The Cattle Killing*. *In* (pp. 205–20) **19144**.

19133. Guzzio, Tracie Church. 'All my father's texts': John Edgar Wideman's historical vision in *Philadelphia Fire*. *In* (pp. 175–89) **19144**.

19134. Jahn, Karen F. Will the circle be unbroken? Jazzing story in *Hoop Roots*. *In* (pp. 57–70) **19144**.

19135. Julien, Claude Fernand Yvon. Figures of life in *Fatheralong*. *In* (pp. 17–29) **19144**.

19136. Lewis, Leslie W. *Philadelphia Fire* and *The Fire Next Time*: Wideman responds to Baldwin. *In* (pp. 145–59) **19144**.

19137. Okonkwo, Chris. 'It was like meeting an old friend': an interview with John Edgar Wideman. Callaloo (29:2) 2006, 346–60.

19138. Page, Eugene Philip. 'Familiar strangers': the quest for connection and self-knowledge in *Brothers and Keepers*. *In* (pp. 3–15) **19144**.

19139. Rodriguez, Denise. Homewood's 'music of invisibility': John Edgar Wideman's *Sent for You Yesterday* and the Black urban tradition. *In* (pp. 127–44) **19144**.

19140. Rushdy, Ashraf H. A. 'A lynching in blackface': John Edgar Wideman's reflections on the nation question. *In* (pp. 107–26) **19144**.

19141. Simpson, Tyrone R., ii. 'And the arc of his witness explained nothing': Black *flânerie* and traumatic photorealism in Wideman's *Two Cities*. *In* (pp. 221–39) **19144**.

19142. Sundquist, Eric J. Fly away home: John Edgar Wideman's *Fatheralong*. TriQ (126) 2006, 9–28.

19143. TuSmith, Bonnie. Optical tricksterism: dissolving and shapeshifting in the works of John Edgar Wideman. *In* (pp. 243–58) **19144**.

19144. —— Byerman, Keith E. (eds). Critical essays on John Edgar Wideman. Knoxville: Tennessee UP, 2006. pp. xv, 275.

Elie Wiesel

19145. Hartman, Geoffrey. Elie Wiesel and the morality of fiction. *In* (pp. 107–16) **11969**.

19146. Katz, Steven T.; Rosen, Alan (eds). Obliged by memory: literature, religion, ethics: a collection of essays honoring Elie Wiesel's seventieth birthday. *See* **11969**.

19147. Manseau, Peter. Revising *Night*: Elie Wiesel and the hazards of Holocaust theology. CC (56:3) 2006, 387–99.

Richard Wilbur

19148. Buzan, Mary. Wilbur's *Digging for China*. Exp (64:2) 2006, 107–9.

19149. Gwynn, R. S. Haunted palaces, trembling strings. *See* **11018**.

James Wilcox

19150. Pastoor, Charles. Moments of grace in James Wilcox's *Modern Baptists*. Ren (58:3) 2006, 211–20.

Laura Ingalls Wilder

19151. Adkison, Jennifer Dawes. 'These is my words' … or are they? *See* **20346**.

19152. Suzuki, Noriko. Japanese democratization and the Little House books: the relation between General Head Quarters and *The Long Winter* in Japan after World War II. CLAQ (31:1) 2006, 65–86.

Thornton Wilder

19153. Knee, Adam. Shadows of *Shadow of a Doubt*. *In* (pp. 49–64) **13181**.

19154. Konkle, Lincoln. Thornton Wilder and the Puritan narrative tradition. Columbia; London: Missouri UP, 2006. pp. xxiii, 301.

19155. Radavich, David. Wilder's dramatic landscape: alienation effect meets the Midwest. AmDr (15:1) 2006, 43–61.

Kate Wilhelm

19156. Lukin, Josh. Cold War masculinity in the early work of Kate Wilhelm. *In* (pp. 107–29) **13537**.

John Lawton Wilkinson (b.1953)

19157. Milne, Drew. The art of wit and the Cambridge Science Park. *In* (pp. 170–87) **13732**.

Sylvia Wilkinson

19158. McLennan, Rachael. Unpacking 'something dark': narrating Southern female adolescence in Jill McCorkle's *The Cheer Leader*, Sylvia Wilkinson's *Bone of My Bones* and Thulani Davis's *1959*. *See* **17309**.

Charles Williams (1886–1945)

19159. McLaren, Scott. Hermeticism and the metaphysics of goodness in the novels of Charles Williams. Mythlore (24:3/4) 2006, 5–33.

Joan Williams

19160. Hickman, Lisa C. William Faulkner and Joan Williams: the romance of two writers. Foreword by Richard Bausch. *See* **15814**.

19161. Holladay, Cary. Remembering Joan Williams. ArkR (37:2) 2006, 84–92.

Jonathan Williams (b.1929)

19162. Beer, John (introd.). To Jonathan Williams. *See* **18206**.

Tennessee Williams

19163. Bak, John. A dying Gaul: the signifying phallus and Tennessee Williams's *Three Players of a Summer Game*. MissQ (58:1/2) 2004/05, 41–73.

19164. Bak, John S. 'May I have a drag … ?': Mae West, Tennessee Williams, and the politics of a gay identity. JADT (18:3) 2006, 5–32.

19165. —— *Vestis virum reddit*: the gender politics of drag in Williams's *A Streetcar Named Desire* and Hwang's *M. Butterfly*. SAtlR (70:4) 2005, 94–118.

19166. Fisher, James. 'Angels of fructification': Tennessee Williams, Tony Kushner, and images of homosexuality on the American stage. *In* (pp. 5–27) **16962**.

19167. Haake, C. Allen. Exorcizing blue devils: *The Night of the Iguana* as Tennessee Williams's ultimate confessional. MissQ (58:1/2) 2004/05, 105–18.

19168. Heintzelman, Greta; Howard, Alycia Smith. Critical companion to Tennessee Williams. (Bibl. 2005, 20189.) Rev. by Len Berkman in NETJ (16) 2005, 136–8.

19169. Isaac, Dan (ed.). *Candles to the Sun*: a play in ten scenes. Foreword by William Jay Smith. New York: New Directions, 2004. pp. xxxii, 117. Rev. by Brian Parker in ModDr (49:1) 2006, 137–42.

19170. Jenckes, Norma. Structure of feeling in Tennessee Williams's *The Night of the Iguana* and Edward Albee's *A Delicate Balance*. SAtlR (70:4) 2005, 4–22.

19171. Kolin, Philip C. The fission of Tennessee Williams's plays into Adrienne Kennedy's. SAtlR (70:4) 2005, 43–72.

19172. —— 'It's hard to be human': the ironies in Tennessee Williams's *Tent Worms*. NCL (36:1) 2006, 9–12.

19173. —— Williams's *The Municipal Abattoir*. Exp (64:2) 2006, 100–3.

19174. —— (ed.). The Tennessee Williams encyclopedia. (Bibl. 2005, 20192.) Rev. by Mark Zelinsky in TJ (58:1) 2006, 162–3; by Shirley Kagan in MidQ (47:2) 2006, 198–200; by Kimball King in SoLJ (39:1) 2006, 137–8; by Garry MacIver in JAStud (40:1) 2006, 182–3; by Felicia F. Campbell in PCR (17:2) 2006, 117–18.

19175. McDaniel, L. Bailey. Reel Italian: melodrama, Magnani, and alternative subjects in *The Rose Tattoo*. LitFQ (34:4) 2006, 274–84.

19176. Moschovakis, Nicholas; Roessel, David (eds). *Mister Paradise* and other one-act plays. Foreword by Eli Wallach and Anne Jackson. London; New York: Penguin, 2006. pp. xxxvi, 245. (Penguin modern classics.) Rev. by Brian Parker in ModDr (49:1) 2006, 137–42.

19177. Powers, W. Douglas. Lifted above Tennessee Williams's *Hot Tin Roof*: Tony Kushner's *Angels in America* as Midrash. SAtlR (70:4) 2005, 119–38.

19178. Radavich, David. You *can* go home again: Tennessee Williams's *A Lovely Sunday for Creve Coeur.* MidM (33) 2005, 7–21.

19179. Saddik, Annette J. 'You just forged ahead': image, authenticity, and freedom in the plays of Tennessee Williams and Sam Shepard. SAtlR (70:4) 2005, 73–93.

19180. Tarver, Milton. Entropic commonalities: the affective presence of Tennessee Williams in the drama of Lanford Wilson. SAtlR (70:4) 2005, 23–42.

19181. Thornton, Margaret Bradham (ed.). Notebooks. New Haven, CT; London: Yale UP, 2006. pp. 856.

19182. Voss, Ralph F. Tennessee Williams's *Sweet Bird of Youth* and William Inge's *Bus Riley's Back in Town*: coincidences from a friendship. AmDr (15:1) 2006, 62–73.

19183. Waters, John (introd.). Memoirs. New York: New Directions, 2006. pp. xix, 274, (plates) 64. (New Directions paperbooks, 1048.)

19184. Xu, Huaijing. The encryption of the theme of homosexuality in Tennessee Williams's plays. FLS (120) 2006, 55–61. (In Chinese.)

William Carlos Williams

19185. Chatlos, Jon. Automobility and lyric poetry: the mobile gaze in William Carlos Williams' *The Right of Way*. JML (30:1) 2006, 140–54.

19186. Churchill, Suzanne W. The little magazine *Others* and the renovation of modern American poetry. *See* **13722**.

19187. Copestake, Ian D. (ed.). Rigor of beauty: essays in commemoration of William Carlos Williams. (Bibl. 2004, 20215.) Rev. by Theodora Rapp Graham in Mod/Mod (13:3) 2006, 593–5.

19188. Dennison, Julie. Williams and H.D. figure it out: reconceiving the childbirth metaphor in 'his' *Paterson*, 'her' *Trilogy. See* **15532**.

19189. Driscoll, Kerry. Gendered poetics. WCWR (25:2) 2005, 55–9 (review-article).

19190. Giles, Todd. A comprehensive William Carlos Williams bibliography: 1994–2004. WCWR (25:2) 2005, 75–114.

19191. Huehls, Mitchum. Reconceiving perceiving: William Carlos Williams' world-making words of *Kora in Hell: Improvisations*. Paideuma (33:1) 2004, 57–88.

19192. Kaplan, Harold. Poetry, politics, and culture: argument in the work of Eliot, Pound, Stevens, and Williams. *See* **15693**.

19193. Lowney, John. William Carlos Williams and modern poetry: from Modernism to modernisms. WCWR (25:2) 2005, 39–54 (review-article).

19194. MacGowan, Christopher. Poet to poet: four books of correspondence. WCWR (25:2) 2005, 5–18 (review-article).

19195. Marsh, Alec. Figure 5: five studies of William Carlos Williams from the 1990s. WCWR (25:2) 2005, 61–74 (review-article).

19196. Morris, Daniel. William Carlos Williams: *Paterson*. *In* (pp. 478–85) **11788**.

19197. Perricone, Christopher. The aspiration to the condition of touch. PhilL (30:1) 2006, 229–37. (*The Dance*.)

19198. Peterfy, Margit. 'These things astonish me beyond words': wordplay in William Carlos Williams's poetry. Connotations (14:1–3) 2004/05, 87–108.

19199. Reeves, Gareth. A Modernist dialectic: Stevens and Williams in the poetry of Charles Tomlinson. *See* **18652**.

19200. Rizzo, Sergio. Remembering race: extra-poetical contexts and the racial Other in *The Red Wheelbarrow*. JML (29:1) 2005, 34–54.

19201. Robillard, Valerie. Dismantling the virgin: Modernism and the sacred feminine. *In* (pp. 181–200) **3415**.

19202. Smith, Caleb. Williams's *Pastoral ('When I Was Younger')*. Exp (64:3) 2006, 153–6.

19203. Smith, Joyce Caldwell. Cubist strategies: from Williams's *Red Wheelbarrow* to Caldwell's *Yellow Girl*. *In* (pp. 77–91) **15001**.

19204. Tomlinson, Charles. Objectivism: William Carlos Williams and Basil Bunting. *In* (pp. 133–45) **16284**.

19205. Vescia, Monique Claire. Depression glass: documentary photography and the medium of the camera eye in Charles Reznikoff, Geocrge Oppen, and William Carlos Williams. *See* **17908**.

19206. Wallace, Emily Mitchell. 'Hares and hounds': critical guides to Williams. WCWR (25:2) 2005, 19–38 (review-article).

David Williamson

19207. Gilbert, Helen. Millennial blues; racism, nationalism, and the legacy of empire. *In* (pp. 12–28) **12360**.

Henry Williamson

19208. Gregory, John (ed.). *Stumberleap* and other Devon writings: contributions to the *Daily Express* and *Sunday Express* 1915–1935. Longstanton, Cambs.: Henry Williamson Soc., 2005. pp. x, 170. Rev. by David Macfarlane in HWSJ (42) 2006, 93–4.

19209. Harris, Will. Henry Williamson as educational thinker. HWSJ (42) 2006, 61–6.

19210. Macfarlane, David. Phillip Maddison and the Decca trench gramophone. HWSJ (42) 2006, 67–76.

19211. Matthews, Hugoe. Henry Williamson: a bibliography. Tiverton, Devon: Halsgrove, 2004. pp. 232.

19212. Williamson, Anne. A dual heritage. HWSJ (42) 2006, 5–34. (Williamson's German ancestry.)

Jack Williamson

19213. Nelson, Dale. Is Lewis' Ransom Trilogy indebted to Yank magazine science fiction? *See* **17194**.

Meredith Sue Willis

19214. Maillard, Keith. Gaining the higher ground: an appreciation. AppH (34:4) 2006, 38–45.

19215. Moore, Phyllis Wilson. Meredith Sue Willis: writing her own dispatch. AppH (34:4) 2006, 10–14.

'August Wilson' (Frederick August Kittel) (1945–2005)

19216. Beidler, Philip D. 'King August': August Wilson in his time. MichQR (45:4) 2006, 575–97.

19217. Bryer, Jackson R.; Hartig, Mary C. (eds). Conversations with August Wilson. Jackson; London: Mississippi UP, 2006. pp. xxii, 260. (Literary conversations.)

19218. Elam, Harry J., Jr. The past as present in the drama of August Wilson. (Bibl. 2005, 20238.) Rev. by Keith Clark in ModDr (48:2) 2005, 448–52; by Harvey Young in TJ (58:1) 2006, 150–1; by David Krasner in TRI (31:1) 2006, 103–4; by Sandra G. Shannon in TheatreS (47:1) 2006, 111–14.

19219. Koprince, Susan. Baseball as history and myth in August Wilson's *Fences*. AAR (40:2) 2006, 349–58.

19220. Radavich, David. African American drama from the Midwest. *See* **16489**.

Edmund Wilson

19221. Dabney, Lewis M. Edmund Wilson: a life in literature. (Bibl. 2005, 20246.) Rev. by Ray Robertson in BkCan (34:8) 2005, 18–20; by Leonard Kriegel in SewR (113:4) 2005, 642–7; by Morris Dickstein in TLS, 3 Mar. 2006, 3–4; by Chilton Williamson, Jr, in Chronicles (30:3) 2006, 26–8; by Dean Flower in HR (59:3) 2006, 509–16; by Peter Heinegg in ANCW (194:1) 2006, 25–6.

19222. Dickstein, Morris. The human interest: Edmund Wilson, from bohemian to moral barometer. TLS, 3 Mar. 2006, 3–4 (review-article).

19223. Flower, Dean. Justice to Edmund Wilson. HR (59:3) 2006, 509–16 (review-article).

19224. Kriegel, Leonard. The man of letters in the modern world. SewR (113:4) 2005, 642–7 (review-article). (Arts and letters.)

Guthrie Wilson (1914–1984)

19225. Millen, Julia. Guthrie Wilson: soldier, writer, educator. Wellington, New Zealand: First Edition, 2006. pp. 214.

Lanford Wilson

19226. Tarver, Milton. Entropic commonalities: the affective presence of Tennessee Williams in the drama of Lanford Wilson. *See* **19180**.

Steven Edmund Winduo (b.1964)

19227. Wood, Briar. In spirits' voices: an interview with Steven Winduo. JPW (42:1) 2006, 84–93.

Yvor Winters

19228. Beer, John (introd.). Three letters. *See* **18205**.

19229. Tracy, D. H. Bad ideas. *See* **15356**.

Jeanette Winterson

19230. DeLong, Anne. The cat's cradle: multiple discursive threads in Jeanette Winterson's *Oranges Are Not the Only Fruit*. LIT (17:3/4) 2006, 263–75.

19231. Ellam, Julie. Jeanette Winterson's family values: from *Oranges Are Not the Only Fruit* to *Lighthousekeeping*. CritS (18:2) 2006, 79–88.

19232. Letissier, Georges. Hyphologie et pharologie dans *Lighthousekeeping* de Jeanette Winterson. EtBr (30) 2006, 157–75.

19233. Monti, Silvia. Fisicità e amore nella narrativa di Henry Miller e Jeanette Winterson. *See* **17530**.

19234. Onega, Susana. Writing, creation and the ethics of postmodernist romance in Jeanette Winterson's *Boating for Beginners*. RANAM (39) 2006, 213–27.

19235. Onega Jaen, Susana. Jeanette Winterson. Manchester; New York: Manchester UP, 2006. pp. 256. (Contemporary British novelists.)

19236. Staveley, Helene. 'It's not power, it's sex': Jeanette Winterson's *Power Book* and Nicole Brossard's *Baroque d'aube*. ESCan (30:4) 2004, 120–38.

Tim Winton

19237. O'Reilly, Nathanael. Rejecting and perpetuating the anti-suburban tradition: representations of the suburbs in *The Tax Inspector*, *Johnno*, and *Cloudstreet*. *See* **15034**.

Owen Wister

19238. Francus, Marilyn. Calamity Jane? Austen and Owen Wister's *The Virginian*. Persuasions (27) 2005, 219–33.

19239. Green, Paul. A history of television's *The Virginian*, 1962–1971. Foreword by Frank Price. Jefferson, NC; London: McFarland, 2006. pp. x, 290.

19240. Hovey, Kenneth Alan. Wister's 'life among the lowly' and anglocentrism. WAL (39:4) 2005, 395–419.

P. G. Wodehouse

19241. Ramsay, Allan. The green baize door: social identity in Wodehouse: part two. ContRev (286:1668) 2005, 39–46. (*Adds to* bibl. 2004, 20266.)

19242. Taves, Brian. P. G. Wodehouse and Hollywood: screenwriting, satires, and adaptations. Foreword by Richard Briers. Jefferson, NC; London: McFarland, 2006. pp. 220.

19243. White, Laura Mooneyham. Another response to *'Across the pale parabola of joy': Wodehouse Parodist*. Connotations (14:1–3) 2004/05, 177–82. (*Response to* bibl. 2005, 20274.)

George C. Wolfe

19244. Vélez, Andrew. George C. Wolfe. *In* (pp. 56–9) **12245**.

Swain Wolfe

19245. Wolfe, Swain. The boy who invented skiing: a memoir. Basingstoke: Macmillan; New York: St Martin's Press, 2006. pp. 287.

Tom Wolfe (b.1931)

19246. Weingarten, Marc. The gang that wouldn't write straight: Wolfe, Thompson, Didion, and the New Journalism revolution. *See* **15501**.

Tobias Wolff

19247. O'Gorman, Farrell. Tobias Wolff's *Back in the World*: American dreamers, American desert, saving word. CritW (48:1) 2006, 71–89.

Jade Snow Wong

19248. Madsen, Deborah L. Chinese American writers of the real and the fake: authenticity and the twin traditions of life writing. *See* **13949**.

19249. —— The Oriental/Occidental dynamic in Chinese American life writing: Pardee Lowe and Jade Snow Wong. *See* **13950**.

George Woodcock

19250. Antliff, Mark; Antliff, Allan (introds). To George Woodcock. *See* **18202**.

Margaret L. (Margaret Louisa) Woods (1856–1945)

19251. Stanford, Donald E. A critical study of the works of four British writers: Margaret Louisa Woods (1856–1945), Mary Coleridge (1861–1907), Sir Henry Newbolt (1862–1938), R. C. Trevelyan (1872–1951). Ed. by R. W. Crump. *See* **9497**.

Leonard Woolf

19252. Glendinning, Victoria. Leonard Woolf. New York: Simon & Schuster, 2006. pp. 464. Rev. by Mark Bostridge in TLS, 20 Oct. 2006, 24; by Claire Messud in NYTB, 10 Dec. 2006, 16.

19253. Gooneratne, Yasmine (ed.). *The Village in the Jungle*: revised and annotated in accordance with the original manuscript. Lewiston, NY; Lampeter: Mellen Press, 2004. pp. xv, 273. (Studies in British literature, 93.)

19254. Ondaatje, Christopher. Woolf in Ceylon: an imperial journey in the shadow of Leonard Woolf, 1904–1911. (Bibl. 2005, 20295.) Rev. by Nick Smith in BkCan (34:7) 2005, 13–15; by Kim A. Wagner in TLS, 31 Mar. 2006, 27.

19255. Reynier, Christine. Image as text in Leonard Woolf's *Quack, Quack in Politics*. EtBr (31) 2006, 41–54.

19256. Roy, Anindyo. Civility and empire: literature and culture in British India, 1822–1922. *See* **8712**.

Virginia Woolf

19257. Alley, Henry. *Mrs Dalloway* and three of its contemporary children. PLL (42:4) 2006, 401–19.

19258. Alwes, Karla. Virginia Woolf and the modern epic. *In* (pp. 55–68) **3395**.

19259. ANDRÉS, ISABEL M. Is it in his feet? The role of cripple and dismemberment in *Jacob's Room*. VWM (70) 2006, 26–7.

19260. ANDRINGA, ELS. Penetrating the Dutch polysystem: the reception of Virginia Woolf, 1920–2000. PT (27:3) 2006, 501–68.

19261. BALDT, ERIKA. Abjection as deviance in *Mrs Dalloway*. VWM (70) 2006, 13–15.

19262. BENZEL, KATHRYN N.; HOBERMAN, RUTH (eds). Trespassing boundaries: Virginia Woolf's short fiction. (Bibl. 2005, 20308.) Rev. by Kathryn Simpson in WSA (12) 2006, 273–8.

19263. BENZIMAN, GALIA. 'Dispersed are we': mirroring and national identity in Virginia Woolf's *Between the Acts*. JNT (36:1) 2006, 53–71.

19264. BESNAULT-LEVITA, ANNE. *'Perhaps silence is better'*: de quelques paradoxes du silence littéraire. EtBr (30) 2006, 13–26.

19265. BLACK, NAOMI. Virginia Woolf as feminist. (Bibl. 2005, 20313.) Rev. by Maria DiBattista in ELT (49:1) 2006, 85–8.

19266. BRIGGS, JULIA. Virginia Woolf: an inner life. (Bibl. 2005, 20317.) Rev. by Stephen Wade in ContRev (288:1680) 2006, 109–10; by Helen Southworth in WSA (12) 2006, 240–2.

19267. CAUGHIE, PAMELA L. Virginia Woolf: *To the Lighthouse*. *In* (pp. 486–98) **11788**.

19268. CHAPMAN, WAYNE K. (ed.). Virginia Woolf's illnesses. By Douglass W. Orr. (Bibl. 2005, 20324.) Rev. by Vara Neverow in VWM (69) 2006, 17–18.

19269. CLARKE, STUART N. (ed.). Translations from the Russian. Southport, Lancs.: Virginia Woolf Soc. of Great Britain, 2006. pp. xxix, 290. Rev. by Lisa Shahriari in TLS, 20 Oct. 2006, 33.

19270. COUSTILLAS, PIERRE. Where 'Affable Hawk' stepped in; or, How Desmond MacCarthy roamed on Gissing's trail for over three decades. *See* **10185**.

19271. CRAWFORD, NICOLAS. Orientalizing Elizabeth: empire and deviancy in *Mrs Dalloway*. VWM (70) 2006, 20–6.

19272. CURTIS, ANTHONY. Virginia Woolf: Bloomsbury & beyond. London: Haus, 2006. pp. 250. Rev. by Julia Briggs in TLS, 20 Oct. 2006, 25.

19273. DALGARNO, EMILY. Virginia Woolf: translation and 'iterability'. YES (36:1) 2006, 145–56.

19274. DAVISON, SARAH. Catching Mrs Brown: Max Beerbohm's influence on Virginia Woolf's *Mr Bennett and Mrs Brown*. NQ (53:3) 2006, 353–5.

19275. DE GAY, JANE. Virginia Woolf's novels and the literary past. Edinburgh: Edinburgh UP, 2006. pp. viii, 231.

19276. DE KEUKELAERE, SIMON. What is deviated transcendency? Woolf's *The Waves* as a textbook case. Contagion (12/13) 2006, 195–218.

19277. DEUTSCH, HELEN. Had I been born a hero. *See* **7424**.

19278. DOYLE, LAURA. Transnational history at our backs: a long view of Larsen, Woolf, and queer racial subjectivity in Atlantic Modernism. *See* **17012**.

19279. FERNALD, ANNE E. Virginia Woolf: feminism and the reader. Basingstoke; New York: Palgrave Macmillan, 2006. pp. xii, 223.

19280. Ferrante, Allyson Salinger. The feminist fantastic: uncovering what was hidden within. VWM (70) 2006, 27–8.

19281. Fluet, Lisa. Hit-man Modernism. *In* (pp. 269–97) **12024**.

19282. Froula, Christine. Virginia Woolf and the Bloomsbury avant-garde: war, civilization, modernity. (Bibl. 2005, 20354.) Rev. by Helen Southworth in VWM (68) 2005/06, 22–3; by Mark Hussey in MFS (52:3) 2006, 742–5.

19283. Fulton, Lorie Watkins. 'A direction of one's own': alienation in *Mrs Dalloway* and *Sula*. AAR (40:1) 2006, 67–77.

19284. Fusini, Nadia. Possiedo la mia anima: il segreto di Virginia Woolf. Milan: Mondadori, 2006. pp. 352. (Scrittori italiani e stranieri.) Rev. by Maria Nadotti in Indice (2006:6) 18.

19285. Glitz, Rudolph. Young Rose Pargiter's eminently Victorian adventure. VWM (68) 2005/06, 10–15.

19286. Goldman, Jane. The Cambridge introduction to Virginia Woolf. Cambridge; New York: CUP, 2006. pp. xi, 157. (Cambridge introductions to literature.)

19287. Gruber, Ruth. Virginia Woolf: the will to create as a woman. New York: Carroll & Graf, 2005. pp. x, 176. Rev. by Jean Mills in VWM (69) 2006, 14–15; by Judy Suh in WSA (12) 2006, 242–6.

19288. Gualtieri, Elena. From *A Room with a View* to the Fascist spectacle: Bloomsbury in Italy. *See* **15958**.

19289. Hall, Sarah M. Before Leonard: the early suitors of Virginia Woolf. London; Chester Springs, PA: Owen, 2006. pp. 304, (plates) 16.

19290. Hancock, Kami A. Deviant snapshots: re-visiting *Jacob's Room*. VWM (70) 2006, 10–11.

19291. Henderson, Diana E. Collaborations with the past: reshaping Shakespeare across time and media. *See* **5324**.

19292. Horsman, Alan. 'A bite medicinally': Leslie Stephen and Virginia Woolf's eighteenth-century essays. *In* (pp. 226–34) **8374**.

19293. Hsieh, Lili. The other side of the picture: the politics of affect in Virginia Woolf's *Three Guineas*. JNT (36:1) 2006, 20–52.

19294. Humm, Maggie. Snapshots of Bloomsbury: the private lives of Virginia Woolf and Vanessa Bell. London: Tate Gallery, 2006. pp. x, 266. Rev. by Lindsay Duguid in TLS, 17 Mar. 2006, 11; by Thaine Stearns in VWM (70) 2006, 38.

19295. Jump, Harriet Devine. 'One cry for justice': Virginia Woolf reads Mary Wollstonecraft. *In* (pp. 41–60) **13735**.

19296. Klitgård, Ida. On the horizon: a poetics of the sublime in Virginia Woolf's *The Waves*. (Bibl. 2004, 20354.) Rev. by Jessica Fisher in WSA (12) 2006, 235–9.

19297. Krouse, Tonya. Sexual deviancy in *Mrs Dalloway*: the case of Septimus Smith. VWM (70) 2006, 15–16.

19298. Kukil, Karen V. (ed.). Woolf in the real world: selected papers from the Thirteenth International Conference on Virginia Woolf, Smith College, Northampton, Massachusetts, 5–8 June 2003. Clemson, SC: Clemson

Univ. Digital Press, 2005. pp. x, 222. Rev. by J. J. Wilson in VWM (70) 2006, 36–7.

19299. Lackey, Michael. The literary Modernist assault on philosophy. *See* **17046**.

19300. Landon, Lana Hartman; Smith, Laurel. Early works by modern women writers: Woolf, Bowen, Mansfield, Cather, and Stein. Lewiston, NY; Lampeter: Mellen Press, 2006. pp. vi, 298.

19301. Lanone, Catherine. Art and the 'second darkness'. CVE (62) 2005, 109–20.

19302. Le Bail, Anne-Sophie. *'I saw them as solid globes of crystal'*: modélisation du réel dans quelques nouvelles de Virginia Woolf. EtBr (30) 2006, 27–39.

19303. Lilienfeld, Jane. 'To have the reader work *with* the author': the circulation of knowledge in Virginia Woolf's *To the Lighthouse* and Toni Morrison's *Jazz*. MFS (52:1) 2006, 42–65.

19304. Lorentzen, Eric G. Foucault's normalizing judgment, deviancy and Woolf's *Mrs Dalloway*. VWM (70) 2006, 11–12.

19305. Louvel, Liliane. Vanessa Bell and Virginia Woolf: an artist and a critic? CVE (62) 2005, 53–67.

19306. Lowe, Gill. A brief history of the *Hyde Park Gate News*, the family newspaper of the Stephen children. VWM (68) 2005/06, 15–17.

19307. —— (ed.). *Hyde Park Gate News*: the Stephen family newspaper. (Bibl. 2005, 20383.) Rev. by Dinah Birch in TLS, 10 Feb. 2006, 3–4.

19308. McQuade, Molly. Woolf's verb impersonators (and other deviants). VWM (70) 2006, 6.

19309. Maier, Sarah E. Symbolist Salomés and the dance of Dionysus. *See* **11614**.

19310. Metz, Walter. Woody's Melindas and Todd's stories: complex film narratives in the light of literary Modernism. *See* **19713**.

19311. Mills, Jean. The unbounded whole: Harrisonian ritual structures in Virginia Woolf's *Night and Day*. VWM (69) 2006, 6–7.

19312. Monod, Sylvère (ed. and trans.). Middlemarch. Preface by Virginia Woolf. *See* **10041**.

19313. Paccaud-Huguet, Josiane. The moment of being & the voice of melancholy in Virginia Woolf's *The Waves*. EREA (4:1) 2006, 28–36.

19314. Palusci, Oriana. *'The London Blitz'*: uno sguardo di genere. *In* (pp. 281–97) **7343**.

19315. Park, Sowon S. Suffrage and Virginia Woolf: 'the mass behind the single voice'. RES (56:223) 2005, 119–34.

19316. Parrott, Jennifer. 'Slaves of the imagination': Sir Walter Scott in the works of Virginia Woolf. VWM (70) 2006, 32–4.

19317. Pierce, David. Joyce and company. *See* **16752**.

19318. Porter, Ryan. Symbols of the nation in *Mrs Dalloway*. VWM (70) 2006, 18–20.

19319. Raschke, Debrah. Modernism, metaphysics, and sexuality. *See* **15301**.

19320. Reviron, Floriane. Blooomsbury and the cinema: practice and theory of a new form of expression. CVE (62) 2005, 69–91.

19321. Reynier, Christine. Image as text in Leonard Woolf's *Quack, Quack in Politics*. *See* **19255**.

19322. Ronchetti, Ann. The artist, society, and sexuality in Virginia Woolf's novels. (Bibl. 2004, 20400.) Rev. by Andrea P. Zemgulys in WSA (12) 2006, 290–2.

19323. Rosen, Jody R. Deviation and acceleration: time in the story and narrative of *Orlando*. VWM (70) 2006, 29–30.

19324. Rosenbaum, S. P. Virginia Woolf and Vanessa Bell: memoirs of Julian. CVE (62) 2005, 167–203.

19325. Rosner, Victoria. Modernism and the architecture of private life. (Bibl. 2005, 20409.) Rev. by Sally Greene in VWM (69) 2006, 19; by Christopher Reed in WSA (12) 2006, 231–4.

19326. Rumbarger, Lee. Housekeeping: women Modernists' writings on war and home. WS (35:1) 2006, 1–15.

19327. Saloman, Randi. 'Charles Lamb is dead': Arnold Bennett's *Journalism for Women* and *A Room of One's Own*. VWM (68) 2005/06, 10.

19328. Sanchez Cuervo, Margarita Esther. Split thought: masculine *vs* feminine in Woolf's essays. VWM (70) 2006, 6–8.

19329. Sarsfield, Rachel. From the chrysalis to the display case: the butterfly's 'voyage out' in Virginia Woolf. *In* (pp. 87–111) **3203**.

19330. Shail, Andrew. 'She looks just like one of we-all': British cinema culture and the origins of Woolf's*Orlando*. CritQ (48:2) 2006, 45–76.

19331. Skrbic, Nena. Wild outbursts of freedom: reading Virginia Woolf's short fiction. (Bibl. 2005, 20428.) Rev. by Alice Staveley in WSA (12) 2006, 250–4.

19332. Smith, Amy. Bad religion: the irrational in *Mrs Dalloway*. VWM (70) 2006, 17–18.

19333. Son, Youngjoo. Here and now: the politics of social space in D. H. Lawrence and Virginia Woolf. *See* **17057**.

19334. Southworth, Helen. The intersecting realities and fictions of Virginia Woolf and Colette. (Bibl. 2005, 20431.) Rev. by Patricia Laurence in VWM (68) 2005/06, 20–2; by Kathryn Laing in WSA (12) 2006, 286–9.

19335. Stelmach, Kathryn. From text to tableau: ekphrastic enchantment in *Mrs Dalloway* and *To the Lighthouse*. StudN (38:3) 2006, 304–26.

19336. Sullivan, Melissa. 'All art, all waifs, & strays', and the English great house in *Between the Acts*. VWM (69) 2006, 8–13.

19337. Szasz, Thomas. 'My madness saved me': the madness and marriage of Virginia Woolf. New Brunswick, NJ: Transaction, 2006. pp. xv, 154.

19338. Taylor, Chloë. Kristevan themes in Virginia Woolf's *The Waves*. JML (29:3) 2006, 57–77.

19339. Tyler, Lisa. The loss of roses: mother–daughter myth and relationships between women in *Mrs Dalloway*. WVUPP (52) 2005, 60–9.

19340. Utell, Janine. Leaving her father's house: Sackville-West's *Saint Joan of Arc* and Woolf's *Three Guineas*. *See* **18397**.

19341. Uzundemir, Özlem. Challenging gender roles through narrative techniques: Virginia Woolf's *To the Lighthouse*. VWM (70) 2006, 8–10.

19342. Veyu, Ernest L. Estrangement and non-conformism: the case of Lily Briscoe. VWM (70) 2006, 12–13.

19343. Villa, Sara. Woolf's deviant canon. VWM (70) 2006, 34–5.

19344. Walkowitz, Rebecca L. Virginia Woolf's evasion: critical cosmopolitanism and British Modernism. *In* (pp. 119–44) **12024**.

19345. Wallace, David. Periodizing women: Mary Ward (1585–1645) and the premodern canon. *See* **7165**.

19346. Weinstein, Arnold. Recovering your story: Proust, Joyce, Woolf, Faulkner, Morrison. *See* **16787**.

19347. Westman, Karin E. 'For her generation the newspaper was a book': media, mediation, and oscillation in Virginia Woolf's *Between the Acts*. JML (29:2) 2006, 1–18.

19348. Whitworth, Michael H. Virginia Woolf. (Bibl. 2005, 20439.) Rev. by Stephen Wade in ContRev (288:1681) 2006, 243–5; by Meg Albrinck in VWM (70) 2006, 37–8; by Urmila Seshagiri in WSA (12) 2006, 278–82.

19349. Williams, Lisa. Letters to Virginia Woolf. Lanham, MD: Hamilton, 2005. pp. 80. Rev. by Sally A. Jacobsen in VWM (70) 2006, 42.

19350. Yates, Andrea L. Deviancy as a way of life: *The Years* as critique. VWM (70) 2006, 30–2.

Cornell Woolrich (1903–1968)

19351. Renzi, Thomas C. Cornell Woolrich: from pulp *noir* to *film noir*. Jefferson, NC; London: McFarland, 2006. pp. viii, 371.

Baron Wormser

19352. Wormser, Baron. The road washes out in spring: a poet's memoir of living off the grid. Hanover, NH; London: UP of New England, 2006. pp. 199.

Herman Wouk

19353. Brown, Kathleen A. 'Vestments of civil life' in *Caine Mutiny* and *Attack*. *See* **12811**.

C. D. (Carolyn D.) Wright (b.1949)

19354. Wright, C. D. Cooling time: an American poetry vigil. Port Townsend, WA: Copper Canyon Press, 2005. pp. 108. Rev. by Jeff Gundy in GaR (60:2) 2006, 423–33.

Charles Wright (b.1935)

19355. Francini, Antonella. Charles Wright: breve storia dell'ombra. PoesiaM (206) 2006, 2–13.

19356. Gardner, Thomas. A door ajar: contemporary writers and Emily Dickinson. *See* **9865**.

19357. GIANNELLI, ADAM (ed.). High lonesome: on the poetry of Charles Wright. Oberlin, OH: Oberlin College Press, 2006. pp. xxiii, 388. Rev. by Fred Chappell in AppH (34:4) 2006, 80–6.

19358. HAHN, ROBERT. The mockingbird's chops: Charles Wright in Italian. Parnassus (29:1/2) 2006, 349–69.

Doug Wright

19359. SCHIAVI, MICHAEL R. The tease of truth: seduction, verisimilitude (?), and spectatorship in *I Am My Own Wife*. TJ (58:2) 2006, 195–220.

19360. STANESCU, SAVIANA. Doug Wright: 'we love to see power subverted'. TDR (50:3) 2006, 100–7.

Harold Bell Wright

19361. SMITH, ERIN A. Melodrama, popular religion, and literary value: the case of Harold Bell Wright. AmLH (17:2) 2005, 217–43.

James Arlington Wright (b.1927)

19362. BLY, ROBERT; WRIGHT, ANNE (eds). Selected poems. New York: Farrar, Straus, & Giroux, 2005. pp. xxxiii, 138. Rev. by Peter Campion in Parnassus (29:1/2) 2006, 272–91.

19363. CAMPION, PETER. 'I have a secret with myself': James Wright's Classicism. Parnassus (29:1/2) 2006, 272–91 (review-article).

19364. CORBETT, WILLIAM. Misjudging James Wright. Brick (77) 2006, 68–71.

19365. FLAJŠAŘ, JIRÍ. Wright's *Today I Was Happy, So I Made This Poem*. Exp (64:2) 2006, 97–100.

19366. KITCHEN, JUDITH. The letter of the life. *See* **17272**.

19367. MASON, DAVID. The inner drama of James Wright. HR (58:4) 2006, 667–74 (review-article).

19368. VAN NESS, GORDON. 'The fiercest hearts are in love with a wild perfection': the James Dickey/James Wright correspondence. *See* **15496**.

19369. WRIGHT, ANNE; MALEY, SAUNDRA ROSE (eds); BLUNK, JONATHAN (asst ed.). A wild perfection: the selected letters of James Wright. (Bibl. 2005, 20454.) Rev. by Peter Campion in Parnassus (29:1/2) 2006, 272–91; by David Mason in HR (58:4) 2006, 667–74; by Shawn Holliday in AppH (34:2) 2006, 94–6; by Judith Kitchen in GaR (60:3/4) 2006, 760–74.

Judith Wright

19370. CLARK, GARY. The two threads of a life: Judith Wright, the environment and Aboriginality. Antipodes (20:2) 2006, 155–62.

19371. GALLAGHER, KATHERINE. Towards reconciliation: inspiration and leadership – Oodgeroo of the Tribe Noonuccal (1920–1993) and Judith Wright (1915–2000). Agenda (41:1/2) 2005, 37–48.

19372. MCCANN, A. L. The literature of extinction. Meanjin (65:1) 2006, 48–54.

Richard Wright (1908–1960)

19373. Allred, Jeff. From eye to we: Richard Wright's *12 Million Black Voices*, documentary, and pedagogy. AL (78:3) 2006, 549–83.

19374. Binggeli, Elizabeth. Burbanking bigger and Bette the bitch. AAR (40:3) 2006, 475–92.

19375. Chander, Harish. The politics of exclusion in *A Passage to India* and *Native Son*. *See* **15952**.

19376. Demirtürk, E. Lâle. Reinscribing the racial subject in 'public transcript': Richard Wright's *Black Boy* (*American Hunger*). A/B (20:2) 2005, 268–81.

19377. Ellis, Aimé J. 'Boys in the hood': Black male community in Richard Wright's *Native Son*. Callaloo (29:1) 2006, 182–201.

19378. Hicks, Scott. W. E. B. Du Bois, Booker T. Washington, and Richard Wright: toward an ecocriticism of color. *See* **15574**.

19379. Jacobs, Tom. Poeticizing the political image: Caldwell, Bourke-White, and the recasting of phototextual expression. *In* (pp. 92–113) **15001**.

19380. JanMohamed, Abdul R. The death-bound-subject: Richard Wright's archaeology of death. (Bibl. 2005, 20465.) Rev. by Jeffrey Atteberry in MFS (52:3) 2006, 731–4; by Rolland Murray in Novel (39:2) 2006, 299–302.

19381. Johns, Gillian. Reading for the comic and the tragic in modern Black fiction; or, Reflections on Richard Wright's change of heart from *Lawd Today!* to *Native Son*. CLAJ (49:3) 2006, 249–82.

19382. Kinnamon, Keneth. Richard Wright: an annotated bibliography of criticism and commentary, 1983–2003. Jefferson, NC; London: McFarland, 2005. pp. 493.

19383. Leiter, Andrew B. Sexual degeneracy and the anti-lynching tradition in Erskine Caldwell's *Trouble in July*. *In* (pp. 203–22) **15001**.

19384. Mullen, Bill V. Richard Wright: *Native Son*. *In* (pp. 499–506) **11788**.

19385. Relyea, Sarah. Outsider citizens: the remaking of postwar identity in Wright, Beauvoir, and Baldwin. *See* **14557**.

19386. Tan, Huijuan. James Baldwin's literary patricide and African American literature turn. *See* **14560**.

19387. Wallach, Jennifer Jensen. Building a bridge of words: the literary autobiography as historical source material. *See* **17717**.

Ronald Wright (b.1948)

19388. Smith, Eric D. A voyage to future pasts: the vengeance of other time in Ronald Wright's *A Scientific Romance*. CritW (48:1) 2006, 58–70.

Elinor Wylie

19389. Hively, Evelyn Helmick (ed.). Selected works of Elinor Wylie. Kent, OH; London: Kent State UP, 2005. pp. xvi, 238. Rev. by Si Wakesberg in BRev (26:1) 2006, 25.

19390. Wakesberg, Si. The sound of Elinor Wylie's poetry. BRev (26:1) 2006, 25 (review-article).

Philip Wylie

19391. Schwartz, Richard A. Family, gender, and society in 1950s American fiction of nuclear apocalypse: *Shadow on the Hearth*, *Tomorrow!*, *The Last Day*, and *Alas, Babylon*. JAC (29:4) 2006, 406–24.

Hisaye Yamamoto

19392. Izzo, Donatella. Le forme della violenza: il modernismo politico di Hisaye Yamamoto. *In* (pp. 125–64) **11954**.

Lois-Ann Yamanaka (b.1961)

19393. Cheung, Floyd. The language of mourning in Lois-Ann Yamanaka's *Blu's Hanging*. CLAJ (49:3) 2006, 305–12.

19394. Chiang, Mark. Autonomy and representation: aesthetics and the crisis of Asian American cultural politics in the controversy over *Blu's Hanging*. *In* (pp. 17–34) **11849**.

19395. Inserra, Incoronata. Spreading traditions: Lois-Ann Yamanaka's *Bildungsroman*. *In* (pp. 197–226) **11955**.

19396. Luangphinith, Seri. Homeward bound: settler aesthetics in Hawai'i's literature. TSLL (48:1) 2006, 54–78.

19397. Russell, Emily. Locating cure: leprosy and Lois-Ann Yamanaka's *Blu's Hanging*. MELUS (31:1) 2006, 53–80.

19398. Suzuki, Erin. Consuming desires: melancholia and consumption in *Blu's Hanging*. MELUS (31:1) 2006, 35–52.

19399. Vastolo, Manuela. '*The real and the fake*': autobiografia, fiction e rappresentatività. *In* (pp. 36–59) **11954**.

Karen Tei Yamashita (b.1951)

19400. Hsu, Ruth Y. The cartography of justice and truthful refractions in Karen Tei Yamashita's *Tropic of Orange*. *In* (pp. 75–99) **11995**.

Dori Jones Yang

19401. Chiu, Monica. The cultural production of Asian American young adults in the novels of Marie G. Lee, An Na, and Doris (*sic*) Jones Yang. *See* **17095**.

Arthur Yap (b.1943)

19402. Goh, Robbie B. H. Imagining the nation: the role of Singapore poetry in English in 'emergent nationalism'. *See* **18765**.

John Yau

19403. Mar, Christina. The language of ethnicity: John Yau's poetry and the ethnic/aesthetic divide. *In* (pp. 70–85) **11849**.

V. M. (Victor M.) Yeates (1897–1934)

19404. Ridler, Jason S. Depleting humanity. WLA (18:1/2) 2006, 222–40.

Jack B. Yeats (1871–1957)

19405. Lloyd, David. Republics of difference: Yeats, MacGreevy, Beckett. FDR (1) 2005, 43–69.

19406. Wilson, James Matthew. Thomas MacGreevy reads T. S. Eliot and Jack B. Yeats: making Modernism Catholic. *See* **15722**.

W. B. Yeats

19407. Allison, Jonathan. War, passive suffering, and the poet. SewR (114:2) 2006, 207–19.

19408. Bacigalupo, Massimo. 'Forth on the godly sea': the Mediterranean in Pound, Yeats and Stevens. *In* (pp. 31–49) **12076**.

19409. Balinisteanu, Tudor. The spectator's pleasure: Yeats's *Long-Legged Fly*. IFR (32:1/2) 2005, 11–20.

19410. Bell, Vereen M. Yeats and the logic of formalism. Columbia; London: Missouri UP, 2006. pp. ix, 201.

19411. Berryman, John. A visit to Ezra Pound in St Elizabeth's Hospital, 1948. *See* **18078**.

19412. Boitani, Piero; Johnson, Anthony (eds). L'opera poetica. Milan: Mondadori, 2005. pp. clxii, 1652. (I Meridiani.)

19413. Bullen, J. B. W. B. Yeats, Byzantium and the Mediterranean. *In* (pp. 17–30) **12076**.

19414. Chapman, Wayne K. Joyce and Yeats: Easter 1916 and the Great War. *See* **16670**.

19415. Doggett, Rob. Deep-rooted things: empire and nation in the poetry and drama of William Butler Yeats. Notre Dame, IN: Notre Dame UP, 2006. pp. xi, 188.

19416. Dwan, David. Abstract hatred: Yeats and the counter-revolutionary paradigm. LitH (15:1) 2006, 18–36.

19417. Gould, Warwick; Toomey, Deirdre (eds). Mythologies. (Bibl. 2005, 20496.) Rev. by Peter McDonald in TLS, 21 Apr. 2006, 3–4.

19418. Harper, Lisa. Courting the muse: Dorothy Wellesley and W. B. Yeats. *In* (pp. 211–28) **3405**.

19419. Harper, Margaret Mills. Wisdom of two: the spiritual and literary collaboration of George and W. B. Yeats. Oxford; New York: OUP, 2006. pp. xii, 382.

19420. Hickman, Miranda B. The geometry of Modernism: the Vorticist idiom in Lewis, Pound, H.D., and Yeats. *See* **17215**.

19421. Howard, Ben. Audacious Ireland. *See* **15045**.

19422. Ingelbien, Raphael. Symbolism at the periphery: Yeats, Maeterlinck, and cultural nationalism. CLS (42:3) 2005, 183–204.

19423. Kinsella, Thomas. Readings in poetry. *See* **6093**.

19424. Lapisardi, Frederick S. Staging Yeats in the twenty-first century: a reception history. Lewiston, NY; Lampeter: Mellen Press, 2006. pp. x, 387, (plates) 13.

19425. Larrissy, Edward. W. B. Yeats: *The Tower* (1928). *In* (pp. 507–15) **11788**.

19426. McDonald, Peter. Ghosts abounding: W. B. Yeats: unable to leave the dead alone. TLS, 21 Apr. 2006, 3–4 (review-article).

19427. Macrae, Alasdair. Professor Derry Jeffares: an appreciation. *See* **14210**.

19428. Markey, Anne. The discovery of Irish folklore. *See* **9667**.

19429. Moran, James. Staging the Easter Rising: 1916 as theatre. *See* **12338**.

19430. Nolan, Emer. Modernism and the Irish Revival. *In* (pp. 157–72) **11829**.

19431. O'Brien, Eugene. Rereading the canon: towards a literary redefinition of Irishness. *In* (pp. 113–33) **12189**.

19432. O'Connor, Laura. Haunted English: the Celtic Fringe, the British Empire, and de-anglicization. Baltimore, MD; London: Johns Hopkins UP, 2006. pp. xviii, 240.

19433. O'Donoghue, Bernard. The reality of courtly love. *In* (pp. 7–24) **3836**.

19434. O'Gorman, Francis. Dickens and Yeats's *The Municipal Gallery Revisited*. NQ (53:3) 2006, 355–6.

19435. O'Hara, Daniel T. Bringing out the terror: James Purdy and the culture of vision. *See* **18164**.

19436. O'Neill, Michael. 'The all-sustaining air': Yeats, Stevens, Rich, Bishop – responses to Romantic poetry. *In* (pp. 143–62) **13735**.

19437. —— (ed.). A Routledge literary sourcebook on the poems of W. B. Yeats. (Bibl. 2004, 20509.) Rev. by Jacqueline Genet in EA (59:2) 2006, 247–8.

19438. Paterson, Adrian. 'An imagined music': Yeats, music and the Irish tradition. *In* (pp. 135–69) **12189**.

19439. Pilný, Ondřej. A 'home of ancient idealism'? W. B. Yeats and the Irish Dramatic Movement. LittPr (16:31) 2006, 3–20.

19440. Pinsky, Robert. Peace, poetry and negation. Raritan (26:1) 2006, 171–80.

19441. Russell, Richard. Talking with ghosts of Irish playwrights past: Marina Carr's *By the Bog of Cats … See* **15046**.

19442. Russell, Richard Rankin. Reading John McGahern's *The Barracks* through Yeats's *Down by the Salley Gardens*. *See* **17341**.

19443. —— The Yeatsian refrain in Paul Muldoon's *Moy Sand and Gravel*. *See* **17669**.

19444. Ryan, Rory. The full or the dark: an analysis of phases 1 & 15 in Yeats's system. YER (23:2) 2006, 2–20.

19445. Santesso, Aaron. *Responsibilities*: H.D. and Yeats. *See* **15542**.

19446. Sayers, William. Gat-toothed Alysoun, gaptoothed Kathleen: sovereignty and dentition. *See* **16766**.

19447. Singh, Sukhbir. Echoes of Shakespeare's Sonnet 116 in Yeats's *The Indian to His Love*. NCL (36:3) 2006, 6–8.

19448. Smith, Peter J. Rome's disgrace: the politics of rape in Shakespeare's *Lucrece*. *See* **6059**.

19449. Spangler, Matthew. 'Haunted to the edge of trance': performance and orality in the early poems of W. B. Yeats. NewHR (10:2) 2006, 140–56.

19450. Tracy, D. H. Bad ideas. *See* **15356**.

19451. Woudhuysen, H. R. Last words from the rhymers. TLS, 1 Dec. 2006, 33.

Laurence Yep

19452. Woo, Celestine. Bicultural world creation: Laurence Yep, Cynthia Kadohata, and Asian American fantasy. *In* (pp. 173–86) **11849**.

19453. —— Toward a poetics of Asian American fantasy: Laurence Yep's construction of a bicultural mythology. LU (30:2) 2006, 250–64.

19454. YEP, LAURENCE. Paying with shadows. LU (30:2) 2006, 157–67. (Dreams and imagination.)

Frank Yerby

19455. JARRETT, GENE ANDREW. 'For endless generations': myth, dynasty, and Frank Yerby's *The Foxes of Harrow*. SoLJ (39:1) 2006, 54–70.

Anzia Yezierska

19456. COKLIN, LJILJANA. Between the Orient and the ghetto: a modern immigrant woman in Anzia Yezierska's *Salome of the Tenements*. Frontiers (27:2) 2006, 136–61.

19457. JIROUSEK, LORI. Ethnics and ethnographers: Zora Neale Hurston and Anzia Yezierska. *See* **16526**.

Emily Hilda Young (Mrs Daniell)

19458. BRIGANTI, CHIARA; MEZEI, KATHY. Domestic Modernism, the interwar novel, and E. H. Young. *See* **13432**.

Rafi Zabor

19459. ZABOR, RAFI. I, Wabenzi: a souvenir: vol. 1, Aporia. New York: Farrar, Straus, & Giroux, 2005. pp. 480.

Adam Zagajewski (b.1945)

19460. HIRSCH, EDWARD; ZAGAJEWSKI, ADAM. Edward Hirsch and Adam Zagajewski: a conversation. *See* **16435**.

Roger Zelazny

19461. NIZALOWSKI, JOHN. An interview with Roger Zelazny. NYRSF (18:7) 2006, 1, 6–7.

Musaemura Zimunya

19462. DUBE, BEVELYN. Re-imagining the prostitute in society: a critique of the male writer's perspective in Zimbabwean literature. *In* (pp. 45–59) **12216**.

Zitkala-Ša (Gertrude Bonnin) (1876–1938)

19463. DEROSA, ROBIN. Critical tricksters: race, theory, and *Old Indian Legends*. *In* (pp. 167–95) **2149**.

19464. IRVIN, AMANDA. Out-of-body experiences in the texts of Zitkala-Ša and Gertrude Bonnin. PemM (38) 2006, 80–6.

19465. RIFKIN, MARK. Romancing kinship: a queer reading of Indian education and Zitkala-Ša's *American Indian Stories*. GLQ (12:1) 2006, 27–59.

19466. STROMBERG, ERNEST. Resistance and mediation: the rhetoric of irony in Indian boarding-school narratives by Francis La Flesche and Zitkala-Ša. *In* (pp. 95–109) **2149**.

Pamela Zoline (b.1941)

19467. PAPKE, MARY E. A space of her own: Pamela Zoline's *The Heat Death of the Universe*. *In* (pp. 144–59) **13537**.

Louis Zukofsky

19468. BERNSTEIN, CHARLES. Louis Zukofsky: an introduction. FLS (118) 2006, 113–21.

19469. GOLSTON, MICHAEL. Petalbent devils: Louis Zukofsky, Lorine Niedecker, and the Surrealist praying mantis. Mod/Mod (13:2) 2006, 325–47.

19470. SCROGGINS, MARK (introd.). To Louis Zukofsky. *See* **18214**.

19471. VAN HULLE, DIRK. Growth and the grid: organic *vs* constructivist conceptions of poetry. *See* **15720**.

Jan Zwicky (b.1955)

19472. FURLANI, ANDRE. Jan Zwicky: lyric philosophy lyric. CanL (191) 2006, 48–68.

TWENTY-FIRST CENTURY

GENERAL

19473. Anon. Notable Latino writers. *See* **11730**.

19474. Alam, Fakrul (ed.). South Asian writers in English. *See* **11734**.

19475. Aldama, Frederick Luis. Spilling the beans in Chicanolandia: conversations with writers and artists. *See* **11737**.

19476. Atkinson, William. The perils of world literature. *See* **11749**.

19477. Atwood, Margaret. Moving targets: selected critical prose, 1982–2004. *See* **11751**.

19478. Avalos, Hector. Strangers in our own land: religion in contemporary Latina/o literature. *See* **11753**.

19479. Baker, Barbara (ed.). The way we write: interviews with award-winning writers. *See* **11755**.

19480. Banerjee, A. (ed.). Humanistic interpretations of modern British and American writers: essays in literary criticism. *See* **20011**.

19481. Bona, Mary Jo; Maini, Irma (eds). Multiethnic literature and canon debates. *See* **11783**.

19482. Byle, Ann E. (comp.). The making of a Christian bestseller: an insider's guide to Christian publishing. Grand Haven, MI: Faithwalk, 2006. pp. xv, 237.

19483. Carolan, Trevor. Down in the valley: contemporary writing of the Fraser Valley. Victoria, B.C.: Ekstasis, 2004. pp. 160. (Archetype west, 1.) (Writing in British Columbia, 1.) Rev. by Trevor Carolan in Amphora (137) 2004, 25–7.

19484. Cart, Michael; Jenkins, Christine A. The heart has its reasons: young adult literature with gay/lesbian/queer content, 1969–2004. *See* **11811**.

19485. Carvalhão Buesca, Helena. Literature's loss of status. Which status? Whose status? *In* (pp. 21–32) **14093**.

19486. Castro, Brian. Making oneself foreign. *See* **13090**.

19487. Chlebek, Diana (comp.). Annual bibliography of Commonwealth literature 2005: Canada. JCL (41:4) 2006, 31–54.

19488. Cutter, Martha J. Lost and found in translation: contemporary ethnic American writing and the politics of language diversity. *See* **11846**.

19489. Czarnecki, Kristin. 'A house made with stones / full of stories': anthologizing Native American literature. *In* (pp. 61–82) **11783**.

19490. Davis, Rocío G.; Lee, Sue-Im (eds). Literary gestures: the aesthetic in Asian American writing. *See* **11849**.

19491. Davis, Todd F.; Womack, Kenneth. Postmodern humanism in contemporary literature and culture: reconciling the void. *See* **11850**.

19492. Decker, Jeffrey Louis. Saint Oprah. *See* **11852**.

19493. Durso, Patricia Keefe. It's just beginning: assessing the impact of the Internet on US multiethnic literature and the 'canon'. *In* (pp. 197–218) **11783**.

19494. Dwyer, June. Canon-openers, book clubs, and middlebrow culture. *In* (pp. 167–82) **11783**.

19495. Elam, Harry J., Jr; Jackson, Kennell (eds). Black cultural traffic: crossroads in global performance and popular culture. *See* **11876**.

19496. Emenyonu, Ernest N., *et al.* (eds). New women's writing in African literature: a review. *See* **11879**.

19497. Evans, Patrick. 'Pakeha-style biculturalism' and the Maori writer. *See* **11882**.

19498. Ferguson, Roderick A. African American masculinity and the study of social formations. *See* **11887**.

19499. Goebel, Walter; Schabio, Saskia (eds). Beyond the Black Atlantic: relocating modernization and technology. *See* **11911**.

19500. Goldsmith, Kenneth. Paragraphs on conceptual writing. *See* **11912**.

19501. Gourevitch, Philip (introd.). The *Paris Review* interviews: vol. 1. *See* **11913**.

19502. Gunnars, Kristjana. Stranger at the door: writers and the act of writing. *See* **11919**.

19503. Hamilton, Stephen (comp.). Annual bibliography of Commonwealth literature 2005: New Zealand. JCL (41:4) 2006, 141–59.

19504. Hasselstrom, Linda M.; Collier, Gaydell; Curtis, Nancy (eds). Crazy Woman Creek: women rewrite the American West. Boston, MA: Houghton Mifflin, 2004. pp. xxix, 305. Rev. by Beth Kalikoff in WAL (41:2) 2006, 223–4.

19505. Huang, Guiyou (ed.). The Columbia guide to Asian American literature since 1945. *See* **11947**.

19506. Ikin, Van; Jorgensen, Darren (comps). Annual bibliography of Commonwealth literature 2005: Australia. JCL (41:4) 2006, 5–29.

19507. Johnson, Sarah Anne. The very telling: conversations with American writers. *See* **11962**.

19508. Katrak, Ketu H. Politics of the female body: postcolonial women writers of the Third World. *See* **11968**.

19509. Kearney, Richard. Navigations: collected Irish essays, 1976–2006. *See* **11972**.

19510. King, Bruce. To be or not to be diasporic: Alas, poor India! I knew her. *See* **11976**.

19511. Krumrey, Diane. Displacing the nation: contemporary literature by and about immigrants. *See* **11982**.

19512. Lang, John (ed.). Appalachia and beyond: conversations with writers from the Mountain South. *See* **11983**.

19513. Mackean, Ian (ed.). The essentials of literature in English, post-1914. *See* **12016**.

19514. Maeder, Beverly (ed.). The seeming and the seen: essays in modern visual and literary culture. *See* **12023**.

19515. Montes, Rafael Miguel. Generational traumas in contemporary Cuban American literature: making places = *haciendo lugares*. *See* **12040**.

19516. Musila, Grace (comp.). Annual bibliography of Commonwealth literature 2005: Central and East Africa. JCL (41:4) 2006, 73–89.

19517. Narayan, Shyamala A. (comp.). Annual bibliography of Commonwealth literature 2005: India. JCL (41:4) 2006, 91–120.

19518. Padley, Steve. Key concepts in contemporary literature. Basingstoke; New York: Palgrave Macmillan, 2006. pp. xiv, 218. (Palgrave key concepts.)

19519. Perera, S. W. Annual bibliography of Commonwealth literature 2005: Sri Lanka. JCL (41:4) 2006, 215–29.

19520. Pichaske, David. Where now 'Midwestern literature'? MidQ (48:1) 2006, 100–19.

19521. Pilný, Ondřej; Wallace, Clare (eds). Global Ireland: Irish literatures for the new millennium. Prague: Litteraria Pragensia Books, 2005. pp. 241.

19522. Poddar, Prem; Johnson, David (eds). A historical companion to postcolonial literatures in English. *See* **12088**.

19523. Rangno, Erik V. R. Contemporary American literature: 1945–present. *See* **12105**.

19524. Richards, Phillip. Black heart: the moral life of recent African American letters. *See* **12110**.

19525. Rigal-Cellard, Bernadette. Le mythe et la plume: la littérature indienne contemporaine en Amérique du Nord. *See* **12112**.

19526. Scafe, Suzanne (comp.). Annual bibliography of Commonwealth literature 2005: the Caribbean. JCL (41:4) 2006, 55–72.

19527. Schlote, Christiane. Interpreters of transnationalism: South Asian American women writers. *See* **12135**.

19528. Scott, Helen. Caribbean women writers and globalization: fictions of independence. *See* **12140**.

19529. Shamsie, Muneeza. Annual bibliography of Commonwealth literature 2005: Pakistan. JCL (41:4) 2006, 161–80.

19530. Slocombe, Will. Nihilism and the sublime postmodern: the (hi)story of a difficult relationship from Romanticism to postmodernism. *See* **12151**.

19531. Talib, Ismail S. (comp.). Annual bibliography of Commonwealth literature 2005: Malaysia and Singapore. JCL (41:4) 2006, 121–39.

19532. Tatum, Charles M. Chicano and Chicana literature: *otra voz del pueblo*. *See* **12181**.

19533. Updike, John. The end of authorship. *See* **935**.

19534. Uricchio, William; Kinnebrock, Susanne (eds). Media cultures. Heidelberg: Winter, 2004. pp. viii, 298. (Publikationen der Bayerischen Amerika-Akademie, 5.)

19535. Warren, Crystal (introd.). Annual bibliography of Commonwealth literature 2005: South Africa. JCL (41:4) 2006, 181–214.

19536. Watkin, William. On mourning: theories of loss in modern literature. *See* **12211**.

19537. Weiss, Bettina (ed.). The end of unheard narratives: contemporary perspectives on Southern African literatures. *See* **12216**.

THEATRE

19538. Aston, Elaine; Harris, Geraldine (eds). Feminist futures? Theatre, performance, theory. Basingstoke; New York: Palgrave Macmillan, 2006. pp. xiii, 243. Rev. by Laura Baggaley in TLS, 7 July 2006, 32.

19539. Bennett, Claire-Louise. Embodying individualism, re-imagining community: Irish theater in 2005. NewHR (10:3) 2006, 137–44.

19540. Bennett, Stuart (ed.). Theatre for children and young people: 50 years of professional theatre in the UK. Foreword by Wolfgang Schneider. *See* **12241**.

19541. Bennett, Susan. Theatre audiences *redux*. *See* **12242**.

19542. Brisbane, Katherine. Not wrong – just different: observations on the rise of contemporary Australian theatre. *See* **12252**.

19543. Brown, Rich. Moisés Kaufman: the copulation of form and content. *See* **16808**.

19544. Brustein, Robert. Millennial stages: essays and reviews, 2001–2005. New Haven, CT; London: Yale UP, 2006. pp. xviii, 282.

19545. Bryer, Jackson R.; Davison, Richard A. (eds). The art of the American musical: conversations with the creators. *See* **12256**.

19546. Chansky, Dorothy. North American Passion plays: 'the greatest story ever told' in the new millennium. TDR (50:4) 2006, 120–45.

19547. Colborn-Roxworthy, Emily. Trading 'earnest drama' for prophecy: performing Japanese American internment after 9/11. JDTC (20:2) 2006, 25–48.

19548. Davis, Hugh H. I was a teenage classic: literary adaptation in turn-of-the-millennium teen films. *See* **12465**.

19549. Ebrahimian, Babak A. The cinematic theater. Lanham, MD; London: Scarecrow Press, 2004. pp. xiii, 141. Rev. by Season Ellison in TJ (58:4) 2006, 711–12.

19550. Elam, Harry, Jr; Alexander, Robert (eds). The fire this time: African American plays for the 21st century. New York: Theatre Communications Group, 2004. pp. xxxiv, 595. Rev. by David Krasner in AAR (40:1) 2006, 185.

19551. Fensham, Rachel, *et al.* The dolls' revolution: Australian theatre and cultural imagination. *See* **12281**.

19552. Godiwala, Dimple (ed.). Alternatives within the mainstream: British Black and Asian theatres. *See* **12294**.

19553. Grant, Mark N. The rise and fall of the Broadway musical. *See* **12295**.

19554. Gray, Nelson. Birds, trees, stones, and politics: agency and ecology in some recent B.C. performances. JDTC (20:2) 2006, 185–200.

19555. Greene, Alexis (ed.). Women writing plays: three decades of the Susan Smith Blackburn Prize. Foreword by Emilie S. Kilgore. Introd. by Marsha Norman. *See* **12297**.

19556. Greenfield, Mandy. First-person singular: female writers embrace the one-person play. *In* (pp. 158–69) **12297**.

19557. Harvie, Jen. Staging the UK. *See* **12306**.

19558. Herrington, Joan. Building the base. *See* **12307**.

19559. Hischak, Thomas S. Enter the playmakers: directors and choreographers on the New York stage. *See* **12308**.

19560. Kruger, Loren. Geographical acts: place, performance, and pedagogy. *See* **12319**.

19561. Luckhurst, Mary (ed.). A companion to modern British and Irish drama, 1880–2005. *See* **12324**.

19562. MacDonald, Gwynn. Engaging social issues, expressing a political outlook. *In* (pp. 104–14) **12297**.

19563. Magelssen, Scott. Making history in the second person: post-touristic considerations for living historical interpretation. *See* **17966**.

19564. Maufort, Marc. 'Listen to them cry out from their dreaming': Blak Inside and the search for an Aboriginal stage aesthetic. *See* **12332**.

19565. Ozieblo Rajkowska, Bárbara; Narbona-Carrión, María Dolores (eds). Codifying the national self: spectators, actors, and the American dramatic text. *See* **12350**.

19566. Rogerson, Margaret. REED *York*: volume 3, 'The revivals'. *In* (pp. 132–61) **3913**.

19567. Román, David. Performance in America: contemporary US culture and the performing arts. *See* **12355**.

19568. Rosenthal, Cindy. Ellen Stewart: La Mama of us all. *See* **12356**.

19569. Schafer, Elizabeth; Smith, Susan Bradley (eds). Playing Australia: Australian theatre and the international stage. *See* **12360**.

19570. Ullom, Jeffrey. Attempting a modern Marinetti: the controversial 'call for manifestos'. TT (16:2) 2006, 167–82.

CINEMA

General

19571. Abel, Marco. Own your lack! New Lacanian film theory encounters the real in contemporary cinema. *See* **12390**.

19572. Aldama, Frederick Luis. Race, cognition, and emotion: Shakespeare on film. *See* **6013**.

19573. AlSayyad, Nezar. Cinematic urbanism: a history of the modern from reel to real. *See* **12396**.

19574. Andrew, Geoff. Film directors A–Z: a concise guide to the art of 250 great film-makers. *See* **12397**.

19575. Andrews, David. Soft in the middle: the contemporary softcore feature in its contexts. Columbus: Ohio State UP, 2006. pp. xvi, 334.

19576. Bell-Metereau, Rebecca. The capital shape of science fiction heroes to come. *In* (pp. 110–29) **12661**.

19577. Belton, John. American cinema, American culture. *See* **12409**.

19578. Benshoff, Harry M.; Griffin, Sean. Queer images: a history of gay and lesbian film in America. *See* **12411**.

19579. Berg, Charles Ramirez. A taxonomy of alternative plots in recent films: classifying the 'Tarantino effect'. FilCr (31:1/2) 2006, 5–61.

19580. Boggs, Carl; Pollard, Leslie Thomas. The Hollywood war machine: US militarism and popular culture. Boulder, CO: Paradigm, 2006. pp. xii, 276.

19581. Bordwell, David. The way Hollywood tells it: story and style in modern movies. *See* **12425**.

19582. Brereton, Pat. Hollywood utopia: ecology in contemporary American cinema. *See* **12428**.

19583. Britton, Wesley Alan. Onscreen and undercover: the ultimate book of movie espionage. *See* **12429**.

19584. Brodie, Ian. A journey through New Zealand film. *See* **12430**.

19585. Campbell, Russell. Marked women: prostitutes and prostitution in the cinema. *See* **12436**.

19586. Carroll, Noël; Choi, Jinhee (eds). Philosophy of film and motion pictures: an anthology. *See* **12440**.

19587. Cashill, Robert. All things Kong-sidered. *See* **12924**.

19588. Chennault, Ronald E. Hollywood films about schools: where race, politics, and education intersect. *See* **12443**.

19589. Codell, Julie F. (ed.). Genre, gender, race, and world cinema. *See* **12447**.

19590. Dave, Paul. Visions of England: class and culture in contemporary cinema. *See* **12464**.

19591. Desilet, Gregory E. Our faith in evil: melodrama and the effects of entertainment violence. *See* **12470**.

19592. Desmond, John M.; Hawkes, Peter. Adaptation: studying film and literature. *See* **12471**.

19593. Dickenson, Ben. Hollywood's new radicalism: war, globalisation and the movies from Reagan to George W. Bush. *See* **12474**.

19594. Dillon, Steven. The Solaris effect: art & artifice in contemporary American film. Austin: Texas UP, 2006. pp. xiii, 265.

19595. Dorsky, Nathaniel. Devotional cinema. *See* **12483**.

19596. Dresner, Lisa M. The female investigator in literature, film, and popular culture. *See* **13459**.

19597. Emmons, Mark. Film and television: a guide to the reference literature. *See* **12493**.

19598. Exum, J. Cheryl (ed.). The Bible in film – the Bible and film. *See* **12494**.

19599. Ezra, Elizabeth; Rowden, Terry (eds). Transnational cinema. *See* **12495**.

19600. Feil, Ken. Dying for a laugh: disaster movies and the camp imagination. *See* **12498**.

19601. Felleman, Susan. Art in the cinematic imagination. *See* **12499**.

19602. Fowler, Catherine; Helfield, Gillian (eds). Representing the rural: space, place, and identity in films about the land. *See* **12506**.

19603. Franklin, Daniel P. Politics and film: the political culture of film in the United States. *See* **12507**.

19604. Gallagher, Mark. Action figures: men, action films, and contemporary adventure narratives. *See* **12513**.

19605. Giannetti, Louis; Eyman, Scott. Flashback: a brief history of film. *See* **12519**.

19606. Gormley, Paul. The new-brutality film: race and affect in contemporary Hollywood culture. Bristol; Portland, OR: Intellect, 2005. pp. 220.

19607. Grindley, Carl James. Arms and the man: the curious inaccuracy of medieval arms and armor in contemporary film. *See* **12530**.

19608. Hayward, Susan. Cinema Studies: the key concepts. *See* **12534**.

19609. Held, Jacob M.; South, James B. (eds). James Bond and philosophy: questions are forever. *See* **15903**.

19610. Hentges, Sarah. Pictures of girlhood: modern female adolescence on film. *See* **12540**.

19611. Horowitz, Josh. The mind of the modern moviemaker: 20 conversations with the new generation of filmmakers. *See* **12550**.

19612. Horsley, Jake. Dogville *vs* Hollywood. *See* **12551**.

19613. Indick, William. Psycho thrillers: cinematic explorations of the mysteries of the mind. *See* **12555**.

19614. Iyer, Pico. The end of happy endings? NYTM, 8 Feb. 2004, 20–1.

19615. Jeffers, Jennifer M. Britain colonized: Hollywood's appropriation of British literature. *See* **12560**.

19616. Johnston, Robert K. Reel spirituality: theology and film in dialogue. *See* **12562**.

19617. Joslin, Lyndon W. Count Dracula goes to the movies: Stoker's novel adapted, 1922–2003. *See* **12563**.

19618. Kavka, Misha; Lawn, Jennifer; Paul, Mary (eds). Gothic N.Z.: the darker side of Kiwi culture. *See* **11971**.

19619. Keller, Alexandra. From Stella Dallas to Lila Lipscomb: reading real motherhood through reel motherhood. *See* **12572**.

19620. King, C. Richard; Leonard, David J. (eds). Visual economies of/in motion: sport and film. *See* **12575**.

19621. Kolker, Robert. Film, form, and culture. *See* **12579**.

19622. Kowalski, Dean A. The new millennium Bond and *yin–yang* Chinese cosmology. *In* (pp. 215–27) **15903**.

19623. Leonard, David J. Screens fade to black: contemporary African American cinema. Westport, CT; London: Praeger, 2006. pp. x, 217.

19624. Leonard, Richard. Movies that matter: reading film through the lens of faith. *See* **12595**.

19625. Letort, Delphine. Femme fatale / femme assassine dans le film noir: dévier le stéréotype. Cycnos (23:2) 2006, 147–59.

19626. Lichtenfeld, Eric. Action speaks louder: violence, spectacle, and the American action movie. Foreword by Richard Slotkin. *See* **12597**.

19627. Littger, Stephan (ed.). The director's cut: picturing Hollywood in the 21st century: conversations with 21 contemporary filmmakers. London; New York: Continuum, 2006. pp. xxv, 330.

19628. LOPATE, PHILLIP (ed.). American movie critics: an anthology from the silents until now. *See* **12598**.

19629. LOTT, M. RAY. Police on screen: Hollywood cops, detectives, marshals, and rangers. *See* **12600**.

19630. LUHR, WILLIAM; LEHMAN, PETER. Experiment in terror: dystopian Modernism, the police procedural, and the space of anxiety. *In* (pp. 175–93) **12661**.

19631. MCCREADIE, MARSHA. Women screenwriters today: their lives and words. *See* **12602**.

19632. MCFARLANE, BRIAN. The heart of things. Meanjin (63:1) 2004, 48–53. (Balance between special effects and human interest.)

19633. MALTBY, RICHARD; STOKES, MELVYN (eds). Hollywood abroad: audiences and cultural exchange. *See* **12613**.

19634. MARTIN, ADRIAN. Empathy connection. *See* **19711**.

19635. MARUBBIO, M. ELISE. Killing the Indian maiden: images of Native American women in film. *See* **12622**.

19636. MAST, GERALD; KAWIN, BRUCE F. A short history of the movies. *See* **12623**.

19637. MITCHELL, CHARLES P. Filmography of social issues: a reference guide. *See* **12631**.

19638. MORAN, ALBERT; VIETH, ERROL. Film in Australia: an introduction. *See* **12633**.

19639. MORT, JOHN. Read the high country: a guide to western books and films. *See* **3490**.

19640. MUSTAZZA, LEONARD. The literary filmography: 6,200 adaptations of books, short stories and other nondramatic works. *See* **12641**.

19641. NIEMI, ROBERT. History in the media: film and television. *See* **12645**.

19642. PAIETTA, ANN C. Saints, clergy, and other religious figures on film and television, 1895–2003. *See* **12651**.

19643. PARISH, JAMES ROBERT. Fiasco: a history of Hollywood's iconic flops. *See* **12653**.

19644. PHILLIPS, JOHN. Transgender on screen. *See* **12656**.

19645. POMERANCE, MURRAY (ed.). Cinema and modernity. *See* **12661**.

19646. POWRIE, PHIL; DAVIES, ANN; BABINGTON, BRUCE (eds). The trouble with men: masculinities in European and Hollywood cinema. *See* **12663**.

19647. PRAMAGGIORE, MARIA; WALLIS, TOM. Film: a critical introduction. *See* **12664**.

19648. RAW, LAURENCE. Adapting Henry James to the screen: gender, fiction, and film. *See* **10594**.

19649. RICHARDSON, MICHAEL. Surrealism and cinema. *See* **12675**.

19650. ROSENSTONE, ROBERT A. History on film / film and history. *See* **12679**.

19651. SEMMERLING, TIM JON. 'Evil' Arabs in American popular film: Orientalist fear. *See* **12692**.

19652. SHAKI, FEMI OKIREMUETE. Modernity and the African cinema. *See* **12693**.

19653. Sharrett, Christopher. False criticism: cinema, bourgeois society, and the conservative complaint. *In* (pp. 130–51) **12661**.

19654. Sheridan, Earl. Conservative implications of the irrelevance of racism in contemporary African American cinema. JBlaS (37:2) 2006, 177–92.

19655. Simon, John. John Simon on film: criticism, 1982–2001. Introd. by Bruce Beresford. *See* **12698**.

19656. Simpson, Paul; Roddis, Helen; Bushell, Michaela (eds). The Rough Guide to cult movies. *See* **12699**.

19657. Sison, Antonio D. Screening Schillebeeckx: theology and Third Cinema in dialogue. Foreword by Robert J. Schreiter. *See* **12700**.

19658. Slocum, J. David (ed.). Hollywood and war: the film reader. *See* **12702**.

19659. Tasker, Yvonne (ed.). Action and adventure cinema. *See* **12716**.

19660. Thomson, David. The new biographical dictionary of film. *See* **12721**.

19661. Tibbetts, John C.; Welsh, James Michael. The encyclopedia of novels into film. *See* **12722**.

19662. Valantin, Jean-Michel. Hollywood, the Pentagon and Washington: the movies and national security from World War II to the present day. *See* **12725**.

19663. Vaughn, Stephen. Freedom and entertainment: rating the movies in an age of new media. *See* **12726**.

19664. Vineberg, Steve. High comedy in American movies: class and humor from the 1920s to the present. *See* **12727**.

19665. Wayne, Mike (ed.). Understanding film: Marxist perspectives. *See* **12733**.

19666. Wexman, Virginia Wright. A history of film. *See* **12736**.

19667. Williams, Linda (ed.). Porn studies: proliferating pornographies on/screen: an introduction. *See* **12739**.

19668. Williams, Linda Ruth. The erotic thriller in contemporary cinema. *See* **12740**.

19669. Wilson, Eric G. Secret cinema: gnostic vision in film. *See* **12743**.

19670. Wood, Jason. 100 American independent films. *See* **12745**.

19671. Wood, Robin. Personal views: explorations in film. *See* **12747**.

Individual Films

21 Grams (2003)

19672. Newman, Michael Z. Character and complexity in American independent cinema: *21 Grams* and *Passion Fish*. *See* **13005**.

About Schmidt (2002)

19673. Woodward, Kathleen. Performing age, performing gender. NWSAJ (18:1) 2006, 162–89.

Adaptation (2002)

19674. SMITH, DAVID L. The implicit soul of Charlie Kaufman's *Adaptation*. PhilL (30:2) 2006, 424–35.

The Alamo (2004)

19675. THOMPSON, FRANK. Reprinting the legend: the Alamo on film. FilmH (36:1) 2006, 20–5.

Along Came Polly (2004)

19676. ROTH, LUANNE. Beyond *communitas*: cinematic food events and the negotiation of power, belonging, and exclusion. *See* **12775**.

American Splendor (2003)

19677. SPERB, JASON. Removing the experience: simulacrum as an autobiographical act in *American Splendor*. Biography (29:1) 2006, 123–39.

Barbershop (2002)

19678. CHAPPELL, BEN. Bakhtin's barbershop: film as folklorist. WF (64:3/4) 2005, 209–29.

Bride & Prejudice (2004)

19679. MCFARLANE, BRIAN. Saying what other people mean. *See* **9054**.

19680. WILSON, CHERYL A. *Bride and Prejudice*: a Bollywood comedy of manners. LitFQ (34:4) 2006, 323–31.

Bridget Jones's Diary (2001)

19681. FERRISS, SUZANNE. Narrative and cinematic doubleness: *Pride and Prejudice* and *Bridget Jones's Diary*. *In* (pp. 71–84) **19862**.

19682. MABRY, A. ROCHELLE. About a girl: female subjectivity and sexuality in contemporary 'chick' culture. *In* (pp. 191–206) **19862**.

19683. MAZZA, CRIS. Who's laughing now? A short history of chick lit and the perversion of a genre. *In* (pp. 17–28) **19862**.

19684. SÉLLEI, NÓRA. Bridget Jones and Hungarian chick lit. *In* (pp. 173–88) **19862**.

Brokeback Mountain (2005)

19685. BARRA, ALLEN. Larry McMurtry: writing westerns from *Hud* to *Brokeback Mountain*. *See* **17381**.

19686. BAVARO, VINCENZO. Il *closet* e la finestra; ovvero, '*What's love got to do with it?*': note su *Brokeback Mountain*. *See* **18146**.

19687. MCFARLANE, BRIAN. Brokeback and Outback. *See* **13049**.

Catch Me If You Can (2002)

19688. POMERANCE, MURRAY. Nothing sacred: modernity and performance in *Catch Me If You Can*. *In* (pp. 211–31) **12661**.

Chicago (2002)

19689. STRIFF, ERIN. Mimicry and murder: female impersonation in *Chicago*. *See* **15660**.

Cinderella Man (2005)

19690. ZIRIN, DAVE. Crass slipper fits *Cinderella Man*. *In* (pp. 195–201) **12575**.

Coach Carter (2005)

19691. Sexton, Jared. The field of fantasy and the court of appeal: on *Friday Night Lights* and *Coach Carter*. *In* (pp. 103–20) **12575**.

A Cock and Bull Story (2005)

19692. Porton, Richard. In praise of folly: an interview with Michael Winterbottom. Cineaste (31:2) 2006, 28–31.

Crash (2004)

19693. Hsu, Hsuan L. Racial privacy, the L.A. ensemble film, and Paul Haggis's *Crash*. FilCr (31:1/2) 2006, 132–56.

The Da Vinci Code (2006)

19694. Martin, James. Saints or assassins? Opus Dei and *The Da Vinci Code*. *See* **20197**.

19695. Reidy, Maurice Timothy. Fiction trumps fact: why do so many people believe *The Da Vinci Code* is true? *See* **20198**.

A Day without a Mexican (2004)

19696. Marambio, John L.; Tew, Chad. Clash in paradise: a fantasy theme analysis of *A Day without a Mexican*. JAC (29:4) 2006, 475–92.

Elephant (2003)

19697. Tubrett, Dion. Seeing *Elephant*. Cineaction (67) 2005, 65–72.

The Final Cut (2004)

19698. Stewart, Garrett. Vitagraphic time. Biography (29:1) 2006, 159–92.

Friday Night Lights (2004)

19699. Sexton, Jared. The field of fantasy and the court of appeal: on *Friday Night Lights* and *Coach Carter*. *In* (pp. 103–20) **12575**.

Ginger Snaps Films (2001–2004)

19700. Miller, April. 'The hair that wasn't there before': demystifying monstrosity and menstruation in *Ginger Snaps* and *Ginger Snaps Unleashed*. WF (64:3/4) 2005, 281–303.

Girl with a Pearl Earring (2003)

19701. Safit, Ilan. Animating vision: visual adaptation in *Girl with a Pearl Earring*. Comparatist (30) 2006, 52–67.

A Good Woman (2004)

19702. McFarlane, Brian. Saying what other people mean. *See* **9054**.

The Hours (2002)

19703. Alley, Henry. *Mrs Dalloway* and three of its contemporary children. *See* **19257**.

In America (2002)

19704. Mulrooney, Jonathan. Rough magic: *In America*. ShB (24:1) 2006, 29–45.

Kill Bill (2003–)

19705. Jordan, Jessica Hope. Women refusing the gaze: theorizing Thryth's 'unqueenly custom' in *Beowulf* and the bride's revenge in Quentin Tarantino's *Kill Bill*. *See* **3748**.

The Lord of the Rings (2001–2003)

19706. Atkins, Barry. Games. *In* (pp. 151–61) **18793**.

19707. Eaglestone, Robert (ed.). Reading *The Lord of the Rings*: new writings on Tolkien's trilogy. *See* **18793**.

19708. Langford, Barry. Time. *In* (pp. 29–46) **18793**.

19709. Saxey, Esther. Homoeroticism. *In* (pp. 124–37) **18793**.

19710. Shieff, Sarah. Well-laundered elves: purity and degeneration in *The Lord of the Rings*. *In* (pp. 111–19) **11971**.

Lost in Translation (2003)

19711. Martin, Adrian. Empathy connection. Meanjin (64:4) 2005, 49–53.

19712. Mitchell, Sebastian. Oliver Goldsmith's *The Deserted Village*: past, present, and future. *See* **7848**.

Melinda and Melinda (2004)

19713. Metz, Walter. Woody's Melindas and Todd's stories: complex film narratives in the light of literary Modernism. FilCr (31:1/2) 2006, 107–31.

Monster (2003)

19714. Michlin, Monica. *Monster*: ambiguous depiction of the female killer. Cycnos (23:2) 2006, 179–95.

Monster's Ball (2001)

19715. Holland, Sharon P. Death in black and white: a reading of Marc Forster's *Monster's Ball*. Signs (31:3) 2006, 785–813.

Monsters, Inc. (2001)

19716. Freeman, Elizabeth. *Monsters, Inc.*: notes on the neoliberal arts education. NLH (36:1) 2005, 83–95.

The Mother (2003)

19717. McFarlane, Brian. Mothers: some kids do 'ave 'em. Meanjin (63:4) 2004, 40–5.

Mulholland Dr. (2001)

19718. Panek, Elliot. The poet and the detective: defining the psychological puzzle film. *See* **12978**.

My Big Fat Greek Wedding (2002)

19719. Roth, LuAnne. Beyond *communitas*: cinematic food events and the negotiation of power, belonging, and exclusion. *See* **12775**.

O (2001)

19720. Deitchman, Elizabeth A. Shakespeare Stiles style: Shakespeare, Julia Stiles, and American girl culture. *In* (pp. 478–94) **5537**.

One Night the Moon (2001)

19721. Langton, Marcia. Out from the shadows. *See* **19757**.

The Passion of the Christ (2004)

19722. Bartchy, S. Scott. Where is the history in Mel Gibson's *The Passion of the Christ*? *In* (pp. 76–92) **19731**.

19723. Brintnall, Kent L. Mel Gibson's *The Passion of the Christ* and the politics of resurrection. ELN (44:1) 2006, 235–40.

19724. Davis, Walter A. Death's dream kingdom: the American psyche since 9-11. London; Ann Arbor, MI: Pluto Press, 2006. pp. xx, 279. Rev. by Nathan Abrams in JAStud (40:3) 2006, 656.

19725. Edelheit, Joseph A. *The Passion of the Christ* and congregational interfaith relations. *In* (pp. 159–63) **19731**.

19726. Edelman, Samuel. Deicide *déjà vu*: Mel Gibson's film *The Passion* – an attack on forty years of Jewish–Christian dialogue. *In* (pp. 124–8) **19731**.

19727. Egan, Joe. Brave heart of Jesus: Mel Gibson's postmodern Way of the Cross. Blackrock, Co. Dublin: Columba Press, 2004. pp. 155.

19728. Feldman, Louis H. Reflections on Mel Gibson's *The Passion of the Christ*. *In* (pp. 93–107) **19731**.

19729. Fredriksen, Paula (ed.). On *The Passion of the Christ*: exploring the issues raised by the controversial movie. Berkeley; London: California UP, 2006. pp. xxiii, 284.

19730. Garber, Zev. The Jewish Jesus: a partisan's imagination. *In* (pp. 63–9) **19731**.

19731. —— (ed.). Mel Gibson's *Passion*: the film, the controversy, and its implications. West Lafayette, IN: Purdue UP, 2006. pp. 184. (Shofar monographs in Jewish Studies.)

19732. Haas, Peter. The quest of the historical Jesus revisited: Gibson's *The Passion of the Christ*. *In* (pp. 57–62) **19731**.

19733. Hödl, Klaus. How Austrians viewed *The Passion of the Christ*. *In* (pp. 39–44) **19731**.

19734. Holderness, Graham. 'Animated icons': narrative and liturgy in *The Passion of the Christ*. LitTheol (19:4) 2005, 384–401.

19735. Holdredge, Richard. Mel Gibson's *The Passion of the Christ* and the *via media*. *In* (pp. 45–53) **19731**.

19736. Jacobs, Steven Leonard. *The Passion of the Christ*: who said what and what did they say? *In* (pp. 144–53) **19731**.

19737. Kozlovsky-Golan, Yvonne. Gibson's *Passion*. *In* (pp. 21–30) **19731**.

19738. Libowitz, Richard. Gibson's *Passion* on a Catholic campus. *In* (pp. 134–9) **19731**.

19739. Moore, James F. Mel Gibson's *The Passion of the Christ*: a Protestant perspective. *In* (pp. 140–3) **19731**.

19740. Morey, Anne. The languages of *The Passion*. ELN (44:1) 2006, 241–5.

19741. Mork, Gordon R. Dramatizing the Passion: from Oberammergau to Gibson. *In* (pp. 117–23) **19731**.

19742. Neusner, Jacob. Crucifixion in rabbinic context: juridical or theological? *In* (pp. 108–13) **19731**.

19743. PAWLIKOWSKI, JOHN T. Gibson's *Passion*: the challenges for Catholics. *In* (pp. 129–33) **19731**.

19744. PIZZATO, MARK. A post-9/11 Passion play. ELN (44:1) 2006, 247–52.

19745. PRINCE, STEPHEN. Beholding blood sacrifice in *The Passion of the Christ*: how real is movie violence? FilmQ (59:4) 2006, 11–22.

19746. ROBERTSON, STUART D. A view from the pew on Gibson's *Passion*. *In* (pp. 154–8) **19731**.

19747. WHEELER, PENNY. Gibson at the crossroads. *In* (pp. 13–20) **19731**.

19748. WINOKUR, MARK. Costume Jewry: *South Park*'s Holocaust of the Passion. ELN (44:1) 2006, 253–7.

19749. YOUNG, GORDON D. History, archaeology, and Mel Gibson's *Passion*. *In* (pp. 70–5) **19731**.

19750. ZUCKERMAN, BRUCE. Where are the flies? Where is the smoke? The real and super-real in Mel Gibson's *The Passion*. *In* (pp. 31–8) **19731**.

Pride & Prejudice (2005)

19751. HUDELET, ARIANE. Chorégraphies implicites et explicites: la danse dans *Pride and Prejudice*, du texte à l'écran. *See* **9031**.

19752. MCFARLANE, BRIAN. Saying what other people mean. *See* **9054**.

19753. WEISSER, SUSAN OSTROV. Charlotte Brontë, Jane Austen, and the meaning of love. *See* **9205**.

The Proposition (2005)

19754. MCFARLANE, BRIAN. Brokeback and Outback. *See* **13049**.

The Quiet American (2002)

19755. BUSHNELL, WILLIAM S. Paying for the damage: *The Quiet American* revisited. *See* **13022**.

19756. KERR, DOUGLAS. *The Quiet American* and the novel. *See* **16205**.

Rabbit-Proof Fence (2002)

19757. LANGTON, MARCIA. Out from the shadows. Meanjin (65:1) 2006, 55–64.

The Ring (2002)

19758. GENOSKO, GARY. Phatic (dys)functions: the shifting contour of the TV screen. *In* (pp. 13–24) **11781**.

Seabiscuit (2003)

19759. KRUSE, HOLLY. Media, marketing, and memory: sport promotion and *Seabiscuit*. *In* (pp. 203–26) **12575**.

Storytelling (2001)

19760. METZ, WALTER. Woody's Melindas and Todd's stories: complex film narratives in the light of literary Modernism. *See* **19713**.

The Three Burials of Melquiades Estrada (2005)

19761. WHITT, MARGARET EARLEY. An O'Connor redemption in Tommy Lee Jones's *The Three Burials of Melquiades Estrada*. *See* **17851**.

The Tracker (2002)

19762. LANGTON, MARCIA. Out from the shadows. *See* **19757**.

Vanilla Sky (2001)

19763. HERBERT, DANIEL. *Sky*'s the limit: transnationality and identity in *Abre los Ojos* and *Vanilla Sky*. FilmQ (60:1) 2006, 28–38.

19764. WILSON, D. HARLAN. Terminal constructedness and the technology of the self in Cameron Crowe's *Vanilla Sky*. Extrapolation (47:2) 2006, 259–79.

We Were Soldiers (2002)

19765. PRATS, ARMANDO JOSÉ. Last stand at the Ia Drang Valley: memory, mission, and the shape of victory in *We Were Soldiers*. AQ (62:2) 2006, 99–144.

X-Men Films (2000–)

19766. DENISON, RAYNA. (Trans)national x-factor: Patrick Stewart, Britishness and the promotion of *X-Men*. CritS (18:3) 2006, 65–82.

RADIO, TELEVISION, INTERACTIVE MEDIA

19767. ANON. Filmography: film and television adaptations of Thomas Hardy. *In* (pp. 196–201) **10349**.

19768. AKASS, KIM. Throwing the baby out with the bath water: Miranda and the myth of maternal instinct on *Sex and the City*. *See* **13263**.

19769. —— MCCABE, JANET (eds). Reading *Six Feet Under*: TV to die for. London; New York: Tauris, 2005. pp. xxii, 249.

19770. —— —— Reading *The L Word*: outing contemporary television. Introd. by Sarah Warn. London; New York: Tauris, 2006. pp. xxxi, 247. (Reading contemporary television.) Rev. by Matt Warman in TLS, 16 June 2006, 33.

19771. ALLINGHAM, PHILIP. Screening the flashback: three ways of opening *The Mayor of Casterbridge*. *In* (pp. 124–39) **10349**.

19772. BANERJEE, MITA. Vikrams of change: the suspended transnational presence of the Indian on *Friends*. Amst (51:3) 2006, 411–23.

19773. BECKER, RON. Gay TV and straight America. *See* **13270**.

19774. BEIRNE, REBECCA CLARE. Embattled sex: rise of the Right and victory of the queer in *Queer as Folk*. *In* (pp. 43–58) **13336**.

19775. BOOKER, M. KEITH. Drawn to television: primetime animation from *The Flintstones* to *Family Guy*. *See* **13274**.

19776. BRODERICK, JAMES F. The literary galaxy of *Star Trek*: an analysis of references and themes in the television series and films. *See* **13276**.

19777. CARTMEL, ANDREW. Through time: an unauthorised and unofficial history of *Doctor Who*. *See* **13279**.

19778. CHAPMAN, JAMES. Inside the Tardis: the worlds of *Dr Who*: a cultural history. *See* **13280**.

19779. CLARK, DOROTHY G. Hyperread: children's literature, CD-ROMs, and the new literacy. LU (30:3) 2006, 337–59.

19780. CONWAY, RICHARD J. A trip to the queer circus: reimagined masculinities in *Will & Grace*. *In* (pp. 75–84) **13336**.

19781. COPPA, FRANCESCA. Writing bodies in space: media fan fiction as theatrical performance. *In* (pp. 225–44) **19868**.

19782. Crawley, Melissa. Mr Sorkin goes to Washington: shaping the President on television's *The West Wing*. *See* **13291**.

19783. Davis, Glyn; Dickinson, Kay (eds). Teen TV: genre, consumption, identity. *See* **13293**.

19784. D'hulst, Lieven. Can new technologies save the (teaching of) literary history? *In* (pp. 237–46) **14093**.

19785. Dotson, Daniel. Portrayal of mathematicians in fictional works. *See* **11867**.

19786. Dunleavy, Trisha. Ourselves in primetime: a history of New Zealand television drama. *See* **13298**.

19787. Edgerton, Gary R.; Rose, Brian G. (eds). Thinking outside the box: a contemporary television genre reader. *See* **13299**.

19788. Emmons, Mark. Film and television: a guide to the reference literature. *See* **12493**.

19789. Erisman, Fred. *Stagecoach* in space: the legacy of *Firefly*. Extrapolation (47:2) 2006, 249–58.

19790. Espenson, Jane; Yeffeth, Glenn (eds). Finding serenity: anti-heroes, lost shepherds and space hookers in Joss Whedon's *Firefly*. (Bibl. 2005, 20809.) Rev. by Jenness Crawford in NYRSF (18:5) 2006, 21–2.

19791. Fearn-Banks, Kathleen. Historical dictionary of African American television. *See* **13303**.

19792. Foster, Guy Mark. Desire and the 'big Black sex cop': race and the politics of sexual intimacy in HBO's *Six Feet Under*. *In* (pp. 99–112) **13336**.

19793. Geraghty, Lincoln. A network of support: coping with trauma through *Star Trek* fan letters. *See* **13308**.

19794. Gray, Herman. Where have all the Black shows gone? *In* (pp. 311–25) **11876**.

19795. Haridakis, Paul M. Men, women, and televised violence: predicting viewer aggression in male and female television viewers. ComQ (54:2) 2006, 227–55.

19796. Harris, Margaret. Taking bearings: Elizabeth Gaskell's *North and South* televised. *See* **10153**.

19797. Harzewski, Stephanie. The limits of defamiliarization: *Sex and the City* as late heterosexuality. *See* **13317**.

19798. Hellekson, Karen; Busse, Kristina (eds). Fan fiction and fan communities in the age of the Internet: new essays. *See* **19868**.

19799. Hipsky, Martin. Post-Cold War paranoia in *The Corrections* and *The Sopranos*. *See* **15988**.

19800. Jones, Robert. From shooting monsters to shooting movies: Machinima and the transformative play of video game fan culture. *In* (pp. 261–80) **19868**.

19801. Juul, Jesper. Half-real: video games between real rules and fictional worlds. *See* **13334**.

19802. Keller, James R.; Stratyner, Leslie (eds). The new queer aesthetic on television: essays on recent programming. *See* **13336**.

19803. Kelley, Wyn. 'Lying in various attitudes': staging Melville's Pip in digital media. *In* (pp. 337–53) **10823**.

19804. Kelly, David. In its own light: a view of the BBC's *North & South*. *See* **10155**.

19805. Knox, Simone. Reading the ungraspable double-codedness of *The Simpsons*. *See* **13340**.

19806. Littger, Stephan (ed.). The director's cut: picturing Hollywood in the 21st century: conversations with 21 contemporary filmmakers. *See* **19627**.

19807. Lotz, Amanda D. Redesigning women: television after the network era. *See* **13343**.

19808. Lury, Karen. Interpreting television. *See* **13345**.

19809. McAllister, Ken S. Game work: language, power and computer game culture. *See* **13347**.

19810. McCabe, Janet. Claire Fisher on the couch: discourses of female subjectivity, desire, and teenage angst in *Six Feet Under*. SFO (3:1) 2004.

19811. —— Akass, Kim (eds). Reading *Desperate Housewives*: beyond the white picket fence. London; New York: Tauris, 2006. pp. xxii, 247. (Reading contemporary television.)

19812. McCoy, Amanda. Equal before and under the law: rethinking the marginality in *This Is Wonderland*. *In* (pp. 187–95) **18943**.

19813. McFadden, Margaret. 'We cannot afford to keep being so straight-minded': fighting the religious Right on *The L Word*. *In* (pp. 113–29) **13336**.

19814. McGonigal, Jane. SuperGaming: ubiquitous play and performance for massively scaled community. *See* **19043**.

19815. Magoulick, Mary. Frustrating female heroism: mixed messages in *Xena*, *Nikita*, and *Buffy*. *See* **13350**.

19816. Martin, Cathlena; Taylor, Laurie. Playing in Neverland: *Peter Pan* video-game revisions. *In* (pp. 173–93) **14616**.

19817. Martinez-Sierra, Juan José. Using Bourdieu to approach the concept of television as an instrument of social reproduction in the US: the paradox of *The Simpsons*. *See* **13354**.

19818. Mitchell, Danielle. Straight and crazy? Bisexual and easy? Or drunken floozy? The queer politics of Karen Walker. *In* (pp. 85–98) **13336**.

19819. Monroe, Shawnthea. Not-so-desperate: fantasy, fact, and faith on Wisteria Lane. St Louis, MO: Chalice Press, 2006. pp. ix, 116.

19820. Montemurro, Beth. Charlotte chooses her choice: liberal feminism on *Sex and the City*. *See* **13360**.

19821. Moore, Barbara; Bensman, Marvin R.; Van Dyke, Jim. Prime-time television: a concise history. *See* **13361**.

19822. Mustazza, Leonard. The literary filmography: 6,200 adaptations of books, short stories and other nondramatic works. *See* **12641**.

19823. Newman, Kim. *Doctor Who*. *See* **13367**.

19824. Niemi, Robert. History in the media: film and television. *See* **12645**.

19825. Paietta, Ann C. Saints, clergy, and other religious figures on film and television, 1895–2003. *See* **12651**.

19826. Parry-Giles, Trevor; Parry-Giles, Shawn J. The prime-time Presidency: *The West Wing* and US nationalism. *See* **13372**.

19827. Pateman, Matthew. The aesthetics of culture in *Buffy the Vampire Slayer*. *See* **13373**.

19828. Pereen, Esther. Queering the straight world: the politics of resignification in *Queer as Folk*. *In* (pp. 59–74) **13336**.

19829. Powell, Neil. Mr Boythorn's canary. *See* **9804**.

19830. Raley, Amber B.; Lucas, Jennifer L. Stereotype or success? Prime-time television's portrayals of gay male, lesbian, and bisexual characters. JHo (51:2) 2006, 19–38.

19831. Relke, Diana M. A. Drones, clones, and alpha babes: retro-fitting *Star Trek*'s humanism, post-9/11. *See* **13376**.

19832. Rogerson, Margaret. Prime-time drama: *Canterbury Tales* for the small screen. *See* **4439**.

19833. Ryan, Marie-Laure. Avatars of story. *See* **13381**.

19834. Schiappa, Edward; Hewes, Dean E.; Gregg, Peter B. Can one TV show make a difference? *Will and Grace* and the parasocial contact hypothesis. JHo (51:4) 2006, 15–37.

19835. Sheehan, Helena. The continuing story of Irish television drama: tracking the tiger. *See* **13386**.

19836. Short, Sue. Misfit sisters: screen horror as female rites of passage. *See* **12696**.

19837. Smith, Valerie. Meditation on memory: Clark Johnson's *Boycott*. AmLH (17:3) 2005, 530–41.

19838. Snauffer, Douglas. Crime television. *See* **13391**.

19839. Stein, Louisa Ellen. 'This dratted thing': fannish storytelling through new media. *In* (pp. 245–60) **19868**.

19840. Tropp, Laura. 'Faking a sonogram': representations of motherhood on *Sex and the City*. *See* **13398**.

19841. Turner, Cristy. Fabulousness as fetish: queer politics in *Sex and the City*. *See* **13399**.

19842. Vaughn, Stephen. Freedom and entertainment: rating the movies in an age of new media. *See* **12726**.

19843. Wilson, Sherryl. 'No need for fear or secrets': Ruth Fisher and grotesque realism in *Six Feet Under*. SFO (3:1) 2004.

19844. Winokur, Mark. Costume Jewry: *South Park*'s Holocaust of the Passion. *See* **19748**.

19845. Wyn, Johanna. Youth in the media: adult stereotypes of younger people. *In* (pp. 23–34) **2798**.

FICTION

19846. Acheson, James; Ross, Sarah C. E. (eds). The contemporary British novel. *See* **13409**.

19847. Anderson, Douglas A. The mainstreaming of fantasy and the legacy of *The Lord of the Rings*. *In* (pp. 301–15) **18804**.

19848. Betz, Phyllis M. Lesbian detective fiction: woman as author, subject, and reader. *See* **13424**.

19849. Bharat, Meenakshi (ed.). Desert in bloom: contemporary Indian women's fiction in English. *See* **13425**.

19850. Bigge, Ryan. The new geographers. *See* **13426**.

19851. Busse, Kristina. My life is a WIP on my LJ: slashing the slasher and the reality of celebrity and Internet performance. *In* (pp. 207–24) **19868**.

19852. Connor, Tom. The state of the story. WD (86:6) 2006, 24–7, 52.

19853. Deardorff, Donald Lee, ii. Hero and anti-hero in the American football novel: changing conceptions of masculinity from the nineteenth century to the twenty-first century. *See* **8630**.

19854. Donadio, Rachel. Promotional intelligence. *See* **923**.

19855. —— Under Western eyes. NYTB, 11 June 2006, 35.

19856. Dresner, Lisa M. The female investigator in literature, film, and popular culture. *See* **13459**.

19857. Driscoll, Catherine. One true pairing: the romance of pornography, and the pornography of romance. *In* (pp. 79–96) **19868**.

19858. Dube, Bevelyn. Re-imagining the prostitute in society: a critique of the male writer's perspective in Zimbabwean literature. *In* (pp. 45–59) **12216**.

19859. Eagleton, Mary. Figuring the woman author in contemporary fiction. *See* **13462**.

19860. English, James F. (ed.). A concise companion to contemporary British fiction. *See* **13466**.

19861. Falzone, P. J. The final frontier is queer: aberrancy, archetype and audience-generated folklore in K/S slashfiction. *See* **13302**.

19862. Ferriss, Suzanne; Young, Mallory (eds). Chick lit: the new woman's fiction. London; New York: Routledge, 2006. pp. ix, 272. Rev. by Carol-Ann Farkas in JPC (39:5) 2006, 902–3.

19863. Finder, Joseph. Where have all the strivers gone? *See* **13471**.

19864. Finney, Brian. English fiction since 1984: narrating a nation. *See* **13472**.

19865. Foster, Thomas. The souls of cyberfolk: posthumanism as vernacular theory. *See* **13478**.

19866. Gregson, Ian. Character and satire in postwar fiction. *See* **13489**.

19867. Harzewski, Stephanie. Tradition and displacement in the new novel of manners. *In* (pp. 29–46) **19862**.

19868. Hellekson, Karen; Busse, Kristina (eds). Fan fiction and fan communities in the age of the Internet: new essays. Jefferson, NC; London: McFarland, 2006. pp. vi, 290.

19869. Hoffman, Daniel. Returns from the grave: the spirit of Poe in contemporary fiction. *See* **11022**.

19870. Johnsen, Rosemary Erickson. Contemporary feminist historical crime fiction. *See* **13511**.

19871. Kaplan, Deborah. Construction of fan fiction: character through narrative. *In* (pp. 134–53) **19868**.

19872. Karpovich, Angelina I. The audience as editor: the role of beta readers in online fan-fiction communities. *In* (pp. 171–88) **19868**.

19873. Lackner, Eden; Lucas, Barbara Lynn; Reid, Robin Anne. Cunning linguists: the erotics of *Words/Silence/Flesh*. *In* (pp. 189–206) **19868**.

19874. Leavis, L. R. Current literature 2003: 1, New writing: novels and short stories. EngS (86:4) 2005, 325–34.

19875. Ley, James. When the past isn't the past: a role for fiction in Australia's history wars. TLS, 19 May 2006, 23.

19876. Little, Judith A. (ed.). Feminist philosophy and science fiction: utopias and dystopias. *See* **13543**.

19877. MacDonald, Marianne. Harry Potter and the fan-fiction phenomenon. *See* **18350**.

19878. McGill, Robert. Everybody knows: community and the Canadian short story. *See* **13550**.

19879. Mazza, Cris. Who's laughing now? A short history of chick lit and the perversion of a genre. *In* (pp. 17–28) **19862**.

19880. Moore, Lewis D. Cracking the hard-boiled detective: a critical history from the 1920s to the present. *See* **13565**.

19881. Morgan, Gwendolyn A. The intervention of false medieval authorities as a literary device in popular fiction: from Tolkien to *The Da Vinci Code*. *See* **13566**.

19882. Morgan, Speer. Is the short story dead? MR (29:3) 2006, 5–8.

19883. Moseley, Merritt (ed.). Booker Prize novels, 1969–2005. *See* **13567**.

19884. Najita, Susan Y. Decolonizing cultures in the Pacific: reading history and trauma in contemporary fiction. *See* **13569**.

19885. Palmer, Christopher. Big Dumb Objects in science fiction: sublimity, banality, and modernity. *See* **13572**.

19886. Pattee, Amy. Commodities in literature, literature as commodity: a close look at the Gossip Girl series. CLAQ (31:2) 2006, 154–75.

19887. Philips, Deborah. Women's fiction 1945–2005: writing romance. *See* **13579**.

19888. Primorac, Ranka. The place of tears: the novel and politics in modern Zimbabwe. *See* **13584**.

19889. Richardson, Brian. Unnatural voices: extreme narration in modern and contemporary fiction. *See* **13588**.

19890. Scott, A. O. In search of the best: what is the best work of American fiction published in the past 25 years? *See* **13599**.

19891. Shaw, Tina; Ross, Jack (eds). Myth of the 21st century: an anthology of new fiction. Auckland: Reed, 2006. pp. 137.

19892. Simpson, Paul. The Rough Guide to cult fiction. *See* **13610**.

19893. Stasi, Mafalda. The toy soldiers from Leeds: the slash palimpsest. *In* (pp. 115–33) **19868**.

19894. Staunton, Irene (ed.). Writing now: more stories from Zimbabwe. *See* **13618**.

19895. Stein, Louisa Ellen. 'This dratted thing': fannish storytelling through new media. *In* (pp. 245–60) **19868**.

19896. Sturgis, Amy H. Re-imagining Rose: portrayals of Tolkien's Rosie Cotton in twenty-first-century fan fiction. *See* **18834**.

19897. Sullivan, Joanna. Redefining the novel in Africa. *See* **13624**.

19898. Wetherell, Rodney. Subtopia or Sunnyside? Meanjin (65:2) 2006, 174–80.

19899. Wilhelmus, Tom. Ah, England. *See* **13641**.

19900. Woledge, Elizabeth. Intimatopia: genre intersections between slash and the mainstream. *In* (pp. 97–114) **19868**.

19901. Yashinsky, Dan. Suddenly they heard footsteps: storytelling for the twenty-first century. Toronto: Knopf Canada, 2004. pp. xviii, 317.

19902. Yuen, Wong Kin; Westfahl, Gary; Chan, Amy Kit-Sze (eds). World weavers: globalization, science fiction, and the cybernetic revolution. *See* **13653**.

LITERATURE FOR CHILDREN

19903. Clark, Dorothy G. Hyperread: children's literature, CD-ROMs, and the new literacy. *See* **19779**.

19904. de Manuel, Dolores; Davis, Rocío G. Editors' introduction: critical perspectives on Asian American children's literature. *See* **13660**.

19905. Donelson, Kenneth L.; Nilsen, Alleen Pace. Literature for today's young adults. (Bibl. 1993, 10750.) Boston, MA: Pearson / Allyn & Bacon, 2005. pp. xvii, 478. (Seventh ed.: first ed. 1980.)

19906. Gebel, Doris (ed.). Crossing boundaries with children's books. *See* **13667**.

19907. Hatfield, Charles. Comic art, children's literature, and the new comics studies. *See* **69**.

19908. Johnson, Joanna Webb. Chick Lit Jr: more than glitz and glamour for teens and tweens. *In* (pp. 141–57) **19862**.

19909. Jones, Katharine. Getting rid of children's literature. *See* **13675**.

19910. Latrobe, Kathy Howard. Ten English authors for young adults. *See* **13678**.

19911. Leeper, Angela. Poetry in literature for youth. *See* **13679**.

19912. MacCann, Donnarae. The sturdy fabric of cultural imperialism: tracing its patterns in contemporary children's novels. *See* **20231**.

19913. Overstreet, Deborah Wilson. Not your mother's vampire: vampires in young adult fiction. *See* **13684**.

19914. Thongthiraj, Rahpee. Negotiated identities and female personal space in Thai American adolescent literature. *See* **13691**.

POETRY

19915. Barr, John. American poetry in the new century. Poetry (188:5) 2006, 433–41.

19916. Bennett, Charles. Current literature 2003: New writing: poetry. EngS (86:4) 2005, 325–34.

19917. Bertram, Vicki. Gendering poetry: contemporary women and men poets. *See* **13704**.

19918. Brennan, Michael. 'A moment along the way': a venture in publishing Australian poetry. *See* **13707**.

19919. Broom, Sarah. Contemporary British and Irish poetry: an introduction. *See* **13714**.

19920. Burnside, John. Mind the gap: on reading American poetry. *See* **13718**.

19921. Clanchy, Kate. Gendering poetry. *See* **13723**.

19922. Constantine, David. A living language. (Bibl. 2005, 20916.) Rev. by Sasha Dugdale in PNRev (31:5) 2005, 89–90.

19923. Cowan, T. L. Punk rock clit lit: reading toward a punk poetics in *Bent on Writing: Contemporary Queer Tales.* CanP (57) 2005, 103–21.

19924. Dennis, Oliver. City limits. *See* **13737**.

19925. Frost, Elisabeth A.; Hogue, Cynthia (eds). Innovative women poets: an anthology of contemporary poetry and interviews. *See* **13748**.

19926. Gabbin, Joanne V. (ed.). Furious flower: African American poetry from the Black Arts Movement to the present. *See* **13749**.

19927. Gery, John. Katrina and her poets. Callaloo (29:4) 2006, 1541–2. (Hurricane Katrina.)

19928. Gilbert, Alan. Another future: poetry and art in a postmodern twilight. *See* **13751**.

19929. Guinness, Selina (ed.). The new Irish poets. Newcastle upon Tyne: Bloodaxe, 2004. pp. 336. Rev. by Chris Jennings in BkCan (34:5) 2005, 35.

19930. Gundy, Jeff. Form and range. *See* **13761**.

19931. Hamilton-Emery, Chris. Outtakes and upsurges: starting Salt Publishing. *See* **735**.

19932. Hart, Jonathan. Poetry in the age of theory and technology. *In* (pp. 175–88) **14093**.

19933. Heiss, Anita. Black poetics. *See* **13767**.

19934. Kent, Alan M. (ed.). The dreamt sea: an anthology of Anglo-Cornish poetry, 1928–2004. Foreword by John Hurst. *See* **13789**.

19935. Kimberley, Emma. Textual implications of ekphrasis in contemporary poetry. *In* (pp. 89–99) **3407**.

19936. Kirsch, Adam, *et al.* Ambition and greatness: an exchange. *See* **13791**.

19937. Kolin, Philip C.; Swartwout, Susan (eds). Hurricane Blues: poems about Katrina and Rita. Cape Girardeau: Southeast Missouri State UP, 2006. pp. 184.

19938. Levin, Dana. The heroics of style: a study in three parts. APR (35:2) 2006, 45–7.

19939. Longenbach, James. The resistance to poetry. (Bibl. 2005, 20928.) Rev. by David Garrison in SAtlR (70:4) 2005, 155–60.

19940. McCooey, David. Surviving Australian poetry: the new lyricism. *See* **13804**.

19941. McFee, Michael. Seven questions about Southern poetry. *See* **13807**.

19942. Maio, Samuel. Creating another self: voice in modern American personal poetry. *See* **13810**.

19943. Manhire, Bill. Letter from Wellington. *See* **13811**.

19944. Middleton, Peter. Distant reading: performance, readership, and consumption in contemporary poetry. (Bibl. 2005, 20930.) Rev. by Brooke Horvath in AL (78:2) 2006, 402–4; by Liz Jones in ANQ (19:4) 2006, 62–6; by V. Nicholas LoLordo in AmBR (27:5) 2006, 7–8; by Jeff Gundy in GaR (60:2) 2006, 423–33; by Brian McHale in ConLit (47:3) 2006, 472–82.

19945. Mitchell, Margaretta K. The face of poetry: portraits. Ed. by Zack Rogow. Foreword by Robert Hass. *See* **13816**.

19946. Orr, David. A toast to the happy couplet. *See* **13826**.

19947. Ostriker, Alicia. Holocaust poetry: another view. *See* **13827**.

19948. Owen, Catherine, *et al.* Inviting the incubus, kissing the succubi: the muse in Canadian women's poetry, 2005. Toronto: League of Canadian Poets, 2006. pp. 51. (Living archives of the Feminist Caucus.)

19949. Patton, Christopher. Sensuous analysis: the art of reading poetry. *See* **13835**.

19950. Perloff, Marjorie. Can a contemporary poet write about the Holocaust? *See* **13839**.

19951. Pugh, Christina. Humor anxiety. *See* **13841**.

19952. Rees-Jones, Deryn (ed.). Modern women poets. *See* **13847**.

19953. Starnino, Carmine (ed.). The new canon: an anthology of Canadian poetry. Montreal: Signal, 2005. pp. 326. (Signal eds.) Rev. by John Lofranco in Arc (57) 2006, 96–9.

19954. Stein, Julia. The New West in contemporary Western working-class poetry, 1990–2005. *See* **13860**.

19955. Zhang, Benzi. Of nonlimited locality/identity: Chinese diaspora poetry in America. *See* **13882**.

19956. Zwiep, Mary. Sufficient unto our day: recent Irish poetry. SewR (114:3) 2006, 463–72 (review-article).

PROSE

19957. Alonso, Pilar. Discourse strategies for global topic construction in complex written texts: evidence from comment articles. *See* **2472**.

19958. Callus, Ivan. (Auto)thanatography or (auto)thanatology? Mark C. Taylor, Simon Critchley and the writing of the dead. *See* **13889**.

19959. Carlson, Douglas. The uses of adversity: American nature writing in despair. GaR (59:4) 2005, 932–44 (review-article).

19960. Corbella, Walter. Strategies of resistance and the problem of ambiguity in Azar Nafisi's *Reading 'Lolita' in Tehran*. Mosaic (39:2) 2006, 107–23.

19961. Corona Marzol, Isabel. Coming out of the closet 'six feet under': textual silences and the social construction of the family stage in the obituary genres. *See* **2481**.

19962. de Gregorio Godeo, Eduardo. Critical discourse analysis as an analytical resource for Cultural Studies: exploring the discursive construction of subject positions in British men's magazines' problem pages. *See* **2485**.

19963. Dirks, Una. Critical discourse analysis of the Iraq conflict in the British and German 'quality' press. *See* **2487**.

19964. Germano, William. Passive is spoken here. *See* **2495**.

19965. González Rodríguez, María José. Tracing context in the discourse of the media: features of language-in-use in the British press. *See* **2496**.

19966. Hammond, Jeffrey. The talking Blues. 4thG (8:1) 2006, 115–24.

19967. Johnson, Amanda. Passage to Indonesia. Meanjin (64:4) 2005, 60–9.

19968. Marín Arrese, Juana I.; Núñez Perucha, Begoña. Evaluation and engagement in journalistic commentary and news reportage. *See* **2513**.

19969. Mason, Oliver; Platt, Rhiannon. Embracing a new creed: lexical patterning and the encoding of ideology. *See* **2047**.

19970. Oha, Obododimma. Well, it is WELL: language and human interest in a virtual community. *See* **2519**.

19971. Sarat, Austin; Hussain, Nasser. The literary life of clemency: pardon tales in the contemporary United States. TriQ (124) 2006, 169–92.

19972. Stuart, Keith. Towards an analysis of academic weblogs. *See* **2533**.

19973. Valdeón, Roberto A. The discursive construction of anti-European sentiment in the *times.co.uk* texts. *See* **2537**.

BIOGRAPHY AND AUTOBIOGRAPHY

19974. Caws, Mary Ann. Walking (even now) with Carolyn. SFO (4:2) 2006.

19975. Davis, Rocío G. Asian American autobiography for children: critical paradigms and creative practice. *See* **13927**.

19976. Duncan-Jones, Katherine. Live with me: obstacles and opportunities in the latest biography of John Donne. *See* **6713**.

19977. Goldman, Lawrence. A monument to the Victorian age? Continuity and discontinuity in the Dictionaries of National Biography 1882–2004. *See* **8899**.

19978. Hardy, Barbara. Writing a critic's biography. *See* **10025**.

19979. Harrison, Brian. Comparative biography and the *DNB*. CompCrit (25) 2004, 3–26.

19980. Holland, Peter. Shakespeare and the *DNB*. *In* (pp. 139–49) **5353**.

19981. Kozuka, Takashi; Mulryne, J. R. (eds). Shakespeare, Marlowe, Jonson: new directions in biography. *See* **5353**.

19982. McKinley, James. Subject: Robert Graves: random notes of a biographer. *See* **16190**.

19983. Moore-Gilbert, Bart. The *Confessions* of Saint Augustine: roots and routes of postcolonial life writing. *See* **13953**.

19984. Nelson, Alan H. Calling all (Shakespeare) biographers! Or, A plea for documentary discipline. *In* (pp. 55–67) **5353**.

19985. Nye, Mary Jo. Scientific biography: history of science by another means? *See* **13955**.

19986. Tridgell, Susan. Communicative clashes in Australian culture and autobiography. *See* **13964**.

19987. Van Dyne, Susan R. The problem of biography. *In* (pp. 3–20) **18038**.

19988. van Niekerk, Annemarié. A leaking of categories: *Rachael, Woman of the Night*. *In* (pp. 19–44) **12216**.

19989. Whitlock, Gillian. Autographics: the seeing 'I' of the comics. *See* **18586**.

19990. Wright, Laura. Praising the subject: new South African autobiography. AfSR (49:3) 2006, 49–57.

RELATED STUDIES

19991. Culler, Jonathan. In need of a name? A response to Geoffrey Harpham. NLH (36:1) 2005, 37–42.

19992. Escoffery, David S. (ed.). How real is reality TV? Essays on representation and truth. Jefferson, NC; London: McFarland, 2006. pp. vi, 281.

19993. Gonick, Marnina. Between 'Girl Power' and 'Reviving Ophelia': constituting the neoliberal girl subject. *See* **13977**.

19994. Graves, James Bau. Cultural democracy: the arts, community, and the public purpose. *See* **13978**.

19995. Gumbrecht, Hans Ulrich. Slow and brilliant: reactions to Geoffrey Galt Harpham's diagnosis of the humanities today. NLH (36:1) 2005, 131–9.

19996. Harpham, Geoffrey Galt. Beneath and beyond the 'crisis in the humanities'. NLH (36:1) 2005, 21–36.

19997. Hedin, Benjamin. The religion of now. *See* **13981**.

19998. MacCabe, Colin, *et al.* Multiculturalism after 7/7: a *CQ* seminar. CritQ (48:2) 2006, 1–44.

19999. McCormick, John. On taste. *See* **13984**.

20000. Specht, Mary Helen. The emerging critical power of cool. *See* **13995**.

20001. Steiner, George. A new literacy. *See* **13996**.

20002. Stewart, Susan. Thoughts on the role of the humanities in contemporary life. With a response by Geoffrey Galt Harpham. NLH (36:1) 2005, 97–109.

20003. Terzo, Leonardo. Ground Zero e le macerie culturali dell'Occidente. ConLett (45) 2006, 197–211.

20004. van Elteren, Mel. Imperial gestures in portrayals of US culture as a 'universal culture'. *See* **14000**.

LITERARY THEORY

20005. Ackerman, Alan. Liberalism, democracy, and the twentieth-century American theater. *See* **12233**.

20006. Alderson, David. Back to the future. *See* **14006**.

20007. Anderson, Linda. Autobiography and the feminist subject. *In* (pp. 119–35) **14277**.

20008. Arac, Jonathan. Global and Babel: two perspectives on language in American literature. *See* **3173**.

20009. ARMSTRONG, NANCY. What feminism did to novel studies. *In* (pp. 99–118) **14277**.

20010. ASANTE, MOLEFI KETE; MAZAMA, AMA (eds). Encyclopedia of Black Studies. *See* **14013**.

20011. BANERJEE, A. (ed.). Humanistic interpretations of modern British and American writers: essays in literary criticism. Lewiston, NY; Lampeter: Mellen Press, 2006. pp. xii, 312.

20012. BAUER, DALE M. Master thoughts. *In* (pp. 186–97) **20098**.

20013. BAUGH, EDDIE. Confessions of a critic. *See* **14636**.

20014. —— Literary theory and the Caribbean: theory, belief and desire; or, Designing theory. *See* **14019**.

20015. BELSEY, CATHERINE. Culture and the real: theorizing cultural criticism. London; New York: Routledge, 2005. pp. xv, 172. (New accents.) Rev. by John Coyle in EJES (10:2) 2006, 199–203; by Alessandra Marzola in SStud (34) 2006, 161–9.

20016. BENZON, WILLIAM L. Literary morphology: nine propositions in a Naturalist theory of form. PsyArt (10) 2006.

20017. BERENSMEYER, INGO. Between the canons: John Banville's reception in national and international contexts. *In* (pp. 291–309) **12189**.

20018. BESSIÈRE, JEAN. The facticity of the literary work. Trans. by Yves Gilonne. *See* **14022**.

20019. BLODGETT, E. D. Reflections on the scholar's art. *In* (pp. 1–14) **3394**.

20020. BOYD, BRIAN. Fiction and theory of mind. PhilL (30:2) 2006, 590–600 (review-article).

20021. —— Theory is dead – like a zombie. *See* **14025**.

20022. BROOKS, JOANNA. Working definitions: race, ethnic studies, and early American literature. *See* **14028**.

20023. BROSMAN, CATHARINE SAVAGE. O literature, thou art sick: the consequences of theory. Chronicles (30:7) 2006, 28–30.

20024. BUELL, LAWRENCE. The future of environmental criticism: environmental crisis and literary imagination. (Bibl. 2005, 21005.) Rev. by Travis V. Mason in CanL (191) 2006, 155–7; by Ursula K. Heise in ConLit (47:2) 2006, 289–98.

20025. CAO, SHUNQING. The construction of a new paradigm of Comparative Literature Studies. *See* **14035**.

20026. CASTILLO, SUSAN. Narratives of blood. EAL (41:2) 2006, 339–45 (review-article).

20027. CASTLE, GREGORY. Literary theory. *See* **14039**.

20028. CASTRONOVO, RUSS. Theme for African American literature B. *In* (pp. 29–39) **20098**.

20029. CHANDRA, SARIKA. From the boardroom to cocktail parties: 'great' books, multiethnic literature, and the production of the professional managerial class in the context of globalization. *In* (pp. 183–96) **11783**.

20030. CHAUDHURI, SHOHINI. Feminist film theorists: Laura Mulvey, Kaja Silverman, Teresa de Lauretis, Barbara Creed. *See* **14043**.

20031. Chiang, Mark. Autonomy and representation: aesthetics and the crisis of Asian American cultural politics in the controversy over *Blu's Hanging*. *In* (pp. 17–34) **11849**.

20032. Chiwengo, Ngwarsungo. The stepsister and the clan: when the native teaches African American literature. *In* (pp. 154–69) **20098**.

20033. Chow, Rey. Poststructuralism: theory as critical self-consciousness. *In* (pp. 195–210) **14277**.

20034. Cobley, Evelyn. Hard going after theory. *See* **14050**.

20035. Connor, Kimberly Rae. Truth and talent in interpreting ethnic American autobiography: from White to Black and beyond. *In* (pp. 209–22) **20098**.

20036. Cuddy-Keane, Melba. Global Modernism. *In* (pp. 558–64) **11788**.

20037. Davis-Undiano, Robert Con. *World Literature Today* goes back to the future. *See* **14060**.

20038. Day, Gary. Beyond management culture: the experience of English. *See* **2483**.

20039. Dean, Paul. Current literature 2004: II, Literary theory, history and criticism. EngS (86:6) 2005, 545–57.

20040. Deane, Seamus. Edward Said (1935–2003): a late style of humanism. *See* **14062**.

20041. DeRosa, Robin. Critical tricksters: race, theory, and *Old Indian Legends*. *In* (pp. 167–95) **2149**.

20042. DeSoto, Aureliano Maria. On the trail of the Chicana/o subject: literary texts and contexts in the formulation of Chicana/o Studies. *In* (pp. 41–60) **11783**.

20043. Dever, Carolyn. Strategic Aestheticism: a response to Caroline Levine. *See* **10127**.

20044. D'hulst, Lieven. Can new technologies save the (teaching of) literary history? *In* (pp. 237–46) **14093**.

20045. Docherty, Thomas. Aesthetic democracy. Stanford, CA: Stanford UP, 2006. pp. xix, 185. Rev. by Erik S. Roraback in EREA (4:2) 2006.

20046. Domínguez, César; Wiersma, Mark D. Literary emergence as a case study of theory in comparative literature. Trans. by Carla Dechant. CLCWeb (8:2) 2006.

20047. Donadio, Rachel. Keeper of the canon. *See* **14075**.

20048. Durso, Patricia Keefe. It's just beginning: assessing the impact of the Internet on US multiethnic literature and the 'canon'. *In* (pp. 197–218) **11783**.

20049. Eagleton, Terry. Making a break. *See* **13463**.

20050. Edelman, Lee. No future: queer theory and the death drive. (Bibl. 2005, 21022.) Rev. by Michael Cobb in Criticism (47:1) 2005, 119–30; by Andrea Fontenot in MFS (52:1) 2006, 252–6; by Antonis Balasopoulos in JAStud (40:2) 2006, 425–6.

20051. Eeckhout, Bart. Why would the spatial be so special? A critical analysis of the spatial turn in American Studies. *See* **14080**.

20052. Erickson, Jon. The ghost of the literary in recent theories of text and performance. *See* **3435**.

20053. Eshelman, Raoul. After postmodernism: performatism in literature. Anthropoetics (11:2) 2005/06.

20054. Estok, Simon. An introduction to Shakespeare and ecocriticism: the special cluster. *See* **5295**.

20055. Evans, Ruth. The afterword of origins: a response. *See* **4321**.

20056. Fenner, David E. W. Why modifying (some) works of art is wrong. APQ (43:4) 2006, 329–41.

20057. Ferguson, Roderick A. African American masculinity and the study of social formations. *See* **11887**.

20058. Figueira, Dorothy M. (ed.). Cybernetic ghosts: literature in the age of theory and technology. *See* **14093**.

20059. Fish, Stanley. 'There is nothing he cannot ask': Milton, liberalism, and terrorism. *In* (pp. 243–64) **7033**.

20060. Fitz, Karsten; Gessner, Ingrid. Publications in American Studies from German-speaking countries: 2005. Amst (51:2) 2006, 263–98.

20061. Flannery, Eóin. Morning yet on *Field Day*? Ireland, *Field Day* and postcolonialism. *In* (pp. 41–62) **12189**.

20062. Franco Carvalhal, Tania. The future of literary studies: technologies of the image or technologies of writing? *In* (pp. 167–74) **14093**.

20063. Frank, Adam. Some avenues for feeling. *See* **14100**.

20064. Friedman, Susan Stanford. Periodizing Modernism: postcolonial modernities and the space/time borders of Modernist Studies. *See* **11895**.

20065. Garren, Samuel B. The honeysuckle and the camellia: a reader-response theory of literary interpretation. *See* **17122**.

20066. George, Rosemary Marangoly. Feminists theorize colonial/postcolonial. *In* (pp. 211–31) **14277**.

20067. Georgianna, Linda. Vernacular theologies. *See* **3851**.

20068. Gervais, David. 'English' and criticism. *See* **14112**.

20069. Gilroy, Paul. Postcolonial melancholia. *See* **14121**.

20070. Giraldi, William. A conversation with Sven Birkerts. MR (29:2) 2006, 28–41.

20071. Gordon, Scott Paul. A new latitude in the culture wars. *See* **7260**.

20072. Gould, Philip. What we mean when we say 'race'. EAL (41:2) 2006, 321–7.

20073. Greaney, Michael. Contemporary fiction and the uses of theory: the novel from structuralism to postmodernism. *See* **13487**.

20074. Guerin, Wilfred L., *et al.* A handbook of critical approaches to literature. *See* **14135**.

20075. Guran, Letitia. US American comparative literature and the study of East–Central European culture and literature. CLCWeb (8:1) 2006.

20076. Gustafson, Sandra M. (comp.). Historicizing race in Early American Studies: a roundtable with Joanna Brooks, Philip Gould, and David Kazanjian. EAL (41:2) 2006, 305–11.

20077. Harpham, Geoffrey Galt. The character of criticism. *See* **14139**.

20078. Harris, Oliver. Not Burroughs' final fix: materializing *The Yage Letters*. *See* **14955**.

20079. Hart, Jonathan. Poetry in the age of theory and technology. *In* (pp. 175–88) **14093**.

20080. Harwood, Britton. Chaucer on the couch: the Pardoner's performance and the case for psychoanalytic criticism. *In* (pp. 47–57) **4310**.

20081. Hegeman, Susan. Culture, patriotism, and the habitus of a discipline; or, What happens to American Studies in a moment of globalization? *See* **14147**.

20082. Heng, Geraldine. Pleasure, resistance, and a feminist aesthetics of reading. *In* (pp. 53–72) **14277**.

20083. Herman, Luc; Vervaeck, Bart. Handbook of narrative analysis. (Bibl. 2005, 21054.) Rev. by Caragh Wells in MLR (101:4) 2006, 1074–5.

20084. Hoy, David Couzens. Critical resistance: from poststructuralism to post-critique. *See* **14155**.

20085. Iser, Wolfgang. How to do theory. *See* **14161**.

20086. Iuliano, Fiorenza. Sovversioni materiche: corpi e politiche del corpo nella teoria culturale contemporanea. Àcoma (32) 2006, 7–27.

20087. Jay, Paul. Locating disciplinary change: the afterlives of area and international studies in the age of globalization. *See* **14168**.

20088. Jones, Katharine. Getting rid of children's literature. *See* **13675**.

20089. Kazanjian, David. 'When they come here they feal so free': race and Early American Studies. EAL (41:2) 2006, 329–37.

20090. Kumar, Nita N. The color of the critic: an intervention in the critical debate in African American theory on interpretive authority. *In* (pp. 134–44) **20098**.

20091. Lethbridge, J. B. Recuperating the return to history. *In* (pp. 15–57) **5100**.

20092. Levine, Caroline. Scaled up, writ small: a response to Carolyn Dever and Herbert F. Tucker. *See* **14194**.

20093. Li, Dingqing. Borrowing, integration, creation: the localization of Western literary criticism and the construction of Chinese literary criticism: an interview with Professor Hu Yamin. FLS (118) 2006, 1–7. (In Chinese.)

20094. —— Ethical literary criticism and the construction of humanistic spirit. *See* **14199**.

20095. Lieb, Michael. Returning the Gorgon Medusa's gaze: terror and annihilation in Milton. *In* (pp. 229–42) **7033**.

20096. —— Labriola, Albert C. (eds). Milton in the age of Fish: essays on authorship, text, and terrorism. *See* **7033**.

20097. Loewenstein, David. *Samson Agonistes* and the culture of religious terror. *In* (pp. 203–28) **7033**.

20098. Long, Lisa A. (ed.). White scholars / African American texts. New Brunswick, NJ: Rutgers UP, 2005. pp. xiv, 247. Rev. by John C. Gruesser in AAR (40:3) 2006, 598–601.

20099. Lynn, Steven. Texts and contexts: writing about literature with critical theory. (Bibl. 1995, 3641.) Harlow; New York: Longman, 2005. pp. xiv, 290. (Fourth ed.: first ed. 1994.)

20100. McCabe, Susan. Whither sexuality and gender? 'What that sign signifies' and the rise of queer historicism. PCP (41) 2006, 26–31.

20101. Mackinnon, Lachlan. Where's Steptoe? *See* **14208**.

20102. May, Theresa J. 'Consequences unforeseen …' in *Raisin in the Sun* and *Caroline; or, Change*. JDTC (20:2) 2006, 127–44.

20103. Miall, David S. Empirical approaches to studying literary readers: the state of the discipline. BH (9) 2006, 291–311.

20104. Miller, Gavin. National confessions: queer theory meets Scottish literature. *See* **11149**.

20105. Moody, Nickianne. Feminism and popular culture. *In* (pp. 172–91) **14277**.

20106. Moss, Laura. Playing the monster blind? The practical limitations of updating the Canadian canon. *See* **3353**.

20107. Mullin, Katherine. Modernisms and feminisms. *In* (pp. 136–52) **14277**.

20108. Murphy, Neil. Political fantasies: Irish writing and the problem of reading strategies. *In* (pp. 63–88) **12189**.

20109. O'Brien, Eugene. Rereading the canon: towards a literary redefinition of Irishness. *In* (pp. 113–33) **12189**.

20110. O'Neill, Michael. Criticism as cross-reference. NQ (53:3) 2006, 357–60.

20111. Onufer, Petr. An interview with Terry Eagleton. *See* **14247**.

20112. Page, Ruth E. Literary and linguistic approaches to feminist narratology. *See* **14249**.

20113. Parr, Katherine. Integrating women's writing into the canon: women poets of Young Ireland. *In* (pp. 235–65) **12189**.

20114. Pease, Donald E. The extraterritoriality of the literature for our planet. ESQ (50:1–3) 2004, 177–221.

20115. Pelan, Rebecca. Literally loose cannon or loosening the literary canon. *In* (pp. 89–109) **12189**.

20116. Perloff, Marjorie. Modernism now. *In* (pp. 571–8) **11788**.

20117. Piccinato, Stefania. The beginning of African American Studies in Italy. *See* **14258**.

20118. Poovey, Mary. Mediums, media, mediation: response. VS (48:2) 2006, 249–55.

20119. Portelli, Alessandro. Between Rome, Harlem, and Harlan. *In* (pp. 145–53) **20098**.

20120. Pozorski, Aimee L. An interview with trauma pioneer Cathy Caruth. ConnR (28:1) 2006, 77–84.

20121. Pritchard, William H. Possibilities for Wordsworth. *See* **11705**.

20122. Pye, Gillian. Comedy theory and the postmodern. *See* **3374**.

20123. Rabaka, Reiland. The souls of Black radical folk: W. E. B. Du Bois, critical social theory, and the state of Africana Studies. *See* **15581**.

20124. Rath, Sura P. What would Said say? Some reflections on tradition, imperialism, and globalism. *In* (pp. 95–110) **14238**.

20125. Ray, Robert B. Film Studies and the problems of the new century. NER (27:4) 2006, 106–20.

20126. Reed, Walter L.; Duke, Marshall P. Personalities as *dramatis personae*: an interdisciplinary examination of the self as author. CK (11:3) 2005, 502–13.

20127. Rodas, Julia Miele. Mainstreaming Disability Studies? *See* **8498**.

20128. Rooney, Ellen. The literary politics of feminist theory. *In* (pp. 73–95) **14277**.

20129. —— (ed.). The Cambridge companion to feminist literary theory. *See* **14277**.

20130. Ross, Charles Stanley. Nabokov and world literature. *See* **17714**.

20131. Rudrum, David. On the very idea of a definition of narrative: a reply to Marie-Laure Ryan. Narrative (14:2) 2006, 197–204. (Dialogue.)

20132. Ryan, Marie-Laure. Semantics, pragmatics, and narrativity: a response to David Rudrum. Narrative (14:2) 2006, 188–96. (Dialogue.) (*Responds to* bibl. 2005, 14996.)

20133. Sarker, Sonita. Afterword: Modernisms in our image … always, partially. *See* **12130**.

20134. Savoy, Eric. Subjunctive biography. *See* **10603**.

20135. Scanlan, J. T. A celebration. *See* **7328**.

20136. Schneider, Rebecca. Intermediality, infelicity, and scholarship on the slip. TheatreS (47:2) 2006, 253–60.

20137. Schoene, Berthold. Queer politics, queer theory, and the future of 'identity': spiralling out of culture. *In* (pp. 293–302) **14277**.

20138. Searle, Leroy. Literature departments and the practice of theory. *See* **14289**.

20139. Shawcross, John. Remarks for a discussion of *Intentionality and the New Traditionalism*: some liminal means to literary revisionism. ExRC (32:1) 2006, 38–49.

20140. Shen, Dan. How stylisticians draw on narratology: approaches, advantages and disadvantages. *See* **14293**.

20141. Shiu, Anthony Sze-Fai. On loss: anticipating a future for Asian American Studies. *See* **14295**.

20142. Simpson, James. Confessing literature. ELN (44:1) 2006, 121–6.

20143. Spiridon, Monica. Literature is dead, long live literature: a challenge to literary theories. *In* (pp. 79–86) **14093**.

20144. Spivak, Gayatri Chakravorty. World systems & the creole. Narrative (14:1) 2006, 102–12. (Dialogue.)

20145. Staten, Henry. Tracking the 'native informant': cultural translation as the horizon of literary translation. *In* (pp. 111–26) **3191**.

20146. Stephens, Michelle. At the borders between: a reply to critics. SmAx (10:2) 2006, 276–86.

20147. Stone, Marjorie; Thompson, Judith. Taking joint stock: a critical survey of scholarship on literary couples and collaboration. *In* (pp. 309–33) **3405**.

20148. Sullivan, James D. Writing about Gwendolyn Brooks anyway. *In* (pp. 198–208) **20098**.

20149. Suzuki, Mihoko; Dufault, Roseanna (eds). Diversifying the discourse: the Florence Howe Award for Outstanding Feminist Scholarship, 1990–2004. *See* **14313**.

20150. Taggart, Andrew J. The function and value of literature and literary studies reconsidered. *See* **14316**.

20151. Takada, Yasunari. A Shakespearean distance: Europe, modernity and traditional values. *See* **5439**.

20152. Temple, Christel N. Rescuing the literary in Black Studies. *See* **12184**.

20153. Thompson, Helen (ed.). The current debate about the Irish literary canon: essays reassessing *The Field Day Anthology of Irish Writing*. *See* **12189**.

20154. Tucker, Herbert F. Tactical formalism: a response to Caroline Levine. *See* **9269**.

20155. Tyson, Lois. Critical theory today: a user-friendly guide. (Bibl. 1999, 14805.) London; New York: Routledge, 2006. pp. xiv, 465. (Second ed.: first ed. 1999.)

20156. Uricchio, William; Kinnebrock, Susanne (eds). Media cultures. *See* **19534**.

20157. Vannini, Simona. The second coming of the author. *See* **14326**.

20158. Varma, Rashmi. On common ground? Feminist theory and critical race studies. *In* (pp. 232–60) **14277**.

20159. Vasvári, Louise O. Queer theory and discourses of desire. CLCWeb (8:1) 2006.

20160. Venturino, Steven J. Inquiring after theory in China. B2 (33:2) 2006, 91–113.

20161. Veric, Charlie Samuya. On the potential of failure. AmQ (58:1) 2006, 255–64 (review-article).

20162. Wake, Paul; Malpas, Simon (eds). The Routledge companion to critical theory. *See* **14330**.

20163. Wang, Haiyan. The past and future of American Vietnam War literature studies in China. *See* **12209**.

20164. Watson, Jay. Introduction: situating Whiteness in Faulkner Studies, situating Faulkner in Whiteness Studies. *See* **15839**.

20165. Watson, Nicholas. Cultural changes. *See* **3894**.

20166. Weed, Elizabeth. Feminist psychoanalytic literary criticism. *In* (pp. 261–82) **14277**.

20167. Westfahl, Gary. Science fiction and the playing fields of Eaton. *See* **3518**.

20168. Williams, R. John. 'Doing history': Nuruddin Farah's *Sweet and Sour Milk*, Subaltern Studies, and the postcolonial trajectory of silence. *See* **15793**.

20169. Xu, Jing. An interview with Professor Harold Bloom. *See* **14350**.

20170. Yuan, Xianlai. Christian culture and the history of Western literature: an interview with Prof. Liu Jian-jun. *See* **14353**.

AUTHORS

Daniel Alarcón (b.1977)

20171. Alarcón, Daniel. The writing life. BkW, 23 July 2006, 10.

Monica Ali (b.1967)

20172. Ali, Monica. The writing life. BkW, 25 June 2006, 10.

20173. Cormack, Alistair. Migration and the politics of narrative form: realism and the postcolonial subject in *Brick Lane*. ConLit (47:4) 2006, 695–721.

Moniza Alvi (b.1954)

20174. Padel, Ruth. The journey or the dance? On syllables belonging to each other. *See* **9885**.

Laurie Halse Anderson (b.1961)

20175. Latham, Don. Melinda's closet: trauma and the queer subtext of Laurie Halse Anderson's *Speak*. CLAQ (31:4) 2006, 369–82.

Neshani Andreas (b.1964)

20176. Orford, Margie. Transition, trauma, and triumph: contemporary Namibian women's literature. *In* (pp. 159–73) **12216**.

20177. Weiss, Bettina. An approach to homoerotic female desire in *Three Moments in a Marriage*, *The Purple Violet of Oshaantu*, and *A Question of Power*. *In* (pp. 117–44) **12216**.

Jennifer Armstrong (b.1961)

20178. Levy, Michael. 'The sublimation of real life': malls, shopping, and advertising in recent young adult SF. *See* **14434**.

Tash Aw (b.1973)

20179. Barta, Peter I. In search of knowledge: voicing the void in Tash Aw's *The Harmony Silk Factory*. Intertexts (9:2) 2005, 105–15.

20180. —— The postcolonial novel: an interview with Tash Aw. Intertexts (9:2) 2005, 117–22.

Anita Rau Badami (b.1962)

20181. Rajan, Gita. Poignant pleasures: feminist ethics as aesthetics in Jhumpa Lahiri and Anita Rau Badami. *In* (pp. 104–20) **11849**.

Anurima Banerji

20182. Tagore, Proma. 'The asymmetrical geography of my heart': forms of queer diasporic desire in Anurima Banerji's *Night Artillery*. CanP (57) 2005, 7–34.

Larissa Behrendt (b.1969)

20183. Prentice, Chris. From liminality to reconciliation: the politics of Aboriginal women's life-narratives. *In* (pp. 277–96) **8374**.

Kate Bernheimer

20184. Bernheimer, Kate. This rapturous form. *See* **13422**.

Gurpreet Kaur Bhatti (b.1968)

20185. Bhatti, Gurpreet Kaur. The freedom to create. *In* (pp. 197–8) **12297**.

Malorie Blackman (b.1962)

20186. Wilkie-Stibbs, Christine. The 'other' country: memory, voices, and experiences of colonized childhoods. CLAQ (31:3) 2006, 237–59.

Jessica Blank (b.1975)

20187. Blank, Jessica; Jensen, Erik. Living justice: love, freedom, and the making of *The Exonerated*. New York: Atria, 2005. pp. xiii, 303.

Marianne Bluger (1945–2005)

20188. Carter, Terry Ann. Red lights and chartreuse fronds: the tanka poetry of Marianne Bluger. Arc (57) 2006, 68–75.

Peter Boyle (b.1951)

20189. Johnson, Andrew. Peter Boyle and the art of poetry. Antipodes (20:1) 2006, 72–9.

Dan Brown (b.1964)

20190. Brown, Kevin. 'Tis pity she's a whore: the revision of Mary Magdalene in contemporary fiction. *See* **12254**.

20191. Davis, J. Madison. The mysterious popularity of the arcane. *See* **9934**.

20192. Eagleton, Terry. A response. *See* **14079**.

20193. Erb, Peter C. The Schwenkfelder Code: did Dan Brown's religious background contribute to the anti-Catholicism and rigorous individualism of his novel? ANCW (194:20) 2006, 14–16.

20194. Griffith-Jones, Robin. *The Da Vinci Code* and the secrets of the Temple. Grand Rapids, MI; Cambridge: Eerdmans, 2006. pp. xii, 130. Rev. by Bernard Hamilton in TLS, 9 June 2006, 37.

20195. Haldane, John. Fiction's enigma innovations: the art of the thriller. *See* **14888**.

20196. Kennedy, D. James; Newcombe, Jerry. The Da Vinci myth *vs* the Gospel truth. Wheaton, IL: Crossway, 2006. pp. 156.

20197. Martin, James. Saints or assassins? Opus Dei and *The Da Vinci Code*. ANCW (194:20) 2006, 10–12.

20198. Reidy, Maurice Timothy. Fiction trumps fact: why do so many people believe *The Da Vinci Code* is true? ANCW (194:20) 2006, 9–12.

20199. Smoley, Richard. Forbidden faith: the Gnostic legacy from the Gospels to *The Da Vinci Code*. *See* **3400**.

Pamela Brown (b.1948)

20200. McCredden, Lyn. 'untranscended / life itself': the poetry of Pam Brown. ALS (22:2) 2005, 217–28.

Jill Conner Browne (b.1953)

20201. Boyd, Elizabeth B. Ya yas, grits, and sweet potato queens: contemporary Southern belles and the prescriptions that guide them. *In* (pp. 159–72) **19862**.

Moira Buffini (b.1967)

20202. Greene, Alexis. New voices: Moira Buffini, Sarah Ruhl, and Rukhsana Ahmad. *In* (pp. 219–40) **12297**.

Augusten Burroughs (b.1965)

20203. Burroughs, Augusten. Magical thinking: true stories. New York: St Martin's Press, 2004. pp. xii, 268. Rev. by Catherine Humble in TLS, 22 Sept. 2006, 33.

20204. —— Possible side effects. New York: St Martin's Press, 2006. pp. ix, 291. (Memoirs.)

20205. —— Running with scissors: a memoir. New York: St Martin's Press, 2006. pp. 304.

Nancy Butcher

20206. Levy, Michael. 'The sublimation of real life': malls, shopping, and advertising in recent young adult SF. *See* **14434**.

Laurie Wagner Buyer (b.1954)

20207. Buyer, Laurie Wagner. Spring's edge. Ashland, OR: Story Line Press, 2004. pp. 320.

Bridget Carpenter

20208. Carpenter, Bridget, *et al.* Crossing borders: a conversation with Bridget Carpenter, Lynn Nottage, Dael Orlandersmith, and Diana Son. *In* (pp. 115–26) **12297**.

Lan Samantha Chang (b.1965)

20209. Ellis, Sherry. Memories that reach back into consciousness: an interview with Lan Samantha Chang. *See* **17235**.

Memory Chirere

20210. Muponde, Robert. 'The eyes of a buck': figuring the child in the Zimbabwean short story in English. *In* (pp. 99–116) **12216**.

Lawrence Chua (b.1966)

20211. Sohn, Stephen Hong. 'Valuing' transnational queerness: politicized bodies and commodified desires in Asian American literature. *In* (pp. 100–22) **11995**.

Basil B. Clark

20212. Huglen, Mark E. (commentary); Brock, Bernard L. (afterword). Poetic healing: a Vietnam veteran's journey from a communication perspective. (Bibl. 2005, 21179.) Rev. by David Beard in QJS (92:2) 2006, 232–5.

Lynn Coady (b.1970)

20213. Wyile, Herb. As for me and me arse: strategic regionalism and the home place in Lynn Coady's *Strange Heaven*. CanL (189) 2006, 85–101.

Neil Cross (b.1969)

20214. Cross, Neil. Heartland. London: Scribner, 2005. pp. 326. (Memoirs.)

Angie Cruz (b.1972)

20215. Maldonado, Sheila. A conversation. InR (28:1) 2006, 139–46.

Mitch Cullin (b.1968)

20216. Cawelti, John G. Sherlock Holmes: the case of the perpetual detective. *See* **9928**.

Julia Darling (1956–2005)

20217. Padel, Ruth. The journey or the dance? On syllables belonging to each other. *See* **9885**.

Rana Dasgupta (b.1971)

20218. Bhatt, Shakti. 'India seems a greater abstraction to me than Europe': a conversation with Rana Dasgupta. JPW (42:2) 2006, 206–11.

Olena Kalytiak Davis (b.1963)

20219. Sadoff, Ira. Olena Kalytiak Davis and the retro-new. APR (35:4) 2006, 11–15.

Siddhartha Deb (b.1970)

20220. Bhatt, Shakti. Against forgetting: a conversation with Siddhartha Deb. JPW (42:2) 2006, 201–5.

Michelle de Kretser (b.1958)

20221. Scott, Barry. The beauty and the menace. Meanjin (63:2) 2004, 97–107.

Brian DeVido (b.1972)

20222. Vanderwerken, David L. Man to man: Brian DeVido's *Every Time I Talk to Liston*. Aethlon (23:2) 2006, 25–31.

Unity Dow (b.1959)

20223. Gagiano, Annie. Entering the oppressor's mind: a strategy of writing in Bessie Head's *A Question of Power*, Yvonne Vera's *The Stone Virgins* and Unity Dow's *The Screaming of the Innocent*. *See* **16305**.

Frances O'Roark Dowell (b.1964)

20224. Leeper, Angela. 'Spreading out all the rocks and treasure and creepy crawlies': an interview with Frances O'Roark Dowell. NCLR (15) 2006, 39–45.

Debra Magpie Earling (b.1957)

20225. Haladay, Jane. 'It just seemed to call to me': Debra Magpie Earling's self-telling in *Perma Red*. AICRJ (30:1) 2006, 53–65.

Will Eno (b.1965)

20226. Silverstein, Marc. 'A word by which you will be revealed': the problem of language in Will Eno's monologues. AmDr (15:2) 2006, 61–90.

Louisa Ermelino

20227. Barone, Dennis. 'We've always been different': Louisa Ermelino's Spring Street trilogy and Italian American women's writing. CritW (48:1) 2006, 19–30.

Ramabai Espinet (b.1948)

20228. Mehta, Brinda. Engendering history: a poetics of the *kala pani* in Ramabai Espinet's *The Swinging Bridge*. SmAx (11:1) 2006, 19–36.

Edward Falco (b.1948)

20229. Esposito, Scott. Well-crafted transformations: an interview with Edward Falco. ChattR (26:2/3) 2006, 165–71.

Vicki Feaver (b.1943)

20230. Sensi, Giorgia; Porster, Brenda. Vicki Feaver: la fanciulla che ritrovò le sue mani. PoesiaM (209) 2006, 39–52.

Anton Ferreira

20231. MacCann, Donnarae. The sturdy fabric of cultural imperialism: tracing its patterns in contemporary children's novels. ChildLit (33) 2005, 185–208.

Jon Paul Fiorentino (b.1975)

20232. Wills, Deborah. 'The flesh continuing': pain, poetry and the therapeutic landscape. *See* **17236**.

Paul S. Flores (b.1972)

20233. Palaversich, Diana. The politics of drug trafficking in Mexican and Mexico-related *narconovelas*. Aztlan (31:2) 2006, 85–110.

Nick Flynn (b.1960)

20234. Lemon, Alex. It ain't *Tuesday with Morrie*: an interview with poet and memoirist Nick Flynn. BRev (26:2) 2006, 5, 26.

Marvin Francis (b.1955)

20235. Cariou, Warren. 'How come these guns are so tall': anti-corporate resistance in Marvin Francis's *City Treaty*. StudCanL (31:1) 2006, 148–58.

Gina Gionfriddo

20236. Durang, Christopher, *et al.* Joking aside: a conversation about comedy with Christopher Durang, Gina Gionfriddo, Sarah Ruhl, and Wendy Wasserstein. *In* (pp. 181–90) **12297**.

Gary Mex Glazner (b.1957)

20237. Glazner, Gary Mex. How to make a life as a poet. New York: Soft Skull Press, 2006. pp. 253.

Kenneth Goldsmith (b.1961)

20238. Bergvall, Caroline. Stepping out with Kenneth Goldsmith: a New York interview. OpL (twelfth series) (7) 2005, 86–93.

20239. Christie, Jason. Sampling the culture: 4 notes toward a poetics of plundergraphia and on Kenneth Goldsmith's *Day*. OpL (twelfth series) (7) 2005, 69–74.

20240. Drucker, Johanna. Un-visual and conceptual. *See* **19060**.

20241. Goldsmith, Kenneth. Paragraphs on conceptual writing. *See* **11912**.

20242. Morris, Simon; Britton, Howard. Sucking on words: a conversation between the artist Simon Morris and the psychoanalyst Dr Howard Britton, using the academic methodology for transcription. OpL (twelfth series) (7) 2005, 140–51.

20243. Perloff, Marjorie. 'Moving information': on Kenneth Goldsmith's *The Weather*. OpL (twelfth series) (7) 2005, 75–85.

20244. Peters, Carl. The medium means nothing. OpL (twelfth series) (7) 2005, 110–16.

20245. Schuster, Joshua. On Kenneth Goldsmith: the avant-garde at a standstill. OpL (twelfth series) (7) 2005, 102–9.

20246. Wershler-Henry, Darren. Uncreative is the new creative: Kenneth Goldsmith not typing. OpL (twelfth series) (7) 2005, 152–9.

Rigoberto González (b.1970)

20247. González, Rigoberto. Butterfly boy: memoirs of a Chicano *mariposa*. Madison; London: Wisconsin UP, 2006. pp. xii, 207. (Writing in Latinidad.)

Sara Gran (b.1971)

20248. Burke, Robert. Turning the world upside down: an interview with Sara Gran. BRev (26:3) 2006, 7, 24.

Jessica Grant (b.1972)

20249. Schagerl, Jessica. 'This is what to read': Jessica Grant's *Making Light of Tragedy*. OpL (twelfth series) (6) 2005, 13–30.

Jaki Shelton Green (b.1953)

20250. Mickle, Mildred R. An interview with Jaki Shelton Green, winner of the 2003 North Carolina Award in Literature. Ob3 (6:1) 2005, 9–27.

Jane Green (b.1968)

20251. Umminger, Alison. Supersizing Bridget Jones: what's really eating the women in chick lit. *In* (pp. 239–52) **19862**.

Richard Greenberg (b.1958)

20252. Witchel, Alex. A dramatic shut-in. NYTM, 26 Mar. 2006, 46–51.

Darren Greer

20253. Greer, Darren. Strange ghosts: essays. Toronto: Cormorant, 2006. pp. 174.

Lara Gularte

20254. Freitas, Vamberto. Da poesia de Lara Gularte: escavações da história imaginada. GavB (26/27) 2005/06, 23–35.

Mark Haddon (b.1962)

20255. Cawelti, John G. Sherlock Holmes: the case of the perpetual detective. *See* **9928**.

20256. Murray, Stuart. Autism and the contemporary sentimental: fiction and the narrative fascination of the present. *See* **16455**.

E. Lynn Harris (b.1955)

20257. Sikorski, Grace. Stepping into the same river twice: the tragic sexual mulatto and subversion of the inside/outside dialectic in the novels of E. Lynn Harris and Alice Walker. *In* (pp. 183–95) **11883**.

Sonya Hartnett (b.1968)

20258. Wilkie-Stibbs, Christine. Borderland children: reflection on narratives of abjection. *See* **15860**.

Louise Hawes (b.1943)

20259. Morgan, Lisa. 'Skill and caring and, yes, passion': Louise Hawes's formula for writing fiction. NCLR (15) 2006, 73–81.

Philip Heldrich (b.1965)

20260. Heldrich, Philip. Out here in the out there: essays in a region of superlatives. Minneapolis, MN: Mid-List Press, 2005. pp. 190.

William Haywood Henderson

20261. Kenney, Jay. Land of inspiration: a walk through the writing career of novelist William Haywood Henderson. BRev (26:3) 2006, 23–4.

Dara Horn (b.1977)

20262. Meyers, Helene. Jewish gender trouble: women writing men of valor. *See* **16155**.

Silas House (b.1971)

20263. Blythe, Hal; Sweet, Charlie; Rahimzadeh, Kevin. The sacred and secular in *Clay's Quilt*. NCL (36:1) 2006, 6–9.

20264. Hatchett, Judith. 'Solemn judge' or source of spirit: Silas House's presentation of Pentecostalism. KenPR (20) 2005, 20–4.

20265. House, Silas. No Bible-beating allowed. *In* (pp. 152–61) **11940**.

Jeanne Wakatsuki Houston (b.1934)

20266. Chen, Fu-Jen; Yu, Su-Lin. Reclaiming the Southwest: a traumatic space in the Japanese American internment narrative. JSwest (47:4) 2005, 551–70.

Siri Hustvedt (b.1955)

20267. Dallmann, Antje. ConspiraCities and creative paranoia: Ellis's *Glamorama*, Hustvedt's *The Blindfold*, and Whitehead's *The Intuitionist*. *See* **15728**.

Erik Jensen (b.1970)

20268. Blank, Jessica; Jensen, Erik. Living justice: love, freedom, and the making of *The Exonerated*. *See* **20187**.

Liz Jensen (b.1959)

20269. Stewart, Victoria. 'The big war outside and the little war at home': anamnesis and the Second World War in recent British fiction. *See* **15991**.

Judy Jordan (b.1961)

20270. Turner, Daniel Cross. New Fugitives: contemporary poets of countermemory and the futures of Southern poetry. *See* **15398**.

Lally Katz (b.1978)

20271. Troup, Cynthia. 'Space to see things': an interview with Lally Katz. Antipodes (20:1) 2006, 84–7.

Sue Monk Kidd (b.1948)

20272. Emanuel, Catherine B. The archetypal mother: the Black Madonna in Sue Monk Kidd's *The Secret Life of Bees*. WVUPP (52) 2005, 115–22.

20273. Terry, Laura. Concealing and revealing: painting the Southern literary landscape. OvR (33:1/2) 2006, 11–70.

Haven Kimmel (b.1965)

20274. Kimmel, Haven. She got up off the couch, and other heroic acts from Mooreland, Indiana. New York: Free Press, 2006. pp. xiv, 304.

'Sophie Kinsella' (Madeleine Wickham) (b.1969)

20275. Scanlon, Jennifer. 'How did she know?': confessional narratives of an online interpretive community. Storytelling (5:4) 2006, 237–47.

20276. Van Slooten, Jessica. Fashionably indebted: conspicuous consumption, fashion, and romance in Sophie Kinsella's Shopaholic trilogy. *In* (pp. 219–38) **19862**.

Lisa Kron

20277. Dias, John. In conversation: on *Well*. Dramatist (8:5) 2006, 44–7.

20278. Kron, Lisa. A straight line. *In* (pp. 51–5) **12245**.

Stephen Kuusisto (b.1955)

20279. Kuusisto, Stephen. Eavesdropping: a life by ear. New York; London: Norton, 2006. pp. xiv, 186.

Neil LaBute (b.1963)

20280. Wood, Gerald C. (ed.). Neil LaBute: a casebook. London; New York: Routledge, 2006. pp. xv, 162. (Casebooks on modern dramatists.)

Jake Lamar (b.1961)

20281. Grassian, Daniel. Passing into post-ethnicity: a study of Danzy Senna's *Caucasia*. *See* **20332**.

Siew Mei Lau (b.1968)

20282. Holden, Philip. Writing conspiracy: race and rights in two Singapore novels. *See* **14582**.

Bryony Lavery (b.1947)

20283. Woddis, Carole. Women's imaginations: experimenting with theatrical form. *In* (pp. 170–80) **12297**.

Shawna Lemay (b.1966)

20284. Anon. An interview with Shawna Lemay. PJCL (45) 2005/06, 21–2.

'J. T. LeRoy' (Laura Albert) (b.1980)

20285. Pancake, Ann. Virtual hillbilly: musings on JT LeRoy by a flesh-and-blood West Virginian. AppH (34:3) 2006, 35–45.

David Lindsay-Abaire (b.1975)

20286. Bossler, Gregory. In conversation with David Lindsay-Abaire. Dramatist (8:5) 2006, 10–15.

Beth Lisick (b.1968)

20287. Lisick, Beth. Everybody into the pool: true tales. New York: Regan, 2005. pp. x, 227.

Sheryl Luna (b.1965)

20288. Pérez, Emmy. An interview with Sheryl Luna. InR (28:1) 2006, 97–101.

Alexander McCall Smith (b.1948)

20289. Gualtieri, Claudia. *The Africa that is not*: la serie *The No. 1 Ladies' Detective Agency* di Alexander McCall Smith. Culture (18) 2004, 259–73.

20290. Mekgwe, Pinkie. 'All that is fine in the human condition': crafting words, creating Ma-Ramotswe. RAL (37:2) 2006, 176–86.

Bernice L. McFadden (b.1966)

20291. McFadden, Bernice. The writing life. BkW, 19 Mar. 2006, 10.

Jon McGregor (b.1976)

20292. Toplu, Şebnem. Fluidity of the city and solid individual dramas: Jon McGregor's *If Nobody Speaks of Remarkable Things*. *In* (pp. 107–20) **3307**.

Patrick McGuinness (b.1968)

20293. Miller, Chris. Choosing who one is. PNRev (31:5) 2005, 69–72.

Patrick Mackie (b.1974)

20294. Welton, Matthew. Unnecessary angels: Patrick Mackie, Jeremy Over, and their use of Wallace Stevens. *See* **18658**.

Diane McKinney-Whetstone (b.1954?)

20295. Tettenborn, Éva. Beyond the boundaries of the Blues: Diane McKinney-Whetstone's *Blues Dancing* as middle-class Blues narrative. CritW (48:1) 2006, 44–57.

Emma McLaughlin (b.1964) and Nicola Kraus (b.1974)

20296. Hale, Elizabeth. Long-suffering professional females: the case of nanny lit. *In* (pp. 103–18) **19862**.

Jeff Mann (b.1959)

20297. Burack, Cynthia. Mountain Mann: a biographical sketch. AppH (34:3) 2006, 10–12.

20298. Friedman, Michael Shannon. An appreciation of his literary work. AppH (34:3) 2006, 28–31.

20299. Pendarvis, Edwina. Writing a new world. AppH (34:3) 2006, 22–3.

Lee Martin (b.1955)

20300. Swanson-Davies, Linda B. Interview with Lee Martin. GT (60) 2006, 24–39.

Daniel (Daniel Philippe) Mason (b.1976)

20301. SWANSON-DAVIES, LINDA B. Interview with Daniel Mason. GT (53) 2005, 187–203.

Jane Mead (b.1958)

20302. WILLIAMSON, ALAN. Cynicism. *See* **16253**.

Ana Menéndez (b.1970)

20303. KANDIYOTI, DALIA. Consuming nostalgia: nostalgia and the marketplace in Cristina García and Ana Menéndez. *See* **16047**.

Christopher (Lyall) Merrill (b.1957)

20304. CASTRO, JAN GARDEN. Christopher Merrill: an interview. APR (33:1) 2004, 41–2.

Richard K. Morgan (b.1965)

20305. SCHWETMAN, JOHN D. Romanticism and the cortical stack: cyberpunk subjectivity in the Takeshi Kovacs novels of Richard K. Morgan. PCP (41) 2006, 124–40.

Phaswane Mpe (1970–2004)

20306. ATTREE, LIZZY. Reshaping communities: the representation of HIV/AIDS in literature from South Africa and Zimbabwe. *In* (pp. 61–79) **12216**.

Raman Mundair

20307. BARFIELD, STEVEN. 'Jewelinthecrown.co.uk': Orientalism's strange persistence in British South Asian writing. *In* (pp. 111–20) **14238**.

Rona Munro (b.1959)

20308. WODDIS, CAROLE. Women's imaginations: experimenting with theatrical form. *In* (pp. 170–80) **12297**.

Joanna Murray-Smith (b.1962)

20309. SHIM, JUNG-SOON. Performing emotion interculturally: the Korean production of *Love Child*. ADS (49) 2006, 20–31.

20310. —— Translating emotions for the local audience. *See* **6072**.

20311. TAIT, PETA. Embodying love: mother meets daughter in theatre for cultural exchange. ADS (49) 2006, 32–9.

An Na (b.1972)

20312. CHIU, MONICA. The cultural production of Asian American young adults in the novels of Marie G. Lee, An Na, and Doris (*sic*) Jones Yang. *See* **17095**.

Vivienne Ndlovu

20313. ATTREE, LIZZY. Reshaping communities: the representation of HIV/AIDS in literature from South Africa and Zimbabwe. *In* (pp. 61–79) **12216**.

Philip Nikolayev (b.1966)

20314. THAYIL, JEET. 'The diaspora of poets': a conversation with Philip Nikolayev. JPW (42:2) 2006, 195–200.

Lynn Nottage (b.1964)

20315. Carpenter, Bridget, *et al.* Crossing borders: a conversation with Bridget Carpenter, Lynn Nottage, Dael Orlandersmith, and Diana Son. *In* (pp. 115–26) **12297**.

JudyLee Oliva (b.1952)

20316. Stanlake, Christy. JudyLee Oliva's *The Fire and the Rose* and the modeling of platial theories in Native American dramaturgy. ModDr (48:4) 2005, 819–41.

Jeremy Over (b.1961)

20317. Welton, Matthew. Unnecessary angels: Patrick Mackie, Jeremy Over, and their use of Wallace Stevens. *See* **18658**.

David Peace (b.1967)

20318. Hart, Matthew. An interview with David Peace. ConLit (47:4) 2006, 546–69.

Allison Pearson (b.1960)

20319. Hewett, Heather. You are not alone: the personal, the political, and the 'new' mommy lit. *In* (pp. 119–39) **19862**.

Katie Peterson (b.1974)

20320. Hillman, Brenda; Peterson, Katie. Hermetic memory: an exchange on Dickinson between two poets. *See* **9868**.

Beth Powning (b.1949)

20321. Powning, Beth. Edge seasons: a memoir. Toronto: Knopf Canada, 2005. pp. 232.

Andy Quan (b.1969)

20322. Quan, Andy. Found in translation? Meanjin (63:2) 2004, 172–80.

Peter Robb (b.1946)

20323. Nowak, Robert. Punk patrician. Meanjin (63:1) 2004, 192–6.

Anthony D. Robles (b.1964)

20324. de Jesús, Melinda L. 'The sound of bamboo planted deep inside them': reclaiming Filipino American history and identity in *Lakas and the Manilatown Fish*. LU (30:2) 2006, 202–17.

Meg Rosoff (b.1956)

20325. Wilkie-Stibbs, Christine. The 'other' country: memory, voices, and experiences of colonized childhoods. *See* **20186**.

Sarah Ruhl

20326. Durang, Christopher, *et al.* Joking aside: a conversation about comedy with Christopher Durang, Gina Gionfriddo, Sarah Ruhl, and Wendy Wasserstein. *In* (pp. 181–90) **12297**.

20327. Greene, Alexis. New voices: Moira Buffini, Sarah Ruhl, and Rukhsana Ahmad. *In* (pp. 219–40) **12297**.

Trish Salah

20328. Woodland, Malcolm. Refraining from desire: Trish Salah's *Ghazals in Fugue*. CanP (57) 2005, 35–51.

Marjane Satrapi (b.1969)

20329. Tensuan, Theresa M. Comic visions and revisions in the work of Lynda Barry and Marjane Satrapi. *See* **14618**.

20330. Whitlock, Gillian. Autographics: the seeing 'I' of the comics. *See* **18586**.

Danzy Senna (b.1970)

20331. Dagbovie, Sika Alaine. Fading to White, fading away: biracial bodies in Michelle Cliff's *Abeng* and Danzy Senna's *Caucasia*. *See* **15184**.

20332. Grassian, Daniel. Passing into post-ethnicity: a study of Danzy Senna's *Caucasia*. MidQ (47:4) 2006, 317–35.

Matthew Sharpe (b.1962)

20333. Ellis, Sherry. Interview with Matthew Sharpe. GT (58) 2006, 115–25.

Craig Sherborne (b.1952)

20334. Bird, Carmel. A history of violence. Meanjin (65:2) 2006, 210–15 (review-article).

20335. Sherborne, Craig. Hoi polloi. Melbourne: Black, 2005. pp. 197. (Memoir.) Rev. by Carmel Bird in Meanjin (65:2) 2006, 210–15.

Makeda Silvera (b.1955)

20336. Davis, Andrea. Translating narratives of masculinity across borders: a Jamaican case study. *See* **18254**.

20337. Kim, Christine. Postcolonial romance, ghostly love stories, and *The Heart Does Not Bend*. Mosaic (39:2) 2006, 57–73.

Amy Sohn (b.1973)

20338. Kiernan, Anna. No satisfaction: *Sex and the City*, *Run Catch Kiss*, and the conflict of desires in chick lit's new heroines. *In* (pp. 207–18) **19862**.

Diana Son (b.1965)

20339. Carpenter, Bridget, *et al.* Crossing borders: a conversation with Bridget Carpenter, Lynn Nottage, Dael Orlandersmith, and Diana Son. *In* (pp. 115–26) **12297**.

20340. Green, Amy S. Whose voices are these? The arts of language in the plays of Suzan-Lori Parks, Paula Vogel, and Diana Son. *In* (pp. 143–57) **12297**.

Shelagh Stephenson (b.1955)

20341. Raby, Gyllian. From pre-Luddites to the Human Genome Project: smashing frames in Shelagh Stephenson's *An Experiment with an Air Pump*. *In* (pp. 137–50) **11781**.

Mark Sullivan (b.1961)

20342. Sullivan, Mark. On writing what won't be read. NER (27:3) 2006, 41–52.

Peta Tait (b.1953)

20343. Dike, Fatima, *et al.* Beyond the USA, beyond the UK. *In* (pp. 199–218) **12297**.

Richard Terrill (b.1953)

20344. Morrill, Donald. Writing, jazz, and the 'ultimate plot of life': a conversation with Richard Terrill. TRev (26) 2004, 24–33.

Monique T. D. Truong

20345. Bavaro, Vincenzo. Politiche di gender e soggettivazione nazionale nell'America asiatica. *In* (pp. 60–93) **11954**.

Nancy E. Turner (b.1953)

20346. Adkison, Jennifer Dawes. 'These is my words' … or are they? GPQ (26:1) 2006, 13–25.

Susan Vreeland (b.1946)

20347. Lanone, Catherine. Pain, paint and popular fiction: *The Passion of Artemisia* by Susan Vreeland. EtBr (31) 2006, 191–209.

20348. Lent, Tina Olsin. 'My heart belongs to Daddy': the fictionalization of baroque artist Artemisia Gentileschi in contemporary film and novels. LitFQ (34:3) 2006, 212–18.

Chris Ware (b.1967)

20349. Raeburn, Daniel. Chris Ware. New Haven, CT; London: Yale UP, 2004. pp. 112. (Monographics.) Rev. by Hillary Chute in MFS (52:4) 2006, 1014–27.

Mary Yukari Waters (b.1965)

20350. Ellis, Sherry. Interview with Mary Yukari Waters. GT (57) 2006, 225–37.

Sarah Waters (b.1966)

20351. Costantini, Mariaconcetta. 'Faux-Victorian melodrama' in the new millennium: the case of Sarah Waters. CritS (18:1) 2006, 17–39.

20352. Letissier, Georges. Le texte victorien à l'âge postmoderne: jouvence ou sénescence? *Fingersmith* de Sarah Waters et le mélodrame victorien. CVE (63) 2006, 277–93.

20353. Wilson, Cheryl A. From the drawing-room to the stage: performing sexuality in Sarah Waters' *Tipping the Velvet*. WS (35:3) 2006, 255–305.

Louise Welsh (b.1965)

20354. Miller, Gavin. Aesthetic depersonalization in Louise Welsh's *The Cutting Room*. JNT (36:1) 2006, 72–89.

Colson Whitehead (b.1969)

20355. Dallmann, Antje. ConspiraCities and creative paranoia: Ellis's *Glamorama*, Hustvedt's *The Blindfold*, and Whitehead's *The Intuitionist*. *See* **15728**.

20356. Grassian, Daniel. Passing into post-ethnicity: a study of Danzy Senna's *Caucasia*. *See* **20332**.

20357. Liggins, Saundra. The urban gothic vision of Colson Whitehead's *The Intuitionist* (1999). AAR (40:2) 2006, 359–69.

Gina Ferris Wilkins ('Gina Ferris', 'Gina Wilkins') (b.1954)

20358. Livingston, Eric. The textuality of pleasure. NLH (37:3) 2006, 655–72.

Crystal E. Wilkinson (b.1962)

20359. Brosi, George. Crystal Wilkinson: a Black Appalachian treasure. AppH (34:2) 2006, 8–12.

20360. Burriss, Theresa. Crystal Wilkinson: enticing readers to stretch. AppH (34:2) 2006, 37–43.

20361. Grubbs, Morris A. Crystal Wilkinson: an interview. AppH (34:2) 2006, 13–23.

Mark Winegardner (b.1961)

20362. Criniti, Steve. Baseball is America: the game of imperialism in Mark Winegardner's *The Veracruz Blues*. CritW (47:4) 2006, 389–406.

INDEXES

INDEX OF AUTHORS AND FILM DIRECTORS

INDEX OF SCHOLARS
including compilers, editors, translators and reviewers.